O9-BUC-969

THE NINTH MENTAL MEASUREMENTS YEARBOOK

Volume I

EARLIER PUBLICATIONS IN THIS SERIES

EDUCATIONAL, PSYCHOLOGICAL, AND PERSONALITY TESTS OF 1933 AND 1934

EDUCATIONAL, PSYCHOLOGICAL, AND PERSONALITY TESTS OF 1933, 1934, AND 1935

EDUCATIONAL, PSYCHOLOGICAL, AND PERSONALITY TESTS OF 1936

THE NINETEEN THIRTY-EIGHT MENTAL MEASUREMENTS YEARBOOK

THE NINETEEN FORTY MENTAL MEASUREMENTS YEARBOOK

THE THIRD MENTAL MEASUREMENTS YEARBOOK

THE FOURTH MENTAL MEASUREMENTS YEARBOOK

THE FIFTH MENTAL MEASUREMENTS YEARBOOK

TESTS IN PRINT

THE SIXTH MENTAL MEASUREMENTS YEARBOOK

READING TESTS AND REVIEWS

PERSONALITY TESTS AND REVIEWS

THE SEVENTH MENTAL MEASUREMENTS YEARBOOK

TESTS IN PRINT II

ENGLISH TESTS AND REVIEWS

FOREIGN LANGUAGE TESTS AND REVIEWS

INTELLIGENCE TESTS AND REVIEWS

MATHEMATICS TESTS AND REVIEWS

PERSONALITY TESTS AND REVIEWS II

READING TESTS AND REVIEWS II

SCIENCE TESTS AND REVIEWS

SOCIAL STUDIES TESTS AND REVIEWS

VOCATIONAL TESTS AND REVIEWS

THE EIGHTH MENTAL MEASUREMENTS YEARBOOK

TESTS IN PRINT III

CHIEF EDITORIAL ASSOCIATE

Debra A. Funk

PRODUCTION AND SECRETARIAL

Linda L. Murphy
Susan M. Woolard

PROFESSIONAL ASSOCIATES

Jane Close Conoley
Jack J. Kramer

THE NINTH MENTAL MEASUREMENTS YEARBOOK

Edited by

JAMES V. MITCHELL, JR.
Director, The Buros Institute of Mental Measurements

Volume I

The Buros Institute of Mental Measurements
The University of Nebraska–Lincoln
Lincoln, Nebraska
1985
Distributed by The University of Nebraska Press

Copyright 1985 and published by the Buros Institute of Mental Measurements of The University of Nebraska–Lincoln, 135 Bancroft Hall, Lincoln, Nebraska 68588–0348. All rights reserved. No part of this publication may be reproduced in any form nor may any of the contents be used in an information storage, retrieval, or transmission system without the prior written permission of the publisher.

LC 39-3422
ISBN 910674–29–9

Manufactured in the United States of America.

The paper used in this publication meets the minimum requirements of American National Standard for Information Sciences—Permanence of Paper for Printed Library Materials, ANSI Z39.48-1984.

Note to Users

The staff of the Buros Institute of Mental Measurements has made every effort to ensure the accuracy of the test information included in this work. However, the Buros Institute of Mental Measurements and the Editor of *The Ninth Mental Measurements Yearbook* do not assume, and hereby expressly and absolutely disclaim, any liability to any party for any loss or damage caused by errors or omissions or statements of any kind in *The Ninth Mental Measurements Yearbook*. This disclaimer also includes judgments or statements of any kind made by test reviewers, who were extended the professional freedom appropriate to their task; their judgments and opinions are their own, uninfluenced in any way by the Buros Institute or the Editor.

All material included in *The Ninth Mental Measurements Yearbook* is intended solely for the use of our readers. None of this material, including reviewer statements, may be used in advertising or for any other commercial purpose.

To the memory of

OSCAR KRISEN BUROS

TABLE OF CONTENTS

PREFACE

At the beginning of the preface for *Tests in Print III*, which was the first volume published by the Buros Institute of Mental Measurements after its relocation at The University of Nebraska–Lincoln, I paid the following tribute to Oscar Buros:

> The publication of *Tests in Print III* is both a sad and a significant milestone. It is sad because it marks the first publication in this series that was not edited by Oscar Krisen Buros, who passed away in 1978. It is significant because it represents a determination to continue the work of the founder and to insure contributions of like kind and importance in the future. For over 40 years Oscar Buros was the editor and publisher of *The Mental Measurements Yearbooks*, *Tests in Print*, and separate monographs covering specific areas of testing. *The Mental Measurements Yearbooks*, containing critical reviews by professionals of all commercially published tests in English, quickly achieved a reputation for integrity, scholarship, and professional responsibility. Under his leadership the *Yearbooks* and other Institute publications became an invaluable resource for test users throughout the world. They also became a prime force in stimulating increased awareness of the necessity for improvement in the construction, validation, and use of tests. As an unabashed crusader for better tests and the more effective use of tests, Oscar Buros made an immense impact on the field of testing that should be felt for some time to come.

It is in the context of this historically important contribution that the new Buros Institute is pleased to present *The Ninth Mental Measurements Yearbook*. This yearbook is the 26th publication in the larger series, listed on an earlier page, that includes all *The Mental Measurements Yearbooks*, the *Tests in Print* volumes, and the various monographs covering special areas of testing. An historical account of the series is presented in the Introduction to *The Eighth Mental Measurements Yearbook* and will not be repeated here. Explanation of the nature, scope, and unique features of this *Ninth Mental Measurements Yearbook* will be presented in the Introduction to follow.

The new Buros Institute of Mental Measurements owes an immense debt of gratitude to Luella Buros, the widow of Oscar Buros and his lifelong companion in Institute activities. It was Luella Buros who provided the official and contractual sanction for the transfer of the Buros Institute to The University of Nebraska–Lincoln, and it was she who provided the office equipment, inventory, and other resources of the previous Buros Institute and also the gifts and encouragement that meant so much to an organization in transition. She has honored her husband and their work together in a way that will have consequential and lasting effects for test users everywhere. It is impossible for words alone to express appreciation commensurate with what she has done for us. We shall try to express our continuing gratitude through actual deeds appropriate to the history and traditions of the Buros Institute and its founder.

A work of the magnitude of *The Ninth Mental Measurements Yearbook* requires intensive and seemingly endless effort. The usually unsung heroes and heroines of such an effort are the ones who should be mentioned first. These are the members of the Buros Institute office staff who are full-time in the trenches from day to day and who have the talent, staying power, commitment, and loyalty to accomplish those endless tasks in accordance with high standards of excellence. Included in this group are Debra Funk, Chief Editorial Associate, Linda Murphy, Secretarial Specialist, and Susan Woolard, Clerical Assistant III. They are my working companions in an immense undertaking, and I am deeply grateful for their contributions to the present work.

Another deep debt of gratitude is owed to the many professional people who consented to write test reviews for this yearbook. The success of the entire endeavor is greatly dependent on their willingness to take time from their busy schedules to provide their expertise in the form of a well-reasoned review. They have accomplished their assignments extremely well, and they cannot be thanked enough.

During the 1984–85 academic year I welcomed to the Buros Institute two people who serve half-time with the Institute and half-time with the school psychology program. They are Dr. Jane Conoley and Dr. Jack Kramer. My thanks go to Dr. Conoley and Dr. Kramer for their significant contributions to such activities as our annual symposium on testing, information and dissemination projects, cooperative arrangements for reviews of computer-based software, editing, and other activities of the Buros Institute. They will also have a major role in the selection of reviewers for the next *Mental Measurements Yearbook*.

Graduate students also play an important role in Institute work. Their assignments are diverse, critical, and often under pressure of time or schedule. We have had some excellent graduate student support from Stephen Axford, Clark House, Michael Kavan, Mark Lukin, Sherral Miller, Christopher Milne, John Olson, Carol Speth, and Ruth Tomes.

The effective use of computer technology has been a hallmark of this yearbook, and much of the credit for that should go to some outstanding personnel in our university Computing Center. Mark Meyer and Charles Sundermeier have been of inestimable help in working with us closely to meet our publication needs and to conduct the cooperative problem-solving and trouble-shooting activities necessary to accomplish the task well.

Our gratitude is also extended to our National Advisory Committee, consisting of Luella Buros, T. Anne Cleary, Roger Lennon, Ellis Page, Daniel Reschly, Lyle Schoenfeldt, Richard Snow, Julian Stanley, and Frank Womer, who not only provided the benefit of their wisdom and professional experience, but also did so in a way that was both supportive and congenial. We also give our thanks to the Departmental Advisory Committee, consisting of Roger Bruning, David Dixon, Terry Gutkin, Kenneth Orton, Wayne Piersel, Barbara Plake, Royce Ronning, Toni Santmire, and Steven Wise. The Buros Institute is part of the Department of Educational Psychology, and this committee has not only provided help and support for our publication efforts, but has also been very instrumental in planning our annual symposium and editing the papers included in the symposium books. Stephen Elliott and Joseph Witt, former members of the Buros Institute professional staff, should also be thanked for their contributions to earlier phases of the work for this yearbook. We also thank The University of Nebraska Foundation for the fiscal support that was so important to our earlier development. Also important to our development have been administrators of The University of Nebraska–Lincoln and The University of Nebraska Press, whose support, consultation, and administrative assistance have been appreciated on many occasions. Acknowledgment should also be made of the role of Cecil Reynolds in initiating efforts to bring the Buros Institute to The University of Nebraska. A very special expression of gratitude should go to my wife, Margaret, who knows far better than anyone else the investment of time, effort, and emotion that goes into a work of this magnitude; our partnership was as central to this effort as it is to everything else in our lives.

James V. Mitchell, Jr.

INTRODUCTION

The Ninth Mental Measurements Yearbook is the 26th publication of the Buros Institute of Mental Measurements. These 26 publications may be classified into three general categories:

1. *Mental Measurements Yearbooks (MMY)*
2. separate monographs covering specific areas of testing (e.g., *Personality Tests and Reviews, Vocational Tests and Reviews*, etc.)
3. *Tests in Print (TIP)*

The *Mental Measurements Yearbooks,* of which nine have now been published, consist of descriptive listings, references, and critical reviews of commercially published tests in English. The separate monographs are collections of those listings, references, and critical reviews pertaining to a specific area that have appeared in all Institute volumes to date. *Tests in Print* consists of descriptive listings and references, without reviews, of commercially published tests that are in print and available for purchase. It also serves as a comprehensive index to the contents of all of the *Mental Measurements Yearbooks* published to date. Criteria for inclusion of a test in *TIP* and *MMY* are quite different. The criterion for inclusion of a test in *TIP*, as previously indicated, is simply that the test is in print and available for purchase. Criteria for inclusion of a test in the *MMY* are that the test be either new or revised since the last *MMY* published by the Institute, or that the test has generated 20 or more references since that last *MMY* (optional). The publications in the series are interlocking volumes with extensive cross-referencing requiring their coordinated use as a system.

It is in this context that *The Ninth Mental Measurements Yearbook*, the present and newest addition to the series, is now made available to the public. Descriptive and explanatory information about this newest publication is presented below.

THE NINTH YEARBOOK

The Ninth Mental Measurements Yearbook, like the eight earlier yearbooks in the series, is designed to assist test users in education, psychology, and industry to choose more judiciously from the many tests available.

The series was initiated in 1938 to fill the great need for frank evaluations of tests by competent reviewers. The objectives of this *Ninth Mental Measurements Yearbook* are to provide: (*a*) factual information on all known new or revised tests published as separates in the English-speaking countries of the world; (*b*) candidly critical test reviews written specifically for the *Yearbook* by qualified professional people representing a variety of viewpoints; and (*c*) comprehensive bibliographies, for specific tests, of references which have been examined for their relevance to the particular tests.

In previous editions of the *Yearbooks*, Oscar Buros, who was editor of the series for 40 years until his death in 1978, also listed the following objectives, which he referred to as his "crusading" objectives: (*a*) to impel test authors and publishers to publish higher quality tests with detailed information on their validity and limitations; (*b*) to foster in test users a greater awareness of both the values and limitations involved in the use of standardized tests; (*c*) to stimulate test reviewers and others to consider more thoroughly their own values and beliefs in regard to testing; (*d*) to suggest more discerning methods to test users of arriving at their own appraisals of tests in light of their particular values and needs; and (*e*) to make test users aware of the importance of being suspicious of all tests—even those produced by well-known authors and publishers—which are not accompanied by detailed data on their construction, validation, uses, and limitations.

All of these objectives continue to have relevance to the field of testing today. In addition to these historic objectives, the present editor would like to add an objective which has always been implicit in these earlier objectives but which deserves emphasis in its own right as well: to provide a consumer service to the professions and to the public that will result in the more effective choice and use of tests for the benefit of both those who use the tests and those who take them. This emphasis on consumer service to the professions and to the public will be a continuing high priority objective to the present editor in the future work of the Buros Institute of Mental Measurements.

Like the other yearbooks in the series, *The Ninth Mental Measurements Yearbook* is a completely new publication which supplements earlier volumes. Although the major coverage is for tests new or revised since the publication of *The Eighth Mental Measurements Yearbook* (1978), older tests which have generated bibliographies of 20 or more references for *Tests in Print III* (1983) are often listed and, in some cases, reviewed.

The contents of *The Ninth Mental Measurements Yearbook* include (*a*) a comprehensive bibliography of commercially available tests, primarily new or revised, published as separates for use with English-speaking subjects; (*b*) critical test reviews by well-qualified professional people who were selected by the Buros Institute professional staff on the basis of their preeminence and/or potential in the field they represent; (*c*) comprehensive bibliographies, for specific tests, of references related to the construction, validity, or use of the tests in various settings; (*d*) a stage-setting, state-of-the-art review by Dr. Anne Anastasi, a leading figure in the field of measurement, on "Mental Measurement: Some Emerging Trends"; (*e*) a test title index with appropriate cross-references; (*f*) a classified subject index which also describes the population for which each test is intended and provides multiple classifications for tests where appropriate; (*g*) a publishers directory and index, including addresses and test listings by publisher; (*h*) a name index which includes the names of all authors of tests, reviews, or references; (*i*) an index of acronyms for easy reference when a test acronym is known but the full title is not; and (*j*) an innovative score index which refers readers to tests featuring particular kinds of scores which are of interest to them.

The Ninth Mental Measurements Yearbook also continues some innovations that were first introduced in *Tests in Print III* (1983). The organization of the volume is encyclopedic in nature, with the tests being ordered alphabetically by title. Thus if the title of a test is known, the reader can locate the test immediately without having to consult the Index of Titles. The test classifications continue to appear in the Classified Subject Index, but the new organization permits some tests to be included in more than one classification, a feature which provides flexible classification faithful to reality and a Classified Subject Index of optimum use to the reader.

The page headings reflect the encyclopedic organization. The page heading of the left-hand page cites the number and title of the first test listed on that page, and the page heading of the right-hand page cites the number and title of the last test listed on that page. All numbers presented in the various indexes are test numbers, not page numbers. Page numbers, important only for the Table of Contents, are indicated at the bottom of each page.

TESTS AND REVIEWS

The Tests and Reviews section is the heart of any *Mental Measurements Yearbook*. This section presents extensive listings for 1,409 tests, 1,266 test reviews by 660 reviewers, and 6,056 references for specific tests.

TESTS

Table 1 presents statistics on the number and percentage of tests in each of the 16 major classifications. It should be recognized, however, that it is not unusual for a test to be classifiable into more than one category, and the Classified Subject Index, to be described later, does indeed classify tests into more than one category. The Table 1 classifications are based upon first-choice classifications.

The total number of tests, 1,409, is 19.0% higher than the number in *The Eighth Yearbook*. Of this total 645, or 45.8%, are in the two categories of Personality and Vocations.

A few minor changes in the classifications of tests have been made since *The Eighth Yearbook*. The most important of these is the addition of two new categories—Developmental and Neuropsychological—to the list of categories. The addition of these two categories is due to the substantial increase in the number of tests published in both of these areas since the last yearbook. The field of testing is typically in a dynamic, changing state, and changes in the classificatory schema are occasionally necessary to reflect more accurately the most current conditions in the field.

The percentages of new and revised or supplemented tests in each major classification are shown in Table 2. Approximately 70.5% of the tests are new tests and/or tests not previously listed in an *MMY*, and 17.5% are tests that have been revised

TABLE 1

TESTS BY MAJOR CLASSIFICATIONS

Classification	Number	Percentage
Personality	350	24.8
Vocations	295	20.9
Miscellaneous	139	9.9
Languages	134	9.5
Intelligence and Scholastic Aptitude	100	7.1
Reading	97	6.9
Achievement	68	4.8
Developmental	56	4.0
Mathematics	46	3.3
Speech and Hearing	39	2.8
Science	26	1.8
Motor/Visual Motor	23	1.6
Neuropsychological	14	1.0
Fine Arts	9	.6
Multi-Aptitude	8	.6
Social Studies	5	.4
Total	1,409	100.0

TABLE 2

NEW AND REVISED OR SUPPLEMENTED TESTS BY MAJOR CLASSIFICATIONS

Classification	Number of Tests	Percentage		
		New	Revised	Total
Achievement Batteries	68	64.7	29.4	94.1
Fine Arts	9	44.4	22.2	66.6
Intelligence and Scholastic Aptitude	100	54.0	26.0	80.0
Languages	134	85.8	7.5	93.3
Mathematics	46	73.9	21.7	95.6
Miscellaneous	139	78.4	12.2	90.6
Motor/Visual Motor	23	65.2	17.4	82.6
Multi-Aptitude	8	37.5	50.0	87.5
Neuropsychological	14	100.0	0.0	100.0
Personality	350	72.3	16.9	89.2
Reading	97	66.0	23.7	89.7
Science	26	34.6	57.7	92.3
Social Studies	5	40.0	40.0	80.0
Speech and Hearing	39	76.9	12.8	89.7
Vocations	295	66.8	14.6	81.4
Developmental	56	82.1	12.5	94.6
Total	1,409	70.5	17.5	88.0

or supplemented since being listed in an *MMY*. The percentage of new tests ranges from 34.6 for science tests to 100 for neuropsychological tests. Readers can determine which tests are new and which are revised by consulting the Index of Titles. *Tests in Print III* should be consulted for information about other tests.

The principal criteria for the inclusion of a test in an *MMY*, as indicated earlier, are that the test be either new or revised since the last *MMY*. However, a limited number of tests not meeting either of these criteria are included because they are widely used, have generated a large number of references in the literature (20 or more in *TIP III*), or should otherwise be brought to the attention of test users.

A strong effort has been made to identify and include *all* commercially published tests in English that are new or have been revised since the publication of the last *MMY*. It is important to emphasize this, because a common misconception is that a test must meet some minimal standards to be included in an *MMY*. Nothing could be further from the truth. The *Mental Measurements Yearbooks* are a service to the professions and to the public, and such a service obviously has as much or more obligation to provide information about poor tests as about good tests. The Buros Institute tries to include all new or revised tests in each *MMY*, provide carefully selected reviewers with the opportunity for independent evaluation, and then let *MMY* readers judge for themselves.

TEST REVIEWS

The Ninth Mental Measurements Yearbook contains 1,266 original reviews, written by 660 reviewers, of 1,409 tests. This represents an increase of 41% more original reviews than appeared in *The Eighth Mental Measurements Yearbook*, and an increase of 36% more reviewers, both very substantial increases.

Table 3 presents statistics on the review coverage for the various test classifications. More than half (56.1%) of the 1,409 tests listed in this yearbook have at least one review, and approximately one-third (33.6%) have two or more reviews. The low percentage for science tests is attributable almost entirely to the appreciable number of American Chemical Society tests that were included but not reviewed. Coverage for most categories is quite extensive.

Since there are too many new and revised tests to permit all to be reviewed, some tests have had to be given priority over others. The highest priority has been given to tests sold commercially in the United States. Some tests have not been reviewed because (*a*) they were published too late; (*b*) competent reviewers could not be located; (*c*) persons who agreed to review did not meet their commitment; or (*d*) reviews were rejected as not meeting minimum *MMY* standards.

The selection of reviewers was done with great care. The objective was to secure reviewers who represent various viewpoints among testing and subject specialists and who would write critical reviews competently, judiciously, and fairly. Reviewers were identified by means of extensive searches of the professional literature, by attendance at professional meetings, by recommendations from leaders in various professional fields, by previous performance on earlier *MMY* reviews, and through what might best be described as general professional

TABLE 3
ORIGINAL TEST REVIEWS IN THE *9TH MMY*

Classification	Number of Reviews	Number of Tests Reviewed	Percentage of Tests: 1 or More Reviews	Percentage of Tests: 2 or More Reviews
Achievement Batteries	96	53	77.9	63.2
Fine Arts	6	3	33.3	33.3
Intelligence and Scholastic Aptitude	117	71	71.0	44.0
Languages	143	97	72.4	34.3
Mathematics	51	31	67.4	43.5
Miscellaneous	116	75	54.0	28.8
Motor/Visual Motor	20	12	52.2	34.8
Multi-Aptitude	12	7	87.5	62.5
Neuropsychological	20	12	85.7	57.1
Personality	366	229	65.4	39.1
Reading	119	71	73.2	49.5
Science	4	2	7.7	7.7
Social Studies	4	3	60.0	20.0
Speech and Hearing	21	15	38.5	15.4
Vocations	119	76	25.8	14.6
Developmental	52	33	58.9	33.9
Total	1,266	790	56.1	33.6

knowledge. These reviewers represent an outstanding array of professional talent, and their contributions are obviously of critical importance in making this and other *Yearbooks* the important resources they are.

In order to make sure that persons invited to review would know what was expected of them, the following "Suggestions to *MMY* Reviewers" was enclosed with each letter of invitation:

1. Reviews should be written with the following major objectives in mind:

a) To provide test users with carefully prepared appraisals of tests for their guidance in selecting and using tests.
b) To stimulate progress toward higher professional standards of test construction by commending good work, by censuring poor work, and by suggesting improvements.
c) To impel test authors and publishers to present more detailed information on the construction, validity, reliability, norms, uses, and possible misuses of their tests.

2. Reviews should be concise, approximately 600 to 1,200 words in length. The average length of the reviews should not exceed 1,000 words except for reviews of achievement batteries, multifactor batteries, and tests for which a literature review is made. Longer reviews require the approval of the Editor.

3. Reviews should be frankly critical, with both strengths and weaknesses pointed out in a judicious manner. Descriptive comments should be kept to the minimum necessary to support the critical portions of the review. Criticism should be as specific as possible; implied criticisms meaningful only to testing specialists should be avoided. Reviews should be written primarily for the rank and file of test users. An indication of the relative importance and value of a test with respect to competing tests will help test users to choose tests more wisely. *It should be emphasized that if a reviewer considers a competing test better than the one being reviewed, the competing test should be specifically named.*

4. Criteria employed for the evaluation of a test should be those generally accepted and endorsed by the professional community. One very useful source of such criteria is the document entitled *Standards for Educational and Psychological Tests*, which was prepared by a joint committee of the American Psychological Association, the American Educational Research Association, and the National Council on Measurement in Education. The *Standards* are reprinted in *Tests in Print II* (1974), edited by Oscar K. Buros.

5. If a test manual gives insufficient, contradictory, or ambiguous information regarding the construction, validity, and use of a test, reviewers are urged to write directly to authors and publishers for further information. Test authors and publishers should, however, be held responsible for presenting adequate data in test manuals—failure to do so should be pointed out. If information not available to the test buyer is used in the review, the source of information should be clearly indicated.

6. The *MMY* office will furnish reviewers with the test entries which will precede their reviews. Information presented in the entry should not be repeated in reviews unless needed for evaluative purposes.

7. The use of sideheads is optional with reviewers.

8. Each review should conclude with a paragraph presenting a concise summary of the reviewer's overall evaluation of the test. The summary should be as explicit as possible. Is the test the best of its kind? Is it recommended for use? *If other tests are better, which of the competing tests is best?*

9. *A separate review should be prepared for each test.* Each review should begin on a new sheet. Clearly indicate the test and forms reviewed. Your name, title, and address should precede each review, e.g.: John Doe, Professor of Education and Psychology, University of Maryland, College Park, Maryland. The review should begin with a new paragraph immediately afterward.

10. All reviews should be typed using double spacing. A copy should be retained by the reviewer, and the original and one high quality reproduction should be sent to the Editor.

11. If for any reason a reviewer thinks he/she is not in a position to write an objective and unbiased review of a particular test, he/she should request the Editor to substitute another test.

12. Reviewing a test is an important professional responsibility, and reviewers are chosen for their competence and their willingness to assume individual responsibility for their statements. Joint authorship of reviews or other kinds of collaboration is acceptable only under unusual circumstances and with the express permission of the Buros Institute of Mental Measurements.

13. To secure better representation of various viewpoints most tests will be reviewed by two or more persons. Overlapping non-critical content in reviews may be deleted. Reviews will be carefully edited, but no substantive changes will be made without the reviewer's consent. Review proofs will be submitted to reviewers for checking.

14. The Editor reserves the right to request changes in or to reject any review which does not meet the minimum standards of the *MMY* series.

15. Submission of a review to another publication source or presentation at a professional meeting prior to publication in the *MMY* is prohibited without the written permission of the Editor.

16. Each reviewer will receive a complimentary copy of *The Ninth Mental Measurements Yearbook.*

Readers of test reviews in *The Ninth Mental Measurements Yearbook* are encouraged to exercise an active, analytical, and evaluative perspective in their reading of the reviews. Just as the reviewer evaluates a test, the reader should evaluate critically what the reviewer has to say about the test. The reviewers selected are outstanding professionals in their respective fields, but it is inevitable that their reviews also reflect their backgrounds and individual perspectives. The *Mental Measurements Yearbooks* are intended to stimulate analytical thinking about the selection of the best available test for a given purpose, not the passive acceptance of reviewer judgment. Active, analytical reading is the key to the most effective use of the professional expertise offered in each of the reviews.

REFERENCES

This yearbook lists a total of 6,056 references on the construction, validity, and use of specific tests. This figure may be slightly inflated because a reference involving more than one test may be listed under each of the tests in question, or because of overlap between the "Test References" section and the "Reviewer's References" section for a given test. The "Reviewer's References" section is new to the *Mental Measurements Yearbook* series; this new feature groups the reviewer's references in one convenient listing for easy identification and use by the reader. Of the total of 6,056 references, 4,758 are included under "Test References," and 1,298 are included under "Reviewer's References."

All references listed under "Test References" have been selected by Buros Institute staff searching through hundreds of professional journals. Because of the great proliferation of tests in recent years, it was decided to increase test and review coverage but to limit the increase in references by not including theses and dissertations. There is ample justification for this in the fact that the findings from theses and dissertations, if worthwhile, usually find their way into the journal literature.

As has been traditional with Buros Institute publications, all references are listed chronologically and then alphabetically by author within year. These reference listings are believed to be fairly complete through midyear 1984. The format for references in journals is author, title, journal, year, volume, and page numbers; for books it is author, title, place of publication, publisher, and year. A large number of additional references are listed in *Tests in Print III*, which was published in 1983.

Table 4 presents the 50 tests in this yearbook that generated the largest number of references. Within the table the tests are also rank-ordered according to number of references. This table refers only to those references listed under "Test References." The Minnesota Multiphasic Personality Inventory continues to reign supreme as a generator of references, as it did for *TIP III*, the *8th MMY*, and cumulatively throughout the history of Institute publications. The Wechsler scales also continue to hold their ground. A comparison of test ranks with parallel data presented in *TIP III* and the *8th MMY* reveals many consistencies in ranking but also some inconsistencies that can lead to interesting hypotheses about reasons for changes. The references are unquestionably valuable as additions to our cumulative knowledge about specific tests, particularly as supplements to in-house studies, and are also a valuable resource for further research.

INDEXES

As mentioned earlier, *The Ninth Mental Measurements Yearbook* includes six indexes which should be invaluable as aids to effective use: (*a*) Index of Titles, (*b*) Index of Acronyms, (*c*) Classified Subject Index, (*d*) Publishers Directory and Index, (*e*) Index of Names, and (*f*) Score Index. Additional comment on these indexes will be presented below.

Index of Titles. Since the organization of this *9th MMY* is encyclopedic in nature, with the tests ordered alphabetically by title throughout the two volumes, the test title index does not have to be consulted to find a test for which the title is known. However, the title index has some features which make it useful beyond its function as a complete title listing. First, it includes cross-reference information that is useful for tests with superseded or alternative titles or tests which are commonly (and sometimes inaccurately) known by multiple titles. Second, it provides information on which tests are new or revised. It is important to keep firmly in mind that the numbers in this index, like those for all *9th MMY* indexes, are *test numbers* and not page numbers.

Index of Acronyms. Some tests seem to be better known by their acronyms than by their full titles. The Index of Acronyms can provide very useful help in such instances; it refers the reader to the full title of the test and to the relevant descriptive information and reviews.

Classified Subject Index. The Classified Subject Index classifies all tests listed in *The Ninth Mental Measurements Yearbook* into 17 major categories: Achievement, Developmental, English, Fine Arts, Foreign Languages, Intelligence and Scholastic

TABLE 4
REFERENCE FREQUENCIES
FOR THE 50 TESTS IN THE *9TH MMY*
GENERATING THE LARGEST NUMBER OF REFERENCES

Test	Number of References	Rank
Minnesota Multiphasic Personality Inventory	339	1
Wechsler Intelligence Scale for Children—Revised	299	2
Wechsler Adult Intelligence Scale—Revised	291	3
State-Trait Anxiety Inventory	158	4
Bem Sex-Role Inventory	121	5
Peabody Picture Vocabulary Test—Revised	117	6
Wide Range Achievement Test, 1978 Edition	103	7
Eysenck Personality Inventory	91	8
Halstead-Reitan Neuropsychological Test Battery	79	9.5
Rorschach	79	9.5
Present State Examination	71	11.5
Matching Familiar Figures Test	71	11.5
Progressive Matrices	67	13.5
Sixteen Personality Factor Questionnaire	67	13.5
Bender-Gestalt Test	65	15
SCL-90-R	61	16.5
California Psychological Inventory	61	16.5
Tennessee Self Concept Scale	60	18
Profile of Mood States	58	19
Thematic Apperception Test	51	20
General Health Questionnaire	50	21
Wechsler Memory Scale	49	22.5
The Job Descriptive Index	49	22.5
Multiple Affect Adjective Check List	47	24
Personality Research Form	42	25.5
Bayley Scales of Infant Development	42	25.5
Stanford-Binet Intelligence Scale, Third Revision	41	28.5
The Luria-Nebraska Neuropsychological Battery	41	28.5
Jenkins Activity Survey	41	28.5
Group Embedded Figures Test	41	28.5
The Adjective Checklist	39	31.5
Peabody Individual Achievement Test	39	31.5
Piers-Harris Children's Self-Concept Scale (The Way I Feel About Myself)	38	33
Illinois Test of Psycholinguistic Abilities, Revised Edition	37	34
Wechsler Preschool and Primary Scale of Intelligence	33	35
Eysenck Personality Questionnaire	32	36.5
Coopersmith Self-Esteem Inventories	32	36.5
College Board Scholastic Aptitude Test and Test of Standard Written English	31	38.5
Revised Behavior Problem Checklist	31	38.5
Benton Visual Retention Test, Revised Edition	30	40.5
Metropolitan Achievement Tests, 5th Edition (1978)	30	40.5
McCarthy Scales of Children's Abilities	29	43
Comprehensive Tests of Basic Skills, Forms U & V	29	43
Iowa Tests of Basic Skills, Forms 7 and 8	29	43
ACT Assessment Program	27	45.5
Kit of Factor Referenced Cognitive Tests	27	45.5
Personal Orientation Inventory	24	47
Fear Survey Schedule	23	49
The Draw-A-Person	23	49
Embedded Figures Test	23	49

Aptitude, Mathematics, Miscellaneous, Multi-Aptitude Batteries, Neuropsychological, Personality, Reading, Science, Sensory-Motor, Social Studies, Speech and Hearing, and Vocations. Many of these categories are further subdivided into subcategories. New to this edition of the *MMY* is a table for the Classified Subject Index showing the various categories and subcategories and where they are located in the Index. Each test entry includes test title, population for which the test is intended, and test number. The Classified Subject Index is of great help to readers who seek a listing of tests in given subject areas. The Index provides for multiple listing of tests for which alternative classifications are possible, a feature which further extends the range of tests that are brought to the attention of a reader with particular subject interests. The Classified Subject Index represents a very useful starting point for readers who know their area of interest but do not know how to further focus that interest in order to identify the best test(s) for their particular purposes.

Publishers Directory and Index. The Publishers Directory and Index includes the names and addresses of the publishers of all tests included in the *9th MMY* plus a listing of test numbers for each individual publisher. This index can be particularly useful in obtaining addresses for specimen sets or catalogs after the test reviews have been read and evaluated. It can also be useful when a reader knows the publisher of a certain test but is uncertain about the test title, or when a reader is interested in the range of tests published by a given publisher.

Index of Names. The Index of Names is an analytical index indicating authorship of a test, test review, excerpted review, or reference. Reading of the instructions preceding the index is essential. Forenames have been reduced to initials in accordance with common practice. Since authors are not always consistent in the way they list their names on publications, two or more listings may refer to the same person. On the other hand, the use of initials instead of forenames increases the probability that the citations for two or more persons will be listed together. When such ambiguities involve the names of test authors or reviewers, they can be resolved by referring to the cited material, where the names are given exactly as reported in the source.

Score Index. The Score Index is a new, innovative feature being introduced for the first time in *The Ninth Mental Measurements Yearbook.* As its name implies, it is an index to all the scores that can be obtained from all the tests in the *9th MMY.* Test titles are sometimes misleading, and even test content is sometimes difficult to define with precision. But test scores represent operational definitions of the variables the test author is trying to measure, and as such they often define test purpose and content more adequately than whatever else is available. When someone is searching for a particular kind of test, the search purpose is usually defined in terms of finding a test that measures a particular variable of interest or perhaps several such variables. Test scores and their associated labels can often be the best operational definitions of the variables of interest. Hence the inclusion of a Score Index represents another effort to help the test user find the test that best fits his or her needs. It is in fact a detailed subject index based on the most critical operational features of any test—the scores and their associated labels.

HOW TO USE THIS YEARBOOK

Some Practical Advice. A reference work like *The Ninth Mental Measurements Yearbook* can be of far greater benefit to a reader if a little time is taken to become familiar with what it has to offer and how one might most effectively use it to obtain the information wanted. The first step in this process is to read the Introduction to the *9th MMY* in its entirety; the Introduction has been kept as brief and simple as possible to encourage such reading. The second step is to become familiar with the six indexes and particularly with the instructions preceding each index listing. The third step is to make actual use of the book by looking up needed information. This third step is simple enough if one keeps in mind the following possibilities:

1. If you know the title of the test, use the alphabetical page headings to go directly to the test entry.
2. If you don't know, can't find, or are unsure of the title of a test, consult the Index of Test Titles for possible variants of the title or consult the appropriate subject area of the Classified Subject Index for other possible leads or for similar or related tests in the same area. (Other uses for both of these indexes were described earlier.)
3. If you know the author of a test but not the title or publisher, consult the Index of Names and look up the author's titles until you find the test you want.
4. If you know the test publisher but not the title or author, consult the Publishers Directory and Index and look up the publisher's titles until you find the test you want.
5. If you are looking for a test that yields a particular kind of score, but have no knowledge of which test that might be, look up the score in the Index of Scores and locate the test or tests that include the score variable of interest.
6. Once you have found the test or tests you are looking for, read the descriptive entries for these tests carefully so that you can take advantage of the information provided. A description of the information provided in these test entries will be presented later in this section.
7. Read the test reviews carefully and analytically, as described earlier in this Introduction. There is a wealth of useful insight to be gained from reading these reviews, and you are well advised to take the time and make the effort to read them thoroughly and with understanding.
8. Once you have read the descriptive information and test reviews, you may want to order a specimen set for a particular test so that you can examine it firsthand. The Publishers Directory and Index has the address information needed to obtain specimen sets or catalogs.
9. The Buros Institute of Mental Measurements also offers an online computer data base service through Bibliographic Retrieval Services (BRS). The search label for the Institute data base is *MMYD*. Coverage begins with *The Eighth Mental Measurements Yearbook* (1978), and the data base provides a vehicle for regularly scheduled updates (typically monthly updates) to the material included in the 8th and 9th yearbooks. As a means for insuring the most current information possible, the combination of the *Mental Measurements Yearbooks* and the online data base service constitutes a remarkable resource for test users.
10. The Buros Institute also sponsors the annual Buros-Nebraska Symposium on Measurement and Testing, usually during the month of April. The first three symposia have included speakers of national and international renown in measurement, and each symposium has been very well received. The presentations are later published in book form. Readers of this yearbook are cordially invited to attend the symposia and to examine the symposium books for their relevance to their purposes as test users.

Making Effective Use of the Test Entries. The test entries include extensive and useful information. For each test, descriptive information is presented in the following order:

a) TITLES. Test titles are printed in boldface type. Secondary or series titles are set off from main titles by a colon. Titles are always presented exactly as reported in the test materials. When the titles on the test booklet and manual differ, the title on the test booklet or the author's preferred title (if different) is given as the preferred title of the test. In such instances the title on the manual may be given in italics in the body of the descriptive entry. When no definitive title is found in the test materials, a title is assigned by the editor and enclosed in brackets.

b) DESCRIPTIONS OF THE GROUPS FOR WHICH THE TEST IS INTENDED. The grade, chronological age, or semester range, or the employment category is usually given. "Grades 1.5–2.5, 2–3, 4–12, 13–17" means that there are four test booklets: a booklet for the middle of the first grade through the middle of the second grade, a booklet for the beginning of the second grade through the end of the third grade, a booklet for grades 4 through 12 inclusive, and a booklet for undergraduate and graduate students in colleges and universities. "First, second semester" means that there are two test booklets: one covering the work of the first semester, the other covering the work of the second semester. "1, 2 semesters" indicates that the second booklet covers the work of the two semesters. "Ages 10–2 to 11–11" means ages 10 years 2 months to 11 years 11 months; and "grades 4–6 to 5–9" means the sixth month in the fourth grade through the ninth month in the fifth grade. Commas are used to separate levels. "High school and college" denotes a single test booklet for both levels; "High school, college" denotes two test booklets, one for high school and one for college.

c) DATE OF PUBLICATION. The inclusive range of publication dates for the various forms, accessories, and additions of a test is reported.

d) ACRONYM. When a test is often referred to by an acronym, the acronym is given in the test entry immediately following the publication date.

e) SPECIAL COMMENTS. Some entries contain special notations, such as: "for research use only"; "revision of the ABC Test"; "tests administered monthly at centers throughout the United States"; "subtests available as separates"; and "verbal creativity." A statement such as "verbal creativity" is intended to further describe what the test claims to measure. Some of the test entries include factual statements which imply criticism of the test, such as "1980 test identical with test copyrighted 1970" and "no manual."

f) PART SCORES. The number of part scores is presented along with their titles or descriptions of what they are intended to represent.

g) RELIABILITY AND VALIDITY DATA. When reliability and/or validity data are absent or limited, a statement is included to inform the reader of the deficiency.

h) NORM DATA. When norm data are absent or limited, a statement is included to inform the reader of the deficiency.

i) INDIVIDUAL OR GROUP TEST. All tests are group tests unless otherwise indicated.

j) FORMS, PARTS, AND LEVELS. All available forms, parts, and levels are listed.

k) PAGES. The number of pages on which print occurs is reported for test booklets, manuals, technical reports, profiles, and other nonapparatus accessories. Blank pages and pages containing only material not related to the test (e.g., advertising pages and pages containing only printer's marks) have not been counted. Self-covers have been counted only when the cover is not duplicated by a title page inside.

l) MACHINE SCORABLE ANSWER SHEETS. All types of machine scorable answer sheets available for use with a specific test are reported.

m) COST. Price information is reported for test packages (usually 20 to 35 tests), answer sheets, all other accessories, and specimen sets. The statement "$17.50 per 35 tests" means that all accessories are included unless otherwise indicated by the reporting of separate prices for accessories. The statement also means 35 tests of one level, one edition, or one part unless stated otherwise. Quantity discounts and special discounts are not reported. Specimen set prices include specimen sets of all levels, all editions, all parts—but not all forms—unless otherwise indicated. Because test prices can change very quickly, the year that the listed test prices were obtained is also given. Foreign currency is assigned the appropriate symbol. When prices are given in foreign dollars, a qualifying symbol is added (e.g., A$16.50 refers to 16 dollars and 50 cents in Australian currency).

n) SCORING AND REPORTING SERVICES. Scoring and reporting services provided by publishers are reported along with information on costs. In a few cases, special computerized scoring and interpretation services are given in separate entries immediately following the test.

o) TIME. The number of minutes of actual working time allowed examinees and the approximate length of time needed for administering a test are reported whenever obtainable. The latter figure is always enclosed in parentheses. Thus, "50(60) minutes" indicates that the examinees are allowed 50 minutes of working time and that a total of 60 minutes is needed to administer the test. A time of "(40–50) minutes" indicates an untimed test which takes approximately 45 minutes to administer, or—in a few instances—a test so timed that working time and administration time are very difficult to disentangle. When the time necessary to administer a test is not reported or suggested in the test materials but has been obtained through correspondence with the test publisher or author, the time is enclosed in brackets.

p) AUTHOR. For most tests, all authors are reported. In the case of tests which appear in a new form each year, only authors of the most recent forms are listed. Names are reported exactly as printed on test booklets. Names of editors are generally not reported.

q) PUBLISHER. The name of the publisher or distributor is reported for each test. Foreign publishers are identified by listing the country in brackets immediately following the name of the publisher. The Publishers Directory and Index must be consulted for a publisher's address.

r) CLOSING ASTERISK. An asterisk following the publisher's name indicates that an entry was prepared from a firsthand examination of the test materials.

s) FOREIGN ADAPTATIONS. Revisions and adaptations of tests for foreign use are listed in a separate paragraph following the original edition.

t) SUBLISTINGS. Levels, editions, subtests, or parts of a test which are available in separate booklets are sometimes presented as sublistings with titles set in small capitals. Sub-sublistings are indented and titles are set in italic type.

u) CROSS REFERENCES. For tests which have been previously listed in a Buros Institute publication, a test entry includes—if relevant—a final paragraph containing a cross reference to the reviews, excerpts, and references for that test in those volumes. In the cross references, "T3:467" refers to test 467 in *Tests in Print III*, "8:1023" refers to test 1023 in *The Eighth Yearbook*, "T2:144" refers to test 144 in *Tests in Print II*, "7:637" refers to test 637 in *The Seventh Yearbook*, "P:262" refers to test 262 in *Personality Tests and Reviews I*, "2:1427" refers to test 1427 in *The 1940 Yearbook*, and "1:1110" refers to test 1110 in *The 1938 Yearbook*. In the case of batteries and programs, the paragraph also includes cross references—from the battery to the separately listed subtests and vice versa—to entries in this volume and to entries and reviews in earlier yearbooks. Test numbers not preceded by a colon refer to tests in this yearbook; for example, "see 45" refers to test 45 in this yearbook.

If a reader finds something in a test description which is not understood, the descriptive material presented above can be referred to again and can often help to clarify the matter.

A reader using the *9th MMY* as effectively as it can be used will find it a comprehensive source of important information and understanding impossible to find elsewhere. From such effective use can come substantive gains in the selection, use, and interpretation of commercially published tests.

MENTAL MEASUREMENT: SOME EMERGING TRENDS

ANNE ANASTASI
FORDHAM UNIVERSITY

[Note. As the new editor of the Mental Measurements Yearbooks, *I have decided that each yearbook should include a stage-setting, state-of-the-art review of the field of testing and measurement by a person with acknowledged preeminence in the field. Such a review would not only provide a context for summarizing current trends but would also point to promising directions for the future. For those with little background in testing, it would serve as a helpful introduction and a source of structure for making effective use of the* 9th MMY. *For those with more extensive backgrounds in testing, it would also serve as a stimulus to creative thought about the present status and possible future of testing through conceptual interaction with one of the leading figures of the field. I would hope that it would also be perceived by everyone as a well-deserved honor to be invited to prepare such a review for the* Yearbook.

Dr. Anne Anastasi is certainly the quintessential choice to be the very first person to prepare this review. Dr. Anastasi's contributions to measurement are so extensive as to be beyond the scope of this short introduction to describe. They are also very well known. Not as well known, perhaps, is the fact that she was a valued and supportive friend of Oscar Buros throughout his career as editor of the Mental Measurements Yearbooks, *and that she is the only person who has prepared test reviews for each of the nine* Mental Measurements Yearbooks. *Needless to say, I am delighted that she has accepted our invitation to write this review.—Ed.]*

Where are we today in our continuing efforts to solve long-standing problems in the construction and use of tests? Which current trends in mental measurement appear especially viable as indicators of future growth? In trying to answer these questions, I have chosen a few developments that I perceive as particularly significant. These developments fall quite naturally under three headings: the role of the test user, technical methodology of test construction, and substantive interpretation of test scores.

Role of the Test User

Tests as Tools

A conspicuous recent trend in mental measurement is the increasing recognition of the part played by the test user. Common criticisms of testing and popular antitest reactions are often directed, not to characteristics of the tests, but to misuses of the tests in the hands of inadequately qualified users in education, industry, clinical practice, and other applied contexts. Many of these misuses stem from a desire for shortcuts, quick answers, and simple routine solutions for real-life problems. All too often, the decision-making responsibility is shifted to the test; the test user loses sight of the fact that tests are tools, serving as valuable aids to the skilled practitioner, but useless or misleading when improperly used.

The increasing focus on the responsibility of the

test user is evidenced in the successive editions of the set of test standards published by the American Psychological Association and prepared jointly with two other associations concerned with testing (American Educational Research Association and National Council on Measurement in Education). In the editions published in 1954, 1966, and 1974, increasing attention was devoted to test use. The role of the test user becomes especially prominent in the 1985 edition, where it is demonstrated in several ways. The title has now been changed from *Standards for Educational and Psychological Tests* to *Standards for Educational and Psychological Testing*. The substitution of "testing" for "tests" in the later title reflects the broadened scope of the *Standards*; it calls attention to the process of test use in addition to the technical qualities of the tests themselves. The organization and content of the latest *Standards* fully support this orientation. One section (5 chapters) covers technical standards on test construction and evaluation; three sections (11 chapters) are devoted to standards for the use of tests in different professional applications and their use with special populations, as well as standards for test administration, scoring, and reporting and for protecting the rights of test takers.

Test publishers, as well as test-related committees of national professional associations, have also been giving increasing attention to the key role of the test user. Some of the major test publishers are making special efforts to improve their communication with test users, to provide the necessary information for proper test selection and score interpretation, and to help guard against common misuses of tests. Test publishers are beginning to assume some responsibility for cautioning users against popular misconceptions about what tests are designed to do and what their scores mean. Attention is also being given to spelling out more fully in test manuals the necessary qualifications of test users for different kinds of commercially available tests. It appears likely that in the years ahead we shall see cooperative action in meeting these problems of test use, action that will involve both test publishers and national professional associations.

Functions of the Test User

By test user, as contrasted to test constructor, I mean essentially anyone who has the responsibility for choosing tests or for interpreting scores and using them as one source of information in reaching practical decisions. Many test users serve both of these functions. Examples of test users include teachers, counselors, educational administrators, testing coordinators, personnel workers in industry or government, clinicians who use tests as aids in their practice, and many others in an increasing number of real-life contexts. Anyone who chooses tests or uses test results needs some technical knowledge for the proper understanding of tests. If a test user, in this sense, lacks adequate background for this purpose, he or she should have ready access to a properly qualified supervisor or consultant.

The interpretation of test scores calls for knowledge about both the statistical properties of scores and the psychological characteristics of the behavior assessed by the tests. Apart from an understanding of different types of scores, such as percentiles, standard scores, and deviation IQs, the test user needs to be familiar with the standard error of measurement (*SEM*), which serves as a corrective against the tendency to place undue reliance on a single measurement. So important is the *SEM* for this purpose, that the College Board now includes data on the *SEM* and a simple explanation of its use, not only in brochures distributed to high school and college counselors, but also in the individual score reports mailed to test takers. Even more important for test interpretation is the evaluation of score differences, as in multi-score batteries, gain scores, etc. Such evaluation requires data on the statistical significance of score differences, the intercorrelations of the scores to be compared, and the differential validity of score patterns.

Besides correct statistical interpretation, the proper use of test scores involves an adequately informed substantive interpretation. The latter requires knowledge about the behavior domain that the tests are designed to assess, including the conditions that influence the development of relevant cognitive and affective traits. It is in this connection, too, that we hear the oft-repeated caution that a test score cannot be interpreted in isolation; it needs confirmatory data from other sources, as well as information about the individual's experiential history and about the particular contexts for which the individual is assessed. Failure to observe this caution accounts for many current misuses of tests and for much popular mistrust of testing.

Clinical Use of Tests

The use of tests in clinical assessment exemplifies to a high degree the need for both statistical and substantive expertise in the interpretation of test scores. The term "clinical assessment" is conventionally used in a broad sense to designate any methodology involving the intensive study of individual cases. Thus, clinical procedures are applied not only by psychologists working in clinics but also by those who function in counseling centers, schools, and industry (especially in the assessment of personnel for high-level jobs). Information derived from interviewing and from case histories is combined with test scores to build up an integrated picture of the individual. Under these conditions, the test user has available certain safeguards against overgeneralizing from isolated test scores.

The effectively functioning clinical examiner

engages in a continuing cycle of hypothesis formation and hypothesis testing about the individual case. Each item of information—whether it be an event recorded in the case history, a comment by the client, or a test score—suggests a hypothesis about the individual that will be either confirmed or refuted as other facts are gathered. Such hypotheses themselves indicate the direction of further lines of inquiry. It should be borne in mind that even highly reliable tests with well-established validity do not yield sufficiently precise results for individual diagnosis. Hence it is understandable that clinicians as a group tend to be more receptive than other psychologists to psychometrically crude instruments, which may nevertheless provide a rich harvest of leads for further exploration.

From another angle, the availability of numerical scores from clinical instruments does not assure accuracy of interpretation; it may create only an illusion of objectivity and quantification. Such instruments are not designed for routine application but require test users with considerable psychological sophistication. The interpretive hazards inherent in clinical instruments are not limited to the misuse of tests by inadequately qualified examiners; they also occur in the rapidly proliferating computerized scoring systems that provide narrative interpretations of test performance. First, these systems must demonstrate the reliability and validity of their score interpretations, through the publication of adequate supporting data. Second, they can serve only as aids to the trained clinician, not as a substitute for the clinician. The special problems presented by commercially marketed computerized systems of narrative score interpretation have aroused widespread concern on the part of clinical practitioners, committees on testing, and national professional associations. Serious attention is being given to the formulation of workable guidelines for the effective utilization of such interpretive services.

Technical Methodology of Test Construction

Broadening Applications of Psychometric Methodology

The increasing emphasis on qualified test users has not diminished the concern for psychometrically sound instruments; on the contrary, there are promising signs of a growing psychometric orientation in fields that began with a qualitative focus, uncontrolled procedures, and subjective interpretations. These operating conditions often characterized the assessments conducted by clinical psychologists and psychiatrists prior to the 1970s. There are now numerous indications that both clinical researchers and practitioners are becoming aware of the need for detailed empirical norms and of the advantages of evaluating their techniques for such psychometric properties as reliability, validity, and the statistical discriminativeness of score patterns. These concerns are illustrated by a comprehensive, long-term project on the Rorschach, involving standardization of administration and scoring procedures, the collection of extensive normative data, and the investigation of reliability and construct validity of several scored Rorschach variables. Other examples are provided by recent efforts to integrate individualized clinical exploration with the use of psychometric data in sophisticated diagnostic interpretation of intelligence test performance.

Another clinical area that began in an antitesting mood and has moved toward the recognition of psychometric standards is that of behavioral assessment. Because of the rapid growth of behavior therapy and behavior modification programs, the development of assessment techniques to meet the needs of these programs had lagged far behind at the outset. Makeshift procedures and crude techniques were prevalent. Many practitioners, moreover, regarded behavioral assessment as fundamentally irreconcilable with the traditional psychometric approach. In the 1970s, however, several leaders in behavior therapy presented thoughtful and convincing arguments demonstrating that behavioral assessment must meet traditional psychometric standards with regard to standardization of materials and procedures, normative data, reliability, and validity. And some progress has been made in implementing these goals in the development of special procedures suitable for behavioral assessment.

Still wider applications of psychometric methodology can be found in the burgeoning field of health psychology. New types of psychometric instruments are being developed as aids in general medical practice and in public health programs. In their construction, some of these instruments have employed highly sophisticated psychometric procedures. The available instruments range widely in nature and purpose. One example is a self-report inventory designed to provide medical practitioners with information about a patient's characteristic coping styles, attitudes toward illness and treatment, and other personality tendencies that may significantly influence the patient's reaction to treatment, as well as the course of his or her illness.

Another application of psychometric techniques is exemplified by health status measures. One such instrument, developed by an interdisciplinary team, represents an effective cooperative enterprise of high technical quality. The instrument consists of a detailed inventory that can be filled out by the respondent or by an interviewer. In either case, the patient indicates which statements describe his or her actual performance or state of health on that day. Within each category, the individual statements cover the full range of possible response, from normality to complete dysfunction. Instruments such as these are beginning to serve a useful function, not only in health research, but also in the treatment of individual patients and in the administration and evaluation of public health programs.

Evolving Approaches to Test Validation

Some current developments in mental measurement reflect trends discernible in American psychology as a whole. Notable among these trends is an increasing interest in theory and a movement away from the blind empiricism of earlier decades. This theoretical orientation is exemplified by the growing emphasis on constructs in the analysis of personality and ability, as well as in the increasing use of construct validation. The term "construct validity" was introduced into the psychometric vocabulary in the first edition of the test *Standards*, published in 1954 by the American Psychological Association. The discussions of construct validation that followed—and that continue with undiminished vigor—have served to make the implications of its procedures more explicit and to provide a systematic rationale for their use. In psychometric terminology, a construct is a theoretical concept closely akin to a trait. Constructs may be simple and narrowly defined, such as speed of walking or spelling ability; or they may be complex and broadly generalizable, such as mathematical reasoning, scholastic aptitude, neuroticism, or anxiety.

It is being recognized more and more that the development of a valid test requires *multiple procedures*, which are employed sequentially, at different stages of test construction. Validity is thus built into the test from the outset, rather than being apparently limited to the last stages of test development, as in traditional discussions of criterion-related validation in test manuals. The validation process begins with the formulation of trait or construct definitions, derived from psychological theory, prior research, or systematic observation and analyses of real-life behavior domains. Test items are then prepared to fit the construct definitions. Empirical item analyses follow, with the selection of the most valid items from the initial item pools. Other appropriate internal analyses may then be carried out, including factor analyses of item clusters or subtests. The final stage includes validation and cross-validation of various scores and interpretive score combinations through statistical analyses against external, real-life criteria.

The overemphasis on purely empirical procedures during the early decades of this century arose in part as a revolt against the armchair theorizing that all too often served as the basis for so-called psychological writings of the period. But empiricism need not be blind; nor does theory need to be subjective speculation. Theory *can* be derived from an analysis of accumulated research findings and can in turn lead to the formulation of empirically testable hypotheses. Tests published since the 1970s show increasing concern with theoretical rationales throughout the test development process. A specific example of the integration of empirical and theoretical approaches is provided by the assignment of items to subtests on the basis of logical as well as statistical homogeneity. In other words, an item is retained in a scale if it had been written to meet the specifications of the construct definition of the particular scale and *also* was shown to belong in that scale by the application of statistical procedures of item analysis.

Tests are rarely, if ever, used under conditions identical with those under which validity data were gathered. Hence some degree of generalizability is inevitably required. When standardized aptitude tests were first correlated with performance on presumably similar jobs in industrial validation studies, however, the validity coefficients were found to vary widely. Such findings led to widespread pessimism regarding the generalizability of test validity across different situations. Until the mid-1970s, "situational specificity" of psychological requirements was generally regarded as a serious limitation in the usefulness of standardized tests in personnel selection. More recently, research with newly developed statistical techniques has demonstrated that much of the variance among the validity coefficients reported for industrial samples may be a statistical artifact resulting from small sample size, criterion unreliability, and restriction of range in employee samples. The subsequent accumulation of empirical evidence suggests that the validity of ability tests can be generalized far more widely across occupations than had heretofore been recognized.

In the assessment of personality traits, on the other hand, situational specificity plays a more significant part. For example, a person may be quite sociable at the office, but shy and reserved at social gatherings. An extensive body of empirical evidence has been assembled showing that individuals exhibit considerable situational specificity in several nonintellective dimensions, such as aggression, social conformity, dependency, and rigidity. Part of the explanation for the higher cross-situational consistency of cognitive than of affective functions may be found in the greater uniformity and standardization of the individual's reactional biography in the cognitive domain. Schooling is a major influence in the standardization of cognitive experience. The formal school curriculum, for example, fosters the development of broadly applicable cognitive skills in the verbal and numerical areas. Personality development, in contrast, occurs under far less uniform conditions. Moreover, in the personality domain, the same response may elicit social consequences that are positively reinforcing in one type of situation and negatively reinforcing in another. The individual may thus learn to respond in quite different ways in different contexts.

From the standpoint of personality test development, one can identify situationally linked traits, as illustrated by the familiar test anxiety inventories. Such inventories cover essentially a trait construct that is restricted to a specified class of situations, namely, those involving tests and examinations. Constructs such as test anxiety can be identified by aggregating observations *within* the situationally defined behavior domain, thereby cancelling out error variance as well as specificity that is irrelevant to the construct definition.

Item Response Theory and Adaptive Testing

Statistical techniques of item analysis have played an important part in test construction since the early days of standardized testing. These techniques have traditionally been concerned with the measurement of difficulty level and discriminative value of items. The first is based on percentage of persons giving the correct response (or in noncognitive tests, the keyed response), which is usually converted to a sigma distance from the normal curve mean; the second is based on the difference in total test score (or score on some external criterion) between those passing and those failing the item; this relation is often expressed as a biserial correlation.

It is apparent that both types of item measures are restricted to the samples from which they were derived and are generalizable only to populations that these samples adequately represent. For many testing purposes that require sample-free item measures, the procedure employed until recently was some variant of Thurstone's absolute scaling. This procedure requires the inclusion of a set of common anchor items across any two samples, in order to work out a conversion formula for translating all item values from one sample to another. A chain of linked sample values can be employed whereby all item values are expressed in terms of one fixed reference group.

With the increasing availability of high-speed computers, more precise mathematical procedures are gradually being adopted to provide sample-free measurement scales. These procedures were originally identified under the general title of "latent trait models." There is no implication, however, that such latent traits exist in any physical or physiological sense, nor that they cause behavior. They are statistical constructs derived from empirically observed relations among test responses. A rough initial estimate of an examinee's latent trait is the total score obtained on the test. In order to avoid the false impression created by the term "latent trait," some of the leading exponents of these procedures have substituted the term "item response theory" (IRT), which is now gaining usage within psychology.

By whatever name they may be called, these procedures utilize three parameters: item discrimination, item difficulty, and a lower-asymptote or "guessing" parameter corresponding to the probability of a correct response occurring by chance. Some simplified procedures, such as the Rasch model, use only one parameter, the difficulty level, on the assumption that item differences in the other two parameters are negligible or can be eliminated by discarding items. This assumption, however, has to be empirically verified for each test. IRT is gradually being incorporated in large-scale testing programs, such as the College Board's Scholastic Aptitude Test.

One of the most important applications of IRT is to be found in computer-administered adaptive testing. Also described as individualized, tailored, and response-contingent testing, this procedure adjusts item coverage to the responses actually given by each examinee. As the individual responds to each item, the computer chooses the next item on the basis of the individual's response history up to that point. This procedure is essentially similar to what the examiner does when administering individual intelligence tests, such as the Stanford-Binet. Adaptive testing achieves the same objective in less time, with far greater precision, and without one-to-one administration by a trained examiner. Exploratory research on computerized adaptive testing has been in progress in various contexts. Its operational use is under consideration in several large-scale testing programs in both civilian government agencies and military services.

Substantive Interpretation of Test Scores

Insofar as the substantive interpretation of test scores requires knowledge about the behavior domain assessed by the test, it is appropriate to look into the present status of relevant substantive areas. For this purpose, I have chosen topics pertaining to intellectual abilities, where popular misconceptions about test scores have been especially prevalent.

Reanalyses of Intelligence

Current statistical techniques of *factor analysis* grew out of early investigations of the nature and composition of human intelligence. Following the development of Thurstone's techniques of multiple factor analysis and his identification of some ten "primary mental abilities," there was a rapid proliferation of factors, in which several of Thurstone's primary abilities were broken down into narrower group factors. One way of coping with the growing multiplicity of factors is exemplified by Guilford's structure-of-intellect model. The three dimensions of this model correspond to operations, content, and products. Any test can be classified along all three dimensions. The model provides a possible total of 120 cells, in each of which at least one factor is expected, although some cells may contain more than one. The number of anticipated factors in this model is admittedly large; but Guilford argued that human nature is exceedingly complex and a few factors could not be expected to describe it adequately.

Another schema for classifying factors uses a hierarchical model. This model resembles an inverted genealogical tree: at the top is a general factor; at the next level are broad group factors, similar to some of Thurstone's primary mental abilities; these major group factors subdivide into narrower group factors at one or more levels; the specific factors are at the bottom level. Different theories focus on one or another level of this hierarchy. No one level, however, need be regarded as of primary importance; rather, each test constructor or test user should select the level most appropriate for his or her purpose. This solution corresponds to what is actually done in practice. For example, if we want to select applicants for a difficult and highly specialized mechanical job, we would probably test fairly narrow perceptual and spatial factors that closely match the job requirements. In selecting college students, on the other hand, a few broad factors, such as verbal comprehension and numerical reasoning, would be most relevant.

A word of caution should be added regarding the general factor found in a particular battery. This factor has often been loosely described as Spearman's *g*. Actually, it represents only the general factor common to the tests in that battery. To conclude from such an analysis that a given test is heavily loaded with Spearman's *g* is thus misleading. It would be more meaningful to say that the general factor identified in that battery is heavily loaded with what that test measures, which can be specified by examining the content of the test (e.g., verbal comprehension, mechanical aptitude, or whatever).

Factor analysis is no longer regarded as a means of searching for *the* primary, fixed, universal units of behavior, but rather as a method of organizing empirical data into useful categories through an analysis of behavioral uniformities. Like the test scores from which they are derived, factors are descriptive, not explanatory; they do *not* represent underlying, causal entities. There is an increasing accumulation of data showing the role of educational, cultural, and other experiential conditions in the formation of factors. It is not only the level of performance in different abilities but also the way performance is organized into distinct traits that is influenced by the individual's experiential history.

Another approach to the analysis of intelligence is that followed by *cognitive psychology*. Since the 1950s, cognitive psychologists have been applying the concepts of information processing to describe what occurs in human problem-solving. Computer programs have been designed to carry out these processes and thereby simulate human thought. In the 1970s, some cognitive psychologists began to apply these information-processing and computer-simulation techniques more specifically to an exploration of the abilities assessed by intelligence tests. A major feature of this approach is its focus on processes rather than end-products in problem solving. Analyzing intelligence test performance in terms of common cognitive processes should strengthen and enrich our understanding of what the tests measure. Moreover, assessing individuals' performance at the level of specific information-processing skills should eventually make it possible to pinpoint each person's sources of difficulty and thereby enhance the diagnostic use of tests. This, in turn, should facilitate the tailoring of training programs to individual needs.

At the same time, we must guard against attaching excess meanings to the emerging terms of cognitive psychology. Basic cognitive skills do not necessarily represent fixed or innate properties of the organism, any more than do IQs or primary mental abilities. Moreover, it is unlikely that intelligence tests will change drastically in content as a result of information-processing analyses. If these tests are to continue to serve practical needs, they must maintain a firm hold on the intellectual demands of everyday life.

Where do current intelligence tests fit into this picture? Clearly, no one test measures all of human intelligence; there are many kinds of intelligence. Each culture or other experiential context demands, fosters, and rewards a different set of abilities, which constitute intelligence within that context. Research in cross-cultural psychology provides a rich store of examples to illustrate this fact. The unqualified term "intelligence" is thus too broad to designate available intelligence tests. These tests can be more precisely described as measures of academic intelligence or scholastic aptitude. They measure a kind of intelligent behavior that is both developed by formal schooling and required for progress within the academic system. To help us define the construct assessed by these tests, there is a vast accumulation of data derived from both clinical observations and validation studies against academic and occupational criteria. The findings indicate that the particular combination of cognitive skills and knowledge sampled by these tests plays a significant part in much of what goes on in modern, technologically advanced societies. In our interpretation of intelligence test scores, the concept of a segment of intelligence, albeit a broadly applicable and widely demanded segment, is replacing that of a general, universal human intelligence.

Aptitudes, Achievement, and Developed Abilities—with Implications for Coaching

The terms "aptitude" and "achievement" are still burdened with excess meanings that may lead to misinterpretation of test results. Certain misleading connotations date from the early days of testing, when it was widely assumed that achievement tests measure the effects of learning, whereas aptitude tests measure so-called innate capacity or potentiality, independently of learning. This approach to testing reflected a simplistic conception of the operation of heredity and environment that prevailed in the 1920s and early 1930s.

It is now widely accepted that all cognitive tests measure *developed abilities*, which reflect the individual's learning history. Instruments traditionally labeled as aptitude tests assess learning that is broadly applicable, relatively uncontrolled, and loosely specified. Such learning occurs both in and out of school. Instruments labeled as achievement tests, on the other hand, assess learning that occurred under relatively controlled conditions, as in a specific course of study or standardized training program; and each test covers a clearly defined and relatively narrow knowledge domain.

A second genuine difference between aptitude and achievement tests relates to their use; achievement tests are used primarily to assess current status, aptitude tests to predict future performance. It should be noted, however, that all cognitive tests show only what the individual can do at the time, i.e., current status. How, then, can aptitude tests predict later progress? They can do so by indicating to what extent the individual has acquired the prerequisite skills and knowledge for a designated criterion performance. Moreover, under certain circumstances, traditional achievement tests can also serve as effective predictors of future performance. For example, an achievement test in arithmetic is a good predictor of subsequent performance in an algebra course. Aptitude and achievement tests are not sharply differentiated with regard to either specificity of knowledge domain or test use. They fall along a continuum of developed abilities, differing only in degree.

Once we recognize that all cognitive tests measure developed abilities, questions about test coaching can be reformulated in meaningful terms. The basic question is not how far test scores can be improved by special training, but how such improvement relates to intellectual behavior in real-life contexts. To answer this question, we must differentiate among three approaches to improving test performance; and we must consider how each approach affects the predictive validity of tests. The first is *coaching*, narrowly defined as intensive, short-term, massed drill, or "cramming," on items similar to those in the test. Insofar as such coaching raises test scores, it is likely to do so without corresponding improvement in criterion behavior. Hence, it thereby reduces test validity. A second approach, illustrated by the College Board booklet, *Taking the SAT*, is designed to provide *test-taking orientation* and thereby minimize individual differences in prior test-taking experience. These differences represent conditions that affect test scores as such, without necessarily being reflected in the broader behavior domain to be assessed. Hence, these test orientation procedures should make the test a more valid instrument by reducing the influence of test-specific variance. Finally, *training in broadly applicable cognitive skills*, if effective, should improve the trainee's ability to cope with subsequent intellectual tasks. Insofar as both test scores and criterion performance are improved, this kind of training leaves test validity unchanged while enhancing the individual's chances of attaining desired goals.

Test Bias and Cultural Diversity

The reformulation of the coaching question in terms of the relation between test performance and criterion performance is also helpful in examining the widely debated question of test bias. Test publishers have been making serious efforts to ensure that their tests are free from cultural bias against any group with which the tests will be used. Essentially, this means that the tests should be equally valid for such groups and should not underpredict the criterion performance of any group. In terms of the familiar regression model, these two goals refer to the avoidance of slope bias and intercept bias of the regression lines, respectively. Extensive research on the test performance of both adults and children against educational and occupational criteria has demonstrated that these conditions are satisfactorily met by most current ability tests.

From a broader viewpoint, all testing should be considered within a framework of cultural diversity. No test is—or should be—culture-free, because human behavior is not culture-free. We live in a pluralistic society, not only within large heterogeneous nations such as the United States, but also within the broader, worldwide society. Increasing international contacts require some reconceptualization of mental measurement. Each test should be fitted into this broad framework. For practical testing purposes, the most effective tests are likely to be those developed for clearly defined purposes and for use within specified contexts. Although these contexts will vary in breadth, none is likely to cover the entire human species. The important point is to identify the locus and range of cultural (or other experiential) context for which any given test is appropriate and then to keep both the use of the test and the interpretation of its scores within those contextual boundaries.

Tests and Reviews

[1]

A.I. Survey. Job applicants; 1982; also called Alienation Index Survey; no data on reliability; no norms; 1 form ('82, 3 pages); administration manual (no date, 5 pages); 1984 price data: $3 per 25 surveys; scoring template may be leased for $15 per year; administration time not reported; Robert W. Cormack and Alan L. Strand; Psychological Systems Corporation.*

[2]

AAHPERD Health Related Physical Fitness Test. Ages 6–17; 1980; 4 tests: Distance Run, Skinfolds, Sit-Ups, Sit-and-Reach Test; manual (77 pages); personal fitness record (4 pages); cumulative fitness record (4 pages); class composite record (1 page); superior fitness award certificate (1 page); 1983 price data: $.15 per cumulative fitness record; $.15 per personal fitness record; $.10 per class composite record; $.25 per superior fitness award certificate; $3.95 per manual; $4.25 per specimen set; administration time not reported; American Alliance for Health, Physical Education, Recreation and Dance.*

TEST REFERENCES

1. Ford, H. T., Jr., Puckett, J. R., Drummond, J. P., Sawyer, K., Gantt, K., & Fussell, C. Effects of three combinations of plyometric and weight training programs on selected physical fitness test items. PERCEPTUAL AND MOTOR SKILLS, 1983, 56, 919–922.
2. Pissanos, B. W., Moore, J. B., & Reeve, T. G. Age, sex, and body composition as predictors of children's performance on basic motor abilities and health-related fitness items. PERCEPTUAL AND MOTOR SKILLS, 1983, 56, 71–77.

[3]

AAMD Adaptive Behavior Scale. Mentally retarded and emotionally maladjusted ages 3–adult, grades 2–6, ages 3-3 to 17-2; 1969–81; ABS; formerly published by American Association on Mental Deficiency (AAMD); ratings in 21 or 24 areas: independent functioning, physical development, economic activity, language development, numbers and times, domestic activity (*a* only), vocational activity, self-direction, responsibility, socialization, violent and destructive behavior, antisocial behavior, rebellious behavior, untrustworthy behavior, withdrawal, stereotyped behavior and odd mannerisms, inappropriate interpersonal manners, unacceptable vocal habits, unacceptable or eccentric habits, self-abusive behavior (*a* only), hyperactive tendencies, sexually aberrant behavior (*a* only), psychological disturbances, use of medications; individual; 2 editions; 1984 price data (for *a* and *b*): $15 per 10 tests; $9 per manual; $14.50 per specimen set; [30–120] minutes; Kazuo Nihira, Ray Foster, Max Shellhaas, and Henry Leland; Publishers Test Service.*

a) [STANDARD VERSION]. Ages 3–adult; 1 form ('75, 26 pages); manual, 1975 revision ('74, 26 pages).

b) PUBLIC SCHOOL VERSION. Grades 2–6; no data on reliability; 1 form ('75, 26 pages, same as *a* except for deletion of items not applicable to schools); manual ('75, 184 pages); manual by Nadine Lambert, Myra Windmiller, Linda Cole, and Richard Figueroa.

c) SCHOOL EDITION. Grades 3-3 to 17-2; revised format, scoring, and profiling procedures; "simplified" administration; increased standardization sample; 5 factors from 21 scores: personal self-sufficiency, community self-sufficiency, personal-social responsibility, social adjustment, personal adjustment, plus a comparison score; 1 form ('81, 15 pages); administration manual ('81, 88 pages); diagnostic manual ('81, 75 pages); assessment booklet ('81, 15 pages); instructional planning profile ('81, 3 pages); diagnostic profile ('81, 3 pages); $17 per 20 tests; $7.25 per 20 profiles; $9.75 per manual; $22 per specimen set; manuals and profiles by Nadine Lambert and Myra Windmiller.

See T3:6 (55 references); for reviews by Morton Bortner and C. H. Ammons and R. B. Ammons, see 8:493 (25 references); see also T2:1092 (3 references); for reviews by Lovick C. Miller and Melvyn I. Semmel of an earlier edition, see 7:37 (9 references).

TEST REFERENCES

1. Lambert, N. M. Contributions of school classification, sex, and ethnic status to adaptive behavior assessment. JOURNAL OF SCHOOL PSYCHOLOGY, 1979, 17, 3–16.

2. Carsrud, A. L., Carsrud, K. B., Dodd, B. G., Thompson, M., & Gray, W. K. Predicting vocational aptitude of mentally retarded persons: A comparison of assessment systems. AMERICAN JOURNAL OF MENTAL DEFICIENCY, 1981, 86, 275–280.

3. Matson, J. L., DiLorenzo, T. M., & Esveldt-Dawson, K. Independence training as a method of enhancing self-help skills acquisition of the mentally retarded. BEHAVIOUR RESEARCH AND THERAPY, 1981, 19, 399–405.

4. Wimmer, D. Functional learning curricula in the secondary schools. EXCEPTIONAL CHILDREN, 1981, 47, 610–616.

5. Campbell, V., Smith, R., & Wool, R. Adaptive Behavior Scale differences in scores of mentally retarded individuals referred for institutionalization and those never referred. AMERICAN JOURNAL OF MENTAL DEFICIENCY, 1982, 86, 425–428.

6. Conroy, J., Efthimiou, J., & Lemanowicz, J. A matched comparison of the developmental growth of institutionalized and deinstitutionalized mentally retarded clients. AMERICAN JOURNAL OF MENTAL DEFICIENCY, 1982, 86, 581–587.

7. Matson, J. L. Independence training vs modeling procedures for teaching phone conversation skills to the mentally retarded. BEHAVIOUR RESEARCH AND THERAPY, 1982, 20, 505–511.

8. Matson, J. L., & Andrasik, F. Training leisure-time social-interaction skills to mentally retarded adults. AMERICAN JOURNAL OF MENTAL DEFICIENCY, 1982, 86, 533–542.

9. Spreat, S. The AAMD Adaptive Behavior Scale: A psychometric review. JOURNAL OF SCHOOL PSYCHOLOGY, 1982, 20, 45–56.

Review of AAMD Adaptive Behavior Scale by STEPHEN N. ELLIOTT, Associate Professor of Psychology, Louisiana State University, Baton Rouge, LA:

The AAMD Adaptive Behavior Scale, School Edition (ABS-SE) is an improved version of the original AAMD Adaptive Behavior Scale, Public School Version (ABS-PSV) (1975) and is designed to measure children's personal independence and social skills. Adaptive behavior is a critical component in the diagnostic classification of mentally retarded and is defined as "the effectiveness or degree with which the individual meets the standards of personal independence and social responsibility expected for his or her age and cultural group." The authors of the ABS-SE have done an excellent job operationalizing the first half of this definition in the form of a detailed behavior inventory. The second portion of the adaptive behavior definition implies the need for normative information with respect to sex and cultural group differences. The original version of the ABS provided such information; however, the influence of sex and ethnicity on the revised ABS has been shown to be minimal and thus is not highlighted.

The authors list nine changes in the revised ABS from the 1975 version. Of these, the most significant changes concern (*a*) an increase in the size and representativeness of the standardization sample, (*b*) an extension of the age norms downward to 3 years and upward to 17 years, (*c*) the development of factor scores, and (*d*) the inclusion of an interpretive guide for parents. These changes have ensured the ABS will remain the most comprehensive, standardized measure of adaptive behavior available. A detailed examination of these changes and critical features of the ABS-SE follow.

ITEMS AND ADMINISTRATION. The ABS-SE consists of 95 items which are conceptually clustered into 21 domains (e.g., independent functioning, physical development, economic activity, responsibility). A factor analysis of the domains resulted in a five-factor solution. The factors are labeled: Personal Self-Sufficiency, Community Self-Sufficiency, Personal-Social Responsibility, Social Adjustment, and Personal Adjustment. The first three factors are arranged virtually in a developmental progression from least complex to most complex. Skills assessed by the Personal Self-Sufficiency factor typically develop early in life and are amenable to training. In contrast, skills assessed under the Community Self-Sufficiency and Personal-Social Responsibility factors are more complex forms of behavior and require a child to generalize skills. Skills assessed by the two remaining factors are relatively independent of age.

The test can be administered as a first-person or third-party assessment. Use of the third-party method is desirable if the primary language of the informant is not English or his/her reading skills are below average. The item format varies among four types: items with hierarchically ordered responses that involve selecting the one best response; items that require selecting all applicable statements from a pool of five or six responses; items that require selecting all applicable statements from a pool of five or six responses and then subtracting the number selected from the total in the pool; and items that require a response characterizing the frequency with which a described behavior occurs. Multiple responses are possible for approximately 60% of the items. In addition, the items are displayed somewhat irregularly in a 15-page assessment booklet. The combination of varying item format and lengthy display requires careful attention to ensure responses to all items and to carry out the appropriate summing of item, subdomain, and domain scores. No evidence is provided to indicate that the accuracy of first-party and third-party administrations differs; however, my experience with the instrument would suggest that unless the respondent is familiar with the ABS, it is best to complete at least a portion of the assessment booklet under the third-party or interview arrangement. Most of the items are written in behavioral or objective terms; however, an occasional item is vague and subjective. For example, the response of "Eats too fast or too slow" (item 4) is confusing, and the response "Interacts with others imitatively (little interaction)" (item 53) is vague. One unique feature of all the items in the 11 domains clustering under the Social Adjustment and Personal Adjustment factors is the opportunity to "personalize" the inventory. This is done by adding a description of a behavior of concern that fits within a given subdomain so its frequency of occurrence can be rated.

STANDARDIZATION AND NORMS. The ABS-SE was standardized on a sample of 6,523 individuals in California and Florida ranging in ages from 3 through 17 years. A significant portion of the sample ($n = 2,135$) came from the standardization sample of the original ABS-PSV. Individuals sampled were classified (prior to and independent of standardization procedures) into one of three groups: Regular, EMR, or TMR. The TMR group may not be representative of the typical TMR population since all individuals sampled were in school and able to function away from home. Individuals from various racial/ethnic groups (i.e., black, white, Spanish-surnamed, other) and locales (i.e., rural, suburban, urban) were included. Although the sample represents only two states, the size and diversity of the sample are very good compared to other adaptive behavior scales.

Standardization data for the ABS-SE represents teachers' responses to all items on the ABS-PSV. This is an atypical procedure, but because the items are identical in content for both versions, it is not a problem. Separate norms are provided for the three reference groups for students aged 3 through 17, with the following exceptions: no EMR norms for students 3 through 6 and no norms for regular students in the 16- to 17-year-old age range. These omissions are not serious, but with little additional effort could have been avoided.

The development of separate norms for males and females and for children from different ethnic groups was a unique feature of the original ABS; however, this revision does not offer such norms. The authors conclude that "the small number of significant sex and ethnic differences on item and domain scores did not justify separate sets of norms." Unfortunately, the database for this decision is not presented. Instead, the authors refer the interested user back to the sex and ethnic norms of the original ABS, a less than satisfactory recommendation when issues of test bias are at stake.

SCORES AND SCORING. Three main types of scores are derived from the item response scores. These are Domain scores ($n = 21$), Factor scores ($n = 5$), and Comparison scores ($n = 1$). The Domain score is simply the summation of all items within a given domain, the Factor score is the summation of the Domain scores within a given factor, and the Comparison score is a weighted summation of three Factor scores (i.e., Personal Self-Sufficiency, Community Self-Sufficiency, and Personal-Social Responsibility). Thus, there is a reductive and summative progression in score derivation that results in a score that compares a child to same-aged peers in either Regular, EMR, or TMR reference groups.

Obtaining the Factor scores is a rather laborious eight-step process involving several score transformations and data transfers from the Assessment Booklet to the Diagnostic Profiles. If instructional recommendations are desired, then scores also must be transferred to the Instructional Planning Profile. Although somewhat cumbersome, the scoring process results in the most meaningful and useful information of any behavior rating instrument I have used. The tables for Comparison Score Distributions are particularly informative for making classification comparisons and illustrating to parents how their child compares to others.

RELIABILITY AND VALIDITY. Reliability data is quite limited for a revision of an established, well conceptualized test. The only form of reliability data documented in the technical manual is the internal consistency of each factor via the coefficient alpha technique. With the exception of the Personal Adjustment Factor, the coefficient alphas are high (range .71 to .97). The omission of test-retest and interrater reliabilities is a major concern for a test that can be administered to several parties (i.e., teachers, parents, guardians) and, in the case of a handicapped child, possibly several times over the course of a few years.

Two types of validity data are presented in the ABS-SE manual: (*a*) data on the relationship between adaptive behavior ratings and intelligence test performance and (*b*) data on the predictive power of the ABS for accurately classifying normal and mentally retarded children. With respect to intelligence, most of the 21 ABS domains have low to moderate correlations with IQ test performances. Noticeable exceptions were observed between IQ and the Language Development domain (r ranging from .39 to .63 depending on age group) and IQ and the Numbers and Time domain (r ranging from .33 to .62).

The capacity of the ABS to classify children accurately into categories labeled Regular, EMR, and TMR was scrutinized by the test's authors. They reported discriminant function analysis data that indicated the test does an excellent job of making the dichotomous classification between Regular and Retarded, but only a modest job of discriminating between EMR and TMR. Of course, this test would never be used alone to make such classification/diagnostic decisions. Thus, in sum, it has very good validity data to substantiate its use in screening and placement decisions.

CONCLUSIONS. The ABS-SE is far superior to any other test of adaptive behavior currently on the market. This includes the ABIC (Adaptive Behavior Inventory for Children, which is part of the System of Multicultural Pluralistic Assessment) and the CABS (Children Adaptive Behavior Scale). The test is well developed, comprehensive, and results in a plethora of diagnostic and instructional information. The reliability information is limited in nature, but the validity data is strong given the purposes of the instrument. The manuals are detailed and provide excellent resource guides for teachers and parents. In sum, the ABS-SE was constructed with sensitivity and insight into the needs of test consumers and handicapped children.

[4]

A.C.E.R. Advanced Test B40. Ages 13 and over; 1940–83; 1 form ('82, 6 pages, identical with test copyrighted in 1965); manual ('83, 11 pages, identical with manual published in 1966 except for minor editorial changes, addition of supplementary data and an introduction to the test); 1983 price data: A$2.80 per 10 tests; $2.80 per manual; $1.15 per score key; $4.20 per specimen set; 55(65) minutes; Australian Council for Educational Research [Australia].*

See T2:323 (6 references) and 7:328 (4 references); for a review by C. Sanders, see 5:296 (3 references).

Review of A.C.E.R. Advanced Test B40 by HARRIET C. COBB, Psychology Department, James Madison University, Harrisonburg, VA:

The ACER Advanced Test B40 was developed by the Australian Council for Educational Research "for use as a research instrument for selection purposes at the advanced adult level." The original form of the instrument was constructed by adapting items from the Otis Higher C Test. The test contains 77 items which have remained substantially unchanged since they were published in 1945. Additional normative data for the test were collected in 1965 and again in 1978. The current version of the manual contains these data together with test instructions and descriptions derived essentially from the 1945 version of the manual. The publishers do suggest that caution be observed in the interpretation of results, since there are no normative data on a current sample of the adult population.

The B40 requires exactly 55 minutes for administration. Raw scores from the test are converted to IQ scores utilizing the original normative data. A correction factor is provided for students below the age of 18 years. Reliability data presented for the instrument indicate a split-half coefficient of .89 with an N of 74 cases. Predictive validity data (1943 sample) are presented in which scores on the B40 are related to the academic success (Honours, Pass, Fail) of college students. Additional data are presented in the manual on mean scores and standard deviations for two samples of students 15 years and older tested in 1978. These two samples had 211 and 321 subjects respectively. A KR20 coefficient of .85 was calculated for each of these samples.

Like the Otis Higher C Test, the B40 is quick and easy to administer and score. Reliabilities reported are adequate although based on remarkably small samples. The caveat suggested by the publishers that this instrument is appropriate primarily for research purposes is well taken. The B40 does not conform to commonly accepted procedures for establishing reliability and validity. Sample sizes are too small and are not well described. Virtually no validity data of any meaningful nature are presented. At least one study (Adcock & Webberley, 1971) has suggested that the instrument does not measure reasoning and word gestalt. Certainly a test of the "*g*" factor ought to measure reasoning as one of its primary attributes. From an applied standpoint, the test has little to offer. The manual is inadequate and does not describe in any detail the construction of the test, the rationale for the selection of the items, nor the statistical procedures for validation. Inspection of individual items on the test suggests very unusual choices in item construction.

In summary, the B40 is marginally useful for research and poor for practical application without further validation of the instrument. Unfortunately, the B40 is a likely candidate for misuse and misinterpretation, since the publishers state in the manual that it "has been widely used for research and selected purposes."

REVIEWER'S REFERENCES

Adcock, C. J., & Webberly, M. Primary mental abilities. THE JOURNAL OF GENERAL PSYCHOLOGY, 1971, 84, 229–243.

[5]

ACER Advanced Tests AL and AQ (Second Edition) and BL-BQ. College and superior adults; 1953–82; 2 tests; 2 forms; manual ('82, 22 pages); 1984 price data: A$3 per 10 tests; $.77 per score key; $8.80 per manual; $13.10 per specimen set; Australian Council for Educational Research [Australia].*

a) TEST AL-BL. Linguistic; Forms A, B, ('78, 4 pages); 15(25) minutes.

b) TEST AQ-BQ. Quantitative; Forms A, B, ('78, 4 pages); 20(30) minutes.

See T3:21 (1 reference) and T2:324 (3 references); for a review by Duncan Howie, see 5:295.

Review of ACER Advanced Tests AL and AQ (Second Edition) and BL-BQ by HARRIET C. COBB, Psychology Department, James Madison University, Harrisonburg, VA:

The ACER Advanced Tests AL-AQ and BL-BQ are alternate forms structured to measure general intellectual ability. The tests were developed by the Australian Council for Educational Research for use with students in Years 11 and 12, college students, and superior adults in Australia. Each of the parallel forms contains a linguistic component including verbal analogies, vocabulary, similarities, and verbal reasoning. The tests also contain a quantitative component which measures number sequences, arithmetic reasoning, and number matrices. Administration time is approximately 25 minutes for the linguistic section and 30 minutes for the quantitative section.

The publishers suggest that the tests be used as a means of providing ability data for the counseling of students in the selection of coursework. They also indicate that the tests may be used for vocational counseling and in job selection where work requires initiative and judgment. Norms are provided in several forms including IQs, IQ ranges (based on standard error of measurement), and percentile ranks.

Directions for administration of the tests are clear and concise and require strict adherence to procedures. Considerable care is taken in the manual to provide information which will maximize test performance and minimize error variance. The test can be easily hand scored, with raw scores being interpreted through the use of multiple norms tables provided in the manual.

The current version of the ACER is a revision of the 1954 edition. Items in the new version have been revised to reflect more modern content. Standardization was based on five groups and included students ranging from 15 years old through the college level. An approximately equal number of students in the standardization sample took the AL-AQ and BL-BQ alternate forms. Subsample sizes range from 212 to 348. Samples were also drawn from 10 colleges throughout Australia, but insufficient data were derived from these samples to produce normative information.

Reliability data are presented in the form of KR20 coefficients for each of the subsamples. These coefficients range from a low of .84 to a high of .91. Alternate form reliabilities are also presented and range from .50 to .84 with typical subtest reliabilities in the .70s.

Information on construct validity is presented in the manual in the form of a principal components factor analysis of the subtests. This analysis suggests the presence of two group factors defined by high loadings for the verbal and quantitative subtests, respectively. No data are presented on concurrent validity.

The AL-AQ and BL-BQ have a number of weaknesses. The tests appear to be too short to measure with any power the factor structure described by the publishers. In addition, the alternate form reliability is below that expected for tests of this type. Given that the expressed purpose of the test is to predict performance in academic and job placements, the absence of criterion and predictive validity data is a significant flaw.

The AL-AQ and BL-BQ do possess a number of relative strengths, including good internal reliability and normative data. The reporting of IQ scores in ranges is especially appealing, given the measurement error commonly associated with tests of this type. Care has been taken to standardize this instrument with established statistical procedures. For the user of the instrument, however, interpreting the meaning of data derived from it is difficult without clear predictive and concurrent validity information. It appears that the AL-AQ has not changed significantly since its first standardization in 1954; therefore, its use in counseling students for coursework or job selection is questionable. Further research for determining predictive validity, concurrent validity, and improving reliability is highly recommended.

Review of ACER Advanced Tests AL and AQ (Second Edition) and BL-BQ by LELAND K. DOEBLER, Assistant Professor of Counseling and Educational Psychology, University of Montevallo, Montevallo, AL:

The stated purpose of the ACER Advanced Tests AL-AQ and BL-BQ is to measure general intelligence as demonstrated by the ability to see relationships and solve problems. The instruments are group tests designed for use with students in years 11 and 12 and first year students in colleges of advanced education (CAE) and technical and further education colleges (TAFE) in Australia. The two forms, A and B, each have a linguistic section and a quantitative section, presented in separate booklets. While separate scores are available for each section, the publishers caution against overinterpretation of subtest scores, suggesting that both sections are measures of Spearman's general ability factor (*g*). Each section contains 29 items. The time limit for the linguistic section is 15 minutes while that for the quantitative section is 20 minutes. The linguistic section consists of verbal analogies, vocabulary, similarities, and verbal reasoning. The quantitative section consists of number sequences, arithmetic reasoning, and number matrices. The tests are highly verbal, containing no perceptual material. As a result, the publishers caution that the tests would be inappropriate for individuals who are linguistically or culturally disadvantaged.

The publishers are to be commended for the very clear directions for administering the tests. These directions not only clearly specify the procedures to be followed, but also very nicely convey the importance of following those procedures exactly. Also commendable is the section of the manual dealing with interpretation of the scores. The types of scores reported on the tests are defined and the limitations of those scores openly discussed.

As with the earlier edition of these tests, the technical information section of the manual is strong, although there are some gaps in the information provided and the narrative is occasionally confusing. One example of this occurs under the heading of standard error of measurement. The reader is told that standard errors of measurement for the 15-year-old sample and the TAFE sample were calculated based upon KR-20 reliability coefficients and are reported in Table 19. On turning to Table 19, however, one finds *SEM* based on KR-20 reported not only for those samples, but also for the Year 11 sample, the Year 12 sample, and the CAE sample. This leaves the reader wondering what was different about the 15-year-old and the TAFE sample that caused them to be singled out in the text. However, this and other flaws in the technical data section are minor and the section is generally quite thorough.

KR-20 coefficients indicate good reliability, with all coefficients being above .70 and 80% of them (including full scale) being .80 or above. The standard error of measurement for the full scale is approximately 3 raw score points for all samples reported. The efforts of the publishers to define *SEM* and explain its application are praiseworthy. Alternate forms reliability coefficients are also reported and indicate adequate reliability.

The discussion of validity focuses primarily on construct validity. Intercorrelations of the ACER Advanced Test AL-AQ and BL-BQ with several other ACER tests are reported for the 15-year-old sample. While these correlations are consistently high, their value may be questionable since the same publishers were responsible for all of the tests. Also reported are the results of a factor analysis, which supports the contention of the publisher that the test is measuring a general ability factor. The first principal component accounts for 83% of the non-error variance on Test AL-AQ and 84% of the non-error variance on Test BL-BQ.

With regard to criterion-related validity, the authors state that no studies are yet available correlating results of this revised edition of Test AL-AQ or Test BL-BQ with scholastic achievement. In light of the nature of the tests and their suggested uses this is a major deficiency. This reviewer is not willing to attribute predictive validity to these tests based upon studies with the previous edition (1955).

In summary, this reviewer finds the ACER Advanced Tests AL-AQ and BL-BQ to be adequate tests of the general mental ability factor. The development and standardization of the tests are clearly documented and the technical information is adequately presented. The one glaring deficiency is the lack of any criterion-related validity data, although the publishers seem to suggest that this deficiency will be remedied in the near future. Until this information is provided, however, the tests should be used with extreme caution in situations where prediction of future performance is important. Since the standardization samples consisted entirely of Australian students and the results may be influenced by culture, any use of these tests outside of Australia should be preceded by the establishment of local norms.

[6]

ACER and University of Melbourne Music Evaluation Kit. Beginning of secondary school; 1976–79; MEK; criterion-referenced; 40 specific objectives in 7 areas: pitch discrimination (6 objectives), discrimination in the length of sounds (5), volume discrimination (10), tone colour discrimination (2), patterns recognition (6), identification of instruments and instrumental groups (5), knowledge of musical signs and symbols (6); no norms; no suggested standards of mastery; test administered by tape cassette; 1 form ('76, 34 sheets); handbook and report ('79, 163 pages); answer key ('76, 35 pages); 1982 price data: A$50 per complete kit; $14 per handbook and report; (105–140) minutes in 7 sessions; Jennifer Bryce and Max Cooke (test); Australian Council for Educational Research [Australia].*

[7]

ACER Checklists for School Beginners. Age 5; 1974–77; ratings by parents and teachers in 5 areas: social development, emotional development, motor skills, memory and attention, language skills; individual; forms for teacher ('74, 4 pages), parent ('74, 3 pages); manual ('77, 31 pages); 1984 price data: A$7.55 per 30 teacher's checklist and class record form; $6.75 per 30 parent's checklists; $.77 per class record form; $7.20 per manual; $7.70 per specimen set; parent's checklist available in Arabic, Greek, Italian, Maltese, Serbo-Croatian, Spanish, and Turkish; administration time not reported; Helga A. H. Rowe; Australian Council for Educational Research [Australia].*

Review of ACER Checklists for School Beginners by PATRICIA NOLLER, Lecturer in Psychology, University of Queensland, Australia:

The ACER Checklists for School Beginners were designed to provide early assessment of children starting school to aid teachers in "minimizing the influence of already existing problem areas and warding off potential difficulties which might have a negative effect on the growth and development of the school beginner." The checklists are designed to provide qualitative assessment rather than quantitative scores as provided by a "test."

Forms are provided for both teachers and parents to fill out. Both forms are attractively presented and easy to read. The Parent form is available in seven languages apart from English. Unfortunately, none of these languages is Asian, and given the present level of Asian immigration (particularly Vietnamese), consideration could well be given to the production of the Parent form in Asian languages. The Parent form provides a valuable adjunct to the assessment process since the questions generally relate to areas of which the teacher would have no knowledge. Using the Parent form of the Checklist may also be a good way of opening communication between parent and teacher.

The Teacher form allows for three administrations of the Checklist, but the format of the form could increase the likelihood that later administrations will be confounded by the results of earlier ones. A better system would allow earlier data to be folded out of sight when a new assessment was being conducted. Of course, while such a system would increase the validity of the assessments, it could also increase the cost of the forms.

Teachers are also provided with a class record sheet so that data for the whole class can be summarised on a single form. Teachers can use this form to pinpoint strengths and weaknesses which are common to the whole class, as well as to identify individual children who are developmentally behind the other members of the group.

The manual provides clear scoring criteria for each item, with information for each item regarding what is being measured (to aid teachers in their planning) and the conditions under which a minus should be scored. Information is also provided about factors to be aware of when using the checklist with particular subgroups. For some items (e.g., motor skills) the manual also provides information about how the teacher might make the relevant observations in order to obtain the required data.

The mean percentage of children passing the items is about 82%, and there are very few items which are passed by fewer than 50% of children (5 for the 1974 sample and 3 for the 1975 sample). Thus it would seem that the checklist is most suitable for identifying the small number of children who cannot pass the items and thus may have emotional or developmental problems.

Very little information is given with regard to the validity of the checklist. We are told that for a small group of children results on the checklist were compared with reports by teachers, the teachers making their reports before completing the checklist. The resulting correlation was .8, with content analysis showing that the teachers used criteria in their reports that were very similar to those used in the checklist. However, it is not at all clear what was correlated with what. More information is clearly needed if the user is to make a considered assessment of the validity of the checklist. No attempt was made to assess the predictive validity of the checklist, and this could also be a worthwhile exercise.

Kuder-Richardson data indicate that the Teacher Checklist has moderate internal consistency. A comparison of data from children tested in 1974 with a similar sample collected in 1975 indicated a fair degree of stability of mean scores with different groups from similar target populations.

Some attempt to assess inter- and intra-rater reliability would have been appropriate. It would seem feasible that teachers could be asked to fill out the checklist for the whole class, and then repeat the process within a short space of time so that there would be minimal opportunity for maturation to occur. Also, since classes at the grade 1 level sometimes involve an open plan classroom and two teachers, it may be possible to use some of these classes to have children rated by both teachers in order to assess inter-rater reliability.

Factor analysis data is also provided in the manual and there is clearly high correspondence between analyses of the 1974 data and the 1975 data. However, the five factors do not correspond well with the five subsections in the checklist. My own attempt at naming the factors resulted in the following: I–Language and Memory, II–General Behavioural Maturity, III–Social Skill, IV–Responsibility, V–Motor Skill. The question arises as to whether it would be better to maintain the current subsections and headings (since they make conceptual sense), remove the subsection headings altogether, or regroup and rename the subsections using the factor loadings. Personally I favour the latter alternative.

In summary, the ACER Checklists for School Beginners would seem to be useful assessment devices for teachers to help them identify likely problem children, and to plan their general classroom activities in the first grade. However, more research needs to be carried out to establish reliability and validity.

Review of ACER Checklists for School Beginners by JUDY A. UNGERER, Lecturer, School of Behavioural Sciences, Macquarie University, North Ryde, New South Wales, Australia:

The ACER Checklists for School Beginners is an instrument for assessing skills needed by young children for adapting to and profiting from school experience. The Checklists are based on observations of children during regular school activities, and they provide an efficient means for screening school beginners for developmental lags and experiential deficits. The Checklists are not intended for children with special difficulties, but rather are oriented toward identifying unevenness in the development and experience of ordinary children which may place them at risk for school problems.

The items comprising the Checklists assess functioning in five domains: Social Development, Emotional Development, Motor Skills, Memory and Attention, and Language Skills. The items assess specific achievements (e.g., "Tells full name on request," "Hops on one leg," "Can draw a reasonably straight line of about 10 cm in length") and provide information concerning children's styles of learning and interacting with the social environment (e.g., "Shows an attitude of enquiry," "Joins readily in play and in class activities," "Not over-aggressive"). This latter emphasis constitutes a particular strength of the ACER Checklists. An awareness of children's styles or approaches to academic and social situations is essential for designing effective learning programs and for facilitating adaptation to the school environment. It is important to understand not only what children know and do not know, but also how they go about acquiring information in order to maximize learning potential. The Checklists also underscore the importance of social and emotional development for successful entry into school. Particularly in the early years, cognitive skills alone are not sufficient to ensure optimal school functioning.

The Checklists are designed to assess what most children can and should be able to do upon first entering school. This is reflected in the fact that during experimental use of the Checklists in 1974 and 1975 with large samples of children (1,833 and 1,638 children, respectively), most items were passed by a minimum of 75% of the sample. However, there were several items in the Memory and Attention and Language Skills categories which were more difficult and were passed by considerably fewer children. It is inappropriate to consider these more difficult items as skills one would expect to find in the large majority of school beginners. Users of the scale should be aware of these differences in item difficulty when interpreting their findings.

The data comparing large samples of children in 1974 and 1975 indicate consistency from year to year in the percentages of children passing each item. In addition, profiles of performance across items were not significantly different, except in the oldest group of children aged more than 70 months. Inspection of the means and standard deviations for the different categories of items by age group indicates that the oldest group in 1974 was particularly deviant and generated scores much lower than the younger groups in that year. The differences between the scores of the same age groups in 1975 was considerably less. It appears that the 1974 sample may have included a disproportionately large number of low functioning children in the oldest age group. The validity of the Checklists' norms (i.e., means) for children older than 70 months is questionable.

No reliability data are reported for independent observers rating the same child. Although many of the Checklists' items are objective, there also are many requiring judgments which could be expected to vary from person to person (e.g., "Not unduly shy," "Does not make undue emotional demands on the teacher"). Reliability data comparing independent observers is essential for judging the true reliability of the scale.

Validity data comparing teachers' reports with Checklists' ratings are presented too briefly to permit assessment of the adequacy of the data. However, construct validity for the Checklists was demonstrated using factor analytic techniques. In addition, assessment of skills within the school setting provides considerable face validity for the instrument.

There is a Parent version of the Checklists which has been translated into seven languages, but discussion of this component of the Checklists is vague. The author states that the Parent Checklists can be a useful tool for initiating dialogue between the parent and teacher concerning the child, but no further information concerning the Parent Checklists is provided. Therefore, the practical significance of the Parent Checklists is unclear.

In summary, the ACER Checklists for School Beginners provides an efficient and sensitive means for screening school beginners for developmental lags and experiential deficits. The particular strengths of the Checklists are the focus on children's styles for learning and for social interaction in the school setting. Although reliability and validity data for the Checklists could be improved, they are sufficient to warrant use of the scales with reasonable confidence.

[8]

ACER Chemistry Item Collection: Year 12 (Chemtic). Grade 12; 1980–81; 1 form ('80, 63 pages, includes manual, answer sheet, and 7 unit chemistry tests); supplement ('81, 73 pages, includes 7 unit chemistry tests which supplement the original form); separate answer sheets may be used; 1983 price data: A$13 per form; $13 per supplement; administration time not reported; Australian Council for Educational Research [Australia].*

Review of ACER Chemistry Item Collection: Year 12 (Chemtic) by J. A. CAMPBELL, Seeley W. Mudd Professor of Chemistry, Harvey Mudd College, Claremont, CA:

The 225 items in the collection and the 317 items in the supplement are essentially all included in the Australian Chemistry Test Item Bank, which is also reviewed in this volume (101). The format and the information presented are essentially identical so that the only reason for buying this particular set would seem to be the somewhat lower cost. The evaluation presented in the other review should give adequate guidance to both sets once one allows for the fact that this set has slightly over 500 items in it and the more complete set has 2,000. Readers should refer to this more comprehensive review for additional information.

Review of ACER Chemistry Item Collection: Year 12 (Chemtic) by FRANK J. FORNOFF, Educational Testing Service, Princeton, NJ:

This publication contains 542 test questions assembled to permit Victorian secondary-school chemistry teachers to assemble diagnostic and achievement tests for use with a new curriculum. American teachers of both high school and introductory college courses will find most of the questions usable in their courses.

Most of the questions are provided with four choices, though other question formats are represented. Each question is presented with an accepted answer and a percentage correct based on administration to rather small samples of Australian high school students. The data may not be very useful to American teachers.

I found a surprisingly large percentage of questions that were a little different from questions with which I am familiar. On the other hand, the percentage of questions for which I thought the correct answer had not been recorded, the choices offered were too similar, or the Australian use of chemical terms differed from American usage, is not large.

Most of the questions in this collection have been included in the Australian Chemistry Test Item Bank, which receives a comprehensive review in this edition of the *Mental Measurements Yearbook* (101). Readers should refer to this review for additional information.

[9]

ACER Class Achievement Test in Mathematics. Grades 4–5, 6–7; 1976–79; CATIM; "based upon an 'Australia-average' syllabus"; criterion-referenced; 4 item classification areas: knowledge, computation, application, understanding; no data on reliability and validity; no norms, authors recommend establishment of local norms; 2 levels; separate answer sheets must be used; Australian Council for Educational Research [Australia].*

a) CATIM YEAR 4/5. Grades 4–5; 1979; 1 form (8 pages); teacher's manual (26 pages); class analysis chart; 1983 price data: A$.90 per test and answer strip sheet; $.35 per answer strip sheet; $1 per class analysis chart; $3.15 per teacher's manual; $5.40 per specimen set; (45) minutes.

b) CATIM YEAR 6/7. Grades 6–7; 1976–79; 1 form ('76, 8 pages); teacher's manual ('77, 26 pages); class analysis chart; price and time information same as *a*.

TEST REFERENCES

1. Marjoribanks, K. The relationship of children's academic achievement to social status and family environment. EDUCATIONAL AND PSYCHOLOGICAL MEASUREMENT, 1982, 42, 651–656.

Review of ACER Class Achievement Test in Mathematics by ROBERT W. CEURVORST, Statistician, Market Facts, Inc., Chicago, IL:

The Class Achievement Test in Mathematics (CATIM) was developed by the Australian Council for Educational Research. Two levels are reviewed here: one for grades 4 and 5, and the other for grades 6 and 7. The two levels are similar with respect to the kinds of skills tested. Each is a 45-item multiple-choice test, with three or four alternatives per item, and is based on an "Australian-average" syllabus; each is aimed at a broad assessment of the degree of progress of each student. This is as far as the authors of the test manual go in describing the rationale and development of the tests.

The test manual states that CATIM is not a norm-referenced test; hence, no normative data is provided. It is difficult to refer to CATIM as criterion-referenced, since no mention is made of any attempts to relate performance on the test to any other criteria. In fact, no validity or reliability information of any type is reported, a rather serious shortcoming. The authors recommend establishment of local norms, particularly item difficulties, to provide an interpretive framework for the test scores. Although this suggestion is a sound one, it does not relieve the test developers of the responsibility of providing users with information concerning test validity and reliability.

CATIM can be administered in a single class period (about 45 minutes), but the test is not speeded. Only about half of the items at either grade level require the student to count, add, subtract, multiply, or divide. Most of the remaining items involve finding patterns in a series of numbers, working with geometric figures (comparing sizes, mentally assembling shapes, etc.), measurement, and telling time. Six items at level 6/7 test simple counting skills, which seem like too many for students at this level; interestingly, there are only four items of this type at level 4/5.

Some of the items test skills that can be only loosely classified as math skills. At level 4/5, for example, one item presents five shapes and asks the student to determine which of four composite shapes can be built using all of them. Another item requires the pupil to identify one shape out of four that is different. One item at level 6/7 asks the student to determine the value of X in the expression "$68X - 226 = X58$." It is unlikely that the student would encounter such a problem in real life; a straightforward subtraction problem (e.g., "$684 - 226 = X$" or "$X - 226 = 458$") would be more realistic.

In some places, the foreign origin of the test becomes evident. For example, "meter" is spelled "metre" and the word "dearer" is used to connote "more expensive." The term "fraction" is used to refer to both fractions (e.g., $^1/_5$) and decimal numbers (0·2). When decimals appear, they are raised instead of at the bottom of the line, as in American style. Also, spaces are used instead of commas in printing numbers in the thousands (e.g., "1 057" instead of "1,057"). Although these characteristics may not appreciably affect test scores, an "Americanized" version with more standard notation would be more appropriate for use in the United States.

The teachers manual classifies test items by content area (counting and place value, whole numbers, common fractions, money, area, time, etc.) and by the level of thinking required (knowledge, computation, application, understanding). The distinctions among the latter categories are not as clear as the authors of the test manual would have the user believe. In level 4/5, for example, three items ask the student to determine what fraction of a figure is shaded; two are classified as understanding and one as computation. Two items ask which one of four shapes is different—one classified as application and one as computation. An item asking how many 10-cent coins make $1.50 is classified as application, whereas asking how much was spent if 45 cents in change is received from $2.00 is described as computation. A more useful classification of items would be by content area and type of math skill(s) involved (counting, addition, division, measurement, etc.).

Students record their answers on answer strips approximately 11/16 in. x 19 1/4 in. These strips are designed to be fastened side by side on a "Class Analysis Chart" on which the answer key appears. This layout simplifies the required hand scoring, since the teacher can read across a row (i.e., across students) and mark any answers that do not match the keyed response. In so doing, one can get a good idea of the difficulty of each item. In addition to simplifying scoring, the Class Analysis Chart can be used to search for patterns of strengths and weaknesses when the answer sheets are arranged, or grouped, according to some relevant criterion (e.g., some estimate of overall ability or math ability). The manual suggests arranging answer strips in order of the CATIM total score. However, this requires either (*a*) scoring the tests before attaching the strips to the chart (thus partially defeating the purpose of the chart) or (*b*) detaching and rearranging strips after scoring. Nevertheless, the answer strip/Class Analysis Chart format is potentially helpful for the user.

SUMMARY. CATIM is an Australian test designed to assess math skills of students in grades 4/5 and 6/7. Some of the items, however, test spatial relations rather than math skills, and the notation used in the tests is nonstandard for the U.S. Anyone considering using CATIM should insure that the scope of skills tested matches what is desired. The lack of documentation regarding test development, validity, and reliability, as well as some ambiguity in the item classification scheme, suggests that the CATIM has not been very carefully developed. For these reasons, CATIM is not recommended as a test of math proficiency for fourth through seventh graders.

Review of ACER Class Achievement Test in Mathematics by DAVID J. KRUS, Associate Professor of Education and Director, University Testing Services, Arizona State University, Tempe, AZ:

The ACER Class Achievement Test in Mathematics (CATIM) test series was intended to survey the mathematical skills of children in the Australian school system. The Australian nomenclature for grades/years of schooling is that "the years of schooling [are] called Year 1 to Year 12, with the final year of secondary schooling being called year 12, and numbering downward through primary school to Year 1." Reviewed here are years 4 through 7, the tests for 4/5 and 6/7 grades being printed in separate booklets with different content, but otherwise following the same format.

The CATIM test series provides information about students' performance in sections on counting and place values, whole numbers and money, fractions (both common and decimal), measurement of time (two sections), temperature, length, weight, mass, circumferences, perimeters, areas, volumes, and graphs and spatial relations. Test items in each section were also classified with respect to the "nature of the thinking process required to answer the item." These item classification categories were selected as knowledge, computation, application, and understanding. The items classified into the knowledge category require the student to define some of the main concepts of the formal arithmetic system including frequently used computational symbols and conventional terminology. The items in the computation category were aimed at direct testing of computational skills. A strength of the CATIM test series is the presentation of a number of items in the application category that measure students' ability to apply their knowledge to a cluster of reasonable, real-life problems. Students' ability to generalize acquired knowledge and to identify main principles and relationships was measured by several items in the understanding category.

Scoring of the CATIM test involves use of a "class analysis chart." This large (16 1/2 in. x 23 1/4 in.) spreadsheet was designed to be used with answer sheets that are 19 1/4 inch perforated strips with adhesive strips on the back side. All answer sheets obtained from a typical classroom of up to 35 students can be attached to a single class analysis chart. To facilitate interpretation of the visual information provided by this chart, strips may be grouped according to students' previous background, their ability, or in simple alphabetical order.

A conversion table for interpretation of the performance of a typical class in terms of percentages has been provided; however, the ACER's intent was to avoid norm-referenced, peer-group-based comparisons of students and to guide the teacher to concentrate on problem areas in the measured content categories.

Unfortunately, as is usually the case, this stress on criterion-referenced test construction was interpreted by the test authors as a license to avoid computation of reliability indices, and neither internal consistency nor test-retest reliability coefficients are provided.

In the same vein, the authors recommend the construction of local norms (not as an addition to provided norms, but in lieu of them). They also recommend the establishment of local validity criteria, based on the teacher's continuing observation of student classroom performance.

Examination of the test booklets suggests that the test items were carefully constructed. However, the direct adaptation of this test series outside of Australia would pose a difficulty, since the coins in the money section are not familiar to American students, all measurements are metric, and the temperature measurements imply the Celsius scale. Also, the recent transition from dial to digital time measurements is not captured by the test questions in the time section.

Despite these relatively minor shortcomings, the CATIM appears to be a carefully designed criterion-referenced measurement instrument with an interesting format and a potential for quick identification of a student's problem areas. Its use outside of the Australian school system would necessitate modification of the contents of some items. This otherwise promising test series would definitely benefit if its authors would develop appropriate norm tables providing a frame of reference for local norms. Demonstration of the validity and reliability of this test package should be a high priority of the CATIM authors in the subsequent editions of this test.

[10]

ACER Early School Series. Age 5–5 ¹/₂ -year-old school beginners; 1981; ESS; criterion-referenced; estimation of cognitive development and maturity for early identification of children who may be at risk of developing learning disabilities; handbook entitled *Early Identification and Intervention*; 10 tests; no reading or verbalizations required by examinees; handbook (153 pages, contains general manual); 1983 price data: A$43 per complete kit including 5 copies of each test, 1 directions for administration for each test, 1 score key for each test, and handbook; $1.40 per directions for administration for any one test; $9.70 per handbook; Helga A. H. Rowe; Australian Council for Educational Research [Australia].*

a) TESTS OF AUDITORY ANALYSIS SKILLS. 2 tests.

1) *Auditory Discrimination Test.* Includes same types of sound-contrasts used in the Wepman Test; 1 form (8 pages); directions for administration (16 pages); $5.60 per 10 tests; $.84 per score key; (20–25) minutes.

2) *Recognition of Initial Consonant Sounds Test.* Authors recommend administering in several sessions; directions for administration (16 pages); prices same as for *a*1 above; (15) minutes for every 4 items.

b) CONCEPTUAL SKILLS TESTS. 2 tests.

1) *Number Test.* 1 form (7 pages); directions for administration (10 pages); prices same as for *a*1 above; (12–20) minutes.

2) *Figure Formation Test.* Provides rough indication of child's general intellectual maturity; 1 form (11 pages); directions for administration (7 pages); $8.40 per 10 tests; $1.15 per score key; (5) minutes.

c) LANGUAGE SKILLS TESTS.

1) *Tests of Syntax.* 5 tests; $2.80 per 10 tests for any one test; $.56 per score key for any one test; (3–15) minutes per test.

(*a*) Preposition Test. 1 form (4 pages); directions for administration (8 pages).

(*b*) Pronouns Test. 1 form (4 pages); directions for administration (8 pages).

(*c*) Verb Tense Test. 1 form (4 pages); directions for administration (7 pages).

(*d*) Negation Test. 1 form (3 pages); directions for administration (7 pages).

(*e*) Comprehension Test. 1 form (3 pages); directions for administration (7 pages).

2) *Word Knowledge Test.* Designed to identify children unable to comprehend a sample of English words which many Australian teachers would expect from 5-year-olds; 1 form (11 pages); directions for administration (9 pages); prices same as for *b*2 above; (15–20) minutes.

[11]

ACER Higher Tests. Grades 9 and over; 1944–82; formerly called ACER General Ability Test: Advanced M; "general intelligence"; 2 parts yielding 3 scores: linguistic, quantitative, total; reliability data for 15-year-olds only; norms for grades 9 and 13 only; 2 parallel forms: Forms ML-MQ (2nd edition), PL-PQ, ('82, 4 pages); manual ('81, 36 pages); 1984 price data: A$3 per 10 tests; $.77 per key; $7.55 per manual; $11.85 per specimen set; 15(25) minutes for Section L (linguistic), 20(30) minutes for Section Q (quantitative); Australian Council for Educational Research [Australia].*

See T3:28 (2 references), T2:325 (1 reference), and 6:432 (1 reference); for a review by C. Sanders, see 5:297.

Review of ACER Higher Tests by ERIC F. GARDNER, Margaret O. Slocum Professor of Psychology and Education Emeritus, Syracuse University, Psychology Department, Syracuse, NY:

The ACER Higher Tests M (2nd edition) and P are spiral omnibus aptitude tests patterned after the Otis but offer separate linguistic and quantitative scores. The previous edition of this test, ACER Higher Test M, was last reviewed in Buros' *Fifth Mental Measurements Yearbook* by C. Sanders, Professor of Education and Dean of the Faculty, University of Western Australia, Nedlands, Australia. The review was highly favorable in terms of the quality of its construction and manuals. The total test and subtests were judged to be reasonably valid and reliable but were criticized for lacking females in the normative sample at the upper end of the scale.

ACER Higher Tests ML-MQ (2nd edition) and PL-PQ maintain the same high quality items contained in their predecessors. The manual is, in general, well written and contains important information about the construction and technical characteristics of the tests. Detailed instructions for administration and scoring are presented. The ML-MQ (2nd edition) and PL-PQ were designed to be parallel in format and in item type. Both forms M and P have a linguistics (L) section and a quantitative (Q) section which are presented in separate booklets. However, as the manual states, "While Test P is designed as a parallel test to Test M, it is not an exact equivalent in content and difficulty level." However, this caveat is not mentioned during the description of the tests but only as an explanation for the usual lower estimates of reliability associated with the lack of test form parallelism. It would have been helpful to the reader to have mentioned this fact after the first sentence of the introduction, "The ACER Higher Test ML-MQ and Test PL-PQ are parallel forms of a group test designed to measure general intellectual ability." Nevertheless, the appropriate procedures have been followed and presented in the manual (e.g., there are separate norms for each test including separate IQs and other derived scores).

Norms are obtained from a sample of 15 1/2-year-olds from 40 secondary schools in New South Wales and a second set of norms from students in 20 Australian technical and further education institutions. Adjustments are made for IQs for ages from 13.0 through 17.6. No details are given regarding the way the derived values were obtained for the other age cohorts, but apparently some sort of extrapolation was used. It would have been desirable to obtain normative data directly from other age cohorts. The norms are apparently appropriate for an Australian population. The extent to which the IQs obtained would be appropriate for other groups such as those in the United States is questionable. At least no comparative data were presented.

The authors do present data that are not common among aptitude tests yielding verbal and quantitative scores. That is, they discuss the reliability of the differences between these scores as well as the reliability of each individual test score itself. Reliability coefficients (KR20) are in the low .90s, showing a consistency with other types of aptitude tests using somewhat similar item types. Alternate forms reliability coefficients for the 15 1/2-year-old sample are also presented, and they range between .83 and .90 for the entire test and .64 and .88 for the verbal or quantitative scores separately.

A rather detailed discussion of validity is presented including comments on each of the three kinds: content, construct, and criterion-related. No data are presented correlating performance on Revised Test M or Test P with scholastic achievement. The results of several studies conducted in 1949–53 with the earlier edition of Test M are presented in the manual. Evidence of construct validity is provided by correlation coefficients for Revised Test M and Test P with several other tests of general ability. The correlation coefficients between the verbal scores of Test M and P are higher than those between the verbal and the quantitative. Further evidence of construct validity is provided by a factor analysis in which the major portion of the variance was accounted for by a single factor, supporting the use of a single score for each form. A second factor was shown to be bipolar, supporting the use of a verbal and quantitative score. Correlation coefficients for the two tests and their subtests with the Otis range from .73 to .85. This evidence of concurrent validity is what would be expected in view of the origin and general quality of the new tests.

CONCLUSION. In general, the ACER Higher Tests contain the types of items which have been used successfully since the early Otis Aptitude Tests. In the manual, the writer discusses validity more thoroughly than is common for such tests, presents a minimum amount of empirical validity data, presents both Kuder-Richardson and comparable forms reliability coefficients, discusses the reliability of a difference, and stresses the importance of knowing and using the standard error of measurement in interpreting both individual scores and difference scores. Since the tests are aptitude tests, it is surprising there is no evidence of predictive validity. This may be forthcoming later but is badly needed. Normed on 15 1/2-year-olds and a group of first year students in technical institutions in Australia, the normative group has been carefully selected and is appropriate for Australian populations. No evidence is given showing the comparability of the Australian norms and norms in other countries such as the United States and Great Britain. It is a quality test and, in view of the experience with its predecessor, is undoubtedly a highly useful instrument in Australia.

Review of ACER Higher Tests by SHARON L. WEINBERG, Professor of Educational Statistics, SEHNAP, New York University, New York, NY:

The ACER Higher Tests ML-MQ and PL-PQ, published by the Australian Council for Educational Research, are "parallel forms of a group test designed to measure general intellectual ability" in students in educational Year 9 or higher, young people who have left school, and adults. Because the test is intended primarily to predict scholastic achievement, the test is restricted to a variety of verbal and quantitative material. Items covering the ability to see relationships and to solve problems are included in the test, but items covering non-verbal perceptual material related to general cognitive ability are not included. The test is organized into two separate sections presented in two separate test booklets—a linguistic section (ML) and a quantitative section (MQ). Test ML and its parallel form, PL, each consist of 34 items including verbal analogies, vocabulary, similarities, and verbal reasoning. Test MQ and its parallel form, PQ, each consist of 34 items including number series, arithmetic reasoning, and number matrices. Administration time for the complete test is given as 1 hour. While separate scores are available for each section, the manual makes it clear that they are not intended as measures of distinct abilities. Rather, they are to "be regarded as substantially measures of the same general ability" factor as described by Spearman's *g*. The ACER Higher Tests, Forms ML-MQ are a revision of the Higher Test M originally prepared by the Australian Council for Educational Research in 1944. In the revision the publisher has sought to update norms which were no longer believed to be accurate and to update content as well. Forms PL-PQ were developed as new parallel forms of the revised M tests. For a review of the earlier test see C. Sanders (5:297).

ITEM QUALITY. While the items appear to be well written, no real data are provided regarding the original item analysis used for item selection. We are told that a pool of 320 items (which appears to include the original ML-MQ items) was administered in four trial forms (presumably 80 per form) "to students in Years 10, 11, and 12 in a number of state high and technical schools and independent schools (Catholic and non-Catholic)." Items which met a "satisfactory" level of discrimination were selected to define the two final forms, which consisted of 34 items each. More information regarding what constitutes a "satisfactory" level of discrimination seems warranted. Moreover, while we are told that item difficulties were calculated, they are not reported in the manual.

NORMS. The revised tests have been standardized on 1,737 fifteen-year-old students enrolled in New South Wales secondary schools and on close to 400 first year students enrolled in Australian TAFE (technical and further education) institutions. All schools were selected randomly, with the probability of selection being a function of the school's enrollment size. Because sampling was limited to students, the normative sample does not represent the other two groups of individuals for whom the test is intended, namely, young people who have left school and adults. Furthermore, because a breakdown by sex, race, or culture is not provided, we do not know the extent to which the normative sample represents the student group.

IQs, percentile ranks, and stanines are available for the 15-year-old sample (noted 15 years 6 months); percentile ranks and stanines are available for the first year TAFE students. The IQ score is a deviation IQ, comparing an individual's standing to others of his/her norm group. To obtain the IQ score of an individual whose age is not exactly 15 years 6 months, the manual provides age correction tables. Unfortunately, these tables are based on a 1955 standardization of Test M. Considering that the test has been revised to update inaccurate norms, one must seriously question the utility and validity of the age correction values provided.

RELIABILITY. Kuder-Richardson estimates of internal consistency reliability for the total test are very high for both the 15-year-old and TAFE students, ranging from .91 to .93. Alternate forms reliability, computed on a subset of the 15-year-old sample ($N = 202$), are, as expected, somewhat lower, ranging from .83 to .90. While Test P is designed to be a parallel form of Test M, the manual notes that Test P "is not an exact equivalent in content and difficulty level." Hence, the claim of parallel forms must be viewed with a certain degree of caution.

VALIDITY. Since the ACER Higher Tests are primarily intended to predict scholastic achievement, it is disappointing to read that "no studies are as yet available correlating performance on the Revised Test M or Test P with scholastic achievement." While correlations with scholastic achievement are reported in the manual, they are based on studies carried out in 1949 using the original test. Hence, they are of limited value in assessing the validity of the current, revised version.

Correlations are reported between the total score on the revised Tests M and P and the revised ACER Advanced Test B40, the Otis Higher Test, Form A, and the Standard Progressive Matrices Test based on the current standardization sample. Both Tests M and P correlate quite respectably with the former two tests (from .83 to .86), but only .50 (Test M) and .57 (Test P) with the latter test.

A principal components analysis on the 15-year-old normative sample was carried out on both M and P forms. Factorially, Forms M and P appear to be equivalent. Before rotation, a general factor accounts for 60% of the total variance in each form, with patterns of loadings being generally similar across forms. After rotation, the variance divides into a verbal and quantitative factor, each accounting for about 35% of the variance.

SUMMARY AND CONCLUSION. While there may be a need in Australia for a standardized group intelligence test with sound psychometric properties, without a more complete set of validation and standardization data, the ACER Higher Tests ML-MQ and PL-PQ cannot be recommended to fill this need. This reviewer would like to urge the publisher to continue efforts to amass the kind of supporting evidence that would be needed to endorse the use of the ACER in Australia. Without cross-cultural norming and standardization data, the ACER Tests cannot be recommended for use outside Australia.

[12]

ACER Intermediate Test F. Ages 10–15; 1980–82; based upon a revision of ACER Intermediate Tests A and D; 1 form ('80, 7 pages); manual ('82, 56 pages); scoring key ('82, 2 pages); 1983 price data: A$.55 per test; $1.15 per scoring key; $7.40 per manual; $9.10 per specimen set; 30(50) minutes; manual by Marion M. de Lemos; Australian Council for Educational Research [Australia].*

[13]

ACER Intermediate Test G. Ages 10–15; 1980–82; based on a revision of the still-in-print ACER Intermediate Tests A and D; general reasoning ability; 1 form ('80, 7 pages); manual for administration and interpretation ('82, 48 pages); not available to government schools; 1984 price data: A$.60 per test; $1.30 per scoring key; $8.15 per manual for administration and interpretation; $10.40 per specimen set; 30(50) minutes; manual by Marion M. de Lemos; Australian Council for Educational Research [Australia].*

Review of ACER Intermediate Test G by DON B. OPPENHEIM, Director of Institutional Research, Rutgers, The State University of New Jersey, New Brunswick, NJ:

This test is designed to be a test of general reasoning ability for students from 10 to 15 years of age. It is based on a revision of ACER Intermediate Tests A and D, retaining selected items from these tests as well as from earlier versions of the test. In addition to the retained items, items were modified and new items were prepared for trial forms. After an extensive trial administration, final forms were prepared based on traditional as well as Rasch model item statistics, the specification of items by item type, and a desire to have enough easy and very difficult items. The test has a somewhat heavier emphasis on quantitative reasoning than is typical in group intelligence tests.

The manual for the test is very complete and readable, providing technical information in a very understandable form. Directions for administering the test are specific and clear. The norming procedure is well described. Alternate form reliability as well as an internal consistency measure are reported for each approximately half-year age range as well as across all ages. The alternate form reliabilities range from .87 to .92, while the measure of internal consistency, Cronbach alpha, ranges from .94 to .96, high enough to justify use for individual decision making. The interpretation of the standard error of measurement, which ranges from 3.16 to 3.32, is discussed. The manual wisely indicates in several places that important decisions require other evidence of a student's ability in addition to a single test score. While criterion-related validity data are unavailable, reasonable claims are made for content validity. Construct validity is reported in terms of correlations with the Australian Adaptation of the Otis-Lennon School Ability Test, fairly regular increases in scores with age, and the results of several factor analyses. The evidence seems to support the contention that the test measures a general factor corresponding to the Spearman *g* factor.

An unusual aspect of the test is that while the general format is that of 4- or 5-choice multiple choice questions, a number of the quantitative reasoning items do not provide choices and ask the student to determine and write his or her answer. Since answers are written directly in the test booklet rather than on a machine-scorable answer sheet, the student-generated responses can be scored as easily, using the key provided, as can the answers for the multiple choice items. However, the fact that all scoring must be done by hand would make large test administrations burdensome, both in determining raw scores as well as in converting scores to the corresponding deviation IQ scores.

A second criticism is the complete lack of information given either to the test administrator or to the student regarding guessing. With the majority of the items being multiple choice with no correction for guessing, it clearly would be advantageous, for these items, to guess in cases when the correct answer is unknown. No consideration is given to this issue in the manual and its instructions.

Finally, while the test appears to have had an appropriate norming in Australia in 1980, potential users in the United States are warned that there are no United States norms. This is not a criticism of the test, which was developed and normed to be used in Australia. Rather, it is a caution that while the test is short, reliable, and valid, and therefore may be considered for use elsewhere, its routine use outside of Australia would be inappropriate without more local data.

[14]

ACER Listening Test. Ages 10, 14; 1981; 2 levels; no data on reliability; 1984 price data: A$56.40 per complete kit including 35 answer booklets, teachers handbook, analysis chart, and cassette; $1.30 per answer booklet; $5 per analysis chart; $3.80 per teachers handbook; Australian Council for Educational Research [Australia].*

a) FOR 10-YEAR-OLD STUDENTS. Ages 10; 10L; 6 scores: comprehending words and statements, understanding instructions, comprehending passages, comprehending conversation, comprehending in different situations, total; 1 form; answer booklet (11 pages); analysis chart (9 pages); teachers handbook (26 pages); (30–35) minutes.

b) FOR 14-YEAR-OLD STUDENTS. Age 14; 14L; 6 scores: same as for *a* above; 1 form; answer booklet (12 pages); analysis chart (11 pages); teachers handbook (25 pages); (35–40) minutes.

Review of ACER Listening Test by ROGER A. RICHARDS, Professor of Communication and Chairman of the Department, Bunker Hill Community College, Boston, MA:

This Australian test makes a favorable first impression. Partly because the need for a good listening test is so great and partly because this one does several things quite well, it is greeted with high hopes. Upon probing a bit, however, we find its appeal to be largely superficial.

The ACER Listening Test (ACERLT) is offered primarily as a mastery test. Its basic purpose is underscored by the authors' statement that "where deficiencies in student performance are revealed, the specific ability a student does not possess is identified by the nature of the assessment." Unfortunately, this tautology reveals not only the test's purpose but also its clumsiness and lack of depth.

Among this test's virtues is the use of a cassette tape to assure both ease and uniformity of administration. Since the tester only starts and stops the tape at designated points, variations introduced by individual test administrators—a defect in many listening tests—are minimized.

A second virtue is the quality of the tape. The pacing is lively but not rushed, and the sound is of good quality. The reading is generally clear and refreshingly free of stiltedness or the affectation of over-acting. (For use outside Australia the tape obviously would need to be re-recorded in appropriate accent and dialect.)

A third strength of the ACERLT is its content. Material has been well selected. The use of an actual radio broadcast in one section and of everyday situations in others should make the test seem quite natural for most students.

A further virtue is the attempt to facilitate diagnosis by testing for mastery. The test is organized by major skills, and a number of subskills are identified for scoring. An elaborate chart (more about that later) is provided for recording the many derived scores. At a time when teachers at all levels tend to be concerned with mastery, this approach is welcome. Unfortunately, it is the intention, rather than the execution, that is to be commended, for the test's actual diagnostic value is very limited.

These assets are heavily outweighed by a number of serious shortcomings:

(1) The most glaring limitation is the absence of validity, reliability, test-development, norming, or other basic data. The user wanting such information is forced to seek out two separate publications. (And outside Australia the needed books are very difficult to find.) This error of omission can scarcely be excused. If the publisher has any expectation of winning acceptance for the test, some summary of the cited works must be provided. Otherwise, the ACERLT deserves to languish in disuse.

(2) Although the test is packaged in two forms (Form 10L, consisting of 47 items; and 14L, of 49 items), more than three-fourths of the items (37) appear on both forms. Given this fact, is it legitimate to refer to the separately printed versions as two "forms"?

(3) The population to whom this test should be administered is by no means clear. The titles of the two forms are unambiguous enough: "ACER Listening Test for 10-Year-Old Students" and "ACER Listening Test for 14-Year-Old Students." But this clarity is muddied by the Teachers Handbook. To their credit, the authors anticipate questions concerning how the test can be administered to all 10- or 14-year-olds when the grade levels are not based strictly on age. Under the heading "Year Level" they offer this explanation: "The majority of 10-year-old students would be contained in Year 5, but Year 4 and Year 6 would also contain a number of students at this age level. Thus the test would be suitable at these latter Year levels provided the intended age was kept in mind when student performance was assessed." A similar passage extends Form 14L to Years 8 through 10. The trouble is that we are given absolutely no guidance on how "the intended age" should be "kept in mind." There are no data about performance by students in grades 4 and 6 (who, incidentally, may be as young as 8 or as old as 12) or those in grades 8 and 10 (who may be as young as 12 or as old as 16). On the contrary, the only available statistics—"item facilities" (the percentage of the tested population who answered each item correctly)—"were calculated using a student population of 1,289 10-year-olds" and "1,303 14-year-olds."

(4) A troubling characteristic of the test is that it is so easy. Almost half the items (20 of 47 on Form 10L and 21 of 49 on 14L) have reported facility scores of 95% or higher, while the median score is approximately 88% for Form 10L and 90% for Form 14L. For Form 14L the median score equals the maximum score on two sections, exceeds the cutoff (or mastery) score on four of the five sections, and equals the cutoff score for the fifth section. Furthermore, of the 10 items included in Section A, Words and Statements of Form 14L, six have facility scores of 100%, three of 99%, and one of 95%. And only four items on each form were answered correctly by fewer than 50% of the students in the tryout population.

The test's intended use as a mastery instrument apparently accounts for its easiness. Although the works detailing the test's construction were not supplied for review purposes, this reviewer did locate a companion volume dealing with ACER's tests of "literacy" and "numeracy" (the listening test is said to measure "oracy"). Of those tests the authors say: "they did not seek to discriminate between students at the upper end of the performance scale as is common in selection tests. Nor were they designed to suit the average student by extending the range of scores as widely as possible as is appropriate for normative testing. These tests attempted to distinguish between students with regard to their level of performance on essential tasks and thus to discriminate between students at the lower end of the ability scale."

The problem is that this approach does not fit reality. Listening is not like the alphabet or multiplication table. It is not learned fairly well at an early age and retained thereafter by the vast majority of students. On the contrary, both everyday observation and the bulk of listening research attest to the widespread inability of people to listen accurately. It does not make sense, therefore, to base a listening test for 5th- and 9th-graders on the assumption that all but a few of them have mastered the covered skills. Only those who accept that fallacious assumption will find this test usable. In fact, widespread use of the ACERLT would do great harm. Because it is so easy, most students would achieve high scores. These high scores, in turn, would deceive teachers into concluding that their students know how to listen. The neglect of listening in the curriculum would thus be perpetuated.

(5) The archaic, time-consuming scoring procedures make the usability of the ACERLT close to nil. The tester is required to record each answer for every student on a large, multi-page Analysis Chart and then to record each section score on the detachable last page of the chart. Beyond that, the computation of subscores is so cumbersome that it is difficult to imagine any busy teacher having time to do it. Computerization would, of course, be ideal; but short of that, other common techniques could reduce the sheer drudgery inflicted upon teachers.

(6) Some of the test's questions do not seem to measure good listening habits. Among them are those that are answerable on the basis of common sense by students who might not have even heard the passages upon which they are ostensibly based. At the opposite extreme, other questions are too "picky." After listening for the general sense of a passage, one is tricked by a question so specific that even a good listener might not have caught the answer. A practice question supplies an example. A passage reads as follows: "The chilling sound of nature out of control. A sound that people in the southern part of Western Australia hope they won't hear again for a long long time." Now, there are three important ideas here—the eeriness of the sound, the source of the sound, and the desire not to hear the sound again. The question, unfortunately, does not deal with any of those ideas but instead asks, "Which part of Western Australia was mentioned?" We could well argue that a poor listener has a better chance of getting this question right by becoming fixated on trivia than has a good listener who pays attention to the larger message.

(7) The most serious failing of the ACERLT is its lack of a sound theoretical base. The section titles reflect the skills which the authors apparently believe make up the construct known as "listening." These skills are (*a*) Comprehending Words and Statements, (*b*) Understanding Instructions, (*c*) Comprehending Passages, (*d*) Comprehending Conversation, and (*e*) Comprehending in Different Situations. These five areas do not appear to be based on sound logic, for the categories are by no means discrete. "Comprehending Words and Statements" overlaps all four other skills. And what is the difference between "Understanding Instructions" and "Comprehending Passages"? Are instructions not made up of passages? And what would it mean if we found that a student had mastered "Understanding Instructions" but had failed to master "Comprehending Words and Statements"?

Suffering from the same problems and illogic are the eight subskills: (1) Comprehending Words, (2) Comprehending Statements, (3) Comprehending Literal Meaning, (4) Comprehending Implied Meaning, (5) Identifying Audience, (6) Identifying Purpose, (7) Making Critical Judgments, and (8) Recognizing Emotive Language. Again, there is much overlap. Isn't recognizing emotive language part of making critical judgments? How can one make critical judgments without comprehending both literal and implied meaning? And how can comprehending either literal or implied meaning occur without also comprehending words and statements? The problem intensifies when we look at the five main sections of the test to which the specified tasks are assigned. "Comprehending Literal Meaning" and "Comprehending Implied Meaning," for example, are listed under Section C—"Comprehending Passages."

Many similar objections could be raised, but they would all point to the same fatal flaw: the lack of an integrated theory of listening to undergird the framework of the test. Three separate dimensions are addressed: units of discourse (words, statements, passages); contexts (conversation, "different situations"); and decoding processes (distinguishing literal from implied meaning, identifying audience, identifying purpose, etc.). These dimensions have been meaningfully integrated by various communication theorists, but no reference is made to any of their work. The dimensions of listening are, rather, treated as a formless hodge-podge.

CONCLUSION. Despite the foregoing recitation of unacceptable features, this reviewer hopes that the ACER Listening Test can be recycled into something quite useful in both Australia and the rest of the English-speaking world. Certainly its use cannot be recommended at this time. In its present form it shows only a potential.

REVIEWER'S REFERENCES

Bourke, S. F., & Keeves, J. P. AUSTRALIAN STUDIES IN SCHOOL PERFORMANCE: VOLUME III, THE MASTERY OF LITERACY AND NUMERACY. Education Research and Development Committee Report No. 13. Canberra: Australian Government Publishing Service, 1977.

[15]

ACER Mathematics Profile Series. Grades 4–10; 1977–83; MAPS; no data on reliability and validity; norms for non-representative students only, publisher recommends use of local norms; 5 tests; teacher's handbook, experimental edition for each test (dates same as for test, 16–48 pages); score key for tests *a, b, c, d,* (dates same as for test, 2 pages); answer and record sheet for test *a, b, c, d,* (dates same as for test, 1 page); self-scoring answer sheet for review test ('83, 1 page); 1983 price data: A$.56–$1.70 per test; $1.40 per 10 answer and record sheets; $.45 per review test answer sheet; $.97 per score key; $5.10–$8 per teacher's handbook; $6.35–$10.80 per specimen set; Greg Cornish and Robin Wines; Australian Council for Educational Research [Australia].*

a) OPERATIONS TEST. Grades 4–10; 1978; 1 form (7 pages); 5 overlapping levels (grades 4, 5–6, 7–8, 8–9, 9–10) in a single booklet; (30–50) minutes.

b) SPACE TEST. Grades 5–10; 1978; 1 form (34 pages); 4 levels (grades 5–7, 7–8, 8–9, 9–10) in a single booklet; (30–50) minutes.

c) MEASUREMENT TEST. Grades 7–10; 1979; 1 form (19 pages); 3 levels (grades 7–8, 8–9, 9–10) in a single booklet; (30–50) minutes.

d) NUMBER TEST. Grades 7–10; 1980; 1 form (15 pages); 3 levels (grades 7–8, 8–9, 9–10) in a single booklet; (30–50) minutes.

e) REVIEW TEST. Grades 7–10; 1983; items chosen from each of the four longer tests in the series; used to select the appropriate test to administer; 1 form (11 pages); (60–80) minutes.

Review of ACER Mathematics Profile Series by JEFFREY K. SMITH, Associate Professor of Educational Statistics & Measurement, Rutgers University, New Brunswick, NJ:

The ACER Mathematics Profile Series is a remarkably ambitious attempt to effect a confluence of current educational, psychological, and psychometric theory in a series of measures of mathematics ability. It is difficult to assess the success of this undertaking since so little technical information is provided in support of the intended interpretations of test results.

The Series is designed to measure the development of mathematical ability and contains four tests. Each of the tests is broken into three or four units of increasing difficulty. Students would typically respond to 20 to 32 items on any given test in the Series. The particular items taken by a student would be determined by his/her age and a teacher estimate of ability. The Operations test consists of equations such as "44 x 125 = 125 x ?" as stems and four options are given to complete the equation. The first 20 items cover elementary mathematical operations using small numbers; the second 20 items are the same problems with large numbers; the final 20 items use letters in place of numbers. The Number test consists of 90 multiple choice items in three units covering areas such as natural and rational numbers, logarithms, ratios and percentages. The item format might best be described as "word problems," and there is frequent use of graphs and other visual displays. The Measurement test consists of 90 multiple choice items in three units covering areas such as statistics, money, area, volume, time, and measurement systems. Again, the word problem format is used and about half of the problems involve interpretation of visual displays. The Space test consists of 128 multiple choice items in four units covering areas such as topology, shapes, solids, location, and spatial transformations. Almost every item involves interpretation or manipulation of a visual display.

The quality of the items is probably the strongest aspect of the Series. Especially in the areas of Number, Measurement, and Space, the items are challenging without being tedious or obscure. In fact, many items on the Number and Measurement tests look like Scholastic Aptitude Test mathematics items with slightly lessened difficulty. As a whole, the Series appears to be measuring the development of quantitative thinking as opposed to mastery of a curriculum. It should be noted that the Series has a distinctly Australian flavor: items refer to maps of Australia, kangaroos, games of "noughts and crosses" (tic tac toe), etc.

Although the tests which comprise the Series appear to be commendable, the supporting technical material clearly is not, and this failing casts a long shadow on the utility of the Series as a whole. In the pure sense of the term, there is no technical manual for the Series at all. There are Teacher's Handbooks for each test which contain some technical information, but not enough to make a judgment on the technical adequacy of the Series. For example, no information is given on the nature of the sample used to estimate the item and test statistics. There are no technical data given nor procedures detailed on item construction, refinement, or final selection. There are no data which reflect on validity whatsoever, not even a table indicating how strongly the tests correlate with one another.

What is presented is a lengthy exposition on the Rasch model of test analysis which was used to develop the Series. The Rasch model seems quite appropriate to be used here (over traditional reliability measures) and the tests compare well to other measures in terms of reliability. (The Rasch procedures do not yield a single index of reliability.)

The lack of validity evidence is always regrettable, but it is especially so with the ACER Series. The reason for this is the elaborate and bold interpretations which are presented for the scores derived from the measures. It is argued that the scores are indicative of the student's cognitive developmental level according to Piagetian stage theory. Having determined the developmental level from the test, the Teacher's Manual then describes how teachers should structure instruction for students at different levels. Instructional activities are categorized according to a modification of Bloom's taxonomy of educational objectives. An example of the results of following the advice of the manual would be the prescription of one set of activities for enhancing reasoning or creativity for the "formal operational" student, and a different set for the "concrete operational" student.

All of the contentions made for the interpretation of scores from the ACER Series may be true. There is, however, scant evidence that any of them are. This unfortunate situation precludes giving a favorable recommendation to the Series. It is unfortunate because the tests themselves are quite attractive and would appear to allow for the monitoring of the development of quantitative reasoning in adolescents. The ACER Series appears to have great potential, but none of it will be realized until claims are backed up with data. The Series can be recommended for research purposes, but not yet for educational practice.

[16]

ACER Mathematics Tests: AM Series. Grades 4–6; 1969–79; 14 tests; no validity data; manual ('79, 382 pages); separate answer sheet must be used except for computation part of *d, f, g*; 1982 price data: A$1.25 per 10 answer sheets; $.60 per scoring key; $13 per manual; $31.50 per specimen set; (30) minutes; Australian Council for Educational Research [Australia].*

a) TEST AM 1: NUMERATION, COUNTING, AND NUMBER PATTERNS. 1 form ('71, 4 pages); $2.50 per 10 tests.

b) TEST AM 2: PLACE VALUE. 1 form ('71, 4 pages); $2.50 per 10 tests.

c) TEST AM 3: SETS. 1 form ('72, 6 pages); $.50 per test.

d) TEST AM 4: WHOLE NUMBERS. 4 parts: mathematical ideas ('71, 4 pages), combined form for mathematical terms, applications ('72, 4 pages), computation ('71, 7 pages); $2.50 per 10 copies of either mathematical ideas or mathematical terms/applications; $.50 per each computation part.

e) TEST AM 5: MONEY. 1 form ('71, 4 pages); $2.50 per 10 tests.

f) TEST AM 6: COMMON FRACTIONS. 4 parts: mathematical ideas ('72, 6 pages), combined form for mathematical terms, applications ('72, 4 pages), computation ('72, 4 pages); $.50 per each mathematical idea part; $2.50 per 10 copies of mathematical terms/applications or computations parts.

g) TEST AM 7: DECIMAL FRACTIONS. 4 parts: mathematical ideas ('72, 4 pages), combined form for mathematical terms, applications ('72, 4 pages), computation ('72, 4 pages); $2.50 per 10 copies of any one part.

h) TEST AM 8: SPATIAL RELATIONS. 1 form ('72, 8 pages); $.50 per test.

i) TEST AM 9: LENGTH. 1 form ('72, 4 pages); $2.50 per 10 tests.

j) TEST AM 10: AREA. 1 form ('74, 4 pages); $2.50 per 10 tests.

k) TEST AM 11: MASS AND WEIGHT. 1 form ('72, 6 pages); $.50 per test.

l) TEST AM 12: CAPACITY AND VOLUME. 1 form ('74, 6 pages); $.50 per test.

m) TEST AM 13: TIME. 1 form ('71, 4 pages); $2.50 per 10 tests.

n) TEST AM 14: GRAPHS. 1 form ('74, 5 pages); $2.50 per 10 tests.

See T3:36 (1 reference).

Review of ACER Mathematics Tests: AM Series by CARL J. HUBERTY, Professor of Educational Psychology, University of Georgia, Athens, GA:

The neatly prepared manual indicates some eight uses of this series of tests—from prognosis to grouping to lesson development. Of course, the usefulness of such tests is a function of the degree of relationship among test content, cognitive skills demand, and local curriculum practices and philosophies. Of the 14 tests, 11 were published in 1971 or 1972, and 3 were published in 1974. As such, some of the content may not be included in some current Australian elementary school curricula. The manual provides a classification of items from all tests according to required cognitive skills: knowledge, computation, understanding, and application. The manual obligingly states, however, that this classification "should be regarded only as a rough guide, and not as a definitive standard." Selecting tests for use by merely looking at titles may be misleading since, as descriptive as the titles may be, they "do not constitute instructions" for item responses.

Directions for administration and for scoring are clearly spelled out. Most items are multiple choice. The norming process was completed in three different years: 1971, 1972, and 1977. All six Australian states were represented in all three years except in 1971 when New South Wales was excluded. The sampling plans appear to have been reasonable. The extent to which the sample is representative, however, may be questionable. Across five states, save New South Wales, nearly 39% of the sets of norms for various tests by grade (or "Year" in Australian terms) are based on fewer than 100 students; about 70% on fewer than 175 students.

The manual includes tables of norms for nearly every test, grades 4 through 6, and each state (except two tests for New South Wales). The tables are fairly easy to read. Generally, raw scores are converted to stanines. However, for some grade norms, raw scores are converted to L (below average), M (average), or U (above average), rather than specific stanines. Because of measurement error, a particular raw score may be associated with more than one derived score (i.e., stanine, L, M, or U). The tables report an estimated probability that a raw score will be associated with a particular derived score. If a raw score is associated with more than one derived score, the student is assigned the one associated with the highest probability. These probability estimates should be made with caution, particularly for those sets of norms based on "small" groups of children. As pointed out above, the number of such small groups is considerable.

The norm tables also report Kuder-Richardson (internal consistency) reliability coefficients. A summary of these values across all tests and all states indicates that approximately 35% are above .80, 48% between .60 and .79, 10% between .40 and .59, and 7% below .40. Thus, the reliability of about 17% of the tests may be considered somewhat questionable. There are also some problems when looking at individual tests, across states. For example, all reliabilities for Tests AM4(II), 6(II), and 7(II) are less than .60. In fact, 22 sets of norms for these tests have reliabilities less than .40. It is interesting to note that all three of these tests concern "mathematical terms." Reliabilities for Tests AM6(III) and 7(III)—which deal with "applications"—range from .80 down to less than .35. On the positive side, Tests AM1, 2, and 4(IV) all have reliabilities above .80; Tests AM4(III), 5, 7(IV), and 14 all have reliabilities above .70; and Tests AM6(IV), 8, 11, 12, and 13 all have reliabilities above .65.

For tests such as these, perhaps the most important type of validity is content validity. This is particularly true in light of the uses for which the tests were designed. The detailed classification of test items with respect to content and cognitive skills should enable a prospective user to make a reasonable assessment of content validity.

SUMMARY. There are several positive features of this series of tests. The content and underlying cognitive skills are fairly well delineated; this should help in selecting relevant tests. Separate state norms are provided. Directions for administration are clearly spelled out. Allowance for measurement error is made in converting raw scores to derived scores. There are, however, some negative features as well. One is the possible uncontemporary test content. A second is the low reliability of some of the tests. Third, small norming groups for some tests render the use of some norm tables somewhat precarious.

Review of ACER Mathematics Tests: AM Series by GLENDA LAPPAN, Professor of Mathematics, Michigan State University, East Lansing, MI:

The ACER Mathematics Tests (AM Series) is a collection of tests for grades 4 to 6. Each test contains 20 to 49 items and requires 30 minutes to administer. The manual claims that these tests are designed "to measure the mathematical skills used by children in solving problems in a large number of topics." In fact there are 14 topics considered. Three of the topics (i.e., whole numbers, common fractions, and decimal fractions) are examined in four parallel ways: Mathematical Ideas, Mathematical Terms, Applications, and Computations. All of the booklets except for three computational tests are reusable. A standard answer sheet is available.

The manual is concise and contains helpful information for the teacher. However, the documentation on the technical aspects of the test is inadequate. There are approximately 600 test items in the 20 booklets. Yet the description of the item selection for so large an undertaking merely tells us that the items "were tested on a sample of school children in Years 3 to 6 (in some cases, Years 3 to 7) and published tests prepared by selecting items with appropriate discrimination between high scorers and low scorers on the test as a whole." Appropriate discrimination is defined to be a phi coefficient significantly different from zero. While this procedure is a useful one, the lack of detail on the original item bank, the size of the sample of school children used, and the proportions of difficult to easy items included makes the procedure suspect.

The collection of test items contains many excellent, creative problems. However, some of these problems do not appear to be appropriate for grade levels 4 to 6. The process of item selection should have addressed the appropriateness for the grades indicated in a much more careful way. One is left wondering how closely these tests actually reflect the curricula of the various Australian states on which norms are provided.

The standardization of the tests was done in clusters at three different times ranging from April 1971 to November 1977. For some unexplained reason the methods of sample selection were different in each of the three standardizations. In 1971 the norms are based on clusters of six children in 20 to 25 schools. In 1972 each norm is based on one child from each of approximately 75 schools. In 1977 each norm is based on clusters of six to seven pupils in approximately 40 schools. Not enough detail is given to make one feel confident that the small numbers of pupils involved actually produced reliable norms. The normative data provided make these concerns seem quite valid. Reliability coefficients (KR20) ranged from .21 to .94 and yet the claim is made that these are "adequate." The lowest reliabilities reported are associated with the 1972 standardization. This could reflect the inadequacy of the sampling procedure or the nature of the tests themselves.

The results of the 1972 testing also raise the question of the appropriateness of the tests for the grade levels indicated. As an example, on the Common Fractions, mathematical terms subtest, AM6(II) consisting of 14 items, for one of the sets of state norms (Year 4, Western Australia), a raw score of 1 puts a pupil in the low or middle grouping; a raw score of 2 or 3 puts a pupil in the middle group; and a raw score of 4 puts a pupil in the middle or upper group. It is hard to see that this test gives any useful information because one would expect students to score in the upper group as a result of guessing alone.

In addition to normative uses of the tests, the developers suggest that the tests might also be used for several other purposes: (*a*) Prognostic (to determine a starting point within a topic before beginning a course of instruction), (*b*) Diagnostic (to suggest some directions for a future teaching program), (*c*) Grouping (to assist in grouping children for differential instruction on a topic or topics), (*d*) Revision (to determine areas which need further instruction), and (*e*) Teacher Guidance (to help a teacher detect inadequacies of his/her presentation of a topic so that instruction might be improved for future groups). All of these suggested uses would require a teacher to analyze the content of the test to determine if it is appropriate for his/her intended use and then to consider carefully the responses of the group of students tested. To aid a teacher in analyzing the tests, two classifications of all the items are included in the manual. The first classification is by content and the second by cognitive skill levels (i.e., knowledge, computational skills, understanding, and applications).

The reviewer has mixed feelings about these nonnormative uses of the tests. On the one hand, this intimate look by a teacher at his/her own pupils for a specific purpose is by far the most potentially valuable of any kind of evaluation. To support this use, ACER has provided a wide range of topics, a classification scheme focusing on content and cognitive development, and an excellent collection of items including many which represent exemplary problem solving situations. On the other hand, the burden on a teacher using the tests for these purposes is very great. The teacher would have to be extremely knowledgeable about test content and would have to spend considerable time analyzing responses. The manual provides no help to a teacher who, for example, is interested in detecting error patterns from student responses.

The printing of the booklets is in some cases poorly done. One diagram, for example, is printed on one page and a question about the diagram is on the back of the same page. In some cases the shading on graphs and diagrams is so light that questions would be impossible to answer. The reviewer must also strongly protest some of the art work. In one case, a racial slur conveyed by a doll shows an amazing lack of sensitivity by the test constructors. Such items should be changed immediately.

In summary, the ACER Mathematics Tests (AM series) contain many excellent items. However, the normative data given for the test should be used with extreme caution. The test constructors should reexamine the appropriateness of the individual tests for grades 4 to 6. Many of the tests seem more appropriate for older pupils. The level of reading required for analyzing many of the items may be beyond pupils in grades 4 to 5. Perhaps the greatest contribution of these tests is the many good examples of items testing both problem solving skills and understanding of concepts in a multiple choice format.

[17]

ACER Mechanical Reasoning Test, Revised Edition. Ages 15 and over; 1951–79; abbreviated adaptation of ACER Mechanical Comprehension Test; 1 form (no date, 7 pages); manual ('79, 21 pages); answer sheet (no date, 1 page); 1983 price data: A$.70 per test booklet; $1.40 per 10 answer sheets; $.85 per scoring stencil; $4.85 per manual; $6.55 per specimen set; 20(25) minutes; Australian Council for Educational Research [Australia].*

See T2:2238 (3 references) and 6:1082; for reviews by John R. Jennings and Hayden S. Williams, see 5:875.

[18]

ACER Paragraph Reading Test. Grades 6–8; 1976–77; no validity data; no norms; 1 form ('76, 8 pages); teachers handbook ('77, 7 pages); separate answer sheets may be used; 1983 price data: A$.56 per test; $1.40 per 10 answer sheets; $.70 per scoring key; $2 per teacher's handbook; $3.40 per specimen set; (35–45) minutes; Australian Council for Educational Research [Australia].*

Review of ACER Paragraph Reading Test by ELFRIEDA H. HIEBERT, *Associate Professor of Curriculum & Instruction, University of Kentucky, Lexington, KY:*

This test, according to information in its manual, is intended to identify poor readers in middle school classrooms at the beginning of the year and is not intended to provide a comprehensive score of reading achievement, to discriminate between poor and good readers, or to measure changes over a period less than a year. The means of identifying poor readers is through a 35-item test. Each item consists of a paragraph of approximately 80 words, followed by one statement about the contents of the paragraph which the student is to complete by selecting one of three choices. Although acknowledging the literature on the need for a variety of question types, the test developers state that this test consists almost solely of factual items because the test is designed to "identify students with reading problems, not to give a comprehensive score on reading ability." They also describe paragraph content as covering a variety of topics and including both narrative and expository text structures.

Item selection was based on the results of administration of a larger pool of items to an unspecified number of students. Items are ordered according to difficulty, with items becoming progressively more difficult. Two practice items are provided and a 1/2-hour time span is suggested, although strict adherence to this time period is not required. Instructions for administration of the measure are succinct and clear. Students are designated as poor readers if their scores fall below a cutoff score of 20. This cutoff score was established by comparing the performances of 179 students on this measure to their teachers' ratings of them as good or poor readers. Sixty-five percent of the poor readers, as categorized by teachers, had a score of 20 or less. Internal consistency of items (KR20) is reported as .88.

There are difficulties in the construction and rationale of this test. The only information verifying that this test fulfills its objective of identifying poor readers was based on teacher ratings. Furthermore, the relationship between such a rough indicator of students' reading ability and performance on this measure was not exceptionally high, with point biserial correlations between students' performances and teachers' ratings in the range from .64 to .89. There is no additional information as to the predictive nature of this test. In other words, it is unclear whether a student classified as a poor reader by this test is a poor reader by other measures of reading performance.

The theoretical orientation underlying this test is even more problematic than the difficulties associated with test construction. The assumption that poor reading is a function of factual comprehension is questionable. For American children at the middle school or junior high level, nationwide test results indicate that poor readers have comparatively more difficulty with inferential than with factual questions (Tierney & Lapp, 1979). No inferencing or higher-level processing is required by this test. Furthermore, the factual nature of the questions would permit children to determine the answer without even reading the paragraph. To characterize a student as a poor reader from an assessment of factual comprehension reflects a narrow conception of reading.

The authors emphasize that the sole purpose of this test is to identify problem readers and not to give a comprehensive measure of reading achievement nor diagnostic information. In most American school systems, it would be presumed that children with reading difficulties will have been identified long before junior high. The test is not aimed at providing any of the information that teachers need at the junior high level such as the degree to which students are having reading difficulties and the areas in which students are having their greatest reading difficulties. One is not even certain as to content areas in which students may be experiencing problems since narrative and expository text are interspersed. The latter problem is confounded by the frequent use of paragraphs that could be described as quasi-expository, in which expository material is conveyed in a narrative format.

There would appear to be little use for this test in American classrooms in that it provides no information not already available to teachers. In fact, since the diagnostic power of this test is based on teachers' rough estimates of children's reading abilities, teachers would be advised to use their own judgment. Any widely used achievement test will give teachers more information about the relative standing of students and the areas in which students require more work.

REVIEWER'S REFERENCES

Tierney, R. J., & Lapp, D. NATIONAL ASSESSMENT OF EDUCATIONAL PROGRESS IN READING. Newark, DE: International Reading Association, 1979.

Review of ACER Paragraph Reading Test by S. E. PHILLIPS, Assistant Professor of Educational Measurement, Michigan State University, East Lansing, MI:

The stated purpose of the ACER Paragraph Reading Test is to identify students with reading problems early in the school year. The manual (Teacher's Handbook) clearly states that the test is designed as a screening device and that it is not designed to provide a comprehensive reading ability score for each student in the class, to discriminate between good and average readers, or to measure growth over time.

In discussing test development, the manual states that since the test is not intended to measure reading comprehension but to identify the poor readers in a classroom (a debatable distinction), the test contains mainly factual items. In the terminology of Bloom's taxonomy, the items fall primarily at the knowledge and comprehension levels with the answers to recall items stated directly in the passage and those at the translation level requiring vocabulary substitutions or slight rewording of the answers given in the passage. Although the manual states that the passages represent the type of material students might read in their school program, no other justification for the selection of passages is given and there is no test blueprint or list of objectives. Some of the vocabulary in the passages may be unfamiliar to students outside Australia (e.g., a ship ran into a punt). Specific qualifications of the item writers are also not given.

A serious flaw in the selection of passages is the underrepresentation of females and the stereotyping of gender roles. The generic "he" is used throughout; the pronoun "she" is used only when a female has been specifically named. If only those passages including characters specifically named by gender are considered, males outnumber females by four to one. Men play active roles including soldiers and hunters and their activities include adventure and danger. Women's roles are isolated and tend to involve domestic tasks. Even animals tend to be male more often than female.

With only one item per passage, the test is somewhat inefficient for the reading time required. Each item has only three alternatives. Given the instructions to students to try to answer every question, this may result in higher proportions of students answering an item correctly by guessing. Final items were selected from a tryout pool based on difficulty (facility) and discrimination. The manual describes an acceptable discrimination level as being significantly different from zero at the 1% level. The author(s) probably mean greater than zero since negatively discriminating items would be undesirable. From the manual, it is also unclear how the upper and lower groups were defined in calculating the discrimination index.

The characteristics of the final tryout samples are described as covering a wide range of socioeconomic levels but no sample or population percentages are provided for comparison. The sample was very small ($n = 179$) and was not geographically representative. No data on sex or ethnic composition is provided.

The manual suggests that the test is slightly easier than others of its kind because the purpose is to spread out scores at the lower end of the distribution. Using the conventional wisdom (appropriate for all students, not just those of lower ability) of a mean difficulty half way between chance and perfect, the target mean difficulty would be 66% [(35/3 + (35–12)/2) 100/35], exactly that reported in the manual for this test. Due to possibilities for guessing, Lord (1952) recommends a slightly higher average test difficulty. These recommendations apply to measurement of all students; to specifically identify those students with reading difficulties an even easier test might be more appropriate.

In the manual for this test, a cutting score of 20 (57%) is suggested based on data collected on the final tryout sample. This value was obtained by examining the test scores of students identified by their teachers as poor readers (i.e., "children who are clearly in need of additional help with their reading"). The manual does not indicate (1) how a "poor reader" was actually defined by teachers (e.g., reading one or two years below grade level), (2) how the lists of good and poor students from the two teachers evaluating the class were combined (e.g., were all names used or only those common to both teacher's lists?), (3) what formula or criterion was used to choose 20 as the cutoff score from the distribution of scores for poor readers, and (4) what percent of the total sample was identified as poor or as good readers. There did appear to be a relationship between rankings and test scores (point biserial correlations ranging from .64 to .89).

Using the mean and standard deviation of raw scores in the final tryout sample and assuming scores were normally distributed (they probably were not), 35% of this group would be identified as needing remediation and further diagnosis of their reading difficulties using the cutting score of 20 [(20–22.73)/7.05=–.39]. Even assuming a nonnormal distribution, the cutoff score is quite close to the mean (less than one half of a standard deviation below the mean) and is likely to identify an excessively large group of students. Cross validation of the cutoff score with a new sample of students would be helpful and special attention should be given to the number of false negatives and false positives.

The manual generally presents good directions for administration and scoring. Standardized directions to be read aloud to the students are provided including two practice exercises that the test administrator works through in detail with the students. The answer sheet is marked by blackening a rectangular space containing the letter of the chosen answer, a format likely to reduce marking errors. A scoring mask would be easier and more efficient than the answer key that is provided for hand scoring. The manual states that there is no precise time limit for the test since it is intended that it be nonspeeded. However, the suggested time of 30–40 minutes allows an average of only one minute per passage/question and may not be enough for slow readers or those who need to refer back to the passage when answering the question. No evidence on completion rates is presented to justify these suggested time limits.

The test score is the number correct with no correction for guessing. No percentile ranks or standard scores are provided. With respect to the recommended cutting score, some evidence of criterion-related validity is presented for the small final tryout sample (percents of good and poor readers above and below the cutting score). No reliability or validity data are reported for the criterion measure (teacher ratings) and the small sample size and lack of cross-validation limit the generalizability of the results. The manual does suggest a grey area of plus or minus 1 standard error of measurement around the cutting score (18–22) where one can't be sure how to categorize students. Users are also cautioned to adjust their interpretations based on knowledge of the class and school since what is poor in one school may be good in another. In keeping with this philosophy it would also be appropriate for the manual to encourage the setting of local cutoff scores based on local validity studies.

Too little information on the test blueprint and item development is provided to adequately judge the content validity of the test. The KR20 reliability and standard error of measurement are reported for the final tryout sample. The internal consistency reliability of .88 is quite acceptable for a screening device. However, the manual suggests that the KR20 coefficient is a good estimator of test/retest reliability; it is probably a lower bound for a test/retest estimate. The manual also discusses a 68% confidence interval for the true score (based on a probably incorrect assumption of normality) but does not clearly describe to the user how to calculate it or how and whether it should be used in test interpretation (except for the discussion of a grey area around the cutting score). Final item difficulties are included in the manual but not discrimination indices.

As an initial screening device for identifying poor readers, the ACER Paragraph Reading Test is potentially useful if the user establishes a local cutoff score based on local validity data. Consideration should be given to revision of the items to provide gender fair treatment, and local studies of completion rates should be undertaken to set time limits consistent with the intent of a power test. In future revisions of the test, consideration should also be given to an appropriate average item difficulty level for identifying poor readers.

REVIEWER'S REFERENCES

Lord, F. M. The relationship of the reliability of multiple-choice tests to the distribution of item difficulties. PSYCHOMETRIKA, 1952, 17, 181–194.

[19]

ACER Physics Unit Tests: Diagnostic Aids. Grades 11–12; 1978–80; collection of 21 separate tests and 21 diagnostic aids corresponding to the tests; 21 tests: Physical Measurement, Vectors, Motion In One Dimension, Motion On a Plane, Dynamics, Work and Energy, Linear Momentum, Oscillations, Gravity and Kepler's Laws, Waves, Light-Reflection and Refraction, Light-Interference Diffraction and Spectra, Models of Light, Kinetic Theory of Gases, Static Charges, Electric Field and Potential Difference, Current Electricity, The Magnetic Field, Induced EMF, Atomic Physics, Quantum Physics; no data on reliability; no norms; 1 form ('78, 131 pages); diagnostic aids ('80, 157 pages); teacher's handbook ('80, 24 pages including answer key); 1982 price data: A$9 per set of 21 tests; $9 per set of 21 diagnostic aids; $2.50 per teacher's handbook; (40) minutes; Graeme Wilmot; Australian Council for Educational Research [Australia].*

Review of ACER Physics Unit Tests: Diagnostic Aids by JOHN COOK, Senior Educational Psychologist, Littlehampton, West Sussex, England:

The ACER Physics Unit Tests were devised in Australia to evaluate progress in physics in the upper part of the school age range: years 11 and 12 in Australia or sixth form G.C.E. "A" level standard in England, corresponding to academically able young people aged 16 to 18 years. For each of the 21 divisions of a physics curriculum there is a multiple-choice test which links to a set of model answers called Diagnostic Aids. In the Aids the student is guided by references to specific pages in a set of standard physics texts (three Australian and two American), where additional information about a question may be obtained. While there is no time limit for the tests, each might be expected to take about 40 minutes to complete.

The contents were chosen relatively recently (1978) to bring up to date earlier materials used in two Australian states. Teachers throughout Australia were requested to report on the major topic areas taught in their schools so that all areas taught in contemporary physics classes could be considered for inclusion. By widening the geographical scope it was anticipated that a common curriculum area would be covered. This seems to have been accomplished well; certainly there are no glaring omissions when compared with similar physics programs taught in England. The number of unit areas is rather arbitrary; as can be seen from the list given in the pre-review notes, however, the 21 units cover a wide range from mechanics to atomic and quantum physics. The importance of a sound mathematical background is recognized throughout the guides and the emphasis is on understanding rather than rote learning and application of formulae. In particular the Unit on Vectors asked many relevant, interesting questions.

Within each unit there are between 25 and 30 questions; for each of these the student is typically required to select from a four-alternatives format. As might be expected from a test that endeavours to be comprehensive, all questions in all units may not be applicable to all students. Teachers should quickly be able to spot the inappropriate question and divert pupils accordingly. The language within each test is clear and unambiguous, and although to the most pedantic observer not all questions state all conditions, they are readily understandable to students of this age. The general layout of the tests in two columns per page is, perhaps, a little cramped, and it might have been clearer to have just one question per horizontal section of the page. However, this layout cuts down the size of the Unit, and it is unlikely that in these relatively short tests students will miss the second column. It may be worth including a warning about the two columns in the introduction to each test, as some students do react adversely to examination pressures.

The Diagnostic Aids linked with each test have a readability level close to what it should be. While the readability level of some school science textbooks is totally beyond the age of the child expected to read the book, an assessment of the Aids with the Fry Readability Chart gives an average of 16 years, and a range from 14.5 years to college level. In any future revision of the Aids it might be possible to lower the readability level further. The answers in each of the Units are accurate and free from all but an occasional error; the errors were related to careless proofreading but nevertheless are likely to confuse some students. However, none of these errors are serious, and they should be readily correctable by teachers as they familiarize themselves with the tests. It has not been possible to assess the list of textbook pages listed as references to the answers in the Diagnostic Aids. Perhaps the addition of a British text would have added to their scope. However, it should not be an insuperable task for a physics teacher in Britain to reference the Aids to the text used in school.

The suggestion is made in the Teachers' Manual that the students complete the test either at home or at school but not long after that part of the curriculum has been covered. Consolidation may occur and any errors made by students may quickly be rectified. The Aids are an integral part of the process. Perhaps another sequence might be considered that might add to the learning potential of the whole. The test should be given as recommended but instead of the Diagnostic Aids being consulted immediately, the list of textbook page numbers, from the Aids, should be extracted. Checks can be made by the students to compare their answers with the textbook. When this has been completed the Diagnostic Aids could compare the model answer with the students' revised work.

Because the ACER Physics Unit Tests are seen as diagnostic, ("aids to learning and not as a final testing of achievement in Physics"), no attempt has been made to standardize them in any normative sense. There are neither norms to compare relative scores nor data on reliability. While both item analysis and content validity are mentioned in the Teachers' Manual, no detail is given. Great care, therefore, needs to be taken before making any interpretation of the results of the tests. Their use should be restricted to diagnostic advice for individual students.

In summary, the ACER Physics Unit Tests are a sound and thorough guide to the physics curriculum of older (16 to 18 years) academically able students. The combination of test linked to model answers and text book references can be a most effective method of reinforcing the material taught. The lack of reliability and validity data should not be forgotten; however, as a learning resource for individual students its use is warmly recommended.

[20]

ACER Review and Progress Tests in Mathematics. Grades 3–6; 1982; RAPT; criterion-referenced; a series of scaled, integrated tests in 4 skill areas (addition, subtraction, multiplication, division); one score on each of 7–12 Progress Tests and 2–4 Review Tests for each skill area; no data on reliability; no norms; suggested standards of mastery; 2 equivalent forms (1 page) for each skill area; class record chart (2 pages); 1984 price data: A$2.50 per 40 Progress Tests; $5 per 40 Review Tests; $.50 per class record chart; $6.50 per manual; administration time not reported; John Izard, Stephen Farish, Mark Wilson, Graham Ward, and Andrew Vander Werf; Australian Council for Educational Research [Australia].*

a) ADDITION. 7 separate Progress Tests and 2 Review Tests; forms A, B, (1 page); manual (49 pages); $9 per specimen set.

b) SUBTRACTION. 8 separate Progress Tests and 2 Review Tests; forms A, B, (1 page); manual (50 pages); $9 per specimen set.

c) MULTIPLICATION. 12 separate Progress Tests and 3 Review Tests; forms A, B, (1 page); manual (59 pages); $10 per specimen set.

d) DIVISION. 7 separate Progress Tests and 2 Review Tests for each level; forms A, B, (1 page); manual (72 pages) $11 per specimen set.

1) *Division Level 1 (for division by one-digit divisors).*
2) *Division Level 2 (for division by two-digit divisors).*

[21]

ACER Short Clerical Test—Form C. Ages 15 and over; 1953–79; 2 scores: checking, arithmetic; 1 form ('66, 4 pages); revised manual ('79, 16 pages); 1983 price data: A$2.80 per 10 test booklets; $1.35 per scoring stencil; $8.25 per revised manual; $9.85 per specimen set; 5(10) minutes per test; Australian Council for Educational Research [Australia].*

[22]

ACER Spelling Test—Years 3–6. Grade 3, 4, 5, 6; 1976–81; no data on reliability; 4 levels: Year 3, 4, 5, 6; Form X, Y, (no date, 1 card) for each level; handbook ('81, 22 pages); class analysis chart (no date, 2 pages); separate answer sheets must be used; 1984 price data: A$15.40 per year package including both Forms X and Y, and 40 answer sheets; $1.30 per test card; $1.15 per class analysis chart; $6.25 per 40 answer sheets; $15.80 per specimen set; (20–30) minutes; Australian Council for Educational Research [Australia].*

Review of ACER Spelling Test—Years 3–6 by RICHARD M. CLARK, Professor of Educational

Psychology, State University of New York at Albany, Albany, NY:

The ACER Spelling Test is designed to measure levels of achievement in third through sixth grade. The test is divided into four parts with each part consisting of 50 words. In this Australian test, words are dictated to the child and the child attempts to spell the word. Most American achievement test batteries include a spelling subtest. However, on American standardized tests the format is usually multiple choice, and the child is asked to indicate which word is incorrect or whether all of the words are spelled correctly.

Do these different methods of assessing spelling lead to the same results? Several researchers (Freyberg, 1970; Croft, 1982; Homenick, 1984) have reported correlations above .80 between spelling measured through dictation and through recognition procedures. Based on these results, either a dictation or a recognition test allows a test user to compare the spelling performance of a child to a reference group. The authors of the ACER indicate that their test results may be used to provide information about the types of errors which each test taker makes. They recommend a supplementary manual designed to help in error analysis and to provide suggestions about corrective teaching. In this regard a dictation test such as the ACER seems to offer an advantage over a multiple choice format. Certainly the complete record of the child's attempts to spell 50 different words provides much more data than can be obtained from a recognition measure in which a child has marked a correctly spelled word as incorrect.

A key factor in a spelling test concerns the selection of the words to which the child is exposed. The maker of a dictation spelling test has available the entire dictionary as possible test items. How does one choose the words to be tested? The authors of the ACER are admirably precise concerning the decisions they have followed. Each 50-word test includes 10 words from the preceeding test, about half homophones and half other forms of commonly mispelled words. The remaining 40 words are drawn from various subject areas (5 words), from the New South Wales spelling list (25 words), and from A Word List for Australian Schools (10 words).

Norming data are also provided in detail. A careful sampling plan is clearly described. For each form of the test information is provided for each word (percent correct at different times of testing). Raw scores for each year are translated into percentile ranks along with a lower and upper limit for each score. Materials are attractive and instructions for administration, scoring, and interpretation are clear and cogent.

An obvious problem for an American user is the fact that the test was developed and normed in Australia. The words chosen for the test seem to cross the cultures. They are words which American children should be able to read and spell, and they might well be selected for an American spelling test. The information provided in the manual allows for interesting cross-cultural comparisons. One could compare on a word by word basis the spelling performance of an American and Australian sample of children. However, considerable research would be necessary in order to equate accurately Australian norms to American norms.

Probably such effort is not warranted for American educators. Spelling subtests are included in most achievement test batteries, and these scores probably provide sufficient norm-referenced data. Spelling programs used routinely in the classroom provide for regular testing via a dictation method, along with suggestions for analysis of spelling errors and for remediation. The ACER Spelling Test exemplifies good test construction characteristics but it should not be transplanted for routine use.

REVIEWER'S REFERENCES

Freyberg, P. S. The concurrent validity of two types of spelling test. BRITISH JOURNAL OF EDUCATIONAL PSYCHOLOGY, 1970, 40, 68–71.

Croft, A. C. Do spelling tests measure the ability to spell? EDUCATIONAL AND PSYCHOLOGICAL MEASUREMENT, 1982, 42, 715–723.

Homenick, M. P. SPELLING: A COMPLEX, TASK-DEPENDENT ABILITY. A dissertation submitted to the State University of New York at Albany, 1984.

[23]

ACER Test of Cognitive Ability. Ages 15 and over; 1978–83; TOCA; general intellectual ability; reliability data and norms for age 15 and first-year college students only; 1 form ('78, 7 pages); preliminary manual for administration and interpretation ('83, 9 pages); score key ('83, 1 card); 1983 price data: A$5.60 per 10 test booklets; $1.15 per score key; $3.40 per manual; $5.10 per specimen set; 55(60) minutes; Australian Council for Educational Research [Australia].*

[24]

Achievement Tests: Grades 1–8. Grades 1, 2, 3, 4, 5, 6, 7, 8; 1980; criterion-referenced; focus is on major reading objectives "directly related to skills tested in the SERIES r Assessment Tests"; 4 scores: comprehension skills, vocabulary skills, decoding skills, study skills; no data on reliability and validity; no norms, acceptable performance defined as 75% for each subtest; 1 form (16 pages); 8 levels; manual (8 pages) for each level; 1984 price data: $7.12 per 10 tests and teacher's manual; administration time not reported; Madeline A. Weinstein; MacMillan Publishing Co., Inc.*

[25]

ACS Cooperative Examination in General-Organic-Biological Chemistry. Nursing and other paramedical and home economics students; 1979; ACS test program is continually updated by retiring an older form of the test upon publication of a new form; 10 scores:

general (part A, part B, total), organic (part A, part B, total), biological (part A, part B, total), part A total; Form 1979 (16 pages); no specific manual; general directions (no date, 4 pages); norms (no date, 4 pages); separate answer sheets must be used; 1984 price data: $18 per 25 tests; $3 per 25 answer sheets; $1 per scoring stencil; $5 per specimen set; 75(85) minutes; Examinations Committee, American Chemical Society.*

[26]

ACS Cooperative Examination in Physical Chemistry. 1 year college; 1946–83; ACS test program is continually updated by retiring an older form of the test upon publication of a new form; 3 subtests, may be administered separately or together; no specific manual; general directions (no date, 4 pages); separate answer sheets must be used; 1984 price data: $18 per 25 tests; $3 per 25 answer sheets; $1 per scoring stencil; $5 per specimen set; Examinations Committee, American Chemical Society.*

a) THERMODYNAMICS. 3 scores: part A, part B, total; Form 1976 ('76, 8 pages); errata sheet (no date, 1 page); norms ('83, 2 pages); 90(100) minutes.

b) CHEMICAL DYNAMICS. 3 scores: part A, part B, total; Form 1981 ('80, 8 pages); norms ('83, 2 pages); 90(100) minutes.

c) QUANTUM CHEMISTRY. 3 scores: part A, part B, total; 1 form ('83, 8 pages); norms ('83, 2 pages); 100(110) minutes.

For a review by Gerald R. Van Hecke of an earlier form, see 8:842 (2 references); see also T2:1826 (2 references), 7:833 (2 references), and 6:904 (1 reference); for a review by Alfred S. Brown, see 3:559.

[27]

ACS Examination in Analytical Chemistry. 1 year college; 1944–82; ACS test program is continually updated by retiring an older form of the test upon publication of a new form; Form 1982 (8 pages); no specific manual; general directions (no date, 4 pages); norms ('82, 2 pages); separate answer sheets must be used; 1984 price data: $18 per 25 tests; $3 per 25 answer sheets; $1 per scoring stencil; $5 per specimen set; 90(100) minutes; Examinations Committee, American Chemical Society.*

See 7:836 (1 reference) and 6:907 (1 reference); for an excerpted review by H. E. Wilcox of an earlier form, see 5:735; for reviews by William B. Meldrum and William Rieman III, see 3:563.

[28]

ACS Examination in Analytical Chemistry, Graduate Level. Entering college students; 1961–81; ACS test program is continually updated by retiring an older form of the test upon publication of a new form; Form 1981–A (7 pages); no specific manual; general directions (no date, 4 pages); norms ('81, 1 page); distribution restricted to graduate schools; separate answer sheets must be used; 1984 price data: $18 per 25 tests; $3 per 25 answer sheets; $1 per scoring stencil; $5 per specimen set; 90(100) minutes; Examinations Committee, American Chemical Society.*

See T2:1815 (1 reference), 7:822 (1 reference), and 6:899 (1 reference).

[29]

ACS Examination in Biochemistry. 1 year college; 1947–82; ACS test program is continually updated by retiring an older form of the test upon publication of a new form; Form 1982 (8 pages); no specific manual; general directions (no date, 4 pages); norms ('82, 2 pages); separate answer sheets must be used; 1984 price data: $18 per 25 tests; $3 per 25 answer sheets; $1 per scoring stencil; $5 per specimen set; 120(130) minutes; Examinations Committee, American Chemical Society.*

See 7:823 (1 reference); for an excerpted review by Wilhelm R. Frisell of an earlier form, see 6:898 (2 references).

[30]

ACS Examination in Brief Organic Chemistry. 1 year college; 1942–84; ACS test program is continually updated by retiring an older form of the test upon publication of a new form; Form 1984B (12 pages); no specific manual; general directions (no date, 4 pages); norms ('79, 2 pages); separate answer sheets must be used; 1984 price data: $18 per 25 tests; $3 per 25 answer sheets; $1 per scoring stencil; $5 per specimen set; 90(100) minutes; Examinations Committee, American Chemical Society.*

[31]

ACS Examination in Brief Qualitative Analysis. 1 year college; 1961–79; ACS test program is continually updated by retiring an older form of the test upon publication of a new form; Form 1977B (8 pages); no specific manual; general directions (no date, 4 pages); norms ('79, 2 pages); separate answer sheets must be used; 1984 price data: $18 per 25 tests; $3 per 25 answer sheets; $1 per scoring stencil; $5 per specimen set; 50(60) minutes; Examinations Committee, American Chemical Society.*

See T2:1818 (4 references); for an excerpted review by W. H. Waggoner of an earlier form, see 6:906 (4 references); see also 4:608 (2 references).

[32]

ACS Examination in General Chemistry. 1 year college; 1934–83; ACS test program is continually updated by retiring an older form of the test upon publication of a new form; Form 1983 (8 pages); no specific manual; general directions (no date, 4 pages); norms ('83, 4 pages); separate answer sheets must be used; 1984 price data: $18 per 25 tests; $3 per 25 answer sheets; $1 per scoring stencil; $5 per specimen set; 110(120) minutes; Examinations Committee, American Chemical Society.*

For a review by Frank J. Fornoff of an earlier edition, see 8:837 (3 references); see also T2:1819 (1 reference) and 7:826 (5 references); for reviews by J. A. Campbell and William Hered and an excerpted review by S. L. Burson, Jr., see 6:902 (3 references); for reviews by Frank P. Cassaretto and Palmer O. Johnson, see 5:732 (2 references); for a review by Kenneth E. Anderson, see 4:610 (1 reference); for reviews by Sidney J. French and Florence E. Hooper, see 3:557 (3 references); see also 2:1593 (5 references).

[33]

ACS Examination in Inorganic Chemistry. 1 year college; 1961–84; ACS test program is continually updated by retiring an older form of the test upon publication of a new form; Form 1981 (8 pages); no specific manual; general directions (no date, 4 pages); norms ('84, 3 pages); separate answer sheets must be used; 1984 price data: $18 per 25 tests; $3 per 25 answer sheets; $1 per scoring stencil; $5 per specimen set; 110(120) minutes; Examinations Committee, American Chemical Society.*

See T3:64 (1 reference), 8:838 (2 references), T2:1820 (1 reference), and 7:827 (2 references); for a review by Frank J. Fornoff and an excerpted review by George B. Kauffman of an earlier form, see 6:903 (1 reference).

[34]

ACS Examination in Instrumental Determinations. 1 year college; 1966–81; ACS test program is continually updated by retiring an older form of the test upon publication of a new form; Form 1981 (12 pages); no specific manual; general directions (no date, 4 pages); norms ('82, 2 pages); separate answer sheets must be used; 1984 price data: $18 per 25 tests; $3 per 25 answer sheets; $1 per scoring stencil; $5 per specimen set; 110(120) minutes; Examinations Committee, American Chemical Society.*

See 7:830 (1 reference).

[35]

ACS Examination in Organic Chemistry. 1 year college; 1942–82; ACS test program is continually updated by retiring an older form of the test upon publication of a new form; Form 1982 (12 pages); no specific manual; general directions (no date, 4 pages); norms ('82, 3 pages); separate answer sheets must be used; 1984 price data: $18 per 25 tests; $3 per 25 answer sheets; $1 per scoring stencil; $5 per specimen set; 115(125) minutes; Examinations Committee, American Chemical Society.*

See 8:840 (3 references), 7:831 (3 references), and 6:905 (4 references); for a review by Shailer Peterson of an earlier form, see 3:558.

[36]

ACS Examination in Organic Chemistry, Graduate Level. Entering college students; 1961–81; ACS test program is continually updated by retiring an older form of the test upon publication of a new form; 5 scores: reactions and synthesis, mechanisms and theory, stereochemistry, spectroscopy and structure determination, total; Form 1981-O (15 pages); no specific manual; general directions (no date, 4 pages); norms ('81, 2 pages); distribution restricted to graduate schools; separate answer sheets must be used; 1984 price data: $18 per 25 tests; $3 per 25 answer sheets; $1 per scoring stencil; $5 per specimen set; 90(100) minutes; Examinations Committee, American Chemical Society.*

See 8:841 (2 references), 7:832 (1 reference), and 6:900 (1 reference).

[37]

ACS Examination in Physical Chemistry for Life Sciences. 1 year college; 1982–83; ACS test program is continually updated by retiring an older form of the test upon publication of a new form; Form 1982-L (8 pages); no specific manual; general directions (no date, 4 pages); norms ('83, 2 pages); separate answer sheets must be used; 1984 price data: $18 per 25 tests; $3 per 25 answer sheets; $1 per scoring stencil; $5 per specimen set; 100(110) minutes; Examinations Committee, American Chemical Society.*

[38]

ACS Examination in Physical Chemistry, Graduate Level. Entering college students; 1961–81; ACS test program is continually updated by retiring an older form of the test upon publication of a new form; 4 scores: thermodynamics, quantum chemistry, dynamics, total; Form 1981-P (8 pages); no specific manual; general directions (no date, 4 pages); norms ('81, 4 pages); distribution restricted to graduate schools; separate answer sheets must be used; 1984 price data: $18 per 25 tests; $3 per 25 answer sheets; $1 per scoring stencil; $5 per specimen set; 150(160) minutes; Examinations Committee, American Chemical Society.*

For a review by Gerald R. Van Hecke of an earlier form, see 8:843 (1 reference); see also 7:834 (2 references) and 6:901 (1 reference).

[39]

ACS Examination in Polymer Chemistry. 1 year college; 1978; ACS test program is continually updated by retiring an older form of the test upon publication of a new form; Form 1978 (8 pages); no specific manual; general directions (no date, 4 pages); norms ('78, 2 pages); separate answer sheets must be used; 1984 price data: $18 per 25 tests; $3 per 25 answer sheets; $1 per scoring stencil; $5 per specimen set; 110(120) minutes; Examinations Committee, American Chemical Society.*

[40]

ACS-NSTA Examination in High School Chemistry, [Advanced Level]. Advanced high school classes; 1963–84; ACS test program is continually updated by retiring an older form of the test upon publication of a new form; Form 1984 Adv (8 pages); no specific manual; general directions (no date, 4 pages); no norms for 1984 Adv form; separate answer sheets must be used; 1984 price data: $18 per 25 tests; $3 per 25 answer sheets; $1 per scoring stencil; $5 per specimen set; 110(120) minutes; sponsored jointly with the National Science Teachers Association; Examinations Committee, American Chemical Society.*

For reviews by Peter A. Dahl and John P. Penna of an earlier form, see 8:844 (1 reference); for a review by Irvin J. Lehmann, see 7:838 (3 references); for reviews by Frank J. Fornoff and William Hered, see 6:909.

[41]

ACS-NSTA Examination in High School Chemistry, [Lower Level]. 1 year high school; 1957–83; ACS test program is continually updated by retiring an older form of the test upon publication of a new form; 3 scores: part I, part II, total; Form 1983 (8 pages); no specific manual; general directions (no date, 4 pages); norms ('83, 6 pages); separate answer sheets must be used; 1984 price data: $18 per 25 tests; $3 per 25 answer sheets; $1 per scoring stencil; $5 per specimen set; 80(90) minutes; sponsored jointly with the National Science

Teachers Association; Examinations Committee, American Chemical Society.*

For a review by Edward F. DeVillafranca of an earlier form, see 8:845 (11 references); see also T2:1830 (3 references); for reviews by William R. Crawford and Irvin J. Lehmann, see 7:837 (9 references); for reviews by Frank J. Fornoff and William Hered and excerpted reviews by Christine Jansing and Joseph Schmuckler, see 6:908 (5 references); for reviews by Edward G. Rietz and Willard G. Warrington, see 5:729.

TEST REFERENCES

1. Gabel, D. L., & Sherwood, R. D. Facilitating problem solving in high school chemistry. JOURNAL OF RESEARCH IN SCIENCE TEACHING, 1983, 20, 163–177.

[42]

ACS Toledo Chemistry Placement Examination. 1 year college; 1959–81; ACS test program is continually updated by retiring an older form of the test upon publication of a new form; 4 scores: general mathematics, general chemical knowledge, specific chemical knowledge, total; Form 1981 (8 pages); no specific manual; general directions (no date, 4 pages); norms ('82, 2 pages); separate answer sheets must be used; 1984 price data: $18 per 25 tests; $3 per 25 answer sheets; $1 per scoring stencil; $5 per specimen set; 110(120) minutes; Examinations Committee, American Chemical Society.*

For a review by Frank J. Fornoff of an earlier form, see 8:853 (3 references); see also T2:1847 (2 references); for reviews by Kenneth E. Anderson and William R. Crawford, see 6:920 (1 reference).

[43]

ACT Assessment Program. Candidates for college entrance; 1959–84; ACT; 3 parts; academic tests administered 5 times a year (February, April, June, October, December) at centers established by the publisher; interest inventory and student profile section completed locally as part of registration for the academic tests; supervisor's manual of instructions ('84, 23 pages); counselor's handbook ('84, 34 pages); registration procedures ('84, 32 pages, including 1-page interest inventory and 6-page student profile section); registration folder ('84, 4 pages); technical report ('73, 412 pages); highlights of technical report ('73, 30 pages); norms ('83, 130 pages); interpretive booklet ('84, 13 pages); using ACT in advising ('84, 7 pages); statement of policies ('79, 26 pages); using ACT on campus ('84, 42 pages); 1984 price data: examination fee, $9.50 per candidate; fee includes reporting of scores to candidate, high school, and 3 colleges; special editions available for administration to the handicapped; American College Testing Program.*

a) ACADEMIC TESTS. 1959–84; 5 scores: English usage, mathematics usage, social studies reading, natural sciences reading, composite; Forms 24B ('83, 37 pages), 25E ('83, 38 pages); new forms published annually; 160(210) minutes.

b) ACT INTEREST INVENTORY, (UNISEX EDITION). 1973–84; UNIACT; a component of the ACT Career Planning Program; 6 scores: science, creative arts, social service, business contact, business detail, technical; 1 form ('84, 1 page is registration procedures booklet); technical report ('81, 92 pages); $5 per technical report.

c) STUDENT PROFILE SECTION. 1964–84; survey inventory of admissions/enrollment information, educational plans/interests/needs, special educational needs/interests/goals, college extracurricular plans, financial aid, background information, factors influencing college choice, high school educational information, high school extracurricular activities, out-of-class accomplishments, evaluation of high school experience, information about educational opportunities; 1 form ('84, 6 pages in registration procedures booklet).

See T3:76 (76 references); for a review by John R. Hills, see 8:469 (208 references); see also T2:1044 (97 references); for a review by Wimburn L. Wallace of an earlier program, see 7:330 (265 references); for reviews by Max D. Engelhart and Warren G. Findley and an excerpted review by David V. Tiedeman, see 6:1 (14 references).

TEST REFERENCES

1. Ohlson, E. L., & Mein, L. The difference in level of anxiety in undergraduate mathematics and nonmathematics majors. JOURNAL FOR RESEARCH IN MATHEMATICS EDUCATION, 1977, 8, 48–56.

2. Hollandsworth, J. G., Jr., Glazeski, R. C., Kirkland, K., Jones, G. E., & VanNorman, L. R. An analysis of the nature and effects of test anxiety: Cognitive, behavioral, and physiological components. COGNITIVE THERAPY AND RESEARCH, 1979, 3, 165–180.

3. Sawyer, R., & Maxey, J. The validity of college grade prediction equations over time. JOURNAL OF EDUCATIONAL MEASUREMENT, 1979, 16, 279–284.

4. Templer, D. I. Death anxiety and mental ability. ESSENCE, 1979, 3, 85–89.

5. Bruch, M. A. Relationship of test-taking strategies to test anxiety and performance: Toward a task analysis of examination behavior. COGNITIVE THERAPY AND RESEARCH, 1981, 5, 41–56.

6. Campion, M. A., & Lord, R. G. A control systems conceptualization of the goal-setting and changing process. ORGANIZATIONAL BEHAVIOR AND HUMAN PERFORMANCE, 1982, 30, 265–287.

7. Dillon, R. F., & Donow, C. The psychometric credibility of the Zelniker and Jeffrey modification of the Matching Familiar Figures Test. EDUCATIONAL AND PSYCHOLOGICAL MEASUREMENT, 1982, 42, 529–536.

8. Domer, D. E., & Johnson, A. E., Jr. Selective admissions and academic success: An admissions model for architecture students. COLLEGE AND UNIVERSITY, 1982, 58, 19–30.

9. Fowler, B. F., & Ross, D. H. The comparative validities of differential placement measures for college composition courses. EDUCATIONAL AND PSYCHOLOGICAL MEASUREMENT, 1982, 42, 1107–1115.

10. Frazier, D. J., & DeBlassie, R. R. A comparison of self-concept in Mexican American and non-Mexican American late adolescents. ADOLESCENCE, 1982, 17, 327–334.

11. Grabe, M. Effort strategies in a mastery instructional system: The quantification of effort and the impact of effort on achievement. CONTEMPORARY EDUCATIONAL PSYCHOLOGY, 1982, 7, 327–333.

12. Jarjoura, D., & Brennan, R. L. A variance components model for measurements procedures associated with a table of specifications. APPLIED PSYCHOLOGICAL MEASUREMENT, 1982, 6, 161–171.

13. Karmos, J. S., Bryson, S., & Tracz, S. Equations for predicting special students who will earn degrees. JOURNAL OF INSTRUCTIONAL PSYCHOLOGY, 1982, 9, 139–144.

14. Moss, C. J. Academic achievement and individual differences in the learning processes of basic skills students in the university. APPLIED PSYCHOLOGICAL MEASUREMENT, 1982, 6, 291–296.

15. Rugg, E. A. A longitudinal comparison of minority and nonminority college dropouts: Implications for retention improvement programs. PERSONNEL AND GUIDANCE JOURNAL, 1982, 61, 232–235.

16. Sypher, H. E., & Applegate, J. L. Cognitive differentiation and verbal intelligence: Clarifying relationships. EDUCATIONAL AND PSYCHOLOGICAL MEASUREMENT, 1982, 42, 537–543.

17. Taylor, K. M. An investigation of vocational indecision in college students: Correlates and moderators. JOURNAL OF VOCATIONAL BEHAVIOR, 1982, 21, 318–329.

18. Wood, P. H. The Nelson-Denny Reading Test as a predictor of college freshman grades. EDUCATIONAL AND PSYCHOLOGICAL MEASUREMENT, 1982, 42, 575–583.

19. Zagar, R., Arbit, J., & Wengel, W. Personality factors as predictors of grade point average and graduation from nursing school. EDUCA-

TIONAL AND PSYCHOLOGICAL MEASUREMENT, 1982, 42, 1169–1175.

20. Ansley, T. N., & Forsyth, R. A. Relationship of elementary and secondary school achievement test scores to college performance. EDUCATIONAL AND PSYCHOLOGICAL MEASUREMENT, 1983, 43, 1103–1112.

21. Frank, B. M. Flexibility of information processing and the memory of field-independent and field-dependent learners. JOURNAL OF RESEARCH IN PERSONALITY, 1983, 17, 89–96.

22. Gorrell, D. Toward determining a minimal competency entrance examination for freshman composition. RESEARCH IN THE TEACHING OF ENGLISH, 1983, 17, 263–274.

23. Huba, M. E. Relationships among high school size, other high school characteristics, and achievement in the freshman year of college. COLLEGE STUDENT JOURNAL, 1983, 17, 284–293.

24. Knowles, B. S., & Knowles, P. S. A model for identifying learning disabilities in college-bound students. JOURNAL OF LEARNING DISABILITIES, 1983, 16, 39–42.

25. Snyder, V., & Elmore, P. B. The predictive validity of the Descriptive Tests of Language Skills for developmental students over a four-year college program. EDUCATIONAL AND PSYCHOLOGICAL MEASUREMENT, 1983, 43, 1113–1122.

26. Stansfield, C., & Hansen, J. Field dependence-independence as a variable in second language cloze test performance. TESOL QUARTERLY, 1983, 17, 29–38.

27. Taylor, K. M., & Betz, N. E. Applications of self-efficacy theory to the understanding and treatment of career indecision. JOURNAL OF VOCATIONAL BEHAVIOR, 1983, 22, 63–81.

Review of ACT Assessment Program by LEWIS R. AIKEN, Professor of Psychology, Pepperdine University, Malibu, CA:

Begun in 1959 under the direction of E. F. Lindquist, the American College Testing Program (ACT) is based on a similar philosophy and approach as the Iowa Tests of Educational Development (ITED). Today the ACT holds the second position among college admissions tests in terms of the number of students who take it, surpassed only by the Scholastic Aptitude Test (SAT) of the College Entrance Examination Board.

Like the SAT, the ACT program has grown over the years in numbers of tests administered as well as services provided to users. It is now administered five times annually (February, March or April, June, October, December) to over a million students at more than 3,300 centers in the United States and 200 centers in 70 foreign countries. On January 5, 1984, more college-bound students in 28 states took the ACT than any other college admissions test. The basic assessment fee of approximately $10 includes reports of test results to six colleges of the student's choice.

There are three major parts in the ACT Assessment Program: The Academic Tests, the Student Profile Section, and the ACT Interest Inventory. The four Academic Tests are: English Usage Test, Mathematics Usage Test, Social Studies Reading Test, and Natural Sciences Reading Test. The Mathematics Usage Test comprises approximately 30% of the testing time, with the remaining tests measuring both reading skills and applied knowledge in the specific area. Total testing time for the Academic Tests is 2 hours, 40 minutes, but the time for directions increases that to over 3 hours.

The four Academic Tests are described in the brochure, Content of the Tests in the ACT Assessment, as follows:

> The English Usage Test is a 75-item, 40-minute test that measures the students' understanding of the conventions of standard written English in punctuation, grammar, sentence structure, diction and style, and logic and organization. The test does not measure the rote recall of rules of grammar, but stresses the analysis of the kind of effective expository writing that will be encountered in many postsecondary curricula. The test consists of several prose passages with certain portions underlined and numbered. For each underlined portion, four alternative responses, including "NO CHANGE," are given. The student must decide which alternative is most appropriate in the context of the passage....
>
> The Mathematics Usage Test is a 40-item, 50-minute test that measures the students' mathematical reasoning ability. It emphasizes the solution of practical quantitative problems that are encountered in many postsecondary curricula and includes a sampling of mathematical techniques covered in high school courses. The test emphasizes quantitative reasoning, rather than memorization of formulas, knowledge of techniques, or computational skill. Each item in the test poses a question with five alternative answers, the last of which may be "None of the above."...
>
> The Social Studies Reading Test is a 52-item, 35-minute test that measures the comprehension, analytical and evaluative reasoning, and problem solving skills required in the social studies. There are two types of items: the first is based on reading passages, the second on general background or information obtained primarily in high school social studies courses. All items are multiple choice with four alternatives. The items based on the reading passages require not only reading comprehension skills, but the ability to draw inferences and conclusions, to examine the interrelationships and import of ideas in a passage, to extend the thoughts of a passage to new situations, to make deductions from experimental or graphic data, and to recognize a writer's bias, style, and mode of reasoning. The discrete information items ask the students to apply what they have learned in high school social studies courses to familiar, new or analogous problems....
>
> The Natural Sciences Reading Test is a 52-item, 35-minute test that measures the interpretation, analysis, evaluation, critical reasoning, and problem-solving skills required in the natural sciences. There are two types of items: the first is based on reading passages, the second on information about science. All items are multiple choice with four alternatives. The passages concern a variety of scientific topics and problems. Descriptions of scientific experiments and discussions of current scientific theories are the most common formats. The items require the students to understand and distinguish among the purposes of experiments, to examine the logical relationships between experimental hypotheses and the generalizations that can be drawn from experiments, to predict the effects of ideas in a passage on new situations, to

propose alternate ways to conduct experiments, and to judge the practical value of the ideas and theories presented in a passage. The discrete information items ask the students to apply what they have learned in high school science courses to familiar, new or analogous problems. Although these items require the understanding of significant facts, they require only minimal algebraic and arithmetic computations.

New forms of the four Academic Tests are developed each year, involving the services of high school and college teachers who are experts in the specific subject-matter. An item writing assignment consists of specifications for a certain number of items to be written in each of several classification categories, in addition to details on item format and content classifications within categories. Item writers are also provided with a guide concerning contract terms, considerations pertaining to item difficulty and style, and sample items in various classification categories. After being submitted to the ACT staff, the completed items are edited and given preliminary tryouts on representative samples of 350 examinees in several hundred school systems.

A standard score scale is used for reporting scores on the four ACT Academic Tests and the Composite, which is the average of the standard scores on the four separate tests. The scale ranges from 1 to 36; the overall mean standard scores for entering college freshmen in 1982 were 18.2 for English, 17.4 for Mathematics, 17.8 for Social Studies, 21.2 for Natural Sciences, and 18.8 for Composite.

Scaled score equivalents are provided for each form of the test by the equipercentile method based on the score distribution of an anchor form of the ACT. New forms of the tests are equated to older forms by giving both forms to parallel samples of students and then equating the forms by the equipercentile method. In reporting the results for a given test date, a score correction is made so students tested later in the school year will not have an advantage over those tested earlier. As with the SAT Verbal and Mathematical scores, annual declines in mean ACT scores were observed during the 1970s. However, the mean standard scores on the tests appear to have stabilized during recent years.

Internal consistency reliability data of the ACT tests administered in June 1984 were: English Usage (.92), Mathematics Usage (.91), Social Studies Reading (.88), Natural Sciences Reading (.85). The reliabilities of the ACT English and Mathematics scores are quite similar to those of the SAT Verbal (.91) and Mathematical (.90) scores. With respect to errors of measurement on the ACT Academic Tests, the standard score scale was designed originally to yield a probable error of 1.00. Thus, the chances on current versions of the test are approximately 50–50 that a student's true score will fall within one unit of his or her obtained score.

Comparisons of the content of the ACT with the item specifications for the four tests point to a substantial degree of content validity. The predictive validity coefficients vary with the specific test and criterion, the ACT Composite score correlating around .40 to .50 with college freshman grade point averages. The ACT tests also add to the validity of high school grades in predicting college grades. The predictive validity coefficients are essentially the same for disadvantaged and advantaged students, indicating that the tests are not biased.

Although the Academic Tests of the ACT are used extensively for college admissions purposes, the abundant literature provided to secondary schools emphasizes using the tests and other parts of the ACT program in counseling and guidance. The ACT Assessment High School Report contains not only the test results expressed in raw score, standard score, and percentile rank (national and local) form, but also the results of the Student Profile Section and the ACT Interest Inventory. The ACT Assessment Student Report also includes a detailed narrative interpretation of results.

The Student Profile Section (SPS) and ACT Interest Inventory are completed at the time the student applies to take the Academic Tests. The SPS is basically a detailed (192 items) college application blank, including demographic data, high school information, years specific subjects were studied in high school, notable high school accomplishments, work experience, and community service. The ACT Interest Inventory is a 90-item survey of students' preferences in six areas: Science, Creative Arts, Social Service, Business Contact, Business Detail, and Technical. The six interest areas, which correspond to John Holland's typology, consist of 15 three-point items on which students indicate their degree of liking or disliking of something. A Technical Report for the Unisex Edition of the ACT Interest Inventory (1981) and other available ACT literature describe a Map of College Major, a World-of-Work Map, and a Career Family List that can be used by counselors in advising students on their academic and vocational careers (see Using ACT in Advising 1983–1984).

Through its research services to secondary schools and colleges, the American College Testing Program offers a wealth of information for use in individual and institutional decision making. In addition to the standard ACT Assessment College Report, magnetic tape reports, punched card sets for disk storage, and other report media are available. Requests from the general public for information about the ACT Assessment Tests are responded to with as many as nine different brochures. Additionally, more than 40 reports or booklets are provided to institutions requesting details on the validity, norming, and reporting services of the ACT Assessment Program. Other "secure" information concerning the test questions, manuals of administration, technical analysis reports, high school reports, and state and national trend data can also be obtained by qualified persons. Of special interest are issues of the ACT Research Bulletin and ACT Research Report, which describe research on the validity and other psychometric features of the tests. An annually-published College Student Profiles: Norms for the ACT Assessment is also useful for its breakdown of ACT score distributions according to college and student demographic characteristics.

The ACT differs from its closest competitor, the SAT, in a number of ways. First, the SAT is more popular in the East and Far West, whereas the ACT is administered more frequently in the Midwest. Although total testing time for the two examinations is approximately the same, the SAT consists of two parts (Verbal and Mathematical) and a combined score generally is not reported. The ACT also emphasizes reading and other linguistic skills more than mathematics, which constitutes only one of the four tests.

Other differences between the ACT and SAT have to do with scoring: no correction for guessing is employed on the ACT, as it is in scoring the SAT. The SAT also provides, at extra cost, a series of advanced placement tests in specific college subjects. Finally, students are not typically encouraged to retake the ACT, although circumstances may lead them to do so. Retaking the SAT, on the other hand, is apparently fairly common.

In general, both the ACT and SAT assess knowledge and skills acquired in and out of school over a period of years. Although not denying the value of coaching or last-minute review, both the ACT Program and the College Entrance Examination Board have tended to deemphasize the value of coaching in improving one's ACT or SAT scores. In any event, both sets of tests are recognized as well-designed measures of both achievement and aptitude: they reflect past learning, but they also predict future academic performance.

Review of ACT Assessment Program by EDWARD KIFER, Associate Professor of Education, University of Kentucky, Lexington, KY:

When I discuss the "ACTs" with students in measurement classes we typically talk about four test scores, an average or composite of the scores, and how those scores are used to determine whether or not students will be admitted to a college or college program of their choice. For my part, I wish to emphasize technical properties of the tests: do they measure what they purport to measure, are they precise measures, and do they predict well what they are supposed to predict? Students tend to emphasize how they are misused, what a bother it is to take them, and how they might not mean anything anyway. Further discussion might include the so-called test score decline, whether the tests are fair to minorities, and whether or not scores can be raised through intense study or tutoring.

Often a sense of mystery pervades the discussion since none of us knows who writes the test, how the questions are written, who looks at the scores, who really makes selection decisions (could it be a computer?), or whether there are particularly happy or tragic educational consequences for any one person with a specific set of scores. Are the tests merely ritual requirements? Do scores—high, low, or middle—make a difference?

Such conversations merely scratch the surface of what is the ACT. The American College Testing (ACT) Assessment includes academic tests in English, Mathematics, Social Studies, and Natural Sciences. In addition, however, the assessment includes a long Student Profile section that provides background information on students who take the assessment and an Interest Inventory that measures students' preferences and categorizes them into general career or occupational areas.

Thus, the assessment generates hundreds of variables and an incredible amount of information about those who are to enter colleges and universities. The information is used as a foundation for various other programs such as the ACT Research Services to help participating colleges and universities better understand their present student body, the ACT Student Need Analysis Service to help students apply and receive financial aid, the ACT Proficiency Examination Program aimed to give students academic credits for performance on any of 49 available standardized tests, and the ACT Evaluation/Survey Service which is designed to help colleges and universities collect information about their students—future, present, and past.

Money collected from prospective students and institutions of higher education, augmented one assumes through outside grants and contracts, finances an elaborate reporting mechanism which provides information to those who have been tested as well as their high schools, colleges, counselors, and other professionals who deal with test results. Also supported is an extremely elaborate and technically sophisticated research program that focuses not only on the assessment devices themselves but also on issues (e.g., test item bias, test score declines, and fairness in selection practices) which pervade the testing enterprise in today's educational climate.

The American College Testing Program will provide information to help colleges and universities recruit students, provide equal educational opportunities, and simplify their admission systems. Suggested additional uses for the information gathered through the assessment include providing better orientation for students, sorting them into homogeneous ability groups, providing advanced placement and credit by examination, and closely monitoring students to prevent, if possible, their attrition from the institution.

What ACT is, then, is not the four tests and several issues that we talk about in class; it is, instead, a large, well-organized, technically competent, highly computerized business organization with the means to influence substantially who goes to what institution of higher education and what students encounter when they get there.

This review deals mainly with the assessment instruments, their technical properties, score reporting, and the more typical issues surrounding test construction and test use. Yet, it is important to remember that while the ACT touches students directly when they take the test, receive their scores, and talk with a counselor, it may influence indirectly many aspects of their college and university lives. What exactly are those indirect influences and whether they have major consequences for educational and later careers and accomplishments are issues of crucial importance that will be addressed only tangentially.

THE FOUR ACADEMIC TESTS. Although descriptions of the characteristics of the tests have not changed greatly since they were reviewed in *The Eighth Mental Measurements Yearbook* (8:469), what is purported to be measured remains crucial. The following are excerpts from a 1984 edition of Using the ACT Assessment on Campus:

> The English Usage Test (75 items, 40 minutes). This test measures the student's understanding of the conventions of standard written English: in punctuation, grammar, sentence structure, diction and style, and logic and organization. The test does not measure the rote recall of rules of grammar but stresses the analysis of the kind of effective expository writing that will be encountered in many postsecondary curricula....
>
> The Mathematics Usage Test (40 items, 50 minutes). This test measures the student's mathematical reasoning ability. It emphasizes the solution of practical quantitative problems that are encountered in many college courses and includes mathematical techniques typically covered in high school courses. The test emphasizes quantitative reasoning, rather than memory of formulas, knowledge of techniques, or computational skill....
>
> The Social Studies Reading Test (52 items, 35 minutes). This test measures the student's ability to read, analyze, and evaluate social studies materials....items based on reading passages require reading comprehension skills and the ability to draw inferences and conclusions, to examine the interrelationships and import of ideas, to extend ideas to new situations, to make deductions from experimental or graphic data and to recognize a writer's bias, style and mode of reasoning....
>
> The Natural Sciences Reading Test (52 items, 35 minutes). This test measures the student's ability to read, analyze, and evaluate material from the natural sciences....questions...require reading comprehension skills and the ability to understand and distinguish between the purposes of experiments, to examine the logical relationship between experimental hypotheses and the generalizations that can be drawn from the experiments, to predict the effect of the application of ideas to new situations, to judge the practical value of elements in an experiment, and to evaluate proposed alternative ways of conducting an experiment....

As descriptions of what is contained in the tests and as a basis for discussing aspects of the content validity of the tests, these descriptions appear to me to be both reasonable and responsible. It is clear, for example, that the majority of items on each test are written to measure skills other than an ability to remember facts, rules, or specific information. Depending on the test, up to 70% of the items appear to require students to do what might be called more cognitively complex things, that is, to apply knowledge rather than merely recall it. The Social Studies Reading test has rather more of these items than the other tests, while the Mathematics Usage Test has fewer.

An emphasis on one aspect of a test and its construction, in this case on what could be called the behavioral facet, can have unintended consequences for other aspects. For example, there appears to be a heavy emphasis on reading in all of the tests. Whether that leads to the high correlations among them (from .61 to .74 in 1964; and .53 to .68 in 1970 according to the technical manual), apparently has not been investigated systematically. Although the technical manual reports a research study with results suggesting a common thread among the tests, this was interpreted as a general ability dimension rather than a reading dimension. Should, for instance, a standard reading test predict college performance as well or nearly as well as the ACT Assessment, an appropriate question would be "why give four tests if one will do as well?"

More important than the above, I believe, is what appears to be less emphasis on the content dimensions of the tests. The Natural Science and Mathematics tests, in particular, are mixtures of a number of distinct content areas. The technical manual recognizes the problem of interpreting scores from a test that contains equal proportions of distinct content areas—Geometry and Advanced Algebra, for instance. (What should be said about the equal mathematics scores from two students, one of whom had no Geometry and the other no Advanced Algebra?) Yet, the argument concludes with an assumption about uniform mathematics curricula and an emphasis on "mathematics usage ability" rather than mathematics achievement. But such a statement does not square with the content of the items. Included in the tests are items which require solving straightforward simultaneous equations, or doing matrix multiplication, or solving a problem of similar triangles. All of these are clearly anchored in distinct curricular experiences. If there is a paradox about the ACT Assessment tests, it is the content labels given to the tests and the ability interpretations that result from them.

Two other technical matters should be mentioned. First, it should be noted that each of the tests is timed. While this helps to standardize the conditions under which the tests are taken, it presents problems of score interpretations if not all examinees finish. Results from 1968 to 1971, presented in the technical manual, suggest that just over half of the examinees finished the test in the Natural Sciences. About 10% more than that finished in Social Studies. More recent studies suggest higher completion rates for all tests with slightly over 3/4 of the examinees finishing the Social Studies section. These increased completion rates are desirable since speeded tests, when examinees do not finish them, will tend to have artificially inflated reliability coefficients but underestimated standard errors of measurement. This technical issue is further influenced by an ACT policy on guessing which is essentially to encourage it but not to adjust the scores. Both phenomena add noise to scores but make the tests appear technically stronger than they really are.

A test can be no stronger than its individual components—the items. ACTs primary competitor in the college admissions test area is Educational Testing Service's (ETS) Scholastic Aptitude Tests. Hearsay suggests that ACT spends more time and effort writing, trying out, and revising items than does ETS. My view is that the items are, indeed, better. They do not have the clumsy response formats so characteristic of portions of the SATs and are written in straightforward, understandable prose. Both test programs, however, probably overemphasize item discrimination parameters in choosing questions and tend, therefore, to create exaggerated test score differences.

Each of these issues affects measures of reliability, properties typically considered of first importance when evaluating a test. The technical manual, which is dated and should be revised to include evidence from recent research reports, devotes a considerable amount of space to details of a variety of reliability studies. Internal consistency, test-retest, and coefficient alpha statistics are reported for each of the tests. In addition, research reports have estimated variance components to describe more precisely what influences test score differences. Each of these techniques is based on assumptions typically not met in practice and each accounts for different sources of error, so the reported coefficients vary considerably (between .6 an .9). Yet, the most critical observer should be impressed by the amount of time and effort devoted to understanding these properties of the tests and would probably conclude along with ACT that values in the range of .80 to .85 are reasonable estimates of the reliabilities. These are certainly high enough to make the tests potentially usable.

As mentioned above, ACT suggests several ways that test score results may be used. However, since the tests are essentially tools for selection, criterion-related or predictive validity is the crucial property that must be demonstrated. The technical manual summarizes hundreds of studies of the correlations among reported high school grades, ACT scores, and college grades. Although coefficients vary from study to study and institution to institution, typical results are generally well known: high school grades correlate more highly with college grades than do ACT scores with college grades; and a combination of predictors, high school grades and ACT scores, correlates more highly than either alone. A generous estimate of the incremental validity due to addition of ACT scores to a model that includes only high school grades is .1, from a correlation of about .5 to about .6. This represents about a 10% increase (25 to 35) in the amount of variation in college grades that can be explained by this predictor.

Since hundreds of thousands pay about $10.00 or so to sit for the ACT tests each year, one can raise the question of the marginal utility of the test. Is it worth that much money to that many persons for the size of the increase in predictive validity? In this regard, it should be pointed out that while these tests do predict college grades, there is no evidence that they are related to traditional academic goals such as making students more thoughtful, articulate, humane, or better people in their social and occupational lives. Hence, the increase in validity is both small and related to an extremely narrow criterion.

To be fair to ACT their publications are filled with reasonable and accurate discussions of the technical properties of their tests and warnings about how these scores could be misused. If the consumers of these test scores were as deliberate and cautious about drawing inferences about the meaning of the scores as those who write these very good manuals and brochures, I would worry less about potential abuses. A discussion of assessment bias contained in the technical manual is, for example, exemplary and raises important ethical, moral, and political issues related to fair selection of students.

Yet, the fact that such a discussion is in a technical volume and not a separate brochure implies that ACT believes that fair selection is just a technical issue. Nothing could be further from the truth. These test scores carry enormous symbolic value. There are those who confer high or low status on institutions and professions based on ACT scores. One even sees the quality of an education equated with the quantity of an institution's test scores. One searches high and low in the abundant ACT literature for a discussion of test scores and their meanings that would justify such strong interpretations or, preferably, a condemnation of such verbal and logical excesses.

Selective admissions means simply that an institution cannot or will not admit each person who completes an application. Choices of who will or will not be admitted should be, first of all, a matter of what the institution believes is desirable and may or may not include the use of prediction equations. It is just as defensible to select on talent broadly construed as it is to use test scores however high. There are talented students in many areas—leaders, organizers, doers, musicians, athletes, science award winners, opera buffs—who may have moderate or low ACT scores but whose presence on a campus would change it. The important point is that each set of attributes used to select students will produce a unique student body and an arguably different kind of institution and quality of education. A rank order based on talent will not be the same as one based on test scores which in turn will be different from one based on high school grades. Institutions should be reminded of this by any testing organization with such prestige and power.

ACT INTEREST INVENTORY (UNIACT). The ACT Interest Inventory is "intended for use by persons (junior high school students through adults) who are in the early stages of career planning or replanning. The primary purpose of UNIACT is to stimulate and facilitate self/career exploration; that is, the exploration of self in relation to careers."

UNIACT is the fourth edition of this inventory. Each edition is based on previous ones and all are based on the considerable theoretical and empirical work of John Holland. The several versions span almost 20 years; UNIACT, the latest version, is different in that it is designed to eliminate sex-role stereotyping and to be applicable to more diverse populations (the first ACT Interest Inventory was designed for students in grades 8 through 12).

Students respond to 90 activities (e.g., study science or run for the school board) by choosing one of three answers: (1) I would dislike doing this activity (D); (2) I am indifferent (I); or, (3) I would like doing this activity (L). The degree to which they respond positively to discrete sets of 15 items is the basis for giving them a score on each of the Basic Interest Scales: Science, Creative Arts, Social Services, Business Contact, Business Detail, and Technical. A second method of scoring based on the Like and Dislike categories provides a means to locate scores on a grid, one dimension of which goes from Data to Ideas and the second from Things to People.

These scores provide a means to place a person's reponses in categories to form a basis for exploring career and occupational interests. ACT provides a way to locate these categories on a World-of-Work map, a pie whose wedges are job clusters and whose dimensions are defined by the Things to People and Data to Ideas coordinates. While my verbal description may be difficult to understand, ACT solves such a problem with an effective graphic called the World-of-Work map. It portrays persons' scores in an easy-to-read manner and summarizes concretely the results of a series of complex and sophisticated statistical analyses of scores.

In its guides to use and interpretations of these data, ACT quite rightly emphasizes their tentative and exploratory nature. They point out that other factors (grades, test scores, motivation, college major) influence crucially what occupations are available and who will be considered acceptable for them.

The Technical Report for UNIACT is recent, well-organized, and thorough. Standard empirical evidence (various measures of reliability and validity) that one would expect is available and easily perused. Internal consistency measures for the separate interest scales range from about .8 to .9. As one would expect, the test-retest or stability estimates are slightly lower over a 6-week time span and substantially lower (.5 to .6) over a 4-year span. These results compare favorably to technical details reported for the major competing interest measures such as the Strong-Campbell and the Kuder. As with other interest inventories, the evidence about the precision of the measurement can be rather easily summarized: the longer between test administrations, the more the scores change; and the younger the person who takes the test, the larger the score changes on a second administration.

The validity evidence reported by ACT is what one would expect from an organization so blessed with technical expertise. Although the technical manual gives various labels to the validity studies, taken as a whole it is construct validity that is being established. As was mentioned earlier, the instrument has a theoretical basis in the work of John Holland and has undergone extensive study and revision during its two decades of existence. While it is impossible in this review to do justice to Holland's work, it is important to note the crux of what he suggests. Stated at the most superficial level, he believes that one can classify academic majors and occupations by those things and activities typically emphasized within them and that persons can judge whether or not they belong in that major or occupation by the extent to which they have interests that correspond to what is typically done in the major or occupation. For instance, scientific careers tend to emphasize investigative activities while social service careers emphasize helping others; if one wanted to do something in biology, then his or her interests should be investigative; if one wanted to become a teacher then one should be interested in providing social service.

I believe the validity evidence is fairly summarized by the following: The scales have intercorrelations of modest size (from about .1 to .5), suggesting a kind of discriminant validity. They tend to correlate substantially with similar scales from other instruments (from about .4 to .9), indicating a type of convergent validity. With the exception of the Science scale where the correlations are modest (around .2), they tend not to correlate with high school academic performance. If one defines groups of persons by academic major, occupation, or occupational preference and then asks whether Holland's theory of what their interests should be corresponds on the average to their measured interests, one finds about 90% agreement, thus providing support for consistency between Holland's definitions and their empirical consequences. If one defines criterion groups by Holland's categories and then asks if each person's highest interest score is in the group that Holland's theory would suggest, one finds, depending on the study, that anywhere from about 35 to 50% of the individuals are correctly classified. Finally, if one takes persons who do not change their mind about their academic major from precollege to graduation and then place their majors in Holland's categories, the average interest score is highest on the scale that is most appropriate, is higher on the most appropriate scale than is any other group's scores, and those who remain in the academic major have higher average scores in the appropriate category than those who change or leave the major.

There is a sufficient amount of technical evidence about UNIACT to make me believe that it is as good as its principal competitors. It is important to reiterate what ACT says about its use. It is meant to be a basis for helping persons who are undecided about a career to begin an exploration of various options. From my point of view any other use would be a misuse. All interest inventories have an insular quality about them. There is no way to capture with paper and pencil tests most aspects of what life in a particular career or occupation might be like. Dreadful routines, boring meetings, intense pressure, joyful experiences, political in-fighting, petty quarrels, a sense of accomplishment, perks, pleasant occasions, funny experiences, and thousands of other daily occurrences cannot be captured by responding to 90 statements. If there were such a thing as the typical member of an occupation, it would take more than 15 sentences to describe him or her and the descriptions might not be appropriate for any other person who shared the occupation.

The real questions are whether people in general need these types of instruments in order to think about careers, and if they do, are these the best ways to approach the topic?

THE STUDENT PROFILE SECTION. The Student Profile Section (SPS) "allows prospective students to present themselves as individuals with unique abilities, aspirations, accomplishments, and needs"; it is a questionnaire designed to gather information about students on a variety of subjects. There are 192 questions about the student's background (e.g., name, gender, racial-ethnic group), educational and vocational plans (program of study, degree goal, etc.), out-of-class accomplishments (athletics, leadership, music, etc.), factors influencing the choice of college (who provides advice and what kind of college or university is considered desirable), and special needs such as financial aid or remedial education.

Information from the profile is then compiled and reported in various forms to students who take the test, institutions to which those same students have sent their scores, and the secondary schools from which the students will be graduated. If there is one outstanding aspect of the ACT assessment I believe that it is the quality of its reporting procedures. Reports sent back to the students are nicely formatted, present important information about test scores in an easily understood manner, and give a computer narrative that "individualizes" the report. Information sent back to the secondary school provides data about students in that school as well as norms and trend data from which it would be possible to make comparisons from year to year. Colleges and universities can, upon request, receive information about the grades, high school records, predicted grades of their prospective students, and a wide variety of other research and reporting services. The information can be compiled in almost any manner to provide institutions of higher education with information to be used in recruiting, selecting, placing, and following students through their college years.

The amount of research done on the technical properties of the student profile section of the ACT assessment appears to be both less and less recent than that on either the academic tests or the interest inventory. Evidence that is presented suggests the information given by students is, for the most part, accurate (for a subset of the items there was an average of about 90% agreement according to a 1973 study) and reasonably stable (test-retest correlations ranged from about .7 to .9 with longer periods between tests showing the lowest reliabilities). It would appear that the information is sufficiently accurate to provide reasonable aggregates or profiles for an institution.

For all parts of the assessment, ACT provides normative data on a large number of variables. There are charts for test scores by ethnic group, high school grades by college major, and factors influencing college choice, to name but a few of the 100 odd norms that are published. Although ACT uses the label "national norm" on occasion, that title can be misleading. The norms are built on students from all over the United States, but those students are not a random sample of United States students. Students who take the ACTs choose to take them and are not by any means a random sample. They tend to be more often, for instance, from the midwest and rather less often from the northeast, than would be true if the sample were representative.

CONCLUSION. ACT is a well developed, broad, and expertly supported information collection and dissemination agency. It has developed sophisticated assessment devices and has used them effectively to provide information to students and schools. It is clearly aware of at least a subset of issues surrounding testing (e.g., item bias, selection bias, careers that are gender-stereotyped) and has responded in technically competent ways to those issues.

Yet, while reading the ACT material I was taken by the extent to which any testing issue that was raised was addressed as mainly a technical one. If interest inventories are biased, change the items; if minorities score lower, have a panel judge the items; if selection is a problem, generate a model. Seldom is there a discussion of what might be at stake educationally when tests have inappropriate properties or are used unwisely. ACT seems unaware of how powerful the information it generates could be and how influential the organization might be.

As testing becomes more and more emphasized in education, it is important to start to look at the impact of testing on the students and institutions that are being served. It would be possible for a student to be tested from cradle to grave, sorted and sifted into and out of curricula, denied access and opportunities, and have his or her talent thwarted on the basis of test scores. With the ACT, a student could be recruited, admitted, assigned to classes, placed in a major, and followed throughout college through the use of assessment service information and little else. What impact would such a scenario have on the student or the institution? No one knows those answers and testing organizations are not asking such questions. They should be.

[44]

ACT Evaluation/Survey Service. High school, college; 1979–83; ESS; for measurement of groups, not individuals; no data on reliability; 2 levels; American College Testing Program.*

a) SECONDARY SCHOOL LEVEL. High school; 1979–83; 2 surveys; user's guide ('83, 33 pages); 1983 price data: $5 per 25 surveys; $8 per normative data report for each survey; $3.50 per user's guide; $4.50 per specimen set including a sample report; scoring service, $50 institutional reporting/handling fee plus $.45 per student; (15–25) minutes.

1) *High School Student Opinion Survey*. 1980; student's perceptions in 6 areas: high school environment, occupational preparation, educational preparation, high school characteristics, additional questions, comments and suggestions; 1 form (4 pages).

2) *Student Needs Assessment Survey*. 1979; students' satisfaction with the high school and students' personal and educational needs in 5 areas: career development, life skills development, knowing myself, educational planning, getting along with others; 1 form (4 pages).

b) POSTSECONDARY SCHOOL LEVEL. College; 1979–82; 9 surveys; user's guide ('81, 43 pages); 1983 price data: $5 per 25 surveys including 25 major/occupation code lists except the Withdrawing/Nonreturning Student Survey (Short Form); $3.25 per 25 Withdrawing/Nonreturning Student Survey (Short Form); $8 per normative data report for Alumni Survey or Student Opinion Survey; $4 per item catalog for selecting additional local questions; $3.50 per user's guide; $5 per specimen set including a sample report; scoring service, $50 institutional reporting/handling fee plus $.45 per student; (15–25) minutes.

1) *Adult Learner Needs Assessment Survey*. 1981; 1 form (4 pages).

2) *Alumni Survey*. College graduates; 1981, 1 form (4 pages).

3) *Alumni Survey (2-Year College Form)*. 2-Year college graduates; 1981; 1 form (4 pages).

4) *Entering Student Survey*. 1982; 1 form (4 pages).

5) *Student Opinion Survey*. 1981; 1 form (4 pages).

6) *Student Opinion Survey (2-Year College Form)*. 1981; 1 form (4 pages).

7) *Survey of Postsecondary Plans*. Prospective students; 1982; 1 form (4 pages).

8) *Withdrawing/Nonreturning Student Survey*. Students withdrawing prior to completing a degree or program; 1979; 1 form (4 pages).

9) *Withdrawing/Nonreturning Student Survey (Short Form)*. Students withdrawing prior to completing a degree or program; 1981; 1 form (2 pages).

Review of ACT Evaluation/Survey/Service by RODNEY T. HARTNETT, Research Associate, Office of Institutional Research, Professor, Graduate School of Education, Rutgers, The State University of New Jersey, New Brunswick, NJ:

Along with the Educational Testing Service, the American College Testing Program (ACT) is recognized as one of the two largest producers of college entrance examinations. Less well known, however, is the fact that both of these national agencies provide various other measurement-related services to secondary schools, institutions of higher education, and other educational organizations and agencies. The ACT Evaluation/Survey Service (ESS) is an excellent example of one of these non-admissions-testing services.

Available since 1979, the ESS is not one instrument, but, instead, a fairly extensive package of survey instruments and scoring services designed to assist educational institutions to gain a better understanding of their students and programs. The various components of the ESS are intended to be used primarily to provide group-reported information to (and about) schools and colleges; they are not intended to provide information about individuals. As a result, in passing judgment on the ESS the psychometric criteria by which more traditional instruments are evaluated are not particularly important, and, in some cases, even inappropriate.

The ESS has two distinct "families" of services, one for secondary schools and one for colleges and universities. The secondary school program consists of two instruments, the High School Student Opinion Survey, designed to explore the perceptions of students regarding the characteristics and environment of the school, and the Student Needs Assessment Survey, designed to explore the educational, career-related, and personal needs of the students. The college and university program is more elaborate. Intended to be particularly useful in connection with institutional research, self-study, and planning, the college-level ESS consists of nine instruments: an Adult Learner Needs Assessment Survey, to determine perceived educational and personal needs of adult students; an Alumni Survey (both a 4-year and 2-year college form), to assist in the evaluation of the impact of the college on students; the Entering Student Survey, to provide college personnel with various educational and background information about their entering students; the Student Opinion Survey, (again, both a 4-year and 2-year college form), to obtain student perceptions of the college's programs and services; a Survey of Postsecondary Educational Plans, to evaluate the plans of prospective students still in high school; and, finally, a Withdrawing/Nonreturning Student Survey (both a regular length and short form), to help determine why students drop out of college. Most of these questionnaires are four pages in length and require between 20–25 minutes to complete. All answers are recorded directly on the surveys, which are machine-readable forms.

The format of all the ESS questionnaires are consistently neat and attractive, the instructions brief and clear. In appearance the questionnaires clearly reflect the efforts of professionals with experience in instrument development. Questionnaire content was determined on the basis of entirely rational (i.e., non-empirical) procedures, mainly discussions with professional educators and reviews of previous questionnaires and research. The content of most of the questionnaires in the series will be familiar to those who have done research on college students or educational environments. In fact, one might wonder about the advantages of using the various questionnaires in the ESS service, given the availability of many similar locally-developed instruments for these same purposes. One answer is that the ESS includes the associated advantage of user norms or relevant comparison data. Thus, for example, users will not only learn something about why students leave their college (which they could learn with their own "home-grown" instrument), but will also be able to compare reasons given by their withdrawing students to those given by students withdrawing from other institutions. Unfortunately, very little information about comparison data is provided in the ESS User's Guide, either for the secondary school or college services. The secondary level guide simply notes that "User norms...are available for both...ESS survey instruments," but no details are given. Similarly, the college-level user guide indicates that "User norms...are available for several of the ESS survey instruments." Sample comparison data are provided in the ESS Specimen Set for the Student Opinion Survey, and does include useful item distribution data based on 102 institutions.

Most of the information in the User's Guides has less to do with the ESS instruments themselves than with suggestions for how to carry out research with them. Excellent practical advice is given about selecting student samples, how to obtain high response rates, using graphics in interpreting survey results, and other matters that are important in conducting meaningful self studies. This emphasis once again reflects the fact that the ESS is not a traditional instrument designed for individual assessment, but a package of measurement services designed to describe institutions. It should not be surprising, then, that the content of the ESS User's Guides resemble that of the manual for the ACT Institutional Self-Study Service Survey, which was the predecessor to the ESS. Very little information about item-selection techniques, reliability, or validity is reported. The secondary school guide, in fact, contains virtually no information about these topics, arguing that the validity of the instruments lies in the items themselves, which deal directly with important aspects of the secondary school. Readers wishing more information about reliability and validity of the secondary school measures are invited to contact ACT. Limited reliability information is reported in the college-level guide in the form of percent of similar item responses on two administrations of the Student Opinion Survey. The data reported do suggest a high degree of stability in student responses; unfortunately, these findings are based only on the Student Opinion Survey and thus tell us nothing about the reliability of the other college-level ESS instruments.

The authors correctly argue that traditional indices of reliability are inappropriate for the ESS measures, but one would hope for more in the way of percent agreements on two administrations. Also, a number of validity questions could and should be addressed. Do schools that receive poor student ratings of their physical facilities in fact compare unfavorably with other schools? Did students who cited unchallenging courses as a major reason for withdrawing from college have different records of performance than remaining students? How do alumni who give high ratings to the college differ from those who are less positive?

The ESS instruments have much to recommend them. They are comprehensive, flexible, and straightforward. To the extent that many schools and colleges have a need for and use such measurement services their value increases, for increased use would probably translate into greater availability of relevant comparison-group information. Such comparison information, especially if coupled with a backup series of technical reports dealing with validity questions, would make the ESS attractive indeed. Interested schools or colleges would then have to decide if these advantages justify the cost of using ESS rather than their own measures.

[45]

ACT Proficiency Examination Program. College and adults; 1964–83; PEP; designed to meet need for "examinations that measure subject matter proficiency attained primarily outside typical classrooms....to award credit or to make other decisions concerning student proficiency"; test administered up to 6 times annually (February, March, May, June, October, November) at centers established by the publisher; 49 tests (31 objective, 7 essay, 11 objective and essay); 3 types of scores: standard scores, letter grades (A, B, C, D, F), and pass-fail grades; candidate registration guide ('82, 15 pages); user's guide ('83, 20 pages); technical handbook ('83–'84, 109 pages); study guide ('80–'82, 4–15 pages) for each test; new essay questions are prepared for each testing period; 1985 examination fee: $40 to $235 per test (fee includes reporting of scores to the candidate and one college); 180(210) minutes except as listed below; all tests developed and in the case of the essay tests graded by the faculty committee from The University of the State of New York; American College Testing Program.*

a) ACCOUNTING. 5 tests.
1) *Level* 1. Objective; 6 credits; fee, $50.
2) *Level* 2. Objective/essay; 9 credits; fee, $125; 240(270) minutes.
3) *Level* 3, *Areas* 1, 2, *and* 3. Essay; 3 tests; 12 credits if all tests are passed; fee, $125 per area.

b) ADULT NURSING. Objective; 8 credits; fee, $40.

c) AFRO-AMERICAN HISTORY. Objective; 6 credits; fee, $40.

d) AMERICAN HISTORY. Objective/Essay; 6 credits; fee, $60.

e) ANATOMY AND PHYSIOLOGY. Objective; 6 credits; fee, $40.

f) BUSINESS ENVIRONMENT AND STRATEGY. Objective/essay; 6 credits; fee, $125; 240(270) minutes.

g) COMMONALITIES IN NURSING CARE, AREAS 1 AND 2. Objective; 2 tests; 4 credits per area; fee, $50 per area.

h) CORRECTIVE AND REMEDIAL INSTRUCTION IN READING. Objective; 9 credits; fee, $40.

i) CRIMINAL INVESTIGATION. Objective; 3 credits; fee, $40.

j) DIFFERENCES IN NURSING CARE. Areas 1, 2, and 3. Objective; 3 tests; 4 credits per area; fee, $50 per area.

k) EARTH SCIENCE. Objective/essay; 6 credits; fee, $60.

l) EDUCATIONAL PSYCHOLOGY. Objective; 3 credits; fee, $40.

m) FINANCE. 3 tests.
1) *Level* 1. Objective; 9 credits; fee, $50.
2) *Level* 2. Objective/essay; 9 credits; fee, $125; 240(270) minutes.
3) *Level* 3. Essay; 12 credits; fee, $235; 420(450) minutes.

n) FOUNDATIONS OF GERONTOLOGY. Objective; 3 credits; fee, $40.

o) FRESHMAN ENGLISH. Objective/essay; 6 credits; fee, $60.

p) FUNDAMENTALS OF NURSING. Objective; 10 credits; fee, $40.

q) HEALTH RESTORATION, AREAS 1 AND 2. Objective; 2 tests; 4 credits per area; fee, $50.

r) HEALTH SUPPORT, AREAS 1 AND 2. Objective; 2 tests; 4 credits per area; fee, $50.

s) HISTORY OF AMERICAN EDUCATION. Objective/essay; 3 credits; fee, $60.

t) INTRODUCTION TO CRIMINAL JUSTICE. Objective; 3 credits; fee, $40.

u) MANAGEMENT OF HUMAN RESOURCES. 3 tests.
1) *Level* 1. Objective; 6 credits; fee, $50.
2) *Level* 2. Objective/essay; 9 credits; fee, $125; 240(270) minutes.
3) *Level* 3. Essay; 12 credits; fee, $235; 420(450) minutes.

v) MARKETING. 3 tests.
1) *Level* 1. Objective; 3 credits; fee, $50.
2) *Level* 2. Objective/essay; 9 credits; fee, $125; 240(270) minutes.
3) *Level* 3. Essay; 12 credits; fee, $235; 420(450) minutes.

w) MATERNAL AND CHILD NURSING. 2 tests.
1) *Associate Degree*. Objective; 6 credits; fee, $40.
2) *Baccalaureate Degree*. Objective; 8 credits; fee, $40.

x) NURSING HEALTH CARE. Objective; 4 credits; fee, $50.

y) OCCUPATIONAL STRATEGY, NURSING. Objective; 4 credits; fee, $50.

z) OPERATIONS MANAGEMENT. 3 tests.
1) *Level* 1. Objective; 9 credits; fee, $50.
2) *Level* 2. Objective/essay; 9 credits; fee, $125; 240(270) minutes.
3) *Level* 3. Essay; 12 credits; fee, $235; 420(450) minutes.

aa) PHYSICAL GEOLOGY. Objective; 3 credits; fee, $40.

bb) PROFESSIONAL STRATEGIES, NURSING. Objective; 4 credits; fee, $50.
cc) PSYCHIATRIC/MENTAL HEALTH NURSING. Objective; 8 credits; fee, $40.
dd) READING INSTRUCTION IN THE ELEMENTARY SCHOOL. Objective; 6 credits; fee, $40.
ee) SHAKESPEARE. Objective/essay; 3 credits; fee, $60.

TEST REFERENCES

1. Suddick, D. E., & Collins, B. A. A validation of the use of the American College Testing Proficiency Examination Program for advanced upper division placement of nursing students graduated from hospital-based (diploma) nursing programs. EDUCATIONAL AND PSYCHOLOGICAL MEASUREMENT, 1982, 42, 1177–1179.

[46]

Action Research Skill Inventory. Adults in organizational settings; 1981; skill development checklist; "assessment of the research process skills of trainers, consultants, researchers, and managers and others interested in the practical application of scientific methodology"; 3 scores (current skill, desired skill, difference) in each of 16 areas measuring specific action research behaviors; no data on reliability or validity; no norms; 1 form (7 pages, contained in manual); manual (20 pages, including checklist); 1984 price data: $3 per inventory; $4 per manual; administration time not reported; Robert C. Preziosi; Development Publications.*

[47]

Activities For Assessing Classification Skills, Experimental Edition. Ages 7–8 and slow learning children, 9–12 and advanced younger children; 1979; 4 scores: additive classification, class inclusion, cross-classification, matrices and intersections; no data on reliability of additive classification and cross-classification; no norms; 2 levels; Forms A (ages 7–8 and slow learning children, 21 pages), B (ages 9–12 and advanced younger children, 21 pages); manual (56 pages); 1983 price data: £2.45 per pad of tests; £3.95 per manual; £1.45 per class record form; (50–70) minutes; Rachel Gal-Choppin; NFER-Nelson Publishing Co. [England].*

[48]

Adaptive Behavior Inventory for Children. Ages 5–11; 1982; ABIC; component of the System of Multicultural Pluralistic Assessment; interview questionnaire for use with parent or most knowledgeable adult; 6 scales: Family, Community, Peer Relations, Nonacademic School Roles, Earner/Consumer, Self-Maintenance; individual; Record Form (2 pages); manual (121 pages, interview questions in English and Spanish); 1983 price data: $26.50 per complete kit including 25 record forms, manual, and scoring keys; $7 per 25 record forms; $15 per manual; (40–50) minutes; Jane R. Mercer and June F. Lewis; The Psychological Corporation.*

See T3:2387 (9 references) for ABIC and related references.

TEST REFERENCES

1. Scott, L. S., Mastenbrook, J. L., Fisher, A. T., & Gridley, G. C. Adaptive Behavior Inventory for Children: The need for local norms. JOURNAL OF SCHOOL PSYCHOLOGY, 1982, 20, 39–44.

Review of Adaptive Behavior Inventory for Children by JAMES E. JIRSA, School Psychologist, Madison (Wisconsin) Metropolitan School District, Madison, WI:

PURPOSE. The Adaptive Behavior Inventory for Children (ABIC) assesses a child's role behavior in a variety of nonschool settings including the home, community, and neighborhood in order to provide a multidimensional view of the child based on the family's perspective and norms. The inventory is considered by its authors to be a method for addressing the American Association on Mental Deficiency definition of retardation, which includes subaverage intellectual functioning and adaptive behavior deficits evident during the developmental period.

ADMINISTRATION AND SCORING. The manual provides necessary and useful administration and scoring information in a logical and straightforward manner. The record form is explained and includes examples of age calculation, which is very useful for interviewers not familiar with this process. The ABIC interview consists of 242 questions, the first 35 of which are asked of all respondents while the remainder are age-dependent and subject to baseline/ceiling rules.

Twenty-four items are used as a "Veracity" measure. These questions are deliberately placed at inappropriate mastery age levels throughout the interview and serve to alert the interviewer to the potential for unreliable information being obtained when 1 (Emergent Role) and 2 (Mastered Role) responses are offered by the respondent. This is a useful ABIC feature.

Each ABIC interview response is scored according to five possibilities: 0 (Never), 1 (Sometimes), 2 (Often), N (No Opportunity/Not Allowed), and DK (Don't Know). A problem with this approach is that while the "N" response lowers the adaptive behavior score, it does not provide a way to explain or qualify why there is no opportunity. Cultural tradition or socioeconomic considerations may limit a child's opportunity, but additional factors in the home, over and above culture and SES, may be operating which the interviewer would be unable to tap and use within the ABIC format. There is also no method for determining a child's motivation for learning certain adaptive behaviors, whether or not the opportunity is provided, or if the child is or is not allowed to perform the behavior(s) in question.

A completed ABIC profile based on scaled scores provides a graphic representation of the child's functioning in the six areas assessed; a total average score is also plotted. A possibly confusing comment in the manual refers to the lowest 3% of the profile distribution as "At Risk," and indicates that this area is shaded red on the profile bars. When the ABIC is used as a stand-alone procedure, separate from the SOMPA, the profile is a part of the ABIC record form and the at-risk population is designated by blue shading.

The use of a profile to display results is considered a very appropriate procedure. Many adults, when presented with unfamiliar assessment information in a strictly numerical fashion, tend to miss much of the accompanying verbal explanation in an effort to assimilate all the numbers. It is also possible with the ABIC to provide parents and others with age-equivalent findings based on raw scores. The profile and age-equivalent scores should encourage clear communication among the respondent, agency representatives if they are involved, and school staff.

Although the interview may be completed in approximately one hour, the scoring process involving six templates together with raw score conversion, profiling, and a thorough rechecking, could easily be expected to double that estimate. If the recommendation that the interview be conducted in the home is followed, travel time must also be considered.

STANDARDIZATION AND TECHNICAL DATA. The manual contains a brief summary of the ABIC standardization process and related technical data and refers the user to the SOMPA Technical Manual. The Technical Manual contains a great deal of pertinent information which documents that the ABIC is a well standardized adaptive behavior assessment strategy.

The ABIC items were generated by interviewing parents of retarded children, other parents specifically recruited and paid for the task, and through the authors' previous research. The initial item pool was pretested with 1,259 parents and tentative decisions regarding the age placement of each item were made. An item analysis of the final standardization sample compared responses by socioeconomic level, ethnic group membership, and sex of the child. Although confounded by socioeconomic status, significant differences related to ethnicity were found in 141 questions; the differences in terms of sex and socioeconomic status were not considered significant since they tended to balance out.

The final standardization sample consisted of responses from 2,085 interviews: 696 Black respondents, 690 Hispanic, and 699 White. While equal ethnic group representation in the standardization sample is thereby demonstrated, equal representation certainly does not exist in the California population where the research was conducted, nor is it likely to exist in any other location where the ABIC would be used. In addition, although the Duncan Socioeconomic Index was used to determine family socioeconomic status, these data are not reported; thus ABIC users are unable to determine to what extent, if any, the standardization sample matches the local population. Users are advised, therefore, that ABIC findings may seriously under- or overestimate adaptive behavior.

Reliability of the ABIC is very good; split-half (odd-even) data are provided for the Total Score and for each ethnic group at each age level from 5 to 11 years. A standard error of measurement statistic is provided for each reliability coefficient, a commendable practice. Total Score reliabilities for the entire standardization sample and for each ethnic group were .95 or higher. The separate scale reliabilities varied from .76 (Peer Relations at 11–0) to .92 (Community at ages 10–0 and 11–0).

In terms of validity, the authors argue that the usual practice of correlating the inventory scores with measures of intelligence, achievement, aptitude, or school performance is inappropriate because the ABIC is designed to assess the degree to which a child successfully meets the expectations of others in the social systems measured. However, the ABIC does not offer any method for developing information regarding those expectations or for making judgments regarding adaptive behavior on the basis of such comparisons. The SOMPA Technical Manual provides ABIC/WISC-R correlations which range from .05 (Performance IQ and Earner/Consumer) to .19 (Verbal IQ and Nonacademic School Roles).

SUMMARY. The ABIC is a well standardized approach to the assessment of adaptive behavior. The manual is clear in most respects and comprehensive, which should result in minimal interviewer error. The ABIC profile for displaying results should be helpful in communicating with parents and others and would allow the interviewer to analyze the patterns presented, both initially and longitudinally if desired. The two primary disadvantages of the ABIC involve, first, the possibility of lowering the scores of some children who are not allowed or do not have the opportunity to engage in certain behaviors without the interviewer being able to determine why there is no opportunity or why the behavior is not allowed. Secondly, the ABIC norms may not be applicable or appropriate for use nationwide. Given these cautions, the ABIC is nevertheless recommended for use since it represents a significant improvement over other instruments in the field, such as the Vineland Social Maturity Scale, in the assessment of adaptive behavior.

Review of Adaptive Behavior Inventory for Children by BENSON P. LOW, Clinical Instructor, Department of Psychiatry & Behavioral Sciences, University of Washington, Seattle, WA:

The Adaptive Behavior Inventory for Children (ABIC) is a useful measure of role functioning in elementary school children, and despite some relatively minor shortcomings, is worthy of inclusion in assessments of developmentally delayed and possibly retarded children.

On the minus side, the ABIC suffers from a lack of normative data on Asian children and Native-American children—a truly unfortunate omission, since the developers of the ABIC and its parent instrument, the System of Multicultural Pluralistic Assessment (SOMPA), originally sought to provide psychometricians with a broader basis for measuring intellectual competence and adaptive behavior in minority children.

Another noteworthy drawback is the limited presentation of psychometric data in the ABIC manual. Some data are provided regarding split-half reliability, and these figures are quite acceptable from a psychometric standpoint. There is, however, no data presented on construct or predictive validity. The reader is referred to the SOMPA Technical Manual, which I find frustrating and puzzling, since the ABIC is marketed independently of the SOMPA, and since the ABIC manual itself contains the enjoinder that "the technical characteristics of the ABIC...need to be understood by all users."

The ABIC also contains some scoring guidelines which are not as clear as they could be. For example, the ABIC yields a "Veracity" score which is to be used in detecting invalid protocols. The manual gives a guideline for determining when a protocol is "suspect," but gives no further clarification on when to eliminate completely the questionable protocol. There are specific cutoff points for discontinuing test administration, but no rationale for the establishment of these criteria.

In all fairness to the test authors, the technical data provided in the SOMPA Technical Manual give a more complete description of the way the ABIC was constructed. Split-half and interobserver reliability coefficients were quite acceptable. The scales showed a high degree of intercorrelation, which suggests that users exercise caution in interpreting various scale patterns, since there is a substantial amount of shared variance among the scales (i.e., the scales are not factorially pure, but they are still useful from a practical standpoint).

Finally, the authors adopted a somewhat circular definition of predictive validity, urging that the ABIC's validity be assessed as to its "ability to reflect accurately the extent to which the child is meeting the expectations of the members of the social systems covered in the scales" (SOMPA Technical Manual, 1979). The authors provide no external data in support of the ABIC's accuracy in measuring role behavior. The nature of the instrument makes such an omission perhaps less glaring, but the authors will need in the future to provide some substantial and credible external validation of the ABIC.

On the positive side, the ABIC seems to be a reliable and adequately normed measure of adaptive behavior for Black, Hispanic, and White children ages 5 through 11. It measures the conceptually important domain of adaptive behavior or role functioning, and is both a necessary and useful companion piece to traditional IQ tests in the intellectual assessment of developmentally "suspect" children in general, and in the assessment of Black or Hispanic children in particular. The ABIC extends and further differentiates the concept of intellectual competence, as the individual role scales reflect. More specifically, the instrument items themselves are more extensive than those found in predecessors such as the Vineland Social Maturity Scale, and the scale scores have obvious, practical teaching and evaluation uses for children who may be at risk.

On balance, despite the relatively minor drawbacks enumerated above, the ABIC appears to be a reliable and useful measure of adaptive behavior for Black, Hispanic, and White children ages 5 through 11. I encourage its use in developmental and intellectual assessments of such children.

REVIEWER'S REFERENCES

Mercer, J. R. SYSTEM OF MULTICULTURAL PLURALISTIC ASSESSMENT: TECHNICAL MANUAL. New York: The Psychological Corporation, 1979.

[49]

Adaptive Functioning Index. Ages 14 and over in rehabilitation or special education settings; 1971–78; AFI; ratings by staff; 3 subtests; no validity data; no norms; individual; administration manual ('76, 43 pages); program manual ('78, 198 pages); standardization manual ('77, 42 pages); target workbook ('77, 12 pages); program workbook ('77, 19 pages); record index ('71, 2 pages); workbooks and program manual not necessary for test administration; 1983 price data: $55 per complete kit; $5.20 per 10 target workbooks; $5.20 per 10 program workbooks; $4.95 per administration manual; $4.95 per standardization manual; $16 per programs manual; administration time not reported; Nancy J. Marlett and E. Anne Hughson (program workbook and target workbook); Vocational and Rehabilitation Research Institute [Canada].*

a) SOCIAL EDUCATION TEST. 9 scores: reading, writing, communication, concept attainment, number concepts, time, money handling, community awareness, motor movements; 1 form ('71, 16 pages); $5.20 per 10 tests.

b) VOCATIONAL CHECK LIST. 12 scores: basic work habits (independence, making decisions, use and care of equipment and materials, taking direction), work skills (speed of movement, ability to follow instructions, competence, skill level), acceptance skills (appearance, attendance/punctuality, self-expressions, relations with co-workers); 1 form ('71, 8 pages); $3.40 per 10 tests.

c) RESIDENTIAL CHECK LIST. 15 scores: personal routines (cleanliness, appearance and eating, room management, time management, health), community awareness (transportation, shopping, leisure, budgeting, cooking and home management), social maturity (communication, consideration, getting friends, keeping friends, handling problems); 1 form ('71, 8 pages); $3.40 per 10 tests.

d) ADAPTIVE FUNCTIONING OF THE DEPENDENT HANDICAPPED. Profoundly handicapped of all ages; checklist; 20 scores: nursing care (medications, body tone, medical care, observation for injury, feeding), physical development (head, legs, body, hands or feet, movement), awareness (eye contact, contact with his world, contact with people, communication, contact with things), self help (feeding, eating, washing, dressing, toileting); $5.20 per 10 tests.

TEST REFERENCES

1. Hull, J. T., & Thompson, J. C. Predicting adaptive functioning among mentally ill persons in community settings. AMERICAN JOURNAL OF COMMUNITY PSYCHOLOGY, 1981, 9, 247–268.

Review of Adaptive Functioning Index by NADINE M. LAMBERT, Professor of Education, University of California, Berkeley, CA:

The Adaptive Functioning Index (AFI) was designed to be used by teachers, supervisors, and nurses for assessing the adaptive behavior functioning of adolescents and adults who are characterized by inadequate intellectual functioning and/or social disadvantage.

The AFI consists of three separate assessment units—the Social Education Test, the Vocational Check List, and the Residential Check List. Each one provides a basis from which an educational and rehabilitational plan is to be developed.

Measures from the Social Education Test are derived from nine subtests: reading, writing, communication, concept attainment, numbers, time, money, community, and motor movements. These are administered individually to the subject, or based on observations of performance. The Vocational Check List contains three sets of ratings on Basic Work Habits, Work Skills, and Acceptance Skills. The Residential Check List also has three sets of ratings including behaviors reflecting personal routines, community awareness, and social maturity. Altogether, the contents of the three scales on the Adaptive Functioning Index are similar to contents of other adaptive behavior assessments.

SOCIAL EDUCATION TEST. The subtests on reading include items on letter naming and recognition, social sight vocabulary, word location, oral readings, recall, and comprehension for a total score of 20 points. For the writing test, the subject completes an application form that requires the subject to print letters, write his or her name, write a sentence after dictation, write a full sentence to describe leisure time activities, and then to complete the application form independently. To compute a score on communication, the examiner makes observations of conversation, speech, understanding directions, and sentence and grammatical development. The concept attainment test requires the ability to discriminate colors, shapes, and to find things that are alike, knowledge of directional concepts, concepts of amount, and conservation of quantity. In the Number Concepts test, the subject must answer correctly questions about counting by units and twos, about height and weight, and measuring the length of the test kit. In this section, knowledge of arithmetic concepts is assessed by 11 problems in addition, subtraction, multiplication and division.

The Time and Money sections of the test contain 20 questions, each on basic concepts. The concepts are sequential order, clock and calendar time, and computing time passages. To succeed on the money test, the subject must have acquired concepts of coin values, money equivalents, collecting coins for money values, and making change.

The Community Awareness section contains a miscellany of items such as name of a newspaper, places of interest in the subject's locale, costs of stamps and movies, and items about work such as minimum wage, payroll deductions, and labor unions. The final section is scored by accounting for observations of posture and gait, gross eye-hand coordination, and balance.

When the Social Education Test is complete, the examiner computes the total score and enters the score for each test on the "AFI Wheel," which is a pictographic summary of scores providing the examiner with a picture of the strengths and weaknesses of the subject's performance.

VOCATIONAL CHECK LIST. The first of two behavior check lists is presented after detailed instructions on objectivity of observation, control of rater bias, standards for comparison (community at large vs. residential setting) and checks on the reliability of ratings.

The Vocational Check List includes sections on Basic Work Habits, Work Skills, and Acceptance Skills such as appearance, punctuality, self-expression and relations with co-workers.

The values of the total observation record for vocational behaviors are then entered on the AFI Wheel to depict abilities as observed by the rater.

RESIDENTIAL CHECK LIST. The rater evaluates the subject's personal routines of cleanliness, appearance, eating habits, room and time management, and health. In addition, ratings of community awareness including transportation, shopping, budgeting, and home management. The section on social maturity requires evaluation of communication skills, consideration of others, getting and keeping friendships, and resolving personal problems. When scores on this section have been computed, the values are again entered on the AFI Wheel.

CONSTRUCT EVALUATION OF THE AFI. To compute the assessment of individuals with limited ability, both assessment of mental ability and evaluation of adaptive behavior are necessary. Adaptive functioning, though correlated with measures of ability, is not synonymous with intelligence. The Standardization Manual for the AFI presents the results of a factor analysis of the WAIS and the

Social Education and Vocational Check List. Five factors ranging from 8% to 34% of explained variance were derived. The author labeled the first factor an "Educational" factor (34% of common factor variance), with which scores from the WAIS subtests and the Social Education Test were highly correlated. Other factors were identified as Nonverbal, Motor Skills; Intelligence; Vocational; and Community Awareness. The factor analysis offers some support, therefore, for a multidimensional concept of adaptive functioning. When factor analysis of the AFI units was done, three main factors, each representing the Social, Vocational and Residential sections of the AFI, were defined as well as three additional factors labeled Personal Routines, Decision Making, and Manual Work Skills.

The two factor analyses presented in the Standardization Manual support the unique contribution of the AFI to the assessment process, and in turn offer some evidence of the construct validity of the tests. Other evidence for the validity of the AFI, such as content validity or predictive validity, is not available. Moreover, evidence of the relationship of the scores on the AFI units and specific educational and rehabilitational programs is not provided.

RELIABILITY ESTIMATES OF THE AFI. Several tables reporting interrater reliabilities for different samples are provided. For the Social Education Test, they range from .83 (community) to .98 (money). For the Vocational Check List, interrater reliabilities range from .54 to .83 for untrained observers, and from .61 to 1.00 for trained observers. The interrater reliabilities for the Residential Check List varied from .64 to .94. The better prepared the raters and the more knowledge they had of the trainees, the higher the interrater reliabilities.

Acceptable levels of test-retest reliabilities were obtained for each of the three tests, with values of .97 to .99 for the Social Education Test, .91 to .97 for the sections of the Vocational Check List, and .93 to .96 for the sections of the Residential Check List.

NORMATIVE DATA. To compare scores earned by an individual on the subtests of the Social Education Test and the units of the Vocational and Residential Scales, the Standardization Manual reports means and standard deviations for several reference groups. For comparison of an individual's scores on the Social Education Tests, the manual offers data from nine groups of subjects in different types of training centers. There are three groups for comparison of scores on the Vocational Check List and four comparison groups of subjects on the Residential Check List. The user will have to derive measures reflecting standard deviation units as deviations from the mean of the selected comparison groups. No values in scales scores or percentiles are presented in the manual.

APPLICATIONS TO REHABILITATION PROGRAMMING. The author suggests making a frequency distribution of scores of a group of subjects in a training program. This provides reference points from which to determine those subjects whose functioning is below the group norm and for whom programming in specific skills is desirable. Although the Rehabilitation Programs Manual provides methods for developing a training program, sequencing steps in learning, and reinforcing target performance, there are few linkages offered to match up performance levels on the AFI with specific program modules.

CRITIQUE. The AFI provides a set of tests and observation check lists for evaluating adaptive behavior in an educational or rehabilitation setting. Training the staff member to use the scale would be necessary, since the instructions do not provide step-by-step detailed procedures. In addition, training the examiner and/or rater to a specific criterion level of agreement between two observers would insure reliability of the assessment.

Validity of the AFI is inferred from the factor analyses. Comparison of scores with independent criteria are not available. The use of the scale should be limited to planning rehabilitation programs rather than to providing normative data for comparison of an individual's scores to a national or provincial standard.

Review of Adaptive Functioning Index by DAVID J. MEALOR, Assistant Professor of School Psychology, University of Central Florida, Orlando, FL:

The Adaptive Functioning Index (AFI) was developed to assess adaptive behaviors in adolescent and adult mentally retarded persons as they began a rehabilitative training program directed toward independent community functioning. This instrument was also designed to monitor change as the individuals moved through the training program and provides a developmental series of training goals, incentive systems, and a uniform system of reporting.

The AFI consists of three "program units"—social education, vocational, and residential—which can be used separately, in pairs, or as a set. The Social Education section is an objective test with criteria for correct/incorrect responses and taps skills in reading, writing, communication, concept attainment, numbers, time, money, community, and motor movement. The Vocational Check List consists of 82 skills considered necessary for a person to function successfully in competitive employment. The Residential Check List is a checklist of 150 skills necessary for independent functioning in the community including skills in personal grooming, community awareness, and social skills. Both checklists allow several opportunities to rate an individual on each specific skill.

The AFI may be administered by direct service personnel (teachers, nurses, trainers, etc.). Specific guidelines for test administration are given in the manual. The manipulatives for the index are well organized. The AFI attempts to use the testing information for establishing specific training goals and provides a Rehabilitation Programs Manual as part of the system to assist in planning. The instrument provides for the monitoring and recording of behavior over time. The language for the examiner and examinee is easy to comprehend; however, the format for the record form is visually distracting and requires the examiner to coordinate the scoring form, question booklet, and administration manual. The individual record forms (which also contain test questions) are visually confusing and cluttered. No suggested time limit is given for the entire test and the length of the testing session may be determined by the examinee's attention span. All information is transferred to the Adaptive Functioning Index Wheel, which is a pictograph of the examinee's profile. The AFI Wheel is very distracting visually and is unable to stand alone as a representation of the examinee's profile. The manuals provide little assistance in clarifying this form.

The standardization procedures are poorly defined. Specific demographic characteristics are not presented. The author gives an overview of various schools or institutional settings but provides no information as to how people were selected to be included in the AFI standardization. There is no mention of the validity of the scale. Reliability is reported for both inter-rater and test-retest reliability. The reliability studies were conducted with wide disparity between both age and IQ levels. This heterogeneity of the sample may help produce spuriously high reliability coefficients. With unequal sample sizes for the three sections it has to be assumed that different groups were represented in the standardization of the index. This fact may lead to difficulty in the interpretation of the AFI especially in attempting to compare a person's performance to others.

The items on this test appear to be appropriate for an adaptive rating scale and would provide meaningful information about an examinee. With increased emphasis on deinstitutionalization, this instrument may allow for the evaluation of the present status and progress of mentally handicapped persons. However, the manuals may confuse the reader. It is often difficult to determine whether the author is referring to the testing procedures, establishing training goals, or monitoring mastery. Possibly these three areas should be addressed as separate entities. The complexity of the system coupled with the inadequate attempt at standardization appear to be drawbacks to this system and may impede widespread acceptance.

[50]

Additional Personality Factor Inventory—#2. College and adults; 1975–80; APF2; 10 scores: fear of being socially unacceptable, hope, general activity, anxiety-state, existential realization, involvement, unusuality, dislikes-annoyances, external control, rigidity; no data on reliability and validity; norms consist of means and standard deviations; 1 form ('80, 6 pages); no specific manual, combined information sheets (no date, 8 pages) for this and Howarth Personality Questionnaire and Howarth Mood Adjective Checklist; combined technical report (no date, 16 pages) for this test, plus the two previously listed; separate answer sheets must be used; price data available from author; (25–35) minutes; Edgar Howarth; the Author.*

Review of Additional Personality Factor Inventory—#2 by AUKE TELLEGEN, Professor of Psychology, University of Minnesota, Minneapolis, MN:

Since 1969 the author of this inventory has been engaged in the development, through factor-analytic methods, of a comprehensive set of self-report personality measures. Starting with a large item pool of over 4,000 items representing significant concepts and measures in the psychological literature (e.g., authoritarianism, internal-external control, rigidity), the author has developed 10 "mainstream" factor scales and 20 additional or "adjunct" scales. The 10 mainstream factors have been incorporated in the earlier published Howarth Personality Questionnaire (HPQ). Of the adjunct factors the 10 most prominent ones (in terms of the variance accounted for in the original item pool) make up the Additional Personality Factor Inventory—#2 (APF2), while the remaining 10 scales have been assembled in the Individuality Inventory. The full list of APF2 scales, which are our main concern here, is as follows: Fear of Being Socially Unacceptable, Hope, General Activity, Anxiety State, Existential Realization, Involvement, Unusuality, Dislikes-Annoyances, External Control, and Rigidity.

Jointly the author's 30 factor scales are aimed "to cover a large part of the individual difference variance in the temperament domain for predictive purposes." The author also indicates that compared to older questionnaires (such as the 16PF, CPI, Guilford-Zimmerman) his scales are intended "to more accurately represent general personality factors (of which there may ultimately turn out to be close to thirty)."

Do Howarth's inventories indeed afford comprehensive, state-of-the-art-and-science self-portrayals? Some observers would rather see evaluative questions of this sort specified and answered within a well-articulated theoretical framework, possibly one advanced by the test author (even if the conception were to be a disputable one). It may well be, however, that no personality inventories in existence today are theory-linked in any but the loosest senses of the terms "theory" and "linked." In the case of the APF2 and the two other related instruments, a defensible alternative approach was taken—an eclectic one aimed at capturing, without major omissions, dimensions considered important by contemporary personality researchers. Again, an assessment of how well that objective was achieved is not easy. The field of personality assessment is not known for its consensus on how to characterize personality (and if such a consensus were to come about, some of us would be alarmed). The author himself does not present a systematic case that these inventories indeed mirror current consensual personality-descriptive emphases.

My own impression is that several of the APF2 scales do represent significant variables, some of which are related though not necessarily equivalent to well-known measures. Thus, although the APF2 External control scale obviously claims Rotter's I-E scale as its ancestor, the two scales are not necessarily interchangeable. The author himself encourages the reader to form a conception of what his scales represent through inspection of the actual items. The reader who does this will find that the factor-analytic process can result in measures that are coherent and distinct in content (so much so in the present case that I could readily detect four item misplacements in the booklet relative to the scoring key).

The test booklet plus scoring key are in fact by far the most informative components of the APF2 material currently available. Although means and standard deviations on a few college samples, and correlations with some scales in the author's other inventories are reported, no percentile- and *T*-score tables, internal consistencies, test-retest reliabilities, tables of scale intercorrelations, data on higher-order factor structure, correlations with other familiar instruments, or other data bearing on validity are included in the accompanying material. In brief, a manual in the usual sense is lacking. Perhaps the author is primarily interested in making his scales known and available to a wider circle of researchers, which would be a justifiable intention considering the sustained effort that must have gone into the development of the APF2 and its companion inventories. But in the absence of a more detailed manual, the broader conceptual significance, empirical status, and practical usefulness of the APF2 cannot be very well determined. I recommend it only for research purposes.

[51]

Adelphi Parent Administered Readiness Test. First grade entrants; 1982; AP.A.R.T.; 10 subtest scores: concept formation, letter form recognition, writing ability, knowledge of numbers, comprehension and memory, visual reception, visual memory, immediate auditory sequential memory, recognition of facial expressions of emotions, creative ability; individual; 1 form (14 pages); instructions for parents (18 pages); background information for school personnel (8 pages); 1983 price data: $24.95 per set of materials including 10 test booklets; (20–30) minutes; Pnina S. Klein; Mafex Associates, Inc.*

Review of Adelphi Parent Administered Readiness Test by JAMES MCCARTHY, Professor of Education, University of Wisconsin-Madison, Madison, WI:

The Adelphi Parent Administered Readiness Test (A P.A.R.T.) is designed to be individually administered and scored by the preschooler's parent. It takes about 20 minutes to administer. The school psychologist and/or other school personnel provide a 30-minute introductory training session for parents after which child and parent are paired off while the school personnel observe and offer aid if necessary.

According to the author, the A P.A.R.T. is designed to meet needs for: (1) an easily administered school readiness evaluation that leads to practical recommendations, (2) parent involvement in evaluation as a first step in building a home-school team, and (3) a measure that can be administered in a language other than English. In addition, it was designed to provide a way of discriminating between children with learning disabilities and those with language problems. Four of the 10 subtests are directly related to tool subjects the children will encounter starting with first grade; the remaining subtests (e.g., Visual Reception, Concept Formation) were included because theory and research suggested their predictive validity.

TEST CONSTRUCTION. The test was created by Pnina Klein, former head of the Learning Disabilities Clinic at Adelphi University, now at Bar Ilan University in Ramat-Gan, Israel. The test was administered to 198 kindergarten children ranging from 5 years 2 months to 6 years 3 months. Following initial item analyses the revised instrument was administered by school personnel to 383 kindergarten children from New York inner city and suburban area schools. No detail is provided on sampling procedures or on the criteria used for determining a stable sample size. About 1 month later, the test was readministered by the respective parents.

RELIABILITY. Pearson product moment correlations between school personnel and parent administered subtests were computed. These ranged from .54 to .83 with a median of about .64. These statistics were seen as supporting the reliability of parent testing. However, only correlations between parent administered tests AND retests would unequivocally provide evidence of the reliability of parent administered tests; also, the magnitude of the published correlations is generally below rule-of-thumb standards. Further support for the test-retest reliability of the parent administered A P.A.R.T. is needed as well as information on the internal consistency reliability of the respective subtests. No standard errors are reported. Subtest standard error data are needed not only to make judgements about the test's precision but as an aid in the interpretation of test scores.

VALIDITY. A P.A.R.T. subtests, excluding the subtests of Creative Ability and Recognition of Facial Expression of Emotions, correlated .61 with the Metropolitan Readiness Test. Additional support for the test's concurrent validity was derived from correlations of each A P.A.R.T. subtest (except Recognition-of-Facial-Expression of Emotions) with some logical existing instrument (e.g., the Torrance Test of Creative Abilities [Form D] correlated .54 [*N* =383] with the Creative Ability subtest of A P.A.R.T.). These various coefficients ranged from .43 to .85, with a median of about .60. Such validity information on a newly developed test is most welcome; it helps to interpret test results.

However, additional validity information is needed. The rationale for the test's content validity should be expanded, clarified, and supported with a series of test objectives or a test blueprint. Support for the predictive validity of A P.A.R.T. is needed to demonstrate that children scoring high on A P.A.R.T. in the beginning of the school year are actually "doing well" in school by the end of the school year as contrasted with those who score low on the A P.A.R.T.

NORMS. Using data from the 383 standardization subjects, the author classified subtest performance as "poor" when it fell below the 2.5th percentile, as "below average" when it fell between the 2.5th and 16th percentile, and "average" when it fell above the 16th percentile. Although these are only rough classifications for children's relative standings, the matters of sample stability and especially sample representativeness must be addressed before the test norms can be regarded as useful.

ADMINISTRATION AND TEST MATERIALS. Although instructions for the administration and scoring of the A P.A.R.T. are clear, many important related points are neglected. For example, there are no instructions for whether the subject should guess or not; on the need—even for parents—to establish and maintain rapport; on the splitting of testing into several periods; on physical arrangements; and on the need to avoid cuing, to mention a few.

Recording instructions as well as scoring directions and criteria seem adequate. The recording form should have space for information like the child's name and birthdate, date of testing, examiner, and describing the behavior of the child during testing.

The test materials themselves are black on white sketches: numbers, letters, figures, and so on. These are not as attractive to this reviewer as the colorful, well packaged American Guidance materials. Still, A P.A.R.T.'s materials are large and legible and probably adequate.

The technical manual is a seven-page pamphlet providing information on rationale, test objectives, and standardization; it is written for school personnel. But the manual is incomplete in a number of ways and would probably not meet the criteria of the *Standards for Educational and Psychological Tests* (APA, 1974) for such publications. As already noted, omissions on the recording form, in instructions to the examiner, and in technical data appear to be the chief problems.

THE PARENT AS EXAMINER. Perhaps the employment of the parent as an examiner is an idea whose time has come, but it may prove to be a burden for psychometry in general and the A P.A.R.T. in particular. Many years of instructing college students in assessment and testing have left this reviewer with the conviction that only the most extraordinary parent can achieve in a few minutes of instructions what many intelligent and motivated college students master only with difficulty over a semester's time. The direct testing of basic skills by the teacher (e.g., Boehm's Test of Basic Concepts), or perhaps the use of parents as participants in assessment under the direction of school personnel (e.g., the Development Indicators for the Assessment of Learning) may describe the present limits of parents as examiners. The natural rapport and common language and culture between parent and child, as well as the current zeitgeist of parent participation, are almost irresistible factors in drawing parents into testing. However, parents' lack of technical training and their difficulty in maintaining impartiality appear as considerable barriers to their employment as examiners. A P.A.R.T. carries the burden of this dilemma.

SUMMARY. A P.A.R.T. is a school readiness test administered by parents. A major problem with the 1982 version of this test is the lack of technical data from which to evaluate the test's technical quality. Additionally, information relating to sampling procedures and standardization sample characteristics is insufficient to determine the type of children for which the A P.A.R.T. is appropriate. Specific data on test-retest reliability and internal consistency reliability are required as well. No standard error data are given. While concurrent validity data are supplied, support for both content and predictive validity is lacking. No rationale is given for characterizing subjects' performance as "poor," "below average," and "average." Nor can interpretation of these characterizations of performance be made until more is known about subtest statistics and sampling procedures.

A second major problem lies in the use of parents as examiners of their own child. The lack of technical training and difficulty in maintaining an objective attitude toward the subject are major obstacles.

In the view of this reviewer, additional research is required before the A P.A.R.T. can be employed for its stated purposes; at a minimum this includes (*a*) provision of technical data on the test's reliability, validity, standard error, and sample characteristics, and (*b*) evidence that for this test, at least, parents have been sufficiently well prepared as technically adequate and unbiased examiners of their own children.

REVIEWER'S REFERENCES

American Psychological Association, American Educational Research Association, and National Council on Measurement in Education. STANDARDS FOR EDUCATIONAL AND PSYCHOLOGICAL TESTS. Washington, DC: American Psychological Association, 1974.

Review of Adelphi Parent Administered Readiness Test by BARTON B. PROGER, Coordinator of Program Evaluation Services, Division of Special Education, Montgomery County Intermediate Unit 23, Norristown, PA:

OVERVIEW. The Adelphi Parent Administered Readiness Test, or A P.A.R.T., purports to seek greater involvement of parents in testing their own children for school readiness and in providing intervention in the home, where necessary. These notions have a great degree of appeal in current thought, but the reviewer asks both parents and professionals to consider whether or not this is the "desired direction," as the test author would have us believe.

THE TEST. A P.A.R.T. consists of three booklets: one for the test itself, one for parents, and one for the professionals. The information is clearly presented and easy to understand.

The test has 10 subparts: (1) Concept Formation has eight items, four pictures to an item. The child must select the item which does not go with the others. (2) Letter Form Recognition has eight items. The child looks at the stimulus letter and then must select the correct one from four choices. (3) Writing Ability consists of five figure reproduction tasks and three word copying tasks. (4) Knowledge of Numbers has five dot-counting activities. (5) Visual Perception presents a detailed picture to the child and asks her/him to say every object s/he sees. (6) In Visual Memory, the parent uses the same picture as in Visual Perception, removes the picture, and then asks the child to recall all the items in the picture. (7) Comprehension and Memory verbally presents two short stories and asks the child four simple factual questions about each story. (8) Auditory Sequential Memory presents eight number sequences verbally to the child, going from a series of two digits up to five digits. (9) Recognition of Facial Expressions of Emotion requires the child to listen to 10 situational verbal statements. For each item (situation) the child then looks at four faces (happy face, sad face, angry face, regular face—not happy, not sad) and draws a line under the face most appropriate to the emotion inherent in the situation. (10) Creative Ability has two tasks. The first asks the child to draw as many different objects as possible which have circles in them or somehow look like circles. The second asks the child to tell the parent as many things as possible which have squares in them.

The test is offered as a first-grade readiness screening device. The 10 tasks do tap such activities. However, judging from the content of both kindergarten and first-grade programs, the reviewer feels the test tasks are somewhat simplistic for the majority of students in public schools today. Further, some of the items have problems. Using the same picture stimulus in Visual Memory as in Visual Perception would seem to have some undesirable carryover effects. I question the value of Auditory Sequential Memory—reminiscent of the Illinois Test of Psycholinguistic Abilities. While on the surface it seems relevant, I do not think the wealth of relevant research has borne out any value for this kind of test in actual practice.

ADMINISTRATION AND SCORING. Since the test author believes in involving parents in the testing of their child and in the subsequent educational/remediational activities, the parents become the test administrators. Klein suggests that the school invite parents of kindergarten children to come to the school about 4 to 6 months before entering first grade. This would normally mean from about March to May of the kindergarten year.

Klein suggests that the parent(s) and child come to the school for three different phases of the testing process. First, there is a 30-minute orientation session for the parents. School officials would lead the parents through the test instructions and exercises. What happens to the child in the meantime is unclear. Presumably, the children should be kept totally separate to avoid disrupting the parent orientation session and to avoid having pre-exposure to the test tasks. No practical suggestions are given. Specific guidelines on what types of precautions to keep in mind, things to avoid when administering the items, and other typical subjects of sound test administration are not covered at all in the professional booklet of A P.A.R.T. The reviewer cannot see how any valid results can arise from a testing process which is so vaguely described and left so open to endless variations in local school practice. This is a major—if not fatal—flaw in the A P.A.R.T. process. One gathers from the tone of the professional booklet that testing is a straightforward procedure which can be learned in a few minutes by the totally uninitiated individual.

The second phase of the A P.A.R.T. process is to have the parent and child go into testing immediately following the 30-minute parent orientation. If the children have been kept in a separate play or babysitting area, how mentally calm and ready will they be for such a structured and formal task as testing? While Klein does suggest that parents be cautioned against "helping" their child with any given test item, the reviewer still wonders how objective and attentive to standardized procedures a parent could be in such a hastily implemented process. No details are given on the actual test situation. Assuming a fair number of parent-child pairs show up for this testing session, the school is left up in the air over whether the tests are to be given in large group settings (in a classroom or cafeteria), although clearly the test is officially individually administered. How does one avoid the potential bedlam and almost certain general distraction which will result from placing even a few child-parent pairs in the same area? These practical school logistics are totally ignored by Klein in the professional booklet and left to the inventiveness of local school officials.

The third phase of the test process is the scoring of results. This is to occur in a large-group parent setting. Again, because of the lack of structure given by Klein, the reviewer can only assume that the children are to be kept in a separate babysitting area.

TECHNICAL DATA. Apart from the many reservations of the reviewer about A P.A.R.T., the professional booklet does present some interesting data. Separate correlations for each subtest are given for 383 children who were given the test first by teachers and, 1 month later, by parents. Because most of the coefficients are in the .50s and .60s, there is a substantial amount of unexplained variance, which to this reviewer only reinforces his fears of invalidity of the entire test administration process.

Klein also presents correlational data with other instruments (ITPA, WRAT, PPVT, and Torrance Form D). However, because of the validity problems inherent in at least two of these outside criteria (ITPA and WRAT), and because the coefficients are again mostly in the .50s and .60s, the results are not overly encouraging.

The reviewer is unable to determine from the professional booklet how this test was researched and devised in a technical sense. The only statement given is that "A population of 198 kindergarten children, 103 girls and 95 boys, ranging in age from 5 years 2 months to 6 years 3 months participated in the initial item analysis and construction of the test." Just what type of "item analysis" used is unknown.

The traditional notions of reliability are not addressed at all.

One of the stated objectives of A P.A.R.T. in the professional manual is "To provide a practical way of identifying specific learning disabilities and discriminating between children with learning disabilities and children with language problems." There is no validation evidence whatsoever to show the usefulness of A P.A.R.T. for these two purposes. In fact, given the pervasive looseness of the concept of learning disabilities by many authors of tests and of instructional strategies, A P.A.R.T. does a disservice to parents who may be overly worried about their children's normal developmental lags at this early age level.

The other six objectives of this test are not as blatantly inappropriate as the one just cited. However, even these other, more routine objectives of A P.A.R.T. are devoid of validation in the professional manual (e.g., "To provide parents with direct information about their child's profile of learning abilities").

In any screening test for readiness problems which purports to identify specific problems or to discern the child as one who is learning disabled, there must be extensive validation evidence of the ability of the instrument to do such tasks. For instance, for screening there must be formal discrimination studies which use already known groups of normal children, children with learning disabilities, and perhaps children who are merely somewhat late in developing these first-grade readiness skills.

USE OF RESULTS. This is the area of A P.A.R.T. most frightening to this reviewer. Klein maintains that active parent participation is a necessity for successful schooling of any child. The reviewer does not differ. However, the reviewer sees no place in the testing process for parents who have been given only 30 minutes of training—or, for that matter, any degree of training. The test performance data becomes so questionable in terms of validity as to become next to useless. The misleading home implications which could be put to inappropriate use are appalling.

Klein also alludes to the necessity of intervention (presumably of the early type, at this kindergarten/first-grade level) to avoid school failure. However, most early intervention theory and practice emphasize the preschool years at home, well before the timelines upon which A P.A.R.T. is based.

In the professional manual Klein says, "Two critical points were established for every subtest, one for the 2.5th percentile and the other for the 16th percentile. All scores falling below the 2.5th percentile are considered 'poor,' all scores falling between the 16th and the 2.5th percentiles are considered 'below average.' All scores above the 16th percentile fall into the 'average' category." In the parents' manual these percentiles are translated into specific scores. How one can justify these cutoff points for practical decisions about whether or not to provide remediation to a child is puzzling to this reviewer. For example, I know of no test user who would consider a student "average" who is at the 20th percentile.

Nowhere in the professional manual or in the parents' manual was the reviewer able to find how continuity between any parental intervention at home and the teacher's in-school efforts is to be achieved. It is a well-known fact that without such careful coordination, the home efforts can often be counterproductive to the school's work.

SUMMARY. The reviewer appreciates the author's concern for parental involvement in the schooling of their children. However, asking parents to become competent test administrators, interpreters of test results and cutoff points, and providers of appropriate remediation at home is overly ambitious and ill-placed. The issuance of A P.A.R.T. in a clearly premature fashion without adequate validation and carefully designed technical studies, is unjustifiable. The reviewer advises against the use of A P.A.R.T. until appropriate technical evidence is provided. In the meantime, many other school readiness tests characterized by more thorough developmental procedures can be used by school personnel to inform parents in an appropriate manner about their children's readiness for first grade.

[52]

The Adjective Checklist. Grades 9–16 and adults; 1952–80; ACL; 37 scales: Number of Adjectives Checked, Number of Favorable Adjectives, Number of Unfavorable Adjectives Checked, Communality, Achievement, Dominance, Endurance, Order, Intraception, Nurturance, Affiliation, Heterosexuality, Exhibition, Autonomy, Aggression, Change, Succorance, Abasement, Deference, Counseling Readiness, Self-Control, Self-Confidence, Personal Adjustment, Ideal Self, Creative Personality, Military Leadership, Masculine Attributes, Feminine Attributes, Critical Parent, Nurturing Parent, Adult, Free Child, Adapted Child, High Origence-Low Intellectence, High Origence-High Intellectence, Low Origence-Low Intellectence, Low Origence-High Intellectence; norms consist of means and standard deviations; 1 form ('80, 3 pages); manual ('80, 113 pages); profile (no date, 1 page); 1984 price data: $5 per 25 checklists; hand scoring stencils must be prepared locally; scoring service, $2.50 or less per test; $3 per 25 profiles; $11.50 per manual; $12 per specimen set; (15–20) minutes; Harrison G. Gough and Alfred B. Heilbrun, Jr.; Consulting Psychologists Press, Inc.*

See T3:116 (117 references), 8:495 (202 references), and T2:1094 (85 references); for reviews by Leonard G. Rorer and Forrest L. Vance, see 7:38 (131 references); see also P:4 (102 references).

TEST REFERENCES

1. Brown, N. W. Personality characteristics of black adolescents. ADOLESCENCE, 1977, 12, 81–87.

2. LaRussa, G. W. Portia's decision: Women's motives for studying law and their later career satisfaction as attorneys. PSYCHOLOGY OF WOMEN QUARTERLY, 1977, 1, 350–364.

3. Megargee, E. I., & Bohn, M. J., Jr. A new classification system for criminal offenders IV: Empirically determined characteristics of the ten types. CRIMINAL JUSTICE AND BEHAVIOR, 1977, 4, 149–210.

4. Welsh, G. S., & Baucom, D. H. Sex, masculinity-femininity, and intellingence. INTELLIGENCE, 1977, 1, 218–233.

5. Wolk, S., & Brandon, J. Runaway adolescents' perceptions of parents and self. ADOLESCENCE, 1977, 12, 176 187.

6. Coplin, J. W., & Williams, J. E. Women law students' descriptions of self and ideal lawyer. PSYCHOLOGY OF WOMEN QUARTERLY, 1978, 2, 323–333.

7. Gendreau, P., Grant, B. A., & Leipciger, M. Self-esteem, incarceration and recidivism. CRIMINAL JUSTICE AND BEHAVIOR, 1979, 6, 67–75.

8. Small, A. C., Gross, R. B., & Batlis, N. C. Sexual identity and personality variables in normal and disturbed adolescent girls. ADOLESCENCE, 1979, 14, 31–44.

9. White, M. S. Measuring androgyny in adulthood. PSYCHOLOGY OF WOMEN QUARTERLY, 1979, 3, 293–307.

10. Cartwright, R. D., Tipton, L. W., & Wicklund, J. Focusing on dreams: A preparation program for psychotherapy. ARCHIVES OF GENERAL PSYCHIATRY, 1980, 37, 275–277.

11. Lazzari, R., & Gough, H. G. Adjective Check List self and ideal self correlates of MMPI profiles classified according to the Meehl-Dahlstrom rules. JOURNAL OF CLINICAL PSYCHOLOGY, 1980, 36, 905–910.

12. Moore, C. D., & Handal, P. J. Adolescents' MMPI performance, cynicism, estrangement, and personal adjustment as a function of race and sex. JOURNAL OF CLINICAL PSYCHOLOGY, 1980, 36, 932–936.

13. Niebuhr, R. E., Bedeian, A. G., & Armenakis, A. A. Individual need states and their influence on perceptions of leader behavior. SOCIAL BEHAVIOR AND PERSONALITY, 1980, 8, 17–25.

14. Rapin, L. S., & Cooper, M. Images of men and women: A comparison of feminists and nonfeminists. PSYCHOLOGY OF WOMEN QUARTERLY, 1980, 5, 186–194.

15. Abbott, A. A. Factors related to third grade achievement: Self-perception, classroom composition, sex, and race. CONTEMPORARY EDUCATIONAL PSYCHOLOGY, 1981, 6, 167–179.

16. Bessmer, M. A., & Ramanaiah, N. V. Convergent and discriminant validity of selected need scales from The Adjective Check List. PSYCHOLOGICAL REPORTS, 1981, 49, 311–316.

17. Kurdek, L. A., Blisk, D., & Siesky, A. E., Jr. Correlates of children's long-term adjustment to their parents' divorce. DEVELOPMENTAL PSYCHOLOGY, 1981, 17, 565–579.

18. Abrami, P. C., Perry, R. P., & Leventhal, L. The relationship between student personality characteristics, teacher ratings, and student achievement. JOURNAL OF EDUCATIONAL PSYCHOLOGY, 1982, 74, 111–125.

19. Budoff, M., & Siperstein, G. N. Judgments of EMT students toward their peers: Effects of label and academic competence. AMERICAN JOURNAL OF MENTAL DEFICIENCY, 1982, 86, 367–371.

20. Castelnuovo-Tedesco, P., Weinberg, J., Buchanan, D. C., & Scott, H. W., Jr. Long-term outcome of Jejuno-ileal bypass surgery for superobesity: A psychiatric assessment. THE AMERICAN JOURNAL OF PSYCHIATRY, 1982, 139, 1248–1252.

21. Heilbrun, A. B. Psychological scaling of defensive cognitive styles on the Adjective Check List. JOURNAL OF PERSONALITY ASSESSMENT, 1982, 46, 495–505.

22. Heilbrun, A. B., Jr. Cognitive factors in early counseling termination: Social insight and level of defensiveness. JOURNAL OF COUNSELING PSYCHOLOGY, 1982, 29, 29–38.

23. Heilbrun, A. B., Jr. Tolerance for ambiguity in female clients: A further test of the cartharsis model for predicting early counseling dropout. JOURNAL OF COUNSELING PSYCHOLOGY, 1982, 29, 567–571.

24. Jones, E. E., & Zoppel, C. L. Impact of client and therapist gender on psychotherapy process and outcome. JOURNAL OF CONSULTING AND CLINICAL PSYCHOLOGY, 1982, 50, 259–272.

25. Kornblau, B. The Teachable Pupil Survey: A technique for assessing teachers' perceptions of pupil attributes. PSYCHOLOGY IN THE SCHOOLS, 1982, 19, 170–174.

26. Lukin, P. R., & Ray, A. B. Personality correlates of pain perception and tolerance. JOURNAL OF CLINICAL PSYCHOLOGY, 1982, 38, 317–320.

27. Mossholder, K. W., Bedian, A. G., & Armenakis, A. A. Group process-work outcome relationships: A note on the moderating impact of self-esteem. ACADEMY OF MANAGEMENT JOURNAL, 1982, 25, 575–585.

28. Parnas, J., Schulsinger, F., Schulsinger, H., Mednick, S. A., & Teasdale, T. W. Behavioral precursors of schizophrenia spectrum: A

prospective study. ARCHIVES OF GENERAL PSYCHIATRY, 1982, 39, 658–664.
29. Robinson, B. E. Sex-stereotyped attitudes of male and female preschool teachers as a function of personality characteristics. PSYCHOLOGICAL REPORTS, 1982, 50, 203–208.
30. Siperstein, G. N., & Chatillon, A. C. Importance of perceived similarity in improving children's attitudes toward mentally retarded peers. AMERICAN JOURNAL OF MENTAL DEFICIENCY, 1982, 86, 453–458.
31. Suinn, R. M. Intervention with Type A behaviors. JOURNAL OF CONSULTING AND CLINICAL PSYCHOLOGY, 1982, 50, 933–949.
32. Vardy, M. M., & Kay, S. R. The therapeutic value of psychotherapists' values and therapy orientations. PSYCHIATRY, 1982, 45, 226–233.
33. Baucom, D. H., & Danker-Brown, P. Peer ratings of males and females possessing different sex-role identities. JOURNAL OF PERSONALITY ASSESSMENT, 1983, 47, 494–506.
34. Bhana, K. Sex trait stereotypes of adults across different life periods. INTERNATIONAL JOURNAL OF PSYCHOLOGY, 1983, 18, 539–544.
35. Cartwright, R. D. Rapid eye movement sleep characteristics during and after mood-disturbing events. ARCHIVES OF GENERAL PSYCHIATRY, 1983, 40, 197–201.
36. Franzoi, S. L. Self-concept differences as a function of private self-consciousness and social anxiety. JOURNAL OF RESEARCH IN PERSONALITY, 1983, 17, 275–287.
37. Frary, R. B., & Ling, J. L. A factor-analytic study of mathematics anxiety. EDUCATIONAL AND PSYCHOLOGICAL MEASUREMENT, 1983, 43, 985–993.
38. Gibb, G. D., Bailey, J. R., Best, R. H., & Lambirth, T. T. The measurement of the obsessive-compulsive personality. EDUCATIONAL AND PSYCHOLOGICAL MEASUREMENT, 1983, 43, 1233–1238.
39. Hagen, B. H., Powell, C., & Adams, R. Influence of personal and academic experiences on formation of attitudes toward mentally retarded adults. PERCEPTUAL AND MOTOR SKILLS, 1983, 57, 835–838.

Review of Adjective Check List by PHYLLIS ANNE TEETER, Assistant Professor of Educational Psychology, University of Wisconsin-Milwaukee, Milwaukee, WI:

The Adjective Check List (ACL) was initially designed as an instrument "for use by observers in describing others," but has evolved as a method of self-description in the personality domain. The authors suggest that the ACL can also be used "to characterize the ideal self, a future or past self, a legendary personage, a geographical region, a commercial product, an idea, a belief, a theory, or almost any other thing." The ACL incorporates both idiographic and normative techniques to provide a comprehensive descriptive method of personality assessment. The ACL allows the individual to select salient adjectives reflecting personality characteristics or attributes, and the selection of one descriptor does not influence subsequent selections. The ACL was developed by Harrison Gough at the Institute of Personality Assessment and Research in Berkeley in 1949, was first published in 1965, and has recently been revised in 1980 by Gough and Alfred Heilbrun.

Portions of Cattell's original trait list was incorporated into the checklist, which was later expanded to include words reflecting the theories of Freud, Jung, Mead, and Murray. Presently the 300-item form has been formulated into 37 separate scales for interpretation. Four subtests compose the Modus Operandi Scale, including variables measuring: (1) the number of adjectives checked, (2) the number of favorable adjectives checked, (3) the number of unfavorable adjectives checked, and (4) the pattern of responses (Communality). Fifteen Need Scales are provided, including: (5) Achievement, (6) Dominance, (7) Endurance, (8) Order, (9) Intraception, (10) Nurturance, (11) Affiliation, (12) Heterosexuality, (13) Exhibition, (14) Autonomy, (15) Aggression, (16) Change, (17) Succorance, (18) Abasement, and (19) Deference. The Topical Scale dealing with interpersonal and social dispositions was derived from nine subtests: (20) Counseling Readiness, (21) Self-Control, (22) Self-Confidence, (23) Personal Adjustment, (24) Ideal Self Scale, (25) Creative Personality, (26) Military Leadership, (27) Masculine Attributes, and (28) Feminine Attributes. In 1978, Kathryn Williams developed 5 new scales based on Eric Berne's theory of Transactional Analysis to measure primary ego states: (29) Critical Parent, (30) Nurturing Parent, (31) Adult, (32) Free Child, and (33) Adapted Child. Finally, the last 4 scales investigate creativity (origence) and intelligence (intellectence) as relevant dimensions of personality: (34) High Origence, Low Intellectence; (35) High Origence, High Intellectence; (36) Low Origence, Low Intellectence; and, (37) Low Origence, High Intellectence.

The manual provides extensive interpretive guidelines for each scale. To provide additional descriptive information, data obtained from a panel of 4 to 10 observers describing 345 males and 242 females on the California Q-Sort method were correlated with ACL scales. For example, Q-sort items which correlated highly with high scores on the Favorable Scale were: "has social poise and presence," "appears socially at ease," "is turned to for advice and reassurance," and "has a high aspiration level for self." Although the adjectives which comprise each scale were derived by different methods and observers, the entire 37 scales were subsequently normed on the same population.

The ACL can be administered in either a group or individual format. Directions are clear, simple, and succinct. Although not mentioned in the manual, low reading abilities are likely to affect test responses. The ACL can be scored by hand or commercial computer scoring is available from the Consulting Psychologists Press. Raw scores can be converted to standard *T*-scores using tables provided in the manual. Conversion tables are available for five normative subgroups based on sex and the number of adjectives selected. The test manual also reports raw score means and standard deviations for the normative sample.

The latest 1980 edition of the ACL was normed on a sample of 5,238 males and 4,144 females. Subjects were selected from populations of high school students, college students, graduate students, medical students, delinquents, psychiatric patients, and other adults. Most of the student subjects were drawn from California, delinquents from New York and California, psychiatric patients from a midwest hospital, and other adults from unspecified regions. The authors do report that the sample was arbitrarily selected, and that "they may not adequately represent general population trends." They further suggest that the sample does represent a heterogeneous group based on age, education, occupation, intelligence, and social status. However, inspection of the sample breakdown indicates that these variables were not equally represented. For example, 2,275 males were college, graduate, or medical students. Also, the adult group seemed to overrepresent professional groups, such as: "actors, architects, business executives, mathematicians, military officers, nurses, police officers, prison guards, research scientists, and writers." Although not indicated in the manual, test users are cautioned against interpretation of test responses for individuals not adequately represented in the normative group. Also, there are no age norms presented, which makes it difficult to determine how this variable affects interpretation of individual profiles.

Alpha coefficients were calculated on a sample of 588 females and 591 males. Although this sample is sufficiently large, the authors did not indicate how the sample was drawn. Alpha coefficients for males ranged from a high of .95 on the Favorable Scale and a low of .56 on the Succorance and Change Scales, with a median value of .76. Coefficients were highest for females on the Favorable Scale (.94) and lowest for the Counseling Readiness Scale (.53), with a median coefficient of .75. Test users are advised to be conservative in their interpretations of scales falling below these median values, as these subtests are less reliable and are prone to measurement error unrelated to the traits or characteristics under study.

Test-retest correlations were derived from a sample of 199 males (100 military officers, 29 college students, and 70 premedical students) after a 6-month interval. Test-retest correlations were highest for the Aggression Scale (.77) and lowest for the High Origence-Low Intellectence Scale (.34), with a median of .65. A sample of 45 female college students were retested on the ACL after a 12-month period. The longer test-retest interval and the smaller sample size makes it difficult to directly compare the stability of the ACL for males and females. The test-retest correlations for the females were highest for the Exhibition Scale (.86) and lowest for the Feminine, High Origence-High Intellectence, and High Origence-Low Intellectence Scales (all .45), with a median of .71. The authors are justified in their explanation that the relatively low test-retest coefficients on some scales are related to "changes in the individuals tested as well as error in the instrument of measurement." They further conclude that "respondents of a cheerful, outgoing, and active temperament will tend to give similar self reports at different times, whereas respondents who are more conventional, subdued, and phlegmatic will be less consistent in the accounts they give of themselves." These final conclusions should be viewed as tentative, as they were based on data from 100 military officers with the 1965 ACL edition. Also, test-retest data for the 1980 ACL edition were conducted on a sample not wholly representative of the normative group, so generalizations concerning the stability of self-descriptions to the general population are not warranted.

Factor analysis of the 37 scales resulted in a similar 6-factor solution for both males and females. These results indicate that the scales are highly related and probably should be interpreted in clusters rather than as 37 independent personality factors. For example, Factor 1, labeled Potency, had high positive loadings for the Achievement, Endurance, Order, Adult, and Low Origence-High Intellectence Scales and a negative loading for the Adapted Child Scale. Individuals scoring high on this factor were described as "resourceful, resolute, and goal-oriented."

Although the ACL can be used for a variety of purposes, "The ACL is also intended for use in the appraisals of individuals." Profile sheets are available, where *T*-scores are plotted with a mean of 50 and a standard deviation of 10. The authors advise test users to first investigate the Modus Operandi Scales to determine the reliability of the protocol. Protocols with less than 20 or more than 250 responses "should be very cautiously interpreted." Also, the Communality Scale is used to determine if responses are unreliable or random. Scores above 60 and below 40 on the remaining scales "have major weighting in the interpretation." Scores are then checked for discrepancies; that is, a difference of 10 or more points on 2 scales which are usually related would "require further exploration." However, test users are not provided with specific information as to how these discrepancies should be interpreted. Finally, scores on the Transactional Analysis and the Origence-Intellectence Scales are analyzed. The authors refer test users to the manual for descriptive and analytic information. Although the manual contains a great deal of descriptive material, it is presented separately under the 37 scales with little information concerning how specific "scale" characteristics are related. Profiles are presented for six individual case studies without reference to "diagnostic signs, profile patterns, or particular configurations" that might be relevant. Research in this area seems essential before the clinical usefulness of this test can be determined.

In summary, the 1980 Edition of the ACL is a 300-item instrument designed as a descriptive method of personality assessment. Although the checklist is arranged into 37 scales, the scales are highly related and should be interpreted in clusters rather than as measures of independent personality factors. Alpha coefficients are respectable and moderately high for half of the scales, but for those subtests with lower reliabilities interpretation should be more conservative. Test-retest information is somewhat limited because of the special samples used. More information concerning the stability of the ACL on a more representative group is needed. Validity information is provided in terms of correlations between ACL scales and several tests, including the scales of the California Psychological Inventory and the MMPI. In general, the ACL appears to be a well developed and relatively reliable instrument. However, further research is needed to determine the clinical utility of this instrument for diagnosis and personality assessment in psychological and counseling settings.

Review of Adjective Checklist by JOHN A. ZARSKE, Private Practice, Flagstaff, AZ:

The 1980 edition of the Adjective Checklist (ACL) represents the first major revision of this instrument since it was first published in 1965. The 1980 revision introduces 15 new scales and presents normative data for a large number of subjects while retaining the same 300-item format initially made available in 1952. The Adjective Checklist may be administered individually or to a group and can be either hand or computer scored. The manual provides a useful and well organized historical description of the ACL and case illustrations which clarify the nature and purpose of the test for the user.

The primary purpose of the ACL has always been heuristic in nature. As the authors point out, the ACL was originally developed for use by observers at the Institute for Personality Assessment and Research (IPAR) in describing individuals. However, as the ACL has evolved over the past two decades, its primary use has been in the area of self-description. The instrument appears to be quite applicable to the assessment of self-concept. The format and nature of the ACL also make it applicable for many other uses, as documented by an extensive bibliography accompanying the manual and test materials.

The primary strength of the ACL has been, and remains, that of a research instrument tied to theoretical developments in the area of personality. While it was initially related to needs theory, the current format demonstrates a more diverse application. Although the 1980 revision includes a new series of scales derived from Berne's Model of Transactional Analysis, the primary application remains theoretical as opposed to clinical in nature. Indeed, use of the ACL would probably not result in any practical diagnostic or therapeutic benefit, except perhaps as a pre- and posttreatment measure of the patient's self description. As such, researchers and theoreticians are likely to find the test more interesting and useful than would a practicing clinician.

NORMS. Approximately 9,400 male and female subjects are included in the normative sample used to determine raw score to standard score conversions. As the authors point out, the male and female samples are ad hoc and arbitrary in composition, calling into question the degree to which the samples approximate the general population. The sample is composed mainly of students of varying levels (i.e., high school, college, graduate, and medical) and consequently the norms appear most applicable for researchers working with subjects from these various categories. However, even within the various sample groupings, the authors fail to provide a description of socioeconomic level, ethnic mix, and age level. Delineation of such characteristics certainly would aid the test user and improve the interpretations to be derived from the scoring of the ACL. No cautions are made by the authors in this regard.

RELIABILITY. The authors provide reliability data based upon internal consistency and retest data. Of these two measures, the sample used to compute test-retest data for females was very small ($N = 45$) and restricted only to college students. As such, generalizability of such reliability data to other groups included in the standardization sample is difficult to achieve. Further reliability studies employing greater *N*s from the various groups employed in the standardization sample would improve the psychometric characteristics of the instrument. Reliability coefficients for the various scales show wide variation (.34 to .95); however, median values in the mid 70s attest to generally adequate reliabilities for most of the scales.

VALIDITY. In reviewing the manual, one will not find a specific section dedicated to the analysis of the validity of the ACL. The appendix provides correlational data on the Minnesota Multiphasic Personality Inventory (MMPI) and California Personality Inventory (CPI) as well as several other test instruments, and the authors provide a brief section on factor analysis of the various scales. However, no attempt is made to summarize this data in terms of the ACL's validity as a personality measure. As a result, the reader is forced to search the text of the manual for support of the test's construct validity. Certainly the authors could greatly improve the manual by providing an organized description of the evidence for the test's validity for each of the different types of inference for which it is being recommended (historiography, environmental psychology, assessment of stereotypes, and assessment of the ideal self, among others). Correlational data presented in the appendix simply establishes that the ACL does not correlate very strongly with the MMPI, CPI, and several other measures. Further correlational studies with other self-concept measures would enhance the psychometric quality of this test. In addition, it would seem fruitful to show data regarding the correlation of the ACL with standardized intelligence scales, as even cursory inspection of the adjective list immediately suggests that a minimum level of reasoning and understanding is required of the examinee in order to guarantee valid interpretation of the derived scores.

In summary, the Adjective Checklist is of greatest utility to researchers and theoreticians interested in the study of the self-concept. It appears particularly applicable for researchers interested in self-descriptions and the relationship between such descriptions and ratings of individuals by trained observers. Its applicability for clinical diagnosis and treatment planning has yet to be established. The authors could improve the manual by providing a more organized approach to the test's construct validity and a clear rationale for the test's applicability in the variety of research situations for which it is recommended.

[53]

Adolescent Separation Anxiety Test. Ages 11–18; 1972–80; provides a measure of emotional and personality patterns which adolescents show in reaction to separation experiences; formerly titled Separation Anxiety Test; 28 scores: 18 association responses (rejection, impaired concentration, phobic feeling, anxiety, loneliness, withdrawal, somatic, adaptive reaction, anger, projection, empathy, evasion, fantasy, well-being, sublimation, intrapunitive, identity stress, total), plus 10 derived response patterns (attachment, individuation, hostility, painful tension, reality avoidance, concentration impairment and sublimation, self-love loss, identity stress, absurd responses, attachment-individuation balance); no validity data, reliability data for association responses only; norms for response patterns only, no description of normative population; individual; separate forms for boys and girls ('80, 27 pages); manual, Vol. 1, A Method for the Study of Adolescent Separation Problems ('80, 201 pages); Vol. 2, Separation Disorders ('80, 207 pages); recording/scoring form ('80, 2 pages); pattern summary chart ('80, 2 pages); 1985 price data: $3 per test of either form; $6 per 60 evaluation sheets (30 record/scoring forms and 30 summary charts); $7.95 per manual; $8.95 per Vol. 2; administration time not reported; Henry G. Hansburg; Krieger Publishing Co., Inc.*

Review of Adolescent Separation Anxiety Test by BRENDA BAILEY-RICHARDSON, Administrator of Psychological Services, Savannah-Chatham County Board of Public Education, Savannah, GA:

The purpose of the Separation Anxiety Test is to assist in the diagnosis of adolescents' attitudes toward separation. The test consists of 12 India ink drawings depicting separation situations common in childhood as well as more stressful situations associated with trauma. The subject responds to each drawing by indicating if the situation has occurred to them, and if not, if they could imagine how the child in the picture would feel. Boys' and girls' forms differ only in regard to the sex of the child in each picture. The subject must read and choose which of 17 statements most accurately describe the child's feelings. The 17 statements were selected to characterize the fundamental reactions of adolescents to separation (i.e., rejection, impaired concentration, phobic feelings, anxiety, loneliness, withdrawal, somatic, adaptive reaction, anger, projection, empathy, evasion, fantasy, well being, sublimation, intrapunitive, identity stress). Responses are analyzed both quantitatively and qualitatively. Quantitative scores include the number of responses for each of the 17 selected reactions, the number of responses for each picture, the total number of responses for each of the 12 pictures, the percentage of the item responses over the total number of responses, and the percentage of the picture responses over the total number of responses. Qualitatively, the responses for each of the 17 reactions are further grouped into the following factors relating to ego functions: attachment, individuation, hostility, painful tension, reality avoidance, concentration impairment and sublimation, self-love loss, identity stress, absurd responses, and attachment-individuation balance.

Volume I includes background information about the test, an explanation of the factors, studies of the various separation pictures, and seven case studies. Volume II further defines the factors and related research with eight case studies. The Separation Anxiety Test obviously reflects many years of research into the effects of separation. The pictures feature a wide range of separation situations some of which would be more familiar to children who are involved with a child care agency than they would be to the average child.

Directions are not clear in regard to the amount of time necessary for administration or to the age ranges for which material is appropriate. The manual includes directions for children and for adults although all norms are from children 11 to 14 years of age. Statements for responses to each picture are said to reflect the "dominant modes or patterns of reacting to separation," but statements even to mild situations such as a mother putting a child to bed seem to be of a negative nature.

Perhaps the author points out the major problem with the test when he notes that it meets but a "few of the statistical and experimental standards for the test method." For example, the reliability study was conducted with an early version of the test on an unreported number of adolescents. Validation is derived largely from clinical practice and the user is encouraged to concentrate on studying the test method itself, the conceptual framework, and the tentative formulations which have been derived from studying the data. The normative data which is available is minimal and not all was collected with the present version of the test. Data are presented from the administration of the test to 157 children between the ages of 11 to 14 years. Few characteristics of these children are noted, with the exception of their school or residential placement. Many of the tables are organized according to schools or placement setting (i.e., P.S. 194; J.H.S. 62; St. John's; Richmond Hill-Far Rockaway). The author is obviously very familiar with the backgrounds of these communities but the user would not be and would find it impossible to make comparisons on this basis.

Using Volume I alone, interpretation of test results would be virtually impossible. Although Volume II includes parameters on various factors there is no explanation about how these criteria were derived.

The manual suggests using the Separation Anxiety Test for making placement decisions about children. Due to the lack of adequate normative data this would be highly questionable at this time. The scale does bear definite promise for research and development. It must be noted that with appropriate revision and development this instrument would be extremely useful in many clinical situations.

Review of Adolescent Separation Anxiety Test by CAROLYN S. HARTSOUGH, *Associate Research Educator, University of California, Berkeley, CA:*

PURPOSE. Having spent considerable time perusing the two 200-page documents accompanying the Adolescent Separation Anxiety Test, I still failed to turn up an explicit statement regarding the author's intended uses of the test. The closest thing to a statement of purpose I was able to find comes from the preface to the manual wherein the author concludes that it is his "hope that this method will come into wider use in clinical settings as well as in research because of its capacity to detect disorders related to separation experiences."

ITEM FORMAT AND SCORING. The test consists of 12 pictures illustrating typical separation experiences, 6 supposedly mild in stimulus value (e.g., child transferring to a new classroom) and 6 strong in stimulus value (e.g., mother going to the hospital). Accompanying each picture are 17 possible reactions that an adolescent might theoretically have to separation situations. These "fundamental reactions which characterize the adolescent response to separation" were derived by the author from extensive reviews of the work of Bowlby, Mahler, Ainsworth, Winnicott, Freud, Harlow, White and others. In an administration of the test, the respondent is asked to select as many of these 17 reactions as describe how the child in the picture is feeling. Quantitative scores consist of (1) the number of responses to each of the 17 selected reactions, (2) the number of responses to each picture, (3) the total number of reactions for 12 pictures, (4) the percentage of the item responses over the total number of responses, and (5) the percentage of picture responses over the total responses. In addition, several derived pattern scores can be obtained from sums of responses to subgroups of the 17 reactions.

INTERPRETATION. According to the author, "a total personality reaction pattern of separation experiences can best be accomplished....[by utilizing] both the theoretical framework presented in Chapter 1 [of the manual], the many different characteristics of the Separation Anxiety Test Method, his own clinical experience and training, and the case material presented in [the manual]." Unfortunately no guidelines are provided regarding either the relative weights that should be assigned these various components of the interpretive process or the minimum level of research or clinical training needed even to attempt such an interpretation. A so-called norm table is provided but for the derived pattern scores only. Moreover, no explicit information is given about how to use the norm table or about the characteristics of the normative group. Even more grievous is the author's pronounced inclination to make claims about the meaning of scores without reference, except for clinical impression, to any substantiating data. The following example gives a flavor of the sort of interpretive commentary that goes on for some 50 pages of the manual. Describing a pattern of responses indicating possible "separation hostility," the manual explains: "A dominance of projection as a medium of hostility expression is obviously a paranoid reaction and should be considered as serious, especially on mild pictures. If this pattern is accompanied by a high percentage of individuation responses, we postulate a paranoid personality." Such an interpretation would not have been "obvious" to this reviewer, certainly not based on the evidence provided. What proportion of children obtaining such a response pattern would have been concurrently diagnosed as displaying a "paranoid reaction" by some external criterion? Objective data that could be used to support such asserted relationships are either totally lacking or presented in such a way that their relevance is obscured.

RELIABILITY AND VALIDITY. Internal consistency coefficients for 16 of the reaction scores are the only reliability data provided. These coefficients range from .34 for the projection reaction to .74 for the somatic reaction. Although marginally acceptable, such coefficients are a woefully incomplete response to the reliability issue. Estimates of the short and long term stability of the various scores as well as some evidence on the consistency of diagnoses achieved by different testers would provide a more compelling argument in favor of the test's use. As for validity, none of a quantitative nature is reported. In the author's own words, "The validity of this technique has been largely verified by clinical experience."

SUMMARY. This is a recently published test although one that apparently has been in the process of development since the late 60s. To my knowledge, this instrument is the only one currently published that deals directly with the measurement of separation anxiety. One wishes, therefore, that as much attention had been given to compliance with conventional standards of technical reporting as was given to the developmental effort. Moreover, the manual and accompanying monograph are written and organized in such a way that one cannot easily find even so rudimentary a fact as the author's intended purpose of the test. Interestingly, the author alludes to many studies wherein the instrument has already seen use. One senses that much of the data necessary for judging the substantive and technical merits of the test already may be available. If such information were presented in a form adhering to the guidelines set forth in the *Standards for Educational and Psychological Tests,* this summary might read very differently. As it stands, this test is guardedly recommended for research uses only. Little justification is found at the present time for recommending its use in clinical diagnosis.

[54]

The Adult Personality Inventory. Adults; 1982–84; API; based upon the 16PF Questionnaire; "individual differences in personality, interpersonal style, and career/life-style preferences"; 25 scores: 7 personality scores (extraverted, adjusted, tough-minded, independent, disciplined, creative, enterprising), 8 interpersonal style scores (caring, adapting, withdrawn, submissive, hostile, rebellious, sociable, assertive), 6 career/life-style scores (practical, scientific, aesthetic, social, competitive, structured), and 4 validity scores (good impression, bad impression, infrequency, uncertainty); 1 form ('84, 12 pages); decision-making worksheet ('84, 6 pages); decision-making worksheet descriptive booklet ('84, 12 pages); manual ('84, 73 pages); 1985 price data: $15 per 25 reusable test booklets; $6.50 per 50 answer sheets; $9.75 per 25 decision-making worksheets; $2.75 per decision-making worksheet descriptive booklet; $9.50 per manual; $13.55 per introductory kit (includes 1 test booklet, answer sheet, decision-making worksheet, manual, and prepaid processing form); scoring service, $16 or less per test; (55–65) minutes; Samuel E. Krug; Institute for Personality and Ability Testing, Inc.*

Review of The Adult Personality Inventory by BRIAN BOLTON, Professor, Arkansas Rehabilitation Research and Training Center, University of Arkansas, Fayetteville, AR:

The Adult Personality Inventory (API) is a self-report questionnaire that measures 21 traits associated with normal personality functioning. The API was designed for use with nonpathological populations in industrial personnel offices, counseling centers, and human development programs. The API can best be described as an updated version of the well-known Sixteen Personality Factor Questionnaire (16 PF), with Cattell's normal personality sphere re-oriented to facilitate assessment applications in career counseling and personal growth settings. Samuel Krug was a graduate student under Raymond B. Cattell and subsequently became director of the Institute of Personality and Ability Testing.

Construction of the API began with the entire 16 PF item pool, 564 items from the current versions of Forms A, B, C, and D. Separate factor analyses of the items composing each of the 16 scales ultimately resulted in the final set of 324 API items, which were allocated as follows: 30 items to measure intelligence, 18 items each for the other 15 scales, and 24 items for two of the validity scales. A carefully conducted confirmatory factor analysis of 80 item-parcels from the API and Form A of the 16 PF demonstrated that the API accurately measures Cattell's normal personality sphere.

During the construction of the API, all of the 16 PF items that survived the initial factor analyses were rewritten. The criteria employed in recasting the items were: retention of the original content, simplification of phrasing and expression, and incorporation of a standard response format (generally true, uncertain, generally false). The net result of item rewriting was minimum item length and a fourth-grade reading level. The 30 ability items are equally represented by vocabulary, arithmetic, and verbal reasoning items.

For what should be obvious reasons, the API is not scored on the 16 primary scales of the normal sphere. (The author's goal was not to develop another form of the 16 PF.) So that continuity with the 16 PF tradition would be maintained, the API is scored on the five major second-stratum factors of the normal personality sphere: Extraverted, Adjusted, Tough-Minded, Independent, and Disciplined. The final two Personal/Motivational scales are Creative, which was developed from data for highly innovative and productive artists and scientists, and Enterprising, which was constructed using need for achievement (nAch) scales in two standardized instruments.

The second and third sets of scales that compose the API are probably most parsimoniously viewed as new partitions of the normal personality sphere, at the level of the 16 primary factors. In fact, the psychometric foundation of the API guarantees that the eight Interpersonal Style scales (Caring, Adapting, Withdrawn, Submissive, Hostile, Rebellious, Sociable, Assertive) and the six Career/Life Style scales (Practical, Scientific, Aesthetic, Social, Competitive, Structured) lie within the 16 PF domain.

Although the derivation and construction of the API interpersonal scales are not adequately explained in the accompanying manual, the eight scales appear to have substantial resemblance to interpersonal scales developed by Leary and Wiggins. One questionable feature of the API interpersonal scales concerns the high correlations between several pairs of scales (e.g., Sociable and Rebellious [.81] and Hostile and Caring [–.80]). While these relationships are consistent with the circular interpersonal model, the pairs of scales are virtually identical after the correlations are disattenuated.

The six API career scales were identified through a multiple discriminant analysis of 73 occupational groups using the 16 PF primary scales as predictor variables. As can be observed, the six career scales are very similar to Holland's occupational themes. This correspondence in conjunction with the strong empirical support that has accumulated for Holland's types confers immediate validity upon the API scales. Even though each of the API career scales is completely predictable from the 16 PF primary scales (and probably from the five second-order personality factors), the new vocationally oriented vectors should be more useful to practitioners working in personnel and counseling settings.

In addition to the 21 trait scales that are scored on the API, four response-style or validity scales are scored. Good Impression indicates the extent to which "faking good" tendencies may be operating while Bad Impression measures the extent of "faking bad" tendencies. When scores on these scales are two or more standard errors above average, scores on the trait scales are adjusted appropriately. The Infrequency scale is comprised of API items with endorsement frequencies below 10% and the Uncertainty score is simply the number of times that the respondent used the "uncertain" option.

The API cannot be hand-scored. The reason for this appears to be that the 21 trait scales are scored using multiple regression equations that suitably combine the 16 primary factors and translate the estimated trait scores into sten scores. In addition to the sten profiles for the trait scales, the computer-generated API report presents horizontal bar graphs depicting the examinee's performance. Only the seven personality scales are accompanied by individualized scale interpretations. The interpersonal scale results are summarized in a brief paragraph and the career scales are just described in general terms.

Because the manual provides thorough descriptive information for the 21 traits, including true- and false-keyed items, high- and low-score self-descriptions, high- and low-scoring occupations, and positive and negative test correlates, users of the API could generate their own interpretation of an examinee's scores if they wished to do so. This possibility could be made available by the publisher if the scoring service included an option to purchase only the profile of 21 adjusted trait scores. For API users specializing in personnel selection and classification, a decision-making procedure has been developed that facilitates profile analysis.

The single outstanding weakness of the manual is the absence of essential technical information. An intercorrelation matrix of all 25 scales would enable the user to understand the relationships among the four sets of scales. Correlations of the 25 scales with the 16 PF primary traits would document the reorientation of the API within the normal personality sphere. Although the normative procedure seems to be excellent (incorporating the 16 PF norms through an equating process), details about the procedure and the demographic characteristics of the male and female norm groups are not given. Finally, an adequate test-retest reliability study should be conducted; however, preliminary evidence suggests that the API is sufficiently reliable for the recommended applications.

In summary, the Adult Personality Inventory is a modern version of the 16 PF that was designed to assess 21 normal personality traits of adults. The API can be completed by almost all adults and the resulting profile of scores is relevant in a variety of counseling and personnel situations. The manual provides extensive information about the scales, enabling users to interpret the profile in considerable depth. A technical supplement describing test construction procedures and presenting psychometric characteristics of the instrument would be a useful addition.

[55]

The Adult Self Expression Scale. Adults; 1974–75; ASES; assertiveness; no data on reliability; norms consist of means and standard deviations; 1 form ('74, 2 pages); scoring instructions (no date, 1 page); self-scoring answer sheet ('75, 1 page); 1983 price data: $.60 per test; $.40 per self-scoring answer sheet; administration time not reported; Melvin L. Gay, James G. Hollandsworth, Jr., and John P. Galassi; Adult Self Expression Scale.*

See T3:122 (2 references).

TEST REFERENCES

1. Emmelkamp, P. M. G. Agoraphobics' interpersonal problems: Their role in the effects of exposure in vivo therapy. ARCHIVES OF GENERAL PSYCHIATRY, 1980, 37, 1303–1306.

2. Shaffer, C. S., Shapiro, J., Sank, L. I., & Coghlan, D. J. Positive changes in depression, anxiety, and assertion following individual and group cognitive behavior therapy intervention. COGNITIVE THERAPY AND RESEARCH, 1981, 5, 149–157.

3. Cyr, D. J., & Bourque, P. Evaluation of an assertiveness training program in a maximum security correctional setting. CANADIAN JOURNAL OF CRIMINOLOGY, 1982, 24, 51–59.

4. Emmelkamp, P. M. G., & Mersch, P. P. Cognition and exposure in vivo in the treatment of agoraphobia: Short-term and delayed effects. COGNITIVE THERAPY AND RESEARCH, 1982, 6, 77–88.

5. Petrie, K., & Rotheram, M. J. Insulators against stress: Self-esteem and assertiveness. PSYCHOLOGICAL REPORTS, 1982, 50, 963–966.

6. Soto, E., & Shaver, P. Sex-role traditionalism, assertiveness, and symptoms of Puerto Rican women living in the United States. HISPANIC JOURNAL OF BEHAVIORAL SCIENCE, 1982, 4, 1–19.

7. Fishel, A. H., & Jefferson, C. B. Assertiveness training for hospitalized, emotionally disturbed women. JOURNAL OF PSYCHOSOCIAL NURSING AND MENTAL HEALTH SERVICES, 1983, 21(11), 22–27.

8. LaFromboise, T. D. The factorial validity of the Adult Self-Expression Scale with American Indians. EDUCATIONAL AND PSYCHOLOGICAL MEASUREMENT, 1983, 43, 547–555.

Review of The Adult Self Expression Scale by PHILIP H. DREYER, *Professor of Education and Psychology, Claremont Graduate School, Claremont, CA:*

The Adult Self Expression Scale (ASES) is a measure of assertiveness which is defined as "the action of declaring oneself; of stating, This is who I am, what I think and feel...an active rather than a passive approach to life" (Fensterheim, 1971, p. 233 as quoted by Gay, Hollandsworth, & Galassi, 1975, p. 340). This scale is based upon the College Self-Expression Scale, which in turn used items from Lazarus (1971), Wolpe (1969), and Wolpe and Lazarus (1966). The authors state that the ASES is appropriate for use with "adults in general" and that it can be used to counsel individuals having problems with assertiveness, to screen applicants for assertiveness training programs, and to measure assertiveness behavior in research.

The scale consists of 48 questions which ask about such behaviors as asking favors, refusing unreasonable requests, expressing opinions, expressing positive feelings, standing up for one's rights, and taking the initiative without undue anxiety. Questions also address interpersonal relations with authority figures, parents, the public, and intimate others. Subjects respond by making a check on a 5-point continuum from "0" ("almost always") to "4" ("never or rarely"). Instructions direct the respondent to "indicate how you generally express yourself in a variety of situations...Your answer should not reflect how you feel you ought to act or how you would like to act." Twenty-five of the items are positively worded, while 23 are negatively worded. Twenty-three items are stated hypothetically (e.g., item 22: "If food which is not to your satisfaction was served in a good restaurant, would you bring it to the waiter's attention?"), so that good reading skill is required in order for scores to be valid. Scoring is facilitated by a duplicate answer form which automatically converts negative responses to their proper score for easy tabulation. Scores have a potential range of 0 to 192; the mean score for 640 adults used as a standardization sample was 115 with a standard deviation of 20.

The authors present retest reliability coefficients of .88 for 2 weeks ($N = 60$) and .91 for 5 weeks ($N = 63$) obtained from two English classes at a community college in North Carolina where the average age was 25.

Validity studies were conducted using 464 community college students who ranged in age from 18 to 60. The ASES correlated significantly with a number of the scales of the Adjective Check List, including Number of Favorable Adjectives Checked, Self-Confidence, Lability, Achievement, Dominance, Affiliation, Heterosexuality, Exhibition, Autonomy, Aggression, and Change. In addition, scores of high and low assertive students as measured by the ASES were compared with the Self-Confidence scale of the Adjective Check List, the internal anxiety or emotionality score from the Taylor Manifest Anxiety Scale, and the internal and external locus of control of reinforcement score taken from the Rotter Locus of Control Scale. These analyses indicated that the Self-Confidence Score of the Adjective Check List and the Manifest Anxiety Score significantly discriminated the low and high assertive students as measured by the ASES, but that the Locus of Control measure did not. The authors also report a study of concurrent validity which found that the ASES scores of a sample of 32 college students seeking personal adjustment counseling were significantly lower than a comparison group of 60 students in English classes who had not sought counseling (Gay et al., 1975).

Finally, the authors report a multitrait-multimethod study of validity using four groups of adults—38 students in a technical arts class, 35 graduate students in counseling, 26 patients at a psychiatric hospital, and 64 convicted male felons at a state penitentiary—who were administered the ASES along with other self-report measures of dominance and abasement, the Rathus Assertiveness Schedule, and peer ratings of assertiveness. From this study they concluded that the ASES has "moderately strong convergent validity and moderate discriminant validity" (Hollandsworth, Galassi, & Gay, 1977).

Two comments about these validity studies seem appropriate. First, while the ASES asserts that it is to be used with "adults in general," most of the samples studied describe students under the age of 30. For example, 77% of the 460 community college students used in the original study (Gay et al., 1975) were under age 30. In the second study (Hollandsworth, 1977), 73 subjects were adult students and 90 were institutionalized mental patients or felons. Thus there is a need to continue the development of the instrument by establishing norms for larger groups of non-student adults, especially middle-aged and older samples. Particular attention should be paid in these studies to subjects' reading skill and their ability to read the rather long and complex questions which make up the ASES. Second, while scores for women are reported and do not appear to be significantly different from men's, it would be helpful to have more data about sex differences in responses to the ASES. Such information could be useful to those counselors working with women's groups and researchers interested in the relationship of assertive behaviors to family history and socialization experiences.

Overall, the Adult Self Expression Scale seems to be a promising research instrument. It seems well grounded in theories of personality and interpersonal behavior and appears to be carefully constructed, with more than the usual detail given to its validity. In order to truly be useful for "adults in general," however, the scale needs to be standardized with a wider sampling of adults of various ages and occupations. As a counseling tool, the ASES seems interesting and useful, especially if the counselor takes care that clients can read and understand the items in the ASES, and if the counselor is prepared to develop his or her own norms for interpreting scores.

REVIEWER'S REFERENCES

Wolpe, J., & Lazarus, A. A. BEHAVIOR THERAPY TECHNIQUES: A GUIDE TO THE TREATMENT OF NEUROSES. New York: Pergamon Press, 1966.

Wolpe, J. THE PRACTICE OF BEHAVIOR THERAPY. New York: Pergamon Press, 1969.

Lazarus, A. A. BEHAVIOR THERAPY AND BEYOND. New York: McGraw-Hill, 1971.

Gay, M. L., Hollandsworth, J. G., Jr., & Galassi, J. P. An assertiveness inventory for adults. JOURNAL OF COUNSELING PSYCHOLOGY, 1975, 22, 340–344.

Hollandsworth, J. G., Jr., Galassi, J. P., & Gay, M. L. The Adult Self Expression Scale: Validation by the multitrait-multimethod procedure. JOURNAL OF CLINICAL PSYCHOLOGY, 1977, 33, 407–415.

Review of The Adult Self Expression Scale by GOLDINE C. GLESER, Professor Emerita of Psychology, University of Cincinnati, Cincinnati, OH:

The Adult Self Expression Scale (ASES) is a 48-item self-report measure of assertiveness. Responses are scored on 5-point Likert scales ranging from "almost always" to "rarely or never." Twenty-five items are positively worded while the remaining 23 are negatively worded. The original item pool from which the present test items were drawn was designed according to a two-dimensional descriptive model of assertiveness. One dimension specified interpersonal situations in which assertive behavior might occur (i.e., interaction with parents, the public, authority figures, friends, intimate relations, and a global situation). The second dimension specified seven behaviors that might occur in these situations, such as expressing personal opinions, refusing unreasonable requests, taking the initiative, expressing positive and negative feelings, and asking favors of others. Forty of the 42 cells thus generated are represented by at least one item in the final scale. The scale can be self-administered and self-scored.

Information on test construction, norms, reliability, and preliminary validation studies are contained in an article by the test authors in the Journal of Counseling Psychology, (Gay, Hollandsworth, & Galassi, 1975). Means and standard deviations were obtained on 464 subjects from a large community college in North Carolina. These are tabulated separately by sex, four age groupings, and by marital status. Males were significantly higher than females on the scale. A factor analysis of the items yielded 14 factors, accounting for 55.9% of the variance. Four factors pertained to interpersonal situations and the remainder involved types of assertive behavior, with three types of assertiveness represented by two factors each. The large number of factors obtained suggests that assertiveness is a broad and rather heterogeneous construct. If additional samples yield such a large number of factors, further investigation of their structure seems warranted, with the possibility that items be clustered into subscales.

Test-retest reliability coefficients of .88 and .91 were obtained at 2-week and 5-week intervals with samples of 60 and 63 subjects respectively drawn from college English classes. Additional test-retest reliability coefficients for a 1-week interval were collected on three small samples from college evening classes and from a psychiatric inpatient ward, in connection with a multitrait-multidimensional study by Hollandsworth et al. (1977). These ranged from .81 to .89. Thus it seems fairly well established that the ASES has adequate short-term stability.

Validation efforts to date have emphasized construct validation strategies. The ASES correlated .88 with the College Self-Expression scale for all subjects and .79 for married subjects 30 years of age or older. This was interpreted as indicating that the ASES may be more appropriate for adults in the general population than is the college version of the test. A correlation of .77 was obtained with the Rathus Assertiveness Schedule, a 30-item self-report instrument, on a sample of 64 male prisoners. Subjects seeking personal adjustment counseling scored significantly lower on the scale than did students in an English class who were not seeking counseling.

In the college sample positive correlations of .44 were found with the Gough Adjective Check List scores of Self-Confidence and of Dominance, .34 with Achievement, and .36 with Exhibition; whereas negative correlations were found with Abasement (–.50), Succorance (–.37), and Deference (–.36). The correlation with Aggression was only .23. Further studies of the constructs of Assertiveness, Dominance, Abasement, and Aggression using the multitrait-multimethod procedure indicated significant convergence between self ratings and peer ratings for all four measures in two samples, and only between self ratings and staff ratings of Assertion for a psychiatric inpatient sample. Self-rated Assertiveness was positively correlated with Aggression and Dominance and negatively with Abasement in all samples, both within and across methods, but discrimination between Assertion and Aggression was not as clear as had been hoped. No correlation was found in a male prison sample between self-rated Assertiveness and ratings of previous assaultive behavior as gleaned from criminal records. However, a correlation of .34 was obtained with self-reported Assaultiveness on the Buss-Durke Hostility Inventory.

The systematic structure and broad range of the ASES as well as the data available to date indicate that the ASES is a promising instrument for research on Assertiveness and for identification of clients who might benefit from assertive training procedures. The possible development of subscales along with additional concurrent and predictive validation research could enhance its usefulness in clinical counseling.

REVIEWER'S REFERENCES

Gay, M. L., Hollandsworth, J. G., Jr., & Galassi, J. P. An assertiveness inventory for adults. JOURNAL OF COUNSELING PSYCHOLOGY, 1975, 22, 340–344.

Hollandsworth, J. G., Jr., Galassi, J. P., & Gay, M. L. The Adult Self Expression Scale: Validation by the multitrait-multimethod procedure. JOURNAL OF CLINICAL PSYCHOLOGY, 1977, 33, 407–415.

[56]

Advanced Reading Inventory. Grade 7 through college; 1981; ARI; 3 reading level scores (independent, instructional, frustration) for each of 3 parts (graded word lists, graded reading passages with questions, cloze tests); no data on reliability; no norms; Forms A and B for each part; manual (164 pages, includes Forms A and B of the graded word lists, graded reading passages with questions, cloze tests, answer sheets, and performance sheets, all which much be duplicated); 1984 price data: $10.44 per manual; administration time not reported; Jerry L. Johns; Wm. C. Brown Co. Publishers.*

[57]

Advanced Test Battery. Personnel at graduate level or in management positions; 1979–83; ATB; "designed for use in the selection, development, or guidance of personnel at graduate level or in management positions"; subtests available as separates; 2 levels; manual ('79, 87 pages); profile chart ('80, 2 pages); practice test ('82, 4 pages); distribution restricted to persons who have completed the publisher's training course or members of the Division of Occupational Psychology of the British Psychological Society; separate answer sheets must be used; 1984 price data: £12 per 50 practice tests; £12 per 50 profile charts; £18 per manual; £70 per specimen set; Roger Holdsworth (VA3, NA4, manual), Peter Saville (VA1, NA2, manual), Gill Nyfield (manual), Dave Hawkey (DA5, ST7, DT8), Steve Blinkhorn (VA3), and Alan Iliff (NA4); Saville & Holdsworth Ltd. [England].*

a) LEVEL 1. 1979–80; higher order aptitudes; 3 tests.

1) *Verbal Concepts*. 1980; VA1; 1 form (no date, 6 pages); administration card (no date, 2 pages); £21 per 10 question booklets; £25 per 50 answer sheets; £5 per scoring stencil; £5 per administration card; 15(20) minutes.

2) *Number Series*. 1980; NA2; 1 form (5 pages); administration card (no date, 2 pages); £21 per 10 question booklets; £25 per 50 answer sheets; £5 per scoring stencil; £5 per administration card; 15(20) minutes.

3) *Diagramming*. 1980; DA5; no data on validity; 1 form (14 pages); administration card (3 pages); command sheet (2 pages); £30 per 10 question booklets; £25 per 50 answer sheets; £5 per scoring stencil; £5 per administration card; £20 per 10 command sheets; 20(25) minutes.

b) LEVEL 2. 1979–83; higher order aptitudes in a work context; 4 tests.

1) *Verbal Critical Reasoning*. 1983; VA3; 1 form (9 pages); administration card (no date, 2 pages); £30 per 10 question booklets; £25 per 50 answer sheets; £5 per scoring stencil; £5 per administration card; 30(35) minutes.

2) *Numerical Critical Reasoning*. 1979–83; NA4; 1 form ('83, 7 pages); administration card (no date, 2 pages); data card ('79, 2 pages); £30 per 10 question booklets; £25 per 50 answer sheets; £5 per scoring stencil; £5 per administration card; £20 per 10 data cards; 35(40) minutes.

3) *Spatial Reasoning*. 1979–81; ST7; no data on validity; 1 form ('79, 8 pages); administration card ('81, 2 pages); £14 per 10 question booklets; £14 per 50 answer sheets; £3.50 per scoring stencil; £3.50 per administration card; 20(25) minutes.

4) *Diagrammatic Reasoning*. 1979–81; DT8; no data on validity; 1 form (no date, 6 pages); administration card ('81, 2 pages); £14 per 10 question booklets; £14 per 50 answer sheets; £3.50 per scoring stencil; £3.50 per administration card; 15(20) minutes.

[58]

Affective Domain Descriptor Program. Ages 6–18; 1978; ADD; "a useful tool in helping teach students an awareness of acceptable and unacceptable behaviors for the classroom"; based on monitoring positive behaviors rather than negative ones; 9 behavioral factors: attends to task, emotionally responsive, participates socially, emotional control, need for adult contact, ability to delay, socially non-aggressive, ethical behavior, cooperation, plus a daily average; no data on reliability and validity; no norms; individual; 1 form; manual (24 pages); 1984 price data: $39.95 per set including 15 sets of cards; administration time not reported; Richard D. Goeman and Deirdre A. Hestand; B. L. Winch & Associates.*

Review of Affective Domain Descriptor Program by RANDALL M. JONES, Research Specialist, Department of Family and Community Medicine, College of Medicine, The University of Arizona, Tucson, AZ:

The Affective Domain Descriptor Program (ADD) is described as a versatile behavior modification technique which utilizes state of the art methodologies. By refocusing teacher attention from negative to positive/appropriate student behaviors within the classroom, providing immediate individualized feedback, and gradually shifting external behavior monitoring to student self-monitoring, teachers can eventually increase their teaching time as a result of less time needed for discipline. Unfortunately, as attractive as this may seem, this outcome is not likely to be achieved with the ADD program.

Many of the criticisms leveled against therapeutic outcome research are readily generalizable to the ADD program. Most obvious is the operationalization of the "target behaviors." Although Goeman and Deirdre have provided behavioral examples for each of the nine "behavioral factors" emphasized in the ADD program, it is doubtful that interobserver consensus would ever approach acceptable levels. Consider the following examples, one for each of the nine behavioral categories: Attends to Task (the student has an acceptable attention span); Emotionally Responsive (the student is not withdrawn and does not daydream); Participates Socially (the student is not timid, shy, or withdrawn); Emotional Control (the student is calm and in control of his/her emotions); Need for Adult Contact (the student seeks out adults for reasons other than to get their negative attention); Ability to Delay (the student thinks before acting); Socially Non-Aggressive (the student does not tend to dominate peers); Ethical Behavior (the student is honest); Cooperation (the student feels capable).

These examples represent a random sample from a pool of 37 presented as "specific behaviors that may be observed" within the ADD program. Clearly, most require a tremendous inferential leap (e.g., "acceptable" attention span, does not daydream, the student is "calm," the student seeks adults for other "reasons," the student "thinks," the student "feels"); while others are not likely to change drastically over a 2-hour interval (the student is not "withdrawn," the student is not "timid," the student is "honest," the student does not tend to "dominate" peers). All of these "behavioral" indicators are anecdotal in nature, and many will not change over the course of months, let alone hours.

The constant referral to "hours" stems from the instructional packet that describes the ADD program. In order to effectively implement the program, teachers are required to write each student's name on a separate sheet, to monitor each student's behavior (on each of the nine dimensions), and to meet individually with each student four times throughout the day to provide feedback. The program developers recommend a fixed-interval schedule (every 2 hours) to ensure continuous feedback. (Although not mentioned by the developers of the ADD program, most behaviorists contend that a variable-ratio schedule of reinforcement would yield more positive and longer lasting results.) At the end of the day, teachers are required to graph behavioral change for each student. The graphs are supplied in the program package. In the average classroom, teachers who wish to implement the ADD program will have to complete the following tasks for 20 to 30 students daily: write names, meet four times daily, and graph daily behavior change. This modern-day approach, in contrast to the more traditional method of modifying the behavior of two or three students a couple of times daily, is supposed to allow "the teacher to increase the time spent in teaching as a result of less time used to manage behavior."

Although empirical evidence supporting the effectiveness of the ADD program is nonexistent, two "testimonials" are provided in the program description: Miraculously, the program is a "viable tool in measuring and evaluating areas in the affective domain"; it "forces staff at particular periods of the day to relate to and evaluate the student. This communication has in many instances been the sole cause of a student's emotional growth"; "Four times a day I discuss with each child his specific behavior problems which helps the child remember what areas of behavior need improvement, while still rewarding or commending the child for excelling in other areas of behavior."

Logistically, the ADD program cannot possibly increase time teaching when it requires so much work to implement. If it is so fantastic, as indicated in the testimonials, why haven't program developers provided empirical evidence supporting their contentions? If it were my choice, I'd buy a pad of graph paper, an introductory psychology text, target specific problematic behaviors, and work on them only. I doubt if the majority of students in a class need a behavior modification program (particularly one that has yet to demonstrate reliability, validity, and effectiveness).

Review of Affective Domain Descriptor Program by GERALD R. SMITH, Professor of Education, Indiana University, Bloomington, IN:

The Affective Domain Descriptor Program (ADD) is a ponderous title for what appears to be a rather crude procedure. The manual's claim that it is the "most up-to-date approach to behavior modification" seems exaggerated at best in the face of missing data and documentation to substantiate this claim.

The manual, in the form of a notebook, is well organized and easy to follow. The two tools that a user employs to administer the instrument—the ADD card and data sheet—are explained carefully and clear examples are presented. The manual's failure to include page numbers is a nuisance and makes it difficult to use with a large group of teachers, as in inservice training.

While the manual's statement that ADD does not "require an in-depth knowledge of behavior modification theories and/or techniques" is true, many users will encounter difficulty with the operational definitions for the nine behavioral categories. In some cases the criteria are stated in non-behavioral terms. Under "ethical behavior," for example, one of the criteria is "the student is honest," but this statement does not describe a behavior which the teacher can observe.

The criteria for making judgments about whether a child is exhibiting the behaviors are not always clear. Under "Attends to Task," for example, two of the three criteria—"stays with activities for a reasonable time" and "is not easily distracted"—suggest a prolonged period of observation. Moreover, it is not clear how the user arrives at that judgment. Is the pupil "not easily distracted" if he or she attends only to loud stimuli, only to friendly stimuli, only to adult stimuli, or to all three of these if they are persistent? Given the manual's limited discussion of how the user is to make such judgments, it is likely that each user will employ different criteria each time he or she records a child's behavior. This procedure could and probably would lead to wide variations in the observations of a given teacher to a given student at different times and of different teachers to the same student at the same time.

The reader will recognize that we have just raised reliability and validity issues for which the manual provides no data. In short, the manual does not help the user to reach an informed judgment of the utility of the instrument for specific purposes. Also, there are no norms and no scale scores. The section entitled "The ADD Program in Action" does provide two testimonial letters from a teacher and an instructional counselor, but no data accompany these letters and no references are given as the sources of such data.

Since one of the nine behavioral categories is "Ethical Behavior," it is somewhat ironic that the instrument's use raises ethical issues. While ADD suggests that teachers may provide feedback to pupils if they wish to do so, it does not suggest that pupils and teachers should reach agreement on the behavior they wish to work on. The judgment of what to change and how extensively to change the pupil's behavior is left entirely to the teacher. ADD is recommended for use with special education students, including the autistic, emotionally disturbed, and multiple handicapped. Since these children may not be capable of reaching judgments of appropriate use for themselves, it is imperative that the manual include statements about appropriate use and misuse of ADD.

In summary, ADD is a simplistic instrument designed to appeal to those who want simple answers to complex problems. It is the reviewer's judgment that users cannot make accurate judgments about pupil behavior without more carefully prescribed and tested criteria. Under the circumstances, the lack of reliability and validity data, as well as other forms of systematic analysis and evaluation, should lead potential users to approach this instrument with some skepticism. Its ease of use is matched only by its potential for misuse.

[59]

Affective Perception Inventory. Grades 1–3, 4–8, 9–12; 1979–80; API; ratings by self and others; 9 scales: Self Concept, Student Self, Reading Perceptions (Form P)/Perceptions in Language Arts (Form I)/English Perceptions (Form A), Arithmetic Perceptions (Form P)/Mathematics Perceptions (Forms I, A), Science Perceptions, Social Studies Perceptions (Form P, I)/Perceptions in Social Services (Form A), Perceptions in the Arts, Sports and Games Perceptions (Form P)/Perceptions in Physical Education (Forms I, A), School Perceptions; 3 levels labeled Form P, I, A; composite test manual ('80, 113 pages, combines primary, intermediate, and advanced level manuals); 1985 price data: $3 per booklet of 9 scales including self-report forms and ratings by others; $3 per separate test manual; $7.50 per composite test manual; Spanish, French, and Italian editions available; (40–60) minutes; Anthony T. Soares and Louise M. Soares; SOARES Associates.*

a) FORM P—PRIMARY LEVEL. Grades 1–3; Form P ('79, 14 pages, ratings by self); ratings by others ('79, 22 pages); manual ('80, 58 pages).

b) FORM I—INTERMEDIATE LEVEL. Grades 4–8; Form I ('79, 17 pages, ratings by self); ratings by others ('79, 18 pages); manual ('80, 58 pages).

c) FORM A—ADVANCED LEVEL. Grades 9–12; Form A ('79, 22 pages, ratings by self); ratings by others ('79, 22 pages); manual ('80, 58 pages).

Review of Affective Perception Inventory by ROSA A. HAGIN, Professor of Psychological and Educational Services, Fordham University-Lincoln Center, New York, NY:

The Affective Perception Inventory is a multilevel measure consisting of nine scales for measuring feelings about the self relative to specific subject areas or classroom experiences: self as a person, self in the role of a student, and self in the environment of school and in interacting with people who are a part of an educational setting. According to the authors, its primary purpose is for research. However, it is also suggested for use in identifying problem areas within individual students and to determine congruence of self-ratings and ratings by others. English, Spanish, French, and Italian language translations of the inventories are available and a German version is being planned. Standardization data are available only for the English language version, although the most recent composite test manual states that validation data "should be available by January 1980—and the scales ready for distribution—after relevant populations have been sampled and the resultant analysis has been completed."

An unusual feature of this inventory is the provision of parallel forms that permit self-ratings as well as peer or teacher ratings. Items are paired between the two forms to permit examination of the congruence between self perception and the perceptions of others. Unfortunately, some items deal with feelings, preferences, fears, worries, thoughts, and impulses that cannot be observed directly and can only be inferred from behavior. This represents a serious threat to the validity of its use as a measure of congruence.

Directions for administration and scoring are reasonably straightforward. However, no evidence of readability levels is presented, although it is suggested that items may be read to respondents with reading or language difficulties. A further threat to validity may be in the vocabulary of the primary level inventory, some words of which may be beyond the understanding of young children. Scoring is based on algebraic summation of ratings, which can be profiled on the basis of stanine scores provided in the manual. No information is given concerning the derivation of these stanines or the reference group on which the original data were obtained.

The inventory appears to have been developed over a period of several years, with copyright dates listed as 1975 and 1979, and the test manuals dated 1980. The composite manual appears to be just that—a collection of the material from the primary, intermediate, and advanced level manuals, lists of references and presentations, and even newsletters sent out by the authors, who apparently publish the inventory for themselves. Various parts of this manual appear to have been written at different times. As might be expected, the style of the manual is uneven, with much of the material presented in an outline format that does not answer all the questions that potential test users might have.

Although the authors present a brief description of the theoretical foundations of the inventory, they give no information concerning the development of the items other than to state that the "initial trait pool was yielded out of extensive research by Cattell, Guilford, Eysenck, and others." They also drew upon their own measure, the Self Perception Inventory. After a criterion assessment period with a variety of experts (also not described further), the inventory was field tested on a total sample of 698 subjects from two classrooms at each level grades 1 through 12. The location of these classrooms is not described, nor are the ethnic characteristics of the subjects.

Reliability estimates of the individual scales, based on Rulon's split-half method, range from .61 to .94. The authors present evidence of convergent validity based on a comparison of self- and peer-ratings with coefficients of agreement ranging from .76 on School Perceptions to .26 for Arts. Evidence of discriminant validity is based on a clustering of self concept, student self, and language art scores quite distinctly from scores for mathematics, science, and social studies. Discriminant analyses derived three functions subsequently labeled "Academic Self," "School Self," and "Humanistic Self." These analyses also provided evidence of separation by grade level and gender.

The Affective Perception Inventory fails to meet most of the standards regarded as essential for educational and psychological tests. The manual provides neither a rationale for item selection nor an explanation of procedures and results of item analyses. Although there are brief directions for administration and scoring of the inventory, there is little assistance given to the user for correct interpretation of results or avoidance of misuse. Evidence of reliability and validity is limited. The lack of information concerning the standardization sample makes it difficult for potential users to make informed decisions about the use of this inventory either in research or in counseling individuals.

Review of Affective Perception Inventory by GERALD R. SMITH, Professor of Education, Indiana University, Bloomington, IN:

The Affective Perception Inventory (API), based to some extent on an earlier instrument called the Self Perception Inventory (SPI), is in widespread use, if one can judge from the number of languages (Spanish, French, Italian, and English) in which it has been printed.

The authors adopt the view that the API provides evidence of at least three dimensions of self-perception: a generic self or *g* factor, specific self perceptions which are situation-relevant or role-dependent (*s* factors), and a combination of these first two which the authors call a multidimensional or *m* factor. However, the data they present do not represent as precise a test of this construct as one would like. They mention the need for factor analysis to determine the clustering of self-concept traits but apparently have not yet carried out (or at least have not reported) such an analysis. Therefore, while the data derived from the API remain encouraging, further analysis must be completed.

Except at the primary level, the items of the API consist of polar pairs (e.g., happy vs. unhappy) with four spaces between the pairs. The respondent is asked to check the appropriate space. At the primary level there are only two spaces. For the most part, this format is easy to follow and respond to. Stanine scores have been determined to aid in the interpretation of the various scales, and these are helpful.

However, the API manual presents no data on the "readability" of the items, and the length of time required to administer it—5 minutes per scale—may result in response fatigue, especially in younger children. The manual does suggest that the instrument may be administered in two sessions to reduce fatigue, but it presents no evidence that the fatigue effect has ever been studied. This would be useful information for potential users.

The authors take for granted that the items are acceptable items to ask children in the context of the school, and since many of the items are related to school subjects or school as a whole, this assumption may be reasonable. Still, where items such as "I am a relaxed person" vs. "I am a nervous person" are asked of children, parents may become rightfully concerned. Yet, the manual provides little evidence of how the API has been received by parents or guidance for users on how to deal with such issues. The authors should address the ethical issues raised by instruments like the API by discussing parent approval and including sample forms for this purpose.

Technical data on the API has been provided in many forms by the manual. Using Rulon's (1939) split-half method, reliability coefficients were calculated for each of the three groups (self, peers, and teachers) on each of nine scales. Generally these coefficients are quite reasonable (.61 to .94) for this type of instrument.

Self-ratings were correlated with peer ratings and again with teacher ratings as measures of validity. Coefficients for the self-peer ratings ranged from .76 on the school perceptions scale to .38 on the arts scale. Most of the remaining coefficients fell between .49 and .55. The self-teacher correlations were generally lower, ranging from .74 on the student self scale to .30 on the arts scale. These are respectable if not exceptional validity coefficients. A plausible case is made as well for discriminant validity.

The API has been criticized (see Long, 1969) for its tendency to produce a positive response set in less able groups (e.g., disadvantaged and poor achievers). Osgood, Suci, and Tannenbaum (1957) and Greenberg (1970) provide support for this observation. While the criticism seems warranted, response set is not sufficiently serious in its effects to undermine the usefulness of the API, and it can be examined to determine the likelihood of its presence in any study using the instrument.

In summary, the authors have used and reported on the API in a number of contexts. Their view is that the instrument provides evidence of three dimensions of self-concept: a general (*g*) factor, specific (*s*) factors which are situation relevant, and a multidimensional (*m*) factor which is a combination of the first two. The technical data on reliability and validity give the instrument credibility and the authors' claims appear restrained and responsible. But factor analysis, which the authors mention is needed but which is not reported, would be a useful addition.

While the API has been criticized for its tendency to elicit higher ratings in less able groups, the magnitude of these distortions is not judged to be unduly serious, but response set bias should be examined in any use of the API, especially when comparing less able to more able groups.

REVIEWER'S REFERENCES

Rulon, P. J. A simplified procedure for determining the reliability for a test of split halves. HARVARD EDUCATIONAL REVIEW, 1939, 9, 99–103.

Osgood, C. E., Suci, G. J., & Tannenbaum, P. H. THE MEASUREMENT OF MEANING. Urbana, IL: University of Illinois Press, 1957.

Long, B. H. Critique of Soares and Soares' "Self-Perceptions of Culturally Disadvantaged Children." AMERICAN EDUCATIONAL RESEARCH JOURNAL, 1969, 6, 710–711.

Greenberg, J. W. Comments on self-perception of disadvantaged children. AMERICAN EDUCATIONAL RESEARCH JOURNAL, 1970, 4, 627–630.

Soares, A. T., & Soares, L. M. Critique of Soares and Soares' "Self-Perceptions of Culturally Disadvantaged Children"—A Reply. AMERICAN EDUCATIONAL RESEARCH JOURNAL, 1970, 7, 631–635.

[60]

Affective Sensitivity Scale. Persons in the helping professions; 1980; ASS; consists of a series of filmed encounters between 2 or or more persons; 16 scores: between, within, adult, child, male, female, total, affection, anger, confusion, distrust, fear/anxiety, guilt/shame, happiness, helplessness, sadness; Form D, E, (31 pages); preliminary mimeographed manual (30 pages); 1984 price data: $375 per 16mm color sound film, examiner's manual, and test; 23(35) minutes for Form D, 24(35) minutes for Form E; Norman Kagan and John Schneider; Mason Media, Inc.*

Review of Affective Sensitivity Scale by DONALD A. LETON, Professor of Education, Department of Counselor Education, University of Hawaii, Honolulu, HI:

The test authors have theorized five sequential phases of therapeutic empathy as follows: (1) perceiving the affective state of the other, (2) experiencing or resonating the other's emotions, (3) attaining an awareness of the other's message or emotional state, (4) labeling the message, and (5) communicating an understanding to the other. This appears to be a convenient theory because the authors use it to discount the low correlations among various empathy and affective sensitivity scales, inferring that different scales assess different phases of empathy.

The item stimuli are brief movie scenes of interactions (interpersonal encounters) from 8 seconds to 2 minutes long. The scenes are taken from a wide variety of interactions, including doctor-patient, friend-friend, teacher-student, counselor-counselee, and psychotherapist-patient interactions. Although the number and time length of the interactions are reported and there is a consideration of Black and White skin colors, there are many other stimulus variables which are not detailed. These include: the focal distance of the "other" from the empathist; the gestural and postural aspects of nonverbal messages; whether the other is frontally facing the viewer or moving toward or away from the empathist; the dress, attractiveness or other physical features of the persons; the loudness and other voice characteristics of the participants; and the use of adverbs and adjectives in the verbal communications. In addition to the length of the scenes these variables may be critical for aspects of perception.

It would seem advisable to obtain laboratory definitions of the five hypothesized components of empathy, to objectify their existence and to separate their occurrences, in the same manner that components are tested in cognitive process theory. This might provide direction to the scaling or measurement of reciprocal affect processes.

The response procedure consists of selecting one or several sentences, from three choices, to describe the feeling of the "other" person or the empathist. Some of the single sentences are punctuated with dashes, as if there might be a pause in the oral rendition of the clauses. Other choices include two or three brief sentences. Some sentences are terminated with one to three exclamation marks; others with periods or question marks. A few words are underlined, to suggest phonemic stress. The composition and punctuation of the sentences are variable; and these structural features could contribute to error choices, independent of the literal content.

Although semantic differential ratings and open-ended response procedures were tried in previous experimental development, these were summarily rejected without comparisons of the response yields from the three procedures. The printed multiple-choice response procedure was chosen, for statistical reasons. To require that the respondent read two to six sentences in the response choices is not situationally representative of oral empathic communication. It could also have an interfering effect on the oral transmission of empathy. An empathic person could conceivably have an accurate proprioception of the resonant affect, and could make an appropriate oral response; but the intervening act of reading sentences with unusual punctuations could lead to incorrect choices of printed sentences.

The Affective Sensitivity Scale (Form C) was first developed in the 1960s. The filmed interaction scenes have not been changed; however, four other experimental versions were evaluated between 1974 and 1980 before the development of the present D-80 and E-80 forms. The correlations of the equivalent forms ranged from .60 to .67, and the test-retest correlation of Form E-80 was .62. The scale yields six sensitivity subscale scores: Between persons, Within persons, Adult, Child, Male and Female, and one total score. The alpha coefficients for subscale scores on the two forms range from .38 to .63.

Key words in the correct and incorrect responses for the two forms have been classified into nine emotional categories: (1) Affection, (2) Anger, (3) Fear and Anxiety, (4) Confusion, (5) Shame and Guilt, (6) Distrust, (7) Happiness, (8) Helplessness, and (9) Sadness. The emotional accuracy scores are the percentages of correct and incorrect response choices in each of the nine emotional categories. The numbers of choices available for the nine emotional categories in the separate forms are not sufficient to reliably assess types of emotional empathy; however, the use of both forms improves the possibility of obtaining reliable results.

Although the 1977 and 1980 versions of the Affective Sensitivity Scale have been administered to thousands of students, they were primarily college students. The student samples were from counseling, nursing, medicine, social work and teaching; the professional samples were physicians, psychotherapists, counselors and teachers; and paraprofessionals included mental health aides. The clinical validity of the A.S.S. for the development of profiles of empathy for types of persons and for types of emotions is tenuous. The emotional accuracy scores have not been validated on external criteria; however, personality tests and socio-interactional behavior data could provide bases for validation studies.

On the first page of the manual the authors write, "Despite the amount of work which has already gone in to the scale we view it as essentially experimental. There is much we do not know about some of the most basic psychological mechanisms involved." Potential users should be aware of the knowledge boundaries that prevail and also be aware of the possible value of the scale for experimental studies.

[61]

Affects Balance Scale. Adults; 1975; ABS; 2 scores: positive, negative; no data on reliability and validity; no norms; 1 form (2 pages); no manual; 1983 price data: $26 per 100 tests; $16 per 100 Score Profile-B (male & female); administration time not reported; Leonard R. Derogatis; the Author.*

TEST REFERENCES

1. Derogatis, L. R., & Meyer, J. K. A psychological profile of the sexual dysfunctions. ARCHIVES OF SEXUAL BEHAVIOR, 1979, 8, 201–223.
2. Derogatis, L. R., Abeloff, M. D., & Melisaratos, N. Psychological coping mechanisms and survival time in metastic breast cancer. JAMA, 1979, 242(14), 1504–1508.
3. Hoehn-Saric, R., Merchant, A. F., Keyser, M. L., & Smith, V. K. Effects of clonidine on anxiety disorders. ARCHIVES OF GENERAL PSYCHIATRY, 1981, 38, 1278–1282.

4. Lang, J. G., Munoz, R. F., Bernal, G., & Sorensen, J. L. Quality of life and psychological well-being in a bicultural Latino community. HISPANIC JOURNAL OF BEHAVIORAL SCIENCE, 1982, 4, 433–450.
5. Snow, R., & Crapo, L. Emotional bondedness, subjective well-being, and health in elderly medical patients. JOURNAL OF GERONTOLOGY, 1982, 37, 609–615.
6. Stock, W. A., & Okun, M. A. The construct validity of life satisfaction among the elderly. JOURNAL OF GERONTOLOGY, 1982, 37, 625–627.

[62]

AH Vocabulary Scale. Ages 9–11, 12–14, 15–16 and sixth formers, college of education students, university graduates; 1978–79; AHVS; scale consists of six 40-word sets which may be given in pairs (tests for ages 15 and over are available in combined format only); 5 levels labeled Tests P and Q (ages 9–11, '79, 6 pages each), Q and R (ages 12–14, '79, 6 pages each), RS (15–16 and sixth formers, '79, 11 pages), ST (college of education students, '79, 11 pages), TU (university graduates, '79, 11 pages); manual ('78, 47 pages); separate answer sheets must be used; 1983 price data: £5.80 per 25 test booklets; £1.50 per key for any one set; £4.40 per 25 answer sheets; £4.65 per manual; £7 per specimen set; (20–30) minutes per set; A. W. Heim, K. P. Watts, and V. Simmonds; NFER-Nelson Publishing Co. [England].*

Review of AH Vocabulary Scale by RIC BROWN, Associate Professor of Education, California State University, Fresno, CA:

The AH Vocabulary Scale was developed on the premise that vocabulary tests are useful adjuncts to verbal and non-verbal tests of reasoning and may aid in the assessment of groups ranging from reticent adolescent to psychiatric patients.

The rationale given by authors for the development of yet another vocabulary scale is twofold. First, they assert that too many tests have words that have gone "out of fashion" or have become too common. The authors state that they have endeavored to avoid use of such words. A second assertion is that most vocabulary tests concentrate on words described as literary or non-technical. In the current test, scientific words and words with Gaelic, Far Eastern, and African stems have been included.

The AH Vocabulary Scale differs from other vocabulary tests in that there is no gradient of difficulty within a set of words. The words in all six sets are described as fairly difficult and are arranged in alphabetical order within each set. However, the six sets are of increasing levels of difficulty. In the easiest set, words such as "combat" and "ponder" are included. The hardest set includes words such as "apostasy," "encomiastic," and "rebarbative."

The three 40-item sets (P, Q, R) seem to yield enough variability for use with younger students (ages 9 to 14). The authors suggest that the 80-item sets (RS, ST, TU) are preferable for older subjects in terms of yielding a wider range of scores. Because of the increased level of difficulty of sets, the 80-item sets are arranged in terms of alternating pages. For example, on test TU, 8 words from test T are followed by 8 words from test U. This is done to prevent respondents from encountering the more difficult 40 words from test U all at one time at the end of the test.

The procedures for administering and scoring tests are clearly stated. The question book and answer sheets provided are easily used and include several practice items. Each word has six alternatives presented. However, the respondents are also allowed to provide their own definition, if desired. The instructions allow very liberal guidelines for scoring such answers as correct.

Reliability data are presented in the form of split-half correlations and KR-21 coefficients. Based on samples of 100 respondents at each age level (11 years, 14 years, 17 years, university students, and university graduates), split-half coefficients are in the .70 to .90 range across all 80-word tests (.50 to .80 for the 40-word tests).

KR-21 coefficients in the range of .60 to .90 were found for the various forms utilizing the same groups upon which the norms were based (each age 9 to 18, college of education students, other graduate students, and miscellaneous adults). Extensive validity data is presented by the authors. Correlations ranging from .50 to .75 are shown between the various vocabulary tests and variables such as non-verbal ability, reading, math, and standard tests of intelligence.

Tables of norms are provided showing means, standard deviations, and sample sizes of the various groups. Additionally, for data at each age level, score ranges are presented for the upper 10% through the lowest 10%. As expected, scores consistently increase with the age level of the subjects.

In the general discussion section of the test manual, several points are made by the authors. First, they assert that although the scale is highly correlated with intelligence, it is not an intelligence test. Secondly, they suggest that the scale may be a valuable aid for identification of "all around" students. This is because of the literary and technical words on the scale.

Overall, the AH vocabulary scales appear to be well-developed tests of vocabulary. Reliability and validity data indicate technically-sound scales. Directions and scoring instructions are clear and extensive norm tables are provided.

Two points need to be made. First, all tests were developed and normed in the late 1970s on respondents in England. Therefore, generalizability of the norms needs to be considered. Secondly, users may find the words from sets R to U extremely difficult. Users will need to exercise care in selecting tests appropriate for intended respondents.

Review of AH Vocabulary Scale by ROBERT B. FRARY, Professor and Assistant Director for

Research and Measurement, Learning Resources Center, Virginia Polytechnic Institute and State University, Blacksburg, VA:

The AH Vocabulary Scale consists of six 40-item progressively more difficult tests. They may be administered singly or in pairs representing adjacent difficulty levels and are suitable for upper elementary school through advanced graduate level examinees. Response format is multiple-choice with the provision that examinees may write an answer if they believe none of the choices is suitable or simply if they prefer to do so. Norms are based on samples of students in England. Use outside of the United Kingdom or without the provision for written answers would make the norms largely inapplicable.

The character of the items on these tests deserves special mention. The stimulus words are extremely varied in origin and application, unlike the mostly literary, nonscientific words found in other vocabulary tests. The distractors are also worthy of note; rarely does one see such clever choices. For the stimulus, accretion (on the next to highest level test), one distractor is inhabitant of Crete. For posterity, the choices are behind, good fortune, awarded after death, collection of mail bags, future generations, and great haste. Apiary brings forth collection of monkeys, home of bees, big cage for birds, chimpanzee's swing, mimicry, and circus. Acumen has among its distractors hothouse plant and ace pilots. It would be fun to teach vocabulary using the potential malapropisms suggested by almost every item in these tests.

Even the lowest level test has words that would challenge the brightest 9- to 11-year-olds, (e.g., ingenious, dialect, and aviary). The highest level has words that do not appear in most dictionaries (e.g., pusket, encomiastic, donga). Variant spellings may confuse some examinees, especially at the higher levels (e.g., mommet rather than maumet). If administered according to directions permitting written responses, scorers would have to be fully conversant with the range of meanings one might attach to such words.

The manual for this scale is extremely complete and well written. Split-half reliability estimates for the 40-item tests range from .54 to .88, with the lower coefficients associated with tests probably too difficult for the subjects sampled. The 80-item tests (two adjacent 40-item tests combined) yielded reliability estimates ranging from .74 to .90. Correlations between scores from adjacent 40-item tests ranged from .67 to .82.

Substantial evidence concerning validity is reported in the manual, including over 200 separate validity coefficients. These suggest virtually no relationship between vocabulary scores and achievement in certain vocational areas to very strong relationships between vocabulary and intelligence or some areas of academic achievement. In addition, mean scores for well-defined samples of examinees vary as would be expected given their academic levels and pursuits.

This scale should receive serious consideration in case of any need to measure vocabulary, especially if a wide range of ability is involved. Results might be even more reliable and valid if the option of writing in answers were eliminated, as there is some possibility that scorer misjudgement may introduce error components into scores. In addition, of course, use of written answers precludes machine processing of responses.

[63]

AH1 Forms X and Y. Ages 7–11 for classroom purposes and 5–11 for research; 1977; downward extension of AH2/AH3; perceptual reasoning; 5 scores: series, likes, analogies, differents, total; Form X, Y, (18 pages); manual (28 pages); 1983 price data: £8.95 per 25 test booklets; £2.95 per answer key; £5.45 per manual; £9.95 per specimen set; 12(40) minutes; A. W. Heim, K. P. Watts, and V. Simmonds; NFER-Nelson Publishing Co. [England].*

Review of AH1 Forms X and Y by FRANK R. YEKOVICH, Associate Professor of Educational Psychology, The Catholic University of America, Washington, DC:

The AH1X and AH1Y are parallel forms of a test of perceptual reasoning ability. The test is group administered and takes about 45 minutes to complete. It has four subtests—Series, Likes, Analogies, and "Differents" (Differences)—which are administered in fixed order. Each subtest is comprised of 4 practice items and 12 test items. Half of the items are drawings of symbols (e.g., squares, arrows) while the remainder are drawings of real world objects (e.g., humans, trucks). The test is multiple-choice and the child must choose one alternative that best fits the conditions displayed by the question stem. For instance, the stem of one question depicts two birds, each in flight. The child must pick the one bird (from six alternatives) that is also flying. The manual presents most of the information that a user needs in order to use the test properly. The introduction section of the manual gives a lucid and concise description of the test. The remaining sections present clearly the necessary information on administration, scoring, psychometric measures, and norming. Further, the psychometric and norming sections are generally complete, with a few exceptions to be discussed below. Since the test was developed and normed in England, American users may find some of the administration instructions awkward, but the authors point out that minor wording changes will not invalidate the test.

Potential users should be aware of several questionable characteristics of the test, however. First, the AH1 is billed as a test of perceptual reasoning.

Exactly what do the authors intend by this term? The authors state: "we use the term 'perceptual' to indicate the nonverbal nature of AH1." At another point, they say: "The generally close association found between AH1 and the other criteria—verbal, non-verbal, and mathematical—suggests that AH1 is testing something fairly basic, which is common to all or most cognitive tasks for young children." Thus, perceptual reasoning is supposedly akin to some fundamental cognitive dimension. Indeed, the validation section of the manual shows that total scores on the AH1 correlate with several diverse measures of cognitive ability. The problem is that the authors do not tell us what *is not* "perceptual reasoning," (i.e., what abilities *do not* correlate with the AH1). If the AH1 is to be diagnostically useful, a tester must be able to use it to rule out certain possibilities and focus on others. Since the AH1 correlates with both verbal and non-verbal reasoning, as well as with reading age, isolation of specific reasoning deficits may be difficult.

Whether or not the AH1 is comparable to tests such as the Raven Progressive Matrices remains a question also, since the manual does not name the tests against which the AH1 was validated. Thus, for instance, it is not clear whether scores on the AH1 are measures of general intellectual functioning or of a more specific reasoning component.

Another area of question on the AH1 concerns the subtests. The manual reports no intercorrelations among the four subtests and no correlations of subtest scores with total scores. Additionally, no subtest reliabilities are given. Thus, the authors present no statistical evidence for the independence or stability of the subtests. Lacking this information, the user should be cautious in interpreting subtest scores in isolation. Further, until additional reports are available, the use of subtest scores to develop "reasoning profiles" also seems unwarranted.

Finally, the user should note three minor potential problems with the AH1. First, the authors point out that long test-retest intervals (7 to 11 months) lead to slightly lower reliability coefficients than short intervals (5 weeks). This difference may be suggestive of developmental factors that affect reasoning ability. Second, the authors do not report any sex-related measures, and as a consequence the user should be careful in making comparisons across gender. Third, the standard error of measurement is slightly high and appears to fluctuate in magnitude with various test-retest intervals. As a result, the user should avoid using narrow ranges of percentile ranks.

In summary, the AH1X and AH1Y are generally well developed and appear to tap some general reasoning ability. However, the potential user should use caution in interpreting what the test actually measures. The statistical support for the test is good although the utility of the subtests will remain questionable until further justification is presented.

[64]

AH2/AH3. Ages 9 and over; 1974–78; 4 scores: verbal, numerical, perceptual, total; Forms AH2, AH3, ('75, 28 pages); manual ('78, 47 pages); separate answer sheets must be used; 1985 price data: £22.95 per 25 reusable tests; £4.85 per 25 answer sheets; £1.95 per scoring stencils for AH2; £3.70 per scoring stencils for AH3; £.95 per key for examples; £5.95 per manual; £12.45 per specimen set; 28(45) or 42(65) minutes; A. W. Heim, K. P. Watts, and V. Simmonds; NFER-Nelson Publishing Co. [England].

See T3:149 (14 references) and 8:175 (1 reference).

TEST REFERENCES

1. Bamber, J. H., Bill, J. M., Boyd, F. E., & Corbett, W. D. In two minds-arts and science differences at sixth-form level. BRITISH JOURNAL OF EDUCATIONAL PSYCHOLOGY, 1983, 53, 222–233.

[65]

AH4 Group Test of General Intelligence. Ages 10 and over; 1955–84; 1 form ('75 15 pages); revised manual ('70, 18 pages); data supplement ('84, 18 pages); separate answer sheets must be used; 1985 price data: £9.75 per 25 tests; £2.15 per 25 answer sheets; £1.75 per answer key; £2.75 per manual; £2 per data supplement; £4.95 per specimen set; 20(30–45) minutes; A. W. Heim, K. P. Watts (test), V. Simmonds (test), and Anne Walters (data supplement); NFER-Nelson Publishing Co. [England].*

See T2:331 (20 references); for a review by John Nisbet, see 7:331 (12 references); for a review by John Liggett of the original edition, see 6:506; for a review by George A. Ferguson, see 5:390 (11 references).

[66]

AH5 Group Test of High Grade Intelligence. Ages 13 and over; 1968–84; "highly intelligent pupils and students"; 3 scores: verbal and numeric, diagrammatic, total; 1 form ('84, 7 pages); answer sheet ('68, 2 pages); marking key (no date, 2 pages); manual ('83, 21 pages); 1985 price data: £6.55 per specimen set (includes test booklet, answer sheet, marking key and manual); £7.95 per 25 test booklets; £2.70 per 25 answer sheets; £5.25 per manual; £1 per marking key; 40(60) minutes; A. W. Heim; NFER-Nelson Publishing Co. [England].*

TEST REFERENCES

1. Gill, R. W. T. A trainability concept for management potential and an empirical study of its relationship with intelligence for two managerial skills. JOURNAL OF OCCUPATIONAL PSYCHOLOGY, 1982, 55, 139–147.

[67]

Ahr's Individual Development Survey. Grades K–1; 1970; AIDS; screening test completed by parent to identify possible learning or behavior problems; 3 major sections: the family, the child, the school; no data on reliability and validity; no data concerning establishment of norms; manual ('70, 8 pages); booklet ('70, 8 pages); 1985 price data: $10 per manual and 35 booklets; $2 per specimen set; A. Edward Ahr; Priority Innovations, Inc.*

Review of Ahr's Individual Development Survey by CAROL A. GRAY, Associate Professor and

Director, Clinical Services and Research Center, Educational Psychology, University of Washington, Seattle, WA:

The Ahr's Individual Development Survey (AIDS) is basically a retrospective questionnaire directed at the parents of kindergarten or first-grade children. The parents are asked to respond to a number of items grouped into three categories: the family, the child, and the school. The response format ranges from a request for a narrative about the child's temperament to birth weight in pounds and ounces. There are no directions for interpreting the responses other than a brief list of developmental milestones on the back page of the manual. It should be noted that the accuracy and relevance of some of these milestones is questionable.

The author indicates that the survey was developed as a first step in a screening program to identify children who have learning and/or behavioral problems. The rationale for using this kind of a parent report survey seemed to be twofold. The first reason given was that eliciting information from parents communicated to the parents a "sincere wish to know about their child's development." The second reason was that the parents should be seen as a good source of information about the developmental status of their children.

Although the intentions of the author appear to be good, there is little else one can say in a positive vein about this instrument. AIDS fails to pass any test one might wish to apply from psychometric quality through clinical usefulness. Probably the most devastating weakness is the fact that there is no evidence that any of the information gathered has any predictive validity in terms of either short or long term educational, developmental, or behavioral outcomes for a child. There is, as a matter of fact, evidence that much of the information gathered is not predictive of much of anything.

The authors make the statement that data should not be collected only to sit and gather dust. In fact, they emphasize the point that information should only be elicited if there is a goal in mind. They then proceed to ignore their own admonishments by having us collect information for which there are no guidelines for interpretation, and for which there are no recommendations for application.

The manual accompanying the survey is basically seven pages of platitudes marked by spelling errors. The table on page seven (developmental milestones) does not reflect the actual content of the survey, a point the authors admit in their discussion. There is no evidence of reliability, validity, or any of the basic information that one would like to have in a manual. There are no guidelines for "scoring" or interpreting the individual items on the survey. Nor are there any samples of responses that might be useful from a clinical point of view.

In summary, this is a survey that cannot be recommended for use as a screening device. It cannot even be recommended for use as a structured interview because of the lack of any rationale for the questions being used.

[68]

Alberta Essay Scales: Models. High school English teachers; "a means for checking writing skills against standards prevailing in 1964"; 1 form (no date, 38 pages); technical report (no date, 24 pages); 1983 price data: $8.50 per test; $8 per technical report; Verner R. Nyberg and Adell M. Nyberg; University of Alberta [Canada].*

See T3:151 (1 reference).

Review of Alberta Essay Scales: Models by STEVE GRAHAM, Assistant Professor of Special Education, University of Maryland, College Park, MD:

The Alberta Essay Scales reportedly represent a standard, based on writing samples collected in 1964, against which the current compositions of 12th-grade students can be compared. According to the authors, the instrument can be used to assist teachers in the task of grading compositions and monitoring progress. Students' essays are evaluated by matching them to a carefully selected and sequenced set of "model" compositions. Essentially, the examiner attempts to match the student's essay as closely as possible with one of the models. The student's score on the essay is the number value of the most similar model.

The instrument differs from other composition scales in that two different sets of models (rather than one) are provided. One set is used to measure the mechanical aspects of writing, while the other deals with writing style and content. Both of these scales are defined by model essays representing achievement at four stanine levels (i.e., 2, 4, 6, 8). The rationale for including two scales is based on empirical evidence. The variables presumably measured by the style-content scale and the mechanics scale were only moderately correlated ($r = .47$). Consequently, it appears that the two scales measure different attributes. In addition, it was the stated intention of the test developers to construct a composition scale which would weight mechanical attributes and style-content variables equally. However, when the variables from both scales were combined, it was found that mechanics accounted for approximately 74% of the total score variance (Nyberg, 1968). Thus, the construction of a single scale would have resulted in an instrument which primarily measured mechanics.

Although there were several notable omissions, the steps and procedures used to develop the instrument were sufficiently documented. Initially 8,020 students enrolled in English 30 (grade 12 academic English) in the Alberta high schools wrote essays on the topic of advertising at the end of the academic school year. One hundred and three of these essays (of 400 to 500 words in length) were randomly selected and scored by two committees of English teachers under the direction of the Examinations Branch of the Alberta Department of Education. One committee repeatedly graded the essays for proficiency in mechanics (e.g., spelling, punctuation, sentence errors, etc.) and used a deduction system. Each essay was first awarded 125 points and, subsequently, a predetermined number of points were deducted each time a particular error was encountered. The second committee used a bonus system and repeatedly scored each essay on style and content. Points were awarded on the basis of competence in 16 different areas (e.g., originality, order, vocabulary, etc.). Instructions and criteria for scoring essays were clearly specified and each committee was monitored to insure that directions were followed. The data generated by each committee was converted into stanines (the process was never clearly delineated) and a representative essay for stanines two, four, six, and eight were selected for each scale. Selections were made on the basis of two criteria: (1) the standard deviation of the model essay was relatively low and (2) the mean score assigned to the model was near the middle of the stanine level.

A critical examination of the information presented on test development reveals that the Alberta Essay Scales exhibit at least three significant limitations. First, the models do not represent the full range of quality found in most 12th-grade classrooms. A normal distribution cannot be assumed, since sample selection was limited to essays which met predetermined criteria (e.g., 400–500 words in length). Second, the normative population is not adequately defined. Data on subjects' experiential background, achievement levels, sex, race, intelligence, etc. are not provided. As a result, it is impossible to determine if acculturation between a prospective testee and the normative population is comparable. Third, it appears that the authors presume that their instrument is an equal-interval scale since the unit of measurement is stanines. Nevertheless, it is not readily apparent that increments between any two adjacent scores are equivalent.

The manual provides no directions for eliciting essays. This is an unfortunate oversight since the performance of a testee is evaluated in terms of the performance of the normative population. Available evidence indicates that writing performance can be influenced by a variety of assignment variables: teacher directions, choice of topic, mode of discourse, source of stimulation, and the intended audience (Graham, 1982). If the procedures for securing an essay from a testee are significantly different from those used to obtain the model compositions, the norms may be useless.

The manual does provide detailed directions for scoring essays. The score for mechanics is determined by: (1) counting the number of errors in the target essay, (2) converting the tally to a frequency, and (3) locating the model with a similar error rate. One drawback to this approach is that the student's score can be affected by the examiner's knowledge of correct usage. Style and content are scored by having the examiner read the target essay to obtain a general impression. The examiner then locates the model that comes nearest to creating the same impression. It should be noted that the procedures for scoring an essay are different from the procedures used to select and determine a model's position on the scale. However, the procedures do not differ substantially and should, therefore, yield similar results.

The authors should be commended for attempting to promote scoring accuracy through proper orientation and training. Each model is accompanied by a brief commentary stating its attributes and a table which shows how it was scored. The manual also includes a series of training exercises which provide both practice and feedback. Nonetheless, prospective examiners who are relatively inexperienced in evaluating written compositions will probably require additional experiences in order to develop precision.

Finally, it is evident that the Alberta Essay Scales have not been adequately validated. Evidence concerning concurrent, predictive, and construct validity is notably absent. Although the authors claim that the instrument evidences "a degree of content validity," the only proof offered to support this proposition is that the variables used to score the models are essentially the same as those developed by two English specialists in Alberta. The manual does present data on inter-rater reliability. The mean reliability coefficients for mechanics and style-content were .78 and .77, respectively. The manual contains no information on test-retest reliability or intra-rater reliability.

To summarize, one of the primary strengths of this instrument was the development and incorporation of two separate scales. This reviewer was also favorably impressed by the completeness of the scoring guide and the inclusion of training activities. Nevertheless, several significant shortcomings were noted. Directions for soliciting essays were not specified. The standardization group was not adequately defined and may not be representative. There was insufficient psychometric data to support the authors' claims of reliability and validity. Therefore, the Alberta Essay Scales: Models is a relatively untried test and should be viewed as an experimental edition which needs to be further validated.

REVIEWER'S REFERENCES

Nyberg, V. THE RELIABILITY OF ESSAY GRADING. Paper presented at the Sixth Annual Canadian Conference on Educational Research. Quebec City, Canada, 1968.

Graham, S. Composition research and practice: A unified approach. FOCUS ON EXCEPTIONAL CHILDREN, 1982, 14, 1–16.

Review of Alberta Essay Scales: Models by PAMELA A. MOSS, Research Associate, Department of Instructional Studies, School of Education, University of Pittsburgh, Pittsburgh, PA:

The Alberta Essay Scales (AES) were designed to be used by 12th-grade English teachers to provide general impression scores for student compositions. There are two scales: one for "style-content" and one for "mechanics." Each scale contains 9 (1–9) levels, which are anchored by a single model essay each at levels 2, 4, 6, and 8. The authors state that the AES can be used for longitudinal comparisons and that they "represent a standard, based on written composition at the twelfth grade level in 1964, against which more current compositions can be compared with a high degree of objectivity."

In order to evaluate this statement, it is necessary to know something about the development of and the suggested techniques for using the AES. The AES, which bear a 1977 publication date, were derived from a subset of scored essays drawn from an essay test administered to 8,020 12th-grade students in Alberta, Canada, in 1964. A "random sample" of 103 essays had been chosen from among those essays written on the most popular of the two topics assigned, "Advertising," and eliminating essays that were less than 400 to 500 words in length. These 103 essays were then scored for content and style by 21 raters using an analytic scale containing 16 separate variables and for mechanics by 27 raters essentially counting errors in each of 6 categories. Subsequently, the AES authors derived the scales by computing stanines for the 103 essays. The models which represent stanine levels 2, 4, 6, and 8 were selected to reflect two criteria: (*a*) the standard deviation of the scores given by the raters for that essay was relatively low, and (*b*) the mean score given by the raters was near the middle of the stanine interval. The model essays provide the primary definition for the levels of the scale. In other words, to understand what a score of 6 on the "content-style" scale means, the user must read the model essay for level 6. Odd numbered levels indicate essays that are slightly better or slightly worse than the models anchoring the even numbers.

To apply the "content-style" scale, the user is instructed to read the essay to be graded in order to form a general impression (focusing on the 16 content and style variables used in the 1964 scoring) and then to match that essay with the model essay that comes nearest to creating the same impression. To apply the mechanics scale, the user has two options: (*a*) to count the number of errors per 100 words and compare this error rate to the range of error rates reported for each of the stanines, or (*b*) to put a "red dot" next to each error both on the essay to be graded and on the mechanics model essays and compare the frequency of the red dots to find the model that has the most similar frequency of dots. The manual contains brief training instructions and a set of sample essays on which users can practice.

For the content-style scale, the statement that the AES enable longitudinal comparisons with 12th-grade standards in 1964 is untenable. First, the sample from which the scale was derived was small (slightly more than 1% of the sample of 1964 essays) and restricted in terms of topic and length, thus limiting its representativeness. Second, there is absolutely no empirical evidence presented in the manual supporting the scales' use for longitudinal comparisons. The only empirical data which even concerns this issue is a 1977 reliability study using six raters each to rate 83 papers. The authors report the data in terms of correlation coefficients—but correlation coefficients are not useful evidence of inter-rater reliability for a scale designed for longitudinal comparisons. The important reliability issue is whether the raters can agree on a score for each paper—not whether they can rank order papers in the same way. Percent agreement among raters would be the more informative reliability coefficient here. Third, longitudinal comparisons, as used here, imply that holistic or general impression scores given to a set of papers at one time can be equated with scores given to another set of papers at a different time by a different set of raters. There are no empirical studies of which I am aware that would support this notion. One method that has been used to equate holistic-type scores randomly mixes papers on identical topics from different test administrations, and raters score the papers from both administrations simultaneously, according to the current scoring rubric, without knowledge of which administration produced them. Comparisons between past and present performance can then be made in terms of present criteria; nothing can be said, however, about the present performance in terms of past criteria (which is the claim of the AES authors). The statement regarding longitudinal comparisons with 1964 standards has somewhat more validity in terms of the mechanics scores. One can certainly count errors from two sets of papers, compare the relative frequencies, and transform these frequencies to the mechanics scale. However, given the lack of representativeness of the sample discussed above, differences can hardly be described as above or below 1964 standards.

Ignoring the statements about longitudinal comparisons, the question remains whether or not these scales can be useful to teachers for grading 12th-grade compositions. Throughout the scoring and technical manuals, the authors use the word "composition" without ever being more specific, thus implying that these scales are designed to be used with any 12th grade composition. The authors do not take into account the fact that different topics make different demands. In developing criteria for evaluating essays, one needs to take into account the rhetorical purpose, the intended audience, the form, and the time limits specified by the essay prompt. Most other essay scales (see Cooper, 1977, for a review) focus on a particular rhetorical purpose (e.g., persuasion or personal expression) and provide more than one example at each score point. For a teacher using the AES, how informative is it to know that a student wrote an essay similar to an essay on a completely different topic, perhaps with a different rhetorical purpose, with time guidelines and audience unspecified? The AES are also limited in the range of the writing ability represented. Many of the compositions which 12th grade teachers might encounter today will be well below and some well above the levels represented in these scales. Scores of 1 and 9 might encompass a wide range of performance levels, making the scores particularly uninformative in these cases. The use of essay models to provide mechanics scores seems unnecessarily tedious. One does not need a model to identify and count errors.

That the most recent reference to essay scales in the AES technical manual is dated 1966 is not surprising. Essay scales are not in vogue at present. Other methods of assigning holistic scores to writing samples have been found generally to be more efficient and reliable. I can find nothing to recommend about the Alberta Essay Scales. They are a poor example of their genre: the accompanying documentation demonstrates a lack of awareness or concern for issues that are important to consider in assessing writing performance, and the information presented in the manual is confusing and misleading.

REVIEWER'S REFERENCES

Cooper, C. R. Holistic evaluation of writing. In C. R. Cooper and L. Odell (Eds.), EVALUATING WRITING: DESCRIBING, EDITING, JUDGING. Urbana, IL: National Council of Teachers of English, 1977.

[69]

Alcohol Dependence Scale. Problem drinkers; 1984; revision of the Alcohol Use Inventory; title on test is Alcohol Use Questionnaire; 1 form (6 pages); user's guide (39 pages); 1984 price data: $6.25 per 25 questionnaires; $14.25 per user's guide; $15 per specimen set; (5–10) minutes; J. L. Horn, H. A. Skinner, K. Wanberg (test), and F. M. Foster (test); Addiction Research Foundation.*

[70]

Alphabet Mastery. Second semester kindergarten to 2.5, second semester kindergarten and over; 1975; no scores, standards of mastery determined by examiner; no data on reliability and validity; no norms; 2 levels; no manual (instructions for administration and scoring included on test); test booklets reusable if special accessories, available from publisher are used; 1982 price data: $2.50 or less per form; $4 per accessories (eradicator fluid and sponge); administration time not reported; Enid L. Huelsberg; Ann Arbor Publishers, Inc.*

a) LEVEL 1: MANUSCRIPT. Second semester K to 2.5; 1 form (35 pages).

b) LEVEL 2: CURSIVE. Second semester K and over; 1 form (35 pages).

Review of Alphabet Mastery by MICHAEL D. SMITH, Associate Professor of Special Education and Communication Disorders, Western Carolina University, Cullowhee, NC:

Alphabet Mastery: Level I & Level II serves both as a test of emergent writing skills (penmanship) and as a basic program of writing instruction emphasizing the recognition and reproduction of alphabetic symbols. Level I has as its focus manuscript letter symbols. It is designed to be used with children between the second semester of kindergarten and the second semester of the second grade. Level II has as its focus the writing of isolated cursive letter symbols. It is designed to be used with children in the second semester of kindergarten and beyond. A test—more precisely a pretest—is administered prior to the onset of each of the two levels of writing instruction. To measure the overall effectiveness of instruction that is prescribed on the basis of pretest results, a posttest is administered. The pretest and posttest are sensitive to degrees of orthographic complexity, principally as they affect letter formation and legibility within upper case and lower case lettering systems. Six degrees of orthographic complexity are specified, ranging from the least complex (O,L,X,K) to the most complex (G,Q,P,D,B).

Alphabet Mastery, then, is a test of letter formation and legibility that is linked directly to a program of writing instruction. The most attractive feature of Alphabet Mastery consists of its sensitivity to orthographic complexity. Additionally, Alphabet Mastery provides a setting wherein young children are challenged to be their own evaluators. For example, provisions are made to engage children in the assessment of their progress toward letter mastery.

The disadvantages of Alphabet Mastery lie mainly in the dearth of substantive information on test development, construction, and implementation. Far too little information is provided on how Alphabet Mastery is to be effectively used. No concrete guidelines are given as to how pretest and posttest performances are to be evaluated. Except for what is implied by the use of the term "mastery," nothing is said about quantitative performance criteria.

Much of the potential of the focus on orthographic complexity in relation to letter formation and legibility is lost because the method by which performance is scored is not made explicit. Although standard models of manuscript and cursive letter symbols are provided, literally nothing is said about what constitutes an acceptable match or approximation of a standard letter form. Consequently, whatever is done is terms of evaluation of test performance will be essentially subjective and imprecise. What is judged to be an acceptable letter match or reproduction for one evaluator may be judged to be unacceptable or deficient by another evaluator. Ambiguity of this sort detracts significantly from the potential of Alphabet Mastery.

Persistent attempts have been made elsewhere to objectify the assessment of early writing skills through the use of various rating scales. A practical set of scales for both manuscript and cursive writing appeared, for example, in Freeman's (1958) Evaluation Scales for Guiding Growth in Handwriting. With the exception of kindergarten, the grades covered by Freeman's scales are equivalent to those covered by Alphabet Mastery. It is critical to note that Freeman's scales are designed to be applied to brief, contextually-based samples of writing (passage form) rather than to isolated letter samples such as those used under Alphabet Mastery. Sampling practices of the former sort are more functional and more revealing of the status of letter formation and overall legibility in children's early attempts at writing. Additionally, information obtained from careful analyses of contextually-based writing samples permits the formulation of substantial predictions of children's early performance on controlled reading tasks (Sealey, Sealey, & Millmore, 1979). This position contrasts with that adopted by Alphabet Mastery, wherein it is claimed that performance in the recognition, naming, and reproduction (writing) of isolated letter symbols is the "only known predictor of later success in reading."

The utility of formal evaluation scales like those of Freeman's has been underscored by Otto, McMenemy, and Smith (1973). Reliable and competent use of existing scales, however, very often calls for considerable training and experience on the part of an evaluator. A viable alternative and a concrete extension of various rating scales has emerged out of Salzberg, Wheeler, Devar, and Hopkins' (1971) innovative application of specially treated materials which utilize latent images to assess young children's letter formation and writing legibility.

To summarize, at first sight Alphabet Mastery appears to have considerable potential as a device used to measure emergent writing skills. However, due in large part to the absence of substantive information on how Alphabet Mastery is to be used and, most importantly, how performance is to be evaluated and interpreted, it does not serve as an improvement of or viable option to materials previously available.

REVIEWER'S REFERENCES

Freeman, F. A. EVALUATION SCALES FOR GUIDING GROWTH IN HANDWRITING. New York: Zaner-Bloser, 1958.

Salzberg, B. H., Wheeler, A. J., Devar, L. T., & Hopkins, B. I. The effects of intermittent feedback and intermittent contingent access to play on printing of kindergarten children. JOURNAL OF APPLIED BEHAVIOR ANALYSIS, 1971, 4, 163–171.

Otto, W., McMenemy, R. A., & Smith, R. J. CORRECTIVE AND REMEDIAL TEACHING. Boston: Houghton Mifflin Company, 1973.

Sealey, L., Sealey, N., & Millmore, M. CHILDREN'S WRITING: AN APPROACH FOR THE PRIMARY GRADES. Newark, DE: International Reading Association, 1979.

Review of Alphabet Mastery by SALLY ANITA WHITING, Psychologist, Deaf/Hard of Hearing, Covina-Valley Unified School District, Covina, CA:

This test, evaluating mastery of the letters of the alphabet, was developed in 1975 and consists of two booklets—a manuscript form which covers second semester kindergarten to grade 2.5, and a form for cursive letters designed for "second semester kindergarten and beyond."

On both forms, some 25 pages provide spaces for a student to fill in missing letters, to copy letters from models provided, or to print/write the entire alphabet on the gold-colored workbook sheets. No rationale is offered for the arrangement of letters, nor is there explanation of procedures to follow, presentation to students, etc. Each of the two forms has bar graphs (four for manuscript and six for cursive) so that the educator may record "Mastery Response." The teacher is advised to cover any model of the alphabet which appears in the classroom, no mean task if this is displayed as it usually is, above and along the blackboard. Booklets are reusable if a special eradicator is purchased. The teacher establishes criteria for successful reproduction of a letter and decides when students have individually met these criteria.

The sole rationale provided by the author for the development of this combination test and workbook is that "Being able to recognize, name and reproduce the letters of the alphabet is the only known predictor of later success in reading." In the opinion of this reviewer, this explanation is simply not sufficient to justify expenditure of such time on the part of both teacher and student. A basic assumption, inherent in design, must be that practice makes perfect—and practice the student will—over and over and over, honing his memory for a particular letter, while the educator, in turn, graphs and charts each student's progress.

Could it be that there might exist, within a teacher's repertoire, other simpler, equally efficient ways to teach the alphabet? Or, to put it another way, is this test really necessary? In the opinion of this reviewer, it is not.

[71]

Alternate Uses. Grades 6–16 and adults; 1960–78; revision of Unusual Uses; spontaneous flexibility; reliability and validity data for grades 6, 9, and adults only; Forms B, C, ('60, 3 pages); manual for Forms B and C ('78, 23 pages); scoring guide ('60, 3 pages) for each form; 1984 price data: $8 per 25 tests; $1 per scoring guide; $4 per manual; $5 per specimen set; 12(20) minutes; Paul R. Christensen, J. P. Guilford, Philip R. Merrifield, and Robert C. Wilson; Sheridan Psychological Services, Inc.*

See T3:157 (21 references), 8:235 (32 references), T2:542 (94 references), and 6:542 (7 references).

TEST REFERENCES

1. Hocevar, D. Intelligence, divergent thinking, and creativity. INTELLIGENCE, 1980, 4, 25–40.
2. Gilchrist, M. B. Creative talent and academic competence. GENETIC PSYCHOLOGY MONOGRAPHS, 1982, 106, 261–318.
3. Shmukler, D. A factor analytic model of elements of creativity in preschool children. GENETIC PSYCHOLOGY MONOGRAPHS, 1982, 105, 25–39.

Review of Alternate Uses by EDYS S. QUELLMALZ, Acting Associate Professor of Education, Stanford University, Stanford, CA:

The Alternate Uses test by Guilford et al. is proposed as one measure of flexible, divergent, and/or creative thinking. There are two forms of the test, Forms B and C. Form A was discontinued for reasons not discussed by the authors. Each form presents six common items, a suggested use, and blanks for examinees to list six additional uses. Eight minutes are allowed for completion of the test. Scoring guides for judging acceptable and unacceptable responses are supplied for items on each form. Materials provided for the review included test Forms B and C (copyright 1960) and the Manual of Instruction and Interpretation.

The test manual of instructions and interpretations leaves much to be desired. It provides little or no information about the theory base or rationale for the test or its construction. Most importantly, the manual does not offer guidelines for score interpretation.

The introduction defines the test as a measure of flexible thinking yet fails to explain adequately how the concept fits into Guilford's broader category of divergent thinking (encompassing, we are told, 29 abilities), or how the concept relates to other conceptualization of divergent/flexible/creative thinking. For example, why only six items? Why common items? Why are only six blanks provided, discouraging additional proposed uses?

The manual then provides brief descriptions of administration and scoring procedures and refers users to the instructions on the test forms and the scoring guides for each form.

The remainder of the manual, pages 2–13, includes estimates of reliability; information on construct validity; evidence of validity; relationships with other personability traits, race, and socioeconomic status; and tables of test norms.

In their discussion of reliability estimates, the authors fail to provide interrater agreement statistics, a serious omission for a constructed response test. Information on construct validity is based primarily on factor analyses. A series of factorial studies involve Alternate Uses and other measures of divergent thinking, cognitive fluency, and originality and creativity. However, in view of current cognitive research on the highly domain-specific skills involved in task performance, some form of componential analysis of the knowledge and procedures involved in generating alternative uses would seem to be a necessary addition to evidence of construct validity. For example, the fact that blacks scored higher than whites on an item involving a newspaper was attributed to the fact that blacks had had more unusual uses for newspapers in their homes than whites. If Alternate Uses is proposed as a measure of creativity, it would be necessary to distinguish newly proposed uses from previously experienced uses, i.e., to disentangle background experience from creativity.

A final problem with the manual is its failure to explain score summation and interpretation. Tables of norms do not explain how "C" scores are derived from raw scores of 1–36. Nowhere does the manual suggest how raw or derived scores might be used.

In sum, the construct measured, the rationale for the measurement method, and the use of the results are seriously underexplained. Furthermore, data documenting the technical quality of the test are incomplete. Potential users of this test should question seriously the correspondence between knowledge tapped by Alternate Uses and processes they wish to measure.

[72]

Analytic Learning Disability Assessment. Ages 8–14; 1982; ALDA; score of fail, weak or solid in 77 unit skill subtests; individual; 1 form; testing book (227 pages); manual (164 pages); findings and recommendations for the classroom teacher (10 pages); score formulation worksheet (2 pages); 1984 price data: $75 per complete kit; $13.50 per 20 testing forms; (105) minutes; Thomas D. Gnagey and Patricia A. Gnagey; Facilitation House.*

Review of Analytic Learning Disability Assessment by MARCIA B. SHAFFER, School Psychologist, Steuben-Allegany BOCES, Bath, NY:

The creators of the Analytic Learning Disability Assessment (ALDA) have a noble and unarguable purpose. "To be less than 'average,'" they say, "has subtly come to mean less than 'good,' that is, 'less valued.'" They would like to alleviate this situation, hoping that the "'ALDA idea' helps make being below average an acceptable and legitimate condition within the mainstream of our schools." They then expand upon their philosophy, which is essentially that children's learning is founded on "functional processes which students use as they actually go about classroom learning activities." These processes, for ALDA's purposes, are grouped into Unit Skills, with the intent of discovering which Unit Skills a given child may be able to use, and basing his/her educational program on the findings.

The Gnageys, in addition to aiming at the individualization which is the dream of every sensible educator, have approached their self-imposed task with total integrity and admirable ethics. They have delineated qualifications for those who use their assessment, including how much training and experience should precede independent administration. Their statistics are painstakingly complete. They have made a sedulous, although not entirely successful, effort to establish reliability and validity. Their directions as to testing environment and proper procedures are models of detail and caution.

Unfortunately, ALDA's flaws outnumber its virtues. The editing of the manual is of inexcusably poor quality. Commas and apostrophes are frequently omitted. Words are printed with uneven spacing. There are numerous spelling errors. In the table of contents, for instance, the word "termonology" [sic] appears; throughout the book, forms of the verb "assume" often have a double "m." All of this occurs in a style of printing which is difficult enough to read that the user could not refer to instructions without giving total attention to the manual.

The test itself is fulsome. There is too much of everything: too many words of explanation; too much equipment provided, including colored pencils for indicating different scoring categories; too many Unit Skills (77 of them, relating to the most minute particulars of reading, mathematics, spelling and handwriting, plus clusters which deal with classroom coping skills); too many pages in the test booklet, making it unwieldy to handle; too many numbers in the complicated tables with their very small print. The vocabulary becomes cloying (e.g., "thruput" may be descriptive, but it is so contrived a word as to seem ridiculous). Directions throughout the manual are complete to the last exhausting act or word of the assessor. Some of the instructions are downright obfuscating (e.g., "To fill in the cells, refer to the lower subsection of the Cluster Summary Section of the Scoring Form for the G scales and to the Tabulation Strip for the Unit Skills scores [for Unit Skills, interpret Solid to be Y, Weak D and Fail N for this Track Analysis Summary Chart]"). Even the model with which the ALDA originated is overly elaborate. Joseph Wepman and Charles Osgood, circa 1935, separately developed simple, understandable models of learning which still provide a suitable framework for the contemplation of learning disabilities. The Gnageys' model is an unnecessary extravagance.

The writers assure readers of their manual that administration, scoring, and reporting on the ALDA consumes only 1 hour and 45 minutes. They do not take into account how long it would take an examiner to memorize 77 Unit Skills, plus other combinations of skills, and to learn to mark the "score formulation worksheet." It is not easy to imagine administering the ALDA automatically.

The information promised by the ALDA is not worth the effort of mastering its administration and the reporting of results. Use of a battery of traditional tests like the WISC-R, the Detroit Tests of Learning Aptitudes, and the Bender Visual Motor Gestalt Test will give some of the same results. Further familiarity with a child's ways of learning or failing to learn can be obtained just as the Gnageys gathered the data from which the ALDA grew: by meticulous observation of the child himself.

[73]

Ann Arbor Learning Inventory. Grades K–1, 2–4; 1977–82; no data on reliability and validity; no norms; adequacy levels reported after each test plus remediation suggestions; individual; 2 levels; 1983 price data: $.50 per test; $4 per manual; (60) minutes; Waneta B. Bullock and Barbara Meister; Ann Arbor Publishers, Inc.*

a) LEVEL A. Grades K–1; 1978–82; 1 form ('82, 24 pages); manual ('82, 61 pages).

b) LEVEL B. Grades 2–4; 1977–82; 1 form ('82, 16 pages); manual ('82, 57 pages).

Review of Ann Arbor Learning Inventory by THOMAS B. BRADLEY, Department of Special Education, Shippensburg University, Shippensburg, PA:

The Ann Arbor Learning Inventory is one of a new wave of tests that bridge the gap between assessment and instructional practice. This individually administered inventory is intended for elementary age students from kindergarten to grade 4 (or older children who are functioning at these levels). The inventory is designed to provide teachers with information regarding the child's competencies or deficiencies in visual discrimination, visual motor coordination, auditory and visual sequential memory, auditory discrimination, and comprehension skill areas. The inventory consists of a series of brief tests which are administered to a child. If the number of errors on a particular test exceeds a specified level, it is claimed that a remedial effort is indicated.

Suggestions for remedial instruction and recommended instructional materials (published by Ann Arbor Publishers) immediately follow each test. This feature is a strong asset and makes the test especially valuable where materials produced by Ann Arbor Publishers are in use. However, a more "generic" approach in which instructional materials were recommended on the basis of their characteristics or in which the materials and products of several publishers were recommended would have insured wider applicability for this inventory. In districts that do not use and do not plan to purchase instructional materials from Ann Arbor Publishers, there is little justification for purchase of this inventory.

The two manuals that accompany the inventory are not test manuals in the typical sense. As expected, the manuals do provide clear and explicit directions on administering the tests and generally clear instructions on scoring. They contain, however, no technical data on the statistical characteristics of the test, no comments on validity, and only a brief description of the children for whom the test is appropriate.

Administration of the Ann Arbor Learning Inventory is highly structured. The tester is provided with scripts to read or recite to the testee for most of the tests in the inventory. This structure may give the tester an impression that the administration procedures are standardized. That impression may be reinforced further by the generally detailed directions for scoring items. However, this impression would be misleading because no other facet of the testing situation is described in the manuals. Some questions among many that one might ask include the following: (1) Is the inventory to be administered in the classroom, clinic, office, or home?, (2) May a parent be present?, (3) What efforts at building rapport with the child are required?, (4) What qualifications are required?, (5) How much prompting, if any, is acceptable?, and (6) Can the inventory be administered piecemeal if the child's attention span is clearly inadequate? None of these questions are answered.

When a school psychologist or educator uses a test to obtain information upon which to base a young child's educational program, it is vital that the information derived from assessment processes reliably reflect the child's strengths and deficiencies. The absence of reliability and validity data has already been noted. Salvia and Ysseldyke (1981) and Nunnally (1978) suggest that the more important the use to which test results will be put, the higher the reliability coefficients should be. As a rule of thumb, reliability coefficients above .80 are generally considered minimally acceptable and above .90 are considered desirable for educational planning.

A survey of reliability data from other tests with formats similar to the Ann Arbor Learning Inventory is revealing. Tests of auditory discrimination are generally satisfactory (often above .90). However, reliability coefficients for tests of visual discrimination (range=.29 to .74), visual motor coordination (range=.29 to .39), auditory sequential memory (range =.61 to .86), and visual sequential memory skills (range=.12 to .50) rarely have achieved the .90 criteria discussed above. It is widely accepted that the lower reliabilities are associated with tests for younger children and higher reliabilities are associated with tests for older groups of children. The Ann Arbor Learning Inventory is designed for grades K to 4, a group of younger children. We would expect, then, that the various tests of the Ann Arbor Learning Inventory would be estimated best by the lower end of the ranges of reliability coefficients reported above. If such extrapolations are justified, and in the total absence of data specific to this test, this inventory should be used for purposes of educational planning only with considerable caution. Diagnoses derived from the tests should be confirmed by the results of structured, systematic, direct observation and informal assessment procedures before test results are used as a basis for educational planning.

In summary, the Ann Arbor Learning Inventory has many positive characteristics that recommend it to schools that use instructional materials published by Ann Arbor Publishers. However, even for that limited audience its value appears limited. If the authors and publishers were to generate acceptable reliability and validity data, if the manuals were enhanced to describe better the target population, and if standardized administration procedures were described in considerable detail, its value for consumers of Ann Arbor Publishers' instructional programs might be considerable. If recommendations of instructional materials were from a wider range of publishers, the inventory might then enjoy a much broader market than is currently the case.

REVIEWER'S REFERENCES

Nunnally, J. C. PSYCHOMETRIC THEORY, 2nd ed. New York: McGraw-Hill, 1978.

Salvia, J., & Ysseldyke, J. E. ASSESSMENT IN SPECIAL AND REMEDIAL EDUCATION, 2nd ed. Boston: Houghton Mifflin, 1981.

Review of Ann Arbor Learning Inventory by KATHRYN CLARK GERKEN, Associate Professor of Human Development, University of Texas at Dallas, Richardson, TX:

The rationale underlying the development and possible use of the Ann Arbor Learning Inventory is unclear. What information is provided by the manual suggests that the test is designed to evaluate certain "central processing areas" so that a teacher can teach to modality strengths and remediate specific central processing deficits. The reasoning underlying an assessment instrument should be described clearly, but there is only a hint of the theoretical base for the inventory and no data are provided to support this base. Thus one is left with an unclear picture of what he/she is measuring and why he/she is measuring it. One is even left in a quandry about the age levels for which the Inventory is appropriate. The manual for Level A (K through 1) contains no statement as to whether the inventory should be given to all students in grades K through 1, or only those having specific problems. From what is written in the manual for Level B (grades 2 through 4), one would assume that you would give the inventory to any student in grades 2 through 4 and to older students who are having difficulty keeping up with the work at their grade level. It is not always clear whether the inventory should be administered to groups of students or individual students and whether all tests should be given to all levels of children. Nor is it specified whether the inventory should be administered in one or more sessions.

The directions for administering each specific test are often unclear. Sometimes general directions are given to the instructor, but no specific instructions are provided concerning what should be said to the student. Even the directions given to the instructor lack specificity. For example, how fast should one present aural sequential memory items? Children who are given this inventory or any assessment instrument deserve to understand why they are being assessed and understand the tasks presented. Yet, most of the time, they are not even given a simple introduction to a new test such as "listen carefully."

The instructions for scoring the inventory are generally clear; thus there should be few scoring errors. However, improvement is needed here also. There is no explanation in the manual for Level A indicating that the number in parentheses after the scoring indicates the level at which a student may have difficulty. Neither manual makes it clear whether that number implies no differentiation for grade level, and occasionally there is a discrepancy between that number and the written explanation regarding scoring. Occasionally one also encounters very ambiguous scoring directions. For example, two items on Test 15, Level B, require the student to draw pictures. Yet no criteria are presented for evaluating these pictures and the instructor is simply told that a child in grades 2, 3, and 4 should be able to do the test with accuracy. Another major problem regarding scoring is that no rationale is provided for the cutting scores. No specific guidelines or cautions are provided for interpreting the scores. If a student makes more errors than the cutoff point, does he/she need remediation? If so, how often and how long, etc.? The remediation section contains general suggestions as well as suggestions for using specific materials from Ann Arbor Publishers. No evidence of the efficacy of the materials is provided.

This inventory does not purport to be a norm-referenced instrument; thus there are no norms reported. However, even for a mastery or content-referenced assessment instrument, evidence of reliability and validity is needed. None is provided in the manuals. Ideally, retesting within a relatively short time interval (before any remediation has taken place) with parallel forms of the inventory should take place in order to obtain a reliability coefficient. Even if parallel forms are not available and it is impractical to do retesting, then at least evidence of internal consistency should be provided.

If the authors believe the instrument has content validity, they need to provide additional information regarding the development and field testing of the instrument. Although the authors do provide definitions at the end of the manual for specific problems such as rotation, reversal, closure, directionality, etc., they also need to define the labels for each section of the inventory in operational terms. In addition, if they believe that the instrument measures a theoretical variable (central processing deficits) then justification and interpretation of that variable should be fully stated.

The authors must provide some evidence that evaluating and remediating students' task-competencies in the areas measured by the inventory leads to positive changes in the students' proficiency levels. The manual for Level A indicates that the Ann Arbor Learning Inventory is not for labeling, but rather to give in-depth information on a group of students. With the limited information available to the test buyer, there is no evidence that deficits in central processing areas will be decreased or that positive changes will occur in practical skill areas such as reading, writing, or arithmetic.

In summary, although the Ann Arbor Learning Inventory is a compact, relatively inexpensive and easy-to-score instrument, this reviewer believes it is of limited value in its present form. Additional information regarding the development, rationale, reliability, and validity must be provided. Neither the reasoning underlying the test, nor the nature of the competency areas it is intended to measure are clearly described. A classroom teacher might find the use of informal phonic inventories, informal reading inventories, and informal math inventories more beneficial since they would be based on specific grade level materials. It is not clear how the content or the cutoff criteria for the Ann Arbor Learning Inventory were determined.

The Brigance Diagnostic Inventories offer more comprehensive, content-referenced assessment information than the Ann Arbor Learning Inventory. This reviewer believes the Ann Arbor Learning Inventory would be a useful tool only for a very experienced instructor who is very familiar with children's normal developmental patterns in such areas as visual discrimination and visual motor coordination. Even then it should only be used as an informal inventory of the specific areas covered in the instrument, with no promise that remediation of these skills will transfer directly to daily classroom work. The instructor would save time and money by simply doing error pattern and/or task analysis of the required classroom work.

[74]

The ANSER System—Aggregate Neurobehavioral Student Health and Educational Review. Ages 3–5, 6–11, 12+; 1980–81; series of questionnaires to be completed by parents, school personnel, and students; for use with children possessing learning and/or behavioral problems; no scores: parent questionnaire covers 11 areas (family history, possible pregnancy problems, newborn infant problems, health problems, functional problems, early development, early educational experience, skills and interests, activity-attention problems, associated behaviors, associated strengths), school questionnaire covers educational setting and program, special facilities available, results of previous testing and 3 checklists (performance area, activity-attention behavioral observations, associated behavioral observations); no reliability, validity, or norms data in test materials; individual; 4 forms; 3 levels; interpreter's guide ('80, 45 pages); 1983 price data: $5.50 per interpreter's guide; $5.50 per specimen set; no administration time reported; Melvin D. Levine; Educators Publishing Service, Inc.*

a) FORM 1. Ages 3–5; 2 questionnaires: parent, Form 1P ('81, 18 pages), school, Form 1S ('81, 10 pages); $7.50 per 12 copies of Form 1P; $5.75 per 12 copies of Form 1S.

b) FORM 2. Ages 6–11; 2 questionnaires: parent, Form 2P ('80, 19 pages), school, Form 2S ('80, 10 pages); $7.50 per 12 copies of Form 2P; $6.50 per 12 copies of Form 2S.

c) FORM 3. Ages 12+; 2 questionnaires: parent, Form 3P ('80, 20 pages), school, Form 3S ('80, 12 pages); $7.50 per 12 copies of Form 3P; $6.50 per 12 copies of Form 3S.

d) FORM 4. Ages 9+; self-administered student profile; no scores, 10 developmental areas: fine motor, gross motor, memory, attention, language, general efficiency, visual-spatial processing, sequencing, general academic performance, social interaction; 1 form ('80, 8 pages); $5.75 per 10 profile forms.

Review of The ANSER System—Aggregate Neurobehavioral Student Health and Educational Review by ROBERT G. HARRINGTON, Assistant Professor in Educational Psychology & Research, The University of Kansas, Lawrence, KS:

There is a need for an assessment device which will permit systematic collection, comparison, and interpretation of data from various members of a multidisciplinary team regarding the formulation of a referred child's problem behaviors. The ANSER System is intended to accomplish this task, but for a variety of reasons it is unsuccessful in meeting some of the most basic psychometric standards. The stated purpose of the ANSER System is to provide information regarding the educational history, health, development, and current behavior of children who have been experiencing school adjustment and learning problems. By comparing responses to a variety of Likert-type questionnaire items and open-ended questions from parents, school personnel, and sometimes the child (when he/she is nine years old or over) the ANSER System attempts to provide insights about the nature of the referral problem from various ecological perspectives. Each form of the scale is further grouped according to age ranges so that responses supposedly can be based on age-appropriate observations of child behavior. The questionnaires are intended for use by such diverse professionals as school personnel, counselors at guidance centers, independent mental health practitioners, doctors and nurses.

At the core of the problem with the ANSER System is that the manual provides absolutely no data on any form of reliability or validity. The questionnaires have not been standardized. There are no norms tables. No criterion data are presented. Consequently, it is impossible to judge the extent to which the ANSER System fulfills its primary objective of specifying the factors contributing to children's problem behaviors. Three studies reported by the author subsequent to the publication of this test fail to provide any further substantial documentation of the scales' psychometric properties. The results are interpreted freely in these reports via visual analysis of graphic and tabular data presentations without the benefits of inferential statistical methods.

Essentially the ANSER System is a clinical tool for conducting an unstructured interview. The examiner's manual appears to deal with this lack of psychometric rigor by simply directing users to two pages of precautions. For example, one caveat states flatly, "The Self-Administered Student Profile has not been standardized or tested as a screening instrument. Use in this manner is therefore entirely experimental and unvalidated. If it is to be used on 'normal populations' of children, it should be done with caution, since normative data are not yet available." This precautionary statement seems to lack meaning since there are no precautions an examiner can take to avoid the hazards of over-interpretation or misinterpretation involved in using an instrument lacking the essential prerequisites of sound test development. In essence, it is unclear exactly what the scales measure and how they are to be used.

Review of specific item content reveals that many of the questionnaire items are vague and undefined. For example, one item on Form 1P (ages 3–5) requires the parent to check those age ranges during which their child experienced "feeding difficulty." No mention is made about the length, severity, or circumstances of the problem. Such questions need to be operationally defined in terms of target behaviors. Some items are organized into subscales such as Activity-Attention Problems (Form 1P, ages 3 to 5). The origin of the items for this particular scale is unknown. Furthermore, these items have been grouped based on face validity of item content and not on item clusters resulting from factor analysis. The scales are supposed to permit the examiner to judge the developmental age-appropriateness of a child's current behaviors in various domains based on the child's ability to pass items. Unfortunately, the assignment of developmental ages to specific items has not been supported by norm-referenced or criterion-referenced research data. In some instances, the authors suggest that a composite score could be obtained for a particular subscale like Activity-Attention Problems (Form 1P, ages 3 to 5) by weighting the Likert-type responses and summing the ratings. Higher scores would indicate less propensity toward attention problems. Of course, this informal approach to scoring a subscale is completely invalid and unreliable. Furthermore, there is a danger that such scores could be misinterpreted by consumers as being based on norms and mislead them in developing remediation programs.

An Interpreter's Guide accompanies the ANSER System. It is unclear, however, how most users, other than those with medical training, would interpret the psychoeducational significance of certain items involving pregnancy problems, such as "has bleeding during second three months" (Form 3P, ages 12+) or child health problems such as "rashes or skin problems" when the child was 4 to 6 months old (Form 3P, ages 12+). The Interpreter's Guide does not stipulate the qualifications needed for examiners to interpret the highly complicated relationships between some of these medical disorders and current behavior problems exhibited by the child. In fact, not one complete example of how the contents of these scales could be used to assist in the formulation of a case is presented in the manual. The burden falls on the examiner's own clinical acumen. The Interpreter's Guide does suggest a series of clinical questions which can be asked at a follow-up interview, and does point out multiple levels of interpretation. However, because of the lack of research support, this type of interpretive advice is necessarily unfounded and over-generalized.

In summary, many uses for the ANSER System are proposed, but validity evidence is provided for none. Studies of the concurrent, construct and eventually the predictive validity of this instrument are needed. Before this instrument could be recommended for use, evidence of the reliability of scale scores and profile interpretations must be demonstrated. An alternative is Brown and Hammill's Behavior Rating Profile (BRP). Like the ANSER System, the purpose of the BRP is to provide an ecological evaluation of children's behaviors. Unlike the ANSER System, however, the BRP is a well-standardized, highly reliable, experimentally validated, and norm-referenced test. Since the BRP is norm-referenced, it is possible to determine whether a child is exhibiting behaviors which are not age-appropriate and in which settings the child is viewed as deviant. For these reasons, the Behavior Rating Profile would be preferable to the ANSER System for those users seeking an ecological approach to behavioral assessment.

Review of The ANSER System—Aggregate Neurobehavioral Student Health and Educational Review by KENNETH W. HOWELL, Chairperson, Department of Special Education, Arizona State University, Tempe, AZ:

According to the manual, the Aggregate Neurobehavioral Student Health and Educational Review (ANSER) System "is an attempt to integrate data" in a variety of areas (education, health, development, and behavior) and from a variety of perspectives (parents, school personnel, and child). The system is actually a series of questionnaires, some of which have numerous subdivisions. Information for the ANSER is obtained by interviewing key individuals and the results are recorded on separate forms. Forms are provided for different age groups (3 to 5, 6 to 11, and 12+) and data sources (parent, school, student). The inclusion of a self administered student profile (available only for ages 9+) is a definite strength. Although the content of the profile has questionable utility, the idea of utilizing self-report data is a good one. In general, students and peers have been ignored as data sources in educational and psychological assessment.

The primary criticism of The ANSER System is its lack of technical information. While the manual does caution against certain interpretations, the system's structure and description necessitates evidence of construct and content validity that is not supplied. The system's subdivisions are not defined adequately and in some cases items are clearly repetitive across subdivisions. For example, school questionnaire Form 1S has a subsection for noting the relative occurrence of various problematic behaviors. The behaviors listed in this subsection, titled Behavioral Observations (Associated), are categorized into affect-dependent, social withdrawal, somatic, and social-aggressive. Items in the affect-dependent category include two which ask about the relative extent to which a child "appears sad or worried" and "lacks confidence," while items categorized as social withdrawal ask if the child "is timid or passive with other children" and "seems anxious during group activities." These items appear very similar and in the absence of data the user is forced to draw conclusions from appearances.

The manual supplies no empirical evidence of reliability or validity. In the one instance where normative data is supplied to guide interpretation, the normative sample is inadequately described. In addition, no evidence is given regarding the definitions of the various subdivisions or the constructs which should tie them together. In the absence of support for the unification of these multiple components it is hard to accept the system as an exercise in integration. This impression is compounded by the absence of a record form for actually summarizing the results.

The ANSER seems to rely heavily on current psycho-educational mythology. There are frequent references to cognitive, affective and/or perceptual traits such as impulsivity, emotional liability, and visual-spatial processing. This needless preoccupation with hypothesized constructs makes the instrument seem presumptuous given its lack of validation. Although the terms themselves are popular, they are not well defined. The undefined usage of a term implies a level of general agreement about meaning and implication that does not exist in this case. Giving these titles to components of the ANSER does not replace the need for validation information to clarify what the items in the components are supposed to be measuring and what treatments, if any, should be related to them.

In summary, the ANSER is a lengthy, non-validated exercise which imposes hypothetical formats on data collection but does not supply a procedure for summarizing or interpreting the data collected.

[75]

Applied Knowledge Test. Ages 14–18; no date on test materials; AKT; a companion test to the Occupational Interest Rating Scale although it can be used independently; 4 subtest scores: mathematics, English, science, spatial relationship; no data on reliability and validity; norms consist of means and standard deviations; 1 form (8 pages); manual (6 pages); 1984 price data: £4.40 per 25 tests; £.10 per overlay key; £.30 per manual; £1.45 per set of 6 tests, manual, and marking keys; 55(65) minutes; M. A. Brimer; Educational Evaluation Enterprises [England].*

Review of Applied Knowledge Test by YONG H. SUNG, Chairman of Executive Committee, HEI-KI DONG, Research Director, and STEVEN GOLDMAN, Research Psychologist, Ball Foundation, Glen Ellyn, IL:

The Applied Knowledge Test (AKT) was developed by M. A. Brimer for academic and vocational guidance in high school. Although the author claims that the AKT can be used independently, the AKT is a companion test to the Occupational Interest Rating Scale. The Applied Knowledge Test consists of four subtests ranging in length from 25 items to 30 items, with an administration time of 15 minutes for each of the first three tests and 10 minutes for the last test. The four subtests are Mathematics, English, Science, and Space. All four subtests are essentially power tests, although all of the subtests are timed.

In discussing construction of the test, the author states that item tryout, revision, and item analysis were all utilized in its construction. Although the author appeared to use Rasch's one parameter model for item calibration, it is very hard to evalute its soundness due to the lack of statistical data. The subtests of the AKT are highly intercorrelated with each other. The correlations range from .47 to .67 with the exception of the Space test. It seems apparent from these correlations that three of the subtests are not factorially independent of each other. In addition, item difficulty appears to be a problem, since the mean scores of the three tests are extremely low.

There is no data in the manual on the reliability of the four subtests. This is obviously a crucial consideration for any test and should be included in any future manual. Therefore, test users use the AKT at their own risk.

The major technical deficiency of the AKT is a very serious lack of validity data. If the purpose of the tests is to provide vocational and academic counseling to young people of ages 14 and above, validity data should include criterion-related validity evidence indicating how effectively success in academic and vocational areas is predicted by AKT scores.

The AKT scores are reported as four "scale scores" ranging from 0 to 8. In addition, the manual also provides items (in three tests—Mathematics, English, and Science) corresponding with the scale score level of 3 to 8 as determined by Rasch item calibration methods. However, this item response data appears to be inconsistent with the "scale scores" conversion table.

In summary, a serious problem with the AKT is the difficulty of finding relevant data. As data are generated on the AKT, they should be provided to users and documented in the manual. It appears that the AKT was published prematurely and could render a disservice to its users. More time should be spent in gathering and documenting relevant data on the reliability and validity of the AKT before it is recommended for operational use.

[76]

Appraisal Report For Management Personnel. Employees and salesmen; no date on test materials; ratings by managers in 3 areas: human factor, performance factor, performance and growth and potential; no data on reliability and validity; no norms; individual; 1 form (no date, 12 pages); supplemental form for sales managers (no date, 4 pages); no manual; 1983 price data: $6 per 25 inventories; $3 per 25 supplemental forms for sales managers; administration time not reported; Stevens, Thurow and Associates.*

[77]

Apraxia Battery for Adults. Adult patients; 1979; ABA; "to verify the presence of apraxia in the adult patient and to gain a rough estimate of the severity of the disorder"; 6 subtests not available as separates: Diadochokinetic Rate, Increasing Word Length, Limb Apraxia and Oral Apraxia, Latency and Utterance Time for Polysyllabic Words, Repeated Trials Tests, Inventory of Articulation Characteristics of Apraxia; no reliability or validity data; no norms; individual; 1 form; manual (23 pages, plus 12 test plates); response record sheet (6 pages); 1984 price data: $42.95 per manual and 40 tests; $9.95 per 40 tests; (20) minutes; Barbara Dabul; C.C. Publications, Inc.*

Review of Apraxia Battery for Adults by NORMA COOKE, Neuropsychologist, Department of Neurology, Baylor College of Medicine, Texas Medical Center, Houston, TX:

Apraxia can be defined as a disorder in the ability to carry out purposeful voluntary movements although, as Dejerine pointed out in 1914, it is much easier to say what apraxia is not rather than what it is. Apraxias are not due to paralysis or paresis of the motor systems, aphasia, dementia, or ataxia. Upon clinical examination apraxias may be divided into kinetic, ideomotor, ideational, or constructional depending upon the nature of the patient's inability to perform certain movements.

Unlike its title suggests, the Apraxia Battery for Adults is not a comprehensive clinical examination of praxis. Instead the test is limited to an evaluation of one form of apraxia, apraxia of speech. This disorder is an inability to perform the purposeful movements necessary for language expression (in the absence of aphasia).

The Apraxia Battery for Adults (ABA) was designed specifically to diagnose and provide information for remediation of apraxia of speech. The first test of its kind, the ABA contains five subtests that examine the output deficits usually associated with apraxia of speech, as well as one subtest concerned with identifying the presence or absence of associated limb and oral apraxia. Although other tests in print (e.g., the Porch Index of Communicative Ability) have been used to determine the presence of apraxia of speech, the ABA is the only instrument currently available that attempts to set some guidelines for assessing the severity of the disorder.

The first two subtests, Diadochokinetic Rate and Increasing Word Length, examine changes in frequency of articulation errors with increasing word length and increasing demands on the ability to sequence phonemes. The third subtest, Limb Apraxia and Oral Apraxia, examines not only limb and oral performance but also scores for the "searching behaviors" often exhibited by apraxic patients. The fourth subtest, Latency and Utterance Time for Polysyllabic Words, distinguishes the latency in responding from the time required to complete an oral response. The Repeated Trials Test (subtest five) examines changes in performance with practice, and Inventory of Articulation Characteristics of Apraxia (subtest six) is a checklist for characteristics of output and errors during spontaneous speech and oral reading.

Based on the scores obtained on each subtest, the author provides guidelines for verifying the presence and severity of apraxia. These guidelines, based on very limited norms (40 subjects, 17 of whom were apraxic) include (1) a very broad statement as to the range of scores in which a patient might benefit from remediation tactics targeted specifically to apraxic behaviors, and (2) a dichotomous ("mild to moderate" and "severe to profound") profile score sheet which the author accurately describes as "a relatively crude measure of severity." No reliability or validity data are provided.

The entire battery requires about half an hour to administer. In terms of content, it covers most of the areas generally agreed on by current authors to be typical components of apraxic speech. The most outstanding feature of the ABA is that it is the only test in print that attempts to systematically measure these components. The manual also provides a subtest-by-subtest description of prospective treatment strategies.

In its present form, the ABA is useful primarily to the speech-language pathologist who distinguishes between therapeutic approaches to apraxia of speech and traditional language therapies. Until some standardization guidelines become available, the potential of the ABA for documenting the relative severity of apraxia of speech with respect to an apraxic population and determining what constitutes significant improvement with therapy remains unrealized. However, the structure of the instrument and rationale behind it appear sound, and its ultimate usefulness awaits only the outcome of appropriate field testing.

REVIEWER'S REFERENCES

Dejerine, J. SEMIOLOGIE DES AFFECTIONS DUE SYSTEME NERVEUX. Paris: Masson, 1914.

[78]

Aptitude Assessment Battery: Programming. Programmers and trainees; 1967–82; AABP; distribution restricted to employers of programmers, not available to school personnel; no manual; validation studies available on request from publisher; 1984 price data: $85 per test including the evaluation and detailed report; French, Spanish, and left-handed editions available; (210–270) minutes; Jack M. Wolfe; Wolfe Personnel Testing Systems, Inc.*

See 7:1087 (1 reference).

[79]

Aptitude Tests for Policemen. Prospective police officers; 2 tests; distribution restricted to civil service commissions or other competent municipal officials; administration time not reported; McCann Associates, Inc.*

a) POLICEMEN TEST. 7 scores: the ability to learn verbal skills, the ability to learn quantitative skills, total learning ability, interest in police work, common sense in police situations, sense of public relations in the performance of police duties, total; Forms 62, 70 (each in 2 booklets); instruction manual available; separate answer sheets must be used; price data available from publisher; scoring service available.

b) OBSERVATION TEST. "Tests the candidates ability to observe obvious and deduced facts about a picture of an accident scene"; separate answer sheets must be used; 1984 price data: $20 per 10 or less sets of test materials; $1.25–$1.70 per each additional set of test materials.

[80]

Arlin Test of Formal Reasoning. Grades 6–12 and adults; 1984; ATFR; "individual's ability to use the eight specific concepts associated with (Piaget's) stages of formal operations"; profiles individual as "concrete, high concrete, transitional, low formal, or high formal"; 9 scores: volume, probability, correlations, combinations, proportions, momentum, mechanical equilibrium, frames of reference, total; norms for grades 6–12 only; 1 form (15 pages); answer sheet (1 page); scoring template (1 page); manual (31 pages); 1984 price data: $38 per complete kit including 35 test booklets and 35 answer sheets; $20 per 35 test booklets; $6 per 35 answer sheets; $4.50 per hand-scoring template; $10 per manual; scoring service, $1.50 or less per student ($35 minimum); (45–50) minutes; Patricia Kennedy Arlin; Slosson Educational Publications, Inc.*

Review of Arlin Test of Formal Reasoning by TONI E. SANTMIRE, Associate Professor and Chair, Department of Educational Psychology, University of Nebraska-Lincoln, Lincoln, NE:

The increasing utilization of concepts derived from developmental psychology, particularly Piagetian psychology, in research and educational practice has made it imperative that easily usable methods for assessing developmental status be available which provide a common definition of status across applications. The method of the clinical interview employed by Piaget and his school (e.g., Inhelder & Piaget, 1958; Piaget & Inhelder, 1969) to establish the existence of levels of cognitive development involves the use of specially trained interviewers conducting individual interviews. It is time consuming and unnecessarily cumbersome for applications in which only an assessment of developmental status is required. What is needed is a test which gives consistent results, is valid in relation to the assessments obtained by the clinical interview, and which is easily administered to groups. The Arlin Test of Formal Reasoning (ATFR) was designed to meet these needs.

CONTENT VALIDITY. Inhelder and Piaget (1958) utilize a series of clinically administered tasks which provide the basis for their descriptions of the differences between concrete and formal operational thinking. Any test purporting to assess levels of concrete and formal thinking should be designed so that the constructs of the test relate to those of the theory.

The ATFR yields two types of scores. One is an overall index of cognitive level which is determined by the total number of items for which the formal operational response was chosen. The total score range is divided into five levels which, according to the manual, are based on the descriptions developed in Inhelder and Piaget (1958) to categorize the levels of thinking demonstrated on their clinically administered tasks.

However, the levels defined in the ATFR are not consistent with those in Inhelder and Piaget. There are six levels described in the theory, IA, IB, IIA, IIB, IIIA, and IIIB, with the first two, describing performance of preoperational children, usually combined into one. Those designated by II represent concrete operations and those by III represent formal operations. The description of the lowest level of the ATFR, *Concrete,* does not correspond to or distinguish between the IB and IIA levels in the Inhelder and Piaget scheme. Since the ATFR *High Concrete* level looks much like IIB in the Inhelder and Piaget scheme on face interpretation, it is presumed that the two lower Piagetian levels are being "lumped together" in the ATFR *Concrete* level. Thus, preoperational thinking is being lumped with early concrete operational thinking. There is also the problem of how the ATFR *Transitional, Low Formal,* and *High Formal* levels relate to the IIIA and IIIB levels of the theory. For Inhelder and Piaget, IIIA seems to be a transitional period in which the beginnings of formal reasoning are supported by grouping and physical experimentation to test unsystematically generated hypotheses. From the description, this corresponds most closely to the ATFR *Transitional* level. Theoretically, Stage IIIB is a period of systematic generation and testing of hypotheses based on prior conceptual analysis, and would most closely correspond to the ATFR *High Formal* level. Where the ATFR *Low Formal* level fits is not clear.

Another theoretical difficulty with the total score of the ATFR arises from the fact that an item is only recorded as "correct" if the "formal" alternative is chosen. Thus, a score of "1" (assuming nonguessing) is indicative of at least some level of formal reasoning on the particular formal reasoning item that was so scored. Therefore, a total score of

"1" should not be taken as indicative of concrete functioning, as it would be according to the scoring procedures of the test. Instead, it should be taken to indicate some beginning functioning in the formal mode.

It is even more ironic that an individual who guesses would score "8," or *High Concrete,* while individuals doing their best and giving formal responses on four items, a score of "4," would be classified at the *Concrete* level. This is possible due to the fact that distractors for the items were constructed to represent the different types of response that individuals of different stages of development typically give in the interview situation (Arlin, 1982). Thus, an individual who was basically concrete operational might be expected to prefer those distractors which are typically generated by concrete operational children, and would then score a "0." The scoring system does not allow any way to weight the score by level of distractor chosen.

The second type of score generated by the ATFR is a score on eight subconcepts presumed to be components of formal operations. These are referred to as Volume, Probability, Correlations, Combinations, Proportions, Momentum, Mechanical Equilibrium, and Frames of Reference. There are four items for each of these subconcepts, and the profile of scores on these subconcepts is presumed to give evidence about the pattern of strengths and weaknesses within individuals.

According to Inhelder and Piaget, an important characteristic of formal operations is its holistic character. Although several tasks were used in the assessment of formal operations, and each was designed to highlight a different characteristic or scheme of such thinking, it was not intended to imply that these were tests of distinct skills which are "component" skills of formal operations. Each one of these characteristics or schemes is made possible by the construction, as a totality, of the group of logical operations which Piaget calls the "INRC group." That is, use of the group of logical operations as a whole underlies each of the characteristics of formal operations, and it is not the case that individuals who are "formal" in the sense of having constructed the logical structure will exhibit some of these schemes and not others. They are all made possible by the whole. On the other hand, it is true that individuals do evidence formal operations in some problems and not others before the final abstraction of the INRC group from the problems to which it is applied (Piaget, 1972). From a theoretical perspective this should not necessarily be regarded as development of the particular characteristic of formal operations which is best shown by that problem. According to Piaget (1972), such performance may be more reflective of that individual's experience with that content area than the particular thinking skill involved. This should disappear when the INRC group becomes consistently abstracted out of the content as the individual becomes "formal operational."

From this perspective, it is theoretically meaningless to try to assess "components" of formal operations. The evidence that assessments of formal operations are plagued by problems with consistency of performance across similar items, traditionally viewed as problems with item difficulty (Neimark, 1975), is consistent with this theoretical interpretation.

CONSTRUCT VALIDITY AND RELIABILITY. A study examining the discriminant validity of the ATFR using a multi-trait multi-method matrix was cited as evidence of the construct validity of the test (Arlin, 1982). In this study seven components were assessed using an earlier version of the ATFR and by clinical interviews. The components constituted traits and the administration constituted methods for that purpose. Although the correlations in the matrix were low, the general conditions for discriminant validity were met. That is, the two methods yield scores which are correlated in such a way as to indicate that they are, at least roughly, measures of the same things. The measures of the schemes also exhibited a pattern of intercorrelations which suggest that they are relatively independent.

The choice of the total score ranges which define the different ATFR levels is problematic from a strictly psychometric point of view. In particular, the score range of 15–17 points for the *Transitional* level is smaller than the standard error for the total score, whose estimates range from 2.20 to 2.28. No discussion of any empirical or theoretical basis for the ranges selected for the different levels is presented in the manual. The *Transitional* level may be of questionable psychometric value although it is a theoretically meaningful construct.

Relatively low indices of internal consistency are reported for the ATFR. This is particularly true for the concept subscales. The small number of items in these scales make lower levels of internal consistency inevitable; however, some of these coefficients appear to be so low as to call into question the relative usefulness of the subscales as indicators of possession of the particular concept. This is also support for the existence of the type of task heterogeneity suggested by theory.

SUPPORT MATERIALS. The manual and other materials supplied with the test appear to be relatively easy to understand and use. The test is easily administered and scored. Arriving at subtest scores is somewhat cumbersome by hand, but computer scoring should eliminate that difficulty. The test booklets are attractive. Although the test has been checked for readability, there did appear to be some words used which might not be in the common vocabulary of some students. The extensive data base used to develop and revise items suggests that this is probably not a problem for middle class populations. Extension of use to lower class and minority populations should be done with caution until other normative data are gathered as discussed in the manual.

OVERALL EVALUATION. Oddly enough, even with the shortcomings of the ATFR as discussed above, the concept of formal operational reasoning is probably robust enough that the total score assessment provided by the ATFR is reasonably well correlated with level of formal operational functioning. It should be noted however, that the test is not a good indicator of concrete functioning. That is, any score above "0" on the ATFR may be indicative of some formal functioning. It is probable that this test will correlate to some degree with other measures, such as the Test of Logical Thinking, but there will be no assurance that they measure the same thing, or may be considered operationalizations of formal operations. Part (subconcept) scores are to be avoided until further evidence of their validity is available.

Despite its shortcomings, the ATFR is a step in the direction of obtaining some sort of standardized assessment of something approaching formal operations which can be generalized across situations; as such, it is useful. Its theoretical and psychometric shortcomings really should be addressed before it is used as anything other than this.

REVIEWER'S REFERENCES

Inhelder, B., & Piaget, J. THE GROWTH OF LOGICAL THINKING: FROM CHILDHOOD TO ADOLESCENCE. New York: Basic Books, 1958.

Inhelder, B., & Piaget, J. THE EARLY GROWTH OF LOGIC IN THE CHILD: CLASSIFICATION AND SERIATION. New York: Norton, 1969.

Piaget, J. Intellectual evolution from adolescence to adulthood. HUMAN DEVELOPMENT, 1972, 15, 1–12.

Neimark, E. D. Intellectual development during adolescence. In F. D. Horowitz (Ed.), REVIEW OF CHILD DEVELOPMENT RESEARCH. (Vol. 4, pp. 541–594). Chicago: University of Chicago Press, 1975.

Arlin, P. K. A multi-trait multi-method validity study of a test of formal reasoning. EDUCATIONAL AND PSYCHOLOGICAL MEASUREMENT, 1982, 43, 103–109.

[81]

Armed Services Vocational Aptitude Battery. High school (some seniors must be included); 1967–82; ASVAB; an aptitude battery designed for use both in high schools and to select and classify all enlistees at the Armed Forces Examining and Entrance Stations (AFEES) across the country; tests administered and scored without charge by Department of Defense personnel; copies of the ASVAB results for students in the 11th and 12th grades are furnished to the local recruiting stations of each of the armed services; 12 subtests: General Information (GI), Numerical Operations (NO), Attention to Detail (AD), Word Knowledge (WK), Arithmetic Reasoning (AR), Space Perception (SP), Mathematics Knowledge (MK), Electronics Information (EI), Mechanical Comprehension (MC), General Science (GS), Shop Information (SI), Automotive Information (AI), combinations of which produce 6 composite scores: verbal (WK+GS), math (AR+MK), perceptual speed (3AD+NO), mechanical (SP+MC), trade technical (AI+EI+SI), academic ability (WK+RC); Forms 5a, 5b, 5c, ('76, 62 pages, all forms are identical except for order of items); counselor's guide ('80, 25 pages); technical supplement to counselor's guide ('80, 97 pages); student information booklet ('80, 34 pages); profile (no date, 2 pages) presents composite scores only, although raw scores for subtests are provided to schools; separate answer cards must be used; specimen set free; 135(165) minutes; United States Military Enlistment Processing Command.*

See T3:202 (8 references); for a review by David J. Weiss, see 8:483 (4 references); see also T2:1067 (1 reference).

TEST REFERENCES

1. Cook, T. M., Novaco, R. W., & Sarason, I. G. Military recruit training as an environmental context affective expectancies for control of reinforcement. COGNITIVE THERAPY AND RESEARCH, 1982, 6, 409–428.

2. Kass, R. A., Mitchell, K. J., Grafton, F. C., & Wing, H. Factorial validity of the Armed Services Vocational Aptitude Battery (ASVAB), Forms 8, 9 and 10: 1981 army applicant sample. EDUCATIONAL AND PSYCHOLOGICAL MEASUREMENT, 1983, 43, 1077–1087.

3. Moreno, K. E., Wetzel, C. D., McBride, J. R., & Weiss, D. J. Relationship between corresponding Armed Services Vocational Aptitude Battery (ASVAB) and computerized adaptive testing (CAT) subtests. APPLIED PSYCHOLOGICAL MEASUREMENT, 1984, 8, 155–163.

Review of Armed Services Vocational Aptitude Battery by R. A. WEITZMAN, Associate Professor of Psychology, Naval Postgraduate School, Monterey, CA:

Introduced in 1976 as a single Department of Defense (DoD) test battery to replace separate batteries used since 1972 by the individual military services, the Armed Services Vocational Aptitude Battery (ASVAB) (Forms 5, 6, and 7) consists of 12 subtests used not only in six different combinations to classify military personnel for training and job assignments, but also in a special combination called the Armed Forces Qualification Test (AFQT) to select applicants for military service. Intended for use especially with high school students, Form 5 of the ASVAB has both facilitated recruitment efforts and provided a basis for vocational counseling. The DoD has developed and made available normative, reliability, and validity information about Form 5 in relation to high school populations. The July 1980 Technical Supplement to the Counselor's Guide reports KR 20 values having a median of .82 for the subtests and .92 for the composites. The same source presents results of a number of validity studies; typical is the median correlation of .73, corrected for restriction in range, of the appropriate selector composite of ASVAB Form 6 or 7 with final school grade in 51 Navy entry-level vocational schools. Likewise typical are full-ASVAB (Form 5) multiple correlations with final vocational course grades for high school seniors ranging from .58 (shorthand, females) to .86 (business math, males). Though formally equivalent to Form 5, ASVAB Forms 6 and 7 have been restricted to inservice use.

The AFQT, scored as Word Knowledge + Arithmetic Reasoning + Space Perception (WK + AR + SP), has been a special object of attention among test experts. The reason for this attention is a miscalibration of the test that led to the acceptance into military service of many applicants who otherwise would have been rejected. The equipercentile method of calibration used was supposed to assign as a score to each person tested his or her percentile standing on the Army General Classification Test in the 1944 reference population of some 11,694,229 officer and enlisted personnel. On the basis of this score, a person is classified into one of the five AFQT categories: I (93–100), II (65–92), III (31–64), IV (10–30), and V (1–9). In peacetime, the services do not accept Category V persons and have on average attempted to maintain the Category IV persons below 21%. As a result of the miscalibration, however, the Army in 1979 reported that it had only 9% Category IV persons when correction of the miscalibration later showed this value to be actually 46%.

Recognition of the AFQT miscalibration has motivated not only studies leading to its correction but also extensive efforts to assure appropriate calibration of the new ASVAB Forms 8, 9, and 10, implemented in October 1980. From 1950 to 1960, AFQT forms were calibrated directly back to the 1944 AGCT; except for the initial (incorrect) calibration of the ASVAB Forms 5, 6, and 7, the 1959 AFQT Form 7A served subsequently as an intermediate link in the chain of calibration back to the 1944 AGCT. The correction of the miscalibration of ASVAB Forms 5, 6, and 7 restored this function to AFQT Form 7A, and AFQT Form 7A retains this function in the calibration of ASVAB Forms 8, 9, and 10. The DoD efforts to assure the appropriate calibration of these new ASVAB forms do not end here, however. In 1980, at a cost of some $6,000,000, the DoD established as a new reference population the national probability sample of 12,686 civilian and military men and women between the ages of 14 and 22 on January 1, 1979, who were participating in the five-year National Longitudinal Survey of the United States Department of Labor. ASVAB Form 8A was administered to 11,914 members of this group between July and October of 1980, a completion rate of 94%. The combination of ASVAB and NLS data available on this group comprises a study called the Profile of American Youth (Office of the Assistant Secretary of Defense, 1982). The NLS data include family, education, employment, health, income, military service, residence, and attitude information on each individual. The new reference population thus ought to make ASVAB Forms 8, 9, and 10 considerably more useful than their predecessors, both for military selection and classification and for high school counseling and guidance.

The new ASVAB forms contain a different set of subtests, 10 instead of 12, and different subtest combinations including in particular a new subtest combination for the AFQT, defined as Word Knowledge + Paragraph Comprehension + Arithmetic Reasoning + 1/2 Numerical Operations (WK + PC + AR + 1/2 NO). (Paragraph Comprehension is a new subtest.) The intention in the development of these forms was to improve not only the calibration of the AFQT but also the predictive validities of all the subtest combinations. Space perception, in particular, is missing from the new ASVAB and from the new AFQT. Test development used new item-response theory as well as traditional methods of item analysis. The recommendation to former, current, and prospective civilian users of the ASVAB is thus not to use Form 5 but to use whichever of Forms 8, 9, and 10 becomes generally available. For users with purely normative concerns, these new ASVAB forms have no peer.

REVIEWER'S REFERENCES

Office of the Assistant Secretary of Defense (Manpower, Reserve Affairs, and Logistics). PROFILE OF AMERICAN YOUTH. March, 1982.

[82]

Assessing Reading Difficulties: A Diagnostic and Remedial Approach. Children in primary school and over; 1980; 3 error scores: last sound different, middle sound different, first sound different; no data on reliability; no description of normative population; individual; 1 form (1 page); manual (40 pages); 1983 price data: £1.75 per test sheets; £2.15 per manual; no administration time reported; Lynette Bradley; Macmillan Education [England].*

Review of Assessing Reading Difficulties: A Diagnostic and Remedial Approach by RUTH GARNER, Associate Professor of Reading Education, University of Maryland, College Park, MD:

Assessing Reading Difficulties is a mix of very good auditory discrimination diagnostic tips and somewhat confusing pieces of information presented in a lengthy manual that, though overlong in many segments, also has some serious informational gaps.

The strengths of this diagnostic tool include the following: a clear statement of the intended test-taker population (students of whatever age who are almost non-readers); an explicit statement of the need for test users to augment test data with information from other sources, including teacher-observation records; cautions about misinterpreting auditory acuity problems as discrimination problems, or anxiety as non-proficiency; and inclusion of both suggestions for remediation and a general suggestion of referral for further assessment by extra-classroom specialists.

In addition, as a tool to assess students' ability to categorize orally-presented words by determining "the odd word out of four spoken words" (e.g., "rub" in the set "sun"—"gun"—"rub" —"fun"), the test seems straightforward in administration. Provision for an anxiety-reducing warm-up is made. Generally the script for individual presentation of test items is clear. There are some minor exceptions (e.g., "This next lot is a bit different. Let us have a practice first"). Such a sentence might need to be altered to avoid constructions unfamiliar to test takers. A space for the observational notes of the test administrator is provided in a convenient spot just to the side of the word lists on the test sheet. A "set" for adjusting test-taker attention from last-sound-different to middle-sound-different to first-sound-different is given. Scoring appears to be straightforward. The entire test seems to be long enough for sufficient sampling of auditory discrimination strengths and weaknesses, without being so long as to induce fatigue in students.

There are, however, some problems with the test. The introduction is treatise-like and overlong, and the best statement of test purpose appears on page 32 of the manual, long after it might serve a useful introductory function. Mention of spelling throughout the introductory material confuses a potential test user about decoding/encoding processes to be assessed. Critical informational gaps are in the areas of: (1) development details (we do not get sufficient information about the 400 five-year-old children on whom the test was normed, and we get no details about the system for selection of words for the test); and (2) technical adequacy information (given the manual statement of predictive strength of the somewhat related Wepman screening test, it seems a bit odd that no quantitative comparisons of performance were made for a selected sample of students).

Because of the lack of technical information, it is difficult to know if one should recommend this test in preference to the older Wepman test to assess auditory discrimination facility. There is no doubt, though, that students of measurement and of reading could benefit from reading Bradley's long manual for the purpose of learning the care that must be taken to exclude extraneous variables from a testing situation. Bradley is obviously aware that lack of practice on an unfamiliar task, hearing acuity barriers, intense test anxiety, and inappropriate mind set for the task at hand can deflate performance in auditory discrimination (or a multitude of other phenomena, for that matter). Her concerns are well grounded in the psychological and educational literature, and her efforts to combat intrusion of "noise" variables into performance should be applauded.

[83]

Assessment in Infancy: Ordinal Scales of Psychological Development. Birth to age 2; 1975–82; 6 scales: The Development of Visual Pursuit and the Permanence of Objects, The Development of Means for Obtaining Desired Environmental Events, The Development of Imitation, The Development of Operational Causality, The Construction of Object Relations in Space, The Development of Schemes for Relating to Objects; no norms; individual; record forms for the Užgiris-Hunt Scales ('82, 32 pages); manual ('75, 270 pages); 1983 price data: $10 per 15 record forms for the Užgiris-Hunt Scales; $17.50 per manual; Ina Č. Užgiris and J. McV. Hunt; University of Illinois Press.*

Review of Assessment in Infancy: Ordinal Scales of Psychological Development by ARLENE C. ROSENTHAL, Educational and Counseling Psychology, University of Kentucky, Lexington, KY:

The scales were developed to identify an infant's developmental level for each of six highly specific cognitive functions. Each of the scales reflects a logically derived developmental sequence and orderly progression of cognitive organization. Development of the scales was strongly influenced by the work of Jean Piaget and his "method clinique." Items consist of situations chosen for their ability to reveal the dominant aspects of successive steps in a developmental sequence. An infant's cognitive development is inferred from behavioral observations which purportedly represent successively higher levels in an ordinal, invariant sequence. An infant can be described in terms of the level of cognitive organization achieved in each of the six branches of psychological development. The test authors have gallantly undertaken the task of obtaining empirical evidence for the validity of the ordinal, invariant sequence of cognitive development they propose. The authors recommend the use of the scales for the purpose of discovering differential rates of development associated with the various childrearing practices. This implies that the conditions for achieving a given level of development can be fostered by environmental manipulations. The scales have implications for both the research and applied areas.

The test manual is a 263-page book which is divided into three parts. The first part is textbook quality and nicely summarizes various conceptualizations of cognitive development. Support for the dissociation between developmental milestones and chronological age (i.e., stage concept) is provided and lays a foundation for a focus on sequence versus stages in development. This portion of the manual could easily be used as recommended reading for students of developmental psychology. Part II of the manual describes the process of test construction from inception to final form. Part III provides specific directions for administering the scales and is considered by the authors (and reviewer) to be essential for test administration. There is a chapter devoted to each of the six scales. One chapter provides general test directions and lists the testing material required. Another chapter is devoted to proper utilization of the Record Form.

The record forms are available under separate cover from the University of Illinois Press. Soundfilms and videocassettes are available for illustrative purposes (for purchase or rent), one for each scale. The record form is composed of three portions. The examination form is used to record whether the infant achieves given criterion (i.e., critical) behaviors for each situation. Critical actions, which reflect achievement of a given step in a developmental sequence, are listed in boldface type. A summary form for each scale provides a summary of the infant's achievement and provides room for examiner observations of the infant. A summary assessment form visually portrays the infant's achievements across all scales to give an overview of his/her functioning. A sample record form is also provided.

The manual nicely illustrates the differences between the scales and traditional measures of infant development. The scales assess highly specific psychological abilities over time versus sampling broad domains of behavior (e.g., motor, social). The scales assume hierarchical organization of a number of abilities versus incremental progress in a "unitary" competence which is expressed as an intelligence or developmental quotient or mental age. Items in the scales represent qualitatively different entities whereas traditional tests assume that success on all items is equivalent, and all items contribute equally to the final quantitative score. The scales are not age bound in that the focus of concern is on ordinal development and not to compare an infant with his/her age group. A global score lacks implications for the development of environmental interventions to foster infant development; in contrast the scales provide a foundation for the development of such interventions. Unfortunately, the role played by factors such as cognitive style (e.g., adaptability, moodiness, intensity of response, persistence, etc.) in cognitive development is ignored. These factors are particularly germane because they strongly influence an infant's response set, which serves as the data base for the development and validation of the scales.

Given its stated purposes, the paucity of psychometric data may or may not be considered a weakness. The examiner must be judicious in his/her use of the test and in its interpretation, particularly since norms are not provided. The reviewer suggests that examiners have a solid background in developmental and cognitive psychology and in the voluminous works of Piaget, a great deal of experience using Piaget's "method clinique," and familiarity with the situations from each of the six scales. Test administration is standardized to the extent that each examiner reads the same manual, although the examiner is encouraged to vary the details of the situation to match individual differences and maximize responding. The variation, however, must meet the essential requirement of the task.

Based on a sample of 84 infants between 1 month and 24 months, reliabilities are reported as percentages of agreement. The mean reliability between raters across 157 infant actions was 96.1, and between sessions (over 48 hours) the mean reliability was 79.9. The authors made no attempt at obtaining a representative sample; infants came from graduate student and faculty families at the University of Illinois. No validity coefficients are reported; the authors state that items have "intrinsic validity." A scalogram analysis was performed on each scale to determine whether the scales actually represent ordinal scales. Green's Index of Consistency (I) was used to make this determination. Each of the scales met the criterion considered to form a scale. The quantitative "substrate" used to determine I is unclear since nowhere on the record form are there any quantitative indices. Further, measures of ordinality and scalogram analysis are controversial.

To summarize, the scales serve a highly specific function not captured by traditional tests of infant development. The examiner's purpose(s) for use of the scales should be concordant with the stated purpose(s) of the scales. The lack of psychometric data is not critical if the scales are used for the appropriate reasons. Widespread use of the scales is not recommended; their use is geared to a narrow focus versus the broader focus of traditional tests to obtain a benchmark of developmental status. It is admirable that the authors seek to obtain empirical evidence for constructs typically evaluated in a qualitative way.

[84]

Assessment in Mathematics. Primary and lower secondary school children; 1980–81; criterion-referenced; 5 areas: number, measure, shape, probability and statistics, relations; no data on reliability or validity; no norms; no suggested standards of mastery, child's success or failure determined by teacher; 1 form (no date, 87 pupils' photocopy masters); teacher's book ('81, 44 pages); record card ('80, 4 pages); 1982 price data: £10.95 per teacher's book and pupils' sheets; £2.95 per 25 record cards; no administration time reported; R. W. Strong, Coordinator, Somerset Local Education Authority; Macmillan Education [England].*

Review of Assessment in Mathematics by FRANK BROADBENT, Associate Professor of Education, Syracuse University, Syracuse, NY:

Assessment in Mathematics is an individual criterion-referenced assessment comprised of 85 photocopy masters for assessing basic arithmetical skills. The test includes a manual which describes the construction and use of the assessment system and provides complete notes for using all 78 tests. The materials were developed by the Somerset Education Authority in Great Britain as a resource for the classroom teacher.

The materials are keyed to a single set of *Guidelines in Mathematics*. The manual suggests that the "individual assessments aim to meet the objectives common to most mathematical schemes of work [sic] and some rearrangement of the suggested order is quite possible to suit local needs." In the United States the objectives would reflect knowledge acquired during kindergarten through about grade 7 and in England "the reasonably able child of eleven (the potential top 20–25% of pupils, not necessarily gifted mathematicians)" should be able to perform competently on these objectives.

The set of 87 photocopy master pupil sheets are of excellent quality and are printed on good white card stock. They are clear, well-illustrated and appealing. The use of metrics, hovercraft, and digital clocks illustrates how up-to-date the masters are. One excellent feature is the combining of computation and problem solving on one sheet. Behavioral objectives provided for each sheet reflect from one to three levels of competency. This three-level hierarchy can be illustrated with a subtraction sequence. On level one the child completes problems with the teacher. On level two, students work through the 20 problems on their own using manipulatives. The third level is a timed test which does not allow the use of manipulatives. The items which involve apparatus or manipulatives require materials that are either readily available or easy to make.

Items are not designed for rank ordering of children in terms of ability. Instead, they are used to assess an individual child's skill and understanding of mathematics. The manual suggests that teachers use the items only when they are confident that a child will be successful at the level of the assessment because "too narrow a range of experiences may result in a high assessment score, but will not necessarily mean that a child has benefited mathematically." Teachers are encouraged to use their own judgement in determining time limits, mastery level, and when to provide assistance to individual children.

The approach represented by this assessment program is preferred to the more common practice of assessing individual objectives and should do much to avoid overtesting and allow more flexibility in classrooms. Hopefully this will result in the development of more lasting skills and a better understanding of concepts. The test developers should be applauded for such a fine system and it is hoped that others will follow their lead.

Assessment of problem solving is an area that could be strengthened. No effort is made to assess children's vocabulary, logic, problem solving, or heuristics. In the next revision these omissions should be corrected. Perhaps a problem solving section could be added. While other weaknesses could be mentioned, it should be pointed out that these assessment materials are probably superior to 90% of the materials available to teachers.

Use of these materials in non-British classrooms is limited for a variety of reasons. For example, the decimal notation, the use of the pound sterling rather than the dollar, and the spelling of many words would increase the difficulty of items for children in the United States. Some words are also uncommon in American usage. These include parcels (for scale weights), bungalows, and anticlockwise. Americans will also have difficulty with the use of the metric system for all measurement. These factors should not discourage administrators or teachers from using Assessment in Mathematics as a model which schools should emulate in developing their own assessment programs in mathematics. Similarly, the Assessment in Mathematics materials would be valuable for inservice education and for teachers who are developing their own classroom assessment materials.

Review of Assessment in Mathematics by LINDA JENSEN SHEFFIELD, Associate Professor of Education, and Mathematics, Northern Kentucky University, Highland Heights, KY:

Assessment in Mathematics was developed by the Somerset Local Education Authority in Great Britain to provide a record of the mathematics progress of individual pupils. The 87 photocopy masters in this packet are designed to test 44 objectives for numbers (including operations with whole numbers, fractions and decimals), 24 measurement objectives, 13 shape objectives, 4 probability and statistic objectives and 4 relation objectives. No criteria for success are listed other than a statement indicating that objectives are expected to be mastered by the top 20–25% of 11-year-olds. The manual suggests that teachers utilizing the instrument rearrange the order of objectives to match their own curricula.

The objectives listed for each of the five sections are not typically written in behavioral terms. In most cases, no criterion for success is provided and terms such as understand and consider are used frequently. The manual admits to the difficulty of assessing the understanding of concepts but states that the problem cannot be ignored simply because it is difficult. Other objectives reflect acquired knowledge, skills, and applications, which are easier to assess.

The manual recommends that testing not be attempted until the teacher is confident that the child will be successful. Each teacher must decide on the degree to which a child is successful on each objective. Although the length of time required for a child to complete a given exercise may indicate his or her competence, no time limits are suggested.

One of the strengths of this package is the fact that the students are tested on the concrete and pictorial as well as the abstract level. Teachers are asked to provide simple manipulatives such as chips, dot cards, a balance beam, base 10 units, strips, squares, and attribute blocks, for several activities. In some cases children may use the worksheets individually and in other cases the teacher interviews the child orally. Applications of concepts are also tested through a variety of simple word problems. The testing of concepts concretely, the use of oral interviews and the testing of applications are commendable practices.

The instrument also includes a good variety of topics. Each operation is tested conceptually before any algorithms are checked. Both comparison and take-away subtraction problems are included as are both measurement and partition types of division. Recent topics such as flow charts and digital clocks are also assessed.

One danger with a single instrument to test the total elementary math curriculum is that it is difficult to test mastery of any topic in depth. For example, fractional concepts, ordering fractions, equivalent fractions, addition of like fractions, fractional parts of a set, and mixed numerals are all tested on a single page. Such testing can only give a teacher a very general assessment of pupil progress.

Once the teacher has assessed the student and come to some decision about level of competence, no suggestions are provided to the teacher about the utilization of this knowledge. No remediation is suggested, presumably because a child is given the instrument only if he or she can be reasonably expected to master it. Apparently, if a student masters a topic he or she proceeds either to the next topic in a subarea or to a topic in another subarea which is at the same level.

The format of the test is good. Teachers may duplicate the masters one at a time as needed. The pictures are attractive and pages are not crowded with too many examples.

The British instrument may cause some slight problems for users in the United States. Money activities are in pence and pounds, British spellings such as learnt and tonnes are used and decimals are written with the decimal point at midline rather than at the bottom of the line. The number track used has no zero, unlike a typical number line.

The Somerset Local Education Authority is to be applauded for this work. It is an important part of a package of materials aimed at providing a continuous, coherent record of pupils' math progress. Other school districts or local education authorities might learn from this effort. It must be remembered, however, that this was developed by one local education authority to meet its own goals and objectives. No attempts have been made to develop norms, define levels of success, or to check the reliability and validity of the instruments. Teachers should decide which specific sections of this package meet their own goals and objectives.

[85]

Assessment in Nursery Education. Ages 3–5; 1978; ANE; assessment by teacher's observation and performance tasks; assessment in 5 areas: social skills and social thinking, talking and listening, thinking and doing, manual and tool skills, physical skills; no norms; 1 form; manual (174 pages); colour selections booklet (7 pages); individual record sheet (2 pages); 1985 price data: £17.95 per teachers's pack of complete testing materials including manual and colour selection book; £4.20 per 30 record forms; £1.35 per colour selection booklet; administration time not reported; Margaret Bate and Marjorie Smith; NFER-Nelson Publishing Co. [England].*

Review of Assessment in Nursery Education by ROBERT P. ANDERSON, Professor of Psychology, Texas Tech University, Lubbock, TX:

The Assessment in Nursery Education scales (ANE) provide a method for assessing the development and performance of 3- to 5-year-old nursery school children. The scales were developed in Great Britain and represent a project organized by the British National Foundation for Educational Research. The ANE scales are not representative of the type of inventory or rating scales (e.g., Alpern & Boll Developmental Profile) utilized in North American (U.S./Canadian) schools. Thus, utilization of these scales in a context other than the country where they were developed would require a considerable modification of the users' expectations for a utilitarian rating system.

The scales are meant to provide a measure of progress for nursery school children. At the same time, one is cautioned in the manual that "the structure of the assessment should not be taken for or used as a developmental guide." Unlike some of the rating systems being used in early childhood education programs, the results derived from a sample of children do not form "a syllabus or constitute prescriptions for a nursery programme." In essence, the scales are not yoked to any particular concept or theory of child development nor should the results be used to develop or plan individual educational plans. The scales simply measure the current status of a child on five empirically derived dimensions or, if used as a repeated measure, they assess the progress of a child on these dimensions.

The following areas of assessment are covered: (1) Social Skills and Social Thinking, (2) Talking and Listening, (3) Thinking and Doing, (4)

Manual and Tool Skills, and (5) Physical Skills. Each of these primary areas is further divided into subareas (subscales) with a variable number of items in each subarea.

The method of assessment is by naturalistic observation of children in their nursery school environment and by their performance on a series of individually administered test tasks. The children are expected to be rated and tested on the items by their teachers and, if necessary, by a psychologist or other professional personnel. In order to be involved in the rating of children an evaluator would need to have a thorough knowledge of the 179-page manual, 143 pages of which are devoted to the assessment procedures and descriptors of performance.

A shortened version of the scale is provided in what is labeled the Colour Selections. The Colour Selections refer to four levels (Red, Blue, Orange and Green) which approximate developmental stages; however, these levels are not age related. Each stage or level has two sets of items taken from the five primary areas. These two item sets represent an alternative choice of items and materials. For normal administration of the shortened version only one item is taken from each area for each of the stages or levels.

If the Colour Selections are not used, and the evaluator wishes to use a broader range of items, he/she is encouraged to pick out items for ratings from the total sample of items. The net result of this rather haphazard method of item selection is that there is likely to be little uniformity in item selection from one administration to the next, and results from assessment in one center may not be comparable to results from a neighboring center.

A limited amount of printed material for the performance measures came with the assessment kit. The majority of the paraphernalia needed for the assessment must be provided by the examiner. Unfortunately for the North American consumer, some of the essential equipment is not readily available in toy stores under the brand names given in the manual (e.g., "Little Froebel wooden figures"). The amount of paraphernalia needed for a complete assessment is considerable. One effect of this informal method of gathering test material is that the assessment procedures cannot be standardized across groups.

The manual is quite complete in the section devoted to administration and scoring. However, scoring in a measure of this type is always subject to examiner bias. The record sheet cannot be interpreted without a thorough reading of the manual. Thus, training of persons who do the assessments is critical if the instrument is to provide any useful data.

The test manual provides no normative data. A profile obtained on a child cannot be tied to developmental ages nor can it be compared to the extremes or means of some standard population. Very limited data is provided on reliability. The one reliability study reported used 32 children. Basically reliability was measured as interrater agreement on scoring 16 items from the total scale. Complete scoring agreement was achieved on 54% of the items.

Two types of validity were reported. Content validity is assumed from evidence that a group of persons apparently agreed on what should be covered in the scales. A minimal amount of concurrent validity data was presented in the manual. The validity study used a subset of 16 items. Ratings on these items were related to the five McCarthy Scales and teachers' ratings on undesignated areas of performance. Thirty-two children were involved in the sample. Non-traditional statistics (Cramer's V) were used to demonstrate an association between the Assessment items and the independent criteria.

In summary, the standardization, normative, validity, and reliability data and the general content of the manual do not meet the criteria set forth in *Standards for Educational and Psychological Tests* (1974).

After careful perusal of the manual it is apparent that considerable effort was directed toward developing the rating system. However, it is equally apparent that the authors were psychometrically naive and seem not to be aware of the standards expected by test/rating scale consumers who are familiar with the American Psychological Association criteria for psychological tests. These scales cannot be recommended for use by schools and/or agencies who hope to provide a developmentally meaningful assessment of nursery age children. At best the scale can be designated as a for-research-purposes only type of instrument.

Review of Assessment in Nursery Education by PHYLLIS L. NEWCOMER, Professor of Education, Beaver College, Glenside, PA:

This instrument is useful for informal or criterion-referenced assessment; it is not a standardized, norm-referenced test. The materials are designed to record the development of children (aged 3 to 5) receiving a nursery education. Assessment in five areas is conducted through direct observation and by having children perform specific tasks. Items in each area are purported to be arranged in order of progressive difficulty. Also, groups of items are said to be independent of one another.

The test manual provides the consumer with detailed .information pertaining to the use of the instrument (i.e., when to test, how to integrate testing into the nursery day, what to expect from testing, and so forth). It is also noted that the entire test is not to be used with every child. Instead, the teacher is to select the areas or specific items that are to be administered to each child. A short form of the battery entitled The Colour Selections is provided to help teachers decide which items should be administered.

The Social Skills Scales, which are to be administered before any other scale, include six areas: independence, conversation skills, relations with other children, relations with staff, concentration, and behavior in an adult-directed group. Each area has nine items that range from exhibiting the trait (score 1.0) to lacking the trait (5.0).

Social Thinking has four groups of tasks which the child must perform. They involve: knowledge of self and family (11 items), knowledge of other people and socially acceptable behavior (11 items), ideas on time and growth (11 items), and understanding of non-present time (5 items). Pictures of model people involved in this selection are provided but must be mounted on cards, colored, laminated, and cut out. Tasks range from easy ("What is your name?") to difficult ("Can you make a pretend family from these people?"). In this section as in all others, the teacher is provided with guidelines called "Descriptors of Performance" for evaluating the child's response.

Talking and Listening contains eight groups of tasks: speech production (2 items), and language to create imaginary experiences (1 item) are based on observation, while talking about a picture (6 items), reconstructing a story (2 items), using books (1 item), and predicting a simple problem (1 item) are performance tasks. Auditory discrimination (6 items) and listening and remembering (4 items) are a mixture of observation and performance.

Thinking and Doing involves seven groups: ability to classify (8 items), counting (6 items), knowledge of quantity, measurement and order (13 items), identification by touch (3 items), problem solving (3 items), knowledge of properties of objects (2 items), and knowledge of another's point of view (7 items). To test these skills, as well as most others throughout the test battery, the teacher must gather together various equipment (e.g., logiblocks in 3 colors, little wooden figures, etc.).

Manual and Tool Skills contains 10 groups of performance tasks which can be used with small groups: building blocks (4 items), linked construction (4 items), jigsaws (4 items), printing (1 item), pencil (5 items), scissors (6 items), hammer (4 items), clay and modelling tool (4 items), pouring (3 items), and threading, winding and buttoning (3 items).

Finally, Physical Skills contains seven areas of items which may be administered to groups: balance (9 items), bodily coordination (6 items), agility (6 items), agility and confidence (4 items), eye and hand/leg coordination (8 items), strength (4 items), and coordination of movements with another person (4 items). Elaborate equipment such as a balance bar, climbing cube, barrel, rope ladder, and so forth is required for certain of these tasks.

As can be readily seen from the description of these areas, this assessment battery closely resembles a thorough, well conceived nursery school curriculum. Items were developed from observation of nursery programs and from input by an advisory group that included nursery school teachers. Materials were field tested in nursery schools. The instrument is quite comprehensive—in fact it is so comprehensive that many nursery teachers may shrink from attempting to use it. Speculation of the time involved to administer one section, not to mention the entire instrument (the authors provide no time estimates), suggests that it is not a very functional tool. The authors recommend testing with selected groups of items; however, the teacher is hard pressed to know where to begin the assessment. Although a short form is provided, there is no empirical substantiation of the extent to which its stages (items from each category) predict performance on the entire battery.

Also, there is the question of the age appropriateness of the tasks. The teacher has no way of knowing if a child's inability to perform a task represents typical behavior for his/her age group or suggests a problem. Although tasks are said to be arranged sequentially, there is no objective basis for their arrangement.

The empirical data reported are not encouraging. The publisher provides a study of interrater reliability for selected test items which reveals only 54% agreement between raters. Also provided is a validity study comparing children's ratings on selected items with items from the McCarthy Scale Tests. The results show 63% agreement in ratings. Investigations involving predictive validity, such as correlating children's performance on these scales with variables measured when they are older (i.e., school success, social and emotional development, motor development, etc.), are lacking.

In summary, this instrument seems most useful as a curriculum guide for nursery teachers. It is far too cumbersome to consider as an assessment tool for each specific nursery school student.

[86]

The Assessment of Aphasia and Related Disorders, Second Edition. Aphasic patients; 1972–83; this second edition contains revised scoring procedures for the Boston Diagnostic Aphasia Examination and a Supplementary Test entitled the Boston Naming Test; 2 tests; no data on validity; norms consist of means and standard deviations; individual; manual ('83, 111 pages plus Boston Diagnostic Aphasia Examination booklet); 1984 price data: $27.50 per complete kit; Harold Goodglass with the collaboration of Edith Kaplan and other authors listed below; Lea & Febiger.*

a) BOSTON DIAGNOSTIC APHASIA EXAMINATION. 44 scores: severity rating, fluency (articulation rating, phrase length, verbal agility), auditory comprehension (word discrimination, body part identification, commands, complex material), naming (responsive, confrontation, animal, body part), oral reading (word reading, oral sentence), repetition (words, high-probability sentences, low-probability sentences), paraphasia (neologistic distortion, literal, verbal, extended), automatized speech (sequences, reciting), reading comprehension (symbol discrimination, word recognition, oral spelling, word picture matching, sentences and paragraphs), writing (mechanics, serial writing, primer-level dictation, written confrontation naming, spelling to dictation, sentences to dictation, narrative writing), music (singing, rhythm), parietal (drawing to command, stick memory, total fingers, right-left, arithmetic, clock setting, 3-dimensional blocks) plus 7 ratings: melodic line, phrase length, articulatory agility, grammatical form, paraphasia in running speech, word finding, auditory comprehension; 1 form consists of booklet ('83, 27 pages) and set of 16 stimulus cards; $15 per 25 booklets; $4 per set of stimulus cards; (75–150) minutes.

b) BOSTON NAMING TEST. 1 form ('83, 64 pages); scoring booklet ('83, 8 pages); $7.50 per test booklet; $6 per 25 scoring booklets; administration time not reported; Sandra Weintraub.

See T3:308 (28 references) of *a* only; for reviews by Daniel R. Boone and Manfred J. Meier of *a* only, see 8:955 (1 reference).

TEST REFERENCES

1. Borod, J. C., Goodglass, H., & Kaplan, E. Normative data on the Boston Diagnostic Aphasia Examination, Parietal Lobe Battery, and the Boston Naming Test. JOURNAL OF CLINICAL NEUROPSYCHOLOGY, 1980, 2, 209–215.

2. Cummings, J., Hebben, N. A., Obler, L., & Leonard, P. Nonaphasic misnaming and other neurobehavioral features of an unusual toxic encephalopathy: Case study. CORTEX, 1980, 16, 315–323.

[87]

Assessment of Basic Competencies. Ages 3+–15 years; 1981; ABC; criterion-referenced; 3 subtests; reliability data for grades K–8 only; manual (206 pages); training manual (32 pages); 2 response forms: diagnostic edition (12 pages), developmental edition (12 pages); training materials (transparencies, tape) are available; 1983 price data: $414 per starter set, including all materials necessary for administering all 3 subtests; $13.50 per 20 response forms of either type; $24 per manual; prices for training package available upon request; (120) minutes in 3–4 sessions; Jwalla P. Somwaru; Scholastic Testing Service, Inc.*

a) INFORMATION PROCESSING. 1 form in 3 booklets: observing skills (271 pages), organizing skills (217 pages), relating skills (221 pages); $125 per set of materials, including manual, 3 reuseable tests, 20 diagnostic and 20 developmental response forms.

b) LANGUAGE. 1 form in 5 booklets: understanding words (217 pages), comprehending expressions (217 pages), producing expressions (217 pages), reading (185 pages), decoding (187 pages); $210 per set of materials including manual, 5 reuseable tests, 20 diagnostic and 20 developmental response forms.

c) MATHEMATICS. 1 form in 3 booklets: knowing numbers and operations (219 pages), understanding concepts (207 pages), solving problems (205 pages); price same as for *a* above.

Review of Assessment of Basic Competencies by PETER W. AIRASIAN, Professor of Education, Boston College, Chestnut Hill, MA:

The Assessment of Basic Competencies is a battery of 11 individually administered tests intended to assess competencies for school learning in three domains: information processing (3 tests), language (5 tests), and mathematics (3 tests). Each test has one form containing either 85 or 100 items. The items in each test are scaled and calibrated according to latent trait theory, so that no examinee need take all of the items in a test in order to obtain an ability estimate. The manual is contradictory regarding for whom the tests are appropriate, suggesting at one point that pupils classified as learning disabled, emotionally disturbed, language disordered, and educationally mentally retarded are prime candidates for the battery and at another that "children with the range of abilities usually found in the mainstream" are the intended examinees. It does seem unlikely that one would want to take the estimated 3 hours per examinee to administer these tests to most pupils in the mainstream, especially since much of the information obtained could be more easily obtained from a group test. Other suggested uses of the tests, such as those for the assessment of various special populations, go beyond the interpretations that this battery can provide in its present form.

INTERPRETATIVE MATERIALS. The test manual varies substantially in level of difficulty, clarity of presentation, and detail. For example, the rationale provided for the particular skills included in the tests is brief and non-specific. Skills are not tied explicitly to school curricula, except for the general note that in language and mathematics, "the content of the items followed closely the content of curricular materials generally used in schools." Better documentation of this claim is required. The manual does caution users to compare the test items to the examinees' curriculum before making decisions on the basis of the test data, a wise caution for all achievement test users. The directions for test administration are generally clear and straightforward. Some prior preparation is required to administer this battery, though not nearly as much as for the Binet or Wechsler.

Section 5 of the manual, "From diagnosis to instruction," describes instructional methods and resources associated with the 11 areas tested by the battery. The information provided here may be of interest to practitioners, and it is novel to see test content related to curriculum materials and instructional strategies, but it also must be noted that the strategies and materials suggested in the manual are general ones which are not tied explicitly to every skill area covered by the tests. The suggestions provided are just that—suggestions, not validated approaches which have been shown to improve pupil learning.

ITEMS. The description of item development is sketchy. The manual does not indicate who wrote the initial set of items or the basis on which the initial set was culled down to those ultimately field tested. Approximately 1,900 pupils between the ages of 3+ and 15 responded to the items during field testing and calibration. This is a relatively small number, particularly since item sampling procedures restricted the number of pupils who took any given test item to about 190 pupils. At the lower age levels and at the ninth grade, the numbers in the tryout/calibration sample were considerably smaller (generally less than 100) than at other age and grade levels, making inferences at these extreme levels relatively imprecise.

The items across the 11 tests are largely, though not exclusively, of the selection variety. Examinees are shown a picture, read a passage, or given a problem and asked to indicate the correct response from a limited set of choices. While such items help make scoring more objective, the structured format lessens substantially the diagnostic richness of the individualized testing situation. Examinees have very little interaction with the test administrator, save to indicate their response choice. A group testing context could provide similar information to that provided by this individualized assessment battery.

For the most part, the test items measure the skills they were intended to measure. However, some of the mathematics items do not set the problem well for younger examinees (e.g., "Which container holds more sugar than either of the other two?" instead of, for example, "Which container holds the most sugar?"). The reading items have a few limitations, particularly those which use pictures to set the question and to provide the response alternatives for the examinees. Some of the pictures permit more than one interpretation. Also, it is difficult to use pictures to represent words such as "hesitate," "reunion," and "poised." Item 60 in the Producing Expressions test is keyed wrong. In the Decoding test, an examinee's ability to identify nonsense words depends substantially on the clarity of the test administrator's pronunciation, but the test directions offer no pronunciation guidelines for the administrator.

NORMS. The battery provides the user a choice of two response forms to score the assessment: a diagnostic form, which focusses upon the skills examinees have mastered, and a developmental form, which focusses upon the level at which examinees perform in the difficulty scale of the items. The response form selected does not affect test administration.

Since testing is adapted to the level of each examinee according to general guidelines in the administration directions, arriving at a test score for each examinee involves finding a basal item and a ceiling item for the examinee and using these indices plus the examinee's item response pattern to derive a raw score on the test. The manual suggests that appropriate interpretations of the results can be made at four levels: individual items, skill clusters, total test, and broad domain. The manual also indicates that the test has not been used in the diagnostic-prescriptive mode. Thus, no evidence is available regarding the validity of item and skill cluster level interpretations.

The raw score on a test can be converted into a Level of Competence. The Level of Competence represents the examinee's location in the developmental sequence of skills assessed by a test, as determined by the latent trait calibration of the items. The manual states that the latent trait approach permits all the items in a given test to be placed on a single ordered scale, such that the performance of different examinees can be placed on the same scale, even if the items the examinees take are themselves different. The three parameter logistic model was used in the item calibration for this battery. The Level of Competence score for an examinee can be converted into the following norm-referenced indices: developmental age, grade equivalent, and percentile rank. Percentile ranks, in turn, can be converted into standard scores and normal curve equivalents. Each Level of Competence is reported with a 75% confidence band around it, a commendable reminder to the user about measurement error.

The adequacy of the norms and the Level of Competence scale depend upon the adequacy of the latent trait calibration, and this, in turn, depends upon the adequacy of the norming/calibration sample. In considering such adequacy, three factors are relevant: sample size, sample representativeness, and cross validation. The sample was stratified by region, type of community, race, and sex. The norming/calibration groups were not balanced by geographic region, and weighting was performed to attain statistical balance. The type of weighting is not described. Each test was administered to a total of about 1,900 pupils between the ages of 3+ and 15. Although not stated explicitly, it appears that a single group of about 1,900 pupils took all the tests in the battery, rather than different groups taking different tests. At any given grade or age level, item calibration values for a test are based upon the performance of approximately 65 subjects, a very small number, especially for estimating the C, or guessing parameter, in the three parameter model.

The norming/calibration sample was composed of subjects who were "in the mainstream of education." This group was selected "on the rationale that the test battery would eventually be used on children with the range of abilities usually found in the mainstream." This argument is lacking, since the manual devotes considerable attention to the use of the test results in making inferences about pupils who are decidedly not in the mainstream and since the mass of mainstream pupils are more easily examined via other, group tests. If inferences are desired about emotionally disturbed or educable mentally retarded pupils, the norming/calibration sample must include a sizable number of such pupils.

Finally, two presumed benefits of latent trait item calibration are that item statistics are "sample free" and that comparable ability estimates can be obtained for different examinees using different sets of items from the calibrated scale of items. Each of these properties is desirable, but neither is a guaranteed by-product of statistical analysis, particularly in the case of this battery, which used a small calibration sample and suggests inferences about populations underrepresented in the norming/calibration sample. The manual provides no evidence that the sample-free and person-free properties are valid for the tests in this battery. Such validation information is particularly warranted for the reasons suggested above.

VALIDITY AND RELIABILITY. The main evidence for the reliability of the tests in the battery is a series of test-retest studies (3- to 4-week intervals) carried out at grades K, 2, and 6. The scores analyzed were the latent trait ability estimates. Reliability coefficients ranged from .76 to .98, with most of the coefficients in the .85 and higher range. These are high reliabilities. No reliability information is provided at the skill or skill cluster level of scoring, and users should not assume high reliability for these subscores.

Evidence pertaining to three types of validity is presented in the manual. The manual suggests that the construct validity of the battery is shown by the intercorrelation pattern among the 11 tests: moderate to high correlations among tests within one of the three general domains in the battery and "not so high" correlations among tests belonging to different domains. This pattern is by no means clear in the data presented, and while it is true that the correlations among tests in a domain are moderate to high, so are many of the correlations among tests across domains. No convincing evidence is presented to validate that a test purporting to measure basic competencies for school learning does measure basic competencies, or that a score scale termed "Level of Competence" provides a valid description of the construct the test measures.

The discussion of content validity needs more specificity to provide sufficient evidence of the content validity of the tests in the battery. Criterion-related validity was examined by correlating performance on the battery with other indices of school achievement and ability. The tests correlate moderately (.30s to .50s) with the SRA Assessment Survey at grade 2, and somewhat higher (.60s to .80s) with the SRA Assessment Survey at grade 6, the Wide Range Achievement Test for a group of grade K to 8 pupils, teachers' ratings, age, grade level, and WISC age. The individual tests in the battery do correlate with other commonly used indices of school achievement and ability. Overall, however, more validation work needs to be done on the tests in the battery.

SUMMARY. Much necessary background and justification work pertaining to this battery of tests has been left undone or unexplained. The manual requires more detail, both of a substantive and technical nature. The advantages of individually administering a set of tests which contain primarily selection-type items need to be explicated and documented. The content validity of the tests vis-à-vis school curriculum emphasis needs more documentation. More work needs to be done in the norming/calibration process, since interpretations of the various scales and norms provided depend heavily upon the adequacy of the item calibration. The validity of the battery needs to be demonstrated in all areas and for all groups the manual suggests it is appropriate to make inferences about. At this stage in its development, the Assessment of Basic Competencies cannot be recommended strongly for use.

Review of Assessment of Basic Competencies by JOSEPH E. ZINS, Assistant Professor of School Psychology, University of Cincinnati, Cincinnati, OH:

The Assessment of Basic Competencies is a battery of psychoeducational tests designed to be individually administered to students who are experiencing learning difficulties. An objective of the test battery is to provide an alternative to current assessment practices by overcoming some of the shortcomings commonly found in other instruments. The Assessment contains 11 tests within three domains: Information Processing, Language, and Mathematics.

Skills assessed in the Information Processing domain include observation (obtaining meaning from what is seen in the environment), organization (deriving conceptual meaning from what was observed), and relational thinking/reasoning. These skills are viewed as being essential to the acquisition of competencies in the Mathematics and Language domains. The 11 skills assessed in the battery were chosen for inclusion because of their relevance to learning in the school. No attempt was made to measure a single overall unitary ability.

The Assessment has its theoretical basis in Gagne's (1968) cumulative learning model, and the hierarchy of items in each scale was designed to reflect the progression of learning complexity generally found in each of the domains. It provides information about a student's level of performance (competence) along a developmental sequence. The results are intended to lead to the development of specific instructional programs.

The battery was designed within the context of the latent trait model developed by Birnbaum (1968), and this aspect deserves special mention. Latent trait models specify the relationship between a child's observed test performance and the unobservable traits or abilities that are presumed to underlie his/her performance. These models have received increased attention in recent years, and they may provide a framework for resolving some measurement problems as well as helping to "explain" examinee test performance (Hambleton & Cook, 1977).

The test manual is complex and could have been written in a much clearer and more organized manner. In addition, the guidelines for scoring items as correct or incorrect usually contain only one or two possible answers with no instructions as to how variations should be scored. A very helpful training manual is included which should facilitate efforts to train novice test administrators who could give the Assessment under the supervision of an assessment specialist.

The manual includes a section on test interpretation. Depending upon the purpose of the evaluation, there are several levels at which the instrument can be interpreted: item (each is based on a specific skill), skill cluster, subtest, or domain level. Furthermore, it can be used as a diagnostic, criterion-referenced instrument or to provide normative data.

There is a strong emphasis upon the use of a developmental perspective in test interpretation. It includes, for example, provisions for obtaining a developmental age and locating a person's level of competence along a developmental sequence. Although changes in cognitive skill development with age are commonly acknowledged in measurement, contemporary research in cognitive psychology emphasizes that individual children may be functioning at very different cognitive levels in different areas at any given age (Flavell, 1982). One outcome of the age equivalents may be the unnecessary stigma associated with a low score, or undue expectations for a child scoring at a higher level. Numerous other criticisms of the developmental approach have been advanced in the literature.

The Assessment of Basic Competencies also emphasizes the use of grade equivalent scores rather than standard scores or percentiles. Since these grade equivalent scores are not curriculum-referenced in any way, their use could lead to misunderstanding and error. Appropriate cautions about the use of developmental ages and grade equivalents are needed.

The manual suggests that the developmental age or grade equivalent be used to determine learning disabilities and mental retardation. There appears to be no empirical basis for such an approach. Rather than overcoming some of the problems associated with the use of the ability-achievement discrepancy to identify learning problems, the Assessment appears to generate a new set of problems in this area.

Some suggested exercises and additional resources which may be helpful in remedial activities in the various areas addressed by the Assessment are included in the manual. Users are cautioned, however, that the various exercises and resources are of varying quality.

Psychometric criteria were carefully considered in the development of the Assessment, and the use of the latent trait model is important as part of this development. A brief overview of test development is presented, and although the manual mentions that a technical manual with a more thorough explanation of test development is available, this reviewer was unable to obtain one from the publisher.

The individual test items were carefully written, reviewed, and revised. However, the procedures used in determining the content of the Information Processing tests were not empirical. Rather, the items reflect the "author's perception of the sequence of skills that would demonstrate competence in the clusters."

The Language and Mathematics domains were developed to reflect the content of school curricular materials, although the rationale and procedures used for item selection are not clearly defined. Apparently, no systematic attempt was made to review textbook series, curricular syllabi, statements of curriculum experts, and national committees, etc.

It is difficult to determine a clear relationship between these items and areas that are relevant to school learning and to diagnostic information which would be useful for the design of instruction. Furthermore, the test emphasizes the importance of the "developmental sequence," but does not describe how the items were designed to fall into such a sequence.

A large stratified random sample of over 20,000 children was included in the norming, and a reasonable attempt was made to match the sample with the current U.S. population (although a number of Canadian children were included). However, at ages three and four a small number of children were tested on several items, and there is no reliability data on this age group. As a result, caution should be exercised when using the Assessment at this level.

Some evidence of the test's reliability is presented for grade levels K, 2, and 6, and for grades K to 8 combined. Based upon this data, test-retest reliability (3- to 4-week intervals) was excellent for both the broad domains (.95–.96) as well as for the 11 subtests (.88–.95).

A number of validity studies are reported in the manual. Evidence for construct validity is not complete at this time. Particularly in need of clarification is the Information Processing domain. For example, at grade 6 the intercorrelations among the subtests are relatively high and suggest overlap among them.

Documentation of content validity is weak. Essentially, it consists of subjective judgments made by professionals in special education, and it appears to be largely based upon face validity. Criterion-related validity was evaluated in terms of correlations of the Assessment battery with several other measures. The correlations reported were generally satisfactory.

In summary, it appears that the Assessment has a number of positive attributes including the use of the latent trait model, a large normative sample, and indications of good reliability. However, the emphasis on the developmental indices, the limited evidence of validity, and the lack of a clear relationship between item content and curricular material weakens its attractiveness. This reviewer cannot recommend it without reservation. A test such as the Woodcock-Johnson Psycho-Educational Battery appears to deserve prior consideration before any decision is made to adopt the Assessment of Basic Competencies.

REVIEWER'S REFERENCES

Birnbaum, A. Some latent trait models and their use in inferring an examinee's ability. In F. M. Lord & M. R. Novick (Eds.), STATISTICAL THEORIES OF MENTAL TEST SCORES. Reading, MA: Addison-Wesley, 1968.

Gagne, R. M. Contributions of learning to human development. PSYCHOLOGICAL REVIEW, 1968, 75, 177–191.

Hambleton, R. K., & Cook, L. C. Latent trait models and their use in the analysis of educational test data. JOURNAL OF EDUCATIONAL MEASUREMENT, 1977, 14, 75–96.

Flavell, J. H. Structures, stages, and sequences in cognitive development. In W. A. Collins (Ed.), THE CONCEPT OF DEVELOPMENT. Hillsdale, NJ: Erlbaum, 1982.

[88]

Assessment of Coping Style. Grades K–8, 9–12; 1981; ACS; manual title is *Analysis of Copying Style*; revision of the School Picture-Story Test; 12 scores: 3 externalized (attack, avoidance, denial), 3 internalized (attack, avoidance, denial), for both authority and peer interaction sources; no norms; 2 levels labeled Forms C, Y; manual (119 pages plus test); individual record form (4 pages), group response form (1 page); separate answer sheets must be used for group administration; 1984 price data: $7 per package of 25 individual record forms; $7 per package of 100 group response forms; $19.95 per set of transparencies for either level; $19.95 per manual; (10–20) minutes; Herbert F. Boyd and G. Orville Johnson; Charles E. Merrill Publishing Co.*

Review of Assessment of Coping Style by GERALD L. STONE, Professor of Counseling Psychology, and Co-Director, Stroud Center for Educational Services, College of Education, University of Iowa, Iowa City, IA:

According to the authors, "the Assessment of Coping Style is...specifically designed for use by educators for the identification of the coping styles being used by young children, preadolescents, and adolescents to deal with problems primarily related to interpersonal relationships with peers and authority (teachers, principals, etc.)." This projective test consists of 20 figure drawings of children (Form C) or youth (Form Y) in various school settings interacting with peers (10 figures) or an authority figure (10 figures). The respondent's task is to select a response from among the six coping style statements (external attack, avoidance, and denial; and internal attack, avoidance, and denial) that is thought to represent the feelings of the child or youth in the drawing. Responses for each coping style are summed and recorded on a record sheet yielding various summary (authority, peers, and total responses) and combination scores (e.g., avoidance plus denial equals withdrawal responses). After the various coping style summaries have been completed, the diagnostician conducts an inquiry concerned with the most commonly used coping style in order to obtain information relevant to planning intervention strategies. The authors provide a manual, *Analysis of Coping Style: A Cognitive-Behavioral Approach to Behavior Management*, that includes information relevant to the assessment and treatment of children with behavior disorders.

The authors indicate that the Assessment of Coping Style represents the continued development and revision of the School Picture-Story Test. Pictures have been continually redrawn and the format altered from a free response situation ("make up a story") to a more structured arrangement (selection of one statement from six provided statements). All previous instruments, designed primarily for research purposes, have been unpublished. The latest revision consists of a number of redrawn pictures and rewritten statements. The latest statements were rewritten to conform to coping styles based on cognitive and behavioral theories emphasizing perceptions of the source of the problem (internal and external perceptions) and basic reactions to problems (attack, avoidance, and denial). These statements were generated from 23 teachers (regular classroom, emotionally disturbed, or learning disability specialists) who were asked to submit verbal statements, made by children in their classes, that reflected attack, avoidance, or denial coping styles. The authors selected items from these statements, added "normal" responses, and conducted various field trials. From these trials it became evident that "normal" responses were too obvious and eliminated the use of other responses. Moreover, such findings led to a reexamination of the theoretical model, resulting in the articulation of the basic premise: that nondisturbed persons will use the six coping styles selectively and will not use one style to the exclusion of the others.

In addition, the authors present interjudge agreements for three judges on the coping style response statements, indicating perfect agreement on 102 of the 120 statements. There is little indication that such agreement indices were subject to replication or that the chance agreement level was considered.

Several approaches to reliability were considered. The authors point to many problems with reliability assessments of their procedure, including the brevity of the measure and the small number of items. The authors do report an attempt at test-retest reliability, but the results were not satisfactory; in explanation the authors argue that some of the students were less receptive to the second testing. In spite of the arguments, reliability should be assessed and reported.

The validity of the instrument was demonstrated through the use of contrasting groups. Comparisons were made between a nondisturbed population (395) and five categories (special education class, resource room, alternative school, day school for delinquents, and a group home) of children with problems ($N=203$). The difference between the normal and criterion group elementary school children is especially evident when a cutoff is set, indicating that elementary school children with problems tend to select a large number of responses from one coping style. The data show little evidence of validity for secondary school students.

Norms have not been systematically developed, but the authors suggest that eight or more responses may serve as a useful guideline.

In summary, the authors should be credited with attempts to continue to update their instrument. The latest version incorporates coping styles, a contemporary trend in health and psychological practices. Also, the authors have developed a useful manual that includes suggested interventions classified by coping method; however, the linkage of coping method and treatment suggestions needs empirical documentation. In the light of the weak evidence and lack of published cross-validation studies, it seems premature at this time to adopt the Assessment of Coping Style as a method of identifying children with behavior disorders.

Review of Assessment of Coping Style by JOHN A. ZARSKE, Private Practice, Flagstaff, AZ:

The Assessment of Coping Style is the outcome of 20 years of research with children who experience learning and behavioral problems. The current edition represents the third revision of the School Picture-Story Test, which was initially published in 1954 and revised in 1961 and again in 1969, when it was renamed the School Attitude Inventory. The Assessment of Coping Style retains the same basic format of the 1961 and 1969 revisions in requiring the child to select one of several statements which he or she feels is descriptive of the feelings of a main character depicted pictorially in a variety of social situations. The current version features redrawn pictures and new statements selected to conform with Boyd's Model of Coping. The reader is provided with considerable background information in the manual regarding the development of this particular model of coping styles. According to Boyd's system, the Assessment of Coping Style yields a discrimination of the child's preferred mode of coping from among six alternative styles (i.e., externalized attack, externalized avoidance, externalized denial, internalized attack, internalized avoidance, and internalized denial).

As the Assessment of Coping Style is based upon the cognitive-behavioral approach to childhood behavioral problems, users unfamiliar with such approaches are at a distinct disadvantage in using the Assessment of Coping Style. The authors describe their tests as being a useful addition to the special education decision making process, particularly as this relates to affective educational planning. Specifically, the authors state that the purpose of their test is to identify coping styles used by young children, preadolescents, and adolescents to deal with problems related to interpersonal relations with peers and authority figures. Thus, the authors assume that Boyd's six coping styles have a direct effect upon interpersonal relations with both peers and adults. Unfortunately, specific support of such a hypothesis is not presented by the authors. According to the assessment system proposed by Boyd, the outcome of a given assessment leads to a selection of various intervention programs specifying types of learning and assignments to be given to the child, kinds of study and work groups within which the child should be included, types of class participation recommended, and guidelines for development of a physical environment. The various intervention programs are specifically selected dependent upon the particular coping strategy of the child as identified by the Assessment of Coping Style. The manual provides a lengthy list of intervention options for each of the six various coping styles. Unfortunately, no empirical validation of the various intervention approaches is provided by the authors. Specifically, the authors fail to provide research support to demonstrate that different coping styles require different types of interventions.

The authors recommend the test for use by "educators." They also indicate that little specialized training is required to utilize the Assessment of Coping Style. However, in reviewing the list of interventions recommended by the authors, one finds that the test user is asked to employ such strategies as behavioral contracting, reinforcement of proper models of behavior, and utilization of other aspects of both cognitive and behavioral modification approaches. Certainly, any serious intervention utilizing such technologies would require an individual of considerably more advanced training than the typical regular classroom teacher. It is therefore of concern that the authors suggest the system may be used by educators who have no particular training in clinical or educational psychology.

NORMS. While no specific norms are provided for the Assessment of Coping Style, the authors report a series of "field tests" whereby the various items selected for inclusion in the scale were submitted to a group of educators and judges to determine their relevance to the coping model put forth by Boyd. No listing of such judges was provided by the authors. As such, one cannot make a judgement regarding the expertise of the panel who allegedly reviewed the various items. The "field testing" employed a sample of 445 regular classroom children in grades 2 through 12 who attended both private and public schools. These subjects were tested in a group situation. However, the instructions for administration of the Assessment of Coping Style also provide guidelines for individual administration. No specific normative data is provided to support the use of the test as an individually administered procedure. In addition, no specific information was reported by the authors regarding the socioeconomic status nor geographic location of subjects used in field testing. While the test has been some years in development, the lack of norms calls into question its widespread use as a clinical tool. It appears that the current scale would best be used on an experimental basis.

VALIDITY. The authors hold that the test's validity is empirically demonstrated by its ability to discriminate a normal or non-disturbed population from a disturbed population. They cite one particular "field test" where the instrument performed admirably in distinguishing between five groups of special children. Unfortunately, the *N*s for the various groups varied considerably ($N = 25$ to 56). In addition, while the test may be able to discriminate normal from disturbed youngsters, evidence for its construct validity is certainly not demonstrated by this fact. The point is that the authors tend to confuse overall test validity with this one particular type of validity. Additional information regarding the validity of the Assessment of Coping Style as an aid in intervention planning should be provided by the authors. While the interventions suggested in the manual seem to have adequate face validity, hard data needs to be developed to insure relevance of the Assessment of Coping Style for diagnosis of coping skills and subsequent intervention planning.

RELIABILITY. The authors report that for various reasons, a test-retest model of reliability was chosen for the Assessment of Coping Style. Individuals from a small sample were retested 3 hours after the initial testing. Test-retest data indicated wide variation in responses between the first and second administrations. Such an outcome raises very serious questions regarding the reliability of the instrument. This is particularly of concern as the authors seem to encourage the test user to employ the instrument in educational planning for special education students and as a pre- and posttreatment measure of the child's progress. Given the unreliability of the scores of the test, its use for diagnostic/intervention purposes and for program evaluation is questionable at best.

In summary, the Assessment of Coping Style represents an attempt to develop an assessment and intervention tool based upon a particular theoretical model of coping strategies. The authors failed to provide research to support linking the various coping styles identified through the test with specific intervention strategies. In addition, the test manual fails to report norms and adequate support of the validity and reliability of the test. Consequently, the Assessment of Coping Style does not appear to be suitable for its recommended use as an educational planning and goal setting device in special education programs. The test may have some utility as an experimental device for researchers interested in the particular model of coping put forth by Boyd. It is not recommended for widespread use by clinicians interested in diagnostic and treatment planning.

[89]

Assessment of Fluency in School-Age Children. Ages 5–18; 1983; AFSC; "criterion-referenced"; assessment includes classroom observation, parent interview, teacher evaluation of child's speech, multi-factored evaluation of child, and post-therapy; multi-factored evaluation assesses 5 areas: automatic speech, cued speech, spontaneous speech, physiological components, interview with student/assessing attitudes; no data on reliability and validity; no norms; individual; assessment of fluency (no date, 8 pages); parent interview (no date, 2 pages); teacher evaluation (no date, 2 pages); dismissal from therapy program (no date, 1 page); resource guide ('83, 220 pages); 1983 price data: $32.50 per complete set including 32 of each form; $8 per 32 assessment of fluency forms; $2.25 per 32 parent interview forms; $2.25 per 32 teacher evaluation forms; $2.25 per 32 dismissal from therapy program forms; $14.75 per resource guide; (45) minutes for student evaluation, (15) minutes for classroom observation, (30) minutes for parent interview, (15) minutes for teacher evaluation; Julia Thompson; Interstate Printers & Publishers, Inc.*

[90]

Assessment of Intelligibility of Dysarthric Speech. Adolescent and adult dysarthric speakers; 1981; AIDS; 6 scores: single word intelligibility (transcription, multiple choice), sentence intelligibility (transcription, speaking rate, rate of intelligible speech, communication efficiency ratio); individual; 1 form; stimulus materials (101 pages); manual (49 pages plus answer sheets and profiles which may be duplicated); 1984 price data: $64.95 per complete set; administration time not reported; Kathryn M. Yorkston and David R. Beukelman; C.C. Publications, Inc.*

[91]

The Assessment of Phonological Processes. Ages 2–9; 1980; leads to the identification of patterns in child speech; 10 occurrence scores: syllable reduction, cluster reduction, prevocalic singleton omissions, postvocalic singleton omissions, stridency deletion, velar deviations, liquid deviations (2 scores), nasal deviations, glide deviations; no reliability or validity data; norms consist of means for ages 3–7 only; individual; 1 form; manual (53 pages); recording form (1 page); analysis of phonological processes (3 pages); phonological analysis summary (2 pages); screening form (1 page); several additional items needed for administration must be supplied by examiner; 1982 price data: $24.95 per complete set; $2.50 per 48 recording forms; $7.50 per 48 analysis of phonological processes forms; $3.75 per 48 phonological analysis summary forms; $3.75 per 96 screening forms; (20–30) minutes; Barbara Williams Hodson; Interstate Printers & Publishers, Inc.*

TEST REFERENCES

1. Hodson, B. W., Chin, L., Redmond, B., & Simpson, R. Phonological evaluation and remediation of speech deviations of a child with a repaired cleft palate: A case study. JOURNAL OF SPEECH AND HEARING DISORDERS, 1983, 48, 93–98.

Review of The Assessment of Phonological Processes by SHELDON L. STICK, Professor of Speech Pathology and Audiology, The University of Nebraska-Lincoln, Lincoln, NE:

The Assessment of Phonological Processes is not an easy test to use. It has a complicated scoring system, and to fully administer the instrument requires at least 20 minutes and another 30 to 60 minutes for analysis of the data. Thus, on the basis only of the time element involved this test is not likely to have wide appeal. Typically the professionals who would be using this instrument cannot afford such an extensive commitment of time with one such instrument on one patient. It seems likely that usage of this test would be limited to situations allowing for extensive time commitments on detailed evaluations, or in research work. Such circumstances would seem to fit in with the author's apparent intent for developing the instrument: to assess severe articulation problems of children who have spent inordinate lengths of time in treatment without showing appreciable improvement.

The instrument was developed from a distinctive feature analysis model, which allows a practitioner to cull out the commonalities across phonemes. Thus, as in language treatment when efforts are directed toward determining cognitive hierarchies or semantic intent inherent in concepts, the notion of using distinctive feature analysis for speech sounds enables a practitioner to determine whether a child is correctly utilizing key processes such as: obstruents, fronting, affrication, vowelization, and numerous others. The intent is to learn which rules or strategies are missing in the child's phonological processes and teach them instead of attempting to teach specific sounds. The model seems to be well grounded in the sense it avoids encouragement of teaching a child splinter skills, but, instead, focuses on apparently underlying processes that would facilitate generalization.

The author has allowed for evaluating the basic phonological processes involved in speech sound production. Among children with severe phonological disorders the five processes that emerge most frequently are: syllable reduction, cluster reduction, obstruent singleton omission (particularly in the post vocalic position), stridency deletion, and velar deviation (particularly in the fronting position). To aid the examiner the author has defined 10 major terms associated with phonological production (i.e., sonorents, cluster reduction, and post vocalic obstruent singleton omissions). Also, there are explanations for 12 miscellaneous phonological processes (i.e., backing epenthesis, and coalescence), 5 types of sonorent deviations (liquids, nasals, and glides), 6 types of assimilation (i.e., regressive progressive, and alveolar), 4 types of articulatory shifts (i.e., substitution, dentalization, and lateralization), and other patterns or preferences (i.e., reduplications and/or diminuitives).

When summarizing a child's phonological processes the practitioner needs to transfer information from the recording sheet to an analysis form. Afterward, all the checks noted in the respective columns are totaled and recorded in the appropriate places on a third form, the summary sheet. Percentage of occurrence scores for each of the basic phonological processes is determined by dividing the total number of occurrences by the total possible occurrences specified for each of the respective processes. No doubt a skilled clinician would be able to transfer information rapidly from the first to the second to the third sheet and determine the appropriate percentage score. However, even an experienced clinician might become somewhat uncertain because, according to the author, there are conditions possible wherein a child could have errors and still earn a score above 100%.

The primary concern in selection of stimuli was that the items be within the vocabulary of preschoolers. Special attention was given to the motivational value of the stimuli; consequently most are three dimensional instead of pictures and all assess more than one phonological process. The author's objective is to elicit spontaneous speech production, but she recognizes there are limitations in procuring stimuli for all speech sounds. Therefore, some stimuli are modeled.

When purchasing the kit one receives the manual, recording forms containing the target phonetic transcriptions for the 55 stimuli words in the full test, an analysis form that allows a practitioner to specifically identify the various processes according to the information transferred from the recording form, a summary form that contains the information on percentages of occurrence for the various major phonological processes, and a screening form that allows a practitioner to check the 20 most common phonological processes. Of interest is that clinicians are to gather a test kit, supplemented with pictures, according to the stimuli presented in the manual. The author's rationale for declining to provide the necessary stimuli is that the total kit would tend to become too expensive.

When testing children, the author suggests that the stimuli be placed in three or four small boxes. Such a procedure presumably would build in short rest periods and assist the clinician in locating target words on the recording form. The stimuli for eliciting the 55 target responses include 49 objects, 3 body parts (thumb, nose, and mouth), and 3 crayons. During the testing a child is instructed to select a toy from one of the boxes, hold it up high, produce its name "loud and clear," and then replace it in the box. During that time the clinician is to transcribe accurately each utterance and, when possible, audio record each utterance for later verification. This procedure allows all American English consonants to be assessed at least twice: all prevocalically and all postvocalically except for /w/, /j/, /h/, which are elicited only in prevocalic positions. Also, 31 consonant clusters are assessed, 4 of them containing 3 elements.

The screening version uses 17 items plus the body parts thumb and teeth to elicit a total of 20 responses. Fifteen of the target stimuli are contained in the 55-item test. The author reported that the screening items were selected with two considerations in mind: (1) items that would be most likely to be available in homes or professional environments; (2) items that would provide the most information in the shortest period of time.

Normative data is presented on 60 preschool children; presumably all were developing normally. There is no information on how the subjects were selected so it must be presumed (though risky) that they were developing without known neurological, emotional, or sensory deficits. The manual indicates that the statistical data presented allows for comparisons of percentage of occurrence scores which would then lead toward identifying intervention entry points and priorities. The author states that there is additional statistical data available but that it needs to be requested; this is an unacceptable position because it hinders proper evaluation of the instrument and evaluation of the data gathered from testing subjects. It is noteworthy that the standardization population was reported to be 60 four-year old children. However, the author reports that adaptations have been made to the test so it can be used with mentally retarded adults and adult apraxics, but there is no indication as to how such modifications were made nor is there any indication regarding the types of performances such subjects produce. Furthermore, it was stated that while the original intent of the instrument was for use with preschool children having multiple misarticulations, it has been used successfully with children between ages 2 and 9. No information was presented on the different age groups.

When interpreting the results obtained from using the Assessment of Phonological Processes the author suggests that the 40th percentile is an appropriate cutoff point. If processes are displayed less often than 40% of the time, presumably they are not likely to require intervention. Five examples are given to show how the results can be interpreted with regard to the mean scores of the 60 subjects used in the normative sample. Also, the manual contains a figure comparing the 60 four-year-old children with 60 children, between the ages of 3 and 7, referred because they had "essentially unintelligible" speech. The author stated that the greatest differences between the two groups occurred on: cluster reduction, stridency deletion, and liquid deviation. The fourth and fifth greatest differences respectively were on velars and then final consonants.

It is worthwhile to reflect upon the reported underlying premise to the development of this instrument. The author set out to develop a test that would provide practitioners with information in a short period of time that could be used for designing systematic treatment programs for children with phonological disabilities. Accountability is to be determined by comparing pretreatment and posttreatment scores. It is questionable whether any but the most sopohisticated clinicians, and among that group only those who can devote extensive blocks of time to testing, would be able to understand and use this test. The model upon which the test was predicated has face validity. Regrettably, there is no reported information on any other type of validity or reliability, and the manner by which the norms were gathered must be considered suspect. It is not reasonable for a responsible professional to use norms for 4-year-olds on 2- and 3-year-olds; yet that is what the author recommends.

Without additional information on the normative process and better norms for the stimuli used, clinicians should be guarded when considering use of this test. Assessment of the phonological processes involved in speech production is a complex task and the manual to this test clearly points out that fact. If a revised manual is distributed it should contain many more examples of how to score the performances. According to the manual preface, the underlying goal of this instrument is to "provide information as quickly as possible which will aid in designing a more efficient and a more effective remediation program for the individual who has a phonological disorder." In its present form The Assessment of Phonological Processes is not endorsed for such a purpose.

[92]

Assessment of Qualitative and Structural Dimensions of Object Representations. Adolescents and adults (patients and normals); 1981; AQSDOR; subjects' descriptions of significant figures (e.g., parents) rated by judges; ratings in 4 areas: personal qualities, degree of ambivalence in description, length of description, conceptual level; no data on validity; norms consist of means and standard deviations, no description of normative population; no reading by examinees; rating form (1 page included in manual); manual (53 pages); 1982 price data: $5 per set of testing materials; (5) minutes per description; Sidney J. Blatt, Eve S. Chevron, Donald M. Quinlan, and Steven Wein; Sidney J. Blatt.*

Review of Assessment of Qualitative and Structural Dimensions of Object Representations by CLIFFORD H. SWENSEN, Professor of Psychological Sciences, Purdue University, W. Lafayette, IN:

The development of the concept of the object has been an increasingly important topic in developmental psychology and in psychoanalytic theory. This test was designed to measure certain qualities of the object as conceptualized by the subject, and the developmental level of that concept. The test is specifically designed to measure aspects of the subjects' conceptualization of important other persons in the subjects' lives, the subjects' parents in particular.

The subject is given 5 minutes to describe a specific important other person, such as the father or the mother. This description may be written or it may be verbal. These descriptions are then rated for personal qualities of the person described, degree of ambivalence toward the person expressed within the description, the length of the description, and the conceptual level of the description.

Twelve personal qualities of the person being described are rated on a 7-point scale. These personal qualities are: affectionate, ambitious-driving, malevolent-benevolent, cold-warm, degree of constructive involvement, intellectual, judgmental, negative-positive ideal, nurturant, punitive, successful, weak-strong.

In addition, the degree of ambivalence toward the person being rated is rated on a 3-point scale, and the length of the description is rated on a 7-point scale.

The 14 variables listed above compose the "qualitative" characteristics of the scale, which, when factor analyzed, produced three factors (Nurturance, Striving, and Verbal Fluency), which account for 77% of the variance of the test.

In addition, the test is scored for five levels of object representation, the levels derived from developmental and psychoanalytic theory.

Unfortunately, the test, as presented in the manual, contains many practical and psychometric problems. The first problem is that although the 14 qualitative characteristics of the test are to be scored on 7- or 3-point scales, no examples are given to define the points on those scales. Presumably the scores on these scales should be combined to provide scores on the three factors which produce most of the variance in the test, but no normative data are presented for the factor scores.

The only normative data that are presented are for 87 female and 40 male "college students." No further description of the normative sample is provided. The only reliability data that are presented are the correlations of the ratings among three judges, who are called an "expert rater," a "trained rater," and an "untrained rater." No further description is contained of the characteristics, training, or experience of these raters. The ratings themselves were obtained from only 28 cases.

The manual does contain 27 examples of descriptions at the different levels of object representation, presented in sequence from the lowest to the highest level. These examples also contain ratings of the other characteristics, but the manner in which these are presented would make it very difficult to use them in practice.

No validation data are presented.

As this test is presented, it cannot be recommended for use. Based on material that is presently available, it should be viewed as a very preliminary report on an experimental instrument that is in the early stages of development. The test needs to have more explicit definition of the points on the scales for rating the qualitative aspects of the test, it needs description of necessary training for the effective use of the instrument, it needs reliability and normative data from a variety of different kinds of samples, and it needs validity data.

Based on the material currently available, it is not clear what useful purpose the test might serve. It would appear that it could be used to assess the level of object representation, but if that is the purpose for which it is to be used, better instruments are available. For example, the Sentence Completion Test developed by Loevinger (1976; Loevinger & Wessler, 1970) to measure ego development was derived from the same theoretical sources in developmental psychology and psychoanalysis, and is scored so as to provide assessment of stages of ego development which appear to be defined in terms very similar to the definition of levels of object representation. Extensive reliability, validity, and normative data are available for the Sentence Completion Test, which has been found useful in a wide variety of different kinds of research projects.

REVIEWER'S REFERENCES

Loevinger, J., & Wessler, R. MEASURING EGO DEVELOPMENT, 2 vols. San Francisco: Jossey-Bass, 1970.

Loevinger, J. EGO DEVELOPMENT. San Francisco: Jossey-Bass, 1976.

[93]

Assessment of Reading Growth. Grades 3, 7, 11; 1979–1980; tests of reading comprehension based on National Assessment of Educational Progress; no data on reliability and validity; 3 levels: Level (Age) 9/Grade 3 ('79, 6 pages), Level (Age) 13/Grade 7 ('79, 8 pages), Level (Age) 17/Grade 11 ('80, 8 pages); manual ('80, 4 pages); 1984 price data: $8 per 30 tests and manual; Jamestown Publishers.*

a) LEVEL 9. Grade 3: 1979; 3 scores: literal comprehension, inferential comprehension, total; 1 form; (50) minutes.

b) LEVEL 13. Grade 7; 1979; 3 scores: literal comprehension, inferential comprehension, total; 1 form; (50) minutes.

c) LEVEL 17. Grade 11; 1980; 3 scores: literal comprehension, inferential comprehension, total; 1 form; (42) minutes.

Review of Assessment of Reading Growth by DARRELL L. SABERS, Professor of Educational Psychology, The University of Arizona, Tucson, AZ:

The Assessment of Reading Growth (ARG) consists of three tests of reading comprehension, each having 18 items on literal comprehension and 18 items on inferential comprehension. Although the manual says the ARG tests may be administered to any student of any age, they are compilations of released items from the 1971 National Assessment of Educational Progress and thus have norms only for ages 9, 13, and 17.

The ARG items share the advantages and disadvantages of the NAEP items. The major advantage is that the items are clearly written and are relatively free from technical flaws. A positive aspect of ARG, not shared by all reading comprehension tests, is that a student must be able to comprehend the reading passage in order to answer the items.

Two problems associated with the compilation of the released items are evident in the ARG. The first is the inefficiency of having to read an entire passage in order to answer a single item. In the level nine test, a reading passage is repeated four or five times with only one item asked after each presentation. The effect of this repetition on the item norms is not addressed in the manual.

The second problem with these items is the use of "I don't know" as an option with all the choice-type items. Data from NAEP indicate a systematic bias resulting from use of this distractor. There are two examples at level nine where the DK distractor is especially unjustified. One test item (no. 14) asks the student what happened first in a story. Because there is no way for the reader to know which of two options (a or d) is correct, the actual answer should be "don't know." Naturally, the DK distractor is not keyed even though in this case it is correct. Another item (no. 34) asks the student for his/her opinion.

The effort to preserve the integrity of the NAEP items is evident. Even minor changes, such as reordering the options within an item, were not made. As a result, although there are four or five options (in addition to DK) for each of the 104 multiple choice items, option a is keyed only 10 times.

The directions have four obvious flaws. First, there is not a complete congruence between the directions the teacher reads to the students and the directions the students are to read at the same time. Although the differences in these directions are slight, students attending to the directions may be distracted. Students should be reading the same words that the teacher is reading. Second, the directions indicate that all the items will be multiple choice when in fact there are items (one at level 13 and three at level 17) that are not multiple choice. Third, no mention is made that there is a DK distractor included in the items, and from reading the directions one could not discern that such an option existed. Last, there are no guidelines for the teacher to follow when the students ask how much time is allowed or how much is remaining. The students are told only "Don't rush, but don't waste time" with regard to time limits.

The manual is inadequate in more than directions for administering the test. Reliability is completely ignored. Validity information is meager, and found only in the table of specifications that indicate how each item is categorized. Validity appears to be assumed in the one sentence that says "Each test covers most of the reading comprehension skills tested in the National Assessment of Educational Progress and found on most standardized reading comprehension tests."

Two statements are made about the potential use of ARG. They say: "The total score is most useful to teachers or administrators who want a single score to indicate how well their students are comprehending....These tests allow teachers or administrators to compare their students with the nation on the same items used in the National Assessment of Educational Progress." Will many teachers or administrators be interested in administering an entire examination in order to compare the performance of their students with 1971 norms on the NAEP items?

The manual overstates the usefulness of the norms. "Instead of just giving grade levels and percentiles, the tests are normed in a manner that provides reference points or averages for the nation and for different types of school settings. It might be more fair, for example, to compare inner city students with other inner city students or suburban schools with other suburban schools. The tests also are more diagnostic than the usual standardized tests because they give the national percent of success for each item for each level." Actually, these norms are not that unusual, nor are the tests diagnostic.

The norms may be useful for comparing the performance on an individual item for one group with the NAEP group; however, for a reading comprehension test they are rather suspect in that only averages are given. There is no measure of dispersion included, and the only comparison allowed is to those averages.

To present the norms on NAEP items as grade norms is misleading at best. The NAEP sampling plan shows the procedure used so that age norms rather than grade norms would result for NAEP data. Also, although the NAEP assessments were taken at various times of the year (e.g., March and April for age 17, October to December for age 13), all norms are referred to as mid-grade norms in the ARG manual.

Because the tests do not adequately accomplish their purported goal, one could be very harsh in judging their validity. Yet because the items are exceptionally well written, the tests could be useful. Given that the national norms are already invalid for use at any grade level, local norms need to be established. Before obtaining norms, however, the directions should be corrected and the DK distractor eliminated. At grade level three (and one case at grade seven), all items based on a given passage should immediately follow that passage to provide more efficient testing. These changes would result in a very good test ready for norming. However, anyone looking for a test of reading comprehension in order to compare students to national norms is advised to look elsewhere.

[94]

Assessment of Skills in Computation. Junior high school; 1978–79; ASC; Form A ('78, 30 pages); examiner's manual ('78, 15 pages); technical manual ('79, 31 pages); separate answer sheets (CompuScan, Scoreze self-scoring) must be used; 1983 price data: $29.40 per 35 tests including examiner's manual; $6 per 50 CompuScan answer sheets; $8 per 25 Scoreze answer sheets; $4.75 per acetate scoring stencil for use with machine-scorable answer sheets; $.50 per class summary sheet; $3.75 per examiner's manual; $4.75 per technical data; $7.50 per specimen set; scoring service, $.66 and over per student ($100 minimum); (100) minutes in 2 sessions; Los Angeles Unified School District; CTB/McGraw-Hill.*

Review of Assessment of Skills in Computation by ROBERT W. CEURVORST, Statistician, Market Facts, Inc., Chicago, IL:

Assessment of Skills in Computation (ASC) is a test designed to measure the ability of students in grades 7 through 9 to solve the types of problems encountered in everyday living. The format of ASC makes it one of the better tests available for this purpose. It contains 18 displays of "real-life" situations, with four multiple choice questions per display. The test is divided into two sections of 36 items each and is designed to be administered in periods of at least 50 minutes on two consecutive days. Form A of the test is reviewed here; according to the manual, at least two parallel forms (B and C) should also be available.

The displays include such things as advertisements for merchandise on sale, a recipe, a sales chart for a candy drive, a map of a bike path, a weekly budget, and plans for building shelves. One third of the displays involve money; all but one of these show prices of various items. The displays provide essentially the same amount and kind of information that would be available to students in comparable real situations. Test items require the student not only to perform calculations but also to decide which calculations are appropriate for each question. For example, students are asked to determine the amount of money saved when clothing is purchased on sale, to compare cost per ounce of various containers of juice, to determine the yield of dry milk when reconstituted according to directions, to calculate the average lap time required for a student to match a school record for a 1-mile run, and to find a person's average weight over seven days. Word problems of this type are more realistic than questions like "72 – 46=?" and should be better indicators of student performance outside the classroom.

Instructions for administering and scoring the test are clear, except on one point. Raw scores are computed as the number of items answered correctly (no correction for guessing is applied), but nowhere in the instructions are students advised to guess if they are unsure of an answer.

The procedures followed in developing ASC are sound and included testing of an initial version containing 120 items (30 displays) and a "content review by instructional and evaluation experts." The technical manual also includes grade levels from two sources for 50 words used in the test, indicating that some care was taken to insure that the vocabulary in ASC is appropriate for seventh through ninth graders.

Normative data on Form A are based on test scores obtained from over 35,000 seventh graders and an unreported number of eighth and ninth graders in the Los Angeles Unified School District in the second month of the 1978–79 school year. Users of ASC should develop local norms if the test is used at other times during the school year or in other areas of the country.

Means, standard deviations, standard errors of measurement, and KR-20 reliabilities for the total test and for each display, as well as item difficulties and item correlations with total scores and with scores for each display, are reported for each grade level and separately for Black and Hispanic groups in the seventh grade. Total test reliability is a respectable .93–.94 for each grade, and .82 and .89 for seventh grade Blacks and Hispanics, respectively. The standard error of measurement is about 3.6 points, or 5% if test scores are expressed as percent correct.

Mean scores in the norm sample ranged from 44% correct for seventh graders to about 55% for ninth graders, so the test is not an easy one. In fact, only about one third of the seventh graders in the norm group answered more than half of the items correctly, and only 12% managed to get more than 70% of the items right. The test is significantly more difficult for Blacks (mean score of 31%) and Hispanics (mean score of 39%) in the seventh grade, so the decision to present norms separately for those groups was a good idea. It would have been better had they presented norms for Blacks and Hispanics for each grade level, at least for total test scores.

Since the computations required in Form A are themselves not unusually difficult, one is led to suspect that the generally low scores stem from students not knowing which calculations are appropriate. This, of course, is valuable information that can only be obtained with "word problems." It also suggests that mathematics instruction must be concerned as much with when to do what as with how to do it.

The authors recommend that ASC initially be administered early in grade 7 so that remedial instruction can be implemented during the next two to three years of junior high school. (ASC instructional materials are available from the publisher.) The difficulty of the test at this level must be taken into consideration if the test is to be used for diagnostic purposes (e.g., to identify students needing special/supplementary instruction).

The technical manual includes tables classifying test items by the skill(s) being measured (e.g., dividing whole numbers, adding fractions, converting scales, etc.) and by content area (e.g., interpreting graphs, pricing, measurement of time, area, or volume). Means, standard errors of measurement, and KR-20 reliabilities are reported, by grade level, for these groupings of items as well. These item classification tables are useful for interpreting student performance, since several items measure multiple skills.

A problem that arises with tests of this type is that a student may answer items incorrectly for any of several reasons. In general terms, a student may (*a*) apply the wrong operation(s) and/or (*b*) make a computational error. It is usually as important to know *why* a student missed an item as to know that (s)he got it wrong. However, the test manuals do not address this issue at all. The inclusion of a brief (one-line) rationale for each distractor used in the test would be a valuable addition to the manual. This information would enable a teacher to more easily identify a student's particular weaknesses or sources of error. As useful as such information could be, few, if any, test manuals provide it.

One section of the ASC technical manual seems to be of limited utility, at best. That section reports relative frequency distributions of the responses to each item in the 120-item "tryout edition." Although the items and alternatives are labeled only as "1A," "1B," and so on, it is evident that the order of the items and response alternatives does not match Form A. As a result, for users of Form A there is little to be learned from this table. A similar table for Form A would have been better, but not really necessary given the extensive normative data provided.

SUMMARY. ASC is a well-designed test of math proficiency for students in grades 7 through 9. Composed essentially of "word problems" in an attractive format, it is aimed at assessing student performance in realistic situations. The test was carefully developed, as evidenced by a longer tryout version, a thorough content review, and attention to the vocabulary used. ASC possesses good internal consistency reliability and should provide a reasonably good indication of how well students can apply their math skills in everyday situations. Potential drawbacks are its length (at least 100 minutes, or about two class periods) and the fact that it is somewhat difficult, particularly for seventh graders. If you are searching for a test that goes beyond assessment of computational accuracy, and you are willing to devote two class periods to testing, then ASC deserves your consideration.

Review of Assessment of Skills in Computation by KARL R. WHITE, *Associate Professor of Special Education and Psychology and Co-Director of the Early Intervention Research Institute,*

Exceptional Child Center, Utah State University, Logan, UT:

According to the Technical Manual, "The Assessment of Skills in Computation (ASC) is a diagnostic, evaluative instrument that measures the ability of junior high school students to undertake the tasks in computation that are required to function effectively in everyday living." The test contains 18 sets of problems (each with four multiple-choice items) which assess a wide range of basic arithmetic skills with whole numbers, fractions, decimals, percentages, graphs, maps, weights and measures, and time. The test is relatively new, with initial development done in 1978 with 2,548 seventh- and ninth-grade students in the Los Angeles Unified School District. Since then, three parallel forms of the test have been developed. Although the impetus for developing the test grew out of concerns about "minimum competencies," the ASC is designed primarily for the early identification of instructional needs rather than the certification of minimum competencies.

TEST DEVELOPMENT. Although the manual states that the particular items included in the ASC were based on "an extensive review of the types of problems in computation that students are likely to encounter in daily life...and an intensive content review by instructional and evaluation experts," no information is provided about the specifics of this process. The range and types of items included in the ASC seem reasonable enough, but as it is now, this decision must be based on a logical analysis of the content rather than any empirical evidence or knowledge of a systematic development process. Such a logical analysis is made easier by the inclusion of excellent tables in the technical manual showing the number of items related to each of the "enabling skills" (e.g., adding, subtracting, multiplying, or dividing with whole numbers, decimals, etc.) and content areas (e.g., graphs, measurement, business, etc.).

Construction and selection of items appears good except for three relatively minor flaws. First, the developers were appropriately concerned about whether an assessment of computational skills might be confounded with a student's reading ability since all of the problems include some reading. In spite of "a concerted effort to control the vocabulary" in the test at or below the sixth-grade level, 10 out of 18 problems in the ASC contain words above the sixth-grade level. Secondly, the ASC does an excellent job of identifying the areas in which students are having difficulty but does not provide specific information about the nature of the difficulty, as could be done if careful attention were given to the types of distractors used for each item. It is frequently unclear whether distractors were systematically chosen, or whether they are just "wrong answers." More attention to the distractors would have made what appear to be quite good items even better from a diagnostic point of view. Finally, even though the test is not a traditional, norm-referenced standardized achievement test, the difficulty index and point biserial correlations of several items raise questions about why they were retained in the test. For example, point biserial correlations between the item and the total test on one item range from –.12 to .05 with a median of –.10 and a median difficulty of .06. Data such as these suggest that two or three items may be ambiguously worded, misleading, or measuring a different construct.

ADMINISTRATION PROCEDURES AND NORMS. Directions for administering and scoring the test are generally quite good; a minor exception is that students are not given any directions on whether to guess. The class summary sheet provides an excellent procedure for immediately identifying not only which items but also what skill areas are missed by each student. The handscoring stencils are easy to use and a scoring service is available. The SCOR-EZE form should be avoided (at least if the examination packet is representative) because it would be relatively easy for an enterprising student to figure out the system and get all answers correct without having mastered the material.

One substantial problem in interpreting test scores is that items within a problem are not always independent of each other. In other words, a student who misses the first item in a problem would almost always miss several of the other items in that problem because a correct answer to items 3 and 4 requires knowledge of the correct answer to item 1. Norms per se are not included in the technical manual, presumably because the authors view this as a criterion-referenced rather than a norm-referenced test. The manual does include a raw score frequency distribution for students in the Los Angeles Unified School District during the Fall, 1978 administration (N=35,578, all in grade 7). Although not absolutely essential, additional norm-related information would be helpful in interpreting the test. At least demographic information on the Los Angeles sample and separate raw score frequency distributions for various subsamples (e.g., boys/girls) would assist users in interpreting scores and establishing pass/fail scores when needed.

RELIABILITY AND VALIDITY. What information is available in the Technical Manual about the reliability and validity of the ASC is reassuring; unfortunately, however, many critical gaps exist. Total test internal consistency coefficients (KR 20) and standard errors of measurement are reported for the total sample for each grade level (.93 or .94) and for Blacks (.82) and Chicanos (.89). In the seventh grade, similar tables are given for each "enabling skill" and content area. Because different methods of computing reliability account for different sources of error variance, test-retest and parallel forms estimates of reliability really should be reported.

Evidence of the test's validity is limited to information about content validity in the various tables which show which items test which enabling skills and content areas. If we assume that all of the critical computational skills "required to function effectively in everyday living" are represented in the test, then these tables contain convincing information that each of the enabling skills and content areas are represented by sufficient numbers and balance of items. The more critical question of whether all of the most important functional skills have been included is unfortunately left to a logical analysis by each individual user. Validity studies of how important the skills tested in the ASC really are in everyday functioning would be very nice to have but are admittedly somewhat expensive and difficult to conduct. However, since one of the primary purposes of the ASC is to identify students needing remedial instruction, it seems essential to have additional information on how effective it is for this purpose.

SUMMARY. The Assessment of Skills in Computation (ASC) is the type of test which could be very useful for junior high school teachers and administrators. It appears to have been carefully and logically constructed, is relatively short and easy to administer, and addresses an area of growing concern (i.e., minimum competencies needed for everyday living). What data are available on reliability and validity are encouraging, but not enough. In its present form, the ASC is promising, but not convincing. Although many local education agencies have developed or are in the process of developing similar types of measures, there are few, if any, readily available measures which have been standardized and carefully refined. If more data can be collected on reliability and validity, and if the minor problems in administration, scoring, and interpretation can be resolved, the ASC would make a valuable contribution.

[95]

Attitude Toward School. Elementary, secondary school students; 1977; IOX objectives-based tests; for group assessment only; 35 tests (spirit masters for local duplicating) including the School Sentiment Index; 2 levels; administration time not reported; tests developed under the direction of Elaine L. Lindheim and Caren M. Gitlin; IOX Assessment Associates.*

a) ELEMENTARY. Grades K–6; School Sentiment Index and 10 other tests in five areas: learning, peer social behavior, class operations, classroom physical environment, school subjects; test set also includes an equivalent set of tests appropriate for pre-readers; 1 form (45 spirit masters); manual (22 pages); 1983 price data: $9.95 per test set.

b) SECONDARY. Grades 7–12; School Sentiment Index and 12 other tests in six areas: learning, peer social behavior, class operations, classroom physical environment, school subjects, learning methods and stimuli; 1 form (25 spirit masters); manual (14 pages); 1983 price data: $9.95 per test set.

Review of Attitude Toward School by MARY ELIZABETH HANNAH, Associate Professor of Psychology, University of Detroit, Detroit, MI:

Attitude Toward School is a substantial revision of a collection of instruments designed to assess "students' attitudes toward or perceptions of factors related to school and instruction." Three versions are available: secondary, elementary, and elementary-prereading. Each version includes the School Sentiment Index, which was published in the original collection and which contains the following subscales: Teachers: Mode of Instruction; Teachers: Authority and Control; Teachers: Interpersonal Relationships (all combined into one scale in the elementary-prereading version); Peers; School Subjects (elementary-prereading version only), Structure and Climate; and School in General. In addition, other areas such as orientation toward learning or subject matter preferences can be measured by using separate instruments. Further, each of these other areas can be assessed using a direct approach in which the questions are clear-cut and therefore subject to faking or an indirect approach where the purpose of the questions is more disguised. For example, to assess perception of pupil social interaction, in the direct approach students answer a series of questions concerning the way students treat each other, while in the indirect approach they are to project themselves into an imaginary television show about a school and answer questions about student interaction. However, there is no research available on the equivalence of the data obtained using these two approaches and, as the authors note, each approach may assess different aspects of the areas being investigated.

All scales are designed for the assessment of group (e.g., class) attitudes and perceptions and hence should not be used in an individual psychological assessment. Further, no normative data are available and interpretative information is limited to statements that high scores are indicative of positive attitudes or perceptions. It appears from reading the manual that the authors believe that each teacher has his or her own standards concerning the degree to which positive attitudes in a particular area are important and that these standards should be used to determine the adequacy or inadequacy of the areas assessed.

While reliability data are not presented for any of the other instruments, such information is available for the School Sentiment Index. Test-retest reliability over a 2-week interval ranged from .35 to .85 for the subscales and .87 for the Total Index for the elementary version, and from .62 to .81 for the subscales and .49 for the Total Index for the secondary version. Since the majority of coefficients fall below .70, the stability of the School Sentiment Index seems subject to question. Information is also available on internal consistency (Kuder-Richardson 20). At the elementary level subscale coefficients range from .42 to .76 and at the secondary level from .68 to .79. In addition, internal consistency estimates for the Total Index are reported as .80 and .88 for the elementary and secondary versions, respectively.

The major advantage of the Attitude Toward School collection of instruments is that it provides a set of measures that assess the same dimensions from kindergarten through 12th grade. However, given the lack of validity data and the low score stability, researchers working in this realm might better choose separate instruments for elementary and secondary levels (e.g., Classroom Environment Scale), instruments which have more empirical data supporting their technical adequacy.

Review of Attitude Toward School by RICHARD M. WOLF, Professor of Psychology and Education, Teachers College, Columbia University, New York, NY:

These two sets of instruments were constructed by staff members of IOX Assessment Associates in Los Angeles. IOX has developed a general approach to instrument development, notably in the achievement area, that involves a three-step process: (1) identification of the domain to be tested, (2) preparation of a general and an amplified description of the characteristic and the envisaged instrument, and (3) the preparation of the actual items to measure the identified attribute. IOX personnel have found this approach to work well in generating highly focused achievement measures that can be used as objectives-referenced and/or criterion-referenced tests in a classroom setting. The present set of instruments represents an attempt to extend this approach to the measures of attitudinal dimensions related to schooling.

The resulting instruments are intended to measure attitudes on five dimensions at the elementary school level and six at the secondary. The common dimensions are: (1) learning, (2) peer social behavior, (3) class operations, (4) classroom physical environment, and (5) school subjects. The additional dimension measured at the secondary school level only is learning methods and stimuli. Each instrument is on a ditto master for easy duplication. The instruments are designed to assess attitudes and perceptions at the class level only. Users are cautioned not to use the instruments for individual measurement. All measures are selected response instruments except for one at each level of schooling that calls for a short essay on the part of the student. Scoring keys for the selected response measures and a general guide for holistic essay scoring are contained in the manual accompanying the set of instruments at each level of schooling. (There is also a set of measures included at the elementary level that is intended for use with pre-reading groups.)

Inspection of the items comprising the instruments at the various levels shows no obvious defects. However, one expects to see more information about instruments than a general description and scoring keys or guides. Conspicuously absent is any information relating to the quality of the items and how they perform, validity, norms, and other interpretative material. Reliability information is presented for only one of the measures, the School Sentiment Index, but there is no description of the sample of schools on which the results are based nor any indication as to whether classes or schools were used as the unit of analysis. If schools were used as the unit of analysis, there is no statement about the likely effects of combining data across grade levels within school levels. If classes were used as the unit of analysis then results should be reported by grade level. Unfortunately, the manual is so lacking on specific information about such matters that the reliability data are suspect. The tables that present the reliability data contain so many questionable items of information that the accuracy of the results is in doubt. The sample sizes (whatever they are—schools, classes, or individuals) are greater for test-retest estimates of reliability than for internal consistency estimates Also, the test-retest estimates of reliability are almost always higher than the internal consistency estimates. While this is possible, it is somewhat implausible. Given such deficiencies, it hardly seems worth reporting the reliabilities for the School Sentiment Scale; these reliabilities, for group measures, are generally unimpressive.

In summary, the Attitude Toward School scale developed by IOX represents an attempt to extend an approach to the development of attitude scales that was developed for the production of focused achievement measures. Such an extension may or may not be warranted. Unfortunately, no evidence is presented to justify the use of these instruments.

[96]

Attitude Toward School K–12. Grades K–3, 4–6, 7–12; 1972; "an IOX measureable objectives collection"; criterion-referenced; utilizes direct self-report, inferential self-report, and observation; no validity data; no norms; 3 levels; manual (190 pages, includes all items necessary for administration); 1983 price data: $11.95 per manual; IOX Assessment Associates.*

a) PRIMARY. Grades K–3; 11 objectives: school sentiment (6 objectives: comprehensive, teacher, school subjects, social climate, peers, general), a picture choice, compliance with assigned tasks, school attendance, school conduct (compliance with school rules), school tardiness; (10–20) minutes per objective.

b) INTERMEDIATE. Grades 4–6; 15 objectives: school sentiment (same as *a* above), subject area preference, imagine that, the story, looking back, the school play, compliance with assigned tasks, school attendance, school conduct (compliance with school rules), school tardiness; (10–20) minutes per objective.

c) SECONDARY. Grades 7–12; 16 objectives: school sentiment (same as *a* above), subject area preference, what would happen, imagine that, take your pick, high school on T.V., class attendance, class tardiness, grade level completion, school conduct (same as *b* above), unwillingness to transfer; (10–20) minutes per objective.

See T3:222 (1 reference).

Review of Attitude Toward School K–12 by ALICIA SKINNER COOK, *Department of Human Development and Family Studies, Colorado State University, Fort Collins, CO:*

The Attitude Toward School K–12 instrument (revised edition) was designed to measure the attainment of instructional objectives in the affective domain. This collection of objectives is based on a criterion-referenced approach to evaluation. Individual items were developed to measure the stated objectives. These affective educational objectives are stated separately in the test manual for primary, intermediate, and secondary levels. At each level, attainment of the objectives is said to occur if a specified percentage of the items on a subscale are answered in a positive direction. Designed for educational rather than clinical purposes, the test is appropriate only for group assessment and not for individual assessment.

While the developers of the instrument report that this type of measure has "high content validity," no validity data are provided. The assumed validity of the items measuring each objective appear to be based largely on the judgment of "members of the IOX staff as well as external consultants." No predictive or concurrent validity is mentioned.

During the revision of the original items, field testing was employed with a larger number of students (1,229 in total) representing a wider socioeconomic range than in the original item development procedures. This field testing was undertaken to obtain reliability data and to determine the ability of items to discriminate among students. Statistical criteria were set for judging the appropriateness of items. Findings resulted in the deletion or modification of a large number of the original items and the addition of several new measures.

The test manual contains internal consistency correlations and stability estimates. The range of correlations obtained on the internal consistency index for each subtest are as follows: secondary level, .45 to .88; intermediate level, .46 to .80; and primary level, .42 to .70. Test-retest reliability coefficients based on a 2-week interval are as follows: secondary level, .49 to .86; intermediate level, .53 to .90; and primary level .35 to .97. The test manual states that reliability data are not provided for the two versions of A Picture Choice subtest at the primary level "due to computer irregularities in the data analysis." Because of the low correlations obtained for the primary level measures, it is suggested that these be used with extreme caution. The developers of the instrument stress, however, that because the measures in the test reflect affective rather than cognitive goals, lower indexes of stability than commonly desired should be anticipated at all levels.

Although a purpose of the test is to measure attitude change following educational intervention, no data have been reported from studies of this type. Also, while some of the subtests are based on observation, no interrater reliability has been established for these items. Because the test is criterion-referenced, instead of norm-referenced, no normative data are available.

The scoring procedures described in the manual are clear. In the case of large samples, machine scoring is possible. Otherwise, hand scoring is feasible but appears to be somewhat time-consuming.

This instrument has merit for use by local school districts in assessing the achievement of instructional objectives in the affective domain. However, use of specific subtests would presume that the objectives to which they refer have been adopted by the particular school district. Pre- and postmeasures would be needed to assess the effect of an intervention program. In the test manual, the test developers give the user considerable flexibility in modifying, adding, or deleting items to make them more suitable for their educational needs. However, they fail to warn the user that doing so will invalidate the statistical work that has been done on these measures and, if modified greatly, the user cannot assume that the statistical data reported in the manual will be applicable to their sample.

The instrument has limited research application at this time for several reasons. First of all, the paucity of validity and reliability data make research use questionable. Also, as mentioned previously, no normative data are available. Even if additional statistical data were collected on the items, it shows little promise for widespread use in research since it was designed for evaluation of specific objectives within an educational context. The test manual states that the items on the instrument will be "in a continual process of revision" as more information is gained in this area.

In conclusion, little research has been done on instrument development in the affective domain of learning because of the difficulty in identifying and measuring appropriate educational outcomes in this area. Unfortunately, there is little literature on school attitudes per se to guide individuals in this process. The Attitude Toward School K–12 instrument represents a significant beginning step in assessing this important aspect of educational attainment.

Review of the Attitude Toward School K–12 by RICHARD L. SIMPSON, Professor of Special Education, University of Kansas, Lawrence, KS:

The Attitude Toward School K–12 (ATS) consists of a set of group-oriented affective instructional objectives and related measurement items. Because this compilation of objectives has few counterparts, it must be considered unique. In fact, this distinction appears to be its primary strength.

While the authors claim that the validity of this criterion-referenced instrument has been established, both the procedure for doing so and the accompanying data are lacking. Thus, the direct self-report items for which "high content validity" is claimed remain unsupported. Users are told that measurement items reflect congruence with various attitude-toward-school objectives. Again, however, empirical support for this claim is absent. Because of limited knowledge about the psychological composition of attitude constructs in general, and the complexity of factors composing attitude toward school in particular, this issue is extremely significant. In spite of other strengths, this underlying shortcoming of the ATS must be recognized as a serious deficiency.

Within the framework of a criterion-referenced strategy, users of the ATS collection are apprised that the system is able to accommodate changes in measurement items (e.g., "Items may be deleted, modified, or added to make the measure more suitable for a given educational need"). Although perhaps consistent with its criterion-referenced approach, and in spite of minimal cautions, ("care must be taken when modifying or adding items that the meaning of the learner's response remains consistent with the objective to be assessed"), this aspect of the ATS further compounds its standardization and validity problems.

Furthermore, reliability data are sketchy and unimpressive. While this flaw may be attributed, to some extent, to the abstract and amorphous nature of attitude, it becomes intensified in combination with the other weaknesses previously described.

Only limited guidance is presented regarding the uses of the ATS. Consequently, in instances where users do not select the ATS for a previously determined purpose, or where they are searching for options for using the system, they will receive little if any aid from the manual.

The ATS objectives (categorized according to student grade level and measurement format—direct self-report, inferential self-report, or observational), are written in an easily comprehensible form. Yet, even if the validity of the measurement items designed to assess the various objectives could be assumed, the absence of norms makes the interpretation of results a matter of conjecture. Further, the simplistic strategy for interpreting group results (i.e., "To obtain an average score for a group of students for a particular subject area, sum the individual students' scores and divide by the number of students in the group") fails to make reference to such issues as standard deviation, special circumstances, the potential influence of pretesting and posttest outcomes, the degree to which pretest/posttest changes constitute significant differences, etc. Consequently, the value of the measurement component is highly questionable.

Though the observational items potentially provide for increased objectivity, they suffer from some of the same weaknesses as the direct and inferential self-report items. There are no norms for directly observed responses. Neither are there strategies for making comparisons in the absence of norms. Assumptions underlying particular attitude concepts are simplistic (e.g., high school students who drop out of school tend to have negative attitudes), and a number of underlying assumptions are either faulty or unsubstantiated. Further, a lack of operational definitions for target behaviors raises questions regarding acceptable interobserver reliability.

To summarize, instruments such as the Attitude Toward School K–12 are badly needed in the evaluation of affective programs and school-related attitudes. Nevertheless, the methodological deficiencies of the ATS reduce its potential impact. Consequently, consumers should be apprised that while the ATS objectives may contain many positive features, the measurement items do not attest to the worth of the system.

[97]

Attitudes Related to Tolerance 9–12. Grades 9–12; 1971; "an IOX measureable objectives collection"; criterion-referenced; utilizes direct self-report, indirect, and observation; 13 objectives: personal perspective (2 objectives), policy choice, group description scale, interaction attitude index, social reactions—specific populations (Caucasian-Negro), contemporary image, situation reaction, ethnic attitude, sociometric techniques, observation form, unobtrusive measure (2 objectives); no reliability and validity data; no norms; manual (125 pages, includes all items necessary for administration); 1984 price data: $10.95 per manual; (10–30) minutes per objective; IOX Assessment Associates.*

Review of Attitudes Related to Tolerance 9–12 by CHRISTOPHER PETERSON, Associate Professor, and JAMES T. AUSTIN, Graduate

Assistant, Department of Psychology, Virginia Polytechnic Institute and State University, Blacksburg, VA:

Attitudes Related to Tolerance 9–12 is a set of objectives and measures "related to the somewhat ambiguous construct of 'tolerance for the values and opinions of others.'" Intended for use with secondary school students, these objectives and measures embody a so-called criterion-referenced approach in which the congruence between a defensible objective and responses to items measuring that objective is assessed. In this case the objectives are 13 different ways of tolerating what other people believe, and the respective measures involve self-report questionnaires, sociometric devices, and behavioral observations. The manual contrasts this approach with a norm-referenced approach in which test items are used to compare and contrast individuals with respect to whatever these items measure.

Our reaction to Attitudes Related to Tolerance 9–12 is somewhat tolerant and somewhat intolerant. Our tolerance at times is enthusiasm, for several reasons. First, the criterion-referenced approach encourages the test user to examine his or her purpose. Measures are regarded as a means to an end, and the end is clear.

Second, both the objectives and their measures closely resemble those developed over the years by social psychologists interested in assessing prejudice (e.g., Cook & Selltiz, 1964). Although these parallels are not made explicit in the manual, we have some confidence that Attitudes Related to Tolerance 9–12 partly shares the construct validity accumulated in the social psychological literature for similar measures. For instance, the Contemporary Image Survey presents favorable and unfavorable statements about ethnic groups, and respondents are asked to indicate the degree to which these statements apply to members of these groups. This questionnaire is analogous to one validated earlier by Selltiz, Edrich, and Cook (1965).

Third, a number of reasonable caveats are contained in the manual. The user of Attitudes Related to Tolerance 9–12 is cautioned to employ as many appropriate measures as possible, to recognize the value connotation of the term tolerance, to be wary of the limits of self-report, and so on.

Our intolerance results from what is not said in the manual about potential problems in the interpretation of scores yielded by Attitudes Related to Tolerance 9–12. Such issues are touched upon but not in enough detail. The uncritical use of these measures might result in specious conclusions with unfortunate consequences. Although "criterion-referenced" measures make sense on one level, on another level they do not. What is the significance of a particular departure from a given objective? These scores do not have an absolute meaning. Only when compared to other scores are they interpretable. Thus, the dichotomy between criterion-referenced and norm-referenced approaches is false. The manual should provide norms so that users of these measures can assess whether a particular group of secondary school students is relatively tolerant, relatively intolerant, or whatever. In a similar vein, we suspect that some users will administer these measures repeatedly to the same group of students. No caution is provided regarding possible threats to validity from repeated testing (Campbell & Stanley, 1966).

The manual observes in general terms that the measures are imperfectly related to tolerance, but we believe that specific cautions should have been raised with respect to the particular kinds of measures utilized. Factors unrelated to tolerance or intolerance might substantially affect scores, and the user of these measures should be alerted to them. Thus, self-report measures may reflect social desirability, acquiescence, confusion, and so on. Sociometric measures may reflect attractiveness, similarity, propinquity, and so on. Behavioral observation measures may also reflect a variety of determinants, not the least of which is bias on the part of the observer. Insufficient mention is made in the manual that behavioral observation is a difficult-to-master assessment technique, requiring careful description of the concrete behaviors to be rated, extensive training of observers, and continuous reliability checks (Kazdin, 1981).

Also, the manual does not describe in any detail the field testing of these measures. The statement is made that "on the basis of the empirical data obtained from initial field testing, all items have been systematically revised." What does this mean? How are data employed to revise a criterion-referenced test?

Finally, in-depth discussion of whether or not "tolerance" is a unitary phenomenon seems warranted. Recent opinions in social psychology, buttressed by research, hold that general attitudes do not exist. Rather, specific attitudes with pertinence to specific behaviors are the focus of current attention (Ajzen & Fishbein, 1977). We would be surprised if the various measures of Attitudes Related to Tolerance 9–12 converged in the characterization of particular students. Accordingly, users should be careful to consider which specific objectives are of concern. The respective measures of these objectives should then be used, subject to the cautions we have raised.

In sum, Attitudes Related to Tolerance 9–12 is a set of self-report questionnaires, sociometric devices, and behavioral observation techniques that assess the degree to which secondary school students approach a variety of objectives reflecting tolerance for the beliefs and opinions of others. These measures are similar to those developed over the years by social psychologists interested in measuring prejudice, and they probably have state-of-the-art reliability and validity. The manual alerts the user to potential pitfalls in the use and interpretation of these measures, but we believe that more detail is needed. An extended example of the use of the objectives and their measures in an actual high school would have been valuable. Attitudes Related to Tolerance 9–12 will not be used for trivial purposes, and to the degree possible, the potential user should be protected from erroneous conclusions.

REVIEWER'S REFERENCES

Cook, S. W., & Selltiz, C. A multiple-indicator approach to attitude measurement. PSYCHOLOGICAL BULLETIN, 1964, 62, 36–55.

Selltiz, C., Edrich, H., & Cook, S. W. Ratings of favorableness of statements about a social group as an indicator of attitude toward the group. JOURNAL OF PERSONALITY AND SOCIAL PSYCHOLOGY, 1965, 2, 408–415.

Campbell, D. T., & Stanley, J. C. EXPERIMENTAL AND QUASI-EXPERIMENTAL DESIGNS FOR RESEARCH. Chicago: Rand McNally, 1966.

Ajzen, I., & Fishbein, M. Attitude-behavior relations: A theoretical analysis and review of empirical research. PSYCHOLOGICAL BULLETIN, 1977, 84, 888–918.

Kazdin, A. E. Behavioral observation. In M. Hersen & A. S. Bellak (Eds.), BEHAVIORAL ASSESSMENT: A PRACTICAL HANDBOOK (pp. 101–124). New York: Pergamon, 1981.

[98]

Attitudes Toward Mainstreaming Scale. Adults; 1980; ATMS; 1 form (1 page); no manual; brief (1 page); 1982 price data: $7 per 100 tests; administration time not reported; Joan D. Berryman, W. R. Neal, Jr., and Charles Berryman; University of Georgia.*

See T3:224 (3 references).

TEST REFERENCES

1. Green, K., & Harvey, D. Cross-cultural validation of the Attitudes Toward Mainstreaming Scale. EDUCATIONAL AND PSYCHOLOGICAL MEASUREMENT, 1983, 43, 1255–1261.

Review of Attitudes Toward Mainstreaming Scale by MARY ELIZABETH HANNAH, Associate Professor of Psychology, University of Detroit, Detroit, MI:

The Attitudes Toward Mainstreaming Scale (ATMS) consists of 18 statements designed to assess attitudes of school personnel (teachers, administrators, non-teaching staff) toward the placement of handicapped students in regular education classrooms. Statements relating to mainstreaming in general and the mainstreaming of physically impaired, sensory impaired, speech impaired, mentally retarded, and behavior disordered students are included. Statements concerning the mainstreaming of learning disabled students were not included due to the difficulty involved in constructing such items. Since this group of children constitutes the largest group of mainstreamed children, this is a serious omission. Disabilities are identified by label and description. While such a procedure doubtlessly promotes clarity, it also may limit generalizability to the disabilities as described. The respondent's task is to rate each item on a 6-point scale (Strongly Agree to Strongly Disagree).

The statements were selected from an original pool of 22 items by means of a principal components factor analysis with VARIMAX rotation applied to the responses of 161 students enrolled in a special education course. Results were then cross-validated on a second similar sample ($N=164$). Three factors were identified: learning capacity (8 items dealing with disabilities that do not hinder learning); general mainstreaming (7 items concerning mainstreaming in general and children typically mainstreamed [e.g., educably mentally retarded and behavior disordered]); and traditional limiting disability (3 items covering handicapped children who have not typically been mainstreamed [e.g., the deaf, blind and physically handicapped in wheelchairs]).

Materials consist of a one-page form containing the directions and items and an additional sheet describing the ATMS and references pertaining to its development and technical characteristics. While the references are useful, a summary of the major findings and norms might be more beneficial to potential users. The directions for administration are clear and consistent with the authors' aim of developing a test that can be given without training. However, no directions for scoring are included. Hence it is unclear whether numerical scores for each item are summed or whether factor loadings from the original sample are utilized in computing total and factor scores.

At present, norms are available on responses collected from 2,549 Georgia teachers and other certified personnel. Data on this group is reported in the form of mean scores and standard deviations for the total scale, factors, and each item. Standard scores and percentiles for raw score equivalents are not available.

Split half reliabilities for the original sample ($N=161$) are reported as .92; coefficients alpha for the original sample and for the cross-validation sample ($N=164$) were .88 for both. In addition, coefficients alpha for the factors for both samples range from .76 to .84. Thus, the ATMS appears to be internally consistent. No information on test-retest reliability is reported so that the stability of the scores over time is subject to question.

Other than the factor analyses discussed previously, which could be regarded as construct validity evidence, no information on other forms of validity is available. Since attitudes are often not related to actual behavior, information on concurrent validity would be particularly useful; for example, how do scores relate to the nature of the interaction between handicapped children and teachers?

In sum, in an area where there is a dearth of instruments to measure attitudes towards this socially important phenomenon, the Attitudes Toward Mainstreaming Scale is a welcome addition. The

ATMS should be useful to researchers wishing to assess a school's readiness to mainstream handicapped children, to evaluate the effectiveness of intervention strategies, or to determine the correlates of positive or negative attitudes in this area. However, the ATMS would also benefit from further technical development, particularly development resulting in normative data on a national sample and information on concurrent validity.

Review of Attitudes Toward Mainstreaming Scale by MICHAEL D. ORLANSKY, Associate Professor of Special Education, Department of Human Services Education, The Ohio State University, Columbus, OH:

The Attitudes Toward Mainstreaming Scale (ATMS) is designed to measure attitudes toward the integration of handicapped students into regular classes, a process colloquially referred to as "mainstreaming." The authors state that the ATMS may be useful in establishing "a national baseline of attitude toward mainstreaming," and in determining the effectiveness of teacher education programs or other activities presumably intended to increase knowledge and foster positive attitude change toward students with various special needs. These goals are commendable, considering the previous lack of instruments that could be reliably used for such purposes.

This instrument appears on a single page which presents instructions and then 18 statements regarding the integration of handicapped students into regular classroom settings. Respondents indicate their degree of agreement or disagreement by rating each statement on a 6-point Likert-type scale. Fourteen statements refer to specific areas of exceptionality (e.g., "Deaf students should be in regular classrooms"), while the remaining 4 statements probe the feasibility of teaching handicapped and nonhandicapped students in regular classes (e.g., "In general, mainstreaming is a desirable educational practice"). The manual offers brief background information, reliability and validity data, and instructions for administering, scoring, and interpreting the scale.

The authors note that it was their intent to design a brief, easily administered attitude instrument that would be usable with subjects who are not necessarily educators of exceptional children (the validation sample consisted of 323 "preservice and inservice students from 17 teaching fields"). The ATMS appears to meet these needs adequately. I found that a group of teachers completed the scale in an average time of 2 1/2 minutes, and had no apparent difficulty in understanding the instructions or terminology. Some users took exception to the phrases, "educable mentally retarded students" and "students confined to wheelchairs." It would be preferable to incorporate terms consistent with current professional usage and concern for the dignity of persons with handicaps, such as "students with mild mental retardation" and "students who use wheelchairs for mobility."

A potentially serious drawback of the ATMS is evident when one examines the distribution of items. Of the 14 statements designed to assess attitudes toward the integration of students with particular disabilities, 9 refer to visual, hearing, physical and health impairments. The ATMS includes only two items on speech impairments, two on behavior disorders, one item on mental retardation, and no statements at all on specific learning disabilities. As any recent census of the population served in special education programs reveals, the latter categories of exceptionality represent the overwhelming majority of students who are considered handicapped or exceptional. It is unfortunate that the authors' concern for brevity evidently resulted in a less-than-thorough consideration of attitudes toward many students who are most likely to be integrated into regular classrooms for all or part of the school day.

I would suggest that any future revisions of the ATMS be expanded to assess attitudes toward a broader and more representative range of students with disabilities, as indicated above. It would also be helpful if the rather ambiguous term "mainstreaming" were de-emphasized in favor of more precise descriptions of the extent to which these hypothetical handicapped students are to be integrated into regular classes.

The ATMS can be recommended for use as a rapid and convenient means of assessing a limited dimension of attitudes toward the integration of students with disabilities. It is hoped that educational programs seriously interested in encouraging positive attitudes toward handicapped students will supplement the ATMS with additional written and performance-based measures.

[99]

Attitudes Toward Working Mothers Scale. Adults; no date on test materials; AWM; norms consist of means and standard deviations; 1 form (4 pages, mimeographed); scoring instructions (1 page); mimeographed paper on construct validation of AWM scale (23 pages); 1983 price data: free of charge; administration time not reported; Toby J. Tetenbaum, Jessica Lighter, and Mary Travis; Toby J. Tetenbaum.*

TEST REFERENCES

1. Tetenbaum, T. J., Lighter, J., & Travis, M. Educators' attitude toward working mothers. JOURNAL OF EDUCATIONAL PSYCHOLOGY, 1981, 73, 369–375.

Review of Attitudes Toward Working Mothers Scale by MARK W. ROBERTS, Associate Professor of Psychology, Idaho State University, Pocatello, ID:

The proportion of women in the labor force has increased steadily for many decades. Millions of modern American children have working mothers. Such facts are clearly discrepant with the traditional perception of women as wives and mothers. If an individual believes that normal child development is best achieved by a traditional mother, that individual may impact negatively on the modern working mother and/or her children. The Attitudes Toward Working Mothers Scale (AWM) was constructed to measure adult beliefs about working mothers and the effects of maternal employment on the family.

The original AWM item pool consisted of 45 statements: 34 endorsed the benefits of traditional mothering; 11 supported a working mother role (Tetenbaum, Lighter, & Travis, 1983). For example, item 21 reads, "Mothers who stay home tend to be more patient and warmer than mothers who go to work." Subjects are asked to respond to each item on a 7-point scale with options ranging from "Disagree Strongly" to "Agree Strongly." The authors did not indicate how the items were generated. The 45 items were administered to a sample of 526 adults attending a graduate school of education in New York City. Data were subjected to a factor analysis. Since a unidimensional scale was desired, only items loading on the common factor were retained. The reliability of the subsequent 32-item scale was quantified by determining the item-test correlations (which ranged from .48 to .74) and scale internal consistency (coefficient alpha: .94 for females, .95 for males). Test reliability would, therefore, seem quite adequate. Unfortunately, such single measurement reliability indices are limited to quantifying interitem consistency and subject consistency to items and may be inflated by temporal sampling errors. Subject consistency across time on the AWM (e.g., test-retest reliability) is currently unknown. Further, the reliability statistics were obtained from the original sample, rather than a cross-validation sample. Therefore, the effects of subject sampling errors may also be spuriously contributing to the reliability statistics. Finally, all 11 items supporting working mothers were deleted by the item analysis strategy. Consequently, the final 32-item AWM Scale may be reactive to acquiescence response sets.

The 32-item AWM Scale was validated by the contrasted group criterion method (Tetenbaum et al., 1983). Female members of the National Organization for Women ($N=81$) were clearly more favorable toward working mothers on the AWM ($t=15.6$) than female members of the Right to Life Organization ($N=73$). Second, working subjects within the two organizations were consistently more positive toward employed mothers than those subjects who did not work. Third, female participants in the original graduate school sample, and in a second sample of suburban educators ($N=330$), significantly favored working women relative to male participants in the study (Tetenbaum, Lighter, & Travis, 1981). Finally, two additional, theoretically relevant contrasts were found in the two educational samples: younger teachers were more positive toward working mothers than older teachers; school counselors and school psychologists were more positive toward employed mothers than either teachers or administrators. The finding that teachers were more traditional in their attitudes than counselors was interpreted as potentially detrimental to children.

The AWM does not appear to measure the same cognitive dimension as scales assessing attitudes toward feminism (Tetenbaum et al., 1983). An additional sample of 60 education graduate students completed the AWM, the Attitudes Toward Women Scale—Short Form, the FEM Scale, and the Feminism II Scale. Discriminant validity coefficients between the AWM and the feminism measures were –.09, –.16, and –.25, respectively, with only the latter coefficient attaining significance ($p < .05$). (Negative correlations are a function of AWM scoring procedure.) The same sample of subjects also completed the Marlowe-Crowne Social Desirability Scale. The correlation with the AWM was .03. Unfortunately, this low correlation does not indicate that the AWM is unaffected by acquiescence response sets, as asserted by the AWM authors (Tetenbaum et al., 1981; Tetenbaum et al., 1983). It does suggest that the AWM does not measure the tendency to endorse socially desirable, yet unlikely items, or the converse.

The AWM represents a good initial effort to measure attitudes about the effects of maternal employment on the mother and family. The scale appears to measure a unidimensional cognitive construct. Total scale scores discriminate several theoretically relevant known groups. The scale does not appear to remeasure attitudes toward modern feminism. It is the only scale of its kind and is clearly relevant for research in diverse areas of social science. It is hoped that future research projects with this instrument will address the technical problems of temporal stability, acquiescence bias, and cross-validation of test statistics. Of critical importance will be efforts to validate the AWM Scale against criterion measurements involving the overt social behavior of those (e.g., employers, teachers) who affect the lives of working mothers and their children.

REVIEWER'S REFERENCES

Tetenbaum, T. J., Lighter, J. L., & Travis, M. Educators' attitudes toward working mothers. JOURNAL OF EDUCATIONAL PSYCHOLOGY, 1981, 73, 369–375.

Tetenbaum, T. J., Lighter, J., & Travis, M. The construct validation of an Attitudes Toward Working Mothers Scale. PSYCHOLOGY OF WOMEN QUARTERLY, 1983, 8, 69–78.

Review of Attitudes Toward Working Mothers Scale by CHARLES WENAR, Professor of Psychology, The Ohio State University, Columbus, OH:

The Attitudes Toward Working Mothers Scale (AWM) is a highly specialized, narrowly focused assessment technique. The authors begin by pointing out that scales evaluating attitudes toward the feminine role do not concentrate specifically on the mother-as-worker; therefore the need for the AWM. Furthermore, their study of discriminant validity shows that the correlation of AWM with three general measures of attitudes toward women, while statistically significant, account for only 3%, 1%, and 6% of the variance. Yet in subsequent discussions the authors tend to undermine their own case: in explaining a number of their empirical findings, such as men and Hispanics holding more traditional views of working mothers, they rely at times on studies of general attitudes toward the feminine role. Intuitively, it would seem reasonable to suppose that attitudes toward working mothers would be closely related to attitudes toward the feminine role in general rather than being compartmentalized. Thus, the need for a specialized test is not convincingly demonstrated and additional data would be desirable.

The Scale is narrowly focused as the name implies, treating primarily mothers-as-workers rather than working women in general. Most of the items are "children" oriented or "family" oriented. Thus, the scale does not encompass attitudes toward working women who are not mothers nor, within the context of working mothers, is much attention paid to the father or, for that matter, to the capabilities of the mother to do a job well.

The AWM has certain psychometric shortcomings. The source of the items comprising the scale is not mentioned. Reliability is measured only in terms of internal consistency whereas it would be highly desirable to have test-retest reliability also; in these changing times, investigators might well be interested in change in attitudes toward working mothers and should know how much variability is due to the AWM itself. Finally, both the basic factor analysis study and the "norms" for individual items are derived from a highly selected population—students attending a graduate School of Education. Since the authors have used the AWM with a more diverse population, it is hoped that they will eventually accumulate sufficient data to publish norms which are more representative than are the present ones.

Overall, the authors have done a conscientious job of constructing an instrument to evaluate attitudes toward working mothers (not working women as the title of the mimeographed paper states). Their validation studies have been ingenious and there is preliminary evidence of fruitful application. The narrowness of the AWM's focus is compensated for by its brevity. While test-retest reliability is needed as well as more representative populations for factor analytic studies and for norms, AWM may be used in its present form provided that investigators are aware of its limitations.

[100]

Auditory Discrimination Test. Ages 5–8; 1958–73; ADT; "ability to recognize the fine differences that exist between the phonemes used in English speech"; individual; orally administered; 2 forms; 2 editions; 1983 price data: $7.10 per 25 tests (specify form); $3.20 per manual; (5–10) minutes; Joseph M. Wepman; Western Psychological Services.*

a) ORIGINAL EDITION. 1958; Forms 1, 2, (2 pages); manual (4 pages).

b) 1973 REVISION. 1958–73; Forms 1A, 2A, ('73, 1 page); manual ('73, 10 pages).

See T3:226 (31 references), 8:932 (74 references), and T2:2028 (82 references); for a review by Louis M. DiCarlo of the original edition, see 6:940 (2 references).

TEST REFERENCES

1. Lyon, R., & Watson, B. Empirically derived subgroups of learning disabled readers: Diagnostic characteristics. JOURNAL OF LEARNING DISABILITIES, 1981, 14, 256–261.

2. Goldberg, T., & Benjamins, D. The possible existence of phonemic reading in the presence of Broca's aphasia: A case report. NEUROPSYCHOLOGIA, 1982, 20, 547–558.

3. Helper, M. M., Farber, E. D., & Feldgaier, S. Alternative thinking and classroom behavior of learning impaired children. PSYCHOLOGICAL REPORTS, 1982, 50, 415–420.

4. Kramer, V. R., & Schell, L. M. English auditory discrimination skills of Spanish-speaking children. THE ALBERTA JOURNAL OF EDUCATIONAL RESEARCH, 1982, 28, 1–8.

5. Eskenazi, B., & Diamond, S. P. Visual exploration of non-verbal material by dyslexic chilidren. CORTEX, 1983, 19, 353–370.

6. Prior, M. R., Frolley, M., & Sanson, A. Language lateralization in specific reading retarded children and backward readers. CORTEX, 1983, 19, 149–163.

[101]

Australian Chemistry Test Item Bank. Grades 11–12; 1982; consists of nearly 2,000 multiple choice items to assist teachers in preparing diagnostic and achievement tests; 2 volumes; no manual; 1983 price data: A$39 per complete set; $21 per volume if purchased separately; edited by C. Commons and P. Martin; Australian Council for Educational Research [Australia].*

a) VOLUME 1. Items in 14 areas: atomic structure, electronic structure, the periodic table, the mole and chemical formulae, molecular compounds, infinite arrays, gases, solutions, surfaces, stoichiometry, heat of reaction, chemical equilibrium, reaction rates, acids and bases; 1 form (199 pages).

b) VOLUME 2. Items in 12 areas: redox reactions, electrochemical cells, electrolysis, measurement and chemical techniques, carbon chemistry, silicon chemistry, nitrogen chemistry, phosphorus chemistry, oxygen chemistry, sulfur chemistry, halogen chemistry, metals; 1 form (197 pages).

Review of Australian Chemistry Test Item Bank by J. A. CAMPBELL, Seeley W. Mudd Professor of Chemistry, Harvey Mudd College, Claremont, CA:

These two volumes of 2,000 items effectively meet most of the requirements of a teacher looking for assistance in evaluating chemistry students. The coverage is both wide and deep. The questions are clear. Each question has been pre-tested and the results are included in the volumes. There is a sufficient number of items so that the set could be used over several years without the necessity for repetition, thus allowing variation in level from year to year as the teaching emphases and the nature of the student body vary.

There is a useful introductory section on methods for using the test bank. Possible uses, test preparation, item selection, writing additional test items, and the nature of the symbols and chemical nomenclature are all discussed. This three-page section should be very useful for any person using the work. The only suggestion with which this reviewer would disagree is that one should ensure that no item supplies a correct response for another item. There are many advantages in allowing the students to learn to apply what they have just observed to the next question or question series.

It is unfortunate that the item selected to explain a typical use has a less than satisfactory suggested answer. It would seem reasonable that this is why the "facility" index is only 20. (As used here, this means that 20% of the students answered the question appropriately.) The question asked is, "The most abundant product from the reaction of 2 mol of chlorine with 1 mol of methane in ultraviolet light is likely to be...." Then four choices of carbon compounds are given plus HCl. The suggested correct answer is HCl. On the other hand, many chemists would say that this is a by-product, not a product, of this reaction. The question could be made clear by making the first part of it read, "The most common molecule produced from the reaction of ...." It is problems like this that make objective tests very difficult to evaluate, to design for one's own students, and to grade in such a fashion that they truly represent the knowledge the students have accumulated in the course.

There is a detailed index of the contents of each of the 14 sections constituting the Item Bank. This makes finding the desirable questions a much simpler matter than is sometimes true. Each volume contains an index to both volumes, and this further simplifies the search.

It is clear that a great deal of thought, effort, and intelligent planning has been employed in organizing and presenting the questions. Almost any teacher interested in using this type of test item would find these two volumes a very valuable source. The great majority of the questions are along conventional lines and emphasize the fundamentals that most chemistry teachers believe are important at this level. The level itself corresponds to grades 11 and 12 in Australia and to approximately first-year college level (or advanced placement in high school) tests in the United States. In some areas the U.S. standard is surpassed, as for example in the area of surface chemistry and the use of electrophiles and nucleophiles for interpreting carbon chemistry. In other areas the most common U.S. level is not covered. For example, Latimer diagrams are not used nor is there much discussion of the transition metals and their chemistry, especially the nature of paramagnetism, color, and interpretation of the formation of transition metal complexes. But it is true that in most of the areas covered there are some imaginative questions which even teachers with great experience in test design will find stimulating.

This reviewer has never yet seen an objective test in which there were not some trivial items which should be changed to clarify the questions. Typically there are also several items which are seriously wrong. This collection has a smaller fraction of each of these than others which have been observed. There was no attempt to read and evaluate all 2,000 questions but several hundred were examined and it seems clear that about 1 in 20 could be considerably clarified. And 25% of that group need appreciable changes. The nature of the "trivial" clarifications would depend a great deal on the teacher and how the course had been taught. Furthermore, the changes would be minor for most teachers, and they could easily be done as part of the process of reproducing the items for the test.

Most of the serious changes result from too great a reliance on conventional chemistry as it has been taught for the last 20 years. It is very clear that a very competent group of teachers worked on this test, but the quality would have been further improved by involving some university teachers more acquainted with the current emphases in chemistry.

A typical example of the more serious type of problem is in the section on catalysis. One of the questions has as a response to "Addition of a catalyst to a chemical reaction" the excellent completion "allows the reaction to proceed by an alternative pathway." After all, the initial reaction continues even in the presence of a catalyst so that an alternative pathway is bound to give an overall faster rate. Unfortunately, in many of the test items there is a great emphasis on the statement that a catalyst lowers the activation energy. It is well established now that many enzyme catalysts actually raise the activation energy but, also raising the entropy of activation, tremendously increase the rate of reaction. These increases are, of course, greater than those obtainable by any catalyst developed by humans in their test tubes. The time has come when we must, even at the beginning level, begin to realize the importance of these changes.

One of the great changes in introductory chemistry in the last years has been an increased emphasis on kinetics. This is an excellent idea because real chemistry in terms of modern explorations is not so much stoichiometry of the reaction (as in the past), but in the mechanism. However, as with many other changes, this one has been introduced too fast by persons who are not well acquainted with the field. This leads to serious errors. There is in this set of test items a group of excellent questions on kinetics and mechanisms. There are also some very bad mechanisms (mostly involving much too complicated changes to occur in a single step) and misinterpretations of the likely kinetics of the situations. These are mentioned here not primarily to degrade this fine collection of questions, but to encourage both the authors and the users of these items to become more current on methods of approaching these subjects even at the introductory level.

One area which is not discussed at all is currently of great controversy in much of the world—Gibbs free energy and entropy. None of these test items seemed to mention either of these terms explicitly. The only reference found was to the word "disorder" in terms of why an endothermic reaction might occur. Many teachers would ardently agree that entropy and free energy are terms which can well be left out of introductory courses. It is more difficult to see why the ideas of spontaneity and available work as influenced both by energy transfer and tendency of chemicals to spread out or become disordered should be omitted. After all, the idea of exothermicity determining spontaneity was disposed of before the beginning of the 20th century.

There are so many good features in these test items that there is no point listing by number, or in any other way, those items which could be appreciably improved. Instead, it should be observed that there is a fine set of questions on laboratory methods and techniques, and there is frequent use of graphs and figures and some actual data. Essentially all the numerical problems can be done without a calculator or any external arithmetic help. Every effort seems to be made to encourage students to use their heads to arrive at a solution rather than to rely on external calculations. The most common method is to give several possible combinations of the data and merely ask the student to collect the right ones rather than making it necessary to do arithmetic to compare the student's answer with the answers given.

There are some unusual features which might easily be improved and which for the most part do not seriously handicap the use of the book. There is no standard number of alternative responses. The most common set is 4, but there are also 3, 5, and 6 answers from time to time. Furthermore, several questions allow the student to select one or more equally good responses rather than a single one. This clearly increases problems with answer sheets. It would also be helpful if the answers and the evaluation of each item in terms of its "facility" were not printed so close to the question. If they were slightly more removed it would be easier to photocopy the questions for inclusion in an examination. There is one problem on significant figures which was found, but in general there is little if any attention devoted to the importance of significant figures and to their use in solving problems. This is somewhat mitigated by the fact that students are not expected to do arithmetic. However, it might be possible for the students to learn more about significant figures if they were used more consistently in problem statements and suggested solutions.

For many secondary teachers there are also too few everyday examples in chemistry. Most of the problems are based on very conventional chemistry and tend to remind one of the statement that "if it weren't for hydrochloric and acetic acid, silver chloride, ammonia, and nitrogen dioxide it would be impossible to teach freshman chemistry." In much of the world there is a very great effort to introduce more interesting examples into the problems and it would be gratifying to see this represented in more of the test items.

With respect to photocopying, it would also be easier if the material were in a spiral bound, rather than rigidly bound, book, or the sheets were 3-hole punched so they could be removed and then replaced in the process of assemblying an exam.

For the most part, SI units are used so that some teachers will be unhappy that pascals, not atmospheres, appear in gas problems, and litres are almost never mentioned in volumetric problems.

In summary, this is a fine set of questions, with primary emphasis on the more conventional side of chemistry but still with a pleasant number of stimulating examples. The coverage is both wide enough and deep enough and the number great enough to serve as a productive source of items. Furthermore, the items are arranged, indexed, and evaluated in such a way that it is easy to assemble an examination for almost any area. Both the depth and breadth of coverage are sufficient that the great majority of introductory chemistry courses could be adequately evaluated with the items in this test bank. And, of course, as much photocopying as needed is allowed as long as the materials are then not sold for a profit.

Review of Australian Chemistry Test Item Bank by FRANK J. FORNOFF, Educational Testing Service, Princeton, NJ:

This publication is a collection of questions from which many tests can be assembled. A user selects the items that fit the particular needs of the moment. For each item there is a percentage correct—to one significant figure—based on the performances of Australian 12th graders. If an item had a biserial coefficient of less than .15 from the same administrations, this fact is also reported. These data may not be very useful for American test assemblers.

The questions are arranged by content areas. The questions classified into an area cover a good breath of the relevant topics in the area and a fair range of question difficulty. Most of the questions have four choices with one correct answer, but other formats are represented, and there are some questions designed to have more than one correct answer.

I was favorably impressed by the percentage of the questions that asked about familiar topics in ways that were unfamiliar to me. The availability of a periodic table during the administration of tests assembled from the collection must be considered. Some questions were designed to be used when the table is not available. The difficulties of others will depend on whether or not a table is in sight.

The questions make clear that a few chemical terms are different for Australian students than for Americans, but the number is not large. The number of questions that I considered to be defective (i.e., questions where the answer may be incorrectly recorded or where the distinction between two choices is more subtle than I like) is small. However, there are enough questions in the total collection that a teacher who builds tests from the collection should consider the chemical accuracy of the questions and the appropriateness of the chemical vocabulary as well as the fit of the questions to the topic being considered.

Faculty members of first chemistry courses in most colleges and universities will find many of the questions appropriate for their use.

Most of the questions from ACER Chemistry Item Collection: Year 12 (Chemtic), also reviewed in this edition of the *Mental Measurements Yearbook*, are included in this publication.

[102]

Australian Item Bank. Grades 8–12; 1978; AIB; teaching and evaluation materials in multiple choice format; 3 item banks; no norms; 1983 price data: A$100 per complete set; Australian Council for Educational Research [Australia].*

a) MATHEMATICS ITEM BANK. 1 form in 2 books, Book 1—arithmetic, algebra (324 pages), Book 2—abstract algebra, relations and functions, analysis, geometry, trigonometry, applied math, statistics and probability (462 pages); handbook (94 pages); $40 per mathematics item bank materials.

b) SCIENCE ITEM BANK. 1 form in 3 books, Book 1—physics and astronomy (332 pages), Book 2—earth sciences and chemistry (299 pages), Book 3—biology (220 pages); handbook (102 pages); $40 per science item bank materials.

c) SOCIAL SCIENCE ITEM BANK. 1 form (471 pages); handbook (35 pages); $20 per social science item bank materials.

Review of Australian Item Bank by PATRICIA NOLLER, *Lecturer in Psychology, University of Queensland, Australia:*

Development of an item bank is inevitably a monumental task, and the present example is no exception. The Australian Item Bank, covering three basic high school subject areas (science, mathematics, and social science) has involved the compilation of over 3,000 items suitable for students over eight states or territories and at least five different educational systems each with its own curriculum.

The main requirements of an item bank are comprehensiveness, ease of use, and accurate information about the items in the bank. Each of these issues will be taken up separately.

COMPREHENSIVENESS. In each of the basic areas the item bank is clearly comprehensive, with a large number of major relevant topics being covered in each area. Not only is a large range of content categories included, but items also vary with regard to the cognitive process involved in reaching the solution. For example, mathematics items are classified as involving recall, computation, comprehension, application, or analysis; while science items are classified as involving knowledge, comprehension, application, and higher processes. The Social Science Item Bank includes items involving eight different skills broadly classified under the headings of researching the problem, processing the data, and applying the findings. However, subcategories differ widely with regard to the number of items included, the range of difficulty level involved in the items, the percentage of items which have been trial-tested (and thus include data on difficulty level), and the range of different cognitive processes involved in answering the items.

EASE OF USE. The Australian Item Bank is made up of three manuals and six attractive loose-leaf binders (in a different colour for each of the three basic areas), which enable pages of questions to be easily removed for photocopying, and extra pages of questions to be added as necessary. Most subcategories (or units) begin on a new page, and this means that new items can generally be filed with other questions on the same topic.

A hierarchical numbering system is used to indicate the category, subcategory, etc. to which an item belongs, and, as a result, each item has a six (mathematics and science) or seven (social science) digit number as its unique identifier. In addition, other numbers or codes are also presented to indicate the particular cognitive skill being tested, the difficulty of the item, and the correct answer. As there are no headings at all throughout the item bank to indicate the beginning of categories or subcategories, teachers wishing to use the item bank may find that they spend a lot of time referring back to the content classifications, at least initially, as well as to the codes for the other information. Certainly ease of use could have been improved by greater use of headings and of verbal codes. It may be that the compilers considered that the use of headings would limit the ease of photocopying the items. Such a consideration would seem to be secondary to increasing the ease of use of the items, particularly since items would generally need to be cut and headings could easily be removed.

Users are also advised to rely on the abridged content codings in the front of each volume rather than those in the manual since in some instances the codes provided in the manual contain more numbers than are actually used in the unique identifiers, and users may become confused. For example, science content classifications are listed in the manual as though they are specific to five digits, but only three of these digits are actually used in the identifying numbers. Relying only on the instructions at the beginning of each volume makes the item bank considerably easier to use.

For both the science and social science volumes of the item bank, items are given alternative classifications when this is appropriate. However, it is unclear how teachers would find these items unless they went searching through related areas. A better system could be to list the numbers of other appropriate items at the end of each topic. In the social science volume an index is provided which partly solves the problem.

A further problem is created by the fact that different numbering systems are used in each of the basic areas. However, since the main differences are between the social science items and other items the problem may not be too serious, since different teachers would likely be using the social science bank from those using the other volumes.

ACCURACY OF INFORMATION ABOUT ITEMS. While many of the items in the item bank have been pretested so that the difficulty level (facility) of the items could be calculated, there are also many items which have not been pretested, although such items have been "subjected to rigorous review and editing sessions aimed at improving quality and removing possible ambiguities" (see Foreward to manuals). A relatively small sample ($N = 300$) has been used for pretesting the items and no data is presented regarding whether any attempt was made to ensure that students of varying levels of ability participated in the trials. Schools may have provided only their best students for the trials and difficulty levels would be affected by such a procedure.

The manuals provide some interesting information for users about the various ways the items can be used—for achievement tests, for diagnostic tests to pick up areas where students are having problems, as tests designed to evaluate teaching methods, or as groups of questions to stimulate class discussion. Some basic techniques of test construction are also presented and users are encouraged to set clear goals for tests, and to set up content/process grids so that they can ensure an appropriate spread of items for each content area over each type of process as far as possible. Item analysis procedures are also provided so that teachers can conduct their own trials on their own students and can efficiently file information about each question.

All in all, the Australian Item Bank should prove a valuable resource for teachers in the areas of mathematics, science, and social science. The item bank is comprehensive and provides indications of the difficulty level (facility) of the items; for teachers who are prepared to spend the time getting to know the system, it should prove relatively easy to use.

[103]

Australian Second Language Proficiency Ratings. Adolescents and adults; 1982–84; ASLPR; "criterion-referenced"; ratings by teachers; 4 subscales: Speaking, Listening, Reading, Writing; no norms; individual; 1 form ('82, 26 pages); manual ('84, 62 pages); mimeographed technical data paper ('82, 174 pages); mimeographed article ('82, 41 pages); 1984 price data: A$2.50 per manual; $60 per video set which introduces and illustrates the test; French, Italian, and Japanese versions ('82) available; administration time not reported; D. E. Ingram and Elaine Wylie; Australian Department of Immigration and Ethnic Affairs [Australia].*

[104]

Australian Test for Advanced Music Studies. Tertiary education entrance level; 1974–78; ATAMS; 3 tests, 4 scores: 3 scores listed below plus total; report and handbook ('78, 97 pages); separate answer sheets must be used; 1980 price data: A$2.50 per set of tests; $25 per set of tapes; $.50 per set of keys; $5 per report and handbook; (180) minutes; test by Doreen Bridges and Bernard Rechter with the assistance of Jennifer Knight; Australian Council for Educational Research [Australia].*

a) BOOK 1: TONAL AND RHYTHM MEMORY AND MUSICAL PERCEPTION. 1 form ('74, 11 pages and 1 7/8 ips tape recording); 43(55) minutes.

b) BOOK 2: AURAL/VISUAL DISCRIMINATION, SCORE READING AND UNDERSTANDING OF NOTATION. 1 form ('74, 19 pages and 1 7/8 ips tape recording); 48(53) minutes.

c) BOOK 3: COMPREHENSION AND APPLICATION OF LEARNED MUSIC MATERIAL. 1 form ('74, 10 pages and 1 7/8 ips tape recording); 40(45) minutes.

See T3:233 (1 reference); for a review by Roger P. Phelps, see 8:91.

Review of Australian Test for Advanced Music Studies by RICHARD COLWELL, Professor of

Music and Education, University of Illinois at Urbana, Urbana, IL:

The Australian Test for Advanced Music Studies was developed to screen prospective music majors for Australian colleges and universities; therefore its content and criterion-related validity should be better assessed and interpreted through examination of the Australian context. Entrance to the study of music in Australia is based on a rigorous preparatory program. A music syllabus is published by the Board of Senior School Studies which is as demanding as many U.S. college music history and theory sequences. Content validity data offered in the ATAMS manual must be judged knowing that the high school seniors tested had completed not only this rigorous course of study but had taken rigorous aural tests that included the ability to hear cadences, harmonic progressions, and texture. Content validity for Australian students would likely be less applicable in other settings.

ATAMS was designed to contrast with the Australian Music Examinations Board test, a test based largely on eighteenth and nineteenth century European music and which measures the student's ability to identify the "elements" of music. That this objective was attained is a major accomplishment. ATAMS is interesting to take, uses a wide variety of music, has some objectives for everyone, and is likely to be accepted on face value by the music profession. No table of specification appears to have been used, however, to aid in selection or weight of the various skills tested. Knowledge of music terminology is an objective that is not tested separately. The student must know and apply terminology in answering; thus, failure to answer a question correctly could be due to lack of aural skills or to inadequate knowledge to label the stimulus heard.

The stated uses of the test are: (*a*) as an adjunct to existing selection procedures, (*b*) as a diagnostic instrument, (*c*) as an evaluation of the progress of students, and (*d*) "as an objective measure which can be used with students transferring between different institutions and states." Supporting data in the manual are inadequate for any use except as an adjunct to selection procedures. With only a single question on some aural skills, any diagnostic interpretation (use *b*) would be tentative at best. Use *c* would be risky as the test has not been given to students with limited musical training, and no investigation has been conducted controlling the amount or type of training to allow the user to interpret "progress." It is not clear what use would be made of test data for students transferring between institutions (use *d*). Even the evidence of the test's usefulness in selecting students for tertiary study is thin; data are based on a sample of 68 advanced music students. This nonrandom group consisted of postgraduate music students and undergraduates, these students scoring significantly better than high school seniors. The primary test author reported (in private correspondence) that Australian colleges using the test appear to be satisfied with the test when the data are used to differentiate among students. She does not believe, however, that systematic data have been gathered. Administration of the test to 138 University of Illinois music students tends to confirm the hypothesis that older students do better. The gain by American students which occurred in the first two years was more likely from sample mortality than a systematic treatment. Range of scores was stable, hinting at the influence of aptitude. This facet was not investigated by the test developers.

The data provided in the test manual come from two administrations of the test, 1974 and 1975. Unfortunately the sample size in 1975 (the only group to take the published test) was only 279, slightly more than half the size of the 1974 group ($N = 461$).

Internal reliability (KR 20) is adequate, typically ranging from .78 to .82 (with one exception), for each of the three test "books." An American student sample yielded approximately the same level of reliability.

The test manual carefully describes the rationale used in the test construction and compares ATAMS with other published tests. The manual, however, has some rather serious omissions, the most egregious being the lack of any report of standard error, a requisite when the results are to be used for individual rather than group measurement. The test is not criterion-referenced (no mention of cutoff scores) and the authors emphasize discrimination. No norms are provided, however, limiting its use as a norm-referenced test. Test data and interpretations are consistently for group measurement, which puts the manual in conflict with the stated purposes and uses. Item analysis data are provided only for the total sample, not by the subgroups used to establish the validity of the test: keyboard versus nonkeyboard, experienced versus less experienced, and male versus female.

A sex difference was found in favor of the males but a two-way ANOVA was not conducted. Major instrument, state, and experience, however, were compared using ANOVA. The authors inspected the impact of aural training on test scores and concluded that training makes little difference. Had they properly used total means rather than the means of the five separate states, the conclusion would have changed. The authors decided not to systematically compare first year students with advanced students because of a difference in sample size, 68 and 279. It does not appear, however, that any ANOVA assumption would have been violated. Some statistical treatments cited in the manual should have been omitted due to inadequate sample size. Data based on sample sizes of 5 and 8 may mislead the reader. No statement is made concerning results of factor analysis.

Selection of items for the test was strongly influenced by results of the item analysis. There were times, however, when a desire to measure a particular skill became more important than the data, e.g., (*a*) on page 54 of the manual, the authors provide a weak justification for inclusion of items with negative discrimination; (*b*) inter-item correlations would have provided better data for decisions; (*c*) a wide range of music was retained contrary to data that indicated the test would be more discriminating had familiar music been used; and (*d*) the authors suggested that pianists are apparently less able than other music students to transfer concepts to unfamiliar music. More information is needed, however, before any such conclusions can be drawn.

A rather capricious decision was made to weight one third of the items in Book 1. The authors state that "items which required subjects to compare a number of musical examples or to attend to several aspects of one example were given twice as much weight." This means that Book 1 with 30 items has 40% of the total score. Questions in Book 2 require that students will "hear in the mind two themes printed in the question book and will recognize and identify material derived from these themes, in each of three short extracts from the work in which they all occur." In Book 3 questions included "listen to two short jazz examples, and indicate whether one or both use the chord progression of the twelve-bar 'blues,' printed in Roman figures in the question book." These questions appear to be as complicated as a question that requires a student to "indicate which of three examples of ethnic music are likely to be performed by the same ethnic group from the same country," which is a weighted Book 1 question.

With item analysis so critical to their decision making process, it is surprising that the authors were satisfied when 10 of the 30 items in Book 1 had a discrimination index lower than .2. When Book 1 item analysis data are compared with the total score for Book 1 only, there are still seven items with discrimination less than .2.

A major concern must be the independence of the three books in this test battery and the independence of the battery from extant measures. The reported correlation between ATAMS and the Aliferis Music Achievement Test, College Entrance Level is .733. This is surprisingly high. Any prospective user must consider that the Aliferis test requires less than 50 minutes to administer while *each* of the three books of ATAMS requires 50 minutes.

The authors report that the correlation between Book 3 and the total battery is .88. Using students as the basis of the inter-test correlations, correlation coefficients were obtained of .51 between Books 1 and 2; .53 between 1 and 3; and .73 between 2 and 3. Use of items (computed by this reviewer) rather than students raises the correlation among the three books to .97 with Spearman and .87 with Kendall. Book 1, which does not require the use of music, and which evaluates one's ability to remember music (i.e., memory for phrases and patterns) does appear to have sufficient independence; the high correlation between Books 2 and 3 raises serious questions about the amount of information gained in relation to the testing time expended. Even though the authors suggested that 16 different skills are evaluated in Book 2 and 13 more in Book 3, they have music in common.

Factor analysis computed on the 138 responses obtained at the University of Illinois provides evidence that there are some good factor structures in the test. In Book 3, one obtains interval as a factor for the first 6 questions and a rather strong interval loading for the first 10. Meter/phrases is strong for questions 16 and 17, and a cognitive historical knowledge factor is present in questions 24–27.

The ATAMS is an attractive test and is likely to be accepted as a valid achievement test by the practicing music educator. The test does have many strengths but it appears to be unnecessarily redundant. In music listening tests, one or two items do provide more stable information than can be obtained with one or two cognitive questions in other subjects, yet the large number of skills measured is a concern. Additional data are needed before the ATAMS test user can be sure what it is that he/she is testing and how valid the resulting scores are for making decisions on an individual's music capacity and/or past attainment.

Review of Australian Test for Advanced Music Studies by WALTER L. WEHNER, Professor of Music and Director, Graduate Studies in Music, University of North Carolina at Greensboro, Greensboro, NC:

The Australian Test For Advanced Music Studies is a relatively recent (1974) musical achievement test designed to measure musical experiences of graduating high school students or entering college students. The criteria used for the development of the test includes: (*a*) the necessity for developing a completely objective test (no questions requiring either respondents or markers to make value judgments); (*b*) the utilization of questions based on musical material in a musical context; (*c*) music selected to represent a wide range of periods and cultures and performed by a variety of voices/instruments, (*d*) emphasis placed on aural abilities, (*e*) for learned musical material, a focusing on questions related to abilities to conceptualize, apply, and generalize knowledge of and about music; and finally, (*f*) exclusion of material relating to the testing of factual knowledge only. By using the criteria indicated above, test content was developed that required respondents to demonstrate ability to (*a*) read music, understand the printed score, and correlate sounds with their notation; (*b*) recognize aurally such musical elements as scales, basic chords, tonality, and durational aspects like meter, note values, tempo, etc.; (*c*) comprehend and apply terminology in common use; (*d*) demonstrate oral recognition of instruments, mode of performance, sound sources, instrumental combinations, principles of organization, and stylistic characteristics of well-known composers, and same/different styles of unfamiliar music; and (*e*) utilize aural imagery and memory.

The test is divided into three parts called "Books." In Book I, questions are included to test musical skills and abilities related to aural imagery and memory, both tonal and rhythmic; and perception of instrumental timbre, inner or lower parts in a musical texture, and likenesses/differences between music of various periods and styles. It is mentioned that this section requires no knowledge of notation or musical terminology and that the results may give some indication of the potential of students who have had little formal musical education. This element may be one of the more significant aspects of the test, since most of the achievement measures of the past required extensive musical training prior to testing.

Book II includes testing which measures score reading and aural-visual discrimination ability, the ability to read and understand musical notation, and to hear in the mind the sounds represented by visual symbols.

Book III measures comprehension and application of learned musical material (including aural recognition of intervals, scale patterns, tonality, triadic chords and the dominant seventh and time signatures), presented in a musical context; aural discrimination between sonata/concerto/symphony/quartet, etc.; and between styles of particular composers.

In addition to the usual Western music emphasis in achievement tests, this test contains examples of contemporary music including blues and jazz, folk music, ranges of styles including Renaissance music along with vocal and instrumental music of various types and combinations. It measures musical experiences of a variety of kinds, and this alone can make it a valuable test for the more broadly educated high school student or the entering college student. Also, actual musical examples are used rather than electronically produced sounds, which have been questioned with respect to relevancy of purpose in musical achievement testing.

The technical data in the Report and Handbook include thorough coverage of the reliability and validity of the test. Included are inter-test correlations, reliability coefficients (KR 20), validity coefficients with other tests, and an analysis of variance which provides evidence of significant discrimination between advanced music students and those of lesser experience.

The ATAMS has various qualities which are superior to other music achievement tests, and its use should prove to be beneficial to the entire field of music achievement testing. The recordings are excellent—clear and distinct. The directions are easily understood, with examples demonstrating each new exercise. Probably the test will have much use in the United States.

[105]

Autism Screening Instrument for Educational Planning, (First Edition). Preschool and school aged severely handicapped and autistic; 1978–80; ASIEP; 5 subtest scores: autism behavior checklist, sample of vocal behavior, interaction assessment, educational assessment of functional skills, prognosis of learning rate; individual; 1 form; examiner's manual ('80, 123 pages); student scoring and record form booklet ('80, 6 pages); 1984 price data: $176 per complete kit; additional manuals, data forms, etc., may be purchased upon request; administration time not reported; David A. Krug, Joel R. Arick, and Patricia J. Almond; ASIEP Education Co.*

TEST REFERENCES

1. Scanlon, C. A., Arick, J. R., & Krug, D. A. A matched sample investigation of nonadaptive behavior of severely handicapped adults across four living situations. AMERICAN JOURNAL OF MENTAL DEFICIENCY, 1982, 86, 526–532.

Review of Autism Screening Instrument for Educational Planning, (First Edition) by LAWRENCE J. TURTON, Professor of Speech Pathology, Indiana University of Pennsylvania, Indiana, PA:

The Autism Screening Instrument for Educational Planning (ASIEP) was designed to assist educators in the process of identifying autistic children and developing an appropriate educational plan in conformity with P.L. 94–142. It is divided into five sections: Autism Behavior Checklist, Sample of Vocal Behavior, Interaction Assessment, Educational Assessment of Functional Skills, and Prognosis of Learning Rate. The authors describe it as an educational extension of a medical diagnosis of autism; as an instrument to prescribe a program for a child who is educationally placed after the diagnosis. They also argue that the ASIEP can be used to differentially diagnose autism from other handicaps, especially other severe handicaps.

The ASIEP is one of the finest examples of a checklist instrument available today. The meticulous care with which Krug, Arick, and Almond developed this instrument is a model for all professionals who set out to design a systematic observation tool for difficult-to-test (and treat) children. Indeed, it has value not only as an educational programming tool for autistic children, but also as an instructional guide for college-level faculty teaching prospective educators and school psychologists. The items contained in each section are a comprehensive list of autistic-like behaviors and can be used to teach college students the characteristics of autism, how to assess behavioral patterns, and how to determine their relative importance. The authors have demonstrated very clearly that severe learning problems can be reliably assessed and analyzed. They are to be commended for their efforts.

The manual is a prototype of how to develop a standardized checklist. The original items for the Autism Behavior Checklist were selected from the existing literature on the characteristics of autism. All references and sources are clearly indicated by their authors. The preliminary set was evaluated by a small sample of professionals, refined, standardized on a sample of checklists completed by 1,049 professionals, refined again, and re-standardized on a total sample of 2,002 completed checklists. A final list of 57 behavioral characteristics evolved from this process.

Data are available on content validity, concurrent validity, criterion-related validity, and reliability for each section. Most of the statistical results conform to the *Standards for Educational and Psychological Tests.* Cutoff scores are presented for the Autism Behavior Checklist (ABC) and for each of the other sections relative to the ABC values. The testing results can be quickly and easily interpreted by an educator and the items in the list can then be used for educational programming.

Krug, Arick, and Almond repeatedly stress the fact that the ASIEP should be administered by a trained examiner. Although they do not specify the discipline, this reviewer interprets that comment to mean a school psychologist or an experienced teacher of autistic children, not a novice. They provide clear, explicit instructions in the manual for administering each section of the test and specific scoring standards that should be readily understandable to anyone familiar with the behaviors of autistic children. A Practice Videotape is available from the authors for training an examiner to score the Interaction Assessment section. The summary profiles are easy to interpret and to use for comparing a child's performance levels to the expected patterns for autistic children.

There are some minor shortcomings to the ASIEP. The scoring sheets for the Autism Behavior Checklist and the Sample of Vocal Behaviors are each compressed into one page by using extremely small, single-spaced print. Double-spacing and larger print would ease the examiner's task when actually confronted with a child. The plastic toys in the kit will undoubtedly require frequent replacement.

The ASIEP is recommended for clinical use without qualification. It is a remarkable instrument because it clearly demonstrates that severely handicapped children can be reliably and validly assessed in a school setting. Despite the fact that it is labelled as a screening instrument, it comprehensively assesses the developmental behaviors that are of greatest importance to the classroom teacher; the data can be used to develop coherent instructional programs for the children. The authors are to be commended for their efforts in test development and should be given a special nod of appreciation by educational personnel.

Review of Autism Screening Instrument for Educational Planning, (First Edition) by RICHARD L. WIKOFF, Professor of Psychology, University of Nebraska at Omaha, Omaha, NE:

PURPOSE AND NATURE OF THE TEST. The Autism Screening Instrument for Educational Planning is an individually administered instrument designed for use at the public school level to identify autistic children. There are actually five separately standardized scales. The Autism Behavior Checklist is to be used for identification of the autistic child and the other four subscales are recommended to determine a child's functioning level. The subscales can be used for diagnosis, placement, planning programs, and analysis of progress of autistic children.

The Autism Behavior Checklist contains 57 behavior descriptors which are to be marked if they are descriptive of the child. It takes from 10 to 20 minutes to administer. The items are weighted according to how predictive they are of autism. Five subscores and a total score are determined by adding the weights. The scores are recorded on a profile in order to make comparisons against several groups including: autistic, normal, deaf-blind, severely mentally handicapped, and severely emotionally disturbed.

The sample of Vocal Behavior subscale takes about 30 minutes to complete. During this time the examiner records all vocalizations which occur. Several categories are scored by counting frequencies of certain types of vocalizations.

The use of the Interaction Assessment subscale requires a second person in addition to the examiner to code responses. This subscale uses a time sampling technique. Cues are given by a tape recorder to indicate when the child's behavior should be observed. The type of interactive behavior manifested at specific times is recorded on an interaction profile data sheet. About 12 minutes is required for the administration of this part of the inventory.

The child's functioning level in five areas can be assessed using the Educational Assessment subscale. These five areas are: In-Seat activity, Receptive Language, Expressive Language, Body Concept, and Speech Imitation. Various stimuli and commands similar to those used in the Bayley Mental Development Scales are used to elicit responses. Correct responses are recorded with a 1 and incorrect responses are given a 0. The score for each area is the count of the correct responses. Administration of this subscale requires 10 to 20 minutes.

Several sessions are required to administer the Prognosis of Learning Rate subscale. Each session lasts about 15 minutes. There is a pre-training session in which the child is taught hand shaping. This is followed by up to four learning sessions. Finally, a posttest is given. The number of correct and incorrect trials is to be recorded during each of these periods. Raw scores are the number of correct responses. These can be converted into percentile ranks.

PRACTICAL EVALUATION. The instrument comes with a kit which contains the manual, record forms, and various materials used in administering the subscales. These are all contained in a cardboard box which is inconvenient to open and close and which would wear out rather quickly. The manual is reasonably well designed and appears to be durable. The content is logically organized. For each subscale there are four sections: Introduction, Administration, Interpreting the Results, and Educational Application. Standardization data are given for each subscale in an appendix.

The inventory would not be difficult to administer but would require some training and prior practice with the scales. The authors recommend that the examiner be a "professional" person who has had several weeks of experience with the child being assessed. They do not explain what "professional" means, but it is assumed that it refers to a person who works with autistic children such as a teacher, therapist, and so forth. The directions are at times rather general and extensive, but are stated clearly enough that they can be easily followed. Scoring is simple. In most cases it involves counting or recording the occurrence of a behavior. The test has face validity and encourages rapport.

TECHNICAL EVALUATION. In order to get a sample of autistic children, professionals were solicited for their cooperation and they administered the scales and returned them to the authors. In the initial study 1,049 Autism Behavior Checklists were returned. This included: 100 normals, 423 severely mentally retarded, 254 emotionally disturbed, 100 deaf-blind, and 172 autistic children. Two additional studies were reported. The sample size for the other subscales ranged from 115 to 177. In some cases more than one study was reported. While the sample is not random, it is probably as representative as one can get for such a limited population.

Norms are provided for each of the subscales. The Autism Behavior Checklist utilizes profile comparisons for different age groups. Percentiles are provided for each of the other subscales.

The reliability of the subscales was based on small samples in some cases, but was impressive. Split-half reliability for the Autism Behavior Checklist was .94. There was 95% interrater agreement on the scoring. The other subscales had reliabilities ranging from .81 to .97, with interrater agreements ranging from 84 to 100%.

Content validity was assured by comparison of items with previously developed checklists, by review of professionals, and by chi-square analysis. For the Autism Behavior Checklist, concurrent validity was assessed using analysis of variance to compare autistic children against several other groups. The results were highly significant. What the authors called criterion-related validity was assessed by counting the number of persons in a second independent sample whose behavior checklist scores were within one standard deviation of the mean for the first sample. Criterion-related validity was determined for the Sample of Vocal Behavior subscale by correlation with the Autism Behavior Checklist and with the Sequenced Inventory of Communication Development (SICD). A multiple correlation of the subparts with the Autism Behavior Checklist was .49. The correlation with SICD was .81. The validity of the other scales was inadequately treated. The authors discussed what they call cross-validity, but their meaning is not the same as that defined by current psychometric theory. They are referring to correlations between various subscales of the inventory. The weakest part of the manual is the discussion of validity. Further studies are needed.

SUMMARY. The Autism Screening Instrument for Educational Planning was developed for the identification and evaluation of autistic children within public schools. It would be useful for identifying autistic preschool children, also. Of the five scales included in the instrument, the best subscale is the Autism Behavior Checklist. It was standardized on a much larger sample and its validity and reliability are better documented. Its major weakness is in its interpretation. Neither percentiles nor standard scores are provided. Raw scores are interpreted using profile comparison and cutoff scores are suggested. The sample sizes of the other subscales are inadequate and incomplete technical data are provided. However, they have promise. They have a sound theoretical basis and the minimal information provided is impressive. In spite of these problems, the scale might be used cautiously by trained professionals. However, further studies related to validity and reliability are needed.

[106]

Ball Aptitude Battery. Senior high school and adults; 1981; BAB; for vocational guidance and employee placement decisions; profile of 12 skill ability tests: Clerical, Idea Fluency, Inductive Reasoning, Word Association, Writing Speed, Paper Folding, Vocabulary, Ideaphoria, Finger Dexterity, Grip, Shape Assembly, Analytical Reasoning; standard scores used for comparisons with norms from standardized sample; administration by qualified BAB-trained users; administrators manual (42 pages); technical manual (38 pages); scoring manual provided only to qualified users; price data available from publisher; (5–15) minutes for most tests, (180) minutes for battery; Yong H. Sung, Rene V. Dawis, and Thomas E. Dohm; Ball Foundation.*

TEST REFERENCES

1. Dohm, T. E., & Sung, Y. H. CONCURRENT, DIFFERENTIAL, AND CONSTRUCT VALIDITIES OF THE BALL APTITUDE TESTS. Technical Report No. 5. Wheaton, IL: Ball Foundation, June, 1980.

2. Sung, Y. H., & Dawis, R. V. Level and factor structure differences in selected abilities across race and sex groups. JOURNAL OF APPLIED PSYCHOLOGY, 1981, 66, 613–624.

3. Dohm, T. E., & Sung, Y. H. THE CONSTRUCT VALIDATION OF THE BALL APTITUDE BATTERY. Paper presented at meeting of the American Psychological Association, Washington DC, August, 1982.

4. Sung, Y. H., & Dawis, R. V. ACTIVITIES AS DETERMINERS OF ABILITIES AND INTERESTS. Paper presented at meeting of the American Psychological Association, Washington, DC, August, 1982.

5. Sung, Y. H., Dawis, R. V., & Dohm, T. E. ABILITY TEST PERFORMANCE AND TEST VALIDITY DIFFERENCES AMONG SEX AND ETHNIC GROUPS. Paper presented at the Multi-Ethnic Conference on Assessment, Tampa, FL, March, 1982.

Review of Ball Aptitude Battery by PHILIP G. BENSON, Assistant Professor of Psychology, Auburn University, Auburn, AL:

The Ball Aptitude Battery (BAB) is a relatively new multiple aptitude test battery that was published by the Ball Foundation in 1976. Twelve tests are included, two of which (Finger Dexterity and Grip) yield separate scores for right and left hands. Thus, a total of 14 scores are derived from the complete battery.

The publishers have developed reasonably good technical and administrator's manuals to accompany the BAB. For example, the Administrator's Manual gives normative data for each test broken down into 24 separate sample groupings. Some of the groups are somewhat small, especially for adult age groups, but overall the data are sufficient for typical applications of the BAB. The Administrator's Manual also includes good information for giving instructions, answering questions during testing, etc. Since the BAB is only available to administrators trained by the Ball Foundation, standardization is reasonably well assured.

The Technical Manual is acceptable, but possibly less helpful than the Administrator's Manual. Its major shortcoming is that the level of expertise assumed for users is unclear. In places it seems to be appropriate for relatively unsophisticated readers, while at other places it seems somewhat more advanced. Readers who can comprehend the entire manual are likely to feel portions are simplistic; readers who do not feel they are being "talked down to" are likely to have difficulty comprehending some portions of the manual.

The clearest competitor for the BAB is likely the Differential Aptitude Tests (DAT); however, the two are not strictly comparable. In particular, the DAT has eight tests which are more focused on cognitive abilities; the psychomotor tests of the BAB (i.e., Finger Dexterity, Grip) are distinctive. In general, the BAB has tests of considerable variety, which theoretically should aid in differential prediction from the complete battery. However, greater empirical verification of this last feature is necessary before definitive statements can be made.

Numerous studies have been conducted on the BAB through the Ball Foundation. To date, the research is of good quality and reasonably supportive of the BAB. In the opinion of this reviewer, a greater emphasis on occupational settings for this research, and less on educational settings, would be useful.

The Ball Foundation has taken the position, stated in the Administrator's Manual, that "selection and placement of individuals by an organization [using the BAB] must be supported by research and must be based on data collected in the organization itself." Thus, potential users and researchers with interests in validity generalization or synthetic validation may have difficulty in obtaining the BAB for such use. The appropriateness of this stance by the publisher is best evaluated by individual test users, as either position can be argued.

Overall, the BAB is a reasonable test battery. The DAT has a greater wealth of supporting data, and for this reason it may be preferable unless the unique tests of the BAB seem of particular interest. In any case, additional research on the BAB, especially by individuals not affiliated with the Ball Foundation, would be a useful contribution.

Review of Ball Aptitude Battery by WILBUR L. LAYTON, Professor and Chair, Department of Psychology, Iowa State University, Ames, IA:

The authors of the Ball Aptitude Battery (BAB) deserve both commendations and condolences. The development of a new multiaptitude test battery to compete with the Differential Aptitude Tests, the Comprehensive Ability Battery, and other well established aptitude tests is a commendable and ambitious undertaking. However, condolences are offered because the task of developing a new test battery is arduous and complex, and requires a long time for the development process.

Emphasis should be placed on development because the reviewed test battery is still in the process of evolving. The test authors began with 15 tests. Three tests (Tonal Memory, Pitch Discrimination, and Hand and Eye Dominance) were eventually deleted. Another test, Numerical Ability, recently has been added to the BAB. However, this test is being researched and no data on it is available to this reviewer.

What guided the selection of specific tests to be developed is not clear. Previous research and definition of aptitudes would suggest that verbal, numerical, spatial, mechanical, and perceptual aptitudes, along with dexterity measures, would be the first to be considered for inclusion. For unknown reasons the authors decided to delay construction of numerical tests.

The Technical Manual begins with an excellent presentation, "The Concept of Aptitude and Its Measurement." The authors begin with the concept of "skill" and proceed to a technical definition of "aptitude": "A skill is an identifiable, repeatable response (or behavior) sequence that is manifested by the individual under the eliciting demand of a 'task'....A task is a demand on the individual either to produce a certain product or outcome, or to proceed (that is, to behave) in a prescribed manner. The demand can come from the environment or from the self. In a sense, the task defines the skill in that the skill is the individual's response to the task....our ability measurements can be used to estimate the individuals' potential standing on the skill, in short, their skill potential. Potential for a skill is what we mean by aptitude."

After the theoretical definition of aptitudes the test authors looked to the work of Johnson O'Connor (1935). O'Connor believed that aptitudes are demonstrated in a person's performance on selected work samples. Several of the first tests tried out for possible inclusion in the Ball Aptitude Battery were either adapted or modified from O'Connor's work. No further rationale for the inclusion of specific aptitudes is given.

The authors are to be commended for the concern shown throughout test development about possible sex and racial differences in their tests.

Data for item analyses were obtained on a heterogeneous sample of 1,600 individuals. The standardization samples were derived from a testing of about 1,000 high school students from 20 high schools in Illinois and 16 high schools in Texas. A subsample of 600 students was selected to make up the standardization sample. It consisted of 100 Black females, 100 Black males, 100 Hispanic females, 100 Hispanic males, 100 White females, and 100 White males. Furthermore, each sex-ethnic group was chosen so that all groups would be similar in socioeconomic status.

A standard score scale with a mean of 100 and standard deviation of 20 was adopted. The standard scores are linear transformations from raw score means and standard deviations of the total standardization sample. The excellent Administrator's Manual presents raw score to standard score conversions for each test and norm tables of percentiles corresponding to standard scores for each test for each of 24 norm groups including the several subgroups of the standardization sample.

Detailed scoring procedures are not described in the Administrator's Manual. A separate scoring manual is available only to qualified users who have been trained to administer the BAB.

RELIABILITY. Test-retest reliabilities for the BAB tests are reported in the Technical Manual. The reliability of the Vocabulary test was estimated through the use of alternate forms. All reliability estimates are based on a sample of 261 persons with 6-week intervals between testings. Reliability coefficients for males and females and the total sample are given. However, standard errors of measurement are given only for the total sample. It would be desirable to have standard errors for the various subgroups for which norms are given because there are considerable differences in test-retest reliability for males and females. For example, the reliability of the Word Association test is .82 for males and .51 for females. The Writing Speed reliability is .63 for males and .77 for females. Standard errors would be significantly different. There may be further differences for other subgroups. The reliabilities for the total group vary from .64 for Word Association to .98 for Vocabulary (Alternate Forms). Four of the coefficients are in the .85 to .98 range; six are in the .70s, and two are .64 and .69. For males, the coefficients range from .63 to .97. For females, they range from .51 to .98. The four tests with high reliabilities are satisfactory for use in making decisions about individuals. The remainder should be used with caution. Further investigation of the reliabilities of the tests is needed for the obvious reason that test-retest estimates confound characteristics of tests and of persons.

VALIDITY. The Technical Manual includes useful discussion of various kinds of validity such as construct and practical validity. The authors have investigated practical validity through concurrent validity studies relating the BAB to academic performance of high school students. As one might expect, the Vocabulary test had the highest relationship to overall grades. Multiple correlations between grade criteria and from three to four of the BAB tests range from .33 to .54. These correlations are no better than what would be expected from a good scholastic aptitude test. Correlations between BAB tests and the American College Tests (ACT) treated as achievement tests are somewhat higher, with Vocabulary and Analytical Reasoning yielding the highest correlations. Evidence of the validity of the

BAB in differentiating occupational groups is presented, but so far the evidence for the differential validity of BAB is promising but meager. Much more research is needed.

The construct validity of the BAB has been investigated by factor analytic studies of sex and racial groups and through correlational studies with the BAB and the Differential Aptitude Tests (DAT) and the Comprehensive Ability Battery (CAB).

The factor analyses were done separately on samples of female, male, Black, Hispanic, Illinois, and Texas high school students. The same procedure was used for each group: a principal axis solution with iteration to obtain the final communality estimates, and orthogonal rotation to a varimax criterion. Similar factors appear to be defined for each of the subgroups. However, further analyses, especially confirmatory factor analyses, should be carried out. The factorial purity of the individual tests is not yet established. The Vocabulary test is not factorially pure. It might define a general factor. It has significant loadings on four to five factors across the several subgroups.

The convergent and discriminant validities of the tests are not established by the correlational studies of the BAB with the DAT and CAT, contrary to statements in the Technical Manual. As indicated, the Vocabulary test correlates highly with other tests, including tests usually not thought of as verbal. The Analytical Reasoning test correlates significantly with verbal and spatial tests and numerical ability. The Clerical Test correlates only .19 with the DAT Clerical Speed and Accuracy Test but correlates .70 with the CAB Perceptual Speed and Accuracy Test. The results indicated are only examples of some of the complex relationships between the BAB tests and other tests. The authors need to develop the rational basis for the specific relationships found in order to extricate the implications for the construct validities of the several BAB tests. It is not specifically clear what aptitudes the tests define and measure. The tests show promise but more links in the nomological net need to be forged.

Overall, the BAB reflects a worthwhile efort. The addition of the numerical measures should extend its practical validity. Additional validity studies are needed, especially in the vocational area. The construct validities of the tests (i.e., what aptitudes do they define?) need much more research attention. However, the authors are to be commended for the high quality of their work to date and for their attention to sex and racial differences. The BAB should be used cautiously in counseling and in personnel work pending further research. It is recommended for research, especially in the study of individual differences.

REVIEWER'S REFERENCES

O'Connor, J. STRUCTURAL VISUALIZATION. New York: Human Engineering Laboratories, 1935.

[107]

Bankson Language Screening Test. Ages 4–8; 1977; BLST; 17 subtest scores: semantic knowledge (body parts, nouns, verbs, categories, functions, prepositions, colors/quantity, opposites), morphological rules (pronouns, verb tenses, plurals/comparatives/superlatives), syntactic rules (subject-verb agreement/negation, sentence repetition/judgement), visual perception (visual matching/discrimination, visual association/sequencing), auditory perception (auditory memory, auditory sequencing/discrimination); individual; 1 form (75 pages including instructions for administration and interpretation, score sheet, and profile sheet); 1985 price data: $27 per complete set; $13 per 25 score sheets and 25 profile sheets; (20–30) minutes; Nicholas W. Bankson; University Park Press.*

TEST REFERENCES

1. Fujiki, M., & Willbrand, M. L. A comparison of four informal methods of language evaluation. LANGUAGE, SPEECH, AND HEARING SERVICES IN SCHOOLS, 1982, 13, 42–52.

Review of Bankson Language Screening Test by BARRY W. JONES, Associate Professor of Communicative Disorders, San Diego State University, San Diego, CA:

The Bankson Language Screening Test (BLST) is described by the author as a screening instrument to assess the psycholinguistic and perceptual skills of children. The purpose of the instrument is to identify children in need of language remediation and to determine which aspects of language need to be tested in greater detail. The test is administered on a one-to-one basis and all of the information necessary to give the test is included in the test manual. It takes approximately 25 minutes to administer and consists of a battery of 17 nine-item subtests assessing the expressive language of children between the ages of 4–1 and 8–0 years. These subtests are organized into five categories: (1) semantic knowledge (eight subtests), (2) morphological rules (three subtests), (3) syntactic rules (two subtests), (4) visual perception (two subtests), and (5) auditory perception (two subtests). Although the test was developed to provide an assessment of more than a single aspect of language behavior, it should be noted that 47% of the test assesses semantic knowledge and that approximately 18% assesses morphological rules. The three remaining areas (syntactic rules, visual perception, and auditory perception) each contain approximately 12% of the test items. It is evident, therefore, that although the test does assess more than a single component of language, its primary emphasis is on semantic knowledge.

The inclusion of items assessing visual and auditory perception is also of interest for a "language screening" test. The Visual Perception Subtest appears to be an enabling factor for the test taking strategies associated with this instrument and the Auditory Perception Subtest could be viewed as an enabling factor for language acquisition and not as a component of language. The relationships of these factors to language should be of continued interest to researchers but the relevance of their content validity to a language screening test could be questioned.

Although the BLST was designed to be a test of expressive language, the author did provide stimuli for assessing receptive language in seven of the eight semantic knowledge subtests. However, the summary statistics (means and standard deviations) and the normative data (percentile scores by age levels) are based only on responses to the expressive language stimuli.

The test was normed on 637 children between the ages of 4–1 and 8–0 years from semi-rural areas near Washington, DC. Eighty percent of the subjects were White, 18% were Black, and 2% represented other nationalities. Test-retest reliability for 70 subjects was established at .94, with the retest occurring 1 week after the initial administration. The Kuder-Richardson internal reliability index (KR-20) yielded .96. These reliability coefficients suggest that the overall instrument consistently measured the subjects' performances.

The author established the concurrent validity of the test in two ways. First, the validity of the total test was demonstrated by correlating the scores of 70 subjects on this instrument with their performances on the Peabody Picture Vocabulary Test ($r = .54$), the Boehm Test of Basic Concepts ($r = .62$), and the Test of Auditory Comprehension of Language ($r = .64$). Second, the scores of 18 children on the eight Semantic Knowledge subtests were correlated with their performances on the Boehm Test of Basic Concepts ($r = .82$), and their performances on the Morphological Rules and Syntactic Rules subtests were correlated with their scores on 100-utterance language samples scored according to the Developmental Sentence Scoring criteria ($r = .76$) proposed by Lee (1974). The author did not, however, address the question of concurrent validity for the Visual and Auditory Perception categories of the BLST.

In addition to concurrent validity, the author should have established the predictive validity of the BLST. As Bankson has indicated, the purpose of the test "is to screen for children who may need language remediation, and to determine appropriate areas for further language testing." Further, he suggested that children who score below the 30th percentile on his norms need additional language assessments and that those who score below the 15th percentile should receive language therapy. Those who score between the 16th and 30th percentiles should be, according to the author, candidates for classroom enrichment activities. Studies to support the validity of these decision criteria should have been conducted and reported in the test manual.

The author provided two tables for interpretations of children's responses to the test stimuli. The first consists of mean raw scores and standard deviations for each of the 17 subtests at 6-month age intervals. Since the reliabilities and validities were not reported for any of the individual subtests of this battery, one should not attempt to establish client profiles for any of the 17 variables. Client's scores on these subtests should be used only as gross approximations for which one might suggest further diagnostic testing.

The second table consists of percentile ranks corresponding to raw scores on the overall test. These, too, are presented in 6-month age intervals. The reliability and validity information provided by the author in the test manual suggests that the data in this table are more important than the table previously described for the screening of individuals who may be in need of further language assessment or remediation.

In summary, there is a need for a language screening test assessing more than a single component of language. The BLST is a step in the right direction; most screening tests assess only one aspect of language. Although the predictive validity of the test has not been established, the concurrent validity indices for the total test indicate that it could be used if interpreted cautiously. The test user should realize that only the total test score is potentially useful for screening purposes and that the reliability and validity of the individual subtests have not yet been established.

REVIEWER'S REFERENCES

Lee, L. DEVELOPMENTAL SENTENCE ANALYSIS. Evanston, IL: Northwestern University Press, 1974.

[108]

The Barclay Classroom Assessment System. Grades 3–6; 1971–83; BCAS; formerly The Barclay Classroom Climate Inventory (BCCI); for the early detection of learning-related and socio-affective problems of child functioning in the classroom; teacher, peer, and self ratings in classes of 10 to 40 students; computer printout consists of classroom summary (lists children who may need special attention for suspected problems in classroom relationships and learning), individual reports (more detailed report for each student), and group data tables (lists raw scores and classroom average scores); report based on 47 scores: 5 self-competency scores (artistic-intellectual, outdoor-mechanical, social-cooperative, enterprising, total), 7 group nomination scores (artistic-intellectual, outdoor-mechanical, social-cooperative, enterprising, reticence, disruptiveness, total), 9 vocational preference scores (outdoor-mechanical, intellectual-scientific, social, conventional, enterprising, arts, conservative, status, total), 12 teacher rating scores (personal adjustment positive, personal adjustment negative, social adjustment positive, social adjustment negative, work habits and attitudes positive, work habits and attitudes negative, total teacher rating positive, total teacher rating negative, external-predictable, external-unpredictable, internal-predictable, internal-unpredictable), 7 self-rated reinforcer scores (self-stimulating, esthetic, intellectual or task-oriented, family-oriented, conventional, male peer group, female peer group), classroom climate index, and 6 factor scores (task-order achievement, control-predictability, reserved-internal, physical-activity, sociability-affiliation, enterprising-dominance); 1 form; evaluation booklet ('81, 4 pages); students in my class sheet ('82, 2 pages); manual ('83, 141 pages plus test); 1982 price data: $120 per introductory kit including 35 evaluation booklets; $3.60 per evaluation booklet including scoring service by the publisher; $1.50 per students in my class sheet; $9.50 per manual; (30–40) minutes; James R. Barclay; Western Psychological Services.*

See T3:239 (5 references); for a review by Richard M. Wolf, see 8:502 (10 references).

TEST REFERENCES

1. Barclay, J. R., Phillips, G., & Jones, T. Developing a predictive index for giftedness. MEASUREMENT AND EVALUATION IN GUIDANCE, 1983, 16, 25–35.

Review of The Barclay Classroom Assessment System by NORMAN A. BUKTENICA, Professor and Chair, Education Department, Moorhead State University, Moorhead, MN:

The Barclay Classroom Assessment System (BCAS), formerly entitled the Barclay Classroom Climate Inventory (BCCI), is reported to be a "system for evaluating individual differences in a classroom setting." While the BCAS might adequately identify some individual differences it is not an assessment instrument of classroom climate in any literal sense. One might be disappointed if expecting such an inventory because naturalistic or ecological observations of classrooms are not part of the procedure. The BCAS provides data on individuals from three perspectives—self report, peer response, and teacher ratings. It should also be noted that the BCAS is in a somewhat transitional state; since 1982 it has been published by Western Psychological Services. The new title and new publishing company represent changes in format only, since the items are unchanged and the norms remain the same as those in the 1978 BCCI.

The self-reporting portion of the BCAS is composed of 174 items that are in three scales or groupings. In the first scale there are 72 items intended to reflect vocational interest by the student. The second scale is made up of 40 items that are supposed to be indicative of how children perceive their personal competence in skill areas (e.g., writing poetry, knowing a lot about cars, and doing well on tests). The third scale is composed of 52 items that are intended to measure behavioral interest. The peer nomination portion is composed of 28 items on which the children are asked to indicate from a class list the child who can do best on a variety of activities/behaviors. In the third portion of the BCAS the teacher is asked to indicate from a list of 61 adjectives the ones that apply to each student.

The theoretical rationale for the BCAS is reported by the author to be behavioral phenomonology that is based on the measurement of environmental press by Pace and Stern (1958), inferences from Holland's (1966) theory of vocational development and personality, and research application of social learning theory as explicated by Bandura (1977). The rationale is clearly stated and seems sound, but there appear to be some conceptual leaps and content gaps when the author states that the instrument "represents an integrative theory of individual differences based on the interaction of structural components (intelligence and emotional characteristics) with environmental forces that include nurturance, expectations and opportunity." This is evident as one examines the degree of congruence between the items and constructs. For example, the items do not represent a measure of intelligence (unless a "*g*" factor is inferred as pervading all behavior), and measurement of nurturance or opportunity is difficult to infer from the instrument items.

The BCAS is a complex procedure involving multi-method and multi-trait assessment of individual differences. Although the procedure has been simplified by combining the inventory items and the "answer sheet" into one optical scanning Evaluation Booklet, the complexity of the procedure seems to present some problems for administration. Each student is given a numbered list of all the students in the class that is used for coding the peer nominations. Young, immature and developmentally-delayed children would have difficulty with the mechanics of responding to the inventory. Reading the items to a child might make it a very different task, and such practice in a group would present many problems. Computer scoring and generation of individual reports is an advantage but may add to the expense of the process.

Results of the self-report, peer nominations, and teacher scales yield 32 "independent short scales." "Four of these are self-report scales relating to a child's own estimate of his skills. Six scales refer to basic sociometric choices about the peer group judgment of skills. In addition, there are 10 scales relating to interests in and knowledge about the environment and vocations. There are four scales which comprise the teacher rating input and eight scales that relate to the child's interests, reinforcers and satisfaction with school." The self-report scales appear to be composed of from 6 to 15 items each. Students are classified as being high or low on the scales and the implications are listed separately for boys and girls.

Through the use of multi-method multi-trait factor analysis (Campbell & Fiske, 1959), six factors have been identified by the BCAS: (*a*) achievement-motivation, (*b*) control-stability, (*c*) introversion-seclusiveness, (*d*) energy-activity, (*e*) sociability-affiliation, and (*f*) enterprising-dominance. On the basis of these factors the computerized individual and group report "provides a description of each student in the classroom and information about the way the teacher and peer group describe each student."

There are a number of favorable and some questionable aspects of the BCAS that are worthy of mention and are not noted in other parts of this review. First, it has heuristic value which is evidenced by approximately 50 studies reported. Second, there is some evidence to suggest that the BCAS is useful for district-wide needs assessment and response to exceptional children. A diagnostic index is generated that is reported to be useful in identifying "gifted" and learning disabled children (Barclay, Phillips, & Jones, 1979). Kehle and Barclay (1979) and Rutledge (1974) report some utility of the BCAS for educational or group counseling interventions for mentally handicapped students. Third, results of the inventory, when shared with children, have changed their assertiveness and their feelings about self-competencies (Church, 1972). Fourth, it is appropriate to drop father's occupation as the SES indicator, but no other SES indices are noted and only race is reported as a socio-cultural-ethnic indicator. Fifth, the teacher completing the adjective check list on the same form as that completed by the children is a major source of possible contamination. Sixth, it would be helpful to have an item analysis reported in order to determine how and why items were selected and retained. Seventh, there is a definite sex bias in use of pronouns throughout the manual. The male pronoun is always used in reference to the child, principal, and school psychologist, while "she" is used in reference to the teacher. Eighth, for some unexplained reason, the author uses selected scales in the tables reporting statistical data.

Standardization data are based on a sample of 5,424 children (2,590 females, 2,834 males), in third through sixth grades in inner city urban schools, mid-class suburban schools, and rural schools in California, Ohio, Oklahoma, Pennsylvania, Texas, Wisconsin, Kentucky, Indiana, Georgia, and West Virginia. The sample included approximately 1,400 Black, 600 Spanish-American, and 250 American Indians. There is an absence of sampling procedure description and other demographic information.

The reliability studies reported in the manual indicate a Cronbach's Alpha ranging from .54 to .93 for the major BCAS scales, and .69 for males and .66 for females for the self-total scale that is supposed to reflect a child's estimate of his/her self-competency. These correlations are based on a sample (not specified how selected) of 473 boys and 493 girls in third through fifth grades and using 24 of the 32 scales. A test-retest exploration from October to May revealed a range of correlations from .34 to .77 for 12 of the scales based on a sample of 305 third graders and 533 fourth and sixth graders. Test-retest correlations for the six factor scores over a six-month period reveal correlations from .58 to .79.

Evidence for validity of the BCAS is given in narrative form; it is an appeal for recognition of face validity "based on the assumption...that there is some degree of correspondence between the real attitudes and feelings of people and what they respond to on a structured item." Concurrent validity is reported on the basis of correlations that are statistically significant from .01 to .10 (actual correlations not reported) between the BCAS and various behavioral ratings, preference tests, personality inventories, grade point averages, and achievement tests for various sized groups ranging from 29 to 502 children and as few as five substitute teachers who rated behavior. Predictive validity is reported in summary form from a number of multiple regression equations obtained between the BCAS scales and factor scores with achievement and social adjustment characteristics. This procedure revealed multiple correlations ranging from .34 to .71 with a sample size of 430 and grade level not reported. A study by Tapp (1972) revealed "clear convergent and discriminant validity for four male and two female factors," while the remaining factors "tended to lack some degree of validity, and...discriminant validity should be reviewed." Once again, the magnitude of the correlations and the demographic characteristics were not provided.

One final question about the BCAS relates to the proposed interventions or prescriptions that are made on the basis of the results. One wonders about the data base for making such recommendations. There is precious little evidence presented to indicate to what extent a given prescription will be effective for an individual or classroom. Furthermore, the printout that is returned to the school states that children show a pattern on the BCAS that is similar to gifted, learning disabled, or handicapped students, and yet there are no data reported for such labeled groups.

The content of the BCAS manual, and supporting data, raise several questions and issues related to the adequacy and utility of the instrument. Given the nature of the process and content, one wonders if it is an individual assessment instrument rather than a classroom assessment system. There is also a question of possible bias and contamination of teacher ratings because of using the same Evaluation

Booklet used by the student. Although the publisher's information refers to 20 years of research and refinement of the system, there are several changes in format but no changes in content over the past decade as reported by the author. The issue of a perceived conceptual leap from the rationale to the use and justification of some scales purporting to measure classroom climate needs to be addressed. There are a series of issues that arise related to standardization, reliability, and validity including: (*a*) there is no clear description of the sample or the sampling procedures; (*b*) the reprocessing of the original 1972–73 standardization data has led to some changes in format, but virtually no changes in content; (*c*) reliability and validity are reported on selected scales with no explanation for the selection, or the reason for not using, all scales; (*d*) very small subsamples are used for determining reliability and validity with no explanation given for the process of sampling; and (*e*) questions could be raised about presenting levels of significance rather than correlation coefficients in concurrent validity and multiple regression analyses.

The BCAS has been developed over a span of more than 10 years, but some fairly serious questions continue to be raised about its format, content, reliability, validity, and applicability. It seems that its use in school systems should be recommended only with extreme caution and with careful consideration of the questions and concerns that were raised above.

REVIEWER'S REFERENCES

Pace, C. R., & Stern, G. G. An approach to the measurement of psychological characteristics of college environments. JOURNAL OF EDUCATIONAL PSYCHOLOGY, 1958, 49, 269–277.

Campbell, D. T., & Fiske, D. W. Convergent and discriminant validation by the multitrait-multimethod matrix. PSYCHOLOGICAL BULLETIN, 1959, 56, 81–105.

Holland, J. L. THE PSYCHOLOGY OF VOCATIONAL CHOICE. Boston: Ginn & Co., 1966.

Church, J. S. Effects of individual and group cue-reinforcement counseling as interventional techniques for modifying elementary classroom behaviors. Ph.D. dissertation, University of Kentucky, 1972.

Tapp, G. S. Convergent and discriminant validity of the Barclay Classroom Climate Inventory. Ph.D. thesis, University of Kentucky. DISSERTATION ABSTRACTS INTERNATIONAL, 1972, 33, 6189A.

Rutledge, P. B. Effects of short-term multiple treatment group counseling on social interaction perceptions of isolate rejectees in the fifth and sixth grades. Unpublished Ph.D. dissertation, University of Kentucky, 1974.

Bandura, A. SOCIAL LEARNING THEORY. Englewood Cliffs, NJ: Prentice Hall, 1977.

Kehle, T. J., & Barclay, J. R. The impact of handicapped students on other students in the classroom. JOURNAL OF RESEARCH AND DEVELOPMENT IN EDUCATION, 1979, 12(4), 80–91.

Barclay, J.R., Phillips, G., & Jones, T. Developing a predictive index for giftedness. MEASUREMENT AND EVALUATION IN GUIDANCE, 1983, 16, 25–35.

Review of The Barclay Classroom Climate Inventory by GALE M. MORRISON, Assistant Professor in Special Education, University of California, Santa Barbara, CA:

[Note: The Barclay Classroom Climate Inventory is the earlier version of The Barclay Classroom Assessment System—Ed.]

The Barclay Classroom Climate Inventory (BCCI) is an assessment tool with the intended purpose of identifying children who may be experiencing problems in social relationships and learning in the classroom. Extensive interpretations and analysis of child characteristics are provided in a complicated computerized printout recommended for use by teachers, principals, counselors, school psychologists, and social workers. Information in the inventory is taken from the following sources: (*a*) 72 vocational interest items (self-rated), (*b*) 24 self-concept type items, (*c*) 51 items concerning saliency of reinforcers (self-rated), (*d*) 28 peer-related items, and (*e*) teacher choice of relevant adjectives (61 possible adjective descriptions).

The BCCI is one of the few inventories available which recognizes the ecological importance of evaluating children from peer and teacher perspectives in addition to the child's orientation. The consideration of these alternative perspectives is the greatest strength of the BCCI. However, the potential of the inventory to provide meaningful information is lessened by the tendency for the advertising and conclusions to go much beyond what is reasonably interpreted from available data. Minimal support from pertinent theoretical and clinical literature is given for the link between data collected and interpretations given. For example, conclusions are made concerning teacher expectations based on adjective checklist information. No information is given on what data patterns correspond to specific interpretations. Unexplained leaps from data to interpretation are characteristic of self and peer ratings also.

Additionally, information is needed on the meaningfulness of the one standard deviation cutoff for high and low on various characteristics. For example, do high or low scores on achievement motivation, artistic skills, or intellectual-scientific interest correspond to some psychologically or behaviorally meaningful differences?

The feedback provided in the computer printouts is difficult to decipher and understand. Extensive use is made of abbreviations and codes for a multiplicity of scales and factors. Specific information is needed on item-scale and item-factor correspondence. From what little information was provided on this correspondence, it appeared as though there was item overlap (on scales and factors that were treated independently) and item exclusion (failure to use some items at all). Obviously more information is needed on scale and factor construction in general.

The format of the BCCI manual is somewhat confusing. Much space is devoted to extolling the potential of the inventory and very little space to descriptions of its psychometric characteristics (the main source of any confidence that might be placed in the assessment procedure). A series of tables are provided toward the back of the manual for which no explanations are provided.

At several points in the manual, reference is made to the fact that the inventory's significance is subject to the accuracy and validity of self, peer, and teacher input. The severity of this problem is perhaps understated. Self-report data (especially those related to self-concept or self-esteem) have classically been subject to problems of conceptualization and validity (Wells & Marwell, 1976). Similarly, questions have been raised concerning the psychometric strength of peer ratings (Kane & Lawler, 1978). Certainly user caution is warranted.

Another serious issue is possible bias inherent in informant sources. Consistent differences for BCCI subscales are noted for sex, SES, and grade level. More information is needed on the significance of these biases and what modifications or adjustments, if any, are needed in BCCI analysis and feedback methods. For example, do scoring procedures take into account the teachers' tendencies to rate girls more positively? What are the implications of this tendency for interpretation of data patterns?

Concurrent validity was determined by correlating selected BCCI Scales with the Kuder Preference Record, The Children's Personality Questionnaire, The California Test of Mental Maturity intelligence score, The Raven's Progressive Matrices, The Iowa Test of Basic Skills, behavioral ratings, and grade point average. No explanation was given for choosing the particular selection of BCCI scales used in these correlations. Of some concern is the timing of the various testings. Although some subscales of the BCCI show moderate (at best) stability, one might expect some day-to-day variations in peer-student-teacher interactions and perceptions. Given such variations, the meaningfulness of behavioral ratings taken 3 months after BCCI administration could be questioned.

No explanations are given for the pattern of significant correlations found between the BCCI and the various other instruments. Such an analysis would be both helpful and interesting for test users.

Predictive validity support was provided by predicting subscale scores on the Barclay Learning Needs Inventory (BLNI) from BCCI factor scores and predicting various academic achievement scores from another selection of BCCI scales. These predictions are made through the use of multiple regression procedures. Some analysis and explanation were given for the prediction of the affective-social learning problem scores (BLNI) but none for the prediction of the achievement scores. Further explanations and comparisons would be helpful; with the data in its present form, however, comparisons between affective and achievement prediction would be difficult due to the use of different subsets of predictors from the BCCI.

One paragraph in the BCCI manual was devoted to construct validity. Given the importance of construct validity for any assessment procedure, more attention to this matter is warranted. It might be noted here that Barclay provides no comparisons with other more traditional constructs of classroom climate.

Internal consistency and test-retest reliabilities were provided for various subsets of factors and scales of the BCCI. Internal consistency reliability coefficients ranged from .53 to .93; test-retest coefficients ranged from .34 to .77. In general, these reliabilities would not be considered high enough to provide secure conclusions or predictions about individual students. It seems very risky to put much confidence in the highly specific characterizations of students that the BCCI provides. This risk is exacerbated by the current zeitgeist of conservatism in labelling students and exposing them to the potentially negative effects of altered expectations and treatment.

Specific note should be made of the fact that for every reliability and validity study cited, a different subset of scales or factors of the BCCI was used. This situation makes comparisons difficult if not impossible and provides little coherent or consistent information about the psychometric properties of the BCCI.

The standardization sample was described briefly with no evidence of its representativeness with respect to age, SES, or ethnicity. Norms are provided at the back of the manual for males and females. No breakdowns were given for the age and SES variables that showed systematic differences on the BCCI.

In summary, the BCCI offers a potentially useful sampling of perceptions of a child's functioning in a classroom. The report on the psychometric properties of this inventory was scant and poorly organized. What evidence does exist suggests that the computerized interpretations provided to test users (at some cost) go much beyond what is warranted by the extent and quality of information sampled.

REVIEWER'S REFERENCES

Wells, L. E., & Marwell, G. SELF-ESTEEM: ITS CONCEPTUALIZATION AND MEASUREMENT. Beverly Hills, CA: Sage Publications, 1976.

Kane, J. S., & Lawler, E. E. Methods of peer assessment. PSYCHOLOGICAL BULLETIN, 1978, 85, 555–586.

[109]

Barclay Learning Needs Assessment Inventory. Grades 6–12 and college; 1975–79; BLNAI; self-report learning problems checklist and ratings by peer, parent, teacher, or counselor; 7 scores: self-competency, group interaction, self-control, verbal skills, energy and persistence, cognitive-motivation, attitude; 1 form ('75, 2 pages); manual ('79, 63 pages); 1984 price data: answer sheet and scoring service, $1.20 per test; $3.50 per manual; $5 per specimen set; score report, to be given to student, consists of 1 page printout yielding profiled scores and narrative statements comparing self-ratings and ratings by other; [40–50] minutes; James R. Barclay; Educational Skills Development, Inc.*

For a review by Rodney T. Hartnett, see 8:503 (1 reference).

Review of Barclay Learning Needs Assessment Inventory by MARLA R. BRASSARD, Assistant Professor of Educational Psychology, University of Georgia, Athens, GA:

"How do I see myself? How do I compare with my peers? How valid is my own judgement compared with that of someone who knows me well?" These are the questions that this 82-item inventory attempts to assess for students relative to their self-reported learning problems. Computer scoring, the use of an important other as a rater in addition to self-report, and behavioral prescriptions tailored to the learner's needs are commendable features of this test. Unfortunately, because of technical inadequacies the Barclay Learning Needs Assessment Inventory (BLNAI) fails to meet its useful and ambitious objectives.

Published originally in 1975 as an experimental instrument, the BLNAI received a justifiably harsh review in *The Eighth Mental Measurements Yearbook*. Technical problems noted were as follows: (*a*) reliability—unreported in a number of instances and generally low when reported; (*b*) validity—evidence for any kind of validity was judged to be very weak; (*c*) standardization sample—described only by sex and grade level, with the latter usually lumped together (e.g., sixth through ninth grades were in one group); (*d*) norms—only percentile norms were provided, and an estimated standard error of measurement based on average reliability made the 95% confidence interval so large as to be useless in prediction.

The deficiencies noted above apply equally to the 1979 non-experimental revision. In fact, it is difficult to discern how the experimental and non-experimental editions differ. The material that has been added appears to provide more evidence of the inventory's lack of construct validity, as well as commentary and analyses that may mislead test users. Evidence of limited construct validity is provided by a factor analysis which demonstrates that six of the seven scales load highly and solely on one factor. Furthermore, for self ratings, all the scales show significant correlations with the social desirability measure (range=–.68 to –.94).

The potentially misleading material is illustrated in the following examples. For instance, the scale intercorrelations are quite high and significantly related to one another (range=.59 to .90, median=.77). The author attributes this, not to poor scale construction or the presence of a global factor, but to evidence suggesting that the more "threatening and negative the environment of learning, the higher the intensity of problems," which results in "a global state of perceived tension." In other words, the intercorrelations are not evidence of limited empirical support for scale independence, but rather an empirical finding that bad learning experiences result in an individual feeling globally inadequate as a learner. Sound test and subscale construction require empirical validation of scale independence as the first priority. Any interpretations about the meaning of scales are inappropriate if this precondition is not satisfied.

Misleading in the same manner is the author's inclusion of an analysis of variance, canonical correlations, and discriminant analysis plots of each sex by grade level (the graduate female group has an *N* of 5). These analyses are followed by comments on how the groups differ on the various scales, and interpretations of the resultant "developmental trends." Although the author reminds the reader that the data are cross sectional, the technical deficits of the inventory make the information presented of questionable validity. Thus, the commentary and the inclusion of the additional analyses may mislead test users who do not closely examine the technical features of this instrument.

In summary, the original reviewer's judgement of the 1975 experimental edition of the BLNAI was: "Unless major revisions and improvements are made, the Barclay inventory cannot provide information that is useful to anybody." The present author believes that the changes made in the interval since the first edition's publication have affected the appearance, and that minimally, but not the substance of the inventory. Thus, the revision does not provide any basis for changing the original reviewer's negative evaluation of the BLNAI.

[110]

Bar-Ilan Picture Test for Children. Ages 4–16; 1982; "semi-projective interview"; no scores; guidelines for analysis in 8 areas: emotional makeup, motivation, interpersonal behavior and areas of conflict, attitudes of teachers-parents towards testee, attitudes of peers and siblings towards testee, degree of mastery and feeling of competence, quality of thinking process, activity; no norms; individual; 1 form (9 drawings, 6 of which have different versions for boys and girls); manual (45 pages); 1984 price data: US$25 per set of 15 drawings; $9 per manual; administration time not reported; Rivkah Itskowitz and Helen Strauss; Dansk psykologisk Forlag [Denmark].*

[111]

Barsch Learning Style Inventory. Grades 7–12 and college; 1980; manual title is *Spelling Plus*; 3 scores: visual preference, auditory preference, tactual preference;

no data on reliability and validity; no norms; 1 form (4 pages); manual (76 pages); 1984 price data: $6 per 25 tests; $6 per manual; 5–10 minutes; Jeffrey Barsch and Betty Creson (manual); Academic Therapy Publications.*

Review of Barsch Learning Style Inventory by JOHN BIGGS, Professor of Education, University of Newcastle, N.S.W. Australia:

Since receiving this Inventory and accompanying manual, this reviewer has been beset with confusion. My first confusion arose because the Barsch Learning Style Inventory (BLSI) appears to have no connection with the Learning Style Inventory of Canfield, likewise reviewed in the *Ninth MMY*, apart from the title and a superficial overlap in the Mode Scale of the latter. My second confusion arose because the manual for the BLSI is entitled *Spelling Plus*, and I thought I might have been sent the wrong manual. Not so. The manual contains 13 chapters, 2 of which deal briefly with the BLSI, describing its instructional use, and alluding to "the brink of an instruction revolution" of which the present package is undoubtedly meant to represent the vanguard. The rest is truer to the title. Chapter 1 gives a brief history of spelling itself, then of its pedagogy. Chapters 4 through 13 deal with various aspects of the teaching of spelling.

The BLSI itself is a 24-item checklist of preferences for visual, auditory, or tactile modalities when in a learning or performance situation. Presumably, the modality receiving the greatest number of preferences indicates a student's preferred modality of learning: I say "presumably" because the inventory form "is to be used in conjunction with other diagnostic tools to help you determine some of the ways you are best able to learn. Discuss your scores with someone who is qualified to interpret them." The minor detail of telling the "someone who is qualified" how to arrive at such interpretations is not, however, to be found in the form itself or the manual.

All that notwithstanding, the theory is that the method of teaching spelling should match the student's preferred learning style (or mode): "If a student is a visual learner, he should try to remember words by placing a mental picture in the learner's head....If an individual's primary sense is auditory, it will help to listen to spelling words....For those students who are tactual learners, it will help to write the spelling words over and over again." Some suggestions then follow in chapter 4 for teaching spelling in each of these three modes. The remaining chapters appear to have little or nothing to do with modes of presentation; they present fairly conventional material on tests, dictionary skills, vocabulary, and syllabification rules.

Then a third confusion develops. The authors appear to have two commodities to market—a Learning Style Inventory and a spelling program—and they have decided to wrap them up in the same package. They have not, however, adequately explained to the practitioner how to integrate the two, or even how to obtain the student's preferred mode from the BSLI. The mysteriously derived preference scores are of unknown reliability and of unknown validity, whether factorial, content, or construct. There are no studies reporting that matching presentation mode with preferred learning style does lead to better acquisition of spelling, and no details on text construction or norming procedures.

The authors apparently constructed and used the BLSI and the spelling program at Ventura Community College, California. Until the general reader has some evidence of the success which they had, and of the success which others independently have also had, he or she should remain completely skeptical. Certainly there is nothing contained within the materials reviewed here suggesting that the expense and trouble of acquiring and using the BSLI would be justified. The absence of any technical information on the inventory itself says very clearly: caveat emptor.

Review of Barsch Learning Style Inventory by JAYNE A. PARKER, School Consultant, Children and Youth Services Program of Washington County Mental Health, Montpelier, VT:

The purpose of Spelling Plus, which contains the Learning Style Inventory, is, according to the authors, "to assist the student at the secondary or community college level who is having difficulty with spelling material at or above the fifth-grade level. It is designed to lead the teacher to some unique observations about the world of spelling." The major portion of the booklet consists of the Learning Style Inventory and exercises intended for the remediation of some forms of learning difficulties encountered by the secondary and college level student.

The first chapter of the booklet contains information describing the history of spelling, beginning with the ancient Semites and the Phoenicians, and ending with more contemporary information. This initial chapter also includes a segment on the character of the language. The material presented is interesting, but does not seem wholly relevant to the authors' stated purpose.

Chapter 2 introduces learning styles, and contains brief descriptions of the visual, auditory, and tactual learning styles. A number of characteristics for each of these learning styles is listed. For example, individuals whose strongest learning style is visual "are good at art and visualization projects," "are skillful and enjoy developing and making graphs and charts," and so on. Auditory learners "have good listening skills," "move lips when reading to themselves," etc. Characteristics of those who possess a tactual learning style include "frequently play with coins in their pockets," and "bear down extremely hard with pen or pencil when writing." The breakdown of learning styles into visual, auditory, and tactual areas seems to artificially compartmentalize the process of learning. The existence of a mixed learning style and the interaction of the different sensory modalities and perceptual processes in learning are not addressed.

Following a brief discussion of temporal style or timing pattern, the remainder of chapter 2 provides information about the role of brain functioning in the learning process, and bilateral brain processes. The discussion of material is simplistic and superficial, with a page and a half devoted to assisting the reader in gaining an understanding of neurological research findings. Brain pattern and learning style are basically segmented into two areas: students who "are very left cerebral hemisphere dominated," and those who "function best using the right cerebral hemisphere." It is advised that spelling instruction be designed to address the needs of these two types of learners, though this concept is not mentioned in later sections describing remedial techniques. The segment headed "Bilateral Process and Learning Style" discusses how a learner could be encouraged to "stimulate both sides of the brain," (i.e., by writing with both hands at the same time). Obviously, the information does not reflect the complexity of neurological functioning and its relationship to the learning process, and is apt to be misleading. There is no mention made of the nature of most learning styles (which requires both brain hemispheres) or of the manner in which brain hemispheres function in an interdependent, not mutually exclusive, fashion. The authors would do well to include a bibliography, but, other than noting Robert Ornstein's *The Psychology of Consciousness*, there are no references provided.

The Learning Style Inventory appears in chapter 3. This self-administered instrument consists of 24 statements (e.g., "can remember more about a subject through listening than reading"; "follow written directions better than oral directions") to which the individual responds in terms of rating categories of "often," "sometimes," and "seldom." The items are then scored, according to the degree of response and type of item, and totalled to achieve Visual Preference, Auditory Preference, and Tactual Preference Scores. There are no guidelines to assist in response selection (i.e., how one should differentiate the terms "often," "sometimes," and "seldom"), and it is possible for two individuals who function quite similarly to have very different profiles because of response style. Once the Preference Scores are obtained, the individual discovers whether he or she is a visual, auditory, or tactile learner by noting a high score for one of these modalities. Again, there is an absence of guidelines to aid in determining the significance of scores. (Essentially, these Preference Scores could range from 8 to 40. Is a score of 20 considered "high"?) Additionally, there is no indication as to what would constitute a significant deficit within one of these learning channels. The authors seem to infer that there is a single modality which will be stronger than the other two. There is no discussion concerning the significance of two scores which are fairly close in magnitude. The manual contains no reference to test construction, normative sample, or validity and reliability of the scale. Thus, it is not possible to determine whether, in fact, the inventory is able to discriminate the preferred modalities of learners.

The remaining 10 chapters present various learning strategies for areas such as spelling, dictionary skills, writing skills, and vocabulary development. The authors' intent is to aid teachers in developing an instructional program. However, there does not seem to be a connection made between the Learning Style Inventory and the suggested techniques. With the exception of a brief presentation on spelling and memory strategies, there is no discussion concerning which methods would benefit an auditory, visual, or tactual learner, and it would be difficult to prescribe activities for a particular type of learner. Several of the activities seem to utilize a multimodal approach, though the rationale for this type of orientation is barely mentioned.

While the instructional material has been developed for high school and community college level students, many of the activities seem to be more appropriate for younger children, and some of them are remedial in nature, such as methods for eliminating reversals. There is some question concerning the appropriateness of attempting to remediate learning disabilities (rather than developing compensatory skills) after an individual has reached a certain age level, usually by the end of elementary school. This type of activity may not be of benefit for older students. Other exercises seem more appropriate for the intended age level, but the entire instructional program seems rather limited in scope and applicability to high school and college level classes. Some of the techniques described are of questionable usefulness for any age level, such as having the student chew gum while learning difficult material (to reduce muscular tension), having the student associate a smell (vanilla extract) with a word being studied in an attempt to incorporate the sense of olfaction in the learning process, and a method called "tongue-steering," which is reminiscent of what one does when concentrating on threading a needle. (The authors claim that researchers have some interest in using the tongue to aid memory, but there is no documentation that this is a serious consideration.) Other activities, such as exercises for alphabetizing a list of words, and syllabication and spelling rules, would not seem to be of any greater benefit than a basic language curriculum or grammar text, and certainly the number of useful exercises provided is limited.

In general, the usefulness of both the Learning Style Inventory and the instructional programming techniques is questionable. While it may prove interesting to discover which (if any) of the learning styles described may apply to oneself (assuming that the scale is able to make this determination), the depth and applicability of the program would not appear to be of great value. Students within the age level for which the material is intended would, assuming the existence of a learning problem significant enough to warrant such attention, benefit from a comprehensive evaluation under the special education procedures mandated by PL 94–142. It is unlikely that such a student would not be identified by the time he or she completed high school. However, a student in college who has not previously been identified as learning disabled would do well to seek a professional evaluation. Teachers who are interested in incorporating spelling lessons within their content area curricula may be able to adapt some of the techniques described, but overall, the material that is included in Spelling Plus is basically a superficial treatment of a quite ambitious undertaking.

[112]

Basic Achievement Skills Individual Screener. Grades 1–12 and post high school; 1983; BASIS; 3 or 4 scores: mathematics, reading, spelling, writing exercise (optional); individual; record form (14 pages); content booklet (69 pages); manual (232 pages); 1984 price data: $30 per examiner's kit including 2 record forms; $17.50 per 25 record forms; $12.50 per content booklet; $17.50 per manual; (50–60) minutes; The Psychological Corporation.*

Review of Basic Achievement Skills Individual Screener by ROBERT E. FLODEN, Associate Professor of Teacher Education and Educational Psychology, College of Education, Michigan State University, E. Lansing, MI:

The Basic Achievement Skills Individual Screener (BASIS) is an individually administered test of achievement in four basic skill areas: mathematics, reading, spelling, and writing. It is designed to be administered in less than an hour to students working at levels from grade 1 through grade 8. The writing test, which is optional, takes about 10 minutes of that hour.

The manual cites two specific advantages of the BASIS. First, the brief individual administration, predominantly of items the student answers correctly, is intended to reduce the inhibiting effects of test anxiety. Second, the test is designed to provide criterion information tied to grade level placement and textbook assignment, in addition to normative information.

The test was also designed to be an efficient general achievement test. The single hour required to administer the BASIS compares favorably with the five or so hours required for a comprehensive achievement battery. The manual suggests that the test results can be used for a wide range of purposes, including beginning diagnosis for special students, placing transfer students, conducting program evaluations, and conducting research.

Directions for administration and scoring are explicit, detailed, and clear. For each area except writing, the tester begins with items likely to be easy for the student. A cluster of 6–8 items associated with a single grade level is administered. If the student meets the criterion for that level (50–83% depending on subject and grade), the cluster for the next higher grade level is administered; if the student does not meet the criterion, testing in that area stops. The student's raw score is the total number of items answered correctly, with credit for all items at levels lower than the starting level. For the writing test, the tester asks the student to write for 10 minutes about a favorite place. The tester scores this writing sample holistically, using examples provided, as either below, at, or above grade level.

Clear, detailed descriptions are given of item development, item selection, and collection of norm data. Because the test is short, only a narrow range of content can be covered in any subject. The test designers tried to test "the essence" of each area, but many educators may find crucial omissions. Mathematics is restricted to computation and word problems requiring simple computation (misleadingly called "problem solving"); spelling words were culled from lists of grade-level words. In reading the designers restricted attention to comprehension. The Mathematics and Spelling tests correspond to the emphases of many curriculum series, while the Reading test emphasis on comprehension matches suggestions of researchers that have yet to become common in basal series.

Selecting content to match the common content of curriculum materials makes sense if the test is to be used for placement within a curriculum—it is an indication of where the child should be placed to avoid duplication or omission of topics universally taught. But for describing the child's achievements or evaluating a program, the omission of all conceptual understanding of mathematics, all use of measuring instruments, and all geometry is a serious problem.

The test designers took many steps to eliminate problems of bias. They deserve special praise for selecting the typeface and layout most readable for the learning disabled or visually handicapped. The developers claim they found no differences in test results "that could be attributed to race, language, or sex." The analyses conducted to look for such attributions were not described, an unfortunate omission given the continuing debate about how to determine item bias.

The manual offers a small, familiar set of derived scores, clearly presented in tables for each age level and grade level. The limitations of grade-equivalent scores are discussed, and they are displayed in a table that also includes percentile ranks. For a test with grade-level placement as a primary purpose, grade-equivalent scores should have been completely omitted; it will be easy to mistake the grade-equivalent score for a grade placement recommendation, even when the manual takes pains to make the distinction.

For use as a general achievement measure, reliability is high for such a short test. Based on data for three grade levels, test-retest reliabilities for reading and spelling tests range from .80 to .95, those for mathematics from .74 to .82.

If the test is to be used for grade level placement, however, the statistic of interest would be some measure of the occasion-to-occasion variation in grade-level recommendation. No such statistic is presented. The test manual presents concurrent validity data comparing the grade and text students were in to the grade and text level the test results would indicate. Unfortunately, what is presented is not the percent of students whose recommended placement would match their actual placement, but whether the recommended placement was within one grade level of actual placement. Even high percentages here are not very informative, since the placement question is more likely to be deciding between third and fourth grade than deciding between third and fifth.

Content validity is clearly documented for the narrow range of content tested in mathematics and spelling but is more problematic for comprehension. The passages for the cloze items comprising the comprehension test were constructed on the basis of the readability of the words in the passages. Complexity of sentences or difficulty of ideas was not considered. Thus, the grade level differences in comprehension may be more a matter of vocabulary knowledge than of ability to understand inherently difficult reading material.

In sum, this test would serve reasonably well as a quick initial screening device for grade level placement. Its content is well matched to the common core of textbook material in mathematics, spelling, and vocabulary. The concurrent validity with grade or text placement is not high enough for this to serve as the only basis of placement, however, especially given the difficulty students may experience trying to change a placement after it has been made. As a general achievement test to be used for evaluation or research, the content coverage is restricted, so it should be used only when that narrow range of skills is what the researcher or evaluator intends to measure. Inspection of the validity studies summarized in the manual suggests that there is interest in using the test with students with a variety of handicaps. The individual testing format may help students who would be anxious or inattentive in a group testing situation, though the test developers do nothing to substantiate this claim.

Review of Basic Achievement Skills Individual Screener by RICHARD E. SCHUTZ, Executive Director, Southwest Regional Laboratory for Educational Research and Development, Los Alamitos, CA:

The Basic Achievement Skills Individual Screener (BASIS) is a test instrument that should make men like Alfred Binet, Leonard Ayres, and Oscar Buros stand up in their graves and cheer. In an hour's testing time it tells you all you need to know about an individual's basic skills in mathematics, reading, spelling, and writing.

You can interpret the results functionally in terms of grade-by-grade 1 through 8 instructional performance in each school subject. This permits you to place a student in the most appropriate instructional working grade. You can also derive as much clinical information about a student's error patterns as the state of psychological/pedagogical understanding of the subject provides.

You can also interpret the results statistically in terms of the normative scale or scales of your choice. For Math, Reading, and Spelling the alternative scales are grade norms (percentile rank, stanine, or grade equivalent) at each grade from 1 to post-high school; age norms (percentile rank, stanine, or age equivalent) for ages 6 to 18; standard score; normal curve equivalent; and Rasch scaled score. The writing exercise ("Write about your favorite place," timed for 10 minutes) is rated above, below, or at average in terms of an "average sample" composition at each grade from 3 through 8.

The test carries impeccable psychometric credentials. The test manual reflects full and complete sensitivity to the *Standards for Educational and Psychological Tests.* The description of the test development and the presentation of technical data in the manual is elegantly brief, lucid, and comprehensive—exactly what psychometricians expect but rarely effect.

The testing materials, including a manual, Content Booklet, and Student Record Form, reflect great sensitivity to human factors in both design and execution. The Content Booklet is a single 6 in. by 9 in. heavy stock, spiral-bound booklet containing the reading passages, which the student reads aloud, and the readiness items, which the student responds to orally or by pointing. The manual is the same shape and size as the Content Booklet, and includes all the information required to understand, administer, and interpret the results of the test. The Record Form is a 14-page 8 1/2 in. by 11 in. newsprint booklet on which the student works the mathematics problems, writes the dictated spelling words, and does the writing exercise. The Record Form also provides pages for tallying, analyzing, and recording the results for each skill subject. Thus, with the manual and Content Booklet that are together less than an inch thick and a thin Record Form, you have all you need for every individual you have reason to test. The instrument is expertly engineered.

How is so much provided with such economy of effort and excellence of product? The trick is to test what constitutes basic skills instruction grade-by-grade—nothing more or less. What constitutes such instruction was determined by looking directly at graded textbook series in crafting the items for mathematics and spelling, looking largely at graded word lists in crafting the cloze items in reading, and selecting a single topic for the writing exercise. What you get is instrumentation that is fully and fundamentally grounded in basic schooling of basic achievement skills—extraneous and irrelevant excesses do not intrude.

In administering the instrument for Mathematics, Reading, and Spelling, you start the testing session at the grade level where the student reaches or exceeds the criterion score for that level: This typically means starting two grade levels below the student's age-grade, dropping back as many grades as necessary to establish the base grade. The student receives credit for all items below that lowest level. Testing then proceeds to the grade level where the student fails to attain the criterion score for that level. In this adaptive sequence, you tap what the student can do, and stop. With 6–8 items at a grade level, the administration in each subject is completed expeditiously. Because all of the responses are of a direct performance nature, the artifacts of multiple-choice tests do not confound the results.

The fact that the instrument must be individually administered is not nearly as restricting as it might appear. Administration is so straightforward that it could be administered by nearly any high school student and by most sixth graders with minimal coaching in how to handle the mechanics. (This assertion is supported empirically by the table of grade norms.) Certainly, virtually every teacher is capable of administering the instrument. Overall, the effort involved in administering, scoring, and analyzing the results for BASIS for a group of students compares favorably with the effort involved in using a typical group test.

Although the publisher modestly coined the test title BASIS as an acronym for "Basic Achievement Skills Individual Screener," in my view a much broader meaning is warranted. I would use BASIS as "the basis" for testing basic skills achievement. BASIS gives students an opportunity to register the basics that schools teach grade-by-grade through grade 8. If all basic skills achievement tests were to do this, they would all look much like BASIS. That BASIS is different tells you a lot about basic skills testing.

A careful examination of the substance of BASIS also tells you a lot about the structure and nature of basic skills instruction within and across school subjects and within and across grade levels. The reality of basic skills instruction is reflected in BASIS.

When you take an operationalized look at basic skills instruction via BASIS, your likely conclusion will be, "There's not all that much to it." If that's the conclusion you draw, you will have the basic skills "problem" pretty much solved. There will undoubtedly be aspects of what you see that don't look good to you. In each subject there is room for "improvement." If and when you change the reality of basic skills instruction, there will be reason to change BASIS accordingly. Meanwhile, BASIS provides a sound basis for doing what the instrument purports to do, and more.

[113]

Basic Economics Test. Grades 4–6; 1980–81; BET; substantive revision of the Test of Elementary Economics; Form A, B, ('80, 8 pages); manual ('81, 32 pages plus an answer sheet which may be duplicated locally and scoring key); 1984 price data: $6 per 25 tests; $3 per manual; 50(60) minutes; John F. Chizmar and Ronald S. Halinski; Joint Council on Economic Education.*

For reviews by Mary Friend Adams and James O. Hodges of an earlier edition, see 8:901 (1 reference).

[114]

Basic Educational Skills Test. Grades 1.5–5; 1979; BEST; for detecting children who are at risk academically; 3 tests: Reading, Writing, Mathematics; no reliability and validity data; no norms; individual; 1 form; manual ('79, 48 pages); separate answer sheets must be used; 1984 price data: $18 per test plates; $6 per 25 recording forms; $7.50 per manual; $7.50 per specimen set; (15–20) minutes per test; Ruth C. Segel and Sandra H. Golding; Academic Therapy Publications.*

Review of Basic Educational Skills Test by MARY KAY CORBITT, Assistant Professor of Mathematics and Curriculum and Instruction, University of Kansas, Lawrence, KS:

The Basic Educational Skills Test (BEST) is designed as an informal screening device to identify children (grades 1.5 through 5) who are not performing at appropriate academic levels. The individually administered test consists of subtests in reading, writing, and mathematics, each of which contains 25 questions and requires 15–20 minutes to complete. Test administration and scoring require no special training.

The test manual is divided into three major sections: the introductory section that delineates the theoretical framework underlying the test, question-by-question descriptions of the three subtests, and four sample protocols. No reliability or validity data are presented nor are reliability and validity mentioned anywhere in the test materials.

The theoretical basis that led to the development of this test is described in a section of the manual titled "How the Child Learns." The authors support a theory of learning that suggests that information is received through a learner's "sensory channels" or "modalities" (auditory, haptic [touch and movement], speech, and visual) and then processed. If the learner has a disorder in one or more of these modalities, learning is adversely affected. Consequently, identification of modality disorders with respect to specific academic tasks can enable the teacher to provide instruction specific to each learner.

The subtests are constructed to reflect basic concepts of reading, writing, and mathematics believed essential to success in each of these areas. If the child cannot successfully complete the task of a test item, the examiner checks the "No" column on the recording form, and then indicates which of the four modalities is involved. For example, on the mathematics test, "Symbols" is an identified component of mathematics, and specific haptic, speech, and visual characteristics are identified as affecting success on the task.

Scoring consists of counting the number of checks in the "No" column. Children receiving from 26 through 50 "No" checks on all three tests are said to need remedial help, while those receiving 51 through 75 checks need "further evaluation." The accompanying information on modalities is supposed to be useful in identifying learning disorders that the teacher should consider in planning instruction.

There are many problems with the BEST. The first area of concern is with the directions (more precisely, the lack of directions) for administering, scoring, and interpreting the results. Little information is given to guide the examiner in conducting the test. For example, there is no information on upper time limits, or testing conditions, or even when the questions are to be read to the student or read by the student (both procedures are acceptable). The manual implies that the test administrators need no special training, but this assumption seems faulty. Little direction is given on deciding the correctness of a student's answer, and even less direction is given to help the untrained person identify the modality disorder(s) accompanying an incorrect response. Finally, although the manual indicates that following screening the teacher should use the appropriate "educational strategies" to address a student's deficiencies, absolutely no guidance is given to indicate what strategies are appropriate, nor is reference made to how a teacher could access such information.

The major problems with the BEST, however, are in the items themselves. First, there is no mention of how specific concepts under the major content areas of reading, writing, and mathematics were identified. The mathematics component, for example, consists of a hodgepodge—concepts of time, space, symbols, counting, place value, logic—with no attempt made to order the components hierarchically or to validate the appropriateness of the identified components. The choice of tasks (test items) is equally bewildering. Some tasks are inappropriate for the concept (e.g., the following item is supposed to assess a child's knowledge of the concept of zero: "How many days are there in a week? How many days from today is a week from today? What day will it be a week from today?"). Other items are clearly inappropriate for the age levels of the students (e.g., asking youngsters to interpret the statement "Don't put all your eggs in one basket").

A third concern with the items is in the identification of modalities that presumably accompany success or failure on an item. It is not at all clear how such identifications were made, or why, in some instances, seemingly parallel tasks have different sets of accompanying modalities. Since no information is presented on how the test items were developed and since no item analysis data are given, a potential test user can only guess at the developers' intentions.

Despite the developers' statement that this test is to be used only as an initial screening device and that results are to be interpreted as indicative of need for further evaluation, the usefulness of this test seems questionable. Given the poor content structure of the three areas and the overall low item quality, as well as the lack of documentation and instructions for administering, scoring, and interpreting the test, it is this reviewer's opinion that the BEST should not be seriously considered as a test option.

Review of Basic Educational Skills Test by LISA FLEISHER, Assistant Professor of Educational Psychology, New York University, New York, NY and CHARLES SECOLSKY, Teacher of Mathematics, James Madison High School, Brooklyn, NY:

The Basic Educational Skills Test is an individually administered test designed for screening and diagnosing children who may have problems in reading, writing, and mathematics, and for prescribing instructional activities. It is intended for children at grade levels ranging from the end of first through fifth grade.

The test is presented using flip charts and contains 75 items divided into reading, writing, and mathematics subtests of 25 items each. Each item has from one to seven parts. The items are read by the student with assistance from the examiner when necessary. The examiner indicates that the child has answered each question correctly or incorrectly by placing a check mark in the YES column or NO column of the recording form. Aside from this, little instruction is given for administering the test. The test manual does not include information on the extent to which the examiner should assist the child (e.g., whether or not the examiner should repeat or explain questions the child does not at first comprehend). Also, although all parts of an item need to be answered correctly for the item to be counted as correct, the criteria used to decide whether or not a child answered a particular part correctly are not always specified. For example, the first part of Item 18 of the reading subtest asks the child to form as many different words as he or she can by joining prefixes and suffixes to the word "act." The second part asks the child for the meaning of each word formed. However, the manual does not indicate how many words the child needs to form and define.

The test is criterion-referenced, with items and tasks purportedly derived from research in psychology, neurology, pediatrics, and education. Each of the three general skill areas (Reading, Writing and Mathematics) are broken into requisite subskills (e.g., Figure-Ground, Gross-Motor Control, Memory, Number Facts). In most cases, the manual provides a short descriptive statement after the name of each requisite skill. The items associated with each requisite skill are listed below each statement. In addition, the manual outlines the modality areas (auditory, haptic, speech, visual) assumed to be involved in learning each of the subskills and how children can learn despite deficiencies in one or more modality areas. A recording form is also provided that allows the teacher to categorize errors according to the modality involved in receiving and processing a task so that a prescriptive program can be outlined for the child.

While the attempt to add theoretical and practical significance is commendable, it presents problems as well. The test is designed for use by teachers or parents. Some of these teachers or parents may not have had the training necessary for understanding the systems or processes associated with incorrect responses emitted by the child nor the background for understanding some of the technical language contained in the manual or for using such knowledge to design appropriate instructional activities.

The most serious problem with the test is the lack of reported reliability and validity evidence. The authors contend that an 8-year-old child who does not answer at least two-thirds of the 25 items in each subtest correctly is highly at risk; a child who responds incorrectly on from 13 to 16 items is moderately at risk, while failure on approximately one-third of the items suggests the need for careful monitoring. The manual offers no rationale to support this classification scheme nor evidence of the reliability of classificatory decisions.

Further, the small number of items for some requisite subskills (e.g., Arithmetic Operations) does not adequately represent the variety of subskills encompassed by each requisite skill area and thus prevents valid diagnoses. Similarly, the names for some requisite skills have different meanings from the short statements on the importance of each requisite skill contained in the manual. For example, in the psychoeducational literature, the term Figure-Ground typically refers to the ability to distinguish relevant from irrelevant features of an environment. The test manual, however, states that Figure-Ground is the ability to recognize "parts of a whole in a variety of combinations for attacking new words." Therefore, the use of this expression to communicate the nature of a child's learning deficiency without specifying how the term should be interpreted can be misleading. In addition, no judgment data are provided on the perceived match between items and the domains from which the items were derived or on the technical quality of the items. Such data would serve to support the validity of diagnoses.

Finally, the manual suggests that the test can be used to diagnose deficiencies associated with each modality area. Such diagnoses may be limited for prescribing instructional activities for particular learning dysfunctions, however, since the efficacy of differential diagnosis/prescriptive teaching and modality matching procedures has yet to be supported empirically.

For these reasons, the use of the test should be restricted to alerting the teacher or examiner to children who may have serious learning difficulties rather than for prescribing instructional activities based on specific diagnoses. Students found to be at risk or in need of careful monitoring should receive a more complete evaluation. However, the lengthiness of the test would suggest that its value is limited even for the purpose of screening.

[115]

Basic Inventory of Natural Language. Grades K–6, 7–12; 1977–79; BINL; 3 scores: fluency, level of complexity, average sentence length; individual; 2 levels: Forms A, B, (grades K–6), C, D, (grades 7–12); instructions manual ('79, 79 pages); individual oral score sheet ('77, 1 page); individual oral language profile ('77,

1 page); class oral language profile ('77, 1 page); story starter posters (no date, 20 posters); talktiles ('79, 80 picture cards); 1984 price data: $55 per complete kit of any one form and level including materials to test 400 students; $5 per 100 individual oral score sheets; $.15 per class oral language profile card; $36 per set of 20 pictures; $12.50 per instructions manual; scoring service available; administration time not reported; Charles H. Herbert; CHECpoint Systems, Inc.*

See T3:251 (1 reference).

TEST REFERENCES

1. Stansfield, C. W. Basic Inventory of Natural Language test review. THE MODERN LANGUAGE JOURNAL, 1978, 62, 64.

Review of Basic Inventory of Natural Language by THOMAS W. GUYETTE, Director of Speech Pathology, Children's Rehabilitation Unit, The University of Kansas Medical Center, Kansas City, KS:

The Basic Inventory of Natural Language (BINL) is a criterion-referenced test which is designed to assess language dominance and language proficiency in school age children. The language profile yielded by the BINL includes a fluency score (i.e., the total number of words used in the sample), an average sentence length score (i.e., the total number of utterances divided into the total number of words used), and a level of complexity score (i.e., derived from scoring the language sample for certain grammatical structures). The BINL can be hand scored or a special scoring sheet is provided for computer scoring.

In the BINL a language sampling approach is used. Before administering the test it is recommended that the students receive practice sessions for between 1 to 5 days. Students should also become habituated to the presence of a tape recorder so this does not inhibit their language sample. Stimulus materials in the test kit are used to elicit a language sample. This sample is then scored according to directions presented in the manual.

There are two criticisms relating to administration and scoring of the BINL language sample. First, the test requires that a sample be only 10 utterances long. A 10-utterance sample would not appear to be large enough to meet the requirement of a "representative" sample. An adequate size for a language sample is usually recommended to be between 50 and 100 utterances per sample (Darley & Moll, 1960; Crystal, Fletcher, & Garman, 1976; Leonard, 1972). Bloom and Lahey (1978) have recommended as many as 200 utterances per sample. In any case, the use of a 10-utterance sample would appear to fall far below the number needed to obtain a representative language sample. The author makes no attempt to argue for the equivalence of the 10-utterance sample with larger samples.

A second criticism involves the scoring of implied meaning in the sample. For example, if the child says "on the table" in response to the question "Where are the toys?", then he is to be given credit for the sentence "The toys are on the table." However, if he is not responding to a question then he does not get credit for the implied subject and verb. The use of implied meanings is considered in the analysis of language complexity but not in assessing overall fluency. The primary criticism is that the BINL does not give explicit instructions on how to reconstruct these implied meanings. Also, no data are presented that would indicate that this can be done reliably between two observers.

The BINL manual presents cutoff scores in the following categories: Non-English Speaking, Limited English Speaking, Fluent English Speaking, and Proficient English Speaking. Cutoff scores are provided in these four categories across the grades K through 12. The first problem with these cutoff scores is that the author presents no data to validate them. The reader is left to wonder how these ranges and cutoff points were established. It is also unclear how this test differentiates children across different grade levels. For example, there is essentially no difference between the cutoff points for children in the third, fourth, fifth, sixth, seventh, and eighth grades. Of what value is a test designed for school age children that does not distinguish between children's linguistic level in the third through eighth grades?

Three pieces of information are presented in support of the validity of the BINL. First, the author correlates the average sentence length attained in his test to the level of complexity score on his test. The correlation coefficients were relatively small ($r = .26$ to .43). A second piece of evidence presented in support of the validity of the BINL is an unpublished study. The third piece of evidence is derived by using the BINL to score the complexity of paragraphs in the Gilmore Oral Reading Test. The results suggest that the BINL average complexity level steadily rises as the level of the Gilmore Oral Reading Test paragraphs gets more difficult. In conclusion, there is little evidence presented to argue for the validity of this test.

One of the most damaging arguments against the use of the BINL is suggested by the nonlinearity of the BINL with increases in grade level. Data on the frequency distribution of BINL scores across grade levels are presented. The BINL scores increased steadily from kindergarten to the sixth grade. However, the scores of 7th, 8th, 9th and 10th graders are below that of the 5th and 6th graders. The score of the 11th grader is essentially the same of the 6th grader. No explanation for these results is provided.

Two studies of the reliability of the BINL were presented. Both studies focus on comparing the results of the first five sentences with the results of the second five sentences. The results show a high correlation between the first five sentences and the second five sentences in the 10-sentence sample. This result, however, leaves the reader wondering how the 10-sentence sample would compare with the results obtained from a larger sample. Also, since the test is designed to demonstrate progress in the acquisition of linguistic skills, it would be important to know how much variation in test scores is related to different administrations across time. Reliability data is lacking in this area.

In summary, problems in the scoring, reliability, and validity of the BINL have been presented. Until better reliability and validity data are presented and until the issue of the representativeness of a 10-utterance sample is settled I would not recommend using this test.

REVIEWER'S REFERENCES

Darley, F., & Moll, K. Reliability of language measures and size of language sample. JOURNAL OF SPEECH AND HEARING RESEARCH, 1960, 3, 166–173.

Leonard, L. What is deviant language? JOURNAL OF SPEECH AND HEARING DISORDERS, 1972, 37, 427–447.

Crystal, D., Fletcher, P., & Garman, M. THE GRAMMATICAL ANALYSIS OF LANGUAGE DISABILITY: A PROCEDURE FOR ASSESSMENT AND REMEDIATION. London: Edward Arnold, 1976.

Bloom, L., & Lahey, M. LANGUAGE DEVELOPMENT AND LANGUAGE DISORDERS. New York: John Wiley and Sons, 1978.

[116]

Basic Language Concepts Test. Ages 4–6 1/2 and "older language deficient children"; 1967–82; BLCT; revision of Basic Concept Inventory; criterion-referenced; 5 scores: receptive language, expressive language (sentence repetition, answering questions), analogy skills, total; individual; student score sheet (6 pages); manual ('82, 87 pages); 1983 price data: $27.95 per manual and 40 score sheets; $5.25 per 40 score sheets; (15–20) minutes; Siegfried Engelmann, Dorothy Ross, and Virginia Bingham; C.C. Publications, Inc.*

[117]

Basic Number Diagnostic Test. Ages 5–7; 1980; 13 scores: reciting numbers, naming numbers, copying over, copying underneath, writing numbers in sequence, writing numbers to dictation, counting bricks, selecting bricks, addition sums with objects, addition sums with numerals, subtraction sums with objects, subtraction sums with numerals, total; no validity data; age-norms only apply to score ranges; individual; 1 form (8 pages); manual (14 pages); 1983 price data: £3.50 per 20 tests; 85p per manual; £1.25 per specimen set; (15–25) minutes; W. E. C. Gillham; Hodder & Stoughton Educational [England].*

Review of Basic Number Diagnostic Test by MARY MONTGOMERY LINDQUIST, *Professor of Mathematics Education, National College of Education, Evanston, IL:*

The main purpose of this test is to provide diagnostic information on basic number skills. There is no doubt that the instrument could provide diagnostic information. If the examiners follow and extend the hints on observing and probing, they could learn a great deal. If only the total score is noted, then little, in comparison to what may have been learned, will be known. It is a shame that the recording device leans so heavily on number. More useful information as to type of error or method of solving could easily be recorded. For example, if the error in copying numbers is a reversal or objects were used to solve the addition problems, this would be useful information to note.

The test is excessive in some areas. For example, it requires copying the numbers 1 through 20 below a sample of the number. A sampling of the 20 numbers would tell us as much. If children can copy 13, they can copy 3. If they can copy 8 and 12, they can copy 18. Likewise, it is not necessary to give all the numbers from 1 through 20 to see if children can write the number when it is given to them orally. This is especially true when one loses, in the scoring procedure, the exact numbers that are missed.

The whole test is weighted heavily on writing. Thirty of the items could be missed if a child had difficulty in writing; and yet they may have the underlying concept for many items. For example, a child may be able to recognize the proper symbol for a number given orally, but not be able to write it. Likewise, a child may be able to find sums and differences, but not be able to write them. Since the writing of numbers was tested, these other 19 items whose correct response depends upon writing (even though allowances were made in the scoring for counting correct intent in the writing) are misleading.

There are number concepts, deemed basic by many, that are not included. There are no items in which a child, given a number symbol, is required to show with objects (or pictures) what the symbol represents. Likewise, there are no items in which a group of objects are shown and the child has to tell which symbol represents how many. Research has shown that these skills are not automatically obtained even if the skills on this test have been. There are no items to identify which number is more or less or the ordinals. There are no items that test any knowledge of place value or grouping, both of which are basic to the understanding of two-digit numbers. Of course, these omissions are the developer's prerogative, but the consumer should be aware of these missing skills.

This brings us to the second purpose: the test was designed to be used in conjunction with the Basic Number Screening Test. The manual suggests that if children score below 7 years on the screening test, they should be given this diagnostic test. Yet a child could answer correctly every item of the diagnostic test and not be able to do any of the items on the screening. There is a large gap between the two tests, mainly in the areas of place-value, ordering, and mastery of basic addition and subtraction facts. No information is given in the manual about whether this instrument has been found to be helpful if used after the screening test.

The third purpose, to tell whether a child's number skills are "satisfactory for his age-level," is questionable. This is due partly to the lack of content validity but also due to the way the norms for age levels were found. The norms were made from a relatively small sample in a small geographic area. While the manual cautions that these are "Approximate norms" only, they represent very unstable data. For example, children could jump from age 6 to 7 if they used objects to solve the addition and subtraction problems. It is a shame that this third purpose was included; it clouds the main purpose and appears to have led to scoring procedures based on numbers rather than on profiles.

The test itself is clear and the manual is written in an easy, unsophisticated style. The spaces for the child to write answers is small and the wording of the questions is delightfully British. If these were of concern to examiners, they could easily modify them by having children write answers on another piece of paper and by rewording the questions.

While reliability is reported (.93, Spearman's rho), there is no report of validity or of procedures used in test construction. There is no justification for the scoring procedure. In many cases it takes five correct responses for a child to obtain any score on an item. This is especially true of naming and items involving the writing of numbers. A child who incorrectly names 3, 9, 13, and 19 while correctly naming all the other numbers (1–20) would score no points. A child who incorrectly names 16 through 20 could score 3 points. There is some logic to the scoring, but it is not explained or justified.

Although the test is relatively inexpensive and some information could be obtained, this reviewer does not recommend it because of the reasons stated above.

[118]

Basic Number Screening Test. Ages 7–12; 1976–80; "number age" norms only; Forms A ('80, 4 pages), B ('79, 4 pages); manual ('79, 14 pages); 1982 price data: £1.65 per 20 tests; 70p per manual; 95p per specimen set; (20–35) minutes; W. E. C. Gillham and K. A. Hesse; Hodder & Stoughton Educational [England].*

Review of Basic Number Screening Test by MARY MONTGOMERY LINDQUIST, Professor of Mathematics Education, National College of Education, Evanston, IL:

The stated purpose of this test is "to give a quick assessment of a child's understanding of the basic principles underlying the number system (number concepts) and the processes involved in computation (number skills)." The 30 items do include both concepts and skills; however, the skill items do not assess understanding of processes, but instead test computational skills alone. The test consists of reasonable, straightforward items relating to operations with whole numbers (adding and subtracting to 3-digit numbers, multiplying and dividing by a 1-digit number), and fraction concepts. No reading is required.

The two forms of the test appear to be parallel, but no item analysis was reported. In some exercises the level of the two forms differs. For example, Form A asks the child to show one-fourth of a set, while the parallel item on B includes the much easier task of asking the child to show one-half of a set. The alternate forms are designed so they can be administered to a group at the same time to discourage student cheating.

Test items are open-ended rather than multiple-choice. At times, the child is required to mark a number or a picture, or to compute an answer. The exact type of response is clearly indicated by the examiner's question. However, having a varying number of items in each section and having a variety of types of responses make it difficult to know where some items begin and end.

The amount of time allotted for the test is left to the discretion of the examiner. Children are told they can return to unfinished items at the completion of the entire test. However, since many of the concept items require a restating of the question, this suggestion is questionable.

The wording of the questions would have to be modified for children in the United States, but the skills assessed would be appropriate. The placement of the decimal point in the one item involving decimal numbers would also be confusing. Administering and scoring the test is described simply and accurately in the manual. It suggests that a more comprehensive test be given following initial screening; however, it does not specify how to determine which test should be used.

Age equivalent scores are provided. These are related to the average raw score performance of each specific age group. While the developers admit age scores have technical limitations, they suggest that such scores are a meaningful indication of whether or not a child is performing satisfactorily. There is no implication that children who have an age equivalent score of 11 years, for example, can do all the mathematics that the average 11-year-old can do. Age equivalent scores could be a source of confusion for parents if the scores were interpreted in this manner. Technical data concerning the test are from a sample of over 3,000 students from one English city. Alternate form reliability of .93 was reported. A validity coefficient of .82 was obtained between teacher rankings and test scores.

This is an appealing test that could be a useful first step in diagnosing mathematics problems. However, it could be strengthened by tying it explicitly to further diagnostic procedures. Also, a more careful analysis of the different types of arithmetical problems could have been undertaken, and tests could have been constructed specifically to fit the types. If the developers assumed that the scores do this automatically, because of the hierarchical nature of mathematics, then this should have been stated explicitly. However, it is doubtful that this is the case. I cannot recommend using this test as a sole measure of arithmetic without knowing more about how the results have been and can be used.

Review of Basic Number Screening Test by MARILYN N. SUYDAM, Professor, Mathematics Education, The Ohio State University, Columbus, OH:

The usefulness of this test is questionable. Its main purpose is "to help identify the child whose number attainments are low for his age or who is failing to make continued progress," thus directing attention to children "whose difficulties need to be explored individually and in detail." However, it would seem that such a child could be identified by the teacher in the course of ongoing instruction as readily as by this test. Moreover, the test fails to focus on specific weaknesses a child might have.

The test contains 15 number concept items and 15 number skill items. It is not immediately apparent which are concept items and which are skill items, and the test developers do not divulge this information. No indication is given of the objectives of individual items. However, this could be viewed as irrelevant, since the scoring does not take type of item into consideration, nor is any diagnostic information provided. We know only that the content spans basic facts (5 items), computational algorithms (11 items), place value (3 items), fractions (4 items), decimals (1 item), sequence (3 items), and patterns (3 items). Of most concern is why only a single item pertains to decimals. Additional measures must be used to assess other curricular goals such as problem solving, yet even the focus on number operations is limited.

The content was determined by the authors' (*a*) "understanding of the development of children's number concepts," (*b*) "appreciation of the changing nature of mathematics in schools," and (*c*) "practical experience and detailed discussion with class-teachers." The latter believeably influenced choice of content, but it is difficult to assess the contribution of the first point and even less possible to discern the role of the second point. In this age of readily available computing tools, a test on which half of the items could be solved more efficiently with a calculator scarcely reflects a changing curriculum.

Directions for administration cover (albeit briefly) everything from where to place children with hearing or sight difficulties to the usual injunction not to alter instructions. One of the longest paragraphs concerns precautions to avoid having children copy each others' answers. One wishes that the space were devoted to information about the test itself.

Instructions for the children are clear and worded naturally. However, the format is likely to cause some difficulty because from one to three items are presented in a given space. One modification of the directions would be necessary for American users: "sum" is used with any operation, not only addition. Use of the dot in midline for decimals would make one item per form meaningless for most American children. On the answer page, interestingly, the decimal point is placed on the line.

The test was standardized in mid-year on 3,042 children aged 7.5 to 11.5 years in 15 schools in Nottingham (England). No characteristics of the norm group are provided. In view of this limited, local sample, the resulting age norms cannot be presumed to generalize to children in other communities and schools.

A satisfactory Pearson product-moment correlation coefficient of .93 was obtained by correlating scores on the two forms administered 1 week apart. No other measure of reliability was determined, nor is internal consistency even discussed.

Since the test directly samples the content it measures, validity was assumed "not to be a serious problem." Feedback from teachers and children after item tryouts aided in determining whether an item was acceptable. Whether any statistical item data were used is not specified. In addition, an unknown number of teachers in one school rated their students on a 7-point scale before the test was administered, and these ratings were correlated with the test scores. The correlation (Spearman's rho) averaged .82, which was considered "very satisfactory"; it is, however, difficult to affirm this.

The manual provides no information to help teachers interpret the test results, diagnose a child's needs, or plan instruction. The test is simply a measure, intact in and of itself. The manual consists only of 2 pages on the purpose, nature, construction, and standardization of the test; 5 pages of instructions for administration; 2 pages on scoring; and 1/3 page of norms. The manual provides age equivalent scores which reflect the average score of norm group members at each age level. What to do with these scores is the user's problem.

SUMMARY. The limited scope of the test, the limited data, and the lack of attention to interpretation of results are serious drawbacks to the usefulness of this test. Teachers might well find that they know as much as the test reveals about the numerical competency of their students. The age norms provided may be simply a number to store in records. Users who want a test which will promote instructional goals in addition to assessing status might better turn elsewhere.

[119]

Basic Reading Inventory, Second Edition. Reading level grades K–8; 1978–81; BRI; 3 reading level scores (independent, instructional, frustration) for each of 3 subtests (Word Recognition in Isolation, Word Recognition in Context, Comprehension); no data on reliability; no norms; individual; Form A, B, C, (no date, 16 pages in spirit duplicating masters, suggested that one form be used for a silent reading measure, one for an oral reading measure, and one for a listening measure or posttest); manual ('81, 154 pages); price data available from publisher; administration time not reported; Jerry L. Johns; Kendall/Hunt Publishing Co.*

Review of Basic Reading Inventory, Second Edition, by GUS P. PLESSAS, Professor of Education, California State University, Sacramento, Sacramento, CA:

Designed for classroom use, the Basic Reading Inventory is an informal test to ascertain performance levels of students in reading for purposes of placement and diagnosis. Included in the manual are guidelines for qualitative interpretation of test results to evaluate students' reading competencies in word attack and comprehension. A series of graded word lists and graded passages make up the test. Comprehension questions follow each reading passage.

Of particular importance to the user of the Basic Reading Inventory is the manual that accompanies the test material. The manual contains underlying assumptions and background information along with testing instructions that enhance understanding of the Basic Reading Inventory. Directions for administering the test and recording reading performances are easy to follow. Practical aids for analyzing and summarizing test results are given.

The variety of possible assessment modes is a positive feature of the Basic Reading Inventory, especially in the hands of a skillful examiner. Graded word lists provide the option of timed and untimed presentations of words for comparison purposes. Similarly analytic data may be secured from testing when the three alternate forms of the test are employed as oral and silent reading measures as well as a listening measure. Although such comparisons are time consuming, a reading specialist may obtain much useful information from them.

Of practical utility to reading appraisal are the suggested techniques for analyzing not only the types of errors made in decoding unfamiliar words during oral reading but also the significance of such errors in the light of graphic and/or context cues.

The use of informal reading inventories as reading assessment tools is not without problems, and the Basic Reading Inventory is no exception. First, criteria for evaluating reading performances on an informal inventory inevitably are subjective. Consider, for example, the author's statement in the preface of the manual: "As an informal test, the Basic Reading Inventory makes no statistical claims to validity and reliability." Thus, questions about test reliability or validity cannot be answered by consulting research data about the Basic Reading Inventory, because such research data are not provided. There is no evidence concerning equivalency of test forms either under oral reading, silent reading, or listening test conditions. There are no test-retest reliability data and no internal consistency data, even for the comprehension items. Nor is it known whether one form of the test is consistently easier than are the alternate forms or whether certain questions on comprehension are typically harder to answer than others.

Second, to discern patterns of difficulty in comprehension, the Basic Reading Inventory contains comprehension checks to assess noting facts and main ideas, making evaluation and inference, and vocabulary. Lacking correlation data, a test user is not in a position to validate the independence of each skill to be appraised. Do evaluation and inference questions, for instance, assess discrete abilities? Does each type of comprehension check provide valid information? If not, how can one have confidence in test results that purport to indicate strengths and weaknesses in comprehension? Can such a diagnostic profile become a prescription for instruction?

Third, in the Basic Reading Inventory reading rate is measured on each graded passage of approximately 100 words by dividing by the time a student takes to read the passage. Difficulty levels of materials have a definite impact on reading speed. What rate values can be assigned to a student who struggles through a difficult passage? What rate is valid when reading speed may differ from passage to passage in terms of difficulty?

Fourth, performances on the Basic Reading Inventory are based on one set of material. If it differs from reading selections that are used for instruction, a teacher should be careful in linking inventory results with instructional decisions. Best results are obtained from inventories when test material is the same as classroom material. In this way, curricular validity of the evaluation process is strengthened for mapping teaching strategies.

Fifth, since the Basic Reading Inventory is not a normed device, the quality of interpretation of performances will depend on an examiner's experience, knowledge, and judgment about testing and teaching reading. Informal tests require too much subjective thinking to ascertain the competence with which a student reads. For example, counting repetitions and determining significant miscues are largely judgmental matters. In the final analysis, the evaluation outcome may indeed vary from examiner to examiner.

In sum, for the reading clinician or diagnostician the Basic Reading Inventory can be a useful tool to assess reading performances, especially among children who have reading disabilities. For the regular classroom teacher the use of graded instructional passages from basal readers would serve as well or better than the use of the Basic Reading Inventory for appraisal and placement purposes.

[120]

Basic School Skills Inventory—Diagnostic. Ages 4–0 to 6–11; 1983; BSSI-D; 7 scores: daily living skills, spoken language, reading, writing, mathematics, classroom behavior, total; individual; pupil record form (2 pages); picture book (36 pages); manual (70 pages including inventory); 1984 price data: $42 per complete kit including 50 pupil record forms; $12 per 50 pupil record forms; $15 per picture book; $18 per manual; (20–30) minutes; Donald D. Hammill and James E. Leigh; PRO-ED.*

For reviews of an earlier edition by Byron R. Egeland and Lawrence M. Kasdon, see 8:424 (2 references).

Review of Basic School Skills Inventory—Diagnostic by WILLIAM J. WEBSTER, Special Assistant to the Superintendent—Research, Evaluation, and Information Systems, Dallas Independent School District, Dallas, TX:

The Basic School Skills Inventory—Diagnostic (BSSI-D) is a readiness test that was designed to provide measures of early abilities of children in six areas: daily living skills, spoken language, reading, writing, mathematics, and classroom behavior. It was designed for use with children who are between the ages of 4 and 6 years 11 months, or with children who are older but function within the 4 to 6 developmental range. The BSSI-D is recommended by the authors for use in identifying children who are significantly below their peers in early abilities related to the aforementioned six areas, in revealing specific strengths and deficits in the assessed areas, and in documenting progress resulting from intervention in the respective areas. Thus, the authors posit both a norm-referenced and criterion-referenced application for the test.

The 1983 edition of the BSSI-D consists of six subtests comprising a total of 110 items. The test is rather unique in that it consists of different mixtures of teacher and student responses depending on each specific situation. Therefore, it must be administered by someone who has a great deal of first-hand information about the child being tested. For this reason the manual recommends that it be administered by classroom teachers and their aides, diagnostic teachers, and other school personnel who see the child on a continuing instructional basis.

The rationale for the BSSI-D is based on the author's argument that most readiness tests lack content, concurrent, and construct validity. The BSSI-D is advanced as focusing directly on academic, linguistic, and cognitive behaviors of concern rather than on hypothetical prerequisite processing abilities for which adequate measures do not currently exist. This reviewer is not convinced that the BSSI-D possesses this strength, since the items do not appear to be logically related in any systematic manner to specific important academic, linguistic, and cognitive behaviors.

There is no time element specified for the administration of the BSSI-D. The examiner is instructed to score items that measure examinee abilities with which the examiner is familiar without testing the examinee. For those behaviors that the examiner has not had the opportunity to observe from prior interactions with the examinee, direct testing of the behavior is required. The manual suggests that actual test administration should not take more than 30 minutes. Thus, the BSSI-D purports to be a norm-referenced test but does not require standard administration procedures (i.e., any two examinees are not likely to take the test under the same conditions). This procedure makes the interpretation of scores relative to norms most difficult.

The apparent lack of standard test administration procedures is exacerbated by the lack of clear and specific items and scoring procedures for many of the exercises. Many of the items are open to differences in interpretation, which would again tend to contribute to error variance in scoring the test.

Each of the six subtests yields a raw score which can be converted to percentiles or standard scores (mean of 10 and standard deviation of 3) through the use of a series of tables presented in the manual. The total test yields a score called the Composite Skill Quotient. This quotient ranges from 50 to 150 with a mean of 100 and a standard deviation of 15. The authors state that the Composite Skill Quotient yields a global measure of basic skills. A pupil record form is supplied by the publisher for recording and interpreting test performance.

Despite the apparent limitations enumerated above, the BSSI-D appears to be quite reliable as measured by indices of internal consistency. Coefficient alphas for each of the six subtests at each of three grade levels vary from a low of .82 to a high of .97, with the total test reliability being in the .96 to .97 range. Alternate form reliability is reported in the .88 to .92 range. The alternate form used is the

BSSI-S, the screening version of the inventory, since no specific alternate form of the BSSI-D exists.

The most important measure of reliability for an instrument that requires rater observation is a measure of interrater reliability. If interrater reliability is not high, then the whole concept of norm-referencing this test is in danger. Doubt about the examiner's ability to administer the test under a standard set of conditions could be somewhat alleviated by a measure of interrater reliability that is sufficiently high to suggest that two raters, following the instructions in the manual, could reach similar independent conclusions about the same child by administering the BSSI-D. Unfortunately, no measure of interrater reliability is reported.

The authors posit content validity on the basis of the fact that teachers supplied the information by which the items were originally selected; that the 1983 edition of the BSSI-D was twice field-tested and revised on the basis of teacher opinion; and that, for the most part, the BSSI-D is completed by teachers and therefore is to some extent a measure of teachers' perceptions of children's abilities and basic skills. That is, the content of BSSI-D is based on the professional beliefs of teachers concerning what is important for children to be able to do. Content validity appears assured although the apparent lack of an underlying test paradigm presents some concerns.

Criterion-related validity was measured by correlating the BSSI-D scores with teacher ratings of readiness and school achievement. This approach appears tantamount to correlating the BSSI-D with itself since the BSSI-D is also, in many cases, a composite of teacher ratings of readiness and school achievement. Since the BSSI-D is a test of readiness, it would seem that the most appropriate measure of criterion-related validity would involve a longitudinal study investigating the capacity of the BSSI-D to predict student success on a respected measure of educational achievement at a later grade. Since no such study is reported, the jury is still out regarding the criterion-related validity of the BSSI-D.

Construct validity was investigated by examining the degree of age differentiation evidenced by the test, the degree of interrelationships among the subtests, the ability of the test to differentiate between "normal" and learning-disabled children, and the discriminating power of the individual items on the test. All four areas of investigation yielded results that were posited by the authors to support the construct validity of the test. This reviewer would tend to agree, although the difficulty levels on some of the subtests make norm-referenced applications questionable.

The publisher made an effort to norm the test on a representative group of children. The BSSI-D was standardized on a sample of 376 children, between the ages of 4–0 and 6–11, residing in 15 states. Information presented by the publisher on the norm group suggests that the sample was not representative of the population of the United States in terms of white-collar versus blue-collar occupation of parents but was relatively close in such areas as sex, urban versus rural, race, and geographic area with the exception that the South was greatly overrepresented and the West underrepresented. No information is given on the number of students tested at various ages.

The BSSI-D was revised and restandardized in 1983 and many improvements in technical documentation were made from the 1976 edition. There is little doubt that the problems inherent in reliably and validly measuring the readiness or achievement levels of young children are many, and that perhaps a series of standardized exercises similar to those included in the BSSI-D represent a potentially powerful approach to overcoming many of those problems. However, the questionable nature of the norms combined with the lack of important interrater reliability and criterion-related validity data dictate that the BSSI-D be used with care. Since the norm conversions are the basis for most uses of the test, be they norm-referenced or criterion-referenced, the usefulness of this test for its intended purposes is largely yet to be demonstrated.

[121]

Basic School Skills Inventory—Screen. Ages 4–0 to 6–11; 1983; BSSI-S; short form of the Basic School Skill Inventory—Diagnostic; individual; answer and record sheet (4 pages); fact sheet (6 pages); 1984 price data: $14 per complete kit including 50 answer and record sheets; (5–10) minutes; Donald D. Hammill and James E. Leigh; PRO-ED.*

Review of Basic School Skills Inventory—Screen by LELAND K. DOEBLER, Assistant Professor of Counseling and Educational Psychology, University of Montevallo, Montevallo, AL:

The stated purpose of the Basic School Skills Inventory—Screen (BSSI-S) is to provide a quick, easy method of identifying children who are "high risk" candidates for failure in the schools. The instrument is designed for use with 4- and 5-year-olds and with 6-year-olds who have exhibited a deficit in basic school skills. In effect, then, BSSI-S can be thought of as an indicator of readiness ability.

The BSSI-S consists of 20 items selected from the 110 items which make up the Basic School Skills Inventory—Diagnostic. Items were chosen based upon their discrimination index and difficulty level. Ordinarily the instrument will be completed by the child's classroom teacher, who is instructed to read each item and respond "Yes, the child can do this," "No, the child can't do this," or "I don't know if the child can or can't do this." If the response is "yes," a 1 is recorded on the answer sheet, while if the response is "no" a zero is recorded. If the examiner cannot respond, he/she then tests the child with the examination procedures which accompany the item. While the authors are to be commended for the thorough explanations accompanying the items, there is an inherent weakness in this scoring procedure. The subjective nature of the scoring makes the items highly vulnerable to the halo effect. This vulnerability is further enhanced by the fact that the teachers are encouraged to respond based upon experience without actually testing. What is actually being measured, then, is the teacher's opinion of the child's ability. This may or may not correspond to the child's actual ability. In addition, there are several items requiring judgements that could vary widely from teacher to teacher. While a "yes" or "no" can easily be assigned to a question such as "Can the child tell you his/her correct address?," a question such as "Is the child's vocabulary appropriate for his/her age?," is dependent upon the teacher's interpretation of the word "appropriate." Other questions such as "Can the child progress through the normal activities of the school day without seeking an inordinate amount of attention from the teacher?" and "Does the child find something acceptable to do after completing his/her work?" reflect not only the teacher's definitions of "inordinate" and "acceptable," but also the teacher's level of tolerance. Again, wide variations are likely, thus allowing a child who might be classified as "at risk" by teacher A to be found perfectly normal by teacher B.

The standardization of the BSSI-S was conducted on a sample of 376 children between the ages of 4–0 and 6–11. Unfortunately further breakdown of the sample by age is not provided. The sample is broken down with regard to the characteristics of sex, residence, occupation of parents, race, and geographic area. In comparing the standardization sample with the United States population one finds that the South is greatly overrepresented in the sample while the Northeast and West are seriously underrepresented. In addition, children of blue-collar workers make up 61% of the sample as opposed to 36% of the population, while children of white-collar workers make up only 28% of the sample but account for 51% of the population. These inbalances in sample selection may limit the usefulness of this instrument in many school districts.

Scores are reported in terms of percentiles and standard scores with a mean of 100 and a standard deviation of 15. The use of this particular scale may lead some parents to equate scores on the BSSI-S with an IQ. It is very important therefore that users of this instrument make clear to parents that this is not the case. The authors consider any child who scores more than one standard deviation below the mean (standard score below 85; percentile below 16) to be a high risk. While this is a convenient cutoff point, very little evidence is presented to validate this claim. To their credit, however, the authors do caution the user to try to obtain confirming evidence from other sources before classifying the child as high risk.

Validity is discussed in terms of content, construct, and criterion-related validity. Content validity is claimed based upon the method of selection of the items. This would seem to assume the validity of the BSSI-D from which the items are drawn. No evidence of this is presented, however, in the "Fact Sheet" which serves as the manual for the BSSI-S. Evidence of construct validity is adequate, although the sample in the study designed to establish diagnostic validity was rather small. It is, however, with regard to criterion-related validity that the most serious questions are raised. Scores on the BSSI-S are correlated with the subtests of the BSSI-D. This reviewer questions the usefulness of that information. Since the items of the BSSI-S are drawn from the BSSI-D, it is not surprising that significant correlations are reported between the two. Much more useful information could be obtained by correlating the BSSI-S scores with some subsequent measure of academic performance. Finally, with regard to criterion-related validity, the authors report a significant correlation ($p < .001$) between the BSSI-S and teacher ratings. This raises the question of the need for the BSSI-S. It does not seem to be making a significant contribution to the identification of high risk students beyond that of a simple teacher rating.

Reliability data are reported as KR-21 and alternate forms coefficients with the BSSI-D serving as the alternate form. While these coefficients are all in the acceptable range, one must question the lack of any estimate of the stability of the scores. In light of the subjective nature of the scoring pointed out earlier in this review, acceptable test-retest and interrater reliabilities would also be very reassuring. Lacking those coefficients, however, this reviewer cannot declare this to be a reliable test.

In summary, this reviewer finds little evidence on which to recommend the use of this instrument. The standardization sample is not well chosen with regard to the population, and evidence is lacking on the stability of the scores over time or across examiners. The authors' attempts to establish criterion-related validity suggest that this instrument contributes little beyond that of a simple teacher rating to the identification of high risk students. Should a measure of readiness be required, this reviewer would suggest that consideration be given to a more well established instrument such as the Metropolitan Readiness Test. This instrument seems to be one more example of the sacrifice of quality assessment to the gods of quick and easy.

[122]

Basic Skills Assessment. Grades 7 and over; 1977–81; BSA; tentative norms are for total scores, grades 8, 9, and 12 only, publisher recommends use of local norms; 4 tests; tests *a*, *b*, and *c* are available in a combined booklet for Forms A and B; user guide ('81, 77 pages); directions for administering the multiple-choice tests (*a*, *b*, *c* below, '77, 8 pages); technical manual ('78, 48 pages); separate answer sheets must be used except with *d*; 1985 price data: $61.25 per 35 combined booklets; $16 per 100 NCS answer sheets; $4.50 per set of 5 scoring stencils; $4 per user guide; $1 per directions for administering multiple-choice tests; $4 per technical manual; $7.50 per specimen set; scoring service available for test *a*, *b*, *c*, $.65 and over per student; (40–60) minutes; National Consortium of School Districts and Educational Testing Service; CTB/McGraw-Hill.*

a) READING. 3 scores: literal comprehension, inference-evaluation, total; Form A ('77, 23 pages), B ('78, 23 pages), C ('79, 23 pages); $26.25 per 35 tests.

b) A WRITER'S SKILLS. 5 scores: spelling, capitalization-punctuation, usage, logic-evaluation, total; Form A ('77, 12 pages), B ('78, 12 pages), C ('79, 12 pages); $24.50 per 35 tests.

c) MATHEMATICS. 3 scores: computation, applications, total; Form A ('77, 11 pages), C ('79, 11 pages); $24.50 per 35 tests.

d) WRITING SAMPLE, A DIRECT MEASURE OF WRITING. Form A ('77, 10 pages); manual for scoring the writer's sample ('79, 18 pages); $17.85 per 35 tests; $3.75 per directions for administering; $3.75 per manual for scoring the writing sample.

Review of Basic Skills Assessment Program by BARBARA S. PLAKE, Associate Professor of Educational Psychology, University of Nebraska, Lincoln, NE:

According to page 1 of the User Guide, the Basic Skills Assessment (BSA) "is a secondary-level testing program that offers schools a systematic method of certifying whether or not future high school graduates have met each school's specific standards of performance in the basic skills of reading, writing, and mathematics." The BSA is also billed as a means for helping teachers identify students in grades 8 through 12 who need additional help in developing their reading, writing, and mathematics skills, and as a national testing program designed to help secondary schools establish minimum competencies for students in grades 7 through 12. In addition, in the pamphlet entitled Guidelines for Using Basic Skills Assessment, two additional uses are suggested: (*a*) as a tool to monitor students' progress in basic skills, and (*b*) as a means of evaluating the effectiveness of educational programs that focus on the areas tested. Thus, the program purports to serve a variety of purposes and be appropriate for several uses. These are ambitious objectives for any testing program to try to accomplish.

There are four tests in the program: Reading, Mathematics, A Writer's Skills, and a Writing Sample. The first three contain multiple-choice items while the Writing Sample provides a direct measure of writing. The three multiple-choice tests can be administered in any combination, but the Writing Sample is designed to supplement the multiple-choice measure of writing obtained from A Writer's Skills test. The test program is designed to allow for two modes of testing: secure and nonsecure. Secure tests, probably used for certification and minimum competence/mastery decisions, are revised every semester and are carefully controlled. These tests are available from Educational Testing Service (ETS). CTB/McGraw-Hill has nonsecure versions available which may be reused within a school system as needed or desired.

The Basic Skills Assessment Program has several supporting documents, ranging in style from catchy advertisement brochures to highly specific technical manuals. There seems to be a document for virtually every purpose and audience, from quick overviews to in-depth analyses. The documentation is well organized, clearly presented, and well written from both a technical and user's standpoint. The documentation provides clear and concise information on what are considered to be valid uses of the testing program and specifies examples of misuses of the tests. In many cases, users are reminded of the social and political implications of certification decisions. Special documentation is provided for establishing local cutoff scores and for scoring the Writing Sample.

The BSA appears to have been developed from an identification of a need for such an assessment tool by representatives of school districts from across the nation. Working with a consortium of school districts, ETS identified the basic skills areas to be addressed in the instrument. Results of a national survey and advice from representatives of school districts were used to finalize the component skills to be assessed. Once developed, a series of analyses were performed to determine the quality of the instruments. A careful sampling procedure was employed to obtain appropriate levels of representation from school districts in terms of geographical and socioeconomic factors. Test analyses indicate that the subscales are neither totally distinct nor redundant. Total test scores for Reading, A Writer's Skills, and Mathematics tests have internal consistency reliability estimates (KR-20) of .94, .94 and .92, respectively. Subscales within each of these tests have somewhat lower reliability values, ranging from .73 to .91. No evidence is provided for stability indices of reliability. No reliability estimates or item data were given for the Writing Sample test.

Although of questionable relevance, the manual gives a rationale for including normative information. Based on the carefully derived norming sample, both entry-level (grades 8 and 9) and exit-level (grade 12) norms are provided. The scale selected for the reported scores has a mean of 150 and a standard deviation of 25. A scale equating method will be used to permit comparison of performance on all forms of a particular test.

With regard to validity, the Technical Manual provides strong evidence for content validity of the tests, citing the use of literature review, school district personnel, and a national survey to identify the component skills to be assessed in the BSA. Concurrent validity is addressed by means of a contrasting group method whereby teachers of students in the norming group were asked to identify their judgment of the status of each student on each of the three tests as (*a*) clearly does not require help in mastering these skills, (*b*) not certain, and (*c*) definitely requires remedial help in mastering the skills measured by the test. Based on the results of separate frequency distributions for the groups identified as (*a*) and (*c*) for each test, concurrent validity was assumed to be established. In a follow-up analysis, the results were less conclusive. Although the test distributions showed substantial differences between 9th and 12th graders in Reading, much less difference was revealed for 9th- and 12th-grade distributions in Mathematics. Some of the subscales show very little mean score differences between 9th and 12th graders: Computation, 3 points; Applications, 6 points; Literal Comprehension, 2 points; Spelling, 1 point. All of these differences are well within usual chance-determined limits. Although plans were discussed for further research of the concurrent and predictive validity of the tests, none were reported in the specimen set provided for review.

A variety of score reports are available which provide information on student performance on the total test and on specific item clusters, such as norm-based information yielding percentile ranks for both entry-level and exit-level norms. Reports that are available as options include item-based information for each student, showing whether the item was answered correctly, incorrectly, or omitted. Such detailed information is of questionable validity and utility, since no claims are made that the test yields individual diagnostic information at the item level. This information may suggest to the naive test user that conclusions about competencies at the item level are reasonable. Unlike other instances where the documentation is clear about potential misuses of data, the manual fails to caution against the use of this individual item performance for decision-making purposes. Since the information is not valid for such purposes, one wonders why this option is available.

The lack of remedial instructional information is possibly the biggest weakness in the program. Because subscales within tests have reliabilities which are, in general, too low to be used for individual decisions, it is not possible to determine prescriptive instructional information about an individual who has been identified as needing remedial help. Although the documentation strongly makes the case for follow-up remediation programs, information provided by this assessment tool is not valid for making specific recommendations for individuals.

On the whole, however, this assessment program appears to be well designed, well documented, and expertly developed and analyzed. Although the purposes of the program are ambitious and challenging, for the most part the BSA program seems to have faced these challenges, and the result is a test that is sensitive to user needs, goals, and purposes.

Review of Basic Skills Assessment by MICHAEL M. RAVITCH, Director of Medical Education, Associate Professor of Education, Northwestern University, Chicago, IL:

The Basic Skills Assessment Program (BSA) was developed to respond to concern about the preparedness of high school graduates. We are all familiar with sensational reports of high school graduates who can neither read nor write and with less publicized cases of graduates who are marginally prepared for the demands of life. The BSA is intended for use early in high school to detect students who are unlikely to be minimally "competent" at graduation and for use at the end of high school as an exit examination, to catch students who still need help.

The framework of the test, developed by Educational Testing Service (ETS) staff and an advisory group of 12 representatives from school systems, colleges, and departments of education, has three major skill areas: reading, mathematics, and writing. Answer sheets can be hand scored or returned to ETS. The basic scoring service provides a student roster with raw scores, scaled scores, and national percentiles. One section of this report is listed in alphabetical order, while another section is listed in descending rank order based on students' scaled scores. Reports can be prepared separately for each test and for subgroups of students. If requested, scores can be given for item clusters. In addition to these machine-scorable multiple-choice tests, there is a writing sample which presents examinees with a standard set of writing tasks; responses to the writing sample must be judged locally, at the school or district level. The tests are displayed clearly. Examinees should have little difficulty following instructions and carrying out the test-taking task.

Any new test deserves a hard look, particularly a new type of test. The fact that the developer is one of the (deservedly) most highly respected testing corporations does not diminish the need for caution. In particular, users must judge whether the content of these tests is appropriate, since no information on predictive validity is provided. For example, the reading test provides subscores for literal comprehension and for inference and evaluation. Reading items can be grouped by content clusters: forms, charts, maps, prose. Items can also be grouped by content (the context in which the task represented in the items might be found in real life): consumer (telephone directory, loan agreement, guarantee, advertising, operating guides, product information), learner (newspaper or magazine, narrative fiction, dictionary, school catalog, cartoon, book or periodical titles), citizen (editorial, tax form, driver's application form, law, political propaganda, community resources), protector (medicine label directions, product warnings, nutritional information, first aid information, road map), and producer (job application, description of benefits, bus schedule, want ads, work-related information). One could argue whether all items are equally important for assessing reading competency. Should understanding a cartoon, medicine label directions, and road maps be given equal weight?

Interpretation of the BSA may cause school personnel to ask an interesting question—if students do poorly, should the curriculum be modified to give students more experience in "real life" tasks in mathematics and reading? The test developers deliberately selected tasks judged to be part of life—the objective was to see if students are prepared for the usual tasks in life, not to predict success in academics beyond high school. Thus, items are not intended to represent high school curricula, but school districts in which students perform poorly on the BSA must consider whether a life-oriented curriculum is needed, or only a strengthening in the three Rs.

Are the items, themselves, good items? Most items seem to be clear and unambiguous, with a few exceptions. For example, one reading question presents a label (for an insecticide), and asks what the appropriate container is for holding the mixed spray; three responses are food containers and so are wrong (could lead to accidental poisoning), but the remaining answer is "an empty paint can"—and paint residue could dissolve in or react with the insecticide solution and cause damage to plants, food consumers, or spray equipment. Item construction is difficult, and it should not surprise us that a test, in spite of a good development team using due caution and extensive tryout and review, should nonetheless have a few questionable items.

The manuals for the BSA are well written and informative. Useful information is provided on development of the tests, descriptive statistics and norms, and validity of the tests. The reliability (KR-20) of each of the three tests was above .90 at each of the three grade levels tested (8, 9, 12). Mean scores by students in higher grades were above those in lower grades. The relatively high reliabilities of subscales within tests and associated small standard errors of measurement lend confidence to interpretations teachers may want to make based on these subscales.

The discussion of validity is candid and appropriate, yet troubling—and at the same time a model of what should be presented. The discussion argues for the content validity of the tests, pointing out that such validity is necessarily subjective since it is based on judgments of the extent to which the content is appropriate and sufficient. ETS went to considerable effort to include educators and specialists from a variety of groups. Regardless, a careful review of test content is required before a school district can reach conclusions about content validity. Concurrent validity was assessed by the relationship between test performance and teachers' assessments of the competence of students being tested. These results strongly supported the BSA's ability to distinguish extreme groups of students (students definitely requiring remediation; students definitely not requiring remediation). Unfortunately, no information is given about the middle group of students, for whom teachers were uncertain regarding need for remediation. Teachers probably do not need tests to help them with students who are clearly succeeding or clearly failing. Spotting borderline students (in teachers' judgments) and discriminating those who need remediation from those who do not is a task to which the BSA might be addressed, but no guidance is given on such discriminations. No information is given on the predictive validity of the tests—what is the relationship between BSA scores and performance in life? Indeed, to what criteria is the test related?

If school systems decide they need an external assessment of competency in the three Rs, the Basic Skills Assessment Program deserves careful consideration. The examination and accompanying manuals bear witness to the quality one expects from good test developers, but the major considerations have to be whether the content is appropriate for the intended uses and, if so, whether criteria for competency should be based on national norms (provided), local judgment (guidance provided), or predictive validity (unknown). This test battery is a good effort at a new and difficult problem.

[123]

Basic Skills Inventory. Grades K–1, 1–2, 2–3, 3–4, 5–6, 7–8, 9–10, 11–12; 1980–82; BSI; "a set of ready-made general achievement assessment instruments designed to test common objectives or minimum competencies"; 3 subtests: Reading, Language Arts, and Mathematics which may be ordered singly or as combined booklets; combined booklets available for grades 4–6, 7–9, and 10–12 only; 8 levels; examiners manuals: primary edition ('80, 6 pages), reusable booklet edition ('80, 4 pages); test coordinator's handbooks: primary edition, reusable booklet edition, ('80, 4 pages); technical report ('83, 204 pages); machine-scorable answer sheet ('80, 2 pages); identification sheets ('80, 2 pages) for teacher/group, school; student report ('80, 1 page); self scoring profile (no date, 3 pages); answer sheets must be used for grades 4–12; price data available from publisher; (45) minutes per subtest; Los Angeles County Office of Education.*

a) READING.

1) *Grades K–1.* Scores from 3 major areas: phonetic analysis, vocabulary, comprehension; 2 forms: Level A (no date, 8 pages), Level I ('81, 16 pages).

2) *Grades 1–2.* Scores from 5 major areas: phonetic analysis, structural analysis, vocabulary, comprehension, study skills; 2 forms: Level B (no date, 8 pages), Level II ('81, 16 pages).

3) *Grades 2–3.* Scores from 5 areas: same as 2 above; 2 forms: Level C (no date, 8 pages), Level III ('81, 16 pages).

4) *Grades 3–4.* Scores from 5 areas: same as 2 above; 1 form labeled Level IV ('81, 12 pages).

5) *Grades 5–6.* Scores from 5 areas: same as 2 above; 1 form labeled Level V ('81, 16 pages).

6) *Grades 7–8.* Scores from 4 major areas: structural analysis, vocabulary, comprehension, study skills; 1 form labeled Level VI ('81, 15 pages).

7) *Grades 9–10.* Scores from 4 areas: same as 6 above; 1 form labeled Level VII ('81, 16 pages).

8) *Grades 11–12.* Scores from 4 areas: same as 6 above; 1 form labeled Level VIII ('81, 15 pages).

b) LANGUAGE ARTS.

1) *Grades K–1.* Scores from 3 major areas: language analysis, conventions, expression/comprehension; 2 forms: Level A (no date, 8 pages), Level I ('81, 12 pages).

2) *Grades 1–2.* Scores from 3 areas: same as 1 above; 2 forms: Level B (no date, 8 pages), Level II ('81, 12 pages).

3) *Grades 2–3.* Scores from 3 areas: same as 1 above; 2 forms: Level C (no date, 8 pages), Level III ('81, 12 pages).

4) *Grades 3–4.* Scores from 4 major areas: spelling, punctuation, sentence structure, verb usage; 1 form labeled Level IV ('81, 11 pages).

5) *Grades 5–6.* Scores from 4 areas: same as 4 above; 1 form labeled Level V ('81, 11 pages).

6) *Grades 7–8.* Scores from 4 areas: same as 4 above; 1 form labeled Level VI ('81, 11 pages).

7) *Grades 9–10.* Scores from 4 areas: same as 4 above; 1 form labeled Level VII ('81, 11 pages).

8) *Grades 11–12.* Scores from 4 areas: same as 4 above; 1 form labeled Level VIII ('81, 11 pages).

c) MATHEMATICS.

1) *Grades K–1.* Scores from 3 major areas: comprehension, computation, application; 2 forms: Level A (no date, 12 pages), Level I ('81, 16 pages).

2) *Grades 1–2.* Scores from 3 areas: same as 1 above; 2 forms: Level B (no date, 12 pages), Level II, ('81, 16 pages).

3) *Grades 2–3.* Scores from 3 areas: same as 1 above; 2 forms: Level C (no date, 11 pages), Level III ('81, 16 pages).

4) *Grades 3–4.* Scores from 4 major areas: basic operations, basic operations with decimals, basic operations with fractions, applications; 1 form labeled Level IV ('81, 11 pages).

5) *Grades 5–6.* Scores from 4 areas: same as 4 above; 1 form labeled Level V ('81, 11 pages).

6) *Grades 7–8.* Scores from 4 areas: same as 4 above; 1 form labeled Level VI ('81, 11 pages).

7) *Grades 9–10.* Scores from 5 areas: same as 4 above plus comprehension of geometric formulas; 1 form labeled Level VII ('81, 11 pages).

8) *Grades 11–12.* Score from 5 areas: same as 4 above plus application and comprehension of geometric formulas; 1 form labeled Level VIII ('81, 11 pages).

Review of Basic Skills Inventory by GARY J. ROBERTSON, Director, Test Division, American Guidance Service, Circle Pines, MN:

The Basic Skills Inventory (BSI) is a series of 24 separate tests (8 tests each in Reading, Language Arts, and Mathematics) designed to provide "basic skills achievement information" for pupils in grades 1 through 12. Each of the eight tests, or levels, within the three BSI content areas contains 50 items drawn from a bank of about 2,000 items assembled by the Los Angeles Test Development Center from test materials previously used by the National Assessment of Educational Progress, the California Statewide Assessment Program, or other state or federally funded item development projects.

A major reason for assembling BSI was the need to provide national norms for the item bank. Since different subsets of items could theoretically be selected from the bank by different users to measure different instructional objectives, a method of obtaining national normative data for various configurations of items was needed. Each of the twenty-four 50-item tests developed from the item bank was designed to provide item calibration data which would ultimately be used as the vehicle for deriving national norms. Item response theory (specifically, the Rasch one-parameter latent trait model) was viewed as offering the technology to achieve these objectives.

If the developers of the BSI had elected to pursue the single goal of assembling subsets of items to calibrate and norm the larger item bank, their effort might well receive higher marks. The decision to use the BSI as an off-the-shelf norm-referenced achievement battery with criterion-referenced interpretive features was a mistake. The final product underscores once again the difficulty of developing a single measure that serves adequately both norm-referenced and criterion-referenced needs. The BSI Technical Report lists 10 uses of the test which range from providing broad baseline achievement data to "individual assessment of basic skill competency," "pupil diagnosis for prescriptive instruction," and "identification of curricular strengths and weaknesses," among others. The naivete of such claims is readily apparent: the 50-item tests in each of the three content areas (Reading, Mathematics, Language Arts) span a range of one-to-two school grades and contain items measuring from 14–35 objectives with an average of 1–3 items per objective. A single global score in each content area constitutes the norm-referenced yield for each test.

ITEM QUALITY AND FORMAT. Use of a single test format for measuring different types of skills leads to some problems. Directions must be given for each item in the test, which increases reading load and is less efficient than placing similar types of items in a subset with a single set of directions. The reading load in the Language Arts tests, in particular, troubled this reviewer (correlations between Reading and Language Arts ranged from .68–.87, with a median of .78). Examples of problem items are "Choose the sentence with incorrect capitalization" (four different sentences follow); or "Choose the correct number of words that should be capitalized in the following sentence" (a sentence follows in which the student must both identify capitalization errors and keep a cumulative count). Items such as the latter illustrate a related problem: a confounding of the abilities required to answer a specific item. Format of the language arts tests in the major group achievement batteries is far superior to that used in BSI.

Reading passages in BSI are, for the most part, interesting and age appropriate. Most items are passage dependent; some items are confusing because they lack a clear statement of the problem in the stem. Mathematics items seem generally satisfactory. Items in Levels I, II, and III requiring coin identification may penalize some students with perceptual problems.

STANDARDIZATION. BSI was standardized nationally, fall and spring, in 83 school districts on a sample of approximately 50,000 pupils, grades 1 through 12. A stratified multi-stage procedure was employed; stratification variables were geographic region and school size. Response rate is not provided so assessment of the quality of the norming procedure is difficult. Post hoc analysis of the standardization sample school districts revealed fairly close agreement with national census statistics on most demographic variables of interest. Standardization procedures for BSI seem as defensible as those for most major achievement batteries. Use of a socioeconomic stratification variable could have improved the efficiency of the sampling plan.

INTERPRETATION. Scaled scores, within-grade fall and spring percentile ranks, and NCEs are provided for norm-referenced interpretation. No clear method of criterion-referenced interpretation is presented. A sample computer printout suggests that a skills breakdown based on the Rasch ability estimate could be obtained; however, lack of well-designed "finished" computer generated interpretive reports and accompanying user manuals leaves the area of interpretation open.

Norms development for the BSI was based on distributions of scaled scores (Rasch ability estimates) and appears well done. The test characteristic curves provided in the Technical Report seem to be in agreement with what one would expect from tests such as these. Inspection of the norms tables (which are not clearly labeled with level designations) reveals considerable variability in the level of difficulty of the tests at the grade levels targeted for their use. Spring median raw scores in Reading, for example, range from 64% of the items correct in grades 5 and 11 to 88% correct in grade 1. Mathematics is most troublesome, with the fall median ranging from 27% of items correct in grade 5 to 56% of items correct in grade 10. In grades 6 through 12, raw score gains at the 50th percentile, fall to spring, typically range between 1 and 2 raw score points. Thus, the sensitivity and consequent appropriateness of these tests for use in a pre-post program evaluation context, a recommended use of BSI, is questionable. Results of a study designed to investigate effects of drawing samples of easy and hard items on Rasch ability estimates (i.e., the item bank concept) showed prediction errors of 2–3 raw score points on 50-item tests. The consequences of using item bank performance estimates with their associated error for pre-post evaluation where fall-to-spring growth averages 1, 2, 3, or even 4 raw score points are obvious.

USE OF IRT TECHNOLOGY. The area where the BSI materials are outstanding is in their application of Rasch item response theory. Those sections of the Technical Report describing the linking of items to common ability scales and the vertical equating of the eight BSI levels are excellently written in a concise, easily understood style. These sections are a valuable primer on the use of Rasch technology to scale items and test scores. A major value of the BSI effort was that of demonstrating the correct application of Rasch IRT to the development of a norm-referenced test.

RELIABILITY. Both KR 20 and split-half reliabilities are provided by grade for the fall and spring standardization samples. For fall testing, median KR 20 coefficients are in the high .80s for language and mathematics and in the low .90s for reading;

split-half coefficients are slightly lower (mid .80s) for all three tests. For spring testing, KR 20 coefficients are in the low .90s for all three areas; split-half coefficients are somewhat lower and fall in the mid .80s. Generally, the KR 20 coefficients are excellent and at a level where individual performance can be interpreted with confidence. The split-half values generally run lower than would be expected from the level of the KR 20 values and may reflect idiosyncrasies in the way the content was subdivided into halves. Split-half values fall below those for total Reading, Language, and Mathematics composites from the major achievement test batteries.

VALIDITY. Content validity of the BSI would need to be determined by the individual user based upon curricular emphases. BSI content was based upon a broad national survey of textbooks and curricula. Specifications for each content area are given in the Technical Report. The information provided is not as detailed as that from the leading achievement batteries. For example, items are not assigned to content categories in the blueprint, and thus users will have difficulty in classifying content by the objectives listed. Examination of the Technical Report suggests that BSI developers have selected content objectives carefully. In addition, 12 consultants from throughout the U.S. reviewed all items and content specifications before the tests were finalized.

SUMMARY. The idea of providing a bank of calibrated achievement test items from which subsets can be drawn to match local curricular emphases is not new. Some test publishers already offer such a program (e.g., CTB/McGraw-Hill Objective Referenced Bank of Items and Tests). The BSI advances the concept by demonstrating the application of item response theory, specifically the Rasch latent trait model, to the problem of item and test score scaling and related norms generation. Thus, the main contribution of the BSI lies in providing an excellent, concise primer of procedures for the use of item response theory in such an item banking enterprise. BSI is not competitive with other achievement batteries whose strength lies in their ability to provide, in a cost-effective manner, information for a number of different uses, including those claimed by BSI. To make BSI a viable commercial product would require an extensive overhaul, with a full complement of interpretive materials and computerized reporting services. To undertake such an effort would be foolhardy in view of the excellence of current achievement batteries and the highly competitive nature of the market.

Review of Basic Skills Inventory by VICTOR L. WILLSON, Associate Professor of Educational Psychology, Texas A & M University, College Station, TX:

The Basic Skills Inventory evolved from an item bank in reading, language arts, and mathematics developed by the Los Angeles County School District. The sources for items included National Assessment of Educational Progress released items, California State Department developed items, and items from various state and federal projects, resulting in a total of about 2,000 items. A parallel development led to the generation of objectives for basic skills assessment, using curriculum guides, textbooks, and experts from throughout the United States. The items were then matched to objectives, modifying them on the basis of test reviewers' recommendations. A set of 24 tests was produced, three content areas at eight levels, which spans grades K.5 to 12.9, with about one and one half grades per level. Scope and sequence charts are provided for grades K–3, 4–6, 7–9, and 10–12, but all are quite rudimentary. The final forms are also packaged in multigrade tests, also labelled Levels I, II, and III, combining the three content areas. Grades 4–6, 7–9, and 10–12 are the three levels for these forms. This is a bit confusing, since the eight cross-grade forms are also termed Levels I to VIII.

Norm samples for the tests appear to be reasonably representative of the U.S. population. While there are small variations from U.S. averages the sample appears to have been capably drawn and similar to those drawn by other major test developers. An attempt was made to test the same population in the spring and next fall for vertical equating purposes between adjacent levels of the tests. The sizes for these samples are about one fourth (typically 500–600) those of the full norm samples at each grade (1,300–2,800).

Reliabilities for the 24 tests at fall and spring administrations are reported as KR-20 and split-half coefficients. They are acceptably high for reading (all but 2 of 24 KR-20 coefficients over .90), but for language arts 9 of 24 KR-20 coefficients are below .90, all above .84. Half the KR-20 coefficients for mathematics are below .90, with a fifth-grade sample having a .78 value. Since all forms are 50 items in length, this might be due to differential difficulty. An examination of the median performance on the mathematics tests shows that for the fifth-grade sample, the median difficulty for the fall testing was 13 items correct of the 50 possible. The fourth-, fifth-, sixth-, and seventh-grade tests for the fall all exhibit this very great difficulty along with lower reliabilities. Even the spring scores for these grades generally average below half the number possible correct. I suggest that these forms have technical difficulties that may render them unacceptable for many school districts.

It is also unfortunate that the test developers fail to use generalizability theory where it is so obviously applicable. The test sample was carefully stratified, and much better information could be obtained from variance components than from the traditional reliability coefficients. This criticism can be made of most test developers yet today, however.

Content validation is supported by content specialists' review of the items. Since the items were developed before the objectives, it is always worrisome that items were forced into some niches for which better items might have been written. Construct validity evidence is presented in the form of intercorrelations among the content areas by grade, a rather weak form of evidence. As part of the latent trait modelling performed on the test scores, evidence of unidimensionality is presented with eigenvalues for the first principal components (or principal factors) for each test. (It is left unspecified whether a principal components or principal factors analysis was performed.) The first component typically consumed about 20% of the total variance. Moreover, first components tended to be about four times as large as the second, giving some evidence for unidimensionality. No other validity data are provided.

Adjacent levels of the tests were equated vertically using Rasch (one parameter) latent trait models. This procedure appears to have been competently performed, given the current state of knowledge on equating. A common ability scale was produced with a grade 1 mean (fall) of 321, a grade 12 mean (fall) of 639, and a standard deviation of about 50 points (range 48.17–66.25) at all grade levels. A validity study of the vertical equating was performed with easy, hard, and comparable (but new) forms of the tests at each level. The results showed that equating of ability scores between forms was reasonably good for items of similar difficulty but becomes poorer for easier or harder forms, a finding well supported in the literature.

Item difficulty and discrimination are presented for each item by grade for fall and spring. Equating tables are presented in the technical manual for conversions between raw scores, ability scale scores, percentile rank scores, and normal curve equivalent scores. These are sufficient for use by school district test specialists.

A scoring service by Intran Corporation provides a range of summaries by grade and subject matter, by student within grade, and by classroom. The latter reports item data by student in a prediction format that could be useful, but no indication is given as to the method of prediction. Student scores on this summary are given in the ability metric based on the Rasch model. The difficulty with this scale is to explain it to teachers and parents in a useful way. The developers do not seem to have spent much effort on information of this kind for either group.

The quality of the booklets is adequate except for some of the primary grade materials, in which drawings, especially of coins, are not always good. Some forms are printed in green and will prove troublesome for children with color vision problems.

The Basic Skills Inventory has been reasonably well developed, and with the exception of mathematics tests for the upper elementary levels, might be quite useful for a school district to consider if it wishes to test basic skills comprehensively across the entire school population and obtain a single ability score. This may prove most effective for out-of-level testing, as has been noted for tests based on latent trait methods. A school district considering this set of tests must examine carefully the items to determine if they are consistent with local objectives and sequencing.

[124]

Basic Visual-Motor Association Test. Grades 1–9; 1982; BVMAT; visual memory; no reliability, validity and norms data for grade 1; individual administration recommended for grade 1; 2 parts labeled Forms A, B, (1 page); manual (45 pages); 1983 price data: $19.50 per complete battery including manual, pad of 25 forms, and quick scoring acetate; $12.50 per specimen set; 3(5) minutes per part; James Battle; Special Child Publications.*

Review of Basic Visual-Motor Association Test by BURKE H. BRETZING, Psychologist, Washington School District, Phoenix, AZ:

The Basic Visual-Motor Association Test (BVMAT) is purported to be a screening device employed by psychologists, counselors, and teachers to diagnose learning problems in children, grades 1 through 9. It is primarily a test of visual memory and takes 10–15 minutes to administer and score. The author indicates that the BVMAT measures the following skills: recall of visual symbols, visual sequencing ability, visual association skills, visual-motor ability, visual-integrative ability, and symbol integration skills.

The test seems fairly easy to administer, and can be given in groups for grades 2 through 9. The task is basically one of matching to sample and consists of the letters A through J, each with a corresponding symbol. Form A employs upper case letters, and Form B lower case. The general format is very similar to coding on the WISC-R. Examinees are instructed to complete sample items after studying the key. Children are then given 3 minutes to place the appropriate symbols with each letter for a total of 60 items. Instructions are similar for group and individual administration. Materials consist of protocols with Form A on one side and Form B on the other, and a scoring key. Students may earn a total of 60 points with a time bonus for a perfect score.

Tables are provided from which percentile ranks and *T*-scores may be obtained. The author reports that individuals scoring two standard deviations below the mean typically have weak visual memory and may suffer from "dyslexia and neurological dysfunctioning." Two case studies are provided in the manual to illustrate the usefulness of the BVMAT in screening.

The test was normed on 124 boys and girls, grades 2 through 9 in 18 schools in a large metropolitan public school district. Subjects were subsequently grouped by age into four categories and percentile and *T*-score tables were developed accordingly, apparently using additional students, with *N* ranging from 153 to 235. Nothing was indicated about the representativeness of these norming groups.

Correlations for test-retest reliability range from .47 to .98, with only the 8th- and 9th-grade category at a qualitatively acceptable level (.98). The next highest correlation was .82 for grades 1 through 3.

In discussing content validity, the author simply states that "experts" support the point that visual memory affects reading and academic achievement, but no specific studies are cited. In support of concurrent validity a correlation of .69 with the Bender-Gestalt is reported. Correlations with the WISC-R are also provided; however, specific subtest values are not. Information about the correlation between the BVMAT and the Coding subtest would be interesting. Correlational studies are cited which link the BVMAT (visual memory) and reading, spelling, and arithmetic.

In general, the manual appears to be well laid out and directions are simple and clear. Tables are easily accessible and scoring presents no problem. The author concludes that because visual memory and related skills are so crucial to the reading process, tests like the BVMAT are an important asset for diagnosing deficits which may impede learning. He asserts that what sets the BVMAT apart from other similar instruments is the use of letters as stimulus items. Although this is the case, this reviewer questions the necessity and advisability of using letters as a measure of visual memory.

Employing more meaningful stimuli may allow subjects to make paired associations which could confound results and would be less likely with another format. Success in this task may also be a function of familiarity with the letters themselves, therefore resulting in confusion with long-term memory skills, especially for younger, developmentally delayed students. If a particular student has mastered these 10 letters in alphabetical order, this task will be simpler, visual memory notwithstanding. A similar argument could be stated for a test with numerical stimuli. Finally, the author argues that the BVMAT correlates highly with arithmetic ability, as well as reading and spelling. If a test using letter stimuli correlates highly with number usage (higher even than reading values) it does not seem as if the case for letter has been established. The Coding subtest on the WISC-R may be just as comprehensive, and test-retest reliability values are comparable.

In conclusion, the BVMAT is a simple, brief measure of visual memory using letter stimuli in a matching to sample task. The manual is well organized, but average reliability coefficients are low, and validity data is limited. Sufficient justification is not provided to make this reviewer, as a school psychologist, wish to employ the BVMAT as a supplementary measure to other instruments. It seems that the Coding subtest on the WISC-R is equally comprehensive, and shows less chance of confounded results due to meaningful stimuli. If the BVMAT is used as a diagnostic tool, caution should be applied by having supporting evidence from other measures, as illustrated by the author.

Review of Basic Visual-Motor Association Test by H. LEE SWANSON, Associate Professor, Department of Special Education, University of Northern Colorado, Greeley, CO:

The purpose of the Basic Visual-Motor Association Test (BVMAT) is to provide a nonverbal reproduction test in order to measure the short-term visual memory of children having learning difficulties. The test is also purported to measure visual sequence, visual association, visual-motor, visual-integrative, and symbol integration skills. The test can be administered individually or in groups for grades 2 through 9. Both test forms (A and B) include as presentation stimuli the first 10 letters of the alphabet. The child's task is to write the appropriate symbols associated with letters of the alphabet in boxes under timed conditions. Test scoring includes one point for each item filled in correctly. Bonus points are awarded for perfect performance. Raw point scores are converted to percentile ranks and *T*-scores. Case studies are presented in the manual which illustrate the diagnostic use of the test.

The test has several deficiencies, but only three major deficiencies will be detailed. First, the construct validity of the test is nonexistent. Five obvious problems related to construct validity include: (*a*) the test has no heuristic value since it fails to provide a clear descriptive analysis of the normed children's learning problems, (*b*) the amount and extent of child learning and behavior problems the author purports the test measures is not supported by data in the manual, (*c*) the comparability of this test to previously constructed tests of the same theoretical orientation is inferior, (*d*) subjecting this test to empirical evaluation is not easily accomplished since there is no clear determination of the normed sample, and (*e*) evidence of the degree to which the test includes items that have already been empirically confirmed is sorely lacking. In general, the author fails to provide a comprehensive theoretical rationale for the test. In addition, current experimental findings would question whether this test could in fact measure visual memory. For example, "automaticity" or other constructs may account for variance in test performance.

Most critically, the manual fails to present evidence on the construct (short-term memory) for which the test is recommended. Instead the author presents information on the concurrent validity of the BVMAT with the Bender Visual-Motor Gestalt Test ($r = .67$), suggesting that the "construct" may be confounded with several motoric and/or perceptual variables. The author goes on to report correlations with the WISC-R scores in which he concludes "that IQ is associated with visual memory, and that both variables are associated with achievement." Since these correlations are low ($r = .16$ thru .31), one might question what the test is measuring. After correlating the BVMAT with Schonell's Graded Word Reading Test (.39 Form A, .46 Form B), Schonell's Graded Word Spelling Test (.69 Form A, .72 Form B) and Monroe-Sherman Arithmetic Computation Test (.60 Form A, .62 Form B), the author goes on to state that the "BVMAT is at least as effective as—if not more (sic) effective than—the other criterion measures listed, for predicting subjects' skills in reading, spelling, and arithmetic." Such claims are clearly unwarranted. We know nothing about the validation sample in terms of socioeconomic status, ethnic origin, demographic variables, or psychological characteristics. Although the test was intended "to assist in the identification and diagnosis of learning problems in children and youth," the potential user is not even sure if such children were included in the validation sample.

Second, the manual fails to include estimates of the standard error of measurement. This information is necessary in order to allow the consumer to judge whether the scores are sufficiently dependable for the intended purpose of the test. Efforts to compute such measures are confounded since the tables (i.e., 1 and 2) in the manual fail to provide adequate descriptive information. Only by referring back to earlier pages would the reader be able to determine how reliability coefficients were determined. Test-retest reliability for Form A was determined from a sample of 274 boys and girls, ages 7 through 15, in one metropolitan school district. Correlation coefficients for four age groupings were: .82 (6–5 to 8–6 CA), .72 (8–7 to 10–6 CA), .47 (10–7 to 12–6 CA), and .98 (12–7 to 15–6 CA). The low correlation coefficient for the second oldest group is not explained. Test-retest reliability for Form B is similar to Form A. Test-retest interval times between both forms was 48 hours. Is this because the same subjects are used for both Form A and B? We are never told! Again, the procedural variables and normed samples used to determine reliability coefficients were so poorly described that the test consumer cannot judge the applicability of the data reported.

Finally, the child's visual-motor speed, association of symbols, ability to learn shapes, ability to learn unfamiliar tasks, and ability to learn symbols and shapes and to recreate them can be assessed in many contemporary tests. For example, this test has little advantage over the coding subtest of the WISC-R. In fact, sampling, validity, and reliability are more appropriately documented in the latter test. The author justifies his test by suggesting "most available tests of visual memory require the test subject to recall and reproduce designs rather than letters." However, the rationale of why letters would be more sensitive to short-term memory deficits than recalling digits, shapes, and objects is not substantiated. No empirical evidence has been provided that this measure is superior to competing measures in identifying learning problems.

In summary, I do not recommend the use of this test. The author overstates the value of the test, norms do not appear representative of the subtypes of children with learning problems for which the test was intended, theoretical constructs are poorly developed, and the test tells us less about learning processes than competing measures.

[125]

Battelle Developmental Inventory. Birth to 8 years; 1984; BDI; designed to assess developmental strengths and weaknesses; individual; 30 profile scores: adult interaction, expression of feelings/affect, self-concept, peer interaction, coping, social role, personal-social total, attention, eating, dressing, personal responsibility, toileting, adaptive total, muscle control, body coordination, locomotion, gross motor score, fine muscle, perceptual motor, fine motor score, motor total, receptive, expressive, communication total, perceptual discrimination, memory, reasoning and academic skills, conceptual development, cognitive total, total; 1 form; examiner's manual ('84, 162 pages); manual for personal-social domain ('84, 86 pages); manual for motor domain ('84, 95 pages); manual for adaptive domain ('84, 59 pages); manual for communications domain ('84, 88 pages); manual for cognitive domain ('84, 74 pages); manual for screening test ('84, 108 pages); 1984 price data: $95 per complete set; $20 per 15 scoring booklets; $10 per 15 screening test booklets; (60) minutes; Jean Newborg, John R. Stock, Linda Wnek, John Guidubaldi, and John Svinicki; DLM Teaching Resources.*

[126]

Bayley Scales of Infant Development. Ages 2–30 months; 1969–84; BSID; revision consists of a manual supplement, which provides clarifications of the directions for administration and scoring; 2 scores: mental, motor, plus 30 behavior ratings; the mental and motor scales "draw heavily upon" the California First-Year Mental Scale, the California Preschool Mental Scale, and the California Infant Scale of Motor Development; no data on validity of motor scale; no data on predictive validity of mental scale; individual; 1 form; manual ('69, 185 pages); manual supplement ('84, 31 pages); record booklets: mental scale ('69, 8 pages), motor scale ('69, 4 pages), infant behavior ('69, 6 pages); 1984 price data: $250 per complete set including all necessary equipment, 25 each of 3 record forms, manual, and carrying case; $18 per 25 combined record forms; $10.50 per 25 mental scale forms; $7.50 per 25 motor scale forms; $7.50 per 25 infant behavior forms; $15 per manual; replacement parts price list available from publisher; (45–90) minutes for mental and motor scales; Nancy Bayley, Leanne Rhodes (manual supplement), and Ben C. Yow (manual supplement); The Psychological Corporation.*

See T3:270 (101 references); for a review by Fred Damarin, see 8:206 (28 references); see also T2:484 (11 references) for reviews by Roberta R. Collard and Raymond H. Holden, see 7:402 (20 references).

TEST REFERENCES

1. Appelbaum, A. S. Developmental retardation in infants as a concomitant of physical child abuse. JOURNAL OF ABNORMAL CHILD PSYCHOLOGY, 1977, 5, 417–423.

2. Jason, L. A. A behavioral approach in enhancing disadvantaged children's academic abilities. AMERICAN JOURNAL OF COMMUNITY PSYCHOLOGY, 1977, 5, 413–421.

3. Koski, M. A., & Ingram, E. M. Child abuse and neglect: Effects on Bayley Scale scores. JOURNAL OF ABNORMAL CHILD PSYCHOLOGY, 1977, 5, 79–91.

4. Berk, R. A. The discriminative efficiency of the Bayley Scales of Infant Development. JOURNAL OF ABNORMAL CHILD PSYCHOLOGY, 1979, 7, 113–119.

5. Armstrong, K. A. A treatment and education program for parents and children who are at-risk of abuse and neglect. CHILD ABUSE & NEGLECT, 1981, 5, 167–175.

6. Berger, J., & Cunningham, C. C. The development of eye contact between mothers and normal versus Down's syndrome infants. DEVELOPMENTAL PSYCHOLOGY, 1981, 17, 678–689.

7. DeFries, J. C., Plomin, R., Vandenberg, S. G., & Kuse, A. R. Parent-offspring resemblance for cognitive abilities in the Colorado Adoption Project: Biological, adoptive, and control parents and one-year-old children. INTELLIGENCE, 1981, 5, 245–277.

8. Hardy-Brown, S., Plomin, R., & DeFries, J. C. Genetic and environmental influences on the rate of communicative development in the first year of life. DEVELOPMENTAL PSYCHOLOGY, 1981, 17, 704–717.

9. Lewis, M., & Brooks-Gunn, J. Visual attention at three months as a predictor of cognitive functioning at two years of age. INTELLIGENCE, 1981, 5, 131–140.

10. Londerville, S., & Main, M. Security of attachment, compliance, and maternal training methods in the second year of life. DEVELOPMENTAL PSYCHOLOGY, 1981, 17, 289–299.

11. Marcus, J., Auerbach, J., Wilkinson, L., & Burack, C. M. Infants at risk for schizophrenia: The Jerusalem Infant Development Study. ARCHIVES OF GENERAL PSYCHIATRY, 1981, 38, 703–713.

12. McGowan, R. J., Johnson, D. L., & Maxwell, S. E. Relations between infant behavior ratings and concurrent and subsequent mental test scores. DEVELOPMENTAL PSYCHOLOGY, 1981, 17, 542–553.

13. Pastor, D. L. The quality of mother-infant attachment and its relationship to toddlers' initial sociability with peers. DEVELOPMENTAL PSYCHOLOGY, 1981, 17, 326–335.

14. Ramey, C. T., & Haskins, R. The modification of intelligence through early experience. INTELLIGENCE, 1981, 5, 5–19.

15. Rode, S. S., Chang, P. N., Fisch, R. O., & Sroufe, L. A. Attachment patterns of infants separated at birth. DEVELOPMENTAL PSYCHOLOGY, 1981, 17, 188–191.

16. Wilson, R. S. Mental development: Concordance for same-sex and opposite-sex dizygotic twins. DEVELOPMENTAL PSYCHOLOGY, 1981, 17, 626–629.

17. Bee, H. L., Barnard, K. E., Eyres, S. J., Gray, C. A., Hammond, M. A., Spietz, A. L., Snyder, C., & Clark, B. Prediction of IQ and language skill from perinatal status, child performance, family characteristics, and mother-infant interaction. CHILD DEVELOPMENT, 1982, 53, 1134–1156.

18. Goodall, E., & Corbett, J. Relationships between sensory stimulation and stereotyped behaviour in severely mentally retarded and autistic children. JOURNAL OF MENTAL DEFICIENCY RESEARCH, 1982, 26, 163–175.

19. O'Connor, S., Vietze, P., Sherrod, K., Sandler, H. M., Gerrity, S., & Altemeier, W. A. Mother-infant interaction and child development after rooming-in: Comparison of high-risk and low-risk mothers. PREVENTION IN HUMAN SERVICES, 1982, 1(4), 25–43.

20. Ollendick, T. H., Shapiro, E. S., & Barrett, R. P. Effects of vicarious reinforcement in normal and severely disturbed children. JOURNAL OF CONSULTING AND CLINICAL PSYCHOLOGY, 1982, 50, 63–70.

21. Poresky, R. H., & Henderson, M. I. Infants' mental and motor development: Effects of home environment, maternal attitudes, marital adjustment, and socioeconomic status. PERCEPTUAL AND MOTOR SKILLS, 1982, 54, 695–702.

22. Prater, R. J. Functions of consonant assimilation and reduplication in early word productions of mentally retarded children. AMERICAN JOURNAL OF MENTAL DEFICIENCY, 1982, 86, 399–404.

23. Ruddy, M. G., & Bornstein, M. H. Cognitive correlates of infant attention and maternal stimulation over the first year of life. CHILD DEVELOPMENT, 1982, 53, 183–188.

24. Seifer, R., & Sameroff, A. J. A structural equation model analysis of competence in children at risk for mental disorder. PREVENTION IN HUMAN SERVICES, 1982, 1(4), 85–96.

25. Siegel, L. S. Reproductive, perinatal, and environmental factors as predictors of the cognitive and language development of preterm and full-term infants. CHILD DEVELOPMENT, 1982, 53, 963–973.

26. Barnard, K. E., & Bee, H. L. The impact of temporally patterned stimulation on the development of preterm infants. CHILD DEVELOPMENT, 1983, 54, 1156–1167.

27. Bayley, N., & Hunt, J. V. Are test materials toys? A reply to Ridenour and Reid. PERCEPTUAL AND MOTOR SKILLS, 1983, 57, 1270.

28. Cohen, S. E., & Parmalee, A. H. Prediction of five-year Stanford-Binet scores in preterm infants. CHILD DEVELOPMENT, 1983, 54, 1242–1253.

29. Crawley, S. B., & Spiker, D. Mother-child interactions involving two-year-olds with Down syndrome: A look at individual differences. CHILD DEVELOPMENT, 1983, 54, 1312–1323.

30. Crnic, K. A., Ragozin, A. S., Greenberg, M. T., Robinson, N. M., & Basham, R. B. Social interaction and developmental competence of preterm and full-term infants during the first year of life. CHILD DEVELOPMENT, 1983, 54, 1199–1210.

31. Hogg, J. Sensory and social reinforcement of head-turning in a profoundly retarded multiply handicapped child. THE BRITISH JOURNAL OF CLINICAL PSYCHOLOGY, 1983, 22, 33–40.

32. Lasky, R. E., Tyson, J. E., Rosenfeld, C. R., Priest, M., Krasinski, D., Heartwell, S., & Gant, N. F. Differences on Bayley's Infant Behavior Record for a sample of high-risk infants and their controls. CHILD DEVELOPMENT, 1983, 54, 1211–1216.

33. Libb, J. W., Myers, G. J., Graham, E., & Bell, B. Correlates of intelligence and adaptive behavior in Down's Syndrome. JOURNAL OF MENTAL DEFICIENCY RESEARCH, 1983, 27, 205–210.

34. Matheny, A. P., Jr. A longitudinal twin study of stability of components from Bayley's Infant Behavior Record. CHILD DEVELOPMENT, 1983, 54, 356–360.

35. Motti, F., Cicchetti, D., & Sroufe, L. A. From infant affect expression to symbolic play: The coherence of development in Down syndrome children. CHILD DEVELOPMENT, 1983, 54, 1168–1175.

36. Moxley-Haegert, L., & Serbin, L. A. Developmental education for parents of delayed infants: Effects on parental motivation and children's development. CHILD DEVELOPMENT, 1983, 54, 1324–1331.

37. Plomin, R., & DeFries, J. C. The Colorado Adoption Project. CHILD DEVELOPMENT, 1983, 54, 276–289.

38. Ridenour, M. V., & Reid, M. Inspection of the Bayley mental scale test materials for potential hazards of choking, aspiration, and ingestion when used outside of test situation. PERCEPTUAL AND MOTOR SKILLS, 1983, 57, 1077–1078.

39. Siegel, L. S. Correction for prematurity and its consequences for the assessment of the very low birth weight infant. CHILD DEVELOPMENT, 1983, 54, 1176–1188.

40. Wilson, R. S. The Louisville Twin Study: Developmental synchronies in behavior. CHILD DEVELOPMENT, 1983, 54, 298–316.

41. Benjamin, G. A. H., Kahn, M. W., & Sales, B. D. Developmental differences in infants and policy on undocumented Mexican American parents. HISPANIC JOURNAL OF BEHAVIORAL SCIENCES, 1984, 6, 145–160.

42. Capute, A. J., Palmer, F. B., Shapiro, B. K., Wachtel, R. C., Ross, A., & Accardo, P. J. Primitive reflex profile: A quantitation of primitive

reflexes in infancy. DEVELOPMENTAL MEDICINE AND CHILD NEUROLOGY, 1984, 26, 375–389.

[127]

Behavior Analysis Forms for Clinical Intervention. Behavior therapy clients; 1977–81; 2 volumes; Joseph R. Cautela; Research Press.*

a) BEHAVIOR ANALYSIS FORMS FOR CLINICAL INTERVENTION. 1977–79; 36 plans, questionnaires, scales, forms, schedules, and data forms in areas such as client history, motivation for change, reinforcement, and social performance; manual ('79, 164 pages including all tests); 1984 price data: $28.95 per manual.

b) BEHAVIOR ANALYSIS FORMS FOR CLINICAL INTERVENTION: VOLUME 2. 1981; 59 questionnaires, scales, forms, schedules, and data forms in areas such as reinforcers for specific populations, surveys of phobic or relationship reactions, and guidelines for clients; manual (244 pages including all tests); $29.95 per manual.

Review of Behavior Analysis Forms for Clinical Intervention by MARY LOU KELLEY, Assistant Professor of Psychology, Louisiana State University, Baton Rouge, LA:

Behavior Analysis Forms for Clinical Intervention (Volumes I and II) contain a large variety of self-report inventories, behavior monitoring forms, and client handouts for use primarily in clinical practice by behavior therapists. The forms are to be employed in gathering client interview data in a structured manner. As the author points out in the introduction to Volume I, the forms contained in the two volumes are not intended to be psychological tests with accompanying norms, etc.

The two volumes contain approximately 100 forms and handouts for assessing a wide variety of client problems. Forms contained in Volume I are divided into four groups: general, process, technique, and specific. For one of the two "general" forms the client provides detailed demographic and background information. The other "general" form presents a list of problems that might be encountered by adults and asks the client to check which problems he/she "needs to learn" to remediate. "Process forms" are completed by the therapist and are used to record such things as target problems, clinical status, and the client's motivation to change. The "technique forms" are designed to "provide information for implementation of the therapeutic strategies." These include forms that survey clients' reinforcers and fears. For example, the Children's Reinforcement Survey Schedule lists potential reinforcers for children. The child is asked to indicate how much he or she likes each item. The section of Volume I entitled "specific forms" consists of questionnaires designed to obtain specific information on the behaviors targeted for change. For example, the Pain Survey Schedule (PSS) requires the client to describe or rate the characteristics and location of pain as well as environmental events associated with the occurrence of pain.

Forms contained in Volume II, as in Volume I, are intended to aid in the evaluation of a variety of behavior problems. They range from questionnaires about phobias (e.g., Agoraphobia Behavior Survey Schedule) to forms about marital problems to surveys about potential reinforcers (e.g., Reinforcement Survey Schedule for the Visually Impaired). Volume II also contains a variety of forms for use as therapist aids such as the Case Presentation Form and the Guidelines for Timeout handout.

The questionnaires and behavior monitoring forms contained in the two volumes have several positive features. In general, the forms could be useful, adjunctive tools to clinicians. For example, the reinforcement survey schedules might be used to prompt clients to specify enjoyable activities that may not have been generated without such prompting. Furthermore, a number of the questionnaires may provide useful prompts to student therapists regarding information to obtain from clients with specific problems.

In spite of the positive features of the two volumes, there are several problems with the packaging and presentation of the forms that hinder their potential utility. First, the forms seem to be arranged in a less than systematic fashion. For example, forms for assessing various marital problems appear scattered throughout the two volume series. Second, very little information is provided on what types of clients might complete each form. Very minimal instructions are provided to clients on how to complete the individual forms. In addition, no systematic rationale was presented for the inclusion of forms on one type of problem over another. For example, the author includes a form for evaluating a client's dental history and fears, but does not include a form for gathering information about medical history and fears. Finally, some of the forms appear to cover trivial content. Examples include the Homosexual Client Session Interview Report Form, the Covert Response Cost Survey Schedule, and the "Homework" form which asks only for name and date and then provides 10 blank spaces (which I assume are for recording homework assignments given to a client).

Although the author states that the forms are not intended to be tests, there are problems with the almost total lack of research on the reliability and validity of the forms. One does not know, for example, if the reinforcers listed on a form are those commonly enjoyed by the people who complete the instrument. The author provides no data on whether the various forms measure what they intend to measure or how the forms relate to any other instruments. Finally, as implied previously, some of the forms appear lacking in face validity. Thus, while some forms might be useful in certain circumstances, the instruments also could be misused.

In sum, the various instruments presented in Behavior Analysis Forms for Clinical Intervention, Volumes I and II contain over 100 self-report inventories and clinical process aids. While the forms may have some clinical utility, there are several problems with the instruments: (*a*) the forms do not appear to be presented in a useful order in the manuals, (*b*) the author provides insufficient information on how to administer the instruments, and (*c*) there is a lack of psychometric evidence supporting the validity and reliability of the forms.

Review of Behavior Analysis Forms For Clinical Intervention by FRANCIS E. LENTZ, JR., Assistant Professor of School Psychology, Lehigh University, Bethlehem, PA:

These various forms were developed by the author and his colleagues for utilization in behavioral assessment within the context of clinical interventions. Permission is given to copy all forms. The (extremely limited) narrative accompanying the forms and reviewer examination of other referenced publications indicate that most of these forms have been used (and developed) during the practice of behavior therapy by the author and his colleagues. According to the author, the forms are to be interpreted within a behavioral assessment model rather than a traditional personality assessment model. In keeping with this model, the forms are intended to structure data collection, either by interview or self-report, and to allow specific identification of target behaviors, identification of antecedents and consequences surrounding them, and selection of efficacious procedures for treatment.

In judging validity, a behavioral assessment model would emphasize close correspondence of derived measures to behavior within environmental settings. These forms are certainly oriented this way, requiring responses about overt or covert behaviors, situations, and client preferences surrounding these. The serious problem with these forms is the almost complete lack of any data within the manual relating to any measurement qualities of these various forms. While there are extensive lists of references accompanying the manuals, examination of over 40 of these revealed most were opinion papers or anecdotal case reports. Even within this nontraditional assessment model, empirical data are necessary to guide user behavior. While the forms do have apparent face validity, and the developer is well known in the field of behavior therapy, basic measurement questions remain unanswered. Even used as suggested—to collect structured client data allowing a behavior analysis—much remains unknown, such as possible effects of assessment through interview versus client self-completion, the relationship to actual levels of behaviors, reactivity, stability over time, and efficacy in choosing procedures. Further, very scanty information is provided for user interpretation of responses within a behavior therapy format.

An examination of references and other more current literature reveals some relevant published research. Two of the reinforcement surveys, the Reinforcement Survey Schedule (RSS) and the Childrens Reinforcement Schedule (CRS), appear to have only moderate stability (.45 to .80) over periods from 1–5 weeks (Kleinknecht, McCormick, & Thorndike, 1973; Cautela & Brion-Meisels, 1979). The RSS appears to have a coherent factor structure for college students, which may help in identifying families of possible reinforcers (Baron, DeWaard, & Galizio, 1981). A useful study was found relating to one of the forms for identifying problem behaviors, an abbreviated Social Performance Survey Schedule (Monti, 1983). Results indicated a low to moderate interrater reliability and a low to moderate relationship between self-completed forms, self ratings, clinical interviews (not using the forms), and staff ratings. These studies are in no way conclusive but strongly suggest the need for research into the basic measurement qualities and their implications for users. Further, it is almost certain that different forms are differentially valid for different populations (age, educational levels, etc.), and for different purposes, certainly prohibiting blanket adoption of all forms by potential users. A final problem is that many forms would be difficult to quantify, and thus their use in research or treatment evaluation may be problematic.

On the positive side, many of these forms may provide a useful vehicle for standard collection of intake data and keeping of clinical records, especially for clinicians who rely primarily on clinical interviews and self-report. The reinforcement schedules may be especially useful in allowing desirable client input when establishing interventions involving contingencies. Clinicians following a behavioral model will undoubtedly be careful about naive reliance on self-report data (although that is certainly a source that must be tapped in any assessment). Further, it is reasonable that data collected may be more reliable when the interview is standardized, a feature provided by many of these forms. Finally, the focus on environment, overt or covert behavior, and client preferences for situations and procedures is refreshing.

Even given the positive points, it is difficult to recommend these forms, except as potentially very useful instruments in need of empirical investigation. Certainly, it would be essential for future editions to provide a clear analysis of research data for each form rather than simply listing potentially useful research in a reference list. Further, clear information about development, guides for interpretation, and warnings about potential biases and unknown qualities must be explicitly provided for the manual to be useful. Given all these problems, it is recommended that great caution be taken with these forms and that users realize that their adoption of a form is based rather completely on their professional opinion unsubstantiated by empirical evidence.

REVIEWER'S REFERENCES

Kleinknecht, R. A., McCormick, C. E., & Thorndike, R. M. Stability of stated reinforcers as measured by the Reinforcement Survey Schedule. BEHAVIOR THERAPY, 1973, 4, 407–413.

Cautela, J. R., & Brion-Meisels, L. A children's reinforcement survey schedule. PSYCHOLOGICAL REPORTS, 1979, 44, 327–338.

Baron, A., DeWaard, R., & Galizio, M. Factor-analytically derived subscales for the Reinforcement Survey Schedule: Reinforcer preference as a function of drug use and sex. BEHAVIOR MODIFICATION, 1981, 5, 203–220.

Monti, P. M. The social skills intake interview: Reliability and convergent validity assessment. JOURNAL OF BEHAVIOR THERAPY & EXPERIMENTAL PSYCHIATRY, 1983, 14, 305–310.

[128]

Behavior Evaluation Scale. Grades K–12; 1983; BES; criterion-referenced; ratings by teachers or other school personnel; "provides educationally relevant information about the behavior of students"; 6 scores: learning problems, interpersonal difficulties, inappropriate behavior, unhappiness/depression, physical symptoms/fears, total (behavior quotient); no norms; suggested standards of mastery; individual; 1 form; student record form (6 pages); data collection form (6 pages); manual (24 pages); 1984 price data: $40 per complete test kit including manual, 50 student record forms, and data collection form; $28 per 50 student record forms; $20 per 25 data collection forms; $12 per manual; (10–20) minutes; Stephen B. McCarney, James E. Leigh, Jane A. Cornbleet (manual and student record form), and Michele T. Jackson (data collection form); Educational Services; distributed by PRO-ED.*

Review of Behavior Evaluation Scale by J. JEFFREY GRILL, Associate Professor of Special Education, University of South Alabama, Mobile, AL:

Of all disabilities which may afflict school-age children, behavior disorders (BD) (e.g., emotional disturbance, emotional conflict, social maladjustment) may be the least susceptible to accurate quantification via tests. Several available rating instruments attest to both the difficulties in attempting an objective measurement of deviant behaviors in school-age children and the multitude of limitations on such attempts.

In a single rating instrument, the authors of the Behavior Evaluation Scale (BES) have provided a simple-to-use, yet sophisticated and carefully developed tool for screening, evaluating, or charting the progress of students in grades K through 12 who are suspected of being behaviorally disordered. Clearly, the BES is state-of-the-art instrumentation.

Like most rating instruments, the BES consists of statements descriptive of behaviors exhibited by youngsters. For each of the 52 statements, the observer, typically the teacher, must assign a rating ranging from 1, "Never or Not Observed" to 7, "Continuously Throughout the Day." The protocol, a single folded sheet which provides six pages, is easily and quickly completed by the teacher who knows the child. Direct observation is not necessary during completion of the form, although knowledge of the child's behavior, obtained from daily or frequent classroom contact, is essential.

Ratings are then recorded on the page labelled Data Summary Sheet, which provides spaces for ratings of items grouped according to five subscales, each of which represents a major characteristic of serious emotional disturbance as defined in the Federal regulations which accompany PL 94–142, the Education for All Handicapped Children Act. The subscales include: Learning Problems, Interpersonal Difficulties, Inappropriate Behaviors, Unhappiness/Depression, and Physical Symptoms/Fears. Each rating is multiplied by a weight of from 1 to 3 (indicating the severity of the problem). Within subscales these weights are summed to obtain a raw score which is converted to a Standard Score having a mean of 10 and a standard deviation of 3. Standard Scores may be plotted on the front page of the protocol, and a BES quotient ($M = 100$; $SD = 15$) may be obtained from Table B.

These relatively simple procedures belie the sophistication of the BES and the thoroughness of its development. Careful reading of the manual reveals only minimal and minor shortcomings, a serious adherence to APA *Standards for Educational and Psychological Tests,* and an almost religious devotion to clarity. In short, the BES and accompanying manual are "user-friendly," providing both unusual power and ease of use for an instrument of this type.

Apparently the BES was developed to satisfy two criteria: congruence with public school reality, and also with the Federal definition of "seriously emotionally disturbed children." An initial pool of 47 items describing typical behaviors of BD children was presented to 80 special education teachers in Missouri. Changes of items recommended by this group resulted in a revised scale of 50 items, which the authors assigned, on the basis of face validity, to each of the five subscales.

The revised scale was presented to 104 Missouri teachers who each evaluated one typical child and one suspected of or already referred for "serious behavioral problems in the classroom." These teachers also were asked to evaluate the BES on several criteria. Final revision resulted in a scale of 52 items. Weightings for items were obtained from 240 teachers (K through 12) in Missouri, and ultimately were collapsed from a range of 1 to 9 to a range of 1 to 3. Field testing included several item analyses and seems to have been thorough.

Medians and "ranges of discriminating powers" (i.e., point-biserial correlations) for items in the five subscales all exceed a criterion of .30, except for the ranges for Interpersonal Difficulties (.14 to .77) and Inappropriate Behaviors (.20 to .82). These data seem to be derived from the normative sample, but this is not directly stated.

The normative sample consisted of 311 unselected teachers who rated a randomly selected group of 1,018 students across 13 grade levels (K through 12) in 10 states. Teachers and students were generally equally distributed across grade levels. The student sample was representative of national demographic characteristics with regard to residence (urban/rural) and parents' occupations (white collar/blue collar/other, not stated). Boys were slightly overrepresented; Black students were somewhat underrepresented as were students from the Northeast and the West. Nonetheless, the normative sample approximated national demographic characteristics.

Both internal consistency (coefficient alphas) and test-retest reliability are reported. Internal consistency coefficients, presumably derived from the normative sample, all exceed .80, except for Unhappiness/Depression (.76) and Physical Symptoms/Fear (.77). Test-retest reliability, derived from 15 teachers who rated 57 students (with at least one teacher at each grade level), is reported at .97 or greater for each subscale.

The authors judge content validity to be evident because of the careful selection and field testing of the items and because of the demonstrated internal consistency of the subscales. Criterion-related validity is demonstrated through correlations of each subscale of the BES with scores on the Behavior Rating Profile obtained on a sample of 25 elementary and 24 secondary grade students previously diagnosed as behaviorally disordered. Only subscale 4 of the BES (Unhappiness/Depression), which does not rate behaviors measured on the Behavior Rating Profile, does not achieve statistical significance. This same sample was compared to 49 students randomly selected from the normative group. Results of this study revealed significant differences ($p < .001$) between groups on all subscales. The authors offer these results as evidence of construct validity because they demonstrate the adequacy of the BES to differentiate between "normal" and "behaviorally disordered" children.

Overall, the Behavior Evaluation Scale is a highly usable and useful instrument, adequate to achieve all the purposes delineated in the manual: screening, assessing/diagnosing, developing Individual Educational Plans, documenting progress, and collecting research data for students suspected of or identified as exhibiting behavior problems in school. The BES is easy to use and to score; insofar as possible with behavior rating scales, it provides clearly objective items which result in reliable and valid data. The BES manual could easily become a model of clarity for reporting technical data and for clarity of administration, scoring, and interpretation directions. Based on its careful development, both practical and theoretical, its wide applicability, and its reliability and validity, the BES should become the instrument of choice for those who evaluate children's classroom behavior.

Review of Behavior Evaluation Scale by LESTER MANN, Chairman and Professor, Special Education Department, Hunter College, NY, and LEONARD KENOWITZ, Director, Department of Program Services, The Woods Schools, Langhorne, PA:

The Behavior Evaluation Scale (BES) is intended to assist "school personnel in reaching and documenting decisions regarding diagnosis, placement and programming" for pupils with "behavior/emotional disturbance," and for use as a general behavior rating scale with "any" student. It consists of 52 items based on behavioral observations, and takes 10–20 minutes to administer per student.

The BES presumes to provide information for "six primary purposes": (1) to screen for behavior problems, (2) to assess the behavior of individual students, (3) to assist in the diagnosis of behavior/emotional disturbance, (4) to develop individual educational plans for students needing special education services, (5) to document student progress, and (6) to obtain data for research purposes.

Each of the BES's 52 items are assigned to one of 5 subscales, though in unequal numbers (because some types of negative behaviors are less usually observed than others). These subscales represent components (characteristics) of Bower's widely used definition of behavior disturbance. These components are: (1) an inability to learn which cannot be explained by intellectual, sensory, or health factors; (2) an inability to build or maintain satisfactory interpersonal relationships with peers and teachers; (3) inappropriate types of behavior or feelings under normal circumstances; (4) a general pervasive mood of unhappiness or depression; or (5) a tendency to develop physical symptoms or fears associated with personal or school problems.

The negative behaviors described in each item are rated on a scale of 1 to 7, depending on how frequently these behaviors are observed. A test item thus receives a score of 1 if a negative behavior is "never or not observed," and a score of 7 if observed "continuously throughout the day." The scored items are weighted 1–3 on the basis of "severity and intensity." The raw scores for each of the subscales are independently computed by adding the appropriate weighted item scores, and then translated into standard scores.

Subscale standard scores from 7–13 are to be interpreted as "normal" or statistically average or typical. Those less than 7 or greater than 13 are "considered to be statistically deviant or atypical" in respect to the subscale's characteristics. A "Behavior Quotient," derived from all the subtest standard scores, provides "a global index of a student's behavior in all the areas measured within the total scale."

The BES is interpreted on three levels: (1) total scale analysis, for a comparative estimate of a student's overall behavior; (2) subscale analysis, to determine a pupil's normality or atypicality in terms of subscale criteria; and (3) item analysis, to be used as a guide in educational planning.

Much care appears to have gone into the development of the BES. It has, however, serious technical deficiencies that belie the authors' claims that "both validity and reliability of the instrument have been clearly established for its stated purposes."

The norms for the BES are based on small and inadequately described samples. A total of 311 teachers rated 1,018 regular classroom students, grades K through 12 and apparently selected at random, from regular classrooms in 10 states that were deemed to represent appropriately the four major geographical regions of the United States. The samples are described as being demographically adequate. The coefficients obtained from such limited data can provide but unstable estimates of the parameters studied and can only result in limited generalizability. Surprisingly, we are not informed whether any of the samples include behaviorally disturbed children. Apropos of this and the authors' own contention that 2%–5% of school children have behavior problems, information about distribution characteristics (i.e., skewness and kurtosis) necessary for proper interpretation of the BES are not provided. The authors' finding that there were no meaningful differences in scores across grade levels for any of the BES measures, while suggesting to them that "the behavioral constructs measured by the BES are not developmental or cumulative," is more likely to be an artifact of inadequate norming procedures.

Nor are the BES reliability data adequate. Its internal consistency coefficients average .87 and do not appear sufficient to support using the scale for diagnostic and placement purposes. Test-retest reliability coefficients exceeding .97 are reported, but are based on observations made 10 days apart, too short a time to test the stability of the characteristics being assessed, and likely to be influenced by memory factors. There is a complete lack of information concerning interrater reliability, a particularly serious omission, since raters assessing behavioral problems have often been found to disagree significantly.

In validating the BES, its authors have focussed upon the validity of the total scale. Their defense of total scale validity is in terms of the trinity of content, criterion-related, and construct validity. The first, based upon careful item selection, is adequate. The claim to criterion-related validity, however, rests on a single study that found a modest (.64) statistically significant correlation between the BES and the Behavior Rating Profile (BRP), a little known instrument whose properties are not explained. This is hardly the path to glory in validation. Claims for the scale's construct validity also rest on meager grounds. The total scale is dependent (again) on its correlation with the BRP and its ability, in another study, to discriminate in a statistically significant fashion between small groups of behaviorally disturbed and non-behaviorally disturbed pupils. Support for the construct validity of the subscales derives entirely from their intercorrelations, which the authors believe confirm them both as measures of "the general construct of behavior" and of "different aspects" of the construct. There is no evidence to support the practical utility of the scale's weighting system.

Among other criticisms, the BES scoring system is poorly guided by criteria like "less than once a week," and "approximately once a month"; and many of the scale items are not behavioral in any concrete sense of the term. Observations that the student "deliberately makes false statement," or "exhibits unwarranted self-blame or self criticism" hardly constitute the "highly precise and objective quantifier" which the authors claim them to be.

To conclude, the BES is a worthwhile effort, but it cannot be recommended for diagnostic or placement decisions about school children with behavior problems, nor do its individual items appear precise enough to guide educational planning. Until technically improved, it can more appropriately be used to gather useful information to support decision making or for research purposes.

[129]

Behavior Rating Instrument for Autistic and Other Atypical Children. Autistic and atypical children; 1977; BRIAAC; 9 scores: relationship to an adult, communication, drive for mastery, vocalization and expressive speech, sound and speech reception, social responsiveness, body movement, psychobiological development, total; no norms; individual; record form (15 pages); manual (11 pages); total score sheet (2 pages); suggested individual plan (2 pages); descriptive guide (8 pages); 1983 price data: $165 per complete set; $37.50 per 25 report forms; $38 per 200 individual scale score sheets; $10.50 per 25 total score sheets; $10.50 per 25 interscale profiles; $32.50 per 25 descriptive guides; $10.50 per 25 suggested individual plans; $32.50 per manual; 120

minutes (minimum); Bertram A. Ruttenberg, Beth I. Kalish, Charles Wenar, and Enid G. Wolf; Stoelting Co.*

See T3:272 (1 reference).

Review of Behavior Rating Instrument for Autistic and Other Atypical Children by EDWARD WORKMAN, Assistant Professor of Psychology, University of Tennessee at Chattanooga, Chattanooga, TN:

The Behavior Rating Instrument for Autistic and Other Atypical Children (BRIAAC) is a behavioral observation and rating system designed to assess the behavior of children characterized as "autistic" or behaviorally "atypical." According to the test manual, the latter category includes children characterized by "disintegrative psychosis" with borderline development during the first two and one-half years of life, followed immediately by the development of severe emotional dysfunction. The system is designed to be used in natural environments by raters who have received adequate training. Adequate training is defined in the BRIAAC manual as 40–80 hours of supervised practice in the use of the system.

The BRIAAC involves the naturalistic observation of a target child for a minimum of 2 hours. These observations form the basis for the observer's ratings of the child's behavior. Ratings are made on eight scales: (I) Relationship to an Adult, (II) Communication, (III) Drive for Mastery, (IV) Vocalization and Expressive Speech, (V) Sound and Speech Reception, (VI) Social Responsiveness, (VII) Body Movement (active and passive), and (VIII) Psychobiological Development. A composite score (Cumulative Total Score) is also available. Each scale describes 10 levels of functioning, with level 1 indicative of severe autistic behavior and level 10 indicative of behavior which is considered average or typical for a 3- to 4-year-old child.

On a given scale, the observer distributes 10 points across the various levels, based upon the proportion of time a child spends engaging in the behaviors described at a particular level. As such, the BRIAAC is basically a behavioral event recording system wherein the behavioral events are weighted in terms of their adaptive value (levels) and proportion or relative frequency of occurrence within the child's behavioral repertoire. Each scale generates a score derived from multiplying points by the level at which they are awarded and summing across levels. The BRIAAC manual provides detailed scoring aids (including examples) for all levels of each scale.

The BRIAAC is a direct behavioral measurement system, and the manual contains no normative information. Although norms are not necessarily required for the interpretation of observational data, they would facilitate the use of the BRIAAC as a diagnostic tool (Helton, Workman, & Matusek, 1982). Specifically, quantitative norms would allow the user of the BRIAAC to compare an observed child to a relevant within-group norm to ascertain, statistically, the relative severity of the child's behavioral difficulties. This reviewer strongly recommends the development of norms in future extensions of the BRIAAC.

Two studies of the reliability of the BRIAAC are reported in the manual. In the first, interrater reliability was assesed by having teams of three to five raters observe a total of 113 children. Spearman rank correlations between scores of the eight BRIAAC scales ranged from a high of .93 on Body Movement to a low of .84 on Vocalization. The average correlation across all eight scales was .88. This suggests that the BRIAAC exhibits adequate interrater stability for raters who are trained rather extensively.

A second reliability study focused on the temporal stability of the BRIAAC. Twenty-two moderately retarded preschoolers were assessed twice with a 1-month interval. Test-retest reliability coefficients ranged from a low of .67 on Mastery to a high of .93 on Psychobiological Development. The reliability for the sum of all scales was .95. However, the average coefficient across reported scales was .75. Clearly the temporal stability of several BRIAAC scales leaves something to be desired.

Several lines of validity evidence are proposed in the BRIAAC manual, including content, concurrent, construct, and factorial validity. In an attempt to develop content validity in the BRIAAC, the authors had items revised by a broad, multidisciplinary group of experts. However, the specific procedures for item examination and revision are not reported. Clear evidence of content validity is, therefore, not presented.

As evidence of concurrent/criterion-related validity, BRIAAC scores of 26 autistic/atypical children were correlated with a single clinician's ratings of the severity of each child's disturbance. Significant moderate positive correlations were obtained for Total Scores, Relationship, Vocalization, and Sound and Speech Reception. A correlation of .83 was found for Mastery. Although these data are suggestive of concurrent validity, it should be noted that they are based on a study involving only one expert's ratings as the criterion.

In another study investigating the concurrent/criterion validity of the BRIAAC, 35 retarded children were contrasted with 32 autistic children. The latter group, as predicted, received lower scores on four of five scales utilized including Relationship, Communication, Vocalization, and Psychobiological Development. These results strongly suggest the "contrasted groups" criterion validity of at least four BRIAAC scales.

Evidence for construct validity is presented in terms of what the BRIAAC authors label "discontinuity scores." These are scores which reflect the number of unscored levels within a range of scored levels. As such, discontinuity scores represent inverse measures of clustering. The logic behind the use of discontinuity scores lies in the notion that mastery of levels within a scale should, theoretically, reflect continuous rather than discontinuous development. Low discontinuity scores, therefore, are purported to suggest that the BRIAAC provides valid measures of factors which exhibit developmental continuity. With the exception of Psychobiological Development, BRIAAC scales exhibit discontinuity scores lower than .50, indicating that the ordering of levels is quite continuous. Psychobiological Development, however, exhibits a discontinuity score of 2.32, indicating the possibility of serious construct validity problems with that scale.

In a study of the factorial validity of the BRIAAC, the authors conducted a factor analysis with varimax rotation. The results indicated the presence of a single complex factor which the authors tentatively label "Reality Testing." Clearly, further research is needed on the factorial structure of the BRIAAC in order to articulate more coherently the entities it measures. This reviewer would strongly suggest that further factor analytic studies utilize procedures which are compatible with the authors' assumption of an oblique factorial structure. Varimax rotation assumes orthogonal factors, which appear to contrast with the author's theoretical model of the BRIAAC structure. It seems that oblique rotations would be more appropriate in future research.

In summary, the BRIAAC appears to represent a major improvement over commonly used "homemade" behavioral observation systems. Historically, behavioral observation systems have been seriously lacking in systematic evidence of their reliability and validity characteristics (Kent & Foster, 1977), and this cannot be said of the BRIAAC. Although much further research is needed to better articulate the psychometric properties of the BRIAAC (especially temporal stability, factorial structure, and normative properties), it appears to offer a viable measurement technology to those pediatric professionals who work with autistic and other atypical children. However, as the authors indicate, the BRIAAC itself does not represent an integrated assessment system, and should be used only as one part of an overall assessment battery with adequate cross-checks for valid interpretation.

REVIEWER'S REFERENCES

Kent, R., & Foster, S. Direct observational procedures: Methodological issues in naturalistic settings. In A. Ciminero, K. Calhoun, and H. Adams (Eds.), HANDBOOK OF BEHAVIORAL ASSESSMENT. New York: John Wiley and Sons, 1977.

Helton, G., Workman, E., & Matuszek, P. PSYCHOEDUCATIONAL ASSESSMENT: AN INTEGRATIVE APPROACH. New York: Grune and Stratton, 1982.

[130]

Behavior Rating Profile. Grades 1–12; 1978; BRP; ecological approach to behavioral assessment; 5 checklists: student rating scales (home, school, peer), teacher rating scale, parent rating scale, plus 1 sociogram score; manual ('78, 37 pages); student rating scales ('78, 4 pages); parent rating scale ('78, 2 pages); teacher rating scale ('78, 2 pages); profile form ('78, 2 pages); 1983 price data: $18 per 50 student rating forms; $12 per 50 teacher or parent rating forms; $12 per 50 profile forms; $18 per manual; $67 per kit of 25 of each form and manual; (5–30) minutes; Linda L. Brown and Donald D. Hammill; PRO-ED.*

See T3:273 (1 reference).

TEST REFERENCES

1. Nunn, G. D., Parish, T. S., & Worthing, R. J. Concurrent validity of the Personal Attribute Inventory for Children with the State-Trait Anxiety Inventory for Children and the Behavior Rating Profile-Student Scales. EDUCATIONAL AND PSYCHOLOGICAL MEASUREMENT, 1983, 43, 261–265.

Review of Behavior Rating Profile by THOMAS R. KRATOCHWILL, Professor of Educational Psychology, The University of Arizona, Tucson, AZ:

The Behavior Rating Profile (BRP) was designed for children who range in age from 6–5 through 13–6 years and/or who are in grades one through seven. The norms have recently been extended upward through students age 18 (Hammill, personal communication, August 1981). The authors consider the BRP an ecological/behavioral assessment device in that it allows an examination of children's behaviors in a variety of settings from different perspectives.

The BRP Student Rating Scales include three self-ratings (covering the areas of Home, School, Peer) and are completed by the child. Items from each of the three scales are intermingled in one 60-item instrument. The student is asked to classify each item as "True" or "False" (e.g., on the school scale the student would respond to the item "I can't seem to concentrate in class").

The Teacher Rating Scale is completed by one or more of the child's regular or special education teachers. The 30 items on this scale are descriptive sentence items in which the respondent is asked to rate a child on some problem behavior (e.g., "Has nervous habits") in terms of four categories, ranging from "Very much like the student," "Like the student," "Not much like the student," to "Not at all like the student."

The Parent Rating Scale is completed by the mother or father (or both) or guardian. These individuals are required to rate 30 items (e.g., "Takes orders from parents unwillingly") on categories similar to those used in the Teacher Scale.

The final component of the BRP is the Sociogram in which pairs of stimulus questions are listed and the teacher selects one pair to ask of the child and his/her classmates (e.g., "Which of the girls and boys in your class would you least like to work with on a school project?"). Each student in the class is then asked to nominate three of his/her classmates for each question.

CONSIDERATIONS IN USE OF THE BEHAVIOR RATING PROFILE. The BRP must be evaluated in terms of methodological and conceptual characteristics that have emerged in the professional literature on the use of checklists and rating scales (Spivack & Swift, 1973; Sandoval, 1977; Walls, Werner, Bacon, & Zane, 1977; Evans & Nelson, 1977; Ciminero & Drabman, 1977; McCulloch, 1979; Kratochwill, 1982; Saal, Downey, & Lahey, 1980; Severson, 1971). Kratochwill and Sanchez (1981) provided a critique of the BRP, and the remainder of this review is based on their formulations.

POSITIVE FEATURES OF THE BRP. The BRP has some positive features for assessment in applied settings. First, it is economical in cost, effort, and clinician time relative to other assessment approaches and rating scales. The BRP can be administered in separate components or in its totality, depending on the nature of the problem and the desired comprehensiveness of assessment. The Sociogram is the most time-consuming to administer relative to other components. Second, the BRP is designed so that a relatively comprehensive picture of the problem(s) can be obtained. The "ecological/behavioral" assessment provides a broad sampling in different settings by different raters. Third, the diverse range of questions asked and the environments and individuals sampled allow the rater to identify problems that may be missed through other assessment methods. The scale shares an advantage with other checklists and rating devices in that it may help identify the child's problem(s). Fourth, the data obtained from the BRP are generally easy to quantify. Also, the directions for the scoring of the BRP are straightforward and do not require extensive training. Fifth, the BRP may be a convenient means of obtaining social validity data for therapeutic outcomes in behavioral intervention programs (cf. Kazdin, 1977; Wolf, 1978). Finally, since the BRP contains normative data from a large sample, it may be very useful in evaluating the nature and scope of intervention programs (Kratochwill, 1982).

DATA OBTAINED. Assessments may be ordered along a continuum of directness representing the extent to which the device and/or procedure (*a*) measures the behavior of relevance, and (*b*) measures it at the time and place of its natural occurrence (Cone, 1982). The BRP is an indirect strategy because the rater is asked to rate the child based upon past observations of the child's behavior. Thus, the behavior of clinical interest (e.g., stealing, lying) may or may not be involved, but the rating occurs subsequent to it. This feature of rating scales is used to distinguish them from direct observation methods which assess the target behavior at the time and place of its natural occurrence.

Rating scales should be confirmed by independent validation of the problem, preferably through direct assessment methods (e.g., tests, direct observation, self-monitoring). Several types of validity issues are important here. First, concurrent validity should be established by direct measurement of actual behaviors as they occur in their natural environment. The BRP authors report acceptable concurrent validity with other rating scales, which are also indirect measures of behavior. Predictive validity with actual measures of behaviors is desirable and should be determined, but the BRP does not yet have this type of validity information. Second, "Diagnostic Validity" (as labeled by the authors) is a useful supplement to conventional measures. Diagnostic validity is utilized "to determine whether the BRP can be used to discriminate between groups of students who are known or suspected to evidence varying degrees of behavior problems." Data from one standardized sample of the BRP provided this type of information.

Recently Reisberg, Fudell, and Hudson (in press) examined comparisons of respondents on a group of 15 "mild to moderate" behaviorally disordered students. Ratings on the BRP were completed by parents, three different teachers, and the students themselves. Results of the study showed that the parents rated students lower than other respondent groups and that only parents rated students outside the "normal" range. Regular classroom teachers rated the students higher than either the students' special education teacher or a paraprofessional. Also, students' self-ratings were found to be consistently higher than other respondents. Results of this study are similar to the original validation data of Brown and Hammill (manual) in which parents rated subjects lower than either teacher or self-ratings and students provided higher self-ratings than other respondents.

ITEM SELECTION. The manual provides a rather clear description of how items for the BRP were selected. The initial item pool was established through two procedures: (1) Existing checklists and related assessment devices were reviewed. (2) Parents ($N = 41$) of children classified as emotionally disturbed, parents ($N = 56$) of children classified as learning disabled, and teachers ($N = 6$) of emotionally disturbed pupils were asked to describe in writing the behaviors that seemed to be characteristic of their handicapped children.

Subsequent to field testing, an item analysis was performed that focused on an examination of item validity. The analysis of the item validity appears acceptable, based on Guilford's (1956) criteria. The statistically significant median correlations (point biserial) ranged from .43 to .83 for the grade levels two through seven.

ITEM CONTENT. The final determination of item content in the BRP was made based on statistical criteria (i.e., validity coefficients). Such criteria may yield considerable variability in the nature of the final items included and the corresponding inference called for. For example, on the Parent Scale one would expect vast differences between the items "Violates curfew" and "Has too rich a fantasy life." When the rater is interested in examining various problematic behaviors for the design of an intervention program, specific and relatively noninferential items are preferred. Yet, few if any of the published rating scales provide operational definitions of the items. Some items in the BRP come close to meeting this criterion (e.g., item 13 on the Parent Rating Scale: "Is self-destructive; pulls out his/her own hair, scratches self to point of drawing blood, etc."). Although providing operational definitions most likely reduces inference regarding the behavior to be rated (McCulloch, 1979), the degree of inference introduced into a particular item and its relation to reliability and validity still awaits empirical testing.

POSITIVE/NEGATIVE ITEM CONTENT. The BRP items are generally worded to detect the presence of problems or negative behaviors, and this is true across the parent, teacher, and student scales. On the other hand, the BRP Sociogram may yield a positive outcome because items are not negatively worded. It should be stressed, however, that although the items (stems) in the BRP are negatively worded, the rater has the option to respond "Not at all like" the child. A large number of responses in this category would allow the inference that the person completing the form is reporting the domain of behaviors rated as nonproblematic for the student.

RATING BEHAVIORS. The BRP is an improvement over many scales on dimensions of how the respondent is required to rate the presence or absence of a behavior (problem), and the kinds of categories employed to code these activities. However, instructions will cause some variability in the quality of data obtained. For example, it is not clear exactly how long the person completing the scale should observe the child before conducting the rating. Even the statement on the rating profile itself, "Which of these behaviors are you concerned about at this particular time and to what extent do you see them as problems?" may be perceived quite differently across raters. Also, some raters may have known the child for years and could rate behaviors occurring over this period. A problem such as "Disrupts the classroom" may be occurring for months, while "Swears in class" may be a more recent problem. Yet, the BRP would not be sensitive to the discrimination of duration of those behaviors occurring over a several-month period of time versus those occurring relatively recently. The rating procedure on the BRP contrasts with the Walker Problem Behavior Identification Checklist (Walker, 1976) which delineates a specific time period (e.g., "respond by circling the number to the right of the statement if you have observed that behavioral item in the child's response pattern during the last two-month period"). The clinician using the BRP should take into account this aspect of rating by requesting respondents to provide additional information on what time period was used in their assessments or specify this time period prior to the school rating.

A related concern is the situation in which the behavior to be rated occurs. Although most of the behaviors on the Teacher Scale would presumably be rated on the basis of behavior observed in the classroom (e.g., "Swears in class," "Doesn't follow class rules"), some behaviors may be rated based on behavior observed outside of the classroom situation (e.g., "Steals," "Bullies other children"). Thus, the clinician must determine the specific situation in which the problem occurs since such information has important implications for the design of intervention programs.

A final concern with the format is that the BRP does not provide specific information on frequency, intensity, and duration of particular behaviors. The clinician must use the general categories (i.e., "Very much like the student" versus "Not at all like the student") to seek out leads for various dimensions of actual behavior.

RATING FORMAT. The BRP requires that the respondent complete all items on a given child at one time. Rating the child in this fashion has the possibility of establishing a negative set (or halo effect) across specific items (McCulloch, 1979; Severson, 1971). Yet, most scales are constructed in this manner and it remains an empirical issue to determine if different rating formats would help eliminate such potential bias. In the absence of data on this issue, it is desirable for the rater to examine the child with other assessment devices to ascertain positive behaviors.

SUMMARY. As an indirect measure, the BRP has definite positive characteristics. First, the separate components or the complete set can be administered depending on the purpose and the degrees of comprehensiveness desired. Thus, when all the components are used, the behavior of a child or adolescent is sampled across various situations or environments, by several respondents, with a wide array of items or questions. Furthermore, the BRP is easy to score and quantify without special training, and it is accompanied by a clearly written manual.

The BRP has use in the evaluation of intervention programs when administered as a pre-post measure or in repeated assessment; however, this remains to be empirically demonstrated. The BRP also has potential as a measure for evaluating the social validity of behaviorally oriented programs. Since the BRP was designed to overcome some of the shortcomings of other rating scales, it is a welcome addition to the assessment options for use with school-age children. Realistically, its potential will only become empirically evident as forthcoming research with the profile appears.

REVIEWER'S REFERENCES

Guilford, J. P. FUNDAMENTAL STATISTICS IN PSYCHOLOGY AND EDUCATION. New York: McGraw-Hill, 1956.

Severson, R. A. The rationale and development of teacher-completed behavior rating scales. In J. Feldhusen (Chair), ASSESSMENT AND MANAGEMENT OF AGGRESSIVE AND DISRUPTIVE BEHAVIOR IN THE CLASSROOM. Symposium conducted at the meeting of the National Council on Measurement in Education, New York, February 1971.

Spivack, G., & Swift, M. Classroom behavior of children: A critical review of teacher-administered rating scales. JOURNAL OF SPECIAL EDUCATION, 1973, 1, 55–89.

Walker, H. M. WALKER PROBLEM BEHAVIOR IDENTIFICATION CHECKLIST. Los Angeles: Western Psychological Corporation, 1976.

Ciminero, A. R., & Drabman, R. S. Current developments in the behavioral assessment of children. In B. B. Lahey and A. E. Kazdin (Eds.), ADVANCES IN CLINICAL CHILD PSYCHOLOGY (Vol. 1). New York: Plenum Press, 1977.

Evans, I. M., & Nelson, R. O. Assessment of child behavior problems. In A. R. Ciminero, K. S. Calhoun, and H. E. Adams (Eds.), HANDBOOK OF BEHAVIORAL ASSESSMENT. New York: Wiley, 1977.

Kazdin, A. E. Assessing the clinical or applied significance of behavior change through social validation. BEHAVIOR MODIFICATION, 1977, 1, 427–452.

Sandoval, J. The measurement of the hyperactive syndrome in children. REVIEW OF EDUCATIONAL RESEARCH, 1977, 47, 293–318.

Walls, R. T., Werner, T. J., Bacon, A., & Zane, T. Behavior checklists. In J. D. Cone and R. P. Hawkins (Eds.), BEHAVIORAL ASSESSMENT: NEW DIRECTIONS IN CLINICAL PSYCHOLOGY. New York: Brunner/Mazel, 1977.

Wolf, M. M. Social validity: The case for subjective measurement or how applied behavior analysis is finding its heart. JOURNAL OF APPLIED BEHAVIOR ANALYSIS, 1978, 11, 203–214.

McCulloch, R. Behavior rating scales: Contexts and criticisms. National Association of School Psychologists, COMMUNIQUE, 1979, Nov., 6–7.

Saal, F. E., Downey, R. G., & Lahey, M. A. Rating the ratings: Assessing the psychometric quality of rating data. PSYCHOLOGICAL BULLETIN, 1980, 88, 413–428.

Kratochwill, T. R., & Sanchez, D. Review of Brown, L. L. & Hammill, D. D. Behavioral Rating Profile: An ecological approach to behavioral assessment, Austin, Texas: PRO-ED, 1978. JOURNAL OF SCHOOL PSYCHOLOGY, 1981, 19, 283–288.

Cone, J. D. The behavioral assessment grid (BAG): A conceptual framework and a taxonomy. In C. R. Reynolds & T. B. Gutkin (Eds.), HANDBOOK OF SCHOOL PSYCHOLOGY. New York: Wiley, 1982.

Kratochwill, T. R. Advances in behavioral assessment. In C. R. Reynolds and T. B. Gutkin (Eds.), HANDBOOK OF SCHOOL PSYCHOLOGY. New York: Wiley, 1982.

Reisberg, L. E., Fudell, I., & Hudson, F. Comparison of responses to the Behavior Rating Profile for mild to moderate behaviorally disordered subjects. PSYCHOLOGICAL REPORTS, 1982, 50, 136–138.

Review of Behavior Rating Profile by JOSEPH C. WITT, Associate Professor of Psychology, Louisiana State University, Baton Rouge, LA:

The Behavior Rating Profile (BRP) offers four methods of assessing the behavior of elementary school children: self-ratings, teacher ratings, parent ratings, and a sociogram. The student self-ratings, which are termed The Student Ratings, are completed by the student and yield separate scores for behavior at home, in school, and with peers. The Student Rating Scale is a 4-page booklet containing 60 items, such as "I seem to get into a lot of fights," which require the student to respond "True" or "False." The Teacher Rating Scale and The Parent Rating Scale each contain 30 instances of problem behaviors which require that the respondent classify the behavior into four categories ranging from "Very Much Like the Student," to "Not At All Like the Student." The fourth component of the BRP is a sociogram which is a unique feature not found in other behavior rating systems. Unlike the other three components, the sociogram is not a rating scale or checklist. Instead, it is a peer nominating technique in which all students in the target child's class are asked to nominate three children with whom they would most like to associate and three with whom they would like least to associate. Each of the four components of the BRP can be used separately or in combination with any of the other BRP measures. The primary advantage of the BRP over other similar rating scales is its ecological emphasis. With the BRP, one can assess the behavior of a child from several different perspectives. The ability to quantify parent and peer data are especially welcome features.

The items on the three scales were selected through a three-step process. First, existing rating scales were reviewed for item content and format. Second, parents and teachers of emotionally disturbed and learning disabled children were asked to list characteristics common to those children. These two steps yielded 306 items which, in step three, were reduced to the present 120 by administering the BRP to 154 children, 7 of their teachers, and 86 of their parents. The exact criteria used to determine item selection are unspecified. All that is known is that point biserial correlations (i.e., item with total score) for the final 120 items ranged from .00 to .91. The inclusion of items with correlations below .30 is questionable because it is likely they may be measuring something different from the scale as a whole (Guilford, 1956).

Despite its name, the items on the BRP frequently do not describe specific behaviors. For example, on The Teacher Rating Scale, the respondent is directed to indicate whether or not the student "is self-centered." Because of the lack of behavioral specificity, the meaning of an item could vary depending on the interpretation of the respondent. A further implication of this problem is that it would be unwise to use many of the so-called behaviors as targets for behavioral intervention. This is contrary to the authors' recommendation that the BRP could be used "in establishing goals for change." What would be the target behavior if the child "is lazy" or "has too rich a fantasy life?"

A major deficiency of the BRP is that it does not contain a sample of positive or appropriate behaviors.

This is problematic because in most situations it is important to identify a student's strengths and assets, as well as weaknesses. Further, appropriate behavior is more than simply the absence of deviant behavior (Ciminero & Drabman, 1977). Interventions directed toward decreasing inappropriate behavior frequently do not lead to increases in appropriate behavior (Evans & Nelson, 1977). Thus, to design interventions from the negative traits identified by the BRP may be a waste of time. A final problem with using exclusively negative items is that raters may develop a negative response set.

Another difficulty involves the rating format, which does not allow for an accurate assessment of the frequency, duration, intensity, or recency of the behaviors being rated. Users may find they want to use the Walker Problem Behavior Checklist or utilize observational data rather than the BRP because it is impossible to determine how recently a behavior rated "Very Much Like the Student" has occurred.

The reading level required to comprehend the items is difficult to assess and this information should be provided in the manual. At what point, and under what conditions, should the items be read to a child?

The manual for BRP is well written and comprehensive, and instructions for administration and interpretation of the scales are clear. Therefore, naive users could master the scale easily. Most pertinent standardization and normative data are contained in the manual. Raw score conversions to scaled scores are printed in the manual and are based upon normative data from a "large unselected" sample of 1,326 students, 645 teachers, and 847 parents in 11 states. The primary weakness of the manual is that it seems to be over-zealous in describing potential uses of the BRP.

In terms of reliability, internal consistency data are presented but unfortunately test-retest and interrater reliabilities were not reported. Coefficient Alpha was reported for each of the BRP scales across three grade level ranges. With the exception of The Teacher Rating Scale, on which reliabilities were excellent, most of the internal consistency data were barely adequate with coefficients consistently below .90 and a few dipping into the .70s. The results of one published study, using children known to be experiencing learning and behavior problems, corroborate the reliability data reported in the manual (Brown, Hammill, & Sherbenou, 1981). This reviewer advocates the reporting of a much more stringent test of reliability for behavior rating scales. Not only should test-retest and interrater reliabilities be reported but also data on the degree of rater agreement on individual items, not just total scores. Reliability figures for total scores and for internal consistency may be quite high while agreement on individual items could be low.

The manual described information relevant to concurrent and construct validity. The BRP was related to other measures of child behavior in one study conducted by the test authors. Although the correlations reported are adequate, the numbers are based upon only 27 children and an enthusiastic endorsement of concurrent validity awaits additional research. Further, the real test of concurrent validity should be to relate the BRP to the direct observation of behavior. No such information is provided. The diagnostic value of the BRP was evaluated by comparing the ratings of students believed to be normal with three groups of children diagnosed as "disturbed." Self-ratings appeared to have no diagnostic utility because the ratings of both the disturbed and normal individuals were in or near the normal range. However, parent and teacher ratings accurately classified the two groups.

Despite the fact that parents' ratings were consistently lower than teachers' or self-ratings, I was surprised to read in the manual that there is diagnostic utility in examining discrepancies between teacher, parent, and self-ratings. If users are to utilize such discrepancies in the profiles of students, they should be aware that parent ratings were consistently lower than teacher or self-ratings.

Previous factor analyses of various scales and combinations of rating scales suggest that common childhood behavior problems cluster into four large groups including problems of conduct, personality, inadequacy-immaturity, and socialized delinquency (Evans & Nelson, 1977). Items from the BRP provide an adequate assessment of only the conduct problem category. The sample of items measuring socialized delinquency or personality problem factors is almost nonexistent.

The inclusion of both positive and negative choices on the sociogram is commendable because it is possible to distinguish between children who are isolated or ignored by peers and those who are disliked. However, the effectiveness of this peer nomination technique is influenced by how well the children in a class know each other (Morrison, 1981). Thus, the sociogram may be inappropriate for some children in special education who are assigned to a classroom on a part-time basis.

The primary advantage of all behavior rating scales is that they are economical and easy to administer and score in contrast to direct behavioral observation which is time consuming and may require specialized training. Some of this time saving advantage may be lost if the entire BRP is used because it may be one of the most lengthy and time consuming of all the behavior rating scales to administer and score. Users under time constraints may consider using only a portion of the BRP or selecting another rating scale.

In summary, the BRP has many redeeming qualities but its usefulness in clinical settings is untested. The capability of sampling behavior across a variety of settings using several respondents is a marked improvement over other rating scales. However, because of the lack of clinical data and the limitations mentioned here, the BRP should presently be confined to use only as an adjunct measure in the identification of children who are behaviorally deviant.

REVIEWER'S REFERENCES

Guilford, J. P. FUNDAMENTAL STATISTICS IN PSYCHOLOGY AND EDUCATION. New York: McGraw-Hill, 1956.

Ciminero, A. R., & Drabman, R. S. Current developments in the behavioral assessment of children. In B. B. Lahey & A. E. Kazdin (Eds.), ADVANCES IN CLINICAL CHILD PSYCHOLOGY (Vol. 1). New York: Plenum Press, 1977.

Evans, I. M., & Nelson, R. O. Assessment of child behavior problems. In A. R. Ciminero, K. S. Calhoun, & H. E. Adams (Eds.), HANDBOOK OF BEHAVIORAL ASSESSMENT. New York: John Wiley, 1977.

Brown, L., Hammill, D. D., & Sherbenou, R. J. The reliability of four measures of children's behavior with deviant populations. BEHAVIORAL DISORDERS, 1981, 180–182.

Morrison, G. M. Sociometric measurement: Methodological considerations of its use with mildly handicapped and nonhandicapped children. JOURNAL OF EDUCATIONAL PSYCHOLOGY, 1981, 73, 193–201.

[131]

Behavior Rating Scale. Grades K–8; 1970–75; ratings by teachers; no validity data; no norms; 3 forms (no date, 2 pages, forms differ only in number of rating categories); no manual; 4 research articles ('72–'75, 5–24 pages, 2 of the articles include the scale); 1984 price data: free upon request from publisher; administration time not reported; Patricia B. Elmore and Donald L. Beggs; Patricia B. Elmore.*

TEST REFERENCES

1. Forehand, R., Griest, D. L., & Wells, K. C. Parent behavior training: An analysis of the relationship among multiple outcome measures. JOURNAL OF ABNORMAL CHILD PSYCHOLOGY, 1979, 7, 229–242.

2. O'Dougherty, M., Wright, F. S., Garmezy, N., Loewenson, R. B., & Torres, F. Later competence and adaptation in infants who survive severe heart defects. CHILD DEVELOPMENT, 1983, 54, 1129–1142.

Review of Behavior Rating Scale by JAYNE A. PARKER, School Consultant, Children and Youth Services Program of Washington County Mental Health, Montpelier, VT:

The Behavior Rating Scale by Elmore and Beggs is part of a package of materials which describes their research efforts and findings. As such, the authors do not seem to promote their materials as a test in and of itself. Practitioners who are interested in a discussion related to the consistency with which teachers rate individual students over time and the relationship between teachers' perception of the importance of traits and their corresponding rating style will find the information well documented and pertinent to those issues.

Use of the Behavior Rating Scale as an evaluation tool, however, would be problematic. The rating scale consists of 16 items reflective of traits such as aggressiveness, responsibility, cooperativeness, gregariousness, etc. The authors include three response forms based on 5-, 7-, or 9-point scales ranging from "strongly agree" to "strongly disagree." A characteristics scale is also included. However, there are no instructions for utilizing these materials, since they relate only to the research conducted by the authors. Furthermore, the items on the Behavior Rating Scale are fraught with general terms and are of such brevity that clarity of meaning and interrater consistency seem unlikely. Examples of items are "demands the teacher's attention," and "is disobedient." One major problem with the scale is that one teacher's perception of problematic attention seeking behaviors and disobedience, for example, may include minor infractions which would be ignored or considered unimportant by the teacher in the next classroom. It would be helpful if future research investigated results obtained when the items are clarified by providing specific examples of type, duration, frequency, and intensity of behaviors.

Test-retest reliability coefficients of the items of the scale over a 2-week interval were unacceptably low, prompting the authors to state that "teacher's ratings of pupil personality traits over a short period are not consistent" (Elmore & Beggs, 1975). These findings were then the source of several further research questions that the authors thought should be addressed to teacher use of all such behavior rating scales. Thus any consideration of the Elmore and Beggs scale should be related to the research context in which it was employed and for which it was intended.

A practitioner who wishes to utilize a behavior rating scale for the rating of children in the classroom will find that the Behavior Rating Scale by Elmore and Beggs is of limited usefulness. This is due, in part, to the absence of data concerning the sample of children rated and the lack of demographic data concerning the teachers who did the ratings and the type of academic environment in which the behaviors occurred, which thereby reduces applicability of the scale. Further, items relate to qualitative aspects of behavior and are not particularly conducive to establishing standardization of assessment. Such generalities do not lend themselves to evaluating frequency, intensity, or duration of behaviors (which might be a more objective approach). This may contribute to interrater and test-retest inconsistency, and will also adversely affect the diagnostic value of the scale. There are no criteria provided to aid in identifying children who are in need of further evaluation or services. Interpretation seems to be entirely subjective, and there is no scoring system. The small number of items do not lend themselves to a factor analytic approach, which would serve to identify specific and empirically defined areas of behavior. A more desirable type of rating scale might be one which includes a larger number of items assessing specific behaviors, with a scoring system based on factor analysis, such as Cassell's Child Behavior Rating Scale. The reader is also referred to the School Psychology Review, Volume XII, No. 3, Fall 1983 (Hynd, Hanson, Kaufman, & Schakel, 1983), entitled "Personality Assessment: The Rating Scale Approach" for a more comprehensive discussion of the rating scale procedure.

As a final comment, the authors' advice to the practitioner who contemplates the use of this type of assessment is sound and deserves to be reiterated. Teachers may formulate responses on the basis of an isolated incident, rather than general behavior, and "it would seem imperative that the elementary counselor determine as quickly as possible the generality of the behavior problem. If the behavior problem is specific to a single episode, the counselor should not have the responsibility of dealing with the observed behavior. The counselor should only be involved after the general nature of the behavior problem has been established." It might be added that a rating scale procedure should comprise one component of a more comprehensive evaluation, and that a child exhibiting behavioral anomalies should not be labelled or diagnosed on the basis of a single assessment tool or when a generalized behavioral disturbance has not been documented.

REVIEWER'S REFERENCES

Elmore, P. B., & Beggs, D. L. Consistency of teacher ratings of pupil personality traits in a classroom setting. MEASUREMENT AND EVALUATION IN GUIDANCE, 1975, 8(2), 70–74.

Hynd, G. W., Hanson, D., Kaufman, N., & Schakel, J. A. (Eds). Personality assessment: The rating scale approach. SCHOOL PSYCHOLOGY REVIEW, 1983, 12.

[132]

Behavioral Academic Self-Esteem. Preschool–grade 8; 1982; BASE; ratings by teachers or parents; 6 scores: student initiative, social attention, success/failure, social attraction, self-confidence, total; norms consist of means and standard deviations; individual; 1 form (4 pages); professional manual (40 pages); separate answer sheets may be used; 1983 price data: $5 per 25 tests; $9.50 per 50 machine scorable answer sheets; $7.50 per manual; scoring service available from The Center for Self-Esteem Development, 699 Channing Ave., Palo Alto, CA 94301; (5) minutes; Stanley Coopersmith and Ragnar Gilberts; Consulting Psychologists Press, Inc.*

TEST REFERENCES

1. Johnson, B. W., Redfield, D. L., Miller, R. L., & Simpson, R. E. The Coopersmith Self-Esteem Inventory: A construct validity study. EDUCATIONAL AND PSYCHOLOGICAL MEASUREMENT, 1983, 43, 907–913.

Review of Behavioral Academic Self-Esteem by HERBERT W. MARSH, Senior Lecturer, Department of Education, University of Sydney, Sydney NSW 2006 Australia:

Behavioral Academic Self-Esteem (BASE) consists of 16 third-person declarative statements such as "This child is willing to undertake new tasks" and "This child readily expresses opinions" that are responded to by teachers who have observed a child's classroom behaviors for a minimum of 5–6 weeks on a daily basis. Teachers rate how frequently a child behaves in a particular way, using a five-category scale which varies from "Never" to "Always." Thus, BASE measures inferred self-esteem rather than the more traditional approach of measuring self esteem based on the respondents' self-reports. While there is disagreement, researchers often question the appropriateness of measuring self-esteem with observational ratings; although the authors suggest that "to measure self-esteem most thoroughly, the Self-Esteem Inventory developed by Coopersmith (1967) may be used with BASE" (Coopersmith & Gilberts, 1982, p. 111–112), no findings are presented to support this suggestion nor even to determine the extent of agreement between the two instruments.

The 16 BASE items are grouped into five subscales that are based on Coopersmith's (1967) Behavior Rating Form, and on his theory and research. However, Coopersmith did not specifically emphasize separate factors of academic self-esteem, and so the theoretical basis of the test is not clear. Furthermore, while the inferred self-esteem is based upon classroom observations, the content of the items and even the labels assigned to the subscales appear to reflect social or general self-esteem rather than academic self-esteem. The authors stress the interpretation of individual student profiles based on the five subscales and even on the 16 individual items. However, the five subscales are substantially correlated with each other (mean $r = .59$), all but one of the subscales are based on only two or three items, and reliability estimates for the subscales are not presented. Furthermore, the anecdotal discussion of what different profiles might mean is insufficient as a basis for the interpretation of the profiles. Consequently, even though the briefly summarized results of factor analyses may support the separation of the scales, the interpretation of individual student profiles is clearly not justified.

Psychometric support for the BASE comes primarily from ratings of over 4,000 children from grades K through 8, but the description of the analyses that are based upon it are insufficient. In the reliability section the authors present item-total correlations, but no internal consistency estimates of reliability for either the total score or for the subscales. A coefficient alpha of .89 was computed by the reviewer for the total score, based on material in the manual, but this estimate is likely to be inflated since the total sample includes both sexes and a wide range of ages, and the inferred self-concepts on this instrument vary with sex (girls are evaluated more favorably) and age (younger children are evaluated more favorably). Consequently, while the total score may be sufficiently reliable to justify the interpretation of individual student scores, the separate subscales probably are not.

Subscale and total scores are classified into high, moderate, and low self-esteem groups, and more detailed norm tables are also available for transforming the total score into percentile ranks. "Moderate" self-esteem is defined as scores that fall within plus or minus one standard deviation of the mean. The authors interpret this to mean that 68% of the scores will be classified as "moderate," but this figure will vary somewhat depending on how closely the response distribution for the score fits a normal curve. Separate classification tables are presented for males and females, and these may be justified even though the mean total scores differ by only .2 of a standard deviation. However, the authors also suggest that there are substantial grade differences, and yet separate classification tables are not presented for different age groups.

Users may also elect to have the BASE computer-scored, and to obtain interpretative materials that include statistical data for specified groups such as a classroom, grade levels, or school districts. Computer scoring also results in a more detailed comparison of student profiles for individual items and subscale scores, but since the interpretation of these profiles may not be justified, this additional advantage is dubious and further encourages the overinterpretation of the scores. No information is presented about the cost of computer scoring.

One indication of the validity of the BASE ratings was determined by correlating the ratings with scores from the Comprehensive Test of Basic Skills (CTBS). Total scores from the two tests consistently correlated about .50 in grades 2 through 6. The authors emphasize that the BASE scale Student Initiative score correlates more highly with the CTBS total score than other BASE scales, but offer no rationale as to why this should be expected. In fact, this scale consists of six items while other scales contain no more than three items, and so this finding might only reflect differing scale reliabilities. While it is encouraging that the BASE ratings by teachers are correlated with achievement scores, the purpose of the test is not to measure academic performance and so this finding must be interpreted cautiously. Superior academic achievement may be indicative of a high self-esteem and thus support the validity interpretation, but it may also mean that teachers just assume that brighter students have high self-esteem and that their perceptions are unduly influenced by levels of academic achievement (see Marsh & Parker, 1984).

As another possible indication of validity, the self-ratings by a group of 27 students (sex, age, and details of the study are not specified) were compared with self-esteem inferred from teacher ratings. Student ratings of Social Attraction were significantly correlated with teacher ratings for each of the BASE subscales (not just the Social Attraction subscale) and with the total score, but other correlations generally failed to reach statistical significance and not even the two total scores were significantly correlated. These findings suggest that the teacher ratings may not reflect student perceptions of their own self-esteem, except, perhaps, in the nonacademic area of Social Attractiveness. This study illustrates a possible danger in using inferred self-esteem, though the small sample size and the paucity of detail make interpretations hazardous and further research of this type is needed. In other research the authors indicate that when two different teachers rated the same children, correlations between the two total scores were high (.71), but not when ratings by teachers and parents were compared (.36). This led the authors to conclude that ratings by nonteachers should be used cautiously, but it also shows that the BASE total score does generalize across ratings by different teachers.

In summary, the most salient feature of the BASE is its reliance on teacher ratings to infer student self-esteem rather than the responses by the students themselves; researchers would disagree as to whether this constitutes a strength or a weakness. However, even as a measure of inferred academic self-esteem, I cannot recommend BASE. The research that has been done with BASE is not adequately described in the manual and important data for evaluating the test are omitted. It is also disappointing that none of this research has apparently been published in refereed journals. The limited validity research does suggest that the teacher ratings are related to academic achievement, but there is little indication that they are related to student self-esteem. Furthermore, the content of BASE does not appear to reflect academic characteristics and focuses instead on general or social self-esteem. The authors' emphasis on the interpretation of individual student profiles is not supported, and it seems unlikely that five separate areas of self-esteem can be measured with only 16 items. The authors have not been sufficiently candid about the limitations of BASE, and many of the suggested uses and applications are not supported by any research. Multitrait-multimethod research, as described by Shavelson, Hubner, and Stanton (1976), is needed to demonstrate that BASE ratings are substantially correlated with other indicators of self-esteem and distinct from other constructs. In fairness to the authors, they indicate that this version of the BASE is an "experimental edition," and so it is reasonable to hope that future editions will be improved.

REVIEWER'S REFERENCES

Coopersmith, S. THE ANTECEDENTS OF SELF-ESTEEM. San Francisco: W. H. Freeman, 1967.

Shavelson, R. J., Hubner, J. J., & Stanton, G. C. Self-concept: Validation of construct interpretations. REVIEW OF EDUCATIONAL RESEARCH, 1976, 46, 407–441.

Coopersmith, S., & Gilberts, R. G. BEHAVIORAL ACADEMIC SELF-ESTEEM: A RATING SCALE. Palo Alto, CA: Consulting Psychologists Press, 1982.

Marsh, H. W., & Parker, J. W. Determinants of student self-concept: Is it better to be a relatively large fish in a small pond even if you don't learn to swim as well? JOURNAL OF PERSONALITY AND SOCIAL PSYCHOLOGY, 1984, 47, 213–231.

Review of Behavioral Academic Self-Esteem by DALE H. SCHUNK, *Assistant Professor of Educational Psychology, College of Education, University of Houston, Houston, TX:*

Behavioral Academic Self-Esteem (BASE) assesses children's academic self-esteem on five factors: self-initiative, social attention, success/failure, social attraction, and self-confidence. These were derived from factor analyses of the Coopersmith Behavior Rating Form (BRF). BASE includes 16 items; most were drawn from the BRF as revised to describe academic behaviors. Each of the BASE factors is measured with 2–3 items except for student initiative (6 items). BASE is easy to complete, although the authors recommend that raters have at least 5–6 weeks of classroom experience with the children to be rated. Children are rated on 5-point scales ranging from 1 (Never) to 5 (Always).

The scoring manual contains descriptions of each factor to show how high and low self-esteem children would be expected to differ. In general, higher factor scores and total scores indicate higher academic self-esteem, but there are exceptions. As the authors point out, some children high in self-esteem may be rated lower on social attention items (e.g., speaking in turn, talking appropriately about school accomplishments, cooperating with others) to the extent that they are active and show enthusiasm for learning. Similarly, some high self-esteem children are assertive and do not passively accept criticism, which will yield lower scores on success/failure items. Thus, interpreting factor scores and the total score is not a straightforward procedure and the scoring manual, at times, adds to the confusion. In the sample base profile, for example, the high self-esteem child's total score is lower than the high self-esteem minimum score in the table of norms, and four of the five factor scores are lower than the minimum scores for boys (three of five for girls).

Although the authors state that the primary function of BASE is to differentiate between children of high and low self-esteem, given the preceding considerations BASE seems more appropriate for identifying the low self-esteem child. Of the five factors, student initiative seems the most important. This factor is assessed with the most items and was extracted first in factor analyses from independent samples. Children low in self-esteem would be expected to be rated low on initiative.

NORMS. Over 4,000 children in grades K through 8 were administered BASE, and the three self-esteem categories (high—moderate—low) were established using 3,055 subjects. Factor intercorrelations are based on 732 boys and 815 girls. The normative group is not nationally representative, because children's families resided in the San Francisco—Oakland Bay area, and socioeconomic status ranged from lower middle to upper middle class. It is not clear why other socioeconomic levels (i.e., lower, upper) were excluded. The sample includes students in regular classes as well as special education students and those enrolled in gifted programs. Ninety percent of the students were rated by regular classroom teachers, and the remaining 10% by aides and remedial/special education teachers. Norms also are included for preschoolers (4-year-olds), although the small sample size (150) renders these questionable.

RELIABILITY. Internal consistency coefficients are based on correlations of individual items with the total score and range from .37 to .76 with a mean z transformation correlation of .61. Intercorrelations of factor scores with the total score range from .71 to .94 with means of .83 for boys and .84 for girls. Interrater reliability was computed on 216 students and reported as .71. Test-retest reliability coefficients are not reported, which is a serious omission.

VALIDITY. The authors contend that construct validity of BASE derives from Coopersmith's self-esteem theory and that the five factors reflect those personality traits most germane to academic self-esteem. Factor analyses show that the student initiative factor is the most powerful, because it accounts for 34–60% of the total variance.

The authors' systematic approach to the generation of factors and items is laudable and ought to enhance validity; however, further empirical evidence is necessary to substantiate their claim. Correlations of BASE with other self-esteem instruments are not reported, which is particularly surprising in light of the contention that using BASE in conjunction with Coopersmith's Self-Esteem Inventory should provide "reliable, consistent, and thorough information about a child's self-esteem." For such a short instrument, BASE yields too many scores; except possibly for student initiative, factors seem incompletely represented. More information is needed on the validity of the five factors to warrant profile interpretations.

SUMMARY. The construct validity of BASE is presently inadequate. The measure has face validity given its theoretical derivation, and its ease of completing and scoring make it appealing. The student initiative factor seems best substantiated, although test-retest reliability coefficients, nationally representative norms, and additional measures of construct validity are needed. BASE seems most useful for identifying the low self-esteem student, and could be used in research to chart improvement over time or to compare experimental groups. It also seems appropriate for program evaluation, but its diagnostic use by classroom teachers should be corroborated by further evaluation.

[133]

Behavioral Deviancy Profile. Ages 3–21 with social and emotional problems; 1980; BDP; ratings by mental health and/or educational staff in 4 major areas: physical and motor development, cognitive development, speech and language, social and emotional development; no norms; individual; 1 form (9 pages); instruction manual (27 pages); 1982 price data: $12 per complete set including 15 profiles and record sheets; $9 per 15 profile forms and record sheets; $4 per manual; administration time not reported; Betty Ball and Rita Weinberg; Stoelting Co.*

Review of Behavioral Deviancy Profile by ROY P. MARTIN, Professor of Educational Psychology, University of Georgia, Athens, GA:

The stated purpose of the Behavioral Deviancy Profile is to "assess the degree of deviancy or disturbance of children with social and emotional problems." Such a purpose might suggest an instrument designed to assess types of social or emotional deviance, and the extent of deviance compared to some norm group. Such an interpretation of the purpose of this instrument would be incorrect. The Behavioral Deviancy Profile is a rating scale in which a mental health professional rates 18 different categories of behavior, including physical growth, sensory perception, motor activity, intelligence, language, relationship with mother, and "ego-self" behavior. Ratings are made of specific behaviors, and then these ratings are totaled and averaged for each category. The ratings are not compared to any normative group; instead their interpretation is based on the internal norms of the rater, who indicates if the behavior is severe, moderate, mild or average. Thus, this instrument seems designed to allow for the recording of impressions of professional mental health workers regarding the overall functioning of children with social-emotional problems. As such, the Behavioral Deviancy Profile can hardly be considered a measurement device. It provides a format for recording subjective impressions.

The weakness of this approach is that it puts enormous faith in the cognitive capacities of the raters. The raters must be able to rate, for example, whether a child's fine motor development is a mild, moderate, or severe problem, or no problem; and must be able to do this for children ranging in age from preschool through adolescence. This assumes the person doing the rating has had a large amount of experience with persons at all these ages, knows how much variation is present within any age for normal persons for the behavior being rated, can remember all this information in order to use it for "normative" purposes, has had enough experience with the target child in order to mentally compute his/her status on the variable in question, and can then compare the behavior of the target child to the accumulated mental "norms." This is, of course, what is called for when any caretaker makes a subjective judgment about a child. However, the problems with clinical judgment are well known. Norm-referenced, psychometrically sound assessment devices are an antidote to some of the problems of clinical judgment. This points out a second problem with the Behavioral Deviancy Profile; it is presented in the manual as a means of objectifying the assessment process. "The Behavioral Deviancy Profile documents changes objectively by using the profile prior to and then after intervention." In fact, it is only a recording device for clinical impressions. It objectifies the process only in a very limited sense. Thus, the manual is misleading.

In addition, the manual for the Behavioral Deviancy Profile is inadequate. There is no statistical evidence that the ratings of subcategory behaviors are correlated (internal consistency reliability), that different raters provide similar ratings (interrater reliability), or that ratings over short periods of time are comparable (test-retest reliability). Further, no validity data of any kind are provided. All of these types of data are relevant even to a device designed to record clinical impressions. Finally, the rating options for each item of the device are confusing. Each item is rated on a 7-point scale ranging from −3 through 0 to +3. The label given −3 is "Severe—absent, very retarded, or regressed." The label given +3 is "Severe—extreme or excessive manifestation, very accelerated." It appears the ratings, in part, are to be made on the basis of amount of behavior exhibited, or at least amount relative to age appropriateness. However, having both ends of the scale labeled "Severe" is confusing. Further, the manual indicates that a "0" rating is considered normal, and that ratings are averaged without regard to sign. Later in the manual the authors state that plus ratings should not be rated as deviant unless they are negatively affecting the child's functioning. It appears that the developers of this device simply did not take the time to design a rating strategy that could be applied consistently across the various areas of functioning the device is designed to assess.

Given all criticisms mentioned above, the conclusion that the Behavioral Deviancy Profile is of limited value is inescapable.

Review of Behavioral Deviancy Profile by DAVID H. REILLY, Professor and Dean, School of Education, University of North Carolina at Greensboro, Greensboro, NC:

The Behavioral Deviancy Profile is "an instrument designed to assess the degree of deviance or disturbance of children with social and emotional problems." The purpose of this instrument is to provide a global and objective assessment of children with such problems. The intent is to provide a method for comparing deviancies of physical, psychological, and social factors in a child before and after intervention.

Four major areas of study are included in the Profile. These are: (1) physical and motor development, (2) cognitive development, (3) speech and language, and (4) social and emotional development. Included in these four major areas are 18 subareas to be rated. Each of these 18 areas has 2 to 14 factors to be rated. No information is provided as to how the 18 areas were developed and what relationship they have to the four major areas.

A child's behavior is rated on each of these factors along a continuum ranging from plus three to minus three with zero indicating no deviancy. Two aspects of behavior for each area are to be considered: the severity or amount of behavior, and the length of time the behavior has existed. A total of 236 different behaviors are to be rated.

It is not clear how these 18 major areas and 236 factors are grouped within the four major areas of the Profile. Neither is it apparent how the length of time the behavior has existed is to be utilized in the rating scale or the extent to which this aspect of behavior relates to deviancy away from the mean.

A record booklet is provided for use with each child. Each factor is indicated on the booklet and each rater is to indicate his/her rating for each of the 236 items, rating the child's deviancy from the norm either in terms of a plus rating or a minus rating. It is stated by the authors that plus ratings are not to be rated as deviant unless they negatively affect the child's functioning. They assume a norm of behavior from which deviancy produces behavioral maladjustment. However, no provision is made on the summary graph for indicating positive or negative direction. Only a scale from 0–3 is provided, and it is difficult to tell whether the behavior rated was in a positive or negative direction.

For each area to be rated the rater provides a rating of 0–3 for all behaviors which are indicated. The ratings for such subareas are totaled and divided by the number of factors rated to provide an average deviancy rating for each of the 18 areas. A simple line graph is provided for indicating the degree of deviancy from the assumed norm for each of the 18 areas.

It is also possible to provide ratings in terms of tenths, although the lack of precise directions makes it difficult to judge the difference, for example, between a rating of 2.2 and 2.4. Lack of specific directions and criteria are a major problem in utilizing this instrument.

A glossary is provided for definition of terminology, but as explained in the manual, the glossary definitions are not to be used as a final arbiter of decisions. Other definitions of the terms are permissible. The manual warns, however, that definitional consistency is important to provide greater reliability for the judgements made. Yet a major flaw of the instrument is the lack of precise definition of glossary terms.

Another major defect of the Profile is that some of the factors to be rated are either/or situations and others exist on a continuum. It is difficult to reconcile these two types of items on a 7-point scale.

Still a further defect in the glossary is the lack of specific criteria and explanation for many of the definitions. For example, under the area of Cognition appears the subarea of "Organization of thought," which is defined as "concept formation, categorizing, and generalizing." This type of definition provides wide latitude in rating a child, and no specific criteria are provided for establishing a degree of deviancy from a presumed norm. Such lack of clearly specified criteria will probably have unfortunate consequences for reliability and validity.

No information related to reliability and validity were provided with the exception of a statement in the manual which indicated that as staff become more experienced and proficient the reliability becomes very high. It was indicated that an analysis of the ratings of one group (no descriptive data provided) yielded reliability coefficients of .90 and above for all items except number two. Since all areas in the manual are defined either by roman numeral or by letter, it is unclear to what the number 2 refers. Further, the test is supposed to be usable for children having social and emotional problems who range in age from preschool through adolescence. The lack of data regarding the impact of age differences on effective use of the instrument make it difficult to judge its usefulness with such a wide age range. Inspection of the items would suggest that it would be most useful with preteens.

Some of the 18 areas are more easily observable than others (e.g., playing with peers). Others, particularly areas called "Ego-Self" and "Superego-Conscience," are more difficult to observe in terms of behavior. For example, under Ego-Self subarea C is Fantasy, defined as an imagined sequence of events or mental images. Three subareas subsumed under this area include "bizarre," the "ability to distinguish fantasy from reality," and "appropriateness." Since fantasy is an internal process it is difficult to see how this would be rated from observations of behavior. Numerous other similar difficulties exist with other areas.

In summary, the Behavior Deviancy Profile is designed to be used by mental health personnel, educators, and other professionals working with children with social and emotional problems. A number of severe problems exist with the Profile, most notably in terms of definition of items, directions for utilizing the rating scale, and the lack of reliability and validity data. Interested parties would be well advised to examine closely the difficulties of using the Profile and what useful data might be forthcoming from the time expended. A number of other instruments are probably more appropriate and less difficult to utilize in assessing these aspects of children's behavior.

[134]

Behaviordyne Retirement Service. Pre-retirees and people in retirement; 1982; BRS; 5 areas: leisure, health, housing, finances, legal issues; no data on reliability; no norms; 1 form (8 pages); report (161 pages); 1983 price data: $25 per test including report and scoring service; (30) minutes; John H. Lewis; Behaviordyne, Inc.*

[135]

Behaviour Assessment Battery, Second Edition. Profoundly handicapped children; 1982; book containing a battery of instruments to provide assessment in developing teaching and training programs; 13 separate tests: Reinforcement and Experience, Inspection, Tracking, Visuo-Motor, Auditory, Postural Control, Exploratory Play, Constructive Play, Search Strategies, Perceptual Problem Solving, Social, Communication, Self-Help Skills; interrater reliability only for Postural Control and Self-Help Skills; no norms; individual, 1 form (96 pages, plus rationale, guidelines for use and interpretation, and score sheets and lattices all in one book); no separate manual; testing materials must be assembled locally; 1984 price data: £8.45 per book; (120–150) minutes in several sessions; Chris Kiernan and Malcom C. Jones; NFER-Nelson Publishing Co. [England].*

[136]

Behaviour Problems: A System of Management. Grades K–12; 1984; BPSM; behaviour checklist for use with disruptive children; forms for recording behaviour in 8 areas: classroom conformity, task orientation, emotional control, acceptance of authority, self-worth, peer relationships, self responsibility/problem solving, other; no data on reliability; no norms; individual; behaviour checklist/monthly progress chart (2 pages); daily record (1 page); manual (16 pages); 1985 price data: £13.75 per complete set (including manual, 50 daily records, and 10 behaviour checklist/monthly progress charts); £4.50 per 50 daily records; £3.50 per 10 behaviour checklist/monthly progress charts; £5.95 per manual; Peter P. Galvin and Richard M. Singleton; NFER-Nelson Publishing Co. [England].*

[137]

Bem Sex-Role Inventory. High school and college and adults; 1978–81; test is titled Bem Inventory; self-administered; 3 scores: femininity, masculinity, femininity-minus-masculinity difference; short and long form ('78, 2 pages), short form consists of first 30 items only; manual ('81, 37 pages); 1983 price data: $3 per 25 inventories; $.75 per scoring key; $7.50 per manual; $5 per instructions for setting up a Computer Scoring Program; $8 per specimen set; (10–15) minutes; Sandra Lipsitz Bem; Consulting Psychologists Press, Inc.*

TEST REFERENCES

1. Falbo, T. Relationships between sex, sex role, and social influence. PSYCHOLOGY OF WOMEN QUARTERLY, 1977, 2, 62–72.

2. LaTorre, R. A. Gender role and psychological adjustment. ARCHIVES OF SEXUAL BEHAVIOR, 1978, 7, 89–96.

3. Calway-Fagen, N., Wallston, B. S., & Gabel, H. The relationship between attitudinal and behavioral measures of sex preference. PSYCHOLOGY OF WOMEN QUARTERLY, 1979, 4, 274–280.

4. Dailey, D. M. Adjustment of heterosexual and homosexual couples in pairing relationships: An exploratory study. THE JOURNAL OF SEX RESEARCH, 1979, 15, 143–157.

5. Gilbert, L. A. An approach to training sex-fair mental health workers. PROFESSIONAL PSYCHOLOGY, 1979, 10, 365–372.

6. Hooberman, R. E. Psychological androgyny, feminine gender identity and self-esteem in homosexual and heterosexual males. THE JOURNAL OF SEX RESEARCH, 1979, 15, 306–315.

7. Powell, G. N., & Butterfield, D. A. The "good manager": Masculine or androgynous? ACADEMY OF MANAGEMENT JOURNAL, 1979, 22, 395–403.

8. Sadd, S., Miller, F. D., & Zeitz, B. Sex roles and achievement conflicts. PERSONALITY AND SOCIAL PSYCHOLOGY BULLETIN, 1979, 5, 352–355.

9. Welch, R. L. Androgyny and derived identity in married women with varying degrees of non-traditional role involvement. PSYCHOLOGY OF WOMEN QUARTERLY, 1979, 3, 308–315.

10. Widom, C. S. Female offenders: Three assumptions about self-esteem, sex-role identity, and feminism. CRIMINAL JUSTICE AND BEHAVIOR, 1979, 6, 365–382.

11. Antill, J. K., & Russell, G. A preliminary comparison between two forms of the Bem Sex-Role Inventory. AUSTRALIAN PSYCHOLOGIST, 1980, 15, 427–435.

12. Bray, J. H., & Howard, G. S. Interaction of teacher and student sex and sex role orientations and student evaluations of college instructions. CONTEMPORARY EDUCATIONAL PSYCHOLOGY, 1980, 5, 241–248.

13. Cunningham, J. D., & Antill, J. K. A comparison among five masculinity-femininity-androgyny instruments and two methods of scoring androgyny. AUSTRALIAN PSYCHOLOGIST, 1980, 15, 437–448.

14. Fleck, J. R., Fuller, C. C., Malin, S. Z., Miller, D. H., & Acheson, K. R. Father psychological absence and heterosexual behavior, personal adjustment and sex-typing in adolescent girls. ADOLESCENCE, 1980, 15, 847–860.

15. Fleming, M. Z., Jenkins, S. R., & Bugarin, C. Questioning current definitions of gender identity: Implications of the Bem Sex-Role Inventory for transsexuals. ARCHIVES OF SEXUAL BEHAVIOR, 1980, 9, 13–26.

16. Gabrenya, W. K., Jr., & Arkin, R. M. Self-monitoring scale: Factor structure and correlates. PERSONALITY AND SOCIAL PSYCHOLOGY BULLETIN, 1980, 6, 13–22.

17. Gerson, M. The lure of motherhood. PSYCHOLOGY OF WOMEN QUARTERLY, 1980, 5, 207–218.

18. Good, P. R., & Smith, B. D. Menstrual distress and sex-role attributes. PSYCHOLOGY OF WOMEN QUARTERLY, 1980, 4, 482–491.

19. Ho, R., & Zemaitis, R. Behavioural correlates of an Australian version of the Bem Sex-Role Inventory. AUSTRALIAN PSYCHOLOGIST, 1980, 15, 459–466.

20. Koffman, S., & Lips, H. M. Sex differences in self-esteem and performance expectancies in married couples. SOCIAL BEHAVIOR AND PERSONALITY, 1980, 8, 57–63.

21. Moore, S. M., & Rosenthal, D. A. Sex-roles: Gender, generation, and self-esteem. AUSTRALIAN PSYCHOLOGIST, 1980, 15, 467–477.

22. Rim, Y. Sex-typing and means of influence in marriage. SOCIAL BEHAVIOR AND PERSONALITY, 1980, 8, 117–119.

23. Rowland, R. The Bem Sex-Role Inventory and its measurement of androgyny. AUSTRALIAN PSYCHOLOGIST, 1980, 15, 449–457.

24. Spence, J. T., & Helmreich, R. L. Masculine instrumentality and feminine expressiveness: Their relationships with sex role attitudes and behaviors. PSYCHOLOGY OF WOMEN QUARTERLY, 1980, 5, 147–163.

25. Uguccioni, S. M., & Ballantyne, R. H. Comparison of attitudes and sex roles for female athletic participants and nonparticipants. INTERNATIONAL JOURNAL OF SPORT PSYCHOLOGY, 1980, 11, 42–48.

26. Vedovato, S., & Vaughter, R. M. Psychology of women courses changing sexist and sex-typed attitudes. PSYCHOLOGY OF WOMEN QUARTERLY, 1980, 4, 587–590.

27. Walfish, S., & Myerson, M. Sex role identity and attitudes toward sexuality. ARCHIVES OF SEXUAL BEHAVIOR, 1980, 9, 199–203.

28. Banikiotes, P. G., Neimeyer, G. J., & Lepkowsky, C. Gender and sex-role orientation effects on friendship choice. PERSONALITY AND SOCIAL PSYCHOLOGY BULLETIN, 1981, 7, 605–610.

29. Brehony, K. A., & Geller, E. S. Relationships between psychological androgyny, social conformity, and perceived locus of control. PSYCHOLOGY OF WOMEN QUARTERLY, 1981, 6, 204–217.

30. Cardell, M., Finn, S., & Marecek, J. Sex-role identity, sex-role behavior, and satisfaction in heterosexual, lesbian, and gay male couples. PSYCHOLOGY OF WOMEN QUARTERLY, 1981, 5, 488–494.

31. Carlsson, M. Note on the factor structure of the Bem Sex-Role Inventory. SCANDINAVIAN JOURNAL OF PSYCHOLOGY, 1981, 22, 123–127.

32. Dunn, P. K., & Ondercin, P. Personality variables related to compulsive eating in college women. JOURNAL OF CLINICAL PSYCHOLOGY, 1981, 37, 43–49.

33. Feinberg, R. A., & Workman, J. E. Sex-role orientation and cognitive complexity. PSYCHOLOGICAL REPORTS, 1981, 48, 246.

34. Feldman, S. S., Biringen, Z. C., & Nash, S. C. Fluctuations of sex-related self-attributions as a function of stage of family life cycle. DEVELOPMENTAL PSYCHOLOGY, 1981, 17, 24–35.

35. Fischer, J. L., & Narus, L. R., Jr. Sex roles and intimacy in same sex and other sex relationships. PSYCHOLOGY OF WOMEN QUARTERLY, 1981, 5, 444–455.

36. Gaa, J. P., & Liberman, D. Categorization agreement of the Personality Attributes Questionnaire and the Bem Sex Role Inventory. JOURNAL OF CLINICAL PSYCHOLOGY, 1981, 37, 593–601.

37. Gillen, B. Physical attractiveness: A determinant of two types of goodness. PERSONALITY AND SOCIAL PSYCHOLOGY BULLETIN, 1981, 7, 277–281.

38. Gilroy, F. D., Talierco, T. M., & Steinbacher, R. Impact of maternal employment on daughters' sex-role orientation and fear of success. PSYCHOLOGICAL REPORTS, 1981, 49, 963–968.

39. Gonzalez, C. T., & Williams, K. E. Relationship between locus of control and sex-role stereotyping. PSYCHOLOGICAL REPORTS, 1981, 48, 70.

40. Hinrichsen, J. J., Follansbee, D. J., & Ganellen, R. Sex-role—Related differences in self-concept and mental health. JOURNAL OF PERSONALITY ASSESSMENT, 1981, 45, 584–592.

41. Lueger, R. J., & Evans, R. G. Emotional expressivity and sex-role perceptions of repressors and sensitizers. JOURNAL OF PERSONALITY ASSESSMENT, 1981, 45, 288–294.

42. Lutes, C. J. Early marriage and identity foreclosure. ADOLESCENCE, 1981, 16, 809–815.

43. Marwit, S. J. Assessment of sex-role stereotyping among male and female psychologist practitioners. JOURNAL OF PERSONALITY ASSESSMENT, 1981, 45, 593–599.

44. Merluzzi, T. V., & Merluzzi, B. Androgyny, stereotypy and the perception of female therapists. JOURNAL OF CLINICAL PSYCHOLOGY, 1981, 37, 280–284.

45. Moore, D., & Nuttall, J. R. Perceptions of the male sex role. PERSONALITY AND SOCIAL PSYCHOLOGY BULLETIN, 1981, 7, 320–325.

46. Owie, I. Influence of sex-role standards in sport competition anxiety. INTERNATIONAL JOURNAL OF SPORT PSYCHOLOGY, 1981, 12, 289–292.

47. Powell, G. N., Butterfield, D. A., & Mainiero, L. A. Sex-role identity and sex as predictors of leadership style. PSYCHOLOGICAL REPORTS, 1981, 49, 829–830.

48. Ratliff, E. S., & Conley, J. The structure of masculinity-feminity: Multidimensionality and gender differences. SOCIAL BEHAVIOR AND PERSONALITY, 1981, 9, 41–47.

49. Shaw, J. S., & Rodriguez, W. Birth order and sex-type. PSYCHOLOGICAL REPORTS, 1981, 48, 387–390.

50. Spillman, B., Spillman, R., & Reinking, K. Leadership emergence: Dynamic analysis of the effects of sex and androgyny. SMALL GROUP BEHAVIOR, 1981, 12, 139–157.

51. Steinman, D. L., Wincze, J. P., Sakheim, B. A., Barlow, D. H., & Mavissakalian, M. A comparison of male and female patterns of sexual arousal. ARCHIVES OF SEXUAL BEHAVIOR, 1981, 10, 529–547.

52. Strahan, R. F. Remarks on scoring androgyny as a single continuous variable. PSYCHOLOGICAL REPORTS, 1981, 49, 887–890.

53. Taylor, D. Social desirability and the Bem Sex-Role Inventory. PSYCHOLOGICAL REPORTS, 1981, 48, 503–506.

54. Volentine, S. Z. The assessment of masculinity and femininity: Scale 5 of the MMPI compared with the BSRI and the PAQ. JOURNAL OF CLINICAL PSYCHOLOGY, 1981, 37, 367–374.

55. von Baeyer, C. L., Sherk, D. L., & Zanna, M. P. Impression management in the job interview: When the female applicant meets the male (chauvinist) interviewer. PERSONALITY AND SOCIAL PSYCHOLOGY BULLETIN, 1981, 7, 45–51.

56. Adams, C. H., & Sherer, M. Sex-role orientation and psychological adjustment: Comparison of MMPI profiles among college women and housewives. JOURNAL OF PERSONALITY ASSESSMENT, 1982, 46, 607–613.

57. Antill, J. K., & Cunningham, J. D. Comparative factor analyses of the Personal Attributes Questionnaire and the Bem Sex-Role Inventory. SOCIAL BEHAVIOR AND PERSONALITY, 1982, 10, 163–172.

58. Antill, J. K., & Russell, G. The factor structure of the Bem Sex Role Inventory: Method and sample comparisons. AUSTRALIAN JOURNAL OF PSYCHOLOGY, 1982, 34, 183–193.

59. Basow, S. A., & Crawley, D. M. Helping behavior: Effects of sex and sex-typing. SOCIAL BEHAVIOR AND PERSONALITY, 1982, 10, 69–72.

60. Batlis, N., & Small, A. Sex roles and Type A behavior. JOURNAL OF CLINICAL PSYCHOLOGY, 1982, 38, 315–316.

61. Bernard, L. C. Sex-role factor identification and sexual preference of men. JOURNAL OF PERSONALITY ASSESSMENT, 1982, 46, 292–299.

62. Clarey, J. H., & Sanford, A. Female career preference and androgyny. THE VOCATIONAL GUIDANCE QUARTERLY, 1982, 30, 258–264.

63. Etaugh, C., & Weber, S. Perceptions of sex roles of young and middle-aged women and men. PERCEPTUAL AND MOTOR SKILLS, 1982, 55, 559–562.

64. Evans, R. G. Defense mechanisms in females as a function of sex-role orientation. JOURNAL OF CLINICAL PSYCHOLOGY, 1982, 38, 816–817.

65. Evans, R. G., & Dinning, W. D. MMPI correlates of the Bem Sex Role Inventory and Extended Personal Attributes Questionnaire in a male psychiatric sample. JOURNAL OF CLINICAL PSYCHOLOGY, 1982, 38, 811–815.

66. Gackenbach, J. Collegiate swimmers: Sex differences in self-reports and indices of physiological stress. PERCEPTUAL AND MOTOR SKILLS, 1982, 55, 555–558.

67. Glass, C. R., Merluzzi, T. V., Biever, J. L., & Larsen, K. H. Cognitive assessment of social anxiety: Development and validation of a self-statement questionnaire. COGNITIVE THERAPY AND RESEARCH, 1982, 6, 37–55.

68. Goldberg, S., Blumberg, S. L., & Kriger, A. Menarche and interest in infants: Biological and social influences. CHILD DEVELOPMENT, 1982, 53, 1544–1550.

69. Gruber, K. J., & Powers, W. A. Factor and discriminant analysis of the Bem Sex-Role Inventory. JOURNAL OF PERSONALITY ASSESSMENT, 1982, 46, 284–291.

70. Hamby, C. L. Dental hygiene students: Stereotypically feminine. PSYCHOLOGICAL REPORTS, 1982, 50, 1237–1238.

71. Harackiewicz, J. M., & DePaulo, B. M. Accuracy of person perception: A component analysis according to Cronbach. PERSONALITY AND SOCIAL PSYCHOLOGY BULLETIN, 1982, 8, 247–256.

72. Henschen, K. P., Edwards, S. W., & Mathinos, L. Achievement motivation and sex-role orientation of high school female track and field athletes versus nonathletes. PERCEPTUAL AND MOTOR SKILLS, 1982, 55, 183–187.

73. Jackson, A. D. Militancy and black women's competitive behavior in competitive versus noncompetitive conditions. PSYCHOLOGY OF WOMEN QUARTERLY, 1982, 6, 342–353.

74. Kane, M. J. The influence of level of sport participation and sex-role orientation on female professionalization of attitudes toward play. JOURNAL OF SPORT PSYCHOLOGY, 1982, 4, 290–294.

75. Kimlicka, T. M., Wakefield, J. A., Jr., & Goad, N. A. Sex-roles of ideal opposite sexed persons for college males and females. JOURNAL OF PERSONALITY ASSESSMENT, 1982, 46, 519–521.

76. Korabik, K. Sex-role orientation and impressions: A comparison of differing genders and sex roles. PERSONALITY AND SOCIAL PSYCHOLOGY BULLETIN, 1982, 8, 25–30.

77. Korabik, K. The effects of sex-typed trait descriptions on judgments of likeableness. SOCIAL BEHAVIOR AND PERSONALITY, 1982, 10, 157–161.

78. Kranau, E. J., Green, V., & Valencia-Weber, G. Acculturation and the Hispanic woman: Attitudes toward women, sex-role attribution, sex-role behavior, and demographics. HISPANIC JOURNAL OF BEHAVIORAL SCIENCES, 1982, 4, 21–40.

79. Lamke, L. K. The impact of sex-role orientation on self-esteem in early adolescence. CHILD DEVELOPMENT, 1982, 53, 1530–1535.

80. Lamke, L. K., & Bell, N. J. Sex-role orientation and relationship development in same-sex dyads. JOURNAL OF RESEARCH IN PERSONALITY, 1982, 16, 343–354.

81. Lee, A. G. Psychological androgyny and social desirability. JOURNAL OF PERSONALITY ASSESSMENT, 1982, 46, 147–152.

82. Lohr, J. M., & Nix, J. Relationship of assertiveness and the short form of the Bem Sex-Role Inventory: A replication. PSYCHOLOGICAL REPORTS, 1982, 50, 114.

83. Long, V. O. Ending of the perpetuation of sex-role stereotypes in our schools: A possible consequence of psychological androgyny. PSYCHOLOGY IN THE SCHOOLS, 1982, 19, 250–254.

84. Myers, A. M., & Gonda, G. Empirical validation of the Bem Sex-Role Inventory. JOURNAL OF PERSONALITY AND SOCIAL PSYCHOLOGY, 1982, 43, 304–318.

85. Nordholm, L. A., & Westbrook, M. T. Job attributes preferred by female health professionals, before and after entering the work force. PERSONNEL PSYCHOLOGY, 1982, 35, 853–863.

86. Price-Bonham, S., & Skeen, P. Black and white fathers' attitudes toward children's sex roles. PSYCHOLOGICAL REPORTS, 1982, 50, 1187–1190.

87. Ridley, C. A., Lamke, L. K., Avery, A. W., & Harrell, J. E. The effects of interpersonal skills training on sex-role identity of premarital dating partners. JOURNAL OF RESEARCH IN PERSONALITY, 1982, 16, 335–342.

88. Robinson, B. E., & Skeen, P. Sex-role orientation of gay fathers versus gay nonfathers. PERCEPTUAL AND MOTOR SKILLS, 1982, 55, 1055–1059.

89. Robinson, B. E., Skeen, P., & Flake-Hobson, C. Sex role endorsement among homosexual men across the life span. ARCHIVES OF SEXUAL BEHAVIOR, 1982, 11, 355–359.

90. Roe, M. D., & Prange, M. E. On quantifying the magnitude of sex-role endorsement. JOURNAL OF PERSONALITY ASSESSMENT, 1982, 46, 300–303.

91. Shapiro, D. H., Jr., Shapiro, J., Walsh, R. N., & Brown, D. Effects of intensive meditation on sex-role identification: Implications for a control model of psychological health. PSYCHOLOGICAL REPORTS, 1982, 51, 44–46.

92. Sinnot, J. D. Correlates of sex roles of older adults. JOURNAL OF GERONTOLOGY, 1982, 37, 587–594.

93. Taylor, S. E., & Falcone, H. Cognitive bases of stereotyping: The relationship between categorization and prejudice. PERSONALITY AND SOCIAL PSYCHOLOGY BULLETIN, 1982, 8, 426–432.

94. Waterman, A. S., & Whitbourne, S. K. Androgyny and psychosocial development among college students and adults. JOURNAL OF PERSONALITY, 1982, 50, 121–133.

95. Welch, R. L., & Huston, A. C. Effects of induced success/failure and attributions on the problem-solving behavior of psychologically androgynous and feminine women. JOURNAL OF PERSONALITY, 1982, 50, 81–97.

96. Yanico, B. J. Androgyny and occupational sex-stereotyping of college students. PSYCHOLOGICAL REPORTS, 1982, 50, 875–878.

97. Zeff, S. B. A cross-cultural study of Mexican American, Black American, and White American women at a large urban university. HISPANIC JOURNAL OF BEHAVIORAL SCIENCES, 1982, 4, 245–261.

98. Bledsoe, J. C. Factorial validity of the Bem Sex-Role Inventory. PERCEPTUAL AND MOTOR SKILLS, 1983, 56, 55–58.

99. Briere, J., Ward, R., & Hartsough, W. R. Sex-typing and cross-sex-typing in "androgynous" subjects. JOURNAL OF PERSONALITY ASSESSMENT, 1983, 47, 300–302.

100. Downing, N. E., & Nevill, D. D. Conceptions of psychological health: The role of gender and sex-role identity. THE BRITISH JOURNAL OF SOCIAL PSYCHOLOGY, 1983, 22, 171–173.

101. Farmer, H. S., & Fyans, L. J., Jr. Married women's achievement and career motivation: The influence of some environmental and psychological variables. PSYCHOLOGY OF WOMEN QUARTERLY, 1983, 7, 358–372.

102. Feather, N. T., & Said, J. A. Preference for occupations in relation to masculinity, femininity, and gender. THE BRITISH JOURNAL OF SOCIAL PSYCHOLOGY, 1983, 22, 113–127.

103. Goodman, S. H., & Kantor, D. Influence of sex-role identity on two indices of social anxiety. JOURNAL OF RESEARCH IN PERSONALITY, 1983, 17, 443–450.

104. Ireland-Galman, M. M., & Michael, W. B. The relationship of a measure of the fear of success construct to scales representing the locus of control and sex-role orientation constructs for a community college sample. EDUCATIONAL AND PSYCHOLOGICAL MEASUREMENT, 1983, 43, 1217–1225.

105. Jackson, L. A. The perception of androgyny and physical attractiveness: Two is better than one. PERSONALITY AND SOCIAL PSYCHOLOGY BULLETIN, 1983, 9, 405–413.

106. Kimlicka, T., Cross, H., & Tarnai, J. A comparison of androgynous, feminine, masculine, and undifferentiated women on self-esteem, body satisfaction, and sexual satisfaction. PSYCHOLOGY OF WOMEN QUARTERLY, 1983, 7, 291–294.

107. Kleinke, C. L., & Hinrichs, C. A. College adjustment problems and attitudes toward drinking reported by feminine, androgynous, and masculine college women. PSYCHOLOGY OF WOMEN QUARTERLY, 1983, 7, 373–382.

108. Lippa, R., Valdez, E., & Jolly, A. The effects of self-monitoring on the expressive display of masculinity-femininity. JOURNAL OF RESEARCH IN PERSONALITY, 1983, 17, 324–338.

109. Murstein, B. I., & Williams, P. D. Sex roles and marriage adjustment. SMALL GROUP BEHAVIOR, 1983, 14, 77–94.

110. Payne, F. D., & Futterman, J. R. "Masculinity," "Femininity," and adjustment in college men. JOURNAL OF RESEARCH IN PERSONALITY, 1983, 17, 110–124.

111. Rea, J. S., & Strange, C. C. The experience of cross-gender majoring among male and female undergraduates. JOURNAL OF COLLEGE STUDENT PERSONNEL, 1983, 24, 356–363.

112. Rooney, G. S. Distinguishing characteristics of the life roles of worker, student, and homemaker for young adults. JOURNAL OF VOCATIONAL BEHAVIOR, 1983, 22, 324–342.

113. Ross, M. W. Societal relationships and gender role in homosexuals: A cross-cultural comparison. THE JOURNAL OF SEX RESEARCH, 1983, 19, 273–288.

114. Sethi, A. S., & Bala, N. Relationship between sex-role orientation and self-esteem in Indian college females. PSYCHOLOGIA, 1983, 26, 124–127.

115. Shapiro, J., McGrath, E., & Anderson, R. C. Patients, medical students, and physicians' perceptions of male and female physicians. PERCEPTUAL AND MOTOR SKILLS, 1983, 56, 179–190.

116. Stokes, K., Kilmann, P. R., & Wanlass, R. L. Sexual orientation and sex role conformity. ARCHIVES OF SEXUAL BEHAVIOR, 1983, 12, 427–433.

117. Williams, S. W., & McCullers, J. C. Personal factors related to typicalness of career and success in active professional women. PSYCHOLOGY OF WOMEN QUARTERLY, 1983, 7, 343–357.

118. Bassoff, E. S. Relationships of sex-role characteristics and psychological adjustment in new mothers. JOURNAL OF MARRIAGE AND THE FAMILY, 1984, 46, 449–454.

119. Belcher, M. J., Crocker, L. M., & Algina, J. Can the same instrument be used to measure sex-role perceptions of males and females? MEASUREMENT AND EVALUATION IN GUIDANCE, 1984, 17, 15–23.

120. Downey, A. M. The relationship of sex-role orientation to death anxiety in middle-aged males. OMEGA, 1984, 14, 355–367.

121. Kiecolt-Glaser, J., & Dixon, K. Postadolescent onset male anorexia. JOURNAL OF PSYCHOLOGICAL NURSING, 1984, 22, 11–20.

Review of Bem Sex-Role Inventory by RICHARD LIPPA, Associate Professor of Psychology, California State University, Fullerton, Fullerton, CA:

The Bem Sex-Role Inventory (BSRI) separately assesses psychological femininity and masculinity, and thereby admits the possibility of identifying "androgynous" individuals—those whose personalities embrace both "feminine" and "masculine" traits. The BSRI, originally published in 1974, differs from earlier instruments in that it does not assume that femininity and masculinity form a single, bipolar dimension, but rather that they are conceptually and empirically distinct. Since 1974 other comparable instruments have appeared; most notable among these are the PAQ (Spence, Helmreich, & Stapp, 1974), the ANDRO Scale (Berzins et al., 1978), and an adjective checklist measure (Heilbrun, 1976). The BSRI remains, however, perhaps the most utilized of all "androgyny" scales. A computerized reference search carried out in January, 1984, yielded 432 research studies employing the BSRI.

The original form of the BSRI (Bem, 1974) asks respondents to rate themselves on 20 stereotypically feminine traits (e.g., "affectionate," "compassionate," "warm"), on 20 stereotypically masculine traits (e.g., "assertive," "has leadership abilities," "dominant"), and 20 filler items. In developing the BSRI, Bem selected these feminine and masculine traits from a much larger pool; feminine traits were those which were rated by 100 college students as being significantly more desirable for women than men in American society, whereas masculine traits were rated as more desirable for men than women. "Filler" items were originally chosen to assess subjects' social desirability of response, but this interpretation was later discarded due to the psychometric inadequacies of this scale.

Bem originally conceived of androgyny as the difference between assessed femininity and masculinity, and thus devised a scoring system which was based on computing a *t*-ratio for the difference between total femininity and masculinity. In the 1981 test manual, Bem tells how to compute a difference score based on standardized *T*-scores for femininity and masculinity, but at the same time recommends that researchers generally use median-split classifications of subjects (based on either the research population or the normative sample used in developing the BSRI) rather than classifications based on difference scores. A major advantage of the BSRI and similar measures over previous instruments is the possibility of separately analyzing the effects and correlates of femininity and masculinity. Thus researchers should generally not collapse the separate information provided by assessed femininity and masculinity.

Much of the normative data provided in the professional manual for the BSRI is based upon a 1973 sample of 279 females and 444 males, and a 1978 sample of 340 female and 476 male Stanford University undergraduates. Additional normative data are provided for small samples of non-Stanford Black undergraduates, White undergraduates, Hispanic undergraduates, psychiatric inpatients, and several groups of individuals in age categories different from the typical undergraduate. The original Stanford samples, while adequate for the purposes of test development and analysis, may be less adequate for providing the normative data needed to classify subjects in other research populations. Bem notes in the BSRI manual that the decision to use medians based on the original normative population or based on a particular research population is a matter of the individual researcher's judgment.

Numbers of validation studies suggest that the BSRI femininity and/or masculinity scales are correlated with gender-related behaviors. For example, studies have shown relations between BSRI scores and conformity, nurturance and interpersonal sensitivity, the avoidance of "cross-sex" behaviors, nonverbal femininity and masculinity, styles of social interaction, and the cognitive processing of gender-related information. The reader should see Taylor and Hall (1982) for a recent meta-analysis of studies which have investigated the relationship between assessed femininity, masculinity, and "male-typed" and "female-typed" dependent measures. The same analysis also provides evidence that measures of psychological health and adjustment seem to be more related to assessed masculinity than femininity.

Psychometrically, the BSRI displays good internal consistency and reliability. Bem reports the following coefficient alphas: for females, .75 for the Femininity scale and .87 for the Masculinity scale; for males, .78 for Femininity and .87 for Masculinity. Alphas for the short BSRI are comparable for the Masculinity scale, and higher for the Femininity scale. The BSRI has good test-retest reliability, and empirically the Femininity and Masculinity scales do prove to be virtually uncorrelated. The BSRI manual presents little evidence of the discriminant validity of the BSRI scales other than that they seem to be uncorrelated with social desirability as measured by the Marlowe-Crowne Scale.

The BSRI has been subjected in its relatively brief life to intense methodological testing and scrutiny, including many factor analytic investigations. (The BSRI manual cites some of the most noteworthy of these studies.) Generally, these factor analyses point to the same conclusion: The BSRI scales are not factorially pure. However, Bem argues that this finding is not necessarily inconsistent with the original rationale and development of the scales; society's stereotypes are not necessarily consistent. Typically factor analyses of BSRI items show two masculinity factors which can be labeled "Dominance/Aggression" and "Self-Reliance/Personal Control," a femininity factor which can be labelled "Interpersonal Sensitivity and Warmth," and finally a fourth factor often correlated with biological sex which is defined by three BSRI items: "Masculine," "Feminine," and "Athletic."

To increase the internal consistency of the BSRI scales, Bem developed a short form which includes 30 items, half the number in the original BSRI. The items, "feminine," "masculine," and "athletic," were discarded from the short version as were other items which showed poor item-total correlations with the Femininity and Masculinity scales. The short form scales correlate strongly (around .90) with the corresponding scales of the original BSRI. One important point should be noted about the short form: Several items were deleted from the femininity scale which were relatively socially undesirable (e.g., "gullible," "flatterable," "childlike"). Because of their removal, absolute scores on the Femininity scale of the short BSRI are often significantly higher than those on the long form. Thus absolute scores and medians for the two forms are not comparable.

The BSRI remains one of the major instruments for the independent assessment of psychological femininity and masculinity. It has generated considerable research and controversy, and undoubtedly will continue to do so. The short form of the BSRI promises to solve some of the psychometric problems of the long form, and thereby aid researchers in studying the effects of masculinity and femininity on behavior and cognition. Perhaps availability of the short BSRI will help researchers to move beyond revisionistic methodological research to more substantive research about femininity and masculinity.

REVIEWER'S REFERENCES

Bem, S. L. The measurement of psychological androgyny. JOURNAL OF CONSULTING AND CLINICAL PSYCHOLOGY, 1974, 42, 155–162.

Spence, J. T., Helmreich, R., & Stapp, J. The Personal Attributes Questionnaires: A measure of sex-role stereotypes and masculinity-femininity. JSAS CATALOG OF SELECTED DOCUMENTS IN PSYCHOLOGY, 1974, 4, 43.

Heilbrun, A. B., Jr. Measurement of masculine and feminine sex role identities as independent dimensions. JOURNAL OF CONSULTING AND CLINICAL PSYCHOLOGY, 1976, 44, 183–190.

Berzins, J. I., Welling, M. A., & Wetter, R. E. A new measure of psychological androgyny based on the Personality Research Form. JOURNAL OF CONSULTING AND CLINICAL PSYCHOLOGY, 1978, 46, 126–138.

Taylor, M. C., & Hall, J. A. Psychological androgyny: Theories, methods, and conclusions. PSYCHOLOGICAL BULLETIN, 1982, 92, 347–366.

Review of Bem Sex-Role Inventory by FRANK D. PAYNE, Associate Professor of Psychology, San Jose State University, San Jose, CA:

In constructing the Bem Sex-Role Inventory (BSRI), Bem did not use traditional scale construction techniques, such as item-total correlations or factor analysis, nor, apparently, was she guided by any clearly articulated theory about the nature of masculinity and femininity. Instead, she began by selecting roughly 200 personality characteristics that seemed to be positive in value and masculine or feminine in tone. She then asked a small sample of Stanford undergraduates to rate the desirability of each characteristic in American society either for a man or for a woman. Any item that female and male raters judged as more desirable for a woman than for a man became a candidate for inclusion in the "Femininity" scale, and just the reverse for the "Masculinity" scale. Bem does not specify how the final 20 items for each scale were selected, except that she attempted to make the absolute social desirability of the Femininity scale similar to that of the Masculinity scale by including "a number of feminine attributes somewhat lower in social desirability (e.g., gullible, childlike, shy)."

One of the major controversies that has surrounded the BSRI—a controversy that unfortunately has escaped the notice of many users of the instrument—is exactly what it is measuring. Bem's position is quite clear. She views the scales as indices of global femininity and masculinity that reflect the degree to which respondents use "cultural definitions as idealized standards of femininity and masculinity for evaluating their own personality and behavior." Unfortunately, there is no convincing evidence from Bem or anyone else that the instrument somehow transcends its limited content to deal with this form of "gender-based schematic processing." The limited validity data that Bem presents simply indicates some tendency for self-description on the BSRI to agree with overt conduct. For example, Bem found that individuals of either sex who scored high on Masculinity and low on Femininity actually tended to behave independently and with low nurturance, which fits with the way they described themselves on the BSRI. That is comforting to know, of course, but it does not prove that the BSRI scales are tapping the deeper processes that Bem says they are.

The content of the scales does not cover a full range of the ways in which males and females differ stereotypically in American society. Instead the items deal primarily with a much more circumscribed, but nonetheless important, domain, which in the case of the Masculinity scale has been described as "dominance" (Wiggins & Holzmuller, 1981), "dominance-poise" (Tellegen & Lubinski, 1983), or "instrumentality" (Spence, 1983)—independence, decisiveness, self-assertiveness; and in the case of the Femininity scale as "nurturance," "nurturance-warmth," or "expressiveness"—emotionality and awareness of others' feelings. Although it is not yet clear which of these more specific terms is most appropriate, any of them appear better than Masculinity and Femininity, because they more accurately reflect the actual content of the scales.

Due to the way in which the BSRI was constructed, the scales also suffer from another major problem—they are factorially complex. A number of factor analyses by others have demonstrated this, and Bem herself reports the results of an exploratory two-factor solution that confirms it as well. Although Bem does not acknowledge it, this has been particularly troublesome for the Femininity scale, which is a combination of socially desirable "expressive" traits and a hodgepodge of socially undesirable characteristics (e.g., "shy," "flatterable," "gullible," "soft-spoken," "childlike"). Recent research (Payne & Futterman, 1983; Silvern & Ryan, 1979) has demonstrated that the latter items often behave just the opposite of the "expressive" items and tend to lower correlations with many external variables.

Interestingly, the "Short Form" of the BSRI, which Bem describes simply as "a refinement of the Original BSRI" and "a convenience in scoring," does not suffer from these faults. Bem developed the Short BSRI, first, by selecting those items from the Original scale that had high loadings in a two-factor exploratory factor analysis, and, second, by culling those items further primarily on the basis of item-total-score correlations. What emerged from this sound psychometric approach appears to be relatively pure measures of "assertiveness-dominance" or "instrumentality" (Masculinity) and "nurturance-interpersonal warmth" or "expressiveness" (Femininity). Recent research involving the Short BSRI (Lubinski, Tellegen, & Butcher, 1983) indicates a pattern of correlations with other variables highly similar to that of Spence and Helmreich's measures of instrumentality and expressiveness (the Personal Attributes Questionnaire [PAQ]), and, indeed Spence (1983) recently has referred to it as "in essence, another PAQ." The Short BSRI therefore is not just a short form of the Original BSRI; it is a psychometrically superior, factorially purer index of "instrumental" and "expressive" traits. It should be chosen over the Original BSRI, and not just for "convenience in scoring."

A final major controversy regarding the BSRI has to do with how scores on the two scales should be combined. Bem originally proposed that if the Femininity raw score exceeded the Masculinity raw score at a statistically significant level, the individual should be labeled "feminine," if the reverse, "masculine," and if the difference was small and not statistically significant, "androgynous." Spence, Helmreich, and Stapp (1975), however, pointed out that this procedure lumps together two quite different kinds of individuals—those who score low on both scales and those who score high on both. Consequently in 1977 Bem renounced her earlier difference score in favor of the approach of Spence et al., which involves a median-split on both scales and produces a fourfold classification ("masculine," "feminine," "androgynous" [above the median on both], and "undifferentiated" [below on both]). In the present manual, Bem continues to advocate the median-split technique, but she goes on to describe a "hybrid" technique that involves a combination of both approaches. She states that the "median-split method is recommended for most purposes because it is much simpler to execute," implying that if one wishes to be more rigorous, the hybrid method is superior. The user should be aware, however, that this is not necessarily true. In many cases the median-split approach is better. Indeed, the most rigorous and sophisticated approach of all is to avoid categorizing people into any simple fourfold typology and instead use the full range of both scales in hierarchical multiple regression.

On balance, the "Short," but not the original, BSRI provides promising indices of the degree to which people describe themselves as having a global "instrumental," "dominant," or "assertive" disposition and "expressive" or "nurturant" tendencies. If one is interested in these stereotypically sex-linked dispositions—and there is accumulating evidence that these tendencies correlate importantly with various indices of adjustment—the Short BSRI deserves consideration. It has generally good test-retest and internal consistency reliability, and, although the validity data are meager, enough research has been done by Bem and others to indicate that it has promise as a research device. The researcher is cautioned, however, not to rely on the normative data reported in the manual, since they were obtained entirely from Stanford undergraduates.

REVIEWER'S REFERENCES

Spence, J. T., Helmreich, R., & Stapp, J. Ratings of self and peers in sex role attributes and their relation to self-esteem and conceptions of masculinity and femininity. JOURNAL OF PERSONALITY AND SOCIAL PSYCHOLOGY, 1975, 32, 29–39.

Silvern, L. E., & Ryan, V. L. Self-rated adjustment and sex-typing on the Bem Sex-Role Inventory: Is Masculinity the primary predictor of adjustment? SEX ROLES, 1979, 5, 739–763.

Wiggins, J. S., & Holzmuller, A. Further evidence on androgyny and interpersonal flexibility. JOURNAL OF RESEARCH IN PERSONALITY, 1981, 15, 67–80.

Lubinski, D., Tellegen, A., & Butcher, J. N. Masculinity, femininity and androgyny viewed and assessed as distinct concepts. JOURNAL OF PERSONALITY AND SOCIAL PSYCHOLOGY, 1983, 44, 428–439.

Payne, F. D., & Futterman, J. R. "Masculinity," "Femininity," and adjustment in college men. JOURNAL OF RESEARCH IN PERSONALITY, 1983, 17, 110–124.

Spence, J. T. Comment on Lubinski, Tellegen, and Butcher's "Masculinity, femininity, and androgyny viewed and assessed as distinct concepts." JOURNAL OF PERSONALITY AND SOCIAL PSYCHOLOGY, 1983, 44, 440–446.

Tellegen, A., & Lubinski, D. Some methodological comments on labels, traits, interactions, and types in the study of "Femininity" and "Masculinity": Reply to Spence. JOURNAL OF PERSONALITY AND SOCIAL PSYCHOLOGY, 1983, 44, 447–455.

[138]

Bench Mark Measures. Ungraded; 1977; developed primarily to be used in conjunction with the Alphabetic Phonics curriculum, but can also be useful as instruments to measure any student's general phonic knowledge; no reliability or validity data; no norms; individual in part; 1 form (26 pages); 3 levels in 4 areas: alphabet and dictionary skills, reading, handwriting, spelling; 1 form (26 pages); administrator's guide (16 pages); summary sheet (6 pages); skeleton dictionary (Anna Gillingham and Bessie Stillman, '56, 79 pages); graph of concepts and multisensory introductions (16 pages); spirit duplicating master (1 page); test cards (56 cards); set of three-dimensional letters; sheet of block capitals (1 page); 1982 price data: $55 per complete kit including 24 summary sheets; $10 per 24 summary sheets; $1.25 per graph; (30–60) minutes; Aylett R. Cox; Educators Publishing Service, Inc.*

Review of Bench Mark Measures by DAVID J. CARROLL, School of Education, University of the West Indies, Bridgetown, Barbados, West Indies:

This is a test of the "secondary" language skills—knowledge of the alphabet, a range of basic letter-sound correspondences, handwriting and spelling. Most of the test is intended for individual administration, and the remainder for use with individuals or small groups. It is intended to produce a profile of these four areas, and is criterion-referenced; each of the levels is described in terms of its content, and errors and differences in level are intended to indicate need for instruction.

The test has been developed over a number of years, and this is reflected in the quality and comprehensiveness of the materials and instructions. The test jacket contains everything that the intending administrator will need, except students and pencils. The materials seem to be of good quality and durability. The test battery is very complex, and intending users are recommended not to embark on it without thorough preparation, or the intention of making repeated use of it. The general organisation is, however, clear and practical, with a record sheet for each student which serves both as a score sheet for the actual testing, and as a more general record sheet. Instructions for administration are clear and explicit; they include preparation, procedure, and what the administrator should say, and take account of most of the likely doubts. They need to be studied carefully before one embarks on first administration. Instructions for marking and the completion of the evaluation are similarly full and practical, and should make the task as objective as can reasonably be hoped.

It is stated in the Guide that substantial work has been done in the development of the measures through item analysis, and revision has occurred as a result of experience and comment; mention is also made of comparison with other tests leading to concurrent validation. However, none of this is actually reported in the test package; neither is any data reported about the stability of the profiles on retest. This is to be regretted in what is otherwise a very sound manual. Clearly, one would not expect the same data to be provided for a test of this kind that one would expect with a group test of general academic ability; but one is surely entitled to expect something, especially when it is clear that some work has been done.

In this reviewer's opinion, therefore, the test is sound, practical, and as easy to administer as can be expected given the type of pupil for whom it is intended. It will be suitable for use wherever the "Alphabetic Phonics" curriculum or the sequence of training in sounds and combinations underlying it is used. There is no evidence given that the materials have been tried out with other pupils who have not been taught with this kind of curriculum, and therefore there is no assurance that the sequences in the test are in a "natural" order of difficulty—although there is a clear gradient of complexity across the three stages of the test. Intending users, however, who do not follow the "Alphabetic Phonics" curriculum might wish to try out the test to see how well the sequencing reflects "natural order." This is made easier by the clear and explicit Graph of Concepts and Multisensory Introductions supplied with the test package.

However, it should be made clear that the test is deeply committed to a model of language teaching and learning which may not be shared by all who might think of using it. First, the curriculum starts with the elements—the alphabet—and works up towards combinations—blends, etc.—of increasing complexity. Second, rules are supplied—spelling principles and "Syllable Division Formulas"—by a process of guided discovery, and the student is encouraged to apply them. Third, there is emphasis on "sounding every vowel as coded and including obscure consonants," constructing texts to embody the features being taught, to the effective disregard of other features which are typically present in natural language, and so on. Fourth, there is emphasis on sequentiality—using only what has been taught or is being taught, in the production of materials.

These principles are those of the "Alphabetic Phonics" curriculum. They are aimed at developing a powerful "monitor" (to use Krashen's term), something in the student's mind which enables the student to process consciously and carefully the language he/she is faced with, so as to "get it right." The relationship between this and an "acquired" system is still far from clear, but the distinction is definitely a reality. If a curriculum were focussing on the acquired system primarily, it would be essentially problem-centred, focussing on natural language use, and creating a need to understand or say, in order to achieve some non-linguistic goal. This implies a non-linguistic syllabus—because if a teacher or student has linguistic goals stated, he/she will go for them—and this will lead to simplification as a reaction to what can and cannot be understood, rather than to a priori grounds of complexity, "peripheral" exposure to unknown language before it is introduced, and so on. This kind of teaching has been attempted in English as a second or foreign language (e.g., at the Regional Institute of English, Bangalore, South India), but its principles have not yet been made explicit for first-language work.

However, given that there are these two basic possibilities, there are several implications for testing. Most testing procedures do not test actual language use, but the correlates of language use, things that fluent natives can do with language, without any prior training. If these same things are used both to teach and to test, then there is no guarantee that successful performance on the test means what it meant in the absence of tuition. Development of the "monitor" will have outstripped the acquired competence formerly associated with it. Therefore, we may say that if a test is to be of this kind, it should be entirely dissociated from similar teaching—i.e., that it should be used with "acquisitionist" teaching—and that if it is used with "synthetic" teaching, it can serve only the very limited purpose of seeing whether the pupil has understood the surface level of the teaching. And any summative evaluation must be based upon considerations of whether, and at what stage, the student can use these rules, etc. to solve real-life problems.

In these terms, the present test cannot be said to be searching. It is based upon exactly the same principles as the "Alphabetic Phonics" curriculum—it is concerned in part with knowledge ABOUT language, reciting the alphabet, putting letters in sequence, making sounds for "nonsense" words, and so on. The student is asked to exemplify his knowledge of phonetics in reading words that he cannot possibly have any understanding of, which are furthermore decontextualised; and when connected text is brought in, it comes as phrases in level 1, sentences in level 2, and paragraphs in level 3. These pieces of text are constructed to include particular phonetic difficulties, and to be simple in every other respect. They are lexically very complex, but structurally very simple—few complex sentences, almost no tenses other than simple present, and propositionally deficient. Thus, the test is an effective test of the skills taught in a particular kind of curriculum, and of whether they have been mastered at the conscious level, but it is in no sense a test of whether the student can exploit his phonic knowledge in a context of use.

[139]

[Bender-Gestalt Test]. Ages 4 and over; 1938–77; individual; the original Bender-Gestalt is listed as *a* below; the modifications listed as *b-h* consist primarily of alterations in administration procedure, new scoring systems, or expanded interpretive procedures, rather than changes in the test materials; *c* and *d* provide, in addition, for use of the materials as projective stimuli for associations.

a) VISUAL MOTOR GESTALT TEST. Ages 4 and over; 1938–46; VMGT; no reliability data; 1 form ('46, 9 cards); manual ('38, 187 pages); directions for administration ('46, 8 pages); 1983 price data: $4 per set of cards and directions; $10 per manual; (10) minutes; Lauretta Bender; American Orthopsychiatric Association, Inc.*

b) THE BENDER GESTALT TEST. Ages 4 and over; 1951; BGT; utilizes same test cards as *a*; scoring sheet (1 page); manual (287 pages); 1982 price data: $11 per 50 scoring sheets; $26.50 per manual; (10) minutes; Gerald R. Pascal and Barbara J. Suttell; Grune & Stratton, Inc.*

c) THE HUTT ADAPTATION OF THE BENDER-GESTALT TEST. Ages 7 and over; 1944–77; HABGT; no reliability data on scored factors; 1 form ('60, 9 cards, same as *a* except for modification in 1 design); manual, third edition ('77, 280 pages); record form ('77, 4 pages); scoring template ('70, 1 page plus directions); Atlas ('70, 290 pages); 1982 price data: $9 per set of cards; $18.50 per 25 record forms and template; $25 per manual; $20.50 per atlas; (45–60) minutes; Max L. Hutt; Grune & Stratton, Inc.*

d) THE BENDER VISUAL MOTOR GESTALT TEST FOR CHILDREN. Ages 4–12; 1962; utilizes same test cards as *a*; manual (92 pages); record form (4 pages); 1983 price data: $7.10 per 25 record forms; $10.40 per manual; (10) minutes without associations; Aileen Clawson; Western Psychological Services.*

e) THE BENDER GESTALT TEST FOR YOUNG CHILDREN. Ages 5–10; 1963–75; a developmental scoring system; utilizes same test cards as *a*; manual ('64, 206 pages); research and application supplement ('75, 220 pages); score sheet ('66, 2 pages); 1982 price data: $14.50 per 100 score sheets; $23.50 per manual; $25 per supplement; administration time not reported; Elizabeth Munsterberg Koppitz; Grune & Stratton, Inc.*

f) THE WATKINS BENDER-GESTALT SCORING SYSTEM. Ages 5–14; 1976; WBSS; utilizes same test cards as *a*; manual (137 pages); record form (2 pages); 1984 price data: $6 per 50 record forms; $10 per manual; $10 per specimen set; administration time not reported; Ernest O. Watkins; Academic Therapy Publications.*

g) THE TWO-COPY DRAWING FORM. Ages 4 and over; 1964; 1 form (1 page plus backing sheet); 1983 price data: $9.80 per 25 forms; Western Psychological Services.*

h) THE CANTER BACKGROUND INTERFERENCE PROCEDURE FOR THE BENDER GESTALT TEST. Ages 4 and over; 1966–70; BIP; also called BIP Bender Test; 1984 price data: $16.50 per 25 tests; $11.50 per manual; Arthur Canter; Western Psychological Services.*

See T3:280 (159 references), 8:506 (253 references), and T2:1447 (144 references); for a review by Philip M. Kitay, see 7:161 (192 references); see also P:415 (170 references); for a review by C. B. Blakemore and an excerpted review by Fred Y. Billingslea, see 6:203 (99 references); see also 5:172 (118 references); for reviews by Arthur L. Benton and Howard R. White, see 4:144 (34 references); see also 3:108 (8 references).

TEST REFERENCES

1. Fish, B. Neurobiologic antecedents of schizophrenia in children. ARCHIVES OF GENERAL PSYCHIATRY, 1977, 34, 1297–1313.

2. Hoy, E., Weiss, G., Minde, K., & Cohen N. The hyperactive child at adolescence: Cognitive, emotional, and social functioning. JOURNAL OF ABNORMAL CHILD PSYCHOLOGY, 1978, 6, 311–324.

3. Lesnik-Oberstein, M., van der Vlugt, H., Hoencamp, E., Juffermans, D., & Cohen, L. Stimulus-governance and the hyperkinetic syndrome. JOURNAL OF ABNORMAL CHILD PSYCHOLOGY, 1978, 6, 407–412.

4. Raskin, A., Gershon, S., Crook, T. H., Sathananthan, G., & Ferris, S. The effects of hyperbaric and normobaric oxygen on cognitive impairment in the elderly. ARCHIVES OF GENERAL PSYCHIATRY, 1978, 35, 50–56.

5. Bradley, P. E., Battin, R. R., & Sutter, E. G. Effects of individual diagnosis and remediation for the treatment of learning disabilities. CLINICAL NEUROPSYCHOLOGY, 1979, 1(2), 25–32.

6. Craig, P. L. Neuropsychological assessment in public psychiatric hospitals: The current state of the practice. CLINICAL NEUROPSYCHOLOGY, 1979, 1(4), 1–7.

7. Freeman, M. J. The need for an organismic therapy in hospitalization. CLINICAL NEUROPSYCHOLOGY, 1979, 1(3), 39–43.

8. Lacks, P. B. The use of the Bender Gestalt Test in clinical neuropsychology. CLINICAL NEUROPSYCHOLOGY, 1979, 1(3), 29–34.

9. Reynolds, W. M. Psychological tests: Clinical usage versus psychometric quality. PROFESSIONAL PSYCHOLOGY, 1979, 10, 324–329.

10. Rieder, R. O., & Nichols, P. L. Offspring of schizophrenics III: Hyperactivity and neurological soft signs. ARCHIVES OF GENERAL PSYCHIATRY, 1979, 36, 665–674.

11. Bigler, E. D., & Ehrfurth, J. W. Critical limitations of the Bender Gestalt Test in clinical neuropsychology: Response to Lacks. CLINICAL NEUROPSYCHOLOGY, 1980, 2, 88–90.

12. Hall, R. C. W., Gardner, E. R., Stickney, S. K., LeCann, A. F., & Popkin, M. K. Physical illness manifesting as psychiatric disease: II. Analysis of a state hospital inpatient population. ARCHIVES OF GENERAL PSYCHIATRY, 1980, 37, 989–995.

13. Hartlage, L. C., & Telzrow, C. F. The practice of clinical neuropsychology. CLINICAL NEUROPSYCHOLOGY, 1980, 2, 200–202.

14. Whitehouse, D., Shah, U., & Palmer, F. B. Comparison of sustained-release and standard methylphenidate in the treatment of minimal brain dysfunction. THE JOURNAL OF CLINICAL PSYCHIATRY, 1980, 41, 282–285.

15. Carsrud, A. L., Carsrud, K. B., Dodd, B. G., Thompson, M., & Gray, W. K. Predicting vocational aptitude of mentally retarded persons: A comparison of assessment systems. AMERICAN JOURNAL OF MENTAL DEFICIENCY, 1981, 86, 275–280.

16. Corotto, L. V., Hafner, J. L., & Curnutt, R. H. The use of a modified administrative procedure (MAP) for the Bender-Gestalt Test with schizophrenic patients and normals. JOURNAL OF CLINICAL PSYCHOLOGY, 1981, 37, 824–827.

17. Fabian, J. J., & Jacobs, U. W. Discrimination of neurological impairment in the learning disabled adolescent. JOURNAL OF LEARNING DISABILITIES, 1981, 14, 594–596.

18. Goldstein, P. K., O'Brien, J. D., & Katz, G. M. A learning disability screening program in a public school: Pediatrics, screening, learning disability. THE AMERICAN JOURNAL OF OCCUPATIONAL THERAPY, 1981, 35, 451–455.

19. Grunau, R. V. E., Purves, S. J., McBurney, A. K., & Low, M. D. Identifying academic aptitude in adolescent children by psychological testing and EEG spectral analysis. NEUROPSYCHOLOGIA, 1981, 19, 79–86.

20. Hariprasad, M. K., Nadler, I. M., & Eisinger, R. P. Hemodialysis for uremic schizophrenics: No psychiatric improvement. THE JOURNAL OF CLINICAL PSYCHIATRY, 1981, 42, 215–216.

21. McCraw, R. K., & Pegg-McNab, J. Effect of test order on Rorschach human and movement responses. JOURNAL OF PERSONALITY ASSESSMENT, 1981, 45, 575–581.

22. Tsai, L., & Tsuang, M. T. How can we avoid unnecessary CT scanning for psychiatric patients? THE JOURNAL OF CLINICAL PSYCHIATRY, 1981, 42, 452–454.

23. Voorhees, J. Neuropsychological differences between juvenile delinquents and functional adolescents: A preliminary study. ADOLESCENCE, 1981, 16, 57–66.

24. Wiener-Levy, D., & Exner, J. E., Jr. The Rorschach EA-ep variable as related to persistence in a task frustration situation under feedback conditions. JOURNAL OF PERSONALITY ASSESSMENT, 1981, 45, 118–124.

25. Abbott, D., Rotnem, D., Genel, M., & Cohen, D. J. Cognitive and emotional functioning in hypopituitary short-statured children. SCHIZOPHRENIA BULLETIN, 1982, 8, 310–319.

26. Adams, R. L., Boake, C., & Crain, C. Bias in neuropsychological test classification related to education, age, and ethnicity. JOURNAL OF CONSULTING AND CLINICAL PSYCHOLOGY, 1982, 50, 143–145.

27. Armstrong, B. B., & Knopf, K. F. Comparison of the Bender-Gestalt and revised Developmental Test of Visual Motor Integration. PERCEPTUAL AND MOTOR SKILLS, 1982, 55, 164–166.

28. Breen, M. J. Comparison of educationally handicapped students' scores on the revised Developmental Test of Visual-Motor Integration and Bender-Gestalt. PERCEPTUAL AND MOTOR SKILLS, 1982, 54, 1227–1230.

29. Delaney, R. C. Screening for organicity: The problem of subtle neuropsychological deficit and diagnosis. JOURNAL OF CLINICAL PSYCHOLOGY, 1982, 38, 843–846.

30. Dunn, F. M., & Howell, R. J. Relaxation training and its relationship to hyperactivity in boys. JOURNAL OF CLINICAL PSYCHOLOGY, 1982, 38, 92–100.

31. Field, K., Bolton, B., & Dana, R. H. An evaluation of three Bender-Gestalt scoring systems as indicators of psychopathology. JOURNAL OF CLINICAL PSYCHOLOGY, 1982, 38, 838–842.

32. Gordon, M. Central placement of Bender figure A by clinic-referred and non-referred children. PERCEPTUAL AND MOTOR SKILLS, 1982, 54, 1241–1242.

33. Kales, A., Constantin, R. S., Bixler, E. O., Caldwell, A., Cadieux, R. J., Verrechio, J. M., & Kales, J. D. Narcolepsy-Cataplexy: II. Psychosocial consequences and associated psychopathology. ARCHIVES OF NEUROLOGY, 1982, 39, 169–171.

34. Karr, S. K. Bender-Gestalt performance of Sierra Leone West African children from four sub-cultures. PERCEPTUAL AND MOTOR SKILLS, 1982, 55, 123–127.

35. Obrzut, J. E., Hansen, R. L., & Heath, C. P. The effectiveness of visual information processing training with Hispanic children. JOURNAL OF GENERAL PSYCHOLOGY, 1982, 107, 165–174.

36. Redfering, D. L., & Collins, J. A comparison of the Koppitz and Hutt techniques of Bender-Gestalt administration correlated with WISC-R performance scores. EDUCATIONAL AND PSYCHOLOGICAL MEASUREMENT, 1982, 42, 41–47.

37. Sattler, J. M., & Gwynne, J. Ethnicity and Bender Visual Motor Gestalt Test performance. JOURNAL OF SCHOOL PSYCHOLOGY, 1982, 20, 69–71.

38. Skeen, J. A., Strong, V. N., & Book, R. M. Comparison of learning disabled children's performance on Bender Visual-Motor Gestalt Test and Beery's Developmental Test of Visual Motor Integration. PERCEPTUAL AND MOTOR SKILLS, 1982, 55, 1257–1258.

39. Spero, M. H. Psychotherapeutic procedure with religious cult devotees. THE JOURNAL OF NERVOUS AND MENTAL DISEASE, 1982, 170, 332–344.

40. Stewart, R. C., Lovitt, R., & Stewart, R. M. Are hysterical seizures more than hysteria? A Research Diagnostic Criteria, DSM-III, and psychometric analysis. THE AMERICAN JOURNAL OF PSYCHIATRY, 1982, 139, 926–929.

41. Tamkin, A. S., & Kunce, J. T. Construct validity of the Weigl color-form sorting test. PERCEPTUAL AND MOTOR SKILLS, 1982, 55, 105–106.

42. Tejani, A., Dobias, B., & Sambursky, J. Long-term prognosis after H. influenzae Meningitis: Prospective evaluation. DEVELOPMENTAL MEDICINE AND CHILD NEUROLOGY, 1982, 24, 338–343.

43. Wagner, E. E., & McCormick, M. K. Relationships between WAIS verbal versus performance decrements and Bender-Gestalt errors. PERCEPTUAL AND MOTOR SKILLS, 1982, 54, 1259–1263.

44. Wright, D., & DeMers, S. T. Comparison of the relationship between two measures of visual-motor coordination and academic achievement. PSYCHOLOGY IN THE SCHOOLS, 1982, 19, 473–477.

45. Ysseldyke, J. E., Algozzine, B., Shinn, M. R., & McGue, M. Similarities and differences between low achievers and students classified learning disabled. JOURNAL OF SPECIAL EDUCATION, 1982, 16, 73–85.

46. Caskey, W. E., Jr., & Larson, G. L. Relationship between selected kindergarten predictors and first and fourth grade achievement test scores. PERCEPTUAL AND MOTOR SKILLS, 1983, 56, 815–822.

47. Connelly, J. B. Comparative analysis of two tests of visual-fine-motor integration among young Indian and non-Indian children. PERCEPTUAL AND MOTOR SKILLS, 1983, 57, 1079–1082.

48. Dana, R. H., Feild, K., & Bolton, B. Variations of the Bender-Gestalt Test: Implications for training and practice. JOURNAL OF PERSONALITY ASSESSMENT, 1983, 47, 76–84.

49. Finch, A. J., Jr., Spirito, A., Garrison, S., & Marshall, P. Developmental differences in Bender-Gestalt recall of children with learning and behavior problems. PERCEPTUAL AND MOTOR SKILLS, 1983, 56, 87–90.

50. Hinkle, J. S. Comparison of reproductions of the Bender-Gestalt and Memory-for-Designs by delinquents and non-delinquents. PERCEPTUAL AND MOTOR SKILLS, 1983, 57, 1070.

51. Huhtaniemi, P., Haier, R. J., Fedio, P., & Buchsbaum, M. S. Neuropsychological characteristics of college males who show attention dysfunction. PERCEPTUAL AND MOTOR SKILLS, 1983, 57, 399–406.

52. Incagnoli, T., & Kane, R. Developmental perspective of the Gilles de la Tourette Syndrome. PERCEPTUAL AND MOTOR SKILLS, 1983, 57, 1271–1281.

53. Liemohn, W. Rhythmicity and motor skill. PERCEPTUAL AND MOTOR SKILLS, 1983, 57, 327–331.

54. Manshadi, M., Lippman, S., O'Daniel, R. G., & Blackman, A. Alcohol abuse and attention deficit disorder. THE JOURNAL OF CLINICAL PSYCHIATRY, 1983, 44, 379–380.

55. Marecek, J., Shapiro, I. M., Burke, A., Katz, S. H., & Hediger, M. L. Low-level lead exposure in childhood influences neuropsychological performance. ARCHIVES OF ENVIRONMENTAL HEALTH, 1983, 38, 355–359.

56. Mermelstein, J. J. The relationship between rotations on the Bender-Gestalt Test and ratings of patient disorientation. JOURNAL OF PERSONALITY ASSESSMENT, 1983, 47, 490–491.

57. O'Dougherty, M., Wright, F. S., Garmezy, N., Loewenson, R. B., & Torres, F. Later competence and adaptation in infants who survive severe heart defects. CHILD DEVELOPMENT, 1983, 54, 1129–1142.

58. Porrino, L. J., Rapoport, J. L., Behar, D., Sceery, W., Ismond, D. R., & Bunney, W. E., Jr. A naturalistic assessment of the motor activity of hyperactive boys: I. Comparison with normal controls. ARCHIVES OF GENERAL PSYCHIATRY, 1983, 40, 681–687.

59. Robin, R. W., & Shea, J. D. C. The Bender Gestalt Visual Motor Test in Papua New Guinea. INTERNATIONAL JOURNAL OF PSYCHOLOGY, 1983, 18, 263–270.

60. Roe, K. V., & Roe, A. Schooling and cognitive development: A longitudinal study in Greece. PERCEPTUAL AND MOTOR SKILLS, 1983, 57, 147–153.

61. Stellern, J., Marlowe, M., Cossairt, A., & Errera, J. Low lead and cadmium levels and childhood visual-perception development. PERCEPTUAL AND MOTOR SKILLS, 1983, 56, 539–544.

62. Vardy, M. M., & Kay, S. R. LSD psychosis or LSD-induced schizophrenia?: A multimethod inquiry. ARCHIVES OF GENERAL PSYCHIATRY, 1983, 40, 877–883.

63. Weinstein, E. S. Sex differences in early Bender-Gestalt Test performance. PERCEPTUAL AND MOTOR SKILLS, 1983, 57, 301–302.

64. Richman, L. C., & Eliason, M. Type of reading disability related to cleft type and neuropsychological patterns. CLEFT PALATE JOURNAL, 1984, 21, 1–6.

65. Storandt, M., Botwinick, J., Danziger, W. L., Berg, L., & Hughes, C. P. Psychometric differentiation of mild senile dementia of the Alzheimer type. ARCHIVES OF NEUROLOGY, 1984, 41, 497–499.

Review of The Watkins Bender-Gestalt Scoring System by KENNETH W. HOWELL, Chairperson, Department of Special Education, Arizona State University, Tempe, AZ:

The Bender-Gestalt test and its modifications is one of the most frequently discussed and enduring instruments available. As noted in previous editions of this yearbook the test, while extraordinarily popular, has limited clinical value (Kitay, 1972). The Watkins scoring system will probably support the test's continued popularity while further disguising whatever value the instrument may have.

The Watkins system consists of 42 items, many of which were taken from the Developmental Bender Scoring System by Koppitz (1963). According to the manual, items included in the system were retained after standardization because they discriminated between "normal" and "LD" children. The process of item selection and scoring is inadequately described, and a direct comparison to the Koppitz system is difficult.

The manual states that the Watkins scoring system was developed to determine the presence of visual-perceptual problems in children. Given that statement it seems logical to assume that the test should be expected to categorize students into "problem" and "no problem" groups. The assumption embodied in the manual is that such a categorization according to visual-perceptual ability has treatment implications. This is an example of the common assumption that aptitude–treatment interactions exist and can be utilized for guiding remedial activities.

The aptitude-treatment interaction assumption lacks treatment verification although it is a popular one in special education and school psychology. Two excellent reviews of the subject which deal directly with the visual-perceptual construct and the Bender-Gestalt (but not the Watkins system) were presented by Coles (1978) and Arter and Jenkins (1979). These reviews point out the absence of a substantiated relationship between Bender-Gestalt scores and the construct of visual perception as well as the absence of a substantiated causative relationship between the use of visual perception measures and academic improvement.

In the only attempt to link the scoring system to the domain of visual perception the Watkins manual states that the correlation of total error score with IQ is statistically significant but low. (The actual level of significance is not supplied.) In a classic non sequitur it then states that this low correlation with IQ shows that the test is NOT a measure of intelligence and therefore IS a measure of the development of the "neural-visual-perceptual system." Of course, a variety of competing explanations could account for the lack of a significant relationship because finding out what something is not doesn't tell you what it is. No attempt was made to relate Watkins scores to other measures of visual perception.

It is an error to attempt to draw treatment implications from classification statements. The Watkins manual contains 60 pages of case studies in which treatment recommendations based on the Watkins' scoring system and interpretation of the Bender-Gestalt are modeled. These treatment recommendations include repeated references to perceptual modality constructs (e.g., "his ability to learn through the auditory modality," and "utilize mainly a haptic auditory approach to teach him reading"). No outcome data supporting these treatment recommendations are supplied. In fact, the only validity evidence presented deals exclusively with the test's ability to classify students as learning disabled.

Watkins' request that we accept treatment recommendations based on the scoring system rests on his finding that the scoring system discriminated between normal and "learning disabled" subjects (the criteria for "learning disability" placement is not supplied). The author attempts to build a construct validity argument from this finding by stating, "Of course, one of the major reasons why children have learning disabilities is that they have visual-perceptual problems."

As presented the categorization study is flawed in that it compares the scores of normal, presumably unreferred students to those of learning disabled students. The critical diagnostic comparison is, of course, between referred populations, not referred populations and normal populations. In order to accept treatment recommendations on the basis of this data a practitioner must accept that: other referred students would not have scored the same as the learning disabled students; the Watkins system summarizes visual-perception; all learning disabled students have visual-perceptual problems; all individuals with visual-perceptual problems learn in similar predictable ways; and visual-perceptual problems are so related to school achievement that information about them can be used to guide instruction.

In addition to the pervasive issue of validity there are a number of technical inadequacies in the manual. Standardization and validation populations and techniques are inadequately described. Scores and interpretation procedures are similarly vague. For example, in order to facilitate interpretation a table presents scores by age which indicate the presence of mild, moderate, and severe visual-perceptual problems. No explanation of the mild, moderate, and severe subdivision construct is presented nor is it explained how the scores were divided.

In general, this reviewer believes the use of ability measures to guide instructional decision making continues to be a time consuming and misdirected exercise. While the literature on the Bender-Gestalt and its various related systems has impressive bulk, it does not have the kind of empirical support that treatment decisions deserve. The ability of the Watkins or any other system to categorize students who have already been recognized by the referral process tells us nothing about the treatment of those students. Until experimental studies with appropriate controls show that students actually learn more as a result of employing the Watkins' scoring system, it remains a theoretical exercise and it should not be recommended for other than research purposes.

REVIEWER'S REFERENCES

Koppitz, E. M. THE BENDER GESTALT TEST FOR YOUNG CHILDREN. New York: Grune & Stratton, 1963.

Kitay, P. M. Review of the Bender-Gestalt Test. In O. K. Buros (Ed.), THE SEVENTH MENTAL MEASUREMENTS YEARBOOK (2 vols). Highland Park, NJ: The Grypon Press, 1972.

Coles, G. S. The Learning-Disabilities Test Battery: Empirical and social issues. HARVARD EDUCATIONAL REVIEW, 1978, 48, 313–340.

Arter, J. A., & Jenkins, J. R. Differential diagnosis-prescriptive teachers: A critical appraisal. REVIEW OF EDUCATIONAL RESEARCH, 1979, 49, 517–555.

Review of The Hutt Adaptation of the Bender-Gestalt Test by JEROME M. SATTLER, Professor of Psychology, San Diego State University, San Diego, CA:

The second revision of the Hutt Adaptation of the Bender-Gestalt, like the former ones, contains nine designs similar to those used by Bender. The designs in the Hutt adaptation are more uniform in size. Interpretations are based on both objective and projective approaches, but the projective approach is stressed. This revision is similar to the prior ones, with the exception of some changes in the scoring criteria and a revised recording form.

In the projective approach, information is sought about the individual's style of adaptation, cognition, affect, areas of conflict, defensive methods, and maturational characteristics. A perceptual-motor test like the Bender-Gestalt, Hutt believes, may tap earlier levels of meaningful and conflictual experience and be less open to distortion than verbal tests. Hutt assumes that the individual's visual-motor reproductions reflect conscious, preconscious, and unconscious determinants.

To use the Bender-Gestalt as a projective instrument, three phases are recommended: (1) a copy phase, (2) an elaboration phase, and (3) an association phase. In the copy phase, designs are copied directly from the card. In the elaboration phase, the designs are drawn again in any way that would make them more pleasing to the individual. In the association phase, the individual is asked to indicate what the original designs and the elaborated designs look like or suggest. A testing-of-limits phase (tailoring extra-testing procedures to reveal possible reasons for the individual's performance) is also recommended.

Interpretations derived from the projective approach must be seriously questioned. Reliability and validity data are sparse. While Hutt's book, *The Hutt Adaptation of the Bender-Gestalt Test* (1977), which discusses this revision, is rich in clinical lore, the projective approach will likely be unacceptable to many clinicians. These include those who question (*a*) the psychoanalytic approach to personality assessment and (*b*) the wisdom of generating hypotheses about personality based on visual-motor reproductions (e.g., "The atypical placement of figure A supports the hypotheses of ego disturbance and of fearfulness in interpersonal relations") (p. 199).

The objective approach is on somewhat firmer ground, but it is still hampered by questions of reliability and validity. Two scales, the Psychopathology Scale and the Scale for Perceptual Adience-Abience, plus a configurational analysis approach, can be included in the objective approach. The focus is on the individual designs as well as on the organization of the designs.

The Psychopathology Scale, a global measure of the degree of psychopathology, contains 17 factors, with almost all factors scored on a 1- to 10-point scale. The weights appear to follow from a commonsense approach, rather than being based on empirical data. Examples of the scoring criteria are contained in An Atlas for the Hutt Adaptation of the Bender-Gestalt Test (Hutt & Biggy, 1970), but not in the 1977 text/manual.

The norms are extremely limited and poorly described. In addition to a normal group of 140 individuals (80 individuals who were screened for evidence of disturbance and 60 unselected college students), there were six groups with various forms of psychopathology. Means and standard deviations, but not standard scores, are provided for each group. Interscorer reliability is reported to be .96 for two experienced scorers and .90 for one experienced and one inexperienced scorer. With a group of hospitalized patients, test-retest reliability over a 2-week period yielded correlations of .87 and .83 for males and females, respectively. The Psychopathology Scale distinguishes psychotic individuals from those who are normal, but it fails to distinguish chronic schizophrenics from those with brain damage. This may be a critical weakness in the scale.

The Scale for Perceptual Adience-Abience, which is more experimental than the Psychopathology Scale, focuses on the individual's perceptual orientation or perceptual style (openness [approach] vs. closedness [avoidance]). Many of the items overlap with those on the Psychopathology Scale, with one study reporting a correlation of .69 between the two scales. The 12 factors on the Scale for Perceptual Adience-Abience have various ranges of scores, with the largest being +2 to −2. The norms consist of five of the same seven groups used for the Psychopathology Scale norms. While validity data are sparse, there is some evidence that the scale has limited construct validity.

In the configurational analysis approach, specific signs are listed and weighted for five clinical groups (brain damage, schizophrenias, depression, psychoneuroses, and mental retardation). Critical scores suggestive of the condition are given for each of the five groups. This approach attempts to distinguish psychiatric groups from one another, but it lacks sufficient validity.

The Hutt system for interpreting the Bender-Gestalt places most of its emphasis on the projective aspects of test interpretation. While the text/manual offers numerous hypotheses and examples for interpreting personality dynamics based on the individual's visual-motor reproductions, there is little empirical justification for using this approach. In fact, naive readers following the Hutt approach may be lulled into thinking that they can appraise personality and make diagnoses solely on the basis of Bender-Gestalt reproductions. While the Psychopathology Scale is on firmer psychometric ground, further reliability and validity data are needed. However, this scale appears useful for screening purposes. The Scale for Perceptual Adience-Abience needs more research before it is used. There is little justification for using the configurational analysis approach for purposes of differential diagnosis.

Overall, the Hutt system provides some useful guidelines for the assessment of visual-motor ability; however, it should be used with extreme caution, if at all, as a projective technique for the assessment of personality.

REVIEWER'S REFERENCES

Hutt, M. L., & Gibby, R. G. AN ATLAS FOR THE HUTT ADAPTATION OF THE BENDER-GESTALT TEST. New York: Grune & Stratton, 1970.

Hutt, M. L. THE HUTT ADAPTATION OF THE BENDER-GESTALT TEST. New York: Grune & Stratton, 1977.

[140]

Benton Visual Retention Test, Revised Edition. Ages 8 and over; 1946–74; BVRT; manual title is *Revised Visual Retention Test*; 2 scores: number correct, error; individual; Forms C, D, E, ('55, 10 cards) in a single booklet; manual ('74, 98 pages); record blank ('74, 1 page); 1984 price data: $17 per set of cards, 50 record blanks, and manual; $4.75 per 50 record blanks; $8.75 per cards; $8.25 per manual; 5(10) minutes; Arthur L. Benton; The Psychological Corporation.*

See T3:283 (27 references), 8:236 (32 references), T2:543 (71 references), and 6:543 (22 references); for a review by Nelson G. Hanawalt, see 5:401 (5 references); for reviews by Ivan Norman Mensh, Joseph Newman, and William Schofield of the original edition, see 4:360 (3 references); for an excerpted review, see 3:297.

TEST REFERENCES

1. Freeman, M. J. The need for an organismic therapy in hospitalization. CLINICAL NEUROPSYCHOLOGY, 1979, 1(3), 39–43.

2. Hartlage, L. C., & Telzrow, C. F. The practice of clinical neuropsychology. CLINICAL NEUROPSYCHOLOGY, 1980, 2, 200–202.

3. Ponsford, J. L., Donnan, G. A., & Walsh, K. W. Disorders of memory in vertebrobasiler disease. JOURNAL OF CLINICAL NEUROPSYCHOLOGY, 1980, 2, 267–276.

4. Vincente, P. J. Neuropsychological assessment and management of a carbon monoxide intoxication patient with consequent sleep apnea: A longitudinal case report. CLINICAL NEUROPSYCHOLOGY, 1980, 2, 91–94.

5. Copeland, A. P., & Hammel, R. Subject variables in cognitive self-instructional training. COGNITIVE THERAPY AND RESEARCH, 1981, 5, 405–420.

6. Gregson, R. A. M., Free, M. L., & Abbott, M. W. Olfaction in Korsakoffs, alcoholics and normals. BRITISH JOURNAL OF CLINICAL PSYCHOLOGY, 1981, 20, 3–10.

7. Ruff, R. L., & Volpe, B. T. Environmental reduplication associated with right frontal and parietal lobal injury. JOURNAL OF NEUROLOGY, NEUROSURGERY, AND PSYCHIATRY, 1981, 44, 382–386.

8. Schaeffer, J., Andrysiak, T., & Ungerleider, J. T. Cognition and long-term use of ganja (cannabis). SCIENCE, 1981, 213, 465–466.

9. Varney, N. R. Letter recognition and visual form discrimination in aphasic alexia. NEUROPSYCHOLOGIA, 1981, 19, 795–800.

10. Watson, C. G., Gasser, B., Schaefer, A., Buranen, C., & Wold, J. Separation of brain-damaged from psychiatric patients with ability and personality measures. JOURNAL OF CLINICAL PSYCHOLOGY, 1981, 37, 347–353.

11. Zaidel, D. W., & Rausch, R. Effects of semantic organization on the recognition of pictures following temporal lobectomy. NEUROPSYCHOLOGIA, 1981, 19, 813–817.

12. Aaron, P. G., Baker, C., & Hickox, G. L. In search of the third dyslexia. NEUROPSYCHOLOGIA, 1982, 20, 203–208.

13. Arenberg, D. Estimates of age changes on the Benton Visual Retention Test. JOURNAL OF GERONTOLOGY, 1982, 37, 87–90.

14. Goldberg, T., & Benjamins, D. The possible existence of phonemic reading in the presence of Broca's aphasia: A case report. NEUROPSYCHOLOGIA, 1982, 20, 547–558.

15. Laursen, P., & Netterstrom, B. Psychological functions of urban busdrivers exposed to exhaust gases: A cross sectional study of urban busdrivers in Denmark. SCANDINAVIAN JOURNAL OF PSYCHOLOGY, 1982, 23, 283–290.

16. Marsh, G. G., & Hirsch, S. H. Effectiveness of two tests of visual retention. JOURNAL OF CLINICAL PSYCHOLOGY, 1982, 38, 115–119.

17. Penk, W. E., Charles, H. L., Patterson, E. T., Roberts, W. R., Dolan, M. P., & Brown, A. S. Chronological age differences in MMPI scores of male chronic alcoholics seeking treatment. JOURNAL OF CONSULTING AND CLINICAL PSYCHOLOGY, 1982, 50, 322–324.

18. Skinner, H. A., & Allen, B. A. Alcohol dependence syndrome: Measurement and validation. JOURNAL OF ABNORMAL PSYCHOLOGY, 1982, 91, 199–209.

19. Skinner, H. A., Glaser, F. B., & Annis, H. M. Crossing the threshold: Factors in self-identification as an alcoholic. BRITISH JOURNAL OF ADDICTION, 1982, 77, 51–64.

20. Brandt, J., Butters, N., Ryan, C., & Bayog, R. Cognitive loss and recovery in long-term alcohol abusers. ARCHIVES OF GENERAL PSYCHIATRY, 1983, 40, 435–442.

21. Eskenazi, B., & Diamond, S. P. Visual exploration of non-verbal material by dyslexic children. CORTEX, 1983, 19, 353–370.

22. Guy, J. D., Majorski, L. V., Wallace, C. J., & Guy, M. P. The incidence of minor physical anomalies in adult male schizophrenics. SCHIZOPHRENIA BULLETIN, 1983, 9, 571–582.

23. Josiassen, R. C., Curry, L. M., & Mancall, E. L. Development of neuropsychological deficits in Huntington's Disease. ARCHIVES OF NEUROLOGY, 1983, 40, 791–796.

24. Marecek, J., Shapiro, I. M., Burke, A., Katz, S. H., & Hediger, M. L. Low-level lead exposure in childhood influences neuropsychological performance. ARCHIVES OF ENVIRONMENTAL HEALTH, 1983, 38, 355–359.
25. Speedie, L. J., & Heilman, K. M. Anterograde memory deficits for visuospatial material after infarction of the right thalamus. ARCHIVES OF NEUROLOGY, 1983, 40, 183–186.
26. Boller, F., Passafiume, D., Keefe, N. C., Rogers, K., Morrow, L., & Kim, Y. Visuospatial impairment in Parkinson's Disease: Role of perceptual and motor factors. ARCHIVES OF NEUROLOGY, 1984, 41, 485–490.
27. Kljajic, I. The predictive utility of a significantly lower WAIS PIQ with psychiatric inpatients. JOURNAL OF CLINICAL PSYCHOLOGY, 1984, 40, 571–576.
28. Pears, E., Bowman, R., Kincey, J., & Gautam, R. Does prostacyclin prevent cognitive deficits after open heart surgery? PSYCHOLOGICAL MEDICINE, 1984, 14, 213–214.
29. Sanchez-Craig, M., Annis, H. M., Bornet, A. R., & MacDonald, K. R. Random assignment to abstinence and controlled drinking: Evaluation of a cognitive-behavioral program for problem drinkers. JOURNAL OF CONSULTING AND CLINICAL PSYCHOLOGY, 1984, 52, 390–403.
30. Storandt, M., Botwinick, J., Danziger, W. L., Berg, L., & Hughes, C. P. Psychometric differentiation of mild senile dementia of the Alzheimer type. ARCHIVES OF NEUROLOGY, 1984, 41, 497–499.

[141]

The Ber-Sil Spanish Test. Ages 5–12, 13–17; 1972–77; reliability and validity data for elementary level only; individual; 2 levels; picture book ('76, 103 pages); 1985 price data: $75 per combination elementary and secondary test kit including 50 tests of each level; $25 per book of picture plates; $9 per cassette tape; $14 per manual; Marjorie L. Beringer; Ber-Sil Co.*

a) ELEMENTARY LEVEL, 1976 REVISED EDITION. Ages 5–12; 5 scores: vocabulary, response to directions, writing, geometric figures, draw a boy or girl; 1 form ('76, 4 pages); manual ('76, 61 pages); $45 per elementary kit including 50 tests; $5 per 50 tests; $14 per translations for available languages; Cantonese, Mandarin, Korean, Persian, Ilokano, and Tagalog editions available; (30) minutes.

b) SECONDARY LEVEL, EXPERIMENTAL EDITION. Ages 13–17; 4 scores: vocabulary, dictation of sentences, draw a boy or a girl, mathematics; 1 form ('77, 8 pages); manual ('77, 49 pages); $45 per secondary kit including 50 tests; $8 per 50 tests; (45) minutes.

Review of The Ber-Sil Spanish Test by GIUSEPPE COSTANTINO, Research Associate, Hispanic Research Center, Fordham University, Bronx, NY, and Chief Psychologist, Lutheran Medical, Mental Health Center, Brooklyn, NY:

In light of recent litigation challenging the "differential" validity of standardized tests for diverse ethnic groups, several states, such as California and New Jersey, have mandated that children who are "limited-English-proficient" be tested for language dominance before they are administered a traditional intelligence test. The Ber-Sil Spanish Test, Elementary and Secondary Levels, has been developed to assess receptive language, ability to understand and follow directions, and visual motor coordination of elementary school children; and to assess vocabulary, grammar, punctuation and spelling, and basic math of children in grades 7 through 11. The test presents a systematic effort to assess Spanish-speaking school-age children in their dominant language, thus endeavoring to obviate the biases of traditional intelligence and educational tests. The manual, 1976 revised edition, for grades K through 6 includes limited validity and reliability data and norms for the vocabulary/receptive language, Section 1, only; whereas the manual for grades 7 through 11 is an Experimental Edition without psychometric data.

In developing this culture and language sensitive test, the author has patterned the instrument on the traditional Peabody Picture Vocabulary Test, the Goodenough-Harris Draw-a-Person Test, and cognitive motoric tasks. Recognizing the dual bias of the Peabody, (both unfamiliarity with the pictorial stimuli and the differential meaning of Spanish and English words symbolizing the same object), the author has created, with the assistance of a professional artist, objects, animals, and persons which more closely resemble the cultural environment of Spanish-speaking children in Southern California. The words representing the drawings are in Spanish. The drawings are professionally executed and attractive for children. The content appears to be familiar to Spanish-speaking children of diverse nationalities. The pictures are organized according to levels of difficulty of words; however, this is mistakenly referred to as evidence of the content validity of the test. The analysis seems to be adequate. Criterion-related validity has not been assessed because the author felt that there is not a valid standardized test to assess the Hispanic child. However, face validity of the test is favorably reported, based on critiques by 45 school psychologists. The reliability data reported are difficult to interpret, since only standard error of measurement and variance statistics are reported. Despite the fact that a test-retest study was conducted, the manual does not report the stability coefficient. Furthermore, no evidence is presented of internal consistency reliability.

Section II provides an informal assessment of perceptual motor functioning, such as sensory-motor integration, directionality, laterality, body-spatial organization, gross motor development, and auditory skills. These cognitive sensory motor tasks give a somewhat comprehensive view of the child's cognitive and psychomotor development. Since there are no norms for these developmental tasks, the assessment is only qualitative in nature.

Section III assesses handwriting, copying geometric forms, and drawing a person. Although the author provides general guidelines for scoring according to developmental stages, again there are no norms. Therefore, the assessment is qualitative in nature.

The directions for the administration of the three sections of the test are standardized, instructions are precise, and tape recorded instructions are available. The scoring and interpretation for the vocabulary section is objective and is referenced to broad categories of percentile equivalents. The interpretation is facilitated by the fact that vocabulary strengths and weaknesses can be assessed for both home and community/school environments. The profile presented is somewhat sketchy and needs to be organized along strength-weakness parameters in order to be diagnostically and instructionally useful.

The development of the Ber-Sil Spanish Test for the Secondary Level shows the same cultural sensitivity as the test for the Elementary Level. The criteria for the selection of the 100-word vocabulary are valid. Although validity and reliability data are not reported, helpful normative data are provided such as percent of correct responses, quartile equivalents for raw scores, and mean scores for ages 13 to 17. Interpretation would be facilitated, however, if percentile conversion were provided. The addition of Dictation provides a more comprehensive assessment of the pupil's ability with the receptive and written language, and the norms for spelling errors and punctuation seem to be adequate. The author states that the picture book is also used for the secondary level. But how the picture book is actually used seems to be unclear to the reader; illustrative examples should be presented.

The inclusion of math in this test is also important, and the problems seem to be differentiated according to increasing difficulty corresponding to grade levels. The scoring, however, gives only approximate grade level.

The secondary version of the Ber-Sil Spanish Test is designated as an experimental edition; thus the present critique is meant to provide guidelines for a later, standardized edition.

A minor comment, but still worth making, is that the author should use non-sexist language in the manual, especially at the elementary level.

SUMMARY. This language and culture sensitive test constitutes a systematic effort to assess language dominance in Hispanic children, thus endeavoring to obviate the biases of traditional intelligence and educational tests. However, a more comprehensive standardization is necessary if this test is to become an unbiased test for assessing intellectual-cognitive functioning in LEP children.

Review of The Ber-Sil Spanish Test by JACLYN B. SPITZER, Chief, Audiology and Speech Pathology Section, Veterans Administration Medical Center, West Haven, CT, and Assistant Clinical Professor of Surgery (Otolaryngology), Yale University, New Haven, CT:

The Ber-Sil Spanish Test was developed to meet an urgent need for evaluation procedures for the accurate identification and placement of Spanish-speaking elementary and high school age children in California. As a result of pressure imposed by a sizeable influx of Hispanic children of various national backgrounds and by consequent legislative changes, it became mandatory for the child to be evaluated to determine his dominant language, so that subsequent intelligence tests could be administered "in the primary home language in which the minor is most fluent and has the best speaking ability and capacity to understand" (California Education Code, Section 6902.6)

In the manual for the elementary school version, the authors indicate that the test was designed to be used as a pre-placement instrument for evaluating bilingual children in the California educational system, and to obtain information similar to that from the Peabody Picture Vocabulary Test (PPVT), but with lexical control superior to previously existing translations of the PPVT. In addition to the vocabulary assessment in Section I, the test is further composed of two sections aimed at evaluating comprehension and motor encoding ability to follow simple directions (Section II) and obtaining a quick sampling of visual-motor ability via writing samples and figure drawing (Section III). The major strength of the test is that it is well planned for administration by non-Spanish-speaking examiners by use of a coordinated pre-recorded stimulus test tape and picture book. There are, however, several very troublesome problems concerning validation data, reporting, and test construction which undermine the application of the Ber-Sil.

The attempted validation study is poorly reported, and not described in any other known published source. Throughout the manual, percentages of children are described as to their national origin or test performance, but the actual numbers involved are unclear; also unclear is whether there was a single validation study or several sub-studies. The protocol is not described, and valuable insights are omitted regarding the test environment, circumstances, and determinants for subject inclusion or exclusion (other than being a Spanish-speaker), if such existed. The data reported as the cross-validation of the Ber-Sil do not qualify as cross-validation of any sort, but are, rather, a simple listing of the percentages of children by birthplace included in the sample. Cross-validation of the test needs to be demonstrated by way of measured congruence with other, established criterion measures as well as the interrelation of performances of subjects of various origins. An item- (word-) analysis as a function of national background is needed to demonstrate the test's applicability to the heterogenous California resident populace. Correlation of the Ber-Sil with the WISC-R, Leiter, and Binet scales is alluded to in the manual, but not reported concretely for the subsample on whom it was feasible to evaluate with both the psychological and Ber-Sil batteries. In the absence of other forms of external validity indicators, the authors rely heavily on expert opinion and testimonials by test users, who do indeed attest to the practicality of the measure.

An important omission in the manual is an overt statement as to intended users of the test, although there appears to be covert assumption that "counselors" or school psychologists will be the evaluators. The latter point should be clarified since unqualified examiners may misuse the tool, especially for sections where trained observational skills (re: motor coordination, Section II) or interpretive skills (re: figure drawing, Section III) are required.

The elementary-level manual gives several erroneous impressions regarding the application of the Ber-Sil. It is suggested that the measure may serve as a screening for auditory "acuity" (i.e., as a hearing screening). It is well established that any hearing screening procedure using speech stimuli has an unacceptable false-negative rate, due to the great likelihood of children with mild hearing loss or high frequency hearing loss being able to process sufficient speech information to pass. Therefore, in an inner city and/or Hispanic sample shown repeatedly to have a high prevalence of conductive (middle ear) hearing disorders, use of speech-based hearing screening is especially dangerous. Using the Ber-Sil, as suggested, to screen for auditory figure-ground disorders is also problematic, since the test environment in the school may be sufficiently noisy to cause children with conductive or high frequency hearing loss to perform poorly. Among the testimonials presented in the manual, there is comment that "Playground noises do not seem to interfere with administration" without further comment regarding required test environment by the authors; to attribute failure on the Ber-Sil to possible auditory figure-ground dysfunction may imply subsequent misevaluation or misclassification, especially where noise background cannot be adequately controlled.

Positive aspects of the test's elementary version must be emphasized. The Ber-Sil does provide a stimulus set that can be administered by someone with no knowledge of Spanish. The picture book is well illustrated and the speaker on the test tape provides well articulated speech and well controlled speech (in terms of vocal effort and rate). The tape does have audible background sound, indicating non-professional recording techniques, but the overall noise level is acceptable for the intended use. A table of recommended follow-up evaluation procedures, based on Ber-Sil findings, is provided. The elementary version would be much strengthened by additional validation study, adequate cross-correlational examination, and reorganization of the manual.

Regarding the secondary version, the authors make it quite clear that it is an experimental version and that further evaluation of the test is needed. The four sections are intended to screen receptive vocabulary (I), written language skill including specific surface structure characteristics (II), figure drawing with its many possible ramifications (III), and mathematical level (IV) for placement purposes.

In attempting to use the same set of illustrations for Section I as for the elementary version, while also increasing the level of sophistication of the vocabulary chosen, several problems occur. Some of the illustrations fall short of the stimulus meaning, there are instances of poor choice of foils, and some very fine visual discriminations are required. An item-error analysis will be vital for this Section. The authors suggest using the PPVT for comparison purposes to determine language dominance; hence, correlational data are also needed.

Section II requires the subject to write dictated sentences of length varying from 4 to 13 words, with consequent varying load on auditory memory. The latter sentences are to be graded for grammatical, spelling, and punctuation errors with a straightforward point-per-error grading system suggested. The authors might consider a more weighted grading approach, giving greater import to certain types of errors over others. Section III requires figure drawing; the comments made for the elementary version are also pertinent for the secondary.

The secondary-level test tape contains motor noise from the recorder used, and the authors should consider re-recording at this early stage in test development.

The Ber-Sil is available in translation to several other languages. The present reviewer cannot comment on the appropriateness of the lexicon for the widely dispersed origins and cultures for which translations have been made. It must be questioned whether the initial principle in test construction (using "scenes and experiences a Southern California Spanish-speaking child might encounter") permits the materials to be equally applicable to children from China, Iran, Korea, and the Phillipines.

In summary, the Ber-Sil Spanish Test has, in both its elementary and secondary versions, design flaws which are remediable through further experimental investigation. The test does provide a means for the non-Spanish speaker to screen receptive vocabulary, and, in a holistic manner, other aspects of receptive language, motor skills, and mathematical level (secondary version only). In its present form, the Ber-Sil must be used with great caution, and its relationship to other measures and to the outcome of subsequent, diagnostic evaluation are entirely unknown.

[142]

Bessell Measurement of Emotional Maturity Scales. Ages 5–11; 1978; MEM; ratings by teachers; 63

measures of behavioral functioning in 4 component areas: awareness traits, relating traits, competence traits, integrity traits; individual; 2 forms: short (2 pages, 70 items), full scale (4 pages, 237 items); teacher's manual (51 pages); prescriptive booklet (43 pages); separate answer sheets must be used; 1985 price data: $.55 per full scale booklet; $5.95 per teacher's manual; $24.50 per complete maturity kit; scoring service, $1.89 or less per test (scoring must be done by publisher); (8–15) minutes for short form, (20–45) minutes for full scale; Harold Bessell; Psych/Graphic Publishers.*

Review of Bessell Measurement of Emotional Maturity Scales by LINDA WHITE HAWTHORNE, Associate Professor of Special Education, Georgia State University, Atlanta, GA:

The Bessell Measurement of Emotional Maturity Scales (MEM) is a rating scale whose purpose is to identify deficient areas of emotional development in children so that appropriate interventions can be provided. The scale is composed of 237 items, with 189 "basic" items and 48 items "which are repeated among the four component subscales." Items were selected on the basis of Bessell's own theory of personality development, which equates emotional immaturity with neurotic functioning and emotional maturity with healthy functioning. The items are grouped into traits, with each trait being composed of 3 to 40 items. Traits are stated as descriptive phrases (e.g., "Being responsible," and "Becoming more likable"). The traits are further grouped into four component areas: Awareness, Competence, Relating, and Integrity. There is a short form of the test with 70 items grouped in the same four component areas. Since no data are presented relative to the merits of this short form nor its relationship to the standard form, it will not be evaluated further. At this point, its credibility has not been established.

To use the MEM, the teacher rates the students on the 237 items. According to the manual, this can be done in 30 to 35 minutes. Each item is rated using a 4-point scale, "rarely," "sometimes," "often," and, "very often." These descriptors are operationalized for the rater. Raters are instructed to "not compare the child as you rate him or her with other children of the same age. Rate only on the basis of how often the behavior appears." This does not seem reasonable given the nature of many of the items. For example, consider the item "Uses a rich vocabulary to describe feelings." How can "richness" of vocabulary be taken into account if there is not basis for comparison? The test author often refers to the items as behavioral descriptions, but many of them are very subjective and not stated in behavioral terms. A few examples include, "Is genuine," "Is sincere," and "Enjoys people more than material things."

Answer sheets must be mailed in for computerized scoring. The manual includes samples of the results that are returned. Four options are available, two for individual children and two for groups. One of the individual reports includes a Rater Internal Consistency Score that tells how many of the 48 repeated items were rated in the same category, high or low. The manual says that the score indicates the "degree of confidence that may be held in the rating." Unfortunately, the score is of little help since the test user is not provided with assistance in interpreting it. He is merely given a ratio such as 39/48 indicating how many of the 48 items were rated in the same way.

The construction of the scale, its norms, reliability, and validity all have technical problems. Items were selected on the basis of the professional judgment of the author and teachers, and they lack adequate empirical support.

The MEM was standardized on children ages 5 to 11 who lived in San Diego, California. The norm group contained 494 males and 522 females. According to the manual, the subjects reflect the ethnic distribution of the 1970 U.S. Census for three groups: Caucasians, Blacks, and Hispanics. Approximately one half of the subjects were from the lower socioeconomic class and the rest from the middle class. Although the sample is large, it cannot be assumed to represent the U.S. population in terms of geographic location, socioeconomic level, nor even race. Obviously, a more representative sample is desirable. Also, data to support combined norms for the various groups should be presented.

Two studies of inter-rater reliability and one study of intra-rater reliability are presented in the manual. All three are inadequately reported and flawed with technical problems. For these studies the 4-point scale was collapsed into a 2-point scale. Ratings were considered to be either high (often or very often) or low (rarely or never). For the two inter-rater studies, two team teachers rated 45 and 30 children from combined 4th, 5th, and 6th grades. The data reported are percentage of agreement (high/high or low/low) of ratings for subjects and for items. For individual subjects in the two studies, the mean percentages of agreement across all items were 78 and 81. For individual items, the mean percentages of agreement were 77 and 80. For the intra-rater study, 28 kindergarten children were rated 6 weeks apart by the same teacher. Again, the high/low ratings were used. Mean percentage of agreement was 95 for both subjects and items. The most salient problems with these studies were found in all three. The teachers used as raters were not adequately described. Further, all of the reliability data are based upon the ratings of only three teachers and small numbers of subjects. It is possible to obtain very biased data from such small samples. The agreement data are probably inflated since the 4-point scale was collapsed into a 2-point one, lessening the chance for disagreement. All of the data presented are for items, yet programming from the MEM is based on ratings of traits. Reliability data should have been presented for traits, and the data expressed as a relative excess or deficit over the amount of agreement expected by chance.

Validation of the MEM is also poor. Validity data are needed to substantiate the author's claims for the use of the instrument, viz., "rating periodically and maintaining the Cummulative Records assures that every important developmental trait can be reviewed and overall good development can be assured." It is doubtful that such grandiose claims could ever be validated; however, the data provided are, at best, a minimal attempt at validation. Only one type of validity data is presented, and that relates to the developmental nature of the traits. Data from the normative group are presented to show that for 4 of the 63 traits raw score means tend to increase with age. There are no data to indicate if items cluster into traits or if traits cluster into the four component areas in which they have been placed. In fact, the 48 repeated items often appear in more than one component area. No criterion-related data are provided, so it is not known how scores on the MEM relate to other developmental scales or measures of adjustment. In summary, no form of validity has been adequately established for the MEM.

Beyond the technical problems with the selection of items, norming of the instrument, reliability, and validity of the scale, I have several other concerns. Bessell views immaturity as neurosis, not a popular position. Nevertheless, given his use of the term with the scale, this raises the possibility of a first-year teacher with a bachelors degree in elementary education and minimal, if any, training in psychology being in the position of asserting that a student is neurotic based upon his or her ratings. A further concern is that normal behavior is equated with average behavior. If a student scores in the lower quartile on a trait, that trait (e.g., "Waiting willingly") may be targeted for intervention. Theoretically, one-fourth of all children rated on an item may be targeted for intervention. Further, it is quite likely that some traits may have one adaptive or developmental value at one age and quite a different one at another age (i.e., at one age warrant intervention, and at another, not). This is not taken into account with the scale. Because of the numerous problems inherent in the instrument, it cannot be recommended for general use.

Review of Bessell Measurement of Emotional Maturity Scales by JUNE M. TUMA, Professor of Psychology, Louisiana State University, Baton Rouge, LA:

The Bessell Measurement of Emotional Maturity Scales (MEM) is a behavioral rating scale designed to provide a description of the emotional development of children between the ages of 5 and 11. The logic for the development of the scale is that a good self-concept and need gratification facilitate learning. Components measured by the scale are derived from theories of Freud, Adler, Reich, Robert W. White, Horney (Awareness, Relating, Competence) and Horney and Cleckley (Integrity).

FORMAT. The scale includes 237 items (Full Scale; or 70 items on the Short Form) to be rated by the child's teacher. The scoring service provides within 2 weeks a Report Profile which lists areas of 63 traits needing attention and an Individual Prescriptive summary which gives prescriptions for intervention. Printouts of ratings of children within the same class who have the same needs (the lowest 25%) permit grouping of children with similar needs, and a School Summary (giving ratings of all children evaluated at the school) is also available. Cumulative Record Sheets (6-year charting forms) are also included in the test packets.

Instructions in the Teachers Manual are presented in language teachers can understand. Teachers are instructed on the method of determining an individual child's deficient areas from the printouts. The Prescriptive Booklet describes 11 methods the teachers can use to promote development of emotional maturity in specific traits identified by the rating scale (e.g., giving one-to-one time; challenging or criticizing always in the context of supportive understanding, giving advice, etc.). The author recommends rerating 3 times per year to track the child's progress and to maintain Cumulative Records yearly.

The author gives several cautions in using the scale. He recommends waiting 2 months into the school year before attempting the ratings to permit sufficient familiarity with the child. Because of the time for evaluation, he also recommends that no more than 5 full scale ratings or 12 short form ratings should be attempted at one sitting. He also encourages teachers to use classroom time rather than free time to make ratings.

ITEM SELECTION. Bessell developed a list of 1,350 behavioral descriptions covering what he believed to be the full spectrum of emotional maturation. From this original list, items that did not differentiate between the more and less mature child or that were semantically confusing were eliminated. Each item was then rated by 55 classroom teachers on its discriminatory power, which further reduced the item pool to 642 items. Criterion for retention of an item was being evaluated two-thirds of the time or better as defining a difference between the more and the less emotionally mature child. This pool was further reduced by removing those items which measured essentially the same behavior. Remaining were the final 189 basic items describing behavior in the four major components of concern.

Unlike most teacher rating scales, the items are couched in a positive direction (e.g., listens attentively, accepts own limitations graciously, uses self-control, etc.). Thus, high scores indicate greater emotional maturity and vice versa.

The Full Scale (237) items includes 48 repeated items which are dispersed among the four component subscales to provide a Rater Internal Consistency. This score is the ratio of same-scored items to the total number of repeated items.

A four-place scale of "rarely," "sometimes," "often," and "very often" was chosen. However, the computer printouts only give results on a 2-point scale, "high" and "low," thus reducing the sensitivity of the results. Although the manual states that numerical scores were assigned to the various frequency ratings, no specifics are provided.

STANDARDIZATION. The 189 items were standardized by age and sex. Normal children in grades kindergarten through six ($N=1,520$) from San Diego County were rated by 55 teachers. To achieve ethnic composition similar to the 1970 U.S. Census the final normative group consisted of 1,016 children.

Means and percentile distributions were calculated for each test item separately for each sex at each age, after ethnic balancing. The number of items representing each trait varies between 3 and 40, according to the author. However, no information is given in the manual concerning which items make up the 63 traits. It does, however, give information about the traits that make up the components.

VALIDITY. The author presents as evidence of validity (1) the increase in raw score means on the four components with age, (2) teachers' estimates of the items' power to discriminate between mature and immature behavior (accomplished on the normative sample), and (3) reasonably high agreement between team teachers. No studies are reported on criterion groups to determine if the scale can discriminate between independently categorized mature and immature children.

OBJECTIVITY. Two studies are reported in the manual. Two team teachers independently rated 45 and 30 children, respectively, from two combined 4th-, 5th-, and 6th-grade classes. The percentage of agreement between the two raters separating children into high and low maturity children for the two groups was 78% (ranging from 47%–99%) and 81% (ranging from 56%–99%). Percentage of agreement between the two ratings of items for the two groups was 77% (ranging from 43%–96%) and 80% (ranging from 52%–98%).

RELIABILITY. One study reports that the same teacher rated 28 kindergarten children 6 weeks apart with a percentage of agreement on the children of 75%–100% ($M=95\%$). Percentage of agreement on the 189 items was 64%–100% ($M=95\%$). No other age groups were studied.

CRITIQUE. The MEM is a rationally constructed, theory-oriented rating scale which yields four components of emotional maturity and 63 traits. Scale construction methodology appears weak in that no criterion groups were used to determine the validity of the items, traits or components, nor is there any description given of how the items were determined to contribute to each trait and component. If, as the author states in the manual, factor analytic studies are accomplished, perhaps more confidence can be placed in the construction of the test. At the present time, however, the structure of the test is suspect.

Validity data presented by the manual are also weak, consisting mainly of relationships between increasing scores with age and stability of scoring across items, children, and between raters. All ages are not included in these studies, sex differences are not reported, and criterion groups were not used. However, preliminary reliability data appear promising and good normative data are given which permit comparison of ratings on the items by a given child of a particular age. The comparisons are limited by the fact that the normative children were drawn from one geographical area.

Further utility of the ratings is restricted by grouping the 4-point scale into a 2-point scale of either high or low. There are no cutoff scores indicated to permit evaluation of the scores. While the preventive focus of tying the scale to the prescriptive booklet is encouraging, no rationale is presented in the instructions and the methods are rather vague and general. No outcome studies are reported and the author seems to ask that his recommendations for intervention be taken on faith.

The advantages of the scale are that the items are couched in positive language and thereby encourage teachers to look for positive rather than negative features of a particular child's behavior. Further, the prescriptive methods recommended are humanistic and stress the development of a child's coping abilities rather than focusing on the elimination of undesirable behaviors (as with most scales and intervention strategies). Overall, the scale has to be regarded as being in an infant stage of development. The full potential of the approach is probably not at this time obvious because of either inadequately reported or incompletely developed scales, inadequate demonstration of validity of the scale, and incomplete development of the prescriptive methods. Further work on the scale and methods of remediation seem indicated before the full usefulness of this approach can be evaluated.

[143]

Bessemer Screening Test. Ages 8–14; 1981; BST; identifies "children who are at risk for learning problems"; 7 scores: name writing, human figure drawing, word knowledge, design copying, math, total, emotional indicators; 1 form; record booklet (4 pages); manual (27 pages); scoring sheet (2 pages); 1984 price data: $12 per complete test; $4.75 per 15 student booklets; $4.75 per 30 scoring sheets; $3 per manual; 10(15) minutes; Evelyn V. Jones and Gary L. Sapp; Stoelting Co.*

[144]

Bieger Test of Visual Discrimination and Visual Discrimination of Words Training Program. Nonreaders and poor readers in grades K–2; 1982; 7 subtests covering 3 areas: larger and lesser contrasts in letters and words, orientation reversal in letters and words, sequence reversal in words; mastery objectives for each subtest; Form A, B, (8 pages); instruction manual (38 pages); workbook (20 pages); 1983 price data: $19 per complete set including 15 tests of each form; $9 per 15 tests of each form; $6 per workbook; $5 per manual; (30–40) minutes; Elaine Bieger; Stoelting Co.*

TEST REFERENCES

1. Bieger, E. Effects of two different training programs on visual discrimination of nonreaders. PERCEPTUAL AND MOTOR SKILLS, 1983, 56, 1009–1010.

Review of Bieger Test of Visual Discrimination and Visual Discrimination of Words Training Program by LINNEA C. EHRI, Professor of Education, University of California, Davis, CA:

The Bieger Test consists of three letter discrimination subtests and four word discrimination subtests plus a visual discrimination training program. Test items require students to select which of four letters or words in a row matches the sample on the left. The purpose of the test is to distinguish and remediate poor readers having visual discrimination difficulties. I have several concerns about this test. Unless future research reveals that these are groundless, the value of the test remains doubtful.

Evidence regarding the test's reliability consists of showing that most students' scores did not change much upon retesting. However, this is not the information consumers need to know. Percentages in the high-consistency category (0–5% change) are misleading because they include students with perfect or near perfect scores on the test. Since this is a domain-referenced test, close-to-perfect performance is expected except in those students having visual discrimination problems. What the manual should report is the reliability of the test in classifying readers as having visual discrimination difficulties, specifically, the extent to which readers diagnosed as having difficulties according to scores on one form of the test are diagnosed similarly on the other form or upon retesting with the same form.

Evidence indicating the value of visual discrimination training for remediating reading difficulties is not provided in the manual. What is provided is an experimental study showing that students completing Bieger's training program outperformed a control group on Bieger's visual discrimination test, which is not a reading but a visual matching task. Although results of the study indicated that the training program was more effective than a control program, it is not clear that the reason was because it improved subjects' ability to perceive word parts. Rather the advantage may have resulted from improved test-taking skill. Students given Bieger's training program practiced circling the correct match for targets in a row of distractors and in addition practiced crossing out the incorrect items. In contrast, students in the control group merely practiced circling the correct match. It may be that having to perform both responses taught Bieger-trained subjects to look at ALL the distractors in a row before selecting their answer. According to my teacher informants, failure to consider all the alternatives is a common source of error among young children taking multiple choice tasks such as this one. Until evidence is presented showing that this training program actually remediates reading difficulties, its demonstrated effectiveness remains narrow and limited.

My main objection to the Bieger tests is that it is derived from an incorrect view of reading disability. Vellutino (1980) reviews much research indicating that strictly visual perceptual processes do not account for poor readers' difficulties in learning to read. Rather poor readers' lack of knowledge of the letter-sound coding system is at the core of their difficulties. Our research also supports this (Ehri & Wilce, 1979, 1983, in press). The reversal and orientation errors exhibited by poor readers in processing printed words arise not from visual processing deficits but rather from an inability to conduct accurate, left-to-right analyses of spellings as maps for pronunciations. Causes of deficient analyses include inadequate knowledge of letter shapes and their sounds (hence b's, d's and p's are confused), and inability to segment pronunciations into a sequence of sounds (hence "grit" and "girt" are confused). Once a reader learns how print tracks speech, such perceptual errors disappear. However, Bieger's training program does not teach this skill.

The purpose of a test such as Bieger's should be to identify readers who confuse visually similar letters and word spellings when they READ them, not when they simply look at them to find visual matches. A completely adequate letter test would be one that assesses whether readers know that similarly shaped letters have separate identities and what these identities are. A completely adequate word test might assess students' skill in identifying which of several visually similar spellings is the word being pronounced by a tester. This sort of task would be more useful for identifying students whose reading is affected by a failure to process letters and letter sequences accurately. Because Bieger's test items have been carefully constructed to detect visual confusions, the test could be modified to assess reading difficulties arising from visual sources. This possibility needs investigating.

In sum, the Bieger test fails to supply information about the reliability of the test in distinguishing readers that have visual discrimination difficulties. Evidence regarding the effectiveness of the training program for remediating the READING difficulties of poor readers is not provided. The test focuses only on the ability to match letter stimuli to a sample. A better testing and training program would be one that assesses and treats visual discrimination difficulties involved in reading print.

REVIEWER'S REFERENCES

Ehri, L. C., & Wilce, L. S. The mnemonic value of orthography among beginning readers. JOURNAL OF EDUCATIONAL PSYCHOLOGY, 1979, 71, 26–40.

Vellutino, F. R. DYSLEXIA: THEORY AND RESEARCH. Cambridge, MA: The MIT Press, 1980.

Ehri, L. C., & Wilce, L. S. Development of word identification speed in skilled and less skilled beginning readers. JOURNAL OF EDUCATIONAL PSYCHOLOGY, 1983, 75, 3–18.

Ehri, L. C., & Wilce, L. S. MOVEMENT INTO READING: IS THE FIRST STAGE OF PRINTED WORD LEARNING VISUAL OR PHONETIC? Paper presented at the National Reading Conference, Austin, TX, December, 1983.

Review of Bieger Test of Visual Discrimination and Visual Discrimination of Words Training Program by SUSAN P. HOMAN, *Assistant Professor of Reading Education, University of South Florida, Tampa, FL:*

The Bieger Test of Visual Discrimination attempts to identify the nature of a non-reader's or a poor reader's visual discrimination problem. As often happens when dealing with a hypothetical construct, much of the basis for both the Bieger Test of Visual Discrimination, and the Discrimination of Words Training Program associated with it, are founded on untested theory.

The author hypothesizes that a child must be able to perceptually and visually discriminate letters and words to read. In addition, she theorizes that visual discrimination problems can be divided into three areas: (l) contrast of features of letters, (2) orientation reversal in letters (e.g., b-d confusion), and (3) sequence reversal in words (e.g., was-saw confusion).

The Bieger Test of Visual Discrimination is a criterion-referenced test made up of two forms with seven subtests each. Test I consists of 26 items measuring visual discrimination of letters with large contrasts. Test II has 17 items and measures visual discriminations of letters with lesser contrasts. Test III has 10 items and measures visual discrimination of almost identical letters. Test IV has 13 items and measures visual discriminations of words with large contrasts. Test V, with 12 items, measures visual discrimination of words with lesser contrasts. Test VI, with 11 items, measures visual discrimination of words with orientation transformations. Test VII, with 23 items, measures visual discrimination of word sequencing.

The mastery levels and adequate performance levels have apparently been arbitrarily set for each subtest. The directions and scoring procedures are clear.

If, in fact, the hierarchy of visual discrimination skills hypothesized for all non-readers and poor readers with visual discrimination problems exists, then the Bieger Test of Visual Discrimination may help identify where visual discrimination instruction and practice should begin. The Discrimination of Words Training Program, as stated in the manual, should help children with visual discrimination problems. After training, experience, and familiarity, a child will demonstrate improvement on visual discrimination skills.

This author is almost a believer. It is unfortunate that both the field test studies on the Bieger Test of Visual Discrimination and the two experiments using the Discrimination of Words Training Program involved such small sample sizes.

Limited information is given concerning the children involved in the studies, only that they were "diagnosed as needing reading remediation." Since no other information is given concerning the sample, it is not possible to know if any total non-readers participated in the field tests. Since the test is specifically aimed at non-readers and poor readers, some non-readers should have been included. The author reports changing items on both test forms based on the item analysis of the field test data; however, no mention is made of field testing the revised items.

Validity information is totally theoretical with no attempt to validate statistically the construct involved. Parallel form and test-retest reliability studies were conducted; however, again very small sample sizes were used. The number of students taking the two tests ranged from 23 to 29. No information was given concerning the subjects involved in the parallel form or test-retest reliability studies. Results clearly support subtests I, II, and IV as being reliable in terms of both parallel forms and test-retest reliability; subtests III and VII appear less stable; for subtests V and VI, in some instances, 25% to 32% of the subjects' scores differed on test-retest or parallel form reliability by as much as 16% to 20%.

Two experimental studies involving the Discrimination of Words Training Program are reported. The first study had only 13 children in each treatment group. The second study had only 10 children in each group. Individual growth was measured by pre- and posttesting using the Bieger Visual Discrimination Test. This leads me to question whether the Discrimination of Words Training Program helps visual discrimination problems, or simply improves scores on the Bieger Visual Discrimination Test.

In summary, the Bieger Test of Visual Discrimination may, indeed, be a valid way to determine the nature of visual discrimination problems. However, the background provided in the test manual is weak. While I believe in and support the theoretical bases that led Dr. Bieger to develop this test, additional reliability and validity information is needed to support its use as a diagnostic instrument. Additional research is also needed on the Discrimination of Words Training Program to determine its effectiveness in remediating visual discrimination problems, and more importantly, its effect on student reading ability.

[145]

Biemiller Test of Reading Processes. Grades 2–6; 1981; BTORP; 5 scores: letters, story #1, word list #1, story #2, word list #2; individual; 1 form (6 pages); manual (18 pages); test administration booklet (6 pages); record sheet (1 page); stop watch necessary for administration; 1982 price data: $2.10 per test booklet; $3.25 per 35 record sheets; $1.80 per test administration booklet; $3.50 per manual; $10.35 per examiner's kit including 35 record sheets; administration time not reported; Andrew Biemiller; Guidance Centre, University of Toronto [Canada].*

Review of Biemiller Test of Reading Processes by MAURINE A. FRY, Professor of Educational Psychology, Arizona State University, Tempe, AZ:

The Biemiller Test of Reading Processes (BTORP) is intended to quickly identify individual differences in three kinds of reading processes: (*a*) the ability to identify letters quickly; (*b*) the ability to identify words quickly; and (*c*) the ability to use context to facilitate word identification.

The test is intended for use with children from grades 2 through 6 and is based on the premise that oral reading speed, particularly the time required to read letters, words, and text, can provide information about the status and probable progress of children in learning to read.

Test materials are spiral-bound in a 6 x 9-inch folder and include the following: (*a*) a passage of 50 typewritten, lower-case letters, (*b*) a primer-level text passage, (*c*) a list of 50 typewritten words drawn from primer-level vocabulary, (*d*) a middle-elementary level text passage, and (*e*) a middle-elementary level list of 50 words. In addition to these materials, the examiner will need a stopwatch.

Directions for the test are simple and easy to follow. The problems of accurately recording reading time, however, indicate the examiner would need some training and experience. It is important to keep the child reading. For example, the author states, "If the child pauses over a word or rereads a line, stop the stopwatch until the child is reading words she/he has not read before." In addition, "If there are more than three delay-type errors (as opposed to misreadings without stopping), the data will be invalid, and testing should be stopped." This is a lot for a novice to remember when seconds count.

If the timing is accurate, scoring should present no problem. Scoring is explained in the manual and is clearly presented on the front of the Individual Record Form.

Interpretation of the scoring in the manual is by percentile (90th, 75th, 50th, 25th, and 10th) for each grade group 2 through 6, for each story, each word list, the letters, Word List 1 minus letters, and Word List 2 minus letters. Interpretive statements seem reasonable, e.g., for story times, "children at or above the 50th percentile for their age group are doing reasonably well and should give little cause for concern."

The primary diagnostic information, according to the author, comes from the difference between word and letter times. "Children whose difference between word and letter times is below the 50th percentile for their age group are clearly making less use of orthographic structure to facilitate their reading than their more able peers." The author is rightfully cautious in terms of how children learn to use orthographic structure. He only suggests that reading practice must be a necessary, if not sufficient, condition for remediation and suggests amounts of practice that might be appropriate for two levels of performance. For children who read text slowly when the difference between word and letter times is small, general oral language development is recommended.

Appendix A of the manual describes the standardization sample, which was composed entirely of Canadian children. Appropriate descriptive information for the children and their performance is provided. Other than the stability of letter time from grades 2 to grade 3, the correlations of the time measures over a 1-year period are quite high (.66 to .89).

More information regarding the BTORP will undoubtedly become available as it is used. At the moment, it seems a reasonable supplement, both in terms of time and expense, to the typical reading achievement battery. The BTORP provides unique, but related, and probably helpful information in planning reading instruction for an elementary child.

Review of Biemiller Test of Reading Processes by RONALD E. REEVE, Associate Professor of

Education, University of Virginia, Charlottesville, VA:

This test assesses speed of naming letters, words in isolation, and words in text. Materials consist of one page of 50 typewritten, lower-case letters; two pages of 50 typewritten words (one page of "primer" level vocabulary, the other at "middle-elementary" level); and two pages of short text passages (one page at primer level and the other at middle-elementary level). A stopwatch is needed since precise times for completing the five tasks are the only scores utilized.

Serious problems exist with practically every aspect of this test, beginning with the theoretical and practical rationale. The stated rationale for the test is that, "the time required to read passages of letters, words, and text...can provide a substantial amount of information about the status and probable progress of children learning to read." A major question must be raised about the extent to which letter naming, word calling, and oral reading are "reading processes."

The first task, letter naming, is not required to read words—it is not a reading skill. The author provides data showing moderate correlations between speed of letter naming and reading scores on the Gray Oral Reading and Metropolitan Achievement Tests, and he states that letter reading time is a useful diagnostic measure. However, he concedes that no type of practice can speed up letter reading. Then in what way is it diagnostically useful?

If one accepts the definition of reading as the extraction of meaning from print, the second task (called "word reading") is, at best, a quasi-reading skill. Reading requires recognizing words in semantic and syntactic context, not at random. The Biemiller Test provides no way of analyzing what phonic or structural cues are used to decode words not recognized on sight. Therefore its diagnostic significance is nil. Since there is no assessment of whether the subject knows a word's meaning, this task is an act of word recognition or word calling, not of reading.

The third type of task, oral "reading" of short passages, also must be questioned. There is no assessment of comprehension; once again one cannot determine if the subject has extracted any meaning from the passage. This, then, may be only a word calling task for some children. Also, no analysis of errors is performed. Apparently, it is assumed that an error is an error. This assumption is inconsistent with miscue analysis approaches which have been standard practice for years in the assessment of oral reading.

Given the shortcomings of the content and construct validity of this test, it may be superfluous to evaluate technical adequacy. In the interest of comprehensiveness, however, it should be noted that the test is technically lacking as well. Norms are based on 340 children from 17 schools in a very restricted geographic area of Canada. Schools reportedly were selected to represent a range of socioeconomic areas, but no supportive evidence is provided. The sample was restricted to Canadian-born children, but it included "many" children who spoke other languages than English at home. Thus the representativeness of the sample cannot be ascertained.

Virtually no reliability data are presented, so one cannot know how confident to be of the obtained scores. The one assessment of stability reported was a test-retest study with a one year interval. Not surprisingly, the "reading time" measures showed varying degrees of stability across that interval, ranging from .57 to .89.

Two concurrent validity studies are reported in the manual. One study found correlations ranging from –.48 to –.79 between reading time measures and Gray Oral Reading scores. The other study related the reading time measures of the Biemiller Test to the reading comprehension score of the Metropolitan Achievement Test. The resulting correlations ranged from –.01 to –.77.

Test materials are attractive, and instructions to the child are simple. However, the administration may be tricky. Since small differences in time result in very different interpretations, an accurate assessment of speed is important. The examiner is told to "keep the child reading" by telling the child the present word and the next word if pauses occur, and by not counting the time elapsed if the child rereads a line. The occurrence of more than three delay type responses or the skipping of more than 10 words are said to invalidate the results. Use of these procedures appears to require considerable examiner judgment, which of course would add to the variability in obtained scores.

In summary, the Biemiller Test of Reading Processes is inadequate to marginally adequate from a technical point of view. Its critical shortcoming lies in its lack of content validity. The test does not assess reading at all, but rather measures speed of performing two aspects of word recognition (of isolated and connected words) and one reading-like behavior (letter naming). No assessment of comprehension is done, and no qualitative evaluation of word recognition (e.g., miscue analysis) is performed. What are the teaching implications? The author admits that speed cannot be altered, so he suggests (without a rationale) simply increasing the amount of daily reading for low scoring children. The same recommendation could be made for any child. What useful diagnostic-prescriptive information do you have after giving the test that you did not have before?

[146]

Bilingual Oral Language Test. Grades 7–12; 1976–78; BOLT; designed to measure oral language skills in English or Spanish; verbal responses scored as correct or incorrect by comparing them to suggested scoring standards, and total correct is translated to one of five proficiency levels in English or Spanish: Level I (non-English/non-Spanish speaking), Level I-S (supplement to Level I), Level II (very limited English/very limited Spanish speaking), Level III (limited English/limited Spanish speaking), Level IV (English/Spanish speaking); individual; 2 forms varying in content labeled English ('75, 5 pages), Spanish ('76, 5 pages); manuals, English version ('76, 15 pages), Spanish version ('77, 15 pages); technical reports, English version ('77, 44 pages), Spanish version ('78, 44 pages); answer sheets, English ('77, 4 pages), Spanish ('77, 4 pages); 1983 price data: $25 per examiner's kit in either English or Spanish including 30 answer sheets, manual, picture booklet, class record chart, and summary sheet; $.50 per answer sheet in either language; $9 per picture booklet in either language; $.50 per class record chart; $.50 per summary sheet; $9 per manual in either language; Sam Cohen, Roberto Cruz, and Raul Bravo; Bilingual Media Productions (BMP), Inc.*

Review of Bilingual Oral Language Test by CHARLES STANSFIELD, Associate Director/Language Programs, Educational Testing Service, Princeton, NJ:

The Bilingual Oral Language Test (BOLT) is an oral language proficiency and dominance test instrument designed for use with Hispanic children up through the secondary school level.

Section I of the BOLT asks for demographic data on the student. It consists of only four questions separately requesting name, grade level, date of birth (e.g., When were you born?), and language spoken in the home. If the student answers three or more of these questions correctly, the examiner goes on to Section II. If not, testing is discontinued and the student is classified at level I.

Section II consists of items numbered consecutively from 1–20, representing proficiency levels II, III, and IV. The examiner begins with proficiency level III which includes items 6 through 13. If the student answers six of the eight items correctly, the examiner proceeds to items 14 through 20 which pertain to level IV of proficiency. If the student answers less than six of the level III questions correctly, items 1 through 5 of section II are administered. These items make up level II of proficiency. If the student correctly answers at least four of these questions, he/she is placed at proficiency level II. If the student misses more than one, he/she is classified at level I. If a plausible answer is given in another language to six or more of the first 13 questions in Section II, the student is classified at level I-S. Level I-S is a "Supplement" to level I. It permits identification of students who can understand a second language, but do not speak it. In order to place at level IV, the student must correctly answer six of the eight level III questions and six of the seven level IV questions. As is apparent, the classification system is somewhat complex. It could be simplified for teachers by use of a flow chart.

Questions in Section II are based on three 8 1/2 x 11 inch drawings, representing an urban setting, a home-family setting, and a neighborhood. These settings appropriately correspond to common sociolinguistic domains of language usage. Noticeably absent is a picture of a classroom setting representing an educational domain of language usage.

The questions are based on the people, objects, actions and events portrayed. Successful responses invoke a variety of pragmatic language tasks, i.e., naming, locating, identifying, describing, excusing, and hypothesizing. The examiner writes each response on the answer sheet and analyzes it after the test has been completed. The answer sheet tells the examiner which language element to look for. The responses are analyzed for morphological and syntactic correctness. Some of the elements tested are mastery of pluralization, possessive pronoun formation, and word order inversion in questions. Tense structures tested include the progressive "ing" suffix, future tense, past tense, "would have," and "could have."

The manual for administering and scoring the BOLT uses common correct and incorrect responses as a scoring guide. The wrong answer cited for item 17 seems to be an acceptable use of ellipsis in everyday speech: "How could the boy have gotten the cat down by himself? Right Answer: He could have gotten a ladder. Wrong Answer: By getting a ladder."

The Spanish version of the test is also based on three drawings, appropriately representing home, neighborhood and school domains of language use. The dialect employed is standard Mexican Spanish.

The first of three versions of the BOLT-English was pilot tested in 1976 on 177 bilingual secondary school students in the San Francisco Bay area. The scores obtained on the pilot version were compared with teacher ratings using descriptions of overall language proficiency corresponding to each level. Subsequently, changes were made in the test pictures, items, and item groupings. A second version of the test was then administered to 3,070 students. This was followed by further refinement of the pictures and the item groupings. The third and present version was administered to 1,037 students. Test scores correlated .90 with teacher classifications of children's proficiency. This measure of concurrent validity was reduced to .86 when corrected for chance agreements, given that a five level proficiency scale was used for ratings.

A group of 100 students were selected for retesting in order to determine the test-retest reliability of the final form. The coefficient for raw scores over two administrations was .97. For the same group of examinees, the KR 20 estimate of internal consistency was .94. It is noteworthy that the sample of students investigated was not randomly selected. Instead, the students were selected to form four equal groups of 25 for each level of language classification.

The Spanish version of the test was similarly constructed and field tested in California during 1976–1977. The first version was field tested on 495 Chicano and Latin-American students, and the second and final Spanish version was administered to 663 students. The concurrent validity coefficient (Pearson's product moment) with teacher classification of children's proficiency was .92, while the Kappa coefficient of agreement corrected for chance was .89. For the BOLT-Español the test-retest reliability coefficient for a group of 100 students not randomly selected was .91, and the KR 20 measure of internal consistency was .97.

In judging the overall quality and uniqueness of the BOLT, one immediately notices its similarity to the Bilingual Syntax Measure (BSM). Both tests focus on syntax, involve elicited natural responses to questions based on pictures, and have the same number and types of proficiency levels (BSM level II and BOLT level I-S measure comprehension only). Each instrument contains a picture booklet, answer sheet where responses are recorded, separate administration manuals written in Spanish and English, a class record, etc. A distinct advantage of the BOLT is that responses in another language may add to the student's score at the lower levels. On the other hand, the BOLT demands correct interpretation of the picture, even though this is a nonlinguistic skill. The BSM scoring procedure evaluates language usage only, and ignores incorrect interpretations of the content. Finally, the quality of the printing in the BOLT technical manuals is wanting. In spite of some limitations, the test can be recommended for general language proficiency assessment purposes. It can be used with students in grades 7 through 12 and possibly for some intermediate school grades as well. It should not be used below the fifth-grade level due to the cognitive difficulty of some of the questions, particularly those which involve hypothesizing.

[147]

Bilingual Syntax Measure II. Grades 3–12; 1978; BSM II; upward extension of the Bilingual Syntax Measure; second-language oral proficiency with respect to syntactic structures in English and Spanish; 2 editions (English, Spanish), both of which may be administered as an indicator of language dominance; scoring for each edition consists of assigning child to one of six proficiency levels ranging from no speaking or comprehension of the language to proficient (Level 1: no English/no Spanish, Level 2: receptive English only/receptive Spanish only, Level 3: survival English/survival Spanish, Level 4: intermediate English/intermediate Spanish, Level 5: proficient English I/proficient Spanish I, Level 6: proficient English II/proficient Spanish II); individual; 1 form; picture booklet ('77, 9 pages); student response booklet ('78, 8 pages) for each edition; manual ('78, 11 pages) for each edition; technical handbook ('80, 33 pages); 1983 price data: $82.50 per complete set including 35 student response booklets for each edition, class records, technical handbook, and expanding envelope; $23 per package of 35 student response booklets of either edition; $22.50 per picture booklet; $2.50 per manual; $7.50 per technical handbook; $1.50 per class record sheet; $10 per expanding envelope; (10–15) minutes for each edition; Marina K. Burt, Heidi C. Dulay, and Eduardo Hernandez Ch.; The Psychological Corporation.*

TEST REFERENCES

1. Morrison, J. A., & Michael, W. B. The development and validation of an auditory perception test in Spanish for Hispanic children receiving reading instruction in Spanish. EDUCATIONAL AND PSYCHOLOGICAL MEASUREMENT, 1982, 42, 657–669.

Review of Bilingual Syntax Measure II by EUGENE E. GARCIA, Director/Professor, Center for Bilingual/Bicultural Education, Arizona State University, Tempe, AZ:

With the continued increase of Spanish speaking students in public schools, and the substantial increase of bilingual programs for these children beyond the first (K through 3) years of schooling, several instruments have been developed to estimate linguistic proficiency in both Spanish and English. The Bilingual Syntax Measure II (BSM II) is one of those measures aimed at assisting educational personnel to determine such linguistic proficiency for children and adolescents in grades 3 through 12.

The BSM II is purposely patterned after the Bilingual Syntax Measure (BSM), developed for children in grades K through 3. The focus of examination with both Spanish and English is oral syntactic ability, "extracted" from students by their responses to colorful cartoon representations designed for the production of specific linguistic structures. Syntactic structures have been placed in a hierarchical order based on the results of a study involving 775 children in grades 3 through 12. Hierarchies were developed for 25 preselected syntactic structures (each represented by one test item) based on a paired comparative analysis of these 25 syntactic attributes. The resultant hierarchy is used to assign students to one of six levels of proficiency in each language. (The higher the level, the more language proficient the student is presumed to be.)

Like the BSM, the authors of BSM II assume a theoretical conceptualization of language proficiency which is based on syntactic (or structural) proficiency. Alternative theories would recommend a much different approach to the measurement of language proficiency, especially in older children and young adults where social functions of language may overshadow strict syntactic abilities. Yet, the authors provide a clear description of their position, and no attempt is made to suggest their product offers more than a measure of language restricted to the structural dimensions. If a potential user is interested in this type of measure, it is clearly a candidate for serious consideration.

Beyond the theoretical constraints, the potential user of the BSM II should be aware of other pragmatic concerns. First, it is not easy to administer or score this test. Prerequisite knowledge of Spanish and English linguistic morphology and syntax is necessary. I do not believe this instrument can be administered, scored and interpreted by the classroom teacher. Second, the products of the BSM II do not provide clear diagnostic information regarding syntactic ability; it is more likely to be useful in determining the grouping of students in differential instructional programs. Third, the test relies on cartoon representations to produce linguistic responses. This cartoon approach may not be as appropriate for the "testing" of adolescents as it is for the testing of younger children. Last, the emphasis on oral language without attention to literacy suggests that the test is less useful for older students where curriculum is dominated by reading and writing as opposed to oral language academic tasks.

Test-retest reliability is provided for a sample of 85 students. Although including only a small number of students at each grade level, this data does provide positive data on test reliability. No correlations with other language measures are reported.

Review of Bilingual Syntax Measure II by SYLVIA SHELLENBERGER, Director of Psychology and Education, The Medical Center of Central Georgia, Department of Family Practice, Associate Professor, Mercer University School of Medicine, Macon, GA:

Court regulations requiring school districts to assess all students whose primary language is not English spurred the development of tests to measure language proficiency such as the Bilingual Syntax Measure II (BSM II). These guidelines necessitate not only assessment of a student's English proficiency but also a determination of whether children are stronger in English, their primary language, or comparably skilled in both languages. Educational services are to be determined on the basis of the assessment outcomes. The BSM II has two sets of proficiency categories which the authors report to be consistent with federal regulations. The test is an efficient way of classifying students according to these guidelines. However, the BSM's assessment of syntax alone to determine language proficiency defines a very narrow view of language. For example, the categorization of a child as "balanced bilingual" means only that the child's grammar, as assessed on the Spanish version of the test, was comparable to his/her grammar on the English version of the test. Such classifications provide only a modicum of information useful in diagnosis or program planning. Though the limited scope of the test is clearly stated in the manual and technical handbook, it is not put forth in score reports as would be desirable.

The BSM II does accomplish its primary purpose, i.e., assessment of proficiency of syntax in Spanish and English. The test is colorful and interesting and even a hesitant child is likely to enjoy it. The mode of response is simple and obvious. Several items are asked before a response is scored, allowing the child time to warm up to the test. The test is also easy for the examiner to administer and score. The manual's directions, discussions, and descriptions are clear and complete for the most part. One aspect of administration which may be confusing for novice examiners is the directions for details the examiner is to point out in certain pictures. The cues are not as explicit as they should be. Scoring is simple and objective, and conversion from raw scores to interpreted scores is easily accomplished. Nevertheless, it would have been helpful to have a place on the scoring sheet for evolving the obtained scores into cluster scores; the paragraph explanations for this process are unwieldy.

The story and the cartoon-like pictures in the BSM II appear to be free of stereotypes or bias. Some of the visual stimuli, however, are misleading. A few of the objects which are to be the focus of the test question are drawn distant and small. Several pictures are so cluttered with detail that the target object is not easily distinguishable. Family members are very similar in appearance and therefore are difficult to identify. Despite the authors' intent to ask questions which would guide the student through the beginning, middle, and ending of a story, some of the questions are extraneous and distract from the flow of the scenario.

In terms of the validity group for the test, the authors maintain that a randomly selected sample was not essential. In any case, the sample should be representative of the national population of students for whom the test was designed. Population density characteristics, for instance, are not discussed. The majority of the sample was composed of Mexican-American children with a small number of children from Puerto Rican or Cuban backgrounds. These limiting factors should be clearly stated in the test handbook.

While little sound evidence of predictive or concurrent validity is presented, the test manual does address certain aspects of construct and content validity. The theoretical basis underlying the measure and the procedures employed in selecting and ordering items are described in detail. Notwithstanding, questions of a more general and primary nature are not considered. For example, the reason for selecting syntax alone for representing language is not explained. Nor do the authors outline the means of sampling from the performance domain of syntax.

The test manual states that "items that elicited responses reflecting multiple linguistic structures varying greatly in difficulty were considered ambiguous and were rejected." However, no criteria for the elimination process are provided. Although the authors contend that the items remaining were found to be within an acceptable range of difficulty, no data are provided and no range of difficulty stipulated. In fact, some items now included elicited no responses on field testing or elicited responses other than that desired. This writer's experience suggests that both the picture and accompanying question for these particular items are not readily understood. The process the authors used to determine item difficulty and to form subclusters is explained in detail. Along with the process, though, should come a rationale and validation for the particular cutoff scores selected. Also lacking is a discussion of how parallel the difficulty levels are for the English and Spanish forms. Parallelism of the two versions is implied, but not validated.

While reliability estimates are more acceptable than those of the BSM I, they still do not consistently reach .90, as would be desirable for a test of this sort. Coefficients based on internal consistency scores of clusters and totals range from .80 to .90 on the English version and .71 to .82 on the Spanish version. Test-retest correlations from .82 to .96 are reported. Sufficient details for this reliability study have not been provided. For example, while it is stated that different examiners administered the test, no mention is made of interrater reliabilities.

In summary, the BSM II is a carefully prepared instrument with substantial theoretical justification for its design. As a rapid screening instrument, it will efficiently classify bilingual students. With the advantage of being colorful and pleasing to children, it is at the same time easy for the examiner to administer and score. Further research regarding the reliability and validity of the instrument is needed. For the present, however, the instrument appears to be adequate for categorizing bilingual children according to their proficiency in one aspect of language, i.e., syntax.

[148]

Bilingual Two Language Battery of Tests. All students having any proficiency; 1983; "criterion-referenced"; "the battery is two sessions in one year (Pre-Post) for three school years—each session is a Native Language sitting followed by an English Language sitting"; languages included are Spanish, Italian, Portuguese, Vietnamese, French; 4 or 5 scores: phonetics, comprehension, writing, total, oral proficiency (optional); no data on reliability; no norms; test administered by tape cassette; student booklet (12 pages); teacher's test manual (109 pages); profile (2 pages); 1983 price data: $12 per 25 student booklets; $5 per 50 profiles; $10 per tape cassette of any one native language; $15 per manual; 21(31) minutes for each sitting; Adolph Caso; Branden Press, Inc.*

[149]

Biographical and Personality Inventory. Delinquent youths; 1971–82; BPI; a measure of recovery potential; 4 scores: amenability, estimated length of treatment, behavior classification, general drug use/addiction-proneness; no data on reliability; individual or group administered; Forms A (for boys), B (for girls), ('82, 22 pages); manual ('82, 9 pages); separate answer sheets must be used; 1982 price data: $.80 per test; $4 per 50 answer sheets; $2 per manual; (45–60) minutes; Ron Force; Test Systems International, Ltd.*

[150]

Biographical Inventory Form U. Grades 7–12; 1976–78; replaces earlier Alpha Biographical Inventory (7:975); 6 scores: academic performance, creativity, artistic potential, leadership, career maturity, educational orientation; 1 form ('76, 17 pages); manual ('78, 20 pages); separate answer sheets must be used; 1982 price data: $30 per 35 tests; $.04 per answer sheet; $10 per specimen set; (60) minutes; Institute for Behavioral Research in Creativity.*

Review of Biographical Inventory Form U by CHRISTOPHER BORMAN, *Professor of Educational Psychology, Texas A&M University, College Station, TX:*

The Biographical Inventory—Form U is an assessment instrument consisting of 150 multiple choice items designed to obtain and analyze information about an individual's characteristics and background. Form U is the latest in a series of more than 20 Biographical Inventory forms dating back to 1959 when Form A was developed. This instrument (Form U) was designed for use with students in grades 7 through 12. There is no time limit for Form U, but the manual states that most students should be able to complete the inventory in an hour.

The Biographical Inventory—Form U was developed primarily to help identify talents which are typically difficult to measure. The manual gives descriptions of the six scores which the inventory yields, with a brief sketch of the students who would score high in each area. The descriptions are concise and well written and should be useful to counselors, teachers, and other professionals who are responsible for interpreting the scores to students. In most cases the score descriptions seem consistent with the theory and research behind the constructs being measured: (1) Academic Performance, (2) Creativity, (3) Artistic Potential, (4) Leadership, (5) Career Maturity, and (6) Educational Orientation.

This reviewer has some concerns with a statement included in the Career Maturity description. The description is consistent with theory and research on career maturity with the exception of a sentence that says that students who are career mature will "plan to decide what to do about a job before their last year in high school." A high school student may have engaged in considerable career exploration and planning but postpone specific decisions about a job until attending college or some other type of post-secondary educational experience. This individual may have a high level of career maturity but not be ready to make a decision. The statement in the manual about making a decision on a job before the last year of high school is misleading and represents an inappropriate criterion for judging career maturity.

The directions provided in the inventory booklet for administering Form U are straightforward. One criticism which can be made about the directions is the very limited information on how to enter the personal information requested on the answer sheet. Scoring keys are not available, and the inventory must be scored by sending the answer sheets to the publisher for a computerized scoring service which the manual says becomes quite expensive on a cost per person basis if the group is small. It is recommended in the manual that the answer sheets be retained until enough have accumulated to yield an acceptable cost per person. This is a disadvantage to using the Biographical Inventory, and the publisher needs to adjust costs to make them uniform no matter how many answer sheets are sent or provide scoring keys for the inventory to be hand scored. Also, the manual does not report the rationale and evidence in support of computer-based interpretation of scores.

Form U scores are reported as percentile ranks, with raw scores appearing in parentheses following the percentile rank for each score. The distributions of a sample of students in grades 4 through 6, 7 through 9, and 10 through 12 from several school districts in rural areas of Utah are used in the computation of percentile ranks. There is no evidence that this Utah sample is a representative sample of students in grades 4 through 12 that would be appropriate for normative comparisons by users.

The reliabilities of the six scores of Form U are reported in the manual; the reliability estimate used was coefficient alpha, a measure of internal consistency. The reliabilities were computed on the Utah data group for the various grade levels, and the reliability coefficients were moderately high (ranging from .77 to .91). Since internal consistency reliability is only a measure of homogeneity, it would also be helpful to have a measure of test-retest reliability. As stated in the manual, the Biographical Inventory is measuring talents which are typically difficult to measure, and information on the stability of scores over time would be helpful to test users.

Form U scores were originally developed through empirical keying procedures against independent criterion measures. Various performance measures such as evaluated products, teacher ratings, and awards were used as independent standards against which the biographical items were validated and selected. Items which showed a significant relationship with the performance measures were retained. The origins and developmental history of each of the six scores are reviewed briefly in the test manual. Descriptions are given on how the scores for each of the six scales were cross-validated, but very limited and incomplete data are given on these validity studies. All of the validity studies reported are on earlier forms of the scales comprising Form U. The exact combination of items assembled in Form U have not yet been validated as a set against any criterion measures, and the manual states that there is no direct evidence that the present form has validity against representative criteria. The manual states, "All that can be said is that the items, in general, have been highly selected, and, on the basis of the extensive past research evidence, could be expected to have predictive utility in identifying talents." The manual cautions that Form U should be used as a research tool or should be supplemented with other data until more information about the instrument is available. One table in the manual gives data on the interrelationships among the six Form U scores. With a few exceptions, the correlations are small, indicating that Form U is measuring relatively independent talents with the different scores.

Although this instrument is based on almost 20 years of research on biographical information by members of the staff of the Institute for Behavioral Research in Creativity, very limited validity evidence is presented in the manual. Validity evidence based on the current form of each of the six scales comprising Form U is needed. The norm sample, students in grades 4 through 12 from rural school districts in Utah, raises questions in the reviewer's mind about the representativeness of the sample if the instrument is being distributed nationally. It is recommended that the Biographical Inventory—Form U be used with caution until more validity evidence and a well planned norm sample become available. In the meantime, this reviewer recommends the use of such instruments as the Torrance Tests of Creative Thinking and the Career Development Inventory to measure at least some of the attributes which the Biographical Inventory attempts to assess.

Review of Biographical Inventory Form U by COURTLAND C. LEE, Associate Professor of Education, University of North Carolina, Chapel Hill, NC:

The Biographical Inventory Form U consists of 150 multiple-choice items designed to gather information about an individual's characteristics and background. The items refer to areas such as childhood activities and experiences, academic experiences, attitudes, interests, values, self-descriptions, and sources of derived satisfactions and dissatisfactions. The inventory content appears relatively free of ethnic and gender biases.

Form U is presented in a rather basic-looking booklet with detailed instructions. An empirical keying procedure was used in selecting items and developing the six scores of the inventory. Items were selected and keyed against performance criteria for a variety of independent samples (e.g., NASA scientists and engineers, gifted and talented high school students). The alternatives for each inventory item are weighted +1, 0, or −1, depending on their degree of relationship to these performance criteria. Raw scores are derived by subtracting the summed negative alternatives from the summed positive alternatives and adding a constant of 100. This process is greatly facilitated by optical scanning and computer scoring. The manual provides no scoring key, however, so no information is provided on how the item alternatives are actually weighted.

The manual provides scant normative data. Raw score means at various grade levels for rural student samples in Utah and Kentucky as well as a talented sample in Pennsylvania are presented with non-statistical comparisons across samples. However, there is no indication as to whether this data represents normative information. It seems apparent that these means are presented to support a claim that the inventory has considerable range in identifying student characteristics and sensitivity with respect to identifying outstanding characteristics. This claim is questionable given the sample sizes presented (approximately 1,000 in each case) and the fact that the manual presents no evidence of statistically significant differences among the samples.

One reliability study on the Utah student sample, using coefficient alpha as a measure of internal consistency, is reported. Reliability coefficients range from .91 for the academic performance score for grades 7 to 12, to .77 for the educational orientation score for grades 4 to 6. Although the manual states that these reliabilities indicate that Form U can be used with no difficulty, particularly at the upper grades, the limited nature of the sample from which these coefficients were derived makes this a tentative assertion. The case for the reliability of Form U would be strengthened with more extensive data, including test-retest reliability information.

Validity issues for the inventory can at best be considered suggestive. As mentioned previously, inventory scores were developed through empirical keying procedures with a variety of independent samples. There appears to have been variation in items and scoring from sample to sample. Significantly, the manual points out that Form U, as a whole, has yet to be validated against criterion measures. Therefore, there is no evidence of criterion-related validity for the total scale.

Intercorrelations among the Form U raw scores for the total Utah samples (grades 4 through 11) are presented in the manual. Modest correlations are found between scores that appear to measure the same construct, such as Creativity and Artistic Potential. However, most correlations are limited, suggesting that different constructs are being measured with the different scores.

In summary, the manual states that the Biographical Inventory Form U has a legacy of research and development behind it. However, there is merely a suggestion of this evidence reported in the manual. In terms of the evidence presented, this inventory at best appears to be an experimental instrument in the process of becoming. Given its stated purpose and the questions raised about technical aspects of Form U, it is the opinion of this reviewer that the inventory would best serve to supplement data from other psychoeducational measures in making counseling or teaching decisions about adolescents. Its major strength would appear to be its potential usefulness, in concert with other assessment techniques, in identifying unusual creative or leadership potential.

[151]

Bi/Polar Inventory of Core Strengths. Managers and adults in organizational settings; 1977–82; ratings by self and others; Form C available for research purposes only; 8 patterns of core strengths: administrator, control manager, college professor, inventor, trainer, public relations person, entrepreneur, promoter; Form A ('77, 2 pages, for self-ratings), B ('77, 2 pages, for ratings by up to 5 others); analysis of core strengths ('82, 2-page computer report plus 13 pages of interpretive materials); manual ('78, 33 pages); 1984 price data: scoring service, $30 per analysis; $20 per analysis (non-profit organization); administration time not reported; J. W. Thomas, Clyde C. Mayo (manual), and T. J. Thomas (interpretive materials); Bi/Polar, Inc.*

[152]

Birth to Three Developmental Scale. Birth to 3 years and older children suspected to fall below the 3-year age level developmentally; 1979; criterion-referenced; designed for early identification of developmental delay; 4 behavioral categories divided into 6-month age intervals: oral language (comprehension, expression), problem solving, social/personal, motor; no norms, item chosen only if

80% of standardization sample responded correctly; individual; 1 form (5 pages); manual (66 pages); assessment summary (1 page); 1983 price data: $20 per 50 each of five scoring forms and assessment summary; $38 per manual and 50 of each scoring form and assessment summary; administration time not reported; Tina E. Banks and Susan Dodson; DLM Teaching Resources.*

Review of Birth to Three Developmental Scale by BONNIE W. CAMP, Professor of Pediatrics and Psychiatry, University of Colorado Medical School, Denver, CO:

This is an 85-item scale with approximately 15 items at each of six age levels between birth and three years. The items are divided into five scales (language comprehension, language expression, problem solving, social/personal, and motor), and all items are scored for each child. Construction of the scale was based on data obtained from 357 children aged 4 1/2 months to 36 months with approximately 20 children per age category from each of three states: California, Tennessee, and Utah. The sample was evenly divided between males and females, rural and urban communities, and included children of varying ethnic background and socioeconomic status. Data are presented on the reliability of scoring protocols (inter-rater reliability); these reliabilities range from .88 to .99. Items were selected for each age if they were passed by 80% (i.e., 16 children) at that age.

In developing this scale, the authors attempted to separate language comprehension, language expression, and problem solving; to eliminate the use of oral directions and/or oral responses to non-verbal items; and to select stimulus items that could be designated as culture fair. The background data describing how this was accomplished was apparently prepared under contract with the U.S. Office of Education, but are not presented for review in the test manual. No data are provided concerning test-retest reliability.

Even more problematical than test-retest reliability, however, is the question of validity, which is handled in its entirety by describing the subjects, who the examiners were, and how items were selected for inclusion in the scale. No data are presented either for comparing the results from this test concurrently with other methods of assessing developmental delay or for describing any kind of predictive validity.

The design of the test materials involves printing each scale on a separate, color-coded sheet of paper. This means that material for each child must be assembled from 6 different pads (including a summary sheet). Items are scored as pass, emerging or fail, blank, not observed or refused, and a summary score on each scale is used to derive an age-equivalent score for that scale. These age-equivalent scores are then compared with the child's chronological age to identify discrepancies and possible referral/treatment cases. No standards are presented for determining what represents minor developmental delay or delay requiring referral. Apparently this is to be done by visual inspection of how much the age-equivalent score is below the chronological age. The entire guide to interpretation is contained in the following sentence: "When all five subscales are administered and scored the examiner can view the child's profile on the Assessment Summary form, and determine whether the child's performance indicates delay in one or more categories of development warranting referral or treatment outcomes."

In general, it is difficult to tell what the test measures since no data are offered to substantiate the authors' statements regarding interpretation of the test, the populations for whom it is proposed, or even the skills required for administration. (The test is recommended for use by individuals without specialized training, yet all examiners were graduate students or speech pathologists.) The reader is warned that the scale is neither a measure of intelligence nor a norm-referenced test yielding a mental age. As it stands, however, test construction is about the level of the 1937 Stanford-Binet before it was validated. The main differences are that for the 1937 Stanford-Binet, more children were examined at each age to determine item selection and items were selected if 50% of the children passed each item instead of 80%. The age-equivalent scores on the present scale are derived in a manner very similar to the Stanford-Binet mental age. According to the small amount of substantive information in the manual, test construction has not gone much further and few of the assertions are backed up by any data.

Because of problems in test construction and interpretation, it is impossible to determine how useful this scale is likely to be in clinical situations. Certainly the effort to simplify items, clarify the context of test items, and create a culture-fair examination is to be applauded. However, much more basic work needs to be done before it will be clear how this test should be used. It is doubtful that the authors have fully considered the implications of recommending widespread use by untrained examiners of an untimed, 6-page scale with 85 items which may identify well over 20% of the population as delayed. Perhaps the scale will have its greatest immediate value in assessing baseline performance of handicapped children and writing and monitoring performance objectives for them. For the present, however, more background research needs to be completed before the scale can be recommended for any clinical use.

[153]

Bloom Sentence Completion Survey. Students ages 6–21, adults; 1974–75; BSCS; attitudes toward important factors in everyday living; 8 scores: age-mates (student)/people (adults), physical self, family, psychological self, self-directedness, education (students)/work (adults), accomplishment, irritants; individual; 1 form; 2 levels: student, adults, ('75, 2 pages); student instruction manual ('74, 30 pages); adult instruction manual ('74, 62 pages); analysis record sheet ('75, 1 page); 1984 price data: $24 per complete set including 30 tests; $12.75 per 30 tests and record sheets; $12 per manual; [20–30] minutes; Wallace Bloom; Stoelting Co.*

Review of Bloom Sentence Completion Survey by ALLEN K. HESS, Associate Professor of Psychology, Auburn University, Auburn, AL:

The Bloom Sentence Completion Survey (BSCS) purports to portray a person's attitudes in eight areas: People, Physical Self, Family, Psychological Self, Self-Directedness, Work, Accomplishment, and Irritants. Five items tap each of the eight areas for a total of 40 sentence completion stems. The items tapping an area are spaced throughout the test so, for example, the "People" domain's items are: 1—Other people usually ______, 9—Most people my age ______, 17—If other people my age ______, 25—People are slow to ______, and 33—Most men or women ______. An Analysis Record, or score sheet, is available on which to record whether a response to a stem shows a positive, neutral, or negative attitude. The scores are added for an area and the net total, which can range from −5 to +5, shows the attitude of the respondent in that area. Since the "Irritant" area was found to range between −4 and −5, it is not scored, but the responses are recorded on the bottom of the sheet. The manual provides anywhere from 0 to 15 scoring examples for each type of response (plus, neutral, minus, or query further) for each stem. It appears to be a useful training manual for scorers, though more examples would help. Yet the BSCS manual only reports, "it was rare that their [technicians'] scoring differed on more than two items with that of the instructor. This, over .90 correlation, indicated high interrater reliability." Furthermore, the manual presents as test reliability evidence the fact that the composite score range of 77 points (based on the seven scoreable areas) shifted only .2719 points in some 3 years over different respondents. Essentially, scant evidence for scorer reliability and no evidence whatever of test-retest reliability are provided.

While Ebbinghaus first used the sentence completion test to measure intelligence in 1897, most sentence completion forms since then have originated as screening devices for military personnel or for students. It is no surprise that Bloom developed his measure on Lackland Airforce Base (Texas) trainees between 1976 and 1979. Since 1 of 10 trainees came directly from high school, Bloom decided to extend the test to create a Student form. This form has 24 stems common to the Adult form, 5 stems differing only in a minor way, and 11 different stems. The "Work" area is replaced by "Education" on the Student form. Scoring materials and reliability are the same for both forms.

VALIDITY. Bloom claims to measure attitudes but, as with virtually all sentence completion forms, this one is used to assess emotional adjustment broadly stated, or fitness for service. The main claim to validation is the 15-point difference between trainees who were screened and returned to duty versus those who were recommended for discharge. Yet criterion contamination vitiates this claim since the BSCS was used in determining return to duty versus discharge. Moreover, no data regarding the hit-miss rates are presented nor are data shown regarding sample overlap. A second claim in the manual addresses the need for less subjective data to support third party payment claims for psychological treatment. The BSCS manual presents two responses from one person who attended a workshop as evidence of personality change, plus a negative correlation between the BSCS and trait anxiety (STAI). Essentially no validity data are provided. Other sentence completion forms are available which have considerably more validity research supporting them.

Normative data (means and standard deviations only) based on 9,897 trainees are provided for the BSCS Adult form for each scale and the Composite Score, as are percentile ranks for each scale, based on 207 trainees. The BSCS Student form manual provides means and standard deviations for the scales for 1,090 trainees, 23 Special Education students, and 97 children in residential institutions. No other data (personality, intelligence, mental status, socioeconomic status, race, gender, or age) are provided. This absence makes the norms close to useless.

A PERSPECTIVE. It seems that Taube in 1916, Kelley in 1917, Payne in 1928, and Tendler in 1930 formed the first wave of sentence completion authors. They were followed by Rohde in 1946, Sacks in 1949, Forer in 1950, Rotter in 1950, and Holsopple and Miale in 1954. Research has shown some of their tests to be quite reliable (interrater and test-retest) and valid, as reviewed by Goldberg (1965). Goldberg's masterful review concludes that sentence completion forms are valuable, particularly compared to other types of tests. But why and how they work is unclear. Test authors seem unconcerned with a theoretical basis for their tests, and most of their research can be considered as pilot studies. Tests which have sound scoring systems seem undynamic and not clinically useful, particularly compared to multifactor inventories. Yet with some clients, sentence completion tests can render the most telling responses in a cost-effective fashion. Perhaps the ambiguity of the method as being halfway between a projective test and a questionnaire provides us with a clue as to the status of sentence completion tests generally and the BSCS in particular. The sentence completion method's flexibility, simple construction, ease of administration, ability to tap various areas (though always relating to emotional maladjustment), and generally high scorer reliabilities all lend to development of new forms (though most tests employ a common set of stems). Each seems associated with a specific population and a particular set of criteria. With each we start at ground zero, and do not seem to build toward a refined and integrated sentence completion methodology. It is within this perspective that the BSCS settles in to take its place as another sentence completion form.

REVIEWER'S REFERENCES

Goldberg, P. A. A review of sentence completion methods in personality assessment. JOURNAL OF PROJECTIVE TECHNIQUES AND PERSONALITY ASSESSMENT, 1965, 29, 12–45.

Review of Bloom Sentence Completion Survey by CHARLES A. PETERSON, Director of Training in Psychology, Veterans Administration Lakeside Medical Center and Assistant Clinical Professor of Psychiatry and Behavioral Sciences, Northwestern University Medical School, Chicago, IL:

QUESTION: What has forty stems, but only one Bloom and smells like a rose? ANSWER: The Bloom Sentence Completion Survey (BSCS), the youngest sprout in a garden already overcrowded with both stems and weeds. Rooted by Ebbinghaus, nurtured by Binet and Simon, pruned by Jung, hybridized by Freud ("What comes to mind when you think of 'x'...?") and propagated by Rotter, the sentence completion method has grown to become one of the most frequently used tests in clinical psychology (Lubin, Larsen and Matarazzo, 1984).

The BSCS is unambitiously designed to reveal global (positive, negative, and neutral) attitudes about everyday life. The 40 stems elicit the subject's attitudes toward the following eight domains of psychological concern: People, Physical Self, Family, Psychological Self, Self-Directiveness, Work, Accomplishment, and Irritants. Dependent on the subject's test-taking attitude and defense effectiveness, as well as the examiner's theoretical affinity, data relevant to other areas of psychological functioning may be obtained. The 40 stems are brief and a bit bland, but seem a faithful incarnation of the author's construct, "everyday living." The items are thoughtfully arranged in sequential order: After the first eight items, the eight domains are successively repeated (e.g., attitudes about People are elicited by items 1, 9, 17, 25, 33). This facilitates the examiner's perusal of content areas. The stems are a mixture of first (75%) and third (25%) person reference, satisfying both the "identification" and "displacement" schools of thought. Subjects write their answers on a two-sided answer sheet, which offers approximately 12 inches of writing space for each item.

ADMINISTRATION AND SCORING. Unlike many sentence completion tests, which seem destined to be completed in isolation for anonymous psychometrists, the BSCS has role-required the participation of the clinician. First, the answer sheet must be prepared prior to administration. Three items must be pre-edited, following which the subject will respond to, variously, "wife or mother," "men or women," "husband or father," or "boys or girls." Subjects may feel that the BSCS has been specially tailored for them. Sounding very much like a therapist teaching a patient how to free associate, the tester provides some clinically focused instruction on how to respond to the BSCS items. Tester and subject rehearse a sample stem, followed by the first item, after which the tester says "That's fine. Write it down just as you said it." The tester remains involved by noting total response time, as well as long latencies which might signal heightened concern. Finally, after the items have been "answered," the tester conducts an inquiry on unanswered, incomplete, ambiguous and unscoreable items, attempting to extend and clarify the subject's initial response.

Scoring is done on a separate Analysis Record Sheet and summed across all the stems in the various categories. Answers are scored as either "+" ("positive, favorable, or well-disposed"), "–" ("negative, unfavorable, or ill-disposed"), or "0" ("concrete or objective description, a response that does not fit the dichotomy or a completely tangential one"). The maximal range of scoring is, therefore, from −5 to +5, a range of 11 points. Due to the limited range of scores obtained in the normative sample, the "Irritants" category is not scored; nevertheless, the responses are noted for their diagnostic and therapeutic significance. Once all the responses have been tabulated and scored, the examiner can inspect the Analysis Record Sheet and determine the subject's hedonic calculus. The BSCS is easily scored. The manual provides numerous clear examples for each of the stems (again excluding the Irritants category). Nevertheless, scoring is not a rote, mechanical procedure, nor is it a clinical free-for-all. The examiner must understand the rationale for each attitudinal category. To avoid a global scoring set, the examiner is encouraged to use the Analysis Record Sheet, rather than the answer sheet.

RELIABILITY AND VALIDITY. Interrater reliability is easily achieved and is reported to be over .90 for trained high school educated technicians. This is a very believable figure, given the clear scoring criteria, numerous examples, and the eschewal of inference in scoring. The validity data are less impressive, but promising. Basically, the BSCS has been validated against the criterion of retention versus discharge from the U.S. Air Force for psychological reasons. Using a less than blind design, the BSCS "composite scores" (arithmetic totals of +, –, and o responses) were shown to differentiate between the two groups. Correlations with the State-Trait Anxiety Inventory were predictably negative: the more positive the attitudes, the less the anxiety. The manual reports that BSCS scores have been compared with other psychological tests, such as the MMPI, but does not report the statistical analyses. The manual concludes with nine tables which sum considerable impressive normative research, some with samples as large as 10,000! It is clear that the author is committed to the validation process, even if much of the research on the BSCS is tucked away in obscure, difficult-to-access journals.

SUMMARY. Sentence completion tests are touted generally for their nonthreatening nature, their face valid appeal to the subject, their ability to sample a broad range of psychological concern, and their economy of clinician time. Sharing in all these virtues, the BSCS may be additionally commended for its palpable clinical "feel," its clever organization, the ease and meaningfulness of scoring, as well as its promising psychometric beginnings. Notwithstanding user inertia, the BSCS should blossom to become one of the most widely used and most respected sentence completion tests. It seems well suited to assess the psychopathology of everyday life.

REVIEWER'S REFERENCES

Lubin, B., Larsen, R. M., Matarazzo, J. D. Patterns of psychological test usage in the United States: 1935–1982. AMERICAN PSYCHOLOGIST, 1984, 39, 451–454.

[154]

Bloomer Learning Test. Grades 1–11 and adults; 1978–81; BLT; "describes academic difficulties on the basis of a pattern of strengths and weaknesses in various learning processes"; 20 subtest scores: activity, response integration, boredom, visual short-term memory, auditory short-term memory, visual apprehension span, impulse, stimulus complexity, serial learning, recall, relearning, learning set, free association, emotional ratio, paired associate learning, paired associate decrement, interference, concept recognition, concept production, problem solving, yielding 3 IQ scores (simple learning, problem solving, full learning); no norms for part scores; 1 form; manual ('78, 185 pages); test stimuli ('78, 358 pages); stimulus cards (no date, 8 cards); student record form ('80, 4 pages); answer form ('81, 16 pages); 1984 price data: $78 per set of testing materials; $31.50 per test stimuli; $2.50 per key; $18.75 per 25 answer forms; $9.75 per 25 student record forms; $22.75 per manual; (55–75) minutes in 2 sessions; Richard H. Bloomer; Brador Publications, Inc.*

Review of Bloomer Learning Test by EDWARD EARL GOTTS, Chief Psychologist, Huntington State Hospital, Huntington, WV:

The construction, validation, and standardization of the Bloomer Learning Test (BLT) represented an enormously ambitious undertaking for an individual test developer whose work was not supported by a major test publisher or any other major organization. The results are, likewise, impressively oversize and innovative (i.e., the manual reports multiple construct validity studies, includes many normative analyses and tables, and attempts to relate the overall effort to a model of human learning). To attempt so much is not merely quixotic, for the goal is commendable if impossible to attain.

The literature review—in fact the entire manual—unfortunately omits all essential citations, credits, and linkages to the rich research tradition from which it was so freely drawn. Brevity cannot pardon this oversight. Several studies of the BLT, as reported in its manual, appear not to have been reported elsewhere. In consequence of this, the author has overburdened the manual's users with a plethora of detail. Yet in several instances the detail presented, although excessive, is not sufficient to support independent replication or full examination of the individual studies. Thus, the manual seems closer in design and detail to a lengthy technical document, and it does not serve as a tidy, test-user's guide.

For the above and other reasons, the manual's organization and flow pose significant weaknesses. Although it claims to cover test administration, the detailed procedures for this actually appear instead interspersed within the book of test stimuli. The manual fails to direct the user's attention to this fact. A more significant and less user-correctable flaw in test administration is the format of the Answer Form itself (i.e., the respondent must often search through the booklet to locate the correct page and section, with the attendant risk of confusion, delay, and invalidity). In the face of this, it is difficult to understand the author's optimism regarding ease of administration to groups, especially with younger respondents, even in the smaller groupings recommended at those levels. It is impossible to imagine how the "behavioral signs" observations could be completed during group administration, nor is this issue addressed.

Test scoring is only briefly covered, although by studying the manual plus a separate Scoring Key (that is not adequately referenced in the manual) plus the Scoring Form and Student Record, a knowledgeable test user will be able to reconstruct the procedures. Thus it is apparent that this kit could have benefitted in numerous ways from expert peer review and professional editing prior to publication.

Taken together, the evidence for reliability, criterion-related validity, and construct validity is impressive and generally relevant. One puzzling point is the absence of evidence on the learning abilities of the mentally retarded, whereas gifted and disabled learners are well considered. While norms are presented by grade level, test-retest reliability has been reported for the overall sample only. The adequacy of the author's conception of a model of human learning to predict the inherent structure of learning processes sampled by the battery is not altogether convincing; although the author expresses general satisfaction with the result, it is evident that there remains much to be learned from a number of largely undiscussed divergences of the BLT's results from the model's predictions.

The author's approach to normative sampling was unconventional, (*a*) being conducted in the Northeast only, probably with many cluster samples being included (i.e., from 87 school districts); and (*b*) proceeding by grade level rather than by age. In some respects it must, by the author's estimate, be called an opportunity sample (i.e., sampling was constrained by "availability...and willingness of teachers and administrators to cooperate"). He has attempted to offset sampling limitations by various procedures, but the true extent of sampling quirks is unknown because of incomplete reporting. Moreover, the oldest group for which norms are reported (i.e., grade 11 through adults) contained only 211 cases, raising doubts about the BLT's claimed applicability to adults.

Some of the normative data, as presented, appear unusually schematic to represent actual group data points. One example is the appearance in the manual of a very schematic appearing "Learning Set" curve. Group results in some instances seem incredibly high, as for 5th and 6th graders, who are shown having a "Recall" after 48 hours of over 50% of a 12-item word list to which they had been briefly exposed (i.e., 4 trials) without advance notice that they would be retested. Similarly, a perfectly flat curve for Serial Learning from grade 6 through adult at about 75% seems highly exceptional in view of the usual variations found in cross-sectional comparisons of behavioral/psychological measures. The foregoing mastery level seems implausibly high also. Without replication, some of the foregoing seeming anomalies of data appear to result from (*a*) sampling artifacts, (*b*) possible errors in reporting, or (*c*) other unexplained sources.

Test interpretation is focused on practical recommendations to teachers for working with students manifesting strengths and weaknesses in each area measured by the BLT. These suggestions are presented authoritatively and with considerable specificity. The desire to provide teachers specific guidance cannot be faulted, but corroborative evidence or research is not cited to back up the validity of the suggestions made. At best these suggestions would appear to be clinical hunches and hypotheses about what should be tried and what may work—unless the author has also undertaken an unreported monumental program of remediation research. If I am correct that these are hunches based on clinical experience, it would seem prudent to present them as approaches that "may work" or are "worth trying," but let the user "be aware."

To sum up my remarks and offer some conclusions, I admit that I have been freely and sharply critical of some aspects of the BLT. Nevertheless, I admire the vision and ambition of Dr. Bloomer's work. He has undertaken single-handedly to replace the traditional reliance on the IQ test with an alternative—a norm-referenced battery based on an articulated model of human learning. If this were wholly successful, the result would prove nothing short of revolutionary in mental testing. The notion has strong intuitive appeal and certainly deserves considerable further work by others, preferably using the BLT materials. Although I have taken exception to this battery on several counts, the fact remains that much has been accomplished, including the creation of a standardized instrument for studying individual differences in learning. I hold strong reservations about using the BLT normatively, in view of the sampling limitations. Nevertheless, I can commend its use experimentally. Attention to some of the issues and points raised in this review will, I hope, facilitate the use and improvement of the BLT (e.g., illuminate its use as an individual versus a group test; establish its practical applicability in classroom settings; cause its manual to be streamlined and the Answer Form reorganized and simplified; and clarify its data base and linkages to the human learning literature).

[155]

The Boder Test of Reading-Spelling Patterns. Grades K–12 and adult; 1982; "a diagnostic screening test for subtypes of reading disability"; 3 reading scores (reading level, reading age, reading quotient) plus 2 spelling scores (known words correct, unknown-word/good phonetic equivalents); individual; reading test form (13 word lists of 20 words each); spelling test form (1 page); prereading form (2 pages); manual (142 pages plus all forms); sentences for use in dictating the known words (14 pages); reading test: examiner's recording form (8 pages); 1982 price data: $55 per complete set; (10–30) minutes; Elena Boder and Sylvia Jarrico; Grune & Stratton, Inc.*

TEST REFERENCES

1. Aaron, P. G., Baker, C., & Hickox, G. L. In search of the third dyslexia. NEUROPSYCHOLOGIA, 1982, 20, 203–208.

2. Smith, M. O. Test review: The Boder Test of Reading-Spelling Patterns. JOURNAL OF READING, 1983, 27, 22–26.

Review of The Boder Test of Reading-Spelling Patterns by FREDRICK A. SCHRANK, *Assis-*

tant Professor of Education, University of Puget Sound, Tacoma, WA:

This test is designed to be a practical, direct diagnostic and screening procedure intended to (1) differentiate specific reading disability, or developmental dyslexia, from nonspecific reading disability through an analysis of reading and spelling performance alone; (2) classify dyslexic readers into one of three subtypes on the basis of reading-spelling patterns; and (3) provide prognostic and remedial implications for the four reading disability subtypes identified by the test. Based on the hypothesis that the same cognitive strengths and weaknesses underlie reading and spelling, the authors of the test purport to offer a rationale for new approaches to prescriptive remediation. The battery consists of an oral reading test (based on a series of graded word lists) and a written spelling test (based on the results of the reading test).

The authors were too ambitious in their undertaking. One instrument simply cannot meet both needs of screening for reading disability and diagnosis of subtypes of developmental dyslexia through reading and spelling performance alone. Although the test contributes criteria for at least two types of dyslexia (dysphonetic and dyseidetic), the categories of "borderline" and "undetermined" are less distinct and less prescriptive. The authors suggest that the test may be used as a screening device in classroom groups, but no norms are provided for this type of administration.

An interdisciplinary appeal for use of this test is made to professionals in psychology, education, neurology, neuropsychology, medicine, school nursing, and speech therapy. Touted as simple and easy-to-administer by all, the administration procedures are convoluted—involving a complex set of instructions and contingencies which leave the examiner with many questions about procedures. It would actually require a great deal of clinical or teaching experience in the field of reading disabilities (or ambitious self-study) to understand and interpret this test.

There are definite strengths to this test. Unprecedented in the field, it provides the first qualitative analysis of reading and spelling together as interdependent functions. The concepts which underlie the test are in line with current research evidence in cognitive psychology and neuropsychology. The two cognitive functions of gestalt vs. analytic are basic to the two standard methods of initial reading instruction (phonemes vs. whole words).

A number of peculiarities may lead examiners to question this test. Computation of the reading quotient is based on an adaptation of Binet's "mental age" formula and is subject to the same types of criticisms which have given way to new forms of computation and terminology in intelligence testing. Use of the mental age concept is actually suggested for computation purposes (reading quotient vs. mental age), which is an outdated concept in psychoeducational assessment. Even the term "dyslexia," which is often viewed as a nonprescriptive label, may be offensive to many (see Bateman, 1971). Concomitant with the archaic nomenclature, the authors of the test have ignored all that has been developed in recent years in analysis of spelling error patterns (see Frith, 1980).

Data presented in the manual show high test-retest reliability for classifications of reading level, correctly spelled known words, good phonetic equivalents, and subtype classification. These statistics are reported for age and sex, but not for race. No information on standard error of measurement is reported. These data are reported only for children and adults examined by Dr. Boder in private and clinical settings. In general, more and better data on reliability and validity are needed.

Studies reported in the manual support the thesis that the three discernable subtypes of reading disability identified through this test are specific entities. Upon investigation of these studies, however, much of the data comes from unretrievable sources such as personal communication, unpublished doctoral dissertations, or data-gathering techniques with samples reported as "essentially random."

This test may best be described as an individually-administered reading disability screening test which provides information which may be used for prescriptive reading instruction. Plaudits to the authors for this unprecedented venture; encouragement to them also to fine-tune this instrument (and its research base) in future editions.

REVIEWER'S REFERENCES

Bateman, B. (Ed.). LEARNING DISORDERS. Seattle: Special Child Publications, 1971.

Frith, U. (Ed.). COGNITIVE PROCESSES IN SPELLING. London: Academic Press, 1980.

Review of The Boder Test of Reading-Spelling Patterns by TIMOTHY SHANAHAN, *Assistant Professor of Education, College of Education, University of Illinois at Chicago, Chicago, IL:*

The Boder Test of Reading-Spelling Patterns (BTRSP) is a clinical screening device used for identifying individuals with reading problems; for differentiating cases of "developmental dyslexia" from non-specific reading problems; and for classifying those identified as dyslexic into three subgroups, each requiring specific remedial instruction. The BTRSP goes beyond typical individual surveys of reading ability, such as the Wide Range Achievement Test (WRAT), in attempting to specify the nature of the reading problems identified. As with such surveys, it requires no special test administration training.

The term "dyslexia" is fraught with controversy (Critchley, 1970; Critchley & Critchley, 1978; Harris & Sipay, 1980; Stauffer, Abrams, & Pikulski, 1978). Many reading authorities avoid this term, although it is used widely in special education and by many physicians (the major author of the BTRSP is a medical doctor). The term dyslexia is often avoided because it can imply that learning is impeded by a neurological deficit or defect (Harris & Hodges, 1981). The inference of a neural disorder on the basis of limited reading ability alone is circular, injudicious, and possibly harmful. Despite this danger, the BTRSP results in labels such as "developmental dyslexia," "dysphonetic," and "dyseidetic." The test manual indicates that no definitive diagnosis of dyslexia should be made on the basis of the BTRSP. It also demonstrates how to arrive at such a classification and it repeatedly refers to subjects as dyslexic on the basis of these test results alone.

The outcome classifications are not only certain to be controversial, they are probably misleading and unnecessary. Nomenclature such as dyslexia refers to the etiology of reading problems. However, the BTRSP is not a test of the underlying causes of reading difficulty. "Dysphonetic," for example, is used to refer to individuals suffering from a "cognitive deficit" in the "auditory analytic function." What this jargon means is that the individual does not evidence a knowledge of, or an ability to apply, phonics. The BTRSP automatically designates such an individual as being cognitively deficient. However, the source of the lack of knowledge could be pedagogical, a possibility not addressed adequately. Whatever the problem source, neurological or pedagogical, the test results would recommend the same remedial instruction or would lead to the same referral for additional neuropsychoeducational analysis, so nothing is gained by the inference of causation.

The BTRSP results in a "reading level" designation of questionable value. This reading level is based upon word list reading only, with no consideration of comprehension ability. The reading level designation is not based upon any adequate normative sample. The test manual is forthright concerning these limitations. There are other important problems with this designation that are not mentioned. Reading level, as used in this test, is identical in interpretation to the grade equivalent score, the use of which was condemned by the 1981 Delegates Assembly of the International Reading Association. Such reading levels are commonly confused with the instructional level, which is the level at which an individual should be taught in order to obtain maximum learning progress. The BTRSP reading level, which is based on a 50% performance criterion, is almost certain to overestimate the instructional level, possibly by several years. The misuse of this unnecessary test result can only lead to confusion, frustration, and limited learning.

Many potential test users might simply avoid the BTRSP because of its liberal use of etiological jargon. This would be unfortunate. The BTRSP provides a superior instrument for differentiating sight vocabulary and phonics problems. Using an informal reading inventory format, this test shows isolated words to the testee in a 1-second flashed presentation. In order to respond the individual must rely on memory, the critical aspect of sight vocabulary. The flashed presentation minimizes the use of phonics to decode the word, but it does not entirely prevent the individual from applying some phonics knowledge. Thus, a sight word problem might be obscured by a superior phonics ability coupled with a good short-term visual memory. The BTRSP lists are uniquely designed to avoid this possibility. Half of the words in each list are readable through the application of simple sound-symbol correspondences, the others include more complex spelling pattern-pronunciation relationships. This design is unique in that sight vocabulary knowledge is evaluated using words that cannot be easily sounded, and phonics skills are assessed through the use of unknown words that can be sounded out. Spelling performance is used to supplement these results.

The test construction appears to be as careful as it is innovative. Words were selected on the basis of reasonable criteria from widely accepted sources. The manual is highly readable although somewhat repetitive. The statistical data for this clinical measure are generally supportive, but limited in scope. Test-retest reliability estimates and internal consistency statistics for reading level are usually in the high .90s. Somewhat lower reliability estimates were obtained for scores on correctly spelled known words (.76) and good phonetic equivalents (.89). These results are based only on small samples of 30–54 subjects each.

Validation information was obtained from four independent studies (three of them unpublished, two of them doctoral dissertations) which found a significant relationship between the BTRSP classifications and performance on relevant processing measures. The strengths of these relationships were not reported, but it appears that they were not especially strong. One of the studies found that the BTRSP failed to identify 9% of the subjects who were experiencing reading problems, and it had an 18% false positive outcome (i.e., subjects experiencing no reading problems but identified as dyslexic by the test). These are not entirely encouraging results for an individually administered test, particularly with the most general classification outcome provided by this measure.

As a quick screening device to be used to compare individuals on general reading performance this test is probably neither better nor worse than other available surveys (i.e., Slosson Oral Reading Test, Peabody Individual Achievement Test, WRAT, etc.), though it lacks their thorough standardizations. As a device for indicating the cause of reading problems or for specifying reading levels, it is both inadequate and misleading. As an analytic tool for identifying sight word and phonics analysis problems, it is superior to the word lists accompanying the typical informal reading inventory. It provides no validation support for such decisions, although it seems plausible that sight vocabulary and phonics ability could be assessed with this test. What is needed is a comparison of the classification results of the BTRSP with the results of other tests of these abilities, or better yet an examination of the progress of subjects instructed on the basis of the BTRSP's classification scheme. Until such support is available it is suggested that it would be prudent to avoid the unfortunate terminology of the BTRSP, and to use this test only in conjunction with other more complete reading measures.

REVIEWER'S REFERENCES

Critchley, M. THE DYSLEXIC CHILD. Springfield, IL: Charles C. Thomas, 1970.

Critchley, M., & Critchley, E. A. DYSLEXIA DEFINED. Springfield, IL: Charles C. Thomas, 1978.

Stauffer, R. G., Abrams, J. C., & Pikulski, J. DIAGNOSIS, CORRECTION AND PREVENTION OF READING DISABILITIES. New York: Harper & Row, 1978.

Harris, A. J., & Sipay, E. R. HOW TO INCREASE READING ABILITY, (7th ed). New York: Longman, 1980.

Harris, T. L., & Hodges, R. E. A DICTIONARY OF READING AND RELATED TERMS. Newark, DE: International Reading Association, 1981.

[156]

The Booklet Category Test. Adolescents and adults; 1979–81; BCT; booklet version of the Halstead Category Test; diagnosis of brain damage; no data on reliability; no norms; individual; 1 form ('79, 216 pages); manual ('79, 21 pages); scoring and recording form ('81, 4 pages); 1983 price data: $95 per kit including BCT, manual, and 25 scoring forms; $15 per 50 scoring forms; $5 per manual; administration time not reported; Nick A. DeFilippis and Elizabeth McCampbell; Psychological Assessment Resources, Inc.*

Review of The Booklet Category Test by RAYMOND S. DEAN, Director of Neuropsychological Assessment Laboratory, Assistant Professor of Medical Psychology, Washington University School of Medicine, St. Louis, MO:

This test is a booklet version of the Category Test originally introduced by Halstead (Halstead & Settlage, 1943) and revised by Reitan (1969) as a subtest within the Halstead-Reitan Neuropsychological Battery. The research with the Category Test has shown it to be a useful predictor of general neurological dysfunction, but it is rarely viewed as a tool in localization of neuropathology (Reitan, 1974).

In the original, revised version of the test (Reitan, 1969), adult (greater than 15 years of age) subjects are visually presented 208 items in a semiautomated format. As an individual test, patients are seated behind a viewing screen and must attempt to abstract the organizing principle or concept (e.g., location, shape, color, etc.) involved in seven groups of stimuli. The testee responds in a nonverbal fashion by depressing one of four keys. This mode of response is seen as important for it allows examination of higher order functions in dysphasic patients. An important part of the original, revised test involves the immediate auditory feedback on the correctness of each item via a bell or buzzer. Thus, the patient attempts to test hypotheses about the nature of the principle that overrides the consideration of other attributes. The number of errors made by the subject is recorded as a measure of the individual's ability to profit from experience. Difficulties exist in interpretation because it is unlikely that any two subjects would exhibit the same pattern of positive and negative feedback (Dean, 1982). Because of the complex nature of the task and feedback mode, it has never been clear exactly what the Category Test measures (Dean, 1982). The Category Test is often seen as a rather complex concept formation test that is not especially difficult for normal subjects, but requires abstraction ability that is often diminished in subjects with cortical damage. According to Reitan and Davison (1974), the purpose of the test is to "determine the ability of the subject to profit from both negative and positive experience as a basis for altering his [sic] performance."

The Booklet Category Test is a printed adaptation of the Category Test and does not require the rather elaborate and stationary equipment necessary in the Halstead-Reitan version. The original 208 slides have been reproduced on 8 x 11-inch sheets of paper and are presented in a binder. The instructions are basically the same as that for the Category Test, with the exception that rather than depressing keys, the subject must respond by pointing to a number from one to four which indicates his or her decision. Feedback as to the correctness of the response is given verbally by the examiner rather than by bells and buzzers. Although the authors view verbal feedback offered by the examiner as "less threatening" to the subject, it may well serve to threaten testing rapport with some patients. The portability of this booklet version of the test represents its major advantage over that of the expensive and stationary nature of the Category Test. The materials consist of a large three-ring binder containing stimuli, protocol for recording responses, and a cardboard response panel with numbers one through four printed on it.

Relatively minor criticisms involving the materials are the lack of durability of the paper on which the stimuli are printed, the rather unwieldy size of the binder, and the lack of clear demarcation between sets of stimuli. On the positive side, the protocol represents a vast improvement over that of the original version in that the keyed responses and distractors are reproduced in miniature. This should reduce errors in administration and scoring.

Directions for the administration and scoring of tests are presented in a straightforward manner in the manual. Other than the modifications necessary for the new response mode congruent with the booklet format, the instructions remain the same as those offered by Reitan (1969). While not stated in the present manual, one must assume that this booklet form of the Category Test is similar to the original and is meant to assess adults 15 years and older.

Assuming a rather empirical stance with respect to constructs measured by the booklet form (i.e., neurologically impaired vs. neurologically non-impaired), the manual relies primarily upon the corpus of research developed with the Category Test (see Reitan & Davison, 1974). The manual reports the correlations between the Booklet Category Test and the Category Test to range from .91, for 30 normal students, to .76, for a heterogeneous group of 38 psychiatric patients. The authors report similar discriminations between normals and alcoholics for both versions of the test. While promising, these data are less than sufficient in establishing the equivalence of the two tests. Although the relationship between the Category Test and the booklet version may be viewed as an estimate of its stability-equivalence, no formal reliability data are reported. The manual also lacks any standardization or normative data, and, in fact, the reader is referred to the rich research base which has evolved for the Category Test as the basis for interpretation of the booklet version. The authors seem to recognize the scant psychometric support for the test and state they are making it available to stimulate further research with the measure. Such a justification seems psychometrically questionable when offering the measure on a large scale basis for clinical use.

Very little information is provided on interpretation. The authors rely upon Reitan's (1955) impairment criterion of 50 errors established with the Halstead-Reitan version as a guide to interpreting performance on this form of the test. While the author reviews two investigations with the same 30 normal subjects (DeFilippis, McCampbell, & Rogers, 1979; McCampbell & DeFilippis, 1979), means and standard deviations are not offered in the manual. Ideally, the manual should supply data on normal individuals with an adequate number of cases throughout the life span. This seems important because of the degree to which neuropsychological batteries are relied upon to distinguish dementia from normal aging. Moreover, the 50 error criterion has been shown to be least trustworthy for ages 50 and above (Bak & Greene, 1980). Hence, interpretation of the results of the test is a rather tenuous procedure without benefit of normative data. On balance, it should be noted that a number of psychologists view neuropsychological procedures to be controlled experiments with interpretations more dependent upon the skills of the psychologist than psychometric properties of the measures (e.g., Lezak, 1976; Luria, 1965).

In short, the Booklet Category Test offers a promising adaptation of the Halstead-Reitan version which reduces equipment cost and increases the portability of the test. Such a refinement would remove one of the most common objections to the use of the Halstead-Reitan Neuropsychological Battery. Although some promising data exist, the lack of rudimentary validity, reliability, and normative data indicate that development of the measure is still in the experimental stage. The test, as it stands, may be utilized as a basis for further standardization or research, but it cannot be recommended for general clinical applications.

REVIEWER'S REFERENCES

Halstead, W. C., & Settlage, P. D. Grouping behavior of normal persons and of persons with lesions of the brain. ARCHIVES OF NEUROLOGY AND PSYCHIATRY, 1943, 49, 489–503.

Reitan, R. M. An investigation of the validity of Halstead's measures of biological intelligence. ARCHIVES OF NEUROLOGY AND PSYCHIATRY, 1955, 73, 28–35.

Luria, A. R. Neuropsychology of the local diagnosis of brain damage. CORTEX, 1965, 1, 2–18.

Reitan, R. M. MANUAL FOR ADMINISTRATION OF NEUROPSYCHOLOGICAL TEST BATTERIES FOR ADULTS AND CHILDREN. Indianapolis: Author, 1969.

McCampbell, E., & DeFilippis, N. A. The development of a booklet form of The Category Test: A preliminary report. CLINICAL NEUROPSYCHOLOGY, 1972, 1, 33–35.

Reitan, R. M. Methodological problems in clinical neuropsychology. In R. M. Reitan and L. A. Davison (Eds.), CLINICAL NEUROPSYCHOLOGY: CURRENT STATUS AND APPLICATIONS. N.Y.: Wiley, 1974.

Reitan, R. M., & Davison, L. A. Clinical Neuropsychology: CURRENT STATUS AND APPLICATIONS, N.Y.: Wiley, 1974.

Lezak, M. D. NEUROPSYCHOLOGICAL ASSESSMENT. N.Y.: Oxford University Press, 1976.

DeFilippis, N. A., McCampbell, E., & Rogers, P. Development of a booklet form of The Category Test: Normative and validity data. JOURNAL OF CLINICAL NEUROPSYCHOLOGY, 1979, 1, 339–342.

Bak, J. S., & Greene, R. L. Changes in neuropsychological functioning in an aging population. JOURNAL OF CONSULTING AND CLINICAL PSYCHOLOGY, 1980, 48, 395–399.

Dean, R. S. Neuropsychological Assessment. In T. Kratochwill (Ed.) ADVANCES IN SCHOOL PSYCHOLOGY—VOL. 2. New Jersey: Lawrence Earlbaum, Inc., 1982.

Review of The Booklet Category Test by THOMAS A. HAMMEKE, Assistant Professor of Neurology & Psychiatry, Medical College of Wisconsin, Milwaukee, WI:

Measures of concept formation have had a long-standing tradition in the study of behavioral sequelae of brain injury. Tests that require subjects to shift responses (hypotheses) regarding novel test stimuli based on feedback of their performance have been found to be particularly sensitive to cerebral dysfunction. The Halstead Category Test (HCT), first developed by Halstead in 1943 and later revised by Reitan in 1969, is a prime example. The HCT has been used extensively in the study of brain-behavior relationships in the context of a battery of neuropsychological measures (Halstead-Reitan Battery).

Unfortunately, the HCT requires costly and largely nonportable equipment (i.e., slide projector, rear projection screen, and auditory feedback device), making it impractical to use in many research and clinical settings. DeFilippis and McCampbell developed the Booklet Category Test (BCT) to eliminate these drawbacks and make the test more widely available.

In developing the test, the authors gave particular attention to making the BCT as comparable to the Reitan version as possible. The size, color, and patterns of stimulus materials are identical. Seven subtests are retained. Only minor modifications in instructions are made to accommodate use of a booklet rather than projection screen, and use of auditory-verbal feedback ("correct" or "incorrect") in place of auditory-nonverbal feedback (bell or buzzer) in the original version. A manual response is retained, although pointing instead of flipping a toggle switch is required. Scoring remains the summation of errors across 208 trials. As with the HCT, a short-form is available that uses a regression formula to predict total score from performance on the first four subtests.

The results of two studies are available to provide preliminary evidence of equivalency between the booklet and Reitan versions of this test. High correlation (.91) between the tests is reported in a neurologically normal, college student sample. Slightly lower correlations were found in an alcoholic (.80) and a mixed brain-injured, psychiatric sample (.76). The lower correlation in the psychiatric sample was not found to be different from the simple test-retest correlation with the HCT, indicating that further documentation of equivalency in this sample is limited by test-retest reliability. While the studies are supportive of equivalency between the measures, sample sizes are small. Further documentation of equivalency is desirable before research on the HCT can be assumed to apply uniformly to the BCT.

Normative and reliability data, correlation with demographic variables, and optimal cut-off scores for diagnosis in various populations have not been established. Thus, to date, one is forced to rely on concurrent data from studies using the HCT to ascertain the test's characteristics and interpretive and diagnostic value. While an extensive body of research on the HCT is available, the test manual provides only a nominal review of this information.

Studies of the HCT have reported adequate split-half reliability in mixed neurological and psychiatric samples (r =.98); (Shaw, 1966) and schizophrenic patients (r =.90); (Klonoff, Fibiger, & Hutton, 1970). Test-retest reliability has been studied in several clinical populations with testing intervals ranging from 3 weeks to 1 year. All reported correlations have been significant and range from .60 in a sample of young, healthy males to .96 in patients with diffuse cerebrovascular disease (Matarazzo, Wiens, Matarazzo, & Goldstein, 1974). Intermediate values have been reported for chronic schizophrenic (r =.72); (Klonoff et al., 1970) and mixed psychiatric patients (r =.93); (MacInnes, Forch, & Golden, 1981). Significant practice effects are also reported or implied, which are most apparent in non-neurological populations (Matarazzo et al., 1974; Matarazzo, Wiens, Gallo, & Klonoff, 1976; DeFilippis, McCampbell, & Rogers, 1979). The practice effects made only minor changes in diagnostic classification ("normal" vs. "abnormal") when used with a battery of diagnostic tests (Matarazzo et al., 1976). These studies, taken together, document adequate reliability of the HCT when applied to a range of clinical populations.

The diagnostic value of the HCT in the context of a battery of neuropsychological measures has been addressed in numerous investigations. The test has repeatedly been found to be extremely sensitive to brain dysfunction, particularly diffuse and anterior brain injury. Wheeler, Burke, and Reitan (1963) reported up to 90% effectiveness in discriminating brain-injured from normal individuals. Less promise has been shown in separating brain-injured from mixed psychiatric and pseudoneurologic groups, and in lateralizing and localizing cerebral dysfunction (Boll, 1978).

In summary, preliminary evidence suggests that the BCT is a less expensive and more portable version of the HCT. The BCT appears to tap higher-level cognitive functions, as well as more elementary visual and auditory perceptual skills, making it a sensitive measure of brain dysfunction and possibly useful as an initial screening tool. However, the BCT's psychometric characteristics and full diagnostic value have yet to be established. While considerable concurrent information in this regard is available on the HCT, the BCT manual does not provide a review of this research. The HCT studies are encouraging, but more information on diagnostic validity in various clinical populations is clearly needed. In addition, age and education adjustments in scores or cutoffs will likely be necessary before more accurate clinical interpretation of test performance can be made. Until such information is available, interpretation must be made with caution. As with the HCT, the BCT will likely prove to be a valuable component in a comprehensive study of higher cognitive functions. Used by itself, the test will not enable a detailed description of neuropsychological deficits, nor lateralize or localize injury. More detailed studies on qualitative patterns of test performance (e.g., frequency of perseverative vs. nonperseverative errors, etc.) may also further our understanding of brain-behavior relationships assessed by this instrument.

REVIEWER'S REFERENCES

Wheeler, L., Burke, C. J., & Reitan, R. M. An application of discriminant functions to the problem of predicting brain damage using behavioral variables. PERCEPTUAL AND MOTOR SKILLS, 1963, 16, 417–440.

Shaw, D. J. The reliability and validity of the Halstead Category Test. JOURNAL OF CLINICAL PSYCHOLOGY, 1966, 22, 176–180.

Klonoff, H., Fibiger, C. H., & Hutton, G. H. Neuropsychological patterns in chronic schizophrenia. JOURNAL OF NERVOUS AND MENTAL DISEASE, 1970, 150, 291–300.

Matarazzo, J. D., Wiens, A. N., Matarazzo, R. G., & Goldstein, S. G. Psychometric and clinical test-retest reliability of the Halstead impairment index in a sample of healthy, young, normal men. JOURNAL OF NERVOUS AND MENTAL DISEASE, 1974, 158, 37–49.

Matarazzo, J. D., Matarazzo, R. G., Wiens, A. N., Gallo, A. E., & Klonoff, H. Retest reliability of the Halstead impairment index in a normal, a schizophrenic, and two samples of organic patients. JOURNAL OF CLINICAL PSYCHOLOGY, 1976, 32, 338–349.

Boll, T. J. Diagnosing brain impairment. In B. B. Wolman (Ed.), DIAGNOSIS OF MENTAL DISORDERS: A HANDBOOK. New York: Plenum, 1978.

DeFilippis, N. A., McCampbell, E., & Rogers, P. Development of a booklet form of The Category Test: Normative and validity data. JOURNAL OF CLINICAL NEUROPSYCHOLOGY, 1979, 1, 339–342.

MacInnes, W., Forch, J. R., & Golden, C. J. A cross-validation of a booklet form of the Halstead-Reitan Category Test. CLINICAL NEUROPSYCHOLOGY, 1981, 3, 3–5.

[157]

Brazelton Neonatal Assessment Scale. Ages 3 days to 4 weeks; 1973; BNAS; also called Brazelton Behavioral Assessment Scale; 47 scores: 27 behavioral items, 20 elicited responses; data on reliability of scores based on prepublication version; no norms; individual; 1 form; manual (70 pages plus 8-page scoring booklet); additional score sheets must be produced locally; 1984 price data: $13 per manual; (20–30) minutes; T. Berry Brazelton and others; distributed by J. B. Lippincott Co.*

See T3:311 (31 references); for a review by Anita Miller Sostek, and an excerpted review by Stephen Wolkind, see 8:208 (15 references).

TEST REFERENCES

1. Als, H., Tronick, E., Lester, B. M., & Brazelton, T. B. The Brazelton Neonatal Behavioral Assessment Scale (BNBAS). JOURNAL OF ABNORMAL CHILD PSYCHOLOGY, 1977, 5, 215–231.

2. Egeland, B. Preliminary results of a prospective study of the antecedents of child abuse. CHILD ABUSE & NEGLECT, 1979, 3, 269–278.

3. Keefer, C. H., Tronick, E., Dixon, S., & Brazelton, T. B. Specific differences in motor performance between Gusii and American newborns and a modification of the Neonatal Behavioral Assessment Scale. CHILD DEVELOPMENT, 1982, 53, 754–759.

4. LaVeck, B., & Hammond, M. A. Performance on the motor scale of the McCarthy Scales of Children's Abilities as related to home environment and neonatal reflexes. PERCEPTUAL AND MOTOR SKILLS, 1982, 54, 1265–1266.

5. Lester, B. M., Als, H., & Brazelton, T. B. Regional obstetric anesthesia and newborn behavior: A reanalysis toward synergistic effects. CHILD DEVELOPMENT, 1982, 53, 687–692.

6. Meares, R., Penman, R., Milgrom-Friedman, J., & Baker, K. Some origins of the "difficult" child: The Brazelton Scale and the mother's view of her new-born's character. THE BRITISH JOURNAL OF MEDICAL PSYCHOLOGY, 1982, 55, 77–86.

7. Barnard, K. E., & Bee, H. L. The impact of temporally patterned stimulation on the development of preterm infants. CHILD DEVELOPMENT, 1983, 54, 1156–1167.

8. Greene, J. G., Fox, N. A., & Lewis, M. The relationship between neonatal characteristics and three-month mother-infant interaction in high-risk infants. CHILD DEVELOPMENT, 1983, 54, 1286–1296.

9. Streissguth, A. P., Barr, H. M., & Martin, D. C. Maternal alcohol use and neonatal habituation assessed with the Brazelton Scale. CHILD DEVELOPMENT, 1983, 54, 1109–1118.

[158]

Brief Hopkins Psychiatric Rating Scale. Psychiatric patients; 1978; B-HPRS; rating scale for recording scaled judgements in 9 dimensions: somatization, obsessive-compulsive, interpersonal sensitivity, depression, anxiety, hostility, phobic anxiety, paranoid ideation, psychoticism; no data on reliability or validity; no norms; individual; 1 form (2 pages); no manual; 1983 price data: $26 per 100 tests; administration time not reported; Leonard R. Derogatis; the Author.*

[159]

Brief Index of Adaptive Behavior. Ages 5–17; 1984; BIAB; ratings by teacher or parent; 4 scores: independent functioning, socialization, communication, total; 1 form (2 pages, including instructions); manual (10 pages); 1985 price data: $5 per 20 response sheets; $3.50 per manual; $4 per specimen set; administration time not reported; R. Steve McCallum, Maurice S. Herrin, Jimmy P. Wheeler, and Jeanette R. Edwards; Scholastic Testing Service, Inc.*

[160]

The Brief Symptom Inventory. Psychiatric patients and nonpatients; 1975–82; BSI; essentially the brief form of the SCL-90-R; self-report inventory of patient's psychological symptom status; 9 primary dimension scores (somatization, obsessive-compulsive, interpersonal sensitivity, depression, anxiety, hostility, phobic anxiety, paranoid ideation, psychoticism), plus 3 global indices (global severity index, positive symptom distress index, positive symptom total); 1 form ('74, 1 page); manual ('82, 48 pages); 1983 price data: $24 per 100 tests; (7–10) minutes; Leonard R. Derogatis and Phillip M. Spencer; Leonard R. Derogatis.*

TEST REFERENCES

1. Derogatis, L. R., & Meyer, J. K. A psychological profile of the sexual dysfunctions. ARCHIVES OF SEXUAL BEHAVIOR, 1979, 8, 201–223.

[161]

Brigance Diagnostic Assessment of Basic Skills—Spanish Edition. Grades preschool–6; 1984; criterion-referenced; 102 tests in 10 areas: readiness, speech, functional word recognition, oral reading, reading comprehension, word analysis, listening, writing and alphabetizing, numbers and computation, measurement; no data on reliability; no norms; no suggested standards of mastery; individual; 1 form (234 pages including directions for administration and scoring); assessment record book (27 pages); assessment class record book (34 pages); 1983 price data: $89 per complete set including 10 record books; $15.95 per 10 record books; $6.95 per class record book; administration time not reported; Albert H. Brigance; Curriculum Associates, Inc.*

[162]

Brigance Diagnostic Comprehensive Inventory of Basic Skills. Grades K–9; 1983; CIBS; "criterion-referenced"; 198 specific-objective tests in 7 areas:

readiness, reading, listening, research and study skills, spelling, language, math; no data on reliability; no norms; no suggested standards of mastery for 29% of the tests; individual; alternate forms (A and B) for 51 of the tests; manual (14 pages plus 682 pages of tests); record book (35 pages); comprehensive class record book (51 pages); reading, readiness, individual, mathematics, (3 pages) objectives forms; 1983 price data: $99 per inventory and 10 record books; $15 per 10 record books; $6.95 per comprehensive class record book; $15.95 per 30 objective forms; preview excerpts free of charge; specific time limits are listed on many tests, others are untimed; Albert H. Brigance; Curriculum Associates, Inc.*

Review of Brigance Diagnostic Comprehensive Inventory of Basic Skills by CRAIG N. MILLS, Administrative Officer, Bureau of Accountability, Louisiana Department of Education, Baton Rouge, LA:

The Brigance Diagnostic Comprehensive Inventory of Basic Skills is designed to monitor individual student progress through an objectives-based curriculum. According to the manual, the Inventory may be used for all students in grades K through 9. A major thrust of the materials, however, is the assessment of special education students.

The record-keeping system that accompanies the Inventory appears to be very good. The class record book allows a teacher to keep an organized and easily interpreted record of student performance on the skills included in the Inventory. A student record book allows the teacher to maintain an extremely detailed record of performance on each student's progress. In fact, the amount of information that may be recorded for each student would probably overwhelm a classroom teacher with 30 students. On the other hand, such detailed record keeping may be extremely useful to a special education teacher who is likely to have fewer students, but greater individualization of instruction than the regular teacher.

At the beginning of each section of the tests (word analysis, number facts, etc.) a brief description is provided. The description includes the purpose for including the skills, a brief description of how the assessment is to be conducted, and other information as appropriate (use of multiple forms, alternate methods of assessment, source material, etc.). The tests are organized efficiently for individual administration. The ring binder holding the tests may be opened to allow the student to view the items while the administrator views the questions, answers, and directions.

One of the "features" claimed of the Inventory is that the tests are criterion-referenced. While the tests are objective-referenced, they are not criterion-referenced. Criterion-referenced tests have come to be defined as those developed to measure a clearly defined domain of content. Domain definition is typically given by the use of item or domain specifications that clearly specify acceptable content, stimulus material, format, and acceptable response options. Such content descriptions are not available with the Inventory, and no statements are made indicating that they were used in test development.

Another "feature" is that the objectives are text-referenced. Grades at which skills (and levels within skills) are most frequently targeted for mastery are noted throughout the Inventory. Unfortunately, however, specific placement of skills in various popular texts is not referenced. The result is that users will have to determine the exact match beween the suggested grade placement in the Inventory and that of the textbooks they are using. Since some content review of major texts would be necessary to determine grade placement of objectives, the provision of that data would have been useful. Users would probably need to perform a content review of any assessment instrument under consideration, particularly a flexible system that allows use of some objectives and not others. However, in the case of the Brigance, for which the author already has conducted such research, it would have been a great aid to potential users if they could have benefited from the author's work.

No data on item quality are provided. In fact, it is not clear from the manual whether items were actually administered to students during the field test. According to the manual, field test editions were circulated to obtain information on the addition, deletion, and sequencing of skills, content validity, and other changes that would enhance publication. Even in these areas, no data regarding the critiques are presented. Instead, a very general statement is made that recommendations for revisions were reflected in the present edition of the Inventory. A tabulation of the comments and critiques or, at a minimum, a listing of additions and deletions should be available. The tabulation would be of interest to those assessing the process of test development. The summary of changes would be helpful to those who have used a previous edition and who wish to assess the degree to which modifications enhance or detract from the usefulness of the Inventory in their situation.

No validity data are reported. The manual refers to assessment of content validity, but the results of that assessment are not presented. No mention is made of construct validity. No reliability information is provided. Two forms are provided for approximately 25% of the objectives and administrators are encouraged to use them as equivalent forms, but no data are provided as evidence that the forms are, in fact, parallel.

When cutoff scores are provided, the manner in which they were established is not clear. Cutoffs range from 50% to 100% for mastery. Unfortunately, no discussion is provided regarding standard-setting method, validity of the classifications, or the reliability (consistency) of the decisions.

Application of cutoff scores is not clear in all cases. In reading comprehension, for example, a cutoff of 80% (four items correct out of five) has been established. However, administration of the alternate form is suggested for students who answer three items correctly. If the student responds correctly to four items on the second test (a combined 70% score) the manual suggests giving credit for reading comprehension at that grade level. Optional questions are also included for each passage. Information is not provided, however, as to how answers to optional questions should factor into decisions. It is thus unclear what the intended cutoff really is. Further, there is no information on the extent to which classifications are stable across administrations or test forms. Data regarding the congruence between classifications using the Inventory and other instruments (other tests, teacher ratings, etc.) are also lacking.

SUMMARY. The Brigance Diagnostic Comprehensive Inventory of Basic Skills appears to provide a flexible assessment system with good record-keeping capabilities to accompany an objectives-based instructional program. However, the lack of information on item quality, content and construct validity, standard-setting methods and rationale, alternate form reliability, and decision consistency and validity severely limit the generalizability of results obtained, and therefore, the usefulness of the tests.

Review of Brigance Diagnostic Comprehensive Inventory of Basic Skills by MARK E. SWERDLIK, Associate Professor of Psychology, Illinois State University, Normal, IL:

The Brigance Diagnostic Comprehensive Inventory of Basic Skills is designed for use with a wide age range of students enrolled in pre-kindergarten through grade nine. The test focuses on 203 clearly defined academic skill sequences in the areas of readiness, reading (including reading comprehension), listening, research and study skills, spelling, language, and math.

Performance on the Brigance is interpreted by referencing the behavioral objective for which the items were written. Objectives are unambiguous and arranged in an ordinal hierarchy so that acquisition of lower level skills are prerequisite to the attainment of higher level skills. Brigance objectives are easily translated into instructional goals.

The Brigance Inventory is useful in the development of individualized instructional programs for normal students and those with special needs to meet the requirements of Public Law 94–142 mandating Individualized Educational Plan (IEP) development. In addition to instructional planning, results from the Brigance can be used for determining the effectiveness of an instructional program, for assessing minimal competence and skills required for promotion, placement, or graduation, and for screening purposes in kindergarten and first grade.

The Brigance is easy to administer and includes complete and clear directions. These directions reflect the feedback of professionals who have used the test during field testing, and feedback received by the test author during workshops and conferences. The test format and test materials are attractive, easy to use, and well organized. The test can be easily administered by school psychologists, learning disability specialists, educational diagnosticians, classroom teachers, and paraprofessionals who have also had training in rapport building. The test manual specifies the examiner's role and responsibilities and includes a useful list of do's and don'ts for more effective use.

Although the entire test is quite long and very time consuming to administer, the test author advises that the examiner not administer the entire inventory, but rather administer selected subtests based on their relevancy to the presenting problems and appropriate to the skill level of the subject. Further, examiners are told to start the subject one year below their grade placement. Test administration is also facilitated by the permission given by the publisher to reproduce student pages that require written responses.

Brigance test items are also easy to score objectively. Multiple options are available to the test user for reporting test results. These options include a comprehensive class record book to report results by class and grade. Only mastery/nonmastery on each skill sequence can be recorded on the pupil record form and class record. Summary scores for each area are not available.

Grade placement scores are provided for the Inventory, even though the author cautions the test user on their use and suggests they should only be used to quickly identify students' global skill and achievement levels. However, the calibration of the grade level scores is too gross for classification purposes, and they do not allow for the precise measurement of the extent of a child's difficulty in an academic area. It is unclear how the grade placement scores were determined. Rather than grade placement scores, test users should report results in terms of objectives attained. It should be noted, however, that the test author does not specify how the performance standards or criterion levels were determined.

The number of items written for each objective appears appropriate to accurately measure each pupil's ability and distinguish between those who have and have not achieved the criterion for that objective. However, no reliability data are reported in the manual. At a minimum, alternate form reliability estimates should have been provided for the 51 skills having two forms. Further, the test author should have provided test-retest reliability data in the form of percentage agreement of mastery-nonmastery of particular objectives on two or more administrations of the test.

The most important type of validity for a test such as the Brigance is content validity. This type of validity provides information as to the congruence between test content and the skill domains identified in the test. According to the test author, experts judged the content of the Brigance items and evaluated them as representing the domains the test is intended to measure. Further, the author indicates that items were chosen through review of the most recently published texts of several widely used basal series, syllabi, and state guidelines. Information on item selection is incomplete; test users are not informed of how the experts were chosen or how items were selected for the final form of the inventory. Finally, items were selected solely by these experts rather than the more preferred method of selecting a random sample of the item population.

No data are presented in the manual comparing scores on the Brigance to scores on other measures believed to be related to the inventory. The test user has no information as to how other examinees performed on the test by geographic region, sex, age, etc. The field testing procedure employed in the development of the Brigance is not described in any detail, and it is unclear how it contributed to the development of the inventory.

However, because behavioral objectives are precise, the test user can determine how well the instrument will measure locally established objectives. The test user must make the judgment at the local level to determine if objectives measured by the test items are congruent with local curriculum objectives. Due to the great diversity in reading curriculum, the reading skill area on the Brigance is better supplemented with more curriculum-based assessment using the actual reading series used in a district. Because no information is presented on item analysis, it is difficult for the test user to determine how test questions meet the requirements of measuring a particular objective and how well the items do in differentiating between those pupils who have and have not mastered a particular objective.

In summary, the Brigance is a well constructed inventory that is easy to administer and score and covers a wide age range. It assesses a broad range of academic skill areas. Although the Brigance is recommended for use, it does not tell the test user how good or poor a subject's achievement is in each of the skill areas. The Brigance should therefore be used in conjunction with good norm-referenced tests. However, the Brigance can yield very useful information that is easily translated into individualized educational programs for normal pupils and students with special needs.

[163]

Brigance Diagnostic Inventory of Basic Skills. Grades K–6; 1976; IBS; criterion-referenced; 141 specific-objective tests in 4 areas: readiness (24 tests), reading (word recognition, 6 tests; oral reading, 3 tests; word analysis, 19 tests; vocabulary, 5 tests), language arts (handwriting, 3 tests; grammar mechanics, 3 tests; spelling, 5 tests; reference skills, 9 tests), mathematics (grade level; numbers, 13 tests; operations, 17 tests; measurement, 25 tests; geometry, 8 tests); no data on reliability; norms (no description of derivation) for 10 tests; no suggested standards of mastery for 65% of the tests; individual; 1 form; response booklet (15 pages); manual (4 pages plus 162 pages of tests); 1985 price data: $69.95 per examiner's kit including manual, test, and 10 student record booklets; $11.95 per package of 10 student record booklets; complete specimen set not available, however preview excerpts free of charge; Spanish edition available; specific time limits are listed on many tests, others are untimed; Albert Brigance; Curriculum Associates, Inc.*

See T3:313 (1 reference).

Review of Brigance Diagnostic Inventory of Basic Skills by CORINNE ROTH SMITH, *Director, Psychoeducational Teaching Laboratory, Syracuse University, Syracuse, NY:*

The Brigance Diagnostic Inventory of Basic Skills is a criterion-referenced measure of academic readiness, reading, language arts, and math skills ranging from kindergarten through sixth-grade levels. It is also appropriate for academic assessment of older students functioning below sixth-grade academic levels. Each of the inventory's tests has a suggested administration format which, like the items, can be varied according to the school's curriculum and the assessment needs of the student. While test items are conveniently presented by flipping loose leaf pages and writing with overhead marking pens on plastic sheets, the format becomes tedious if overtesting occurs. Since the purpose of the inventory is to assess whether an individual has gained competence in a specific skill and which objectives require instruction, Brigance wisely warns to limit testing to only those tests that tap the skills in question. The inventory does an excellent job of meeting this objective by breaking skills into their component parts, thereby indicating specific criteria that have been mastered and those that remain instructional objectives. For example, contrary to standardized measures that judge letter mastery by asking the student to point to only five or six letters, the Brigance inventory asks the student to visually discriminate, read, and write all upper and lower case letters. It is particularly amenable to task analysis procedures that further clarify test performance: e.g., point to letters when named by examiner, alter oral reading passage administration in order to assess silent reading or listening comprehension.

Readiness skills assessed by the inventory include: color naming; visual discrimination of shapes, letters, and short words; copying designs; drawing shapes from memory; draw a person; gross motor coordination; recognition of body parts; following directional and verbal instructions; fine-motor self-help skills; verbal fluency; sound articulation; personal knowledge; memory for sentences; counting; alphabet recitation; number naming and comprehension, letter naming; writing name, numbers and letters. The criteria evaluated by these subtests are common objectives within kindergarten curricula, thereby offering the kindergarten teacher information on exactly what to teach. Again, the test format is quite boring for young children, may not hold their attention, and may not elicit maximum effort. Therefore, it is suggested that examiners retain the evaluation items and general administration instructions, but creatively vary the testing format. For example, alphabet blocks, a blackboard, or a flannel board could be used to assess particular objectives in a far more exciting manner.

The reading tests evaluate word recognition, oral reading and comprehension, oral reading rate, word analysis (auditorily and while reading), meaning of prefixes, syllabication, and vocabulary. Language arts tests assess cursive handwriting, grammatic mechanics, spelling and reference skills. Besides operations through division of fractions and decimals, math tests assess rote counting, writing numerals in sequence, reading number words, ordinal concepts, numeral recognition and writing to dictation, counting in sets, Roman numerals, fractions, decimals, measurement (money, time, calendar, linear/liquid/weight measurement, temperature) and two and three dimensional geometric concepts. Again, performance on any of these tests is directly translatable into instructional objectives.

In contrast to its status as one of the most comprehensive elementary grade-level, criterion-referenced instruments, the Brigance inventory is on shaky grounds in determining a student's grade level performance on the tested skills. Though the test author claims that the measure can be used for grade placement decisions, the inventory cannot reliably and validly accomplish this. It has no norms to validate the sequence, difficulty level, or percent correct criteria for items within tests. Nor does it offer any data on the reliability of student performance or validity of placement decisions based on this performance.

The grade equivalency of the inventory's items was determined by researching the grade level at which a skill is first introduced by the majority of four school texts. Word recognition grade levels were assigned with the additional perusal of existing word lists. The sequence of readiness test items was selected from various developmental scales. Since the names of most of these selection materials are not reported by the author, nor has research been conducted using the inventory, there is no way to make even gross validity and reliability estimates. One must keep in mind that the Brigance inventory's item selection procedure combines the errors of the original sources.

Field testing on level and order of item difficulty did occur in California and Boston, but neither the child-based data nor reliability and validity figures are reported in the test. Apparently three unpublished 1970–75 versions of the inventory led to revisions based on the responses of 66 California teachers and curriculum specialists in 23 California schools. While such face validity is desirable, the absence of further validity and reliability data becomes a significant problem when Brigance suggests that test results be used for determining grade levels for instruction in reading, math, and spelling; for identifying learning disabilities; and for determining specific sequences for instruction. These purposes for evaluation cannot be validly fulfilled without determination of test reliability and validity relative to a standardization or research sample.

In spite of the suggestion in the Brigance inventory that grade-level scores be used for placement in instructional groups, its use should be reserved for evaluation of whether specific competencies have been mastered. Many far more efficient, norm-referenced instruments exist for the purpose of making grade equivalency determinations: e.g., Peabody Individual Achievement Test, Woodcock-Johnson Psychoeducational Battery, Woodcock Reading Mastery Tests, Test of Written Language, Key Math. On the other hand, the Brigance inventory's word recognition, spelling, and math grade-level scores could prove useful in an informal manner in deciding which other competencies to test, within which difficulty ranges to begin an informal reading inventory in the student's actual classroom texts, or whether to refer a child for a complete diagnostic evaluation. Noneducators (physicians, optometrists, speech pathologists, developmental pediatricians) may find these and some of the readiness tests to be convenient, gross aids to referral decisions, especially considering that no specialized test administration training is required.

An additional value of the Brigance inventory is in demonstrating to a teacher how to construct his or her own criterion-referenced instrument. It offers the teacher an excellent model for pretesting and posttesting for mastery of actual classroom curriculum objectives.

In summary, the Brigance is a criterion-referenced measure of readiness, reading, language arts, and math skills that is well-suited to determining mastery of very specific teaching objectives. Due to lack of validity and reliability information as well as a normative or research sample, it is not appropriate for making decisions that compare children against one another or specific academic materials (e.g., class or reading group placement). It is valuable in that it helps determine what has and has not been learned, highlights very specific instructional objectives, requires no testing expertise, is modifiable, is adaptable to task analysis procedures, and can help in a gross way with referral decisions. As Brigance emphasizes, the measure is best used in conjunction with evaluation of the student's classroom products, classroom observation, and scrutiny of actual curricular goals.

Review of Brigance Diagnostic Inventory of Basic Skills by JOSEPH C. WITT, Associate Professor of Psychology, Louisiana State University, Baton Rouge, LA:

The Brigance Diagnostic Inventory of Basic Skills (BDIBS) is a criterion-referenced achievement test which is designed to measure four curricular areas: readiness, reading, language arts, and mathematics. It is individually administered, and like other criterion-referenced tests, can be used to assess the presence or absence of specific skills within learning hierarchies. In addition, the publisher asserts that the test is comprehensive enough to be used as an instructional management system. Forms are provided so that, at a glance, a teacher would have a record of each child's cumulative performance over time and could use that as a basis for determining specific areas of instructional need.

The BDIBS contains subtests designed to measure over 200 behavioral objectives representing 140 skill sequences. Each subtest is designed to answer the question, "Has the student mastered this skill adequately, or is additional instruction needed?"

The test is contained in a plastic ring binder that is designed to be laid open and placed between an examiner and a student during testing. The specific instructions for administering a subtest are contained on the page facing the examiner while the test stimuli face the child. The examiner's page also contains instructions for discontinuing the test, time limits, grade-level scores and an instructional objective for the subtest or area being assessed. A separate student record booklet is used to record the student's responses. The design of the student booklet is commendable because it is organized so that the skills generally range from easy to difficult, and a teacher can ascertain quickly the next skill in an instructional sequence. In addition, the booklets can be used several times, which not only decreases cost but allows for the formative evaluation of each skill assessed. The test is attractive in appearance and very easy to use and transport. Plastic tabs make it easy to access subtests for specific skills. Ease of access is important because it is unlikely that all the test would be given.

Two potential problems with test administration were detected. First, the guidelines on where to begin testing are imprecise. The manual recommends testing begin at a level where "the student can experience success 90% of the time." No further information is provided on how to determine this a priori. A second problem is that the publisher recommends using teacher aides or other paraprofessionals to administer the test. This may be unwise because observations and interactions during testing provide a rich array of information which may be lost to an untrained eye. Further, many aides simply lack the technical knowledge to administer some of the items (e.g., distinguishing the voiced from the unvoiced "th" sound).

Many items are termed "text-referenced" because they were selected by examining "the more commonly used texts to determine the grade level at which a skill is first introduced by a majority of texts." The exact texts and the process used in the text-referencing process are not specified. For example, "waiting" and "early" are placed at the fourth-grade level on the spelling subtest because those words were first introduced at the fourth-grade level in all of the texts surveyed during test development. The readiness scales were referenced to "commonly used developmental scales." Not all of the items are text-referenced and the criteria used for selecting the unreferenced items are not specified. Further, it is difficult or impossible to determine which items are text-referenced and which are not.

The grade equivalent scores available on the BDIBS were derived from the text referencing process and not from a norm group. The word recognition subtest provides an illustration of the arbitrary nature of some aspects of test development. The grade equivalent table for this subtest was constructed to yield a score three months below the grade equivalent score the same student would be expected to earn on the Wide Range Achievement Test. The process for doing this and the rationale for selecting "three months below" are not provided.

The greatest deficiency of the BDIBS is the complete absence of data concerning reliability and validity. The time is past when criterion-referenced tests are subject to less stringent criteria than norm-referenced tests (Hambleton & Eignor, 1978). Technical information, which is typically presented in a test manual, is contained in a four-page introduction and a two-page appendix to the 320-page test. These short sections provide directions for administering the test and describe briefly some aspects of test development. The information reflects a lack of careful attention to detail and most technical psychometric data are incomplete or missing. Reliability, for example, is not mentioned. Since reliability is a function of test length, I suspect the reliability figures will be adequate because each of the skills are measured by a number of items. The manual does not discuss the important issue of "error" in test scores or possible sources of error. It is necessary to know the stability of a child's performance on an objective especially if important educational decisions are to be made on that basis. The fact that the publisher suggests a flexible administration format and advocates the use of paraprofessionals as test administrators may increase measurement error. Thus, a student's mastery level may be attributable to factors irrelevant to the student's mastery level of achievement. This possibility is not addressed in the descriptive materials provided with the test.

As with reliability, the authors provided no technical data with respect to validity. The information which is provided pertains only to content validity, which was assessed by asking "66 teachers and other curriculum personnel" if any changes were needed in the test and if the test was relevant to their students. The exact number of "other" people surveyed and the process utilized were not specified. With respect to content validity, the breadth of the items is certainly impressive. However, most of the items measure objectives taught prior to the end of second grade. This is because each lower level mechanical skill (i. e., phoneme-grapheme correspondence) merits a separate objective, while higher level conceptual skills are almost ignored. Reading comprehension, math application, and other conceptual skills are assessed inadequately, especially in comparison to a norm-referenced test such as the Iowa Test of Basic Skills where conceptual objectives reflect skills much closer to the outcome expected after the seven years of reading and math instruction. The assumption is made that if children master each of the subskills in the hierarchy, then they will be able to read or compute. This assumption may be faulty on two counts. First, unless higher level conceptual skills are taught specifically, they may not be acquired. Second, some children can learn to master the terminal objective without going through the drudgery of mastering each component skill. Reading, for example, involves the integrated, strategic use of many skills, but an instructional system such as the one based upon the BDIBS, appears to encourage teaching skills in isolation from reading. Even if most children follow the developmental sequence of skills utilized by the BDIBS, and this assumption is questionable, it is difficult to justify only one skill sequence for use with *all* children. For example, in arithmetic, research does not indicate that worksheet decimal addition aids or enhances the learning of the *concept* of the decimal system and its application to addition (Poplin & Gray, 1980). The point is that teachers using the BDIBS should not use it in a lock-step fashion and should not continue to focus energy on unmastered skills with children who can function effectively on higher level skills. In other words, it may be logical to bypass some skills in the hierarchy, but the author of BDIBS does not address this possibility.

Some validity issues also arise with respect to the behavioral objectives provided for each subtest on the BDIBS. The most important, but unanswered, question is whether students classified as mastering an objective perform better than children who did not master the objective on some external criterion measure. A separate but related issue relates to the cutoff scores used within each objective which dictate whether or not a child has mastered that objective. Children who achieve above the cutoff score are assumed to have mastered the objective, and those who perform at a level below the cutoff score are targeted for additional instruction on that objective. Unfortunately, no empirical evidence and no rationale are offered for the selection of cutoff scores. Similarly, there is no evidence for the validity of a particular cutoff score.

In summary, the BDIBS does have a number of commendable qualities which include good content validity, ease and flexibility in administration, and an excellent format for reporting results and record keeping. However, there is a looseness about this instrument which one does not expect to find in commercially prepared tests. The most critical problem is a lack of attention to practically every important technical detail in test development. The BDIBS will be of greatest value to teachers, school psychologists, and educational diagnosticians who wish to conduct informal assessments of specific skills to supplement instructional observations. Because of a lack of technical data, the test should not be used for diagnosis or classification of students.

REVIEWER'S REFERENCES

Hambleton, R. L., & Eignor, D. P. Guidelines for evaluating criterion referenced tests and test manuals. JOURNAL OF EDUCATIONAL MEASUREMENT, 1978, 15, 321–327.

Poplin, M., & Gray, R. A conceptual framework for assessment of curriculum and student progress. EXCEPTIONAL EDUCATION QUARTERLY, 1980, 1, 75–86.

[164]

Brigance Diagnostic Inventory of Early Development. Ages 0–7; 1978; IED; criterion-referenced; 98 skills tests in 5 areas: motor skills (pre-ambulatory motor skills, 4 tests; gross motor skills, 13 tests; fine motor skills, 9 tests; self-help, 11 tests); speech-related skills (pre-speech, 3 tests; speech and language skills, 10 tests); general knowledge and comprehension (13 tests); written language skills (readiness, 5 tests; basic reading skills, 11 tests; manuscript writing, 7 tests); math (12 tests); no data on reliability; individual; 1 form; developmental record book (23 pages); manual (23 pages plus 245 pages of tests); 1983 price data; $57.95 per examiner's kit including manual, test, and 10 student record booklets; $12.95 per package of 10 student record booklets; excerpts free of charge; specific time limits are listed on a few tests, others are untimed; Albert Brigance; Curriculum Associates, Inc.*

Review of Brigance Diagnostic Inventory of Early Development by STEPHEN J. BAGNATO, Developmental School Psychologist, Assistant Professor of Child Psychiatry, Milton S. Hershey Medical Center, Pennsylvania State University College of Medicine, Hershey, PA:

DESCRIPTION. The Brigance Diagnostic Inventory of Early Development (IED) is actually the "developmental analysis" section of a continuous assessment system which spans the birth to 18 years age range. This system also includes the inventories of Basic and Essential Skills. With the recent and continuing emphasis on providing early intervention services to handicapped infants and preschoolers, the IED has many effective qualities that help to guide individualized assessment and programming. Constructed by a school psychologist, it is based on a developmental task-analytic model, combines norm- and criterion-based elements, and links assessment and curriculum goal planning.

The IED surveys the age range from birth to 7 years while analyzing 98 skill sequences within 11 major developmental domains. Because of its broadband survey of multiple developmental processes, the IED is a truly comprehensive and goal-based measure of child functioning throughout the infancy-early childhood period.

The IED requires no special administration techniques, although a firm grounding in developmental theory should be viewed as essential for accurately interpreting a child's behaviors. Teachers and developmental specialists can effectively administer the scale using its durable, flip-card format for displaying assessment material. The author notes that common objects in the classroom or home can be used to supplement the test. Evidence of a child's optimal performance can be derived from multiple sources (e.g., parent interview, observations, diagnostic teaching, and pragmatic modifications of tasks). It is stressed that "If adaptations provide a more valid assessment of particular skills, use them, since the Inventory is not a norm-referenced test." Moreover, the IED allows a variety of response styles (e.g., verbal, pointing, eye localization, paper-pencil behaviors) to help accommodate certain dysfunctions. The scale is given by selecting specific tasks according to the child's age, functional level, and the purpose for the assessment. Performance is scored by circling completed tasks and making qualitative comments about performance. Similarly, each skill sequence is defined by a span of developmental ages at which learning of a skill typically emerges and is mastered by most children. A system of color-coding with pencils is suggested as a practical guide for monitoring periodic reassessments of the child's developmental progress. This developmental task-analytic format effectively merges assessment, goal-oriented teaching, and progress evaluation. The availability of a computerized method of creating Individualized Educational Program's (IEP's) with the Brigance makes the scale highly valuable in an ongoing early intervention program.

NORMS. The IED is a multifactor developmental measure which effectively blends norm- and criterion-referenced curricular qualities, yet has no self-contained normative base, itself. As with most commercially available developmental curricula, item placement and skill sequencing on the IED were accomplished by reviewing traditional scales and resources (e.g., Gesell, Bayley, Griffith, White, Lavatelli) in order "to establish and validate the skill sequences and the developmental ages." Specific references regarding item placement are listed clearly before each assessment subdomain. This procedure shows painstaking work and is a model for criterion-based test construction. Moreover, the final edition of the scale was field-tested by over 100 developmental specialists in a variety of clinical and educational settings in 16 states, which supports the measure's quality and practicality.

TECHNICAL ADEQUACY. The major limitation of the IED, as with most criterion-referenced measures, is the absence of basic research data on reliability and validity in the manual section (e.g., test-retest reliability, concurrent validity). Content validity appears to be and should be adequate; yet, a much more solid technical base needs to be established with wider use of the measure. Moreover, data from independent research studies which employ the IED should be cited and annotated in the manual.

CRITIQUE. Because of its broad survey of developmental processes and its merger of norm- and criterion-based features, the IED is one of the best and most practical of the newly marketed, criterion-referenced developmental batteries. Several features highlight its excellent qualities. The IED "links" assessment and intervention elements in one format. This is accomplished by arranging developmental tasks in a hierarchical manner and matching appropriate objectives to these assessment tasks for each subdomain (e.g., social speech, classification, visual discrimination, puzzles). In this format, pre-ambulatory and general motor skills are broken down quite well into 17 subdomains. Next, the graphics to illustrate each task and the standardized directions for administration serve to make the tasks highly interesting and motivating. The drawings and stimuli are detailed and colorful, which make visual discriminations more reliable. Also, the IED offers a flexible system of scoring the presence, absence, and quality of responses by emphasizing that performance data should be collected across multiple sources (e.g., observation, interview, judgment, elicited performance). This feature increases the likelihood that emerging, situation-specific skills can be checked and recorded. The inclusion of drawings or pictures of the skills to be observed serves to effectively increase the likelihood of more precise and reliable assessments, especially in the motor domain.

Despite the scale's obviously effective features, some practical limitations need to be noted. Unlike comparable scales such as the Uniform Performance Assessment System (UPAS) and the Early Intervention Developmental Profile (EIDP), the IED presents certain task analyses which are not always sufficiently narrow enough to accommodate the functional capabilities of severely and multihandicapped infants and young children. The Language, Perceptual, and Fine Motor skill areas are indicative of this. In addition, the scale lacks a sufficiently detailed assessment of separate auditory and visual functions. Perhaps revisions of the scale will establish distinct subdomain sequences for these sensory processes. Next, while the matched assessment-programming objectives are crucial, the objectives are exactly the same as the assessment tasks and encourage "teaching to the test" and, thus, the development of non-functional splinter skills. Objectives which emphasize teaching a "cluster" of related skills or processes (e.g., visual focusing, tracking, grasp and reach) would appear to remedy this difficulty. Finally, a unique dimension would be added to the IED if specific suggestions were offered for adapting assessment tasks to circumvent the impact of various developmental dysfunctions (visual, auditory, neuromotor) and, thereby, provide diagnostic guides to teachers for the most effective modes of presenting learning materials and tasks.

SUMMARY. The IED is one of the best available criterion-based measures of developmental functioning in a non-curricular format. It is easy to use, motivating for children, and effectively fulfills a variety of assessment purposes (e.g., assessment, goal-planning, progress evaluation). However, its use with young severely and multihandicapped children needs to be viewed critically since other scales are more appropriate for such children (e.g., Uniform Performance Assessment System). In addition, even though it is a criterion-based measure, basic reliability and validity data must be generated to guide consumers. Nevertheless, few assessment systems merge assessment and individualized goal-planning for young children as well as the IED.

Review of Brigance Diagnostic Inventory of Early Development by ELLIOT L. GORY, Psychology, Getz School for the Developmentally Disabled, Tempe, AZ:

The Brigance Diagnostic Inventory of Early Development (IED) is a criterion-referenced test for use with infants and children whose developmental level ranges from birth through six years. The developmental nature of this skill-based assessment device also permits ready use with older, but developmentally delayed individuals. According to information stated in the test instructions, the IED is useful in defining a child's profile of strengths and weaknesses on a wide variety of developmental tasks, as a record keeping system of a child's progress, and as a tool for developing instructional objectives in planning a child's educational program. The instrument also is useful in making diagnostic/referral decisions and as a communication method for use with parents and program staff in describing a child's abilities and needs within a developmental framework.

Eleven functional domains, with subdomain sequences, make up the IED (see inventory description above). The skill sequences within each domain area are arranged in difficulty via a combined developmental/task analytic hierarchy. IED areas are representative of the major areas of function in early childhood and can yield a truly representative profile of a child's behavior. The only exception is the conspicuous absence of a social-emotional domain with attendant skill sequences. This important information must be obtained by other supplementary methods, e.g., observation, parent/staff report, or the use of a subtest from another scale such as the AAMD Adaptive Behavior Scale.

The test consists of an examiner's ring-bound manual with durable, hard plastic covers and separate, paper-bound record booklets. These items are durable, distinctive, and easily transportable. Various manipulatives (e.g., balls, bean bags, toys, etc.) are not supplied in the test kit and provide the test user an opportunity to reduce cost by independently purchasing this equipment or by using items commonly available in schools and homes. Manual instructions include exceedingly clear directions, examples, and illustrations. A fairly comprehensive list of "do's" and "don'ts" makes a handy checklist for users who may be new to developmental or criterion-referenced assessment. With a minimum of review and practice, psychologists, speech therapists, occupational/physical therapists, and teachers are able to administer, score, and interpret the test. General data gathering methods employed by a user of the IED include observation, parent or teacher report, and a child's test performance. Response requirements for children include a wide range of behaviors such as simple reflexes, pointing, verbalization, and paper/pencil performance. The manual includes frequent encouragement and some suggestions for adapting the test procedure to accommodate children who may be physically and/or mentally handicapped.

During direct assessment of many areas, especially pre-academic and readiness skills, the tab-indexed manual is placed flat and open on a table between the examiner and child. When a page is turned, the child is presented with a page of visual stimulus material for accomplishing a task, and the examiner is presented with a page of directions for administering the task. This format, similar to the test procedure used with the Peabody Picture Vocabulary Test—Revised (PPVT-R), significantly contributes to the test user's ability to quickly put the instrument into use with a minimum of transferring attention from test manual to test task. The child's performance, whether directly observed or by parent/teacher report, is recorded in the accompanying record book. Test behavior is scored by circling tasks mastered and writing qualitative comments about the child's performance, test situation, or test adaptations that the examiner may wish to note. Developmental age levels where skills are typically mastered are indicated beside most test items in the record book. Use of a different color pencil for each administration of the test with a given child is suggested as a means for effective and easy visual representation of progress and accomplishment over time. This suggestion also permits savings to the test user by permitting use of the same record book over repeated assessments of the same child. Depending on a child's ability and selection of areas to be assessed, test administration may take 30 to 90 minutes. In practice, frequently only selected domain areas of interest are examined and the entire test is not administered. This suggested practice, and beginning a skill sequence at a child's estimated ability level, provide a means to reduce test administration time.

The IED is truly a criterion-referenced test, and test construction and interpretation of results are appropriate for this kind of measure. Task items in the test were selected on the basis of a careful literature review in which age norms for various skills were specified. References used to set developmental levels at which various skills typically are mastered are available in the test manual. This method of norm-referencing test items has been used, reasonably, in lieu of specific normative studies. No formal validity or reliability studies exist at this time. Test-retest reliability studies, possibly necessitating the development of an alternate test form, are suggested as a means to enhance the credibility of this worthwhile test. Also, more specific suggestions are needed for validating information derived from parent report. The author suggests that the principal use of the Inventory is to identify skill areas where a child may need more practice or training. Indeed, a major strength of this test is the ease and clarity with which test results on specific skills and skill areas may be translated into training objectives that are consistent with the curricula of many preschool, primary, elementary, and special education programs for the developmentally disabled.

In conclusion, the Brigance Diagnostic Inventory of Early Development is a developmentally sequenced criterion-referenced test appropriate for children and developmentally disabled clients whose functional age levels range from birth to 7 years. Except for lack of a social-emotional skill domain, the test is very comprehensive and assesses 11 major skill domains. Developmental ages at which skills are typically mastered are defined adequately on the basis of a thorough literature review. Reliability information is needed to enhance the credibility of this instrument. Ease of administration, versatility in administration methods, and clarity of behavioral information gained make the IED one of the best devices for use with the developmentally young. The IED should receive widespread use by preschool, elementary school, and special education staff interested in child assessment outcome products that are relevant to curriculum, intervention, and educational program planning.

[165]

Brigance Diagnostic Inventory of Essential Skills. Grades 4–12; 1981; IES; criterion-referenced; 10 rating scales and 180 specific-objectives; 191 tests in 4 areas: reading (word recognition grade placement, 1 test; oral reading, 5 tests; reading comprehension, 9 tests; functional word recognition, 6 tests; word analysis, 9 tests), language arts (reference skills, 5 tests; schedules and graphs, 3 tests; writing, 7 tests; forms, 2 tests; spelling, 8 tests), mathematics (math grade placement, 2 tests; numbers, 4 tests; number facts, 4 tests; computations of whole numbers, 6 tests; fractions, 9 tests; decimals, 6 tests; percents, 4 tests; measurement, 15 tests; metrics, 16 tests; math vocabulary, 3 tests), life skills (health and safety, 6 tests; vocational, 23 tests; money and finance, 11 tests; travel and transportation, 10 tests; food and clothing, 10 tests; oral communication and telephone skills, 7 tests); no data on reliability; individual in part; Forms A and B for 6 of the tests all in the same book; response booklet (42 pages); manual (31 pages plus 361 pages of tests); 1983 price data: $99.95 per examiner's kit including manual, tests, and 10 student record books; $16.95 per package of 10 student record books; complete specimen set not available, however preview excerpts free of charge; specific time limits are listed on many tests, others are untimed; Albert Brigance; Curriculum Associates, Inc.*

Review of Brigance Diagnostic Inventory of Essential Skills by PAULA MATUSZEK, Assistant Professor of Educational and Counseling

Psychology, University of Tennessee, Knoxville, TN:

The Brigance is a very detailed criterion-referenced test aimed primarily at secondary school students and designed to assess basic skills that are seen as necessary for successful functioning as an adult.

The test is divided into 26 general areas, such as Food and Clothing. These overall areas are in turn divided into more detailed skills, such as Food Vocabulary, Basic Recipe Directions, and Foods for a Daily Balanced Diet. There are 191 individual skills in all. Each skill is introduced separately, with directions, a skill analysis, related skills, and educational objectives related to the skill. In addition, each major area is introduced with a discussion of purpose, methods of assessment, grade levels, and other information relevant to that section. Most subtests are individually administered. About half can also be administered in a group. Ten skills, in areas such as Speaking Skills and Self-Concept, are measured through teacher rating forms.

Like most criterion-referenced tests, the Brigance lacks any kind of national norms. According to the manual, the items were developed by an extensive review of relevant literature, and field tested in a variety of sites. Materials were tested for relevance, content validity, and needed changes. Most skills were assessed by the field sites as having moderate to high relevance and high content validity. One subtest (Roman Numerals), which was not rated as highly relevant, was dropped; several were modified. The manual provides a partial list of field sites; in all, sites were drawn from 26 states and two Canadian programs. Some skills, such as Word Recognition Grade Placement, also list texts which provided the source for item content. Others are stated to be the level at which a skill is normally taught, without providing references. A few, such as the metric skills, indicate that there is little uniformity in the grade at which skills are introduced. It is suggested throughout the manual that local expectations and standards are more important in interpretation than the grade levels provided in the manual.

The assessment of reliability and validity for criterion-referenced instruments is an issue at present. Many of the methods used for typical norm-referenced tests seem inappropriate for criterion-referenced instruments. However, it cannot automatically be assumed that criterion-referenced instruments are reliable; while a test as detailed as the Brigance may minimize error due to sampling, all the other sources of error that contribute to unreliability are applicable. Both test-retest reliability and in some cases alternate form reliability could easily be calculated for many skill areas on the Brigance, and would provide useful and appropriate information. A study by Lindsey (1983) compared the Brigance Reading and Math Grade Level tests to the Wide Range Achievement Test (WRAT) and the Peabody Individual Achievement Test (PIAT) and found that Brigance grade levels for both these areas are higher than the PIAT, and that Brigance math scores are also higher than the WRAT. The grade level scores on the WRAT and PIAT are not necessarily more appropriate measures, but it is clear that the scores cannot be used interchangeably.

Except for the rating scales, the most appropriate form of validity for the Brigance is content validity; the manual provides some information regarding this area, and the user can judge the test for appropriate content for the expected use. Some additional information on the sources of grade levels and the results of the field study, and substantial additional validation of the rating scales, would be desirable. The most questionable skills on the Brigance in terms of validity are the rating scales. These were reviewed for content validity, and references for the item sources are given, but no formal studies of the technical adequacy of these scales were carried out. At a minimum, studies of inter-rater reliability and concurrent validity would be desirable. The manual is clear on the limited validity of these scales, and the author has been sensitive to their possible misuse. Thus, for instance, the standard record book has no place to record the results of these scales, and the instructions indicate that it is probably unwise to keep any permanent record of them. This approach is preferable to nothing, and the areas measured are probably of enough relevance to warrant the use of rating scales in spite of their validity problems. Nonetheless, it would certainly be desirable to see better technical data on these areas.

Overall, the Brigance Diagnostic Inventory of Essential Skills is a carefully designed, very detailed assessment tool. The manual is well arranged for easy administration, and it is easy to give only a part of the test. The manual provides suggestions for use, objectives, references, and other helpful information. It can form a useful part of an overall teaching program, especially as part of an Individual Educational Plan for a child whose high school education is focused on acquiring basic skills. The very broad scope of the test allows educators to choose those areas relevant to their own programs and students. The author of the Brigance clearly recognizes the limitations of criterion-referenced tests, and the manual is explicit in warning against some possible misuses of the results.

The Brigance cannot be used as part of a single assessment session; the overall administration time for the entire instrument would be many hours. In addition, some subtests require that the tester know the child fairly well. Some entire areas, such as Travel and Transportation and Vocational, are limited in their scope, and are intended largely for informal planning. Its usefulness is more within a classroom framework than within the more typical diagnostic framework of an individual assessment. For classification it has little utility, since neither norms nor reliability data are provided. Its use is also primarily with children (or adults) for whom minimum survival skills are the educational goal. It would be inappropriate for high school students functioning at an average level or above.

REVIEWER'S REFERENCES

Lindsey, J. D. Comparison of educably mentally retarded students' Brigance, PIAT AND WRAT achievement scores. JOURNAL FOR SPECIAL EDUCATORS, 1983, 19(3), 66–71.

Review of the Brigance Diagnostic Inventory of Essential Skills by PHILIP A. SAIGH, Associate Professor of Education, American University of Beirut, Beirut, Lebanon:

The Inventory of Essential Skills is a criterion-referenced measure that consists of 191 skill sequences and 10 rating scales. The instrument was designed to accommodate the assessment needs of secondary programs that cater to students with "special needs." In constructing and field testing the instrument, the author drew on more than 20 years of professional experience, knowledge gained through developing the Inventory of Early Development and the Inventory of Basic Skills, consultations with interested personnel, and an extensive review of the literature. The record book-manual also indicates that 103 skill sequences were field tested by more than 100 participants from 55 programs in 26 states and 2 Canadian locations.

A detailed examination of the Inventory revealed that it has two major sections and that the first section involves a sequential arrangement of subtests that reflect reading, writing, spelling, and mathematics skills that are appropriate for grades 4 through 11. The second section presents a series of interrelated subtests that are intended to measure adaptive behaviors pertaining to health, safety, employment, money, finance, travel, nutrition, and clothing. In doing so, the author drew on a rich array of life-related tasks (e.g., filling out an IRS 1040 form, using a pay telephone, or reading a road map). Interspaced within the second section are a number of rating scales that purport to assess attitudes or traits that are not readily amenable to observational recording techniques (e.g., attitudes toward job interviews).

Addressing procedures for administering the Inventory, the record-manual advises users to identify and assess discrete skills at specified levels of achievement in lieu of administering the Inventory in its full length, inasmuch as the scope of the Inventory is too comprehensive (375 pages) for normal administration. It is further advised that personnel trained in criterion-referenced testing and curriculum development are best suited to supervise the use of the Inventory. Twenty-one recommendations are offered to facilitate the use of the Inventory and standardized administrative procedures are listed throughout. Paradoxically, it is proposed that "the Inventory of Essential Skills, a criterion-referenced test, does not require rigid administrative procedures usually used in comparing students."

Viewed from a more comprehensive perspective, criterion-referenced testing has justifiably enjoyed a considerable degree of utility since the early 1960s. Nevertheless, it should be recalled that the ultimate value of a test is gauged by its ability to generate reliable and valid information. It is unfortunate to observe in this regard that the record-manual of the Inventory of Essential Skills is conspicuously void of psychometric data. Of course, it may be argued that criterion-referenced testing may present discrete measurement problems (e.g., mastery reduces variability and increased homogeneity attenuates coefficients). This argument is tenuous, however, as a number of strategies have been formulated to facilitate the psychometric analysis of criterion-referenced tests.

In conclusion, it is readily apparent that a great deal of time and effort went into the development of this inventory. It is also evident that the use of this instrument should be precluded in special education settings until its psychometric properties have been empirically demonstrated.

[166]

Brigance K & 1 Screen for Kindergarten and First Grade. Grades K, 1; 1982; no reliability or validity data; no norms; individual; 1 form; 2 levels; manual (80 pages, includes observation and rating forms which can be reproduced locally); pupil data sheet (3 pages) for each level; 1983 price data: $24.95 per manual (test) and one each sample pupil data sheet; $11 per 30 pupil data sheets and 1 class summary record folder; administration time varies depending upon administrator and student; Albert H. Brigance; Curriculum Associates, Inc.*

a) KINDERGARTEN. Grade K; 13 scores: personal data response, color recognition, picture vocabulary, visual discrimination, visual-motor skills, gross motor skills, rote counting, identification of body parts, follows verbal directions, numeral comprehension, prints personal data, syntax and fluency, total.

b) FIRST GRADE. Grade 1; 14 scores: personal data response, color recognition, picture vocabulary, visual discrimination, visual-motor skills, draw a person (body image), rote counting, recites alphabet, numeral comprehension, recognition of lower case letters, auditory discrimination, prints personal data, numerals in sequence, total.

Review of Brigance K & 1 Screen for Kindergarten and First Grade by ANN E. BOEHM, Professor of Psychology and Education, Teachers College, Columbia University, New York, NY:

The Brigance K & 1 Screen was developed as a brief (10 to 20 minute) screening instrument to provide a picture of overall development in five basic areas: language development, motor ability, number skills, body awareness, and auditory and visual discrimination. The Screen is to be used to rank or group children who are high, average, or lower than their local reference group in order to contribute to readiness decisions, to make placement decisions, and to serve as an indicator for more comprehensive evaluation or referral for special services. The Pupil Data Sheet includes sections where the assessor can indicate a summary rating and a recommendation for placement. Children scoring either higher or lower than the local average may be referred for more comprehensive evaluation which may include use of either the Brigance Diagnostic Inventory of Early Development (1978; birth to age 7) or the Diagnostic Inventory of Basic Skills (1977; K through grade 6) to assist teachers in developing appropriate and challenging curricular goals. Furthermore, items for the 17 skill areas (12 at the K level and 13 at the grade 1 level) were selected from, and may duplicate, items in these two more comprehensive batteries. Thus, information obtained from prior use of either of these instruments may be recorded on the Screen and vice versa. A table references items to each of the comprehensive inventories for quick referral or follow-up assessment.

The test claims to be both criterion- and curriculum-referenced so that results can be translated into curriculum objectives. There are no norms. The stated rationale is that readiness is a continuous process that cannot be reflected by a norm-referenced score. Here lies the most fundamental problem with the otherwise carefully prepared materials, since one use of the test is to review the score and use it in arriving at readiness or placement decisions. Yet no predictive validity or reliability data are presented, each of which is essential to making such decisions.

In contrast to the Brigance diagnostic inventories to which items are referenced, the K & 1 Screen does not lead directly to instructional objectives. Clearly one can develop objectives by referring to identical items on the other two comprehensive instruments and using the format provided to translate results. This procedure, however, requires the availability of the other instruments and is a cumbersome process.

The author repeatedly and advisedly cautions that screening involves a team effort and that pupil performance on the Screen needs to be supported by other information. Materials are suggested for "Screening Observations" on the part of the assessor and for both parent and teacher observation/rating procedures appropriate for children entering kindergarten and grade 1. It would have been useful if the author also had provided the user with data as to the likelihood of false positive and negative decisions. Specific correlations with other measures, including the skill mastery information from the suggested parent and teacher observations/ratings, would have been useful as well.

The manual materials are clear both for the administrator and the pupil. Helpful procedural information is provided for pre-administration planning (scheduling, room arrangements, alternate procedures); for administration (possible observations and supplemental assessments); and for post-administration evaluation (reasons for low scores, sources of errors made by pupils, and suggestions to help identify causes for incompatibility of data). Specialized training in test administration is not required; paraprofessionals with training and supervision can assist in the process. Child responses are recorded on a grade-appropriate, one-page Pupil Data Sheet with three attached carbon copies. Point values are assigned to each skill area, which result in a composite score of 100 used for ranking or grouping pupils. Pupil responses are objectively checked. The scoring criteria, time limits, and cutoff points are all clearly presented. The items in each skill area are weighted, but the rationale employed for assigning weights is not specified. Examinee materials are large and clear except for two visual discrimination tasks which present 10 items per page.

The scores of all pupils tested in the local group are to be ranked from highest to lowest and divided into three groups. An individual pupil's score is then checked as to whether it is higher, average, or lower than this local reference group. The author recommends that pupils scoring below 60 be evaluated in detail. "Advanced Assessments" in five areas are recommended for use with pupils scoring 95% or above. The results of the "Advanced Assessments" are not included on the Pupil Data Sheet.

Skill areas included on the Screen were selected through a review of the literature as those "having the greatest predictive validity for success in kindergarten and first grade" and supported by the field testing and user requirements. The bibliography included was not referenced to specific skills. Both content and predictive validity are implied but not supported by evidence provided in the manual. The technical portion of the manual could have presented more comprehensive documentation.

Content validity is also suggested through concurrence of user opinion. During extensive field testing in 53 schools in 14 states, users rated and critiqued the appropriateness of the content for screening. A summary of the percentage of raters viewing skill areas as appropriate by grade level is the only field test data presented in the manual. It is unfortunate that this field testing was not used to produce reliability and validity information. The areas covered by the Screen provide the user with helpful information related to important aspects of early school learning.

In summary, the Brigance K & 1 Screen is a carefully presented set of items in 17 skill areas which are to be used to help make curriculum and placement decisions. Using it to make curriculum decisions is justified, since the teacher can decide whether the areas covered match local goals. Readiness and placement decisions are more problematic, despite the caution that the Screen should be used in the context of other information. Evidence of predictive validity necessary to make placement decisions is not presented. Reliability data are totally lacking. Given the acknowledged variability of young children, at least test-retest reliability data should have been provided. Thus, while the Brigance K & 1 Screen can prove a useful brief screening instrument covering important early skills, it should be used cautiously when making grouping or placement decisions. Until validity and reliability data are provided, users might better turn to instruments that provide such information.

Review of Brigance K & 1 Screen for Kindergarten and First Grade by DAN WRIGHT, School Psychologist, Ralston Public Schools, Ralston, NE:

The Brigance K & 1 Screen is the newest in a series of criterion-referenced inventories by the same author. Although it covers an age range already overlapped by two previous instruments, it is designed more specifically for screening students entering kindergarten and first grade. As the test description indicates, it provides a basis for shallow inquiry into a broad range of skills.

Administration of the test should be within the ability of anyone with training in individual assessment, although examiners may encounter some problems. Directions and scoring criteria are vague on several of the subtests, it may be easy to select the wrong level on some, and the record forms the examiner must use are cramped. Considerable latitude allowed in presentation decreases the extent to which students will encounter comparable experiences. A further difficulty for the students is that many of the stimulus pages present too much information, or contain items that are too small. More than one stimulus page per subtest would have been preferable.

Unfortunately, a more in-depth analysis of this test is rendered moot by the complete absence of relevant technical information. There is no discussion of how items were selected and field-tested, no evidence that they are adequately representative of their respective domains, and no information on their reliability or discriminability. There are no reliability estimates of any kind for subtest or total scores. Although the manual encourages that students at each level be assigned to one of four categories based on group results, it is not very helpful on how such standards should be derived. Studies on criterion-related and decision validity are necessary to support recommendation of such classification. It appears that because the test is "criterion-referenced," the author feels absolved of any need to support its psychometric adequacy.

Additionally, the manual describes uses for the test which are too broad. In the brief section on its features and rationale, it encourages or implies the test can be used for screening, placement, instructional planning, and pupil evaluation. Few tests are adequate for all these purposes, and the author has yet to support the adequacy of this one even for screening.

In summary, the Brigance K & 1 Screen is a screening device of unproven merit with a high potential for misuse. Users will be left with data of unknown meaning with which to make unsupported decisions. No screening at all would be preferable to the use of this test at this time.

[167]

Brigance Preschool Screen. Ages 3–4; 1985; BPS; evaluates basic readiness skills and development; criterion-referenced; no data on reliability; no suggested standards of mastery; separate data sheets for age 3 and age 4 (1 page); screen (assessment book, 90 pages and 10 blocks); 1985 price data: $11.95 per 30 age 3 data forms; $39.95 per 120 age 3 data forms; $12 per 30 age 4 data forms; $40 per 120 age 4 data forms; $29.95 per screen; (10–15) minutes; Albert H. Brigance; Curriculum Associates, Inc.*

a) AGE 3. 12 scores: personal data, identifies body parts, gross motor skills, identifies objects, repeats sentences, visual motor skills, number concepts, builds tower with blocks, matches colors, picture vocabulary, plurals, total.

b) AGE 4. 12 scores: personal data, identifies body parts, gross motor skills, tells use of objects, repeats sentences, visual motor skills, number concepts, builds tower with blocks, identifies colors, picture vocabulary, prepositions and irregular plural nouns, total.

[168]

Bristol Achievement Tests. Ages 8–0 to 9–11, 9–0 to 10–11, 10–0 to 11–11, 11–0 to 12–11, 12–0 to 13–11; 1969–82; BAT; 3 tests available as separates; Forms A, B, ('82, 7–8 pages); 5 levels; administrative manual ('82, 30 pages) for each level; interpretive manual ('69, 84 pages); profile ('69, 2 pages) for each form; 1985 price data: £5.55 per 25 tests; £3.25 per 25 profiles; £5.55 per teacher's set (without interpretive manual) of any one level (must be purchased to obtain administrative manual); £4.75 per interpretive manual; NFER-Nelson Publishing Co. [England].*

a) ENGLISH LANGUAGE. 6 scores: word meaning, paragraph meaning, sentence organisation, organisation of ideas, spelling and punctuation, total; 50(55) minutes for levels 1–3, 40(45) minutes for levels 4–5; Alan Brimer and Herbert Gross.

b) MATHEMATICS. 6 scores: number, reasoning, space, measurement, arithmetic laws and processes, total; 55(60) minutes; Alan Brimer.

c) STUDY SKILLS. 6 scores: properties, structures, processes, explanations, interpretations, total; 50(55) minutes; Alan Brimer, Margaret Fidler, Wynne Harlen, and John Taylor.

For reviews by G. A. V. Morgan and A. E. F. Pilliner of an earlier edition see 7:4. For a review of the English Language subtest, see 169 and 7:185; the Mathematics subtest, see 170 and 7:453; and the Study Skills subtest, see 171 and 7:776.

Review of Bristol Achievement Tests by F. G. BROWN, Professor of Psychology, Iowa State University, Ames, IA:

The 1982 edition of the Bristol Achievement Tests is a revision of the 1969 edition of the test. The extent of the revision, however, is unclear from the published materials accompanying the test. An advertising flyer mentions "extensive editorial, design, and statistical work," but the Interpretive Manual (IM) makes no mention of any revision. The Administrative Manual briefly notes that the Pupil Forms were redesigned and that changes were made in a small number of questions and instructions. It also states that as data from 7,500 pupils in 50 schools collected in 1982 showed that there were high correlations between the original and revised forms, no changes were made in the original statistical information. Thus the data presented in the current IM (which is still dated 1969) is presumably from the original edition of the test.

The battery consists of three tests—English Language, Mathematics, Study Skills—each of which is divided into five subsections. The tests are designed to be "balanced measures of basic skills and concepts in school achievement" but are not intended to completely represent the school curriculum. Rather "the tests focus deliberately on skills and conceptual strategies of knowing rather than upon the content of knowledge." The five levels of the battery are organized by a combination of age and level of schooling (i.e., grade). Within each test, the same objectives are measured at every level, although the relative emphasis varies among levels.

Items were originally written on the basis of psychological, pedagogical, and curriculum considerations. The item tryout and selection procedures were carefully and appropriately done and used large samples (331 to 706 pupils for each part by level sampling cell). Particularly noteworthy is the fact that item statistics were obtained for both the designated age level and adjacent levels. Items on the two forms were then matched for content and process. The authors did not, however, describe the tryout sample, only stating that it was representative in terms of ability and curriculum range.

Details on the selection of the standardization sample are also sketchy, but the authors state it was representative of England and Wales in terms of school size, school type, and urban/rural location. The standardization samples were sufficiently large ($N = 1,072$ to 1,265 per level) and, with one exception, contained about equal numbers of males and females. When necessary, groups were weighted to approximate the distribution of English school children more closely.

The means on the two forms differ, often significantly, with scores on Form B higher than those on Form A. This is expected as Form A is designed for beginning of the school year testing and Form B for retesting later in the year. These mean differences were corrected for when scores were transformed to standard scores. There were also significant sex differences on many of the tests.

The English Language test measures understanding the meanings of words from context, comprehension of prose, effectiveness of expression, organization of ideas, and punctuation and spelling. The Mathematics test covers the concept of number, sets and inferences, spatial relations, measurement, and arithmetic laws and processes. The Study Skills test assesses the skills and concepts used in environmental, physical, and biological sciences. Topics covered include properties of materials, structures, sequences and trends, explanations, and interpretations.

The Study Skills test, and parts of the Mathematics test, make extensive use of pictorial materials. Item quality is generally good and often inventive. For example, comprehension of prose is tested by having students supply the words needed to make a coherent passage rather than by having them answer questions about what they have read. Some items use a multiple-choice format but most require pupils to supply an answer. On all tests several questions frequently are based on a single common situation or example, such as a map, graph, table, or schematic drawing. With the exception of several English subtests, the individual items are not interdependent.

Responses are made in the test booklet, a format that requires hand scoring by the teacher. Teachers are also responsible for transforming the raw scores into the various derived scores. These scoring procedures are described in the manual, but are time consuming and open to a variety of clerical errors.

Scores on the three major sections are reported as standard scores (mean = 100, standard deviation = 15) and as percentile ranks. The standard scores are based on norm groups having a 2-month age range. Decile scores are reported for the subsections within each test. An expected error range, based on the standard error of measurement, is incorporated into the score reporting procedure. The manual also describes a procedure for obtaining predicted achievement level scores using scores on the words in context section of the English test as the estimator.

A strength of the manual is the many helpful suggestions—and cautions—for interpreting scores. The section on levels of confidence and educational decision making is particularly good. The IM even includes a nine-page short course in educational measurement to help test users better understand the psychometric principles underlying testing. On the other hand, the Student Profile sheet is quite complex, and although it is clearly explained in the manual, it will probably appear overwhelming when first using the test. The authors are also somewhat inconsistent in their recommendations regarding interpretation of subtest scores, in places pointing out their diagnostic value and in other places cautioning that they may easily be misinterpreted.

The only reliability data reported are the correlations between forms over a 2-week interval, using data from the standardization sample. The coefficients for the test scores are acceptably high (.92 to .95), with the exception of Study Skills levels 4 and 5 (.88 and .83, respectively). The correlations among subtests are lower, with median coefficients of .81 for the English and Mathematics subtests and .73 for the Study Skills subtests. No internal consistency reliability coefficients are reported, but standard errors of measurement are reported for all scores.

The intercorrelations among the tests are relatively high, in the .80s for levels 1 through 3 and somewhat lower at higher age levels.

An obvious weakness of the test is the lack of validity evidence. Although the care taken in developing the test lends some support for its content validity, no detailed studies or data regarding validity are reported. Even the content validity must be taken on faith as no item-by-item content/skill classification of items is presented in the manual. No correlations with other measures or achievement criteria are reported. The original IM (dated 1969) promised that validity data would be forthcoming, but no additional evidence or data appear in the current manual. The authors need to provide more empirical and logical support for the validity of the battery.

SUMMARY. The Bristol Achievement Tests have many good features. The item quality is good, the test appears to have been carefully standardized, the available reliability evidence is good, and the manuals are useful. The major weaknesses are the scoring procedures and the lack of validity evidence. As with any achievement test, the potential user's main question should be: How well does the content of the test reflect my curriculum? As the test was designed for use in England, potential users in other countries may not find the desired content match. Test developers, however, would be well advised to study the desirable features of the test and incorporate them into their tests.

[169]

Bristol Achievement Tests: English Language. Ages 8–0 to 9–11, 9–0 to 10–11, 10–0 to 11–11, 11–0 to 12–11, 12–0 to 13–11, 1969–82, 6 scores: word meaning, paragraph meaning, sentence organisation, organisation of ideas, spelling and punctuation, total; Forms A, B, ('82, 7–8 pages); 5 levels; administrative manual ('82, 30 pages) for each level; battery interpretive manual ('69, 84 pages); battery profile ('69, 2 pages) for each form; 1985 price data: £5.55 per 25 tests; £3.25 per 25 profiles; £5.55 per teacher's set (without interpretive manual) of any one level (must be purchased to obtain administrative manual); £4.75 per interpretive manual; 50(55) minutes for levels 1–3, 40(45) minutes for levels 4–5; Alan Brimer and Herbert Gross; NFER-Nelson Publishing Co. [England].*

For a review by Ralph D. Dutch of an earlier edition, see 7:185. For reviews of the complete battery, see 168 (1 review) and 7:4 (2 reviews).

Review of Bristol Achievement Tests: English Language by ROY A. KRESS, Professor Emeritus of Psychology of Reading, Temple University, Philadelphia, PA:

The revised edition of this 1969 test represents only "re-designed Pupil Forms and changes to a small number of questions and instructions." Apparently this new edition has not been restandardized. Instead, it was "trialled alongside the original edition in 50 schools, utilizing 7,500 pupils, during March and April 1982." However, none of the statistical data obtained in this administration has been made available and "no ammendments have been made to the original statistical information." The normative scales published in the Administrative Manuals are the same as those for the 1969 editions and the Interpretive Manual still carries a 1969 copyright. Thus, Ralph D. Dutch's review in *MMY* 7:185 would seem appropriate for the current edition as well.

Although the Interpretive Manual contains no new data pertinent to the revised edition, it is an excellent publication and section 3, "Understanding Achievement Tests," should be of great value to the teacher interested in educational measurement. However, one wonders why, in the elapsed time between the first and revised editions, no attempt has been made to establish validity evidence for this test. The author refers to the need for external criteria but none have been provided. Since the original raw score data reveal statistically significant differences between boys and girls on four of the test batteries one also wonders why the authors did not establish separate norms, especially at Level 1, where the significance was at the 1% level of confidence.

This reviewer found the concept of "error limits" expressed in the use of the profile sheets an interesting one and much like the "percentile band" used in some American tests. However, the procedure to be followed to identify the "error limit" range for each subtest is complicated and itself subject to examiner error. Further, the procedure suggests that the results obtained in such group achievement testing have significant diagnostic value for the individual child. Such is not the case. While this reviewer would not quarrel with the interpretation placed on the sample case presented, he would insist that there are several other possible interpretations; that to single out one of those possibilities and act solely upon it for that child is a dangerous practice indeed. The use of group administered achievement tests for individual diagnostic purposes is a questionable educational procedure.

Another interesting procedure advanced in the profile sheet is that of computing an expected score for each subtest based upon a measure of the subject's reading level. The reading level is obtained by scoring the subject's performance on the Word Meaning subtest. Thus reading ability is essentially defined as vocabulary knowledge. The procedure has a great deal of merit but is limited by this quite narrow definition of reading based upon the subject's Word Meaning score.

Each of the five subtests is concerned with some aspect of the reading process. The Word Meaning subtest attempts to get at vocabulary knowledge through the use of similar meanings. However, the synonym to be identified is placed in a different context from that used for the stimulus, thus modifying the similarity of the basic meaning (e.g., "The rose-petal was as *soft* as velvet" [a simile]; "With a gentle touch she smoothed the silk cushion"). The subject is to identify that "gentle" in the second sentence means the same as "soft" in the first. Subtests two and three, which cover paragraph meaning and sentence organization, are essentially word identification tests involving a modified type of cloze procedure in which the subject must supply a word from his own experience and oral language background which will fit in the blank space provided. In most instances the initial or first two letters of the word required are provided (e.g., i... for "ice"; fl... for "float"). Subtest four deals with organization of ideas by requiring the subject to recognize sequence in a story and identify structures which make up complete sentences. Subtest five is concerned solely with spelling and punctuation although it should be recognized that knowledge of the latter is also important in the reading process.

In general, this reviewer would not suggest the use of this test, except on an experimental basis, until validity has been established. In any event, it should be used for group measurement and comparison only, never as an individual diagnostic test. The Interpretive Manual is its greatest strength.

[170]

Bristol Achievement Tests: Mathematics. Ages 8–0 to 9–11, 9–0 to 10–11, 10–0 to 11–11, 11–0 to 12–11, 12–0 to 13–11; 1969–82; 6 scores: number, reasoning, space, measurement, arithmetic laws and processes, total; Forms A, B, ('82, 7–8 pages); 5 levels; administrative manual ('82, 30 pages) for each level; battery interpretive manual ('69, 84 pages); battery profile ('69, 2 pages) for each form; 1985 price data: £5.55 per 25 tests; £3.25 per 25 profiles; £5.55 per teacher's set (without interpretive manual) of any one level (must be purchased to obtain administrative manual); £4.75 per interpretive manual; 55(60) minutes; Alan Brimer; NFER-Nelson Publishing Co. [England].*

For a review by Kenneth Lovell of an earlier edition, see 7:453. For reviews of the complete battery, see 168 (1 review) and 7:4 (2 reviews).

Review of Bristol Achievement Tests: Mathematics by F. G. BROWN, Professor of Psychology, Iowa State University, Ames, IA:

This test is one of three major sections of the Bristol Achievement Tests, the others being English Language and Study Skills. The current forms are a revision of an earlier version of the test. The extent of the revision is unclear from materials accompanying the test, but presumably the revisions were relatively minor.

There are five levels of the test, organized by a combination of age and level of schooling. The same five topics—number, reasoning, space, measurement, and arithmetic and algebraic operations—are represented at each level, although their relative emphasis varies across levels. These five parts are identified by headings within the test and pupils are instructed to move to the next section at designated times, even if they have not completed the previous part. Scores are reported for each part and for the total test.

The authors state that the items were chosen on the basis of psychological, pedagogical, and curriculum considerations, and that they were designed to stress understanding of concepts and reasoning more than computational accuracy. The most marked difference occurs between levels 3 and 4 (between primary and secondary levels). Levels 1 through 3 are heavily influenced by Piagetian thought and use concrete examples; the upper levels introduce more abstract concepts and problem solving.

Responses to all items are written in the test booklet, a procedure that requires hand scoring and thus raises the possibility of clerical errors. Most items require pupils to supply an answer, although some items require a choice between alternatives or a true/false decision. Many of the items are grouped into sets based on a common diagram, map, or problem. Most items are clearly written and challenging; some use interesting and unusual formats. There are a minimum of directions and practice items, which may present problems for less able pupils.

The primary emphasis in Part 1, Number, is on the conservation of number. "Domino" items, where pupils identify which adjacent domino faces are mismatched, are included in levels 1 through 4. This format is used because the problems can be solved without using numeral names. A second major emphasis is on the use of different bases. At lower levels this is measured by "gate" problems (which involve partitioning objects into sets with remainders); at upper levels more traditional base problems are used. Other items measure the concepts of relative magnitude and serial position.

Part 2 focuses on a thought process, Reasoning, rather than on a content area. Items at levels 1 through 3 all involve set operations, such as addition and partitioning of sets. The upper levels include inference, approximation, and necessary information items. This last format asks pupils to indicate which of several bits of information are necessary to reach a stated conclusion.

Part 3, Space, emphasizes spatial orientation and the conservation of area. The former is tested by items requiring identification of parts of a divided figure, the latter by items involving comparisons of portions of different geometric figures. Levels 4 and 5 introduce navigation problems, geometric concepts, and properties of solids.

Levels 1 through 3 of Part 4, Measurement, stress linear measurement but also include some items on time and relative speed. The items are written so that the answer can be obtained by estimation, thus emphasizing the process rather than computations. Most of the problems, however, can also be solved computationally. Interpretation of graphs and tables is introduced at level 3, the measurement of area at level 4, and the measurement of solids at level 5.

Part 5, Arithmetic and Algebraic Operations, again stresses operations rather than computational accuracy. This is accomplished by using problems involving simple numbers and ones where the pupil indicates the operation rather than the result (e.g., 3 __ 2=6). Another emphasis, from level 3 on, is on problems involving the ability to recognize different ways of expressing the same quantity.

The test appears to have been carefully constructed and standardized, though details of these procedures are not reported in the manual. Items were selected on the basis of their difficulty and discrimination power in a tryout sample.

Total scores are reported as standard scores (mean 100, standard deviation 15) and as percentile ranks. Part scores are reported as deciles to minimize the risk of overinterpretation. Standard errors of measurement are reported for each score and incorporated into the score profile.

Raw scores on the two forms differ, which is to be expected as Form A was developed for beginning of the year testing and Form B for testing later in the year. Corrections for these differences were used when developing the standard scores. There are also sex differences in total scores at each level. Girls score higher at level 1, although not significantly so; boys score higher at every other level, with five of the eight differences being significant.

The only reliability data reported are interform correlations. These are acceptable (.92 to .94) for total scores. The median interform reliabilities for the parts are in the low .80s except for Part 4 (median interform correlation of .69).

The median correlations among different parts range from .60 to .70, with correlations tending to be higher at upper age levels. The correlations of total Mathematics scores with scores on the English and Study Skills tests are also quite high, around .80. These relatively high correlations raise questions about the diagnostic use of the test. The authors recognize this problem but suggest that scores can be used for diagnosis, especially when differences are large.

The major weakness of the test is the absence of any validity data. The manual promises that some is forthcoming but none is given. Although the content and skill assessed by each item is relatively obvious, the authors should have included this information in the manual. It would also be interesting to know how scores on the test, and its parts, relate to other measures of mathematical ability and achievement and to success in math and science courses.

SUMMARY. The test appears to be a good measure of pupils' understanding of the concepts, principles, and reasoning involved in mathematics. The items are of good quality and will be challenging and interesting to pupils. The major weakness of the test is the lack of validity data. Although the test should be used with caution as a diagnostic measure, the total score should provide a good indication of pupils' mathematical ability when used in situations where the test content matches the mathematics curriculum of the school.

[171]

Bristol Achievement Tests: Study Skills. Ages 8–0 to 9–11, 9–0 to 10–11, 10–0 to 11–11, 11–0 to 12–11, 12–0 to 13–11; 1969–82; 6 scores: properties, structures, processes, explanations, interpretations, total; Forms A, B, ('82, 7–8 pages); 5 levels; administrative manual ('82, 30 pages) for each level; battery interpretive manual ('69, 84 pages); battery profile ('69 2 pages) for each form; 1985 price data: £5.55 per 25 tests; £3.25 per 25 profiles; £5.55 per teacher's set (without interpretive manual) of any one level (must be purchased to obtain administrative manual); £4.75 per interpretive manual; 50(55) minutes; Alan Brimer, Margaret Fidler, Wynne Harlen, and John Taylor; NFER-Nelson Publishing Co. [England].*

For a review by Elizabeth J. Goodacre of an earlier edition, see 7:776. For reviews of the complete battery, see 168 (1 review) and 7:4 (2 reviews).

Review of Bristol Achievement Tests: Study Skills by KENNETH J. SMITH, Professor of Reading, The University of Arizona, Tucson, AZ:

Some of the problem of reviewing this test may lie in a language barrier between the authors and the reviewer, for it was very difficult for this reviewer to determine the purpose of the test. Although the title indicated that this was a "study skills" test, the content had little to do with what are considered to be study skills in the United States. In fact, this appears to be more like an aptitude test, plus perhaps a cognitive measure, particularly in science areas. Nowhere is there anything like note taking, outlining, or previewing. Instead, items call upon children to perform tasks from reading to spatial relations. Furthermore, the scientific knowledge required to answer many of the items is considerable, often probably of more importance than any "study skill" required in order to answer the question successfully. The following comment in the Interpretive Manual is revealing: "The most frequent comment from teachers who have used the tests is their surprise that, despite the absence in their curriculum of skills and content relevant to the tests, children perform well on them."

The Interpretive Manual is not a bad tutorial on test analysis. Unfortunately, however, this test does not come off too well. Even though this is the second edition of the test, we are told that statistical data on validity are not yet available and are asked in the meantime to accept "rational" validity. That's exactly what was said for the first edition, published 15 years ago.

There are five "subtests," with from 10 to 15 items per subtest. One cannot be surprised, therefore, that standard error of measurement results for subtests are not very good. Given a mean score of 100 and a standard deviation of 15, standard errors range as high as 9.87 for part scores and 6.15 for total scores, with the error becoming consistently worse as the levels of the tests progress from lower to higher.

More comments could be made concerning administration, scoring, etc., but they seem pointless in view of the fact that the use which could be made of the results seems obscure. The authors merely comment that, "It attempts to represent the underlying skills and understandings without prescribing the curriculum's form or content." No further recommendations in terms of application of findings are made. Therefore, this test cannot be recommended for diagnostic or other purposes having to do with "study skills" or anything else.

[172]

The British Ability Scales. Ages 2.5–17; 1977–83; BAS; 24 scales in 6 major areas yielding 4 IQ scores: general, visual, verbal, short-form; individual; record form one—summary ('78, 4 pages); manual 1—introduction and rationale ('83, 215 pages); manual 2—technical and statistical information ('83, 239 pages); manual 3—directions for administration and scoring ('78, 194 pages); manual 4—tables of abilities and norms ('78, 90 pages); supplement to manual 4 ('78, 139 pages); 1983 price data: £139 per complete set excluding manuals 1 and 2; £76 per complete school age scales (ages 5–17); £70 per supplementary pre-school and early school scales (ages 2.5–8); £45 per set of supplementary materials (to turn school age set into a complete set); £3.20 per 25 record forms one; £16.50 per manual 3; £6.50 per manual 4; £3.45 per supplement to manual 4; Colin Elliott, David J. Murray (test and manuals 3 and 4), and Lea S. Pearson (test and manuals 3 and 4); NFER-Nelson Publishing Co. [England].*

a) SPEED OF INFORMATION PROCESSING. Ages 8–17; 1977–78; 1 form consists of 2 parts: Booklet B, C, ('77, 13 pages); record form two ('78, 1 page); £2.20 per 25 booklets; £2.80 per 25 record forms two; 6.5(10) minutes.

b) REASONING. Ages 5–17; 1977–78; 4 scale scores; record form three ('78, 2 pages); £2.80 per 25 record forms three; administration time not reported.

1) *Formal Operational Thinking*. Ages 8–17; 1 form ('78, 12 cards); £2.45 per set of 12 cards.

2) *Matrices*. Ages 5–17; 1 form consists of 5 test booklets from which appropriate booklet(s) will be selected; Booklet B, C, D, E, F, ('77, 15–19 pages); £8.50 per 10 of each booklet.

3) *Similarities*. Ages 5–17; 1 form.

4) *Social Reasoning*. Ages 5–17; 1 form.

c) SPATIAL IMAGERY. Ages 4–17; 1977–78; 4 scale scores; record form four ('78, 2 pages); £2.80 per 25 record forms four.

1) *Block Design*. Ages 4–17; 2 scale scores: level (ages 4–17), power (ages 5–17); 1 form ('77, 19 pages); £1.20 per booklet; £2.65 per set of 9 cubes; 17.5(20) minutes for level score, 6.5(10) minutes for power score.

2) *Rotation of Letter-Like Forms*. Ages 8–14; 1 form ('77, 23 pages); £1.95 per booklet; 60p per wooden doll; administration time not reported.

3) *Visualization of Cubes*. Ages 8–17; 1 form ('77, 27 pages); £1.95 per booklet; £3.60 per set of 4 cubes; administration time not reported.

d) PERCEPTUAL MATCHING. Ages 2.5–9; 1977–78; 3 scale scores; record form seven ('78, 2 pages); £2.80 per 25 record forms seven; administration time not reported.

1) *Copying*. Ages 4–8; 1 form ('77, 20 pages); £1.40 per booklet.

2) *Matching Letter-Like Forms*. Ages 5–9; 1 form ('77, 34 pages); £2.35 per booklet.

3) *Verbal-Tactile Matching*. Ages 2.5–8; 1 form; £6.60 per white bag containing objects; £2.30 per

green bag containing objects; £1.75 per demonstration bag containing objects.

e) SHORT TERM MEMORY. Ages 2.5–17; 1977–79; 5 scale scores; record form five ('78, 2 pages); 1983 price data: £2.80 per 25 record forms five.

1) *Recall of Designs*. Ages 5–17; 1 form ('77, 24 pages); £1 per booklet; 5 seconds exposure per item up to 19 items.

2) *Immediate Visual Recall/Delayed Visual Recall*. Ages 5–17; 2 scale scores: immediate, delayed (15–30 minutes after immediate recall); 1 form ('79, 1 card); 80p per card; 2 minutes per exposure.

3) *Recall of Digits*. Ages 2.5–17; 1 form; up to 34 digits read at half second intervals.

4) *Visual Recognition*. Ages 2.5–8; 1 form ('77, 40 pages); £2.65 per booklet; 5 seconds exposure per item up to 17 items.

f) RETRIEVAL AND APPLICATION OF KNOWLEDGE. Ages 2.5–17; 1977–82; 7 scale scores; record form six ('78, 4 pages); £3.20 per 25 record forms six.

1) *Naming Vocabulary*. Ages 2.5–8; 1 form ('77, 18 pages); £3.75 per booklet; administration time not reported.

2) *Word Reading*. Ages 5–14; 1 form ('77, 1 card); £1 per card; administration time not reported.

3) *Verbal Comprehension*. Ages 2.5–8; 1 form; £1.30 per picture of teddy bear; £2.40 per box of toys; £6.40 per inset tray; administration time not reported.

4) *Word Definitions*. Ages 5–17; 1 form; administration time not reported.

5) *Verbal Fluency*. Ages 3.6–17; 1 form ('77, 6 pages); £1 per booklet; administration time not reported.

6) *Basic Arithmetic*. Ages 5–14; 1 form ('82, 2 pages); £1.45 per 25 disposable sheets; administration time not reported.

7) *Early Number Skills*. Ages 2.5–8; 1 form ('77, 9 pages); £1.95 per booklet; £2.35 per set of 12 cubes; administration time not reported.

TEST REFERENCES

1. Elliot, C. D., & Murray, D. J. The measurement of speed of problem solving and its relation to children's age and ability. BRITISH JOURNAL OF EDUCATIONAL PSYCHOLOGY, 1977, 47, 50–59.

2. Johnston, R. S. Phonological coding in dyslexic readers. THE BRITISH JOURNAL OF PSYCHOLOGY, 1982, 73, 455–460.

3. Thomson, M. E. The assessment of children with specific reading difficulties (dyslexia) using the British Ability Scales. THE BRITISH JOURNAL OF PSYCHOLOGY, 1982, 73, 461–478.

4. Hay, D. A., & O'Brien, P. J. The La Trobe Twin Study: A genetic approach to the structure and development of cognition in twin children. CHILD DEVELOPMENT, 1983, 54, 317–330.

5. Rodgers, B. The identification and prevalence of specific reading retardation. BRITISH JOURNAL OF EDUCATIONAL PSYCHOLOGY, 1983, 53, 369–373.

Review of The British Ability Scales by SUSAN EMBRETSON (WHITELY), Professor of Psychology, University of Kansas, Lawrence, KS:

The British Ability Scales (BAS) are an individually administered intelligence test that yield three major intelligence scores—general, visual, and verbal—as well as a short-form score. Since the age range for the test is 2 1/2 to 17 1/2 years, the test potentially competes with the WISC-R and the Stanford-Binet. However, the test has greater scope than either of them (23 scales!) and has greater flexibility in score interpretation, due to operationalizing a latent trait model in test development. The author expects that its main strength will be for ipsative assessments in the "broader diagnostic assessment context, for the purpose of generating and testing hypotheses regarding a child's relative strengths and weaknesses in ability."

The 23 scales on the test were carefully selected to reflect major theoretical advances during its major developmental phase in the middle 1970s. A typical test administration may utilize as few as four scales for a short-form IQ or all of the scales appropriate for a given age level. Although all scales are appropriate for multiple age levels, only one scale—Recall of Digits—is appropriate for all ages. The scales are classified into five general areas as follows: (1) Reasoning (Formal Operations, Similarities, Matrices, and Social Reasoning), (2) Spatial Imagery (Block Design Level and Power, Rotation of Letter-Like Forms, and Visualization of Cubes), (3) Perceptual Matching (Copying, Matching Letter-Like Forms, and Verbal-Tactile Matching), (4) Short-Term Memory (Immediate and Delayed Visual Recall, Recall of Designs, Recall of Digits, and Visual Recognition), and (5) Retrieval and Application of Knowledge (Basic Number Skills, Naming Vocabulary, Verbal Comprehension, Verbal Fluency, Word Definitions, Word Reading, and Conservation Items).

In contrast to other individual intelligence tests, the British Ability Scales include several tests that are based on developmental theory. These include an operationalization of Piagetian variables in Formal Operations and Conservation Items, Olver and Hornsby's (1966) concept equivalence theory in the Similarities scale, and Kohlberg's (1969) theory of moral reasoning in the Social Reasoning scale. Many other scales are discussed in terms of contemporary theories, but they are not derived so directly from them.

The test development procedures for the BAS represent the best contemporary psychometric practice. The 23 scales were developed to fit the Rasch latent trait model. The Rasch model is an item response model that predicts the encounter of a particular person with a specified item. The latent trait model gives psychometric respectability to the clinical practice of selecting item subsets to be appropriate for the ability level of the examinee. The Rasch model permits great flexibility in equating scores between different subsets. Although measurement error depends on the appropriateness of the subset, comparable ability estimates may be obtained from any item subset. The examiner receives a standard error of measurement for each score, given the item subset, to aid score interpretation.

The item-free ability estimates, along with the individual measurement errors, greatly enhance the diagnostic potential of the scales. For example, change measurements and scale differences may be compared directly to expectation by measurement error. Furthermore, unusual response patterns may be detected by comparing the items that are passed or failed to expectation from the item response prediction by the Rasch model. The Rasch model also permits great flexibility in extending the scales; other researchers may link new items to the scales since the item difficulties are reported on the answer sheets.

Although the psychometric basis of the BAS is sophisticated, the administration and scoring procedures are well designed, so as to minimize examiner bias. The norms were very carefully constructed to constitute a representative sample of Great Britain. Of 113 school districts in Great Britain, 75 districts participated in the norming. Children were stratified for sex and age, but otherwise were selected randomly. The norms give both *T* scores and centiles corresponding to the Rasch ability scores within the appropriate age groups.

Interesting features of the BAS are two systems to guide the interpretation of scale differences. First, the scale scores are compared to expectation by measurement error for the scores, which is available through the Rasch model calibrations. Second, the scores are compared to expected values from regressing one scale on the other. The probability of the score, given the other scale, is reported. Unfortunately, the probability depends on which scale is taken as the dependent variable (i.e., the probability of obtaining the higher *T* score, given the lower *T* score, is not equal to the converse probability). This illuminates nicely a familiar regression paradox. Unfortunately, the examiner is placed in the untenable position of sometimes interpreting one scale score as unusual, compared to a second scale, but the second score is not unusual as compared to the first scale! The authors should seek a system of interpreting scale differences that does not depend on the arbitrary direction of prediction.

Despite the excellent beginning in test development, the BAS currently have only the most meager data on reliability and validity. The amount of data presented on these topics in the manuals is more appropriate for a research instrument than a published test that appeals to a wide market. Although the normative sample provided extensive data for goodness of fit for the Rasch model and internal consistency, the data on stability and scorer reliability are clearly inadequate. Exactly one study each is reported on score stability and on scorer reliability, with *N* s of 60 and 50 respectively.

The lack of validity data is even more serious. Extensive factor analyses on the scales from the normative data are available and are quite useful. However, only five studies of correlations of BAS with other measures are reported, and the sample sizes are small (20 to 88 subjects). Although the results are positive, they are by no means adequate.

Since the BAS contains 23 separate scales, differential validity is a major issue. However, only two studies are reported on scale profiles. Again, the data appear positive, but the studies are by no means adequate.

It is alarming that in the discussion of future developments of the BAS it is "hoped" that the users will begin to publish the needed studies on reliability and validity. Although clearly the users, particularly researchers, will provide many such studies, this reviewer believes that the publisher should be responsible for some large scale reliability and validity studies prior to extensive marketing. The test has real potential to be a major intelligence test. The required technical data cannot be left to happenstance.

In summary, the BAS is an individual intelligence test with greater scope and psychometric sophistication than the major American individual tests. The test development procedures and norms are laudatory. It could easily become the major instrument in studies of individual differences in intelligence. However, the current data on reliability and validity are inadequate. The test is not suitable for routine ability assessment until such data become available.

REVIEWER'S REFERENCES

Olver, R. R., & Hornsby, J. R. On equivalance. In J. S. Bruner, R. R. Olver, & P. M. Greenfield (Eds.), STUDIES IN COGNITIVE GROWTH. London: Wiley, 1966.

Kohlberg, L. Stage and sequence: The cognitive developmental approach to socialization. In D. A. Goslin (Ed.), HANDBOOK OF SOCIALIZATION THEORY AND RESEARCH. Chicago: Rand McNally, 1969.

Review of The British Ability Scales by BENJAMIN D. WRIGHT, Professor of Education, and MARK H. STONE, MESA Research Associate, MESA Psychometric Laboratory, University of Chicago, Chicago, IL:

The British Ability Scales (BAS) is a significant advance in mental measurement. It comes from the coordinated labors of scores of British educators and psychologists over two decades and has been put together by unusually effective and versatile psychometric methods. Its form and function are a model for contemporary test builders and a preview of the future of test construction.

The BAS is similar in design and purpose but superior in construction and scope to the Stanford-Binet, Wechsler, and Kaufman batteries. Like them, it provides the basic scales from which IQ measures are estimated. Two additional scales, Basic Number Skills and Word Reading, estimate school achievement. Two more, Formal Operational Thinking and Conservation, are Piaget variables.

The BAS kit is handsomely housed in a well-made carrying case containing everything needed including four unusually comprehensive manuals. The materials of wood and heavy paper are more serviceable and attractive than the plastic materials used by competing batteries. The four manuals provide 740 pages of relevant and useful information. They not only explain how the BAS scales were made and how to use them, but Manuals 1 and 2 provide an excellent introduction to the Rasch psychometric methods used to build the BAS item banks and to set up the subtest equations, score interpretations, and response quality control. Manuals 1 and 2 are texts on modern psychometric method. They belong on the required reading list of any course on mental measurement.

THE BAS ITEM BANKS. The 23 age-graded BAS scales measure the compass of mental abilities in children and adolescents. Each scale is built into an explicit and versatile definition of an important variable of mental development. Twenty-one of these carefully developed and operationalized variables are Rasch calibrated item banks (there are more than 500 calibrated items). These item banks transport the BAS beyond the provision of a battery of useful tests to the foundation of a system of mental measurement.

Rasch psychometric method brings the BAS many advantages not found in other batteries. Among immediate alternatives only the Kaufman mentions Rasch methods. But the Kaufman manual contains no explanation nor evidence of Rasch use. Rasch psychometrics make the BAS far more than a collection of standardized tests. They make the BAS a measuring system open to revision and enrichment.

Examiners have always wanted the opportunity to add or delete items without losing the benefits of standardization. The BAS invites this kind of examiner participation and enables it in a practical way. Examiners can use the BAS subtests provided in Manual 3 or they can use the Rasch calibrated BAS items listed in Manual 2 to form their own subtests or they can mix calibrated BAS items and their own new items to form combination tests, all without losing contact with the norms laid out in Manual 4.

OPERATIONAL DEFINITIONS OF MENTAL VARIABLES. When a pool of test items written to indicate a particular mental variable has been fitted to a latent scale, their calibrations on this scale serve several important and useful functions. The BAS item banks provide an explicit operational definition of each mental variable. Each variable is marked out by an ordered series of calibrated items. If we picture a variable as a line with a direction pointing toward more difficult, then the BAS items benchmark positions along this line according to their calibrated difficulties. The relative positions of the items along the scale from easy to hard spell out what the variable is all about. The ordered organization of the items from easy to hard provides a content-based, substantive picture of the variable.

This picture is important because the story it tells must fulfil our theoretical expectations. The items expected to be "easy" must be at the easy end of the variable and the items expected to be "hard" at the hard end. Otherwise the test item data do not cooperate with our idea of what we are trying to do and so fail the first question of test item fit: Do the content and relative positioning of these items fulfil our intentions? Does this set of items have construct validity?

BUILDING ITEM BANKS. The BAS item banks lay the foundation for further bank building. They invite enrichment, extension, linking with other comparable scales, and challenge. This is because the examiner is free to add his/her own items, whether borrowed from another scale or newly constructed, and then, by administering these items in the company of BAS items, to find out whether the items fit with the BAS items and thus measure the same variable the BAS items embody. The opportunity to add new items enables an examiner to enrich any region of the BAS variable in which he or she wants more items available than the BAS provide. It also allows the extension of the BAS variable in either direction by adding new items that are easier or harder than those provided.

CONNECTING THE BAS TO OTHER TESTS AND NORMS. If an examiner wishes to connect a BAS measure with a score on a similar variable from another battery so as to compare results or make contact with other norms, this can be done, too. Examiners wishing to anchor BAS measures to local tests and norms need only include a few suitably chosen calibrated BAS items in their own tests, calibrate the resulting compound tests, and use the resulting calibrations of the BAS linking items to determine whether a valid connection can be made and, if it can, to make it.

CONDUCTING NEW RESEARCH ON BAS VARIABLES. Should an examiner be research-minded and wish to revise the BAS definition of a particular variable, he/she can introduce new items which sharpen or challenge the interpretation implied by the BAS items and investigate the merits of the revision. This is done by administering a new test composed of both new and BAS items to a suitable sample of children and calibrating the two kinds of items together. If the new calibrations of the BAS items do not form a linear link with their published BAS item difficulties, then the challenge items have upset the BAS variable definition. If, on the other hand, they do, then those new items which fit the calibration can be located on the BAS variable and used accordingly.

MEASURING CHILDREN. A child's test score on any selection of BAS items, when transformed into an ability estimate, can also be thought of as a position on a line—the same line built up and defined by the calibrated items. This positioning of the child places the child among the items he/she has passed and failed. In addition to the child's ability measure we also have the child's pattern of successes and failures. This allows us to evaluate the quality of performance and, should irregularities occur, to detect and diagnose them.

PRE-EQUATED MULTIPLE TEST FORMS. The BAS item banks enable the composition of a wide variety of pre-equated tests. Because the items have been calibrated onto a common scale, the scores from any test composed of some of these items point to positions on this scale which have the same meaning no matter which set of items are selected. The authors of the BAS have used this property of the 21 item banks to offer BAS users equated series of age-graded subtests for 16 of the BAS variables. There are four vertically equated age-graded subtests for the Speed of Information Processing, Basic Number Skills, and Word Reading scales.

TAILORED TESTING. The BAS item banks also provide an objective basis for individualized testing. An examiner can tailor selection of calibrated BAS items to the performance of the child being tested. Then, by noting the bank difficulties listed in Manual 2 of the items chosen and following either the PROX (simple calculation) or UFORM (simpler table look-up) procedures on pages 143–151 of *Best Test Design* (Wright & Stone, 1979), the examiner can equate the score the child obtains on this individualized test to a measure (and its standard error) on the mental variable defined by that BAS item bank.

MASTERY PROFILING. The behavior called for by each BAS item when coupled with its calibrated position along the line of the BAS variable tells what it means in expected performance when a child is measured to be at a particular point on the variable. This enables the construction of a criterion-based mastery profile to go with each child's score. Once we have a child's test score we can transform it into his/her position on the variable defined by the whole bank of items. Then we can estimate the expected success rate on any calibrated item, including items not attempted. This allows us to identify those items so easy for the child that he/she has mastered them, say, to the extent that the expected rate of success exceeds 90%. We can also identify those harder items with which the child is still so struggling that the expected success rate is only 50%. Additionally, we can identify those items so very hard for the child as to be unconstructive and perhaps even provocative of abnormal behavior, like guessing and resignation, because the expected success rate is, say, less than 20%. This rate-of-success indexing of the relation between the measure on a BAS variable implied by a child's score and the calibrations of the BAS items produces a mastery profile for each child's performance which spells out in detail exactly what the child can be expected to do and just how well.

QUALITY CONTROL AND PERFORMANCE DIAGNOSIS. The calibrated BAS items also enable a detailed analysis of the plausibility of each child's response pattern. We expect children to do well on items which are easy for them and not so well on items which are hard for them. When a child deviates from this expectation the performance surprises have diagnostic value. Manuals 1 and 2 provide useful explanations and illustrations of how to implement this kind of response pattern validation. There is also a useful chapter on the detection of item bias in Manual 2.

BRITISH NOTATION. Can British test materials be used with American children? We found two notational conventions on the BAS arithmetic worksheet which might annoy some Americans. The operation sign for short division is inverted and decimals are vertically centered. These British conventions are easily explained, but why not provide an American worksheet?

BRITISH LANGUAGE. We also found two examples of British language which might distract some Americans. One Similarities item asks for the communality shared by "cod," "shark," and "pilchard." In Word Reading and Definition "-ize" is spelled "-ise" in "emphasize" and "ostracize." None of these minor cultural differences will make any difference in BAS results.

BRITISH NORMS. Can British norms be used to evaluate American performances? The absence of norms labeled "American" will fret some examiners. But American norms for the Stanford-Binet are used routinely in Britain, and the WISC standardization provided by the Scottish Council for Research and Education is so close to the American that British psychologists continue to use the American norms.

More to the point, if there are any differences between British and American norms, they are less than the cultural and regional differences within the United States. Any examiner seriously interested in local norms will make the effort to accumulate those local norms. Fortunately, the construction of local norms is easier than textbooks imply. We need only determine whether "our" children develop faster or slower than the BAS age curves expect. That can be done by giving small sets of well-chosen BAS items to small samples of age-stratified children and using the BAS regression on age and the combined replications of items and children within age to see if there is an age shift large enough to matter.

PSYCHOMETRIC TECHNIQUE. Some of the simple techniques necessary to take advantage of the opportunities for building on the BAS system are not spelled out in the BAS manuals. We hope Colin Elliot will remedy this shortcoming in his next edition of Manual 2—Technical Handbook. In the meantime, examiners can obtain the missing pieces from *Best Test Design* (MESA Press, 5835 Kimbark Ave., Chicago, IL 60637) where the steps necessary to calibrate, link, build new forms, evaluate item and person fit, diagnose performance irregularities, and construct mastery profiles are explained and illustrated.

CONCLUSION. The BAS was developed and produced with unusual care. Its four manuals are models of what examiners should receive when purchasing a battery of this magnitude. They provide examiners with ample evidence of the construct validity and internal consistency of the scales. We do not consider any of its minor British specifics to be an impediment to American use. The lack of American norms will be misunderstood by some as a barrier to using the BAS with American children. Potential users should not avoid the BAS on this account. Local norms are easy to develop. National American norms, when they emerge, will be indistinguishable from the British norms now provided.

REVIEWER'S REFERENCES

Wright, B. D., & Stone, M. H. BEST TEST DESIGN: RASCH MEASUREMENT. Chicago, MESA Press, 1979.

[173]

British Picture Vocabulary Scales. Ages 2.5–18; 1982; BPVS; adapted from 1981 edition of Peabody Picture Vocabulary Test for UK use; measures receptive vocabulary; not available for sale in the USA; individual; 2 forms: long (156 items) for detailed assessment, short (38 items) for rapid screening; long form test plates (165 pages); short form test plates (40 pages); plastic folding stand; long form test record (6 pages); short form test record (4 pages); manual (73 pages); 1983 price data: £18.95 per packet containing manual, long form test plates, short form test plates, 25 long form test records, 25 short form test records, stand; £3.85 per 25 long form test records; £3.25 per 25 short form test records; £3.45 per manual; (10–20) minutes (long form); (5–15) minutes short form; Lloyd M. Dunn, Leota M. Dunn, Chris Whetton, and David Pintillie; NFER-Nelson Publishing Co. [England].*

[174]

Bruininks-Oseretsky Test of Motor Proficiency. Ages 4–5 to 14–5; 1978; revised edition of The Oseretsky Tests of Motor Proficiency; 3 scores: gross motor composite, fine motor composite, battery composite; individual; 2 forms: short (3 pages), and long (6 pages), short form is used in situations that require only a survey of general motor proficiency; student test booklet (8 pages); manual (153 pages); other test materials (e.g., two chairs, clipboard, gym mat or carpeted surface, stopwatch) must be supplied by examiner; 1984 price data: $117.50 per test kit including 25 student booklets and 25 individual record forms; $7.50 per 25 individual record forms (complete and short form); $3.50 per 25 individual record forms (short form); $8.25 per 25 student booklets; $17 per examiner's manual; (45–60) minutes for long form, (15–20) minutes for short form; Robert H. Bruininks; American Guidance Service.*

See T3:324 (3 references), and T2:1898 (15 references) for references of an earlier edition; for a review by Anna Espenschade, see 4:650 (10 references); for an excerpted review, see 3:472 (6 references).

TEST REFERENCES

1. Fine, D. L. Test review: Bruininks-Oseretsky Test of Motor Proficiency. JOURNAL OF EDUCATIONAL MEASUREMENT, 1979, 16, 290–292.

2. Cantor, S., Trevenen, C., Postuma, R., Dueck, R., & Fjeldsted, B. Is childhood schizophrenia a cholinergic disease?: I. Muscle morphology. ARCHIVES OF GENERAL PSYCHIATRY, 1980, 37, 658–667.

3. Beitel, P. A., & Mead, B. J. Bruininks-Oseretsky Test of Motor Proficiency: Further verification with 3- to 5-yr.-old children. PERCEPTUAL AND MOTOR SKILLS, 1982, 54, 268–270.

4. Broadhead, G. D., & Church, G. E. Discriminant analysis of gross and fine motor proficiency data. PERCEPTUAL AND MOTOR SKILLS, 1982, 55, 547–552.

5. Brunt, D., & Broadhead, G. D. Motor proficiency traits of deaf children. RESEARCH QUARTERLY FOR EXERCISE AND SPORT, 1982, 53, 236–238.

6. Walker, E., & Green, M. Motor proficiency and attentional-task performance by psychotic patients. JOURNAL OF ABNORMAL PSYCHOLOGY, 1982, 91, 261–268.

7. Pissanos, B. W., Moore, J. B., & Reeve, T. G. Age, sex, and body composition as predictors of children's performance on basic motor abilities and health-related fitness items. PERCEPTUAL AND MOTOR SKILLS, 1983, 56, 71–77.

Review of Bruininks-Oseretsky Test of Motor Proficiency by DAVID A. SABATINO, Dean, University of Wisconsin-Stout, Menomonie, WI:

It is rewarding to see a most capable researcher adopt and improve upon an instrument which was first translated from Portuguese to English 35 years ago (Doll, 1946). Indeed, this test was revised in 1948 at the Lincoln State School (Lincoln, Illinois) and used to generate both individual diagnosis and research for a goodly number of years. The present revision retains a very old conceptual model of observable motor traits, but with improved directions for administration and updated assessment procedures.

EASE OF ADMINISTRATION. The test is complete except for stopwatch, clipboard, two chairs, and a table. The metal carrying case is strong, yet relatively light in weight, and even includes a balance beam.

The test items are administered easily requiring 45 minutes for administration of the full scale. A short form, or screening test, requires 20 minutes. The test manual is thorough, with diagrams and easy-to-read instructions. No special training is required, and the author suggests that persons from many different disciplines in various settings can successfully administer the test.

EASE OF SCORING. Standard scores and age equivalents are provided for each subtest. Standard scores, percentile ranks, and stanines are provided for: (1) a gross motor composite, (2) a fine motor composite, and (3) a total battery composite. The standard scores for the composites are expressed as a normalized standard score with a mean of 50 and a standard deviation of 10.

STANDARDIZATION. The standardization included 765 non-handicapped subjects drawn according to stratified sampling procedures sensitive to culture and other contributing factors. Since the test will be used with specialized populations, a small sampling of handicapped students was also included. Bruininks reports a large difference in mean battery composite scores in favor of the normal (non-handicapped) in comparison with the mildly retarded (22 points), the moderately-severely retarded (32 points), and the learning disabled (10 points).

RELIABILITY. Battery composite test-retest coefficients of .89 and .86 are reported for grades 2 and 6 respectively for the long form, with parallel coefficients of .87 and .84 respectively for the short form. Subtest retest correlations for grades 2 and 6 range from .29 to .89, and have a mean value of .70.

VALIDITY. Limited validity evidence is reported. The comprehensive nature of this test, and a resurgence of interest in motor development, should generate widespread research applications. Currently, a formal motoric screening device is unavailable, and limited information is available on motor development or motor growth with most exceptional populations. In short, Bruininks has developed a practical diagnostic instrument with great appeal to the interested researcher.

Bruininks and Bruininks (1977) reported a group comparison study using 55 learning disabled and 55 normal subjects. They contrasted the performance of the two groups, subdividing them by age. Significant differences were observed between the overall motor performance of the learning disabled and normal subjects, in favor of the normal subjects. Interestingly enough, non-learning disabled children showed little subtest variability, while learning disabled students showed extensive subtest variability. The learning disabled group performed more poorly on fine-motor, gross-motor, and total test scores. There was also a significant difference between age groups. These differences occurred primarily on the strength and upper limb speed subtests.

SUMMARY. What then is the current utility and future research application for this test? This instrument may not be the only game in town, but it certainly is the most outstanding one in this area. It is a well developed, well standardized, usable motor test that is useful to professionals from several disciplines. Clinically it fills a void; those diagnosticians attempting to develop a systematic assessment procedure to describe learner characteristics of this nature now have a reliable means of doing so. Moreover, researchers interested in motor development and motor performance with various populations should find it a rich source of data.

REVIEWER'S REFERENCES

Doll, E. A. (Ed.). THE OSERETSKY TESTS OF MOTOR PROFICIENCY. Translation from the Portuguese Adaptation. Circle Pines, MN: American Guidance Service, 1946.

Bruininks, V. L., & Bruininks, R. H. Motor proficiency of learning disabled and nondisabled students. PERCEPTUAL AND MOTOR SKILLS, 1977, 44, 1131–1137.

[175]

Burt Word Reading Test, New Zealand Revision. Ages 6–0 to 12–11 years; 1981; revision and New Zealand standardization of The Burt Word Reading Test; provides an estimate of word recognition skills for 110 words; individual; 1 form ('81, 1 card, identical with 1974 revision except for word order); manual ('81, 10 pages); 1983 price data: NZ$.25 per card; $1.50 per manual; untimed; original test by Cyril Burt; 1938 revision by P. E. Vernon; 1974 revision by Scottish Council for Research in Education; current revision by Alison Gilmore, Cedric Croft, and Neil Reid; New Zealand Council for Educational Research [New Zealand].*

TEST REFERENCES

1. Davidoff, J. B., Beaton, A. A., Done, D. J., & Booth, H. Information extraction from brief verbal displays: Half-field and serial position effects for children, normal and illiterate adults. THE BRITISH JOURNAL OF PSYCHOLOGY, 1982, 73, 29–39.

2. Kashani, J. H., McGee, R. O., Clarkson, S. E., Anderson, J. C., Walton, L. A., Williams, S., Silva, P. A., Robins, A. J., Cytryn, L., & McKnew, D. H. Depression in a sample of 9-year-old children: Prevalence and associated characteristics. ARCHIVES OF GENERAL PSYCHIATRY, 1983, 40, 1217–1223.

Review of Burt Word Reading Test, New Zealand Revision, by MARK W. AULLS, Associate Professor, Educational Psychology and Elementary Education, Reading Centre, McGill University, Montreal, Quebec, Canada:

The Burt Word Reading Test, New Zealand Revision, is an individually administered, norm referenced measure. The authors describe it as a measure of an aspect of a child's word recognition skills. No further explanation is provided of what aspect of word recognition skill the test measures. The source and criteria for selecting the 110 words used to assess word recognition skill are not mentioned in the test manual. Thus it is impossible to infer what the word recognition vocabulary of a student with a given raw score means because of the lack of information about how the words were selected. In order to offer a meaningful interpretation of the test's raw scores, Equivalent Age Band (EAB) scores were derived for the raw scores from 20 to 80.

The EAB scores are norm referenced scores. Each EAB is a 6-month age band associated with each raw score from 20 to 80. It enables the test user to describe a student's word recognition skill as being the same as the mean score obtained by students in half year intervals between 5 years, 10 months of age and 12 years, 9 months of age. Thus EAB scores do not directly estimate what type or frequency of words a child knows. The only meaning they provide is an indication of a student's score relative to the performance of all other students who took the same test. As the authors stress, any other interpretation of the EAB score such as calling it a "reading age" score is simply unwarranted.

The authors of the Burt claim that five types of instructional decisions can be made with the test's score. First, they state in the Teachers' Manual, "The test, used in conjunction with other data about each child, should help teachers make a broad estimate of a child's reading achievement." The authors also emphasize that an EAB score may be used to provide a guide to selecting suitable graded reading material. Third, they suggest test information can be used for making decisions about instructional groupings. Finally, the authors claim the test's record of pronunciation errors will provide preliminary diagnostic information about the source of a child's reading problem. Sufficient guidelines, however, are not provided in the Teachers' Manual to clearly explain the rationale or steps the teacher follows to use the test scores or the record of pronunciation errors for any of the preceding instructional decisions. More importantly, the authors offer no related research or technical data to demonstrate that the test offers valid information for making any of the preceding five instructional decisions. Quite plainly, there is no reason to believe the Burt EAB score should be used for any other instructionally relevant decisions than to identify students who may drastically vary from the 1980 New Zealand age group and class norms in the number of words recognized on the Burt Test.

The Burt is individually administered. However, norm referenced score interpretations require that standardized test administration procedures be followed. Therefore, these procedures must be clearly spelled out in the test manual in order to assure that all students arrive at a total raw score under essentially the same testing conditions. Several administration procedures are emphasized repeatedly in the Teachers' Manual and are critical to the EAB score reliability. First, every student must receive an equal chance to read and respond to all 110 words on the list. Unless this condition is fulfilled, internal consistency estimates of reliability cannot be used. Therefore, it is imperative that any unnecessary cues or aids to a word other than the child's own knowledge be excluded from the test administration procedure. The procedure given in the Teachers' Manual for recording students' responses to each word should be unobtrusive. Unfortunately, no evidence is provided to demonstrate that the recording procedure recommended is in fact unobtrusive. The procedure appears potentially to offer considerable feedback to most children regarding whether or not their response to a word is correct. Since the child controls the word presentation and response pace, she or he is especially likely to give considerable attention to what the examiner reports.

The estimate of a student's word recognition skill is based on whether or not words are accurately pronounced. Speed is not recorded. The criteria for a correct pronunciation is current usage. Consonants, vowels, and accents must all be correct. The authors also suggest concessions should be made for children with speech defects, various dialects, or whose native language is not English. This is a wise suggestion, but its implementation is difficult to assess. Technical data should provide information regarding the extent to which examiners typically vary from one another in judging the responses of one child and the extent to which one examiner is consistent in scoring the same student at different points in time. At the present time, the reliability of this test in judging students who have dialects or a different native language than the examiner may be very questionable. In fact, the Teachers' Manual reports a difference between the performance of European and non-European student populations. Part of these differences may be accounted for by scoring biases as well as other cultural or school-based factors in New Zealand (Nash, 1980).

Technical information is provided on the reliability and validity of the Burt. Internal consistency reliability is provided for three of the 60 half-year age groups. While the KR 20 coefficients are impressively high (.96, .97, .97), a sample of ages from only three age groups is not sufficient. Test-retest reliabilities are given for only seven of the 60 half-year age groups. Again those reported are unusually high (.95 to .99). The reliability data presented does suggest the Burt provides consistency of measurement for Equivalent Age Band scores.

Only concurrent validity is reported for the Burt. A student's score on the Burt was found to be somewhat related to his/her comprehension and vocabulary score on the PAT reading achievement test. Also the score appears to be highly related to the scores on two word recognition tests used in New Zealand. However, one of the word recognition tests (Fieldhouse, 1952) was strongly criticized by Rayner and Wheeler (Buros, 1959) and has very outdated norms. This suggests that recent changes in the 1980 revised Burt may not have changed markedly the meaningfulness of scores from the test. It also warrants repeating that concurrent validity offers no evidence for the content validity of the test or functional validity for the uses of the EAB score for placing students in materials, for grouping students, or for estimating reading achievement.

In conclusion, the information provided by the Burt is basically irrelevant to most reading instructional decisions teachers wish to make. It does provide a global norm referenced estimate of an aspect of word recognition skill. However, the EAB scores are based on relatively small samples of New Zealand schools, and within each age group no consideration has been given to SES, urban-rural schools, and European and non-European influences on the EAB score distribution. Therefore, teachers of minority linguistic or cultural groups should not use the Burt test. An alternative New Zealand reading measure to consider is Clay's Sand test (1972).

REVIEWER'S REFERENCES

Fieldhouse, A. E. ORAL WORD READING TEST. Educational Books, 1952.

Buros, O. K. THE FIFTH MENTAL MEASUREMENTS YEARBOOK. Highland Park, NJ: The Gryphon Press, 1959.

Clay, M. M. SAND: CONCEPTS ABOUT PRINT TEST. New Zealand, Heinemann Educational Books Ltd., 1972.

Nash, R. Primary education in rural New Zealand: Current issues and developments. NEW ZEALAND JOURNAL OF EDUCATIONAL STUDIES, 1980, 15(1), 3–14.

Review of Burt Word Reading Test, New Zealand Revision, by JOHN ELKINS, Reader in Special Education, Schonell Educational Research Centre, University of Queensland, St. Lucia, Qld., Australia:

The Burt Word Reading Test has been widely used in British Commonwealth countries for more than 50 years. The New Zealand Revision is the most recent restandardization of the test, incorporating a reordering of the set of 110 words and the compilation of age norms for New Zealand children. As the authors note, oral reading of isolated words provides a limited sampling of reading skills, and fails to tap the use of semantic and syntactic clues available when reading prose. Therefore, a score on this test should not be interpreted as a measure of overall reading achievement, but rather as an indication of word recognition and decoding skills. The manual also points out that clinical insights into a subject's word recognition skills may be obtained through examination of faulty attempts to pronounce the stimulus words. Users are urged to interpret Burt scores in the light of other indices of reading, such as oral reading fluency and reading comprehension.

The manual provides information about the nature of the test and the purposes for which it may be used. Administration procedures are clearly described, and criteria for interpreting responses are provided for most situations. A minor criticism is that the word "accent," which is used for syllabic stress within words, may be misinterpreted as dialect difference. Detailed information is provided on the calculation and interpretation of derived scores called Equivalent Age Bands, in which the standard error of measurement is incorporated. This is a valuable device to compel teachers to recognize measurement error. However, researchers will need to estimate age equivalents as the midpoint of the band. Separate norm tables are provided for boys and girls as well as the usual combined group. The sex differences are quite large (e.g., a raw score of 22 places boys 7 months ahead of girls, while a raw score of 79 places boys a full year ahead of girls on age equivalent scores). Although Maori and Polynesian children scored "marginally but consistently" lower than Pakeha (European) children, separate norms are not provided for ethnic groups.

Not all technical information which has been obtained is reported in the manual. Item difficulty and discrimination indices are referred to but not tabulated, though items differing substantially in rank order from the 1974 Scottish restandardization are presented. No reasons are given as to why item difficulty order differs across countries or in time. Tables of means and standard deviations are presented for 6-month age levels from 6 to 12 years, and by grades from J2 to Form II (roughly U.S. grades 1 through 7). Test-retest reliability and KR-20 internal consistency measures are extremely high (.95 to .99), and the standard error of measurement is about three raw score points and also three months on the derived scale. This correspondence prompted an examination of the norm table revealing that in the lower half of the age range, each item did correspond to one month on the age equivalent scale. Above about 8 years, each item corresponded to a slightly higher age equivalent range, and above 11 years, each item was equivalent to two months. This observation is of some historical interest, as it illustrates the persistence of the attempt in early British word reading tests to select stimulus words such that each word represented one month on a reading age scale. The manual points out that the assumption of a uniform gradation of word difficulty has not been maintained in this revision of the Burt test (though the empirical results are equivalent over half the range of the test). The question of the growth of reading vocabulary cannot be addressed with the present test. A future edition of this test should provide latent trait analyses of the stimulus words. However, unless words are sampled from some domain, it will be difficult to construct a useful measure of growth in reading vocabulary (Davies & Williams, 1974). The content validity of the test is thus limited, and relies heavily upon historical precedent. One might ask whether teaching to the test (a not uncommon behavior among teachers) might not limit the utility of this test, given that the stimulus words are so well known. Concurrent validity measures are presented which show coefficients above .90 with other word reading tests, and mostly above .70 with group reading vocabulary, reading comprehension, and scholastic aptitude.

In summary, the New Zealand Revision of the Burt Word Reading Test is a well constructed test, limited mostly by its continuing orientation towards the traditional use of the Burt test—the individual assessment of word recognition ability in reading diagnosis and evaluation of remedial programs. A fresh approach to the construction of word reading tests using domain-referenced item definition and latent trait scaling seems indicated.

REVIEWER'S REFERENCES

Davies, P., & Williams, P. ASPECTS OF EARLY READING GROWTH. Oxford: Basil Blackwell, 1974.

[176]

Buswell-John Diagnostic Test for Fundamental Processes in Arithmetic. Pupils doing unsatisfactory work in arithmetic; no date on test materials; to discover how children work through arithmetic problems; no scores; no reliability or validity data; no norms; individual; 1 form (4 pages); manual (31 pages); teacher's diagnostic chart; 1982 price data: $10.40 per 35 tests; $.88 per manual; $1.76 per specimen set; (15–20) minutes; G. T. Buswell and Lenore John; Allen House.*

Review of Buswell-John Diagnostic Test for Fundamental Processes in Arithmetic by FRANK W. BROADBENT, Associate Professor of Education, Syracuse University, Syracuse, NY:

This chart was the forerunner of modern diagnostic tests in arithmetic. Buswell and John believed that a distinction needed to be made between diagnosing and testing. In the early part of this century they conducted an extensive study of children's errors in the four fundamental arithmetical operations which led to the development of this chart. In line with the behaviorist psychology of their time, they viewed children's errors mostly as the result of poor habits. These habits are recorded by the teacher directly on the Teacher's Diagnostic Chart, as the child does "all of his thinking aloud" for each example. The habits, which are different for each process, include such things as "Lost place in column," "Subtracted minuend from subtrahend," and "Grouped too many digits in dividend."

The materials developed to assist teachers in diagnosis are comprised of a Pupil's Work Sheet consisting of graded examples of computation in the four fundamental processes, a Teacher's Diagnostic Chart which lists from 24 to 35 of the "habits," and a thirty-one page Manual of Directions which explains how to use the chart and gives illustrations of each work habit. The tests for each operation require approximately 15 to 20 minutes to administer. The manual is very clear on how to administer the chart and use it for diagnosis, but remediation is covered with the statement "Improvement in arithmetic may be expected to follow as soon as the teacher specifically determines poor habits of work and gives specific instructions for substitution of better habits." Implementation of these instructions is left completely up to the teacher.

This groundbreaking Diagnostic Chart is presently of little use. Today the emphasis in computation is on understanding rather than efficiency. Other educators who have further developed Buswell and John's ideas are Ashlock (1975) who has emphasized the detection and elimination of more conceptually-oriented error patterns and Weaver (1955) who has encouraged teachers to use "little interviews" to study children's thinking during computation. Bitter, Englehardt, and Wiebe (1977) have produced a set of materials called Math H.E.L.P., that include specific suggestions for remediation in computation. These materials and others similar to them could be considered the modern equivalent of Buswell and John's Diagnostic Chart.

REVIEWER'S REFERENCES

Weaver, J. F. Big dividends from little interviews. THE ARITHMETIC TEACHER, 1955, 2, 40–47.

Ashlock, R. M. ERROR PATTERNS IN COMPUTATION: A SEMI-PROGRAMMED APPROACH, SECOND EDITION. Columbus, OH: Charles Merrill, 1975.

Bitter, G., Englehardt, J., & Wiebe, J. MATH H.E.L.P. Saint Paul, MN: EMC Corporation, 1977.

Review of Buswell-John Diagnostic Test for Fundamental Processes in Arithmetic by LINDA JENSEN SHEFFIELD, Associate Professor of Education and Mathematics, Northern Kentucky University, Highland Heights, KY:

This instrument consists of 40–50 exercises which assess each of the four basic operations (i.e., addition, subtraction, multiplication, division). Each set of exercises involves whole number computations only and is organized in order of approximate difficulty from basic facts up to exercises involving 7-digit numbers. The instrument is designed to be used individually with children having difficulty in computation. The manual suggests that a teacher choose one operation and have the child work from the beginning until the problems become too difficult. No time limits were established for the test, but the manual indicates administration normally requires 15–20 minutes. Children are asked to "think aloud" as they work.

Although the materials have no copyright date, many features of the instrument seem to date it. The manual states that the ultimate goal should be "the ability to use the fundamental operations accurately, rapidly and with understanding." The fundamental operations apparently refer only to computations with whole numbers. No coverage is given to other aspects of elementary mathematics which have been common since the "new math" of the 1960s, the "back to basics" math of the 1970s or the "problem solving" math of the 1980s. The use of the terms "carrying" and "borrowing" and the references to the teacher as "she" and the students as "he" also date the materials.

Although the test purports to assess work methods in arithmetic, it is clear that the instrument is designed to identify "habits" which interfere with computational speed and accuracy. As the pupil works through the exercises, the teacher checks off those habits, from a list of approximately 30, that are observed in the pupil's performance. The habits are not necessarily all bad. "Some of the habits are poor simply because they are time-consuming and uneconomical." Presumably this includes several habits which demonstrate that the child has a good understanding of the processes of computation, result in a correct answer, but may not be as rapid as traditional algorithms. For example, habit a-11 is "splits numbers into parts." The example is "27 and 8 equals,—27 and 3 equals 30 and 5 equals 35." Even though this demonstrated that a student understands the associative property, it is not a recommended procedure. Other habits of this type are: derived unknown combination from a familiar one, used scratch paper, depended on visualization, based subtraction on multiplication combination, multiplied by adding, used long division form for short division and used short division form for long division. Even though these methods may reflect some understanding of the processes, they are discouraged because they are time-consuming. Clearly, the goal is the rapid use of traditional algorithms.

No norms are provided and data on reliability and validity are missing. The authors state that the items were arranged in approximate order of difficulty after testing them on 500 children in Chicago. The habits are those which were observed in at least 5 of another sample of 250 Chicago children and are listed from the most to least frequently observed. This data could be useful to a classroom teacher who wishes to present computation exercises in a logical sequence. The process of individually diagnosing students as they think aloud is highly recommended and the habits listed give the teacher a good idea of expected responses.

One glaring omission of this diagnostic instrument is the lack of any prescriptive procedure. Although suggested remedial measures were collected from 70 teachers, they are not included in the manual due to space limitations. The manual states that these suggestions are available in a supplementary monograph. However, it is stated that "improvement in arithmetic may be expected to follow as soon as the teacher specifically determines poor habits of work and gives specific instructions for the substitution of better habits."

Overall, this instrument seems to have limited usefulness. It tests one aspect of an elementary math curriculum, computational speed and accuracy with whole numbers using traditional algorithms. No problems utilizing concrete or pictorial work is provided and applications are never mentioned. The individual oral interviews are commendable and the habits identified are useful if speed and not understanding is the goal. Specific suggestions for working with children displaying these habits and behaviors would enhance the usefulness of the instrument. Teachers wishing this type of information might turn to a book such as *Error Patterns in Computation* by Robert B. Ashlock (1982), which provides not only analyses of errors but also contains suggestions for instruction. In addition, problems involving place value, fractions, decimals, and whole number computation are also included. Teaching suggestions focus on understanding and include many concrete manipulatives. These features are both missing from the Buswell-John Diagnostic Test.

REVIEWER'S REFERENCES

Ashlock, R. B. ERROR PATTERNS IN COMPUTATION. Columbus, OH: Charles E. Merrill, 1982.

[177]

C-PAC: Clinical Probes of Articulation Consistency. Ages 5 and over; 1981; C-PAC; 2 scores for consonant and vocalic R probes, vowel and diphthong probes have only a single word and sentence score; no reliability or validity data; no norms; individual; 1 form (1 page for each phoneme); examiner's manual (21 pages plus adult storytelling tests, training words, and posttests); storytelling manual (51 pages); 1983 price data: $45 per complete C-PAC Program including examiner's manual, spirit master articulation probes, and storytelling manual; $15.95 per 44 additional spirit master articulation probes; $14.95 per examiner's manual; (5) minutes for each of 23 consonant probes and the 1 vocalic R probe, (1–2) minutes for vowels and diphthongs; Wayne Secord and Roxie M. Ball (storytelling manual); Charles E. Merrill Publishing Co.*

Review of C-PAC: Clinical Probes of Articulation Consistency by RICHARD J. SCHISSEL, Associate Professor and Coordinator, Speech Pathology-Audiology Program, University of Arkansas-Fayetteville, Fayetteville, AR:

The C-PAC is described in the examiner's manual as a "comprehensive set of articulation measures" applicable with subjects kindergarten through adulthood. The measures consist of 23 consonant probes and one vocalic R probe. Additional probes examine 12 vowels and 4 diphthongs. The consonant probes are intended to assess consistency of production in single words and across word boundaries. Each consonant is examined by syllabic function in a wide variety of English phonetic contexts.

The C-PAC utilizes an imitation and delayed imitation format. The storytelling manual contains an illustrated story (four pictures per story) for each of the 23 consonant probes, one for the vocalic R and one for all vowels and diphthongs (25 total stories). For each story, which contains 10 to 20 examples of the target phoneme in a variety of contexts, the examiner shows the pictures to the child and reads the story from the card facing her. The child retells the story and the examiner records correct and incorrect productions of the target phoneme on the probe sheet. The author stated that the stories were constructed to allow easy repetition by children over the age of four.

The probes also may be administered imitatively. In this case the examiner reads each probe stimulus word or word pair, the subject responds, and the examiner records the response. Probes also may be administered through a reading mode for adults and children who can read.

The complete C-PAC kit includes an examiner's manual, a spiral bound easel-type storytelling manual, and probes. The probes are packaged in a set of 44 spirit duplicating masters usable with any standard ditto machine (15 spirit master probes are duplicates of the frequently misarticulated sounds). In addition, 30 different probes of some sounds are included in the manual for use as posttests. According to the author, the C-PAC has multiple uses including: determining where to begin therapy, identifying facilitating phonetic contexts, determining the direction of therapy, creating measurement strategies, measuring multiphonemic production, facilitating and teaching patterns of context generalization, measuring the effectiveness of therapy, and posttesting.

The reviewer believes that this kit is best considered to be, and used as, a collection of therapy materials. In this context the author did a commendable job of developing lists of single words, two-word combinations, reading and story passages which do provide opportunities for production of target phonemes in an extensive array of phonetic contexts. With the exception of a few procedural concerns and methodological questions, I would recommend the kit for such use and would characterize it as well designed, easy to use, and unquestionably extensive. The inclusion of spirit master probes also was a nice and thoughtful touch. However, the failure of the C-PAC to meet even the most minimal standards for education and psychological tests makes it useless for any type of assessment task.

The C-PAC is not titled as, nor is it claimed to be, a "test." The author provides no norms and there is no data on reliability or validity. I have two very serious concerns regarding this situation. First, the manual is quite misleading. While it does not claim to be a test, in the first paragraph alone of the manual are the following statements: "[C-PAC] is a comprehensive set of articulation measures"; "provides an in-depth picture of articulation consistency"; "C-PAC examines phoneme production not just in isolation or in syllables." Such descriptors are found throughout the manual and all clearly imply that the C-PAC is to be used to measure something. It is quite probable that this is the way it will be used.

Related to the first, my second concern is that the author seems to believe that since the material is not considered a test, and is designed for use in therapy, he is under no obligation to provide reliability or validity data. However, it is clear from a reading of the manual and, particularly from the stated uses of the C-PAC, that it is intended to measure something. The author tells us that this something is articulation consistency but provides no data to support his contention. A user of this material has no idea what is being measured, how much reliance can be placed on the results, how stable the measurements are, whether there is any agreement between independent scorings under operational conditions, or whether there is any relationship between alternate forms (probe and posttest scores). To use the C-PAC for its stated purposes a speech-language pathologist would need at least this much information.

Given the absence of reliability and validity data, the reviewer cannot recommend the C-PAC as anything other than a nicely packaged collection of therapy stimulus materials. I further would suggest that all claims made in the manual for the purposes and uses of the material be disregarded until documentation for them is provided.

[178]

The CAHPER Fitness Performance II Test. Ages 7–17; 1966–80; 6 scores: speed sit up, standing long jump, flexed arm hand, shuttle run, 50 metre run, endurance run; no reliability data; largely individual; 1 form; manual ('80, 90 pages, English and French); 1984 price data: $6.95 per manual; administration time not reported; Canadian Association for Health, Physical Education and Recreation [Canada].*

See T3:599 (1 reference), T2:919 (2 references), and 7:599 (1 reference).

[179]

CAI Study Skills Test. College-bound high school seniors and college freshmen; 1981–83; SST; based upon Effective Study Test; "procedure for measuring a student's knowledge about efficient study behavior and effective scholastic motivation"; 11 scores: time management, memory improvement, note taking, textbook reading, examination taking, report writing, oral reporting, scholastic motivation, interpersonal relations, concentration improvement, total (study effectiveness); norms for total score only, standards of mastery for 10 study skills areas; 1 form ('81, 8 pages); manual ('83, 16 pages); answer-profile sheet ('81, 4 pages); microcomputer editions available for administration; 1984 price data: $.85 or less per reusable test booklet; $.35 or less per answer-profile sheet; $5 per set of 2 scoring stencils; $1.50 per manual; (55) minutes; William F. Brown and Bernadette Gadzella; Effective Study Materials.*

[180]

California Achievement Tests, Forms C and D. Grades K–0 to K–9, K–6 to 1–9, 1–6 to 2–9, 2–6 to 3–9, 3–6 to 4–9, 4–6 to 5–9, 5–6 to 6–9, 6–6 to 7–9, 7–6 to 9–9, 9–6 to 12–9; 1957–78; CAT/C & D; subtests in reading and mathematics for Levels 11–19 available as separates; 2 forms for Levels 13–19; 10 overlapping levels; coordinator's handbook ('78, 95 pages); technical bulletin 1 ('79, 161 pages), 2 ('80, 113 pages); class management guide ('78, 177 pages); locator test 1 for grades 1–6, 2 for grades 6–12, ('77, 7 pages); practice tests ('77, 2 pages each for Levels 11–13 and 14–16); separate answer sheets (CompuScan, IBM 1230, Scoreze) must be used with Levels 14–19; 1983 price data: $20 per multi-level examination kit (Form C only); $12 per primary (grades K–3) kit; $12 per intermediate (grades 4–6) kit; $12 per secondary (grades 7–12) kit; $8 per class management guide; $4.75 per coordinator's handbook; $4.75 per technical bulletin; CTB/McGraw-Hill.*

a) LEVEL 10. Grade K–0 to K–9; 10 scores: listening for information, letter forms, letter names, letter sounds, visual discrimination, sound matching, total, mathematics, alphabet skills, visual and auditory discrimination; 2 editions; Form C examiner's manual ('77, 42 pages); norms book ('78, 22 pages); $3.75 per examiner's manual; $3.35 per norms book; (160–180) minutes in 2 or 3 sessions.

1) *Hand Scorable Booklet.* Book 10C ('73, 22 pages); scoring key ('77, 3 pages); $24.50 per complete battery including 35 tests.

2) *CompuScan Machine Scorable Booklet.* Book 10C ('73, 24 pages); $35.35 per complete battery including 35 tests; scoring service, $1.05 and over per student ($100 minimum).

b) LEVEL 11. Grades K–6 to 1–9; 9 scores: phonic analysis, reading vocabulary, reading comprehension, total, language expression, mathematics computation, mathematics concepts and applications, total mathematics, total; 2 editions; Form C examiner's manual ('77, 35 pages); norms book ('78, 28 pages); prices same as for Level 10; (130–140) minutes in 2 or 3 sessions.

1) *Hand Scorable Booklet.* Book 11C ('77, 22 pages); scoring key ('77, 3 pages).

2) *CompuScan Machine Scorable Booklet.* Book 11C ('77, 22 pages).

c) LEVEL 12. Grades 1–6 to 2–9; 13 scores: phonic analysis, structural analysis, reading vocabulary, reading comprehension, total, spelling, language mechanics, language expression, total language, mathematics computation, mathematics concepts and applications, total mathematics, total; 2 editions; Form C examiner's manual ('77, 42 pages); norms book ('78, 31 pages); prices same as for Level 10; (175–195) minutes in 2 or 3 sessions.

1) *Hand Scorable Booklet.* Book 12C ('77, 28 pages); scoring key ('77, 4 pages).

2) *CompuScan Machine Scorable Booklet.* Book 12C ('77, 27 pages).

d) LEVEL 13. Grades 2–6 to 3–9; 13 scores: same as for *c*; 2 editions; Form C examiner's manual ('77, 60 pages); norms book ('78, 47 pages); prices same as for Level 10; (175–195) minutes in 2 or 3 sessions.

1) *Hand Scorable Booklet.* Book 13C ('77, 32 pages); scoring key ('78, 8 pages).

2) *CompuScan Machine Scorable Booklet.* Book 13C ('77, 31 pages).

e) LEVEL 14. Grades 3–6 to 4–9; 12 scores: reading vocabulary, reading comprehension, total reading, spelling, language mechanics, language expression, total language, mathematics computation, mathematics concepts and applications, total mathematics, total, reference skills; Book 14C, 14D, ('77, 53 pages); Form C and D examiner's manual Levels 14–19 ('77, 43 pages); norms book ('78, 47 pages); scoring key for Levels 14–19 Forms C and D ('78, 7 pages); $36.05 per 35 reusable test booklets; $10 per 50 CompuScan complete battery answer sheets; $31.50 per 50 sets of IBM 1230 answer sheets; $24 per 25 sets of Scoreze answer sheets; $14.25 per set of IBM 1230 hand-scoring stencils; $3.75 per examiner's manual; $3.35 per norm book; CompuScan scoring service, $.66 and over per student ($100 minimum); (190–210) minutes in 2 or 3 sessions.

f) LEVEL 15. Grades 4–6 to 5–9; 12 scores: same as for *e*; Book 15C, 15D, ('77, 53 pages); Form C and D examiner's manual same as for *e*; norms book ('78, 53 pages); scoring key same as for *e*; prices and time same as for Level 14.

g) LEVEL 16. Grades 5–6 to 6–9; 12 scores: same as for *e*; Book 16C, 16D, ('77, 57 pages); Form C and D examiner's manual same as for *e*; norms book ('78, 53 pages); scoring key same as for *e*; prices and time same as for *e*.

h) LEVEL 17. Grades 6–6 to 7–9; 12 scores: same as for *e*; Book 17C, 17D, ('77, 58 pages); Form C and D examiner's manual same as for *e*; norms book ('78, 53 pages); scoring key same as for *e*; prices and time same as for *e*.

i) LEVEL 18. Grades 7–6 to 9–9; 12 scores: same as for *e*; Book 18C, 18D, ('77, 60 pages); Form C and D examiner's manual same as for *e*; norms book ('78, 61 pages); prices and time same as for *e*.

j) LEVEL 19. Grades 9–6 to 12–9; 12 scores: same as for *e*; Book 19C, 19D, ('77, 59 pages); Form C and D examiner's manual same as for *e*; norms book ('78, 70 pages); scoring key same as for *e*; prices and time same as for *e*.

See T3:344 (68 references); for reviews by Miriam M. Bryan and Frank Womer of the 1970 edition, see 8:10 (33 references); for reviews by Jack C. Merwin and Robert D. North of the 1957 edition, see 6:3 (19 references); for a review by Charles O. Neidt, see 5:2 (10 references); for reviews by Warren G. Findley, Alvin W. Schindler, and J. Harlan Shores of the 1950 edition, see 4:2 (8 references); for a review by Paul A. Witty of the 1943 edition, see 3:15 (3 references); for reviews by C. W. Odell and Hugh B. Wood of an earlier edition, see 2:1193 (1 reference); for a review by D. Welty Lefever and an excerpted review by E. L. Abell, see 1:876. For reviews of subtests, see 8:45 (2 reviews), 8:257 (1 review), 8:719 (2 reviews), 6:251 (1 review), 5:177 (2 reviews), 5:468 (1 review), 4:151 (2 reviews), 4:411 (1 review), 4:530 (2 reviews, 1 excerpt), 2:1292 (2 reviews), 2:1459 (2 reviews), 2:1563 (1 review), 1:893 (1 review), and 1:1110 (2 reviews).

TEST REFERENCES

1. Evertson, C. M., Emmer, E. T., & Brophy, J. E. Predictors of effective teaching in junior high mathematics classrooms. JOURNAL

FOR RESEARCH IN MATHEMATICS EDUCATION, 1980, 11, 167–178.

2. Knifong, J. D. Computational requirements of standardized word problem tests. JOURNAL FOR RESEARCH IN MATHEMATICS EDUCATION, 1980, 11, 3–9.

3. Cicchelli, T. Effects of direct and indirect instruction patterns and prior achievement on post course achievement. JOURNAL OF INSTRUCTIONAL PSYCHOLOGY, 1982, 9, 176–189.

4. Evertson, C. M., & Emmer, E. T. Effective management at the beginning of the school year in junior high classes. JOURNAL OF EDUCATIONAL PSYCHOLOGY, 1982, 74, 485–498.

5. Merkel, S. P., & Hall, V. C. The relationship between memory for order and other cognitive tasks. INTELLIGENCE, 1982, 6, 427–441.

6. Powers, S., & Crowder, C. Redundancy in the California Achievement Test. EDUCATIONAL AND PSYCHOLOGICAL MEASUREMENT, 1982, 42, 1253–1257.

7. Sandoval, J. Light's Retention Scale does not predict success in first-grade retainees. PSYCHOLOGY IN THE SCHOOLS, 1982, 19, 310–314.

8. Tallmadge, G. K. An empirical assessment of norm-referenced evaluation methodology. JOURNAL OF EDUCATIONAL MEASUREMENT, 1982, 19, 97–112.

9. Ulrey, G. L., Alexander, K., Bender, B., & Gillis, H. Effects of length of school day on kindergarten school performance and parent satisfaction. PSYCHOLOGY IN THE SCHOOLS, 1982, 19, 238–242.

10. Young, E. D., & Exum, H. A. Upward bound and academic achievement: A successful intervention. JOURNAL OF COLLEGE STUDENT PERSONNEL, 1982, 23, 291–299.

11. Ysseldyke, J. E., & Algozzine, B. Bias among professionals who erroneously declare students eligible for special services. JOURNAL OF EXPERIMENTAL EDUCATION, 1982, 50, 223–228.

12. Crowell, D. C., Hu-pei Au, K., & Blake, K. M. Comprehension questions: Differences among standardized tests. JOURNAL OF READING, 1983, 26, 314–319.

13. Douglas, P., Powers, S., & Choroszy, M. Factors in the choice of higher educational institutions by academically gifted seniors. JOURNAL OF COLLEGE STUDENT PERSONNEL, 1983, 24, 540–545.

14. Genesee, F., & Lambert, W. E. Trilingual education for majority-language children. CHILD DEVELOPMENT, 1983, 54, 105–114.

15. Gottesman, R. L., Croen, L. G., Cerullo, L. G., & Nathan, R. G. Diagnostic intervention for inner-city primary graders with learning difficulties. THE ELEMENTARY SCHOOL JOURNAL, 1983, 83, 239–249.

16. Kochnower, J., Richardson, E., & DiBenedetto, B. A comparison of the phonic decoding ability of normal and learning disabled children. JOURNAL OF LEARNING DISABILITIES, 1983, 16, 348–351.

17. Miller, L. B., & Bizzell, R. P. Long-term effects of four preschool programs: Sixth, seventh, and eighth grades. CHILD DEVELOPMENT, 1983, 54, 727–741.

18. Osako, G. N., & Anders, P. L. The effect of reading interest on comprehension of expository materials with controls for prior knowledge. NATIONAL READING CONFERENCE YEARBOOK, 1983, 32, 56–60.

19. Powers, S., Thompson, D., Azevedo, B., & Schaad, O. The predictive validity of the Stanford Mathematics Test across race and sex. EDUCATIONAL AND PSYCHOLOGICAL MEASUREMENT, 1983, 43, 645–649.

Review of California Achievement Tests, Forms C and D, by BRUCE G. ROGERS, Associate Professor of Educational Psychology and Foundations, University of Northern Iowa, Cedar Falls, IA:

The California Achievement Tests, Forms C and D, (CAT/C & D) is a traditional series of achievement tests, primarily covering reading, mathematics, and language skills from kindergarten through grade 12. Begun almost 50 years ago, the overall purpose has remained constant, while a continuous evolution has occurred in testing with respect to content validity, test bias, individualized testing, and normative data.

The CAT/C & D is described by its authors as "a comprehensive information system for educational evaluation." In this context, "comprehensive" means pre-reading, reading, spelling, language, mathematics, and reference skills. Educators who define "comprehensive" to include such areas as social studies and science may want to examine instruments such as the Comprehensive Tests of Basic Skills or the Stanford Achievement Tests, but they should keep in mind that reviewers in previous editions of the *Mental Measurements Yearbook* did not bless these additional areas with unmixed accolades. Perhaps that is one reason the CAT authors choose to retain the limited focus.

With the current emphasis on individualized testing, the CAT now consists of separate levels for each grade from kindergarten through grade nine, with the stated intent "to make functional level testing both possible and practical." An optional pretest can be used in determining which level is most appropriate for a particular child, but it must be used with considerable teacher judgment.

The test booklets have an attractive format. The print size is appropriate for the grade level and the exercises are neatly laid out on the page. The reading levels of the exercises and passages have been checked with widely used readability formulas. Some of the pages with reading passages, however, contain pictures which may be distracting. Since the pupils are not being tested on their interpretation of pictures, time spent looking at the pictures may detract from time spent on the test.

As with other major test batteries, content validity was of paramount importance in test development. Curriculum guides were requested from all states and "the objectives were thoroughly reviewed." From this analysis, a list of 98 objectives (called Category Objectives) was prepared and classified by grade level. These objectives can be helpful to potential users in making a comparison with their own local curriculum guides; however, they are subject to certain criticisms. First, no information is given on how many guides were used or how the analysis was conducted. Such matters are likely to be of concern to potential users, and an explanation would be helpful. Second, although most of the objectives are stated in terms of observable behavior (e.g., with verbs such as *match* and *select*), some are not (e.g., with verbs such as *understand* and *obtain information*), and it is thus ambiguous as to what criteria guided the authors in the phrasing of these objectives. Third, while the list of objectives for each test provides a useful outline, it might be even more indicative of what the test measures if it were expanded into a two-way content-by-process outline. Finally, a reviewer of the previous edition of CAT suggested that an outside group of curricular experts should be used to establish content relevance, but if the authors took that suggestion, it was not reported in the technical manuals.

The Category Objectives were used to construct the test items, which were then reviewed for bias and administered to a tryout group that was reasonably representative of the various parts of the nation. The resulting item analysis followed good professional practice and is well described in the manuals. On the basis of these data, final test forms were prepared for standardization.

STANDARDIZATION AND NORMS. The standardization procedure was based on a national probability sample, stratified in terms of public and Catholic schools, geographical region, size of school district, and socioeconomic status. The success of such a sampling plan depends upon the willingness of the selected schools to participate, but in usual practice not even half of the first choice schools agree to participate (Baglin, 1981). Unfortunately, the manuals do not report how many of the 359 schools that actually participated were first choice, second choice, etc. When the demographic data on the schools is compared with U.S. Census data, reasonably good agreement is shown, but some difficulties are apparent. While it is obvious by inspection that the reported family income for the CAT schools is less than that reported in the census data, the authors dismiss this discrepancy by explaining that it is a result of lack of knowledge by the school principals who supplied the data, rather than a lack of representativeness of the sample. A widely held alternative explanation is that poorer districts are more likely to participate than wealthy districts because of the financial incentives (Baglin, 1981); but there is no mention of this possibility in the manuals.

The norming was done in both the fall and spring of the 1976–77 school year, permitting a wide variety of data to be made available to users. Percent of correct responses are given for each item and show a consistent increase from fall to spring. The norm tables show interpolated values at three times during the year. For recipients of ESEA Title 1 funds, interpolated norms are available at approximately weekly intervals to comply with legal requirements. For schools which have unusual student populations, special norms can be generated by computer from data that was collected from schools with similar populations in the standardization sample.

The description of the standardization sample is quite complete. It appears that a reasonable attempt was made to achieve a proportionate representation of special education students, Blacks, Hispanics, and Catholic school students. The standardization procedure represents an exemplary effort to conform to the Standards for Educational and Psychological Tests (1974), and overall, the resulting normative data seem quite adequate.

To report to students, parents, teachers, and administrators, schools may select from a variety of derived scores, including national percentiles, grade equivalents, normal curve equivalents, scale scores, anticipated achievement scores, and category objective scores. Of these, only percentiles and category objective scores are recommended by the authors for communicating with students and parents. For the teacher, category objective scores are particularly recommended for determining priority areas of instruction. Grade equivalent scores are interpreted with caution, but no recommendations are given for their use; scale scores are instead recommended to administrators for plotting the growth in achievement for groups. Normal curve equivalents are recommended for Title 1 evaluation purposes and for comparing performances on two different tests. The anticipated achievement scores (predictions based primarily on scores from the Short Form Test of Academic Aptitude) are described, but no discussion is given of their proper interpretation. Considering the potential dangers that can occur through the improper use of underachievement and overachievement labels, it would seem most useful to remedy this omission.

In the norm tables, derived scores are generated for every raw score value, including those below the chance level on the test. But the interpretation of scores in the chance range is problematical. For a pupil who guessed on all of the items, the score has little meaning, and for another who just refused to respond to most of the items, the score cannot be meaningfully compared with those of pupils who seriously attempted the items. In light of the Standards (D5.4), it would probably be better to indicate such scores as uninterpretable.

Each Category Objective produces a score labeled "Derived Objectives Mastery Score." This transformation represents a first attempt by the CAT authors to grapple with the thorny problems of mastery scores. One cause of concern arises from the reported reliability estimates for the raw score on the category objectives. Since they are based on so few items, these estimates are quite low, seldom reaching .70. Psychometricians repeatedly advise against interpreting scores with so little evidence of stability. In order to increase this reliability, the authors adopted a Bayesian inference model, wherein the prior information is the examinee's score on the remainder of the items in that test containing the Category Objective. The procedure proved effective in increasing the reliabilities, most to above .70; however, there are two disadvantages associated with this procedure. First, few users have any conception of Bayesian inference (but for those desirous to learn, the manual presents a simple example). Second, strange results can occur. If a student failed half the items on an objective, but did very well on the remainder of that particular test, a passing score could be reported, on the rationale that the poor score in the one area was a sampling error. Now the statisticians may all nod in agreement, but the average teacher will wonder if this was a case of legerdemain. Nonetheless, the authors are to be commended for their effort, and it is hoped that future psychometric developments will further increase the acceptability of these types of scores. Indeed, these scores, and the other types of scores available, constitute one of the strengths of the CAT/C & D.

RELIABILITY. Reliability measures are reported for each subtest at each level. For internal consistency, KR20 estimates are used. These values are highest for the mathematics sections, moderate for the reading sections, and lowest for the spelling and language parts. Parallel-form correlations are presented for time intervals of about 3 weeks and 6 months. If the assumption is made that there should be at least as much true score variance as error variance in a set of scores (reliability greater than .71), then almost all of the tests at every level will be considered satisfactory. The exceptions tend to be in the primary grades; teachers in these grades should interpret scores with considerable caution. Previous reviewers have criticized the use of subsection scores because of their low reliability. With the use of the Bayesian technique, this limitation is somewhat alleviated, although the resulting scores should still be interpreted with considerable caution. Standard error of measurement values are reported, but for the KR20 coefficients only. Since the importance of parallel-forms reliability is emphasized in the Standards (F1.1, F1.2), users might find it helpful to have corresponding standard errors reported for these reliability figures also.

The reading tests are structured to measure the skills most likely taught at each grade level. While well planned, they are also susceptible to some criticism. For the CAT items measuring Letter Sounds at the kindergarten level, the teacher says a word and the pupils select a letter representing the sound at the beginning of the word. This is not what the child does when reading aloud, and reading teachers may wonder if there is evidence to indicate that the two processes are equivalent. Unfortunately, no evidence is presented nor is the problem acknowledged in the manuals.

The interpretations of the vocabulary test results are enhanced by the use of three methods of evaluation: using synonyms, antonyms, and words within the context of a sentence. The reading comprehension tests were checked for readability and interest, yet two areas of possible criticism should be mentioned. First, while these exercises test both recall of specific facts and main concepts, the relative emphasis appears to be more with the former than the latter. Second, some of the items may be answerable without reading the passage. The manual gives no indication as to whether the passages were empirically tested for this possibility.

Each item in the spelling tests for grades 4 through 6 presents a sentence with two underlined words and the student is to indicate whether either word is misspelled. Does this measure the same thing as a dictated test? Why are two words underlined rather than only one? It is not unrealistic to expect that these types of questions will arise in the minds of perceptive teachers, and it would be helpful if they were addressed in the manual.

The items in the mathematics tests are described as representing a middle ground between rote memory and understanding. Junior high school teachers who emphasize exact computational skills (e.g., adding three 3-digit numbers) will find a compatible emphasis in these tests, while those who stress estimation skills may find a lack of that concentration in these tests. More detailed analyses of the contents of the reading and mathematics subtests will be found in Schell (1980) and Mercer (1978), respectively.

MANUALS AND SUPPORTING LITERATURE. Five manuals are available to help test users properly administer the entire testing program. The Class Management Guide is appropriately subtitled "A Teacher's Guide to Interpreting and Using Test Information." It describes procedures for using the test results in establishing instructional priorities and instructional activities for each category objective. While the size of this volume (170 pages) is likely initially to overwhelm the busy teacher, it should prove to be an efficient classroom resource when accompanied with appropriate inservice education. The Examiner's Manuals give detailed instructions for administering the tests at each level. The instructions to be read to the student and the descriptions of what the student is to do are printed in different colors. The Test Coordinator's Handbook, primarily designed to be used by testing directors, covers the organization of a testing program and the training of proctors to administer the tests.

Technical Bulletins 1 and 2 are concerned with validity, standardization, norming, reliability, and bias studies. While some sections of these manuals are well written, certain parts could be improved. Any manual should be written to be understood by the intended audience, and since the Technical Bulletins are intended primarily for directors of testing, a small sample of directors should be used as a tryout group, and requested to prepare constructive criticisms. The section on scaling, in particular, is likely to cause difficulty. On a positive note, the discussion of test bias is very readable.

The advertising brochure is in good ethical taste. A brief description is given of the purpose of the test, the individual report, and the classroom summary sheet. As would be expected, all the statements were positive and laudatory, but none were found to be deliberately misleading. Some, however, like "criterion-referenced," might be confusing. The Standards (Sec. D) point out the confusion surrounding the popular usage of the term "criterion-referenced," and carefully explicate the distinction between that and the term "content-referenced." The score interpretations of the CAT aptly fit the definition of the term "content-referenced," but confusion is perpetuated by the use of the term "criterion-referenced" in both advertisements and manuals. It would be helpful to users if the Standards were more closely followed in this regard.

Basically, the CAT contains separate levels for each elementary grade, reflecting the perception that students typically learn the basic skills in an orderly sequence throughout elementary school. However, since some students will not have mastered the basic skills by the end of grade 8, many districts administer a type of minimal competency measure during high school. The CAT level for grades 9 through 12 combined is certainly worthy of consideration for this purpose, but the interpretation of the scores may prove controversial. While there is the possibility of misinterpretation of grade equivalents at any level, it is particularly likely for high school students. In elementary school, every child is essentially presented the same curriculum at the same rate, so grade equivalents can be viewed in terms of the curriculum covered in any particular grade. But in high school, this progressive curricular frame of reference no longer holds and the interpretation of grade equivalents is much more problematical. In accordance with the Standards (D5.2.3), users would probably be well advised to ignore grade equivalents at the high school level and rely instead on percentile norms and scale scores. Of course, for many high school students, these tests will be considered too easy, and not relevant to the courses they are studying. Teachers who desire to measure educational progress beyond the basic skills may want to consider instruments explicitly designed for that purpose, such as the Iowa Tests of Educational Development.

The CAT authors substantially extended the data on bias in this edition. During the development phase, the items were submitted to representatives of various ethnic and cultural groups (selected for their expertise with some phase of the education of minority students), and the item tryout data from black students were separated out and analyzed. This information was used in the final revision of the test. The data appears to support the modest claim that bias was eliminated where possible, but the authors admit that some bias against Blacks and Hispanics probably remains in the tests. The integrity of the CAT is improved by this admission of imperfection, as reported in the Technical Bulletin, and it would be further enhanced by similar statements in the Teacher's Guide and the advertisements.

Recipients of ESEA Title 1 funds are required to evaluate their projects using a prescribed model. A special handbook was prepared by the authors to show how the CAT data, when properly gathered and analyzed (using the company's computer scoring services), could be used to fulfil the legal requirements. The reader is referred to the User's Guide by Tallmadge and Wood (1981) for further details. (The source is incorrectly listed in the handbook. Users should contact an appropriate official in their own state department of education to determine how the Guide is distributed in their state.)

SUMMARY. The CAT series has long been regarded as a well-developed achievement series whose authors are responsive to suggestions for improvement. The CAT/C & D continues this tradition, and is suitable for schools that emphasize the "three Rs" across the elementary grades. Scores on the subtests at the lower levels appear to have larger error components and should be interpreted accordingly. Scores on the category objectives at all levels also need to be interpreted with sufficient caution. At the high school level, users may question whether the test designed for grade 9 is appropriate for the other three grades. Despite the criticisms and cautions cited in this review, these tests do appear to have been carefully developed and normed. Educators desiring to obtain a good measure of the three basic skills areas, and who find the test specifications compatible with their own overall objectives, should consider the CAT/C & D as potential tests for their schools.

REVIEWER'S REFERENCES

STANDARDS FOR EDUCATIONAL AND PSYCHOLOGICAL TESTS. Washington, DC: American Psychological Association, 1974.

Mercer, M. The content of two mathematics achievement subtests. SCHOOL SCIENCE AND MATHEMATICS, 1978, 78, 669–674.

Schell, L. M. California Achievement Tests: Reading (Test Review). JOURNAL OF READING, 1980, 23, 624–628.

Baglin, R. F. Does "nationally" normed really mean nationally? JOURNAL OF EDUCATIONAL MEASUREMENT, 1981, 18, 97–107.

Tallmadge, C. K., & Wood, C. T. USER'S GUIDE: ESEA TITLE 1 EVALUATION AND REPORTING SYSTEM (revised edition). Mountain View, CA: RMC Research Corporation, 1981.

Review of California Achievement Tests, Forms C and D, by VICTOR L. WILLSON, Associate Professor of Educational Psychology and Director, Research Assistant Laboratory, College of Education, Texas A&M University, College Station, TX:

The California Achievement Tests, Forms C and D are entirely new tests developed to replace the

CAT/70, the previous edition in a series that now has a 50-year history. The CAT C and D are intended to measure basic skills in six content areas: reading aptitude (at the kindergarten level), reading, spelling, language, mathematics, and reference skills. There are 10 tests for Form C, designed to test students from entry in kindergarten to the end of grade 12. Form D has 7 tests that are parallel to the upper 7 tests of Form C. Each test (except those for grades K.0–K.9) is intended to measure pupil achievement over a 1.3 grade equivalent range, beginning with the sixth month of one grade and extending to the ninth month of the following grade. This allows for a 3-month overlap between the tests, so that one may use two different tests to assess pupil progress at the end of the school year. One would select the level on the basis of student characteristics, since one level will give a high ceiling, and the other a low floor.

A major change in CAT C and D is the stated purpose of the tests to function as either norm-referenced or criterion-referenced tests. This psychometric feat of legerdemain is apparently intended as a marketing device to attract those school districts that have rejected norm-referenced testing. Since it is so important it will be tackled first. In the original conception of criterion-referenced testing test items are derived from sampling the objectives of a content domain. There is no evidence that this method was used in the CAT C and D. Objectives for the CAT were selected in a systematic way from reviews of state and major city curriculum guidelines and from two CRT instruments. There is no hint that any sampling took place. In the domain model of criterion-referenced testing a student's score represents the percentage of objectives that the student has mastered. These are not the scores reported in the CAT C and D. The other approach to CRT is based on the concept of mastery or passing a criterion score. The critical issue is the selection of the cutoff. The authors of the CAT C and D have answered the question by telling us that a score of .80 (indicating 80% of the items for an objective group answered correctly) is mastery, with 65% to 79% partial mastery, and below 65% nonmastery. Items, however, were selected on the basis of traditional classical true score theory criteria and further subjected to ethnic bias analyses to further restrict range of difficulty. It is indefensible for the test publishers to present the tests as criterion-referenced when they were developed in the classical framework. There is no validation of the mastery scores nor evidence for decision-consistency of the cutoff scores. The developers are to be commended on the use of the Bayesian model to construct an estimated true score for each category of objectives, but the caveat given that each user must define mastery is just too obscure, placed as it is in the second Technical Bulletin.

As classically developed norm-referenced tests the CAT C and D are excellent. The content areas, expanded from the 1970 tests, have been developed to fit well with most school curricula and reflect mainstream objectives. A sampling by me of items from throughout the tests failed to produce any items that could be considered obscure or unusual. Content review for ethnic and sex bias was extensive. Item tryout was employed to further refine the item pool. The test manuals provide placement of each item into objective categories. Information given concerning cognitive level of the items is not very clear. While I do not insist that any particular taxonomy be used, information regarding an item's intended level within the test in which it is placed would have been helpful. At a minimum a differentiation between recall and manipulation items should have been provided. The authors do provide their own classification tables, but they are not very helpful in this regard.

The sampling of students nationwide appears to be good. Public and parochial school samples were drawn. A criticism made about the sampling frame of the 1970 tests was that the largest metropolitan school districts were underrepresented. The developers included a separate cell in the CAT C and D sampling frame for the 25 largest cities in the U.S.A., an adequate response to the criticism. A major plus for the sample used to norm the CAT C and D is that a large percentage of the sample was tested both fall and spring. In the fall these students received the Form C test, and in the spring the samples were split so that some received the same form, some the intended parallel test in Form D, and some the next higher level tests for Forms C and D. This allowed equipercentile equating of forms, still the method of choice in equating. Also, subsamples at each grade were retested after about three weeks. Grades K through 2 were readministered Form C, while grades 4 through 12 received first Form C and then Form D.

The 3-week grades K through 2 stability estimates for reading, language, and mathematics total scores are all in the .80–.90 range with a .72 for Total Reading at grade 1 (Form C). Subtest score stabilities range from .35 to .93. Alternate form total score 3-week reliabilities are all above .80, while subtest reliabilities vary from .53 to .95, generally above .70. Alternate form reliabilities for the reference skills subtests are uniformly and surprisingly low, in the .68–.76 range between grades 4 and 11. This is probably due to the haphazard way such objectives are introduced from district to district. The fall to spring reliabilities within Form C increase with grade level from the .60–.70 range in grades K through 1 to the mid .80s for grades 2 through 12. The cross form reliabilities are only a point or two below the Form C test-retest reliabilities at every grade 3 through 12. The reference skills tests continue to have low values in the .64–.76 range. Internal consistency coefficients tend to be higher, in the .90s, reflecting the item analyses performed to obtain homogeneous subtests. The reference skills subtests have reliabilities in the high .80s. The reliabilities are adequate at all levels and for all forms.

Norm tables and summary statistics are well presented but divided among four manuals: class management, test coordinator, and two technical supplements. The only real disappointment was the lack of observed difference distributions for the fall to spring testings of Form C, which would be quite useful for many school districts. I recommend that they be provided as a supplementary set of tables.

Additional tables are available for a variety of purposes, including Title I evaluation usage and predicted achievement based on the CTB/McGraw-Hill Short Form Test of Academic Aptitude (SFTAA), either in grade equivalent or standard score form. The regressions are based on concurrent administrations of the tests. Standard errors are provided as well as cross-validation data from selected samples at each grade. The comments of Womer (8:10) about the CAT 70 and the SFTAA still apply. If one finds them useful the predicted scores are available.

Administration of the tests is straightforward using the administration manuals. I administered all forms for grades K through 3 with convenience samples. Children enjoyed the tests and had no difficulty taking them.

This test is as good as any test available for its purpose as a norm-referenced multilevel basic skills test. All major technical issues have been carefully addressed. Results for grades K through 1 tend to be somewhat poorer than for the remaining grades, but overall the battery will provide users with a good, interpretable test. Both forms seem equally usable. The criterion-referenced use for the test does not seem defensible due to the methods for item and test development.

[181]

The California Child Q-Set. Children; 1980; CCQ; for an upward extension see The California Q-Set; Q-Sort rating of children by teachers and counselors in 9 categories, ranging from extremely uncharacteristic to extremely characteristic; no data on reliability and validity; no norms, use of norms not recommended; 1 form (100 cards); instruction sheets (5 pages); 1984 price data: $6 per Q-set deck including instructions; (35–60) minutes; Jeanne Block and Jack Block; Consulting Psychologists Press, Inc.*

See T3:348 (2 references).

Review of The California Child Q-Set by ALFRED B. HEILBRUN, JR., Professor of Psychology, Emory University, Atlanta, GA:

The California Child Q-Set (CCQ) is not a psychological test in the conventional meaning of the term. Norms, technically required to qualify as a test, are not provided by the developers and, in fact, are not recommended for the use of this psychometric instrument. The CCQ is better described as an assessment technique, a set of operations from which an overall picture of a child's personality characteristics can be generated. The procedures do include some of the important properties of a test such as a standard set of items to be judged by the rater as more or less descriptive of the target child. There are also fairly specific instructions furnished to the rater regarding how the judgments are to be reached.

The normless quality of this Q-sort procedure follows logically from the fact that as recommended for use there is no score to be normed. Ipsative ratings of 100 characteristics presumably provide a description of an individual child's personality that cannot profitably be compared normatively with other children. Interpretation, according to the developers' instructions, requires review of the judgments regarding the child's characteristics not only on an item-by-item basis but more profitably in terms of item constellations that offer more complex, integrative, and critical insights about the child. I would take issue with the conclusion that ipsative (within-person) ratings cannot be used in a normative way to compare one person with another. Experience with the Edwards Personal Preference Schedule, an ipsative self-rating technique used normatively, teaches us that the two assessment approaches can be blended. In the last analysis, the CCQ user will settle the issue of whether purely ipsative child assessment occurs. I doubt whether it is even possible. Can a judgement about how characteristic some attribute is for a child be made without some mental comparison of that child to other children?

Since no information regarding validity or reliability of the CCQ is made available in the user's guide, current evaluation must rest heavily upon the presumed potential of this Q-sort and the deceptively simple and readily understandable steps provided users for rendering their judgements. It is important to note as well that personality measurement in children presents formidable obstacles, especially in the decreasing availability of reliable self-report procedures as younger ages are considered. The CCQ is a welcome addition to the assessment tools that can be employed with children. Time should provide more palpable evidence of whether the potential of this instrument is illusory or real as critical questions are answered. Are meaningful predictions from CCQ sorts possible? Do different raters agree in their sorts as they describe the same child?

As this is a psychometric technique that maximizes the involvement of its user, the real source of validity is less the instrument than the person using it. Skills are involved in translating knowledge about children into descriptive priorities and then organizing these decisions into a meaningful interpretation of personality dynamics. Not everyone is capable of performing these difficult activities well. All that can be asked of the instrument is that it provide the opportunity for capable judges to organize their observations of a child in an effective way.

The fact that the CCQ is not a formal test does offer some advantages, although these may be more vital to the researcher than the practitioner. For one thing, the user could effect a different distribution of sorts than that recommended by the developers. A more or less normal distribution of judgments regarding trait applicability (i.e., the ubiquitous bell-shaped distribution) could be introduced rather than the prescribed rectangular sort. The CCQ also could prove valuable (as Q-sorts with adults have) in describing a variety of stereotypes involving children—the "ideal child," the "disturbed child," etc. Finally, this technique would be an interesting way to compare judges' observations rather than concentrating on the observed child. Many possibilities come to mind such as isolating discrepant observations of parents as they describe their child or as a married couple describes an ideal prospective child. These discrepancies could prove useful in resolving or avoiding child-rearing conflicts between parents.

[182]

California Psychological Inventory. Ages 13 and over; 1956–75; CPI; 18 or 24 scores: dominance (Do), capacity for status (Cs), sociability (Sy), social presence (Sp), self-acceptance (Sa), sense of well-being (Wb), responsibility (Re), socialization (So), self-control (Sc), tolerance (To), good impression (Gi), communality (Cm), achievement via conformance (Ac), achievement via independence (Ai), intellectual efficiency (Ie), psychological-mindedness (Py), flexibility (Fx), femininity (Fe), 6 additional scores included when scored by the publisher (empathy, independence, managerial interests, work orientation, leadership, social maturity); 1 form ('56, 12 pages); manual ('75, 36 pages); profile ('57, 2 pages); separate answer sheets (hand scored, prepaid CPI or NCS machine scored) must be used; 1983 price data: $10 per 25 tests; $7 per 50 hand scored answer sheets and profile; $32.50 or less per 10 prepaid CPI answer sheets; $5.50 per 50 NCS answer sheets; $15 per set of scoring stencils; $4 per manual; $2.25 per specimen set; NCS scoring service available: $2 or less per test (daily service), $.95 and over per test (weekly service); French, German, Italian, and Spanish editions available; (45–60) minutes; Harrison G. Gough; Consulting Psychologists Press, Inc.*

See T3:354 (195 references); for a review by Malcolm D. Gynther, see 8:514 (452 references); see also T2:1121 (166 references); for reviews by Lewis R. Goldberg and James A. Walsh and an excerpted review by John O. Crites, see 7:40 (370 references); see also P:27 (249 references); for a review by E. Lowell Kelly, see 6:71 (116 references); for reviews by Lee J. Cronbach and Robert L. Thorndike and an excerpted review by Laurance F. Shaffer, see 5:37 (33 references).

TEST REFERENCES

1. Cohen, P. A., & Sheposh, J. P. Audience and level of esteem as determinants of risk taking. PERSONALITY AND SOCIAL PSYCHOLOGY BULLETIN, 1977, 3, 119–122.

2. Gilstein, K. W., Wright, E. W., & Stone, D. R. The effects of leadership style on group interactions in differing socio-political subcultures. SMALL GROUP BEHAVIOR, 1977, 8, 313–331.

3. Haskell, S. D. Desired family-size correlates for single undergraduates. PSYCHOLOGY OF WOMEN QUARTERLY, 1977, 2, 5–15.

4. Judd, L. L., Hubbard, B., Janowsky, D. S., Huey, L. Y., & Attewell, P. A. The effect of lithium carbonate on affect, mood, and personality of normal subjects. ARCHIVES OF GENERAL PSYCHIATRY, 1977, 34, 346–351.

5. Kendall, P. C., Deardorff, P. A., & Finch, A. J., Jr. Empathy and socialization in first and repeat juvenile offenders and normals. JOURNAL OF ABNORMAL CHILD PSYCHOLOGY, 1977, 5, 93–97.

6. Megargee, E. I., & Bohn, M. J., Jr. A new classification system for criminal offenders IV: Empirically determined characteristics of the ten types. CRIMINAL JUSTICE AND BEHAVIOR, 1977, 4, 149–210.

7. Welsh, G. S., & Baucom, D. H. Sex, masculinity-femininity, and intelligence. INTELLIGENCE, 1977, 1, 218–233.

8. Anderson, C. R., & Schneier, C. E. Locus of control, leader behavior and leader performance among management students. ACADEMY OF MANAGEMENT JOURNAL, 1978, 21, 690–698.

9. Judd, L. L. Effect of lithium on mood, cognition, and personality function in normal subjects. ARCHIVES OF GENERAL PSYCHIATRY, 1979, 36, 860–865.

10. Vaughn, R. L. Behavioral response to vasectomy. ARCHIVES OF GENERAL PSYCHIATRY, 1979, 36, 815–821.

11. Aronow, E., Rauchway, A., Peller, M., & De Vito, A. The value of the self in relation to fear of death. OMEGA, 1980–1981, 11, 37–44.

12. Butt, D. S. Short scales for the measurement of sport motivations. INTERNATIONAL JOURNAL OF SPORT PSYCHOLOGY, 1980, 10, 203–216.

13. Butt, D. S., & Schroeder, M. L. Sex-role adaptation, socialization and sport participation in women. INTERNATIONAL JOURNAL OF SPORT PSYCHOLOGY, 1980, 11, 91–99.

14. Cunningham, J. D., & Antill, J. K. A comparison among five masculinity-femininity-androgyny instruments and two methods of scoring androgyny. AUSTRALIAN PSYCHOLOGIST, 1980, 15, 437–448.

15. King, G. D., McGowen, R., Doonan, R., & Schweibert, D. The selection of paraprofessional telephone counselors using the California Psychological Inventory. AMERICAN JOURNAL OF COMMUNITY PSYCHOLOGY, 1980, 8, 495–501.

16. Logan, D. D., & Kaschak, E. The relationship of sex, sex role, and mental health. PSYCHOLOGY OF WOMEN QUARTERLY, 1980, 4, 573–580.

17. Ross, H. G. Matching achievement styles and instructional environments. CONTEMPORARY EDUCATIONAL PSYCHOLOGY, 1980, 5, 216–226.

18. Schut, B., Hutzell, R. R., Swint, E. B., & Gaston, C. D. CPI short-form incorporating MMPI shared items: Construction, cross validation comparison. JOURNAL OF CLINICAL PSYCHOLOGY, 1980, 36, 940–944.

19. Wardell, D., & Yeudall, L. T. A multidimensional approach to criminal disorders: The assessment of impulsivity and its relation to crime. ADVANCES IN BEHAVIOUR RESEARCH AND THERAPY, 1980, 2, 159–177.

20. Falk, R., Gispert, M., & Baucom, D. H. Personality factors related to black teenage pregnancy and abortion. PSYCHOLOGY OF WOMEN QUARTERLY, 1981, 5, 737–746.

21. Kupst, M. J., & Schulman, J. L. The CPI subscales as predictors of parental coping with childhood leukemia. JOURNAL OF CLINICAL PSYCHOLOGY, 1981, 37, 386–388.

22. Kurdek, L. A., Blisk, D., & Siesky, A. E., Jr. Correlates of children's long-term adjustment to their parents' divorce. DEVELOPMENTAL PSYCHOLOGY, 1981, 17, 565–579.

23. Levin, J., & Karni, E. S. A note on the interpretation of the factor pattern of the California Psychological Inventory. JOURNAL OF PERSONALITY ASSESSMENT, 1981, 45, 430–432.

24. Martin, J. D., Blair, G. E., Dannenmaier, W. D., Jones, P. C., & Asako, M. Relationship of scores on the California Psychological Inventory. PSYCHOLOGICAL REPORTS, 1981, 48, 151,154.
25. Tarte, R. D. Contrafreeloading in humans. PSYCHOLOGICAL REPORTS, 1981, 49, 859–866.
26. Watkins, D., & Astilla, E. Antecedents of personal adequacy of Filipino college students. PSYCHOLOGICAL REPORTS, 1981, 49, 727–732.
27. White, M. C., De Sanctis, G., & Crino, M. D. Achievement, self-confidence, personality traits, and leadership ability: A review of literature on sex differences. PSYCHOLOGICAL REPORTS, 1981, 48, 547–569.
28. Aries, E. J. Verbal and nonverbal behavior in single-sex and mixed-sex groups: Are traditional sex roles changing. PSYCHOLOGICAL REPORTS, 1982, 51, 127–134.
29. Cross, D. T., & Burger, G. Ethnicity as a variable in responses to California Psychological Inventory items. JOURNAL OF PERSONALITY ASSESSMENT, 1982, 46, 153–158.
30. Forgac, G. E., & Michaels, E. J. Personality characteristics of two types of male exhibitionists. JOURNAL OF ABNORMAL PSYCHOLOGY, 1982, 91, 287–293.
31. Furnham, A., & Henderson, M. A content analysis of four personality inventories. JOURNAL OF CLINICAL PSYCHOLOGY, 1982, 38, 818–825.
32. Gilchrist, M. B. Creative talent and academic competence. GENETIC PSYCHOLOGY MONOGRAPHS, 1982, 106, 261–318.
33. Goldsmith, R. E., & Goldsmith, E. B. Dogmatism and self-esteem: Further evidence. PSYCHOLOGICAL REPORTS, 1982, 51, 289–290.
34. Gorenstein, E. E. Frontal lobe functions in psychopaths. JOURNAL OF ABNORMAL PSYCHOLOGY, 1982, 91, 368–379.
35. Grube, J. W., Kleinhesselink, R. R., & Kearney, K. A. Male self-acceptance and attraction toward women. PERSONALITY AND SOCIAL PSYCHOLOGY BULLETIN, 1982, 8, 107–112.
36. Gruber, D. L., & Shupe, D. R. Personality correlates of urinary hesitancy (paruresis) and body shyness in male college students. JOURNAL OF COLLEGE STUDENT PERSONNEL, 1982, 23, 308–313.
37. Heilbrun, A. B., Jr. Cognitive models of criminal violence based upon intelligence and psychopathy levels. JOURNAL OF CONSULTING AND CLINICAL PSYCHOLOGY, 1982, 50, 546–557.
38. Kodman, F. Personality traits of black belt karate instructors. SOCIAL BEHAVIOR AND PERSONALITY, 1982, 10, 173–175.
39. Koziey, P. W., & Davies, L. Broken homes: Impact on adolescents. THE ALBERTA JOURNAL OF EDUCATIONAL RESEARCH, 1982, 28, 95–99.
40. Kozma, R. B. Instructional design in a chemistry laboratory course: The impact of structure and aptitudes on performance and attitudes. JOURNAL OF RESEARCH IN SCIENCE TEACHING, 1982, 19, 261–270.
41. Lorr, M. On the use of cluster analytic techniques. JOURNAL OF CLINICAL PSYCHOLOGY, 1982, 38, 461–462.
42. Orpen, C. Effect of job involvement on the work-leisure relationship: Correlational study among bank clerks and police officers. PSYCHOLOGICAL REPORTS, 1982, 50, 355–364.
43. Raine, A., Roger, D. B., & Venables, P. H. Locus of control and socialization. JOURNAL OF RESEARCH IN PERSONALITY, 1982, 16, 147–156.
44. Robinson, B. E. Sex-stereotyped attitudes of male and female preschool teachers as a function of personality characteristics. PSYCHOLOGICAL REPORTS, 1982, 50, 203–208.
45. Rule, W. R., & Traver, M. D. Early recollections and expected leisure activities. PSYCHOLOGICAL REPORTS, 1982, 51, 295–301.
46. Sher, K. J., & Levenson, R. W. Risk for alcoholism and individual differences in the stress-response-dampening effect of alcohol. JOURNAL OF ABNORMAL PSYCHOLOGY, 1982, 91, 350–367.
47. Sid, A. K. W., & Lindgren, H. C. Achievement and affiliation motivation and their correlates. EDUCATIONAL AND PSYCHOLOGICAL MEASUREMENT, 1982, 42, 1213–1218.
48. Steinberg, R., & Shapiro, S. Sex differences in personality traits of female and male master of business administration students. JOURNAL OF APPLIED PSYCHOLOGY, 1982, 67, 306–310.
49. Watkins, C. E., Jr. A decade of research in support of Adlerian psychological theory. INDIVIDUAL PSYCHOLOGY, 1982, 38, 90–99.
50. Bernstein, I. H., Garbin, C. P., & McClellan, P. G. A confirmatory factoring of the California Psychological Inventory. EDUCATIONAL AND PSYCHOLOGICAL MEASUREMENT, 1983, 43, 687–691.
51. Lifton, P. D. Measures of autonomy. JOURNAL OF PERSONALITY ASSESSMENT, 1983, 47, 514–523.
52. Martin, L. M., Rodgers, D. A., & Montague, D. K. Psychometric differentiation of biogenic and psychogenic impotence. ARCHIVES OF SEXUAL BEHAVIOR, 1983, 12, 475–485.
53. Procidano, M. E., & Heller, K. Measures of perceived social support from friends and from family: Three validation studies. AMERICAN JOURNAL OF COMMUNITY PSYCHOLOGY, 1983, 11, 1–24.
54. Repapi, M., Gough, H. G., Lanning, K., & Stefanis, C. Predicting academic achievement of Greek secondary school students from family background and California Psychological Inventory scores. CONTEMPORARY EDUCATIONAL PSYCHOLOGY, 1983, 8, 181–188.
55. Schmidt, B. J. The learning styles of students related to individualized typewriting instruction. THE DELTA PI EPSILON JOURNAL, 1983, 25, 41–51.
56. Carbonell, J. L. Sex roles and leadership revisited. JOURNAL OF APPLIED PSYCHOLOGY, 1984, 69, 44–49.
57. Carbonell, J. L., Moorhead, K. M., & Megargee, E. I. Predicting prison adjustment with structured personality inventories. JOURNAL OF CONSULTING AND CLINICAL PSYCHOLOGY, 1984, 52, 280–294.
58. James, S. P., Campbell, I. M., & Lovegrove, S. A. Personality differentiation in a police-selection interview. JOURNAL OF APPLIED PSYCHOLOGY, 1984, 69, 129–134.
59. Myers, M. B., Templer, D. I., & Brown, R. Coping ability of women who become victims of rape. JOURNAL OF CONSULTING AND CLINICAL PSYCHOLOGY, 1984, 52, 73–78.
60. Paterson, C. R., Dickson, A. L., Layne, C. C., & Anderson, H. N. California Psychological Inventory profiles of peer-nominated assertives, unassertives, and aggressives. JOURNAL OF CLINICAL PSYCHOLOGY, 1984, 40, 534–538.
61. Waddell, K. J. The self-concept and social adaptation of hyperactive children in adolescence. JOURNAL OF CLINICAL CHILD PSYCHOLOGY, 1984, 13, 50–55.

Review of California Psychological Inventory by DONALD H. BAUCOM, Associate Professor of Psychology, University of North Carolina, Chapel Hill, NC:

A questionnaire recently sent to all clinical psychology programs in the United States and Canada with full accreditation from the American Psychological Association included the question, "In your opinion, with what five objective personality measures should the clinical Ph.D. candidate be familiar?" The California Psychological Inventory (CPI) was included in the list of 49% of the respondents, placing it second in endorsement only to the Minnesota Multiphasic Personality Inventory (Piotrowski & Keller, 1984). A search of Psychological Abstracts also indicated that the CPI was the second most frequently used personality inventory in research with adolescents from 1969–1973 (LeUnes, Evans, Karnei, & Lowry, 1980). Thus, the CPI apparently has gained the respect of many academic clinical psychologists, and it is an increasingly popular research tool. Still a personality inventory must not be selected because of popularity or respect by others. It is essential to understand what the inventory assesses and the logic underlying the constructs if appropriate use is to be made of an inventory.

The focus of the 18 basic CPI scales is interpersonal behavior or social interaction. Consequently, the concepts chosen for assessment are "folk concepts—aspects and attributes of interpersonal behavior that are to be found in all cultures and societies, and that possess a direct and integral relationship to all forms of social interaction" (Gough, 1968). That is, by measuring such constructs as socialization, social presence, and responsibility, the inventory attempts to assess constructs which are among those likely used by people in evaluating typical social interaction. Consequently it is intended for use primarily with normal individuals. This direct mapping of scale constructs onto the way people think about social interaction is one of the great strengths of the inventory. The CPI is not based on esoteric constructs which bear little resemblance to the way most people think about social behavior. It should also be noted that the CPI scales do not purport to measure personality traits. Instead the scales have two major purposes: (*a*) to predict what people will say and how they will behave in defined situations and, (*b*) to identify people who will be described and talked about in certain ways by observers and people who know them well.

At the same time, the reliance on folk constructs has resulted in what some may see as a lack of coherence. First, there was no major personality theory underlying the selection of the constructs. Gough developed a set of scales for the CPI which he felt assessed a broad range of constructs related to social behavior. This absence of an underlying personality theory is neither an inherent strength nor a weakness of the test. There are various philosophies for scale construction, and Gough has chosen one. Second, the CPI has also been criticized because the scales are correlated with each other. Again, however, the goals of the inventory must be understood. If the purpose of the inventory had been to develop independent scales which maximally account for the variance in respondents' answers, then perhaps an orthogonal factor analytic approach would have been the method of choice for scale construction. The CPI's purpose, on the other hand, was to assess folk concepts. If these folk concepts are correlated with each other in people's minds, then the CPI scales would logically show corresponding correlations. Still, Gough and his colleagues are presently developing structure scales which are independent of each other and which deal with the metathemes of the inventory—role, character, and psychological competence. However, these scales are currently unpublished, so their utility is unknown.

In addition to what the scales are intended to measure, their actual utility must be evaluated. First, Gough as well as others have conducted numerous construct validational studies of the scales. Although generalizations about all 18 scales must be made cautiously, accumulated evidence indicates that the scales generally measure what their titles suggest. Summarizing well over 1,000 references is not possible, but many of the correlations between individual CPI scales and relevant external criteria fall in the .2 to .5 range. Such relationships are typical in personality research, and extremely high correlations are unlikely to be found since the scales are developed to assess rather broad behavioral tendencies. They were not constructed in a way to predict specific behavior to a high degree of accuracy in narrowly defined situations; instead the scales show moderate relationships to a wide range of criteria. This phenomenon is known in test theory as the bandwidth-fidelity dilemma.

Research to date with the CPI has been extremely diverse. It includes such varied topics as predicting successful job performance in a variety of fields such as law enforcement (e.g., Mills & Bohannon, 1980), managerial potential (Gough, 1984), and nursing (e.g., Miller, 1965); school performance (e.g., Pfeifer & Sedlacek, 1974); behavioral medicine including Type A coronary-prone behavior (e.g., Musante, MacDougall, Dembroski, & Van Horn, 1983); and alcohol and drug abuse (e.g., McGuire & Megargee, 1974); and autonomic activity and reinforcement as related to socialization (e.g., Waid & Orne, 1982). Investigations of various American ethnic groups have also been conducted including American Indians (e.g., Mason, 1973), Blacks (e.g., Cross & Burger, 1982), Chinese Americans (e.g., Fong & Peskin, 1969), Japanese Americans (e.g., Blane & Yamamoto, 1970), and Mexican Americans (e.g., Mason, 1971). The notion of folk concepts relevant to a particular culture is a meaningful idea. However, in the CPI Gough intended to develop scales for folk concepts which have universal meaning. Consequently, translating the CPI into several languages as noted above has been essential. A vast accumulation of data will be necessary to determine whether these folk concepts are applicable to all cultures and societies, but investigations have already been conducted in Japan, Israel, Romania, Italy, France, Poland, Yugoslavia, Greece, Germany, and Taiwan as well as in the United States.

A major area in which additional research evidence is needed is profile interpretation. Not only must the meaning of each scale be understood, but the interaction among scale scores and resulting configural patterns of scales must be investigated if the potential richness from a multiscale inventory is to be maximized. In 1972, Megargee noted that only a small percentage of the 153 pairs of CPI scales had been investigated with almost no studies investigating larger constellations of scales. Twelve years later, there are numerous correlates of individual scales, but still little data are available to guide the interpretation of CPI configural patterns. In the CPI Manual, Gough proposes what appears to be a meaningful approach to profile interpretation, yet the lack of empirical investigations in this arena limits the conclusions one can reach.

One can ask why so little empirical data exist relevant to profile interpretation, when it seems integral to understanding CPI results. One reason may be that empirical investigation of profile configurations of the CPI's 18 scales is extremely complex. Second, as suggested above, many investigations employing the CPI have had foci other than achieving increased understanding of the CPI.

While the results of such studies may be of importance to the topics addressed, they are unlikely to provide findings useful for general CPI profile interpretation. Much more research focused directly on profile configurations will need to be conducted in order to provide the user with the information needed to confidently interpret CPI profiles. Meanwhile, Megargee's *CPI Handbook* (1972) along with the CPI Manual and "An Interpreter's Syllabus for the CPI" (Gough, 1968) provide vital information that is currently available regarding profile interpretation of the CPI.

It should be noted that at the present time, Gough is revising the CPI scales, so the item content will vary somewhat from the current scales. In addition, a new CPI Manual is being prepared. Of course, at this time the strengths and weaknesses of the revised scales remain unknown.

In summary, the CPI is a popular personality inventory, and a vast amount of data is mounting based on the CPI in its current form. The CPI's popularity likely results in part from the ease with which respondents understand the items, and the appeal of folk concepts to a wide range of investigators. Findings indicate that the scales generally measure what their titles suggest, but an increased focus on profile configurations is one major research direction for the future. Gough is already undertaking such efforts by investigating configural patterns with his yet unpublished structure scales. The CPI is not a perfect instrument, yet even critics of the test have not been able to point to a superior instrument for measuring similar constructs. In this reviewer's opinion, Gough is to be commended for his several decades of commitment to personality research and the fruits yielded thus far from the CPI. All indications are that its utility is likely to increase even more as additional data are collected on the scales.

REVIEWER'S REFERENCES

Miller, D. I. Characteristics of graduate students in four clinical nursing specialties. NURSING RESEARCH, 1965, 14, 106–113.

Gough, H. G. An interpreter's syllabus for the California Psychological Inventory. In P. McReynolds (Ed.), ADVANCES IN PSYCHOLOGICAL ASSESSMENT (Vol. 1). Palo Alto, CA: Science and Behavior Books, 1968.

Fong, S. L. M., & Peskin, H. Sex-role strain and personality adjustment of China-born students in America.\ JOURNAL OF ABNORMAL PSYCHOLOGY, 1969, 74, 563–567.

Blane, H. T., & Yamamoto, K. Sexual role identity among Japanese and Japanese-American high school students. JOURNAL OF CROSS-CULTURAL PSYCHOLOGY, 1970, 1, 345–354.

Mason, E. P. Stability of differences in personality characteristics of junior high school students from American Indian, Mexican, and Anglo ethnic backgrounds. PSYCHOLOGY IN THE SCHOOLS, 1971, 8, 86–89.

Megargee, E. I. THE CALIFORNIA PSYCHOLOGICAL INVENTORY HANDBOOK. San Francisco, CA: Jossey-Bass, 1972.

Mason, E. P. An Indian migrant child. In M. F. Freehill (Ed.), DISTURBED AND TROUBLED CHILDREN. Flushing, NY: Spectrum, 1973, 69–93.

McGuire, J. S., & Megargee, E. I. Personality correlates of marijuana use among youthful offenders. JOURNAL OF CONSULTING AND CLINICAL PSYCHOLOGY, 1974, 42, 124–133.

Pfeifer, C. M., Jr., & Sedlacek, W. E. Predicting Black student grades with nonintellectual measures. JOURNAL OF NEGRO EDUCATION, 1974, 43, 67–76.

LeUnes, A., Evans, M., Karnei, B., & Lowry, N. Psychological tests used in research with adolescents, 1969–1973. ADOLESCENCE, 1980, XV, 417–421.

Mills, C. J., & Bohannon, W. E. Personality characteristics of effective state police officers. JOURNAL OF APPLIED PSYCHOLOGY, 1980, 65, 680–684.

Cross, D. T., & Burger, G. Ethnicity as a variable in response to California Psychological Inventory items. JOURNAL OF PERSONALITY ASSESSMENT, 1982, 46, 153–158.

Waid, W. M., & Orne, M. T. Reduced electrodermal response to conflict, failure to inhibit dominance behaviors, and delinquency proneness. JOURNAL OF PERSONALITY AND SOCIAL PSYCHOLOGY, 1982, 43, 769–774.

Musante, L., MacDougall, J. M., Dembroski, T. M., & Van Horn, A. E. Component analysis of the Type A coronary-prone behavior pattern in male and female college students. JOURNAL OF PERSONALITY AND SOCIAL PSYCHOLOGY, 1983, 45, 1104–1117.

Piotrowski, C., & Keller, J. W. Psychodiagnostic testing in APA-approved clinical psychology programs. PROFESSIONAL PSYCHOLOGY: RESEARCH AND PRACTICE, 1984, 15(3), 450–456.

Gough, H. G. A managerial potential scale for the California Psychological Inventory. JOURNAL OF APPLIED PSYCHOLOGY, 1984, 69, 233–240.

Review of California Psychological Inventory by H. J. EYSENCK, Institute of Psychiatry, University of London, England:

The California Psychological Inventory has been on the market for approximately 30 years, and is extremely well-known. Its 18 scores are divided into four classes: measures of poise, ascendancy, self-assurance and inter-personal adequacy; measures of socialization, responsibility, intra-personal values, and character; measures of achievement potential and intellectual efficiency; and measures of intellectual and interest modes. Many of the items were taken from the Minnesota Multiphasic Personality Inventory, and quite generally the items themselves resemble those used in many other scales. The purpose of the CPI scales is stated by the author as follows: "Each scale is designed to forecast what a person will say or do under defined conditions, and to identify individuals who will be described in characteristic ways by others who know them well or who observe their behavior in particular contexts. The scales are grouped for convenience into four broad categories, bringing together those having related implications. The underlying logic here is interpretational, not factorial, i.e., these four categories do not necessarily constitute psychometric entities."

It is difficult to understand what is meant by this opposition between convenience and interpretational logic, as contrasted with factorial logic. Factorial logic demands that items or scales correlating highly together should be grouped together, as having related implications and interpretations. But this is precisely what Gough apparently intended to do without benefit of correlational analysis! It is difficult to see what alternative criteria he would have, other than perhaps some kind of commonsense interpretation which is far removed from scientific evidence.

Gough returns to the argument on a later page where he states that: "In interpreting scores on the Inventory, it is imperative to keep in mind the basic purpose of each scale, which is to identify individuals who will (*a*) behave in a certain way and (*b*) be described in a characteristic manner. The scales are not intended to define traits or to specify psychometric factors; validation, therefore, should address itself to the degree to which the Inventory can forecast behavior and identify individuals who are perceived in characteristic ways. Factor analyses, although of interest in delineating the internal structure of the Inventory, are not of very particular relevance to the validational claims advanced for the test." Again, it is difficult to understand just what Gough is trying to say. To state that dominance, or sociability, or tolerance, or responsibility are not "traits" is not a statement which is self-explanatory; these have always been taken for traits, and it is difficult to see what Gough is after in denying that he so regards them.

Neither is it obvious why he should have avoided a factor analytic study of the intercorrelations between the items which are chosen to describe the specific behavior he is intending to define; surely the items chosen to make up the Dominance scale must be internally consistent and different from those making up the Tolerance or the Responsibility scale, and what better way is there of measuring the degree of internal coherence than correlational or factorial analysis? It seems to this reviewer, at least, that the author has eschewed a duty to demonstrate statistically that his otherwise subjective and arbitrary choices of scales and items to make up these scales are indeed justified.

This criticism is more than a simple preconceived preference for statistical analyses of the factor-analytic kind. Reynolds and Nichols (1977) have carried out factor-analytic studies of the CPI and have shown (as other have before them) that the matrix of intercorrelations gives rise to two major factors similar to or identical with neuroticism-stability and extraversion-introversion. This suggests that this may be all the scales are measuring. Further analyses were done to test this particular hypothesis by comparing predictions of diverse criteria based alternately on these two factors and on the full set of 18 scales. The outcome was a very simple one; predictions from 18 scales did not add significantly to the prediction from the two factors! Here we have have a test of Gough's postulates on his own grounds, i.e., using the kind of criterion he is concerned with, but making a useful and valuable comparison between the subjectively chosen combinations of items constituting his 18 scales, and a mathematically much more rigorous way of combining scales. The outcome is certainly counter to Gough's claims, and hence must throw doubt on the adequacy of the CPI.

This argument rests on a practical level, but there is a much more important scientific level which is involved in this debate. There are in existence and in use hundreds of inventories, and thousands of scales, all making use of the same item pool, more or less, and differing only in the way the items are arranged, aggregated, and scored. Of the making of questionnaires, there appears to be no end, and psychologists do not seem to realize that in this way we would never be able to build up any kind of paradigm, any agreed system of measurement or model of personality. All is subjectivity, individuality, and confusion! Factor analysis is one important way of imposing some degree of order on this field, and attempting to reach agreed conclusions along methodologies. Gough's refusal to accept this discipline, which he does not attempt even to justify in terms of any kind of acceptable statistical or philosophical argument, leads us straight into a situation where personality models, different inventories, and choice of scales are subject to a kind of Dutch auction, rather than a scientific debate which might result in a universally acceptable conclusion. Many of the scales of the CPI do, of course, resemble well-established factorial scales, and it seems quite likely that they will have reasonable psychometric consistency coefficients, although others may not. On the principle that all possible information should be given the user, the absence in the manual of item intercorrelations and factorial analyses is to be deplored, particularly as no rational argument is advanced to justify it. In the absence of such supporting evidence of internal validity, it is difficult to recommend the test to prospective users.

REVIEWER'S REFERENCES

Reynolds, C. H., & Nichols, R. C. Factor rates for the CPI: Do they capture the valid variance? EDUCATIONAL AND PSYCHOLOGICAL MEASUREMENT, 1977, 37, 907–915.

[183]

California Test of Personality. Grades K–3, 4–8, 7–10, 9–14, adults; 1939–53; CTP; 15 scores: self-reliance, sense of personal worth, sense of personal freedom, feeling of belonging, withdrawing tendencies, nervous symptoms, total personal adjustment, social standards, social skills, anti-social tendencies, family relations, school relations or occupation relations (adult level), community relations, total social adjustment, total adjustment; Forms AA, BB, ('53, 8 pages); 5 levels; manual ('53, 32 pages); profile ('53, 1 page); separate answer sheets (IBM 1230) may be used for grades 4 and over; 1984 price data: $17.50 per 35 tests, 35 profile sheets, examiner's manual, scoring key, and class record sheet; $11.50 per 50 answer sheets; $5.25 per hand-scoring stencils; $17 per specimen set; (45–60) minutes; Louis P. Thorpe, Willis W. Clark, and Ernest W. Tiegs; CTB/McGraw-Hill.*

a) PRIMARY. Grades K–3; 1940–53.

b) ELEMENTARY. Grades 4–8; 1939–53.

c) INTERMEDIATE. Grades 7–10; 1939–53.
d) SECONDARY. Grades 9–14; 1942–53.
e) ADULT. Adults; 1942–53.

See T3:357 (22 references), 8:516 (67 references), T2:1123 (196 references), P:29 (73 references), and 6:73 (49 references); for a review by Verner M. Sims, see 5:38 (93 references); for reviews by Laurance F. Shaffer and Douglas Spencer and an excerpted review by Earl R. Gabler of the original edition, see 3:26 (27 references); for reviews by Raymond B. Cattell, Percival M. Symonds, and P. E. Vernon and an excerpted review by Marion M. Lamb of the elementary and secondary levels, see 2:1213.

TEST REFERENCES

1. Evans, A. L. Personality characteristics and disciplinary attitudes of child-abusing mothers. CHILD ABUSE & NEGLECT, 1980, 4, 179–187.

2. Thomson-Rountree, P., & Woodruff, A. E. An examination of Project AWARE: The effects on children's attitudes toward themselves, others, and school. JOURNAL OF SCHOOL PSYCHOLOGY, 1982, 20, 20–31.

Review of California Test of Personality by ROSA A. HAGIN, Professor, Division of Psychological and Educational Services, Fordham University, Lincoln Center, New York, NY:

The California Test of Personality is a multi-level self-administering questionnaire designed by the authors to "identify and reveal the status of certain highly important factors in personality and social adjustment." The manual indicates that total or section scores are less useful than reactions to individual items (based on yes-no responses) that reveal tendencies to think, feel, and act in a manner that reveals undesirable individual adjustments. In keeping with the objective of individual guidance, a major part of the manual presents methods for classifying and treating the adjustment difficulties detected by the questionnaire. The test is intended for group administration with quantitative scoring based on percentile norms derived from approximately three to four thousand school or adult education students at each level. No rationale is presented for the selection of standardization samples nor the ethnic distribution of the normative subjects (85% Caucasian, 15% various minority group members). Norms are based on the assumption that some general standard of adjustment exists in each personal and social area tapped by the test.

Reliability data are presented in terms of Kuder-Richardson coefficients. The coefficients range from .51 to .97 for the subtests and from .88 to .96 for the total score. Intercorrelations suggest considerable overlap of sections of the test. Validity data provided by the authors is minimal; related research is presented more in the form of testimonials to the use of the test than in any objective review of research applications. Content validity was based on (1) judgments of items by professionals in the field, (2) correlation of teacher ratings and student responses, and (3) factor analyses and multiple correlation studies of the norming samples. The obviousness of the items raises questions about fakability, although the authors maintain that the wording of items in behavioral terms limits this possibility. The language of the items appears dated, with such terms as "your folks" and "mean boys and girls" used.

In summary, there is little to recommend this test for either research or clinical uses. The current edition of the test (1953 Revision) appears dated in terms of rationale, content, language, statistical characteristics, research support, and therapeutic approach.

[184]

Callahan Anxiety Pictures. Ages 5–13; 1978; CAP; norms consist of means and standard deviations; 1 form (40 cards); manual (18 pages); price data available from publisher; administration time not reported; Roger J. Callahan; Sunset Distributors.*

Review of Callahan Anxiety Pictures by JULIEN WORLAND, H. Edison Child Development Research Center, Department of Psychiatry, Washington University School of Medicine, St. Louis, MO:

PURPOSE AND RATIONALE. The Callahan Anxiety Pictures (CAP) is a 40-item projective test to measure anxiety in children. A child's responses to the black and white silhouettes presented on cards purportedly represent the "degree of threat which the child attributes to relatively unstructured aspects of the environment." Callahan states that the child who perceives a great deal of threat is commonly described as anxious by clinicians. It should be noted that children can perceive threat without necessarily experiencing anxiety. The test might better be labelled as a test of perceived threat.

ADMINISTRATION AND SCORING. Administration instructions are similar to other projective tests. The child is asked to respond to what he or she sees in each picture. Suggestions for minimal probes are presented in the manual, which should present few problems for standardized administration.

Scoring is carried out by assigning a score of 0, 1, 2, or 3 to each response, a weighting of the degree of threat in the response given. For example, zero is assigned if the response has "no threat quality for most children in our culture"; a score of 2 is given if the response is from a group of five specific examples of threatening perception; and the highest score, 3, is given when a response scored otherwise as a 2 is enhanced in its threat value ("Indian with a scalp"). Examples are given. For example, a policeman is scored zero, a tiger is scored one, an Indian is scored 2 (but a female Indian is scored 1), and a witch with a little boy is scored 3. What would we score "Mr. T"? Generalizing the examples to novel responses might prove quite difficult.

INTERPRETATION, VALIDITY, AND RELIABILITY. These topics get only short treatment in the manual. A contrast between the scores of public school children ($M=23.01$, $SD=7.60$) vs. those of children in a psychiatric hospital ($M=29.82$, $SD=10.15$) forms the basis on which the author asserts that scores above 30 "may...be taken to indicate a high degree of anxiety." Since the psychiatric population remains undescribed, this assertion is debatable.

Interscorer reliability is reported for the protocols of 30 11- and 12-year-old mentally retarded youngsters. While the reported interscorer reliability is very respectable for projective tests (.90), one wonders whether the verbal limitations of mentally retarded youngsters might have elevated scoring accuracy. Test-retest reliability is not presented, other than a 4- to 6-week stability study for a single group of boys in a residential training school. Again, while quite favorable (.85), sample limitations present a serious obstacle to accepting this as a solid estimate of stability.

Few validity data are presented. Reported differences between children in public school and children in psychiatric hospitals on this test do not offer support for its use as a measure of anxiety or that the test may be used as a "quantification of anxiety levels." Other offered evidence of validity is flawed by being performed with different items in one case and with a different test in another case. The reported association of the CAP with Wechsler Digit Span is intriguing; but Digit Span scores are affected by factors other than anxiety (Kaufman, 1979, pp. 70ff), again leaving scant evidence that this test measures what it purports to measure.

CRITIQUE. (1) The name of this test is possibly misleading; it might better be labeled a test of perceived threat. (2) The limitation that this is a test for use in assessing children is never explained. Why could it not also be considered as a test for adults? (3) Reliability and validity are not established. (4) What is the need of a projective test for anxiety or perceived threat? Clinicians usually find that anxious children (and adults) are easily identified by interview. Researchers of anxiety in children might find the child version of the Manifest Anxiety Test (Reynolds & Richmond, 1978) more acceptable. (5) The author mentions but does not carefully consider the possibility that perceptions (or responses) could be subject to interference by defense mechanisms. A protocol filled with butterflies and day lilies might emerge from a defensive but very anxious, bright child. (6) The manual offers no advice on the range of individual differences within which the test is appropriate. Is it appropriate for the retarded? For the very bright? For children with perceptual handicaps? If so, would the same cutoff score be appropriate?

SUMMARY. The CAP is a 40-item projective instrument of uncertain reliability and validity that perhaps measures anxiety. Further research is necessary to establish that it is a reliable and valid measure of anxiety in children.

REVIEWER'S REFERENCES

Kaufman, A. S. INTELLIGENT TESTING WITH THE WISC-R. New York: Wiley, 1979.

Reynolds, C. R., & Richmond, B. O. What I think and feel: A revised measure of children's manifest anxiety. JOURNAL OF ABNORMAL CHILD PSYCHOLOGY, 1978, 6, 271–280.

[185]

Cambridge Kindergarten Screening Test. Grade K; 1984; CKST; "designed for screening only"; measures levels of speech and language functioning; 13 subtests: Articulation, Discrimination, Vocabulary, Association/Categorization, Object/Function, Action/Agent, Color Concepts, Number Concepts, Commands/Spatial Relations, Memory for Commands, Digit Repetition, Diadochokinesis, Story Sequencing/Language; no data on reliability and validity; no norms; individual; 1 form ('84, 37 pages); screener's manual ('84, 10 pages); 1984 price data: $35 per set; (20) minutes; Ann M. Shahzade; DLM Teaching Resources.*

[186]

Camelot Behavioral Checklist. Mentally retarded; 1974–77; CBC; ratings by parents, ward attendants, and teachers; 11 scores: self help, physical development, home duties, vocational behaviors, economic behaviors, independent travel, numerical skills, communication skills, social behaviors, responsibility, total; item norms only; 1 form ('74, 8 pages); manual, second edition ('77, 37 pages); item profile ('74, 1 page); score profile ('74, 1 page); program bibliography ('79, 78 pages, optional); 1983 price data: $.50 per test including profiles; $4 per manual; 25–35 minutes; Ray W. Foster; Camelot Behavioral Systems.*

See 8:517.

Review of Camelot Behavioral Checklist by ELLIOT L. GORY, Psychology, Getz School for the Developmentally Disabled, Tempe, AZ:

The Camelot Behavioral Checklist is a criterion-referenced and norm-referenced test designed to assess the adaptive behavior of mentally retarded individuals. Though age is not specified in the manual, inspection of the content of the test items indicates that the Camelot is most useful for moderately mentally retarded clients from late adolescence through adulthood. Several uses of the test are suggested in the manual, and these fit reasonably into the design of the individual booklets used to record scores: (*a*) A profile is generated that includes skills that a client has mastered and skills in which a client requires further training to achieve mastery. (*b*) The test can be used as a progress record over time with subsequent administrations. (*c*) Classification and program planning decisions can be made on the basis of a domain score profile and total adaptive behavior score.

The Camelot Behavioral Checklist consists of 40 skill subdomains organized into 10 major domains of behavior: Self Help (e.g., grooming, bathing, toilet use); Physical Development (e.g., walking, posture, sensory development); Home Duties (e.g., house cleaning, cooking, clothing care, yard care, applicance use); Vocational Behavior (e.g., work related skills, job skills); Economic Behavior (e.g., shopping, money handling, credit use); Independent Travel (e.g., transportation, travel skills); Numerical Skills (e.g., time, arithmetic skills); Communication Skills (e.g., receptive language, expressive language, reading, writing, telephone use); Social Behaviors (e.g., spectator activities, participation, interaction with others); and Responsibility (e.g., social responsibility, response to emergencies, security).

The subdomains, including 399 test items, provide a representative survey of skills required for the mentally retarded adult to successfully adapt to society.

The test consists of a manual, checklist record book, and bibliography of skill training guides and programs. The paper-bound manual includes information about construction of the scale, test uses, administration and interpretation guidelines, reliability, and validity. Instructions for test administration are sufficiently clear that, with a minimum of practice, teachers, aides, and other direct care staff can begin use of the test. Also included are summaries with references on the item selection procedure, a reliability study, a construct validity study, and the method of item difficulty calculation. Though a reference for an intercorrelation study of the Camelot with eight psychometric instruments is provided, an expanded discussion of this procedure in the manual would be helpful to potential test users to gauge validity. Administration of the Camelot typically involves consideration of each item in the checklist record book by an individual familiar with the client and/or on an interview basis with a person who has had opportunity to frequently observe the client in a variety of situations. Test time may vary from 30 to 45 minutes. To actually test the client on each test item is both impractical timewise and unnecessary. As a typical administration of the Camelot relies heavily on an informant's memory of observed instances of a client's behavior, cautions stated in the manual about using client behavior that has actually been observed are particularly judicious. Comparing results with those obtained from an independent administration of the scale by a second individual who is familiar with the client is suggested as a practical method of enhancing reliability. This is especially recommended because particular test items frequently give little or no information about the circumstances under which a behavior has been observed or is to be tested (e.g., knows holidays, doesn't overuse credit, prepares food requiring no mixing).

Test items are scored on a simple yes/no basis by circling either "can do" or "needs training." For most effective use of the test, the user should supplement this scoring procedure by noting other possibilities relevant to the display of a behavior, such as whether the client has had an opportunity to perform the behavior and whether the item/behavior consists of something that the client "can do but refuses to do." Also the scoring procedure provides no opportunity to note at what level of independence the behavior is performed (e.g., mastery, requires verbal prompts, requires gestural prompts, etc.). This latter consideration would be helpful and, in most cases, necessary in planning an effective prescriptive program based on test results. Once all items have been scored, the results can be transferred to an item profile page. This page visually represents which skills a client has mastered and provides a method to compare the client's behavior within a subdomain to the performance of individuals used in the item norming sample. On another page in the checklist record booklet, subdomain data can be converted so that performance on each of the 10 major domains may be graphically illustrated and compared to the performance of individuals used in the norming process. Similarly, a total adaptive behavior score can be derived and compared to the percentage of the test population with scores equal to or lower than the corresponding score obtained for a particular client.

The separate manual of references, listing training programs and guides that can be used in developing prescriptive training/educational plans based on test results, is recommended only for test users new to task analysis and for those who do not already have access to one or two common prescriptive activity guides (e.g., The Portage Project Checklist, the APT Skill Assessment, etc.). This "Skill Acquisition Program Bibliography," as it is called, is the most expensive single item in an otherwise inexpensive test, and is not recommended for purchase.

In conclusion, the Camelot Behavioral Checklist is a criterion-referenced and norm-referenced adaptive behavior scale for use with moderately retarded individuals from late adolescence through adulthood. The test domains are a representative survey of skills required for successful, socially competent functioning in society. The Camelot is inexpensive and the comprehensiveness of its item domains, ease of administration, quick scoring, and simple format for test result interpretation are its best features. The scale can be used to profile skills that a client has mastered, make comparisons to a norm sample, and measure progress. Usefulness as a prescriptive instrument is limited by ambiguity about the circumstances under which a behavior is observed and by no direct method to record or score the level of independence at which a behavior is displayed. Despite this shortcoming, the Camelot Behavioral Checklist is recommended for use as a viable method to assess a wide range of adaptive behavior.

[187]

Canadian Achievement Tests, Form A. Grades 1.6–2.9, 2.6–3.9, 3.6–4.9, 4.6–5.9, 5.6–6.9, 6.6–7.9, 7.6–9.9, 9.6–12.9; 1981–83; CAT, Form A; criterion-referenced; subtests available as separates; 8 overlapping levels; test coordinator's handbook ('82, 69 pages); directions for test coordinators (no date, 15 pages); class management guide ('83, 157 pages); technical bulletin ('83, 80 pages); diagnostic profile sheet ('81, 4 pages); brochure for parents (no date, 12 pages); separate answer sheets must be used for grades 3.6–12.9; 1984 price data: $42.85 per 35 reusable test booklets of any one level (grades 3.6–12.9); $9.85 per 25 u-score answer sheets of any one level; $13.15 per 50 CanScan answer sheets of any one level (grades 3.6–12.9); $19.80 per 100 student diagnostic profile sheets of any one level; $10 per test coordinator's handbook; $12.50 per class management guide; $12.50 per technical bulletin; $4.15 per additional examiner's manual of any one level; $3.80 per norms tables of any one level; $12.95 per specimen set of primary (grades 1.6–3.9), junior (grades 3.6–6.9), or senior levels (grades 6.6–12.9); $24.10 per multi level specimen set; scoring service, $.95–$1.20 per student for basic service (additional reports available); Canadian Test Centre/McGraw-Hill Ryerson Ltd. [Canada].*

a) LOCATOR TESTS. Grades 2–6, 6–12; short vocabulary and mathematics tests that can be used to help determine an appropriate level of the CAT, Form A; 2 scores: reading vocabulary, mathematics; 1 form ('81, 5 pages) for each of 2 levels; directions ('81, 11 pages); $11.55 per 35 tests of either level (includes directions and 35 answer sheets); $11 per 50 additional answer sheets; (22) minutes.

b) LEVEL 12. Grades 1.6–2.9; 9 subtests: reading (phonic analysis, structural analysis, reading vocabulary, reading comprehension), spelling, language (mechanics, expression), mathematics (computation, concepts and applications); machine-scorable, hand-scorable editions, ('81, 26 pages); practice test ('81, 2 pages, for Levels 12 and 13); examiner's manual ('81, 42 pages); norms tables ('82, 29 pages); $42.85 per 35 machine scorable tests; $29.65 per 35 hand-scorable tests; $4.35 per 35 practice tests; (190) per complete battery.

c) LEVEL 13. Grades 2.6–3.9; subtests same as for *b* above; machine scorable, hand scorable editions, ('81–'82, 26 pages); examiner's manual ('81, 39 pages); norms tables ('82, 29 pages); prices same as for *b* above; (198) minutes for complete battery.

d) LEVEL 14. Grades 3.6–4.9; 8 subtests: reading (vocabulary, comprehension), spelling, language (mechanics, expression), mathematics (computation, concepts and applications), reference skills; 1 form ('81, 51 pages); practice test levels 14–16 ('81, 2 pages); examiner's manual levels 14–19 ('81, 42 pages); norms tables ('82, 29 pages); separate u-score answer sheets for spelling and language, mathematics, reading and reference skills; $5.80 per 35 practice tests levels 14–16; (202) minutes for complete battery.

e) LEVEL 15. Grades 4.6–5.9; subtests same as for *d* above; 1 form ('81, 52 pages); norms tables ('82, 29 pages); answer sheets and time same as for *d* above.

f) LEVEL 16. Grades 5.6–6.9; subtests same as for *d* above; 1 form ('81, 56 pages); norms tables ('82, 29 pages); answer sheets and time same as for *d* above.

g) LEVEL 17. Grades 6.6–7.9; remaining data same as for *f* above.

h) LEVEL 18. Grades 7.6–9.9; subtests same as for *d* above; 1 form ('81, 56 pages); norms tables ('82, 35 pages); answer sheets and time same as for *d* above.

i) LEVEL 19. Grades 9.6–12.9; subtests same as for *d* above; 1 form ('81, 57 pages); norms tables ('82, 41 pages); answer sheets and time same as for *d* above.

Review of Canadian Achievement Tests, Form A, by LILLIAN A. WHYTE, Professor of Educational Psychology & Special Education, University of Alberta, Edmonton, Alberta, Canada:

The Canadian Achievement Tests, Form A include several ancillary publications, three of which are considered in this review. The publications are: the Technical Bulletin containing the bulk of the technical information available, to date, for the test concerning standardization, norming, reliability, and validity; the Test Coordinator's Handbook describing the nature, development, and content of the tests and providing guidelines for supervising a testing program and interpreting the results; and the Class Management Guide, a teacher's guide for interpreting and using the norm-referenced and criterion-referenced information provided by the tests. There is some repetition of information included in the three publications.

The Canadian Achievement Tests, Form A constitute a unique approach to educational evaluation, since they merge two approaches to achievement measurement: norm-referenced assessment and criterion-referenced assessment. Functional level testing is facilitated by the Locator Tests, which aid the teacher in selecting the best level of the test for individual pupils. The publishers claim the narrow grade range sampled at each test level makes it possible to measure more of the skills taught at a given grade level.

Provincial and school district curriculum guides, major textbooks, and the objectives of several criterion-referenced testing programs were used as the basis for writing test or category objectives. Educational objectives were termed category objectives because each subsumes two or more related skills and items were written to measure these objectives. This review will consider the content of the tests, standardization procedures, and technical data.

TEST CONTENT. The major content areas included in the tests are Reading, Spelling, Language, Mathematics, and Reference Skills, and each content area measures numerous skills in that area. The range of skills tested is commendable, particularly in mathematics. This reviewer has found no other mathematics test which samples such a wide variety of skills related to mathematics concepts and applications. This type of diagnostic information is invaluable in planning remedial programs for individual students.

Unfortunately, the number of items in each area assessed is frequently insufficient to provide the detailed data necessary for individualized educational programming. For example, in the Reading Test only 11 items are provided to assess structural analysis skills which are used to assess knowledge of affixed words, including both inflected forms (6 items) and derived forms (5 items). This is true of Levels 12 and 13, the only two levels where decoding skills are assessed. Phonic analysis is constrained in a similar manner. The Spelling Tests are organized around the phoneme-grapheme-morpheme approach. The category objectives follow the broad groupings of consonants, vowels, and morphemic units. The number of items included to assess this variety of objectives ranges from 16 to 18 per level.

If the publishers' claims that the test can serve as a criterion-referenced test are to be justified, this limitation should be corrected and data provided to validate the usefulness of the test for individualized programming. Fortunately, not all the tests are constrained in this way; for example, the number of items for Reading Comprehension ranges from 20 to 40, with a wide variety of comprehension skills sampled.

STANDARDIZATION PROCEDURES. Norms are based on normative data obtained by (*a*) stratified random sampling of school districts by geographic area and degree of urbanization, (*b*) random sampling of schools within districts, and (*c*) achieving a high participation rate. Socioeconomic characteristics of the sample were ascertained by questionnaire. Norms are intended to apply to all Canadian schools in which English is the language of instruction.

While standardization procedures are elaborate, separate norms by geographic region, sex, socioeconomic level, etc., are not presented, at least not in the publications reviewed. Other limitations in the standardization data involve the proportion of minority groups within the sample. For example, in the overall total sample of 76,485 students, just over 1,000 of those tested were identified as learning disabled. Obviously, there is a higher percentage of learning disabled children in the school population than this sample would indicate. Furthermore, the publishers do not recommend using the test for children functioning more than one grade level below age expectations, a condition found frequently with exceptional children. It is questionable whether the test should be used with these students.

Finally, it appears that only 95 native children, all enrolled in elementary schools, and 65 children with English as a second language were included in the standardization. This figure does not reflect the true situation in Canadian schools and the publishers state that data for these groups may not be complete.

TECHNICAL DATA. Several methods were applied to ensure content validity for the tests. The development and writing of category objectives played an important part in establishing content validity. The category objectives are designed to measure the basic skills that are common to all curricula.

All norming of the eight levels of the Canadian Achievement Tests was based on a single, equal-interval scale of standard scores describing the range of performance from grades 1.7 through 12.7. Both mean and median scores are presented. A peculiarity of the norming results for mean grade score norms is the tendency for norms at each level to range from .1 to .7 above the expected grade level from grades 1.7 to 6.7, while the differences are in a negative direction in grades 10.7 through 12.7. If medians are used, these discrepancies do not exist; therefore, the median is recommended as the best reference point to use.

Reliability estimates for the normed sections of the tests are presented. Means, standard deviations, and KR 20s for each category objective measured at each level are also provided. The KR 20 reliability coefficients in some cases are very low. However, test-retest reliability estimates are planned for a later date.

The Canadian Achievement Tests, Form A are recommended for several reasons. They provide Canadian educators with national Canadian norms. They provide two important types of information, norm-referenced and criterion-referenced, and do so with a minimum of testing. There are excellent forms for summarizing and meaningful reporting of results. Directions and procedures for interpreting results are clear and concise. The criterion-referenced assessment does have some limitations for individual programming, but these can be overcome by using subtests from other test batteries (e.g., in assessment of reading decoding skills), when this is necessary for individual children.

[188]

Canadian Occupational Interest Inventory. Grades 9–12 and adults; 1981–82; COII; 5 factor scores: things/people, business contact/scientific, routine/-creative, social/solitary, prestige/production; no norms; 1 form ('82, 17 pages); administration, scoring, and interpretation manual ('82, 49 pages); technical manual ('82, 118 pages); profile aid chart ('82, 1 page); profile ('82, 1 page); separate answer sheets must be used; 1983 price data: $20.50 per 25 test booklets; $3.25 per scoring key; $7.95 per 35 answer sheets; $7.95 per 35 profiles; $7.95 per 35 profile aid charts; $10.95 per glossary of interests; $8.50 per administration, scoring and interpretation manual; $9 per technical manual; $9.25 per specimen set; French edition available; (30–50) minutes; Luc Begin, J. A. Gordon Booth (manuals), and Luc Lavallee (test and technical manual); Nelson Canada [Canada].*

Review of Canadian Occupational Interest Inventory by RICHARD W. JOHNSON, Associate Director of University Counseling Service and Adjunct Professor of Counseling and Guidance, University of Wisconsin-Madison, Madison, WI:

The Canadian Occupational Interest Inventory (COII) measures interests in 10 areas derived from research conducted by William Cottle (1950). The 10 areas correspond with the 10 interest fields used to code occupations in the Canadian Classification and Dictionary of Occupations (CCDO). By using the COII in conjunction with the CCDO, counselors may compare interest patterns of individuals with those specified for workers in different occupations.

ITEMS AND SCALES. The COII consists of 70 forced-choice triads scored on five bipolar scales. Interest activities were grouped together in triads to make the interest areas easier to identify. Bipolar scales were constructed because Cottle's research indicated that most of the variance in interest and personality inventories could be accounted for by means of five bipolar factors. For each scale, respondents must choose between 14 pairs of triads that represent opposite ends of the scale.

SCORING. The five bipolar factor scales are hand scored to indicate preferences in 10 interest areas. Because of the bipolarity of each scale, the interests which one can demonstrate are limited. If a person likes activities represented by both ends of a bipolar scale, his or her score will fall in the middle of the scale. For example, a person may be interested in both business and science; however, it would be impossible to show both types of interests on the Business Contact-Scientific scale. The use of bipolar scales artificially restricts the type and range of interests which an individual may reveal.

No norms are available. Mean scores from studies reported in the technical manual show large sex differences on both the Things-People and the Social-Solitary scales. Separate sex norms should be available to take such sex differences into account. If not, sexual stereotypes associated with social conditioning will be reinforced. Men will be encouraged more often to pursue occupations associated with "things" or "solitary" activities while women will be counseled more frequently to consider "people" or "social" occupations.

RELIABILITY. The five scales possess an adequate degree of internal consistency (median correlation=.87) based on studies cited in the manual. Scores on the scales appear to be relatively stable over short time periods. The median correlations for test-retest studies ranged from .85 to .89 for various groups tested over intervals of 11 to 28 days. The two versions of the COII (English and French) were equally reliable.

VALIDITY. Although the scales were based on constructs derived from factor analytic research, they lack factorial purity. With the exception of the Routine-Creative scale, scores on the scales were substantially intercorrelated. Scores on the Things-People scale correlated highly with scores on the Social-Solitary, Prestige-Production, and Business Contact-Scientific scales (median correlations= –.74, –.61, and –.51, respectively) in three studies reported in the manual. High correlations also occurred between scores on the Social-Solitary scale and scores on both the Business Contact-Scientific and Prestige-Production scales (median correlations=.51 and .47, respectively). The magnitude of these correlations indicates considerable overlap in the constructs tapped by the interest scales.

Scores on the COII scales were moderately intercorrelated with scores for comparable scales on the Kuder Preference Record-Vocational in most cases. Low correlations were found between the Routine, Creative, and Production factors and the Kuder scales for both English-speaking and French-speaking subjects.

The authors mention only one study (Farrell, 1977) in which the validity of the COII in differentiating among workers in various occupations was investigated. No data from the study were presented. The study itself, an unpublished master's degree thesis, is not readily available for review.

SPECIAL CONCERNS. The groundwork in applying Cottle's bipolar factors to job descriptions was undertaken by the U.S. Employment Service in preparing the 3rd Edition (1965) of the *American Dictionary of Occupational Titles* (DOT). Recent research conducted by the U.S. Employment Service indicates that the bipolar factors do not adequately represent interests found within various occupations (Droege & Hawk, 1977; Droege & Padgett, 1979). First, one-half of the 10 factors (Prestige, Production, Routine, Things, and People) could not be replicated satisfactorily in their work. Second, all of the factors, as they measured them, were positively intercorrelated. No evidence of bipolarity could be found. Based on their research, they decided not to use the Cottle system of classifying interests in the 4th Edition (1977) of the DOT. They replaced the 5 bipolar factors with 12 unipolar factors as the means of classifying occupations in the *Guide to Occupational Exploration*, a companion volume of the DOT (4th Ed.). A new test, the USES Interest Inventory, was developed to measure interests in each of these 12 areas. Their research suggests that the COII is based on an obsolete system.

SUMMARY AND RECOMMENDATIONS. The COII is most appropriate for use with the CCDO. It suffers from several major disadvantages which restrict its value in other situations. First, the 10 interest factors upon which the COII is based do not appear to describe sufficiently the types of interests found in work situations. Second, because of the bipolarity of the scales, clients are limited in the types of interests that they can express. Third, scant normative data are provided. Fourth, little research has been conducted on the empirical validity of the instrument.

Counselors who wish to use an interest inventory to aid clients in career planning should use the Strong-Campbell Interest Inventory or the Kuder Occupational Interest Survey, Form DD, in place of the COII. If they wish to relate the scores directly to job definitions or to a comprehensive job classification scheme, the U.S. Employment Service Interest Inventory would appear to be a better choice.

REVIEWER'S REFERENCES

Cottle, W. C. A factorial study of the Multiphasic, Strong Kuder, and Bell inventories using a population of adult males. PSYCHOMETRIKA, 1950, 15, 25–47.

Droege, R. C., & Hawk, J. Development of a U.S. Employment Service Interest Inventory. JOURNAL OF EMPLOYMENT COUNSELING, 1977, 14, 65–71.

Farrell, A. R. THE CONCURRENT VALIDITY OF THE CANADIAN OCCUPATIONAL INTEREST INVENTORY. Unpublished master's thesis, University of Saskatchewan, Saskatoon, 1977.

Droege, R. C., & Padgett, A. Development of an interest-oriented occupational classification system. VOCATIONAL GUIDANCE QUARTERLY, 1979, 27, 302–310.

[189]

Canadian Tests of Basic Skills. Grades K.2–1.5, K.8–1.9, 1.7–2.6, 2.7–3.5, 3, 4, 5, 6, 7, 8, 9, 10, 11, 12; 1955–84; CTBS; Canadian adaptation of Iowa Tests of Basic Skills; 3 batteries; manual for administrators, supervisors and counsellors ('84, 138 pages); profile ('81, 2 pages); profile chart for averages ('81, 1 page); 1984 price data: $5.25 per 35 profiles; $2.65 per 10 profile charts for averages; $14.95 per manual for administrators, supervisors and counsellors; original test by E. F. Lindquist, A. N. Hieronymus, and others; adaptation by Ethel M. King and others; Nelson Canada [Canada].*

a) PRIMARY BATTERY: LEVELS 5–8. Grades K.2–1.5, K.8–1.9, 1.7–2.6, 2.7–3.5; 4 levels; teacher's guide for Levels 5 and 6, 7 and 8, ('82, 67–106 pages); report to parents ('81, 4 pages); $22.95 per 25 test booklets; $10.50 per scoring masks; $5.25 per 35 reports to parents; $6.85 per teacher's guide; $7.15 per specimen set.

1) *Level* 5. Grades K.2–1.5; 6 scores: listening, vocabulary, word analysis, language, mathematics, total; Form 5 ('81, 16 pages); (150) minutes in 6 sessions.

2) *Level* 6. Grades K.8–1.9; 7 scores: listening, vocabulary, word analysis, reading, language, mathematics, total; Form 5 ('81, 20 pages); (205) minutes in 8 sessions.

3) *Level* 7. Grades 1.7–2.6; 17 scores: listening, vocabulary, word analysis, reading (spelling, capitalization, punctuation, usage, total), language total, visual materials, references, work study total, math (concepts, problems, computation, total), total composite; Form 5 ('81, 29 pages); (285) minutes in 11 sessions.

4) *Level* 8. Grades 2.7–3.5; 17 scores: same as for Level 7; Form 5 ('81, 29 pages); (285) minutes in 11 sessions.

b) MULTILEVEL BATTERY: LEVELS 9–14. Grades 3, 4, 5, 6, 7, 8; 15 scores: vocabulary, reading, language (spelling, capitalization, punctuation, usage, total), work study skills (visual materials, references, total), mathematics (concepts, problems, computation, total), composite; 6 overlapping levels in a single booklet; Form 5, 6, ('81, 96 pages); teacher's guide ('82, 98 pages); item norms ('82, 8 pages) for each level; pupil report folder ('81, 4 pages); separate answer sheets must be used; $5.25 per test booklet; $9.15 per 35 hand scorable answer sheets; $9.90 per 35 machine scorable answer sheets; $6.65 per set of scoring stencils; $2.40 per item norms booklet; $5.25 per 35 pupil report folders; $8.50 per teacher's guide; $14 per specimen set; scoring service, $.99 per pupil ($50 minimum); 244(295) minutes in 8 sessions.

c) HIGH SCHOOL MULTILEVEL BATTERY: LEVELS 15–18. Grades 9, 10, 11, 12; 6 scores: reading, mathematics, written expression, using resources, composite, applied proficiency skills; 4 overlapping levels in a single booklet; Form 5 ('81, 65 pages); teacher's guide ('82, 49 pages); item performance analysis ('83, 6 pages); separate answer sheets must be used; prices and scoring same as for Multilevel Battery: Levels 9–14 except $24.75 per 100 machine scorable answer sheets; 160(190) minutes in 2 sessions.

See T3:363 (15 references) and 8:11 (1 reference); for a review by L. B. Birch of the earlier edition of *b*, see 7:6.

[190]

The Canfield Time Problems Inventory. Management and administrative personnel; 1980; TPRI; a measure of why individuals waste time; 4 scores: priorities, planning, delegation, self-discipline; no data on reliability and validity; norms consist of means and standard deviations, no description of norm group; 1 form (8 pages, includes profile and scale interpretations); manual (12 pages); 1983 price data: $1.50 per test (15 minimum); $2.50 per manual; $9.95 per specimen set; (20–30) minutes; Albert A. Canfield; Humanics Media.*

Review of The Canfield Time Problems Inventory by JEANETTE N. CLEVELAND, Assistant Professor of Psychology, Colorado State University, Fort Collins, CO:

The Canfield Time Problems Inventory is a 48-item inventory developed to identify why individuals waste time, as opposed to how people waste time. The test developers state that the inventory typically has been used in workshops or seminar settings, but also can be used for individual self-study purposes in business, industry, and government. The manual clearly suggests that the inventory is not designed for selection or placement purposes.

The 48 items in the inventory were selected from a pool of over 200 items collected over a 2-year period. The manual indicates that these items were most representative of 200 time problems encountered by management and administrative personnel.

However, no criteria are given for the selection of the 48 items which compose the inventory. In addition, there is no description of how well the domain reflecting time problems was represented by the original 200 items.

The items in the inventory reflect four major dimensions of time wasting behaviors: priorities, planning, delegation, and self-discipline. Although the manual provides intercorrelations among the four dimensions (ranging from .50–.75), there is no documentation of the reliability of the scores on each of the dimensions. In addition, documentation is lacking on the method (whether statistical or clinical) used to assign items to dimensions.

The inventory is self-administered. Material describing and explaining each of the four dimensions accompanies the inventory. In scoring the inventory, a value is assigned to each of the five possible responses and the individual simply totals the scores by major section. The answer sheet is provided with the inventory and is divided into four columns, each reflecting one of the major dimensions of time problems.

Individuals construct their own profiles using the total score for each of the dimensions. Percentile information is presented with the profile, based on scale means and standard deviations obtained from a sample of 79 individuals. The characteristics of the norm group are not described. Although the profile provides individuals with some normative information about their scores, the intended interpretation of the scores is ipsative. Individuals are instructed to examine the comparative height of the profile points in each of the four scales. The higher the point in one's own profile, the more likely that it represents an area of potential for improving time management.

The Canfield Time Problems Inventory claims to identify why individuals waste time. Time problems are assessed in four major dimensions. The user, however, is not provided with the information necessary to assess the criteria used in deriving the four dimensions from the 48 items. The inventory may actually reflect not four, but three, two, or one time problem dimension. The nature of the inventory and the stated purpose of the inventory implies that if time problems could be successfully identified and understood, then job performance or satisfaction would increase. No data are reported relating time problem scores with job performance or satisfaction. Given these limitations, the inventory is not recommended for its intended use in seminars until developers have demonstrated that the inventory assesses what it claims to assess and that the construct of time problem management relates to individual performance or satisfaction.

Review of The Canfield Time Problems Inventory by LYLE F. SCHOENFELDT, Professor of Management, Texas A&M University, College Station, TX:

For all of us who have wondered where the time goes, the Canfield Time Problems Inventory is designed to assist in identifying the reasons why we waste time. The Inventory consists of 48 items, 12 each to measure the extent to which individuals are effective (or ineffective) in four areas: priorities, planning, delegation, and self-discipline. The Inventory is designed for self-administration and self-scoring, and is recommended for use in conjunction with workshops or seminars on time management.

According to the manual, the 48 items were selected from some 200 over a period of nearly 2 years. The specific procedures for developing and selecting items are not discussed. Each item is rated on a 5-point scale with the anchors labeled "not at all," "a little," "some," "quite a lot," and "nearly perfectly." One problem is that the anchors are not equally suited to all items, with the "nearly perfectly" anchor being most frequently out of place. For example, the "nearly perfectly" option does not really fit the item, "I frequently find that I have to spend more time getting something done than I had anticipated." The author intends that the examinee decide the extent to which the item describes his or her behavior (i.e., "not at all" to "nearly perfectly"), but there are some ambiguities as to how the items relate to this scale (i.e., which end of the scale is really descriptive of one's typical behavior). Another problem is one common to inventories of typical behavior; for most respondents, the time wasting behaviors indicated by the 48 items occur "some" of the time, hence this would be the frequent answer of choice.

The answer sheet is a double-thickness set, and responses print through to a scoring sheet. The four scale scores are derived by assigning weights of 0, 1, 3, 5, and 8, respectively to responses "not at all" through "nearly perfectly." A low score indicates less of a problem; the higher the score, the more likely it represents an area of potential improvement. The profile sheet includes a translation of raw scores to percentiles and presents a short description of each scale. The manual, which is unlikely to be available to most examinees, cautions that profiles tend to be near the top or near the bottom of the sheet, but that the key issue is "the comparative height of the profile points on each of the four scales" for the particular individual completing the Inventory. The explanation offered for the warning that the percentile scores do not indicate that one person has a bigger problem than another is the tendency for people to see problems (items) differently on a self-report instrument. Another caveat offered in the manual, but not as part of the scale descriptions on the answer sheet, concerns the potential inapplicability of the delegation scale for those who do not supervise.

The 12-page (double spaced) manual includes seven sections, with over 5 pages essentially repeating the description of the scales on 1 page of the profile segment of the answer form. The covers of the manual and of the answer form indicate that the survey "is based on the experience of hundreds of people." No information is given on the examinees used to construct the norms, or the reliability or validity of the inventory. Two tables present the means/standard deviations and intercorrelations, and both are based on 79 examinees. Three of the scale intercorrelations are in the 70s, and three in the 50s. On the basis of this limited data, there is the suggestion that a single, general factor may underlie the effective use of time, thus calling into question the four dimensions presented.

The information on the development of The Canfield Time Problems Inventory leaves much to be desired, and the data supporting its technical adequacy is nonexistent. For these reasons it is difficult to know whether the Inventory deserves more deference than the typical Sunday supplement test. On the other hand, the Canfield could be of value in providing those involved in the ever popular time management workshops with a basis for self-examination and discussion, although even on this point no information is offered to support its value.

[191]

CAP Achievement Series. Grades preschool–K.5, K.0–1.5, 1.0–2.5, 2.0–3.5, 3.0–4.5, 4.0–5.5, 5.0–6.5, 6.0–7.5, 7.0–9.5, 9.0–11.5, 11.0–12.9; 1980–82; 1–2 forms ('80); teacher's manual for Levels 4–6 ('81, 45 pages), Levels 7–12 ('80, 104 pages), Levels 13–14 ('81, 22 pages); directions for administration ('80, 15–24 pages) for each level with Levels 13–14 in a single booklet; technical manual ('81, 103 pages); norms booklet ('81, 18–61 pages) for each level with Levels 13–14 in a single booklet; answer key ('80, 4–16 pages) for each level with Levels 9–12 and 13–14 in a single booklet; practice tests available for grades 1–3 and 4–8; 1983 price data: $3.40 per 35 practice tests including directions for administration (grades 1–3); $4.80 per 35 practice tests including directions for administration (grades 4–8); $1.30 per answer key; $5.90 per 35 student records; $1.90 per directions for administration; $2.85 per norms booklet; $5.90 per technical manual; $6.30 per teacher's manual; $10.60 per test review kit for either Levels 4–8 or 9–12; several different scoring options available; John W. Wick and Jeffrey K. Smith; American Testronics.*

a) LEVEL 4. Grades preschool–K.5; 4 scores: reading, mathematics, language, total; 1 form ('80, 24 pages); $35.20 per 35 tests including 1 directions for administration; administration time not reported.

b) LEVEL 5. Grades K.0–1.5; 4 scores: same as for Level 4; 2 editions; administration time not reported.

1) *Machine scorable booklets.* 1 form ('80, 24 pages); $35.95 per 35 tests including 1 directions for administration.

2) *Hand scorable booklets.* 1 form ('80, 24 pages); $26.50 per 35 tests including 35 pupil records, class analyzer, and 1 directions for administration.

c) LEVEL 6. Grades 1.0–2.5; 4 scores: same as for Level 4; 2 editions; prices same as for Level 5; administration time not reported.

1) *Machine scorable booklets.* 1 form ('80, 29 pages).

2) *Hand scorable booklets.* 1 form ('80, 29 pages).

d) LEVEL 7. Grades 2.0–3.5; 12 scores: word attack, reading (vocabulary, comprehension, total), mathematics (concepts, computation, total), language (spelling, capitalization and punctuation, grammar, total), basic skills total; 2 editions; (130–140) minutes.

1) *Machine scorable booklets.* Forms A, B, ('80, 31 pages); $35.95 per 35 tests including 1 directions for administration.

2) *Hand scorable booklets.* Forms A, B, ('80, 32 pages); $26.50 per 35 tests including 35 pupil records, class analyzer, and 1 directions for administration.

e) LEVEL 8. Grades 3.0–4.5; 13 scores: same as for Level 7 plus problem solving included in mathematics; 2 editions; prices same as for Level 7; (130–140) minutes.

1) *Machine scorable booklets.* Forms A, B, ('80, 31 pages).

2) *Hand scorable booklets.* Forms A, B, ('80, 32 pages).

f) LEVEL 9. Grades 4.0–5.5; 13 scores: reading (vocabulary, comprehension, total), mathematics (computation, concepts, problem solving, total), language (spelling, capitalization and punctuation, grammar, total), reference and study skills, basic skills total; Forms A, B, ('80, 40 pages); separate answer sheets must be used; $34.50 per 35 reusable tests including 1 directions for administration; $6.90 per 35 answer sheets; 180(190) minutes.

g) LEVEL 10. Grades 5.0–6.5; 13 scores: same as for Level 9; Forms A, B, ('80, 40 pages); separate answer sheets must be used; prices and time same as for Level 9.

h) LEVEL 11. Grades 6.0–7.5; 13 scores: same as for Level 9; Forms A, B, ('80, 34 pages); separate answer sheets must be used; prices and time same as for Level 9.

i) LEVEL 12. Grades 7.0–9.5; 13 scores: same as for Level 9; Forms A, B, ('80, 39 pages); separate answer sheets must be used; prices same as for Level 9; 210(220) minutes.

j) LEVEL 13. Grades 9.0–11.5; 8 scores: reading, mathematics, language, basic skills total, English, writing, social studies, science; 1 form ('80, 31 pages); separate answer sheets must be used; prices same as for Level 9; 120(130) minutes.

k) LEVEL 14. Grades 11.0–12.9; 8 scores: same as for Level 13; 1 form ('80, 31 pages); separate answer sheets must be used; prices same as for Level 9; 120(130) minutes.

TEST REFERENCES

1. Dolan, L. J. Validity analyses for the School Attitude Measures at three grade levels. EDUCATIONAL AND PSYCHOLOGICAL MEASUREMENT, 1983, 43, 295–303.

Review of CAP Achievement Series by GARY W. PETERSON, Associate Professor of Education and Research Associate, Center for Educational Technology, The Florida State University, Tallahassee, FL:

The overarching purpose of the Comprehensive Assessment Program (CAP): Achievement Series, according to the Technical Manual, is to provide an assessment of basic skill areas from pre-kindergarten through grade 12. More specifically, the authors assert that it can be used to evaluate the status of individuals, to plan for instructional improvement, to monitor student progress, and to evaluate program effectiveness. The purpose and potential uses of the CAP Achievement Series place it as a rival among other well established and notable school and district level achievement batteries such as the Comprehensive Tests of Basic Skills, Metropolitan Achievement Test, Iowa Tests of Basic Skills, and Curriculum Referenced Tests of Mastery. Nevertheless, a theme that emerges from the reading of the technical and teachers' manuals is that CAP Achievement series seeks to assess readiness for instruction. In this way it appears to be highly criterion-referenced in its approach to item development and in the nature of information reported pertaining to student and classroom achievement. Emphasized throughout is the term "developmental" in the sense that items are constructed according to tasks prescribed both by developmental psychological theories and by typical classroom experiences.

If it is true that the test battery is principally a criterion-referenced instrument, then the establishing of content validity becomes an extremely important issue. For this purpose 330 instructional objectives were derived from most frequently taught instructional objectives, reviews of textbooks and supplementary materials, curriculum guides from large cities, materials from the International Reading Association, National Council of Teachers of English and National Council of Teachers of Mathematics, as well as formative reviews by teachers, testing personnel and CAP authors and editors. The objectives are classified according to broad skill domains (Reading, Math, and Language) and items are clustered according to each objective. The objectives and test items can be easily reviewed by curriculum coordinators and teachers at each of the 11 levels of the tests to determine the correspondence between the skills measured on the test and the skills fostered in the curriculum.

With respect to the development of items, norms, and scales, 4,000 items were retained from an initial pool of 10,000 that met test specifications for Rasch analysis standards, discriminability, difficulty, proportional responses to distractors, goodness of fit on statistical bias analysis, and readability. Norms were established from a random sampling of 634 schools and 4,177 classrooms from 157 public and 16 Catholic school districts in 1979 and 1980. The sample of districts is somewhat overrepresented from the North Central Region (41.6% actual to 27.3% expected according to national student distribution) and underrepresented from the North East Region (14.2% actual to 22.4% expected). The sample of districts is, however, representative nationally in terms of SES. Further, in order to adjust for potential effects of misrepresentation, student scores were adjusted according to classroom, school, and district sampling variation. Equal interval score (EIS) scales were developed using the Rasch latent-trait model. Item difficulty values and person-ability estimates were generated for each raw score point on every content area test at each level. Each CAP Achievement Series level was equated with the adjacent levels using common items with the Rasch analysis. Parallel forms for levels 7–12 (grades 2.0 through 9.5) were also developed and validated using the Rasch analysis.

Reliabilities are provided for Content Areas (Reading, Math, Language) and for the first order of subtests using the KR 20 formula. Short term test-retest reliability would be warranted particularly in the lower grade levels to confirm the stability of the item domains. Generally, the content area reliabilities are in the .80–.95 range while most of the subtests are in the .70–.85 range with some subtests occasionally dipping into the .50s and .60s at the lower grade levels. Even though intercorrelations are reported among the subtests, factor analytic studies would be helpful in determining the relative independence of constructs measured.

The CAP Achievement series adequately meets requirements for practicality and feasibility. The tests can be administered in components to meet classroom teachers' needs. Levels 13–14, the high school years, can be administered in 1- or 2-hour blocks to conform to class scheduling. Nine indices of achievement are reported for each subscale so that teachers, program evaluators, curriculum planners, and parents may interpret the results. The indices include raw scores, percent correct, local percent correct, national percentiles, local stanines, national stanines, grade equivalents, normal curve equivalents, and equal interval scores. Reports supplied by the publishers include the Group Diagnostic Report, Individual Student Profile, Group Item Analysis, Classroom Organizer, Home Report, School and District Administrator Summary, Evaluator's Summary, Student Labels, Frequency Distribution, Student Name and Number List and Scored Magnetic Tapes. The administrators' manuals are clearly written and easy to follow and the test booklets can be easily read by the children.

Thus far the critique has focused on the purposes of the test, its technical qualities, and practical concerns. The ultimate selection of a school or district level achievement test, however, depends on the correspondence between the testing needs of a school district and the attributes of a variety of interlocking tests to meet them. Such needs typically include program accountability, teacher accountability, diagnosis of group learning needs, curricular placement, academic promotion, identifying students with special needs such as the gifted or those with special learning disabilities, and instructional improvement.

With respect to this last function, the CAP Achievement Series could be potentially a very strong candidate among its rivals provided content validity requirements have been sufficiently addressed at the local school and classroom levels. The authors of the test have made a concerted effort to counteract the "smile and file" response so often expressed among teachers. Extensive diagnostic/prescriptive information is provided at four levels of analysis: (1) area (Reading, Mathematics, Language); (2) subtest; (3) item cluster (objective); and (4) individual item. The capability exists from the information provided to individualize instruction so that material is neither redundant nor offered before any child is ready. However, making inferences from information provided at the item cluster or individual item level should be made along with data from other observations since the reliabilities and validity may be uncertain. Finally, the results can also be used to classify individuals within classrooms according to reading, language, and mathematics development if homogeneous achievement grouping is the order of the day in a given school or district.

Because the item pools were designed to assess readiness for achieving instructional objectives at a given grade level rather than to discriminate among learners, the test may not be particularly effective in identifying gifted or accelerated learners. We only know how a student performs against certain grade level objectives. For example, at the early grade levels, the subtests were designed to appear to be easy for the average child. At levels 7–12, mathematics concepts appear on the test only after they have been typically introduced. In problem-solving tasks, reading and math concepts are presented 2 years behind when they are typically presented. Therefore the test appears to serve the function of assessing individual readiness for instruction better than determining whether an individual or group has excelled beyond national norms. Other achievement tests designed specifically to differentiate levels of achievement among students along broad ability lines might be more suitable if a school or district wished to demonstrate how far beyond national norms its students might have attained.

Since norms are provided both at the entry of a level (2 months into the school year) and at the exit (8 months), the CAP Achievement Series could be used to assess student and classroom progress against specific instructional objectives during a school year. Again, provided that teachers and curriculum planners have established validity of objectives and modes of testing, such information can be integrated into the ongoing formative development of instructional process. Therefore, if there is a bottom line, the CAP Achievement Series may well be the best among its rivals in terms of its potential for relating to the improvement of instruction, for curricular placement, and for monitoring student growth against specific criteria. It may not fare as well as others as a measure of growth in more general cognitive abilities or in terms of how generic abilities are distributed across groups of learners.

Review of CAP Achievement Series by JOHN H. ROSENBACH, Professor of Educational Psychology, Chair, School Psychology Program, State University of New York at Albany, Albany, NY:

Achievement Series, one of seven components of the CAP, is an extraordinarily ambitious effort to "provide the capability for continuous measurement of students in pre-kindergarten through grade twelve." To enhance the notion of continuity of assessment, the concept of "Basic Skills" (Reading, Language, and Mathematics), ordinarily associated with the elementary years, is carried through grade 12. To achieve continuity, the authors developed a continuous scale (Equal Interval Scores), "spanning all eleven levels of the Achievement Series." This scale, which purportedly measures equal units of educational growth, represents, depending on one's point of view, either state-of-the-art or beyond-state-of-the-art psychometric techniques.

Although the Series is presented as a package, and the publishers would undoubtedly prefer that it be used as a school-wide, K through 12 battery, it can also be viewed, perhaps more conventionally, as three or four separate batteries: Levels 4, 5, and 6 (preschool through grade 1); Levels 7 through 11 (grades 2 through 6); Level 12 (grades 7, 8, and perhaps 9); and, Levels 13 and 14 (through grade 12). Such a breakdown reflects not only more typical differences in test use as instructional programs change, but acknowledges certain realities with respect to norms. Few school districts sponsor pre-kindergartens and, across the country, kindergarten practices are widely varied from none, to part-time, to full-time. Similarly, beyond grade 9, instructional programs become more sharply differentiated and student populations change as dropout rates increase. Thus, one can place a bit more confidence in the representativeness of norms for grades 1 through 8 than either at very early ages or at the high school level, when school districts, as is the case here, are the basic units of the norm sample.

All of this is said as a preface to this reviewer's opinion that the Achievement Series is of questionable value as a continuous measure of K through 12 educational development, while at the same time offering some attractive possibilities as a more conventional achievement test, particularly for grades 2 through 6.

OVERVIEW. In general, the steps taken to develop and norm this test series are impressive and represent just about every concern and advancement in contemporary psychometrics. The authors began the project by identifying 330 instructional objectives that are considered to be common to most American schools. School personnel, curricular materials from various professional organizations, and curriculum specialists were the sources for the objectives, which are listed in detail in the Teacher's Manuals. Based on these objectives, an item pool of over 10,000 was generated by a writing team selected to balance gender, ethnicity, geographical regions, and professional backgrounds. Moreover, this team was trained to avoid writing items that would favor a gender, include cultural stereotypes, or be culture-laden. (A reading of a sample of items seems to confirm that these goals were met.) Following editorial selection and three tryout phases with 80,000 students, about 4,000 items survived. Further steps were then taken to modify reading level and vocabulary range to the appropriate grade levels.

The final standardization sample consisted of 157 public and 16 Catholic schools drawn from all 50 states and the District of Columbia. A total of just under 130,000 students was involved. Testing was done in the fall and spring, with the majority of students tested in the fall. Care was taken to draw samples that roughly approximate national percentages with respect to geographic region, socioeconomic level, size of school district, race, and bilingualism.

The test materials, including the various manuals, are presented in the usual professional manner of major test publishers: the materials include a plethora of booklets, attractively packaged, with various suggestions to teachers as to score use, and pages and pages of tables. The user has a choice of some or all of 13 score reports, ranging from information on individual students, to classroom data, to home reports, to grade, school, and district summaries. One additional feature that could prove helpful is the "Inventory of Teacher Concerns," a structured observation form. The Inventory is designed to focus the teacher's attention on a student's (or group's) strengths and weaknesses. Although it is not part of the test, strictly speaking, it comes with the Series.

RELIABILITY AND VALIDITY. The various subscale (composed of subtests) and total test reliabilities (KR-20) are well within acceptable limits and comparable to those reported in similar batteries. Not surprisingly, the reliabilities are somewhat low at the pre-K and kindergarten levels, but from grade 2 and up the reliabilities for the Reading scale and for the total test are typically .95 or higher. However, individual subtests, particularly Spelling and Grammar, occasionally drop to the low .50s, and the user should be cautioned against overinterpreting subtest scores.

Validity, as usual, is a somewhat different matter. Typical of achievement tests, the primary claim to validity is based on content analysis by experts. Empirical validity is derived solely from internal characteristics and from correlations with the companion Developing Cognitive Abilities Test (DCAT), another component of the CAP. The question of how high an ability or aptitude test should correlate with an achievement test is, of course, unanswerable. But clearly there has to be a limit for at some point the tests simply do not provide independent information. The Achievement Series and the DCAT may well be approaching this limit since the majority of correlations between their total scores fall between .85 and .90. The important issue is the construct validity of the instruments; if the achievement test is primarily a measure of some general intellectual ability, and only secondarily a measure of school learning, then its use as an indicator of instructionally induced change, either with individuals or groups, is markedly restricted. Two conspicuous examples of this problem at the subtest level occur with Mathematics and Social Studies at grade 12, where the reliabilities for the two subtests are reported at .88 and .83, respectively, while the correlation with the DCAT are .83 and .81. In other words, just about all the reliable variance in these subtests can be explained on the basis of the abilities test. Although no factor analytic results are presented, it's probably fair to guess, based on the magnitudes of intercorrelations, that the Achievement Series like so many other achievement batteries, taps heavily into some general mental ability factor. This fact should be taken into consideration by the test user.

SCORES. In addition to the usual array of scores (i.e., grade equivalents, with their presently well-publicized limitations; percentiles; and stanines) the reader is presented with Equal Interval Scores (EIS) and Normal Curve Equivalents (NCEs). The EIS are particularly susceptible to misinterpretation (reinforced in the manuals) because they imply that an educational/psychological construct (e.g., Mathematics) develops continuously (and, perhaps, linearly) from an early age (4) through adolescence and, further, can be measured in equal units across those ages. The authors go so far as to claim that a difference of any magnitude means the same at any point on the scale (e.g., 100–115 is the same as 600–615), which "is particularly useful in assessing a student's growth over a number of years and in evaluating the effectiveness of a new instructional technique." Such a claim goes well beyond the demonstrated efficacy of such scales. Most studies of the development of human characteristics show negatively accelerated growth curves, with most development occurring relatively early in the life of the characteristics in question. And even the data presented in the Series' manuals confirm this pattern. I plotted average EIS scores by grade and found a decidedly curvilinear relationship. For example, the average increment in EIS from grade 1 to grade 2 was 79 points, whereas it was 24 from grade 5 to 6 and 13 from grade 9 to 10. Given these data, it is hard to see how the author's contentions can be substantiated. I can only recommend that users of the Series pay little, if any, attention to the EIS.

With respect to the Normal Curve Equivalent scores (NCE), the manual is virtually useless. Unless the consumer is sophisticated as to its use, or is willing to research its meaning, this score is probably better ignored.

Of grave concern to this reviewer is the uncritical inclusion of an Anticipated Grade Equivalent score which is provided for each student, if the Series is used in conjunction with the DCAT. This type of score (i.e., predicting achievement scores from ability test scores) is simply another version of the under- and overachievement concept, which has been widely and seriously criticized in the psychometric literature. A major test publisher should, at the very least, acknowledge the questionable status of this concept and warn the consumer about the psychometric problems inherent in its use.

LEVELS. Although strong claims are made as to the continuous nature of the scales, there appear to be breaking points especially (and not surprisingly) between grades 1 and 2 and between the upper grades and high school. The lower levels stress readiness and pre-skill development in a manner consistent with most tests that are designed for 4- to 6-year-olds. At the high school level the items reflect a greater subject matter orientation in keeping with the nature of the curriculum, and with the exception of Reading and some language areas, hardly fall within the usual definition of basic skills. This is not to say the Series has no place in high school assessment, but rather that a school staff, if it is to adopt the battery, should have a clear plan as to how the information is to be used.

The middle levels are more in keeping with the usual concept of basic skills, and it is this portion of the battery that is most likely to be a serious competitor to other major test series. However, as in the case of any achievement battery, a school district should study the content of the test to determine to what extent the objectives and items are consistent with the school's own curriculum.

STRENGTHS OF THE ACHIEVEMENT SERIES. The authors have done a commendable job in presenting the test content (objectives and items), together with relevant statistics, to be of potential value to school staff. Each item in the entire battery is presented with respect to the objective it measures, along with its difficulty level. Thus, teachers and other professional staff have a rich resource to turn to for diagnostic purposes—assuming, of course, that the scores are available and used within a short period of time. The information that is provided can be used to isolate individual as well as group strengths and weaknesses and, presumably, as a basis to modify instruction. Furthermore, the Teacher's Manual contains a variety of helpful guides for the classroom teacher. But the prospective user should be warned that a full implementation of the materials contained in the Achievement Series will require a major commitment in both time and energy. In a sense, the suggested uses of the Series present problems not unlike those encountered in many do-it-yourself kits. The directions seem simple enough until one embarks on the project, and then the task seems both endless and impossible. To exploit fully the potential application of the Series will require not only a dedicated professional staff but one that has ample time at its disposal.

SUMMARY. As an effort to provide a continuous assessment of educational development from pre-K through grade 12, the Achievement Series is of questionable value. As a more traditional achievement battery, particularly for grades 2 through 6, it offers some attractive possibilities. It appears to be well-normed, items have been carefully selected with respect to objectives and to avoid potentially controversial cultural issues, and item information can be of practical assistance to classroom teachers. Full usage of the test results may, however, demand more time and energy than the typical school can or is willing to afford. A prospective user is well advised to examine the test's content (objectives and items) to decide whether the Series meets local needs.

[192]

Career Adaptive Behavior Inventory. Disabled students ages 5–15; 1980; CAB; ratings by parents, teachers, or other professionals in 10 major categories: academics, communication, interest, leisure time, motor, responsibility, self-concept, self-help, socialization, task performance; no reliability data reported in manual; no norms; 1 form (6 pages); manual (26 pages); activity book (84 pages); 1983 price data: $6 per 25 rating forms; $10 per activity guide; $7.50 per manual; [30] minutes; Thomas P. Lombardi; Special Child Publications.*

Review of Career Adaptive Behavior Inventory by BOB ALGOZZINE, Professor of Special Education, University of Florida, Gainesville, FL:

The Career Adaptive Behavior Inventory is a checklist of 120 items grouped in 10 clusters: Academics, Communication, Interest, Leisure Time, Motor, Responsibility, Self-Concept, Self-Help, Socialization, and Task Performance. The author indicates in the CAB manual that "anyone who is in a position to observe and know the student" may use the device. Ratings of the actual test items are obtained through "direct observation and/or memory of individual target students" using a six-point scale. A rating of 0 is assigned if the student is unable to perform/exhibit the "behavior" listed in the items; ratings of 1 to 5 are assigned according to the extent to which the student performs/exhibits the behavior (i.e., 1=1 to 20% of the time, 2=21 to 40% and so on). It is recommended that several "trials" of the "behavior" be solicited to facilitate assignment of ratings from number of trials completed successfully (e.g., 3 of 5=60%=rating of 3).

According to discussion presented in the manual, the degree of reliability of the CAB ratings is determined by use of the following code: memory (1), observation (2), combination of memory and observation (3). According to the author (and this system), the highest score possible in this type of rating is 36 for each category and 360 for the entire CAB. Three reliability score groups are included in the manual: Most=category scores between 26 and 36 and CAB total scores between 260 and 360; Average=category scores between 11 and 25 and CAB total scores between 110 and 259; Least=category scores below 10 and total scores below 109. This means that the "most" reliable scores are those obtained mostly from a combination of memory and observation.

A table is provided for use by "teachers, counselors, psychologists, and therapists in determining the strengths and weaknesses of individuals and groups" evaluated with the CAB. Scores of 44–60 in each category (440–600 Total Score) are to be interpreted as strengths, 21–43 in each category (210–439 Total Score) are believed to be average scores, and category scores of 0–20 (0–209 Total Score) are weaknesses. No data are provided indicating the basis for these scoring criteria.

The basis for including items in the scale was "their relationship to the generic skills required in preparation for the world of work," and no other validity data are stated or implied in the manual. No conventional reliability data are provided by the author, although it is indicated that "reliability in the CAB is directly related to the accuracy of procedures used by the rater." Summary data from 35 developmentally disabled students evaluated in 1978 constitute the only norm-like values in the manual; they are provided more to illustrate the effectiveness of the Career Models Project, which included activities from the Career Adaptive Behavior Inventory Activity Book, than to be useful as norms.

The Career Adaptive Behavior Inventory is an assessment device of limited technical adequacy and practical value. The technical limits are obvious; an assessment device with inadequately developed and/or described norms, reliability, and validity can at best be considered technically inadequate. The practical limits of this inventory are in part due to the nature and kind of items which comprise it and in part due to the simplistic link implied between diagnostic use and intervention planning.

With regard to items, some are much more observable than others. For example, it is relatively easy to "see" and count the extent to which an individual "identifies coins and paper currency (up to $10.00)" or "tells time" with some degree of accuracy. It is more difficult, perhaps impossible, to tell if that same individual "enjoys general cleaning duties (mopping, polishing, dusting)" or "plans use of time" adequately. Similarly, the scoring system implies that each item in a category is considered as important as each other item (i.e., each is weighted the same in scoring); large degrees of skill difference exist among items in all the categories. For example, reading and understanding simple directions is a higher level skill than naming the days of the week in succession, yet both are similarly weighted in scoring the CAB Academics category.

Perhaps the greatest failing of the CAB is inherent in the simplistic assumption that scores on the inventory can be used to plan interventions. Treatment of areas of weakness (among the 10 CAB categories) is accomplished through use of the Career Adaptive Behavior Inventory Activity Book. It includes 360 (3 for each of the 120 CAB items) activities for use as "examples, or starting points, designed for the creative teacher to build upon" in planning remedial programs. In evaluating these materials, one wonders, first, how to know if a student is "willing to engage in new activities" to a satisfactory degree. Then, if not, how having that "student participate in physical education activities specially designed for minimum failure (e.g., playing volleyball with balloons, having a wheelchair race, etc.)" can be considered sound pedagogy in any diagnostic/prescriptive sense.

The CAB materials appear to be the products of a Title IV-C project of limited scope. Practitioners may find the listing of 120 items useful as a source of ideas on what to look at in clients. The psychometric characteristics as well as the selective nature and unbalanced kind of items in each category of the inventory severely limit the usefulness of it as an assessment device. Finally, making effective use of the suggestions provided for "creative" teachers is perhaps a better way to use the CAB materials than using them as a basis for diagnostic/prescriptive programming.

Review of Career Adaptive Behavior Inventory by JOHNNY L. MATSON, Associate Professor of Learning and Development, Northern Illinois University, DeKalb, IL:

The Career Adaptive Behavior Inventory (CAB) is designed to assist teachers in improving the developmentally disabled student in 10 areas. These categories include academics, communication, interest, leisure time, motor ability, responsibility, self-concepts, self-help, socialization, and task performance. Twelve specific behaviors are listed under each of these categories. The CAB has been primarily developed for use with elementary school-age disabled students but is suggested for use with children 3 through 15 years of age. The scale is rated by a significant other utilizing a six-point scale for each item.

It is suggested that the CAB be used for both assessment and treatment purposes. To aid in meeting these goals an "activity book" is provided along with the test manual and scoring sheets. Activities are based on an operant conditioning model (e.g., task analysis of items and use of contingent reinforcements). Three tasks (perceptual-motor, social-emotional, and cognitive) are described for each of the 120 items from the test.

The concept and general rationale for this adaptive behavior test are good. However, a number of problems exist with respect to this assessment instrument that make it less than optimal. First, this reviewer was hard pressed to determine why the word "career" was included in the title of an instrument designed primarily for children, and which covers such a broad list of behaviors well out of the purview of prevocational or vocational skills. Even more importantly, acceptable reliability, validity or normative data are not provided. Thirty-five students were tested, from 5 to 17 years old and ranging from severely to mildly retarded. Such a small and exceedingly heterogeneous group hardly tells us anything about the scale. Therefore, those who choose to use this instrument must rely on face validity.

[193]

Career Assessment Inventories for the Learning Disabled. Learning disabled elementary school grades and over; 1983; CAI; 3 tests; no data on reliability and validity; no norms; individual; 2 forms; manual (58 pages); 1984 price data: $7 per 25 Attributes/Ability Inventories; $3 per 25 Interest Inventories; $15 per manual; $15 per specimen set; (10–15) minutes per test; Carol Weller and Mary Buchanan; Academic Therapy Publications.*

a) ATTRIBUTES INVENTORY. 6 scores: realistic, investigative, artistic, social, enterprising, conventional; 1 form (4 pages).
b) ABILITY INVENTORY. 6 scores: verbal understanding, conversation, visual, spatial, fine motor, gross motor; 1 form (in same booklet as *a*).
c) INTEREST INVENTORY. 6 scores (in same areas as *a*); may be orally administered; 1 form (2 pages).

Review of Career Assessment Inventories for the Learning Disabled by COURTLAND C. LEE, Associate Professor of Education, University of North Carolina, Chapel Hill, NC:

The Career Assessment Inventories for the Learning Disabled (CAI) is designed to be used by counselors and other educators who work with learning disabled children and adults. The rationale for its development centers around the need for new approaches to career counseling and training for learning disabled people given the fact that a large number of them are characteristically unemployed and/or underemployed. The results of the CAI can be used to facilitate important aspects of career development for learning disabled individuals.

The CAI is a comprehensive battery designed to assess personality characteristics, psychomotor abilities, and interests. The data collected is then used to select appropriate career options from a job finder in the manual.

The instrument was developed using John Holland's model of personality types and the literature on learning disabilities as the basis for item selection. The authors state that CAI development began with interviews of unspecified teachers of learning disabled students about their perceptions of existing career inventories. From these interviews appears to have come the major aspect of the CAI which differentiates it substantively from other career assessment inventories—a focus on the learning strengths and weaknesses inherent in learning disabilities.

The focal point of the CAI is a reasonably well written manual that provides specific information on the three inventories that comprise the instrument, basic information on its development, administration and scoring procedures, a job finder, the use of results with the job finder and in career education, and case studies that illustrate possible CAI profiles.

Two response sheets are included with the CAI. One includes both the Attributes Inventory and the Ability Inventory, and the other contains the Interest Inventory. The Attributes Inventory and the Ability Inventory are observational instruments designed to be completed by a teacher or counselor after a suggested 1- to 3-hour period of observing an individual. The Interest Inventory is completed by the examinee.

In terms of content and results, the Attributes Inventory and the Interest Inventory appear similar to any number of career inventories that assess personality characteristics and interests. The Attributes Inventory consists of six attribute sections each with 11 descriptors. An observer numerically rates an individual from "most like" to "least like" for each descriptor. The attribute scores are derived by totalling the points for the descriptors under each of the six sections. This produces a ranking of attributes which is recorded on the front of the inventory booklet. An attribute summary box allows the observer to record the highest and second highest rankings as the primary and secondary attributes. Other than the observational technique, the Attributes Inventory has little to distinguish it from other inventories for identifying behavioral and personality characteristics using Holland's career typology model.

Likewise, the Interest Inventory is reminiscent of instruments such as Holland's Vocational Preference Inventory. The inventory contains 72 jobs from the job finder grouped according to the six attributes. The examinee checks one of three categories, "interested," "uninterested," or "unfamiliar," in preferential response to each job. Responses are then totaled for each attribute in the three categories. The attributes that receive the highest and second highest number of "interested" scores are identified as the primary and secondary attribute categories with respect to occupational interests. This information is recorded on the response sheet.

One feature that appears to distinguish the Interest Inventory from others of its genre, however, is the fact that its range of occupations appears somewhat limited. This is no doubt due to its having been developed, in part, from the literature on job possibilities for the learning disabled.

It is the Ability Inventory of the CAI that seems to represent a significant departure from most career assessment instruments. It was specifically designed to measure unique ability characteristics of individuals with learning disabilities. The Ability Inventory measures the level of difficulty in auditory, visual, and motor abilities. The manual provides good operational definitions of difficulties found in these three areas.

In assessing abilities, an observer rates an individual on 10 characteristics in each of six ability categories in comparison to other people making career choices from 1 ("very poor") to 6 ("excellent"). Ratings are totaled to provide a score for each ability section. Scores are then transferred to an ability profile on the response sheet. A profile summary allows for the interpretation of abilities as average or low. The fact that an individual can be rated as "excellent" on a characteristic, indicating skill that far exceeds expectations for most people, raises the question as to why the authors did not include a "high" category for score interpretation.

Importantly, the authors have realized that career decisions should not be made on the basis of the results of a single inventory. Therefore, the attributes and ability booklet contains a section for recording other data (e.g., scores from intelligence and achievement measures, results from physical examinations, an individual's history, scores from adaptive behavior scales) that should prove helpful in producing a comprehensive individual career profile.

The data collected with the three inventories is intended to be used with the Job Finder. The Job Finder contains career options that have been catalogued according to attributes and abilities. The authors have outlined a four-step procedure for identifying appropriate career options based on CAI results in the manual.

The major concern this reviewer has about the CAI is the fact that no technical information has been provided for the instrument. A thorough reading of the manual reveals no normative data or reliability and validity information. The manual has a brief paragraph about a field test that was conducted with the CAI. This research appears to have been conducted in an effort to improve items, instructions, and scoring procedures for the instrument. One particular technical aspect that seems crucial to report is interrater reliability for the attributes and ability measures, given their observational format.

The lack of such crucial information is interesting, considering the extensive effort that seems to have gone into explaining the purpose and developing the practical aspects of this instrument. Without such important technical information, it is difficult to consider the CAI as anything more than an experimental assessment tool.

In summary, the CAI represents an important attempt to meet the neglected career development needs of the learning disabled. The attributes and interest inventories appear to be consistent with Holland's career typology model of career choice as seen in similar career assessment instruments, while at the same time making allowances for learning disabilities with their observational procedures. The assessment of abilities shows an appreciation for the unique psychomotor aspects associated with learning disabilities. Additionally, the use of inventory data with the Job Finder seems to be a systematic attempt to facilitate realistic job exploration on the part of learning disabled examinees. However, this reviewer is somewhat disturbed by the lack of technical data for the CAI. In its present form, the CAI can only be cautiously recommended for supplemental use, in conjunction with more established career assessment inventories, as a tool for facilitating career exploration among the learning disabled.

[194]

Career Decision Scale. Grades 9–12 and college; 1976–80; 1 form ('76, 4 pages); manual ('80, 80 pages); 1983 price data: $5 per 25 scales; $4.95 per manual; (10–15) minutes; Samuel H. Osipow, Clarke G. Carney (scale), Jane Winer (scale), Barbara Yanico (scale), and Maryanne Koschier (scale); Marathon Consulting & Press.*

TEST REFERENCES

1. Cesari, J. P., Winer, J. L., Zychlinski, F., & Laird, I. O. Influence of occupational information giving on cognitive complexity in decided versus undecided students. JOURNAL OF VOCATIONAL BEHAVIOR, 1982, 21, 224–230.

2. Fuqua, D. R., & Hartman, B. W. A behavioral index of career indecision for college students. JOURNAL OF COLLEGE STUDENT PERSONNEL, 1983, 24, 507–512.

3. Rogers, W. B., Jr., & Westbrook, B. W. Measuring career indecision among college students: Toward a valid approach for counseling practitioners and researchers. MEASUREMENT AND EVALUATION IN GUIDANCE, 1983, 16, 78–85.

4. Taylor, K. M., & Betz, N. E. Applications of self-efficacy theory to the understanding and treatment of career indecision. JOURNAL OF VOCATIONAL BEHAVIOR, 1983, 22, 63–81.

Review of Career Decision Scale by LENORE W. HARMON, Professor of Educational Psychology, University of Illinois, Champaign, IL:

The Career Decision Scale (CDS) was introduced in 1976. Judging from the amount of research on the scale itself and research utilizing it as a measure of indecision, it has been greeted with considerable interest.

Administration and scoring are simple and straightforward. The first two items concern certainty of choice of career and major. They are negatively related to items 3 through 18, where a high score indicates indecision.

Two-week test-retest reliabilities of .90 and .82 and a six-week test-retest reliability of .70 are reported.

Validity is evidenced by the fact that a number of studies show greater decidedness after exposure to career planning interventions. The most impressive of these (Taylor, 1979) utilized an untreated control group. Pre- and posttest measures over eight months showed the career planning group to be initially less decided (they volunteered for the career planning experience) and to have become significantly more decided. After the intervention they were no different from the initially more decided control group.

Scores on the CDS have also been related to locus of control, career maturity, grade level, ability, anxiety level, fear of success, sex, and another measure of career decidedness by Holland and Holland. Some of the results regarding locus of control, ability, and sex, are apparently inconsistent, but in general the results indicate that the construct of career decidedness as measured by the CDS is quite clearly and reasonably defined. The originally reported factor structure has not been completely replicated in subsequent analyses, and Osipow has cautioned responsibly against the use of factor scores in clinical applications of the CDS.

Norms are presented for undecided college freshmen by sex ($N=138$ males, 130 females), college students by year and sex (*N*s range from 31 to 76), and high school students by year and sex (*N*s range from 132 to 251). Total CDS scores among college students do not differ by sex, year, age, or college of enrollment.

SUMMARY. The CDS is extremely well developed and researched for such a relatively new inventory. It clearly fills a need to assess both individuals in career counseling and groups. It may prove useful in assessing groups when career interventions are being contemplated. It has already proved useful in evaluating interventions. It is highly recommended for these uses. The manual is a model of clarity and completeness. The potential user will find a wealth of information there. Additionally, the cost is reasonable and it can be administered quickly.

REVIEWER'S REFERENCES

Taylor, K. M. THE EFFECTS OF A RESIDENTIAL CAREER EXPLORATION PROGRAM ON THE LEVEL OF CAREER DECIDEDNESS OF COLLEGE STUDENTS. Unpublished data. Ohio State University, Columbus, 1979.

Review of Career Decision Scale by DAVID O. HERMAN, Vice President, Measurement Research Services, Inc., New York, NY:

Of the 19 items of the Career Decision Scale, all but three are concerned with the barriers that prevent one from making career decisions. The respondent indicates on a four-point scale the degree to which each statement describes him- or herself. The sum of self-ratings on these 16 items provides the indecision score. The first two items are statements reflecting certainty about choosing a career and a school major and, accordingly, the sum of ratings on these two items is a certainty score. Item 19 is an unscored open-ended item that allows the respondent to add his or her own self-description.

The manual for the Career Decision Scale does not directly suggest appropriate uses for the inventory, but the senior author states that it may be used to review an individual client's career decision problems as an aid to initiating counseling dialogue, and that it may be administered in a program evaluation context to groups of students before and after career counseling interventions (Osipow, personal communication, April, 1983).

The manual summarizes a great deal of empirical research with the Scale that will be helpful to prospective users. For instance, it appears that four factors run through items 3 through 18, though the nature of some of the factors varies somewhat from one study to another. Test-retest coefficients with the supporting means and standard deviations are given for high school and college groups, for individual items as well as for total scores. The items range widely in retest stability. Retest coefficients for the scale as a whole are reported in the range of .70 to .90. Estimates of internal consistency are not reported.

Percentile norms are presented for high school and college samples, and for a group of adults seeking continuing education. Inspection of the norms suggests that levels of career indecision decrease over the high school and college years, and that sex differences in the scores are insignificant for all groups studied.

A number of studies establish that indecision scores decrease following career counseling interventions, and that while indecision scores in general decrease over time, they decrease more for treated than for untreated groups. Another type of validity information is reflected in the relationships that are demonstrated between scores on the Scale and measures of such variables as locus of control, knowledge about careers, and strength of commitment to a college major.

In summary, the Career Decision Scale seems quite suitable for either of its major purposes—as a springboard for discussion in individual counseling sessions, and as an outcome measure in program evaluation. Its brevity, comprehensiveness, and extensive research support are important strengths of the inventory. It also appears to have little or no direct competition.

[195]

Career Development Inventory [Consulting Psychologists Press, Inc.]. Grades 8–12, college; 1979–81; CDI; measures vocational maturity; 8 scores: career planning, career exploration, decision making, world-of-work information, knowledge of preferred occupational group, career development attitudes, career development knowledge and skills, total; norms for grades 9–12 only; 2 levels: School Form (grades 8–12, '79, 15 pages), College and University Form (college, '81, 15 pages); user's manual ('81, 29 pages); separate answer sheets must be used; 1984 price data: $17 per 25 reusable tests; $12.50 per 50 answer sheets; $24 per 10 prepaid answer sheets; $8 per manual; $10 per specimen set; scoring service, $2.50 or less per test for answer sheets without prepayment feature; (55–65) minutes; Donald E. Super, Albert S. Thompson, Richard H. Lindeman, Jean P. Jordaan, and Roger A. Myers; Consulting Psychologists Press, Inc.*

Australian adaptation: Years 8–11; 1983; norms for ages 14 and Year 11 only; 1 form (19 pages); manual (80 pages); 1985 price data: A$1.95 per student booklet; $2.75 per 10 answer sheets; $2.25 per score key; $9.90 per manual; $14 per specimen set; Jan Lokan; Australian Council for Educational Research [Australia].*

TEST REFERENCES

1. Lokan, J. J., & Biggs, J. B. Student characteristics and motivational and process factors in relation to styles of career development. JOURNAL OF VOCATIONAL BEHAVIOR, 1982, 21, 1–16.

2. Phillips, S. D., Strohmer, D. C., Berthaume, B. L. J., & O'Leary, J. C. Career development of special populations: A framework for research. JOURNAL OF VOCATIONAL BEHAVIOR, 1983, 22, 12–29.

3. Healy, C. C., & Mourton, D. L. The Self-Directed Search Personality Scales and career maturity. MEASUREMENT AND EVALUATION IN GUIDANCE, 1984, 17, 3–14.

4. Jepsen, D. A., & Dustin, R. A simulated measure of adolescent career information-seeking behavior. MEASUREMENT AND EVALUATION IN GUIDANCE, 1984, 17, 32–39.

Review of Career Development Inventory [Consulting Psychologists Press, Inc.] by JAMES W. PINKNEY, Associate Professor of Counseling, East Carolina University, Greenville, NC:

The Career Development Inventory (CDI) uses a multiple choice format to assess components of career development and career maturity. There are two forms: a School Form and a College and University Form. The two forms are closely parallel, with minor item changes in the College and University (CU) form to make it more relevant to higher education. The 120 items are divided into two parts: a general assessment of career planning constructs, and a specific assessment of the respondent's "most Preferred" occupational group (PO). The 20-item scales for career planning (CP), career exploration (CE), decision making (DM), and world-of-work information (WW) are also reported in combination as an assessment of career development attitudes (CP and CE) and of career development knowledge (DM and WW); then all four scores are combined into a total score which "approaches a measure of career or vocational maturity." The 40-item PO scale is a two-step process. The respondent first reacts to 100 occupational titles arranged in 20 occupational groups with the option of adding titles of interest. A forced choice is then made of 1 occupational group as most preferred by the respondent, and the 40 items are then answered in terms of respondent knowledge about the chosen occupational group. Each occupational group has a separate scoring key developed from objective occupational information or opinions of expert judges. Items are written in unisex terms consistently throughout the inventory (with two exceptions).

Based on Super's theoretical model, the CDI is presented as a measure of four of his five dimensions of career maturity (CP, CE, DM, and WW). The CDI does not assess reality orientation, the fifth dimension. The authors refer to a long history of development and research going back to the Career Planning Study, and suggest the CDI is now ready for group assessment, individual counseling, research, and program planning and evaluation. How reasonable these potential uses of the CDI actually are is difficult to assess since the CDI Technical Manual will not be published until the summer of 1984, even though the 1981 CDI User's Manual frequently refers to it. Given a long history of development, one would think the potential user should have easy access to all the available information rather than just the User's Manual (and a supplement for the CU form).

The administration and scoring section of the User's Manual is good but raises some questions. The instructions are well done and thorough. Steps for standardized administration are clear, information necessary for accurate scoring is accented, and directions for how to handle common problems (such as what to do with questions) are included. Scoring is done by machine and hand scoring is not recommended. There are some attractive options offered (at a cost), which include specifying various combinations of summary reports for groups, the opportunity to develop local norms, and a response analysis by item for the attitude scales. A question not addressed is that of respondents (especially testwise ones) going for "high" scores regardless of what they truly think or do, nor is there anything in the instructions dealing with this issue. The CP and CE scales are particularly vulnerable on this point.

Another question concerns the need for machine scoring. The authors offer differential item weights and the need for 20 keys on the PO scale as reasons, but only one scale (CE) has item weights, matching a key to an occupational cluster is not difficult, and the other scales are a simple total sum of item scores. My impression was that hand scoring would be reasonable and would have real advantages such as immediate feedback and the opportunity to examine individual items as a resource for counseling.

A final question concerns the authors' suggestion that a profile of percentile ranks may be helpful in discussing the CDI with students. This is certainly true, but surely machine scoring procedures could easily generate such a profile so as to save user time. An individual report now consists of brief scale descriptions with standard scores and percentiles from the appropriate norm group. There is room on the report for a profile, and a simple profile would seem like a reasonable expectation as part of the machine scoring procedures.

Percentile norms are reported by sex and grade for both the School form and the CU form. Scale statistics are also reported by sex and grade, as well as by major field for college students and by career focus for high school students. Norms for the School form are based on a nationwide sample of 5,039, while the CU norms are based on a sample of 1,345. This information is clearly presented, shortcomings in the sampling are noted, and test users are encouraged to consider local norms. The suggestion about local norms is not an idle one since the scoring arrangements are available (at a cost) and convenient for producing local norms. In addition, the CU Supplement to the User's Manual provides a clear description of how to construct local norms.

I would consider the norms and scale scores to be a strong point for the CDI with two cautions. First, the answer sheets can be scored for 7th and 8th graders, junior college students, and graduate students, but no norms or scores are provided for these groups. In fact, the authors directly state that the PO scale may be too difficult for most 10th graders even though the reading level is aimed at 8th graders. Second, the norms for the CU form are based on much smaller *N*s (one cell has an *N* of 71) than the School form. This reflects the developmental history of the forms; the CU form is newer and less work has been done with it.

Both Cronbach alpha coefficients and standard errors of measurement (SEM) are reported in the User's Manual. The internal consistency of the CDI is generally good (median values from .78 to .89), except for the DM scale (.67) and the PO scale (.60). The user is cautioned about using these two scales with individuals, although the authors assume the other reliabilities are strong enough for use with individuals. The latter is a matter of opinion.

Some problems arise for the potential user because of a respectable start at reporting reliability but inadequate follow-through. SEM values are only reported by grade for the School form and the user is left to calculate values for other groups. For the CU form the authors offer an average alpha of .75 as adequate for individual counseling, then suggest caution for a combined scale with an overall alpha of .75. In fairness, these problems may well be covered in the Technical Manual. But the Technical Manual should be available! A more distressing issue is the absence of information on the stability of the CDI, which would be critical for any assessment dealing with development and maturation. Stability of the CDI scales is "based on data from previous forms of the CDI and strongly suggests the CDI scores are highly stable over periods of up to six months." It is also indicated that "further evidence of such stability" is included in the Technical Manual. However, no data on stability are reported in the User's Manual and one wonders what the author means by "further evidence of such stability" when the evidence is again unavailable.

Both content validity and construct validity are discussed in the User's Manual. Unfortunately, the discussion of content validity turns out to be face validity as determined by expert judges. The authors do offer clear, theory-related definitions of what content the scales attempt to measure but little else. No information is provided about how domains were defined, what process produced scale items, or anything else related to content validity.

The DM scale serves as an example of the CDI's problems with adequate content validity. The scale is a series of vignettes about hypothetical students, and the respondent is to select the best career decision from a list of four responses for each vignette. The authors assert that a range of levels and types of occupations are covered, but no information is provided about how the range was determined, what the range is, how items were selected, how the performance domain was defined, or how the "best" answer was determined. The extent to which personal performance or knowledge can be estimated from what hypothetical others should do would also benefit from elaboration.

The CDI's case for construct validity is stronger, although again one is referred to the Technical Manual. Both the factor structure of the CDI and scale differences among subgroups suggest the CDI has utility for assessing career maturity.

Criterion-related validity is assigned by the authors to future research with the CDI. This seems strange for an instrument clearly intended to be predictive, but unfortunately is not unusual. A review of the literature did find two studies supportive of the CDI's criterion-related validity.

In summary, what is available on the CDI is encouraging. When and if the Technical Manual becomes available, many of the missing pieces may be filled in concerning construction, stability, reliability, and validity. It is unfortunate that an instrument claiming a long history of developmental work has such a limited amount of available supporting data.

[196]

Career Exploration Series. Grades 9-college and adults; 1979–81; CES; self-administered and self-scoring interest inventories for 6 areas: agriculture-conservation-forestry, business-sales-management-clerical, consumer/home economics-related fields, design-performing arts-communication, industrial-mechanics-construction, scientific-mathematical-health; no data on reliability; no norms; 6 booklets: AG-O ('79, 19 pages), BIZ-O ('79, 18 pages), IND-O ('79, 18 pages), CER-O ('81, 19 pages), DAC-O ('81, 18 pages), SCI-O ('79, 18 pages); user's guide (no date, 4 pages); 1983 price data: $42.50 per 35 reusable booklets; $1.35 per reusable booklet; $.20 per additional answer insert folders (one comes with each test booklet); user's guide free with each order; $7.50 per specimen set; (45–60) minutes; Arthur Cutler, Francis Ferry, Robert Kauk, and Robert Robinett; CFKR Career Materials, Inc.*

Review of Career Exploration Series by BRUCE R. FRETZ, Professor of Psychology, University of Maryland, College Park, MD:

The Career Exploration Series is a set of six inventories designed for students who want to identify specific jobs that fit their self-reported educational goals and interest areas. The most unique feature of these inventories, in addition to their high face validity, is that in completing the series students can acquire a wide range of information about occupational tasks, pay levels, and job prospects. However, since each of the six booklets requires 45 to 50 minutes to complete, this series is much more time consuming than other interest inventories when used by students who have yet to focus upon a specific interest area. For these students, Holland's Self-Directed Search or the Strong-Campbell Interest Inventory would be a more appropriate beginning. The Career Exploration Series is best suited for further exploration of career choices once a major occupational area of interest has been identified.

Standard reliability and validity data are not reported for these recently developed inventories. To develop the series, the authors report having used consultants and also provide references that purport to give some indication of the content validity of the measures. The only other psychometric information provided for these instruments is made available by the authors in the form of field test reports. These describe percentages of responses to the various types of questions, as well as students' reports of their satisfaction with the results obtained.

Rather than a manual, a user's guide is provided for the administration of the series. In this guide the authors explain their intention to provide interest inventories that focus on specific occupational fields which: (1) offer a favorable job outlook, (2) are related to specific vocational programs in our educational system, and (3) employ a large percentage of the total labor force in America. No further explanation is given as to how the authors decided on the six inventoried occupational areas. Even though each of these is a logically coherent area, the six are not congruent with any well-recognized system of occupational classification.

Each of the six booklets has basically the same structure. The first section ascertains the level of the students' educational aspirations. In the second section, students are asked to select the kinds of job activities they prefer. In five of the six booklets, students indicate which one of the listed job activity categories is most attractive. In the business area, for example, one chooses the most preferred activity from the list of direct sales, clerical-office work, work with computers and machines, consultant/educational work, and creative work. Unique to the consumer economics booklet is a format requiring students to indicate on a 3-point scale how much they would like to work with data, people, and things.

In the third section of each booklet, students are asked to make a one to three rating of their own interests and skills. For example, in the industrial occupations booklet, respondents rate their interests in problem-solving, the use of tools and machinery, repetitious work, hazardous work, outdoors work, physical stamina, precision work, and creativity.

Once these first three sections are completed, the student has indicated his or her choices pertaining to 10 to 12 different variables, depending on the booklet, related to job preference. These choices are then compared to the corresponding ratings of one to three on each of the same variables, determined by the authors, for 60 different occupations in the booklet's domain. The number of matches between the student's preferences and the given variables for each occupation is then counted to determine how appropriate each career choice might be for the individual. Unfortunately, this task is quite repetitive, and could cause less motivated students to either fail to complete it or to complete it hurriedly.

Interestingly, this monotonous human task is ideal for a computer application. The authors might well modify the series such that after the student has indicated her or his choices for the basic ratings developed through the first three sections, a computer could scan the 60 occupations in each of the areas and provide a listing of the jobs best suited to the student's ratings. This would reduce administration time to a matter of minutes, and could be easily incorporated into the growing repertoire of microcomputer programs available in many schools.

Once the job matching task is completed, students have a list of jobs potentially appropriate for them, based on educational aspirations, task preferences, and interests and skills. Each job listed also gives specific duties entailed, salary range, occupational outlook, and related jobs. Using summary sheets, students are encouraged to consider related as well as high match jobs.

The lack of any studies of predictive validity for these measures, even in terms of whether or not a greater degree of career choice certainty is achieved by using them, leaves potential users totally on their own intuition as to whether or not the measures will be helpful or not.

In sum, for students who already have a focused area of career interest, and who wish to select specific jobs in which they might seek training or employment, these measures offer some exploratory merit. However, because of the lack of standard reliability and validity data, the only known benefits that can be anticipated from these measures is that sufficiently motivated students will report that they found the inventories helpful.

Review of Career Exploration Series by ROBERT B. SLANEY, Associate Professor of Psychology, Southern Illinois University, Carbondale, IL:

Each of these six instruments has a similar format and consists of two major parts: a reusable booklet and an insert. The booklets include directions for responding to self-assessment questions concerning educational goals, preferred job activities, and a number of relevant work interests that are rated on three-point scales. Sixty job titles are listed that have been coded according to the education needed for entry, the major job activities, and the work interests that are represented. Finally, sources to write to for additional information are provided for the listed job titles.

Each of the six booklets has an accompanying insert that lists the same 60 job titles along with their major duties, pay ranges, general outlook for employment, and a number of related occupations. The inserts also contain space at the top for recording the responses to the self-assessment questions that are contained in the booklets. After completing the self-assessment questions, respondents compare their responses with the ratings that are provided in the booklet for each of the 60 jobs. These ratings use the same dimensions that were used for the self-assessment questions. The number of matches for each job title are recorded on the insert and the job titles with the most matches are given particular consideration in the final section of the insert. This section, labelled "Job Research—Putting It All Together for Decision-Making," consists of four parts: (*a*) a review of the matches, (*b*) a listing of preferred jobs, (*c*) a narrowing of the field, and (*d*) further exploration.

There is no manual for these instruments. The four page "User's Guide" contains all the information that is provided and, therefore, many questions are unanswered. For example, it is unclear how the six occupational areas that were selected were chosen and whether they are supposed to represent selected areas or the entire world of work. Perhaps the most surprising initial question that arises is whether respondents are to take one booklet, several, or all six. If only one is taken, who decides which one and what is the basis for this decision? If the respondents decide, do they base their choices on the apparent topics? Although most of the titles are relatively clear, what it is that constitutes "Consumer Economics and Related Occupations" seems an exception. If several booklets are taken, the question of making sense of all of the results becomes an issue. If all of the booklets are responded to, the task takes a great deal of time and tedium becomes a problem. The above issues and questions, as well as many others, are simply not addressed.

Given that a choice is made, the instructions are clearly presented in the nicely printed and illustrated booklets. The issues and questions that are raised for self-assessment certainly seem relevant and well chosen, i.e., they do seem to possess considerable face validity. Relative to the reading level and time required, the User's Guide states that "The reading level of the questions and directions in CES instruments are [sic] sufficiently easy to enable 90% of those taking the instruments to complete the questions and job research in a 45–50 minute period." Although the meaning of this statement may not bear close inspection, the language used in the booklets does seem simple, clear, and articulate. The appropriate age levels are said to be 9th grade through adults, although how this was determined is unclear.

In a statement that does bear closer inspection, the User's Guide notes that: "The CES instruments are EXPLORATORY only. They are not designed as tests. The occupational coding system provides a way to see relationships and will help the student to sort out preferred jobs, but, as with any interest inventory, measurement cannot be precise and valid for all people."

This disclaimer about the instruments being only exploratory, although not to be taken seriously, may serve a useful function by helping to separate two major aspects of these instruments—the measurement aspect and the intervention aspect. Dealing with each of these aspects separately should lead to a clearer understanding of the strengths and weaknesses of the instruments.

Relative to the intervention aspect, some very responsible decisions and suggestions for career exploration have been made. For example, the authors chose the specific occupations for sound reasons, they raise relevant questions and issues, they provide germane, accurate, and up-to-date information on a sizeable number of job titles, and they make useful suggestions for gathering additional information. These aspects of the instruments appear to be quite promising for career exploration exercises.

However, it would be a very serious mistake to commend the intervention or exploratory aspects of the instruments without noting that the matching of the self-assessment ratings with the ratings that are provided on the job titles is extremely basic to these instruments. This matching process raises fundamental questions about these instruments that focus on issues that are basic to psychological measurement.

One question that is raised concerns the source of the ratings of the job titles that appear in the booklets. This issue is not discussed and the need for reliability and validity studies on these ratings is simply not mentioned. Similarly, the lack of reliability and validity studies on the self-assessment ratings is not even acknowledged, nor are the issues surrounding possible sex differences even raised. Another issue that at least deserves some consideration is the procedure used for scoring the matched ratings. At present, all of the separate items receive equal weight although it seems highly unlikely that they are of equal importance to all subjects. It is also unclear why 3-point scales were chosen, especially when only exact matches are counted. At the very least some acknowledgement that the authors have considered these latter issues would be reassuring. Clearly, it is not adequate to state that the instruments "are exploratory only." Measurement issues are central for these instruments and, in fact, determine which occupational titles will be explored.

It should be clear that a great deal of basic research is needed on these measures. The first priority should be studies that address reliability and validity issues. When these studies are adequately performed for each of the instruments, the results should be compiled in a manual which addresses the issues raised above and others concerning instrument development and use. Until this basic work is performed, it would be premature to recommend that these measures be used in career exploration.

[197]

Career Guidance Inventory. Grades 7–13 students interested in trades, services, and technologies; revision in examiner's manual only; 1972–79; CGI; 25 scores: 14 engineering related trades (carpentry and woodworking, masonry, mechanical repair, painting and decorating, plumbing and pipefitting, printing, tool and die making, sheet metal and welding, drafting and design, mechanical engineering, industrial production, civil and architectural engineering, electrical engineering, chemical and laboratory) and 11 nonengineering related services (environmental health, agriculture and forestry, business management, communications, data processing, sales, transportation services, protective services, medical laboratory, nursing, food service); 1 form ('72, 15 pages); manual ('79, 7 pages); separate answer sheets must be used; 1983 price data: $1.25 per test; $20 per 25 self-scoring answer sheets and profiles; $1 per manual; $3 per specimen set; administration time not reported; James E. Oliver; Educational Guidance, Inc.*

For a review by Bert W. Westbrook, see 8:996.

Review of Career Guidance Inventory by JAMES B. ROUNDS, JR., Assistant Professor of Counseling and Educational Psychology, The State University of New York at Buffalo, Buffalo, NY:

The Career Guidance Inventory (CGI), developed for use with students in high schools, trade schools, and junior colleges, was devised as a measure of 25 interest areas in nonprofessional fields. The manual suggests that the CGI is to be used by counselors in the guidance of students making vocational decisions.

The inventory has so many negative features that only those that seriously affect the score interpretations will be mentioned. These relate to the scale construction procedures, method of scoring, normative score interpretations, absence of validity data, and the limited reliability data. Some of these negative features are due to the omission of explanatory information and to inaccuracy of reporting in the revised 1979 manual, but most are due to the lack of research data. (The manual does not contain a single reference.)

A major problem is the arbitrary selection of the 25 vocational interest areas and the misleading implication that the scales actually measure interest in these organized work-related areas. The rationale for selection of the 25 areas is vague: "they encompassed the semiprofessional curricula offered in secondary and post-secondary schools." The 25 vocational interest areas vary in breadth, depth, and level of generality, and thus cannot be meaningfully compared. Several interest scales (e.g., Sales, Business Management) include a narrow set of work activities which can be performed in different industries and organizations; other scales (e.g., Masonry, Plumbing and Pipefitting) include work activities involved in only a few occupations; and the remaining areas (e.g., Communications) include a broad, diverse set of occupational activities. The CGI's forced-choice format notwithstanding, these interest areas simply cannot be meaningfully compared.

The manual does not offer an analysis of the item content. Definitions of the interest areas, procedures used to generate and sample items, and data on the internal structure of the inventory are omitted. The manual claims that 24 statements are included in each scale when in fact there are only 20 statements per scale, and these are not always unique. At least 3 scales (the reviewer examined 5 of the 25 scales in detail) have less than 20 statements per scale: Carpentry and Woodworking and Food Service scales, 19 statements; Communications scale, 18 statements. Repetition of the scale statements (e.g., 2 of the 18 statements appear twice) accounts for the discrepancy. Intended or unintended, it is indefensible and the test booklet should be corrected immediately.

The item statements are a mixture of occupational titles, school subjects, and work activities, which probably introduces error variance. Many of the items are redundant ("Work as a bricklayer," "Work as a stone setter," "Work as a brick mason for a contractor"), thus obtaining scale homogeneity at the loss of generality. Some of the item statements may be incorrectly keyed. For example, the statement "Sell radio commercial time to businesses" may be more appropriately keyed on the Sales scale rather than the Communications scale. The apparently heterogeneous item content of the Communications scale (e.g., "Learn to operate radio broadcasting equipment," "Be a movie actor") may preclude meaningful score interpretations. An incomplete block design was used to assemble the statements in a paired format. This forced-choice format eliminates a general like-dislike response bias dimension. It does not control for desirability unless statements with similar endorsement or preference frequency are assigned to the same pairs—which the CGI fails to do.

The inventory itself consists of a 14-page reusable test booklet listing 250 pairs of statements and a 1-page, self-scoring answer sheet on which the respondent places an "x" in a box to indicate which of the two statements is "of greater interest." Each statement includes a number from 1 to 25 in parentheses; the "x" is placed in the same-number row on the answer sheet as that appearing at the end of the statement. The directions for this task are not easy to follow, and the administration information in the manual is insufficient as well. Mistakes in marking the answer sheet are all too likely, given the complexity of that task, and the scoring key appears on the test forms, raising the possibility that responses to the inventory will be affected by its presence.

The claim that the "current revisions to this Examiner's Manual are designed to provide additional information consistent with recommendations implementing Title IX of the Educational Amendment to the National Education Act" is undercut by the manual's failure to provide norms. Provided instead are arbitrary normative interpretations printed on the test profile. For example, raw scores from 1 to 3 are "very low," 4 to 6 are "low," and so on to raw scores of 18 to 20 labeled as "very high." The basis for the cutting points is not given in the manual; in fact, the interpretative statements are not even mentioned in the manual. These normative interpretations are also puzzling in that the item format results in ipsative scores and the manual notes correctly that ipsative scores can only indicate relative strength of the interest field, not absolute strength.

Although the seven-page manual has other irritating features (e.g., no sample profiles and no systematic discussion of how to interpret the scores), the most serious are the absence of validity data and the presence of inadequate reliability data. While the manual claims the inventory has content validity, no explanation or reference to evidence is attempted. Only one type of reliability data is presented: split-half correlations with a Spearman-Brown correction to obtain the full-test reliability estimates. Although 21 of the 25 scales have acceptable internal consistency estimates, these estimates are inflated by item redundancy. The estimates are based on a group of 100 junior college students, the sex composition of which is not specified. Given what is known about sex differences in vocational interest item endorsements, analyses must be conducted separately for females and males. Finally, no test-retest correlations are presented.

Fortunately, there are other more reliable and valid inventories, similar in purpose to the Career Guidance Inventory and based upon more extensive empirical research. They include: the Career Assessment Inventory, patterned after the Strong Vocational Interest Blank and designed specifically for individuals seeking work that does not require a 4-year college degree; the Self-Directed Search, a self-administered, self-scored measure of Holland's six occupational types; the Jackson Vocational Interest Survey, which consists of 289 pairs of statements describing occupational activities and provides scores pertaining to work roles and styles; and the Minnesota Importance Questionnaire, a measure of 20 work-related rewards in which an individual's scores are compared to occupational reinforcer patterns to predict satisfaction in over 180 skilled trades, technical, and service occupations. A user who wants to have a measure of nonprofessional interests would be better advised to use any one of the above inventories.

CONCLUSION. The author should withdraw the Career Guidance Inventory from publication until the scale content is corrected and the normative interpretations are removed from the profile. Once these corrections are made it is recommended that research be directed at building an empirical base for score interpretations. Under no circumstances should the CGI be used in counseling or guidance until adequate normative, reliability, and validity evidence is presented and a revised manual is published providing accurate and adequate information for use of the inventory.

[198]

Career Interests Test. Young persons and adults; 1971–83; 6 scores: outdoor-physical, scientific-theoretical, social service, aesthetic-literary, commercial-clerical, practical-technical; norms consist of means and standard deviations; 1 form ('71, 4 pages); manual ('83, 17 pages); 1984 price data: £2.25 per 25 tests; manual and scoring key free on request with order; 75p per specimen set; (30) minutes; Educational & Industrial Test Services Ltd. [England].*

Review of Career Interests Test by CHRISTOPHER BORMAN, Professor of Educational Psychology, Texas A&M University, College Station, TX:

The Career Interests Test was developed as a simple and easy-to-administer instrument to be used with young persons and adults. It is designed to identify the basic occupational interests of individuals. There is no time limit for completion of the test, but the manual states that most test subjects should be able to complete the instrument within a half hour. The instrument was originally published in 1971, but the test and manual were revised in 1983. The original version of the Career Interests Test had separate forms for males and females, but the current form is unisex. The 1971 manual did not include any data on the test, but there are tables in the 1983 test manual giving data on the intercorrelations of the six scales comprising the instrument, means and standard deviations for the scales, correlations with ability measures, one concurrent validity study, and data on the internal consistency of the instrument.

The Career Interests Test comprises four lists, each containing 5 job titles representative of each of six scales—a total of 30 in each list. For each of the four lists respondents are asked to mark the 15 jobs that they would like to do and the 15 jobs that they would not like to do. The respondents are then requested to choose the 6 jobs they would like to do even better than the others and the 6 jobs they would like even worse than the others. Finally, the test subjects are requested to mark the 1 job that they like best and the job that they like least in each of the four lists. The test manual explains that since the Career Interests Test uses a "forced choice" technique of construction, there is no need for norms. The intensities with which the various interests are held by test subjects are compared. The manual states, "As has already been indicated, actuarial norms are meaningless in the context of an interest test." This reviewer disagrees with the statement and sees the absence of norms as a serious weakness of the instrument.

This instrument was developed in England and is published by an English company. If the Career Interests Test is going to be used widely in the United States, this reviewer believes that a special version of the instrument should be developed for use in the United States because a number of the job titles are not representative of occupations in the United States.

Six categories of interest are indicated by the Career Interests Test: (1) Outdoor-Physical, (2) Scientific-Theoretical, (3) Social Service, (4) Aesthetic-Literary, (5) Commercial-Clerical, and (6) Practical-Technical. Descriptions of each of these six scales are given in the manual, which should aid in the interpretation of the scores. It is this reviewer's opinion that the first four scales are very similar to John Holland's personality orientations and environmental models of Realistic, Investigative, Social, and Artistic. The remaining two scales (Commercial-Clerical and Practical-Technical) relate to Holland's Conventional category. The only one of Holland's six personality types missing from the Career Interests Test is the Enterprising category.

The directions for administering and scoring the Career Interests Test are clear, and the chances for errors are limited. A scoring key giving detailed instructions comes with the instrument. The raw scores for each of the six interest categories are translated into scale scores that run from 1 to 20 with a mean of 10. This scoring scale assumes equal means and variances for each of the six interest categories, but means and standard deviations for a sample of 325 subjects reported in the test manual indicates differences among the six interest categories. Therefore, there is a certain amount of error involved in converting all of the raw scores to the same 1–20 scale. The manual states that the instrument is unisex, but the means and standard deviations reported in the manual for the same sample of 325 subjects indicates differences in performance between males and females—another potential for error in the interpretation of the scores.

The original test manual (1971) did not give any reliability data, but the 1983 revision gives data from one study of internal consistency (split-half), with the coefficients for each of the scales ranging from .77 to .86. This reliability study used 80 subjects but no information is given on who the subjects were—a shortcoming for all studies reported in the test manual. No information is reported on test-retest reliability of the Career Interests Test; this is an important piece of missing data on the instrument, because one of the most useful types of reliability evidence for an interest inventory is consistency over time.

The most serious shortcoming of the Career Interests Test is a lack of evidence of predictive validity. This absence of predictive validity is a condition common among interest inventories, but it is a serious weakness because interest inventories are based on the assumption that predictions can be made from the scores. One study of concurrent validity is reported in the manual; the Career Interests Test is compared to the Rothwell-Miller Interest Blank, and the correlations between comparable scales on the two instruments are fairly high. The problem with this concurrent validity study is that little is known about the quality of the Rothwell-Miller because reviews are not readily available on the instrument.

This reviewer does not recommend use of the Career Interests Test at this time because of almost no validity data on the instrument and only one reliability study (a study of internal consistency). Another serious weakness is the lack of norms for the instrument. The manual states that this interest inventory is unisex, but data reported in the manual indicate differences in performance between males and females. Other interest inventories such as Holland's Self Directed Search, the Kuder General Interest Survey (Form E), the Ohio Vocational Interest Survey, and the Interest Determination, Exploration, and Assessment System (IDEAS) would be far better to use in situations where the Career Interests Test might be considered.

Review of Career Interests Test by DAN ZAKAY, Senior Lecturer, Department of Psychology, Tel Aviv University, Israel:

GENERAL DESCRIPTION. The Career Interests Test (CIT) is designed as a tool for determining the relative career interests of young persons and adults. In its present form the test is unisex. Six categories of career interests are indicated by CIT: (1) Outdoor-Physical, (2) Scientific-Theoretical, (3) Social Service, (4) Aesthetic-Literary, (5) Commercial-Clerical, (6) Practical-Technical. The six categories are quite independent of each other, as is reflected by the intercorrelations among them. The test is composed of four lists of 30 jobs each. In each list 5 jobs are representative of each category. Test subjects can complete the test by following the instructions which appear on the test form. However, it should be ensured that test subjects understand their task well because in cases of errors or even of a slight deviation from the instructions, it is necessary to do the test all over again. This is a point of weakness. The test subject is required in the first phase to choose from each list those jobs which s/he would like to do and those which s/he would not like to do. This is done in a forced choice method so that 15 jobs must be chosen in each category. In the second phase the test subject is required to choose from each list the 6 jobs which s/he would like to do even better than others and the 6 jobs which s/he would like even worse. This procedure repeats itself for a third time in which only one job of each type is chosen. The administration of the test takes about 20–30 minutes. A manual is available.

SCORING. The scoring can be done by hand by using a scoring key. The scoring is quite simple and is based on adding the number of jobs from each interest category which were liked and subtracting the number of jobs which were rejected. However, scoring might be tedious and confusing. It is therefore recommended to use a computer program which is available from the publisher or can be easily programmed by a lay programmer.

The raw score in each category of career interest can range from +44 to −44. The raw scores obtained should be translated into "scale scores" by referring to a table given in the manual or the scoring key. However, no rationale is given for this translation, and this is a major flaw in the manual which should be corrected.

VALIDITY. Only concurrent validity evidence is presented, and it is based on correlations between each of the six interest categories and the categories of the Rothwell-Miller Interest Blank. The validity coefficients are reasonable for four categories, ranging from .74 to .83. The validity coefficients for the Social-Service and Practical-Technical categories are moderate (.54 and .55 respectively). However, construct validity tells almost nothing about the utility of CIT, and what is needed is research to determine its predictive validity.

INTERNAL CONSISTENCY. A measure of internal consistency is given by a correlation between two parts of the test, similar to a split-half correlation. This is done by comparing the scores obtained for each category in list 2 + list 3, and list 3 + list 4. The results are moderate to high reliabilities (.77 to .86). However, a test-retest reliability is required as well, especially since it is recommended to administer the test a second time in case of an error in the first administration.

INTERPRETATION OF THE "SCALE SCORES." The interpretation is based on the profile of scores obtained, from which it can be determined if there is a positive interest or an aversion toward a specific category, etc. However, in some cases the interpretation is not unequivocal. This is especially true for complex profiles in which two strong positive interests are associated with one or more strong aversions. This situation calls for further development and refinement of the CIT. No norms are available; although information about means and standard deviations is given, the information is based on a small N and cannot serve as norms. This makes the interpretation of scores even more difficult. In terms of the meaning of the scores, it should be kept in mind that the CIT scores are mainly reflective of interest-attitudes based on stereotyped social norms and do not reflect the needed abilities. Hence, the interest pattern should be used in conjunction with an adequate assessment of the fundamental ability structure of the person, as is correctly mentioned in the manual.

SUMMARY. The CIT can be used as a guidance tool, but in a limited way. It should be remembered that the CIT does not measure abilities but only attitudes. The scores of the CIT are not easy to interpret because of the lack of sound norms and because the interpretation of a complex profile is ambiguous. The predictive validity of the test is not known. A counselor who is well aware of all these limitations might use the CIT as one source of information to be utilized with other sources in the guidance process.

[199]

Career Maturity Inventory. Grades 6–12; 1973–78; CMI; machine-scorable edition incorporating Counseling Form and Competence Test available for adults; 3 tests; manual ('78, 54 pages); handbook ('78, 46 pages); profile ('78, 2 pages); separate answer sheets (CompuScan, IBM 1230) must be used; 1984 price data: $55.30 per 35 sets of 3 tests; answer sheets: $6.50 per 50 CompuScan, $11.50 per 50 IBM 1230; $21 per set of 4 IBM 1230 scoring stencils; $15 per 100 profiles; $5.15 per handbook; $4.25 per manual; $8.25 per specimen set; scoring service ($100 minimum): $.91 and over per student for 3 tests, $.88 and over per students for any 1 test; John O. Crites; CTB/McGraw-Hill.*

a) ATTITUDE SCALE, SCREENING FORM A-2. 1 form ('78, 7 pages); $24.15 per 35 tests; (30) minutes.

b) ATTITUDE SCALE, COUNSELING FORM B-1. Extension of the Attitude Scale, Screening Form A-2; 5 career decision-making scores: decisiveness, involvement, independence, orientation, compromise; validity data based on an earlier, shorter version; 1 form ('78, 7 pages); $24.15 per 35 tests; (40) minutes.

c) COMPETENCE TEST. 5 scores: self-appraisal, occupational information, goal selection, planning, problem solving; Form A-1 ('78, 38 pages); $40.25 per 35 tests; (120) minutes.

See T3:374 (48 references); for reviews by Martin R. Katz and Donald G. Zytowski, and an excerpted review by Garth Sorenson, see 8:997 (152 references); see also T2:2103 (35 references).

TEST REFERENCES

1. Dillard, J. M., & Campbell, N. J. Influences of Puerto Rican, Black, and Anglo parents' career behavior on their adolescent children's career development. THE VOCATIONAL GUIDANCE QUARTERLY, 1981, 30, 139–148.
2. Gardner, D. C., Beatty, G. J., & Bigelow, E. A. Locus of control and career maturity: A pilot evaluation of a life-planning and career development program for high school students. ADOLESCENCE, 1981, 16, 557–562.
3. Wiggins, J. D., & Moody, A. A field-based comparison of four career-exploration approaches. THE VOCATIONAL GUIDANCE QUARTERLY, 1981, 30, 15–20.
4. Alvi, S. A., & Khan, S. B. A study of the criterion-related validity of Crites' Career Maturity Inventory. EDUCATIONAL AND PSYCHOLOGICAL MEASUREMENT, 1982, 42, 1285–1288.
5. Guthrie, W. R., & Herman, A. Vocational maturity and its relationship to Holland's theory of vocational choice. JOURNAL OF VOCATIONAL BEHAVIOR, 1982, 21, 196–205.
6. Alvi, S. A., & Khan, S. B. An investigation into the construct validity of Crites' Career Maturity model. JOURNAL OF VOCATIONAL BEHAVIOR, 1983, 22, 174–181.
7. Burkhead, E. J., & Cope, C. S. Career maturity and physically disabled college students. REHABILITATION COUNSELING BULLETIN, 1983, 27, 142–150.
8. Chodzinski, R. T., & Randhawa, B. S. Validity of Career Maturity Inventory. EDUCATIONAL AND PSYCHOLOGICAL MEASUREMENT, 1983, 43, 1163–1173.
9. Kapes, J. T., & Baker, G. E. Exploring the effects of industrial arts on career maturity in grades seven through twelve: A synthesis of cross-sectional and longitudinal methods. JOURNAL OF INDUSTRIAL TEACHER EDUCATION, 1983, 20(2), 18–35.
10. Khan, S. B., & Alvi, S. A. Educational, social, and psychological correlates of vocational maturity. JOURNAL OF VOCATIONAL BEHAVIOR, 1983, 22, 357–364.
11. Krebs, E. A study of the relationship of moral development and social interest to vocational maturity of adolescents. CONTEMPORARY EDUCATION, 1983, 54, 299–305.
12. Palmo, A. J., & Lutz, J. G. The relationship of performance on the CMI to intelligence with disadvantaged youngsters. MEASUREMENT AND EVALUATION IN GUIDANCE, 1983, 16, 139–148.

[200]

Career Problem Check List. Ages 14–17; 1983; CPCL; no scores, 7 areas: problems at school or college, problems in making decisions, problems at home, problems in obtaining specific occupational information, problems in applying for a job or for a course, problems in starting work, problems outside work; 1 form (4 pages); manual (16 pages); 1983 price data: £7.95 per 40 checklists; £3.95 per manual; (10–15) minutes; A. D. Crowley; NFER-Nelson Publishing Co. [England].*

Review of Career Problem Check List by NICHOLAS A. VACC, Professor, and JAMES PICKERING, Doctoral Student, Counselor Education, University of North Carolina, Greensboro, NC:

The Career Problem Check List (CPCL), developed in Great Britain, is based on items written by career officers (counselors) and career teachers, and open-ended questionnaires completed by students. The instrument has had several revisions based on analyses of data collected from "several hundred" secondary-school and college students; exact figures, however, are not reported. Designed for 14- to 17-year-old students, the instrument is composed of frequently encountered, career-related problems. Students are asked to (*a*) underline problems they are experiencing, (*b*) circle problems that are of most concern to them, and (*c*) complete three open-ended questions (e.g., "What type of work would you like to do when you leave school or college?").

The CPCL's 100 items are classified into seven generic problem areas: (*a*) school and college, (*b*) decision-making, (*c*) home, (*d*) obtaining specific occupational information, (*e*) applying for a job or education, (*f*) beginning work, and (*g*) outside work. No criterion or method is reported for the selection of items or the assignment of generic problem areas. Also, some categories seem incomplete (e.g., there is no mention of values in the school and college area nor is the skill of resume writing mentioned in the area of applying for a job or education).

The CPCL is designed to aid counselors in rapidly identifying difficulties experienced by students making career plans. The author reports that CPCL is an alternative to pre-interview questionnaires that are directed toward collecting information concerning a student's or client's hobbies and work interest, questionnaires typically used to identify the type of work for which an individual is best suited. The CPCL differs from pre-interview questionnaires by purportedly permitting individuals to indicate problems for which they are seeking clarification during a counseling session. It is also intended as an aid to the counselor in forming student groups to discuss common problem areas.

The CPCL's value within counseling programs has not been empirically documented by the author. Yet to be answered are questions such as under what conditions is the instrument most helpful? When would its use be inadvisable? Is it an effective method for establishing groups? How much time, if any, is saved by using the CPCL?

Because the CPCL does not produce scores, analysis is primarily directed to the individual items and the clustering of themes within areas. The author indicates that determining general and specific themes is a skill that is acquired through use of the CPCL, but information should be included concerning the type of training or experience needed before a person becomes skilled and whether the novice user should be required to receive supervision in analyzing the checklist. Individuals who mark a large number of items may be in greater need of assistance, but such determination is inapplicable because there exists no frame of reference. Norms are not included and there is no presentation of data concerning factors that may contribute to the selection of a large number of items, such as the author's suggestion on page 3 that anxiety about the whole process of leaving school may influence an individual's selection of items. Counselors are encouraged to check how many items are underlined, what kind of items are selected, and whether or not any unusual items are selected. However, what constitutes an unusual item is unclear. The author is commended for emphasizing the importance of allowing individual students or clients to explain how they interpreted items, but application of the same recommendation to group work is not mentioned.

The manual and advertisements need to state the specific audience for whom the CPCL is intended. If the CPCL is intended for use in the United States, a serious problem exists with wording in some items that may be unfamiliar because of (*a*) different grammatical structures; (*b*) inapplicable content (e.g., the reference to a National Insurance number card in item 73); and (*c*) uniquely British phrases (e.g., "being laid-off or made redundant" in item 90).

The CPCL is more content-referenced than norm-referenced. Because there are no derivative scores, a student's or client's responses are directly interpreted. The manual provides response frequencies for 510 students to be used not as norms, but as a guide only. This is well advised by the author because the sample is small and the information reported is inadequate for making comparisons. The author also cautions that responses between schools vary according to areas of the country, which suggests that perhaps national and local demographic norms are needed for sex, race, socioeconomic status, and grade level.

In summary, the major problems with the CPCL seem to be (*a*) a cultural bias toward students in Great Britain, (*b*) vague or incomplete information concerning its technical development, and (*c*) a lack of references to support its use. Aiding counselors and clients with an easy-to-use, time efficient instrument for identifying difficulties experienced in making career plans is a good idea, but the CPCL needs further development before it can be recommended. More information is needed concerning item development, norms, reliability, and validity. Until more empirical data are available, the manual and announcements as well as advertisements for the CPCL should temper claims of the instrument's effectiveness in meeting its purpose. For example, the publishing house reports that the CPCL is a "comprehensive approach....provides an in-depth analysis....(and) can also be employed to monitor the success of career guidance programmes." At this time we do not believe these claims are justified.

[201]

Career Profile System. Life insurance agents and candidates; 1983; selection tool to predict "candidate's chances of success as an insurance sales representative"; total score only; no data on reliability; no norms; 2 editions: insurance, financial services; 2 levels: initial (for unexperienced candidates), advanced (for experienced candidates); 1 form for each level (20–24 pages, reuseable questionnaire); answer sheet (2 pages); manual (18 pages); distribution restricted to home offices of member life insurance companies; 1983 price data: $5 per questionnaire (specify edition/level); $1,000–$1,200 (depending on level) per per 100 answer sheets (includes computer scoring service and a 4-page report on candidates scoring above cutoff); $4 per manual; $12 per administrator's kit; English-speaking Canada and French-speaking Canada editions available; other system materials available from publisher; (55–65) minutes; Life Insurance Marketing and Research Association, Inc.*

[202]

Career Skills Assessment Program. High school and college students; 1977–79; CSAP; experimental edition; 6 tests; validity data not reported in manual, available in separate research report for *b, c, d,* below; no norms; manual ('78, 114 pages); directions for administering ('78, 22 pages); technical report ('79, 151 pages); sound filmstrip kit (no date); separate answer sheets must be used; 1983 price data: educator's starter set: $25 per set of 25 exercise booklets, response sheets, and self-instructional guides for any one test; $13.50 per 25 reusable exercise booklets for any one test; $13.50 per 25 sets of response sheets and guides for any one test; $48.50 per sound filmstrip kit; $4 per manual; $6 per specimen set; scoring service, $.33 per student (minimum of 100 per content area); (70–90) minutes per test; Career Skills Assessment Program of The College Board.*

a) SELF EVALUATION AND DEVELOPMENTAL SKILLS. 1977–78; 5 scores: understanding individual differences, evaluating individual characteristics and test results, changing personal characteristics and behavior, locating and interpreting information about self, applying knowledge about self to career opportunities; 1 form ('77, 21 pages); self-instructional guide ('78, 18 pages); response sheet ('77, 3 pages).

b) CAREER AWARENESS SKILLS. 1977; 4 scores: relating abilities/values/needs/and experience to career choices, locating/evaluating/and interpreting information for career choices, knowing facts about career opportunities, finding out about educational requirements for occupations; 1 form (15 pages); guide (15 pages); response set (3 pages).

c) CAREER DECISION–MAKING SKILLS. 1977; 7 scores: defining the problem, establishing an action plan, clarifying values, identifying alternatives, discovering probable outcomes, eliminating alternatives systematically, starting action; 1 form (23 pages); guide (19 pages); response sheet (3 pages).

d) EMPLOYMENT SEEKING SKILLS. 1977; 5 scores: anticipating job prospects, finding and interpreting facts and sources on available jobs, identifying appropriately written letters/resumes/and applications, describing appropriate appearance and behavior as one is interviewed and evaluated for a job, evaluating when a specific job fits a person's needs and interests; 1 form (19 pages); guide (15 pages); response sheet (3 pages).

e) WORK EFFECTIVENESS SKILLS. 1977–78; 7 scores: identifying employer and employee responsibilities, developing effective work habits, achieving effective working relationships with co-workers, managing work situation to achieve personal satisfaction, giving and receiving supervision effectively, advancing on the job, planning job changes; 1 form ('78, 19 pages); guide ('78, 18 pages); response sheet ('77, 3 pages).

f) PERSONAL ECONOMICS SKILLS. 1977; 7 scores: figuring your paycheck and income tax, understanding personal banking procedures, purchasing goods and services and paying bills, insuring yourself and your possessions, borrowing and using credit, understanding investment procedures, understanding basic economic ideas; 1 form (23 pages); guide (19 pages); response sheet (3 pages).

See T3:375 (1 reference).

TEST REFERENCES

1. Krumboltz, J. D., Scherba, D. S., Hamel, D. A., & Mitchell, L. K. Effect of training in rational decision making on the quality of simulated career decisions. JOURNAL OF COUNSELING PSYCHOLOGY, 1982, 29, 618–625.

Review of Career Skills Assessment Program by JEFFREY H. GREENHAUS, Department of Management & Organizational Sciences, Drexel University, Philadelphia, PA:

The Career Skills Assessment Program (CSAP) was designed to help institutions (primarily schools and colleges) plan, implement, and/or evaluate career development programs, and to help individuals enhance their career development skills. In order to accomplish these objectives, The College Board has developed six subtests, each of which measures proficiency in a career skill content area: (*a*) Self-Evaluation and Development; (*b*) Career Awareness; (*c*) Career Decision-Making; (*d*) Employment-Seeking; (*e*) Work Effectiveness; and (*f*) Personal Economics. Each of the six content areas is, in turn, comprised of more specific skills relevant to the particular area.

Each subtest was designed to be administered during approximately one class period, and institutions may use one, several, or all of the subtests in the CSAP. Each subtest packet includes: (*a*) reusable test booklets that contain 60–70 items; (*b*) self/machine scorable response sheets; and (*c*) self-instructional guides (to be used by students) that discuss skills in the content area (often with dialogues and stories illustrating the application of the skills), explain the preferred response to each item, and suggest sources of additional information.

I should indicate at the outset my perception that the CSAPs strengths considerably outweigh its limitations. The major strengths of the CSAP, in my opinion, are the rigorous manner in which it was developed and the explicitness of its documentation.

First, the procedure used to identify the six career skill content areas and their requisite skills was systematic and thoroughly described in the handbook. The content domains were specified in consultation with experts from a five-state Career Education Consortium and were based, in part, on lists of career education objectives, recommendations of professional organizations, and the career development literature. Although not necessarily exhaustive, the six career skill areas are thought to be "useful for achieving a personally satisfying career." This was not an exercise in arm-chair scale development.

In addition, the items written to assess each of the specific skills were reviewed by subject-matter experts, checked for possible bias against members of minority, cultural, and gender groups, and assessed for reading difficulty level. The handbook contains detailed descriptions of item and scale characteristics. (Although I assume the subject-matter experts reached consensus on the preferred response for each item, the procedure was not specified in the handbook.)

The procedures by which domains and skills were identified and items were written provide support for the content validity of the CSAP. The six content areas seem to represent significant elements of the career management process, and the items within each subtest appear to be representative of the career skill domain. To the extent to which items are representative, subtest scores can be used to draw appropriate inferences regarding students' proficiency in that domain.

However, since content domains can vary across different situations, no measurement operation is content valid in all circumstances. An institution's career education program may emphasize specific career skills that only partially overlap with the skill areas assessed by the CSAP. Therefore, The College Board provides a manual for institutions to conduct local content validity studies. This detailed manual enables an institution to specify its career education objectives and programs, and to determine the relevance of the CSAP to its own needs. Such analyses may lead some institutions to use only certain parts of the CSAP and to determine where supplementary assessment techniques will be necessary.

Another strength of the CSAP is the quality of the written material. I think most students will find the exercises and the self-instructional guides interesting. Furthermore, the guide's inclusion of explanations for each item can provide a sense of understanding and closure that one doesn't often find in measuring devices of this kind. In fact, I feel the self-instructional guide is an integral part of the CSAP.

Finally, The College Board should be commended for identifying some of the major limitations and potential abuses of the CSAP. Cautious institutions should benefit from the caveats and suggestions offered in the handbook.

The primary limitation of the CSAP, in my opinion, is that it lacks evidence of criterion-related validity. Thus, a student's score on a particular subtest does not necessarily predict his or her successful application of that career skill but rather assesses the student's current knowledge regarding that area. For example, a high score on the Self-Evaluation and Development subtest does not indicate that the student has a clear and accurate appraisal of him/herself or that the student will make an appropriate career choice. Rather, it suggests that the student possesses the skills, knowledges, or abilities to develop self-awareness to apply such knowledge in career decision-making situations. Knowledge and effective action are not identical and, to its credit, this limitation of the CSAP is acknowledged in the handbook.

In sum, my overall appraisal of the CSAP is quite positive. Institutions should find the CSAP useful in assessing students' current proficiencies in the six career skill areas and in suggesting areas in which curricula and programs may be needed. Institutions with ongoing career education programs can use the CSAP to monitor students' proficiencies before and after exposure to the programs.

From a student development perspective, the CSAP seems promising. However, the self-instructional guide appears essential to the learning process, and coordination of the CSAP with counseling and/or career education classes would maximize a student's benefit from the CSAP. Follow-up, in other words, is essential.

These factors place a responsibility on institutions to know what they want to accomplish regarding career education, to assess students' proficiencies, and to follow-up student assessment with effective programs. The enhancement of career skills seems particularly important in these times of rapidly changing technologies and job opportunities and alternative lifestyles. I feel the CSAP can be a useful vehicle for institutions to face this challenge.

Review of Career Skills Assessment Program by JAMES D. WIGGINS, Coordinator, Agency and School Counseling Programs, University of Delaware, Newark, DE:

Six content modules, whose titles are noted above, are presented in true "College Board" testing fashion for assessment purposes. Each module is presented through the reading of an exercise booklet, with assessment then based on answers to 60–70 multiple-choice questions. Answer sheets may be machine- or self-scored. A follow-up self-instructional guide accompanies each exercise booklet.

The Career Skills Assessment Program (CSAP) offers a great deal of information for counselor and student alike. Unfortunately, it is packaged in such a format that it is unlikely to spark much interest in either group in the secondary schools with which this reviewer is familiar. This opinion is based on recent studies with various career assessment, exploration, and selection programs in a variety of schools (Wiggins & Moody, 1982). Most students are simply not interested in programs that are general in nature; it is difficult to convince them that "this is for your own good." Also, although modules may be skipped, the overall assessment procedures necessary to complete parts of the CSAP do not encourage self-initiated further career exploration. The CSAP would need to be coordinated by a very skilled counselor or teacher in order not to be downright boring.

The namby-pamby characters found in the exercise booklets were actually irritating to this reviewer. Real people don't express themselves in such a fashion and most students dislike such condescension.

On the plus side, the informational sections of the CSAP are thoroughly and accurately presented although the same data may be found in a number of other references. The guides also offer explanations for each "best response" assessment question. While these are factual, they seem of limited value (e.g., few students are interested in finding out who assists bricklayers in their work—unless the students are specifically interested in the construction field). If they do have such interests, they usually know answers to questions posed in the CSAP by the time they reach secondary school age.

The sheer amount of material presented may be misleading. A program that is for everyone may be of limited value to any one person. The publishers seem to have ignored the vital question, "What do students want and what will they use in career assessment areas?" Many persons simply want assurance that their tentative career choices are reasonable. A smaller number want to explore more occupations—often in a specific career area. Still others have career-connected personal and emotional concerns such as lack of family support for career choices, doubts as to ability, and financial limitations. While most students are interested in skill and occupational information related to their expressed interests, few are interested in the total occupational world. Forcing them to do the CSAP exercises would only prove that we can make career assessment as boring as any badly-taught academic subject.

Statistical data presented shows adequate reliability coefficients for studies reported. No evidence is presented regarding criterion-related validity. A major weakness is noted by the publisher; each CSAP measure is highly correlated with a measure of verbal ability. This may be a "principal factor influencing performance."

Better choices than the CSAP abound for individual assessment and exploration. These include The Self-Directed Search and the Career Maturity Inventory. The need for interest and career skills assessment seems self-evident in an ever-changing world. However, the CSAP is not a true assessment instrument; it is more of a reading test. Other methods of skills assessment, such as work samples related to specific occupations, would seem to offer more to students than the CSAP.

REVIEWER'S REFERENCES

Wiggins, J. D., & Moody, A. A field-based comparison of four career-exploration approaches. VOCATIONAL GUIDANCE QUARTERLY, 1982, 30, 15–20.

[203]

Carlson Psychological Survey. Criminal offenders; 1981–82; CPS; 5 scale scores: chemical abuse, thought disturbance, anti-social tendencies, self-depreciation, validity; 1 form ('81, 14 pages); manual ('82, 32 pages); score sheet ('81, 1 page); profile ('81, 1 page); 1983 price data: $15 per examination kit including 10 question and answer booklets, 10 scoring sheets, and 10 profiles; $14 and less per 25 question and answer booklets; $4.25 and less per 25 scoring sheets; $4.25 and less per 25 profiles; $8 per manual; [10–20] minutes; Kenneth A. Carlson; Research Psychologists Press, Inc.*

Review of Carlson Psychological Survey by H. C. GANGULI, Professor and Head, Department of Psychology, University of Delhi, Delhi, India:

The author considers this test as "a psychometric instrument intended primarily for individuals accused or convicted of crimes, or otherwise referred for socially deviant behaviour." It has four scales referred to as Chemical Abuse, Thought Disturbance, Antisocial Tendencies, and Self-Depreciation and also an added Validity scale.

Through actual administration of this test to subjects, this reviewer has noted the following: (*a*) Minimum time required for taking the test will be 6 to 8 minutes for subjects of grade 8 or higher education. Time for writing marginal comments will be extra and variable. (*b*) The language and format are such that the test can be administered to subjects with reading skills as low as grade 4. (*c*) Response alternatives are well thought out and respondents do not have much difficulty in fitting their answers to these. (*d*) Respondents tend to look upon the CPS as a "neat" instrument because there are not too many items, language is simple and easily understood, and the test format and the booklet are artistic and esthetically pleasing. Respondent acceptance of this test is likely to be high, and at the end it leaves a feeling in the subject that the instrument is intended to be helpful to him.

For the user, the primary intent of the CPS is for initial assessment and classification of incarcerated male adults and secondarily for non-incarcerated offenders on probation. The scoring procedure is simple; it involves summation of the scale values of the alternatives checked (1 to 5) and then transposing these raw scores to the profile sheet provided. The author has provided 18 profile "Types" or score patterns based on multivariate analysis. The Type for an obtained CPS profile can be established with help of a Reference Guide (Appendix B), and then the characteristics of the subject can be read out from the description of the Type given in the Manual. For each Type, the user has the following information available: descriptive summary of the subject's personality, need for psychiatric treatment, motivation for treatment, and probable institutional adjustment. Predictions are also provided regarding the intrainstitutional security status most appropriate for these subjects, possibility of parole violation, and post-release adjustments.

Although the Profile Sheet, with standard scores and percentile scores for each of the four scales, provides useful information, the average user is most likely to check out the Profile Type of the subject and make assessments on the basis of the Type descriptions provided. Here there are several points that deserve mention. First, the Types will not cover about 30% of the subjects, as noted in the validation study. The tendency of the practical-minded user in these cases will be to interpolate. For example, a subject with a score of 12 on Chemical Abuse, 30 on Thought Disturbance, 34 on Antisocial Tendencies, 11 on Self-Depreciation, and 5 on Validity does not fit into any Type. Shall we place him in Type 7 or shall we simply note that he has a standard score of 51 on Thought Disturbance and that his test-taking attitude tends to be somewhat "careless or facetious" as indicated by a 65 standard score on Validity? Second, the number of subjects on which each Type is based tends to be rather small. It varies from 5 subjects for Type 2 to 34 subjects for Type 13. Through discriminant analysis, however, the author has been able to establish that these are highly distinct, non-overlapping types ($p < .001$). This reviewer notes that the standardization sample consists of 412 adult male subjects, all inmates in an Ontario correctional center, and appreciates the difficulty of having still larger sample sizes. Nevertheless, the point that 7 out of 18 Types are based on 10 or less subjects deserves mention.

The manual gives 25 Tables, some of which could be collapsed (e.g., Tables 2 and 3), or shortened (e.g., Table 6 or 7). The test-retest reliability values ($N = 32$), with an interval of 2 weeks for the four scales, range from .87 to .92; for the Validity scale, it is .49. Faking studies indicate that the "CPS appears susceptible to faking." Motivation in taking the test thus becomes an important factor in determining its usefulness. Correlations between the CPS and MMPI scales and intergroup comparison of scores between correctional officers and offenders, as well as data on offenders from three different prisons, are illustrative of the author's painstaking psychometric analyses. However, this reviewer feels that presentation of these statistics in a simpler and more meaningful manner would greatly enhance the value of the manual.

The selection of the four content areas of Chemical Abuse, Thought Disturbance, Antisocial Tendencies, and Self-Depreciation has been made on the basis of review of "descriptive phrases and adjectives actually being used to describe incarcerated individuals" in psychological, psychiatric, and social work reports. But one wonders why some measures of hostility and anger or rage have not been included. Considerable research has been going on in these areas since about 1960, and some of these would be most appropriate for the purpose of the CPS. Affect Disturbances is an important area and should not be omitted. The major weakness of this instrument thus lies in the choice of areas. The instrument can be more useful if it combines such areas as drug use with an integrated measurement of disturbances in thought, affect, and motor behavior. Some contemporary research in personality and clinical psychiatry has been neglected, somewhat unjustifiably.

In summary, the CPS is a psychometrically sound instrument for measuring certain aspects of the personality of adult males incarcerated in correctional centers for purposes of assessment and providing possible psychological help. However, the author might usefully explore the inclusion of items relating to traits like hostility, which is receiving increasing attention from personality psychologists. Making the test more comprehensive without losing its essential simplicity for the type of subjects and users it is intended for is a difficult but challenging task for the author. More meaningful presentation of tables in the manual and clear instructions to the user for interpretation of scores, particularly when qualified psychologists may not be available, are some of the other improvements suggested.

[204]

Carrow Auditory-Visual Abilities Test. Ages 4–10; 1981; CAVAT; 2 batteries; no reliability data for entry test; individual; entry test (100 pages); manual (173 pages); scoring booklet (8 pages); entry test scoring booklet (4 pages); 1983 price data: $85 per set of testing materials including 1 test book each for auditory, visual, and entry tests, 15 copies of each scoring booklet, 1 tape cassette and manual; $17 per 15 copies of each of all 3 scoring booklets; (90) minutes for entire battery, (5) minutes per subtest; Elizabeth Carrow-Woolfolk; DLM Teaching Resources.*

a) VISUAL ABILITIES BATTERY. 5 subtests: visual discrimination matching, visual discrimination memory, visual-motor copying, visual motor memory, motor speed; 1 form (459 pages); scoring booklet for subtests 3–5 (20 pages).
b) AUDITORY ABILITIES BATTERY. 9 subtests: picture memory, picture sequence selection, digits forward, digits backward, sentence repetition, word repetition, auditory blending, auditory discrimination in quiet, auditory discrimination in noise; 9 subtests; 1 form (235 pages); cassette tape for subtests 13 and 14.

Review of Carrow Auditory-Visual Abilities Test by CURTIS DUDLEY-MARLING, Assistant Professor, University of Colorado at Denver, Denver, CO:

DESCRIPTION AND PURPOSE. The Carrow Auditory-Visual Abilities Test (CAVAT) is a norm-referenced, individually administered test of perceptual, memory, and motor skills appropriate for use with children between four and ten years of age. The CAVAT also includes an Entry Test which is used to determine which CAVAT subtest groups, if any, should be administered. The major purposes of the CAVAT are to aid in the identification of language/learning problems and to provide a detailed analysis of suspected perceptual problems. The author of the CAVAT, Elizabeth Carrow-Woolfolk, cautions that this battery should be part of a more comprehensive assessment program but that it can be very helpful in determining children's learning styles. Unlike the authors of many other perceptual tests, Carrow-Woolfolk does not recommend that the results of the CAVAT be used to develop remedial perceptual programs. In fact, she cautions against teaching the tasks used to assess perceptual-motor skill.

TEST CONSTRUCTION. The development of the CAVAT was the result of a thorough, rigorous process. The perceptual areas which comprise the various subtests of the CAVAT were selected on the basis of research relating these areas to language and learning problems and the testability of these areas. An effort was also made to limit the CAVAT to tasks involving recognition, discrimination, recall, and synthesis output. The motor speed subtest was included to rule out a motor problem in the event children performed poorly on subtests requiring motor responses.

The pilot version of the CAVAT, including test items, standardization procedures, and so on, emerged from years of field testing and peer review. The pilot form of the CAVAT was administered to 140 normal and 70 clinical children. An item analysis was performed on this data to determine items to be included in the final version of the CAVAT.

Items for the Entry Test were selected from the total auditory and visual abilities batteries on the basis of their representativeness and their discriminative power.

ADMINISTRATION AND SCORING. Administration procedures detailed in the CAVAT manual are thorough, clear, and concise. Scoring guidelines are also very clear and include a sufficient number of examples. Instructions to subjects and guidelines for determining ceiling levels, recording responses, and scoring are conveniently repeated in the test books.

The CAVAT overcomes the difficulties of many other auditory discrimination tests by presenting items on audio tape. This insures standard pronunciation for all test administrations. Another useful feature of the CAVAT is the graduated scoring system for the Visual-Motor Copying, Visual-Motor Memory, and Sentence Repetition subtests. For example, the CAVAT scoring of digit repetition is done on a continuum. Within each item, points are awarded for each sequence of two digits, if there are no digits omitted or included between them. Bonus points are awarded for correct sequences of four or more digits.

NORMING. The norming sample is representative of the U.S. population along the dimensions of race, sex, geographic distribution, and socioeconomic status. The sample included a total of 1032 children from four regions and 17 states.

The norming version of the test included only a subset of items from the entire CAVAT. For subtests that had items fitting the Rasch Model, a subset of items was chosen for norming. The entire subtest was administered for subtests not fitting this model.

RELIABILITY. The CAVAT manual presents test-retest and split-half reliability data. Split-half reliabilities were calculated for each subtest (except motor speed) and range from .72–.95. The test-retest interval ranged from six to eight weeks. The test-retest correlation for the entire CAVAT is .94. The correlation coefficients for the individual subtests range from .28–.86. Nine of the 14 subtests have reliabilities below .70. Low test-retest reliability is a problem that has plagued most perceptual-motor tests (Arter & Jenkins, 1979). Reliability coefficients for the CAVAT subtests are higher than most tests of this genre but may be too low for purposes of making individual diagnostic decisions. No reliability data is provided for the Entry Test.

VALIDITY. Carrow-Woolfolk argues that the CAVAT possesses four types of validity: content validity, construct validity, criterion-related validity, and sex and ethnic validity.

Chapters of the CAVAT manual describing the test, test development, and its theoretical bases are cited in support of the CAVAT's content validity.

The primary support for construct validity rests on the ability of the CAVAT subtests to discriminate between age levels and between clinical and normal groups at statistically significant levels.

In an attempt to establish criterion-related validity CAVAT subtests were correlated with selected subtests of the Detroit Tests of Learning Aptitude. CAVAT subtests correlate very well with many of the Detroit Tests. However, Carrow-Woolfolk herself questions the Detroit Tests as criterion measures since little data is available on the reliability of this test. This statement undermines any claim of criterion-related validity.

In order to determine the appropriateness of the CAVAT norms for both males and females, *t*-test comparisons were performed comparing males and females on each subtest. No differences were found. Additionally, ethnic groups were compared by age and by subtest to the subtest means for the overall sample. A large number of comparisons were performed and only a relatively small number were statistically significant. Carrow-Woolfolk asserts that since there were no apparent patterns to these statistically significant comparisons, and since there were fewer statistically significant differences than would be expected by chance, the CAVAT is valid for use with Blacks and Hispanics. However, while there are fewer significant differences than would be expected by chance alone it cannot be argued that these obtained differences are, in fact, chance events. Additionally, sample sizes for these comparisons were very small, 6 to 11 subjects per cell for Blacks and Hispanics. It is arguable that, if differences do exist between the subtest performance of Blacks and Hispanics and subtest means from the overall sample, there may not have been sufficient statistical power to identify these differences. A larger study with sufficiently large sample sizes representing different ethnic groups will have to be conducted in order to support the "ethnic validity" of the CAVAT.

RECOMMENDATIONS. The CAVAT is technically a good test, but it is not certain the information it yields makes it worth the effort. The CAVAT avoids the dubious claims of most other perceptual tests that the diagnosis of perceptual deficits leads directly to efficacious remedial programming which will positively influence academic performance. Carrow-Woolfolk makes the more modest claim that the CAVAT will assist in the identification of language/learning problems and will identify children's learning styles. Whether the identification of children's learning styles positively influences instruction is still an empirical question, and even if the identification of learning style is valuable, it may be that teacher observation is as reliable and valid a procedure for doing so as any test.

In conclusion, the CAVAT is a well constructed test accompanied by a superbly detailed manual. The major technical limitation of the CAVAT is the relatively low test-retest reliabilities of many of its subtests. Therefore, CAVAT users should be cautious about making any individual diagnostic decisions based on the CAVAT subtests. However, low test-retest reliability is a problem common to most perceptual tests, and if perceptual abilities are going to be assessed, the CAVAT may be the most comprehensive and well constructed test available.

REVIEWER'S REFERENCES

Arter, J. A., & Jenkins, J. R. Differential diagnosis-prescriptive teaching: A critical appraisal. REVIEW OF EDUCATIONAL RESEARCH, 1979, 4, 517–555.

Review of Carrow Auditory-Visual Abilities Test by JOHN SALVIA, Professor of Special Education, The Pennsylvania State University, University Park, PA:

The Carrow Auditory-Visual Abilities Test, CAVAT, is a norm-referenced, individually administered device intended to assess the perceptual abilities of children between the ages of 4 and 10 years. The 332 test items are arranged into five visual and nine auditory subtests. The first two subtests (visual-discrimination matching and visual-discrimination memory) are arranged in multiple-choice formats and differ primarily in memory demands. The contents of these subtests include discrimination of form, number, size, pictures, directionality, closure, figure-ground, form-space patterns, form-order patterns, and letter-order patterns. The next two subtests, visual-motor copying and visual-motor memory, differ only in one component of the content (the memory subtest additionally assesses closure). Both subtests require the child to draw, and both assess the perception of form, number, directionality, form space, form order, and letter order. Within these four subtests, all of the different components of contents (e.g., form or number) are tested. No rationale is offered for blocking the content of the subtests or for obtaining subtest scores that sum across components that are usually thought to represent different psychological demands. The remaining subtests are more usual in their construction.

Raw scores on each subtest can be converted to percentile ranks or *T*-scores. Raw scores can also be aggregrated into 15 different unweighted composites (clusters) and into battery (visual, auditory, and total) scores. (Unweighted composites are usually undesirable since they are actually weighted by the variability of the components, and only subtests with equal variances carry equal weights in the composites.)

The CAVAT was standardized on 1032 children ranging in age from 4 to 10 years of age. Seventeen states in four geographic regions were sampled; representative schools within representative communities were selected. Children were then selected on the basis of age, sex, and race. Neither data on the socioeconomic makeup nor urban-rural breakdown of the normative sample are presented. The final sample underrepresents minorities by about 20%. Seven of the subtests were normed using latent-trait theory; the remaining seven were standardized by administering the battery to the entire normative sample.

Test-retest reliability (stability), internal consistency, and interscorer agreement (for three subtests that require drawing) are reported in the manual. The stability coefficients are based on the performances of 39 children whose ages are not reported. However, one may assume that the ages vary, since only one coefficient per subtest was used to compute SEMs for all age groups. (If the ages vary, reliability estimates will be inflated since raw scores covary with age on the CAVAT.) Stability estimates for each subtest range from .28 to .86, with only 3 of the 17 coefficients being greater than .79. The composite scores are more reliable, but the reliability for the auditory battery is less than .90. Internal consistencies are reported for each of the seven ages for 13 subtests (subtest 5 is timed). Corrected odd-even correlations range from a low of .11 to a high of .96. Of the 91 coefficients, 16 are .90 or greater while 48 are .79 or less. The manual also contains substantially higher estimates of internal consistency, but these estimates are based on pooling the seven age groups and should be disregarded. Interscorer agreement appears to be excellent. The manual's treatment of difference scores is inadequate on two counts. First, no data on the reliability of differences are presented even though the interpretation of profile differences is recommended; second, the standard deviation of *T*-scores is incorrectly recommended as the standard deviation in evaluating differences between *T*-scores. No reliability data on cluster scores are reported.

The careful sampling of items for the subtests, especially in the visual battery, demonstrate concern for content validity. Minimal evidence for construct validity is presented. Scores covary with age as would be expected for developmental abilities. Mean battery scores for children previously identified as having perceptual handicaps were significantly lower on the CAVAT than the means of the normative sample. (Neither the degree of overlap in the distributions nor other factors potentially responsible for the differences were considered.) No data are presented to support claims of usefulness in planning educational activities. Criterion-related validity is generally lacking although a few modest correlations with the Detroit Tests of Learning Aptitude are presented. Some data are presented to indicate that race and sex differences are nonsignificant; of the 432 age *x* sex *x* ethnicity comparisons that were made, only 16 were statistically significant.

Included in the specimen kit is an "entry" test designed to assess if a child should be tested with all or part of the CAVAT and composed of items from each subtest except motor speed, auditory discrimination in quiet, and auditory discrimination in noise. No reliability data are presented for the entry test. Correlations between the entry test and visual battery, auditory battery, and total test for a sample of 125 children from the norm sample were .77, .89, and .91 respectively. These correlations are probably inflated since the age of the sample varied across the entire age range. No data on false positives and false negatives are presented. The cutoff points below which testing with the CAVAT is recommended are arbitrarily selected and unvalidated.

In summary, the CAVAT is a comprehensive test of perceptual abilities to be used in identifying children with problems. The adequacy of the norms is unestablished. Subtest reliabilities are generally inadequate for making important educational decisions about children; data on the reliability of other scores recommended for use in assessment are absent (i.e., clusters and difference scores). Validity rests on CAVAT's content validity. CAVAT should probably be considered an experimental test although it is not labeled as such.

[205]

Caso Test for Limited English-Speaking Students. Limited English-speaking students ages 8–12 living in an English-speaking setting; 1970–71; CTLESS; ratings in 3 areas: phonetics, comprehension, picture generating response; no data on reliability and validity; no norms; 1 form ('79, 10 pages, included in booklet with manual); manual ('79, 4 pages); answer sheet booklet ('79, 15 pages); 1982 price data: $.50 per answer sheet booklet; $1.50 per manual; (24–30) minutes; Adolph Caso; Kaso Industries, Inc.*

Review of Caso Test for Limited English-Speaking Students by ALAN GARFINKEL, Associate Professor of Foreign Language Education, Purdue University, West Lafayette, IN:

The Caso Test for Limited English-Speaking Students features 120 items intended for 8- to 12-year-old elementary school students of English as a second language. It is apparently designed to measure achievement in English and to function as a diagnostic tool. A maximum of 34 minutes is allowed for completion. Three subscores provide evaluations of abilities to spell and recognize initial consonants and vowels, to comprehend written and spoken passages and recognize relationships between words, and to write answers in response to questions based on illustrations. A total raw score of 140 points is possible. The test is hand scored.

Since the manual provides no information on norms, reliability, and validity, one is left with only the test items themselves as sources of information on validity.

Often enough an experienced teacher can read the items and be satisfied that at least the content contributes to one's confidence in the validity of the test. Such is not the case here. The items contain one awkward error after another. Whether one uses incorrect English in an attempt to test students' abilities to distinguish between correct and incorrect English is a pedagogical question open to discussion. However, there can be no discussion of an absolute requirement for clearly written, correct, and unambiguous instructions and stimuli. The Caso test has several such failings. We can start with the clumsily worded title, which one supposes is intended to be reminiscent of language in The Federal Register that refers to students of "limited English proficiency" (LEP). The reading passage misuses prepositions. The listening passage includes incorrectly spelled words. The instructions for one of the sections use incorrect grammar. The illustrations for the section titled "Picture Generating Response" (whatever that may mean) are quite ambiguous. This ambiguity will lead to an unnecessarily wide range of correct responses that makes it even more difficult to score a test that is already excessively difficult to score. One can only shudder at the thought of grading 150 Caso tests.

The usual approach to evaluating a test of this kind would be to look for signs of reliability and validity. In their absence, one might say that there is no evidence that the test in question is bad and that one might make a case for using it by reading the items for content, clarity, estimated difficulty, etc. There is no way to do that for the Caso test because of readily observed shortcomings in construction. The author says that future editions of the test are contemplated. There is not enough apparent content validity to warrant purchase and use of the current edition. Nonetheless, there is enough creativity in the test's construction to consider a subsequent edition if the author is able to demonstrate reliability and validity while remedying stylistic flaws. This is the absolute minimum a prospective purchaser should demand of a commercial test. If that minimum cannot be realized, the Caso test cannot be recommended. Although the S-D Primary ESL Inventory (reviewed elsewhere in this volume) is intended for adults of foreign background who function at grade levels 1 to 7, it is to be preferred to the current edition of the Caso Test for Limited English-Speaking Students.

Review of Caso Test for Limited English-Speaking Students by DIANA S. NATALICIO, Dean, College of Liberal Arts, The University of Texas at El Paso, El Paso, TX:

The goals of the Caso Test for Limited English-Speaking Students are stated as: "(1) to see to what extent the students know English, (2) to place them in appropriate programs, (3) to discover language weak and strong points, (4) to help discover handicaps and disabilities, and (5) to evaluate rates of progress." These ambitious goals are to be achieved via a 34-minute test which is divided into three parts (Phonetics, Comprehension, and Picture Generating Response) whose content, it is claimed, permits assessment of the skills of: oral comprehension and verbalization, written comprehension and composition, reading ability, and oral/written creativity and imagination. The test contains both oral and written stimuli; all subject responses are written. An Answer Sheet booklet is available to record subject responses, which are scored on the basis of a point system presented as part of the Administration Instruction Sheet.

The Phonetics section of the Caso consists of four subsections: (1) Initial Consonant Recognition, 20 dictated words (ranging from "fall" to "zodiac"), whose initial letters are to be written by subjects on the answer sheet; (2) Initial Vowel Recognition, a 10-item analogue to the initial consonant task, with words ranging from "owl" to "eternal"; (3) Initial Two-Letter Recognition, a 10-item task requiring students to write the first two letters of words such as "ghost" and "cow"; and (4) a 20-item spelling test consisting of words ranging from "ball" to "security," "giraffe," and "candor." The Comprehension section consists of three subsections: (1) Word-Lexical Relations, which requires subjects to select a pair of opposites from three-word sets (5 items), to select a pair of synonyms from three-word sets (5 items) and to select the two words in each of 10 three-word sets which "function similar to the words in parentheses," (e.g., couch sofa/divan/chair); (2) Reading Comprehension, a short paragraph (on squirrels) followed by 5 multiple-choice questions; and (3) Listening Comprehension, a short paragraph presented orally followed by 5 multiple-choice questions. The final major section of the Caso, Picture Generating Response, presents subjects with three picture sets about each of which 10 questions are to be answered in complete written sentences. The questions range from descriptive ("What is presented in picture 1?") to inferential ("Who do you think the person may be in picture 5?") to experiential ("What other kinds of tools have you seen?" "Where could you buy this tool?").

This test has all the earmarks of an ad hoc instrument designed for a specific program whose generalizability to other settings is severely limited. Such tests may well permit the assessment of some aspects of language proficiency for purposes of placement or monitoring pupil progress, but almost any sample of subjects' language performances could serve equally well. In gross terms, then, the Caso Test may provide information about the performance of any given group of 8- to 12-year-old

English-as-second-language learners on the tasks included therein, but there are no bases for determining how such performances compare to those recorded elsewhere (there are no norms), nor guidelines for interpreting the meaning of scores on the various subsections of the test in terms of overall English language proficiency. For example, being able to spell words (or identify the initial consonant or vowel spellings of these words), which accounts for 40 of 140 total possible points on the CASO, is not an obviously appropriate means of assessing phonetic awareness or knowledge. Recognizing two words similar to "couch" or "lion" seems only peripherally related to comprehension. Scoring itself is also a problem. In the final section (Picture Generating Response), which requires complete sentence written responses to 30 questions, one-word answers receive 1 point and complete sentence answers only 2, with 1/2 point deducted for each spelling and grammar error contained in each complete sentence answer. It would appear that a student might actually be penalized for complete sentence responses which contain major (minor?) spelling and grammar errors, and the poor speller is obviously not going to perform well on the Caso since Parts I and III both lean heavily on correct spelling (100 of 140 points).

Caso suggests that there are three limitations of his test: "(1) Not all parts of the test can be administered to all students; (2) It does not test specific grammar points; (3) The content may not always be familiar." To these must be added the fact that the test requires literacy on the part of the subjects to be tested (a requirement which eliminates its use for the placement of preliterate pupils), the fact that there is no explanation provided for the inclusion of specific items and item types, and, most importantly, the fact that this test provides no information concerning validity, reliability, or performance norms. At best, this is a test likely to be appropriate only to the setting for which it was designed (or which the author had in mind in creating it). It should definitely be regarded as "not for export."

[206]

CGP Self-Scoring Placement Tests in English and Mathematics. Students entering postsecondary institutions with open-door policies; 1972–79; also called Self-Scoring Placement Tests in English and Mathematics; self-scoring edition of the achievement/placement tests (Form UPG) in the Comparative Guidance and Placement Program (CGP); 6 tests ('72); may be used independently or in combination with full or modified CGP Program; student usually takes 4 tests (reading, written English expression, and 2 mathematics tests in prescribed combinations depending on amount of algebra studied) but single tests may be administered; subtests available as separates; publisher recommends use of local norms; using and interpreting scores on the CGP self-scoring placement tests ('79, 23 pages); score summary sheet ('76, 1 page); separate answer sheets (self-marking) must be used; 1985 price data: $19 per 25 reusable test booklets; $20.75 per 25 self-scoring answer sheets; 90(105) minutes; published for The College Board by Educational Testing Service.*

a) SELF-SCORING ENGLISH PLACEMENT TESTS. 2 tests; 25(30) minutes per test.

1) *Written English Expression Placement Test.* 1 form ('72, 8 pages, same as sentences test of CGP).

2) *Reading Placement Test.* 1 form ('72, 8 pages, same as reading test of CGP).

b) SELF-SCORING MATHEMATICS PLACEMENT TESTS. 4 tests usually administered in following pairs: computation and applied arithmetic for students with less than 1 year of high school algebra, computation and elementary algebra for students with 1 year, elementary and intermediate algebra for students with more than 1 year; 20(25) minutes per test.

1) *Computation Placement Test.* 1 form ('72, 6 pages, same as Mathematics Test C, Part I, of CGP).

2) *Applied Arithmetic Placement Test.* 1 form ('72, 6 pages same as Mathematics Test C, Part 2, of CGP).

3) *Elementary Algebra Placement Test.* 1 form ('72, 5 pages, same as Mathematics Test D, Part 2, of CGP).

4) *Intermediate Algebra Placement Test.* 1 form ('72, 5 pages, same as Mathematics Test E, Part 2, of CGP).

For reviews by Ronald K. Hambleton and J. Thomas Hastings, see 8:7. For reviews of subtests, see 8:61 (1 review) and 8:289 (1 review). For reference to reviews of the CGP Program, see 8:475.

[207]

Character Assessment Scale. Adult; 1980–83; CAS; self report; measures character strengths and weaknesses "founded on biblical principles"; 25 scores: 8 moral resource scales (truth, respect, concern, anger, money, time/energy, sexuality, body/health), 8 character strength scales (honesty, humility, peacemaking, resourcefulness, enthusiasm, sexual integrity, physical fitness, compassion), 8 character weakness scales (denial, envy, vanity, resentment, greed, laziness, lust, gluttony), total morality index; norms consist of means and standard deviations; 1 form ('80, 4 pages); answer sheet ('80, 2 pages); feedback sheet (no date, 4 pages); manual ('83, 34 pages); 1984 price data: $15 per 25 test booklets; $5 per 25 answer sheets; $7.50 per 25 feedback booklets; $10 per manual; administration time not reported; Paul F. Schmidt; Institute for Character Development.*

[208]

Characteristics Scale. Grades K–8; 1970–75; ratings by teachers; no validity data; no norms; 1 form (no date, 2 pages); no manual; 4 research articles ('72–'75, 2 articles include the scale); price data available from publisher; Patricia B. Elmore and Donald L. Beggs; Patricia B. Elmore.*

[209]

Chart of Initiative and Independence. Mentally handicapped adults; 1980; CII; assessment of environmental opportunities available to clients and their current and potential use of those resources; ratings by staff; no scores; no data on reliability or validity; no norms;

individual; 1 form, 4 formats: individual assessment format (3 pages, assesses present behavior), development programme format (3 pages, assesses future behavior), residential policy format (3 pages, assesses residential policy), preliminary assessment format (2 pages, short form of individual assessment to be used by social workers); complete manual (67 pages); manual of activities (10 pages); preliminary assessment manual (9 pages); 1985 price data: £3.45 per 25 individual assessment forms; £3.45 per 25 development programme forms; £.85 per residential policy form; £3.95 per 25 preliminary assessment forms; £1.25 per manual of activities; £1.05 per preliminary assessment manual; £5.45 per complete manual; administration time not reported; I. Macdonald and T. Couchman; NFER-Nelson Publishing Co. [England].*

Review of Chart of Initiative and Independence by MORTON BORTNER, Professor of Psychology & Education & Director of Clinical Training, Yeshiva University, New York, NY:

This assessment procedure consists of three separate rating scales which are concerned with the behavior of mentally retarded adults. The three formats are entitled: (1) Individual Assessment Format, (2) Development Programme Format, and (3) Residential Policy Format. The purpose of these evaluative summaries is to describe social competence in areas of function presumed to underlie the capacity to adjust to living arrangements requiring increasing levels of skill ranging from hospital wards through community living. This is done by assessing both the level of the client's behavior and the level of available environmental opportunities. Environmental opportunities, in turn, are seen as reflecting staff expectations (i.e., if you expect less from a client you will tend to create circumstances that prevent him from testing his upper limits). This conclusion is asserted to be based on the authors' own research, which they indicate was completed in a setting where decisions regarding client placement was a central issue. Unfortunately, the authors do not provide either references to published work or data of any kind which would help the reader to evaluate the basis for the conclusion that circumstance and staff expectations play such a vital role in determining the functioning level of the client.

Levels of behavior are assessed, based on observations reported by either staff or parents, according to "Modes." A Mode is a category of functioning which ranges on a continuum from complete passivity, which defines a client who needs to be told or shown what to do if he is to act at all (Mode A), through various intermediary stages, to Mode E, which defines a client who does not require monitoring and who is capable of independent action. In addition, this assessment requires that the rater estimate the "present potential" of the client, and that this inference be an "explicit statement of your intuition." However, the authors offer no bases for objectifying such intuitions.

All of the above defines the essential features of the first section, "The Individual Assessment Format." The second section of the procedure, "The Development Programme Format," is a repetition of the first section except that instead of looking at present behavior, potential, and level of opportunity, the focus is on future behavior, potential, and level of opportunity. Thus, it is an estimate of how far a client may be expected to progress. The third section, the "Residential Policy Format," refers to assessment, not of individuals, but of policy. It is, in effect, an attempt to evaluate the context in which clients live.

No information is provided to substantiate the validity of the "Modes" used to define varying levels of competence. The Modes are labels for complex levels of behavior which are hierarchically ordered from passive to active. The complexity of these Modes would be expected to militate against uniform interpretations by different staff, but no empirical evidence is offered to suggest that these categories can be interpreted uniformly.

Finally, case studies are offered as examples of how these assessments were used. However, no empirical data are offered to confirm whether this instrument helped in achieving the goals for which it was intended. Moreover, the case examples, while interesting as social histories, are psychologically incomplete insofar as they do not report objective data on the intellectual status of the client, and leave open the question as to whether these rating scales are more suitable for any particular category of mental retardation.

It is not possible to compare individual ratings with any normative sample, since normative data are not provided, and indeed would be difficult to collect since raters are encouraged to invent their own items as long as they adhere to the general categories or Modes suggested by the authors.

In summary, this assessment procedure is concerned with rating the behavioral status of the retarded client in a given social context, but the importance of this special approach is not verified. In addition, an intuitive estimate of potential functioning is encouraged without any attempt to introduce consistent guidelines by which such judgements could be made reliably by the same person on different occasions or by different persons at any given time. It is noteworthy that the concept of reliability is never discussed in the manual.

It is not possible to say whether this instrument is effective, since the necessary data are neither reported nor acknowledged as relevant. Moreover, none of the standard concerns of test construction are reported. The validity, reliability, and objectivity of the constructs and items used to evaluate the client's behavior remain unknown.

Review of Chart of Initiative and Independence by WAYNE C. PIERSEL, Associate Professor of Educational Psychology, University of Nebraska, Lincoln, NE:

Assessment instruments are usually designed to serve either of two functions. The traditional assessment function is to assist in identification, classification, or placement decisions regarding individuals or groups of individuals. Such instruments usually provide an array of derived normative scores that are used in the decision making process. The second function of assessment instruments is to facilitate the organization, management, and evaluation of treatment or intervention programs applied to individuals or groups of individuals. This purpose necessitates describing the individual's current skill or competence level and developing training objectives and goals that can be monitored. To accomplish this second activity requires an instrument that is sufficiently fine grained and sensitive to reflect progress in specific skills. The instrument must be tailored to the individual concerned and to the situation.

Just as nature abhors a vacuum, so does the publishing field. Until the late 1960s and early 1970s there were very few assessment instruments of either type that could be utilized with the severely and profoundly handicapped. The severely and profoundly mentally retarded were an especially neglected clientele in terms of assessment instruments fulfilling the second assessment function. The Chart of Initiative and Independence (CII) represents one of many recent attempts that have been made to fill this void in program planning, organization, management, and evaluation for individual mentally retarded clients. The CII attempts to assess and monitor specific behaviors of individuals in particular learning environments. Other scales that are also intended to be employed with the severely and profoundly mentally retarded (e.g., Vineland Social Maturity Scale and AAMD Adaptive Behavior Scale) are more general and designed to provide normative data, thus sacrificing the fine grained analysis and tailored fit to specific training situations that is necessary for day-to-day monitoring of change.

The stated purpose of the CII is to provide staff working directly with mentally retarded clients a method to evaluate their work and the development of the clients in their care. The CII was developed for the purpose of providing a direct measure of an individual client's progress. It is designed to provide information on: (*a*) the behavior and expectations of staff, (*b*) opportunities available for clients to acquire selected behaviors, and (*c*) institutional policies that facilitate or inhibit client progress. The CII can be employed to record: (*a*) the assessment of environmental opportunities available to clients and (*b*) the assessment of a client's present and potential future use of these available resources. The present version of the CII was developed specifically for use with mentally retarded adults. The manual is divided into four sections including: (*a*) an introduction, (*b*) description of the Individual Assessment Format (IAF), (*c*) description of the Development Program Format (DPF), and (*d*) description of the Residential Policy Format (RPF). The manual also contains a list of suggested behavioral descriptions by category that can be used in developing the assessment activities for each of the three assessment formats. The goal of these three assessment formats is to provide the assessors (staff), who work with the clients, information that will be useful in planning and assessing a client's progress in the program.

It is important to note that the CII is not a test in the traditional framework of a norm-referenced test nor is it a criterion-referenced test. The CII is not a behavior rating scale nor an observational system. Rather, the CII is a process for gathering information. The CII consists of three types of charts or assessment formats and a list of suggested behaviors or activities that are intended to provide a structure for gathering information. The assessment charts are blank and must have the behaviors or activities to be observed and rated entered on each chart by the assessor. The CII is a structured observational rating system requiring the assessor to develop or select behaviors that are of importance to the individual being assessed. After completing each of the charts with the behavior or activities to be observed, the assessor enters a subjective rating in a variety of categories for each of the three formats. The completed CII theoretically guides the assessor in appraising relevant client behaviors and important aspects of the training environment.

The assessment process utilizes three separate record forms or formats. The Individual Assessment Format (IAF) consists of a form on which to rate a client's behavior, the level of opportunity offered in the environment to perform that behavior, and the client's present, potential, and optimum modes of functioning. The Development Program Format (DPF) is to be used as a target chart (i.e., a statement of where you expect the client to be at the end of a stated period of time such as three months). The Residential Policy Format (RPF) is intended to be a general assessment of the institution's or agency's policy as it pertains to expectations regarding client behavior. The manual states that this format is designed to reflect staff expectations of client behavior. The RPF chart is designed to reflect the minimal level of acceptable competence for each stated behavior and to indicate the minimal level of opportunity or assistance that will be provided for each behavior. Taken together, these three assessment charts are intended to provide staff with a comprehensive picture of a client's current skill level, what a client is expected to achieve, the circumstances for performance, and the time period to accomplish intended goals.

The intent of the CII is certainly laudable. To the extent that an organization does not have the necessary structure and knowledge to organize, plan, conduct, and evaluate client progress, the CII formats do provide such a structure within which to accomplish this end. A major advantage of the CII is the delineation of behaviors to be observed, circumstances under which the behaviors are to occur, opportunities for the client to engage in the behaviors, and degree of potential usefulness of the behaviors for the client's habilitation.

There are a number of difficulties and limitations inherent in the CII. The CII manual is difficult to read and utilize. Minimal information is given on how to construct and implement the various assessment formats. For example, only two paragraphs are devoted to explaining the preparation, use, and interpretation of the DPF. No information is provided on the reliability of the development of the charts across staff nor are any data provided on the reliability of the judgements made in completing each of the formats. There is no indication of any type of validity for the CII. Conceivably, different individual assessors could derive very different sets of charts or arrive at very different subjective ratings using previously completed charts. Although the process outlined is sensible, this reviewer questions whether the manual or the forms provide individuals with sufficient information to implement the three assessment procedures. Most importantly, utilization of the various assessment formats requires considerable knowledge of behavior, programming, observation skills, and evaluation procedures. In essence, naive individuals could not utilize the charts effectively, and knowledgeable professionals will have developed the necessary forms and procedures to fit their institution's unique situation, with developed treatment plans available that specify much of the content that the CII formats are designed to identify.

There are a number of systems available that have developed the assessment procedures, companion curriculum, and related treatment plans in a much more detailed, integrated, and useful package. Such systems as the Portage Guide to Early Education and the Behavioral Characteristics Progression represent two examples of systems that include comprehensive assessment procedures for determining client skill level. These systems also include detailed teaching procedures, curriculum suggestions, and a mechanism for systematic evaluation of client progress. The Balthazar Scales of Adaptive Behavior (BSAB) represent another observational system with similar goals to the CII. The BSAB scales represent a more reasonable approach to the fine grained analysis that the CII is attempting. Psychometric data on reliability and validity are available for the BSAB. The CII manual does not make clear that the system is neither an observational system nor a rating system. In short, the CII does not have the advantages of a behavior checklist nor the advantages of direct observation systems. It does have all of the disadvantages of systems that combine observation approaches and rating scale procedures, require staff to develop instrument content, and utilize subjective assessor perceptions.

[210]

Checklist/Guide to Selecting a Small Computer. Individuals selecting a small computer for a business; 1980; ratings of "essentials" or "nice-to-have" characteristics in 10 areas: display features, keyboard features, printer features, controller features, software, word processing, service, training, miscellaneous, costs; no reliability or validity data; 1 form (33 pages, includes all materials for administration); 1983 price data: $5 per checklist; administration time not reported; Wilma E. Bennett; Pilot Books.*

Review of Checklist/Guide to Selecting a Small Computer by DOUGLAS B. EAMON, Associate Professor of Psychology, University of Houston-Clear Lake, Houston, TX:

Although many readers will find this checklist useful for selecting a business computer, it will be less informative for practitioners or educators whose principal use of computers will be as an adjunct to test administration and scoring.

The questions which comprise the checklist tend to be quite specific, and range from very important considerations (e.g., "281. How reliable is the system?"), to seemingly trivial ("95. Is the keyboard low enough so pencils won't roll under it?").

There are several virtues to the checklist approach to evaluating a small computer: (1) It forces the prospective computer user to examine the computer in some detail, or at least obtain detailed information from a sales representative. (2) It suggests consideration of a number of potential strengths and weaknesses in a system which may not be immediately evident. (3) It requires the user to make decisions about the desirability of various features; this approach may reduce the persuasiveness of demonstrations of attractive but "gimmicky" features only marginally related to the planned use of the computer.

At the same time, there are several weaknesses in the approach. One important weakness is that the checklist employs an "atomistic" evaluation of the various subcomponents of the computer rather than an integrative evaluation based on the interrelations among the various components. As in other complex systems, a well-designed computer whole is more than the sum of its parts. Unfortunately, a customer using this checklist could end up with a computer whole which is less than the sum of its parts.

The failure to emphasize the integrated nature of a computer system is particularly obvious in considerations of "software" (the programs to be run). Although over one third of the questions pertain to software, the usefulness of the questions is limited. Fifty-seven questions constitute a list of types of software (general ledger, accounts receivable, accounts payable, etc.); the checklist user is simply to indicate with a mark whether the vendor can supply it. With the exception of a separate 18-question section on word processing, little attention is given to evaluation of the programs themselves, apparently under the assumption that if the program exists, it will take care of the user's needs. Such is rarely the case; among the most critical decisions to be made in implementing a computer system are those regarding the selection of the best possible software which will do the job required. There are a great many considerations involved in these decisions, and they are of the utmost importance. Indeed, many experts suggest that the best strategy for selecting a computer is to first select the software packages needed, and then find a hardware configuration which will handle them.

Another weakness is that many of the questions require responses not easily characterized by a check mark indicating presence or absence of the feature described. Question 281 cited above, for example, asks the checklist user to indicate with a check mark the computer's reliability. Clearly, some sort of rating scale or quantitative description would be more appropriate for such a question.

Whatever the form of the question, the "essential/nice-to-have" categories assume at least some knowledge of the relative importance and potential use of the various features. Such information may not be available to a first-time computer user. The "essential/nice-to-have" distinction also assumes that any feature is at least worthwhile (though it may not be important enough to play a role in the decision); experienced computer users may wish to supplement these two categories with a third: "don't want."

The format of the evaluation, with blanks for each question corresponding to three vendors, suggests that the end result of the evaluation will be the selection of a single vendor from which the entire system (display, keyboard, main computer, peripheral storage devices, printer, software, service, and even training) will be obtained. There are many companies which specialize in peripherals and software compatible with a variety of computers. It is often advisable to construct a computer system by selecting components from several different vendors; such a possibility does not become apparent with this checklist.

Among the most serious problems this reviewer finds with the checklist is its lack of focus on the intended use of the computer, the time needed to implement the programs, and the problems of converting from existing procedures to a computerized one. Investment in a computer system with the expectation that existing problems can be solved if only they can be "computerized" usually ends up wasteful of both time and money, frequently compounds the problems, and almost always involves unforseen complications and additional frustration and difficulties.

Were the reader now to tally the number of "check marks" described above, it would be concluded that Bennett's Checklist/Guide is not a particularly useful source. Such a conclusion would be quite wrong. In spite of its weaknesses, I can recommend this little booklet very highly for a prospective computer purchaser. The 332 questions brought together here enumerate so many considerations, large and small, as to make it a valuable source and certainly well worth its very modest purchase price. Used with caution, judiciously supplemented with an integrative analysis of the requirements of the purchaser and a careful evaluation of the software to be implemented, this booklet could be of great help in the selection of nearly any business computer.

Review of Checklist/Guide to Selecting a Small Computer by C. MICHAEL LEVY, Professor of Psychology, University of Florida, Gainesville, FL:

The lofty aim of this checklist/guide is to enable decision makers, who are assumed to be computer novices, to make the best possible choice in selecting a small business computer. The materials suffer on so many levels that this aim cannot even be approximated.

The volume is divided into two major parts: the checklist and a glossary. Bennett intended to avoid jargon in the checklist that would confound her audience, and resorted to the glossary when this goal became infeasible. But the glossary was remarkably elaborated to include nearly four times the number of technical terms used in the checklist. While a good and reasonably complete glossary could benefit the intended audience, this glossary is neither particularly good nor reasonably complete. Several of the definitions are incorrect (e.g., ASCII, magcard reader, Real Time Systems, utilities, window), misleading (e.g., array, BASIC, core storage, function keys, host), circular (e.g., software), or superfluous (audit trail, BTU, chassis, halon, risk analysis). Many extremely important terms are absent (e.g., cache memory, electronic spread sheet, file, escape, multitasking, PASCAL, record, UNIX, user group, virtual storage, Winchester). Sadly, nearly 60% of the technical terms used in the checklist were omitted from the glossary including, for example, compiled language, emulation software, mask painted on, operating system, page forward, and telecommunications.

One major part of the uselessness of this guide relates to the massive changes within the industry that have occurred since Bennett formulated this volume. At that time the term small computer system evoked images of minicomputers; now, the primary association would probably be microcomputer. The sole reference to microcomputer in this volume occurs, however, in the glossary rather than the checklist: "A small computer which differs from a minicomputer in that only one person uses it and it has less capacity." Both of these assertions were false within a year of Bennett's writing them. While this is but one example, history has largely made this publication obsolete.

As a consequence, the intended audience will probably be unable to use the checklist in any useful way. Could a more sophisticated user—a systems analyst, data processing manager, or professional consultant—use the checklist to compare the products of several vendors to help in the winnowing process? The answer is: dubious.

For starters, the checklist is not as task-oriented as is usually necessary for determining the computing needs of a company. Word processing is a large task but it is given as much attention as capabilities that are not usually major items of concern, such as printer features. Electronic mail, energy management, inventory control, and accounting operations are as prominently featured as such questionable "general business procedures" as Morse code, musical scores, and teachers' logs. Consideration of the absolutely vital concept operating system is relegated to the "software" category, along with games and data base management.

Some potential users will be put off by the fact that, while the Table of Contents includes display features, keyboard features, software, costs, etc., it has no section dealing specifically with the computer. The astute reader will infer that, by default, the appropriate checklist heading is controller features, in spite of the fact that the glossary entry for controller would suggest otherwise.

Overcoming these limitations by careful editing would not necessarily yield a useful checklist. The checklist format is entirely appropriate when products are compared along binary dimensions (e.g., "Are graphics available?") or even when comparisons are required along certain continuous scales (e.g., "How heavy is the CRT?" "How much power does it use?"). Many important comparisons (e.g., "How does it store information?" "How reliable is it?") are ill-suited to the checklist format.

Unquestionably, the majority of the problems raised here could have been avoided by a modest field test or peer evaluation. The seemingly intractable problems related to the rapid pace of technological change in this area require a more complex set of solutions, the most elemental of which is a plan for an annual revision/update.

[211]

Child and Adolescent Adjustment Profile. Children and adolescents seen in mental health centers; 1977–81; CAAP; pre- and posttreatment ratings by significant other; 5 scores: peer relations, depending, hostility, productivity, withdrawal; pretreatment posttreatment change norms provided; manual ('81, 18 pages); profile ('78, 2 pages); scale ('79, 2 pages); 1983 price data: \$4.50 per 25 scales including profiles; \$5 per manual; \$5.50 per specimen set; (10) minutes; Robert B. Ellsworth and Shanae L. Ellsworth (scale and manual); Consulting Psychologists Press, Inc.*

Review of Child and Adolescent Adjustment Profile by ROBERT H. DELUTY, Assistant Professor of Psychology, University of Maryland Baltimore County, Baltimore, MD:

The Child and Adolescent Adjustment Profile (CAAP) was designed to be used by parents, teachers, therapists, and probation officers to evaluate how often during the preceding month a given child exhibited each of 20 behaviors. By summing the ratings for the four behaviors associated with each factor, scores for the five adjustment dimensions are obtained.

Items selected for the CAAP were: (1) "highly clinically relevant" for measuring adjustment, as judged by a group of clinicians working with children and adolescents; (2) sensitive to pre-post treatment change and to differences between groups known to differ in adjustment; and (3) internally consistent, temporally reliable, and characterized by stable and high factor loadings. Although the scale's development is psychometrically commendable, the studies assessing and reporting its reliability and validity are fraught with problems.

Ellsworth found that the internal consistency of the five CAAP dimensions ranged from .80 (Peer Relations) to .90 (Productivity); unfortunately, no information is provided about the reliability sample other than that it consisted of 157 people. Test-retest correlations ranged from .78 (Dependency) to .89 (Hostility). Although Ellsworth claims that these correlations "are all quite high," the fact that three dimensions had correlations less than or equal to .81 after only a 1-week test-retest interval leads one to conclude that the CAAP's temporal consistency is rather modest.

Ellsworth assessed the interrelationships among the CAAP dimensions and concluded that they "are largely independent of each other." This conclusion is remarkable, given that a substantial number of intercorrelations are quite large and would likely have reached high levels of statistical significance had tests of significance been conducted (e.g., Withdrawal correlated –.55 with Peer Relations, –.69 with Productivity, and .52 with Dependency).

To assess inter-rater reliability, correlations were obtained between ratings of parents and probation officers for 25 "offenders," and between ratings of parents and teachers for 18 normal children. None of the correlations in the latter study were significant, while only correlations for Dependency, Hostility, and Withdrawal achieved significance in the former study. To determine whether the CAAP does indeed have acceptable inter-rater reliability, rather than compare the ratings of two adults who have very different kinds of relationships with the same child, one should compare the ratings of either both parents, or of teachers with comparable student contact, or of objective classroom observers.

The major problems with the CAAP, however, involve its validation. Ellsworth compared the parent ratings of children "referred to Mental Health Centers for counseling," children on probation, and "normal" children. The lack of information regarding the types of children included in each of these groups is striking. There is no information regarding the MHC children's age, sex, SES level, reason for referral, diagnosis, or type of treatment received. In the case of the probation group, not only are there no demographic data presented, but we are never informed from what the children are on probation and why they were put there. Ellsworth reports that the "normals" were all from single parent families and were "screened" for emotional/learning problems. Why he chose for his "normal" population a group of children with only one parent is not explained, nor is his screening procedure discussed in any detail. Thus, given the information provided by Ellsworth, it is impossible to know whether the MHC, Probation, and Normal groups are at all comparable in terms of such critical dimensions as age, sex, parentage, and socioeconomic level; differences between the groups, therefore, might not reflect actual differences in adjustment levels but, rather, differences along these demographic dimensions. Furthermore, the composition of the MHC and Probation groups is so unclear and the nature of the treatment received by the MHC children so unspecified, that both the normative scores and the pre-post treatment change norms reported by Ellsworth are largely uninterpretable; likewise, scores for the "normal" group must be interpreted and used with great caution given their atypical parentage and the unclear screening procedure.

For the record, for four of the CAAP dimensions (all but Dependency), parent ratings of the "normal" group indicated significantly better adjustment ($p < .01$) than did ratings of the pretreatment MHC, posttreatment MHC, and Probation groups. "Normal" children had significantly lower Dependency ratings ($p < .01$) than did the pretreatment and posttreatment groups, but did not differ significantly from Probation children. Although these findings are encouraging, the failure to control for critical extraneous variables leaves one very unsure as to the CAAP's validity and clinical utility.

Ellsworth also examined developmental differences within his "normal" group by comparing the ratings of children aged 3 to 5, 6 to 12, and 13 to 19. Although the oldest group was rated least "dependent" while the youngest group was rated least "productive," there is no indication whether these differences were statistically significant. No significant sex differences were obtained on the five CAAP dimensions as rated by parents, although girls were perceived as more "productive" than boys by their teachers. Ellsworth comments that these findings "are consistent with what one would expect." Not at all! The absence of sex differences on all five parent ratings and on four teacher ratings is very surprising, given the findings of Gesten (1976) that girls had consistently higher, teacher-reported, personal and social competence scores than boys, and the consistent findings of Deluty (1979, 1983) that boys obtain significantly higher aggressiveness ratings and lower submissiveness ratings than girls.

In conclusion, the five CAAP dimensions appear to be internally consistent and to have modest test-retest reliabilities. Due to the paucity of information regarding the samples used in the reliability and validity studies, the reliability coefficients, normative scores, and pre-post treatment change norms cannot be used or interpreted with confidence. Ratings are not available for "normal" two-parent children, and the age range for which the CAAP is appropriate is never specified. In light of its psychometrically-sound development, however, it is recommended that the CAAP not be abandoned prematurely, but rather that its inter-rater reliability, convergent and discriminant validity, and clinical utility be assessed using clearly delineated samples in internally valid studies.

REVIEWER'S REFERENCES

Gesten, E. L. A health resources inventory: The development of a measure of the personal and social competence of primary-grade children. JOURNAL OF CONSULTING AND CLINICAL PSYCHOLOGY, 1976, 44, 775–786.

Deluty, R. H. Children's Action Tendency Scale: A self-report measure of aggressiveness, assertiveness, and submissiveness in children. JOURNAL OF CONSULTING AND CLINICAL PSYCHOLOGY, 1979, 47, 1061–1071.

Deluty, R. H. Children's evaluations of aggressive, assertive, and submissive responses. JOURNAL OF CLINICAL CHILD PSYCHOLOGY, 1983, 12, 124–129.

Review of Child and Adolescent Adjustment Profile by DAVID R. WILSON, Coordinator of Psychology Services and Research & Evaluation, Brewer-Porch Children's Center, The University of Alabama, University, AL:

The Child and Adolescent Adjustment Profile (CAAP) consists of 20 items that have been classified by factor analysis into five areas of adjustment. It is intended to be used by parents, teachers, counselors, probation officers, and other treatment staff, and it is easily administered and scored, with each adjustment factor summed on the scale itself. Once summed, scores are transferred to a profile sheet which aids in detecting high and low levels of adjustment. A unique addition is the inclusion of change norms which can be used as a standard for gauging a child's response to treatment. These norms are in the form of tables from which standard scores ($M=50$; $SD=10$) can be determined from pre- to posttreatment changes in raw score values.

The development of the scale began with 292 items selected from previous studies as well as input from clinicians. No further detail about these studies or clinicians is provided. It would be helpful to know if existing behavior rating scales and checklists were used and whether the entire behavior domain of interest was adequately sampled. Using a sample of 147 "referred" and 115 "non-referred" children, these 292 items were rated by parents using a true-false format. At this stage, three criteria were used to select items: the items should differentiate between referred and non-referred children, each item should have a sufficient factor loading, and it should be judged to be of clinical importance. The 115 items which met the first two criteria were evaluated by clinicians (no detail), and 69 items were judged to be clinically relevant. The 55 items which best measured six factors were selected for further study.

These 55 items were rated by 248 raters (parents of 89 referred children, 34 probationers' parents, 39 normals, 49 probation officers, and 37 teachers). These items were screened for their sensitivity to pre-post treatment differences in Mental Health Center children as well as for sensitivity to group differences (normals vs. delinquents vs. referred). The items meeting these criteria (detail lacking) were factor analyzed to search for factors consistent across four groups (ages 6 to 11, 12 to 18, boys, girls), and this resulted in the dropping of one factor—the Anxiety-Depression factor. Finally, 20 items were selected for the final version based on the magnitude of the factor loadings and reliability (both internal consistency and test-retest). The five factors are Peer Relations, Dependency, Hostility, Productive, and Withdrawn.

Analyses based on parent ratings using approximately 203 normals (detail lacking) revealed that the dimensions are largely independent, with the highest correlation being .42 between dependency and hostility. Teacher ratings were found to be more interrelated. The scale was found to have an acceptable level of internal consistency, with coefficient alphas for the five factors ranging from .80 to .90. Test-retest stability over a period of one week was also acceptable, with a range from .78 to .89.

Validity data for the CAAP scale is lacking. The author presents no correlations with existing measures, nor is there any mention of previous factor analytic work on child behavior. This is a serious omission. It is possible that other scales and previous factor analytic research was used during the development of the scale and that the manual simply neglects to mention this. The scale's utility as well as its validity would be increased if the author had taken the time to relate it to the existing body of knowledge.

The manual suggests that the scale is valid based on data regarding its discriminant validity. Data are presented demonstrating the CAAP scores differentiate among groups which are known to differ from each other in adjustment. This approach is a welcome one, but this reviewer cannot definitely state that discriminant validity was actually established for the CAAP. There is a paucity of detail, as well as confusion regarding which sample of children was used for which stage of the development of the scale, but it seems that at least a portion of the same sample was used during the item selection phase, and then again to provide support for discriminant validity. It is not legitimate to use a sample to select items based on their ability to discriminate among known groups, and then cite that same data (whole or in part) as evidence for discriminant validity. There is a need for the collection of more data to cross-validate this scale. This would be true even if totally separate samples had been used.

The manual includes extensive instructions regarding the filling out of the scale, along with some setting-specific instructions which may be of little interest to some test users. The scale is very easy to administer, score, and profile. Clinical staff or parents should have no trouble using it. The norms provided are standard score norms based on a sample which included 203 parent ratings. By placing raw scores on the profile sheet, *T*-scores are automatically derived, based on the child's standing relative to this normative sample. One side of the profile sheet is for the school rating, and the other is for use in the home or community. These norms are seen as a start, but are inadequate. A more comprehensive normative sample, and one which is more adequately described, would be helpful.

The developers have also attempted to increase the utility of the test through the inclusion of change norms. The inclusion of these change norms is an excellent idea, but their application here is inadequate. These norms are based on a sample of 90 youngsters who were seen for a mean of 4.8 sessions of unspecified mental health center treatment. The suggestion is made that these norms can be used to gauge progress that is made in a variety of settings, but this is questionable. For example, should these norms (which may be specific to only this mental health center) be used as a standard of comparison for children involved in six months of day treatment? The use of these standardized residual scores, which take into account the fact that pre and post scores will be correlated, is a vastly superior approach to that of reliance on simple change scores. The author is to be commended for encouraging reliance on the former, and pointing out the problems with the latter. But these norms would be more useful if they had been developed using a larger sample and varied settings.

In sum, the CAAP scale is a potentially valuable instrument for use in a mental health center, or other child treatment programs. It is simple to fill out, score, profile, and interpret, and it does tap some important dimensions of child behavior. But the user should be extremely careful about placing much reliance on either the standard norms or the change norms because of the limited sample on which both of these were developed. One recommendation would be for users to develop their own program-specific norms and change norms. Children's treatment programs are so different that it is unrealistic to expect change norms to be relevant to all of them. Perhaps the author could include some instructions regarding the development of these types of norms in a future edition of the manual. Any program which deals with a large group of children, and has the capacity to accumulate data, should consider this option. The CAAP scale, when interpreted in this fashion, could be a valuable part of a program evaluator's collection of measures.

[212]

Child Anxiety Scale. Grades K–5; 1980; CAS; tape cassette; 1 form; manual ('80, 27 pages); separate answer sheets must be used; 1985 price data: $19.45 per complete kit including 50 answer sheets; $7.25 per cassette tape; $3.75 per scoring key; $6.10 per 50 answer sheets; $2.70 per manual; (15) minutes; John S. Gillis; Institute for Personality and Ability Testing, Inc.*

Review of Child Anxiety Scale by SUSANNA MAXWELL, Associate Professor of Educational Psychology, Northern Arizona University, Flagstaff, AZ:

The Child Anxiety Scale (CAS), a 20-item self-report questionnaire, was developed to enable the "early detection of emotional problems." The manual suggests the scale might be useful for large screening programs in schools and clinics as well as for monitoring anxiety over time. The construction of the CAS was based on a second-order anxiety factor identified in the much longer Early School Personality Questionnaire (ESPQ) created by Coan and Cattell (1966). Using this anxiety factor as the criterion against which the validity of CAS items could be determined, 20 items from a pool of 320 were chosen based on their factor loadings on the ESPQ anxiety factor. While an advertising brochure for the CAS states that the questions are based on "extensive studies of the form anxiety takes in the self-reports of 6 to 8 year olds," the manual contains no information about the source of the item pool. Information about the author's interpretation of the construct of anxiety beyond the reference to its factor structure is also missing from the manual.

In addition to the brief explanation of the development of the scale, the test manual contains clear and simple directions for administration and scoring. The answer sheets contain no words, only red and blue circles for the child's response and pictures to aid in the identification of each item (butterfly, spoon, etc.). A simple scoring key yields a single raw score which reflects responses to high anxiety items. An audio cassette tape containing the instructions and questions is available to simplify administration and standardization. Since the items indicating high anxiety have been randomly switched from side to side (red circle to blue circle), the child who has a tendency to mark only the first or only the second answer is readily identified. However, the test author has not included a lie scale or any control for a socially desirable response set. While the picture answer sheet and the oral questions make this an easily administered scale for young children, some children in 4th and 5th grades may find the presentation too elementary.

Separate norm tables are presented for grade level K through 5 and age 5–0 to 12–11. Though the author found a tendency for females to score higher on the CAS, he states that the difference was not large enough to warrant separate norm tables for males and females. These separate data are not included in the manual. The grade and age norm tables are constructed so that raw scores may be converted into two types of standard scores—stens or percentiles.

The standardization sample for the CAS contained 2,105 children (1,097 boys and 1,008 girls). This sample is described by geographic region, community size, and racial ethnic distribution (88.5% White, 10.2% Black, .9% Spanish-American, .4% Other). Because of disproportionately large sampling from the Midwest, an analysis of 30 children randomly drawn from each of the four regions was conducted; results did not demonstrate significant differences among the regions. However, the manual also includes a table which reveals that 44% of the sample was drawn from communities under 2,500 while 75% came from communities under 50,000. No data are included to address similarities or differences between the CAS scores of rural and urban children.

Reliability data on the CAS are good, with immediate test-retest reliability coefficients for first through third grades ($N = 127$) ranging from .82 (first grade) to .92 (third grade). However, the number of children in each separate grade is not included. One week test-retest results with 78 children (age not specified) gave a coefficient of .81. The Kuder-Richardson 20 coefficient for internal consistency was .73 for a sample of 343 children (mean age 6.5).

While factorial validity data for the CAS are adequate, there is a significant lack of criterion-related validity. No correlational studies between the CAS and clinical or teacher ratings of anxiety are presented, nor are correlations between the CAS and other anxiety scales mentioned. Few studies tying the CAS to external criteria are cited and those few have questionable results. Hypothesizing that a community with a large number of armed forces personnel would have children with higher CAS scores because of family mobility, Ells (1979) found a significant relationship between the CAS and "attitudes toward moving," but not mobility per se. No information is given regarding the characteristics of this sample or how attitudes toward moving were determined. A study by Elder (1978) examining differences between CAS scores of single parent and two parent children failed to reveal differences. The test author explains that in the one parent families there was a tendency for children to give more extremely high or extremely low scores so that it was impossible to distinguish between the truly low anxious children and those children who were using denial. In spite of this admission of an implied weakness in the CAS, the author cites another example (part of the standardization data) where 34 children with "speech handicaps, learning disabilities, educable handicaps, and emotional problems" scored below average in their self-reports of anxiety. Yet in this case the author claims that "early detection and intervention strategies had made an important impact upon the psychological well-being of these children." Denial is not mentioned as a possible interpretation.

In summary, the CAS is an attractive, easy-to-administer, easy-to-score scale. The manual contains clear norm and conversion tables. The brightly colored picture format of the answer sheets and the oral presentation of the 20 questions would seem most appealing to children under 8 or 9 years of age though the norms extend through 12 years. Like most self-report questionnaires, the CAS is open to faking. Though the standardization sample was of sufficient size, 50% came from communities under 5,000 and 75% under 50,000. Further research is needed to determine if there are differences between anxiety levels as measured by the CAS in rural communities and more urban communities. In the meantime, test users from large communities should interpret the norms cautiously. Reliability data are adequate for the CAS but criterion-related validity is seriously lacking. Until such data are available, the CAS might best be used as a research instrument. Because of its brevity and appeal to young children, the CAS is a promising screening device. But until criterion-related validity is established, the State-Trait Anxiety Inventory for Children, General Anxiety Scale for Children, and revised Children's Manifest Anxiety Scale might prove more useful diagnostic instruments even though they are not completely similar in age level and intent.

REVIEWER'S REFERENCES

Elder, M. I. CHILDHOOD ANXIETY AND PARENTAL FAMILY BACKGROUND. Unpublished B. A. Thesis, St. Thomas University, 1978.

Ells, P. RELOCATION, FATHER ABSENCE AND ANXIETY IN ELEMENTARY SCHOOL CHILDREN FROM MILITARY AND CIVILIAN FAMILIES. Unpublished B. A. Thesis, St. Thomas University, 1979.

Review of Child Anxiety Scale by F. E. STERLING, *Psychological Associate, Department of Psychology, Central Louisiana State Hospital, Pineville, LA:*

In response to the expressed concern of the Task Force on The Mental Health of Children for early detection and treatment of emotional and behavior disorders, J. S. Gillis has attempted to develop a reliable measuring device appropriate for use with young children. The Child Anxiety Scale (CAS) was designed to be brief, easily administered, and easily scored. As a result of earlier factorial investigations, 20 items were extracted from the Early School Personality Questionnaire (ESPQ) item pool which evidenced high loadings on a general second-order factor pattern labeled Anxiety, which has also been found to exist among older aged groups (Gillis & Cattell, 1979).

Administration of the 20-item instrument is facilitated by an administrator who introduces the subjects to the tasks and operates an audio tape machine by which the stimulus items are presented. Maximum amount of administration time required is under 20 minutes, with taped presentation of the items being just under 15. Response sheets are similar to those employed in the administration of the ESPQ, having numbered rectangles with different pictures in the middle of each, flanked by a red dot on the left and a blue dot on the right. Responders are instructed to mark an "X" over the colored dot which signifies the appropriate response of the child to the presented items. To guard against yea-saying response sets, several items are reflective items presented in apparently random order. A clear scoring template is provided to facilitate rapid, easy scoring. The test manual provides scoring norms for converting raw scores into both sten scores or percentiles for children ages 5 years, 0 months through 12 years, 11 months and for grades K through 5.

The 20 items constituting the CAS appear to correlate well with the designated "pure anxiety factor," with item correlations ranging from .17 to .49 ($N = 251$). Correlations between items and total scale scores range from .14 to .45 ($N = 343$). Test-retest reliability coefficients for 127 children in grades 1, 2, and 3 were .82, .85, and .92 respectively for these class groups. Another sample of children produced a 1-week test-retest coefficient of .81. Congruence coefficients between the factor pattern proposed by Krug, Scheier and Cattell (1976) and the factor pattern used in the construction of the CAS were .81 ($p < .01$) and .74 ($p < .05$) respectively for the two independent samples.

The above data support the notion that the CAS has respectable statistical reliability and factorial validity. The factorial validity that is provided for the potential user of this testing instrument appears to satisfy Gillis' nomothetic operational definition of anxiety as "a stable pattern of weights on specified primary personality traits." The CAS manual presents cross-validation data reflecting factor loadings of the ESPQ primary factors on the second-order factor of anxiety for two separate groups with *N*s of 192 and 251 respectively. Factors C, D, H, and O all have the expected high loadings; however factor F (Sober versus Enthusiastic) and factor G (Expedient versus Conscientious), excluded by operational definition, also load appreciably on the second order factor (–.56 and –.27 respectively) for the larger of the two groups. The demography of these respective groups is not revealed, and it may be that these high loadings are reflections of a coincidental group characteristic. It seems important to consider that what is being called anxiety may be exemplified by fluctuating factorial components across age or other groupings, and that factorial stability may be demonstrated only within verified demographic parameters.

As is the case with the development of testing instruments designed to measure relatively uncharted domains, external criteria pose a difficult problem. Such is the case with the CAS. A previous investigation (Ells, 1979) had suggested that family relocation may have an upsetting influence on children. The CAS was administered to 292 children in a community which to a large extent was comprised of military personnel considered to have a higher than average probability for frequent relocation. A significant relationship between CAS scores and attitudes toward moving, although not with mobility per se, was found. The relationship alluded to is assumed to imply frequency of relocation. If these assumptions are true, then we can conclude that the higher the CAS score the more negatively individuals viewed family relocation. Actual frequency of relocation (if mobility implies this) did not significantly covary with CAS scores beyond chance expectancy. Inferring the relative presence of anxiety from attitudinal scores (the psychometric parameters of which are undisclosed) appears to tax the limits of scientific inference.

Parental separation and divorce were also hypothesized as generators of anxiety in children. Elder (1978) administered the CAS to a group of children living with only one parent and also to a control group, the results of which revealed no significant difference between the CAS scores of the two groups. These unexpected results were subjected to some interesting, after-the-fact, and perhaps heuristically speculative explanations which should be investigated, but the results as they stand are hardly supportive of the criterion-related validity of the CAS.

CAS scores obtained from children from six different classrooms revealed a significantly higher mean score for a classroom identified as one with "special problems...for an extended period of time." The investigator was unable to explore the nature of those special problems due to issues of confidentiality, an unfortunate circumstance which may have prevented the discovery of a valid and reliable criterion against which the CAS validity could be compared.

A similar disappointment followed an investigation to determine a relationship between CAS and high, middle, and low academic achievers. Although no significant findings were obtained for this achievement breakdown, there was a statistically significant tendency for teachers to make no comments at all on their report forms about high CAS scores. No substantive data is provided which would clarify whether this finding was a reflection of a student as opposed to a teacher variable.

Finally, Gillis reports that a group of special education students in grades K through 4 ($N = 34$) with verified speech and education handicaps, learning disabilities, and emotional problems scored significantly lower on the CAS than the national CAS norm group. From this finding it was concluded that early detection and intervention had "an important impact upon the psychological well-being of these children." Such a conclusion may be correct; however, the suggested inference that this finding represents relative freedom from anxiety as measured by the CAS appears unwarranted given the current stage of the test's development.

In summary, the CAS is a brief screening instrument to identify anxiety in children in grades K through 5. Although the CAS may evidence respectable factorial stability for some clearly defined primary factors within some groups, the intrusion of incidentally significant loadings of other primary factors within other groups suggest the need for further validity investigations with varying age groups of young children. Additionally, more soundly based investigations aimed at establishing criterion-related validity should be required before this screening instrument can be recommended for general use in applied settings.

REVIEWER'S REFERENCES

Krug, S. E., Scheier, I. H., & Cattell, R. B. HANDBOOK FOR THE IPAT ANXIETY SCALE. Champaign, IL: Institute for Personality and Ability Testing, Inc., 1976.

Elder, M. I. CHILDHOOD ANXIETY AND PARENTAL FAMILY BACKGROUND. Unpublished B. A. Thesis, St. Thomas University, 1978.

Ells, P. RELOCATION, FATHER ABSENCE AND ANXIETY IN ELEMENTARY SCHOOL CHILDREN FROM MILITARY AND CIVILIAN FAMILIES. Unpublished B. A. Thesis, St. Thomas University, 1979.

Gillis, J. S., & Cattell, R. B. Comparison of second order personality structures at 6–8 years with later patterns. MULTIVARIATE EXPERIMENTAL CLINICAL RESEARCH, 1979, 4, 93–99.

[213]

Child Behavior Checklist. Ages 4–18; 1980–83; individual; 4 forms; manual ('83, 243 pages); 1983 price data: $25 per 100 forms; $25 per 100 revised child behavior profiles including hand scoring instructions; $4 per scoring templates; $18 per manual; $4 per sample packet including one of each form and profile with hand scoring instructions; computer programs available for computer scoring; Thomas M. Achenbach and Craig Edelbrock; Thomas M. Achenbach.*

a) CHILD BEHAVIOR CHECKLIST. Ages 4–16; CBCL; ratings by parents; 5 scale scores: social competence (activities, social, school), behavior problems (internalizing, externalizing); 1 form ('81, 4 pages); revised child behavior profile ('82, 2 pages) for girls aged 4–5, 6–11, 12–16, boys ages 4–5, 6–11, 12–16; instructions for hand scoring the revised child behavior profile (no date, 10 pages); administration time not reported.

b) TEACHER'S REPORT FORM. Ages 6–16; TRF; ratings by teacher; 5 scale scores; same as for *a*; 1 form ('80, 4 pages); child behavior profile—teacher's report version ('82, 2 pages) for boys ages 6–11; instructions for hand scoring the profile ('82, 4 pages); administration time not reported.

c) DIRECT OBSERVATION FORM. Ages 4–16; DOF; ratings by a trained observer; 2 scores: behavior problems, on-task score; self-explanatory form ('81, 3 pages); (10) minutes for each observation.

d) YOUTH SELF-REPORT FORM. Ages 11–18; YSR; ratings by self; 2 scales: social competence, behavior problems; 1 form ('81, 4 pages): administration time not reported.

TEST REFERENCES

1. Kazdin, A. E., Esveldt-Dawson, K., & Loar, L. L. Correspondence of teacher ratings and direct observations of classroom behavior of psychiatric inpatient children. JOURNAL OF ABNORMAL CHILD PSYCHOLOGY, 1983, 11, 549–564.

2. Last, J. M., & Bruhn, A. R. The psychodiagnostic value of children's earliest memories. JOURNAL OF PERSONALITY ASSESSMENT, 1983, 47, 597–603.

3. Mash, E. J., Johnston, C., & Kovitz, K. A comparison of the mother-child interactions of physically abused and non-abused children during play and task situations. JOURNAL OF CLINICAL CHILD PSYCHOLOGY, 1983, 12, 337–346.

4. Reed, M. L., & Edelbrock, C. Reliability and validity of the Direct Observation Form of the Child Behavior Checklist. JOURNAL OF ABNORMAL CHILD PSYCHOLOGY, 1983, 11, 521–530.

5. Lemoine, R. L. The Louisiana Mental Health Client-Outcome Evaluation Project: An initial progress report. COMMUNITY MENTAL HEALTH JOURNAL, 1984, 20, 90–100.

Review of Child Behavior Checklist by B. J. FREEMAN, Associate Professor of Medical Psychology, Department of Psychiatry, UCLA School of Medicine, Los Angeles, CA:

The Child Behavior Checklist (CBCL) was designed to address one of the most serious problems in clinical child psychopathology—that of defining child behavior problems empirically. In the development of the CBCL much more attention has been paid to its psychometric properties than is usually the case. It is based on a careful review of the literature and carefully conducted empirical studies.

The CBCL is designed to assess in a standardized format the behavioral problems and social competencies of children, ages 4 to 16 years, as reported by parents. It can be self-administered or administered by an interviewer. It consists of 118 items related to behavior problems which are scored on a 3-point scale ranging from not true to often true of the child. There are also 20 social competency items used to obtain parents' reports of the amount and quality of their child's participation in sports, hobbies, games, activities, organizations, jobs and chores, friendships, how well the child gets along with others and plays and works by him/herself, and school functioning.

As noted by the authors, the value of any checklist rests on its ability to distinguish between children who have problems and those who do not. In order to identify syndromes of behavior problems, factor analytic studies were conducted on CBCLs completed by parents of children referred for outpatient mental health services. Separate analyses were done for each sex and ages 4 to 5, 6 to 11, and 12 to 16. These analyses identified the following descriptive scales: Schizoid/Anxious, Depressed, Uncommunicative, Obsessive-Compulsive, Somatic Complaints, Social Withdrawal, Hyperactive, Aggressive, and Delinquent. Subsequently, both parts of the CBCL were normed on a sample of 1,300 children and *T*-scores derived. This permits comparison of any child's profile to the norms of the defined scales.

Several forms of reliability are reported in the manual. Individual item intraclass correlations (ICC) of greater than .90 were obtained "between item scores obtained from mothers filling out the CBCL at 1-week intervals, mothers and fathers filling out the CBCL on their clinically-referred children, and three different interviewers obtaining CBCLs from parents of demographically matched triads of children." In addition, stability of ICCs over a 3-month period were .84 for behavior problems and .97 for social competencies. Test-retest reliability of mothers' ratings were .89. Some differences were found between mothers' and fathers' individual ratings.

In addition to the CBCL completed by parents, supplementary data forms are provided for obtaining data from different sources. The Teacher's Report Form (TRF) is designed to obtain the teacher's assessment of many of the same problems that parents rate on the CBCL. A scoring profile for boys 6 to 11 is available and research is continuing on generating profiles for the other age/sex groups.

The Direct Observation Form (DOF) is designed for use by an experienced observer who observes the child for 10-minute periods in the classroom or other group activity. The DOF includes many of the same behaviors as the TRF but uses 4-step rating scales geared to 10-minute samples of behavior. It also provides for scoring of on-task behavior in 1-minute intervals. High correlations are reported between total DOF problem scores obtained by pairs of observers after minimal training. No normative data are yet available for the DOF.

The Youth Self-Report (YSR) is designed to obtain self-ratings from 11- to 18-year-olds on most of the CBCL social competencies and behavior problems. The authors report the preliminary research indicated good stability for self-ratings over a 6-month period and low but statistically significant agreement with ratings by parents and a clinician. Standardized scoring profiles and normative data are as yet not available on the YSR.

The CBCL has several advantages. It is well documented psychometrically with adequate reliability and validity; focuses on a child's competencies as well as behavior problems; is easily administered and can be scored without the use of a computer; provides a well-written manual; and can provide cross-situational data when used in conjunction with the TRF, DOF, and YSR. In addition, since the CBCL is based on empirical research, it can easily be utilized in a variety of research settings.

The major disadvantage of the CBCL is that it is primarily based on parental report and has the limitations of all such measures. The authors have addressed this problem by providing other forms to generate cross-situational data. However, to date the supplementary measures have not been subjected to the same rigorous psychometric analyses as the CBCL.

In summary, the CBCL is probably one of the better checklists currently available. It is based on empirical research and appears to have adequate reliability and validity. It can be easily utilized by persons who are relatively unsophisticated in the use of psychometric tests to identify behavior problems in children. However, a word of caution is in order. Any checklist is only as good as the clinician who uses it.

Review of Child Behavior Checklist by MARY LOU KELLEY, *Assistant Professor of Psychology, Louisiana State University, Baton Rouge, LA:*

The Child Behavior Checklist (CBCL) is a rating scale consisting of 118 behavior problem items and 20 items that assess the amount and quality of children's activities, social interactions, and school performance. As stated in the manual, the CBCL "is designed to obtain parents' descriptions of their children's behavior in a standardized format." The instrument is not to be used to make diagnostic inferences. The instrument is intended for use with children aged 4 to 16. The items are written at a 5th-grade reading level and generally are worded in a nontechnical, colloquial way.

The behavior problem items of the test were derived from the clinical and research literature, through consultation with various child care professionals, and from actual case records. Parents rate the degree to which each item "describes their child currently or within the last 6 months," using a 3-point rating scale (0=not true, 1=somewhat or sometimes true, 2=very true or often true). While the majority of the items describe overt behavior (e.g., disobedient at home, gets teased a lot), some of the items require the parent to make inferences about the child's feelings or thoughts (e.g., feels worthless or inferior, feels he or she has to be perfect).

The social competence portion of the test requires parents to list sports, activities, and organizations in which their child participates and then to rate the quality and/or amount of time the child spends in each activity as compared to same-aged peers. The social competence scale also obtains information on the amount and quality of peer interaction, quality of family interaction, and current and past school performance.

In addition to the CBCL, the Teacher Rating Form (TRF), the Youth Self-Report (YSR) and the Direct Observation Form (DOF) have been developed to obtain supplementary information. The new instruments are similar to the CBCL in content and format. However, the items for each test vary somewhat from the CBCL depending on the purpose of the instrument. For example, on the YSR, items naturally are worded in the first person, several items have been eliminated as they are unlikely to be reported by youths aged 11 to 16, and other items have been modified slightly. On the TRF more emphasis is placed on evaluating current and past academic performance and on evaluating behavior problems likely to be observed by a teacher. At this date, scoring profiles are available for the TRF only. However, scoring profiles for the DOF and the YSR are in the process of being developed. The manual describes all three supplementary tests. Preliminary studies supporting the reliability and validity of the supplementary instruments have been conducted.

The manual which accompanies the text is well written. The authors describe the purposes, conceptualization of, and rationale for the CBCL in a manner that is informative yet not overly technical. The authors provide much detail on the construction and psychometric properties of the test yet do so in a way that is clear and understandable. Throughout the manual, the authors provide logical, succinct rationales for the use of various psychometric procedures. Given the level of detail and clarity of the manual, the rationale for and psychometric properties of the CBCL are understandable and informative to professionals with varying backgrounds in test construction.

The manual provides adequate information on the administration and scoring of the CBCL. The authors' writings reflect their sensitivity to the potential uses and misuse of the CBCL in both clinical and research settings. Particularly relevant to users of the CBCL is the chapter on commonly asked questions about the instrument and the appendix which describes hand scoring procedures. While all information relevant to the administration and scoring of the CBCL is included, the information is somewhat scattered throughout the manual. The manual might be more useful if a separate chapter on the administration of the test was included.

The CBCL is one of the best standardized instruments of its kind. As described in the manual and elsewhere, separate principal component analyses have been conducted on data obtained on clinic-referred male and female children at three age levels (4 to 5, 6 to 11, 12 to 16). For each age/sex group eight or nine factors were obtained; items loading highest on each factor were used to form behavior problem scales. In addition, second order factor analyses yielded two broad band groupings (labelled Internalizing/Externalizing) for each sex/age group. Normative data, obtained from parents of 1,300 children, were used to derive scaled *T* scores for each age/sex group. Both the clinical and normative samples were heterogeneous with respect to race and socioeconomic status and were proportionate to the composition of the general U.S. population.

From the normative data, Achenbach & Edelbrock have constructed easy-to-use profile sheets for each of the six sex/age groups. Each profile sheet groups behavior problem scales according to their loadings on the Internalizing/Externalizing factors. The social competence scales (Activities, Social, and School) also have normalized *T* scores and are included in the CBCL profiles. In addition to hand scoring the CBCL, programs for computer scoring the test are available from Dr. Achenbach.

As pointed out in the manual, hand scoring of the CBCL on the Child Behavior Profile requires that the instructions be carefully followed. Several items require the test administrator to question parental responses to insure that accurate readings are obtained. Without the required questioning, high *T* scores on several scales can be obtained inaccurately. Furthermore, several scales are labelled using psychiatric terminology (e.g., Schizoid). Achenbach and Edelbrock provide rationales for the use of such terminology and take great care to caution the reader against misinterpreting elevated *T* scores as diagnostic labels. However, use of psychiatric terminology appears unnecessary and potentially damaging if used in a summary fashion in test reports without appropriate qualification. Nonetheless, with appropriate completion and scoring of the test, as well as with careful, accurate interpretation of the results, the profiles provide a useful and efficient method of summarizing parental responses.

The psychometric properties of the CBCL have been extensively evaluated and are discussed in detail in the manual. Intraclass correlation coefficients were computed to assess test-retest reliability, interparent agreement, and inter-interviewer reliability of item scores; all coefficients on these assessments were above .90. Furthermore, correlational studies conducted with scale scores, total problem scores, and competence scores indicated good test-retest reliability, score stability, and mother-father agreement.

With regard to the validity of the CBCL, several studies have supported the construct validity of the instrument. Tests of criterion-related validity using clinical status as the criterion (referred/non-referred) also support the validity of the instrument. Importantly, demographic variables such as race and SES accounted for a relatively small proportion of score variance. Furthermore, using the 90th percentile of the behavior problem scores and the 10th percentile of the social competence scores in the nonclinical samples as cutoff points, the misclassification rate on the behavior problem scale was 9.8% for nonreferred children and 25.9% for referred children. Misclassification was higher when the social competence scores were used (9.9% for nonreferred children and 42.9% for referred children). However, as Achenbach and Edelbrock describe, the discriminative power of the test can be improved when the two scores are used together.

The CBCL is one of the best if not the best instrument of its kind. The test is comprehensive both in breadth of content and in the age range for which it is intended. The test is inexpensive and is very easy to administer and score. Use of the CBCL yields much information both to the clinician and to the researcher. Achenbach and his colleagues have constructed and evaluated the psychometric properties of the CBCL in a scholarly and comprehensive manner. Further, the test items are relatively noninferential. In my opinion, the CBCL is an exemplary test and I would recommend its use over any other similar test. While the supplementary tests which currently are being evaluated will likely prove to be equally useful, additional studies are needed to establish their psychometric strength.

[214]

The CHILD Center Operational Assessment Tool. Regular or special classroom students; 1971–77; OAT; criterion-referenced; assesses and identifies children with special educational needs; no data on reliability and validity; no norms; 4 tests; 1983 price data: $6 per specimen set, includes one reading/spelling test, spelling manual, and instructions book; administration time not reported; The Child Center; the Author.*

a) READING/SPELLING TEST. 1971–77; both forms are to be used together; 3 areas: primary learning abilities, phonic encoding-decoding, structural analysis encoding-decoding; 2 forms: reading ('71, 16 pages), spelling ('71, 23 pages); spelling manual ('71, 20 pages); reading/spelling instructions book ('77, 35 pages); $.95 per spelling manual; $3.50 per instructions book.

b) MATH TEST. 1971; 2 forms; $.95 per form.

1) *Basic Concepts.* 4 areas: numeration, basic operations, place value, fractions; 1 form (15 pages); student cards (13 cards); $.95 per set of cards.

2) *Operational Skills.* 6 areas: addition and subtraction, multiplication, division, fractions, decimals, percents; 1 form (25 pages); manual (3 pages); $.95 per manual.

c) LANGUAGE TEST. 1971; 3 areas: memory and sequencing, auditory discrimination, similarities; 1 form (12 pages); examiner cards (40 cards); $.95 per test; $.95 per set of cards.

d) BEHAVIORAL QUESTIONNAIRE. 1971; ratings by teachers; 8 scores: learning, liability, coordination, self-esteem, concentration, inappropriate involuntary behavior, motor expression, school attitude; 1 form (4 pages); score form (2 pages); $.95 per questionnaire and score form.

Review of The CHILD Center Operational Assessment Tool by WILLIAM L. HEWARD, Professor of Education, The Ohio State University, Columbus, OH:

Any sample of behavior can be used to assess present levels of performance and to make inferences about future performance. The Operational Assessment Tool (OAT) samples a variety of behaviors in the academic areas of Reading/Spelling, Mathematics, and Language. In addition, a behavior rating form is provided for the teacher to complete. The extent to which the OAT may be considered a test, however, depends on the user's expectations of a test. On the surface, the instrument has the trappings of a test—items grouped into subtests, directions for administration, stimulus materials, record forms, and scoring instructions. On another level, the instrument claims to have content validity. Although the term "validity" is never used by the author in describing its construction, the author describes the development of the tool as based on a task-analysis of reading (no similar claim is made for mathematics), administration of the tests to "several hundred children in experimental and control groups," computer analysis which verified "the task analysis levels as specific skill clusters and determined which items in each subtest were the most reliable indicators of mastery," and "retesting in experimental and control groups." On still another level, the test includes criterion scores for each subtest within each content area, both for use in determining deficit skills and discontinuing the subtest.

However, the instrument has severe limitations as a test. Not one specific reference is made to any of the research mentioned as supporting the test's design; not one piece of concrete data is provided on the tryout sample, the performances of students in the tryouts, the types of analyses performed, the basis for establishing the criterion scores, or the results of test-retest studies. (In fact, the mention of experimental and control groups suggests a research design for measuring the effectiveness of curricular or instructional programming, not test construction.) Not one piece of evidence is given to justify the discontinuation of testing in some subtests but not in others, other than a general reference to "research." These criticisms, by the way, refer to the paucity of information included for the Reading/Spelling tests—literally no information is provided to the user of the math, language, and behavior rating tools. Not one sentence is devoted to the intended age or grade levels of the students for whom any of the tests are intended, nor is there any attempt even to suggest the approximate curriculum levels of the content sampled by the various tests. Worse, the OAT tests are recommended for use as repeated measures of student progress, despite the fact that the examiner is encouraged to provide feedback on the items during testing.

It is difficult to argue that these tasks are really "tests" at all. Rather, they are the kind of informal measures that any practicing teacher can develop (and probably already has developed) in a matter of a few hours. Moreover, the items selected by the practicing teacher would probably provide a more relevant evaluation of the teacher's own curriculum sequences and priorities. But to leave the matter at that might imply that there is value in the "criterion-referenced" aspects of the OAT. In fact, the OAT is the type of instrument that has given criterion-referenced tests a somewhat dubious reputation over the years. None of the standards by which competent testmakers design, evaluate, and refine a good criterion-referenced test have been followed (or at least documented) by the authors of the OAT. No information on test specifications, no support for the varying numbers of items across subtests, no data to support the assignment of criteria, no definition of "mastery" other than the meeting of the arbitrary criterion—none of this can be found in the materials that comprise the OAT. While these are not necessarily expectations that one has of informal instruments prepared by classroom teachers, they are legitimate demands of an instrument describing itself as a "test" and being offered for sale.

In spite of these fundamental inadequacies of the OAT, let us suppose that a teacher has purchased the tests. The teacher must then learn how to give, score, and interpret the test. The teacher begins by reading the administration directions given for the Reading/Spelling tests, only to encounter such admonitions as "Do not let 'creeping failure' set in!" Moreover, the teacher is instructed to abandon the common practice of avoiding correction or feedback during testing. In fact, the teacher is told that "The test is designed to be a positive, non-threatening experience for the child and frequent feedback is a must." No further mention is made, however, of what the feedback should consist of or how it should be provided. Similarly, in the Expressive Language subtest, the following direction is given: "In order to encourage the child to give his best response if a poor one is elicited, the tester may use a phrase such as 'that's true, but in what other ways are they alike?'" The literal meaning of this direction, coupled with the assignment of different score values depending on the quality of the response (e.g., citing the conceptual class to which a pair of objects belongs earns 3 points, while citing a physical property or characteristic of the objects earns 1 point), makes it conceivable that a student making adequate initial responses could earn lower total point-values than the poorer student who is prompted for second responses. Scoring of the OAT is straightforward, although the Expressive Language test requires some subjective judgments and the Behavioral Questionnaire requires the examiner to respond to 60 questions but, for no apparent reason, ignores 22 of them in totaling the child's score. Interpretation of the scores is left completely to the teacher, except for the overall guideline to teach all the skills on which the child is below criterion. No suggestions for error analysis are given, nor are recommendations for further testing included for any of the subtests. The stated purpose of the Behavioral Questionnaire is "to lead to better teaching strategies," but absolutely no information is given about how to interpret scores in ways that might lead to those teaching strategies.

It is obvious that this reviewer does not feel the OAT merits serious consideration as a test. For the purpose of systematically assessing academic skill levels with criterion-referenced measures, the series of test batteries by Brigance (Curriculum Associates) or the batteries by Howell, Zucker, and Morehead (Charles E. Merrill Publishing) offer far more. The teacher seeking a series of informal classroom measures would do as well to create his or her own items.

Review of The CHILD Center Operational Assessment Tool by DAVID H. REILLY, Professor and Dean, School of Education, University of North Carolina at Greensboro, Greensboro, NC:

The major purpose of this test is to assess a child's mastery along a continuum of skills which must be mastered in order to read and spell effectively. The instrument is criterion-referenced with the criteria being the aforementioned continuum. The test author indicates that the instrument was developed with a research design base, and that the test was administered to several hundred children in experimental and control groups in order to verify that the skill clusters in each subtest were the most reliable indicators of mastery. Unfortunately, this is the only information provided with respect to the development of the test. Absolutely no data regarding the norm groups, reliability, or validity are provided. This seriously detracts from the usefulness of the test. Inspection of the test does suggest that the reading and spelling portions are primarily readiness instruments appropriate for nursery through first grade.

The math portions of the test deal with basic concepts and operational skills. No norm group, reliability or validity data are provided. These portions of the test go significantly beyond the apparent age suitability of the reading/spelling test but again the lack of relevant information for norm groups and appropriate test populations is lacking and makes it difficult, if not impossible, to specify appropriate age levels for the test.

The tests were apparently designed to be utilized by teachers in the classroom situations of teaching reading, spelling, and math. Specific reference is made to the criterion-referenced nature of the test and the fact that when a student does not achieve mastery the testing is to be terminated and teaching is to take place until mastery is achieved. This presumably relates only to the reading and spelling portions; no mention of this is made with respect to the math teaching, but since the format for the math test is the same as that for reading and spelling it is assumed that the same principle applies.

The test comes with different colored paper for the math, reading, and spelling portions. The instructions for administration and the test booklet itself are in separate packages held together by one staple. This makes it quite likely that with fairly moderate use the material may come apart and be lost or destroyed. The sets of cards which are to be used with various portions of the test are of similarly poor quality. One set of cards is held together with string and two sets of cards are held together only by one rubber band. Again the opportunity for loss and/or destruction is quite likely.

The quality of the test is quite poor with many of the designs and pictures difficult to understand and obviously hand drawn. The general appearance of the test is rather amateurish and keeping track of all the materials could present a formidable problem. Further, the instructions for the different subtests, particularly spelling, are difficult to follow. The instructions for the first four pages of the test are presented on one page while the student portion is on separate pages. Assuring that the instructions and the student's response will be geared to the same page could present a considerable problem. Also, some editing would seem to be required on various sections of the test. For example, on the spelling criterion test, Visual Perception, Part C—Letter Discrimination, the instructions state that the student is to circle the word in each row that is different. However, the first two items of the test are letters, not words, and this could present a problem to some students.

Directions for the administration of the test are provided with each of the test booklets. A more comprehensive manual is provided which provides most of the information related to how to use the instruments. This manual does suffer from excessive detail and appears to be largely focused on an introductory course in reading about readiness. It could be improved considerably by omitting much of the detail related to teaching, by focusing on the administration of the test, and by providing considerably more information with respect to the norm groups, reliability, validity, and outcome data after the teaching programs have been implemented. There are apparently packaged teaching programs which are associated with each of the test instruments but these were unavailable for review.

The tests themselves can apparently be of aid to the classroom teacher although significant individual time would have to be spent on administering the reading tests as well as portions of the spelling test. It is questionable whether a regular or special classroom teacher would want to devote as much time to the assessment as is presumably necessary to test all children in a classroom. Other instruments which provide essentially the same data and have more information regarding validity, reliability, and norm group characteristics are available.

In summary, this test is poorly manufactured, lacks any information related to norm group characteristics, reliability, or validity data. It would seem to require excessive classroom time for a teacher to administer and utilize when other instruments with better technical information are so readily available.

[215]

Child Development Center Q-Sort. Ages 1.5 to adult; 1968; CDCQ; manual title is *A Method for Assessing Personality Development for Follow-Up Evaluations of the Preschool Child*; sorting of personality characteristics by mental health workers, psychologists, psychiatrists, social workers, or specially trained teachers; reliability and validity data for pre-schoolers only; no scores as such, but correlations possible with age-typical sort, age-ideal sort, and statistically normal sort; 6 overlapping levels (toddlers, 1.5–3 years; preschool, 3–4.5 years; kindergarten, 4.5–6.5 years; school age; adolescence; maturity) in 113 sort deck cards; manual (61 pages); record form (no date, 1 page); age ideal form (no date, 1 page); distribution cards (no date, 48 cards); 1984 price data: $35 per complete set including 30 record forms for any one level; $7.50 per 30 record forms plus age ideal for each sex for any one level; $16 per sort deck cards; $11 per distribution cards including all age levels; $10.50 per manual; Frances Fuchs Schachter, Allan Cooper (manual), and Rona Gordet (manual); Stoelting Co.*

See T3:394 (1 reference).

Review of Child Development Center Q-Sort by MICHAEL L. REED, Western Psychiatric Institute and Clinic, University of Pittsburgh School of Medicine, Pittsburgh, PA:

This instrument is composed of 113 child characteristics which are listed on cards and sorted into categories by clinicians or other trained mental health workers. Each card contains an upper statement and a lower statement, which express the child characteristics in a negative (i.e., Is distractible, cannot concentrate) and a positive (i.e., Can concentrate even under distracting circumstances) manner. Overlapping subsets of the item pool are used for children in the following age groups: toddler (1.5 to 3 years), preschool (3 to 4.5 years), kindergarten (4.5 to 6.5 years), school age, adolescent, and maturity.

To use the Q-sort, child characteristics are sorted into seven categories which follow a normal distribution. Categories 7, 6, and 5 are used if the upper statement on the card reflects a "highly salient," "somewhat salient," or "salient" characteristic for the target child. Categories 1, 2, and 3 are used if the lower statement on the card reflects a "highly salient," "somewhat salient," or "salient" characteristic for the target child. Category 4 is used when neither statement is true for the child. Clinicians may evaluate children in two ways: by comparing them against the typical child of the same age (yielding an age-typical sort), or by comparing them against the ideal, or perfectly healthy, child of the same age (yielding an age-ideal sort). The similarities and differences between the Q-sorts of target children and those of standard age-typical or age-ideal children are used as an index of psychopathology.

Reliability estimates for the CDCQ were derived from two sources. First, case records were obtained for 8 clinically referred and 8 normal preschool children. Four clinicians completed Q-sorts based on the age-typical criteria. The intersorter correlation for individual sorters was .62, and this increased to .77 and .83 based on composite sorts of 2 and 3 clinicians, respectively. Second, 6 clinicians and 6 preschool teachers were asked to construct sorts for age-typical and age-ideal boys and girls at the toddler, preschool, and kindergarten age levels. Mean intersorter reliabilities ranged from .65 to .76 across the age and gender groups, and reliabilities ranged from .95 to .97 when composite sorts were used. Reliability estimates based on mythical cases and clinical records are difficult to interpret and these findings should be viewed with caution. Test-retest reliability data are needed and additional intersorter reliability data (preferably based on actual cases) are needed given the small sample size and limited age range.

Case records for the 8 clinically referred and 8 normal preschool children were also used to estimate validity for the CDCQ. Two clinicians, who were blind to the children's clinical status, completed sorts separately for each child. Clinician sorts for the 8 clinic children were negatively correlated with the standard age-ideal sort (average $r = -.22$), and clinician sorts for the 8 normal children were positively correlated with the standard age-ideal sort (average $r = .24$). These findings support the discriminant validity of CDCQ-sorts for preschool children, but the correlations are not robust and, given the small sample size, results should be interpreted with caution. Discriminant validity data for children in other age groups and data estimating predictive validity are needed.

A strength of the CDCQ is that separate item pools have been developed for children at different ages, yielding sorts which are age appropriate. This instrument may be useful as a descriptive tool; however, the sorting and scoring procedures are complex and time consuming. An additional concern is that categories derived from the sorting procedures overlap. This is because the upper and lower statement on each card may be either positive or negative. As a result categories which should reflect opposite ends of a continuum (7 and 1, 6 and 2, 5 and 3) contain both positive and negative statements with the same degree of saliency. The sorting procedures would yield more meaningful categories if the upper statement on each card was consistently positive and the lower statement was consistently negative (or vice versa). The categories would then contain child characteristics ranging from the most salient strength to the most salient weakness. This information might be useful in targeting areas for intervention and for identifying children's competencies. Given the lack of compelling reliability or validity evidence and the problem of overlapping categories, the CDCQ, in its present form, is not recommended for use.

Review of Child Development Center Q-Sort by JUDY A. UNGERER, Lecturer, School of Behavioural Sciences, Macquarie University, North Ryde, New South Wales, Australia:

The Child Development Center Q-Sort (CDCQ) is a methodology for the longitudinal assessment of personality development across five age levels—Toddler, Preschool, Kindergarten, School Age, and Adolescence-Maturity. The Q-sort consists of items reflecting "the basic dimensions of personality." It is not a pathological symptom checklist. Items for the Q-sort were carefully adapted from Block's (1961) California Q-sort and supplemented by other sorts, input from clinical experts, and psychoanalytically oriented diagnostic guides. The authors describe the CDCQ as eclectic in orientation, but there is a strong psychoanalytic bias in item content and interpretation. For example, items assess personality functioning in the areas of Independence-Dependence, Affect, Heterosexual Matters, Ego, Superego, and Relations with People, the Self, and Inanimate Objects. Most items are worded to "denote manifest behavior or conscious feeling. However, for the major motivational systems—including hostility, dependency, generalized anxiety, anxiety about the self, and anxiety about the body—items were included to specify unconscious or latent levels." A commendable effort is made to control for the biasing effects of the positive/negative value of specific items by equalizing the number of positively and negatively biased items at each age level. However, situational inconstancy of behaviour is poorly assessed. Separate items for specifying behavior "at home" and "outside the home" are included only for the dimensions docile/negative and domineering/submissive.

The clearest advantage of the CDCQ is its ability to reduce into manageable form large masses of descriptive data. In addition, the CDCQ can be applied longitudinally without loss of sensitivity. New items are added at each developmental phase, permitting the assessment of newly emerging functions as well as new meanings accruing to earlier functions.

The major disadvantage of the CDCQ is its currently limited potential for interpretation. There are no reliable norms at any age level, and, therefore, no quantitative assessment of developmental deviation can be made. The authors provide examples of composite sorts for the age-ideal child (relative to the typical child of the same age), the age-typical child (relative to the typical child of any other age), and the statistically normal child for males and females separately at the preschool level, but these are based on too few cases to be used as developmental norms. The age-ideal and age-typical composite Q-sorts were generated by only six and five sorters, respectively, while the statistical norm composites were based on samples of only four children each. No other composite Q-sorts or statistical norms are presented. The authors suggest that the age-ideal and age-typical conceptual sorts are more appropriate measures of normality than the statistical norm, since statistical norms are strongly influenced by sample characteristics. However, statistical norms are widely used in developmental assessments, and when carefully generated, are not subject to significant sample selection biases. In addition, statistical norms are less influenced by theoretical orientation than the age-ideal conceptual Q-sort and are no more influenced by sampling biases or theoretical orientation than the age-typical conceptual Q-sorts. Statistical norms are more costly and difficult to generate, but they are the preferred basis for defining normality in the general population.

Interpretation of the CDCQ is further limited by the authors' failure to provide a clear developmental model for conceptualizing the item groupings. A psychoanalytical model is most appropriate for this assessment, but only one example is given as to how such a model could be used (i.e., to identify reaction formation). The authors' claim that personality typologies can be derived from the CDCQ lacks substance without more explicit discussion of item interpretation.

Reliability data on real children are minimal, and are reported only for a preschool sample of 16 children, 8 clinical and 8 control children matched loosely for age and socioeconomic factors. The Q-sorts were based on extensive written reports of each child's current and past functioning, which included data from mothers' interviews, teachers' interviews and reports, psychological tests, observation reports, and reports of interviews with the child. Each case was rated by three sorters. The mean intersorter correlation for both clinical and control groups was .62, indicating considerable between-sorter variability. The precise meaning of this variability is unclear since the correlation is a very coarse measure of reliability. A statistic which compares the absolute value of category assignment for each item across raters would provide a more informative index of between-sorter variability. The reliability for composite sorts based on three sorters was considerably higher ($r = .83$) than for sorts generated by single individuals. However, the use of composite sorts markedly reduces the efficiency of the measurement instrument. It is important to note that the protocols used in the reliability studies were extensive, and application of the CDCQ to less robust data sources may lead to significant reduction in reliability. No criteria for specifying the adequacy of a data record for use with the CDCQ are provided, although these clearly are needed.

Validity data for the CDCQ also are minimal. Validity was assessed by correlating the real Q-sorts for each of 16 preschoolers with three "normal" sorts for the same age group (i.e., age-ideal, age-typical, and statistically normal). The real-normal sort similarities then were correlated with clinical rankings of adjustment for the 16 children. The validity correlations for the age-ideal, age-typical, and statistically normal comparisons were .75, .77, and .47, respectively. Thus, the CDCQ may have some validity since children who approximate the age-ideal, age-typical, or statistically normal child are more likely to be judged well adjusted by clinicians. However, these results should not be emphasized too strongly because of the questionable reliability of the norms used in the validity computations.

To summarize, the CDCQ can be used as a tool for synthesizing large amounts of data derived from a psychoanalytic perspective. Its usefulness is currently limited to descriptive accounts of personality functioning, since no adequate norms which would enable quantitative assessments of developmental deviation are available. Means for developing personality typologies from the CDCQ have not been adequately specified, and the longitudinal usefulness of the measure remains to be tested. Considerable development of the measure is necessary before reliability and validity of the measure can be assured.

[216]

Children of Alcoholics Screening Test. Children of alcoholics; 1981–82; CAST; questions about experiences with an alcoholic parent; 1 form ('81, 2 pages); preliminary test manual ('82, 18 pages); 1983 price data: $15 per complete set including test, manual, and validity studies; administration time not reported; John W. Jones; Camelot Press.*

Review of Children of Alcoholics Screening Test by SUSANNA MAXWELL, Associate Professor of Educational Psychology, Northern Arizona University, Flagstaff, AZ:

The Children of Alcoholics Screening Test (CAST) is a 30-item self-report inventory which is accompanied by a "preliminary" test manual. A primary goal of the CAST is to aid in the identification of "at risk" children of alcoholics in schools and clinics so that they can receive appropriate preventive and therapeutic treatments. The items are to be answered "yes" or "no" and ask the child about "(*a*) psychological distress associated with a parent's drinking, (*b*) perceptions of drinking-related marital discord between their parents, (*c*) attempts to control a parent's drinking, (*d*) efforts to escape from the alcoholism, (*e*) exposure to drinking-related family violence, (*f*) tendencies to perceive their parents as being alcoholic, and (*g*) desire for professional counseling." The test items came from experiences of children of clinically-diagnosed alcoholics receiving treatment as well as published case studies.

The test author provides a strong rationale for the development of the CAST, pointing out that no other such measure exists even though a 1981 report from the U.S. Department of Health and Human Services noted that only 5% of the school-aged children of alcoholics in the United States are identified and receive treatment. Stating that "no family member escapes unscathed from an alcoholic family system," the author feels that even children who appear to be well adjusted in childhood are at risk for problems later in life.

Though the need for the CAST is well presented, the specifics of administration, interpretation, and psychometric properties are less clear. The manual does not specify administration time or age range though it states that children 9 years of age and older can usually complete it without assistance while younger ones may need to have the questions read aloud "and sometimes interpreted to them." Because the score reflects the number of "yes" responses, the CAST is open to "faking," an interpretive caution mentioned in the manual.

Reliability data include only split-half (odd vs. even) coefficients. A Spearman-Brown reliability coefficient of .98 was computed in each of three separate samples. But while internal consistency is important, the need for test-retest reliability data seems critical with such emotionally charged questions. Since the author has stated that children 8 and younger may need the items "interpreted," the user must be able to judge the impact of such an intervention on the child's responses before labeling the CAST "a very reliable screening test" as the author has done.

Only two validity studies have been conducted with the CAST to determine if it can discriminate children of alcoholics from the general population of children, and one of these studies was composed of 81 adults (mean age 26.4). The single study of latency-age and adolescent children contained 97 children of alcoholics and a control group of 118 randomly selected children. There are no additional data regarding the characteristics of the sample. Chi-square analyses showed that all 30 CAST items significantly discriminated children of alcoholics from control group children. The author found that 100% of the children of alcoholics scored 6 or more compared to 23% of the control group, so he suggests using a score of 6 to identify children of alcoholics while a score of 2 to 5 diagnoses "children of problem drinkers or possible alcoholics." Jones does not provide information regarding a corroborative diagnosis of those control children scoring 6 or above. This reviewer would urge extreme caution in adopting the diagnostic criteria recommended by Jones. Not only are there no data in the manual regarding sex and ethnic differences, but there are no distinctions made for different age groups. Danielle L. Spiegler (1983) has found that young children tend to have mildly unfavorable attitudes toward alcohol but by ages 9 and 10 they have become increasingly more negative. Yet from 10 to 14 their attitudes are progressively less severe. Such developmental trends, hypothesized to correspond to Kohlberg's stages of moral development, may significantly influence a child's response to some CAST items.

In addition to its use as a screening instrument, the test author suggests the CAST may be used as a counseling tool, a research measure, and an aid in the evaluation of a parent for possible alcoholism using the viewpoint of the children. This last suggestion seems potentially imprudent within an unpredictable and highly stressed family situation. Nevertheless, the CAST could be used effectively within a family counseling situation.

In summary, the CAST seems most promising for use in a therapeutic relationship. While the author has effectively outlined the need for a screening measure to identify "at-risk" children of alcoholics, he has not provided sufficient reliability and validity data to justify the widespread use of the CAST as such a device. Until more research establishes reliable diagnostic criteria which address any age, sex, racial or ethnic differences, scores on the CAST should be interpreted with extreme caution.

REVIEWER'S REFERENCES

U.S. Department of Health and Human Services. THE FOURTH SPECIAL REPORT TO THE CONGRESS ON ALCOHOL AND HEALTH. Washington, DC: U.S. Government Printing Office, 1981.

Spiegler, D. L. Children's attitudes toward alcohol. JOURNAL OF STUDIES ON ALCOHOL, 1983, 44, 545–552.

Review of Children of Alcoholics Screening Test by BARRIE G. STACEY, Senior Lecturer in Psychology, University of Canterbury, Christchurch, New Zealand:

The Children of Alcoholics Screening Test (CAST) consists of 30 items dealing with pre-adult and adult children's attitudes, feelings, behavior, and experiences pertaining to their parents' use of alcohol. All 30 questions are answered by the testee checking either "Yes" or "No." Administration time would probably range from 5 to 15 minutes. The Yes answers are summed to yield a CAST score; a score of 0 indicates no reported experience of alcohol misuse, a score of 6 or more suggests at least one alcoholic parent, and the top score of 30 represents multiple severe experiences with parental alcohol abuse. The test is meant for older children, adolescents, and adults. With some help, it could be administered to individuals who have reading difficulties. CAST was developed to aid in the identification of "at risk" children of alcoholics, especially in schools and clinics. It is also recommended as a counseling tool, an aid in the evaluation of parental alcoholism, and a research tool.

The preliminary manual presents information about the development, reliability, and validity of the CAST. The test items were derived from the clinical work of the author and from published case studies of the children of alcoholics. The items were judged to be face valid by an unspecified number of alcohol counselors and adult children of alcoholics. The reliability and validity information was obtained from two small studies, one based upon 215 older children and adolescents, and the other upon 81 adults. The author obtained split-half reliability coefficients of .98, and interpreted them as demonstrating "the CAST is a very reliable screening test." However, the test may not be so reliable over time. But given the objective and easy way of scoring the test, marker judgement on scoring is not a potential source of unreliability.

With reference to validity, the author found that the children of alcoholics differed significantly from control group children for the total CAST score and for all 30 items. Further, no children of alcoholics obtained scores of 5 or less, whereas about three-quarters of the controls obtained scores of 5 or less. The author stated that "some children might have been motivated to 'fake good' on the CAST" without discussing this issue. In addition, he did not consider the sizeable minority of controls who obtained CAST scores from 6 to over 20. The size of this minority suggests the CAST may have limited value as a screening device and, possibly, as a research tool in the population at large.

The author's claim that "the CAST appears to be a highly valid and reliable screening tool that can discriminate children of alcoholics from the general population" is not warranted by the modest results of two small studies. A good deal more systematic work is needed on the reliability and validity of the test. It would be useful to have some general population norms and some special group norms. The overlap of CAST high scores from the children of alcoholics and the offspring of non-alcoholics needs to be examined. At present, the test is at the pioneering stage. But it may well prove useful to those concerned with the children of alcoholics.

In the reviewer's part of the world it would not be possible to use the CAST in schools. This probably applies in some other places as well. Any text which openly questions the young about their parents' alcohol use and its detrimental impact on the whole family would be unacceptable to the system. An item such as "Did you ever argue or fight with a parent when he or she was drinking?" would simply generate criticism of the would-be test user by administrators and teachers. The author of the CAST may be excessively optimistic in regarding it as a promising research tool for use with pre-adults in any institution given the political sensitivity of some family issues. CAST would appear to be most immediately useful in clinical and counseling settings where problem drinking or alcoholism is known or suspected.

[217]

Childrens Adaptive Behavior Report. Ages 5–11; 1982; CABR; "a developmental interview guide"; ratings by parent, teacher, or other informant in 5 areas: language development, independent functioning, family role performance, economic-vocational activities, socialization; no data on reliability and validity; no norms; individual; 1 form (14 pages, includes directions, test, and summary sheet); 1984 price data: $1 per form; administration time not reported; Richard H. Kicklighter and Bert O. Richmond; Humanics Limited.*

Review of Childrens Adaptive Behavior Report by FRED DAMARIN, Associate Professor of Psychology, The Ohio State University, Columbus, OH:

The Childrens Adaptive Behavior Report (CABR) provides 35 open-ended questions for interviewers who are seeking information about a child's adaptive behavior from parents, teachers, or other informants. Seven questions are allotted to each of the five areas covered by the report. Following each question set the informant and the interviewer make separate estimates on five-point scales of the child's adaptive behavior in the area just covered. The options run from "far below average for age" through "about average for age" to "very superior for age."

The two sets of scores are separately profiled and then summed into separate informant and interviewer composite ratings that are each expressed in three categories, "below average for age," "average," and "above average for age." Six blank lines are provided for an "analysis of report" and there are additional spaces for ratings of rapport and the adequacy of the information provided by the informant.

The instructions for interpreting the results begin with the claim that the CABR provides both "subjective and objective data on the child's level of adaptive functioning." The claim is false; the CABR provides only subjective data. Objectivity in tests means that different scorers arrive at the same evaluation of the performance, but the CABR does not take even the first step toward providing for such objectivity. It is not merely that the instrument lacks a manual, scoring standards or norms; the items are not scored at all. There is no necessary connection between anything the informant says and any subsequent rating by either the informant or the interviewer. The items serve as a standardized prelude to purely impressionistic ratings by both parties. The informant's subjective ratings may be clinically important but time expended in interviewing is usually expected to produce more adequate data from the interviewer. As it is, there is no guarantee that different interviewers will produce anything like the same ratings, even when they are exposed to precisely the same sets of responses from the same informants.

While the instrument supposedly works with teachers or "other informants," many questions call for the kinds of information that only a parent is likely to have. Teachers, for example, would be unlikely to know about the child's first attempts to talk, the age at which eating utensils were first used, or when a child first played outside the house without supervision. Items calling for parental knowledge seem more prominent on topics like independent functioning and role performance in the family than on topics like economic and vocational activities and socialization.

Many items seem to be worded in ways that could enhance attitudinal biases in the informant's recall or reporting of the child's behavior. Many items present several questions about interrelated behaviors that differ in maturity. The first independent functioning item, for example, asks how old the child was when s/he "first used eating utensils, scissors, dressed self, toileting, etc." The span of difficulty levels allows a caretaker with a favorable (or unfavorable) bias to dwell selectively on the child's strong (or weak) points while avoiding reference to countervailing evidence. The interviewer is not encouraged to probe the informant's account and may actually be discouraged from doing so by such comments as, "listening skills may be a more important aspect of the communication process than talking."

The CABR might be considered for research on factors that produce systematic differences between the informant's and the interviewer's ratings of the same children. The effects of informant-interviewer differences in socioeconomic status, ethnic status, race, or in prior knowledge of such data as the child's IQ might be investigated in this way, providing the five ratings intercorrelate highly enough to make the total score reliable.

Insofar as the school psychologist, counselor, or clinician is expected to produce normative information about a child's adaptive behavior, either the Vineland Social Maturity Scale or the AAMD Adaptive Behavior Scale is preferable to the CABR. The CABR not only lacks norms, it may be unnormable in its present form. Moreover, the alternative instruments seem likely to produce a more comprehensive picture of the child's adaptive problems because they ask more questions and questions that are simpler and more direct than those used in the present report.

Review of Childrens Adaptive Behavior Report by CARL L. ROSEN, *Professor of Education, Kent State University, Kent, OH:*

The Childrens Adaptive Behavior Report (CABR) is a non-standardized guided interview procedure designed either to independently provide information on adaptive behavior or to supplement information on adaptive behavior obtained from other sources. Administration involves recording key comments from the responses of an informant (parent, teacher, etc.) to seven questions for each of five adaptive behavior domains, and then obtaining separate ratings of the child's level of functioning for each domain from both informant and interviewer.

One booklet contains all materials: a one-page discussion of the instrument, a summary sheet for recording basic information (on the child, informant, interview setting, rapport, adequacy of information, etc.), a profile for entering the two sets of ratings for each of the five domains, and the 35 questions arranged by behavioral area with spaces under each for the recording of key comments.

Because of quick administration and a seemingly simple interpretive procedure, the CABR appears to be a convenient interview guide; however, there are many problems with the instrument. In fact, the instrument in its current state reflects few signs of adherence to minimal standards of instrument construction. There is little indication of serious attention to basic design characteristics important to the systematic collection of psychologically relevant variables.

First, there is a lack of specificity as to the exact function of the instrument and the types of situations, children, and decisions for which it is designed. The one-page discussion is inadequate for these purposes and the user will be hard-pressed even with repeated readings to derive such information.

Second, the authors provide no definition of adaptive behavior, the underlying construct of the procedure. In the absence of any definition, different terms referring to the construct are used interchangeably in the test description (child's functioning, competence, developmental history, performance, etc.). The user cannot determine from the description what the authors mean by the term.

Third, the content of the instrument does not represent a comprehensive array of relevant adaptive behavior dimensions since two areas important to a comprehensive understanding of the child—the physical and affective areas—are not directly or adequately sampled. In addition, many of the question stems seem simplistic and unsophisticated in content and wording (e.g., "How well does ________ read and write? Is ________ often creative in ideas? How well can ________ handle money? Is ________ usually happy or unhappy?"). Information is not provided on the source of domain identification or on the criteria for question selection and construction. Four of the domains bear similar if not identical titles to several major areas measured in the Adaptive Behavior Scales published by the American Association on Mental Deficiency. One is left to wonder how the domains were identified and what were the criteria for question construction.

Fourth, inadequate guidance is provided in the booklet for the administration, analysis, and interpretation of the kinds of information obtainable from the CABR. Whether psychological instruments are designed for quantitative or for qualitative data collection methodologies, authors of published tests are responsible for providing users with basic information, data, and assistance necessary for effective professional utilization. For example, the "clinical insight" suggested as required for the interpretation of subjective responses from informants is not illustrated, effective interview techniques which are said to be required are only minimally outlined, and examples of how to contrast informant with interviewer ratings in a systematic way are not provided. It is also difficult to justify not providing well-designed guidelines on developmental and behavioral descriptions which are age appropriate to aid the user in analysis and interpretation of responses. In light of what we know about growth and development of elementary-aged children, without specific information on significant developmental landmarks, inferences extracted from responses to questions by any but the most well-trained observers could be rather loose. Profile comparisons based upon arbitrarily determined ratings could be, at the least, unproductive.

Indeed, there is little justification for profile development with this instrument, since this involves unassisted and subjectively derived numerical ratings for which no information is available on either validity or reliability. The lack of information on the empirical validation of inferences from the CABR, informant consistency, or interrater reliability leaves the user with little basis for determining what degree of confidence should be placed in the instrument.

In summary, while adaptive behavior is a worthwhile construct to examine, the guided interview procedure of the CABR cannot be recommended in its current state for sole use in making decisions involving children. Only well-trained and experienced clinicians can utilize this procedure; these same clinicians might preferably devise their own interview questions to supplement information obtainable from better designed standardized instruments such as the Adaptive Behavior Scales and the Manchester Scales of Social Adaptation.

[218]

Childrens Adaptive Behavior Scale. Ages 5–10; 1980; CABS; 6 scores: language development, independent functioning, family role performance, economic-vocational activity, socialization, total; norms consist of means and standard deviations from a sample of mildly retarded children; individual; manual ('80, 18 pages); student record booklet ('80, 12 pages); test cards ('80, 20 cards); 1984 price data: $1 per student record booklet; $14.95 per manual; $19.95 per specimen set of 5 student record booklets, 1 manual, and 1 set of test cards; (30) minutes; Bert O. Richmond and Richard H. Kicklighter; Humanics Limited.*

See T3:395 (1 reference).

Review of Childrens Adaptive Behavior Scale by THOMAS R. KRATOCHWILL, Professor and Director, School Psychology Program, Department of Educational Psychology, The University of Wisconsin-Madison, Madison, WI:

The Childrens Adaptive Behavior Scale (CABS) is designed for use with children age five (5–0) years through 10 years (10–11). It is administered directly to the child and measures from other informants are not necessary for use of the scale. The CABS consists of five specific domains, with the number of items within a set varying from 16 to 30. The specific domains include the following: language development (LD), independent functioning (IF), family role performance (FRP), economic-vocational activity (EVA), and socialization (S).

CONSIDERATIONS IN USE OF THE CHILDRENS ADAPTIVE BEHAVIOR SCALE. With the increase in development and use of adaptive behavior measures, a variety of methodological and conceptual issues have been elucidated (e.g., Coulter & Morrow, 1978; Reschly, 1982). However, before discussing the specific issues, some positive features of the CABS should be mentioned. First of all, the CABS appears to be economical in clinician and client time. The CABS takes about 30–40 minutes to administer. In contrast, such instruments as the Adaptive Behavior Scale—Public School Version (ABS–PS) take considerably more time (Oakland, 1979). Second, the CABS is designed for use in an educational setting. Other measures such as the

Vineland Social Maturity Scale or the Adaptive Behavior Scale were not developed for use in educational settings. Thus, the CABS appears to have some definite advantages here, at least at a conceptual level. Finally, the CABS is administered directly to the child. This is in contrast to other measures that require a respondent (e.g., teacher, parent) to provide information on the child. Thus, the CABS appears to have some conceptual and practical advantages over other measures of adaptive behavior.

DATA OBTAINED. As noted above, the CABS requires direct assessment of the child by a trained examiner, usually in a one-to-one setting. This may be a definite improvement over other adaptive behavior measures that depend on self-report data from informants gathered retrospectively (Mealor & Richmond, 1980). Nevertheless, it cannot be assumed that data obtained from the child in a one-to-one setting with an examiner will be reflective of "adaptive" performance outside of that testing situation. Information obtained on the CABS should be confirmed by obtaining direct samples of behavior in other natural settings (e.g., home, community). This is an important issue inasmuch as a primary reason for obtaining measures of adaptive functioning is to go beyond individual testing situations. This is an especially relevant issue when considering that some of the item content of the CABS is similar to that included within intelligence tests (see below).

ITEM SELECTION. There is no one agreed-upon definition of adaptive behavior in the professional literature. Indeed, conceptions of what adaptive behavior is, such as that reflected in the AAMD manual, have changed over time (Reschly, 1982). The authors of the test take into account the working definition proposed by Coulter and Morrow (1978), wherein "the manner in which persons perform the tasks expected of their particular age group can be broadly conceived as their adaptive behavior." This conception is not at variance with many other common definitions offered (e.g., Sattler, 1982). Guided by this definition, the authors developed their five domains based on the following considerations (Kicklighter, 1981): (1) social, developmental, and adaptive behavior scales, checklists, and tests were reviewed; (2) behavioral/performance indications were extracted and grouped by domain affiliation and chronological age parameters; (3) the various behavioral domains were selected on the basis of the research literature and on the judgment of the authors with reference to evaluative utility and measurement feasibility; (4) skills, concepts, and/or knowledge tapped by each group of performance indicators were analyzed; (5) test items were constructed for selected indicators in each of the domains; (6) the various test items (approximately 50 per domain) were submitted to "expert" judges for rating; (7) items surviving the ratings were included in the test.

In this process there was apparently no specific test to determine whether the items falling within a particular domain were hierarchially ordered or if items in all domains were highly related to items in another domain.

NORMS. The CABS was administered to 250 mildly retarded children in the South Carolina and Georgia public schools. Nevertheless, these data are quite limited, considering the purpose of the scale. More extensive norms based on different groups and geographical regions will be necessary for more effective use of the CABS as a measure of adaptive behavior. However, the authors do emphasize that "local norms" should be developed. This is a useful strategy and will complement already existing normative data.

VALIDITY. Information on the validity and reliability of the CABS is available from the authors (Richmond, personal communication, 1981). In addition, several studies have also been published.

Some issues relevant to validity have already been discussed under the heading of item content. Decisions regarding the item domains represent validity concerns. Currently it is unclear if the domain would hold up to specific validation of the items. In addition to these measures the internal relationship among the domains was investigated (Kicklighter, 1981). The intercorrelation of the five domains of the CABS and total score was calculated for a sample of 60 EMR students and 60 children classified as slow learners. The domain scores are generally highly correlated.

The authors also report more conventional validity information in the manual. Generally, the correlations between the CABS and other commonly used measures of adaptive behavior, such as the Adaptive Behavior Scale (Lambert, Windmiller, Cole, & Figueroa, 1974), are positive and significant. Yet, examination of these correlations shows that they are not high. The authors' rationale for this is that the CABS measures the child's adaptive behavior (i.e., through the child's responses to an examiner), whereas the other measures obtain data through parent and teacher reports of child performance. However, it must again be stressed that the various scales may each be measuring different aspects of the child's behavior through different assessment methods in different settings. Thus, it is difficult to speak of "better" measures in the abstract. Correlations with actual child functioning in the natural environment will be necessary to further establish the validity of the CABS, as well as other established measures of adaptive behavior.

RELIABILITY. Test-retest reliability at two week intervals ($N = 36$) yielded correlations of .98 or .99 for all domains and the total score. Coefficient alpha values for the CABS were as follows: Total score, .94; FRP, .74; S, .79; LD, .64; EVA, .78; IF, .86. In addition to this information, KR-21 reliability coefficients for a sample of EMR children (*N* = 250) were as follows: LD, .63; S, .72; FRP, .76; EVA, .79; IF, .83; and Total Score, .93. Thus, the CABS appears to have adequate reliability.

SUMMARY AND CONSIDERATIONS. The CABS appears to be a useful addition to the existing measures of adaptive behavior. One of the most unique aspects of the CABS is that it provides a direct assessment of the child's behavior in a one-to-one testing situation. This is in contrast to other existing measures of adaptive behavior that depend on retrospective self-report data from parents or other caretakers.

My review suggests that individuals using the CABS should consider the following issues. First, the CABS still has rather limited data on norming, reliability, and validity. Psychometric research is currently in progress, and in the future we should know more about the scale on these dimensions. Second, the CABS should likely be supplemented by other measures of adaptive functions to obtain a broader picture of performance across settings and individuals. This could be accomplished through use of other available instruments as well as direct observation of children in various environments. A major rationale for this is that no single existing test or scale can fully assess adaptive behavior appropriate to all situations (Kazdin & Matson, 1981).

Adaptive behavior is an important assessment area in psychology and education. The CABS was designed to overcome some of the limitations of other scales. In this regard it is an important addition to the literature. However, its utility will be more clearly elucidated as empirical work on its characteristics becomes more fully explored.

REVIEWER'S REFERENCES

Lambert, N., Windmiller, M., Cole, L., & Figueroa, R. AAMD ADAPTIVE BEHAVIOR SCALE: PUBLIC SCHOOL VERSION 1974 REVISION. Washington, DC: American Association on Mental Deficiency, 1975.

Coulter, W. A. & Morrow, H. W. ADAPTIVE BEHAVIOR: CONCEPTS AND MEASUREMENTS. New York: Grune & Stratton, 1978.

Oakland, T. Research on the ABIC and ELP: A revisit to an old topic. SCHOOL PSYCHOLOGY REVIEW, 1979, 8, 209–213.

Mealor, D. J. & Richmond, B. O. Adaptive behavior: Teachers and parents disagree. EXCEPTIONAL CHILDREN, 1980, 46, 386–389.

Kazdin, A. E. & Matson, J. L. Social validation in mental retardation. APPLIED RESEARCH IN MENTAL RETARDATION, 1981, 2, 39–53.

Kicklighter, R. H. Testing as a strategy in the measurement of adaptive behavior. Unpublished manuscript, 1981.

Richmond, B. O. Personal communication, September, 1981.

Reschly, D. J. Assessing mild mental retardation: The influence of adaptive behavior, sociocultural status, and prospects for nonbiased assessment. In C. R. Reynolds and T. B. Gutkin (Eds.) THE HANDBOOK OF SCHOOL PSYCHOLOGY. New York: Wiley, 1982.

Sattler, J. M. ASSESSMENT OF CHILDREN'S INTELLIGENCE AND SPECIAL ABILITIES. Boston: Allyn and Bacon, 1982.

Review of Childrens Adaptive Behavior Scale by CORINNE R. SMITH, Director, Psychoeducational Teaching Laboratory, Syracuse University, Syracuse, NY:

The Childrens Adaptive Behavior Scale (CABS) is a norm-referenced instrument for the evaluation of adaptive behavior skills in 5- to 10-year-old children. In contrast to other adaptive behavior scales that obtain their data through parent or teacher interviews, the items of the CABS are administered directly to the child. The CABS consists of five domains, each requiring verbal responses to orally administered questions: language development, independent functioning, family role performance, economic-vocational activity, and socialization. Every item is administered to every child, with 30 minutes being the approximate testing time.

The CABS was standardized on a sample of 250 mildly mentally retarded (EMR) children (IQ range 55–70) from South Carolina and Georgia. Fifty children were included at each age level from ages 6 through 10. Given the small and unrepresentative standardization sample (i.e., no breakdown for socioeconomic factors, race, urban acculturation, primary language and culture), the norms may not be representative of the general population of mildly retarded children. Therefore, the authors rightly urge test users to develop their own local norms. The normative data contain large standard deviations on individual subtests at each age level. Therefore, reporting a range of age scores is recommended for individual domains, rather than using a precise age equivalent score. The most emphasis should be placed on the total test score.

Test-retest data gathered at a two-week interval on a sample of 36 black, nonretarded children yielded reliability coefficients ranging from .98 to .99 for individual domains and the total score. This sample consisted of only three males and three females at each age level from ages 5 through 10.

The purpose of the CABS is to provide a nonbiased assessment that distinguishes those children who are retarded in all aspects of development from those who test within retarded ranges on intelligence measures but whose adaptive skills are not in the retarded ranges. Because the latter child (Grossman, 1973) has adequate ability to cope with the natural and social demands of the environment, he or she is not considered retarded. The use of CABS for making this type of differentiation was supported in one study of 30 black EMR children (for whom socio-cultural differences can result in IQ scores which are not representative of true cognitive abilities). These children had higher socialization, family role performance, economic vocational activity and total CABS scores, than did 30 white EMR students (Bailey, 1978).

Despite some promising research using the CABS, the test user is cautioned about using the CABS scores alone for such important decisions as "Is a child retarded or not?" and "Exactly what should I emphasize in my curriculum?" due to the small and unrepresentative normative sample, the lack of test-retest data on retarded children, and the low, albeit significant validity coefficients. For example, comparisons of the performance of EMR children (IQ 50–69) with that of slow learners (IQ 70–89) revealed significantly higher mean scores for the latter group, as would be expected. Though this research offers valuable validity data, it should be noted that the mean differences between groups on the total or domain scores is so slight as to have little practical significance with respect to making judgements about an individual child. This same study (Bailey, 1978) also found a sex effect in the economic-vocational activity domain, with males obtaining a higher mean score. Elsewhere, Kicklighter, Bailey, and Richmond (1980) reported that IQ was related differentially to CABS scores for different categories of children. They found a significant correlation between CABS scores (economic activity, socialization and total score) and full scale IQ's on the Wechsler Intelligence Scale for Children—Revised for an EMR sample but not for a slow learner group.

Further validity research using the CABS normative sample suggests CABS domain scores are significantly correlated with chronological age, as would be expected. The correlations, however, account for only 16 percent to 24 percent of the total variance, thereby indicating that the test is tapping many factors besides chronological age and adaptive ability. Correlations between CABS subtest scores and an interview-format adaptive-behavior measure (AAMD Adaptive Behavior Scale), though significant in 42 of 60 possible comparisons, are of such low magnitude that the tests are clearly tapping different skills. Finally, though the authors state that the domains are "relatively independent," no factor analytic studies have been conducted to evaluate whether each CABS domain actually represents a skill independent of the other domains.

Until further validity and reliability studies are conducted and the normative sample is expanded, the test user remains uncertain as to the precise skills and abilities that the CABS is tapping. The test user, then, is also on questionable grounds in interpreting a low score in one domain as indicating a need to strengthen that particular ability, or a high total test score as definitely indicating that a child is not retarded. The authors wisely advise the test user to seek corroborating evidence for such judgements from parent/teacher interviews and further observational data.

Particular caution seems appropriate when testing children whose poor performance on intelligence measures may be due to language disabilities. The verbal format of the CABS may not permit the child to demonstrate his or her true understanding of everyday living skills, thereby underestimating adaptive skills and adjustment potential. Thus, alternative observational and parent or teacher interview measures of adaptive behavior (e.g., Revised AAMD Adaptive Behavior Scale, the revised Vineland Social Maturity Scales, Mercer's Adaptive Behavior Inventory for Children) are recommended for language disabled children, as well as those for whom English is not the primary language.

In summary, the CABS is a norm-referenced measure of adaptive behavior that holds promise for identifying children whose poor performance on an intelligence test is not indicative of true adaptive potential. The authors urge creation of local norms and use of corroborative observation and interview data in making important decisions based on CABS performance. Certainly a larger and more nationally representative normative population and test-retest reliability data on a sample of retarded children are needed. Furthermore, norms on typical learners, and a breakdown of the normative population by socioeconomic factors, race, urban acculturation, primary language, and culture would facilitate test interpretation. At this point, individual CABS items are best used as criterion-referenced indices for instructional planning, while the domain scores should be ignored. CABS total scores are best used to suggest additional assessment questions.

REVIEWER'S REFERENCES

Grossman, H. J. (Ed.). MANUAL ON TERMINOLOGY AND CLASSIFICATION IN MENTAL RETARDATION. Washington, DC: American Association on Mental Deficiency, 1973.

Bailey, B. S. Differential perceptions of children's adaptive behavior. Unpublished doctoral dissertation, University of Georgia, 1978.

Kicklighter, R. H., Bailey, B. S., & Richmond, B. O. A direct measure of adaptive behavior. SCHOOL PSYCHOLOGY REVIEW, 1980, 9, 168–173.

[219]

Children's Apperception Test. Ages 3–10; 1949–80; no data on reliability and validity; no norms; individual; 3 editions; short form record blank ('74, 6 pages); checklist ('74, 2 pages); 1983 price data: $40.50 per set of test materials for all 3 editions including 25 record blanks and 30 checklists; $15 per set of test and manual for any one edition; $6 per 25 record blanks; $6 per 30 checklists; (15–20) minutes; Leopold Bellak, Sonya Sorel Bellak, Mary R. Haworth (checklist), and Marvin S. Hurvich (manual for *c*); C.P.S., Inc.*

a) CHILDREN'S APPERCEPTION TEST. 1949–80; CAT; 1 form ('80, 10 cards); revised manual ('80, 22 pages, esentially the same as the 1974 edition manual except for the inclusion of the checklist, the addition of 2 short paragraphs, and 5 additional references in the bibliography).

b) CHILDREN'S APPERCEPTION TEST—SUPPLEMENT. 1952–74; CAT-S; 10 pictures, one or more of which may be presented in addition to the regular CAT; 1 form ('74, 3 cards); manual ('74, 10 pages).

c) CHILDREN'S APPERCEPTION TEST (HUMAN FIGURES). 1965–74; CAT-H; designed to be "equivalent" to the regular CAT cards; 1 form ('65, 10 cards); manual ('65, 14 pages).

See T3:396 (1 reference), T2:1451 (23 references), and P:419 (18 references); for reviews by Bernard I. Murstein and Robert D. Wirt, see 6:206 (19 references); for reviews by Douglas T. Keeny and Albert I. Rabin, see 5:126 (15 references); for reviews by John E. Bell and L. Joseph Stone and excerpted reviews by M. M. Genn, Herbert Herman, Robert R. Holt, Laurance F. Shaffer, and Adolf G. Woltmann, see 4:103 (2 references).

TEST REFERENCES

1. Passman, R. H., & Lautmann, L. A. Fathers', mothers', and security blankets' effects on the responsiveness of young children during projective testing. JOURNAL OF CONSULTING AND CLINICAL PSYCHOLOGY, 1982, 50, 310–312.

Review of Children's Apperception Test by CLIFFORD V. HATT, *School Psychologist and Private Practice, Virginia Beach, VA, and Adjunct Assistant Professor of Psychology, Old Dominion University, Norfolk, VA:*

The Children's Apperception Test (CAT) is a projective technique consisting of a series of 10 pictures depicting anthropomorphic animals in a variety of situations which require the 3- to 10-year-old child to make up a story related to the pictures presented. The purpose is to facilitate an understanding of a child's thoughts, needs, drives, and feelings regarding important relationships, situations, and conflicts that the child is currently experiencing at both a conscious and unconscious level. It is considered a downward extension of the Thematic Apperception Test (TAT), which is more suitable for adults and adolescents. According to the authors, animals are used in the pictures because children may more readily identify themselves with animals than humans, and animals are more culture-free and less structured in regard to sex or age than human figures. Concern over the relative merits of animal versus human figures led to a human modification of the CAT (CAT-H) in which human figures were substituted for animals with slight variations in the context of the pictures. No clear advantages of human over animal forms have been suggested by the research cited in the manuals, with the exception for children between ages 7 to 10 who have a mental age beyond 10 years (Bellak & Hurrich, 1966). It is speculated that these children find the animal pictures too childish and respond more favorably to the human forms. In addition, a supplement (CAT-S) consisting also of 10 animal pictures of specific situations was developed to elicit children's responses to issues of physical activity, physical injury, competition, body image, sexual conduct, or classroom situations. The manuals for the three forms are supplemented by a book (Bellak, 1975) that elaborates on theoretical rationale, administration, interpretation, and clinical uses.

When evaluating the CAT according to psychometric standards of test construction, this projective technique suffers from the typical problems associated with many other projectives (Anastasi, 1976). Administration and scoring are not standardized, which allows for considerable subjectivity and variability in these processes. Scoring and interpretive aids have been provided like the Bellak Recording and Analysis Blank, which may summarize key areas of interpretation, and Haworth's Schedule of Adaptive Mechanisms in CAT Responses, which attempts to provide a rough quantitative and qualitative evaluation of children's responses. However, categories of analysis tend to be too general and allow too much individual interpretation. This tends to lead to poor scorer reliability. There is little, if any normative data available, poor coefficients of internal consistency and retest reliability, and inconclusive validation. In sum, the CAT is psychometrically inadequate.

Despite this fact, the CAT and similar techniques are frequently used and given emphasis in training programs (Prout, 1983). In a recent analysis of thematic picture techniques, Obrzut and Cummings (1983) question the appropriateness of using psychometric standards for evaluating projective techniques in general and the TAT and CAT in particular.

They state that "because of the unique characteristics of projective techniques (e.g., differing number of responses, rarity of many categories, interrelatedness of responses, each test's sensitivity to different interpersonal variables), they provide poor psychometric data but rich ideographic data" (Obrzut & Cummings, 1983, p. 417). They suggest that the nature of the traits and characteristics purportedly measured are motivational and emotional in nature, and, therefore, issues related to consistency over time (test-retest reliability) and even internal consistency (split-half reliability) may not be applicable. Emotions and motivations may not be expected to be stable over time nor was the CAT designed to have equivalent pictorial stimuli.

It is clear that a projective technique like the CAT, being based on psychodynamic theory, will be questioned by others of different theoretical orientations. However, as Kerlinger (1973) suggests, "all methods of observation and measurement must satisfy the same scientific criteria," and projective techniques, being considered as a method of observation and measurement, "must be subjected to the same type of reliability testing and empirical validation as any other psychometric technique." It has been suggested that the psychometric properties of the CAT and similar projectives could be improved by scoring the stories produced through content analysis, "a method of studying and analyzing communications in a systematic, objective, and quantitative manner to measure variables" (Kerlinger, 1973, p. 525). In addition, providing a standardized situation and verbalized instructions for administration, objective criteria for interpretation, and development of equivalent alternate forms may provide closer adherence to standard test construction principles (Obrzut & Cummings, 1983).

New trends in the use of projective techniques in clinical assessment suggest a more narrow, more focused, psychometrically refined approach in keeping with the previously mentioned concerns and a contrasting "wide-band," interview approach involving conversational transactions and quantitatively-scored "communication deviances" (Korchin & Schuldberg, 1981). This second approach, which views the CAT more as a clinical tool than a psychometric instrument, can provide a much wider range of response (but with lesser dependability), be an effective "ice-breaker" to establish therapeutic rapport, be less susceptible to faking (Anastasi, 1976) and provide rich, valuable material for psychotherapeutic interventions.

In summary, the CAT can be viewed as a useful clinical tool with children 3 to 10 years of age. Considerable training and skill are required for administration and interpretation. The CAT has poor psychometric properties, but could be improved in this regard by developing standardized administration and scoring procedures and equivalent alternate forms.

REVIEWER'S REFERENCES

Bellak, L., & Hurvich, M. A human modification of the Children's Apperception Test. JOURNAL OF PROJECTIVE TECHNIQUES, 1966, 30, 228–242.

Kerlinger, F. N. FOUNDATIONS OF BEHAVIORAL RESEARCH (2nd ed.). New York: Holt, Rinehart and Winston, 1973.

Bellak, L. THE THEMATIC APPERCEPTION TEST, THE CHILDREN'S APPERCEPTION TEST, AND THE SENIOR APPERCEPTION TECHNIQUE IN CLINICAL USE (3rd ed.). New York: Grune & Stratton, 1975.

Anastasi, A. PSYCHOLOGICAL TESTING (3rd ed.). New York: Macmillan, 1976.

Korchin, S. J., & Schuldberg, D. The future of clinical assessment. AMERICAN PSYCHOLOGIST, 1981, 36, 1147–1158.

Obrzut, J. E., & Cummings, J. A. The projective approach to personality assessment: An analysis of thematic picture techniques. SCHOOL PSYCHOLOGY REVIEW, 1983, 12, 414–420.

Prout, H. T. School psychologists and social-emotional assessment techniques: Patterns in training and use. SCHOOL PSYCHOLOGY REVIEW, 1983, 12, 377–383.

Review of Children's Apperception Test by MARCIA B. SHAFFER, School Psychologist, Steuben-Allegany Board of Cooperative Educational Services, Bath, NY:

The Children's Apperception Test (CAT), the Children's Apperception Test Supplement (CAT-S), and the Children's Apperception Test—Human Figures each consists of a series of pictures about which children are asked to tell stories. It is hypothesized that the stories will be projections of the children's own feelings. The CAT, according to its creator, is "a method of investigating personality by studying the dynamic meaningfulness of the individual differences in perception of standard stimuli." Like most projective techniques, it provides dubious psychometric data but rich information regarding the unique emotional reactions of an individual child. It has been proposed that such tests as the CAT "may be most valid when used as a type of structured clinical interview" (Obrzut & Cummings, 1983, p. 418), but that viewpoint is by no means in accord with the intent of Leopold and Sonya Bellak, originators of the CAT. The manuals contain no hint of any intended use other than the traditional clinical interpretation and utilization.

Prospective purchasers of the CAT should be cautioned that each of its three editions has a separate and distinct manual. The CAT manual, most recently revised in 1980, contains a brief history of the test; an account of its "nature and purpose"; directions for administration; description and interpretation of anticipated responses; a few samples of stories; and a copy of the recommended recording and analysis blank. The CAT-S manual explains its purpose and administration; has a short segment on interpretation and a discussion of norms; but no "objective" data worthy of the adjective, except with regard to card IX. CAT-H is accompanied by a manual which devotes most of its 12 pages to studies on the relative virtues of animal versus human subjects in drawing responses from children. No definitive conclusion can be reached. This manual also provides the nearest thing to norms which the Bellaks et al. offer.

Since they contain almost no overlapping information, it would be best to buy all of the manuals, even if one does not plan to use all three sets of pictures.

The CAT, in all of its editions, relies heavily on conjecture. The CAT manual states that "The pictures were designed to elicit responses to feeding problems specifically, and oral problems generally." It continues in this vein, with no genuine evidence to tell us whether the expected verbal responses and feeling are actually evoked. However, if the results of research used as references in the manuals were gathered together and presented in a direct, succinct manner, the CAT might have a respectable data base to support the assumptions on which it rests.

In addition to lacking organized comments on the CAT's basic premises, the manuals present no developmental norms. There is no way to know what responses are typical of what ages. The texts are replete with remarks about the availability and value of all three editions to research, suggestions that research would be welcome, and even cognizance of the need for research. But the CAT has been around for more than 30 years, and no systematic effort apparently has been made to validate common interpretations of children's responses or to delineate typical themes for children at specific stages of growth.

Projective techniques are generally interpreted on the basis of widely accepted theories of personality, ego psychology, and cognitive development. The CAT manuals, especially the original, clearly indicate that a knowledge of such theories is fundamental to understanding the stories. Yet there is no suggestion that sale of the pictures should be restricted, no recommended proscription in terms of the training of those who administer the CATs, no explanation that responses should be interpreted only by persons trained in the theories from which the idea of projection emanates. The CAT manual avers that it "may be profitable in the hands of the psychoanalyst, the psychiatrist, the psychologist, the social worker, and the teacher, as well as the psychologically trained pediatrician." Certainly all of these people may be able to use the results, but somewhere in each of these manuals should be a warning that these pictures are not like other "tests." Knowing how to administer a test is a necessary, but not sufficient, background for users of the CAT. Their stories should be interpreted only by persons schooled in the appropriate theories.

In short, the manuals are in need of revision and additions, which could add significantly to the value and integrity of the CATs. Whether or not such improvements are made, the CAT has no salient rival. Over the years, other "picture story tests," such as the Educational Apperception Test and the infamous Blacky Pictures, have appeared. None has had conspicuous success. Despite the shortcomings mentioned above, the CAT remains what it has been for 3 decades: a classic of its genre.

REVIEWER'S REFERENCES

Obrzut, J., & Cummings, J. The projective approach to personality assessment: An analysis of thematic picture techniques. SCHOOL PSYCHOLOGY DIGEST, 1983, 12, 414–420.

[220]

Children's Depression Scale. Ages 9–16; 1978; CDS; 8 scale scores: depressive (affective responsive, social problems, self-esteem, pre-occupation with own sickness and death, guilt, total depression), positive (pleasure, total positive); individual; 2 forms (1 form administered to child and 1 form administered to either parents, sibling, teacher, or relative of child); manual (72 pages); record booklet (4 pages); 3 sets of cards (1 child form, 1 adult form for boys, 1 adult form for girls); 1983 price data: A$47.25 per complete set including 25 record forms; $8.20 per manual; $.35 per record form; administration time not reported; Moshe Lang and Miriam Tisher; Australian Council for Educational Research [Australia].*

See T3:397 (1 reference).

Review of Children's Depression Scale by HOWARD M. KNOFF, Assistant Professor of School Psychology, State University of New York at Albany, Albany, NY:

According to its manual, the Children's Depression Scale (CDS) was published as a research edition based on preliminary evidence of its validity and clinical usefulness. While there is a great need for well-developed diagnostic techniques to evaluate childhood depression, the CDS may have been prematurely published—even as a "research edition." Its theoretical, standardization, and psychometric characteristics symbolize the difficulties of test development in this area; yet it seems fair to say that these challenges could have been met more effectively before publication. The authors' admission that the CDS requires further study and research is not followed with admonitions suggesting limited clinical and diagnostic use in the field but with a statement encouraging its use as a clinical instrument. Thus, the CDS could be abused by practitioners who need a technique to assess childhood depression and who are willing to overlook its serious technical limitations.

The CDS Manual could be divided logically into three major sections providing (*a*) a review of the childhood depression literature, the authors' definition of depression, and a rationale for the CDS's development; (*b*) a description of the CDS's administration, scoring, and interpretation; and (*c*) technical information, including the CDS's normative data and discussions of its reliability and validity. Generally, the manual provides extremely brief, potentially misleading, discussions and descriptions across these three sections.

The "literature review" is undefined in purpose and organization and appears more as a brief description of some isolated theoretical and research studies. To be a true review it could be strengthened by in-depth analyses of the theoretical perspectives of depression—including the learned helplessness and cognitive perspectives—and a stronger emphasis on childhood depression vis-a-vis childhood development and maturation. The interpretation section consists mainly of brief analyses of case studies with little background information on the clients or pre/post-treatment comparisons and results. The manual provides minimal direction for an empirically derived, objective way to analyze and use the CDS's subscales and total scores. Finally, descriptions of the normative sample and some technical data are not detailed enough. For example, the control group which is used for the scale's normative data and interpretation is described in less detail than an "experimental, depressed" sample which was used to validate the Scale. And the factor analysis which would support the CDS construct validity is discussed in one paragraph with no statistical tables showing the various item and subscale loadings. On a positive note, the administration procedures and scoring directions are well written and easy to understand.

Technically, the CDS is weakest in two important areas: test development and standardization. The six subscales were developed originally on "theoretical or logical grounds" and were maintained in the published version even though the factor analysis suggested that a single dimension accounted for most of the items. Items were selected based on the agreement of seven expert judges, rather than through a more empirical approach, for example, of item analysis with depressed and non-depressed samples. Further, the ratings of two judges were excluded when they showed relatively poor agreement between themselves and the other judges.

The standardization or control group sample consisted of an extremely small sample of 22 boys and 15 girls from Australia who were matched with the "experimental, depressed" sample on age, sex, school, and year. The normative data from this control sample were collapsed into one set of "children's decile scores" which are used for all CDS analyses and interpretations despite the fact that (*a*) girls consistently scored higher than boys on the CDS subscales, (*b*) younger children's CDS scores tended to differ from older children, (*c*) children from higher socioeconomic status (SES) levels scored higher than those from middle SES families or lower SES homes, and (*d*) the cross-cultural utility of the CDS was not evaluated or discussed. Even the statistical analyses across some of the demographic variables were not strong. For example, when analyzing the age variable, the children's data were separated into two groups, either older or younger than 14 years. Given the small sample size, it was impossible to separate the data into groups representing a single chronological age, a procedure that is suggested by the depression literature and would be possible with a larger normative sample. These statistical results and concerns make the normative data questionable for both statistical and interpretive use. This is also true for the parent control group sample and "parent decile scores," based on 37 parents of the control group children, which were collapsed and are used in a norm referenced manner to analyze the data of parents who complete the CDS.

The "experimental, depressed" group consisted of "relatively severe cases of school refusal" who are considered "depressed" by the authors because "there is some evidence...that depression is an important component of school refusal." This sample of 25 boys and 15 girls is recommended as a comparison group to the control group during interpretation to permit a finer discrimination amongst the CDS subscales. Again, sample size, diagnostic and clinical purity, and cross-cultural concerns make any resulting conclusions questionable. Because of all these standardization concerns, the validity data reported in the manual also are limited and questionable for practical use.

Despite these weaknesses, the CDS does provide some administrative contributions. Because each item is printed on a separate card, the child can focus separately on items, minimizing any response bias or carryover effect from a previous item. Further, the game-like format of placing each card in one of five boxes can increase attention, motivation, and task validity. Finally, the two forms of cards make the CDS a more flexible diagnostic tool with self-report and parent or significant other-rating options and comparisons, respectively.

The authors seem well aware of the CDS's limitations and weaknesses. When summarizing the interpretations section, they stated that "our knowledge at this early stage of the development of the CDS is insufficient for us to give a clear statistical basis for interpretation....the user of the CDS is encouraged to interpret the results he obtains with flexibility....it is most important that the data obtained from the CDS be considered within the context of all other knowledge of the child which is available and interpret accordingly." In their suggestions for future research, they suggest replication of the CDS on a large scale with separate decile tables for sex and age and with better item analysis, factor analytic, and psychometric investigations. In a sense, the authors have written a research monograph but published it as a clinical and diagnostic tool. Published in its present format, however, it could be purchased and inappropriately used by the non-discriminating practitioner.

To summarize, the CDS was published as a research edition in the hopes of acquiring additional test development and validation data. Nonetheless, its publication was premature in its present form—its standardization samples are demographically unclear in places and are too limited for statistical and diagnostic utility, and the scale's preliminary item and factor analyses did not guide the test development and format. With additional investigation and data, this scale has great potential in the childhood depression area. At this time, however, it would be used inappropriately for anything other than its own improvement.

Review of Children's Depression Scale by F. E. STERLING, Psychological Associate, Department of Psychology, Central Louisiana State Hospital, Pineville, LA:

The Children's Depression Scale (CDS) was designed by Lang and Tisher to provide a quantitative index of the clinical symptom of childhood depression (ages 9 through 16) as it relates to: Affective Response, Social Problems, Self-esteem, Preoccupation with own sickness and death, Feelings of Guilt, and Pleasure. The CDS consists of 66 items designed to sample the above factors. The first five factors (48 of 66 items) are represented as subscales each contributing to a total score intended to represent a quantitative level of depression. The remaining 18 items were designed to reflect the respondent's ability to experience pleasure.

The testing procedure requires the respondent to sort cards into five categories which are scored on a scale of 1 to 5. The stimulus cards present affirmative statements which the subject places in one of five small slotted boxes (provided as a part of the test kit), which have printed on them the qualitative judgments: "Very Wrong, Wrong, Don't Know/Not Sure, Right, and Very Right." The items are printed on cards of different colors, each color representing one of the factors. The colors are pastel in hue and were selected both to facilitate scoring and to make the test set more aesthetically appealing. Two similar sets of cards are provided for the use of a parent and/or other adults to use in the assessment of the child's depression. Cards provided for the adults are the same in every respect as those given to the children, except that the wording of one set is phrased in the third person male singular and the other in the third person female singular. Scoring of the sorted cards is always in the pathological direction, with 5 being the highest possible score per item, 1 the lowest.

Norms are based on relatively small samples of "normal" (*N*) children ($N=37$) and adults (parents of the "normal" children; $N=37$) and are presented in the form of decile scores. These norms provide the standard against which all respondents are compared. In addition to these normative data, means and standard deviations of CDS scores obtained from a group of "depressed" (*D*) children ($N=40$), parents of that group ($N=40$), and a group of children drawn from a child's psychiatric clinic (*C*) ($N=19$) are presented. The manual stresses that the depressed group was selected first and the normal controls were matched to this group on age, sex, school, and year.

The *D* group consists of a sample of "relatively severe cases of school refusal," since the authors' review of the literature suggested that depression appeared to play a major role in school refusal. In addition to meeting the requirement for school refusal (as well as other operational criteria), psychiatric readings were obtained on each of the children in group *D* utilizing a 7-point bipolar (Happy vs. Unhappy) scale. Ratings were provided by clinicians who knew the children in group *D* well.

The authors appear to have invested a great deal of conscientious effort into the selection of items to represent the universe of content being measured. The literature provided few examples of research related to childhood depression, a relatively new area of investigation. Items gleaned from the literature were presented to a group of depressed clinic patients who were asked to comment on the expressive adequacy of the generated items. These comments offered by the clinical patients were utilized for item modification in this first stage of item development. Following this operation, 7 judges (child psychiatrists) were asked to select items which clearly distinguished between depression, anxiety, or neither. The pool of items consisted of the 18 positive items, rephrased to be similarly worded to the 48 depression items, all of which were intermingled with 75 items from the Sarason Anxiety Scales, the latter also reworded so as to be structurally indistinguishable from the 48 depression items. There was a high degree of agreement between 5 of the 7 judges with respect to their being able to single out items reflecting anxiety and depression, as opposed to those which appeared to be reflecting neither. Of the 66 CDS items, 5 judges agreed on 35 as reflecting depression (53%) and 4 judges agreed on another 18 items (27%). Based on the judges' ratings it was concluded that the CDS was in fact measuring depression.

In order to address concurrent validity, the authors correlated CDS scores with 13 of the scores of an unstated form of one of the IPAT multi-factor personality inventories. The sample consisted of 77 subjects (presumably those subjects who constitute groups *D* and *N*). Results of this investigation revealed that CDS-D scores were significantly correlated with 11 of the 13 primary factors ($p<.05$). Additionally, the second order factors Exvia (Avoid Social Interaction), Anxiety, and Neuroticism were all significantly correlated with CDS-D scores ($p<.01$). These three second-order factors are purportedly indicative of anxious social withdrawal and neurotic maladaptation. These findings raise questions about the ability of the CDS to discriminate between groups of anxious and depressed children.

As evidence of construct validity the authors present tables of the results of *t*-test comparisons of the various children and parent groups. Based on these results the authors have concluded that the CDS is capable of discriminating between the various categories of children and between the levels of depression perceived by the parents of the children of the *D* and *N* groups. Finally, the responses of all children and adults utilized in the normative study ($N=226$) were factor analyzed. The first general factor accounted for 32% of the variance, suggesting to the test authors that the CDS items were tapping a single factor.

Based on the above analysis, it is evident that the effort invested in the development of the CDS by the authors is considerable. It is refreshing to read these authors describe their manual as a "Research Edition," and while it is agreed that a reliable instrument which can provide a valid index of depression in children is needed, a great deal more effort will be required before the CDS should be utilized in applied settings. The comments below are intended to be constructive suggestions, offered in the hope that the authors will complete the task of constructing and refining their instrument.

First, a practical suggestion or two. Since children are not always seen for evaluation under optimum environmental conditions (such as complete freedom from extraneous noises or adequate lighting, etc.), modification of test administration procedures and materials might result in a better instrument. Based on several administrations of the CDS, this reviewer found that when working under low illumination, preliminary sorting of the cards required extra care to prevent confusing either the yellow (Self-esteem) or the white (Sickness/Death) with the cream colored cards (Miscellaneous D). The same care was required in distinguishing the pale blue (Guilt) from the pale aqua (Miscellaneous P) cards. No scoring errors were made, but the scoring took slightly longer than would have been required if all cards had been clearly distinguishable. When parents and children are in the office, it is often desirable to be able to provide immediate feedback. Anything that would facilitate this process would be most helpful.

While on the subject of the stimulus cards, it is believed that administration and scoring would be facilitated by making this a paper and pencil task. With items printed on a test form, much as they are now on the record form, the respondent could indicate his/her response to each item by making a check mark in the appropriate column. The examiner could then sum down each column within each subscale and sum across columns to derive a subscale score. Totaling the subscale scores will then produce the overall *D* and *P* scores. Two forms, one for a child and one for an adult, would be required, but a reduction in paraphernalia would result in a more manageable and probably less expensive test. The authors may wish to supplement the above procedure by having the child respondent "read along" as items are presented audibly by means of a cassette tape player. These procedures would not only facilitate ease of administration and scoring, but there would be the added benefit of standardized presentation. The audible presentation would insure that respondents understand all items, irrespective of different levels of reading proficiency.

Two other practical suggestions relate to the specific wording of items. If this instrument is to be employed cross-culturally, item content should be carefully evaluated and vernacularisms should be removed or modified. Southern U.S. children typically do not comprehend item 65: "I feel I'm a beaut person" or the word "keen" (item 8). The other practical suggestion relates to the frequent use of such qualifiers as often, most of the time, sometime, always, and never. Since the respondent must make judgments about whether an item is a Right vs. Very Right or Wrong vs. Very Wrong description of him/herself, it may be that simplification of items will reduce erroneous responses due to "qualification overload." Based on the correlations between the CDS and the scores of the multi-factor IPAT inventory, one might suspect that anxious, neurotic, and socially withdrawn children might be susceptible to this phenomenon and the reduction of its effect might reduce error.

The data provided in the manual suggest that the authors' prodigious efforts may have been compromised by inadequate sampling, inappropriate statistical manipulations, and/or incorrect reporting. A sample of 37 subjects is woefully inadequate. It certainly appears that norms expressed as z or T scores would result in ease of collaboration with other researchers. The authors have provided means and standard deviations (unfortunately carried out only one decimal place) for all groups participating in the study. The reported data, however, are sometimes confusing and perplexing.

It is not this reviewer's intent to second guess the authors or to take apart their work in a piecemeal fashion, but closer examination of their data in an attempt to understand confusing or unexplained statistical inferences has caused some concern over the reporting and appropriateness of certain statistical analyses. Table 15 provides an example of one such point of concern. For the subtest Self-esteem, the reported t value is -2.48 and is shown by the authors to be nonsignificant. The subtest Sick/Death ($t = -2.20$) and Guilt ($t = -1.95$) are reported to be significant at the .03 and .05 levels, respectively, although both were of lesser magnitude than the Self-esteem t value. With 66 degrees of freedom a t value of 2.2 would not be significant at the .03 level nor would $t = 1.95$ achieve a .05 significance level. Similarly, this reviewer's evaluation of data presented in Table 7 of the manual (too lengthy to describe here) suggests both inappropriate use of statistical procedures by the authors and results using correct procedures that are at variance with results presented in the table.

Consideration of the samples utilized in the normative study suggest further that there are some sampling procedures which are also a matter of concern. The school-refusing children appear to have been a relatively intact group. Were they in an institutional setting, being treated for their school refusal by a child psychiatrist "who knew the child[ren] well"? A conservative interpretation of this selection process suggests that rater judgments of "Happy or Unhappy" by these same clinicians might reflect rater bias, had they known the clinical history of each of the children in the *D* group. While one must sympathize with all investigators over the problems of obtaining subjects, research design safeguards (e.g., appropriate sampling, blind ratings, tests for magnitude of effects, etc.) tend to maximize the usefulness of a sample. Within the same vein, since the same raters were employed in judging the merits of the test items (as appears to have been the case) those same biases held with respect to the children might be reflected in the items selected to describe the perceived clinical status of those children. This problem would only increase the potential for artificially biasing the instrument used to measure various dimensions of that specific group of subjects. A scale "designed" (even in error) to fit a specific group will perform well in discriminating that group from others, whether the other groups are randomly selected or not. Such an artifice limits the test's generalizability to other groups presumed to possess some measure of the characteristics of the group to which the instrument has been fitted. The relatively high correlations between the CDS and the 16PF primary and second-order factors, especially the latter, suggest that the CDS is measuring too much. While a measuring instrument must attempt to encompass all the lower order components of the higher order construct, it must at the same time exclude those components which fail to contribute to the higher order construct. I fear that the CDS is lacking in this last aspect of the defining operation.

In summary, it is believed that the CDS has a relatively good conceptual beginning, and I would like to encourage the authors to resume their activities in refining their instrument. It is believed that some of the suggestions above, if followed, will result in the development of a much more useful and robust instrument.

[221]

Children's Embedded Figures Test. Ages 5–12; 1963–71; CEFT; revision of the Goodenough-Eagle modification of the Embedded Figures Test; individual; 1 form ('71, 25 cards plus demonstration and practice materials); no specific manual; combined manual ('71, 32 pages) for this and Embedded Figures Test and Group Embedded Figures Test; score sheet ('71, 1 page); 1984 price data: $20 per set of testing materials including 50 score sheets; $5 per 50 score sheets; $5.25 per manual; [15–30] minutes; Stephen A. Karp, Norma Konstadt (test), and manual coauthors Herman A. Witkin, Philip K. Oltman, and Evelyn Raskin; Consulting Psychologists Press, Inc.*

See T3:398 (34 references), 8:519 (53 references), and T2:1127 (14 references); for a review by Sheldon A. Weintraub, see 7:53 (15 references); see also P:36 (7 references) and 6:746 (2 references).

TEST REFERENCES

1. Ghuman, P. A. S. An exploratory study of Witkin's dimension in relation to social class, personality factors and Piagetian tests. SOCIAL BEHAVIOR AND PERSONALITY, 1977, 5, 87–91.

2. Lega, L. I. A Columbian version of the Children's Embedded Figures Test. HISPANIC JOURNAL OF BEHAVIORAL SCIENCES, 1981, 3, 415–417.

3. Gargiulo, R. M. Reflection/impulsivity and field dependence/independence in retarded and nonretarded children of equal mental age. BULLETIN OF THE PSYCHONOMIC SOCIETY, 1982, 19, 74–77.

4. Swyter, L. J., & Michael, W. B. The interrelationships of four measures hypothesized to represent the field dependence-field independence construct. EDUCATIONAL AND PSYCHOLOGICAL MEASUREMENT, 1982, 42, 877–888.

5. Ackerman, P. T., Dykman, R. A., & Ogelsby, D. M. Sex and group differences in reading and attention disordered children with and without hyperkinesis. JOURNAL OF LEARNING DISABILITIES, 1983, 16, 407–415.

6. Burlingame, K., Hardy, R. C., & Eliot, J. Study of horizontal line-mazes. PERCEPTUAL AND MOTOR SKILLS, 1983, 57, 1103–1109.

7. Sneider, C., & Pulos, S. Children's cosmographies: Understanding the earth's shape and gravity. SCIENCE EDUCATION, 1983, 67, 205–221.

8. Brown, R. T., & Wynne, M. E. Attentional characteristics and teachers ratings in hyperactive, reading disabled, and normal boys. JOURNAL OF CLINICAL CHILD PSYCHOLOGY, 1984, 13, 38–43.

[222]

Children's Personality Questionnaire, 1975 Edition. Ages 8–12; 1959–1979; CPQ; test booklet title is What You Do and What You Think; 14 scores: reserved vs. warmhearted (A), dull vs. bright (B), affected by feelings vs. emotionally stable (C), undemonstrative vs. excitable (D), obedient vs. assertive (E), sober vs. enthusiastic (F), disregards rules vs. conscientious (G), shy vs. venturesome (H), tough-minded vs. tender-minded (I), vigorous vs. circumspect individualism (J), forthright vs. shrewd (N), self-assured vs. apprehensive (O), uncontrolled vs. controlled (Q3), relaxed vs. tense (Q4); Forms A, B, C, D, ('75, 8 pages); manual ('75, 28 pages); technical handbook ('79, 77 pages, data from 1972 handbook and norm tables previously published separately); profile-answer sheet ('73, 2 pages); profile ('73, 1 page); separate answer sheets (hand scored, OpScan) may be used; 1982 price data: $9 per 25 tests; $3 per scoring key for test booklet; $6 per 50 machine or hand scored answer sheets; $7 per 50 answer profile sheets; $6 per scoring key for answer sheet; $6 per 50 profile sheets; $1.95 per manual; $6.25 per technical handbook; $14.80 per professional examination kit; $2.95 per specimen set (without handbook and scoring key); OpScan scoring service, $3.80 or less per test; computer interpretation service, $10 or less per subject; German and Spanish editions (Forms A and B, '63) available; (45–60) minutes for each form; Rutherford B. Porter and Raymond B. Cattell; Institute for Personality and Ability Testing, Inc.*

South African editions available from Human Sciences Research Council in Pretoria, South Africa.

See T3:400 (16 references); for a review by Harrison G. Gough, see 8:520 (46 references); see also T2:1129 (60 references) and P:38 (14 references); for reviews by Anne Anastasi, Wilbur L. Layton, and Robert D. Wirt of the 1963 edition, see 6:122 (2 references).

TEST REFERENCES

1. Ghuman, P. A. S. An exploratory study of Witkin's dimension in relation to social class, personality factors and Piagetian tests. SOCIAL BEHAVIOR AND PERSONALITY, 1977, 5, 87–91.

2. Harris, W. J., Drummond, R. J., & Schultz, E. W. An investigation of relationships between teachers' ratings of behavior and children's personality traits. JOURNAL OF ABNORMAL CHILD PSYCHOLOGY, 1977, 5, 43–52.

3. Willis, J., & Seymour, G. CPQ validity: The relationship between Children's Personality Questionnaire scores and teacher ratings. JOURNAL OF ABNORMAL CHILD PSYCHOLOGY, 1978, 6, 107–113.

4. Growe, G. A., & Levinson, S. A reexamination of the validity of the Children's Personality Questionnaire. JOURNAL OF ABNORMAL CHILD PSYCHOLOGY, 1980, 8, 435–439.

5. Marjoribanks, K. Ecological correlates of children's subjective school outcomes. CONTEMPORARY EDUCATIONAL PSYCHOLOGY, 1981, 6, 323–333.

6. Steinhausen, H. Chronically ill and handicapped children and adolescents: Personality studies in relation to disease. JOURNAL OF ABNORMAL CHILD PSYCHOLOGY, 1981, 9, 291–297.

7. Cattell, R. B., Schuerger, J. M., & Klein, T. W. Heritabilities of ego strength (Factor C), super ego strength (Factor G), and self-sentiment (Factor Q3) by Multiple Abstract Variance Analysis. JOURNAL OF CLINICAL PSYCHOLOGY, 1982, 38, 769–779.

8. Harris, W. J., & King, D. R. Achievement, sociometric status, and personality characteristics of children selected by their teachers as having learning and/or behavior problems. PSYCHOLOGY IN THE SCHOOLS, 1982, 19, 452–457.

9. Karnes, F. A., & Wheery, J. N. Concurrent validity of the Children's Personality Questionnaire O Factor as suggested by the Piers-Harris Children's Self-concept Scale. PSYCHOLOGICAL REPORTS, 1982, 50, 574.

10. Ackerman, P. T., Dykman, R. A., & Ogelsby, D. M. Sex and group differences in reading and attention disordered children with and without hyperkinesis. JOURNAL OF LEARNING DISABILITIES, 1983, 16, 407–415.

11. Karnes, F. A., & Wherry, J. N. CPQ personality factors of upper elementary gifted students. JOURNAL OF PERSONALITY ASSESSMENT, 1983, 47, 303–304.

Review of Children's Personality Questionnaire, 1975 Edition, by STEVEN KLEE, Senior Child Supervisor, Department of Psychiatry, Beth Israel Medical Center, New York, NY:

The Children's Personality Questionnaire (CPQ) was designed to yield a general assessment of personality for children ages 8 to 12. Fourteen primary factors and four second-order factors are measured. The CPQ has been designed to be useful in predicting various aspects of behavior including academic achievement, tendency towards delinquency, leadership potential, and need for clinical help.

The CPQ addresses an age range which has been difficult to assess. Children 8 to 12 vary greatly in their ability and willingness to verbalize their experiences and concerns about their functioning. Previous attempts to assess personality functioning at this age level have largely relied upon parental report. In contrast, the CPQ provides a more direct, self-report format. However, potential users should be cautioned that despite the relatively simple wording of items, children at the lower age ranges may require a good deal of administrative assistance.

Administration and scoring of the CPQ is relatively simple and straightforward. Scoring is accomplished through the use of a stencil key or through the more recently available computer scoring service. Administration time is given at approximately 50 minutes per part (each form has 2 parts), and it is suggested that this be given in two sessions for younger children.

In general, the CPQ appears to have been extensively studied with regard to reliability and validity issues. One week test-retest correlations ranged from a low of .28 to a high of .87, indicative of moderate short term consistency in CPQ responding. The internal consistency (KR-21) of factor scales, however, was not very high, implying less correlation between items than would be desirable.

Four parallel forms of this questionnaire have been developed. This is a great advantage for repeated testing in both clinical and research settings. Unfortunatley, the correlation of scales across forms is not always high, casting some doubts as to the equivalency of the four forms. The authors do advise administering two separate forms to each child and using the composite scores. Such a procedure alleviates some of the reliability problems within and between forms while adding significantly to the administration time.

The handbook that accompanies the CPQ provides a good description of the various factors and how to interpret high and low scores on these 14 individual scales. While these descriptions are helpful, there is less clarity as to how to interpret the overall CPQ profile. Part of this problem is addressed by the numerous validity studies which provide CPQ profiles for such diverse subject samples as low and high achievers, delinquents, and personality disorders. Despite these studies, the potential user may still have difficulty understanding various combinations of factor scores, as well as interpreting the overall CPQ profile.

Given the fact that extensive normative data and tables are provided, it is surprising that no information is given regarding the demographics of the normative sample. Specifically, it would have been useful to know such factors as the number of subjects sampled, their age and sex breakdown, and where they were recruited. Although it is assumed that these norms represent a non-clinical population, this too should have been made explicit.

Overall, the CPQ offers a self-report sampling of personality for an age range that is difficult to assess. The goal is to provide an assessment of 14 separate factors from which future functioning can be predicted. Despite some difficulties with reliability and some uncertainty in interpreting questionnaire profiles, this measure appears to have potential usefulness for both clinical assessment and research.

Review of Children's Personality Questionnaire, 1975 Edition, by HOWARD M. KNOFF, Assistant Professor of School Psychology, State University of New York at Albany, Albany, NY:

The Children's Personality Questionnaire (CPQ) is the second within a series of four personality inventories which includes the Early School Personality Questionnaire (for ages 6 through 8), the Jr.-Sr. High School Personality Questionnaire (for ages 12 through 17), and the Sixteen Personality Factor Questionnaire (for adults). Based on Cattell's theoretical beliefs that there are objectively determined source traits that comprise one's personality structure and that these traits are consistent across the lifespan, all four personality inventories maintain the same order, labels, and descriptions of the 14 primary traits. The CPQ comes with a 28-page manual which serves "as a brief summary of the main points involved in administering, scoring, and using test information" and a 77-page handbook which carries a 1975 copyright, yet is identified as a 1979 edition on the title page. The manual is extremely brief, does not discuss the technical and psychometric aspects of the test as thoroughly as the handbook, and cannot be used to fully score or interpret the test's raw data (e.g., there are no tables to convert the data into either standard or percentile scores). Thus, the handbook, which will be a major focus of this review, is the only comprehensive source amongst the CPQ materials, and the CPQ authors appropriately urge examiners to consult it for all significant questions and concerns.

The CPQ comes in four different forms (A through D), with each form containing 140 items—10 for each primary factor. Each form is divided into two sections (e.g., A1 and A2) to help at those times when the test's administration must be broken into two or more testing sessions. The authors' recommendation to administer two (A+B, C+D) or all four (A+B+C+D) forms to children for the most accurate personality assessment is well-taken; the test's reliability coefficients (both test-retest and internal consistency) are noticeably higher with combined administrations. This practice also can increase the examiner's diagnostic "comfort level" as interpretations become based on 20- or 40-item factors rather than just 10-item factors. Raw data are transformed easily into "*n*-stens" (10–category standard scores), "*s*-stens" (10–category normalized standard scores), and percentiles using tables in the handbook. These standard score tables are separated by sex and are organized for single or multiple form (A+B, C+D, A+B+C+D) administrations. Administration and scoring directions and procedures are clear and concise.

Children completing the CPQ (ages 8 through 12 or approximately grades 3 through 7) should have few difficulties given the organization and format of both the administration forms and the computer answer sheet. The reading and comprehension levels of some items, especially those written in the negative sense, may present problems for younger or academically weaker students. Thus, as suggested, examiners should closely proctor the test's administration and be available to clarify confusing items. Examiners who wish to administer only one form of the CPQ, regardless of their format similarities, should be aware that the forms may not be comparable. CPQ equivalence coefficients evaluating alternate-form reliability between Forms A and B and Forms C and D, respectively, were very low. For example, correlations of .28 for Factor H and .23 for Factor O existed in the Form A vs. B comparisons; and correlations of .20 for Factor O, .21 for Factor J, and .29 for Factor H were reported for the Form C vs. D comparisons. Additionally, the correlations for the other form comparisons (e.g., A vs. C, B vs. D) are not presented, nor are these form differences or their implications for administration and interpretation discussed.

The CPQ and the handbook have numerous weaknesses in the area of test interpretation. Descriptions of the test's development, specifically item selection, are not presented; the handbook only details the "principles" of test design and construction for a "good" test. Factor analytic data demonstrating construct validity is incomplete (e.g., missing analyses for the individual forms) and difficult to interpret (e.g., nowhere is the sample of 836 boys and girls described). The normative sample used to create the standard score tables also is never described—except for another discussion of "basic principles of sampling and construction of norm tables" in Appendix D. The descriptions of the 14 primary source traits do not facilitate a clinical understanding of a child aged 8 through 12. This is because some of the descriptions are drawn directly from the Manual for the Jr.-Sr. High School Personality Questionnaire (1960), and because the research studies cited are primarily from the 1960s. The interpretive section, "Criterion Relations Useful in Educational, Clinical, and Social Psychology," from which the authors hope to demonstrate "concrete validity," is also dated, although somewhat more clearly written and diagnostically useful. Thus, even if the normative data were adequate, interpretive suggestions are not necessarily geared to the CPQ's stated age ranges, nor does the handbook clearly facilitate a diagnostic understanding of the child from the data. Regardless of the theoretical belief in 14 stable factors, the CPQ handbook does not report any comprehensive empirical support nor does it describe the data necessary to fully evaluate and critique the CPQ's technical adequacy.

Finally, the handbook's description of the primary traits through their "technical names" is difficult to follow. With such terms as "sizothymia," "phlegmatic temperament," "threctia," "zeppia," and "coasthenia," the notion that labels can facilitate professional communication and understanding is severely tested. The handbook does a far better job of explaining the traits when behavioral descriptors and more contemporary psychological and diagnostic concepts are used.

In summary, it is very difficult to evaluate the usefulness of the CPQ for the field. The handbook contains many psychometric and descriptive gaps that frustrate an objective evalutation. The CPQ needs to be validated as a tool independent of its three sister tools, and its interpretation should focus on characteristics of the 14 factors specific to its stated ages 8 through 12. The CPQ authors apparently did not take advantage of their 1979 revision process to update their references, to strengthen their interpretation sections, and to edit the handbook's sometimes overbearing tone and attitude. It is unfortunate when texts from the 1950s and 1960s are referred to as "current textbooks in psychology and personality." The CPQ may be a useful tool to some practitioners and researchers; the published test materials, however, need to guide, discuss, and demonstrate that usefulness.

[223]

Chromatic Differential Test. Grades 1–12 and college and adults; 1970–72; CDT; "an objectively scored projective measure of attitudes towards persons and institutions"; 20 or more constructs in 5 areas: preference, emotions, persons, institutions, self concept; Form D ('70, 1 page); scoring sheet (no date, 1 page); handbook ('72, 28 pages); personal interpretation booklet for grades 1–2, older elementary, secondary, college, adults, ('71, 7–9 pages); 1983 price data: $22 per 12 overlays for 12 basic constructs; $.50 per personal interpretation booklet; $2.50 per handbook; rental of tests and supplies for group administration available; (10–15) minutes; A. B. Sweney; Test Systems International, Ltd.*

[224]

CIRCUS. Nursery school-grade K.5, K.5–1.5, 1.5–2.5, 2.5–3.5; 1972–80; a battery designed "to diagnose the instructional needs of individual children and to monitor and evaluate early education programs"; for an upward extension see Sequential Tests of Educational Progress, Series III; 1–2 forms; each of the tests has a teacher's edition which includes directions for administering; 4 levels; manual and technical report ('79, 98 pages); norms booklets (individual norms tables, group norms tables, anticipated posttest score tables) are available; 1985 price data: $6 per manual and technical report; $7.50 per specimen set of basic assessment measures of any one level (without manual and technical report); $20 per complete specimen set of either A or B (without manual and technical report); scoring service available as listed below for booklets and answer sheets (answers must be transcribed locally to machine scored answer sheets); Educational Testing Service; CTB/McGraw-Hill.*

a) CIRCUS A. Nursery school-grade K.5; 1974–79; 14 tests (2 basic assessment measures [7, 10], and 12 additional measures), 2 scales for teacher ratings of pupils, and a questionnaire for teacher ratings of the educational environment; CIRCUS A and B user's guide ('75–'79, 8–43 pages) for each test; practice sheet ('74, 2 pages) and directions ('74, 2 pages); $2.50 per 25 practice tests and directions; $15 per 100 NCS answer sheets; answer sheet scoring service (except for 12): $.30 and over per pupil per test, $1.10 and over per pupil per basic assessment package; booklet scoring service (except for 1, 2, 3, 12, 14): $.90 and over per pupil per test, $2.35 and over per pupil per basic assessment package; (30–40) minutes per test.

1) *Activities Inventory.* Ratings by teachers; 4 ratings (frequency, complexity, adult help, peer group structure) for each of 15 activities: physical-motor (4), academic (4), role playing-fantasy (4), music-art (3); 1 form ('76, 3 pages); $2 per 10 inventories including user's guide.

2) *CIRCUS Behavior Inventory.* 3 ratings by teachers: following procedures, enjoyment, talking; 1 form ('74, 1 page); $2 per 10 inventories including user's guide.

3) *Copy What You See: Perceptual-Motor Coordination.* 1 form ('76, 4 pages); $8.75 per 25 tests including teacher's edition and user's guide.

4) *Do You Know?: General Information.* 1 form ('76, 18 pages); $18.75 per 25 tests including teacher's edition and user's guide.

5) *Educational Environment Questionnaire.* EEQ; ratings by teachers in 3 areas: class, school, program; 1 form ('74, 12 pages); $.60 per questionnaire; scoring service, $1.25 per questionnaire (minimum of 5 questionnaires).

6) *Finding Letters and Numbers: Letter and Numeral Recognition and Discrimination.* 4 scores: capital letters, lower-case letters, numbers, total; 1 form ('76, 12 pages); $18.75 per 25 tests including teacher's editions and user's guide.

7) *How Much and How Many: Quantitative Concepts.* 4 scores: counting, relational terms, numerical concepts, total; 1 form ('76, 27 pages); $19.25 per 25 tests including teacher's edition and user's guide.

8) *How Words Sound: Auditory Discrimination.* 4 scores: consonants (initial, final), medial vowels, total; 1 form ('76, 24 pages); $18.75 per 25 tests including teacher's edition and user's guide.

9) *How Words Work: Aspects of Functional Language.* 4 scores: verb forms, prepositions/negation/ conjunctions, syntax, total; 1 form ('76, 15 pages); $18.75 per 25 tests including teacher's edition and user's guide.

10) *Listen to the Story: Comprehension, Interpretation, and Recall of Oral Language.* 3 scores: comprehension, interpretation, total; 1 form ('76, 15 pages); $18.25 per 25 tests including teacher's edition and user's guide.

11) *Look-Alikes: Visual Discrimination.* 3 scores: complex matching, reversals, total; 1 form ('76, 28 pages); $18.75 per 25 tests including teacher's edition and user's guide.

12) *Make a Tree: Divergent Pictorial Production.* Construction of a tree using paper mosaics; 3 scores: appropriateness, unusualness, difference between 2 constructions; 1 form; $7.80 per 20 test books including 5 packages of stickers and a teacher's edition.

13) *Noises: Discrimination of Real-World Sounds.* 1 form ('74, 14 pages plus tape cassette); $7.80 per 10 test books including tape cassette and teacher's edition.

14) *Say and Tell: Productive Language.* 11 scores: description (3 scores), functional language (5 scores), narration (3 scores); individual; 1 form: Part 1 (familiar items provided by examiner), 2 ('74, 73 pages), 3 ('74, 4 pages); performance guide ('74, 11 pages); $10.50 per complete set including 10 performance guides.

15) *See and Remember: Visual and Associative Memory.* 1 form ('76, 34 pages); $34 per 25 tests including teacher's edition and user's guide.

16) *Think it Through: Problem Solving.* 4 scores: problem identification, classification, solution evaluation and time sequence, total; 1 form ('76, 28 pages); $24.75 per 25 tests including teacher's edition and user's guide.

17) *What Words Mean: Receptive Vocabulary.* 4 scores: nouns, verbs, modifiers, total; 1 form ('76, 22 pages); $18.75 per 25 tests including teacher's edition and user's guide.

b) CIRCUS B. Grades K.5–1.5; 1974–79; 12 tests (3 basic assessment measures [6, 7, 14] and 9 additional measures), a scale for teacher ratings of pupils, and a questionnaire for teacher ratings of the educational environment; CIRCUS A and B user's guide ('75–'79, 8–43 pages) for each test; practice sheet ('74, 2 pages) and directions ('74, 2 pages); $2.50 per 25 practice tests and directions; $15 per 100 NCS answer sheets; answer sheet scoring service (except for 12): $.30 and over per pupil per test, $.65 and over per pupil per basic assessment package; booklet scoring service (except for 1, 2, 9, 10): $.90 and over per pupil per test, $2 and over per pupil per basic assessment package; (30–40) minutes per test.

1) *Activities Inventory.* Ratings by teachers; 4 ratings (frequency, complexity, structure preference, situational preference) for each of 9 activities: physical (2), language (2), number, science, classroom citizenship, music-art (2); 1 form ('76, 3 pages); $2 per 10 inventories including a user's guide.

2) *Copy What You See: Perceptual Motor Coordination.* 1 form ('76, 4 pages); $8.75 per 25 tests including teacher's edition and user's guide.

3) *Do You Know?: General Information.* 1 form ('76, 9 pages); $18.75 per 25 tests including teacher's edition and user's guide.

4) *Educational Environment Questionnaire.* EEQ; ratings by teachers in 3 areas: class, school, teacher; 1 form ('76, 11 pages); $.60 per questionnaire; scoring service, $1.25 per questionnaire (minimum of 5 questionnaires).

5) *Finding Letters and Numbers: Letter and Numeral Recognition and Discrimination.* Details same as *a* 6.

6) *How Much and How Many: Quantitative Concepts.* 7 scores: counting, numerical concepts, adding and subtracting, subtotal, mathematical concepts, conservation, subtotal; 1 form ('76, 23 pages); $19.25 per 25 tests including teacher's edition and user's guide.

7) *Listen to the Story: Comprehension, Interpretation and Recall of Oral Language.* 4 scores: comprehension, interpretation, vocabulary, total; 1 form ('76, 14 pages); $18.25 per 25 tests including teacher's edition and user's guide.

8) *Look-Alikes: Visual Discrimination.* 1 form ('76, 27 pages); $18.75 per 25 tests including teacher's edition and user's guide.

9) *Make a Tree: Divergent Pictorial Production.* Details same as *a* 12.

10) *Say and Tell: Productive Language.* 11 scores: description (2 scores), functional language (5 scores), narration (4 scores); individual; 1 form: Part 1 (familiar items provided by examinee), 2 ('76, 58 pages), 3 ('76, 3 pages); performance guide ('76, 12 pages); $10.50 per complete set including 10 performance guides.

11) *See and Remember: Visual Memory.* 1 form ('76, 47 pages); $34 per 25 tests including teacher's edition and user's guide.

12) *Things I Like: Interests and Preferences.* 2 scores: verbal/nonverbal, group/individual; 1 form ('76, 10 pages); $17.15 per 35 tests including teacher's edition and user's guide.

13) *Think It Through: Problem Solving.* 3 scores: word problems, patterns, mazes; 1 form ('76, 18 pages); $18.75 per 25 tests including teacher's edition and user's guide.

14) *Word Puzzles.* 5 scores: sounds, consonants (beginning, ending), whole words, total; 1 form ('76, 16 pages); $18.25 per 25 tests including teacher's edition and user's guide.

c) CIRCUS C. Grades 1.5–2.5; 1979–80; 9 tests (3 basic assessment measures [3, 4, 7] and 6 additional measures), and a questionnaire for teacher ratings of the educational environment; CIRCUS C and D user's guide ('79–'80, 11–49 pages) for each test; practice sheet ('79, 2 pages) and directions ('79, 2 pages); 2 editions of basic assessment booklets: hand-scorable, machine-scorable; $20.30 per 35 hand-scorable basic assessment booklets including teacher's edition and user's guide; $32.20 per 35 machine-scorable basic assessment booklets including teacher's edition and user's guide; $14 per 35 hand-scorable individual test booklets including teacher's edition and user's guide (except as listed below); $2.50 per 35 practice tests and directions; scoring service, $.65 and over per pupil per test, $.95 and over per pupil per basic assessment booklet; (30–40) minutes per test.

1) *Do You Know?: General Information.* 1 form ('79, 8 pages).

2) *Educational Environment Questionnaire.* Details same as for *b* 4.

3) *Listening.* Form X, Y, ('79, 8 pages).

4) *Mathematics.* 4 scores: numerical and mathematical concepts, computation, relational concepts, total; Form X, Y, ('79, 8 pages).

5) *Oral Reading.* Individual; 1 form ('79, 4 pages).

6) *Phonetic Analysis.* 1 form ('79, 8 pages).

7) *Reading.* Form X, Y, ('79, 13 pages).

8) *Say and Tell: Productive Language.* Details same as for *b* 10.

9) *Things I Like: Interests and Preferences.* Details same as for *b* 12.

10) *Think It Through: Problem Solving.* 3 scores: word problems, patterns, mazes; 1 form ('79, 12 pages); $14.35 per 35 hand-scorable test booklets including teacher's edition and user's guide.

d) CIRCUS D. Grades 2.5–3.5; 1979–80; 10 tests (4 basic assessment measures [3, 4, 7, 11] and 6 additional measures) and a questionnaire for teacher ratings of the educational environment; CIRCUS C and D user's guide ('79–'80, 11–49 pages) for each test; practice sheet ('79, 2 pages) and directions ('79, 2 pages); 2 editions of basic assessment booklets: hand-scorable, machine-scorable; $22.40 per 35 hand-scorable basic assessment booklets including teacher's edition and user's guide; $34.65 per 35 machine-scorable basic assessment booklets including teacher's edition and user's guide; $14 per 35 hand-scorable individual test booklets including teacher's edition and user's guide (except as listed below); $2.50 per 35 practice tests and directions; scoring service same as for *c*; (30–40) minutes per test.

1) *Do You Know?: General Information.* 1 form ('79, 8 pages).

2) *Educational Environment Questionnaire.* Details same as for *b* 4.

3) *Listening.* Details same as for *c* 3.

4) *Mathematics.* 4 scores: same as for *c* 4; Form X, Y, ('79, 8 pages).

5) *Oral Reading.* Individual; 1 form ('79, 4 pages).

6) *Phonetic Analysis.* 1 form ('79, 8 pages).

7) *Reading.* Form X, Y, ('79, 12 pages).

8) *Say and Tell: Productive Language.* Details same as for *b* 10.

9) *Things I Like: Interests and Preferences.* Details same as for *b* 12.

10) *Think It Through: Problem Solving.* Details same as for *c* 10.

11) *Writing Skills.* 4 scores: spelling, word structure, capitalization and punctuation, total; Form X, Y, ('79, 12 pages).

See T3:404 (5 references); for reviews by Sueann Robinson Ambron, William L. Goodwin, and excerpted reviews by James Raths and Lilian G. Katz, and Rochelle Selbert Mayer, see 8:7A (3 references).

TEST REFERENCES

1. Snyder, S. D., & Michael, W. B. The relationship of performance on standardized tests in mathematics and reading to two measures of social intelligence and one of academic self-esteem for two samples of primary school children. EDUCATIONAL AND PSYCHOLOGICAL MEASUREMENT, 1983, 43, 1141–1148.

Review of CIRCUS by LEWIS R. AIKEN, Professor of Psychology, Pepperdine University, Malibu, CA:

The CIRCUS achievement test battery is a downward extension of the Sequential Tests of Educational Progress (STEP III) (CTB/McGraw-Hill). There are four grade levels of CIRCUS: Preprimary A for preschool through K.5, Preprimary B for K.5 through 1.5, Primary C for 1.5 through 2.5, Primary D for 2.5 through 3.5. The A and B levels were published in 1974 and 1976, respectively, and the C and D levels in 1978.

The four levels of the CIRCUS tests, which are based on the results of several child development research projects conducted by Educational Testing Service (ETS), were designed to measure not only the traditional scholastic areas of language and mathematics but other areas such as productive language and interests. Selection of the "circus" theme, designing the test materials, and administering the tests themselves was done with an awareness of the interests and abilities of preschool and primary school children and the convenience and capabilities of teachers. Before writing the actual items, test specifications concerned with the content and types of items were drawn up, although no detailed information or tables of specifications are presented in the manual. Three preliminary forms of each test were tried out, from which two final forms emerged. Items were also analyzed for sex- and ethnic-group bias.

The various measures comprising the CIRCUS (and STEP) battery are grouped into three categories: Basic Assessment Measures, Other Measures, and Measures for Special Purposes. The "Basic Assessment Measures" (Listening Comprehension, Mathematics Computation and Concepts at all four levels; Pre-reading and Reading Vocabulary & Comprehension at levels B through D; Writing Skills at Level D only) assess more fundamental skills. Parallel forms of each test are available at Levels C and D. Tests in the "Other Measures" category (Phonics, General Knowledge, Problem Solving, Perceptual-Motor Coordination, Visual Memory, Visual Discrimination, Letter and Numeral Recognition, Receptive Vocabulary, Auditory Discrimination, Functional Language, Discrimination of Real World Sounds) are also available at different levels but are not meant to be administered to all children. Only one of the 15 tests in the "Basic Assessment Measures" and "Other Measures" categories requires oral answers and must therefore be administered individually. Even when the groups are small, however, group administration of the other A- and B-level tests seems neither as reliable nor valid as individual administration. Teachers are encouraged to select the tests from the "Other Measures" category which will answer their specific educational questions.

The CIRCUS "Measures for Special Purposes" (Educational Environment Questionnaire, Say and Tell, Oral Reading, Things I Like, Make a Tree, Activities Inventory), some of which assess cognitive and others affective variables, are designed to supplement the achievement tests in the "Basic Assessment Measures" and "Other Measures" categories. The Educational Environment Questionnaire and Activities Inventory, both of which are filled out by the teacher, provide background information for interpreting a child's test scores. The Things I Like inventory, consisting of 26 items concerning classroom activities and group settings, can also provide useful interpretive information on the students.

The 1979 CIRCUS Manual and Technical Report lists three basic uses of CIRCUS test data: program evaluation, individual assessment, pretesting and posttesting. Matters such as the selection of measures, test administration and scoring, and test interpretation are also discussed briefly in the manual and in the User's Guide for specific tests. A variety of statistical tables are available for assisting in test score interpretation: summaries of mean scores of groups of children who took the tests; the percentages of children answering each item correctly; written interpretations of total scores and subscores; individual norms tables listing the mid-percentile ranks of scores by grade and time of testing; tables of mid-percentile ranks and stanines by the domains (subsets of items) of Reading, Mathematics, Writing Skills, and Phonetic Analysis; group norms tables listing mid-percentile ranks by grade and testing time; expectancy tables indicating relationships between scores on various levels.

Four separate reviews of Levels A and B of CIRCUS were included in *The Eighth Mental Measurements Yearbook* (8:7A). Among the advantages of CIRCUS noted by Sueann Ambron are: CIRCUS scores are not combined into total scores; users can select CIRCUS tests to suit their programs, time, and finances; CIRCUS achievement measures can be linked to measures of the educational environment (by means of the Educational Environment Questionnaire). The fact that the CIRCUS tests are both "criterion-referenced," providing verbal comments on competency levels, as well as "norm-referenced," was also deemed an advantage. However, more negative than positive comments were made by the reviewers. The tests were criticized as being too long (requiring too much testing time) for preschoolers, having directions that many children were unable or unwilling to follow, creating boredom and a tendency to cheat in the children, providing no information on content validity, being difficult if not impossible to administer on a group basis, having many modest alpha coefficients and no test-retest reliability coefficients, containing poor and unappealing art work, and failing to include tests of fine and gross motor coordination. The majority of the reviewers did compliment the ETS staff on its attempt to extend group achievement testing to the preschool level, but it was concluded that the results were far from satisfactory. Statements such as "a significant addition to the literature on testing young children," "a promising start in providing multiple measures of competency in assessing preprimary and K-1 children," and "the idea of developing...sentence reports is a good one," were among the positive conclusions. One reviewer concluded, however, that "the data in the Manual and Technical Report do not support the claims made for CIRCUS," while another emphasized the fact that "the CIRCUS measures come across to most children as tests, and not, as the authors had hoped, as 'interesting puzzles.' "

The 1979 CIRCUS Manual and Technical Report does not really address the criticisms made by the four reviewers with respect to levels A and B, although one could argue that some of the criticisms are nitpicking. For example, a test of perceptual-motor coordination ("Copy What You See") is included among the "Other Measures" at levels A and B. In any event, certain criticisms, such as those concerning lengthy testing sessions and the failure of children to follow the instructions, would not be expected to apply as strongly to the older examinees taking the C and D forms. Children in grades 1.5 to 3.5 have had more experience with testing than preschoolers and kindergartners. Primary school children tend to be less distractible and conforming in school situations, and have a greater tendency to follow the test directions and rules by trying to do one's best and not looking on other students' test papers. Nevertheless, group testing even at grade levels 2 and 3 should be approached carefully and patiently by the teacher.

An examination of the test booklets for levels C and D indicates that they are well-designed (the monkey doesn't look like a dog!). Admittedly, although the tests are untimed, estimated testing time is still rather long—40 minutes for each of the three or four tests in the "Basic Assessment Measures," 30–40 minutes for each of the three tests in the "Other Measures" category, and 15–20 minutes for each of the "Special Purpose Measures." It is also recommended that a Practice Test be given before each test in the first two categories.

Several hours would be needed to administer all measures in the CIRCUS battery, but the teacher is encouraged to follow the guidelines in chapter 5 of the manual and select the subset of tests that best meet his or her particular needs. None of the tests is particularly difficult to administer, no special training being required. But even a teacher who has had one or more courses in educational testing should read carefully the User's Guide for each selected test and the manual before beginning the actual process of test administration, scoring, and interpretation of results. Scoring is straightforward, raw scores being converted to standard scores, percentile ranks, and stanines. Domain Score Tables, Verbal Report Tables, Item Data Tables, and Group Norms Tables are also included in the User's Guide for each test.

Chapter 6 of the CIRCUS manual devotes a great deal of space to a discussion of Grade Level Indicators (GLIs), which are similar to grade-equivalent scores but limited to on-level testing. Cautions concerning the use of the GLIs and what they are intended and not intended to do are given, but teachers will have to read pages 25–26 of the manual very carefully in order not to misinterpret this new system of scoring. Certainly, the entire manual is worthwhile reading for teachers, and should be supplemented with expert interpretation and perhaps even a CIRCUS workshop.

Even more uses are suggested for CIRCUS levels C and D than for levels A and B. Uses of test results for individual diagnosis and placement are stressed, but applications in curriculum design and modification are also considered. As might be expected, there are a few oversights. For example, standard errors of measurement but not reliability coefficients are given in Table 5 of the manual. Also, the amount of assistance that teachers will need in order to select and administer the tests and interpret the results is somewhat minimized. Among the positive features, however, are standardization samples for the C and D forms that were selected to be representative of a national population of children at the appropriate grade levels, and parallel forms for the tests that were carefully equated.

Information on the concurrent, content, predictive, and construct validity of the C and D forms and procedures for obtaining this information are briefly discussed in chapter 9 of the manual. Pages 72–86 of the manual contain detailed statistical data (means, standard deviations, correlations) concerning the reliability and validity of the test and domain scores. An examination of these tables provides more support for the psychometric adequacy of levels C and D than for levels A and B. The reliabilities of the CIRCUS tests are adequate for differentiating among groups and in some cases individuals.

With respect to the predictive validity of the tests, the correlations between scores on CIRCUS A and B, B and C, and C and D range from .34 to .77 when uncorrected for attentuation and from .51 to .99 when corrected for attenuation. The second set of coefficients is higher than the first because of the moderate reliabilities of many of the tests. In any event, the predictive validity coefficients point to a modest level of predictive accuracy of the test scores at one level compared to those at a higher level. This is not surprising when one realizes that not only are cognitive abilities more consistently measurable at the primary than at the preschool level, but that those abilities also change qualitatively during early childhood and especially after a child enters school.

Review of CIRCUS by GLYNN LIGON, Director, Office of Research and Evaluation, Austin Independent School District, Austin, TX:

CIRCUS is an impressive selection of achievement tests for preschool to grade 3 students. (STEP III is the sister test for grades 3 through 12.) A questionnaire for teacher ratings of the educational environment is also available for all four levels. CIRCUS A and B include scales for teacher ratings of pupils. There are 14 student tests at Level A, 12 at Level B, 9 at Level C, and 10 at Level D.

Although a large number of tests are available in CIRCUS A and B, for longitudinal comparisons across grade levels four test areas can be used. Continuous assessment from prekindergarten through grade 12 is available in Listening Comprehension (Listen to the Story, CIRCUS A and B; Listening, CIRCUS C and D; Listening, STEP III E-J) and in Mathematics Computation and Concepts (How Much and How Many, CIRCUS A and B; Mathematics, CIRCUS C and D; Math Basic Concepts and Math Computation, STEP III E-J). Writing Skills begins at the beginning of grade 3 (CIRCUS D) and continues through grade 12 (STEP III E-J); and Reading begins at the end of kindergarten (Prereading, CIRCUS B) and continues through grade 12 (Reading, CIRCUS C and D; Reading, STEP III E-J). The other CIRCUS tests are more domain- or skill-referenced measures that might be influenced more by local curriculum differences. Choices among them are intended to be made on the basis of a local need for assessment in a specific area.

A key factor for any school system considering CIRCUS is time. The user of CIRCUS must be willing to invest substantial time in choosing among the many available tests, training teachers to administer the tests, administering them, and interpreting the results. At the prekindergarten level, the question to be addressed is whether this time investment nets information about students that is significantly more useful than the less formal observations and tests a teacher normally uses.

In selecting an achievement test, matching what is tested with what is taught is critical. The specimen sets, teacher's guides, and Manual and Technical Report do not contain enough well-specified descriptions of the measured skills to allow easy comparisons with local curriculum. To understand many of the skills tested, one must study the actual items on the test. This is a common difficulty encountered on most standardized tests. The CIRCUS is particularly complex and difficult to analyze for the skills being measured.

The major question about CIRCUS A and B (or any other standardized test for young children) is one of validity and reliability. How much do the verbal directions and teacher-read items measure receptive language skills rather than the intended content of the test? Correlations among various CIRCUS A and B tests are sufficiently high to suggest a common ability factor. Of concern in administration is the occurrence among young test takers of calling out answers and looking around at the work of others. Both problems occurred during the norming. Practice materials are provided and recommended, but in reality they are a necessity. In fact, users should consider several practice sessions for very young children with special emphasis on marking answers, not calling out answers, and working independently. An investment of time by the teacher is required to prepare the students for a valid testing. Moreover, a substantial investment of time is probably necessary to prepare teachers to give CIRCUS A and B—to be able to read the items with ease and to be able to manage a group-testing situation with very young children. Raw scores, percentiles, standard scores, and grade level indicators (GLI) are available. The first three are common and have their traditional advantages and disadvantages. GLI scores (available for Levels C and D only) are somewhat unique to the CIRCUS/STEP tests and are a response to the misinterpretations and misuses of grade equivalents (GE). A lengthy discussion, albeit a justification, for GLI scores rather than GE scores is provided by the authors. The only real difference between the two is that GLI scores are not extrapolated beyond the most extreme empirical norming dates. Therefore, one might have more confidence in the proper interpretation of available GLI scores. Unfortunately, without extrapolation, GLI scores above and below the most extreme empirical norming date are shown as the most extreme GLI with a + or –. For the fall of grade 3 on Level D of the Reading Test, this means that only one third of the students get a precise GLI and all the others get a 3.5+ or a 2.5–. How useful is it to report a score with such a limiting floor and ceiling?

For districts with existing GE criteria for programs and services, the GLI scores may be too restricted in range. Teachers, counselors, and principals who use GE scores tend to use them more for interpreting scores for students more than a year from grade level. A 3.5+ for all students at or above the 59th percentile (Reading, Level D) may not be very useful. If GE scores are desired, GLI scores will probably be a disappointment.

An attractive marketing feature of the CIRCUS is sentence reports that translate raw scores into statements such as "Evidences a fairly broad range of general knowledge." This type of reporting might be useful to teachers and counselors who are studying test scores for their implications. Too often time does not allow school staff to interpret the numbers for individual students into more useful terminology. Users should, however, determine on their own whether the range of scores used for each sentence report is appropriate. For example, should 80% of the kindergarten and first-grade students in the norming sample be considered to have a "broad" or "fairly broad" range of general knowledge? Can a teacher actually translate these sentences into instructional strategies? Probably not.

Sentence reports are unique to performance on each test rather than a vehicle for relating skills across test areas. This is in line with the authors' intent to avoid composite or total scores, thus not predetermining which combination of tests will be chosen by each user.

Some reviewers may consider the artwork for the CIRCUS items to be marginal in quality. Using the Peabody Picture Vocabulary Test—Revised as an industry standard, the CIRCUS items are noticeably less realistic, less attractive, and less crisp. Because the norming sample dealt with the same illustrations, it is questionable that this would have any impact on reliability of measurement in the practical setting; however, some students may have their thinking distracted by some of the less realistic drawings.

CIRCUS norms appear to be technically sound, with the authors taking care to sample carefully from all sections of the country. As with any standardized test, the low participation rate of those schools initially selected can bias the norms. The CIRCUS participation rate is unreported in the 1979 Manual and Technical Report. For tests designed for prekindergarten and kindergarten students, there is an additional bias introduced by the nature of the students who enroll. Not all children attend school below grade 1. No nonschool children were included in the norming.

Caution must be advised when interpreting scores on the CIRCUS because of the self-selected nature of prekindergarten and kindergarten students from which norms are derived. This is important not only for interpreting CIRCUS A and B scores but for comparing them to CIRCUS C and D, which were normed on a population of students affected by compulsory attendance laws.

According to the most recent (1979) technical report, CIRCUS A was normed in 1972–73; CIRCUS B in 1975; CIRCUS C and D in 1976–77. Longitudinal comparisons across test levels would be affected by any changes in national achievement from 1972 to 1977. Based on the dramatic improvement in early school achievement during the 1970s, longitudinal comparisons using 1972 and 1977 norms could be greatly misleading.

Testing preschoolers, especially in a group setting, should be expected to be difficult and to require an investment in preparation time. The design of CIRCUS offers no relief from this challenge. The two most attractive features of CIRCUS are the continuous assessment available in four areas through grade 12 with CIRCUS/STEP III, and the wide range of skill areas for which prekindergarten and kindergarten tests are available.

[225]

The Clarke Reading Self-Assessment Survey.

Grades 11–12 and college freshmen; 1978; SAS; self-administered, self-scored; 15 scores: reading (speed, comprehension, interpretation, total), organization of facts and ideas (word lists, concept, diagrams, paragraph parts, total), writing skills (word usage, sentence structure, writing mechanics—punctuation, research and writing, total), total; no data on reliability and validity; no norms; individual; 1 form ('78, 31 pages, includes instructions for administration and scoring); no manual; 1983 price data: $4 per survey; (60) minutes; John H. Clarke and Simon Wittes; Academic Therapy Publications.*

Review of The Clarke Reading Self-Assessment Survey by ROBERT M. WILSON, Professor of

Education, University of Maryland, College Park, MD:

The Clarke Reading Self-Assessment Survey (SAS) is essentially a self diagnosis instrument of ten skills that the authors contend are essential for academic success in high school and college. The booklet indicates, however, that its most effective use is as a counseling tool. I agree. In fact, to expect a student to use the SAS to develop a self diagnosis is loaded with problems.

Since each test section is designed to measure a specific academic skill area, the SAS is, in fact, a criterion-referenced test. As such the use of combined scores or total scores, as recommended, is meaningless. For example, the combining of scores from Reading Speed, Reading Comprehension, and Reading Interpretation into a total Reading Score is suspect. Of further concern is the manner of weighting the various subtests. For example, Reading Speed has a maximum score of 13 while Reading Comprehension has only 10 for a maximum score. One interpretation of such a weighting is that how fast one reads is more important than how well one understands what has been read.

The small number of items for each of the subtests raises serious concerns about reliability. No reliability data are given, but when one measures Reading Comprehension with five multiple choice items and Reading Interpretation by five items, then reliability concerns are present.

Reading Interpretation is assessed through the use of one poem, followed by five questions. To suggest that a student can self-assess his or her reading interpretation in such a manner may be more misleading than helpful. Certainly there is more to reading interpretation than responding to five questions about a single poem.

By using the Score Chart the student is able to generate three part scores and a total score. There is no explanation for the use of the total score. On the last page there are suggestions for the use of the part scores, using cutoff procedures. How the cutoff scores for part scores were obtained is not explained and appear to be arbitrary.

Through the use of weighted scores and the multiplication of part scores by 3 (no reason given) a maximum score of 99 or 108 is obtainable for each part of the SAS. For example: Part 2, Organizing Facts and Ideas, has three sections. Section A, Word Lists, has seven items which are weighted by two making a score of 14 possible. Section B, Concept Diagrams, has six items weighted by two making a score of 12 possible. Section C, Paragraph Parts, has five items weighted by 2 making a score of 10 possible. These three section scores are added and multiplied by a weight of 3 making a possible score of 108 for Part 2.

That score of 108, by now, loses all meaning. There is no explanation for the different weightings given the various subtests but, obviously, those weightings effect the total part score. The use of the common multiplication factor of 3 increases the weight attributed to each of the subtest scores, but there is no explanation for the adding of further weight to already questionable scores.

There are important high school/college study skills that the SAS leaves unassessed. Some of those are summarizing, note taking, rereading to locate information, underlining, and student generated questions. Of course no instrument can assess every aspect of learning; however, I would recommend consideration of the inclusion of some of these important study skills.

It would seem to me that the SAS should be used only with a counselor and then with great caution. To think of letting a high school senior make interpretations from data such as these is dangerous. I would recommend a rethinking of the use of the SAS and an expansion of the advice to students and counselors, including a rationale for the scoring system and the cutoff scores. As presently constituted, the SAS might well lead students to believe they need a tutor or a specific course erroneously.

[226]

The Class Activities Questionnaire. Students and teachers grades 6–12; 1981–82; CAQ; students' perceptions of the classroom situation as compared to the teacher's intended and predicted classroom situation; 21 factors in 5 dimensions: lower thought processes, higher thought processes, classroom focus, classroom climate, student opinions; 1 form ('81, 2 pages); manual ('82, 52 pages); 1984 price data: $16.95 per 30 questionnaires including computer scoring of the completed forms; $6.95 per manual; $7.50 per specimen set; (20–30) minutes; Joe M. Steele; Creative Learning Press, Inc.*

TEST REFERENCES

1. Kusimo, P. S., & Erlandson, D. A. Instructional communications in a large high school: Its impact on effectiveness. NASSP BULLETIN, 1983, 67, 18–24.

Review of The Class Activities Questionnaire by ROBERT W. HILTONSMITH, Assistant Professor of Psychology and Education, Syracuse University, Syracuse, NY:

The growth of interactional approaches to assessment problems in both psychology and education has spawned the development of an increasing number of instruments designed to assess the characteristics of settings in which human behavior occurs. An especially fertile ground for the emergence of these instruments has been the school classroom (and, to a lesser extent, the school building itself). A common assumption here is that classroom psychosocial characteristics, or "social climate," can be reliably inferred from the perceptions of students and teachers, and that this perception of social climate has direct or indirect impact on the behavior occurring in the classroom. A sizeable body of research has accumulated in two major areas: (1) the factors, such as classroom size, curriculum, etc., that influence classroom environment, and (2) the effects of perceived classroom climate on student cognitive and affective behavior. At the same time, many measures designed to describe and quantify classroom climates have appeared, most prominently the Learning Environment Inventory and the Classroom Environment Scale. Both of these measures draw on Murray's early work in needs-press theory, and acknowledge the influence ("press") that environments exert on the expression of internalized personality characteristics ("needs"). The Class Activities Questionnaire (CAQ) is yet another instrument which adopts this general theoretical framework.

The CAQ is designed for students at the sixth-grade level or above, although the author cautions that the items may be too difficult for many sixth graders. Both students and teacher respond to 27 statements about their classroom social and instructional climate on a four-category Likert scale, from strongly disagree to strongly agree. Provision is made for an additional 20 teacher-generated statements and also for open-ended comments about class strengths and weaknesses. The scale is administered in group format and all responses are made on a machine-scoreable answer sheet. Teachers complete the CAQ in two ways: an ideal response, as they wish their classrooms to be, and a predicted student response, as they predict their students will rate the classroom environment. Scoring sheets are returned to a "scoring center" for scoring—no scoring directions are included in the manual. General guidelines and an example are offered to assist in interpretation of the scores.

The 27 items on the CAQ purport to measure five major dimensions of classroom climate. The first two, Lower Thought Processes and Higher Thought Processes, comprise a Cognitive Scale that is keyed to seven levels of a Taxonomy of Intellectual Abilities derived by the author from Bloom's Taxonomy of Educational Objectives. The third dimension, Classroom Focus, is a very general dimension that assesses "how the group and teacher interact and work together." The fourth, Classroom Climate, assesses affective dimensions of classroom atmosphere, including excitement and involvement of students, warmth, tolerance, and openness. Finally, the Student Opinions dimension is a summary of the aforementioned open-ended comments about perceived class strengths and weaknesses. Within these five dimensions are 21 factors or scales, which typically contain two items each (though several contain just one item).

The manual reports both reliability and validity data that are generally derived from a series of studies done over a dozen years ago. Reliability estimates are tied to the CAQ's scoring procedure, which dictates that only those scales are scored for which the assessed group's proportion of consistent responses (both in the direction of agree or disagree) for paired items on the scale reaches .66. Scales with a smaller proportion of consistent responses are considered "inconclusive." The author claims that "due to the method of scoring a more relevant indicator of test reliability is the degree of consensus in responding to paired items." Using this definition of reliability, a sample of 131 classes was administered the CAQ. All CAQ factors but one (the Memory factor on the Lower Thought Processes section of the Cognitive Scale) received consistent responses from approximately two-thirds or more of the students. Additional reliability data for this sample was estimated using the Horst formula for estimating reliability from within-class and between-class variance. This resulted in reliability estimates for four CAQ factors (excluding the open-ended Student Opinions) ranging from .76 to .88. Finally, a pilot study of six classes over a 2-week interval produced generally acceptable test-retest reliability coefficients of .67 to .91 in the four CAQ subscales noted above.

Validity data is often far less adequate than reliability data for even the best social climate measures, and the CAQ is no exception. The author presents evidence that the items have face validity as well as content validity, at least in terms of their perceived appropriateness for the seven-level taxonomy used in the two cognitive scales. The manual is unclear as to CAQ interscale relationships, stating only that "scales were in general appropriately related." Evidence for construct validity is derived from four sources: (1) a "high level of agreement indicated by hundreds of teachers and administrators regarding the relevance of the activities included in the CAQ to important aspects of instructional climate in the classroom," (2) factor analyses of the CAQ done by the author, (3) a cross-validation of factorial validity, and (4) observational studies of classrooms and evidence that profiles vary "in expected ways." Again, this evidence is at best incomplete and is derived from a group of studies completed in Illinois and California in the late 1960s and early 1970s. No recent evidence is presented in the manual, although the author alludes to "an accumulating body of evidence that supports the construct validity of the CAQ." Correlational studies with major instruments of this type do not appear to be available. No support is provided for the major contention of the author that the CAQ, by describing the instructional setting climate, "helps the teacher reexamine purposes and better match behaviors to the purposes."

In summary, the CAQ provides a quick measure of classroom instructional climate as perceived by students and the teacher. Through its theoretical heritage in both Murray and Bloom's work, it links up with a rich body of research in social and instructional climate. Like several other measures of its type, such as the Classroom Environment Scale, it provides a measure of the discrepancy between teacher goals and students' perception of actual instructional climate. But like several of its better known brethren, the CAQ falls short psychometrically, particularly in predictive validity. The link between process variables noted on the CAQ and actual classroom outcomes is unclear. Until this information is provided, it is preferable to use measures such as My Class, the Learning Environment Inventory, and the Classroom Environment Scale, which have by no means solved the validity problem but have accumulated far greater research literatures to use in interpreting the results.

[227]

Classroom Learning Screening. Grades 1, 2, 3, 4, 5, 6; 1980; 2 derived scores (performance, learning) from each of 3 learning channels (see/write, hear/write, see/say) in math, spelling, and reading; 1 form (92 pages of spirit duplicating masters, includes all levels); 6 levels corresponding to each grade plus 3 gradations (easy, typical, hard) per level; handbook (55 pages); stimulus cards (12 pages); correction key cards (17 pages); cassette for timing and for administering hear-write spelling lists; 1982 price data: $59.95 per kit of testing materials including spirit duplication masters, stimulus cards, and cassette; 1(5) minutes per task for 10 consecutive school days; Carl H. Koenig and Harold P. Kunzelmann; Charles E. Merrill Publishing Co.*

Review of Classroom Learning Screening by JACK KRAMER, Associate Professor of Educational Psychology, University of Nebraska-Lincoln, Lincoln, NE:

According to the Classroom Learning Screening (CLS) handbook, children tested with this instrument receive direct, repeated measurement on materials which are representative of those which teachers use on a daily basis. This assessment yields data which can be used to calculate current performance levels and learning rate. It is suggested that as a result of this type of assessment we are better able to identify children in need of remedial assistance, reduce the influence of cultural factors in educational decision making, develop individual instructional objectives, plan group instruction, and compare children to themselves across "learning channels." Unfortunately, inspection of the CLS reveals little evidence that it can be used to accomplish any of these objectives.

According to the handbook, one of the most innovative aspects of the CLS is the measurement of children's performance in different "learning channels." Learning channels, as used on the CLS, refer to the input (see and hear) and output (write and say) combinations used in the completion of a particular task. There are three learning channels assessed on the CLS: see/write, hear/write, and see/say. It is interesting to note, however, that there is a complete learning channel-task overlap on this instrument: math skills are assessed through the see/write channel, spelling through the hear/write channel, and reading through the see/say channel. The handbook fails to acknowledge the potential problems involved as a result of this overlap, nor does it supply any empirical support for the use of these specific learning channels. For example, how are we to reliably differentiate between skill deficits and channel weaknesses (i.e., is a low score due to poor multiplication skills or see/write channel deficiencies)? Although no adequate answer is provided, the handbook does not fail to suggest repeatedly that the CLS can be used to plan specific instructional objectives and to determine learning channel strengths and weaknesses. It is as if constant reference and repetition are believed to be enough to overcome inappropriate design and insufficient empirical support.

Before proceeding with the actual administration, the examiner must first familiarize him/herself with the materials and procedures of the CLS. This is no easy task and the handbook is of limited help. At each grade level (1 through 6), and for each learning channel (3), there are three levels of tasks (easy, typical, hard). In addition to having to familiarize oneself with the instructions provided for different tasks, the examiner must also: prepare a "Screening Tabulation Sheet" for each student, a "Class Ranking Sheet" for the class, three "Channel Ranking Sheets" for the class, and weave through a baffling set of scoring and interpretation instructions. And that's before beginning two weeks of testing and data analysis. More specifically, the CLS requires that 1-minute measures of children's performance be taken for 10 consecutive school days on the same three tasks. Two of the tasks (see/write-math and hear/write-spelling) are group administered while the third (see/say-reading) must be administered individually.

The handbook suggests that the entire assessment process (for a class of 25 pupils) would take less than 20 hours over a 2-week period. This figure appears to be, at best, a conservative estimate. For example, it is doubtful that a teacher could complete the administration of the CLS in approximately one-half hour per day as suggested in the manual. It is conceivable that a teacher could complete the actual administration in 30–40 minutes (two group tasks requiring one minute each and one individual task requiring one minute); however, it is presumed that the teacher would need to have some time to distribute materials, move from one task to another, direct other students not currently involved in the testing, and to collect materials at the completion of testing. The estimates of 30–45 minutes of daily scoring and "a few hours" at the conclusion of the assessment process are also believed to be inadequate. It takes almost that long to read and understand the scoring instructions, let alone to carry out the actual calculations. Finally, the 20-hour estimate assumes that the entire class will be administered the same sets of materials. The handbook provides instructions on how to determine appropriate child/task matches; however, it does not suggest the relative likelihood of being able to administer the same set of tasks to an entire class. If some tasks are found to be too easy (or difficult) for some students (per the handbook's guidelines), the examiner will be required to administer additional (i.e., different) tasks to these children, which will only increase the amount of time involved in testing. In short, it is believed that in almost all instances the administration and scoring of the CLS will take considerably longer than the handbook suggests.

As indicated earlier, the examiner must determine the appropriate level of difficulty of each task for each student. Examples of the types of tasks available in each channel are as follows: Grade 2, See/Write: Easy—write add facts sums 0–5, Typical—write add facts sums 0–9, Hard—write subtract facts top number 1–5; Grade 4, Hear/Write: Easy—write words (first word "going"), Typical—write words (first word "horse"), Hard—write words (first word "almost"); Grade 6, See/Say: Easy—say words (first word "ache"), Typical—say words (first word "human"), Hard—say words (first word "wisdom").

There is no explanation provided regarding the choice of content. It is presumed that there was an attempt to pick tasks that were age appropriate; however, the description of the specific rationale and decision-making process is absent. It is clear, however, that individuals are tested over a narrow range of skills (remember that the same tasks are administered on each of the 10 days of testing) and that the design of individualized instructional programs based on such a limited sample of content would be problematic.

Examiners hoping for detailed, standardized instructions will be disappointed. In fact, the handbook explicitly states that instructions need not be presented as indicated, as long as the examiner is consistent from day to day. Not only may the examiner vary the instructions, s/he is provided with four alternatives for timing the test and the option of providing "a dry run" practice session. This amount of variability in the administration process certainly leads one to question the meaningfulness of much of the data presented in regard to the standardization sample. If the sample is not broken down on the basis of these differences in administration procedures (and it is not) how can one compare a particular sample to the normative group? No mention is made anywhere in the handbook regarding the impact of these different procedures on performance, and one is not ever sure how the test was actually administered to the standardization sample.

Following administration, the teacher/examiner compiles performance and learning scores for each student in each learning channel, a class ranking for each channel, and an overall class ranking. The handbook suggests five specific ways in which the performance and learning data can be used: (1) performance levels can be compared to suggested proficiency levels, (2) learning measures for the three learning channels can be compared to determine the "best bet" learning channel, (3) children with learning problems can be referred for diagnostic evaluation, (4) appropriate individualized instructional programs can be developed, and (5) each child's learning environment can be modified accordingly.

In no instance is there any data presented which validates the use of the CLS in the manner described above. The specific meaning and utility of proficiency levels, learning channels, and learning rates remain unclear. (The manner in which proficiency levels were determined is never specified.) How is a teacher to determine which children to refer for further testing? Can individualized programs be developed on the basis of such limited content sampling? What is the effect of using CLS to design environmental modifications? Can "best bet" learning channels really be determined and instructional programs designed based on the CLS data? Although the handbook suggests positive outcomes, no documentation is provided for these claims.

Finally, the information provided in regard to the normative group is inadequate and believed to be of no help in the interpretation of the data generated with the CLS. Most of the sample came from four locations in the state of Washington and no attempt was made to stratify the group on the basis of sex, race, geographic region, or parental occupation. Limited information concerning reliability and validity is presented in the manual and most of that material is of little value in evaluating the CLS. For example, the only data presented related to reliability is one vague statement about interobserver reliability and one test-retest study of 54 third graders. More is written about validity; however, it is not enough. The manual argues for the content validity of the CLS because "it is a direct measure repeated under the same conditions for 10 consecutive school days" when, of course, these factors have nothing to do with content validity. Data which appear to be supportive of the use of the test in prereferral screening and nondiscriminatory assessments are selectively reported. Due to the limited information provided in the handbook, these studies cannot be objectively evaluated. If these studies are truly supportive of the use of the CLS in the manner described, one wonders why a more complete presentation of the data was not provided.

SUMMARY. The notion of being able to measure children in terms of both current performance level and learning rate is an appealing idea that has gained increased attention in the literature. Although others may document the value of this type of assessment, the CLS, unfortunately, fails in its attempt to operationalize these goals in a manner that provides useful information to teachers, schools, or parents. In the end, the CLS has been found to be time consuming, to assess a narrow range of skills, to have inadequate normative data, and to lack reliability and validity data which support its many claims of usefulness. As a result it cannot be recommended for use under any conditions.

Note: The Buros Institute of Mental Measurements has a policy prohibiting members of its staff from conducting test reviews for Institute publications. Dr. Kramer is now a member of the Institute staff. However, this review was solicited and written before Dr. Kramer became a member of the Institute staff, or before he was even considered for such a position.

Review of Classroom Learning Screening by JOSEPH E. ZINS, Assistant Professor of School Psychology, University of Cincinnati, Cincinnati, OH:

Classroom Learning Screening (CLS) was designed to be an easily administered, systematic tool for use in identifying children's learning difficulties in math, spelling, and reading. It attempts to identify children who may need additional assistance to succeed in school and to assess their performance over time. It uses a repeated measures design and purports to provide information upon which instructional strategies may be based. The authors claim that it has certain non-discriminatory characteristics and that it assesses tasks based upon a "typical curriculum." It is designed to be administered by a classroom teacher, with some components administered in a group and others individually. While exemplary goals have been established for the instrument, they are accomplished with varying degrees of success.

The test attempts to screen a child's academic skills in writing letters and numbers, saying letters and sounds, oral reading, answering math facts, and spelling. These skills are measured through three "learning channel combinations": (*a*) seeing and saying (usually an oral reading task), (*b*) seeing and writing (usually a math task), and (*c*) hearing and writing (usually a spelling task). By assessing these channels, a teacher is supposed to obtain data about the most effective manner in which to instruct a child.

The CLS takes brief (1-minute) measures of a child's performance on the same three tasks for 10 consecutive school days. As a result of these repeated measures, both performance and learning statements are obtained. "Learning" is based upon a comparison of the child's change in performance (average ending performance minus average beginning performance).

For an entire class, the instrument would require approximately one-half hour of classroom time each day in order to administer the group and the individual items. A minimum of 30 to 45 minutes of additional time is required for daily scoring, in addition to several hours at the conclusion of the testing for ranking, etc. Overall, 20 hours of teacher time are required for a class of 25 to 30 students, which appears to be a prohibitive amount of time for a "screening" measure.

The CLS manual has many significant omissions. There is a paucity of information which would assist a potential user in making an informed decision about the merits of the instrument. Furthermore, this reviewer was unable to obtain additional descriptive information from the publisher.

The development of the test is not clearly described, although the manual mentions that, "Perhaps the most significant aspect of the CLS is the fact that it has been used with literally tens of thousands of children before its publication." However, sufficient descriptions of these results are not found in the manual. At no time do the authors state how the content of the test was determined, although they claim that it is based upon a "typical curriculum." Users are cautioned to compare the test contents carefully to the course content and objectives of their local curriculum.

Administration directions are generally clear as are the scoring procedures. The instructions adequately prepare the examinee for the test. Levels of difficulty for the items are given, although again, one is left to speculate about how these were determined.

The repeated measures approach, while necessarily being time consuming, might be considered a strength of the test. Rather than basing the results on a single performance, average performance is ascertained over 10 days' time. Average beginning performance is compared to average ending performance, the result being the child's learning or change in performance. The authors suggest that one may "predict" future performance based upon this measure of change, erroneously assuming that learning proceeds by equal increments from day to day for all children.

The theoretical basis for choosing the three "learning channels" is not described. A full explanation and discussion of the reasoning underlying this aspect of the test is needed. Furthermore, the manual does not contain any references which would be helpful in understanding the theoretical basis of the test. Similarly, the interpretive section is vague and most likely would be of minimal value to the classroom teacher.

Another major shortcoming is the lack of empirical evidence supporting the instrument. More care could have been taken in describing the technical aspects of the CLS. The population upon which the norms are based is not adequately described (e.g., no mention of sex, parental occupation, socioeconomic level, rural/urban, etc.). Approximately 4% of the sample was Black, but 11.6% was not specified. Although the normative data is based upon a large number of children (nearly 9,000), most of them were from a single state (Washington), which may severely bias the results. Apparently, no attempt was made to obtain a stratified random sample.

Reports of reliability and validity are essentially lacking. The one brief test-retest study (10-day interval, $N = 54$) reports a correlation of .90 for subtraction and .86 for see-say words. A study of predictive validity indicated that the CLS correctly identified 91% of the pupils who subsequently were referred for special services one year later. Unfortunately, the descriptions of both of these studies are vague and the results of other investigations are not cited in the manual. Furthermore, this reviewer was unable to locate additional references to the test in the research literature or obtain them from the publisher. A solid case is not built for the nondiscriminatory aspects of the instrument.

In conclusion, these major deficiencies in a nationally distributed, commercially available instrument seem unwarranted today, particularly when clear guidelines are available to authors and publishers in the Standards for Educational and Psychological Tests and in other sources. It would appear that publication of this instrument was premature. There does not appear to be sufficient reason for recommending the CLS in its present stage of development. The authors have not presented sufficient data about its development and psychometric properties to enable an intelligent evaluation of its merits. It does not meet the expectations developed in the introductory sections of the manual.

[228]

Classroom Reading Inventory, Fourth Edition. Grades 2–8, high school and adults; 1965–82; CRI; 6 scores: independent reading level, instructional reading level, frustration reading level, hearing capacity level, word recognition, comprehension; no data on reliability; no norms; individual in part; Forms A, B, C, ('82, 33 pages), D ('82, 38 pages, for use with high school and adults); manual ('82, 170 pages includes all forms); price data available from publisher; (24) minutes for each form; Nicholas J. Silvaroli; Wm. C. Brown Co., Publishers.*

For a review of an earlier edition by Marjorie S. Johnson, see 8:749; see also T2:1618 (1 reference); for an excerpted review by Donald L. Cleland, see 7:715.

[229]

The Claybury Selection Battery. Patients and staff regarding psychological and psychiatric treatment; 1982; catalog uses the title Claybury Assessment Battery; self-administered questionnaires to help allocate patients to treatment and to select therapists; 3 questionnaires; norms consist of means and standard deviations; manual (12 pages); 1983 price data: £3.75 per 50 questionnaires; £3.50 per set of 3 answer keys; £4.65 per manual; administration time not reported; T. M. Caine, D. J. Smail, O. B. A. Wijesinghe, and D. A. Winter; NFER-Nelson Publishing Co. [England].*

a) DIRECTION OF INTEREST QUESTIONNAIRE. Patients and staff; DIQ; 1 form (2 pages).

b) TREATMENT EXPECTANCIES QUESTIONNAIRE. Patients; TEQ; 1 form (1 page).

c) ATTITUDES TO TREATMENT QUESTIONNAIRE. Staff; ATQ; 1 form (1 page).

Review of The Claybury Selection Battery by JULIAN FABRY, Chief of Rehabilitation Psychology, Immanuel Medical Center, Omaha, NE:

The Claybury Selection Battery consists of three questionnaires, standardized answer sheets for each questionnaire, scoring templates, and a manual. The materials for this battery can be obtained from NFER-Nelson, the British publisher, with British currency only.

The battery is based on the premise that a patient's expectancies and the attitudes of staff are the major determinants of the outcome of treatment for psychological therapies. The authors argue that these expectancies and attitudes are part of an individual's more general attitudes and adjustment strategies which reflect an individual's personal style. They therefore believe that the assessment of the patient's and therapist's personal style can provide a more rational and systematic framework for treatment. To this end, the authors developed the Direction of Interest Questionnaire (DIQ), the Treatment Expectancies Questionnaire (TEQ), and the Attitudes to Treatment Questionnaire (ATQ), which comprise the battery. The DIQ is considered a concise measure of the Jungian concept of libidinal flow, i.e., inward/outward direction of interest, or intraversion/extroversion. It is a 14-item, forced-choice questionnaire designed to distinguish between an individual's interests in what appears to be theoretical ideas versus an interest in practical facts.

The TEQ is a 15-item factor analytically-derived scale which attempts to measure a patient's expectancies and attitudes which may be favorable to either small group psychotherapy or those associated with a more medical or behavioral management approach. A 19-item factor analytically-derived scale, the ATQ, is an attempt to measure staff attitudes which distinguish between the organic approach represented by general hospitals and a more psychological, therapeutic community approach to patient care. The questionnaires can be administered either to individuals or a group. Each of the questionnaires can be administered and scored within a 10- to 20-minute period. Scoring is relatively easy and convenient with the plastic template which covers the standardized answer sheet.

Validity and reliability information is presented in the technical data section of the manual. Criterion-related validity was established for the DIQ by utilizing known groups of subjects from various occupations who theoretically had either an inner direction of interests or a more practical outer direction. The mean scores on the DIQ are presented for the various occupational groups. In addition, comparisons of DIQ scores of various occupational groups of comparable intellectual ability and educational attainment are presented. Some significant differences were found between occupational groups. For example, psychiatrists and general hospital doctors were found to differ significantly on this assessment. A correlation of .81 was reported between the DIQ and the Myers-Briggs S/N scale. Significant differences in DIQ and TEQ scores were found between different patient groups receiving group versus behavior therapy. Mean ATQ scores are presented in table form to demonstrate the difference between physical treatment and therapeutic community oriented hospitals for selected samples of doctors, nurses, and various patient groups.

A test-retest reliability coefficient of .84 was obtained for 42 occupational therapy students on the DIQ for a three-month interval. No test-retest reliability was undertaken for the TEQ due to the author's premise that treatment expectancies are not static and therefore would be subject to many influences and changes. A coefficient of .79 was determined for the ATQ on a sample of 52 psychiatric and general hospital nurses retested after approximately one year.

The authors propose that individuals with high DIQ and low TEQ scores are expected to respond to small group treatment, whereas low DIQ and high TEQ scorers should respond to behavior therapy. They further propose that a clinician use the TEQ and the DIQ, along with the Wilson-Patterson Attitude Inventory (a measure of conservatism-radicalism), in order to achieve greater treatment selection accuracy. They indicate that a composite score can be obtained by adding the TEQ and the Wilson-Patterson Attitude Inventory C-scale scores and then subtracting the score on the DIQ. It is suggested that the composite score is highly predictive of treatment response. They report cutoff scores of 47 as a means of separating group psychotherapy improvers from non-improvers. Higher cutoff points are also proposed that yield a greater proportion of patients who improve in therapy. The authors believe that the Claybury Selection Battery offers a wide clinical application in addition to those previously mentioned.

The battery does offer a seemingly rational and somewhat empirically validated means of matching people with therapeutic processes and environments which hopefully would diminish defensiveness and frustration and foster cooperation and follow-through. However, there is little evidence of the adaptability of the battery to use in the United States. It also suffers from its relative newness and the potential difficulty that U.S. users may have in purchasing it from a British publishing company with British currency. Although it is seemingly eclectic in approach, its foundation is in Jungian concepts and is therefore primarily psychodynamic. To date, the research substantiating its utility is with small samples differentiating individuals with preferences for small group psychotherapy versus a more organic management approach. Its utility with various individual approaches to psychotherapy remains to be investigated. A multitrait-multimethod matrix validation would help to insure the battery's validity.

Review of The Claybury Selection Battery by GEORGE P. PRIGATANO, Head, Section of Neuropsychology, Department of Neurosurgery, Presbyterian Hospital, Oklahoma City, OK:

The Claybury Selection Battery addresses an important question for psychotherapists. Can self-reported interests and expectations about psychological treatments be used to select the type of therapy a patient should receive? Unfortunately, this battery is not sufficiently developed to strongly endorse its use at this time, but is may be helpful in certain clinical settings and research projects. This review will focus on its methodological strengths and weaknesses and suggest guidelines, based on the data reported in the test manual, regarding its applicability. The potential user of this battery is also encouraged to review the text, *Personality Styles in Neurosis* by Caine, Wijesinghe, and Winter, which provides a more complete discussion of the theoretical and empirical basis for this battery.

The battery consists of three questionnaires: Direction of Interest Questionnaire (DIQ), the Treatment Expectancies Questionnaire (TEQ), and the Attitudes to Treatment Questionnaire (ATQ).

The first two questionnaires are completed by the patient. They are coupled with the C Scale of the Wilson-Patterson Attitude Inventory and used to classify patients as most likely benefiting from small group psychotherapy versus behavioral therapy.

The DIQ and the TEQ are based on theoretical notions concerning introversion/extroversion and personal beliefs about the nature of psychopathology. It is argued that individuals who are introspective are likely to see themselves needing an insight-oriented approach to treatment and expect to participate actively in the solution to their psychological problems.

Conversely, extroverted types of individuals are assumed to want an expert to take responsibility for their treatment and see themselves as participating very little in guiding the course of treatment.

The ATQ was designed to assess therapists' attitudes concerning the nature of treatment. The ATQ is not used to assign patients to one or the other treatment condition. It serves only to make explicit therapists' orientations and thereby to facilitate a matching of therapists with patients on the basis of their attitudes.

The strengths of the DIQ and the TEQ are that they are empirically derived questionnaires, easily administered and scored, and are based on clinically relevant constructs in psychology. They also relate to an important question for the clinician practicing psychotherapy. The DIQ has reasonable test-retest reliability ($r = .84$) and concurrent validity with its parent scale: the Myers-Briggs' S-N Scale ($r = .81$). The DIQ also has been given to a wide range of individuals in an attempt to provide construct validation for the notion of introversion/extroversion interest patterns as they relate to vocational choices. The TEQ has been given to a moderate number of subjects and is shown to correlate with whether or not patients are assigned to small group psychotherapy or behavior therapy. There is also some tentative evidence that TEQ and DIQ scores are related to outcome from group psychotherapy and behavior therapy, but small sample size and inadequate cross-validation make these findings tentative. The ATQ has modest test-retest reliability ($r = .79$). Finally, the manual also reports on the relationship of age, sex, and intelligence as potentially confounding variables influencing DIQ, TEQ, and ATQ scores.

The weaknesses of this battery include the following: No reliability data is reported for the TEQ. Even though the authors give a rationale for this, unless it can be established that patient treatment expectations are a stable phenomena prior to treatment assignment, this construct cannot be considered a valid basis for treatment assignment. Second, reported interest patterns do not fully support the introversion/extroversion concepts suggested by the authors. For example, introversion is supposed to relate to religious interests, while extroversion is supposedly related to interests in such fields as biochemistry. Yet, in the data reported in the manual, research biochemists and theology students make very similar scores on the DIQ. This weakens the conceptual basis of this test and questions its use in vocational counseling, a secondary purpose suggested by the authors.

Third, the utilization of present scoring procedures provides a potential response bias. TEQ and ATQ agreement with the statements supposedly reflects an organic or behavioral approach. The tendency on the part of some individuals simply to endorse items (i.e. acquiesence response set) might give a spuriously high elevation on these measures. Also the number of items on the DIQ ($n = 14$) and TEQ ($n = 15$) are small. This questions the internal reliability of these scales. It would be helpful to have split-half reliability coefficients on each of these measures.

Finally, in this reviewer's opinion, there is a potential conceptual confusion underlying this battery. The organic approach and behavioral approach are "lumped" together. Many behavioral therapists expect their patients to participate actively in setting goals and solicit their cooperation in identifying what would be reasonable steps to accomplishing these goals. The organic approach is perhaps less flexible, more authoritarian, and asks only that the patient comply with prescribed treatment regimes.

There is an absence of sufficient validity data. Much of the data reported in the manual reflects whether or not the patient has been assigned to a treatment condition rather than whether scores on the DIQ and TEQ actually make a difference in terms of treatment outcome once patients have been assigned. Future research studies should focus on the predictive validity of this battery.

There is also an inadequate consideration of the base rate problem. While cutoff scores are suggested for placement of patients in one or the other treatment group, the misclassification ratios based on a larger pool of subjects are missing and are desperately needed to utilize this as a clinically sensitive measure.

The potential areas in which this battery may presently be applied include the following: (1) clinical settings where initial screening of treatment expectations is helpful in order to assign patients to different types of therapy, (2) research settings where the goal is to predict responsiveness to an authoritarian versus nonauthoritarian approach to treatment, (3) research which attempts to look at the relationship of introversion/extroversion as it relates to various psychological treatments, and (4) studies which attempt to evaluate a therapist's expectations as they relate to some parameter involved in research.

The battery is the first step to helping psychotherapists plan treatment choices for patients. However, in its present form, it has limited clinical usefulness.

[230]

Clerical Task Inventory. Clerical and/or office personnel; 1980; CTI; "an inventory of standardized statements of tasks frequently performed by clerical and/or office personnel," divided into 13 performance domains; no data on reliability; no norms; Form C (10 pages); separate answer sheet may be used; no manual; 1984 price data: $15 per 10 inventories; administration time not reported; C. H. Lawshe; University Book Store.*

[231]

Clifton Assessment Procedures for the Elderly. Ages 60 and over; 1979–81; CAPE; assesses cognitive and behavioral competence of the elderly; 2 tests plus combination short version; 9 scores yielding a cognitive, behavioural, and overall dependency grade; norms consist of means and standard deviations; authors recommend administering both tests concurrently, however, they can be used separately; manual ('79, 34 pages); report form ('79, 2 pages); distribution restricted to persons professionally involved in the care of the elderly; 1983 price data: £1.85 per 20 report forms; £3.25 per manual; £4 per specimen set; administration time not reported; A. H. Pattie and C. J. Gilleard; Hodder & Stoughton Educational [England].*

a) COGNITIVE ASSESSMENT SCALE. CAS; revision of Clifton Assessment Schedule; 4 scores: information/orientation, mental ability, psychomotor (adaptation of Gibson Spiral Maze), total; 1 form ('79, 2 pages); £1.85 per 20 tests (CAS); £2.75 per 20 Mazes.

b) BEHAVIOUR RATING SCALE. BRS; shortened version of Stockton Geriatric Rating Scale; 5 scores: physical disability, apathy, communication difficulties, social disturbance, total; 1 form ('79, 2 pages); £1.85 per 20 tests.

c) SURVEY VERSION. Short version of CAPE for quick assessment; consists of informational/orientation scale of the CAS and the physical disability scale of the BRS; 1 form ('81, 1 page); instruction sheet ('81, 2 pages); £1.50 per 20 tests plus instruction sheet.

See T3:471 (1 reference).

TEST REFERENCES

1. Pattie, A. H. A survey version of the Clifton Assessment Procedures for the Elderly. BRITISH JOURNAL OF CLINICAL PSYCHOLOGY, 1981, 20, 173–178.

2. Moore, V., & Wyke, M. A. Drawing disability in patients with senile dementia. PSYCHOLOGICAL MEDICINE, 1984, 14, 97–105.

Review of Clifton Assessment Procedures for the Elderly by ALICIA SKINNER COOK, Associate Professor of Human Development and Family Studies, Colorado State University, Fort Collins, CO:

The Clifton Assessment Procedures for the Elderly (CAPE) was designed to assess the cognitive and behavioral competence of elderly persons. It consists of the following two measures: The Cognitive Assessment Scale (CAS) and the Behavior Rating Scale (BRS). It is recommended that results on these two scales be combined to produce an overall measure of functional competence; however, these instruments can also be used separately. Intercorrelations between subtests on the CAS and BRS show that these instruments are measuring overlapping disabilities rather than one single dimension.

The Cognitive Assessment Scale consists of three subscales measuring information/orientation, mental ability, and psychomotor functions. The Information/Orientation subtest consists of 12 items asking such basic orientation questions as "What is your name?" and "What year is it?" Because the test was developed in Great Britain, a few of the items would need to be modified for American samples. For example, Item 7 reads "Who is the Prime Minister?" The phrase "of Great Britain" would need to be added to indicate what country is referred to in the item. (This item is followed by the question "Who is the President of the United States of America?") The Mental Abilities subtest of the CAS consists of four measures relating to the skills of counting, saying the alphabet, reading, and writing. (Supplemental material for the reading task are included in the test packet and contain printed words of varying sizes and difficulty levels.) Performance on this subtest shows retention of these skills as well as attention and concentration levels. The Psychomotor subtest on the CAS is a measure of fine motor performance and hand-eye coordination. This subtest consists of the Gibson Spiral Maze with amended administration and scoring criteria. All of the measures of the CAS can be administered by a variety of professionals who work with the elderly.

The second major measure composing the CAPE, the Behavior Rating Scale, consists of 18 items. Each item relates to a specific observable behavior that is rated from 0 to 2. The ratings on the items are to be completed by an individual familiar with the subject's behavior. Subscale scores are available for the following areas: physical disability, apathy, communication difficulties, and social disturbance. The total on the BRS provides an overall measure of behavioral disability level.

All scores obtained on the CAS and BRS are translated into dependency grades from A to E, with each grade representing different levels of functional impairment. The levels range from "no impairment in mental functioning and no significant behavioral disability" (Grade A) to "severe impairment/maximum dependency" (Grade E). The test manual provides a table for conversion of scores to grades. It also includes further differentiation of Grades D and E.

The Clifton Assessment Procedures for the Elderly is an outgrowth of considerable research conducted during the past decade. Normative data are provided for both the CAS and BRS and is based on groups ranging from elderly living independently in the community to elderly persons who are institutionalized. Reliability and validity data are reported separately for the CAS and BRS. Correlation coefficients for elderly acute psychiatric patients for a test-retest interval of four days ranged from .79 (Psychomotor subtest) to .89 (Mental Ability). Among a "non-pathological" group of elderly, test-retest reliability coefficients for a six-month period ranged from .69 (Psychomotor subtest) to .84 (Information/Orientation subtest). Impressive predictive and comparative validity data for CAS are also presented in the manual. On the BRS, interrater reliability coefficients on the subscales and individual items are reasonably high, but lower than on the CAS. Results from five separate studies show BRS subscale coefficients to be primarily in the .70 to .91 range with the exception of the Communication Difficulties subtest. This subtest contained an interrater reliability range of only .45 to .72. Concurrent and construct validity data on the BRS are presented in the test manual.

The CAPE offers a useful tool for assessing the functional status of the elderly. It is a short, easy-to-administer instrument suitable to a wide range of functional ability levels. However, it will yield limited information on the nonimpaired elderly. It should be emphasized that it is not an intelligence test, nor does it purport to be so.

The CAPE is one of the few functional status scales available that classifies individuals according to objective criteria. It has applications in clinical assessment, research, and identification of patients for rehabilitation purposes. Specifically, functional status assessment can be valuable in determining the impact of disease on the elderly. It can also be used effectively in determining the effects of an intervention program, as a basis for priorities in service provision, and as a criterion in decisions regarding appropriate placements for the functionally impaired elderly.

Review of Clifton Assessment Procedures for the Elderly by K. WARNER SCHAIE, Professor of Human Development and Psychology, The Pennsylvania State University, University Park, PA:

The last few years have seen several attempts to develop brief assessment instruments for the evaluation of cognitive status and behavioral functioning in elderly persons that are suitable for administration by minimally trained personnel and that, in particular, can be used with nursing home residents and other marginally functioning elderly (Schaie & Stone, 1982). The CAPE consists of two parts: A Cognitive Assessment Scale (CAS) and a Behavior Rating Scale (BRS) which represents a shortened version of the Stockton Geriatric Rating Scale. The Cognitive Assessment Scale in turn has three parts: An information/orientation test with 12 questions assessing current information and orientation; a mental ability test which involves counting, saying the alphabet, reading words scaled from easy to difficult, and writing the subject's name; and a psychomotor test that is a modification of the Gibson Spiral Maze.

The authors have indeed succeeded in devising an instrument which could be taught quickly to relatively unsophisticated mental health and medical personnel, and which has only moderate scoring difficulty. Based on very small samples (*N*s of 38 and 39 respectively), the magnitudes of test-retest reliability coefficients reported for the CAS for intervals of several days and over a six-month period are not impressive, but are minimally acceptable. Similarly, interrater reliabilities for the BRS (number of raters are not reported) seem minimally acceptable. However, there are some serious problems with the test's validity, and it is likely that it might be misapplied and results misinterpreted unless used by a trained psychological examiner who has experience in working with the elderly.

To begin with, there are some obvious face validity problems. On the information/orientation test American users could readily substitute the Stars and Stripes for the Union Jack, but what would substitute for the Prime Minister, since inquiry about the President of the United States is already a standard question? The authors do not seem aware of the fact that errors in repeating the alphabet are a common occurrence in many well-functioning community elderly, may be related to level of education, and are not necessarily a function of pathology. Likewise errors on the Gibson maze under the authors' scoring instructions would in many subjects reflect adequacy of visual correction or the presence of slight arthritic conditions rather than cognitive ability.

What is most disturbing is that the manual does not clearly reveal how the final grading system (dependency levels from A to E) were arrived at, or how the cutoff scores for the various tests are related to these grades. The normative data consist of interquartile ranges for several samples ranging in size from 50 to 100 which are not clearly described beyond the label of "social services," "chronic functional," "acute organic," and so on. In addition there are means and standard deviations for quite small samples that are described equally poorly. A .90 correlation is reported between the CAS information/orientation score and the Wechsler Memory Scale. Since the latter is thought to be quite obsolete, this finding does not necessarily speak well for the Clifton Procedures. Other validation procedures, always on very small samples, suggest large group overlaps and create doubts about the predictive validity of the scale. The manual reports non-equivalence of factorial structure for BRS among homogeneous populations, but nevertheless claims that its present subscales are satisfactory for the evaluation of general behavioral competence. Age norms are reported for small samples of ill-described characteristics, and should probably not be relied upon.

In sum, the Clifton Procedures have all the trappings of an attractive brief assessment procedure for the marginal elderly. The manual provides enough information, however, to suggest that its publication was premature in that not enough test construction efforts have been made to create a scale of high reliability and validity. The ability section is too primitive to permit differential diagnoses, and the normative data are inadequate and often misleading. At the present time the objectives for this procedure are more likely to be met by the Duke University OARS instrument (Pfeiffer, 1980).

REVIEWER'S REFERENCES

Pfeiffer, E. The psychosocial evaluation of the elderly patient. In E. W. Busse & D. G. Blazer (Eds.), HANDBOOK OF GERIATRIC PSYCHIATRY. New York: Van Nostrand Reinhold, 1980.

Schaie, K. W., & Stone, V. Psychological assessment. In C. Eisdorfer (Ed.), ANNUAL REVIEW OF GERONTOLOGY AND GERIATRICS. VOL. 3, New York: Springer, 1982.

[232]

Clinical Analysis Questionnaire. Ages 16 and over; 1970–80; CAQ; 37 scores (listed below): 28 primary factor scores and 9 second-order factor scores; no norms for second-order factors; Form A ('70, 16 pages); 2 parts in 1 booklet; manual ('80, 86 pages); record folder ('80, 5 pages); separate answer sheet, machine or hand scored ('71, 2 pages); 1982 price data: $17.50 per 25 tests; $8 per 50 answer sheets; $6 per set of scoring stencils; $6.90 per 25 record folders; $7.90 per manual; $9.15 per specimen set; CAQ Interpretation Report $4.70–$16 per report depending on number requested; Spanish edition available; (120) minutes for both parts; Samuel E. Krug; Institute for Personality and Ability Testing.*

a) PART II (NORMAL PERSONALITY TRAITS). Shortened version of the Sixteen Personality Factor Questionnaire; the regular version of the 16PF may be substituted; 16 primary factor scores: warmth (A), intelligence (B), emotional stability (C), dominance (E), impulsivity (F), conformity (G), boldness (H), sensitivity (I), suspiciousness (L), imagination (M), shrewdness (N), insecurity (O), radicalism (Q1), self-sufficiency (Q2), self-discipline (Q3), tension (Q4), plus 5 second-order factor scores: extraversion (Ex), anxiety (Ax), tough poise (Ct), independence (In), superego strength (Se).

b) PART II (THE CLINICAL FACTORS). 12 primary factor scores: hypochondriasis (D1), suicidal depression (D2), agitation (D3), anxious depression (D4), low energy depression (D5), guilt and resentment (D6), boredom and withdrawal (D7), paranoia (Pa), psychopathic deviation (Pp), schizophrenia (Sc), psychasthenia (As), psychological inadequacy (Ps), plus 4 second-order factor scores: socialization (So), depression (D), psychoticism (P), neuroticism (Ne).

See T3:472 (11 references); for a review by Douglas McNair, see 8:522 (7 references); see T2:1131 (1 reference) and 7:54 (1 reference).

TEST REFERENCES

1. Wardell, D., & Yeudall, L. T. A multidimensional approach to criminal disorders: The assessment of impulsivity and its relation to crime. ADVANCES IN BEHAVIOUR RESEARCH AND THERAPY, 1980, 2, 159–177.

2. Birenbaum, M., & Zak, I. Contradictory or complementary? Reassessment of two competing theories of the structure of attitudes. MULTIVARIATE BEHAVIORAL RESEARCH, 1982, 17, 503–514.

3. Bolton, B. Issues in validity research on the 16 PF. PSYCHOLOGICAL REPORTS, 1982, 50, 1077–1078.

4. Skinner, N. F. Personality characteristics of volunteers for painful experiments. BULLETIN OF THE PSYCHONOMIC SOCIETY, 1982, 20, 299–300.

Review of Clinical Analysis Questionnaire by GEORGE GUTHRIE, Professor of Psychology, The Pennsylvania State University, University Park, PA:

The Clinical Analysis Questionnaire (CAQ) has been developed in the tradition of the 16 PF and by the same organization. Part I of CAQ is an abbreviated, simplified version of the 16 PF, measuring the same 16 factors with half of its items the same as those in Form A of the 16 PF. Final item selection appears to have been a matter of judgement, selecting from items that had been identified in earlier analyses.

Part II consists of 144 items measuring 12 factorially defined clinical dimensions. This part was designed to measure dimensions of pathology and to perform functions such as those done by the MMPI. Development of these scales is not described in the manual except to say that items were successively refined in six factor-analytic validation studies. Nothing is indicated about the populations used in the development of the scales. The factor analyses apparently yielded seven depression scales, including hypochondriasis, suicidal depression, agitation, anxious depression, low energy depression, guilt and resentment, and boredom. In addition, there are scales called paranoia, psychopathic deviation, schizophrenia, psychasthenia, and inadequacy. Although several names sound like those of the MMPI, the correlations with MMPI scales are very low.

Test-retest reliabilities range from .51 to .74 in Part I and from .67 to .90 in Part II. The author of the manual argues that validity be defined as the correlation of a scale with the underlying factor it is designed to measure. Given this definition, validity coefficients are high, often higher than reliability. But this is not the usual meaning of validity.

The manual also presents mean profiles of samples of schizophrenics, neurotics, personality disorders, substance abusers, child abusers, and homosexuals. However, no evidence is offered that one could use these mean profiles to diagnose individual patients.

If someone were attempting to use the CAQ in a clinical setting, as the name of the test implies, it would be difficult to know what clinical significance to attach to each scale. Interpretations in the manual are largely repetitions of the contents of some of the items. While mean profiles for various clinical groups are presented it is far from clear how much differentiation of groups could be achieved using profiles alone. But that is really not the question the scales are designed to answer. The scales are not expected to correspond with clinical types.

Each clinical scale has only 12 items, a number that must inevitably limit the degree that scales correlate with external variables such as diagnosis. This can be overcome with Part I by giving additional forms of the 16 PF, but this remedy is not available for Part II.

As described in the manual, the CAQ should probably be seen as a research device, especially as it purports to measure various aspects of the depression that is an aspect of many different syndromes of psychopathology. However, a clinician needs to know what scales imply in the behavior and personal experience of the patient. More work needs to be done with populations of patients to develop interpretations that are meaningful to clinicians. Finally, it would be important to know the extent to which the factors remain stable when the tool is used with a large sample of disturbed people.

[233]

Clinical Evaluation of Language Functions—Diagnostic Battery. Grades K–12; 1980–83; CELF; measures language functions in areas of phonology, syntax, semantics, memory, and word finding and retrieval; 15 scores: word and sentence structure, word classes, linguistic concepts, relationships and ambiguities, oral directions, spoken paragraphs, word series, confrontation naming, word associations, model sentences, formulated sentences, processing speech sounds, producing speech sounds (blends, final, initial); individual; 1 form ('80, 16 pages); manual ('80, 104 pages); technical manual ('83, 123 pages) for this and the CELF Screening Tests; 2 stimulus manuals; audiotape for administration training; 1983 price data: $89 per examiner's kit including test manual, two stimulus manuals, audiocassette, and 12 score forms; $9.95 per package of 12 score forms; $10 per technical manual; (60–120) minutes; Eleanor M. Semel and Elisabeth H. Wiig; Charles E. Merrill Publishing Co.*

TEST REFERENCES

1. Wiig, E. H., Semel, E. M., & Nystrm, L. A. Comparison of rapid naming abilities in language-learning-disabled and academically achieving eight-year-olds. LANGUAGE, SPEECH, AND HEARING SERVICES IN SCHOOLS, 1982, 13, 11–23.

2. Wiig, E. H., Becker-Redding, U., & Semel, E. M. A cross-cultural, cross-linguistic comparison of language abilities of 7- to 8- and 12- to 13-year-old children with learning disabilities. JOURNAL OF LEARNING DISABILITIES, 1983, 16, 576–585.

Review of Clinical Evaluation of Language Functions-Diagnostic Battery by DIXIE D. SANGER, Assistant Professor of Speech Pathology and Audiology, University of Nebraska-Lincoln, Lincoln, NE:

The Clinical Evaluation of Language Functions (CELF) assesses morphological, semantic, syntactical, and phonological aspects of language processing and production abilities in children and adolescents. The purpose of the subtests, testers' qualifications, and time requirements are explicitly explained in the examiner's manual. Specific suggestions for test administration are outlined to facilitate accurate results. The format of the test is attractive, clearly designed, and free from distractions. The pictures accompanying the stimuli are unambiguous and easy to interpret. An audiotape provides examiners with suprasegmental aspects of speech to use as models for presenting the oral stimuli in the CELF. These models help control for variations which can spuriously alter test scores. It is clear that the authors are sensitive, evidence insight, and are objective about the different features of their test. They point out positive attributes, but also caution examiners about certain limitations of their battery. These include cautions about the use of the audiotape, interpretation of results, and use of the CELF as the only measure of a child's abilities.

The test design is supported by research theory documented in the examiner's manual. Each of the 11 subtests, which probe selected dimensions of word meanings, sentence structure, and recall and retrieval, are clearly described and developed. This also holds true for the two supplementary subtests designed to examine aspects of processing and production at the level of phonology. The items allow the examiner to differentiate the performance of language and learning disabled children from academically achieving children. Additionally, they are systematically controlled to allow the examiner to investigate vocabulary, conceptual development, syntactical complexity, or length as a variable that affects a child's performance.

Organized and concise instructions are provided for administering and scoring each of the subtests. The test includes a number of positive features viewed as valuable attributes in assessing children and planning remedial programs. First, all subtests use a consistent scoring format to indicate the accuracy of a subject's response and whether a correct response occurred after the first or second presentation of the stimulus sentence. Second, the test items are presented in the score forms to provide ease in administration, scoring, interpretation, and later reference. Third, explicit criteria are provided for discontinuing the subtests upon presentation of the trial items or if the child responds incorrectly on five consecutive items. Fourth, raw scores can be compared to criterion scores at the child's grade level. Fifth, error analysis grids accompany most subtests to allow for an evaluation of error patterns. Utilization of these grids allows the phonological, semantic, or syntactic structures tested to be quickly examined and a response pattern to be identified. These grids facilitate a systematic approach for scoring and remedial planning. Sixth, methods and principles for informal and formal extension testing are associated with most of the subtests and provide a way to explore the nature and extent of the problem along with possible variables which contribute to the child's performance below criterion for his or her grade level. Seventh, the examiner's manual is complete with rationale for test designs, administration and scoring, standardization and test norms, and theory-based data and research to support the inclusion of the 13 subtests. A complete set of appendices describes topics such as extension testing, dialectal variations in the use of word formation rules, and dialectal variations in the use of sentence structures.

The Clinical Evaluation of Language Functions (CELF) was standardized concurrently with the standardization of the CELF Screening Tests. The authors indicate a primary goal of the CELF Diagnostic Battery was to establish criteria for determining which children should be recommended for extension testing. The 1980 manual reports that 159 children from different groups were used to establish these criteria. Although one might be quick to criticize the normative procedures, prior consideration should be given to the authors' own precautionary statements. First, the authors suggest that examiners can set higher grade-level criteria for certain subtests after they have gained some experience with the battery. Second, the criteria are considered experimental and, therefore, are not intended to be final. Third, additional norms are being developed. Examiners are urged to supplement the findings with other formal and informal observations.

Additional test data provided includes intertest correlation coefficients, relationships among components of the CELF Screening Tests and CELF Diagnostic Battery, and concurrent validity evidence involving several other speech and language tests. Test-retest reliability coefficients for the combined subtests indicated excellent stability of performance over a 6-week interval ($r = .96$). As with most standardized measures, individual subtests should be administered as a total battery for maximum reliability. Additional data would be beneficial to document the reliability and validity of the Diagnostic Battery, and reportedly these data have been collected and will be available soon. However, this should not be interpreted erroneously to suggest negative impressions toward the CELF. Rather, the theory upon which the measure is developed and the vast amount of linguistic information to be gained from a subject's performance far exceed any concerns about the technical data available on the test at this time.

In summary, the test is attractive and instructions for administering and scoring the CELF are explicit and provide the examiner with accurate linguistic behavioral observations about a child's strengths and weaknesses. The scoring allows for responses to be recorded on error analysis grids to evaluate possible error response patterns. Most impressive is the theory and research upon which the test is developed and the variety of useful psycholinguistic data it can provide. The authors appropriately report cautions in administering and interpreting the results of the test and point out that the CELF should be supplemented with other measures to plan remedial or compensatory programs. Finally, the development and design of this test reflects an enormous amount of planning on the part of the authors and can provide a wealth of valuable language processing and production information for diagnosis, extension testing, assessment, and intervention purposes.

[234]

Clinical Evaluation of Language Functions, Elementary and Advanced Screening Tests. Grades K–5, 5–12; 1980–83; CELF; a screening measure of language processing and production abilities, developed and standardized with the CELF-Diagnostic Battery; individual; 2 levels; manual (93 pages including 34 picture stimuli for Advanced Level) same for both levels; technical manual ('83, 123 pages) for this and CELF-Diagnostic Battery; 1983 price data: $10 per technical manual; Eleanor M. Semel and Elisabeth H. Wiig; Charles E. Merrill Publishing Co.*

a) ELEMENTARY LEVEL. Grades K–5; 3 scores: processing, production, total; 1 form (4 pages); $18.95 per examiner's kit including 25 score forms; $6.95 per package of 25 score forms; (10–15) minutes.

b) ADVANCED LEVEL. Grades 5–12; 3 scores: processing, production, total; 1 form (4 pages); $18.95 per examiner's kit including 25 score forms; $6.95 per package of 25 score forms; (10–15) minutes.

Review of Clinical Evaluation of Language Functions, Elementary and Advanced Screening Tests, by LINDA M. CROCKER, Associate Professor, Foundations of Education, University of Florida, Gainesville, FL:

The CELF Screening Tests are designed to serve as the initial tests in a hierarchical testing program for students with potential language disability. Recommended use is for identification of children who require in-depth diagnostic testing. Items for the language processing subtest (elementary level) consist of simple instructions to the examinee, predicated by the phrase "Simon says." At the advanced level, the language processing subtest requires recognition of features of playing cards and their arrangements. The language production subtests include word and sentence repetition, phrase completion, alphabet and calendar knowledge, and counting skills.

No formal definition of the construct of "language ability" is offered (although reference is made to a textbook by the test authors which presumably provides this information). Items were selected which discriminated among children at different age levels. Since items from a general intelligence test would meet this same criterion, it would be desirable to know more about the authors' theoretical definition of language ability. Furthermore, no theoretical rationale is presented for the types of items used as an operational definition of this trait. Thus it seems fair to question whether items on this test measure only language ability and whether they represent a comprehensive (or adequate) sampling of behavior from the domain of oral language function. This is a critical point since children who pass the screening measure probably would be exempt from further testing.

The test manual is clearly written and well-organized. Instructions for administration are concise and easy to follow. Examinees to whom I administered these tests reacted favorably to the "game" format of the item presentation and generally enjoyed the testing session. Since the advanced battery uses pictures of playing cards, it is possible that some examinees or their parents might find this format offensive. Potential users should also consider the possibility of cultural bias when testing examinee subpopulations who may not be familiar with this type of material.

The CELF tests can be quickly and easily scored. Separate norm tables are provided for each grade level, and the standardization sample is described in some detail. Percentile rank norms for some grade levels are based on relatively small samples (e.g., 56 fifth graders and 84 kindergartners). The suggested cutoff scores for further referral have been arbitrarily set at the 15th percentile rank for the total score and the 10th percentile rank for subtests. No logical or empirical rationale is offered for this cutoff, and it seems questionable to use normative cutoffs based on such small standardization samples. To illustrate, with these norm tables and cutoffs, a first grader who answers only four items correctly on the language production subtest would fail the screening, but a third grader who answers these same four items correctly (and no others) would pass the screening.

Internal consistency estimates fluctuate widely from grade to grade (from .47 for fifth graders to .91 for third graders). Stability data are reported only for grades three and eight. Thus users should not assume that the tests are equally reliable at all grade levels. The issue of the tests' reliability at the cutoff score has not been addressed. This is a serious deficit in a screening measure.

Like many new tests, the CELF screening measures appear to have been published before sufficient validity data were martialled. No evidence of either content or construct validity is presented in the test manual. Criterion-related validity data are low to moderate correlations with other tests of language development (e.g., the ITPA). Relatively high correlations demonstrate that the CELF Screening Tests are good predictors of performance on the CELF Diagnostic Scales, published by the same authors. But do the scores on other diagnostic tests constitute reasonable and sufficient criteria for validating a screening measure? Presumably a language screening measure is given to identify those with language development problems which inhibit academic or social performance, not simply to predict their performance on other functional language tests. Data on the relationship between test scores and classroom performance in language related areas would be more appropriate evidence of these tests' usefulness.

In summary, the positive points of the CELF Screening Tests include: ease of administration and scoring, favorable examinee reactions, adequate internal consistency and stability estimates at selected grade levels, and coordination with a larger diagnostic testing system developed by the same authors. Weaknesses of these tests include: questionable procedures for establishing norms and cutoff scores, uneven reliability across grade levels, and little evidence of the types of validity and reliability most appropriate for a screening measure. Potential test users are cautioned that "language disability" is a term which is diversely defined by various test developers, educators, and clinicians. Careful inspection of test-item content is advised before selecting this or any screening test in this area, to confirm whether the test authors' definition of the trait conforms to user expectations and needs. This test is not recommended as the sole or primary screening measure for identifying students with language disability.

Review of Clinical Evaluation of Language Functions, Elementary and Advanced Screening Tests, by JON F. MILLER, Professor, Communicative Disorders, University of Wisconsin-Madison, Madison, WI:

The Clinical Evaluation of Language Functions, (CELF), Elementary and Advanced Screening Tests, was designed to identify potential language processing and production disabilities in school-age children, grades K to 12. These tests also can be used in conjunction with the CELF Diagnostic Battery. The tests' authors define language disabilities as disorders of comprehension at the word or sentence levels, deficits in immediate recall of spoken digits, words, sentences, and oral directions, word finding problems, and dysnomia. Thus, according to the authors, the CELF Screening Tests specifically identify language disorders associated with learning disabilities.

Test items were selected on the basis of the authors' clinical and research experience with learning disabled children rather than from any particular theory or model of language performance. The items were classified as one of two types, processing or production. Processing items include measures of a variety of linguistic features including: (*a*) "phoneme discrimination," (*b*) "sentence formation rules," (*c*) "interpretation of words," "logical relationships among sentence components and linguistic concepts," and (*d*) "retention and recall of word and action sequences." Production items measure: (*a*) "agility and accuracy in phoneme production," (*b*) "ability to recall, identify and retrieve words and concepts," (*c*) accuracy in serial recall, and (*d*) "immediate recall of model sentences." According to the authors, the total item pool will identify children with language disorders without sex or racial bias and contains a progression of difficulty across age levels. The items selected provide a good representation of language characteristics evaluated in both comprehension and production.

The standardization sample was stratified for sex, SES, racial background, geographic region, and grade level. The sample is too small for the number of variables included in the sample, resulting in uneven distribution in some categories. For example, there are only 25 males at the fifth-grade level and six Afro-Americans at the kindergarten level included in the sample for the elementary level test. A more serious limitation of the standardization sample was the decision to include only normal children. The resulting range of "normal" performance on these tests is restricted and will result in an increased number of false positives, i.e., normal children identified as having a possible language disorder. This overidentification has the benefit of reducing false negatives, i.e., identifying children with disorders as normal, but adds an increased number of children requiring complete diagnostic evaluation.

Measures of concurrent validity comparing performance with three criterion measures, the Illinois Test of Psycholinguistic Abilities (ITPA), the Detroit Test of Learning Aptitude (DTLA), and the Northwestern Syntax Screening Test (NSST), resulted in low but significant correlations for both elementary and advanced tests. The relationship among components of the screening tests and the CELF Diagnostic Battery revealed generally high and significant correlations. Evaluating agreements and disagreements between the screening and diagnostic battery on 28 second-grade children resulted in 86% agreements between the two measures. One child who met screening criteria failed to meet criteria on the Diagnostic Battery, which resulted in a false negative rate of just over 3% on middle class children. While these data show some relationship between abilities measured by the screening tests and other measures of language abilities, the tests show greatest overlap with the CELF Diagnostic Battery. The face validity of these tests is strong, based on the authors' research and clinical experience. Given the target population (children with language disorders associated with learning disabilities), it is not surprising that correlations with other oral language tests are low.

These tests show good test-retest reliability (mean $r=.77$) in three evaluations of 81 children. Internal consistency measures and inter-test relationships demonstrate consistent, evenly constructed item pools. The subjects of these studies are primarily middle class and do not adequately reflect the stratification sample, particularly for race and socioeconomic levels.

In summary, the CELF Screening Tests are well constructed to detect language disorders associated with learning disabilities in school-age children. These tests perform best in conjunction with the CELF Diagnostic Battery. They are expensive to use in terms of administration time and the potential number of false positives identified. The reliability data are inadequate with respect to size of sample and population characteristics of the subject pool, including sex, race, socioeconomic status, grade level, and geographical distribution. These tests, however, remain the best of their kind available to date.

[235]

Clinical Language Intervention Program. Grades K–8; 1982; CLIP; criterion-referenced; progress checklist for developing individualized language intervention programs; item scores in 4 areas: syntax, semantics, memory, pragmatics; no data on reliability and validity; no norms; individual; 1 form (12 pages, progress checklist); picture manual (186 pages, book of stimulus pictures); language activities manual (131 pages, resource/activities workbook); professional's guide (336 pages); 1983 price data: $140 per complete program (includes 12 progress checklists, picture manual, language activities manual, and professional's guide; $9.95 per 12 progress checklists; $85 per picture manual; $12.95 per language activities manual; $22.95 per professional's guide; administration time not reported; Eleanor Semel and Elizabeth H. Wiig; Charles E. Merrill Publishing Co.*

[236]

Clinical Record Keeping System. Adults and children; 1980–83; a collection of 25 record keeping forms: clinical interview technique (adults/children, marriage/family), mental health checkup, neuropsychological screening exam, relationship satisfaction survey, health history, progress note method (adults/children, marriage/family), treatment plan and review (adults/children, marriage/family), crisis intervention record, clinical notes, thermal biofeedback, quit smoking now, weight control, awards for kids, children's mental health record, consent and request for release of information, QSN progress chart, career path strategy, learning opportunity method, psychological consultation in hospital, professional service survey, discharge summary and aftercare, health insurance claim form; various instructional material available; 1984 price data: varies from $12–$15 per pad of 25–50 of each form; various authors; The Wilmington Press.*

[237]

Cloze Reading Tests. Ages 8–0 to 10–6, 8–5 to 11–10, 9–5 to 12–6; 1982; CRT; 3 levels: Level 1 (ages 8–0 to 10–6), Level 2 (ages 8–5 to 11–10), Level 3 (ages 9–5 to 12–6), (4 pages); manual (16 pages); 1982 price data: £2.25 per 20 tests; £2 per manual; £3 per specimen set; 35(45) minutes; D. Young; Hodder & Stoughton Educational [England].*

Review of Cloze Reading Tests by ESTHER GEVA, *Senior Research Officer, The Ontario Institute for Studies in Education, Toronto, Canada:*

The Cloze Reading Tests series were designed to provide continuity in assessing reading comprehension in grades six through the first half of grade nine. The series consists of three booklets corresponding to three reading levels. At each level the test consists of 16 to 17 unrelated paragraphs, which represent a good mixture of expository and narrative styles. On each line one word has been omitted, and altogether students have to fill in 70 words.

Most cloze reading tests require students to fill in every *n*th content word. This test, on the other hand, focuses on that aspect of reading comprehension which is reflected in the more demanding task of having to complete function words. Children have to "cloze" the test by completing items such as the correct form of the copula, prepositions, pronouns, relative pronouns, conjunctions, and definite and indefinite articles. In other words, they have to attend to form in addition to meaning. In most cases, in order to be able to fill in correctly such linguistic categories the reader has to take into account the context of one or two sentences, notice (consciously or unconsciously) the linguistic category which has been deleted, and select the most appropriate lexical item to "cloze" the text. For instance, in "Mark's dad has a van. He uses ____ to move people," the skilled reader will realize that the omitted word should correspond to "van" in the previous sentence and select the pronoun "it" to complete the text. Task demands, however are not equal for all items. For instance, consider the sentence "He had a message that people wanted to hear and, ____ addition, he used words that were easy [for] uneducated audiences to understand." The word "in," which is necessary to complete the conjunction "in addition," may be filled in by sophisticated readers without having to attend to textual meaning. Such an item does not seem to involve the same task demands as do most other items. In other words, it is not clear whether all items in the test measure reading comprehension or whether they also measure linguistic competence and lexical familiarity. In his introduction to the manual the author explains the rationale for this test by arguing that asking readers to fill in words such as "of" or "to" "provides a convenient method of testing reading skills that make use of, but transcend, the recognition of printed forms and the knowledge of the meaning of words." Unfortunately, the author does not define clearly what these "other skills" are that are presumably measured by the test. Furthermore, it is not clear what he means by his statement that "it is the best readers who can rectify [omissions] because they have the best grasp of the whole."

As stated in the manual, flexibility in test administration is facilitated by the fact that practice examples, instructions to students, and time allocation are identical for all three levels. The author also points out that this permits testing at the same time of students of different ages and/or differing reading levels. The tests are simple enough for classroom teachers to administer. However, the manual does not state clearly when teachers should use different test levels to test students of the same age. The exact word scoring method is used and the manual provides a key for scoring. The test in its present form is not machine scorable. Directions for scoring procedures are clearly stated.

The manual includes three tables with "reading quotients" for use with each test level. As the author points out, the reading quotients (which are actually standardized scores) permit useful comparison of the reading abilities of children of different ages who are in the same class. He suggests that quotients may be useful for school records of individual students. In order to determine students' reading quotients, the teacher must first determine the chronological ages of the children and then consult the appropriate table of reading quotients.

If the purpose of administering the test is to allocate students to reading groups, it is recommended that the raw scores be converted to "reading ages," using Table 4 in the manual.

The information provided in the manual concerning the development of the test is sketchy and difficult to comprehend. The standardization of each test level was based on over 900 students. Altogether, 19 schools said to represent "national standards" in Great Britain were used. The reading age norms are based on the main sample ($N = 929$ to 968 depending on level) as well as two additional samples (Ns$=93$ and 121). These two additional samples were used for calibration and for confirming extrapolations from the main samples.

The Kuder Richardson Formula 20 was used to calculate reliability. The reliability coefficients of

.94 for each of the three levels are more than satisfactory.

To provide information about test validity the manual includes four tables with intercorrelations between the three levels of the tests as well as correlations between these tests and the NFER Reading Tests, an oral verbal intelligence test (COVIT), two spelling tests, and two mathematics tests. These correlations are based on samples of 88–119 students, which presumably were drawn from the main samples. The correlations between the cloze reading tests and these latter tests range from .67 to .90. The author however, does not provide any rationale for having chosen these particular tests to validate the cloze reading tests. The author is frank in stating that "interpretations [of these correlations] are not entirely without difficulties" but no discussion of these tables is provided. Yet, he concludes that "the tables provide strong evidence for the validity of the tests."

Finally, the author refers in the manual to tests such as the NFER, SPAR and OVIT. It would have been helpful if full references and a brief description of these tests had been included for the naive reader who is not familiar with these tests.

In sum, not enough information is provided in the manual about what this test purports to measure, about test development, test validity, and the interpretation of test results. At the same time the test is easy to administer, it is reliable, and most important, it focuses on an important component of reading comprehension which has not been addressed in previously published reading tests.

[238]

Clyde Mood Scale. Normals and schizophrenics; 1963–83; CMS; to measure human emotions and behavior which are influenced by stress or drugs by self ratings or ratings by others; 6 scores: friendly, aggressive, clear thinking, sleepy, depressed, jittery; individual; 1 form (no date, 1 page); manual ('83, 16 pages); 1984 price data: $.10 per scale; $3 per manual and 1 scale; (5–15) minutes; Dean J. Clyde; Clyde Computing Service.*

See P:41 (12 references); for a review by David T. Lykken of the original edition, see 7:55 (13 references).

Review of Clyde Mood Scale by CYNTHIA M. SHEEHAN, *Director of Research, Department of Clinical Services, St. Mary's Child Care Agency, Syosset, NY:*

The Clyde Mood Scale (CMS) is a revised version of a checklist of 48 adjectives "designed to measure human emotions and behavior which are influenced by certain conditions (such as stress) or by drugs (such as antidepressants)." Each of the adjectives (e.g., "grouchy," "reckless") is rated on a 4-point scale anchored by "extremely" and "not at all." The scale is designed to provide the user with six factor scores labeled: Friendly, Aggressive, Clear-Thinking, Sleepy, Depressed, and Jittery.

From the information provided in the manual, it is not entirely clear what the nature and extent of the revisions are since the last edition. It is stated that the factors entitled "Depressed" and "Jittery" were previously described as "Unhappy" and "Dizzy," respectively. From this reviewer's examination of early research findings, it appears also that a previous format utilizing a deck of 52 IBM cards has been discarded, although this is not stated in the manual.

The scale lends itself to self-ratings or ratings by a variety of different personnel. The manual does, however, warn that proper interpretation of the scale requires knowing the "type of person" who made the rating because, for example, "schizophrenic patients often rate themselves as being very clear thinking, but...doctors and nurses do not agree." It seems only reasonable to this reviewer that such judgements required of a seriously disturbed or psychotic population would have serious consequences for the psychometric properties of the scale.

The manual describes a statistical comparison in which groups of items for both 500 self-rated and 500 other-rated checklists were subjected to separate factor analyses. The six largest factors appeared to be almost identical for the two groups; thus only one scoring key is provided, which is to be used for both self-ratings and ratings by others.

Although a variety of personnel qualified by "reasonable intelligence and familiarity with the instructions," (e.g., secretaries, nurses, research assistants, psychologists, and psychiatrists) are stated to have successfully administered the scale, the manual provides only a scant amount of evidence in support of this assertion. Correlation coefficients range from .32 to .91 between pairs of same-skill raters (i.e., 2 doctors, 2 nurses). Since the simplicity of the scale does lead one to believe that it may be appropriately used by a variety of personnel, it would be helpful to see data on interscorer agreement across skill levels (i.e., secretary/psychologist).

The scoring of the scale is best accomplished through computer scoring offered by the publisher. Steps for calculating the scores are provided, but they appear to be time consuming and cumbersome because of a complex weighting system.

Means and standard deviations are provided for the six factors for a variety of groups ($N = 100$ to 446) described only as "newly-admitted schizophrenics," "normal males," etc. It is to the credit of the scale's author that the manual cautions that the user's norm group will probably differ from those reported. The norms provided are to give "a rough idea of how normals mark the items" with "some schizophrenics [shown] for comparison." Local norms can and probably should be established. It would be a grievous error to assume that the reported norms are to be generalized to user-specific populations.

With the intended limited use of the scale, the validity data appropriately focus on how well this scale differentiates stressed or drugged groups from control or placebo groups. The difficulty is that the data reported in the manual reflect only one specific study in which the effects of phenothiazines on schizophrenics was evaluated. Doctors, nurses, and patients using the CMS misclassified cases at a rate of 20%–27%, depending on rater classification. Despite the author's statement that "hundreds of scientific articles have reported on the use of the Clyde Mood Scale in research," the only additional data reported in support of the scale's validity consists of references on 19 research studies related to 14 drugs or conditions, such as "antianxiety drugs" or "sleep." The reader is required to search out and evaluate the study or studies relevant to the particular drug or condition of interest. Given the data provided, the manual's statement that the reader may conclude from the information reported above that "the Clyde Mood Scale is a valid measure in a wide variety of situations" is unsupported. It is likely the CMS differentiates certain types of stresses or drug groups better than others but data addressing this issue are not discussed in the manual. Even after a search of the literature for relevant information, this reviewer remains unconvinced of the scale's validity. A summation of the data for the most common uses of the scale would be a welcome addition to the manual, as would some convergent or discriminant validity information in relation to other behavior rating scales.

The only reliability data reported is the aforementioned correlation between same skill-level raters. The limited sample size and lack of descriptive data, such as drug or condition rated, make these data unsuitable for evaluating scale use for a particular experimental interest or the uses of the scale in general.

The explicitly stated purpose of the CMS is to provide a quantifiable description of various emotions and behaviors. There is no assumption of the scale's relation to particular personality constructs, and so clinical significance of the scores is appropriately limited by the author to the circumstances surrounding the rating.

Ease of administration makes this an attractive instrument for quantifying behaviors within the context of a controlled research setting. In order to feel confident in using this instrument, however, the investigator must be willing to be active in establishing local group norms, investigating or establishing validity and reliability standards for use with the condition or drug of interest, and assessing the impact of the rater (self/other) on any clinical interpretation to be made from the scale. Those willing to expend the energy may find the CMS an aid to their research. Those unwilling to address these issues should not consider using the CMS.

[239]

The Clymer-Barrett Readiness Test, Revised Edition. Grades K–1; 1966–83; CBRT; formerly called Clymer-Barrett Prereading Battery; 4 scores: visual discrimination, auditory discrimination, visual-motor coordination, total; short screening form consisting of 2 of the 6 subtests yields a single score; Forms A, B, ('83, 16 pages); class record ('83, 2 pages); manual ('83, 40 pages) for each form; 1983 price data: $14.50 per 25 tests including manual and class record; $2 per manual; $3 per specimen set; (90) minutes in 3 sessions, (30) minutes for short form; Theodore Clymer and Thomas C. Barrett; Chapman, Brook & Kent.*

See T3:482 (5 references) and T2:1699 (2 references); for reviews by Roger Farr and Kenneth J. Smith of an earlier edition, see 7:744 (2 references).

Review of The Clymer-Barrett Readiness Test, Revised Edition, by JAMES MCCARTHY, Professor of Education, University of Wisconsin-Madison, Madison, WI:

The Clymer-Barrett Readiness Test (CBRT) is designed to measure skills necessary for success in beginning school instruction, especially instruction in reading. A teacher completed check list (Readiness Survey) directs attention to eight general areas of behavior basic to readiness (e.g., oral language skills, listening, social and emotional development). For a rapid assessment of readiness, a short form consisting of two of the test's six subtests is recommended. Children with vision, hearing, or other handicaps may be tested individually. The individual record forms and class record provide a way for organizing and summarizing results for both individual students and classes.

TEST CONSTRUCTION. The CBRT is an updated revision of the Clymer-Barrett PreReading Battery (1966). Like its predecessor, the CBRT stresses reading skills. It is said to measure skills and understandings required in elementary classrooms during reading instruction and those skills and understandings known to be essential to first-grade readiness. Considering the experience and background of the authors, there is little reason to expect this is not the case. However, no further information is supplied in the manual on the selection of content or the preparation and selection of items.

RELIABILITY. Internal consistency reliability figures are based on 188 pupils, drawn at random, one from each of the 188 classrooms of the norming group ($N = 5{,}565$). These split-half reliabilities, corrected by the Spearman-Brown formula, were .97 for the Full Form test (6 subtests); .96 for the Short Form test (subtests 1 and 3, Recognizing Letters and Beginning Sounds); .97 for the Visual Discrimination Combined Scores (subtests 1 and 2, Recognizing Letters and Matching Words); .90 for the Auditory Discrimination Combined Scores (subtests 3 and 4, Beginning Sounds and Ending sounds); and .94 for the Visual-Motor Coordination Combined Scores (subtests 5 and 6, Completing Shapes and Copy-A-Sentence). Internal consistency correlation coefficients for Visual Discrimination, Auditory Discrimination, Visual-Motor Coordination, Total Score/Short Form, and Total Score/Full Form were supplied for the following special groups: kindergarten pupils tested in May, $N = 120$ (midwestern school system); first graders, bilingual/rural, $N=63$ (southwestern school system); first graders, low ability/rural, $N=52$ (White schools); first graders, low ability/rural, $N=28$ (Black schools); and first graders, mixed ethnic/deprived, $N=111$ (large metropolitan schools). Coefficients ranged from .89 to .98 with a median of .96. Equivalent form reliability coefficients, based upon data from 2,468 pupils, are reported for each of the six subtests and Total Score/Full Form; these range from .57 to .92 with a median of .76. No test-retest reliabilities were reported in the manual. Raw score standard errors of measurement based upon internal consistency reliabilities were given for Visual Discrimination, Auditory Discrimination, Visual-Motor Coordination, Total Score/Short Form, and Total Score/Full Form; these were, respectively, 3, 3, 2, 3, and 4.

VALIDITY. Evidence for concurrent validity of the CBRT is found in the correlation between it and other readiness tests. The authors report the range of such correlations to be from about .55 to .80, indicating a communality with other tests accepted as assessing school readiness. Similarly, expected moderate correlations between the CBRT (Total Score/Full Form) and tests of intelligence (Binet L-M, Pintner-Cunningham, California Test of Mental Maturity, Kuhlman-Anderson) ranged from .43 to .55 for IQ scores and from .46 to .63 for mental ages.

Evidence for predictive validity was obtained from cooperating school systems which administered the CBRT in the fall and a standardized reading test in the following spring. Correlation coefficients for the Total Score/Full Form CBRT (fall) and reading subtests from the Gates, Stanford, Gates-MacGinitie, and Metropolitan Achievement Tests (following spring) ranged from .40 to .69 with a median of .61.

The usual evidence for content validity (i.e., listing of test objectives or presentation of a test blueprint) was not provided. Although the authors state that the major support for content validity derives from the similarity in the skill focus of the CBRT and elementary classroom reading activities, no supporting evidence is given that this, in fact, is the case.

The authors feel that evidence supporting construct validity is found in the relative lack of correlation between the subtests. For a group of 816 pupils, subtest intercorrelations ranged from .02 to .45 with a median of .21.

NORMS. Form A of the CBRT was standardized on 5,565 public school pupils, all tested in approximately the 3rd week of first grade. The sampling consisted of 50 community schools drawn from regions of the United States, distributed in proportion to each region's population. Proportional weighting for larger states was accomplished by selecting two or more schools therein. Results from 44 participants in 32 states were lost during the data collection process but the authors feel this introduced no significant bias. In addition to test data, information on school system size, socioeconomic nature of the school neighborhood, pre-first-grade school experiences, ages of children, and psychometric scores were gathered. This information was used to adjust raw score distributions to ensure their representativeness of a typical entering first-grade population. First-grade norms for Form B were based on an equating study in which the elementary schools of a "large and typical midwestern city" were divided into two groups of approximately equal size based on socioeconomic, demographic, achievement, and psychometric data. One group ($N = 1,517$) received Form A of the CBRT while the other ($N = 1,613$) received Form B. Form B distribution curves were equated to those of Form A through adjusting differences in means and standard deviations when such differences were significant. There are no kindergarten norms as such. The authors recommend use of published beginning first-grade norms and cite appropriate cautions.

ADMINISTRATION AND TEST MATERIALS. The administration instructions are clearly written and provide practice items preceding each subtest. Pictures are nicely executed and words are printed in manuscript. In all, it seems to be the kind of test a teacher could administer with relative ease and that pupils would find interesting. Scoring for the first four subtests is well keyed and objective. The last two subtests require scoring words and figures copied by the pupil; scoring principles and correct/incorrect models are provided.

Raw scores for the Total Test (Full or Short Form), and for the combined scores of subtests one and two, three and four, and five and six can all be translated into percentile ranks and/or stanines.

SUMMARY. The CBRT is the kind of school readiness test I would select if I were still teaching. It is well packaged, provides clear directions for the teacher and instructions for the pupils, and can be scored objectively. The test is psychometrically impressive. It has high internal consistency reliability and usefully small standard errors. The concurrent and especially predictive validity data are supportive. The norms, especially for Form A, appear to be based upon a stable and representative sample of beginning first graders. But nothing is perfect. The CBRT should provide some data on test-retest reliability, especially for the time period the test needs to be stable (fall to following spring). In addition, support for content validity should be provided; this is more important now than for the predecessor test which assessed *only* reading readiness as contrasted with the present version designed to measure *school* readiness with an emphasis on reading readiness. Finally, for the purpose of intra- and intertest comparison, standard scores or *T*-scores would be very useful and are directly derivable from the percentile ranks the CBRT already employs.

On balance, the CBRT appears to be a reliable and valid instrument for assessing school readiness (particularly reading readiness), with user-friendly characteristics.

Review of The Clymer-Barrett Readiness Test, Revised Edition, by BARTON B. PROGER, Coordinator of Program Evaluation Services, Division of Special Education, Montgomery County Intermediate Unit 23, Norristown, PA:

OVERVIEW. The Clymer-Barrett Prereading Battery of the late 1960s has now been issued in a revised edition of 1983. The new test, the Clymer-Barrett Readiness Test (CBRT), continues its earlier three components of visual discrimination, auditory discrimination, and visual-motor coordination. The manual is exceptionally well-written, easy to understand, and specific yet clear in all topics addressed. The test booklets for Forms A and B are well organized, pleasing in appearance, and generally reflect overall quality of production.

Forms A and B are said to be equivalent and appear from the data to be so. The Visual Discrimination section consists of two subtests: Recognizing Letters (35 items) and Matching Words (20 items). The two subtests of the Auditory Discrimination section are Beginning Sounds (20 items) and Ending Sounds (20 items). The Visual-Motor Coordination section also has two subtests: Completing Shapes (20 items) and Copy-a-Sentence (7 possible points). Finally, if time is a problem, there is the Short Form, which uses only the two subtests of Recognizing Letters and Beginning Sounds. Directions for administration, scoring, and interpretation are quite clear. Proper precautions are offered.

TECHNICAL DATA. On the whole, the reviewer was impressed with the technical merits of the CBRT. As with any device, however, there are some puzzling aspects. Both positive and negative features will be covered in this part of the review.

Reliability coefficients (split-half, corrected) for Visual Discrimination, Auditory Discrimination, Visual-Motor Coordination, Total Score/Short Form, and Total Score/Full Form are all in the .90s, quite acceptable. Norming was based on 5,565 first-grade students in 188 classrooms. This reviewer would have preferred coefficient alpha data reported for internal consistency reliability, rather than split-half (odd-even) coefficients.

It is commendable that the authors carried out five studies for Form A on the reliability of the CBRT with "atypical groups." The five "atypical groups" were kindergartners in a midwestern school system; first graders in a bilingual, rural, southwestern school system; first graders in a low-ability, rural white system; first graders in a low-ability, rural, black system; and first graders in a "mixed-ethnic, deprived, large metropolitan school system." With the sole exception of an .89, all coefficients were again in the .90s.

The manual of the CBRT contains a clear discussion of validity. The discussion emphasizes content validity, construct validity, and predictive validity. The reviewer has no arguments with the authors' claims of content validity.

Some encouraging finds are also reported for construct validity. The intercorrelations among Form A's six subtests are all low (.02 to .45), indicating that CBRT's subtests are each tapping relatively independent aspects of the school readiness areas of behavior. Also, the reviewer is glad to see that the correlations between the CBRT Form A subtests and short form and full form totals, on the one hand, and various measures of first-grade intelligence (Stanford-Binet, Form L-M; Pintner-Cunningham; California Test of Mental Maturity; Kuhlman-Anderson), on the other hand, are not very high (generally in the .30s, .40s, and .50s). Thus, while some aspects of intelligence are involved in whatever skills CBRT is tapping, the CBRT task performances cannot, on the whole, be explained by intelligence only.

The manual also groups correlations of CBRT with other readiness measures under construct validity. However, no details are given of these studies. One is told only that "The reported correlations have ranged from .55 to .80." The reviewer is also puzzled by the authors' claim that "Validity evidence based upon high correlations between two tests of the same general type is not appropriate in judging the validity of the CBRT." While the authors may have a strong case to make in this regard, we do not know what it is. Further, even if this is the case, just what stronger evidence of outside, recognized criteria can the authors provide to assure us of solid construct validity?

The reviewer was generally satisfied with the content and construct validity sections of the manual. The predictive validity section is also clearly written and contains relevant data. The authors in Tables 6 and 7 present correlational data between the fall first-grade CBRT scores and various reading achievement test scores in spring of first grade. Achievement was measured by the Stanford Achievement Test, Gates Primary Reading Test, Gates-MacGinitie Reading Test, and Metropolitan Achievement Test. The results generally range from the .30s to the .70s. One interesting finding is that the CBRT Short Form fared just as well as the CBRT Full Form.

The last part of the manual's discussion on technical data treats the equivalence of CBRT Form A and Form B. Means and standard deviations on the two forms are given. Table 8 presents equivalency data for the "preliminary" versions of Forms A and B, while Table 10 presents similar information for the final versions. From this information Forms A and B do seem to posssess equivalency. Yet, the reviewer is puzzled by Table 9, which presents the correlations of each subtest of Form A with its counterpart on Form B. With the exception of the subtest on Recognizing Letters (.92), the correlations are rather moderate (.57 to .79). Perhaps part of the answer is to be found in the introductory section in the manual on "Some Questions and Answers." In this section the authors claim that "Traditionally, Form B is designated as a beginning or basic test and is used for testing prior to first grade. In some schools Form A is reserved for testing in first grade and is regarded as an advanced test. But to repeat, either form can be, and has been, successfully used at any time during either grade." The reviewer asks why Form A is considered an "advanced test." Is there something inherently different about the tasks represented in the items of Form A? There is some lack of consistency in the authors' discussion.

While the data presented in the manual on the technical aspects of CBRT were very helpful to the reviewer, exactly the same information and narrative were presented in the manual on Form B of CBRT. In other words, the technical data were generated only on Form A. If, as the authors claimed on Page 1, Form B is really the basic predictive version of CBRT, then this reviewer would have spent most of his technical efforts on Form B. At any rate, the reviewer would want separate sets of data on both Forms A and B.

The reviewer wishes that in any test related to school tasks, the publisher would provide still another aspect of validity: diagnostic validity. Regardless of whether the test is group-administered or individually administered, it would be quite useful to know whether or not children who are already known to exhibit deficiencies in the specified tasks can be successfully identified by the test in question. In the case of CBRT, since instructional grouping is a stated purpose of the test, one could have asked the teachers in the 188 classrooms to rank order their students in terms of overall spring reading ability. Regardless of size of a classroom group, these rankings could then be translated into thirds or quarters for each classroom to allow comparability of competency groupings across classrooms, school systems, etc. Then a multiple discriminant analysis could be performed. The state of the art in validating a test for its stated practical purposes (e.g., instructional grouping, or identification of performance weaknesses) never seems to address directly the needed data to judge the adequacy of the test. In this regard, CBRT is no better, nor any worse, in its validation efforts than any other major test of its type.

INTERPRETATION OF RESULTS. As with all sections of the manual, the CBRT carefully and thoroughly addresses all necessary issues. Proper precautions are put forward at all points in the manual. One is told how to interpret percentile rank results, stanine results, and what these mean in terms of prognosis for success. The manual is exemplary in these respects.

SUMMARY. The CBRT is a competently designed revision of an already established test. The reviewer considers the norming and validation of the CBRT quite acceptable. The use of test results is put forward in a fashion which should be useful to all practitioners, with suitable cautionary notes. The new CBRT should continue to prove to be a useful readiness instrument.

[240]

Cognitive Abilities Test, Form 3. Grades K–1, 2–3, 3–12; 1954–83; CogAT; Form 1 is still available; class record folder (no date, 4 pages); technical manual ('82, 44 pages); development of 1982 norms for the ITBS, TAP, and CogAT ('83, 30 pages); 1984 price data: $5.95 per 35 class record folders; $8.45 per technical manual; $6 per examination kit; Robert L. Thorndike and Elizabeth Hagen; Riverside Publishing Co.*

a) PRIMARY BATTERIES. Grades K–1, 2–3; 1979–83; 2 levels: labeled Primary Battery, Level 1 and Primary Battery, Level 2; 3 editions: hand-scorable ('79, 16 pages), MRC machine-scorable ('79, 16 pages), NCS machine-scorable ('79, 16 pages); examiner's manual ('83, 60 pages) for Levels 1 and 2; practice test ('79, 4 pages) for Levels 1–2; examiner's manual for practice test ('79, 8 pages); scoring key ('78, 1 page); $18 per 35 hand-scorable tests (includes examiner's manual, scoring key, and materials needed for machine-scoring); $51.75 per 35 NCS tests (includes NCS directions for administration); $10.56 per 100 practice tests (includes directions for administration); $.99 per scoring key; $5.49 per examiners manual; scoring service, $.68 and over per test ($50 minimum); (50–60) minutes in two sessions.

b) MULTILEVEL EDITION. Grades 3–12; 1978–83; separate level editions also available; 3 scores: verbal, quantitative, nonverbal; 1 form ('78, 73 pages); 8 overlapping Levels A (grade 3), B (4), C (5), D (6), E (7), F (8–9), G (10–11), H (12) in a single booklet;

examiner's manual ('83, 108 pages); practice test ('79, 4 pages); MRC answer sheets ('78, 2 pages); NCS answer sheets ('78, 4 pages); $3.24 per complete battery test; $10.56 per 100 practice tests; $13.50 or less per 35 MRC answer sheets; $72 per 250 NCS answer sheets; $6 per MRC scoring mask; $4.95 per examiner's manual; scoring service, $.45 and over per test ($50 minimum); (130–140) minutes in three sessions.

See T3:483 (32 references) for references to an earlier edition; for reviews by Kenneth D. Hopkins and Robert C. Nichols, see 8:181 (12 references); for reviews by Marcel L. Goldschmid and Carol K. Tittle and an excerpted review by Richard C. Cox of the primary batteries, see 7:343.

TEST REFERENCES

1. Fennema, E. H., & Sherman, J. A. Sex-related differences in mathematics achievement and related factors: A further study. JOURNAL FOR RESEARCH IN MATHEMATICS EDUCATION, 1978, 9, 189–203.

2. Stayrook, N., & Corno, L. An application of generalizability theory in disattenuating a path model of teaching and learning. JOURNAL OF EDUCATIONAL MEASUREMENT, 1979, 16, 227–237.

3. Lee, L. A., & Karnes, F. A. Correlations between the Cognitive Abilities Test, Form 3, and the Ross Test of Higher Cognitive Processes for gifted children. PERCEPTUAL AND MOTOR SKILLS, 1983, 56, 421–422.

4. McGivern, J. E., & Levin, J. R. The keyword method and children's vocabulary learning: An interaction with vocabulary knowledge. CONTEMPORARY EDUCATIONAL PSYCHOLOGY, 1983, 8, 46–54.

5. Sherman, J. Factors predicting girls' and boys' enrollment in college preparatory mathematics. PSYCHOLOGY OF WOMEN QUARTERLY, 1983, 7, 272–281.

Review of Cognitive Abilities Test, Form 3, by CHARLES J. ANSORGE, Associate Professor of Educational Psychology, University of Nebraska-Lincoln, Lincoln, NE:

Form 3 of the Cognitive Abilities Test (CAT) is for use in kindergarten through grade 12. A primary battery is available for kindergarten and grades 1 and 2. There are two levels of this battery for testing from the second half of kindergarten through grade 2. Only a single score is provided for the primary battery although there are subtests for relational concepts, object classification, quantitative concepts, and oral vocabulary included.

There is also a multilevel edition of three batteries (verbal, quantitative, and nonverbal) available for use in grades 3 through 12. The verbal subtests (vocabulary, sentence completion, verbal classification, and verbal analogies) contain items which are similar to those found in other tests of verbal ability. The quantitative subtests (quantitative relations, number series, and equation building) were designed to show that quantitative abilities are related to achievement in mathematics and some sciences. The nonverbal subtests (figure analogies, figure classification, and figure synthesis) are entirely pictorial or diagrammatic. The authors admit that tests in this battery are not expected to predict success in school as well as tests in the other two batteries. They believe these tests may have special utility in appraising abstract intelligence for students who may have some reading disability.

ITEM SELECTION. Item selection for the primary battery involved administering questions to 250–300 students in each of grades K, 1, 2, and 3. For the multilevel battery a similar procedure was followed with students in grades 4, 6, 8, 10, and 12. Only those items with satisfactory discrimination based on biserial correlations were selected. No data are supplied regarding difficulty or discrimination for individual items, only means for the subtests. These means are based on 2,500–7,700 students. Mean difficulty of the primary battery subtests have *p*'s typically in the .70s and .80s, which seem to be appropriate for this level, but five out of seven subtests of the verbal and quantitative batteries have *p*'s in the .40s or low .50s for grade 3, which seems too difficult.

ADMINISTRATION AND SCORING. The primary test is given without a time limit. Items are presented one at a time with the rate of presentation determined by the person administering the test. The manual indicates that each of the subtests can be administered in 12–16 minutes, about appropriate for this level. The three sections of the multilevel edition are timed with 34 minutes allowed for the 100 verbal battery items, 32 minutes for the quantitative battery, and 32 minutes for the 80 items on the nonverbal battery. Suggestions are provided regarding scheduling the CAT test for both young children and also older children. A testing span of 2 to 3 days is recommended.

The two primary levels of the test provide for a single score while the multilevel tests yield separate scores for the verbal, quantitative, and nonverbal batteries.

NORMS AND STANDARDIZATION. The standardization of the CAT occurred in 1977 and 1978 and was done concurrently with the Iowa Tests of Basic Skills (ITBS) and the Tests of Achievement and Proficiency (TAP). Considerable care was exercised in the norming process. Three major stratification variables were used in the selection of the sample (size of enrollment of school districts, geographic region, and community socioeconomic status, determined from the 1970 census). An effort was also made to ensure that the racial-ethnic composition of the standardization sample was representative of the racial-ethnic composition in the country.

The raw score for each pupil was converted into a "Universal Scale Score" following a prescribed procedure and these scores in turn can be transformed into standard age scores (SAS). These are normalized standard scores with a mean of 100 and a standard deviation of 16. Also available are grade percentile ranks, NCE's and stanines for age groups, and percentile ranks and stanines for grade groups. Interpolation was used to provide fall, winter, and spring norms. Two tables of norms are available, one based on data collected in 1978 and the other in 1981.

RELIABILITY. The K-R 20 reliability estimates for both the primary batteries and the multilevel edition are quite high, ranging from .89 to .96. Some data were also provided for the retest reliability of the multilevel edition. When retesting with the same form after an interval of 6 months the obtained reliabilities ranged from .76 to .94. Test-retest reliabilities were also reported for over 4,000 pupils who were administered Form 1 of the multilevel edition in grades 5, 7, and 9. Correlations between grades ranged from .73 to .87 for the verbal, quantitative, and nonverbal batteries.

ETHNIC AND SEX DIFFERENCES. An effort was made to minimize ethnic differences in the development of the test. Identified samples of majority and minority students were administered all final-tryout items. Any items that revealed unusual patterns of difficulty between groups were removed from the test. The manual states that the authors of the test attempted to eliminate sex-biased language in test items.

Information is presented regarding ethnic group means (White, Black, Hispanic, and Asian) on the CAT test for grades 7, 9, and 11. Black students averaged about 15 SAS units lower on the verbal battery, slightly more on the quantitative battery, and a little less on the nonverbal battery. Hispanic students also tended to be lower than White students across the test batteries and grade levels. Some means for the Asian group were higher than the White students (as much as 8 points) and some were lower (as much as 5 points).

Comparative scores for the two sexes were presented for grades 3 through 11. At nearly every level and test battery the means for the girls were higher. The exception was in grades 7, 9, and 11 where the boys had higher means than the girls on the quantitative battery.

CORRELATIONS AMONG BATTERIES. Correlations among the verbal, quantitative, and nonverbal batteries produced some interesting results which clearly supported a substantial amount of overlap among the three batteries. A median correlation of .78 was reported between the verbal and quantitative battery across the grades with the same value reported between nonverbal and quantitative. Only the median verbal and nonverbal correlation was lower (r =.72). Since there is little uniqueness offered by the quantitative battery an argument may be presented for deletion of this battery from the CAT although the test authors recommend use of all batteries because differences in performance of students may reveal special information to assist teachers. A strong case does not seem to be made for doing this, however.

VALIDITY. Information regarding the content, criterion-related, and construct validity of the CAT is provided. Concurrent correlations of the CAT batteries and (ITBS) subtests for grade 3 through 8 are high, as are the correlations between the CAT batteries and (TAP) subtests in grades 9 through 12. Correlations are the highest between the verbal battery and the ITBS and TAP subtests (.70s to .80s).

Correlations of the CAT with grade point average at the end of the year were determined for four ethnic groupings and also sex groupings for grades 7, 9, and 11. Correlations ranged from .31 to .63 for the ethnic groups and .40 to .61 for the sexes. There did not appear to be a clear trend as to which battery was best in the prediction.

Construct validity was reported by determining correlations of the CAT multilevel batteries with the Stanford-Binet for 550 individuals tested in the 1971–72 school year. The correlations were substantial (.65–.75).

SUMMARY. Form 3 of CAT was built of the same types of items and of the same specifications as the previous forms. It has several new features which distinguish it from its predecessors including shorter directions for administration, new scoring service reports, and a manual which now includes information to assist teachers and counselors in interpreting test score patterns in practical terms. The CAT has high reliability and its criterion-related validity is also very high. A careful standardization procedure was followed to establish norms. Both 1978 and 1982 norms are available for the primary and the multilevel batteries.

[241]

Cognitive Diagnostic Battery. Psychiatric and retarded patients; 1982; CDB; 5 tests; individual; record form (4 pages); manual (120 pages); 1984 price data: $42.95 per complete kit including 50 of each record form; $9.50 per 50 record forms; $4.50 per 50 span of attention test forms; $10 per manual; Stanley R. Kay; Psychological Assessment Resources, Inc.*

a) COLOR-FORM PREFERENCE TEST. CFP; 2 scale scores: color-form scale, identity scale; 1 form (40 cards); (3–5) minutes.

b) COLOR-FORM REPRESENTATION TEST. CFR; 1 form (21 cards); (3–5) minutes.

c) EGOCENTRICITY OF THOUGHT TEST. EOT; 1 form; (1–3) minutes.

d) PROGRESSIVE FIGURE DRAWING TEST. PFDT; 8 scores: 7 drawing scores (vertical line, circle, cross, square, triangle, tree, diamond), and a derived mental age score; 1 form (7 cards); (1–3) minutes.

e) SPAN OF ATTENTION TEST. SOA; 1 form (1 page); (1–7) minutes.

Review of Cognitive Diagnostic Battery by JOHN L. FISK, Clinical Neuropsychologist, Windsor Western Hospital Centre, Windsor, Ontario, Canada:

The Cognitive Diagnostic Battery consists of five individual tests which are designed primarily to discriminate and differentiate between intellectual subnormality (retardation) and abnormality (psychiatric disorder) in psychiatric populations. The battery attempts to circumvent some of the more obvious difficulties inherent in standard IQ scales (*e.g.*, absolute range restriction, academic and/or verbal requirements, etc.) by utilizing a developmental framework as opposed to cross-sectional standardization based on largely normal, non-clinical populations. As the author correctly points out, evaluation derived by reference to the normal curve is often of limited value to any pathological grouping with a non-normative distribution.

The battery is composed of: (1) Color Form Preference Test (CFP)—which requires the matching of comparison cards to a standard card by utilizing color and/or form cues; (2) Color Form Representation Test (CFR)—requiring a judgment of similarity as to which of three comparison cards can be matched to a standard on the basis of color, form, or neither cue; (3) Egocentricity of Thought Test (EOT)—involving a hierarchical series of inquiries to determine developmental level of socialized thinking; (4) Progressive Figure Drawing Test (PFDT)—requiring the subject to draw seven figures in ascending order of difficulty; and (5) Span of Attention Test (SOA)—requiring the subject to circle in a specific order a series of 500 *X*s arranged in a 25 x 20 matrix.

In contrast to many standard measures of IQ, this battery has the advantage of being administered in a relatively short time period (15–20 minutes), which is an important consideration given the typical problems with respect to attentional deployment, restlessness, and other untoward characteristics of some psychiatric patients. Administration of the tests is relatively straightforward and clearly described in the test manual. Scoring is quite simple although the author does not provide specific examples for the Progressive Figure Drawing Test which, despite relatively clear rules, is open to variant interpretation. The performance characteristics of the test battery (no necessarily correct answers) render it suitable for repeat administration, which might be useful to those individuals interested in measurement of treatment effects.

With respect to statistical properties, the manual outlines the following in sufficient detail: the characteristics of the normative sample; measures of reliability for each of the five tests on the basis of both split-half and test-retest data; and an evaluation of discriminative, criterion-related, and construct validity. The normative sample is composed of 97 schizophrenics, 88 mentally retarded psychotics, and 198 non-psychotic individuals. Criteria for these classifications are defined in the manual. On the basis of the data presented, the reliability indices for all five tests would seem to indicate substantial consistency. Reliability studies are briefly described and appropriately referenced for those interested in specific details. Discriminative validity studies are also described and, where appropriate, referenced. The results of several investigations utilizing this battery have been compared with data obtained from measures of psychometric intelligence, psychiatric disturbance, and developmental disorder. A number of appendices present details on such matters as item analysis, item difficulty, and correlations with other measures.

The guidelines for clinical interpretation are sufficient as far as they go. Prototypic analysis is stressed and illustrated with four case studies. However, the manual does not provide any information regarding possible errors of interpretation which potentially might be encountered. Furthermore, the author makes no recommendations regarding populations for whom the battery would be clearly inappropriate. For example, the test would not seem to be appropriate as a measure of type or degree of "organicity." At the same time, the author does make clear that the battery should not be viewed as a substitute for a clinical interview.

In summary, the Cognitive Diagnostic Battery appears to be a potentially useful instrument which would be helpful in rendering decisions regarding diagnosis, placement, and mode of treatment in psychiatric populations. The relative ease of administration and scoring suggests that it could be most helpful as a screening instrument or as a supplemental evaluation in those cases where there are questions regarding the cognitive functioning of the patient. However, in this reviewer's opinion, this battery should not be viewed as a complete substitute for more extensive assessment of cognitive functioning in such populations.

Review of Cognitive Diagnostic Battery by ARTHUR B. SILVERSTEIN, *Professor of Psychiatry, University of California, Los Angeles, CA:*

The Cognitive Diagnostic Battery (CDB) is presented as a method for assessing and differentiating among aspects of cognitive dysfunction, more specifically, for distinguishing between intellectual subnormality (as in mental retardation) and intellectual abnormality (as in schizophrenia). The differential diagnosis of these conditions has obvious implications for treatment, but existing tests were not designed for that purpose. According to the author of the CDB, they tend to overestimate the scores of severely retarded individuals and to underestimate the scores of actively psychotic persons, thus blurring the distinction between them. Moreover, existing tests do not take a developmental perspective, nor do they focus on the qualitative aspects of performance, both of which are said to be critical for accurate diagnosis.

The CDB comprises five tests, each taking from 1 to 6 minutes to administer; the total administration time is usually between 15 and 20 minutes. On the Color-Form Preference Test (CFP), the subject's task is to select the optimal match to a standard card on the basis of color, form, neither, or both cues. The Color Form Representation Test (CFR) is an upward extension of the CFP that introduces the further option of matching on the basis of figural representation. The Egocentricity of Thought Test (EOT), based on the early work of Piaget, taps the ability to distinguish left from right from the subject's own viewpoint, the viewpoint of the examiner, and relative to other objects. The Progressive Figure Drawing Test (PFDT), based on studies by Gesell, Buhler, and Terman and Merrill, involves copying a series of simple designs, from a vertical line to a diamond. On the Span of Attention Test (SOA), the subject is to circle each *X* on a page filled with *X*s.

To date, the CDB has been administered, in whole or in part, to approximately 400 subjects: about 100 schizophrenics, almost as many retarded psychotics, and about 200 nonpsychotic individuals (children, adults, and elderly persons). The bases of sample selection are clearly described, and the demographic features of each group are summarized in a table. Provisional norms are offered for the various groups. Scores between the 25th and 75th percentiles are classified as "normal" for a particular group. Scores at or below the 5th percentile for nonpsychotic adults are considered "defective." Scores at or above the 95th percentile for each of the clinical groups are regarded as suggestive evidence against the corresponding diagnosis.

Successive chapters of the manual are devoted to each test in turn. The chapters discuss test development, describe the tests, provide details of administration and scoring, outline the normative standards, and present data on reliability and validity. The reliability data include both corrected split-half (where appropriate) and test-retest correlation coefficients. Reliability indices corresponding to the latter are also reported, but these may lead the unwary into believing that a test is more reliable than it actually is: a reliability coefficient of .67 translates into a reliability index of .82. The validity data take several different forms: the ability of the tests to differentiate the nonpsychotic from the clinical groups, and for the latter, to distinguish among the different subtypes of schizophrenia and levels of retardation; correlations with mental age and a wide variety of other measures; and sensitivity to therapeutic change, specifically, the schizophrenics' responsiveness to drug treatment. Both the reliabilities and validities appear generally satisfactory. Intercorrelations among the tests should be reported, but they are not.

One chapter of the manual deals with the clinical interpretation of performance on the battery. A table summarizes characteristic patterns for nonpsychotic persons (adults and elderly individuals), schizophrenics (classified by subtype and various prognostic criteria), and retarded psychotics (categorized by level of retardation), and the accompanying text discusses the distinctive features of the various groups. Four case illustrations are offered to demonstrate the application of the CDB to various clinical problems (e.g., the differentiation between schizophrenia and mental retardation). A number of appendices present, in addition to the normative data, a variety of information on the five tests, including predicted mental ages, item analyses, distributions of scores by schizophrenic subtype and level of retardation, and correlations with scores on other tests and rating scales.

It is easy to criticize the CDB for the inadequacies of the normative data: the small sample sizes (especially when the nonpsychotic group is broken down by age, and the clinical groups by schizophrenic subtype or level of retardation); the narrow sampling base; and the omission of at least one essential group of subjects—nonpsychotic mentally retarded individuals. Moreover, although the justification for including each test in the battery is set forth, there is no overarching theoretical rationale for the inclusion of just these tests. (In fairness, the same can be said about the items of the Stanford-Binet or the subtests of Wechsler's intelligence scales.) Nevertheless, the CDB appears to be a promising instrument for the purpose for which it is intended. Caution should be exercised in employing it for making clinical decisions, but on the basis of the very encouraging results reported thus far, it certainly appears worthy of further research to establish more conclusively its utility for evaluating the nature and degree of intellectual pathology.

[242]

Cognitive Skills Assessment Battery, Second Edition. Pre K–K; 1974–81; CSAB; criterion-referenced; 98 item scores (49 consist of plus or minus) in 18 areas: basic information (4 scores), identification of body parts (4 scores), color identification (4 scores), shape identification (4 scores), symbol discrimination (10 scores), visual-auditory discrimination (6 scores), auditory discrimination (6 scores), number knowledge (10 scores), letter naming (2 scores), vocabulary (6 scores), information from pictures (4 scores), picture comprehension (4 scores), story comprehension (4 scores), multiple directions (4 scores), large muscle coordination (4 scores), visual-motor coordination (6 scores), memory (8 scores), response during assessment (8 scores); individual; 1 form; card manual ('81, 113 pages); response sheet ('81, 4 pages); assessors manual ('81, 62 pages); 1983 price data: $48.95 per testing materials including 30 response sheets;

$8.50 per 30 response sheets; $3.50 per assessors manual; $3.95 per specimen set (without card manual); (20–25) minutes; Ann E. Boehm and Barbara R. Slater; Teachers College Press.*

See T3:484 (2 references); for reviews by Kathryn Hoover Calfee and Barbara K. Keogh, see 8:797.

Review of Cognitive Skills Assessment Battery by ESTHER E. DIAMOND, *Educational and Psychological Consultant, Evanston, IL:*

The Cognitive Skills Assessment Battery (CSAB) was developed to provide teachers of kindergarten and prekindergarten children "with information regarding children's progress relative to teaching goals in the cognitive and physical-motor areas." This individually administered battery, revised in 1981, surveys children's performance in five such areas: orientation toward one's environment, discrimination of similarities and differences, comprehension and concept formation, coordination, and immediate and delayed memory.

Although described as a criterion-referenced test, criterion levels are not set, and total scores are not obtained. Instead, a profile is obtained of each child's skills on the basis of performance of each task within each goal area, as well as a profile of the skills of a class as a whole. The teacher presumably can use the results to match instruction to pupil and class needs.

The second edition, according to the authors, responds to critical user comments regarding the first edition; these comments are not summarized but to some extent may be inferred from the changes made. Some items were redrawn, color production was improved, and directions to teachers were clarified. As examples of such clarification, it is now indicated in the Assessors Manual that the eight blocks needed for some number knowledge tasks are not included in the CSAB materials and must be provided by the assessor, and that a sweep-second watch is needed.

The four components of the CSAB are a two-sided Card Easel, used to present the tasks to the child; an Assessors Manual, which gives information about the rationale and construction of the CSAB, as well as instructions for administration and scoring; field test data, and suggestions for use of the results; a Pupil Response Sheet, on which both the child's responses and the teacher's evaluation of the child during assessment are recorded; and a Class Record Sheet, on which the responses of each child and the class as a whole are recorded.

The Card Easel is an attractive and well-constructed piece of equipment, with one side of the easel presenting the task to the child while the other side presents the examiner's instructions and scoring procedures for the task with a reduced replica of the task, where appropriate. A racial/ethnic mix of children is presented, and the drawings of objects are all quite clear and easily identified. None of the objects appear to have a regional, geographic, or social class bias.

There are two methods for coding a child's responses: plus or minus, or by three levels of competency. The assessor also codes the child's behavior during a task, on a scale of 1 to 4, on eight behaviors such as task persistence, attention span, and attention to directions. Visual-Motor Coordination responses are scored separately for kindergarten and prekindergarten children. At the kindergarten level particularly, distinctions between plus and minus responses given in the Assessors Manual seem rather arbitrary for some of the Visual-Motor Coordination items. An intermediate level of correctness might present a more accurate picture of the child's ability.

The CSAB was field tested with 860 prekindergarten and kindergarten children in early fall of 1979 and with 558 prekindergarten and kindergarten children in late spring of 1980. Samples were representative of lower and middle socioeconomic status (SES), and of a variety of community sizes and types across the country. The Assessors Manual presents breakdowns by sex, ethnic background, language spoken in the home, average school income, and a number of other demographic variables. A breakdown of percentage of children responding to each option, by grade and SES, is also given. No data are given on sex differences in performance; such data might have been particularly helpful in noting developmental differences and in making comparisons with findings such as those of Maccoby and Jacklin. As expected, percentages of correct responses are greater for middle than for lower SES children. The ceiling effect described in the *Eighth Mental Measurements Yearbook* review by Calfee (8:797) is still present in this edition; there are many items that were answered correctly by more than 90% of the children tested.

The Assessors Manual expresses several wise cautions regarding use of the results: The assessor is counseled that what may appear as a "weakness" in a child's performance may simply be a matter of lack of exposure to the particular learning area and may be unrelated to ability. Translation or use of some other mode of presentation, such as pantomime, is suggested for children with non-English-speaking backgrounds or minimal English language facility; if neither of these alternatives is possible, administration of the CSAB may not be appropriate. Teaching to the test or permitting the CSAB to "set goals" would, the user is warned, "limit the variety of learning experiences prekindergarten and kindergarten children ought to have." Finally, the user is cautioned to consider carefully use of the CSAB as a pre-post measure of a program's effectiveness. "For many children, improved performance in some areas occurs as a result of their general development rather than as a result of a specific program." This is sound advice for evaluators everywhere who use pre-post models indiscriminately, especially with early childhood interventions.

Percentage of agreement between test and retest over a 2- to 3-week period is given as evidence of reliability—80% overall at the prekindergarten level and 85% overall at the kindergarten level. Agreement of assessor observations was 40% at the prekindergarten level and 79% at the kindergarten level. Samples for the study were very small—16 prekindergarten and 32 kindergarten children. There is no information regarding the standard deviation or the standard error of measurement; this omission, together with the small sample size, raises serious questions about the instrument's reliability.

As content validity evidence, the authors cite the procedures used to determine the skill areas and tasks to be included—review of curricular materials, teacher interviews, classroom observations, reviews of existing tests, review of the relevant research literature, and field testing. However, since curricula vary among schools, the authors caution that the CSAB has content validity only for those teachers who include among their curricular goals the areas covered in the battery. The fact that a number of the competencies included were listed by only one teacher, and a number of others by only two or three, makes the content validity argument less convincing.

Overall, the CSAB appears to be a useful instrument for purposes of rough, informal assessment of children's developmental level in the five areas represented. Any attempt to go beyond this type of assessment and make more in-depth inferences cannot be justified until there is stronger evidence of validity and reliability. The items seem attractive and non-threatening, and most children should enjoy responding to them. The Assessors Manual provides many helpful suggestions and caveats for wise use of the test results; the caveats, in particular, should be heeded by the user.

Review of the Cognitive Skills Assessment Battery by SUSAN EMBRETSON (WHITELY), Professor of Psychology, University of Kansas, Lawrence, KS:

The Cognitive Skills Assessment Battery (CSAB) is an individually-administered test of the cognitive skills that are relevant to kindergarten and first grade curricula. The test is purported to have criterion-referenced validity for assessing skills in five major areas: (1) Orientation Toward One's Environment, (2) Discrimination of Similarities and Differences, (3) Comprehension and Concept Formation, (4) Coordination, and (5) Immediate and Delayed Memory.

The test content appears very similar to teaching materials that are presented to preschoolers and kindergartners. It contains identification and discrimination items such as color, shape, and symbols; picture comprehension and story comprehension items; letter naming, and so forth. The instructions are geared for administration by a psychometrically unsophisticated examiner, such as a teacher or an aide. Although examiner judgment is required for scoring performance "levels" for some items, the scoring instructions appear relatively uncomplicated.

Items were selected by an informal process to represent the criterion skills that were gleaned from examining curricular materials, classroom observations, interviewing teachers, and reviewing the research literature. However, exact item selection criteria are not given in the manual. This is a definite shortcoming, since item content is a major issue for criterion-referenced tests.

The CSAB normative sample consists of about 1,000 (total) prekindergarten and kindergarten children. The authors present data on the sex, ethnic background, native language, economic background, and community size for the normative sample. Although it is maintained that the sample represents the range of socioeconomic levels that are found nationally, neither information on sample selection nor national data for comparing the sample characteristics are presented. Presumably this sample is *not* representative, since only sixteen communities participated in the norming study.

The major normative data is presented for item responses. Mean scores on similar items related to goal area are also presented, but not standard deviations. The examiner is encouraged to interpret performance by goal area, in terms of mastery. According to the manual, "The individual teacher is best equipped to define the level of mastery appropriate for determining a child's competency in a given area." Thus, the interpretation of performance into competencies is unusually vague for a cognitive test.

Reliability data is provided from a single study of score stability over 2 to 3 weeks for 48 children. Average item agreement is 80%. Although the results from this study appear promising, one study on stability is not adequate. Other studies, with samples that vary in ethnic background, socioeconomic level, and other major characteristics, are clearly needed.

Stability is not the only type of reliability that is relevant to the CSAB. Since relatively unsophisticated examiners administer the CSAB, scorer reliability is particularly crucial. Unfortunately, no data are given. Internal consistency reliability is also relevant, at least for items within a goal area. Again, no results are presented.

One validity study is given in the manual. The content of the CSAB items is compared to 51 teachers' lists of competencies that are considered prerequisite to kindergarten and first grade. It was found that 85% of the listed competency areas were measured by CSAB.

Traditional validation studies are sorely lacking for CSAB. Correlations of CSAB with other tests of cognitive skills and achievement in kindergarten and first grade are highly relevant to the test's validity. Furthermore, studies of convergent and discriminant validity, group differences, and experimental studies also should be included.

Although the CSAB attempts to assess important preschool skills, it contains little useful technical data. The term "criterion-referenced" seemingly is used as a dispensation for normal technical standards for psychological tests. Neither newer psychometric methods for criterion-referenced and mastery tests nor more traditional psychometric methods are even considered as relevant. Yet, many questions which require psychometric answers could be generated. For example, do the particular item types represent adequately the "competencies" that they intend to measure? How well do the selected items represent their intended domains? Is mastery over the item domain uniform (i.e., correlated) or specific? What is mastery level? What is the score distribution? How do the measurements relate to attempts to change the cognitive skill area by educational intervention? Are the skills really prerequisite to kindergarten and first grade curricula?

In summary, the CSAB seeks to fulfill a definite need in assessing skills that are prerequisite to grade school. However, little psychometric development accompanies the instrument to evaluate its quality. Thus, this reviewer cannot recommend the test for routine assessments.

[243]

College Board English Composition Test with Essay. Candidates for college entrance; 1943–84; test administered each December at centers established by the publisher; 3 scores: essay, multiple-choice, total; no data on validity; no specific manual; English composition test with essay booklet ('79, 12 pages); mimeographed test analysis booklet ('83, 21 pages); 1984 price data: $17.50 per candidate; 60(65) minutes; program administered by The College Board and Educational Testing Service.*

For reviews on the College Board Achievement Test in English Composition (without essay) by David P. Harris and Leo P. Ruth, see 8:46 (2 references); see also T2:64 (1 reference) and 7:188 (10 references); for reviews by Charlotte Croon Davis, Robert C. Pooley, and Holland Roberts of earlier forms, see 6:287 (6 references); see also 5:204 (14 references); for a review by Charlotte Croon Davis (with Frederick B. Davis), see 4:178 (6 references). For reviews of the testing program, see 6:760 (2 reviews).

Review of College Board English Composition Test with Essay by DALE P. SCANNELL, Dean, School of Education, University of Kansas, Lawrence, KS:

Measuring student writing skills reliably, validly, and in a way acceptable to College Board patrons has been an elusive and time-consuming goal for the College Board during the past 40 years. After using various combinations of multiple-choice (M-C) and writing sample formats and a completely M-C format for several years, the Board responded in 1977 to general concerns about the erosion of high school student writing skills by re-introducing a 20-minute essay as a part of one English composition test. Because of costs, the composition test with essay is used only once each year, in the December administration; in all other national test administrations the M-C test is used.

The English Composition Test with Essay (ECTwE) includes two parts: Part A, which is the writing exercise; and Part B, which is in multiple-choice format. Part B is divided into three sections. The first includes 30 items covering problems of grammar, usage, diction, and idiom. The second section includes 25 items covering correctness and effectiveness of expression. The final section, interestingly, includes 15 items of the same type and focus as those in the first Part B section. All parts of the test are in one booklet, and examinees use one answer sheet for both the essay and objective exercises.

The time limit for the test is 60 minutes. Examinees begin with Part A, the essay. Examinees are advised that they will have 20 minutes for the essay and that those who have not already started Part B must do so when the supervisor announces that 20 minutes have elapsed. Examinees then are told they have 40 minutes remaining and if they finish Part B early they may spend the remaining time on either part.

This reviewer finds the directions to examinees concerning the use of time to be somewhat equivocal. The directions say, "Note that you are responsible for spending the proper amount of time on each part; the calling of time is merely a reminder." Yet earlier the directions say, "When [the] announcement is made, you must stop work on Part A and you must go on to Part B." Although examinees should be capable of following these directions, the conflicting statements may cause uncertainty or doubt at a time when full attention should be given to the relevant task.

The essay question in the form examined seems appropriate and challenging for the intended use of this test. Of equal importance, the topic seems likely to produce essays which differ qualitatively, and thus provide potential for scores at all points on the scale. Examinees are directed to plan and write an essay, agreeing or disagreeing with a statement provided and supporting their opinion with specific examples from personal experience or knowledge. Effective writing is noted as more important than the quantity written, but examinees are advised to cover the topic adequately.

Essays are scored by trained readers who use holistic scoring. Prior to the actual grading of essays, workshops are conducted using examples of the essays written by examinees. Great care is taken to ensure that the graders are using constant standards. Evidence collected by the College Board suggests that reasonable success in this regard has been achieved.

Each essay is read independently by two readers who assign a grade on a scale of 1 to 4, 0 being used only for essays which are off-topic. If readers split 4–1, 3–1, or 4–2, a third grading occurs. The score on the essay is the sum of the two readers' scores and is weighted so that it contributes one-third to the total score on the test.

As noted earlier, Part B is in multiple-choice format. The first 30 items and the last 15 are based on sentences which may contain errors in grammar, usage, diction, and idiom. Four parts of each sentence are underlined, labeled A to D. Examinees are to select the one part in which an error occurs or select E, meaning no error.

The balance among types of composition errors covered in these 45 sentences is quite good. However, it should be noted that the format presents different types of errors within a given sentence. Thus, examinees will be judging, for example, a possible grammar error versus a potential usage error rather than selecting the best alternative for a given writing situation.

Items 31–55 require examinees to select one of five ways to express an idea most effectively. A sentence is provided and the critical part is noted by underlining. Examinees are to decide whether the stimulus sentence or one of the alternatives most effectively phrases the underlined portion of the sentence. The 25 sentences sample different types of common composition problems.

The multiple-choice part of the test is formula scored, rights minus one-fourth of wrongs. Even so, the directions for the test make no reference to correction for guessing and provide no guidance to examinees for earning their best score. The only reference to formula scoring is in a separate publication. The absence of appropriate instructions is a weakness of this test.

Materials provided, in addition to the test booklet, include the "ATP Guide for High Schools and Colleges," the "Student Bulletin," a booklet prepared by the Chief Reader titled "The English Composition Test with Essay," an unpublished statistical report, "Test Analysis of College Board Achievement Examinations, English Composition Test with Essay, December 1982 Administration 3EBE," and a pre-publication draft of a new "Admissions Testing Program (ATP) Technical Handbook." The last item lacked the chapter on predictive validity that was being edited at the time of review.

These materials are appropriate and useful for the intended audiences. The information provided includes orientation for prospective examinees, guidelines for potential users of test data, and psychometric information for users and test reviewers.

The analysis of the December 1982 ECTwE provides the most appropriate technical information for assessing the test form provided to the reviewer. Several important characteristics are described below.

MEASURES OF TEST DIFFICULTY. The mean raw scores for Form 3EBE based on total examinees are 5.58, 32.34, and 59.21 for the Essay, Multiple-Choice, and Composite respectively; with standard deviations of 1.28, 12.52, and 16.39 for these scores in the same order. (The Composite or total score is determined by multiplying the Essay score by 4.841 and adding the Multiple-Choice score.) The Essay scores are slightly above the mid score of the scale and the M-C mean is slightly below the midscore of 35. Both averages fall in the middle range of possible scores. The ranges of earned scores and the percent of scores near the M-C chance score are appropriate.

SPEEDEDNESS OF TEST. Elaborate analyses are presented. For this form 65.6% of the examinees completed the entire M-C test, 80% completed 65 of the 70 items, and 96.7% completed at least 75% of the items. It is the reviewer's opinion that the test rewards students who take exams quickly. Examinees are given slightly more than 30 seconds per M-C item and only 20 minutes to plan, organize and write an essay.

RELIABILITY. The Dressel adaptation of the K-R 20 for formula-scored tests yielded reliability coefficients of .84 (Usage), .73 (Sentence Correction), and .88 (Multiple-Choice). Reliability for the essay is estimated to be between .45 and .70. The lower bound figure is based on results of an experiment, and the upper bound is the Spearman-Brown estimate based on a correlation of .54 between first and second readings of the essays and after adjudication of the two readings. The coefficients for the M-C Part B are quite good for a selective group of examinees, and a 40-minute time limit; the intercorrelation between grades on two readings of the essay is somewhat disappointing. The coefficient for the total score, .85–.89, is satisfactory given the nature of the test and the group taking the test.

This test provides a good measure of editing skills and an example of a student's writing skills. The psychometric qualities are generally quite good. Test directions need improvement, and users should be aware that the test favors examinees who work rapidly. The test is a useful tool for college admissions and placement purposes.

Review of College Board English Composition Test with Essay by JOHN C. SHERWOOD, Professor of English, University of Oregon, Eugene, OR:

A test of this character inevitably invites a whole complex of controversies. Some of them are basically political: on that score I shall only observe that, for better or worse, the Test with Essay is definitely a test of what most of us call standard English, what some would call middle-class English, and what might better be called textbook English, since few even of the middle classes can produce it without considerable training. For the consumer who accepts this state of affairs, of more immediate concern is the question as to what skills are actually being tested; are tests of this character really tests of the student's ability to write or merely of his adeptness at proofreading? The present instrument is of special interest since it combines the usual multiple-choice questions with an actual writing sample. As a matter of convenience, let us consider the two elements separately at first, though they are combined to produce the final score.

In judging the essay section we need to show a certain amount of charity, for the inherent difficulties are obvious. There are the time limitations, which mean that the student is performing as if on a midterm rather than on an outside assignment. There are the twin problems of unpredictable performance on the part of students and of unpredictable grading on the part of instructors. In my judgment the testers have done as well as could be expected. It may be disconcerting that the student must work under limitations not only of time but also of space, the room allotted on the answer sheet being such that handwriting must be kept to a "reasonable size." The essay topic is one that many of us would avoid on a regular assignment, since it invites pompous platitudes, but it is one on which any tolerably educated person would have ideas and for which he or she could easily furnish illustrations, even under pressure. Especially reassuring is the account of the scoring procedures. Grading is to be "holistic," to measure the total impression given by the passage rather than the minutiae, and considerable care is taken to see that the graders are not only holistic but also reasonably consistent with each other. Altogether this is a very good try at obtaining a usable score from a writing sample.

The multiple-choice section will present few surprises to the experienced test user. In spite of the assaults it had to endure from the structural linguists back in the 50s, the old textbook grammar is very much alive, and woe to the college-bound senior who does not have some conception of it, even in its more pedantic aspects. Whatever its value for effective communication, whatever its relationship to actual usage, it is dear to the hearts of test-writers, and the reason is easy to see: it is eminently suited to multiple choice, machine-graded testing. It may be very hard to test in this way for originality and organization; it may take a good deal of ingenuity to test for logic and transitions; but testing for agreement is simplicity itself, provided everyone concerned accepts the validity of the textbook rules. The tendency to test what is most testable rather than what is most important is all too obvious in this section. Two concessions are in order. Many of the items involve questions of idiom, where memorizable rules may not apply and the student's feeling for language must take over; and the majority of the bad examples not only are technically faulty but also impair readability and even comprehension. Still, there seems an excessive preoccupation with agreement and parallelism, possibly also with dangling constructions; reference, the most troublesome error in practice, comes in fourth. Finally, the student who has mastered the art tested here could certainly write elegant sentences, but there would be no assurances that he could assemble them into an acceptable composition. It is sometimes tempting to feel that much of the activity in teaching and testing is more like a series of ceremonies in honor of literacy than like an effective system for bringing literacy about.

So where does the profession stand? As our educational system is constructed, it is absolutely necessary to do some sort of rating of high school seniors to determine college entrance and placement after entrance. Rating solely on the basis of writing samples would be intolerably expensive, and there is no assurance that the result would be completely reliable as a predictor of college performance. We seem to be resigned to the multiple-choice test, nourishing the hope that the scores will more or less correlate with active writing skills, a hope which is supported by some statistical evidence. As for the test now being reviewed, I would myself be happier if the multiple-choice section were expanded from a consideration of largely stylistic matters to include such testable issues as logic and transitions. At the same time, there is the writing sample, and there is some assurance that it will be consistently scored. The combination of the two sections could well give us as reliable a predictor as is now available.

[244]

College Board Scholastic Aptitude Test and Test of Standard Written English. Candidates for college entrance; 1926–84; SAT, TSWE; test administered 7 times annually (January, April, May, June, October, November, December) at centers established by the publishers; 3 scores: verbal, mathematical, standard written English; verbal subscores (reading, vocabulary) also available; 9 new forms issued annually; 2 tests in a single booklet; guidelines on the uses of College Board test scores and related data ('81, 8 pages); guide to the College Board validity study service ('82, 58 pages); technical handbook ('85); Admissions Testing Program guide ('83, 31 pages); student bulletin ('83, 32 pages); taking the SAT ('83, 63 pages); test and technical data ('80, 36 pages); SAT question and answer booklet ('83, 24 pages); test analysis of SAT ('84, 36 pages); test analysis of TSWE ('84, 17 pages); using the TSWE ('83, 6 pages); 1984 price data: examination fee, $11 per candidate; 180(240) minutes; program administered by The College Board and Educational Testing Service.*

See T3:501 (152 references), 8:182 (217 references), and T2:357 (148 references); for reviews by Philip H. DuBois and Wimburn L. Wallace of an earlier form, see 7:344 (298 references); for reviews by John E. Bowers and Wayne S. Zimmerman, see 6:449 (79 references); for a review by John T. Dailey, see 5:318 (20 references); for a review by Frederick B. Davis, see 4:285 (22 references). For reviews of the testing program, see 6:760 (2 reviews).

TEST REFERENCES

1. Bernstein, B. E., Effect of menstruation on academic performance among college women. ARCHIVES OF SEXUAL BEHAVIOR, 1977, 6, 289–296.

2. Templer, D. I. Death anxiety and mental ability. ESSENCE, 1979, 3, 85–89.

3. Alderman, D. L. Language proficiency as a moderator variable in testing academic aptitude. JOURNAL OF EDUCATIONAL PSYCHOLOGY, 1982, 74, 580–587.

4. Bejar, I. I., & Wingersky, M. S. A study of pre-equating based on item response theory. APPLIED PSYCHOLOGICAL MEASUREMENT, 1982, 6, 309–325.

5. Benbow, C. P., & Stanley, J. C. Consequences in high school and college of sex differences in mathematical reasoning ability: A longitudinal perspective. AMERICAN EDUCATIONAL RESEARCH JOURNAL, 1982, 19, 598–622.

6. Bridgeman, B. Comparative validity of the College Board Scholastic Aptitude Test—Mathematics and the Descriptive Tests of Mathematics Skills for predicting performance in college mathematics courses. EDUCATIONAL AND PSYCHOLOGICAL MEASUREMENT, 1982, 42, 361–366.

7. Decker, W. D. An investigation of the procedures used to assign students to remedial oral communication instruction. COMMUNICATION EDUCATION, 1982, 16, 131–140.

8. Dempster, F. N., & Cooney, J. B. Individual differences in digit span, susceptibility to proactive interference, and aptitude/achievement test scores. INTELLIGENCE, 1982, 6, 399–416.

9. Resnick, H., Viehe, J., & Segal, S. Is math anxiety a local phenomenon? A study of prevalence and dimensionality. JOURNAL OF COUNSELING PSYCHOLOGY, 1982, 29, 39–47.

10. Sanford, T. R. Predicting college graduation for black and white freshman applicants. COLLEGE AND UNIVERSITY, 1982, 57, 265–278.

11. Wood, P. H. The Nelson-Denny Reading Test as a predictor of college freshman grades. EDUCATIONAL AND PSYCHOLOGICAL MEASUREMENT, 1982, 42, 575–583.

12. Alexander, K. L., & Pallas, A. M. Private schools and public policy: New evidence on cognitive achievement in public and private schools. SOCIOLOGY OF EDUCATION, 1983, 56, 170–182.

13. DeVito, A. J., Tryon, G. S., & Carlson, J. F. Scholastic aptitude decline and changes in study habits and attitudes. JOURNAL OF COLLEGE STUDENT PERSONNEL, 1983, 24, 411–416.

14. Grossman, F. M., & Johnson, K. M. Validity of the Slosson and Otis-Lennon in predicting achievement of gifted students. EDUCATIONAL AND PSYCHOLOGICAL MEASUREMENT, 1983, 43, 617–622.

15. Hess, J. H., Grafton, C. L., & Michael, W. B. The predictive validity of cognitive and affective measures in a small religiously oriented liberal arts college. EDUCATIONAL AND PSYCHOLOGICAL MEASUREMENT, 1983, 43, 865–872.

16. Higgins, A. S. Student financial aid and equal opportunity in higher education. COLLEGE AND UNIVERSITY, 1983, 58, 341–361.

17. Hogrebe, M. C., Ervin, L., Dwinell, P. L., & Newman, I. The moderating effects of gender and race in predicting the academic performance of college developmental students. EDUCATIONAL AND PSYCHOLOGICAL MEASUREMENT, 1983, 43, 523–530.

18. Houston, L. N. The comparative predictive validities of high school rank, the Ammons Quick Test, and two Scholastic Aptitude Test measures for a sample of black female college students. EDUCATIONAL AND PSYCHOLOGICAL MEASUREMENT, 1983, 43, 1123–1126.

19. Johnson, T. F., & Butts, D. P. The relationship among college science student achievement, engaged time, and personal characteristics. JOURNAL OF RESEARCH IN SCIENCE TEACHING, 1983, 20, 357–366.

20. Levine, M. V., & Drasgow, F. The relation between incorrect option choice and estimated ability. EDUCATIONAL AND PSYCHOLOGICAL MEASUREMENT, 1983, 43, 675–685.

21. McCornack, R. L. Bias in the validity of predicted college grades in four ethnic minority groups. EDUCATIONAL AND PSYCHOLOGICAL MEASUREMENT, 1983, 43, 517–522.

22. Peterson, J. M., & Lansky, L. M. Success in architecture: A research note. PERCEPTUAL AND MOTOR SKILLS, 1983, 57, 222.

23. Raymond, M. R., & Roberts, D. M. Development and validation of a foreign language attitude scale. EDUCATIONAL AND PSYCHOLOGICAL MEASUREMENT, 1983, 43, 1239–1246.

24. Savage, T. V. The academic qualifications of women choosing education as a major. JOURNAL OF TEACHER EDUCATION, 1983, 34, 14–19.

25. Taylor, K. M., & Betz, N. E. Applications of self-efficacy theory to the understanding and treatment of career indecision. JOURNAL OF VOCATIONAL BEHAVIOR, 1983, 22, 63–81.

26. Tracey, T. J., Sedlacek, W. E., & Miars, R. D. Applying ridge regression to admissions data by race and sex. COLLEGE AND UNIVERSITY, 1983, 58, 313–317.

27. Zak, P. M., Benbow, C. P., & Stanley, J. C. Several factors associated with success as an undergraduate chemistry major. COLLEGE AND UNIVERSITY, 1983, 58, 303–312.

28. Zeleznik, C., Hojat, M., & Veloski, J. Long-range predictive and differential validities of the Scholastic Aptitude Test in medical school. EDUCATIONAL AND PSYCHOLOGICAL MEASUREMENT, 1983, 43, 223–232.

29. Dukes, F., & Gaither, G. A campus cluster program: Effects on persistence and academic performance. COLLEGE AND UNIVERSITY, 1984, 59, 150–166.

30. Serwatka, T. S., Hesson, D., & Graham, M. The effect of indirect intervention on the improvement of hearing-impaired students' reading scores. THE VOLTA REVIEW, 1984, 86, 81–88.

31. Stricker, L. J. Test disclosure and retest performance on the SAT. APPLIED PSYCHOLOGICAL MEASUREMENT, 1984, 8, 81–87.

Review of College Board Scholastic Aptitude Test and Test of Standard Written English by SANFORD J. COHN, Deputy Director, The Johns Hopkins University Center for the Advancement of Academically Talented Youth, and Lecturer in Psychology, The Johns Hopkins University, Baltimore, MD:

The College Entrance Examination Board's Scholastic Aptitude Test (SAT) is designed to offer a measure of the developed verbal and mathematical abilities of high school candidates for college entrance. Verbal and mathematical scores are reported separately. The SAT is intended to provide objective information about student abilities to use in conjunction with such other means of assessment as the high-school record, letters of recommendation, essays, and portfolios to determine admissibility to a college or university. The SAT and the Test of Standard Written English (TSWE), a measure of the student's developed skills in the correct use of the English language, are administered jointly in a 3-hour testing session six times a year at more than 3,800 test administration sites (500 of which are located in 100 foreign countries on six continents).

Each form of the SAT consists of six equal sections of 30 minutes duration: two are verbal, two are mathematical; one is the Test of Standard Written English, and one is reserved for research to gather information for equating different forms of the test, for pretesting items to determine their psychometric characteristics and their overall utility for future tests, and for conducting other research.

The verbal sections consist of four different item types: antonyms, analogies, sentence completions, and reading comprehension. Since 1974, in addition to the total verbal score, students have also received a vocabulary subscore based on the antonyms and analogies and a reading subscore based on the sentence completion and reading comprehension items. Each verbal section contains all four types of items. Item content is drawn from a variety of substantive areas spanning the humanities and the sciences.

The mathematical sections include only two distinct kinds of items: regular mathematics items and quantitative comparisons. The latter type offers four choices, requires special directions, and demands evaluation of the relative size of two expressions or quantities. Formal courses in algebra and Euclidean geometry are not prerequisite to the SAT mathematical section; rather knowledge of basic arithmetic processes, introductory algebra, and geometry form the item content.

The Test of Standard Written English (TSWE) evolved in the 1970s as a result of the sense, shared by American educators and the general public, of a "writing crisis" developing among students. The TSWE was designed for colleges to determine whether or not their applicants possess the writing skills college course work requires of them. Because those students who have deficiencies in their use of the conventions of the English language were the targets of this test, it is much easier than the verbal and mathematical sections of the SAT. It is intended to help place entering students in freshmen writing courses of varying difficulty and demand. Two types of items are included in the TSWE: usage and sentence correction. Usage items require recognition of writing that does not follow the conventions of standard written English; sentence correction items not only require recognition of unacceptable phrasing, but also choice of the best way of rephrasing the offending sentence component.

The sixth section of the SAT, called the "variable" section because its content changes from form to form, contains questions that do not contribute to the student's score, but serve to provide information necessary to equate differing forms of the test (past, present, and future), to try out items for use in future tests, or to gather information relevant to other research. Items in this section are made to appear indistinguishable from items in the other five operational sections of the SAT.

SCORING. The SAT/TSWE consists entirely of multiple-choice items with usually five choices per item (with the exception of four choices in the quantitative comparison items). Since 1953 raw scores have been determined by the formula (Number Right)—(Number Wrong)/(k − 1), where k = the number of choices. Prior to that time, even though test directions had discouraged (and continue to discourage) strictly random guessing, number right scoring had been used. The change to formula scoring resulted from a concern that students who were more comfortable with guessing were likely to earn higher scores under those conditions. Unless students are given explicit directions to mark every item, it was considered unethical not to use the formula correction for guessing.

Scores reported to students and to test users are scaled scores, computed in such a way as to be comparable across different forms of the tests and across different groups of test takers. The SAT scale ranges from 200 to 800, with the final digit always 0. For the reading and vocabulary subscores of the SAT-Verbal section, the trailing zero is dropped and a two-digit score is reported. These two subscores are reported on a scale ranging from 20 to 80 that corresponds to the 200 to 800 scale used for the total verbal score. Similarly, a two-digit score is reported for the TSWE, but the highest possible score is 60+, because of the relative easiness of the test.

The process for equating the SAT scores relies on a complex linkage of each form of the SAT to one or more previous forms. For all intents and purposes, efforts to make all forms of the SAT parallel succeed by adherence to well defined test specifications that include the distribution of item content, the distribution of item difficulties, and the average of item-test correlations.

RELIABILITY. Reliability of SAT scores is based primarily on an internal consistency estimation, using an adaptation (Dressel, 1940) of the familiar Kuder-Richardson 20 for use with formula scores. Typical internal consistency reliability coefficients exceed .90. Test-retest correlations average approximately .87 for both the mathematical and verbal sections. Internal consistency reliability coefficients for the vocabulary and reading subscores hover around .85; for the TSWE, around .88. The median test-retest reliability for the TSWE is .82.

VALIDITY. Both the SAT and TSWE are intended to help college admissions officials select and place students. Students with high SAT scores should tend, then, to get higher grades in college than those with lower scores. Since 1964, when The College Board initiated its Validity Study Service to examine how well SAT scores correlate with such external criteria as college grades and other predictors in admissions, more than 3,500 studies have been conducted at 750 colleges. Such investigations have shown that SAT scores are indeed correlated with college performance.

Studies other than criterion-related validity studies, focusing on content or construct validity, have also been conducted. For example, the language of the SAT, the vocabulary employed in its items, is consistent with that experienced in college study. The most difficult SAT items were found not to have been constructed from verbal obscurities. In spite of the fact, moreover, that the difficulty level of the reading passages was found consistently near college level, the corrected readability grade-level has varied from 6th to 10th grade. Careful attention has been paid, in addition, to ensure that item content has not become obsolete over the years. Analyses of items to remove cultural bias and sexist language have also been performed at both psychometric and psychological levels. Reviews of test items by committees of college and high-school faculty have been undertaken to find and remove those that might contain language potentially offensive to certain subgroups.

Studies of the effects of sizable amounts of coaching (57 hours for the verbal section, 19 hours for the mathematical section) on SAT performance have found that such efforts tend to increase scores by an average of 15 scaled points (less than 2 additional raw score points), the same figure found to characterize the effect resulting from prior experience taking the SAT. Extensive materials are provided without cost, moreover, to anyone who has signed up to take the SAT to ensure a consistent degree of "testwiseness" across all groups. One pamphlet, entitled Taking the SAT, not only offers detailed descriptions about each item type, but also contains a complete form of the SAT for practice. Recent legislation requiring disclosure of forms used in specified administrations of the SAT in New York has resulted in The College Board's release of 10 retired forms of the examinations. A highly motivated student has more than 30 hours of practice, then, to prepare for taking the SAT, if he or she chooses to do so. While studies have shown that such practice does not yield vast increases in scores, it does aid the student in feeling more comfortable while taking the test.

Despite the fact that the SAT was originally designed for use with culminating high-school students, since 1972 it has also been found valuable in identifying junior high school age youths who reason extremely well mathematically and/or verbally. Initially used for this purpose by the Study of Mathematically Precocious Youth (SMPY), the SAT serves as the basis of Talent Searches conducted by several universities across the nation and in several foreign countries. In 1984 more than 75,000 seventh and eighth graders took the SAT as Talent Search participants. Reports of short-term and longitudinal studies conducted since 1972 suggest that the SAT provides a firm indicator of precociously developed reasoning abilities in both the mathematical and verbal areas.

SUMMARY. The SAT remains the best documented instrument of its kind. Detailed manuals describing all phases of its administration, use, and interpretation ensure maximum likelihood of standardized test conditions, in spite of its widespread use and multiple administration sites. State-of-the-art techniques of equating test forms and scoring and reporting test results make its use convenient and accessible to all. Meticulous test security practices and required reporting of irregularities in test administration make it practically immune to cheating and other forms of abuse. A multitude of studies concerning its reliability and validity have been and continue to be conducted. Careful attention on the part of the SAT publisher, Educational Testing Service, to its value as a supplement to other measures for evaluating applicants for college admission serves to enhance the probability of its appropriate use.

Other test batteries exist for assisting college admissions personnel in selecting applicants, in particular the American College Testing Program's four-part test battery and the University of Washington Pre-College Test. These tests rely more heavily, however, on the student's having taken specific course work than the SAT does, which consequently makes them less aptitude tests than achievement tests.

REVIEWER'S REFERENCES

Dressel, P. L. Some remarks on the Kuder-Richardson reliability coefficient. PSYCHOMETRIKA, 1940, 5, 305–310.

Review of College Board Scholastic Aptitude Test and Test of Standard Written English by LEE J. CRONBACH, Fellow, Center for the Study of Youth Development, Stanford University, Stanford, CA:

The context of admissions testing changed radically in the late 1960s, when student protesters made the Scholastic Aptitude Test (SAT) a symbol of elitism, technocracy, the unhappy fate of minorities, and much else. Even prior to those events, the College Board had come to see test takers as well as colleges as clients, and had begun to modify procedures to help students understand their scores and to reduce risks of scoring error, misuse of scores, and bias. Now the fine orientation booklet, Taking the SAT, introduces each type of test item, suggests tactics that use time efficiently, and provides a practice examination with key. For institutional users, a document entitled Guidelines on the Uses of College Board Test Scores and Related Data (1981) stresses the importance of informing test takers about intended uses of scores, and discourages uses for which scores are not well suited. Colleges are urged not to require applicants to take the SAT if the scores will play little part in the decision to admit.

Since colleges want all editions of the Scholastic Aptitude Test to provide equivalent information, change in the test since 1960 has been slight. The techniques used in test development have become more complex and more subtle. Even so, the new Technical Handbook (Donlon, 1985) tells essentially the same story as its 1971 predecessor, except as it offers additional insight into what makes for good and poor scores. One fact in the Handbook is newsworthy because of the furore about the "decline of SAT" in self-selected samples: Norms for the preliminary SAT for representative high-school juniors show no downward trend from 1960 to 1983.

The Test of Standard Written English (TSWE), added in 1974, is not intended for use in admissions. TSWE aims to give a dependable basis for assigning each enrollee to appropriate instruction in English. Each item asks the student to identify which segment of a sentence is faulty or to choose a best wording. Success requires an ear for lucid, well-formed sentences; grammatical rules and conventions play a lesser role. "The most important concern [in evaluating a placement test] should be content validity" as judged by the local faculty, we are told. (This is questionable, as judgments about likely predictors often prove to be wrong.) TSWE would meet that standard only halfway. Instructors value what TSWE measures, but they value at least equally things these items cannot measure, notably organization between and within paragraphs.

Only 80% of the true-score variance comes from whatever writing samples measure (Breland & Gaynor, 1979). TSWE scores of blacks average 1.2 *SD* below those of whites, compared to a difference of 0.7 *SD* on essay writing; males' scores overlap scores of females more on TSWE than on the essay (Breland & Griswold, 1982). The two kinds of writing test differ, then, on a variable having important correlates.

On empirical validity for placement, the Handbook says nothing relevant. The needed justification is a demonstrated statistical interaction between TSWE scores and the instructional options, carried out for the courses of each college separately. When a uniform measure of writing ability is collected following the alternative courses of instruction, regression coefficients onto the initial placement score should differ from course to course. (Additional considerations enter a full interpretation.) Although the Guide to the College Board Validity Study Service (1982) presents this logic, the chapter is riddled with questionable statements and emphases. If we take the available evidence (Breland, Conlon, & Rogosa, 1976; Breland, 1977) at face value, TSWE will not improve placement decisions in most colleges.

For SAT, ingenious items were developed so as to discriminate validly among candidates of the highest calibre. In general, difficulty is achieved by requiring precise and complex thought. Analogy and antonym items do not bring in rare words; they ask for close comparisons among plausible answer options. Few mathematics items ask for content knowledge above the eighth-grade level, and the four geometric theorems that examinees may need to know are laid out in the orientation booklet. Each question arises out of a novel configuration of elementary facts; the student has to find a line of attack and move unerringly through several logical steps. The reading items are less impressive. Difficulty is achieved by presenting poorly written selections and by requiring convoluted thought processes not usual in college reading.

Antonym and analogy items provide a vocabulary subscore; sentence completions and questions on column-long text selections provide a reading subscore. Reporting the subscores appears to be a bad idea. The ATP (Admissions Testing Program) Guide (1983) that serves most interpreters as a manual warns that a 9-point difference on the 60-point scale is necessary to be "certain" (!) that one ability exceeds the other. (The standard error of the difference is near 6.) No evidence is offered that the subscores are distinctive, their true scores correlate higher than 0.9, and the group factors linking item types within subscores are weak (Rock & Werts, 1979).

The combination of SAT with high school rank predicts college grades as well as can be hoped for. Ten years ago, SAT was being charged with systematically "underpredicting" the grade averages of Blacks and Hispanics. Research has not supported that charge, though technical problems of comparing regressions make the research equivocal (Linn, 1983). The Validity Study Service will analyze local predictive validity (with no fee) for any college that provides criterion data; its Guide (1982) explains such studies admirably. In proposing to develop formulas from 75 cases, however, the Guide is insensitive regarding validity generalization, robust statistics, and Bayesian reasoning. Small colleges, the ones most dependent on the Service, will rarely gain by fitting formulas to their limited data. Overrefinement mars some technical documents; here is an example: Data from a large freshman class in Year 1 yielded a formula used for Year-2 selection. In Year 2 the validity is 0.542. A fresh formula derived from Year-2 data has validity 0.545 (shrunken R); therefore the new formula is said to be "preferable." Because of truncation, the difference of 0.003 is fallacious as well as miniscule.

The scaling that keeps the meaning of the 600-point Verbal (V) and Mathematical (M) scales stable has always been as precise as available psychometric theory permitted. Recent SAT equating is based on item response theory, with the hope that the small departures from equivalence found in some past years will be eliminated. When variance from one testing to another is recognized as error, the standard error of V is approximately 34; of M, 37. SAT documents warn readers about measurement error but say too little about variation over occasions; my estimates are calculated from deeply buried numbers (Donlon, 1985, Table 3.17). A college should not regard one applicant as a better prospect than another on the basis of a 30-point score difference; facts other than those scores should be used to choose between the two.

The package of tests and services is excellent, apart from the doubtful utility of TSWE. If schools and colleges come to understand the import of the Guidelines, admissions testing will be subject to little legitimate criticism, save from those who have philosophical objections. Reasoning about psychometric matters is not uniformly excellent in the documentation, but the SAT proper has no major fault.

A college considering this system or the competing American College Testing Program can choose among many alternative packages of services and can tailor its own pattern of utilization. What one college values may not benefit another or may be too costly to its applicants; hence a general statement comparing the two programs is inappropriate. The scores have comparable predictive validity. Colleges need more of the information that could be derived from examinees who take both SAT and ACT, and the test sponsors should collaborate to provide it. Unless a college has a compelling reason to rely on one of the two programs, it probably should advise applicants that scores from either battery will be equally welcome; comparatively few candidates would then have to take both.

REVIEWER'S REFERENCES

Breland, H. M., Conlon, G. C., & Rogosa, D. A PRELIMINARY STUDY OF THE TEST OF STANDARD WRITTEN ENGLISH. Princeton, NJ: Educational Testing Service, 1976.

Breland, H. M. A STUDY OF COLLEGE ENGLISH PLACEMENT AND THE TEST OF STANDARD WRITTEN ENGLISH. RDR-76-77, No. 4. Princeton, NJ: Educational Testing Service, 1977.

Breland, H. M., & Gaynor, J. L. A comparison of direct and indirect assessments of writing skill. JOURNAL OF EDUCATIONAL MEASUREMENT, 1979, 16, 119-128.

Rock, D. A., & Werts, C. E. CONSTRUCT VALIDITY OF THE SAT ACROSS POPULATIONS—AN EMPIRICAL CONFIRMATORY STUDY. RDR 78-79, No. 5. Princeton, NJ: Educational Testing Service, 1979.

GUIDELINES ON THE USES OF COLLEGE BOARD TEST SCORES AND RELATED DATA. New York: College Entrance Examination Board, 1981.

Breland, H. M., & Griswold, P. A. Use of a performance test as a criterion in a differential validity study. JOURNAL OF EDUCATIONAL PSYCHOLOGY, 1982, 74, 713-721.

GUIDE TO THE COLLEGE BOARD VALIDITY STUDY SERVICE. New York: College Entrance Examination Board, 1982.

ATP GUIDE FOR HIGH SCHOOLS AND COLLEGES. New York: College Entrance Examination Board, 1983.

Linn, R. L. Predictive bias as an artifact of selection procedure. In H. Wainer and S. Messick (Eds.), PRINCIPLES OF MODERN PSYCHOLOGICAL MEASUREMENT. Hillsdale, NJ: Erlbaum, 1983.

Donlon, T. F. (Ed.). THE TECHNICAL HANDBOOK FOR THE COLLEGE BOARD SCHOLASTIC APTITUDE TEST AND ACHIEVEMENT TESTS. New York: College Entrance Examination Board, 1985.

[245]

College-Level Examination Program. 1-2 years of college or equivalent; 1964-84; CLEP; "a way for earning college credit for what you have learned," tests administered monthly (except February and December) at centers throughout the United States; 2 series of examinations; 1984 rental and scoring fee: $30 per test; fee includes reporting of scores to the candidate and one college; program administered for the College Entrance Examination Board by Educational Testing Service.*

a) CLEP GENERAL EXAMINATIONS. 1964-84; 5 tests: English Composition, Humanities, Mathematics, Natural Sciences, Social Sciences and History; separate answer folders must be used; 90(100) minutes per test.

b) CLEP SUBJECT EXAMINATIONS. 1964-84. 30 tests; most tests have an optional essay supplement which is scored by the college; separate answer sheets must be used; 90(95) minutes per test, 90(95) minutes for essay supplement.

1) *Business*. 5 tests.
- *a*) Computers and Data Processing.
- *b*) Introduction to Management.
- *c*) Introductory Accounting.
- *d*) Introductory Business Law.
- *e*) Introductory Marketing.

2) *Composition and Literature*. 5 tests.
- *a*) American Literature.
- *b*) Analysis and Interpretation of Literature.
- *c*) College Composition.
- *d*) English Literature.
- *e*) Freshman English.

3) *Foreign Languages*. 3 tests.
- *a*) College French, Levels 1 and 2.
- *b*) College German, Levels 1 and 2.
- *c*) College Spanish, Levels 1 and 2.

4) *History and Social Sciences*. 11 tests.
- *a*) American Government.
- *b*) American History I: Early Colonization to 1877.
- *c*) American History II: 1865 to the Present.
- *d*) Educational Psychology.
- *e*) General Psychology.
- *f*) Human Growth and Development.
- *g*) Introductory Macroeconomics.
- *h*) Introductory Microeconomics.
- *i*) Introductory Sociology.
- *j*) Western Civilization I: Ancient Near East to 1648.
- *k*) Western Civilization II: 1648 to the Present.

5) *Science and Mathematics*. 6 tests.
- *a*) Calculus with Elementary Functions.
- *b*) College Algebra.
- *c*) College Algebra-Trigonometry.
- *d*) General Biology.
- *e*) General Chemistry.
- *f*) Trigonometry.

See T3:506 (7 references); for reviews by Paul L. Dressel, David A. Frisbie, and Wimburn L. Wallace of an earlier program, see 8:473 (15 references); for reviews of the General Examinations, see 8:8 (2 reviews); for reviews of the separate Subject Examinations, see 8:43 (1 review), 8:44 (1 review), 8:64 (1 review), 8:65 (1 review), 8:66 (1 review), 8:255 (1 review), 8:256 (1 review), 8:297 (1 review), 8:365 (1 review), 8:460 (1 review), 8:832 (1 review), 8:847 (1 review), 8:911 (1 review), 8:919 (1 review), 8:1119 (1 review), and 8:1120 (1 review); see also T2:1050 (4 references); for reviews by Alexander W. Astin, Benjamin S. Bloom, and Warren G. Findley, see 7:664 (7 references).

TEST REFERENCES

1. Arnold, L., Calkins, E. V., & Willoughby, T. L. Can achievement in high school predict performance in college, medical school, and beyond? COLLEGE AND UNIVERSITY, 1983, 59, 95–101.

[246]

College Student Experiences. College; 1979–81; quality of effort students put into the opportunities offered by the college environment; 4 areas: college activities, opinions about college, college environment, estimate of gains; norms consist of means for college activities area only (available in monograph, Measuring Quality of Effort); 1 form ('79, 8 pages); information booklet ('81, 16 pages); 1985 price data: $175 participation fee (includes normative report, summary computer report, tape); $.40 per test plus information booklet; Intran scoring service, $1 per test; administration time not reported; C. Robert Pace; Higher Education Research Institute of the University of California, Los Angeles.*

TEST REFERENCES

1. Michael, J. J., Nadson, J. S., & Michael, W. B. Student background and quality of effort correlates of reported grades, opinions about college, and perceptions of magnitudes of cognitive and affective attainment by students in a public comprehensive university. EDUCATIONAL AND PSYCHOLOGICAL MEASUREMENT, 1983, 43, 495–507.

Review of College Student Experiences by ROBERT D. BROWN, Professor of Educational Psychology, University of Nebraska, Lincoln, NE:

The College Student Experiences questionnaire is a standardized self-report survey of how students spend their time and the nature and quality of their activities. Besides collecting background information from students it provides scaled scores on 14 dimensions of college activities, eight dimensions of the college environment, and 18 estimates of gains during college. Suggested institutional uses include self-studies for purposes of program evaluation, resource allocation, and faculty and staff discussions. Potential research uses include investigations pursuing a wide range of questions on the relationships between quality of student experiences and institutional characteristics. The manual suggests the questionnaire be administered after about two-thirds and not later than three-fourths of the way through the academic year. Administration takes 30 to 45 minutes. All questionnaires are centrally processed.

The major part of the questionnaire is the Quality of Effort scale, an activities checklist. Students respond by checking "never," "occasionally," "often," or "very often" to activities in 14 clusters of mostly 10 items: Library Experiences; Course Learning; Art, Music, Theater; Science Lab Activities; Student Union; Athletic and Recreation Facilities; Dormitory or Fraternity/Sorority; Experiences with Faculty; Clubs and Organizations; Experiences in Writing; Personal Experiences; Student Acquaintances; Topics of Conversation; and Information in Conversation. A unique and important characteristic of the Quality of Effort scales is that they are Guttman scales, which means that items are arranged in a hierarchy and it is assumed that participation in a high activity is qualitatively different than participation in a lower activity. This attempt alone makes the instrument and research related to it a valuable addition for theorists and practitioners attempting to understand student development. For the most part, the items concern process rather than outcomes.

The measures of College Environment include eight, one-item rating scales. Four relate to various aspects of students' development and four to relationships among people at the college. Students respond on a seven-point scale with one end defined as "strong emphasis" and the other end as "weak emphasis."

Eighteen educational goals make up the Estimate of Gains scale with students responding, "very little," "some," "quite a bit," and "very much" to indicate the extent they feel they have gained or made progress.

The College Student Experiences questionnaire offers institutions and researchers an instrument to assess objectively dimensions of college life that have been only sporadically measured. It measures students' level of and the quality of involvement in a broad range of campus activities including curricular and co-curricular. The convenience of having these measures in one instrument along with students' self-reported characterizations of the college environment and their estimates of personal gains is a major accomplishment. Many institutional studies and research efforts have had to rely on quickly constructed home-made instruments. The College Student Experiences questionnaire provides researchers with an instrument for further studies of college student life and development that could make comparisons across studies more meaningful.

The process used to develop the questionnaire was psychometrically sound and the arguments for its validity well documented. This is particularly true for the Quality of Effort scales. As indicated in the manual, the items for each scale correlated significantly with each other and each item correlates with the total score for its scale. Alpha reliability coefficients ranged from .79 to .90. A factor analysis indicated a dominant factor in every scale accounted for at least 70% of the variance. There was an adequate range of scores on each scale and about half of the scales had a mean near the middle of the distribution.

The results of factor analysis of the three scales tells almost as much about college life as they do about the scales. Subscale scores of the Quality of Effort scale correlated with each other from .06 to .60 with a median of .30. Factor analysis of the Quality of Effort scales resulted in three factors: Personal Relationships, Group Facilities, and Academic-Intellectual Activities. Artistic activities and science lab activities remained distinct and did not fit in the three major factors.

The College Environment items correlated with each other from .02 to .59 with a median of .24. Factor analysis yielded two factors: Supportive Relationships and Intellectual, Cultural, and Esthetic Emphasis.

The Estimate of Gains items correlated with each other from –.04 to .78 with a median of .23. Factor analysis yielded four factors: Personal and Interpersonal Understanding, General Education, Intellectual Competencies, and Understanding Science.

The pattern of the intercorrelations and the factors are generally congruent with theoretical constructs about student life, and the pattern of responses lends support to the hierarchial nature of the Quality of Effort scales.

The College Student Experiences questionnaire represents a significant step forward in providing institutions and researchers with a picture of what students do during the college year. But this is a long way from where research in this area needs to go and what needs to be done to make this approach more comprehensive and valuable.

Unfortunately, items assessing the College Environment and Estimate of Gains are almost entirely perceptual and for the most part not behaviorally specific. Students are asked, for example, to indicate their college's emphasis on "being critical, evaluative, and analytical," rather than responding to behavioral descriptions of that characteristic. The Estimate of Gains questions also ask for student perceptions of gains, (e.g., developing good health habits and physical fitness) rather than responses to specific behavioral indices. The Quality of Effort items focus on what the student has done, which is to be applauded, but the other scales request mainly perceptions of sometimes vague generalizations.

The test author discusses past studies supporting the credibility of student self-reports. This evidence is helpful as is the pattern of correlations, reported differences among types of institutions, and other indices of construct and content validity. This should not forestall, however, future efforts to provide evidence of predictive validity related to measures independent of the College Student Experiences questionnaire. The same is true for reliability. The alpha coefficients are adequate but test-retest reliability is also necessary. Little or no information is provided in the basic manual regarding reliability of the College Environment or the Estimate of Gain scales.

The rationale for focusing for the most part on students' use of facilities and other opportunities for learning and development in a college setting seems appropriate, as the goal is to look at the process of learning rather than the product. Yet, when scales such as self-understanding are included, some users will wish the test developer had gone somewhat further and included opportunities and experiences related to spirituality, intimacy, career development, and other developmental goals. This problem illustrates the difficulty of making distinctions between process and product when studying college student life.

In summary, the College Student Experiences questionnaire is a valuable addition to the instruments available for institutional research, program evaluation, and researchers studying student life. It combines a variety of scales useful for documenting students' activities, their perceptions of the college environment, and self-reported measures of gains. Research reported thus far indicates the scales are internally reliable and have good construct and content validity. Direct indications of concurrent or predictive validity are lacking. The information provided by the College Student Experiences questionnaire should be particularly useful when combined with additional questions of particular interest or relevance to a specific institution. Anyone studying college student life should consider this instrument in lieu of constructing their own home-made version.

Review of College Student Experiences by JOHN K. MILLER, Associate Dean for Graduate Studies and Associate Professor, Graduate School of Education and Human Development, University of Rochester, Rochester, NY:

In this reviewer's judgment extravagant claims to psychometric quality accompany a dubious rationale for the theoretical relevance and practical value of the College Student Experiences questionnaire. The instrument is based essentially on two premises: (1) that the quality of the college experience is a direct function of the quality of efforts individuals expend on its pursuit, and (2) that quality of effort may be indexed by the frequency with which a student exploits campus facilities and opportunities designed to promote the attainment of educational goals. Items deemed relevant to assessing the quality of college experience are organized under two broad categories, a College Activities section (145 items) and an Estimate of Gains section (18 items). Three additional sections are devoted to personal Background Information (16 demographic items), Opinions about College (3 items), and The College

Environment (8 items describing institutionally favored social styles and value orientations).

The College Activities section is divided into 14 topical scales measured, with two exceptions, by ten items each. Seven scales relate to use of campus facilities (library, classroom, recreational, etc.); and seven relate to use of personal/social opportunities afforded by college life (faculty contacts, writing experience, conversational activity, etc.). On each item respondents rate on a four-point scale (very often, often, occasionally, never) their performance of activities that vary in the demands they make on personal time, energy, and commitment. Quality of effort devoted to an area of activity, along with the quality of college experience, purports to vary with the frequency of more or less demanding activities.

In the Estimate of Gains section one records perceptions of personal accomplishment, from very much to very little, in the attainment of various goals: vocational, aesthetic, personal, social, literary, and scientific.

The only published source of norms and technical information for the instrument, aside from a brief bibliography of dissertations and conference presentations, is a research monograph written from a perspective that is unmistakably promotional in nature. It pursues its claim to psychometric plausibility through a potpourri of analyses on data sampled from 13 institutions, including 8 California colleges and universities ($N=3{,}123$) and 5 other institutions in the east and midwest ($N=1{,}228$).

Item data for the College Activities section were analyzed only with respect to relationships among items logically defined as indices of the same scale. Relatively high values are consistently reported for all scales: median inter-item correlations of .26–.47, median item-total (scale score) correlations of .46–.67, and internal consistency statistics (coefficient alpha) of .79–.90. Moreover, intra-scale item factor analysis results supporting a claim to single-factor purity for all scales are reported. In fact, the incredible claim is made that, for each activity scale, between 70% and 100% of item variance is explained by a single factor. It is also implied that response frequencies for the items on each scale, without reference to intra-individual response patterns, are indicative of success in the construction of Guttman-like scales. The author concludes that the activities scales measure highly homogeneous constructs with items that successfully distinguish different levels of quality of effort. It must be noted that not only is it inappropriate to interpret the item analysis results as evidence of construct relevance, but that the homogeneity of the scales in this case might well be substantially heightened as an artifact of the questionnaire's physical features. The items of each scale are located together, share a common label, and are ordered according to a transparent logic regarding similarity of content and difficulty of the activities they describe.

Validity evidence cited in the report is of two kinds, direct and indirect. Direct evidence is flawed by its exclusive appeal to evidence that is internal to the instrument itself. Face validity, based upon the logical relationships among the literal meanings of items on the same scale, is obvious. In addition, the generally modest to moderate correlations among the activity scales are taken as evidence of their differential construct validity. Somewhat inconsistently, on the other hand, factor analysis is used to group scales according to more broadly defined constructs that actually appear to account for a relatively small amount of scale variance. Criterion-related validity claims are based upon relationships observed between quality of effort (activities scales) and self-ratings of perceived educational attainment. Four dimensions of self-perceived progress were derived by factor analysis of the 18 Estimate of Gains items. Multiple regression of each of these factors on the activities scales was performed in two different ways. First, the increase in R-squared attributable to all 14 activities scales was assessed, after taking Background Variables, College Satisfaction, and College Environment ratings into account. Inexplicably, the author ascribes importance to increases of .10–.15 in R-squared, that are attributable to no less than all 14 activities scales taken together. Second, in stepwise regression of gains estimates on all activities scales, background variables, satisfaction, and environment ratings, individual activities scales emerged in each case as the one or two most powerful "predictors" of gains measures. As a group, however, the other activities ratings accounted for only slight additional increases in R-squared. It is difficult, therefore, to understand the author's apparent satisfaction with validity evidence that is unimpressive in its magnitude and questionable in its relevance.

Indirect evidence adduced in support of the questionnaire's validity as a "quality of effort" measure is based principally on appeals to consistency between questionnaire results and widely documented trends in the general college population. For example, the verified accuracy of information that similarly constructed instruments elicit from respondents is cited as a basis for the credibility of data obtained by the College Student Experiences questionnaire. Similarly, arguments for construct validity are based on consistency between observed response variations on the activities scales and conventional wisdom about student interest and behavior patterns. Such assertions, however, beg the question, since the issue is not the accuracy of student responses, but the hypothetical relevance of those responses to an underlying dimension of behavior, "quality of effort," which is further presumed to affect the attainment of educational objectives.

It must be concluded that claims advanced in support of the psychometric quality of the College Student Experiences questionnaire are overstated. The benefit of explaining student behavior in terms of such psychological constructs as "quality of effort" and "quality of experience" remains tenuous. The basis for this instrument's attractiveness as a source of information remains, quite simply, its ability to elicit student perceptions about their involvement in various aspects of college life. And for that purpose the development of an elaborate theoretical model seems neither necessary nor particularly advantageous.

[247]

Communication Abilities in Daily Living. Aphasic adults; 1980; CADL; individual; 1 form; picture book (44 pages); manual (125 pages); scoring booklet (16 pages); 1982 price data: $75.95 per complete kit including 10 scoring booklets; $7.95 per 10 scoring booklets; $14.50 per manual; (30–50) minutes; Audrey L. Holland; PRO-ED.*

[248]

The Communication Screen. Ages 2–10 to 3–9, 3–10 to 4–9, 4–10 to 5–9; 1981; preschool speech-language screening tool; performance rated as pass, suspect, or fail; limited reliability and validity data; individual; 1 form; 3 levels: 3-year ('81, 2 pages), 4-year ('81, 2 pages), 5-year ('81, 2 pages); manual ('81, 32 pages); picture card ('81, 2 pages); 1983 price data: $10 per complete set including manual, 25 test forms, and laminated picture sheet; $3 per 25 test forms (specify level); (5) minutes; Nancy Striffler and Sharon Willig; Communication Skill Builders.*

Review of The Communication Screen by LINDA M. CROCKER, Associate Professor, Foundations of Education, University of Florida, Gainesville, FL:

As the title denotes, The Communication Screen is primarily intended for identification of preschoolers who may have delayed speech or language comprehension. The test is not designed for diagnostic purposes. Items require demonstration of language comprehension skills as well as verbal expression. Verbal expression is assessed in terms of sentence length, intelligibility, and fluency through informal observations by the examiner. Language comprehension includes more structured items such as naming objects, following instructions, digit memory, sentence repetition, and comprehending actions in pictures.

The test can be easily administered (probably within 2 to 5 minutes per child). No special psychometric or clinical training is needed. Some advance practice is necessary for smooth administration, since preparation and manipulation of additional materials are required. One undesirable feature of the manual is that the examiner's questions are not separated or highlighted within the instruction paragraph for each item. In addition, the examiner must elicit some spontaneous conversation from the examinee to judge language expression. Thus reliable, accurate judgements of examinee verbal expressions may depend heavily upon the quality of rapport established between examiner and examinee.

Scoring instructions are generally simple and criteria for referral are explicitly stated. For some items, examiner prompting would seem appropriate (e.g., when a 4-year-old child gives his/her first but not last name), but instructions for prompting are not provided; nor are they specifically prohibited. This may result in nonstandard administration or unnecessarily high failure rates. Consequently, efficiency of the screening process will be reduced. One uncommon and commendable feature of the manual is that it contains brief reviews of other available speech and language screening measures.

The authors describe only a preliminary standardization sample of 133 children. No item analysis data are discussed or presented. The validity and reliability evidence for this test are sparse. Furthermore, there is no evidence that the tests have been successfully used by others than the authors or graduate students under their supervision. This is a critical shortcoming in a test designed for use by a broad spectrum of educational or allied health personnel.

In summary, the main strengths of The Communication Screen are that it was developed by clinicians, can be quickly administered, and easily scored. Its weaknesses are the degree of arbitrary judgement required by the examiner, and lack of adequate data to demonstrate that the test scores are objective (from rater to rater), stable, or valid. With more standardization and validation effort, The Communication Screen may have the potential to become a useful addition to preschool assessment techniques. Without this substantiating data, publication of this test seems to have been premature. As such, the usefulness of this test for other than research purposes is questionable.

Review of The Communication Screen by MARY ELLEN PEARSON, Associate Professor of Special Education, Mankato State University, Mankato, MN:

PURPOSE. The Communication Screen (TCS) was designed as a screening instrument of general language development to identify children between 2–10 and 5–9 years who are high risk for a speech-language problem. The authors carefully state that the test is for screening purposes only, and children who are identified as at risk by TCS should be evaluated by a speech-language specialist to determine if a delay exists, the extent of the delay, and programming goals. TCS subtests measure a variety of areas of speech-language development including phonology, semantics, and syntax, as well as imitation, comprehension, production, and memory.

The authors' goal was to develop a screening measure which could be quickly and easily administered and interpreted by a variety of people who are not speech-language specialists, but who work with young children. This goal has been realized in many aspects of the TCS. The instrument is administered in 5 minutes, yet it is efficient in that a variety of measures of language are included. A one sheet form is provided for each of three age groups (i.e., 3-, 4-, and 5-year-olds). This form and the manual are readable, understandable, well organized, and easily filed. The directions are clear, and the authors carefully include directions for criterion performances where they are needed. The testing time can be shortened by stopping when it is clear a child has reached or cannot reach criterion. The final determination of pass/fail/suspect (follow and re-screen) is clear (with the exception of the Verbal Expression subtest) to the non-professional and is easily reached by following the manual directions.

The disadvantages of TCS include the one year intervals for determining pass/fail/suspect. The rapid growth of language during the 2–10 to 5–9 years warrants a more discrete breakdown of age groups. The picture stimulus card is acceptable but uninteresting, and one wonders if the spoon and baby (doll?) are clear to the child. Additional problems with TCS involve standardization, validity, reliability, and the Verbal Expression subtest.

STANDARDIZATION. Because TCS was developed for administration by personnel other than speech-language clinicians, standards for administration must be carefully explained. The authors do provide clear and understandable directions for administration and scoring for most of the test, but more detail is needed for the Verbal Expression subtest. Less critical standardization questions are also raised concerning objects the examiner must provide. Although the objects are common and easy to acquire, they are not standard (e.g., the size, shade, wrapping on color crayons). More standard procedures should also be provided for repetition of questions and praise.

VALIDITY. The validity data provided for TCS are very limited. The authors state that items and age norms are based on developmental norms and authors' judgment. The authors need to provide the potential user with more detailed information concerning the validity of the items and age norms for the test, and a firmer rationale for the inclusion of processing abilities such as memory.

The predictive validity of the test has been addressed to some extent by the authors. Speech-language clinicians administered TCS and a battery of speech-language assessments to 133 children. TCS was between 95% and 100% effective in identifying children who were identified as delayed on the battery. However, the battery included some tests which themselves do not have demonstrated validity and which have subtests with the same content as TCS. Consequently, in the future TCS should be given to many more children and their scores compared to other assessment batteries. In addition, the predictive validity of TCS must be demonstrated for personnel who are not speech-language specialists.

RELIABILITY. The reliability data provided by the authors of TCS are also limited. Twenty-two children were tested and then re-tested by different examiners. The percentage of agreement was 100% for all but one subtest on one of the three forms; this subtest provided 91% agreement. The initial data, although limited, provide high interrater reliability scores. More data need to be provided because the initial scores were obtained on only 22 children and were obtained by the authors. Striffler and Willig are aware of the need for more data, especially with non-speech-language clinicians, and have indicated through personal communication that they are collecting more information.

VERBAL EXPRESSION SUBTEST. Most of TCS is designed to facilitate its use by non-speech-language personnel; however, the Verbal Expression subtest in all three forms contains two sections that will require substantial data to demonstrate that the non-speech-language specialist can reliably and validly identify at risk children.

In the first section, Sentence Length, the examiner must determine the average number of words in the sentences produced orally by the children. Much responsibility is put on the child and the examiner in this subtest. The child is in a clinical setting where verbalizations are not encouraged, but is expected to verbalize at his or her level of competence. The examiner is expected to test, converse, listen, and count average number of words without training or a written corpus.

In the second section of Verbal Expression, called Intelligibility, the examiner is expected to determine whether or not the child is 75 to 80% intelligible for the 3-year-old form, 90% for the 4-year-old form, and 100% for the 5-year-old form. Even with training this is a difficult task, and the authors need to provide data confirming this can be done by groups of people who work with young children. An appendix of sounds and ages when the sounds are acquired is provided, but its relationship to a determination of intelligibility or understandability is unclear.

SUMMARY. There is a need for a screening level language assessment to be administered by personnel who work with young children but who are not trained in speech and language. TCS meets many of the necessary criteria for such an assessment (cost, time, ease of administration, organization, clarity); however, TCS lacks any validity and reliability data to support use by persons not trained in speech and language. The limited data that are provided were gathered from administrations by speech-language clinicians, and with more data like those the instrument may be recommended in the future for screening by clinicians. It is recommended that this instrument not be used by other personnel until validity and reliability data are provided, particularly for the Verbal Expression subtest.

[249]

Communication Sensitivity Inventory. Managers; 1970–78; CSI; 4 scores: feeling response, challenge response, more information response, recommendation response; face validity only; no description of normative population; 1 form ('78, 6 pages); instrument administration guide ('78, 4 pages); fact sheet (no date, 2 pages); 1982 price data: $40 per 10 inventories, fact sheet, and administration guide; (10–20) minutes; W. J. Reddin and Ken Rowell; Organizational Tests Ltd. [Canada].*

[250]

Community College Goals Inventory. Community colleges; 1979–81; CCGI; helps define goals, establish priorities, and direct planning; 20 areas: outcome goals (general education, intellectual orientation, lifelong learning, cultural/aesthetic awareness, personal development, humanism/altruism, vocational/technical preparation, developmental/remedial preparation, community services, social criticism), process goals (counseling and advising, student services, faculty/staff development, intellectual environment, innovation, college community, freedom, accessibility, effective management, accountability); no data on reliability; 1 form ('79, 11 pages); instructions for administering (no date, 4 pages); summary data report-sample pages (no date, 8 pages); comparative data report ('81, 20 pages); 1983 price data: $.65 per inventory; scoring service, $1.75 per inventory ($200 minimum); (45) minutes; ETS Community and Junior College Programs; Educational Testing Service.*

Review of Community College Goals Inventory by HAZEL M. CRAIN, Professor of Vocational Education, University of Nebraska-Lincoln, Lincoln, NE:

The Community College Goals Inventory (CCGI) is designed as a tool to assist community colleges in planning by helping to define goals and to set priorities. The instrument covers 20 areas considered common to community college planning and allows for an institution to add 10 items which it considers unique to its needs. Information questions allow the responses to be grouped by faculty, students, administrators, board members, advisory committee members, and community members as well as other demographic data. Examination of each subgroup's responses is useful and comparisons of the subgroups could provide essential information for the planning process.

The inventory consists of 90 goal statements which cover 20 areas relating to both outcome goals and process goals. Outcome goals are divided into the areas of General Education, Intellectual Orientation, Lifelong Learning, Cultural/Aesthetic Awareness, Personal Development, Humanism/Altruism, Vocational/Technical Preparation, Developmental/Remedial Preparation, Community Services, and Social Criticism. Areas included as process goals are Counseling and Advising, Student Services, Faculty/Staff Development, Intellectual Environment, Innovation, College Community, Freedom, Accessibility, Effective Management, and Accountability. Responses to the goals are indicated on 5-point scales of importance in two different ways: "How important is the goal at this institution at the present time?" and "how important should the goal be at this institution?" Goals included appear adequate for community colleges which are particularly focused on academic or transfer programs. The content specified most often is general education with emphasis upon the basic mathematics, science, and English areas. Only four goals relate directly to vocational/occupational education though other general goal statements would apply to all students or all programs. Community colleges which have a strong mission in vocational education would need to design additional goal statements to obtain adequate information needed for planning. The 10 spaces provided in the instrument for such additions would meet that need. Similarly, answers to the information questions would have to be utilized to accurately identify subgroups of vocational students and teachers because of the limited and inappropriate categories provided for major fields of study. Though there are limitations for vocational education, the provisions for additional items are adequate and the limitations do not diminish the usefulness of the CCGI for use by community colleges with wide variations of missions. Similar adjustments could be made for foci other than vocational education. Such built-in accommodation for additions makes the CCGI flexible for effective use by a variety of institutions.

The CCGI is an 11-page booklet which combines goal statements and answer spaces. It can be completed in approximately 45 minutes. The directions to the respondent are clear and concise. Instructions for Administering the Community College Goals Inventory are also easy to follow and include directions necessary to use the scoring and summarizing services available from ETS. Sample pages from a CCGI Summary Data Report along with a description of what is provided give an excellent overview of the service so that an institution can choose to buy the service or to handle the data on-site.

Scoring and a summary data report can be obtained at a stated cost, though that is not required in order to purchase the tests. The summary provides means and standard deviations for the responses to each item on both the "Is" and "Should Be" ratings. Data are provided for the total and subgroups in ranked format of high to low means as well as ranked in goal area discrepancies. The most recent Comparative Data Report is included with the institution's report. The Report summarizes data from a variety of 74 institutions from 31 states and Canada. Such a report is interesting but does not provide data for use in local planning. It may be more useful for institutions with common missions to share data within a state to allow comparisons of responses in regard to more common goals. It would be particularly useful for institutions to share in common the additional goals that may be added to the CCGI in order to generate specific and fruitful inter-institutional comparisons.

The CCGI was developed to meet the needs of community colleges more precisely than could be done with the previous instrument, the Institutional Goals Inventory, which is more appropriate for four-year institutions. ETS has also developed the Small College Goals Inventory. Certainly these adaptations to type, mission, and size of institutions provide an opportunity to select the most appropriate instrument. The CCGI is particularly useful for community colleges with specific needs largely unmet by what was earlier available.

[251]

Community Living Observational System. Severely and profoundly mentally retarded persons living in group homes; 1977; CLOS; codings by a trained observer in 14 separate classes of behavioral events; no norms; individual; 1 form (1 page); manual (37 pages, includes all materials necessary for test administration); 1982 price data: $.75 per manual; (5) minutes; Valerie Taylor and Daniel Close; Rehabilitation Research and Training Center in Mental Retardation.*

See T3:541 (1 reference).

Review of Community Living Observational System by RICHARD L. SIMPSON, Professor of Special Education, University of Kansas, Lawrence, KS:

The Community Living Observational System (CLOS) purports to provide a means of observing and analyzing the behaviors and interactions of severely and profoundly retarded individuals assigned to group living situations. The system is specifically designed to assess responses and interactions that occur during unstructured periods.

In spite of its lack of norms, the CLOS has two primary strengths. First, this naturalistic observational system allows for direct analysis of specific and meaningful responses to various stimuli. Hence, as a descendant of experimental analysis of behavior strategy, the CLOS encompasses many of the assumed virtues of other behavioral observation techniques. Second, because of a paucity of more traditional instruments, the CLOS serves to fill an otherwise critical void in the assessment of retarded individuals living in community settings.

In spite of its general strengths, several aspects of the CLOS require further explanation and refinement. In particular, little information is presented on how or why the 14 target behaviors were selected. It is not apparent whether the behaviors were empirically derived or simply assumed to be significant target responses for retarded persons. While the coding system may encompass all possible leisure-time responses of severely and profoundly retarded persons, as the manual claims, clarification is required regarding the manner in which the response categories were selected. Without such information the validity of the instrument cannot be assumed. This issue is further clouded by such information in the manual as, "The code is flexible, however, and may be adapted to a variety of settings and program needs." This statement raises further questions regarding the conditions, if indeed empirical, surrounding the selection of the behavioral categories.

The issue of arriving at acceptable levels of interobserver reliability also appears problematic. Without more detailed explanations of such behaviors as "attending to someone" and "interacting with others in an appropriate manner," it is questionable whether acceptable levels of reliability can be obtained without rewriting or redeveloping the behavioral descriptors and categories. Further, since the system is designed to assess leisure-time activities, one must question the social validity of certain types of coding directives. For example, if a person is appropriately involved in an independent free-time activity (e.g., watching television, drawing) and fails to comply with a somewhat inappropriate peer command, it must be considered whether such a response may not actually be more "normal" than mere compliance. However, the observation system does not allow for such nuances of behavior.

Even though a description of the data collection procedures is provided, it is rather complex and hence generates a number of questions. Further, while the interactions between subjects and their environment often provide valuable information, the recording system used is confusing and difficult. Consequently, users not familiar with this type of methodology may need to be made aware of the complexity of the task as well as potential interobserver reliability problems.

The manual refers to the assumed value of the data generated through the CLOS; however, aside from very general comments, no suggestions are presented for how to employ CLOS data either for program evaluation or individual client analysis purposes. Consumers are assumed to know how collected data will be used.

In summary, the Community Living Observational system is a naturalistic observation method which may be used to evaluate and aid in the decision making about retarded persons assigned to group living situations. Users of the system who are inexperienced with this type of procedure, including the ability to make modifications and to extrapolate from the information presented in the manual, may encounter difficulty in effectively applying the system.

[252]

Community Living Skills Screening Test, Second Edition. Adult developmentally disabled; 1975–81; CLSST; original edition called Independent Living Screening Test; criterion-referenced assessment plus a prescriptive remediation strategy; 174 behavioral skills in 10 behavioral domains: personal maintenance, dressing and clothing care, eating and food management, social behavior, expressive skills, home living, money management, time awareness and utilization, recreation and leisure skills, community awareness and utilization; norms consist of means and standard deviations; individual; 1 form ('80, 112 pages); quick screening test recording form ('81, 2 pages); standardization manual ('80, 43 pages); screening test materials ('80, 74 pages); baseline and skill acquisition record ('80, 2 pages); remediation manual ('80, 408 pages); 1982 price data: $35 per complete set; $4.50 per quick screening test; Robert L. Schalock and Linda Sweet Gadwood; Mid Nebraska Mental Retardation Services.*

TEST REFERENCES

1. Schalock, R. L., Harper, R. S., & Carver, G. Independent living placement: Five years later. AMERICAN JOURNAL OF MENTAL DEFICIENCY, 1981, 86, 170–177.

Review of Community Living Skills Screening Test by JEAN DIRKS, Psychologist, Southgate Regional Center for Developmental Disabilities, Southgate, MI:

The Community Living Skills tests and remediation manual are designed to assess and train the skills which developmentally disabled clients will need for living in non-institutional settings such as group homes, foster family homes, staffed apartments, or independent housing. The assessment part is made up of the Community Living Skills Screening Test (Second Edition), which covers 174 items in ten areas, and its abridged version which is called the Community Living Skills Quick Screening Test. For all but 1 of the 10 subtest areas (Social Behavior), inter-observer reliability is between .79–.92, with correlations between .80–.97, with the same exception, between the subtests of the shorter and longer test versions. Normative data are available for both test versions.

In general, the longer version (Community Living Skills Screening Test) is clearly worded in terms of procedures and criteria for individual test items. However, it is fairly time-consuming to administer due to its length (174 items) and because individual test items often require multiple observation periods. (Sample: "Observe if client puts dirty clothes in hamper daily [morning or evening] for 2 weeks," or "Observe client while preparing a casserole" [franks and beans, tater tot casserole, or tuna casserole].)

The Quick Screening Test, on the other hand, is preferable due to its relative brevity of administration. It covers between 41–69 items depending on the client's level, and it permits some verbal report from staff, rather than depending entirely on direct tester-client observation. In general, the Quick Screening Test is a very useful assessment instrument. There are some drawbacks but these can be remedied if the tester observes certain precautions. The drawbacks stem from the division of the Quick Screening Test into three parts. The test was constructed by subdividing the 174 items on the longer test into three non-overlapping subsets, with the lower level being intended for clients in an institution or ICF/MR setting, the medium level being for clients in group homes or extended family settings, and the high level being for clients in staffed apartments. The authors of the test suggest that remedial training should be instituted in test areas where there are major deficits, and that the client should be considered for transfer to the next least restrictive living environment when she/he has mastered the majority of skills at the level of the test that was administered.

These suggestions are troubling, however, since the low level test items—which include toileting, shaving, nail care, knife usage, household cleaning, making small purchases, earning money, etc.—are in many cases so advanced that they should not be used as exit criteria for transfer out of an institution. Similarly, many retarded clients who actually are living successfully at this time in group homes will not have mastered the majority of skills at the lower test level, and certainly will not be able to do most of the medium level skills. (Medium level skills include taking one's own temperature, demonstrating first aid, washing clothes, preparing three meals, controlling own money for a week, etc.) Thus the test authors' direction to use the low level subset of the Quick Screening Test for institutional clients, and the medium level for group home clients, does not appear entirely appropriate. These problems can be remedied if the tester gives both low and medium levels to group home or foster family clients, and if any one test level is not considered a hard-and-fast prerequisite for transfer to a particular environmental setting.

In addition to the tests, the Community Living Skills kit also includes a remediation manual which consists of diverse procedures and plans designed to train clients on the skills listed in the tests. Many of the plans are taken from current research reports and have been used previously with retarded clients. In general, the plans are quite helpful and can be used by trainers either "as is" or with editing to make them briefer. However, consultation with a speech therapist, occupational therapist, or psychologist is advisable before applying plans respectively for language, cerebral palsy clients, or reduction of maladaptive behaviors. Such consultation would insure that speech goals, limb positions, and psychological techniques for behavior control are tailored to meet the needs and characteristics of the individual client.

Because of the priority that is given in community placement to clients without maladaptive behaviors, it is unfortunate that the remediation manual gives only scant attention to maladaptive behaviors. Although psychological techniques for reducing maladaptive behaviors are defined in the remediation manual, there are no sample plans that apply these techniques to aggression, self-abuse, or other major maladaptive behaviors. In addition, references to the use of a locked time-out room or statements that "initial administration of the punishment should be at full intensity rather than escalating the intensity with each successive occurrence" could easily be misinterpreted and need qualification. In order to properly safeguard clients' rights while reducing maladaptive behaviors, the trainer should thus consult a psychologist when drawing up plans for maladaptive behaviors.

In conclusion, the remediation manual and the abridged test (Community Living Skills Quick Screening Test) are both recommended by this reviewer. Although they have some drawbacks, the drawbacks can be ameliorated if the precautions noted here are kept in mind. Both the remediation manual and the Quick Screening Test have the advantage of being applicable to low functioning as well as high functioning clients, and both appear to be feasible for use in real-life situations.

[253]

Comparative Guidance and Placement Program. Entrants to postsecondary institutions; 1954–79; CGP; a battery of background, abilities and interest measures which may be administered at any time by participating colleges; full program or modified program (excluding Comparative Interest Index and Special Abilities tests) may be administered; Form UPG ('72, 55 pages); descriptive booklet (no date, 8 pages); administrator's handbook sent to coordinator in each participating institution; technical handbook ('79, 38 pages); CGP: what it's like ('79, 20 pages); using your CGP report ('79, 23 pages); separate answer sheets (NCS) must be used; 1985 price data: rental and scoring service, $6.25 per student for full program, including scored answer sheet and individual score report, $5.75 per student for modified program, including scored answer sheet and individual score report, $8 for reusable test booklet and $.50 for answer sheet for local scoring; 164(185–250) minutes for full program, 90(110–150) minutes for modified program; program administered for the College Entrance Examination Board by Educational Testing Service.*

a) INTEREST AND BACKGROUND INVENTORIES. Questions are on battery answer sheet and may be completed earlier at home by the student to lessen administration time.

1) *Biographical Inventory.* Modification of the Student Descriptive Questionnaire; yields an academic motivation score; (15) minutes.

2) *Comparative Interest Index.* Revision of Academic Interest Measures; 11 scores: mathematics, physical sciences, engineering technology, biology, health, home economics, secretarial, business, social sciences, fine arts, music; (25) minutes.

b) ACHIEVEMENT/PLACEMENT TESTS. For self-scoring editions (which may be used independently or with the full or modified program), see 1103, 1104, and 1105; 5 scores: reading, sentences, mathematics (part 1, part 2, total); student takes one of three 2-part mathematics tests: Test C (computation, applied arithmetic) for students with less than 1 year high school algebra, Test D (computation, elementary algebra) with 1 year, Test E (elementary algebra, intermediate algebra) with more than 1 year; 90(100) minutes.

c) SPECIAL ABILITIES. 3 scores: year 2000 (ability to follow directions), mosaic comparisons (perceptual speed and accuracy), letter groups (inductive reasoning); 34(40) minutes.

See T3:543 (3 references); for a review by Norman Eagle of an earlier edition, see 8:475 (18 references); see also T2:1052 (8 references); for reviews by C. Robert Pace and H. Bradley Sagen of an earlier program, see 7:666.

[254]

Comprehension of Oral Language. Grades K–1; 1962–73; parallel editions in English and Spanish; no data on reliability and validity; no norms; test is orally administered; Form A ('62, 8 pages), B ('73, 8 pages); directions for administering and scoring (no date, 8 pages); 1985 price data: $11 per 20 tests; $7.50 per specimen set; [30–35] minutes; H. Manuel; Wilma Dolezal.*

TEST REFERENCES

1. Gerken, K. C. Language dominance: A comparison of measures. LANGUAGE, SPEECH, AND HEARING SERVICES IN SCHOOLS, 1978, 9, 187–196.

Review of Comprehension of Oral Language by RICHARD P. DURAN, Research Scientist, Educational Testing Service, Princeton, NJ:

The Comprehension of Oral Language test is a group administered instrument useful in assessing children's receptive skills for spoken Spanish and English. The instrument is intended for use with kindergarten and early school grade children. The test is offered in parallel Spanish and English forms with pre- and posttest forms available in both languages. A test consists of 3 practice items and 35 regular test items. Items consist of three or four sentences read aloud by the examiner. Each item asks children to identify a particular drawing in a strip of five figure drawings that corresponds to the item described orally. A child's score on the test is the total number of correct identifications out of the 35 items presented. The English or Spanish administration manual for the test indicates that examiners should be satisfied beforehand that children to be tested have adequate mental maturity to meet the cognitive and linguistic demands of the group testing procedure. The administration manual suggests that the test may also be individually administered.

The drawings included in the test booklets are of familiar objects and situations, with the exception of one strip of drawings which is of geometrical figure outlines. There are line drawings, for example, of everyday household objects, animals, plants, outdoor and indoor scenes, and people carrying out identifiable actions. By 1982 cultural standards, the characteristics of the pictures are beginning to appear somewhat dated; this is most noticeable in the clothing worn by people depicted in figure drawings. Overall, however, the objects, scenes, and actions depicted in the pictures ought to be interpreted as was intended by children who are familiar with U.S. life. Recent immigrant children to the U.S., however, may have difficulty identifying some drawings. For example, on one item children are asked to identify a picture of "something that is ugly." The correct response is a picture of what appears to be a collection of grocery bags sitting askew on a pile of rubbish. The picture may be ambiguous in what it depicts due to the quality of the line drawings and particularly for children who lack cultural familiarity with the U.S.

The oral language which children must understand in order to respond correctly to items involves basic vocabulary and simple to moderately difficult syntax. Items which involve comprehension of relative clauses, as in "Darken the circle under the white rabbit that has very big ears," or "Darken the circle under the kitten which is following its mother" may be particularly difficult for very young children. The relative clause structures which are involved are not only demanding grammatically, they often also require that children be skilled in interpreting to what or to whom pronouns refer in preceding item information. The point raised is not a criticism of the test per se, since children who are able to respond to items of this kind are demonstrating essential oral comprehension skills.

Occasionally, test items require that children make inferences based on pragmatic knowledge rather than on information made explicit in the oral text of an item. For example, one item asks children to identify a picture depicting what happened as a result of a situation where a flower pot sat on a table in a room with an open window and with the wind blowing hard. The correct answer is a drawing of an overturned, partially shattered flower pot. An item of this sort would appear to be questionable for inclusion in a test of elementary oral receptive skills. Failure on this item could result from an inappropriate inference and not only from poor oral comprehension.

While the examples which have been discussed are presented in English, the corresponding phenomena occur likewise in the Spanish versions of tests. The Spanish versions of test items have an accurate correspondence to English versions of the same items. The language demands are very similar, if not identical, across the two languages for the same item. The vocabulary occurring in Spanish and English version items appears to be of equivalent difficulty.

There are a number of shortcomings which limit the immediate utility of the test. The directions for administering and scoring the test include no information on the reliability and validity of the tests, nor is there any indication of where such information may be obtained. Only superficial information or advice is given on how to interpret performance on the test. Mention is made in the directions that some test items were drawn from the Tests of General Ability and the Tests of Reading, Levels 1 and 2, produced by the same test publisher. No information is given on the oral linguistic proficiency criteria which were used in selecting items; this lack of mention suggests the possibility that there may not have been a deliberate sampling frame or sampling schema for choosing test items.

Other instruments such as the Language Assessment Scales (Level I and II) or the Bilingual Syntax Measure, which assess production as well as reception of oral Spanish and English, may be more useful than the present test. The present test is useful as a quick, group administered test of basic oral receptive skills. It should not be used in an isolated fashion to make educational decisions involving placement of children in monolingual or bilingual programs. Other instruments and other sources of information on children's language facility should augment use of the current test for placement or diagnostic purposes.

Review of Comprehension of Oral Language by ROBERT RUEDA, *Associate Professor, Department of Special Education, Arizona State University, Tempe, AZ:*

The Comprehension of Oral Language test (COL) was designed by the publisher "to assist in the appraisal of a child's language ability in the early stages of formal instruction," and to "provide an estimate of the ability to understand short verbal expressions presented orally."

The test is administered orally in either a group or individual format. The COL is comprised of 35 items contained in a test booklet provided to each examinee. For each item, there is a row of five drawings. The first drawing in the row is used by the examiner to focus the child's attention on the appropriate row, e.g., "Now look at the dog and the other pictures in that row." The child's task is to darken the circle underneath the correct drawing in response to the examiner's instructions, e.g., "Darken the circle under the scissors." The child's score is simply based upon the number of questions answered correctly.

This test would seem to be appealing based upon its simplicity and ease of administration. Nevertheless, there are major as well as minor problems related to the technical aspects of the test construction and the actual testing materials. In general, the major flaws of this test are related to omissions of critical information on the part of the publisher. For example, there is no accompanying technical manual, other than what is contained in the Directions for Administering and Scoring. In evaluating a test of this type, one would want to know the how, when, where, and why of the construction of the test, as well as information on reliability, validity, and norming procedures and data. Unfortunately, none of this information is available to the user of this test. The only information of this nature, contained in the directions booklet, is a statement that many of the items in the COL have been taken or adapted from other ability and reading tests in the series published by this company.

Although the question of validity is a key issue for any test, the question of reliability, especially alternate-form reliability, is also critical information for a test with supposedly parallel forms. Again, no such information has been provided. This lack of information is also true with respect to norms or other interpretative information; test interpretation remains uncertain.

Examination of the testing materials indicated that a wide variety of skills may be involved in a successful performance on this test. The type of items range from identifying single words, e.g., "Darken the circle under the scissors," to relational concepts, e.g., "Robert...left his shoes under the table. Darken the circle under the picture that shows him where they are," to counting skills, e.g., "Darken the circle under the third rabbit." Clearly, the items are not homogenous in nature, and therefore a rationale for the inclusion of various items is desirable. This would be important for theoretical as well as for interpretive purposes.

An additional potential problem is that discrimination skills appear to be heavily involved in successfully answering some of the items. For example, in item 32 (Form A), the four pictures of various geometric shapes require careful discrimination for selecting the appropriate answer. The same is also true of item 7 (Form B) which depicts representations of four rabbits. It is very possible that these discrimination aspects of the test may be problematic for very young children and confound the interpretation of a child's performance.

The COL test also comes in two parallel forms (Form A and Form B) in Spanish. The items and the instructions appear to be direct translations of the English version of the test. Although the Spanish speaking population in the United States is extremely heterogeneous, it seems that this was not accounted for in the test construction, procedures for administration, and interpretation of performance. Again, the information is simply not provided, and there are no precautionary statements about possible misuses of this test with Spanish speaking students. This is a serious omission given present controversies related to the testing and education of children who speak a language other than English.

In sum, although this is a quick and easily administered measure, lack of relevant information of a technical nature precludes recommendation of its practical use in clinical or educational settings. This instrument appears to be basically untested.

[255]

Comprehensive Ability Battery. Ages 15 and over; 1975–82; CAB; 20 scores listed below; 4 test booklets; norms for high school only; manual ('82, 7 pages); preliminary scoring suggestions and keys available on request; separate answer sheets (OpScan) must be used except with *d*; 1982 price data: $11 per 50 sets of answer sheets; $2 per manual; $5 per specimen set; scoring service (for *a* - *c* only); A. Ralph Hakstian and Raymond B. Cattell; Institute for Personality and Ability Testing, Inc.*

a) CAB-1. 4 scores: verbal ability, numerical ability, spatial ability, speed of closure; 1 form ('75, 17 pages); $16.50 per 25 booklets; 21.75(30) minutes.

b) CAB-2. 5 scores: perceptual speed and accuracy, inductive reasoning, flexibility of closure, rote memory, mechanical ability; 1 form ('75, 15 pages); $19 per 25 booklets; 20(35) minutes.

c) CAB-3/4. 5 scores: memory span, meaningful memory, spelling, auditory ability, esthetic judgment; memory span and auditory ability administered by tape cassette; 1 form ('75, 17 pages); $16.50 per 25 booklets; price of tape not yet determined; (25–30) minutes.

d) CAB-5. 6 scores: spontaneous flexibility, ideational fluency, word fluency, originality, aiming, representational drawing; 1 form ('75, 22 pages); $30 per 25 booklets (not reusable); 32(40) minutes.

See T3:547 (5 references); for reviews by John B. Carroll and Robert M. Thorndike, see 8:484 (3 references).

Review of Comprehensive Ability Battery by ROBERT C. NICHOLS, State University of New York at Buffalo, Buffalo, NY:

The manual and test materials for the Comprehensive Ability Battery (CAB) have not changed since the 1976 edition, although additional norms were added in 1982. Thus, the cogent comments in the reviews by Carroll and by Thorndike in the *Eighth MMY* (8:484) still apply. Briefly, the CAB measures most of the recognized ability factors with 20 short subtests averaging about 5 minutes each. The test materials are well prepared, and the reliabilities are generally acceptable for such short tests. The 31-page manual, however, contains only minimal information about the construction, factorial composition, and external validity of the tests. The manual's brief descriptions of the 20 abilities that are measured by the CAB suggest relationships with occupational and other criteria that are wholly unsupported by any evidence and are based, apparently, on face validity. The norms added to the manual in 1982 provide percentiles relative to a reference group of over 2,000 high school students, although scores for only about half the group are available for some subtests. Little additional information is given about the normative group. Even the critical information about age or grade level is missing. Additional norm tables for some of the subtests are provided for smaller samples of Canadian high school students, first year college students, and young male prisoners. The differences among the means for these groups are about what would be expected, except that the Canadian high school students average about half a standard deviation above the U.S. high school students on most subtests. The manual wisely recommends that local norms be developed for any extensive use of the CAB.

The CAB is similar to the Kit of Factor Referenced Cognitive Tests that is available for experimental use from the Educational Testing Service. For many users the CAB may be preferable because it is available in nicely printed test booklets with machine-readable answer sheets, scoring keys, and profile forms; while the ETS Kit is simply a collection of subtests that the user must reproduce for himself. The absence of information about the meaning of the CAB scores, however, makes it, like the ETS Kit, a collection of factor referenced tests for experimental use.

Who, then, aside from researchers studying the structure of human abilities, can make good use of the CAB? Many users of tests seem to believe, explicitly or implicitly, that there is more to intellect than Spearman's *g*, and that the non-*g* part is the more interesting if not the more important. These users are often frustrated by tests that yield only a single score, such as an IQ, and they are little placated by the common practice of dividing the global score into parts based on verbal and nonverbal content. Such test users are, no doubt, responsible for the popularity of such multi-aptitude batteries as the Differential Aptitude Tests, in which the shape of the profile is much more apparent than its elevation. The CAB allows this bias to be pushed to the limit by providing scores for virtually every widely recognized ability factor, including those measured with somewhat longer subtests by the DAT. The CAB makes good use of the bandwidth-fidelity trade-off: It sacrifices a little in the reliability of individual subtests to achieve a lot in breadth of coverage.

The diversity of scores provided by the CAB is seductive. Surely all of these data contain more information than can be summarized by a single score. Surely it is better for prediction to measure the components of intelligence separately and then to combine them with appropriate weights, either statistical or intuitive, than to depend on the arbitrary weighting inherent in a factorially-complex, single-score test. Although such assertions have a self-evident quality that seems in accord with common sense, there is little solid evidence that they are true. In fact previous studies have had great difficulty in finding any evidence at all that the predictive validity of multi-aptitude tests exceeds that of general ability tests, even in situations where it might be expected to do so. The CAB manual does not include any. That is why the battery must be considered experimental.

The little evidence included in the manual does not support the differential validity of the subtests. The CAB includes an Academic Aptitude score, which is a weighted composite of the verbal, numerical, inductive reasoning, associative memory, and spelling subtests. One would not administer the CAB just for this composite, but it is free if the five subtests are given for other purposes. The composite is a good general academic aptitude measure with an average correlation with overall grades of .63 in five high schools. This general score has a higher correlation with achievement in five specific subject-matter areas than the best single subtest with the exception of math achievement, which is somewhat better predicted by the numerical subtest. This latter result is not specific validation for the numerical subtest, since its correlation with achievement in French and in English are almost as high.

One might expect the general Academic Aptitude Composite to predict academic achievement well, while the more specific measures might do better with other, more specific, criteria of achievement. Perhaps they might, but the manual gives no evidence of this; and the test authors have chosen academic achievement as the only non-test criterion to include as evidence of the validity of the CAB.

The challenge for those making experimental use of the CAB or similar tests is clear: Show that the 20 factor scores, or some subset of them, are significantly superior to the Academic Aptitude Composite (or IQ) for some worthwhile purpose. The CAB seems well suited for this kind of applied research on multi-aptitude measurement. If it is successful, the widespread faith in differential aptitudes will be vindicated. If it is not, we can soon return to a simpler concept of intelligence for applied work.

There is a final, lingering suspicion that should be mentioned. Reviewers of other multi-score tests, such as the DAT, often comment that, in spite of the rhetoric of differential abilities in the test manuals, the correlations among the subtests are so high that little differential measurement in fact exists. The CAB manual contains the usual differential rhetoric, but it does not contain the correlations among the subtests! Let us hope that this is just an oversight that will be corrected with a table of suitably low correlations in the badly needed revision of the manual.

Review of Comprehensive Ability Battery by KARL R. WHITE, Associate Professor of Special Education and Psychology and Co-Director of the Early Intervention Research Institute, Exceptional Child Center, Utah State University, Logan, UT:

The Comprehensive Ability Battery (CAB) was developed to "provide investigators with an economical vehicle for assessing a wide range of the important ability constructs." Building on Thurstone's conceptualization of primary mental abilities, the battery provides short tests of 20 primary mental abilities which are supposedly well established from existing research and reflect "currently accepted views of the number and nature of the psychological constructs involved." The test was designed for general use (including academic and occupational counseling) and was developed in response to the authors' perception that there did not exist a "carefully standardized test series by which to evaluate these abilities." A major advantage of the CAB, according to the authors, is the relatively brief administration time for each of the subtests.

The foregoing description of the CAB, taken from the test manual, is somewhat misleading. Although the battery does include the generally recognized primary mental abilities, it also includes measures of abilities that are not so well established as the manual implies (e.g., auditory ability, esthetic judgment, aiming, and representational drawing). Most of the items in the remaining subtests are similar to existing tests such as the Differential Aptitude Tests (DAT), the Primary Mental Abilities Test, and the French Kit of Reference Tests. Because some of these tests (particularly the DAT) are already well established, a potential user of the CAB must decide whether the CAB represents a major improvement in terms of technical quality, type of information provided, or usability.

DEVELOPMENT OF THE CAB. Very little information is given in the 1982 version of the manual about the procedures for selecting factors to be included, writing or selecting items, or setting time limits. Supposedly, items were included only if there was research which clearly identified the item with the factor being measured and if items were independent of all factors except the one they were designed to measure. Factor analyses during the developmental stage supposedly demonstrated "the clear distinguishability of the 20 ability factors." Unfortunately, the manual only includes vague assurances that these criteria were met. What evidence is available in the research literature (most of which is not referenced in the 1982 manual) should make the reader skeptical. For example, I was unable to find any reference to item level factor analyses to demonstrate that items load only on the factor they were intended to measure. Factor analyses of the 20 subtests (not included in the test manual) are often substantially correlated; the Numerical Ability factor correlates .44 with Spatial Ability, .40 with Perceptual Speed and Accuracy, .48 with Inductive Reasoning, and .42 with Word Fluency. The two "large scale studies" on which the developmental work resulting in the final battery was done consisted of only 343 adults and 280 high school students near Edmonton, Alberta. Apparently, there was no effort to cross-validate the factor analytical results of the first study, and the sample sizes are somewhat small for the analyses conducted. No mention is made of how decisions were made to eliminate items from the original pool, no intercorrelation matrix of the factors is presented in the manual (a serious omission given the nature of the test), and samples used in the developmental work are clearly not representative of the populations for which the test is intended.

ADMINISTRATION PROCEDURES AND NORMS. As intended by the authors, subtests of the CAB are relatively short (the longest working time is 6 1/2 minutes). Administration instructions are adequate (the only major weakness is the need for the examiner to switch back and forth between the manual and the test booklet to read instructions during the test), and the test materials look professional. Scoring instructions are generally quite good except for several of the non-machine-scorable subtests (e.g., Spontaneous Flexibility) where scorers will have some trouble deciding what should be counted as a correct answer. Sample items and directions for examinees are occasionally somewhat confusing, but sufficient so that good test administrators would not have major difficulty if they are alert to potential problems.

Norms for the CAB are completely inadequate. Given the fact that the CAB was developed because the authors believed there was "no carefully standardized test" to evaluate primary mental abilities and their intent that the test be useful for general academic and occupational counseling of high school students, this is somewhat surprising. Interim norms included in the 1976 manual were based on up to 1,148 students. Current norms included in the 1982 manual are based on up to 2,351 students. In neither case is the reader given sufficient information about the type of students included. The only information given in the 1982 manual is that the norms are based on a "sample of Canadian and United States high school students." Comparison of the two sets of norms reveals disturbing inconsistencies which should make the reader skeptical about either set unless more information is available. For example, a Verbal Ability Score of 12 for males was at the 66th percentile in 1976 but only the 48th percentile in 1982. A Numerical Ability score of 10 for males was at the 65th percentile in 1976 but only the 46th percentile in 1982. Discrepancies between the Canadian and U.S. samples are even greater. A Verbal Abilities score of 12 on 1982 norms was at the 31st percentile of Canadian norms but the 56th percentile of U.S. norms.

RELIABILITY AND VALIDITY. The 1976 CAB manual makes numerous references to reliability and validity data that will be available in the near future. Unfortunately, no additional data are included in the 1982 manual. The lack of adequate data on reliability and validity is the test's most serious flaw. While previous reviewers (see 8:484) could be more charitable since the CAB was at that time recently developed (and more data were supposedly forthcoming), one cannot in good conscience recommend the CAB as a general use battery given the weaknesses in currently available data about reliability and validity.

The manual reports internal consistency coefficients (KR-20) and split half reliabilities for all 20 subtests. Seventeen of the 20 tests are timed, and at least eight of the tests have a significant speed component. It is well known that internal consistency and split half procedures are inappropriate for speeded tests. Although the authors discount the possibility that the estimates in the manual are inflated, the four subtests for which both test-retest reliability (average r =.75) and split-half reliability (average r =.88) are available show clear evidence that inflation is present. One is also concerned that there are several subtests for which the reported reliabilities are quite variable—Perceptual Speed and Accuracy (.58 to .96), Mechanical Ability (.30 to .72), Esthetic Judgment (.44 to .71), and Spontaneous Flexibility (.43 to .87). Even given the short nature of the test, the lower end of these ranges would be unacceptable for many of the individual purposes for which the test is supposedly designed.

The validity of the CAB for the purposes for which it was designed has not yet been established. Numerous correlation coefficients between the CAB and school achievement and IQ scores are presented. Some of these are reasonably satisfactory, but numerous questions remain. For example, no predictive or concurrent validities of any kind are given for 9 of the 20 subtests. Correlations between the CAB and Otis IQ scores should have been corrected for shrinkage (which would have reduced the correlation from .60 to .48). No correlation between CAB scores and occupational success are reported.

A more serious problem is that the description of the various subtests makes many unsubstantiated claims such as the following: "[Meaningful Memory] can be expected to be highly relevant for success in most academic endeavors" and "Inductive Reasoning Ability is important to success in...courses and occupations in mathematics or mathematics-related pursuits." Data presented in the manual shows that many of these claims are not well supported. For example, the correlations between Meaningful Memory and Overall School Achievement range from .19 to .30 with a median of .22. The correlation between Inductive Reasoning and Math Achievement ranges from –.07 to .48 with a median of .21. In addition to the weak correlations between CAB subtests and factors with which they should correlate, there are relatively strong correlations between factors and criteria that are counterintuitive. For example, the median correlation of Numerical Ability with French is .52 and with English .44.

"Direct concept validities," which the authors refer to "as the correlation between the test and the pure factor which it is supposed to measure," range from .72 to .98 with a median of .88. Although of satisfactory magnitude, they are of little use in making judgments about the CAB's validity for the purposes for which it was designed for two reasons. First, as the authors note, the coefficients represent the upper limit which is possible, not the actual correlation obtained with any criterion. Secondly, several of the direct concept validities exceed the theoretically possible square root of the reliability coefficient.

SUMMARY. The CAB represents an effort to develop a better test of primary mental abilities from what was then available. From the data that are available, some of the subtests included in the CAB are not well established or generally accepted, the normative samples are of unknown composition and provide inconsistent data, most reliability estimates are inappropriate for speeded tests such as many of the CAB subtests, and validity data are sparse and sometimes logically inconsistent. If additional data were collected, many of these problems might be solved. Until such data are collected, however, people interested in a test of primary mental abilities are better off using a test such as the Differential Aptitude Tests.

[256]

Comprehensive Language Program. Mental ages 0–5; 1981; a prescriptive teaching tool composed of planning, assessment, and teaching components; behavior ratings in 8 areas: attending, manipulation of objects, mimicking, matching, identifying, labeling, following directions, word combinations; individual; profile checklist (8 pages); administrator's manual (21 pages); profile manual part 1, part 2, (35–37 pages); lesson plan manual (23 pages); lesson plan class record sheet (2 pages); lesson plan booklets (42–156 pages) for each of the 8 areas; 1984 price data: $190 per complete set including 20 profile checklists and 20 record sheets; $13.50 per 20 profile checklists; $5 per 20 record sheets; $8.95–$32.95 per lesson plan booklet; $7.65 per lesson plan manual; $19 per profile manual (parts 1 and 2); $7.65 per administrator's manual; $17 per specimen set; Peoria Association for Retarded Citizens; Scholastic Testing Service, Inc.*

Review of Comprehensive Language Program by RICHARD M. CLARK, Professor of Educational Psychology, State University of New York at Albany, Albany, NY:

The Comprehensive Language Program is designed for use with children and adults who are developmentally delayed and who are functioning below the level of a typical 5-year-old. The program was developed over a 10-year period by the staff of the Peoria Association for Retarded Citizens.

Is the Comprehensive Language Program a test? According to its developers, it is a guide for curriculum and for instruction. It is also described as a tool for determining the best level at which to begin prescriptive teaching. It can be used for assessments that can pinpoint areas of deficiency for each student. It can be used to assist planning and teaching as well as for assessment. However, the authors don't call it a test for very good reasons. At its current stage of development, the Comprehensive Language Program lacks many of the qualities that one associates with a standardized measurement instrument.

The assessment component of the program has elements in common with criterion-referenced tests. Data are provided about eight developmental areas. Certain items marked with an asterisk are presented first. If the asterisked item is passed then the final criterion behavior for the area has been achieved and the rest of the items in the section can be skipped. Results are recorded on a checklist.

The test administrator is encouraged to make comments concerning handicapping conditions, behavior that might influence test taking performance, and behaviors that might reveal understanding even though the item is missed. After the checklist is complete a profile graph is made. The number correct in each subarea is circled, and a line is drawn to connect the circles. The left side of the graph is scaled for the percentage correct. The number of items in the subareas ranged from 2 to 40. For the 2-item subtest, "word-combinations," scores of zero, 50%, or 100% are the only ones possible. No data are presented concerning reliability.

According to the Profile Manual, the eight areas that are assessed are "arranged developmentally." Thus, one should expect the profile to be elevated on the left side and to decline on the right side—a scaling notion. Again, no data are presented to support the developers' contentions. One is told to identify major areas of strengths and deficiencies by looking at the percent correct in each subsection. However, users are enjoined to pay careful attention to just which items are answered and missed, within each subsection, and to the comments section. The authors suggest that the same profile graph be used for three assessments of the same individual so that a visual display of improvements will be available. Color coding of the profile line is recommended.

Users of the Comprehensive Language Program will find no discussion of reliability, no empirical data concerning item difficulty or item clusters, no direct validity data or discussion of validity, and no suggestion of a norm. Rather, users will find a program for language development in which skills are clearly articulated, means of assessing skills clearly described, and ways of teaching suggested.

The program is described as "a grass roots" effort in which those working with the clients of the Peoria Association are responsible for the product. It appears that no one has looked at the product from the perspective of test construction. Perhaps someone should. If the program suggestions are worthwhile, as they appear to be, then efforts might be made to look at the data that might have been produced in Peoria or in other places where the program has been used. Until such work is done, interpretations based on this instrument are more art than science.

Review of Comprehensive Language Program by JOHN A. COURTRIGHT, Associate Professor of Communication and Assistant Director for Academic Computing, Cleveland State University, Cleveland, OH:

Perhaps the most salient question surrounding the Comprehensive Language Program (CLP) is whether it should be viewed (and thus reviewed) as a "test" in the sense that word is normally used. As its title would suggest, the CLP is designed to provide a complete program of instruction for individuals (primarily children) who possess "significant speech and language delays....which have resulted from mental retardation, brain damage, cerebral palsy, visual impairment, hearing impairment, cultural deprivation, hyperkinesis, or learning disabilities."

The CLP consists of three clearly delineated components: Planning, Assessment, and Teaching. The Planning Component entails little more than reading the brief Administrator's Manual, which is excessively succinct and fails to provide the information necessary to evaluate adequately the materials on assessment.

The Teaching Component comprises the bulk of the CLP. The authors' description of this component as "a prescriptive teaching" tool is most accurate. The substance of the material taught, as well as the order and method of instruction, is rigidly prescribed, with little room for flexibility or innovation on the part of the teacher. Whether this approach to remediation for language delayed or disordered children is the most appropriate and successful is an important question in its own right, but will not be pursued further in this review.

The Assessment Component consists of a two-part Profile Manual and an assessment checklist. The manual introduces the eight sections which comprise the assessment procedures, as well as the subsequent Teaching Component: (1) attending, (2) manipulation of objects, (3) mimicking, (4) matching, (5) identifying, (6) labeling, (7) following directions, and (8) word combinations. These sections are referred to as "developmental areas," although the authors make a point of stating that their sequence is not meant to represent the order of language development.

The Profile Manual, much like the Administrator's Manual described earlier, offers absolutely no information about the reliability or validity of the items in the sections; nor does it provide any rationale for the test items which were included. Given the objective nature of many of the items (e.g., "Student looks at the teacher on his right side (or left) when she says his name"), serious concern about reliability seems unnecessary. Accuracy of measurement and thus reliability will almost certainly be quite high.

The complete absence of any discussion of either content or predictive validity, on the other hand, is much more problematic. There is absolutely no way to discern why certain items were included and others were not. This problem is compounded by the method prescribed for administering the several sections of the test.

Each of the sections (except V and VI) of the assessment component contains one or more "asterisked" items. These are to be administered at the beginning of each section. If the child responds appropriately, no more items in this section need be administered and the child is credited with a perfect score for that section of the assessment component. Sections V and VI (Identifying and Labeling, respectively) employ a slightly different procedure, in which a "hierarchy" of abilities is described: (1) labeling pictures, (2) labeling objects, (3) identifying pictures, and (4) identifying objects.

The implicit assumption throughout the test is that the items in a section define a cumulative scale (e.g., in the spirit of a Guttman scale), with the asterisked items being the most difficult. The same assumption clearly guides the use of the hierarchy in Sections V and VI. Hence, if a child can respond accurately to a higher-order (e.g., asterisked) item, it is assumed that he or she will certainly respond correctly to the remaining, less difficult items.

The validity of the entire test, therefore, rests on the accuracy of this basic assumption. Unfortunately, the test materials contain no discussion of the procedures by which this assumption was implemented for each section, nor are there empirical data which would support the validity of those procedures.

The authors seem to disavow the responsibility for supplying such a theoretic and/or empirical rationale by inserting the caveat that the CLP "was not a research oriented project, but was developed at the 'grass roots' level through direct work with individuals who have significant speech and language delays." Be that as it may, the authors' lack of interest in a research orientation does not alleviate the need for some basic information about the construction and performance of the assessment instrument.

The authors continue their description of the CLP by stating, "Since 1972, speech and language therapists, educators of the deaf, and psychologists have worked as a team to develop CLP." This quotation is relevant, for it allows one to infer (not that inference is sufficient) that the content validity of the individual items in the eight sections is acceptable. To the extent that a variety of qualified professionals contributed to the selection process, then the items are likely to represent the domain of interest. Nevertheless, the crucial assumption that the items in each section are cumulative (at least with respect to the asterisked items) remains unaddressed and unverified. In short, what you see is what you get or, perhaps more appropriately, caveat emptor.

In summary, the assessment procedures of the CLP are clearly without the information and description necessary to document their reliability and validity. Those whose primary interest falls in the realm of precise evaluation and placement, therefore, are advised to look elsewhere for a testing instrument to fulfill those needs. The current documentation which accompanies the CLP is woefully inadequate for that purpose.

In fairness, however, one must ask how relevant these obvious deficits in the assessment procedures are to the purpose of the entire program. Recall that the bulk of the CLP is devoted to the "Teaching Component." Moreover, a reasonable assumption is that the children who receive this instruction are profoundly delayed or disordered in their language abilities. Accordingly, an exact assessment of these abilities may be neither possible nor necessary for the children to benefit from the CLP. To the extent that the children's language abilities are enhanced (even slightly!) on any of the eight dimensions of the instrument, the CLP will most likely have served the purpose for which it was intended.

[257]

Comprehensive Test of Adaptive Behavior. Birth–21 years; 1984; "evaluate how well a retarded student is functioning in the environment"; behavior checklist, and survey for adult informant; more comprehensive version of the Normative Adaptive Behavior Checklist; 31 scores in 6 skill areas: 5 self-help skills (toileting, grooming, dressing, eating, subtotal), 7 home living skills (living room, kitchen-cooking, kitchen-cleaning, bedroom, bath and utility, yard care, subtotal), 7 independent living skills (health, telephone, travel, timetelling, economic, vocational, subtotal), 4 social skills (self-awareness, interaction, leisure skills, subtotal), 3 sensory and motor skills (sensory awareness, motor, subtotal), 4 language and academic skills (language concepts, math skills, reading and writing, subtotal), total; individual; 1 form (12 pages, record form); parent/guardian survey (16 pages); test manual (96 pages); technical manual (183 pages, identical to technical manual for Normative Adaptive Behavior Checklist); 1984 price data: $29 per complete set; $12.95 per 12 record forms and parent/guardian surveys; $9.95 per test manual; $6 per CTAB/NABC technical manual; separate answer sheets and a computerized scoring system for the record form, consult test manual for details; administration time not reported; Gary L. Adams and Jean Hartleben (parent/guardian survey); Charles E. Merrill Publishing Co.*

[258]

Comprehensive Tests of Basic Skills, [Forms U & V]. Grades K–0 to K–9, K–6 to 1–6, 1–0 to 1–9, 1–6 to 2–9, 2–6 to 3–9, 3–6 to 4–9, 4–6 to 6–9, 6–6 to 8–9, 8–6 to 12–9; 1968–82; CTBS; previous edition (Forms S and T) still available; subtests in reading (grades K–6 to 12–9) and mathematics (grades K–6 to 12–9) available as separates; partial batteries are available without science and social studies (grades 1–6 to 12–9); Forms Y (all levels), V (levels D-J); 9 levels; both machine scored (CompuScan not requiring use of separate answer sheets) and hand scored tests are available through level E; manual for each level with levels F-J in a single book ('81, 38–45 pages); coordinator's handbook ('81, 103 pages); class management guide ('82); preliminary technical bulletin ('82, 172 pages); norms book for each of primary, intermediate, and secondary levels, ('81, 59 pages); profile ('81, 2 pages); practice tests ('81, 2 pages) available for levels A-G; locator tests 1 (grades 1–6, '77, 7 pages), 2 (grades 6–12, '77, 7 pages) available; separate answer sheets (CompuScan, IBM 1230, Scoreze) must be used at levels F-J; 1984 price data: $13 per 100 practice tests; $11.20 per 35 locator tests; $3.25 per locator tests manual; $15 per 100 profile sheets; $.55 per class record sheet; $8.75 per class management guide; $5.25 per technical bulletin; specimen sets: $22 per Form U multilevel examination kit; $13.25 per primary (grades K–3), intermediate (grades 4–6), or secondary (grades 7–12) examination kit; Spanish edition (CTBS Español) available; CTB/McGraw-Hill.*

a) LEVEL A. Grades K–0 to K–9; 6 scores: reading (visual recognition, sound recognition, vocabulary, oral comprehension, total), mathematics concepts and applications; Form U ('81, 19 pages); $20.30 per 35 hand scored tests; $29.75 per 35 CompuScan tests; scoring service, $.96 per student ($100 minimum); (102) minutes.

b) LEVEL B. Grades K–6 to 1–6; 6 scores: reading (word attack, vocabulary, oral comprehension, total), language expression, mathematics concepts and applications; Form U ('81, 22 pages); $26.60 per 35 hand scored tests; $39.90 per 35 CompuScan tests; scoring service, $1.10 per student ($100 minimum); (109) minutes.

c) LEVEL C. Grades 1–0 to 1–9; 8 scores: reading (word attack, vocabulary, reading comprehension, total), language expression, mathematics (mathematics computation, mathematics concepts and applications, total); Form U ('81, 28 pages); prices same as for *b*; (172) minutes.

d) LEVEL D. Grades 1–6 to 2–9; 14 scores: reading (word attack, vocabulary, reading comprehension, total), language (language mechanics, language expression, total), mathematics (mathematics computation, mathematics concepts and applications, total), total, spelling, science, social studies; Form U, V, ('81, 47 pages); $29.05 per 35 hand scored tests; $45.50 per 35 CompuScan tests; scoring service, $1.25 per student ($100 minimum); (251) minutes.

e) LEVEL E. Grades 2–6 to 3–9; 14 scores: same as for *d*; Form U, V, ('81, 47 pages); prices same as for *d*; (279) minutes.

f) LEVEL F. Grades 3–6 to 4–9; 14 scores: reading (vocabulary, reading comprehension, total), language (language mechanics, language expression, total), mathematics (mathematics computation, mathematics concepts and applications, total), total, spelling, science, social studies, reference skills; Form U, V, ('81, 77 pages); $40.25 per 35 reusable tests; answer sheets: $11 per 50 CompuScan, $34 per 25 sets of Scoreze; $21 per set of IBM hand-scoring stencils; scoring service, $.76 per student ($100 minimum); (313) minutes.

g) LEVEL G. Grades 4–6 to 6–9; 14 scores: same as for *f*; Form U, V, ('81, 78 pages); prices and time same as for *f*.

h) LEVEL H. Grades 6–6 to 8–9; 14 scores: same as for *f*; Form U, V, ('81, 78 pages); prices and time same as for *f*.

i) LEVEL I. Grades 8–6 to 12–9; 14 scores: same as for *f*; Form U, V, ('81, 77 pages); prices and time same as for *f*.

See T3:551 (59 references); for reviews by Warren G. Findley and Anthony J. Nitko of an earlier edition, see 8:12 (13 references); see also T2:11 (1 reference); for reviews by J. Stanley Ahmann and Frederick G. Brown and excerpted reviews by Brooke B. Collison and Peter A. Taylor (rejoinder by Verna White) of Forms Q and R, see 7:9. For reviews of subtests of earlier editions, see 8:721 (1 review), 8:825 (1 review), 7:685 (1 review), 7:514 (2 reviews), and 7:778 (1 review).

TEST REFERENCES

1. Conklin, J. E., Burstein, L., & Keesling, J. W. The effects of date of testing and method of interpolation on the use of standardized test scores in the evaluation of large-scale educational programs. JOURNAL OF EDUCATIONAL MEASUREMENT, 1979, 16, 239–246.

2. Slinde, J. A., & Linn, R. L. A note on vertical equating via the Rasch model for groups of quite different ability and tests of quite different difficulty. JOURNAL OF EDUCATIONAL MEASUREMENT, 1979, 16, 159–165.

3. Bell, C., & Ward, G. R. An investigation of the relationship between Dimensions of Self-Concept (DOSC) and achievement in mathematics. ADOLESCENCE, 1980, 15, 895–901.

4. Diaz, J. O. P. Reading and self-concept of Hispanic and non-Hispanic students. JOURNAL OF INSTRUCTIONAL PSYCHOLOGY, 1980, 4, 127–136.

5. Knifong, J. D. Computational requirements of standardized word problem tests. JOURNAL FOR RESEARCH IN MATHEMATICS EDUCATION, 1980, 11, 3–9.

6. Clawson, T. W., Firment, C. K., & Trower, T. L. Test anxiety: Another origin for racial bias in standardized testing. MEASUREMENT AND EVALUATION IN GUIDANCE, 1981, 13, 210–215.

7. Soenksen, P. A., Flagg, C. L., & Schmits, D. W. Social communication in learning disabled students: A pragmatic analysis. JOURNAL OF LEARNING DISABILITIES, 1981, 14, 283–286.

8. Behuniak, P., Jr., Gable, R. K., & Archambault, F. X., Jr. The validity of categorized proficiency test scores. EDUCATIONAL AND PSYCHOLOGICAL MEASUREMENT, 1982, 42, 869–876.

9. Bryant, B. K. An index of empathy for children and adolescents. CHILD DEVELOPMENT, 1982, 53, 413–425.

10. Dombrower, J., Favero, J., King, M., Dombrower, E., & Michael, W. B. The criterion-related validity of two tests hypothesized to represent left brain and right brain function for a group of elementary school children. EDUCATIONAL AND PSYCHOLOGICAL MEASUREMENT, 1982, 42, 927–933.

11. Dziuban, C. D., & Mealor, D. J. Validity of a primary screening device as a predictor of subsequent academic achievement. PERCEPTUAL AND MOTOR SKILLS, 1982, 54, 1053–1054.

12. Gross, A. L. Predicting academic achievement over a one-year period. EDUCATIONAL AND PSYCHOLOGICAL MEASUREMENT, 1982, 42, 371–375.

13. Holmes, S. E. Unidimensionality and vertical equating with the Rasch model. JOURNAL OF EDUCATIONAL MEASUREMENT, 1982, 19, 139–147.

14. Leinhardt, G., Seewald, A. M., & Zigmond, N. Sex and race differences in learning disabilities classrooms. JOURNAL OF EDUCATIONAL PSYCHOLOGY, 1982, 74, 835–843.

15. Low, B. P., & Clement, P. W. Relationships of race and socioeconomic status to classroom behavior, academic achievement, and referral for special education. JOURNAL OF SCHOOL PSYCHOLOGY, 1982, 20, 103–112.

16. Muller, D., Foster, G., & Wooden, S. Academic achievement of sixth graders matched for intelligence but not for self-concept. PSYCHOLOGICAL REPORTS, 1982, 51, 273–274.

17. Nimmer, D. N. The use of standardized achievement test batteries in the evaluation of curriculum changes in junior high school earth science. SCIENCE EDUCATION, 1982, 66, 45–48.

18. Smith, M., III, Stuck, G. B., & Johnston, D. R. The identification of students likely to fail The North Carolina Competency Tests. EDUCATIONAL AND PSYCHOLOGICAL MEASUREMENT, 1982, 42, 95–104.

19. Tallmadge, G. K. An empirical assessment of norm-referenced evaluation methodology. JOURNAL OF EDUCATIONAL MEASUREMENT, 1982, 19, 97–112.

20. Valencia, R. R. Predicting academic achievement of Mexican American children: Preliminary analysis of the McCarthy Scales. EDUCATIONAL AND PSYCHOLOGICAL MEASUREMENT, 1982, 42, 1269–1278.

21. Weinstein, R. S., Marshall, H. H., Brattesani, K. A., & Middlestadt, S. E. Student perceptions of differential teacher treatment in open and traditional classrooms. JOURNAL OF EDUCATIONAL PSYCHOLOGY, 1982, 74, 678–692.

22. Croft, D. B., & Franco, J. N. Effects of a bilingual education program on academic achievement and self-concept. PERCEPTUAL AND MOTOR SKILLS, 1983, 57, 583–586.

23. Crowell, D. C., Hu-pei Au, K., & Blake, K. M. Comprehension questions: Differences among standardized tests. JOURNAL OF READING, 1983, 26, 314–319.

24. Fulmer, S., & Fulmer, R. The Slingerland Tests: Reliability and validity. JOURNAL OF LEARNING DISABILITIES, 1983, 16, 591–595.

25. Griffing, P., Steward, L. W., McKendry, M. A., & Anderson, R. M. Sociodramatic play: A follow-up study of imagination, self-concept, and school achievement among black school-age children representing two social-class groups. GENETIC PSYCHOLOGY MONOGRAPHS, 1983, 107, 249–301.

26. Payne, B. D., Smith, J. E., & Payne, D. A. Sex and ethnic differences in relationships of test anxiety to performance in science examinations by fourth and eighth grade students: Implications for valid interpretations of achievement test scores. EDUCATIONAL AND PSYCHOLOGICAL MEASUREMENT, 1983, 43, 267–270.

27. Roberts, K. T., & Ehri, L. C. Effects of two types of letter rehearsal on word memory in skilled and less skilled beginning readers. CONTEMPORARY EDUCATIONAL PSYCHOLOGY, 1983, 8, 375–390.

28. Schell, L. M. Test review: Comprehensive Tests of Basic Skills (CTBS, Form U, Levels A-J). JOURNAL OF READING, 1984, 27, 586–589.

29. Slavin, R. E., Leavey, M. B., & Madden, N. A. Combining cooperative learning and individualized instruction: Effects on student mathematics achievement, attitudes, and behaviors. ELEMENTARY SCHOOL JOURNAL, 1984, 84, 409–422.

Review of the Comprehensive Tests of Basic Skills, Forms U and V, by ROBERT L. LINN, Professor of Educational Psychology and Psychology, University of Illinois, Urbana-Champaign, IL:

Forms U and V of the Comprehensive Tests of Basic Skills (CTBS) are the third edition of this popular achievement test battery. The new edition has retained many of the features of the previous edition, Forms S and T, and the Total Reading, Total Language, Total Mathematics, and Total Battery scores Levels D through J of Form U have been equated to Form S. However, there are several notable changes other than the obvious updating expected when an achievement test is revised. The coverage and number of levels of the test in the early grades has been expanded. Six levels of Form U span grades K through 4, compared to only 4 levels for Form S. Some changes have been made in item classification (e.g., the separation of whole numbers, decimals, and fractions into subclasses within each of the four computation operations), some content categories have been added (e.g., application of consumer skills), and some new item formats have been added (e.g., the use of a context sentence for spelling items).

Although the changes in number of forms, content coverage, and item formats are important, the most dramatic change was the switch from traditional analytical techniques to item response theory (IRT) for purposes of item analysis, item bias studies, test construction, scaling, equating, and estimation of standard errors of measurement. The user now has an option of traditional number-correct scores or item-pattern scores based on the three-parameter logistic IRT model. Although the correlations between number-correct and item pattern scores are quite high, differences greater than a full standard deviation can occur on rare occasions for a particular subtest (see Yen, in press). For this and other reasons it is clear that the reliance on IRT is more than a cosmetic change or a mere technical nicety. Hence the advantages and disadvantages of this approach will be considered in several of the sections of this review.

FEATURES. The CTBS has a number of desirable features. The test materials have obviously been carefully edited and the test booklets have clear illustrations and are easy to read. The Examiner's Manuals provide good explicit directions for administration. A wide range of score reporting systems are available. Options include locator tests to select an appropriate level of the CTBS for a student, practice tests for familiarizing students with the test format, and combination services for combining CTBS results with other CTB/McGraw-Hill tests (Test of Cognitive Skills, PRI Reading Systems, and Diagnostic Mathematics Inventory). A Class Management Guide which provides many suggested activities to help students learn the tested objectives is also available.

TEST CONSTRUCTION. The test objectives were specified following the usual approach of reviewing textbooks and curriculum guides from state departments of education and large school districts. Comparisons were also made to other recently published CTB/McGraw-Hill tests. A pool of tryout items two or three times as large as needed for the final version of the tests was developed using an objective by process table of specifications. Vocabulary difficulty was controlled for target grades using standard sources and reading passages were subjected to analysis using familiar readability formulas. Item writers and editors were directed to follow guidelines on "multiethnic publishing," "equal treatment of the sexes," and "fair representation of disabled people." Panels representing various ethnic groups were asked to review the tryout materials for "appropriateness of language, subject matter, and representation of people." As part of the item tryout, teachers were also asked to review the materials and provide comments.

Statistics produced from the tryout data included estimates of the item parameters of the three-parameter logistic model, indices of model fit for each item, indices of item bias based on a comparison of item location parameters, and results of distractor analyses. The statistical results were combined into an "overall quality index." An "automatic test selection" computer program provided an initial starting place for test selection which approximated the minimum standard error of measurement curve for a test within the editorial constraints for minimum number of items for each objective. The test was then refined by editors who focused on test content. However, the editors were aided in this task by an interactive computer display which provided immediate feedback on the changes in statistical properties of the test when items were replaced.

The Preliminary Technical Report conveys the impression that the item selection process was highly sophisticated and technologically advanced. But the reader is left with some unanswered questions. Did the editorial constraints apply to the process categories as well as the objectives? To what extent was final selection determined by the estimated item discrimination parameter, which was the most heavily weighted statistic in the overall quality index? How close was the starting test selected by the automatic test selection program to the final test?

Answers to questions such as the above could have important implications for interpretation. Traditional methods of constructing achievement tests have often been criticized for an overreliance on statistics. Such criticisms take on new force in the context of IRT. As argued by Traub and Wolfe (1981, p. 383), "to limit our conception of achievement...to only those items that fit a unidimensional latent trait model is to narrow our emphasis too much." Thus, it seems important to know the degree to which indices of item discrimination and of model fit determined the selection of items.

VALIDITY. Although part 2 of the Preliminary Technical Report runs 65 pages and is entitled "Validity," evidence supporting the validity of the interpretations and suggested uses of the various scores is rather scanty. A brief description of each test is given followed by a description of the test development process that was summarized in the preceding section. The "statistical data related to validity" consist of a list of the number of items and the percentage of students in the norming sample "who demonstrated mastery of each objective at a given grade and level." Bayesian estimates of proportion correct within a category are used with a .75 mastery criterion for each objective. The next 15 pages report the estimated item location parameters. Finally, 30 pages of tables reporting intercorrelations of the Form U subtests along with the Test of Cognitive Skills and intercorrelations of Forms S and U subtests are presented without interpretive comment. All of the reported results have potential value, but they leave some important validity issues unaddressed.

For example, the Class Management Guide suggests that the computer-generated Class Grouping Report, which lists students who have not mastered or who have only "partial knowledge" of an objective, can be useful in organizing a class into skill groups. This may be useful, but no evidence is presented to support the validity of this use. As another example, the claim is made that the new item format used for the spelling test measures "spelling in a way that is not affected by reading comprehension or vocabulary knowledge." It is unclear what evidence supports this claim or how it is reconciled with the slightly higher correlations reported between Total Reading and Spelling scores on levels D through G of Form U than were obtained on the comparable levels of Form S.

In fairness, it should be noted that the validity evidence for the CTBS is comparable to that provided by publishers of several similar batteries. Content validity is understandably considered primary and content validation is generally viewed as a matter of judgment. Test coordinators are appropriately advised to check the content validity of the tests "by reviewing the content organization and objectives as well as the actual test items." This advice is fine as far as it goes, but it seems insufficient for using the tests for instructional purposes such as grouping or for reasonable interpretation of more complicated score reports such as the discrepancy between observed and anticipated achievement scores.

RELIABILITY. Conventional reliability estimates are not reported in the Preliminary Technical Report but KR-20 coefficients are promised when the Final Technical Report is produced. Though one might wonder why KR-20s for a test normed during the 1980–81 school year were not included in the 1982 Preliminary Technical Report, their absence is no great loss. Standard errors of measurement are of much greater value than KR-20s, and with regard to the former statistics the CTBS results are more comprehensive and potentially useful than those provided by most of the publishers of achievement test batteries. Standard errors of measurement are reported as a function of scaled score based on the IRT results. This is a distinct advantage over a single estimate for each test accompanied by the common, but obviously false, assumption that errors of measurement have a constant variance throughout the score range.

The detailed reporting of standard errors of measurement by level of scaled score clearly reveals the range of scores where the results are most dependable. With IRT scoring on the level E Reading Comprehension test it can be seen, for example, that the scaled scores are most dependable between about 530 and 640 (standard errors between 12 and 22). A scaled score of 723, on the other hand, has a standard error of 65 and a score of 423 has one of 93. These differences, which are fairly typical, have important implications for interpretation.

Traditional estimates of alternate form reliabilities are not available since the two forms were administered to separate samples. Comparisons of the IRT standard errors of measurement curves for Forms U and V can be made, however, and these suggest that the two forms provide quite comparable measurement over a given score range. These comparisons would be facilitated if the Technical Report included figures showing joint plots of the standard error curves or plots of relative efficiency curves. Nonetheless, it would be desirable to have alternate form reliabilities because it would be possible to have identical standard error curves for uncorrelated tests.

No estimates of score stability are provided. This same shortcoming was noted in Nitko's (8:12) review of Forms S and T.

NORMS. The fall and spring norms are based on a combined sample of approximately 250,000 students, which yielded between 3,028 and 18,992 students for a given combination of grade, test level, and testing date. The sample design was appropriate and standard procedures were used for replacing schools that refused to participate. No information is given on non-participation, however. Hence, it is not possible to reach any firm conclusions regarding representativeness. Unlike some of the competitive test batteries, no school or district norms are provided.

SCALES. The usual array of percentile, stanine, grade equivalent, and normal curve equivalent scores are provided. The crucial score from a technical perspective, however, is the scale score. The scale score, which has a possible range of 1 to 999, was derived from the IRT scaling. It is the scale that is used for equating forms and articulation across levels of the test. According to the Test Coordinator's Handbook, "Scale scores are units of a single, equal-interval scale that is applied across all levels of CTBS U and V regardless of grade or time of year of testing." These scores are considered "especially appropriate for various statistical purposes" including the tracking of "year-to-year growth of individual students or groups."

Previous editions of the CTBS used Thurstone scaling to place levels of the test on a common scale. Thurstone scaling, or a variant of it, is the most widely used approach of major test publishers to the problem of creating a common scale across levels of a test. Once having been scaled in this way the scores obtained from different levels of the test are treated as equivalent. Some have also claimed, as CTB/McGraw-Hill did for Forms S and T, that the result is an "equal-interval scale." The equal-interval claim for this, or any other, test scale is questionable (see Angoff's 1971, p. 510 quotation of personal communication from Lord). The notion that the test levels are "vertically equated" is also questionable (e.g., Slinde & Linn, 1977).

IRT scaling provides an approach to scaling that may be particularly appropriate for the task of vertical equating (Lord, 1975; Slinde & Linn, 1977), though Kolen's (1981) results favored a conventional equipercentile equating. The question of equal intervals seems beyond resolution. Certainly, it cannot be resolved by a comparison of the IRT scale to some other putatively equal-interval scale. Nonetheless, the properties of the CTBS scale scores are sufficiently different from other more familiar scales that questions must be raised.

A pervasive finding for scale scores that span multiple levels of a test is that the variability of the scores tends to increase with grade level. The putatively equal-interval scales of Form S is typical in this regard. The Form U scale score, on the other hand, shows just the opposite trend. For example, the Total Battery standard deviations for the sample of students who took both Forms S and U in the fall of 1981 were 57, 75, and 107 on Form S in grades 2, 6, and 10 respectively (see Tables 37, 41, and 45 of the Preliminary Technical Report). The corresponding Form U standard deviations were 74, 44, and 37. Yet both scales have been called equal-interval.

The point of the above comparison is not to try to reach a conclusion that one scale correctly represents reality while the other one does not. However, the difference has important implications for interpretation, and the decreasing standard deviation across levels of Form U is intuitively surprising. For example, a student who has a scale score of 446 on the Math Concepts/Applications Test in the fall of grade 2 would have a percentile rank of 10. To maintain the same percentile rank in the spring, the student would have to gain 64 scale points to 510. On the other hand, a student who was at the 90th percentile in the fall would only need to gain 20 scale points, from 648 to 669, to maintain his or her percentile rank of 90. To continue to hold their own over the summer, the lower scoring student would have to gain an additional 21 scale points compared to only 4 points for the higher scoring student. These results are contrary to much that has been written about the relative rate of growth of highly able and less able students (see Hoover, 1983 for more detailed analysis of the scale properties).

Simple comparisons of the Form U scale scores to number-correct scores also seem to yield strange results. On Level C a student who correctly answers 60% of the items on the Math Concepts/Applications Test would get a scale score that is 79 points higher than a student who answered 40% of the items correctly. In contrast, Form J would yield a scale score difference of only 18 points between students with 60% and 40% correct answers. Should one conclude that learning an additional 20% of the content of Level C is equivalent to roughly 4 times the growth of learning an additional 20% of the content of Level J?

Such a conclusion seems implausible. However, it should be noted that Yen (1983) has argued that reasons can be found to explain either decreasing or increasing standard deviations. She also gave an example of a post-hoc explanation of the decreasing standard deviations obtained for the CTBS scaled scores across levels.

ANTICIPATED ACHIEVEMENT SCORES. It has become common practice for publishers of major achievement test batteries to use an aptitude test in conjunction with their achievement tests to compute predicted achievement scores and discrepancy scores. CTB/McGraw-Hill is no exception in this regard. The Test of Cognitive Skills can be used to compute "anticipated achievement scores" to which the obtained achievement can be compared. There is nothing unusual about the computation of anticipated achievement scores. However, erroneous claims are made about the statistical significance of the difference between the obtained and anticipated scores due to a misinterpretation of the standard error of estimate. The standard error of estimate is used to compute "80% confidence intervals" around an anticipated score and an observed score outside this interval is flagged as a "significant difference." It would be appropriate to indicate that the flagged differences fall in the upper or lower 10% of the distribution of differences. But it is inappropriate to say that the difference is statistically significant.

SUMMARY. Despite the above criticisms for the lack of evidence in some areas and the serious reservations regarding the scale scores, the CTBS has many positive features. It is a highly professional product that offers some unique advantages such as score specific standard errors of measurement. It is worthy of careful consideration by schools seeking a comprehensive achievement test battery for any of the grades K through 12. Although the properties of the scale scores may be considered unreasonable, this may be more of a concern for longitudinal research purposes and in situations where scaled scores are used in evaluations (e.g., as part of a Chapter 1 evaluation) than for the many more common uses of an achievement test battery. Indeed it is the other scores that typically get the most use: percentile ranks and grade equivalents for reporting to parents and school boards, normal curve equivalents for Chapter 1 evaluations, and objective mastery scores for planning instruction.

REVIEWER'S REFERENCES

Angoff, W. H. Scales, norms, and equivalent scores. In R. L. Thorndike (Ed.), EDUCATIONAL MEASUREMENT, SECOND EDITION. Washington, DC: American Council on Education, 1971.

Lord, F. M. A SURVEY OF EQUATING METHODS BASED ON ITEM CHARACTERISTIC CURVE THEORY. (ETS RB 45–13) Princeton, NJ: Educational Testing Service, 1975.

Slinde, J. A., & Linn, R. L. Vertically equated tests: Fact or phantom? JOURNAL OF EDUCATIONAL MEASUREMENT, 1977, 14, 1–10.

Kolen, M. J. Comparison of traditional and item response theory methods for equating tests. JOURNAL OF EDUCATIONAL MEASUREMENT, 1981, 18, 1–11.

Traub, R. E., & Wolfe, R. G. Latent trait theories and the assessment of educational achievement. In D. C. Berliner (Ed.), REVIEW OF RESEARCH IN EDUCATION, 1981, 9, 377–435.

Hoover, H. D. The most appropriate scores for measuring educational development in the elementary schools: GE's. Paper presented at the

Annual Meeting of the American Educational Research Association, Montreal, 1983.
Yen, W. M. Use of the three parameter logistic model in the development of a standardized test. In R. K. Hambleton (Ed.), APPLICATIONS OF ITEM RESPONSE THEORY. Vancouver, British Columbia: Educational Research Institute of British Columbia, 1983.
Yen, W. M. Obtaining maximum likelihood trait from number-correct scores for the three-parameter logistic model. JOURNAL OF EDUCATIONAL MEASUREMENT, in press.

Review of Comprehensive Tests of Basic Skills by LORRIE A. SHEPARD, Associate Professor of Education, University of Colorado, Boulder, CO:

The Comprehensive Tests of Basic Skills comprise a well-known, widely used standardized achievement test battery. The new CTBS-U is among the leading achievement batteries to be considered for adoption by school districts. Although there are hundreds of achievement tests there are only a half-dozen batteries that have all of the features desirable for an entire testing package. When school districts select one of these batteries, they are virtually purchasing a testing program. It is not out of laziness that test directors do not piece together a unique testing program from many sources. Rather, the technical benefits of using an intact package will almost always outweigh the attractions of separate tests. Some of these benefits include multi-level tests with both articulated content and norms, practice tests and ancillary materials, and co-normed school aptitude measures.

The primary purpose of this review is to judge the CTBS as a comprehensive testing program. Which strengths or weaknesses are so compelling that they argue for or against the selection of this package? In the past, practitioners have frequently been dissatisfied with reviews in the Mental Measurements Yearbook because they were not conducive to comparative evaluation. Sometimes this occurred because reviewers addressed their measurement colleagues on esoteric points and did not make clear how serious criticisms were in judging the overall quality of the test. In this review I will distinguish between minor criticisms and those issues that are key to choosing this test among its competitors. Minor criticisms imply things the publisher should work on in the future or problems to watch out for when using the test.

CONTENT VALIDITY. The match between test content and local curriculum should be the most important consideration in selecting an achievement test. The developers of CTBS-U have done the hard work of surveying state and local curriculum guides and textbook series to determine which objectives are most often taught in each subject at each grade level. Developers of all of the major standardized tests attempt to do this. As a general rule, the more recent the test, the more up-to-date it will be in reflecting changes in instructional materials. The changes in the new version of CTBS reflect recent trends in the interests and emphases of subject area specialists. Nevertheless, there will always be different degrees of fit between the inferred common curriculum and local objectives.

The typical procedure for selecting a test battery is to form a committee of teachers to review several tests. Such a committee will find the table of item classification useful. In it the items at each test level are categorized by subobjective (e.g., word attack: diphthongs—variant vowels) and by cognitive process (i.e., whether the item requires recall, understanding, inferential reasoning, or evaluation). Thus we are assured that the tests measure more than just rote learning—something we can expect from all the better achievement tests. These blueprints give a good overview of the test content but it will be difficult to distinguish major tests on this basis—they all look alike. To choose a test, teachers should scrutinize tests at the item level. This does not mean that a bad item makes a bad test. It does mean that the match between test content and instruction should be judged by studying the array of items rather than content descriptions. In rating each test, teachers might be asked to report what is taught but not tested, what is tested but not taught, and to identify familiar content that is asked in unfamiliar ways. Once the two or three most likely candidates have been identified it is even desirable to administer each battery to a sample of students. One school district made a final choice about instructional fit by correlating tryout test scores with teacher judgments about degree of student mastery on the district's objectives (Hopkins, Kretke, Martin, & Averill, 1978).

Because the judgment of content validity must be idiosyncratic to local curricula, I cannot rank one battery above another on this single most important criterion. My overall impressions of the content are quite favorable, however. CTBS-U is an improvement over the previous Form S. A commendable effort has been made to reduce the effect of reading on performance in other content areas; there is essentially no reading required in math concepts through level C (1.0–1.9). New item types such as vocabulary in context enhance the logical validity of the test. For the youngest children (level A), every trick of effective test administration has been included. For example, there are plenty of practice items, never more than five items per page (counting practice), and item-locator pictures. At the upper levels the material looks challenging. The task demands for inference and problem solving are evident. Thus, it is not a basic skills test in the narrowest sense.

MULTI-LEVEL TESTS. There are nine levels of CTBS-U to assess achievements from kindergarten through 12th grade. Multi-level tests are an important feature because they allow closer tailoring of test difficulty to each child's level of performance. A generation ago, test levels spanned a greater grade range and really measured accurately only the middle ranking children. Now, with finer gradations in the levels of tests, especially in the early elementary years, more accurate assessment can be obtained without burdensome increases in test length. Several levels are available in all the best achievement tests. For example, the grade coverage of the 1982 Stanford Achievement Test is nearly identical to the CTBS, with six levels spanning 1.5 to 9.9. The 1980 Sequential Tests of Educational Progress begin at grade 3.5 but provide slightly denser coverage in upper elementary and junior high with six levels, 3.5 to 12.9. The 1982 Iowa Test of Basic Skills provides different starting and stopping points for a total of ten levels K.1 to 9.9.

The positive feature of multiple test levels can be a mixed blessing, however. More responsibility is now placed on the test director and classroom teacher to make sure that each child is tested with the appropriate level. Multilevel tests can actually be detrimental if only the child's nominal grade placement is considered. Because the tests are now narrower it would be easier to miss measuring a child entirely (i.e., all of the items are too easy or too hard). In the Test Coordinator's Handbook, out-of-level or functional level testing is explained briefly. Locator tests are provided to use first to decide which levels are appropriate for different students. These tests are short and can also serve as practice tests to orient students to the actual testing. Or, once teachers are familiar with test content and difficulty, they can use their judgment to select the appropriate test level.

Although the publishers represent best practice by gearing the test materials for functional level testing, they should say more in a more obvious place to ensure that this is how the tests are actually used. For example, more should be said to the test coordinators about the logistics of level selection (e.g., teachers will have to identify the levels needed before materials can be distributed), and the individual Examiner's Manuals should carry a warning to first determine the child's correct test level. This involves some risks for the publisher because it will highlight the inconvenience of functional level testing for the early grades. Because Levels A through E involve some oral administration they cannot be given concurrently; children taking different levels have to be regrouped. The improved test information as well as the reduced anxiety when children do not have to take too-difficult tests should be worth the logistical headaches. Since out-of-level testing is only beginning to be common practice, the publisher has responsibility for educating test users. If the test levels are not used properly, the benefits of multiple levels will not be realized.

ITEM RESPONSE THEORY (IRT). Advertisements for CTBS-U and V emphasize that the application of IRT is one of the most important attractions of the new edition. Item Response Theory is a "major innovation in measurement technology,...which has been under development, study, and refinement for forty years." While this statement is true, it is not true that the use of IRT for achievement tests has a forty-year history. The use of latent trait models with achievement tests is very recent and is controversial. One debate has to do with whether achievement domains fit the assumptions of the statistical model (or might be distorted when made to fit). Conceptually, the question asked, for example, is whether all math computation items are measuring the same trait. (What if examinees have been taught some of the skills but not all of them?)

What relevance does this technical debate among measurement specialists have to do with the basic question, i.e., should school districts buy this test? To address this question, the use of IRT has to be separated into three distinct stages: the use of IRT in test development, IRT scoring, and IRT scaling.

IRT used in test development means that when items were tried out they were analyzed using the three-parameter logistic model. Just as with classical test theory, items might be rejected or revised if they were not in the expected difficulty range or did not discriminate between high and low examinees. Additionally, under IRT the items also had to meet a criterion of model fit. (Readers should be aware that many more items are likely to satisfy the three-parameter model used by CTBS than would be true had they used the one-parameter, Rasch model.) Whenever statistical criteria are used to select items there is the potential for distortion of the content domain. However, this is not a serious problem for the CTBS-U and should not be a major consideration in deciding whether to adopt the test. The final content should be judged on its merits. The statistical constraints would have the effect of limiting the types of items within each subdomain. Since it looks as if more item types have actually been added compared to the earlier version, this does not appear to be a problem.

IRT scoring refers to the computer estimation procedure whereby examinees are given a "pattern" score based on a weighted combination of the item responses. Basically, the program locates both items and examinees along the same score continuum; items are located by difficulty and examinees by an approximation of their total score. In estimating the pattern score, each examinee is given different amounts of credit for items he/she gets right. Especially, if an examinee with very low achievement gets a hard item correct, it will not be counted very much because knowing that answer is inconsistent with the examinee's overall level of knowledge.

Here is where the technical debate can have practical significance. If in a local district a particular subset of items has been taught that is not typically taught at that grade level nationally, the model will "disbelieve" student correct answers and will not give full credit for what they know. Because the IRT content domains are relatively homogeneous and because most curricular areas are fairly uniformly sequenced nationally, this phenomenon would happen rarely and should only have small effects on scoring. Therefore, it may be more a hypothetical concern than a pragmatic one. In any case, it is not a reason not to buy the test since traditional scoring—i.e., simply counting the number correct—is available. If an incongruence were suspected at a particular grade level, district coordinators could check on relative standing by both scoring methods. (Note that small and unsystematic irregularities between the two scoring methods are to be expected.) Ideally, the publishers will worry more about this problem and make available to users both person and school "fit statistics" which signal when the pattern of item responses is unusual.

IRT scaling refers to the procedures by which scores from different test levels are transformed to a continuous, purportedly equal-interval, scale. This new standardized metric permits the reporting of classroom averages for students who took different tests or the assessment of gain from one level of the test to another. IRT scale scores are the basis for all of the other derived scores available for CTBS-U. "Traditional" scale scores are not available for the new edition of the test. Because there are two sets of norms available, some practitioners believe that the scale scores for traditional scoring are based on traditional scaling. This is not the case; both sets of norms are IRT-derived norms.

A potentially serious logical flaw has been identified in the CTBS IRT achievement scales (see Hoover, 1984). Unlike other scales and contrary to our experience with individual differences in schools, the IRT metric shows a pattern of decreasing variances as grade level increases. Correspondingly, there is less year-to-year growth as grade level increases, and to remain at the 90th percentile requires less gain than to remain at the 10th percentile. Psychometricians at CTB/McGraw-Hill have argued that this pattern could be what one might expect from a basic skills test where students at higher levels had already mastered the basics. This explanation cannot account, however, for the deceleration in the upper elementary grades nor does it really fit with the content of this test. The effort that went into testing higher-order cognitive skills leaves plenty of room for growth in the upper test levels. The disturbing scale property is more plausibly an artifact of the scaling method. For example, had the IRT model assumed one underlying normal distribution spanning all the grades, it would be possible that when two adjacent test levels were equated the larger (upper-grade) variance would necessarily be shrunk and the smaller variance stretched. What actually accounts for the scaling distortion is not well understood and is just beginning to receive attention from researchers.

How serious are these scaling problems to the consumer? We do not know yet. So long as the method is internally consistent, the scores should give a reasonably accurate picture of gains across short spans of the scale. Furthermore, many users do not rely on scale scores for test interpretation, preferring to use within-grade percentiles, normal-curve equivalents, or grade-equivalents. Although these scores were derived from the IRT scale scores because they were normed separtately at each test time and level, they do not have the same problems as the continuous IRT scale. The most likely problems with the IRT scale will arise when users try to take advantage of functional level testing or evaluate growth across time. There are some unknowns involved, then, in adopting the desirable content of CTBS-U but with IRT scaling. In the next two years we can expect both the publishers and other researchers to provide not only better theoretical explanations of scale properties but also empirical evidence that pictures of achievement gains are not artifactual. If the arguments in support of IRT scaling do not become more compelling, the publisher always has the option of providing traditional (Thurstonian-equipercentile) scaling where at least the pitfalls are better understood.

OTHER TECHNICAL ISSUES. Traditional reliability data are not available in the Preliminary Technical Report; however, we can infer from the intercorrelations and reported IRT standard errors that the tests are adequate in this regard. The national standardization and norming procedures were extensive. Sample attrition (which we can infer from collapsed cells in the sampling frame) is always a problem; however, we can expect these national data to be as representative as for any other major test. The norming was done twice a year to improve the accuracy of norms, which is now a standard practice. Users can further ensure the accuracy of normative interpretations by planning their own testing period to correspond to one of the standardization times, either early October or late April. CTBS-U is a very well-developed test, as are the other major achievement batteries. The practitioner can then safely ignore these technical points in choosing among the leading tests.

TEST OF COGNITIVE SKILLS (TCS). The Test of Cognitive Skills (TCS) replaces the Short Form Test of Academic Aptitude and includes four subtests: Sequences, Analogies, Memory, and Verbal Reasoning. When the publisher's scoring service is used, the

TCS can be used in conjunction with age and grade to predict achievement. The "anticipated achievement" scores are based on multiple regression equations derived from the standardization sample. The availability of a co-normed aptitude measure is one of the positive features of a well-developed battery. When anticipated achievement scores are compared to actual achievement, teachers or parents may be alerted to significant areas of underachievement. If the same area is flagged for many students, it may signal a curricular deficiency.

The TCS is more appropriate for program evaluation purposes than for making important diagnostic decisions about individual children. For example, it would be useful to have a relatively curriculum-free measure to equate schools on academic aptitude. It is not, however, a good individual measure of intellectual functioning. Disabilities that affect achievement are very likely to affect the paper-and-pencil aptitude measure. In fact, the TCS correlates between .60 and .82 with CTBS total score. Especially, the TCS should not be used to compute severe discrepancies to identify the learning disabled.

ESPAÑOL AND SERVS. CTBS Español carries the CTBS name but was not developed with the same level of care and effort as the English achievement battery. It is a translated version of the CTBS reading and mathematics tests. Although some care was taken to make the content comparable, bilingual teachers sometimes find individual items to be stilted or less familiar than the corresponding English item. Content validity should be the key issue in deciding whether to use CTBS Español.

The availability of the Spanish/English Reading and Vocabulary Screening test (SERVS) is a very desirable feature. It can be used to determine the child's dominant language for subsequent testing and at the same time to give practice with test taking. A screening measure is especially important since often teachers erroneously assume that if children are silent or do not speak English well, they are necessarily more fluent in Spanish.

The norms for CTBS Español are problematic. They were developed by using a biliterate sample to convert the CTBS English norms. Thus, the "percentiles...are not norms for the CTBS Español; rather, assuming a basic competency in both English and Spanish, they are estimates of the percentile a student with a given raw score on CTBS Español would have received if CTBS/S had been taken." This is nonsense. Although it may be reasonable to ask how a child would have done in math on the English version (or at least math computation since this involves only translated directions), it is meaningless to say that because a child has a certain level of reading comprehension in Spanish that this would also be his level of English reading comprehension if he only could speak and read English. For program evaluation or individual placement decisions one would never use these substitute norms as evidence of English reading proficiency. Using the converted norms to judge the level of Spanish reading achievement rests on spurious assumptions, e.g., assuming that in bilingual children vocabulary development proceeds at the same rate in the dominant language as it would if only one language were being learned. In the manual, the assumption is also stated that biliterate examinees (used in the equating) should have the same expected score for both versions of the CTBS, but this ignores the differential effect of school language on reading comprehension. In fact, the raw score means for the equating samples follow a pattern that contradicts the assumption. For the English and Spanish versions of the math test the means are similar; for the reading test the means for the English version are consistently higher by about a half standard deviation. Either Español reading is much harder or the biliterate sample cannot be expected to read as well in Spanish. The norms can also not be taken to mean relative standing among bilingual or Spanish-speaking students in the United States because representative samples were not selected for this purpose.

SUMMARY. CTBS-U is one of the best developed standardized achievement test batteries available. The choice between it and the few other major batteries with similar features should be made on the basis of content match with local curriculum. The traditional technical features are excellent; multilevel tests, twice-a-year national standardization samples, and a co-normed aptitude measure represent best measurement practice. These features do not, however, differentiate the CTBS from other leading batteries. The only problem area for use of CTBS-U is the application of Item Response Theory scaling. The unexpected growth patterns reflected by the scale are not yet understood. Interpretation of amount of achievement gain for low- versus high-scoring examinees could be misleading but within-grade normative statements are not affected.

REVIEWER'S REFERENCES

Hopkins, K. D., Kretke, G., Martin, L., & Averill, M. DISTRICT TESTING REPORT, 1977–78. Boulder, CO: Boulder Valley School District, 1978.

Hoover, H. D. The most appropriate scores for measuring educational development in the elementary schools: GE's. EDUCATIONAL MEASUREMENT: ISSUES AND PRACTICE, 1984, 3(4), 8–14.

[259]

Computer Aptitude, Literacy, and Interest Profile. High school students and adults; 1984; CALIP; 7 scores: aptitude (estimation, graphic patterns, logical structures, series, total), interest, literacy; 1 form; test booklet (16 pages); manual (56 pages); answer booklet (4 pages); 1984 price information: $45 per complete test including manual, 50 answer booklets, and 10 test booklets; $18 per 50 answer booklets; $12 per 10 test booklets; $18 per manual; 2(7) minutes for estimation aptitude subtest, (60) minutes for complete battery; Mary S. Poplin, David E. Drew, and Robert S. Gable; PRO-ED.*

[260]

[Computer Programmer Test Package]. Applicants for computer programming jobs, computer programmers; 1981–84; 2 tests; research summary ('84, 9 pages); 1984 price data: $30 per complete set (includes all materials listed below plus research summary); Industrial Psychology, Inc.*

a) APTITUDE PROFILE TEST. Applicants for computer programming jobs; "screening and selection of those applicants most likely to succeed in the programming area"; 5 subtests: Office Terms, Numbers, Judgment, Parts, Perception; 1 form ('81, 4 pages for each subtest); profile sheet ('84, 1 sheet); test examiner's manual ('84, 4 pages); scoring stencil ('81, 1 sheet); scoring stencil for parts subtest ('84, 1 sheet); $10 per instruction kit (includes all aptitude profile material); $6 per set of subtests and profile sheet; 30(40) minutes.

b) PERFORMANCE APPRAISAL SCALE. Computer programmers; 1984; "objective evaluation of programmer's work performance"; ratings by supervisor; item scores only; no data on reliability and validity; 1 form (4 pages); instruction manual (4 pages); norms sheet (1 page); $10 per instruction kit (includes 3 performance appraisal scales, manual, norms sheet); $17 per 20 performance appraisal scales; administration time not reported.

[261]

Comrey Personality Scales. Ages 16 and over; 1970; CPS; 10 scores: trust vs. defensiveness (T), orderliness vs. lack of compulsion (O), social conformity vs. rebelliousness (C), activity vs. lack of energy (A), emotional stability vs. neuroticism (S), extraversion vs. introversion (E), masculinity vs. femininity (M), empathy vs. egocentrism (P), validity check (V), response bias (R); Form A (6 pages); profile (2 pages); manual (40 pages); only norms based upon college students and friends; separate answer sheets must be used (Digitek, hand scored); 1983 price data: $9.50 per 25 tests; $6.50 per 50 Digitek answer sheets; $5.75 per 50 hand scored answer sheets; $4 per 50 profiles; $2.50 per manual; $3 per specimen set; (30–50) minutes; Andrew L. Comrey; EdITS/Educational and Industrial Testing Service.*

See T3:558 (22 references); for a review by Edgar Howarth, see 8:527 (27 references); for reviews by R. G. Demaree and M. Y. Quereshi, see 7:59 (20 references).

TEST REFERENCES

1. Cole, R. E., Johnson, R. C., Ahern, F. M., Kuse, A. R., McClearn, G. E., Vandenberg, S. G., & Wilson, J. R. A family study of memory processes and their relations to cognitive test scores. INTELLIGENCE, 1979, 3, 127–138.

2. Berard, S., & Hoiberg, A. The Physical Conditioning Platoon: Two years later. JOURNAL OF CLINICAL PSYCHOLOGY, 1980, 36, 900–905.

3. Hoiberg, A., Berard, S. P., & Watten, R. H. Correlates of obesity. JOURNAL OF CLINICAL PSYCHOLOGY, 1980, 36, 983–991.

4. Comrey, A. L., & Montag, I. Comparison of factor analytic results with two-choice and seven-choice personality item formats. APPLIED PSYCHOLOGICAL MEASUREMENT, 1982, 6, 285–289.

5. Montag, I., & Comrey, A. L. Comparison of certain MMPI, Eysenck, and Comrey personality constructs. MULTIVARIATE BEHAVIORAL RESEARCH, 1982, 17, 93–97.

6. Montag, I., & Comrey, A. L. Personality construct similarity in Israel and the United States. APPLIED PSYCHOLOGICAL MEASUREMENT, 1982, 6, 61–67.

7. Gibb, G. D., Bailey, J. R., Best, R. H., & Lambirth, T. T. The measurement of the obsessive-compulsive personality. EDUCATIONAL AND PSYCHOLOGICAL MEASUREMENT, 1983, 43, 1233–1238.

8. Zamudio, A., Padilla, A. M., & Comrey, A. L. Personality structure of Mexican Americans using the Comrey Personality Scales. JOURNAL OF PERSONALITY ASSESSMENT, 1983, 47, 100–106.

[262]

Concept Formation: The Assessment and Remediation of Concept Deficit in the Young Child. Ages 3–8; 1978; no data on reliability and validity; no norms; manual (57 pages); 1984 price data: $8.95 per manual; (10) minutes; Elizabeth Tabaka-Juedes; Communication Skill Builders.*

TEST REFERENCES

1. Reeves, W. H. Perception and conceptual thinking in language disabled children. JOURNAL OF THE ASSOCIATION FOR THE STUDY OF PERCEPTION, 1978, 13(1), 24–29.

Review of Concept Formation: The Assessment and Remediation of Concept Deficit in the Young Child by J. P. DAS, Professor of Educational Psychology and Director, Centre for the Study of Mental Retardation, The University of Alberta, Edmonton, Canada:

In the introduction to the manual for this program the manual is described as a manual of activities for remediating concept deficits in retarded children who are functioning at least at the kindergarten level. The manual is also meant to help normal preschoolers. The first step in using the manual for a specific child entails the assessment of the child's concept knowledge. The author recommends the use of Boehm's Test of Basic Concepts for this purpose. A total of 36 concepts are given in the manual for training purposes. For each of the concepts, a list of activities is prescribed.

There is no significant theoretical background given which might have guided the author in her choice of the 36 concepts and the design of activities. However, the approach followed by Bereiter and Engelmann has been adopted for teaching. Essentially it entails four distinct steps, which are: (1) introducing the concept, (2) following directions, (3) responding to yes-no questions, and (4) responding to wh- questions. The author describes activities which are geared to each one of these four "phases." At the end of the fourth phase, the author claims that the child should have learned the concept. Although no operational definition of successful learning is given, the author mentions that the child can do all of the following things: object manipulation, picture interpretation, and work sheet tasks.

Due to space limitations, illustration of the activities relating to one concept only is given here to make some general observations about the inadequacies of this program. Let us examine the teaching of the concept "first, second, and third" as instances of order. The training consists of spatial positioning, arranging a sequence of narratives, role playing (act out the three following activities in sequence—Tom ate breakfast, Tom woke up, Tom dressed), and a sequence of three errands to be run by the character in a story (first Tom has to do this, then he has to do this, then he has to do this). It is all very clearly described, but one is immediately aware of the fact that the author has not taught the concept of order. In all of these activities, order is confounded with spatial positioning.

Without spatial cues, can the child order a series of events? It is not possible to learn a purely temporal order through the activities prescribed by the author. As an alternative illustration of temporal order, let me suggest a task in which the child looks at a box with three windows arranged in a row. There are three familiar pictures which appear in these windows, in a specific temporal order. First, the middle window is lighted up, showing the picture, then the left window is lighted up, then the right window is lighted up. The presentation is brief for each window, so that the subject does not have more than 1 second to view each picture. Then the subject is asked to show to the tester which picture was the second one. Would the subject be able to do this successfully after going through the training recommended by the author?

The criticism, then, of concepts like first, second, and third is twofold; the author should have consulted the psychological literature in regard to: (1) learning particular concepts, and (2) the learning of general concepts. In regard to the second point, the object of teaching concepts is not so much the achievement of mastery in doing the activities related to the specific concepts, but the facilitation of transfer. In other words, could it be assumed that after having gone through the training program for the 36 concepts described in the manual, the child can spontaneously learn other concepts more easily? There is no awareness on the part of the author that this indeed is the aim of training programs in concept learning.

From another point of view, the activities themselves seem to be mostly syntagmatic in nature, inasmuch as they ask children to act out the concept. However, paradigmatic associations should also be learned, so that the child is able to label the concept learned with another word, or learn to understand the concept in a superordinate-subordinate context. Teaching of paradigmatic associations, then, would facilitate the comprehension of the concept in a way which is different from teaching syntagmatic associations, as the manual does.

The manual does not describe validation studies for the training program; has it been tried on the retarded population, and if so, has there been a general improvement in the child's ability to learn concepts?

To sum up, the manual is a collection of activities relating to 36 common concepts used at the kindergarten level. The concepts are not at all an exhaustive set of those that are required or should be learned by the time the child reaches a kindergarten class. There is also no suggestion to the effect that subsequent concept learning for the children would be easier for those who have followed the training program described in the manual. However, the manual does offer 36 activities. If a teacher does not have the time to think up better ones, then he/she might certainly find these activities useful.

Review of Concept Formation: The Assessment and Remediation of Concept Deficit in the Young Child by FRANK R. YEKOVICH, Associate Professor of Educational Psychology, The Catholic University of America, Washington, DC:

The author states that this instrument "has been designed as a remedial approach for those children who exhibit a deficiency or delay in the development of basic concept knowledge." Although aimed at remediation for retarded children, the Concept Formation instrument can be used with preschool, kindergarten, and young elementary school children who are expected to be deficient. The activities in the manual are for the assessment and remediation of concept deficits. Consequently, my comments will be addressed in turn to each of these two topics.

With respect to assessment, the author provides in the manual a modified version of the Boehm Test of Basic Concepts (BTBC). According to the author's instructions, the test materials may consist of any set of available objects; however, the recommended objects include a set of eight small wooden cubes and an elevated box with open ends. A scoring worksheet is also included in the manual. The test consists of asking the child to perform 36 individual manipulations of the blocks using verbal commands such as, "Put a block *in* the box,...*under* the box." The child receives a pass or fail score for each item.

The format of this concept assessment test raises several questions which the manual does not address. First, the original BTBC is a paper and pencil test whereas the current test is an object manipulation test. The author fails to remark on the comparability of the two versions. Further, the author reports no norms, reliability checks, or validation statistics for the modified version, and does not provide concurrent validation with the BTBC. Second, the BTBC is a 50-item test whereas the Concept Formation test contains 36 items. The author states that the current items were chosen using a criterion of frequency of occurrence, but does not define "frequency of occurrence" procedurally. Thus, the user cannot be certain about the content validity of the test. Third, the administration procedure for the test is not detailed. There are no instructions for setting up the test (e.g., whether the tester should sit across a table facing the student) and no standard instructions for administration. Fourth, the scoring criteria are equally ill-defined (e.g., what boundaries constitute correct and incorrect placement of the blocks). In short, the manual presents an incomplete test of concept knowledge. A potential user would be better off using the more widely known BTBC.

The other major purpose of the Concept Formation package is to provide an approach to the remediation of concept deficit. The manual presents sets of instructional activities for the 36 concepts and relations contained in the test described above. For each concept, the author includes (*a*) the name of an activity, (*b*) the materials needed for completing the activity, (*c*) the instructional technique, and (*d*) variations on the activity. Often the author provides several instructional activities for each concept. The instructional activities are imaginative and appealing. The instructional techniques appear sound, based on their descriptions in the manual. However, there is no formal treatment given to the development of the activities or to the instructional approaches adopted by the author. For instance, the author does not describe any systematic method for the construction of each activity. Ideally, the instructional techniques should be grounded in sound principles of learning and retention. The author does not address this point nor does she justify her particular methods over competing alternatives. These problems would not be severe if the author presented results of a formal evaluation of the activities. However, no such data are included in the manual. The author hints at one simple form of evaluation; the scoring worksheet from the test contains columns for pre- and post-instructional assessment, thus allowing the calculation of gain scores. Statistical treatment on such gain scores would provide some measure of the effectiveness of the particular instructional approach. Still a more complete evaluation is in order.

The serious user should also note that each activity does not contain a description of standard procedure. Thus, the user has great flexibility in his/her instructional approach. This flexibility may actually hamper an accurate assessment of how much concept knowledge has been gained from the instruction.

In summary, the Concept Formation instrument needs further development and testing, and the manual needs to be expanded accordingly. I recommend the use of the BTBC as an alternative assessment instrument. Finally, the remediation exercises are probably useful to teachers and/or testers, but these users should be aware of the fact that the instructional materials have not gone through any formal evaluation.

[263]

The Conley-Vernon Idiom Test. Hearing and deaf children reading levels grades 1–6; 1975; no data on reliability and validity; Forms A, B, (6 pages); administration and norms (4 pages); 1984 price data: $10 per specimen set; administration time not reported; Janet E. Conley and McCay Vernon; Janet E. Conley.*

[264]

Content Inventories English, Social Studies, Science. Grades 4, 5, 6, 7, 8, 9, 10, 11, 12; 1979; CI; screening instrument to determine general reading and study skills; 3 reading levels: independent, instructional, frustration; no data on reliability and validity; no norms; 1 form consisting of 3 parts: cloze placement tests, group reading inventories, and related skills and attitude survey instruments; 6 levels (grades 7, 8, 9, 10, 11, 12) in English, 9 levels (grades 4, 5, 6, 7, 8, 9, 10, 11, 12) in Social Studies and Science, in a single booklet; manual (240 pages including all levels of all tests which may be reproduced locally); 1984 price data: $9.95 per test materials; (30–50) minutes for each part; Lana McWilliams and Thomas A. Rakes; Kendall/Hunt Publishing Co.*

Review of Content Inventories English, Social Studies, Science, by KATHRYN H. AU, Educational Psychologist, Kamehameha Schools/Bernice Pauahi Bishop Estate, Honolulu, HI:

These highly informal inventories were designed to give information to classroom teachers about students' reading and study skills as they would be applied to the three subject areas listed above. Classroom teachers are supposed to gain information to support their use of a diagnostic-prescriptive approach to instruction.

Given this view of the potential users of the test and the overall purpose the results are supposed to serve, this review will focus on two questions. First, how likely are these tests to provide diagnostic information useful to classroom teachers? Second, how practical would it be for classroom teachers to use these tests?

READING TESTS: CLOZE PLACEMENT INVENTORIES. These are billed as an optional first step in the teacher's screening of a group. Students write their answers directly in blanks in the passage; administration would pose no difficulty at all. However, the manual does not state the method used to establish the difficulty of the passages (one per grade level), to select their particular content, or to determine which words would be deleted. Nor can this information be readily inferred.

It would be simple and take little time for teachers to follow the stated scoring procedures. Unfortunately, though, one would doubt the validity of the results. According to the instructions and scoring key, the only response that can be counted as correct is the exact word used by the author. Such a scoring procedure would be valid if the students' responses were so constrained by the context that only one response would be likely and acceptable, both in terms of meaning and grammar. This simply is not the case. There are many blanks which can be filled acceptably with two or even three common words. Teachers would have to take the time to examine all "incorrect" student responses to determine if truly improper substitutions had been made.

READING TESTS: GROUP READING INVENTORIES. These tests, too, would be easy to administer. Students read a passage and write answers to 14 questions designed to cover the following categories: understanding main ideas, using context, understanding details, and making inferences. Category definitions can vary greatly from passage to passage. For example, one passage, while centering on a single topic, essentially consists of a listing of facts. In this case, a main idea question has to do with naming the topic. With another passage a main idea question has to do with giving the purpose of the text, and this information is stated in a single sentence. What this means is that teachers would have to look at each question to determine the type of reading comprehension skill students were actually asked to use.

The scoring of students' responses would be extremely time consuming. There are many questions where the scoring key indicates only that answers will vary, and in these cases, samples of answers indicative of various difficulties would have been helpful. It seems likely that teachers could obtain higher quality diagnostic information if they simply had students attempt to read a passage from their textbook and answer some questions. The same amount of time would be required to administer and score this assignment, and the information obtained would be more directly relevant to the course of study. Because of the internal inconsistencies in category definitions pointed out above, it is doubtful that teachers will want to model their own tests after those presented here, as the authors suggest they might.

STUDY SKILLS TESTS. The study skills assessed are the following: using book parts, locational skills, ability to organize and retain information, ability to read and interpret graphic aids, and ability to read for different purposes. There are also surveys for assessing students' attitudes, habits, and interests. Tests are not marked for different grade levels, although there are easier and more difficult versions of some of the tasks. The tests are highly diverse in concept and difficulty and teachers would want to pick and choose carefully, depending upon their specific program of instruction.

The tests most likely to give good diagnostic information are those that are open-ended and likely to be revealing of students' abilities to absorb and make use of verbal information (e.g., the advanced level of the summarizing test). However, these are also quite difficult to score and interpret. For these tests, it would have helped greatly if the authors had presented sample answers to illustrate the different types of student weaknesses which might be revealed.

SUMMARY. In summary, the reading comprehension tests do not seem to be particularly well constructed. In response to the two questions posed initially, some diagnostic information might be obtained, but only if teachers were willing to go through a great deal of trouble. The study skills tests are varied and might be of interest to teachers searching for assessment ideas. They are a diverse and conceptually unintegrated package and each test should be examined in terms of its match to teachers' goals for student learning. Again, the information likely to be of greatest diagnostic value would require considerable teacher time and effort to obtain.

[265]

Continuing Education Assessment Inventory. Mentally retarded adolescents and adults; 1975; CEAI; criterion-referenced; designed for "mentally retarded individuals who have not as yet reached minimal development in vocational independence and/or adequate independence in personal and social skills"; ratings in seven areas: independence, leisure time, prevocational, self-care, mobility, communication, personal and social development; no data on reliability and validity; no norms; individual; 1 form (27 pages, consists of individual ratings sheets for each area); manual (37 pages, shows examples of all testing materials); personal data sheet (1 page); progress/program chart (1 page); quarterly progress/program chart (1 page); 1984 price data: $3.50 or less per inventory depending on number ordered; $6 or less per manual depending on number ordered; administration time not reported; Gertrude A. Barber, Beth Lane, Shirley Johnson, and Alfred P. Riccomini; Barber Center Press, Inc.*

Review of Continuing Education Assessment Inventory by RODNEY T. HARTNETT, Research Associate, Office of Institutional Research, Professor, Graduate School of Education, Rutgers, The State University of New Jersey, New Brunswick, NJ:

The Continuing Education Assessment Inventory (CEAI) is designed to measure the development of somatic, personal, social, and vocational capabilities of mentally retarded teenagers and adults. Competencies in seven types of functioning are assessed (see descriptive entry preceding this review), with the seven being further subdivided into 34 specific skill areas. Independence competencies, for example, are subdivided into eight more specific skills: laundry, kitchen, cooking, washing dishes, ironing, numbers, shopping, and measuring concepts in cooking. Self-care competencies are further subdivided into: eating habits, personal grooming, restroom habits, and dressing skills. Similar skill breakdowns are given for each of the seven major competencies. Finally, each of the 34 skill areas are further subdivided into 455 specific skills. Specific laundry skills, for example, include: recognizes those items in need of washing, uses appropriate soap in washing clothing, uses proper washer settings, etc. Specific eating habits include: uses spoon correctly, chews with mouth closed, demonstrates proper table manners, etc. On each of these skills raters are asked to indicate whether the subject has attained mastery, approached mastery, or given an inadequate or inappropriate response.

Virtually no useful information pertaining to the development or use of the CEAI is provided. No hint is offered as to how the seven major competencies were identified. (They are similar to, but far from identical with, those of the Vineland Social Maturity Scale and the Adaptive Behavior Scale of the American Association on Mental Deficiency.) Nor is there any clue about the method for identifying the 34 large skill areas. Under the major competency area of Leisure Time, to give just one example, how was it determined to include skills dealing with aquarium maintenance rather than a number of other leisure time activities?

Neither is there any information about the reliability of the measures. At the very least one would have expected some suggestions for raters or some general guidelines to be used in scoring the CEAI. There are none, and one is only left to wonder about the extent to which different raters agree on their assessments of an individual's skills.

Validity information is likewise absent. No attempts at age differentiation, comparison of normals with mental retardates, or comparison of CEAI scores with other expert opinion were apparently made. Users are simply left with a list of skills organized into seven general categories, and a rating scale to employ in recording their judgments of basic functioning.

The CEAI is, properly, a criterion-referenced measure, and thus no norms information is given. Still, it would have been useful to have some information regarding the distribution of performances on the CEAI skills. What percentage of young people diagnosed as mentally retarded score at what level on each skill at the time of first testing? What progress can be reported about their attainment of these important developmental skills?

Finally, the user's manual is beset with numerous typographical and spelling errors, incorrectly hyphenated words, and other such nuisances. One error is so glaring that it is embarrassing: the consistent misspelling of the word "rudements" [sic] in the instructions for scoring a skill level that is inadequate. In a scale to be used to assess basic competencies, such an egregious error is pathetically ironic.

In the absence of more information about the CEAI—particularly the rationale behind its development and scale construction, its reliability and validity—it cannot be recommended for anything other than research at this time. It does not compare favorably with several already-available measures designed for the assessment of the mentally retarded.

[266]

The Cooperative Institutional Research Program. College freshmen and transfer and part-time students; 1980–81; CIRP; test entitled Student Information Form; no data on reliability or validity; national norms reported annually; 1 form ('81, 4 pages); information booklet ('80, 24 pages plus test); national norms for Fall 1980 (no date, 158 pages); 1985 price data: $.80 per test plus $175 basic institutional charge (scoring service included); (40) minutes; Alexander W. Astin, Margo R. King, and Gerald T. Richardson; Higher Education Research Institute of the University of California, Los Angeles.*

Review of The Cooperative Institutional Research Program by HARVEY RESNICK, Director, Career Development and Placement Center and (adjunct) faculty member, Department of Psychology, University of Hartford, West Hartford, CT:

The Cooperative Institutional Research Program Student Information Form (SIF) is a 40-minute, 4-page multiple-choice survey. It is completed by college freshmen in participating institutions of higher education. In 1982, 267,185 freshmen at 492 colleges and universities completed and returned the SIF. The SIF is part of an ongoing longitudinal study on higher education begun in 1966 by the American Council on Education.

The survey is designed to provide each institution with a detailed profile of information regarding new students entering the institution and also the larger population of new students entering various other institutions of higher education across the nation. Information collected from each student includes a broad range of demographic characteristics including parents' income, education, and background; secondary school background; finances, including questions about how and who will cover educational expenses; orientation to college—objective and subjective information about student's application to college and expectations relating to college; aspirations, including questions about college major and career choice; attitudes and values about current education; and the option of up to 10 local questions developed by the participating institution. In all the SIF includes more than 150 items clustered into 40 areas. For example, the 1981 SIF had 31 items on social and political attitudes which students were asked to respond to on a 4-point Likert-type scale from (1) Disagree Strongly to (4) Agree Strongly.

Both regional and national normative data for comparable types of institutions are provided to each institution. Elaborate care has been taken to develop a stratified design including 38 different groupings of institutions stratified by factors such as (1) type (e.g., 2- vs. 4-year), (2) control (e.g., public, private, denominational), (3) racial makeup of student body (e.g., predominantly black colleges), and (4) academic selectivity level. Selectivity is defined by an estimate of the mean for entering freshmen of the Verbal and Mathematical score of the SAT (or ACT composite converted to equivalent SAT). Because of disproportionate sampling of institutions within each strata (e.g., in 1980 11 of 113 Protestant 4-year colleges with an SAT mean of less than 875 participated compared to 28 of 49 Protestant 4-year colleges with SAT mean of 1,050 or more), the student data are differentially weighted. Extensive care is taken to provide differential weighting that corrects not only for disproportionate sampling within and across strata but also corrects for disproportionate rates of student response within institutions.

The SIF serves two separate functions. First, it allows for individual institutions to profile both the entering class and subgroups within the entering class. Second, it is the basis of input data for longitudinal research and comparative national trend analysis in American higher education. The SIF data have been part of several very important national studies on dropouts, education and work, student development, and minorities.

It would appear that the SIF has been offered for the use of individual institutions as a secondary purpose, trailing far behind its original purpose for a national survey and longitudinal research base. As noted by a previous reviewer (Hood, 8:397), the report is presented in a format that would intimidate all but the undaunted researcher. The data are returned to the institution with no interpretation, no narrative explanations, and no guidelines for how to present the data meaningfully to any of the potentially numerous university and college constituencies interested in this information. The potential exists now more than ever before to use these data for planning and research purposes along with other student data available at each institution. Yet, there are no examples of reports, guidelines for use, or cautions about such use. This would appear to be a serious omission, limiting the most effective use of these data to those institutions with the resources most ready to translate this data set into useable information. An institutional users guide and better formatting would go a long way to correct this deficiency.

Extensive information is available about the sampling procedures and weighting procedures; yet nothing is said about the reliability or validity of the data. This reviewer could locate only one study dealing with the stability of SIF items (Boruch & Creager, 1972). As students become more concerned about the image they present to college officials and about the possible use and misuse of such survey data, there is more reason to be concerned about both the validity and reliability of these self-report data. Questions must be raised also about both individual and institutional differences in the validity and reliability of data for such matters as student finances, academic achievement, and specific political and social practices. The authors deal only with a narrow subset of technical issues, focusing principally on sampling, but provide little information about other equally important measurement issues.

The SIF remains the most useful instrument for defining the interests, aspirations, and backgrounds of entering college students. The SIF has the potential to be even more useful than it currently is if the Cooperative Institutional Research Program staff would attend to the issue of making the information more accessible, and would also provide clearer guidelines about its potential uses for the individual institution. Approximately 90% of the users in any recent year elect to participate again in the following year. Yet, only 18.5% of the institutions invited to participate in 1982 accepted the invitation. This reviewer believes that percentage would be much higher if the results were presented in a more "user friendly" format.

REVIEWER'S REFERENCES

Boruch, R. F., & Creager, J. A. A note on stability of self-reported protest activity and attitudes. MEASUREMENT AND EVALUATION IN GUIDANCE, 1972, 5(2), 332–338.

[267]

Coopersmith Self-Esteem Inventories. Ages 8–15, 16 and above; 1981; SEI; norms consist of means and standard deviations, no norms for adults; 2 levels labeled Forms; manual ('81, 22 pages); 1984 price data: $5.50 per manual; $6 per specimen set (both forms, no scoring keys); (10–15) minutes; Stanley Coopersmith; Consulting Psychologists Press, Inc.*

a) SCHOOL FORM. Ages 8–15, 6 scores: general self subscale score, social self-peers subscale score, home-parents subscale score, school-academic subscale, total self score, lie scale score; separate answer sheets may be used; $5 per 25 tests; $9.50 per 50 machine scorable answer sheets; $2 per scoring key; scoring service available from The Center for Self-Esteem Development, 669 Channing Ave., Palo Alto, CA 94301.

b) ADULT FORM. Ages 16 and above; 1 form (2 pages); $3.25 per 25 tests; $1.25 per scoring key.

TEST REFERENCES

1. Bedeian, A. G., & Zarra, M. J. Sex-role orientation: Effect on self-esteem, need achievement and internality in college females. PERCEPTUAL AND MOTOR SKILLS, 1977, 45, 712–714.

2. Rosenberg, B. S., & Gaier, E. L. The self concept of the adolescent with learning disabilities. ADOLESCENCE, 1977, 12, 489–498.
3. Kokenes, B. A factor analytic study of the Coopersmith Self-Esteem Inventory. ADOLESCENCE, 1978, 13, 149–155.
4. Fischer, B. J., & Bersani, C. A. Self-esteem and institutionalized delinquent offenders: The role of background characteristics. ADOLESCENCE, 1979, 14, 197–214.
5. Strathe, M., & Hash, V. The effect of an alternative school on adolescent self-esteem. ADOLESCENCE, 1979, 14, 185–189.
6. Diaz, J. O. P. Reading and self-concept of Hispanic and non-Hispanic students. JOURNAL OF INSTRUCTIONAL PSYCHOLOGY, 1980, 4, 127–136.
7. Dorr, D., Stephens, J., Pozner, R., & Klodt, W. Use of the AML scale to identify adjustment problems in fourth-, fifth-, and sixth-grade children. AMERICAN JOURNAL OF COMMUNITY PSYCHOLOGY, 1980, 8, 341–352.
8. Houtz, J. C., Denmark, R., Rosenfield, S., & Tetenbaum, T. J. Problem solving and personality characteristics related to differing levels of intelligence and ideational fluency. CONTEMPORARY EDUCATIONAL PSYCHOLOGY, 1980, 118–123.
9. Seginer, R. The effects of cognitive and affective variables on academic ability: A multivariate analysis. CONTEMPORARY EDUCATIONAL PSYCHOLOGY, 1980, 5, 266–275.
10. Watkins, D., & Astilla, E. Self-esteem and causal attribution of achievement: A Filipino investigation. AUSTRALIAN PSYCHOLOGIST, 1980, 15, 219–225.
11. Buell, G., & Snyder, J. Assertiveness training with children. PSYCHOLOGICAL REPORTS, 1981, 48, 71–80.
12. Craparo, J. S., Hines, R. P., & Kayson, W. A. Effects of experienced success or failure on self-esteem and problem-solving ability. PSYCHOLOGICAL REPORTS, 1981, 48, 295–300.
13. Held, L. Self-esteem and social network of the young pregnant teenager. ADOLESCENCE, 1981, 16, 905–912.
14. Johnson, L. S., Johnson, D. L., Olson, M. R., & Newman, J. P. The uses of hypnotherapy with learning disabled children. JOURNAL OF CLINICAL PSYCHOLOGY, 1981, 37, 291–299.
15. Leung, J. J., & Sand, M. C. Self-esteem and emotional maturity in college students. JOURNAL OF COLLEGE STUDENT PERSONNEL, 1981, 22, 291–299.
16. Riffee, D. M. Self-esteem changes in hospitalized school-age children. NURSING RESEARCH, 1981, 30, 94–97.
17. Bleck, R. T., & Bleck, B. L. The disruptive child's play group. ELEMENTARY SCHOOL GUIDANCE AND COUNSELING, 1982, 17, 137–141.
18. Fair, T. C., & Lawlis, G. F. Self-concept and verbal behavior in a small-group social situation. JOURNAL OF CLINICAL PSYCHOLOGY, 1982, 38, 292–298.
19. Gold, P. C., & Johnson, J. A. Entry level achievement characteristics of youth and adults reading below fifth grade equivalent: A preliminary profile and analysis. PSYCHOLOGICAL REPORTS, 1982, 50, 1011–1019.
20. Gordon, M., & Tegtmeyer, P. F. The egocentricity index and self-esteem in children. PERCEPTUAL AND MOTOR SKILLS, 1982, 55, 335–337.
21. Hawkins, D. B., & Gruber, J. J. Little League baseball and players' self-esteem. PERCEPTUAL AND MOTOR SKILLS, 1982, 55, 1335–1340.
22. Kawash, G. F. A structural analysis of self-esteem from preadolescence through young adulthood: Anxiety and extraversion as agents in the development of self-esteem. JOURNAL OF CLINICAL PSYCHOLOGY, 1982, 38, 301–311.
23. Knight, G. P., Nelson, W., Kagan, S., & Gumbiner, J. Cooperative-competitive social orientation and school achievement among Anglo-American and Mexican-American children. CONTEMPORARY EDUCATIONAL PSYCHOLOGY, 1982, 7, 97–106.
24. Lazarus, P. J. Correlation of shyness and self-esteem for elementary school children. PERCEPTUAL AND MOTOR SKILLS, 1982, 55, 8–10.
25. Rotheram, M. J., Armstrong, M., & Booraem, C. Assertiveness training in fourth- and fifth-grade children. AMERICAN JOURNAL OF COMMUNITY PSYCHOLOGY, 1982, 10, 567–582.
26. Tesing, E. P., & Lefkowitz, M. M. Childhood depression: A 6-month follow-up study. JOURNAL OF CONSULTING AND CLINICAL PSYCHOLOGY, 1982, 50, 778–780.
27. Benner, E. H., Grey, D. H., & Gilberts, R. A construct validation of academic self-esteem for intermediate grade-level children. MEASUREMENT AND EVALUATION IN GUIDANCE, 1983, 16, 127–134.
28. Cox, T. Cumulative deficit in culturally disadvantaged children. BRITISH JOURNAL OF EDUCATIONAL PSYCHOLOGY, 1983, 53, 317–326.
29. Demo, D. H., & Savin-Williams, R. C. Early adolescent self-esteem as a function of social class: Rosenberg and Pearlin revisited. AMERICAN JOURNAL OF SOCIOLOGY, 1983, 88, 763–774.
30. Farmer, H. S., & Fyans, L. J., Jr. Married women's achievement and career motivation: The influence of some environmental and psychological variables. PSYCHOLOGY OF WOMEN QUARTERLY, 1983, 7, 358–372.
31. Johnson, B. W., Redfield, D. L., Miller, R. L., & Simpson, R. E. The Coopersmith Self-Esteem Inventory: A construct validity study. EDUCATIONAL AND PSYCHOLOGICAL MEASUREMENT, 1983, 43, 907–913.
32. Patten, M. D. Relationships between self-esteem, anxiety, and achievement in young learning disabled students. JOURNAL OF LEARNING DISABILITIES, 1983, 16, 43–45.

Review of Coopersmith Self-Esteem Inventories by CHRISTOPHER PETERSON, Associate Professor of Psychology, and JAMES T. AUSTIN, Graduate Assistant, Department of Psychology, Virginia Polytechnic Institute and State University, Blacksburg, VA:

The Coopersmith Self-Esteem Inventories (SEI) are three self-report questionnaires intended to measure "the evaluation a person makes and customarily maintains with regard to him- or herself." Each questionnaire presents respondents with generally favorable or generally unfavorable statements about the self, which they indicate as "like me" or "unlike me." The School Form is a 50-item inventory to be used for 8- to 15-year-old children. It may be broken into four subscales pertaining to different self-esteem domains: peers, parents, school, and personal interests. The School Form is accompanied by an 8-item Lie Scale to assess defensiveness. The School Short Form contains the 25 items from the School Form with the highest item-total correlations. The Adult Form is an adaptation of the School Short Form for individuals over 15 years of age.

The Coopersmith Inventories have much to recommend them as measures of self-esteem. They are among the best known and most widely used of the various self-esteem measures (Johnson, Redfield, Miller, & Simpson, 1983). They are brief and easily scored. They are reliable and stable, and there exists an impressive amount of information bearing on their construct validity. Finally, these measures are straightforwardly based on a general theory of self-esteem and its relationship to academic performance. One of the interesting aspects of the SEI manual is a brief discussion of how to boost the self-esteem of students.

These measures do have some drawbacks, however, some of them endemic to all measures of self-esteem and self-concept (Crandall, 1973; Wylie, 1974). Most basically, researchers have been unable to agree on the precise meaning of self-esteem. In the SEI measures, this disagreement is reflected in several ways. "Self-esteem" is defined unidimensionally (see above), but the School Form is composed of subscales. Personal standards of evaluation are assumed, but some of the items seem to reflect assessment by others (e.g., "People usually follow my ideas").

Relatedly, there is not enough evidence that different self-esteem measures tap the same underlying construct. Some recent research has shown that the Coopersmith questionnaires indeed converge with other self-report measures of self-esteem (e.g., Johnson et al., 1983), but there is less indication that they diverge from measures of conceptually distinct constructs (e.g., Cowan, Altmann, & Pysh, 1978).

Also, self-esteem and self-concept are usually regarded as multidimensional, but it is not clear what this means (see an extended discussion of this point by Fleming & Courtney, 1984). The different factor analyses reported in the SEI manual yield different structures. Further, the SEI manual presents no evidence for differential validity of the four subscales, probably because it has proven difficult to obtain (cf. Shavelson, Hubner, & Stanton, 1976).

Finally, measures of self-esteem may be confounded by social desirability biases, tendencies to answer questions in terms of social appropriateness rather than "true" self-esteem (Wells & Marwell, 1976). Crandall (1973) reported substantial correlations of .44 and .75 between the SEI and the social desirability scales of Marlowe-Crowne and Edwards, respectively. At this time, social desirability is not itself well understood. Nonetheless, that it may confound measures of self-esteem should not be ignored.

There are several more specific problems with the SEI, and these involve possible clinical uses of the measures. First, the provided norms could be based on better defined samples. We suspect that teachers may use these measures to make decisions about individual students, and we doubt that the norms are sufficient for such clinical use. Similarly, the user of the SEI is cautioned to supplement scores with additional observations and information, but no clear guidelines are provided about how to do this. In light of a recent study showing that teacher-completed scales of behaviors indicating self-esteem have little relationship to students' self-report of self-esteem (Benner, Frey, & Gilberts, 1983), this recommendation must be better explained.

Second, detailed instructions are not provided about how to use the Lie Scale that accompanies the School Form. The user is told that high scores may indicate defensiveness, but we were left wondering just what is a "high" score and what is the evidence linking such a score to defensiveness or to lying, behaviors with different denotations and connotations.

Third, at least some discussion seems warranted in the manual of the fact that the validating research has regarded SEI scores as a continuous variable, while the recommended uses of SEI scores typically regard SEI scores in terms of cutoff values.

In sum, we find the Coopersmith self-esteem measures to possess enough reliability and validity to recommend their use in research. These questionnaires share some problems in common with most measures of self-esteem and self-concept. Additionally, there is reason to be careful about the clinical use of these questionnaires. Differential validity of the subscales needs to be established, guidelines for use of the Lie Scale need to be provided, and the cutoff values contained in the manual need to be justified.

REVIEWER'S REFERENCES

Crandall, R. The measurement of self-esteem and related constructs. In J. P. Robinson & P. R. Shaver (Eds.), MEASURES OF SOCIAL PSYCHOLOGICAL ATTITUDES (2nd ed., pp. 45–167). Ann Arbor, MI: Institute for Social Research, 1973.

Wylie, R. C. THE SELF-CONCEPT: A REVIEW OF METHODOLOGICAL CONSIDERATIONS AND MEASURING INSTRUMENTS (2nd ed., Vol. 2). Lincoln: University of Nebraska Press, 1974.

Shavelson, R. J., Hubner, J. J., & Stanton, G. C. Self-concept: Validation of construct interpretations. REVIEW OF EDUCATIONAL RESEARCH, 1976, 46, 407–441.

Wells, L. E., & Marwell, G. SELF-ESTEEM: ITS CONCEPTUALIZATION AND MEASUREMENT. Beverly Hills, CA: Sage, 1976.

Cowan, R., Altmann, H., & Pysh, F. A validity study of selected self-concept instruments. MEASUREMENT AND EVALUATION IN GUIDANCE, 1978, 10, 211–221.

Benner, E. H., Frey, D. H., & Gilberts, R. A construct validation of academic self-esteem for intermediate grade-level children. MEASUREMENT AND EVALUATION IN GUIDANCE, 1983, 16, 127–134.

Johnson, B. W., Redfield, D. L., Miller, R. L., & Simpson, R. E. The Coopersmith Self-Esteem Inventory: A construct validation study. EDUCATIONAL AND PSYCHOLOGICAL MEASUREMENT, 1983, 43, 907–913.

Fleming, J. S., & Courtney, B. E. The dimensionality of self-esteem: II. Hierarchical facet model for revised measurement scales. JOURNAL OF PERSONALITY AND SOCIAL PSYCHOLOGY, 1984, 46, 404–421.

Review of Coopersmith Self-Esteem Inventories by TREVOR E. SEWELL, Associate Dean, College of Education, and Professor of School Psychology, Temple University, Philadelphia, PA:

The Self-Esteem Inventories (SEI) were designed to assess self-esteem in children and adults. The School Form, which incorporates a lie scale as an index of defensiveness, consists of 58 items. The Adult Form is actually an adaptation of the School Short Form of 25 items. The theoretical rationale on which the scale is based has generated a classroom intervention program in addition to its clinical and research applications. A central factor in the development of the SEI is the belief that self-esteem is significantly associated with effective functioning. Presumably, it is on the merits of this theoretical reasoning coupled with limited empirical evidence of a significant relationship between school performance and self-esteem that an instructional program is promoted.

The manual is lucidly written and the theoretical orientation of the author is well integrated into the purpose and rationale of the scale.

In terms of technical adequacy, there is a conspicuous lack of any systematic attempts to establish technical support based on a standardization sample. The reliability and validity data are drawn from a number of independent studies from which generalization must be approached with extreme caution. Nevertheless, reliability data based on a number of studies are impressive. Internal consistency data by KR 20 range from .87 to .92 for grades 4 to 8.

Similarly, although validity data are reported in the manual, the evidence is not convincing. In specific areas in which validity needs to be documented, one is forced to accept the summarized conclusions of studies attesting to the validity of the SEI without the benefit of the actual quantitative information. It is indeed paradoxical that the support for concurrent validity was established by correlation of the SEI with achievement and intelligence tests rather than other measures of self-concept. Based on the supporting data, the predictive validity is also questionable. The lie scale, which is negligibly correlated with other subscales (–.02 to –.12), is the best predictor of reading achievement (.39). The General Self subscale correlation of .35 is also significant but there is no evidence that the other subscales are significantly related to achievement. No reliability or validity data are presented for the Adult Form.

A fundamental concern of this reviewer is that the SEI is built on a psychometric model, yet the normative data must be considered grossly inadequate for clinical interpretation. More specifically, there are several tables of means and standard deviations from which one can be expected to make comparative analysis. The lack of a central body of information to serve as the necessary reference group for the interpretation of scores is best reflected in the fact that the means for males from several samples range from 57 to 81.3. Similar discrepancies in means are reported based on sex, ethnicity, social class, and grade levels. Thus it is possible that any given score could conceivably result in a wide range of interpretation based on the sample one chooses to use as the reference group. The strong recommendation in the manual to develop and utilize local norms for clinical interpretation seems highly necessary, but the concept of local norms must be seen as contributing to accurate assessment under condition where acceptable technical standards are already established.

Most disconcerting is the inadequate normative data to support the notion that the SEI can validly differentiate the four categories embedded in the total SEI score: General Self, Social Self-Peers, Home-Parents, School-Academic. The only available data for interpretative purposes are based on a fairly restrictive sample of predominantly low-income and minority children. This is perceived as a critical limitation of the scale since Coopersmith advanced as a central feature of the definition of self-esteem the notion that one's overall appraisal of his/her self-esteem may not be reflective of one's self-appraisal under different role-defining conditions.

CONCLUSION. The format of the test is attractively presented and the general directions for administration and scoring are straightforward and uncomplicated. The theoretical rationale and purposes of the SEI are based on sound reasoning and are succinctly and logically presented. However, the justification for an instructional program is not clearly demonstrated. The notion that "self-esteem is significantly associated with personal satisfaction and effective functioning" does not seem sufficient to promote a classroom program without strong empirical support. Furthermore, the general technical quality of the scale constitutes a fundamental weakness in that acceptable reliability and validity standards cannot be inferred from the diverse samples utilized. The interpretation of the SEI for clinical use would be difficult for even the most sophisticated clinician. The recommendation that behavioral ratings be administered along with the SEI is an excellent one. However, the manual also points out the lack of a significant relationship between any of several self-concept scales and behavioral observational ratings. Perhaps the need for supplementary measures to enhance the clinical value of the SEI reflects the uncertainty and inadequacy of the norm structure of the scale.

In general, the SEI does not merit a recommendation for clinical use in the context of individual assessment. I agree that the applicability for research purposes seems virtually limitless, and the scale can be highly recommended for this specific purpose.

[268]

Coping Inventory. Ages 3–16, adults; 1985; measures adaptive behavior; 2 levels; 9 scores: 3 scores (productive, active, and flexible) for coping with self (total), coping with environment (total), plus adaptive behavior index (total); norms consist of means and standard deviations; individual; administration time not reported; Shirley Zeitlin; Scholastic Testing Service, Inc.*

a) SELF-RATED FORM. Adults; self-report ratings of adaptive behavior; no data on reliability and validity; self-rating form (7 pages); manual (27 pages); 1985 price data: $10 per 10 inventories; $5 per manual; $9 per specimen set.

b) OBSERVATION FORM. Ages 3–16; ratings of adaptive behavior by adult informant; observation form (9 pages); manual (75 pages); $15 per 20 inventories; $10 per manual; $14 per specimen set.

[269]

Cornell Critical Thinking Tests. Grades 4–12, 13 and over; 1961–83; CCTT; 1 form; 2 tests; manual ('83, 50 pages); separate answer sheets may be used; 1984 price data: $.80 per test; $.03 per answer sheet; $2.50 per manual; $3.50 per specimen set; (50) minutes; Robert H. Ennis, Jason Millman, and Thomas N. Tomko (manual); Illinois Thinking Project, University of Illinois.*

a) LEVEL X. Grades 4–12; 1 form ('82, 17 pages, identical to 1971 edition except for minor format and wording changes).
b) LEVEL Z. Grades 13 and over; 1 form ('82, 13 pages, identical to 1971 edition except for minor format and wording changes).

See T3:606 (7 references), T2:1755 (2 references), and 7:779 (10 references).

TEST REFERENCES

1. Modjeski, R. B., & Michael, W. B. An evaluation by a panel of psychologists of the reliability and validity of two tests of critical thinking. EDUCATIONAL AND PSYCHOLOGICAL MEASUREMENT, 1983, 43, 1187–1197.

[270]

Cornell Medical Index—Health Questionnaire. Ages 14 and over; 1949–56; CMI; a questionnaire for use by physicians in collecting medical and psychiatric information from patients; no data on reliability; price data available from publisher; French Canadian and Spanish editions available; (10–30) minutes; Keeve Brodman, Albert J. Erdmann, Jr., and Harold G. Wolff; Cornell University Medical College.

See T3:609 (33 references), 8:530 (46 references), and T2:1145 (42 references); for reviews by Eugene E. Levitt and David T. Lykken, see 7:61 (32 references); see also P:49 (77 references).

TEST REFERENCES

1. Buglass, D., Clarke, J., Henderson, A. S., Kreitman, N., & Presley, A. S. A study of agoraphobic housewives. PSYCHOLOGICAL MEDICINE, 1977, 7, 73–86.
2. Piper, W. E., Debbane, E. G., & Garant, J. An outcome study of group therapy. ARCHIVES OF GENERAL PSYCHIATRY, 1977, 34, 1027–1032.
3. Friedmann, E., Katcher, A. H., & Brightman, V. J. A prospective study of the distribution of illness within the menstrual cycle. MOTIVATION AND EMOTION, 1978, 2, 355–368.
4. Lin, K., Tazuma, L., & Masuda, M. Adaptational problems of Vietnamese refugees: I. Health and mental health status. ARCHIVES OF GENERAL PSYCHIATRY, 1979, 36, 955–961.
5. Millon, T., Green, C. J., & Meagher, R. B., Jr. The MBHI: A new inventory for the psychodiagnostician in medical settings. PROFESSIONAL PSYCHOLOGY, 1979, 10, 529–539.
6. Masuda, M., Lin, K., & Tazuma, L. Adaptation problems of Vietnamese refugees: II. Life changes and perception of life events. ARCHIVES OF GENERAL PSYCHIATRY, 1980, 37, 447–450.
7. Chiriboga, D. A., & Pierce, R. C. The influence of stress upon symptom structure. JOURNAL OF CLINICAL PSYCHOLOGY, 1981, 37, 722–728.
8. Hartmann, E., Russ, D., Van Der Kolk, B., Falke, R., & Oldfield, M. A preliminary study of the personality of the nightmare sufferer: Relationship to schizophrenia and creativity? THE AMERICAN JOURNAL OF PSYCHIATRY, 1981, 138, 794–797.
9. Piccione, P., Tallarigo, R., Zorick, F., Wittig, R., & Roth, T. Personality differences between insomniac and non-insomniac psychiatry outpatients. THE JOURNAL OF CLINICAL PSYCHIATRY, 1981, 42, 261–263.
10. Schill, T., Toves, C., & Ramanaiah, N. UCLA Loneliness Scale and effects of stress. PSYCHOLOGICAL REPORTS, 1981, 48, 257–258.
11. Zorick, F. J., Roth, T., Hartze, K. M., Piccione, P. M., & Stepanski, E. J. Evaluation and diagnosis of persistent insomnia. THE AMERICAN JOURNAL OF PSYCHIATRY, 1981, 138, 769–773.
12. Baum, S. K. Loneliness in elderly persons: A preliminary study. PSYCHOLOGICAL REPORTS, 1982, 50, 1317–1318.
13. Ludwig, A. M., & Forrester, R. L. ...Nerves, but not mentally. THE JOURNAL OF CLINICAL PSYCHIATRY, 1982, 43, 187–190.
14. Tableman, B., Marciniak, D., Johnson, D., & Rodgers, R. Stress management training for women on public assistance. AMERICAN JOURNAL OF COMMUNITY PSYCHOLOGY, 1982, 10, 357–367.
15. Piper, W. E., Debbane, E. G., Bienvenu, J. P., & Garant, J. A comparative study of four forms of psychotherapy. JOURNAL OF CONSULTING AND CLINICAL PSYCHOLOGY, 1984, 52, 268–279.

[271]

Cornish Test of Motor Planning Ability. Ages 6–12; 1980; 7 scores: imitative crawling, rope A, rope B, jumping jacks, throw-clap-catch, dominant strength, total; norms consist of means and standard deviations; individual; 1 form (7 pages, mimeographed); development of a test of motor-planning ability (4 pages, reprint of journal article); 1983 price data: $4.50 per reprint of journal article; (10–20) minutes; Suzanne V. Cornish; Easter Seal Rehabilitation Center.*

TEST REFERENCES

1. Cornish, S. V. Development of a test of motor-planning ability. JOURNAL OF AMERICAN PHYSICAL THERAPY ASSOCIATION, 1980, 60, 1129–1132.

Review of Cornish Test of Motor Planning Ability by ALIDA S. WESTMAN, Professor of Psychology, Eastern Michigan University, Ypsilanti, MI:

This test purports to measure motor-planning ability in order to diagnose apraxia, "a disorder of sensory integration interfering with the ability to plan and execute skilled, non habitual motor tasks." Apraxia is said to be a "frequent problem in children with minimal brain dysfunction" and learning disabilities. As the author acknowledges, the test measures only gross motor skills. These are elementary ones of the limbs and torso only; they do not include the face (except for looking behavior), bilateral motion with different movements of each hand (except for the limb motions of crawling), sequencing of different but continuous motions with one object, or sequencing with more objects. These exclusions and the exclusion of fine motor skills, which are essential for elementary school tasks, make this test unsuitable for those interested in the child's ability to learn in school.

Any other purpose of the test becomes unclear when it is observed that the stated criterion of using "skilled, non habitual motor tasks" was not in fact followed (except for dominant hand strength) if non-habitual means not-a-habit or new to the child. Even the instructions acknowledge that the child probably will know jumping jacks on verbal command. Similarly, most children have tried to jump over things such as chalk lines or cracks rather than a rope, or tried to move like a dog, cat, or other animal rather than a crawling tester, etc.

Children with apraxia more frequently have problems understanding instructions; yet, despite the author's claim that there is an item using physical demonstration (Rope A) rather than verbal instruction (Rope B), the instructions for each item are verbal with physical demonstrations required or provided only if needed.

The instructions to the tester at times are unclear and the expectations of the child may be denied. In imitative crawling, it is unclear where the child is to be in order to see the limbs of the tester clearly, and whether the child is faced with a perspective or mirror-image problem. How to determine the dominant hand for strength testing also is not mentioned. Goodness of form (e.g., how high the jump in the jumping jack or how well the limbs move and with what degree of coordination) does not matter, only the speed of execution of the basic pattern, however sloppy. The child may not agree with this criterion. In contrast, the child has to move the whole length of the rope in the rope tasks or be penalized, yet the importance of this is not pointed out clearly to the child and the demonstrating tester need not do so. Effect of pressure to perform as fast as possible is never mentioned. Also not mentioned is whether peers are permitted to be present.

Validation, reliability, the scoring sheet and example, and interpretation also leave something to be desired. The children tested for purposes of task selection were all normal and primarily but not exclusively Caucasian and from middle-income families, and the results have not been validated with another sample. Furthermore, as the author points out, other groups have to be tested for normative data as well. In addition, some of the original and the final items are too easy or boring for children 10 years of age and older. With the original items, zero variability started to appear at 9 years of age, and with the final items, older children are sometimes so variable as to cause heterogeneity of variance on the tasks (e.g., on the rope tasks). The criterion for selection of the final items remains unclear. They were chosen on the basis of clinical intuition, and, as the author points out, what aspect of motor functioning they test remains to be established. No reliability data are provided except for intertester reliability by three testers on three children, and this was very good (.97). The score sheet needs further work, and so does the example. On the score sheet, the score for imitative crawling looks as if it has to be divided by 16 when it has to be subtracted from 16, and the equation for calculating "S" has an equal sign where a plus sign was intended. The example has a multiplication error for calculating dominant strength. Interpretation of the percentage of what is expected of a child of a particular age is yet to be devised.

In summary, this test is not useful for those interested in learning in the classroom or learning new, skilled motor tasks. The validity and reliability are unclear. In addition, the instructions need to be clarified, and expectations of the child need to be incorporated.

[272]

Corrective Reading Mastery Tests. Students grades 4–12 and adults in the Corrective Reading Program; 1980–81; criterion-referenced; 6 tests; no data on reliability and validity; no norms; Siegfried Engleman and Linda Garcia Olen; Science Research Associates, Inc.*

a) COMPREHENSION A: THINKING BASICS. 1980; 19 scores: deductions, classification, true-false, description (I, II), same (I, II), analogies (I, II), inductions (I, II), statement inference, definitions, basic evidence, opposites, animal facts (I, II), calendar facts, poems; 1 form (6 pages); examiner's manual (11 pages); 1984 price data: $17.85 per set, includes 20 tests and manual; (25–40) minutes.

b) COMPREHENSION B: COMPREHENSION SKILLS. 1980; 2 subtests; examiner's manual (13 pages); 1984 price data: $35.65 per set, includes 20 tests and manual; (20–40) minutes per subtest.

1) *Test* 1. To be completed after lesson 70 of Comprehension B; 17 scores: deductions (I, II), basic evidence, analogies, contradictions (I, II), body systems, body rules, sentence combinations (I, II), parts of speech, subject-predicate, definitions (I, II), statement inference, writing directions, following directions; 1 form (8 pages).

2) *Test* 2. To be completed at end of Comprehension B; 16 scores: basic evidence (I, II), contradictions, similies, body rules, economic rules, statement inference (I, II), following directions, definitions, sentence combinations, subject-predicate, sentence analysis, writing directions, editing, writing paragraphs; 1 form (7 pages).

c) COMPREHENSION C: CONCEPT APPLICATIONS. 1981; 2 subtests; examiner's manual (15 pages); price data same as for *b* above; (20–30) minutes per subtest.

1) *Test* 1. To be completed after lesson 70 of Comprehension C; 17 scores: deductions (I, II), basic evidence, argument rules, contradictions (I, II), maps/pictures/graphs, basic comprehension passages, supporting evidence, definitions, editing (I, II), combining sentences, writing directions, filling out forms, identifying contradictory directions, information; 1 form (8 pages).

2) *Test* 2. To be completed at end of Comprehension C; 19 scores: main ideas, morals, specific-general, visual-spatial organization, outlining, deductions, argument rules (I, II), ought statements, contradictions, words or deductions, maps/pictures/graphs, supporting evidence, editing, combining sentences, definitions, meaning from context (I, II), information; 1 form (10 pages).

d) DECODING A: WORD-ATTACK BASICS. 1980; 14 scores: word identification (short and long vowels, sound combinations, final blends, initial blends, consonant digraphs, irregular words), sentence reading (time, errors), dictation (sound dictation, spelling from dictation), word completion (rhyming dictation, word completion), workbook skills (matching completion, circle game); 1 form (7 pages); examiner's manual (11 pages); price same as for *a* above; (35–40) minutes.

e) DECODING B: DECODING STRATEGIES. 1980; 2 subtests; examiner's manual (12 pages); price data same as for *b* above; (10–15) minutes per subtest.

1) *Test* 1. To be completed after lesson 60 of Decoding B; 12 scores: word identification (short-vowel words, consonant digraphs, ed endings in short-vowel words, word endings s and ing, word endings er and est, sound combinations ea/ar/ai, sound combinations ol/or/oa/ow, irregular words, vowel-conversion words), story reading (rate, accuracy, comprehension); 1 form (4 pages).

2) *Test* 2. To be completed at end of Decoding B; 13 scores: word identification (short-vowel words, ed endings and contractions, s and es endings, other endings, irregular words and difficult discriminations, vowel-conversion words, difficult multisyllabic words, sound combinations ou/al/ar/igh/tch, sound combinations ir/ur/er/io/wa, combinations orel/soft c/g/tion/ure, story reading (rate, accuracy, comprehension); 1 form (4 pages);

f) DECODING C: SKILL APPLICATIONS. 1980; 2 subtests; examiner's manual (12 pages); price data same as for *b* above; (10–15) minutes per subtest.

1) *Test* 1. To be completed after lesson 69 of Decoding C; 13 scores: word identification (sound combinations ou/ai/ur, sound combinations ir/er/ar/al, sound combinations oi/ee/ea/au/aw, sound combinations ure/tion, soft c and soft g, affixes un/dis/ex/ly, affixes pre/ly/re/ex, difficult words, words with endings), vocabulary (vocabulary words), story reading (rate, accuracy, comprehension); 1 form (4 pages).

2) *Test* 2. To be completed at end of Decoding C; 11 scores: word identification (sound combinations, prefixes, suffixes ible/able/by/less/ness, suffixes ial/tion/ure, affixes, endings, difficult words), vocabulary (vocabulary words), story reading (rate, accuracy, comprehension); 1 form (4 pages).

Review of Corrective Reading Mastery Tests by ESTHER GEVA, Senior Research Officer, The Ontario Institute for Studies in Education, Toronto, Canada:

The Corrective Reading Mastery Tests consist of two series of tests, one dealing with various aspects of decoding and the other dealing with comprehension.

The tests were designed to be used as posttests, after students have completed the appropriate sections of the SRA decoding or comprehension programs. These carefully prepared tests constitute a criterion-referenced measure. In other words, they include a sample of all of the skills practiced in the program. The tests are geared towards mastery learning, and some of the items are taken verbatim from the program; but a few require students to apply principles to new sets of data (e.g., pronouncing correctly the affix in the word "generally"). Each series consists of three tests representing a gradual development in the type of skills tested. The Decoding tests deal with various aspects of decoding words in isolation as well as literal comprehension of connected discourse. The Comprehension tests deal with a large array of important cognitive and linguistic skills such as deductions and inductions, inferencing, sentence combining and editing, writing directions, and interpreting charts.

Instructions for the administration and scoring of the tests are very clear. Furthermore, very precise suggestions are provided for diagnosis and remediation. The "pass" criterion for each skill varies, so that for some skills one error is allowed, but for others no errors are allowed. For instance, if a student or a group of students has failed any of the five "true-false" judgements in the "comprehension A: Thinking Basics" test, specific guidelines are provided for those lessons of the Decoding or Comprehension program which should be reviewed.

Unfortunately, no information is provided about the construction of the tests or their reliability and validity. Since the tests were designed to sample "all the comprehension objectives in the program," we may assume that the tests are valid in terms of their content (i.e., the tests measure explicitly what has been taught). However, no information is provided about the relationships between student performance on these decoding and comprehension tests and other related reading tests. This problem is especially serious since the test items are very closely related to the program itself.

Another methodological problem arises from the fact that the number of items which measure each skill varies widely and is sometimes very small. For instance, in the "Comprehension B: Comprehension Skills" test, a student's mastery in combining subordinate and coordinate sentences is measured with three items (Skill "9"), and his or her skill in word Definitions (Skill "13") is measured with five items. The small number of items may reduce the reliability with which each skill is being measured.

Finally, a careful examination of test items points to some weak items. For example, in the final section of the "Decoding C: Skill Applications" test, students are required to read a short narrative and answer a number of comprehension questions. One of the questions ("How did the light change underwater?") may be interpreted as a complicated question focussing on the process of light change, while the test writers intended the successful reader to find in the text the answer "glimmering blue." The next question requires students to "Name two kinds of coral they saw." Once again the term "kinds" is not precise and may be misleading since the text does not deal with "kinds" of coral, but with shapes (i.e., corals that look like the "brain" and like "fans"). Such items seem to be unreliable since they may be interpreted in different ways by different readers and the test writers did not provide any information on item analysis.

Finally, one of the criteria for scoring the Comprehension tests is that the first word in a student's written response should be capitalized and the response should have appropriate "midsentence punctuation." While capitalization and punctuation are important skills, there is doubtful rationale for using such a stringent criterion when the focus of the test is on high level reading comprehension skills.

To conclude, reservations are raised with regard to certain scoring procedures, the reliability of some test items, and lack of information about validity.

However, the tests were carefully designed to assess student learning of all the skills taught in the Corrective Reading programs; as such, they fulfill their purpose.

[273]

Cosmetology Student Admissions Examination. Prospective cosmetology students; 1977–80; CSAE; 5 scores: interests, word analogies, comprehension and reasoning, manual dexterity, total; 1 form ('79, 20 pages); manual ('79, 21 pages); statistical supplement ('80, 16 pages); evaluation sheet (no date, 1 page) for dexterity; remedial work guide (no date, 1 card); 1985 price data: $15.71 per 12 tests and evaluation sheets; $5 per 50 work guide cards; $7.14 per manual; (25–35) minutes; Anthony B. Colletti; Keystone Publications.*

[274]

Counseling Services Assessment Blank. College and adult counseling clients; 1968–79; CSAB; for evaluation services provided by counseling agencies; 3 problem-goal areas: vocational, personal, educational; 1 form ('68, 2 pages); manual ('79, 67 pages); price data available from publisher; James C. Hurst, Richard G. Weigel, and Martha L. Butler (manual); Rocky Mountain Behavioral Science Institute, Inc.*

See T3:618 (2 references) and T2:857 (3 references).

Review of Counseling Services Assessment Blank by LEE N. JUNE, Professor and Director of the Counseling Center, Michigan State University, East Lansing, MI:

The Counseling Services Assessment Blank (CSAB) provides a relatively quick method for university counseling services to collect demographic information, obtain clients' perceptions of counseling needs, and assess their views of the effectiveness of the agency in meeting those needs. Most counseling agencies in a university or college setting provide assistance for career, personal, and occasionally educational concerns, deliver such service in an individual and group format, and make use of various tests/inventories. The CSAB is useful because it includes items which attempt to assess and evaluate each of these areas.

Sample letters to facilitate returns of the CSAB are provided. Such detail is useful and may serve as a guide in helping to standardize the survey procedure and increase return rates.

The norming group ("narrative data" as described in the manual) consists of the entire client populations of 49 American universities from 1968 to 1975. Data are presented in such a manner that comparisons can be made according to size of institution, sex of respondents, type of presenting problems, etc. Such data tend to accurately reflect the populations which university and college counseling agencies serve. Missing, however, are normative data on other kinds of institutional variables (e.g., urban or non-urban, residential or commuter, geographical location, and racial composition).

Given that racial differences have often been found regarding presenting problems, the demographic data would be more complete if such information were included. In the absence of this information and the lack of such an item on the CSAB, it is recommended that users gather these data locally.

Test-retest reliability data are considered adequate. Face and content validity, though not labelled as such in the manual, are likewise adequate. The only type of validity specifically mentioned is construct validity but support for it is sketchy. Evidence of other types of validity are scanty and difficult to assess. The manual continually presents claims for validity in a global sense—a clear violation of one of the standards for educational and psychological tests. Further, there is the tendency to relate validity issues fairly exclusively to items within the CSAB. This is in the form of stating that because problem A was listed and change (gain) occurred or did not occur on item X, this supports or does not support validity. This is unfortunate, given that the nature of the CSAB would allow more direct opportunities for gathering and presenting clearer information on the various types of validity.

At several points, the explanation of the data in the manual becomes overly speculative. While certain of the hypotheses presented are obviously necessary in an attempt to explain the data, this may occur too often. This is particularly evident in the explanation of male-female differences, number of sessions attended, and gain scores. Such speculations often went far beyond the data.

A subtle discrepancy occurs between the recommended use of the CSAB in the manual and the accompanying descriptive materials. The manual describes the CSAB as having been developed for university counseling services while the additional inserted descriptive material suggests that it be used for counseling agencies more generally. Since the normative data is exclusively from university counseling services, it is recommended only for this population. If others utilize it, it should be done purely on an experimental basis until such additional normative data are provided.

Overall, the CSAB has much potential as an instrument to obtain a demographic description of users, description of problems, perception of gains, and a general assessment of how a counseling service is viewed. Since counseling services need to evaluate themselves periodically, and since there are basically no other instruments for this purpose that are as comprehensive, the CSAB could be very useful when used with the proper precautions. One major precaution is that an agency should not consider that it has completed a comprehensive evaluation on the basis of this instrument alone. This is particularly critical given the validity issues mentioned earlier and the fact that it is administered only after termination. Thus, other appropriate measures should be utilized along with the CSAB. Nevertheless, in spite of the several negatives, the CSAB shows promise. It is hoped that a prompt revision will correct the problems mentioned in this review and thus make the CSAB a valuable tool for counseling services.

Review of Counseling Services Assessment Blanks by MARLENE W. WINELL, Senior Counselor, University Counseling Center, Colorado State University, Fort Collins, CO:

This instrument is a client self-report inventory measuring client demographics, self-diagnosis in terms of the Missouri Diagnostic Classification Plan (reasons for coming to counseling and causes for these issues), client-perceived growth as a result of counseling, and an evaluation of services. The format is short, clear, and amenable to easy data collection. Data analysis procedures are not specifically described, but an insert to the manual provides a suggested computer coding format.

The manual provides detailed information on the development of the instrument, validity and reliability information, sample letters to increase mailing returns, and evaluative findings. There appears to be support for the psychometric properties and usefulness of this instrument.

However, two problems have occurred with using the CSAB in at least one counseling center's experience. First, the results of evaluation were uniformly positive over a period of years, thereby providing the reassuring knowledge of a job well done but no useful detail. Second, it was not possible to tell from the data exactly who or what the clients were evaluating. For example, it was learned that one client might be judging the intake counselor instead of the therapist assigned. Or when evaluating the center, one person might judge the receptionist, another the testing staff. In conclusion then, the instrument gathers important demographic data and some interesting information on self-diagnosis and growth. In terms of agency evaluation, it appears to need work in the direction of more specificity.

[275]

Counselor Effectiveness Rating Instrument. Counselors; 1965; CERI; ratings of 28 criteria of counselor effectiveness; no data on reliability and validity; no norms; 1 form (5 pages); no manual; 1982 price data: $.50 per instrument; administration time not reported; Marjorie Wasserburger; Developmental Reading Distributors.*

[276]

Counselor Rating Scales (Short Form). Subjects in counseling experiments; 1978; for research use only; ratings by subjects in 3 areas: first impressions, helpfulness of counselor, helpfulness for specific problems; no data on reliability and validity; no norms; 1 form (no date, 5 pages); no manual; price data available from publisher; administration time not reported; Thomas F. Cash; the Author.*

[277]

Couple's Pre-Counseling Inventory. Married couples beginning counseling; 1972–83; SCPI; revision of the Marital Pre-Counseling Inventory; 13 areas: general and specific happiness with the relationship, caring behaviors, communication assessment, conflict management, moods and management of personal life, sexual interaction, child management, willingness to change, marital history, goals of counseling, personal and relationship change goals, other changes, general commitment to the relationship; norms consist of means and standard deviations; 1 form ('83, 12 pages); counselor's guide ('83, 29 pages); 1983 price data: $16.95 per set including 25 inventories and a counselor's guide; administration time not reported; Richard B. Stuart; Research Press.*

See T3:1373 (1 reference).

Review of the Couple's Pre-Counseling Inventory by LEE N. JUNE, Professor and Director of the Counseling Center, Michigan State University, East Lansing, MI:

The Stuart Couple's Pre-Counseling Inventory (SCPI) is a revision of the Marital Pre-Counseling Inventory which was originally published in 1973. Comparing the two, I believe that the SCPI is a major improvement over the original. The improvements and/or changes are as follows: (1) The SCPI is now based on a standardization sample. (2) Nonmarried heterosexual as well as homosexual couples are included, and thus it is labelled as a couple's inventory rather than merely a marital inventory. (3) The various sections are specifically labelled. (4) The ordering of items is different. (5) While many of the former items are still included, there are various word changes. (6) Many of the former items have been dropped and several new items have been added. (7) The accompanying manual is more extensive and is much better written than the earlier edition.

The SCPI is presented by the author as: "a useful tool in planning and evaluating relationship therapy based on the principles of social learning theory. As a pencil-and-paper instrument completed by clients prior to the start of therapy, it provides therapists with the information needed to make necessary plans for the content of the first session as well as a tentative plan for the full treatment process. Readministration of the full Inventory or subscales drawn from it during or after treatment is useful in evaluating therapeutic success." Viewing the SCPI purely from the perspective of its stated purpose, I judge that it is true to its billing. It can be a useful tool in planning, evaluating, and conducting research or relationship therapy. However, users need to be fully aware that the instrument is related to a very specific theoretical orientation—social learning theory. This may be either a strength or weakness depending upon one's own perspective and theoretical orientation.

This reviewer is impressed with the author's explicitness in stating some of the inventory's major limitations. For example, it is clearly stated in the manual that: (1) The standardization sample is small (60 couples) and is limited to clients voluntarily seeking counseling in a mental health clinic or private practice. (2) Some of the alpha coefficients are modest. (3) Further statistical work is needed on the instrument. (4) Test reliability data are incomplete. (5) Other assessment tools should be used in conjunction with the SCPI.

While these limitations are explicitly stated, the following properties are presented as major advantages: (1) The SCPI content is related to an intervention theory (social learning). (2) Conventionalization (i.e., the tendency of couples to express only socially desirable responses) is reduced because items were selected to minimize this possibility. (3) The SCPI relies upon descriptive assessments thus minimizing negative inferences which are often associated with trait descriptions. (4) The instrument relies heavily on identifying the constructive aspects of interactions in a strength-oriented assessment rather than a pathology-oriented framework. (5) Its reading level is low. (6) Its assessments are multidimensional (13 scales) because marital satisfactions or dissatisfactions are multifaceted.

In addition to the above, the SCPI includes items from other instruments which have relevance to couple assessment and intervention. It also allows couples, in some cases, to indicate how they see or expect their partner to respond.

As one reviews the literature on marital and couple counseling, therapy and assessment, one encounters immediately a variety of conceptual approaches and assessment devices/instruments. In such a context the SCPI has much to offer particularly from a research and theoretical point of view. Some major advantages of the SCPI are that its author has been active in the field for some time, has written extensively on the subject, and has developed a tool consistent with a theoretical viewpoint (social learning theory) which has both idiographic and research utility.

Given the measurement inadequacies (mentioned clearly by the author), the SCPI needs further work before it can be recommended as an adequate psychometric instrument. Improvements need to occur particularly in regard to sample size, reliability and validity data, and more detailed demographic information on the standardization sample. This observation is not altered by the author's promise that "this test sample is being expanded, and when practical, users of the SCPI will receive by mail a statistical update of instrument properties based upon analysis of the responses of these additional couples." Overall, little evidence of reliability and validity is presented in the current revision. These are major flaws. However, the SCPI is recommended as an aid in the assessment and conceptualization of the counseling process and as a research tool. Though there are numerous other marital/couple instruments available, no specific competing instrument is recommended. This position is taken primarily because the usefulness of instruments in this area must also be viewed not only in terms of psychometric adequacy but also in terms of specific use intended and the nature of one's theoretical viewpoint.

Review of Couple's Pre-Counseling Inventory by MARLENE W. WINELL, Senior Counselor, University Counseling Center, Colorado State University, Fort Collins, CO:

The Couple's Pre-Counseling Inventory is an assessment tool designed "for the planning and evaluation of relationship-enhancement therapy based upon the principles of social learning theory." It is not meant to be an objective, thorough measurement of relationship strengths and weaknesses. There is a strong emphasis on positive elements, based on the type of treatment for which the instrument is designed, namely strategies to build positive interactions. Stuart states that pathology-oriented assessment was avoided because of possible iatrogenic effects and cites research on negative trait labeling and the need to increase couples' satisfaction as well as relieving distress. The SCPI is designed to model a positive approach to problems and provide optimism. For example, one section asks for "ten things that your partner does that please you" and then "three things that you would like your partner to do more often."

The instrument is descriptive and directed toward current interaction patterns rather than personality traits or attitudes. With the exception of a half page on marital history, the SCPI is ahistorical. This instrument would thus be useful to a clinician whose treatment methods are congruent with Stuart's approach. Otherwise the discontinuity would be highly confusing and possibly disturbing. The SCPI very clearly primes a couple for therapy; it is stated that it is "intended to socialize clients into action-oriented therapy."

To the extent that this is acceptable to the potential user, there are a number of segments that appear effective. In addition to forcing clients to be specific and positive about behavioral requests, the instrument requires some attention to self-responsibility. For example, after rating the relationship on 15 dimensions (e.g., sex, communication, finances), the client is asked to suggest ways in which changes in his/her own behavior might improve satisfaction. A level of empathy is also elicited with a question about specific changes one's partner would like to see. In addition, there are sections related to personal management (e.g., work, health) and self-improvement goals. This appears to be a strength of the instrument, since it is generally recognized that while relationship satisfaction affects personal satisfaction, the reverse is also true and merits attention.

Finally, there are sections on "willingness to change" and commitment to the relationship. These constructs are valid ones to assess and perhaps thought provoking for the client. However, several items were worded very poorly to the point of annoyance. For example, the respondent is forced to choose between "If our relationship fails, I know that I will soon find another partner who offers as much as my current partner," and "...I might never find another partner..." For some reason, this section does not provide any scales and the options are uncomfortably loaded. Aside from the clients' experience with these items, the rationale for this section is confusing. The client who scores highest on "willingness to change" is the one who is pathologically needy (this scale has a high negative correlation with self-esteem). Stuart discusses variables of power and investment that are detected by this scale, providing clinically useful data. However, the method of ascertaining this seems backward. Perhaps a more direct scale of willingness to change would be better, with attention to specific domains of interaction.

The SCPI is not exclusively devoted to positive dimensions, and this makes the instrument more generally applicable. In the rating scales and a few of the open-ended questions, clients can express their dissatisfactions. The conflict management section allows detection of physical violence—an area that would require immediate intervention.

This instrument is long. While being readable, the 12 pages require considerable time and motivation to complete. On the other hand, the experience can be valuable, amounting to a therapy session of its own if taken seriously. As Stuart says, the particular way this inventory is completed also provides clinical data. For some clients it would probably help to provide coaching ahead of time since the task is demanding and wording may be unfamiliar. For example, for the list of "caring behaviors" requested, it would help to define more explicitly and give examples.

The manual provided with the SCPI gives a rationale for item selection that is sometimes related to research interests and sometimes to clinical purposes. It appears that the author is trying to make the instrument useful for both. However, this is confusing and makes the instrument long. For example, health status was an item included "because marital success has been shown to be very closely related to health status" (no clinical purpose stated). Then there are questions such as those about children's roles in parental conflict that were included because "these issues should be addressed at an appropriate point in treatment" (no research data cited). Is this a research instrument or a clinical assessment tool? Perhaps the manual could be revised to explain more clearly which parts are for what purpose.

As it is now, Stuart reports norms and alpha coefficients for some of the scales and also data from other research. The SCPI is based on responses of 60 couples with "statistically reliable and clinically valid responses." The sample size is small (as Stuart admits) and the latter statement totally unexplained. There is no test-retest data and no report of validity studies. The author states that follow-up data were obtained from 19 couples but does not give any information about how this was done. Additional psychometric work is in progress, the manual states, and will be distributed to test users.

As for the clinical purposes stated, Stuart provides interesting research evidence much of the time. Occasionally, however, the item selection and treatment recommendations appear to be personal judgments. The chief example is the section on caring behaviors. High scores here relate to providing and perceiving a balance between "instrumental" and "expressive" behaviors. This is said to indicate investment in the relationship but no evidence for this is offered.

The manual thus provides a curious mix of research data on couples, scoring instructions, and treatment recommendations. These are not necessarily contradictory but they could be more explicitly presented, perhaps with subheadings. There is virtually nothing said about test administration. Since this tool is so closely related to treatment process, comments along this line could be quite helpful.

In summary, this instrument appears to have considerable potential. The scales tap a wide range of dimensions, including positive and negative elements. Clinical use would not be limited to behavior therapy but the data collected is present-oriented and descriptive of interaction patterns rather than "deeper" dynamics. The positive focus is strong and the emphasis on taking responsibility a definite plus. Particularly good are the sections devoted to articulating both personal and relationship goals. The optimism created by the instrument's design provides HOPE, a necessary ingredient for successful therapy.

[278]

Course-Faculty Instrument. Business faculty and courses; 1976; CFI; 1 form (no date, 2 pages to be reproduced locally); no manual; reprints containing information regarding development, validation, attributes, and correlates are available; 1982 price data: $1 per test; $15 per package of reprints; administration time not reported; Richard D. Freedman and Stephen A. Stumpf; New York University.*

See T3:621 (7 references).

TEST REFERENCES

1. Freedman, R. D., & Stumpf, S. A. Student evaluations of courses and faculty based on a perceived learning criterion: Scale construction, validation, and comparison of results. APPLIED PSYCHOLOGICAL MEASUREMENT, 1978, 2, 189–202.

Review of Course-Faculty Instrument by RABINDRA N. KANUNGO, Professor, McGill University, Faculty of Management, Montreal, Quebec, Canada:

Student evaluations of courses and instructors in educational institutions fulfill three major functions. First, they provide information to students for course and instructor selection. Second, they provide feedback to instructors for improving their courses and classroom teaching behavior. Third, they provide data to administrators on faculty and curriculum related planning and decisions. The Course-Faculty Instrument (CFI) is developed to fulfill the above functions. Although the CFI is one among hundreds of such instruments currently in use, it clearly stands out as one of the best researched instruments, satisfying the stringent criteria of valid text construction and standardization.

The CFI was developed in 1976 and during the last five years several studies by the authors of the instrument and their associates have appeared in various journals. These studies have reported psychometric properties of the instrument, particularly with reference to its construct validity, convergent and discriminant validity, and external generalizability. Since the CFI does not have a manual containing all the information reported in these articles, the psychometric properties of the instrument may remain unknown to potential users. However, users may refer to a paper by Freedman and Stumpf (1978) for the basic information on CFI scale construction and validation.

The CFI consists of 38 items. The construct validity of each item is determined by its relation to "perceived student learning," a criterion of teaching effectiveness. On the basis of factor analyses, the items are grouped under seven factorially simple dimensions: subject functionality (four items), subject affect (four items), subject difficulty (three items), instructor in class (eight items), instructor in general (five items), graded assignments/exams (seven items), and text required readings (seven items). Each dimension is highly correlated with the criterion of "perceived student learning" (median $r = .53$), but is relatively independent of other dimensions (median $r = .23$). The internal consistency reliability of each dimension is quite acceptable (median coefficient alpha=.82 with $N = 1,332$ students). A factor analytic replication provides evidence for stability of these dimensions in two different samples (median coefficient of congruence=.98). Factorial analysis of the seven dimensions suggests the existence of two general factors, instructor and course. These two general factors are relatively independent (median $r = .19$ for the three subject dimensions with the two instructor dimensions), suggesting that students can discriminate between the course and instructor dimensions.

Besides establishing dimensionality and stability of the CFI, the authors also report some coursewise cross-validation data. "Two instructor dimensions (instructor in class and instructor in general) and a graded assignments dimension predicted 83% of the variance in a three-item overall instructor rating ($N = 47$ courses). Three subject dimensions (functionality, affect, and difficulty) predicted 70% of the variance in a three-item overall course rating" (Stumpf & Freedman, 1979).

The convergent and discriminant validity of the CFI is also demonstrated using multitrait-multimethod analysis (Campbell & Fiske, 1959). Such analyses supplemented by further confirmatory analysis of variance suggest not only satisfactory convergent and discriminant validity of the CFI, but also its superiority over another similar measure called the Course Evaluation Instrument (CEI) reported by Schwab (1974). An inspection of variance components reveals that while both the CFI and CEI have similar convergent validity (variance component for CFI=.44, and CEI=.43), the CFI has higher discriminant validity (.39 vs. .15), lower method bias (.08 vs. .17), and lower error term (.18 vs. .35).

An examination of the nomological network of the CFI shows further evidence of its construct validity. It appears that students' ratings of instructors are more strongly related to "intrinsic" factors (as measured by the two instructor dimensions and one grading dimension) than to "extrinsic" factors such as sex, class size, etc. However, the CFI measures seem to be influenced by "expected grades" in a course, particularly when between-class comparisons are made. For this reason, some caution should be exercised when between-class results are used by administrators for pay, promotion, and tenure decisions. The best way to overcome this problem would be to perform covariance analyses on the data, using "expected grades" as a covariate.

The CFI seems to be a valid instrument when applied to students in a wide range of academic settings (business school, liberal arts, graduates, undergraduates, military students specializing in science and engineering). In these diverse settings, the CFI demonstrates similar measurement properties, and therefore further validity generalization of the CFI is quite promising.

A number of uses of CFI-based data have been suggested by the authors. For instance, data on the three subject dimensions, graded assignment dimension, and text dimension of the CFI can be useful for specific course design and development. Furthermore, by aggregating data on specific courses in given disciplines, one can compare the relative effectiveness of programmes in various disciplines in any given school. Since the validity generalization of the CFI extends to different institutions, similar courses and programs can be compared across institutions. Finally, the CFI can be used for the purpose of faculty self-development and administrative decisions regarding curriculum planning and human resource management. The format of the CFI questionnaire is simple and straightforward. The scoring procedure appears quite easy and the authors claim that the instrument can be completed within 5 minutes.

In summary, the CFI is a reliable, valid, and quick measure of students' perception of their learning environment. It has multiple usages from which educational institutions might benefit immensely. However, its major weakness lies in the lack of a manual describing the psychometric properties of the CFI, its administration and scoring procedures, and normative data (standardized score conversion table) from the samples so far studied. The instrument may be of better use if the authors can address the practitioner's needs in a more meaningful manner.

REVIEWER'S REFERENCES

Campbell, D. T., & Fiske, D. W. Convergent and discriminant validation by the multitrait-multimethod matrix. PSYCHOLOGICAL BULLETIN, 1959, 56, 81–105.

Schwab, D. Development of the CEI: Scale construction and initial testing. CEI Report No. 1, University of Wisconsin-Madison: Graduate School of Business and Industrial Relations Research Institute, 1974.

Freedman, R. D., & Stumpf, S. A. Student evaluation of courses and faculty based on a perceived learning criterion: Scale construction, validation, and comparison of results. APPLIED PSYCHOLOGICAL MEASUREMENT, 1978, 2(2), 189–202.

Stumpf, S. A., & Freedman, R. D. Expected grade covariation with student ratings of instruction: Individual versus class effects. JOURNAL OF EDUCATIONAL PSYCHOLOGY, 1979, 71, 293–302.

Review of Course-Faculty Instrument by CHARLES K. PARSONS, Assistant Professor of Management, Georgia Institute of Technology, Atlanta, GA:

This instrument is to be used for evaluating course content and instructors in business school curricula, although there appears to be no reason why the same scales could not be used for other curricula. The authors cite a number of reasons for the need to develop reliable and valid measures of instructor performance. One reason is that many schools are basing administrative decisions about faculty, at least in part, on class performance. Student evaluations of class performance are one source of such data. Another reason for valid data is the need to make relative statements about strengths and weaknesses of existing courses and programs in order to focus attempts to improve. A third reason concerns the possibility of inter-institution comparisons in order to make statements of institutional effectiveness. Finally, the authors imply that faculty development could result from the feedback of these results to individual instructors.

The authors make the point that evaluation data should be valid before it is used for any purpose. They then provide an extensive array of research to support their claims that the CFI fits the usual scientific and professional criteria for reliability and validity.

INSTRUMENT DEVELOPMENT. The authors developed the instrument by sampling from the rater population: about 100 graduate students in business. These students provided critical incidents, descriptive phrases or adjectives of positive or negative experiences on five dimensions. The dimensions were Instructor in Class, Subject Matter, Text and/or other Required Reading, Graded Assignments and Examinations, and Instructor in General (Freedman & Stumpf, 1978).

From the original item pool, item selection was based on how well an item discriminated between a class that a student had had, a self-reported "high" learning experience, and a self-reported "low" learning experience. Scales were then based on those items which contributed to coefficient alpha. Factor analyses were conducted on both the scale development sample and a replication sample ($N = 1{,}332$). The factor analysis yielded seven factorially simple dimensions. The Subject Matter items represent three factors: subject functionality, subject affect, and subject difficulty. There was also high congruence between the factor structures and a median coefficient alpha of .82. In the two samples, the median scale intercorrelation was .23 (Freedman & Stumpf, 1978). Various rating formats have also been compared. The instrument shows convergent-discriminant validity across three different response format methods, with a three-response format judged as superior.

In the current version, responses are Yes, No, or ? (cannot decide) to the descriptive phrases. The simplicity of this approach and the fact that it yielded the superior psychometric properties for the scales is an advantage of the CFI. The psychometric properties of the instrument (coefficient alpha and factor structure) were also stable across four diverse educational institutions at both the graduate and undergraduate levels. The mean score differences across the institutions were very small when perceived learning was partialed out. This means that the perceived learning criterion is accounting for virtually all of the systematic variance in the CFI scales, and other non-learning, institutional factors are negligible.

FREEDOM FROM BIAS. There is typically some concern whether or not the scores on a course/faculty evaluation instrument reflect no more than expected grades on the part of the student. The CFI has been subjected to careful scrutiny in this area. When individual scores are the level of analysis, the CFI scales correlate with expected grade in the range of −.14 to .17 (Freedman & Stumpf, 1978). When the class is the level of analysis the correlations are somewhat higher, as is the case with many other instructor/course evaluation instruments (Stumpf & Freedman, 1979). The scales were also validated against overall student evaluations of instructor and course. When the class is the unit of analysis, the multiple correlation was .85 for instructor and .81 for the course. These values were upheld in a cross validation sample.

Likewise, in a study of the factors of sex, teacher experience, teacher rank, proportion of students taking the course as a requirement, class size, and teacher publications, Freedman, Stumpf, and Aguanno (1979) found that perceived learning accounted for virtually all of the systematic variance in the CFI scales. This means that these external factors do not influence ratings except to the extent that they are consistent with variation in perceived learning.

Overall then, it appears that the CFI is a psychometrically sound instrument for measuring student reactions to the instructor and course material. However, several drawbacks should be mentioned, only to point out that further research would be advisable and beneficial (which the authors also advise).

First and foremost, the criterion chosen for validation (self report of perceived student learning), though reasonable and important, is deficient in capturing or measuring the concept of teacher/course effectiveness. By way of analogy, one should consider the development and validation of the Job Descriptive Index (JDI) (Smith, Kendall, & Hulin, 1969) as a measure of job satisfaction. The adjectives and descriptive phrases and the response format used in the JDI are very similar to the CFI. It is not claimed that the JDI measures organizational effectiveness but rather job satisfaction, which may be but one element of organizational effectiveness. This reviewer would suspect that a good deal of variance in the CFI is also satisfaction or affect that may or may not be highly related to learning effectiveness. Of course, this assertion is subject to empirical verification. One approach would be to use student ratings of their liking for the course as a criterion and determine the relation between the CFI scales and this criterion. To the extent that correlations, regression weights, etc. are highly similar, questions could be raised concerning the earlier validation results. It is true that some of the authors' findings ruled out some logical contaminants such as required/not required course, sex of the teacher, experience, etc. as contaminants of the ratings. This reviewer's comments are not intended to discourage potential users of the CFI, but only to point out that the criterion used for validation is deficient in some respects.

Another shortcoming of the instrument would appear to be its usefulness for instructor development. For example, scores on the scale, Instructor in Class, may be reported as poor, but the instructor learns little about the causes of the poor ratings. The items themselves provide little guidance. For instance, if the majority of the students found the instructor "not enjoyable," the instructor learns little about how to become more enjoyable. This problem could only be addressed by a more behavioral approach to effectiveness measurement where the behaviors that are seen as effective are more clearly specified. Interestingly, the development of the CFI began with the use of critical incidents which may have had many behavioral referents, but internal psychometric properties of the instrument may have been maximized by adopting the affective terms.

In summary, this reviewer is quite pleased and confident that the CFI is a positive step towards evaluations of professors and courses. The criterion deficiency mentioned above can certainly be addressed by future research.

REVIEWER'S REFERENCES

Smith, P. C., Kendall, L. M., & Hulin, C. L. THE MEASUREMENT OF SATISFACTION IN WORK AND RETIREMENT. Skokie, IL: Rand McNally, 1969.

Freedman, R. D., & Stumpf, S. A. Student evaluations of courses and faculty based on a perceived learning criterion: Scale construction, validation, and comparison of results. APPLIED PSYCHOLOGICAL MEASUREMENT, 1978, 2, 189–202.

Freedman, R. D., Stumpf, S. A., & Aguanno, J. C. Validity of the Course-Faculty Instrument (CFI): Intrinsic and extrinsic variables. EDUCATIONAL AND PSYCHOLOGICAL MEASUREMENT, 1979, 39, 153–158.

Stumpf, S. A., & Freedman, R. D. Expected grade covariation with student ratings of instruction: Individual versus class effects. JOURNAL OF EDUCATIONAL PSYCHOLOGY, 1979, 71, 293–302.

[279]

A Courtship Analysis. Dating and engaged couples; 1961–79; unscored counseling and teaching aid; 12 areas: habits, religion, health, common interests, sex attitudes, adaptability, background, sense of humor, ambition, money, relationship, marriage; no data on reliability and validity; no norms, author recommends use of local norms; 1 form ('79, 7 pages); combined manual ('79, 11 pages) for this and 297; 1984 price data: $5 per 10 tests; $1 per manual; administration time not reported; Gelolo McHugh; Family Life Publications, Inc.*

For a review by William R. Reevy of the original edition, see, 6:675.

Review of A Courtship Analysis by ANDREW CHRISTENSEN, Associate Professor of Psychology, University of California, Los Angeles, CA:

A Courtship Analysis is not really a test or measurement procedure, in that it is not a systematic basis for making inferences about people. As the manual acknowledges, "it is not a scorable test, and is not designed to predict success or failure" (or anything else for that matter). Rather, it is a "counseling and interviewing aid." "It is designed to acquaint counselees and students with the complexity of relationships through a survey of some of the most important aspects of relating."

The questionnaire was developed through the author's work with 91 young married men and women. These subjects were well educated and presumably happily married. They listed traits and behaviors of a courtship partner and conditions of courtship that they thought were important positive and negative factors in later adjustment to marriage. An item was included in A Courtship Analysis if at least 10 of the subjects mentioned the topic.

What evolved from these procedures were 150 items of the form "My courtship partner..." (e.g., "strives to keep promises," "enjoys being with me," etc.). The subject responds by indicating which statements are true or false or questionnable or inapplicable. The items are divided into 12 subcategories and are presented in the questionnaire in these categories: habits, religion, health, common interests, sex attitudes, adaptability, background, sense of humor, ambition, money, relationship, and marriage. For some inexplicable reason, these category titles are abbreviated on the questionnaire itself with letters such as "ha" for habits, "sa" for sex attitudes, and "r" for relationship. The respondent cannot easily understand these abbreviations and would likely be puzzled or suspicious of them.

The author suggests that the questionnaire captures some of the most important aspects of relating and that all items have some validity for use in studies of individual courtships. It would be hard to argue strongly against these qualified suggestions, since the items have considerable "face validity." However, the important point is that the author has provided no research basis for determining which items or which categories are more important than others. Currently, the item "My courtship partner has regular physical and dental checkups," which is in the health category, has equal status with the item "My courtship partner is interested in and likes most of the things I like," which is in the common interests category.

The author is generous in his suggestions for possible uses of the instrument. He discusses its use in premarital counseling, marriage counseling, and individual counseling plus teaching situations in the classroom. Generally, the instrument is to be used as a stimulus material for discussion. Certain variations are offered (e.g., completing the measure for past as well as current relationships or completing the measure for an ideal relationship). As stimulus material, A Courtship Analysis might be useful in generating discussion as the author envisions. It is unlikely to be harmful, unless it distracted the discussion away from the most important issues. The crucial point is whether it is necessary or even useful. Perhaps counseling sessions dealing with relationships should focus on the presenting problems of the couple or individual. Perhaps classroom discussions of courtship should focus on topics generated by the students. Young people don't ordinarily have difficulty coming up with topics to discuss about male-female relationships.

Since its development in the early 1960s, A Courtship Analysis has proven to be a popular instrument. The author notes that the original version was used with more than a quarter of a million young people. However, changes in such factors as drug use, sexuality, and economic and sex role expectations made the author revise the questionnaire in 1979. Seventeen new items were added, which hardly capture these changes. For example, no items specifically address drug use; sex roles are addressed by two items about supporting the partner in his/her career. Most importantly, the revisions were not based on research emanating from the widespread use of the test. One wishes the author would take seriously the following quote from the Standards for Educational and Psychological Tests (APA, 1974): "When a test is widely used, the developer has a greater responsibility for investigating it thoroughly and providing more extensive reports about it than when the test is limited in use. Large sales make research financially possible. Therefore, the developer of a popular test can add information in subsequent editions of the manual."

SUMMARY. A Courtship Analysis was designed as an aid for counseling relationships and for leading classroom discussions of relationships. While the items have a certain face validity, no empirical data indicate the importance of the items or support its usefulness as a counseling or discussion aid. Counselees, students, teachers, and counselors can probably generate their own discussion material in a more efficient and cost-effective manner.

REVIEWER'S REFERENCES

American Psychological Association, American Educational Research Association, & National Council on Measurement in Education. STANDARDS FOR EDUCATIONAL AND PSYCHOLOGICAL TESTS. Washington, DC: American Psychological Association, 1974.

[280]

Creativity Assessment Packet. Grades 3–12; 1980; CAP; consists of 2 tests and a rating instrument to be used by parents and teachers; manual (24 pages); 1983 price data: $19.95 per complete set; Frank Williams; D.O.K. Publishers, Inc.*

a) TEST OF DIVERGENT THINKING. 6 scores: fluency, flexibility, originality, elaboration, title, total; 1 form (4

pages); 20(25) minutes for grades 6–12, 25(30) minutes for grades 3–5.
b) TEST OF DIVERGENT FEELING. 5 scores: curiosity, imagination, complexity, risk-taking, total; 1 form (7 pages); (10–20) minutes.
c) THE WILLIAMS SCALE. Ratings by teachers and parents; 1 form (4 pages); (20–30) minutes.

Review of Creativity Assessment Packet by FRED DAMARIN, Associate Professor of Psychology, The Ohio State University, Columbus, OH:

The Creativity Assessment Packet (CAP) contains the germs of good ideas, but the author seems to be out of contact with the research literature in the field, as reviewed most recently, for example, by Kogan (1983). The CAP presents three instruments—a drawing test, a questionnaire, and a rating form—all of which are intended to measure creativity in persons in the 3rd through 12th grades. The three instruments appear to measure the same or related creative traits and the author would seem to be in a position to offer multitrait-multimethod validation. That term is never mentioned, however, and the concept itself may not be grasped. One's initial sense of new opportunities offered by the tests dwindles further upon more thorough examination of the test material and the manual.

The manual is nicely printed but poorly written. There is a dangling modifier in the first sentence. The word "to" is overused as a preposition and the word "attributing" is used where "contributing" is meant. Verbal descriptions of the scoring of the drawing test are uninterpretable but they suggest that multiplication is involved, whereas the worked-out example uses only the conventional addition of item scores. A paragraph describing the interpretation of the test scores contains references to score "pairs," but one can only guess at the meaning of this reference.

The scales in the CAP were apparently devised to assess the effects of the author's pedagogical system for increasing the creativity of school children. Those desiring further information are referred to the author's book (Williams, 1969). This is the only explicit reference to any publication in the manual. Guilford's factor analytic research is mentioned as an inspiration for the author's drawing test. This test is said to measure divergent thinking factors involving both left and right brain tasks. The author, however, misidentifies one of Guilford's factor codes and shows scant familiarity with the type of tests used in the relevant locations in the Guilford model. References to other research studies of creativity are absent, and the author seems unaware that his recommended testing procedures come down heavily on one or another side of hotly debated issues. Some authorities insist, for example, that creativity measures should be given a playful, game-like setting; others say that standardized testing procedures will do. The author's own test instructions urge the children to work fast at being creative. The instructions require children to attempt each drawing in turn without skipping around. They represent the distinctly unplayful end of the continuum.

A close inspection of the drawing test suggests that Guilford's labels have been applied to testing procedures that Guilford would not use. The first drawing test score is called "fluency." This is a very important label for, as Kogan (1983) notes, the primary focus of attention in children's creativity research for the past 15 years has been ideational fluency. Fluency is the production of multiple responses to a single stimulus. The CAP presents twelve 3 x 3 inch frames containing one to four straight or curved lines and requests the child to sketch an object or picture in each frame. The "fluency" score is a simple count of items attempted (while working under instructions not to skip around). No evidence is presented to show that this type of score correlates with any test that measures fluency in the usual sense of that term.

The drawing test supposedly measures "originality" as well. This important label usually stands for some index of the novelty or infrequency of the subject's responses. In the CAP drawing test, however, "originality" means the tendency to draw both inside and outside the stimulus lines that are provided. Evidence about the relationship between this score and novelty of responses is not offered.

One additional point deserves attention: the fluency, flexibility, originality, elaboration, and title scores on the drawing test are all obtained from the same 12 items. This practice usually raises the correlations among the scores spuriously and guarantees a higher coefficient alpha for the battery than investigators using different items on each test are likely to obtain.

The second test in the packet is a questionnaire entitled "Exercise in Divergent Feeling" that contains 50 multiple choice items. It features a four category response format with options defined (roughly) as "yes," "maybe," "no," and "don't know," which (on positively worded items) are weighted 2, 1, 1 and −1. According to the author, the "don't know" response counts negatively because indecisiveness is not a creative trait! Nothing is said about response sets, but acquiescence is likely to be a bigger problem in the two scales where most of the items are keyed "yes" than in the two that are nicely balanced. A final issue in this questionnaire is content validity. The reviewer found it difficult to anticipate the correct assignment of many items to their respective scales. The scales seem poorly differentiated and this, along with response set variance, could cause the four scales to intercorrelate highly and defeat attempts to interpret the scores as profiles.

The final instrument in the CAP is the Williams Scale, a rating form on which parents or teachers can enter their impressions of the children on eight of the nine dimensions assessed by the drawing test and questionnaire. Four free response items are included in this scale.

The test manual presents means and standard deviations for both the component scores and total scores on both the drawing test and the questionnaire, but only for the total score on the rating form. Some of these data seem internally inconsistent. Adding the means for the drawing test subscores does not produce the mean for the drawing test total score. In addition, there is a "Pupil Assessment Matrix" which supposedly converts raw scores on the scales into standard score profiles, but some conversions are crude and inaccurate. Different results can sometimes be obtained from the table than by computing standard scores with the actual means and standard deviations. No explicit information whatsoever is given about the size or composition of the norm group. A subsequent section of the manual gives information on reliability and validity from a sample of 256 students in grades 3 through 12. The normative data may or may not be based on the same sample; the manual does not say.

Test-retest reliabilities over a 10-month period are characterized vaguely as "in the sixties." The values for individual scales are not given and no other form of reliability is presented. The validities of the two "performance tests" are said to be .71 and .76, but absolutely nothing is said about what the author did to obtain these numbers. High correlations are also claimed between pupil test performance and parent and/or teacher ratings, but nothing is said about whether parents or teachers or both were used to obtain the data. One other high validity coefficient was claimed but its meaning is even more ambiguous than those just repeated.

There is only one circumstance in which this reviewer would use the CAP in research, and that is as part of a test of Wallach's (1971) hypothesis that many creativity tests are really measures of susceptibility to experimenter-demand characteristics. The creative child who resists being tested for creativity may do very poorly on tests in which he is instructed to draw pictures in squares one at a time (no skipping around) and is penalized for answering "don't know" to ambiguous questions. If one wants to measure Guilford's divergent production factors, why not use the Creativity Test for Children from Guilford's own laboratory? If one wants to measure creativity, why not study the literature on the topic thoroughly and make a discriminating choice among the existing instruments for your own situation?

REVIEWER'S REFERENCES

Williams, F. E. CLASSROOM IDEAS FOR ENCOURAGING THINKING AND FEELING. Buffalo, NY: D.O.K. Publishers, 1969.

Wallach, M. A. THE INTELLIGENCE/CREATIVITY DISTINCTION. Morristown, NJ: General Learning Press, 1971.

Kogan, N. Stylistic variation in childhood and adolescence: Creativity metaphor and cognitive style. In P. H. Mussen (Ed.), HANDBOOK OF CHILD PSYCHOLOGY, Vol. III. New York: Wiley, 1983.

Review of Creativity Assessment Packet by CARL L. ROSEN, Professor of Education, Kent State University, Kent, OH.

The Creativity Assessment Packet (CAP) contains three instruments described as measuring "a different set" of abilities, as a "whole new way" of viewing children's skills, and as a collection which evaluates "the most important factors" of creativity, etc. Many claims and proclamations are made, but the well-packaged and presented materials provide a facade for a set of instruments that can be critiqued on at least four grounds. First, the effort to establish a conceptual base for the instruments is tenuous. It is acknowledged in the manual that four of the five factors (Flexibility, Fluency, Originality, and Elaborative Thinking) scored in the CAP Test of Divergent Thinking (DT) are derived from Guilford's work. The author's model appears to be the source of the four affective factors (Risk-Taking, Complexity, Curiosity, and Imagination) in the Test of Divergent Feeling (DF). The rationale, however, for the development of the instruments in this packet is vague and discursive. There is no specific tie-in with Guilford's or the author's model, no discussion of the actual methods used for instrument construction, no presentation of the principles guiding the selection of tasks, and no criteria nor information from field trials on how items and scoring protocols were designated.

Second, it seems difficult to justify, without experimental data on construct validation, how the CAP can be used to screen, identify, and diagnose creative abilities when the only pupil production test in the collection, the DT, is essentially a picture sketching task (similar to Activity 2, Booklet B, in the Thinking Creatively With Pictures subtest of the Torrance tests). One of the major problems in constructing creativity tests is to provide a broad variety of production tasks to insure that adequate sampling of this complex construct is accomplished. While the CAP manual proclaims a "multiple approach" for assessing creativity, the self-report task of the DF and the observations from the rating scale cannot nullify the narrowness of DT test content. The addition of a verbal score for assigning titles to the pictures is not sufficient.

A third area of concern involves the claim that the packet is designed to provide a "practical" method for evaluating creative potential. Administration times do indeed seem economical. However, the assertion that scoring of the DT and DF tests for a class of 25 pupils will take "approximately an hour or less" may be misleading. The manual does not provide information from the standardization sample as to how many of the 12 incomplete frames in the DT are completed, on the average, by different age groups. The scoring of the completed sketches in this test is subjective, requiring the examiner to follow protocols and examples for deriving five scoring decisions per picture. Careful scoring of each picture produced by 25 students might require more than 1 hour. If 25 older students, for example, were to provide sketches for all 12 frames, one would need to assess 300 pictures at the rate of 5 per minute just to finish scoring the DT in an hour. Scoring of the DF test also appears to be less efficient than is apparent. The scoring templates provided have placed item numbers awkwardly in the middle of the punched answers. Holes punched for scoring are only for answers which earn 2 points. No holes are punched for 1 point or minus 1 point responses. The "factor code," which indicates which of four affective areas each item relates to, is poorly placed in the last of four columns. The fourth and most serious concern is with the quality of technical information supplied in the manual. Administration and scoring of the two pupil tests and the rating scale yields three total scores and nine subscores. The obtained scores are to be interpreted from one table of means and standard deviations undifferentiated by age and grade and a separate pupil "matrix" which provides all possible scores in intervals across a continuum. These norms are derived from quite a small sample ($N=256$) with no information provided as to the selection process used to identify norm group. The group is described as "a mixed sample of students in grades 3 through 12." Without a description of the characteristics of the normative sample, interpretation of scores is uncertain. The reader is also required to be content with two validity coefficients (.71 and .76) independent of description. Authors of published tests are expected to adequately report the basis of validity claims. Correlations of .59, .67, and .74 between the sample's test scores and adult ratings of creativity suggest that both sets of instruments are measuring somewhat similar attributes, but this is not an adequate demonstration of validity.

In conclusion, the CAP contains a technically uncertain set of instruments whose usefulness is limited by a lack of appropriate information as to validity and reliability. The manual's inadequate treatment of the standardization process, including the absence of information on the normative sample, makes it clear that the user cannot approach normative data with any degree of confidence. Given these problems and the exaggerated claims made for the uses of these instruments, the CAP cannot be recommended for use. For more fully developed tests of creativity, consider the Creativity Tests for Children and the Torrance Tests of Creative Thinking.

[281]

Creativity Checklist. Grades K–graduate school; 1979; CCh; "objective, self-report, eight-item instrument developed specifically to identify overt creativity observed by at least one other person"; no data on reliability; no description of normative population, norms consist of a possible breakdown of scores by level of creativity in the setting; 1 form (2 pages); manual (4 pages); 1983 price data: $8.75 per complete set including 30 record forms; $6.50 per 30 record forms; $4.75 per manual; 15(20) minutes; David L. Johnson; Stoelting Co.*

Review of Creativity Checklist by PATRICIA L. DWINELL, Coordinator of Evaluation and Testing, Division of Developmental Studies, University of Georgia, Athens, GA:

When first viewing the Creativity Checklist (CCh) and the manual, one cannot help but wonder, "Is this all there is?" Both the instrument and manual are limited in volume and content.

The Creativity Checklist itself consists of two pages; one page presents eight characteristics of creativity, the other page is used to record the extent to which the observed characteristics are exhibited. Using Torrance's (1970) definition of the processes by which creativity takes place, and the author's definition of creativity as a spontaneous productive act within a social interaction setting, the author has developed a checklist of eight behaviors which he believes are characteristic of the creative person. These behaviors can be observed by others in various group settings such as meetings and classrooms, and scored on a 5-point scale ranging from "never" to "consistently" according to the frequency of the behavior. A creativity score for an individual is obtained by summing the scores. Descriptions of the characteristics are given in the record form; they include such observed characteristics as sensitivity, fluency, flexibility, resourcefulness, constructional skill, ingenuity, independence, and positive self-referencing behavior.

The manual consists of four pages. However, two of the pages are sample pages of the record form. Approximately one and one-fourth pages actually relate to the instrument. This reviewer finds a number of inappropriate terms and phrases in this manual. First of all, the manual is described as an instruction manual. Any instructions given in the manual are negligible, and the one-sentence instruction on the second page of the form could have been written more clearly. A number of questionable terms also appear in the second paragraph of the manual. For example, the description of the CCh as an "objective, self-report" instrument is misleading. Other than a caution to make an "effort to reduce bias," no instructions are given to ensure objectivity. Furthermore, "self-report" implies that persons report on themselves, although nowhere in the manual is this kind of reporting suggested. In addition, the phrase "can be administered quickly by one's self" must refer to the checklist user since this is not a self-administered instrument. Finally, the term "test" is used. At best, the checklist is an assessment device used to record observed cues to creative behavior.

No norms are given to guide the user in interpreting the scores obtained by observers. Instead, the author presents one possible breakdown of the scores by level of creativity and suggests that users establish their own criteria based on performance in the setting. This absence of standardization suggests that creative behavior interpreted as low or average through use of the CCh in one setting may be considered as moderate or high in another setting.

Use of this instrument requires great reliance on the skills of the users not only for interpretation of the data but also for training of observers and establishment of reliability and validity. The author claims that "one in-service training session and sharing of examples of creative behavior observed in the setting is sufficient to maintain intercoder reliabilities in the .70 to .80 range." However, evidence to support this statement is not given; in the absence of well described procedures for establishing reliability estimates, and with evidence limited to this kind of vague generalization, credibility of reliability evidence becomes an issue. Test-retest reliability evidence is not presented.

To demonstrate the validity of the checklist, correlations are reported between the CCh and the Torrance Tests of Creative Thinking verbal total scores ($r=.56$), the Remote Associates Test ($r=.51$), and the Pre-conscious Activity Scale ($r=.51$). Again, references to support these correlations are not given in the manual. Two additional studies which are cited to support the validity of the instrument contained extremely small sample sizes.

The manual contains seven references, one of which is a 70-page technical report available from the publisher. Only two references are readily available to the test user and only one of these directly relates to the Checklist.

Publication of the Creativity Checklist appears to be premature. Although the author is to be credited for his endeavor to develop a checklist by which observed creative behavior can be identified, he presents little evidence to support its use as a screening, identification, or evaluation instrument. Nevertheless, the items in the checklist represent rather salient characteristics and, used as a quick didactic device to observe behavior, may be useful.

REVIEWER'S REFERENCES

Torrance, E. P. ENCOURAGING CREATIVITY IN THE CLASSROOM. Dubuque, IA: William C. Brown Co., 1970.

Review of Creativity Checklist by LINDA WHITE HAWTHORNE, Associate Professor of Special Education, Georgia State University, Atlanta, GA:

The manual describes the Creativity Checklist (CCh) as an objective, self-report checklist. It is none of the three. It is a subjective, observation-based rating scale. It consists of eight items prefaced with the statement, "The creative person is able to:...." The items that follow are rated on a scale ranging from "never" (1) to "consistently" (5). These ratings are to be based on "the respondent's observations of each person's social interactions in a given setting (classroom, activity, training session, meeting, etc.)." Unfortunately, most items do not delineate specific behaviors to be observed. They consist of rather vague references to abilities. For instance, the first item is "Perceive the subtle, ambiguous, and complex features of the setting-OBSERVED sensitivity or preference for complexity." Other abilities referred to in the items include fluency, flexibility, resourcefulness, constructional skill, ingenuity and productiveness, independence, and positive self-referencing.

The four-page manual (two of the pages are reproductions of the protocol) is flawed with numerous inaccurate and confusing statements and is technically inadequate. It does not state an age or grade range for which the CCh is appropriate. The stated purpose of using the instrument is not clear. Although the manual states that it was "developed specifically to identify overt creativity," it does not state the purpose of identifying creativity. To screen for creative students? To identify creative students for placement purposes? To measure the effects of intervention? The author's use of the term "creativity" also is confusing. He states that the instrument was developed on the basis of two definitions. The first he credits to E. Paul Torrance: "Creativity takes place within a process of becoming sensitive to or aware of problems, deficiencies, or gaps in knowledge; of bringing information together into new relationships; of defining the difficulties in identifying missing information; of searching for solutions; of testing them; and in communicating results." The second definition of creativity is the author's own. In stark contrast to Torrance's definition, the author defines creativity as an "unexpected, positive self-referenced, or productive act emitted spontaneously by a person within a social interaction setting." The author makes no attempt to link Torrance's cognitive definition with his own social-interaction definition.

Directions for rating subjects on the test's eight items are very limited. The manual states that items are rated on a 1-to-5 scale and then summed to obtain a total score. It is stated that the CCh typically requires less than 15 minutes per "test."

Each protocol provides space to record ratings of up to 26 subjects in a single setting. Is the rating of a single subject considered a test or the rating of multiple subjects within a single setting? Even if a test is limited to a single subject, it is unlikely that within 15 minutes an observer could observe an adequate sample of the numerous abilities described in the items. The manual states that the observer should sample as many settings and content/activity areas where creativity may be observed, but it does not give adequate guidelines for structuring the observations. For instance, if a subject is observed in multiple settings, should multiple ratings be done or should a single rating take into account behaviors in various settings? The manual cautions that every effort should be made to reduce bias and maintain high reliability, yet it does not provide suggestions for helping the rater to accomplish these goals. Further, the items are on one side of the protocol and the space for rating them is on the other side—a very inconvenient format requiring the rater to continually flip back and forth.

The CCh is not normed, but a table is provided that lists intervals of total scores and corresponding descriptors of levels of creativity. For instance, scores of 34 to 40 correspond to a "high" level of creativity. No data or rationale is provided for the table. The author simply offers it as "one possible breakdown of CCh scores by level of creativity in the setting." It is questionable that the raw scores can be interpreted in the same manner across all age groups.

The author does not report reliability data. He merely states that "Typically, one in-service training session and sharing of examples of creative behavior observed in the setting is sufficient to maintain intercoder reliabilities in the .70 to .80 range." Inter- and intra-rater reliability data are critical for any observation-based instrument, but they are especially vital to the CCh since most of the items are not stated in behavioral terms and are very open to different interpretation.

In estimating the CCh's validity, the author refers to numerous correlational studies. None of the studies are adequately described in the manual. The problem is compounded by the fact that the studies referred to in the manual are (*a*) not available (studies done by the author's students), or (*b*) not actually reported in the reference cited, or (*c*) not referenced at all. An example of the third problem is reflected in the following quote from the manual: "High mean product-moment correlations have been reported for the CCh with the Torrance Tests of Creative Thinking (TTCT) verbal total scores ($r = .56$), the Remote Associates Test (3 studies, $r = .51$), and the Preconscious Activity Scale (3 studies, $r = .51$)." No references are cited for the studies and no descriptions of the validation samples are provided. It would be pointless to review the correlational data presented since none of it is substantiated adequately. Suffice it to say that the validity data in the manual is inadequate.

Given the technical and conceptual problems of the CCh, there is no reason to recommend it over unaided observation. No normative data is provided, validity studies are not adequately described nor referenced well enough to be evaluated, no reliability data is provided, and the conceptual basis for the instrument is two different, if not disparate, views of creativity. Although the author's idea of viewing creativity within a social-interaction framework is an interesting one, the CCh in its present state does not appear to be a viable instrument for exploring it.

[282]

Cree Questionnaire. Adults; 1957–81; CQ; creativity and inventiveness; 14 scores: overall creative potential, plus 13 technical dimension scores grouped under four broad headings (social orientation, work orientation, internal functioning, interests and skills); no reliability data; no description of normative population; Forms A ('81, 9 pages), B ('81, 9 pages); score sheets, separate for each form ('80, 3 pages); interpretation and research manual ('80, 51 pages); 1984 price data: $15 per 25 tests of either form; $2.50 per 25 score sheets; $6 per manual; $10 per specimen set; (15–20) minutes; T. G. Thurstone, J. J. Mellinger, and Peter W. B. Goddard (manual); London House Management Consultants, Inc.*

See T2:1149 (1 reference) and P:53 (3 references); for reviews of an earlier edition by Allyn Miles Munger and Theodor F. Naumann, see 6:84.

Review of Cree Questionnaire by JANET M. STOPPARD, Associate Professor of Psychology, University of New Brunswick, Fredericton, New Brunswick, Canada:

"The Cree Questionnaire is a semi-disguised, psychological test designed to assess an individual's creative-innovative potential." Since last reviewed (see 6:84) this test has undergone a number of revisions. The Cree Questionnaire itself, consisting of 145 items (answered Y, ?, or N) remains unchanged, but an alternative form is now available. The manual (revised 1980) states that availability of an alternative form "decreases the possibility of learned responses if the questionnaire has to be readministered." However, the utility of the alternative form seems limited by the fact that the 145 items are identical in the two forms, and only minimal changes in item order are apparent. The manual provides scoring keys for the newly added technical dimensions as well as for the Overall Creative Potential (OCP) score. The 13 technical dimensions were derived from a factor analytic study (Furcon, 1965) of Cree responses of 1,016 males from a variety of professional, administrative, sales, and other occupational backgrounds. The technical dimension scores appear to offer an alternative mode of interpretation to that based solely on the OCP score. According to the manual, the 13 dimensions (factors) are grouped under the four broad headings of Social Orientation, Work Orientation, Internal Functioning, and Interests and Skills. While these groupings seem to have some face validity in terms of the content of the items making up the dimensions under each heading, the generally low intercorrelations among the dimensions would suggest that there is little empirical basis for the groupings. Prospective users should also note that scoring systems for the technical dimensions and OCP score diverge in many instances, so that the OCP is relatively independent of scores on the dimensions. Not surprisingly, intercorrelations between dimension and OCP scores, reported for men in four occupational groups (managers, administrators, salesmen, and policemen), while reaching significance for eight of the dimensions, are of a relatively low order and in some cases are zero or negative.

In addition to describing the original development of the scale, the technical information provided in the manual now includes data on the relationship between Cree scores and scores on a variety of self-report questionnaires (47 subscores), verbal-perceptual tests (3 scores), and job performance indices for men in managerial, administrative, sales, and police occupations. In general, with a few exceptions, the correlations reported are low. Scores for OCP and a few of the technical dimensions were positively correlated with a history of school achievement, involvement in extracurricular activities, and participation and leadership in group activities. OCP scores were also found to correlate with perceptual closure flexibility, impulsiveness, extraversion, being excitable, and having a high energy level. Measures of work interest, verbal ability, and emotional health showed only a few significant associations with Cree scores.

A number of more recent validity studies are reported in which aspects of work performance are used as criterion variables. OCP and dimension scores have been found to produce significant multiple correlations with salary in a sample of managerial staff, and to be among those variables in a larger test battery which contribute to the predictor equations for ratings of overall job performance, salary, and tenure in executives and engineers. Furthermore, OCP scores of managerial workers have been found to differ significantly as a function of status in the management hierarchy, with top level managers obtaining higher scores.

Despite the additional research findings included in the revised manual which are offered as support for the validity of the Cree Questionnaire, the serious limitations of the test identified by previous reviewers have not been rectified. Data on reliability are still absent; no attempt has been made to cross-validate the original findings (carried out in the mid-50s) on which the item selection was based; and no information is provided about the demographic characteristics of the group used as a basis for deriving the norms. The revised manual seems to have been published without careful proofreading: a number of inconsistencies are present between the text reference to tabulated data and the tables themselves.

The test developers' attempts to expand the scope of research relevant to the validity of the scale should be commended. However, the nature of the validity data presented does little to strengthen faith in the claim that the test provides a measure of creative potential. Rather, the test might more appropriately be treated as a measure of "managerial potential." Except for the original study, now 30 years old, in which Cree items were selected on their ability to discriminate between inventive and noninventive engineers, subsequent studies have not directly addressed the validity of the test for assessing creative potential. Given the problems (conceptual and empirical) inherent in specifying creative processes independently from knowledge of creative products, the development of a test of creative potential is fraught with difficulties, ones which the Cree test shows few signs of having tackled.

As it stands, this test would appear to have some limited utility in research on management potential and behaviour, but the male-bias incorporated in its construction precludes its use for job selection or other applied purposes without major modifications.

REVIEWER'S REFERENCES

Furcon, J. E. CREATIVE PERSONALITY: A FACTOR ANALYTIC STUDY. Unpublished master's thesis, De Paul University, Chicago, 1965.

[283]

Criterion Test of Basic Skills. Grades K–8; 1976; criterion-referenced; no data on reliability; no norms; mastery defined as 90–100% correct; instructional level, 50–89% correct; frustration level, 0–49% correct; no information presented in support of increasing difficulty levels (student takes only subtests beginning with 2 mastery scores and ending with 2 frustration scores) or relevancy to grade levels; individual; 1 form; 2 tests; manual (96 pages); stimulus cards (35 pages); record sheet (4 pages) for each test; 1984 price data: $33.50 per set of testing materials including manual, stimulus cards, 25 record sheets for each test, and 25 math problem sheets in a vinyl folder; $6 per 25 reading or arithmetic record sheets; $3.50 per 25 math problem sheets; $6 per stimulus cards; $12 per manual; $12 per specimen set; (10–15) minutes per test; Kerth Lundell, William Brown, and James Evans; Academic Therapy Publications.*

a) READING. 19 specific-objective subtests in 6 areas: letter recognition (3 subtests), letter sounding (4), blending and sequencing (3), special sounds (6), sight words, letter writing (2); 1 form (23 cards).

b) ARITHMETIC. 26 specific-objective subtests in 11 areas: counting, numbers and numerals (4 subtests), addition (3), subtraction (3), multiplication (2), division (2), money measurement (2), telling time (2), symbols, fractions (3), decimals and percents (3); 1 form (9 cards); problem sheet (2 pages).

See T3:635 (1 reference).

[284]

Criterion Validated Written Tests for Fire Company Officer, Lieutenant and Captain. Prospective lieutenants and captains; 4 subtests and total: Supervisory Knowledge and Ability, Fire Attack Knowledges, Fire Extinguishment Knowledges, Fire Chemistry and Physics Knowledges, total; 3 forms: Forms 1, 2, A; test administration instructions available; candidate study guide available; separate answer sheets must be used; distribution restricted to civil service commissions, city managers, and other responsible officials; 1983 price data: rental and scoring service, $450 for the first 5 candidates when test is used for one rank only; $9.75–$27 for each additional candidate when test is used for one rank only ($450 minimum); $540 for the first 5 candidates when one form is used for two ranks at the same time; $11.70–$32.40 for each additional candidate when one form is used for two ranks at the same time ($540 minimum); 210(230) minutes; McCann Associates, Inc.*

[285]

Critical Reasoning Test Battery. Students and employees ages 15 and over; 1981–83; CRTB; used to assist students in subject and career choices and employers with the selection of job candidates; subtests available as separates; 3 tests; manual ('83, 71 pages); profile chart ('83, 2 pages); distribution restricted to persons who have completed the publisher's training course or members of the Division of Occupational Psychology of the British Psychological Society; separate answer sheets must be used; 1984 price data: £45 per 10 reusable test booklets including 3 tests; £20 per 50 answer sheets for each test; £3.50 per scoring stencil; £7.50 per 50 profile sheets; £3.50 per administration card; £12 per manual; £34 per specimen set; Peter Saville, Roger Holdsworth, Gill Nyfield (tests), David Hawkey (NC2, DC3), Susan Bawtree (manual), and Ruth Holdsworth (manual); Saville & Holdsworth Ltd. [England].*

a) VERBAL EVALUATION. 1982–83; VC1; 1 form ('82, 10 pages); administration card ('82, 2 pages); 30(35) minutes.

b) INTERPRETING DATA. 1982–83; NC2; 1 form ('82, 6 pages); administration card ('82, 2 pages); data card ('82, 2 pages); £11 per 10 data cards; 30(35) minutes.

c) DIAGRAMMATIC SERIES. 1982–83; DC3; 1 form ('82, 6 pages); administration card ('82, 2 pages); 20(25) minutes.

[286]

Croft Readiness Assessment in Comprehension Kit. Children for whom diagnostic information in reading readiness is needed; 1978; CRAC-Kit; designed to be used with the five readiness subtests of the Cooper-McGuire Diagnostic Word-Analysis Test; provides the "directions and record-keeping system for measuring performance on oral and written language readiness" in addition to pattern readiness; 3 subtests; no reliability or validity data; no norms; individual; 3 forms for each subtest consist of concrete objects, pictures, and oral directions or stories; 2 levels; teacher's guide (34 pages); individual record card (2 pages); other materials must be supplied by examiner; 1984 price data: $199 per kit (includes 4 boxes of materials, class record charts and individual record cards, teacher's guide); administration time not reported; Marion L. McGuire and Marguerite J. Bumpus; Croft, Inc.*

a) ORAL LANGUAGE READINESS. Relates oral language with experience at all levels of abstraction; 3 scores: concrete, semi-abstract, abstract; no reading by examinees.

b) COMPREHENSION READINESS. Recognizes, at sight, "words that have recurred frequently in his language-experience stories and classroom activities"; scores same as for *a* above.

c) PATTERN READINESS. Ages 5 and over only; 4 parts: classification, sequence, causation, comparison, scores same as for *a* above within each part.

Review of Croft Readiness Assessment in Comprehension Kit by JERRY D. HARRIS, Associate Professor of Educational Psychology, Arizona State University, Tempe, AZ:

The Croft Readiness Assessment in Comprehension Kit (CRAC-Kit) is one of the assessment components in Reading Comprehension Skills, an instructional program for teaching reading comprehension. The authors state that most standardized tests of reading readiness are useful in determining which pupils are ready for initial reading instruction but fail to provide information which is helpful in designing a readiness program for those who are not. The CRAC-Kit, an informal assessment procedure, is intended to provide such information.

When used in conjunction with the Cooper-McGuire Diagnostic Word-Analysis Test, the CRAC-Kit is thought by the authors to provide a comprehensive view of the child's readiness skills. The Teacher's Guide which serves as a manual also includes appendices with suggestions for assessing general readiness and readiness for word analysis, but the clear focus of the CRAC-Kit is on comprehension.

Assessment with the CRAC-Kit involves determining which of 19 readiness objectives a child has mastered. Three objectives concern oral language readiness, four deal with written language readiness, and twelve concern pattern readiness. Test stimuli are both oral and visual; responses are oral or motoric. Stimuli were selected so as to represent concrete (e.g., balls or other toys), semi-abstract (i.e., pictures), and abstract (i.e., oral statements or questions) levels of functioning.

A large array of stimulus materials are included in the CRAC-Kit. The materials are for the most part attractive and likely to appeal to 5-year-olds. This appeal with its associated effect on children's task orientation is one of the more commendable features of the CRAC-Kit. Ease of administration is another.

Less commendable is the attention given by the authors to the technical adequacy of this measure. The CRAC-Kit is purported to measure objectives corresponding to skills which are essential if children are to comprehend what they read. No empirical evidence is presented or cited to support this assertion. No data are presented to demonstrate that CRAC-Kit performance and performance on other reading measures, administered concurrently or at a later time, are associated to any degree or that teaching for mastery of the 19 objectives facilitates subsequent reading comprehension.

Data concerning the reliability of the CRAC-Kit are also lacking in the manual. This omission is particularly noteworthy because so few items comprise the measure. For many objectives, on each administration of the test only one item is given to determine attainment or non-attainment. For example, to be credited with mastery of sequence patterns at the semi-abstract level (Objective PR5), a child needs only to determine the correct order of three pictures which tell a story—an item which will be answered correctly 17% of the time on the basis of random guesses. For this and for other objectives, three items are included in the CRAC-Kit, but the authors recommend that only one be given on each administration.

The three items for each objective are said to be equivalent measures of the objective. This claim is unsubstantiated and appears questionable. For example, the three items which assess classification of concrete objects vary in the number of objects to be classified, the number of classes to be formed, the number of dimensions by which classification is possible, and the salience of those dimensions.

Another shortcoming of the CRAC-Kit is that scoring standards or criteria are inadequate. For example, on comparison items the child is presented with two objects (or pictures or words) and is asked how the two are alike and different. For the nine items of this type, sample responses are presented in the scoring guide for only four. In other parts of the CRAC-Kit such as the classification and sequence portions, it is unclear on a number of items whether a correct motor response suffices or needs to be accompanied by a correct oral response.

Other considerations for the potential user of the CRAC-Kit include: (*a*) no norms are provided; (*b*) the clarity of the exposition in the Teacher's Guide is quite variable; and (*c*) the price is much greater than that of most readiness measures.

In summary, the CRAC-Kit is not purported to be a standardized test of reading readiness. Rather, its authors view it as a semi-structured system for determining whether or not 19 pre-reading skills in the area of comprehension have been mastered. Nonetheless, lack of data bearing on reliability and validity and inadequate scoring standards severely limit the utility of the CRAC-Kit in its present form.

Review of Croft Readiness Assessment in Comprehension Kit by ANNETTE B. WEINSHANK, Teacher-Collaborator and Project Coordinator, Institute for Research on Teaching, Michigan State University, East Lansing, MI:

There are numerous test batteries available for assessing the general phonics skills believed to underlie the decoding process, including auditory discrimination of letter sounds, auditory blending ability, letter recognition and visual matching, sound-letter relationships, and word recognition. Measures of comprehension readiness, however, are not commonly found in reading readiness batteries. The Croft Assessment in Comprehension Kit (CRAC-Kit) is an exception since it contains directions and materials for assessing 18 comprehension reading objectives. The authors claim that when the Kit is used with five readiness subtests of the Cooper-McGuire Diagnostic Word-Analysis Test (available separately), a comprehensive picture of a child's readiness skills for comprehension as well as decoding results.

The CRAC-Kit purports to test three types of comprehension readiness skills: oral language, written language, and pattern recognition. Within each type there are three levels of proficiency to be demonstrated: concrete, semi-abstract, and abstract. Oral language readiness is evaluated by having children talk about objects (concrete level), pictures (semi-abstract level), and experiences (abstract level). Written language readiness is tested using language experience stories centered on current situations (concrete level), pictures (semi-abstract level), and past or future situations (abstract level). No special materials or procedures are provided for either the oral or written language readiness tests. The teacher is responsible for choosing appropriate stimulus materials and for evaluating performance.

The CRAC-Kit contains stimulus materials only for testing pattern recognition. Four large color-coded boxes of materials each cover one of the following four patterns: classification (understanding how objects, pictures, and words belong in classes or sets); sequence (ordering objects, pictures, and words along a continuum with respect to time, space, etc.); causation (suggesting possible causes or outcomes or images); and comparison (noting meaningful differences between objects or images). Each pattern box contains three complete sets of stimulus materials, with each set containing objects, picture cards, and cards for oral presentations to evaluate, in turn, concrete, semi-abstract, and abstract comprehension readiness. One set is chosen as a pretest, a second for practice in the event the pretest is not passed, and the remaining set is used as a posttest. On the outside of each box are printed the contents and instructions for their use.

Using the classification pattern box as an example, we see that the student is asked to choose three objects, pictures, or names that belong to the same class, then label them and tell why they belong together. Concrete classification skills are tested using: three foam balls, one foam cube, and one rubber ball (set one); three plastic fruits and three plastic vegetables (set two); and three each of plastic knives, forks, and spoons (set three). The objects for each set are packaged in transparent zip-lock pouches. Semi-abstract classification readiness is tested using pictures of people and clothing (set one); furniture and toys (set two); and birds and animals (set three). Finally, abstract classification skill is tested through oral presentation of lists of clothing (set one); flowers (set two); and parts of buildings (set three).

There are technical difficulties with the materials themselves. The zip-lock pouches containing the objects are identified as to set number only, with a small gummed sticker pasted on the outside of the pouch. Half of the stickers peeled off during the examination process; this could leave an undifferentiated array of stuffed animals, beads, balls, wooden shapes, toy furniture, etc. lying around that would have to be traced back to the proper pattern box and pouch. The picture cards have no identification whatever. Should they be scattered, they too would have to be traced back to where they belong by reading the contents printed on the side of each box. Only the cards used for verbal presentations are permanently marked both as to pattern name and set number. Overall, it is hard to see why a kit composed of five and dime quality toys, laminated cards, a class record form, and a teacher's guide should come to almost $200.00.

More serious, however, are the educational problems associated with the CRAC-Kit. There are no normative data provided. How do large groups of 4- and 5-year-olds tend to perform on the various tasks? What could be considered as average performance? The publishers imply that *(a)* these materials and procedures are reliable (i.e., that their use will consistently identify those students who need help in mastering specified comprehension readiness skills), and that *(b)* they are valid (i.e., that treating weaknesses identified by testing with the Kit will prevent subsequent comprehension problems when reading instruction is actually begun). However, the authors offer no empirical evidence whatever on either *(a)* the reliability of these measures in diagnosing comprehension readiness deficiencies, or *(b)* any correlational evidence linking successful practice using the readiness materials with subsequent reading performance. Ryan and Ledger (1982) suggested that the comprehension requirements of non-reading tasks, particularly listening tasks, may not be as closely related to reading comprehension as previously thought. They report on the use of pictograph sentences to assess the level of semantic integration abilities in young children and note that children who were not able to integrate semantically across a pictorial sequence were nevertheless quite capable of integrating oral language forms.

In sum, the CRAC-Kit attempts to redress the imbalance in readiness test batteries between phonics and comprehension skills. Regrettably, what has resulted is an overpriced, technically flawed comprehension kit whose claims are not supported by an empirical documentation and whose assumptions are being challenged by current research.

REVIEWER'S REFERENCES

Ryan, E., & Ledger, G. Assessing sentences processing skills in prereaders. In Hutson, B. (Ed.), ADVANCES IN READING/LANGUAGE RESEARCH VOLUME 1, Greenwich, CT: Jai Press, Inc., 1982.

[287]

Crown-Crisp Experiential Index. Normal and psychoneurotic adults; 1979; CCEI; formerly published under the title Middlesex Hospital Questionnaire; designed to obtain the diagnostic information typically gained in a formal clinical psychiatric examination; 7 scores: free-floating anxiety, depression, hysteria, phobic anxiety, obsessionality, somatic anxiety, total; 1 form (4 pages); manual (32 pages); distribution restricted to qualified persons; 1983 price data: £2.25 per 20 tests; 85p per scoring template; £2.25 per manual; £3 per specimen set; (5–10) minutes; Sidney Crown and A. H. Crisp; Hodder & Stoughton Educational [England].*

See T3:639 (22 references); for reviews by H. J. Eysenck and Lester M. Libo, see 8:615 (26 references); see also T2:1279 (8 references); for a review by D. F. Clark, see 7:103 (5 references).

TEST REFERENCES

1. Bulpitt, C. J., Dollery, C. T., & Hoffbrand, B. I. The contribution of psychological features to the symptoms of treated hypertensive patients. PSYCHOLOGICAL MEDICINE, 1977, 7, 661–665.

2. Hafner, J., & Milton, F. The influence of propranolol on the exposure in vivo of agoraphobics. PSYCHOLOGICAL MEDICINE, 1977, 7, 419–425.

3. Milton, F., & Hafner, J. The outome of behavior therapy for agoraphobia in relation to marital adjustment. ARCHIVES OF GENERAL PSYCHIATRY, 1979, 36, 807–811.

4. Birtchnell, J. Women whose mothers died in childhood: An outcome study. PSYCHOLOGICAL MEDICINE, 1980, 10, 699–713.

5. Parkes, K. R. Social desirability, defensiveness and self-report psychiatric inventory scores. PSYCHOLOGICAL MEDICINE, 1980, 10, 735–742.

6. Bland, K., & Hallam, R. S. Relationship between response to graded exposure and marital satisfaction in agoraphobics. BEHAVIOUR RESEARCH AND THERAPY, 1981, 19, 335–338.

7. Harris, B. "Maternity blues" in East African clinic attenders. ARCHIVES OF GENERAL PSYCHIATRY, 1981, 38, 1293–1295.

8. Wilkinson, I. M., & Blackburn, I. M. Cognitive style in depressed and recovered depressed patients. BRITISH JOURNAL OF CLINICAL PSYCHOLOGY, 1981, 20, 283–292.

9. Kogeorgos, J., Fonagy, P., & Scott, D. F. Psychiatric symptom patterns of chronic epileptics attending a neurological clinic: A controlled investigation. BRITISH JOURNAL OF PSYCHIATRY, 1982, 140, 236–243.

10. Kumar, A., & Vaidya, A. K. Neuroticism in short and long sleepers. PERCEPTUAL AND MOTOR SKILLS, 1982, 54, 962.

11. Elliott, S. A., Rugg, A. J., Watson, J. P., & Brough, D. I. Mood changes during pregnancy and after the birth of a child. THE BRITISH JOURNAL OF CLINICAL PSYCHOLOGY, 1983, 22, 295–308.

12. Hafner, R. J., Badenoch, A., Fisher, J., & Swift, B. A. Spouse-aided versus individual therapy in persisting psychiatric disorders: A systematic comparison. FAMILY PROCESS, 1983, 22, 385–399.

13. Zeitlin, C., & Oddy, M. Cognitive impairment in patients with severe migraine. BRITISH JOURNAL OF CLINICAL PSYCHOLOGY, 1984, 23, 27–35.

Review of Crown-Crisp Experiential Index by ANTHONY J. DEVITO, *Assistant Director, Counseling Center, Fordham University, Bronx, NY:*

The Crown-Crisp Experiential Index (CCEI) was originally published as the Middlesex Hospital Questionnaire and reviewed under that title in previous editions of MMY. The CCEI consists of 48 items requiring about 10 minutes to complete and yielding scores on six dimensions of neurosis. Some of the items are dichotomous and others are on a 3-point scale. The CCEI may be administered individually or in groups. The test items—questions of the type usually used in a psychiatric interview—survived the psychometrically sound test development procedures. The manual accompanying the test has many worthwhile features, which include detailed discussion of its construction and summaries of studies using the instrument.

Each subscale seems to have sufficient concurrent criterion-related validation information. The primary empirical validation evidence, summarized in Figure 1 of the manual, shows that each subscale, individually, differentiates normals from neurotics. Although the point is not made in the manual, one can conclude that the total neuroticism score will also differentiate normals from neurotics. The subscales do not, however, have discriminative validity in the criterion-related sense. For example, all subscales, except hysteria, differentiated depressives from normals. One would be much more satisfied if the depressive scale alone differentiated depressives from normals.

In contrast to criterion-related validity, the construct validity evidenced by factor analytic studies (Alderman, Mackay, Lucas, Spry, & Bell, 1983; Bagley, 1980) tends to support the retention of the six subscales. However, the evidence for a general factor of neurosis is even more persuasive. While the factor analytic results are encouraging, they are not substitutes for positive evidence of the criterion-related discriminative validity of the subscales. Therefore, from the practical point of view, the instrument would appear to be eminently appropriate for the diagnosis of neurosis, but not very useful for differential diagnosis in terms of subscale dimensions.

In view of the construct and empirical validity evidence for the total neuroticism score discussed previously, the manual and profile sheet should emphasize and have more information about the total score. The total score for neuroticism is barely mentioned in the manual and there is no mention of how it is to be interpreted. Nowhere can a measure of variability of the total score be found. Furthermore, the profile sheet does not have provisions for this total. Also, the variability of the subscale data represented in the profile sheets should be reported and possibly even represented on the profile sheet.

Most of the reliability information contained in the manual is quite adequate. However, one of the studies, purported to demonstrate the instrument's reliability, flies in the face of the definition of reliability (i.e., "consistency of scores obtained by the same person" Anastasi, 1982, p. 102). The test authors cite a study in which three independent groups of subjects were compared on each subscale as evidence for the reliability of the scales.

The test authors have taken measures to eliminate response sets and have provided relatively convenient scoring procedures. The manual contains thorough discussions of the influence of age, sex, and social class on scores. The probable biasing influence of social desirability and faking on scores is not, however, adequately addressed.

In evaluating its use in places other than Britain, one should consider that the instructions and three or four items might not be understood by other English-speaking persons (e.g., Americans). Fortunately, these difficulties can be easily remedied in future versions of this instrument. More serious may be variations in diagnostic customs and the psychiatric diagnostic manuals of the respective countries.

There is no other instrument known to this reviewer to give as valid and reliable global measure of neuroticism in such a brief period of time as the CCEI. Competing instruments the user may wish to consider, depending upon the testing application, are: the Minnesota Multiphasic Personality Inventory, the Millon Clinical Multiaxial Inventory, the Cornell Medical Index, the Eysenck Personality Questionnaire, the State-Trait Anxiety Inventory, and the Mooney Problem Check Lists.

Perhaps the best summary of this instrument is given by the authors themselves: "It is important not to assume that a simple instrument such as the CCEI is anything other than a brief, conveniently administered, reasonably valid and reliable measure of personality for use in research and screening." In the opinion of this reviewer, it is at the very least an aid in diagnosis and assessment of neuroticism. With better normative data for the total score, it would be an extremely useful index of neuroticism. As yet, the evidence presented for the empirical validity of the subscales is not persuasive except insofar as the subscale scores contribute to the total score.

REVIEWER'S REFERENCES

Bagley, C. The factorial reliability of the Middlesex Hospital Questionnaire in normal subjects. BRITISH JOURNAL OF MEDICAL PSYCHOLOGY, 1980, 53, 53–58.

Anastasi, A. PSYCHOLOGICAL TESTING (5th ed.). New York: Macmillan, 1982.

Alderman, K. J., Mackay, C. J., Lucas, E. G., Spry, W. B., & Bell, B. Factor analysis and reliability studies of the Crown-Crisp Experiential Index (CCEI). BRITISH JOURNAL OF MEDICAL PSYCHOLOGY, 1983, 56, 329–345.

Review of Crown-Crisp Experiential Index by DOUGLAS S. PAYNE, Assistant Professor of Psychiatry, Medical College of Georgia, Augusta, GA, and Director of Psychology Department, Georgia Regional Hospital, Augusta, GA:

The Crown-Crisp Experiential Index (CCEI) is meant to be a brief paper and pencil psychiatric screening instrument. The authors suggest the following three uses for the CCEI: (1) to compare identified populations, (2) to screen for psychoneurotic traits and symptoms, and (3) to determine if an individual or group has changed due to a particular intervention. The CCEI requires only the 5–10 minutes claimed for administration. The authors recommend that a clerk may administer and score the CCEI, which would probably take less than 5 minutes with practice, but they do not suggest what level of training is necessary in order to interpret the CCEI.

The CCEI consists of 48 items divided into six scales of eight items each. Each scale has a range of scores from 0 to 16 and was developed on a theoretical basis to measure symptoms and/or character traits of a particular neurotic type. In general, many of the scales are lacking in validity by the authors' admission. For example, the authors report that the Hysteria scale fails to differentiate conversion hysterics from normals or matched controls. They further reported that this was not surprising since "only a minority of the patients with conversion symptoms show a 'hysterical' personality pattern" and that this scale best correlated with extraversion. Perhaps they should have renamed the scale, since it has shown little discriminative power and its name is misleading. The validity of the Phobic Anxiety scale was heavily dependent on the particular phobic symptoms (a scale of eight items is not capable of sampling a broad enough domain of phobic objects). The Somatic scale was supposed to identify patients diagnosed for hypochondriasis or having a functional psychosomatic complaint. Although there were insufficient numbers of these patients to determine whether this scale discriminated between them and normals, many people with other diagnoses scored high on it, indicating a lack of discriminative ability for the Somatic scale. The other subscales appear to be capable of differentiating groups of psychiatrically identified groups from normals, but not necessarily from other psychiatric groups.

The reliability figures for test-retest studies are in the lower range of acceptability, .68 to .77, for most of the subscales, but two studies of split-half reliability showed that the reliability of the Phobic Anxiety, Obsessional, Somatic, and Depression scales was inadequate. The manual includes no norms showing percentile or standard score equivalents. Most of the data presented in the manual compares different diagnostic groups. If one compares the descriptive data presented for several groups, however, it then becomes apparent that there may be more than 50% overlap within one standard deviation of the means of many of the scales. For example, a group of depressed patients had a mean of 9.7 and a standard deviation of 3.4 on the Obsessional scale while a group of patients diagnosed as having an obsessional neurosis had a mean of 11.4 with a standard deviation of 2.8. These results would indicate that the use of the CCEI would result in a large number of misclassifications if one concretely interpreted the scale scores. Another example of this is that females having an obsessional neurosis had a mean of 10.2 on the Depression scale, while those suffering from depression had a mean of 9.4! Thus, the CCEI would seem to have limited usefulness in distinguishing between diagnostic groups. This is further exemplified in the failure of the CCEI to distinguish between schizophrenics and normals. While the CCEI was not designed to be sensitive to psychotic symptomatology, it is suggested by the authors that it be used as a general screening instrument. Due to the presence of psychotic people among those seeking mental health assistance, the CCEI would seem to be inadequate for this task.

Some further criticisms of the CCEI may be in order. The items are fairly blatant in their intent, so without any validity scale to measure defensiveness, it is not possible to determine the extent to which a test taker tried to present a good image. It is generally accepted that even people seeking mental health assistance are going to exhibit some defensiveness. Two factor analytic studies of the CCEI found only three factors, indicating that the six scales are not independent. This result would argue for development of a profile analysis, which has not been done. The CCEI contains some unfamiliar language for most United States citizens (e.g., tick for mark and Underground for subway). The authors state that the CCEI was designed to determine one's general emotionality or neuroticism and to provide the six subscale scores. However, neither information on how to compute this general neuroticism score nor related research is presented.

The CCEI manual is thorough and presents a fair description of the CCEI and CCEI research. It includes some thoughtful comments for scoring. There are many research studies described in the manual which would be helpful to the researcher in deciding whether the CCEI would be useful in his/her particular investigations.

In summary, the CCEI attempts to perform several functions: discriminate diagnostic groups, provide research data, and screen patients psychiatrically. It fails to meet the requirements for discriminating diagnostic groups because of the general elevation of all scales for neurotic test takers. It is, however, capable of discriminating between certain psychiatric populations and groups of normals. The CCEI may have some research value but only for the more reliable scales. Because of its inability to discriminate psychotic individuals from normals and the large variation in individual scores, regardless of diagnostic type, the CCEI is inadequate as a screening instrument. The only value it would have clinically is to provide some information through examination of the specific answers of those patients who answered as honestly as they could. However, low subscale scores on the CCEI should certainly not be taken as a clean bill of mental health.

[288]

CSMS Science Reasoning Tasks. Ages 10–16 and older children and adults; 1977–79; criterion-referenced; assessment of ability to use concrete and formal reasoning strategies; 7 tests; no description of normative population; general guide ('78, 26 pages); other test materials must be supplied by examiner; 1985 price data: £3.10 per general guide; £3.45 per mini specimen set; £7.45 per full specimen set; (35–50) minutes per test; M. Shayer, H. Wylam, P. Adey, and D. Küchemann; NFER-Nelson Publishing Co. [England].*

a) SPATIAL RELATIONSHIPS. Manual ('79, 4 pages); £1.75 per manual.

b) VOLUME AND HEAVINESS. 1 form ('79, 4 pages); manual ('79, 4 pages); £3.95 per 25 tests and manual.

c) THE PENDULUM. 1 form ('79, 4 pages); manual ('79, 5 pages); £3.95 per 25 tests.

d) EQUILIBRIUM IN THE BALANCE. 1 form ('79, 3 pages); manual ('79, 6 pages); £4.45 per 25 tests and manual.

e) INCLINED PLANE. 1 form ('79, 4 pages); manual ('79, 5 pages); £4.45 per 25 tests and manual.

f) CHEMICAL COMBINATIONS. 1 form ('79, 4 pages); manual ('79, 8 pages); £6.45 per 25 tests and manual.

g) FLEXIBLE RODS. 1 form ('79, 4 pages); manual ('79, 6 pages); £5.95 per 25 tests and manual.

[289]

CTBS Readiness Test. Grades K–0 to 1–3; 1973–77; originally developed as readiness measure (CTBS/S, Level A) of the CTBS Series; 11 scores: alphabet skills (letter forms, letter names, total), listening for information, letter sounds, visual and auditory discrimination (visual discrimination, sound matching, total), language, total, mathematics; Form S ('77, 23 pages); examiner's manual ('77, 75 pages); user's handbook for the Reading Readiness Report of Skill Mastery ('77, 36 pages); answer key ('77, 3 pages); 1983 price data: $40.25 per 35 machine-scorable tests, examiner's manual, and user's handbook; $29.40 per 35 hand-scorable tests, examiner's manual, and user's handbook; $3.75 per examiner's manual; $4.75 per user's handbook; $7.50 per specimen set; scoring service, $1.05 per student ($100 minimum); (159–216) minutes; CTB/McGraw-Hill.*

Review of CTBS Readiness Test by STEPHEN J. BAGNATO, Developmental School Psychologist, Assistant Professor of Child Psychiatry, Milton S. Hershey Medical Center, Pennsylvania State University College of Medicine, Hershey, PA:

DESCRIPTION. The CTBS Readiness Test-Level A, Form S is the initial segment of McGraw-Hill's continuous group achievement battery entitled The Comprehensive Tests of Basic Skills, Expanded Edition, covering the K through 12 grade range. The CTBS/Readiness Test surveys the acquisition of various reading readiness processes and skills across the K through 1.3 range. This broad screening survey consists of 8 tests involving 168 assessment tasks which sample such skill clusters as Letter Forms and Names, Listening for Information, Letter Sounds, Visual Discrimination, Sound Matching, Language, and Mathematics. The primary purpose of the CTBS Readiness Test is to identify students who have not acquired the skills necessary for success in beginning reading. The Reading Readiness Report of Skill Mastery is a classroom summary report and profile which analyzes and displays the child's proficiency within each skill cluster. Deficit skills are then assigned a rank, based upon the predictive value of the items for success in reading; the rankings emphasize the skill's relative priority for instructional planning. Both machine- and hand-scorable versions are available.

NORMS. The entire CTBS/S (K through 12) was standardized on a large, randomly selected sample of students representative of the various regions and states across the U.S. Levels A and B of the CTBS/S appear to have undergone substantial emphasis in this standardization. In April 1972, a pre-standardization edition was normed on 1,300 children in an effort to establish time limits and to analyze the functional range of the CTBS/S items. Based upon this preliminary analysis, changes were made in item content. Finally, two groups of children comprised the standardization samples for Levels A and B of the CTBS/S. A pre-post group of 2,830 students consisted of children who took the CTBS/S Level A in April and May of their kindergarten year (1975) and the CTBS/S Level B in April and May of first grade (1976). In addition, norming was accomplished on 3,547 children who were administered the CTBS/S Level A in September and October of first grade (1975) and CTBS/S Level B in April and May of first grade (1976).

TECHNICAL ADEQUACY. The CTBS/S provides information on scoring, interpretation, and basic background research which support its use. Three categories of derived scores help the teacher to summarize and interpret child performance data across eight individual subtests: cluster scores, summary scores, and expected scores. Cluster Skill scores are reported for each cluster (e.g., letter forms, visual discrimination, language, sound matching) in terms of raw scores, performance level (for categories "proficient," "not proficient," and "needs additional diagnosis"), and a relational rank (i.e., rankings to highlight instructional needs). Summary scores are reported in the form of percentiles, stanines, and standard scores (i.e., mean of 50 and standard deviation of 21). These normal curve equivalents (NCE) are based on the CTBS/S standardization data for Total Readiness, Total Language, and Total Mathematics clusters, and compare a child's performance with a national sample of students in the second month of first grade. Finally, expected scores derived from multiple regression analyses help to predict probable performance levels from pretesting on the CTBS/S Level A at the start of grade 1 to posttesting on the CTBS/S Level B at the end of grade 1. It is encouraging to see that McGraw-Hill has dispensed with the concept of grade equivalent scores, particularly at the kindergarten level, since they tend to portray misleading information about child functioning and skill levels. However, it is emphasized that the cutoff scores which determine the level of proficiency may lead to misclassifications.

Supporting research for the CTBS/S is basic and is included in the User's Handbook. Content validity was addressed by conducting workshops on appropriate item content to be measured and by surveying the literature on prerequisite reading skills. Individual items were written and reviewed by a group of preschool and primary teachers as well as curriculum and testing specialists. A correlation of .77 between the CTBS/S and the Metropolitan Readiness Test is offered as evidence of construct validity. Data on predictive validity show a correlation of .76 between the CTBS/S Total Prereading score at the beginning of first grade and the Gates-MacGinitie Total Reading score at the end of first grade. A comparable predictive relation between the CTBS/S Level A and Level B ($r = .73$) is cited as supporting evidence for these overlapping test levels. No evidence on test-retest or alternate form reliability of the CTBS/S is reported in the manual. However, internal consistency data in the form of KR-20 coefficients for the cluster scores range from .30 to .92, with a mean of .66.

CRITIQUE. The CTBS/S Level A is a carefully designed group readiness measure which effectively samples a variety of critical skill-processes for learning to read. The format of the CTBS shows careful thought in terms of administration procedures and effective presentation of information. For example, practice tests are included within the test format to ensure that children are familiar with the prerequisite behaviors for taking a test and responding to precise directions. Moreover, the emphasis on standardized administration procedures helps to ensure the reliability of assessment for each child. For example, for grade levels K through 1.0, it is recommended that only 15 students be included in the room during testing to reduce distractions. Perhaps provision should be made also to test individually those children who score low in proficiency in order to rule out the impact of a group situation on performance, rather than attributing poor performance immediately to deficit skills. Also, both the directions to examiners and the graphic illustrations for students are clear and effectively presented.

However, it is possible that the response mode required to complete each task may be somewhat difficult for certain students. Specifically, children with visual limitations or perceptual-motor delays will have difficulty exerting enough control or precision to color in the circles below each correct answer, unlike the more global "checking" response required on an individual measure such as the Boehm Test of Basic Concepts.

One of the most effective features of the CTBS/S is the coding of subtest skill clusters to instructional materials available through McGraw-Hill. These include such criterion-referenced guides as the System for Teacher Evaluation of Prereading Skills (STEPS), the Prescriptive Reading Inventory (PRI), and the Diagnostic Mathematics Inventory (DMI).

SUMMARY. The CTBS/S Level A is an effective group diagnostic measure of prerequisite reading readiness skills. For a diagnostic screening measure, its coverage is broad but its analysis is detailed. Children's performances on the scale are clearly profiled through a format which highlights areas in need of specific instruction. Both the norms and reliability and validity data appear adequate for diagnostic comparisons among children to identify those lacking readiness for beginning reading instruction. However, because of the potential for misidentification, it is recommended that children who score low during group diagnosis be assessed individually through followup assessment to confirm or refute the original estimates.

[290]

Culture Fair Intelligence Test. Ages 4–8 and mentally retarded adults, 8–14 and average adults, grades 9–16 and superior adults; 1933–73; CFIT; formerly called Culture Free Intelligence Test; test booklet title is Test of *g*: Culture Fair, formerly Test of *g*: Culture Free; 3 levels; manual ('73, 26 pages) for Scales 2 and 3; technical supplement ('73, 31 pages) for Scales 2 and 3; 1985 price data: $2.80 per manual for Scales 2 and 3; $3.50 per technical supplement for Scales 2 and 3; $4.65 per specimen set of Scales 2 and 3 (without technical supplement); Spanish edition of Scales 2 and 3 available;

Raymond B. Cattell and A. K. S. Cattell (Scales 2 and 3); Institute for Personality and Ability Testing.*

a) SCALE 1. Ages 4–8 and mentally retarded adults; 1933–69; identical with Cattell Intelligence Tests, Scale 0: Dartington Scale; individual in part; 1 form ('50, 12 pages); handbook with 1967 supplementation ['69, 15 pages]; $22.55 per complete kit including 25 test booklets, classification cards, scoring key, and handbook; $10 per 25 tests; $8.60 per set of cards for classification test; $1.50 per scoring key; $2.25 per handbook; $4.25 per specimen set; materials for following directions test must be assembled locally; (22–60) minutes.

b) SCALE 2. Ages 8–14 and average adults; 1949–73; Forms A ('57, 8 pages), B ('61 edition, 8 pages); recording (reel-to-reel) available for individual untimed administration of Form A; separate answer sheets may be used; $9 per 25 tests; $1.05 per key for answer sheets; $1 per key for test booklets; $4.50 per 50 answer sheets for either form, $5.50 per 50 for both forms; $25 per tape; 12.5 (30) minutes.

c) SCALE 3. Grades 9–16 and superior adults; 1950–73; Forms A ('63, 8 pages), B ('61, c1950–61, 8 pages); separate answer sheets may be used; $9 per 25 tests; $1.55 per key for answer sheets; $1 per key for test booklets; $4.50 per 50 answer sheets; (30) minutes.

See T3:643 (51 references), 8:184 (38 references), and T2:364 (61 references); for reviews by John E. Milholland and Abraham J. Tannenbaum, see 6:453 (15 references); for a review by I. MacFarlane Smith of *a*, see 5:343 (11 references); for reviews by Raleigh M. Drake and Gladys C. Schwesinger, see 4:300 (2 references).

TEST REFERENCES

1. Gupta, B. S. Dextroamphetamine and measures of intelligence. INTELLIGENCE, 1977, 1, 274–280.

2. Cattell, R. B., & Horn, J. L. A check on the theory of fluid and crystallized intelligence with description of new subtest designs. JOURNAL OF EDUCATIONAL MEASUREMENT, 1978, 15, 139–164.

3. Carlson, J. S., & Wiedl, K. H. Toward a differential testing approach: Testing-the-limits employing the Raven Matrices. INTELLIGENCE, 1979, 3, 323–344.

4. Johnson, D. L., & Danley, W. Validity: Comparison of the WISC-R and SOMPA Estimated Learning Potential scores. PSYCHOLOGICAL REPORTS, 1981, 48, 123–131.

5. Undheim, J. O. On intelligence I: Broad ability factors in 15-year-old children and Cattell's theory of fluid and crystallized intelligence. SCANDINAVIAN JOURNAL OF PSYCHOLOGY, 1981, 22, 171–179.

6. Undheim, J. O. On intelligence II: A neo-Spearman model to replace Cattell's theory of fluid and crystallized intelligence. SCANDINAVIAN JOURNAL OF PSYCHOLOGY, 1981, 22, 181–187.

7. Vilkki, J. Changes in complex perception and memory after three different psychosurgical operations. NEUROPSYCHOLOGIA, 1981, 19, 553–563.

8. Heilbrun, A. B., Jr. Cognitive models of criminal violence based upon intelligence and psychopathy levels. JOURNAL OF CONSULTING AND CLINICAL PSYCHOLOGY, 1982, 50, 546–557.

9. Lawson, A. E. The nature of advanced reasoning and science instruction. JOURNAL OF RESEARCH IN SCIENCE TEACHING, 1982, 19, 743–760.

10. Stanley, G., Smith, G., & Powys, A. Selecting intelligence tests for studies of dyslexic children. PSYCHOLOGICAL REPORTS, 1982, 50, 787–792.

11. Hains, A. A., & Ryan, E. B. The development of social cognitive processes among juvenile delinquents and nondelinquent peers. CHILD DEVELOPMENT, 1983, 54, 1536–1544.

12. Pyszczynski, T., & Greenberg, J. Determinants of reduction in intended effort as a strategy for coping with anticipated failure. JOURNAL OF RESEARCH IN PERSONALITY, 1983, 17, 412–422.

13. Fu, L., & Edwards, H. P. Mathematics achievement: Effects of language of instruction and teachers' use of new curriculum materials. CANADIAN JOURNAL OF BEHAVIOURAL SCIENCE, 1984, 16, 120–129.

[291]

Culture-Free Self-Esteem Inventories for Children and Adults. Grades 3–9, adults; 1981; 3 forms; manual (64 pages); 1984 price data: $51 per complete set including 25 of each form, scoring acetates, 25 machine-scored answer sheets, and oral administration cassette tape; $15 per specimen set; French and Spanish editions available; (15–20) minutes; James Battle; Special Child Publications.*

a) FORM A. Grades 3–9; 60 items yielding 6 scores: general, social/peer related, academics/school related, parents/home related, lie, total.

b) FORM B. Grades 3–9; 30 items yielding same six scores as in *a*.

c) FORM AD. Adults; 40 items yielding 5 scores: general, social, personal, lie, total.

See T3:644 (1 reference).

TEST REFERENCES

1. Ludwig, D. A., Blau, G. J., & Lenihan, M. Note on the internal consistency of Canadian Self-Esteem Inventory for Adults. PSYCHOLOGICAL REPORTS, 1981, 49, 81–82.

Review of Culture-Free Self-Esteem Inventories for Children and Adults by GERALD R. ADAMS, Professor, Departments of Family and Human Development and Psychology, Utah State University, Logan, UT:

The Culture-Free Self-Esteem Inventories for Children and Adults (SEI), formerly called the Canadian Self-Esteem Inventories for Children and Adults, was originally developed out of the belief that educators have been ineffective in serving the developmental needs, both cognitive and affective, of children and youth. The author of the test, James Battle, has argued that there is a particular need to develop an instrument to reliably measure the affective domain of self-esteem. Battle reports having undertaken more than 30 studies to develop a series of valid and reliable self-esteem instruments. He describes the various scales as effective assessments of change in subjective feelings of self-esteem due to intervention strategy efforts.

CONCEPTUAL LIMITATIONS. The introduction provides very limited information on the theoretical underpinnings of self-esteem as a viable developmental construct. Rather, the tests are presented as practical screening devices for identifying children and adults in need of psychological, psychiatric, and educational intervention. While the author recommends the user should be knowledgeable about measurement, self-theory, perceptual psychology, or the psychology of adjustment, he provides no clear conceptualization about how these general fields of study are associated with the SEI and its development as a measure of self-esteem. Likewise, it is unclear why the test is considered culture-free. While the test is available in three languages (English, French, Spanish), no details are provided on how the tests were conceptualized or developed to assure "culture-free" items.

While the SEI scales have some conceptual limitations, they also have certain psychometrically defined strengths. The manual provides numerous tables that summarize the estimated reliability and validity of the scales for use with children and adults.

RELIABILITY ESTIMATES. Reliability estimates are presented in numerous forms: test-retest, alternate forms, and internal consistency. Battle reports strong test-retest correlations (mostly over undesignated lengths of time) for: (*a*) Form A and B with elementary school students in grades three through six (range .79 to .92), and (*b*) Form AD with adults in an educational psychology course (range .79 to .82). Alternate forms correlations between Forms A and B for fifth- and sixth-grade children are reported to be between .80 and .89. Internal consistency estimates (KR 20) range from .66 to .76 for Form A and .54 to .78 for Form AD. In general, the reported estimates of test-retest, alternate forms, and internal consistency are adequate to excellent. Indeed, the test-retest reliability coefficient for a small sample of young adolescents over a 2-year test period was a remarkably high .74.

VALIDITY ESTIMATES. Like reliability, validity estimates were presented in numerous forms (e.g., content, construct/factorial, concurrent, discriminant). Content validity was centered on a definition of self-esteem as "the perception the individual possesses of his own worth." From an original 150 items (Form A), 60 items were selected through factor analysis, with eigenvalues and percent of shared variance unspecified in the manual. Each of the factorially derived subscales showed good internal consistency. Concurrent validity has been established between Coopersmith's Self-Esteem inventory and the SEI (correlations ranging from .66 to .91 for elementary age boys and girls), and between SEI scores and teacher ratings of self-esteem (*r*s ranging from .32 to .39). Discriminant validity was estimated by correlating IQ scores with SEI self-esteem scores. Intelligence was generally unassociated with self-esteem. Higher SEI scores were found to be predictive of high self-perception of ability and lower depression. Comparisons of academically successful versus unsuccessful students reveal that successful students have higher self-esteem.

The several studies presented by the author provide some evidence of content, construct, concurrent, and discriminant validity. However, little information is provided on sampling procedures, and relatively small (and frequently nonrandom) samples were utilized in the studies reported in the manual. While few sex or age differences were observed, the external validity (generalizability) of the SEI is highly questionable. For example, the basic normative population for Form AD consists of students in an educational psychology course.

CONCLUSIONS. One must question whether the SEI is truly a "culture-free" measure of self-esteem. No systematic sampling or norming studies were undertaken to confirm such an assumption. However, the estimates of reliability and validity suggest that the SEI is a promising instrument for measuring self-esteem. The administration is simple, scoring is easy, and the manual materials are useful. The measure provides scores on several subscales that are correlated with the total score. Analyses can be made for subscales or total scores depending upon the researcher/practitioner's interests. Unfortunately, the conceptual or theoretical underpinnings of the SEI are weak and leave the user with a strong need for a better foundation for the instrument. Finally, issues of external validity, sample comparability, and problems in norming lead one to question how broadly applicable the assessment is for use in locations other than Alberta, Canada. I must conclude that the Culture-Free SEI for Children and Adults is a promising assessment of self-esteem that needs further development before one can recommend widespread use in educational, clinical, developmental, or social science research.

Review of Culture-Free Self-Esteem Inventories for Children and Adults by JANET MORGAN RIGGS, Assistant Professor of Psychology, Gettysburg College, Gettysburg, PA:

The Culture-Free Self-Esteem Inventories (SEI) for Children and Adults are designed to assess an individual's perception of self-esteem in general and across a variety of specific domains. The main purpose of these instruments is to identify those children and adults who have low self-esteem and who may be in need of psychological assistance. These inventories can also be used to measure changes in self-esteem, which may be particularly helpful to those interested in assessing the effectiveness of therapeutic intervention. Those who would probably be most interested in administering these inventories would include psychologists, psychiatrists, counselors, and teachers. The inventories can be administered and scored quickly and with relatively little effort on the part of the subject and administrator. The subject simply answers yes or no to a series of questions concerning his or her behavior and feelings. Instructions for the administration and scoring of the inventories and their subscales are quite clear. However, as the author warns, interpretation of scores should be done only in conjunction with someone knowledgeable in the areas of measurement and the psychology of adjustment.

STANDARDIZATION. The Culture-Free SEIs for Children and Adults were standardized on samples of students ranging from grades 3 to 9 and from an educational psychology class, respectively. The appropriate statistics (means, standard deviations, correlations) for all forms are presented. However, no mention is made of the socioeconomic status, race, or cultural background of the samples on which these statistics are based. This is particularly surprising given the fact that these inventories are billed as being "Culture-Free." Indeed, the only evidence presented which relates to this notion is that the protocols for these inventories are available in French and Spanish! While the author assures the reader that each of the stimulus items is culture-free, there is no documentation of this assertion. Furthermore, the author clearly states that the inventories were standardized in the English language.

RELIABILITY. The reported test-retest reliabilities for both of the child forms and the adult form are more than respectable. However, the time lapse between testing times is not reported (with the exception of a group of students in grades 7 through 9 tested on Form A). This makes the interpretation of the reliability coefficients difficult.

OTHER RESEARCH. The author reports that for elementary school children there is no significant correlation between IQ and self-esteem. No parallel research is reported for adults. It would not be particularly surprising if a correlation between IQ and self-esteem did emerge for adults, for whom intelligence might be more integrally related to self-esteem.

The author also describes research concerning the relationship between students' self-esteem and their teachers' ratings of them. Included in the manual is Battle's Teacher Behavior Rating Form, which is to be completed by teachers as an appraisal of a student's success, assurance, and self-confidence. A positive correlation between teachers' ratings and students' self-esteem scores exists for male students, but not for females. In any case, the author suggests that teachers use the Behavior Rating Form to assess their own perceptions of their students on a regular basis.

Research on the relationship between self-esteem and depression, academic success, and brain dysfunction is also presented. It is unfortunate that the author has applied the label of learning disabled to the academically unsuccessful. A deficit of 2 or more years in reading and/or arithmetic does not conform to conventional definitions of learning disabilities. Therefore, the use of this label is rather misleading.

ADMINISTRATION. The author provides classification tables for scores from each SEI form and subscale so that individuals may be classified into one of five categories ranging from very high to very low in self-esteem. The meaning of these classifications is, however, unclear. The author merely reports that while they are "time-tested" and to be used "for diagnostic purposes," they "do not necessarily conform to universally accepted classifications." Therefore, classification of an individual according to this system may not be particularly useful. More illuminating are the tables of percentile ranks which allow the administrator to determine the subject's standing relative to those who participated in the standardization of the scale. However, the usefulness of these tables is severely limited due to the lack of information presented concerning the characteristics of the standardization sample.

CONCLUSION. The Culture-Free SEIs provide a quick and easy-to-administer measure of the self worth of both children and adults. However, before the claim can be made that these inventories are truly culture-free, norms based on culturally diverse samples must be established. Furthermore, the assertion that these inventories can be used to identify students with learning problems is somewhat misleading. While level of self-esteem may be associated with learning problems in some cases, these inventories are designed only to measure self-esteem. As a measure of self-esteem, however, these inventories may prove to be quite valuable to those who want to identify individuals in need of counseling or other assistance.

[292]

Culture Shock Inventory. Adults and older children who expect to work outside their own culture; 1970–78; CSI; 8 scales: lack of western ethnocentrism, cross cultural experience, cognitive flex, behavioral flex, cultural knowledge-specific, cultural knowledge-general, cultural behavior-general, interpersonal sensitivity; 1 form ('70, 3 pages, self scoring); instrument administration guide ('78, 4 pages); fact sheet ('77, 2 pages); 1982 price data: $40 per 10 tests including guide and fact sheet; (10–20) minutes; W. J. Reddin and Ken Rowell; Organizational Tests Ltd. [Canada].*

[293]

Current and Past Psychopathology Scales. Psychiatric patients and nonpatients; 1966–68; CAPPS; rating scale and optional interview guide for use in diagnosing mental illness if any; judgments based upon various sources of information (subject, informant, case records, nurse's reports, etc.); the PEF-D section deals with the patient's current functioning over the past month, the PHS with his past functioning from age 12 up to the past month; computerized psychiatric diagnosis (DIAGNO II) produces for each subject 1 of 46 possible diagnoses, using the official nomenclature of the American Psychiatric Association for 44 of the diagnoses; Form C50 ('68, 11 pages, scales only); Form C51 ('68, 25 pages, scales and interview schedule); no manual; typewritten data sheets; separate answer sheets must be used; 1984 price data: $1 per test; $.20 per answer sheet; fee for editing, coding, key punching, and verifying protocol, $.40 per subject; computerized psychiatric diagnosis is available; (15–30) minutes for scales only, (60–120) minutes for scales with interview guide; Robert L. Spitzer and Jean Endicott; Research Assessment and Training Unit, New York State Psychiatric Institute.*

See T3:645 (23 references); for reviews by William J. Eichman and Raymond D. Fowler, Jr., see 7:62 (3 references); see also P:53A (1 reference).

TEST REFERENCES

1. Wender, P. H., Rosenthal, D., Rainer, J. D., Greenhill, L., & Sarlin, M. B. Schizophrenics' adopting parents: Psychiatric status. ARCHIVES OF GENERAL PSYCHIATRY, 1977, 34, 777–784.

2. Mendlewicz, J., Linkowski, P., & VanCauter, E. Some neuroendocrine parameters in bipolar and unipolar depression. JOURNAL OF AFFECTIVE DISORDERS, 1979, 1, 25–32.

3. Mendlewicz, J., Linkowski, P., & Wilmotte, J. Relationship between schizoaffective illness and affective disorders or schizophrenia: Morbidity risk and genetic transmission. JOURNAL OF AFFECTIVE DISORDERS, 1980, 2, 289–302.

4. Marcus, J., Auerbach, J., Wilkinson, L., & Burack, C. M. Infants at risk for schizophrenia: The Jerusalem Infant Development Study. ARCHIVES OF GENERAL PSYCHIATRY, 1981, 38, 703–713.

5. Parnas, J., Schulsinger, F., Schulsinger, H., Mednick, S. A., & Teasdale, T. W. Behavioral precursors of schizophrenia spectrum: A prospective study. ARCHIVES OF GENERAL PSYCHIATRY, 1982, 39, 658–664.

[294]

Curriculum Referenced Tests of Mastery. Grades 1, 2, 3, 4, 5, 6, 7, 8, 9–10, 11–12; 1983–84; CRTM; academic skills achievement; customized tests available in which the user can tailor the test objectives to meet their curricula; criterion-referenced scores with suggested standards of mastery; norm-referenced scores for reading/language arts and mathematics; objective-referenced scores vary with level and may include the following areas: phonic analysis, structural analysis, vocabulary, life/study reference, literal comprehension, inferential comprehension, critical comprehension, understanding literature, listening, spelling, mechanics, usage, grammar/syntax, proofreading, numeration, whole numbers (addition, subtraction, multiplication, division), decimals, fractions, ratio/proportion/percent, measurement, geometry, problem solving, graphing/statistics/probability, pre-algebra; 10 levels; buyer's guide ('84, 61 pages); reports catalog ('84, 28 pages); technical report ('84, 107 pages); objectives catalog ('83, 105 pages); objectives catalog supplement ('84, 40 pages); separate answer sheets must be used with reusable editions; 1984 price data: $40.25 per 35 machine-scorable tests plus manual for levels E, F, G; $33.25 per 35 reusable tests plus manual for levels G–R; $5.25 per 35 practice tests; $19.95 per 35 survey tests; $7.35 per 35 NCS answer sheets; $89.50 per 500 NCS answer sheets; $7 per 35 self-scoring survey test answer sheets; $4.50 per manual; $4.50 per norms manual; $5.95 per technical report; $5.50 per custom manual; scoring service: $.75 per NCS answer sheet, $1.05 per machine-scorable test; optional reports available for student, teacher, principal, district; Charles E. Merrill Publishing Co.*

a) LEVEL E. Grade 1; 1 form ('84, 28 pages); manual ('83, 22 pages).
b) LEVEL F. Grade 2; 1 form ('83, 32 pages); manual ('84, 23 pages).
c) LEVEL G. Grade 3; 1 form ('83, 16 pages); manual ('84, 22 pages).
d) LEVEL H. Grade 4; 1 form ('83, 23 pages); manual ('84, 23 pages).
e) LEVEL I. Grade 5; 1 form ('83, 23 pages); manual ('84, 22 pages).
f) LEVEL J. Grade 6; 1 form ('83, 24 pages); manual ('83, 22 pages).
g) LEVEL K. Grade 7; 1 form ('83, 30 pages); manual ('84, 23 pages).
h) LEVEL L. Grade 8; 1 form ('83, 32 pages); manual ('84, 23 pages).
i) LEVEL Q. Grades 9–10; 1 form ('84, 17 pages).
j) LEVEL R. Grades 11–12; 1 form ('84, 24 pages).

Review of Curriculum Referenced Tests of Mastery by RANDY W. KAMPHAUS, Assistant Professor of Psychology, Coordinator of School Psychology Training, Eastern Kentucky University, Richmond, KY:

The Curriculum Referenced Tests of Mastery (CRTM) is a new entrant in the competition for the group achievement testing marketplace. The flexibility of the CRTM is likely to be praised; however, its lack of breadth at grades 1 through 8 is likely to make it an ineffective competitor for the ITBS, CTBS, Stanford, Metro, and other more widely used batteries.

The technical manual, called Technical Report 1 by the authors because it is supposed to be the first in a series of technical updates, is a paradox. On the one hand, it gives great detail on the premise behind the CRTM and clearly differentiates it from the major group achievement tests. On the other hand, the manual lacks evidence of reliability and validity for certain forms of the test (e.g., the Survey Tests). The strong point of the CRTM is its flexibility. In addition to the Standard Edition, which is essentially a group-administered test of reading and mathematics achievement for grades 1 through 12, the CRTM offers Survey Tests and Custom Edition Tests. The Survey Tests are designed for use at the beginning of the school year. Teachers can give the Survey Tests, hand score them, and get an idea of the general strengths and weaknesses of the class in these two curricular areas.

A potentially more beneficial option is the opportunity for schools to design their own Custom Edition Tests. This approach takes full advantage of statistics emanating from item response theory models. Essentially, school districts can select their own objectives and mastery criteria and the publisher will use latent trait methodology (essentially Wright's BICAL program) to link the Custom Edition Test's raw scores to those for the Standard Edition, allowing use of the Standard Edition national norms. This is an important contribution because it develops a middle ground between the inflexible group achievement tests currently available and the "home grown" tests developed by municipalities and state education agencies which do not have the expertise or the resources to develop a test properly. This is a very time- and cost-efficient option for state education agencies who are developing their own tests or contracting with test publishers to develop custom tests from the ground up. The Custom Edition of the CRTM allows school districts, in effect, to develop their own custom test of high quality, and not lose the value of still having national norms.

The shortcomings of the CRTM are mostly related to its incompleteness at this time. An equivalent form of the CRTM is under development, but is as yet unavailable. There is no reliability data presented for the individual objectives, which are measured by four items each. There is also no description of the Survey Tests' standardization sample and no reliability data presented for this instrument. The manual states that the match of the Standard Edition to United States Census Bureau Statistics is currently being computed. It is clear from the winter 1983 norming sample that children of Spanish origin are underrepresented (3.3% in the sample versus 9.2% in the population).

Some conclusions drawn in the technical manual are also overstated. At the outset, the authors try to point out how different the CRTM is from other group achievement tests, primarily by saying that they put more emphasis on selecting items by content rather than their discrimination indices or *p*-values. The insinuation is that developers of other group achievement tests all but ignore content validity. This is simply not true. Item selection procedures for the CRTM and competing tests are different, but not to the degree suggested by the CRTM authors. Other group test developers have curriculum experts that ensure that the test content is appropriate, and items that are statistical "clunkers" are retained because they measure content too important to be excluded.

In the final analysis, the difference between the CRTM and other group tests is the content. On this issue the CRTM has advantages and disadvantages. In terms of reading and mathematics achievement, the CRTM does certainly yield more specific domain (criterion) referenced information than its competitors. One has only to look at the list of objectives in the CRTM manual to see that it possesses greater breadth in these areas. This information should be more useful to teachers than the broad band scores currently offered by group achievement tests.

In contrast, the CRTM lacks breadth in that it does not measure science and social studies (until the ninth-grade level) and other areas usually included in other group achievement tests. This will undoubtedly frustrate middle-school science teachers.

In summary, the CRTM is a valuable contribution to the group achievement testing scene because of its flexibility to meet different testing needs and the more detailed information yielded on specific subskills in reading and mathematics, which teachers should find helpful for planning instruction. The CRTM technical data, however, are incomplete at this time, and it does not assess all areas of the curriculum in grades 1 through 8. Is the CRTM a suitable substitute for other group achievement batteries? Probably not, in its current form, but it may be a good substitute for the reading and mathematics portions of another group achievement battery. It may be worthwhile to try out the CRTM and see if teachers find the domain referenced information more helpful. The Custom Edition of the CRTM is an attractive alternative for developing a local reading and mathematics test that also has national norms.

Review of Curriculum Referenced Tests of Mastery by GLYNN LIGON, Director, Office of Research and Evaluation, Austin Independent School District, Austin, TX:

This ambitious new test series spans grades 1 through 12 and covers reading/language arts and mathematics. For grades 9 through 12, subject-referenced tests also cover science and social science. Users have the option of administering the Standard Edition, which measures objectives found by the authors to be most common in their national study of curricula, or creating a Custom Edition, which allows choices of objectives to measure. Survey Tests, grades 2 through 8 only, are designed for beginning-of-the-year, classroom-level estimates. Individual assessment is not recommended with the Survey Tests. Subject-Referenced Edition Tests, grades 9 through 12, are available for English, mathematics, science, and social science. Contract Tests may be designed from the item bank of available items if none of the other formats is suited to a unique situation.

CRTM authors have produced an excellent, textbook-like Technical Manual, which discusses test development issues clearly and in detail. Reviewers selecting achievement tests could use this manual as a valuable source of background on what makes a good test.

CRTM attempts to be both a criterion-referenced test and a norm-referenced test. It does the former admirably and the latter with less reliability than traditional norm-referenced achievement tests. If a criterion referenced measure is needed, CRTM is an excellent candidate—especially if a custom edition is desired. However, the number of options per item ranges from 2 to 4, and this is a disadvantage in competing for reliability with other norm-referenced batteries using 5 options.

The Custom Edition provides the user a choice of objectives, each carefully normed using IRT (Item Response Theory) calibrations. However, potential users should consider several issues. No mention is made in the technical manual of the stability of item logits when item sequences differ on a custom test from those in the norming edition. It is important that items on a custom test appear as nearly as possible in the same location as they appeared when calibrated. Recent work with IRT calibrated item banks has shown a drift in item difficulty when sequence is varied. Many current item banks code the location of items in addition to item calibrations.

Selecting mastery levels on objectives (i.e., 3 out of 4, or 4 out of 4 items correct) is possible, but should be done with care. A fatal flaw of many criterion-referenced tests is a low mastery criterion that produces universal mastery on a pretest. The authors provide a table showing the virtual impossibility of objective mastery by pure guessing, but they missed the point. Few students are pure guessers. The real issue is how many guess just enough to cross over the line between nonmastery and mastery. This is where the small number of items per objective and the small number of choices per item limit the reliability of the mastery designations. A table of hits, false positives, and false negatives would be more enlightening to a buyer.

No time limits are imposed; only suggested times are given. This also makes CRTM as a norm-referenced instrument different from traditional tests. This is a power test, not a speed test. Was the norming sample really given unlimited time by teachers? Will comparisons across schools be influenced by different applications of this untimed feature? Secondary schools in particular are so class-period oriented that allowing a few students to work on long after others have finished is problematic. It should be remembered that CRTM's strength is being objective-based and mastery focused. Its ability to predict future success on timed tests (such as college-entrance exams) is unknown.

In addition to the traditional scores available, there is an option for mastery scores to be counted within cognitive levels. For reading/language arts, the number of objectives mastered may be requested as a scoring option for each of the recognizing, understanding, and reasoning levels. In mathematics the levels of computation, concepts, and problem solving are defined. The authors expect these levels to aid teachers in grouping students, analyzing performance, and adjusting instructional strategies.

Because CRTM has clearly defined the objectives tested and measures each with at least a minimum number of items, a user can select the Standard Edition or a Custom Edition with full knowledge of the skills that will be reflected in the students' scores. This is an advantage over the more general norm-referenced achievement tests that usually have less specific skill definitions.

The technical manual currently contains no mention of the adequacy of the vertical scaling that is necessary for studies across more than two test levels or over more than 2 years. In the creation of Custom Edition tests, the adequacy of comparisons across test levels is a key issue to consider. Manipulation of objectives at each grade level can give closer test-curriculum matches, but can also limit the comparability of scores across grade levels.

An excellent discussion of acceptable and unacceptable item bias is provided and should be read by potential users. An unanswered question is whether it is valid to allow minority reviewers to veto items regardless of their contribution to validity and reliability. More discussion of regional biases would have been helpful. Potential users themselves should review items and objectives for regional bias as part of the objective-selection process.

My favorite feature is the option of designing a unique cover for a custom edition test with one's own district name, test name, superintendent's name, and logo. This local touch is attractive, but in today's world, why would a school system print a superintendent's name on the covers of test booklets to be used more than one year?

[295]

The D.A.L.E. System: Developmental Assessment of Life Experiences. Profound to severely mentally retarded, moderate to mild mentally retarded; 1975–79; DALE; "an inventory to assess competencies in community living"; criterion-referenced; no data on reliability and validity; no norms; individual; 1 form; 2 levels; manual ('78, 136 pages, includes fact sheets, initial contact surveys, rating sheets for each area, and record charts for both levels); 1982 price data: $2.50 or less per inventory for level 1 or level 2 depending on number ordered; $6.50 or less per manual depending on amount ordered; administration time not reported; Gertrude A. Barber, John P. Mannino, and Robert J. Will; Barber Center Press, Inc.*

a) LEVEL 1. Profound to severely mentally retarded; 1979; ratings in 5 areas: sensory motor, language, self-help, cognition, socialization; 1 form (52 pages, includes fact sheet, initial contact survey, rating sheets for each area, and record charts).

b) LEVEL 2. Moderate to mild mentally retarded; 1979; ratings in 5 areas: personal hygiene, personal management, communications, residence/home management, community access; 1 form (59 pages, includes same materials as listed in Level 1).

Review of The D.A.L.E. System: Developmental Assessment of Life Experiences by FRANK M. GRESHAM, Associate Professor of Psychology, Louisiana State University, Baton Rouge, LA:

The D.A.L.E. System is a criterion-referenced mastery testing approach to the assessment of what appears to be adaptive behavior, although the manual does not specifically use the term "adaptive behavior." The stated purposes of the D.A.L.E. System are to assess relative strengths and weaknesses in home and community living skills, prescribe goal plans for remediation of weaknesses based upon assessment results, and to evaluate the effectiveness of remediation procedures.

Since the D.A.L.E. System employs a mastery testing approach, no norms are provided in the manual. The use of a mastery testing approach to the measurement of adaptive behavior is perhaps most useful in terms of utilizing the assessment information for the planning and evaluation of treatment. A strong case for mastery testing of academic achievement has been made by Popham (1978) and others, and the same advantages should hold true for adaptive behavior. Most adaptive behavior scales employ a norm-referenced model in constructing the scales (e.g., the AAMD Adaptive Behavior Scale, Vineland Social Maturity Scale, Adaptive Behavior Inventory for Children, etc.) and typically have meager reliability and validity evidence and poor normative samples.

The D.A.L.E. System does not differ from the more traditional norm-referenced adaptive behavior measures in terms of reliability and validity evidence. In reading the manual, it almost seems as if the authors imply a justification for the use of the inventory simply because the skills being measured are behaviorally defined or operationalized. This is obviously a mistake since reliability and validity are as important for criterion-referenced measures as they are for norm-referenced measures (Hambleton, Swaminathan, Algina, & Coulson, 1978; Popham, 1978; Subkoviak, 1980). The D.A.L.E. System manual presents no data regarding interrater agreement, stability, or internal consistency. We thus have no evidence that raters agree among themselves in rating behaviors, that ratings are stable over time in the absence of treatment, or that specific behaviors making up domains are homogenous. Moreover, there is no evidence presented in the manual that the D.A.L.E. System reliably classifies individuals as masters or nonmasters of specific skills or domains. Subkoviak (1980) emphasizes that an important form of reliability for criterion-referenced measures is the consistency of mastery and nonmastery decisions over repeated testing of the same group. The D.A.L.E. System offers no such evidence for reliability.

Similarly, there is no evidence for validity presented in the manual. Although the specific skills within each domain appear face valid, there is no indication that the items constitute a representative sample of all items from the domain of interest (i.e., content validity). This lack of evidence for content validity in a criterion-referenced scale is perplexing since one of the most important characteristics of criterion-referenced measures is this representative sampling from item domains (Popham, 1978).

Concepts from Generalizability Theory (Cronbach, Gleser, Nanda, & Rajaratnam, 1972) have been used to evaluate the psychometric quality of criterion-referenced measures. Evidence for item and setting generality are particularly relevant for content validity. At this time, we do not know that the items in the D.A.L.E. System representatively sample from domain universes (e.g., sensory-motor, cognitive, etc.), nor do we know that similar ratings would be obtained in different settings in the absence of training.

The D.A.L.E. System also does not provide evidence for construct validity. There is no explicit statement in the manual that the system is a measure of the construct of adaptive behavior. The manual simply states that the D.A.L.E. System assesses a wide spectrum of skills involved in home and community living. The subdomains listed in the scale are similar to most adaptive behavior scales, and specific skills are supposedly listed in order of difficulty, although no data are presented to support the authors' hierarchical sequencing (e.g., scalability analyses).

Sorely lacking in the D.A.L.E. System manual is evidence that the scale can differentiate masters and nonmasters of the domains listed in the D.A.L.E. The extent to which the scale can discriminate masters/nonmasters would be evidence for construct validity (i.e., discriminative efficiency). The D.A.L.E. System lacks this basic form of construct validation.

Another important type of construct validity, especially for rating scales like D.A.L.E. that involve some degree of subjectivity, is convergent validity. In convergent validity, validity is defined by substantial correlation between two or more variables hypothesized to measure or to be related to the same construct, using maximally different methods of measurement (Campbell & Fiske, 1959). Future research with the D.A.L.E. System should utilize assessment methods in addition to the rating method, such as direct observations and interviews with significant others, to assess convergence of assessment information. To the extent that different assessment methods converge or agree there would be evidence of the construct validity of the scale.

The purported value of the D.A.L.E. System is in the specification of target behaviors so that they may be taught by behavioral principles (i.e., operant conditioning). Misstatements and misunderstandings of operant learning theory are evident throughout the manual regarding such concepts as use of reinforcement, schedules of reinforcement, contingency contracting, and confusion of operant learning with other learning theories (e.g., the concept of habit strength from Hullian theory). The sections of the manual that deal with teaching adaptive skills require extensive revision to conform more accurately to the current language and empirical data from the fields of operant learning and applied behavior analysis.

In summary, the D.A.L.E. System represents an attempt to measure adaptive behavior using a criterion-referenced approach. While the specific skills making up the scale appear comprehensive and face valid, the manual presents no reliability and validity data. The D.A.L.E. System may have some utility in the initial stages of assessment for identifying strengths and weaknesses in adaptive behavior. Without any indication of the reliability and validity of the scores, however, users will not be sure what the scores mean. Also, users of the D.A.L.E. System would be well advised to ignore the manual's recommendations for teaching adaptive skills and consult recent texts in the field of applied behavior analysis for guidance on teaching strategies (e.g., Kazdin, 1980).

REVIEWER'S REFERENCES

Campbell, D. T., & Fiske, D. W. Convergent and discriminant validation by the multitrait-multimethod matrix. PSYCHOLOGICAL BULLETIN, 1959, 56, 81–105.

Cronbach, L. J., Gleser, G. C., Nanda, H., & Rajaratnam, N. THE DEPENDABILITY OF BEHAVIORAL MEASUREMENTS: THEORY OF GENERALIZABILITY FOR SCORES AND PROFILES. New York: Wiley, 1972.

Hambleton, R. K., Swaminathan, H., Algina, J., & Coulson, D. B. Criterion-referenced testing and measurement: A review of technical issues and developments. REVIEW OF EDUCATIONAL RESEARCH, 1978, 48, 1–47.

Popham, W. J. CRITERION-REFERENCED MEASUREMENT. Englewood Cliffs, NJ: Prentice-Hall, 1978.

Kazdin, A. E. BEHAVIOR MODIFICATION IN APPLIED SETTINGS (2nd ed.). Homewood, IL: Dorsey Press, 1980.

Subkoviak, M. J. Decision-consistency approaches. In R. A. Berk (Ed.), CRITERION-REFERENCED MEASUREMENT: THE STATE OF THE ART. Baltimore: The Johns Hopkins University Press, 1980.

[296]

DABERON: A Screening Device for School Readiness. Ages 4–6; 1972–82; screening test for school readiness; individual; 1 form; revised manual ('82, 48 pages); report on readiness ('76, 3 pages); record form ('81, 2 pages); 1984 price data: $59.95 per set of testing materials including manual, 25 report on readiness forms, 25 record forms, and 5 classroom summary forms; $9.95 per 25 record forms; $9.95 per 25 report on readiness forms; $24.95 per manual; (20–40) minutes; Virginia A. Danzer, Mary Frances Gerber, and Theresa M. Lyons; ASIEP Education Co.*

[297]

A Dating Problems Checklist. High school and college; 1961–79; DPCL; 7 areas: dating conditions, home-parents-family, personality and emotional self, sex attitudes, social poise, physical self, dating and definite commitments; no data on reliability and validity; no norms, author recommends use of local norms; 1 form ('79, 6 pages); combined manual ('79, 11 pages); for this and 279; 1984 price data: $5 per 10 tests; $1 per manual; (15–30) minutes; Gelolo McHugh; Family Life Publications, Inc.*

For reviews by Clifford R. Adams and Robert A. Harper of the original edition, see 6:676.

Review of A Dating Problems Checklist by ANDREW CHRISTENSEN, Associate Professor of Psychology, University of California, Los Angeles, CA:

A Dating Problems Checklist has been in existence for more than 20 years. From the time of its original version in 1961 to its revision in 1979, more than 250,000 young people used this questionnaire. Given such widespread use, one might hope that a wealth of data had accumulated on the instrument. What dating problems are normative for a particular age group or relationship stage? What dating problems are predictive of relationship failure or success? What dating problems are associated with what types of persons? Unfortunately, the test manual describes no research to answer these or any other questions about the instrument or dating.

The checklist consists of 125 statements about dating (e.g., "I am jealous of my dates" and "Dating makes me nervous"). The respondent indicates whether the statement is true or false and separately indicates whether the condition described is a problem. The items are grouped under the following seven categories: dating conditions; home, parents, family; personality and emotional self; sex attitudes; social poise; physical self; and dating and definite commitments. These categories are indicated on the questionnaire by abbreviations (e.g., "dc" for dating conditions), which are certain to puzzle or confuse the respondent.

The purpose of A Dating Problems Checklist is to be a teaching and counseling aid. "It is designed to help teachers and counselors become acquainted with the dating atmosphere within which their students and counselees exist, as well as focus on individual dating problems." The checklist was designed to overcome the generation gap so that teachers and counselors could facilitate relevant discussion for teenagers today.

One cannot evaluate whether the checklist achieves its goals because no data are offered on the reliability, validity, or utility of the test or its items and no data are offered on its usefulness in counseling or teaching situations. The items have a certain "face validity," but the user has no way of knowing which are the important items or scales, whether some content was overrepresented while some was underrepresented, or whether some important content was left out entirely. Also, it is not at all clear that students, counselees, teachers, and counselors need an instrument to generate discussion or discover what their dating problems are.

The manual is not clear on the scoring of the instrument. Presumably one just adds up the number of true or false statements, yet this is problematic because the items are not all phrased in a consistent direction. Maybe one just totals the number of items marked as a problem. Of course, the precise method of scoring does not matter since there is no way to evalute the scores! But the danger is that users may attempt to evaluate themselves with the instrument. A student who checks off more of the items as problems than another student might believe that he or she is more troubled or disturbed when this may not be the case.

The author suggests some limited research use with the checklist. He acknowledges that there are no standardized statistics for the instrument, but suggests it be used as a survey instrument and results compared to local norms. Apparently he hopes others will do what he has failed to do—develop data on the instrument.

SUMMARY. A Dating Problems Checklist was designed as a teaching and counseling aid. Through its use, the counselor and teacher could become acquainted with the dating atmosphere and the individual dating problems of their counselees and students. No data are reported on whether the checklist captures significant dating problems or whether it aids in classroom or counseling discussions. Because there is no way to evaluate responses to the instrument, users could misinterpret their scores (e.g., assume they have serious problems when they don't or assume they don't have serious dating problems when they do). Furthermore, most counselees, students, teachers, and counselors can probably generate their own discussions of dating problems without the use of any such aid.

[298]

DECAD (Departmental Evaluation of Chairpersons Activities for Development). Departmental chairpersons; 1977–82; DECAD; ratings of departmental chairperson by chairperson and faculty, for evaluation and development; ratings in 5 areas: responsibilities, evaluation summary, administrative methods, characterization of department, diagnostic summary; norms consist of means only; 1 form ('82, 2 pages); chairperson information form ('82, 1 page); DECAD report ('77, 3 pages, individualized results summary); interpretive guide ('77, 12 pages); 1985 price data: 1 report—$50, 2 reports—$80, 3 or more reports—$35 each (includes all materials plus scoring/reporting service); administration time not reported; Center for Faculty Evaluation and Development and Donald B. Hoyt (interpretive guide); Center for Faculty Evaluation and Development.*

[299]

Decision Making Inventory. High school and college students; 1983; DMI; 4 scores: 2 information-gathering styles (systematic, spontaneous), 2 information-analysis styles (internal, external); reliability data for college students only; norms consist of means and standard deviations for college students only; Form H ('83, 1 page); scoring grid (1 page); manual (72 pages); 1984 price data: $6 per 30 inventories; $1 per 2 scoring grids; $10 per manual (includes specimen set); (10–15) minutes; William Coscarelli, Richard Johnson (test), and Jadeau Johnson (test); Marathon Consulting & Press.*

[300]

The Decision-Making Organizer. Grades 9–12, college; 1979–81; DMO; ratings in 5 or 6 areas: self understanding, education, work, barriers to decision making, time use (college), personal time economics (high school), designing occupation (college); 2 levels; 1985 price data: $14.85 per complete set including 20 organizers; $13.75 per 20 organizers; $1.50 per manual; $4 per specimen set (specify level); (10–20) minutes; Anna Miller-Tiedeman and Patricia Elenz-Martin (college level); Scholastic Testing Service, Inc.*

a) DECISION-MAKING ORGANIZER. Grades 9–12; 1979–81; 1 form ('79, 6 pages); manual ('81, 10 pages).

b) DECISION-MAKING ORGANIZER: THE COLLEGE YEARS. College; 1979–81; 1 form ('79, 9 pages); manual ('81, 8 pages).

Review of The Decision-Making Organizer by RHONDA L. GUTENBERG, Consultant, Jeanneret & Associates, Inc., Houston, TX:

The Decision-Making Organizer (DMO) represents an attempt to help both high school and college students develop plans for the immediate, mid-range, and even long-term future. It requires the student to focus on five (for the high school version) or six (for the college version) subject areas and check off or complete sentences that clarify goals, objectives, and obstacles to the decision-making process. The primary use for the DMO is to enable the student (with or without input from a counselor) to "project his or her life using the management concepts of planning, directing, controlling, and improving."

The instrument is based on the Miller-Tiedeman Pyramidal Model of Decision Making which defines four levels in decision making and follow-up. Level 1 consists of Exploration, Crystallization, Choice, Clarification, and Decision. Level 2 is Problem Solving; Level 3 is Solution Using; and Level 4 is Solution Reviewing. The authors of the instrument suggest that it provides the students with insight into the decision-making process. It is the opinion of this reviewer, however, that the decision-making model merely provides a framework for ordering questions in a logical manner (as opposed to an understanding of the process). The fact that questions flow in a hierarchical fashion adds to the usefulness and attractiveness of this instrument in that answers to earlier questions within a particular section aid in responding to later questions.

The DMO is meant to measure a particular state which is subject to change within any given length of time. Therefore, the issue of reliability (over time) is not appropriate. In addition, responses are not quantified, and thus a measure of internal consistency is not viable. Given that the DMO is a counseling/clarification aid, the usual statistical concern about reliability is not as relevant.

The authors explain that the question of validity is whether or not the student understands the decision-making states. It is not so much a matter of understanding the states but rather understanding the questions and being able to answer them truthfully. Once again, the issue of statistical validity does not seem especially applicable given the nature of the DMO.

The DMO is not a test but rather a mechanism for assisting students in defining goals. As such it appears to be a useful tool. It is not possible to judge how helpful this instrument is without considering the individual using it as well as the person providing the student with related assistance and interpretation. It does seem to be a very good starting point for clarifying major goals.

Review of The Decision-Making Organizer by CAROLINE A. MANUELE, Assistant Professor, Division of Psychological and Educational Services, Counseling and Personnel, Graduate School of Education, Fordham University, NY:

The Decision-Making Organizer is described by its authors as a "self-monitoring guide to the decision-making processes encountered during the college years." The questions in the Organizer ask students to provide information about their thoughts, feelings, choices, and actions with respect to different life-choice areas (self-understanding, education, work, decision-making barriers, time use, designing employment, and life management by objectives).

The questions in each area on the form are grouped into categories which are designed to correspond to the different levels and styles of the Miller-Tiedeman Pyramidal Model of Decision-Making, which includes Exploration, Crystallization of Choice, Clarification, Decision (Level 1); Problem-Solving (Level 2), Solution Using (Level 3) and Solution Reviewing (Level 4). For example, next to a series of questions which asks students about the advantages and disadvantages of the occupations they are considering is the label Clarification, which falls under Level 1 in the model. If students are able to positively answer a question or a series of questions in any given category, they are assumed to be in a specific stage of the career decision-making process.

To better understand the purposes and nature of this form, it is important for users to know that the Organizer is not a test. Data on the form is not quantifiable, rated, or summed in any way to provide a score, profile, or ranking. Rather, it is an individual's record of what s/he has chosen or learned about the choices s/he needs to make. The authors suggest that the form can be filled out individually by students, used by the counselor as an interview tool, or group administered and discussed in the context of a career-life planning course.

The major problem with this form, which relates to how it can best be used, is that it is difficult to ascertain how individuals could realistically determine, from the form, where they are in the decision-making process. First, the questions in the specific decision-making category are either too few or not varied enough to provide sufficient information for placing an individual in a given stage of the process (e.g., several questions on obtained occupational information are meant to imply that the individual is in the Crystallization stage of decision-making). Second, there is a great deal of overlap in the type of information that is elicited under the different areas of the form (e.g., the advantages and disadvantages of choice of occupations and work are asked about under each of the areas of self-understanding, work, and decision-making barriers). Third, the form does not provide a way of summarizing or organizing all the information included in its six pages in a manner which would be easily understood and interpreted by the student.

All of this means that the assistance of a counselor is needed to interpret and make some subjective judgements, from the information elicited, about where the individual may be in the decision-making process. It is unlikely that students using the form alone, without assistance, would be able to interpret in any meaningful way what the information implies about their career development needs. The Organizer is probably best used as an activity in individual or group career counseling sessions where students can be provided with instruction about the meaning of the decision-making concepts in the model and given assistance with determining how the information is related to their own particular status in decision-making. The manual includes suggestions from the authors on how the Organizer can be used and related to different topics usually covered in a career planning course. Without counselor assistance the form is more of a record of information, and the counselor might like to use it as such to help keep track of individual students' plans and activities.

In the manual the authors state that the amount of time required to complete the Organizer depends on the reading ability of the student, but that the average reader can do it in 10 minutes. This time is probably greatly underestimated because students usually have not thought or done that much about their future school and career plans. Most likely, many students would need to take more time to reflect on the meaning of the questions and may need assistance with deciding what information to put down on the form. Students with literacy problems would require even more time and assistance with both reading and replying to the questions.

The manual also includes sections on validity and reliability. In these sections the authors state that the validity question is whether or not students understand the current state of their decision-making. This may be an accurate validity question to pose about the Organizer but the form does not seem to provide, as the authors claim, a design that really provides the information to answer this question. Mastery of the basic concepts of decision-making and the "self-monitoring" of the decision-making process would require more effort and learning than what is available through the use of the Organizer.

The reliability issue posed by the authors is whether or not an individual considers the state of his or her decision-making to be stable. This would be very difficult to ascertain in any student at one period of time (such as when the student is filling out the form) and probably would best be determined by a counselor who has an opportunity to observe a student's behavior over time. Thus with both of these questions the reliability and validity of any given student's comprehension of and participation in decision-making is not an issue of the form itself but an issue related to the conditions under which the form should be used.

Basically the Decision-Making Organizer is a simple self-report form that asks students for information about their future education and career plans. Additional issues such as time management and barriers to decision-making are also addressed. Used alone it would not seem to add a great deal to a student's understanding of where they are in the decision-making process. With counselor assistance and more information about decision-making concepts it may be useful to students.

[301]

Decoding Inventory. Grades 1 and over; 1979; DI; "screening measure designed to assess student performance in auditory and visual discrimination, phonics, structural analysis and use of context clues"; initial screening measure used to decide appropriate level to be administered to the individual student; no data on reliability and validity; no norms, mastery objective: 80% correct on each part of each level; individual; 1 form (7 cards in manual consisting of items to be administered for all 3 levels); manual (22 pages plus recording pad which may be reproduced locally and test cards); 1985 price data: $7.95 per test including all levels; administration time not reported; Lyndon W. Searfoss and H. Donald Jacobs; Kendall/Hunt Publishing Co.*

a) LEVEL R—READINESS. Students whose performance was less than 50% on specified parts of Level 1; 2 parts: auditorily discriminating words, visually discriminating words.

b) LEVEL 1—BASIC. Reading level grades 1–3; 8 parts: naming letters, hearing initial consonants, hearing final consonants, hearing initial consonant clusters, pronouncing vowel and consonant clusters, hearing syllables, dividing shorter words into syllables, using context clues.

c) LEVEL 2—ADVANCED. Reading level grades 4 and over; 7 parts: hearing syllables, pronouncing vowels and consonant clusters, hearing initial consonant clusters, hearing final consonants, hearing initial single consonants, dividing longer words into syllables, using context clues.

Review of Decoding Inventory by MARY E. CURTIS, Assistant Professor of Education, Harvard University, Cambridge, MA:

As stated by its authors, the primary purpose of the Decoding Inventory is "to isolate the various word identification skills after a student's weakness in applying a decoding strategy is discovered."

Nine of the subtests in Levels 1 and 2, as well as the initial screening measure, use nonwords in order to "assure that a student must apply a decoding skill, rather than be able to respond from previous knowledge of the word." The authors' description of the creation of the nonwords, however, indicates a major weakness in the test. They began with words that were above the intended grade levels of the test (e.g., the Level 1 nonwords were created from 4th- to 6th-grade words). Next, they substituted graphemes and attached affixes that are "easy" and "difficult" (based on publishers' lists and clinical data). The result is what the authors call "mutilated words," and include items like "glestment," "lingulation," and "grodiment" (from the initial screening measure), and "toub" and "loim." In addition, the test includes several words such as "task," "rook," "curd," "torpedo," and "holocaust," although students are instructed that these too are "nonsense words."

The use of synthetic words in tests of decoding has often been advocated as a way to distinguish between skills in word analysis and sight word vocabulary knowledge. However, the procedure used for creation of the nonwords on this test, along with the "mutilated words" that result, seriously limit its application. Extensive research is available concerning the order in which word analysis skills and knowledge are usually taught and mastered. Given this research, one has to wonder why the authors chose to use the procedure that they did.

With the exception of a letter naming subtest in Level 1, Levels 1 and 2 are identical with regard to the skills assessed. Three of the subtests require that the student give the letter names of the consonant sounds that are heard in nonwords that are read by the tester. Although this skill is required in spelling rather than decoding, no mention is made of this in the manual. Level 1 subtests consist of all one-syllable nonwords, while Level 2 nonwords are predominantly two and three syllables.

Two subtests in each level assess skill in syllabication. One subtest requires students to indicate the number of syllables heard in a set of nonwords, while the other requires them to mark the locations of syllables. Again, the only difference between the levels appears to be in the number of syllables.

Only one of the subtests in each level requires the students to read the nonwords. All of the items are one-syllable: Level 1 has 15 items and Level 2 has 20 items. Many of these nonwords contain high frequency vowel and consonant clusters, thus providing some valid information about students' skill in decoding. However, items such as "neeg" and "gawt" are of little apparent value.

Each level concludes with a subtest that assesses knowledge of the meanings of ambiguous words. The words are presented first in isolation and then in context. Students who give a meaning for an isolated word that does not fit the context to follow receive one point. Those who give the meaning that fits the upcoming context receive two points. Students then read the contexts and define the words again. These definitions are scored in the same way. The authors maintain that a comparison between the isolated and context scores indicates whether or not students are using context to establish word meaning. Why this subtest is part of an inventory of decoding skills is unclear, since the tester is instructed to pronounce the words for the students if they cannot be correctly read.

The third level, Level R, is given to those students who experience difficulty on the Level 1 letter naming and phoneme-grapheme subtests. It consists of same/different judgments on auditorially presented words and visually presented letters and words.

In summary, the Decoding Inventory yields very little diagnostic information about a student's decoding knowledge and skills. It includes only one subtest at each level that assesses the student's ability to actually read the nonwords aloud. In addition, no reliability or validity data are included in the manual. Although the levels are assumed to be appropriate for differing levels of readers, the primary difference between them is in terms of number of syllables. Related skills, such as spelling and syllabication, are assessed with items that have questionable validity. In addition, the presentation of words as nonsense words could be confusing to some students. It is doubtful that classroom teachers (the intended users) would find the time spent in individualized administration to be of any more value than an informal analysis of their students' oral and reading skills.

Review of Decoding Inventory by NEIL H. SCHWARTZ, Assistant Professor of Educational Psychology, Northern Arizona University, Flagstaff, AZ:

The Decoding Inventory may be of interest to those test users who view the act of reading as a process that encompasses a constellation of subordinate decoding skills for the identification of words. However, the instrument should be used judiciously because it yields levels of skill proficiency which may or may not reflect directly upon inadequacies of reading.

The 22-page manual contains an introduction, description, and rationale for the inventory, along with the test materials and instructions for administration, scoring, and interpretation. The introduction makes a clear statement of definition for the test. It also clearly delineates the individuals for whom the instrument is intended to be used. However, while the description of some of the inventory's levels are clear, other levels and the entire rationale of the inventory are vague and non-substantive. Taken together, the purpose of the instrument becomes confusing, contradictory, and open to misinterpretation. For instance, the authors state that the inventory is "designed to assess student performance in auditory and visual discrimination, phonics, structural analysis, and use of context clues." They go on to inform the test user that the initial screening level of the instrument contains words "formulated to include common phonic and structural elements" to be "used to obtain a preliminary estimate of a student's decoding ability." Yet, the test authors warn the user in their rationale that "the appearance of an isolated word identification skill deficiency with the Decoding Inventory does not necessarily indicate a decoding strategy weakness." Apparently, according to the test authors, a testee can be proficient with various decoding skills but not be able to apply them.

Beyond being contradictory, the rationale and description of the inventory levels are misleading. The test authors state that Level R will "assess readiness for phonics and structural analysis instruction." Level 1 (Basic) and Level 2 (Advanced) carry no description. They are defined only by the subtests which are included under them. This presents a serious problem of possible misinterpretation by the test user. Each subtest would probably be interpreted as measuring a specific decoding skill. (Of course, this is likely in light of the title of the instrument and the initial description of the test.) However, the authors state that the subtests are actually measuring abilities that "are not specific to decoding unknown words...but are significant because of the way most students are required to learn the decoding skills." Much of the ambiguity of the instrument could have been avoided had the authors defined their theoretical position of reading and highlighted limitations of the test's utility for purposes of screening. As it is now, the manual falls significantly short of such a condition. The rationale was included as an afterthought. It appears for the first time in the 1981 edition, and is placed obscurely after the administration procedures and answer key.

The instrument has still other serious failings—particularly its technical characteristics. First, there is no description explaining the development of the test. Secondly, while there is a brief, but generally vague, explanation for the inclusion of subtests, there is no rationale explaining why various subtests are contained in some levels of the inventory and not others or why some easier subtests are placed at more advanced levels but are absent from levels preceding. Third, the authors have adequately explained the method for constructing the nonsense words; however, they have not described adequately the criteria or theoretical basis upon which the items (nonsense words) were chosen and placed in various subtests or levels of the instrument. The authors tell only that the stimulus words were derived from actual words "selected from grade level lists above their intended level of application," with substitutions of easy and difficult graphemes and affixes selected from comparisons between "charts of leading reading text publishers and...decoding error compilations from...client records of a local reading clinic."

Finally, the test fails to offer any statements or data relative to reliability or validity. It also contains no norms. Since the scores obtained on subtests are percentages correct to subtest totals, a test user may be deceived in assuming that the type of measurement yielded by the instrument is criterion-referenced. However, criterion-referenced tests measure the development of particular skills in terms of absolute levels of mastery. The instrument fails as a criterion-referenced test for two reasons. First, close inspection of the subtests and the instrument's rationale reveals that the authors are undecided whether they are measuring decoding skills or the abilities that underlie those skills. Secondly, if it can be assumed, for the moment, that the subtests measure skills rather than abilities, a testee's performance, if 100% correct on a particular subtest, does not necessarily reflect mastery because there is no data on the stimulus items themselves. Therefore, it can only be concluded that the instrument is a norm-referenced screening device intended to measure something about decoding. The authors do support this conclusion because they offer the test user three levels of score interpretation: 80%–100%: skill established; 50%–79%: practice only indicated; and, 0–49%: basic remedial or developmental instruction necessary. Unfortunately, without norms, it is unclear how these cutoff scores have been determined. In addition, without validity or reliability data, test users have no basis for: (*a*) predicting a testee's future performance in reading, or (*b*) deciding if a testee's performance is an accurate assessment of decoding in the first place.

The instrument is intended for screening purposes only and can be administered quickly and efficiently. In fact, one of its redeeming qualities is that its directions for administration and scoring are extremely clear and simple to follow. However, it must be remembered that the Decoding Inventory suffers from several serious flaws in both its theoretical foundation and technical adequacy. Therefore, if one is inclined to use the instrument, it should be used prudently.

[302]

Deductive Reasoning Test. Candidates for graduate scientists and higher level professional occupations; 1972–73; DRT; no data on predictive validity; norms for only CSIR graduate applicants and research scientists; 1 form ('72, 11 pages); manual ('73, 19 pages); separate answer sheets must be used; 1983 price data: R4,00 per test; R2,00 per 25 answer sheets; R3,00 per scoring stencil; R8,00 per manual; (40–50) minutes; J. M. Verster; National Institute for Personnel Research [South Africa].*

Review of Deductive Reasoning Test by LLOYD G. HUMPHREYS, Professor, Department of Educational Psychology and Psychology, University of Illinois, Urbana-Champaign, Champaign, IL:

This is supposed to be a test of deductive reasoning. The items all follow the format of the classical syllogism. It is designed to measure individual differences in samples from populations representing high levels of general intelligence such as graduate scientists. Although a statement appears in the manual that the test is not recommended for groups having less than a high school education, the level indicated in this statement refers to South African educational norms. The test is probably too difficult for a United States college applicant population.

Highly satisfactory (high eighties to low nineties) internal consistency estimates of reliability are reported. Because the time limit for the test is reasonably generous for the number of items included (i.e., 36), whether the limit be the 45 minutes that appears in the printed directions or the 40 minutes found in the manual, these internal consistencies are probably sound. There are two norm groups: 160 male and female research scientists and 152 applicants for such positions. These are also the samples for whom the internal consistency coefficients were computed.

There is little in the manual concerning the validities of the test. Test scores were entered in a correlational and factor analytic study along with scores for a number of reference tests, but the reference tests did not have sufficient numbers of items appropriately difficult for the population sampled. Based upon the factor analysis the author reported a high percentage of specific variance that he attributed to deductive reasoning. Experience has shown that the syllogistic format is quite sensitive to specific training in logic. Certain courses in philosophy and in mathematics affect scores on items of this type. This may be especially true for nonsense content syllogisms and those that contain contrafactual materials.

This test can hardly be recommended for general use. It has an adequate ceiling for high levels of talent, but a good deal more is known about Terman's Concept Mastery test, the Miller Analogies, or the Graduate Record V and Q scores. Additional research is required to make the test useful for personnel selection purposes. Even for research purposes one would have to take on faith the author's suggestion that specific variance in this test is accounted for by deductive reasoning.

Review of Deductive Reasoning Test by ROBERT P. MARKLEY, Professor of Psychology, Fort Hays State University, Hays, KS:

The creator of the Deductive Reasoning Test (DRT) attempted to accomplish two goals. The first was to provide a selection tool to be used in making personnel decisions in high level jobs where deductive reasoning would be a skill important to success. Selection of research scientists and high level managers was intended. A second goal was to obtain a factorially pure measure of a hypothesized deductive reasoning component of intelligence.

The test, consisting of 36 syllogisms, is long and appears formidable to the test taker. Subjects would have to be highly motivated to get through this test. It is hard work. I suspect that an error analysis would show fatigue and distractibility effects. The items cover various types and forms of syllogisms. It would be interesting to students of cognition to know if there are systematic differences in item difficulty. Subscale scores for different item types would be informative, but are not provided.

The differential data on employment groups are inadequate. The test manual presents norms for 160 research scientists and for 152 applicants for graduate research scientist positions. The education level for these groups is not clearly specified. The mean for the scientist group is markedly higher ($M = 23.43$ vs. $M = 20.82$) than the applicant group. However, no differences exist in the variability of the two groups. The possible contribution of age and life experience differences to the group difference make for interesting future research. It is not clear what the phrases "graduate research scientists" and "graduate applicants for employment" as used in the test manual really mean. Ph.D. psychologists in my department were able to top out the test (34 or more out of 36 items correct). I also gave the DRT to seventeen first semester graduate students in an MS psychology program. This graduate group had a mean score of 24 with a range from 15 to 34 and an *SD* of 5.5. My students' data look much like the scientists' data presented in the test manual.

No data relating the test scores to job performance are reported. There is no indication in the test manual that skill in deductive reasoning, even if this test did measure it, contributes to successful job performance or that high scorers on this test did better than low scorers at anything other than taking the test. No data relating the test to other measures of intellectual ability are reported. A preliminary unpublished study with 14 measures of intellectual ability is referenced but no correlations are presented by the test manual. The test author reports that a factor analysis failed to yield a pure deductive reasoning factor although there was evidence he considered suggestive of such a construct.

Some minor quibbles: The test manual suggests that 40 minutes be allowed for completion of the test. The test booklet indicates that there will be 45 minutes to do the test. Also the vocabulary occasionally betrays the test's cultural origins (e.g., cricketers, chimneypots, paediatricians).

I do not know why one would want to use this test, unless one were an instructor of logic. It would not seem to be an improvement over omnibus intellectual ability tests that tap several intellectual factors. It might be useful for future research to discover whether scores on this, or a similar test, relate to high level cognitive achievements. If I were hiring a research scientist I would certainly select that person on the basis of previous accomplishments and not on the basis of a high score on the DRT.

[303]

Defense Mechanism Index. Ages 16 and over; 1965–71; DMI; 25 scores: 12 defense scores (compensation, rationalization, negative affect, positive affect, perceptual defense, autism, projection, repression, phantasy, paleologic, dissociation, reaction formation), 13 conflict scores (aggression vs. fear of retaliation, blame avoidance vs. blame acceptance, dominance vs. submission, dependency vs. independency, expression vs. suppression of sex, deferred vs. immediate gratification, faith in God vs. faith in men, homosexuality vs. heterosexuality, individuality vs. conformity, judgement vs. action, kindness vs. selfishness, expression of love vs. fear of rejection, total); tentative norms; Form E ('70, 7 pages); handbook and interpretation manual ('70, 39 pages); profile (no date, 2 pages); separate answer sheets must be used; 1984 price data: $.75 per test; $10 per 100 answer sheets; $10 per 100 profiles; $5 per manual; (50–70) minutes; Arthur B. Sweney and Jerold May; Test Systems International, Ltd.*

Review of Defense Mechanism Index by H. THOMPSON PROUT, Assistant Professor of Educational Psychology and Statistics, State University of New York-Albany, Albany, NY:

Although the test manual does not clearly indicate uses for the Defense Mechanism Index

(DMI), the authors of this instrument clearly have clinical utilization in mind for their scale. The authors allude to psychodynamically-oriented clinicians' and practitioners' need for more psychometrically valid measures of the variables important in their professional work. Yet, the authors are ambiguous concerning whether or how the instrument should be used clinically, and they also do not detail potential research uses. Their general purpose for developing the scale is worthy—to provide more objective measures of key psychodynamic variables. The authors clearly indicate that this has been a problem in the psychodynamic literature, particularly with projective tests that claim to assess these variables. Indeed, the elusive and subjective nature of these variables has been the source of constant criticism of psychodynamic theory.

The authors have made a concerted effort to tie the test to this one particular theoretical orientation. Needless to say, this is a positive aspect of the scale for those of this orientation, but does limit the use for other practitioners. Related to this, the authors have provided "operational" definitions of the defense and conflict subscale variables. These are in relatively more detail and depth than in most tests of this nature. The definitions themselves, however, seem a bit ambiguous and confusing, a characteristic often seen in the writings of psychodynamic theorists. The definitions would probably not be considered to be "operational" definitions by those with more empirical and/or behavioral orientations. Nonetheless, this attempt to better conceptualize and operationalize psychodynamic theory is encouraging and commendable.

From a test development viewpoint, however, the scale has a number of deficiencies. There is virtually no description of item development and validation procedures. While likely tied to theory and the authors' definitions, it is not clear how the items were generated, tested, and assigned to scales. Each defense mechanism scale and each conflict scale, respectively, have an equal number of items. Each item is scored twice, once in the defense mechanism direction and once in the conflict direction. With equal numbers of items on the scales, this has allowed the authors to develop a very "neat" scoring procedure. Items are scored across rows for the conflict scores and down columns for defense mechanism scores. Admittedly, this provides an easy and attractive scoring package. Unfortunately, it also suggests that items were selected and scales developed to fit into the neat package for scoring, administration, etc., and not in terms of how the particular items contributed to the scale. This reviewer knows of no well-regarded multi-scale personality measure that just happened to end up with equal numbers of items on scales through generally accepted statistical validation procedures. The authors note that the scales were not factor-analytically derived, but were factor-analytically verified; yet, no data or statistical procedural description is provided for this. Thus, the inclusion of specific items on scales and the scales themselves are suspect at best.

The statistical data that is provided could best be termed as incomplete and lacking in detail. Several reliability and validity tables are presented, but the manual lacks clear explanation of the data and how it was produced. In general, these sections are poorly organized and confusing. For example, the manual refers to a "stability" measure of reliability, but does not detail the time frame and procedures for obtaining what appears to be a test-retest correlation. Validity studies include a concurrent measure of defense mechanisms which produced generally adequate correlations (e.g., .25 to .70) for variables of this nature, and two studies which found differences between two clinical samples and normals on several of the subscales. These latter two studies suggest that the measure is probably assessing some type of adjustment or psychopathology variables. However, the validation of this instrument, as presented in the manual, seems to be only in its incipient stages.

Finally, the norms of the DMI are presented in the manual as "Temporary Norms." Since the publication date of this test is 1970, one wonders why the "temporary" label has not been removed and/or the norming updated and completed. Practically, it is difficult to have much faith in norms labeled as temporary. Further, the norms simply refer to "General Population Males" or "General Population Females." No other descriptive data are provided for these norming groups, thus leaving the generalizability of the obtained norm-referenced scores of questionable value.

In summary, the authors of the DMI are to be commended for their attempt to operationalize and make measurable the often hazy and elusive psychodynamic theoretical and clinical variables. They have made a strong effort to tie the scale to theory and define variables. The preliminary validity data suggest that some type of clinical variable is being measured, although whether it coincides with the variables hypothesized by the authors is still in question. However, the DMI has a number of deficiencies that limit its usefulness in practice. The face validity of the measure would obviously have appeal for psychodynamically oriented clinicians who wish to be more empirical in their professional work. But because of the item selection problems noted, incomplete validity data, "temporary" norms, etc., the measure is not recommended for general clinical application. Nonetheless, cautious use of the instrument in research may be warranted.

Review of Defense Mechanism Index by ARLENE C. ROSENTHAL, Research Associate,

Department of Allied Health Education and Research, University of Kentucky, Lexington, KY: The purpose of this test is to measure and demonstrate the presence of defense mechanisms to "gain greater clarity into the structure of personality" and to measure concepts "helpful to the practitioner, as well as to the theoretician." The authors acknowledge that the test in no way exhausts either the universe of conflicts or defense mechanisms that are possible in human functioning.

The test is comprised of a battery of subtests or scales—12 defense scales and 12 conflict scales. The defense scales are divided into two sets, adaptive and maladaptive, in terms of their relation to psychological adjustment in "our culture as it is now constituted." This implies that the scales may have limited generalizability. This is particularly distressing given that the normative sample is not described with respect to cultural variables. They report that the adaptiveness of a particular defense may change with changes in cultural values.

For the conflict scales, each conflict is expressed in terms of its strength. Thus conflict scaled scores reflect the degree to which there is conflict; an average score reflects equal attraction or revulsion to the two extremes (e.g., Dominance vs. Submission). This contrasts with more traditional measures where the score is associated with the expression of a behavior. A low conflict score is equated with conflict resolution. The conflict score does not reveal the direction of the conflict. For example, on the scale "Expression vs. Repression of Sexual Needs," a low conflict score can be equated with resolutions in either direction, promiscuity or celibacy. The authors suggest that the scales have clinical utility although it would seem more helpful if the scales could reveal the direction, as well as the strength, of the conflict. Measures were chosen, in part, for their relevance to current clinical theory and practice.

Each of the 12 conflicts and defenses are briefly described. The paragraphs devoted to each have an anecdotal flavor. Describing the "Expression vs. Repression of Sexual Need" scale, they state: "Our world is said to be within the grip of a Sexual Revolution. This may be true but there are many Victorian vestiges which remain." While defense mechanisms are varied and complex, they are described herein in a rambling and discontinuous manner.

The examinee responds to each of 288 items by either agreeing or disagreeing (strongly or moderately). Items were selected both for their theoretical underpinnings and empirically through item analysis. A sample item is "It's not safe to trust anyone too much." Empirical data for this process is not contained in the manual but can be obtained from the authors.

The items are presented to the examinee in an eight-page booklet. The front page lists the instructions and two examples are provided. The items are interspersed and not grouped by scale. This diminishes the opportunity for the examinee to discover relationships between the items (i.e., lessens the tendency towards response sets). To determine which conflict and defense scale an item belongs to, the examiner must refer to the answer sheet. The answer sheet has been cleverly arranged so that defense items appear in columns and conflict items appear in rows. The items for each column/row are then summed to obtain the raw score. Responses are rated on a 4-point scale (0–3). Scoring can be done with or without the use of stencils.

The raw scores are converted to sten scores using the appropriate norms table. The sten score for each conflict and defense scale is plotted on a profile sheet. There is a profile sheet for the conflict scales and one for the defense scales.

Norms for males ($N = 510$) and females ($N = 423$) are presented separately because "significant differences between males and females have been found from large studies." Presumably these differences were statistical, but this is not indicated. The reader must wonder for which scales these differences were obtained. Norms are reported for Form E, and temporary norms are available for Forms C and F on smaller samples. No information is provided with respect to the representativeness of the normative sample, for example, on demographic indices.

The test may be administered individually or in a group. The time required is approximately 1 hour. Standardized test instructions are provided in the manual and the authors emphasize the importance of following test administration guidelines.

The authors report four types of reliability coefficients for the defense scales and three types for the conflict scales. The reviewer finds the reliability coefficients of little value because of methodological weaknesses (e.g., no time intervals are reported for test-retest reliability; alternate form reliability is reported with an "experimental" measure that is itself of questionable psychometric merit). The remaining measures of reliability are labeled "communality" and "saturation," and it is unclear what these coefficients convey. Thus they will not be reported here.

The authors acknowledge the paucity of validity data although they do report concurrent validity of the defense scales with a rating scale (1966) developed specifically for such concurrent validation. The subject sample is not described, and the validity of the validating scale is also suspect.

Validity of the conflict scales derives from a 1969 comparative study between normal and delinquent boys, but again the samples aren't described. Means are given for each of the groups and results of multiple *t*-tests are given. A predictive validity study is described for one of the alternate forms (Form C), in which the DMI was used to discriminate between college students and mental hospital patients.

To summarize, the DMI is an index which purportedly attempts to quantify conceptual psychodynamic entities (e.g., defenses). There is not only a lack of recent research on the scales, but even the research cited is poorly done and any accurate conclusions are precluded. There are 36 references cited, and 35 of them are before 1970. The manual is poorly written and not of scholarly quality. The test yields little of value to the theoretician but perhaps somewhat more for the clinician as a rough estimate of a client's internal states.

[304]

The Defining Issues Test. Grades 9–12 and college and adults; 1979; DIT; experimental forms for research use only; short (4 pages), and long (7 pages) forms; "principled morality" score and "stage" scores; revised manual (78 pages); accessories not necessary; companion book entitled *Development in Judging Moral Issues* (optional, available from Minneapolis: University of Minnesota Press); separate answer sheets may be used; 1985 price data: $10 per manual; (15–30) minutes for short form, (30–40) minutes for long form; James R. Rest; Minnesota Moral Research Projects.*

See T3:666 (8 references).

TEST REFERENCES

1. Sumprer, G. F., & Butter, E. J. Moral reasoning in hypothetical and actual situations. SOCIAL BEHAVIOR AND PERSONALITY, 1978, 6, 205–209.

2. Tjosvold, D., & Johnson, D. W. Controversy within a cooperative or competitive context and cognitive perspective-taking. CONTEMPORARY EDUCATIONAL PSYCHOLOGY, 1978, 3, 376–386.

3. LaRue, A., & Olejnik, A. B. Cognitive "priming" of principled moral thought. PERSONALITY AND SOCIAL PSYCHOLOGY BULLETIN, 1980, 6, 413–416.

4. Olejnik, A. B., & LaRue, A. A. Affect and moral reasoning. SOCIAL BEHAVIOR AND PERSONALITY, 1980, 8, 75–79.

5. Parish, T. S. The relationship between factors associated with father loss and individuals' level of moral judgment. ADOLESCENCE, 1980, 15, 535–541.

6. Simmons, D. D. Purpose-in-Life and the three aspects of valuing. JOURNAL OF CLINICAL PSYCHOLOGY, 1980, 36, 921–922.

7. Leahy, R. L. Parental practices and the development of moral judgment and self-image disparity during adolescence. DEVELOPMENTAL PSYCHOLOGY, 1981, 17, 580–594.

8. Marlowe, A. F., & Auvenshine, C. D. Greek membership: Its impact on the moral development of college freshmen. JOURNAL OF COLLEGE STUDENT PERSONNEL, 1981, 23, 53–57.

9. Muehleman, T., & Barrett, T. Preference for moral reasoning and conflict compromise theory. PSYCHOLOGICAL REPORTS, 1981, 48, 501–502.

10. Cohen, E. R. Using the Defining Issues Test to assess stage of moral development among sorority and fraternity members. JOURNAL OF COLLEGE STUDENT PERSONNEL, 1982, 23, 324–328.

11. Dickinson, V., & Gabriel, J. Principled moral thinking (DIT-P% scores) of Australian adolescents: Sample characteristics and family correlates. GENETIC PSYCHOLOGY MONOGRAPHS, 1982, 106, 25–58.

12. Kay, S. R. Kohlberg's theory of moral development: Critical analysis with The Defining Issues Test. INTERNATIONAL JOURNAL OF PSYCHOLOGY, 198 17, 27–42.

13. Nichols, M. L., & Day, V. E. A comparison of moral reasoning of groups and individuals on the "Defining Issues Test." ACADEMY OF MANAGEMENT JOURNAL, 1982, 25, 201–208.

14. Poole, M. E., Gelder, A. J., & Dickinson, V. M. Turntaking in family interaction. PSYCHOLOGICAL REPORTS, 1982, 51, 236–238.

15. Pratt, M. W., & Royer, J. M. When rights and responsibilities don't mix: Sex and sex-role patterns in moral judgment orientation. CANADIAN JOURNAL OF BEHAVIOURAL SCIENCE, 1982, 14, 190–204.

16. Simmons, D. D. Is there compassion in principled moral judgment? PSYCHOLOGICAL REPORTS, 1982, 50, 553–554.

17. Hains, A. A., & Ryan, E. B. The development of social cognitive processes among juvenile delinquents and nondelinquent peers. CHILD DEVELOPMENT, 1983, 54, 1536–1544.

18. Horan, H. D., & Kaplan, M. F. Criminal intent and consequence severity: Effects of moral reasoning on punishment. PERSONALITY AND SOCIAL PSYCHOLOGY BULLETIN, 1983, 9, 638–645.

19. Krebs, E. A study of the relationship of moral development and social interest to vocational maturity of adolescents. CONTEMPORARY EDUCATION, 1983, 54, 299–305.

20. Pratt, M. W., Golding, G., & Hunter, W. J. Aging as ripening: Character and consistency of moral judgment in young, mature, and older adults. HUMAN DEVELOPMENT, 1983, 26, 277–288.

21. Wilson, J. P. Motives, values and moral judgments. JOURNAL OF PERSONALITY ASSESSMENT, 1983, 47, 414–426.

22. Brabeck, M. Ethical characteristics of whistle blowers. JOURNAL OF RESEARCH IN PERSONALITY, 1984, 18, 41–53.

Review of The Defining Issues Test by ROBERT R. MCCRAE, Research Psychologist, Section on Stress and Coping, Gerontology Research Center, National Institute on Aging, NIH, Baltimore City Hospitals, Baltimore, MD:

James Rest's work on the Defining Issues Test (DIT) is a rare example of test construction at its best. Here a sophisticated theoretical approach to issues in human development and moral judgment is combined with a keen appreciation of psychometric requirements, and both theory and instrument have been shaped and refined by a vigorous program of empirical research. The author has been equally attentive to the practical requirements of the user, providing such features as computer scoring programs and cost estimates for alternative scoring procedures. By requesting copies of the data in return for free use of the test by qualified researchers, Rest has ensured that new findings will continue to influence the future development of the test. If used as intelligently as it was constructed, the DIT will provide valuable information on an important aspect of human development.

It is always incumbent on the user of a test to have sufficient familiarity with the construct it measures to employ the test wisely. That principle applies with more than the usual force to the DIT. Unless the user understands the particular form of moral development measured by the DIT, he or she is likely to draw the wrong inferences from results. The manual for the DIT provides technical information on its use and a summary of conceptualization and supporting evidence, but the potential user is strongly advised to read *Rest's Development in Judging Moral Issues* (1979) before choosing the test. (Researchers with an interest in moral development would benefit from reading that book whether or not they were planning to use the DIT.)

For Rest, moral development is increasing sophistication in the understanding and application of principles for judging fairness. It is measured by an objective test that requires the subject to indicate which of a series of offered statements describes issues that are most relevant to making a decision in regard to a moral dilemma. Numerous studies have been conducted showing that moral judgment as measured by the DIT increases with age and education; that it is related to, but distinct from, general cognitive capacity; that it influences moral behavior—in short, that it conforms to the predictions of the theoretical model it is based on. It is not, however, a good measure of the ability to *produce* moral arguments, nor, certainly, is it a test of morality. As Rest stresses, moral behavior and humanitarian concern are influenced by many factors other than appreciation for abstract principles of justice, and only under specific conditions would one expect moral judgment to predict moral behavior. Similarly, the relations between political or religious ideology and moral judgment are complex, and the finding that certain groups score higher on the DIT does not necessarily mean that their beliefs are in any sense more valid as moral principles.

At a more sophisticated level, the test user must appreciate the differences between Rest's model and test of moral development and that of Kohlberg and his colleagues. In brief, Kohlberg sees development as a series of qualitative shifts to higher stages of moral reasoning, with the individual either occupying a stage, or in transition between adjacent stages. Rest, by contrast, has come to believe that while stages of moral reasoning may be defined logically, individuals operate on many different stages at once, or by turns, and development simply means increasing comprehension and preference for higher stage reasoning. Defining "stage" as an attribute of the reasoning rather than of the person is a major conceptual advance that preserves the qualitative framework so appealing to developmentalists while explaining the ubiquitous finding that individuals tend to straddle several stages.

Because of this conceptual shift, the DIT cannot be construed as a way of diagnosing the stage to which a subject "belongs." The most common scoring algorithm is the percentage of time subjects prefer principled reasoning—from the three highest stages—over all other choices (the P score). This is a somewhat unusual method of indexing development, but is is based on extensive research on alternative methods of scoring. Both manual and book discuss the issue at length, and the manual recommends using both this scoring method and a second, empirically derived weighting scheme (the D score) that may be more sensitive to changes at lower stages of development. The latter method, however, requires computer scoring and correlates .78 with the simpler system, so for many applications the P score should suffice.

Rest also recommends an examination of scores for specific stages, and the creation of profiles for individuals and groups. As he recognizes, individual stage scores are quite unreliable; he does not seem to appreciate sufficiently that in an ipsative scoring system such as his, the unreliability is compounded. Users are advised to interpret any moral judgment profiles with extreme caution, if at all.

The DIT contains two safeguards against invalid responding: an M score that indicates the extent to which the subjects endorse high-sounding but meaningless statements, and a Consistency Check that compares ratings and rankings to see that random responding is not occurring. Rest wisely recommends that analyses be run with and without elimination of cases deemed invalid by these checks, though he often fails to report both analyses in his book. The requirements for consistency, in particular, seem quite rigorous, and the finding that only 5 to 15% of subjects are eliminated by the proposed decision rules implies that most subjects are highly attentive to the requirements of the task—itself an encouraging finding.

Intelligent use of the DIT may require that the researcher also employ other, supplemental measures. In particular, the potential user must be alert to the possible influence of third variables on results. Moral development is—as it ought to be—significantly related to education, intelligence, certain personality variables (like Gough's Tolerance and Achievement via Independence), and some forms of liberal political attitudes. Rest has given persuasive evidence that moral development is not reducible to any or all of these, but one or more of these, instead of moral development, may be responsible for any observed correlation. For example, finding that members of one church score higher on the DIT than do members of another may be attributable to differences in education rather than religious principles. In most research contexts, it would seem to be necessary to measure these other characteristics in addition to moral development to enhance interpretability of the data.

For judicious applications, the Defining Issues Test is a convenient and reliable objective measure of maturity in judging moral issues. It is backed by an impressive series of construct validity studies, and promises to play an enduring role in the exploration of moral development.

REVIEWER'S REFERENCES

Rest, J. R. DEVELOPMENT IN JUDGING MORAL ISSUES. Minneapolis, MN: University of Minnesota Press, 1979.

Review of The Defining Issues Test by KEVIN L. MORELAND, Product Development Manager, NCS Interpretive Scoring Systems, Minneapolis, MN:

The Defining Issues Test (DIT), subtitled in the test manual "An Objective Test of Moral Judgment Development," was developed from the point of view of Kohlberg's (1964) cognitive-developmental theory of moral reasoning. The DIT comprises six moral-dilemma stories taken from the work of Kohlberg (1958) and Lockwood (1970). A multiple choice question about how the protagonist should act follows each dilemma. This question is followed by a series of 12 issues most of which might be considered in deciding how to resolve the dilemma; some of the "issues" are pretentious-sounding nonsense used to detect faking. Test respondents are asked to rate the importance of each issue on a 5-point scale from "great importance" to "no importance." Finally, the test respondent must choose the four most important issues and rank them. Two major complaints have been raised about the format of the DIT (Martin, Shafto, & Van Deinse, 1977). First, the number of issues at each of Kohlberg's stages are unequal, both within and among dilemmas. Second, lower stage issues always appear first, followed by higher stage issues. However, Rest (1979a, chapter 4) presents a convincing rationale for both of these features. Some of the issues have been found to possess undesirable psychometric characteristics (cf. Davison, 1979), possibly because they are ambiguous (Lawrence, 1978). Refinement or replacement of those issues should improve a test that is already quite useful.

The four issues that are deemed most important are used to generate eight scores pertinent to moral development: Kohlberg's stages 2, 3, 4, 5a, 5b, and 6, and two global indexes. An "M" scale that detects "faking good" (McGeorge, 1975) and a Consistency Check on random or careless responding (cf. Panowitsch, 1975) are also commonly scored. An "anti-establishment [scale]...in effect a stage 4 1/2" (Rest, 1979b, p. 5.2) has enjoyed very little use. A number of other means of scoring the DIT have been tried and rejected (cf. Rest, 1979b). In particular, no satisfactory means of stage-typing (a la Kohlberg) has been discovered and the test author recommends against trying to use the DIT for that purpose (Rest, 1979b). Some complaints have also been raised about the way the DIT is scored. Loevinger (1976) found the Principled Morality score—the most frequently used global index—unappealing because it involves only those issues from stages 5a, 5b, and 6. It has subsequently outperformed several more sophisticated indexes in empirical trials (Davison, 1979; Rest, 1979b). Some investigators (e.g., Martin et al., 1977) also feel that standardized scores would be useful. Although not a standard feature of DIT scoring, normative data are now available in the revised DIT manual and elsewhere that permit interested investigators to standardize DIT scores against well-described samples. Moreover, Rest (1975, 1979b) has provided some helpful hints on how to compare profiles of DIT stage scores.

Test-retest reliabilities of the DIT have been reported for three samples and internal consistency for one (Davison & Robins, 1978; see also Davison, 1979; Rest, 1979b). The two global indexes have demonstrated test-retest reliabilities generally in the .70s and .80s over periods ranging from a few weeks to a few months. Cronbach alphas in the high .70s have been reported for the global indexes. The stage scores, not surprisingly, are less reliable. Their test-retest reliabilities are generally in the .50s and .60s with internal consistencies usually in the .50s. Davison (1979) has suggested that scales with reliabilities this low may not be very useful in correlational studies. Unfortunately, no reliability data are available for the M scale, Consistency Check, or the A[ntiestablishment] scale. In view of this and the very small samples used in two of the test-retest reliability studies (see Rest, 1979b, p. 6.2), more investigation of the DIT's reliability is warranted. More reliability data would also lead to more accurate standard errors of estimate for the stage scales, thereby increasing the power of comparisons among stage score profiles.

A number of investigators have used a three-dilemma short form of the DIT for which reliability data are also available. Test-retest reliabilities for the short form average about .08 lower than those for the full test. The picture with regard to internal consistency, being based on only one study, permits only the expectable observation that the three-dilemma scales are not as internally consistent as the longer scales. Rest (1979b) feels that the reliabilities of the short form stage scores are probably too low for those scores to be useful. Data presented in the test manual suggest that the global indexes of moral judgment derived from the short form are likely to be adequate substitutes for their long form counterparts. Short form validity data support this view (e.g., Rest, 1979b). Unfortunately, there is no way to split the test into two parallel forms (see Rest, 1979b).

A wide variety of evidence attests to the DIT's validity. The following can, obviously, only highlight some of the main lines of support emanating from over 200 studies that have included the DIT. Correlations with Kohlberg's measure of moral reasoning and the Comprehension of Moral Concepts Test (Rest, Cooper, Coder, Masanz, & Anderson, 1974) reach as high as the .70s in age-heterogeneous samples, averaging about .50 (cf. Davison, 1979; Rest, 1979a, chapter 6). However, the DIT is not simply a measure of cognitive development. Correlations between the DIT and measures of non-moral cognitive development (e.g., IQ and achievement tests) range only into the .50s and average about .36 (cf. Davison, 1979; Rest, 1979a, chapter 6). Nor is the DIT simply a measure of attitudes, values, or personality. Rest's (1979a, chapter 6) review of about 200 correlations turned up no consistent significant relationships between the DIT and a variety of such measures (see also Davison, 1979). Further evidence of the discriminant validity of the DIT is provided by studies showing that it is related to important real-life criteria, such as deliquency, even when variables like age, IQ, and SES are controlled (McColgan, 1975). Evidence for the construct validity of the DIT is enhanced by several longitudinal studies wherein subjects attribute increasing importance to "higher" moral issues over time (cf. Davison, 1979; Rest, 1979a, chapter 5; Rest, Davison, & Robbins, 1978). It is noteworthy that attempts to enhance DIT scores experimentally, through moral education programs, for example, have been largely ineffective (cf. Lawrence, 1980; Rest, 1979a, chapter 7). A similar lack of change has been noted with other measures of moral development (see, for example, Lawrence, 1980; Lockwood, 1978). Finally, studies of the internal structure of the DIT indicate that the stage scores interrelate in the theoretically predicted manner (Davison, Robbins, & Swanson, 1978; see also Davison, 1979).

In summary, the DIT is the result of careful thought both about moral development and about test construction. It is easy to administer and comparatively easy to score; computer programs for the latter purpose are provided in the test manual. The heuristic value of the DIT is undeniable given the number of studies that have employed it. The results of those studies, while of course leaving room for improvement, suggest that the DIT is at least as valid as other measures of moral judgment. Those adhering strictly to Kohlberg's theory will probably eschew the DIT because it cannot be used for stage-typing and further refinements of the test are unlikely to change that state of affairs. On the other hand, those who find Rest's (e.g., 1979a, chapters 3 and 4) modification of Kohlberg's theory congenial probably could not construct an instrument that would better suit their needs.

REVIEWER'S REFERENCES

Kohlberg, L. THE DEVELOPMENT OF MODES OF MORAL THINKING AND CHOICE IN THE YEARS 10 TO 16. Unpublished doctoral dissertation, University of Chicago, 1958.

Kohlberg, L. Development of moral character and moral ideology. In M. L. Hoffman and L. W. Hoffman (Eds.), REVIEW OF CHILD DEVELOPMENT RESEARCH (Vol. 1). New York: Russell Sage Foundation, 1964.

Lockwood, A. L. RELATIONS OF POLITICAL AND MORAL THOUGHT. Unpublished doctoral dissertation, Harvard University, 1970.

Rest, J. R., Cooper, D., Coder, R., Masanz, J., & Anderson, D. Judging the important issues in moral dilemmas—An objective measure of development. DEVELOPMENTAL PSYCHOLOGY, 1974, 10, 491–501.

McColgan, E. SOCIAL COGNITION IN DELINQUENTS, PRE-DELINQUENTS, AND NON-DELINQUENTS. Unpublished doctoral dissertation, University of Minnesota, 1975.

McGeorge, C. Susceptibility to faking of the Defining Issues Test of moral development. DEVELOPMENTAL PSYCHOLOGY, 1975, 11, 108.

Panowitsch, H. R. CHANGE AND STABILITY IN THE DEFINING ISSUES TEST. Unpublished doctoral dissertation, University of Minnesota, 1975.

Rest, J. R. Longitudinal study of the Defining Issues Test: A strategy for analyzing developmental change. DEVELOPMENTAL PSYCHOLOGY, 1975, 11, 738–748.

Loevinger, J. EGO DEVELOPMENT. San Francisco: Jossey-Bass, 1976.

Martin, R. M., Shafto, M., & Van Deinse, W. The reliability, validity, and design of the Defining Issues Test. DEVELOPMENTAL PSYCHOLOGY, 1977, 13, 460–468.

Davison, M. L., & Robbins, S. The reliability and validity of objective indices of moral development. APPLIED PSYCHOLOGICAL MEASUREMENT, 1978, 2, 391–403.

Davison, M. J., Robbins, S., & Swanson, D. B. Stage structure in objective moral judgments. DEVELOPMENTAL PSYCHOLOGY, 1978, 14, 137–146.

Lawrence, J. A. THE COMPONENT PROCEDURES OF MORAL JUDGMENT-MAKING. Unpublished doctoral dissertation, University of Minnesota, 1978.

Lockwood, A. L. The effects of values clarification and moral development curricula on school-age subjects: A critical review of recent research. REVIEW OF EDUCATIONAL RESEARCH, 1978, 48, 325–364.

Rest, J. R., Davison, M. L., & Robbins, S. Age trends in judging moral issues: A review of cross-sectional longitudinal and sequential studies of the Defining Issues Test. CHILD DEVELOPMENT, 1978, 49, 263–279.

Davison, M. L. The internal structure and the psychometric properties of the Defining Issues Test. In J. R. Rest, DEVELOPMENT IN JUDGING MORAL ISSUES (pp. 223–261). Minneapolis: University of Minnesota Press, 1979.

Rest, J. R. DEVELOPMENT IN JUDGING MORAL ISSUES. Minneapolis: University of Minnesota Press, 1979a.

Rest, J. R. REVISED MANUAL FOR THE DEFINING ISSUES TEST. Minneapolis: Minnesota Moral Research Projects, 1979b.

Lawrence, J. A. Moral judgment intervention studies using the Defining Issues Test. JOURNAL OF MORAL EDUCATION, 1980, 9, 178–191.

[305]

Degrees of Reading Power. Grades 3–4, 5–6, 7–8, 9–12, 12–14; 1979–83; DRP; consists of 2 components: tests to measure student's ability to comprehend prose, and readability analyses of instructional material in print; 5 levels plus practice/screening test; test administration manual ('82, 31 pages); test coordinator's information kit ('83, 8 pages); user's guide ('83, 31 pages); norms booklet ('83, 23 pages); technical manual (no date, 114 pages); readability report-academic year 1982–83 ('82, 170 pages); separate answer sheets must be used; 1983 price data: $5.20 per 40 answer sheets; $3.50 per scoring stencils; $2.50 per test administration manual; $2.50 per user's guide; $5 per norms booklet; $12.95 per readability report-academic year 1982–83; $2.95 per specimen set; scoring service, 60 or more per student ($100 minimum); Touchstone Applied Science Associates; The College Board.*

a) FORM PX-1. Grades 3-14; may be used as a practice test or screening test to select appropriate form for student; Form PX-1 ('79–'80, 6 pages plus answer sheets); $7.50 per 35 tests; (25–30) minutes.

b) FORM PA-8. Grades 3-4; Form PA-8 ('79, 13 pages); $38.00 per 35 tests including test administration manual; (40–60) minutes.

c) FORM PA-6. Grades 5–6; Form PA-6 ('79–'80, 14 pages); $41.50 per 35 tests including administration manual; (50–70) minutes.

d) FORM PA-4. Grades 7–8; Form PA-4 ('79–'80, 14 pages); prices same as for *c*; (50–70) minutes.

e) FORM PA-2. Grades 9–12; Form PA-2 ('79, 14 pages); prices same as for *c*; (50–70) minutes.

f) FORM CP-1. Grades 12–14; Form CP-1A, CP-1B, ('79–'80, 21 pages); $45.50 per 35 tests; administration time not reported.

TEST REFERENCES

1. Hiebert, E. H., Englert, C. S., & Brennan, S. Awareness of text structure in recognition and production of expository discourse. JOURNAL OF READING BEHAVIOR, 1983, 15, 63–79.

Review of Degrees of Reading Power by ROGER BRUNING, Professor of Educational Psychology, University of Nebraska-Lincoln, Lincoln, NE:

The Degrees of Reading Power (DRP) test has as its aim the measurement of reading effectiveness; that is, how well an individual can perform "real life" reading tasks. The builders of the DRP have taken this aim very seriously and have constructed a system unique among reading comprehension measures that directly links test scores to the readability ratings of a large body of text materials (over 2,000 titles in the 1983–84 DRP Readability Report).

The DRP test employs an unusual format, with test items derived from an adaptation of a cloze procedure. Each DRP test consists of prose passages written specifically for the test and ordered by increasing difficulty. Each passage has seven deleted words; for each deletion, five response options are provided. Since the responses are all plausible in the context of the sentence in which the deletion has been made, and since all are familiar words, the authors argue that student selection of correct responses must have its source in passage-level comprehension.

Perhaps the most novel feature of the test, however, is that scores are scaled to the readability of text materials, rather than to grade equivalents or other more common indices. DRP scores of text materials are obtained through a standard readability analysis. A student's scores, given in the same DRP units, are interpreted as the readability of prose (indexed in DRP units ranging from 15 to 100) that can be read with varying levels of comprehension. DRP tables provide a Rasch model based estimate of the readability of materials that can be read at the independent level (P=.90), at the instructional level (P=.75), and at the frustration level (P=.50). Thus, a student's DRP scores reported at, say, 41 at the independent level, 52 at the instruction level, and 63 at the frustration level are taken to indicate that he or she is likely to read prose materials with readability ratings around 41 easily and successfully alone, read those around 52 successfully with appropriate instructional support, and experience frustration in materials rated near 63.

The ability to link test scores directly to the probability of success in reading is obviously an exciting prospect and a significant advance over current practice. At the same time, however, such judgments plainly must be made with considerable caution, recognizing the insensitivity of readability indices to many critical variables in text comprehension such as story structure, use of cohesive devices, and student background knowledge and interest. Also, one must take account of the inevitable presence of error in both test scores and text ratings.

RELIABILITY OF THE DRP. A serious problem for the current evaluation of the DRP is the absence of a technical manual. Although available in draft form to this reviewer, its more general absence keeps most of the available evidence on DRP reliability and validity out of the hands of potential DRP users. Even recognizing that the DRP has had a multi-year and painstaking developmental history that the manual attempts to capture, the situation is clearly inappropriate for a test that is being widely marketed.

The data, as available in the draft form of the manual, indicate that the reliability of the DRP is generally good. The DRP is a relatively long and homogeneous test, and KR-20 coefficients range from .93 to .97 for various forms of the test administered to a statewide sample. For grades 4 ($N=353$) and 6 ($N=250$), alternate forms reliability estimates ranged from .86 to .91. Standard error of measurement decreases systematically from a range of 3.3 to 4.0 DRP units at grade 4 to a low of 2.2 DRP units at grade 12. For students who are in the effective range of the test (i.e., for students who get from 25% to 75% of the items correct), standard errors of Rasch ability estimates are about 2.5 DRP units. In all, the DRP can be regarded as a quite reliable test focused on a homogeneous construct.

VALIDITY OF THE DRP. The technical manual reports high correlations of the DRP with the California Achievement Test-70 (CAT-70) reading comprehension test ranging from .77 (grade 3) to .85 (grade 8) for an urban school sample. In another study, DRP scores were shown to correlate much more highly with CAT Reading Comprehension scores than with CAT Vocabulary scores (.56), as would be expected from a measure of reading comprehension.

For an effectiveness measure, however, convergent-discriminant validation is secondary in importance to its construct and predictive validity, since the major use of the DRP is to predict probabilities of success for students in prose materials of varying difficulties. Scores on the Word Completion Test (WCT), which is psycholinguistically similar to the DRP but with different content and response options (cloze completion items), were found to correlate around .90 with DRP performance for a sample of 5th-grade students from one urban and one suburban school district. In further analyses presented in the technical manual, it is shown that DRP scores forecast performance on the WCT with reasonable accuracy, that the DRP is sensitive to gain, and that by-classroom gains on the DRP are related to the degree of match or mismatch of curriculum materials readability with the reading ability of students in the classes. The match-mismatch data, if they are replicable and especially if shown to apply to individual students, could become particularly important in asserting a role of the DRP in the selection of instructional materials in classrooms, school districts, and states.

GENERAL COMMENTS. As mentioned previously, the absence of the technical manual represents a serious problem, particularly with the considerable attention given to the DRP and its adoption by many school systems. A second lies in the DRP's approach to test administration. According to the test manual, "it is assumed that not every person administering the test will have a copy of this manual." While directions are presented in the front of each test booklet, they do not address vital aspects of test-taking such as completion of answer sheets, guessing, length of the test, or what to do if the test is not completed during a single class period, a fairly common occurrence. For a test with a goal of matching children to instruction and for which norms are now provided, a more rigorous approach to test administration is necessary.

The DRP norms also must be regarded as questionable at this point. While they are not central to the use of the test as an effectiveness measure, one must believe that now that they have been provided, they will be used. They are based on a sample of 34,000 students, grades 4 through 12, "representing national demographic characteristics." No information is given, however, on the source of this sample to permit judgment of its actual representativeness. Norms are also reported at the "mid-instructional level (P=.75)," without any explanation of what this fairly complex concept derived from reading research and from application of the Rasch model might mean. There is great potential for misinterpretation if the norms are used with no more explanation than is currently available.

SUMMARY. The Degrees of Reading Power presents a paradoxical situation to the prospective user. On one hand, the DRP is clearly innovative and technologically advanced, and possesses a link into instructional materials through its scaling and the Readability Report that few if any other tests can claim. This reviewer judges it to be among the best-conceived and carefully constructed measures of reading comprehension available. On the other hand, however, there are insufficient data readily available for users to make informed judgments about the utility of the test, most users will find the test administration instructions unclear, and the norms must be viewed with caution, at least until further information is provided on the characteristics of the norm group. Also, the increasing use of the DRP for making instructional judgments about individual students compels the early gathering and reporting of data on the DRP's utility as a predictor of reading effectiveness in actual classroom settings.

Review of Degrees of Reading Power by GERALD S. HANNA, Professor of Educational Psychology and Measurement, College of Education, Kansas State University, Manhattan, KS:

The Degrees of Reading Power (DRP) is more than a test; it is program having two central components. First are the comprehension tests of nonfiction English prose. Second are systematic readability data for instructional materials. The major payload of the program is the connection between the test scores and the rated readability of materials. This review will focus upon the adequacy of (1) the tests, (2) the readability ratings of instructional materials, and (3) the bridge linking the two.

In the DRP, both readability and reading achievement are weaned from widely misunderstood grade-level values and grade-equivalent scores. Both are expressed in a common DRP scale. The DRP units are based on Bormuth's (1969) mean cloze formula, which employs the common surface variables of mean sentence length, fraction of common words (i.e., on Dale's long list), and mean word length. Since this formula is basic to both major DRP components, its developmental research merits scrutiny.

Bormuth administered short passages with every fifth word deleted to large numbers of students and scored for exact restorations (save spelling). Passages were then assigned mean cloze scores. These passage scores were the dependent variable used to select indicants that were efficient in predicting passages' mean cloze scores via multiple-regression techniques. In a cross-validation study, Bormuth's indicants yielded an R of .92. The DRP materials hail Bormuth's formula for its large, cross-validated R which accounts for 85% of the variance in mean cloze scores across passages. But before being too impressed by the R of .92, one should realize that the students taking these cloze tests varied from grades 4 to 12 and that the research passages ranged from first grade to college level. Thus, the formula is excellent in predicting mean cloze scores across such an enormous expanse of passage difficulties. But how well does it function within a reasonable range of materials that a teacher might consider for an individual student? Much less, certainly. The likely result of the publisher's failure to make this point clear will be user overconfidence in the formula and the program built upon it.

THE TESTS. Each DRP test form consists of several passages of about 325 words each. For each passage, there are precisely seven test items. Each item consists of a simple sentence within the passage that contains a blank space for a missing word. If a test item sentence is taken in isolation, each of the five options is plausible; only when the surrounding text is considered does one and only one alternative stand out as clearly right. This item type seems brilliantly suited to assuring virtually no passage independence.

Although the entire DRP program is rooted in cloze technique, the tests do not employ a cloze format. The developers cited several problems associated with cloze methods. These include the common rigidity in crediting only exact restorations while not crediting equally good or even superior restorations and the method's focus upon comprehension within sentences at the expense of intersentence comprehension. Such limitations of cloze methods may erode the validity of the foundational research upon which the DRP units are based, but not the content validity of the tests.

An important feature of DRP items is that all options are common, high frequency words. Thus item difficulty is more a function of passage difficulty (in contrast to difficulty in comprehending the items) than is true of conventional multiple-choice items. For any test that aspires to provide meaningful criterion-referenced interpretations, it is vital that examinee success be mainly or exclusively attributable to passage difficulty and not to uncontrolled, independent item difficulty. The DRP item type is the best applied approach the reviewer has seen for subduing two obstacles to criterion referencing—item comprehendability and passage independence. This is a refreshing departure from the naivete of most attempts to criterion reference reading comprehension, such as those found in most informal reading inventories, in many minimal competence testing programs, and in customized criterion-referenced test programs offered by several major test publishers.

Even though the DRP tests ingeniously evade two obstacles to criterion referencing, in the reviewer's judgment they are only marginally amenable to criterion-referenced interpretations. Four reasons limit the meaningfulness of criterion referencing. First is the limitation of test content to nonfiction prose. What about fiction and poetry? Interpretations that may not be applicable to fiction seem limited in utility.

Second is the rooting of DRP units in cloze methodology. For reasons mentioned above, DRP developers recognized that cloze technique leaves much to be desired. Yet the criterion-referenced interpretations aspire only to predict examinee success on materials whose cloze difficulty is known.

Third is the lingering extent to which the independent item difficulty may impede interpretation. The DRP Norms booklet reports a correlation between passage readability and mean Rasch item difficulty per passage of .94. This suggests that item difficulty is not wholly irrelevant. Although the problem has been wisely and openly faced and cleverly brought under control, it has not been totally eliminated.

The final and most serious stumbling block to criterion referencing concerns the need for a well defined content domain by which to describe what an examinee can do. The domain of nonfiction English prose is large and ill defined. Although Bormuth showed that all but 15% of the variance in passages' mean cloze scores could be accounted for by surface features, his range of passages was enormous. Within the range of reading materials that a teacher might sensibly consider for a particular student, the total variance would be smaller. Yet the error variance would remain the same. Therefore, a much larger (than 15) percent of the variance in mean cloze scores would not be accounted for; it would be a function of other untapped features of nonfiction prose. Among such ignored characteristics would likely be well chosen examples of difficult concepts, helpful illustrations, beneficial use of headings, use of advance organizers, careful definitions of new terms, and thoughtful sequencing of materials. This reviewer, for one, is not prepared to ignore such variable features of instructional materials.

Collectively these limitations lead to the conclusion that only the surface features of only nonfiction prose is referenced to an inherently limited cloze assessment of passage difficulty. This falls far short of the Users Guide's claim that DRP tests are genuine criterion-referenced measures just as are measures of height and weight. The obstacles to sound criterion referencing of reading comprehension may well be insurmountable. By having subdued the impact of item difficulty, the DRP comes closer to a defensible criterion-referenced measurement approach to reading comprehension than other devices known to the reviewer. Yet it seems reckless to claim that the DRP has achieved a solid criterion referencing of reading comprehension.

In the reviewer's opinion, the DRP tests are highly amenable to norm referencing. To realize this potential, however, a well defined set of normative data is necessary. Rasch calibration of the various test forms provides the potential for sound norm-referenced interpretation of all forms based upon the norming of the scale. All that is needed is a clear description of a relevant reference group.

The Norms Booklet states that "a sample of approximately 34,000 fourth through twelfth graders representing national demographic characteristics" took the norming forms of the test. Conventional socioeconomic data for the participating students are absent. Also lacking is information concerning region of the country and school district enrollment. Data on the sample's ethnicity are provided. The unexplained grade-to-grade variations in reported membership is startling (e.g., the fraction of black examinees ranged from a high of 13.4% in Grade 10 to a low of 4.6% in Grade 11). The only other demographic data reported is the percent of examinees who participated in the National School Lunch Program. Here, too, there are grounds for concern about grade-to-grade fluctuations.

Inspection of the normative data reveals some irregularities in the grade-to-grade gain trends of average scores. Unsmoothed irregularities also appear in the within-grade norms tables. On balance, the reviewer doubts that the normative sample was selected carefully to provide national data or that it can safely be considered to be representative of the country. Consequently the present utility of the DRP tests for norm-referenced interpretations is limited. However, this problem (unlike those concerning criterion-referencing interpretation) are clearly remediable.

Reliability data are difficult to interpret. The User's Manual does not contain adequate detail, while reports in the draft of the overdue technical manual are subject to ongoing revisions. To conserve space, the reviewer will simply offer his rough impression of the tests' reliability based upon those two sources. If reliability were investigated by use of alternate 77-item forms administered a few days apart and if standard errors were computed from the results, then the standard error of measurement would likely be about 5 DRP units. This seems acceptably small in comparison with the standard deviations within grade of 13 to 17 DRP units.

READABILITY RATINGS OF INSTRUCTIONAL MATERIALS. The other major component of the DRP program consists of annual expansions and updates of readability data on books used in school instruction in eight content areas. Bormuth's mean cloze formula is used to assess the readability of three 250- to 300-word samples in each of five sections of each (longer) book. Thus, instructional material for grades 4 through 12 are given readability ratings in DRP units.

Unfortunately, there are fundamental problems. The Readability Report appropriately acknowledges some limitations of readability analyses: "Readability formulas do not measure whether new concepts are defined or whether chapter titles and headings are appropriate. The formulas were never intended to replace editorial or teacher judgment on matters of style and coherence. Formulas do not give any indication of the clarity of exposition or dramatic effectiveness. Indeed, as some critics of these formulas have observed, the formulas would not differentiate between scrambled and coherent prose. The use of all formulas assumes well-developed, organized text. If text is incoherent or has other shortcomings, then all readability formulas will underestimate its difficulty." These issues apply to all attempts to quantify readability on the basis of surface features. In addition to the general problems, four additional issues limit the value of the DRP readability analyses.

First, there is inadequate attention to the reliability of the book ratings. A standard error of measurement might be the most sensible method of making users mindful of imperfect reliability. Unfortunately the Readability Report does not report the standard error with which the readability of whole books is estimated.

Next, meaningful data are lacking concerning the validity with which the formula predicts cloze scores for a reasonable range of books. Although Bormuth achieved good discrimination ($R = .92$) for passages that ranged from Grade 1 to college level, this is largely irrelevant. The appropriate question is, how well does the formula discriminate cloze readability among books that one might sensibly consider for a given student?

Third, the mean cloze formula has been developed and validated against the criterion of mean cloze scores. Thus the limitation of cloze scores, such as insensitivity to intersentence comprehension, may have been "built into" the formula as it was developed to predict cloze scores.

Finally, the mean cloze formula (or any other that is limited to a very few surface features) has the capacity to undermine its own effectiveness. This arises from the fact that the three variables that enter into Bormuth's formula are not the essence of readability; rather, they are mere indicants or correlates of readability. If other things are equal (e.g., if materials are uniformly well written and well edited without special attention to the three indicants), then the formula has utility. But other things cannot be counted upon to remain equal. Indicants are vulnerable to tinkering. Undue attention can be directed to the three surface features. Because the formula uses so few indicant/correlates, it can easily be subverted. Moreover, the more widespread the use of the DRP program, the greater will be the motivation of publishers to misuse its three indicants!

Two external examples may help to illustrate how indicants that function well in original research may, when used for applied work, become misleading. First, consider the Internal Revenue Service's method of selecting tax returns for audit. Research has identified a set of indicant/correlates for identifying suspect returns. If a small set of such characteristics were common knowledge, then dishonest taxpayers could simply avoid that set of indicants and cheat with relative safety in other ways. Appropriate defenses against having useful indicants destroyed by their use include employing many rather than few indicants, occasionally rotating some of the indicants into or out of use, and keeping the current set a secret.

Second, consider Page's (1966) early work on scoring essays by computer. Using a set of surface features such as proportion of uncommon words and fraction of prepositions, a computer could score essays at least as well as could typical teachers. Yet Page recognized that these superficial surface characteristics are not the essence of quality writing; they are mere indicants or correlates of good writing. If it were widely known that a particular short list of indicants was being used to score essays, then students could easily improve their grades by superficial tinkering with these indicant/correlates without materially improving their writing in the process. Recognition of this potential contamination of the indicants led Page to suggest (1) using many indicants (i.e., far more than are incrementally efficient in the foundational multiple-regression analyses) and (2) keeping the current set secure. Thus, "the program may eventually become so complex and consider so many variables that the most efficient way for a student to 'con' the machine is just to write well."

Unfortunately, the developers of the DRP annual readability report did not invoke this kind of prudent, good common sense protective mechanism. If they had, they could have (1) protected their method from contamination and (2) avoided the risk of prompting undesirable editorial practices. The program could have been so complex and considered so many variables that the most efficient way for an author or editor to "con" the program would be simply to write well at the desired level. Instead, it is relatively easy to manipulate the three surface features to alter DRP readability ratings. It is regrettable that the DRP developers exacerbated this problem by failing to confront it.

BRIDGING TEST SCORES AND READABILITY RATINGS OF MATERIALS. Like a suspension bridge, the DRP program aspires to link two discrete elements. At one end is the estimated difficulty of instructional materials, as estimated by use of Bormuth's mean cloze formula and expressed in DRP units. At the other end is the estimated proficiency with which an examinee can read nonfiction prose, estimated by use of the DRP tests with scores expressed in DRP units via Rasch scaling. To the extent that the tests achieve criterion referencing of reading comprehension and to the extent that Bormuth's three surface features capture the essence of readability, the program achieves the desired linkage. As concluded above, neither of these conditions is wholly attained. However, some linkage has been realized.

Two additional problems arise from the linkage process itself. First is the slight incongruence in domains assessed by the DRP components. The tests assess achievement only in nonfiction, while the instructional materials assessed include fiction.

The second linkage feature concerns reliability. Student reading skill is matched with the difficulty of selected books. The adequacy of this match depends jointly upon (1) the test's reliability and (2) the reliability with which the readability of instructional materials is rated. The reliability of the match is thus the reliability of a difference between two scores. The measurement error of the match will be greater than the error of either the test scores or the rated readability of the instructional material. This issue of reliability of the payload is neglected in the DRP materials.

In summary, the DRP tests are judged to be singularly effective in avoiding passage independence. The novel item type is appealing. The tests seem well suited for norm-referenced survey purposes. Reliability appears to be adequate. Less satisfactory is the reference group and its description by which norm referencing is attempted. Also worrisome are the serious obstacles to criterion referencing performance in a domain as ill defined as reading comprehension. Along the same lines, several issues raise doubt about the adequacy with which the readability of instructional material is assessed. Chief among these is the poverty of indicants of readability which may prompt counterproductive practices in the preparation of instructional materials. Such practices can reduce the future utility of the three surface features that are used to assess readability. The linkage between readability of materials and student reading skill is the major payload of the DRP program. Like a suspension bridge, the linkage can be no more secure than the weaker tower. The DRP approach of eliminating grade equivalents and grade-level values and of controlling item difficulty represents substantial progress in bridge building. But the criterion referencing of student reading comprehension and the rating of instructional material's readability were both judged to be marginal. The linkage between the two therefore seems tenuous.

REVIEWER'S REFERENCES

Page, E. G. Grading essays by computer. PHI DELTA KAPPAN, 1966, 47, 238–243.

Bormuth, J. R. DEVELOPMENT OF READABILITY ANALYSES. Final report, Project Number 7–0052, Office of Education, Bureau of Research, U.S. Department of Health, Education, and Welfare, 1969 (ERIC ED 029–166).

[306]

Deluxe Fire Promotion Tests. Prospective firefighters; a "complete service" program; "specially prepared and tailor-made tests to fit the duties and responsibilities involved in your jobs, based on job analysis information"; study book lists and candidate study guides provided to candidates; 5 areas: fire fighting methods and techniques, related fire knowledges and techniques, supervisory methods and techniques, administrative methods and techniques, other related knowledges and abilities; 1983 price data: rental and scoring service, $450 for the first 5 candidates, $9.75–$27 for each additional candidate ($450 minimum); McCann Associates, Inc.*

[307]

Deluxe Police Promotion Tests. Prospective police officers; a "complete service" program; "specially prepared and tailor-made tests to fit the duties and responsibilities involved in your jobs, based on job analysis information"; study book lists and candidate study guides provided to candidates; 6 areas: technical police knowledge—patrol related, technical police knowledge—investigative, supervisory knowledge and ability, administrative knowledges and abilities, legal knowledges, police related abilities; 1983 price data: rental and scoring service, $450 for the first 5 candidates, $9.75–$27 for each additional candidate ($450 minimum); McCann Associates, Inc.*

[308]

Dental Admission Testing Program. Dental school applicants; 1946–84; DATP; formerly called Dental Aptitude Testing Program; tests administered 2 times annually (April, October) at centers established by the publisher; 4 tests, 8 scores: 7 scores listed below plus academic average (average of *a* – *c*); overview ('84, 15 pages); preparation materials for examinees ('80, 64 pages); bulletin for applicants ('83, 20 pages); 1984 price data: examination fee, $25 per student; fee includes reporting of scores to any 5 schools designated at time of application; $1 per additional report ($2 per report requested after examination); 270(330) minutes in 2 sessions; Division of Educational Measurements, Council on Dental Education, American Dental Association.*

a) DENTAL ADMISSION QUANTITATIVE EXAMINATION. 1980; 35(45) minutes.

b) READING COMPREHENSION TEST. 1953–77; 50(60) minutes.

c) SURVEY OF THE NATURAL SCIENCES. 1951–77; 4 scores: biology, inorganic chemistry, organic chemistry, total; 90(100) minutes.

d) PERCEPTUAL ABILITY TEST. 1968–79; 40(50) minutes.

See T3:673 (2 references); for reviews by Robert L. Linn and Christine H. McGuire of an earlier edition, see 8:1085 (7 references); see also T2:2337 (8 references), 7:1091 (28 references), 5:916 (6 references), and 4:788 (2 references).

Review of Dental Admission Test by HENRY M. CHERRICK, Dean, College of Dentistry, University of Nebraska Medical Center, Lincoln, NE:

The Dental Admission Testing Program (DAT) is conducted by the Council on Dental Education of the American Dental Association and has been in operation on a national basis since 1950. Examinations are given twice annually, in October and April, at numerous United States and foreign testing centers. The DAT is designed to measure general academic ability, comprehension of scientific information, and perceptual ability. Test results are one of the major factors considered in evaluating the admission potential of a candidate for dental school.

The present test battery is composed of four sections (Survey of the Natural Sciences, Perceptual Ability, Reading Comprehension, and Quantitative Reasoning) requiring 1/2 day for its administration. The Survey of Natural Science subtest is a 90-minute achievement test consisting of 100 multiple choice test items requiring the simple recall of basic scientific information. The content is limited to those areas normally covered by first year college courses in biology and inorganic and organic chemistry. The three science sections are not separated in the examination booklet. It is important, therefore, that the candidates pace themselves since separate subscores will be given for each section throughout the entire test battery. The Perceptual Ability test is a 40-minute exercise consisting of 90 multiple choice items of the nonverbal perceptual type. They require visual discrimination of two- and three-dimensional objects. The Reading Comprehension section contains a lengthy passage typical of the material that must be read in dental school. The rest is composed of 50 multiple choice items based on the passage. The Quantitative Reasoning subtest is composed of 50 multiple choice questions which measure the candidate's ability to reason with numbers, to manipulate numerical relationships, and to deal intelligently with quantitative materials.

Excellent preparatory materials are available for the Dental Admission Testing Program and include an informational booklet and a manual of previous examinations. Instructions to examiners which precede each subtest are precise, easy to follow, and insure that the testing will be uniform at every center.

The test scores for the Dental Admission Testing Program are reported in terms of standard scores with a mean of 4, a standard deviation of 2, and a range from −1 to +9. In addition, three composite scores are reported: total science (an average of the biology, inorganic chemistry and organic chemistry scores), academic average (an average of quantitative reasoning, reading comprehension, biology, inorganic chemistry, and organic chemistry scores) and perceptual ability.

The American Dental Association provides each dental school abundant analytical data on the Dental Admission Test. Included are: DAT summary statistics of the previous year's test, comparison of DAT and National Board scores, DAT candidate general information, comparison of applicants repeating the Dental Admission Test, and a correlational study of DAT and collegiate GPA versus freshman dental student grades. There is a strong correlation between the performance on the Dental Admission Test and future performance on the National Boards for Dentistry (measure of performance in dental school) and freshman dental school grades. The total science and academic average values for the DAT are the best predictors of National Board scores, with correlations in the range of .40 ($p < .05$). For freshman grades, the same two parameters also approach .40. Schools are also provided an item-by-item analysis of the DAT. Based on an analysis of the results of over 4,700 students who took the exam in 1982, the Kuder Richardson reliability coefficients range from .81 to .91.

Despite all the correlational evidence described above, there are still some questions concerning the reliability of the Reading Comprehension part of the Dental Admission Test. There is a danger that using only a 50-item test covering subject matter could lead to erroneous prediction especially in a student who has some previous background and knowledge in the subject matter covered. Furthermore, there are concerns that the Dental Admission Test may be testing simple academic skills and does not have enough emphasis on more complicated problem solving and psychomotor skills which are more closely aligned with the clinical practice of dentistry. The final concern deals with the possible impact that dental aptitude test preparatory courses might have on test scores and their predictive value. Despite its possible shortcomings, the Dental Admission Test appears to be a well-constructed and well-analyzed examination. It has proven itself as a worthy predictor of dental school performance as measured by freshman dental school grades and performance on the national boards.

Review of Dental Admission Test by LINDA M. DU BOIS, Assistant Professor of Adult Restorative Dentistry, University of Nebraska Medical Center, Lincoln, NE:

The Dental Admission Test (DAT) is an assessment instrument used for supplementing other information in the selection of dental college candidates for admission. The examination is designed for persons who have successfully completed a minimum of 2 years of basic science study at the undergraduate collegiate level.

The DAT is a testing battery of timed multiple-choice tests on Quantitative Reasoning, Reading Comprehension, a Survey of the Natural Sciences, and Perceptual Ability. From the four tests, 10 scores are reported.

Raw scores are based on the number of correct answers and are converted into standard scores with a mean of 4, a standard deviation of 2, and a range from −1 to +9. Scores −1 and +9 are, respectively, less than and greater than 2 standard deviations from the mean. With the exception of certain anchor items, a new form of the test is administered twice a year. The reported scores are, therefore, standard with respect to other scores that have resulted from the same testing date and not from all reported DAT scores.

Anchor items were first used on the DAT in 1981. These items were added to the Survey of Natural Sciences to help keep the DAT consistent from year to year. Each subtest of the Survey of Natural Sciences contains 30 or 40 items, and of these, 7 or 8 are anchor items. One DAT report tabulates the means of the anchor items for each subtest and the overall means through the three Natural Sciences subtests. The overall means appear to be relatively close for different testing dates. The report offers no further information about the problem of variability between testing dates. The reader is evidently supposed to reason that, since the overall means for the anchor items do not show much apparent variation, then the entire measurement scale contains little variation. The conclusion may be true, but several problems exist with the reasoning.

First, the Survey of Natural Sciences contains 100 questions, of which the 1983 item analysis indicated that: 14 were unacceptable because of the point-biserial correlation between item performance and total test performance, 4 were unacceptable because of lack of difficulty, and 14 were unacceptable because they were overly difficult. A total of 27 items was unacceptable. (Five items demonstrated both unacceptable correlations and difficulty.) The Biology, Inorganic, and Organic subtests have 40, 30, and 30 items respectively. Taking into consideration the unacceptable items, the subtest scores are based on very few items in relation to the magnitude of the subject material. The item representation of the subject material could easily change between test administrations.

Second, the Reading Comprehension test is a 50-item instrument that covers a single reading passage, and the topic of the passage changes between testing dates. No data are published to indicate that these different forms are equivalent.

Third, the nature of the group tested changes markedly between the April and October testing dates. The April date has fewer subjects who have taken an alternate form of the DAT at an earlier date. For example, in April of 1983, 15.1% of the test subjects were repeating the examination, while in October of 1983, 29.5% were repeating the test. The DAT publications indicate that, on an average, repeat subjects increase their test scores from 0.43 to 1.28 standard score units. The scores of the repeat subjects are usually below the averages for the entire group. Because the proportion of weaker subjects increases between the April and October testing dates, the increase in scores for repeat test takers may be inflated due to the standard score based on the testing date population, and scores for first-time test takers may also be inflated for the same reason. Conversely, the scale could also be deflated if the increase in the repeat subjects scores more than compensated for the increase in the proportion of repeat subjects.

During 1983, the Kuder-Richardson 20 reliability coefficients ranged from .77 for the October inorganic chemistry score to .92 for the April biology and perceptual ability scores. Test-retest and parallel-form reliability are not reported in the DAT literature. Either of these methods would be better for a timed test like the DAT. The DAT may place too much emphasis on speed.

The reliability coefficient for the Reading Comprehension test may be inflated due to the subject's familiarity with or ignorance of the academic content of the single reading passage. The Reading Comprehension test may measure previous knowledge of the subject matter in addition to reading ability and, as a result, validity could also be compromised.

The DAT literature provides validity data in terms of freshman grades and National Board scores. Correlation coefficients for the freshman grades are tabulated for individual colleges and subjects. These generally range from .00 to .50 with a broad distribution across this range. The correlation coefficients from the National Board scores are based on national averages and range from .10 to .40. Although the validity of the instrument is modest, its documentation is comprehensive and well prepared. As cited, the predictive validity of the DAT is similar to the predental GPA. The apparently low validity coefficients are partially a result of three problems.

First, the DAT is administered to a large group of applicants whereas the correlation studies are subsequently done on a more select group, those who are admitted into dental school. The effect of calculating the validity on a smaller, less variable group is to reduce the value of a validity coefficient.

Second, the distribution of grades may also be restricted. Course grades in professional schools are often tightly clustered leading to smaller correlations and increased variation across colleges. This variation was demonstrated by differences in validity among schools.

Third, the National Board scores used for the correlations came from over 50 different institutions. The variations in curriculum may well increase the influence of error on the validity coefficients and thereby decrease their numerical value.

Recent journal articles have discussed other examinations that have shown greater validity than the DAT for predicting technique grades in individual schools (Suddick, Yance, & Wilson, 1983; Wood & Boyd, 1982). The validity of the DAT for these schools was comparatively low (Wood & Boyd, 1982). National documentation on these examinations is not available, and currently the quality of data about the DAT is far superior.

The literature distributed as part of the DAT program does not, however, include a technical manual that cites item development, treatment of anchor items, and correlations between tests. Accompanying materials do provide extensive background information on candidates, basic statistics, and a useful practice examination for test candidates.

CONCLUSION. The DAT is a well documented, professionally prepared admissions examination. In interpreting the test scores, admissions committees should consider the instrument's mediocre validity and the problems with comparing scores from separate testing dates. The lack of standardization across testing dates is particularly significant during times of changing applicant pool.

REVIEWER'S REFERENCES

Wood, W. W., & Boyd, M. A. The DAT as a predictor of preclinical technique performance. JOURNAL OF THE CANADIAN DENTAL ASSOCIATION, 1982, 48, 599–600.

Suddick, R. P., Yance, J. M., & Wilson, S. Mirror-tracing and embedded figures tests as predictors of dental students' performance. JOURNAL OF DENTAL EDUCATION, 1983, 47(3), 149–154.

[309]

Denver Audiometric Screening Test. Ages 3–6; 1973; DAST; criterion-referenced; to identify children who have a serious hearing loss; 3 ratings for each ear: pass, fail, uncertain; no data on reliability and validity; no norms; individual; 1 form; manual/workbook (34 pages, includes scoring form); training film (16 mm, 64 minutes); training video cassette (3/4 inch U-standard cassette); preschool hearing screening slide-tape available; audiometer must be obtained by the examiner, not available from this publisher; 1984 price data: $2 per 25 test forms; $400 per training film, $55 weekly rental; $175 per training video cassette, $45 weekly rental; $90 per preschool hearing screening slide-tape, $30 weekly rental; $7.50 per manual/workbook; (5–10) minutes; William K. Frankenburg, Marion Downs, and Elyner Kazuk; LADOCA Publishing Foundation.*

Review of Denver Audiometric Screening Test by LEAR ASHMORE, Professor of Speech Communication and Education, The University of Texas at Austin, Austin, TX:

The Denver Audiometric Screening Test (DAST) has a copyright date of 1973. The test, as presented, follows standard procedures for pure-tone identification audiometry as recently reaffirmed by the Committee on Audiometric Evaluation of the American Speech-Language-Hearing Association (ASHA, February, 1984, p. 47–50). One small difference is to be found in the screening level; the committee recommends 20 dB HL and the DAST recommends 25 dB. Both recommend screening frequencies of 1,000, 2,000, and 4,000 Hz. Since the development of the DAST, acoustic immittance measurements have become recommended as part of the screening process, directed particularly toward detection of middle ear disorders (which are fairly common in the 3- to 6-year age range). Since middle ear problems usually are medically or surgically reversible, their detection and treatment in the young child are crucial to the speech and educational development of the child.

If an additional requirement of the review of the DAST is to evaluate the suggested method of training individuals to perform the screening, then some additional comments can be made. It is not clear from the contents of the DAST manual that the purpose is to train nonprofessionals to administer the test, but one would assume that purpose when reading through the instructions. The manual does contain a simple step-by-step procedure for training persons to do screening audiometry. No matter how complete the training, nonprofessionals should not be allowed to do audiometric screening without the close supervision of an audiologist, and this requirement is not stated clearly in the manual. Generally, the training process as described in the manual is thorough and represents the procedures advocated by professionals in audiology.

In summary, the DAST meets the guidelines for pure-tone audiometric screening (with the exception of a 5 dB difference in screening level) as advocated by the Committee on Audiometric Evaluation of the American Speech-Language-Hearing Association. It does not include information on acoustic immittance measurements, which have become recommended procedures for identification audiometry. It also provides procedures for the training of personnel to administer the screening.

REVIEWER'S REFERENCES

Proposed revisions of guidelines for identification audiometry. ASHA, February, 1984, 47–50.

[310]

Denver Community Mental Health Questionnaire—Revised. Mental health clients; 1978; DCMHQ–R; adolescent version (for ages 13–17) also available; 13 scales covering 4 areas: personal distress, alcohol and drug abuse, social and community functioning, client satisfaction; individual; 1 form (9 pages, mimeographed); mimeographed scoring procedures manual (10 pages); extended format for outcome measure (15 pages); scoring sheet (4 pages); price data available from author; (20–30) minutes; James A. Ciarlo; the Author.*

See T3:677 (2 references).

TEST REFERENCES

1. Weissman, M. M., Sholomskas, D., & John, K. The assessment of social adjustment: An update. ARCHIVES OF GENERAL PSYCHIATRY, 1981, 38, 1250–1258.

2. Rumsey, M., & Justice, B. Social correlates of psychological dysfunction. PSYCHOLOGICAL REPORTS, 1982, 50, 1335–1345.

3. Turner, R. M., McGovern, M., & Sandrock, D. A multiple perspective analysis of schizophrenics' symptoms and community functioning. AMERICAN JOURNAL OF COMMUNITY PSYCHOLOGY, 1983, 11, 593–607.

Review of Denver Community Mental Health Questionnaire—Revised, by R. W. PAYNE, Professor of Psychology, University of Victoria, Victoria, B.C., Canada:

The Denver Community Mental Health Questionnaire is a 79-item standardized social history interview designed to be used by "non-professional" level case workers. A modified form can be used as a self-administered questionnaire. The questions cover four general areas—personal distress, alcohol and drug abuse, social and community functioning, and client satisfaction. The questions in each area are subdivided into several scales, there being 13 scales in all. The questions proceed logically from one scale to the next, and from one area to the next.

Standardization data are based, for the most part, on a "random Denver community sample" (Scales 1–11 and 13), while standardization data for Scale 12 (Client Satisfaction) was based on a "sample of 500 Denver Health and Hospitals Mental Health program clients." The raw score for each scale can be converted to a standard score with a mean of 50 and, with some exceptions, a standard deviation of 5. The length of the scales varies considerably, ranging from only two items for the "Interpersonal Aggression—Friends" scale to nine items for the "Psychological Distress" scale. It should be noted that no items score on more than one scale, and the "scales" are merely clusters of questions dealing with the same area, and were derived from a purely logical analysis. For example, the two questions which define the "Interpersonal Aggression—Friends" scale are, "When you are with your friends how often do you argue with them?" (never, seldom, often, constantly), and "When you are with your friends how often do you physically fight?" (never, seldom, often, constantly). The total possible range of raw scores for this scale is only 0 to 6 ("never" is scored 0). Data presented in the manual suggest that the mean raw score for the standardization sample on this scale was between 0 and 1. Thus, although standard score equivalents can be obtained from the table, they are not meaningful for this scale, because the data are so extremely skewed. (The modal raw score was probably 0, so that to say of this standard score distribution that it has a mean of 50 and a standard deviation of 5 is meaningless, since the highest possible standard score is 54, and this is also probably the modal score.) It would have been much more useful to the test user if the authors had done away with the "standard score" table altogether, and merely shown the frequency of each raw score in their standardization sample.

The same general criticism applies to a lesser degree to the "standard" scores for all the other scales. All the distributions seem to be very skewed in the direction of low (i.e., "normal") scores. The main value to the user of scoring the questionnaire at all is surely to allow some comparison to be made between one's particular client and the standardization sample of Denver clients. But this sort of comparison is really not possible without the frequency distribution of all the raw scores for all the scales. This information could easily have been presented in a table of exactly the same size as the table of standard score equivalents given in the manual.

The main value of this test is as a preliminary screening device, and as a rough check on the possible improvement in social adjustment following treatment. The authors provide some evidence that four of the scales are relatively reliable, as assessed by a 2-week test-retest study. The correlation coefficients ranged from only .60 for the two-item "Interpersonal Aggression—Friends" scale to .83 for the "Interpersonal Isolation/Family" scale, a 4-item scale evaluating the extent to which the client socializes with and can depend on other members of his family.

The validity of a measure such as this obviously depends a great deal on whether the clients answer the questions truthfully, or whether they try to make themselves seem more socially acceptable. One study by Ciarlo and Reihman (1977) suggests that the correlations between clients' self-report scores and clinicians' ratings of the same variables may be very low, as only two correlation coefficients over .40 were found for these scales. Of course many of the clients for which this questionnaire is intended are alcoholics or drug abusers, and taking the client's word on his or her own consumption and social behaviour might not be wise. At the very least it would seem important to get independent confirmation of the facts from at least one other informant. This is, of course, not so much due to any shortcomings in this potentially very useful standardized interview, as it is due to the characteristics of many of the clients with which it is used.

REVIEWER'S REFERENCES

Ciarlo, J. A., & Reihman, J. The Denver Community Mental Health Questionnaire: Development of a multi-dimensional program evaluation instrument. In Coursey, R., Spector, G., Murrell, S., & Hunt, B. (Eds.), PROGRAM EVALUATION FOR MENTAL HEALTH: METHODS, STRATEGIES, AND PARTICIPANTS, (pp. 131–167). New York: Grune & Stratton, 1977.

[311]

Denver Developmental Screening Test. Ages 2 weeks to 6 years; 1968–81; DDST; 4 scores: gross motor, fine motor-adaptive, language, personal-social; individual; 1 form, 2 formats: 1968 edition ('68, 2 pages and kit of small objects), revised 1981 edition ('81, 2 pages and kit of small objects, differs from '68 edition only in that the 105 items are arranged in a chronological stepwise order); manual, 1970 ('70, 65 pages); 1984 price data: $34 per complete test package including 100 test forms, and manual; $9 per 100 English test forms; $10 per 100 Spanish test forms (1968 edition only); $17 per kit of small objects; $14 per manual; [15–20] minutes; William K. Frankenburg and Josiah B. Dodds; LADOCA Publishing Foundation.*

See T3:678 (25 references) and T2:492 (6 references); for reviews of an earlier edition by Alice E. Moriarity and Emmy E. Werner, see 7:405 (6 references).

TEST REFERENCES

1. Appelbaum, A. S. Developmental retardation in infants as a concomitant of physical child abuse. JOURNAL OF ABNORMAL CHILD PSYCHOLOGY, 1977, 5, 417–423.

2. Dodge, G. R. A comparison of language screening methods. LANGUAGE, SPEECH, AND HEARING SERVICES IN SCHOOLS, 1980, 11, 214–217.

3. Kirkconnell, S. C., & Hicks, L. E. Residual effects of lead poisoning on Denver Developmental Screening Test scores. JOURNAL OF ABNORMAL CHILD PSYCHOLOGY, 1980, 8, 257–267.

4. Welbourn, A. M., & Mazuryk, G. F. Inter-agency intervention: An innovative therapeutic program for abuse prone mothers. CHILD ABUSE & NEGLECT, 1980, 4, 199–203.

5. Medoff-Cooper, B., & Schraeder, B. D. Developmental trends and behavioral styles in very low birth weight infants. NURSING RESEARCH, 1982, 31, 68–72.

6. Totta, A. R., & Crase, S. J. Parents' and day-care teachers' perceptions of young children's skills. PERCEPTUAL AND MOTOR SKILLS, 1982, 54, 955–961.

7. Karch, D., Rohmer, K., & Lemburg, P. Prognostic significance of polygraphic recordings in newborn infants on ventilation. DEVELOPMENTAL MEDICINE AND CHILD NEUROLOGY, 1984, 26, 358–368.

[312]

Denver Eye Screening Test. Ages 6 months and over; 1973; DEST; criterion-referenced; detects problems in visual acuity and non-straight eyes; 3 ratings for each eye: normal, abnormal, untestable; no data on reliability and validity; no norms; individual; 1 form; 2 parts; manual/workbook (40 pages, includes scoring form); training/proficiency film (16mm color sound); training/proficiency video cassettes (3/4 inch U-standard cassette); preschool vision screening slide-tape and film available; 1984 price data: $2 per 25 test forms; $350 per training/proficiency film, $45 weekly rental; $115 per training/proficiency video cassettes, $40 weekly rental; $290 per preschool vision screening slide-tape and film; $7.50 per manual/workbook; (5–10) minutes; William K. Frankenburg, Arnold D. Goldstein, and John Barker; LADOCA Publishing Foundation.

a) PART 1: VISION TEST. Ages 6 months–2.5 years, 2.5–3, 3 years and over; 3 levels; 3 tests, one test per level.

b) PART 2: TESTS FOR NON-STRAIGHT EYES. Ages 6 months and over; 3 tests.

[313]

Denver Handwriting Analysis. Grades 3–8; 1983; DHA; "criterion-referenced cursive writing scale"; 5 subtests, 7 scores: near-point copying, writing the alphabet (capitals, lower case), far-point copying, total, manuscript-cursive transition, dictation; subskill and performance profiles; no data on reliability; no norms; individual; record form (4 pages); scoring profile (2 pages); wall chart; manual (69 pages); 1984 price data: $21 per kit including 25 record forms and 25 scoring profiles; $8.50 per 25 record forms and scoring profiles; $12.50 per set of manual and wall chart; $12.50 per specimen set; (25–65) minutes; Peggy L. Anderson; Academic Therapy Publications.*

[314]

Denver Prescreening Developmental Questionnaire. Ages 3 months–6 years; 1975–76; PDQ; ratings by parents; criterion-referenced; "designed to detect developmental lags"; no reliability data; no norms; individual; 5 forms ('75, 2 pages), choice of form to be administered depends upon age of child tested; instruction sheet (no date, 2 pages); research article ('76, 10 pages); 1984 price data: $5 per 100 copies of any one form, includes instruction sheet and article; French and Spanish editions available; (2–5) minutes; William K. Frankenburg; LADOCA Publishing Foundation.*

[315]

Depression Adjective Check Lists. Grades 9–16 and adults; 1967–81; DACL; Forms A, B, C, D, E, F, G, (1 page); manual ('81, 34 pages); 1983 price data: $3.75 per 25 tests; $2.50 per scoring key; $2.50 per manual; $3.25 per specimen set; (5) minutes; Bernard Lubin; EdITS/Educational and Industrial Testing Service.*

See T3:681 (46 references), 8:536 (20 references), and T2:1154 (2 references); for reviews by Leonard D. Goodstein and Douglas M. McNair, see 7:65 (3 references); see also P:57 (4 references).

TEST REFERENCES

1. Lubin, B., Millham, J., & Paredes, F. Spanish language versions of the Depression Adjective Check Lists. HISPANIC JOURNAL OF BEHAVIORAL SCIENCES, 1980, 2, 51–57.

2. Natale, M., & Bolan, R. The effect of Velten's mood-induction procedure for depression on hand movement and head-down posture. MOTIVATION AND EMOTION, 1980, 4, 323–333.

3. Lomranz, J., Lubin, B., Eyal, N., & Medini, G. A Hebrew version of the Depression Adjective Check Lists. JOURNAL OF PERSONALITY ASSESSMENT, 1981, 45, 380–384.

4. Lomranz, J., Lubin, B., Eyal, N., & Medini, G. Norms for the revised Hebrew version of the Depression Adjective Check List. JOURNAL OF CLINICAL PSYCHOLOGY, 1981, 37, 378–379.

5. Lubin, B. Additional data on the reliability and validity of the brief lists of the Depression Adjective Check Lists. JOURNAL OF CLINICAL PSYCHOLOGY, 1981, 37, 809–811.

6. Lubin, B., Nathan, M. M., & Nathan, R. G. Comparison of response formats for the Depression Adjective Check Lists. JOURNAL OF CLINICAL PSYCHOLOGY, 1981, 37, 172–175.

7. Lubin, B., Schoenfeld, L. S., Rinck, C., & Millham, J. Brief versions of the Spanish Depression Adjective Check Lists: Some indices of reliability and validity. HISPANIC JOURNAL OF BEHAVIORAL SCIENCES, 1981, 3, 83–89.

8. Roth, A. V., Lubin, B., & Hornstra, R. K. Validation of individual items of the Depression Adjective Check List (Form E) across three populations. JOURNAL OF CLINICAL PSYCHOLOGY, 1981, 37, 375–378.

9. Byerly, F. C., & Carlson, W. A. Comparison among inpatients, outpatients, and normals on three self-report depression inventories. JOURNAL OF CLINICAL PSYCHOLOGY, 1982, 38, 797–804.

10. Caplan, M., Lubin, B., & Collins, J. F. Response manipulation of the Depression Adjective Check List. JOURNAL OF CLINICAL PSYCHOLOGY, 1982, 38, 156–159.

11. Danker-Brown, P., & Baucom, D. H. Cognitive influences on the development of learned helplessness. JOURNAL OF PERSONALITY AND SOCIAL PSYCHOLOGY, 1982, 43, 793–801.

12. Davis, F. W., & Yates, B. T. Self-efficacy expectancies versus outcome expectancies as determinants of performance deficits and depressive affect. COGNITIVE THERAPY AND RESEARCH, 1982, 6, 23–35.

13. Hartz, G. W., Wallace, W. L., & Cayton, T. G. Effect of aerobic conditioning upon mood in clinically depressed men and women: A preliminary investigation. PERCEPTUAL AND MOTOR SKILLS, 1982, 55, 1217–1218.

14. Kramer, M. E., Rosellini, R. A. Universal and personal helplessness: A test of the reformulated model. THE PSYCHOLOGICAL RECORD, 1982, 32, 329–336.

15. Manly, P. C., McMahon, R. J., Bradley, C. F., & Davidson, P. O. Depressive attributional style and depression following childbirth. JOURNAL OF ABNORMAL PSYCHOLOGY, 1982, 91, 245–254.

16. McGaghie, W. C., & Whitenack, D. C. A scale for measurement of the problem patient labeling process. THE JOURNAL OF NERVOUS AND MENTAL DISEASE, 1982, 170, 598–604.

17. Bradley, C. F. Psychological consequences of intervention in the birth process. CANADIAN JOURNAL OF BEHAVIOURAL SCIENCE, 1983, 15, 422–438.

18. Dickstein, L. S., & Whitaker, A. Effects of task outcome and subjective standard on state depression for cognitive and social tasks. BULLETIN OF THE PSYCHONOMIC SOCIETY, 1983, 21, 183–186.

19. Norbeck, J. S., & Tilden, V. P. Life stress, social support, and emotional disequilibrium in complications of pregnancy: Complications of pregnancy: A prospective, multivariate study. JOURNAL OF HEALTH AND SOCIAL BEHAVIOR, 1983, 24, 30–46.

20. Sokoloff, R. M., & Lubin, B. Depressive mood in adolescent, emotionally disturbed females: Reliability and validity of an adjective checklist (C-DACL). JOURNAL OF ABNORMAL CHILD PSYCHOLOGY, 1983, 11, 531–536.

21. Rosenbaum, M., & Palmon, N. Helplessness and resourcefulness in coping with epilepsy. JOURNAL OF CONSULTING AND CLINICAL PSYCHOLOGY, 1984, 52, 244–253.

[316]

Depressive Experience Questionnaire. Adolescents and adults (patients and normals); 1979; DEQ; 3 scores: dependency, self-criticism, efficacy; no data on reliability or validity; norms consist of means and standard deviations; 1 form (4 pages); 1982 price data: $3 per test; administration time not reported; Sidney J. Blatt, Joseph P. D'Afflitti, and Donald M. Quinlan; Sidney J. Blatt.*

See T3:682 (1 reference).

TEST REFERENCES

1. Pargament, K. I., Tyler, F. B., & Steele, R. E. The church/synagogue and the psychosocial competence of the member: An initial inquiry into a neglected dimension. AMERICAN JOURNAL OF COMMUNITY PSYCHOLOGY, 1979, 7, 649–664.

2. Zuroff, D. C., Moskowitz, D. S., Wielgus, M. S., Powers, T. A., & Franko, D. L. Construct validation of the Dependency and Self-Criticism Scales of the Depressive Experiences Questionnaire. JOURNAL OF RESEARCH IN PERSONALITY, 1983, 17, 226–241.

[317]

Derogatis Sexual Functioning Inventory. Adults; 1975–79; DSFI; 12 scores: information, experience, drive, attitudes, psychological symptoms, affects, gender role definition, fantasy, body image, sexual satisfaction, total, patient's evaluation of current functioning; 1 form ('78, 8 pages); manual ('79, 36 pages); separate profiles ('78, 2 pages) males and females; 1982 price data: $25 per 100 tests; $18 per 100 score profiles; $15 per 100 answer sheets; $4 per manual; (45–60) minutes; Leonard R. Derogatis; the Author.*

See T3:683 (6 references).

TEST REFERENCES

1. Derogatis, L. R., & Meyer, J. K. A psychological profile of the sexual dysfunctions. ARCHIVES OF SEXUAL BEHAVIOR, 1979, 8, 201–223.

2. Skrapec, C., & MacKenzie, K. R. Psychological self-perception in male transsexuals, homosexuals, and heterosexuals. ARCHIVES OF SEXUAL BEHAVIOR, 1981, 10, 357–370.

3. Perlman, S. D., & Abramson, P. R. Sexual satisfaction among married and cohabitating individuals. JOURNAL OF CONSULTING AND CLINICAL PSYCHOLOGY, 1982, 50, 458–460.

Review of Derogatis Sexual Functioning Inventory by EDWARD S. HEROLD, Associate Professor, Department of Family Studies, University of Guelph, Guelph, Ontario, Canada:

The Derogatis Sexual Functioning Inventory (DSFI) consists of 10 sections or subscales. Evaluative comment for each of these subscales is presented below.

The information subscale consists of 26 items in a true-false format. Derogatis found significant differences in the amount of accurate sexual information possessed by sexually dysfunctional males and females compared with those not having problems. However, he questions the clinical significance of this finding because the actual differences were small. While a general scale of knowledge items may provide some insight, it is debatable how useful such a scale might be in counselling for specific sexual problems. For some of the questions it is not clear whether the question refers to all instances or most instances and this can affect one's response. The statement "Women who have fantasies during intercourse are dissatisfied with their sex lives" can be answered both true and false because fantasies in some cases may be an indication of dissatisfaction, whereas in other cases they are not. The scale ascertains not only knowledge of factual information, but also attitudes towards aspects of sexual functioning such as whether it is necessary for women to obtain an orgasm during intercourse. One disadvantage of using attitudinal measures as knowledge items is that there are many unique aspects of sexual functioning. The potential danger of these types of items is that someone whose sexual functioning differs from that of the majority may feel he or she is abnormal.

The experience subscale lists 24 sexual behaviors ranging from kissing on the lips to oral-genital sex and different intercourse positions. Subjects are asked to indicate whether they have or have not engaged in each of those behaviors, and if they have, whether they have experienced the behavior within the past 60 days. Certainly clinicians dealing with sexual dysfunctions need to obtain some knowledge of the sexual experience of clients. Some of the items, however, could easily be deleted without affecting the usefulness of the scale. This scale would be more useful if, for each of the behaviours listed, clients were to indicate how much they desired that behavior and how much they enjoyed that behavior. Derogatis reports that dysfunctional men reported fewer sexual experiences than normal men while the same was not true for dysfunctional women.

The sexual drive subscale measures the frequency of intercourse, masturbation, kissing and petting, and sexual fantasies. Additionally, clients are asked to indicate their ideal frequency of sexual intercourse. The combining of kissing and petting into one category is questionable. Petting, in particular, is a general term that could include a diversity of behavior ranging from breast stimulation to oral sex. Derogatis reports significant drive differences for the male groups but not for the female groups.

The attitude subscale consists of 30 items measuring a diversity of liberal and conservative attitudes. In deciding upon a particular therapeutic treatment it is essential that therapists be aware of the value system of the client, and this subscale could be of considerable assistance in this respect. In general, the items are good measures of attitudes although two of the items are clearly sexist. Derogatis did not find significant differences between normals and dysfunctionals for this attitude scale.

The brief symptom inventory measures psychopathology in terms of nine major symptom dimensions and three global indices of distress. While this subscale may measure psychological distress it does not indicate the relationship of the psychological distress to specific sexual dysfunctions. In other words, it would not indicate whether the psychological distress was a cause or a consequence of sexual dysfunction.

The affects or emotions measure represents eight affect dimensions and three global affect indices. The client is asked to indicate his/her emotional feelings during the past 2 weeks.

The gender role measure consists of 30 adjectives reflecting primarily masculine or feminine characteristics. The responses to many of these adjectives can provide useful insight regarding the client's approach to sexual functioning.

The fantasy subscale lists 20 fantasies and asks clients to indicate which of the fantasies they have experienced. Many therapists believe that understanding and dealing with sexual fantasies is an important part of the therapeutic process. Thus it can be most helpful to obtain an understanding of the client's fantasies. The weakness of this scale is that it focuses more on deviant types of fantasies as opposed to the more common types of fantasies. Clients may have difficulty responding to this particular scale not only because it focuses on the more deviant types of fantasies but also because people generally have difficulty in revealing any of their fantasies to others. It would be more helpful to know which are the current fantasies the client has rather than knowing which ones he or she has ever had. Also it would be more useful to know which of the fantasies are the most common ones and also if the fantasies have been discussed with others. Derogatis found that males have a greater diversity of fantasies than females. He also found that while male normals had a greater diversity of fantasies than the dysfunctionals, the opposite was true for females.

The body image subscale consists of 10 items filled out by both sexes and 5 gender-specific items for each of the sexes. Because negative body image can seriously affect sexual functioning, this subscale is a highly useful one.

The satisfaction subscale has 10 items measuring satisfaction with different aspects of sexuality. It provides the therapist with an overall rating of satisfaction. In addition, analysis of specific items by the therapist can help to determine which aspects of sexual functioning appear to be the least satisfying.

Derogatis presents data indicating both high internal reliability as well as high test-retest reliability. However, the validity data based on comparisons of dysfunctionals with normals are ambiguous especially for females. Further research with larger samples is required to confirm validity.

While the test can provide some useful information for the clinician with respect to sexual dysfunctioning, it is not a substitute for detailed interviewing. Clinicians should not present the test to clients until sufficient rapport has been established. Many clients, especially those with serious sexual dysfunctions, may find the test items to be threatening and anxiety-provoking. One means of diminishing this anxiety would be to present only parts of the test at a time rather than a whole test at once. It might also be useful to administer the test again at the completion of therapy so as to obtain more precise indicators of change over time.

Although some therapists may find the test a helpful means of obtaining clinical data, others may prefer to obtain this information through traditional interviewing techniques.

Review of Derogatis Sexual Functioning Inventory by DAVID L. WEIS, Assistant Professor of Home Economics, Cook College, Rutgers University, New Brunswick, NJ:

The Derogatis Sexual Functioning Inventory (DSFI) is a multi-scaled inventory of a group of clinically relevant sexual and personality dimensions. The inventory is composed of 10 sections. These sections generate subscale scores for sexual information, sexual experience, sexual drive, sexual attitudes (liberalism-conservatism), psychological symptoms, general affect, gender role definition, sexual fantasy, body image, and sexual satisfaction. The subscale scores can be summed to form a generalized Sexual Functioning Index. Finally, the DSFI includes a single item which is used to generate a score for the General Sexual Satisfaction Index.

The entire inventory can be expected to take 45–60 minutes to complete. The DSFI is a technician-aided, self-report series of measures and was designed to assess the adequacy of sexual functioning for clinical purposes. Instructions for administering the inventory are included in the packet. Directions for scoring the DSFI are also included; however, these scoring guidelines are often imprecise and confusingly vague.

It should be stressed that the DSFI was designed to assess individual, rather than couple, sexual functioning. This approach gains important information in a self-report test, but does so at the possible expense of a couple. For example, the sexual drive subscale measures the total sexual outlet (frequency of fantasy, masturbation, kissing and petting, and intercourse) of the individual respondent, but it makes no attempt to assess how this outlet is influenced by the relationship with the sexual partner. The DSFI does include a question about ideal frequency of intercourse. However, this item is not used in computing the score for sexual drive, and there are no items pertaining to discrepancies in desire between sexual partners. This point is not intended as a criticism of the DSFI. The author is certainly aware of and forthright about the limitations of his inventory. Potential users of the DSFI should, nonetheless, be cautioned that this instrument does not assess dyadic dynamics.

The author also claims that the DSFI focuses on "current" functioning. In general, this orientation is maintained throughout the test. Most sections ask the respondent to indicate his/her present position or recent experiences. However, both the sexual experience subscale and the sexual fantasy subscale ask the respondent to report lifetime experiences.

One of the strongest features of the DSFI is that is has been subjected to considerable study of its reliability and validity. In fact, it can be fairly stated that the DSFI is one of the most thoroughly studied instruments in the entire realm of sexual research. Normative response patterns were developed separately for males and females by administering the inventory to several hundred heterosexual men and women. As a result, raw scores on the DSFI can be converted to soundly established percentile rankings. In addition, empirical studies have demonstrated that the inventory succeeds in discriminating between sexually dysfunctional and "normal" men and women and also between transsexuals and "normals." Moreover, the empirical studies of the DSFI have been extensively reported in the professional literature. (For the most thorough and descriptive reports, see Derogatis, 1980; Derogatis & Melisaratos, 1979; Derogatis & Meyer, 1979.)

These tremendous strengths should be considered in evaluating the criticisms I will direct at the DSFI. While I do believe that there are several conceptual and measurement problems within the inventory, the already extensive research on the instrument serves to pinpoint these weaknesses and to indicate specifically which areas of the DSFI require further revision. The DSFI is not a perfect instrument, but I can think of no diagnostic test for sexual functioning that is better conceived or more thoroughly researched.

An inspection of the DSFI suggests that there may be conceptual problems with several of the subscales. A number of items within the sexual information subscale appear to measure perceptions of trends within society, more than sexual knowledge or information per se. I have already mentioned that the sexual desire subscale measures sexual outlet rather than assessing a possible discrepancy between desire and outlet. The gender role subscale is patterned after a similar scale by Bem (1974). It is, perhaps, noteworthy that the Bem Sex-Role Inventory itself has been severely criticized in recent years (Gaudreau, 1977; Silvern & Ryan, 1979). Finally, the body image subscale appears to measure several dimensions, such as physical appearance, general physique, genitalia, and physical conditioning.

The statistical analyses of the DSFI reveal these problems acutely. Reliability was tested in two ways: test-retest and internal consistency (Derogatis, 1980; Derogatis & Melisaratos, 1979; Derogatis & Meyer, 1979). The reliability coefficients for the various subscales range from .42 to .97. It is interesting to note that the weakest coefficients (below .70) are those for the subscales discussed above as having conceptual difficulties. Indeed, it can be suggested that further revisions of the subscales for sexual information, sexual desire, gender roles, and body image are necessary. Other reliability coefficients were quite good.

Attempts to demonstrate the validity of the DSFI have yielded mixed results as well. Discriminant analysis has indicated that the inventory succeeds in accurately classifying 77% of dysfunctional and "normal" men and 75% of dysfunctional and "normal" women. These results also reveal, however, that the inventory fails to correctly categorize one-quarter of those who complete the test. This suggests that clinicians should be cautious in interpreting responses to the DSFI and that further discriminative power is needed. While the discriminant analysis indicates that the generalized Sexual Functioning Index (sum of all scores on subscales) is a useful discriminating tool, a factor analysis of subscales reveals again the problems of internal consistency reflected in the reliability testing. The factor structure succeeded in explaining only 52% of the total DSFI variance, and this was achieved by including factors with eigenvalues below 1.0 and factor loadings as low as .35. An additional problem is indicated by the fact that the factor pattern shows the subscales are highly intercorrelated (Derogatis & Melisaratos, 1979), raising serious questions about whether the DSFI actually measures 10 distinct areas of sexual functioning.

To summarize, the DSFI is, in all likelihood, the best composite measure of overall sexual functioning available and certainly the most thoroughly studied. Despite these considerable strengths, the research on the instrument indicates that the DSFI still possesses conceptual weaknesses and problems with internal consistency. I would hope that Derogatis and his associates would work to improve the inventory by increasing its discriminative power, by increasing the reliability of weak subscales (sexual information, sexual drive, gender role definitions, body image), and by further exploring the complex factor structure embedded in the instrument. As now constituted, the DSFI can provide clinicians with a wealth of data which has been shown to be relevant to sexual functioning. However, the existing weaknesses strongly suggest that great caution should be exercised in forming therapeutic conclusions based on those responses.

REVIEWER'S REFERENCES

Bem, S. L. The measurement of psychological androgyny. JOURNAL OF CONSULTING AND CLINICAL PSYCHOLOGY, 1974, 42, 155–162.

Gaudreau, P. Factor analysis of the Bem Sex-Role Inventory. JOURNAL OF CONSULTING AND CLINICAL PSYCHOLOGY, 1977, 45, 299–302.

Derogatis, L. R., & Melisaratos, N. The DSFI: A multidimensional measure of sexual functioning. JOURNAL OF SEX AND MARITAL THERAPY, 1979, 5, 244–281.

Derogatis, L. R., & Meyer, J. K. A psychological profile of the sexual dysfunctions. ARCHIVES OF SEXUAL BEHAVIOR, 1979, 8, 201–223.

Silvern, L. E., & Ryan, V. L. Self-rated adjustment and sex-typing on the Bem Sex-Role Inventory: Is masculinity the primary predictor of adjustment? SEX ROLES, 1979, 5, 739–763.

Derogatis, L. R. Psychological assessment of psychosexual functioning. PSYCHIATRIC CLINICS OF NORTH AMERICA, 1980, 3, 113–131.

[318]

Description of Body Scale. Adolescents and adults; 1980; DOBS; may be rated by an observer; 5 scores: masculinity-femininity of body, consistency of present body description, ideal body description, self-ideal body description difference score, incongruence between present and ideal body description; 1 form (2 pages); preliminary manual (56 pages); 1984 price data: $7.50 per 50 tests; $7 per specimen set; administration time not reported; Carney, Weedman and Associates.*

Review of Description of Body Scale by JAMES J. JUPP, Senior Lecturer in Psychology, Director of Counselling Programmes, School of Behavioural Sciences, Macquarie University, North Ryde, Australia:

The asserted purpose of the Description of Body Scale (DOBS) is to tap conscious views of self and of others concerning aspects of body structure, voice quality, and movement. Specifically the scale attends to the bipolar dimension of body masculinity-femininity rather than to other physical traits more readily described on the basis of objective physical measures (i.e., roundness, linearity, or muscularity), or measures of blood chemistry, attitudes, or social behaviours. The authors of the test suggest that its scores predict such behaviours as drug use, sex role adoption, and propensity to violence.

The Scale provides a simple format employing two identical sets of bipolar statements scored on a connecting 6-point scale which allows, in one form of administration, ratings of perceived present versus ideal body features with respect to voice pitch, walking gait, and five different aspects of the body. Focus is on the face, arms, chest, and waist, those parts of the body typically considered for physical somatotyping. The bipolar items and particularly the addition of those concerned with voice and movement provide reasonable face validity for measurement of the assumed underlying dimension. Indeed the obviousness of the items may be such that testees could easily contrive to produce patterns of response perceived as socially desirable or situationally appropriate which might limit the context in which the scale could be applied. The simple structure of the Scale suggests that test-retest correlations for self, ideal self, or discrepancy between self and ideal would be high because identical performances at different administrations would be particularly easy to achieve. This weakness is less evident when the instrument is used to rate another. When it is used for this purpose, interscorer reliability has been shown to be high (70%+ agreement). However, test-retest reliability has not been formally investigated.

The scores derived directly from the DOBS are: a Present Body Masculinity Self Rating (SB) obtained by the addition of ratings over the seven items of the scale weighted so that high scores indicate greater body masculinity; an Inconsistency of Present Body Perception (KB), which describes the degree of variation of ratings on the separate items about the mean of all seven ratings, thus providing a check for inconsistency or confusion which might invalidate an individual's scale score; Ideal Body Rating (IB) obtained in the same way as the SB rating but ascertained from responses to a different test demand (i.e., "how you would like to be" as opposed to "present situation"); and Incongruence of Present-Ideal Ratings (CB), the calculated discrepancy between SB and IB ratings.

The current DOBS, like previous versions, uses the same seven items, no reference being made by the authors to how these were selected, possibly because of their suitability for both self and other ratings. It is important to note that scores obtained from the current and previous forms are different. The SB rating is common to current and earlier forms. The CB rating is new and replaces the earlier direct rating scale concerned with satisfaction (the SATB Scale). The KB consistency score is also new. Observer rating (OB scores) utilizing the same seven-item formats from which SB or IB scores are obtained is common to new and older forms of the DOBS.

Results from only a small sample of data (*N* =70) relate to scores derived from the form of administration described in the 1980 manual, and these appear to provide only preliminary norms. Most of the results reported by the publishers are concerned with different kinds of scores obtained from different formats of test material and presumably therefore different item endorsement demands (e.g., one older form used a rating scale 1–6 clearly designated masculine versus feminine; another version appears to have used a seven-item scale; the new DOBS makes no reference to the underlying dimension). Thus, even the conceptually similar SB scores, or OB scores, may be empirically different across procedures, and relationships assumed on the basis of earlier scores not necessarily valid for later scores. Clearly the SATB score could not be regarded as in any way equivalent to the CB discrepancy score. The potency of the KB rating remains essentially unexplored.

The authors claim, however, that the classic body structure dimensions of Endomorphy, Ectomorphy, and Mesomorphy are related negatively in the case of the former two, and positively for the latter, to OB, SB, and SATB scores. Loadings from these DOBS scores on factors of body dimensions in the analyses of two data sets from relatively large samples (112 males and 119 females respectively) provided only equivocal support for this view, and then only in the case of males. However, the same pattern of relationship between the body dimensions and OB score (i.e., correlations of .17, –.26, and .15 respectively) were obtained in the analysis of another very large sample of scores. It is also contended that chromatin level is related to DOBS scores, particularly SB, SO and SATB scores. These scores (which, incidentally, did not define their own factor) were found in the analysis referred to above to load .40, –.18 and .68 respectively on a percentage chromatin factor. However, this was the case for females only. DOBS scores for males did not load on this factor. Point biserial correlations of the DOBS scores OB and SB with biological sex (males coded 1 and females coded 2) were –.60 (*N* =388) and –.50 (*N* =143) respectively, reasonable support for the predictive capacity of the scores.

No item-total correlations are reported for the DOB, but there is evidence of moderate intercorrelation among the item scores (2) shoulders, (3) hips, (4) chest, and (5) figure for both SB and OB scoring. However, these relationships are unstable across samples and sex groupings, and the interrelationships of items (1) face, (6) voice, and (7) movement with these items and with each other are erratic. Therefore it is difficult to support with any assurance a view that the separate items define a single dimension. The appropriateness of the use of the total score is consequently questionable, and the implication of relationships to the total score (and there are many reported), is difficult to interpret.

The DOBS presents a novel approach to the measurement of masculinity-femininity. There is some evidence that an older version had some capacity to do this. But the new form, despite an excellent description of the structure and details for scoring, has not been empirically examined. Studies examining characteristics of the older form(s) have been inadequately reported, and tables supporting the text are very poorly labelled. It is generally difficult to find, or to be sure about the exact nature of results supporting the author's contentions; and the presentation of material concerned with the relationships between DOBS scores and a range of attitudes and behaviours gives the impression that a shotgun approach with post hoc rationalization of findings has been employed, rather than a testing of specific and ordered prediction of theoretically sound relationships.

[319]

Design for Math. Grades K–1, 1–2, 2–3, 3–4, 4–5, 5–6, 6 and over; 1975–79; "criterion-referenced"; a mathematics instruction system including placement tests, pre- and postdiagnostic progress tests, and instructional aides; each diagnostic test level contains 14–30 subtests covering specific objectives; no data on reliability; no norms; mastery ratios are given for each subtest; 2 forms ('79, 8 pages); placement test administrator's manual ('79, 18 pages, for all levels); test administrator's manual Forms X and Y ('79, 22–40 pages) for each level; teacher's planning guide ('79, 68 pages); profile card ('79, 2 pages); additional instructional materials available; 1983 price data: $150 per levels A–B kit including 45 placement tests, spirit master pretests (Form X) and posttests (Form Y), 45 profile cards, 45 award certificates, a teachers planning guide, resource file, set of learning sequences, and all necessary manuals; $195 per levels C–D kit including same as for A–B kit; $210 per levels E–G kit including same as for A–B kit; $8.50 per 15 placement tests; $12.50 per 50 profile cards; $7.50 per teacher's planning guide; $3.75 per placement test administrator's manual; $3.75 per manual of any one level; (50–60) minutes for the placement test; Donald A. Kamp, John W. Armenia, Dale H. McDonald, and Lee N. VonKuster; NCS Interpretive Scoring Systems.*

a) LEVEL A. Grades K–1; 14 subtests scores; Forms X, Y, (11 spirit masters): $13 per set of spirit masters; (80) minutes.

b) LEVEL B. Grades 1–2; 25 subtest scores: Forms X, Y, (21 spirit masters); $27.75 per set of spirit masters; (153) minutes.

c) LEVEL C. Grades 2–3; 26 subtest scores; Forms X, Y, (31 spirit masters); $36.50 per set of spirit masters; (177) minutes.

d) LEVEL D. Grades 3–4; 27 subtest scores; Forms X, Y, (24 spirit masters); $28.50 per set of spirit masters; (158) minutes.

e) LEVEL E. Grades 4–5; 25 subtest scores; Forms X, Y, in a single booklet (49 pages); separate answer sheets (spirit masters) must be used; $35 per 15 tests; $5 per set of spirit masters for answer sheets; (137) minutes.

f) LEVEL F. Grades 5–6; 29 subtest scores; Forms X, Y, in a single booklet (53 pages); separate answer sheets (spirit masters) must be used; prices same as for Level E; (180) minutes.

g) LEVEL G. Grades 6 and over; 30 subtest scores; Forms X, Y, in a single booklet (47 pages); separate answer sheets (spirit masters) must be used; prices same as for Level E; (196) minutes.

Review of Design for Math by RONALD A. BERK, Associate Professor of Educational Research, The Johns Hopkins University, Baltimore, MD:

Design for Math is an assessment system that is intended to be used in conjunction with a school's existing mathematics curriculum in grades K through 6. Two types of criterion-referenced tests are employed: (*a*) placement tests and (*b*) diagnostic progress tests. The placement tests serve as screening devices to assist teachers in identifying a student's math ability level. The diagnostic progress tests are administered as pretests (Form X) and posttests (Form Y) to pinpoint a student's math skill strengths and weaknesses. In addition to these tests, there are instructional planning guides, resource files, and learning sequences to facilitate the instructional phase between the pre- and posttests.

The foundation of the entire system is 176 mathematics skills expressed as objectives. They are supposed to represent those skills currently taught nationwide. This initially signals a need for the user to determine the curricular match at the local level. Just how relevant this system is to a particular mathematics curriculum remains to be appraised by the consumer. If the verdict is positive, the next step would be an inspection of the tests to estimate the degree of curricular validity. The usefulness of the system is contingent primarily upon the findings of these two reviews. Although obviously time-consuming tasks, they are essential for all commercially-prepared tests and diagnostic-prescriptive packages.

The mathematics domain of 176 skills is further partitioned into 10 strands that are the major subject areas in elementary mathematics, 7 math ability levels (A–G) which correspond to grades K through 6, and, finally, 43 skill clusters with 5 to 8 clusters at each level, for instructional purposes. This structure is clearly explicated in the Teacher's Planning Guide.

Unfortunately the effort devoted to defining the domain is not apparent in the specifications for the tests. First, there is no documentation linking the domain structure to the placement and diagnostic progress test items. No information is presented on how the items were developed from the structure, the number of items per objective/cluster/level, and the rationale underlying the item generation or selection procedures. For the placement tests, it is stated only that they measure three overlapping levels with one or two items written for most of the computational and place value objectives. Of the 176 diagnostic progress tests measuring the 176 skills, 149 are in paper-and-pencil format and 27 are performance tests which require motor and/or oral responses.

Second, there is no description of the technical adequacy of any of the tests. Once a placement test is administered, score ranges are given to guide the teacher to the appropriate diagnostic test. No justification, empirical or otherwise, is provided for these particular ranges. As screening devices, there is no indication whether the tests function effectively for placement purposes. No indices of decision validity or decision reliability are reported. These problems also characterize the diagnostic progress tests. No explanation is given for how the mastery ratio (e.g., 5/6) or performance standard was set for each test. Furthermore, there is no validity evidence on the accuracy of the mastery-nonmastery classification decisions and no reliability evidence on the consistency of those decisions. The two test forms (X and Y) recommended for pre- and posttesting are claimed to be parallel and interchangeable; yet, no parallel forms reliability coefficients are reported.

Despite these deficiencies in the tests, the authors did exhibit care in delineating the procedures for test preparation, test administration, and scoring. Warm-up tests in spirit-master format were developed to acquaint students with the item formats of the progress tests. Testing conditions and materials are clearly specified. The Test Administrator's Manual provides well-written, readily understandable directions for group administration of the paper-and-pencil tests and individual administration of the performance tests. As criterion-referenced tests, the tests are untimed. However, approximate testing times are suggested for completion of all placement and progress tests. These times should be useful to teachers in scheduling the test administrations. Finally, the tests are hand scorable. This facilitates immediate feedback and decision making. Scoring criteria for individual placement and mastery decisions are indicated.

In addition to the assessment components of the system, there is an instructional component. It consists of directions for using local materials in skill-directed instruction, a resource file containing the cluster's skills and objectives keyed to listings of commercially available basic texts and other instructional materials, and learning sequences based on Piaget's concrete-pictorial-abstract graduated experience theory of learning. The value of these materials seems to reside in the extent to which they are congruent with the local mathematics curriculum and teaching methods. Some of the materials may be adopted and others may not. In any case, the package does not constitute a complete instructional program.

In summary, the lack of documentation on the quality of the placement and diagnostic progress tests renders the system worthless at this time. Since the major phases of the system employ the scores from these tools for individual decisions, the information used to guide the instruction and measure its effects on the students may be very misleading. In other words, the suggested interpretation of the scores may produce results antithetical to one of the primary aims of the program—to facilitate effective and efficient teaching and learning. A technical manual containing the types of data cited previously could furnish the information essential to allay most of these fears.

Review of Design for Math by STEVEN D. ELLIOTT, *Statistician, Market Facts, Inc., Chicago, IL:*

Design for Math is a set of teaching aids for grades K through 6. The set contains seven levels, each of which contains a placement test, instructional materials, and a mastery test. Design for Math is intended to: (*a*) diagnose a student's performance level with respect to various types of problems in mathematics, (*b*) provide instructional materials designed for specific areas of weakness, and (*c*) provide posttests to determine when a skill has been mastered. The tests in Design for Math are criterion-referenced. Posttests are alternate forms of the pretests. No norms are presented; however, mastery ratios are presented for each area.

The instructional materials for Design for Math are based on a logical sequence of learning. A concept is first presented concretely. For example, in order to teach the concept of sorting objects by length, the teacher passes out sets of objects of various lengths. The next step involves presenting the concept pictorially, and in the final step the concept is presented abstractly. By presenting concepts in this fashion, Design for Math allows students to develop an intuitive base for new information.

Design for Math covers 176 skills. Each skill is listed as a behavioral objective in a "Teacher's Resource File," which also contains a list of textbooks covering the objective. Instructional materials are organized in clusters of skills; however, a teacher can present skills individually. Thus, the program can be tailored to fit the needs of each student.

The materials involved in Design for Math are well organized and easy to understand. The teacher is provided with a planning guide, warm–up tests, student profile sheets, as well as the materials previously mentioned. An administration manual is provided for each level. These manuals are very well organized and easy to follow. The tests also appear to be very good. The items are straightforward, and they have face validity.

I contacted the publishers of Design for Math on two occasions in an attempt to get technical data and information about the development of Design for Math. However, I received no response. I do not suspect that Design for Math has major flaws; nevertheless, this information should be available. It would also be interesting to see data on a school system that used Design for Math. I expect that students who used Design for Math would have improved achievement test scores. Comments from teachers who used this system would also be interesting. Design for Math is quite comprehensive. It may require a great deal of a teacher's time when used in conjunction with existing curriculum.

In summary, Design for Math is a well organized, comprehensive system of mathematics instruction. It covers 176 skills areas for grades K through 6. Placement tests, instructional material, and mastery tests are provided. The instructional materials are logically sequenced from concrete exposure to abstract representation. All of the testing and support materials appear to be very good. However, there is no information concerning test development, and no technical data are presented.

[320]

Detroit Tests of Learning Aptitude, (Second Edition). Ages 6–18; 1935–85; DTLA-2; 20 scores: 11 subtest scores (word opposites, sentence imitation, oral directions, word sequences, story construction, design reproduction, object sequences, symbolic relations, conceptual matching, word fragments, letter sequences) and 9 composite scores (verbal aptitude, nonverbal aptitude, conceptual aptitude, structural aptitude, attention-enhanced aptitude, attention-reduced aptitude, motor-enhanced aptitude, motor-reduced aptitude, overall aptitude); individual; 1 form; student response form ('85, 4 pages); examiner record form ('85, 4 pages); manual ('85, 135 pages); summary and profile sheet ('85, 2 pages); 1985 price data: $77 per complete kit including 25 student response forms, 25 examiner record forms, 25 summary and profile sheets, picture book, and manual; $9 per 25 student response forms; $9 per 25 examiner record forms; $6 per 25 summary and profile sheets; $39 per picture book; $19 per manual; $49 per software scoring system; (50–120) minutes; Donald D. Hammill; PRO-ED.*

See T3:691 (20 references); for a review by Arthur B. Silverstein of an earlier edition, see 8:213 (14 references); see also T2:493 (3 references) and 7:406 (10 references); for a review by F. L. Wells of an earlier edition, see 3:275 (1 reference); for reviews by Anne Anastasi and Henry Feinburg and an excerpted review by D. A. Worcester (with S. M. Corey) of an earlier edition, see 1:1058.

TEST REFERENCES

1. Bradley, P. E., Battin, R. R., & Sutter, E. G. Effects of individual diagnosis and remediation for the treatment of learning disabilities. CLINICAL NEUROPSYCHOLOGY, 1979, 1(2), 25–32.

2. Marston, L. E., & Larkin, M. Auditory assessment of reading underachieving children. LANGUAGE, SPEECH, AND HEARING IN SCHOOLS, 1979, 10, 212–220.

3. Schwartz, E. R., & Solot, C. B. Response patterns characteristic of verbal expressive disorders. LANGUAGE, SPEECH, AND HEARING SERVICES IN SCHOOLS, 1980, 11, 139–144.

4. Lyon, R., & Watson, B. Empirically derived subgroups of learning disabled readers: Diagnostic characteristics. JOURNAL OF LEARNING DISABILITIES, 1981, 14, 256–261.

5. Gold, P. C., & Horn, P. L. Achievement in reading, verbal language, listening comprehension and locus of control of adult illiterates in a volunteer tutorial project. PERCEPTUAL AND MOTOR SKILLS, 1982, 54, 1243–1250.

6. Gold, P. C., & Johnson, J. A. Entry level achievement characteristics of youth and adults reading below fifth grade equivalent: A preliminary profile and analysis. PSYCHOLOGICAL REPORTS, 1982, 50, 1011–1019.

7. Sachs, H. K., Krall, V., & Drayton, M. A. Neuropsychological assessment after lead poisoning without encephalopathy. PERCEPTUAL AND MOTOR SKILLS, 1982, 54, 1283–1288.

8. Curley, J. F., & Reilly, L. J. Sensory process instruction with learning disabled children. PERCEPTUAL AND MOTOR SKILLS, 1983, 57, 1219–1226.

9. Hasbrouck, J. M. Diagnosis of auditory perceptual disorders in previously undiagnosed adults. JOURNAL OF LEARNING DISABILITIES, 1983, 16, 206–208.

10. Sneider, C., & Pulos, S. Children's cosmographies: Understanding the earth's shape and gravity. SCIENCE EDUCATION, 1983, 67, 205–221.

11. Zinkus, P. W., & Gottlieb, M. I. Patterns of auditory processing and articulation deficits in academically deficient juvenile delinquents. JOURNAL OF SPEECH AND HEARING DISORDERS, 1983, 48, 36–40.

[321]

Developing Cognitive Abilities Test. Grades 2, 3, 4, 5–6, 7–8, 9–12; 1980–81; DCAT; component of Comprehensive Assessment Program; 6 levels; teacher's manual ('80, 22 pages); directions for administration—Level 2 ('80, 20 pages); directions for administration—Levels 3–12 ('80, 19 pages); technical manual and norms ('81, 124 pages); answer key ('80, 14 pages, all levels in single booklet); 1983 price data: $3.80 per answer key; $3.80 per technical manual; $6.25 per teacher's manual; $19 per test review kit, Levels 2–12; $10.60 per test review kit, Levels 2–8; $10.60 per test review kit, Levels 9–12; Donald L. Beggs, John T. Mouw, John F. Cawley, John W. Wick, Jeffrey K. Smith, Miriam Cherkes, Anne M. Fitzmaurice, and Louise J. Cawley; American Testronics.*

a) LEVEL 2. Grade 2; 4 scores: verbal ability, quantitative ability, spatial ability, total; 2 editions; $5.90 per 35 record sheets; administration time not reported.

1) *Machine Scorable Booklets.* 1 form ('80, 20 pages); $23.40 per 35 tests; scoring service, $.75 and over per test ($100 minimum).

2) *Hand Scorable Booklets.* 1 form ('80, 20 pages); $17.80 per 35 tests.

b) LEVEL 3. Grade 3; 4 scores (verbal, quantitative, spatial, total) in 5 categories (knowledge, comprehension, application, analysis, synthesis); 2 editions; prices same as for Level 2; 50(60) minutes.

1) *Machine Scorable Booklets.* 1 form ('80, 11 pages).

2) *Hand Scorable Booklets.* 1 form ('80, 11 pages).

c) LEVEL 4. Grade 4; scores same as for Level 3; 1 form ('80, 10 pages); separate answer sheets must be used; $18.50 per 35 reusable tests; $7.95 per 35 answer sheets; $8.75 per 35 combination answer sheets for testing with achievement series; $5.90 per 35 record sheets; scoring service, $.65 and over per test ($100 minimum); 50(60) minutes.

d) LEVELS 5–6. Grades 5–6; scores same as for Level 3; Form A ('80, 8 pages); separate answer sheets must be used; prices and time same as for Level 4.

e) LEVELS 7–8. Grades 7–8; scores same as for Level 3; Form A ('80, 8 pages); separate answer sheets must be used; prices and time same as for Level 4.

f) LEVELS 9–12. Grades 9–12; scores same as for Level 3; Form A ('80, 8 pages); separate answer sheets must be used; prices and time same as for Level 4.

Review of Developing Cognitive Abilities Test by LYNN H. FOX, Professor of Education,

Evening College and Summer Session, The Johns Hopkins University, Baltimore, MD:

The unique feature of the Developing Cognitive Abilities Test (DCAT) relative to other aptitude measures is its development of items in terms of Bloom's Taxonomy of Educational Objectives. Schools which develop educational objectives based on that taxonomy may find this categorization of items useful in planning and evaluating instructional programs for individual students. The inclusion of some application items might be viewed by others as a weakness in terms of traditional aptitude assessment. For example, several of the application items on the spatial subtest resemble mechanical reasoning or mathematics and science achievement items more than classical spatial visualization items of the type used on the Revised Minnesota Paper Form Board or the spatial subtest of the Differential Aptitude Test. To illustrate, consider the question of comparing the volume of two solid figures given their relevant dimensions. Such criticism would not bother the publishers since they acknowledge the DCAT differs from more traditional aptitude tests in its focus on "those cognitive abilities that can be altered through instruction."

Reliability as assessed by a measure of internal consistency (KR-20) is fairly high for all levels and forms for both the verbal and spatial subtests. Estimates for the quantitative subtest tend to be lower (e.g., ranging from .60 to .68) for level 5/6 for grades 5, 6, and 7. No test-retest studies are reported. Parallel forms are highly correlated with respect to the composite score but evidence somewhat lower correlations for the spatial subtests. There appears to be a problem of ceiling at grade 12 on the verbal subtest; the mean and median are 21 and 22 for 26 items with a standard deviation of about 5. Thus a perfect score of 26 in grade 12 is ranked at the 95th percentile.

The technical manual provides rather limited evidence of the test's validity. Tables of correlations with the achievement subtests of the Comprehensive Assessment Program Achievement Series are provided. The verbal subtest tends to correlate highly with the verbal achievement subtests, particularly reading. The correlations among mathematics achievement measures and the quantitative and spatial subtests are more modest. Inspection of the items in the verbal and quantitative subtests suggested that the DCAT is similar to other well-developed tests such as the Scholastic Aptitude Test (SAT) and the School and College Abilities Test (SCAT). No studies are reported, however, comparing the DCAT with similar measures. Such research is needed, especially in the case of the spatial subtest.

A great deal of time, effort, and thought appears to have gone into the construction of the DCAT. In time it may well become a widely used and respected measure of developing intellectual abilities. Its potential for diagnostic-prescriptive instructional planning in relationship to the taxonomy could indeed make it more generally useful than other more traditional aptitude measures. At present the reliability and predictive validity studies are not as extensive and impressive as for some other tests such as the SAT and SCAT. This does not negate its potential for immediate use, but more research is needed to establish whether or not the test has predictive powers equivalent to, greater than, or less than more traditional measures. For now, the user should be cautioned about the ways in which this test might be closer to an achievement measure or different from other aptitude measures. In this case different may indeed eventually prove better.

[322]

Developmental Activities Screening Inventory. Ages 6–60 months; 1976–77; DASI; no data on reliability; no norms; no information on how basal age and item-month equivalents were determined; individual; manual ('77, 51 pages); response sheet ('76, 2 pages); some testing materials must be assembled locally; 1983 price data: $99 per complete set including 50 response sheets; $7 per 100 response sheets; (25) minutes; Rebecca F. DuBose and Mary Beth Langley; DLM Teaching Resources.*

TEST REFERENCES

1. Petersen, G. A., & Sherrod, K. B. Relationship of maternal language to language development and language delay of children. AMERICAN JOURNAL OF MENTAL DEFICIENCY, 1982, 86, 391–398.

Review of Developmental Activities Screening Inventory by CARL J. DUNST, Director, Family, Infant and Preschool Program, Western Carolina Center, Morganton, NC:

The Developmental Activities Screening Inventory (DASI) is an informally administered, nonverbal screening instrument designed for use with children functioning between 6 and 60 months of age. The DASI was specifically developed for use with retarded, handicapped, developmentally disabled, and sensory impaired children as a means for translating assessment data into "practical applications for educational programs." This scale was developed as a nonverbal screening tool so that it did not penalize children with auditory impairments or language disorders.

The DASI includes 55 test items divided into nine five-month age groups that typically have six items per group. The manual includes explicit instructions on administration of the test items. Adaptations for administration of test items to visually impaired children are described as part of the administration procedures. The manual presents only one case study to illustrate the procedures involved in administering, scoring, interpreting, and utilizing the assessment results. Procedures for determining basal, ceiling, and a child's "overall" developmental level of performance are not described. The manual sorely needs more descriptive information regarding scoring of DASI results. The potential user of the DASI would also benefit immensely from more illustrative examples and case studies of how results are interpreted and used for intervention purposes. As written, the manual lacks clarity and its potential usefulness is not fully described.

The majority of items on the DASI were presumably taken from existing infant and preschool tests. The items include such varied behaviors as: lifts cup by handle, imitates scribble, builds tower of 3–4 blocks, strings four beads, demonstrates the use of six objects, copies cross, imitates two-step vertical paper fold, identifies five colors by name, and counts to 10. Presumably, the placement of items at particular age ranges was based on age placements of the items on the tests from which they were taken. Because the DASI was not standardized on a representative sample of normally developing children, these ages as well as the developmental levels derived from them must be considered gross estimates of developmental status. The DASI should therefore be considered an experimental scale, and is not recommended for use in determining age-level developmental status in lieu of a better standardized instrument.

Reliability and validity studies with both normal children and children for whom the DASI was developed are essentially lacking. The test manual reports no data relevant for determination of interobserver (scorer) agreement, short- or long-term stability, or internal consistency reliability. A computer literature search of 10 data bases by the reviewer yielded no studies which have examined the reliability of the DASI.

Three investigations have been conducted which have examined the concurrent validity of the DASI. The criterion measures in these studies included the Cattell Infant Intelligence Scale, the Merrill-Palmer Scale of Mental Tests, the Preschool Attainment Record, and the Denver Developmental Screening Test. Validity coefficients ranged from .87 to .97 (median=.92). These coefficients are probably inflated and spuriously high for several reasons. First, the dependent measures in these studies were age levels, and because the subjects tended to cover a wide age range (7 to 74 months in one study), one would expect such high correlations. Correlations with chronological age partialed out would provide a better estimate of the concurrent validity of the DASI. Second, if the items on the DASI were taken from the tests which were used as the criterion measures, the high correlations would, in part, be due to the fact that the DASI and the criterion tests are measuring the same behaviors! The authors interpret the high correlations between the DASI and the criterion measures as evidence for the criterion-related validity of the DASI. This is a misinterpretation of the data. The high correlations are more indicative of prediction of levels of performance; they do not indicate that the DASI and criterion measures are assessing the same behavioral construct.

The ultimate test of the validity of a screening instrument is how well it predicts the presence of the actual problems/deficits it is intended to identify. Yet no such studies have been conducted with the DASI. Until such investigations are undertaken, the DASI must be considered an experimental test that cannot and should not be used for diagnostic screening purposes. Its use must be limited to a rough determination of behaviors which are and are not in a child's repertoire without reference to predictive value. The DASI is the type of test that is sorely needed in assessment and evaluation work with young preschool children who are at-risk for subsequent learning related problems. It is most unfortunate that appropriate attention was not paid to establishing its reliability and validity when the scale was constructed.

SUMMARY. The DASI is a nonverbal screening instrument designed to be used as an assessment tool for identifying appropriate early educational interventions with preschool retarded, handicapped, developmentally disabled, and sensory impaired children. This scale is an unstandardized developmental assessment instrument, and reliability and validity studies with the DASI are essentially lacking. The idea of the development of a nonverbal assessment tool for use with a population often lacking in verbal abilities is a laudable one. However, the scale as it currently exists is psychometrically deficient, and consequently the DASI must be considered an experimental scale which yields only a rough indication of a child's nonverbal behavior competencies. Until properly standardized and validated, its use is perhaps best restricted to an assessment of current behavior capabilities within a narrowly constricted area of development. It is highly recommended that the scale not be used for determining developmental age levels of performance since there is no evidence to support such use.

[323]

Developmental Activities Screening Inventory—II. Birth to 60 months; 1977–84; DASI-II; revision and downward extension of still-in-print Developmental Activities Screening Inventory (DASI); behavior checklist "designed to provide early detection of developmental disabilities"; no data on reliability; no norms; no information on how item-month equivalents are determined; individual; manual ('84, 103 pages); picture cards ('84, 57 cards); other test materials (e.g., formboard, bells) must be supplied by examiner; response form ('84, 2 pages); 1984 price data: $39 per set of testing materials including manual, picture cards and 50 response forms;

$11 per 50 response forms; $19 per manual; $12 per set of 57 picture cards; (25–30) minutes; Rebecca R. Fewell and Mary Beth Langley; PRO-ED.*

TEST REFERENCES

1. Petersen, G. A., & Sherrod, K. B. Relationship of maternal language to language development and language delay of children. AMERICAN JOURNAL OF MENTAL DEFICIENCY, 1982, 86, 391–398.

[324]

Developmental Assessment for the Severely Handicapped. Individuals functioning within the 0–6 year developmental range; 1980; DASH; criterion-referenced; 5 developmental areas: language, sensory-motor, social-emotional, activities of daily living, preacademic; criterion performance levels 1–7; individual; 1 form in 5 booklets: language (38 pages), sensory-motor (31 pages), social-emotional (23 pages), activities of daily living (28 pages), preacademic (47 pages); administration manual (84 pages); comprehensive program record (2 pages); daily plan sheet (1 page); individualized educational plan (4 pages); numerous additional accessories must be supplied by examiner; 1985 price data: $85 per complete kit; $35 per 10 copies of any 1 scale; $15 per 50 individualized educational plans; (120–180) minutes; Mary Kay Dykes; Exceptional Resources, Inc.*

Review of Developmental Assessment for the Severely Handicapped by HARVEY N. SWITZKY, Professor of Learning, Development, and Special Education, Faculty of Special Education, Northern Illinois University, DeKalb, IL:

The purposes of the Developmental Assessment for the Severely Handicapped (DASH) assessment system are to provide a developmentally sequenced, fine-grained, behaviorally defined, criterion-referenced measure of current and developing skills in five skill domains: language, sensory-motor, social-emotional, activities of daily living, and preacademic for severely, multiply handicapped or developmentally young children. The DASH assessment system may be useful in identifying and measuring very discrete changes in behavior in very low functioning individuals so as to pinpoint skills and facilitate training of skills within the Individualized Educational Plan process. The DASH assessment system is one of the best organized assessment/curricular systems commercially available for low functioning children, and it provides a good framework for assessment as well as for intervention. The DASH system provides a complete set of forms for assessment of programming including a history protocol, a cumulative summary sheet of developmental information, a priority intervention worksheet which is used to determine developmental task sequences for intervention, an individualized education plan sheet, a daily plan sheet of individual programs which provides individualized daily behavioral skill goals and the level obtained each day, and a comprehensive program record which can be used to record weekly student progress.

The DASH assessment system is organized around sequences of developmental behavior that nonhandicapped children pass through in our society. Users of this system need to be aware of the controversies regarding the use of the normal developmental model as a basis for the assessment of behavioral skill domains and the setting of curricular behavioral skill objectives for severely handicapped children (Switzky, Rotatori, Miller, & Freagon, 1979; Switzky, 1979; Switzky, 1981) before using the DASH system as the author recommends.

The DASH assessment system has many fine features. The four behavioral skill domains (Language, Sensory-Motor, Social-Emotional, and Activities of Daily Living) provide fine-grained, well defined, developmentally sequenced, behavioral and criterion-referenced "Pinpoint Item Statements" from a developmental age of 2 years to 8 years. Thus there is quite a range of items especially at low levels of development, an aspect of the DASH assessment system important to educators of low functioning children and youth.

The DASH assessment system is a well thought out assessment/curricular approach, i.e., the items for assessment also make up the content of the curriculum. This approach makes the DASH system very easy and compact to use.

The author is very attentive to problems of test reliability and validity and provides good instructions to the test user on how to collect sources of information regarding students in natural ecological settings, i.e., in the living environments where students reside, an extremely important consideration. The DASH system is the only commercially available device that I am aware of that explicitly asks the users to observe individuals in their own environment. The author makes a strong attempt to operationalize the definition of levels of performance of behavioral pinpoints on a 7-point scale of competence and to define explicitly frequencies of behavior.

The DASH can be used for either diagnostic or screening purposes, a very useful feature. For diagnostic purposes, all the items on a pinpoint scale are administered; for screening purposes only a subset of items (items in capital letters) are administered.

The DASH provides a very thorough set of forms and easy-to-use pinpoint scales which are easier to use than the developmental resources on which they are based (i.e., the Bayley Scales of Infant Development, Gesell and Amatruda's Developmental Diagnosis, etc.).

The author also claims that the DASH has good internal consistency and construct validity. The information regarding internal reliability needs to be confirmed in further research. Examination of the pinpoint scales leaves no doubt that they are developmentally based to a high degree.

The author provides very good instructions to users regarding administration. I do not foresee even the most naive user having problems in understanding how the DASH system works.

There are problems in actually using the DASH system, however. The pinpoint scales require relatively experienced and sophisticated evaluation personnel. Users of this system need to have a sound background in developmental and behavioral programming. The sensory-motor pinpoint scale may require the expertise of a registered occupational or physical therapist. The language pinpoint scale may require an experienced speech clinician. The educational model of the author views professional personnel as assessors and program developers, and managers and paraprofessional personnel as the actual instructors and teachers of severely handicapped students. Thus the DASH system may only be useful in agencies and schools organized around this educational model and possessing relatively sophisticated personnel.

Though an attempt is made by the author to operationalize levels of performance of behavioral pinpoints on a 7-point scale of competence, I expect that the middlemost levels of competence may be hard to distinguish from one another. More importantly the author makes no attempt to deal with the problems of behavioral lability of students' behavioral skills, a notorious and difficult problem in assessing the behavioral repertoire of severely handicapped children and youth (Switzky & Rotatori, 1981). There is no built-in check on the consistency of the student's behavioral repertoire over days. (The author does have a 2 out of 3 criterion of item completion in order to determine student basal and ceiling competence on the scales of behavioral pinpoints at an individual assessment.) The concern I have is that a student may fail to perform an item on a single occasion but show competent behavior a few days later. Because it does not require repeated assessment over days, the DASH system may give false low readings.

The DASH system, like other assessment systems for the severely handicapped, provides no real criterion-referenced validity for behavioral items (i.e., how generalizable over persons, places, and objects are the student's responses).

The author's attempt to measure basal and ceiling levels of developmental competence requires a great deal of sophistication on the part of the test user. However, this information provides an empirical operationalization within a developmental model of the operating characteristics of an individual learner. The calculations of a developmental age may provide a very crude index of growth. It would be more appropriate and useful to derive a mastery skill level regarding a particular behavioral goal independent of developmental age. The relevance of developing an overall developmental age which weights equally each developmental pinpoint scale escapes me.

The DASH assessment system is overall a fine assessment/curricular approach for the severely handicapped. It is well designed and thoughtfully organized. School systems and organizations with access to relatively sophisticated and professional personnel will derive the most benefit from the DASH system. In my opinion it is the best commercially published system that is presently available for assessment and curriculum construction for the severely handicapped.

REVIEWER'S REFERENCES

Switzky, H. N. Assessment of the severely and profoundly handicapped child. In D. A. Sabatino & T. L. Miller (Eds.), DESCRIBING LEARNING CHARACTERISTICS FOR SPECIAL EDUCATION INSTRUCTION. Grune & Stratton, 1979.

Switzky, H. N., Rotatori, A. F., Miller, T., & Freagon, S. The developmental model and its implications for assessment and instruction for the severely/profoundly handicapped. MENTAL RETARDATION, 1979, 17, 167–170.

Switzky, H. N. Book review of Curricular Design for the Severely and Profoundly Retarded. Paul Wehman, Human Science Press. AMERICAN JOURNAL OF MENTAL DEFICIENCY, 1981, 85, 441.

Switzky, H. N., & Rotatori, A. Assessment of perceptual-cognitive functioning in non-verbal severely/profoundly handicapped children. EARLY CHILD DEVELOPMENT AND CARE, 1981, 7, 29–44.

Review of Developmental Assessment for the Severely Handicapped by DAVID P. WACKER, Coordinator of Research, Division of Developmental Disabilities, University of Iowa, Iowa City, IA:

The Developmental Assessment for the Severely Handicapped (DASH) is "a criterion-referenced system that provides a means of measuring, programming and tracking skills across five developmental areas: language, sensory-motor, social-emotional, activities of daily living, preacademic." As an assessment instrument, the DASH is intended to be used as "a screening or diagnostic instrument...to determine an overall functioning level or to determine specific strengths and weaknesses in each or all of the aforementioned developmental areas." Evaluation can be completed either through direct observation or through interviews with individuals knowledgeable about the functioning of the child. Each scale is divided into three or four 24-month age ranges (usually beginning at birth), and every item contains an approximate age or age range in which the behavior should occur. The programming component of DASH follows directly from assessment. Results of assessment are entered onto the Cumulative Summary Sheet which serves to facilitate the identification of strengths and weaknesses across the developmental areas. Once these strengths and weaknesses have been identified, the Priority Intervention Worksheet is used to determine training needs. Priorities for instruction are established in the Individualized Educational Plan, and specific intervention strategies are listed on the Daily Plan Sheet. Finally, evaluation of performance is conducted utilizing the Comprehensive Program Record and/or readministration of the five assessment scales. Therefore, DASH is intended to be a comprehensive assessment and programming system for severely and multiply handicapped children who are functioning at or below 96 months.

ASSESSMENT COMPONENT OF DASH. Dykes emphasizes that multiple examples of behavior at very young developmental ages are needed to appropriately evaluate the functioning of multiply or severely handicapped children. In addition, Dykes states that assessments of these children need to be "sensitive to even small behavior changes." In accordance with these recommendations, the greatest number of items in the developmental scales are located in the lower age ranges (e.g., in the Sensory-Motor Scale, 113 items are provided for the 0 through 23 months section; 20 items in the 71 through 96 months section), and scoring of items is conducted on a seven-point scale with "7" indicating the child can complete the task without assistance, and "1" indicating that the child cannot complete the task and resists assistance provided by the examiner.

The major difficulty of the assessment component of the DASH is that the research and development information provided in the Administration Manual is incomplete. Dykes states that research concerning the development of the DASH has been ongoing since 1973, but only one study conducted in 1978 was reported in the Administration Manual. The study reported correlations between the developmental ages achieved with the DASH and the Bayley Scales of Infant Development or the Developmental Activities Screening Inventory (DASI). Subjects were "fifteen severely and multiply handicapped children from two public school classes and from an institution for the retarded." The only other subject information provided was chronological age (between 5 and 16 years). The correlations were .97 for the overall scores, and .98, .91, .86, and .10 for the Social-Emotional, Language, Daily Living, and Sensory-Motor Scales respectively. In interpreting the findings, Dykes states that "Since the Bayley and DASI have been determined to be primarily measures of mental or cognitive abilities, this may account for the somewhat lower correlation with the Activities of Daily Living Pinpoint Scale and the lack of correlation with the Sensory-Motor Pinpoint Scale of DASH."

Several aspects of these data are tenuous or incomplete in establishing the validity of the DASH. For example, the intercorrelations of the scales are not reported and no data are reported which establish the validity of the Sensory-Motor or Preacademic scales. Dykes reports that the "content and construction [sic] validity are regarded as high for the DASH since all item core behaviors appear on other developmental scales for which validity has already been demonstrated." However, most of the developmental scales which Dykes used to select items were not normed on severely and multiply handicapped children, necessitating the need to conduct further validity studies with these items. In addition, no instructions are provided in the Administration Manual regarding how children with motoric or sensory impairments should be scored, except that Dykes states that sign language instructions may be substituted for oral instructions. Even this may cause problems in scoring several of the items in the Language Scale (e.g., "makes several different sounds in one breath"). Since no information is provided regarding how to change the items or scoring procedures for children with motoric or sensory impairments, and no studies are reported which establish the validity of the DASH for individuals with various disabilities, it is premature to state that the DASH is valid with severely and multiply handicapped children. In addition, several aspects of the item composition of the subscales raise concerns regarding what the scales actually measure. Several items within and between scales appear to be very similar. Other items, as Dykes points out, appear to measure general cognitive ability rather than skills specific to a given scale.

With respect to reliability, the only data reported in the Administration Manual is odd-even reliability (.99), presumably across all scales. Further analyses are needed, including reliability estimates for each age-month level and for each of the separate subscales. In addition, the reliability of the seven-point rating scale needs to be investigated across examiners. Several items appear to be difficult to score using this scale (e.g., "does not offer to share possessions with other children"). If a child does not demonstrate this behavior, does he or she receive a "1" and fail the item?

PROGRAMMING COMPONENT OF THE DASH. The major advantages of the DASH over most other instruments are the attempts to provide multiple examples of behavior at young age ranges and the development of a scoring method which attempts to measure the conditions under which behavior occurs. Unfortunately, the validity and reliability of the items and scoring procedures are unknown, making it impossible to evaluate how adequately the DASH can be used as a programming system. However, many of the items appear too general or vague to be translatable into direct programming. In addition, no guidelines are provided concerning when a behavior should be targeted for remediation, or how one should proceed to remediate the behavior. As a result, one is left with assessment data indicating general strengths and weaknesses, which may not be much different than what is provided with any other developmental assessment procedure. Also, if the aim is to teach the test items, the validity of programming may be questionable.

SUMMARY. Data which establish the reliability and validity of the DASH system are needed before the adequacy of the DASH can be evaluated. The preliminary data reported by Dykes indicate that the DASH should continue to be developed, but the use of this system in applied settings appears premature.

[325]

Developmental Communication Inventory. Children functioning at developmental levels from birth to age 5 who are severely communicatively handicapped or speech and language delayed or non-handicapped; 1982; DCI; a component in the Developmental Communication Curriculum program, used to determine the child's eligibility and placement in the program; part 2 consists of a behavior checklist for use in interviewing adult informants; part 1 consists of an observation of child on 16 developmentally sequenced tasks in 5 areas: response to task, attention span, response to teacher, reactions to play experience, planning and structuring of play; no data on reliability and validity; no norms; individual; 1 form consists of 2 parts in a single booklet (21 pages); curriculum guide (138 pages); activity handbook (331 pages); parent news (24 pages); 1985 price data: $65 per complete program including 12 tests and 12 parent news; $12.95 per 12 tests; $12.95 per 12 parent news; $18.95 per activities handbook; $13.95 per curriculum guide; administration time not reported; Rosemarie P. Hanna, Emily A. Lippert, and Ann B. Harris; Charles E. Merrill Publishing Co.*

[326]

Developmental Indicators for the Assessment of Learning—Revised. Ages 2–6; 1983; DIAL-R; revision of still-in-print Developmental Indicators for the Assessment of Learning (DIAL); a screening test to identify children with potential learning problems who require follow-up diagnosis; 4 scores: motor, concepts, language, total; norms consist of means and standard deviations; individual; 1 form; manual (108 pages); directions for administering: motor (12 pages), concepts (8 pages), language (11 pages); score sheet (2 pages); parent information form (2 pages); cutting card (2 pages); some testing materials must be supplied by examiner; optional activity card system available; 1984 price data: $149.95 per set of testing materials including manual; $4.25 per 50 score sheets; $4.25 per 50 parent information forms; $4.25 per 100 cutting cards; $3.95 per set of 3 administration booklets; $8.50 per manual; (20–30) minutes; Carol D. Mardell-Czudnowski and Dorothea S. Goldenberg; Childcraft Education Corporation.*

See T3:696 (2 references); for reviews by J. Jeffrey Grill and James J. McCarthy of an earlier edition, see 8:428 (3 references).

TEST REFERENCES

1. Mardell-Czudnowski, C. D. Validity and reliability studies with DIAL. JOURNAL FOR SPECIAL EDUCATORS, 1980, 17, 32–45.

[327]

Developmental Profile II. Birth to age 9; 1972–80; identical with original 1972 edition except for deletion of items for ages 10–12; ratings in 5 areas: physical, self-help, social, academic, communication; individual; 1 form ('80, 15 pages); manual ('80, 66 pages including test and set of scoring forms); scoring and report form ('80, 7 pages); 1983 price data: $23.50 per manual plus 15 profile and scoring forms; $8.25 per 30 profile and scoring forms; $18.25 per manual; (20–40) minutes; Gerald D. Alpern, Thomas J. Boll, and Marsha S. Shearer; Psychological Development Publications.*

See T3:698 (5 references); for a review by Jane V. Hunt of the original edition, see 8:215 (1 reference).

Review of Developmental Profile II by DENNIS C. HARPER, Associate Professor of Pediatric Psychology, University of Iowa, Iowa City, IA:

The Developmental Profile II (DPII) is a revision of the 1972 Developmental Profile (DP) modified by the authors to reflect user feedback and comply with changing emphases in providing services to handicapped children. It was designed initially as a multidimensional inventory to estimate developmental level in five basic areas: physical skill, self-help, social, academic, and communication. The original DP has enjoyed rather widespread acceptance, as evidenced by its appearance in a variety of research publications. As in the original edition, each subscale has two to three items at each test age in 6-month intervals through 3 years and yearly thereafter until approximately 9 years of age. The ceiling on the DPII has been shortened from 10 to 12 years to 9 years. No specific educational requirements are needed for the interviewer. Scores continue to be presented as age equivalents in each of the five developmental areas, and a ratio IQ equivalent score, IQE, can be computed from the academic scale outcome.

Modification of the DPII consists of deletion of items for ages 10 to 12, clarification and rewording of directions, inclusion of a graphic display of a child's performance (Profile Sheet), removal of sexist language, and the addition of practical assessment suggestions for the user. No additional field testing was completed for the 1980 DPII. Although changes have primarily been cosmetic, they are well thought out and add clarity in format and general instructions.

Item development as described in the original edition (1972) was based upon selection of 318 items from the child development literature placed in an age framework. These 318 items were subsequently standardized on a population of 3,008 normal subjects, excluding those with medical, emotional, or physical impairments. An equal distribution of subjects by age and sex was obtained and evaluated by trained interviewers. Careful attention was devoted primarily to selecting infants and children who were developing normally. The 318 items in the initial pool were examined in the standardization process, and items were retained if they met the guidelines for age discrimination (70 to 80% of the sample passed), and were nondiscriminatory as to sex, social class and race. In the original edition (1972) this standardization review resulted in 217 items across the five scales. In the DPII the items were reduced to 186 by eliminating those at the 10 to 12 year age ranges.

The number of children examined at each 6-month interval below 4 years ranged from 91 to 202, and from 227 to 261 for children 4 to 9 years old. The sample was drawn predominantly from Indiana (2,730 or 91%), 278 or 9% came from Washington, and the majority of families (89%) resided in large urban areas. Racial and social class characteristics of the standardization sample were: 84% white, 14% black, and 2% other; and 80% middle class, 11% upper class, and 9% lower class. Generally these sample frequencies are consistent with national population percentages. The authors note that the DPII is most appropriate for urban white and black children in the Midwest and suggest more cautious interpretation for youngsters from small rural locations.

Accuracy of maternal report in the standardization process was carefully monitored to increase initial reliability and validity of the instrument. This process consisted of a combination of objective and subjective rating scales designed to verify the consistency and accuracy of maternal item reports and eliminate questionable protocols. Several studies were attempted to ascertain various types of validity of the DP. Volunteer mothers of 100 children were asked to report on their child's present development while concurrent direct assessment was attempted on each child. Using approximately 60% of the item pool, the authors revealed 86% average agreement for items over the five basic scales, with no bias for race or sex. It can be concluded that maternal report can be consistent with direct assessment. The authors acknowledge that this percent of agreement may be less accurate when the evaluation is of more personal importance. Two studies are reported in the manual offering information on the correspondence between standard intelligence estimates and the IQE. Fifty-four children (mean IQ=51) were administered the DP, Academic Scale by their teachers. The average correlation between the Stanford-Binet IQ (SBIQ) and the IQE was .85, and 69% of the sample obtained an IQ and IQE within 10 points of each other. Sixteen normal volunteer mothers and children were concurrently administered the Academic Scale and the Stanford-Binet. These normal data revealed that they received lower scores on the IQE as compared to their SBIQ. In summary, these data suggest that the IQE has a tendency to overestimate when sample IQs are low and underestimate with an above average sample. As with most screening instruments, these data also indicate that the DPII may readily misclassify children.

Three studies (two on the DP, one utilizing the DPII) provide further information for the user. Prout, Harper, Snider, and Lindgren (1978), using the DP to contrast maternal and teacher reports on 35 moderate to severely handicapped youth (mean age=13 years, mean IQ=39) in relation to SBIQ, found significant differences between mothers and teachers on the Physical, Self-Help, and Communication Scales. Correlations between the SBIQ and IQE for mothers and teachers were nonsignificant. Extent of agreement between SBIQ and IQE for mothers and teachers were nonsignificant. Extent of agreement between SBIQ and IQE was lower for mothers (57% within 10 points) than for teachers (83% within 10 points). Gradel, Thompson, and Sheehan (1981), using the DP as one tool, evaluated multiple methods of assessment on 60 handicapped children (30 infants, 30 preschoolers) and reported adequate concurrent agreement of the DP with other early standard instruments. The study identified maternal overestimation of development as a common feature of early assessment. Finally, the DPII was compared to the Revised Denver Developmental Screening Test (RDDST) as a screening tool with preschool children (German, Williams, Herzfeld, & Marshall). Results obtained from evaluating 84 children referred for suspected developmental delay with both instruments revealed that accuracy of screening outcome for either instrument is a function of intended diagnostic criteria and that generally the RDDST under-refers fewer children than the DPII, while the DPII over-refers far fewer children.

Interscorer reliability was assessed by the authors, who required 35 teachers to score the report of the same parent interview following an instruction session. This method indicated that 25 of the teachers (71%) had identical scores and no teachers disagreed on more than two test items. Finally, scorer reliability, reporter reliability, and test-retest reliability were assessed on 11 children and mothers. Repeated administration of the DP by two interviewers, alternating parents on 2- to 3-day intervals, revealed that 50% of the test-retest scores were within 1 point and 92% were within 3 points, suggesting very adequate test-retest and inter-interviewer reliability of the DP.

It should be emphasized that, at present, the majority of information verifying the DPII is based upon the original edition (1972); however, the DPII is not substantially different from the earlier version. Since its appearance, research information has accumulated suggesting that this tool can provide a reasonably accurate and brief review of developmental strengths and weaknesses for children from birth to 9 years of age. The DPII appears to meet the more current demands of users by its acknowledgment of P.L. 94–142 and deletion of sexist language. As noted in earlier reviews, the DP is a good instrument to elicit multiple views of a child. When consensus is apparent, programming may proceed with greater confidence. Where discrepancies exist, it should prompt us to identify the sources of these differing perceptions. Discrepancies may not only reflect rater bias, but also observational and functional differences of settings in which we view the child.

The DPII is one of many screening tools available. The present evidence would suggest that the DPII may have advantages over the RDDST when predicting language delay, or when seeking a more moderate outcome rate when one does not want to over-refer. Furthermore, users of the DPII must select the instrument if it coincides with their particular sample characteristics (white, black, midwest, urban).

The developers should be applauded for expending considerable effort in offering a number of practical suggestions based upon their own clinical experience in examining children. The manual, if reviewed carefully, can offer a very appropriate evaluation "mind set" to the inexperienced interviewer. There are numerous graphic displays of where to begin testing, suggested logic and procedures for various assessment decisions, cross-classification of demographic sample characteristics, simple scoring directions, an abbreviated assessment method, clarifications for the user on phrasing questions to elicit more accurate data from respondents, and repeated cautions on over-interpretation of developmental delays. Special recognition should be paid to the authors for their attempt to discuss the question of when a delay is significant. This is followed by a set of tables derived from the authors' clinical experience, offering at least some guidelines for when to refer for further opinions. This would appear a very useful chart for most inexperienced users.

REVIEWER'S REFERENCES

German, M. L., Williams, E., Herzfeld, J., & Marshall, R. M. UTILITY OF THE REVISED DENVER DEVELOPMENTAL SCREENING TEST AND THE DEVELOPMENTAL PROFILE II IN IDENTIFYING PRESCHOOL CHILDREN WITH COGNITIVE, LANGUAGE, AND MOTOR PROBLEMS. Unpublished article available from Children's Evaluation Center of Southern Arizona, 332 S. Freeway, Tuscon, AZ 85745.

Prout, H. T., Harper, D. C., Snider, B., & Lindgren, S. Comparisons between mothers' and teachers' evaluations of developmental status. JOURNAL OF PEDIATRIC PSYCHOLOGY, 1978, 3(2), 57–61.

Gradel, K., Thompson, M. S., & Sheehan, R. Parental and professional agreement in early childhood assessment. TECSE, 1981, 1(2), 31–39.

Review of Developmental Profile II by SUE WHITE, Assistant Professor of Psychology, Case Western Reserve University, School of Medicine, Cuyahoga County Hospital, Cleveland, OH:

The Developmental Profile II (DPII) is a developmental scale of 186 items fairly equally divided into five scales: physical, self-help, social, academic, and communication. Norms are presented for age levels in six-month intervals from birth to 4 years and then at year intervals thereafter. Most age levels contain three items per scale. Criterion for passing an item is whether the child has the skill as judged either by an interviewer directly observing the behavior or by report of the primary caregiver. It is designed to be given by teachers and other trained school personnel.

It appears to provide a means of evaluating some very important areas of development. Historically linked to the Vineland Social Maturity Scale, it attempts to provide five individual scores to determine a child's strengths and weaknesses. The authors repeatedly relate its use to the evaluation and placements of children according to P. L. 94–142 mandates. This particular use is inappropriate, but the DPII could serve as a screening instrument for the five assessed skills. With proper standardization, it could also replace the outdated Vineland in its assessment of socialization and self-help skills in a complete psychological evaluation.

There are major difficulties with the DPII's development. Alpern and Shearer's 1980 revision of the 1972 Developmental Profile is based on clinical feedback from users. As a result, the DPII was shortened, and all items were eliminated beyond nine years chronological age as well as "inappropriate, outdated, or sexist" items. Some of the language was changed to reflect nonsexist terminology, and some directions were clarified. In spite of these changes, however, there is no indication in the description of the standardization sample that the scale was restandardized on a new population. It seems that the norms presented are representative of a 1970 child. The revision date of 1980 is thus misleading if the user is assuming an updated test. The described changes in the test items could have altered children's responses.

In reviewing the 1972 norms, there are further questions raised. One of the author's goals was to present a scale with no bias as a function of sex, race, or social class. This goal was not met. Overall the sex distribution was fairly even (males = 1,527, females = 1,481), but in individual age groups, there were occasional serious discrepancies (i.e., 2 to 2.5 years: 60 males, 35 females). The white/black ratio (84% white, 14% black) was overall fairly equal to the U.S. population percentages. Again in individual age groups, however, the percentages varied from a 69% white and 24% black split at 0 to 6 months to 91% white and 9% black at 6 years. In spite of this range, the authors feel that the scale is "adequately standardized and constructed for valid use with black children." With respect to social class norms, the authors admit that "social class representation was accomplished less formally" than the other parameters. As a result the lower class is presented as 9% of the sample, middle class is 80%, and upper class is 11%, although the ranges vary greatly.

Another question relating to norms concerns the number of children included at each age level. The original goal of a minimum of 200 subjects at each YEAR level was accomplished, but this varies from 222 to 341. In addition, one might assume that because the DPII attempts to present norms for half-year levels from birth to 4 years that those half-year norms should be considered separate and the number of subjects should be equivalent to the number for the year levels. The authors concluded that for these seven half-year levels, the distribution was sufficient for valid use even though they ranged from 91 to 202 subjects per level.

Another problem which is discussed but not made part of the introductory description of the DPII is the fact that the standardization was primarily completed in Indiana (91% Indiana; 9% Washington). The urban population (89% of sample) was from Indianapolis or Seattle. The authors argue that because the test has had nationwide dissemination, it should be useful with urban populations throughout the U.S. This reviewer disagrees. Just because someone buys a test does not mean that it automatically becomes appropriate for the intended population. This issue of applicability should be discussed in the opening remarks.

Several purposes of the DPII appear to be useful ones for the classroom teacher. These include a multidimensional description of a child's development with specific disregard of the child as a "35 IQ" rather than viewing his/her other strengths and weaknesses. In spite of this effort to move away from classifying children by IQs, the DPII provides for an IQ Equivalency Score (IQE) based on only one of the five individual scales. Using the score from the Academic scale, a formula is presented to obtain an IQE score with which to classify and track children into specific programs. The data presented to defend this use were weak. First, scores of 54 retarded subjects were correlated with their IQ score on the Binet. A second study was completed with only 16 normal children. Since there are only two academic items per age level in the first three age levels and three in the remaining, it is not appropriate to determine an IQE score based on such little data. Based on this meager amount of data, IQE scores from the DPII should NOT be used at all.

In summary, the DPII may well have merits in screening young children for determining the need for further evaluation, but the results should not be used for classifying children according to specific programs. The IQE should be eliminated because of its potential for abuse. Further standardization should be undertaken on a more representative, nationwide sample before being used nationwide.

[328]

Developmental Tasks for Kindergarten Readiness. Children prior to kindergarten entrance; 1978; DTKR; 12 subtest scores: social interaction, name printing, body concepts, auditory sequencing, auditory association, visual discrimination, visual memory, visual motor, color naming, relational concepts, number knowledge, alphabet knowledge; individual; 1 form (12 pages); manual (54 pages); materials book (20 cards); 1984 price data: $30 per complete kit including manual, stimulus cards, and 25 record booklets; $18.50 per 25 record booklets; $6 per stimulus cards; $7 per manual; (20–30) minutes; Walter J. Lesiak, Jr.; Clinical Psychology Publishing Co., Inc.*

Review of Developmental Tasks for Kindergarten Readiness by CAROL A. GRAY, Director, Clinical Services and Research Center, University of Washington, Seattle, WA:

The Developmental Tasks for Kindergarten Readiness (DTKR) is described by the author as "an assessment of abilities and skills in preschool children to determine kindergarten readiness." The test was designed to be administered either prior to kindergarten entry or during the early weeks of kindergarten. The test was normed for children in the range of four years, six months to six years, two months of age. The DTKR is actually made up of 12 subtests with separate scores for each and no composite readiness score. This lack of a composite score was designed to discourage the use of the test as a means of deciding whether a child is or is not ready to enter kindergarten. The 12 subtests are drawn from other similar tests, preschool and kindergarten curricula, and standard developmental knowledge. They are clearly oriented toward skills that children might be expected to acquire in a standard preschool experience. Unfortunately, there is no information in the technical part of the manual about whether or not the standardization sample had such an experience and whether it makes a difference in scoring patterns.

The materials for administration include a manual, a spiral bound materials book, and individual test booklets for each child. It is designed to be administered individually by school personnel. The test author states that training (approximately two hours) is advisable prior to administration. The actual time needed for each administration is estimated at 20–30 minutes, with another 30 minutes needed to complete scoring and recording information on the cover sheet of the test booklet. The materials are nicely prepared and appear to be quite durable.

The author takes pains to elaborate his rationale for developing this test and provides a good deal of background information in the opening chapters of the manual. He contends that what is needed is a system of assessing children that provides diagnostic information rather than merely labeling the child. It seems unfortunate that he has included the term "readiness" in the title of the test since it implies that a single readiness score can be extracted. There is, unfortunately, a potential for misuse built into the scoring system. The method of computing and recording individual profile information is cumbersome. The child receives three types of scores for each of the subtests, with the third score recorded in the form of a letter grade. Although the letter grade does not correspond directly to a traditional school grading system, it will be tempting to interpret it that way. Another flaw in the scoring system is the restricted range of norm ratings for some of the subtests in some of the age brackets. The author points out that it is impossible for children to actually receive a "D" in some cases. It appears that in an effort to avoid the use of a numerical scoring system, the author has created a confusing system that may be just as liable to inappropriate interpretation.

The manual is quite explicit in its directions about administration and scoring of most of the subtests although it is somewhat uneven. The major weakness in this area is in "suggestions for interpretation." The weakness would be less serious if the author had not made such an issue of the fact that the greatest strength of this instrument is in the area of diagnostic interpretation. Suggestions for using the information are limited to some rather vague generalizations in Chapter Three (three pages). The section ends by urging the user to consider looking at performance on individual items for clues as to strengths and weaknesses. This is always a risky business since reliability for individual items is typically shaky. The manual would be substantially strengthened by an elaboration of the section on interpretation.

The psychometric qualities of the test receive a great deal of attention in the manual. The author reports that the standardization sample consisted of 2,140 preschool age children. He does point out that there may have been a disproportionate number of low income families represented. At the same time, 90% of the sample was Caucasian. Internal consistency was analyzed using 262 of the sample children. Item analysis revealed that only 4 of the 12 subtests had a majority of items adequately differentiating between high and low performing children, a rather disappointing finding. The split-half reliability data were also disappointing. The split-half reliabilities, uncorrected for length, ranged from .08 to .93, with a mean reliability of .60. These data suggest that some reassessment of the items in each of the subtests is in order. On the other hand, test-retest reliability was a respectable .90 over a two-week period.

The conceptual organization of the subtests was examined using a factor analytic approach as well as by simply looking at the pattern of intercorrelations among subtests. The disappointing results could be the product of some ambiguous items in some of the specific subtests. It seems that if this test as a whole is to be seen as a source of skill specific information for programming purposes, some attention needs to be paid to the subtest structure.

In summary, this test seems to have some strong points. The author has done a thorough job of defining the rationale for the DTKR. His arguments for following a diagnostic/descriptive model are quite convincing, and he appears to have made a sincere effort to create a scoring format that would discourage labeling a child. There are some shortcomings in the scoring system that tend to be more organizational than conceptual.

The greatest problem seems to be in the item makeup of the subtests. Some further work on item analysis is in order. It would seem that this would also possibly lead to a better distribution of predictive power across subtests. In a test that is going to take approximately 30 minutes to administer on an individual basis, it would certainly seem that the user would want to get the most usable information for the investment in time.

Review of Developmental Tasks for Kindergarten Readiness by SUE WHITE, Assistant Professor of Psychology, Case Western Reserve University, School of Medicine, Cuyahoga County Hospital, Cleveland, OH:

While the seeming face validity of the DTKR appears to provide promise of its effectiveness for screening incoming kindergarten students, it has many deficiencies which raise serious questions about its intended use.

The standardization sample of 2,140 preschool children (4 years 6 months through 6 years 2 months) raises issues of representativeness. While the mean age (5 years, 2 months) is representative of children just before their kindergarten year, the inclusion of children who are 6 years and presumably first grade eligible is questioned. No explanation is given of why these older preschoolers are lacking school experience. Also, no indication is given of whether or how children with specific handicapping conditions were excluded from the sample. More information is also needed with reference to demographics, including the children's prior preschool experience and geographic location. The percentage of nonwhite minorities (10%) is lower than the 1970 census figures.

The rationale for the DTKR appears to be valid, but implementation brings to focus several problems. For example, the author's casual attitude towards the selection and training of examiners raises serious concerns. While he recommends that psychologists, teachers, and paraprofessionals are most appropriate for administering the test, he suggests that parents are sometimes suitable, which is highly questionable. Additionally, he feels that adequate training requires about two hours, with each examiner performing only three evaluations before being qualified. Also, no information is provided on the training or reliability of the examiners who administered the DTKR to the standardization population.

Subtest names are misleading, and items are misplaced or confusing (Auditory Association is more of an expressive language task; Auditory Sequencing is more memory; Social Interaction item #11 is body concept (language). Auditory sequence, having two types of items (numerals, words) at each level, may cause response-mode confusion in a child. Also, failure is not reached until a child misses all four items at a level. The score is the highest level reached, regardless of which item at that level is correct. If the DTKR is designed to identify strengths and weaknesses, it falls short in this instance, since performance with numbers and words represent very different tasks.

The child's ability to print his name is scored as part of the Social Interaction subtest, as well as being the only item for Name Printing. This item may be more appropriately placed with Visual Motor skills. A scoring issue with the Body Concepts subtest is that if the examiner must demonstrate the item, the item is considered incorrect. Establishment of a pointing response before the task begins would be preferable.

Visual Motor scoring standards are inadequate in several instances (circle: no "zero" examples; diagonal cross: no degrees of separation, e.g., 90 degrees). Also there is no guideline for judging the location of the point of the triangle.

In relation to scoring in general, several subtests have two-point responses versus zero. With the final score being a percentage of the total possible, one questions this procedure. If it is for ease of computation, fewer errors in computation would occur if conversion tables were provided.

A more practical consideration is the ease of administration. Several subtests are awkward to present (e.g., Visual Memory, Relational Concepts). "Examiner" and "Child" markings on several subtests would assist the examiner in presenting nondirectional items appropriately. Relational Concepts is almost impossible to administer because the examiner must read the instructions from an inverted position. Also, children should be presented with only one task at a time, not two to a page as in Relational Concepts.

Several problems should be noted concerning the statistics for the DTKR. Only 262 of 2,140 protocols were employed to determine internal consistency. Only 121 were used for the Social Interaction scale, which was revised and standardized separately. No sample data were presented for this subscale. Subtest reliabilities as indicated in Table 4 show split-half reliabilities, uncorrected, to range from .08 to .93, an extremely wide variation. A minor note, but indicative when considered with other omissions, is the omission of Visual Discrimination reliabilities from Table 4. The author himself states that all but four tests "failed to have a majority of their items adequately differentiate high and low performers." Test-retest data came from only 93 children in two elementary schools. Demographics were not noted. Half were retested by the original examiner, half by a new one. The reliability coefficients were .92 and .87 respectively. Predictive validity was completed on protocols of 250 children by comparing their scores to Metropolitan Readiness Test scores. Correlations ranged from .20 (Visual Memory) to .62 (total MRT raw score).

It should be clear that the DTKR has many deficiencies. Serious reservations exist which prevent the reviewer from recommending the use of this test for kindergarten screening.

[329]

Developmental Test of Visual-Motor Integration. Ages 2–8, 2–15; 1967–83; VMI; 2 levels; manual ('82, 112 pages); monograph ('67, 46 pages); 1984 price data: $10.98 per monograph and stimulus cards; $9.09 per manual; $4.56 per specimen set (complete test and manual not included); [15–20] minutes; Keith E. Beery and Norman A. Buktenica (test); Modern Curriculum Press.*

a) [SHORT FORM.] Ages 2–8; 1967–82; 1 form ('67, 10 pages, identical with Long Form except for omission of 9 items); $11.31 per 15 tests.

b) [LONG FORM.] Ages 2–15; 1967–82; 1 form ('67, 14 pages); set of 24 stimulus cards available for remedial work; assessment and remediation worksheets ('83, 40 pages); $16.20 per 15 tests; $39.54 per 10 sets of worksheets.

See T3:701 (57 references); for reviews by Donald A. Leton and James A. Rice, see 8:870 (24 references); see also T2:1875 (6 references); for a review by Brad S. Chissom, see 7:867 (5 references).

TEST REFERENCES

1. Ysseldyke, J. E. Aptitude-treatment interaction research with first grade children. CONTEMPORARY EDUCATIONAL PSYCHOLOGY, 1977, 2, 1–9.

2. Fletcher, J. M., & Satz, P. Developmental changes in the neuropsychological correlates of reading achievement: A six-year longitudinal followup. JOURNAL OF CLINICAL NEUROPSYCHOLOGY, 1980, 2, 23–37.

3. Winsberg, B. G., Bialer, I., Kupietz, S., Botti, E., & Balka, E. B. Home vs hospital care of children with behavior disorders: A controlled investigation. ARCHIVES OF GENERAL PSYCHIATRY. 1980, 37, 413–418.

4. Lyon, R., & Watson, B. Empirically derived subgroups of learning disabled readers: Diagnostic characteristics. JOURNAL OF LEARNING DISABILITIES, 1981, 14, 256–261.

5. Abbott, D., Rotnem, D., Genel, M., & Cohen, D. J. Cognitive and emotional functioning in hypopituitary short-statured children. SCHIZOPHRENIA BULLETIN, 1982, 8, 310–319.
6. Armstrong, B. B., & Knopf, K. F. Comparison of the Bender-Gestalt and revised Developmental Test of Visual Motor Integration. PERCEPTUAL AND MOTOR SKILLS, 1982, 55, 164–166.
7. Breen, M. J. Comparison of educationally handicapped students' scores on the revised Developmental Test of Visual-Motor Integration and Bender-Gestalt. PERCEPTUAL AND MOTOR SKILLS, 1982, 54, 1227–1230.
8. Fletcher, J. M., & Satz, P. Kindergarten prediction of reading achievement: A seven-year longitudinal follow-up. EDUCATIONAL AND PSYCHOLOGICAL MEASUREMENT, 1982, 42, 681–685.
9. Goldstein, D. J., Allen, C. M., & Fleming, L. P. Relationship between the Expressive One-Word Picture Vocabulary Test and measures of intelligence, receptive vocabulary, and visual-motor coordination in borderline and mildly retarded children. PSYCHOLOGY IN THE SCHOOLS, 1982, 19, 315–318.
10. Skeen, J. A., Strong, V. N., & Book, R. M. Comparison of learning disabled children's performance on Bender Visual-Motor Gestalt Test and Beery's Developmental Test of Visual Motor Integration. PERCEPTUAL AND MOTOR SKILLS, 1982, 55, 1257–1258.
11. Wright, D., & DeMers, S. T. Comparison of the relationship between two measures of visual-motor coordination and academic achievement. PSYCHOLOGY IN THE SCHOOLS, 1982, 19, 473–477.
12. Ysseldyke, J. E., Algozzine, B., Shinn, M. R., & McGue, M. Similarities and differences between low achievers and students classified learning disabled. JOURNAL OF SPECIAL EDUCATION, 1982, 16, 73–85.
13. Connelly, J. B. Comparative analysis of two tests of visual-fine-motor integration among young Indian and non-Indian children. PERCEPTUAL AND MOTOR SKILLS, 1983, 57, 1079–1082.
14. Liemohn, W. Rhythmicity and motor skill. PERCEPTUAL AND MOTOR SKILLS, 1983, 57, 327–331.
15. Siegel, L. S. Correction for prematurity and its consequences for the assessment of the very low birth weight infant. CHILD DEVELOPMENT, 1983, 54, 1176–1188.

[330]

Devereux Elementary School Behavior Rating Scale II. Grades K–6; 1967–82; DESB II; ratings of problem behaviors by teachers; 10 factor scores (work organization, creative initiative/involvement, positive toward teacher, need for direction in work, socially withdrawn, failure anxiety, impatience, irrelevant thinking/talk, blaming, negative-aggressive), 4 cluster scores (perseverance, peer cooperation, confusion, inattention); norms consist of means and standard deviations; 1 form ('82, 4 pages); manual ('82, 40 pages); 1985 price data: $.30 or less per scale; $2 per manual; (5–10) minutes; Marshall Swift; Devereux Foundation Press.*

For references to an earlier version, see T3:704 (17 references) and T2:1159 (3 references); for a review by William M. Littell, see 7:68 (1 reference); see also P:62 (2 references).

TEST REFERENCES

1. Spivak, G., & Swift, M. "High risk" classroom behaviors in kindergarten and first grade. AMERICAN JOURNAL OF COMMUNITY PSYCHOLOGY, 1977, 5, 385–397.
2. Willis, J., & Seymour, G. CPQ validity: The relationship between Children's Personality Questionnaire scores and teacher ratings. JOURNAL OF ABNORMAL CHILD PSYCHOLOGY, 1978, 6, 107–113.
3. Willis, J., Smithy, D., & Holliday, S. Item level validity of the Devereux Elementary School Behavior Rating Scale. JOURNAL OF ABNORMAL CHILD PSYCHOLOGY, 1979, 7, 327–335.
4. Growe, G. A., & Levinson, S. A reexamination of the validity of the Children's Personality Questionnaire. JOURNAL OF ABNORMAL CHILD PSYCHOLOGY, 1980, 8, 435–439.
5. Winsberg, B. G., Bialer, I., Kupietz, S., Botti, E., & Balka, E. B. Home vs hospital care of children with behavior disorders: A controlled investigation. ARCHIVES OF GENERAL PSYCHIATRY. 1980, 37, 413–418.
6. Larrivee, B., & Bourque, M. L. Factor structure of classroom behavior problems for mainstreamed and regular students. JOURNAL OF ABNORMAL CHIILD PSYCHOLOGY, 1981, 9, 399–406.
7. Ledingham, J. E. Developmental patterns of aggressive and withdrawn behavior in childhood: A possible method for identifying preschizophrenics. JOURNAL OF ABNORMAL CHILD PSYCHOLOGY, 1981, 9, 1–22.
8. Bleck, R. T., & Bleck, B. L. The disruptive child's play group. ELEMENTARY SCHOOL GUIDANCE AND COUNSELING, 1982, 17, 137–141.
9. Emery, R., Weintraub, S., & Neale, J. M. Effects of marital discord on the school behavior of children of schizophrenic, affectively disordered, and normal patients. JOURNAL OF ABNORMAL CHILD PSYCHOLOGY, 1982, 10, 215–228.
10. Giannotti, T. J., & Doyle, R. E. The effectiveness of parental training on learning disabled children and their parents. ELEMENTARY SCHOOL GUIDANCE AND COUNSELING, 1982, 17, 131–136.
11. McKim, B. J., Weissberg, R. P., Cowen, E. L., Gesten, E. L., & Rapkin, B. D. A comparison of the problem-solving ability and adjustment of suburban and urban third-grade children. AMERICAN JOURNAL OF COMMUNITY PSYCHOLOGY, 1982, 10, 155–169.
12. Reynolds, W. M., & Bernstein, S. M. Factorial validity and reliability of the Devereux Elementary School Behavior Rating Scale. JOURNAL OF ABNORMAL CHILD PSYCHOLOGY, 1982, 10, 113–122.

[331]

Diagnosing Abilities in Math. Slow learning children in math; 1980; DAM; no data on reliability; no norms; 1 form consists of 2 parts: timed facts tests in addition, subtraction, multiplication, and division (2 pages) and diagnostic tests covering whole numbers, fractions, and decimals (3 pages); directions for administering and answer key (3 pages); 1983 price data: $22.95 per complete set; (210) minutes; Francis T. Sganga; Mafex Associates, Inc.*

Review of Diagnosing Abilities in Math by DAVID J. KRUS, Associate Professor of Education and Director, University Testing Services, Arizona State University, Tempe, AZ:

The Diagnosing Abilities in Math (DAM) test was intended to be used as a pretest for a series of instructional courses offered by Mafex Associates for slow learners. Placement into these programs in remedial mathematics, advertised as Galactimath 1 and 2, Arithmetic Power, Your Daily Math, Motorcycle Math, etc., called for assessment of elementary arithmetical skills to add, subtract, multiply, and divide whole numbers, fractions, and decimal numbers.

The test consists of two parts. The shorter part ("Timed Facts Test") contains four subtests: Addition (40 items, time limit: 2 minutes), Subtraction (40 items, 2 minutes), Multiplication (32 items, 2 minutes) and Division (48 items, 3 minutes). The addition and multiplication items were constructed using single digit numbers only; both single and double digit numbers were used for construction of items in subtraction and division subtests.

The administration of the longer part ("Diagnostic Test") is estimated to take about 3 hours. This part consists of 12 subtests, each subtest containing five items. As in the first part, four arithmetic operations (addition, subtraction, multiplication and division) are used in problems using whole numbers, fractions, and decimal numbers, the only difference being that the numbers used as test items consist of two to five digits and summands for the addition subtest contain four terms. For example, a typical item in this part asks subjects to add 78 + 3327 + 346 + 10,039 or to multiply 10.004 x 0.075.

No data on validity, internal consistency reliablity, or test stability were given. No norms are provided for the test. The assertion is made that "students should be expected to score 100% for each operation" in the "Timed Facts" part and that "Ordinarily, a student who misses 3 out of 5 problems in any operation should be given work in that area," or some minor problems should be remedied verbally.

The test package does not contain keyed stencils; the dubious "let students do it" scoring strategy is recommended ("redistribute tests randomly for scoring in class"). The author's main concern seems to be that the test proctor should "note those students who subtly or openly use their fingers" so as to discourage this practice by "helping students break this habit." The test comes in a package of ten booklets for each subtest with a list price of $19.95.

In this day and age of ubiquitous electronic calculators, the DAM test puts too much stress on manipulation of large numbers (thousands and tens of thousands). With slight hyperbole, it is possible to describe this test as a collection of random numbers interspersed with decimal points and fraction lines, arranged into summands, minuends, subtrahends, multiplicators, multiplicands, dividends, and divisors. It is likely that a classroom teacher could do equally well or better by constructing an ad hoc test in a matter of minutes.

Review of Diagnosing Abilities in Math by J. LEE WIEDERHOLT, Associate Professor of Special Education, University of Texas, Austin, TX:

The Diagnosing Abilities in Math (DAM) test consists of diagnostic test booklets containing problems on addition, subtraction, multiplication and division, a brief discussion of diagnostic procedures, and the test answer key. All problems are number problems—no word problems are included. No data are presented on the standardization sample, reliability, or validity.

The rationale for the test is stated as follows: "Since instant recall of basic facts is essential for successful performance in testing situations, it is necessary to check students' proficiencies by giving them TIMED facts tests." Thirty minutes is specified for the timed facts tests; three hours for the diagnostic tests. How these times were arrived at is unspecified. On the facts test, 100% is expected; on the diagnostic portion of the test, it is recommended that any student who misses three out of five problems should likely get extra work in that area. Several math programs also published by Mafex are listed on the back of the booklet and it is suggested that the DAM can be used as a pretest to determine the level of the student for these programs.

The lack of data and the fact that all problems are number problems limits the validity of the test. In fact, it is probably just as easy and a great deal less costly for teachers to simply pull a representative sample of math problems from their own curriculum for testing their students.

[332]

Diagnosis: An Instructional Aid: Mathematics, Levels A and B. Grades K–3, 3–8; 1979–80; DIAM; objectives-based diagnostic-prescriptive; consists of a series of diagnostic tests (called probes) and optional survey tests; no data on reliability; no norms; 2 levels; administration time not reported; Science Research Associates, Inc.*

a) LEVEL A. Grades K–3; 2 parts; student record sheet ('80, 1 page, spirit master for local duplicating); prescription guide ('80, 7 pages); teacher's guide ('79, 80 pages); 1984 price data: $127.75 per complete kit including spirit masters for each form of each survey test and 25 copies of each form of each probe test; $6 per specimen set; components may be purchased separately.

1) *Survey Tests.* Provides quick survey of broad areas of mathematical understandings and skills; 3 tests: Numbers and Numerals, Addition-Subtraction-Story Problems, Geometry and Measurement; Forms 1, 2, ('80, 2 pages for each test, spirit masters for local duplicating).

2) *Probes.* Diagnostic tests designed to pinpoint student weaknesses; 28 tests: Comparing Sets, Sets and Numbers (1, 2), 1-Digit Numbers (Counting, Comparing), Ordinal Numbers, 2-Digit Numbers (Place Value and Comparing, Place Value and Counting, Comparing), 3-Digit Numbers (Place Value, Counting and Comparing), 4-Digit Numbers, Addition (1, 2, 3, 4), Subtraction (1, 2, 3), Story Problems (1, 2, 3), Comparisons, Geometry, Measurement, Time, Money (1, 2); Forms 1, 2, ('80, 2 pages for each probe test).

b) LEVEL B. Grades 3–8; 2 levels; student record sheet ('80, 1 page, spirit master for local duplicating); $176.25 per complete Level B kit (Lab B1 and Lab B2) including materials for 25 pupils; $105.70 per complete kit of either Lab B1 or Lab B2 including spirit masters for each form of each survey test, spirit masters for each form of each test of basic facts (for Lab B1 only), and 25 copies of each form of each probe test; $7.30 per specimen set; components may be purchased separately.

1) *Lab B1.* Covers whole number topics as well as easier topics in geometry and measurement; 3 parts; prescription guide ('80, 11 pages); teacher's guide ('80, 79 pages).

(*a*) Tests of Basic Facts. For students suspected of lacking knowledge of basic facts; 4 tests: Addition, Subtraction, Multiplication, Division; Forms 1, 2, ('80, 1 page for each test, spirit masters for local duplicating).

(*b*) Survey Tests. 6 tests: Whole Numbers (Concepts, Addition and Subtraction, Multiplication and Division, Word Problems), Money and Time,

Geometry and Measurement; Forms 1, 2, ('80, 1–2 pages for each test, spirit masters for local duplicating).

(*c*) Probes. 20 tests: Whole Numbers/Concepts (Numbers Through 999, Numbers Through 9999, Numbers Greater Than 10000), Whole Numbers (Addition, Subtraction, Multiplication-1, Multiplication-2, Division-1, Division-2), Whole Numbers/Word Problems (One-Step Word Problems-1, One-Step Word Problems-2, Multiple-Step Word Problems, Extraneous and Insufficient Information Problems), Money (1, 2), Time, Geometric Figures, Geometric Relationships, Measurement (1, 2); Forms 1, 2, ('80, 2 pages for each probe test).

2) *Lab B2*. Covers fractions and decimals as well as the more difficult topics in geometry and measurement; 2 parts; prescription guide ('80, 11 pages); teacher's guide ('80, 95 pages).

(*a*) Survey Tests. 6 tests: Fractions/Concepts, Decimals/Concepts, Fractions and Decimals/Computation, Fractions and Decimals/Word Problems, Rates-Ratios-Percents, Geometric Measurement-Statistics-Probability; Forms 1, 2, ('80, 1–2 pages for each test, spirit masters for local duplicating).

(*b*) Probes. 21 tests: Factors and Multiples, Fractions and Mixed Numerals (1, 2), Decimals (1, 2), Decimals/Fractions/Mixed Numerals, Fractions and Mixed Numerals (Addition and Subtraction, Multiplication and Division), Decimals (Addition and Subtraction, Multiplication and Division), Fraction Word Problems, Decimal Word Problems (1, 2), Rates and Ratios, Percents (1, 2), Special Applications of Percent, Geometric Measurement (1, 2), Bar and Line Graphs, Circle Graphs/Statistics/Probability; Forms 1, 2, ('80, 2 pages for each probe test).

See T3:709 (2 references).

[333]

Diagnostic Achievement Battery. Ages 6–14; 1984; DAB; 13 scores: listening (story comprehension, characteristics), speaking (synonyms, grammatical completion), reading (alphabet/word knowledge, reading comprehension), writing (capitalization, punctuation, spelling, written vocabulary), math (math reasoning, math calculation), total achievement, plus 2 additional composite scores (spoken language, written language) consisting of various combinations of subtests; entire battery or any combination of subtests may be administered; individual; 1 form; manual (81 pages); student booklet (29 pages); student worksheets (4 pages); answer-profile sheet (6 pages); 1984 price data: $52 per test kit including manual, student booklet, 25 student worksheets, and 25 answer-profile sheets; $9 per 25 student worksheets; $13 per 25 answer-profile sheets; $15 per student booklet; $19 per manual; administration time not reported; Phyllis L. Newcomer and Delores Curtis; PRO-ED.*

Review of the Diagnostic Achievement Battery by WILLIAM J. WEBSTER, Special Assistant to the Superintendent—Research, Evaluation, and Information Systems, Dallas Independent School District, Dallas, TX:

The Diagnostic Achievement Battery (DAB) is a nationally standardized, individually administered achievement test that is designed to assess children's abilities in listening, speaking, reading, writing, and mathematics. It was developed in part to provide an instrument that would help educators meet the requirements of PL 94–142. The test was designed to aid educators in identifying those students who are significantly below their peers in the areas of spoken language, written language, and mathematics, and who—as a result—may profit from supplemental or remedial help; to determine the particular kinds of component strengths and weaknesses that individual students possess; and to document students' progress in specific academic areas. The DAB was designed for use with children between the ages of 6 and 14.

The DAB measures three constructs (spoken language, written language, and mathematics), which are comprised of five components (listening, speaking, reading, writing, applied math), which in turn are comprised of 12 subtests (sentence completion, characteristics, synonyms, grammatic completion, reading comprehension, alphabet/word knowledge, punctuation, spelling, capitalization, written vocabulary, math calculation, and math reasoning). The test yields an overall composite score, a construct score for each of the three measured constructs, a component score for each of the five measured components, and a subtest score for each of the 12 subtests. The examiner has the choice of administering the entire test battery or any portion of the test.

Items on the DAB are presented in many standardized formats. Some of them are read aloud to the examinees and the examinees are asked to respond verbally; some require the examinee to read printed matter and respond in writing to specific questions about the material read; some are read aloud to the examinees and the examinees are asked to respond in writing; some require the examinee to look at pictures and write a story; some involve problem solving without aid of paper or pencil; and some involve calculation and writing of answers to mathematical problems. None are presented in the traditional item format of group-administered standardized achievement tests.

The DAB is a norm-referenced test. It yields two kinds of normative information. Tables are provided in the manual for converting raw scores on each of the 12 subtests to percentiles and to standard scores with a mean of 10 and a standard deviation of 3. Standard scores can be summed across subtests to obtain composite scores for component areas, constructs, and total achievement. Composite scores have a mean of 100 and a standard deviation of 15.

The DAB was normed on a sample of 1,756 examinees drawn from 13 states. Characteristics of the sample were generally sufficiently close to the characteristics of the nation as a whole to warrant confidence in using the norms. Lending additional credence to the use of the norms is the fact that the authors of the test have done a better than average job of specifying test administration procedures and scoring criteria. This is particularly important given the unusual nature of some of the items.

The only significant question regarding test administration procedures that is not addressed by the manual is item administration time for the orally presented items. The paper-pencil tests have specified administration times. Perhaps the authors feel that the item administration directions are sufficiently structured so that no time limits need be applied. There is some justification for not specifying times but, to the extent that administration time does vary, error variance will be introduced into the scores.

The reported reliabilities of the various DAB subtests and composite scores are, in general, quite acceptable. Internal consistency measures generally range from the high .70s to the low .90s for the subtests and from the middle .80s to the middle .90s for the composites. Test-retest reliabilities range from the low .80s to the middle .90s for the subtests and generally cluster around the high .90s for the composites. These reliability coefficients further support the previously mentioned observation that the authors have done a better than average job in specifying test administration and scoring procedures for a series of items somewhat difficult to administer and score. One particular problem area—one that is discussed by the authors in the manual—is a series of lower than usual reliabilities recorded when the test was administered to 13-year-olds.

The degree of care that apparently went into the construction of this test would tend to support the content validity of the test. Criterion-related validity was studied by correlating DAB subtest scores with other well known tests of the same or similar abilities. These coefficients were generally acceptable. The authors also did a better than average job of establishing the construct validity of the DAB.

In summary, the DAB appears to be extremely well designed and constructed for an individually administered achievement test. Although no content map per se is included in the manual, all available evidence suggests that a great deal of care went into the selection and validation of the items, subtests, components, and constructs that make up the DAB. Norming was carefully implemented on an adequate sample; reliability was carefully studied and documented; and the validity of the test was studied to a degree not often found in even the most widely used norm-referenced achievement tests. If a test user is in need of an individually administered achievement test, and the content of the DAB measures the content of the user's school curriculum, this test would be a worthy choice for use.

[334]

Diagnostic Analysis of Reading Errors. Adolescents and adults; 1971–79; DARE; "uses the forty-six-item word list of the Wide Range Achievement Test (Spelling, Level II)"; 4 scores: correct, error (sound substitutions, omissions, reversals); 1 form ('71, 2 pages); manual ('79, 59 pages); profile sheet ('79, 1 page); 1983 price data: $16 per 5 answer sheets, 5 profile forms, manual, and scoring template; $9.25 per 50 answer sheets; $9.25 per 50 profile forms; $13.50 per manual with scoring stencil; administration time not reported; Jacquelyn Gillespie and Jacqueline Shohet; Jastak Associates, Inc.*

TEST REFERENCES

1. Saigh, P. A., & Khairallah, S. The concurrent validity of the Diagnostic Analysis of Reading Errors as a predictor of the English achievement of Lebanese students. EDUCATIONAL AND PSYCHOLOGICAL MEASUREMENT, 1983, 43, 1149–1152.

Review of Diagnostic Analysis of Reading Errors by RICHARD L. ALLINGTON, Associate Professor of Education, State University of New York at Albany, Albany, NY:

This test (formerly the Diagnostic Spelling Test) was developed to identify "language-related learning disabilities in classroom-size groups" of adolescents and young adults and to "provide indications of the nature of each...individual's disability." This information is to be obtained from an analysis of errors elicited from administration of a multiple choice word recognition test. Each item is presented with three distractor items. The distractors are nonwords designed to present alternatives "which identify error patterns typically associated with learning disabilities." The three alternative spellings were selected to represent the following categories of errors: (1) sound substitution (nesascity for necessity), (2) omitted sounds (nesscity), (3) reversal (necetisy). Four scores are obtained, a correct response total and a score for each error category.

The test manual presents modest normative data with grade level norms for grades 7 through 12 and separate normative tables for community college students. Age level norms are available for ages 12 through 18. Both the grade level and age norms seem to be based upon a sample of 1,583 students with a majority of subjects seemingly coming from suburban school populations. The number of subjects from which the community college norms were generated is not explicitly noted but a supplemental table lists a sample total of 290. Reliability information is limited. One set of analyses on the performance of 39 high school seniors reports an odd-even item correlation (.51) and a split-half reliability coefficient (.67). A second set of analyses included test-retest comparisons with 41 high school remedial English students. In an immediate retest condition a correlation of .78 is reported, similar to the .81 reported for a delayed retest. In these cases noted the correlations and reliability coefficients are reported for total correct scores. The analyses of the stability of error scores or diagnostic categories are even more limited and these test-retest coefficients are often quite low. Based on the limited data available, one could assume the test provides a consistent total correct score but less can be assumed about the reliability or stability of the error scores or diagnostic categories.

The data on validity of the test is sparse. The authors report that the test discriminated among four groups of students (gifted, regular students, educationally handicapped, and educable mentally retarded) but this was on the basis of total test scores which were ordered, not surprisingly, as in the listing above. The test also discriminated among four categories of community college students, though the mean total score difference between the basic English students and the Speed Reading students is less than 1 raw score unit. Far more convincing data could have been provided with application of a multiple-discriminant function analysis which indicated the number of subjects accurately placed in groups based upon test scores. The authors argue that the increases in total correct scores from grade to grade and the "generally random and even distribution of error scores" reflect the normal increments of growth that provide evidence of construct validity. The comparisons of this test with existing tests is limited primarily to presenting correlations with the WRAT Spelling Test. These correlations are generally high. All in all, the available information on the validity of this test suggests it measures abilities similar to those tapped by the WRAT Spelling Test. Given the high correlation just noted and the format of the test (which requires receptive, not production skills) it seems the original designation as the Diagnostic Spelling Test was more appropriate than the current Diagnostic Analysis of Reading Errors title. This test does not provide a diagnostic analysis of reading errors, at least not in any traditional sense, and the authors seem to admit as much throughout the manual.

The most disconcerting aspects of the manual which accompanies the test, however, are found in the Test Interpretation and Case Studies sections. Though neither reliability nor validity of the error scores were well-established, the authors treat these and the resultant diagnostic categories as truly meaningful data upon which one can base remedial intervention. Even with the modest disclaimers offered the authors overstate the diagnostic value of this test. The analyses of error scores presented in the case studies particularly exceed the established limited discriminating power of this instrument. In addition, seven of the ten case studies represent non-native English speakers and an eighth subject is hearing impaired. Selection of such cases for a test which was developed to identify learning disabilities in the classroom is odd indeed. Rarely, if ever, have English-as-a-Second-Language students been considered prime candidates for learning disability designation based upon an inability to recognize the correct spellings of English words.

In summary, then, this test seems in many respects to be a variation on the WRAT Spelling Test, providing little reliable information beyond a spelling achievement score. As an alternative spelling test, it may prove useful; but its usefulness as a diagnostic test is limited, and it has even less usefulness as a diagnostic test of reading.

[335]

Diagnostic Analysis of Reading Tasks. Grades 2.5 and below, 2.5 and above; 1976; criterion-referenced test comprised of nonsense words for diagnosing problems in encoding, transcribing sounds, and decoding of written symbols; no data on reliability; no norms; 2 levels labeled DART I and DART II; manual (28 pages); 1982 price data: $16 per examiner's kit including manual, directions, DART I and II, and score sheets; $1.50 per pad of 20 score sheets for each form; untimed test; Ethel Steinberg; Slosson Educational Publications, Inc.*

a) DART I. Grades 2.5 and below; item scores in 3 areas: encoding, decoding, auditory screening; 85% correct suggested standard of mastery; Form 1 (1 page), Form 2 (1 page).

b) DART II. Grades 2.5 and above; item scores in 6 areas: encoding (sections A, B), decoding (sections A, B, medial diphthongs and digraphs, irregular letter clusters); 85% correct suggested standard of mastery; Form 3, 4, 5, (1 page).

Review of Diagnostic Analysis of Reading Tasks by JAMES V. HOFFMAN, Associate Professor of Curriculum & Instruction, The University of Texas at Austin, Austin, TX:

My initial problem in reviewing this test came in trying to interpret the title. Task analysis in the jargon of education typically involves the identification of critical components of a learning task. The goal is often to specify the kinds and levels of skills needed to perform the task successfully. The term diagnosis is applied to an assessment of learner characteristics related to a task which, in a deficit model, forms the basis for subsequent instructional activity. The DART has little to do with the former and much to do with the latter. That is, it is a test designed to aid the teacher of reading in diagnosing instructional needs in decoding.

While acknowledging that reading is much more than decoding, the author argues that the process of decoding is the basis of reading and must be overlearned so the reader is free for total involvement in the act of reading and comprehension. The subskills of reading identified as critical to decoding in this test are: phonics, structural analysis, and recognition of useful word parts (presumably syllables). Student performance with nonsense words is used as the sole basis for testing each of these areas. The argument is made that nonsense words force the use of visual clues to convert symbols to sounds. They also eliminate the possibility that the students might have some prior familiarity with the test items.

DART test I is suggested for use with students in grade levels below 2.5 and DART test II for levels 2.5 and above. The 22 nonsense words in DART test I, Section A, purport to test pupil knowledge of 49 sound-symbol relationships. No comprehensive listing of these phonic elements is provided. Nor is any rationale for their selection given. DART test I, Section B, consists of a "gross auditory screening device" which tests for the ability to hear the number of syllables in a word. In what seems to be a contradiction in terms, the author recommends that this section only be given to those youngsters who are having some difficulty with auditory processing. The 30 nonsense words in DART test II purport to cover 71 critical decoding elements (again, these are unspecified). They include blends, digraphs, and even "structural analysis." Sections B, C, and D of test II probe more advanced decoding skills including phonograms and irregular letter sounds.

DART test I, Section A, and DART test II, Sections A and B, can be administered as either an encoding or a decoding task. The encoding task (described as "recall") requires that the student listen to a nonsense word and then write it down. The decoding task (described as "recognition") requires that the student look at a nonsense word and pronounce it. The author recommends that since the encoding test can be group administered and is a more difficult test that it should be administered first to all students as a screening device. Those who fail to perform well on this test can be individually administered the decoding form of the test. There is little empirical evidence in the research literature on reading to suggest that an encoding task of this type has any diagnostic, let alone predictive, value relative to reading acquisition. The decoding task suffers from the same limitation and in addition is one that few would label as "recognition" in nature, given the use of nonsense words.

The directions for administration and scoring tend to be a bit vague at times with respect to individual items. In test II, Section A, the test administrator is free to determine his or her own pronunciations of the nonsense words. In most cases the items are clear, but in others there is room for different interpretations (e.g., drol). Scoring is even more obscure, particularly on the encoding task. For example, "cir" is given as an acceptable encoding of "kur," yet for "rete" no credit is indicated for "reet." It is also not clear how the ability to write or pronounce nonsense words with -ed, -er, and -ing endings assess a student's knowledge of structural analysis.

There is a total absence of data reporting test reliability or validity characteristics, nor is there the suggestion that any data exists. The interpretation of performance by students focuses on the identification of phonic needs based on individual item analysis. On test I, Section A, it is suggested that "those children who get 7 items (not words) or less incorrect (42 items correct) can be considered to have adequate phonic skills to proceed in the developmental reading program at instructional level." It's not entirely clear what the message is in this sentence, but there is the clear danger that the potential user of this test might interpret the prescription to mean not permitting the student to engage in any real reading (real words in real sentences in real texts for real purposes) until he can perform well on a test of this type. To label this a totally unsound practice is to be mild in criticism.

In summary, I can find little in this test that warrants its use. With only a modicum of training, any classroom teacher could prepare test items using nonsense words to assess student knowledge of phonic elements in the manner presented in this test. There is no evidence that items prepared in this manner by a teacher would be any less reliable than those provided in this test, and they would likely be more valid since they would flow from the instructional program the teacher is prepared to offer.

[336]

Diagnostic Guide to DSM III. Adults; 1983; checklist for "clinician generated diagnoses" according to DSM III (does not include child, sexual, or adjustment disorders); 8 axis I scores (organic disorders, substance abuse, psychosis, paranoid, affective, anxiety, somatoform, dissociative), 1 axis II score (personality disorder), and 3 ratings (presence of medical history, severity of psychosocial stressor, highest level of adaptive functioning last year); reliability consists of data on interscorer reliability only; no data on validity; no norms; individual; 1 form (3 pages); answer sheet and summary (1 page); scoring templates (2 sheets); manual (9 pages); 1984 price data: $28 per complete set of testing materials including 10 answer/summary sheets; 10(20) minutes; Joel Butler, Frank Lawlis, and Myrna Niccolette; The Wilmington Press.*

[337]

Diagnostic Reading Inventory. Students grades 3–12 with reading problems; 1977–79; DRI; for reading levels grades 1–8; 5 or 6 subtests: isolated word lists, phrase list (optional), oral reading passages, silent reading passages, listening passages, decoding inventory (2 levels: basic, advanced); no data on reliability or validity; no norms; individual; 1 form ('79, 28 pages); manual ('79, 38 pages); record sheets ('79, 68 pages); 1985 price data:

$10.95 per complete test; administration time not reported; H. Donald Jacobs and Lyndon W. Searfoss; Kendall/Hunt Publishing Co.*

Review of Diagnostic Reading Inventory by KRISTA J. STEWART, Assistant Professor of Psychology and Director of the School Psychology Training Program, Tulane University, New Orleans, LA:

The authors regard the Diagnostic Reading Inventory (DRI) not as a "test" but rather as a controlled observation instrument designed for analyses based upon patterns of responses among reading related tasks. At each grade level of the DRI, general comparison can be made of a student's ability to recognize (timed) and identify (untimed) isolated words, to recognize phrases, to orally read passages, and to define words both with and without the availability of contextual cues. Moreover, specific comparison is possible for the one or more words repeated across all tasks within any given grade level. In addition, oral discrepancies can be evaluated across levels of each task and can be contrasted with decoding skills. Comprehension proficiency for oral and silent reading and for listening can also be compared for skills which have been broken into 20 component types based on a 4 (Character, Event/Action, Object, Locale/Setting) by 5 (Critical, Inference, Interpretation, Literal, Referent) Model of Comprehending.

While the authors are to be respected for their attempts to make all of these comparisons within the context of a single instrument, the DRI suffers from a number of problems. Apparently because the DRI is not conceptualized as a "test," no attempt is made to meet the traditional standards for test instruments. Little information is given on the development of the DRI beyond an indication of the source of stimulus materials. The authors indicate that the reading passages have been selected from "high interest-low readability" books with the readability level for each passage being within .5 of the desired grade level. However, no indication is given as to the method for establishing readability levels nor is mention made of how the performance on these passages compares with performance on any criterion measures.

Because the passages contain "high interest" material which assumes an above grade level maturity of the student, these passages, particularly at the lower level, appear more sophisticated than is typical of first or second grade material. The authors, in fact, indicate that the DRI should be used only with students who are mature third graders or older. This reviewer questions the appropriateness of the term "grade level," however, if indeed the material could not be read by the average student of a particular grade. Because no data are presented indicating how students of various ages or grade levels perform on any of the reading tasks, the novice user of this instrument is left with no idea of what to expect in terms of performance.

Comprehension measures also appear to present certain potential problems. Comprehension questions are of short answer format with 12 questions for each passage at levels 1 through 3 and 20 questions for levels 4 through 8. The task demands placed on the reader by including so many questions would seem to obscure whether the questions are indeed measuring "comprehension" or primarily "memory." Presumably the reason for including the specified number of questions is that 12 types of comprehension are measured at the first three levels (Critical and Referent types are omitted) and 20 types at the latter five levels. However, not each type of comprehension is measured for each passage; also, more of the questions evaluate the four types of Literal comprehension than any of the other components. Again, because no data are given on how readers actually perform on the comprehension tasks, evaluating comprehension skills would be difficult. This reviewer's own attempts at the task, however, suggest that even skilled readers would have problems consistently achieving 100% accuracy on comprehension without looking back at the passages.

Several errors occur in the illustrations in the manual, the most important of which has to do with the construction of a student's "proficiency profile," one of the key sources for interpreting performance on the DRI. The manual indicates that the proficiency profile is to be based upon instructional performance level percentages. However, the illustration in the manual appears to employ independent performance level percentages. This error makes it unnecessarily difficult to understand the explanation of profile construction.

A number of limitations with administration of the DRI should also be mentioned. Little attention is given to describing the population for which the DRI is appropriate and the type of training necessary for the person administering the instrument. The complex nature of the DRI would suggest that only those experienced and highly skilled in reading diagnosis would be able to adequately administer and meaningfully interpret the instrument. Even so, the detailed nature of the scoring would appear to necessitate tape recording the responses, a suggestion which is in fact made in the manual. With respect to administration time, the authors indicate that the DRI should be given over several sessions but give no indication of how long complete administration might be expected to take. Because all tasks are to be started at the first-grade level, administration time for some students might be expected to be particularly long.

Another limitation is that the DRI requires extensive preparation of materials before the instrument can be administered. The user must make 400 word cards, 40 phrase cards, laminate or in some way make durable the 28 pages from the student booklet, reproduce the 68 pages of the recording pad, and establish response criteria for over 400 comprehension questions.

On the more positive side, several pages of the manual are dedicated to interpretation of results and subsequent remediation. The appropriateness and accuracy of the interpretations made from a test which has not been validated, however, must be questioned.

In summary, the authors' goal of creating a test which can be used to compare patterns of responses is a desirable one. However, complexities and time demands in scoring and administration, the lack of any normative data on task performance, and errors in the manual present serious limitations to the use of the DRI.

[338]

Diagnostic Reading Scales. Grades 1–7 and poor readers in grades 8–12; 1963–81; DRS-81; previous edition ('72) still available; 3 derived scores: instructional level, independent level, potential level, plus 12 raw scores: initial consonants, final consonants, consonant digraphs, consonant blends, initial consonant substitution, initial consonant sounds recognized auditorily, auditory discrimination, short and long vowel sounds, vowels with r, vowel diphthongs and digraphs, common syllables or phonograms, blending; individual; 1 form ('81, 32 pages); examiner's manual ('81, 59 pages); technical report ('81, 31 pages); technical bulletin ('75, 23 pages); examiner's record book ('81, 47 pages); tape cassette ('81) for training; 1984 price data: $5.35 per reusable test booklet; $38.50 per 35 examiner's record books; $5.25 per technical report; $4 per tape cassette; $4.25 per examiner's manual; $13.25 per specimen set; (60) minutes for entire battery; George D. Spache; CTB/McGraw-Hill.*

See T3:719 (13 references); for reviews by Nancy L. Roser and Robert L. Schreiner, and an excerpted review by Jerry Stafford of an earlier edition, see 8:753 (15 references); see also T2:1624 (4 references); for a review by Rebecca C. Barr, see 7:717 (7 references); for a review by N. Dale Bryant, see 6:821.

TEST REFERENCES

1. Hebben, N. A., Whitman, R. D., Milberg, W. P., Andresko, M., & Galpin, R. Attentional dysfunction in poor readers. JOURNAL OF LEARNING DISABILITIES, 1981, 14, 287–290.

2. McHugh, L. M., & Buss, R. R. Diagnostic and prescriptive decisions made by specialists and classroom teachers: Quadratic assignment as a reliability measure. NATIONAL READING CONFERENCE YEARBOOK, 1981, 30, 137–143.

3. Gold, P. C., & Horn, P. L. Achievement in reading, verbal language, listening comprehension and locus of control of adult illiterates in a volunteer tutorial project. PERCEPTUAL AND MOTOR SKILLS, 1982, 54, 1243–1250.

4. Leinhardt, G., Seewald, A. M., & Zigmond, N. Sex and race differences in learning disabilities classrooms. JOURNAL OF EDUCATIONAL PSYCHOLOGY, 1982, 74, 835–843.

Review of Diagnostic Reading Scales by RAY R. BUSS, Assistant Professor of Psychology, Louisiana State University, Baton Rouge, LA:

The Diagnostic Reading Scales (DRS) consist of a battery of individually administered tests which are used to estimate the instructional, independent, and potential reading levels of a student. Estimates of these three levels are obtained by assessing the following skills: word recognition, oral reading performance and comprehension (instructional level), silent reading comprehension (independent level), and auditory comprehension (potential level). Additionally, 12 supplementary word analysis and phonics tests may be administered to examine strengths and weaknesses of a particular student. The new, 1981 norms on this measure are for grades 1 through 7, except for the phonics tests, which are normed through grade 4.

SUPPORT MATERIALS. The DRS support materials are very useful and include an examiner's manual, an examiner's cassette, and a technical bulletin. The technical bulletin provides information about the tests' reliability and validity. Test-retest reliability for instructional level was .89. Other reliability and validity data also attest to the instrument's strong psychometric properties. The examiner's cassette is very helpful in learning to administer the DRS. It provides an example of an actual administration of the DRS and excerpts which demonstrate administration to students with special problems (e.g., dialect and nonreader) and administration of the 12 phonics tests. The examiner's manual provides a rationale and description for the tests and information relevant for administering, scoring, and interpreting the results. Generally speaking, it provides adequate instructions, but occasionally it is confusing, difficult to follow, and overly vague.

TESTING MATERIALS. Testing materials include a reusable student's reading book which consists of three lists of words to assess word recognition, two passages at each of 11 graded levels (e.g., preprimer through 7.5) to assess oral and silent reading performance and comprehension, and the 12 supplementary phonics tests. An examiner's record book (one is required for each student) includes the directions for the tests, word lists, passages and accompanying comprehension questions, and the 12 phonics tests. In addition, places to record student oral reading errors and comprehension question responses are provided in the book. Acceptable levels for the number of oral reading errors and comprehension performance, as well as acceptable comprehension responses, are also included in this book. This allows for convenient administration of the DRS. At the end of the examiner's record book, one will find a summary record sheet, a word analysis checklist, and a checklist of reading ability.

WORD RECOGNITION LISTS. Three separate word recognition lists are provided. The primary purpose of these lists is to allow the examiner to determine the level at which to begin assessing instructional reading level. The most severe limitation of the word recognition lists is that the most advanced list only includes words up to grade level 5.5, while passages are normed up to 7.5. The usefulness of these lists for students from the upper grades is minimal if reading levels go above this 5.5 ceiling.

READING PASSAGES. Instructional, independent, and potential reading levels are estimated on the basis of performance on the reading passages. Instructional level is estimated by having the student read a passage orally and then having the student answer comprehension questions about this oral passage. Independent level is estimated by having the student read a passage silently and then having the student answer comprehension questions about this passage. Potential level is estimated by having the student answer comprehension questions from a passage read aloud by the examiner. These definitions lead to several problems, and the interested user should be careful to note this discrepancy. First, the DRS does not use the terms instructional and independent reading levels in the same way that practitioners use them. Hence, the interpretation of reading scores and the use of these terms tends to complicate and confuse matters, and their utility is called into question. Second, the rationale for the concept of reading potential is unclear. While listening comprehension is related to reading, it seems that reading potential has very little utility in the typical classroom reading setting. It just does not say much about what to do with a student during reading instruction. An additional limitation related to these issues is concerned with the low criterion which has been established for comprehension performance. Use of the 60% accuracy criterion for comprehension scores is very low. As a result, a student's reading ability may be overestimated. Most practitioners would expect better performance from a student than 60% correct.

On the other hand, the passages appear to be appropriate in terms of both type and difficulty. First, the passages for the primary grades are narrative in style, while the passages for the upper grades are descriptive or expository in nature. Second, reading difficulty levels appear to be appropriate based on the Spache and Dale-Chall formulas. Generally speaking, the comprehension questions which accompany each passage measure recall of material which the student read or heard. However, in some instances use of prior knowledge may be sufficient to answer the comprehension questions.

WORD ANALYSIS AND PHONICS TESTS. Twelve separate tests, listed in the descriptive entry preceding this review, can be used to assess word attack and phonics skills. The examiner's manual indicates that each test should be reviewed by the examiner to determine which ones are most appropriate for a particular student. Thus, the basic problem with the phonics tests is that there is no standard order for administering them. At first, this might appear to be a minor point, but it seems that auditory discrimination is a necessary condition for performance on the other phonics tests. Similarly, initial and final consonants are some of the initial skills taught in the first grade. Thus, there seems to be an implicit hierarchy of phonics skills which is not reflected in the way the tests are organized or administered.

SUMMARY. The definitions of instructional and independent reading levels in the DRS differ substantially from those in ordinary use. Therefore, results from the DRS are of limited value to practitioners who wish to place a student at appropriate levels for reading instruction. Very low comprehension criterion cutoff scores also limit the utility of this instrument. Therefore, scores may overestimate a student's ability. While the DRS may be administered by anyone who takes the time to learn the instrument, the examiner's manual states that "it is strongly recommended that DRS administrators have clinical experience in reading diagnosis." Moreover, it takes a substantial amount of time to initially learn to administer the DRS and the value in terms of costs and benefits may not warrant this time investment. Finally, the checklists at the end of the examiner's record book which are supposed to aid in identifying a student's strengths and weaknesses are overly vague and general in nature; as a result, they have limited utility for classroom practice. Use of an informal reading inventory, which can be developed by individual users and practitioners to meet their specific needs, may be a better solution for estimating a student's strengths and weaknesses in reading as well as her/his instructional and independent reading levels.

Review of Diagnostic Reading Scales by STEVEN L. WISE, Assistant Professor of Educational Psychology, University of Nebraska, Lincoln, NE:

The Diagnostic Reading Scales (DRS) is an individually administered test designed to be used by reading specialists and school psychologists in the evaluation of oral and silent reading abilities and auditory comprehension. This reviewer is impressed that through two revisions the developer of the DRS has demonstrated a willingness to alter his instrument and accompanying materials in order to produce a more useful and effective test. One is left with the impression that, if needed, the DRS would be further revised. This sensitivity to the needs of test users is too often lacking in test developers.

The latest (1981) revision of the DRS has incorporated a number of changes. Probably the most important change concerns the reassignment of reading grade levels. This change was made in response to frequent criticism that previous versions of the DRS generally overestimated reading ability. The current set of grade levels should prove to be much more useful. A second major change involved the revision of the examiner's manual. Directions for test administration are clearly described, as is information regarding test rationale and development. Further, specific quidelines are given for the interpretation of responses for individuals who speak a nonstandard English dialect. A new addition to the test materials is a 90-minute tape cassette intended to aid examiners in using the DRS. The tape cassette includes excerpts of sample administrations of the DRS. A final major addition to the testing materials is an expanded technical report presenting detailed evidence of reliability and validity.

The DRS yields three reading levels for each student: instructional, independent, and potential. The instructional level, based on oral reading and comprehension, is intended to correspond to the reading grade level at which the student would be placed in a typical classroom. The independent level indicates the student's silent reading comprehension. The DRS definitions of "instructional" and "independent" reading levels differ from most other reading tests. However, the author is forthright in acknowledging this fact in the examiner's manual. The potential reading level, based on the student's auditory comprehension, is intended to measure the reading level that the student should attain as the result of classroom or remedial instruction. The rationale for this third reading level is the most questionable; a clear theoretical link has not been established between auditory comprehension and reading potential. In the case of a student with a relatively high actual reading potential but poor listening skills, the "potential" level indicated by the DRS may be very misleading and may result in the student's potential reading ability being underestimated. Hence it is recommended that users of the DRS interpret the potential level score with caution.

The technical report contains much information concerning the reliability and validity of the DRS. However, this technical report has several problems. First, the information on reliability and validity, while for the most part clearly described, is poorly organized and is consequently tedious to follow. Second, the most recent information reported in the technical report is based on relatively small samples of 534 and 290 students. Finally, a description of test development is erroneously presented as evidence of construct validity. Furthermore, correlations of the DRS with other reading tests, which is evidence of convergent (i.e., construct) validity, is erroneously presented as evidence of concurrent validity. In general, the discussion in the technical report on the validity of the DRS is confusing and incomplete.

In conclusion, the latest version of the DRS represents a substantial improvement over the previous versions. The revised examiner's manual, the training tape cassette, and the guidelines given for testing students who speak nonstandard dialects are all positive features. However, the DRS continues the questionable practice of using auditory comprehension as a measure of potential reading level. The technical report, although full of useful information regarding reliability and validity, is difficult to use. The DRS is an instrument that is getting better, but still has a way to go.

[339]

Diagnostic Screening Test: Achievement. Grades K–13; 1977; 5 scores: science, social studies, literature and the arts, practical knowledge, total achievement; 1 form (8 pages); manual (14 pages); 1983 price data: $11.95 per package of 20 test forms and manual; $19.95 per package of 100 test forms; (5–20) minutes; Thomas D. Gnagey and Patricia A. Gnagey; Facilitation House.*

Review of Diagnostic Screening Test: Achievement by EDWARD F. IWANICKI, Associate Dean of the School of Education and Professor of Educational Administration, University of Connecticut, Storrs, CT:

The Diagnostic Screening Test (DST): Achievement provides teachers, psychologists, and counselors with a quick assessment of student performance for use in planning classroom instruction. The entire battery consists of 108 multiple choice items keyed to graded and developmentally sequenced concepts spanning grades K through 12. The test is most reliable when administered individually at grades K through 1. At grades 2 and above it can be administered either on a group or an individual basis. When administering the test to a group, the examiner reads the items aloud while the students follow and respond on their test forms. The DST: Achievement Test Manual provides clear directions for scoring the test and for interpreting the results. The total test score is a measure of overall achievement in the content areas. The practical knowledge score is an indicator of performance in practical areas relevant to daily living. Interpretation procedures focus on individual subject area scores as well as on comparisons between these scores. Step-by-step interpretation procedures result in classroom recommendations for each pupil. From administration to interpretation, this instrument is packaged well for the school practitioner.

However, there are some major concerns regarding the technical quality of the DST: Achievement

Test. In constructing the subject area subtests, the authors compiled an initial item pool by sampling items from "end of chapter" tests in a variety of science, social studies, and literature series. Items were sampled which assessed those concepts which teachers indicated were first introduced for mastery at a particular grade level. This approach resulted in a 900-item pool that presumably measured both graded and developmentally sequenced concepts in each subject area tested. From this pool, a draft form of the test was constructed and submitted to classroom teachers for review. A second form of the test was developed on the basis of feedback from these teachers and was administered subsequently to 241 pupils in grades K through 12. An item analysis was then conducted and each subject area subtest was compiled. For each subtest three items were selected at each grade level which were answered correctly by at least 60% of the students at that grade level or above, but were not answered correctly by at least 70% of the students at all lower grade levels.

In describing the development of the DST: Achievement Test, the authors provided insufficient information concerning its content validity. No description was provided of (*a*) the K through 12 curricula reviewed, (*b*) the numbers and qualifications of the classroom teachers involved at various stages of the test development process, or (*c*) the specific concepts measured in the subject areas of science, social studies, and literature and the arts. Although the test is intended to measure student performance in terms of a graded and developmentally sequenced series of concepts, the construct validity of this claim was not supported adequately. The authors failed to define their concept of a developmental sequence. Also, the item analysis procedures used to determine the graded difficulty level of the items in the final test form were based on a limited sample, averaging about 20 students per grade level. While the authors had an excellent opportunity to support further the results of their initial field test by replicating their item analysis procedures using their norming population ($N = 3,770$), they chose not to pursue this option. Finally, the test items themselves do not appear to be keyed to graded and developmentally sequenced concepts. Although the final three Science subtest items should measure 11th- or 12th-grade concepts, two of these items tend to measure mere vocabulary rather than science concepts. One of the final items deals with condensation, a concept which is introduced much earlier than the 11th or 12th grade in most science programs. Until these concerns are addressed adequately, the content and construct validity of this instrument is questionable.

Although reliabilities were reported for each subtest score on the DST: Achievement Test for grades 1 through 12 combined, only the reliability of the total test score was reported by grade level. The procedures used to derive these reliability coefficients were not discussed. Since this test is used for diagnostic screening purposes at a particular grade level, the high reliabilities reported across grades have little relevance. The low to moderate reliabilities reported by grade level for the total test score are also irrelevant. Since the results on the subject area subtests are examined individually when a student's performance is interpreted, the reliabilities of these subtests should be reported by grade level.

The consolidation index was introduced early in the interpretation of the results of the DST: Achievement Test. Teachers were shown how this index can be used with a grade equivalent score to assess the consistency of a student's pattern of sequential skill development in a subject area. The intent of this approach could be achieved more simply and effectively by using a developmentally validated grade scale rather than the traditional grade equivalent and a consolidation index. Also, teachers should use extreme caution in following the suggestions in the manual for obtaining estimates of a student's ability from the achievement test results. The data provided to support the validity of such inferences are inadequate. For example, the suggestion that the total test age equivalent score provides a rough estimate of a child's mental age is based on a small sample study ($N = 35$) of students ranging from the primary to the high school grade levels.

In summary, the DST: Achievement Test is a neatly packaged instrument, but further technical information is needed to support its reliability and validity. This test merits review by school personnel seeking an instrument that measures achievement in areas not included in many basic skills tests. Before the DST: Achievement Test is adopted for wide scale use, pilot studies should be conducted to determine whether it provides accurate information for making instructional decisions about the students with whom it will be used.

[340]

Diagnostic Screening Test: Language, Second Edition. Grades 1–12; 1977–80; 8 scores: punctuation, spelling rules, sentence structure, grammar, capitalization, formal knowledge of language, applied knowledge of language, total language; 1 form ('80, 10 pages) manual ('77, 14 pages); 1983 price data: $14 per package of 20 test forms and manual; $25 per package of 100 test forms; (10–20) minutes; Thomas D. Gnagey and Patricia A. Gnagey; Facilitation House.*

Review of Diagnostic Screening Test: Language, Second Edition, by JANICE ARNOLD DOLE, Assistant Professor of Education, University of Denver, Denver, CO:

NATURE OF THE TEST. The Diagnostic Screening Test (DST): Language is a "wide range language test" designed "as a quick, valid method for estimating overall achievement level in written language and more specifically, skill mastery levels in grammar, punctuation, capitalization, sentence structure and formal spelling rules." The test consists of 120 multiple-choice items subgrouped into the above skill areas and hierarchically arranged in order of difficulty. It is designed to be administered to students in grades 1 through 12 in "approximately 10–20 minutes."

ADMINISTRATION AND SCORING. Several problems arise in the administration and scoring of the test. First, the manual lists three different procedures for administering the test: (1) examiner reads questions while student listens only, (2) student reads questions by him or her self, and (3) examiner reads questions while student reads along and marks correct responses. It is recommended that method 3 be used because it is the most "reliable," although no data are provided as to how this was determined. Method 2 is considered "generally reliable" for students beyond grade 4 reading levels, although it is clear that using this method would alter the nature of the test to include measures of vocabulary and reading as well as the skill areas outlined. Method 1 is considered most useful for "kindergarten and early first grade." Two problems arise here: (*a*) the test was not designed to be used at the kindergarten level, and (*b*) first grade and many primary grade students would have difficulty understanding the items on the test or holding in memory the different distractors for each item. In addition, no data are provided as to which procedure or procedures were used for norming the test. Since standardization of a test implies a standard procedure for administration, it is unclear how this test could be justified as a standardized test.

Another problem in the administration of the test is the determination of when to conclude the test. A formula is provided for determining the entry point of the test depending on grade level. The administrator is told to terminate the test when 10 of 13 items in a row are missed. If students are to mark the test booklets themselves, however, the examiner cannot determine when 10 of 13 items are missed except by stopping the student and scoring each item immediately. Otherwise, students would have to respond to most of the 120 items, an activity which would be extremely frustrating and time-consuming to 1 through 6 grade students. The manual is completely unclear on this matter. Lastly, according to the manual, test-taking time should vary from 10 to 20 minutes, but the reviewer's guess is that this is an extremely conservative estimate.

NORMS. The final form of the test was normed on 5,247 students in grades 1 through 12 in schools in "the mid-western and middle southern U.S. ranging from large to small in size." The manual reports no additional characteristics of the standardization sample, nor how schools were chosen. Thus, the description of the norming sample, if not the norming sample itself, must be regarded as completely inadequate.

RELIABILITY. Reliability coefficients are reported for the total test, individual subtests, and grade levels 1 through 12. How these reliabilities were obtained is not reported, nor is the standard error of measurement. While the total test reliability is high (.96), the reliabilities of the subtests within each grade level are not reported. These reliabilities may be adequate at the upper grade levels, but they will be predictably lower at the lower grade levels.

VALIDITY. The manual adequately reports the content validity of the test, which resulted from a "careful sampling of basic language rules" and the selection of "developmentally ordered concepts" found in language text series and verified by classroom language teachers. No data are provided for evaluating predictive or criterion-related validity.

Perhaps the least tolerable aspect of this test is the claim that the obtained diagnostic information can be "immediately translated into practical, helpful classroom learning activities." The scoring sheet lists classroom recommendations such as to "encourage written expression, avoid grading free writing assignments except for content and style." It is unclear how such an instructional implication can be derived from the data collected from this test, since the test does not measure written expression. In addition, the manual states that if the Grammar subtest is 20% or more below the Total Language score, it may be that the student comes from a different socio-cultural environment and needs different instructional content and materials. An examination of the items in that subtest, however, reveals items such as "Which is a demonstrative pronoun?", "Which sentence has the verb underlined?", "Which is used to name a person, place or thing?", "Which has the adjective underlined?" and "In which is the action or state regarded as doubtful or merely desired?". Clearly, these items assess the direct teaching and learning of specific traditional grammar terms and do not reflect grammatical departures of linguistically different speakers.

SUMMARY. The DST: Language is a wide range test designed to measure rote memorization and knowledge of isolated subskills in the mechanics of writing. It is not a "language" test as it claims to be because it does not assess oral language nor the full scope of written language. It cannot be used to diagnose the subskill areas of punctuation, spelling, sentence structure, grammar, and capitalization at the lower grade levels because the items are too few for adequate reliability. No data are reported on the validity of the test as a predictor of oral language or of written expression, nor is there data relating to the criterion-related validity of the test. Additionally, both the interpretation of scores presented in the manual and the classroom recommendations presented on the scoring sheet cannot be derived from the limited data collected from this test. Both the test and the manual must be regarded as inadequate for diagnosing the "language" of students in grades 1 through 12, and consumers are urged to look elsewhere for more reliable and valid instruments.

Review of Diagnostic Screening Test: Language, Second Edition, by EDWARD F. IWANICKI, Associate Dean of the School of Education and Professor of Educational Administration, University of Connecticut, Storrs, CT:

The Diagnostic Screening Test (DST): Language provides teachers, psychologists, and counselors with a quick assessment of student performance for use in planning classroom instruction. The entire instrument contains 120 multiple choice items keyed to graded and developmentally sequenced concepts spanning grades 1 through 12. Although the test can be administered individually in three ways, it is most reliable when the student reads along and marks his or her copy while the examiner reads the items aloud. The DST: Language Test Manual provides clear directions for administering and scoring the test. The Total Test score is a measure of overall achievement in written language. Overall language achievement is divided further into Formal Knowledge and Applied Knowledge. The Formal Knowledge score is a measure of the student's rote knowledge of formal language rules. The Applied Knowledge score is a measure of the student's skill in correct language usage. Step by step procedures are provided for interpreting the test scores. The interpretation process results in classroom recommendations for each pupil.

The DST: Language Test was developed by compiling lists of rules in the areas of punctuation, spelling, sentence structure, grammar, and capitalization through a review of major references on the English language. Then test items were constructed to measure each rule. These items were circulated among experienced language arts teachers to obtain an indication of which concepts were first introduced for mastery at their grade level and which concepts the typical student would have mastered prior to entering that grade. Based on teacher feedback and a survey of the content and specialized vocabulary in current language series, a pilot version of the instrument was developed and administered to 580 students at grades 1 through 12. These students' teachers were also asked to comment on this test form. The final form of the DST: Language Test was compiled by selecting two highly discriminating items at each grade level for each language skill area, one item measuring formal knowledge and the other item measuring applied knowledge. An item was judged as highly discriminating at a particular grade level if it was passed by at least 70% of the students in the next two grades and missed by at least 60% of the students in the two grades immediately prior to that grade level. The final test form was then normed on a sample of 5,247 students in grades 1 through 12.

Although the DST: Language Test Manual contains a description of the test development process, specific information is not provided to support the validity of the instrument. From a content validity perspective, no information is provided regarding the language arts series reviewed or the numbers and qualifications of the "experienced" teachers who participated in the test development process. Also, no information was provided for assessing the representativeness of the student sample employed in the test development process. Although the authors conclude that the test measures a careful sampling of basic language rules in each skill area as they relate to graded and developmentally ordered concepts, no information is provided as to the specific rules and concepts being measured in each skill area across grade levels. Furthermore, if the test does measure a series of graded and developmentally ordered concepts, the authors should have provided evidence to support the construct validity of this claim. While the item analysis procedures employed in the development of the test provided some support for the graded nature of the items, the authors ignored an excellent opportunity to support further the construct validity of their instrument by replicating these item analysis procedures with their substantially larger norming population. In short, other than the authors' claims, the evidence supporting the validity of this test is very limited.

As the validity of the DST: Language Test is examined further, it is important to note that this instrument assesses the student's ability to recognize proper written language usage. Over the years, there has been much debate as to whether a student's ability to recognize proper written language usage is related strongly to his or her ability to apply language skills effectively in producing a written work. Subsequent validity studies should address this issue by correlating DST: Language Test performance with measures of demonstrated writing proficiency.

Although reliabilities were reported for each score on the DST: Language Test for grades 1 through 12 combined, only the reliability of the Total Test score was reported by grade level. The procedures used to derive these reliability coefficients were not discussed. Since this test is used for diagnostic screening purposes at a particular grade level, the moderate to high reliabilities reported across grades have little relevance. The moderate reliabilities reported by grade level for the Total Test score are also irrelevant. Since the results on the language skill subtests are examined individually when a student's performance is interpreted, the reliabilities of these subtests should be reported by grade level.

DST: Language Test performance in a particular area is interpreted using a grade equivalent (GE) score in combination with a consolidation index (CI). The CI is a measure of the consistency of student skill development up to the grade level indicated in the GE. If a high degree of consistency is exhibited, subsequent instruction can proceed at the grade level specified in the GE. If skill development is inconsistent with the level indicated in the GE, teachers are encouraged to focus instruction at the grade level where the student began to encounter skill difficulty. This approach to test score interpretation is disappointing in light of the authors' claim that the test measures graded and developmentally ordered concepts as they relate to the rules of written language in each of five areas. If this is true, then it seems quite logical that the results of a subtest such as Punctuation could be interpreted to obtain information about those punctuation rules the student has mastered, those rules where difficulty is being encountered, and those where no learning has taken place. Such a criterion-referenced interpretation would be more effective than using the GE in combination with the CI.

In summary, according to the authors, the DST: Language Test is an attractive instrument for diagnosing written language skills. However, further evidence concerning the reliability and validity of this test needs to be provided to support these claims. Since no information is provided concerning the specific concepts and rules being assessed by each subtest, it is difficult for a potential user to assess whether the instrument is valid for a particular school setting.

[341]

Diagnostic Screening Test: Math, Third Edition. Grades 1–12; 1980; 31 scores: 5 basic processes scores (addition, subtraction, multiplication, division, total), 6 specialized processes scores (money, time, percent, U.S. measurement, metric measurement, total), 11 consolidation index scores, and 9 concept scores; Forms A, B ('80, 6 pages); manual ('80, 19 pages); 1983 price data: $12 per manual and 20 Form A tests; $21 per 100 tests (specify form); (5–20) minutes; Thomas D. Gnagey; Facilitation House.*

Review of Diagnostic Screening Test: Math, Third Edition, by EDWARD F. IWANICKI, Associate Dean of the School of Education and Professor of Education Administration, University of Connecticut, Storrs, CT:

The Diagnostic Screening Test (DST): Math provides teachers, psychologists, and counselors with a quick assessment of student performance for classroom planning. An optional 9-item pretest can be used to obtain a rough estimate of basic computation skills. The test is divided into a Basic Processes and a Specialized Section. The Basic Processes Section consists of 36 graded and developmentally ordered items. This section yields addition, subtraction, multiplication, and division scores as well as nine supplemental diagnostic measures of student performance on math concepts which transcend basic computation. Computational and conceptual skills in five areas commonly taught in math programs are assessed in the Specialized Section. Each of the 36 items comprising this section are keyed to a grade level. Although the DST: Math Test can be administered individually or to a group, the author advises either individual administration or closely supervised group administration at grades three and below.

The DST: Math Test Manual provides directions for administering and scoring the instrument as well as step by step interpretation procedures. The interpretation process culminates in completing a Classroom Recommendations form for each pupil. While for the most part the directions in the manual are clear, there are some ambiguous sections and some inconsistencies. For example, the manual indicates the Specialized Section utilizes from 37 to 45 items to evaluate student performance, when only 36 items are contained on the test form. Furthermore, it is noted that group administration of the Specialized Section at the lower grade levels has been facilitated by using shapes (star, ball, house) to distinguish among items, but all items on the test form are labelled with a ball. Finally, a misplaced paragraph in the discussion of the scoring procedures for the Specialized Section could lead a user to miscalculate the total score. Due to these problems as well as to the intricacies of scoring and interpreting the results of this instrument, teachers would benefit from some supervised training before using the test.

The author claims the face and construct validity of the DST: Math Test are obvious due to the manner in which the test is developed. Although sufficient information is presented to support the face and content validity of this instrument, adequate data are not provided to substantiate its construct validity. First, the item analysis procedures used to determine the graded difficulty of the items in the final test form were based on a limited sample, averaging less than 25 students per grade level. Second, the construct validity of the DST: Math Test was assessed by comparing DST performance with total math scores on the PIAT and KeyMath. Instead of correlating DST performance with the PIAT and KeyMath scores, a table was presented containing the proportion of students at each grade level whose DST grade equivalent performance was within (plus or minus) 3 months of their performance on the PIAT or the KeyMath. More thorough attention to these issues would have resulted in stronger support for the validity of the DST: Math Test.

The discussion of the reliability of the DST: Math Test was inadequate. It focused on the amount of overall math growth exhibited over a three-month period by a sample of students. The tetrachoric correlation between November and January scores was reported as an indicator of test-retest reliability. Three months is too long a period to use when assessing the stability of a math test. No internal consistency reliability estimates were provided.

The only section which differs between Forms A and B of the DST: Math Test is the Basic Processes Section. In describing the development of this section for Form B, the author noted simply that the procedures followed were basically similar to those used in developing Form A. The two test forms were administered to the same student sample at grades 1 through 12 to assess the equivalency of Forms A and B. The nature of this student sample or the number of students at each grade level was not specified. The generally accepted practice of calculating the Pearson product-moment correlation coefficient between the obtained scores on each form was not followed. Instead, the score distributions for each form were dichotomized. Students were classified as to whether they scored in the top or bottom half of the distribution. Then the tetrachoric correlation between Form A and Form B performance was calculated by grade level and reported as a measure of equivalence. The moderate to high equivalency coefficients reported could be questioned, since dichotomizing the score distribution can result in higher equivalency coefficients than if the obtained scores on each test form were correlated.

The Classroom Recommendations form used to report the results of the DST: Math Test is organized well, especially in summarizing performance on the Basic Processes Section. A table is provided which displays student performance in addition, subtraction, multiplication, and division in terms of the nine major concepts measured by the test. Performance in the major process and specialized skill areas is interpreted using a grade equivalent (GE) score along with a consolidation index (CI). The CI is a measure of the consistency of skill development up to the grade level indicated in the GE. If a high degree of consistency is exhibited, subsequent instruction can proceed at the grade level specified in the GE. If skill development is inconsistent with the level indicated in the GE, teachers are directed to focus instruction at the grade level where the student began to encounter math difficulty. The consolidation index is an interesting feature of this instrument, but users may find it is not worth taking the time to calculate this index. Inspection of the item responses on the Classroom Recommendations form yields the same information for the Basic Processes Section as one would obtain from the CI.

In summary, the DST: Math Test merits review by school personnel seeking an instrument for screening students in mathematics skill proficiency. Since only four items are used to measure each concept across grades 1 through 12, the test is more appropriate for rough screening than for diagnostic purposes. Inadequate technical data are provided to support the reliability and validity of this test. Thus, pilot studies should be conducted before the DST: Math Test is adopted for wide scale use to determine whether this instrument provides accurate information for making decisions about the types of students with whom it will be used.

Review of Diagnostic Screening Test: Math, Third Edition, by STANLEY F. VASA, Associate Professor of Special Education, University of Nebraska-Lincoln, Lincoln, NE:

The author states that the Diagnostic Screening Test: Math is "designed to assist teachers, psychologists and counselors in quickly obtaining diagnostic information which can be immediately translated into practical, helpful classroom learning activities appropriate to each student's individual needs." These claims seem to be unrealistically optimistic. More appropriately, the test may be used as an initial screening tool; but it requires follow-up with further testing or informal analysis of a student's work by the teacher before effective instructional planning can occur.

The test may be administered as a group or individual test. Instructions are clear and concise. No estimates of administration time are provided; however, the amount of time required to complete the 72-item scale will vary with the age of the student. The test is hand scored, using a key provided in the manual. Directions for computing scores and interpreting results are confusing. The author's choice of grade equivalent (GE) scores and consolidated index (CI) scores is based on a very limited number of items (0–7) per grade level, and normative procedures (sample size 250 in grades 1 through 11) are not sufficient to establish GE scores at tenths of a school year. General cautions concerning the use of grade equivalent scores should be observed by the user. The CI scores are used to determine relative mastery of grade level performance rather than mastery of specific skills. This information seems to be of little value in meeting instructional planning needs of individual students.

The author's suggestion of informal analysis of a subject's performance provides the greatest amount of information for instructional purposes. One should note, however, that informal analysis of student mathematical errors to determine patterns may be conducted without the use of the test. Teacher samples of students' work would provide the same information and potentially provide a greater number of trials of various types of problems.

The author utilized a review of major arithmetic series (Addison-Wesley, Ginn, Macmillan, and Houghton Mifflin) and a survey of 80 mathematics teachers to develop the initial items. An experimental edition was then used to conduct an item analysis ($N = 549$ students) allowing elimination of poorly constructed items and arrangement of items into a developmental sequence (K through 12). From this item analysis, each item was assigned a grade level. Items utilized in both the basic and specialized sections of the test deal with performing basic operations (addition, subtraction, multiplication, division), the recall of facts, regrouping, decimals, and fractions. There is a lack of higher-order problem solving or mathematical reasoning in the scale. Although GE scores are provided for grades 1 through 11, items do not reflect secondary mathematics curriculum areas such as algebra and geometry.

The experimental edition of the test (November administration) and the final edition (January administration) were used to establish reliability estimates. An overall reliability of .93 for the scale was reported. No estimates of reliability at various grade levels were provided within the manual. Estimates of the standard error of measurement are not included in the test information. This information, however, is necessary in determining significant discrepancies in the student's performance at various age levels as suggested by the test interpretation instructions. Normative data suggest that performance may vary, particularly at upper grade levels in which fewer items are used in establishing grade level equivalents. Because of the small number of items at each grade level, reliability for individual student diagnosis is suspect.

The author attempted to establish face and construct validity through a discussion of the test's construction and by reporting for each level of the test the percentage of student grade equivalent scores within (plus or minus) three months of their performance on the Peabody Individual Achievement Test and the Key Math Diagnostic Test. Percentages ranged from 61% (grade 1, specialized) to 97% (grade 4, basic). Again, care should be taken to compare test items with adopted curriculum guides to insure curricular validity.

Technical data indicate that the author has taken steps to insure that items represent various developmental sequences in mathematics. The technical data, however, do not support the assignment of grade level equivalents to test subjects or the use of the test as a comparison of inter-student performance.

The use of a screening instrument for instructional planning is questionable. Teacher made informal tests covering local curriculum seem more useful. Use of grade equivalents tend to encourage inter-student comparisons and the use of the test as a norm-referenced test. Use of the test as a norm-referenced scale is not recommended by the author or supported by the norming procedures. Teachers who have experience with mathematics curricula and students' skills at various grade levels would gain little from using the test.

[342]

Diagnostic Screening Test: Reading, Third Edition. Grades 1–12; 1981; identical with Diagnostic Screening Test: Reading ('76) except for the addition of one graded reading passage, a listening comprehension subtest, and an alternate form; 16 scores: comfort reading level, instructional reading level, frustration reading level, comprehension reading level, listening level, phonics/sight ratio, word attack skill analysis (c–v/c, v–r, v–l, v–v, c–v–c, silent e, mix, site, total), and a consolidation index; no data on reliability; individual; Form A, B, ('79, 6 pages); manual ('79, 16 pages); 1983 price data: $12 per 20 tests of Form A and manual; $21 per 100 tests of Form B; (5–10) minutes; Thomas D. Gnagey; Facilitation House.*

For a review by P. David Pearson of an earlier edition, see 8:755.

Review of Diagnostic Screening Test: Reading, Third Edition, by EDWARD F. IWANICKI, Associate Dean of the School of Education and Professor of Educational Administration, University of Connecticut, Storrs, CT:

The Diagnostic Screening Test (DST): Reading provides teachers with a quick, valid assessment of a student's reading skill proficiency. This individually administered instrument yields Comfort, Instructional, and Frustration Word Reading Level scores as well as Reading and Listening Passage Comprehension scores. In addition, eight subtests provide estimates of a student's phonics and word attack skill proficiency. The testing process begins with the administration of pretests in word reading and passage comprehension and proceeds with more extensive testing in these areas. Due to the high correlations between pretest scores and scores on other sections of the DST: Reading Test as reported in the manual, the pretest scores can serve as rough estimates of a student's word reading and passage comprehension performance. Interpretation procedures focus on individual test scores as well as on comparisons between these scores. Step by step interpretation procedures result in classroom recommendations for each pupil.

The directions for administering and scoring the DST: Reading Test are sometimes difficult to follow. Furthermore, some important aspects of the test administration process are not treated adequately. For example, teachers are directed to administer a list of nonsense words as part of the pretest and to scan the student's responses for probable rule-related weaknesses. No guidance is provided as to how these responses should be scanned. Teachers are expected to know they should go back to the first page of the manual, figure out which nonsense word is keyed to a particular rule, and then identify probable rule-related weaknesses. Teachers are also not provided with any criteria for assessing whether a word has been read correctly when administering the word attack sections of the test. Although clear directions are provided for administering the reading comprehension passages, the manual simply directs the teacher to administer the listening comprehension passages in a similar manner. No guidance is provided for selecting appropriately graded listening passages. Due to such problems, teachers should receive some supervised training in the administration and scoring of this instrument before it is used.

In describing the development of the DST: Reading Test, the author provided some information to support its content validity. Although the numbers of teachers and students involved in the test development and validation process were specified, further information for assessing the qualifications and representativeness of these groups was lacking. It was not clear whether the test was normed during a specific month or whether the norms were derived from data accumulated over a longer period. When the construct validity of the DST: Reading Test was assessed by comparing DST performance with SRA and WRAT reading achievement scores, two problems were evident. First, no information was provided as to whether the three tests were administered at about the same time. Second, the usual practice of correlating DST performance with SRA or WRAT scores was not followed. Instead, a table was presented containing the proportion of students at each grade level whose DST grade equivalent scores were within plus or minus 2 months of their performance on the SRA or the WRAT. Attention to such issues would have resulted in stronger support for the validity of the DST: Reading Test.

The word attack sections of Form B of the DST: Reading Test were developed from a list of words computer rated as identical to those in Form A in word attack and grade level difficulty. The author did not elaborate further on this process. The approach used to develop the comprehension passages for Form B was not discussed. When both Forms A and B were administered to 25 students at grades 2, 4, 6 and 8, the correlation between scores on the two forms was .93. This limited study and the incomplete description of the development of Form B do not provide sufficient justification for the equivalence of Forms A and B. Also, no data were provided to support the reliability of the scores obtained when using either Form A or B of the DST: Reading Test.

The DST: Reading Test results are interpreted with primary emphasis on grade equivalent scores. The grade equivalent metric used is based on a nine-month year, rather than on the conventional ten-month year. For example, an increase in reading comprehension scores from 2.0 to 3.0 would represent nine months growth. This approach could be confusing when assessing growth or when summarizing test results for groups.

In summary, the DST: Reading Test has some inadequacies. The directions for administering and scoring the test need some further clarification and elaboration. Also, more comprehensive data are needed to support the validity and reliability of this test. Since reading is a critical area where accurate diagnostic information is required, it is questionable whether this instrument should be considered for adoption. Other individually administered tests such as the Woodcock Reading Mastery Tests have been constructed with considerably more attention to ease of administration and interpretation as well as to technical rigor.

[343]

Diagnostic Screening Test: Spelling, Third Edition. Grades 1–12; 1979; 12 scores: 3 scores (verbal, written, total) in each of 3 categories (phonics, sight, total) plus 3 consolidation index scores; Forms A, B, ('79, 6 pages); manual ('79, 16 pages); 1983 price data: $12 per kit including manual and 20 Form A tests; $21 per 100 tests (Forms A or B); (5–10) minutes; Thomas D. Gnagey; Facilitation House.*

Review of Diagnostic Screening Test: Spelling, Third Edition, by EDWARD F. IWANICKI, Associate Dean of the School of Education and Professor of Educational Administration, University of Connecticut, Storrs, CT:

The Diagnostic Screening Test (DST): Spelling can be administered individually or on a group basis to obtain a measure of spelling proficiency. When administered to a group, the test yields scores on phonics, sight, and total spelling. Additional verbal and written spelling scores are obtained when the test is administered individually. The results of an individual administration can be interpreted to derive further diagnostic information concerning a student's gross and sequential memory ability. The

DST: Spelling Test Manual provides clear directions for administering and scoring the instrument as well as step by step interpretation procedures. The interpretation process results in classroom recommendations for each pupil. Due to the intricacies of administering, scoring, and interpreting the results of this instrument, teachers would benefit from some supervised training in these procedures, especially if the test is to be administered individually.

In describing the development of the DST: Spelling Test, the author provided some information to support its content validity. Although the numbers of teachers and students involved in the test development and validation processes were specified, further information needed to assess the qualifications and representativeness of these groups was lacking. When the construct validity of the DST: Spelling Test was assessed by comparing DST performance with scores on the spelling subtests of the SRA and WRAT, two problems were evident. First, no information was provided as to when the SRA and WRAT were administered. Second, DST performance was not correlated with SRA or WRAT scores. Instead, a table was presented containing the proportion of students at each grade level whose DST grade equivalent performance was within 2 and 3 months of their performance on the SRA or the WRAT. Better attention to such issues would have resulted in stronger support for the validity of the DST: Spelling Test.

The discussion of the reliability of the DST: Spelling Test was inadequate. It focused on the amount of spelling growth exhibited over a three-month period by students who participated in the development of the test at each grade level. No discussion was provided as to how this information could be interpreted as a measure of reliability. No internal consistency or test-retest reliability estimates were provided.

In describing the development of Form B of the DST: Spelling Test, the author noted simply that the procedures followed were basically similar to those employed in developing Form A. The two test forms were administered to the same student sample at grades 1 through 12 to determine the equivalency of Forms A and B. The nature of this sample or the number of students at each grade level was not specified. The generally accepted practice of calculating the Pearson product moment correlation coefficient between the raw scores on each form of the test was not followed. Instead, the score distributions for each form were dichotomized. Students were classified as to whether they scored in the top or bottom half of the distribution. Then the tetrachoric correlation between Form A and Form B performance was calculated by grade level and reported as a measure of equivalence. The moderate to high equivalency coefficients reported could be questioned since calculating a tetrachoric correlation using dichotomized scores can result in higher equivalency coefficients than if the raw scores on each test form were correlated using a Pearson *r*.

When DST: Spelling Test performance is interpreted in a particular area, a grade equivalent (GE) score is used along with a consolidation index (CI). The CI is a measure of the consistency of student skill development up to the grade level indicated in the GE. If a high degree of consistency is exhibited, subsequent instruction can proceed at the grade level specified in the GE. If skill development is inconsistent with the level indicated in the GE, teachers are directed to focus instruction at the grade level where the student began to encounter spelling difficulty. Since the purpose of the test is to diagnose spelling skill proficiency and to identify an appropriate instructional placement, the grade score corresponding to the level at which spelling difficulty is encountered appears to be a more appropriate measure of student performance than use of the GE with the CI.

In summary, the DST: Spelling Test is an attractive option for consideration by school personnel seeking an instrument for diagnosing spelling skill deficiencies. Due to the types of information provided through individual administration, the test is most appropriate for use with pupils experiencing spelling problems or in placing new students at the proper level of instruction. This instrument is superior to the spelling subtests in many basic skill achievement batteries since it assesses the student's ability to spell rather than the ability to discriminate between properly and improperly spelled words. As this instrument is used in local settings, further data should be collected to assess its reliability and validity in light of the technical inadequacies noted.

Review of Diagnostic Screening Test: Spelling, Third Edition, by ROBERT E. SHAFER, *Professor of English, Arizona State University, Tempe, AZ:*

The Diagnostic Screening Test: Spelling (DST) comes complete with a manual and six-page test forms of which pages four and five are to be detached and used as an examiner's worksheet. The manual contains complete, detailed, readable instructions on the administration of a pretest and the test itself, information on scoring, instructions on computation of the consolidation index, which reflects "how solid or spotty a student's knowledge or skill is," and a section on the interpretation of data obtained from the test, which contains a discussion of the roles of visual and auditory sequential memory, gross memory, and the length of memory in any spelling task. Although the section on objectives indicates the test can be used for both group and individual diagnosis, the instructions for the administration of the test clearly presupposes individualized diagnostic situations—something that many classroom teachers would have some difficulty in creating in their classrooms. The directions contained in the manual for scoring, computation of the consolidation index, and interpreting the data are all readable and understandable. A basic problem with tests of spelling ability is that a test of words in isolation heard or read apart from a meaningful context may not be an accurate assessment of an individual's spelling ability. In natural communication situations, listeners and readers use more than memory to comprehend and reproduce meaning; in other words they listen, speak, read, and write meaningful utterances. As the work of Smith (1971) and Goodman (1975) have shown, reading and writing abilities are tied to meaningful contexts and to natural communication situations. This presents a problem for all published spelling tests including the DST, unless ways can be found to devise a test which tests spelling ability in a natural communication context.

Another problem with this test is the division of the words into "phonics words" and "sight words." The test author does not explain what a "sight word" is as differentiated from a "phonics word." A speculation might be that a "phonics word" would be one which would contain a one-to-one phoneme to grapheme relationship. But the inclusion of such words as "fallacy" and "lucidity" on the "phonics word" list would seem to belie that possibility. Nor does the method of test construction shed light on this dilemma since the "initial pool" of spelling words was obtained by having "71 teachers, grades one through twelve submit lists of 100 words typically 'taught' and mastered by average students in that teacher's classroom." No attempt is made to show what an "average" student might be or how the teachers were instructed to select such students. Nor does the test author explain by what criteria the "ten phonics words" and "ten sight words" were selected to be placed on the initial form of the test or by what criteria three of the most "differentiating sight" words and three of the most "differentiating phonics" words were assigned to each level (and ultimately were used to determine grade level). The test author generated "Form B words...by a computer," proposing them "as equivalent to Form A [words] in phonetic and grade level characteristics." The author, however, does not explain what he means by "phonetic" characteristics. Any word or morpheme, when pronounced, would be a phonetic entity in a stream of speech. But how a word can have "grade level characteristics" and further how these could be put together to construct a computer program is not explained. Small wonder that we find "conscientious" being proposed as a 12th-grade word and "pretentious" as a 10th-grade word. The "sight words" for grade six have two words in the same exercise, "belief" and "brief," which require a knowledge of the i–e digraph in English spelling—a rather precise bit of orthographic knowledge to account for such a significant weighting in the test.

Since it would be possible to select words for reading and spelling tests on the basis of several criteria such as frequency of occurrence, phoneme/grapheme correspondence, or occurrence in meaningful contexts, it is surprising that the author did not specify more carefully the precise means of selection from the groups of words which the 71 teachers presented. Each of the students in a particular teacher's class might be at a different level of spelling development (Henderson, Estes, & Stonecash, 1972); therefore, each child's individual spelling development may reflect quite different adaptations of his or her phonological knowledge to orthography (Read, 1975). It would seem highly questionable as to where the "average child" would fall in any teacher's classroom on such a complex intellectual task.

All of the above calls into question both the content validity and the predictive validity of the DST. If "average" children have more difficulty spelling some words than others at various grade levels, it would be advantageous for test makers to attempt to discover what psycholinguistic principles are at work and incorporate these findings in spelling tests rather than relying on teachers' observations of the mythical average.

REVIEWER'S REFERENCES

Smith, F. UNDERSTANDING READING: A PSYCHOLINGUISTIC ANALYSIS OF READING AND LEARNING TO READ. Holt, Rinehart and Winston: New York, 1971.

Henderson, E. H., Estes, T. H., & Stonecash, S. A. An exploratory study of word acquisition among first graders at mid-year in a language experience approach. JOURNAL OF READING BEHAVIOR, Summer, 1972, 4, 21–31.

Goodman, K. (Ed.) MISCUE ANALYSIS: APPLICATIONS TO READING INSTRUCTION. Urbana, IL: National Council of Teachers of English, 1975.

Read, C. CHILDREN'S CATEGORIZATION OF SPEECH SOUNDS IN ENGLISH. Urbana, IL: National Council of Teachers of English, 1975.

[344]

Diagnostic Skills Battery. Grades 1–2, 3–4, 5–6, 7–8; 1976–80; DSB; "criterion- and norm-referenced"; 4 levels; general manual ('77, 48 pages); norms supplement ('80, 6 pages); master content outline ('76, 16 pages); information brochure ('76, 15 pages); pupil score folder ('76, 6 pages); identification form ('76, 2 pages); separate answer sheets (machine scored) must be used (except for Level 12); 1982 price data: $.10 per pupil score folder; $2.50 per general manual; $2 per specimen set; plus 2 price/scoring programs: lease score (all levels) and school purchase (Levels 34, 56, 78); each program has 2 scoring service plans: plan I (includes 3 alphabetical lists, 3 group summaries, 1 set pressure-sensitive labels, 1 test interpretive manual per class, 1 master content outline per class), plan II (3-copy performance profile, 3 group summaries, 1 master content outline per class, 1 test interpretive manual per class), $20 minimum per order for this scoring service;

(150–200) minutes per level; O. F. Anderhalter; Scholastic Testing Service, Inc.*

a) LEVEL 12. Grades 1–2; 2 scores: reading, mathematics; forms A, B, ('76, 24 pages); manual ('76, 23 pages); machine scored test booklets must be used; $2.10 per pupil for lease/score program, plan I (includes machine scored booklets and manual); $2.01 per pupil for lease/score program, plan II (includes machine scored booklets and manual).

b) LEVEL 34. Grades 3–4; 3 scores: reading, language arts, mathematics; forms A, B, ('76, 31 pages); combined manual ('76, 12 pages) for this level and *c*, *d*, below; $1.69 per pupil for lease/score, plan I (includes returnable booklets, answer sheets, and manual); $1.60 per pupil for lease/score, plan II (includes same items as plan I); $.95 per pupil for school purchase, plan I; $.86 per pupil for school purchase, plan II; $26 per 20 test booklets and one manual; $10 per 50 answer sheets.

c) LEVEL 56. Grades 5–6; 3 scores: same as *b* above; forms A, B, ('76, 29 pages); combined manual (same as *b* above); prices same as *b* above.

d) LEVEL 78. Grades 7–8; 3 scores: same as *b* above; forms A, B, ('76, 29 pages); combined manual (same as *b* above); prices same as *b* above.

Review of Diagnostic Skills Battery by JACK J. KRAMER, Associate Professor of Educational Psychology, University of Nebraska-Lincoln, Lincoln, NE:

On the surface the Diagnostic Skills Battery (DSB) has the appearance of a comprehensive test of achievement for individuals in Grades 1 through 8. The materials that one would expect with this type of instrument (general manual, norms supplement, content outline, and general information brochure) are provided with intent to facilitate administration and interpretation of the test battery. In addition, the publisher correctly points out that most school systems today are in need of both norm-referenced and criterion-referenced information for use in planning educational programs. The DSB, according to the general manual, is designed to meet these needs. Unfortunately, closer inspection reveals that the publisher has failed to document this and numerous other assertions.

Concern about adequacy of the DSB in meeting its objectives and the needs of educators must begin with an examination of the methods used to select items for inclusion in the battery. Although the DSB manual reports that "close attention was given to the quality of the items themselves," there is little evidence provided to substantiate this point. In fact, the most extensive analysis of item selection techniques provided is a reproduction (Appendix B—general manual) of the rationale for the items and objectives used in a criterion-referenced test (i.e., Analysis of Skills) published by the same company that publishes the DSB. The authors imply that since the logic for item selection in criterion- and norm-referenced testing is similar, it is permissible to reproduce the material from the other test in lieu of a separate analysis. However, even if this were true (and it is not), most individuals would find the publisher's comments inadequate. For example, at various points throughout the general manual there are vague statements concerning the methods used to select items and objectives. These comments indicate there was "extensive consultation with curriculum specialists, administrators, and classroom teachers at the various levels," and "analysis of the most widely used textbooks." It is also claimed that "secondary sources for objectives included many of the already existing statements of objectives compiled throughout the United States." While any consumer desires this type of information, it is the publisher's responsibility to provide sufficient detail to enable the user to evaluate whether these tasks were carried out in a manner that improves the ability of the instrument to provide information of interest. These concerns fall under the heading of content validity, and it is important to know how many experts were involved, what textbooks, and which lists of objectives. One wonders what rationale guided and what decisions shaped the test content. In all cases that information is lacking.

The general manual implies that it is primarily the test users responsibility to match the DSB with local instructional objectives in order to assess content validity. While it is agreed that each test user should make this type of comparison, it is primarily the publisher's responsibility to see to it that items contained within a test are adequate, representative samples of the skills they are designed to test. The DSB does not live up to this responsibility.

Unfortunately, the problems with the DSB do not end here. It is evident that the publisher has not taken sufficient care to provide an adequate standardization sample. Data from 1976 is provided on less then 10,000 students (405 to 605 for each level when broken down by test form and grade). While the sample does appear to represent adequately the U.S. population in terms of geographic region, there is no data provided which indicate that any systematic attempt was made to stratify the sample in terms of race, type of school, community type (urban-rural), or ability level. In the latter instance (ability level) the manual reports that "school systems which agreed to participate were asked to identify a given number of generally 'average,' 'below-average,' and 'above-average' schools with approximately equal numbers of pupils per grade." While it is certainly possible to question whether this procedure would provide a representative sample, it would at the very least be helpful to know the criteria employed by school districts in making this decision and the numbers of schools of each type used in the standardization studies. Once again these data are unavailable.

Conditions regarding the reliability of the DSB are only slightly better. Reliability estimates for the Battery Composite (.93 to .97), individual test total scores (.83 to .94) and part scores (.54 to .90) do appear to fall in the acceptable range. This would be acceptable, except that the manual goes on to say that the method of calculating reliability (Kuder-Richardson Formula 21) "underestimates reliability for tests in which the items are of varying difficulty, and overestimates reliability for tests that include a large proportion of speed variances. Since all of these tests are essentially power tests, and since all include items of varying difficulty the reliability estimates in these tables are probably lower than would have been obtained through the use of other techniques for analyzing internal consistency." There are at least two serious problems with the foregoing statement: (*a*) If this formula doesn't account for items of varying difficulty, why wasn't a formula used that did (e.g., Kuder-Richardson Formula 20), and (*b*) once again, it is the publisher's responsibility, not the consumer's, to provide evidence that other statistical methods would yield higher reliability estimates than those reported in the manual.

Finally, with respect to reliability issues, the publisher presents no statistical evidence of alternate form reliability although it is acknowledged that this is typically done through a comparison of groups of individuals who take both forms of the test. Instead only a comparison is presented of median raw scores on the two forms. Nor is there any evidence presented to substantiate the claim that use of the same form is appropriate if "sufficient time" elapses between pretesting and posttesting.

Evidence of validity (referred to as preliminary estimates in the DSB general manual) is provided through a comparison of the scores of 777 children on the DSB with those on the Educational Development Series (a norm-referenced test which according to the publisher, Scholastic Testing Services, samples career choices and school and career plans and includes two ability and three to six achievement tests). Although the reported correlations are in the moderate to high range, it should be noted that when broken down by level, grade, and form these calculations were computed on samples which ranged in size from a low of 36 to a high of only 126 children. Furthermore, this data is presented only in narrative form and is not available for detailed inspection.

Finally, it seems doubtful that the DSB could provide objective-referenced information of much use. This is not only a direct criticism of the DSB, but a concern with making inferences about mastery (or lack of mastery) of skills based on a restricted number of items (in this case, two per objective). Furthermore, not only is there a limited number of items but a limited number of objectives as well. It seems logical that the best way to conduct criterion-referenced testing would be for a school district to identify its objectives in each skill area and then to develop tests of those objectives based on the curriculum and materials used in that district. A test like the DSB would almost inevitably fall short of meeting the particular needs of any school district with interest in objective-referenced assessment.

This review has not examined every facet of the DSB. The problems identified, however, are extremely serious and strike at the very heart of what competent test construction is all about. The concerns expressed here include the rationale and method of item selection, the standardization sample, and aspects of both reliability and validity data. As a result, the DSB cannot be recommended for any purpose. There are far too many excellent achievement batteries available (e.g., Stanford Achievement Test, Comprehensive Test of Basic Skills, and Iowa Test of Basic Skills) which offer more to the consumer. The selection of any of these instruments is recommended as being superior to the choice of the DSB.

[Note: The Buros Institute of Mental Measurements has a policy prohibiting members of its staff from conducting test reviews for Institute publications. Dr. Kramer is now a member of the Institute staff. However, this review was solicited and written before Dr. Kramer became a member of the Institute staff, or before he was even considered for such a position.—Ed.]

Review of Diagnostic Skills Battery by R. STEVE MCCALLUM, *Assistant Professor of Psychology, University of Southern Mississippi, Hattiesburg, MS:*

The Diagnostic Skills Battery (DSB) provides consumers with norm-referenced and criterion-referenced achievement data for students in grades 1 through 8. The DSB is a hybrid, representing a mix of characteristics from the publisher's norm-referenced Educational Developmental Series and their criterion-referenced Analysis of Skills (ASK) series. For example, the same master list of objectives serves for the DSB and ASK; however, the number of objectives assessed by the DSB is reduced from the 60 per level listed in the ASK to about 40 for each of the four levels of the DSB. Also, the DSB relies on only two items to test each objective rather than the three required by the ASK tests. A Master Content Outline listing objectives is included and feedback is provided in several formats: (*a*) An Individual Skills Analysis report provides a class list showing pupils' performance on each objective by "+," "–," "p"; class and national percentages of mastery(+), non-mastery(–), and partial mastery(P) are available. (*b*) A Performance Profile combines norm-referenced and objective-referenced reports and provides raw scores, local stanines, and national grade scores and percentiles for Total Reading, three reading subtests, Total Mathematics, two mathematics subtests, Total Language, three languages subtests, and the composite score. Also, the profile provides a "ratio correct," a national percentage correct, and the national percentage of non-mastery of "skill clusters" (grouping of objectives). (*c*) A class record shows all subtest and total scores and the Battery Composite for the classroom group. At the consumers' option, additional normative data can be printed on the class record. (*d*) Pressure sensitive labels are available for cumulative folders, and optional Pupil Score Folders are available for parents. (*e*) A Summary Report is provided and gives frequency distributions, means, and standard deviations for all subtest and total scores and the Battery Composite. This Summary Report also provides comparisons of selected local percentile ranks with national percentile ranks and grade scores.

Except for the grade score, all the scores reported are conventional and from either norm- or criterion-referenced format. The grade score is a modification of the more familiar grade-equivalent score and is actually based on within-grade comparisons which are expressed on a normalized standard score scale, with the mean set equal to actual grade placement, and the standard deviation set to 1.0. Information from the manual suggests that this normalizing transformation provides grade scores which limit extreme (and uninterpretable) grade-placement values and provides additional psychometric qualities. Actually, this score is just another normalized standard score and offers no more information than would any such score. This "Grade" score, like its namesake the grade-equivalent score, does not actually reflect the pupil's grade level functioning. As has been suggested elsewhere, use of the terms grade score or grade equivalent score should be avoided to prevent misinterpretation.

The DSB originally was standardized during the spring of 1976, and again during fall and spring, 1979. The 1979 norms included data from 6,000 pupils (3,000 fall, 3,000 spring) at grades 2 through 8 (N =42,000), with the contribution of each school held constant across the two samples. An effort was made to obtain "representative" schools in various states. Representativeness was determined by previous testing data (schools obtaining approximately median scores on the distribution of school averages in a state), or by recommendation by personnel from state departments of education from other data. Also, a few higher-than-average and lower-than-average schools were included. No mention was made of the stratification criteria used to choose students from these schools designated "other than average." The inclusion of students from four geographical areas approximately reflected the population proportion from those areas and the public school/private school ratio, as indicated in the 1978 edition of the Statistical Abstract of the United States. There was, however, no special effort to stratify by ethnic group or race, or to include handicapped children. According to the manual, estimates of racial composition of various schools were provided via phone conversations with administrators. The following racial breakdown was obtained: White, 84%; Black, 14%; Native American, 1%; and Oriental, 1%. Obviously, systems using the DSB with significant portions of non-middle class, non-average white students should interpret the results cautiously.

Content of the tests was determined by analysis of textbook series and recommendations from school and curricular experts. The item format is multiple choice; four options for each item are included for the first level, and five for the three higher levels. The use of four and five options, rather than three and four, does not seem consistent with the stated need to reduce DSB testing time (from the time allowed on the ASK), especially since very little is gained by adding the options beyond three for the younger students and four for those in grades 3 through 8. In fact, the use of four options on level 1 items may actually confound results and add to error for these young children.

The General Manual of the DSB contains reliability and validity data for the 1976 norms. A brief description of the 1979 norming activities is provided by the publishers in a five-page supplemental booklet. This supplementary booklet does not provide reliability or validity data from the 1979 sample. Data from the 1976 sample were obtained from 9,951 pupils from end of the year testing only. Internal reliability was based on Kuder-Richardson Formula 21 estimates. (The Kuder-Richardson Formula 20 would have been more appropriate since KR–21 provides underestimates when items vary in difficulty.) Respectable reliability estimates for the Battery Composite ranged from .93 to .97, from .83 to .94 for total test scores, and from .54 to .90 (median=.83) for subtests or part scores. Intercorrelations among the various total test scores ranged from .21 to .81, with a median value of .55. The manual provides little discussion of alternate form equivalence. The section dealing with equivalence of forms provides an unsatisfactory discussion of the use of raw score statistics, particularly the median scores, to determine equivalence. The use of raw scores for establishing parallel form equivalence is appropriate only when supplemented with additional data such as correlation coefficients and values from standard score comparisons.

Also, the manual emphasizes the use of raw scores as indices of growth patterns across the forms. Because of differing item difficulty levels from form to form, such a comparison is suspect.

Validity data reported in the manual were obtained from a comparison of the DSB data collected in 1976 and scores from the Educational Developmental Series tests collected in 1975 (*N* =777). The correlations between composites for the batteries ranged from .65 to .97 (median=.90), for Reading .55 to .97, Mathematics .58 to .96, and Language Arts .54 to .98. Additional data from studies comparing the DSB with other batteries were promised, but these did not appear in the updated 1979 supplementary norms booklet.

In summary, the DSB represents an admirable effort to combine norm-referenced and criterion-referenced tests; use of such tests can provide data for making system-wide, school, and individual-student decisions. Collecting norm- and criterion-referenced data simultaneously saves money and time for systems requiring both. The test exhibits significant strengths including a variety of feedback formats, detailed description of test content for instructional programming, and recent normative data. Salient weaknesses, however, are also present and include the use of an easily misunderstood "Grade Score," failure to include enough relevant stratification variables (thereby restricting somewhat the use of normative data), limited use of data to indicate extent of alternate form reliability, and unavailability of the reliability/validity data from the latest normative sampling. In spite of the limitations the test is generally appealing and could offer valuable educational information, especially for "average" schools, i.e., those reflecting the characteristics of the normative sample.

[345]

Diagnostic Spelling Potential Test. Ages 7 and over; 1982; DSPT; individual; 5 subtest scores: spelling, word recognition (sight, phonetic), visual recognition, auditory-visual recognition; Form A-1, B-1, (4 pages, contains first 2 subtests); Form A-2, B-2, (8 pages, contains last 2 subtests); word recognition sheet (2 pages); manual (160 pages); 1984 price data: $6 per 25 tests; $3 per 25 profile sheets; $17.50 per manual including word recognition sheet; $17.50 per specimen set; (25–40) minutes; John Arena; Academic Therapy Publications.*

TEST REFERENCES

1. Blachman, B. A. Test review: Diagnostic Spelling Potential Test (DSPT). JOURNAL OF READING, 1982, 27, 134–138.

Review of Diagnostic Spelling Potential Test by MARCEE J. MEYERS, Associate Professor of Education, University of North Carolina-Wilmington, Wilmington, NC:

OVERVIEW. The Diagnostic Spelling Test (DSPT) is a comprehensive spelling test designed to assess current level of spelling performance and potential for spelling progress. The four 90-item subtests include tasks in spelling dictation, sight word pronunciation, phonetic decoding, identification of correctly spelled words from sets of distractors, and identification of correctly spelled, dictated words from sets of distractors. An information processing approach is used to describe the spelling subskills of discrimination, memory, language generalization, and auditory-visual integration. The DSPT manual clearly describes these purposes, subtests, and spelling characteristics and their underlying theory.

Although the manual is well organized with adequate explanations and examples, a few ambiguities exist. The test, for example, is described as a one-to-one test in one section and a group or individual test in another. In the Word Recognition Subtest directions, it is not clear whether the basal criterion is established with sight recognition responses or phonetic recognition responses, or both. In addition, calculation of the phonetic recognition raw score according to the directions does not yield the raw score obtained in the sample protocol. There are several misprints, including 00-00 as page numbers referred to in the manual; a scoring guide answer of d instead of b; a word misspelled in the technical section; and an entire sentence repeated in the interpretation section. The most serious errors, however, involve inaccuracies on the sample protocols used to clarify administration, scoring, and interpretation procedures. The following errors should be noted: an incorrect raw score in scoring box; seven inaccurately marked responses affecting basal, ceiling, and raw score calculation; and an incomplete birthdate recorded on a sample protocol.

ADMINISTRATION AND SCORING. The instructions for administering and scoring the DSPT are clearly explained with sufficient detail and illustration. Directions to be read to the students for each subtest are concise and easy to understand. All components of the test, including record forms and Word Recognition cards for student use, are well organized and easy to use. Although the manual contains useful suggestions for behavioral observation, additional space for comments should be included on the record form. Directions for scoring and recording are presented with detail and clarity, but likelihood of scoring error is still possible because of the ambiguities, misprints, and sample protocol marking errors previously described.

INTERPRETATION. The DSPT manual presents a set of variables that should be taken into account for the interpretation of test scores. Included in this list of "critical factors" are general intelligence, visual acuity, auditory acuity, and general health. It is true that these factors represent conditions which often have impact on test results; however, diagnosticians usually recommend that these factors be considered and assessed prior to academic testing.

Percentile ranks, standard scores, and grade ratings are clearly defined in the manual. Examples and explanations of these derived scores and related statistical concepts are described in sufficient detail to enable the examiner to make accurate interpretations. The manual also includes a description of appropriate cautions and limitations associated with these scores, which should reduce the likelihood of misinterpretation. In addition, the manual contains an elaborate classification of possible subtest performance. The detailed descriptions of these patterns assist in the analysis of test results and identification of skills for remediation.

In addition to subtest scores, a spelling error analysis is also used to interpret spelling performance and potential. Although error analysis is an excellent diagnostic tool for spelling and other skill areas, the procedures described in the manual seem somewhat limited. Only two categories of errors are recorded: phonetically correct misspellings and "all other errors." A more specific classification—including categories such as errors with vowels, blends, and digraphs—might provide further assistance for the professionals qualified to use this test.

SUGGESTED REMEDIATION. Over 40 pages of the DSPT are devoted to recommendations for guidelines, activities, and materials. The majority of these recommendations are sound, supported in the literature, and appropriate for teaching spelling. The organization of the remedial activities section, a random listing without regard to specific skills, goals, or objectives, would seem to encourage isolated games and tasks rather than a systematic, sequential spelling program. Although it would be possible to match specific activities to test result patterns obtained on the DSPT profile, a more clearly organized classification system based on the possible spelling patterns described in the interpretation section would facilitate use of this chapter.

Three of the specified remedial suggestions are not currently supported by research. One guideline recommends that the teacher should "encourage the use of cursive writing." Although this recommendation may be appropriate in the majority of cases, it is not always the best alternative for certain groups of students (i.e., learning disabled). It is also suggested that with some students, "visual perceptual activities should be profitable," but the empirical literature does not currently support this type of training. In at least three instances, the neurological impress method is recommended, even though its effectiveness has not been clearly established.

All of the items on the lists entitled "Suggested Materials" and "Suggested Tests" are available from Academic Therapy Publications; the selection criterion appears to be somewhat biased and limiting.

DEVELOPMENT AND TECHNICAL DATA. Test construction, standardization, reliability, and validity are discussed in depth. The equating method of standardization is explained and justified for the DSPT in combination with the spelling subtest of the Wide Range Achievement Test (WRAT). It is, however, suggested that the validity of this method depends on the equivalence of anchor and target tests; both tests should measure similar processes. Although this assumption would appear to be true for the dictation task on both tests, the reading subtest of the WRAT and the Word Recognition subtests of the DSPT would appear to be the other two parallel tasks. For the standardization procedures, however, the spelling section of the WRAT was used as the anchor test for each subtest of the DSPT.

The reliability coefficients obtained by the parallel forms method range from .81 to .98, with an overall average of .95 for the subtests at primary, intermediate, and secondary grade categories. Criterion-related validity is based on the relationship of performance on the DSPT subtests to the WRAT spelling subtest. The correlations across three grade levels and for all subtests range from .59 to .93, with the secondary values consistently lower than the primary and elementary, and the spelling subtest values consistently higher than the other subtest values.

SUMMARY. Taken together, the DSPT subtests clearly represent a thorough information processing approach to spelling assessment. The test materials are well organized and easy to use, and an elaborate model for analysis and interpretation is provided. The chief problems with the DSPT grow out of the numerous ambiguities, misprints, and errors still present in the manual. In addition, the remediation section should be tied more closely to the classification of spelling problems suggested in the interpretation section. If this test were to be revised and corrected, it would provide a useful tool for comprehensive spelling diagnosis.

Review of Diagnostic Spelling Potential Test by RUTH NOYCE, Associate Professor, Curriculum and Instruction, The University of Kansas, Lawrence, KS:

The Diagnostic Spelling Potential Test (DSPT) is intended for use by school psychologists and remedial specialists who need a complete profile for diagnosis of strengths and weaknesses in spelling-related skills of students with learning difficulties. The four subtests yield five scores: sight and phonetic recognition, spelling age level, visual recognition, and auditory visual recognition. Although three of the subtests can be used with groups, the test is primarily recommended for individual administration. Instructions are furnished for critical range testing, making completion of the full test possible in one sitting.

By differentiating between students who depend upon memorization and those who use phonetic generalizations, the DSPT measures "spelling potential," as well as present performance, according to the developer. It is emphasized that determination of the phonetic skills students have developed to assist them in learning to spell new words is an important feature of the test. Research support for the premise that good spellers apply generalizations in spelling unfamiliar words is cited in the early pages of the manual, and the stated assumption underlying measurement of "spelling potential" is that application of spelling rules is essential to good spelling.

The Spelling subtest provides information on a student's complete range of spelling skills by requiring the written encoding of spoken words. This score is the primary criterion for determining a speller's age level proficiency as well as the selection of other subtests to be utilized for diagnosing specific deficiencies. The Word Recognition subtest requires a subject to pronounce words, with an immediate response indicating sight vocabulary and a delay of two seconds (or an error corrected) representing phonetic decoding. The Word Recognition protocol yields two scores, one reflecting the speller's automatic familiarity with words and the other indicating the ability to apply spelling rules. The Visual Recognition subtest presents four alternative spellings of a word from which the student is expected to select the correct one, and performance is dependent upon both whole word memory and use of language generalizations. On the Auditory-Visual Recognition subtest a student responds from an auditory stimulus, which may be a difficult task for a speller who depends to a large extent upon phonetic generalizations because a phonetically correct spelling may not be the correct one.

Three derived scores available from the raw subtest scores (standard scores, percentile rank, and grade ratings) are useful in comparing a student's performance to a norm and in detecting strengths and weaknesses across subtests. Included in the manual are directions for conducting a Spelling Error Analysis, a procedure generated from the DSPT rationale that a student whose errors represent phonetically correct spellings has greater "spelling potential" than one whose misspellings show lack of application of phonetic rules.

The Development and Technical Data section of the manual clearly describes the standardization procedures used and presents evidence indicating acceptable reliability. An equipercentile method was used to equate each subtest with the WRAT Spelling subtests, after which scores were aligned in normative scales for ages seven through adult. Reliability data were obtained through the parallel forms method, yielding an average coefficient of .95 and establishing consistency of content between the two forms. Diagnostic validity was examined by testing secondary handicapped learners, resulting in performances below the norms, supporting the contention that the DSPT can identify deficiencies in each skill area.

Words were selected and ordered through the use of difficulty indices published with the 1954 New Iowa Spelling Scale and the 1953 New Standard High School Spelling Scale. The advantages of using high frequency words ranked by difficulty on a spelling scale for a test of this kind, rather than words from grade level lists of spelling series, probably outweigh the disadvantages. However, the use of the old (1954) rather than the 1977 New Iowa Spelling Scale introduces concerns related to datedness and sources of words. For example, "tenement" is no longer a high frequency word, due to societal changes, and most newer word lists include words drawn from children's reading materials as well as from the writing of children and adults. The effectiveness of the DSPT word list for testing the ability to apply phonetic rules is questionable, according to the work of Groff (1961), who found that 75% of the New Iowa Spelling Scale words were non-phonetic.

The test manual provides adequate guidance for easy administration, scoring, and interpretation by testers with minimal experience. The format is good, but its durability and ease of use would be improved with a spiral binding. The present binding is fragile and the book will not stay open without support. In view of the fact that the testers using this instrument are not likely to be the implementers of the remedial spelling instruction prescribed for a student, the inclusion of a 43-page section of remedial activities seems to be an unnecessary addition, increasing the cost of the manual. The remedial techniques suggested merit publishing in an instructional resource rather than in a testing manual.

The DSPT subtests yield an informative profile describing a subject's spelling-related skills. However, the continuing controversy over the usefulness of phonetic generalizations to spellers raises questions about the value of measuring "spelling potential" as it is defined for this test. There is substantial research to negate the theory that children become better spellers by learning phonetic generalizations, due to their limited applicability. It is suspected that an emphasis on spelling rules may even cause them to develop a dependence on consistency, leading to phonetic misspellings of unfamiliar words. Use of the DSPT carries with it the implication that the spelling disabilities of a student with a poor phonetic analysis profile can be remedied by teaching more rules.

If the DSPT is being considered as a tool for measuring present spelling ability, testers are advised to examine the regular battery of tests administered to students in that school setting. A comparison of information from regularly-administered wide range achievement tests, diagnostic reading tests, and informal spelling tests with that from the DSPT is likely to show considerable redundancy. It may not be efficient or economical to use the DSPT as a separate measure in some situations.

REVIEWER'S REFERENCES

Groff, P. J. The New Iowa Spelling Scale: How phonetic is it? ELEMENTARY SCHOOL JOURNAL, 1961, 62, 46–49.

[346]

Diagnostic Spelling Test. Ages 8–12; 1981–82; DST; 9 scores: homophones, common words, proof-reading, letter strings, nonsense words, dictionary use, dictation, total, self-concept; Forms A, B, ('81, 8 pages); teacher's guide ('82, 18 pages); 1984 price data: £4.95 per 25 tests; £3.35 per specimen set (must be purchased to obtain manual); (50–60) minutes; Denis Vincent and Jenny Claydon; NFER-Nelson Publishing Co. [England].*

Review of Diagnostic Spelling Test by GWYNETH M. BOODOO, Assistant Professor of Research and Statistics, University of Texas Health Science Center at Houston, Houston, TX:

The Diagnostic Spelling Test (DST) is designed for the "identification and diagnosis of spelling difficulty in the age range 7+ to 11+." The teacher's guide is incomplete with respect to information on the theory on which the test is based. There are eight subtests: (1) Homophones, (2) Common Words, (3) Proof Reading, (4) Letter Strings, (5) Nonsense Words, (6) Dictionary Use, (7) Dictation, and (8) Self-Concept. The use of these subtests as aids to identify and diagnose spelling difficulties is never justified in terms of any theoretical base or otherwise. Although the authors mention that "the subtests follow established theory and research," it would be invaluable to the test user if the theory was summarized. Further, with the exception of subtest 2, no sources of potential items are given. Procedures used for constructing the final test forms are not described; from the brief technical section, however, it appears that a larger number of items were initially developed. Subtest 8, an affective measure, is called a self-esteem scale; but nothing in the guide helps to show that this was developed in a manner that demonstrates its construct validity as a measure of self-esteem in spelling.

There are two equivalent test forms, and the authors are to be commended for cautioning the test user against raw score gains of less than twice the standard error of the test (7 points) as meaningful. No information is provided as to the equivalence of respective subtests 1–5 on Forms A and B, either in their construction, or by the use of supportive data. The authors do state that "Forms A and B of the Diagnostic Spelling Test are closely matched in content and difficulty."

The directions for administration are clear and easy to follow. Instructions given to the examinees include an example prior to each subtest. The timing of each subtest (with the exception of dictionary use) is flexible. However, the reader is not told how the suggested times (e.g., approximately 5 minutes for homophones) were obtained. Were they the average times allowed the standardization sample?

The procedures for scoring the tests are simple to follow, but the rationale for scoring the dictation test appears arbitrary without further explanation. A total score is obtained for subtests 1–7, with subtest 8 not included, and rightly so, since it purports to measure the affective domain.

Norm tables comprise normalized standardized scores ($M = 100$, $SD = 15$), computed from raw total scores (subtest 1–7) obtained by students in the norm sample. There is a separate table for each age group from 7 years 8 months to 11 years 8 months in monthly increments. This is to be commended since it allows for interpretation of a student's spelling prowess within his age group. There are separate norm tables for Forms A and B with Form A being slightly easier than Form B. The test user should beware of using these tables, since the standardization sample is only vaguely described. The authors state that a more complete technical report is in preparation. All that is said is that "the schools were selected from a larger pool of schools and were chosen to approximate closely a national sample" (UK). This is not enough. Any potential user wishing to use this test should develop local norms. Additionally the number and characteristics of students in the norm sample in each age group are not given; therefore, the basis for interpreting the scores for any student is meaningless. No measures of central tendency or variability are reported. The interpretation of each subtest's total scores for diagnosis is questionable since we know neither the theory nor source of items for the subtest. The authors do suggest ways teachers may carry out remedial work for each subtest.

As with the norming sample, samples used to assess reliability and validity are insufficiently described. Factor analyses yield one factor across the first seven subtests and the authors use this to provide evidence of a unidimensional test. Reliability coefficients are all high and acceptable. Two concurrent validity studies are presented. The first ($N = 422$) compares an earlier form of the test to a free writing sample. The second ($N = 25$) compares

Form A to spelling errors in exercise books, student copying of prose, dictation, and free writing. In none of these cases were the properties of the criteria given.

In addition, the authors claim that the test is "particularly discriminating amongst below average spellers," an unsubstantiated claim. They also advocate comparisons of the results of the DST with other tests. This is invalid, strictly speaking, unless the samples on which all the compared tables are normed are the same or can be shown similar.

In summary, the DST appears to have been published prematurely. In addition to other flaws mentioned above, two major standards of a published test have not been implemented. First, the theory underlying the test is never described nor is the development of the test explained. Thus the content and construct validity of the test for identifying and diagnosing spelling weaknesses in students 7 to 11 years is questionable. Second, samples on which the interpretation of test scores and technical data are based are never described. Test users should proceed with caution before using a test with so many unanswered questions regarding its development.

Review of Diagnostic Spelling Test by PHILIP L. SMITH, Associate Professor of Educational Psychology, University of Wisconsin-Milwaukee, Milwaukee, WI:

The Diagnostic Spelling Test (DST) "was designed for the identification and diagnosis of spelling difficulty in the age range 7+ to 11+." The test is published in two equivalent forms, each of which contains seven subtests plus a dictation task. The DST was designed for group administration and is not timed. Based upon the instruction manual, administration time should normally run 60 to 70 minutes for the entire battery.

The subtest structure was designed around existing theory and research (e.g., Peters, 1967) and includes the following subtests: Homophones (test 1), Common Words (test 2), Proof-Reading (test 3), Letter Strings (test 4), Nonsense Words (test 5), Dictionary Use (test 6), and Self-Concept (test 7). In addition to the seven subtests, a dictation task is included in the battery.

The manual contains a rationale for the inclusion of each of the subtests and also provides a brief description of the meaning and interpretation of low scores on each. In addition, brief descriptions of instructional activities that might be used to strengthen performance in each area are included in the manual. The administration procedures are brief and clear. Scoring procedures are equally straightforward, making the test fairly easy to use for classroom teachers.

For interpretive purposes, normative tables are provided for the total test score. The rationale given for the use of a total score is for the identification of groups or individuals who are poor spellers and to provide an indication of the severity of spelling problems. While the primary purpose of the test appears to be diagnostic, and the use of a total score questionable from this perspective, the subtest correlations provided in the manual suggest that all of the subtests are fairly highly correlated. When self-concept is eliminated, these correlations range from .59 to .88, which suggests one underlying trait as contributing to all subtests. The results of a factor analysis performed by the authors on the first six subtests indicates "a single common factor which accounts for about 70 per cent of the variance between sub-tests." While the authors acknowledge that students who do poorly on one subtest are likely to do poorly on others, this would seem to negate the diagnostic value of the subtest structure of the test, since subtest scatter is likely to be a rare occurrence. The occurrence of any significant subtest scatter may be more an indication of an unreliable subtest than anything else.

The inclusion of a self-concept subscale (which is actually a student self-evaluation of spelling ability) is an interesting feature of the DST. The correlations between this scale and the other six subtests and the dictation task range from .35 to .51. The rationale for its inclusion in the test is based upon the practical importance of self-concept as a construct, and to provide the teacher with evidence that the learner does recognize and appreciate subsequent success in spelling, thus providing a stronger basis for further improvement.

The test was normed on 4,263 children in the appropriate age range from the United Kingdom. Because of this norming population, the use of the norm tables in the United States should be approached with extreme caution. Due to the fact that the test was developed in the United Kingdom, stimuli in the various subtests (such as common words) should be inspected carefully by the potential user for relevance in particular classroom applications. Also, picture stimuli are used in two of the subtests, some of which appear to be subject to ambiguous interpretation by the student and therefore may raise questions as to the validity of incorrect responses in these areas. The authors claim that the alternate forms of the test make the measurement of progress one of its most beneficial uses. Evidence related to the equivalence of the two forms is rather limited, however, with one report of test-retest alternate form correlations of .95 for subtests 1–6 and .72 for subtest 7 ($N = 90$).

Technical information on the DST is somewhat limited. Reliability (sample size unspecified) for both Forms A and B (subtests 1–6) are estimated to be .95 and that for subtest 7 was estimated to be .77. No subtest reliabilities are reported in the manual; however, since each is based upon a relatively small number of items, they can be expected to be somewhat attenuated.

With respect to validity, in addition to the subtest correlations and factor analysis mentioned earlier, two additional studies of validity are reported in the manual. The first of these studies correlated DST subtest scores with spelling errors made in a free writing exercise by 422 children described as "third year junior children." These correlations ranged from .70 (common words subtest) to .51 (dictionary use), with the self-concept correlations in the low .30s. Because of limitations associated with the free writing exercise as a criterion, a second validity study was conducted. The criteria for this second study consisted of spelling errors from four different tasks: free writing, dictation, copying prose, and analysis of classroom exercise books. The study was limited to 25 "third year" students and produced validity coefficients beween the total score of the DST (subtest 1–6) and each of the criteria of .79, .83, .01, and .69, respectively. Correlations of these criteria with the self-concept scale were somewhat lower.

In summary, the DST provides teachers with a relatively short and easy-to-use spelling test. The availability of alternate forms strengthens the test for those users interested in measuring progress. However, the diagnostic value of the test is, at best, questionable since the subscale correlations are very high. In addition, since the norms for the test were developed in the United Kingdom, they may be of little use in the United States. Because of these limitations, potential users are urged to inspect the test thoroughly before deciding to use the test. Finally, after considering these advantages and limitations, one most wonder what advantage the DST provides over traditional classroom measures of spelling proficiency.

REVIEWER'S REFERENCES

Peters, M. SPELLING: CAUGHT OR TAUGHT. London, England: Routledge & Kegan Paul, 1967.

[347]

Diagnostic Tests for Minimal Math Competencies. High school; 1980; student proficiency in 28 specific math competency areas considered essential for successful functioning in daily life; item scores in 28 areas: one-digit one-step addition and subtraction, one-digit one-step multiplication and division, one or more digits/one or more steps addition-subtraction-multiplication-division, elapsed time clocks, elapsed time calendar, equivalent amounts of money and operations on money amounts, fractions—addition and subtraction, fractions—multiplication and division, mixed numbers all operations, determining percents and decimal equivalents from whole numbers and fractions, decimals and percents—addition and subtraction, decimals and percents—multiplication and division, U.S. measures of length, U.S. measures of capacity, U.S. measures of weight, metric measures of length, metric measures of capacity, metric measures of weight, temperature scales, ratios and proportions, areas and perimeters of rectangles, areas and perimeters of plane figures other than rectangles, angles and lines, statistics: averages and the range, line graphs, bar graphs, circle graphs, tables; no data on reliability; no norms; 1 form for each area (1 page) and survey form (4 pages); manual (12 pages); 1984 price data: $14 per set of tests; administration time not reported; Fred Pyrczak and John Longmire; J. Weston Walch, Publisher.*

[348]

Diagnostic Test of Arithmetic Strategies. Grades 1–6; 1984; DTAS; measures and identifies the procedures used to perform arithmetic calculations; no scores, 4 areas: setting up the problem, number facts, written calculation, informal skills; no data on reliability; no norms, use of norms not recommended; individual; 4 forms labeled addition, subtraction, multiplication, division, (4 pages); manual (63 pages); 1984 price data: $49 per complete kit; $9 per 25 tests; $19 per manual; (79–90) minutes; Herbert P. Ginsburg and Steven C. Mathews; PRO-ED.*

Review of Diagnostic Test of Arithmetic Strategies by LAWRENCE M. ALEAMONI, Professor of Educational Psychology, Director, Office of Instructional Research and Development, The University of Arizona, Tucson, AZ:

The Diagnostic Test of Arithmetic Strategies (DTAS) was designed to measure the procedures elementary school students use to perform arithmetic calculation in addition, subtraction, multiplication, and division. It focuses on both successful and unsuccessful strategies and identifies procedures that systematically lead to incorrect responses. It also describes effective strategies, including informal skills like mental addition, that can be used to facilitate instruction.

The purpose of the DTAS is laudable in that it is designed to provide diagnostic feedback to clinicians, teachers, and administrators about the specific strengths and/or weaknesses of the student in the processes of calculation while also documenting student progress in learning calculation and serving as a measure in research projects. All of the problems in Section I of each of the four tests are contained in chapter 2 of the manual and require the test administrator to read each problem to the student, who writes it on the scoring sheet. All of the problems in Section II are printed on the scoring sheet.

The first two pages of the scoring sheet are designed to allow the test administrator to record observations of student performance and the processes that underlie the student's number fact responses. There is no underlying scoring or coding scheme that would allow the clinician, teacher, or administrator to determine any pattern in the student's responses without reading through everything recorded. For example, there are no subscales that can be scored nor profiles of typical student responses to compare against for remediation advice. In fact, to accurately score the students' responses one must have chapter 3 of the manual at hand or committed to memory.

The most important part of the manual is Chapter 4: Interpretation and Remediation. In this chapter, four general principles are presented and discussed to guide efforts at interpretation and remediation. These principles are: (*a*) focusing on specific problems, (*b*) exploiting existing strengths, (*c*) encouraging active learning, and (*d*) using available materials. The rest of the chapter contains specific interpretations and remedial suggestions for each section of the test separately, and assumes that the four subtests of the DTAS (addition, subtraction, multiplication, and division) can be interpreted in the same general way. The principles of interpretation and remediation are well documented and based on recent books and journal articles. However, here again the clinician, teacher, or administrator would need to have chapter 4 at hand or committed to memory in order to interpret the scoring and make remedial suggestions.

The authors, acknowledging that difficulty may be encountered in scoring the DTAS, have presented exercises in the appendix of the manual to provide practice with feedback. In spite of this well designed programmed-instruction exercise, the task of scoring and interpreting the DTAS will be formidable with large numbers of individual students. If one were to use the DTAS with small numbers of individual students (five or less), then some of the problems mentioned above would not be as important.

Although the manual contains an excellent chapter on the rationale and overview of the DTAS, there are no reported reliability or validity studies nor any attempt to address these issues. At the very least some interrater reliability studies could have been conducted to show that the scoring sheets could be used in a consistent manner. In fact, an obvious study would have been to provide evidence on the usefulness of the appendix designed to train scorers for the DTAS. The authors should also have gathered some evidence on (*a*) the usefulness of the problems presented and (*b*) the scoring sheet results.

In summary, the DTAS appears to be a carefully designed and constructed test using current knowledge of arithmetic strategies employed by the elementary school student. The scoring, interpretation, and remediation strategies require a careful reading of and a ready availability of the manual. This test is more akin to an essay test rather than an objective test in its scoring format. Without any reported reliability or validity studies, it is not possible to determine the actual effectiveness of the DTAS.

[349]

Diagnostic Test of Library Skills. Grades 5–9; 1981; DTLS; no data on reliability; no norms; Form A, B, (4 pages); item analysis sheet (1 page); teacher's guide (2 pages); separate answer sheets must be used; 1983 price data: $23.95 per complete set including 50 tests and 100 answer sheets; $14.95 per 50 tests; $9.95 per 100 answer sheets; $.50 per scoring key; $.25 per item analysis sheet; $.50 per teacher's guide; (30) minutes; Barbara Feldstein and Janet Rawdon; Learnco Inc. *

[350]

Diagnostic Tests in Elementary Mathematics. Grades 3–4; 1977; criterion-referenced; item scores only; 3 tests available as separates; no data on reliability and validity; no norms, no suggested standards of mastery; teachers' manual (19 pages); 1984 price data: $13.55 per 35 tests; $4.60 per teachers' manual; administration time not reported; Dorothy M. Horn and Florence Roliff; Ontario Institute for Studies in Education; distributed by Guidance Centre [Canada].*

a) CONCEPTS OF NUMBERS AND NUMERALS. 1 form (7 pages).

b) OPERATIONS: ADDITION AND SUBTRACTION. 1 form (8 pages); facts sheet (2 pages).

c) OPERATIONS: MULTIPLICATION AND DIVISION. 1 form (8 pages); facts sheet (2 pages).

[351]

Diagnostic Word Patterns Tests. Grades 3 and over; 1969–78; criterion-referenced test of sound-symbol relationships in spelling and word recognition; no data on reliability; no norms; no suggested standards of mastery for item and total scores; may be administered orally as a spelling test or visually as a word recognition test; 1 form ('78, 9 tachistoscopic cards); 3 tests; manual ('78, 20 pages); hand tachistoscope for displaying single words ('78); student scoring chart for each test ('78, 1 page); 1983 price data: $3.85 per teacher's manual; $4.40 per set of 9 test cards; $3.80 per 50 individual student charts for either Test 1, 2, or 3; (15–30) minutes; Evelyn Buckley; Educators Publishing Service, Inc.*

a) TEST 1. 1978; no scores, 10 areas: vowel-consonant pattern, vowel-consonant-consonant pattern, consonant-consonant-vowel-consonant pattern, consonant-consonant-vowel-consonant-consonant pattern, generalization for k and ck, common consonant digraphs, adding -ed, generalization for ch and tch, common letter combination patterns, nonphonetic words.

b) TEST 2. 1978; no scores, 10 areas: vowel-consonant-silent e pattern, ai and ay, oa and ow, ea and ee, ie and igh, ou and ow, au and aw, vowel controlled by r pattern, oo, nonphonetic words.

c) TEST 3. 1978; no scores, 10 areas: ea and e, oi and oy, suffixes, 1-1-1 generalization, vowel controlled by r pattern, suffixes, silent-e words with suffixes, two-syllable words with short vowels, two-syllable words with short and long vowels, nonphonetic words.

Review of Diagnostic Word Patterns Tests by PRISCILLA A. DRUM, Associate Professor of

Education, University of California, Santa Barbara, Santa Barbara, CA:

The Diagnostic Word Patterns Tests consist of three lists of 100 words each to be administered to a group as a spelling test in order to measure "basic phonic and word analysis skills of each student in the class." Each list contains 10 different spelling patterns, with each category set of 10 supposedly more difficult than the previous set, so the lists cannot be used as alternate forms. However, since there are 10 words for each category within a list, subtests of 10 containing one exemplar from each category can be used for pre- and posttesting.

Generally, poor readers are poor spellers. Thus there is a relationship between the auditory to visual representation encoding task of spelling and the visual to auditory representation decoding task of word recognition. The problem is that many good readers are also poor spellers, so the relationship between encoding and decoding is not that strong. Also, the research necessary for mapping particular categories of spelling errors to specific word recognition problems has not been done. It is an interesting question, and the words on the lists might be used to pursue the answer. Until appropriate validation studies are conducted, the tester cannot know whether this is a test of phonics knowledge or not.

The lists can be administered individually as a direct test of word recognition, but the tester should ignore the instructions on order of administering the tests. Test 2 is not necessarily harder than Test 1. It depends on the reading curriculum the child has received. Many children in first grade have had instruction on vowel digraphs, vowels controlled by r words, two syllable words containing either long or short vowels, and sight words such as *could*, *young*, and *laugh*. These are examples from list three, which the author states is usually too difficult for end of the year, second grade students. If first graders can name these words, then the task is not too difficult for them. Thus there is a question about the appropriateness of this test for the third- to ninth-grade students suggested by the author.

Since there are no data given in the manual on students' performance, there is no way to examine the appropriateness question for the lists as either a spelling or a word recognition test. What is an adequate performance for a third grader? What do the results mean? All tests including diagnostic, criterion-referenced tests must justify their content and provide standards for performance. Without this minimal information, it is impossible to evaluate the instrument.

Basically, no tester should waste either the time or the money required for examining and using this test. Without validation and scoring criteria, this test simply represents three lists of 100 words each. The tester can create his own lists from the reading curriculum used for instruction. If spelling performance is of interest, The Larsen-Hammill Test of Written Spelling (1976), which provides scoring criteria, would be a better choice.

Review of Diagnostic Word Patterns Tests by PATRICIA HERMAN, Research Assistant, and P. DAVID PEARSON, Professor, Center for the Study of Reading, University of Illinois at Urbana Champaign, Champaign, IL:

Any test can be reviewed from at least two perspectives; one is internal and the other, external. An internal perspective attempts to answer the question, "How well does this test do what it purports to do?" An external perspective asks the broader question, "Is this the kind of phenomenon or behavior that anyone should care about assessing?" Each question will be considered in turn.

The Diagnostic Word Patterns Tests are based upon a subskills approach to reading and spelling. Buckley describes the test as "a quick, graphic method for evaluating the learning gaps in basic phonic and word analysis skills." These gaps are to be identified on the basis of student misspellings and mispronunciations on the three word tests; remediation, Buckley suggests, can occur by helping students learn the very phonics generalizations the tests indicate as gaps for individual students. In choosing to test common words in isolation in order to obtain an unambiguous index of either spelling (encoding) or word identification (decoding) ability, Buckley has selected an approach that has long standing precedence within the reading disability field.

How appropriate are Buckley's word samples? Will they permit the conclusions about weaknesses she claims? For each major vowel pattern (e.g., short e, long a, oi, etc.), a few key consonants and consonant clusters (e.g., k, ck, sh), some syllable relevant patterns, at least for two-syllable words (e.g., cattail, selfish) and a category called nonphonetic learned words (common sight words), Buckley offers a sample of approximately 10 words containing the element in question. Compared to comparable tests, Buckley offers a fairly generous sample for each assessed phonics element.

There are, however, some problems with the word samples she has chosen. First, many errors on her test could result from dialect or second language mismatches. She makes no provision in her manual for modifying test interpretations by incorporating knowledge about student language or dialect history. Second, many of the words she includes in a given sample, especially for short vowels, do not really exemplify the true sound of the vowel (e.g., leg is considered a short e word; bulk, a short u word; spilled and string, short i words; spank, a short a word). In short, she has failed to take into account intraword phonemic variations in creating her sets of words. Third, for some of the syllable relevant patterns in Test 3, she has used an odd criterion for choosing words. For both the two-syllable word pattern with short vowels in each syllable (e.g., selfish) and the two-syllable word pattern with a mix of long and short vowels (e.g., window), she has selected a number of common compound words (e.g., flagship, raindrop). Thus she has created a test which confounds knowledge of syllable patterns with knowledge of compounds and/or knowledge of common sight words (e.g., flag, ship, rain, drop). Any conclusions about performance on these subtests should be conditioned by the admission that there could be multiple explanations of failure or success.

Whether or not her list is basic and represents "words commonly used in reading and spelling by first and second graders (Tests 1 and 2) and by third and fourth graders (Test 3)" is open to question. One craves for even the most rudimentary of descriptive information about the items. In Test 1, we found only three words out of 90 pattern words on Johnson's (1978) list of common first and second grade basal words. According to Johnson, Moe and Baumann's (1983) graded list of 9,000 common English words, 72.2% of the words on Test 2 are above Grade 2 and 52.2% on Test 3 are above Grade 4. Such words cannot be termed common.

Buckley seems to assume that symbol-sound problems in encoding are intimately related to those in decoding. In fact, the only circumstance in which she recommends using the test as an individually-administered word identification test is if a student makes a large number of errors when it is administered as a spelling test. Reading and spelling are not the same processes in reverse: "skill in one does not imply skill in the other" (Read & Hodges, 1982). If any relationship exists, it is likely to be that good readers can be poor spellers; the reverse is unlikely to be true (Frith, 1978). One should be extremely cautious in making any inferences about word identification ability on the basis of spelling performance.

Buckley discourages the use of context sentences in presenting words in the spelling test. Such sentences, she claims, often cause the students to spell another interesting or familiar word in the sentence rather than the target word. We worry that the exclusion of context may leave some words ambiguously specified (*deaf* and *death* are very similar acoustically, as are *leg* and *lake*, *been* and *bin*, and *have* and *half*). Fortunately, Buckley uses no homophones in any of her lists. Further, we believe that the ubiquity of context sentences in most spelling programs creates an expectation in most students that spelling words will be presented in context. Hence the exclusion of context places the students in an unfamiliar and ecologically invalid situation.

Buckley suggests dividing each 100-word test in half to create pre- and postinstructional tests. This is a noble idea; however, the reliability of a five-item test is questionable. More important, since we have no notion of individual item difficulty, the likelihood of obtaining equally difficult half-tests seems low. We think it would be more sensible to administer each entire test pre and post.

The layout of the test is quite useful. Student answers can be recorded on record sheets. The words are arranged on the sheets so that words testing the same generalization are either in rows or along the diagonal. Buckley offers several examples of scoring and interpretation protocols. They should be useful to novice examiners.

Buckley offers broad criteria for passing a test. Missing 50% seems reasonable to alert the teacher to the possibility of trouble. However, her claim that students who miss 10 or fewer words (especially if only a half-test is given) can "handle the curriculum for that grade level" is overestimating the power of the test. There is simply no basis for the claim.

So much for our evaluation of Buckley's tests as a test of (primarily) encoding and (incidentally) decoding knowledge of common phonic patterns. Now the broader question: In the 1980s, can the educational community afford the luxury of administering tests that are at odds with, or at least exhibit ignorance of, recent advances in theory and research about the processes of reading and learning to read? We think not.

Buckley's test, like so many other tests that try to provide information about knowledge of symbol-sound patterns, fails to take into account the fact that word identification or spelling occurs in a context that influences these behaviors in very important ways. We see at least two glaring faults with tests of this ilk.

First, save for the few occasions in which one is reading or composing a random list of words, no one ever has to rely solely on symbol-sound knowledge to complete a spelling or reading task. Both linguistic context (surrounding print) and situational context (classroom, home, etc.) provide many additional clues to help language users solve the problems they must in order to become competent language users. Tests which fail to try to approximate these contexts as faithfully as possible must abide with the criticism that they provide an inaccurate and biased estimate of true performance in real reading and spelling situations. The influence of these contextual factors has been well known for at least a decade and a half. Further, such tests fail to consider the intentionality of both reading and writing; readers and writers in real problem-solving situations do what they do for functional reasons rather than simply to satisfy a teacher or to score well on a test.

Second, such tests fail on the ground of preoccupation with product at the expense of understanding the processes that account for success or failure. Further, by emphasizing product, they force remedial schemes that emphasize getting the correct product when what the student is more likely to need is some help in approaching the task with a different strategy. In Buckley's case, she mentions integrating word pattern learnings and suggests monitoring students' written work to "evaluate and review continually any incorrect sound-symbol relationships and generalizations," but the role of student self-monitoring strategies and student awareness of basic strategies for approaching novel spelling or word identification tasks is ignored. Passing a test is no guarantee students truly "own" the knowledge and will remember to use it appropriately. Read and Hodges (1982) argue that "spelling ability is a product of both word memory and strategies for predicting unfamiliar words." What we need so desperately is some way to assess students' knowledge about strategies for spelling and word identification as well as their ability to monitor how they are able to use those strategies independently.

We do not mean to say that knowing specific word patterns is unimportant. Such knowledge gives students a powerful tool for approaching spelling and word identification tasks. Buckley's test provides an estimate of such knowledge as well as, if not better than, most other tests available. Anyone who uses this test will be getting a decent glimpse into a small corner of a larger picture called literacy. Those who remember that the picture is much larger and who can find informal ways of assessing the whole picture—particularly the contextual, awareness, and monitoring facets—can benefit by the information provided by the Diagnostic Word Patterns Tests.

REVIEWER'S REFERENCES

Frith, U. Spelling difficulties. JOURNAL OF CHILD PSYCHOLOGY AND PSYCHIATRY AND ALLIED DISCIPLINES, 1978, 19, 279–285.

Johnson, D., & Pearson, P. D. TEACHING READING VOCABULARY. New York: Holt, Rinehart & Winston, 1978.

Read, C., & Hodges, R. Spelling. In H. Mitzel (Ed.), ENCYCLOPEDIA OF EDUCATIONAL RESEARCH (5th ed.). New York: The Free Press, A Division of Macmillan Publishing Co., 1982.

Johnson, D., Moe, A., & Baumann, J. THE GINN WORD BOOK FOR TEACHERS. Lexington, MA: Ginn & Co., 1983.

[352]

Differential Aptitude Tests (Forms V and W). Grades 8–12 and adults; 1947–83; DAT; also used as a part of the DAT Career Planning Program; Forms S and T still available; 9 scores: verbal reasoning, numerical ability, total, abstract reasoning, clerical speed and accuracy, mechanical reasoning, space relations, spelling, language usage; no reliability data or norms for adults; Forms V, W, ('82, 57 pages); administrator's handbook ('82, 48 pages); technical supplement ('84, 81 pages); counselor's manual ('82, 42 pages); directions for administration and scoring ('82, 22 pages); explanation of the career planning report summary ('83, 7 pages); student report forms ('82): 6-page report, 1-page report; separate answer sheets (MRC, NCS) must be used; 1985 price data: $60 per 35 tests; answer sheets: $44 per 100 MRC, $57.50 per 100 NCS; $6 per hand scoring key for MRC answer sheets; $19 per 100 6-page report forms; $5.50 per administrator's handbook; $4.75 per counselor's manual; $2.75 per directions for administration and scoring; $10 per technical supplement; $6 per DAT career planning service information packet; $9 per specimen set; scoring service, $.75 and over per student ($50 minimum); 171(225) minutes in 2 or more sessions; George K. Bennett, Harold G. Seashore, and Alexander G. Wesman; The Psychological Corporation.*

See T3:732 (26 references); for reviews by Thomas J. Bouchard, Jr., and Robert L. Linn and an excerpted review by Gerald S. Hanna of earlier forms, see 8:485 (56 references); see also T2:1069 (64 references); for a review by M. Y. Quereshi and an excerpted review by Jack C. Merwin of earlier forms, see 7:673 (139 references); for reviews by J. A. Keats and Richard E. Schutz, see 6:767 (52 references); for reviews by John B. Carroll and Norman Frederiksen, see 5:605 (49 references); for reviews by Harold Bechtoldt, Ralph F. Berdie, and Lloyd G. Humphreys, see 4:711 (27 references); for an excerpted review, see 3:620.

TEST REFERENCES

1. Sherman, J. A., & Fennema, E. Distribution of spatial visualization and mathematical problem solving scores: A test of Stafford's x-linked hypothesis. PSYCHOLOGY OF WOMEN QUARTERLY, 1978, 3, 157–167.

2. Sherman, J. Cognitive performance as a function of sex and handedness: An evaluation of the Levy hypothesis. PSYCHOLOGY OF WOMEN QUARTERLY, 1979, 3, 378–390.

3. Silver, E. A. Student perceptions of relatedness among mathematical verbal problems. JOURNAL FOR RESEARCH IN MATHEMATICS EDUCATION, 1979, 10, 195–210.

4. Dalby, J. T. Hemispheric timesharing: Verbal and spatial loading with concurrent unimanual activity. CORTEX, 1980, 16, 567–573.

5. Gregory, R. J., Alley, P., & Morris, L. Left-handedness and spatial reasoning abilities: The deficit hypothesis revisited. INTELLIGENCE, 1980, 4, 151–159.

6. Sherman, J. A. Predicting mathematics grades of high school girls and boys: A further study. CONTEMPORARY EDUCATIONAL PSYCHOLOGY, 1980, 5, 249–255.

7. Aaron, P. G., Baker, C., & Hickox, G. L. In search of the third dyslexia. NEUROPSYCHOLOGIA, 1982, 20, 203–208.

8. Bander, R. S., Russell, R. K., & Zamostny, K. P. A comparison of cue-controlled relaxation and study skills counseling in the treatment of mathematics anxiety. JOURNAL OF EDUCATIONAL PSYCHOLOGY, 1982, 74, 96–103.

9. McCormick, R. V. The balance effect on the M-space by spacial interaction. THE ALBERTA JOURNAL OF EDUCATIONAL RESEARCH, 1982, 28, 113–121.

10. Pieters, J. P. M., & van der Ven, A. H. G. S. Precision, speed, and distraction in time-limited tests. APPLIED PSYCHOLOGICAL MEASUREMENT, 1982, 6, 93–109. and W)):

11. Riskind, J. H., & Gotay, C. C. Physical posture: Could it have regulatory or feedback effects on motivation and emotion? MOTIVATION AND EMOTION, 1982, 6, 273–298.

12. Sherman, J. Continuing in mathematics: A longitudinal study of the attitudes of high school girls. PSYCHOLOGY OF WOMEN QUARTERLY, 1982, 7, 132–140.

13. Smith, M., III, Stuck, G. B., & Johnston, D. R. The identification of students likely to fail The North Carolina Competency Tests. EDUCATIONAL AND PSYCHOLOGICAL MEASUREMENT, 1982, 42, 95–104.

14. Yates, L. V., & Bailey, L. J. Realism of three types of vocational choices: Expectations, preferences, and fantasies. JOURNAL OF INDUSTRIAL TEACHER EDUCATION, 1982, 19, 59–68.

15. Blatter, P. Training in spatial ability: A test of Sherman's hypothesis. PERCEPTUAL AND MOTOR SKILLS, 1983, 57, 987–992.

16. Harshman, R. A., Hampson, E., & Berenbaum, S. A. Individual differences in cognitive abilities and brain organization, Part 1: Sex and

handedness differences in ability. CANADIAN JOURNAL OF PSYCHOLOGY, 1983, 37, 144–192.
17. Sherman, J. Factors predicting girls' and boys' enrollment in college preparatory mathematics. PSYCHOLOGY OF WOMEN QUARTERLY, 1983, 7, 272–281.
18. Stuckless, E. R., & Walter, G. G. Students hearing impaired from the 1963–1965 rubella epidemic begin to enter college. THE VOLTA REVIEW, 1983, 85, 270–278.
19. Menard, S., & Morse, B. J. A structuralist critique of the IQ-delinquency hypothesis: Theory and evidence. AMERICAN JOURNAL OF SOCIOLOGY, 1984, 89, 1347–1378.

Review of Differential Aptitude Tests (Forms V and W) by RONALD K. HAMBLETON, Professor of Education and Psychology, University of Massachusetts, Amherst, MA:

The Differential Aptitude Tests (DAT) has flourished for almost 40 years as the best known and most popular battery of aptitude tests for high school students and young adults. Interested readers will find DAT test reviews as far back as the third *MMY*. The 1983 version of the DAT comes with not only parallel-form booklets for eight aptitudes, but, as has become customary for test batteries that have existed for a long time, it comes with a plethora of documents such as Administrator's Handbook, Directions for Administration and Scoring, Technical Supplement, Counselor's Manual, Orientation Booklet, Explanation of the Career Planning Report Summary, Career Planning Report, Career Planning Glossary, Scoring Keys, several types of scoring sheets, and more. This reviewer would have benefited from a list of available documents in the specimen set to help organize the 18 different pieces of literature. A considerable amount of time was spent in just sorting through the available documents to find pertinent material.

The eight aptitudes measured by the DAT are as follows: Verbal Reasoning (50 items)—ability to understand concepts in words and to reason with words. This aptitude is measured with verbal analogies with the first and last of four terms missing. Content of the verbal analogies is varied to include items from history, geography, literature, etc.

Numerical Ability (40 items)—ability to understand numerical relationships and have a facility to handle numerical concepts. Items are principally computational in nature so as to avoid less than valid scores due to the confounding of reading comprehension skills with numerical ability when word problems or reasoning problems are used.

Abstract Reasoning (45 items)—ability to understand ideas that are not expressed in words or numbers and to see relationships among objects. Each test item requires the examinee to identify an operating principle in a sequential series of diagrams (for example, the number of circles in the series of diagrams may be increasing).

Clerical Speed and Accuracy (100 items)—this test measures speed and accuracy of response to a simple perceptual task. The stimulus for each item is five sets of pairs of letters with one pair underlined. The examinee's task is to match quickly the underlined pair to one of the five available answer choices.

Mechanical Reasoning (70 items)—ability to understand principles of mechanical operations and the laws of physics as they arise in everyday activities. With each item a pictorial is presented along with a related mechanical problem.

Space Relations (60 items)—ability to deal with concrete objects through visualization. Each test item contains a complicated two-dimensional figure and 4 three-dimensional figures, one of which can be constructed from the two-dimensional figure. The examinee's task is to visualize from a two-dimensional plan what the plan would look like in three dimensions.

Spelling (90 items)—ability to recognize correct and incorrect spellings of common words. Examinees must identify words as correctly or incorrectly spelled.

Language Usage (50 items)—ability to detect errors in grammar, punctuation, and capitalization. Each item contains a sentence with an error that the examinee must locate.

All in all, the tests appear to contain clear directions and acceptable items. I do, however, have two criticisms of the test booklets, one minor and one major. My minor criticism concerns the style used in printing the tests. Quite frankly, the booklets do not have a modern look to them. The choice of paper, the artwork, the lettering, the highlighting, etc., are not of the same quality found in many popular tests. My second criticism is more serious though it is limited to the Mechanical Comprehension Test. The artwork for this test is shamefully old-fashioned. The artwork belongs in a 1940s test, not a test for the '80s. Also, the attempt by the publisher to create a "balanced" racial mix of persons depicted in the artwork by darkening a few faces is embarrassing.

The DAT is principally used to provide high school students and young adults with information that can help these individuals in career planning. The battery is also used in the selection and placement of employees. Normative information for interpreting examinee performance is provided for the eight aptitudes mentioned earlier plus a ninth variable called Scholastic Aptitude, which is a sum of the verbal reasoning and numerical ability test scores.

The 1983 Administrator's Handbook and the 1984 Technical Supplement provide a wealth of important technical information about the test battery. The information is well organized and clearly and thoroughly presented in these two documents. With respect to the percentile and stanine score norms (which are reported for males and females separately), this reviewer would like to draw attention to three shortcomings. First, though an elaborate sampling plan for obtaining the norms groups was described, no statistics are reported of the acceptance rates of schools or school districts contacted to participate in the norming study. Second, while both fall and spring test score norms are reported for grades 8 through 12, the spring norms are based on interpolations from the fall data. In view of the high degree of subjectivity associated with preparing norms based on interpolations around only five data points (as well as smoothing data both within and across grades), more details on how the spring norms tables were prepared would have been desirable. Third, reporting only 23 percentile points in each norms table strikes this reviewer as being less than desirable. The actual number of test score points ranges from 41 to 101 with an average of 64 possible score points per test. More than half the time, multiple test scores were assigned to the same percentile. Providing more percentile points combined with the use of percentile bands based on the standard error of measurement would seem to be a more efficient use of the available information. Certainly, this reviewer's suggestion would be more consistent with present-day measurement practices. Presently, bands for score interpretations are used but the psychometric soundness of a method which involves constructing a band (plus or minus) .5 inches around the percentile point for the examinee on each test can be improved upon. Modernizing the methods used for reporting percentiles and percentile bands would bring the score reporting component up to date.

Reliability estimates for test scores remain high though several of the tests were shortened in the 1983 edition. These corrected split-half reliability estimates, which are reported for each sex and at each grade level, are (with one exception) typically in the low .90s. The one exception is the Clerical Speed and Accuracy Test, where the more correct alternate-form reliability estimates are substituted. These reliability estimates were typically in the .80s.

Validity evidence reported in the Technical Supplement is predominantly of the predictive type where the popular criterion measures are high school achievement scores. The correlations are substantial and reflect the usefulness of each of the tests for predicting high school achievement. Missing from the Technical Supplement, however, are a substantial number of correlations to reflect the predictive validity of the tests using job success measures. Also missing is evidence for the construct validity of the individual tests.

With respect to score profile interpretations, the document Counseling From Profiles (CFP) will be useful. Providing counselors with typical student case histories, profiles, and reasonable courses of action will be of substantial value to them as they carry out their counseling responsibilities. The CFP might easily be expanded in the future to include additional cases, and updated to reflect, for example, the many new careers in the high technology and electronics industries. The counseling documents contain the appropriate cautions about the less-than-perfect validity of test scores, and the need for counselors to interpret test performance and offer career guidance within a broad framework that includes other data available on the examinee (e.g., sex, interests, school achievement scores, teacher evaluations, etc.).

In summary, there is no doubt in this reviewer's mind that the DAT will continue to provide distinguished service in the high schools, armed services, and industry. Still, this reviewer would like to see in the next edition a more modern look to the test battery with special emphasis given to the art work in the Mechanical Comprehension Test. Also, more details about the preparation of test score norms as well as improved norms tables (with more points) would seem to be worthwhile.

Review of Differential Aptitude Tests (Forms V and W) by DARYL SANDER, Professor of Education, University of Colorado, Boulder, CO:

The 1982 revision (Forms V and W) of the Differential Aptitude Tests (DAT) has responded to many of the criticisms of previous reviewers, but a few problems remain unattended to and these may constitute concerns for test users. Since its initial appearance in 1947, the DAT has undergone periodic revisions, each enjoying considerable popularity, and this latest edition promises to be the best.

Substantial revisions have been made on Verbal Reasoning, Numerical Ability, and Mechanical Reasoning, in both item content and sequence. For example, of the 50 items which comprise Verbal Reasoning (Form V), 12 are revisions of items from Form S, 6 are revisions of items from Form T, and 7 are new; thus, half of the content of Verbal Reasoning items is new or newly revised, as well as a change in sequence of items. In Numerical Ability (Form V), about one-third of the items are new or revised, and in Mechanical Reasoning (Form V) slightly less than 20% of the items are new or revised. Less extensive revision was accomplished on other portions of the DAT. Abstract Reasoning, Spelling, and Language Usage were each shortened without appreciable loss of reliability. Across grade levels, and for both males and females, split-half reliabilities with correction for variability of norm groups range from a low of .85 for females on MR to a high of .95 for both sexes on VR + NA. Split-half reliabilities for all nine scales (eight separate tests plus a composite VR + NA) are reported in both the Administrator's Handbook and the Technical Supplement. Standard errors of measurement are also reported in the Administrator's Handbook. Only the Clerical Speed and Accuracy test is speeded, and for it, alternate-form reliability coefficients for Forms V and W by sex and grade levels, corrected for variability of norms groups, are provided; they range from .93 to .97 with a median r =.96. These reliabilities are sufficiently high to assure test users of an acceptably small error of measurement in virtually all cases.

Previous reviewers have noted the lack of evidence of differential validity of the DAT, and this problem remains. Intercorrelations among the tests of Forms V and W are relatively high, except for CSA, and suggest considerable redundancy among the scales and the consequent limitation on the battery's potential to differentially predict academic or occupational criteria.

Although the validity data given in the Technical Supplement for Forms V and W are extensive and exemplary in detail, it is regrettable that little attention is given to predictive validity with respect to post-secondary work. The desirability of predicting course grades is unquestioned. However, career planning by secondary school students requires attention to post-secondary work opportunities, and too little attention is given to the validities of the DAT for this purpose. Virtually all of the validity criteria provided are scholastic in nature, primarily course grades. These need to be treated with caution as distributions of course grades have changed substantially in recent years, and the data upon which these validities are based were obtained in 1980–81. Commendably, the authors of the Technical Supplement make a strong case for users to develop expectancy tables utilizing their own local data. It must be again emphasized that for youth who enter the labor market immediately upon high school completion, or sometimes before, test validity utilizing performance in entry-level jobs as the validity criteria is most appropriate and badly needed.

The practice of converting raw scores into only 23 percentile values remains unchanged for Forms V and W. Since the Individual Report form provides for a band score to accommodate measurement error, it seems unnecessary and unwise to further reduce precision in this manner in the score conversion process. The Administrator's Handbook only notes that this is done "to avoid the appearance of exaggerated precision," but this is not done without some loss of potentially valuable information.

The normative data used for Forms V and W come from 61,000 students in 64 parochial and public school districts throughout the U.S. These districts comprise a sample which is stratified according to (*a*) enrollment size within 4 geographic regions, and (*b*) a socioeconomic index based upon income and educational level of residents in the district as reported in the 1970 Bureau of Census data. An estimated 14.1% of the standardization sample are black students, which compares favorably with national census data, but other ethnic proportions within the sample are not given. The selection of the districts and the differential weighting of the cells within the sample design appear to be more than adequate and are well-described in the Handbook. The advantage of separate norms for each sex for grades 8 through 12 for both Fall and Spring is continued as in previous editions.

Included with the DAT is Counseling From Profiles, a casebook originally published in 1951 and revised in 1977. Excellent case material is provided to assist counselors in the interpretation of multifactor scores. The 29 cases are arranged in three sections based upon the level of the VR + NA composite score. The case data are both current and relevant, are about evenly divided between male and female subjects, and include several with Hispanic surnames. Other ethnic identities are not given, nor are there any specific guidelines pertaining to use of DAT profiles with minority students or those for whom English is a second language. Regrettably, the casebook is lacking any cases involving extremely low, flat profiles. Many counselors would welcome help in the difficult task of interpretation of profiles in which all scores are uniformly very low.

The Career Planning Program (CPP) initially developed in 1973 has also been revised for use with Forms V and W. It provides a computer-printed report based upon DAT scores and other data supplied by students in the Career Planning Questionnaires. The CPP provides meaningful information in easily understood language, and provides excellent reference to other career information resources, particularly the *Guide for Occupational Exploration* and the *Dictionary of Occupational Titles.*

SUMMARY. Despite several criticisms noted above, the DAT is a very fine multi-factor battery, and the new revision ensures continuing popularity with users in the secondary schools. Of the criticisms noted above, the most significant one is the continuing problem of demonstrating differential validity of the tests for different outcomes. An absence of job-related validity studies was also noted. The usefulness of the VR + NA composite score as an indicator of general ability is well-established, and careful interpretations of the other scores can provide valuable information for use in career exploration and decision-making.

[353]

Dimensions of Self-Concept. Grades 4–6, 7–12; 1977–78; DOSC; self-report instrument; 5 factor scales:

level of aspiration, anxiety, academic interest and satisfaction, leadership and initiative, identification vs. alienation; 2 levels labeled Form E (grades 4–6), Form S (grades 7–12), ('77, 4 pages); user's manual ('78, 15 pages, adaptation of technical manual); preliminary technical manual ('77, 37 pages); price data available from publisher; (20–40) minutes; William B. Michael and Robert A. Smith; Los Angeles Unified School District.*

See T3:734 (5 references).

TEST REFERENCES

1. Bell, C., & Ward, G. R. An investigation of the relationship between Dimensions of Self-Concept (DOSC) and achievement in mathematics. ADOLESCENCE, 1980, 15, 895–901.

2. Darakjian, G. P., & Michael, W. B. Comparative validities of standardized academic self-concept scales and achievement test measures and of teacher ratings of citizenship and effort in forecasting performance of junior high school students. EDUCATIONAL AND PSYCHOLOGICAL MEASUREMENT, 1982, 42, 629–641.

3. Antion, D. L., & Michael, W. B. Short-term predictive validity of demographic, affective, personal, and cognitive variables in relation to two criterion measures of cheating behaviors. EDUCATIONAL AND PSYCHOLOGICAL MEASUREMENT, 1983, 43, 467–482.

4. Darakjian, G. P., & Michael, W. B. The long-term comparative predictive validities of standardized measures of achievement and academic self-concept for a sample of secondary school students. EDUCATIONAL AND PSYCHOLOGICAL MEASUREMENT, 1983, 43, 251–260.

Review of Dimensions of Self-Concept by HERBERT G. W. BISCHOFF, School Psychologist, Psychology Resources, Anchorage, AK:

The Dimensions of Self-Concept (DOSC) was developed originally to assist gifted students viewed as having low self-esteem and poor self-concept. The questionnaire was devised for students in an enrichment program in the Los Angeles Unified School District. This self-report instrument may be group administered, self-administered, or administered individually. There are 70 multiple-choice items, with three possible answers per item on the elementary school form and five possible answers on the secondary school form. No time limit is required and authors report administration time to range between 15 and 55 minutes, with an average of 25 minutes needed for completion. Normative data are confined to the Los Angeles City Unified School District. It is unclear who is qualified to administer this instrument, although the authors define its screening and diagnostic purposes as useful for counseling or guidance by teachers, administrators, or counselors.

A technical Preliminary Manual accompanied the specimen set sent for review. The manual included reliability and validity data. Reliability measures based on internal consistency were reported as ranging between .70 and .90 depending on grade level. Test-retest reliability data were unavailable. Concurrent validity data fall short of providing a consistent relationship between the DOSC and indicators of reading comprehension and a locally developed measure of critical thinking. Concurrent validity using other measures of self-concept and/or self-esteem is not reported. No predictive validity data are reported.

Standardization data were collected from about 1,500 children in grades 4th through 6th (Elementary Scale), 7th through 9th (Junior High Scale), and 10th through 12th (Senior High Scale). Relative to each form, the author prepared "three sets of about 30 items for each of the five constructs." The five constructs are (*a*) Level of Aspiration, (*b*) Anxiety, (*c*) Academic Interests and Satisfaction, (*d*) Leadership and Initiative, and (*e*) Identification versus Alienation. These DOSC dimensions are described more fully in the Preliminary Manual. It is unclear how the Junior and Senior High levels of the DOSC were combined to form the current format. The Elementary Form covers grades 4 through 6 and the Secondary Form grades 7 through 12. The forms contain parallel items which vary in wording. While the authors report that the Anxiety Scale reflects the "purest" factor in terms of construct validity, there still remains the question of construct validity for the other dimensions.

The Preliminary Manual provides some suggestions to teachers and counselors for enhancing self-concepts of students relative to the five DOSC factor scales. These suggestions are not available in the User's Manual and users of the DOSC are encouraged to obtain a copy of both the User's and Preliminary Manual.

Suggestions for improvement include the following: (1) The readability level for each form is not reported and clarification is warranted. (2) It would be helpful to prospective users to obtain data reflecting the utility of the DOSC from the perspective of current users. (3) A demonstration item could be included to assist students in completing the forms accurately. (4) Further standardization which includes a broader representation of students is recommended. (5) Suggestions provided to teachers and counselors in the Preliminary Manual should be included in the User's Manual. (6) Although the Glossary of Terms is a helpful appendix item, many of the terms are not used in the manual and other terms which are used have not been included. Perhaps a reader's survey would clarify which terms would be most useful in a future revision.

In summary, this test appears to satisfy the authors' intent to provide a scale which ranks students on five dimensions of self-esteem and self-concept. Applicability beyond gifted students in the Los Angeles area is unknown. Use of this assessment instrument in other areas of the country should be tempered by the limited standardization sample and encouraged only after relevant norms have been established.

Review of Dimensions of Self-Concept by ALFRED B. HEILBRUN, JR., Professor of Psychology, Emory University, Atlanta, GA:

The Dimensions of Self-Concept (DOSC) is intended to be a measure of "non-cognitive" factors associated with self-concept or self-esteem in a school setting. If one ignores the illogic involved in conceptualizing the ways in which children think about themselves as having nothing to do with cognition, the rationale for test development seems promising. What the test developers wished to do was to identify the critical sources of self-esteem within the school experience and construct a measuring instrument that would allow for reliable and valid measurement of these self-esteem factors. Given the availability of such a measure, school personnel would have available a means of identifying children with low self-esteem for whom remedial efforts might counteract difficulties in school learning. Restricting the measurement of self-esteem to factors central to the school experience rather than relying on a more global appraisal has an intuitive appeal when the purpose of the test is confined to engineering optimal school performance.

The five factors measured by the DOSC were selected by the test developers as important to the self-concept of school-age children as well as relevant to the school experience. Their choices—level of aspiration, anxiety (over school work), academic interest and satisfaction, leadership and initiative, and identification versus alienation (relative to the school as an institution)—appear to qualify on both counts. Intuitive appeal is all one can go on in evaluating the developmental rationale for this test, since the technical manual remains remarkably free of any evidence that these are critical self-esteem factors in school children. The test developers also present their own theory of "affectivity in school learning" that attempts to explain and integrate these five factors as they relate to emotionality and deficit performance. Despite this ad hoc theory, even the most basic assumption underlying the test development, that low self-esteem disrupts school performance, remains totally undocumented.

The test manual does include the kind of technical information that should interest the potential user of the DOSC. The 14 items constructed to measure each of the five factors appear to be acceptably homogeneous as evidenced by item-scale correlations. Scale reliabilities ranging between .70 and .90 are reported, but these too are internal consistency figures. Despite the wealth of subjects available in the Los Angeles public schools, test-retest reliability coefficients were not obtained. Certainly the stability of self-reports over time is a major concern when testing children, especially those at the elementary-school age. Norms are provided for both the elementary-school and secondary-school forms of the test. While these may be satisfactory for preliminary norms, their restriction to only Los Angeles school children requires further work. Either they should be expanded so as to be more representative nationally or their current representativeness should be corroborated.

The validity of this test, as judged from the evidence reported in the manual, is a total mystery. The test developers try to extract evidence of "construct" and "concurrent" validity from some rather strange sources. Moderate item-scale homogeneity figures and the fact that no more than two of their scales (on earlier outmoded forms) clustered on factor analysis are somehow construed to be validational in nature. Even more perplexing, the occasional significant correlation of the DOSC scales with tests of reading comprehension and critical thinking is cited as evidence of concurrent validity. There is no explanation of why reading comprehension or critical thinking ability should have anything to do with self-esteem scale scores nor mention made that the significant correlations within two of the factors are inconsistent, being positive for some samples and negative for others.

Worst of all, we are told that no predictive validity evidence is currently available but that efforts are under way to obtain correlations between DOSC factor scores and school grades. The publication of a test without having gathered these correlations, the most primitive data necessary to evaluate its validity, is unfortunate. The ideas for this testing approach originally were published in 1976 and the preliminary manual bears a 1977 date of printing. Unless there are more recent publications of which I am unaware, it must be assumed that the test is being promulgated without critical and readily-accessible evidence of its worth being made available to the potential user. Despite this, the available manual offers eight pages of explicit counseling advice to be used in conjunction with DOSC scores. Until validity evidence is made available, educational specialists who use this children's test of self-esteem in their professional work do so totally at their own risk.

[354]

Distar Mastery Tests. Preschool–grade 3; 1977–78; DMT; criterion-referenced; determines mastery for the Distar reading, language, and arithmetic programs; 6 tests; no data on reliability and validity; no norms; 1984 price data: $35.65 per kit including 25 tests, 25 practice sheets, and examiner's manual (with answer key) for any one test; (30–60) minutes per test; Science Research Associates, Inc.*

a) READING I. 1977; 3 areas: sound recognition, vocabulary, comprehension; 1 form (11 pages); examiner's manual (8 pages); practice sheet (2 pages).

b) READING II. 1978; 5 areas: letter recognition, sound recognition, vocabulary, deductive thinking rules, comprehension; 1 form (13 pages); examiner's manual (14 pages); practice sheet (2 pages).

c) LANGUAGE I. 1978; 7 to 8 areas: description of objects and actions, actions, instructional words, classification, information, applications, shapes, statement

production (optional); 1 form (12 pages); examiner's manual (15 pages); practice sheet (1 page).
d) LANGUAGE II. 1978; 7 to 8 areas: word skills, sentence skills, reasoning skills, directional skills, information, applications, take-homes, statement production (optional); 1 form (12 pages); examiner's manual (11 pages); practice sheet (1 page).
e) ARITHMETIC I. 1978; 9 areas: symbol identification, groups, horizontal addition and algebra addition, horizontal and vertical subtraction, vertical addition, oral story problems, ordinal counting, more-less, written story problems; 1 form (11 pages); examiner's manual (9 pages); practice sheet (2 pages).
f) ARITHMETIC II. 1978; 7 areas: column addition, column subtraction, telling time, multiplying and reducing fractions, measurement, coins, written story problems; 1 form (12 pages); examiner's manual (12 pages); practice sheet (2 pages).

Review of Distar Mastery Tests by JASON MILLMAN, Professor of Educational Research Methodology, Cornell University, Ithaca, NY:

The Distar Mastery Tests are an optional tool for teachers who do not wish to construct their own tests based on the Distar instructional materials. Three test items are used to measure each of the 17 to 23 learning objectives referenced by the six tests. The objectives correspond to material covered by the reading, language, and arithmetic programs.

Although some of the objectives are of general interest (e.g., given a reading selection, the learner will identify a main idea from the story), others are specific to the program (e.g., given a word from lessons 37–100, the learner will identify the corresponding picture). Because the tests are intended for users of the Distar materials to learn which of the program objectives a student has mastered, and not to compare a student's performance with others, it is reasonable that no norms are provided.

How well do the tests serve their intended purpose? This question can be answered by addressing the following concerns:

(1) Are the most important or most representative program objectives being measured? The tests must, by practical necessity, measure only a fraction of the skills covered by the instructional materials. No information is provided, however, about the selection of the objectives for testing. Evidently, users must compare the selected objectives to all of the program objectives and form their own opinions.

(2) Are the measured objectives stated clearly? A positive answer to this question implies that the user can tell what the items used to measure the objectives are apt to look like and thus will know what tasks students who master the objectives can do. Although many of the objectives are stated with adequate clarity for educators familiar with the Distar instructional materials, most leave unclear the level of difficulty of the items, the testing formats, and the content limits of the questions. The user must refer to the individual items to infer what knowledge and skills are being referenced by the objectives.

(3) Do the test items correspond to the objectives? This question is usually answered by submitting randomly ordered sets of items and objectives to judges who are instructed to match the sets. No such information is provided; however, a cursory inspection suggests that the items do measure the objectives with which they are associated.

(4) Are the test items a representative sample of items that could be used to measure the objective? Three items cannot possibly include all ways of measuring a knowledge or skill. But, unfortunately, more often than not the three items are more homogeneous in format and content than the stated objective indicates. For example, none of the vertical addition problems in Arithmetic I involve either carrying (regrouping) or use of more than two addends, although both features are implied by the objective. Likewise, all of the questions about identifying seasons show pictures of trees, a limited context in which to measure the objective. What is truly being measured is mastery of objectives more narrowly conceived than those defined in the Examiner's Manual.

(5) Can one conclude from the student's score that the student has mastered a given objective? Has the student who meets the passing standard by answering all three items correctly mastered the objective, even allowing a restricted definition of the objective? Conversely, has the student who misses one or more of the items not mastered the objective? Of importance in answering these questions are data on whether the objectives a student mastered on one set of three-item subtests are the same objectives the student mastered on a second set of three-item subtests. Such data on the decision consistency of the instrument are not available. However, the seriousness of any misclassifications is apt to be minimal, given that the test information is intended for classroom use, where the need for corrective action is likely to be noticed and where remedial instruction is available.

SUMMARY AND CONCLUSIONS. The Distar Mastery Tests are intended as a convenience for teachers who use the Distar instructional programs and who prefer not to construct their own assessment tests. They are supposed to indicate which of a sample of from 17 to 23 instructional objectives a student has mastered. No norms or scoring services are available. Technical information needed to make a full review of the tests is not available. The user should decide whether the objectives being measured are the same ones they are interested in. Users should also be aware that many of the objectives are measured in rather limited ways. Thus, students might appear to have mastered objectives when, if presented with a more heterogeneous sample of items, they might be considered in need of further instruction.

Review of Distar Mastery Tests by CRAIG N. MILLS, Administrative Officer, Bureau of Accountability, Louisiana Department of Education, Baton Rouge, LA:

The Distar Mastery Tests are designed to be a criterion-referenced evaluation tool designed to accompany the Distar textbooks. Several issues arise, however, that cast doubt on the usefulness of the tests. Among the issues are test development, technical quality of the tests, usefulness of the manuals, and explanation of reports and interpretation of results. Each will be discussed in turn.

TEST DEVELOPMENT. The Distar Mastery Tests are labeled as a "criterion-referenced measurement program." A more accurate definition would be that the tests are objective-referenced. A criterion-referenced test is one that clearly and completely defines the domain of content from which test items are drawn. Such specifications are not provided or referenced for the Distar objectives.

One must assume that the objectives tested are those that comprise the Distar texts, but that point is never made. It is also never made clear whether the tests are designed as end-of-course, end-of-grading period, or end-of-unit tests.

Item development is not explained. Information is not provided concerning who the item writers were, what their qualifications were, what the review process for items was, or whether or not a pilot administration occurred.

TECHNICAL QUALITY. The test examiner's manuals imply that there are multiple forms of all the tests (this reviewer had Form X). However, no information is provided on alternate form reliability, test-retest reliability, or decision consistency across forms. No data regarding item or test validity are reported. No portion of the examiner's manual is devoted to a discussion of item development, pilot testing, or any other aspect of test development.

There is no discussion provided to explain the manner in which cutoff scores were established. In fact, although the tests are referred to as mastery tests, half of the manuals do not even indicate the level of performance required for objective mastery. This information can only be found in the description of the reports that may be obtained if the tests are machine scored, and these descriptions are not included in all manuals.

MANUALS. Several features of the manuals limit their usefulness. First, it appears that all tests are designed for machine scoring, but directions for preparing documents for scoring appear only in the manuals for Language I, Reading II, and Arithmetic II. If all tests are machine-scorable, the manuals for Reading I, Arithmetic I, and Language II should contain directions for preparing documents. If certain tests are not machine-scorable, a discussion of determining mastery status is required. Unfortunately, as mentioned previously, the fact that the cutoff score is 100% is revealed only in the discussion of reports available when tests are machine scored.

Some of the manuals have a section containing directions for completing name and student identification grids for scoring. Unfortunately, no such grids could be located on the tests provided for this review.

Finally, format of the manuals is inconsistent. Test directions that are to be read aloud are supposed to be indented. Each manual has at least a portion of the directions that are not indented. While this is a minor point, it could cause confusion.

REPORTS AND INTERPRETATION OF RESULTS. Four types of reports are available when the tests are machine-scored. The student report is a straightforward listing of the student's mastery status on each objective and an indication of performance on each item. The class list is a useful listing of each student in the class, a summary of individual performance (number of objectives mastered), and class objective performance (number of students mastering each objective). Examples of the other two reports (group reports and mastery distributions) were not provided.

Guidelines for interpreting test results at either an individual student or class level are not provided. This would seem especially important for items requiring oral responses on the student's part. These items, which are intended to assess language production, require an exact structured response from the student. It is not clear from the materials provided how non-conforming but accurate statements are to be interpreted.

It is clear that the Distar Mastery Tests are designed to correspond to the Distar texts. Thus, one can question whether or not users of other texts would even consider the use of the tests. It does not follow, however, that simply because a test has a narrowly defined audience, the responsibilities of the test developer are lessened. In this case, it appears that those responsibilities have not been well met. The total lack of documentation of test development practices and test and item quality, the lack of generalizability of results, and manuals that are not clear, call into question whether or not these tests represent an improvement over tests and other assessments developed by the classroom teacher.

[355]

DMI Mathematics Systems Instructional Objectives Inventory. Grades K.6–1.5, 1.6–2.5, 2.6–3.5, 3.6–4.5, 4.6–5.5, 5.6–6.5, 6.6–8.9; 1983; DMI/MS IOI; "criterion-referenced approach to mathematics assessment and instruction"; 4 areas: whole numbers, fractions/decimals/integers, measurement and geometry, problem-solving and special topics; no data on reliability; estimated norms report available for machine-scored tests; test booklets available in both machine-scorable and hand scorable editions; 1983 price data: $25.50 per 35 hand-scorable tests and manual for levels A–C; $26.25 per 35 tests and manual for levels D–G: $6.30 per 35 locator tests and manual; $5.25 per 35 practice tests; $.50 per class record sheet; $4.20 per 35 individual diagnostic maps; $25 per coordinator's guide; $9.50 per 2 hand-scoring stencils; $8.25 per 25 hand-scorable Scoreze answer sheets; $6 per 50 CompuScan machine-scorable answer sheets for level D; $10 per 50 CompuScan machine-scorable answer sheets for levels E–G; $3.75 per manual; scoring service: $1.17 per student for levels A–D, $.86 per student for levels E–G; John Gessel; CTB/McGraw-Hill.*

a) LEVEL A. Grades K.6–1.5; machine-scorable form (16 pages); manual (25 pages); $27.30 per 35 tests and manual; (53–73) minutes.

b) LEVEL B. Grades 1.6–2.5; machine-scorable form (20 pages); manual (25 pages); $29.75 per 35 tests and manual; (71–91) minutes.

c) LEVEL C. Grades 2.6–3.5; machine-scorable form (16 pages); manual (23 pages); $33.95 per 35 tests and manual; (75–95) minutes.

d) LEVEL D. Grades 3.6–4.5; machine-scorable form (20 pages); manual (25 pages); $33.35 per 35 tests and manual; (93–124) minutes.

e) LEVEL E. Grades 4.6–5.5, 1 form (23 pages); manual for levels E–G (32 pages); (106–131) minutes.

f) LEVEL F. Grades 5.6–6.5; 1 form (23 pages); (128–158) minutes.

g) LEVEL G. Grades 6.6–8.9; 1 form (31 pages); (157–186) minutes.

[356]

Do I Know How to Apply For a Job? Job applicants; no date on test materials; no data on reliability; no norms; 1 form (no date, 12 pages); no manual; 1982 price data: $.72 per test; administration time not reported; Lawrence W. Hess; Bobbs-Merrill Co., Inc.* (Since reviews were received, Bobbs-Merrill, former publisher of this instrument, has informed us that they no longer publish and distribute it.)

Review of Do I Know How to Apply For a Job? by LARRY R. COCHRAN, Department of Counselling Psychology, Faculty of Education, University of British Columbia, Vancouver, British Columbia, Canada:

Do I Know How to Apply for a Job? is a 12-page instructional booklet. There are nearly eight pages of instruction on how to apply for a job; following that is a 52-item test of the material, which is used to check readiness to begin a "job getting campaign." There is no test manual, nor is there a date on the publication.

The instructions for how to apply for a job consist largely of common-sense recommendations and glowing generalities ranging from "It always pays to tell the truth" to keeping one's teeth clean. Inadequacies are evident. First, the instructions are dated. For example, the reader is informed that "hat and gloves add to the appearance of every lady." Second, the instructions do not include current knowledge of how people actually get jobs. Third, the instructions are largely too general to be very useful. Richard Bolles' *What Color Is Your Parachute?* is vastly superior as a guide for job finding. There is little in the instructions that would indicate even a minimal effort to develop a reasonable basis for test construction.

The test consists of 52 questions, most beginning with the phrase "Do I know that...," to which one responds either yes or no. All yes responses indicate knowledge of how to apply for a job, while all no responses indicate lack of knowledge. The questions are defective in a variety of ways. There is typically an obvious right answer. Questions sometimes call for a judgment a person is not in a position to make. For example, how would one know a company's products and their uses if one has not yet decided upon actual places to apply for work? The answer for question 3 is found in question 27. There are ambiguities in some questions. For example, one is supposed to be generally liked. However, question 47 merely asks whether one knows if he or she is generally liked, which could be answered yes by one who is disliked. There are no apparent boundaries on questions, which range from technicalities in applying for a job to conditions for happiness in life generally. The test mixes pertinent questions with those that have little to do with how one applies for a job. For example, must one be generally liked to apply for work? How would knowledge that one might be asked to take a test help in applying for a job? The questions lack a sense of proportion. One question concerns carrying a fountain pen while another concerns an analysis of one's strengths and weaknesses. The trite and the important are combined in a generally disorganized list of questions.

Following the test, one is asked to judge whether he or she is good (top 10%), above average, average, below average, or poor (bottom 10%). There is no basis supplied for making this judgment. There is no clear description of what the test is measuring. There is little basis for making any judgment whatever. It is not just that the test fails to meet some standards for test construction; it fails to meet any standard.

There is no evidence for any form of reliability or validity. There are no norms. There is no explicit scoring system, although it can be assumed one counts the yes responses. There is no warrant for even believing that it adequately tests the eight pages of instruction. Although the author refers to it as a test, it is not a test using any acceptable definition of this term, for it offers no real measure of anything. Rather, it is an ill-contrived checklist dressed up in a test format. The question stems are simply cues for briefly reiterating part of the instructions in a glowing manner.

Review of Do I Know How to Apply For a Job? by BARBARA KERR, Assistant Professor of Educational Psychology, University of Nebraska-Lincoln, Lincoln, NE:

The Do I Know How to Apply for a Job instrument is useful as an engagingly humorous anthropological artifact, but certainly not as a measure of knowledge of job-seeking behaviors. This is an instrument which first subjects the reader to a long series of homilies and mostly unfounded suggestions for applying and interviewing for jobs and then asks a series of recall questions to check for proper memorization of the homilies and unfounded suggestions. Throughout the text, there is the prodigious and incorrect use of quotation marks to emphasize, rather bizarrely, certain points. "Is the 'Future' in the 'Job' or in 'You'?"

The Do I Know How to Apply for a Job instrument is a relic of that semi-mythical time when all employers were "he" and when "ladies" applying for a job were always sure to wear "hat and gloves" and had to be instructed to "Leave the gum at home." It is from a time when all the cues of almost pathological deference to authority were assumed to be the appropriate behaviors of a successful job applicant. It is also an artifact of a period of such extraordinary economic prosperity that job applicants who even took such silly advice as is provided by this instrument could still expect to be employed eventually. The use of this instrument today would seem patronizing to unemployed adults and hilarious to adolescents, and therefore is not advised.

Probably the best information about job-seeking is included in two books, the *Job Club Counselor's Manual* by Azrin and Bezalel (1980) and *What Color is Your Parachute?* by Richard Bolles (1980). Both of these books contain suitable instrumentation for use with job seekers, ranging from self-analyses to check lists of appropriate interview behaviors. *The Job Club Manual*, because it is highly behavioral in orientation and action-oriented in its approach, is very helpful to the counselor working with unemployed, non-college educated adolescents and adults. The techniques, if used properly, have been shown to be about 90% effective in placing minimally educated or unskilled individuals in jobs. The Bolles book, deservedly on the non-fiction best-seller lists for several years, has been useful for counselors working with college educated clients, for whom the rather enterprising, job-creation strategies advocated by Bolles are most actionable.

Both of these books and the instrumentation included in them are respectful of their readers and both show a responsible awareness of the difficulties encountered by the job-seeker in the current economy.

REVIEWER'S REFERENCES

Azrin, N. H., & Bezalel, V. A. JOB CLUB COUNSELORS MANUAL. Baltimore, MD: University Park Press, 1980.

Bolles, R. N. WHAT COLOR IS YOUR PARACHUTE? Berkeley, CA: Ten Speed Press, 1980.

[357]

Dole Vocational Sentence Completion Blank. Grades 7–12; 1952–82; DVSCB; 27 scores in 3 major areas: concerns (problem, achievement, independence, satisfaction, material, vocation, effectiveness, recognition), general emphasis (relaxation, intellectual, active, other people, recreational), specific preference areas (outdoor, mechanical, computational, scientific, persuasive, artistic, literary, musical, social service, clerical, domestic, academic, armed forces, household arts), plus 2 miscellaneous scores (other, omit), and 9 optional categories (peace of mind, security, value, obligation, health, religion, social studies, negative academic, unclassifiable); norms consist of means and standard deviations; 1 form ('74, 2 pages); instruction manual ('79, 34 pages); individual score profile (no date, 1 page); 1983 price data: $5 per 30 tests; $15 per complete set (includes manual, 30 tests, and 30 individual score profiles); $5 per 30 record forms; $6 per manual; (20) minutes; Arthur A. Dole; Stoelting Co.*

Review of Dole Vocational Sentence Completion Blank by WILLIAM BORGEN, Associate Professor and Head, and ROBERT TOLSMA, Assistant Professor, Department of Counselling Psychology, University of British Columbia, Vancouver, British Columbia, Canada:

The Dole Vocational Sentence Completion Blank (VSCB) is a semi-projective instrument which consists of 21 incomplete sentence stems. The sentences are completed by the subject using his or her own words. Responses are scored by assigning them to one or more of 29 standard categories. The category into which the most frequent number of responses is assigned is considered to be a reflection of the topic of most concern to the subject. The VSCB is said by the author to be of use in counseling, rehabilitation, diagnosis, therapy and research. However, because it is designed to tap concerns, preferences, and the subject's stream of consciousness, but not repressed or unconscious material, pathology, or complex personality dynamics, it has little utility as a diagnostic aid for psychotherapeutic purposes.

An instruction manual accompanying the VSCB contains information about the assumptions underlying the development and purposes of the test, psychometric properties, administration and scoring instructions, and how the VSCB can be used in counseling. The only evidence provided by the author regarding the psychometric properties of the instrument is provided in the instruction manual. A mimeographed paper (Dole, 1977) is referenced throughout as a source of studies that the author has conducted regarding the psychometrics of the instrument, but this paper is unavailable from the publisher. While the author indicates in the instruction manual that he has attempted to follow the recommended standards for psychological tests, he recognizes that gaps exist between these standards and what he has been able to provide. The manual should be read carefully since there are implications that the instrument has been developed to a greater extent than the data presented indicates. The work planned by the author to further develop this instrument is necessary to enhance its psychometric credibility.

The author states that the item stems used in the test were selected and developed on the basis of counseling experience and completion analysis. Although studies are cited that might explain the item selection procedure, not all of these citations appear in the reference section of the manual; thus necessary information about the studies could not be obtained. The categories to which subjects' responses are assigned were developed on the basis of logic. Six criteria were used to judge whether a category should be retained. Since a category had to meet only a majority of the six criteria for inclusion, not all categories were retained on the basis of the same criteria. Unfortunately, the specific set of criteria each category met are not given, leaving the user to speculate on the relative adequacy of each category. For example, one of the six criteria is that the category being considered for inclusion be independent of other categories. Since only a majority of criteria was needed for inclusion some categories apparently do not meet the independence criterion. This has very strong implications for scoring because if some categories are not, in fact, independent of one another, then it would be difficult for the scorer to discriminate among them when assigning responses.

The VSCB has been normed on urban and suburban students in grades 7 to 12. However, there are no norms listed in the manual for grade 10 and some of the norming groups for the other grades are small (e.g., $N = 19$). The author suggests that the VSCB be used with college students, adults and a variety of minority groups: blacks, the poor, the retarded, and the psysically disabled, etc. There are no norms presented for these groups.

Inter-scorer agreement and test-retest reliability studies are reported. It is stated that experienced scorers range from 80 to 95% agreement with another. The characteristics of the scorers are unknown (e.g., how many, how much training they had in scoring, and what constituted agreement). A study rank ordering the frequency of items assigned to various categories by two scorers produced a rank order correlation which "exceeded .80." No information is given about the scorers, whether they assigned similar or different items to the same categories, nor what other artifacts in the research design might have contributed to the magnitude of the correlation. A two year test-retest reliability study yielded Pearson product-moment correlations ranging from –.01 to .56. The author explains away these low correlations by indicating that they are a function of changing interest patterns over time. These correlation coefficients are lower than those reported for standardized measures with similar categories such as the Vocational Preference Kuder Record Form CM. It may be that the author's conclusion about the low test-retest reliability coefficients is correct; however, it is also equally plausible that the test itself may not be stable over time.

The author states that in instruments like the VSCB the standard error of measurement is not really meaningful and instead instructs the user in a "rules of thumb" determination as to whether differences in the number of mentions between categories is interpretable. This rule is stated as follows: a "difference of plus or minus two mentions should be interpreted as 'more' or 'less,' with confidence as [sic] 95% likely to hold up." There is no statistical evidence to indicate that score differences can be accurately interpreted in this manner. Using precise numbers such as 95% as if they represent confidence levels based on standard error of measurement is misleading.

Results of six studies are cited as evidence of validity. The purpose of these studies was to establish concurrent and predictive validity. No quantified findings are presented from these studies, only brief interpretations. The information is so meager it must be concluded that the concurrent and predictive validity of the VSCB has yet to be established.

Administration of the VSCB is presented clearly and succinctly in the instruction manual. Sample sentences are given along with hints designed to assure cooperation of people writing the test.

The author claims that "any reasonably intelligent person, irregardless [sic] of psychological experience, can learn to score VSCB in a few hours." He further indicates that two naive student clerks could master the material within about 3 hours. No information is provided as to how long it took them to do the actual scoring of the material. He provides examples of statements that could be assigned to each of the 29 scoring categories. These examples would seem to be vital for anyone to refer to when scoring this test. The author admits that some statements may be scored in more than one category but indicates that most should fit into one. This part of the manual would be improved by having more examples in each category as well as examples of statements that could be scored in two or more categories. Ease of scoring reliably is alluded to by the author but there is no evidence that this in fact is the case. Further, the author provides no information regarding how long it may take to score the instrument. The author cautions that scoring errors, inconsistencies, idiosyncratic responses, and limited range of categories may lower accuracy of measurement far more than occurs with objective inventories. He encourages the use of the VSCB in conjunction with other information about the client, especially other standardized interest inventories. He makes this suggestion when the blank is being used primarily as a counseling tool. However, it would seem to be vital to keep this in mind when using the blank for any purpose. The author recognizes the problem of rating each client's statement within the 29 categories and provides a further list of 8 categories where "errant responses" may be placed. Overall the description of the scoring procedures is disappointing. It would seem that the author would have been better advised to either present more examples to enable the test user to score the instrument more accurately or to have presented the blank as an adjunct to counseling to be used informally as an extension to an interview. As it is he seems to have reached neither goal satisfactorily.

SUMMARY. There are pictures on the cover of the instruction manual which suggest this test is appropriate for different age groups from a variety of different ethnic backgrounds. In fact, this instrument has been normed on relatively small groups of students in grades 7, 8, 9, 11, and 12 representing just a few different ethnic backgrounds. Further, it is not clear how the normative data presented in the instruction manual are to be used in interpretation.

The author presents the VSCB as a psychometric instrument and uses validity and reliability arguments in parts of the manual to bolster his case for its use as a somewhat standardized device. In other parts of the manual he cautions against the use of the instrument in the absence of a counseling interview situation designed to check out the validity of the information gained from the instrument. On the basis of our review his cautions are well founded. Use of this instrument is recommended only as a stimulus for further discussion within the context of a counseling interview.

REVIEWER'S REFERENCES

Dole, A. A. MANUAL FOR VOCATIONAL SENTENCE COMPLETION BLANK. (Revised) Mimeographed Report. Philadelphia: University of Pennsylvania, 1977.

Review of Dole Vocational Sentence Completion Blank by RODNEY L. LOWMAN, Assistant Professor of Psychology, North Texas State University, Denton, TX:

With the exception of McClelland's and Atkinson's work on the need for achievement motive as reflected in the Thematic Apperception Test and Miner's sentence completion methodology, researchers have mostly relied on objective measures to assess vocationally relevant constructs. This practice appears to reflect both prejudice against the "looser" methods and the generally disappointing results obtained when projectives have been employed to predict occupationally-relevant variables. This reviewer, for one, believes that imaginative research with the more powerful wide-band projectives has untapped potential for expanding knowledge of vocational interests and decision making. But while one can be open about the use of projectives in vocational research, standards in the selection of projectives need not be abandoned. Unfortunately, the Dole Vocational Sentence Completion Blank (VSCB) is not a measure likely to open new understandings, either for practice or research.

To date, the VSCB has been primarily used with high school pupils. The test is intended to be a "semi-projective," and, despite its name, is said to be useful in educational, vocational, and other important life decisions. Dole further claims the measure to be of value in counseling, rehabilitation, diagnosis, and therapy—ambitious goals indeed.

"Semi-projective" is a rather infrequently used term in psychological assessment. It appears in this case to refer to combining an open-ended sentence completion format with an objective scoring system. Like most projectives, semi- or otherwise, the measure is claimed to be most valuable as an idiographic measure in diagnosis or counseling. However, the author notes that it is only conscious, not unconscious, concerns and motivations that are tapped by his instrument.

A promising twist to the VSCB is its attempt to objectify the scoring of a sentence completion instrument. Just as Exner has revived interest in removing the excessive and often misleading subjectivity in the scoring and interpretation of the Rorschach, the provision of a scoring system for a sentence completion measure is cause for attention. However, the particular scoring scheme used in the VSCB is something else again. The 29 separate scoring categories are claimed to be independent, based on research reported in an apparently hard-to-obtain 1977 mimeograph. It is difficult to imagine that such scoring areas as achievement, effectiveness, and recognition are orthogonal, or that vocational areas such as computational and scientific are unrelated. Interrater scorer reliabilities for category assignments are claimed to "typically" range from 80 to 95%. Although the author notes that the test is easily scored, it is rather difficult when compared to other, more objective, measures, and such effort should be rewarded with better results.

Normative data were obtained from 8 schools, all junior high or high schools. All but two of the schools were in Philadelphia, and the data were collected in 1960 and 1969. Although an admirable attempt was made to include minority groups, the norms are now hopelessly dated, and are of highly questionable representativeness. Norms are appropriately separated by sex, since there is evidence that many of the scoring categories differ by sex. A more fundamental question plagues the normative data: what specifically does it mean if an individual's number of mentions of an item exceed or are less than those of the normative samples? Does it mean anything, for example, if a person has three mentions on achievement when the normative sample averages one? If so, what? Unfortunately, the test manual provides little guidance on this issue, except for its largely untested assumption that the quantity of mentions of an item signify a probable concern or issue. Similarly, the sparse reliability data on the measure are limited by the recognition that the respondent's concerns may change, so test-retest reliability is of limited usefulness.

The 30-plus years of history of the VSCB is not reflected in a large or impressive body of research data about the instrument. Unfortunately, the few studies done are not easily obtainable, many of them apparently summarized in the aforementioned 1977 mimeo. I wrote both to the test publisher and author requesting copies of unpublished research on the instrument. Since the test author did not respond, and the publisher had no additional information, or even copies of the studies cited in the manual, one must surmise that the reader is to accept on faith the author's extremely brief report in the test manual of the "substantial evidence" that is claimed for one thing or another. Another approach would be to attempt to track down firsthand the published citations in such widely available sources as the Proceedings of Hawaiian Academy of Science (in abstract, no less!), or a test manual available at the University of Hawaii bookstore.

The few validity studies adequately summarized in the test manual present rather mixed results. One set of studies compared results of the VSCB with another Dole product, You and Your Future. In general, the claims for the instrument's validity exceed the number and quality of studies cited in the manual. Both the author and the test publisher are liable to criticism for the paucity of validity evidence available for this commercially marketed product, and for their failure to provide enough information in the test manual on these few studies for readers to draw independent judgements. There is little to suggest that the VSCB in its present form is useable for anything but research purposes.

In short, in attempting to be too many things, this test succeeds in validly and reliably measuring too few. The VSCB may have some use as a rough screen of areas of concern to a client, but even here it is not clear that the test is an efficient measure. Since the VSCB is described as a measure of the conscious concern of the client rather than the unconscious, a clinical interview would probably do as well. As a measure of vocational interests, the VSCB is far inferior to existing measures. Until there is far more convincing evidence of the value of the VSCB, it is best regarded as an example of a measure with better intentions than results.

[358]

The Draw-A-Person. Ages 5 and over; 1963; DAP, 1 form; manual (38 pages plus sample copies of record and interpretive booklets); record booklet (4 pages); interpretive booklet (4 pages); 1984 price data: $7.10 per 25 record booklets; $7.10 per 25 interpretive booklets; $9.70 per manual; [5–10] minutes; William H. Urban; Western Psychological Services.*

See T3:751 (44 references); for reviews by Dale B. Harris and Philip M. Kitay, see 7:165.

TEST REFERENCES

1. Hoy, E., Weiss, G., Minde, K., & Cohen N. The hyperactive child at adolescence: Cognitive, emotional, and social functioning. JOURNAL OF ABNORMAL CHILD PSYCHOLOGY, 1978, 6, 311–324.

2. Fleming, M., Koocher, G., & Nathans, J. Draw-A-Person test: Implications for gender identification. ARCHIVES OF SEXUAL BEHAVIOR, 1979, 8, 55–61.

3. Freeman, M. J. The need for an organismic therapy in hospitalization. CLINICAL NEUROPSYCHOLOGY, 1979, 1(3), 39–43.

4. Henggeler, S. W., & Tavormina, J. B. Stability of psychological assessment measures for children of Mexican American migrant workers. HISPANIC JOURNAL OF BEHAVIORAL SCIENCES, 1979, 1, 263–270.

5. Reynolds, W. M. Psychological tests: Clinical usage versus psychometric quality. PROFESSIONAL PSYCHOLOGY, 1979, 10, 324–329.

6. Rieder, R. O., & Nichols, P. L. Offspring of schizophrenics III: Hyperactivity and neurological soft signs. ARCHIVES OF GENERAL PSYCHIATRY, 1979, 36, 665–674.

7. Fleming, M. Z., Jenkins, S. R., & Bugarin, C. Questioning current definitions of gender identity: Implications of the Bem Sex-Role Inventory for transsexuals. ARCHIVES OF SEXUAL BEHAVIOR, 1980, 9, 13–26.

8. McCauley, E. A., & Ehrhardt, A. A. Sexual behavior in female transsexuals and lesbians. THE JOURNAL OF SEX RESEARCH, 1980, 16, 202–211.

9. Falk, J. D. Understanding children's art: An analysis of the literature. JOURNAL OF PERSONALITY ASSESSMENT, 1981, 45, 465–472.

10. Hjorth, C. W., & Harway, M. The body-image of physically abused and normal adolescents. JOURNAL OF CLINICAL PSYCHOLOGY, 1981, 37, 863–866.

11. Udwin, O., & Shmukler, D. The influence of sociocultural, economic, and home background factors on children's ability to engage in imaginative play. DEVELOPMENTAL PSYCHOLOGY, 1981, 17, 66–72.

12. Abbott, D., Rotnem, D., Genel, M., & Cohen, D. J. Cognitive and emotional functioning in hypopituitary short-statured children. SCHIZOPHRENIA BULLETIN, 1982, 8, 310–319.

13. Duffy, K. G., Beaty, J. W., & DeJulio, S. Size of human figure drawings as influenced by instructions for "sexy" versus "average" drawings and by the status of the experimenter. JOURNAL OF CLINICAL PSYCHOLOGY, 1982, 38, 191–197.

14. Field, K., Bolton, B., & Dana, R. H. An evaluation of three Bender-Gestalt scoring systems as indicators of psychopathology. JOURNAL OF CLINICAL PSYCHOLOGY, 1982, 38, 838–842.

15. Fleming, M., Cohen, D., Salt, P., Robinson, L., & Spitz, J. The use of an animal drawing test in the assessment and disposition of transsexualism. JOURNAL OF CLINICAL PSYCHOLOGY, 1982, 38, 420–424.

16. Gonzales, E. A cross-cultural comparison of the developmental items of five ethnic groups in the southwest. JOURNAL OF PERSONALITY ASSESSMENT, 1982, 46, 26–31.

17. Maloney, M. P., & Glasser, A. An evaluation of the clinical utility of the Draw-A-Person test. JOURNAL OF CLINICAL PSYCHOLOGY, 1982, 38, 183–190.

18. Pontius, A. A. Global spatial relations in face representations shown in "ecological dyslexia" of Australian Aboriginals and in "Western" dyslexics. PERCEPTUAL AND MOTOR SKILLS, 1982, 55, 1191–1200.

19. Spero, M. H. Psychotherapeutic procedure with religious cult devotees. THE JOURNAL OF NERVOUS AND MENTAL DISEASE, 1982, 170, 332–344.

20. Clark, L. A., & Halford, G. S. Does cognitive style account for cultural differences in scholastic achievement? JOURNAL OF CROSS-CULTURAL PSYCHOLOGY, 1983, 14, 279–296.

21. Manshadi, M., Lippman, S., O'Daniel, R. G., & Blackman, A. Alcohol abuse and attention deficit disorder. THE JOURNAL OF CLINICAL PSYCHIATRY, 1983, 44, 379–380.

22. Sims, J., Dana, R. H., & Boulton, B. The validity of the Draw-A-Person test as an anxiety measure. JOURNAL OF PERSONALITY ASSESSMENT, 1983, 47, 250–257.

23. Zucker, K. J., Finegan, J. K., Doering, R. W., & Bradley, S. J. Human figure drawings of gender-problem children: A comparison to sibling, psychiatric, and normal controls. JOURNAL OF ABNORMAL CHILD PSYCHOLOGY, 1983, 11, 287–293.

[359]

Drumcondra Attainment Tests. Grades 2, 3–4, 5–6, 7, 8, 9; 1976–78; 3 subtests at each level except *a*; 6 levels; separate answer sheets must be used for levels III to VI; price data available from publisher; Educational Research Centre [Ireland].*

a) LEVEL I. Grade 2; 1978; manual (63 pages).
1) *Mathematics*. 4 scores: computation, concepts, problem solving, total; Form A (10 pages); (54) minutes.
2) *English*. 4 scores: vocabulary, word analysis, comprehension, total; Form A (12 pages); (45) minutes.

b) LEVEL II. Grades 3–4; 1978; manual (109 pages).
1) *Mathematics*. 4 scores: computation, concepts, problem solving, total; Form A (12 pages); (85) minutes.
2) *Irish*. 5 scores: vocabulary, comprehension, reading total, usage, spelling; Form A (15 pages); (56) minutes.
3) *English*. 7 scores: vocabulary, comprehension, reading total, capitalization/punctuation, usage/grammar, language total, spelling; Form A (18 pages); (64) minutes.

c) LEVEL III. Grades 5–6; 1977; manual (107 pages).
1) *Mathematics*. 4 scores: same as Level II; Form A (12 pages); (105) minutes.
2) *Irish*. 5 scores: same as Level II; Form A (14 pages); (70) minutes.
3) *English*. 7 scores: same as Level II; Form A (20 pages); (102) minutes.

d) LEVEL IV. Grade 7; 1977; manual (87 pages).
1) *Mathematics*. 4 scores: same as Level II; Form A (10 pages); (85) minutes.
2) *Irish*. 5 scores: same as Level II; Form A (16 pages); (59–70) minutes.
3) *English*. 7 scores: same as Level II; Form A (20 pages); (68) minutes.

e) LEVEL V. Grade 8; 1976; manual (87 pages).
1) *Mathematics*. 4 scores: same as Level II; Form A (12 pages); (77) minutes.
2) *Irish*. 5 scores: same as Level II; Form A (20 pages); (84) minutes.
3) *English*. 7 scores: same as Level II; Form A (22 pages); (87) minutes.

f) LEVEL VI. Grade 9; 1978; manual (77 pages).
1) *Mathematics*. 4 scores: same as Level II; Form A (11 pages); (85) minutes.
2) *Irish*. 5 scores: same as Level II; Form A (20 pages); (124) minutes.
3) *English*. 7 scores: same as Level II; Form A (22 pages); (93) minutes.

[360]

Durrell Analysis of Reading Difficulty, Third Edition. Grades 1–6; 1937–80; previous edition still available; 16 to 21 scores: oral reading, silent reading, listening comprehension, word recognition, word analysis, listening vocabulary, sounds in isolation (letters, blends and digraphs, phonograms, initial affixes, final affixes), spelling, phonic spelling of words, visual memory of words (primary, secondary), identifying sounds in words, pre-reading phonics abilities inventories (optional, including syntax matching, letter names in spoken words, phonemes in spoken words, naming lower case letters, writing letters from dictation); individual; 1 form ('80, 15 pages); manual ('80, 63 pages); 1982 price data: $14.50 per examiner's kit, including 5 record booklets, tachistoscope, reading booklet and manual; $4.50 per reading booklet; $12.75 per 35 individual record booklets; $3.85 per tachistoscope; $2 per manual of directions; administration time not reported; Donald D. Durrell and Jane H. Catterson; The Psychological Corporation.*

See T3:766 (14 references) and T2:1628 (18 references); for reviews by James Maxwell and George D. Spache of an earlier edition, see 5:660; for a review by Helen M. Robinson of the original edition, see 4:561 (2 references); for reviews by Guy L. Bond and Miles A. Tinker, see 2:1533; for a review by Marion Monroe, see 1:1098.

TEST REFERENCES

1. Johnson, L. S., Johnson, D. L., Olson, M. R., & Newman, J. P. The uses of hypnotherapy with learning disabled children. JOURNAL OF CLINICAL PSYCHOLOGY, 1981, 37, 291–299.

2. Aaron, P. G., Baker, C., & Hickox, G. L. In search of the third dyslexia. NEUROPSYCHOLOGIA, 1982, 20, 203–208.

3. Marr, M. B. An analysis of text variables in three current reading diagnostic tests. NATIONAL READING CONFERENCE YEARBOOK, 1983, 32, 115–122.

Review of Durrell Analysis of Reading Difficulty, Third Edition, by NANCY L. ROSER, Associate Professor of Curriculum and Instruction, University of Texas at Austin, Austin, TX:

In past reviews, critics have called attention to the scant description of normative data and to the absence of standardization procedures from the administrator's manual for the Durrell Analysis. Thus, claims for the reliability and validity of this enduringly popular diagnostic test were questioned. In preparation for this Third Edition, the publisher surveyed 200 users of the test to determine that new normative data, revised paragraph contents, and "clearing up confusion about certain tests" were priorities.

The structure of the instrument, however, is essentially unchanged. This appears to be true also for the test's content. While the number of paragraphs for oral and silent reading remains the same, the content of some paragraphs is revised slightly, and a few are completely new. Questions which follow the oral paragraphs continue to require the reader to recall explicit information, rather than make inferences, unless they be intersentential ones. For example, the second passage reads, "It began to rain. He [the dog] went under a tree." A question for this content asks: "Why did the dog go under the tree?" The publishers claim to have made a "detailed study" of the paragraphs to update content, to avoid sex and ethnic bias, and to achieve more curricular balance. In some cases, these changes are evident. For example, one paragraph was revised so that mother now fixes her own car, instead of waiting for a man. But in other cases, this detailed study is not so evident. Overall, the dull paragraph content and mundane style could influence a child's performance on the test.

While procedures for administering the test are essentially the same, the consumer will find the manual itself to be much more explicit than the previous edition. The publisher explains that over the years many locally developed manuals containing notes of clarification have been shared with the publisher. As a result, it seems much less in the current manual is left to interpretation or guesswork. The following examples are exceptions, where more guidance for the administrator seems called for: (*a*) In scoring the reader's performance on the Oral Reading paragraphs, the administrator is directed to use judgment so as not to overcount minor errors, as to do so risks termination of the test before the child has read all he or she can. It is further noted that minor errors are "especially common in the first paragraphs that a child reads." It is not clear what minor errors are considered to be. (*b*) Similarly, on the Silent Reading Test, the examiner is told to ignore minor errors in recall. Again, there is no evidence that any two examiners would agree to what constitutes a minor error. (*c*) Procedures for scoring Listening Comprehension direct the examiner to give partial credit if that seems appropriate, but there is neither an example nor explanation of a partially correct answer. (*d*) An assessment of imagery in silent reading is included, based on the assumption that "imagery flow in reading is of great future importance." Yet, the most recent study cited to support that assumption is 1963. The examiner has but a two-option choice to make in the record booklet as a result of assessing imagery: rich flow or poor flow. There is no direction for making or interpreting that decision.

Other revisions in the Third Edition include a new Listening Vocabulary test, new measure of Prereading Abiliites, and some additional word lists for the Word Recognition/Word Analysis subtest. A Sounds in Isolation subtest has been added for the purpose of assessing mastery of sound/symbol relationships, including letters, blends, digraphs, phonograms, and affixes.

The Listening Vocabulary test is unique in the sense that it tests the same words as those in the Word Recognition/Word Analysis lists, permitting comparison of ability to attach meaning to words met earlier in isolation. Meaning is demonstrated by placing the word into one of three designed categories. The manual explains that Listening Vocabulary provides a second index of the child's reading capacity. Capacity is first mentioned in the test of Listening Comprehension. The test consumer should note, however, that the term reading capacity does not carry its usual connotation as the highest level at which the child can listen with understanding. In the Listening Comprehension test, the examiner is directed to read one or two paragraphs aloud to determine "whether or not reading difficulty rests upon lack of comprehension."

Since the Listening Vocabulary imposes no such limit, it is likely that this second index of capacity will allow children, especially younger ones, to demonstrate greater "capacity," since they are read lists of words at increasing difficulty levels, receiving as a score the total number of words categorized correctly. This prediction is supported by the low inter-correlation of these two subtests for primary level readers ($r = .22$), an indication that there is little performance overlap between the two subtests.

The most unusual and questionable test for overall utility is a part of the Prereading Phonic Abilities Inventories. It is called Identifying Letter Names in Spoken Words. Directions state the "letter names can be clearly identified in spoken words when the name appears in the first syllable of the word." For example, the child is asked to say the letter name heard at the beginning of Esther. The correct response is S. This task is so alien to typical instruction that beginning readers are likely to experience confusion.

There is no evidence of the predictive power of this subtest or any of the more typical ones intended for prereaders (e.g., tests of letter names, phonemic awareness, matching spoken sentences with written words) because of the sketchy description of norming procedures. An unidentified number of end-of-year kindergarten children were tested in a group situation and norms derived from their performance. A consumer should consider how useful a comparison of a child's performance will be with norms derived from kindergarten children completing the school year in unspecified districts and of unspecified abilities. When used as a September measure in first grade, four of the subtests of the Prereading Inventory yielded correlations with end of year achievement ranging from .55 to .65, or nearly the same as most group readiness tests.

For the other tests in the Durrell Analysis, norms were obtained from at least 200 children per grade in grades 1 through 6 in five geographic regions of the U.S. In six states, 40 children at each grade were identified for testing who had earned average Metropolitan Reading Test scores (i.e., scores falling within the fourth, fifth, or sixth stanines). It is not stated why a wider range of pupil abilities were not tapped through individual testing, as that would have provided more support for the high and low classifications that the Durrell frequently uses for interpretation. While it is not certain why the numbers were kept low, reference to expense and economics crops up three times in the manual of directions, perhaps in an attempt to be frank or as explanation for the small sample.

The validity of the Durrell Analysis is described in a most unsatisfactory way and is based largely on the test's longevity, the harvest of opinions from experts who use the test, and its stability in content over time. The manual attests to "current professional confidence in its general validity."

Information on reliability is more specific. To gauge reliability for Oral and Silent Reading, a random sample of children from grades 2 through 6 were timed while reading two adjacent paragraphs (the paragraph most suitable for the child and the next more difficult one) and the times correlated. Time and Oral Reading paragraphs correlated .85 and between Silent Reading paragraphs, .80. How these correlations provide a basis for the use of reading time for assigning grade levels is not described. Kuder-Richardson Formula 21 reliability estimates for selected subtests range from .63 for visual memory of words to .97 for intermediate spelling. Subtest inter-correlations for primary level readers range from .22 (Listening Comprehension with Listening Vocabulary) to .94 (Word Analysis with Word Recognition) and for intermediate level readers from .42 (Spelling with Silent Reading) to .96 (Word Analysis with Word Recognition). Scores of the intermediate level children correlate slightly higher with the reading grade scores of the Metropolitan Reading Test than do those of primary children.

In summary, the Durrell Analysis has long served a population of experienced teachers whose primary purpose was to discover and describe weaknesses and faulty habits in children's reading. The manual of directions for the Third Edition is improved, providing clearer procedures for testing. A continuing strength of the test is its sets of behavioral checklists, urging the close observation of individual reader characteristics. The addition of several new subtests makes for an even more complete battery for assessment; yet the major focus of the test continues to be on specific skills. Norming data and standardization procedures are not yet presented satisfactorily. There is still need for establishing the test's validity, for providing data for the Prereading Inventories gathered from individual testing of a broader sample of children, for clarifying the use of time as a reliable aid for assigning reading grade levels, for specificity in the description of the use of read-ability formulas to equate passage difficulty, and for a rationale for subtest inclusion. For the most part, changes in this edition have made the Durrell Analysis easier to administer, but did not significantly influence the examiner's ability to feel confident in its results.

Review of Durrell Analysis of Reading Difficulty, Third Edition, by BYRON H. VAN ROEKEL, *Professor Emeritus, College of Education, Michigan State University, East Lansing, MI:*

This edition is the second revision of a test which in a few years will be observing its 50th anniversary. Preparatory to the revision, the authors: (*a*) obtained the opinions of nearly 200 college professors who use the Durrell Analysis of Reading Difficulty as an integral part of the courses they teach; (*b*) researched the literature (critical reviews, research articles, essays reflecting changing attitudes about the nature of reading, etc.) to provide ideas and approaches for improving the test; and (*c*) solicited reactions from previous users of the test to tentative proposals for changes in the test.

According to the Manual of Directions, the test-users were generous with comment and suggestion and, in general, concurred on the need for: new normative data (which is implicit in a revision), updating and modifying paragraph content, and clearing up confusions about certain subtests. Concensus among the test-consumers supported the retention of most of the subtests from the 1955 edition as well as the addition of a new Listening Vocabulary subtest, new measures of pre-reading abilities, and additional inventories on word analysis. The authors interpreted this as a mandate to update "the familiar Analysis, with verbiage and expense kept to a minimum."

The sum and substance of this effort has produced an instrument whose structure remains essentially unchanged as well as one that retains many of the shortcomings reported in earlier *MMY* reviews—the latter of which might have been avoided had the "jury" included test specialists as well as individuals who qualified merely because they had opted to use the test previously.

The core of the test continues to be two sets of paragraphs, one set for oral and the other for silent reading. Revisions range from minor changes in some of the paragraphs carried over from the previous edition to paragraphs treating completely new subject matter, supposedly to alleviate sex and ethnic bias and promote curricular balance. A number of these changes appear to be primarily cosmetic.

A third set of paragraphs comprises the Listening Comprehension subtest which supposedly provides an estimate of the child's reading capacity. The subtest proceeds on the assumption that an individual's ability to understand paragraphs read aloud by the examiner indicates whether or not reading difficulty stems from inability to comprehend. Accordingly, the rendition of each paragraph is followed by a group of recall questions. What the subtest measures, beyond providing a tally of the number of questions answered correctly, is not clear. A poor showing, for example, could well stem from either language deficits or a lapse in attention.

Norms for the oral and silent reading subtests are expressed in grade equivalents based on speed for each of grades 1 to 6 on three levels (low, medium, and high). Apparently, the middle level is the mean reading time for each paragraph; there is no explanation of how the numerical values of the low and high levels were determined. Unfortunately the authors did not provide data to supply a frame of reference for judging the precision and significance of these test scores.

Comprehension on the oral reading paragraphs is measured by questions which demand only the exercise of rote recall. Performance is judged on the number of questions answered incorrectly. A child earns a rating of "good" when no more than two questions about a paragraph are omitted or answered incorrectly, a rating of "fair" when three questions are answered incorrectly and a rating of "poor" if more than three responses are incorrect. In silent reading the child demonstrates his ability to comprehend by reciting "memories" after each of the paragraphs is read. No questions involving any type of inferential comprehension are provided. Listening comprehension level is scored as the grade level designation of the paragraph where no more than two questions are answered incorrectly. The criteria for rating performance on the comprehension exercises in oral reading and listening appear to be scaled arbitrarily. It would have been a rather simple task to establish more meaningful norms based on the performance of pupils in the standardization group.

Other major subtests deal with word recognition and word analysis; auditory and visual characteristics of letters, affixes, and words; and written spelling. There will be those who argue that some of the skills measured by these subtests are not essential to the acquisition of reading. The argument is moot simply because a consensus of the exact nature of the reading process is nonexistent, to which the recent surge in theoretical models of reading bears witness. Because the essential nature of the components of the word recognition act have not been precisely defined, the authors are to be commended for providing broad coverage of phonic skills.

This reviewer shares little enthusiasm for the new subtests in this edition. In the Listening Vocabulary subtest a child's task is to assign words spoken by the examiner to one of three classification categories based on meaning. Thus, in the first item, the child must classify the word "red" as either "time," "big," or "color," whichever is nearest in meaning. Skepticism about this subtest stems from two sources: (*a*) the belief that tasks such as prescribed here can be performed strictly by association without differentiation among members of a group, and (*b*) the low correlations reported between scores on the Listening Vocabulary subtest and scores on subtests involving measures of comprehension. The Prereading Phonics Abilities Inventories are really adaptations of subtests from the previous edition except for Identifying Letter Names in Spoken Words. The authors' rationale for including the latter is unconvincing.

The validity of the various subtests in the Analysis essentially is content validity. It is based largely on the judgment and competence of the test constructors. It remains for the test-user to decide if the skills and abilities required for successful performance on the various subtests are essential to the acquisition of reading.

The standardization of this edition appears to be much improved. Geographical distribution was attained by drawing a sample of approximately 200 children from each of five widely scattered regional centers. Although a sample of about 1,200 children hardly is a national sample in the usual sense, testing that many children with an individually administered test reflects a substantial effort to provide better norms.

Although several shortcomings of the Durrell Analysis of Reading Difficulty have been noted, in comparison with other similar tests it has some excellent qualities and fewer deficiencies. However, during the lapse of nearly a half century since the origin of the Analysis, there have been a number of developments and refinements in tests and measurements. More adequate normative data could have been provided had the authors chosen to pay more attention to test theory.

[361]

Dyadic Parent-Child Interaction Coding System: A Manual. Children ages 2–7 and their parents; 1981; DPICS; behavioral rating by clinician in 3 standard situations; norms consist of means and standard deviations; 1 form (1 page included in manual); manual (84 pages); accessories not necessary; 1984 price data: $14.50 per manual; (15) minutes coding time; Shelia M. Eyberg and Elizabeth A. Robinson; Shelia M. Eyberg.*

See T3:768 (1 reference).

TEST REFERENCES

1. Eyberg, S. M., & Robinson, E. A. Parent-child interaction training: Effects on family functioning. JOURNAL OF CLINICAL CHILD PSYCHOLOGY, 1982, 11, 130–137.

Review of Dyadic Parent-Child Interaction Coding System: A Manual, by ROBERT J. MCMAHON, *Associate Professor of Psychology, University of British Columbia, Vancouver, British Columbia, Canada:*

The manual for the Dyadic Parent-Child Interaction Coding System (DPICS) describes a system for coding parent-child interaction in a clinical setting. As noted in the manual, the coding system is designed to serve as a component in the assessment of childhood disorders and/or parenting skills, provide a baseline pretreatment assessment of parent-child interaction, serve as a measure of therapy progress, and provide a measure of treatment outcome. It is most appropriate for use with children referred for conduct-disorder (acting-out) types of behavior problems, although this is not explicitly stated in the manual. The parent-child dyad is observed for 5 minutes each in three standard situations that vary in the degree to which parental control is required: Child-Directed Interaction (a free play situation), Parent-Directed Interaction (the parent guides the child's activity), and Clean-Up (the parent attempts to get the child to pick up the toys in the clinic playroom). Most of the manual is a comprehensive description of 24 parent and child behaviors scored in the coding system.

The authors provide an adequate description of the playroom setup (although room size, which has been implicated as a possible setting factor for deviant child behavior in such analogue settings, is not specified) and the procedures to be followed for an observation. Information concerning observer training and the availability of additional training materials (e.g., written exercises, videotapes) which might decrease the likelihood of observer drift was not provided. The descriptions of each behavior are enhanced by multiple exemplars of the behaviors and extensive decision rules for discriminating the scoring of various behaviors. Like all complex observation systems, however, there are some difficult discriminations (e.g., acknowledgement versus unlabeled praise). The behaviors are scored continuously via frequency counts during each 5-minute observation. However, for some non-discrete behaviors (e.g., yelling), the observer is required to make use of a "5-second rule" in which the behavior is scored at the beginning of each 5-second period during which the behavior is occurring. No timing cues are provided to the observers, and they could be scoring several other behaviors simultaneously. This would seem to make accurate coding of these behaviors extremely difficult.

The psychometric data presented in the manual concerning norms, reliability, and validity are quite limited. For example, there are no data reported for the Clean-Up phase of the observation in any of the reports cited in the manual. The sample sizes in the studies are also quite small (e.g., 22 mother-child pairs in the standardization sample). Presumably because of this small sample size, the normative data presented in the manual are not grouped according to age and sex of the child. Clinical decisions concerning the normative basis of observed parent or child behaviors are precluded.

Interrater reliability has been assessed in several investigations, with correlation coefficients ranging from .65 to 1.00. Individual coefficients are not reported, so it is impossible to determine which behaviors are the most reliably scored. There are no test-retest reliability figures, although families were observed twice over a 7-day period during the primary standardization study (Robinson & Eyberg, 1981).

Validation studies have indicated that the DPICS is able to successfully discriminate families of conduct-problem children and those of normal children, neglectful and normal mothers on the basis of maternal verbal behavior, conduct-problem children and their siblings, and fathers and mothers, both in normal and conduct-problem families. It is also sensitive to changes induced by treatment. While such research is commendable and serves a useful clinical function, additional validational studies remain to be performed. Foremost among these is the need to demonstrate that parent-child interaction in a clinic playroom relates in some systematic and meaningful fashion to parent and child behaviors in more naturalistic settings such as the home. This is an empirical question, and it is the authors' responsibility to provide evidence that the DPICS does have this external validity.

With respect to content validity, the authors could have presented rationales for the utilization of the three standard situations (other than that they differ in degree of parental control) and for the selection of particular parent and child behaviors in the coding system. It is not clear from the manual just why these particular tasks and behaviors were chosen. Because this reviewer is familiar with the authors' work, he knows that they operate within a social learning framework. It is not likely that clinicians from other perspectives would find these particular categories as important or define them in the same way.

Given the limited psychometric data on the DPICS, how does it compare with other observational systems of a similar nature? The most widely recognized system for scoring parent-child interactions within a social learning framework is the coding system developed by Gerald Patterson, John Reid, and their associates at the Oregon Social Learning Center (Reid, 1978). This coding system has extensive reliability and validity data. However, it is a very complex system, and observations occur in the home. These factors make it less likely to be of use to the practicing clinician. The Response-Class Matrix (Mash, Terdal, & Anderson, 1973) is clinic-based like the DPICS and uses similar interaction tasks. However, it requires two observers and has been employed primarily in assessment, as opposed to treatment-oriented, studies. Finally, Forehand and McMahon (1981) utilize a coding system that focuses on a much smaller sample of parent and child behaviors. The coding system has been used primarily in naturalistic settings but has also been employed in clinic settings in a manner analogous to the DPICS. Although it has been validated extensively with respect to treatment outcome data and with different populations, its normative sample is quite limited.

In summary, the DPICS is an instrument that holds promise as an assessment device for practicing clinicians who work with young conduct-problem children and their families. It permits the clinician to view parent-child interaction in three different contexts in a brief time period and provides the observer with comprehensive definitions and examples of the various behaviors. However, much more extensive research pertaining to the reliability, validity, and clinical utility of this observation system is needed. On a general level, it must be empirically demonstrated that parent-child interaction in a clinic playroom is a valid measure of such interactions in the home setting. The DPICS is not alone with respect to these requirements since some or all of these criticisms may be applied to the other coding systems noted above. The DPICS is a coding system that is designed for a practicing clinician but which is quite comprehensive in terms of the parent and child behaviors that can be recorded. As such, it is likely to receive wide use.

REVIEWER'S REFERENCES

Mash, E. J., Terdal, L. G., & Anderson, K. The Response-Class Matrix: A procedure for recording parent-child interactions. JOURNAL OF CONSULTING AND CLINICAL PSYCHOLOGY, 1973, 40, 163–164.

Reid, J. B. (Ed.). A SOCIAL LEARNING APPROACH TO FAMILY INTERVENTION. VOL. II. OBSERVATION IN HOME SETTINGS. Eugene, OR: Castalia Publishing, 1978.

Forehand, R., & McMahon, R. J. HELPING THE NONCOMPLIANT CHILD: A CLINICIAN'S GUIDE TO PARENT TRAINING. New York: Guilford Press, 1981.

Robinson, E. A., & Eyberg, S. M. The Dyadic Parent-Child Interaction Coding System: Standardization and validation. JOURNAL OF CONSULTING AND CLINICAL PSYCHOLOGY, 1981, 49, 245–250.

Review of Dyadic Parent-Child Interaction Coding System: A Manual, by PHILLIP S. STRAIN, *Associate Professor of Psychiatry, School of Medicine, University of Pittsburgh, Pittsburgh, PA:*

The Dyadic Parent-Child Interaction Coding System is a direct observational assessment procedure designed to: (*a*) supplement a full psychological evaluation of children 2 to 7 years of age with suspected conduct problems; and, (*b*) serve as an initial and ongoing measure of parent-child interaction within a treatment context.

While a total of 24 standard parent and child behaviors are coded, 2 parent-child interaction patterns are central to the clinical utility of this instrument: (*a*) the parent's response following a child's deviant behavior, and (*b*) the child's response to a parent's command. These two interaction patterns are coded with one parent-child dyad at a time. Observations are conducted in a playroom equipped with a two-way mirror, microphone system, several chairs, and a variety of toys. Observations are conducted from an adjoining room. Total time devoted to a single observational period is 15 minutes, distributed across three, invariant order 5-minute intervals: (*a*) Child-Directed Interaction, in which the child may choose from a variety of available activities; (*b*) Parent-Directed Interaction, in which the parent selects activities and establishes rules for the activities; and (*c*) Clean-up, in which the parent instructs the child to put away all materials.

When viewed as a screening and treatment assessment procedure for problem-behavior children, the Dyadic Parent-Child Interaction Coding System has a number of strong features: (1) The instrument is based upon a direct as opposed to an indirect (e.g., someone's verbal report) assessment of difficult parent-child interactions; (2) The instrument has been found to discriminate between clinical and non-clinical groups; (3) The instrument has been found to be sensitive to intervention effects; and (4) The instrument seems to correspond closely with parent report levels of child problem behavior.

Notwithstanding these positive features, the instrument does have two potentially troublesome characteristics. First, the normative data on parent-child interaction is taken from a small sample ($N = 22$) of families within a limited geographic region. Presumably the normative sample was rather homogeneous in regard to race, socioeconomic status, and educational level. At this point in time it seems prudent to exercise caution when using the normative data for research and clinical identification purposes.

Second, the authors' treatment of test reliability is limited in scope and method. Reliability is considered exclusively in terms of agreement between observers. However, it would also be helpful to know what level of consistency the authors have found across observation sessions with various populations. If, for example, dyadic interaction tends to be quite stable across sessions, then a few samples of behavior can be used with considerable confidence. The method for agreement calculation among observers is also of some concern. Reliability is reported only using correlation techniques on frequency of behavior coded by observers. It is clear from the data that observers do agree quite favorably on number of behaviors coded. Yet, agreement of this kind does not preclude the possibility that observers disagree on the sequence of behavior coded.

In all, the Dyadic Parent-Child Interaction Coding System can be recommended as a valuable adjunct to the clinical assessment of behavior problem children. The instrument developers have compiled a comprehensive manual that should make training in coding procedures a relatively simple exercise.

[362]

Dyslexia Determination Test. Preschool–college; 1980–81; DDT; 6 subtests: dysnemkinesia (Writing of Numbers, Writing of Letters), dysphonesia (Decoding, Encoding), dyseidesia (Decoding, Encoding); no data on reliability and validity; no norms; suggested standards of mastery; individual; Form A, B, decoding words ('80, 23 pages); recording page (no date, 2 pages); examiner's instruction manual ('81, 52 pages); supplemental instructive tape cassette available; 1983 price data: $44.95 per complete kit including 30 recording pages of each form, 60 interpretation recording forms, decoding word book, examiner's instruction manual, and tape cassette; administration time not reported; John R. Griffin and Howard N. Walton; I-MED.*

Review of Dyslexia Determination Test by FRED M. GROSSMAN, Assistant Professor of Special Education and Communication Disorders, University of Nebraska-Lincoln, Lincoln, NE:

The Dyslexia Determination Test (DDT) is described by its authors as a specialized reading, writing, and spelling test that has been clinically developed during the last 10 years. The authors also maintain that the DDT provides educators, optometrists, psychologists, and physicians who are professionally involved in the diagnosis and treatment of specific learning disabilities with an assessment tool to identify individuals (i.e., preschool through college-age) who exhibit dyslexic patterns of responding in the areas of reading, writing, and spelling. In effect, dyslexia is perceived as relating to language disabilities and as such can be used to examine aspects of language difficulties pertaining to reading, writing, and spelling. As a result of evaluation using the DDT, the authors suggest that children with learning disabilities, school personnel, and parents may gain a greater understanding of dyslexic patterns, appropriate therapy and remediational techniques, and prognosis for improvement.

The test is administered for the purpose of identifying three basic types of dyslexia: dysnemkinesia, dysphonesia, and dyseidesia. The authors also discuss four other kinds of dyslexia that are, in effect, combinations of the three basic types. The seven types of dyslexia and other related terms are briefly defined at the beginning of the examiner's instruction manual. Dysnemkinesia is referred to as a "deficit in the ability to develop motor gestalts (engrams) for written symbols," dysphonesia is defined as a "deficit in symbol sound (grapheme-phoneme) integration, and the inability to develop phonetic word analysis synthesis skills," and dyseidesia is a "deficit in the ability to perceive whole words (total configuration) as visual gestalts and match with auditory gestalts." Two subtests are administered to examinees in order to evaluate each of the three basic types of dyslexia, for a total of six subtests in all.

Dysnemkinesia is assessed by requiring the examinee to write the numbers 1–10 and to print the entire alphabet in upper case and lower case letters. An Interpretation Recording Form is used by the examiner to record behavioral observations (e.g., hand preference for writing, pencil grip, omissions of numbers or letters, etc.), the reverse side of which is provided to the examinee to perform the writing tasks. Instructions are in cursive writing in order to prevent copying of some of the letters. The authors chose to ask examinees to print the letters of the alphabet since such a method would increase the likelihood of reversal problems being revealed than if examinees were to write cursive letters. A total score is obtained by counting the number of 1–10 reversals and adding to that the number of alphabet upper case or lower case reversals, whichever is greater. Thus, a total of 10 numbers and 26 letters is used to determine the total number of reversals. Guidelines are provided in the instruction manual to aid the examiner in the determination of reversal problems. Essentially, as a result of their clinical experience, the authors have formulated reversal expectancies based upon grade placement criteria such that a child may be identified as having no reversal difficulties or as experiencing mild, moderate, or marked degrees of dysnemkinesia.

A booklet of word lists is used to evaluate decoding deficits as found in dyseidesia and dysphonesia. Lists range from the preprimer to college level, each including 10 words. Two test forms are provided, with Form A recommended for initial assessment and Form B for retesting. Initially, the decoding test focuses on assessing the examinee's eidetic ability (i.e., sight reading, with no more than 2 seconds allowed for each word). The second part of the decoding portion of the test requires the examinee to attempt to read (allowing 10 seconds per word) those words that he/she was unable to read within the initial 2-second time limit. Ostensibly, such a procedure permits the examinee to use a phonetic, syllabication, or structural analysis approach to aid in the oral reading of words and, thereby, assesses phonetic ability. Directions relating to starting and stopping points (i.e., basal and ceiling levels), general testing procedures, scoring, and recording responses for the eidetic and phonetic sections of the test are clearly delineated in the instruction manual. However, the authors' suggestions for determining the decoding mode of the examinee (i.e., eidetic vs. phonetic) are inadequate.

In fact, the authors state that a qualitative value judgment must be made in order to decide the examinee's decoding mode.

Administration of the DDT concludes with the assessment of encoding (e.g., analysis of eidetic vs. phonetic spelling problems) as it relates to dyseidetic and dysphonetic patterns of reading. According to the authors, analysis of encoding testing should, in most cases, parallel decoding results. That is, an individual experiencing dysphonesia in reading (phonetic reading worse than eidetic reading) will most likely have more difficulty spelling phonetically than eidetically. As with decoding assessment, instructions for administration, recording, and scoring of responses are clearly presented and pose no ambiguity for the examiner. Tables are provided in the instruction manual for determining encoding difficulties as they exist within dyseidetic or dysphonetic dyslexic patterns. Case examples are also presented in order to aid examiners in their decision-making.

In addition to the examiner's instruction manual, word list booklet, interpretation recording forms, and recording forms, an audiotape is available from the authors to supplement the instruction manual. Users are encouraged to purchase the tape cassette as it includes additional information with regard to symptoms of learning disabilities, physiological bases of the proposed seven dyslexic patterns, and interpretation of the test. To the authors' credit, the audiotape contains information which cautions users against administering the DDT in isolation and not as part of a comprehensive test battery. However, a statement of such importance should have been included in the instructional manual in order to prevent possible misuse of the test.

Despite the DDT's apparent face validity, the authors have provided no information regarding standardization and normative data. One would think that after 10 years of investigation and field testing to develop the DDT that the authors would report reliability and validity data; however, such information is not presented in the instruction manual. Despite the notion that "the authors are convinced that the DDT does what it is supposed to do," test users who are more psychometrically inclined will most likely feel uneasy about the absence of statistical data. Similarly, much of the interpretation of results has no statistical base and requires the examiner's qualitative judgment. The authors' brief descriptions regarding treatment/therapy approaches as they relate to specific dyslexic conditions were also formulated as a result of the authors' clinical experiences and, again, lack psychometric validation.

In summary, the Dyslexia Determination Test is an attempt to assess possible dyslexic patterns as they relate to the areas of reading, writing, and spelling. Despite its rather clear presentation of general procedures for administration, recording of responses, and scoring guidelines, the DDT is lacking in terms of standardization sample, reliability data, and validity data. In effect, users are being advised by this reviewer not to use the DDT as an instrument to diagnose dyslexia, as the psychometric properties of the test are essentially unknown. Until further research is conducted using the DDT, use should be restricted to the screening of reading, writing, and spelling difficulties and their relationship to possible dyslexic patterns. Finally, as the authors suggest, the DDT should only be administered as part of a total assessment battery which includes measures of general ability, achievement levels, visual-motor integration, and so on.

[363]

E.I.T.S. Clerical Tests. Applicants for clerical positions; 1983; 3 tests available as separates; no data on reliability and validity; norms consist of means and standard deviations for ages 17–28; 1983 price data: £2.30 per 25 tests; manual free on request with order; 85p per specimen set; Educational & Industrial Test Services Ltd. [England].*

a) CLERICAL TEST 1 (SPEED AND ACCURACY). 3 scores: number checking, name checking, total; 1 form (4 pages); manual (8 pages); 4(9) minutes.

b) CLERICAL TEST 2 (ARITHMETIC). 3 scores: computational skills, arithmetic problem skills, total; 1 form (4 pages); manual (7 pages); 10(15) minutes.

c) CLERICAL TEST 3 (ENGLISH). 4 scores: spelling, grammar, language, letter writing; 1 form (4 pages); manual (11 pages); 11.5(17) minutes.

[364]

E.S. Survey. Job applicants and employees; 1970; "emotional stability and control"; no data on reliability; no norms; 1 form (4 pages); information brief (1 page); 1982 price data: $1.50 per test; $12 per year per scoring template; (5–10) minutes; Robert W. Cormack and Alan L. Strand; Personnel Security Corporation.*

Review of E.S. Survey by JEANETTE N. CLEVELAND, Assistant Professor of Psychology, Colorado State University, Fort Collins, CO:

The stated purpose of the test is to screen applicants and employees for emotional stability and control. The one-page manual states that unstable employees have higher turnover and will be higher security risks than stable employees. This suggests that the survey will be used in selection and placement in such jobs as police and security positions.

The survey is a self-report measure consisting of 100 items. The individual responds to each question with a "yes," "no," or "?". The survey is scored by placing a template on the responses and counting the number of empty boxes. In addition, a "critical factor" score template is provided to identify attempts to bias answers or to "fake good."

In assessing the individual's emotional status, three areas are evaluated. First, the general stability level of the individual is evaluated. The test manual provides guidelines for interpreting stability levels as above average, average, or below average. Second, control questions, which purportedly assess faking, are evaluated. If more than two of the nine control items are not answered appropriately (yes), the individual may be trying to fake the survey. In addition to the overall stability level score and responses to the control questions, an individual's emotional status is evaluated through 21 "key" questions. Regardless of the stability level score (the total test score), responses to each of these individual items are examined. The manual implies that if the individual responds inappropriately to any specific item, the individual's emotional stability is seriously questioned. This method of item interpretation poses serious problems, because responses to individual items may be very unreliable and spurious. Guidelines for the appropriate interpretation and use of the key items are not provided. In addition, no suggestions are made for interpreting the key item responses in conjunction with the total stability score and the control questions.

There is no general description or definition of the domain that the survey purports to assess. Therefore, a user would not have a clear idea of what stability meant to the test developer, nor any means for assessing the extent to which the 100 items adequately tap this construct. No information is given on item generation and development.

No reliability indices are reported for the E.S. Survey. The test scores were correlated with an overall evaluation of stability by professional psychologists and showed a validity coefficient of .87 (N =4,000). Although it is implied that psychologists rated the overall stability of individuals, there is no indication that psychologists rated individuals using the same or similar stability criterion measures. The survey also implies that unstable employees have higher turnover rates and are greater security risks than stable individuals. There is, however, no validity data relating survey scores and turnover measures or security violations.

The 100-item survey concerns sensitive material (assessing the psychological well-being of the individual). In addition, the instructions warn that faking can be scientifically detected. The survey therefore constitutes a potentially serious invasion of privacy. In addition, the instructions, which emphasize the importance of being truthful, along with the sensitive nature of the items, may be a source of anxiety.

The manual claims that the test does not discriminate according to sex, race, age, or ethnic background. However, no data are provided to substantiate this claim of fairness.

In summary, the E.S. Survey claims to assess the emotional stability of individuals. However, no definition or description of emotional stability is provided for users. In addition, test score reliabilities are not reported. The manual suggests that the survey scores relate to turnover and security risks on the job. However, no validity data are provided which demonstrate a relationship between survey scores and these measures. In addition, the sensitive nature of the survey questions along with the warning in the instructions against faking constitutes a possible invasion of privacy. The above limitations pose a serious question concerning the adequacy of the survey especially given its intended use in selection and placement. Therefore, the test cannot be recommended for use in the workplace until additional data are provided on the content of the domain to be tapped, the consistency of the items to assess emotional stability, and the relationship between the survey scores and the designated job criterion measures.

Review of E.S. Survey by JAMES W. PINKNEY, Associate Professor of Counseling, East Carolina University, Greenville, NC:

The Emotional Status Survey (ESS) was designed to screen job applicants and employees for emotional stability and control. The ESS consists of 100 items with a "Yes," (?), or "No" response format. Scoring is done by template (available only on a yearly rental basis) and lower scores indicate more stable emotions. No other information on scoring was provided, nor is any information provided on scale construction or rationale.

The one-page information brief has little value and merely confirms the initial impression of the ESS as an unsubstantiated measure of a poorly defined construct. Administration and scoring are covered in three sentences. There are no norms provided of any kind. "Consistent validity" is claimed by the authors but not supported. The one correlation reported is between total ESS score and "overall evaluations by professional Psychologists." No definition of overall evaluation and no information on the sample makes it impossible to know what this correlation (.87) means for the test user. Similarly, a significant difference in ESS scores for stable and unstable groups is reported but not clarified. The use of "total E.S. scores" is confusing since it implies the existence of subscales. The only reference to any subscales is in a prominent notice on the actual survey that warns of a falsification grading scale to "identify persons attempting to bias test results." This scale is not mentioned in any of the information provided. Reliability data is not available and is not referred to other than the authors' statement that the ESS is highly job related for police and security positions.

The items in the ESS are phrased as short questions and focus on health, interpersonal interaction, and anxiety. The content is strongly reminiscent of the Minnesota Multiphasic Personality Inventory (MMPI), and inspection of the MMPI found many parallel items. There are two major problems with the actual items of the ESS: social desirability and absolute phrasing. Employment related assessment always raises the question of honesty, and the authors are clearly concerned with the issue. Yet many of the items seem grossly transparent as to which response is most desirable. One questions whether warnings and reminders that psychological techniques are being used to detect dishonesty would have an effect for items clearly answerable in the socially desired direction.

This issue seems even more relevant for the items phrased in absolute terms (Have you ever..., Do you always..., Do you ever...). One is hard pressed to imagine who would seriously consider the undesirable option. These issues with item construction raise doubt about the sensitivity of the ESS as a screening instrument. In fact, the ESS may actually measure acquiescence to instructions or honesty rather than emotional status.

Actually completing the ESS was irritating. It requires two signatures (both indicating dishonesty is cause for disqualification), has two separate warnings that dishonesty can be graded, and specifies that one's own handwriting be used. The specification about handwriting is confusing since the instructions state that the respondent print except for the signatures, the position applied for, and the organization offering the position.

In summary, what little information is offered about the ESS is not specific enough to help the test user. The instructions leave one wondering what is being assessed, the authors give no limitations about appropriate uses of the ESS, and there is no manual. The absence of norm groups, reliability data, and validity information are adequate reasons for not recommending the ESS at this time.

[365]

Early Childhood Environment Rating Scale. Early childhood settings; 1980; provides rating scales for the assessment of various environmental characteristics of early childhood facilities; 7 areas: personal care routines of children, furnishings and display for children, language-reasoning experiences, fine and gross motor activities, creative activities, social development, adult needs; no norms; 1 form (44 pages, includes administration instructions); no manual; separate answer sheets must be used; 1985 price data: $7.95 per rating scale; $5.95 per 30 scoring sheets and profile; (120) minutes; Thelma Harms and Richard M. Clifford; Teachers College Press.*

Review of Early Childhood Environment Rating Scale by RICHARD ELARDO, Associate Professor of Education, The University of Iowa, Iowa City, IA:

An instrument with which to measure the environment in a day care center or preschool has been needed for a long time. Reviews of research on day care, for example, often conclude that day care centers are not harmful to children provided they are of the same "high quality" as those university-based centers typically examined in studies of this kind. With at least one notable exception (Honig & Lally, 1975) there are no comparable instruments in the field of early childhood education. Harms and Clifford have been bold enough to put their values on the line and have produced, after 3 years of field testing and revision, a scale which represents their view of "the best" early childhood environment. As such, it meets their criteria for face validity, and probably also content validity. The authors intended to exclude interpersonal relationships from the instrument and to develop a separate test for this, but they found it necessary to include such items as part of the present scale.

I was quite satisfied by the instrument's face validity. For example, professionals in the field generally agree that a room in a day care center should have "softness." This concern is reflected by one item in the present instrument where "softness" is defined as "Soft, comfortable places to eat or rest, rugs, and soft toys." Face validity can be similarly exemplified by other items.

A 7-point item format is used throughout the scale, and several alternate items are provided for rating infant and toddler rooms. The scoring criteria for each item on the scale are well-defined and should allow raters to achieve acceptable levels of reliability. The test booklet also contains an address from which trainees may order two slide tapes to assist them in learning to administer the scale.

Three reliability measures were reported: (*a*) interrater reliability by item for two independent raters in 25 rooms was .94; (*b*) interrater reliability by classroom ranged from .79 to .90; and (*c*) internal consistency for the total scale (Cronbach's Alpha) was .83. Subscale alphas ranged from –.22 to .87, and the authors warn that problems exist with the internal consistency of the subscales, but not with the scale as a whole. Thus, subscale scores should not be used for research or evaluation purposes. Also, the authors caution that reliability has not been established for infant and toddler rooms.

Validity was reported in two areas. First, the developers asked seven experts in early childhood education to rate each item on the scale in terms of its importance to early childhood programs. A total of 78% of the items were rated as highly important and only 1% were considered of low importance. These figures represent an acceptable degree of face validity. Second, the developers asked an undisclosed number of trainers who had been working in 18 early childhood rooms to rate the quality of those rooms according to their own criteria. These rooms were then rated by expert observers using the Early Childhood Environment Rating Scale, and a rank order correlation of .74 was obtained. This provides an indication of the concurrent validity of the scale. Attempts to establish the criterion-related or "predictive" validity of the scale await future studies. Also, while the content validity of the scale is satisfactory, certain additional items could be added to assess other aspects of what is often said to be a "quality" program (e.g., types of discipline used, the consistency among caregivers, and staff morale).

The fact that no norms for the scale are included is puzzling. Perhaps the developers felt that the procedures necessary to establish norms would be too sensitive and controversial: rating one room against another, or the rooms in one center against those in another center.

In summary, I see this scale as a large step forward in the field of early childhood education, and I believe this is the best instrument of its kind. It helps to objectify what experts define as quality in early childhood environments.

REVIEWER'S REFERENCES

Honig, A. S., & Lally, J. R. How good is your infant program? Use an observational method to find out. CHILD CARE QUARTERLY, 1975, 4, 194–207.

Review of Early Childhood Environment Rating Scale by CATHY FULTZ TELZROW, Coordinator, Assessment Project, Cuyahoga Special Education Center, Maple Heights, OH:

The Early Childhood Environment Rating Scale (ECERS) is purported to provide early childhood professionals with a standardized instrument with which to evaluate preschool environments such as nursery schools, day care centers, or Headstart centers. The term, "environments," as defined by the test authors, includes a variety of physical and experiential factors which may affect a child in a preschool setting. The instrument is designed to be completed by a preschool administrator or teacher, or by an independent observer. The authors indicate that the ECERS assesses strengths and weaknesses in the preschool environment which can provide a basis for planned change.

The 37 items on the ECERS are organized into 7 categories: personal care routines, furnishing and display, language-reasoning experiences, fine and gross motor experiences, creative activities, social development, and adult needs. Each of these 7 scales contains from 4 to 7 items. There is no mention in the manual of how these scales were derived nor how the items were associated with them. A separate source (Harms & Clifford, 1983) reported that items were derived from research, evaluations of quality preschool environments, and recommendations from early childhood professionals.

Each item on the ECERS is rated on a 7-point scale. To assist in determining ratings, descriptors are provided for ranks 1 (inadequate), 3 (minimal), 5 (good), and 7 (excellent) for each of the 37 items. Although the manual specifies the criteria for ratings of 2, 4, or 6, a notation repeating these guidelines directly on the rating scale would be useful. The method used for determining the rating descriptors is unspecified. It is apparent that the selection of the 37 items as well as the specific ratings for each item reflect one philosophy of early childhood education. While this philosophy represents a viewpoint that is highly respected and widely held by early childhood professionals, programs operating under different philosophies may be assigned lower scores on ECERS (Bailey, Clifford, & Harms, 1982).

The actual ratings of the 37 items are recorded on three score sheets. These score sheets list the number and abbreviated name of each item, together with the 1–7 rating scale. Ample space is provided beneath each item for additional comments. The items are arranged in a vertical, rather than horizontal, left to right direction. This makes following the items on the score sheet somewhat difficult. An especially useful feature is the "notes for clarification" section, which provides elaboration on selected items, thus facilitating the rating.

Total ratings within each of the seven scales are computed and may be charted on a profile. Although the authors report that a total score can be calculated, it is not apparent from the manual that a total score to reflect an overall environment rating can be calculated. The test user is directed to use the classroom profile to compare different aspects of the preschool environment, to identify areas for modification, and to measure improvement over time. Nevertheless, the manual advises against using scores on individual subscales for research and evaluation because of poor internal consistency.

The authors report three validity studies. The first, which asked seven nationally prominent child care experts to evaluate the importance of the items selected, resulted in a 78% confirmation of the importance of the chosen items. Comparison of the ECERS with ratings of expert observers resulted in rank order correlations of .74, with these being reduced to .70 for less experienced observers.

Reliability coefficients were calculated for classrooms with children above age 22 months only. Interrater reliability by classroom revealed rank order correlations ranging from .79 to .90. Calculation of interrater reliability by item resulted in rank order correlations ranging from .93 to .94. Internal consistency, using Cronbach's Alpha, revealed low reliability coefficients for the subscales, although a coefficient of .83 was obtained for the total scale.

To summarize, the ECERS is one of the few rating scales of preschool environments available which provides systematic and quantitative results. It is completed easily by early childhood teachers and supervisors, and represents a useful tool for professionals, especially for informal or self-evaluation of preschool settings. Because of poor reliability for subtests, and the lack of interpretive guidelines for a total score, it is recommended that the ECERS should be used cautiously for formal program evaluation.

REVIEWER'S REFERENCES

Bailey, D. B., Clifford, R. M., & Harms, T. Comparison of preschool environments for handicapped and nonhandicapped children. TOPICS IN EARLY CHILDHOOD SPECIAL EDUCATION, 1982, 2(1), 9–20.

Harms, T., & Clifford, R. M. Assessing preschool environments with the Early Childhood Environment Rating Scale. In B. Spodek (Ed.), STUDIES IN EDUCATIONAL EVALUATION, 1983, 8.

[366]

Early Identification Screening Program. Grades K, 1; 1982; EISP; developed to screen for children who may experience learning problems; 3 scores: hear-write, see-write, see-say; no norms; individual; 1 form; 2 levels: kindergarten, first-grade, (12 pages); administration and scoring manual (31 pages); see-say letter card (1 page); see-say color card (1 page); Spanish-directions supplement to manual (12 pages); 1984 price data: $10.98 per 15 screening booklets (specify level); $7.95 per manual; $1 per Spanish-directions supplement to manual; $4.95 per specimen set; (20) minutes over a period of 3 days; Baltimore City Public Schools; Modern Curriculum Press, Inc.*

Review of Early Identification Screening Program by JAYNE H. EPSTEIN, Psychologist, Kyrene School District, Tempe, AZ:

The Early Identification Screening Program (EISP) is an individual screening device that is intended to be administered at the beginning of the school year to identify kindergarten and first-grade children who are at risk in terms of vulnerability to learning problems. There are three activities, Hear-Write, See-Write, and See-Say, that tap various auditory, short-term memory, visual, visual-motor, and verbal skills at each of the two grade levels. Screening materials consist of an administration and scoring manual, which is also available in a Spanish version, individual record booklets for each child's responses, two 8 x 10 glossy stimulus cards for the See-Say activity (one for kindergarten and one for first grade), a Class Record Sheet for recording students' scores, and a Ranking Work Sheet for developing class or grade level profiles.

The stimuli for the kindergarten level of each activity are as follows: Hear-Write—shape names (circle, line, square); See-Write—10 simple one- or two-line figures, randomly arranged in four rows; and See-Say—130 randomly arranged, brightly colored, half-inch boxes, utilizing six colors. The stimuli for the first-grade level of each activity are as follows: Hear-Write—numbers; See-Write—lower case letters, randomly arranged in four rows; and See-Say—150 randomly arranged lower case letters.

The presentation format and response requirement for both levels are identical: Hear-Write—the teacher reads the stimuli and the child writes them as quickly as possible on a page of the record booklet that consists of a grid of three-quarter inch squares; See-Write—the child must reproduce the stimuli on a page in the record booklet consisting of four rows of three-quarter inch empty boxes directly under the appropriate corresponding model; and See-Say—the child is presented with an 8 x 10 inch glossy stimulus card and must name the stimuli in order of arrangement as quickly as possible.

Each activity is administered three times, once during each of three separate screening sessions, on 3 consecutive days. Scoring is simply the number of correct responses produced in 1 minute, and an average is computed across the three sessions for each activity. Rationale supporting the number of sessions (three) is not presented in the manual, and averaging over two sessions is allowed if a child misses the third. The manual does caution, however, that the margin of error would be too great if scores from only one session were used. While this contention appears to be reasonable, no supporting rationale or data are presented.

This instrument may be administered by any one or two staff members, but the authors recommend using a team of four to seven individuals for greater efficiency and less classroom disruption. No specific training is required, but the authors suggest a practice session to insure accurate counting and timing of responses. The entire process takes about 20 minutes per child (10 minutes for the first session, which includes one practice activity before each actual screening activity, and 5 minutes for each of the other two sessions). The manual provides specific instructions and suggestions, including diagrams, regarding coordination of screening activities and integration of the process into the regular classroom as a reasonable attempt to minimize disruption in the normal routine. All materials are simple to use and in a convenient format, but noticeably lacking in the record form is a means for recording responses on the See-Say activity. The manual instructs users to keep a mental count, make slash marks, or use a counter to record number correct while keeping track of the time. This procedure is a little cumbersome but becomes more automatic with practice. Some diagnostic information may be lost, however, if a child consistently has difficulty with specific colors or numbers. Additionally, the issue of color-blindness and the possible effects it may have on the kindergarten level of the See-Say activity is not addressed.

The manual provides clear instructions for administration, including exact wording in dark type. No suggestions are offered, however, for dealing with atypical responses, refusals, or inappropriate/irrelevant behavior. Since individuals administering this instrument may not have had extensive testing experience, the absence of specific guidelines may pose serious limitations on the interpretation of the results. Some general scoring guidelines are offered, but only a minimal number of possible correct and incorrect responses are provided as examples. The manual encourages individuals administering the test to determine their own scoring standards as a group, which may be adequate for comparisons of student performance within a specific setting and for a specific purpose as recommended by the developers. The manual also contains suggestions for some specific follow-up practice activities in each of the three general areas.

To summarize the results of the screening program, each child's average scores are recorded on the Class Record Sheet and then ranked with respect to the performance of the other children either within a classroom or grade level. Comparisons can thus be made on a classroom or grade level basis, and the Class Record Sheet can be used in either capacity. The ranks are then totalled across the three activities, and an overall rank of the ranks and a Priority Need List of students is obtained. (A Ranking Work Sheet with detailed instructions on its use is provided for this purpose.)

The authors recommend a cutoff at the lowest 25th percentile for considering a child at risk. They suggest, however, that in order for the instrument to be most relevant to those using it, a different cutoff, or several cutoffs, might be established for specific purposes. In order to assist in interpreting screening results, the manual identifies some specific skills associated with each of the three modalities assessed. Information is also provided regarding assessment focus, strengths, and recommended assessment personnel for further evaluation of children obtaining several possible combinations of scores. The effect of vision or hearing deficits on a child's performance is not addressed.

Development of this program was based on empirical observation of student performance on selected learning tasks. The final version of the activities was developed out of an initial item pool of nine learning tasks (listed in the manual), each of which, according to the authors, reflects an important curricular goal or performance skill that children at this level are expected to attain. While, intuitively, these items would appear to be an important part of any early learning curriculum, the manner of item selection as well as the relationship of items to higher order mental processes or to actual academic skill development is not specifically delineated. A frequency measure was chosen for structuring responses because such measures generally provide a wide range of scores when using only a few test items. The rationale for choosing 1 minute as the response time is not indicated.

The manual contains information on reliability and validity measures based on a sample of 124 kindergarten and first-grade children. This group was randomly selected from an initial subject pool of 558 children from four schools in one large urban school district. The sample is not representative of kindergarten and first-grade children in general; black children are overrepresented (96%) and girls and first graders are slightly favored (53% and 56%, respectively). For this group the instrument was highly reliable across sessions (correlations were significant beyond the .01 level). The nature of the sample poses serious questions regarding the discriminative properties of the tasks and, thus, the usefulness of this instrument to identify characteristically different at-risk children in other settings.

Concurrent validity of the EISP was established through correlations with the Language and Mathematics subtests of the Test of Basic Experience (TOBE), Level I (.37 and .33, respectively), and comparisons with teacher identification of at-risk and low-risk children (agreement=89%). There was a slightly greater number of false positives than false negatives, which is clinically preferable for this type of instrument. Teacher judgment was also used as a measure of predictive validity by comparing end-of-year ratings of children with their earlier performance on the EISP (agreement=93%).

The pattern of low correlation with the TOBE and high agreement with teacher judgment leads this reviewer to question whether the EISP actually measures other factors such as personological and/or learning style characteristics rather than academic aptitude. The absence of longitudinal studies, objective measures of academic performance, and follow-up evaluations of children identified by this instrument as at-risk also leaves a question concerning its value even in the setting in which it was developed.

In summary, the EISP, as the authors intended, allows for quick, easy screening of a large group of children by any staff member or paraprofessional. Cautions by the authors regarding the use of screening results in isolation are well founded, as is their focus on its use for making only in-house comparisons among children. The benefit of using this type of instrument is the availability of a direct comparison and ranking of all children on identical tasks in a neat, concise format. In this reviewer's opinion, the technical adequacy of this instrument has not been demonstrated. There are serious shortcomings in its development, notably in item and response mode selection and in the sample used for field testing and validation. Additionally, the lack of any subsequent validation studies or follow-up of the children in the original study severely limits the usefulness of this instrument.

Review of Early Identification Screening Program by PATRICK J. JESKE, School Psychologist, Apache Junction School District, Apache Junction, AZ:

The Early Identification Screening Program (EISP) was developed by Baltimore City Public Schools and was validated on 124 kindergarten and first-grade students. The racial composition of the standardization sample is not representative of the average school population, being 96% black and 4% white.

The EISP is composed of three separate tests, all of which are administered each day for 3 days. Final scores are derived by averaging the scores that each child obtains over the 3 days of testing. Children who do not take all three tests at least twice cannot receive a meaningful score because the "margin of error is too great." Unfortunately, the authors do not report the standard error of measurement, nor do they mention any measures of internal consistency. They do, however, report high coefficients of stability between the scores obtained on each testing day.

Predictive validity was not determined for the sample that was targeted for study and is only reported for a control group whose composition is not adequately described. Concurrent validity was determined by correlating EISP scores with language and math subtest scores of the Tests of Basic Experience (TOBE) and by comparing EISP scores to teacher judgments. Correlations with the TOBE, although low ($r = .37$ and $.33$), were statistically significant. Teacher judgments found 11% of the children to be misclassified.

The test is difficult to administer since the examiner is required to time the child with a stopwatch while either counting the number of accurate responses the child makes, or while naming figures for the child to draw. Use of a 60-second timer instead of a stopwatch would have made administration much easier. Although the authors recommend that children be given pencils without erasers, they don't require it, which could lead to significant scoring differences. Some of the directions do not seem appropriate. For example, as part of one timed test, children are directed to draw squares, which could cause more prepared students to be penalized for taking the time to correctly draw a figure with four equal sides, while less well prepared students receive credit for hurriedly drawing a four-sided figure with unequal sides. It would probably be better to ask the children to draw boxes instead of squares.

Scoring criteria are not well defined. Even though test administrators are instructed to discuss the scoring criteria with one another, the danger of one person scoring a test differently from another still exists.

After each child's scores have been averaged, all of the scores are ranked. The authors recommend that the lower 25% of the children be considered for some form of educational intervention. However, since means and standard deviations may vary widely from one school to another, they suggest that each school determine its own cutoff.

Although it is suggested by the authors that students scoring at the upper levels be considered for more advanced work or enrichment, doing so would seem to be a misuse of this instrument since validity evidence for such purposes has not been established. The authors caution that results from this instrument should only be used for screening and not for placement purposes. Yet, they seem to contradict that statement when they suggest that student scores on the three modalities be used to aid in planning initial instructional groupings and in developing specific objectives for individual students.

In summary, the EISP can be used to screen children who are in need of further evaluation. However, the value of using this instrument in any school that is not composed primarily of urban black children is unknown since that is the group upon whom this test was standardized. The instrument is difficult to administer properly. The fact that it is not normed means that each school would have to decide arbitrarily its own cutoff score. Its major advantage is that it doesn't take very long to administer (5 to 10 minutes per session). However, even that advantage is somewhat negated by the fact that three sessions of the test have to be administered to each individual three different times over a 3-day period. This test is not recommended for use in most schools. A more useful screening procedure would include one or two brief norm-referenced instruments, behavioral observations, and a brief parental questionnaire.

[367]

Early Learning: Assessment and Development. Ages 5–3 and 5–6 through the first year of school and older children with specific learning difficulties; 1981; 5 areas: movement skills—fine and gross motor, perceptual skills, communication—language and listening skills, learning and memory, emotional and social development; no data on reliability; no norms; individual; 1 form; spirit duplicator masters (9 pages); teacher's handbook (47 pages); class record sheet (5 pages); testing materials must be assembled locally; 1983 price data: £9.95 per complete kit; administration time not reported; Audrey Curtis and Mary Wignall; Macmillan Education [England].*

Review of Early Learning: Assessment and Development by DENNIS DELORIA, Senior Scientist, Mobius Corporation, Alexandria, VA:

Early Learning: Assessment and Development (ELAD) is more like a set of curricular activities than like a test, even though it presents "items" to be used for assessment. Its spirit is that of an informal aid to teachers of children during the school year following an entry age of about 5 years 3 months to 5 years 6 months. The ELAD Manual does not suggest calculating numerical scores and does not present any norms or research involving the test. The only decisions about children suggested by the manual are choosing specific classroom activities that might assist the development of children unable to successfully perform certain of the items.

In keeping with the ELAD Manual's emphasis on the whole child, items and curricular activities are presented in seven skill areas: gross motor, fine motor, visual perception, auditory perception, communication skills, learning and memory, and emotional and social. All told, the manual suggests about 100 items in these skill areas. Items that the authors believe a child aged 5–3 to 5–6 should be able to perform successfully are asterisked. Each set of items has a corresponding set of detailed activities for teachers to use in fostering development in the skill area.

The ELAD consists of a single looseleaf manual, containing cards needed for some of the items, spirit duplicating masters for printing up to 250 of the consumable pages drawn on by the children, and classroom summary sheets to be photocopied for use in recordkeeping. Objects needed for the items are expected to be provided by the teacher. A simple but useful year-long coding system is suggested for tracking children's progress. The manual does not insist on any sort of standardized administration, but rather leaves most of the items open for administration as the teacher finds useful and convenient. Some items are suggested as appropriate for the entire class as a whole, others for use on an individual basis.

In summary, the ELAD has modest aspirations and succeeds at them reasonably well. Its purpose is more oriented toward teacher training than toward child assessment. Teachers searching for classroom activity ideas are likely to find some that are helpful. No major decisions about children are suggested beyond choosing appropriate classroom activities, so the test is not likely to lead to inappropriate consequences for children. Given the low cost and informal nature of the ELAD, it can be considered a useful device for sharpening teacher observational skills and fostering improved teaching activities.

Review of Early Learning: Assessment and Development by WILLIAM B. MICHAEL, Professor of Education and Psychology, University of Southern California, Los Angeles, CA:

Designed to provide an assessment of strengths and weaknesses of children falling primarily between the ages of 5 years 3 months and 5 years 6 months as well as of older children with specific learning disabilities, the set of materials entitled Early Learning: Assessment and Development, is basically a handbook for teachers. It includes five areas: movement skills (fine and gross motor), perceptual skills, communication (language and listening skills), learning and memory, and emotional and social development. For each of these areas, sets and subsets of listed behaviors of children are presented. The teacher checks off whether the behaviors have been exhibited by the child rated. In addition, numerous activities are suggested in which the child may participate to facilitate his or her development of skills associated with each of the five areas. These suggested activities constitute what may be termed a learning package for primary school children, the varied uses of which are dependent upon which behaviors have been checked in the assessment portions of the handbook. It is recommended by the authors that children be observed periodically and that further assessment with the checklists be carried out to afford evidence of personal growth or change.

Within the handbook, instructions are given on how to keep records. Teaching materials on master sheets may be duplicated for use with children for learning purposes. All materials in the handbook are attractively presented.

In the reviewer's judgment, there is little doubt that this handbook can be very helpful to teachers as well as facilitative to the learning process. The major concern or reservation is that the lists of behaviors that teachers check as being present or absent hardly can be considered as scales or tests as typically employed in a controlled and/or standardized operation of psychological measurement, because there is no systematic assignment of points to item statements necessary to generate scores on a continuum. In light of the absence of any quantification of behaviors recorded in the observation process, one questions whether, technically speaking, tests or scales exist that can be reviewed or critiqued in a manner relevant to the traditional objectives of the *Ninth Mental Measurements Yearbook*.

Missing from the handbook is any information concerning such important psychometric characteristics as norms, reliability, and validity. No attempt has been made in a systematic way to prepare a rationale that would permit the generation of a domain of behaviors from which items could be selected in a planned manner to furnish at least a semblance of content validity. In fact, concerns of reliability and validity have not been addressed within the handbook.

In view of the weaknesses that have been cited, this reviewer has serious reservations about whether these rudimentary assessment scales in the form of checklists of children's behaviors have any psychometric utility. Although these checklists may serve a useful informal evaluation function in the classroom, a traditional standardized assessment procedure simply does not exist. Until appropriate research and development activities involving careful consideration of norming, reliability, and validity concerns have been achieved and the results obtained from these efforts have been reported to the potential consumer, this reviewer cannot recommend the handbook for other than informal use in the classroom setting.

[368]

Early Mathematical Language. Children in their first year at school and older children with difficulties in mathematics; 1982; EML; catalog uses the title Assessment of Early Mathematical Language; no data on reliability and validity; no norms; 6 booklets (Book 1 used at the beginning of the child's first year and Books 2–6 used at intervals throughout the child's first year); teacher's handbook (63 pages); record sheet (2 pages); 1982 price data: £3.50 per 6 booklets; £1.25 per 25 record sheets; £1.50 per teacher's handbook; administration time not reported; Margaret Williams and Heather Somerwill; Macmillan Education [England].*

a) BOOK 1—POSITION IN SPACE. 1982; 1 form (16 pages).
b) BOOK 2—NUMBER. 1982; 1 form (16 pages).
c) BOOK 3—LENGTH. 1982; 1 form (16 pages).
d) BOOK 4—WEIGHT AND SHAPE. 1982; 1 form (16 pages).
e) BOOK 5—VOLUME AND CAPACITY. 1982; 1 form (16 pages).
f) BOOK 6—TIME. 1982; 1 form (16 pages).

[369]

Early School Inventory. Kindergarten entrants; 1976; for obtaining information about a child's skills in areas important for early school progress; may be used with bilingual pupils or native English speakers; item scores in 5 areas of development: physical, language, cognitive, social-emotional, parent interview; no data on reliability and validity; no norms; 1 form ('76, 7 pages); no manual; 1984 price data: $12.50 per package of 35 inventories; administration time not reported; Joanne R. Nurss and Mary McGauvan; The Psychological Corporation.*

[370]

Early Screening Inventory. Ages 4–6; 1983; ESI; first introduced as the Eliot-Pearson Screening Inventory; "designed to identify children who may need special educational services in order to perform adequately in school"; individual; 1 form; test and manual (64 pages); score sheet (4 pages); parent questionnaire (4 pages); other testing materials (e.g., colored paper squares, drawing paper, and pencil) must be supplied by examiner; 1984 price data: $39.95 per set of testing materials; $11.95 per set of screening materials; $9.95 per 30 score sheets; $9.95 per 30 parent questionnaires; $10.95 per test and manual; (15–25) minutes; Samuel J. Meisels and Martha Stone Wiske; Teachers College Press.*

[371]

Eating Disorder Inventory. Ages 12 and over; 1983–84; EDI; self-report measure of "psychological and behavioral traits common in anorexia nervosa and bulimia"; 8 subscale scores: drive for thinness, bulimia, body dissatisfaction, ineffectiveness, perfectionism, interpersonal distrust, interoceptive awareness, maturity fears; 1 form ('83, 3 pages); profile form ('84, 1 page); set of scoring keys ('84, 8 sheets); manual ('84, 34 pages); 1984 price data: $22 per complete set (includes 25 test booklets and profile forms); $6.50 per 25 test booklets; $3 per 25 profile forms; $4 per set of scoring keys; $8.50 per manual; (15–25) minutes; David M. Garner, Marion P. Olmsted, and Janet Polivy (test); Psychological Assessment Resources, Inc.*

[372]

Economy Fire Promotion Tests. Prospective fire chiefs, assistant chiefs, battalion chiefs, captains, lieutenants, drivers-engineers; 6 tests; instruction manual available for each test; separate answer sheets must be used; distribution restricted to civil service commissions or other competent municipal officials; 1982 price data: rental service, $200 for the first 5 candidates; $4–$8 for each additional candidate ($200 minimum); administration time not reported; McCann Associates, Inc.*

a) CHIEF. Prospective fire chiefs; 6 areas: extinguishment knowledges, overhaul and salvage and rescue, fire prevention and investigation, supervision, administration, total.
b) ASSISTANT CHIEF. Prospective fire assistant chiefs; 7 areas: before the fire knowledges, extinguishment knowledges, overhaul and salvage and rescue, fire prevention and investigation, supervision, administration, total.
c) BATTALION CHIEF. Prospective fire battalion chiefs; 6 areas: same as for *b* except fire prevention and investigation omitted.
d) CAPTAIN. Prospective fire captains; 5 areas: same as *b* except fire prevention and investigation, and supervision omitted.
e) LIEUTENANT. Prospective fire lieutenants; 4 areas: before the fire knowledges, extinguishment knowledges, supervision, total.
f) DRIVER-ENGINEER. Prospective drivers-engineers; 4 areas: before the fire knowledges, extinguishment knowledges, overhaul and salvage and rescue, total.

[373]

Economy Police Promotion Tests. Prospective police chiefs, captains, sergeants, detectives, lieutenants, assistant chiefs; 6 tests; instruction manual available for each test; separate answer sheets must be used; distribution restricted to civil service commissions or other competent municipal officials; 1982 price data: rental service, $200 for the first 5 candidates; $4–$8 for each additional candidate ($200 minimum); administration time not reported; McCann Associates, Inc.*

a) CHIEF. Prospective police chiefs; 6 areas: other police knowledges, crime investigation, police supervision, police administration, legal knowledges, total.
b) CAPTAIN. Prospective police captains; 7 areas: patrol, other police knowledges, crime investigation, police supervision, police administration, legal knowledges, total.
c) SERGEANT. Prospective police sergeants; 6 areas: patrol, other police knowledges, crime investigation, police supervision, legal knowledges, total.
d) DETECTIVE. Prospective police detectives; 3 areas: crime investigations, legal knowledges, total.
e) LIEUTENANT. Prospective police lieutenants; 6 areas: same as *c* above.
f) ASSISTANT CHIEF. Prospective police assistant chiefs; 6 areas: same as *a* above.

[374]

Edinburgh Reading Tests. Ages 7–0 to 9–0, 8–6 to 10–6, 10–0 to 12–6, 12–0 to 16–0; 1972–81; upward and downward extension plus second editions for Stages 2 and 3 of Edinburgh Reading Tests; 4 levels labeled Stages 1, 2, 3, 4; Hodder & Stoughton Educational [England].*
a) STAGE 1. Ages 7–0 to 9–0; 1977; 5 scores: vocabulary, syntax, sequences, comprehension, total; Forms A, B, ('77, 16 pages); manual ('77, 31 pages); 1982 price data: £4.75 per 20 tests Form A or B; £1.25 per manual; £1.50 per specimen set; (30–55) minutes; test by The Godfrey Thomson Unit, University of Edinburgh, in association with The Scottish Education Department and The Educational Institute of Scotland; manual by D. J. Carroll.
b) STAGE 2. Ages 8–6 to 10–6; 1972–1980; 7 scores: vocabulary, comprehension of sequences, retention of significant details, use of content, reading rate, comprehension of essential ideas, total; no data on reliability for reading rate subtest; Parts 1 (8 pages), 2 (7 pages); manual ('80, 39 pages); profile (1 page); practice test (3 pages); £6 per 20 test booklets; £1.40 per 20 copies of profile sheet; £1.80 per 20 copies of practice test; £1.60 per manual; £2 per specimen set; (40) minutes for Part 1, (35) minutes for Part 2, (30–35) minutes for practice test; test by The Godfrey Thomson Unit, University of Edinburgh, in association with The Scottish Education Department and The Educational Institute of Scotland; manual by M. J. Hutchings and E. M. J. Hutchings.
c) STAGE 3. Ages 10–0 to 12–6; 1973–1981; 6 scores; reading for facts, comprehension of sequences, retention of main ideas, comprehension of point of view, vocabulary, total; Parts 1 ('81, 14 pages), 2 ('81, 7 pages); manual ('81, 39 pages); profile ('81, 1 page); practice test ('81, 3 pages); £7.25 per 20 test booklets, (specify Booklet A or Booklet B); £1.40 per 20 copies of profile sheet; £1.40 per 20 copies of practice test; £1.75 per manual (Booklet A): 75p for (Booklet B); £2.25 per specimen set; (40) minutes for Part 1, (35) minutes for Part 2, (30–35) minutes for practice test; test by Moray House College of Education, in association with The Scottish Education Department and The Educational Institute of Scotland; manual by J. F. McBride and P. C. McNaught.
d) STAGE 4. Ages 12–0 to 16–0; 1977; 6 scores: skimming, vocabulary, reading for facts, points of view, comprehension, total; £6.50 per 20 copies of test booklet; £1.25 per manual; £1.50 per specimen set; 60(70) minutes; test by The Godfrey Thomson Unit, University of Edinburgh, in association with The Scottish Education Department and The Educational Institute of Scotland; manual by D. J. Carroll.

See T3:775 (2 references); for reviews by Douglas A. Pidgeon and Earl F. Rankin of the first editions of Stages 2 and 3, see 8:724.

TEST REFERENCES

1. Rodgers, B. The identification and prevalence of specific reading retardation. BRITISH JOURNAL OF EDUCATIONAL PSYCHOLOGY, 1983, 53, 369–373.

Review of Edinburgh Reading Tests by NANCY L. ROSER, Associate Professor of Curriculum and Instruction, The University of Texas at Austin, Austin, TX:

The second edition of the Edinburgh Reading Tests offers tests at four levels, spanning ages 7 to 16. Only Stages 2 and 3 were previously available. Stages 2 and 3 include practice tests, designed to precede administration of the actual test. It is unclear why Stages 1 and 4 do not. Stage 1 provides alternate forms, but no evidence of their equivalency.

The tests were commissioned by the Scottish Education Department and the Educational Institute of Scotland to serve teachers' assessments of pupil progress in reading. Each test consists of four or more separately timed subtests, "each of which is designed to assess a different area of reading competence." Each of the four separate test administration manuals claims that the tests will provide information regarding organization of group activities as well as information for meeting the instructional needs of individual children. However, it should be noted that the contents of the tests are not directly comparable from one stage to the next. A test of Reading Rate is only included at Stage 2. A test of Use of Context at Stage 2 matches in tasks the tests of Vocabulary at other levels. Further, it is difficult to gauge what is being measured from item inspection nor is the scheme of reading assessment readily discernible.

The test authors admit that it might be expected that subtests would give markedly different assessments of a child, crediting him or her with distinctly greater competence in some aspects of reading than in others. In actuality, the subtests are highly intercorrelated within each stage, ranging from the low .70s to the low .80s. However, when the Reading Rate subtest is entered into the product-moment correlations, its lower average correlation with the other subtests (.45) demonstrates that rate may be a more independent trait.

The relatively high correlations fueled the author's contention that "reading can be thought of as a unified ability, an accomplishment which children tend to be good or bad at as a whole." Nevertheless, elaborate procedures for plotting areas of relative strengths and weaknesses on a profile chart are provided. Rather than offering support for the unified nature of reading, it seems just as likely that the decision underlying the initial selection and building of subtests to measure reading as a unified ability could have been a theoretical one. For example, no subtest assesses phoneme-grapheme correspondence except indirectly, i.e., within context.

The standardization samples were randomly selected from each chosen authority of the state schools in Great Britain. Total sample sizes for each stage averaged about 5,000 children. Raw scores for the total test were converted to deviation quotients, which provide comparison by relating performance of a pupil with that of age mates. For Stages 2 through 4, separate comparison tables are provided for combined English and Welsh and for Scottish children. For Stage 1, separate quotient tables are presented for sex rather than geographic area.

Deviation quotients are based on a normal distribution with a mean of 100 and a standard deviation of 15. They were calculated on the basis of 13 linear regressions of scores upon age at fixed percentiles. These percentiles correspond to quotients at 5-point intervals from 70 to 130. Intermediate quotients were obtained by interpolation, while at later stages, quotients above 130 have an age allowance based on the regression at quotient 130. The authors suggest that it is best to interpret quotients as indication of the percentage of children from the standardization sample obtaining a score no higher. The curtailment of quotients at specified points is indicative of the test's inability to give accurate measurements above and below certain points. The manuals are appropriately cautious in providing interpretive assistance for quotients.

The administration manuals also provide reading ages, a means for relating a child's performance to the age at which such a performance is typical. Reading ages, provided only for total scores, are determined by the median score for each age group. Thus any child, regardless of age, who obtains a certain mid-score is said to have a reading age equal to the chronological age of the group to which that score belongs. All children with a particular subtest raw score achieve the same standardized score, regardless of age and sex. Once again (as with quotients) the "extremes" tend to be less thoroughly tracked: young children will tend toward low subtest standardized scores, while older children obtain higher standardized scores.

Kuder-Richardson 20 reliabilities for the total test ranged from .95 to .97 for all four stages. The content validity was estimated by a steering committee of teacher and reading experts. In addition, subtest inter-correlations were calculated as noted earlier. Unfortunately, no other estimates were made of reliability (such as stability over time) or validity.

The manuals are exemplary in urging cautious interpretation and, in some instances, more thorough data collection before making instructional decisions. Manuals provide rationale for item choices as well as guidance in interpreting the subtests.

United States test consumers will find that unique terminology and variation in phrasing between British and Americans may confuse test takers on some items. It is unlikely that many American children will have had experience with Guy Fawkes' Day, lorries, queues, fortnights, or be able to answer the question "How are they getting on?" with the same perspective with which it was asked. Neither is ambiguity in items unusual, (e.g., "Because it is raining, I must wear my suit/coat/socks/shirt").

In summary, manuals clearly intended for instructors provide straightforward information on test construction, interpretation, and application. Different statistics than are typically provided may make the test consumer want to consider how the test's normative data will be used. The language differences which appear in some test items will doubtlessly also weigh against use by American consumers. Further, there are limited reports of the tests' reliability and validity. Little evidence exists that subtests measure different aspects of reading performance. Overall, the stages concentrate on comprehension, recall, grammar, and experience. It is not particularly a well-defined, broad-based diagnostic tool, but could serve as a general survey of reading achievement.

Review of Edinburgh Reading Tests by BYRON H. VAN ROEKEL, Professor Emeritus, College of Education, Michigan State University, East Lansing, MI:

At the risk of emphasizing the obvious, there may be some merit in reminding the reader that the Edinburgh Reading Tests were produced in Scotland and have a strong British flavor. The latter is significant because early in their development it was reported that these tests were intended for use throughout the English-speaking world. However, British linguistic and stylistic characteristics and metric properties based on the performances of children in England, Scotland, and Wales impose severe limitations on the suitability of the tests for children in the United States.

These tests were conceived under particularly favorable circumstances more than a decade ago. Official sponsorship, the institutional affiliation of the test constructors, and the involvement of a steering committee of teachers and reading experts offered promise of providing a sound basis for assessing achievement in reading acquisition. The fundamental objective of the test constructors was to provide measures which are easy to administer and interpret, and which would afford urgently needed assistance in the teaching of reading. This objective, however, has been only partially achieved.

According to a previous *MMY* review, the original plan was to provide a series of tests in five levels or stages for children of age 7–0 upwards. Subsequently, Stage 2 was first published in 1972, Stage 3 in 1973, and Stages 1 and 4 in 1977. Revisions of Stages 2 and 3 appeared in 1980 and 1981, respectively. Only Stage 1 is available in two parallel forms. The inconstancy reflected in the temporal order of the publication of the four stages, the magnitude of the time lapse among the publication dates, and the construction of parallel forms for Stage 1 only, give rise to an impression that these tests may have grown a bit like Topsy.

Each stage of the tests was normed on two separate samples—one drawn from state schools in Scotland, the other from state schools in England and Wales. Schools and classes within schools were chosen with considerable care so that samples would be proportional to the population and balanced by geographic areas. Conversion tables are provided for expressing total test scores as reading quotients (deviation quotients having a mean of 100 and a standard deviation of 15) and as reading ages (equivalent to the 50th percentile for each age group).

The reading quotient is stressed in each manual as an assessment of the child's overall reading ability compared with the performances of other children of the same age. Teachers are advised to interpret each of the quotients as a point on the distribution below which a certain percent of the scores fall. Despite their similarity to normalized percentiles, reading quotients, we are told, are preferred in order to distribute the test results "according to what is reasonably supposed to be the actual distribution of presently realized ability" and "to ensure that a difference of one point should roughly represent a constant difference in ability at whatever level of score or ability it occurs." There is little evidence to support this rationale.

Reliability was determined by internal consistency measures with the total test reliabilities of all four stages in the range of .95 to .97. Subtest reliabilities are equally as impressive, ranging as follows: .77 to .84 for Stage 1, .81 to .91 for Stage 2, .81 to .95 for Stage 3, and .73 to .91 for Stage 4. Standard errors of measurement are not provided, but it is suggested that "it is reasonable to think of a child's true quotient as lying within plus or minus 3 points of the one he actually obtains."

The validity of tests of this type depends largely upon the competence and skill of the test constructors. Accordingly, this reviewer fully expected that the constructors of these tests, relying on the collective judgement of a steering committee comprised of teachers, reading experts, and university affiliated educational psychologists, would create a well-defined hierarchical domain of reading skills. However, the authors of the manuals failed to address a number of issues pertinent to the validity of the tests. For example, details of the function of the steering committee and the substance of the information provided by it are not revealed. No reason is given for measuring certain reading skills to the exclusion of others nor is mention made of curricular requisites, taxonomies of reading skills, or theoretical models of reading, any of which might have provided a rationale for determining test content. Evidence is not cited to justify the inclusion of items that require the execution of tasks of questionable relevance to the reading act (e.g., items that require the sequencing of a set of sentences displayed in random order). The raising of these issues is not intended to discredit these tests but rather to alert the test user that in the absence of other measures of validity, the validity of these tests must be judged on the relationship of the test content to the objectives of instruction.

The manuals are complete and easy to follow. Included are administrative instructions in an easy step-by-step format, careful advice for the interpretation of test results, prescriptions for instructional options, and technical data. Teachers in the United States may not have the statistical knowledge to understand the concepts involved in the computation and interpretation of the technical data. The test booklets are well done but would have been more convenient to use had the subtests been labeled and numbered to correspond with the administrative instructions. In a few instances item style appears to be cumbersome and inefficient.

Overall, claims for the tests exceed their capabilities. Clearly, the primary function is to provide a general measure of reading achievement, and, as such, the tests probably correlate reasonably well with other general measures of reading achievement. Diagnosis, on the other hand, is portrayed as an ancillary function. However, a very substantial segment of the interpretive information in the manual dwells on detailed procedures for plotting and analyzing individual pupil subtest profiles. Unfortunately, the authors fail to caution the test user about the severe limitations imposed by subtest intercorrelations so high as to call into question the usefulness of the separate subtest scores.

[375]

Educational Abilities Scales. Ages 13–15; 1982–83; EAS; "to assist with the selection of options subjects in the final two years of compulsory schooling"; 10 tests yielding 5 scales: Clerical Aptitude, Mechanical Comprehension, Symbolic Reasoning, Spatial Reasoning, Science Reasoning; no data on validity; 1 form; student's book

('82, 65 pages); manual ('83, 45 pages); profile ('83, 2 pages); answer booklet ('82, 4 pages); 1985 price data: £2.45 per reusable student book; £4.45 per 10 answer booklets; £2.45 per 25 profiles; £4 per 10 developer pens; £5.95 per manual and scoring stencil; £8.95 per specimen set; 150(200) minutes in 2 sessions; Andy Stillman and Chris Whetton; NFER-Nelson Publishing Co. [England].*

[376]

Educational Development Series, [1984 Edition]. Grades K, 1, 2, 3, 4, 5, 6, 7, 8, 9, 10, 11, 12; 1963–84; EDS; a battery of ability and achievement tests and questions on interests and plans; a basic skills battery, a core achievement battery, and a cognitive and basic skills battery are also available; 13 levels; manual of directions ('84, 15–30 pages) for each level; content outline (no date, 3 pages) for each level; 1985 price data: $1.90 per manual of directions; $8 per specimen set of specified grades (K–2, 3–5, 6–8, 9–12); O. F. Anderhalter, R. H. Bauernfeind, V. M. Cashew, Mary E. Greig, Walter M. Lifton, George Mallinson, Jacqueline Mallinson, Joseph F. Papenfuss, and Neil Vail; Scholastic Testing Service, Inc.*

a) LEVEL 10A. Grade K; 1984; 8 scores: 3 cognitive skills (verbal, nonverbal, total), 4 basic skills (reading, language, mathematics, total), battery average; 1 form (30 pages); rental and scoring service, $2.53 per pupil; (160–180) minutes in 5 sessions.

b) LEVEL 11A. Grade 1; 1984; 11 scores: 3 cognitive skills (nonverbal, verbal, total), 4 basic skills (reading, language, mathematics, total), reference skills, science, social studies, battery average; 1 form (47 pages); rental and scoring service, $2.92 per pupil; (280–300) minutes in 5 sessions.

c) LEVEL 12A. Grade 2; 1984; 12 scores: 3 cognitive skills (verbal, nonverbal, total), 4 basic skills (reading, language arts, mathematics, total), reference skills, science, social studies, battery average, school interests; 1 form (51 pages); rental and scoring service, $2.92 per pupil; (295–315) minutes in 5 sessions.

d) LEVEL 13A. Grade 3; 1984; 12 scores: same as for *c* above; 1 form (52 pages); separate answer sheets must be used; tests may be purchased or rented; $27 per 20 tests; $11 per 50 answer sheets; scoring service, $1.15 per pupil; rental and scoring service, $1.89 per pupil; (320–340) minutes in 5 sessions.

e) LEVEL 14A. Grade 4; 1984; 14 scores: 3 cognitive skills (verbal, nonverbal, total), 4 basic skills (reading, language arts, mathematics, total), reference skills, science, social studies, battery average, career interests, school plans, school interests; 1 form (68 pages); separate answer sheets must be used; prices same as for *d* above; (345–365) minutes in 3 sessions.

f) LEVEL 15A. Grade 5; 1984; 14 scores: same as for *e* above; 1 form (68 pages); separate answer sheets must be used; prices same as for *d* above; (345–365) minutes in 3 sessions.

g) LEVEL 15B. Grade 6; 1984; 14 scores: same as for *e* above; 1 form (68 pages); separate answer sheets must be used; prices same as for *d* above; (345–365) minutes in 3 sessions.

h) LEVEL 16A. Grade 7; 1984; 14 scores: same as for *e* above; 1 form (70 pages); separate answer sheets must be used; prices same as for *d* above; (345–365) minutes in 3 sessions.

i) LEVEL 16B. Grade 8; 1984; 14 scores: same as for *e* above; 1 form (70 pages); separate answer sheets must be used; prices same as for *d* above; (345–365) minutes in 3 sessions.

j) LEVEL 17A. Grade 9; 1984; 14 scores: same as for *e* above; 1 form (73 pages); separate answer sheets must be used; tests may be purchased or rented; $28 per 20 tests; $11 per 50 answer sheets; scoring service, $1.15 per pupil; rental and scoring service, $1.89 per pupil; (350–370) minutes in 3 sessions.

k) LEVEL 17B. Grade 10; 1984; 14 scores: same as for *e* above; 1 form (73 pages); separate answer sheets must be used; prices and time same as for *j* above.

l) LEVEL 18A. Grade 11; 1984; 14 scores: same as for *e* above; 1 form (83 pages); separate answer sheets must be used; prices and time same as for *j* above.

m) LEVEL 18B. Grade 12; 1984; details same as for *l* above.

See T3:2325 (1 reference); for reviews by Samuel T. Mayo and William A. Mehrens of forms copyrighted 1976 and earlier see 8:27; see also T2:33 (1 reference); for a review by Robert D. North of forms copyrighted 1968 and earlier, see 7:22.

Review of Educational Development Series by ESTHER E. DIAMOND, Educational and Psychological Consultant, Evanston, IL:

The Educational Development Series (EDS) is a battery of tests that surveys verbal and nonverbal ability, interest in school subjects, educational and career plans, and school achievement in major curriculum areas.

The latest edition, published in 1984, has new norms—Fall and Spring—developed during the 1982–83 school year with a nationally representative sample of 101,575. Eighty-five percent of the sample was white, 13% black, and 2% other. Another 2% were handicapped. The norms were checked in Fall 1983 and Spring 1984 on students tested with the earlier (1975) norms the preceding Fall and Spring; although there were very slight differences, the norms were judged to be essentially equivalent.

There are 13 levels in the 1984 edition, covering kindergarten through grade 12. (Earlier editions had five levels, from lower primary through senior—grades 2 through 12.) There is no indication as to whether earlier editions of the EDS are still being marketed, particularly Forms R, S, T, and U, which carry copyright dates ranging from 1976 to 1980 (with Upper Primary Form T the latest).

Like the earlier editions, the 1984 EDS has 11 parts, although not every part is included at every level. The parts are: (1) My Career Interests, (2) My School Plans, (3) My School Interests, (4) Non-Verbal Skills, (5) Verbal Skills, (6) Reference Skills, (7) Reading, (8) Language Arts, (9) Mathematics, (10) Science, and (11) Social Studies. Language Arts has replaced the English test of the earlier editions, Reference Skills has been added, and the earlier Test 11, Problems in Career Planning, has been dropped. Parts 1, 2, 3, and 6 are omitted from Levels 10 and 11, and Parts 1 and 2 are omitted from Levels 12 and 13. All 13 levels have been coordinated and anchored to an expanded standard score scale, using overlapping items and Rasch item response procedures. Administration times range from approximately 3 hours at the lowest level to approximately 6 hours at the uppermost level. Dividing administration into several sessions is suggested. Machine-scorable booklets are available for kindergarten and grades 1 and 2, as well as for the upper levels.

The basic structure of the new EDS is the same as before, although the number of levels has increased, a new subtest has been added, and test objectives and content have shifted slightly to reflect new developments in world events and science. Content outlines for Reading, Mathematics, and Language Arts at all levels contain objectives representative of those in most current curricula. Each objective is referenced to the items measuring it. There are some instances of only one or two items per objective, although some objectives have as many as 20 items. If a skill is measured by three or fewer items, however, performance on the skill is not reflected in the measurement band on the Performance Profile; only the number of items involved and the number correctly answered are given. B forms are somewhat more difficult than A and are recommended for the higher of each grade pair (5 to 6, 7 to 8, 9 to 10, 11 to 12).

For the most part, the items are well constructed, and the item content—particularly the reading passages—should be of interest to students. Some problems in the earlier battery (e.g., occasional ambiguities in the pictorial non-verbal items, and a number of instances of potential bias where the characters were all white and women were shown only in traditional work roles) seem to have been overcome. The geometric and abstract figures in the Non-Verbal part seem to work better than the earlier mixture of pictures and abstract figures. A random inspection indicates that most of the items are new, although many earlier items have been retained.

There is some overlap between the Verbal Skills items and the Reading items; they are virtually interchangeable. For example, in the Level 10 Verbal Skills test students are asked to mark the picture of the safety pin; in the Reading test, they are asked to mark the picture of the goat. Also, many of the Reading test items, although context-embedded, are vocabulary items, as are the items in the Verbal Skills test. Some of the Language Arts items appear to be more appropriate for Reading, while some of the Reading objectives—for example, compounds, syllables, plurals, and contractions—appear to be more appropriate for Language Arts. (In the upper battery, comparable objectives do indeed appear in Language Arts.)

A variety of scores and score-reporting formats is available. Scores reported include Cognitive Skills—Verbal, Non-Verbal, and Total; Basic Skills—General Assessment (Reading, Language Arts, and Mathematics), and Skills Analysis, which divides each basic skill into two subskill areas; Interests and Present Goals; and Significant Patterns, which identifies students who may be in need of counseling because of conflicts among their achievements, abilities, and school/career plans. Scores for Reference Skills, Science, and Social Studies are reported under "Other Skills and Achievements." A Cognitive Skills Quotient (CSQ) is also reported. Based on Verbal and Non-Verbal scores and age at the time of testing, it "replaces the traditional IQ score" and is to be used as an index of future academic performance. It is described as being similar to a deviation IQ score, designed to be interpreted in the same manner as the traditional IQ. No evidence is offered in support of such interpretation, and use of the CSQ raises some questions about its theoretical basis and its construct validity, as well as the inferences to which its use might lead.

There are 11 types of scores, 6 of which may be included in a given set of reports: standard scores on an expanded standard score scale developed on the basis of the Rasch calibrations; fall and spring national and local percentiles, as well as interpolated January percentiles; national and local stanines; Grade Scores (GSs—"normalized grade equivalent scores," with a limit of 3 years above or below actual grade placement), which compare the student's performance with that of others at the same grade level; Grade Equivalent (GE) scores; raw scores; the CSQ; and the Expected Performance Indicator, based on a comparison between performance on an achievement subtest and on the Cognitive Skills subtests, with a plus or minus indicating any difference of 0.6 or more GS units. Available reports include individual and group Performance Profiles, which provide some diagnostic information; and individual and group item analyses. Two leaflets—one for parents and one for students—provide brief explanations of the meaning of the scores.

It is difficult to justify offering both the Grade Score and the Grade Equivalent score. It must surely be a source of confusion to both parents and teachers, many of whom already have enough difficulty interpreting grade equivalents correctly. In fact, the variety of derived scores, a number of which serve the same purpose, is somewhat akin to a smorgasboard or salad bar with so many offerings that the consumer is totally confused as to which dishes are the wisest nutritional choices. Nevertheless, justification aside, the scores appear to have been carefully and conscientiously derived.

At all stages of test development, the fit of items to the Rasch item response model was a primary consideration. All tests at a given level were equated horizontally on the basis of Rasch item calibrations for a stratified random sample of 1,000 students from the spring standardization at that test level. Tests were equated vertically on the basis of items common to adjacent levels.

Internal consistency (KR 20) reliabilities were mainly in the .80s for kindergarten and grade 1, although they were in the .90s for Cognitive Skills and Basic Skills scores. For the upper grades, reliabilities were mainly in the .90s, except for Science and Social Studies, which were mainly in the .80s. Median reliabilities for subjects across grades ranged from .87 to .98. Reliability information is not given for Parts 1, 2, and 3.

Median intercorrelations of the scores across the 13 EDS levels range from .55 to .74; median of the medians is .68.

Both concurrent and predictive validity studies are reported for the elementary, intermediate, and high school grades. Most of the studies reported were conducted before the current renorming, but the results are most likely generalizable to the present edition. Correlations with the Iowa Tests of Basic Skills (ITBS) were generally in the .70s and .80s, with a high of .87, for related areas or total Grade Equivalent scores. Similar results were obtained with the Stanford Achievement Tests, the Iowa Tests of Educational Development (ITED), the PSAT/NMSQT, the Scholastic Aptitude Test, the American College Test (ACT), and the Sequential Tests of Educational Progress (STEP), except for Reading, Science, and Language Arts in the latter case. Correlations with teacher grades were mainly in the .60s and .70s, with Basic Skills correlating the highest. The Non-Verbal score, interestingly, was the best predictor of grades in vocational subjects. Correlations with teacher recommendations for grade placement were mostly in the .60s. Six studies of students in grade 8 followed up in grades 9, 10, and 11 resulted in median correlations with grade averages ranging from .37 for Non-Verbal to .61 for Mathematics. In another series of studies, EDS scores were correlated with grade point averages for students in grades 9, 10, 11, and 12; correlations ranged from .37 for Non-Verbal in grades 9 and 11 to .70 for Language Arts in grade 9. In general, Basic Skills showed the highest correlations with grade point averages. Correlations with the PSAT/NMSQT were in the .70s for similar subject areas.

Predictive and concurrent validity studies for the 1984 EDS were conducted using the California Achievement Tests (CAT), the Comprehensive Tests of Basic Skills (CTBS), the PSAT/NMSQT, and the College Board SAT and Achievement Tests in Reading, Vocabulary, and Written English. Median correlations across grade levels ranged from .76 to .88 for the CAT, .69 to .79 for the CTBS, .76 to .83 for comparable PSAT/NMSQT scores, and .73 to .84 for comparable College Board scores. Combined correlations with grade 12 grade point averages in two schools ranged from a low of .42 for Science to a high of .61 for Basic Skills.

In summary, the 1984 EDS tests appear to be broadly representative of current school curricula and objectives. Items are generally well constructed and, for the most part, appear to be free from bias—although there is no information about judgmental or statistical bias analyses. Technical information on the development of the tests and on the characteristics of the scores—including their reliability and the validity of the inferences to be drawn—is presented in abundant detail. The publishers have really done their homework! Reliability and validity estimates are at least as adequate as they are for most competitive achievement batteries—and quite possibly more so. The general quality of the tests overall is comparable to that of most widely used batteries. However, one might question the wisdom of some of the score offerings, such as both a Grade Equivalent and a Grade Score, or the Cognitive Skills Quotient with its "is it or isn't it?" IQ score identity. The Interpretive Manual makes a valiant attempt to explain the scores and score reports to the user as honestly and simply as possible, and on the whole the attempt is successful.

[377]

Educational Interest Inventory, Revised Edition. High school and college; 1962–77; EII; 22 scores: literature, music, art, communications, education, business administration, engineering, industrial arts, agriculture, nursing, library arts, home economics, botany, zoology, physics, chemistry, earth science, history and political science, sociology, psychology, economics, mathematics; no high school norms; 1 form ('74, 12 pages); examiner's manual ('77, 14 pages); answer sheet/profiles ('77, 2 pages, self-marking); 1983 price data: $1.25 per test; $20 per 25 answer sheet/profiles; $1 per examiner's manual; $3 per specimen set; [40–60] minutes; James E. Oliver; Educational Guidance, Inc.*

For reviews by Fred H. Borgen and Thomas T. Frantz, see 8:1002 (1 reference); see also T2:2178 (1 reference) and 7:1017 (6 references).

[378]

Edwards Personal Preference Schedule. College and adults; 1953–59; EPPS; 15 scores: achievement, deference, order, exhibition, autonomy, affiliation, intraception, succorance, dominance, abasement, nurturance, change, endurance, heterosexuality, aggression; 1 form ('53, 8 pages); revised manual ('59, 25 pages); separate answer sheets (IBM 805, IBM 1230, NCS, OpScan, hand scored) must be used; no instructions on the use of specific answer sheets; 1984 price data: $12.50 per 25 tests; $11 per 50 IBM 1230 or OpScan answer sheets; $8.75 per 50 IBM 805 or hand scored answer sheets; set of manual and scoring stencils: $5 per hand scored, $15 per IBM 805 hand scored or machine scored; OpScan and IBM 1230 scoring stencils not available; $5 per specimen set; (40–55) minutes; Allen L. Edwards; The Psychological Corporation.*

See T3:780 (70 references), 8:542 (334 references), and T2:1164 (226 references); for reviews by Alfred B. Heilbrun, Jr., and Michael G. McKee, see 7:72 (391 references); see also P:67 (363 references); for reviews by John A. Radcliffe and Lawrence J. Stricker and an excerpted review by Edward S. Bordin, see 6:87 (284 references); for reviews by Frank Barron, Åke Bjerstedt, and Donald W. Fiske and excerpted reviews by John W. Gustad and Laurance F. Shaffer, see 5:47 (50 references).

TEST REFERENCES

1. Pandey, J. Dependency similarity, attraction and perceived helpfulness. SOCIAL BEHAVIOR AND PERSONALITY, 1978, 6, 37–41.

2. Langevin, R., Paitich, D., Ramsay, G., Anderson, C., Kamrad, J., Pope, S., Geller, G., Pearl, L., & Newman, S. Experimental studies of the etiology of genital exhibitionism. ARCHIVES OF SEXUAL BEHAVIOR, 1979, 8, 307–331.

3. Ammons, P., & Stinnett, N. The vital marriage: A closer look. FAMILY RELATIONS, 1980, 29, 37–42.

4. Fisher, S. Personality correlates of sexual behavior in black women. ARCHIVES OF SEXUAL BEHAVIOR, 1980, 9, 27–35.

5. Getter, H., & Nowinski, J. K. A free response test of interpersonal effectiveness. JOURNAL OF PERSONALITY ASSESSMENT, 1981, 45, 301–308.

6. Lange, S., & Coffman, J. S. Integrative test interpretation: A career counselor tool. THE VOCATIONAL GUIDANCE QUARTERLY, 1981, 30, 73–77.

7. Mozdzierz, G. J., & Semyck, R. W. Further validation of the social interest index with male alcoholics. JOURNAL OF PERSONALITY ASSESSMENT, 1981, 45, 79–84.

8. Furnham, A., & Henderson, M. A content analysis of four personality inventories. JOURNAL OF CLINICAL PSYCHOLOGY, 1982, 38, 818–825.

9. Pederson, S. L., Magaro, P. A., & Underwood, C. Personality styles, manifest needs, and the perception of time in college women. JOURNAL OF CLINICAL PSYCHOLOGY, 1982, 38, 346–351.

10. Robinson, B. E. Sex-stereotyped attitudes of male and female preschool teachers as a function of personality characteristics. PSYCHOLOGICAL REPORTS, 1982, 50, 203–208.

11. Zagar, R., Arbit, J., & Wengel, W. Personality factors as predictors of grade point average and graduation from nursing school. EDUCATIONAL AND PSYCHOLOGICAL MEASUREMENT, 1982, 42, 1169–1175.

12. Edwards, J. E., & Waters, L. K. Predicting university attrition: A replication and extension. EDUCATIONAL AND PSYCHOLOGICAL MEASUREMENT, 1983, 43, 233–236.

13. Finkelstein, M. J., & Gaier, E. L. The impact of prolonged student status on late adolescent development. ADOLESCENCE, 1983, 18, 115–129.

14. Lorber, J., & Ecker, M. Career development of female and male physicians. JOURNAL OF MEDICAL EDUCATION, 1983, 58, 447–456.

15. Rule, W. R. Birth order and earliest memory. PERCEPTUAL AND MOTOR SKILLS, 1983, 56, 601–602.

16. Dubey, S. N. Characteristic need patterns of Scheduled caste Indians. PSYCHOLOGIA, 1984, 27, 122–124.

[379]

Effectiveness Motivation Scale. Ages 3–5; 1976; manual title is *Stott-Sharp Effectiveness Motivation Scale*; ratings by teachers; 3 scores: E (strength of effectiveness motivation), W (withdrawal), Q (inconsequence); no data on reliability and validity of W or Q scores; "no normative interpretation of the W or the Q scores is proposed"; norms based on ages 4.5–5; 1 form (8 pages); manual (40 pages); scoring form (1 page); 1984 price data: £6.45 per 25 tests; £2.25 per 25 scoring forms; £5.45 per manual; £5.65 per specimen set; (5–10) minutes; John D. Sharp, D. H. Stott, J. B. Albin (manual), and H. L. Williams (manual); NFER-Nelson Publishing Co. [England].*

Review of Effectiveness Motivation Scale by HERBERT W. MARSH, *Senior Lecturer, Department of Education, The University of Sydney, NSW 2006 Australia:*

The authors define effectiveness motivation "in terms of the ways in which the child finds the outcomes of curiosity, discovery, recognition, production of an effect or change, and exercise of control over his environment reinforcing and productive of further effort." They go on to argue that the "justification for subsuming a multiplicity of behaviours within a single concept is (1) their common result—that of putting the child in the position of acquiring knowledge and skills that will enable him to be more effective in dealing with and understanding his world, and (2) their common basis in positive feelings of competence or enhanced effectiveness and the child's observed enjoyment thereof." Hence the authors see the effectiveness motive as a more comprehensive concept than specific types of motivation (e.g., achievement, aggression, curiosity, manipulation, novelty). The Effectiveness Motivation Scale (EMS) is based on this theoretical understanding of motivation, its relation to cognitive development, and empirical results of several earlier versions of the scale.

ITEMS. The EMS consists of 11 areas of activity (5 areas of individual play, 5 of social, and 1 of general mobility) that are judged by nursery school or kindergarten teachers who have worked directly with a child (3 to 5 years of age) on a day-to-day basis for at least 3 months. For each area there are eight or nine dichotomously scored items, and each item has a scale value between 0 and 4 that reflects the level of motivation that can be inferred from an affirmative response. An example area is "Activities Involving Noise" and three of the items (and their scale values) are "You can hardly get a squeak out of him" (0), "Is nearly always making some racket" (3), and "Listens to noises he makes and experiments with them" (4).

SCORING. For each area the one item with the highest scale value is selected from the affirmatively answered items, resulting in a set of 11 scale values. The total effectiveness (E) score is obtained by summing the scale values for the selected items, and results in a score between 0 and 44. The score is then placed into one of five "score bands," and the authors offer a brief verbal description of characteristics indicative of children who fall in the highest band and of those falling into the second lowest band, and more extensive discussions of those falling into the lowest band. The authors offer no justification for why only the response with the highest scale value is scored, and it would seem that potentially valuable information is lost by ignoring all other responses in each area. The authors also encourage the teachers "to record any reservations which he/she has regarding appropriateness of descriptions" for a particular child, but offer no explanation of how these should be used.

One or more of the items in each area, in addition to having an E-score scale value, are used to define scales labeled Withdrawn and Inconsequent. For example, for the area called Building, the item "Will simply throw the bricks around aimlessly" has a scale value of 1 for the E-scale, but also counts for the Inconsequent scale. However, the authors provide very little information about the Withdrawn and Inconsequent scores. They suggest that no normative interpretations of these scores are justified; no evidence of the reliability or the validity of the scales is presented, and no clear definition of what these scores are designed to measure is offered. I do not recommend the use of the Withdrawn and Inconsequent scales, and they are not discussed further in the review.

NORMS. The normative data is based on 338 British children assessed just before leaving nursery school at age 4.5 to 5, apparently in the late 1960s. The mean E-scores for males and females do not differ significantly and the authors emphasize norms based on the total population, though sex-specific norms are also presented. The actual presentation of the norms is in terms of a crude, visual frequency histogram based on very large category intervals, and the category end-points do not even correspond to the five "interpretive" score bands discussed earlier. While the EMS is designed for use with 3- to 5-year-olds, the normative data are based on 4.5- to 5-year-olds, and the authors present no data to suggest that the norms are appropriate for the wider age range. The normative sample is small, very dated, limited to one geographic region, and there is no indication that it will be applicable for non-British users. Consequently, the norms for this test represent an important weakness and are of questionable utility.

RELIABILITY. The authors present no internal-consistency estimates of reliability, though part-total correlations for a sample of 126 children from the normative group range from .43 to .71 (mean r =.61) for the 11 areas. In a small, unpublished study two "experienced nursery school teachers" each completed the scale independently for 39 Canadian children (ages unspecified), and the two sets of E-scores correlated .91. In a second, even smaller unpublished study an experienced and an inexperienced teacher each rated 20 Scottish children on the EMS, and their ratings correlated only .52, suggesting to the authors that "all teachers completing the scale should have worked directly with the children on a day to day basis for at least three months." In an additional small, unpublished study the authors indicated that test-retest ratings by the same teacher of 20 Scottish children was .95. In summary, it appears that the total E-score for the EMS may be sufficiently reliable to warrant interpretation, but insufficient attention is given by the authors to estimates of reliability. Internal consistency estimates based on the entire normative sample and interrater reliabilities based upon larger, more systematically described studies are clearly needed.

VALIDITY. Part of the EMS normative group was included in a longitudinal study where additional measures involving "problem solving, recognition and discrimination" were collected at the same time as the EMS, and measures of Word Recognition, Comprehension, and Mathematics were collected for many of these children when they were 7 years old. The E-scale correlated .52 with "Caldwell's Preschool Inventory" (which the authors state is correlated "just under" .80 with the Stanford-Binet), .49 with the Visual-Motor Integration Test (which the authors state is similar in rationale to the Bender-Gestalt Test), and .38 with the English Picture Vocabulary Test administered at the same time as the EMS. The E-scale correlated .45, .39, and .44 respectively with Word Recognition, Comprehension, and Mathematics for 77 of the children tested at age 7. The authors suggest that these findings support the predictive value of noncognitive preschool measures, and are an "indirect" source of evidence of validity for the EMS.

Stott and Albin (1975) argue that effectiveness motivation is composed of five components: recognition/discrimination, completion, control, exploration, and effecting change. They devised five experimental tasks designed to reflect the components to varying degrees. One example, the "noise box," was a large wooden box with a number of noise-producing attachments with which children were invited to play. The child's spontaneous play behavior was judged according to willingness to manipulate, number of components manipulated, patterning of effects, and mastery of fear. In two different samples (*N*s of 21 and 61) the total for the five tasks correlated .78 and .74 with the E-scale, while the noise box score alone correlated .72 and .74 with the E-scale. Stott and Sharp suggest that the size of correlations between the E-scale and individual tasks, which range from .16 and .74, "was consistent with the hypothesis of a general factor," but the basis of such a conclusion is unclear. The authors also state that the "correlations were on the whole higher than are usually obtained in the testing of preschool children."

The authors have consistently interpreted the E-score and effectiveness motivation to be a unidimensional, general factor of motivation. They base this conclusion on the finding that each of the 11 EMS items correlates significantly with the other 10 items, and on the consistently positive correlations between the five experimental tasks and the E-scale.

However, they also identify specific components that comprise effectiveness motivation. Their findings certainly suggest that components of effectiveness motivation are correlated, but their claim for a general factor is not justified by their analyses. This issue may or may not be of practical significance, but it is clearly an important theoretical concern.

SUMMARY. Effectiveness motivation as defined by the authors is intuitively and theoretically appealing. The EMS, as a measure of this construct, has some potential strengths and several important weaknesses. On the positive side the EMS seems to be developed according to a reasonable theoretical model, is moderately correlated with cognitive measures, and is substantially correlated with a set of experimental tasks specifically designed to reflect aspects of effectiveness motivation. The demonstration that teacher ratings on the EMS are substantially correlated with a child's performance on a theoretically related task is particularly important. On the negative side, the test items may be dated and were developed for British children, the norms for the test are probably not very useful, and inadequate attention has been given to the determination of reliability estimates. Also, additional research like the Stott and Albin study is needed to examine further the construct validity of the EMS. On the basis of this review I cautiously recommend the use of the EMS for research purposes, and hope that such research will lead to a better understanding of the construct.

REVIEWER'S REFERENCES

Stott, D. H., & Albin, J. Confirmation of a general factor of effectiveness-motivation by individual tests. BRITISH JOURNAL OF EDUCATIONAL PSYCHOLOGY, 1975, 45, 153–161.

Review of Effectiveness Motivation Scale by DALE H. SCHUNK, Assistant Professor of Educational Psychology, College of Education, University of Houston, Houston, TX:

This scale measures preschool children's motivation to achieve effects that serve no social or organic needs. Stott previously showed that effectiveness motivation comprised five categories of behavior: gains in knowledge, recognition and discrimination, control of objects, producing environmental change, and realizing a new arrangement or completing a task. The instrument includes 11 play settings: 5 address individual play (e.g., building and construction, creative play), 5 pertain to social play (e.g., helping others, response to strangers) and 1 assesses general mobility. For each setting there are 8–9 behavioral descriptions from which the rater checks 1 or more as applying to the ratee. Descriptions cover five levels of effectiveness motivation, which are weighted from 0 (low) to 4, and ratings are summed for a total E score. When 2 or more descriptions are checked in the same area, only the highest rating is counted in the total score. Of the 8–9 descriptions for each setting, 1 or 2 also count toward a separate "withdrawn" score (W), and 2 toward a separate "inconsequent" (i.e., impulsive or hyperactive) score (Q).

This instrument is short and easy to complete. It is intended for use by nursery or kindergarten teachers with children aged 3 to 5. The authors recommend that teacher and child be together at least 3 months prior to evaluation.

NORMS. Norms are provided for classifying children into one of five categories of effectiveness motivation (definite deficit, low average, average, high average, strong) based on total E score. The normative data are inadequate. The sample comprises 338 children aged 4.5 to 5 (167 girls, 171 boys); data were collected as part of the Preschool Project of the National Foundation for Educational Research, Slough, on children just prior to their leaving the Slough nursery schools. Although diverse socioeconomic backgrounds are represented, the sample size is too small and is not geographically representative. Norms are not given for children younger than 4.5 years. No norms are provided for W or Q scores; however, based on other data the authors suggest cutoffs worthy of individual follow-up assessment.

RELIABILITY. Each subarea score was correlated with the total E score (minus the subarea score) for part of the normative sample ($N = 126$). Correlations ranged from .43 to .71. Interrater reliability ($r = .91$) is based on a sample of 39 Canadian nursery children. Test-retest reliability ($r = .95$) is computed on a sample of 20 Scottish nursery children after a 2-week delay. This short period may have allowed memory to artificially enhance stability. Although reliabilites are good, samples are too small and limited to draw conclusions.

VALIDITY. Although the authors contend that there are no other tests of effectiveness motivation, they note that it bears similarity to constructs such as competence motivation and internal versus external control; however, correlations of the Effectiveness Motivation Scale with such similar measures are not reported, which is a serious omission. There also is a problem concerning the derivation of items and their weights to reflect degrees of effectiveness motivation. Weights were given on theoretical grounds, but this process is not clearly explained. Although such derivation usually increases validity, inspection of different behavioral descriptors raises questions. In the area of Building, for example, "Ignores the building pieces but has peculiar activities of his own" rates a higher score (2) than, "Will try after some encouragement" (1).

In an effort to strengthen their case for construct validity, the authors present correlations between the total E score and five individual child tasks: noise box, marble sorter, map shapes, matchers game, and persistence form boards. These correlations range from .16 to .78. Presumably these five tasks give the child the opportunity to display one or more of the five component effectiveness motivation behaviors, but the links are not clear.

SUMMARY. This instrument has face validity, and is easy to complete. Its use seems warranted to chart the progress of individual children over time and for research comparing treated with untreated groups. But there are serious drawbacks. The normative sample is small and not geographically representative, reliabilities are suspect, and empirical construct validation is needed using related measures (e.g., locus of control and perceived competence scales). The theoretical derivation is commendable but needs clearer explanation. Until the preceding concerns are addressed the group profiles are best used cautiously.

[380]

Ekwall Reading Inventory. Grades K, 1, 2, 3, 4, 5, 6, 7, 8, 9; 1979; the Quick Survey Word List and the El Paso Phonics Survey are included to "determine if a student has the necessary skills to read material written at an adult level successfully"; mastery objective: 99% correct on word recognition and 90% correct on comprehension, at the independent level; individual; Forms A-oral, B-silent, (1 page for each level in duplicating masters); 10 levels; manual (135 pages); San Diego Quick Word List used to determine reading level, Quick Survey Word List, El Paso Phonics Survey, and summary sheets included in manual and as duplicating masters; 1985 price data: $16.07 per complete set; (11–53) minutes for the word list and the reading passages depending on grade level and student ability, (7–25) minutes for phonics inventory depending on grade level and student ability; Eldon E. Ekwall; Allyn and Bacon, Inc.*

Review of Ekwall Reading Inventory by LYNN S. FUCHS, Assistant Professor of Education and Psychology, Wheelock College, Boston, MA:

The Ekwall Reading Inventory is a set of individually administered tests designed to assess listening comprehension level; independent, instructional, and frustration oral and silent reading levels; and phonics skills. Included in this battery are (*a*) the San Diego Quick Assessment, a graded word list from which initial placement into the reading passages is made; (*b*) the informal reading inventory, including four alternate passages at each level, preprimer (PP) and grades 1 through 9; and (*c*) two phonics tests, the Quick Survey Word List and the El Paso Phonics Survey.

The author states that the Inventory was designed to overcome some weaknesses of previously published instruments. The author seems to have succeeded in some respects. The content of the passages does not appear inappropriately juvenile; the four alternate forms of the passages allow versatility in administration; 10 comprehension questions per passage should enhance reliability; the summary sheet structures quantitative and qualitative observations; and printed materials along with related spirit masters are relatively easy and inexpensive to use. Despite these strengths, there are concomitant weaknesses of which the test user should be aware, including problems with the development of passages and comprehension questions, with the derivation of reading levels from students' reading samples, with the presentation of technical information, and with the inclusion of the two phonics tests.

Passages were developed by adjusting sentence length and percentage of hard words to derive readability scores that conform to expected grade levels. Such passage development is problematic for several reasons. First, it is unclear whether decreasing sentence length actually increases text comprehensibility or places added inference load on readers (Pearson, 1974–1975). Second, two selections with identical formula-based designations can lead to substantially different numbers of errors when read by the same child. Norming passages on representative samples of children probably would provide a more valid basis for grading passages. Finally, description of how passages were adjusted after piloting on a limited student sample is unclear, with no criteria provided to determine how judgments about acceptability were formulated.

Development of comprehension questions in the Inventory also is problematic. No taxonomy is presented to determine how factual and inferential questions were classified. No satisfactory procedure for interjudge agreement on the clarity or correct classification of questions is presented. In fact, some questions that are classified as inferential appear to be textually explicit or factual according to either Pearson and Johnson's (1978) or Barrett's (1976) taxonomy. Additionally, the student is required to perform only the simplest comprehension tasks, (*a*) because almost all questions are detail "wh" questions that are direct syntactic transformations of passage sentences, and (*b*) because there typically is one question per sentence with the order of questions matching that of the passage sentences. Furthermore, there are no inferential questions for the PP or grade 1 passages, with no explanation for the omission provided. Only 10% of the questions for grade 2 through 9 passages are inferential, with one grade 2 passage containing no inferential question. While it is admittedly important that questions be passage dependent, the comprehension tasks required in the Inventory might reflect the real task of reading better if more diverse factual and inferential questions had been included.

Additional problems with the Inventory relate to the derivation of reading levels from students' reading samples. First, directions to examiners and students at times are unclear. Students are directed to try to read all words on the word list page, whereas examiners are instructed to administer a subset of the lists. Directions for finding independent reading level on the San Diego also are confusing: Examiners are told to move students to a lower list if they make *any* errors in order to search for the highest level where no more than *one* error is made. Second, the author describes performance criteria as those most widely accepted; however, widespread consensus on such standards does not exist (Kender, 1969), and evidence (Powell & Dunkeld, 1971) suggests that primary and intermediate students may require different criteria. Furthermore, the author does not employ the traditional Betts criterion for instructional level, and provides the following rationale for using a lower comprehension standard: Without excessive word recognition errors, students tend not to show signs of frustration above 60% comprehension. However, because students' word recognition errors cannot be monitored during silent reading, a lowered comprehension criterion may result in spuriously high silent instructional level placements.

The manual of the Inventory is deficient with respect to technical information. Reliability data are reported with a small *N* spread across 9 grades; no breakdown per grade level is provided; only alternate form (or what the author terms "intrascorer") reliability data are presented. There are no validity data, and there is no mention of other measures against which reading level designations were correlated or demonstrated agreement.

For the two phonics tests, no technical development, no psychometric data, and no references to obtain such information are included in the manual. Furthermore, the test publisher claims to have no relevant data. The Quick Survey Word List, which asks students to read 14 multi-syllabic words with 100% accuracy, is so artificial to the reading process, and seemingly difficult to score, that the omission of technical data makes results based on the instrument difficult to interpret. The El Paso Phonics Survey suffers from similar problems. The student is required to read letter name(s) or vowel representations and a word base in isolation, then combine the parts into nonsense words. Directions are unclear, behavior sampling is poor (one item per phonics skill), and no information is provided on how grade level designations were formulated or how to derive overall scores. It would seem that more realistic information about students' abilities to apply phonographemic relationships might be obtained from scrutiny of oral reading errors.

In summary, the Ekwall Reading Inventory represents a worthwhile attempt to improve upon some previous commercial inventories, especially in the presentation of four alternate forms of passages. Nonetheless, it suffers from serious limitations including problems with the development of passages and comprehension questions, the derivation of reading levels, the presentation of psychometric data, and the inclusion of the phonics tests.

REVIEWER'S REFERENCES

Kender, J. P. How useful are informal reading tests? In A. Beery, T. C. Barrett, & W. R. Powell (Eds.), ELEMENTARY READING INSTRUCTION. Boston: Allyn and Bacon, 1969.

Powell, W. R., & Dunkeld, C. G. Validity of the IRI reading levels. ELEMENTARY ENGLISH, 1971, 48, 637–642.

Barrett, T. C. Taxonomy of reading comprehension. In R. J. Smith, & T. C. Barrett (Eds.), TEACHING READING IN THE MIDDLE GRADES. Reading, MA: Addison-Wesley, 1976.

Pearson, P. D. The effects of grammatical complexity on children's comprehension recall and conception of certain semantic relations. READING RESEARCH QUARTERLY, 1974–1975, 10, 155–192.

Pearson, P. D., & Johnson, D. D. TEACHING READING COMPREHENSION. New York: Holt, Rinehart, and Winston, 1978.

Review of Ekwall Reading Inventory by MARY BETH MARR, Assistant Professor of Education, State University of New York at Albany, Albany, NY:

This test, like other informal reading inventories, is designed to assess reading proficiency in word recognition and comprehension. To achieve this goal the test employs graded word lists, graded passages, and a phonics survey.

Perhaps the strength of this test is its use of a reading level table located at the end of each passage. This table combines word recognition and comprehension performance scores to arrive at one reader level (independent, instructional, frustrational) for the passage, thus enabling the examiner to interpret test performance efficiently and therefore judiciously administer other passages as needed. Other admirable test features include a test manual which in a straightforward and clear manner describes administration and scoring procedures and provides a sample student summary protocol with interpretation to aid the analysis of test performance. The test manual also includes a description of reader behaviors at the independent, instructional, and frustrational reading levels to aid assessment of reading performance. Lastly, test passages are coded in an attempt to disguise the level of difficulty from the student during testing.

The test has two serious limitations: (1) the nature of the passages and corresponding comprehension questions and (2) the data establishing validity of the instrument. Since the test is designed to assess reading proficiency from the preprimer to the ninth-grade level, the passages vary considerably in length, content, and text structure across the grade levels. Like other reading tests, this instrument has controlled for passage difficulty using only a readability formula which uses the number of hard words and sentence length to identify a corresponding reader level. Research in text processing has noted the limitations of readability formulae for test construction and has suggested other text features that need to be considered: topic, number of ideas presented in the test, number of text-based inferences required for comprehension, content structure, etc. (Kintsch & Vipond, 1979; Marr, 1983). These passage limitations are even more pronounced at the lower reader levels.

In addition, the questions used to assess comprehension are unusually restrictive. The author has constructed approximately 10 questions for each passage. Since passages vary in length from 70 to 186 words, the quality of the questions which could be constructed is reduced, particularly at the lower reader levels. Further, the author chooses to emphasize factual questions, typically allowing only one vocabulary and one inferential question for each passage at the third and above grade levels. The author's justification for such a restricted range of questions is a vague reference to research findings regarding the difficulty in constructing comprehension questions and the types of questions teachers typically ask. This justification does not reflect the current status of the research and practice in the field of reading comprehension. Specifically, Pearson and Johnson (1978) provide a systematic method for constructing and categorizing comprehension questions. In addition, the research findings regarding teacher questioning behavior are inconclusive. Guszak found that teachers ask mainly literal questions, as the author notes, but Hare and Pulliam (1980) have found quite the opposite results. Thus, the author's rationale for asking mainly literal comprehension questions is quite suspect. Certainly the test seems less than adequate at assessing comprehension proficiency representative of the reading curriculum demands at the first- through ninth-grade levels. Other informal reading inventories such as the Analytical Reading Inventory has been more successful in overcoming these difficulties by using children's literature and biographical stories as well as a wide range of comprehension questions to approximate real classroom reading demands and adequately assess comprehension performance.

The second significant limitation of this test is the author's vague reference to experimental research to establish the validity of the instrument. Specifically, the author notes the word list was derived from two other authors who tested the list on "over 100 subjects" (La Pray & Ross, 1969) to match word list performance with reading level. Results from this "study" do not report statistical findings with regard to subjects' performance, but report only performance compared with teacher recommendations. The author also studied the performance of 40 subjects from grades one to nine to determine the match between word list performance and passage placement, and was able to accurately place subjects in passages 18% of the time. Further, to establish the validity of the questions the instrument was administered to 60 subjects and adjustments were made "until it was determined that the questions and the levels of the passages were satisfactory." In short, accepted standards for establishing content, criterion-related, or construct validity of this instrument are not evident.

Other minor weaknesses in the instrument include no introduction to the passages nor illustrations to aid the reader in accessing and using prior knowledge to comprehend the text. Also, the phonics survey designed to assess word analysis skills (decoding initial and final consonants, vowels, etc.) is not as comprehensive as other phonic tests such as that which supplements the Spache Diagnostic Reading Scales. Finally, the Quick Survey Word List, designed to assess knowledge of syllabication, vowel rules, and accent generalizations, uses nonsense words such as "pramminciling" and "grantellen" which do not approximate "real words" in the English language and thus pose some question as to the usefulness of this particular measure.

In summary, the Ekwall Reading Inventory has the honorable intent of assessing reading proficiency using a variety of test components. Because of the limitations noted above, however, it does not improve upon or extend the contributions of existing instruments which use interesting and well structured passages, diverse comprehension questions, or varied phonic measures. Thus, while the intrument has the potential to eliminate the current need to use two existing instruments to obtain the same information, as it is currently composed its use is not recommended.

REVIEWER'S REFERENCES

La Pray, M., & Ross, R. The graded word list: Quick gauge of reading ability. JOURNAL OF READING, 1969, 12, 305–307.

Kintsch, W., & Vipond, D. Reading comprehension and readability in educational practice and psychological theory. In L. Nilsson (Ed.) PERSPECTIVES ON MEMORY RESEARCH. Hillsdale, NY: Earlbaum, 1979.

Pearson, P. D., & Johnson, D. D. TEACHING READING COMPREHENSION. New York: Holt, Rinehart, & Winston, 1978.

Hare, V. C., & Pulliam, C. A. Teacher questioning: A verification and an extension. JOURNAL OF READING BEHAVIOR, 1980, 12, 68–72.

Marr, M. B. An analysis of text variables in three current reading diagnostic tests. In J. Niles (Ed.) SEARCHES FOR MEANING IN READING/LANGUAGE PROCESSING AND INSTRUCTION. National Reading Conference, Rochester, NY, 1983.

[381]

El Circo. Ages 4–6; 1980; for use by teachers to assess Spanish-speaking children's comprehension of simple mathematical concepts and basic linguistic structures in both Spanish and English; 5 parts listed below; 1 manual (96 pages) for all parts; 1985 price data: $7.25 per manual; $10.50 per specimen set; Educational Testing Service; CTB/McGraw-Hill.*

a) LANGUAGE CHECK. To assess if a child's Spanish skills are sufficient to take the other measures in Spanish; item scores and mode of response scores (Spanish, English, mixture Spanish-English, nonverbal); administered individually and entirely in Spanish; 1 form (2 pages); $9.30 per examiner's kit including one response stimulus picture, 30 child record forms, and one set of directions; (5–10) minutes.

b) PRACTICE MATERIALS. Item scores; administered in Spanish; 1 form (2 pages); $9.30 per package of 30 practice pages and one set of directions; (5–10) minutes.

c) WHAT WORDS ARE FOR. Item scores in 4 areas: verb tenses, prepositions, possessives, miscellaneous (negations, embedded sentences, active and passive voices, reflexives, indirect objectives); administered mainly in English, only preliminary directions and examples in Spanish; 1 form (20 pages); $26.70 per examiner's kit including 30 test booklets, one teacher's booklet, and two class record forms; (15–20) minutes.

d) CUANTO Y CUANTOS. Item scores in 3 areas: counting, relational terms, numerical concepts; administered entirely in Spanish; 1 form (27 pages); $26.70 per examiner's kit including 30 test booklets, one teacher's booklet, and two class record forms; (15–20) minutes.

e) PARA QUE SIRVEN LAS PALABRAS. Item scores in 4 areas: verb tenses, prepositions, indirect objects, miscellaneous (plurals, adjectival agreement, reflexives, object pronouns, possessives); administered entirely in Spanish; 1 form (23 pages); $26.70 per examiner's kit including 30 test booklets, one teacher's booklet, and two class record forms; (15–20) minutes.

TEST REFERENCES

1. Madrid, D., & Garcia, E. E. Development of negation in bilingual Spanish/English and monolingual English speakers. JOURNAL OF EDUCATIONAL PSYCHOLOGY, 1981, 73, 624–631.

Review of El Circo by EDWARD N. ARGULEWICZ, Assistant Professor of Educational Psychology, Arizona State University, Tempe, AZ:

El Circo Package A is the first three of eight measures which comprise the El Circo Assessment Series. The three subtests of Package A are Cuanto y Cuantos, Para Que Sirven Las Palabras, and What Words Are For. They were developed to assess basic numerical concepts and linguistic structures of Spanish-speaking children in kindergarten through first grade. The tests were thus designed to assess skills necessary for academic success, and in turn, provide information for instructional programming. In this way, the tests also were designed to serve as an evaluation measure of early childhood bilingual programs.

Test instructions for El Circo are written in Spanish and English and are explained clearly so that persons with a minimum of testing experience should readily be able to administer the test after a few practice sessions. However, examiners MUST be able to speak both Spanish and English in order to administer and score all three subtests. Prior to administering the three subtests of Package A, a Language Check may be given in those cases in which there is uncertainty about whether a child is proficient enough in Spanish to understand the directions. Although the Language Check takes only 5 to 10 minutes to administer, it does require that the test administrator have some knowledge of a child's environmental background in order to score the responses correctly.

Each of the three subtests of El Circo was designed to measure discrete skills; deriving a total score for the battery is inappropriate. The Cuanto y Cuantos subtest samples many relational and numerical concepts necessary for teaching mathematical skills. Para Que Sirven las Palabras and What Words Are For subtests measure receptive language ability in Spanish and English, respectively. The two tests are not translations of one another, thus taking into account the differential development in grammatical structures between the two languages. Both tests assess linguistic structures that are considered to be prerequisites to further verbal and cognitive development in young children.

Normative data on El Circo were developed by using the 1970 census information to identify geographical areas in which 5% or more of the population were Spanish speaking. A stratified random sampling was conducted upon urban/rural, distance from Mexico, socioeconomic, and density of Spanish-speaking population variables. Prekindergarten, kindergarten, and first-grade children were then selected from public, private, Catholic, and Head Start schools within the selected counties.

Norms tables provide means, standard deviations, percentile ranks, and stanines converted from total scores on each of the three measures for preschool, kindergarten, and first grade children. These data can be used to interpret a child's score in relation to the national sample. However, a possible shortcoming of constructing the norm tables for grade level is that age may be a stronger influence on some subtest scores than grade. Thus, it is possible that interpreting a child's score to a grade-level reference could result in spuriously higher scores than if he/she were compared to normative data based on age. The El Circo manual also presents tables which provide the percentages of correct responses for each item from the three subtests. These tables were also constructed based upon grade level of children in the normative sample. Here again, the addition of age norms would provide test users with more precise information regarding the developmental levels at which mastery of the skills sampled could be expected.

Since El Circo is primarily a diagnostic instrument, the content validity of the test is a major concern. In this regard, the team of El Circo test developers comprised of bilingual educators, linguists, and early childhood specialists have generated items that adequately sample the basic linguistic and numerical concepts that are generally acquired in early childhood. No formal concurrent or predictive validity data are reported in the manual or have been published at this time. Such information is necessary to determine empirically the relationship between the concepts measured by El Circo and academic achievement.

No stability data are reported in El Circo's manual. However, internal consistency reliability coefficients are reported for the three subtests at each grade level. The reliability coefficients range from .63 for the Para Que Sirven las Palabras subtest for first grade to .83 for the What Words Are For subtest for first grade. Given the diagnostic nature of El Circo, and the consequent heterogeneity of the items, these coefficients tentatively should be considered adequate.

In conclusion, El Circo represents a major advancement in measuring basic language and numerical concepts within a cultural milieu. At the present, its most promising use appears to be in identifying children's strengths and weaknesses in basic concepts and skills which can be used to aid educators in curriculum planning for Spanish-speaking youngsters. El Circo can then also be given as a posttest measure in assessing the success of various educational interventions. Before El Circo can realize its full potential, however, additional validity and reliability studies must be conducted so that consumers can have confidence in its technical adequacy.

Review of El Circo by J. MANUEL CASAS, Assistant Professor in Counseling Psychology, Department of Education, University of California, Santa Barbara, CA:

El Circo—Package A is a long awaited screening battery specifically developed for use with Spanish-speaking children. Package A is comprised of three tests: Cuanto y Cuantos, What Words Are For, and Para Que Sirven Las Palabras. The total battery, when published, will include the tests in Package A as well as eight other tests which teachers will be able to use to obtain information about the perceptual, cognitive, and linguistic skills of individual children. More specifically, the battery will focus on the skills which a child must acquire in order to subsequently succeed at the kindergarten and grade one levels. The information provided is intended to be of use to the teacher for curriculum and instructional planning.

The manual is well designed and provides understandable instructions on administration, scoring, interpretation, and use of test information. In addition, it provides good background information on the procedures which were followed in the development and norming of the battery.

Items in the test booklets consist of pictures that are large and well spaced. The size of the pictures is a positive factor in facilitating the childs' marking of his/her own responses. A practice section is included for each of the tests for the purpose of ensuring that the child understands how to respond appropriately to the task at hand. Children can be tested individually or in groups, depending on age.

Class record forms are included for charting the scores on individual items and for facilitating tabulation of those items most and least frequently missed. In addition, instructions are also given for adapting the record form for comparison of scores obtained at different time periods. A table categorizing the items is of particular value to a teacher in planning curriculum. For example, in Cuanto y Cuantos the items are divided into three categories: counting, relational terms, and numerical concepts.

The section on interpretation of test results appropriately cautions teachers against sole reliance on the test for individual planning purposes and makes suggestions for possible acquisition of supplementary information to more fully understand each child. The suggestions provided reflect the authors' belief that "Test results provide only a piece of the total picture—namely, how a child performs specific tasks under standardized conditions. Therefore, test performance information must be blended with teacher and staff observations, parent information, teacher judgments, and other available performance ratings."

Care is taken to cover details including how to treat omissions and incomplete tests. The standard error of measurement and its relationship to the interpretation of results is explained. In addition, examples of ways to interpret individual cases are provided.

Concepts that were formulated and tested in the development of the Circus series were used as the basis for El Circo. Although some measures are similar in content, the authors warn that scores are not comparable to one another.

Items were translated by three teams representing Cuban-American, Mexican-American, and Puerto Rican cultural groups, each headed by a test development specialist. Items that presented difficult or unfamiliar wording in translation were modified or discarded. A Cultural Advisory Committee composed of prominent Hispanic educators and researchers did a final review of the development of each test and made final recommendations regarding vocabulary options.

As part of the pretesting of items, a study was conducted to address the questions: (*a*) "How can a child's general level of language competency be accurately and efficiently assessed?" and (*b*) "What level of language competence in Spanish is necessary for valid use of EL CIRCO'S tests of nonlanguage skills?"

As a result of the study, a language check screening was incorporated as part of Package A to determine if the child has the minimal level of language proficiency for being tested in Spanish. For the sake of norming, the test was administered solely in Spanish to those who met the criterion level on the language check.

The norming population was systematically chosen, with stratification on the basis of community type, distance from the border of Mexico, density of Spanish-speaking population, and percentage of Spanish-speaking population below poverty level. A complete list of the participating counties and participating school sites is presented. Norms for each of the measures are presented with percentile ranks, means, and standard deviations for each of the preschool, kindergarten, and first grade groups.

Reliability coefficients (internal consistency) for Cuanto y Cuantos and for What Words Are For ranged from .73 to .83 for the various levels, and values of .63 to .67 were found for the Para Que Sirven Las Palabras. The authors suggest that the lower coefficients obtained for the Para Que Sirven Las Palabras may be due to the wide range of language skills that are purposefully covered by this measure.

With respect to El Circo's validity, the authors wisely state: "Content validity is best ensured by entrusting test development to persons well qualified to judge the relationship of test content to teaching objectives. The test development procedures are described in detail in the section DEVELOPING THE TESTS. It is recommended that each test user make an individual judgment of content validity with respect to local instructional practices and educational objectives."

Because of the relative newness of these measures, no published research has been conducted using El Circo measures. The measures are currently being used by Head Start programs throughout the country.

In summary, El Circo appears to be a well designed and carefully developed battery, and as such it is highly recommended as a valuable source of information for helping to screen Spanish-speaking children in the early primary school grades. It is hoped that forthcoming research will help to justify and substantiate this reviewer's recommendation.

[382]

Embedded Figures Test. Ages 10 and over; 1950–71; EFT; field dependence; colored versions of the original black-and-white figures by K. Gottschaldt ('26); individual; Forms A ('50, first 12 figures of the original 24-figure test), B ('50, last 12 figures of the original 24-figure test); norms (except for 2 groups) and reliability data for the 12-figure, 3 minutes-per-figure Forms A and B estimated from the original 24-figure, 5 minutes-per-figure test; norms consist of means and standard deviations; no specific manual; combined manual ('71, 32 pages) for this and Children's Embedded Figures Test and Group Embedded Figures Test; response record ('69, 1 page); 1984 price data: $13 per set of cards and 50 record sheets; $5 per 50 record sheets; $5.25 per manual; (10–45) minutes; Herman A. Witkin and manual coauthors Philip K. Oltman, Evelyn Raskin, and Stephen A. Karp; Consulting Psychologists Press, Inc.*

See T3:794 (88 references), 8:548 (134 references), T2:1169 (149 references), and P:71 (47 references); for reviews by Harrison G. Gough and Leona E. Tyler, see 6:89 (24 references); see also 5:49 (9 references).

TEST REFERENCES

1. Gamer, E., Gallant, D., Grunebaum, H. U., & Cohler, B. J. Children of psychotic mothers: Performance of 3-year-old children on tests of attention. ARCHIVES OF GENERAL PSYCHIATRY, 1977, 34, 592–597.

2. Ludwig, A. M., Bendfeldt, F., Wikler, A., & Cain, R. B. 'Loss of control' in alcoholics. ARCHIVES OF GENERAL PSYCHIATRY, 1978, 35, 370–373.

3. MacVane, J. R., Lange, J. D., Brown, W. A., & Zayat, M. Psychological functioning of bipolar manic-depressives in remission. ARCHIVES OF GENERAL PSYCHIATRY, 1978, 35, 1351–1354.

4. Gabrenya, W. K., Jr., & Arkin, R. M. Motivation, heuristics, and the psychology of prediction. MOTIVATION AND EMOTION, 1979, 3, 1–17.

5. Martin, T. O., & Gross, R. B. A comparison of twins for degree of closeness and field dependency. ADOLESCENCE, 1979, 14, 739–745.

6. Fletcher, J. M., & Satz, P. Developmental changes in the neuropsychological correlates of reading achievement: A six-year longitudinal followup. JOURNAL OF CLINICAL NEUROPSYCHOLOGY, 1980, 2, 23–37.

7. Luborsky, L., Mintz, J., Auerbach, A., Christoph, P., Bachrach, H., Todd, T., Johnson, M., Cohen, M., & O'Brien, C. P. Predicting the outcome of psychotherapy: Findings of the Penn Psychotherapy Project. ARCHIVES OF GENERAL PSYCHIATRY, 1980, 37, 417–481.

8. McCauley, E. A., & Ehrhardt, A. A. Sexual behavior in female transsexuals and lesbians. THE JOURNAL OF SEX RESEARCH, 1980, 16, 202–211.

9. Richardson, A., & Divyo, P. The predisposition to hallucinate. PSYCHOLOGICAL MEDICINE, 1980, 10, 715–722.

10. Grunau, R. V. E., Purves, S. J., McBurney, A. K., & Low, M. D. Identifying academic aptitude in adolescent children by psychological testing and EEG spectral analysis. NEUROPSYCHOLOGIA, 1981, 19, 79–86.

11. Gul, F. A., & Zaid, O. Field dependence and accountants' confidence in decisions. PSYCHOLOGICAL REPORTS, 1981, 49, 949–950.

12. Wender, P. H., Reimherr, F. W., & Wood, D. R. Attention deficit disorder ('minimal brain dysfunction') in adults: A replication study of diagnosis and drug treatment. ARCHIVES OF GENERAL PSYCHIATRY, 1981, 38, 449–459.

13. Campbell, S. B., Szumowski, E. K., Ewing, L. J., Gluck, D. S., & Breaux, A. M. A multidimensional assessment of parent-identified behavior problem toddlers. JOURNAL OF ABNORMAL CHILD PSYCHOLOGY, 1982, 10, 569–592.

14. Streibel, M. J., & Ebenholtz, S. M. Construct validity of perceptual style: Role of stimulus size in the embedded-figures test and the rod-and-frame test. PERCEPTION & PSYCHOPHYSICS, 1982, 31, 128–138.

15. Thomas, H., II. A strong developmental theory of field dependence-independence. JOURNAL OF MATHEMATICAL PSYCHOLOGY, 1982, 26, 169–178.

16. Vardy, M. M., & Kay, S. R. The therapeutic value of psychotherapists' values and therapy orientations. PSYCHIATRY, 1982, 45, 226–233.

17. Zoccolotti, P., & Pizzamiglio, L. Measuring visual disembedding in a tachistoscopic presentation. PERCEPTUAL AND MOTOR SKILLS, 1982, 54, 479–486.

18. Chatterjea, R. G., & Paul, B. Field independence, science achievement and intelligence. PSYCHOLOGIA, 1983, 26, 111–117.

19. Fogliani-Messina, T. M., Fogliani, A. M., & DiNuovo, S. Embedded Figures Test in old age: A psychometric note. PERCEPTUAL AND MOTOR SKILLS, 1983, 56, 284–286.

20. Martin, M. Cognitive failure: Everyday and laboratory performance. BULLETIN OF THE PSYCHONOMIC SOCIETY, 1983, 21, 97–100.

21. Erwin, J. E., & Hunter, J. J. Prediction of attrition in alcoholic aftercare by scores on the Embedded Figures Test and two Piagetian tasks. JOURNAL OF CONSULTING AND CLINICAL PSYCHOLOGY, 1984, 52, 354–358.

22. Fowler, C. J. H., & Fowler, J. F. The consistency of Nigerians' performance on three tasks measuring field dependence. INTERNATIONAL JOURNAL OF PSYCHOLOGY, 1984, 19, 271–278.

23. Woodfield, R. L. Embedded Figures Test performance before and after childbirth. BRITISH JOURNAL OF PSYCHOLOGY, 1984, 75, 81–88.

[383]

Emo Questionnaire. Adults; 1958–78; "designed to assess an individual's personal-emotional adjustment"; 10 diagnostic dimensions: rationalization, inferiority feelings, hostility, depression, fear and anxiety, organic reaction, projection, unreality, sex, withdrawal, plus buffer score; 4 second-order adjustment factors: internal, external, somatic, general; alternate Forms A ('62, 10 pages), B ('78, 11 pages); manual ('77, 126 pages); report form (2 pages); score sheet (1 page); calculation sheet (1 page); separate answer sheets may be used; 1982 price data: $8 per 20 test booklets (Form A or B); $2.50 per scoring templates; $9.50 per manual; $12.50 per specimen set; (30) minutes; George O. Baehr and Melany E. Baehr (test); Human Resources Center, University of Chicago.*

See T2:1170 (1 reference); for reviews by Bertram D. Cohen and W. Grant Dahlstrom, see 6:90 (1 reference).

Review of Emo Questionnaire by ALLAN L. LAVOIE, Associate Professor of Psychology, Davis & Elkins College, Elkins, WV:

The Emo Questionnaire (EQ), originally designed to measure emotional adjustment in clinical settings, was revised in 1959 to make it more appropriate for its current purposes: first, to screen large numbers of job applicants to identify those who will be disruptive, unreliable, or unpredictable; and second, to assist in the placement of specialized personnel for whom it is desirable to have very detailed personality diagnoses.

An examination of the EQ's 140 items reveals some of the underlying content. More than 80 of the items seem to be direct adaptations of MMPI items (e.g., EQ items 30, 31, and 46 are very similar to MMPI items 281, 114, and 187 respectively). Thirty items are called nonthreatening "buffer" items, and were included to reduce the focus on pathology, though some of these seem to be from the MMPI, too. Form B items, on brief inspection, appear to simply be a rearrangement of Form A's. In short, the EQ apparently measures psychopathology, a carryover from its days as the Discontentment Scale.

The test is easy to administer. There are no difficult instructions for clients to understand, there is no time limit, and the manual indicates it requires only 20–30 minutes. Scoring remains cumbersome and unnecessarily complex. In the 20 years since Dahlstrom (6:90) first noted the scoring problems surely something could have been done to simplify the procedure. For screening purposes, only the four second-order factors are routinely scored, a relatively easier task. The scores seem very susceptible to impression management, but, aside from very low scores, the author pays scant attention to the possibility of faking.

Score reliability, assessed by KR20, varies from .70 to .83 for the second-order factors, with a mean of .78. The range for the dimensions is from .59 to .79 with an average of .68. To be useful for either individual interpretation or group screening, the reliabilities should be higher. An illustration is the General second-order factor, with a reliability of .70, a standard deviation of 4.8, and a standard error of measurement of 2.6 points. The 95% confidence interval for a score of 14 would extend down to 9 and up to 19. With the screening cutoff score at 17, this person's score is uninterpretable—should you hire, or not? Only the most extreme scores will be useful, at least for this purpose.

Considerable data have been accumulated to demonstrate the validity of the EQ, though some of the data may actually undermine the conclusion of validity. For example, EQ scores were correlated with MMPI scores. The strongest relationships were between the validity scales of the MMPI (L,F,K) and all of the EQ scales except General. Expected relationships sometimes did not show up, as with the nonsignificant correlation of the two depression scales. This pattern of results suggests that the EQ measures the lie scales of the MMPI rather than the content scales. The test authors should be concerned by this outcome.

The Maudsley Personality Inventory (MPI) was also correlated with the EQ. Scores on Neuroticism correlated strongly and positively with every EQ scale, again with the exception of General. It would seem simpler and more economical to use the shorter MPI than the Emo Questionnaire.

Another validity study examined the ability of the EQ to differentiate the norm group from a hospitalized psychiatric sample. The four second-order factors did this successfully. There is cause for concern, however, because the two samples overlapped considerably; on Internal and General the two groups differed by less than three points. Such large overlaps reduce the chance of accurate prediction of future problems. As the cutoff scores are made more stringent, more and more normals will be classified as potential patients until the false positives outnumber the true positives. The test authors need to attend carefully to this problem, and to demonstrate incremental validity.

Similar criticisms apply to the use of the EQ in distinguishing among various occupational groups. Analyses of variance and *t* tests showed that about one-third of 450 comparisons approach or reach statistical significance, but many of those comparisons involve the hospitalized sample, an inappropriate group on which to test the potential of the EQ for classifying employees. After all, the hospitalized sample cannot be considered as an occupational group. When the comparisons involving them are removed, and a correction for multiple comparisons is made to alpha, a relatively small number of significant distinguishing characteristics is found. The small differences that exist probably could not be used predictively (e.g., on General, the largest difference between groups is the contrast between district sales managers and industrial laborers, where the means differ by less than 2 points while the pooled standard deviation is nearly 4).

The authors demonstrated that EQ scores can more successfully predict job success for police, bus drivers, and feed salesmen. No consistent scale pattern showed up in these studies, but that would be a job for local validity studies in any case. Other factors influenced EQ scores in these studies, including sex, race, and ethnicity (e.g., white non-Spanish bus drivers differed significantly from Spanish on 8 of the 14 scores).

If we consider all the evidence on validity, it would be fair to say that the EQ may have some predictive validity, but it would also be fair to have reservations about its construct validity.

If you are concerned with individual interpretations, the manual provides little help. The only norms are for a large industrial sample collected 25 years ago. Means and standard deviations are available on a variety of other occupational groups, so standard scores could be calculated in reference to them. That is the task of the author of the manual, however, and should have been done if he were concerned with assisting individual diagnosis. No interpretive guidelines are provided, as the manual states that the psychologist has the task of devising a personal approach to the interpretation of EQ results. In short, for this kind of use, it is up to you and the raw scores, some of which are directly useable.

To summarize, the EQ, now a quarter century old, has been used primarily by its creators and primarily for screening. Critical users have not made contributions to the literature as yet, so we have by no means a complete picture of the test. For screening purposes you would be better off using a more widely understood, better documented test that can be scored more easily, has broad norms, and content similar to the CPI or MMPI. And meanwhile we will wait for the authors to correct the deficiencies noted.

Review of Emo Questionnaire by PAUL MCREYNOLDS, Professor of Psychology, University of Nevada-Reno, Reno, NV:

The Emo Questionnaire (EQ) is a promising but largely unproven test. It purports to assay the emotional (thus "Emo") health of individuals across a variety of behavioral and attitudinal areas, including both internal dynamics and the person's relations with the external world. Though in principle suitable for direct clinical applications, the most extensive use of the EQ to date has been in industrial psychology, and the content of the manual leads one to infer that the authors see the test's main application in this area. The EQ is designed to serve either as a general procedure for personality diagnosis or as a screening procedure to identify individuals likely to perform poorly under stress (both require full test administration).

The EQ, a descendant of the earlier Baehr Discontentment Scale, includes 140 items and requires about 30 minutes for administration. A new test manual, an alternate test form, and considerable developmental work leading to changes in test interpretation have been completed since the *MMY6* reviews. The manual adequately describes the background, purposes, administration, scoring and interpretation of the test, plus statistical data available up to 1977, including correlations of test scales with MMPI and Maudsley Personality Inventory (MPI) variables. It is deficient, however, in delineating clinical interpretations of test variables and profiles and in specifying limitations in test applications.

The item format in the EQ is unique. Instead of answering trait-like questions "Yes" or "No," the subject is presented with a series of possible experiences (e.g., "My sleep was fitful and disturbed"; "I felt that I was being plotted against"), and asked to indicate whether there was at least one time within the past month when the indicated experience occurred; the subject then checks "No" or "Yes," and if "Yes," also indicates whether he or she was "Pleased," "Not Affected," "Troubled a Little," or "Troubled Very Much" by the experience. The EQ thus focuses on the subject's current, rather than long-term psychological status. The screening function is based on the four factor scores: Internal Adjustment, External Adjustment, Somatic Adjustment, General Adjustment; the more complete interpretation utilizes the 10 diagnostic scores plus certain information unique to this instrument. The factor scores reflect second-order factors (based on 21 first-order factors) derived from the responses of 1,193 male subjects, including 1,030 gainfully employed men and 163 psychiatric hospital patients. The 10 diagnostic dimensions are each based on 10 items, except for Organic Reaction, which is based on 20; there are also 30 buffer items. These 10 dimensions were evidently derived from rational considerations. Additional information involved in test interpretation includes possible overuse of the "Yes" subcategory "Not affected"; total number of diagnostic items checked "Yes"; and the overall pattern of the subject's responses among the four

"Yes" subcategories. The various raw scores are translated into normalized standard scores, most of them based on the 1,030 subjects used in the original factor analysis. The EQ is rather complicated to score by hand. Machine scoring is possible.

Internal consistency measures (KR-20) reported for the 1,193 subjects noted above range from .59 to .79 for the 10 diagnostic scales, and .70 to .83 for the four factor scales. Many of the intercorrelations among scales are fairly high, although generally not as high as scale reliabilities. Test-retest reliability (stability) coefficients are not available for the EQ, and neither are correlations between the alternate forms. Additional normative and reliability data, especially on cases not involved in the factor derivations and on female subjects, are obviously needed.

The main form of reported validity with respect to the stated test purpose of assessing emotional health appears to consist of comparisons between the 1,030 employed men and the 163 psychiatric patients referred to earlier. By this criterion 7 of the 10 diagnostic scales and all 4 of the factor scales show significant between-group differences at the .01 level or better. While encouraging, these findings are obviously limited. It is not particularly striking that the test distinguishes significantly between gainfully employed men and psychiatric patients, especially when the *N*s are large. The psychiatric sample included various diagnoses, but 75% were schizophrenic reaction. Clearly there is a pressing need to determine whether and in what respects the EQ can distinguish among types and degrees of psychiatric disability. An early study (Pishkin, Olson, & Jacobs, 1961) offers a promising beginning to such research, and more recent reports (Hoffman-Delvaux & Mertens, 1977; 1978) suggest the test may be useful in studying certain somatic disorders. With respect to the identification of worker or management level individuals who have interfering degrees of maladjustment, the preferable criterion groups would seem to consist of specifically indicated maladjusted persons from these groups, rather than psychiatric patients.

The 1,030 subjects in the employed sample represented a variety of occupations, and there were a number of differences on EQ scales among the different occupational groups, suggesting that the test is of potential value in personnel psychology. The instrument has been usefully employed in a large-scale study of bus operators (Baehr, Penny, & Froemel, 1980) and also in selection studies for police patrolmen, supermarket store managers, and marketing personnel. These studies included a number of ethnic minority subjects, and there is some reason to believe that the EQ may be of value in this area. One study (Jones & Boyd, 1968) reported the EQ to be a significant predictor of successful vocational training.

Although it is obvious that a great deal of additional work is needed on the EQ before it can be considered as a serious competitor of such tests as the MMPI, Clinical Analysis Questionnaire (CAQ), and Millon Clinical Multiaxial Inventory (MCMI), the EQ does have a number of features which recommend it to research workers. It is brief and straightforward, and the item format, which focuses on specific experiences within the past month and provides for a range of answers, is an attractive and novel approach. The test's scales, while needing additional empirical support, refer to somewhat different dimensions than those in related inventories.

To sum up, the EQ is a promising and somewhat innovative test. Additional developmental work, particularly with female subjects and with respect to clinical uses of the instrument, are needed. For clinical applications the test must be considered as strictly a research instrument, but its use in occupational psychology, with proper cautions and with specific validations for particular applications, appears justified.

REVIEWER'S REFERENCES

Pishkin, V., Olson, L. O., & Jacobs, D. F. An objective attempt to analyze emotional interactions between psychiatric patients and nursing staff. JOURNAL OF CLINICAL PSYCHOLOGY, 1961, 17, 383–389.

Jones, L. W., & Boyd, E. D. PERFORMANCE RELATED TO INDICATORS OF POTENTIAL OF TUSKEGEE INSTITUTE MDTA TRAINEES. Tuskegee Institute, AL, 1968.

Hoffmann-Delvaux, C., & Mertens, C. Organization of defense mechanisms in patients suffering from myocardial infarction (French). ACTA PSYCHIATRICA BELGICA, 1977, 77, 379–398.

Hoffmann-Delvaux, C., & Mertens, C. Homogeneity of defense mechanisms in a group of infarct patients and impact of these defenses on the expression of their emotions (French). ACTA PSYCHIATRICA BELGICA, 1978, 78, 337–347.

Baehr, M. E., Penny, R. E., III, & Froemel, E. C. A VALIDATION AND ANALYSIS OF SELECTION PROCEDURES FOR MALE AND FEMALE BUS OPERATORS. Chicago, IL: Human Resources Center, University of Chicago, 1980.

[384]

The Employment Barrier Identification Scale. Ages 15 and over; 1982–83; EBIS; to assess potential barriers to employment for CETA participants and others; no data on reliability and validity; no norms; manual ('82, 16 pages); 1984 price data: $30 per 25 scales and manual; [30] minutes; John M. McKee, Susan M. Pirhalla, and Bettye B. Burkhalter; Behavior Science Press.*

[385]

Emporia American Government Test. High school; 1978; EAGT; 1 form (6 pages); key (1 page); manual of directions (2 pages); 1983 price data: $4.75 per 25 tests including manual; $.20 per key; $1.50 per specimen set; (40–60) minutes; Earl Rohrbaugh, Robert Zwier, and David J. Hurt; Bureau of Educational Measurements.*

Review of Emporia American Government Test by HERBERT C. RUDMAN, Professor of Measurement, Evaluation and Research Design,

College of Education, Michigan State University, East Lansing, MI:

The Emporia American Government Test was designed to be used in the secondary schools of Kansas. It replaces an older American Government test that had been used for many years in some Kansas schools. According to a single two-sided sheet that accompanies the test, it "covers theory and factual data concerning government and problems which assess the student's ability to apply his/her knowledge." The test is designed to be used as either a pretest or a summative measure at the end of the course.

The student is asked to respond to 75 items which ostensibly sample the domain of American Government as taught in an 11th-grade high school class. The items are written in a multiple-choice format, and the student chooses the best answer among four options. Students may mark their responses directly on the test or on a separate answer sheet.

Several important issues of test development are considered in this review: (1) validity, (2) reliability, (3) norming procedures used, and (4) test content. These issues were deemed important in light of what appeared to be a norm population that was limited in size and scope, and content that was not well-defined in the peripheral material which accompanied the test.

VALIDITY. A reasonable expectation of a test represented as a measure of academic achievement is some description of its content, and some evidence that that content is a representative sample of the content that students study; in short, a statement of content validity. Unfortunately, the potential user of the Emporia American Government Test will find little or no information on content validity, and none at all on the guiding constructs that led to item development.

The limited information which accompanies this test indicates that its content is "based on the content of current American government courses," but offers no evidence of instructional materials examined, no evidence of the major concepts which drove the development of test items, and offers no conceptual structure of the domain sampled. From a conversation with one of the test developers, this reviewer must conclude that the test content was based solely on the judgments of authors who were social science specialists on the staff of Emporia State University. Judgments of authors are essential, but these judgments would have been strengthened had they supplied potential users with descriptive information about the test's content. A test user should have available specific information about a test's content if estimates are to be made about a student's level of academic attainment based on the results of a specific test.

Although not stated in the descriptive information available, one might assume that the authors relied on "face validity"—the appearance of the test—rather than on content validity to buttress their claim that the test is designed to "assess the student's ability to apply his/her knowledge" to problems of American government content studied in secondary schools. Face validity is a poor basis for making such an inference.

RELIABILITY. A Kuder-Richardson (KR21) reliability of .87 is indicated for the Emporia American Government Test. Since this estimate is based on the assumption that all items are of equal difficulty, this reliability estimate is probably low. Even though no written documentation is available concerning the range of item difficulties, a conversation with one of the test's authors indicated that the items ranged in difficulty from a p value of 25 to one of 75. It would probably have been better to use the KR20 as an estimate of reliability.

NORMING PROCEDURES. The Emporia American Government Test was standardized on 3,572 high school students in 90 secondary schools located in Kansas. The standardization took place in the spring of 1978. Although not stated in the descriptive material which accompanies the test, one of the test's authors indicated to this reviewer that almost all of the schools used in the norm population were small rural high schools. All schools used were volunteered for the project. No evidence is available to indicate how those schools in the norm population are similar or different from those schools which did not volunteer, an important lack of information particularly in the absence of any accompanying demographic information about the norm group. No evidence is available about the ethnic and racial composition of the students used in the norm group, no socioeconomic characteristics are available (educational level of parents, income and the like), and no evidence is presented on population size of communities in which the norm schools were located nor whether the schools included private as well as public schools. The user of this test should be wary of drawing any conclusions concerning the status of knowledge of his or her students. There simply is not enough information supplied to warrant any generalizations to any group not included in the norm population used for this test.

TEST CONTENT. An item count reveals that 62 items (83%) were written as relatively low-order recall exercises, and only 13 (17%) of the items required any kind of higher-order intellectual skill (generalizing, analyzing, drawing inferences, relating isolated facts). The Emporia American Government Test was judged to be poorly balanced in light of its stated objective of assessing "the student's ability to apply his/her knowledge."

Since the Emporia American Government Test was written to replace a similar kind of test that had been used for a number of years, one can safely assume that this test, like it predecessor, will also be used for a long time. Therefore, it would seem to be important that the items used would not be easily "dated" by changing events. A few items are dated even in this new edition.

Several items are based on stereotypes (e.g., "Which of the following is least likely to vote for a candidate of the Democratic Party: 1. a blue collar worker 2. a banker 3. a Jew 4. a black").

It must be said, in fairness to the authors of this test, that the Emporia American Government Test was not envisioned as an assessment to be used on a widespread national basis (although the impetus to develop it, according to one of its authors, came from another state which had—in the past—used its predecessor to help certify teachers). While standards for tests should be applied differentially according to their uses, there still needs to be a striving for excellence in test construction on a local level as well as on a national one. When normally accepted standards of test construction are applied to this test, it seems to fall short in terms of (1) clearly defined purposes for which it should be used, (2) a clearly defined taxonomy of concepts and skills to be measured, and (3) an adequate norm base for general use within the State of Kansas.

[386]

Endeavor Instructional Rating System. College; 1973–79; EIRS; student ratings of courses and instructors; 9 scores: 7 item scores (hard work, advanced planning, class discussion, personal help, presentation clarity, grade accuracy, increased knowledge), and 2 composite scores (student perception of achievement, student-instructor rapport); 1 form ('74, IBM prepunched card); user's handbook ('79, 19 pages); 1985 price data: $.05 per rating card; $2 per handbook; (5–10) minutes; Peter W. Frey; the Author.

See T3:818 (2 references); for a review by Kenneth O. Doyle, Jr., see 8:370 (5 references).

TEST REFERENCES

1. Ames, R., & Lau, S. An attributional approach to the validity of student ratings of instruction. CONTEMPORARY EDUCATIONAL PSYCHOLOGY, 1979, 4, 26–39.

[Note: After the reviews below were received and edited, the Editor was informed that the scoring service was no longer available.—Ed.]

Review of Endeavor Instructional Rating System by DOUGLAS B. EAMON, Associate Professor of Psychology, University of Houston-Clear Lake, Houston, TX:

The brevity of the Endeavor Instructional Rating System (EIRS) may suggest, at first glance, that it is something any educational psychologist with a little computer training could put together in a few minutes of spare time. It most definitely is not.

EIRS is the distillation of a continuing effort (since 1971) to develop a valid and reliable instrument for summative evaluation of teacher performance. The seven 7-point rating items are thoughtfully selected based on considerable empirical research, and the summary information is much more comprehensible than other systems using more items. The authors attempted to exclude, with good reason, items which require the student to judge the professional competence or knowledge of the teacher, and tried to focus on items which the student can observe in a classroom or laboratory setting. One might quarrel with the ability of students to observe whether "Each class period was carefully planned in advance" (usually interpreted to mean that the instructor closely followed the syllabus, daily outline, or textbook), but the overall impression is that the items are as objective as possible given the subjective nature of such evaluations.

The computer card format ("porta-punch" cards) is clear, readable, and easy to use. Use of only seven rating items allows the perforated punch positions to be widely spaced, resulting in a format that is less prone to error through mis–punching or damage to the cards.

The system is impressively documented; 39 references or citations are provided in the 16-page User's Handbook, many of these by the EIRS development team. The Handbook provides a brief history of the development of the system including the rationale for its current format, instructions for administration (to both teachers and administrators), documented evidence of the validity and reliability of the system, a description of the EIRS summary, and guidelines for interpreting the summaries along with a discussion of potential sources of bias.

This last point is a particularly important one. Developers of instructional rating systems are sometimes less cautious in their claims about the generalizability and usefulness of the summaries; EIRS repeatedly warns administrators of known sources of bias in this and other such systems, and suggests specific procedures to reduce these biases. For example, that students in different majors tend to rate instructors differently on some items is addressed by providing "thematic groupings" of courses within which comparisons can more legitimately be made. Unfortunately, this is the only grouping available. It might be equally useful, however, to provide such comparisons for groupings based on class size, course level, required/elective courses, and so on.

Summary information returned after the cards have been processed by the EIRS group is clear and complete. Administrators receive two bound volumes of the entire set of materials, which allows comparison of instructors on two "global" factors (described below) as well as on individual rating items. Included are frequency counts for each possible response to each item, mean item ratings, standard deviations, a histogram showing responses to each item, and a scatter plot with each course located on the two global factors. Individual instructors receive the same information (for their courses), except that the identities of the other instructors are hidden.

The global factors, "Pedagogical Skill" and "Rapport," are weighted sums of mean ratings for selected items. Scatter plots locate each course on these axes. Since all courses in a thematic group are shown (only the particular instructor's course is labelled by name), they can provide an interesting and very usable visual comparison on two principal components of effective instruction. An instructor might, for example, rate high on pedagogical skill but low on rapport, or vice versa. One might hope that such information in an easily digestible form could be used by administrators and faculty committees, who often have a tendency to seek a single numerical value for each instructor.

The rationale for the weightings is, however, not provided. Why is the item "Class discussion was welcome in this course" weighted +.5 on the rapport factor but −.2 on the pedagogical skill factor? Presumably, some sort of statistical procedure was used here, but I wish I knew what it was.

As with any system, there exists the potential for ambiguity and abuse. Psychologists, for example, might wonder in which thematic group their courses should be placed (e.g., physical sciences, health sciences, social sciences, humanities?). Some administrators and committees will continue to use such numerical ratings as the sole evaluation of teacher effectiveness, in spite of the admonitions of the authors. And some will simply use the average of the items, or compute the average of the global factors, in order to arrive at a single value on which all instructors can be scaled, in effect throwing away much of the information as well as the philosophy of EIRS.

Still, the Endeavor system clearly rates as one of the most usable and best instructional ratings systems currently available.

Review of Endeavor Instructional Rating System by ROBERT H. ZABEL, Associate Professor of Administration and Foundations, Kansas State University, Manhattan, KS:

Unlike many other rating systems designed to elicit students' evaluations of classroom instruction, the Endeavor Instructional Rating System (EIRS) is intended only for use in "summative," as opposed to "formative," evaluation. This very short, seven-item form is not designed to be used by faculty as a guide to instructional improvement, but rather by administrators to help them evaluate their faculty's teaching performance.

An attractively prepared User's Handbook addresses the purpose and uses of the system, construction of the form, and directions for administration; reviews studies examining reliability, validity, and possible biases of the instrument; and provides guidelines for interpretation of results.

The questionnaire itself consists of a computer card with seven statements alternately printed on light and dark backgrounds to enhance readability. Students respond to each statement by punching out the perforated "chad" corresponding with their assessment of each statement in relation to the course. The response field consists of seven categories on a frequency dimension (i.e., never=1, seldom=2 or 3, sometimes=4, often=5 or 6, and always=7). Although unsuccessful attempts to provide discriminative labels for the 2 and 3 and the 5 and 6 categories are reviewed, there is no explanation for the decision to retain seven categories rather than five.

On the seventh item ("The course has increased my knowledge and competence in this area"), the rating categories change, with only the extreme points labeled (very little=1 and very much=7). There is no discussion of the possible effects of this switch on possible rating errors or of the difficulty of discriminating among the intervening points on the scale.

The chad punching system has an advantage over optically scanned computer scored evaluation systems in that pencils need not be provided. Disadvantages of this technique are that students are unable to change their ratings and that chad must be disposed of properly.

Ratings are computer scored by Endeavor Instructional Rating Systems and returned to the college/university coordinator for distribution to appropriate administrators and evaluated instructors. The printouts include four copies of the rating summaries of all instructors within the thematic instructional group predetermined by the institution (e.g., academic department, course sections). Included on the first page is a tabular comparison of the ratings on each of the seven items for all instructors within the group. Group means for each item are also provided. A second page provides a scatter-plot of the ratings on two composite factors, "Pedagogical Skill" and "Rapport," for all instructors in the group. Individual instructors receive copies of their own evaluation data only from these two pages.

A third page provides the frequency, mean, and standard deviation on each item for each instructor and calculated, weighted scores for the two factors. Although it appears that these calculated composite scores are based upon previously determined factor loadings, there is no explanation of the item weightings. A fourth page presents a frequency histogram displaying the proportion of students' ratings in each response category. A final page includes tables of the mean ratings for each department and for the entire institution.

The User's Handbook includes considerable detail on the construction of the EIRS. The current seven items have been selected from much longer predecessor forms that have been successively subjected to factor analysis. Based upon these procedures, the relatively small number of items in the present form are purported to be both reliable and representative items for the two composite factors.

A number of published studies relating to the reliability and validity of the instrument are available. They provide some evidence of the stability of ratings over time, the consistency of ratings within classes, and the consistency of ratings of the same instructor by different classes, particularly for items constituting the "Pedagogical Skill" factor. Evidence of reliability of the "Rapport" items is admittedly not as strong.

Issues related to the instrument's content validity have been considered in the manual in the context of deliberate avoidance of ratings of either instructor's professional knowledge or enthusiasm. Based upon cited research, the former is considered a characteristic students are not qualified to judge, and the latter as neutral with respect to pedagogical skill. Criterion validity has been examined by studying correlations between students' ratings and their final exam performance. High median correlations have been found for the "Pedagogical Skill" ratings, with much lower correlations for the "Rapport" items. Lest this be cited as evidence of a simple grade for rating trade-off, contrary evidence is provided of low within class correlations between ratings of some items and grades.

There is some research evidence that students' ratings, especially of the "Rapport" items, are affected by such factors as instructor's grading leniency, class size, class level, instructor's academic rank, and students' majors. Other factors which may affect ratings but have not yet been examined are sex of instructor and student motivation to take the course. Thus, users must exercise caution when interpreting evaluation results and use them only in the context of other information about the instructor's teaching performance.

The major advantages of the EIRS are its brevity, systematic development, well-organized and clearly written "User's Handbook," and diverse presentation of results. Limitations of the instrument include questionable reliability and validity of the "Rapport" items, absence of guidelines for improving instruction, and the absence of norms for courses of similar description, size, level (e.g., undergraduate vs. graduate), instructional format (e.g., lab vs. lecture), and student motivation. Like other standardized teaching evaluation systems, such as the IDEA (Kansas State University) or the Student Instructional Report (Educational Testing Service), the EIRS provides quantitative scores that can easily be used to make comparisons among instructors. However, like the other rating systems, these should not be used in isolation.

[387]

[The Endler Anxiety Scales]. High school and college and normal and institutionalized adults; 1962–80; battery of 3 research instruments based on interactionist personality theory; norms consist of means and standard deviations; no manual; separate answer sheets must be used; price information available from publisher; administration time not reported; Norman S. Endler, J. McV. Hunt, Alvin J. Rosenstein, and Marilyn Okada; Norman S. Endler [Canada].*

a) S-R INVENTORY OF GENERAL TRAIT ANXIOUSNESS. S-R GTA; multidimensional measure of the intensity of trait anxiety; title on test is Inventory of Attitudes Toward General Situations; 1 form ('80, 5 pages).

b) THE PRESENT AFFECT REACTIONS QUESTIONNAIRE IV. PARQ IV; measures the cognitive and physiological aspects of state anxiety; 1 form ('80, 2 pages).

c) THE PERCEPTION OF SITUATIONS RATING FORM. PSRF; subjective perception of anxiety producing situations; 1 form ('80, 2 pages).

[388]

English Language Skills Assessment in a Reading Context. Beginning, intermediate, and advanced students of English as a second language from upper elementary to college and adult students; 1980–81; ELSA; criterion-referenced; 5 tests; no suggested standards of mastery; 3 levels; technical manual ('81, 37 pages); separate answer sheets must be used; 1983 price data: $8.95 per set of testing materials for any one test including 25 tests, 50 answer sheets, and 1 answer key; $3.95 per technical manual; (30) minutes per test; Cecelia Doherty and Donna Ilyin (technical manual); Newbury House Publishers, Inc.*

a) BEGINNING LEVEL. 2 tests: Conversation ('80, 4 pages), Narrative ('80, 4 pages); separate answer sheet/practice test ('80, 2 pages) for each test; Donna Ilyin, Lynn Levy (Conversation test), and Lauri E. Fried Lee (Narrative test).

b) INTERMEDIATE LEVEL. Test and answer sheet/practice test information same as *a* above; Donna Ilyin, Cecelia Doherty (Conversation test), and Lauri E. Fried Lee (Narrative test).

c) ADVANCED LEVEL. Narrative test ('80, 4 pages); answer sheet/practice test ('80, 2 pages); Cecelia Doherty and Donna Ilyin.

[389]

English Skills Assessment. Grades 11–12 and first year of post-secondary education; 1969–82; ESA; ACER adaptation of STEP Series and DTLS by Educational Testing Service and The College Board; 10 or 11 scores: Part I (spelling, punctuation and capitalization, comprehension I, total), Part II (comprehension II, usage, vocabulary, sentence structure, logical relationships [optional], total), total; tentative norms, publisher recommends use of local norms; 1 form consists of 2 parts: Part I ('82, 12 pages) and Part II ('82, 20 pages); interim manual ('82, 46 pages); separate self-scoring answer sheets must be used; 1984 price data: A$1.50 per reusable test booklet of either Part I or II; $12.50 per 20 answer sheets of either part; $6.30 per manual; $10.55 per specimen set; 50(60) minutes for Part I, 60(70) minutes for Part II; Australian Council for Educational Research [Australia].*

Review of English Skills Assessment by JOHN C. SHERWOOD, Professor of English, University of Oregon, Eugene, OR:

The English Skills Assessment Test is an adaptation for Australian use of two ETS batteries: the Sequential Tests of Educational Progress Series II, forms 2A and 2B, for grades 10 through 12, and the Descriptive Tests of Language Skills for College Freshmen. The special character of the test requires a somewhat special approach in the review; we need to consider the test as a response to the needs of a particular group of students and also to consider its general quality as a testing instrument.

The American teacher casually inspecting this test would probably sense nothing unfamiliar about it nor anything specifically Australian; there are no bunyips or billabongs, nor anything else to confuse pommies and other outsiders. On a more careful inspection, however, the teacher would begin to notice usages which could be classified as British. Some are matters of vocabulary ("petrol") or spelling ("humour"), but in neither case would the outsider experience any trouble—the spelling errors offered for correction would be errors in any variety of English. The difference between British and American usage in matters of punctuation and especially in the use of quotation marks could be more troublesome but affects only a few items. In sum, the test offers some advantages for students trained in the British tradition but would not be unusable for students trained in the American. (I am not, of course, expecting to see this test imported for use in New Jersey, but the issue might be relevant in Asia.)

In judging the suitability of the test, however, the potential user has to consider more than the student's educational background; there is what might be called the testing situation. Note, to begin with, that for better or worse the test is intended for both secondary and post-secondary levels; it is for this reason that the adapters combined two American tests. Here is clearly something more than a placement test, a crude instrument for roughly separating the sheep from the goats. According to the adapters, the test can be used to "help teachers choose suitable instruction material for each student," to "identify students who require special assistance," to "determine the content of remedial programs," and to "promote student self-assessment." The test is not, like so many others, simply a test of mechanics; it tests what it calls "logical relationships," as well as "comprehension," or reading, including the reading of literature (which, however, is skimpily represented). There is a faith here not only in classification but also in diagnosis; the test will tell teacher and student not only that something is wrong but exactly what is wrong and what to do about it. Incidentally, the test comes without the massive if unconvincing proofs of validity which usually accompany an ETS product. According to the adapters, "because a test may be valid for one use or purpose and not another, it is the proposed interpretation of the test by the user that should be validated, not the actual test."

As to the quality of the items, I would judge them good or better, though I would note that item 31 under Punctuation cannot be made to produce a satisfactory sentence by any of the suggested alterations. The experienced teacher can always spot the correct answer, provided he or she accepts the implied standards of usage, which are very conservative; some of the issues seem trivial. The range of difficulty is very great, as might be expected when tests intended for different levels are combined. The most interesting items occur in the last two sections, "Sentence Structure" and "Logical Relationships." The first really tests the student's feeling for language and not merely a knowledge of mechanical rules; the second at least begins to get into matters of organization.

This adaptation is not one which can be unequivocally recommended, nor is it to be lightly disparaged. It obviously has advantages for students trained in the British tradition. Beyond this the teacher or administrator must ask some searching questions. Is it wise or necessary to test several levels and a variety of distinguishable issues in a single instrument? Could some of the issues be judged better from writing samples or even course grades? How suitable in practice are such tests for diagnosis? In the end the examiners themselves shift these decisions to the consumer.

[390]

Ennis-Weir Argumentation Test, Level X: An Essay Test of Rational Thinking Ability. Grades 7–12 and college; 1982; EWAT-X; no data on reliability of scores; no norms; 1 form (2 pages); mimeographed manual (17 pages plus test and criteria for grading); criteria for grading (1 page); 1983 price data: $.50 per test booklet and criterion sheet; $1 per manual; 40(50) minutes; Robert H. Ennis and Eric Weir; Illinois Thinking Project, University of Illinois at Urbana-Champaign.*

Review of Ennis-Weir Argumentation Test, Level X: An Essay Test of Rational Thinking

Ability by HERBERT C. RUDMAN, Professor of Measurement, Evaluation, and Research Design, Michigan State University, East Lansing, MI:

The number of available tests and measures is growing, as can be attested to by the briefest of perusals of the indexes of this *Ninth Mental Measurements Yearbook* as well as the contents of all of its illustrious predecessors. There is always room for still another educational or psychological measure, IF it is, (1) useful, (2) needed, (3) valid, (4) reliable, (5) demonstrably accurate, and (6) a contribution to our understanding of human behavior.

The Ennis-Weir Argumentation Test, Level X unfortunately falls short on four of these characteristics (useful, valid, reliable, demonstrably accurate), and its manual fails to demonstrate that the remaining two (needed, a contribution to our understanding of human behavior) have been addressed in any sufficient way. While it is important to be able to measure such higher-order mental skills as logic and criticism, this test is not one that will do that. It offers no strong evidence of reliability, no clear statement of validity, no norms by which to judge whatever logic is measured, and fails to demonstrate that the use of this test will serve as a contribution to our understanding of human behavior.

EWAT-X, as the authors refer to this test, is founded on an interesting but limited premise. The authors state that EWAT-X is a "general test of rational thinking ability in the context of argumentation." In fact, it is neither a "general" test of rational thinking, nor is it a test of "rational" behavior. It is, as the authors make clear a bit further in the manual, a test of how effectively one can evaluate arguments.

The EWAT-X consists of (1) a one-page letter written to the editor of a newspaper urging the adoption of an ordinance which would prohibit overnight parking on public streets; (2) a scoring sheet which contains nine criteria for scoring the EWAT-X and six scores which range from -1 to $+3$; and (3) a 15-page manual which contains short and wholly inadequate descriptions of such vital topics as reliability, validity, the uses to which the test can be put, and the administration and grading of the test. A second part of the manual examines each of the nine paragraphs of the letter and offers some insights into the beliefs of the authors concerning "good" argumentation.

The test is predicated upon a paragraph-by-paragraph analysis of the test-letter with the objective of writing a short essay supporting or refuting each paragraph of the test-letter as well as a summary paragraph evaluating the argument presented. In the words of the authors, "The test is designed to be used in assessing ability to evaluate and respond to arguments as they occur naturally in discussion, disputation, and debate in the real world. It is not a test of formal or deductive argument, nor does it require technical knowledge of such. In comparison with arguments considered in many deductive logic tests, arguments in the real-world require considerable interpretation...require evaluation of content as well as form, often have value dimensions, and do not have mechanical decision procedures. This test is a real world test."

One could reasonably argue that the Ennis-Weir Argumentation Test is not a test at all, but some device that falls somewhere between a psychological measure and an evaluation instrument. It may be a measure of the characteristics of argumentation and an approximation of what the Phi Delta Kappa National Study Commission on Evaluation (1971, p. xxv) defined as evaluation (i.e., "the process of delineating, obtaining, and providing useful information for judging decision alternatives"). It is described by its authors in terms that vacillate between a "correct" judgment of an argument offered in the test-letter, to a rejection of "mechanical decision procedures." All told, it is a difficult measure to score, and almost meaningless to interpret.

TEST USE. The authors offer the test as a discussion-generator in a class that might be discussing "informal logic." They make no claim for a comprehensive survey of this type of logic but do state that most elements of informal logic are contained within the test-letter.

A more startling claim is made for the instrument as a diagnostic tool that could identify "specific areas of reasoning or argumentation with which students may need help." However, one is hard-pressed to find an item-by-item or paragraph-by-paragraph description which clearly enough delineates the concepts embedded within them. Without these conceptual statements, and some norms to accompany them, what kind of diagnosis can be made? How does one judge when something is lacking and the degree of that condition? How does one diagnose, armed with a statement such as the following from the scoring guide which accompanies the EWAT-X? "These criteria are guidelines. Graders should use judgment in awarding points, subtracting for unspecified errors, and adding for unspecified insights."

Another recommended use for the test is as a device for evaluating "effectiveness of instruction" in informal logic. But the next sentence which follows states, "Since there are as yet no norms for the test, it cannot be used to compare a tested group with an untested group."

Probably the most puzzling of all statements is to be found in the last paragraph describing the possible uses of EWAT-X. "The EWAT-X is probably most appropriate for use with high school and college students. However, we have checked its suitability for use with junior high school and grade school students. In the latter case, six sixth grade students...read the directions for taking the test and the letter and were quizzed by their teacher to test their understanding. All of the students were judged able to understand the directions without difficulty, and all were able to paraphrase the contents of the letter accurately. In addition, their teachers reported that the students enjoyed the exercise very much."

There is no indication, however, how the EWAT-X was judged to be most appropriate for high school and college students.

RELIABILITY. Twenty-seven students in one college level course in an unidentified subject were the basis for establishing some measure of the reliability of the EWAT-X. Three raters were used to establish an interrater reliability of approximately .74. Two raters were identified as professors who had taught information logic, and the other rater was a graduate student.

VALIDITY. This reviewer was puzzled by the following statement: "The type of validity most appropriately claimed for EWAT-X is content validity (in the old-fashioned sense)." I have no idea what the "old-fashioned sense" can be. Content validity addresses the question, "Does the content of the test reflect the content of the instructional materials used by the students for the study of this subject?" Content validity in this sense is inappropriate for the EWAT-X.

Construct validity is what should be demonstrated by the authors and it is sorely lacking. Their only discussion of construct validity appears in the following sentence: "While questions of construct validity are certainly appropriate for a test purporting to measure rational thinking ability, claims about the construct validity of the EWAT-X are premature." So it would appear is the publication of this test for public use.

REVIEWER'S REFERENCES

Phi Delta Kappa National Study Committee on Evaluation. EDUCATIONAL EVALUATION AND DECISION-MAKING. Bloomington, IN: Phi Delta Kappa, 1971.

[391]

The Ennis-Weir Critical Thinking Essay Test: An Instrument for Testing/Teaching. High school and college; 1983; "a general test of critical thinking ability in the context of argumentation"; norms consist of means and standard deviations; 1 form (2 pages); manual (23 pages including test); 1984 price data: $.20 per test; $.10 per answer sheet; $2.50 per manual including test; (45) minutes; Robert H. Ennis and Eric Weir; Illinois Thinking Project, University of Illinois at Urbana-Champaign.*

[392]

Enright Diagnostic Inventory of Basic Arithmetic Skills. Grades 1–8; 1983; EDIBA; "criterion-referenced"; 144 skills in 3 areas: whole numbers, fractions, decimals; no norms; 1 form (511 pages plus instructions for administration and scoring); no manual; student workbook (127 pages plus arithmetic record book); arithmetic record book (17 pages); individual progress record for decimals, whole numbers, fractions (1 page); 1983 price data: $79.95 per complete set including 10 arithmetic record books; $13.95 per 10 arithmetic record books; $29.50 per 10 student workbooks; $14.95 per 30 individual progress records; administration time not reported; Brian E. Enright; Curriculum Associates, Inc.*

[393]

Entry-Level Professional Test. Persons entering professional and technical and managerial occupations; 1983; EPT; 4 subtests (Reading Comprehension, Quantitative Reasoning, Tabular Completion, Inference) measuring 3 cognitive abilities (verbal comprehension, quantitative problem solving, reasoning); norms for 3 occupations only, publisher recommends use of local norms; 1 form (43 pages); manual (38 pages); administrator's guide (8 pages); separate answer sheets must be used; price data available from publisher; 180(210) minutes; Psychological Services, Inc.*

[394]

Environmental Language Inventory. Children with severe delay in expressive language; 1974–78; ELI; revision of earlier ('74) edition of ELI; measures what and how to teach a child whose communication is limited to one- and two-word utterances; item scores are derived on 3 dimensions (8 semantic-grammatical rules, utterance length, intelligibility) across 4 communication situations (conversation 1, imitation, conversation 2, free play); individual; 1 form ('78, 11 pages); manual ('78, 60 pages plus instructional programming materials); 1983 price data: $10.95 per package of 12 score forms; $10.95 per manual; (30–45) minutes; James D. MacDonald; Charles E. Merrill Publishing Co.*

Review of Environmental Language Inventory by MARTIN FUJIKI, Assistant Professor of Speech Pathology and Audiology, University of Nevada, Reno, Reno, NV:

The Environmental Language Inventory (ELI) is designed to provide information regarding both the evaluation and treatment of language disordered children. In this respect, the ELI is one of the few tools that focuses upon semantic relationships. However, in utilizing this test, there are a number of issues to consider.

Perhaps the most important point to note is that the ELI must be used within certain distinct limits. For example, consider the population with which the test may be used. It is implied by the manual that this test may be used with a wide range of ages (two years through adult level) and handicaps (mental retardation, cerebral palsy, autism). While this is true, it must be stressed that the critical factor determining the usefulness of the ELI is not age or handicap, but linguistic level of development. This procedure is most useful with children near the two-word level. If the child is beyond this level of development, the ELI is unable to adequately characterize the linguistic system. This limitation stems from the fact that all utterances produced by the child are scored using eight basic two-element semantic-grammatic rules. For example, a two-word combination such as "Daddy go" is characterized as "agent + action." Similarly, longer utterances are also analyzed according to these two element rules. Thus, a sentence such as "He pushed ball here." would be scored as "agent + action, action + object, agent + object, and X + location." Such an analysis ignores the fact that the child is able to produce a single sentence combining four semantic relations (agent + action + object + locative), which more accurately characterizes the child's linguistic system.

Another factor that limits the application of this instrument to individuals at the one- and two-word utterance level is the fact that it examines only eight semantic-grammatic rules. While such an analysis may account for many of the two-word utterances produced by a speaker at the two-word level, it ignores a variety of linguistic data produced by even a moderately more sophisticated speaker. Thus, when the child's linguistic system has developed beyond the two-word level, or when the examiner wishes to gain information about other aspects of language, other methods of analysis may be more profitable. A traditional language sample would be the most obvious procedure to utilize.

Another area of discussion is the scoring system of the ELI. This test produces the following scores: frequency of appearance of the semantic-grammatic rules, mean length of utterance (MLU) of all utterances, MLU for intelligible utterances only, proportion of intelligible words, and frequency of unintelligible multiple-word utterances. Each of these scores may be produced in imitation, conversation, and play.

The MLU and intelligibility scores provide useful information regarding various aspects of the child's language ability. Further, comparisons between contexts (i.e., between imitation and play) may reveal clinically useful information. However, the frequency, proportion, and rank order scores for the semantic-grammatic rules are somewhat more difficult to utilize.

The proportion score has only indirect clinical relevance. The author notes that this score is obtained for experimental purposes and to provide more detail regarding the child's linguistic ability. The same might be said of the rank order scores. For both types of scores it is difficult to judge at what point a difference between observed performance and test norms becomes significant. In fairness to the author, it may be noted that it is not clear that these scores were intended to be used in this manner.

The frequency score provided by the ELI has the strongest implications for clinical intervention. Assuming that the test accurately measures the child's ability, low frequency of occurrence figures may indicate rules with which the child is having difficulty. On this note, the ELI might be strengthened with additional normative data to aid the clinician in deciding when a frequency is significantly low (or different) as to merit clinical attention. Data concerning measures of central tendency and variability would be helpful in this regard. These are not provided by the test manual.

A final point of discussion in this review concerns reliability. The reliability evidence presented in the test manual deals with various aspects of intratest and test-retest reliability. While the data presented are supportive, the data base from which this support is drawn is marginal. All the reliability data are drawn from two studies involving a total of 10 subjects. Five of these subjects were mentally retarded children between the ages of 3 and 7 years at the one- and two-word spontaneous language level. The remaining five subjects were mentally retarded individuals between the ages of 6 and 9 years, with a three- to four-word spontaneous language level. The fact that reliability data require a generalization from mentally retarded individuals to all other types of individuals with whom the test might be used is a matter of concern. This generalization requires the test user to assume that all children to be tested perform in the same manner as mentally retarded children. It is not clear that this generalization can be reliably made. An additional problem is that the subjects are not described in the manual in any more detail than has been reported in this review. Thus, it is difficult to judge how these subjects would compare to any other specific population.

The ELI may be a useful measure when utilized within the limitations noted. As has been stated, the ELI is one of the few tests to focus on semantic relations, and it may be a valuable resource for the examiner in need of such a tool. The examiner may want to utilize the ELI in conjunction with other procedures, or to extend the free play portion of the ELI in order to gain a broader picture of the child's linguistic abilities.

[395]

Environmental Prelanguage Battery. Children with language-delays functioning at or below the single-word level; 1978; EPB; revision of first edition (1975); criterion-referenced; item scores in 14 or 15 areas: foundations in communication (functional play, motor imitation), early receptive language (identifying objects, understanding action verbs, identifying pictures), following directions (optional), nonverbal total, sound imitation, single words (noun imitation, noun production, action verb production, other categories), beginning social conversation (two-word phrase imitation, more word phrase production), verbal total; no data on reliability; no norms, authors provide general age equivalents but do not recommend they be reported with an individual's score; individual; 1 form (14 pages); manual (90 pages including pictorial test stimuli); 1984 price data: $10.95 per package of 12 score forms; $8.95 per manual; administration time not reported; DeAnna S. Horstmeier and James D. MacDonald; Charles E. Merrill Publishing Co.*

Review of Environmental Prelanguage Battery by JOHN T. HATTEN, Professor of Communicative Disorders, University of Minnesota, Duluth, Duluth, MN:

The authors of the Environmental Prelanguage Battery (EPB) indicate that the purpose of the battery is to assess and *train* the prelinguistic skills necessary for the development of spoken language. The adequacy of the battery must be judged relative to the appropriateness of the behaviors the authors select as prerequisite to the development of verbal language, the efficacy of the evaluation procedures, and the scoring and data base of the test.

Although the authors make liberal use of the words "diagnostic" and "test" the battery is neither. It appears to be best described as a structured observational tool and as such it has substantial merit. The authors clearly display their knowledge of children who are difficult to test and provide substantial flexibility in test administration. The examiner is encouraged to seek information from parents, teachers, formal tests, or informal play and observation. Since standardized and structured "tests" are often unsuccessful with young developmentally delayed children this measure offers a useful process to collect information regarding language development.

A unique characteristic of this battery is the attempt to measure the child's teachability of skills being measured. If an item is failed the examiner is instructed to attempt to "train" the behavior and test the skill again. This process helps the examiner to determine how ready the child is to acquire the skill. This procedure is not only useful as an assessment process but also leads directly to language instruction through the use of a companion program, Ready, Set, Go: Talk to Me, which is also published by Charles E. Merrill.

Since this battery measures receptive and expressive language it is curious that it is titled a prelanguage battery. It should more properly be called a pre-syntax battery or an early language battery since many of the behaviors evaluated are linguistic and not prelinguistic in nature.

The selection of skills to be evaluated is vitally important to the value of such an instrument. This reviewer would much prefer assessment of preverbal symbolic play in greater depth than is provided. For example, the procedures described by Westby (1980) or Nicholich (1977) would be more helpful. More extensive measures of cognitive functioning also appear appropriate. Relative to prelinguistic skills, the reviewer would expect to find more extensive evaluation of such early communication skills as mutual referencing, joint play routines, turntaking, parent-child play and communication, and other preverbal communication systems. Since the publication of the EPB a very helpful evaluation process for such skills has been developed by MacDonald and his co-workers. The prelanguage skills measured in the ECOMAPS (1984) program provide the examiner with a much richer evaluation of a child's early prelinguistic communication level. The EBP appears to be rather narrowly focused on preverbal skills and fails to provide adequate information on a child's communication skills, which appear to be much more important to the development of functional language through any modality.

The scoring procedure used by the EPB is generally helpful but appears to be provided somewhat as an afterthought. A particularly helpful aspect is the measurement of the child's rapidity of learning a particular skill, which should provide insight into the readiness for specific learning tasks. Although the objective scoring procedures are provided with no reference to normative data, reliability, or validity, they can be useful in measuring individual progress with a particular child by providing pre- and postintervention accountability data. Information on language age is provided but is clearly intended for information only and is not to be reported as a part of the child's test score.

SUMMARY. The EPB has several unique characteristics which make it of interest to those working with very young preverbal and early verbal children. It adapts easily to the difficult-to-test child, provides direct suggestions for intervention, and it measures how ready the child is to learn various preverbal tasks. The inherent subjectivity which comes with the test flexibility is well worth the risks since the target children are too often misevaluated through strict adherence to formal and unforgiving measures.

The primary difficulty with the EPB appears to be its preverbal rather than prelanguage nature as reflected in the selection of test items. The user is encouraged to go beyond the test and accept it as a part of a total precommunication battery which may include the ECOMAPS (1984) program also published by the author.

REVIEWER'S REFERENCES

Nicholich, L. M. Beyond sensorimotor intelligence: Assessment of symbolic maturity through analysis of pretend play. MERRILL-PALMER QUARTERLY, 1977, 23, 89–99.

Westby, C. E. Assessment of cognitive and language abilities through play. LANGUAGE, SPEECH, AND HEARING SERVICES IN SCHOOLS, 1980, XI, 154–168.

MacDonald, J. D., & Gillette, Y. ECOMAPS, A MANUAL FOR ASSESSING LANGUAGE THROUGH CONVERSATION. Columbus, OH: The Nisonger Center and Speech and Hearing Science Department, The Ohio State University, 1984.

Review of Environmental Prelanguage Battery by SAMUEL KNAPP, Psychologist, Rosalie G. Handler Center, Millersburg, PA:

The Environmental Prelanguage Battery (EPB) tests prelanguage and language skills. It is designed primarily for mentally retarded or language delayed children, but it may also be adapted for use with children with physical handicaps, or for persons with less than one-word vocabularies. The EPB is not a pure diagnostic instrument. Its primary purpose is to serve as the assessment portion of the Environmental Language Inventory (ELI), a comprehensive training program for persons with delayed language or prelanguage skills.

The EPB consists of a nonverbal and a verbal section. The nonverbal section includes foundations of communication skills such as the ability to attend to others, object permanence, gesture communication, and early receptive language development. The verbal section includes single word production and the beginnings of social conversation.

The administrative and interpretative procedures of the EPB reflect the emphasis on prescriptive teaching. For example, the test authors view language as a tool for social communication and believe that assessment and training should involve individuals in the child's environment. The parents are encouraged to be present during the assessment and may even administer some of the items. The presence of the parents has two purposes. First, it helps the child relax and perform at an optimal level. Second, it initiates the parents into the training program (which follows the assessment and requires their participation).

Much of the information gathered in the assessment is used for the training program. The EPB will provide a training level, an estimate of learning potential, and procedures which could maximize the learning progress of the language delayed individuals. The children are administered the test items, and, if they fail an item, an attempt is made to train them on that particular item. The children are then tested to determine the effectiveness of that training. The children receive 3 points for a response which is correct the first time, and 1 point for responses which are correct after training. The examiner learns the current functioning level of the child, their receptiveness to training, and the most effective means of training. Also, the examiner will observe behaviors which can be used in setting up the training program by noticing which behavioral reinforcers improve performance, or how physical handicaps impair performance.

The instructions in the EPB manual are explicit. The test is designed so that the examiner may deviate from standard administrative procedures to accommodate the needs of the children or to capitalize on their particular interests. For example, the examiner may attempt to incorporate test items into the natural play activities of the child.

Despite the explicit instructions in the manual, this reviewer found it helpful to read the Professionals Guide: A Trainers Manual for Ready, Set, Go and the Environmental Language Intervention Program. This manual further explains the rationale and format of the ELI, of which the EPB is an integral part.

According to the EPB manual, it can also be used as a pre- or posttest language assessment tool. The authors, however, acknowledge the limitation of the EPB in this regard. The research commonly found for psychometric tests is not reported and apparently does not exist. The EPB lacks data on reliability and validity and no standardization sample is reported. It provides general age equivalent scores, in months, but contains no developmental quotient or any standard score by which to quantify the child's level of linguistic skills.

In conclusion, the Environmental Prelanguage Battery was developed as a prescriptive component of the Environmental Language Inventory. It should not, however, be considered as a standard language assessment test. It is not appropriate for research purposes or for uses outside of the Environmental Language Inventory because of the lack of standard psychometric data.

[396]

Eosys Word Processing Aptitude Battery. Job candidates; 1983; WPAB; applicable for selection, allocation, and development of word processor operators; 5 independent tests: Verbal Skills (WP1), Checking Skills (WP2), Written Instructions (WP3), Coded Information (WP4), Numerical Computation (WP5); 1 form (39 pages, includes all 5 tests); manual and user's guide (59 pages); administration instructions for WP1, WP3, WP5, (2 pages) and WP2, WP4, (4 pages); command card, WP4 (2 pages); scoring keys (5 sheets); profile chart (1 page); score sheet (1 page); separate answer sheets must be used; 1984 price data: £80 per 10 test booklets including all 5 tests and command card for WP4 (reusable); £40 per set of scoring keys; £30 per 10 sets of answer sheets and profile; £2 per group score sheet; £30 per set of administration instructions; £50 per manual and user's guide; (10) minutes per WP1, WP2, WP5; (12) minutes per WP3; (15) minutes per WP4; Gill Nyfield, Susan Bawtree, Michael Pearn (test), David Hawkey (test), and Emma Bird (manual); Saville & Holdsworth Ltd. [England].*

[397]

ERB Comprehensive Testing Program II. Grades 1–2, 2.5–3, 3.5–6, 6.5–9, 9.5–12; 1974–83; CTP II; aptitude tests include the revised School and College Ability Test (SCAT III); no data on validity for aptitude tests; 2 forms; 5 levels; technical manual ('83, 110 pages); interpretive and normative manual ('84, 138 pages); directions for administration, levels 1 and 2 ('82, 85 pages), levels 3 to 5 ('82, 20 pages); 1983 price information: $4 per interpretive and normative manual; Educational Records Bureau; Educational Testing Service.*

a) ACHIEVEMENT TESTS, LEVEL 1. Grades 1–2; 1974–83; 4 scores: listening, mathematics, reading, word analysis; Forms C, D, ('82, 30 pages, MRC scorable); pilot test ('82, 3 pages); $19 per 20 tests; scoring service, $2.30 per test; (150–220) minutes in several sessions.

b) ACHIEVEMENT TESTS, LEVEL 2. Grades 2.5–3; 1974–83; 5 scores: listening, writing skills, mathematics, reading, word analysis; Forms C, D, (82, 36 pages, MRC scorable); price of test and scoring service same as for Level 1; (200–290) minutes in several sessions.

c) APTITUDE/ACHIEVEMENT TEST, LEVEL 3. Grades 3.5–6; 1974–83; 9 scores: aptitude (verbal, quantitative, total), vocabulary, reading comprehension, mechanics of writing, English expression, mathematics basic concepts, mathematics computation; Forms C, D, ('82, 72 pages); practice test ('83, 8 pages); separate answer sheets must be used; $31 per 20 tests; $11.20 per 50 answer sheets; $3.80 per scoring stencil; scoring service, $2 per test; 270(305) minutes in several sessions.

d) APTITUDE/ACHIEVEMENT TEST, LEVEL 4. Grades 6.5–9; 1974–83; 10 scores: aptitude (verbal, quantitative, total), vocabulary, reading comprehension, mechanics of writing, English expression, mathematics basic concepts, mathematics computation, algebra; Form C ('82, 92 pages), D ('82, 86 pages); answer sheet and price information same as for Level 3; 310(350) minutes in several sessions.

e) APTITUDE/ACHIEVEMENT TEST, LEVEL 5. Grades 9.5–12; 1974–83; 10 scores: aptitude (verbal, quantitative, total), vocabulary, reading comprehension, mechanics of writing, English expression, general mathematics, algebra, geometry; Forms C ('82, 95 pages), D ('82, 94 pages); answer sheet and price information same as for Level 3; 315(355) minutes in several sessions.

Review of ERB Comprehensive Testing Program II by KATHLEEN BARROWS CHESTERFIELD, Research Associate, Juarez and Associates, Los Angeles, CA:

The ERB Comprehensive Testing Program II (CTP II) is a generally well constructed battery of tests which reflects a basic concern on the part of the developers with usefulness for school practitioners such as teachers and administrators. One of the greatest strengths of the program is its focus on the diagnostic purposes of tests. The Directions for Administration provide a clear explanation of the objectives of each of the tests, with a table for each which classifies items by the type of skill being tested. The authors discuss how analysis of the students' performance on these items can serve to identify different types of problems, and at times offer suggestions as to what the teacher might do to remedy particular problems. Also discussed are the limitations of the tests and the reasons for the inclusion/exclusion of items. For example, the authors demonstrate effectively that letter recognition items in the word analysis test at Level 1 are unnecessary, and the importance of supplementing the analysis of the writing test with writing samples is explained. Such explanations can be extremely valuable for teachers in adapting programs to the needs of individual students.

The battery appears to be extremely well normed. There are two groups based on current 1982–83 data to which the performance of individual test takers can be compared—independent schools and suburban schools which are client schools with the ERB—as well as a representative national sample based on earlier data. The variables used to stratify the national sample include geographical region, urban-rural status, ethnic makeup, and socioeconomic status. The CTP II score report can also provide local norms, or such local norms can be established by following the directions given in the Guide to Using Test Results.

The choice of test items is varied and interesting. In the Reading test, the selections reflect the materials that students are likely to read both in school and out of school. Different types of discourse used at Level 2, for example, include poems, personal narratives, and a list of regulations for using a library. At Level 5, students must use reading skills to decipher information from a credit application for a consumer loan. Similarly, consistent with recent theory regarding the reading process, a variety of reading strategies reflecting high order thought processes, as opposed to simple decoding, are tested. Students must make inferences and interpretations such as identification of the author's tone, as well as use the more traditional skills of identifying the main idea of the passage, both implied and stated, and the literal comprehension of details and sequence. The content of the math test reflects a similar relevance and thus pragmatic appeal for the test taker. Items involving graph and table reading are included, for example.

None of the test items appears to be culturally or sex biased. Reading selections focussing on Black Americans, Indians, and Hispanics are included as well as examples of women in non sex-stereotyped roles. The human figures presented in the illustrations at Levels 1 and 2 reflect ethnic diversity.

The test also appears to be relatively easy to administer. A pilot test designed for young students or those inexperienced in test taking is included and the language of the instructions for administering the test is generally clear and straightforward. Printing the instructions to be read aloud to students in italic type, however, may cause some reading difficulties due to the lack of contrast between the two type styles.

The design and format of the test are attractive and clear. At the elementary levels the questions are in bold face to assure readability. In the Mathematics Basic Concepts test illustrations are attractively interspersed with word problems. At the lower levels the illustrations are simple but appealing. The test booklets contain, in addition to question and page numbers, identifying pictures of animals to help students to keep their places.

In summary, the ERB Comprehensive Testing Program can be recommended on the basis of its diagnostic utility to teachers and administrators as well as the relevance of its content, which is appropriate to both the classroom and more informal learning. The form and content of the test items, directions for administration, and explanation of scoring are clear and understandable, making it valuable for a variety of educational situations.

[398]

Estes Attitude Scales: Measures of Attitudes Toward School Subjects. Grades 2–6, 6–12; 1975–81; EAS; 2 levels; manual ('81, 23 pages); 1983 price data: $36 per complete kit including manual, 25 elementary booklets, 25 secondary booklets, 50 secondary answer sheets and set of scoring keys; $15 per manual; (20–30) minutes; Thomas H. Estes, Julie Johnstone Estes, Herbert C. Richards, and Doris Roettger; PRO-ED.*

a) ELEMENTARY FORM. Grades 2–6; 1981; 3 scores: mathematics, reading, science; 1 form (4 pages); $13 per 50 elementary booklets.

b) SECONDARY FORM. Grades 6–12; 1981; 5 scores: English, mathematics, reading, science, social studies; 1 form (2 pages); separate answer sheets must be used; $12 per 50 secondary forms; $12 per 50 secondary profile/answer sheets.

See T3:845 (6 references) and 8:371 (5 references).

TEST REFERENCES

1. Summers, E. G., & McClelland, J. V. A field-based evaluation of Sustained Silent Reading (SSR) in intermediate grades. THE ALBERTA JOURNAL OF EDUCATIONAL RESEARCH, 1982, 28, 100–112.

Review of Estes Attitude Scales: Measures of Attitudes Toward School Subjects by JOHN K. MILLER, Associate Dean for Graduate Studies and Associate Professor, Graduate School of Education and Human Development, University of Rochester, Rochester, NY:

The Estes Attitude Scales were developed to assess the tastes of elementary (grades 3 through 6) and secondary (grades 7 through 12) students for the content and study of basic school subjects. Test materials are simply and attractively designed for convenient, efficient administration and hand-scoring by classroom teachers. The manual is brief, well organized, well written, and generally intelligible to the non-technically oriented user. It is unpretentious in purpose and in its recommendations for use and interpretation; directions for administration, scoring, and use of norms tables are clear and simple; and technical data on test construction, psychometric properties, and norms development are presented in a straightforward and reasonably detailed fashion.

Items require respondents to indicate on a five-point scale (secondary form) or three-point scale (elementary form) their agreement/disagreement with statements that reflect a positive or negative bias toward a particular school subject. Though each scale includes both favorably and unfavorably worded statements, different scales do so to a disproportionate extent.

Scale construction procedures emphasized content relevance and homogeneity of factor structure among items pertaining to the same subject matter. Item selection for the final version of the secondary form was carefully accomplished in stages that successively involved content analysis, item discrimination analysis, and factor analysis with rotation to simple structure (Varimax criterion) of the full inter-item correlation matrix. The elementary form originated with the most discriminating items of the secondary Mathematics, Reading, and Science scales. Vocabulary adaptation of items to the elementary level was empirically validated through several stages of individual interviews and group discussions with independent groups of third grade children. As in the case of secondary scales, the item-selection criterion for the final version of the elementary form was homogeneity of within-scale factor structure. This strategy produced for both forms scales that represent distinct subject matter emphases. Unfortunately, factor structures reported for the final version of the secondary form were not derived from freshly sampled data. They resulted, instead, from analysis of partial data sets from which items with weak or ambiguous factor loadings had been eliminated. This was not the case for the elementary scales, which were administered in final form to an entirely new sample prior to the final factoring.

Reported reliabilities of the internal consistency type (coefficient alpha) are respectable for measures of this kind and ranged from .76 to .93 for scores on the secondary scale and from .76 to .88 on the elementary scale. Coefficients for the secondary form were, like the final factor analyses of item data, based on partial data sets. Failure to present evidence regarding test-retest reliabilities may be the most serious deficiency in the technical properties of the Estes Scales. The stability of any measure purportedly relevant to educational practice, or any other continuous process variable, should be examined carefully. It is important to establish that measures of this kind are not the product of unstable traits or transitory states.

Construct validation of the elementary and secondary forms attended to both convergent and discriminant validity of individual subject matter scales. Extrinsic measures of students' interest in each school subject were obtained from the respondents themselves, from peers, and from teachers. At the secondary level criteria also included respondents' course grades, standardized achievement test scores, and extra-curricular involvement in course-related activities. Though on the whole correlational evidence satisfied conditions favoring both convergent and discriminant validity of individual interest scales, findings were somewhat mixed for the secondary form. In particular, the discriminant validity of English interests was confounded by relatively high correlations between English criterion measures and reading interests. This is hardly a surprising discovery, considering the likelihood that reading interests are relevant in a global sense to other academic interests.

Finally, it must be noted that "national" norms, reported in terms of normalized *T*-scores and percentiles, depend on an inadequate data base for generalization to the school population at large. Distribution of the norms sample by sex, race, and urban vs. rural residence, was proportional to their representation in the national population. However, the size of the combined norms sample for both levels was only 1,815 students (969 at the elementary level and 846 at the secondary level), with geographic representation limited to five states.

In summary, the Estes Attitude Scales appear to have been competently constructed. They evidence a conscientious attempt at compliance with procedural standards for test development. The deficiencies of these measures seem to be principally the result of compromises directly attributable to the authors' limited resources. Although the Estes Scales cannot be recommended as a basis for comparisons with national trends, they could constitute a useful and inexpensive means to less ambitious ends: (*a*) simple description of children's sentiments regarding various aspects of standard curriculum; (*b*) acquisition of affective data relevant to curriculum research and evaluation, especially at the local level; and (*c*) development of local norms for the relative assessment of children's subject matter preferences. Any of these objectives might be accomplished without undue reliance on the instruments' weaker features, while capitalizing in particular on the obvious care and attention to detail that characterized the development of the Estes Scales.

[399]

ETSA Tests. Job applicants; 1959–84; formerly called Apitest; 8 tests: General Mental Ability (1A), Office Arithmetic (2A), General Clerical Ability (3A), Stenographic Skills (4A), Mechanical Familiarity (5A), Mechanical Knowledge (6A), Sales Aptitude (7A), Personal Adjustment Index (8A); publisher recommends use of Tests 1A, 8A, and one other; administrator's manual ('84, 27 pages); technical handbook ('72, 24 pages); 1984 price data: $5 per sample set of any one test; $15 per complete sample set (includes test 1A and 8A, scoring keys, and manual); $2.50 per administrator's manual; $2.25 per technical handbook; manual and technical handbook by S. Trevor Hadley and George A. W. Stouffer, Jr.; tests by Psychological Services Bureau; Employers' Tests & Services Associates.*

For reviews of an earlier version of the ETSA Tests by Marvin D. Dunnette and Raymond A. Katzell, see 6:1025.

[400]

Examination for the Certificate of Proficiency in English. Nonnative speakers of English; 1982–83; ECPE; "for students of English outside of the United States"; administration once a year at 75 sites in 40 countries; candidates who do not pass free preliminary screening test and oral interview are discouraged from paying the $20 examination fee for the main battery of 4 tests; 4 scores: written composition, listening comprehension, multiple-choice cloze reading test, 100-item objective test of grammar-vocabulary-reading comprehension; no data on reliability and validity; no norms; examiner's manual ('82, 16 pages); distribution restricted to ECPE examiners; separate machine scorable answer sheets must be used; 1983 price data: examination fee includes scoring service, $20 per candidate; 130(140) minutes; The English Language Institute of the University of Michigan, Testing and Certification Division.

[401]

Executive Profile Survey. Business executives; 1967–78; EPS; self-administered; computer processing mandatory; 11 profile dimensions: ambitious, self-assertive, enthusiastic, creative, innovative, self-directed, receptive, adaptable, composed, perceptive, systematic; norms based on business executive data base; 1 form ('78, 10 pages); manual entitled *Perspectives on the Executive Personality* ('78, 79 pages); separate answer sheets (included in test booklet) must be used; 1985 price data: $20 per test booklet (not reusable, fee includes computer processing); $10 per manual; $26.50 per specimen set; (60) minutes; Virgil R. Lang and Samuel E. Krug (manual); Institute for Personality and Ability Testing, Inc.*

Review of Executive Profile Survey by WILLIAM I. SAUSER, JR., Associate Professor and Head, Department of Management, Auburn University at Montgomery, Montgomery, AL:

The Executive Profile Survey (EPS) is a self-administered paper-and-pencil test intended to measure 11 dimensions of the occupational self-concept of top-level executives similar to the 2,000 individuals surveyed during the development of the instrument. Clear directions and a well-designed test booklet and answer sheet make the EPS very easy to administer. The EPS cannot be scored manually; the answer sheet must be detached and mailed to IPAT for computer scoring. A computer-generated test report is furnished to the user by return mail. As is appropriate with personality measurement devices such as this, IPAT requires potential users to establish their credentials before purchasing copies of the EPS. All purchasers receive a copy of the test manual with their first order of test booklets. The booklets are not reusable.

The test consists of three parts. The first part is a set of 13 paragraphs, adapted from the book *Varieties of Human Value* by Charles Morris, describing 13 distinctive lifestyles. The test-taker rates his or her preference for each lifestyle on a 7-point scale. The second part consists of 33 short phrases with which the test-taker rates agreement on a 3-point scale. These phrases were adapted from Arthur Brodbeck's attempt to capture "the essence of the inner/other directed orientations" developed by David Riesman in his book *The Lonely Crowd*. The third part is a set of 48 adjectives which the test-taker rates on a 7-point scale as descriptive of his or her personality. These self-descriptions were taken from Erich Fromm's book *Man for Himself*, and were intended to measure Fromm's marketing, hoarding, receptive, and exploitive orientations. The first 13 items in particular require some reflection and thought before answering. The test is not recommended for use with persons with a reading level below the 12th grade.

The test results take the form of five computer-generated pages stapled to a fancy folder. The results themselves consist simply of percentile scores, displayed as bar graphs, showing how the test-taker ranks on each dimension in comparison to the normative sample of 2,000 executives. While the short paragraphs accompanying each graph appear to be individualized interpretations, they are really nothing more than standardized descriptive paragraphs with such words as "low," "very high," or "extremely low" appearing in the blanks of sentences such as "Mr. Smith is ________ on this dimension." The results summary page displays the percentile scores on the 11 dimensions in order ranging from highest to lowest as representative of the test-taker's self-concept. The report provides no evaluative information regarding the test-taker's personality, nor does it contain any speculations about the test-taker's suitability for an executive position. All the report really does is show how the self-concept of the test-taker compares to the norms developed by surveying 2,000 executives.

The manual for the EPS is very well written and contains descriptive information of interest to typical test users as well as technical information intended for sophisticated psychometric theorists. Two major construct validation studies are described in the manual, and the characteristics of each of the 29 subsamples making up the normative base are displayed. The research described in the manual indicates that the 11 EPS dimension scores are reliable and that they are meaningful representations of the test-taker's self-concept. Thus, the EPS may be useful for research and counseling purposes. The validity of the EPS for any purpose other than describing the test-taker's occupational self-concept is not established, however.

The personnel specialist relying on the EPS to provide assistance in selecting high-level executives is likely to be sorely disappointed. On page 3 of the manual, the authors indicate that they "recognized that one of the powerful applications of the Survey lay in its use for selection and management-succession planning," and the brochures used to advertise the EPS certainly imply that it can be used for these purposes. Despite these claims, however, the manual provides no research evidence supporting the validity of the EPS as an executive selection device.

For a personality test such as the EPS to be useful as a selection device, three things must be established: (*a*) the test must be proven to be a valid measure of one or more psychological constructs, (*b*) these psychological constructs must be shown to relate to observable behaviors, and (*c*) these behaviors must be shown to be critical for successful performance of the job in question. Research described in the manual supports point (*a*); the EPS does measure 11 dimensions of occupational self-concept. However, points (*b*) and (*c*) must be established, presumably by the user, before the EPS can be considered a useful selection device.

The research reported in the manual does not establish that any one configuration of EPS scores relates to success as an executive; on the contrary, the 29 subsample profiles include a variety of configurations. (This is consistent with current leadership theory which holds that there is no consistent pattern of personality traits common to all successful leaders.) Furthermore, since no nonexecutives were included in the normative sample, there is no way to determine, without further research, whether the EPS is useful for distinguishing successful business executives from the general population. Given the current state of research with the EPS, how the authors intend it to be used for selection purposes remains unclear. Personnel specialists would probably be more successful in selecting business executives by reviewing applicant's records of past performance and accomplishments, perhaps supplemented with scores from well-constructed assessment center exercises, than by using personality inventories such as the EPS in its present state of development.

In summary, the EPS is a well constructed, easily administered instrument which provides meaningful measures of 11 dimensions of the test-taker's occupational self-concept. The computer-generated report compares the test-taker's self-concept, in terms of percentile scores, with the normative data collected from 2,000 executives. In its present state of development, the EPS appears to be useful as a research instrument; it may also provide data which can lead to greater self-understanding in a counseling context. The EPS should not be used as a selection instrument unless the user has conducted studies indicating that certain patterns of EPS scores reliably predict important job-related behaviors.

[402]

The Experiencing Scale. Counselors and counselor trainees; 1969; "evaluating the quality of patient self-involvement in psychotherapy directly from tape recordings or typescripts of the therapy session"; 2 scores: mode, peak, based on a 7-point rating scale; 1 form; manual in three volumes: Volume I—research and training manual, includes criterion for rating scale (110 pages), Volume II—transcripts of tapes for training sessions (215 pages), Volume III—audio tapes for practice sessions; tape or transcript of session required; 1983 price data: $12 per Volumes I and II; $42 per Volume III; administration time not reported; M. H. Klein, P. L. Mathieu, E. T. Gendlin, and D. J. Kiesler; University of Wisconsin.*

[403]

Expressive One-Word Picture Vocabulary Test. Ages 2–12, 12–16; 1979–83; EOWPVT; verbal intelligence; 2 levels; (10–15) minutes per level; Morrison F. Gardner; Academic Therapy Publications.*

a) [LOWER LEVEL]. Ages 2–12; 1979; individual; 1 form; manual (46 pages); 1984 price data: $41 per test kit including manual, test plates, and 25 record forms; $6 per 25 record forms; $25 per test plates; $10 per manual; $10 per specimen set; Spanish edition ('79) available.

b) UPPER-EXTENSION. Ages 12–16; 1983; 2 forms: individual, group; manual (39 pages); $33.50 per test kit including manual, test plates, and 25 record forms; $6 per 25 record forms; $6 per 50 group administration forms; $17.50 per test plates; $10 per manual; $10 per specimen set; Spanish edition ('83) available.

TEST REFERENCES

1. Goldstein, D. J., Allen, C. M., & Fleming, L. P. Relationship between the Expressive One-Word Picture Vocabulary Test and measures of intelligence, receptive vocabulary, and visual-motor coordination in borderline and mildly retarded children. PSYCHOLOGY IN THE SCHOOLS, 1982, 19, 315–318.

2. Stoner, S. B., & Spencer, W. B. Sex differences in expressive vocabulary of Head Start children. PERCEPTUAL AND MOTOR SKILLS, 1983, 56, 1008.

Review of Expressive One-Word Picture Vocabulary Test [Lower Level] by JACK A. CUMMINGS, Assistant Professor of Educational Psychology, Institute for Child Study, Indiana University, Bloomington, IN:

(Editor's Note: Review for lower level only.)

The test materials for the Expressive One-Word Picture Vocabulary Test (EOWPVT) consist of 110 line drawings. The examinee's task is to give a one-word description of the object(s) pictured in each test plate. The quality of the line drawings is generally mediocre (i.e., some of the pictorial representations appear dated). Although the artistic quality of the drawings is mediocre the pictured objects are recognizable.

Gardner states the purpose of the EOWPVT is "to obtain a basal estimate of a child's verbal intelligence by means of his acquired one-word expressive picture vocabulary, i.e., the quality and quantity of a child's vocabulary based on what he has acquired from home and from formal education." The author continues, "The EOWPVT was developed as a measure of how a child thinks, since the child must identify a single object or a group of objects on the basis of a single concept. The ability to identify a single object or group of objects according to an abstract concept usually indicates that a child's intellectual functioning is developing appropriately." These above statements in conjunction with the use of "deviation IQ scores" and mental ages would give the naive consumer the impression that the EOWPVT is an appropriate tool for assessing a child's verbal intellectual functioning. Obviously verbal intelligence is much more complex (e.g., comprehension of verbal stimuli, elaborate verbal expression, memory for meaningful verbal stimuli, verbal reasoning, etc.). It is the reviewer's opinion that in the section of the manual on interpretation Gardner should have included a stronger caution to the prospective user that the EOWPVT assesses only one aspect of a child's verbal intellectual functioning (i.e., expressive vocabulary). Although the correlation between the EOWPVT and Wechsler Preschool and Primary Scale of Intelligence (WPPSI) Verbal Scale IQ scores is substantial (.73), it should be noted that an individual's total verbal language performance may depart significantly from the estimate provided by the EOWPVT.

ADMINISTRATION AND SCORING. The administration of the EOWPVT is quite straightforward. A basal is established by eight consecutive correct responses while a ceiling is obtained when the child fails six consecutive items. The author suggests that the EOWPVT may be given by counselors, learning specialists, physicians, psychologists, social workers and teachers. Familiarity with psychological and/or educational tests is the only qualification stated by the author. It is the reviewer's opinion that the test author should have restricted the users to persons with at least minimal formal training in measurement and child development. Knowledge of typical child behaviors would increase the likelihood of the examiner eliciting an optimal performance from the child.

In the manual it is unclear whether the examiner may credit a slight mispronouncement. For example, the first item of the test is a picture of a "car." If the preschooler makes an "r" sound substitution or omits the "r" sound, it would have to be assumed that credit would be assigned for the response. Future editions of the manual should address this aspect of scoring children's responses.

STANDARDIZATION. The normative data are based on the testing of 1,607 children living in the San Francisco Bay area. Children from age 2–0 through 11–11 were included in the standardization sample. Generally the sample size for each age level is adequate. A less than satisfactory number of children were sampled in the following age levels: 2–0 to 2–5, 2–6 to 2–11, and 3–6 to 3–11. More than 109 children between the ages of 2–0 and 2–11 should have been sampled because this age range is broken into six levels. In the manual, no data are provided which break down the number of children in these six age levels. On the average it may be assumed that there were approximately 19 children per age level. The small size of the samples for these six age levels between 2–0 and 2–11 should therefore alert the prospective consumer of the EOWPVT that extreme caution should be observed when interpreting the performance of a two-year-old child.

Another issue that should be considered with respect to the standardization is that all the children in the sample were residents of the San Francisco Bay area. The central concern pertains to the generalization of the standardization sample to the country at large. The Peabody Picture Vocabulary Test (PPVT) or the Columbia Mental Maturity Scale (CMMS) were used as anchor measures. Depending on the child's age, one of the above tests was administered and used to insure that the standardization sample included a representative range of children with varying levels of cognitive ability. A "statistical weighting procedure" was then used to ensure representation of the sample into nine IQ categories, resulting in an approximately normal distribution. Thus, the problem associated with a regionally restricted sample may have been avoided by the use of the above anchor tests. There are two basic problems with the anchoring procedures used by Gardner. First it was unfortunate that three different anchor tests were used across age levels: PPVT, ages 2–0 to 3–5; CMMS (1972), ages 3–6 to 9–11; and CMMS (1959), ages 10–0 to 11–11. It is clear that the PPVT and CMMS assess different abilities, hearing vocabulary vs. discrimination and classification. A second problem is the technical adequacy of the norms. The PPVT standardization sample was drawn from the metropolitan area of Nashville, Tennessee, while the CMMS (1959) norms were almost 20 years old at the time of EOWPVT standardization.

RELIABILITY AND VALIDITY. The split-half reliability is reported for each half-year age level between age 2–0 and 5–11, and for each full-year age level between 6–0 and 11–11. The reliability coefficients ranged from .87 to .96. The corresponding SEMs ranged from 3.38 to 5.41 (mean = 100, standard deviation = 15). Only for the age level 2–0 to 2–5 did the coefficient drop below .90. At face value, these data indicate that the EOWPVT could be considered adequate in terms of providing a consistent estimate of a child's expressive vocabulary relative to his/her peers. However, it is unclear in the manual how the split-half reliabilities were calculated. If Gardner presumed that items below the basal were uniformly correct and items above the ceiling were uniformly failed, then the reported correlations may be spuriously high. No data were reported on the test-retest stability of the EOWPVT.

In regard to validation, two types are reported in the manual: content validity, and criterion-related validity. Several efforts were made to establish content validity. Questionnaires on children's word usage were sent to parents of children between the ages of 18 months and 2 years. Words at these and other age levels were selected by "frequency of use." It was not specified which source(s) were employed to determine frequencies of word usage. The reviewer's subjective impression of the selection and representativeness of test items is favorable. The test author appears to have isolated exemplars of concepts which are commonly encountered in a child's environment, regardless of that child's socio-cultural background. It should be noted that this is an "armchair" or subjective analysis. Previous measurement research indicates that empirical evidence is required prior to making definitive judgments regarding item bias. Although Gardner does not report item bias data, a multiple correlation analysis with age and IQ held constant is included in the manual. Gardner states that "only a fraction" of the variance could be explained by the racial-cultural variable (i.e., 12 percent). The term "racial-cultural" reflects the inclusion of persons with Hispanic backgrounds as part of the analysis. The magnitude of the explained variance is dismissed as incidental. The present reviewer believes that the magnitude was sufficient to justify additional investigations into possible racial-cultural item bias. It should be noted that Gardner's use of multiple correlations makes the assumption that the anchor tests (PPVT, CMMS) are not biased. Another problem associated with the standardization was that it took place only in the San Francisco Bay area. Bias could not be detected for the variables of community size (i.e., rural vs. urban children), nor with respect to geographic region of the country.

Criterion-related validity is provided by correlations with the PPVT (.67 to .78), CMMS (.29 to .59), and the WPPSI. The correlations with the PPVT and CMMS were obtained on the standardization sample, while the criterion-related validity of the EOWPVT with the WPPSI was established on a sample of 122 pre-kindergarten children ranging in age from 4–1 to 6–4. The correlation corrected for attenuation between the EOWPVT and the WPPSI Verbal Scale was .73. In reporting the results of this pre-kindergarten study, Table 8 in the manual is misleading. Rather than correlating standard scores for the WPPSI subtests with the EOWPVT the author used mental ages. Due to the width of the age range, this artificially inflated the reported correlations. Hence the reported correlations of the WPPSI subtests with the EOWPVT should be interpreted cautiously.

CONCLUDING COMMENTS. The EOWPVT is a measure of expressive vocabulary. The test should not be construed as a quick substitute for a more comprehensive measure of verbal intellectual functioning. In fact, the EOWPVT assessed only one small part of the domain labeled expressive vocabulary. Since the EOWPVT requires a one-word response, elaborate verbal expression is not sampled. At best, the EOWPVT should be considered either a screening instrument or a supplemental test to be used as one piece of a clinician's battery.

When one compares the EOWPVT to other commercially available brief screening measures, the technical superiority of the Peabody Picture Vocabulary Test—Revised (PPVT-R) is overshadowing. The national standardization, wealth of reliability and validity studies, and the availability of an alternate form makes the PPVT-R a more psychometrically sound choice when selecting a screening measure of vocabulary development. Further research on the test-retest stability and additional criterion-related studies with children of various ability groups and age levels would be necessary before the present reviewer could recommend the use of the EOWPVT.

Review of Expressive One-Word Picture Vocabulary Test by GILBERT M. SPIVACK, Learning Disabilities and Behavior Disorders Specialist, Walton County Board of Education, Monroe, GA:

The Expressive One-Word Picture Vocabulary Test (EOWPVT) is an untimed individual test of expressive vocabulary, designed for children from 2 to 12 years of age. The EOWPVT is administered in 15 minutes or less, and consists of two demonstration and 110 test plates, each plate consisting of hand-drawn figures. Answer sheets indicate starting points by chronological age and correct responses, and also contain spaces on the reverse side to record pertinent behavioral data and recommendations.

The EOWPVT may be administered by classroom teachers as well as by other educational specialists, with the author suggesting only that the examiner be familiar with psychological and/or educational tests, and this test in particular. Test administration requires the examiner to present the figures individually, asking the subject to name the object pictured. Testing begins at an item determined by the child's chronological age, with the subject responding only to those items between his basal (eight consecutive correct) and ceiling (six consecutive error) responses. Only one response is allowed per item, although several items have more than one correct response.

EOWPVT scoring is quick and objective, with raw scores readily translated into Mental Age, Deviation Intelligence Quotient, Percentile, and Stanine rankings. Inspection of the norms tables reveals extrapolated mental ages below age 2–0 and above age 11–11, which facilitates the description of the performance of exceptional children at the lower and upper test ranges. Deviation IQ scores from 55 to 145 are presented, a range that will encompass the vast majority of subjects and will indicate those children who will need further, more in-depth diagnostic testing. Additionally, the use of two month chronological age groupings (through age 3–11), and three month chronological age groupings (through age 11–11) in the Deviation IQ norms tables avoids the large drop that would occur if broader age groupings were utilized.

In developing the EOWPVT, 435 letters were sent to parents of children (ranging from 18 months to 2 years of age) to obtain a list of common words that children learn and use at an early age. As reported in the manual, other words chosen for the EOWPVT are those that are common in the home and those that are usually learned through formal education. A total of 1,249 children were examined in order to obtain raw data for the development of the EOWPVT, while 1,607 children comprised the sample for the gathering of final data. While the author infers that such biases as race, sex, cultural differences, and bilingual idiosyncracies were avoided by the item selection process, this inference should be viewed cautiously in light of the fact that all 1,607 children included in the final standardization sample resided within the San Francisco Bay area.

Reliability coefficients of the EOWPVT were determined through the use of the split-half method. Matching odd versus even items by age level, the author computed internal consistency coefficients, corrected by the Spearman-Brown formula, which ranged from .87 to .96, with a reported mean reliability of .94. The coefficients seem quite adequate and stable across age ranges; however, test-retest data would be appreciated to demonstrate reliability across administrations. Validity data included correlations of .67 to .78 (median=.70) with the Peabody Picture Vocabulary Test (PPVT) and correlations of .29 to .59 (median=.39) with the Columbia Mental Maturity Scale (CMMS). As reported in the manual, these criterion tests were administered concurrently with the EOWPVT as part of the standardization procedure. It is reported that the PPVT was administered to those children ages 2–0 to 3–5, while the CMMS '72 and '59 versions were administered to those children ages 3–6 to 9–11 and 10–0 to 11–11 respectively. The EOWPVT's lower correlations with the CMMS than with the PPVT are justified by the author as an expected outcome, since "The PPVT provides a measure of receptive rather than expressive vocabulary, while the CMMS (1959 and 1972) provides a measure of general reasoning ability, which is largely independent of verbal processes." Although this may offer some justification for the EOWPVT's lack of commonality with a measure of general intelligence, it is this reviewer's contention that stronger indices of criterion-related validity need to be present for those children over the age of 3–6.

From the perspective of the test user, this instrument is to be praised for its brevity and also for the attempt to provide unambiguous scoring criteria. However, the author seems to have gone too far in the attempt to simplify scoring by considering incorrect those alternate responses that occurred infrequently in the EOWPVT standardization. Thus, very bright or culturally different children may be penalized by not receiving credit for atypical (although correct) responses, such as the child that supplies the response "jet" instead of "airplane," or "locomotive" instead of "train." Another concern for the test user relates to the application of EOWPVT results, as this reviewer believes that the author's inferences as to the utility of EOWPVT results seem somewhat overstated. In the test manual it is indicated that the EOWPVT may be used to determine a child's readiness for kindergarten, for grouping in nursery school programs, and by pediatricians as an expressive language measure. While the EOWPVT does provide diagnostically significant information regarding expressive vocabulary, such important decisions as school readiness and placements necessitate a more comprehensive assessment. Thus, the EOWPVT could then be used to complement such measures as the PPVT-R, the McCarthy Screening Test, or the Bender-Gestalt Test.

[404]

Eyberg Child Behavior Inventory. Children ages 2–16; 1978–80; ECBI; ratings by parents or others well acquainted with child on 2 scales: the problem scale, the intensity scale; individual; 1 form (no date, 2 pages); no manual; price data available free of charge from publisher; no administration time reported; Sheila Eyberg; the Author.*

See T3:858 (2 references).

TEST REFERENCES

1. Eyberg, S. M., & Robinson, E. A. Parent-child interaction training: Effects on family functioning. JOURNAL OF CLINICAL CHILD PSYCHOLOGY, 1982, 11, 130–137.

2. Webster-Stratton, C., & Eyberg, S. M. Child temperament: Relationship with child behavior problems and parent-child interactions. JOURNAL OF CLINICAL CHILD PSYCHOLOGY, 1982, 11, 123–129.

3. Eyberg, S. M., & Robinson, E. A. Conduct problem behavior: Standardization of a behavioral rating scale with adolescents. JOURNAL OF CLINICAL CHILD PSYCHOLOGY, 1983, 12, 347–354.

4. Robinson, E. A., & Anderson, L. L. Family adjustment, parental attitudes, and social desirability. JOURNAL OF ABNORMAL CHILD PSYCHOLOGY, 1983, 11, 247–256.

5. Hamilton, S. B., & MacQuiddy, S. L. Self-administered behavioral parent training: Enhancement of treatment efficacy using a time-out signal seat. JOURNAL OF CLINICAL CHILD PSYCHOLOGY, 1984, 13, 61–69.

6. Tobiasen, J. M., & Hiebert, J. M. Parents' tolerance for the conduct problems of the child with cleft lip and palate. CLEFT PALATE JOURNAL, 1984, 21, 82–85.

Review of Eyberg Child Behavior Inventory by MICHAEL L. REED, Western Psychiatric Institute and Clinic, University of Pittsburgh School of Medicine, Pittsburgh, PA:

This 36-item questionnaire is used to obtain ratings of conduct problem and acting out behavior from children aged 2 to 16. Each item is rated on two scales. The Intensity scale reflects the frequency of conduct problems and parents respond on a 1 (never occurs) to 7 (always occurs) scale. The Problem scale identifies behaviors viewed as problematic and parents respond on a simple yes (1) or no (0) scale. Scale scores are derived by summing the ratings across all items.

The Eyberg Child Behavior Inventory (ECBI) reliability estimates were derived for 512 children, aged 2 to 12, referred to a pediatric clinic. Correlations between individual items and scale totals ranged from .31 to .73 for the Intensity scale and .35 to .69 for the Problem scale. Split-half reliabilities were also computed and coefficients averaged .95 and .94 for the Intensity and Problem scales, respectively. Three-week test-retest reliabilities were computed using a subsample of 17 children and ranged from .49 to .90. Summing across items yielded test-retest reliabilities of .86 for the Intensity scale and .88 for the Problem scale. These findings support the internal consistency of the ECBI; however, interrater reliability data are needed and further test-retest data may be desirable given the small sample size.

Validity evidence comes from two sources. For a sample of 2- to 7-year-olds, significant differences in scale means were reported between conduct problem children ($n = 43$) and clinic control ($n = 20$) and nonclinic children ($n = 22$). This finding supports the discriminant validity of ECBI ratings. Conduct problem children showed significant reductions in both intensity and problem ratings following treatment, suggesting the ECBI is sensitive to behavior change and is potentially useful as an outcome measure. For the pediatric sample of 2- to 12-year-olds, the correlation between the Intensity and Problem scales was .75 ($p < .001$). Item intercorrelations averaged .31 for intensity ratings and .29 for the problem ratings, and a principal components factor analysis of intensity ratings yielded positive loadings on a single factor for all items. The scale scores of boys were significantly higher than those of girls, and children previously identified as conduct disordered ($n = 57$) scored higher than the other children sampled (replicating the discriminant validity results). Overall these findings support the internal and discriminant validity of the ECBI.

Validity evidence could be strengthened, however, by examining the relations between ECBI ratings and comparable ratings from other informants and/or other assessment instruments.

Scale means and standard deviations are available for the pediatric sample as are frequency data for the individual behavior problems defining each item. Descriptive statistics were also calculated separately for boys and girls and for children differing in clinical status. These data provide useful benchmarks but they are insufficient for screening purposes. The generalizability of these data is also limited by the fact that parent reports were obtained primarily from minority and low income parents in one pediatric clinic. The ECBI may also be of limited use for some applications in that it taps only behaviors associated with conduct disorder. Conduct disordered children may have behavioral problems in other areas (i.e., depression, social withdrawal), and information about these problems could be useful for treatment planning.

The ECBI has advantages over previously available measures of conduct disorder in that it taps a wide range of acting out behavior and it is easy to administer and score. Information concerning which behaviors are problematic and their frequency of occurrence can contribute to the identification and prioritization of areas for intervention. This approach is useful because some high frequency behaviors (i.e., poor table manners, argues) may not be problematic, while some low frequency behaviors (i.e., steals, wets the bed) may represent serious concerns. Additional reliability and validity analyses could strengthen the ECBI psychometrically, but the existing data for children aged 2 to 12 is supportive and this should not preclude use of the instrument. Reliability and validity data for children older than age 12 are not currently available, and ratings for these children should be interpreted with caution.

The ECBI is recommended for use as a descriptive measure for conduct disordered children but not as a screening instrument or tool for evaluating children characterized by multiple areas of disturbance. An alternative parent rating scale is the Child Behavior Checklist developed by Achenbach and Edelbrock. This instrument has well established reliability and validity, encompasses a broad range of problem behaviors, and has well stratified norms making it useful for screening purposes. Additional alternatives include the Parent Rating Scale developed by Conners and the recently revised Behavior Problem Checklist developed by Quay and Peterson.

[405]

Eysenck Personality Inventory. Adults; 1963–69; EPI; revision of Maudsley Personality Inventory; for revised edition of EPI, see Eysenck Personality Questionnaire; 3 scores: extraversion, neuroticism, lie; no reliability data for lie score; authors recommend use of both forms to obtain adequate reliability for individual measurement; 2 editions (identical except for 3 words and directions); (10–15) minutes; H. J. Eysenck and Sybil B. G. Eysenck.

a) UNITED STATES EDITION. Grades 9–16 and adults; 1963–69; Forms A, B, ('63, 2 pages); manual ('68, 27 pages); adult industrial norms ['69, 1 page]; 1983 price data: $3.75 per 25 test-answer sheets; $2 per set of scoring stencils; $2 per manual; $3 per specimen set; scoring service, $.45 or less per test; Spanish edition ('72) available; a printing with the title Eysenck Personality Inventory is available for industrial use; EdITS/Educational and Industrial Testing Service.*

b) BRITISH EDITION. Adults; 1963–64; norms consist of means and standard deviations for various groups; Forms A, B, ('64, 4 pages); manual ('64, 24 pages); £1.75 per 20 test-answer sheets; £1.25 per scoring key; £1.65 per manual; £2.50 per specimen set; Hodder & Stoughton Educational [England].*

See T3:859 (245 references); for a review by Auke Tellegen, see 8:553 (405 references); see also T2:1174 (140 references); for reviews by Richard I. Lanyon and excerpted reviews by A. W. Heim and James Linden, see 7:76 (121 references); see also P:77 (52 references); for a review by James C. Lingoes, see 6:93 (1 reference).

TEST REFERENCES

1. Buglass, D., Clarke, J., Henderson, A. S., Kreitman, N., & Presley, A. S. A study of agoraphobic housewives. PSYCHOLOGICAL MEDICINE, 1977, 7, 73–86.

2. Green, D. E. Prediction of nursing examination success and attrition in a New Zealand nursing program. SOCIAL BEHAVIOR AND PERSONALITY, 1977, 5, 215–223.

3. Hampson, S. E., & Kline, P. Personality dimensions differentiating certain groups of abnormal offenders from non-offenders. THE BRITISH JOURNAL OF CRIMINOLOGY, 1977, 17, 310–331.

4. Hinton, J. W., & Craske, B. Differential effects of test stress on the heart rates of extraverts and introverts. BIOLOGICAL PSYCHOLOGY, 1977, 5, 23–28.

5. Rutter, B. M. Some psychological concomitants of chronic bronchitis. PSYCHOLOGICAL MEDICINE, 1977, 7, 459–464.

6. Sanderson, H. Dependency on mothers in boys who steal. THE BRITISH JOURNAL OF CRIMINOLOGY, 1977, 17, 180–184.

7. Taylor, F. G., & Marshall, W. L. Experimental analysis of a cognitive-behavioral therapy for depression. COGNITIVE THERAPY AND RESEARCH, 1977, 1, 59–72.

8. Abrams, A. I., & Siegel, L. M. The Transcendental Meditation program and rehabilitation at Folsom State Prison. CRIMINAL JUSTICE AND BEHAVIOR, 1978, 5, 3–20.

9. Best, J. A., Owen, L. E., & Trentadue, L. Comparison of satiation and rapid smoking in self-managed smoking cessation. ADDICTIVE BEHAVIORS, 1978, 3, 71–78.

10. Kilpatrick, D. G., Roitzsch, J. C., Best, C. L., McAlhany, D. A., Sturgis, E. T., & Miller, W. C. Treatment goal preference and problem perception of chronic alcoholics: Behavioral and personality correlates. ADDICTIVE BEHAVIORS, 1978, 3, 107–116.

11. LaTorre, R. A. Gender role and psychological adjustment. ARCHIVES OF SEXUAL BEHAVIOR, 1978, 7, 89–96.

12. Morgan, W. P., & Johnson, R. W. Personality characteristics of successful and unsuccessful oarsmen. INTERNATIONAL JOURNAL OF SPORT PSYCHOLOGY, 1978, 9, 119–133.

13. Thompson, S. C. Detection of social cues: A signal detection theory analysis. PERSONALITY AND SOCIAL PSYCHOLOGY BULLETIN, 1978, 4, 452–455.

14. Abrams, A. I., & Siegel, L. M. Transcendental Meditation and rehabilitation at Folsom Prison. CRIMINAL JUSTICE AND BEHAVIOR, 1979, 6, 13–21.

15. Bachman, J., & Jones, R. T. Personality correlates of cannabis dependence. ADDICTIVE BEHAVIORS, 1979, 4, 361–371.

16. Barlow, D. H., Abel, G. G., & Blanchard, E. B. Gender identity change in transsexuals: Follow-up and replications. ARCHIVES OF GENERAL PSYCHIATRY, 1979, 36, 1001–1007.

17. Bentler, P. M., & Peeler, W. H., Jr. Models of female orgasm. ARCHIVES OF SEXUAL BEHAVIOR, 1979, 8, 405–423.

18. Cantwell, D. P., Baker, L., & Rutter, M. Families of autistic and dysphasic children: I. Family life and interaction patterns. ARCHIVES OF GENERAL PSYCHIATRY, 1979, 36, 682–687.

19. Crisp, A. H., & Stonehill, E. Personality, body weight and ultimate outcome in anorexia nervosa. THE JOURNAL OF CLINICAL PSYCHIATRY, 1979, 40, 332–335.
20. Crookes, T. G. Sociability and behavior disturbance. THE BRITISH JOURNAL OF CRIMINOLOGY, 1979, 19, 60–66.
21. Edman, G., Schalling, D., & Rissler, A. Interaction effects of extraversion and neuroticism on detection thresholds. BIOLOGICAL PSYCHOLOGY, 1979, 9, 41–47.
22. Ogunlade, J. O. Personality characteristics related to susceptibility to behavioral contagion. SOCIAL BEHAVIOR AND PERSONALITY, 1979, 7, 205–208.
23. Rutter, B. M. The prognostic significance of psychological factors in the management of chronic bronchitis. PSYCHOLOGICAL MEDICINE, 1979, 9, 63–70.
24. Shadish, W. R., Jr., & Zarle, T. The validation of an encounter group outcome measure. SMALL GROUP BEHAVIOR, 1979, 10, 101–112.
25. Sturgis, E. T., Calhoun, K. S., & Best, C. L. Correlates of assertive behavior in alcoholics. ADDICTIVE BEHAVIORS, 1979, 4, 193–197.
26. Forsman, L. Habitual catecholamine excretion and its relation to habitual distress. BIOLOGICAL PSYCHOLOGY, 1980, 11, 83–97.
27. Gabrenya, W. K., Jr., & Arkin, R. M. Self-monitoring scale: Factor structure and correlates. PERSONALITY AND SOCIAL PSYCHOLOGY BULLETIN, 1980, 6, 13–22.
28. Gardiner, B. M. Psychological aspects of rheumatoid arthritis. PSYCHOLOGICAL MEDICINE, 1980, 10, 159–163.
29. Harris, R., Yulis, S., & Lacoste, D. Relationships among sexual arousability, imagery ability, and introversion-extraversion. THE JOURNAL OF SEX RESEARCH, 1980, 16, 72–86.
30. Hester, R. K., & Brown, W. R. Eysenck Personality Inventory: A normative study of an adult industrial population. JOURNAL OF CLINICAL PSYCHOLOGY, 1980, 36, 937–939.
31. Kim, J. S. Relationships of personality to perceptual and behavioral responses in stimulating and nonstimulating tasks. ACADEMY OF MANAGEMENT JOURNAL, 1980, 23, 307–319.
32. Kirkcaldy, B. D. An analysis of the relationship between psychophysiological variables connected to human performance and the personality variables extraversion and neuroticism. INTERNATIONAL JOURNAL OF SPORT PSYCHOLOGY, 1980, 11, 276–289.
33. Reid, R. M., & Hay, D. Some behavioral characteristics of rugby and association footballers. INTERNATIONAL JOURNAL OF SPORT PSYCHOLOGY, 1980, 10, 239–251.
34. Rim, Y. Sex-typing and means of influence in marriage. SOCIAL BEHAVIOR AND PERSONALITY, 1980, 8, 117–119.
35. Wardell, D., & Yeudall, L. T. A multidimensional approach to criminal disorders: The assessment of impulsivity and its relation to crime. ADVANCES IN BEHAVIOUR RESEARCH AND THERAPY, 1980, 2, 159–177.
36. Wolff, S., & Chick, J. Schizoid personality in childhood: A controlled follow-up study. PSYCHOLOGICAL MEDICINE, 1980, 10, 85–100.
37. Benjaminsen, S. Primary non-endogenous depression and features attributed to reactive depression. JOURNAL OF AFFECTIVE DISORDERS, 1981, 3, 245–259.
38. Buhrich, N. Psychological adjustment in transvestism and transsexualism. BEHAVIOUR RESEARCH AND THERAPY, 1981, 19, 407–411.
39. Burgess, I. S., Jones, L. M., Robertson, S. A., Radcliffe, W. N., & Emerson, E. The degree of control exerted by phobic and non-phobic verbal stimuli over the recognition behaviour of phobic and non-phobic subjects. BEHAVIOUR RESEARCH AND THERAPY, 1981, 19, 233–243.
40. Butter, H. J. Some physiological and behavioral predictive characteristics of psychiatric patients. JOURNAL OF CLINICAL PSYCHOLOGY, 1981, 37, 52–60.
41. Christensen, L. The relationship between arousal and positive self-presentation. JOURNAL OF PERSONALITY ASSESSMENT, 1981, 45, 263–269.
42. Feingold, A. Testing equity as an explanation for romantic couples "mismatched" on physical attractiveness. PSYCHOLOGICAL REPORTS, 1981, 48, 247–250.
43. Garfinkel, P. E., & Waring, E. M. Personality, interests, and emotional disturbances in psychiatric residents. THE AMERICAN JOURNAL OF PSYCHIATRY, 1981, 138, 51–55.
44. Katz, L. Computer and manual administration of the Eysenck Personality Inventory. JOURNAL OF CLINICAL PSYCHOLOGY, 1981, 37, 586–588.
45. Poole, A. D., Sanson-Fisher, R. W., & German, G. A. The rapid-smoking technique: Therapeutic effectiveness. BEHAVIOUR RESEARCH AND THERAPY, 1981, 19, 389–397.
46. Riggio, R. E., Friedman, H. S., & DiMatteo, M. R. Nonverbal greetings: Effects of the situation and personality. PERSONALITY AND SOCIAL PSYCHOLOGY BULLETIN, 1981, 7, 682–689.
47. Stanaway, R. G., & Watson, D. W. Smoking and personality: A factorial study. BRITISH JOURNAL OF CLINICAL PSYCHOLOGY, 1981, 20, 213–214.
48. Tavormina, J. B., Boll, T. J., Dunn, N. J., Luscomb, R. L., & Taylor, J. R. Psychosocial effects on parents of raising a physically handicapped child. JOURNAL OF ABNORMAL CHILD PSYCHOLOGY, 1981, 9, 121–131.
49. Templer, D. I., Salter, C. A., Dickey, S., Baldwin, R., & Veleber, D. M. The construction of a Pet Attitude Scale. THE PSYCHOLOGICAL RECORD, 1981, 31, 343–348.
50. Thauberger, P. C., Ruznisky, S. A., & Cleland, J. F. Avoidance of existential-ontological confrontation: A review of the research. PSYCHOLOGICAL REPORTS, 1981, 49, 747–764.
51. Throll, D. A. Transcendental meditation and progressive relaxation: Their psychological effects. JOURNAL OF CLINICAL PSYCHOLOGY, 1981, 37, 776–781.
52. Walsh, R. N., Budtz-Olsen, I., Leader, C., & Cummins, R. A. The menstrual cycle, personality, and academic performance. ARCHIVES OF GENERAL PSYCHIATRY, 1981, 38, 219–221.
53. Asso, D., & Braier, J. R. Changes with the menstrual cycle in psychophysiological and self-report measures of activation. BIOLOGICAL PSYCHOLOGY, 1982, 15, 95–107.
54. Bartram, D., & Dale, H. C. A. The Eysenck Personality Inventory as a selection test for military pilots. JOURNAL OF OCCUPATIONAL PSYCHOLOGY, 1982, 55, 287–296.
55. Campbell, J. B., & Hawley, C. W. Study habits and Eysenck's theory of extraversion-introversion. JOURNAL OF RESEARCH IN PERSONALITY, 1982, 16, 139–146.
56. Campbell, J. B., & Reynolds, J. H. Interrelationships of the Eysenck Personality Inventory and the Eysenck Personality Questionnaire. EDUCATIONAL AND PSYCHOLOGICAL MEASUREMENT, 1982, 42, 1067–1073.
57. Credidio, S. G. Comparative effectiveness of patterned biofeedback vs mediation training on EMG and skin temperature changes. BEHAVIOUR RESEARCH AND THERAPY, 1982, 20, 233–241.
58. Danheiser, P. R., & Graziano, W. G. Self-monitoring and cooperation as a self-presentation strategy. JOURNAL OF PERSONALITY AND SOCIAL PSYCHOLOGY, 1982, 42, 497–505.
59. Gudjonsson, G. H., & Haward, L. R. C. Detection of deception: Consistency in responding and personality. PERCEPTUAL AND MOTOR SKILLS, 1982, 54, 1189–1190.
60. Lapierre, Y. D., Tremblay, A., Gagnon, A., Monpremier, P., Berliss, H., & Oyewumi, L. K. A therapeutic and discontinuation study of clobazam and diazepam in anxiety neurosis. THE JOURNAL OF CLINICAL PSYCHIATRY, 1982, 43, 372–374.
61. Lavellee, Y. J., Lamontagne, Y., Annable, L., & Fontaine, F. Characteristics of chronically anxious patients who respond to EMG feedback training. THE JOURNAL OF CLINICAL PSYCHIATRY, 1982, 43, 229–230.
62. Maddi, S. R., Hoover, M., & Kobasa, S. C. High activation and internal orientation as factors in creativity. THE JOURNAL OF CREATIVE BEHAVIOR, 1982, 16, 250–255.
63. Mathew, R. J., & Weinman, M. L. Sexual dysfunctions in depression. ARCHIVES OF SEXUAL BEHAVIOR, 1982, 11, 323–328.
64. Mathew, R. J., Weinman, M. L., Semchuk, K. M., & Levin, B. L. Driving phobia in the city of Houston: A pilot study. THE AMERICAN JOURNAL OF PSYCHIATRY, 1982, 139, 1049–1051.
65. McCrae, R. R. Consensual validation of personality traits: Evidence from self-reports and ratings. JOURNAL OF PERSONALITY AND SOCIAL PSYCHOLOGY, 1982, 43, 293–303.
66. Morrelli, G., Andrews, L., & Morrelli, R. The relation involving personality variables, problem relevance, rationality, and anxiousness among college women. COGNITIVE THERAPY AND RESEARCH, 1982, 6, 57–62.
67. Poole, A. D., Dunn, J., Sanson-Fisher, R. W., & German, G. A. The rapid-smoking technique: Subject characteristics and treatment outcome. BEHAVIOUR RESEARCH AND THERAPY, 1982, 20, 1–7.
68. Schmeck, R. R., & Spofford, M. Attention to semantic versus phonetic verbal attributes as a function of individual differences in arousal and learning strategy. CONTEMPORARY EDUCATIONAL PSYCHOLOGY, 1982, 7, 312–319.
69. Schneider, A., & Gibbins, K. The EPI in research with the aged. AUSTRALIAN PSYCHOLOGIST, 1982, 17, 41–46.
70. Skinner, N. F. Personality characteristics of volunteers for painful experiments. BULLETIN OF THE PSYCHONOMIC SOCIETY, 1982, 20, 299–300.
71. Skinner, N. F. Personality correlates of Machiavellianism: IV. Machiavellianism and psychopathology. SOCIAL BEHAVIOR AND PERSONALITY, 1982, 10, 201–203.
72. Smyth, L. D. Psychopathology as a function of neuroticism and a hypnotically implanted aggressive conflict. JOURNAL OF PERSONALITY AND SOCIAL PSYCHOLOGY, 1982, 43, 555–564.

73. Snyder, M., & Gangestad, S. Choosing social situations: Two investigations of self-monitoring processes. JOURNAL OF PERSONALITY AND SOCIAL PSYCHOLOGY, 1982, 43, 123–135.

74. Tucker, L. A. Weight training experience and psychological well-being. PERCEPTUAL AND MOTOR SKILLS, 1982, 55, 553–554.

75. Webb, N. M. Group composition, group interaction, and achievement in cooperative small groups. JOURNAL OF EDUCATIONAL PSYCHOLOGY, 1982, 74, 475–484.

76. Webb, N. M. Peer interaction and learning in cooperative small groups. JOURNAL OF EDUCATIONAL PSYCHOLOGY, 1982, 74, 642–655.

77. Weinman, M. L., Levin, B. L., & Mathew, R. J. Use of psychological testing in symptom detection in a normal population. PSYCHOLOGICAL REPORTS, 1982, 50, 499–504.

78. Amidon, E., Kumar, V. K., & Treadwell, T. Measurement of intimacy attitudes: The Intimacy Attitude Scale-Revised. JOURNAL OF PERSONALITY ASSESSMENT, 1983, 47, 635–639.

79. Blaz, M. Perceived extraversion in a best friend. PERCEPTUAL AND MOTOR SKILLS, 1983, 57, 891–894.

80. Campbell, J. B. Differential relationships of extraversion, impulsivity, and sociability to study habits. JOURNAL OF RESEARCH IN PERSONALITY, 1983, 17, 308–314.

81. Duckworth, D. H. Evaluation of a programme for increasing the effectiveness of personal problem-solving. THE BRITISH JOURNAL OF PSYCHOLOGY, 1983, 74, 119–127.

82. Feingold, A. Measuring humor ability: Revision and construct validation of the Humor Perceptiveness Test. PERCEPTUAL AND MOTOR SKILLS, 1983, 56, 159–166.

83. Hirschfeld, R. M. A., Klerman, G. L., Clayton, P. J., & Keller, M. B. Personality and depression: Empirical findings. ARCHIVES OF GENERAL PSYCHIATRY, 1983, 40, 993–998.

84. Kazi, M. U., & Piper, M. K. A comparison of personality attributes of science teachers and medical technologists. JOURNAL OF RESEARCH IN SCIENCE TEACHING, 1983, 20, 529–536.

85. Mikel, K. V. Extraversion in adult runners. PERCEPTUAL AND MOTOR SKILLS, 1983, 57, 143–146.

86. Peterson, C. A., & Knudson, R. M. Anhedonia: A construct validation approach. JOURNAL OF PERSONALITY ASSESSMENT, 1983, 47, 539–551.

87. Russell, J., & Wagstaff, G. F. Extraversion, neuroticism and time of birth. THE BRITISH JOURNAL OF SOCIAL PSYCHOLOGY, 1983, 22, 27–31.

88. Smith, B. D., Wilson, R. J., & Jones, B. E. Extraversion and multiple levels of caffeine-induced arousal: Effects on overhabituation and dishabituation. PSYCHOPHYSIOLOGY, 1983, 20, 29–34.

89. Feldstein, S., & Sloan, B. Actual and stereotyped speech tempos of extraverts and introverts. JOURNAL OF PERSONALITY, 1984, 52, 188–204.

90. Fletcher, K. E., & Averill, J. R. A scale for the measurement of role-playing ability. JOURNAL OF RESEARCH IN PERSONALITY, 1984, 18, 131–149.

91. Spotts, J. V., & Shontz, F. C. Drugs and personality: Extraversion-introversion. JOURNAL OF CLINICAL PSYCHOLOGY, 1984, 40, 624–628.

[406]

Eysenck Personality Questionnaire. Ages 7–15, 16 and over; 1975–76; EPQ; revision of the still-in-print Eysenck Personality Inventory (1963–69) and Junior Eysenck Personality Inventory (1963–70); 4 scores: psychoticism (P), extraversion (E), neuroticism (N), lie (L); no data on validity of the revised E, N, and L scales; norms consist of means and standard deviations, 2 editions; 2 levels; (10–15) minutes; H. J. Eysenck and Sybil B. G. Eysenck.

a) UNITED STATES EDITION. 1975–76; manual ('75, 19 pages); 1983 price data: $4.50 per 25 tests; $2.75 per set of scoring stencils for both levels; $2 per manual; $3.25 per specimen set; EdITS/Educational and Industrial Testing Service.*

1) *Junior.* Ages 7–15; norms based on British population; 1 form ('75, 4 pages).

2) *Adult.* Ages 16 and over; 1 form ('75, 4 pages); preliminary American norms ['76, 1 page].

b) BRITISH EDITION. 1975; manual (47 pages); £2.25 per 20 tests; £3 per set of scoring stencils for either level; £1.65 per manual; £2 per specimen set; Hodder & Stoughton Educational [England].*

1) *Junior.* Ages 7–15; 1 form (4 pages).

2) *Adult.* Ages 16 and over; 1 form (4 pages).

See T3:860 (72 references); for reviews by Jack Block, Paul Kline, Lawrence J. Stricker, and Auke Tellegen, see 8:554 (84 references).

TEST REFERENCES

1. Eaves, L. J., & Eysenck, H. J. A genotype-environmental model for psychoticism. ADVANCES IN BEHAVIOUR RESEARCH AND THERAPY, 1977, 1, 5–26.

2. Eysenck, S. B. G., Rust, J., & Eysenck, H. J. Personality and the classification of adult offenders. THE BRITISH JOURNAL OF CRIMINOLOGY, 1977, 17, 169–179.

3. Gossop, M. R., & Kristjansson, I. Crime and personality: A comparison of convicted and non-convicted drug-dependent males. THE BRITISH JOURNAL OF CRIMINOLOGY, 1977, 17, 264–273.

4. Bartol, C. R., & Holanchock, H. A. Eysenck's theory of criminality: A test on an American prisoner population. CRIMINAL JUSTICE AND BEHAVIOR, 1979, 6, 245–249.

5. Loo, R., & Wudel, P. Estimates of fakeability on the Eysenck Personality Questionnaire. SOCIAL BEHAVIOR AND PERSONALITY, 1979, 7, 157–160.

6. Barry, R. J. Electrodermal responses to emotive and non-emotive words as a function of personality differences in affect level. BIOLOGICAL PSYCHOLOGY, 1980, 11, 161–168.

7. Catts, S. V., Armstrong, M. S., Norcross, K., & McConaghy, N. Auditory hallucinations and the verbal transformation effect. PSYCHOLOGICAL MEDICINE, 1980, 10, 139–144.

8. James, A. L., & Barry, R. J. Habituation of electrodermal and respiratory responses to visual stimuli as a function of personality differences in affect level. BIOLOGICAL PSYCHOLOGY, 1980, 10, 253–264.

9. Maqsud, M. Eysenck's theory of personality and child-adult emotional attachments. MOTIVATION AND EMOTION, 1981, 5, 75–83.

10. McGurk, B. J., & Bolton, N. A comparison of the Eysenck Personality Questionnaire and the Psychological Screening Inventory in a delinquent sample and a comparison group. JOURNAL OF CLINICAL PSYCHOLOGY, 1981, 37, 874–879.

11. Raskin, R., & Hall, C. S. The Narcissistic Personality Inventory: Alternate form reliability and further evidence of construct validity. JOURNAL OF PERSONALITY ASSESSMENT, 1981, 45, 159–162.

12. Young, G. C. D., & Martin, M. Processing of information about self by neurotics. BRITISH JOURNAL OF CLINICAL PSYCHOLOGY, 1981, 20, 205–212.

13. Campbell, J. B., & Reynolds, J. H. Interrelationships of the Eysenck Personality Inventory and the Eysenck Personality Questionnaire. EDUCATIONAL AND PSYCHOLOGICAL MEASUREMENT, 1982, 42, 1067–1073.

14. Chapman, L. J., Chapman, J. P., & Miller, E. N. Reliabilities and intercorrelations of eight measures of proneness to psychosis. JOURNAL OF CONSULTING AND CLINICAL PSYCHOLOGY, 1982, 50, 187–195.

15. Goh, D. S., King, D. W., & King, L. A. Psychometric evaluation of the Eysenck Personality Questionnaire. EDUCATIONAL AND PSYCHOLOGICAL MEASUREMENT, 1982, 42, 297–309.

16. Henderson, M., & Furnham, A. Self-reported and self-attributed scores on personality, social skills, and attitudinal measures as compared between high and low nominated friends and acquaintances. PSYCHOLOGICAL REPORTS, 1982, 50, 88–90.

17. Hojat, M. Loneliness as a function of selected personality variables. JOURNAL OF CLINICAL PSYCHOLOGY, 1982, 38, 137–141.

18. Hojat, M. Psychometric characteristics of the UCLA Loneliness Scale: A study with Iranian college students. EDUCATIONAL AND PSYCHOLOGICAL MEASUREMENT, 1982, 42, 917–925.

19. Hood, J., Moore, T. E., & Garner, D. M. Locus of control as a measure of ineffectiveness in anorexia nervosa. JOURNAL OF CONSULTING AND CLINICAL PSYCHOLOGY, 1982, 50, 3–13.

20. Kirkcaldy, B. D. Personality and sex differences related to positions in team sports. INTERNATIONAL JOURNAL OF SPORT PSYCHOLOGY, 1982, 13, 141–153.

21. Montag, I., & Comrey, A. L. Comparison of certain MMPI, Eysenck, and Comrey personality constructs. MULTIVARIATE BEHAVIORAL RESEARCH, 1982, 17, 93–97.

22. Oei, T. P. S., & Jackson, P. R. Social skills and cognitive behavioral approaches to the treatment of problem drinking. JOURNAL OF STUDIES ON ALCOHOL, 1982, 43, 532–547.

23. Philips, C., & Hunter, M. Headache in a psychiatric population. THE JOURNAL OF NERVOUS AND MENTAL DISEASE, 1982, 170, 34–40.

24. Raine, A., Roger, D. B., & Venables, P. H. Locus of control and socialization. JOURNAL OF RESEARCH IN PERSONALITY, 1982, 16, 147–156.

25. Spielberger, C. D., & Jacobs, G. A. Personality and smoking behavior. JOURNAL OF PERSONALITY ASSESSMENT, 1982, 46, 396–403.

26. Thornton, D., & Kline, P. Reliability and validity of the Belief in Human Benevolence scale. BRITISH JOURNAL OF SOCIAL PSYCHOLOGY, 1982, 21, 57–62.

27. Turnbull, M. J., & Norris, H. Effects of transcendental meditation on self-identity indices and personality. THE BRITISH JOURNAL OF PSYCHOLOGY, 1982, 73, 57–68.

28. Elliott, S. A., Rugg, A. J., Watson, J. P., & Brough, D. I. Mood changes during pregnancy and after the birth of a child. THE BRITISH JOURNAL OF CLINICAL PSYCHOLOGY, 1983, 22, 295–308.

29. Eysenck, S. B. G. One approach to cross-cultural studies of personality. AUSTRALIAN JOURNAL OF PSYCHOLOGY, 1983, 35, 381–391.

30. Furnham, A., & Henderson, M. The mote in thy brother's eye, and the beam in thine own: Predicting one's own and others' personality test scores. THE BRITISH JOURNAL OF PSYCHOLOGY, 1983, 74, 381–389.

31. Kline, P., & Cooper, C. A factorial analysis of the authoritarian personality. BRITISH JOURNAL OF PSYCHOLOGY, 1984, 75, 171–176.

32. Stelmack, R. M., Wieland, L. D., Wall, M. U., & Plouffe, L. Personality and the effects of stress on recognition memory. JOURNAL OF RESEARCH IN PERSONALITY, 1984, 18, 164–178.

[407]

The Facial Interpersonal Perception Inventory. Ages 5 and over; 1980; FIPI; 15 scores: total positive self-perception, pleasant-unpleasant (PU), accepting-rejecting (AR), sleep-tension (ST), inconsistency, within factor inconsistency, inconsistency F ratio, total self-ideal, self-perception incongruence, PU incongruence, AR incongruence, ST incongruence, between factor incongruence, within factor incongruence, incongruence F ratio; norms consist of means and standard deviations; 1 form (4 pages); manual, rough first draft (55 pages); 1983 price data: $12.50 per 50 tests; $7 per specimen set; scoring service, $1 per test ($50 minimum); administration time not reported; Joseph J. Luciani and Richard E. Carney; Carney, Weedman and Associates.*

Review of The Facial Interpersonal Perception Inventory by CHARLES D. CLAIBORN, Associate Professor of Educational Psychology, University of Nebraska-Lincoln, Lincoln, NE:

The Facial Interpersonal Perception Inventory (FIPI) purports to assess dimensions of self-perception—or, if instructions are modified, perception of others—by soliciting responses to simplified line drawings of faces displaying different emotional expressions. The authors claim that such a device is "relatively free" of cultural bias, which they (erroneously) equate with social desirability, because the items employ only faces and not words. However, they provide no data to support this assertion.

The development of the FIPI is omitted from the draft of the manual I reviewed, although the authors allude to factor analytic procedures with orthogonal solution. The construction of the basic scales—Pleasant-Unpleasant (PU), Acceptance-Rejectance (AR), and Sleep-Tension (ST)—is based on early research on the perception of emotion, but the description of even these basic scales is not linked to the research from which they apparently emerged. The other variables measured by the FIPI—overall positive self-perception, inconsistency of responding across dimensions, and incongruence of present and ideal self-perception—make sense intuitively, but are not based on any apparent theoretical framework. In fact, the authors indulge in a good deal of unsupported speculation about what these higher order variables mean.

Individuals respond to the FIPI on separate 7-point scales, indicating the extent to which the faces are how they see themselves presently and ideally. The FIPI would seem very easy for adults and most children over five to take, although assistance in following instructions might be needed for younger children. Item scores sum to yield the basic scale scores, and are combined according to formulas provided in the manual to yield all other scores. The scoring by hand is, as the authors state, complicated at first, but it is clearly described. Formulas and tables are provided for converting raw scores to *T* scores, but the norms are inadequate. In particular, the norms for children are based on a very small sample, covering too wide an age range. Thus, interpretation of scores is difficult.

The FIPI is obviously in its infancy. Few reliability and validity data are reported, and they are generally weak. No internal consistencies for PU, AR, ST, or the higher order variables are given. Of the higher order variables, moreover, only incongruence correlates adequately (.75 to .90) with its contributing variables (present-ideal incongruence on PU, AR, and ST). Test-retest reliabilities for PU, AR, and ST are reported without an indication of the time elapsed between testings; they range between .64 and .94 for self-perception. The authors claim that there are no directly comparable measures with which to determine concurrent validity; yet the dimensions tapped by the FIPI do not seem entirely unique in the realm of personality assessment. Their one attempt to establish concurrent validity used the Self Concept Evaluation of Location Form (SELF), developed by one of the FIPI authors to assess the same dimensions as the FIPI, but with adjectives rather than faces. That study employed very small samples and generally failed to find much correspondence between the two instruments. The authors claim, on the basis of one published study, that the FIPI is a good predictor of marital adjustment. This study is only briefly described in the manual.

The authors state in the manual that "the FIPI is a relatively new instrument and, as such, lacks the depth of research needed to firmly establish its reliability and validity." If so (and I agree that it is), its publication is premature unless it simply serves to stimulate research. However, in the draft of the manual I reviewed, the authors seem to think the FIPI ready for a variety of applications. Given the scant information about its psychometric properties, I would urge considerable restraint in using the FIPI or in promoting its use until its reliability, validity, and usefulness in experimental applications are established. I do, however, think that continued development of the FIPI appears worthwhile. The constructs it seeks to measure are meaningful, and the approach to measurement it employs is a creative and potentially fruitful one.

Review of The Facial Interpersonal Perception Inventory by FRED ZIMRING, Professor of Psychology, Case Western Reserve University, Cleveland, OH:

The purpose of The Facial Interpersonal Perception Inventory (FIPI) is to measure the perception of the present and ideal selves and the perception of others. The FIPI consists of 13 cartoon faces which, the authors claim, represent the positive and negative ends of three dimensions: pleasant-unpleasant, acceptance-rejection, and sleep-tension (activation level). The respondent decides which cartoon faces represent how one sees oneself and these choices are seen as falling on the three dimensions. For example, the choices may be high on the pleasant-unpleasant dimension, low on the acceptance-rejection dimension, and high on the sleep-tension dimension. This configuration, the authors say, can be interpreted as "positive perception, but feelings of being closed off or rejecting."

It is claimed that "the FIPI is useful for a wide range of applications including self understanding" (which results from respondents learning their scores on the above dimensions), needs assessment, and evaluation of programs that have as their goals the enhancement of self-perception, clinical assessment, marriage, family, and child counseling. In addition, when family members rate themselves and each other "the status of the entire perceptual system of the family's connotation can be sketched." Using faces as scale items avoids problems that plague other self descriptive scales such as social desirability, desire to please the examiner, misreading, illiteracy, or other inabilities to handle semantic content.

An instrument such as the FIPI can be used in several ways. First, the self (or others) can be described by the items. In a context where the items are faces and not verbal statements, the meaning of the items is given by their position on the three dimensions. Thus, in the above example, the authors assert that choosing particular faces means that the person had "positive perception but feelings of being closed off." Unfortunately, it is impossible to determine the validity of the statement about the meaning of the choice of particular faces. No evidence is given to support the claim that particular faces represent specific dimensions. Also the validity of the authors' statements about the meaning of choosing a face high or low on a particular dimension has not been established. Some correlations were reported with the Self Concept Evaluation of Location Form, which is based on semantic differential dimensions, but these correlations were frequently negative, and even when they were positive they were low and hard to interpret.

Second, a self descriptive instrument can be used to describe the beliefs of the respondent. With the usual self descriptive instrument the person judges whether an item is true of him/her. Even though these descriptions might not be valid behaviorally, they allow for the illumination of the individual's self-beliefs. For example, if an item chosen as self-descriptive was a statement such as "I am nervous" we can conclude that the respondent believes that he or she is nervous. With the FIPI, on the other hand, since the items do not have direct semantic meanings, it is impossible to know what the self belief is when a particular face is chosen. We do not know how a respondent interprets the expression on any particular face, or, indeed, how respondents in general interpret the expressions on the cartoon faces. Thus, the non-verbal nature of the instrument, thought to be an asset, here becomes a liability.

Third, a scale like the FIPI can be used to measure the difference or discrepancy between the present and the ideal selves. This discrepancy has been thought to reflect self esteem or self regard. There is some evidence that the measurement of the self-ideal discrepancy is typically affected by social desirability. It may be that the self-ideal discrepancy measurement resulting from the FIPI, not being affected by social desirability, would be a unique measure. The self-ideal discrepancy can be measured globally, free of content from any one particular dimension. In addition, the authors advocate interpretation of discrepancies on each of the three dimensions. However, as previously mentioned, since the placement of particular faces on particular dimensions has not been determined empirically, the interpretation of particular discrepancies should be avoided.

High test-retest reliabilities (self-perception $r = .64$ to $.94$) are reported from a study wherein 60 married couples were administered the FIPI on two occasions. Unfortunately, the length of time between test administration was not reported. Finally, some evidence is presented concerning the internal consistency of the items.

To summarize, the FIPI is designed to measure the self-perception of present and ideal selves, the discrepancy between the two, and the perceptions of the same variables by others; it does this by means of the choice of cartoon faces which are said to represent three dimensions. However, because of the lack of validation studies, in this early stage of scale development the meaning of the choice of particular faces is unknown and should not be interpreted. Because the choice of cartoon faces probably does not involve social desirability, the FIPI would make an interesting research instrument for the investigation of present-ideal self discrepancy, especially in comparison to self scales using verbal items.

[408]

Family Environment Scale. Family members; 1974–81; FES; a part of The Social Climate Scales (T3:2227); 10 scores: cohesion, expressiveness, conflict, independence, achievement orientation, intellectual-cultural orientation, active recreational orientation, moral-religious emphasis, organization, control, plus a derived nonprofiled family incongruence score; reliability data for Form R only; norms for Form R only; Form R ('74, 4 pages); 2 other forms (not available as separates) may be administered: Form I (ideal family), Form E (expectations), which are rewordings of Form R items and may be requested from the publisher and reproduced locally; manual ('81, 40 pages); combined preliminary manual ('74, 48 pages) may still be used for administering and scoring, however authors strongly recommend use of current manual for interpreting scale results; bibliography ('79, 23 pages, includes studies for Social Climate Scales); separate answer sheets must be used; 1983 price data: $4.25 per 25 tests; $3.25 per 50 answer sheets; $3 per 50 profiles; $1 per scoring key; $5 per manual ('81); $6.25 per specimen set; (15–20) minutes; Rudolf H. Moos and Bernice S. Moos (manual); Consulting Psychologists Press, Inc.*

See T3:872 (14 references); for a review by Philip H. Dreyer, see 8:557 (4 references). For a review of The Social Climate Series, see 8:681.

TEST REFERENCES

1. Penk, W., Robinowitz, P., Kidd, R., & Nisle, A. Perceived family environments among ethnic groups of compulsive heroin users. ADDICTIVE BEHAVIORS, 1979, 4, 297–309.

2. DeFries, J. C., Plomin, R., Vandenberg, S. G., & Kuse, A. R. Parent-offspring resemblance for cognitive abilities in the Colorado Adoption Project: Biological, adoptive, and control parents and one-year-old children. INTELLIGENCE, 1981, 5, 245–277.

3. Forman, S. G., & Forman, B. D. Family environment and its relation to adolescent personality factors. JOURNAL OF PERSONALITY ASSESSMENT, 1981, 45, 163–167.

4. Fowler, P. C. Maximum likelihood factor structure of the Family Environment Scale. JOURNAL OF CLINICAL PSYCHOLOGY, 1981, 37, 160–164.

5. Hardy-Brown, K., Plomin, R., & DeFries, J. C. Genetic and environmental influences on the rate of communicative development in the first year of life. DEVELOPMENTAL PSYCHOLOGY, 1981, 17, 704–717.

6. Pinsker, M., & Geoffroy, K. A comparison of parent effectiveness training and behavior modification parent training. FAMILY RELATIONS, 1981, 30, 61–68.

7. Engfer, A., & Schneewind, K. A. Causes and consequences of harsh parental punishment: An empirical investigation in a representative sample of 570 German families. CHILD ABUSE & NEGLECT, 1982, 6, 129–139.

8. Fowler, P. C. Factor structure of the Family Environment Scale: Effects of social desirability. JOURNAL OF CLINICAL PSYCHOLOGY, 1982, 38, 285–292.

9. Fowler, P. C. Relationship of family environment and personality characteristics: Canonical analyses of self-attributions. JOURNAL OF CLINICAL PSYCHOLOGY, 1982, 38, 804–810.

10. Mitchell, R. E. Social networks and psychiatric clients: The personal and environmental context. AMERICAN JOURNAL OF COMMUNITY PSYCHOLOGY, 1982, 10, 387–401.

11. Robertson, D. U., & Hyde, J. S. The factorial validity of the Family Environment Scale. EDUCATIONAL AND PSYCHOLOGICAL MEASUREMENT, 1982, 42, 1233–1241.

12. Smits, M. R., & Oliver, J. M. Perceptions of university and family environments as functions of depression in university students. COGNITIVE THERAPY AND RESEARCH, 1982, 6, 447–454.

13. Splane, S., Monahan, J., Prestholt, D., & Friedlander, H. D. Parents' perceptions of the family's role in involuntary commitment. HOSPITAL AND COMMUNITY PSYCHIATRY, 1982, 33, 569–572.

14. Billings, A. G., & Moos, R. H. Comparisons of children of depressed and nondepressed parents: A social-environmental perspective. JOURNAL OF ABNORMAL CHILD PSYCHOLOGY, 1983, 11, 463–486.

15. Perry, M. A., Wells, E. A., & Doran, L. D. Parent characteristics in abusing and nonabusing families. JOURNAL OF CLINICAL CHILD PSYCHOLOGY, 1983, 12, 329–336.

16. Rowe, D. C. A biometrical analysis of perceptions of family environment: A study of twin and singleton sibling kinships. CHILD DEVELOPMENT, 1983, 54, 416–423.

17. Spiegel, D., & Wissler, T. Perceptions of family environment among psychiatric patients and their wives. FAMILY PROCESS, 1983, 22, 537–547.

18. Carpenter, P. J. The use of intergenerational family ratings: Methodological and interpretive considerations. JOURNAL OF CLINICAL PSYCHOLOGY, 1984, 40, 505–512.

Review of Family Environment Scale by NANCY A. BUSCH-ROSSNAGEL, Associate Professor of Human Development and Family Studies, Colorado State University, Fort Collins, CO:

The Family Environment Scale (FES) is a 90-item scale, answered in a true-false manner, that measures the social environmental characteristics of all families. The 10 subscales (of nine items each) are grouped into three underlying domains. The Relationship domain includes the Cohesion, Expressiveness, and Conflict subscales; the Personal Growth domain includes the Independence, Achievement Orientation, Intellectual-Cultural Orientation, and Moral-Religious Emphasis subscales; the System Maintenance domain includes the Organization and Control subscales.

The test is relatively easy to administer. The paper and pencil method requires reading, which will exclude participation by some family members (e.g., children). The format of the answer sheet is somewhat confusing because it requires marking an "X" above the item number for true, but putting the "X" below the number for false. With the stencil overlay, scoring is simply a matter of summing the "Xs" within circles in each column. A family average can be calculated for each subscale, and a family incongruence score (across the 10 subscales) can also be obtained.

Although not stated in the FES manual, the assumption behind the series of Social Climate Scales is that environments have unique personalities and that these personalities can be measured just as individual personalities can. In order to gain an initial pool of items tapping family personality, structured interviews with members of different types of families were conducted, and items were adapted from other social climate scales. The final 90-item form has good psychometric properties. The distributions of the items are close to a 50–50 split so that the means of six of the eight-item subscales range closely around 5.5; only the mean for conflict is markedly low at 3.3. The internal consistencies for the 10 subscales range from .61 to .78, and the corrected average item-subscale correlations range from .27 to .44. The 8-week test-retest reliabilities range from .68 to .86, and the 12-month stabilities range from .52 to .89.

Unfortunately, these psychometric properties do not carry over into the evidence for validity. The face validity of the FES is good. The wording of each item reflects not only the subscale, but also the underlying domain. However, no information is provided about the rationale for selecting the 10 subscales which were included or the three underlying domains. (In an examination of the second order factor structure of the German version of the FES, the second order factors grouped the subscales differently than the three underlying domains do). We need to know the relevance of the dimensions assessed by the FES for individual psychological and familial functioning. Such a rationale would be most useful for obtaining some evidence of predictive validity.

Along a similar line, no validity evidence is given for the goal of discriminating between families. While the subscale means of the distressed family sample are different from that of the normal family sample, no indication is given as to which are significantly different. More importantly, there is no basis for predicting on which subscales certain types of distressed families will differ from the normal sample. Such information and its theoretical foundation are necessary before the FES will really be useful for clinical applications.

The norms which are presented limit the usefulness of the FES as well. The norms are based on 1,125 normal and 500 distressed families. According to the manual, "the subsample for normal families includes families from all areas of the country, single-parent and multigenerational families, families drawn from ethnic minority groups, and families of all age groups." However, the breakdown of the sample into the various subgroups is not presented. Although subscale means are presented for families with an older member, for Black and Mexican-American families, for single-parent families, and for families of different sizes, the tables do not present which means are significantly different from "control" families. The authors state "that family size, partners' age, and education should be controlled in comparisons among groups of families," so separate norms and standard score conversion tables for these and other relevant variables should be available.

In summary, the internal psychometric properties of the FES make it one of the best measures available for assessing families. However, use of the FES should be tempered by two factors. First, the lack of background information on the normative samples makes it difficult to assess the comparability of samples. In addition to the breakdowns provided for age, ethnicity, and family size, information about the responses of families from different social classes, from different geographical regions, and with different levels of education would be helpful. Second, the lack of a rationale for the choice of the 10 subscales and three underlying domains makes prediction difficult and limits the clinical utility of the FES. The use of the FES in over 100 research studies documents the importance and need for a psychometrically sound scale of family environment. Additional work on validity and the inclusion of some rationale for subscale selection will enhance the FES for further research and clinical work.

Review of Family Environment Scale by NADINE M. LAMBERT, Professor of Education, University of California, Berkeley, Berkeley, CA:

PURPOSE. The Family Environment Scale (FES) was developed to provide a measure of the social-environmental characteristics of all types of families. There are three forms: the Real Form (Form R), which measures people's perceptions of their conjugal or nuclear family environments; the Ideal Form (Form I), which measures conceptions of ideal family environments; and the Expectations Form (Form E), which measures expectations about family settings. The FES contains 10 subscales assessing three underlying domains: Relationship, Personal Growth, and System Maintenance dimensions.

The items on the FES are naturalistic statements about family environments. Initially the items were constructed from information gathered in structured interviews with members of different types of families. Additional items were adapted from other scales and the total set of items subjected to a variety of item analysis studies. Five psychometric criteria were employed to select items for the final form of the FES. The overall true/false response rate for each item was as close to 50–50 as possible, items correlated more highly with their own subscales than with any other, and each of the subscales had an approximately equal number of items scored true and scored false.

PSYCHOMETRIC PROPERTIES. Data for samples of 1,125 representative and 500 distressed families were collected to provide normative data. The representative sample came from subjects from all areas of the country and included a sample of individuals drawn randomly from census tracts in the San Francisco area. The results for the randomly selected subjects in San Francisco were not different from those of the remainder of the representative group, supporting the authors' contention that the representative sample truly represents families in the country at large. Some of the distressed families were assessed in a psychiatrically-oriented family clinic, and others in a probation and parole department affiliated with a local correctional facility. Additional distressed family subjects were from families of alcohol abusers, of general psychiatric patients, and from families in which an adolescent or younger child was in a crisis situation.

The means and standard deviations for the FES subscales for the representative and distressed families are reported. Analysis of the differences after controlling for socioeconomic factors, age, and education showed that when compared to normal families, the distressed family members rated their families lower on cohesion, expressiveness, independence, and intellectual and recreational orientation, and higher on conflict and control.

RETEST RELIABILITY AND PROFILE STABILITY. Data from 47 family members in nine families who took Form R twice with an intervening 8-week period ranged from a low of .68 for the Independence subscale to a high of .86 for the Cohesion subscale. Test-retest reliabilities over a 4-month and 12-month period were also available. These stability coefficients ranged from .52 for the Independence subscale to .91 for the Moral-Religious Emphasis subscale, indicating a fair amount of stability in the scales over time.

An effort was made to ascertain the stability of the profiles of families for a 4- and 12-month interval. These results showed that the average correlation of the subscale means at time 1 and time 2 were .78 for the 4-month period and .71 over a period of 12 months.

VALIDITY EVIDENCE. Information on the validity of the subscales comes primarily from the evidence of the significance of the difference between the means of representative and distressed families on the subscales. Additionally, studies of the FES profiles of family members varying with respect to age, family size, length of marriage, and educational and occupational status showed differences in subscales depending on these family background factors. As the FES subscales provide reports of perceptions of family members differing with respect to a variety of social characteristics, there is no effort to identify typical or best families. Consequently ideal or prototypic family profiles are not available as criterion evidence against which to correlate family member's perceptions of their families.

ADMINISTRATION AND SCORING. The Form R test items are printed in a reusable booklet designed to be used with a separate answer sheet. The instructions may be read aloud to the subjects to control for any confusion in the meaning of an item or in the answering procedures. The FES also can be administered in a small group situation. A simple scoring key enables the user to compute scores on each of the scales in a straightforward manner.

CLINICAL AND PRACTICAL APPLICATIONS OF THE FES. The FES provides information on family members' perceptions of their family environment, and does not provide norm-referenced data regarding the ideal family. Research or clinical applications of the scale are several. The manual provides examples of how one can study differences between families that are relationship-oriented vs. achievement-oriented, and differences in parent and child perceptions of the family. The authors suggest that changes in family environments over time as a result of therapeutic interventions or reductions in crisis orientation would be a useful application.

By using the Ideal Form or the Expectations Form of the scale (both scales with similar item content, but items that are reworded to reflect either ideal or expectation statements), one has a perspective from which to identify aspects of the family environment that may be the cause of stress, as well as areas where particular changes over time might be desirable.

In addition to these examples of clinical applications of the scales, the authors provide a summary of the variety of research that has been conducted with the FES or its predecessors.

SUMMARY. The FES is a clearly formulated effort to develop a measure of the family environment that can be used with family members to describe differences among their perceptions, or to study differences between families of different types. The normative data provide statistics on the responses of representative and distressed families to the subscales of the FES. The normative data are not meant to be used to obtain values suggesting better or poorer families, but to study differences in family members' perceptions.

Although a great deal of additional research might be required before one could expect to validate particular descriptions of types of family environments, there is sufficient information available to enable the professional psychologist or the family-oriented professional to make practical use of the scale so long as no comparative judgments are made on the relative worth of family environments on the basis of the results from administering the FES.

[409]

Family Relations Test. Ages 3–7, 7–15, adults; 1957–78; FRT; 1978 revision consists of minor changes in the wording of 5 items, changes in administration of the test, and inclusion of normative data; individual; 4 levels; (20–25) minutes; Eva Bene and James Anthony (*a, b*); NFER-Nelson Publishing Co. [England].*

a) CHILDREN'S VERSION. Ages 3–7, 7–15; 1957–78; 1 form; 2 levels; manual ('78, 57 pages); 1985 price data: £42.50 per complete set; £23.95 per set of figures; £5.75 per set of item cards; £2.95 per 25 scoring sheets (specify level); £4.45 per manual; £4.55 per specimen set.

1) *Younger Children.* Ages 3–7; scoring sheet for younger children (no date, 4 pages).

2) *Older Children.* Ages 7–15; scoring sheet for older children ('65, 2 pages); record sheet for older children ('65, 4 pages).

b) ADULT VERSION. Adults; 1965–81; 1 form; 96 item cards; manual ('65, 28 pages); £42.50 per complete set; £5.75 per set of item cards; £23.95 per set of figures; £4.55 per 25 record forms; £4.75 per 25 scoring sheets; £6.55 per manual; £4.85 per specimen set.

c) MARRIED COUPLES VERSION. Married persons and parents; 1976; 1 form; 95 item cards; manual (37 pages); £41 per complete set; £23.95 per set of figures; £5.75 per set of item cards; £4.55 per 25 record sheets; £2.95 per 25 scoring sheets; £4.15 per manual; £4.55 per specimen set.

See T3:874 (33 references), 8:558 (18 references), and T2:1182 (4 references); for an excerpted review by B. Semeonoff of *a* and *b*, see 7:79 (7 references); see also P:81 (2 references); for reviews by John E. Bell, Dale B. Harris, and Arthur R. Jensen of *a*, see 5:132 (1 reference).

TEST REFERENCES

1. Teichman, Y., & Granot, N. Overt and fantasized aggression toward parents by enuretic and honenuretic children. JOURNAL OF ABNORMAL CHILD PSYCHOLOGY, 1977, 5, 379–386.

2. Jacobson, R. S., & Straker, G. A research project on abusing parents and their spouses. CHILD ABUSE & NEGLECT, 1979, 3, 381–390.

3. Rekers, G. A., & Mead, S. Early intervention for female sexual identity disturbance: Self-monitoring of play behavior. JOURNAL OF ABNORMAL CHILD PSYCHOLOGY, 1979, 7, 405–423.

[410]

Fast-Tyson Health Knowledge Test. High school and college; 1970–81; 11 scores: personal health, exercise-relaxation-sleep, nutrition and diet, consumer health, contemporary health problems, tobacco-alcohol-drugs-narcotics, safety and first aid, communicable and noncommunicable diseases, mental health, sex and family, total; reliability data and norms are for total scores, grades 12 and 13 only; Forms A, B, ('81, 8 pages, forms are identical except that subtest items appear in inverse order); general information sheets ('81, 10 pages); administration materials ('81, 5 pages); personal data sheet ('81, 1 page); 1983 price data: $60 per 50 tests of one form; $75 per 25 each of both forms; $2.50 per set of general information sheets (including a sample item from each subtest); 49(50) minutes; Charles G. Fast and Harry L. Tyson, Jr.; Charles G. Fast.*

For a review by James E. Bryan of the 1975 edition, see 8:412.

[411]

Fear Survey Schedule. College and adults; 1964–77; FSS; self-ratings on 108 fears; norms, consisting of means and standard deviations, based on 1964, 73-item edition; 1 form ('69, 3 pages); revised preliminary manual ('77, 11 pages); 1983 price data: $5 per 25 tests; (15) minutes; Joseph Wolpe and Peter J. Lang; EdITS/Educational and Industrial Testing Service.*

See T3:883 (53 references); for a review by Charles D. Spielberger, see 8:559 (32 references); see also T2:1185 (14 references); for a review by R. G. Demaree, see 7:80 (17 references).

TEST REFERENCES

1. Ginsberg, G., & Marks, I. Costs and benefits of behavioural psychotherapy: A pilot study of neurotics treated by nurse-therapists. PSYCHOLOGICAL MEDICINE, 1977, 7, 685–700.

2. Glenn, S. S., & Hughes, H. H. Imaginal response events in systematic desensitization: A pilot study. BIOLOGICAL PSYCHOLOGY, 1978, 7, 303–309.

3. Milton, F., & Hafner, J. The outome of behavior therapy for agoraphobia in relation to marital adjustment. ARCHIVES OF GENERAL PSYCHIATRY, 1979, 36, 807–811.

4. Anderson, M. P., & Borkovec, T. D. Imagery processing and fear reduction during repeated exposure to two types of phobic imagery. BEHAVIOUR RESEARCH AND THERAPY, 1980, 18, 537–540.

5. Sheehan, D. V., Ballenger, J., & Jacobsen, G. Treatment of endogenous anxiety with phobic, hysterical and hypochondriacal symptoms. ARCHIVES OF GENERAL PSYCHIATRY, 1980, 37, 51–59.

6. Woodward, R., & Jones, R. B. Cognitive restructuring treatment: A controlled trial with anxious patients. BEHAVIOUR RESEARCH AND THERAPY, 1980, 18, 401–407.

7. Arrick, M. C., Voss, J., & Rimm, D. C. The relative efficacy of thought-stopping and covert assertion. BEHAVIOUR RESEARCH AND THERAPY, 1981, 19, 17–24.

8. Bland, K., & Hallam, R. S. Relationship between response to graded exposure and marital satisfaction in agoraphobics. BEHAVIOUR RESEARCH AND THERAPY, 1981, 19, 335–338.

9. Evans, P. D. The effects of sex and fear level of subjects on the snake approach behaviour of dyads. BEHAVIOUR RESEARCH AND THERAPY, 1981, 19, 207–214.

10. Johansson, J., & Ost, L. G. Applied relaxation in treatment of "cardiac neurosis": A systematic case study. PSYCHOLOGICAL REPORTS, 1981, 48, 463–468.

11. Liberman, R. P., & Eckman, T. Behavior therapy vs insight-oriented therapy for repeated suicide attempters. ARCHIVES OF GENERAL PSYCHIATRY, 1981, 38, 1126–1130.

12. Ost, L. G., Jerremalm, A., & Johansson, J. Individual response patterns and the effects of different behavioral methods in the treatment of social phobia. BEHAVIOUR RESEARCH AND THERAPY, 1981, 19, 1–16.

13. Chambless, D. L., Foa, E. B., Groves, G. A., & Goldstein, A. J. Exposure and communications training in the treatment of agoraphobia. BEHAVIOUR RESEARCH AND THERAPY, 1982, 20, 219–231.

14. Curtis, G. C., Cameron, O. G., & Nesse, R. M. The dexamethasone suppression test in panic disorder and agoraphobia. THE AMERICAN JOURNAL OF PSYCHIATRY, 1982, 139, 1043–1046.

15. Emmelkamp, P. M. G., & Mersch, P. P. Cognition and exposure in vivo in the treatment of agoraphobia: Short-term and delayed effects. COGNITIVE THERAPY AND RESEARCH, 1982, 6, 77–88.

16. Granell de Aldaz, E. Factor analysis of a Venezuelan Fear Survey Schedule. BEHAVIOUR RESEARCH AND THERAPY, 1982, 20, 313–322.

17. Ost, L. G., Johansson, J., & Jerremalm, A. Individual response patterns and the effects of different behavioral methods in the treatment of claustrophobia. BEHAVIOUR RESEARCH AND THERAPY, 1982, 20, 445–460.

18. Roberts, R. J., & Weerts, T. C. Cardiovascular responding during anger and fear imagery. PSYCHOLOGICAL REPORTS, 1982, 50, 219–230.

19. Sappington, A. A., Burleson, R., Studstill, L., Rice, J., Gordon, J., & Cornelison, K. Reduction of avoidant behavior through the semantic conditioning of a self-related target stimulus. COGNITIVE THERAPY AND RESEARCH, 1982, 6, 315–323.

20. Traub, G. S. Relationship between locus of control and maladaptive fears. PSYCHOLOGICAL REPORTS, 1982, 50, 1249–1250.

21. Yanni, M. I. Y. Perception of parents' behavior and children's general fearfulness. NURSING RESEARCH, 1982, 31, 79–82.

22. Rose, R. J., & Ditto, W. B. A developmental-genetic analysis of common fears from early adolescence to early adulthood. CHILD DEVELOPMENT, 1983, 54, 361–368.

23. Mannion, N. E., & Levine, B. A. Effects of stimulus representation and cue category level on exposure (flooding) therapy. BRITISH JOURNAL OF CLINICAL PSYCHOLOGY, 1984, 23, 1–7.

[412]

Figure Classification Test. Applicants for industrial work with 7 to 9 years of schooling; 1976; 1 form (no date, 38 pages, English and Afrikaans); manual (21 pages, English and Afrikaans); norms supplement (no date, 8 pages, English and Afrikaans); scoring stencil (no date, 1 page); separate answer sheets must be used; price data available from publisher; 60(70) minutes; T. R. Taylor; National Institute for Personnel Research [South Africa].*

[413]

Fine Dexterity Test. Applicants for jobs involving fine motor dexterity; 1983; FDT; 2 scores: finger dexterity, fine tool dexterity; no data on reliability; no norms, publisher recommends use of local norms; 1 form; manual ('83, 10 pages); 1983 price data: £38.20 per complete set; £2.55 per set of spare washers and collars; manual free on request with order; 6(8) minutes; Educational & Industrial Test Services Ltd. [England].*

[414]

Firefighter Selection Test. Applicants for firefighter trainee positions; 1983; FST; measures mechanical comprehension, reading comprehension, report interpretation; no reliability and validity data for complete Form B; no norms, publisher recommends use of local norms; Forms A, B, (32 pages); separate answer sheets must be used; test key (1 page); technical report (23 pages); administrator's guide (5 pages); 1984 price data: leasing fee, $170 per 20 tests, scoring key, administrator's manual, and technical report (minimum order); $3.50 per additional test; $.10 per answer sheet; 150(170) minutes; Psychological Services, Inc.*

[415]

Fireman Entrance Aptitude Tests. Prospective firefighters; covers verbal and quantitative learning ability, interest, common sense and mechanical aptitude; 2 forms: 62A, 70A (each in 2 booklets); instruction manual available; separate answer sheets must be used; distribution restricted to civil service commissions or other competent municipal officials; price data available from publisher; administration time not reported; McCann Associates, Inc.*

[416]

The FIRO Awareness Scales. Grades 4–8, 9–16 and adults; 1957–82; 7 tests; revised manual ('78, 40 pages); 1985 price data: $6 per manual; William C. Schutz and Marilyn Wood (*b*); Consulting Psychologists Press, Inc.*

a) FIRO-B [FUNDAMENTAL INTERPERSONAL RELATIONS ORIENTATION—BEHAVIOR]. Grades 9–16 and adults; 1957–82; 6 scores of behavior toward others: inclusion (expressed, wanted), control (expressed, wanted), affection (expressed, wanted); no high school norms; 1 form ('57, 3 pages, reprinted as a 1977 edition with 1967 copyright); manual supplement ('77, 39 pages); Understanding your FIRO-B Results ('82, 11 pages); $1.50 per set of scoring keys; $1 per Understanding Your FIRO-B Results; $3 per specimen set (without manual); [8–15] minutes; Ed Musselwhite and Diane Schlageter (Understanding Results).

b) FIRO-BC [FUNDAMENTAL INTERPERSONAL RELATIONS ORIENTATION—BEHAVIOR OF CHILDREN]. Grades 4–8; 1972; 6 scores: same as for FIRO-B; 1 form ('72, 3 pages, reprinted as a 1977 edition); $4.25 per 25 tests; $3.75 per set of scoring keys; $4 per specimen set (without manual and scoring keys); administration time not reported.

c) FIRO-F [FUNDAMENTAL INTERPERSONAL RELATIONS ORIENTATION—FEELINGS]. Grades 9–16 and adults; 1957–67; 6 scores of feelings toward others: inclusion (expressed, wanted), control (expressed, wanted), affection (expressed, wanted); 1 form ('67, 3 pages); $4.25 per 25 tests; $5 per set of scoring keys; $5.25 per specimen set (without manual); [8–15] minutes.

d) LIPHE [LIFE INTERPERSONAL HISTORY ENQUIRY]. Grades 9–16 and adults; 1962; retrospective childhood relationships with parents; 12 scores (6 scores for each parent): inclusion (behavior, feelings), control (behavior, feelings), affection behavior-feeling, perceived parental approval; 1 form ('62, 3 pages); $9 per 25 tests; $3.25 per set of scoring keys; $3.75 per specimen set (without manual); [20] minutes.

e) COPE [COPING OPERATIONS PREFERENCE ENQUIRY]. Grades 9–16 and adults; 1962; 5 scores: denial, isolation, projection, regression-dependency, turning-against-self; no data on reliability; separate forms for males, females, (4 pages); $9 per 25 tests; $1 per specimen set (without manual); [20] minutes.

f) MATE [MARITAL ATTITUDES EVALUATION]. Grades 9–16 and adults; 1967–76; 5 scores: inclusion (behavior, feelings), control (behavior, feelings), affection; 1 form ('76, 3 pages, identical with husband and wife forms copyrighted 1967 except for format and wording changes); $4.25 per 25 tests; $1.25 per set of scoring keys; $1.50 per specimen set (without manual); [8–15] minutes.

g) VAL-ED [EDUCATIONAL VALUES]. Grades 9–15 and adults; 1967–77; 12 scores: importance, mind, teacher-student (control, affection), teacher-community (inclusion, control, affection), administrator-teacher (inclusion, control, affection), administrator-community (control, affection); 1 form ('77, 3 pages); $9 per 25 tests; $2.50 per set of scoring keys; $2.50 per specimen set (without manual); [15] minutes.

See T3:890 (45 references), 8:555 (147 references) and T2:1176 (58 references); for a review by Bruce Bloxom, see 7:78 (70 references); see also P:79 (30 references) and 6:94 (15 references).

TEST REFERENCES

1. Andrews, D. A., Farmer, C., Russell, R. J., Grant, B. A., & Kiessling, J. J. The research component of the Ottawa Criminal Court Volunteer Program: Theoretical rationale, operationalization and evaluation strategy. CANADIAN JOURNAL OF CRIMINOLOGY AND CORRECTIONS, 1977, 19, 118–133.

2. Annis, H. M. Group treatment of incarcerated offenders with alcohol and drug problems: A controlled evaluation. CANADIAN JOURNAL OF CRIMINOLOGY, 1979, 21, 3–15.

3. O'Leary, M. R., Donovan, D. M., Chaney, E. F., & Speltz, M. L. Correlates of clinicians' perceptions of patients in alcoholism treatment. THE JOURNAL OF CLINICAL PSYCHIATRY, 1979, 40, 344–347.

4. Katz, L., & Dalby, J. T. Computer-assisted and traditional psychological assessment of elementary-school-aged children. CONTEMPORARY EDUCATIONAL PSYCHOLOGY, 1981, 6, 314–322.

5. Vickers, R. R., Jr., & Hervig, L. K. Comparison of three psychological defense mechanism questionnaires. JOURNAL OF PERSONALITY ASSESSMENT, 1981, 45, 630–638.

6. Akin, G. Interpersonal correlates of Fromm's character types. SOCIAL BEHAVIOR AND PERSONALITY, 1982, 10, 77–81.

7. Shaw, M. E., & Webb, J. N. When compatibility interferes with group effectiveness: Facilitation of learning in small groups. SMALL GROUP BEHAVIOR, 1982, 13, 555–564.

8. Ware, R., Barr, J. E., & Boone, M. Subjective changes in small group processes: An experimental investigation. SMALL GROUP BEHAVIOR, 1982, 13, 395–401.

9. Elliott, T. R., & Byrd, E. K. A pilot study of effects of cardiopulmonary resuscitation training on participants' self-concepts. PERCEPTUAL AND MOTOR SKILLS, 1983, 57, 604–606.

10. Tucker, J. H. Leadership orientation as a function of interpersonal need structure: A replication with negative results. SMALL GROUP BEHAVIOR, 1983, 14, 107–114.

11. Wanat, P. E. Social skills: An awareness program with learning disabled adolescents. JOURNAL OF LEARNING DISABILITIES, 1983, 16, 35–38.
12. Williams, E. U. Adolescent loneliness. ADOLESCENCE, 1983, 18, 51–66.

Review of The FIRO Awareness Scales by PETER D. LIFTON, Assistant Professor of Psychology, The University of North Carolina at Chapel Hill, Chapel Hill, NC:

Schutz's FIRO Awareness Scales are seven self-report questionnaire measures concerned with the assessment of interpersonal relationships. The ultimate purpose of the FIRO is to aid persons in developing an awareness of themselves and of their relations to other people. The FIRO scales assess a person's characteristic behavior toward other people (FIRO-B); a child's characteristic behavior toward other children (FIRO-BC); a person's characteristic feelings toward others (FIRO-F); a retrospective account of a person's childhood relationship with his or her parents (LIPHE); a person's satisfaction with the behaviors and feelings of his or her significant other (MATE); a person's perception of the optimal interrelation among children, teachers, administrators, and the community in a school setting (VALED); and a person's preferred defense or coping style (COPE).

The first six scales yield subscores for the interpersonal dimensions of "inclusion" (the degree to which a person associates with others), "control" (the extent to which a person assumes responsibility or dominates people), and "affection" (the degree to which a person becomes emotionally involved with others). Subscores also are obtained for "expressed" behavior and feelings (how a person interacts with other people), and "wanted" behavior and feelings (how a person wishes others would interact with him or her). These subscales form a 3 x 2 typology defining six theoretically though not empirically discrete categories of interpersonal relationships.

The seventh scale, COPE, measures a preference for either the defense mechanism of denial, isolation, projection, regression-dependency, or turning-against-the-self. How this scale relates conceptually or empirically with the other six FIRO Awareness Scales is uncertain.

The FIRO Awareness Scales are reviewed here critically in terms of traditional issues of psychological measurement (i.e., reliability; and content, criterion-related, and construct validity; cf. Anastasi, 1982; Cronbach, 1984; Gough, 1965). Additional discussion considers the scales' practical utility and their contribution to clinical and counseling psychology.

Information concerning the reliability, validity, and utility of these scales is based primarily on Schutz's FIRO Awareness Scales manual. This well-written document, intended for both experts and laypersons, provides a clear, precise, and user-friendly exposition of the various FIRO scales.

DESCRIPTION OF SCALES. Except for the COPE measure, all other measures consist of single statement items to which persons respond using a 6-point Guttman type scale. A positive consequence of Guttman scaling is high internal consistency. A negative consequence is that only nomothetic comparisons of item responses are meaningful. This, however, is more problematic for therapists than researchers.

The COPE measure describes six hypothetical characters involved in anxiety-provoking situations. Persons rank order five possible responses (defense styles) that each character might employ. This rank ordering approach poses the opposite problem from the Guttman scaling approach. For the COPE scale scores, only idiographic comparisons are meaningful since preference for one defense style precludes preference for the other four.

RELIABILITY. Reliability of the scales is excellent with reproducibility coefficients (being able to accurately predict item responses from scale scores) at least .80, and most exceeding .90. FIRO-B shows good stability over time with test-retest reliability coefficients for its subscales ranging from .71 to .82. However, no test-retest reliability is reported for the other scales, and no indication of reliability is reported for the COPE scale. Such information needs to be provided.

CONTENT VALIDITY. Schutz argues that because of the Guttman scaling technique and high reproducibility coefficients, content validity for all the scales (except COPE) is implied if not established. However, users should keep in mind that the FIRO scales represent an operationalization of Schutz's theoretical model of interpersonal relationships. As such, the content validity is for Schutz's particular domain of interpersonal behavior and feelings. Other persons might choose to define the content of this domain differently.

The content validity of COPE is suspect. The five defense mechanisms "were selected as representative of all coping mechanisms following an extensive analysis of...the psychological literature." Anna Freud (1946) describes over 25 defense mechanisms, Norma Haan (1977) 30 mechanisms. COPE, by only measuring five, probably does not represent adequately the content of the defense mechanism domain.

CRITERION-RELATED VALIDITY. Most of the work on criterion-related validity has been for the FIRO-B. The scale or its subscales successfully differentiate persons in sociable vs. non-sociable occupations, pre- vs. post-Synanon therapy patients, working vs. non-working wives, high vs. low self-esteem adolescent girls, and reticent vs. non-reticent students in beginning college speech courses. These findings and others reported in the test manual strongly suggest the concurrent validity of the FIRO-B.

Most studies of the FIRO-B's predictive validity focus on providing empirical evidence for the theory of "FIRO-B Compatibility"; that is, predicting the compatibility between two persons based on the configuration of their FIRO-B subscale scores. Dyads studied include doctors and patients, therapists and clients, principals and curriculum coordinators, teachers and students, husbands and wives, and supervisors and subordinates. The results suggest some evidence for predictive validity but the overall pattern of results is too mixed to allow for a definitive statement on the issue.

The evidence for the criterion-related validity (both concurrent and predictive) of the other six FIRO scales is inconclusive. Most evidence is based on a study of school administrators (Schutz, 1977). The results for criterion-related validity are promising but more studies with other populations are needed.

CONSTRUCT VALIDITY. The weakest aspect of the FIRO Awareness Scales is their construct validity. Evidence for the scales' convergent validity is minimal. Furthermore, moderate intercorrelations among various subscales within each measure suggest that differentiations of persons by their "FIRO type" (a major theoretical part of the FIRO model) may not be based on meaningful psychological constructs. Slightly better evidence exists for discriminant validity, in particular the FIRO's lack of association with demographic variables (e.g., sex, age, marital status, socioeconomic status). However, a systematic examination of the FIRO Awareness Scales' construct validity in the Campbell and Fiske (1959) multitrait-multimethod matrix tradition is needed.

TARGET POPULATION. The FIRO scales have been administered to a wide variety of persons including students, educators, salespersons, business managers, architects, and medical and military personnel. The test manual provides norms for both combined and distinct subject populations. Thus, the FIRO's practical utility and application appears limitless, at least for non-clinical populations.

CONCLUDING REMARKS. Schutz's FIRO Awareness Scales provide useful information concerning the nature of interpersonal relationships. Of the seven FIRO scales, FIRO-B ranks best psychometrically, COPE poorest. However, even the FIRO-B's scores should be interpreted judiciously. This is due to the less than certain psychological meaning of the "FIRO types" derived from the various FIRO-B subscales. Researchers, clinicians, and counseling personnel should approach these classifications with caution, especially when predicting a person's interpersonal behavior. This cautionary note is particularly important since the 1978 FIRO test material package includes a booklet entitled "Clinical Interpretation of the FIRO-B" (Ryan, 1977). The booklet's clinical predictions may overstep the limits of the psychometric evidence for the FIRO Awareness Scales.

REVIEWER'S REFERENCES

Freud, A. THE EGO AND THE MECHANISMS OF DEFENSE. New York: International Universities Press, 1946.

Campbell, D., & Fiske, D. Convergent and discriminant validity by the multitrait-multimethod matrix. PSYCHOLOGICAL BULLETIN, 1959, 56, 81–105.

Gough, H. G. Conceptual analysis of psychological test scores and diagnostic variables. JOURNAL OF ABNORMAL PSYCHOLOGY, 1965, 70, 294–302.

Haan, N. COPING AND DEFENDING. New York: Academic Press, 1977.

Ryan, L. CLINICAL INTERPRETATION OF THE FIRO-B. Palo Alto, CA: Consulting Psychologists Press, 1977.

Schutz, W. C. LEADERS OF SCHOOLS: FIRO THEORY APPLIED TO ADMINISTRATORS. LaJolla, CA: University Associates, 1977.

Anastasi, A. PSYCHOLOGICAL TESTING (5th edition). New York: MacMillan, 1982.

Cronbach, L. J. ESSENTIALS OF PSYCHOLOGICAL TESTING. New York: Harper & Row, 1984.

[417]

The Fletcher Time-by-Count Test of Diadochokinetic Syllable Rate. Ages 6–13; 1978; no data on reliability and validity; norms consist of means and standard deviations; individual; 1 form (2 pages, includes instructions for administration and scoring); 1984 price data: $11.95 per 150 forms; administration time not reported; Samuel G. Fletcher; C.C. Publications, Inc.*

[418]

Flexibility Language Dominance Test, Spanish/English. Spanish/English bilingual students ages 10 and over; 1978; 3 scores: Spanish total, English total, difference score interpreted according to a 7 level dominance rating system; no norms; 1 form ('78, 4 pages); no specific manual; general directions for administration and interpretation; 1982 price data: $12.75 per complete test set; 12 minutes; Gary D. Keller; Publishers Test Service.*

Review of Flexibility Language Dominance Test, Spanish/English by EUGENE E. GARCIA, *Director/Professor, Center for Bilingual/Bicultural Education, Arizona State University, Tempe, AZ:*

The purpose of this test is to measure linguistic dominance of Spanish/English bilinguals, 10 years of age or older. In doing so it provides a specific measure of Spanish and English performance which is integrated into a relative dominance interpretation. The test's primary focus is Spanish and English lexicon. It requires the test-taker to form Spanish and English words from five nonsense word presentations which have been controlled for number of possible word derivatives in each language (e.g., test-takers are requested to generate Spanish words from the nonsense word MAPURITO within a 60-second temporal period).

The test's major strengths lie in its easy and time-saving administration requirements, and its attempt to measure and arrive at a relative proficiency index. The test's major weaknesses, unfortunately, are significant. First, it relies completely on the measure of language within the domain of lexicon production and does not include morphological or syntactic proficiency information. Moreover, it centers on written measures as opposed to oral production and/or receptive ability in either language. These construct limitations weaken its overall "face" validity and provide a very limited measure (vocabulary only) of linguistic performance confounded with the "writing" ability of the test taker.

A second major weakness is its simplistic evaluation of language dominance. Recent sociolinguistic data with Spanish/English bilinguals suggest that the use of languages may be bound by social contexts. Additionally, regional and ethnic dialect variations may serve to produce social context use or ability differences as well as codeswitching. Neither of these issues is considered by the author of this test.

Lastly, the author cites some limited evidence regarding the reliability and validity of this instrument. This data was generated by an administration of the test to 100 fifth- and sixth-grade students. This is an extremely limited and non-diversified group from which to determine reliability and/or validity estimates.

SUMMARY. The test measures Spanish and/or English lexicon production by requesting the test-taker to form Spanish and/or English words from five resource word presentations (e.g., form as many words as possible in Spanish from the nonsense word MAPURITO.) The test focuses on lexicon production without concern for broader linguistic, pragmatic, and sociolinguistic assessment of language proficiency. No adequate validity or reliability analysis is presently available. Therefore, the instrument is best utilized as a preliminary measure of an individual's lexical knowledge in Spanish and/or English.

Review of Flexibility Language Dominance Test, Spanish/English by SYLVIA SHELLENBERGER, Director of Psychology and Education, The Medical Center of Central Georgia, Department of Family Practice, Associate Professor, Mercer University School of Medicine, Macon, GA:

Designed to measure the language dominance of Spanish/English bilingual students, the Flexibility Language Dominance Test, Spanish/English requires students to construct words from a group of letters. For each series of letters, 1 minute is allowed for forming words in Spanish and 1 minute in English. The author states that dominance can be determined from a difference score (i.e., the English total subtracted from the Spanish total) and students can be classified both in terms of a seven-level rating system and in terms of their relative standing within a testing group. In this reviewer's opinion, however, there is little indication that the ratings and classifications obtained provide a valid indication of language dominance. Concerns center not only in scoring and interpreting the test, but also in administration and stated purpose.

The examiner's manual, consisting of one printed page, lacks a thorough explanation of such basic aspects as the purpose, uses, and limitations of the test. No indication is given as to how the measure was developed, nor who should conduct the test administration. No information is provided on what scores mean and how to use them. Instead, only vague guidelines are given that will likely lead a test user to highly ambiguous, inconsistent results.

Whether the test is appropriate for the stated target population remains unproven. The test is purported to be appropriate for bilingual students 10 years and older, although it is this examiner's experience that many 10-year-olds will have difficulty constructing words in the spontaneous manner required by the test.

The layout of the test booklet is an additional concern. The guide states that the Spanish-English order is to be alternated; however, the test is not printed accordingly. With the habitual impulse to move from left to right, many children will undoubtedly continue to follow the left to right pattern as printed. Furthermore, switching from one language to another may result in score differences not related to dominance. Instead production may be confounded by the extraneous element of switching time. Kolers (1966) and Macnamara (1967) found that switching takes time and that amount of time is unrelated to degree of bilingualism.

The first administrative concern arises with the set of background information questions on the front of the response booklet. The questions are printed in Spanish and are to be asked in Spanish unless the child is known to be English dominant. Then questions may be translated. Since the test is designed to measure dominance, it is assumed that directions in a group administration would be in Spanish. Does this not set the pattern for thinking and writing in Spanish? Furthermore, the items asked appear to be haphazardly chosen. For example, what is the usefulness of knowing the type of work a parent does without knowing if the parent lives with or has contact with the child?

Many important points of administration are not delineated. For example, the language to be used in giving test directions is not specified. The length of time the practice session may continue is not stated nor is the type of input the administrator may have; the more practice and help the child has, the better the test performance is likely to be. Similarly, if the test is administered in group format with an oral practice session, a child is likely to learn from answers given by fellow test-takers, hence improving performance over what could be expected in individual administration. The exact format for the practice session should be explained. In addition, students often ask questions while taking the test; directions do not indicate how the examiner is to respond. To illustrate, no mention is made as to whether a letter listed may be used more than once. Without a script for instructions or answers to common questions, the test cannot be given in a standardized fashion.

A cursory coverage of scoring provides insufficient guidance for the examiner. How to score a word using a letter more than once, or a word formed correctly but listed under the incorrect language heading are just two of the many unclarified scoring dilemmas. Likewise, guidance on interpretation of scores is unsatisfactory. The child with low production will obtain a classification of "balanced Spanish/English bilingual." At the same time that a child's classification is in the balanced category due to limited responses on the test, another child may be classified as balanced as a result of high production in both languages. The close ranking of these two children in terms of their relative standing within a group, holds little meaning either for diagnostic purposes or for program planning. If category labels are always accompanied by Spanish and English totals, production can be judged; however, without totals, the rankings appear meaningless. Furthermore, the test guide does not indicate how the dominance classifications were determined and if they were validated against any criterion.

Data supporting the validity of the test reportedly derive from correlations with the Ambiguous Word Language Dominance Test, Spanish/English, of 100 fifth- and sixth-grade students. However, information regarding the group studied leaves many questions unanswered. For example, which scores and in what manner were the two tests correlated? What is the evidence that this criterion test is effective in determining language dominance? Were the two tests given in counterbalanced order for the validity study? In addition, the manual should supply a description of the study group. There is no indication that the scores obtained correlate with direct measures of bilingual skills. In fact, the test manual is totally lacking in any indication of predictive, concurrent or construct validity.

Test reliability was measured using a test-retest procedure with the group of 100 fifth- and sixth-graders at a six week interval. The correlation coefficient obtained was .87. Again, a thorough description of the study group and an explanation as to which scores were correlated should be provided for the test user.

In summary, the publication of this assessment tool appears premature. Much more specificity in scoring, administering and interpreting the test, more normative data, and more documentation of reliability and validity are needed before this examiner would put credence in information obtained on the Flexibility Language Dominance Test.

REVIEWER'S REFERENCES

Kolers, P. A. Reading and talking bilingually. AMERICAN JOURNAL OF PSYCHOLOGY, 1966, 79, 357–376.

Macnamara, J. The linguistic independence of bilinguals. JOURNAL OF VERBAL LEARNING AND VERBAL BEHAVIOR, 1967, 5, 729–736.

[419]

The Flint Infant Security Scale. Ages 3–24 months; 1974–83; FISS; mental health; no data on reliability; individual; 1 form ('74, 8 pages); revised manual ('83, 14 pages); price data available from publisher; (30–60) minutes; Betty M. Flint; Guidance Centre [Canada].*

For a review by Jane V. Hunt, see 8:560 (1 reference).

[420]

Florida International Diagnostic-Prescriptive Vocational Competency Profile. Adolescents and adults (educable and trainable mentally retarded, specific learning disabled, seriously emotionally disturbed, economically disadvantaged); 1979–80; "designed to evaluate individuals' general functional level and six specific domains of vocational competency"; 7 scores: vocational self-help skills, social-emotional adjustment, work attitudes-responsibility, cognitive-learning ability, perceptual-motor skills, general work habits, total; individual; 1 form ('79, 5 pages); manual ('80, 42 pages); individualized vocational prescription ('79, 4 pages); 1983 price data: $25.50 per complete set including 10 record forms and 10 prescription sheets; $9 per 10 record forms; $9 per 10 prescription sheets; $9 per manual; administration time not reported; Howard Rosenberg and Dennis G. Tosolowski; Stoelting Co.*

Review of Florida International Diagnostic-Prescriptive Vocational Competency Profile by PATRICIA W. LUNNEBORG, Professor of Psychology, University of Washington, Seattle, WA:

The Florida International Diagnostic-Prescriptive Vocational Competency Profile (FIDPVCP) is a set of behavioral rating scales consisting of 70 items which refer to six domains of behavior related to vocational competency. Eight uses of the FIDPVCP are suggested in the manual, beginning with selecting individuals for training programs. The instrument is, however, clearly designed to assess trainees presently enrolled in training programs and simply could not be used under any other circumstances. For example, the Punctuality item refers to observations made over a "randomly selected 4 week period," the Attention Span item refers to paying attention for "an entire 8-hour work day," and the Gross Motor Coordination item refers to a trainee performing tasks at 100%, 50–74%, and less than 25% of the "competitive production rate." Indeed, the authors say that valid and reliable observations are contingent on the length of time clients have spent in training.

The 70 items were written using a literature search, site visits, and interviews with training personnel. Each item has the observer/examiner select from five behaviorally-based statements ranging from level 5 (ready for placement in competitive employment) to level 1 (unable to perform task). These item statements are contained in the manual; scores are entered on a separate record form. The examiner also totals points for the six domains and for a composite score entered on the record form as well. These scores are then put into a scoring table, and the manual consulted again to determine percentile equivalents for a Profile of Strengths and Weaknesses.

Much of the manual is taken up with the actual rating scales, which are very elaborate and specific, particularly at level 5. For example, level 5 of "Ability to maintain a savings account" reads: "Will be able to distinguish deposit and withdrawal slips; will be able to completely fill out both deposit and withdrawal slips; will be able to understand when interest is posted into passbook; will understand what insurance of $100,000 for each account means; will store passbook in safe place in home or vault."

The percentile norms are based on a standardization sample of 100 clients, 10 in each of 10 subgroups (i.e., 5 types of rehabilitation trainees at both secondary and postsecondary levels). This norm group represents a major flaw in the FIDPVCP; there are simply too few subjects in it and the subgroups are too heterogeneous to permit practical use of the norms. For example, the 10 trainable mentally retarded secondary students ranged in age from 13 to 19 and had been in their programs from 1 to 12 months. The 10 trainable mentally retarded postsecondary students were age 20 to 54 and had been in their programs from 4 to 48 months. To use norms based on such a variable sample, particularly outside of Dade County, Florida, would represent a gross misuse of this instrument.

Normative subjects in the 10 groups were rated by different pairs of evaluators all closely associated with the respective training programs. Unfortunately, reliability coefficients are presented only for the composite scores so there is no way of knowing how reliable the six domain scores are. Also unfortunate is the evidence presented for the concurrent validity of the device—the only kind of validity addressed. Each of the two evaluators rank-ordered the 10 students in his/her training group in terms of vocational competency. Following this, the same evaluator filled out the FIDPVCP for the students, whose composite scores were similarly rank-ordered. Then Spearman rank order correlations between the two rankings were performed resulting in two rhos for each of the 10 groups. They are high, ranging from .76 to .96, but spuriously so, inasmuch as the same evaluator made all the judgments that went into each rho.

Finally, an examination of the Profile of Strengths and Weaknesses as a clinical diagnostic-prescriptive device reveals additional weaknesses. The 10 group profiles are diagrammed in the manual, which also says that the strengths and weaknesses revealed in the individual profile will allow an evaluator to "easily translate the data obtained into an individualized vocational training plan." However, the profiles are so flat across the six behavioral domains for any group, it is not at all clear how individualized prescriptions are to be accomplished. The manual would have benefitted from some case studies (e.g., what would one recommend for an economically disadvantaged woman age 40 who scored at the 50th percentile on Self-Help Skills, Cognitive-Learning Ability, and Perceptual Motor Skills, and above the 75th percentile on Social-Emotional Adjustment, Work Attitudes-Responsibility, and General Work Habits?

A further limitation on the use of this instrument is the content of the 70 items. There is no way of handling missing data. If, for example, a training program did not include opportunities to demonstrate finger dexterity, operating power tools and machines, eye-hand-foot coordination, and form discrimination, trainees would rate very poorly on the Perceptual-Motor Skills domain through no fault of their own. The 70 items are very specific and seem tailored to the specific training facilities within which they were developed.

No estimate is given of how long it takes to complete the instrument, but it would appear to require many hours of observations and judgment.

In summary, the FIDPVCP consists of behavioral rating scales to measure six types of vocational competency in five types of rehabilitation trainees. There is no evidence of reliability or validity for the six domain scores and, while the composite scores are reliable, it is the scant evidence of the "diagnostic-prescriptive" utility of the instrument which makes its adoption questionable. Local norms would have to be developed in any case, and one could probably do as well, for a lot less effort and expense, if one used the work sample approach for all of the purposes for which the FIDPVCP was constructed. And even though it is not as vocationally-oriented, the AAMD Adaptive Behavior Scale should be preferred on psychometric grounds as a behavior rating scale, particularly for the secondary level population.

Review of Florida International Diagnostic-Prescriptive Vocational Competency Profile by MI-

CHAEL D. ORLANSKY, *Associate Professor of Special Education, Department of Human Services Education, The Ohio State University, Columbus, OH:*

This instrument represents a promising attempt to incorporate behavioral observation techniques into the realm of standardized vocational testing for students or clients with special needs. The Florida International Diagnostic-Prescriptive Vocational Competency Profile (FIDPVCP) focuses on the observation of 70 "vocationally relevant behaviors" considered necessary for an individual to obtain and keep a job. The evaluator is to rate the student or client on each of the 70 behaviors, using a scale of 1 (Poor) to 5 (Excellent).

The manual contains adequate descriptive information on the development of the instrument, tables for converting raw scores into percentage equivalents, and data on the performance of 100 vocational trainees (50 adolescents and 50 adults) who served as a standardization sample. Interrater reliability and concurrent validity coefficients are reported. However, the instructions for test administration are vague. No specific qualifications of the evaluator are enumerated, and evaluators must determine for themselves "what length of time constitutes an appropriate observation period for their own clientele." The nature of the behaviors evaluated suggests that FIDPVCP would be most relevant for use with individuals who are already participating as trainees in structured vocational programs, such as sheltered workshops, work activity centers, and other vocational rehabilitation facilities. The "International" refers to the university at which the instrument was developed, and should not be misconstrued as an indication of appropriateness for international usage.

Although the emphasis on observable performance is laudable, several items present fairly intricate clusters of positive and negative behaviors which render the corresponding numerical ratings largely meaningless in the absence of detailed comments by the evaluator. For example, the manual's description of a trainee who is to be rated 3 (Average) in the area of Grooming is as follows: "Trainee's clothes are clean, but do not fit properly and are inappropriate for work situation; hair is clean and combed; and facial hair is improperly shaven or cosmetics are inappropriate." Perhaps such tangled items arose from excessive condensing and combining of characteristics regarded as vocationally important.

Other problems noted with the construction of certain test items include a lack of intermediate levels of gradation: a trainee with "slight body odor" may be rated 4 (Good), while the next lower level of performance refers to "strong body odor." Also, the assumptions incorporated into a number of items may make them inapplicable to trainees who are not in traditional assembly line-type vocational training programs in metropolitan areas. One item, for example, assesses the trainee's performance as an operator of power tools and machines, while another (Travel) provides for the trainee who drives an automobile or travels by city bus or taxi, but does not consider the trainee who may need to depend on alternate forms of transportation, such as a car pool or a special transit system for handicapped persons.

Some vocational evaluators, particularly those attuned to the needs of individuals with severe and multiple disabilities, may question this test's inclusion of several skills which usually are not directly related to on-the-job task performance (though admittedly desirable adjuncts for those persons who can achieve them). In this category would fall "Ability to Use Employment Agencies," "Ability to Use a Credit Card," "Leadership Ability," and others. FIDPVCP is not recommended for use with persons who have visual, auditory, physical, or neurological impairments.

The ultimate value of any vocational assessment procedure for persons with special needs should be determined by how useful it is to educators and rehabilitation professionals in planning an effective program of job training and placement. On this score FIDPVCP, like most other instruments which attempt to assess vocational potential, ranks as an unknown quantity. Future follow-up studies of former clients would be helpful in establishing a more substantial dimension of validity for this instrument. The percentages used in reporting trainees' scores on each of the six domains may be helpful to some evaluators in providing a sort of baseline of vocational performance; however, they would appear to be only marginally useful in the difficult and important process of "matching" a particular client to an appropriate job. It should also be pointed out that percentage scores for two of the domains are based on fewer than 10 items, and that the actual percentage range on all domains is from 20% to 100%, since the lowest possible rating a trainee may achieve is one point out of a possible five points.

The test package includes an "Individualized Vocational Prescription" form which should be a worthwhile aid to short-range and longer-range planning within a school or agency setting. Prospective users of FIDPVCP should first carefully review the instrument to see whether it is appropriate to their population and environment. If so, the instrument can be recommended for use in conjunction with work-sample assessments and other approaches to vocational evaluation.

[421]

Florida Kindergarten Screening Battery. Grade K; 1982; FKSB; designed for early detection of reading disability; individual; 1 form; 5 tests: Beery Test of Visual-Motor Integration (VMI), Recognition-Discrimination, Peabody Picture Vocabulary Test—Revised (PPVT-R), Alphabet Recitation, Finger Localization (optional); manual (51 pages); record form (4 pages); recognition-discrimination test (15 pages); 1984 price data: $45 per basic kit including 50 record forms, Recognition-Discrimination Test, Finger Localization Test, and Alphabet Recitation (does not include PPVT-R or Beery VMI); $99 per expanded kit including all items in basic kit plus PPVT-R and Beery VMI; $10 per 50 record forms; (20) minutes; Paul Satz and Jack Fletcher; Psychological Assessment Resources, Inc.*

Review of Florida Kindergarten Screening Battery by EDWARD EARL GOTTS, Chief Psychologist, Huntington State Hospital, Huntington, WV:

The developers of the Florida Kindergarten Screening Battery (FKSB) have undertaken an unusually rigorous program of studies regarding its predictive validity over intervals ranging from 3 to 7 years. Validity is expressed in terms of classification tables that display predictions based on the battery on the one hand and actual outcomes in terms of later reading levels. Comparisons are made between the battery's predictions and those based on teacher judgments, with the former producing smaller numbers of false negatives but greater numbers of false positives. The authors, in discussing the relative merits of the foregoing comparative differences, do not bring their conclusions to as sharp a focus as might be done. With screening procedures we must favor the one which best informs us of those who may be at risk and choose it over the one that more often fails to detect risk, provided that they are about equal in other respects. That is, we can more easily accept a surplus of false positives than false negatives, if the original intent to detect true positives (i.e., potential learning problem children) is a meaningful and worthwhile activity. On balance, then, the screening battery performed better than kindergarten teachers, who had known the children for an entire school year, in the prediction of future reading problems, in the essential sense that it detected more of these, even though it somewhat overselected potential problem cases. The authors deserve greater credit on this count than they claim for their work. Only when identification of false positives carries elevated risks of its own need such caution be exercised. More should also be made of the fact (not discussed by the authors) that the teachers could only make their judgments after knowing the children for a year, so they did not necessarily have available for their use in remedial work during the year so extensive a data base as they did at year's end. Yet the battery could have supplied them such a basis for instruction from the very outset. The authors need to highlight this practical advantage of screening in their manual.

The research handling of construct validity is quite another matter. Here the authors seem not to grasp clearly the conceptual issues involved in establishing validity. Constructs as such are not really discussed. Instead the authors present a factor analysis of a larger source battery from which the present battery was selected. Their interpretation in the manual of this factor analytic study is defective and misleading for the non-specialist in test construction (e.g., a footnote to the factor matrix table suggests that certain problematic tests "clearly loaded on their respective factors," which cannot be supported from the findings presented).

A fundamental issue that perhaps led the authors astray is: What is the proper meaning of construct validity for a screening device? They seem to have decided that construct validity is not very germane when, in their discussion of the inconclusiveness of the factor analysis, they conclude, "These questions are more appropriate for criterion validity analyses," whereupon they move immediately into a discussion of such studies. One gets no sense that they considered whether other constructs or measures, if they had been used, might also have resulted in high rates of risk identification. For example, measures of general ability and of academic readiness have traditionally been used for these predictive purposes and might reasonably be employed to establish concurrent discriminant and convergent validity—which they were not. Because of this omission, it is not possible to know whether ability and readiness measures, which might have been administered at comparable or lesser cost, could have fared as well as did the FKSB, or whether the FKSB would have been superior predictively. Second, since screening is performed at a smaller cost than would be experienced if each child were tested diagnostically (which this battery disavows as its aim), it would have made sense to establish construct validity in terms of the more expensive diagnostic alternative. That is, a screening procedure should correlate well with what might be accepted as a somewhat definitive diagnostic procedure for predicting future reading problems in the kindergarten population. The authors have not examined their battery in relation to such a definitive diagnostic procedure or battery, however. Third, it would be desirable to use the construct word "reading" in the battery title. Fourth, the Finger Localization measure (which is optional) contains in its total score five subparts, two of which are reported to be unreliable; and the authors have failed to check the internal consistency of this disparate item pool while deciding to use its total score only in the final product. Had they refined this test further, it might have performed more satisfactorily in their factor study. Since this part needs to be studied, and it is optional in the battery, I advise against its use until the authors have had a chance to complete development of the Finger Localization Test and to have this published as an addendum to the manual.

Administration instructions are relatively abbreviated, omitting points that will be important to the paraprofessional user who is destined to use it. I advise the user to pay close attention to collating and integrating administration information from the applicable section of the manual with that appearing on the Record Form and also on pages 12–13 of the manual. This is the only way that administration procedures can be fully replicated. In their comments on the Beery VMI the FKSB authors state the stimulus is to be "flat," whereas Beery says "centered and squared." For the Recognition-Discrimination task, the authors state in bold face type that the examiner may repeatedly remind the child about the issue that is to be judged. One must wonder if examiner variation on this point cannot in some instances produce extensive unintentional prompting and coaching, following what the examiner recognizes as inaccurate responses. This matter requires considerable further research. Finally, returning to Finger Localization, the authors need to provide errata for Task III, Bilateral Touch, to clear up contradictory directions: (1) either the child signals an answer by waving or raising the hand(s), and (2) either the backs of the hands or the palms are to be stimulated. A map of the fingertips should be provided to indicate exactly where they are to be stimulated, since receptor ends are not uniformly distributed over the entire surface of the fingertip, and the examiner must know how to replicate the desired procedure of administration.

Reliability studies of measures unique to the battery were conducted by the internal consistency method. Test-retest reliabilities are not reported for these battery-specific measures. Reliabilities are generally acceptable, except as noted earlier for Finger Localization.

The battery (except for the PPVT and Beery VMI portions) cannot be viewed as adequately normed, since all children were drawn from a single school system, and the focus of the bulk of the studies was upon white boys who were disproportionately from higher levels of SES than the general population. The reader should, nevertheless, review the useful cross-validation studies reported in the manual, since they help extend the scope of the battery's predictive uses. Because of the norming inadequacies, however, I must recommend, along with the authors, that local norming studies be conducted.

Although this brief review cannot explore additional matters of potential interest, the manual will generally suffice for introducing these. For example, the user must also have the PPVT and VMI tests; decisions must be made about PPVT vs. PPVT-R; and the Auditory Analysis Test may be added to battery to enhance detection.

My overall evaluation is that the battery represents a promising approach to screening which is only incompletely developed. Its predictive accuracy and reliability appear generally good, but research has not yet sufficiently compared these to alternative approaches. Construct validity of the battery requires considerable additional study. It is true that many commercially available kindergarten screening measures fall far short of this battery's sophistication and validation, but its superiority to these and to more traditional predictors (e.g., ability and readiness) has not been demonstrated directly thus far. Its utility in the hands of paraprofessional users certainly commends it over the elaborate battery developed by the Gesell Institute (i.e., representing, as it does, a lower cost approach). Direct comparison to other reading readiness measures is difficult, since they usually aim at shorter range prediction than is true of the FKSB. The user must pay particular attention to collating the procedures for administering the battery. The manual provides no assistance in using the results for purposes other than prediction.

[422]

Fluharty Preschool Speech and Language Screening Test. Ages 2–6; 1978; 4 scores: identification total, articulation total, comprehension total, repetition total; individual; 1 form ('78, 2 pages, 10 cards); manual ('78, 19 pages); separate answer sheets must be used; some test materials (e.g., hat, paper bag, sock, feather) must be supplied by examiner; 1983 price data: $18 per manual, 10 picture cards, and 100 response forms; $8 per 100 response forms; (6–10) minutes; Nancy Buono Fluharty; DLM Teaching Resources.*

TEST REFERENCES

1. Bee, H. L., Barnard, K. E., Eyres, S. J., Gray, C. A., Hammond, M. A., Spietz, A. L., Snyder, C., & Clark, B. Prediction of IQ and language skill from perinatal status, child performance, family characteristics, and mother-infant interaction. CHILD DEVELOPMENT, 1982, 53, 1134–1156.

Review of Fluharty Preschool Speech and Language Screening Test by NICHOLAS W. BANKSON, *Professor and Chairman, Department of Communication Disorders, Boston University, Boston, MA:*

The purpose of this screening test is to identify children in the 2 to 6 year age range that need comprehensive speech and language evaluations. The instrument includes 35 test items which can be administered in 6 minutes, and allows for a cursory examination of picture identification skills, speech sound articulation, syntactic comprehension, and sentence imitation skills. The test is administered individually and includes the following four sections: (*a*) identification of 15 familiar objects for the purpose of sampling vocabulary skills; (*b*) production of 30 consonant sounds (obtained through the naming of the 15 objects); (*c*) comprehension of 10 sentences, as reflected through a pointing response (e.g., "Show me—The ring is on the bag"); and (*d*) repetition of 10 sentences representing different kernel sentence transformation types. Responses are elicited through object naming (the objects are supplied by the examiner—they don't come with the test), repetition of sentences, and by pointing responses. Items are scored as correct or incorrect, with the scoring of the articulatory responses requiring the examiner to be able to distinguish correct from incorrect phoneme productions for two sounds within a word, and the sentence repetition task requiring knowledge of acceptable and unacceptable alternative responses (these are delineated in the manual). Each correct response receives one point. The child's score on each of the four subtests is then compared with the cutoff scores prescribed for that age level. These scores are delineated for 12 month intervals (i.e., 2, 3, 4, 5, and 6 years) for each of the subtests. A child is considered to fail the screening test if one or more of his four scores fall below the cutoff scores for the child's age group.

This test is easy to administer, containing directions that are simple and clear. Scoring is more complex and requires, in the case of judging articulatory productions, that the examiner have perceptual skills in this area. A strength of the instrument is that specific suggestions are made to the examiner that make allowance for regional and Black dialect in the scoring.

The test manual indicates the instrument was standardized on 2,147 children, ages 2 through 6, from four racial or ethnic backgrounds, three socioeconomic classes, and a variety of geographical areas. Intertester and intratester reliability for the test are acceptable, ranging from .87 to 1.00 for various subtests. However, certain details regarding the validity of the measure are lacking in the manual. For example, the procedure by which the cutoff scores were determined is unclear. It simply indicates the cutoffs were arrived at by correlating scores from the Peabody Picture Vocabulary Test, the Goldman-Fristoe Test of Articulation, and the Northwestern Syntax Screening Test with the screening test scores. Neither percentile norms nor measures of central tendency are presented to allow for interpretation of the relative standing of cutoff scores. Validity of the cutoff scores is, however, supported by a .90 Pearson product-moment correlation between the child's screening test performance (pass/fail) and the implications of his or her speech evaluation (needs therapy/does not need therapy). This correlation was based on a sample of 211 children.

The Fluharty Preschool Speech and Language Test is recommended if a rapid screening measure is desired. While it may not be particularly helpful in pinpointing the specific direction(s) that follow-up diagnostic testing should take, it nonetheless allows the examiner to make a cursory observation of a child's communication skills.

Review of Fluharty Preschool Speech and Language Screening Test by HAROLD A. PETERSON, Director of Hearing and Speech Center, Professor of Audiology and Speech Pathology, University of Tennessee, Knoxville, TN:

The Fluharty scale was designed for use with children 2 through 6 years of age. There are three sections of the test, with four scores to be derived. Section A is scored from the child's identification of 15 common objects which the tester is to supply. Two scores are generated from this section: the correct naming of the objects, and the articulation of 23 consonant sounds contained in the names of the objects. Section B requires nonverbal responses to 10 sentences to illustrate the child's understanding of some basic syntactic structures, and Section C requires repetition of 10 sentences, and is identified as a test of expression. Administration time for the 35-item test is approximately 6 minutes.

Cutoff scores for adequacy of performance are supplied for each of the four subtest areas for children aged 2 to 6 years by one-year separations. A child is considered to have failed the screening test if one or more of the subtest scores fall below the cutoff for his/her age group.

SUBTEST CONTENT. The 15 words in the identification task are common objects and expected to be in most pre-school children's vocabularies, but the words were apparently selected primarily to elicit the articulation of the 23 single-phoneme consonants tested for the articulation score. Fifteen of the test sounds occur in an initial word-position, seven of the fifteen are tested also in medial or final word-positions, which means that the other eight tested consonants appear in the "second position" (medial or final) in the test words.

The Comprehension portion of the test uses 10 questions, statements, or directions to which an action or pointing response is elicited to indicate the child understood. In terms of what the critical elements for identification are, four of the ten would appear to require only identification of an object (leaf, paper, sock, feather), three identifications of an action (open mouth, cough, take), and one item each of locative (on), color identification (yellow), and negative (isn't). In other words, there is relatively little linguistic contrast being sampled. The ten sentences for a measurement of expression show more diversity. They may be categorized as representing: plural, predication, adjective, present progressive, locative, possessive pronoun, negation, indefinite pronoun, imperative, and past tense irregular.

STANDARDIZATION AND INTERPRETATION. The standardization population consisted of 2,147 children, aged 2 through 6 years, representing four racial or ethnic backgrounds and three socioeconomic classes from nine geographical regions. Representation of the racial/ethnic, socioeconomic classifications, geographical regions and sex was not equally distributed, e.g., there are 775 Black children of whom 673 were classed as lower SES; a total of 33 Mexican-American, and 3 Orientals. Statistical ANOVA treatments indicated age differences were significant, but sex and SES were not significant. Essentially this means that 6-year-olds did better than the 2-year-olds. There are no reported levels of significance for differences between age levels. The manual reports that cutoff scores for the test were determined for the five preschool age levels, but it is not clear how these cutoff (adequacy) levels were determined.

The manual reports that the accuracy of the cutoff scores were "verified" by results of the Peabody Picture Vocabulary Test (PPVT), the Goldman-Fristoe Test of Articulation, and the Northwestern Syntax Screening Test (NSST). It is not clear what comparisons were made between the Fluharty Preschool Speech and Language Screening Test and the other instruments. The Peabody is the only one of the three that has normative comparisons for the age ranges covered in the Fluharty. Was the −1 or the −2 *SD* point on the PPVT taken as the adequacy cutoff for comparison with the 10 vocabulary words? Receptive vocabulary within a normal range of talent is usually not expected to correlate with language skill. The Goldman-Fristoe normative comparisons run from ages 6 years to 16 years. For the one age group (6 years) on which there was an overlap what was the adequacy criterion? How could the Goldman-Fristoe possibly be used as a comparative yardstick for ages 2 through 5? The Northwestern Syntax Screening Test norms include ages 3 through 8 and there is some similarity of content between the NSST items and the expressive portion of the Fluharty, but not with the receptive portion. There is little agreement between how items on the receptive portion of the NSST and the repetition portion of the Fluharty are scored. And there is no statement in the Fluharty Test Manual to indicate the level of performance on the NSST which was used to set the cut-off criteria on the Fluharty. Was it the 25th percentile, the 10th percentile, the 3rd percentile?

VALIDITY. The manual's statement of validity is entangled with the same confusions as expressed in the preceding paragraph. The statement is that: "The correlation between each child's screening test performance (pass/fail) and the implications of his or her speech evaluation (needs therapy/does not need therapy) was computed at .897 by the Pearson product-moment correlation."

If Fluharty used a Pearson r, then she would have worked from the magnitude of the z scores rather than the implied either/or (pass/fail) classifications. If she used the categorical judgments of pass or fail and needs or does not need therapy, then she should probably have reported the percentage of agreed judgments with the percentages of false negative judgments. The validity statement as written does not allow for a determination as to whether or not the test has validity.

The test as described has simplicity, and that is a favorable attribute of a screening measure. This simplicity in design and scoring yields a high reliability, which is also in its favor. But given the question as to how cutoff (adequacy/inadequacy) scores were determined, as well as the question of how validity was determined, simplicity and brevity (6 minutes test time) are not sufficient substitutes.

REVIEWER'S REFERENCES

Fluharty, N. B. The design and standardization of a speech and language screening test for use with preschool children. JOURNAL OF HEARING DISORDERS, 1974, 34, 75–88.

[423]

Four Picture Test, Third Revised Edition. Ages 10 and over; 1948–83; FPT; projective; no data on reliability and validity; no norms; 1 form ('83, 4 cards); manual ('83, 26 pages); 1984 price data: Hfl. 85 per set of 4 cards and manual; administration time not reported; D. J. van Lennep; Swets Test Services [The Netherlands].*

See P:431 (3 references); for a review of an earlier edition by S. G. Lee and Johann M. Schepers, see 6:213 (3 references); for reviews by John E. Bell, E. G. Bradford, and Ephraim Rosen of the original edition, see 4:105 (3 references, 1 excerpt).

[424]

Four Relationship Factor Questionnaire. Adults in dyadic relationships; 1973; 4R-F; 4 scores: parental-respect, problem-solving, identification, sexual; norms for college students only; 1 form ('73, 4 pages, includes scoring system); manual (no date, 34 pages); 1985 price data: $30 per 100 test booklets; $5 per manual; (15–25) minutes; Frank G. Lawlis; Test Systems International, Ltd.*

[425]

The Fred Test. Non-native speakers of English; 1983; "a test of oral proficiency for ESL placement"; alternative to The John Test; shortened version available; no norms, publisher recommends use of local norms; individual; 4 scores: comprehension, connected discourse, asking questions, total; 1 form (no date, 3 pages); guide for using (no date, 10 pages); score sheet (1 pages); 1983 price data: $5 per complete set; (10) minutes; Language Innovations, Inc.*

[426]

Frost Self Description Questionnaire: Extended Scales. Ages 9–14; 1972–79; extension of Frost Self

Description Questionnaire; norms consist of means and standard deviations; 3 forms; statistical supplement (no date, 42 pages); price data available from publisher; administration time not reported; Barry P. Frost; Psychoeducational Clinic, University of Calgary [Canada].*

a) FORM 1. 3 scores: externalized aggression, internalized aggression, projective aggression; 1 form (no date, 6 pages); manual ('79, 19 pages).

b) FORM 2. 4 scores: free floating anxiety, body damage anxiety, separation anxiety, worry and tension; 1 form (no date, 7 pages); manual ('79, 39 pages).

c) FORM 3. 5 scores: test anxiety, concentration anxiety, social anxiety, denial, affiliation; 1 form (no date, 8 pages); manual ('79, 34 pages).

Review of Frost Self Description Questionnaire: Extended Scales, by DORCAS SUSAN BUTT, Associate Professor of Psychology, University of British Columbia, Vancouver, Canada:

Originally developed in London, England, for research purposes, the Frost Self Description Questionnaire (1973) eventually came to be used in the Calgary school system as a screening device to "indicate to the psychologist the degree of general emotionality of the child tested, the area in which he [she] has concern (type of anxiety), the level of his [her] externalized, projective and internalized aggression, the degree to which he [she] uses the defence mechanism of denial and to which he [she] is affiliative or submissive." It is supposed to indicate which affective areas the psychologist should investigate further.

In 1979 the author followed with the Frost Self Description Questionnaire: Extended Scales, which "are extensions of the original Frost Self Description questionnaire....They are designed to be used to follow up indications obtained from the FSDQ, or separately." The extended scales are made up of 20 items each. The earlier scales appear to have been made up of less than 10 items each, raising problems with reliability coefficients (since the magnitude of split-half coefficients is partially a function of the number of items in a scale). Although this reviewer is sympathetic to the problem of reliability and test length and in fact favors short scales in spite of low reliability, reliability coefficients do need to be provided. There is no table of reliability coefficients presented in the manuals for either the short or extended scales. Point biserial correlations are reported between test items and subscale scores; although these are suggestive of level of interitem correlation, most users would appreciate a more orthodox presentation of test and item statistics for comparison purposes. In short, these scales are not presented in a systematic manner that would permit ease of administration, scoring, and interpretation.

The number of unattached forms, manuals, test sheets, and factor analytic results which one must study to understand the background to the scales forms a mass of sometimes repetitive and unindexed documentation. This reader is left with the wish that all test producers be required to present their materials, items, scoring systems, and supplemental documentation in a single, indexed, self-contained manual.

Although the identification of clinical styles based upon the psychoanalytic and interpersonal (Leary) theoretical traditions is the worthwhile purpose of the scales, the theoretical statements and their implications for educational settings need clearer and more practical elaboration.

Pages of statistics (means, standard deviations, and factor analytic results by age groupings) are presented for children aged 9 to 14. But there is no substantive discussion of the implications of age and sex variations in the results. The factor analytic stabilities across age groupings, available for inspection but without statistical summary of their consistency, are offered as construct validity. No other validation is offered in spite of the rich opportunity in the school system for behavioral, teacher, and peer ratings; and parental interview data and performance measures. Yet validation statistics are much needed in view of the high correlations between the subscales (e.g., the seven anxiety scales have correlations ranging from .25 to .77 for 13- to 14-year-old females, with 9 out of 21 correlations being over .55). Although loading on a general factor, they are claimed to have important specificity. This needs to be demonstrated.

The reviewer administered the scales to a small number of children (aged 9 and 10 years) and followed with an interview. The children said they enjoyed answering the questions but had great difficulty in interpreting the meaning of some of them. For example, the term "left alone" ("it all depends where I am left"), the term "loud noises" ("does it mean a scary noise or loud music") and "stores" ("there are millions of kinds of stores"), etc. The child's interpretation, of course, determines whether the attached question receives a true or false endorsement.

The scales contain large numbers of buffer items in order to disguise scale content; these items are not used in the scoring. This reviewer has severe doubts about the psychologist's right to use participant's time and concentration for such in vacuo activity and would suggest such buffer items in all tests be made scorable so they will be of use to the participant. At a time when much psychometric sophistication is being questioned and examined (Burisch, 1984), surely such diversionary tactics should be questioned as well.

In short, the reviewer found the Frost Self Description Questionniare: Extended Scales to be promising and the research to date of interest. Substantive validation studies must follow and the practical applications of the scales documented before it can be considered as other than a research instrument.

REVIEWER'S REFERENCES

Burisch, M. Approaches to personality inventory construction: A comparison of merits. AMERICAN PSYCHOLOGIST, 1984, 39, 3, 214–227.

Review of Frost Self Description Questionnaire: Extended Scales, by GEORGE F. MADAUS, Director, The Center for the Study of Testing, Evaluation, and Educational Policy, Boston College, Chestnut Hill, MA:

The Frost Self Description Questionnaire consists of 120 true-false items intended to measure 12 separate constructs at three levels spanning ages 9 through 14. Included in the 120 items are an unspecified number of buffer items relating to the student's interests, hobbies, and preferred adult occupation, which are inserted to obscure the nature of the constructs being assessed. Since each scale contains 20 items, simple arithmetic reveals that items are scored for more than one scale. The implication of this item dependence between scales is not considered in the manual.

The manuals accompanying the scales are totally inadequate to permit a reasonable psychometric or theoretical assessment of the scales. For example, the intended uses are not described. One could infer from the manual that the scales are meant to be group administered but to what end? Are they to be used in counseling situations or for program evaluation? Were the age categories 9 to 10, 11 to 12, and 13 to 14 selected empirically or on some theoretical basis? The construction of the scales, in particular the assignment of items to constructs, is not described anywhere. The items were tried out with school children in Calgary, Alberta. Scale means and standard deviations and score by sex distributions are provided for each age level, but there are no analyses or discussion of the results.

Alpha coefficients are reported for each scale but there are no coefficients of stability offered. Given the age of the intended population, the stability of these constructs is an important but neglected question.

There is no validity information except for correlations between scales and factor analyses of the 12 scales but not of the 120 items. However, there is very little discussion of the correlational data or the tables showing the results of the factor analyses. Readers are left to interpret the tables for themselves. Validity studies for the selected age groups need to be done on a wider sample than just Calgary school children before these scales are used operationally. Much more evidence of the construct validity of the scales is needed.

At best the Frost Self Description Questionnaire is an experimental instrument that needs considerable work and study. The author needs to be more explicit on intended uses and provide much more in the way of validity data and psychometric analyses before any potential user considers it for operational use.

[427]

Fuld Object-Memory Evaluation. Ages 70–90 regardless of language and sensory handicaps; 1977; FOME; 5 scores: total recall, storage, consistency of retrieval, ability to benefit from reminding, ability to say words in categories; individual; 2 forms; record form I, II, (2 pages); instruction manual (24 pages); 1984 price data: $21 per complete kit; $5.75 per 30 record forms; $4 per instruction manual; administration time not reported; Paula Altman Fuld; Stoelting Co.*

Review of Fuld Object-Memory Evaluation by ERIC F. GARDNER, Margaret O. Slocum Professor of Psychology and Education Emeritus, Syracuse University, Psychology Department, Syracuse, NY:

The Fuld Object-Memory Evaluation is the outgrowth of clinical appraisal and research by the author and is based on a modification of Buschke's procedure of selective reminding which allows differential evaluation of storage and retrieval from a single testing occasion. The test, which is still in its developmental stages, was produced while working with numbers of aged adult nursing home residents and community active individuals. It was tried out with successful administrations to young school-aged children.

The test, since it is individually administered on a one-to-one basis, requires, like all individually administered tests, a much longer time to obtain research data. Even taking this restriction into account, the statistics reported in the manual are based on very meager samples. A reliability coefficient (alpha) of .71 was reported although neither the number of cases nor the variability was given. However, small samples selected from similar sources showed large variances which could inflate the reliability index. A number of appropriate studies supplying evidence of validity have been conducted although each of these is based on a very small sample.

The pool from which samples were selected for research and norms was highly restricted, most subjects coming from a senior citizen's center and the immediate community. The normative sample for 70-year-olds and 80-year-olds was described as follows: "All subjects were Caucausian and most were Jewish." Separate norms are given for community residents and nursing home residents although apparently only 15 subjects each were used for the 70- to 79-year-old groups and 17 for the 80- to 89-year-olds.

All the scores obtainable from the Fuld for an 83-year-old woman are given and discussed (partly for illustrative purposes). Throughout the manual, numerous clinical observations supporting some of the research statistics are offered. However, one is constantly aware of the extremely small samples in each case.

Plans are being made to expand some of the validity studies and to perform an alternate form reliability study. Many more data of those types are needed.

There has been considerable thought, extensive clinical observation, and small sample checking of important relationships. However, the sample sizes and representativeness of the 70- and 80-year-old population does not permit one to conclude that much is known about the test's psychometric properties. The instrument can be useful when used by a skilled clinician with the aged population for which it was designed. However, it will be much more useful after the collection of additional data to describe its psychometric properties and to provide more suitable norms.

[428]

The Fullerton Language Test for Adolescents, Experimental Edition. Ages 11–18; 1980; 8 scores: auditory synthesis, morphology competency, oral commands, convergent production, divergent production, syllabication, grammatic competency, idioms; individual; 1 form (8 pages); manual (31 pages); package of tokens varying in shape and color; 1982 price data: $13.25 per 25 scoring forms and profiles; $1.50 per set of stimulus items; $20 per examiner's kit (manual, stimulus items, 25 scoring forms and profiles); $13.25 per 25 scoring forms and profiles; $1.50 per set of stimulus items; $6 per manual; $6.25 per specimen set (without stimulus items); (40–50) minutes; Arden R. Thorum; Consulting Psychologists Press, Inc.*

Review of The Fullerton Language Test for Adolescents, Experimental Edition, by MARGARET C. BYRNE, University of Kansas, Lawrence, KS:

This test has two purposes: (1) to identify language-impaired adolescents, and (2) to encourage research on the language proficiency of this age group. Because most tests have been devised for younger students, there is a paucity of information about the language processing and language use of adolescents.

The test has eight subtests that deal with skills presumed to be needed for the acquisition and use of language. The author points out that the test doesn't cover all skills, but only those that, in his judgment, are the most important. The selection of the eight was based on research studies of adolescent language, commercial assessment instruments that were available, and an analysis of what language skills are necessary. This experimental version was prepared from the results of the administration of a field-study version.

There are two subtests that tap receptive skills and six that measure expressive skills. There is a rationale for each subtest, and some subtests are modelled after sections of other tests such as the Illinois Test of Psycholinguistic Abilities (Auditory Synthesis, Morphology Competency); The Token Test (Oral Commands); and the Stanford Diagnostic Reading Test (Syllabification). The subtests on Divergent and Convergent Production are based on Guilford's model of the Structure of Intellect. The Grammatical Competency subtest is related to Wood's assumptions about linguistic intuitions. The subtest on Idioms emerged from Chafe's reports on idiom usage and other researchers' work on how idioms are learned.

The test takes about 45 minutes to administer. There are separate directions given for each subtest, and scoring is based on one point for each correct answer. Only one subtest, Oral Commands, requires any stimulus materials (tokens). All instructions and subtest items are in the manual. The items are also given on the scoring form.

The interpretation of a set of test results is based on the means and standard deviations of the scores of the normative group. For each subtest the mean, plus or minus a standard deviation or two, is then utilized to determine the category of language performance. For example, Competence Level is above the mean; the Instruction Level includes scores below, at, and above the mean; and the Frustration Level typically includes scores at or lower than one standard deviation below the mean.

The standardization sample included 727 students, 78.6% of whom were White, and the rest Black, Spanish surname, or others. They were from Oregon and California, from cities and rural populations.

The examiners were 45 speech and language specialists in public schools or were graduate students in Communicative Disorders. All were given special training in both the administration and scoring of the subtests.

Reliability was determined through test-retest and split-half procedures. Test-retest coefficients were in the 90s, except for the Divergent Production, Convergent Production, and Oral Commands subtests, which were in the 80s. Split-half reliabilities averaged .76.

Validity was determined in several ways. Content and item validity of each subtest reportedly was based on a theoretical framework; items are also reported to be similar to items in other language tests, which is questionable validity evidence at best. Correlation coefficients among the eight subtests indicated that they were all measuring related language components. A comparison of the performance of a normative sample with a special education group receiving some special services within the schools showed highly significant differences on all eight subtests.

This test was carefully devised and standardized. Its weakness is that of similar language tests. There is no evidence that these are the most important skills needed for normal language users, or that a remedial program to correct these linguistic skills will result in more competent comprehension and production for the individual.

Results on some of the subtests may be due to the directions for administration. On the Auditory Synthesis subtest a pause is to follow the presentation of each sound, but the length of the pause is not mandated. As a result examiners not trained by the author may obtain different results. In discussing potential results on the Convergent Production Task, the author even points out that production of *pore* and *poor* is different in many parts of the country. As a result the final test score will be affected by the pronunciation. The same is true for the items *do* and *dew, blue* and *blew*.

The Idioms subtest is probably the most colloquially based. As a result, scores will be dependent on the environment of the individual. In addition, an understanding of idioms requires cognitive processing. The test results may be providing information about cognition, rather than about language use.

Syllabification skills may be needed in reading, but their relationship to oral language use has not been established.

SUMMARY. This test has no overall theoretical frame of reference. Its subtests are presumed to measure skills that an adolescent needs to process and use language. Although the test has high test-retest reliability, there is no evidence that the subtests as a group are tapping the important processes of language. The information about the language-impaired group whose scores were significantly below those of a normal group is so limited that it is difficult to interpret the results.

[429]

Gates Associative Learning Tests. Grades 1.5–7.0; no date available; 4 scores: visual-visual (2 scores), auditory-visual (2 scores); no data on reliability and validity; no description of normative population; individual; 1 form (no date) consisting of 4 sets of cards (10 cards per set) presenting either a symbol and word or a symbol and object; no manual; directions for administration (no date, 4 pages); 1985 price data: $4 per complete set; administration time not reported; The Reading Clinic, Temple University.*

Review of Gates Associative Learning Tests by RICHARD L. ALLINGTON, Associate Professor of Education, State University of New York at Albany, Albany, NY:

This test is like large four-door family sedans of the past. Just as those automobiles were designed for and met the needs of an earlier era, such is the case with the Gates Associative Learning Tests. Derived from behavioristic theory in an era when many, if not most, learning tasks were considered to be associative learning tasks, this test also presents the laxity of norming procedures more common in earlier eras. Mimeographed material that accompanies the test cards contains no information on test development, reliability, or validity, but provides only directions for administration and a crude norm chart.

The test itself is of simple design. Basically there are two types of associations: visual-visual and visual-auditory. Each type is tested in two formats, with single character visual stimuli and multiple character stimuli. In the visual-visual tasks the subject is presented with non-alphabetic characters and line drawing pictures of objects. The task is to associate the visual elements. In the visual-auditory tasks the examiner pronounces a word while exposing the non-alphabetic visual stimuli.

The stimulus cards present several problems. First, several of the depictions of the objects (e.g., letter, frog) are less than realistic on the visual-visual task cards. This is a serious flaw, for a representation that is not realistic complicates the task as the subject struggles to figure out what object is depicted. Second, several of the objects depicted are outdated (e.g., glass milk bottle, high button shoe) and this too would seem to unnecessarily complicate the associative tasks. Third, the non-alphabetic characters are a strange mixture of geometric designs, common symbols, rotated alphabetic characters, dot patterns, and Hebrew-like characters. In addition, many of these characters seem to float about rather than being strictly arrayed in line for the multiple-character stimuli. Recent research on the non-comparability of task performances by readers with alphabetic and non-alphabetic characters and the use of this hodge-podge of visual stimuli seriously limits the utility of this test.

A more serious limitation, however, is in what one can reliably ascertain from the administration of the test. While the test has been used for a variety of educational purposes, few, if any, applications can be vigorously supported. Of particular note here is the lack of support for using the test as either a general predictor of reading acquisition ability or as a predictor of modality preference in reading acquisition. Some will argue for the diagnostic utility of the test, but rigorous test development should not be expected only of achievement tests. Thus the test is not recommended for diagnostic purposes.

In summary, this test provides an assessment of a limited type of associative learning. Unfortunately, the lack of adequate data on reliability, validity, or diagnostic power severely limits any application of this test.

Review of Gates Associative Learning Tests by NEIL H. SCHWARTZ, Assistant Professor of Educational Psychology, Northern Arizona University, Flagstaff, AZ:

The Gates Associate Learning Tests (GALT) consists of four sets of stimulus cards and a two-page mimeographed description sheet. Upon receipt of these materials, one may have the impression that the description sheet is merely a summary of the manual for the test. It is not. There is no manual. There is no rationale or purpose for the test, either stated or implied, anywhere in the materials. There are no reliability or validity data. While there is a very brief set of norms consisting of grade-equivalence scores, 1.5–7.0, there is no description of the population or procedures for norming. In fact, there is a considerable degree of mystery surrounding the entire test. Had the name "Gates" been absent from the title, this reviewer would have abandoned his search for the test's background and resigned himself to a discussion of the test's inadequate psychometric properties.

As it turns out, Arthur I. Gates developed the Associative Learning Test in 1925. While the test was never formally published, it was described in Gates' book, *The Improvement of Reading*—the most recent edition of which was published in 1947. In his book, Gates described the purpose of the GALT as that of "testing the pupil's ability to learn materials in substantially the manner and similar in form to materials learned in the initial stages of reading." He suggested that the test be used to "estimate a pupil's ability to learn to attach a particular word meaning to a visual item resembling a word."

The GALT contains four subtests—two of which assess associations between two visually-apprehended stimuli (a familiar object and an unfamiliar figure) and two which measure associations between a visually-apprehended unfamiliar figure and its orally-presented concept- or referent-name. In all subtests, the testee is required to learn and remember the figure and its corresponding meaning. According to Gates, the two subtests which are entirely visual "resemble the classroom situation in which the teacher presents a printed word and shows a picture of a dog or a cat or some other object which conveys the word's meaning." The visual-auditory tests are designed to approximate a learning situation where a teacher states the name of a word to the learner after showing it in print. Gates maintains that "both the material and the form of these tests are designed to duplicate an actual experience in learning to recognize and think of the meaning of words."

The rationale underlying the test is a traditional one. It predicates that the acquisition of reading ability is particularly difficult if the reader has difficulty constructing and retaining associations between meaning derived from experience and word forms or printed symbols (Betts, 1945; Bronner, 1917; Resnick & Weaver, 1979). If a reader cannot relate a symbol or a series of symbols in print to a referent, concept or idea, the development of meaning will be severely impeded. Of course, this position is reflective of those contemporary views that subscribe to a direct-access theory of the reading process without phonological recoding (Smith, 1977).

The rationale and purpose of the test may make good sense to some test-users depending upon their theoretical perspective of the reading process. However, it is important to remember that the GALT has virtually no psychometric data with which to judge its adequacy as a measure of associative learning. Without reliability data, test-users have no way of determining whether obtained test scores represent a testee's true score or whether the scores reflect errors of measurement. Likewise, in the absence of any validity data, test-users have little other than the general appearance of the materials and tasks for determining whether the test measures what it is purported to assess. Finally, the test is accompanied by a sheet consisting of a score tabulation matrix and a table of norms reproduced from Gates' text. As mentioned above, no information is provided concerning the nature of the sample upon which these norms were derived. There is also no information offered regarding the procedures that were used for constructing the norms. While it is the case that both sources of information may appear in Gates' *Improvement of Reading*, this reviewer was able to secure only the 1947 edition. It is important to note that the norms appear in the 1936 edition of the text, and both volumes are apparently out of print.

Since the instructions for administration of the instrument are clear, most testers will find little difficulty in administering it. However, based on the foregoing discussion, test users are encouraged to proceed with caution in the interpretation of this test. It is neither suitable for use as a diagnostic device nor for making decisions relative to placement, instructional planning, or program evaluation. It is recommended by this reviewer to be used informally as a screening device for generating working hypotheses relative to a child's inability to read.

REVIEWER'S REFERENCES

Bronner, A. THE PSYCHOLOGY OF SPECIAL ABILITIES. Boston: Bobbs-Merrill, 1917.

Betts, E. A. Classification of reading disabilities. VISUAL DIGEST, 1945, 9, 36–44.

Gates, A. I. IMPROVEMENT OF READING. New York: Macmillan Co., 1947.

Smith, F. Making sense of reading—And of reading instruction. HARVARD EDUCATION REVIEW, 1977, 47, 386–395.

Resnick, L. B., & Weaver, P. A. THEORY AND PRACTICE OF EARLY READING (3 vols.). Hillsdale, NJ: Erlbaum, 1979.

[430]

Gates-MacGinitie Reading Tests. Grades 1.0–1.9, 1.5–1.9, 2, 3, 4–6, 7–9, 10–12; 1926–78; GMRT; first edition of Gates-MacGinitie Reading Tests still available; 7 levels; 2 editions; out-of-level norms available; 1983 price data: $2.91 per manual for any one level; $5.70 per out-of-level norms; $2.28 per examination kit for any one level; scoring service, $.49 and over per student (4 plans, $36 or more minimum depending on plan); Walter H MacGinitie (test and manual), Joyce Kamons, Ruth L. Kowalski, Ruth K. MacGinitie, and Timothy MacKay (manual); Riverside Publishing Co.*

a) BASIC R. Grades 1.0–1.9; 1978; manual (78 pages); (60–70) minutes in 2 sessions.

1) *Hand Scored Edition.* Forms 1, 2, (12 pages); $13.62 per 35 tests.

2) *Machine Scored Edition.* Forms 1M, 2M, (12 pages); $17.19 per 25 tests.

b) LEVEL A. Grades 1.5–1.9; 1978; 3 scores: vocabulary, comprehension, total; manual (70 pages); decoding skills analysis form (6 pages); (20) minutes for vocabulary, (35) minutes for comprehension; remaining details same as Basic R.

c) LEVEL B. Grade 2; 1978; scores same as Level A; manual (75 pages); remaining details same as Level A.

d) LEVEL C. Grade 3; 1978; scores same as Level A; manual (77 pages); remaining details same as Level A.

e) LEVEL D. Grades 4–6; 1978; scores same as Level A; manual (94 pages); time same as Level A.

1) *Hand Scored Edition.* Forms 1, 2, 3, (11 pages); separate answer sheets (self-scored, MRC) may be used; $13.62 per 35 tests; $14.94 per 35 self-scored answer sheets; $8.04 per 35 MRC answer sheets; $2.85 per MRC scoring stencils.

2) *Machine Scored Edition.* Form 1M (11 pages); separate answer sheets (NCS 7010, IBM 1230) may be used; $17.19 per 25 tests; $65.46 per 250 NCS answer sheets; $10.77 per 35 IBM answer sheets.

f) LEVEL E. Grades 7–9; 1978; scores same as Level A; manual (96 pages); time same as Level A.

1) *Hand Scored Edition.* Details same as for Level D.

2) *Machine Scored Edition.* Separate answer sheets (NCS 7010, IBM 1230) must be used; prices same as Level D.

g) LEVEL F. Grades 10–12; 1978; remaining details same as Level E.

See T3:932 (77 references) and 8:726A (34 references); for reviews by Carolyn L. Burke and Byron H. Van Roekel and an excerpted review by William R. Powell of an earlier edition, see 7:689.

TEST REFERENCES

1. Andersen, B. L., Licht, B. G., Ullmann, R. K., Buck, S. T., & Redd, W. H. Paraprofessional reading tutors: Assessment of the Edmark Reading Program and flexible teaching. AMERICAN JOURNAL OF COMMUNITY PSYCHOLOGY, 1979, 7, 689–699.

2. Roberts, R. N., & Tharp, R. G. A naturalistic study of school children's private speech in an academic problem-solving task. COGNITIVE THERAPY AND RESEARCH, 1980, 4, 341–352.

3. Rennie, B. J., Neilsen, A. R., & Braun, C. The effects of typographical cueing on memory for superordinate structures in connected discourse. NATIONAL READING CONFERENCE YEARBOOK, 1981, 30, 169–173.

4. Sawyer, D. J. The relationship between selected auditory abilities and beginning reading achievement. LANGUAGE, SPEECH, AND HEARING SERVICES IN SCHOOLS, 1981, 12, 95–99.

5. Whaley, J. F. Readers' reactions to temporal disruption in stories. NATIONAL READING CONFERENCE YEARBOOK, 1981, 30, 191–195.

6. Creaghead, N. A., & Donnelly, K. G. Comprehension of superordinate and subordinate information by good and poor readers. LANGUAGE, SPEECH, AND HEARING SERVICES IN SCHOOLS, 1982, 13, 177–186.

7. Mitterer, J. O. There are at least two kinds of poor readers: Whole-word poor readers and recording poor readers. CANADIAN JOURNAL OF PSYCHOLOGY, 1982, 36, 445–461.

8. Roberge, J. J., & Craven, P. A. Developmental relationships between reading comprehension and deductive reasoning. THE JOURNAL OF GENERAL PSYCHOLOGY, 1982, 107, 99–105.

9. Ryckman, D. B. Gray Oral Reading Tests: Some reliability and validity data with learning-disabled children. PSYCHOLOGICAL REPORTS, 1982, 50, 673–674.

10. Crowell, D. C., Hu-pei Au, K., & Blake, K. M. Comprehension questions: Differences among standardized tests. JOURNAL OF READING, 1983, 26, 314–319.

11. Hood, J., & Dubert, L. A. Decoding as a component of reading comprehension among secondary students. JOURNAL OF READING BEHAVIOR, 1983, 15, 51–61.

12. McCue, M. Assessment and rehabilitation of learning-disabled adults. REHABILITATION COUNSELING BULLETIN, 1983, 27, 281–290.

13. Stanovich, K. E., Feeman, D. J., & Cunningham, A. E. The development of the relation between letter-naming speed and reading ability. BULLETIN OF THE PSYCHONOMIC SOCIETY, 1983, 21, 199–202.

14. Williams, J. D. Covert language behavior during writing. RESEARCH IN THE TEACHING OF ENGLISH, 1983, 17, 301–312.

15. Duffelmeyer, F. A. The effect of context clues on the vocabulary test performance of word dominant and paragraph dominant readers. JOURNAL OF READING, 1984, 27, 508–513.

Review of Gates-MacGinitie Reading Tests by ROBERT CALFEE, Professor of Education and Psychology, School of Education, Stanford University, Stanford, CA:

According to the advertising flyer from the publisher, the Gates-MacGinitie is "the most widely used reading test in the country." No data are presented to support this claim, but neither is there any reason to doubt it; this battery is a prototype of the contemporary standardized reading test. Seven levels span the range from 1st through 12th grade. Vocabulary and comprehension are measured at each level, with transformations to percentiles, normal curve equivalents, stanines, grade equivalents, and extended scale scores. Parallel forms are available at each level. Attempts have been made to ensure that the battery is appropriate for Title I and Chapter I evaluations, and the tests have been reviewed for bias due to Black English or sexism in language usage. Testing time is short, less than an hour except for Level R. Scoring by hand is feasible, but machine scoring is also available. All things considered, the Gates-MacGinitie is quite adequate for a wide array of uses—program evaluation, special education, grade placement, and research, among others.

A review of this test therefore provides an opportunity to consider the strengths and weaknesses of the standardized test as a device for the assessment of reading skills, with one exception. Unlike several other batteries presently available, the Gates-MacGinitie does not attempt to provide information on specific objectives. I see this as an advantage. The effort to generate criterion-referenced information from a generalized battery generally comes to naught; the number of items and the validity of individual items for measuring a clearly defined skill both fall short in those cases with which I am familiar.

The Gates-MacGinitie is well suited to fulfill the rationale stated at the end of the introduction (where, unfortunately, it may not be noticed). The statement is as follows:

> The basic premise of the Gates-MacGinitie Reading Tests is that it is useful for teachers and schools to know the general level of reading achievement of individual students, through their entire school careers. This information, added to whatever else is known about the student, is an important basis for selecting students for further individual diagnosis and help, for locating students who are ready for more advanced work, for evaluating the general effects of instructional programs, for counseling students, and for reporting to parents and the community.

The purposes listed above are important ones; the greatest problems in the use of tests like the Gates-MacGinitie arise when they are pushed beyond their stated purposes, or when the caveat to search for other sources of information is forgotten.

The Gates-MacGinitie measures a limited domain of reading. In the first edition of the test, speed and accuracy were assessed, along with vocabulary and comprehension (a cloze procedure). Speed and accuracy are now gone, and comprehension is measured by multiple-choice questions. All in all, the revisions of the second edition have led to a version that is quite similar to other reading batteries. These limitations can be understood by examining what is included at each of the levels A through F (grades 1.5 through 12) under the headings of vocabulary and comprehension. Level R is quite different from the other levels and will be discussed separately. Such an examination reveals several points. First, decoding is essential at all levels. The student who is slow or inaccurate in translating from print to sound will do poorly in both Vocabulary and Comprehension. Second, testing is more concentrated in the primary grades than in the later grades. This strategy is sensible if one assumes that reading is to be taught in the elementary school, and that other disciplines dominate in the secondary grades. Indeed, one might reasonably argue that it is inappropriate to assess "reading" in the secondary grades, because reading is not generally taught after about sixth grade.

The third point has to do with limitations of the battery: The materials and the format cover only a small subset of the reading curriculum. Students are expected to do much more in reading than to select a single distinctive alternative from a set of four. In vocabulary, the task is often to decide among similar meanings; fine distinctions are important. In comprehension, it is the ability to integrate the elements of a test that is most vital, not simply the skill of tracking down the answer to a detailed question. Skills of this sort are not assessed by the battery.

Finally, there is the linkage of the battery to the "curriculum." As tests are used increasingly to make significant decisions about students (e.g., competency testing for high school graduation), the question is asked, "Does the test measure what is being taught?" This matter is discussed on page iv and 27–30 of the Teacher's Manual, appropriately enough under the heading of Test Validity. Two steps have been taken to establish curricular validity in this battery. First, standard word lists were consulted in selecting the words for the vocabulary subtest. Second, the texts at each level were selected according to a design that goes from simple stories in the primary grades to expository writing in the various disciplines at the later levels. Some reviewers might find fault with this rather simple approach, because it is not sufficiently rigorous, not adequately linked to specific objectives. I do not have any such concerns. Other limitations on the validity of the test have been noted above; nonetheless, if the test is to be used as a general measure of reading achievement, then the approaches taken to establish curricular validity seem quite reasonable to me.

What are the specific strengths and weaknesses of the Gates-MacGinitie? First we consider some strong points. Both the student's test booklet and the teacher's manual are clearly laid out and easy to work from. The practice tests for students provide an opportunity to become familiar with the format and response demands. The test instructions are detailed but coherent. The content of the teacher's manual is meaty; the section on reliability packs a lot of solid information into a single page.

The discussion of out-of-level testing is especially noteworthy. The tendency in many bureaucratically-driven test programs is to administer the same test level for all students at a particular grade level, regardless of the appropriateness of that level for individual students. An example of this would be sixth graders in a Chapter I program who are given a sixth-grade test because of their grade placement, but whose reading performance may range from second to fourth grade. Not surprisingly, most find the test frustrating, their scores pile up near the chance level, and the scores are statistically untrustworthy. The information in the teacher's manual of the Gates-MacGinitie warns about this situation, and presents alternative strategies.

Now let us consider some of the problems. While some parts of the teacher's manual are exceptional, others confuse or mislead. The discussion of Types of Test Scores falls into the latter category. The intention is laudable, but by the time the teacher has waded halfway through the dozen pages of this section, he or she will very likely retreat in the face of technical detail and inconsistency. The teacher is advised, for instance, that percentiles and grade equivalents cannot be averaged; yet the scoring service provides averages for both of these indices.

Also problematic in the Teacher's Manuals for Levels A and B is the section on Decoding Skills Analysis. This section has two problems. First, the scoring system is well intentioned, but so convoluted that most teachers are unlikely to have the time and energy to untangle the system. Second, the analysis of the English letter-sound system is presented at a level of detail that loses the forest for the trees. Moreover, some of the comments are either misleading or simply wrong. For instance, decoding skills are grouped "in descending order of importance" from initial and final consonants, through initial or final vowels, thence to medial consonants and vowels. If the intention is that the first items on the list are most important to assess, then this listing flies in the face of virtually all research on the topic, which shows that vowels are the major source of problems. In addition, the classification of letter-sound elements bears only passing resemblance to psycholinguistic analyses of this topic. I would suggest that this portion of the battery for the primary grades be disregarded by teachers; there are better ways to assess decoding skills.

Finally there is Level R. This level, which is new with the second edition, "is designed to serve the needs of many programs for which evaluation of reading achievement is required both at the beginning and the end of the first grade." (Recall that Level A requires decoding skills that are not likely to be possessed by many students at the beginning of first grade.) The statement continues, "The test is not only a measure of the general level of reading achievement; it can also be used to identify particular reading skills that individual children or groups of children still need to learn." The rationale differs significantly from that of the other levels, and suffers accordingly. Level R is a long test (65 minutes in two sessions). It is a complex test; the item format and content changes every few items. Despite the complexity, it yields a single standardized score. To be sure, there is a rough breakdown into subtests of letter-sound correspondences, vocabulary, letter recognition, and comprehension, but this breakdown does not appear on the front of the booklet—nor can it be "averaged." The comprehension questions are test-plus-picture format, so that decoding skills are critical. All in all, this level of the battery is a motley that reflects some of the worst aspects of current practice.

The Gates-MacGinitie has a long history, going back to the Gates Reading Tests of 1926. The present edition, as noted at the beginning of the review, reflects the features both positive and negative of contemporary standardized tests of reading. When used for the purposes for which it was designed, this battery should prove quite serviceable; it can't do everything, but it isn't designed for that. Nonetheless, the Gates tests are quite an achievement, and a historical review of this series would provide some interesting insights into our changing conceptions of reading.

Review of Gates-MacGinitie Reading Tests by WILLIAM H. RUPLEY, Associate Professor, Educational Curriculum and Instruction, Texas A & M University, College Station, TX:

The Gates-MacGinitie Reading Tests are norm-referenced and as reported in the manuals "can be used to complement teachers' evaluations and thus can contribute to making sound educational decisions." There are seven levels of the tests, with each level having at least two equivalent forms. Subtests for all levels include Vocabulary and Comprehension; the Basic R level also includes Letter Recognition and Letter Sounds subtests. Normative data—Normal Curve Equivalent scores, percentile rank, stanine, grade-level equivalents, and extended scale scores—can be derived from raw scores for total score, vocabulary subtest, and comprehension subtest for all levels except the Basic R. Normative information for the Basic R level is descriptive due to the fact that the subtests are very short.

Vocabulary subtests for Levels A, B, and C use the identical item format as in the earlier edition. The A and B levels present a picture and a set of four words from which the child is to select the word that describes the picture. Level C requires that the student select from four choices a word or phrase that means most nearly the same as the test word. The item format for levels D through F are identical to C except there are five words or phrases from which the student is to select a response.

Vocabulary words in each test level were selected from a variety of word list sources, which included a list of words found in 16 reading series for grades one, two, and three; Harris-Jacobson Core Words for First Grade; Barnes' Revised Dolch List of 193 Words; Dale List of 769 Words; A Revised Core Vocabulary; and American Heritage Word Frequency Book. Words were selected to characterize those likely to be found in reading materials in the grade range covered by each test level. Also, the authors report that "a balance of nouns, verbs, adjectives, and adverbs was maintained at levels C through F. In levels R, A, and B, the use of pictures to be named precluded testing many adjectives or adverbs."

A criticism by Roekel (7:689) of earlier editions of the Gates-MacGinitie Reading Tests was that approximately 90% of the correct answers for words defined by pictures are nouns. An analysis of the vocabulary items for the revised tests indicates that authors have attended to this earlier criticism. For

Basic R, Form 1 and also for Level A, Form 1, approximately 40% of the correct items are not nouns. Approximately 35% of the correct answers for Level B, Form 1 are not nouns, also. Although the correct answers in these instances are usually verbs, this still reflects a better balance of vocabulary items than was noted in earlier editions of the Gates-MacGinitie tests.

Comprehension subtests vary through test levels for both subject matter content and item format. Comprehension materials for Basic R, Levels A and B, and approximately two-thirds of Level C, were written specifically for the test. Levels D, E, and F use content taken from published sources and are either narrative or story type materials. Item format for Basic R and Levels A and B Comprehension subtests require that the student select the correct picture for a given sentence or sentences. Levels C through F utilize short passages and the student responds to questions about information based on the passages.

At levels R through B, the student in some instances must make fine visual discrimination of the pictures to identify the correct answer. For example, a correct response for item 14 (Comprehension) in Level B, Form 1 requires that the student note the picture where the end seat in the front row is empty. Each response choice depicts some empty theater seats, but only one seat is on the end. In addition, some items in these levels require recognition of grammatical language features to derive the correct response. An illustration of this is item number 13 (Comprehension) in Level B, Form 1: "The girl has a long scarf. The boy has a short one. Which is the boy's?" Four pictures are presented: (1) a long scarf hanging on a hoof, (2) a boy dressed in a coat and tie, (3) a short scarf hanging on a hook, and (4) two boys each dressed in a coat and a tie. The correct answer is picture number three, and such an item may not be a valued measure of comprehension if one defines it as an understanding of ideas represented by written text.

One improvement in the Comprehension subtest for levels R through B is worth noting. In an earlier review, Burke (7:689) pointed out that "answers to many of the questions are built entirely upon one word." An analysis of the Comprehension items for levels R through B did not reveal any question built entirely upon one word. As a result, the focus is more on measuring student's comprehension as opposed to vocabulary knowledge.

The Comprehension subtests for all levels do require some inferencing and abstracting rather than simply recognizing information presented in the passages. Most items appear to be passage dependent and progress in difficulty level within each of the test levels. Higher test levels represent the content found in most public schools, such as social sciences, natural sciences, and the arts.

The teacher's manuals for each level are well written; easy to read; and detail accurately administration, norm interpretation, and technical information. Major sections that are improvements over past editions and ones which users of the test should read carefully are "Interpreting the Test Scores" and "Norms Available for Out-of-Level Testing." Topics addressed in these sections that are major concerns for the interpretation of students' test results are validity and reliability. Validity is discussed in terms of content validity, and guidelines are given for teachers to assess validity of the test in relation to their school's curriculum. Also, procedures used to identify and select Vocabulary words and Comprehension items are presented. Items were submitted to minority consultants to screen for those that might be offensive or inappropriate for minority group members. Twice as many items were used in a tryout as appeared in the final form of the test and attention was given to eliminating elements of test bias. Reliability coefficients for internal consistency (KR20) are presented for each test level and form. Vocabulary reliability coefficients range from .90 to .95 and Comprehension coefficients range from .88 to .94. In addition to technical information about the reliability of the tests, suggestions for teachers are presented to help them judge the accuracy of students' scores. Improvements over earlier editions are the recommendations for how to interpret and use norm-referenced scores for comparing achievements and for determining growth in achievement.

Two strong features of the Gates-MacGinitie Reading Tests are out-of-level testing and recommendations for error analysis. Norms available for out-of-level testing in the teacher's manual are normal curve equivalent scores and percentile ranks. All norms are available through the Riverside scoring service. Several pages in the Teacher's Manual for levels R through C are devoted to qualitative analyses of students' incorrect responses for the Vocabulary subtest. A table of item difficulties is presented (for both Comprehension and Vocabulary) of the percentage of the norming group who answered each item correctly, with an accompanying discussion of how to analyze student's incorrect responses.

This edition of the Gates-MacGinitie Reading Tests is a marked improvement over the first edition. The authors have given attention to past criticism and in most instances have made recommended changes. The teacher's manual is more comprehensive and better written than the manual for the first edition. As a measure of students' reading ability for evaluation purposes the Gates-MacGinitie would function well. However, for the purpose of reading diagnosis it lacks the specificity needed to identify weaknesses; therefore, it would best serve as a survey test to identify students for whom diagnostic testing is warranted.

[431]

Gates-MacGinitie Reading Tests, Canadian Edition. Grades 1.0–1.9, 1.5–1.9, 2, 3, 4–6, 7–9, 10–12; 1978–81; GMRTCE; based on the second edition (1978) of the Gates-MacGinitie Reading Tests; no validity data; 7 levels; out-of-level norms available; 1984 price data: $16.15 per 35 tests (specify level); $1.40 per scoring key; $6.60 per manual (specify level); $6.85 per examination kit (specify level); scoring service, $.82 and over per student ($82 minimum, grades 4–12 only); Walter H. MacGinitie (test and manual), Joyce Kamons, Ruth Kowalski, Ruth K. MacGinitie, and Timothy Mackay (manual); Nelson Canada [Canada].*

a) BASIC R. Grades 1.0–1.9; 1979–80; 1 form ('79, 12 pages); manual ('80, 75 pages); (65) minutes in 2 sessions.

b) LEVEL A. Grades 1.5–1.9; 1979–80; 3 scores: vocabulary, comprehension, total; forms 1, 2, ('79, 13 pages); manual ('80, 60 pages); decoding skills analysis form ('81, 6 pages); $3.25 per decoding skills analysis form; (20) minutes for vocabulary, (35) minutes for comprehension.

c) LEVEL B. Grade 2; 1979–80; scores and forms same as for Level A; manual ('80, 62 pages); remaining details same as for Level A.

d) LEVEL C. Grade 3; 1979–80; scores and forms same as for Level A; manual ('80, 55 pages); time same as for Level A.

e) LEVEL D. Grades 4–6; 1979–80; scores and forms same as for Level A; manual ('80, 82 pages); $9.70 per 35 hand-scorable answer sheets; $25 per 100 machine-scorable answer sheets; time same as for Level A.

f) LEVEL E. Grades 7–9; 1979–80; scores and forms same as for Level A; manual ('80, 80 pages); remaining details same as for Level D.

g) LEVEL F. Grades 10–12; 1979–80; scores and forms same as for Level A; manual ('80, 79 pages); remaining details same as for Level D.

Review of Gates-MacGinitie Reading Tests, Canadian Edition, by MARIAM JEAN DREHER, Assistant Professor of Curriculum & Instruction, University of Maryland, College Park, MD:

The Gates-MacGinitie Reading Tests, Canadian Edition, are survey tests of reading performance. The Canadian Edition is based on the Gates-MacGinitie Reading Test, Second Edition (1978) developed in the United States. Each of the seven levels, which cover grades 1 through 12, includes vocabulary and comprehension subtests. In addition, the first level, Basic R, includes subtest scores for letter recognition and letter "sounds." At all levels, on all subtests, the items are 4-option multiple choices.

For Basic R and Levels A and B, vocabulary is said to be "primarily a test of decoding skills." Students must select the word that goes with a picture from among choices that look and sound rather alike. For most of these items, children can look at the picture, figure out the intended word, and then try to find it among the choices. However, for a few pictures, it is difficult to determine the intended word unless one reads the choices first. For example, one picture shows a group of children in a circle reaching out to another child; the intended word is "include." Such items seem more complex than those which simply require looking for a word which matches a recognized picture. As a result, some children may need to have an example demonstrating the appropriate strategy for such items. But the practice exercises do not include any such items since the teacher identifies the practice exercise pictures for the children. The problem does not arise on Basic R because the teacher tells the children what each picture on the test represents.

For Levels C through F, vocabulary is tested by having students select the correct meaning for a printed word; as a result the vocabulary test for these levels is "primarily a test of word knowledge rather than a test of decoding skills." Thus the vocabulary test for Levels C through F represents a somewhat different skill than what is measured at the lower levels. Although the manuals at each level clearly state what is meant by vocabulary at that level, the use of the term vocabulary throughout could be somewhat confusing especially if longitudinal comparisons in performance are to be made.

The comprehension subtests for Basic R and for Levels A and B require students to select a picture that answers questions or matches the information given in a sentence or a short passage. For Levels C through F, the students must read a passage and answer two or more questions about it. The comprehension subtests at all levels involve both literal and inferential questions, but the percentage of inferential questions increases from 10% on Level A to 45% on Levels D, E, and F. (No figure is given for Basic R, but it appears to include some inferential questions.)

Although the vocabulary and comprehension subtests are said to measure two somewhat different abilities, no information is available in the manual to support this claim. Moreover, the Technical Manual for the Canadian Edition, which would be likely to contain such information, was unavailable as of April, 1984. For the U.S. Edition, the correlation between vocabulary and comprehension subtests is generally high—ranging from .71 to .87. In some cases, the correlation between vocabulary and comprehension subtests was almost as high as correlations between two forms of the same subtest. At Level A, for example, the vocabulary subtests of Form 1 has a .88 correlation with the vocabulary subtest of Form 2; this .88 correlation is not much higher than the correlation of .86 between vocabulary and comprehension subtests on Form 1. When the Technical Manual for the Canadian Edition becomes available similar correlations may be apparent since the Canadian Edition is based on the U.S. Edition. When the information becomes available, therefore, test users may wish to check whether vocabulary and comprehension subtests measure appreciably different abilities.

A Decoding Skills Analysis Form is available for Levels A and B. This form is designed to enable teachers to discover error patterns by having them chart all the vocabulary subtest items that each student misses. But teachers are cautioned that the form will not allow "a definitive statement of problem areas" since performance is based on a "survey test, not a diagnostic test" and as a result "does not test repeatedly the individual decoding skills, and it does not include the full range of skills that a student needs to learn." Thus, since the form can only be used as a basis for further diagnosis, it requires considerable work for little return. As a result, teachers may want to skip the form completely and simply give children who score poorly on the Gates-MacGinitie a good diagnostic test.

For Levels A to F, split-half reliability coefficients for vocabulary range from .85 to .94 and for comprehension from .85 to .92. For Levels B through F, these coefficients are given only for Form 1; for Level A, coefficients are provided only for Form 2. No information is given on reliability for the total scores on each test. There is also no information on alternate-form reliability in the manual. The manual contains a very clear discussion about reliability concerns in test score interpretation. But information on standard error of measurement, which might help test users interpret the scores, is not included.

For the Basic R, reliability is given only for the total test—.87. Although teachers are shown how to break the Basic R scores into the four subtests previously mentioned, and although norms are provided for each of these subtests, no reliability information is provided for them. The norms for the four subtests are described as "very rough" and, indeed, provide only a rating of high, average, or low for students' performance in each of the areas. In addition, teachers are cautioned that the meaning of these ranks will vary greatly depending on the school's curriculum and even on the particular subtest itself. In view of these cautions and the lack of subtest reliability figures (which must be lower than .87 for the whole test), the value and accuracy of the subtest scores for Basic R must be questioned.

The manual presents no statistical data on test validity, but it does attempt to establish content validity by explaining how the items were developed to reflect typical school reading programs. For example, vocabulary items were selected from well-known word lists and from a study of popular reading series. Comprehension items were selected according to a plan which presumably reflects curricular changes by moving from mostly narrative passages on Level A toward increasing percentages of social science, natural science, and arts passages on high levels of the test. But the manual should clarify whether these steps were taken in developing the Canadian Edition or for the U.S. Edition. A comparison of both editions suggests that these steps for establishing content validity were taken for the U.S. Edition. Apparently the only major action in checking content validity for the Canadian Edition was to modify or delete some items based on a screening by Canadian educators. If Canadian reading programs can be assumed to be largely equivalent to those in the U.S., then the steps taken to make the U.S. Edition representative of typical U.S. programs are probably adequate for Canadian programs as well. But if Canadian and American programs diverge, then users ought to be particularly mindful of the manual's statement that a test is only valid if it matches a school's curriculum. The manual makes an excellent recommendation that the test be checked against a series of questions about whether it reflects the same emphases in decoding skills, comprehension questions, and types of written materials as the school's reading program.

Although test users should indeed check whether test content matches their program, additional information on validity ought to be supplied. For example, the Technical Summary for the U.S. Edition does address construct validity by reporting correlations between the U.S. Edition and the Metropolitan Achievement Tests at grades 5 and 8, indicating that the two measure much the same thing. Evidence of stability of students' relative standing over time is also reported. But no such information is yet available for the Canadian Edition. It seems likely that similar construct validity arguments will be made for the Canadian Edition by equating it to the U.S. edition.

To construct the norms, a sample of 46,000 Canadian students was tested. This sample appears to have been carefully selected to be representative of Canadian students. Their scores were compared to the existing U.S. score distributions for the U.S. Edition. This comparison produced a table of differences which was then used to calculate the Canadian norms. February and May norms are provided for Level A; for all other levels, October norms are also given.

The Gates-MacGinitie Reading Tests, Canadian Edition, appear to be worthwhile tests of reading progress, particularly if potential users follow the manual's advice to check the emphases of the tests against their reading curriculum. Each teacher's manual contains complete, clear directions for administering and scoring the tests. The manuals also contain appropriate cautions about possible misinterpretations of derived scores. However, as has been noted, the manuals contain only scanty technical information. Users must rely on inferences made from the Technical Summary of the U.S. Edition since details for the Canadian Edition were not available from the publisher as of April, 1984, despite the passing of several years since the publication of the test.

Review of Gates-MacGinitie Reading Tests, Canadian Edition, by SUSANNA W. PFLAUM, Dean, Honors College, University of Illinois at Chicago, Chicago, IL:

The Gates-MacGinitie Reading Tests were developed for use in Canadian schools by establishing Canadian norms, by correcting spelling to conform to Canadian usage (e.g., "labour" for "labor"), and by substituting some new items that reflected Canadian writers and experiences. This review highlights differences between this Canadian version and the U.S. version.

The Canadian Edition offers no machine scoring service although all other scoring services are available. The norming procedure used 46,000 students from 10 provinces and the Yukon Territory. In provinces with large French-speaking populations, English-speaking students constituted the norming groups. A comparison of the norms at Level B for the U.S. Second Edition and the Canadian Edition, with identical items in each test, reveals that the same raw score gives a slightly lower percentile and grade equivalent in the Canadian than the U.S. Edition. The Canadian Edition presents the standard score as a *T* score. There are no validity data provided. The Kuder-Richardson Formula 20 reliability coefficients range from .85 to .94 (U.S. .88 to .95). Several items in the comprehension subtests of the upper grade forms have a distinctly Canadian or North American content. The appearance of the Canadian Edition is similar to the U.S. The paper is of somewhat lower quality. Subtests are clearly set off from one another.

The Canadian Edition of the Gates-MacGinitie Reading Tests has similar strengths and weaknesses as the U.S. Edition. The use of more appropriate content and the development of Canadian norms provides a much improved battery of reading achievement tests for use in Canadian schools over the U.S. Edition. These characteristics outweigh any disadvantages in paper quality and slightly lower reliability evident in the Canadian Edition.

[432]

Gates-McKillop-Horowitz Reading Diagnostic Test, Second Edition. Grades 1–6; 1962–81; revision of Gates-McKillop Reading Diagnostic Tests; 23 scores: omissions, additions, repetitions, mispronunciations (directional errors, wrong beginning, wrong middle, wrong ending, wrong in several parts, accent errors, total), reading sentences, words-flash, words-untimed, word attack (syllabication, recognizing and blending common word parts, reading words, giving letter sounds, naming capital letters, naming lower-case letters), vowels, auditory (blending, discrimination), spelling; individual; 1 form consists of 2 parts: reading tests ('81, 9 pages), auditory tests/pupil record booklet ('81, 12 pages); manual of directions ('81, 16 pages); 1983 price data: $5.25 per examiner's kit including test materials, 1 pupil record booklet, and manual of directions; $3.50 per set of test materials; $13.50 per package of 30 pupil record booklets; $1.50 per manual of directions; administration time not reported; Authur I. Gates, Anne S. McKillop, and Elizabeth Cliff Horowitz; Teachers College Press.*

For a review by Harry Singer of an earlier edition, see 8:759 (8 references); see T2:1629 (11 references); for reviews by N. Dale Bryant and Gabriel M. Della-Piana, see 6:824 (2 references); for a review by George D. Spache of the earlier edition, see 5:662; for a review by Worth J. Osburn, see 4:563 (2 references); for a review by T. L. Torgerson, see 3:510 (3 references).

Review of Gates-McKillop-Horowitz Reading Diagnostic Test, Second Edition, by PRISCILLA A. DRUM, Associate Professor of Education, University of California, Santa Barbara, Santa Barbara, CA:

The Gates-McKillop-Horowitz test is an individually administered series of subtests that mainly tap word recognition skills. The diagnostician and/or teacher will have to decide which of the subtests provides appropriate information for the pupil to be tested and whether the pupil has had instruction on these skills. In addition, it may be necessary to select tests to measure vocabulary knowledge and listening and reading comprehension. In other words, this test addresses decoding, along with a brief spelling test and a single writing sample. It is not a complete diagnostic package.

The 1981 revision does address certain psychometric criticisms on reliability and norming noted for the 1962 edition of the Gates-McKillop test. The norming sample of 600 children in grades one through six is now described to some extent, with both ethnic and urbanicity stratifications representative of the general school population. Sixty-five percent of the children attended private schools rather than public, and no information is given on the instructional programs in the schools sampled. A norming sample of 600 students in six grades can only suffice as a criterion for performance if we know what instruction the norming children have received. Also, all of the sample children were fluent English speakers, so there are no comparisons for children who are learning English.

Further, we don't know how many children were tested at each grade, although the assumption is that there were 100. In the manual, the average performance by grade is provided for most subtests, but no measures of dispersion are given. A single table presenting means, standard deviations, and the number tested at each grade for each subtest would be most helpful in establishing criteria for diagnostic evaluation. Approximately 5% ($N=27$) of the sample students were retested on the Oral Reading subtest yielding a test-retest reliability of .94. The interrater reliability by two testers on 50 Oral Reading protocols was greater than 90%. The two scorers must have been both knowledgeable and practiced; providing scores while listening to a child read is difficult. Perhaps they listened to tapes, a recommended procedure for these tasks, since the tester is quite busy.

The only concurrent validation compares the Oral Reading subtest scores with silent reading scores from various standardized reading achievement tests. The coefficients range from .68 to .96, with higher correlations at grades one and two than for the upper grades. Since only first and second graders who "were clearly good readers" read the last three paragraphs, the skills tested in the first four paragraphs and those of the comparison silent reading tests likely tap similar beginning reading abilities. But the validity of this test for older and/or better readers may be questionable; at least the validity data provided does not substantiate this use.

The correlations between the various subtests are not given. For almost every subtest, there is a brief note suggesting performance comparison with a different subtest (e.g., the Words: Untimed score should be compared with the score on Words: Flash and the score on Oral Reading). Supposedly, if the child can read paragraphs accurately, but not untimed words, the reader is overly dependent on context. The Words: Flash is described as a sight word test and Words: Untimed as a phonics test, so this comparison is intended to isolate differences between these skills. The question is whether there were patterns in the norm group sample that would substantiate these comparisons.

The tests themselves, however, are interesting and could provide useful information for a well trained, perceptive diagnostician. The seven paragraph passage used for the 20 subscores on Oral Reading is divided into two subtests for the first four and last three paragraphs. Each paragraph increases in vocabulary level, sentence length, and irregular sight-sound correspondences. Whenever the child makes 11 errors on each of two consecutive paragraphs, oral reading is stopped. By the fifth paragraph, such words as gnawed, furious, and estate are included. This is a word recognition in context task, but at the upper level the context may not provide clues for many children. Instead, it becomes a test of higher level phonics skills, which could be useful for older pupils.

The authors have not given any purpose for reading the four phonetically regular sentences. Possibly if the child cannot read the first two paragraphs in Oral Reading, this would prove to be an easier task. The sentences are fairly short (9 to 12 words), all monosyllables, no consonant clusters, five vowel digraphs, and regular CVC and CVCe word patterns. This should be a fairly easy task. If the child successfully reads the four paragraphs in Oral Reading, Part One, the sentence task should be omitted.

Words: Flash and Words: Untimed may or may not examine sight word skills versus phonics skills as the authors suggest, but the two scores do provide a comparison of accuracy under time pressure versus accuracy when there is no pressure. In order to concentrate on the meaning of the message, a child must scan the words with sufficient fluency so that the various phrases can be connected into idea units. If decoding every word is a laborious task, the likelihood is that the child will be unable to grasp much of the content. The timed and untimed word reading tasks together can indicate both ease and accuracy in decoding.

In testing, there is a trade-off on whether to start with the simplest items, thereby providing the children with likely success as motivation for trying, or to start with the hardest items while the child is fresh and attentive. For the Knowledge of Word Parts, the hardest test, reading polysyllabic nonsense words, is administered first. Thus, if the child does well on this task, he or she is assumed to have the skills to successfully master the next five subtests, which are then skipped.

However, some of the later tests, from Knowledge of Word Parts on, suffer from a common problem—how the tester is to score the responses. Nonsense words, particularly polysyllabic ones, can have more than one legitimate pronunciation. There is no key for permissible answers. One can wonder what the correct response is for ACDENGIST or the sounds for x, or c, and q in isolation. The spelling test is scored as number correct, and it is recommended that the examiner perform an error analysis. The general directions for the error analysis include substitutions and counting syllabication errors in longer words. No interpretation of error patterns is discussed.

Finally, why the writing sample is taken is a mystery. From decoding skills, the tester leaps to scoring usage and syntactic encoding errors from a single, brief composition on "any topic." The interpretation offered is that many children have difficulty with syntax, usage, and letter formation, but "children with learning problems seem to have these difficulties more often and for a longer period of time than other children." For the decoding tasks, the relationships between them are noted, and possible error interpretations for specific reading difficulties are given. Until the same thought and explanations are accorded to the Written Expression tasks, this section should be omitted. There are likely error pattern relationships between decoding, spelling, and writing, but this test does not clarify them.

On the other hand, if the tester is knowledgeable, has studied this test and refined the scoring criteria, and is an ambidextrous tester for the Word:Flash task, the contrast between scores for oral reading of paragraphs, timed and untimed words in isolation, and nonsense words could identify specific instructional needs in decoding for particular children. The testing time should be quite short, 15–20 minutes, and the information gained more pertinent to decoding accuracy and fluency than for many other tests, such as the Spache Diagnostic Reading Scales, the Durrell Analysis of Reading Difficulty, or the Woodcock Reading Mastery Tests.

Review of Gates-McKillop-Horowitz Reading Diagnostic Test, Second Edition, by P. DAVID PEARSON, Professor, and PATRICIA HERMAN, Research Assistant, Center for the Study of Reading, University of Illinois at Urbana-Champaign, Champaign, IL:

Unlike many standardized tests, the Gates-McKillop-Horowitz Reading Diagnostic Tests are designed to identify strengths and weaknesses within an individual student rather than to compare performance across students or groups of students. Firmly entrenched within a traditional view of reading diagnosis and remediation, the purpose of these tests, to paraphrase the authors, is to find unique weaknesses that can be used to plan a program of instruction.

Implicit in the rationale for the test is a traditional componential view of the reading process, i.e., that skilled performance in reading rests upon the acquisition of a number of distinct and discrete behaviors, such as acquiring a repertoire of sight words, using context available in a sentence, decomposing words into syllables, blending word parts together to produce whole words, recognizing the sounds and names of individual letters, and hearing likenesses and differences among phonemes (auditory discrimination). Hence the authors provide an oral reading test as an index of overall reading ability, along with discrete tests for each of the assumed component behaviors. Also, they offer an extended discussion of how to use errors made by students on the oral reading test to provide converging evidence about weaknesses in component word identification behaviors.

This review is divided into two parts. First, an evaluation is made of selected subtests in terms of their logical and statistical adequacy. Then some cautionary notes are offered about the whole tradition of diagnostic assessment from which this test, along with a host of others, derives.

The Oral Reading subtest consists of seven paragraphs sequenced by increasing difficulty (the sentences get longer and the words less common). This part of the 1981 version of the test is exactly the same as its 1962 predecessor. On the positive side, the paragraphs are linked together by at least a weak story line (an unresolved conflict between a rat and a dog). On the negative side, certain phrases may strike contemporary readers as strange and unfamiliar (e.g., "what sublime conceit," "aggravate my sensibilities," and "pathetic imbecile").

The authors instruct examiners to allow students to progress through the paragraphs until they have made 11 or more errors on two successive paragraphs; at that point, examiners may assign a reading level to a student by using norm tables. The directions for recording and analyzing errors are quite traditional, with the usual mix of mispronunciations, additions (insertions), omissions, hesitations, and repetitions. They also include self-corrections. Error interpretation focuses on word parts (beginning, middle and end), with a single paragraph admonishing examiners that some errors may reflect attention to context.

The authors report a .94 test-retest correlation for grade placement scores and concurrent validity indices ranging from .96 (in the lower grades) to a low of .68 (in the upper grades) with different standardized reading achievement tests. The interrater reliability ratings (for error classifications) range from 94% agreement for the easier paragraphs to 91% agreement for the harder paragraphs. The population used for both norming and reliability indices consisted of some 600 children (35% public schools and 83% urban).

On balance, the Oral Reading subtest has acceptable empirical characteristics, but suffers from seemingly archaic language (it may only be uncommon) and what is a very limited view of the role of context in oral reading performance.

A new test in the 1981 edition is the Reading Sentences subtest. It consists of four sentences containing "almost entirely phonetically regular [sic]" words (THE and MEAN appear to be the only words not exhibiting a predictable spelling to sound correspondence). It is designed to assess the "extent to which the child uses meaning clues and word-form clues in word recognition." With sentences like, "The mean eel can hide in the weeds in the bay," the face validity of the test becomes questionable. One wonders whether such contexts are sufficiently rich and familiar to measure anyone's penchant for using context.

The Words:Flash and Words:Untimed subtests both consist of lists of unrelated words; the difference, of course, is that the brief exposure in the Flash subtest prevents visual analysis of the words. Hence, the Flash subtest permits an assessment of sight word recognition, while the Untimed subtest permits an assessment of "word-attack skills." After reading this rationale, one expects to find the Flash list composed of fairly common words that one would encounter often in print, with a fair proportion of words exhibiting unpredictable spelling to sound correspondences. Conversely one expects to find the Untimed test, composed of less common words with predictable correspondences. What is found instead is that the Flash list is a subset of the Untimed list. The inclusion of words like THE, HERE, COUNTER and RESTAURANT in the Untimed list leads us to question any predictability criterion. Likewise, the inclusion of words in the Flash list like ILLUSTRIOUS and LAMENTATION leads us to question the commonness criterion. According to our own calculations, using the *American Heritage Word Frequency Book* (Carroll, Davies, & Richman, 1971) as a criterion for frequency, the first several words on each list are very common (about 6,000 occurrences per million), while the remainder represent reasonably uncommon words (about 150 occurrences per million). In short, there are many rare words on the test.

The Syllabication subtest consists of 17 nonsense words such as RIVLOB, FIZBLE, AND ACDENGIST. The authors claim that this subtest, "which is composed of nonsense words of two or more frequently used syllables, determines whether the child can divide a word into syllables and produce an acceptable total word." The test fails on several counts. First the claim of commonality is suspect. Of the 40 syllabic units in these 17 words, only 21 appear in the common phonogram list in *Thorndike's Beginning Dictionary* (Jones, 1969). Second, units like -iv, -iz, la-, and ga-, do not often appear as separate syllables; some sequences are also unrepresentative of real words (e.g., ACDENGIST). Third, since no pronunciation guide is provided, examiners may have difficulty knowing what is acceptable. Fourth and most important, the whole point of syllabication as a word identification strategy is to come up with a pronunciation that approximates a word that is part of one's listening but not necessarily one's reading vocabulary. By filtering possible pronunciations through the constraints provided by the linguistic context of the text and one's listening vocabulary, a reader decides what makes sense. This method of assessment thus misses the whole point of syllabication as a word-attack strategy.

The Recognizing and Blending Common Word Parts subtest is designed to measure a student's ability to "analyze and read one-syllable words containing consonant combinations." It differs from its companion subtests, Reading Words, in two respects: (*a*) Reading Words contains no consonant blends, and (*b*) Reading Words has no backup procedure for breaking a word into parts to see if the student can put it back together. Both tests consist of nonsense words formed from presumably common letter clusters.

What is difficult to understand about these two subtests and the Syllabication subtest is why the authors have chosen to use nonsense words rather than real words. It is understandable why they have avoided common words (the student might be able to recognize them as sight words, thus preventing any assessment of word-attack strategies), but it is difficult to understand why they have avoided rare real words, particularly words one might expect to be in the student's listening but not reading vocabulary. There is no reason for test developers to rely upon nonsense words when they could obtain a more valid estimate of strategy use by using rare real words. In fact, nonsense words prevent students from performing the last critical step in the whole word-attack sequence, namely, checking an hypothesis against one's listening vocabulary.

There are two tests which measure individual letter-sound knowledge, the Giving Letter Sounds subtest (which requires a student to produce the sound of a letter or letter group) and the Recognizing the Visual Form of Sounds subtest (which requires the student to point to the vowel letter that "makes" the sound in a word the examiner pronounces). In relation to the Letter Sounds subtest, it may be questioned why consonants, vowels and a few vowel digraphs were included but several vowel digraphs (oe, ie, and ey), all diphthongs, and all consonant clusters were excluded.

So much for evaluation of the test from an internal point of view. The question should now be raised about whether reading diagnosis ought to proceed from the assumption of discrete component skills focusing on "pieces" of written language that somehow combine to produce the interpretive act of reading. The answer is negative. To assess sheer knowledge of these "pieces" outside the context in which a student is expected to apply that knowledge, i.e., when the student is really reading real text, gives a biased estimate of ability to use that knowledge. Not only does assessment devoid of context prevent the student from using the rich range of resources available in most real text, it also prevents the examiner from getting a picture of how the student is or is not able to marshall resources, skills, and strategies to solve the problem of what the text means.

It is not surprising, therefore, that this review concludes that the Reading Diagnostic Tests, like so many of its peers, should be used only by those who are willing to supplement the information it can provide with much informal diagnosis concerning how students actually use and monitor the strategies they bring to the printed page.

REVIEWER'S REFERENCES

Jones, V. OCCURRENCE OF GRAPHEMES IN THE VOCABULARY OF ELEMENTARY SCHOOL CHILDREN. Northeast Regional Educational Laboratory, September 1969. (ERIC Document Reproduction Service No. ED 040 008)

Carroll, J., Davies, P., & Richman, B. WORD FREQUENCY BOOK. New York: Houghton-Mifflin Co., 1971.

[433]

General Clerical Ability Test: ETSA Test 3A. Job applicants; 1960–84; "measure the general skills required of clerks in routine office work"; norms consist of means and standard deviations; 1 form ('83, 4 pages); scoring key ('83, 1 sheet); for more complete information, see 399; 1984 price data: $12 per 10 tests and scoring key; 30(35) minutes; Psychological Services Bureau; Employers' Tests & Services Associates.*

For reviews of an earlier version of the ETSA Tests by Marvin D. Dunnette and Raymond A. Katzell, see 6:1025.

[434]

General Health Questionnaire. Adolescents and adults; 1969–78; GHQ; "self-administered screening test aimed at detecting psychiatric disorders among respondents in community settings"; 5 scores for scaled form only: somatic symptoms, anxiety and insomnia, social dysfunction, severe depression, total; 3 forms: short ('78, 2 pages identical to 1972 form except for order of questions), long ('78, 4 pages identical to 1969 form), scaled ('78, 2 pages); manual ('78, 31 pages); 1984 price data: £2.45 per 25 short forms; £2.45 per 25 scaled forms; £3.85 per 25 long forms; £4.25 per manual; £4.45 per specimen set; administration time not reported; David Goldberg; NFER-Nelson Publishing Co. [England].*

See T3:941 (34 references) and 8:565 (15 references).

TEST REFERENCES

1. Finlay-Jones, R. A., & Burvill, P. W. The prevalence of minor psychiatric morbidity in the community. PSYCHOLOGICAL MEDICINE, 1977, 7, 475–489.

2. Glass, N. J., & Goldberg, D. Cost-benefit analysis and the evaluation of psychiatric services. PSYCHOLOGICAL MEDICINE, 1977, 7, 701–707.

3. Henderson, S., Davidson, J. A., Gillard, H. N., & Baikie, A. G. An assessment of hostility in a population of adolescents. ARCHIVES OF GENERAL PSYCHIATRY, 1977, 34, 706–711.

4. Mann, A. H. Psychiatric morbidity and hostility in hypertension. PSYCHOLOGICAL MEDICINE, 1977, 7, 653–659.

5. Mann, A. H. The psychological effect of a screening programme and clinical trial for hypertension upon the participants. PSYCHOLOGICAL MEDICINE, 1977, 7, 431–438.

6. Rutter, B. M. Some psychological concomitants of chronic bronchitis. PSYCHOLOGICAL MEDICINE, 1977, 7, 459–464.

7. Wing, J. K., Henderson, A. S., & Winckle, M. The rating of symptoms by a psychiatrist and a non-psychiatrist: A study of patients referred from general practice. PSYCHOLOGICAL MEDICINE, 1977, 7, 713–715.

8. Tennant, C., & Andrews, G. The pathogenic quality of life event stress in neurotic impairment. ARCHIVES OF GENERAL PSYCHIATRY, 1978, 35, 859–863.

9. Goldberg, D. P., & Hillier, V. F. A scaled version of the General Health Questionnaire. PSYCHOLOGICAL MEDICINE, 1979, 9, 139–145.

10. Newson-Smith, J. G. B., & Hirsch, S. R. Psychiatric symptoms in self-poisoning patients. PSYCHOLOGICAL MEDICINE, 1979, 9, 493–500.

11. Rutter, B. M. The prognostic significance of psychological factors in the management of chronic bronchitis. PSYCHOLOGICAL MEDICINE, 1979, 9, 63–70.

12. West, J. E., & West, E. D. Child abuse treated in a psychiatric day hospital. CHILD ABUSE & NEGLECT, 1979, 3, 699–707.

13. DePaulo, J. R., Folstein, M. F., & Gordon, B. Psychiatric screening on a neurological ward. PSYCHOLOGICAL MEDICINE, 1980, 10, 125–132.

14. Gardiner, B. M. Psychological aspects of rheumatoid arthritis. PSYCHOLOGICAL MEDICINE, 1980, 10, 159–163.

15. Harding, T. W., DeArango, M. V., Baltazar, J., Climent, C. E., Ibrahim, H. H. A., Ladrido-Ignacio, L., Murthy, R. S., & Wig, N. N. Mental disorders in primary health care: A study of their frequency and diagnosis in four developing countries. PSYCHOLOGICAL MEDICINE, 1980, 10, 231–241.

16. Jenkins, R. Minor psychiatric morbidity in employed men and women and its contribution to sickness absence. PSYCHOLOGICAL MEDICINE, 1980, 10, 751–757.

17. Jones, R., Goldberg, D., & Hughes, B. A comparison of two different services treating schizophrenia: A cost-benefit approach. PSYCHOLOGICAL MEDICINE, 1980, 10, 493–505.

18. Parkes, K. R. Social desirability, defensiveness and self-report psychiatric inventory scores. PSYCHOLOGICAL MEDICINE, 1980, 10, 735–742.

19. Tarnopolsky, A., Watkins, G., & Hand, D. J. Aircraft noise and mental health: I. Prevalence of individual symptoms. PSYCHOLOGICAL MEDICINE, 1980, 10, 683–698.

20. Andrews, G. A prospective study of life events and psychological symptoms. PSYCHOLOGICAL MEDICINE, 1981, 11, 795–801.

21. Buhrich, N. Psychological adjustment in transvestism and transsexualism. BEHAVIOUR RESEARCH AND THERAPY, 1981, 19, 407–411.

22. Garfinkel, P. E., & Waring, E. M. Personality, interests, and emotional disturbances in psychiatric residents. THE AMERICAN JOURNAL OF PSYCHIATRY, 1981, 138, 51–55.

23. Murray, J., Dunn, G., Williams, P., & Tarnopolsky, A. Factors affecting the consumption of psychotropic drugs. PSYCHOLOGICAL MEDICINE, 1981, 11, 551–560.

24. O'Muircheartaigh, C. A., & Wiggins, R. D. The impact of interviewer variability in an epidemiological survey. PSYCHOLOGICAL MEDICINE, 1981, 11, 817–824.

25. Rabins, P. V., & Brooks, B. R. Emotional disturbance in multiple sclerosis patients: Validity of the General Health Questionnaire (GHQ). PSYCHOLOGICAL MEDICINE, 1981, 11, 425–427.

26. Roy, A. Risk factors and depression in Canadian women. JOURNAL OF AFFECTIVE DISORDERS, 1981, 3, 65–70.

27. Wall, T. D., & Clegg, C. W. Individual strain and organizational functioning. BRITISH JOURNAL OF CLINICAL PSYCHOLOGY, 1981, 20, 135–136.

28. Watkins, G., Tarnopolsky, A., & Jenkins, L. M. Aircraft noise and mental health: II. Use of medicines and health care services. PSYCHOLOGICAL MEDICINE, 1981, 11, 155–168.

29. Benjamin, S., Decalmer, P., & Haran, D. Community screening for mental illness: A validity study of the General Health Questionnaire. BRITISH JOURNAL OF PSYCHIATRY, 1982, 140, 174–180.

30. Cleary, P. D., Goldberg, I. D., Kessler, L. G., & Nycz, G. R. Screening for mental disorder among primary care patients. ARCHIVES OF GENERAL PSYCHIATRY, 1982, 39, 837–840.

31. Cooper, P., Osborn, M., Gath, D., & Feggetter, G. Evaluation of a modified self-report measure of social adjustment. BRITISH JOURNAL OF PSYCHIATRY, 1982, 141, 68–75.

32. Fairburn, C. G., & Cooper, P. J. Self-induced vomiting and bulimia nervosa: An undetected problem. BRITISH MEDICAL JOURNAL, 1982, 284, 1153–1155.

33. Goldberg, D., Steele, J. J., Johnson, A., & Smith, C. Ability of primary care physicians to make accurate ratings of psychiatric symptoms. ARCHIVES OF GENERAL PSYCHIATRY, 1982, 39, 829–833.

34. Hirsch, S. R., Walsh, C., & Draper, R. Parasuicide: A review of treatment interventions. JOURNAL OF AFFECTIVE DISORDERS, 1982, 4, 299–311.

35. Kogeorgos, J., Fonagy, P., & Scott, D. F. Psychiatric symptom patterns of chronic epileptics attending a neurological clinic: A controlled investigation. BRITISH JOURNAL OF PSYCHIATRY, 1982, 140, 236–243.

36. Monroe, S. M. Life events and disorder: Event-symptom associations and the course of disorder. JOURNAL OF ABNORMAL PSYCHOLOGY, 1982, 91, 14–24.

37. Parkes, K. R. Field dependence and the factor structure of the General Health Questionnaire in normal subjects. BRITISH JOURNAL OF PSYCHIATRY, 1982, 140, 392–400.

38. Scott, W. A., & Scott, R. Ethnicity, interpersonal relations, and adaptation among families of European migrants to Australia. AUSTRALIAN PSYCHOLOGIST, 1982, 17, 165–180.

39. Syrotuik, J. M., & D'Arcy, C. Occupational stress, locus of control and health among men in a prairie province. CANADIAN JOURNAL OF BEHAVIOURAL SCIENCE, 1982, 14, 122–133.

40. Vachon, M. L. S., Rogers, J., Lyall, W. A., Lancee, W. J., Sheldon, A. R., & Freeman, S. J. J. Predictors and correlates of adaptation to

conjugal bereavement. THE AMERICAN JOURNAL OF PSYCHIATRY, 1982, 139, 998–1002.

41. Monroe, S. M. Social support and disorder: Toward an untangling of cause and effect. AMERICAN JOURNAL OF COMMUNITY PSYCHOLOGY, 1983, 11, 81–97.

42. Cooper, P. J., Waterman, G. C., & Fairburn, C. G. Women with eating problems: A community survey. BRITISH JOURNAL OF CLINICAL PSYCHOLOGY, 1984, 23, 45–52.

43. Corney, R. H. The mental and physical health of clients referred to social workers in a local authority department and a general practice attachment scheme. PSYCHOLOGICAL MEDICINE, 1984, 14, 137–144.

44. Fairburn, C. G., & Cooper, P. J. Binge-eating, self-induced vomiting and laxative abuse: A community study. PSYCHOLOGICAL MEDICINE, 1984, 14, 401–410.

45. Hoare, P. Psychiatric disturbance in the families of epileptic children. DEVELOPMENTAL MEDICINE AND CHILD NEUROLOGY, 1984, 26, 14–19.

46. Keyes, S. Gender stereotypes and personal adjustment: Employing the PAQ, TSBI, and GHQ with samples of British adolescents. BRITISH JOURNAL OF SOCIAL PSYCHOLOGY, 1984, 23, 173–180.

47. Knuiman, M. W., & Burvill, P. W. A statistical modelling approach to community prevalence data. PSYCHOLOGICAL MEDICINE, 1984, 14, 167–173.

48. Mari, J. J., & Williams, P. Minor psychiatric disorder in primary care in Brazil: A pilot study. PSYCHOLOGICAL MEDICINE, 1984, 14, 223–227.

49. Skuse, D., & Williams, P. Screening for psychiatric disorder in general practice. PSYCHOLOGICAL MEDICINE, 1984, 14, 365–377.

50. Tsoi, M. M., Ho, P. C., & Poon, R. S. M. Pre-operation indicators and post-hysterectomy outcome. BRITISH JOURNAL OF CLINICAL PSYCHOLOGY, 1984, 23, 151–152.

Review of General Health Questionnaire by JOHN D. BLACK, President, Consulting Psychologists Press, Palo Alto, CA:

The General Health Questionnaire (GHQ) is an instrument designed to detect the presence of psychological dysfunction or distress of sufficient magnitude to warrant medical notice. The author recommends that it be answered by patients awaiting their appointments with a physician though it should be equally applicable in a counseling center. The instrument has been the object of much thoughtful work and an excessive fascination with factor analysis.

The original item pool included 140 questions about depression, anxiety, impaired social functioning, and hypochondriacal symptoms, most of them suggested by published inventories such as the Cornell Medical Index, Taylor's Manifest Anxiety Scale, etc. Items were administered to 139 hospitalized psychiatric patients, 135 outpatients, and 100 normals matched for age, sex, and social class.

Careful analysis reduced the number of items to 93, all of which loaded on a general factor that was labelled "severity of psychiatric illness" and accounted for 45.6% of the variance. The questionnaire was further reduced to 60 items. Repeated factor analyses were carried out on the 60-item version and finally resulted in the GHQ-30, a 30-item version that included six rotated factors accounting for 53.5% of the variance, each factor being represented by five items. Apparently no provision has been made for scoring these factors but the fascination with rotating factors continued and finally produced GHQ-28, which has four factors each represented by seven items and can readily be scored without templates.

The four subscales are labeled Somatic Symptoms, Anxiety and Insomnia, Social Dysfunction, and Severe Depression; and they can be summed to obtain an estimate of the severity of psychiatric illness. Not surprisingly, they parallel closely the areas included in the original item pool. The overlap of the subscales is enormous and the Somatic Symptoms subscale is actually less correlated with psychiatric interview ratings of somatic symptoms than it is with interview ratings of anxiety and depression.

Although the respondent uses a 4-point scale, which most people find easier than a true-false format, each item counts either 0 or 1, so scoring is simple. Mean raw scores are available for very large groups of people in Australia, Britain, and Philadelphia. Some data are provided on sex, age, socioeconomic level, and marital status as these affect scores. No percentiles or standard scores are provided but the author suggests "threshold scores" for case identification. On GHQ-28, a score of 4/5 correctly classifies 86.4% of subjects.

Reliabilities based on test-retest (six month interval) range from .51 to .90 for patients judged by themselves or physicians to have changed little during the interval. Internal consistency is very high. No correlations with other questionnaires are given but validity coefficients comparing GHQ-60 with independent clinical assessments in seven studies range from .71 to .88. False negatives (misclassifications of patients as normal) range from 9% to 19%; false positives range from 6% to 27% using 11/12 as the cutting point. As the author points out, cutting points may be altered depending upon one's purpose in classifying subjects.

The counselor, therapist, or physician might find the GHQ provides a timesaving, helpful guide to an initial interview. Although the domains it covers are more limited, it should function somewhat like the Mooney Problems Check List has done for many school and college counselors and it is certainly an improvement over the old Cornell Medical Index. In the United States a few British colloquialisms should be translated (e.g., "possibility that you might make away with yourself," "feeling nervous and strung-up"). This reviewer sees no sense to using the 4 subscales on the GHQ-28 (or the six on the GHQ-30, for that matter), and the original 60-item version allows the patient or client to say more things about himself. As the author points out, the GHQ would be of no value in situations where there is any motivation to minimize problems or "fake good"; it is designed to assist people who want to tell about their problems.

[435]

General Mental Ability Test: ETSA Test 1A. Job applicants; 1960–84; "measures ability to learn"; norms consist of means and standard deviations; 1 form ('83, 4 pages); scoring key ('83, 1 sheet); for more complete information, see 399; 1984 price data: $12 per 10 tests and scoring key; (45–50) minutes; Psychological Services Bureau; Employers' Tests & Services Associates.*

See T3:942 (1 reference); for reviews of an earlier version of the ETSA Tests by Marvin D. Dunnette and Raymond A. Katzell, see 6:1025.

[436]

Geriatric Sentence Completion Form. Ages 60 and over; 1982; GSCF; personal responses in four domains: physical, psychological, socioenvironmental, temporal orientation; no data on reliability and validity; no norms; individual; 1 form (2 pages); manual (13 pages); 1983 price data: $10 per 50 tests including manual; (20–30) minutes; Peter LeBray; Psychological Assessment Resources, Inc.*

Review of Geriatric Sentence Completion Form by RODNEY K. GOODYEAR, Associate Professor of Counseling and Student Personnel Services, Kansas State University, Manhattan, KS, and THOMAS R. COLEMAN, Director, Mental Health Section, Lafene Student Health Center, Kansas State University, Manhattan, KS:

The Geriatric Sentence Completion Form (GSCF) consists of 30 single words or short phrases that examinees are to use as stems for writing sentences expressing their "real feelings." The manual speculates that the instrument is suitable for anyone with a 6th-grade reading level and states that items have been chosen to elicit responses representing four domains: physical (4 items); psychological (13 items); socioenvironmental factors (12 items); and temporal orientation (3 items). Each item (except for 2 items) represents one domain. The psychological and socioenvironmental factors categories are each broken down further, with six and seven subcategories respectively. However, because most subcategories are represented by only 1 or 2 items, it would be inappropriate to place interpretive value on them.

The use of sentence completion items for personality assessment seems to date back to the work of Payne (1928). Items in the test he devised, in their original and revised forms, seem to have provided the basis for later, better known instruments. In fact, Schofield commented that "sets of incomplete sentences have been sired so prolifically that the question of parenthood has drawn amusing attention" (4:130, p. 244). The GSCF seems to continue that tradition; it is difficult to know how many of its items are truly unique. For example, several are identical to those found in Rotter's Incomplete Sentence Blank (ISB), and several other GSCF and ISB items vary only minimally.

What does distinguish the GSCF from other instruments of this genre is its targeted population. Sentence completion instruments have been designed for use with children, with high school students, with college students, and with adults; this instrument extends that range into old age. The manual contends that three GSCF characteristics make it more appropriate for use with an older population than the widely used ISB: (1) brevity (the ISB has 40 items); (2) reference to such socioenvironmental issues as housing ("Where I live..."), transportation ("Travel..."), and income ("Money..."); and (3) reference to death ("Death...").

The GSCF's most severe deficiency, however, is its lack of any suggested scoring system. The manual does note that the examiner should be skilled in the use of projective material. Yet the value of even this means of utilizing the GSCF is difficult to ascertain from the manual, for there is nothing to suggest that the instrument has actually been tried out in a field setting. Moreover, the procedures used to develop and test the items are not described. Although the items appear useful, users could place more confidence in the GSCF if they could know that the items have been developed on the basis of something more than the author's intuition.

The manual does provide five clinical case illustrations. Four of these concern individuals who are at least 79 years old. This seems to raise an issue of applicable range: although the manual reports the instrument to be useful for anyone 60 or older, the physical and psychological environments of a 60-year-old are quite different from those of an 80-year-old. It may be that the items are written in such a manner that the GSCF is equally applicable across the range. However, in the absence of any comparative data this is difficult to know.

Perhaps relatedly, it seems likely that the title of the instrument—printed prominently across the top of the form given examinees—may arouse resistance in some examinees. For example, the 60-year-old seeking help for stresses relating to a pending retirement is unlikely to consider him- or herself to fit a geriatric category.

In summary, the GSCF does offer clinicians an assessment tool that may be useful in working with the elderly. Such tools are certainly needed. Unfortunately, the lack of a scoring system, of any information about item development, and of any suggestion that the instrument has been tried out in actual clinical practice all suggest that clinicians should adopt it with some caution.

REVIEWER'S REFERENCES

Payne, A. F. SENTENCE COMPLETIONS. New York: New York Guidance Clinic, 1928.

Review of Geriatric Sentence Completion Form by DAVID S. NICHOLS, Staff Psychologist, Dammasch State Hospital, Wilsonville, OR:

With what has been called "the graying of America," test developers can anticipate a swelling of demand for instruments more suitable for assessing the patterns of concerns of older clients than those developed in the '40s and '50s. The latter tests, both objective and projective, were typically developed and normed for use with adults in their third and fourth decades. But the adjustment demands of later life are strikingly not those of young adulthood.

Pending the development of a better understanding of personality and psychopathology in latter life, sentence completion methods seem well suited to meet current needs in the area of personality assessment. By informed selection of sentence stems, areas of content relevant to common concerns of older clients can be obtained in standardizeable form to support research inquiry, augment other and possibly less relevant test findings, or simply to use as grist for the interview mill. Relative to other tests, sentence completion tests (SCT) are economical to give and score, easy to modify, and are often seen by examinees as relevant and non-taxing. When they follow structured inventories in a battery, examinees may see incomplete sentences as an opportunity to "make my own test" and rise to this challenge.

The Geriatric Sentence Completion Form (GSCF) presents 30 stems, about a third of which overlap the Rhode (1957) SCT, which appear on two sides of a form with spaces for identification, demographic, and referral information. The provision of large print stems and a generous 13/32 inches of space between them suggests a sensitivity to the special needs of those to whom the GSCF may be administered, but some may take offense at the word "Geriatric" in the form's boldface heading.

The advantages claimed for this blank are three: (*a*) brevity, in that it contains only 30 stems; (*b*) the inclusion of stems which are intended to reveal problem areas of later life (e.g., "My health...," "The government...," "In years past...," etc.), and (*c*) a stem for "Death...," with the odd claim that "This important theme is referenced exclusively in the GSCF." (In fact this stem is included in at least three other SCTs, including that of Rhode [1957].) Naturally, the first two advantages claimed are to some extent conflicting since the addition of more stems germane to the concerns of older people would lengthen the test. The stems which are included appear to have been chosen arbitrarily. The manual contains almost no information on stem selection and whether the stems on the final form were pretested or retained from a larger stem pool.

The seven and one-half page manual (excluding references) is attractively produced and well organized. Following an introductory paragraph are headings for development, structure, administration, and interpretation containing from one to three paragraphs each. Five case illustrations are provided, each of which is offered with completions of up to 10 stems but without commentary on test findings or interpretations.

Although the GSCF is described as a "projective measure," measurement is clearly not an issue. No scoring system is offered, nor are normative, reliability, or validity data presented. Users are simply invited to treat responses as projective material and employ their knowledge of personality and behavior to turn completions into meaningful information about examinees. Thus the GSCF generally fails to meet the *Standards for Educational and Psychological Tests.*

In summary, the GSCF is a custom sentence completion blank which has found a distribution channel. It has no clear advantages over other locally developed custom blanks for use with older clients, and in fact it has far fewer stems referencing content relevant to this group than this reviewer considers desirable.

REVIEWER'S REFERENCES

Rhode, A. R. THE SENTENCE COMPLETION METHOD. New York: Ronald Press, 1957.

[437]

Gesell Preschool Test. Ages 2.5–6; 1980; abbreviated adaptation of the Gesell Developmental Schedules (see 6:522) and the Gesell Developmental Tests (see 7:750); maturity ratings in four basic fields of behavior: motor, adaptive, language, personal-social; no data on reliability and validity; no norms; individual; 1 form; manual ('80, 72 pages); 1985 price data: $68 per test kit (includes all test accessories and manual); $34.50 per set of 50 tests (contains face sheet, cube tests, interview questions, pencil & paper, incomplete man, prepositions, digits, picture vocabulary, comprehension questions, color forms, action agent, formboard, identifying letters & numbers, computation and motor) with minimum order of two sets; $8.50 per copy forms; $7 per 1 in. cubes; $4 per letter and numbers chart; $19 per formboard; $6 per color forms; $5.50 per pellets & bottle; $11 per picture vocabulary; $2.95 per bean bag; $25 for "typical response" cards containing incomplete response set cards and copy form; $11.95 per manual; (30–45) minutes; Jacqueline Haines, Louise Bates Ames, and Clyde Gillespie; Programs for Education, Inc.*

TEST REFERENCES

1. Ball, R. S. The Gesell Developmental Schedules: Arnold Gesell (1880–1961). JOURNAL OF ABNORMAL CHILD PSYCHOLOGY, 1977, 5, 233–239.

2. de Chateau, P. Parent-infant relationship after immediate post-partum contact. CHILD ABUSE & NEGLECT, 1979, 3, 279–283.

3. Dukes, L., & Buttery, T. J. Comparison of two screening tests: Gesell Developmental Test and Meeting Street School Screening Test. PERCEPTUAL AND MOTOR SKILLS, 1982, 54, 1177–1178.

4. Paine, P. A., & Pasquali, L. Effects of intrauterine growth and gestational age upon infants early psychomotor development in Brazil. PERCEPTUAL AND MOTOR SKILLS, 1982, 55, 871–880.

5. Cohen, S. E., & Parmalee, A. H. Prediction of five-year Stanford-Binet scores in preterm infants. CHILD DEVELOPMENT, 1983, 54, 1242–1253.

6. Krakow, J. B., & Kopp, C. B. The effects of developmental delay on sustained attention in young children. CHILD DEVELOPMENT, 1983, 54, 1143–1155.

7. Lewis, D. O., Shanok, S. S., Grant, M., & Ritvo, E. Homicidally aggressive young children: Neuropsychiatric and experiential correlates. THE AMERICAN JOURNAL OF PSYCHIATRY, 1983, 140, 148–153.

8. Paine, P. A., & Pasquali, L. Is motor development really more advanced in Third World infants? PERCEPTUAL AND MOTOR SKILLS, 1983, 57, 729–730.

Review of Gesell Preschool Test by NADEEN L. KAUFMAN, Director Psycho-educational Clinic, California School of Professional Psychology, San Diego, CA:

There are several Gesell Tests. The Gesell Developmental Schedules extend from age 4 weeks to 6 years; despite their lack of updating, they are still used in some clinical settings for infant evaluations. The Gesell School Readiness Test for 5- to 10-year-old children appeared in the mid-1960s and has been used primarily to determine children's school placement in grades K and 1.

Now there is the Gesell Preschool Test for 2- to 6-year-old children, which is really a cross between the other two Gesell batteries. This preschool instrument includes traditional Gesell tasks (e.g., the incomplete man, copy forms, and cube tests) and subtests from other instruments including the Stanford-Binet and Merrill-Palmer. Like all Gesell tests, the preschool battery offers ratings in four primary areas of behavior: motor, adaptive, language, personal-social. From the Gesell vantage point, "adaptive" is similar to cognitive or mental ability, and is measured with tasks that minimize language ability and are intended to be culture fair. It is the personal-social area that closely approximates the contemporary usage of the term adaptive behavior.

The authors of the Gesell Preschool Test propose that it be used to assess the normality of any given child's rate of development, especially when parents suspect a lag; to give parents a clear picture of a child's individual strengths and weaknesses; to evaluate how a child adapts to a new situation; and for "the proper placement of boys and girls in kindergarten and the early primary grades." The latter purpose, according to the authors, is "perhaps the most important of all."

The test authors have long advocated the placement of children in school classes based on developmental age (as determined by the Gesell Preschool Test or Gesell School Readiness Test) instead of chronological age. In view of the claims made for the Gesell battery and the decisions that are currently based on the test profiles, a psychometric evaluation of its properties becomes crucial, more so than for most contemporary instruments.

Unfortunately, the authors do not fulfill their obligation to the consumers of the Gesell Preschool Test. They flagrantly ignore their responsibilities as test makers, and do not report the type of information that is mandated as essential by APA guidelines. The manual and a book which accompanies the manual offer no evidence of internal consistency reliability, stability over time, or empirical validity. Information pertaining to the normative sample is presented in only two brief paragraphs in the preface to the book accompanying the manual. The sample is composed of 40 girls and 40 boys at each 6-month age level from 2 through 6 years, for a total sample of 320 girls and 320 boys. On the positive side, the sample is stratified on the basis of socioeconomic status (parental occupation) in accordance with 1960 census data. On the negative end, however, "nearly all were Caucasians and all resided in the state of Connecticut."

The test materials are attractive and child oriented, especially the formboard, cubes, and beanbag. Most materials seem durable and are professional in appearance. In contrast, test directions are sometimes vague. For example, during administration of the Incomplete Man, children may be "encouraged with either a suggested or direct clue" if they do not complete the "salient" parts. From the perspective of standardized administration, it is unclear exactly what is meant by salient, when to give a suggested (general) or direct (specific) clue, and how many clues to give. In the manual, the history of each test and the norms for scoring it are interspersed with the directions for administration. This can impede a smooth, straightforward administration of the test. Although the authors state that "the Manual should properly stand on its own feet," the scoring of the various items cannot be performed very objectively without using outside sources. The book accompanying the manual is especially needed since a wealth of information for understanding and scoring the preschool test is included in this reference. Whereas the combined use of the manual and supplementary text facilitates scoring most responses, there is still much ambiguity. The scoring system provides for evaluating each test as "succeeds," "performs at a level higher than age expectation," "a questionable success," or "failure." Proper evaluation of questionable successes, in particular, often seems dependent on some degree of training at workshops conducted by The Gesell Institute. Training also seems necessary to understand clinically the distinctive features of item responses that have to be categorized globally as "4 year old behavior," "5 year old behavior," and so forth.

The Gesell Preschool Test is not satisfactory in a psychometric sense. Its norms are unrepresentative, and the directions for administration and scoring, as presented in the manual, do not promote strictly standardized, uniform evaluations from examiner to examiner. The instrument may indeed be reliable and valid, but the authors have made no effort to provide this vital information. The only validity evidence concerns the effectiveness of the Gesell instruments for developmental placement. Whereas this type of validity is probably the most vital in view of how the instrument is used, the evidence provided is not well documented, apparently does not pertain directly to the Gesell Preschool Test, and is largely testimonial in nature.

The authors' goals for the Gesell test are admirable. They want to reduce school failure by basing class placements on development age. They have constructed their test from the theory and developmental research of Arnold Gesell, which gives the instrument a substantial theoretical foundation and supports their claim that they are actually measuring developmental age. However, they seem to think of the Gesell Preschool Test as a clinical system rather than as a conventional psychometric test; furthermore, they have complete faith in the effectiveness of this system for reducing children's failure in school, despite the absence of hard data to document this faith. It is time for users of this clinical system to demand evidence of the psychometric properties of the test, and to demand well-designed studies to show that developmental placement is beneficial to the children directly affected by the educational decisions. It is also time for the authors to heed these demands.

Review of Gesell Preschool Test by JACK A. NAGLIERI, Assistant Professor of Psychology, Ohio State University, Columbus, OH:

The Gesell Preschool Test, published by the Gesell Institute of Human Development, is designed to evaluate motor, adaptive, language, and personal-social behavior of children 2 to 6 years of age. The test kit includes materials for administration and a manual that provides normative guidelines and has directions for giving and scoring the test questions. The authors state that the test is a behavioral evaluation of developmental age, not an intelligence test. The aim of the Gesell Preschool Test is to determine a child's level of maturity or development (which they suggest is largely dependent upon genetic factors) and assign each child an educational placement commensurate with his or her current developmental level of performance. Using this approach a child would not begin school on the basis of chronological age, for example, but would begin when he or she acquired the requisite behavioral skills to succeed in kindergarten.

The Gesell Preschool Test includes tasks such as block building, copying geometric forms (circle, cross, diamond), completing a drawing of a man, repeating digits, picture vocabulary, identifying letters and numbers, tests of basic concepts, motor activities (e.g., skipping, standing on one foot, beanbag catch and throw), and dressing (e.g., ties shoe lace). Each item is scored as "succeeds," "performs above age expectation," "questionable success," or "failure" according to normative guidelines presented for each item. These norms are descriptions of what a typical child at a specific age level can do and are the sole basis for scoring. When every item is scored "a clear summary of just where the child's successes and failures fall" results. However, there is no indication of how many items scored as "questionable" or "failure" are needed to distinguish between a child who is slightly or significantly behind his age mates. Moreover, since no description of the normative sample is included, the test user can only hope that the normative guidelines reflect typical performance and not the performance of some restricted sample of children.

The test authors present little information regarding the normative population or psychometric qualities of the Gesell Preschool Test. In lieu of presenting information on the size, ages, and number of each of the socioeconomic levels and geographic locations of individuals who comprised the normative sample, the Gesell Preschool Test manual presents the Gesell Developmental Schedules and information about what a preschool child can do according to Ilg, Ames, and Haines (1978). Apparently these normative guidelines are based on past experience rather than a carefully constructed standardization sample. Information such as reliability, standard error, etc. are not included. This lack of emphasis on psychometric attributes of the scale leads to a potential for misuse or misinterpretation.

Despite the fact that the test authors suggest the Gesell Preschool Test is a behavioral evaluation which "is not the same thing as an intelligence test," the test items are very similar to and in some cases identical to those found in current IQ tests. The Incomplete Man, Digit Repetition, Calculation, and especially the Picture Vocabulary tests are very similar to those found in the Stanford Binet (the Picture Vocabulary test is exactly the same material used in the Binet). Similarly, the Copy Forms, Digit Repetition, Cube Tests, and Motor activities are highly reminiscent of the McCarthy Scales. Hence, on an item basis, the Gesell Preschool Test is quite similar to standardized measures of intellectual ability. The major difference between the Gesell and current intelligence tests appears to be the lack of emphasis on psychometric properties of the scale (e.g., no standardization sample, no factor analytic results or reliability coefficients).

The Gesell Preschool Test appears to be most appropriate for practitioners who wish to obtain an estimate of performance in areas that appear to be important for school success such as language, adaptive, motor, and personal-social behaviors. The assessment of these skills should be viewed as estimates since a normative sample is ill-defined and the psychometric aspects of the test are not presented. Given the availability of well normed and psychometrically sound instruments that measure language and motor skills (e.g., McCarthy Scales; McCarthy, 1972) and adaptive and personal-social behaviors (e.g., Vineland Adaptive Behavior Scales; Sparrow, Balla, & Cicchetti, 1984), it seems more logical and psychometrically more defensible to choose them over the Gesell Preschool Test.

REVIEWER'S REFERENCES

McCarthy, D. MANUAL FOR THE MCCARTHY SCALES OF CHILDREN'S ABILITIES. New York: Psychological Corp., 1972.

Ilg, F. L., Ames, L. B., Haines, J., & Gillespie, C. SCHOOL READINESS: BEHAVIOR TESTS USED AT THE GESELL INSTITUTE. New York: Harper & Row, 1978.

Sparrow, S. S., Balla, D. A., & Cicchetti, D. V. VINELAND ADAPTIVE BEHAVIOR SCALES. Circle Pines: American Guidance Service, 1984.

[438]

The Gesell School Readiness Test. Ages 4.5–9; 1964–80; formerly called Gesell Developmental Tests; 9 subtests: Interview, Paper and Pencil Test, Cube Tests, Copy Forms, Incomplete Man, Right and Left, Monroe Visual Tests, Naming Animals, Home and School Preferences; individual; 1 form; recording sheet ('78, 1 page); revised manual ('78, 250 pages); directions for cube tests ('80, 8 pages); 1983 price data: $19.95 per set of test materials (test cards, 1 set of 10 recording sheets, 12 three-dimensional objects, and Cube Tests direction booklet); $31.50 per 50 sets of the recording sheets; $22 per set of instructional cards to assist in evaluating responses to the Incomplete Man and Copy Forms subtests; $15.50 per manual; (20–40) minutes; Frances L. Ilg, Louise Bates Ames, Jacqueline Haines, and Clyde Gillespie; Programs for Education, Inc.*

See T3:953 (6 references) and T2:1703 (4 references); for excerpted reviews by L. J. Borstelmann and Edith Meyer Taylor, see 7:750 (5 references).

Review of Gesell School Readiness Test by ROBERT H. BRADLEY, Professor and Director, Center for Child Development and Education, University of Arkansas at Little Rock, Little Rock, AR:

The Gesell School Readiness Test fits well within the Gesell Institute's philosophy that readiness is a matter of maturity or behavioral age rather than chronological age or IQ. The test is primarily intended as a means of helping to place children appropriately in school based on the belief that the number of school failures will be reduced if appropriate placements are made. A broad array of competencies are examined using the Gesell, with perhaps a disproportionate share being given to perceptual-motor capabilities. An important feature of the test is that it is conducted in a generally comfortable, non-threatening style for the child being examined.

The Gesell Test requires a considerable amount of time and clinical expertise on the part of the examiner. The test developers have substantial room for examiner discretion in scoring and interpretation. Given that the criteria to be used in evaluating performance are not always clearly specified in the manual, it is evident that examiners using the Gesell Test will need to be carefully trained.

The writers of the manual for the test indicate that the School Readiness Test might be useful for a number of purposes. However, they provide little specific information with regard to the test's validity in accomplishing each of those purposes. The test developers state that Alan Kaufman is "now checking on the predictive validity of our tests," yet results of those investigations have not been provided. It is critical that a test which is to be used for screening or diagnostic purposes demonstrate discriminant or differential validity for those purposes. The test developers offer no set of cutoff scores that might be useful in making decisions about placements, nor do they provide evidence that students who are placed according to scores on the test really benefit over the long term from such placement. The information gathered on this test is not, in fact, directly relatable to many of the curricular experiences that children are typically involved in. The test developers do provide some evidence that performance on the Gesell Test is valid in terms of agreements with teacher ratings of children's performance at the end of the school year. Using teacher ratings as criteria is not a bad means of evaluating the validity of the test—albeit somewhat limited. As one might expect, the highest level of agreement between Gesell Test scores and later teacher ratings of student performance were those for children at the extremes. As a matter of fact, the .74 correlation between scores on the Gesell Test during preschool years and 6th-grade performance may be overly influenced by extreme scores. Another important limitation of the information provided in the test manual is the failure to include sufficient reliability information (i.e., interobserver agreement, internal consistency estimates, stability coefficients, etc.).

One of the strengths of the Gesell Test manual is that it provides some interesting and informative descriptions of children's performance on each test year by year with comments made with respect to sex differences. These descriptions can be quite useful to those working with children in terms of providing a better understanding of the typical kinds of performances expected by age and sex. The test also provides a format for dealing not only with the competence of children during the test situation but the style with which children handle themselves in the test situation. Unfortunately, the manual does not provide a particularly good framework from which to interpret stylistic differences or suggestions on how to use the information gathered about stylistic differences in making placement decisions. Neither do the authors sufficiently explain why certain items have been included in the test. For example, the authors state that the use of the nondominant hand in children can be very valuable information, but we are given no explanation as to why it is valuable or how one might use this information once obtained. In general, it would be valuable to have some empirical or theoretical framework from which to interpret the information obtained about behavioral style, handedness, and right-left orientation in terms of readiness and placement in school.

The test also appears to have some important weaknesses in terms of its usability in many school settings. First, the norms used for the test are outdated—albeit they are not clearly specified in the manual. Moreover, the norms appear to be restricted by geography, ethnicity, and to a lesser degree, social class. It is doubtful that even the rich descriptive material provided in the manual would be adequate for use in rural southern areas of the country. Second, the context of the test also appears to be outdated. Some of the information appears more appropriate for children who lived 20 and 30 years ago, prior to the advent of TV and near-universal preschool experiences, and who had more frequent early experiences in intact rather than single-parent homes. A good example is the inclusion of vocabulary words such as "palm" and "ring-finger," words more commonly used 20 years ago. Moreover, not all of the children who would take the test will find all of the items comfortable to deal with (i.e., those dealing with working fathers, the use of nondominant hand, and attempts to continue naming animals for a period of 60 seconds, long after they have exhausted their ability to recall individual animal names.)

As one might expect as a result of differences in the content of the various subtests on the Gesell, there are substantial differences in the distribution of performances by age on the subtests. These differences, at least to some degree, may relate to the extent to which biological maturation might account for abrupt improvements in performance in a given domain versus those where a gradual accumulation of knowledge typically is the reason for increases in performance with age.

Overall, the Gesell Test would seem to provide useful information about preschool age and early school age children. It takes a rather extensive look at the performance of children in a number of content areas that are related to readiness for performing well in school. In general, the setting provided should be basically a comfortable one for most children, allowing for a rich interchange with the test examiner. Descriptive information provided in the test manual should allow teachers and other school personnel to get a reasonably good fix on how an individual child stands in terms of what is typical for children of that age. It is a humane approach to testing, one which fits well within an overall philosophy of not thrusting "unready" preschool age children into a highly academic atmosphere. However, in light of weaknesses mentioned above, it is likely that many school systems will choose one of the other well-normed and validated preschool tests requiring considerably less time and less examiner expense.

Review of The Gesell School Readiness Test by EVERETT WATERS, Associate Professor of Psychology, State University of New York, Stony Brook, NY:

School Readiness is the fifth edition of a combined text and manual for the instrument widely known as the Gesell Developmental Tests. It summarizes the Gesell Institute's perspective on school readiness, provides test instructions and norms, and includes a new chapter on current topics (mainstreaming, shortened first grade day, sex differences, etc.).

The instructions for administering the test are clear and detailed. Descriptive information about qualitative differences in performance at different ages and norms in 6 or 12 month intervals are included for each item. The test materials are well designed and well constructed. The full test is too lengthy to be considered a screening instrument for most contexts.

A great deal of extremely detailed descriptive material has been eliminated from this edition of the manual. As a result it is clearer and more useful. Norms have been extended down from 4.5 years to 3, while the ceiling has been lowered from 10 years to nine.

The goal of the test is to determine the developmental level at which a child is currently functioning. The authors emphasize that the test is designed to assess maturity rather than IQ. Accordingly, conventional scoring tables are absent, in favor of tables that present the percent of children at each normed age who give specific responses. Responses given by 50% or more of the normative sample at any age are italicized. There are no explicit procedures for combining subtests into total scores.

While it is easy to determine whether a child's response is modal for his or her age, it is often difficult to evaluate non-modal responses. Many items have constant frequencies across age, others increase or decrease slightly, and others first increase then decrease across age. Moreover, data on the percent of a normative sample giving a particular response do not necessarily help place a particular child precisely at a given age level. Presumably one could assign the child to the lowest age level for which at least 50% gave the same response as the child (assuming at least 50% did so at any age). But it is unclear how to get from here to a recommendation about placement. It is also unclear whether this kind of age equivalent scoring captures what the authors have in mind for developmental assessment. They may very well intend something involving substantially more clinical judgment. In any event, the formal results of the full test would be difficult to convey concisely to a principal, teacher, or parent.

The test's major strengths lie in the presentation of a coherent perspective on school readiness and a well designed and widely familiar set of test materials. The authors explicitly recognize the importance of school readiness programs which involve preschool, prekindergarten, and pre-first grade options for both developmentally disabled and normal but delayed children. Their vision of developmental assessment is as a component rather than a substitute for such programs. They also explicitly grant the validity of teachers' evaluations as guides to placement.

The test's major limitations are (1) lack of data on reliability and stability; (2) limited reference to or availability of validity data other than the authors' own early studies of placement recommendations, teacher recommendations, and later school performance; and (3) limitations in the normative data. According to the authors, it is highly desirable for users to develop local norms by accumulating data over several years. Potential users should take this suggestion seriously because the published norms have not been revised for 20 years and therefore do not take into account a wide range of changes in preschool attendance, television viewing and programing, children's toys, parental employment patterns, etc. Users should also note that the new preschool norms are from lower SES samples than the rest of the norms and thus may overestimate the developmental level of more advantaged subjects.

Another limitation of the test is that it primarily emphasizes cognitive, language, and motor tasks, despite the authors' emphasis on the large component of social development in their concept of school readiness. While the manual goes to considerable lengths to encourage and assist the examiner in using the test situation to make relevant inferences and observations about social maturity, inclusion of sensible questionnaires which recent teachers or parents might complete would have been a useful supplement to the standard items.

Ultimately, any school readiness test faces a difficult challenge. Only a very small proportion of any school population is realistically going to delay school entry or repeat a grade. Children with serious clinical problems will generally be identified prior to or soon after school begins and will be referred for more detailed diagnostic testing. But it is simply difficult (and often unethical) to undertake the research necessary to let us routinely identify otherwise normal children who might profit if parents and schools respected their slower developmental schedules.

In brief, the Gesell package offers a useful perspective, a nice set of broad-band materials, clear instructions, and very valuable descriptive material. Formal scoring is problematic but manageable and the test situation provides enough contact for the examiner to make reasonable clinical judgments about overall readiness. If we were to select a single instrument as the standard across the full range of readiness assessment settings, none could offer everything we might wish for. In this context, the Gesell tests would not be a poor choice.

[439]

Gifted and Talented Screening Form. Grades K–9; 1979–80; GTSF; self-report checklist; 10 talent area scores: academic, creativity, arts (visual, performing, total), intelligence, leadership, psychomotor (athletics, mechanics, total); no norms, author recommends establishment of local norms; 1 form ('79, 2 pages); manual ('80, 6 pages); score key/sheet ('79, 1 page); 1986 price data: $14.25 per complete set including 30 record forms and 30 score key/sheets; $11.50 per 30 record forms; $11.50 per 30 score key/sheets; $4.75 per manual; 10(15) minutes; David L. Johnson; Stoelting Co.*

Review of Gifted and Talented Screening Form by JOSEPH S. RENZULLI, Bureau of Educational Research, University of Connecticut, Storrs, CT:

The attractive cover and handsome spiral binding of this instrument open to reveal a single page manual, (plus sample instrument and scoring form), with only one and one-half sides of this page actually covered with print! The Gifted and Talented Screening Form (GTSF) is mistakenly described as an "objective, self-report instrument"; however, it is intended as a guide for teacher rating rather than self-reporting, and its objectivity is questionable because of an almost total absence of supporting data. Before describing the data that are reported, let us examine some of the obvious deficiencies of this instrument.

The author does not report an underlying theoretical rationale, definition of giftedness, research studies from which the items were derived, or the procedures that were used to develop the items. The scoring procedure yields scores for eight separate "content areas" or "talents", but no factorial studies are reported that might indicate how the content areas were determined. Four of the content area scores are derived from only two items per area.

RELIABILITY AND VALIDITY. Although the 24 items are reported to discriminate between a gifted and non-gifted group, the procedures used to reach this conclusion are not described, and the sample size (40 students per group) ranged across eight grade levels. A split-half reliability of .90 is reported, and individual item correlations with the total composite score ranged from .49 to .69. Correlations with another rating scale (Social Interaction and Creativity in Communication System) are generally in the low positive range, but this single example of a validation study using a relatively unknown instrument does nothing to inspire confidence. The author does make reference to a 70-page Technical Report, and one wonders why some of the content of this report is not included, especially since there is plenty of vacant space between the covers of the handsome spiral bound manual.

SUMMARY EVALUATION. No one expects a rating scale to possess the technical qualifications or supportive data that typically is reported for achievement tests; however, it is inexcusable to offer for public consumption a commercial instrument that is little more than a list of largely unverified generalizations about the characteristics of gifted and talented students. The GTFS lacks the kind of theoretical and research support that would allow me to give it an even minimally favorable evaluation. My only recommendation is that persons looking for a teacher rating scale to assist in the identification of gifted and talented students should be advised to look elsewhere.

[440]

Gochnour Idiom Screening Test: An English Idiom Comprehension Test for the Deaf. Junior high through college level deaf students; 1977; GIST; norms consist of mean scores only; 1 form (6 pages); manual (15 pages); 1984 price data: $4.90 per 20 test booklets and manual; $2.95 per 20 test booklets; $1.95 per manual; (10) minutes; Elizabeth A. Gochnour; Interstate Printers & Publishers, Inc.*

See T3:959 (1 reference).

Review of Gochnour Idiom Screening Test by JILL M. STOEFEN-FISHER, Assistant Professor, Hearing Impaired Program, Department of Special Education, University of Nebraska-Lincoln, Lincoln, NE:

The Gochnour Idiom Screening Test (GIST) is designed to assess deaf students' comprehension of English idioms. It is to be used with deaf students in the seventh grade or above, and can be administered, according to the manual, in less than 10 minutes. Each of the 20 multiple choice items consists of a sentence containing an idiom followed by four other sentences, one of which means the same as the sentence containing the idiom.

One strength of the GIST is in the administration procedures. They are stated very specifically. Separate directions are provided for deaf students who sign and oral deaf students. The directions are parallel, although not identical. The directions for the oral deaf recommend projecting the instructions with an opaque projector. The use of an overhead projector would be preferred as this type can be used effectively in a room with more light. An opaque projector works best in a darkened room, which eliminates speechreading for the oral deaf. Nevertheless, the procedures used in norming the test are specified clearly.

It is rare to find a test with deaf norms. Another strength of the GIST is that the norm group consisted of 620 deaf students in grades 7 through college. The group was comprised of students from "two state schools, three private schools, one major county system, one city school, two junior colleges and two four-year colleges for the deaf." The manual states that "All major geographic regions of the continental United States were represented" although specific localities were not identified. Oral, total communication, and Rochester Method communication modes were represented.

Inspection of the norms for the number of students at each grade level reveals that the number is adequate for grades 7 through 15 (range—30 to 97) but falls off at grades 16 and 17 (11 and 10 respectively). Norms are also given by age, and the number of students per age is adequate for 14-year-olds through 22-year-olds (range—25 to 85), but too small at age levels above or below this to provide meaningful comparisons.

A hearing norm group was also used but no descriptive information (i.e., age, grade, etc.) is provided. The manual simply presents the mean score correct for this group.

One concern about the GIST is that norms are presented in means and standard deviations only. The test user could, provided they had the time and skills, calculate how many standard deviations a particular individual's score varied from the mean in order to make more accurate judgments. It is, however, doubtful that all test users would do this. It would greatly facilitate the test user's decision making process if derived scores (i.e., percentiles, standard scores, stanines) had been provided in the manual for interindividual comparisons.

Although the test consists of 20 items, there is a possible score of 50 because the items are weighted. Item difficulty was based on the frequency with which the idiom occurred in *The Language of Life*, a textbook coauthored by the test developer (Gochnour & Smith, 1973). Items containing idioms which occurred less frequently in this textbook were judged more difficult and given higher point values. Weighting of items is questionable at best and, with this test, appears highly subjective. No difficulty index, which could be obtained from an item analysis of the test, was provided to substantiate the test developer's judgment as to the difficulty of the items.

The content validity of the GIST is highly suspect. As noted, the idioms tested were selected from the idioms used in a textbook, *The Language of Life*. In describing this book, the test manual states "Since conversational-type English is employed [in the text] and each idiom used is identified, the result is a catalog and frequency count of the most familiar idioms in American English." Such a conclusion is unwarranted. To adequately develop a catalog and frequency count of familiar American English idioms would require an analysis of a vast number of printed materials such as is used in the development of word frequency lists. Inspecting the textbook yields no new information on how idioms were selected for inclusion in the book. One can only assume that the choice of idioms was based on the authors' best judgment. While the GIST would have good content validity if it were utilized as a pretest for the textbook, its content validity as a test of the "most familiar idioms in American English" is doubtful.

Promotional material for the test states that it is a "highly valid test of English idiom comprehension" which can assist professionals "in finding appropriate job placement, planning vocational training, and...designing remediation measures for the deaf." The manual, however, provides no guidance for doing this. Does an individual need to have a specific score to succeed in a given job placement? If so, what scores would suggest which jobs? Claims that the test will assist in such decisions, especially those related to job placement, demand that the predictive validity of the GIST be established.

Test-retest reliability was established with 110 subjects. Procedures for establishing this reliability were not provided. The subjects were not described and it is not clear whether they are part of the norm group or a new group of subjects. The time period between testing sessions was not given so it is difficult to estimate the effect of memory. Although the reliability coefficient was high (reported as .9), the above deficiencies make it difficult to accept this test as a reliable instrument. While the procedures for establishing test-retest reliability may have been acceptable, they should be described fully in the manual. It is also recommended that reliability based on internal consistency be established for the GIST. With modern day computers, this is a relatively simple task.

There is another omission of statistical information in the manual. No standard error of measurement is provided, so the user has no way of determining, with any confidence, where an individual's true score might lie.

SUMMARY. The GIST is an easily administered test and one of the few which provides deaf norms. Psychometrically, however, its value is questionable. Content validity is overstated, as it is based solely on the judgment of the developer. Claims are made that it can be used to assist in job placement decisions, but no predictive validity for doing this has been established. Although test-retest reliability was high, insufficient information on how reliability was established produces little confidence in the results. No standard error of measurement was reported in the manual.

Within the reviewer's knowledge, the GIST is the only commercially available test of its kind. Another test, the Conley-Vernon Idiom Test, is available from its developer, Janet Conley, 1105 River Road, Sykesville, Maryland 21784. This test is available in two forms, each consisting of 50 multiple choice items. Idioms tested were randomly selected from *A Dictionary of Idioms for the Deaf* (Boatner & Gates, 1969), which was developed by a number of professionals. Therefore, its validity is based on the judgments of several professionals rather than one or two. Reliability is high ($r = .96$), and percentiles are provided (Conley, 1975, 1976). It is normed on 13- to 20-year-old deaf students, although not on as large or representative a group as the GIST. This test developer does not make the unsubstantiated claims that are made for the GIST. The Conley-Vernon Idiom Test's developer claims, and the results uphold, that the score is related to reading ability. However, she makes no claims about the predictive capacity of her test. This test is recommended over the GIST.

REVIEWER'S REFERENCES

Boatner, M. T., & Gates, J. E. A DICTIONARY OF IDIOMS FOR THE DEAF. Washington, DC: National Association of the Deaf, 1969.

Gochnour, E. A., & Smith, T. B. THE LANGUAGE OF LIFE. Danville, IL: The Interstate Printers & Publishers, Inc., 1973.

Conley, J. E. COMPARISON OF DEAF AND HEARING STUDENTS ON IDIOM COMPREHENSION. Unpublished master's thesis, Western Maryland College, 1975.

Conley, J. E. The role of idiomatic expressions in the reading of deaf children. AMERICAN ANNALS OF THE DEAF, 1976, 121, 381–385.

[441]

Goodenough-Harris Drawing Test. Ages 3–15; 1926–63; revision and extension of the Goodenough Intelligence Test; 1 form ('63, 4 pages); manual ('63, 80 pages); quality scale cards ('63, 24 cards); 1984 price data: $12.50 per 35 tests; $9.50 per set of quality scale cards; $6.50 per manual; $15 per specimen set; (10–15) minutes; Florence L. Goodenough and Dale B. Harris; The Psychological Corporation.*

See T3:964 (52 references), 8:187 (87 references), and T2:381 (93 references); for reviews by Anne Anastasi and James A. Dunn, and excerpted reviews by M. L. Kellmer Pringle, Marjorie P. Honzik, Carol Hunter, Adolph G. Woltmann, Marvin S. Kaplan, and Mary J. Rouse, see 7:352 (158 references); see also 6:460 (43 references) and 5:335 (34 references); for a review by Naomi Stewart of the original edition, see 4:292 (60 references).

TEST REFERENCES

1. Ratusnik, D. L. & Koenigsknecht, R. A. Biracial testing: The question of clinicians' influence on children's test performance. LANGUAGE, SPEECH, AND HEARING SERVICES IN SCHOOLS, 1977, 8, 5–14.

2. Whitehouse, D., Shah, U., & Palmer, F. B. Comparison of sustained-release and standard methylphenidate in the treatment of minimal brain dysfunction. THE JOURNAL OF CLINICAL PSYCHIATRY, 1980, 41, 282–285.

3. Morrison, J. A., & Michael, W. B. The development and validation of an auditory perception test in Spanish for Hispanic children receiving

reading instruction in Spanish. EDUCATIONAL AND PSYCHOLOGICAL MEASUREMENT, 1982, 42, 657–669.

4. Reynolds, C. R. Convergent and divergent validity of the Revised Children's Manifest Anxiety Scale. EDUCATIONAL AND PSYCHOLOGICAL MEASUREMENT, 1982, 42, 1205–1212.

5. Griffing, P., Steward, L. W., McKendry, M. A., & Anderson, R. M. Sociodramatic play: A follow-up study of imagination, self-concept, and school achievement among black school-age children representing two social-class groups. GENETIC PSYCHOLOGY MONOGRAPHS, 1983, 107, 249–301.

6. Popovics, A. J. Predictive validities of clinical and actuarial scores of the Gesell Incomplete Man Test. PERCEPTUAL AND MOTOR SKILLS, 1983, 56, 864–866.

[442]

The Goodman Lock Box. Child suspected of a developmental delay or specific learning disability or behavioral problem with a chronological or mental age 2.5–5.5; 1981; "mental organization and psychomotor competence"; 5 scale scores: competence (total adaptive, total nonadaptive, number unlocked), organization, aimless actions; individual; 1 form; manual (53 pages); record form (4 pages); 1983 price data: $295 per complete kit including 30 record forms; $6 per 30 record forms; $6 per manual; 6.5(10) minutes; Joan F. Goodman; Stoelting Co.*

Review of The Goodman Lock Box by STEPHEN N. ELLIOTT, Associate Professor of Psychology, Louisiana State University, Baton Rouge, LA:

The Goodman Lock Box is a relatively unstructured "test" designed to assess preschooler's ability to control their attention and organize a search for toys in a container with 10 latched compartments. The Lock Box is actually a 32 in. x 10 in. wooden container with 10 compartments, 5 in a row, accessible from only one side of the container and enclosed by small, latched doors. The latches differ (e.g., metal eyelet and rope combination; leather strap and buckle combination; padlock and key; latch and pin mechanism) for each door and have been designed to vary in manipulative difficulty. The author accurately reports that mentally retarded and hyperactive children, in particular, have difficulty controlling attention, inhibiting responses, and using systematic strategies for exploration. Thus, the Lock Box apparently was designed as a norm-referenced test to more completely assess children suspected of mental retardation or hyperactivity.

ADVANTAGES AND SHORTCOMINGS. The Lock Box is unique, can be administered within 10 minutes, presents an activity that most youngsters would enjoy, and does not require a verbal response from a child. In addition, the author's emphasis on assessment of the process rather than the product of attention and search activities is in vogue. Unfortunately, these are the only positive qualities of the test with respect to its stated purpose. The test's shortcomings include an inadequate standardization sample, a complex (and possibly unreliable) observational scoring system, and a price tag of $295.00. The major shortcomings involving the standardization sample and scoring cause one to question the generalizability of the norms. Details of these shortcomings are discussed below.

TEST DEVELOPMENT. The Lock Box was developed in a systematic fashion as part of the author's research program. The test manual adequately documents this development. The bulk of this documentation concerns the development of a reliable scoring system to describe children's explorations of the box.

STANDARDIZATION SAMPLE. This test was standardized over a period of several years with a sample ($N = 405$) of normal, clinical, and retarded children from the Philadelphia area only. This sample was approximately balanced for sex and SES; however, no information was provided concerning race. Nor is evidence provided indicating that hyperactive children were included in the standardization sample, yet the test is designed to assess hyperactive behavior. This is an unfortunate sampling error. Lock Box scores are reported to be highly correlated with age, but not significantly related to sex, SES, or IQ.

SCORING SYSTEM AND INTERPRETATION. According to the author, "it will take several hours of practice to master the coding system." Scores are derived in three areas: Competence, Organization, and Aimless Actions. Competence is the degree of skill demonstrated by a child in lock manipulation. Competence is operationalized by observing the number of latches opened successfully and relative frequency of adaptive to nonadaptive moves a child makes in manipulating a latch. Organization refers to the order or sequence of a child's movements during the test. Organization is operationalized by recording the number of adjacent latches a child approaches sequentially, and any repetition of a pattern of movements once a door is unlatched. Aimless Actions are behaviors that are not coordinated or directed toward the task of unlatching doors to find the concealed toys. Behaviors such as leaving the box and repetitively opening/closing a door are illustrations of Aimless Actions.

Scoring for Competence and Aimless Actions involves using a combination event-interval observation method to record a child's interactions with the locks and toys. Specifically, there are 10 possible lock activities (e.g., unsuccessful attempts to unlock, unlocks, closes without attempting relock) and 9 possible toy activities (e.g., removes toy, adaptive play, shares toy) that are to be coded on a sheet divided according to time units. Scoring for Organization is less complicated, but more arbitrary than for the Competence and Aimless Actions Scales.

The interobserver reliability estimates reported for pairs of examiners who observed a group of 59 normal and handicapped children were very acceptable, ranging from .74 to .99. The agreement between observers was lowest for nonadaptive behaviors and aimless actions. It is assumed the examiners involved were highly experienced and had many hours of practice scoring videotaped test administrations.

A profile analysis comparing a child's performance to a sample of normal children in one of four age groups (24 to 35 months, 36 to 47 months, 48 to 59 months, and 60 to 71 months) results in percentile scores for Competence (Adaptive, Nonadaptive, and Unlocked), Organization, and Aimless Actions. No single, cumulative score is computed for the entire test. The focus of score interpretation, according to the author, is "on low scores (below the 25th and particularly 10th percentiles), for the purpose of the Lock Box is to identify problems rather than strengths. The meaning of high scores—if any—has not been explored."

RELIABILITY AND VALIDITY. The only reliability information presented in the manual was for pairwise interobserver agreement, as previously noted. Although the author argues against the appropriateness of test-retest and split-half reliabilities due to practice and novelty effects, both types of reliability would be useful in sustaining the author's hypotheses, particularly in regard to samples of normal, retarded, and hyperactive children.

As evidence of the test's validity, the author provides data that she interprets as indicating the test discriminates among normal, clinical, and retarded subgroups varying in age. A close examination of the data only partially supports this interpretation. The discriminations between normal and retarded subgroups are quite consistent across the four age groups, but one does not need the Lock Box to make this discrimination given the required use of intelligence and adaptive behavior tests with children.

TEST USAGE. I have major reservations about the use of the Lock Box for purposes of making screening, classification, or educational programming decisions for young children. The test, however, does provide a rich stimulus for research on the development of numerous perceptual-motor and cognitive abilities, including attention to task, spatial memory, and with some modifications of instructions, sequential memory. It is apparent the author recognizes this value of the test, for she discusses the informal use of the Lock Box in detail.

SUMMARY. The Goodman Lock Box is a unique test that undoubtedly would interest a normal preschooler and may be a valuable instrument for researchers investigating children's early cognitive strategy development. The Lock Box, however, does not have a valuable role to play in the assessment of handicapped children other than as an "ice breaking" task. The useful application of information from this test is highly dependent on the examiner's theoretical and practical knowledge of preschoolers' cognitive development. This fact, coupled with the cost and arduous scoring system of the Lock Box, will serve to limit the use of this test. Direct observation methods provide information of lower inference, more educational relevance, and more situational specificity when a child's potential problem is poor attention-to-task or lack of a systematic problem solving approach.

Review of The Goodman Lock Box by KATHLEEN D. PAGET, Associate Professor of Psychology, University of South Carolina, Columbia, SC:

Whenever an instrument for the psychological assessment of young children is grounded in sound psychological principles and a firm understanding of young children, test users should take special note. The Goodman Lock Box is such an instrument. Essentially, it is based on the principle that over the first years of life, children develop a more controlled and organized approach to solving problems and are better able to distinguish and evaluate various aspects of their environment. Also integral to its conceptual framework is an understanding of the importance of play to young children and behavioral observation to proper psychological assessment. Perhaps the most unique aspect of the Lock Box is that it is designed to objectify mental processes and behaviors that are often interpreted subjectively by psychologists.

Despite its conceptual strengths, a practical problem exists that may interfere with the widespread use of the Lock Box. The materials are very expensive, substantially more so than most other preschool assessment instruments, including broad-based diagnostic instruments like the McCarthy Scales of Children's Abilities. The materials consist of a brightly colored large wooden rectangular container with 10 latched compartments, each housing a different toy. Although the purchase price is high, the expense incurred in the development of the materials has made them very enticing to young children, who enjoy the tasks and remain engaged with them.

ADMINISTRATION. During a 6½ minute administration time, the examiner codes all moves made by the child in unlocking the compartments and then engages in a "testing of the limits" procedure. The coded scores reflect the naturally occurring behaviors of the child with little, if any, interaction with the examiner. Thus, the Lock Box could be particularly useful for easing the assessment situation for shy, nonverbal, or noncompliant children. The Instruction Manual contains good descriptions of the behavioral categories and the few instances when the examiner should redirect or intervene with the child. Moreover, the format of the record form facilitates a fairly complex coding process. In addition to the five major scoring categories, four subsidiary scores are calculated for the child's total moves, the relative balance of adaptive and nonadaptive moves, the quality and quantity of play behaviors, and persistence.

The manual contains sample case reports, examples of common errors in coding and scoring, as well as good descriptions of behaviors. While these help to synthesize administration and scoring information, administration of the Lock Box should take place only after substantial practice. Even for psychologists who are trained well in behavioral observation techniques, extensive familiarity with the coding and scoring systems is necessary before a test user can accurately code and score the test within the 20-minute time period mentioned in the manual.

The availability of videotapes and training workshops is mentioned in the manual; however, the high price of the test, in many instances, would preclude the purchase of more materials. Given this practical problem, it is noteworthy that no explicit performance criterion is given in the manual to guide the practice of test users who do not obtain training materials. In the absence of such materials, it is wise for users to videotape practice sessions and the first formal administrations to afford the opportunity for post-evaluation review.

STANDARDIZATION. Examination of the standardization procedures followed in the development of the Lock Box immediately reveals some need for caution when applying the norms to individual cases. The sample size is small, relative to many standardization samples, and the sample was drawn from one metropolitan area. Additionally, information is lacking on the breakdown of the sample by ethnic group, with the socioeconomic characteristics of the children only sparsely described. Thus, the test users must understand that the norms do not represent children nationwide and that sampling bias may exist.

PSYCHOMETRIC PROPERTIES. Because the Lock Box is based on principles of behavioral assessment, traditional methods for determining reliability and validity are not the most appropriate or meaningful. Of most importance with a behavioral assessment device is its accuracy, or its sensitivity to objective and generalizable characteristics of the responses (Cone, 1981). Given this consideration, psychometric data on the Lock Box are adequate; however, procedures that were followed limit generalizability.

Most interobserver reliability estimates reported in the manual are of sufficient size to suggest that consistent scores can be obtained by different observers. Only for the normal group were estimates for two scoring categories lower than Nunnally's (1967) recommended standard of .90 for practical use. While demonstrating consistency among observers, the estimates do not show that observers can be consistent with an acceptable scoring criterion. The use of a calibrator observer (Cone, 1981) to set a criterion would aid in understanding observer accuracy as well as consistency.

Other forms of reliability were not calculated for the Lock Box. Test/retest reliability is not appropriate because responses are dependent on the test's novelty; nor was split-half reliability measured, since changes in tempo and activity make it impossible to divide the administration into equivalent units.

Results of validation procedures suggest that Lock Box scores change with age and that the test discriminates between different groups of problem children. Supplemental validity information should appear in the manual. Concurrent comparisons of the Lock Box with other measures of psychomotor competence and mental organization are needed, as well as predictive comparisons with measures of academic performance. Moreover, before it can be said that the Lock Box meets high standards of accuracy, as well as reliability and validity, comparisons need to be made between behaviors displayed during Lock Box administration with assessments of behavior in other settings, at other times, and while using different observation methods.

SUMMARY. The Goodman Lock Box is a behavioral assessment device that contributes uniquely to the body of assessment instruments available for preschool populations. Because it is conceptually sound and designed to objectify processes that are often interpreted subjectively, it is a valuable supplement to preschool test batteries and screening tests. Despite some limitations mentioned in this review, the Lock Box should be viewed enthusiastically by test users as a trend-setter that adds a new dimension to assessment information traditionally obtained on preschool children.

REVIEWER'S REFERENCES

Nunnally, J. PSYCHOMETRIC THEORY. New York: McGraw Hill, 1967.

Cone, J. D. Psychometric considerations. In M. Hershen and A. S. Bellack (Eds.), BEHAVIORAL ASSESSMENT: A PRACTICAL HANDBOOK. New York: Pergamon Press, 1981.

[443]

Gordon Occupational Check List II. Grades 8–12 and adults; 1961–81; GOCL; "designed for persons seeking education and job training below the college level"; 6 or 12 scores: business, outdoor, arts, technology (mechanical, industrial), service, and 6 optional summarization scores (preceding 6 areas); no norms; 1 form ('80, 6 pages); job title supplement ('80, 2 pages); manual ('81, 19 pages); 1984 price data: $17 per complete set including 35 check lists and 35 job title supplements; $3 per manual; $3.75 per specimen set; (20–25) minutes; Leonard V. Gordon; The Psychological Corporation.*

For reviews by John N. McCall and Bert W. Westbrook of an earlier edition, see 7:1019; for reviews by John O. Crites and Kenneth B. Hoyt of an earlier edition, see 6:1056.

Review of Gordon Occupational Checklist II by DONALD G. ZYTOWSKI, Counseling Psychologist & Professor of Psychology, Iowa State University, Ames, IA:

The Gordon Occupational Checklist II (GOCL II) is described in the manual as a systematic way in which students who are not planning college study may communicate their vocational interests "within defined occupational domains" so that a teacher or counselor can identify relevant sources of more information. The feature that makes this version different from its predecessor is that it has adopted the structure of the U.S. Department of Labor's Guide for Occupational Exploration (GOE), in place of one that roughly paralleled Roe's fields and levels (Roe, 1956). The author has added and revised items to reflect 59 of the GOE's 66 Work Groups, the omitted groups consisting chiefly of occupations that require four or more years of college. Items are organized into six categories: Business, Outdoor, Arts, Service, and Technical, which is split into Mechanical and Industrial because there were so many occupations in this group in the GOE. Although it is difficult to discern the difference in the job titles related to these subdivisions, apparently Mechanical requires more spacial ability and Industrial requires more motor dexterity.

Response format remains as before—from 240 occupational activities, respondents underline those which they "would like to do," and circle those underlined activities that they would like to do "the very most." The manual reports that the average number of items underlined is about 25, and usually one-third of these are circled. Summarization scores in each category consist of the number of items underlined added to the number also circled. Each item is keyed to a job title and its corresponding work group or subgroup in the GOE, so that endorsement of an item can lead to occupational information and to consideration of several additional occupations that are closely related. The items are framed in gender-neutral language, and the author has taken pains to provide suggestions to avoid sex stereotyping in the Checklist's use.

Since individual responses are the basis of interpretation and use, many of the psychometric properties expected of scales are irrelevant to the GOCL II. Nevertheless, material is presented in support of its reliability and validity. Students tend to endorse the same items (although fewer on second administration) over a three-week interval. It would be reasonable to ask for stability data over a year or more, or spanning the interval between school and actual employment.

Data on the independence of the categories are also presented. They reveal a high correlation between Mechanical and Industry—in the .60s—and a similarly high correlation between the Business and Service domains, which might be expected to be more independent. Correlations between .30 and .50 also appear between Technical and Outdoor, and Arts and Service, such as might be predicted from Holland's hexagonal arrangement of his types.

Any device that purports to identify occupations that are to be further explored by the test-taker ought to demonstrate some level of validity: perhaps the occupations suggested should be more likely to result in eventual satisfaction than occupations not suggested. I am especially interested in such validity for the GOCL II because of its reliance on item responses. I have to wonder what high school junior or senior understands, for instance, what it means to "investigate and settle insurance claims." How valid is the endorsement of such an item? Do people who are insurance claims adjusters (the keyed job title) endorse this item? What other occupational activities do they endorse? Do people who say they would like this activity eventually weave their way into occupations that require this and related interests?

On the other hand, a checklist may not require such exacting evidence. Perhaps it serves chiefly as what Holland has called "a rehearsal of aspirations." In this sense its utility may be to help the user appreciate the diversity of things that there are to do in life, how they may be related, and what jobs follow from what activities, all emphasizing that choices are there to be made. Taken from this perspective, the GOCL II would seem to need little more than the qualities which are reported in its manual.

I would only plead that users understand the purpose which they expect the GOCL II to serve, and take care not to exceed its apparent limits. If used as an exploratory device, its comprehensive sampling of occupational activities linked to a comprehensive source of further information makes it possibly one of the best of its kind.

REVIEWER'S REFERENCES

Roe, A. THE PSYCHOLOGY OF OCCUPATIONS. New York: John Wiley, 1956.

[444]

Gordon Personal Profile-Inventory. Grades 9–16 and adults; 1951–78; GPP-I; a combination of the Gordon Personal Profile and the Gordon Personal Inventory; separate booklet editions are still available; combined form ('78, 5 pages); 2 tests; manual ('78, 105 pages); 1984 price data: $32.50 per 35 test booklets, scoring key, and manual; $11 per manual; $15 per specimen set; (20–25) minutes; Leonard V. Gordon; The Psychological Corporation.*

a) GORDON PERSONAL PROFILE. 1953–63; 5 scores: ascendancy, responsibility, emotional stability, sociability, self-esteem; 1 form ('63, 3 pages); manual ('63, 27 pages); scoring key (1 page); $17.50 per 35 test booklets, scoring key, and manual; (15–20) minutes.

b) GORDON PERSONAL INVENTORY. 1956–63; 4 scores: cautiousness, original thinking, personal relations, vigor; 1 form ('63, 3 pages); manual ('63, 20 pages); scoring key (1 page); prices and time same as *a* above.

See T3:966 (6 references), 8:568 (34 references), 8:569 (52 references), T2:1194 (56 references), and P:93 (23 references); for reviews by Charles F. Dicken and Alfred B. Heilbrun, Jr., see 6:102 (13 references) and 6:103 (25 references); for reviews by Benno G. Fricke and John A. Radcliffe and excerpted reviews by Laurance F. Shaffer and Laurence Siegel, see 5:58 and 5:59 (16 references).

TEST REFERENCES

1. Woody, G. E., Mintz, J., Tennant, F., O'Brien, C. P., McLellan, A. T., & Marcovici, M. Propoxyphene for maintenance treatment of narcotic addiction. ARCHIVES OF GENERAL PSYCHIATRY, 1981, 38, 898–900.

[445]

Goyer Organization of Ideas Test. College and adults; 1966–79; GOIT; no data on validity; Form S ('68, 8 pages); no manual; mimeographed report ('79, 24 pages); score distribution sheet (no date, 1 page); separate answer sheets must be used; 1984 price data: $2 per test; (20–40) minutes; Robert S. Goyer; the Author.*

See 8:817 (1 reference).

Review of Goyer Organization of Ideas Test by RIC BROWN, Associate Professor of Education, California State University, Fresno, CA:

The stated purpose of the Goyer Organization of Ideas Test is to measure aspects of adult ability to verbally organize ideas. This purpose is based on the premise that the learning and utilization of categories is one of the most elementary and general forms of cognition. The author provides a theoretical background and offers evidence that the underlying process of organizational skills involves the perception and analysis of stimuli and abstracting cues that lead to synthesis and generalization. The theoretical background and evidence provided the author with the four organization skills upon which the test is based: component (part-whole) relationships, sequential relationships, material to purpose (relevance) relationships, and transitional (connective) relationships.

The present form of the test consists of 30 items of various types that can be completed in about 30 minutes. Some items require the ordering of statements in terms of temporal or logical sequence. For example, one item lists five steps that are part of the process of reflective thought. The respondent is to pick the "most logical way" of ordering the steps from among five alternative orderings. Other items require the selection of main ideas from a series of statements, while other items ask the respondent to select transitional words or phrases to complete statements. It should be noted that a relatively high level of reading ability is required in addition to the underlying organization skill requirements.

The test documentation presents data on the development of four initial forms of the test leading to the present version. All of the versions used the same basic items with slight modifications of stems and foils while manipulating only sequence and number of items on the test. The original items were developed in the late 1950s from other tests and the author's own ideas. All reliability and validity data were obtained using university students from Ohio as respondents.

Split half reliability coefficients in the .70–.80 range are reported for all versions. In terms of validity, speech communication professors were used as expert raters to determine if individual items measured one of the four organization skills. "Majority agreement" was used in place of any formal statistical index of interrater agreement.

In order to assess the scale's relationship to other variables, scores on the original two forms were correlated with the Ohio State Psychological Examination (OSPE). Coefficients of .67 and .73 were found between these two forms of the Goyer test and the OSPE.

In an attempt to find the relationship between knowledge in a subject area (speech communication) and organization skills, 14 items on the test were identified as measuring content from introductory speech courses. Scores from these 14 items correlated substantially (.89) with the total test scores. Because the correlation represents the relationship between part of a test and the total scores on the same test, the generalizability of this finding is questionable in terms of organizing skills and understanding content in general areas.

The current form of the Goyer test is a shortened version of the original forms. While a .72 split-half reliability is reported, no index of relationship was presented between the current form and its longer predecessors.

SUMMARY. In the technical information provided, the author stated three purposes: to develop and validate an instrument to measure the ability to organize ideas verbally (although it is a written test), to develop normative data, and to determine relationships between the ability to organize ideas and other individual indices. From the data presented, only the first of these purposes was even partially accomplished.

Although the test measures something consistently, it is unclear if that something is a generalized organizational skill or the content of an introductory speech communication class.

Except for ranges of scores, no normative data in terms of means and standard deviations are given. The group for which data are given are only described as Ohio freshmen and sophomores.

Evidence of the relationship between organizing skills and other skills is less than convincing. The high correlation between the test and general intelligence (OSPE) may be more a function of the high level of reading ability required than the ability to organize. The content relationship reported was merely a subtest to test correlation.

For the test to be used as a generalized measure of organizational skill, more evidence is needed of how the construct underlying the test relates to other cognitive constructs and also to content knowledge in a variety of areas. At this point, the test is probably best used as a content measure in courses where organizational skills are taught.

Review of Goyer Organization of Ideas Test by ROBERT B. FRARY, Professor and Assistant Director for Research and Measurement, Learning Resources Center, Virginia Polytechnic Institute and State University, Blacksburg, VA:

Development of this test began in the mid-1950s as part of the author's doctoral dissertation. Since then it has progressed through several stages culminating in the present published version, Form S, with a 1968 copyright date. Form S consists of 30 multiple-choice items of the following types: (1) arranging sets of five statements into appropriate order or recognizing the basis for a given order (8 questions); (2) questions about outlining, e.g., identifying where a statement belongs in a given outline or recognizing errors in a given outline (10 questions); (3) choosing the most unifying statement from a group of four statements on a single topic (6 questions); (4) selecting the most appropriate connective word or phrase to insert between two clauses of otherwise complete sentences (5 questions); and (5) selecting the first premise of a syllogism given the second premise and the conclusion (1 question).

As reported by Goyer (1979), the test was developed using methods from classical test theory to enhance internal consistency. Based on responses from 652 unspecified examinees (presumably college students), a split-half reliability coefficient of .72 is reported. This relatively low value suggests that factor analysis might reveal subscales with only moderate intercorrelations, probably based on the item types described above.

The only validity data for this test come from two forms preceding the present published version. These forms had 50 items, as opposed to 30 on Form S, and scores from the same 65 examinees on each form were correlated with their percentile scores (!) on the Ohio State Psychological Examination. Resulting validity coefficients were .67 and .73, remarkably high, given split-half reliability estimates for these forms of .80 and .83. In fact, scores from a good group-administered IQ test might correlate no more strongly with percentile scores from the Ohio State Psychological Examination. This is not meant to say that the Goyer test is simply another measure of intelligence, but performance on it must depend heavily on general intellectual/academic ability.

This test is untimed, and, according to its author's report, it can be administered in about 30 minutes. Its printing is of good quality, and the directions are clear (no correction for guessing). It is probably appropriate for college-bound high school through undergraduate college students. Norms as such do not exist, but the author has produced a score distribution sheet for the sample of 652 mentioned above, from which it can be estimated that the mean score was about 18, with the 5th and 95th percentiles corresponding to scores of about 10 and 25 (out of 30).

This test may be useful for measuring the effect of efforts to upgrade the skills embodied in its items. For other uses, such as diagnosis or comparison of populations, its scores are probably too strongly related to general verbal ability measures to be uniquely useful.

REVIEWER'S REFERENCES

Goyer, R. S. A TEST TO MEASURE THE ABILITY TO ORGANIZE IDEAS. Special Report No. 9 (rev.), Center for Communication Studies, Ohio University, Athens, OH, 1979.

[446]

Graded Naming Test. Adolescents and adults; 1983; GNT; "diagnoses reduced efficiency in language, naming and comprehension functions in brain-damaged patients by presenting 30 black and white pictures for naming by patient"; no data on reliability; individual; record form (2 pages); object picture book (32 pages); manual (12 pages); 1984 price data: £3.45 per 25 record forms; £9.50 per object picture book; £4.50 per manual; administration time not reported; Pat McKenna and Elizabeth Warrington; NFER-Nelson Publishing Co. [England].*

[447]

Graduate Management Admission Test. Business graduate students; 1954–84; GMAT; test administered 4 times annually (January, March, June, October) at centers established by the publisher; 3 scores: verbal, quantitative, total; information bulletin ('83, 38 pages); user's guide ('83, 18 pages); score interpretation guide ('83, 4 pages); technical report on test development and score interpretation (no date, 23 pages); methods of test preparation ('82, 23 pages); separate answer sheets must be used; 1984 price data: examination fee, $30 per student (fee includes reporting of scores to 5 schools); 180–190(240) minutes; Graduate Management Admission Council; Educational Testing Service.*

See T3:973 (6 references), 8:1074 (11 references), and T2:2325 (5 references); for reviews by Jerome E. Doppelt and Gary R. Hanson of earlier forms, see 7:1080 (10 references).

TEST REFERENCES

1. Youngblood, S. A., & Martin, B. J. Ability testing and graduate admissions: Decision process modeling and validation. EDUCATIONAL AND PSYCHOLOGICAL MEASUREMENT, 1982, 42, 1153–1162.

Review of Graduate Management Admission Test by LAWRENCE A. CROSBY, Associate Professor of Marketing, College of Business, Arizona State University, Tempe, AZ:

First administered in 1954 as the "Admission Test for Graduate Study in Business," use of the GMAT has grown to the point that 555 graduate schools of business now require the test for admission. Nearly 600,000 candidates took the test between June 1980 and March 1983. Despite these impressive numbers, consumer groups have raised questions about the validity of the GMAT (and other college admissions aptitude tests). The issue of validity is of no less concern to admissions officers and committees within colleges of business. These users of the test have an ethical and legal responsibility to rely on test scores only if they are meaningfully related to future academic performance and do not unfairly discriminate against certain groups. As a result of this pressure, the Educational Testing Service (ETS) is now required to publicly disclose the contents of its tests.

Earlier reviewers of the GMAT (7:1080) gave a favorable overall evaluation, claiming that it serves the purposes for which it was designed: (*a*) to contribute to the prediction of first-year academic performance, and (*b*) to provide a means of comparing the abilities of a large number of applicants. While the test does appear to have many positive attributes when judged against traditional criteria for test construction, previous conclusions about its usefulness may not be entirely warranted.

Over the years, there has been extensive research on the predictive validity of the GMAT. Validity studies conducted by ETS as well as independent investigations appearing in academic journals have consistently reported modest validity coefficients for the GMAT when used alone, but slightly higher figures when used in combination with undergraduate grades. Figures for 1982–83 indicate a median correlation of .30 between Total GMAT (quantitative & verbal) and first-year grades in MBA or equivalent programs. The multiple correlation of GMAT and undergraduate GPA with first-year grades is slightly higher at .38, although multiple correlations in the mid .40s have been noted previously.

There are important caveats presented regarding these findings, such as a lack of evidence about the validity of the test when taken under nonstandard conditions (e.g., by handicapped persons), by persons whose native language is not English, or for admission to other academic programs (e.g., the PhD). Perhaps the most important warning of all, however, is that the test may be valid or invalid depending on the particular institution involved. Across 150 management schools participating in a recent ETS study, the multiple correlation of GMAT and undergraduate GPA with first-year grades ranged from .12 to .67. While these validity coefficients may be underestimates due to the well-known "restriction of range" effect, it cannot be concluded that the GMAT has predictive validity in all academic environments.

This variability has not gone unnoticed by ETS, which now offers a validity study service. While further research is certainly needed, this service seems to shift much of the responsibility and expense for validation to the participating schools. It is worrisome that only 150 of the 555 schools using the test appear to have taken advantage of the service. This is a situation that would seem to call for further analysis to be conducted by ETS. Studies already completed for individual schools would serve as the units of analysis. Observed correlations between test scores and first-year grades would be one of the dependent variables. Independent variables would be characteristics of the schools' academic programs that might affect the ability of the GMAT to successfully predict subsequent performance. Dissemination of the results would allow schools unable to conduct their own studies to estimate the predictive validity of the GMAT as it applies to their schools.

Procedures described in the test manual provide reasonable assurance that, whatever the test measures, it is consistently measured from year to year. In addition, the test appears to have some face validity, particularly in a section on Practical Business Judgment and in items concerned with the interpretation of charts, graphs, and tables. But evidence is clearly lacking for construct validity. One might argue that predictive validity is enough, and that it really doesn't matter what is measured as long as test scores remove some of the uncertainty about future performance. In the case of the GMAT, however, this argument is flawed. The predictive efficacy of the GMAT for graduate business programs is modest, at best. More information is needed in order to evaluate whether the test adequately measures the constructs it claims are related to success in business programs (e.g., verbal and quantitative abilities). Is it possible that there are subordinate skills within the verbal and quantitative areas that account for success in business programs, or could there be other constructs that are more useful in predicting success in graduate school? More extensive construct validation would help to clear up these problems.

On the positive side, information provided by ETS does show a high degree of internal consistency for the verbal and quantitative sections. Reliability coefficients range from .86 to .93. This high degree of internal consistency, a necessary condition for construct validity, may be partly explained by the large number of items.

In conclusion, scores on the GMAT are predictive of first-year grades at an aggregate level. The relationship is far from perfect, however, and important contextual effects remain unaccounted for. In the absence of data from comparable institutions, use of the GMAT in admissions decisions is recommended only upon completion of a validation study tailored to the programs of an individual school. Admissions committees should not equate test scores with candidates' verbal and quantitative abilities and should be creative in identifying other indicators of potential success in graduate school.

Review of Graduate Management Admission Test by JAMES LEDVINKA, Professor of Management and Psychology, The University of Georgia, and WILLIAM R. BOULTON, Director of Graduate Studies, College of Business Administration, The University of Georgia, Athens, GA:

The Graduate Management Admission Test (GMAT) is an aptitude test designed to predict success in the first year of graduate study in business. The test is sponsored by an organization of 66 graduate business schools known as the Graduate Management Admissions Council. The current version of the test contains eight separately timed sections, each with 20 to 35 questions, and each designed so that about 80% of the examinees will get far enough to attempt the last question in the section. Three sections measure verbal skills, three measure mathematical skills, and the remaining two are reserved for questions being tried out for possible future use.

RELIABILITY AND VALIDITY. The GMAT appears to be an exceptionally well developed test. Reliability figures are impressive: .92 for the GMAT total score, .90 for the verbal part score, and .87 for the quantitative part score (KR-20 coefficients). Validity coefficients are also respectable. Using first year MBA grades as a criterion, the average predictive validity of the GMAT in 32 studies was .30. That compares with a validity coefficient of .24 for undergraduate grades as a predictor of MBA performance. When GMAT and undergraduate grades are combined and weighted optimally, the average validity coefficient increases to .38. These figures are hard to improve upon. Some business schools have discontinued using the GMAT in favor of the Graduate Record Examination, but the GMAT is probably still more popular, and the validity of the GMAT makes it understandable why.

DOCUMENTATION. The documentation provided to examinees is extensive and well written. The information bulletin gives a realistic preview of the test, and the sample items are representative. The score interpretation guide provided when ETS reports scores is straightforward and thorough—its description of reliability and validity is a model of clarity. Taken together, the examinee documents anticipate most of the common concerns and misconceptions. ETS also makes available full form sample tests, accompanied by clear, detailed scoring instructions and test explanations.

In short, ETS has succeeded in being both comprehensive and comprehensible in its documentation to examinees. The curious test-taker can get answers to just about every legitimate question one might have regarding the GMAT. Much the same can be said of the documentation provided to business schools that use the GMAT.

ADEQUACY OF VALIDITY INFORMATION. On balance, we think that the GMAT is the best test available for its purposes. Nevertheless, there are problems, not with the technical adequacy of the test itself but with the information that is provided to help ensure effective use of the test.

More validity information would be particularly helpful. ETS correctly recommends that the GMAT be used in conjunction with other predictors and urges schools to conduct their own validity studies. It even offers a Validity Study Service to assist schools in carrying out those studies. The problem is that ETS requires a sample size of 100 to participate. We understand that ETS allows up to 3 years to accumulate the sample, but still the requirement makes the service unavailable to many graduate business schools.

ETS's concern over sample size is misplaced. For most schools the main purpose of a validity study is not to assess whether the GMAT is valid, but to determine the optimal weights to apply to GMAT scores and other predictors such as undergraduate grade point average. Some set of weights will be used, and weights based on even a small sample would be better than weights devised without benefit of any systematic empirical analysis at all. Of course, schools can carry out their own validity studies, but the schools with the technical expertise to do so are more likely to be those with MBA classes that are large enough to qualify for participation in the Validity Study Service. Ironically, then, ETS's sample size requirement tends to exclude the very schools that are most in need of help with local validation.

In the absence of local validation, other information would be helpful. Schools could use the predictor weights from ETS's previous validity studies. Also, many schools use prediction systems that approximate unit weighting but have no information on the validity of those systems. Unit weighting validity coefficients would help them tell how good their systems are. This kind of information may be available upon special request to ETS, but it should be provided more routinely than that.

USE WITH NON-MBA PROGRAMS. Another information problem lies in the fact that the validity data provided on the GMAT are for MBA admissions only. That leaves the question of whether the test is valid for business-school MA and PhD programs, as well as for graduate management programs in non-business schools such as public administration, education, and social services. Yet some of the GMAT documentation indicates that the test predicts success in the first year of "graduate management school," without differentiating among the varieties of graduate management education available. In many schools there are vast differences between MBA education and the education received by students in other graduate management school programs. Users should consider the possibility that other tests, such as the GRE, might be more valid than the GMAT, particularly for MA and PhD programs that follow a research degree model rather than the more analytic professional degree model followed by the typical MBA program.

USE WITH MINORITIES. A related issue is the optimal use of the GMAT for applicants other than native Caucasians. International students often score low on the verbal section of the GMAT yet do quite well in MBA programs, perhaps due to diligence in overcoming their language deficit. Consequently, some schools have substituted the Test of English as a Foreign Language (TOEFL) for the GMAT verbal score. It would be helpful to know whether the validity for this procedure is any greater than that for the traditional use of GMAT verbal scores.

Likewise, blacks and other native minorities tend to score lower on the GMAT than do whites, and their representation among those who score above a cutoff diminishes dramatically as the cutoff rises. While the GMAT seems no worse than other similar tests in that regard, the test's documentation could be more informative about the problem. Also useful would be separate prediction equations for whites and non-whites, which would help admissions officers quantify the tradeoffs involved in any minority preference policies they might be considering. Such equations would also provide an answer to the key question of whether whites and non-whites with equal GMAT scores are equally likely to succeed in graduate management school.

CONCLUSION. In sum, the GMAT appears to be a model of sound test development and clearly the preferred instrument for the majority of graduate management admissions decisions. Where the GMAT may be weaker is for exceptional situations such as non-MBA programs and non-native applicants. But we find the main problem to lie in user information. We think more information about predictor weights and minority performance should be provided routinely to schools that use the GMAT. The information provided is adequate for those schools who do everything by the book, making admissions decisions in a psychometrically pure multivariate manner without being influenced by affirmative action considerations. Unfortunately, we know of no school that operates in that way.

[448]

Graduate Record Examinations—General Test. Graduate school candidates; 1949–85; GREGT; test administered 5 times annually (February, April, June, October, December) at centers established by the publisher; 3 scores: verbal, quantitative, analytical; information bulletin for candidates ('85, 95 pages); supervisor's manual ('83, 29 pages); guidelines for use (no date, 2 pages); guide ('83, 61 pages); technical manual ('77, 110 pages); data summary report ('83, 112 pages); validity summary report ('83, 47 pages); separate answer sheets must be used; 1984 price data: examination fee, $29 per candidate; fee includes reporting of scores to the candidate, current college, and 3 graduate schools; Braille, large-type and cassette editions available; 210(230) minutes; Educational Testing Service.*

See T3:995 (26 references), 8:188 (45 references), T2:382 (15 references), and 7:353 (43 references); for reviews by Robert L. French and Warren W. Willingham of an earlier edition, see 6:461 (17 references); for a review by John T. Dailey, see 5:336 (7 references); for reviews by J. P. Guilford and Carl I. Hovland, see 4:293 (2 references). For reviews of the GRE program, see 7:667 (1 review) and 5:601 (1 review).

TEST REFERENCES

1. Wild, C. L., Durso, R., & Rubin, D. B. Effect of increased test-taking time on test scores by ethnic group, years out of school, and sex. JOURNAL OF EDUCATIONAL MEASUREMENT, 1981, 19, 19–28.

2. Drasgow, F. Choice of test model for appropriateness measurement. APPLIED PSYCHOLOGICAL MEASUREMENT, 1982, 6, 297–308.

3. Stricker, L. J. Identifying test items that perform differentially in population subgroups: A partial correlation index. APPLIED PSYCHOLOGICAL MEASUREMENT, 1982, 6, 261–273.

4. Ward, W. C. A comparison of free-response and multiple-choice forms of verbal aptitude tests. APPLIED PSYCHOLOGICAL MEASUREMENT, 1982, 6, 1–11.

5. Wolansky, W. D., & Resnick, H. S. Trends and emphases in industrial education doctoral programs. JOURNAL OF INDUSTRIAL TEACHER EDUCATION, 1982, 19(3), 4–19.

6. Broadus, R. N., & Elmore, K. E. The comparative validities of undergraduate grade point average and of part scores on the Graduate Record Examinations in the prediction of two criterion measures in a graduate library school program. EDUCATIONAL AND PSYCHOLOGICAL MEASUREMENT, 1983, 43, 543–546.

7. Levine, M. V., & Drasgow, F. The relation between incorrect option choice and estimated ability. EDUCATIONAL AND PSYCHOLOGICAL MEASUREMENT, 1983, 43, 675–685.

8. Michael, J. J., Nadson, J. S., & Michael, W. B. The prediction of academic achievement in graduate study in education. EDUCATIONAL AND PSYCHOLOGICAL MEASUREMENT, 1983, 43, 1133–1139.

9. Kingston, N. M., & Dorans, N. J. Item location effects and their implications for IRT equating and adaptive testing. APPLIED PSYCHOLOGICAL MEASUREMENT, 1984, 8, 147–154.

Review of Graduate Record Examinations—General Test by SANFORD J. COHN, Deputy Director, The Johns Hopkins University Center for the Advancement of Academically Talented Youth, and Lecturer in Psychology, The Johns Hopkins University, Baltimore, MD:

The College Entrance Examination Board's Graduate Record Examinations—General Test

(GRE) is designed to offer a global measure of the verbal, quantitative, and analytical reasoning abilities acquired by an applicant for graduate study over a long period of time and not related to any specific field of study. Verbal, quantitative, and analytical scores are reported separately. The GRE is intended to provide objective information about student abilities to use in conjunction with such other means of assessment as the college record, letters of recommendation, essays, and portfolios to determine admissibility to graduate study. The GRE General Test is given five times a year at test centers throughout the world; it resembles its counterpart for applicants to college, the Scholastic Aptitude Test (SAT), but is more difficult.

Each form of the GRE consists of seven equal sections of 30 minutes duration: two are verbal, two are quantitative, two are analytical, and one is reserved for research to gather information for equating different forms of the test, for pretesting items to determine their psychometric characteristics and their overall utility for future tests, and for conducting other research.

The verbal sections consist of four different item types: antonyms, analogies, sentence completions, and reading comprehension. Each verbal section contains all four types of items. Item content is drawn from a variety of substantive areas spanning the humanities and the sciences, including items related to practical or everyday life, and human relationships and feelings.

The quantitative sections include three distinct kinds of items: discrete quantitative questions, data interpretation items, and quantitative comparisons. Discrete quantitative items test basic mathematical skills. Some require little more than basic knowledge and manipulation; others focus on reading, understanding, and solving problems of actual or abstract situations. Sets of data interpretation items are based on data presented in charts and graphs and focus on synthesizing information, selecting appropriate information, and determining whether or not sufficient information is provided to solve the problem. Quantitative comparison items offer four choices, require special directions, and demand evaluation of the relative size of two expressions or quantities. They focus on the quick and accurate determination of the relative sizes of two quantities or the sufficiency of information required to make such a decision. Formal courses in algebra and Euclidean geometry are not prerequisite to the GRE quantitative section; rather knowledge of basic arithmetic processes, introductory algebra, and geometry (measurement or spatial visualization) form the item content.

The analytical sections contain two distinct types of items: analytical reasoning items and logical reasoning items. Analytical reasoning items examine the ability to understand a given structure of relationships among fictitious persons, places, things, or events, to deduce new information from the relationships provided, and to evaluate the conditions used to determine the structure of relationships. Logical reasoning items examine the ability to understand, analyze, and evaluate arguments: recognizing the point of the argument and the assumptions upon which it is based, drawing conclusions, inferring missing information, applying principles from one argument to another, and analyzing evidence. The analytical sections were added to the GRE General Test in 1977. Test users are warned, however, to avoid using the analytical scores as a basis for making decisions until experience has provided the necessary validity studies to ensure their utility.

The seventh section of the GRE General Test contains questions that do not contribute to the student's score, but serve to provide information necessary to equate differing forms of the test (past, present, and future), to try out items for use in future tests, or to gather information relevant to other research. Items in this section are made to appear indistinguishable from items in the other six operational sections of the GRE.

SCORING. The GRE General Test is composed entirely of multiple-choice items with usually five choices per item (with the exception of four choices in the quantitative comparison items). Scores are based on the number of correct answer choices selected. Scores reported to students and to test users are scaled scores, computed in such a way as to be comparable across different forms of the tests.

The GRE General Test scale ranges from 200 to 800. Although scaled scores are equated across different forms of the test, percentile ranks provided on the score reports are based on the performance of the current reference group regardless of when the test was taken. The percentile rank of a particular score may vary, then, over the years depending upon the group against which it is compared. Distributions of General Test scores are also provided according to intended graduate major field.

RELIABILITY. Reliability of GRE General Test scores are based primarily on an internal consistency estimation, using the familiar Kuder-Richardson 20. Typical internal consistency reliability coefficients exceed .90 for the verbal and quantitative sections and hover around .86 for the analytical section.

VALIDITY. Publishers of the GRE offer a GRE Validity Study Service to determine the relationships among the GRE scores, undergraduate grade point average, and first-year graduate grade point average. In a report of 246 departments that submitted criterion data on first-year graduate grade point average since the inception of this service in 1979, summaries of score distributions have been provided according to department type: humanities, social sciences, biological sciences, and physical sciences. The average humanities department, for example, demonstrated a higher mean verbal score than any of the other department types. The GRE quantitative score tends, on the other hand, to be more effective in predicting performance in mathematical and physical sciences. In general, validity coefficients for the three sections of the GRE General Test tend to hover around .20 to .30. These correlations are moderate, at best. GRE Subject Tests tend to be better predictors of first-year graduate grade point averages for specific departments than the GRE General Test.

Among a number of important limitations to the accuracy of correlations between GRE General Test scores and first-year graduate grade point averages is the restriction of range that tends to lower correlations substantially. The group of students who are admitted to graduate study and who complete their first year do not include all who applied or who were even admitted. Moreover, the group of students is small, and small samples lead to unstable correlations.

SUMMARY. The GRE remains the best documented instrument of its type. Detailed manuals describing all phases of its administration, use, and interpretation ensure maximum likelihood of standardized test conditions, in spite of its widespread use and multiple administration sites. State-of-the-art techniques of equating test forms and scoring and reporting test results make its use convenient and accessible to all. Meticulous test security practices make it practically immune to cheating and other forms of abuse. Many studies concerning its reliability and validity have been and continue to be conducted. While validity coefficients tend to be small, factors that tend to diminish their size are understood and should be taken into account. Careful attention on the part of the GRE publisher, Educational Testing Service, to its value as a supplement to other measures for evaluating applicants for admission to graduate schools serves to enhance the probability of its appropriate use.

Review of Graduate Record Examinations—General Test by RICHARD M. JAEGER, Professor of Education and Director, Center for Educational Research and Evaluation, University of North Carolina at Greensboro, Greensboro, NC:

The General Test (called the Aptitude Test prior to October, 1982) of the Graduate Record Examinations (GRE) is described by the publisher as a test of developed verbal, quantitative, and analytic abilities that students have acquired over a long period of time. Recommended uses of the test include graduate school admissions decisions and fellowship awards, prediction of applicants' success in graduate school, and guidance and counseling of graduate students in selection of their courses of study.

The test is composed of seven separately timed, 30-minute sections, each in multiple-choice form, and yields three scores. An examinee's performance on two sections containing a mixture of antonym items, analogies items, sentence completion items, and reading comprehension items is used to produce a verbal score. A quantitative score is based on two additional sections that contain items requiring interpretation of sets of data, comparison of the magnitude of two factors, or solution of mathematical "word problems." Although the quantitative problems require no formal mathematics other than high school algebra and elementary visual geometry, the mathematical facility afforded by recent and continuing exposure to college courses in mathematics would provide examinees a clear advantage. An analytic score is derived from two test sections that contain analytical reasoning and logical reasoning items. The analytical reasoning items test examinees' abilities to recognize correct deductions and inferences about the structural relationships among a set of objects, based on given facts concerning the structure. Logical reasoning items test examinees' abilities to discriminate among correct and incorrect conclusions and deductions from stated arguments. A seventh section of the test, used for pretesting experimental items and for test equating, is not scored.

Because the analytic portion of the GRE-General Test was completely revised in October 1981 and limited evidence on the functioning and validity of new test items is available, the publisher considers this portion to be experimental. In all descriptive materials intended for examinees and test users, the publisher advised against the use of analytic scores for decision making. To emphasize this point, normative data on examinees' analytic scores are not provided on routine score reports. This reviewer finds the publisher's decision to include analytic scores on score reports and to provide normative data in the GRE Guide intended for test users somewhat puzzling, in view of the experimental status of the subtest. It appears that the publisher is facilitating use of the analytic scores for decision making while advising against such use.

The GRE General Test enjoys the widespread confidence of persons who make graduate school admissions decisions, as evidenced by more than 180,000 test administrations per year. Explanatory materials provided would-be test users and test-takers inspire such confidence by forthrightly describing the nature and structure of the test, what is known about its psychometric properties, and its apparent limitations. In many ways, the Technical Manual for the GRE is a model of good professional practice as prescribed by the 1974 *Standards for*

Educational and Psychological Tests. The test development process is described completely, as are essential details of test scaling, equating, reliability estimation, and validation. If not always resolved to the satisfaction of this reviewer, important questions concerning the speededness, validity, and appropriateness of the test for minority examinees are raised and addressed by the publisher. Test materials contain refreshing evidence of the publisher's concern about appropriate and inappropriate uses of the test. One characteristic of the Technical Manual that can be faulted is its age. It has not been updated since 1977 despite a major revision of the analytic portion of the test in 1981 and extensive research on the psychometric properties of the test during the last five years.

The Kuder-Richardson Formula 20 reliabilities of a recent (but unidentified) form of the GRE General Test are reported as .93 for the verbal score, .91 for the quantitative score, and .86 for the analytic score. Although the values for the operational portions of the test are quite respectable and support use of the test for individual decision-making, test users should expect reliabilities to be somewhat lower for the subpopulations of examinees that typically apply to particular graduate schools or degree programs. Data summarized by Goodison (1983) show that the standard deviations of scores of examinees intending to major in particular fields are as much as 20% smaller than corresponding standard deviations for the entire examinee population. As earlier reviewers have noted (6:461) it is unfortunate that alternate-forms estimates of reliability are not available for the GRE General Test. Despite the practical difficulties associated with two administrations of a 3¹/₂-hour test, the moderate speededness of the GRE General Test suggests that internal consistency measures might overestimate the true reliabilities of the subtests. Available evidence on the effect of speededness on these reliability estimates is indirect and not totally satisfying.

Virtually every author of a review of the Graduate Record Examinations has commented on the paucity of predictive validity evidence in support of the GRE General Test (4:293; 6:461; 7:667). Unfortunately, currently-available evidence is neither as extensive nor as compelling as would be desired for a test that affects the educational opportunities of as many students as does the GRE. In addition, data provided in the Technical Manual and the GRE Guide are often not clearly identified, making accurate interpretation difficult. Results of validity studies conducted prior to 1971 are summarized in the Technical Manual. Median predictive validity coefficients for the verbal score ranged from .02 to .36 across nine major fields. Corresponding statistics for the quantitative score ranged from .06 to .32. However, in combination with undergraduate grade point averages, the combined predictive validities of the GRE ranged from .32 to .56, and were substantially higher than corresponding coefficients for undergraduate grade point averages alone in most fields. Because labeling and discussion are incomplete, it is not clear whether composite coefficients apply to the GRE General Test alone or include scores on the GRE Subject Tests. The GRE Guide reports median validity coefficients for the verbal and quantitative tests alone, in combination, and combined with undergraduate grade point averages, based on studies conducted during three time periods. It must be a source of some concern to the publisher that median validities show a monotonically decreasing trend as a function of time period despite somewhat larger standard deviations of scores since the early 1970s. In combination, the verbal score, the quantitative score, and undergraduate grade point average had a median multiple correlation of about .45 with first-year graduate grade point average in studies conducted during 1952 to 1972. This figure dropped to about .39 in studies conducted between 1974 and 1976, and to .35 in studies conducted between 1979 and 1981. Burton and Turner (1983) report a median multiple correlation of .34 based on studies conducted during 1981 and 1982. Restriction of range in the most frequently used criterion (first-year graduate grade point average) due to grade inflation is a likely explanation.

Since predictive validity coefficients vary so widely across major fields, subpopulations, and settings, and because available validity evidence has not been organized by the publisher in a way that facilitates generalization to any particular setting, local validity studies of the GRE General Test are absolutely essential. Users must be cautious and judicious in their use of the GRE General Test in making admissions decisions until they have obtained clear evidence that examinees with superior performance on the test exhibit superior performance in the particular programs of study offered by the institution in question. Particular care should be exercised in making inferences based on the test performances of minority examinees. Differences between the mean test performances of black and white examinees are well in excess of a standard deviation on both the verbal and quantitative subtests (Goodison, 1983), and the standard deviations of scores of black examinees are somewhat smaller than those of white examinees, suggesting the possibility of lower validity coefficients. Available evidence in support of the predictive validities of the GRE for minority examinees is limited and indirect.

Of final concern is the utility of the GRE General Test to prospective graduate students. What do they, as examinees, receive as a direct benefit of their $29 payment to sit for the test? To this reviewer, it seems, not much. Students' interpretive reports consist solely of limited norms data. Students receive little information on their relative chances of admission or success in any given graduate program, despite the availability of a four-volume *Directory of Graduate Programs:* 1984 & 1985 that the publisher offers at additional cost. The direct guidance and counseling value of the GRE General Test is unnecessarily limited. Perhaps this is a concern that must be addressed by all publishers of admissions tests that are supported by direct charges to examinees.

In summary, the GRE General test assesses skills that are essential to success in many graduate programs. The subtests are highly reliable and appear to provide modest increments in predictive validity when used in conjunction with undergraduate grade point averages to predict examinees' first-year graduate grade point averages. The most widely used GRE competitor, the Miller Analogies Test, is more restricted in content, shows substantial correlation (typically in the low 80s) with the verbal subtest of the GRE General Test, and does not offer superior validity evidence. The GRE is, perhaps, the best available measure for predicting traditional criteria of graduate students' success. As the publisher states in all supporting documents, it should not be used as the sole determiner of admission to any graduate program.

(It is a pleasure to acknowledge the assistance of Ms. Donna Sundre in preparing this review.)

REVIEWER'S REFERENCES

Burton, N.W., & Turner, N. J. EFFECTIVENESS OF THE GRADUATE RECORD EXAMINATIONS FOR PREDICTING FIRST-YEAR GRADES. Princeton, NJ: Educational Testing Service, 1983.

Goodison, M. B. A SUMMARY OF DATA COLLECTED FROM GRADUATE RECORD EXAMINATIONS TEST TAKERS DURING 1981–1982. Princeton, NJ: Educational Testing Service, 1983.

DIRECTORY OF GRADUATE PROGRAMS: 1984 & 1985. Princeton, NJ: Educational Testing Service, 1984.

[449]

Grammatical Analysis of Elicited Language—Pre-Sentence Level. Hearing impaired children ages 3–6; 1983; GAEL-P; Simple Sentence Level (GAEL-S) and Complex Sentence Level (GAEL-C) also available; 3 sections (readiness skills, single words, word combinations) yielding 3 scores: comprehension, prompted production, imitated production; individual; 1 form; manual (81 pages); score sheet (4 pages); 1985 price data: $275 per complete kit; $5 per 25 score sheets; $15 per manual; administration time not reported; Jean S. Moog, Victoria J. Kozak, and Ann E. Geers; Central Institute for the Deaf.*

[450]

Griffiths Mental Development Scales. Ages 0–2, 2–8; 1951–78; 2 levels; distribution restricted to persons who qualify by attendance at an approved course, details may be obtained from distributor; Ruth Griffiths; Association for Research in Infant and Child Development [England]; distributed by The Test Agency [England]. (United States distributor: Test Center, Inc.)*

a) SCALE 1. Ages 0–2; 6 scores: locomotor, personal-social, hearing and speech, eye and hand, performance, total; individual; 1 form ('54); manual ('54, 229 pages); manual supplement for scales 1 and 2 ('78, 7 pages); record form ('55, 2 pages); record book (no date, 19 pages) for scales 1 and 2; 1983 price data: £58 per set of testing materials including 25 record forms (manual not included); 20p per record form; £6.80 per manual; [20–40] minutes.

b) SCALE 2. Ages 2–8; 7 scores: same as for *a* plus practical reasoning; individual; 1 form ('70); manual ('70, 188 pages); manual supplement for scales 1 and 2 ('78, 7 pages); record book (no date, 19 pages) for scales 1 and 2; 1983 price data: £63 per set of testing materials including a record book (manual not included); 42p per record book; £6.80 per manual; administration time not reported.

For review by C. B. Hindley of Scale 1, see 6:523 (4 references); for a review by Nancy Bayley of Scale 1, see 5:404 (3 references).

TEST REFERENCES

1. Griffiths, R. THE ABILITIES OF YOUNG CHILDREN: A COMPREHENSIVE SYSTEM OF MENTAL MEASUREMENT FOR THE FIRST EIGHT YEARS OF LIFE. London: Child Development Research Centre, 1970.

[451]

The Gross Geometric Forms Creativity Test for Children. Ages 3–12; 1982; 7 scores: form construction, name, action, color, embellishment, communicability, total; norms consist of means and standard deviations; norms for ages 3–6, 9–10, and 15 only; individual; 1 form; record form (no date, 3 pages); instruction manual (43 pages); 1982 price data: $32 per complete set including 30 record forms; $13.50 per 48 felt forms; $11.50 per 30 record forms; $13.50 per instruction manual; administration time not reported; Ruth Brill Gross, Bonnie Lepper Green, and Goldine Cohnberg Gleser; Stoelting Co.*

Review of Gross Geometric Forms Creativity Test for Children by PHILIP E. VERNON, Professor of Educational Psychology, University of Calgary, Calgary, Alberta, Canada:

At first sight the materials for Gross's Geometric Forms (GGF) test appear more attractive for young children, and more suitable for creative manipulation, than most of the nonverbal creative thinking subtests put forward by Torrance, Guilford, Wallach and Kogan, and others. However, one wonders whether the colored felt shapes, to be arranged on a board, may be more tricky for the small fingers of preschool and kindergarten children to handle than would thin plastic cards. Whether the materials also appeal to older children (grade 4 and up) may be queried.

The manual starts with a sensible and useful discussion of the nature of creativity and artistic abilities in children generally (not mature adults), and brings out the difficulties in reaching operational definitions of what to measure, or specifying appropriate criteria for validating any test in this area. This provides the basis for constructing the GGF, and for scoring the designs children produce. Previous tests have chiefly used the verbal medium, and have been applied with time limits, which stress quantity rather than quality of creative ideas. The GGF, like Wallach and Kogan's, is given individually in a game-like situation, without timing. The child is shown how to make a cat's face (from one circle and two triangles), and then urged to make something different of his/her own, using any of the five kinds of pieces and the three colors. Ten such trials are asked for, though children who are less responsive may produce a smaller number. It should be noted that the instructions imply that representations of objects or animals are required, rather than abstract designs which might have more aesthetic merit. But the latter would be more difficult to score objectively.

Each of the 10 trials is recorded by the tester, and scored later under 6 headings: (1) a new construction, not a repetition; (2) a name or title is given; (3) presence of activity (i.e., the object is doing something); (4) spontaneous verbalization of one or more colors; (5) embellishment (i.e., something further, relevant, shapes are added, and named); (6) communicability—clear relation of the constructed form to the name, and evidence of planning. (This is a complex quality, but detailed criteria are listed.)

Each feature is scored only 1 or 0, which appears wasteful when many gradations are possible (especially in 5 and 6). Presumably, though, less coarse scoring would also be more subjective. Thus a total score of 60 is possible, and children in grades 3 and 4 averaged around 30.

Interscorer reliabilities are good, ranging from .87 into the .90s. Also, the internal consistency of the 10 trials reaches about .85 (split half, or Cronbach's alpha). Nowhere are the correlations between the six score categories presented. Quite possibly some features (e.g., [2] Naming) are less effective measures of the total than others; it is entirely arbitrary to weight all of them equally. The authors admit that the stability (repeat reliability) may be low because young children in particular are likely to be quite changeable. This statistic is explored by Cronbach's Generalizability Coefficient, which averages .60 after a gap of about 12 weeks. But the coefficients are based on rather small numbers of 3- to 6-year-olds, and are much lower at 3 years, good at 4, and barely acceptable at 5 to 6. No data at all on reliability are given for children older than 6 1/2. Moreover, the stability for the Form score is low; for Naming and Embellishment, the coefficients are intermediate, and for Communicability quite high. In a 4th-grade group the retest reliability for total score after 1 year was .55.

Some 12 samples of children were tested, but they were too uneven in their age coverage, and doubtfully representative, to make norming possible. There is no evidence of any increase with age beyond 9 years, which seems to bear out the query raised in our opening paragraph as to whether the test is of much use in the upper half of elementary school. Several minor studies showed that type of administration (formal vs. game-like), achromatic vs. colored pieces, socioeconomic status, or race (black vs. white) had no significant effect on scores. Though there were some sex differences, they were inconsistent at different ages. But all such comparisons should be replicated with larger, more representative groups, and including older children.

Various approaches to validation were tried. Six artists were asked to rate the overall creativity of each production by groups of preschool and 3rd-grade children. Their averaged ratings correlated .84 with the total scores already awarded. What was more interesting was the 3rd-grade correlations with separate features: Form (.50), Naming (.29), Embellishment (.75), and Communicability (.61). As suggested earlier, Naming has little creative loading, and Activity and Color were probably even poorer since they are not listed. In the same sample, correlations of the GGF totals with later school Art marks were nonsignificant. But about half the sample were followed up to 7th grade, and here the correlation with Art grades reached .46. This has a probability of less than .05; thus it might or might not be replicated in another, larger, group.

The best result was a correlation of .71 with observational records of creative play among 3- to 5-year pupils in an English school. But here the *N* was only 10. Three comparisons were made at kindergarten, 1st, and 4th grades with a battery of cognitive tests, including some of the WPPSI or WISC subtests, Embedded Figures and Matching Familiar Figures, other tests of curiosity or divergent thinking, and Banta's "Dog and Bone" test of creativity. Seven (out of 29) correlations with GGF reached .31 to .37, but these mostly differed in different age groups. Dog and Bone attained this level in both the younger groups, the Curiosity test in the youngest only; WPPSI only in kindergarten, and EFT only in 1st grade. In the oldest group, all correlations except WISC Comprehension were negligible, and the test was not even related to some of Wallach and Kogan's battery.

Though the authors should be congratulated on their initiative and their extended enquiries into generalizability and validity, it would be difficult to agree with them that the results justify calling the test "a valid measure of creativity." However, they do warn that the test is "experimental and intended to be used primarily for research purposes." It is probably no worse, and possibly better than other tests available for 3- to 9-year-olds. But what is the point of trying to test at such an unstable period? The main practical value of divergent thinking tests is to pick out those upper elementary and secondary students whose cognitive styles differ so markedly from conventional convergent thinking that special enrichment or other methods for encouraging creativity are desirable. But this kind of provision is hardly necessary until schooling becomes more formal in, say, grades 3 to 9. The authors claim that the GGF is suitable for ages 3 to 12, but the data at 4th grade are disappointing, and there is no evidence beyond this level.

In conclusion, the GGF test marks an advance on other published tests for young children. Considerable care has been given to objective scoring, and interscorer reliability and internal consistency are high. But some of the six scorable features of creative productions are of doubtful value; and no norms are available. The repeat reliability over time is barely adequate, and the evidence for validity quite patchy. In the absence of further data, one cannot recommend it for testing beyond grades 3 to 4.

[452]

Group Embedded Figures Test. Ages 10 and over; 1971; GEFT; adaptation of the individually administered Embedded Figures Test; 1 form (18 pages); no specific manual; combined manual (32 pages) for this and Embedded Figures Test and Children's Embedded Figures Test; 1984 price data: $15 per 25 tests; $1 per scoring key; $5.25 per manual; $1.50 per specimen set (without manual); (20) minutes; Philip K. Oltman, Evelyn Raskin, Herman A. Witkin, and Stephen A. Karp (manual); Consulting Psychologists Press, Inc.*

See T3:1013 (88 references); for reviews by Leonard D. Goodstein and Alfred E. Hall, see 8:572 (47 references); see also T2:1201 (3 references); for references to reviews of the individual test, see 8:548.

TEST REFERENCES

1. Adams, V. M., & McLeod, D. B. The interaction of field dependence/independence and the level of guidance of mathematics instruction. JOURNAL FOR RESEARCH IN MATHEMATICS EDUCATION, 1979, 10, 347–355.

2. McLeod, D. B., & Adams, V. M. Aptitude-treatment interaction in mathematics instruction using expository and discovery methods. JOURNAL FOR RESEARCH IN MATHEMATICS EDUCATION, 1980, 11, 180–234.

3. O'Connor, E. J., & Barrett, G. V. Informational cues and individual differences as determinants of subjective perceptions of task enrichment. ACADEMY OF MANAGEMENT JOURNAL, 1980, 23, 697–716.

4. Nummedal, S. G., & Collea, F. P. Field independence, task ambiguity, and performance on a proportional reasoning task. JOURNAL OF RESEARCH IN SCIENCE TEACHING, 1981, 18, 255–260.

5. Ritchey, P. A., & LaShier, W. S., Jr. The relationship between cognitive style, intelligence, and instructional mode to achievement of college science students. JOURNAL OF RESEARCH IN SCIENCE TEACHING, 1981, 18, 41–45.

6. Tobacyk, J. J., Myers, H., & Bailey, L. Field-dependence, sensation-seeking, and preference for paintings. JOURNAL OF PERSONALITY ASSESSMENT, 1981, 45, 270–277.

7. Wareing, C. Cognitive style and developing scientific attitudes in the SCIS classroom. JOURNAL OF RESEARCH IN SCIENCE TEACHING, 1981, 18, 73–77.

8. Allen, M. J., Gargia, M., & Bealessio, L. B. Measurement of Rod-and-Frame Test performance. PERCEPTUAL AND MOTOR SKILLS, 1982, 54, 915–922.

9. Blaha, J. Predicting reading and arithmetic achievement with measures of reading attitudes and cognitive styles. PERCEPTUAL AND MOTOR SKILLS, 1982, 55, 107–114.

10. Docherty, D., & Boyd, D. G. Relationship of disembedding ability to performance in volleyball, tennis, and badmitton. PERCEPTUAL AND MOTOR SKILLS, 1982, 54, 1219–1224.

11. Jacobs, R. L., & Gedeon, D. V. The relationship of cognitive style to the frequency of proctor/student interactions and achievement in a PSI technology course. JOURNAL OF INDUSTRIAL TEACHER EDUCATION, 1982, 19(2), 18–26.

12. Lawson, A. E. The relative responsiveness of concrete operational seventh grade and college students to science instruction. JOURNAL OF RESEARCH IN SCIENCE TEACHING, 1982, 19, 63–77.

13. Loo, R. Cluster and principal components analyses of the Group Embedded Figures Test. PERCEPTUAL AND MOTOR SKILLS, 1982, 54, 331–336.

14. Lusk, E. J., & Wright, H. Baseline data on questions in Group Embedded Figures Test. PERCEPTUAL AND MOTOR SKILLS, 1982, 55, 546.

15. Panek, P. E. Relationship between field-dependence/independence and personality in older adult females. PERCEPTUAL AND MOTOR SKILLS, 1982, 54, 811–814.

16. Reardon, R., Jolly, E. J., McKinney, K. D., & Forducey, P. Field-dependence/independence and active learning of verbal and geometric material. PERCEPTUAL AND MOTOR SKILLS, 1982, 55, 263–266.

17. Stricker, L. J. Interpersonal competence instrument: Development and preliminary findings. APPLIED PSYCHOLOGICAL MEASUREMENT, 1982, 6, 69–81.

18. Weinbaum, J., Fayans, A., & Gilead, S. Consistency across modalities in self/nonself-segregation. PSYCHOLOGICAL REPORTS, 1982, 50, 835–838.

19. Adejumo, D. Effect of cognitive style on strategies for comprehension of prose. PERCEPTUAL AND MOTOR SKILLS, 1983, 56, 859–863.

20. Copeland, B. D. Cognitive style of female university students of visual art. PERCEPTUAL AND MOTOR SKILLS, 1983, 56, 439–442.

21. Copeland, B. D. The relationship of cognitive style to academic achievement of university art appreciation students. COLLEGE STUDENT JOURNAL, 1983, 17, 157–162.

22. Crow, L. W., & Piper, M. K. A study of the perceptual orientation of community college students and their attitudes toward science as they relate to science achievement. JOURNAL OF RESEARCH IN SCIENCE TEACHING, 1983, 20, 537–541.

23. DeSanctis, G., & Dunikoski, R. Group Embedded-Figures Test: Psychometric data for a sample of business students. PERCEPTUAL AND MOTOR SKILLS, 1983, 56, 707–710.

24. Flexer, B. K., & Roberge, J. J. A longitudinal investigation of field dependence-independence and development of formal operational thought. BRITISH JOURNAL OF EDUCATIONAL PSYCHOLOGY, 1983, 53, 195–204.

25. Hughes, R. N. Menstrual cycle influences on perceptual disembedding ability. PERCEPTUAL AND MOTOR SKILLS, 1983, 57, 107–110.

26. Lawson, A. E. Predicting science achievement: The role of developmental level, disembedding ability, mental capacity, prior knowledge, and beliefs. JOURNAL OF RESEARCH IN SCIENCE TEACHING, 1983, 20, 117–129.

27. Lusk, E. J., & Wright, H. Relation of scores on Group Embedded Figures Test and Myers-Briggs Type Indicator. PERCEPTUAL AND MOTOR SKILLS, 1983, 57, 1209–1210.

28. Mahlios, M. C., & D'Angelo, K. Group Embedded Figures Test: Psychometric data on children. PERCEPTUAL AND MOTOR SKILLS, 1983, 56, 423–426.

29. Moran, A. P. An Irish psychometric appraisal of the Group Embedded Figures Test. PERCEPTUAL AND MOTOR SKILLS, 1983, 57, 647–648.

30. Owens, W., & Limber, J. Lateral eye movement as a measure of cognitive ability and style. PERCEPTUAL AND MOTOR SKILLS, 1983, 56, 711–719.

31. Proudfoot, R. E. Hemispheric asymmetry for face recognition: Cognitive style and the "crossover" effect. CORTEX, 1983, 19, 31–41.

32. Reiss, D., & Oliveri, M. E. Sensory experience and family process: Perceptual styles tend to run in but not necessarily run families. FAMILY PROCESS, 1983, 22, 289–308.

33. Schmidt, B. J. The learning styles of students related to individualized typewriting instruction. THE DELTA PI EPSILON JOURNAL, 1983, 25, 41–51.

34. Sheckels, M. P., & Eliot, J. Preference and solution patterns in mathematics performance. PERCEPTUAL AND MOTOR SKILLS, 1983, 57, 811–816.

35. Stansfield, C., & Hansen, J. Field dependence-independence as a variable in second language cloze test performance. TESOL QUARTERLY, 1983, 17, 29–38.

36. Swinnen, S. Role of field dependence in perception of movements. PERCEPTUAL AND MOTOR SKILLS, 1983, 57, 319–325.

37. Thompson, B., Pitts, M. M., & Gipe, J. P. Use of the Group Embedded Figures Test with children. PERCEPTUAL AND MOTOR SKILLS, 1983, 57, 199–203.

38. Windsor, A. Sex and profession as determinants of field dependence. PERCEPTUAL AND MOTOR SKILLS, 1983, 57, 617–618.

39. Zuroff, D. C., Moskowitz, D. S., Wielgus, M. S., Powers, T. A., & Franko, D. L. Construct validation of the Dependency and Self-Criticism Scales of the Depressive Experiences Questionnaire. JOURNAL OF RESEARCH IN PERSONALITY, 1983, 17, 226–241.

40. Reardon, R., & Rosen, S. Psychological differentiation and the evaluation of juridic information: Cognitive and affective consequences. JOURNAL OF RESEARCH IN PERSONALITY, 1984, 18, 195–211.

41. Rierdan, J., & Koff, E. Age at menarche and cognitive functioning. BULLETIN OF THE PSYCHONOMIC SOCIETY, 1984, 22, 174–176.

[453]

Group Environment Scale. Group members and leaders; 1974–81; GES; a part of The Social Climate Scales (T3:2227); 10 scores: cohesion, leader support, expressiveness, independence, task orientation, self-discovery, anger and aggression, order and organization, leader control, innovation; no data on reliability for Forms I and E; no validity data; Form R ('74, 4 pages); Forms I (Ideal) and E (Expectations) (not available in a published version) may be reproduced by qualified investigators upon receipt of a written request; manual ('81, 25 pages); bibliography ('79, 23 pages); separate answer sheets must be used; 1983 price data: $4.25 per 25 reusable tests; $3.25 per 50 answer sheets; $1 per scoring stencil; $3 per 50 profiles; $5 per manual; $1.75 per bibliography; $6.25 per specimen set; administration time not reported; Rudolf H. Moos and Barrie Humphrey (test); Consulting Psychologists Press, Inc.*

For reviews by David P. Campbell and Robyn M. Dawes, see 8:573; see T3:1015 (1 reference); for a review of the Social Climate Scales, see 8:681.

TEST REFERENCES

1. Melnick, J., & Rose, G. S. Expectancy and risk taking propensity: Predictors of group performance. SMALL GROUP BEHAVIOR, 1979, 10, 389–401.

2. Fisher, A. C., Mancini, V. H., Hirsch, R. L., Proulx, T. J., & Stavrowsky, E. J. Coach-athlete interactions and team climate. JOURNAL OF SPORT PSYCHOLOGY, 1982, 4, 388–404.

3. Beutler, L. E., Frank, M., Schieber, S. C., Calvert, S., & Gaines, S. J. Comparative effects of group psychotherapies in a short-term inpatient setting: An experience with deterioration effects. PSYCHIATRY, 1984, 47, 66–76.

4. Schramski, T. G., Feldman, C. A., Harvey, D. R., & Holiman, M. A comparative evaluation of group treatments in an adult correctional facility. JOURNAL OF GROUP PSYCHOTHERAPY, PSYCHODRAMA, AND SOCIOMETRY, 1984, 36, 133–147.

Review of Group Environment Scale by MICHAEL J. CURTIS, Associate Professor of School Psychology, University of Cincinnati, Cincinnati, OH:

The Group Environment Scale is one of the nine Social Climate Scales developed by Moos and his associates and is intended to "measure the social-environmental characteristics of task-oriented, social, and psychotherapy and mutual support groups." The GES includes ten subscales which are reported to "assess three underlying domains, or sets of dimensions: The Relationship dimensions, the Personal Growth dimensions, and the System Maintenance and System Change dimensions."

The Relationship dimensions are reported to assess such characteristics as involvement in and commitment to the group, concern and friendship among members, as well as similar feelings of the leader for the group, and the extent to which freedom of action and expression of feelings are encouraged.

The Personal Growth dimensions are intended to assess such characteristics as the extent to which independent action and expression are encouraged, the encouragement of member revelations and discussions about personal information, and the degree to which the group tolerates and encourages open expression of negative feelings and intermember disagreement.

The System Maintenance and System Change dimensions reportedly assess the degree of formality and structure of the group and the explicitness of group rules and sanctions, as well as the degree to which group-related responsibilities are assigned to the leader and how much the group facilitates diversity and change in its own functions.

The GES includes 90 items which describe aspects of a group setting that reflect an emphasis on "interpersonal relationships (such as the degree of cohesion), on an area of personal growth (such as independence), or on the organizational structure of the group (such as leader control)." Respondents are asked to indicate whether the statements are true or not true of their group. Some examples of the items are: "There is a feeling of unity and cohesion in this group." "The leader doesn't expect much of the group." "Angry feelings are rarely expressed in this group." A scoring template allows for easy scoring of the answer sheet. Individual subscale scores or group averages can be converted to standard scores using tables provided in the manual.

The 1981 Manual is intended to replace the GES sections of the 1974 combined preliminary manual which also included information about the Family Environment Scale and the Work Environment Scale. Although noting that the preliminary manual can still be used for "administering and scoring the GES," the developers go on to state that "it is strongly recommended that users study the current manual before interpreting scale results." If the current manual contributes information which is necessary for the understanding and appropriate interpretation of the GES, then use of the GES sections of the preliminary manual should be emphatically discouraged. Providing added emphasis to this point is the fact that the preliminary manual included interpretive cautions because of the sparse normative data provided therein.

Items seem to have been developed logically and in a manner consistent with the conceptual framework for the larger social climate research series. The 1981 manual provides an explanation of the item development and selection process. The individual items seem to be constructed appropriately for easy use by potential group respondents. Development of the subscales is explained and appears to be sound. The manual provides a reference to be consulted for detailed information about psychometric criteria and item and subscale development. Unfortunately, this represents a general problem with the manual. Rather than presenting the potential user with the data pertinent to consideration of the GES firsthand, it is often necessary to pursue the information in other references. It should be included in the manual for ready examination.

There appears to be no empirical basis for the identification of the three categories or dimensions into which the subscales are grouped. The manual provides no explanation for their identification or use except for what would appear to be a rather arbitrary assignment of subscales. Distinctions between the dimensions are very unclear. For example, the Relationship dimensions and the Personal Growth dimensions are reported to assess the extent to which the group encourages "freedom of action and expression of feelings" and "open expression of negative feelings and intermember disagreement," respectively. Furthermore, the three sets of dimensions fail to contribute in any meaningful way to the functional usefulness of the GES. For example, three illustrative profile interpretations presented in the manual reflect no benefit from reference to the dimensions.

There is progress reflected in the current manual over the earlier preliminary version in terms of the inclusion of some additional normative data. On the other hand, the lack of a sound empirical base continues to be a serious flaw. No validity data are presented. All pertinent normative data relate only to Form R. Data pertaining to Form I are described as "preliminary." No data are reported for Form E. Form E is intended to assess what individuals "expect a group milieu to be like." Form I was developed to assess the types of group settings that individuals "would ideally like." The two forms represent a rewording of the items and instructions for Form R in order to assess the expectations or preferences of individuals in terms of group settings. Although Forms I and E "are not available in a published version....The publisher will usually authorize qualified investigators to reproduce these copyrighted items upon receipt of a written request." Any use of Forms I or E should be for research purposes only. The statement in the manual that "Form E can be useful in group placement to identify the expectations of patients who are about to enter a psychotherapy or mutual support group and to help prepare them for group membership" is shocking in view of the total absence of any normative data or other vital information about the form in the manual.

On face value, the GES appears to be sensible and credible. It benefits from the strong conceptual foundation of the social climate scale series. To those who are experienced in group leadership, the individual items will probably reflect strong face validity. However, there continues to be a lack of adequate empirical evidence to substantiate the functional value of the GES. Practical applications for other than very general purposes would not be justified.

Review of Group Environment Scale by ROBERT J. ILLBACK, Director of Student Services, Fort Knox Dependent Schools, Fort Knox, KY:

The Group Environment Scale, Form R (GES) is a 90-item scale for group members and leaders which purports to measure "social-environmental characteristics of task-oriented, social, and psychotherapy and mutual support groups." It encompasses three basic dimensions: Relationships, Personal Growth, and System Maintenance and System Change. Relationship subscales include Cohesion, Leader Support, and Expressiveness. Personal Growth Subscales include Independence, Task Orientation, Self-Discovery, and Anger and Aggression. System Maintenance and System Change subscales include Order and Organization, Leader Control, and Innovation.

The GES was developed by Moos and associates as part of a series of social climate scales to assess the salient aspects of various environments (such as a group), particularly as they impinge upon and moderate human functioning in that environment. Parallel scales are available to measure similar dimensions in treatment settings, institutions, educational environments and community settings.

Underlying all of these scales is the assumption that settings have unique "personalities," which can be described and measured. The purposes suggested for such measurement are numerous, and include: describing the group environment to both participants and non-participants, comparing the group to other social environments, evaluating changes in the group over time, relating changes in the group to their impact on members and environments external to the group, planning clinical and social interventions, selecting and improving group environments, enhancing clinical case descriptions, increasing person-environment congruence, and making cross-cultural comparisons.

Accompanying the GES are three primary sources of information: the GES Manual, a booklet by Moos entitled *The Social Climate Scales: An Overview*, and an annotated bibliography of relevant research. Additionally, Moos' numerous books and publications are adequately referenced, and these serve as further background (e.g., Moos, 1974). Taken together, these sources provide most of the data necessary to evaluate the GES, and this can be seen as a considerable strength. Also, the manual itself is greatly improved over the 1974 version. It is eminently readable, even for non-measurement specialists, and provides relatively detailed descriptions of the theoretical and practical rationale for the scale, test development procedures, normative characteristics, reliability and validity data, and ongoing research. Suggestions for interpretation are also provided.

Test administration directions are simple and clear. The GES is a straightforward paper and pencil test which can be administered orally to assure understanding. One concern here is the lack of data regarding readability level for the scale, and potential users may wish to review it with this in mind. Scoring is equally simple, and is accomplished with a template overlay. Raw scores are aggregated by subscale and converted to a standard score using tables which are relatively easy to read and understand.

With regard to normative data, the manual describes a sample composed of 130 groups and leaders from 112 groups, a total which includes data from the test development samples. This is a potential problem, as the item pool was substantially larger and less refined during the development phase. A larger problem is the lack of sampling data. The authors do not give the precise number of cases included in the sample, only the number of groups from which scores were obtained. Also, the procedures used for sampling the norm groups are unknown (stratified random versus convenience sample), and the lack of information about the social and cultural characteristics of this group renders interpretation problematic. The manual does provide information which enables users to derive standard scores, and measures of central tendency and variability are given. However, the narrative describing this process is insufficient and may be confusing to some. It is unclear whether the norms tables represent linear transformations or normalized scores.

Two special forms of the scale are described, Form I (Ideal) and Form E (Expectations). Neither is available in published form, but they can be obtained from the authors. Each represents a reworded version of Form R, and they purport to measure ideal and expectancy perceptions of the group, requiring a future-orientation and suspension of the current state of affairs in the group by the respondent. While there may be some face validity to such measurement, there is no compelling evidence for the use of these forms. Means and standard deviations for a sample of 608 are provided for Form I, but there are no other data provided about the essential psychometric characteristics of either form. Moreover, research is needed on the clinical utility and appropriateness of such discrepancy comparisons across forms. Thus, Forms I and E should only be seen as research instruments at this point in time.

With regard to the technical characteristics of the scale, reliability data and some limited validity data are presented. The GES appears to be adequately reliable. Internal consistency data for the 10 subscales (using coefficient alpha) for a sample of 246 respondents reveal subscale values ranging from .62 to .86, with the average in the mid .70s. No value is given for the total scale, but this presumably would be considerably higher. The authors correctly state that these are acceptable. Test-retest reliability coefficients ($N = 63$) at a 1-month interval range from .65 to .87 for the separate subscales, with no value cited for the total scale. However, profile stability studies are cited (Brill, 1979; Duncan & Brill, 1977; and Menard, 1974, 1976) which reveal stability coefficients of .92 at 4 months, .91 at 8 months, .84 at 12 months, and .78 at 24 months.

The adequacy of validation data is another matter. Item-subscale correlations are moderate. The subscales themselves appear to be relatively independent in terms of their reported intercorrelations. The authors also cite the variability of subscale scores across task-oriented, social and recreational, and psychotherapy and mutual support groups in expected directions as evidence of construct validity. However, meaningful and detailed validation studies are not in evidence. Test users must base their decisions about validity on three brief clinical case studies cited in the manual and a small set of difficult-to-retrieve and rather limited studies cited in a reference list. Taken as a whole, none of these contribute to the validation of the scale in a meaningful way. Confidence in the validity of the scale would be enhanced by research relating GES scores to the behavior of members and leaders using observational and/or ethnographic methods. Also, factor analytic research would help to clarify underlying constructs. The authors should more specifically state the limits of interpretation and generalizability imposed by the unavailability of validity data.

Overall, the GES represents a substantial contribution to the technology of group measurement. It is firmly grounded in theory and research, and its potential usefulness is especially significant given the complexity of assessing group and organizational variables. Nonetheless, the utility of the GES is constrained by the lack of validity data and confidence in its generalizability. It should be used cautiously and judiciously, and in conjunction with other measures. More specifically, test users need to be able to conceptualize about social climate and group and organizational functioning, and to recognize what scores on this measure may mean in relation to other individual, group, and organizational data (e.g., behavioral observations, organizational structure). Users will additionally need to decide whether the GES can accurately and meaningfully characterize their particular group(s). It is further recommended that users cautiously evaluate both item and subscale data for their own group(s) in drawing inferences about current status and change, using both norm-referenced and clinically-derived criteria.

REVIEWER'S REFERENCES

Menard, R. Le climat social dans les equipes de reeducation de Boscoville. Groupe de Recherche sur L'Inadaptation Juvenile, University of Montreal, Montreal, Canada, 1974.

Moos, R. H. Evaluating treatment environments: A social ecological approach. New York: Wiley, 1974.

Menard, R. Le climat social dans une institution pour jeunes delinquants: Boscoville. Groupe de Recherche sur L'Inadaptation Juvenile, University of Montreal, Montreal, Canada, 1976.

Duncan, B., and Brill, R. Staff team climates and treatment unit environments. Boys' Farm Research Project, Groupe de Recherche sur L'Inadaptation Juvenile, University of Montreal, Montreal, Canada, 1977.

Brill, R. Development of milieus facilitating treatment. Final report No. 4. Boys' Farm Research Project, Group de Recherche sur L'Inadaptation Juvenile, University of Montreal, Montreal, Canada, 1979.

[454]

Group Inventory for Finding Creative Talent. Grades K–2, 3–4, 5–6; 1976–80; GIFT; overall score plus 3 dimension scores: imagination, independence, many interests; norms consist of means and standard deviations; 1 form ('80, 4 pages) for each of 3 levels: primary, elementary, upper elementary; manual ('80, 17 pages); 1983 price data: $30 per 30 test booklets and scoring service (scoring must be done by publisher); $7 per specimen set; Spanish, French, Hebrew, and German editions available; (20–45) minutes; Sylvia B. Rimm; Educational Assessment Service, Inc.*

See T3:1016 (1 reference).

TEST REFERENCES

1. Rimm, S., Davis, G. A., & Bien, Y. Identifying creativity: A characteristics approach. GIFTED CHILD QUARTERLY, 1982, 26, 165–171.

Review of Group Inventory for Finding Creative Talent by PATRICIA L. DWINELL, Coordinator of Evaluation and Testing, Division of Developmental Studies, University of Georgia, Athens, GA:

The Group Inventory for Finding Creative Talent (GIFT) was designed to screen elementary school students for programs for the creatively gifted by identifying those students with attitudes and values related to creativity. The developer encourages users to combine the results of GIFT with other identification procedures for selecting students for programs.

Three levels of GIFT are available—primary for grades K to 2 (32 items), elementary for grades 3 to 4 (34 items), and upper elementary for grades 5 to 6 (33 items). Twenty-five items are common to each form. Vocabulary appears appropriate; however, the inventory can be read to students who do not have the reading ability and words can be explained. Students give "yes" or "no" responses to personality and biographical statements, some of which are worded in a non-creative direction. Test booklets are attractive and directions are clearly written in each booklet. There is no time limit to complete the inventory.

The manual states that GIFT norms are based on "over 8,000 children stratified according to grade" representing five geographical regions throughout the United States and varied backgrounds such as rural, urban, suburban, minority and white. No other information regarding norms is given in the manual. Inventories must be sent to the publisher for scoring. Percentile scores and Normal Curve Equivalent scores are provided for each student.

Split-half reliabilities were .80, .86, and .88 for primary, elementary, and upper elementary, respectively. For the kindergarten age, the author states that reliability coefficients were not "acceptably high." The test-retest reliability coefficient of .56 over a 6-month interval is disquieting.

To establish content validity, the personality and biographical characteristics were based on descriptions of creative persons given by authors of creativity instruments. All of the instruments researched for characteristics appear appropriate; five of the instruments have been used extensively with children. The main characteristics assessed by GIFT include curiosity, independence, flexibility, perseverance, and breadth of interests. However, no other information is given about the selection of items such as the number of items in each category or the number of personality versus biographical type items.

Criterion-related validity was based primarily on correlating inventory scores with a composite score consisting of three criteria—teacher ratings of creativeness and experimenter ratings of short stories and ratings of pictures. Teachers rated students on their verbal, musical, or artistic expression of creative ideas. The expressions of ideas through stories and pictures were rated according to specific criteria which are presented in the manual. Interrater reliability for stories and pictures ranged between .75 and .96. Validation studies are cited for diverse student populations, both national and international. With the one exception of a small group of primary students, validity correlations ranged between .20 and .54 and were statistically significant. Another cited validity study compares the mean scores of students identified as gifted with those of students designated as "normal." Although the assumption that the gifted students were also creatively gifted may be erroneous, the difference between the scores was significantly different, with the mean scores of gifted students being higher.

GIFT does not appear to be an especially strong instrument for identifying creativity; however, it is brief and easy to administer. When used with other identification procedures it can be considered useful and fairly valid for selecting students of varied backgrounds and cultures to participate in special programs which would encourage creative behavior. The lack of information in the manual regarding norms and the scoring procedure appear to be definite limitations to its use.

Review of Group Inventory for Finding Creative Talent by DAN WRIGHT, School Psychologist, Ralston Public Schools, Ralston, NE:

The specimen set provided by the publisher of the Group Inventory for Finding Creative Talent (GIFT) includes a 12-page manual, samples of response forms for each level, and a reprint of a review of studies involving the GIFT. Response forms are simply 8 1/2 x 11 sheets folded over to make small, 4-page booklets. Students respond to 32 to 34 questions (depending on level) on three pages by filling in small circles marked "yes" or "no." Although users are instructed to read the items to students in grades K to 2, group administration at that level will no doubt involve practical difficulties; users will probably wish to administer this level individually or to small groups.

The GIFT can only be scored by returning the response forms to the publisher. Although this understandably protects the publisher's control of otherwise easily-reproduced response forms, it introduces a potentially annoying delay. The manual indicates a typical administration-to-report lag of one month, but indicates rush handling will be attempted on request. An example of the report of results, requested by the reviewer, consists of a printout of raw scores, percentiles, and normal curve equivalents for the total score for each student, as well as raw scores and stanines for the three dimension scores. Brief guidelines for interpretation are also included.

Apparently a great deal of study has been devoted to documenting the psychometric properties of GIFT, but the currently available manual does not present the results adequately. Very brief reference is made to what may be commendable norms based on 8,000 students, presumably derived to ensure urban-rural, geographical, and minority representation. However, no information is provided regarding selection procedures, proportion of representation, or relevant group differences. Split-half reliability coefficients, based on an unspecified sample and corrected with the Spearman-Brown formula, are minimally acceptable, ranging from .80 to .88 across levels. Test-retest reliability for 30 core items in one study over a 6-month interval was reported as .56.

If the manual's descriptions of norms and reliability are compromised mainly by omission or ambiguity, its treatment of scale validity suffers even more serious difficulties. Most of this difficulty relates to the subjective and ephemeral nature of attempts to define creativity, and leaves the author at cross-purposes. For example, it is claimed that the GIFT measures attributes not assessed by I.Q. or achievement tests; yet the author appeals to small but statistically significant mean differences on the GIFT between samples of "normal" students and those identified as gifted by more conventional criteria as evidence of its validity. Similarly, the author overstates as "modest" the correlations of GIFT scores with teacher ratings of creativity and judges' scoring of students' pictures and drawings for creativity, both methods with serious limitations in themselves. Finally, the GIFT yields three dimension scores, presumably based on the results of factor analytic studies, with no explanation of their derivation or utility.

As a self-report inventory intended to assess creativity with elementary students, the GIFT appears to be alone in its class at this time. A much more extensive manual should be made available to users, with complete information on norms and reliability. More data are sorely needed on criterion-related validity. Although the GIFT presently represents an ambitious and industrious effort in a novel direction, it is at most a screening device of unproven validity, best employed as an adjunct to more conventional methods of identifying children of exceptional ability.

[455]

Group Inventory For Finding Interests. Grades 6–9, 9–12; 1979–80; GIFFI; for screening the creatively gifted; 5 dimension scores: creative arts and writing, challenge-inventiveness, confidence, imagination, many interests; 2 levels: Level I ('78, 4 pages), Level II ('79, 4 pages); manual ('80, 10 pages); 1984 price data: $40 per 30 test booklets and scoring service (scoring must be done by publisher); $7 per specimen set; Spanish and Hebrew editions available; (20–40) minutes; Sylvia B. Rimm and Gary A. Davis; Educational Assessment Service, Inc.*

TEST REFERENCES

1. Rimm, S., Davis, G. A., & Bien, Y. Identifying creativity: A characteristics approach. GIFTED CHILD QUARTERLY, 1982, 26, 165–171.

Review of Group Inventory For Finding Interests by M. O'NEAL WEEKS, Professor of Family Studies, University of Kentucky, Lexington, KY:

"The Group Inventory For Finding Interests (GIFFI) was developed in order to provide an easy-to-administer, reliable, and valid instrument for use in screening junior and senior high school students for programs for the creatively gifted," state the authors in the opening sentence of the manual. Whether this has been accomplished in this inventory is open to debate. To attempt to identify such an elusive trait as "creativity" through the use of a simple, 60-item, Likert-type paper and pencil inventory may require more creativity than one can reasonably expect of any two inventory authors. The GIFFI claims to "identify students with attitudes and interests usually associated with creativity," including independence, curiosity, perseverance, flexibility, breadth of interests, risk-taking, sense of humor, and other such traits and attitudes. To be able to measure a student's possession of all these attitudes with a simple 60-item scale seems unrealistic to this reviewer. Even to a sixth-grader it would seem to be obvious how one "should" answer certain items in order to appear creative. In fairness to the authors, they do point out in the manual that more than one identification procedure should be used to identify creative students, including the GIFFI in combination with the impressions of teachers, parents and/or peers.

There appear to be several incongruences between the manual and the inventories. For example, the teacher's instructions include the option of reading the items to the class if students in the class have reading problems and then one of the items measuring creativity asks for the students' response to the following: "I read a lot of books" (Level 1) or "I read over 20 books a year" (Level 2). Also the manual suggests that GIFFI is useful with all ethnic and SES groups, but several of the items impress this writer as being very middle-to-upper-middle class oriented (e.g., "I like to attend concerts," "I have taken art, dancing or music lessons outside of school because I wanted to," "I own painting and drawing supplies," "My parents read more books than most parents," "My mother or father likes to visit art galleries and museums," "I have both classical and folk music in my record collection."). These and other items seem to reflect a very clear class/culture bias, which may be more what this inventory measures than creativity.

To the developers' credit they do insist in the manual that this and all test scores should be used with caution and should be used to screen children "into" and not "out of" special programs for the gifted. This reviewer appreciates their point but also worries that too many teachers/administrators ignore such admonitions and rely too heavily on such inventories to screen children out as much as to screen them in.

Among the other problems this reviewer has with the GIFFI, two stand out: First, the manual provides no information about scoring and/or interpreting the inventory. Instead, the completed inventories must be mailed to Educational Assessment Service, Inc., to be scored and returned with percentile scores for each student along with Normal Curve Equivalent scores. There is no indication why such a simple, short inventory must be returned to the publishers for scoring. This makes use of the inventory unnecessarily expensive and its use cumbersome and time-consuming. The other problem has to do with the relatively low correlations reported in the criterion-related validity studies. Criterion-related validity was established by correlating inventory scores with outside measures of creativity, mainly teacher ratings of creativity and experimenter ratings of short stories. Depending on the population used, the correlations between these outside measures and the GIFFI ranged from .21 to .68, with most falling below .50. While all the correlations were significantly greater than zero at the .05 level of significance, correlations this low are less than impressive for establishing confidence in the inventory's validity.

The internal consistency of the GIFFI is quite high as measured by the Hoyt reliability correlation (.88 for GIFFI 1 and .94 for GIFFI 2). The authors attempted to establish the construct validity of GIFFI by including items dealing with personality traits of creative individuals as assessed by a number of other creativity measures, including the Starkweather Preschool Tests, Getzels and Jackson Creativity Tests, Torrance Tests of Creativity, Pennsylvania Assessment of Creative Tendency, Creativity Scale of the Adjective Checklist, Children's Reactive Curiosity Scale, and others. However, there is no indication that any research was done to determine relationships between the GIFFI and any of these other inventories. Information on the normative populations is very limited and general in nature. The only specific information includes the *N* of the population and criterion-related validity correlations for different rural, urban, suburban, and small city groupings.

In conclusion, as the developers of GIFFI concede in their manual, "creativity is a subtle characteristic which is difficult to identify." Unfortunately, GIFFI does little to make creativity any more specific or any more identifiable than it has been. The problems cited above plus the total absence of information on how the inventory is scored and interpreted leaves one with the impression that for all their effort the developers of GIFFI have only added their stirring to the already muddied waters of creativity. There is very little to recommend this scale as one that measures what it purports to measure, viz., creativity. Those who need to measure creativity are left to their own creativity in their attempts to do so.

[456]

Group Literacy Assessment. End of junior school and beginning of secondary school; 1981; GLA; 3 scores: proof-reading, fill the gaps, total; 1 form (2 pages); manual (16 pages); 1983 price data: £1.50 per 20 test forms; £1.50 per manual; £1.75 per specimen set; 16(30) minutes; Frank A. Spooncer; Hodder & Stoughton Educational [England].*

Review of Group Literacy Assessment by GAIL E. TOMPKINS, Assistant Professor of Education, The University of Oklahoma, Norman, OK:

The Group Literacy Assessment (GLA) is a short reading and writing test with two sections. A story about two children who help the victim of a car accident is continued through both sections. In the first section, students proofread a story. They are directed to identify and correct the spelling errors. There are two types of spelling errors in the story: (1) homonyms (i.e., ant–aunt, sea–see), and (2) letter changes (i.e., horse–house, expulsion–explosion). The second section involves a modified cloze test. Students are directed to decipher a partially burned letter which, according to the story, belonged to the accident victim. Words and parts of words are missing from the letter. The students are to fill in the missing words to complete the letter.

The purpose of the GLA is to sample children's overall efficiency with written material. The author states that "the rationale of the test reflects recent changes in the assessment of reading, and in the overall approach to literacy." In contrast with traditional reading tests in which students read words in isolation and mark multiple choice answers to isolated sentences, this test involves students with reading and writing in a meaningful context. In this test, students "use and combine perceptual, contextual, and grammatical cues offered by continuous prose. It also tests their ability to note particular details, to carry information in short-term memory, and to make judgments about plausible inferences." The test also provides information about students' achievement in spelling. Furthermore, the author emphasizes the Assessment's value in providing "reasonably accurate information about slower learners."

The Assessment is designed for British students, ages 10 1/2 to 12 1/2, to be used during their transfer from junior to secondary schools. For American children, the GLA seems to be appropriate for use with sixth graders. Some words (i.e., petrol, lorry, ploughed) and phrases (i.e., "you will be very silly" instead of "you will be very sorry") will be unfamiliar to American students. These differences make it difficult for teachers to use this test with American students without making some modifications.

The test is contained on the front and back of a single sheet of paper. The test sheet is well arranged and includes a picture to set the stage for the story. There is a definite attempt to make the test attractive and motivating for all students. There are 36 test items in the first section of the test and 32 items in the second section.

The manual is brief, clearly written, and easy to follow. Adequate directions are provided for administering and scoring the GLA.

The GLA is group-administered. There is a time limit of eight minutes for each of the two sections. According to the manual, the time required to administer the Assessment is less than 30 minutes; the total time to administer and score the test for an average sized class is approximately 1 1/2 hours. Scoring is easily accomplished with the answer sheet provided in the manual. Points are given for each correct answer. Scores for the two sections are combined to provide the raw score. Charts are provided in the manual for translating the raw scores into standard scores (mean of 100, standard deviation of 15) and reading age equivalents. In addition, the reading age scores are divided into four categories. These categories define the limits for students who are (*a*) very competent in literacy skills, (*b*) competent, (*c*) in need of help to become literate, and (*d*) in urgent need of help. According to the manual, students falling into the last two categories should receive additional diagnostic testing and remedial instruction as needed.

Background information on test construction and a list of criteria used in developing test items are included in the manual. The GLA was standardized in 1979–1980 using approximately 7,000 students from a London borough. In order to establish the test's validity, students' performance on the GLA was compared to their performance on one or more of the following tests: Daniels and Diack's Graded Test of Reading Experience, Spooncer's Group Reading Assessment, NFER Sentence Reading 1, and NFER Primary Reading 2. Correlation coefficients ranged from .78 to .86. Reliability was calculated using the split-half method. A sample of 188 students was used. Values of .91 and .92 were found for sections one and two respectively, and a value of .95 was found for the full test. The reading age equivalents were calculated by calibrating raw scores on the GLA with reading ages given by established reading tests using a method of equivalent percentiles.

In summary, the GLA presents an interesting attempt to incorporate new theories about the reading process into a group test. The Assessment seems to accomplish its purpose, which is to sample children's overall literacy skills. The test is cost efficient because the test is contained on a single sheet of paper. In addition, the test can be administered and scored quickly and easily. Unfortunately, because of language differences some modifications are necessary before the GLA can be used with American students.

[457]

Group Mathematics Test, Second Edition. Ages 6.6–8.5 and older underachieving students; 1970–80;

GMT; 3 scores: oral, computation, total; no reliability data or norms for subscores; Forms A, B ('70, 2 pages); manual ('80, 25 pages); 1983 price data: £1.50 per 20 tests; £1.25 per manual; £1.50 per specimen set; (40–50) minutes; D. Young; Hodder & Stoughton Educational [England].*

For a review by John Cook of an earlier edition, see 8:273.

Review of Group Mathematics Test, Second Edition, by MARY KAY CORBITT, Assistant Professor of Mathematics and Curriculum and Instruction, University of Kansas, Lawrence, KS:

The Group Mathematics Test, Second Edition, is designed for use with students in mixed ability classes in the last year of the British Infants school, and with "backward" (underachieving) students (ages 6.6 to 14.10). The purpose of the test is not made explicit, although it is described as intended for "general assessment" purposes, and scores are interpreted as being indicative of the student's knowledge of basic mathematical concepts and skills.

Each of the two forms of the GMT consists of four subtests, two (of 15 exercises each) that are pictorial with questions read aloud by the test administrator, and two (15 exercises each) that consist of written computation exercises. The content tested on the pictorial items includes vocabulary (e.g., twice as many, middle-sized), knowledge of shapes, place value concepts, simple fractions, telling time, students' understanding of addition and subtraction, and simple multiplication and division situations. The written computation subtests, one covering addition and one covering subtraction of whole numbers, range in complexity from exercises testing knowledge of basic number facts to knowledge of algorithms for adding or subtracting two- and three-digit numbers.

The manual that accompanies the test contains explicit instructions for administering and scoring the test. "Standardized" scores, referred to as "mathematics quotients," are found in tables. Derivation of the quotients is not explained, but they are apparently functions of both the raw score on the GMT and the child's chronological age. A separate table of "mathematics ages" is also given, although the author points out the limited usefulness of this scale.

The author suggests that teachers rank children according to raw scores on the GMT to see "if the relative success of the children is in accordance with the teacher's own order of merit." He then suggests ranking them by quotients. Students with low quotients may be in need of remedial help, although the author cautions against automatic assumptions about students' deficiencies. Quotients are recognized as being a useful basis of comparison of students' progress across time, as well as a basis for comparing students within a single class.

The manual provides some information about the groups on which the norms are based, and explains revisions in the norms from the first to the second editions of the test. Norms are given for total scores only. Evidence of "satisfactory" concurrent and predictive validity is claimed by presenting correlations between the GMT and several other standardized tests. These range from .63 to .86. The author indicates that teachers may judge the content validity for themselves, but observes that a general factor (general "intelligence"?) may account for a large portion of variance in GMT scores. Standard errors of measurement are given for various age and score levels and range from 2.5 to 3.2.

The author appears to have adhered to most recommendations about the kind of information that should be included in a test manual, and this attention to detail is commendable. It is unfortunate, however, that the content domain of the test is not better specified than it is, and that no information is given on how the "standardized" scores were derived. These omissions put the potential user in a somewhat uncertain and uncomfortable position regarding interpretation of scores. This problem is compounded if the potential user is unfamiliar with the terminology of English schools (e.g., "infant") and the mathematics curriculum of the corresponding classrooms. These factors perhaps should be considered by potential users in the United States.

Review of Group Mathematics Test, Second Edition, by DOUGLAS H. CRAWFORD, Chairman of Curriculum Studies, Faculty of Education, Queen's University, Kingston, Ontario, Canada:

This second edition of the Group Mathematics Test is unchanged from the first edition of 1970, except that the first two oral items are not scored; they are simply used as practice examples. Many of the comments made in the review in *The Eighth Mental Measurements Yearbook* (8:273) are still appropriate, and generally endorsed by the present reviewer.

The test covers a range of basic mathematical concepts in two sections. The first half is a set of 15 oral questions (including the two practice ones), together with 15 computation questions involving addition of two whole numbers. The second part again has 15 oral questions (slightly more difficult), accompanied this time by 15 "subtraction" computations. The oral questions relate primarily to pictorial situations, which are both varied and interesting; in the judgment of the present reviewer, they have high face validity and should prove enjoyable to the pupil. The test is envisaged as suitable also for "backward" secondary children defined as "pupils in ordinary schools with an expected median quotient of less than 85."

Except for relatively minor points (e.g., the persistence of horizontal format for all computations, and lack of provision for entering chronological age), the layout of the test is clear. The administration and scoring instructions are unambiguous, making the use of the test expeditious and trouble-free for the classroom teacher. Clear procedures for converting from raw scores to either "mathematics ages" or "mathematics quotients" are also provided.

On the debit side, it is surprising that no content changes have been made since the first edition. In particular, elementary school mathematics has been much influenced by the Nuffield Project and at least one graph-related question and possibly one on the geometry of three-dimensional objects might well have been included. For one or two oral questions, lack of clarity is a problem. However, the range and distribution of items, their difficulty levels, and the degree of clarity of the oral section are still highly commendable.

There are two forms of the test, a feature which further facilitates reliable administration of the test. An informal examination of the two forms suggests a high degree of equivalence, which is supported by item analyses carried out during test development.

Standardization of the second edition appears similar to that for the first, being based on some 3,175 cases. The details given, however, are insufficient to evaluate readily how the samples were chosen, or what their size relative to present populations were. Some evidence is adduced "for satisfactory concurrent and predictive validity for the GMT" by reporting correlations of .85 and .86 with two other mathematics tests developed by the same publisher, and with the Non-Readers Intelligence Test (.83). Sample size was very small ($N = 83$) and inferences cannot be made with much certainty. Standard errors of measurement are given for various age and score levels and range from 2.5 to 3.2 Median gains on retesting using the parallel form, again for various age and score levels, ranged from –.1 to 3.6, with a median of 1.5. Because of the small numbers of students tested, these data can only be taken as suggestive.

In summary, the GMT is a useful survey test which covers many of the basic mathematics content areas experienced by children in the 6 to 8 years range. Although unchanged since 1970, it still has high face validity, particularly in the English school system. Its value in this reviewer's judgment is that it is readily administered in one classroom period, is easily scored and interpreted, and can yield a quick and valid indication of the overall attainment of children in this age range. All of these are features that should be of particular value in identifying areas or concepts which need further study or attention. The meaning of the derived scores, however, should be treated with caution in light of inadequate data on the standardization procedures.

[458]

Group Reading Test, Second Edition. Ages 6–5 to 12–10; 1968–80; identical with earlier edition ('68) except for new norms; Forms A, B ('69, 2 pages); manual ('80, 33 pages); 1982 price data: £1.25 per set of 20 tests; 75p per scoring template; £1.25 per manual; £1.50 per specimen set; 13(20) minutes; D. Young; Hodder & Stoughton Educational [England].*

For a review by Ralph D. Dutch of the original edition, see 8:729.

TEST REFERENCES

1. Tizard, J., Schofield, W. N., & Hewison, J. Collaboration between teachers and parents in assisting children's reading. THE BRITISH JOURNAL OF EDUCATIONAL PSYCHOLOGY, 1982, 52, 1–15.

Review of Group Reading Test, Second Edition by PATRICK GROFF, Professor of Education, San Diego State University, San Diego, CA:

The Group Reading Test (GRT), published in England, is said to be suitable for children ages 6–5 to 8–10 and can be used with children to age 12–10 if they are believed to be "below-average." The possible scores on the GRT are translated into "reading ages" from 5–4 to 10–0.

The GRT consists of 45 items presented on the front and back sides of a single 8 x 11-inch sheet. The front side of the GRT includes the first 15 items of the test and appears easy to administer. Here children are led to understand its demands from drawings of objects or animals, the names of which they must select from three-, four-, or five-word multiple choice displays. Items 16 through 45 of the GRT are more difficult for the child to follow for they require the pupil to maintain his or her eye fixations over an 8-inch horizontal span in order to select a word which completes a sentence or is a synonym (e.g., Cows give—mud many more make milk mouse 16). Adding to the perceptual task here is the placement of the numbers of each line on the wrong side, i.e., the right-hand side of the page. The narrowness of the space between each item line, one-eighth of an inch, further adds to the perceptual complexity of the GRT.

The norms of this second edition of the GRT are said to be "new," i.e., "based on surveys carried out between 1974 and 1979 in three widely-separated [geographical] areas" (presumably of England). Three tables of reading quotients are provided in the manual of the GRT for urban and rural children aged: 6–5 to 7–1, 7–0 to 8–1, and for "below-average" pupils ages 8–0 to 12–1. These quotients were derived from the testing of 21,711, 5,560, and 1,867 pupils for each of these age groups, respectively. Comments as to the meaning and usefulness of these tables of quotients are given. Unfortunately, some of the comments are disjointed, poorly phrased, and otherwise unnecessarily difficult for teachers to read and understand.

The validity of the GRT as a true examination of reading ability rests on acceptance of certain of its author's assumptions, especially his thesis that a pupil's ability to recognize words and the ability to select synonyms for them, as such, is the indication of reading ability. Of the 45 items on the GRT, 83% assess pupils' knowledge of word synonyms, or of pupils' ability to match drawings with printed names. In only 12 of the 45 items of the GRT is the pupil even asked to use single-sentence context cues (e.g., The sky is sometimes—bull bible blue bellow bald bluebell). At present, however, there is disagreement that such word identification actually signifies reading ability. Some reading experts therefore would deny that the GRT truly measures reading ability since it does not examine children's abilities to comprehend connected discourse.

The stated validity of the GRT is based, for the most part, on the correlations obtained between its scores and those from other standardized reading tests. These correlations ranged from .69 to .88. The author of the GRT also warns users to attend to the relationship between teachers' opinions as to how well pupils read and their scores on the GRT. If there is an observed discrepancy between these two variables, the teacher is reminded to apply the standard error of measurement of scores of the GRT. It was found that 70% of the scores obtained were within 2.5 points, and 95% were within 5 points of the true scores. In the GRT manual it is reported that teachers' opinions of the reading ability of 80 children were compared with their GRT scores. The r here was very high: .93.

American teachers using the GRT would be faced with one other difficult interpretive problem. Three of the items of the GRT have a multiple choice word that likely would not be familiar to American children. These are "tap" (picture of faucet), "wireless" ("Radio means..."), and "shop" (picture of store). If the American child missed these items his/her GRT reading age score would be reduced three months. It does not appear possible for the teacher to accommodate for this loss by a manipulation of the tables of the GRT.

It is clear that the GRT has both positive and negative features. To its credit the GRT is a well-designed and thoughtfully constructed test. The author of the GRT has been careful in his efforts to standardize its items, and to explain in detail in its manual how this item analysis was accomplished. He presents several tables of statistics that illustrate the extent of the efforts made in this regard. He also paid meticulous attention to item construction and selection, to the reliability problems of specific items, to the effects of immediate retest on gains in scores, and to the GRT's relationship to other current reading tests. Apparently, steps were taken to correct a noted deficiency of the first edition GRT (*MMY*, 8:729), that it did not measure the attainment of good readers in the age range above 10.

The administration of the GRT is short in duration, requiring approximately 20 minutes. It is easy to score; a template is offered for this purpose. The directions for the administration and scoring of the GRT generally are well organized and clearly written. Teachers are instructed in the GRT manual how to interpret scores, and how its scores relate to various other factors of reading diagnosis.

On the other hand, the test has shortcomings which may cause some American reading experts to judge the GRT unacceptable. The test provides no indication of children's abilities to read connected discourse. It thus appears to offer little insight for teachers into children's overall reading competence. The format of the GRT presents perceptual difficulties which may interfere with an accurate assessment of word recognition. And finally, certain of its key words may be unfamiliar to American children, a condition which would tend to lower their scores on the GRT.

Review of Group Reading Test, Second Edition by DOUGLAS A. PIDGEON, Former Head, Reading Research Unit, University of London Institute of Education, London, England:

The review of the first edition of this test (8:729) made two criticisms—defects in the norming of the test and a questioning of its value for the classroom teacher. The new manual attempts to overcome the first criticism by incorporating data from a restandardisation. Whereas the original norms, based on an effective sample of 5,600 pupils, were combined into a single table covering the age range 6–6 to 12–11, the distortion introduced by this procedure has to a large extent been eliminated by the new standardisation in which data from 21,711 infants, 5,560 first-year juniors and 1,867 older pupils, have been used to produce three separate tables, one for each group. The standardisation has been carried out by independently calibrating the original score distributions by means of nationally standardised tests, although details of what these were and how and when they were obtained are not supplied. In accordance with standard British practice the tables are of quotients, or more strictly, of standardised scores having a mean of 100, a standard deviation of 15, and incorporating an age allowance.

The age ranges in the tables overlap and the quotients for a given score and age do not correspond exactly. This is certainly due, as the manual explains, to the fact that pupils do not all achieve a specified age at the same time during the school year and those tested later in the year tend to have slightly higher average scores. The explanation relating to this problem, however, is somewhat confusing since the testing dates for the norming samples are not provided and the reference to the use of other age scales is far from clear. The introduction to the manual probably explains the reason for this by stating that sections dealing with technical points have been written "with some consideration for teacher and students who have no specialist knowledge," hence "there will be too little detail for some students and too much for others." If the result of this procedure leads to confusion and a lack of clarity it is far from satisfactory. In this instance the correctness of the standardisation is probably not in doubt, but it would clearly be better if sufficient information was supplied, in an appendix if necessary, so that a proper judgment can be made.

The norms also include a table of Reading Ages; to allow comparisons, equivalents from four other British tests are given as well: the Salford Sentence Reading Test and the Burt, Schonell, and Vernon word reading tests. The manual, however, provides a caution for the teacher about the use of reading ages, their possible inaccuracies at the lower end of the scale, and their comparison with quotients. In all, including some evidence and explanations about reliability and validity written in a clear and precise style, the manual appears to do most of what should be demanded of it.

The fact that it does little to rectify the second criticism mentioned above is perhaps not unexpected since the test is not, and does not claim to be, in any sense diagnostic. It is simply a relatively cheap, easy to administer and mark, survey instrument. As such its major use is as a screening device and it should perform this function as well as any other similar test. While the manual makes no direct claims for more sophisticated uses, in the new edition there are some routine suggestions offered if large discrepancies occur between test results and teachers' expectations. This should not occur often, since the authors report a correlation of .93 between the test results and teachers' scaled orders of merit. Comments of this kind, however, should not delude teachers into thinking they have here a cheap all-purpose reading test. If they are looking for guidance to improve the reading competencies of their pupils, they will certainly need to look elsewhere.

[459]

Group Shorr Imagery Test. Adults; 1977; GSIT; group form of the Shorr Imagery Test; tape cassette used for administration; record form (4 pages); description sheet (2 pages); manual for the Shorr Imagery Test (no date, 41 pages); monograph In-Depth Interpretation with the Shorr Imagery Test (no date, 73 pages); 1984 price data: $44.50 per complete kit including 25 record forms and 25 score sheets; $5 per 25 record forms and 25 score sheets; administration time not reported; Joseph E. Shorr; the Author.*

[460]

The Guilford-Zimmerman Temperament Survey. Grades 12–16 and adults; 1949–78; GZTS; revision and condensation of 3 tests: Guilford-Martin Inventory of Factors, Guilford-Martin Personnel Inventory, and Inventory of Factors STDCR; 10 scores: general activity, restraint, ascendance, sociability, emotional stability, objectivity, friendliness, thoughtfulness, personal relations, masculinity; 1 form ('49, 8 pages); manual, 1978 revision ('78, 19 pages); profile chart ('55, 1 page); interpretation system manual ('76, 50 pages); interpretation worksheet ('76, 1 page); separate answer sheets (IBM 805) must be used; 1984 price data: $17 per 25 tests; $5.50 per 25 answer sheets; $6 per set of scoring stencils; $4 per 25 profile charts; $5 per interpretation system manual; $4 per 25 interpretation worksheets (specify male or female); $5 per manual; $7 per specimen set (complete test not included); (45) minutes; J. P. Guilford and Wayne S. Zimmerman; Sheridan Psychological Services, Inc.*

See T3:1046 (24 references), 8:574 (72 references), T2:1207 (188 references), P:104 (132 references), and 6:110 (120 references); for a review by David R. Saunders, see 5:65 (48 references); for reviews by William Stephenson and Neil Van Steenberg and an excerpted review by Laurance F. Shaffer, see 4:49 (5 references).

TEST REFERENCES

1. McCauley, E. A., & Ehrhardt, A. A. Sexual behavior in female transsexuals and lesbians. THE JOURNAL OF SEX RESEARCH, 1980, 16, 202–211.

2. Dreher, G. F. The role of performance in the turnover process. ACADEMY OF MANAGEMENT JOURNAL, 1982, 25, 137–147.

3. Maloney, P., Deitchman, R., & Wagner, E. E. Consistency of some personality measures as a function of stage of menstruation. JOURNAL OF PERSONALITY ASSESSMENT, 1982, 46, 597–602.

4. Hirschfeld, R. M. A., Klerman, G. L., Clayton, P. J., & Keller, M. B. Personality and depression: Empirical findings. ARCHIVES OF GENERAL PSYCHIATRY, 1983, 40, 993–998.

Review of The Guilford-Zimmerman Temperament Survey by JOHN B. GORMLY, Associate Professor of Psychology, Rutgers University, New Brunswick, NJ:

The Guilford-Zimmerman Temperament Survey (GZTS) is an example of a personality inventory designed to assess multiple facets of personality. Guilford was the first person to use factor analysis in developing a personality inventory, and the GZTS is a result of over 40 years of successive development of inventories by Guilford and his associates.

The GZTS is a 300-item inventory which measures 10 broad personality characteristics; each characteristic is assessed by 30 statements. There are some real advantages to having such a large number of items for each facet of personality being measured. Using the Emotional Stability subscale as an example, the large number of questions in the subscale is conducive to a broad sampling of responses relevant to the construct of emotional stability, including fluctuations of moods, feelings of loneliness, guilt, and worry. Thus the scale has good content validity for the construct of emotional stability. If the examiner, however, were interested in a more specific aspect of emotional stability, such as cheerfulness versus gloominess, there are seven items within the scale that assess that particular aspect of emotional stability. Thus, while the GZTS measures 10 broad dimensions of personality, the test constructors have identified 62 specific patterns within the 10 scales, and the test user might wish to examine the score patterns for any of these mini-scales within the survey. Although the mini-scales are named in the Manual, the scoring keys are not given, and an interested person would have to contact the publisher for these keys.

More than 500 studies have been published which have included the GZTS; consequently, much is known about the reliability and validity of the scales as well as the relationships between the GZTS and other measures of performance. Guilford, Zimmerman, and Guilford have produced a handbook (1976) which extensively describes most of the published research. People who use this test will find the handbook to be a useful resource. The measures of internal consistency for the 10 scales have reasonable values (mostly in the .80s). The values are large enough to indicate that the scales are each measuring a particular facet of personality, but not so high as to indicate that the scales are measuring narrow characteristics. Score consistency of adults over 1, 2, or 3 years yields correlation coefficients of approximately .67, .54, and .51, respectively. These stability coefficients are surprisingly low, and it is entirely possible that the surprise comes from our intuitive overestimation of the stability of personality. With regard to the relationships between GZTS and other performance, the handbook contains descriptions of many such findings. The profiles of scores on GZTS scales for many reference groups, such as office workers, successful supervisors, and salespeople, are presented in the handbook. These norms for various groups can be useful in practical interpretations of test scores, although most of the profiles are of college students who were in special circumstances (e.g., in teacher training or seeking vocational guidance).

PREDICTING PERFORMANCE AND SELECTING PEOPLE FROM PERSONALITY SCORES. The profiles of scores for various reference groups are of limited value when making decisions about people (e.g., applicants for employment). Each test user must establish that for their particular situation there is a relationship between test scores and performance. An important advantage of the GZTS is that it appears to assess personality in a way that does lead to correlations with other measures of performance.

There are two issues in applied assessment which are frequently discussed as if they were the same, which they are not. These issues are (1) the predictive validity of the personality scores and (2) the predictive utility of the personality scores. Predictive validity refers to the correlation between test scores and performance. A large body of research leads one to expect only small correlations for predictive validity. Predictive utility, on the other hand, is indicated by how well the test score leads to correct decisions about which people are likely to be successful in a particular occupation or situation. Even a small correlation between personality scores and performance can result in substantial increases in correct decisions about people. The distinction between predictive validity and predictive utility is explained more completely in chapter 6 of Wiggins' text on personality and prediction (1973). The many correlations between GZTS and a wide range of performance, then, indicate that this test can be quite useful in making decisions about people.

DESCRIBING PEOPLE FROM PERSONALITY SCALE SCORES. There is a booklet containing an interpretation system to assist the examiner in preparing psychological reports based on GZTS scores. The raw score for each scale is easily converted into a new score that ranges between 1 and 10. Each converted score is represented by statements in the booklet which describe behavioral characteristics of people who score at that particular level on the test. Such a system efficiently yields a literate psychological description of the testee. The interpretation system contains sufficiently diverse statements so that the psychological report can be oriented toward characteristics which are relevant to employment or characteristics which are relevant to personal and social adjustment.

The interpretation system is similar to automated interpretation, which was critically discussed in *The Eighth Mental Measurements Yearbook*. The benefit of this "cookbook" approach to personality description (and prediction) is that the manual was built from an extensive research literature on GZTS and performance. Therefore, the interpretation system is likely to produce a more accurate description of the testee from GZTS scores than the examiner could from GZTS scores. The major problem, however, is that the statements in the interpretation system are generalizations based on small correlations between scale scores and performance, and as such, they are likely to be quite inaccurate in describing individuals.

OVERALL EVALUATION OF THE GUILFORD-ZIMMERMAN TEMPERAMENT SURVEY. The quality of a personality inventory is directly related to the quality of the individual items in the test. The items of the GZTS are excellent. They are brief, straightforward, and cover a wide range of behavior. The test constructors took into consideration the potential for people being defensive while taking the test. They avoided making the survey appear to be an inquisition of the testee by writing all items as affirmative statements. Further, they avoided making the person's response a confession by having the testee respond "Yes," "No," or "?" (uncertain) rather than "True" or "False."

The test is convenient to administer and easy to score by hand. The normative information on scale values for many groups of people is extensive as are the correlates of the scales. The responses can be scored in a way that allows the examiner to investigate whether or not the testees falsified their answers and to examine whether the testees were careless in responding or did not understand the statements. All information about the test is summarized in a readable handbook. The major problem with the test and its supporting material is the interpretation system, which leads the examiner to describe the testee with statements which may be highly inaccurate for the individual case. Overall, however, it is an excellent personality inventory.

REVIEWER'S REFERENCES

Wiggins, J. S. PERSONALITY AND PREDICTION: PRINCIPLES OF PERSONALITY ASSESSMENT. Reading, MA: Addison-Wesley, 1973.

Guilford, J. S., Zimmerman, W. S., & Guilford, J. P. THE GUILFORD-ZIMMERMAN TEMPERAMENT SURVEY HANDBOOK. San Diego, CA: EdITS Publishers, 1976.

[461]

Hahnemann Elementary School Behavior Rating Scale. Elementary school students in both regular and open classrooms; 1975; HESB; ratings by teacher; 14 scores: originality, independent learning, involvement, productive with peers, intellectual dependency with peers, failure anxiety, unreflectiveness, irrelevant talk, disruptive social involvement, negative feelings, holding back/withdrawn, critical-competitive, blaming, approach to teacher, plus 2 added items, inattention, academic achievement; no reliability data; norms consist of means and standard deviations; individual; 1 form (4 pages); manual (52 pages); 1982 price data: $11 per 50 scale forms; $4 per manual; $8.50 per 25 scale forms and manual; [(10) minutes]; George Spivack and Marshall Swift; Department of Mental Health Sciences, Hahnemann Medical College and Hospital.*

[462]

Hahnemann High School Behavior Rating Scale. Grades 7–12; 1971–72; HHSB; ratings by teachers; 13 scores: reasoning ability, originality, verbal interaction, rapport with teacher, anxious producer, general anxiety, quiet-withdrawn, poor work habits, lack intellectual independence, dogmatic-inflexible, verbal negativism, disturbance-restless, expressed inability; no reliability or validity data; individual; 1 form ('71, 4 pages); manual ('72, 48 pages); 1985 price data: $.25 per scale form; $10 per manual and 25 scale forms; $4 per manual; administration time not reported; George Spivack and Marshall Swift; Department of Mental Health Sciences, Hahnemann Medical College and Hospital.*

See T3:1050 (2 references).

TEST REFERENCES

1. Spivak, G., & Swift, M. The Hahnemann High School Behavior (HHSB) Rating Scale. JOURNAL OF ABNORMAL CHILD PSYCHOLOGY, 1977, 5, 299–307.

2. Watt, N. F., Grubb, T. W., & Erlenmeyer-Kimling, L. Social, emotional, and intellectual behavior at school among children at high risk for schizophrenia. JOURNAL OF CONSULTING AND CLINICAL PSYCHOLOGY, 1982, 50, 171–181.

Review of Hahnemann High School Behavior Rating Scale by BERT O. RICHMOND, Professor of Counseling and Human Development Services, University of Georgia, Athens, GA:

The Hahnemann High School Behavior Rating Scale (HHSB) is described by its authors as an instrument to measure "classroom behaviors of junior and senior high school students." Moreover, the HHSB was designed to be used in determining the relationship between student behavior and academic achievement. Eight references, all by one or both of the authors, purport to detail the development and standardization of this instrument. Unfortunately, the most recent of these references bear a 1972 date and are listed as "in press" or as unpublished manuscripts. A major criticism of the test manual is its failure to include more recent research, if available, on the instrument.

The total package for this instrument consists of a manual and a four-page scale on which the teacher rates a student's behavior. The first page of the scale calls for the usual demographic data on student and school and provides rating guidelines for the teacher. The two inner pages of the scale contain the descriptions of behavior to be rated. The first 22 items are scored on a 5-point scale according to how frequently the student exhibits each behavior. The next 20 items are scored on a 7-point scale according to the degree that the student is perceived as possessing the characteristic listed. The final 3 items are also scored on a 7-point scale to indicate the degree to which a student performs certain actions. The manual describes the scale as comprised of "45 overt behavior items," yet one of the 45 items asks to what degree the student is "liked by you as a person."

The final page of the scale contains the HHSB Profile, which allows for plotting the individual student's score on each of 13 factors. There are no data presented in the manual for this factor analysis, although the 13 factors are described as emerging from separate factor analyses of items. Thus, it is not clearly understood whether these are statistical or theoretical factors. Each of the 13 "factors" contain 3 or 4 items whose ratings are added together to obtain a total raw score.

In an initial study to develop the HHSB, 882 ratings were obtained in grades 7 to 12 in suburban public schools, and 672 ratings were obtained for students in special classes for the emotionally disturbed. Students in another sample of 602 7th to 12th graders were also rated, resulting in a total of

2,157 students rated by 155 teachers. The authors indicate that the 13 factors which emerged from these studies of special and regular class students were found to relate to academic achievement.

The ratings of this instrument are to be completed only by a classroom teacher who has known the student long enough or, as the authors state, "over a sufficient period of time." It is intended to be an index of the individual's behavior in a classroom and thereby should be correlated with academic achievement.

There are no data presented on either the validity or reliability of the scale. The manual explains that the first five factors (grouped together under the label Productive Factors) correlate with achievement between .39 and .64, with a mean correlation of .48. It is also noted that these correlations are significant when the effect of IQ is partialed out statistically. There is no information on intercorrelations of factors and a paucity of other statistical treatment provided.

This rating instrument was derived from discussion with teachers of students in regular and special classes. Therefore, it has a certain content validity in that it reflects the student behaviors that teachers associate with academic achievement. It could be improved by obtaining the necessary research evidence to support its validity in relation to external criteria as well as its stability and internal reliability.

An elaborate system of ten profiles is outlined in an effort to identify students who fall into certain profile classifications. This profile system may be best described in the authors own words as, "at present, tentative and subject to further experimentation."

In essence, the strength of the HHSB appears to reside in its attempts to distill from teachers the behaviors of students considered most relevant to academic achievement. These 45 items reflect teacher's perceptions of desired student behavior but often the items are not stated in appropriate behavioral terms. For example, item 39, "Prone to want quick 'black' or 'white' answers to questions" may be more readily a description of a teacher's perception of a student than of a student's behavior. The scale is brief and easily completed; however, the lack of normative and statistical data make it impossible to compare student performance to a normative population.

[463]

Halstead-Reitan Neuropsychological Test Battery. Ages 5–8, 9–14, 15 and over; 1979–81; consists of three neuropsychological test batteries, one for each age level; 1 combined score: Halstead impairment index; manual ('79, 102 pages); interpretive manual for children ('79, 186 pages); price data available from publisher; Ralph M. Reitan; Reitan Neuropsychology Laboratories, University of Arizona.*

a) REITAN-INDIANA NEUROPSYCHOLOGICAL TEST BATTERY FOR CHILDREN. Ages 5–8; 1979–81; 12 tests.

1) *Category.* Projection box with slide projector and slides necessary for administration.
2) *Tactual Performance.* 6-figure board; 3 scores: total time, memory, localization.
3) *Finger Tapping.* Electronic finger tapper necessary for administration.
4) *Matching Pictures.*
5) *Individual Performance.* 4 subtests: Matching Figures, Star, Matching V's, Concentric Squares.
6) *Marching.*
7) *Progressive Figures.*
8) *Color Form.* 2 scores: total time, errors.
9) *Miles' ABC Test of Ocular Dominance.*
10) *Target.*
11) *Aphasia Screening.*
12) *Sensory Perceptual.* 6 subtests: Imperception (Tactile, Auditory, Visual), Tactile Finger Recognition, Finger-Tip Symbol Writing Recognition, Tactile Form Recognition.

b) HALSTEAD NEUROPSYCHOLOGICAL TEST BATTERY FOR CHILDREN. Ages 9–14; 1979; 11 tests.

1) *Category* (similar to *a* above).
2) *Tactual Performance* (same as *a* above).
3) *Seashore Rhythm Test.*
4) *Speech-Sounds Perception.*
5) *Trail Making.*
6) *Finger Tapping.* Manual finger tapping apparatus necessary for administration.
7) *Aphasia Screening.*
8) *Sensory-Perceptual.* 6 subtests: Sensory Imperception (Tactile, Auditory, Visual), Finger Agnosia, Finger-Tip Number Writing, Coin Recognition.
9) *Tactile Form Recognition.*
10) *Grip Strength.* 2 scores: preferred grip, nonpreferred grip; hand dynamometer necessary for administration.
11) *Lateral Dominance.*

c) HALSTEAD NEUROPSYCHOLOGICAL TEST BATTERY FOR ADULTS. Ages 15 and over; 1979; 11 tests: same as *a* above, except Tactual Performance has a 10-figure board for this level.

See T3:1052 (4 references).

TEST REFERENCES

1. Judd, L. L., Hubbard, B., Huey, L. Y., Attewell, P. A., Janowsky, D. S., & Takahashi, K. I. Lithium carbonate and ethanol induced "highs" in normal subjects. ARCHIVES OF GENERAL PSYCHIATRY, 1977, 34, 463–467.

2. Carlin, A. S., Stauss, F. F., Adams, K. M., & Grant, I. The prediction of neuropsychological impairment in polydrug abusers. ADDICTIVE BEHAVIORS, 1978, 3, 5–12.

3. Grant, I., Adams, K. M., Carlin, A. S., Rennick, P. M., Judd, L. L., & Schooff, K. The collaborative neuropsychological study of polydrug users. ARCHIVES OF GENERAL PSYCHIATRY, 1978, 35, 1063–1074.

4. Radford, L. M., Chaney, E. F., O'Leary, M. R., & O'Leary, D. E. Screening for cognitive impairment among inpatients. THE JOURNAL OF CLINICAL PSYCHIATRY, 1978, 39, 712–715.

5. Bigler, E. D. Neuropsychological evaluation of adolescent patients hospitalized with chronic inhalant abuse. CLINICAL NEUROPSYCHOLOGY, 1979, 1(1), 8–12.

6. Bigler, E. D., Tucker, D. M., & Piran, N. Neuropsychological differentiation in a psychiatric late adolescent-young adult population: Preliminary report. CLINICAL NEUROPSYCHOLOGY, 1979, 1(2), 9–14.

7. Craig, P. L. Neuropsychological assessment in public psychiatric hospitals: The current state of the practice. CLINICAL NEUROPSYCHOLOGY, 1979, 1(4), 1–7.

8. DeFilippis, N. A., McCampbell, E., & Rogers, P. Development of a booklet form of the Category Test: Normative and validity data. JOURNAL OF CLINICAL NEUROPSYCHOLOGY, 1979, 1, 339–342.

9. Matarazzo, R. G., Matarazzo, J. D., Gallo, A. E., Jr., & Wiens, A. N. IQ and neuropsychological changes following carotid endarterectomy. JOURNAL OF CLINICAL NEUROPSYCHOLOGY, 1979, 1, 97–116.

10. Rey, A. C., Savard, R. J., Silber, E., Buchsbaum, M. S., & Post, R. M. Cognitive changes and the averaged evoked response in depression. COGNITIVE THERAPY AND RESEARCH, 1979, 3, 263–267.

11. Townes, B. D., Priest, S. R., & Bourke, V. M. Clinical neuropsychology: An evolving field. AUSTRALIAN PSYCHOLOGIST, 1979, 14, 169–174.

12. Warnock, J. K., & Mintz, S. I. Investigation of models of brain functioning through a factor analytic procedure of neuropsychological data. CLINICAL NEUROPSYCHOLOGY, 1979, 1(4), 43–48.

13. Barth, J. T., Sandler, H. M., & Anchor, K. N. Cerebral dysfunction and self-concept in chronic alcoholics. CLINICAL NEUROPSYCHOLOGY, 1980, 2, 28–32.

14. Bigler, E. D. Neuropsychological assessment and brain scan results: A case study approach. CLINICAL NEUROPSYCHOLOGY, 1980, 2, 13–24.

15. Delaney, R. C., Wallace, J. D., & Egelko, S. Transient cerebral ischemic attacks and neuropsychological deficit. JOURNAL OF CLINICAL NEUROPSYCHOLOGY, 1980, 2, 107–114.

16. Grant, I., Reed, R., & Adams, K. M. Natural history of alcohol and drug-related brain disorder: Implications for neuropsychological research. JOURNAL OF CLINICAL NEUROPSYCHOLOGY, 1980, 2, 321–331.

17. Hartlage, L. C., & Telzrow, C. F. The practice of clinical neuropsychology. CLINICAL NEUROPSYCHOLOGY, 1980, 2, 200–202.

18. Hevern, V. W. Recent validity studies of the Halstead-Reitan approach to clinical neuropsychological assessment: A critical review. CLINICAL NEUROPSYCHOLOGY, 1980, 2, 49–61.

19. Loberg, T. Alcohol misuse and neuropsychological deficits in men. JOURNAL OF STUDIES ON ALCOHOL, 1980, 41, 119–128.

20. Miller, W. R., & Orr, J. Nature and sequence of neuropsychological deficits in alcoholics. JOURNAL OF STUDIES ON ALCOHOL, 1980, 41, 325–33

21. Newlin, D. B., & Tramontana, M. G. Neuropsychological findings in a hyperactive adolescent with subcortical brain pathology. CLINICAL NEUROPSYCHOLOGY, 1980, 2, 178–183.

22. Storrie, M. C., & Doerr, H. O. Characterization of Alzheimer Type Dementia utilizing an abbreviated Halstead-Reitan Battery. CLINICAL NEUROPSYCHOLOGY, 1980, 2, 78–82.

23. Townes, B. D., Trupin, E. W., Martin, D. C., & Goldstein, D. Neuropsychological correlates of academic success among elementary school children. JOURNAL OF CONSULTING AND CLINICAL PSYCHOLOGY, 1980, 48, 675–684.

24. Tramontana, M. G., Sherrets, S. D., & Golden, C. J. Brain dysfunction in youngsters with psychiatric disorders: Application of Selz-Reitan rules for neuropsychological diagnosis. CLINICAL NEUROPSYCHOLOGY, 1980, 2, 118–123.

25. Tsushima, W. T., & Popper, J. S. Computerized tomography: A report of false negative errors. CLINICAL NEUROPSYCHOLOGY, 1980, 2, 130–133.

26. Vicente, P., Kennelly, D., Golden, C. J., Kane, R., Sweet, J., Moses, J. A., Jr., Cardellino, J. P., Templeton, R., & Graber, B. The relationship of the Halstead-Reitan Neuropsychological Battery to the Luria-Nebraska Neuropsychological Battery: Preliminary report. CLINICAL NEUROPSYCHOLOGY, 1980, 2, 140–141.

27. Yeudall, L. T., Fromm-Auch, D., & Davies, P. Neuropsychological impairment of persistent delinquency. THE JOURNAL OF NERVOUS AND MENTAL DISEASE, 1980, 170, 257–265.

28. Bolter, J., Veneklasen, J., & Long, C. J. Investigation of WAIS effectiveness in discrimination between temporal and generalized seizure patients. JOURNAL OF CONSULTING AND CLINICAL PSYCHOLOGY, 1981, 49, 549–553.

29. Boyar, J. J. Coping with non-organic factors on neuropsychological examination: Utility of repeated neuropsychological measures. CLINICAL NEUROPSYCHOLOGY, 1981, 3(4), 15–17.

30. Cohen, R., Woll, G., & Ehrenstein, W. H. Recognition deficits resulting from focussed attention in aphasia. PSYCHOLOGICAL RESEARCH, 1981, 43, 391–405.

31. Diamant, J. J., & Hijmen, R. Comparison of test results obtained with two neuropsychological test batteries. JOURNAL OF CLINICAL PSYCHOLOGY, 1981, 37, 355–358.

32. Dodrill, C. B. An economical method for the evaluation of general intelligence in adults. JOURNAL OF CONSULTING AND CLINICAL PSYCHOLOGY, 1981, 49, 668–673.

33. Dye, O. A., Saxon, S. A., & Milby, J. B. Long-term neuropsychological deficits after traumatic head injury with comatosis. JOURNAL OF CLINICAL PSYCHOLOGY, 1981, 37, 472–477.

34. Gordon, N. G., O'Dell, J. W., & Bozeman, N. Variation in neuropsychological performance as a function of sex. THE JOURNAL OF PSYCHOLOGY, 1981, 109, 127–131.

35. Haaland, K. Y., & Delaney, H. D. Motor deficits after left or right hemisphere damage due to stroke or tumor. NEUROPSYCHOLOGIA, 1981, 19, 17–27.

36. Harris, M., Cross, H., & VanNieuwkerk, R. The effects of state depression, induced depression and sex on the finger tapping and tactual performance tests. CLINICAL NEUROPSYCHOLOGY, 1981, 3(4), 28–34.

37. King, M. C. Effects of non focal brain dysfunction on visual memory. JOURNAL OF CLINICAL PSYCHOLOGY, 1981, 37, 638–643.

38. King, M. C., & Snow, W. G. Problem-solving task performance in brain-damaged subjects. JOURNAL OF CLINICAL PSYCHOLOGY, 1981, 37, 400–404.

39. Kinney, M. J., Varga, E., Varga, V., Tarter, R., Sugerman, A. A., Nilsen, S., & Gupta, G. Hemoperfusion for chronic schizophrenia: Preliminary psychiatric results. THE JOURNAL OF CLINICAL PSYCHIATRY, 1981, 42, 174–177.

40. Klesges, R. C., & Fisher, L. P. A multiple criterion approach to the assessment of brain damage in children. CLINICAL NEUROPSYCHOLOGY, 1981, 3(4), 6–11.

41. Leli, D. A., & Filskov, S. B. Actuarial detection and description of brain impairment with the W-B Form I. JOURNAL OF CLINICAL PSYCHOLOGY, 1981, 37, 615–622.

42. Louks, J., & Calsyn, D. A comparison of the Impairment Index and the Average Impairment Rating in the evaluation of the level of performance on the Halstead-Reitan Battery. CLINICAL NEUROPSYCHOLOGY, 1981, 3(4), 1–3.

43. Neuger, G. J., O'Leary, D. S., Fishburne, F. J., Barth, J. T., Berent, S., Giordani, B., & Boll, T. J. Order effects on the Halstead-Reitan Neuropsychological Test Battery and allied procedures. JOURNAL OF CONSULTING AND CLINICAL PSYCHOLOGY, 1981, 49, 722–730.

44. Russell, E. W. The chronicity effect. JOURNAL OF CLINICAL PSYCHOLOGY, 1981, 37, 246–253.

45. Snow, W. G. A comparison of frequency of abnormal results in neuropsychological vs. neurodiagnostic procedures. JOURNAL OF CLINICAL PSYCHOLOGY, 1981, 37, 22–28.

46. Barrett, E. T., Jr., Wheatley, R. D., & Laplant, R. J. A brief clinical neuropsychologic screening battery: Statistical classification trials. JOURNAL OF CLINICAL PSYCHOLOGY, 1982, 38, 375–377.

47. Bolter, J., Gouvier, W., Veneklasen, J., & Long, C. J. Using demographic information to predict premorbid IQ: A test of clinical validity with head trauma patients. CLINICAL NEUROPSYCHOLOGY, 1982, 4, 171–174.

48. Bornstein, R. A. Reliability of the speech sounds perception test. PERCEPTUAL AND MOTOR SKILLS, 1982, 55, 203–210.

49. Calsyn, D. A., Louks, J. L., & Johnson, J. S. MMPI correlates of the degree of generalized impairment based on the Halstead-Reitan Battery. PERCEPTUAL AND MOTOR SKILLS, 1982, 55, 1099–1102.

50. Chavez, E. L., Schwartz, M. M., & Brandon, A. Effects of sex of subject and method of black presentation on the Tactual Performance Test. JOURNAL OF CONSULTING AND CLINICAL PSYCHOLOGY, 1982, 50, 600–601.

51. Chelune, G. J. A reexamination of the relationship between the Luria-Nebraska and Halstead-Reitan Batteries: Overlap with the WAIS. JOURNAL OF CONSULTING AND CLINICAL PSYCHOLOGY, 1982, 50, 578–580.

52. Crosson, B., & Warren, R. L. Use of the Luria-Nebraska Neuropsychological Battery in aphasia: A conceptual critique. JOURNAL OF CONSULTING AND CLINICAL PSYCHOLOGY, 1982, 50, 22–31.

53. Doerr, H. O., & Storrie, M. C. Neuropsychological testing in the People's Republic of China: The Halstead-Reitan Seattle/Changsha Project. CLINICAL NEUROPSYCHOLOGY, 1982, 4, 49–51.

54. Dorman, C. Personality and psychiatric correlates of the Halstead-Reitan tests in boys with school problems. CLINICAL NEUROPSYCHOLOGY, 1982, 4, 110–114.

55. Golden, C. J., Gustavson, J. L., & Ariel, R. Correlations between the Luria-Nebraska and the Halstead-Reitan neuropsychological batteries: Effects of partialing out education and postmorbid intelligence. JOURNAL OF CONSULTING AND CLINICAL PSYCHOLOGY, 1982, 50, 770–771.

56. Hochla, N. A. N., & Parsons, O. A. Premature aging in female alcoholics: A neuropsychological study. THE JOURNAL OF NERVOUS AND MENTAL DISEASE, 1982, 170, 241–245.

57. Miller, V. S., & Bigler, E. D. Neuropsychological aspects of Tuberous Sclerosis. CLINICAL NEUROPSYCHOLOGY, 1982, 4, 26–34.

58. Nichols Hochla, N. A., Fabian, M. S., & Parsons, O. A. Brain-age quotients in recently detoxified alcholic, recovered alcoholic and nonalcoholic women. JOURNAL OF CLINICAL PSYCHOLOGY, 1982, 38, 207–212.

59. Pendleton, M. G., & Heaton, R. K. A comparison of the Wisconsin Card Sorting Test and the Category Test. JOURNAL OF CLINICAL PSYCHOLOGY, 1982, 38, 392–396.

60. Sachs, H. K., Krall, V., & Drayton, M. A. Neuropsychological assessment after lead poisoning without encephalopathy. PERCEPTUAL AND MOTOR SKILLS, 1982, 54, 1283–1288.

61. Shelly, C., & Goldstein, G. Psychometric relations between the Luria-Nebraska and Halstead-Reitan Neuropsychological Test Batteries in a neuropsychiatric setting. CLINICAL NEUROPSYCHOLOGY, 1982, 4, 128–133.

62. Swiercinsky, D. P., & Howard, M. E. Programmatic series of factor analyses for evaluating the structure of neuropsychological test batteries. CLINICAL NEUROPSYCHOLOGY, 1982, 4, 147–152.

63. Tarter, R. E., & Holtzman, A. Neuropsychological and psychopathological sequelae of intractable temporal lobe epilepsy. CLINICAL NEUROPSYCHOLOGY, 1982, 4, 161–164.

64. Wolf, B. A., & Tramontana, M. G. Aphasia Screening Test interrelationships with complete Halstead-Reitan test results for older children. CLINICAL NEUROPSYCHOLOGY, 1982, 4, 179–186.

65. Bornstein, R. A. Reliability and item analysis of the Seashore Rhythm Test. PERCEPTUAL AND MOTOR SKILLS, 1983, 57, 571–574.

66. Chavez, E. L., Trautt, G. M., Brandon, A., & Steyaert, J. Effects of test anxiety and sex of subject on neuropsychological test performance: Finger Tapping, Trail Making, Digit Span and Digit Symbol Tests. PERCEPTUAL AND MOTOR SKILLS, 1983, 56, 923–929.

67. Clemmons, D. C., & Dodrill, C. B. Vocational outcomes of high school students with epilepsy. THE JOURNAL OF APPLIED REHABILITATION COUNSELING, 1983, 14(4), 49–53.

68. Fromm-Auch, D., & Yeudall, L. T. Normative data for the Halstead-Reitan Neuropsychological Tests. JOURNAL OF CLINICAL NEUROPSYCHOLOGY, 1983, 5, 221–238.

69. Gordon, N. G., & O'Dell, J. W. Sex differences in neuropsychological performance. PERCEPTUAL AND MOTOR SKILLS, 1983, 56, 126.

70. Incagnoli, T., & Kane, R. Developmental perspective of the Gilles de la Tourette Syndrome. PERCEPTUAL AND MOTOR SKILLS, 1983, 57, 1271–1281.

71. Josiassen, R. C., Curry, L. M., & Mancall, E. L. Development of neuropsychological deficits in Huntington's Disease. ARCHIVES OF NEUROLOGY, 1983, 40, 791–796.

72. McCue, M. Assessment and rehabilitation of learning-disabled adults. REHABILITATION COUNSELING BULLETIN, 1983, 27, 281–290.

73. Nolan, D. R., Hammeke, T. A., & Barkley, R. A. A comparison of the patterns of the neuropsychological performance in two groups of learning disabled children. JOURNAL OF CLINICAL CHILD PSYCHOLOGY, 1983, 12, 22–27.

74. O'Donnell, J. P. Lateralized sensorimotor asymmetries in normal learning-disabled and brain-damaged young adults. PERCEPTUAL AND MOTOR SKILLS, 1983, 57, 227–232.

75. Selin, C. L., & Gottschalk, L. A. Schizophrenia, conduct disorder and depressive disorder: Neuropsychological, speech sample and EEG results. PERCEPTUAL AND MOTOR SKILLS, 1983, 57, 427–444.

76. Zendel, I. H., & Pihl, R. O. Visual and auditory matching in learning disabled and normal children. JOURNAL OF LEARNING DISABILITIES, 1983, 16, 158–160.

77. Bolter, J. F., Hutcherson, W. L., & Long, C. J. Speech Sounds Perception Test: A rational response strategy can invalidate the test results. JOURNAL OF CONSULTING AND CLINICAL PSYCHOLOGY, 1984, 52, 132–133.

78. Fernandez-Guardiola, A., Jurado, J. L., & Aguilar-Jimenez, E. Evaluation of the attention and sleepiness states by means of a psychophysiological test of reaction time and time estimate in man: Effects of psychotropic drugs. CURRENT THERAPEUTIC RESEARCH, 1984, 35, 1000–1009.

79. Goldstein, G., & Shelly, C. Discriminative validity of various intelligence and neuropsychological tests. JOURNAL OF CONSULTING AND CLINICAL PSYCHOLOGY, 1984, 52, 383–389.

Review of Halstead-Reitan Neuropsychological Test Battery by RAYMOND S. DEAN, Associate Professor of Psychology in Educational Psychology and Director, School Psychology Program, Ball State University, Teachers College, Muncie, IN, and Indiana University School of Medicine, Indianapolis, IN:

Neuropsychological assessment in North America has focused on the development of test batteries that would predict the presence of brain damage while offering a comprehensive view of a patient's individual functions. Numerous batteries have been offered as wide-band measures of the integrity and functioning of the brain (see Dean, 1982, for a review). However, the Halstead-Reitan Neuropsychological Test Battery (HRNB) remains the most researched and widely utilized measure in the United States (Dean, in press b). Originally developed to articulate Halstead's (1947) theory of biological intelligence, the present battery owes much to the efforts of Reitan (1955). Indeed, of the some 27 experimental tasks collected by Halstead (1947), the present battery consists of the 10 tests which have been shown to best discriminate between normals and patients with documented cortical damage (Reitan, 1955). In a rather radical quantitative approach, individual tests of the battery were included or discontinued after a substantive research base had been developed concerning the incremental validity in the differential diagnosis of various forms of neuropathology (Reitan, 1974). This approach, while increasing sensitivity to cortical dysfunction, has compromised the utility of the HRNB as a measure of individual functions (e.g., memory).

The HRNB was developed primarily for adults (ages greater than 15 years). However, the manual reports modifications of the HRNB for children (ages 9 to 14 years) based on the administration of the battery to a sample of successively younger children. This modified version, which is commonly known as the Halstead Neuropsychological Test Battery for Children (HNTB-C), is but a downward revision of the adult battery. That is, although the number and organization of the items of many tests have been altered (and the Wechsler Adult Intelligence Scale replaced with the Wechsler Intelligence Scale for Children), the HRNB and HNTB-C are basically the same.

In its present configuration, the battery includes tests purported to measure elements of memory, abstract thought, language, sensory-motor integration, imperception, and motor dexterity. It should be recognized, however, that the measurement of individual functions to the exclusion of all others is prohibitive. Thus, for example, conclusions of impaired non-verbal reasoning would have to be deferred without evidence of intact non-verbal memory. Clearly, such memory function is a prerequisite to abstract manipulation. With this caveat in mind, individual tests of the HRNB are described in the paragraphs below:

Category Test (Halstead): Visual presentation of slides with underlying concept. Feedback provided as to correctness after depression of one of four levers. Measures concept formation, abstraction, and integration.

Tactual Performance Test (Seguin-Goddard Form Board): Shapes required to be placed in form board without aid of vision (dominant, non-dominant, both hands). Recall of shapes and location of shapes required. Measures tactual discrimination, manual dexterity, kinesthesis, incidental memory, and spatial memory.

Speech-Sounds Perception (Halstead): Individual paralogs presented auditorially are selected from four printed alternatives, total of 60 items. Measures verbal auditory discrimination, auditory-visual integration, and phonetic skills.

Rhythm Test (Seashore Tests of Musical Talent): Identification of 30 pairs of rhythmic beats as being "same" or "different." Measures non-verbal auditory discrimination and auditory perception.

Trail Making Test (A & B) (Army Individual Test Adjutant Generals Office): (*a*) Connect 25 numbered circles in numeric order. Measures motor speed, visual scanning, visual-motor integration. (*b*) Connect 25 numbered or alphabetic circles alternating between numeric and alphabetic order (i.e., 1–A–2–B...). Measures motor speed, visual scanning, visual motor integration, mental flexibility, and integration of alphabetic and numeric systems.

Finger Oscillation Test (Halstead): Measure of number of taps with index finger in 10 seconds for each hand. Dominant, non-dominant scores (mean of five trials for each hand). Measures motor speed and dexterity.

Reitan-Indiana Aphasia Screening Test (Halstead & Wepman; Reitan): Thirty-two items requiring naming, spelling, reading, write, math, calculations, enunciate, identify body parts, pantomime actions, perform acts, draw, shapes, and identify directions. Measures wide-band language and education, nonverbal functions, occupation, and concentration.

Reitan-Klove Sensory Perceptual Examination (Reitan): Accuracy of unilateral and bilateral simultaneous tactile, auditory, and visual imperception, finger localization from tactile stimulation without vision. Tactile number perception on fingertips. Tactile recognition of shapes without vision. Measures lateralized distractibility, sensory perception (visual, auditory, and tactile).

Strength of Grip Test (Hand Dynamometer) (Reitan): Measure of strength of grip. Alternating measures for preferred and nonpreferred hands. Measures motor strength.

Wechsler Intelligence Scale (age appropriate) (Wechsler): Measures general verbal/nonverbal cognitive function, constructs by subtests.

Lateral Dominance (Reitan): Measure of left or right preference for performance task involving hands, arms, legs, eyes, and feet. Measures completeness of hemispheric lateralization.

From the above description it becomes clear that an appreciable number of the individual measures were developed for other than the assessment of neuropsychological functions as such. These measures were adapted and interpretations expanded to include neuropsychological implications. In each case, the constructs described are those purported to be measured in the manual. Dean (in press, b) has argued that functions such as sensory acuity, attention, concentration, and distractibility are implicit constructs measured in these tests. Although such functions play a role in most psychometric efforts, these variables become crucial in neuropsychological assessment, which seeks to make inferences concerning specific brain functions. The cost and size of much of the equipment necessary for the administration of the battery make other than a laboratory setup rather unwieldy. Indeed, the lack of portability is one of the most common objections to the use of the HRNB.

Reitan presents information concerning the administration and scoring of individual tests and allied procedures of the HRNB in a rather slender manual. The manual reports no standardization or normative data as such, but relies upon the corpus of research which has evolved over the past 30 years with the battery (Dean, in press a). Each of the regular tests of the HRNB are examined in the manual with special focus on the origin of the measure and rationale for inclusion in the battery. Moreover, reliability and construct validity are not approached in any systematic fashion. Without standard score transformation data, it is difficult to make any meaningful comparison between scores on individual tests. Because age and other demographic variables are correlated with many neuropsychological functions, interpretation for the individual becomes further complicated. Moreover, most neuropsychologists have relied on cutoff scores (impaired-normal) established from research for interpretation (Dean, in press a). This approach, while familiar in medicine, is rather foreign to the individual difference conceptualization of measurement. On balance, this differential diagnosis stance has served the fledgling specialty of neuropsychology well in gaining credibility in the medical setting.

The manual for the HRNB lacks the basic psychometric documentation needed in interpretation. Moreover, interpretations are more dependent on the psychologist's knowledge and clinical acumen than reported psychometric properties for the battery (Reitan, 1974). Indeed, providing interpretations from any neuropsychological battery which involves inferences concerning localized brain dysfunction requires considerable training in neuropsychology and brain-behavior relationships. In this regard, the "validity" of the HRNB has come from research which has involved the "clinical blind" technique (Dean, 1982). This procedure focuses on the administration and interpretation of test results without knowledge of the patient's case history or present diagnosis (Reitan, 1974). In this way, diagnoses and inferences made on the basis of test results are compared with independently determined neurological information from radiological and/or surgical means. The problem here, of course, is the difficulty in isolating the utility of the battery from the psychologist's clinical acumen (Dean, in press b). Although not reported in the HRNB manual, a number of attempts have been made to provide a more rigorous empirical (mechanical/actuarial) approach to the interpretation of the battery (see Dean, in press b). The Halstead Impairment Index, which is reported in the manual, does provide some aid in interpretation. This summary measure reflects the proportion of the most sensitive tests of the battery which the individual patient has scored in the impaired range. Although of little value in outlining the patient's strengths for individual functions, this index is most sensitive to the more general prediction of brain damage (Reitan, 1959).

Research with the HRNB indicates a sensitivity to cortical dysfunction (see Boll, 1981; Dean, 1982; Reitan, 1974). The battery has been shown to discriminate normal controls from patients with brain damage with considerable accuracy (84–98%). In general, Reitan and his associates (Dikmen & Reitan, 1977; Reed & Reitan, 1963; Reitan, 1955) offer convincing data favoring clearer brain damage localization with the HRNB for acute lesions rather than more chronic neuropathology. When chronic schizophrenics are excluded from consideration, a number of researchers have shown the HRNB to distinguish patients with specific organic pathology from those with psychiatric disorders (see Heaton & Crowley, 1981).

In summary, the HRNB is the most widely utilized method of inferring neuropsychological functioning. The battery has been shown to have a good deal of clinical utility in diagnosing and localizing brain dysfunction. The manual, however, fails to integrate what psychometric data does exist concerning the battery. Moreover, the evidence of utility of the battery rests in a large corpus of research concerning differential diagnosis. Rudimentary data concerning the validity, reliability, and norming procedures are absent from the manual. Interpretation of the battery relies more on the training of the professional in neuropsychology than the development and standardization of specific subscales. The HRNB cannot be recommended for general clinical use without considerable training and familiarity with research on the battery.

REVIEWER'S REFERENCES

Halstead, W. C. BRAIN AND INTELLIGENCE. Chicago: University of Chicago Press, 1947.

Reitan, R. M. An investigation of the validity of Halstead's measures of biological intelligence. ARCHIVES OF NEUROLOGY AND PSYCHIATRY, 1955, 73, 28–35.

Reitan, R. M. The comparative effects of brain damage on the Halstead Impairment Index and the Wechsler-Bellevue scale. JOURNAL OF CLINICAL PSYCHOLOGY, 1959, 18, 281–285.

Reed, H. B. C., Jr., & Reitan, R. M. Intelligence test performances of brain damaged subjects with lateralized motor deficits. JOURNAL OF CONSULTING PSYCHOLOGY, 1963, 27, 102–106.

Reitan, R. M. Methodological problems in clinical neuropsychology. In R. M. Reitan and L. A. Davison (Eds.), CLINICAL NEUROPSYCHOLOGY: CURRENT STATUS AND APPLICATIONS. New York: Wiley and Sons, 1974.

Dikmen, S. J., & Reitan, R. M. Emotional sequelae of head injury. ANNALS OF NEUROLOGY, 1977, 2, 492.

Boll, T. J. The Halstead-Reitan neuropsychology battery. In S. B. Filskov and T. J. Boll (Eds.), HANDBOOK OF CLINICAL NEUROPSYCHOLOGY. New York: Wiley, 1981.

Heaton, R. K., & Crowley, T. J. Effects of psychiatric disorders and their somatic treatments on neuropsychological test results. In S. B. Filskov & T. J. Boll (Eds.), HANDBOOK OF CLINICAL NEUROPSYCHOLOGY. New York: Wiley, 1981.

Dean, R. S. Neuropsychological assessment. In T. Kratochwill (Ed.), ADVANCES IN SCHOOL PSYCHOLOGY (VOL. 2). Hillsdale, NJ: Lawrence Erlbaum, Inc., 1982.

Dean, R. S. Neuropsychological assessment. In J. D. Cavenar, R. Michels, H. K. H. Brodie, A. M. Cooper, S. B. Guze, L. L. Judd, G. L. Klerman, and A. J. Solnit (Eds.), PSYCHIATRY. Philadelphia, PA: J. B. Lippincott Company, in press. (a)

Dean, R. S. Perspectives on the future of neuropsychological assessment. In B. S. Plake and J. C. Witt (Eds.), BUROS-NEBRASKA SYMPOSIUM ON MEASUREMENT AND TESTING: VOL. 2. THE FUTURE OF TESTING AND MEASUREMENT. Hillsdale, NJ: Lawrence Erlbaum, in press. (b)

Review of Halstead-Reitan Neuropsychological Test Battery by MANFRED J. MEIER, Professor and Director, Neuropsychology Laboratory, Department of Neurosurgery, University of Minnesota Medical School, Minneapolis, MN:

This comprehensive neuropsychological test battery has a long and illustrious history of clinical research and application in American clinical neuropsychology. Following its inaugural presentation to the psychological community (Halstead, 1947), and the careful nurturance of concept and application by Reitan (1974), the battery has had perhaps the most widespread impact of any approach in clinical neuropsychology. It seems reasonable to state that in the first half of the period since World War II, during which clinical neuropsychology expanded so remarkably, this approach was the primary force in stimulating clinical research and application in this country. It is a credit to its proponents that this neuropsychological battery remains the most widely applied in clinical settings even while alternative "comprehensive" batteries and highly specialized new neuropsychological assessment procedures are being developed and applied on a wider basis (Goldstein, 1984; Hamsher, 1984).

Reed (1983) has provided a detailed history while Goldstein (1984) presented descriptive information and an analysis of the relationship of this approach to other developments within clinical neuropsychology. The tests that comprise the battery are also described in the manual available from Reitan (1979) and in the many publications that have been generated by this group (Reitan & Davison, 1974). The following narrative assumes familiarity with the battery through the extensive primary sources available in the literature.

The purpose of this battery is to provide the clinician with a data base for inferring the nature, location, and extent of the structural changes in the brain that may underlie and explain the pattern of intact and impaired functions derived from the measures and qualitative information yielded by the battery. The normative base for establishing a profile of individual standard score patterns can be found in a large collection of studies designed to demonstrate validity of the battery to differentiate (1) organic neurological from normal populations, (2) organic neurological from functional psychiatric populations, (3) focal from diffuse neurological disease, (4) regional focal cerebral dysfunctions by major zones, and (5) the etiological conditions associated with individual differences in outcome pattern. The results of these validation studies have been integrated with clinical experience by Reitan and associates for formulating hypotheses about brain-behavioral relationships. These hypotheses are expressed as clinical inferences about the neuropathological substrate that is most congruent with the behavior changes measured by the battery. Reitan's ability to utilize the data to draw such inferences was aptly demonstrated 20 years ago in a formal predictive validity analysis (Reitan, 1964). Subsequently, efforts have been made to objectify the inferential process by means of pattern analysis and the development of diagnostic prediction criteria (Goldstein, 1984). By drawing these inferences independently of the external neurological criteria used in validation research, Reitan and his associates have argued that any significant differences between subgroups, especially at diagnostic levels of significance, favor clinical application. In the initial predictive validity study Reitan clearly demonstrated his effectiveness in drawing these inferences. He had earlier provided demonstrations with individual cases at conferences and workshops, emphasizing the need for extensive supervised experience in the use of the battery. Many people have obtained formal postdoctoral training in the approach. Yet, nobody has formally subjected her/his inferences to analysis in order to replicate Reitan's detailed diagnostic applicability of the battery. This is not to suggest that individuals trained by him do not have comparable clinical skill. His proponents are highly active in many different clinical settings and enjoy high rank and reputation in roles that have been defined as much by Reitan as model as by any other single factor. However, since diagnosis constitutes the major application, it seems appropriate to demonstrate empirically the generalizability of what is widely accepted as valid clinical practice with this battery. Perhaps one reason this has not been done formally is that a fully effective competency in the use of the battery is probably limited to fewer individuals than are actually applying it.

Despite the lack of a comprehensive evaluation of the effectiveness with which the battery is being applied, it seems likely that a substantial number of individuals are competent to generate valid inferences with this approach. Application is complicated by the required 1 day of test administration and additional hours of scoring and report preparation. The traditional emphasis on diagnosis in the interpretive reports, while a worthwhile clinical pursuit, is not the priority referral issue of one or two decades ago before specialized neurological and neuroradiological diagnostic procedures were fully developed. Even in the early days of the battery's application, referring neurologists and neurosurgeons did not depend heavily on the interpretations for establishing diagnoses except perhaps in settings where the extensive medical resources required for sophisticated diagnostic determinations were not available. Battery interpretations were used primarily to confirm or disconfirm diagnoses based on medical grounds. When the battery yielded a disconfirming conclusion, further medical diagnostic procedures were typically introduced before final diagnosis was made. The battery clearly contributed to diagnosis, but not all tests are likely to have contributed equally. Empirical analysis might reveal that validity is enhanced especially by the sensitivity of the aphasia and sensory-motor measures to focal neurological changes, and these measures constitute a relatively small portion of administration time. These measures were derived largely from procedures developed by European and some American neurologists before they came into widespread use as part of the neurological examination. Behavioral neurological procedures are now routinely taught in neurology residency programs so that such aphasia and sensory-motor assessments are characteristically done before the patient is referred for neuropsychological examination. In order to evaluate the current effectiveness and validity of the battery, it is important to ask how much it improves upon the conclusions based on a more cursory behavioral neurological assessment. Furthermore, it seems important to ask whether or not the battery's diagnostic utility exceeds that of a well-conducted neurological exam when the aphasia and sensory-motor assessments of a complete neurological examination are excluded from the battery.

Such diagnostic issues are important perhaps more from a historical point of view since diagnosis is no longer the exclusive, and perhaps not even the primary, purpose of clinical neuropsychological assessment. Expansion of neuropsychological application is occurring primarily in rehabilitation settings where rehabilitation planning, remediation, and retraining are the primary concerns. Batteries that emphasize quantitative variables and do not address in considerable scope and depth the psychological processes affected by CNS lesions are not optimally relevant in such settings. Reitan and his associates acknowledge the need to develop suitable recommendations for rehabilitation based on the battery. However, there is a rapidly expanding literature in clinical and experimental neuropsychology that links the concepts and methods of cognitive psychology, psycholinguistics, and behavioral neurology to the analysis of the psychological processes affected by the underlying pathophysiological conditions in CNS disease. This should ultimately lead to the development of brief screening batteries designed to identify primary deficits, followed by detailed qualitative and quantitative analyses of the affected psychological processes. In turn, this may lead to more effective interventions for the purpose of modifying impaired functions and retraining individuals to compensate for neuropsychological deficits. Some of these developments may well proceed from the Halstead-Reitan battery though it seems unlikely that this will be achieved without considerable progressive revision of the approach to incorporate selected concepts and methods from this growing literature. A salient example of an area requiring revision is memory functioning, which is incompletely assessed by this battery.

The requirements for effective functioning as a clinical neuropsychologist have now been recognized to transcend the application of a particular battery and to include an integrated knowledge of the neuropathological, pathophysiological, neurological and behavioral outcomes of central nervous system involvement. Thus, the essential knowledge and experience for drawing such inferences may well require more than a cursory exposure to the broader contents of these areas. This more extensive factual knowledge and supervised experience is usually available only in formal and structured predoctoral, specialized internship, and postdoctoral training activities. The latter are expanding in number and geographic location quite remarkably, not only to more effectively develop the competencies required to apply batteries of this kind, but also to incorporate knowledge and skills derived from cognitive/experimental psychology, physiological psychology, psychopathology, behavioral neurology, neurolinguistics, developmental psychology, and gerontological psychology that are necessarily a part of the information base for performing competently in clinical neuropsychological roles. Incomplete acknowledgement of the necessity for such preparation has contributed to the widespread use of such procedures by individuals with limited training and has prompted professional organizations like the American Psychological Association (Division 40) and the International Neuropsychological Society to develop formal guidelines and criteria for education, accreditation, and credentialing in this area of practice (Task Force Report, 1981). The American Board of Professional Psychology has begun to examine individuals in the new area of practice of clinical neuropsychology, irrespective of preferred neuropsychological approach. The American Psychological Association has been developing criteria for the identification and recognition of new specialties and special proficiencies, of which clinical neuropsychology will be among the first for consideration should a formal policy be established. These developments are cited to underscore the fact that comprehensive neuropsychological assessment batteries have not been demonstrated to be applicable on the basis of a quickly or easily acquired clinical competency. Required is a body of knowledge and skills that at a minimum incorporates an expanding brain-behavior technological domain for various purposes—diagnosis, prognosis, and rehabilitation planning.

While the Halstead-Reitan battery remains the most widely used and most extensively validated approach for such purposes, it has not been shown to be applicable except in the hands of a highly trained and experienced clinical neuropsychologist with a broad background in clinical neuroscience, basic behavioral sciences, the generic components of applied psychology, and, to an increasing extent, developmental psychology. The Halstead-Reitan battery will no doubt continue to be an important part of clinical neuropsychology but will probably need to undergo further modification and revision to accommodate increased knowledge in these various areas or be replaced by other comprehensive batteries or, more likely, by specialized techniques emerging from the extensive multidisciplinary knowledge explosion occurring in clinical and experimental neuropsychology.

REVIEWER'S REFERENCES

Halstead, W. C. BRAIN AND INTELLIGENCE: A QUANTITATIVE STUDY OF THE FRONTAL LOBES. Chicago: The University of Chicago Press, 1947.

Reitan, R. M. Psychological deficits resulting from cerebral lesions in man. In J. M. Warren and K. Akert (Eds.), THE FRONTAL GRANULAR CORTEX AND BEHAVIOR. New York: McGraw-Hill, 1964.

Reitan, R. M. Methodological problems in clinical neuropsychology. In R. M. Reitan and L. A. Davison (Eds.), CLINICAL NEUROPSYCHOLOGY: CURRENT STATUS AND APPLICATIONS. Washington, DC: V. H. Winston and Sons, 1974.

Reitan, R. M., & Davison, L. A. CLINICAL NEUROPSYCHOLOGY: CURRENT STATUS AND APPLICATIONS. Washington, DC: V. H. Winston and Sons, 1974.

Reitan, R. M. MANUAL FOR THE ADMINISTRATION OF NEUROPSYCHOLOGICAL TEST BATTERIES FOR ADULTS AND CHILDREN. Tucson, AZ: Neuropsychology Laboratory, 1979.

REPORT OF THE TASK FORCE ON EDUCATION, ACCREDITATION AND CREDENTIALING. Atlanta, GA: Board of Governors of the International Neuropsychological Society, February 6, 1981.
Reed, J. The Chicago-Indianapolis group. In G. Goldstein (Chair), HISTORY OF HUMAN NEUROPSYCHOLOGY IN THE UNITED STATES. Symposium conducted at the 91st Annual Convention of the American Psychological Association, Anaheim, CA, 1983.
Goldstein, G. Comprehensive neuropsychological assessment batteries. In G. Goldstein and M. Hersen (Eds.), HANDBOOK OF PSYCHOLOGICAL ASSESSMENT. New York: Pergammon, 1984.
Hamsher, K. de S. Specialized neuropsychological assessment methods. In G. Goldstein and M. Herson (Eds.), HANDBOOK OF PSYCHOLOGICAL ASSESSMENT. New York: Pergammon, 1984.

[464]

The Hand Test, Revised 1983. Ages 6 and over; 1959–83; HT; 41 scores, 24 quantitative scores: interpersonal (affection, dependence, communication, exhibition, direction, aggression, total), environmental (acquisition, active, passive, total), maladjustive (tension, crippled, fear, total), withdrawal (description, bizarre, failure, total), experience ratio, acting out ratio, pathological, average initial response time, high minus low score, plus 17 qualitative scores: ambivalent, automatic phrase, cylindrical, denial, emotion, gross, hiding, immature, impotent, inanimate, movement, oral, perplexity, sensual, sexual, original, repetition; individual; 1 form ('69, 10 cards); scoring booklet ('81, 4 pages); manual ('83, 90 pages plus scoring booklet); 1983 price data: $7.10 per 25 scoring booklets; $12.70 per set of picture cards; $6.40 per manual; (10) minutes; Edwin E. Wagner; Western Psychological Services.*

See T3:1053 (21 references); see also 8:575 (29 references), T2:1470 (15 references), and P:438 (12 references); for a review by Goldine C. Gleser and an excerpted review by Irving R. Stone of an earlier edition, see 6:216 (6 references).

TEST REFERENCES

1. Wagner, E. E., Maloney, P., & Walter, T. Efficacy of three projective techniques in differentiating brain damage among subjects with normal IQs. JOURNAL OF CLINICAL PSYCHOLOGY, 1980, 36, 968–972.
2. McCraw, R. K., & Pegg-McNab, J. Effect of test order on Rorschach human and movement responses. JOURNAL OF PERSONALITY ASSESSMENT, 1981, 45, 575–581.
3. Wagner, E. E., & Heise, M. R. Rorschach and Hand Test data comparing bipolar patients in manic and depressive phases. JOURNAL OF PERSONALITY ASSESSMENT, 1981, 45, 240–249.
4. Wagner, E. E., Maloney, P., & Wilson, D. S. Split-half and test-retest Hand Test reliabilities for pathological samples. JOURNAL OF CLINICAL PSYCHOLOGY, 1981, 37, 589–592.
5. Daniel, F. R., Jr., & Wagner, E. E. Differences among Holland types as measured by the Hand Test: An attempt at construct validation. EDUCATIONAL AND PSYCHOLOGICAL MEASUREMENT, 1982, 42, 1295–1301.
6. Hayslip, B., Jr., & Panek, P. E. Construct validation of the Hand Test with the aged: Replication and extension. JOURNAL OF PERSONALITY ASSESSMENT, 1982, 46, 345–349.
7. Maloney, P., Deitchman, R., & Wagner, E. E. Consistency of some personality measures as a function of stage of menstruation. JOURNAL OF PERSONALITY ASSESSMENT, 1982, 46, 597–602.
8. McGiboney, G. W., & Carter, C. Test-retest reliability of The Hand Test with acting-out adolescent subjects. PERCEPTUAL AND MOTOR SKILLS, 1982, 55, 723–726.
9. McGiboney, G. W., & Huey, W. C. Hand Test norms for disruptive black adolescent males. PERCEPTUAL AND MOTOR SKILLS, 1982, 54, 441–442.
10. Stoner, S., Panek, P., & Satterfield, G. T. Age and sex differences on the Hand Test. JOURNAL OF PERSONALITY ASSESSMENT, 1982, 46, 260–264.
11. Teng, E. L., & Lee, A. L. Right-left discrimination: No sex difference among normals on The Hand Test and the Route Test. PERCEPTUAL AND MOTOR SKILLS, 1982, 55, 299–302.
12. Wagner, E. F. Personality differences as measured by The Hand Test among Holland types for females. PERCEPTUAL AND MOTOR SKILLS, 1982, 55, 710.
13. Branconnier, R. J., Cole, J. O., Ghazvinian, S., Spera, K. F., Oxenkrug, G. F., & Bass, J. L. Clinical pharmacology of bupropion and imipramine in elderly depressives. THE JOURNAL OF CLINICAL PSYCHIATRY, 1983, 44 (5–Section 2), 130–133.
14. McCormick, M. K. T., & Wagner, E. E. Validity of The Hand Test for diagnosing organicity in a clinical setting. PERCEPTUAL AND MOTOR SKILLS, 1983, 57, 607–610.
15. Panek, P. E., & Spencer, W. B. Hand Test personality correlates of aging in institutionalized mentally retarded adults. PERCEPTUAL AND MOTOR SKILLS, 1983, 57, 1021–1022.
16. Stoner, S. B., & Spencer, W. B. Age and sex differences on The Hand Test with children. JOURNAL OF CLINICAL PSYCHOLOGY, 1984, 40, 598–602.

[465]

Hannah-Gardner Test of Verbal & Nonverbal Language Functioning. Ages 3.5–5.5; 1978; screening device for identifying English and Spanish speaking children with language deficits; 7 scores: visual perception, conceptual development, auditory perception, linguistic development, total, nonverbal, verbal; individual; 1 form each for English and Spanish versions; manual (50 pages) includes English and Spanish versions; picture book (17 pages); picture cards (41 cards); score sheet (1 page); price data available from publisher; (25–30) minutes; Elaine P. Hannah and Julie O. Gardner; Lingua Press.*

[466]

Harding Skyscraper. Ages 17 and over with intelligence level in top 1% of population; 1973–75; Form B–C ('73, 4 pages); no manual; 1982 price data: tests rented only; rental and scoring service, $7 per test; (90–120) minutes; C. Chris. Harding; the Author [Australia].*

See 8:189 (2 references).

Review of Harding Skyscraper by DONALD J. TREFFINGER, Professor, Interdisciplinary Center for Creative Studies, State University College at Buffalo, Buffalo, NY:

The Harding Skyscraper test was developed by the Founder of the International Society for Philosophical Enquiry for use as an examination for screening applicants for membership in that organization. It was intended to be a measure of high level intellectual functioning. The test is presumably self-administered, with the direction to "take any reasonable amount of time." The instrument is not lengthy, but appears rather carelessly organized and printed. It is unaccompanied by any empirical research concerning its development or validation, the development of any scales or scoring procedures, or the statistical characteristics of the items. The norms are based on a sample of 644 subjects, about whom no other information was provided. A page of correlation coefficients was received, showing positive correlations of the test with other intelligence tests and asserting that the test-retest reliability of the Skyscraper test was .84. However, no information was provided concerning the nature of any of the studies that yielded these results, so the correlations cannot be interpreted in any meaningful way. No Norms-Technical Manual was provided. A search of the usual literature and written inquiries to the author and his colleagues produced no published research regarding the validity, reliability, or interpretation of this instrument. There is certainly no empirical basis for recommending this instrument to anyone seeking measures of intellectual abilities.

[467]

Harding Stress-Fair Compatibility Test. Adults; 1980; HSFCT; measures compatibility between people; 11 scores: intellective, extraversion, sensitivity, idealism, motivation, awareness, independence, reasonability, objectivity, dominance, compatibility; no data on reliability and validity; provisional norms; 1 form (3 pages); directions and work sheet (2 pages); 1983 price data: $2 per test, initially; $10 for marking and administration; administration time not reported; Chris. Harding; the Author [Australia].*

Review of Harding Stress-Fair Compatibility Test by CHARLES D. CLAIBORN, Associate Professor of Educational Psychology, University of Nebraska-Lincoln, Lincoln, NE:

The Harding Stress-Fair Compatibility Test scarcely warrants a review. It consists of 46 questions, seemingly arbitrary in content, with the expressed aim of "matching" compatible individuals through the mail. Although a "Stress Level Indication" form and "Work Sheet" were among the materials I reviewed, a manual was not included, nor, indeed, was there any explanation of how these supplementary materials are to be used. Thus, what the test measures, how it measures it, and how well it measures it are completely unclear.

Review of Harding Stress-Fair Compatibility Test by DOUGLAS S. PAYNE, Assistant Professor of Psychiatry, Medical College of Georgia, Augusta, GA, and Director of Psychology Department, Georgia Regional Hospital, Augusta, GA:

The Harding Stress-Fair Compatibility Test (HSFCT) is a 46-item instrument, lacking a manual, which is presumably designed to determine whether two people are compatible. It produces data on 10 subscales, which are unnamed on the material routinely sent to test users. Depending upon how it is answered, an item may be scored on as many as five of these subscales. The HSFCT requires approximately 5–10 minutes to complete, but there are no directions provided as to who should administer or interpret this instrument. Apparently, the author intended to have all completed HSFCTs mailed to him for scoring for a fee.

The scoring directions provided for this review of the HSFCT are easily misinterpreted and follow no generally accepted statistical process. Without a rationale for this scoring procedure, it is impossible to say that it is appropriate for increasing the meaningfulness of the scores. The scoring sheets are confusing, e.g., listing a column for Raw Score which is apparently intended for a square root derivation following an arithmetical procedure. There are also other columns of numbers on the scoring worksheets with no clearly indicated purpose. If the reader is able to understand the scoring instructions (I am not sure I was) so that she/he thinks everything has been done correctly, then the resulting scores can be placed into one of 12 levels of compatibility, ranging from Complete Alienation to Optimum Compatibility. Placement in one of these categories is determined by the score on a chi square distribution, and it is not explained how this distribution is related to the operations and products of the scoring sheet or to the stated levels of compatibility. The four highest levels of compatibility listed are from 99.2 to 99.92 percentiles, which is a very restricted range with a probable lack of reliability. The Optimum Compatibility level is achieved by having more similar scores than the level labeled Beginnings of Identity Fusion. This is confusing, as compatibility does not seem to be optimal in the unhealthy sounding range of identity fusion.

The presentation of the HSFCT by the author is utterly inadequate. Lacking a manual, research results, or a described normative procedure, it is impossible to recommend this test as anything but an oddity. By presenting the HSFCT for sale, the author is, essentially, asserting that it can determine levels of compatibility. However, he has neglected to provide any evidence, whether empirical or theoretical, to induce the consumer to believe his assertion.

[468]

The Harrington-O'Shea Career Decision-Making System. Grades 7–12 and adults; 1974–82; CDM; "self-administered and self-interpreted" inventory; 6 scores (arts, business, clerical, crafts, scientific, social) used to identify 3 or more occupational areas, for intensive career exploration, from among 18 clusters (art work, clerical work, customer services, data analysis, education work, entertainment, legal, literary work, management, manual work, math-science, medical-dental, music work, personal service, sales work, skilled crafts, social services, technical) and questions in 5 areas (abilities, future plans, job values, occupational preferences, school subject preferences); manual ('82, 102 pages); 1984 price data: $5.75 per manual; $7 per audiocassette; $2 per specimen set; (40) minutes; Thomas F. Harrington and Arthur J. O'Shea; American Guidance Service.*

a) SELF-SCORED EDITION. 1 form ('82, 12 pages); instructions for administration ('82, 6 pages); interpretive folder ('82, 8 pages); $26.50 per 25 tests; Spanish edition available.

b) MACHINE-SCORED EDITION. 1 form ('81, 4 pages); instructions for administration ('82, 2 pages); 3 scoring reports available: profile report, profile report with group summary report, narrative report; $59.50 per 25 tests with profile reports; $63.25 per 25 tests with profile reports and group summary report; $8 per test with narrative report.

See T3:1059 (3 references); for a review by Carl G. Willis of an earlier edition, see 8:1004.

[469]

Harvard Group Scale of Hypnotic Susceptibility. College and adults; 1959–62; HGSHS; adaptation for group administration of Form A of the Stanford Hypnotic Susceptibility Scale; no data on reliability; Form A ('62, 8 pages); manual ('62, 22 pages); 1984 price data: $12.50 per 25 tests; $5 per manual; $5.50 per specimen set; (50–70) minutes; Ronald E. Shor and Emily Carota Orne; Consulting Psychologists Press, Inc.*

See T3:1063 (57 references), 8:576 (46 references), T2:1212 (19 references), and P:107 (12 references); for a review by Seymore Fisher, see 6:112 (4 references).

TEST REFERENCES

1. Frankel, A. S., Reilly, S., & Lert, A. A style variable in assertion training. COGNITIVE THERAPY AND RESEARCH, 1978, 2, 289–292.

2. Katz, N. W. Hypnotic inductions as training in cognitive self-control. COGNITIVE THERAPY AND RESEARCH, 1978, 2, 365–369.

3. Rivers, S. M., & Spanos, N. P. Personal variables predicting voluntary participation in and attrition from a meditation program. PSYCHOLOGICAL REPORTS, 1981, 49, 795–801.

4. Jones, B., & Spanos, N. P. Suggestions for altered auditory sensitivity, the negative subject effect and hypnotic susceptibility: A signal detection analysis. JOURNAL OF PERSONALITY AND SOCIAL PSYCHOLOGY, 1982, 43, 637–647.

5. Smyth, L. D. Psychopathology as a function of neuroticism and a hypnotically implanted aggressive conflict. JOURNAL OF PERSONALITY AND SOCIAL PSYCHOLOGY, 1982, 43, 555–564.

6. Spanos, N. P., Jones, B., & Malfara, A. Hypnotic deafness: Now you hear it—Now you still hear it. JOURNAL OF ABNORMAL PSYCHOLOGY, 1982, 91, 75–77.

[470]

Hay Aptitude Test Battery. Clerical and plant workers; 1947–82; tape cassette available for administration; 4 tests; manual (no date, 32 pages); 1982 price data: $57 per 25 battery sets; Edward N. Hay; E. F. Wonderlic & Associates, Inc.*

a) THE WARM UP TEST 1. Form C ('78, 2 pages); scoring key ('50, 1 page); $12.50 per 25 tests; 1(6) minutes.

b) NUMBER PERCEPTION TEST. NP; Form A, B, ('77, 3 pages); scoring key (no date, 2 pages); $17 per 25 tests; 4(9) minutes.

c) NAME FINDING TEST. NF; Form C ('79, 2 pages); practice exercises ('77, 2 pages); scoring key ('50, 2 pages); $18 per 25 tests including practice exercises and right and left hand tests; 4(9) minutes.

d) NUMBER SERIES COMPLETION TEST. NS; Form C ('77, 2 pages); scoring key (no date, 2 pages); $17 per 25 tests; 4(9) minutes.

See T2:2132 (2 references) and 5:849 (2 references); for reviews by Reign H. Bittner and Edward E. Cureton, see 4:725 (8 references).

Review of Hay Aptitude Test Battery by ROBERT P. VECCHIO, Associate Professor of Management, University of Notre Dame, Notre Dame, IN:

The Hay Aptitude Test Battery is designed to aid in the selection of clerical workers. Four tests comprise the Battery: (*a*) a 20-item Warm-Up Test (which resembles a general intelligence test), (*b*) Number Perception Test, (*c*) Name Finding Test, and (*d*) Number Series Completion Test. The Warm-Up Test is timed for one minute, while the remaining tests each require four minutes. Ostensibly, the Warm-Up Test is intended to ease the nervous or familiarize the inexperienced test taker. No data are reported which substantiate the claimed benefits of this device. Further, the professed innocence of the Warm-Up Test is belied by the suggestion in the manual that the test can be scored for the number correct (a scoring key is provided), and that the scores on the test have been found to correlate with supervisor ratings of performance for several occupations. Interestingly, the Warm-Up Test is reported as correlating .55 with the Wonderlic Personnel Test. However, any user who may be considering the deceptive use of the Warm-Up Test should recall Principle 8a of the Ethical Principles of Psychologists ("In using assessment techniques, psychologists respect the right of clients to have a full explanation of the nature and purpose of the techniques in language that the client can understand..."). Other than a cursory suggestion of the practical utility of the Warm-Up Test for selection purposes, the manual does not equate the Warm-Up Test with the remaining components of the Battery (i.e., in terms of normative data or discussion).

The Number Perception Test requires that the test taker compare pairs of numbers and identify whether the paired numbers are the same or different. This test is, in essence, a shorter version of part of the Minnesota Clerical Test. Similarly, it suffers from the same defect of having a majority of the numerical discrepancies occur in the last half of each of the paired numbers (Kirkpatrick, 1957). This construction defect could hinder or benefit test takers who exhibit particular response biases (Diaz, 1978). Reliability estimates for this test are not reported.

The Name Finding Test requires that the test taker examine a particular name and remember it well enough to identify it from a group of similar names. This activity resembles the duties performed by bookkeepers or billing machine operators in finding a correct ledger sheet. Like the Number Perception Test, this test involves a simple activity which could be performed with great accuracy if sufficient time were afforded the test taker. For such assessment devices, it is generally accepted that reliability should be estimated from parallel forms or test-retest procedures (Anastasi, 1982). Surprisingly, the manual reports an odd-even reliability coefficient for clerical job applicants. As expected, the coefficient is spuriously high (.94).

The final test in the Battery, the Number Series Completion Test, consists of sets of numbers which are related in accordance with a specific logical rule. For each set, the test taker is required to generate the next two numbers in the sequence. Once again, the reported reliability (.94) is inappropriately taken from an odd-even estimate.

The validity of the three tests is suggested by the results of selected validity studies. Unfortunately, neither references to the representative studies nor specific procedural information on the studies is provided in the manual. Thus, the concerned test adapter can only guess as to whether the reported validity studies were concurrent or predictive in nature. The range of validity coefficients seems adequate (.25 to .62). However, the completeness of the summarized studies is suspect in that a published account of a failure of the Number Perception Test to correlate with performance ratings of clerical workers (Mackinney, 1959) is not tabled with the "success stories."

A further problem involves the manual's imprudent style and careless use of terminology. For example, the phrase "job related" is used repeatedly as a descriptive trait of each test. Yet, the extent of the job-relevance of a test cannot be determined without a careful analysis of a job's components (i.e., "job-relatedness" must be determined in a case-by-case fashion and not by fiat or in an a priori manner).

The manual's norms provide mean performance values by sex. For the Number Series Completion Test, males displayed significantly superior performance relative to females. This difference, however, is not discussed in the manual. Aside from legal concerns, sex differences in performance on clerical aptitude measures are an important issue; an example is the 1981 Elliott report of female superiority on the Minnesota Clerical Test. In addition, the means of the highest and lowest educational groupings of the normative sample differed by somewhat more than one-half standard deviation on all three of the Hay tests, with the more highly educated test takers tending to do better on all measures. This evidence suggests that educational differences need to be controlled before drawing inferences regarding demographic differences. Although racial differences on the tests are not documented or discussed, such differences are perhaps expected because of racial differences in educational attainment.

In summary, the Hays Battery remains a promising collection of tests. In light of the manual's deficiencies, users of these tests must be careful to exercise vigilance for demographic differences and to avoid accepting the manual's favorable statements concerning the utility, reliability, and validity of the tests.

REVIEWER'S REFERENCES

Kirkpatrick, D. L. The Minnesota Clerical Test. PERSONNEL PSYCHOLOGY, 1957, 10, 53–54.

Mackinney, A. C., & Wolins, L. Validity information exchange. No. 12–19, PERSONNEL PSYCHOLOGY, 1959, 12, 482–483.

Diaz, A. P. D. Construction defect in the Minnesota Clerical Test. PROFESSIONAL PSYCHOLOGY, 1978, 9, 7–8.

Elliott, A. G. P. Skill and aptitude in the Minnesota Clerical Test. THE IRISH JOURNAL OF PSYCHOLOGY, 1981, 1, 16–22.

Anastasi, A. PSYCHOLOGICAL TESTING. MacMillan Publishing, New York, 1982.

[471]

Health Problems Checklist. Adult men, adult women; 1984; for "rapid assessment of the health status and potential health problems of clients typically seen in psychotherapy settings"; screening for appropriate medical referrals; no formal scoring system; no data on reliability and validity; no norms; separate forms for men, women, (4 pages); no manual; 1984 price data: $10.95 per combination kit, including 25 men's and 25 women's forms; administration time not reported; John A. Schinka; Psychological Assessment Resources, Inc.*

[472]

The Hearing Measurement Scale. Adults; 1979; HMS; self-administered questionnaire for the assessment of hearing handicap; 8 scores: speech hearing, hearing for nonspeech sounds, spatial localization, emotional response to hearing impairment, speech distortion, tinnitus, personal opinion of hearing, total; norms for men only; 1 form (no date, 6 pages); manual (61 pages); price data available from publisher; (20–40) minutes; William G. Nobel; University of New England [Australia].*

Review of The Hearing Measurement Scale by JUDY R. DUBNO, Assistant Professor of Surgery (Head and Neck), UCLA School of Medicine, Los Angeles, CA:

The Hearing Measurement Scale (HMS) is an instrument which has been devised to measure the hearing handicap of persons with sensorineural hearing loss. The scale was designed to be administered in an interview format, but the authors suggest that a self-administration method may be acceptable. "Hearing handicap" is described as a twofold entity consisting of the hearing impairment and the dysfunctions associated with it, and the listener's response to that impairment. The dysfunctions resulting from sensorineural hearing loss were incorporated in the HMS by dividing the scale into seven subsections. Five of the subsections (speech hearing, hearing for nonspeech sounds, spatial localization, speech distortion, tinnitus) contain questions related to difficulties encountered as a direct result of the hearing loss. The remaining two sections (emotional response to hearing impairment, personal opinion of hearing) evaluate the psychosocial aspect of the listener's hearing handicap, or the person's response to the impairment.

There are several aspects of the construction and validation of the HMS that should be noted. First, the original set of questions used in the HMS were determined from the results of an open-ended questionnaire, administered to a large group of patients seeking hearing aids. In this questionnaire, the patients were asked to make a list of difficulties resulting from their hearing loss in order of importance. These data provided insight into the most commonly reported problems encountered by hearing-impaired adults and thus provides substantial face validity for the resulting HMS. Second, although it is understood that hearing loss affects areas of everyday life other than speech understanding, the HMS is one of only a few tools used to evaluate hearing handicap which includes social, vocational, and emotional areas of inquiry. Third, although there is lengthy administration time required, the test format is simple to understand for both the patient and the administrator. The test manual gives extensive instructions concerning procedures for the interviewer and interviewee, including strategies for cross-referencing and recapitulating. It would be helpful, however, if average test-administration times were provided.

Fourth, there has been extensive experimentation undertaken to evaluate the validity and reliability of the test form, with mostly favorable results. Correlational analyses indicate relationships among test subsections and standard audiometric tests, a high degree of internal consistency, as well as strong relationships to other well-known hearing-handicap scales. A factor analysis provided some construct validity evidence for the scale. Conclusions of several studies utilizing the HMS (as cited in the test manual) indicate that the test may be applicable to many different populations of hearing-impaired individuals, including those over 65. Concerning its use in an aural rehabilitation program, results show higher HMS scores with listeners who wear their hearing aids for long periods of time, and a reduction in HMS scores subsequent to the initial hearing aid fitting.

Several questions remain unanswered concerning the HMS. First, the original form of the test was validated on working-age males with evidence of noise-induced hearing loss. Although there have been additional studies using females, listeners with severe-to-profound hearing loss, or other auditory dysfunctions, including presbycusis, it has not been made clear that the test is valid for these populations. Furthermore, an experiment with a very large population of hearing-impaired listeners has not been undertaken. Second, it is not clear that the reliability of the test is adequate. The test manual presents numerous test-retest correlations which are, in some cases, statistically significant but not as high as might be expected or required. In addition, if the HMS is to be used in an aural rehabilitation program, the test may be administered more than twice; this would require that the reliability analysis cover multiple repetitions of the test in addition to test-retest correlations.

Third, the authors suggest that the test, although designed to be administered in an interview format, could be self-administered. The data pertaining to the test when given in a paper-and-pencil format present sufficiently inconsistent results as to make this method questionable. The unknown aspect of "self-disclosure" and its possible ramifications should be studied further. Finally, the results of the HMS are weighted and modified "to give a valid measure of handicap." Sufficient discussion is not included as to how these weights and modifiers were derived, or how they are used to measure handicap. It is also unclear whether the weights included in the test manual are specifically designed for the original validation group (working males with etiology of noise exposure) or whether they may be used for any hearing-impaired individual.

Despite these several questions that remain unanswered, the HMS could, nevertheless, be a useful tool for the evaluation of hearing handicap. The inclusion of items pertaining to the listener's reaction to the impairment is an important aspect of any handicap measurement device, although it is missing from several well-known scales of this type. The HMS may also be useful as a research tool if used as a subjective validation of audiometric procedures which attempt to evaluate a listener's receptive communicative handicap.

[473]

Henderson-Moriarity ESL/Literacy Placement Test. Adult learners of English as a second language who have minimal or no English skills; 1982; HELP; criterion-referenced; 3 components: intake information/first language assessment, oral English assessment, written English assessment; no data on reliability and validity; individual; 1 form (20 pages, plus instructions for administration and scoring); no separate manual; some testing materials must be assembled locally; 1985 price data: $11.95 per test booklet; administration time not reported; Cindy Henderson, Pia Moriarty, and Mary Kay Mitchell (illustrations); The Alemany Press.*

[474]

Henshaw Secondary Mathematics Test. Grades 9–10; 1980; HSMT; "redesigned from A Diagnostic Test in Basic Algebra and A Diagnostic Test in Basic Geometry"; 10 scores: four processes, set language and solution or truth sets, construction of equations and inequations and formulae, co-ordinates and graphs of relations, simultaneous and quadratic equations and factors, plane and solid figures, transformations—similar figures and symmetry, angles, congruence—chords of circle—tangents, total; no data on reliability and validity; no norms; 1 form (32 pages); manual (27 pages); 1983 price data: A$2 per test; $6.55 per manual; $8.50 per specimen set; administration time not reported; John Henshaw; Australian Council for Educational Research [Australia].*

Review of Henshaw Secondary Mathematics Test by BARRY J. FRASER, Head of School of Curriculum Studies, Western Australian Institute of Technology, Perth, Australia:

This mathematics test is for the junior high school level and covers mainly the areas of algebra and geometry in both the field of conventional and modern mathematics. Items test understanding of mathematical terms and vocabulary together with the application of these to mathematical situations. The test is suitable for group administration, but also could be particularly valuable if administered orally to individual students in the presence of a teacher. The Henshaw test was written by an experienced mathematics teacher and reflects a good understanding of errors commonly made by students.

This test is comprehensive and provides good coverage of the range of topics in algebra and geometry important in mathematics teaching at the junior high school level. It contains 386 items altogether and these are divided among the nine topics listed above. In turn, the nine major sections are subdivided into 46 subsections (as well as a number of extension exercises providing more advanced problems). Consequently, a major merit of this test is that it gives the mathematics teacher access to diagnostic tests for 46 separate topics.

The main purpose of the test is the diagnosis of student errors. Consequently, the manual is devoted almost entirely to describing the common errors reflected in students' answers to each of 386 items in the battery. This discussion of common errors is very detailed and thorough, and is likely to be of considerable use in helping teachers pinpoint their students' specific deficiencies which require remediation. Also, through using this test with students and carefully reading the test manual, many mathematics teachers (especially inexperienced teachers or people in training) could gain valuable insight into students' mathematical reasoning and misconceptions.

Of course, not all subsections of the test would be equally relevant to all students. Because of the diversity of topics covered in the 46 subsections, however, it is likely that most mathematics teachers will find many relevant topics irrespective of the grade level they teach in the junior high school, the specific program or syllabus they are following, or the part of Australia in which their school is located. Moreover, although the test was designed for use in Australia, there appears to be no reason why it would not be suitable for use in other countries.

As the test is intended primarily as a diagnostic tool, it is the student's performance on each individual item which is important rather than the total score for a particular topic. Consequently, it is understandable that the manual for this test does not contain the whole-test statistics (such as the mean, standard deviation, and reliability) usually found in other test manuals. It is surprising, however, that no statistical information about individual items is reported for a suitable sample. Although the author draws on his own experience to identify which questions are usually answered well by most students, the reader would be helped by the reporting of statistics describing the percentage of students from a defined sample obtaining correct answers for each item in the battery.

The detailed discussion of individual items contains numerous implicit or explicit hints to teachers about how to remediate the errors detected. It is likely, however, that many users of the test could appreciate even more attention to possible teaching strategies likely to be useful in helping students overcome their weaknesses.

Although the test's intended purpose is to use responses to individual questions to identify errors, it is still possible that some teachers could make use of students' total scores on sections or subsections of interest to them. For example, teachers could use the total scores of a class of students on several selected subsections to infer whether the class possessed the entry level proficiency needed prior to commencing study of a certain topic. Or the teacher in charge of a school's mathematics department might develop a year's programme for each grade level based in part on information about what topics were generally mastered already and which topics required special attention during the school year. Given that some teachers might find total scores on sections or subsections of the Henshaw test useful for various purposes, the inclusion in the manual of some whole-test statistics (e.g., mean, reliability) could make a worthwhile addition.

Generally the items themselves are well written and represent skills that would be considered salient by mathematics teachers. For example, Topic 6: Plane and Solid Figures, contains 64 well-written items covering the topics of lines, planes and surfaces, types and sizes of angles, supplementary and complementary angles, rectilinear figures, types of triangles, quadrilaterals, properties of parallelograms, circle terms, compass directions, and solids. One exception to the generally high quality of items is the use of some unrealistic examples which could reinforce some children's view that mathematics is of little practical value in real life. For example, Question 3.27 requires the writing of an inequation for a situation in which a father's age is now five times his son's age and, in five years time, the sum of their ages will be more than four times the son's age at that time. Whereas some teachers and students could be fascinated by such questions, it cannot be assumed that the average student will react in this way.

Although reference to "research or experience" is used more than once in the manual, no research studies are cited and no research results are described. In fact, the absence of a bibliography is unhelpful to the interested teachers wishing to read further on diagnosis of students' mathematical errors.

In summary, this diagnostic test consists of well-written items which assess a comprehensive range of topics which are salient in mathematics teaching. The highly detailed discussion of common errors reflects the author's experience as a teacher and is likely to be of great use to others. Additions whose inclusion could improve the manual are a bibliography, data on the proportion of students answering each question correctly, further guidance in methods for remediating the deficiencies diagnosed, and (for those teachers wishing to use student performance on whole sections for certain purposes) some conventional whole-test statistics such as means and reliabilities. The quality of production of the test and manual are uniformly high.

Review of Henshaw Secondary Mathematics Test by RICHARD F. SCHMID, Associate Professor of Education, Concordia University, Montreal, Quebec, Canada:

The Henshaw Secondary Mathematics Test is the product of a beneficial redesign of the Diagnostic Test in Basic Algebra and the Diagnostic Test in Basic Geometry by the same author. A number of new topics and subtopics have been added which broaden the test to encompass the majority of secondary mathematics content. All the previous test's algebra items, and virtually all the old geometry items, reappear unaltered.

It is unfortunate that the word "diagnostic" was removed from the new title, as the test's intended use is explicitly diagnostic; it is not an achievement test. Because it is designed as a diagnostic tool, reliability data and norms are unnecessary. The validity criterion is met via face validity because the individual user must determine what sections are useful, and when. Being a power test, time limits are wisely not supplied.

This test was successfully designed to serve as an aid for instruction and remediation by mathematics teachers. The problems are designed to measure either understanding of mathematical terms and vocabulary, or the capacity to apply terms to mathematical situations. Most questions have two parallel items, and one or both may be used. Administration variations are clearly explained. All the topic sections have a standard set of many items. Most are then followed by extension exercises which may be used for postremedial work and to provide more challenging problem-solving situations. Questions usually test only one process, though some items, especially the extension exercises, are designed to go beyond the obvious, and require intermediate steps. Thus the test is useful for all student ability levels. Topic content tends to span the entire standard secondary curriculum, with no notable omissions. Several of the topics offered are usually not emphasized in North American schools or are not covered at all. This, however, does not create a problem, as the teacher can select only those areas of immediate concern, and continue to do so throughout the ongoing secondary curriculum. In a few cases, the wording in problems may not be familiar to the students, and the user may find it necessary to "translate" the statement to a form to which the students are accustomed.

The test booklet and manual are well printed and bound. The manual is clearly and concisely written. Each topic is introduced with a useful statement on content and purpose. Perhaps the most valuable aspect of the manual is the "common errors" feature. Students' most frequent errors and misunderstandings are listed for every test question. At times, either a fuller explanation is given about the basis of the error, and/or suggestions are made for re-teaching the principle involved. When a large number of errors occurs, re-teaching is strongly recommended before use of further test or extension items.

While this test is well designed and can be an extremely useful diagnostic tool, its flexibility calls for a certain level of conscientiousness on the part of the user. It can be used as an accurate measure of group strengths and weaknesses, but is best applied to individuals once problems are detected. Mathematics is infamous for being acutely frustrating at a personal level, and such problems often call for individual attention.

In summary, the Henshaw Secondary Mathematics Test provides the user with a complete, useful tool for diagnostic purposes. Its use of parallel items for most questions enables a sort of pre- and posttest use ideal for criterion-referenced learning. Remediation is enhanced with an extensive catalog of "common errors" and some suggestions for re-teaching. This test would be an extremely valuable, inexpensive addition to any mathematics teacher's set of learning materials.

[475]

High School Career-Course Planner. Grades 8–10; 1983; CCP; criterion-referenced; self-assessment of job interests to facilitate high school course selection; no scores, 3 areas: occupational interests, occupational titles, high school plan; no data on reliability; no norms; 1 form (6 pages); user's guide (4 pages); 1984 price data: $16 per complete set (includes 35 planners, user's guide, and 2 JOB-O dictionaries); $.40 per planner; (50–60) minutes; CFKR Career Materials, Inc.*

[476]

High School Subject Tests. Grades 9–12; 1980; part of Comprehensive Assessment Program; 15 tests; teacher's manual (93 pages); directions for administration (4 pages) for each test; separate answer sheets must be used; 1983 price data: $21.95 per 35 reusable tests of any one subject including directions for administration; $12.50 per 35 self-scoring answer sheets for any one subject including 1 class analyzer; $9 per 35 machine-scorable answer sheets; $10.15 per 35 class analyzer sheets; $6.50 per teacher's manual; $2.85 per directions for administration for any one subject; $19.40 per specimen set (without manual); $8.80 per mathematics review kit including *a*, *b*, and *c* below; $8.80 per science review kit including *d*, *e*, and *f* below; $9.45 per social studies review kit including *g*, *h*, *i*, and *j* below; $8.80 per English review kit including *k*, *l*, and *m* below; $5.25 per consumer education review kit; $5.25 per health review kit; scoring service, $.55 per student; (30–50) minutes; Louis A. Gatta, Robert B. Adams, Marjorie C. Frey, Melton E. Golmon, Karen J. Kuehner, Vincent F. Malek, and John W. McConnell; Scott, Foresman and Co. Test Division.*

a) ALGEBRA. 1 form (7 pages).
b) GEOMETRY. 1 form (8 pages).
c) GENERAL MATHEMATICS. 1 form (7 pages).
d) BIOLOGY. 1 form (8 pages).
e) CHEMISTRY. 1 form (8 pages).
f) PHYSICAL SCIENCE. 1 form (8 pages).
g) AMERICAN GOVERNMENT. 1 form (8 pages).
h) AMERICAN HISTORY. 1 form (8 pages).
i) WORLD GEOGRAPHY. 1 form (8 pages).
j) WORLD HISTORY. 1 form (7 pages).
k) WRITING AND MECHANICS. 1 form (10 pages).
l) LITERATURE AND VOCABULARY. 1 form (11 pages).
m) LANGUAGE. 1 form (8 pages).
n) CONSUMER EDUCATION. 1 form (8 pages).
o) HEALTH. 1 form (8 pages).

Review of High School Subject Tests by ROBERT K. GABLE, Director, Bureau of Educational Research and Service, Professor, Educational Psychology, and FRANCIS X. ARCHAMBAULT, Professor and Department Head, Educational Psychology, The University of Connecticut, Storrs, CT:

According to the authors, the High School Subject Tests provide both criterion-referenced and norm-referenced information regarding student achievement in specific school subjects. We should first note that, like many of the new "criterion-referenced" tests, the High School Subject Tests should properly be called "objective-referenced" in that, unlike truly criterion-referenced measures, they do not contain the cut scores needed to make mastery classification decisions.

Despite this oversight, comprehensive lists of objectives representing each subject matter area are provided in the Teacher's Manual. If properly presented, such information can be used for individual evaluation and diagnosis as well as for school curriculum analysis. However, although the test items are classified by content area, they are not grouped by objective. For example, the General Mathematics test content area of Computation (Recall and Basic Operations) lists 10 objectives measured by 17 items, but does not list the objective/item matches. Thus, student diagnostic work is more difficult than it would be if the objective/item assignments were included.

Norm tables containing percentiles and standard scores are provided for each subject area for all grades combined. In addition, norms are provided for grades 9 through 12 for the Literature and Vocabulary, Language, and Writing tests. While a total of 28,481 students in a representative sample of 316 schools defined the total norm group, it should be noted that different norm groups were used for each test. As a result, comparisons of scores across different subject matter tests should not be made. Self-scoring answer sheets, which contain directions for scoring and making comparisons with national norms, facilitate local scoring by teachers, aides, or students. Score reports include an individual student record and a class record. The student record enables the scores for each content area (e.g., Cell Biology and Microbiology) within a subject area (e.g., Biology) to be entered on a bar graph which contains national norm information. The percentile rank for the total subject area score is also entered. The "class analyzer sheet" allows the teacher to record each student's content area score, total subject area score, and national percentile rank.

The content validity of the tests is supported by the test development process employed. Subject matter specialists selected the objectives to represent the curriculum in most high schools and developed test items to measure the achievement of the objective. As with any achievement test, users should examine the alignment of the subject test objectives with their local curriculum. The content classification tables and lists of objectives provided in the Teacher's Manual will assist in this task. We note again, however, that the content validity of the specific objective/item matches has not been clearly supported.

These reviewers had several of the subject tests reviewed by university teacher preparation faculty representing the respective subject area. The objectives included in the Literature and Vocabulary, Language, Writing, and Mechanics tests were judged to be appropriate. However, the conventional approach for spelling, employing retrieval/editing skills, is used rather than a more applications-oriented strategy. While the inferential questions in the Literature test are good, these appear to be more literal than inferential.

The objectives included in the General Mathematics, Algebra, and Geometry tests are also appropriate. The General Mathematics test appears quite difficult for grade 9 general math students, however, since a high level of understanding of algorithms instead of basic facts is required. In some cases, test items reflecting stated content area objectives listed in the Teacher's Manual could not be located (e.g., "substitute in formulas" and "compute a square root"). The Algebra test is well developed and reflects the typical content for an Algebra I course. While the Geometry test objectives were well conceived, some objectives are listed for which no test items could be located. Given the emphasis in plane geometry on triangles and their relationships, we would like to have seen more than 15% of the test reflect the Similarity and Congruence content area, as well as more than two items assessing the important congruence concept.

The American History test was found to be quite factual rather than conceptual, and was also judged to be somewhat difficult. On the other hand, the American Government test is mostly conceptual, but also quite difficult. The Geography test is considered to be conceptually strong and difficult, and necessitates good geometric and spatial skills. Finally, the World History test appears to be less conceptual and contains a large amount of trivia. Readers should also note that many schools include American Government and Geography as parts of several courses, which may make these tests quite difficult for some students.

Kuder-Richardson (KR 20) reliability coefficients and standard errors of measurement were calculated for the various subject tests, but are not provided for the content areas included in each subject test. The subject reliability coefficients are quite adequate, ranging from .79 to .94, but since individual score reports will be made at the content area level, the lack of reliability information for the content areas is considered a limitation. The authors properly note that data from more homogeneous local norm groups taking the tests may result in lower reliabilities and larger standard errors of measurement than those reported for the subject tests. Supportive item analysis information is also presented in the form of indices of item difficulty level and item-total biserial correlations ("Discrimination Coefficients"). We do note, though, that the reported discrimination indices are based upon the total set of subject area items and not the respective content areas within the respective subject.

Overall, the High School Subject Tests reflect content area objectives judged to be appropriate for the curriculum of most schools. The tests do provide reasonable norm-referenced data derived from separate norming groups for each subject area. However, although the tests are advertised as criterion-referenced, they neither provide cut-score information nor specify item/objective matches within each content area. The diagnostic value of the instrument is thereby diminished.

[Special appreciation is extended to our colleagues Judy Meagher (Reading), Robert Shaw (Mathematics Education), and Thomas Weinland (Social Studies Education) for their assistance in reviewing the content of the subject tests.]

Review of High School Subject Tests by GARY W. PHILLIPS, Chief, Measurement, Statistics and Evaluation Section, Maryland State Department of Education, Baltimore, MD:

The High School Subject Tests provide end-of-course exams in 15 subject areas. The tests are intended to provide both norm-referenced and criterion-referenced scores. National norms tables are provided (at the total test level) which contain percentile ranks and scaled scores. The national norms tables are based on the performance of 28,481 students from 316 schools. Quartile points are provided for each content-area subscore.

The tests appear to have been well developed and are easy to administer and score. Although sufficiently large sample sizes were used in the norming process there is no information given about ethnic and regional performance. Also there does not appear to have been any attention given to item bias analyses.

The High School Subject Tests are purported to be norm-referenced tests for 15 subject areas. The authors claim the norm-referencing is accomplished by comparing student performance to "extensive norms tables...of a national sample of students." In reading the technical portion of the Teacher's Manual I generally found the norming procedures to be adequate, and the tables provided more than enough information to evaluate the psychometric properties of the tests. The KR-20s were very high at the total test level (only one was below 80). However, no reliability information is given at the objective level.

The major psychometric problem with the tests is that although it is claimed that they are criterion-referenced, no criterion-referenced score is reported (e.g., domain scores, mastery classification, etc.). One reason why such scores are not provided might be because there are not enough items to provide adequate measures of individual objectives. For example, in the World History Test there are only three items measuring anthropology. For this reason the test user should be cautious in making criterion-referenced judgements from the High School Subject Tests. As a general rule of thumb, I would recommend the objective have 15–20 items before any conclusions about content mastery are made.

The derivation of the scale scores and percentile ranks are not sufficiently discussed. Although the manual states the scale score is based on a normalization procedure it does not state which one. It is not clear from the manual whether any type of distributional smoothing has been performed or whether the tests have been vertically equated across grade levels. From these omissions I assume the normalization was accomplished by a simple area transformation, and no smoothing or equating was conducted.

In summary, the High School Subject Tests should be used for the summative evaluation of high school courses. It is recommended that they be used as norm-referenced tests and not as criterion-referenced tests. Of course users of the tests should be familiar with the content breakdown of each test. This is useful in determining the match between course objectives and test content. However, the subskill area scores should not be used for either individual or group criterion-referenced interpretations, because these subskill areas are not measured with a sufficient number of items. Furthermore, the reported scores are not criterion-referenced scores (e.g., domain scores or mastery classification scores).

[477]

Hill Performance Test of Selected Positional Concepts. Visually impaired children ages 6–10; 1981; revision of Concepts Involved in Body Position and Space; 5 scores: ability to identify positional relationships of body parts, ability to move various body parts in relationship to each other, ability to move body in relationship to objects, ability to form object to object relationships, total; individual; 1 form (no date, 6 pages); instructional manual (40 pages); 1984 price data: $14.75 per complete set including 20 record forms: $5.25 per 20 record forms; $11.50 per manual; administration time not reported; Everett W. Hill; Stoelting Co.*

Review of Hill Performance Test of Selected Positional Concepts by HOMER B. C. REED, JR., *Director, Neuropsychology Service, Associate Professor of Pediatrics (Psychology), Tufts University School of Medicine, Boston, MA:*

The Hill Performance Test of Selected Positional Concepts is a highly specialized instrument designed for use with a specific handicapped population. As the title of the test indicates, the instrument is used to examine positional concepts. It is intended for use specifically with blind or partially sighted children between the ages of 6 and 10 years. The target group of children is defined quite narrowly as children who (*a*) are legally blind, (*b*) are congenitally blind, (*c*) are between the ages of 6 and 10 years, (*d*) have basic receptive language abilities, (*e*) are mobile and flexible enough to perform the test items, and (*f*) have knowledge of basic body parts (face, shoulder, eye, ear, back, etc.). The test can be used with multiply handicapped children so long as these 6 requirements are met.

The normative sample identified in the instructional manual consists of 273 youngsters, 64 of whom have additional handicaps and 209 of whom have blindness or partial sightedness as their only handicapping condition. The normative sample also yielded data on (*a*) type of school placement, (*b*) etiology of blindness, (*c*) visual acuity and field, (*d*) reading mode, (*e*) sex, (*f*) chronological age, (*g*) present level of orientation and mobility skills, (*h*) number of instructional hours enrolled in orientation and mobility, (*i*) grade, (*j*) number of years in school, and (*k*) any additional handicaps.

The test is divided into 4 parts. Part 1 requires the child to identify positional relationships of body parts. Part 2 requires the child to demonstrate positional concepts by moving various body parts in relationship to one another. Part 3 requires the child to demonstrate positional concepts by moving the body in relationship to objects, and Part 4 requires the child to form object to object relationships.

A number of useful tables for interpreting test results are included in the instructional manual. Each of the four parts of the test can be scored in terms of the percentile rank achieved by the subject. Data are also provided that identify the percent passing each test item by reading mode. Braille youngsters are separated from youngsters who read large print and from youngsters who read regular print. Each item is also assigned an index of difficulty and an index of discrimination.

The instructions for the examiner to administer the test and to score the test are quite specific and clear. Each item is scored on a 3-point scale depending on whether the child is fully successful in demonstrating the concept, has partial knowledge of the concept, or fails the concept altogether. The materials needed to test the positional concepts are identified and they are materials that are readily available to anyone who would be using this test.

The usefulness of highly specialized psychological tests is always difficult to evaluate, particularly if one is not a full time specialist in that field. Most psychologists, however, are required at some point to evaluate children whose vision is insufficient to permit valid administration of many kinds of tests. Verbal tests certainly do not present any problem in terms of administration or scoring but it is singularly difficult to examine blind or partially sighted youngsters for their spatial abilities. Furthermore, spatial concepts are of extraordinary practical importance since training in orientation and mobilization depends on the child's knowledge of such concepts. Hill's test permits a useful degree of quantification of the partially sighted child's knowledge of positional concepts. The test yields a highly dependable measurement. Information about relationships between test performance and training program outcome is not provided in the instructional manual. Information on content validity as this is inferred from interexaminer agreement is presented. The test items are innately appealing to teachers of visually impaired children and that factor together with the low cost of the instructional manual enhances the attractiveness of the test.

[478]

The Hilton Questionnaire. Adults; 1981; "a measure of drinking behavior"; 1 form (2 pages); user's manual (14 pages); 1984 price data: £2.75 per 25 questionnaires; £2.95 per user's manual; administration time not reported; Margaret R. Hilton; NFER-Nelson Publishing Co. [England].*

Review of The Hilton Questionnaire by GARY W. LAWSON, Associate Professor of Psychology, Director, Doctoral Studies in Chemical Dependency, School of Human Behavior, United States International University, San Diego, CA:

The Hilton Questionnaire is a 32-item instrument that purports to measure for "diagnostic" and "research" purposes "essential features which are generally considered to indicate alcoholism." The title should perhaps be oriented to maladaptive drinking behavior or drinking problems because the questionnaire does not measure the full range of drinking behavior. The author states in the 14-page manual that "there are nevertheless some generally accepted 'signs' and 'symptoms' of alcohol dependence"; yet she does not make it explicit what these are, although the questionnaire items ostensibly were selected to measure them.

Similarly, she goes on to state that there is "a certain progression of symptomatology in the acquisition of dependence." Apparently, the progression reflects problem severity, with alcohol dependence continuous with and representing the most severe kind of problems in general. It seems reasonable to assume that the test author stands by the unitary concept of alcoholism, which downplays individual differences and variability in symptom patterns.

The author selected questionnaire items to cover all stages in the development of alcoholism, reasons for drinking, and consequences of alcohol dependence. She eliminated items found to discriminate criterion groups on the bases of age, sex, social class, and ethnic background.

Results of an initial study of incarcerated drinkers showed that 21 of 30 questionnaire items formed a unidimensional scale of severity, as measured by the Guttman coefficient of reproducibility. After 13 additional face-valid items were added to make a 34-item instrument (later reduced to 32 items) with a frequency response scale, further validation studies were undertaken. Demographic data, a modified quantity-frequency measure of consumption, and scores on the Alcadd Test were also collected. The latter test, though used to exclude alcoholics from a control group, has had a rather undistinguished history in terms of its empirical validity.

In the section describing Subjects, the alcoholic group consisted of currently or formerly hospitalized persons, and persons affiliated with AA. At least 40 of 48 subjects therein would have been exposed to some kind of indoctrination and treatment ideology. Presumably, active drinkers and abstainers were both included in the same group. Curiously, about 25% of the control group was ultimately re-classified on the Alcadd Test as alcoholics; this figure is quite high for what was supposed to be a sample of the general population.

ADMINISTRATION. All alcoholics were asked to reply on the basis of their experience before help-seeking. Thus, responses from this group are retrospective and with reference to an indefinite, unstated, and variable interval preceding the test administration. Administration of questionnaires to alcoholics was done both individually and in groups. Monitored and unmonitored conditions of administration were represented. Subjects affiliated with AA were exclusively volunteers responding in an unmonitored condition. Conditions for controls were similar.

About 37.5% of AA members who might constitute potential participants returned completed questionnaires. Among controls, about 76% of potential participants did so. All hospital-associated alcoholics except one submitted completed questionnaires.

Factor analysis of questionnaire responses revealed four common factors as accounting for 75% of the total variance. Most (86.4%) of the variance accounted for by the four factors was attributable to Factor 1. All questionnaire items loaded significantly on Factor 1. The author elected to discard the remaining three common factors as non-substantive. Apparently no attempt was made to rotate the four original factors. Communality data and item-total correlations supported test homogeneity. The reliability estimate (internal consistency) was quite high (.98).

The author commented on construct validity, concurrent validity for individual items, and empirical validity for the entire questionnaire, as assessed using correlation with external measures. Factorial validity, as one form of construct validity, does not seem sufficiently established through exclusive reliance on alcoholic respondents selected for high-level exposure to institutional or self-help programs of treatment and intervention. The proposition that questionnaires such as Hilton's confound self-attribution and self-identification with alcoholism, as opposed to documented and observable symptomatology, is well known. Hilton's research does nothing to extricate the mentioned sources of variance.

Questionnaire items individually and collectively distinguished between alcoholics and controls. Only *p*-values were reported for the relationships between questionnaire scores and Alcadd scores and measures of quantity-frequency. Sex differences in responding were apparently minimal. Social class differences were observed for three items. Score distributions differed among groups examined, with AA respondents having the highest scores.

Fakeability of responses is discussed and the possibility acknowledged, though limited by confidentiality assurances. No further research in this area is reviewed for the instrument.

Biased sampling of alcoholics is noted as a possibility, and a disclaimer is made as to the representativeness of the current sample relative to the population of alcoholics in general. Small sample size may also be problematic as well as a lack of validation of the initial item pool.

Possible departures from standardized administration of the questionnaire are stated to be an additional source of variance in results. Self selected AA subjects and mail-in protocols further cloud the picture.

The author recommends the questionnaire as a screening tool and an aid to research. Her illustrations of possible uses include assumed sensitivity to genuine change in symptomatology over time, an aspect that was not examined or reported on in the manual.

In summary, the Hilton Questionnaire provides the field no more, and perhaps no less, than other inventories of its kind. For a review of 13 such assessments including the Michigan Alcoholism Screening Test (MAST), perhaps the best known and most frequently used alcoholism screening device, see Jacobson (1976). For more on the MAST see Selzer (1971), Zung (1978), and Skinner (1979).

REVIEWER'S REFERENCES

Selzer, M. L. The Michigan Alcoholism Screening Test: The quest for a new diagnostic instrument. AMERICAN JOURNAL OF PSYCHIATRY, 1971, 127, 1653–1658.

Jacobson, G. R. DIAGNOSIS AND ASSESSMENT OF ALCOHOL ABUSE AND ALCOHOLISM: A REPORT TO THE NATIONAL INSTITUTE ON ALCOHOL ABUSE AND ALCOHOLISM. DHEW Publication No. (ADM) 76–288, 1975.

Zung, B. J. Factor structure of the Michigan Alcoholism Screening Test. JOURNAL OF STUDIES ON ALCOHOL, 1978, 39, 56–67.

Skinner, H. A. A multivariate evaluation of MAST. JOURNAL OF STUDIES ON ALCOHOL, 1979, 40, 831–844.

[479]

The Hoffer-Osmond Diagnostic Test. Mental patients age 13 and over; 1961–81; diagnosis of schizophrenia; 6 scores: total, perceptual, paranoid, depression, ratio, short form; tentative norms only; manual ('81, 40 pages); 1984 price data: $55 per test kit including manual, 145 test cards, 1 test booklet, and 10 answer sheets; (15–20) minutes; Abram Hoffer, Humphry Osmond, and Harold Kelm; Behavior Science Press.*

See T2:1215 (6 references) and P:110 (22 references); for reviews by Maurice Lorr and William Schofield, see 6:114 (6 references).

[480]

The Holtzman Inkblot Technique. Ages 5 and over; 1958–73; HIT; 20–22 scores: reaction time (*a* only), rejection, location, space, form definiteness, form appropriateness, color, shading, movement, pathognomic verbalization, integration, content (human, animal, anatomy, sex, abstract), anxiety, hostility, barrier, penetration, balance (*a* only), popular; 2 formats; separate book entitled *Inkblot Perception and Personality* ('61, 428 pages, not adapted for group administration) serves as overall manual; 1985 price data: $40 for *Inkblot Perception and Personality*; (75) minutes; Wayne H. Holtzman, Joseph S. Thorpe (book), Jon D. Swartz (book), and E. Wayne Herron (book); The Psychological Corporation.*

a) INDIVIDUAL TEST. 1958–73; Forms A, B, ('58, 45 cards); administration and scoring guide ('61, 171 pages reprinted in part from book); record form ('58, 8 pages) for each form; summary sheet ('58, 2 pages); clinical summary sheet ('72, 1 page); workbook ('73, 107 pages); $137.50 per complete set including 45 inkblots, 25 record forms with summary sheet, and scoring guide; $7.25 per 50 record forms.

b) GROUP TEST. 1958–70; administration slides for either form must be constructed locally; no specific manual; group record form ('66, 2 pages); group normative item statistics ('70, 11 pages); norm supplement for computer scored group technique ('68, 27 pages); $7.25 per 50 group record forms; $3.75 per group normative item statistics; $7 per norm supplement for computer scored group technique; Donald R. Gorham (record form).

See T3:1106 (25 references); for a review by Rolf A. Peterson, see 8:578 (96 references); see also T2:1471 (42 references); for excerpted reviews by Raymond J. McCall and David G. Martin, see 7:169 (106 references); see also P:439 (90 references); for reviews by Richard W. Coan, H. J. Eysenck, Bertram R. Forer, and William N. Thetford, see 6:217 (22 references).

TEST REFERENCES

1. Janowsky, D. S., Huey, L., Storms, L., & Judd, L. L. Methylphenidate hydrochloride effects on psychological tests in acute schizophrenic and nonpsychotic patients. ARCHIVES OF GENERAL PSYCHIATRY, 1977, 34, 189–194.

2. Judd, L. L., Hubbard, B., Janowsky, D. S., Huey, L. Y., & Attewell, P. A. The effect of lithium carbonate on affect, mood, and personality of normal subjects. ARCHIVES OF GENERAL PSYCHIATRY, 1977, 34, 346–351.

3. Leon, G. R., Bemis, K. M., Meland, M., & Nussbaum, D. Aspects of body image perception in obese and normal-weight youngsters. JOURNAL OF ABNORMAL CHILD PSYCHOLOGY, 1978, 6, 361–371.

4. Judd, L. L. Effect of lithium on mood, cognition, and personality function in normal subjects. ARCHIVES OF GENERAL PSYCHIATRY, 1979, 36, 860–865.

5. Hayslip, B., Jr. Verbosity and projective test performance in the aged. JOURNAL OF CLINICAL PSYCHOLOGY, 1981, 37, 662–666.

6. Lockwood, J. L., Roll, S., & Matthews, D. B. Two studies of the movement responses in young children: New and highly discrepant norms. JOURNAL OF PERSONALITY ASSESSMENT, 1981, 45, 250–255.

7. Sison, G. F., Fehr, L. A., & Muhoberac, B. P. A projective analysis of guilt: The Holtzman Inkblot Technique. JOURNAL OF PERSONALITY ASSESSMENT, 1981, 45, 23–26.

8. Vilkki, J. Changes in complex perception and memory after three different psychosurgical operations. NEUROPSYCHOLOGIA, 1981, 19, 553–563.

9. Ewing, J. H., Gillis, C. A., Scott, D. G., & Patzig, W. J. Fantasy processes and mild physical activity. PERCEPTUAL AND MOTOR SKILLS, 1982, 54, 363–368.

10. Hayslip, B., Jr. The Holtzman Inkblot Technique and aging: Norms and factor structure. JOURNAL OF PERSONALITY ASSESSMENT, 1982, 46, 248–256.

11. Lockwood, J. L., Roll, S., & Matthews, D. B. Fine points aside: Data are data. JOURNAL OF PERSONALITY ASSESSMENT, 1982, 46, 128–130.

12. Mullen, J. M., Reinehr, R. C., & Swartz, J. D. Performance of forensic patients on the Holtzman Inkblot Technique: A normative study. PERCEPTUAL AND MOTOR SKILLS, 1982, 54, 275–280.

13. Olsen, K., Legg, J., & Stiff, M. Vulnerability of the self: Barrier and penetration scores of depressed patients. JOURNAL OF PERSONALITY ASSESSMENT, 1982, 46, 481–485.

14. Rosegrant, J. Primary process patterning in college students' inkblot responses. JOURNAL OF PERSONALITY ASSESSMENT, 1982, 46, 578–581.

15. Dush, D. M., & Gabriel, R. M. Scale properties of the Holtzman Inkblots. JOURNAL OF PERSONALITY ASSESSMENT, 1983, 47, 350–356.

16. Mullen, J. M., Reinehr, R. C., & Swartz, J. D. Holtzman Inkblot Technique scores of delinquent adolescents: A replication and extension. JOURNAL OF PERSONALITY ASSESSMENT, 1983, 47, 158–160.

17. Swartz, J. D., & Reinehr, R. C. A quick version of administration for the group Holtzman Inkblot Technique. PERCEPTUAL AND MOTOR SKILLS, 1983, 56, 813–814.

Review of The Holtzman Inkblot Technique by BERT P. CUNDICK, Professor of Psychology, Brigham Young University, Provo, UT:

The Holtzman is a well known inkblot test that consists of two alternate forms of 45 inkblots. It can be individually administered or given to groups by utilizing slides. It differs from Rorschach administration in that only one response per card should be elicited and scored. It is scored on 22 variables. The manual provides raw score to percentile conversions on all 22 scores for separate norm groups of college students, average adults, 7th graders, elementary school children, 5-year-olds, chronic schizophrenics, mental retardates, and depressed patients. The manual was published when the test was originally created and has not been revised since. Additional norms and statistical data are available in a later publication by Holtzman and his associates (1961).

Holtzman et al. (1961) reported intrascorer consistency on three examiners after a period of about 3 months. These reliabilities average about .95 on 9 scores. Interscorer consistency is reported for a number of different scorers for various scores. The lowest reported score reliabilities are .57, the highest .99. Intrasubject reliabilities are reported for 15 different groups on all 22 scores. These split-half reliabilities vary widely, but generally range between .50 and .90 with an approximate average in the .70s or .80s. No test-retest reliabilities were found by this reviewer which might furnish information about whether the scores are measuring persisting traits.

As with reliability, information regarding the validity of the HIT does not appear in the manual. The HIT, like some other projective techniques, is like a game in which you are given the materials and the rules, but not the point of the endeavor. The test has not motivated individuals to the extent that the Rorschach has. One does not find a Klopfer, Beck, or Exner, who after researching the test for an extended period, has written a comprehensive volume which gives scoring, interpretation, reliability, and validity information all in one convenient place.

HIT data on older populations was obtained from Hayslip (1981, 1982), who found that factor scores were similar to those obtained on other populations although response length in the elderly was a factor that significantly affected their scores. Data from Lockwood, Roll, and Matthews (1981, 1982) indicated that the standardization norms did not adequately represent the movement score, a finding that was disputed by Swartz, Reinehr, and Swartz (1981).

It appears that test instructions can significantly change test results on the HIT (Krieger & Levin, 1976; Cooney, 1977; Rosegrant, 1982). However, group forms may yield results similar to using the longer test (Swartz & Rienehr, 1983). Interpersonal confrontation also affects responses (Prokop, 1983).

Test scores have been related to a number of different variables. Guilt has been found to inhibit some scores and make respondents less creative (Sison, Fehr, & Muhoberac, 1981). Drug users give responses that are more "inner directed" and more pathological than do controls (Hartung & Skorka, 1980). Comfortable interpersonal distance was found related to 4 scores (Greenberg, Arnow, & Rauchway, 1977). Delinquent groups were found to be significantly different than other criterion groups (Mullen, Reinehr, & Swartz, 1983) as were adult forensic males (Mullen, Reinehr, & Swartz, 1982). Pre-post change in responses have also been found after psychosurgical operations (Vilkki, 1981).

The HIT has an impressive amount of material relating various responses to different norm groups. The reliabilities of the scores appear to be acceptable for an instrument of its type. The norm material is unwieldy and is difficult to use in its present form. The scoring is tedious and time consuming. The validity information is fragmented and found in diverse places. Its popularity does not approach the Rorschach and it has yielded far less research. Its original construction and norm groups were a considerable improvement over the Rorschach, but it appears that the test will never attract a wide following. Tests of visual perception such as inkblot tests tap processes that differ from straight verbal instruments. They will likely always have a place in experimental and practical use, but will have far less use than verbal report inventories such as the MMPI.

REVIEWER'S REFERENCES

Holtzman, W. H., Thorpe, J. S., Swartz, J. D., & Herron, E. W. INKBLOT PERCEPTION AND PERSONALITY. Austin, TX: University of Texas Press, 1961.

Krieger, M. J., & Levin, S. M. Schizophrenic behavior as a function of role expectation. JOURNAL OF CLINICAL PSYCHOLOGY, 1976, 32, 463–467.

Cooney, J. A. Holtzman Inkblot Technique responses of normals and schizophrenics under varied instructional sets. DISSERTATION ABSTRACTS INTERNATIONAL, 1977, 38, 235.

Greenberg, E., Arnow, E., & Rauchway, A. Inkblot content and interpersonal distance. JOURNAL OF CLINICAL PSYCHOLOGY, 1977, 33, 882–887.

Hartung, J., & Skorka, D. The HIT clinical profile of psychedelic drug users. JOURNAL OF PERSONALITY ASSESSMENT, 1980, 44, 237–245.

Hayslip, B., Jr. Verbosity and projective test performance in the aged. JOURNAL OF CLINICAL PSYCHOLOGY, 1981, 37, 662–666.

Lockwood, J. L., Roll, S., & Matthew, D. B. Two studies of movement responses in young children: New and highly discrepant norms. JOURNAL OF PERSONALITY ASSESSMENT, 1981, 45, 250–255.

Sison, G. F., Fehr, L. A., & Muhoberac, B. P. A projective analysis of guilt: The Holtzman Inkblot Technique. JOURNAL OF PERSONALITY ASSESSMENT, 1981, 45, 23–26.

Swartz, J. D., Reinehr, R. C., & Swartz, C. J. The Holtzman Inkblot Technique is not the Rorschach: A reply to Lockwood, Roll and Matthews. JOURNAL OF PERSONALITY ASSESSMENT, 1981, 45, 582–583.

Vilkki, J. Changes in complex perception and memory after three different psychosurgical operations. NEUROPSYCHOLOGIA, 1981, 19, 553–563.

Hayslip, B. The Holtzman Inkblot Technique and aging: Norms and factor structure. JOURNAL OF PERSONALITY ASSESSMENT, 1982, 46, 248–256.

Lockwood, J. L., Roll, S., & Matthews, D. B. Fine points aside: Data are data. JOURNAL OF PERSONALITY ASSESSMENT, 1982, 46, 128–130.

Mullen, J. M., Reinehr, R. C., & Swartz, J. D. Performance of forensic patients on the Holtzman Inkblot Technique: A normative study. PERCEPTUAL AND MOTOR SKILLS, 1982, 54, 275–280.

Rosegrant, J. Primary process patterning in college students' inkblot responses. JOURNAL OF PERSONALITY ASSESSMENT, 1982, 46, 578–581.

Mullen, J. M., Reinehr, R. C., & Swartz, J. D. Holtzman Inkblot Technique scores of delinquent adolescents: A replication and extension. JOURNAL OF PERSONALITY ASSESSMENT, 1983, 47, 158–160.

Prokop, C. K. Responses to interpersonal confrontation: Interactions with human movement and color perception. JOURNAL OF PERSONALITY AND SOCIAL PSYCHOLOGY, 1983, 44, 1297–1303.

Swartz, J. D., & Reinehr, R. C. A quick version of administration for the Group Holtzman Inkblot Technique. PERCEPTUAL AND MOTOR SKILLS, 1983, 56, 813–814.

Review of The Holtzman Inkblot Technique by DAVID M. DUSH, Program Evaluator, Midland-Gladwin Community Mental Health Services, Midland, MI:

The Holtzman Inkblot Technique (HIT) is a multi-variable projective personality test that was designed to overcome psychometric limitations of the Rorschach, yet preserve richness of the projective material elicited. Reviewers have generally found it promising and psychometrically impressive, yet it continues to lag far behind the Rorschach in popularity in both research and clinical applications. More critically, with its 22 variables and complex factor structure, a massive amount of research is needed to establish the HIT's validity and utility, but the pace of HIT research appears to be slowing. For example, an annotated bibliography by Swartz, Reinehr, and Holtzman cited 142 HIT studies from 1973 to 1977, but only 54 from 1978 to 1982.

The strongest suit of the HIT has been its reliability data. The monograph reports interrater reliability of .89 to .99 (median=.98) for 15 variables scored by experienced raters, and quite respectable figures for inexperienced raters. Intrarater, split-half, and test-retest reliabilities are equally impressive. There are numerous other distinctive features and potential assets of the HIT: (*a*) administration is streamlined and standardized; (*b*) the use of 45 inkblots and a potential range of at least 0 to 45 on each variable enhance reliability and scaling properties; (*c*) parallel forms are provided; (*d*) stimulus properties of the blots were varied to provide a wider range of responses to all variables across subjects; (*e*) the scoring of responses for each variable is unidimensional (versus separate scores for CF, FC, C, etc.); (*f*) all variables are at least ordinally scaled; (*g*) only one response per blot is scored, bypassing the troublesome effects of wide variance in the number of responses per subject; (*h*) scoring examples are provided in the manual for all levels of all variables; (*i*) norms are provided for several normal and diagnostic groupings of subjects; (*j*) group, short, and computerized versions of the HIT are available.

A considerable amount of validity, reliability, and normative data has been compiled for the HIT. Much of this has been fully or partly supportive, but the task is formidable and many of the HIT's features remain to be adequately investigated. For example: (*a*) the equivalence of the two forms has received mixed support; (*b*) the equivalence of the group, short, computerized, and individual versions has not been adequately replicated, and the appropriateness of alternatives to individual administration for clinical applications is unclear; (*c*) Space, Sex, Abstract, and Balance are not norm referenced for most groups because of their severely compressed range; (*d*) normative data are uncomfortably old, inadequately stratified across relevant demographics, and of questioned generalizability, particularly to the elderly; (*e*) the factor structure of the variables has received mixed support, and appears to vary across some subpopulations; (*f*) little attention has been given to the scale properties of the variables, such as the tenability of assuming interval or ratio scaling, or the functional relationship between verbal responses and stimulus properties; (*g*) while only one response is allowed per blot, the length of responses is still free to vary, and this has been found to bias several of the variables.

Administration and scoring are rather time consuming, except in computerized versions. Also, while learning to reliably score the HIT is quite simple, learning to use the HIT is not. The manual (with instructions and norms) and the large monograph (with extensive test development data) have not been updated since their appearance in 1961 to reflect the hundreds of studies that have ensued. Hill's guide to clinical interpretation is similarly growing dated. This leaves the careful user to search through the literature and the critical reviews, none of which are comprehensive. Clearly a revision of these materials, if not the test itself, is overdue. Amidst the many factors that may impact the slow growth of the HIT's popularity, updated, comprehensive resource materials for the test are a pressing need at this stage of the test's history.

Another continuing obstacle for the HIT is the lack of ample study of its predictive validity and diagnostic utility. There have been a few encouraging studies of this type, but there remains very little data from realistic clinical applications to determine if the HIT can assist in making valid personality descriptions or diagnostic decisions, and few controlled comparative studies examining the HIT's performance in this respect against alternatives such as the Rorschach or objective tests. The test of the HIT's psychometric advantages must ultimately be made at the level of clinical utility or predictive validity.

In all, the HIT remains a promising projective personality test, clearly warranting serious consideration and further research. In abbreviated, group, and particularly computerized forms, it offers the possibility of practical incorporation of projective assessment in even large investigations. It also appears promising in clinical applications to personality assessment and diagnosis, but the data here remains scant at present. Until such time that revised support materials become available, the user will also benefit from a careful review of the considerable literature that has accrued, particularly in reference to clinical interpretation.

[481]

Home Observation for Measurement of the Environment. Birth to age 3, preschool; 1978–79; HOME; 7 or 9 scores listed below; norms consist of means and standard deviations; group administration not recommended; 2 levels; instruction manual ('78, 42 pages); monograph ('79, 130 pages including all materials needed for administration); 1984 price data: $13 per monograph; $6 per instruction manual; (60) minutes; Bettye M. Caldwell and Robert H. Bradley; the Authors.*

a) LEVEL 1. Birth to 3 years; 7 scores: emotional and verbal responsivity of mother, acceptance of child's behavior, organization of the physical and temporal environment, provision of appropriate play materials, maternal involvement with the child, opportunities for variety, total; 1 form (4 pages).

b) LEVEL 2. Preschool; 9 scores: stimulation through toys and games and reading materials, language stimulation, physical environment, pride and affection and warmth, stimulation of academic behavior, modeling and encouragement of social maturity, variety of stimulation, physical punishment, total; 1 form (5 pages).

See T3:1108 (14 references).

TEST REFERENCES

1. DeFries, J. C., Plomin, R., Vandenberg, S. G., & Kuse, A. R. Parent-offspring resemblance for cognitive abilities in the Colorado Adoption Project: Biological, adoptive, and control parents and one-year-old children. INTELLIGENCE, 1981, 5, 245–277.

2. Hardy-Brown, K., Plomin, R., & DeFries, J. C. Genetic and environmental influences on the rate of communicative development in the first year of life. DEVELOPMENTAL PSYCHOLOGY, 1981, 17, 704–717.

3. Affleck, G., Allen, D., McGrade, B. J., & McQueeney, M. Home environments of developmentally disabled infants as a function of parent and infant characteristics. AMERICAN JOURNAL OF MENTAL DEFICIENCY, 1982, 86, 445–452.

4. Bee, H. L., Barnard, K. E., Eyres, S. J., Gray, C. A., Hammond, M. A., Spietz, A. L., Snyder, C., & Clark, B. Prediction of IQ and language skill from perinatal status, child performance, family characteristics, and mother-infant interaction. CHILD DEVELOPMENT, 1982, 53, 1134–1156.

5. LaVeck, B., & Hammond, M. A. Performance on the motor scale of the McCarthy Scales of Children's Abilities as related to home environment and neonatal reflexes. PERCEPTUAL AND MOTOR SKILLS, 1982, 54, 1265–1266.

6. MacKinnon, C. E., Brody, G. H., & Stoneman, Z. The effects of divorce and maternal employment on the home environments of preschool children. CHILD DEVELOPMENT, 1982, 53, 1392–1399.

7. Medoff-Cooper, B., & Schraeder, B. D. Developmental trends and behavioral styles in very low birth weight infants. NURSING RESEARCH, 1982, 31, 68–72.

8. Poresky, R. H., & Henderson, M. L. Infants' mental and motor development: Effects of home environment, maternal attitudes, marital adjustment, and socioeconomic status. PERCEPTUAL AND MOTOR SKILLS, 1982, 54, 695–702.

9. Siegel, L. S. Reproductive, perinatal, and environmental factors as predictors of the cognitive and language development of preterm and full-term infants. CHILD DEVELOPMENT, 1982, 53, 963–973.

10. Barnard, K. E., & Bee, H. L. The impact of temporally patterned stimulation on the development of preterm infants. CHILD DEVELOPMENT, 1983, 54, 1156–1167.

11. Moxley-Haegert, L., & Serbin, L. A. Developmental education for parents of delayed infants: Effects on parental motivation and children's development. CHILD DEVELOPMENT, 1983, 54, 1324–1331.

12. Plomin, R., & DeFries, J. C. The Colorado Adoption Project. CHILD DEVELOPMENT, 1983, 54, 276–289.

13. Stevens, J. H., Jr. Child development knowledge and parenting skills. FAMILY RELATIONS, 1984, 33, 237–244.

Review of Home Observation for Measurement of the Environment by ANN E. BOEHM, Professor of Psychology and Education, Teachers College, Columbia University, New York, NY:

The Home Observation for Measurement of the Environment (HOME) consists of two inventories designed as screening instruments to describe types of stimulation in the child's home environment that foster cognitive development. Given the extensive research linking socioeconomic status variables with measures of cognitive development in young children, the authors, Caldwell and Bradley, sought to develop procedures more sensitive to environmental influence than gross SES indices. Their ultimate goal was to screen for sources of potential environmental retardation that can lead to remedial intervention. Components of the early environment were included in each of the two HOME inventories based on previous research establishing their relationship to cognitive development. Thus, the content validity of the HOME is supported through an extensive review of the literature.

The HOME Inventory for Families of Infants and Toddlers (birth to age 3) consists of six subscales, whereas the HOME Inventory for Families of Preschool Age Children (age 3 to 6) consists of eight subscales. Items on each subscale were developed to focus primarily on observation which takes place in the home environment. About one-third of the content involves parent (or primary caregiver) report which is elicited to cover transactions not likely to occur between the parent and child at the time of the home visit.

The rationale, background history, and accounts of studies which have employed the two HOME inventories were thoroughly presented, particularly for the HOME Inventory for Families of Infants and Toddlers. Thus a firm basis was established as to the purpose, scope, and utility of these inventories in assessing the quality of stimulation in the environment. This reviewer found the manual highly informative. A brief overview of essential data follows the detailed presentation for each inventory.

Data for earlier versions of both inventories were collected in Syracuse, New York, whereas for the present (1978–1979) version it was collected in Little Rock, Arkansas. Although the data presented on the HOME are not representative of a national sample, the replications of findings reported attest to the utility of the inventories in predicting cognitive functioning. Subscales and items were extracted from the earlier versions through factor and item analysis. Point-biserial correlations of items with their factor scores and the total score were satisfactory. On both inventories items correlated more highly with their factor score than with the total score. The particular technical characteristics of the two inventories will be summarized individually.

HOME INVENTORY FOR FAMILIES OF INFANTS AND TODDLERS. Data on this inventory of 45 items were collected on a sample of 174 families from both welfare and nonwelfare backgrounds. Mean scores tended to increase with age. While total HOME scores did not differ by sex, there was a relationship to selected cognitive measures by sex. The standard error of measurement ranged from .89 to 1.14 for individual subscales and was 2.55 for the total score. Internal consistency reliabilities were acceptable and ranged from .44 to .89 for subscales and was .89 for the total score.

Test-retest reliability, based on a study of 91 families assessed on three occasions (child 6 months, 12 months and 24 months), indicated moderate to high stability (coefficients of .27 to .77 for subtests and .62 to .77 for the total score).

A series of validation studies was presented which document that the HOME correlates with SES measures to a moderate degree, a level desired by the authors since higher correlations would not have supported their goal to develop a measure more sensitive than traditional SES measures to features of the home environment. Furthermore, HOME scores were significantly related to early measures of cognitive development, with HOME scores at 24 months correlating .72 with 36-month Binet IQ scores and sharing "about 40% common variance" with Binet scores at 54 months. Among the subscales, Appropriate Play Materials and Maternal Involvement were correlated most strongly with cognitive measures.

Predictive validity was supported through discriminant analysis of 6-month HOME scores in identifying retardation on 36-month Binet IQ scores. The HOME correctly identified children scoring below IQ 70 at age three 71% of the time and 62% of the time those scoring at IQ 90 or above. Changes in test performance were also predicted, further supporting the conclusion that the HOME had adequate predictive power to identify home environments associated with retarded development. The number of false positives was also high, suggesting that caution needs to be exercised.

Finally, construct validity was supported through a number of studies reported in the literature showing that the HOME discriminated between homes in terms of developmental retardation of children and was associated with language disability and with cognitive measures. HOME scores were related to malnutrition among Guatemalan infants.

INVENTORY FOR FAMILIES OF PRESCHOOL AGE CHILDREN. Data for this 55-item inventory were collected on a sample of 117 families. Means increased only slightly with age. Approximately one-third of the items were passed by 81% of the families. Not passing these items was said to indicate severe environmental lack. No standard error of measurement data were reported. Again, the HOME scores did not differ by sex, nor were sex differences reported on later cognitive or achievement measures. Internal consistency was acceptable and ranged from $r = .53$ to $r = .88$ for subscales and $r = .93$ for the total score.

A small test-retest reliability study, conducted with 33 families when their children were 3 and 4½ years of age, yielded scores that were generally stable over time (coefficients of .05 to .70). Low stability (r below .20) was apparent on only one subscale, Physical Punishment. The authors point to the need for reevaluation over time.

A small number of validation studies were reported for the Preschool HOME with the following outcomes. A moderate relationship was demonstrated between both subscales and the total score to three of five SES indices. Product-moment and multiple correlations between HOME scores and IQ scores at both 3 and 4½ years of age remained stable over time. However, the pattern of HOME subscale score correlations with Binet scores varied over time. Subscale I, Stimulation through Toys, Games and Reading Materials was highly related at both ages. These data were viewed as supporting the usefulness of the inventory as a screening measure.

Based on a small sample, a positive relationship was found between total scores obtained when children were between the ages of 3 and 5 and four SRA Achievement Test scores (Reading, Language Arts, Mathematics, and Composite) obtained between the ages of 6 and 10. Limited evidence is reported on the construct validity of this inventory.

The administrative portion of the manual is presented clearly. The appropriate HOME inventory (birth to age 3; age 3 to 6) needs to be administered during a home visit while the child is awake in order that the observer/interviewer can take account of the interaction between the child and the primary caregiver. The interview is presented in a nonstandard manner so as to place the caregiver at ease and at the same time elicit the desired information. The time required for the home visit is about 1 hour. Detailed suggestions are provided for arranging for the visit and conducting the interview, and cover such details as the warm-up period, lead-in questions for each area covered, and follow-up questions. Useful examples are provided for eliciting information in each area.

Items are scored simply as "yes" or "no" so that judgement is not required as to quality. Items are discussed in detail in order to provide the observer/interviewer with a basis for making the yes-no judgements. A summary of items correct by subscale allows the user to assess the percentile band in which the HOME score falls.

The issue is raised regarding possible distortions that might occur in the observer-caregiver-child interaction. However, no data were presented regarding observer agreement or the consistency of findings over brief time intervals. Certainly, to the extent one observer is obtrusive to the flow of the parent-child interaction, two observers would probably be more so. However, some reference to observer agreement would be useful to potential users, along with the extent of training required to develop reasonable rates of agreement.

In summary, the HOME inventories are useful and well-researched tools for identifying and understanding stimulation aspects of the home environment related to later cognitive functioning as assessed by traditional IQ measures and achievement tests. The data presented indicated that the HOME provides a "sensitive alternative" to traditional SES indices which can reward users with in-depth understanding of the quality of home environments that can lead to intervention where needed. The HOME inventories are recommended for use.

[482]

Home Screening Questionnaire. Ages 0–3, 3–6; 1981; HSQ; parent-answered questionnaire; 3 scores: questions, toy checklist, total; no norms; individual; 2 forms: ages 0–3, 3–6, (4 pages); reference manual (33 pages); 1983 price data: $4.25 per 25 questionnaires; $4 per reference manual; (15–20) minutes; John F. Kennedy Child Development Center; LADOCA Publishing Foundation.*

Review of Home Screening Questionnaire by S. RUBEN LOZANO, School Psychologist, Mesa Public Schools, Mesa, AZ:

Identifying high risk infants due to a deleterious environment in poor American families is the purpose of the Home Screening Questionnaire (HSQ). The birth through 3-year questionnaire has 30 items, the 3- through 6-year-old version has 34 items, and both use the same 50-item toy checklist. The questions were developed from items in the Home Observation for Measurement of the Environment (HOME) Inventory and put in question form. The toy inventory also was developed from the HOME Inventory.

The HSQ has many strong features which make it a useful screening instrument. The test-retest reliability is satisfactory for infants 1 through 3 years old (.82) and 3 through 6 years old (.86) over a period of 4 months. The concurrent validity correlation coefficients with the HOME Inventory were .61 for birth through 3-year-olds and .71 for 3- through 6-year-olds. The questions for the HSQ were carefully developed in three revisions, with resulting acceptable rates of identifying false positives of 14% and 21%, and false negatives of 11% and 7%, for the birth through 3-year-olds and 3- through 6-year-olds, respectively. The usefulness of the HSQ is also seen in its short administration time (20 minutes) and easy reading level (3rd to 4th grade). The clear directions make the administration simple and scoring understandable. The authors clearly describe the limitations of the HSQ in the helpful manual.

The weaknesses of the HSQ arise from the narrow population for whom it can be used. The selection procedure for the standardization sample was not described so the sample cannot be said to be representative of Denver's impoverished let alone that of the United States. The sample also seems highly educated compared to the poor of America. The total percentage of poor heads of households who were high school graduates, had attended college, or graduated from college in the 1980 census was 15%, but in the sample more than 56% were in this category: 0 through 3 group—Mothers 59%, Fathers 67%; 3 through 6 group—Mothers 57%, Fathers 59%. The manual acknowledges that the sample may be nationally unrepresentative due to the higher education of the parents and also due to the ethnicity of the sample. The White and Black families are grossly misrepresented (e.g., in the 1980 census, poor families were about 7% White and 26% Black; in the standardization sample there were 62% White and 4% Black in the 0 through 3 group and 41% White and 8% Black in the 3 through 6 group).

Low test-retest reliability plagues the birth through 3-year form, but the correlation coefficient changes from .62 to .82 when infants under a year of age are excluded. In spite of these data the authors of the HSQ recommend an initial screening at 6 months of age. Waiting 6 more months seems advisable.

The HSQ seems to be an internally valid and reliable screening instrument for infants 1 through 6 years of age, not 0 through 6 as recommended by the authors. Also, it is quick to administer and score. The applicability of the norms is in doubt due to the unrepresentativeness of the standardization sample in terms of Denver's population of poor families, specifically, and America's poor, in general.

[483]

Hopkins Psychiatric Rating Scale. Psychiatric patients; 1974–78; HPRS; rating scale for recording scaled judgements in 17 dimensions: somatization, obsessive-compulsive, interpersonal sensitivity, depression, anxiety, hostility, phobic anxiety, paranoid ideation, psychoticism, sleep disturbance, psychomotor retardation, hysterical behavior, abjection-disinterested, conceptual dysfunction, disorientation, excitement, euphoria; no data on reliability and validity; no norms; individual; 1 form ('78, 4 pages); no manual; 1983 price data: $30 per 100 tests; administration time not reported; Leonard R. Derogatis; the Author.*

TEST REFERENCES

1. Owen, W. L. Analysis and aggregation of CMHC outcome data in a statewide evaluation system: A case report. COMMUNITY MENTAL HEALTH JOURNAL, 1984, 20, 27–43.

[484]

How A Child Learns. Classroom teachers; 1970–71; manual title is *Classroom Analysis of Learning Skills and Disabilities: An Observational Approach*; observation of activities of children which is guided through analysis of children's learning channels and leads to a written prescriptive teaching plan; 4 areas: auditory, visual, verbal, manual; no data on reliability and validity; no norms; individual; 1 form ('70, 4 pages); manual ('71, 29 pages); 1983 price data: $16 per 100 forms; $8.95 per training manual and 20 forms; Thomas Gnagey and Patricia Gnagey (manual); Facilitation House.*

Review of How A Child Learns by GLENN MOE, School Psychologist, Washington Elementary District, Phoenix, AZ:

How A Child Learns is not a test, but rather an observational approach to analyzing the strengths and weaknesses in a child's learning channels: expressive (verbal, manual) and receptive (visual, auditory). The materials consist of recording sheets on which classroom teachers are to make anecdotal notes of approximately 15 behavioral episodes. These episodes are broken into strong, weak, and closed skill areas which are analyzed as to which learning channels were employed by the student. Teachers are then instructed to teach to the child's strengths and to develop weak channels by presenting curriculum material in both strong and weak modalities.

A major problem with this observation system is that it is based on processing notions which are viewed by many as obsolete. Like many tests, How A Child Learns was developed from theories not well grounded in research. Subsequent empirical evidence has not supported the validity or usefulness of a modality training approach in educating special children. Therefore, the value of this observation system is questionable given that the theoretical base on which it was developed has been undermined. For example, the authors state that if caught early, modality deficits can be remediated or weak channels can be strengthened, all in an attempt to improve the child's learning potential. The fact is that few researchers have supported these contentions while most investigators have found that process training does not increase academic achievement.

Regardless of the weakness addressed above, the construction of the scale is extremely inadequate. The manual contains a basic review of information processing, how to record observations of a child's channel preferences, and several practice activities. No evidence exists to indicate that the authors attempted to standardize the instrument. Thus, there is no data on reliability of teachers' observations across time or of separate teachers' observations of the same child. The authors state that 10 to 15 observations should be taken to determine the child's strong and weak learning channels. Without standardization data, how do they know how many observations would be necessary to produce a reliable depiction of the child? The authors also have made the mistake of assuming that if a child is failing in school, it is because of the observed weak or closed channels of processing. This is an oversimplified view of learning which places considerable importance on a once popular "channels" explanation while ignoring the multitude of remaining possible explanations for school failure. Thus, the authors have failed completely in establishing the validity of their scale and in substantiating the premise on which it is based.

In summary, I do not recommend that anyone use How A Child Learns as an observational approach to children's learning. The scale is based on outdated and terribly simplistic assumptions of how children process information. The scale is poorly constructed and the authors fail to demonstrate its validity, reliability, and usefulness to classroom teachers.

[485]

Howarth Mood Adjective Checklist. College and adults; 1979–80; HMACL; 10 scores: aggression, skepticism, egotism, outgoingness, control, anxiety, co-operative, fatigue, concentration, sadness; no data on reliability and validity; no norms; 1 form (no date, 2 pages); no specific manual, combined information sheets ('80, 8 pages) for this and Howarth Personality Questionnaire and Additional Personality Factor Inventory; combined technical report (no date, 16 pages) for this test, plus the two previously listed; separate answer sheets must be used; price data available from author; (25–35) minutes; Edgar Howarth; the Author [Canada].*

TEST REFERENCES

1. Howarth, E., & Hoffman, M. S. A multidimensional approach to the relationship between mood and weather. BRITISH JOURNAL OF PSYCHOLOGY, 1984, 75, 15–23.

Review of Howarth Mood Adjective Checklist by ROBERT R. HUTZELL, Clinical Psychologist, Veterans Administration Medical Center, Knoxville, IA:

Howarth's Mood Adjective Checklist (HMACL) is a research instrument developed for the exploration of changes within a domain of factor analytically derived mood states. The current version of the HMACL is evidently the fourth version (HMACL4). It usually should be completed within 10–15 minutes by normal individuals with average or better intelligence. It can be obtained directly from its author at no charge.

CHECKLIST FORMAT AND MATERIALS. The HMACL4 is printed on a single Question/Answer sheet. In addition to the checklist itself, the face of the Question/Answer sheet has (*a*) blanks for the respondent to report name, date, and sex; (*b*) coded blanks for recording the respondent's scores on each of the 10 purported mood scales; and (*c*) instructions for the 4-point response system by which the respondent is required to mark the adjectives according to how the respondent feels "right now." The response system instructs the respondent to leave the adjective blank "if you definitely do not feel that way," while a response of "1" is made "if you do not feel that way," a response of "2" is made "if you feel that way," and a response of "3" is made "if you definitely feel that way."

The HMACL4 checklist itself consists of 60 adjectives placed in a format of five columns by 12 rows. This arrangement of the adjectives is for scoring convenience, with each column containing all six items for two mood scales. Odd items constitute one mood scale of the column and even items constitute the other. Each scale score is derived by adding the numbers the respondent has assigned to the six items of each scale.

The HMACL4 arrives as a copy of the Question/Answer sheet plus several reprints more or less related to the HMACL. Also included in the package is a fact sheet with (*a*) the scoring instructions, (*b*) a statement claiming that reliabilities are inapplicable, (*c*) no norms (but a statement that local student norms do exist), (*d*) a statement that there is no manual, and (*e*) a statement that the 60 items were derived from a number of studies using the previous 120-item HMACLs with R- and P-technique factor analyses plus "all the available factor solutions in the relevant literature."

CRITICAL EVALUATION. The concept of a brief but inclusive measure of rather transient mood states is intriguing, particularly for research purposes. Seen as positive aspects of the HMACL4 are the relatively short administration time and the ease of scoring. The dimensions of mood putatively measured by the HMACL4 are also seen as a positive in that they evidence much face validity and they are dimensions which likely would be of considerable interest to researchers and clinicians.

An overwhelming deficit of the HMACL is the lack of data supporting the psychometric properties of the instrument. The development of the instrument is not adequately outlined. The HMACL4 appears to have abandoned both the balancing of adjectives and the use of a binary answer format which were incorporated into earlier versions of the HMACL and argued to be advantages over some of the other existing multiple mood adjective checklists; no explanation of the reason for this change is offered in the materials which arrive with the checklist. The author eschews assessment of reliability, although split-half reliability estimates would appear simple to obtain from existing data, and other reliability estimates are equally important. Publications involving the HMACL have been written principally by its author, and they do not offer much additional information about the development, reliability, validity, or utilization of the instrument. One publication (Howarth, 1980), brings into question whether or not some of the mood dimensions (Anxiety, Concentration, Cooperativeness, and Sadness) actually are independent from trait dimensions.

Whether a particular score on one scale of the HMACL indicates a level of mood comparable to the same score on another scale of the instrument is not known. The relationships between the HMACL and other mood scales remain to be ascertained.

At this point, it is not clear that the HMACL has incremental validity over very simple and straightforward questions. An example of such a question might be: "Rate your present level of ______ on a 1 to 10 scale with 1 signifying very little ______ and 10 signifying a very high ______ level."

Lastly, many persons will have difficulty responding to the HMACL4. Some of the adjectives require a rather high reading level (e.g., CONVENTIONAL, INTENT, etc.). The Question/Answer sheet is not professional looking and is not aesthetically pleasing. The coded blanks for the recording of mood scale scores appear odd looking and out of place on the Question/Answer sheet. The 4-point response system is difficult for many respondents to interpret.

SUMMARY. In sum, although a quick and psychometrically sound mood adjective checklist that measures a variety of relevant moods with the same instrument will be valuable, too little statistical information is available to recommend the HMACL for purposes other than to conduct research on the psychometric properties of the instrument itself. Although the HMACL might continue to be useful for factor analytical studies of adjective associations, its use in applied and research settings as an assessment of individuals' mood levels must await further publication of relevant data. Independent investigations designed to assess reliability and validity seem warranted at this point.

It is recommended that potential users of multiple mood adjective checklists approach the HMACL cautiously and consider other such instruments which are available and for which more data are published by the scale developers as well as by independent researchers. Good starting points include the Clyde Mood Scale (for drug studies), Gough's Adjective Checklist (with the researched wording of instructions to assess moods), Nowlis's Mood Adjective Checklist, the Psychiatric Outpatient Mood Scale (for psychiatric outpatients), or Zuckerman's Multiple Affect Adjective Checklist.

REVIEWER'S REFERENCES

Howarth, E. Interrelations between state and trait: Some new evidence. PERCEPTUAL AND MOTOR SKILLS, 1980, 51, 613–614.

[486]

Howarth Personality Questionnaire. College and adults; 1971–80; HPQ; 10 scores: sociability, anxiety, dominance, conscience, hypochondriac-medical, impulsive, cooperative-considerateness, inferiority, persistence, suspicion vs. trust; no data on validity; norms consist of means and standard deviations; 1 form ('73, 6 pages); no specific manual, combined information sheets ('80, 8 pages) for this and Additional Personality Factor Inventory and Howarth Mood Adjective Checklist; combined technical report (no date, 16 pages) for this test, plus the two previously listed; separate answer sheets must be used; price information available from author; (25–35) minutes; Edgar Howarth; the Author [Canada].*

Review of Howarth Personality Questionnaire by ANTHONY J. DEVITO, Assistant Director, Counseling Center, Fordham University, Bronx, NY:

The Howarth Personality Questionnaire (HPQ) is a 120-item test measuring 10 traits or dimensions, 12 items comprising each scale. The written materials provided with the test (Howarth, 1978, 1980) will be referred to as "supplementary materials." The information provided in these supplementary materials is so sketchy and incomplete that one can only conclude that this instrument is still being developed. Much of this review will discuss the information which must be included in a manual before the use of the instrument can be seriously considered. Other sources cited by the test author (e.g., Browne & Howarth, 1977; Howarth & Browne, 1971) were examined to better understand the HPQ.

Howarth relied on his own work and that of Sells, Demaree, and Will (1970) in determining which factors or traits were to be measured. Howarth (1978) claims to have begun with 4,000 items drawn from a number of sources. While the test author does not name the sources in the supplementary materials, he alludes to Browne and Howarth (1977), where 15 sources of items are given. Among the most familiar are the Minnesota Multiphasic Personality Inventory, the Guilford-Zimmerman Temperament Survey, the California Psychological Inventory, the Omnibus Personality Inventory, the Comrey Personality Scales, and the Sixteen Personality Factor Questionnaire. The methodology outlined in Browne and Howarth (1977) involved distilling the 4,000 items by inspection to obtain 20 items for each of the 20 hypothesized factors. The factor analyses to which the test author refers in the supplementary materials were apparently performed on about 400 items. The 10 scales comprising the HPQ are the 10 most reliable of the 20 factors which were hypothesized and which emerged.

The HPQ's main strength is the factor analytic methodology used in its development. Factor analysis was extensively used in construction of the HPQ, and it is one of only a few personality questionnaires whose construction was based on a factor analysis of items, with each item treated as a variable. The author is to be commended for the extensive work done and for the selection of this technology, which is possible with such large numbers of items only since the advent of large-scale computers. The results of the factor analyses should be included in the manual. The only reservation one might have would relate to the appropriateness of factor analysis with dichotomous variables.

According to Anastasi (1982, p. 515), "Homogeneity and factorial purity are desirable goals in test construction. But they are not substitutes for empirical validation." In the case of the HPQ, the factor analyses appear to constitute the only validity evidence, since no additional validity information is provided in the supplementary materials. Empirical validity of the scales should also be demonstrated. It would be worthwhile for the author to provide intercorrelations of the HPQ scales and correlations of the HPQ scales with other instruments known to measure similar constructs. The method used to calculate the split-half reliabilities, ranging from .66 to .84, should be stated so that reliability can be better interpreted. Test-retest reliability information should also be available to the test user.

While the HPQ is technically sophisticated in certain aspects of its development, there are deficiencies which may be obvious even to the naive test taker. The instructions are needlessly detailed, yet do not give the test taker the most basic instructions (i.e., "Mark the Box," etc.). Furthermore, the test taker has no way of knowing that Y, T, N, and F represent "yes," "true," "no," and "false." Another disconcerting feature of this instrument is that the items are not expressed uniformly in the same person. The items "You are troubled by unusual fears or distastes" and "I rarely act without careful consideration" are consecutive. Items are sometimes expressed interrogatively and at other times declaratively. In the opinion of this reviewer, the items should have been rewritten so they are all in the same person (preferably first person singular, to induce involvement) and all of the same sentence type. Furthermore, the items should be written to fit a true/false or yes/no format—not both. All items should have been rewritten prior to the factor analytic procedures. In addition, the manual should include some investigation of bias, especially social desirability and faking.

It is disconcerting to see so many similar items within the same scale. It is redundant to include items 37 ("I always try to follow the golden rule") and 57 ("I always try to do unto others as I would have them do unto me"). The items are indeed very homogeneous within each scale. This homogeneity will necessarily result in higher split-half reliabilities and factor loadings in the factor analyses. The danger here is that one would be measuring a very narrow, limited dimension.

There is no clear statement of the appropriate uses of the instrument or the population for which it was intended. Norm tables include separate Canadian samples of English-speaking college students, French-speaking college students, male army soldiers, and male army officers. The norm tables within the supplementary materials are insufficient in that only means and standard deviations for each of the 10 scales are provided. The following refinements should be included: (*a*) a more detailed norm table (e.g., conversion of raw scores to percentile ranks or standard scores), and/or (*b*) a profile sheet representing normative standing. Consideration should also be given to including other normative groupings such as normal adults.

At this time, the reviewer would recommend this test as a research instrument for use with relatively normal populations. The test user may wish to consider as alternatives to the HPQ the Jackson Personality Inventory and the instruments named previously (from which items were drawn to construct the HPQ). When the manual with the requisite information has been compiled, its suitability for purposes other than research can be considered.

REVIEWER'S REFERENCES

Sells, S. B., Demaree, R. G., & Will, D. P., Jr. Dimensions of personality: I. Conjoint factor structure of Guilford and Cattell trait markers. MULTIVARIATE BEHAVIORAL RESEARCH, 1970, 5, 399–422.

Howarth, E., & Browne, J. A. Investigation of personality factors in a Canadian context: I. Marker structure in personality questionnaire items. CANADIAN JOURNAL OF BEHAVIOURAL SCIENCE, 1971, 3, 161–173.

Browne, J. A., & Howarth, E. A comprehensive factor analysis of personality questionnaire items: A test of twenty putative factor hypotheses. MULTIVARIATE BEHAVIORAL RESEARCH, 1977, 12, 399–427.

Howarth, E. TECHNICAL BACKGROUND AND USER INFORMATION FOR TRAIT AND STATE INVENTORIES. Unpublished manuscript, 1978.

Howarth, E. SCALE DESCRIPTIONS, NORM TABLES AND BIBLIOGRAPHY. Unpublished manuscript. University of Alberta, Department of Psychology, Edmonton, Canada, 1980.

Anastasi, A. PSYCHOLOGICAL TESTING (5th ed.). New York: Macmillan, 1982.

Review of Howarth Personality Questionnaire by STEPHEN L. FRANZOI, Post-Doctoral Fellow, Training Program in Social Psychology, Indiana University, Bloomington, IN:

The most important information about this questionnaire is that there is insufficient information available to properly judge its quality; in two sparse papers the reader is presented with only a description of the subscales comprising the Howarth Personality Questionnaire (HPQ), norm tables for different adult samples (e.g., students, soldiers), and data concerning the subscales' split-half reliabilities. No data are presented to shed very much light on the factor structure of the questionnaire or, more importantly, its validity. Even if the reader were to take the time to find and read some of the articles referenced in one of the two papers provided, he or she would still learn little about the HPQ's factor structure or validity. However, having taken these steps, the reader would discover that in the factor analyses conducted in constructing the HPQ, an adequate amount of sampling of one stable item pool does not seem to have been carried out, and it appears that no attempt has been made to replicate the factor structure of the present version of the HPQ. Further, in constructing the questionnaire items, the ratio of the number of subjects given the questionnaire to the number of items tested at any one time was, on the average, less than 3 to 1. Generally a ratio of 10 to 1 or at least 7 to 1 is considered prudent in scale factoring.

An examination of the actual questionnaire items reveals that there are a total of 120, with each subscale consisting of 12 items. The questionnaire has clear instructions and the items are fairly straightforward. The items consist of relatively brief statements that are answered using a true-false format. While the statements are relatively straightforward, some respondents may become confused by the fact that some items are worded in the first person ("I almost always feel well and strong"), while other items are worded in the second person ("Are your feelings easily hurt?"). Scoring of the separate subscales is easily accomplished using the overlay scoring key.

No information is provided concerning the intercorrelations of the subscales. Split-half reliabilities range between .66 and .84, with an average reliability coefficient of .75, a respectable value.

SUMMARY. The questionnaire is easy to administer and score. However, there is too little information currently available about the scale's factor structure or validity to recommend its use. What information is available concerning scale construction suggests that an adequate sampling of one stable item pool has yet to be carried out or, at the very least, reported to the potential user of the questionnaire. It is clearly up to the author to provide further data before the HPQ can be rated as acceptable.

[487]

Hughes Basic Gross Motor Assessment. Ages 6–12 believed to have minor motor dysfunctions; 1979; BGMA; designed to detect disorders in motor performance; 8 subtests: Static Balance, Stride Jump, Tandem Walking, Hopping, Skipping, Target, Yo-Yo, Ball Handling Skills; individual; 1 form; manual (95 pages); testing materials must be assembled locally; 1984 price data: $12 per manual; administration time not reported; Jeanne E. Hughes; the Author.*

TEST REFERENCES

1. Hughes, J. E., & Riley, A. Basic Gross Motor Assessment: Tool for use with children having minor motor dysfunction. THE JOURNAL OF AMERICAN PHYSICAL THERAPY ASSOCIATION, 1981, 61, 503–511.

[488]

Human Information Processing Survey. Adults; 1984; HIP Survey; "assesses processing preference—left, right, integrated, or mixed [brain functioning]"; 3 scores: right, left, integrated; norms consist of means and standard deviations; 2 forms; administrator's manual (44 pages); 1985 price data: $6.50 per administrator's manual; $8 per specimen set; administration time not reported; E. Paul Torrance, William Taggart (manual), and Barbara Taggart; Scholastic Testing Services, Inc.*

a) RESEARCH EDITION. 1 form (5 pages); profiles form (1 page); response sheet (1 page); $42 per starter set (includes administrator's manual plus 20 copies each of survey, profiles, and response forms); $12 per 20 profiles and response forms.

b) PROFESSIONAL EDITION. 1 form (9 pages); strategy and tactics profiles booklet (4 pages); $25 per starter set (includes administrator's manual plus 10 copies each of survey and strategy and tactics profiles booklet); $20 per 10 surveys plus strategy and tactics booklets.

[489]

Human Loyalty Expressionaire. College and university students; no date on test materials; "measures human loyalty and global awareness"; no data on reliability; no norms; 1 form (6 pages, includes directions for administration and scoring key; no manual; 1983 price data: $7 per questionnaire (may be reproduced locally); administration time not reported; Theodore F. Lentz; Character Research Association.*

[490]

Humanics National Child Assessment Form. Ages 0–3, 3–6; 1982; behavior checklist to be completed by parents or teachers; no data on reliability and validity; no norms; 2 levels; 1984 price data: $.75 per checklist (specify level); administration time not reported; Humanics Limited.*

a) AGES 0–3. Item scores in 5 areas: social-emotional, language, cognitive, gross motor, fine motor; 12 pages (includes directions).

b) AGES 3–6. Item scores in 5 areas: social-emotional, motor skills, language, cognitive, hygiene/self-help; 14 pages (includes directions).

[491]

Hunter-Grundin Literacy Profiles. Ages 6.5–8, 7.10–9.3, 9–10; 1979–80; ratings by teacher in part; 4 to 5 tests: Attitude to Reading (Levels 1 and 2 only), Reading for Meaning, Spelling, Free Writing, Spoken Language; norms for Reading for Meaning and Spelling tests only; 3 levels; 1983 price data: 14p each per Reading for Meaning tests of any one level; 6p each per remaining 4 tests of any one level; 80p each per Spoken Language picture; 17p each per cumulative record; £1.00 per set of classroom board and key; £3.55 per manual of any one level; £16.30 per trial kit of Level 1 including 30 Reading for Meaning tests, 30 spelling tests, 1 manual, 1 key, 1 picture, 1 classroom board, and 1 cumulative record; £11.20 per trial kit of any level 2–5; (3–10) minutes per test of any one level; Elizabeth Hunter-Grundin and Hans U. Grundin; Test Agency [England].*

a) LEVEL 1. Ages 6.5–8; reliability and validity data for Reading for Meaning and Spelling tests only; 1 form ('79, 2–4 pages) for each test; manual (no date, 52 pages).

b) LEVEL 2. Ages 7.10–9.3; no reliability or validity data for Aptitude Scales or Free Writing Scales; 1 form ('80, 2–4 pages) for each test; manual (no date, 48 pages).

c) LEVEL 3. Ages 9–10; no data on reliability or validity for Spoken Language Scales; 1 form ('80, 2–4 pages) for each test; manual (no date, 46 pages).

Review of Hunter-Grundin Literacy Profiles by MARTHA C. BEECH, Assistant Professor, School of Education and Allied Professions, University of Miami, Coral Gables, FL:

The Hunter-Grundin Literacy Profiles are described by the authors as a pioneering effort in the development of a system for monitoring individual pupil progress in language and literacy for children ages 7–10 in England. While three separate forms are packaged, a closer look reveals that only the Reading for Meaning and Spelling Scales are actually different across the three levels. Spoken Language Scales have stimuli and evaluation criteria which are identical for Levels 1 and 2. The Free Writing Scales use stimuli and evaluation criteria which are essentially the same across all three levels.

The tests were standardized on large populations (approximately 2,400 to 2,800 subjects per grade level). The authors claim that these samples represented urban/rural areas and a wide socioeconomic range. While participating school districts are listed in each manual, no specific demographic data are included to support these claims. The age range of the standardization population is given for each level, but there is no breakdown of numbers of subjects at each age level. This would be important in evaluating the norm tables, which give standard scores at 2-month intervals at each level.

The Reading for Meaning Scale uses a modified cloze procedure. To establish validity, performance was correlated with five other well-known reading tests in England. Correlation coefficients ranged from .74 to .87 across the three levels of the test. Kuder-Richardson reliability coefficients were high, ranging from .97 to .98 for the three levels. This test appears to be a good measure of general reading ability, particularly considering its brevity. The visual presentation, with words and lines so widely spaced, may provide some difficulty for students—particularly where the student must select the correct word to complete the sentence.

The Spelling Scale requires that students fill in deleted words from a story which is read to them by the examiner. The context of the story "eliminates, as far as possible, the risk of misunderstandings about the words to be written." As no other standardized spelling test existed in England, the authors correlated the Spelling Scale with the number of words spelled correctly in the Free Writing Scale and reported correlations ranging from .81 to .84 as an indication of criterion-related validity. The Kuder-Richardson reliability coefficients ranged from .90 to .93 for the Spelling Scale. Although very short, this test appears to be a reasonable estimate of the student's spelling skills.

The Free Writing Scale has students "write about the things they see and the things that happen, or might happen, on the way to school." Claims of construct validity are presented by the authors. They report that the reliability of the Free Writing Scales will be dependent on the way the individual teacher scores the test. Fairly detailed evaluation criteria are included and samples of student responses are provided in the manual to assist teachers in a general evaluation of the response. These student response samples are different at each level. The authors point out that the scoring, done initially by teachers, was later "double-checked." Unfortunately no inter-rater reliability estimates are provided. Use of this test is not clearly supported by the material presented in the manual.

The Spoken Language Scale requires the student to tell a story about a picture. The story is rated on five factors, such as enunciation, vocabulary, and imagination. Specific criteria for Grades A through E are provided in the manual, but no examples of student responses are given. There is no suggestion of validity or reliability for this scale. This scale will require further study before its claims of appropriateness can be supported.

Attitudes Toward Reading is assessed at Levels 1 and 2 using a forced choice scale of 1–5 (like very much to dislike very much) for each of the subtests included in the profile. It is doubtful that this simplistic evaluation could provide much useful information to the teacher other than to act as a starting point for further investigation.

The manual also provides information regarding the use of the Scales for diagnostic teaching. Suggestions for interpretation of results and appropriate instructional follow-up are given. These may be useful to stimulate a teacher who is familiar with the procedures described, but are not detailed enough for precise application.

SUMMARY. The Hunter-Grundin Literacy Profiles are a comprehensive system for monitoring the written and spoken language skills of children ages 7 through 10 in England. While the normative sample was large, the information concerning its demographic characteristics is only briefly described in the manual. Two scales, Reading for Meaning and Spelling, appear to have sufficient evidence of validity and reliability to support their use. The remaining three scales, Free Writing, Spoken Language, and Attitude Toward Reading, are only supported by the authors' claims of their usefulness. Further study is recommended for these scales to demonstrate both their technical merits and practical usefulness.

Review of Hunter-Grundin Literacy Profiles by PATRICIA H. KENNEDY, Associate Professor, Arizona State University, Tempe, AZ:

The Hunter-Grundin Literacy Profiles, Levels one to three, are intended to assess pupil progress in several important language and literacy skill areas: attitude toward reading, reading for meaning, spelling, free writing, and spoken language. The Profiles are appropriate for children from age 7 to 10.

The test development and norming of the Profiles were conducted in Great Britain. Consequently, the names of grades and some vocabulary words will not make sense to Americans. Because Scotland has an education system which is separate from that of England and Wales, separate average scores are given for Scotland for the Spelling scales and the Reading for Meaning scales. No scores are given for the American education system.

There are a number of noteworthy aspects of the Profiles. Results are reported in standard scores and in an index called "reading age." Reading age is preferable to the more common index, grade level equivalent, because it has immediate meaning for teachers. Another laudable aspect of the Profiles is that only three scales need to be timed. It is hard for teachers to give timed tests and not raise pupil anxiety.

Seldom do researchers show much interest in attitudes pupils have toward reading, so it was encouraging that the Profiles had a scale assessing that variable. Unfortunately, the method of assessment leaves something to be desired. Of the six items in the "Attitude to Reading" scale, only one directly measured attitude toward reading. The other five served as anchors. The item format requires the pupil to select one face from five graded faces that best reflects the degree of like or dislike of an activity. Discriminating between five similar faces would be particularly difficult for a young child or a learning disabled, distractible pupil. Three faces rather than five would have permitted measurement of the attitude without the complicated discrimination.

Validity was assessed by correlating the Profile scales with European tests unfamiliar to the American professional. Internal consistency reliability coefficients were generally high. No information was presented regarding other reliability indices that would be important to know, such as interrater reliability or test-retest stability over time.

In general, the disadvantages of the Profiles outweigh the advantages. The Profiles are premised on a good method of teaching language development, the cloze technique. One of the main advertised advantages of the Profiles is supposed to be that the teacher can translate a pupil's errors into remedial teaching techniques. This is where the Profiles fall short of the mark. The diagnostic-prescriptive advice is too superficial to be of any real use.

[492]

ICES: Instructor and Course Evaluation System. College students; 1976–78; instructors choose items from a pool of over 450 covering student perceptions of teaching styles, student outcomes, and course characteristics; norms for University of Illinois at Urbana-Champaign only; item catalog ('77, 24 pages), rationale-description, choosing items, interpretive guide, (no date, 4 pages); instructor reports: departmental core items plus instructor-selected items (option 1, 4 pages), instructor-selected items only (option 2, 4 pages), complete forms (option 3, 4 pages); faculty request form (no date, 2 pages); research report (no date, 4 pages); 1985 price data: $.08 per sheet for printing; $.19 per sheet for processing; $2 per user information packet; additional charges for establishing service available from publisher; administration time not reported; Measurement and Research Division, University of Illinois at Urbana-Champaign.*

Review of ICES: Instructor and Course Evaluation System by EDWARD A. NELSEN, Professor of Educational Psychology, Arizona State University, Tempe, AZ:

The Instructor and Course Evaluation System (ICES) is a computer based system that allows users to compile their own questionnaires for student ratings of college instructors and courses. It is described by the developers as having two purposes: "(1) to provide information to instructors who desire to monitor and improve their instruction and (2) to provide information which others might use to help with promotion or similar decisions." To elicit information for course improvement, users are furnished with a catalog comprised of over 450 items, among which they may choose up to 23 objective and 2 essay questions to form a custom instrument. To obtain standard information for comparisons, three objective "global" items are printed on every form. The global items ask students to rate "the course content," "the instructor," and "the course in general" on a 6-point scale ranging from "excellent" to "very poor." Scoring and analysis services are offered via mail at the University of Illinois; or the ICES software package, including the item bank, is available for institutional purchase.

Printed information concerning the ICES includes the Item Catalog, a newsletter series, reports with descriptive statistical information, and an annotated list of research reports. The Item Catalog outlines directions for three modes of structuring questionnaires. One mode consists of instructor selected items only (in addition to the three standard global items). A second mode includes instructor selected items along with a "departmental core" (i.e., any set of items that might be designated by an administrative unit as standard items). Third, users may choose among 10 completely predesigned forms. The items in the Catalog are classified under six broad categories: course management, student outcomes of instruction, instructor characteristics and style, instructional environment, student learning styles and preferences for instruction, and specific instructional settings.

The four newsletters and five descriptive statistical reports are comprised of information that would normally be integrated within a single technical manual. The first newsletter consists of the Item Catalog itself. Another newsletter presents the rationale and description of the ICES, a third offers guidelines for selecting items from the catalog, and the fourth provides directions for interpreting the computer printout of the results for individual faculty. This guide is helpful, because the "faculty reports" are complex and slightly confusing; even with the guide, initial users must study the printout to comprehend all of its facets. Several statistical reports portray norms on each of the global items, separately for faculty and teaching assistants in elective, required, and mixed classes. Newsletter November 4 refers to University of Illinois faculty who have used the form as constituting the norm groups, but the selection and characteristics of the norm groups are not adequately described. No norms are provided for the optional items. Presumably, users will develop norms locally, if they are needed.

There is almost no information pertaining to the reliability or validity of the ICES as a measure of instructional performance. The most needed reliability information concerns consistency of ratings averages for instructors across courses (e.g., across different courses or across the same course taught in different semesters). The most needed validity information concerns relationships of the ratings with alternative indices of teaching performance and effectiveness (e.g., indices of student achievement or observational ratings of teaching performance). Studies have compared instructor evaluations based upon student responses to the ICES objective items with student comments on the ICES open-ended items and with interviews with groups of students. The results revealed moderate to high degrees of congruence between these different types of measures (Braskamp, Ory, & Pieper, 1981; Ory, Braskamp, & Pieper, 1980). However, such data reflect only the extent of consistency across different types of student judgments of the same instructor and course, not the validity of the ICES as a more general index of teaching quality.

Should the ICES be used for decisions about promotion and other personnel matters? Considering the lack of representative norms and the lack of data on the reliability and validity of the global items as indices of teaching quality, I advise caution. An index of students' judgments of their teachers based upon these items alone may not be as informative as one based on a more detailed and structured instrument. Indeed, only one of the three items focuses on the faculty member per se (i.e., "rate the instructor"). The other two items ask the students to evaluate the course, which may not be an appropriate basis for assessing the instructor's performance if important aspects of the course were under others' jurisdiction. Nevertheless, a larger set of items could be used to construct a more comprehensive questionnaire to obtain student ratings of teaching performance (i.e., by establishing a departmental core of items along with local norms). The ICES is conducive to such an approach and could be especially useful for departments in which a standardized instrument is inappropriate because most instruction is specialized or nontraditional (e.g., in studio or laboratory courses). However, if data for personnel decisions are to be based upon classes taught in conventional modes (e.g., lectures and discussions), the established organization of a good standardized instrument would seem to be advantageous.

On the other hand, if the primary purpose of faculty evaluation is to obtain feedback for instructional improvement, then the cafeteria style offerings of the ICES offer distinct advantages. A large variety of content is offered, including both broad and specific items. The computer based system is uniquely comprehensive and flexible. Thus, by custom designing the instruments to focus on teaching issues of particular concern, instructors can obtain information especially relevant to their courses. Further, for instructors who gather data periodically, the contents of the ICES can be varied systematically to elicit elaborative information on successive administrations.

In conclusion, the ICES capitalizes on the capacity of computers to print and process custom-designed faculty rating questionnaires. The comprehensiveness and flexibility of the system are advantageous for obtaining relevant and detailed feedback from students. Improved graphic design of the report would enable users to interpret the feedback more easily. The ICES needs better documentation, norms, reliability and validity studies, and decision-making guidelines before using the results for faculty personnel decisions. Nevertheless, the system offers great potential for future development.

REVIEWER'S REFERENCES

Ory, J. C., Braskamp, L. A., & Pieper, D. M. Congruency of student evaluative information collected by three methods. JOURNAL OF EDUCATIONAL PSYCHOLOGY, 1980, 72, 181–185.

Braskamp, L. A., Ory, J. C., & Pieper, D. M. Student written comments: Dimensions of instructional quality. JOURNAL OF EDUCATIONAL PSYCHOLOGY, 1981, 73, 65–70.

[493]

IDEA. College faculty; 1975–83; student ratings for faculty evaluation and development; 3 or 7 parts to report: evaluation (progress ratings), course description (standard form only), students' self ratings, methods (standard form only), additional questions (standard form only), diagnostic summary (standard form only), summary profile; 2 forms: standard survey form ('81, 1 page), short form (1 response card with 14 items printed on card itself); faculty instruction sheet (no date, 4 pages); interpreting your IDEA report ('75, 6 pages); interpreting your IDEA short form report (no date, 2 pages); IDEA report ('76, 3 pages); IDEA short form report ('82, 1 page); technical report no. 1 ('77, 40 pages); technical report no. 4 ('78, 90 pages); technical report no. 5 ('83, 51 pages); separate response cards must be used; 1984 price data: $.15 or less per response card; no charge for other materials; scoring service, $5 per class for standard form, $3 per class for short form; administration time not reported; Donald P. Hoyt, Richard E. Owens, William E. Cashin (technical reports), Bruce M. Perrin (technical report no. 4), and Akihiro Noma (technical report no. 5); Center for Faculty Evaluation and Development.*

TEST REFERENCES

1. Bray, J. H., & Howard, G. S. Interaction of teacher and student sex and sex role orientations and student evaluations of college instruction. CONTEMPORARY EDUCATIONAL PSYCHOLOGY, 1980, 5, 241–248.

2. Hanna, G. S., Hoyt, D. P., & Aubrecht, J. D. Identifying and adjusting for biases in student evaluations of instruction: Implications for validity. EDUCATIONAL AND PSYCHOLOGICAL MEASUREMENT, 1983, 43, 1175–1185.

Review of IDEA by JOHN C. ORY, Head, Measurement and Research Division, University of Illinois, Urbana-Champaign, Urbana, IL:

The Instructional Development Effectiveness Assessment (IDEA) System is a program involving student rating of classroom instruction and the instructor. As described in the IDEA Technical Report No. 1, IDEA is a family of student rating forms which can be used to provide a source of interpretable information for both evaluation and development decisions. The basic premise of the IDEA system is that there is no one model of effective teaching but that effective teaching could best be recognized by its effect on students.

The IDEA premise is incorporated in the format and content of each of the different IDEA survey forms (e.g., long form, short form). The attempt is to obtain student data addressing three major problems in the assessment of instructional effectiveness: (1) To what extent did students make progress on the instructor's objectives? (2) How was the amount of progress affected by the teaching methods used in the course? (3) How can effects on ratings other than the instructor's teaching be controlled?

There are items on the survey forms addressing each of these three questions. Students report the amount of progress they have made on 10 course objectives. For reporting purposes, faculty indicate the extent to which each of the 10 objectives were emphasized in their course. A second set of items asks students to describe the teaching methods used in the course so that instructors might relate particular methods to low or high progress ratings. Two other sets of items are included to address the third question regarding control of other factors which affect student ratings. Items in these two sets collect information about student affect toward the course (including level of student motivation) and the difficulty of the course. A series of multiple regression analyses conducted over several years has isolated class size (as indicated by the instructor) and level of student motivation (as measured by the item "I had a strong desire to take this course") as variables having a "statistically potent influence on student progress ratings." As will be discussed later, the IDEA system attempts to control for these two factors by establishing appropriate norm groups for classes of comparable size containing students with similar levels of motivation to be in the course.

The IDEA method of reporting results is based on a strategy which requires comparisons across classes. Faculty receive information about their relative standing (e.g., low average, average, high, etc.) as compared to all instructors in the comparison group (all faculty using IDEA, approximately 18,000 classes over 10+ years) and/or to other faculty teaching classes of similar size and with comparable levels of student motivation. The computerized report also identifies teaching weaknesses where students report unsatisfactory progress on course goals and indicate teaching method patterns which are related to the low progress ratings. The reporting system is clearly presented and easy to interpret.

A tremendous amount of quality research went into the development of the IDEA system. It is well documented in the available technical reports. Instructions for using the IDEA system are lengthy but easy to follow, as is the interpretation guide. The costs for using the IDEA system are comparable to other nationally available student rating systems.

While there should be no argument about the quality of this particular student rating system, there may be some disagreement over its basic premise or philosophy. The available student rating systems reflect differences of opinion about the IDEA emphasis on measuring student progress on course objectives. Some systems utilize omnibus forms with a fixed set of items across a wide range of topics, while other systems allow faculty to select items from a catalogue containing items which are grouped by topics (e.g., course management, instructor characteristics). Instructors' preferences for assessing instructional quality through student achievement on course objectives, rather than through other types of responses, will surely affect their opinion of the IDEA system.

Another personal preference which may alter one's evaluation of the IDEA system involves the appropriateness of the norm comparisons. Results are reported as comparisons between an individual instructor and all faculty who have used IDEA (across all schools) or all faculty who have taught courses of similar class size containing students with similar levels of motivation. Some faculty and administrators may prefer being compared to a local norm group, others teaching at their university or college, rather than an aggregate of faculty users teaching at small, medium, and large colleges and universities in the country. The IDEA system does not provide local norm comparisons.

IDEA is a highly respected and popular student rating system in use at over 100 colleges and universities. The system is well documented, easy to administer, and appropriately priced. The reporting of results is especially well designed with a clear presentation of useful information. A recommendation for using the system, however, is somewhat dependent on one's personal preference for evaluating instruction through student progress and one's preference for national rather than local norms.

[494]

Identi-Form System for Gifted Programs. Grades K–12; 1982; rating form for identifying gifted students; "incorporates test, performance and anecdotal data in a total assessment of the child"; ratings in 4 areas: intellectual abilities, creative abilities, personal characteristics, artistic and performing abilities; no data on reliability; no norms, use of norms not recommended; 1 form (2 pages); manual (216 pages); 1984 price data: $19.95 per 25 rating forms and manual; $2.95 per 25 rating forms; Patricia Weber and Catherine Battaglia; D.O.K. Publishers, Inc.*

[495]

Illinois Children's Language Assessment Test. Ages 3–6; 1977; 21 scores: matching colors, recognizing colors, naming colors, matching forms, auditory retention, repetition, auditory comprehension, recognizing objects, naming objects, matching objects to test pictures, stimulability, articulation test, oral musculature, free association (matching, placing), matching objects to test pictures, determining function, explaining pictures, Draw-A-Man, copying geometric forms, total; norms consist of means and standard deviations for all scores except the articulation test and Draw-A-Man which are scored separately; individual; 1 form (15 pages, plus assorted plastic objects and 17 picture cards); instruction booklet (24 pages); 1984 price data: $39.30 per complete set including 12 test booklets; $2.95 per 12 test booklets; (40) minutes; Phyllis B. Arlt; Interstate Printers & Publishers, Inc.*

See T3:1124 (1 reference).

Review of Illinois Children's Language Assessment Test by KENNETH G. SHIPLEY, Associate Professor of Communicative Disorders, California State University, Fresno, Fresno, CA:

The Illinois Children's Language Assessment Test (ICLAT) is an attempt to modify Schuell's "Short Examination for Aphasia" for adult aphasia into a test for evaluating children's language abilities. The author comments that the ICLAT was developed "to evaluate the language performance of children who exhibit a delay or disruption in acquisition of speech and/or language." The author describes the ICLAT as consisting of 18 variables which result in a performance profile in the areas of "expressive, receptive, visual, auditory, symbolic and motor function."

STRENGTHS. One attractive aspect of the test is its focus on a 3- to 6-year age group. There is a relative paucity of diagnostic instruments for practitioners working with this population. This is, as the author points out, an area that should be considered as a high priority because of the importance of optimal language development during the preschool years.

The second major attraction of the test is the use of a binary plus-or-minus scoring pattern which attempts to reduce the need for subjectivity in scoring. A third feature of the test is the use of objects, pictures, and a cute storybook that should be attractive to children.

STRENGTHS WITH LIMITATIONS. The author feels that speech pathologists and special education and regular teachers familiar with testing procedures can use the test. This is probably true for many of the subcategories. However, special training is needed for several test areas. For example, the "Articulation Test" requires the phonetic transcription of errors for any of 79 possible items. Similarly, in the "Oral Musculature" section, it is improbable that persons without specific training in communicative disorders and oral examinations could identify such items as a palatal deviation, or inadequacy of velopharyngeal closure. Some parts of the test, like the "Copying Geometric Forms" sections, require subtle judgments for which some psychometric training would seem desirable.

The standardization of the test was conducted with 240 children from 3 to 6 years of age. Subjects were equally divided by sex at six-month intervals (20 males and 20 females from 3–0 to 3–5, etc.). All subjects were reported to be normal and exhibited a mean IQ of 110 as measured by the Peabody Picture Vocabulary Test. Data from these children provides the bases for the test's mean scores and standard deviations which, in turn, are used to compare the scores you might obtain from a communicatively impaired child.

WEAKNESSES. Major weaknesses are evident in the review of literature, reliability, and validity sections of the manual. The section entitled "Review of Literature and Related Research" is essentially a criticism of five other tests (two for children; three for adult aphasia). The author seems to try to build the case for her test by citing these instruments. Unfortunately, there are many other tests for both children and adults that seem to be ignored. This is particularly noticeable when the author states that "there are three widely used tests for adults with language difficulties...the Eisenson Examination for Aphasia, the Halstead-Wepman Test and the Schuell Short Examination for Aphasia." Practitioners will recognize that even these tests may not be the most widely used when compared with such measures as the PICA, Boston, Sklar, etc. Similarly, there are a number of children's tests other than the ITPA and Bang's Profile, which are cited as the two major children's tests.

Finally, the statements on reliability and validity are, at best, difficult to interpret. While a test/retest reliability of .90 sounds relatively impressive, it is difficult to determine exactly what the author really means when she refers to a test reliability ranging from 0–1.00, with a 1.00 coefficient for 33% of the population, and .50-to-1.00 coefficients for 67% of the group. It is difficult to make sense out of the data as stated. In addition to clarification here, it would have been useful to know whether inter-tester reliability was measured. This would seem especially important since several subtests seem somewhat subject to some tester interpretation.

Validity was measured by comparing ICLAT scores with Peabody Picture Vocabulary Test scores, and a "positive correlation was obtained." However, the degree of relationship is not described. Since a positive correlation could range from .01 to 1.00, this "positive correlation" is essentially uninterpretable. Finally, the author writes that the standardization results were compared to teacher's evaluations of 80 preschool children, but again no results of this comparison are offered.

Readers should also be aware of two other areas that could affect the interpretation of test results.

First, it is suggested that the ICLAT is "moderately low" with respect to cultural bias. This was reportedly accomplished by avoiding certain items that would contribute to bias. The test was then administered to a group of black children, and the results judged by "a panel of blacks." Again, however, there is no information provided about the children tested, or about the panel members (e.g., number of judges, knowledge about testing, etc.). Although we know nothing about them, the judges apparently found that four subtests contain possible cultural bias, and seven subtests contain moderate-to-little cultural bias. There is no indication of which subtests contain these potential contaminants.

Second, the potential user should be aware that not all of the 18 identified variables have a one-to-one correspondence with what is actually tested. For example, the stimulability subtest probably measures an aspect of diadochokinetic (rapid articulator movement) skill, rather than stimulability in the sense of eliciting an errored sound. Another variable is described as mean length of response (MLR). Speech-language pathologists use MLR to evaluate children's syntactic and morphologic language abilities. There is, however, no subtest for this. The "Explaining Pictures" subtest could be adapted for this purpose, but no instructions for determining MLR are offered.

In summary, this reviewer cannot recommend the use of this test in its present form. The information provided (e.g., on validity, reliability, cultural bias, literature, etc.) leaves the reader with more questions that answers. Needless to say, this does not enhance a tester's confidence when making important decisions about children's abilities. While the ICLAT scores would probably identify a child who requires special attention, this could be said of many tests and many professionals' informal observations. It would seem as beneficial to use instruments like the Peabody Picture Vocabulary Test, Test for Auditory Comprehension of Language, Receptive-Expressive Emergent Language, etc., for assessing children's language abilities.

[496]

Illinois Test of Psycholinguistic Abilities, Revised Edition. Ages 2–10; 1961–68; ITPA; 11–13 scores: auditory reception, visual reception, visual sequential memory, auditory association, auditory sequential memory, visual association, visual closure, verbal expression, grammatic closure, manual expression, auditory closure (optional), sound blending (optional), total; individual; 1 form ('68); manual ('68, 134 pages); record form ['68, 16 pages]; visual closure picture strips ['68, 5 pages]; 1984 price data: $110 per set of testing materials including manual, 25 record forms, and 25 visual closure picture strips; $12.50 per 25 record forms and sets of picture strips; $10 per manual; (45–60) minutes; Samuel A. Kirk, James J. McCarthy, and Winifred D. Kirk; University of Illinois Press.*

See T3:1126 (145 references); for reviews by James Lumsden and J. Lee Wiederholt, and an excerpted review by R. P. Waugh, see 8:431 (269 references); see also T2:981 (113 references); for reviews by John B. Carroll and Clinton I. Chase, see 7:442 (239 references); see also 6:549 (22 references).

TEST REFERENCES

1. Camp, B. W., Blom, G. E., Hebert, F., & van Doorninck, W. J. "Think aloud": A program for developing self-control in young aggressive boys. JOURNAL OF ABNORMAL CHILD PSYCHOLOGY, 1977, 5, 157–169.

2. Duchan, J., & Baskervill, R. D. Responses of black and white children to the Grammatic Closure Subtest of the ITPA. LANGUAGE, SPEECH, AND HEARING SERVICES IN SCHOOLS, 1977, 8, 126–132.

3. Klinge, V., Rennick, P. M., Lennox, K., & Hart, Z. A matched-subject comparison of underachievers with normals on intellectual, behavioral and emotional variables. JOURNAL OF ABNORMAL CHILD PSYCHOLOGY, 1977, 5, 61–68.

4. Witkin, B. R., Butler, K. G., & Whalen, T. E. Auditory processing in children: Two studies of component factors. LANGUAGE, SPEECH, AND HEARING SERVICES IN SCHOOLS, 1977, 8, 140–154.

5. Rabe, M. B., & Matlin, M. W. Sex-role stereotypes in speech and language tests. LANGUAGE, SPEECH, AND HEARING SERVICES IN SCHOOLS, 1978, 9, 70–75.

6. Rennick, P. M., Klinge, V., Hart, Z., & Lennox, K. Evaluation of intellectual, linguistic, and achievement variables in normal, emotionally disturbed, and learning disabled children. ADOLESCENCE, 1978, 13, 755–766.

7. Bradley, P. E., Battin, R. R., & Sutter, E. G. Effects of individual diagnosis and remediation for the treatment of learning disabilities. CLINICAL NEUROPSYCHOLOGY, 1979, 1(2), 25–32.

8. Crawford, J. H., & Fry, M. A. Trait-task interaction in intra- and intermodal matching of auditory and visual trigrams. CONTEMPORARY EDUCATIONAL PSYCHOLOGY, 1979, 4, 1–10.

9. Rieder, R. O., & Nichols, P. L. Offspring of schizophrenics III: Hyperactivity and neurological soft signs. ARCHIVES OF GENERAL PSYCHIATRY, 1979, 36, 665–674.

10. Baker, L., Cantwell, D. P., & Mattison, R. E. Behavior problems in children with pure speech disorders and in children with combined speech and language disorders. JOURNAL OF ABNORMAL CHILD PSYCHOLOGY, 1980, 8, 245–256.

11. Hartlage, L. C., & Telzrow, C. F. The practice of clinical neuropsychology. CLINICAL NEUROPSYCHOLOGY, 1980, 2, 200–202.

12. Leong, C. K. Cognitive patterns of "retarded" and below-average readers. CONTEMPORARY EDUCATIONAL PSYCHOLOGY, 1980, 5, 101–117.

13. Mattison, R. E., Cantwell, D. P., & Baker, L. Dimensions of behavior in children with speech and language disorders. JOURNAL OF ABNORMAL CHILD PSYCHOLOGY, 1980, 8, 323–338.

14. Winsberg, B. G., Bialer, I., Kupietz, S., Botti, E., & Balka, E. B. Home vs hospital care of children with behavior disorders: A controlled investigation. ARCHIVES OF GENERAL PSYCHIATRY, 1980, 37, 413–418.

15. Green, A. H., Voeller, K., Gaines, R., & Kubie, J. Neurological impairment in maltreated children. CHILD ABUSE & NEGLECT, 1981, 5, 129–134.

16. Kavale, K. Functions of the Illinois Test of Psycholinguistic Abilities (ITPA): Are they trainable? EXCEPTIONAL CHILDREN, 1981, 47, 496–510.

17. Kavale, K. The relationship between auditory perceptual skills and reading ability: A meta-analysis. JOURNAL OF LEARNING DISABILITIES, 1981, 14, 539–546.

18. Lyon, R., & Watson, B. Empirically derived subgroups of learning disabled readers: Diagnostic characteristics. JOURNAL OF LEARNING DISABILITIES, 1981, 14, 256–261.

19. Stilwell, J. M. Relationship between development of the body-righting reaction and manual midline crossing behavior in the learning disabled: Sensory integration, postural reflex development. THE AMERICAN JOURNAL OF OCCUPATIONAL THERAPY, 1981, 35, 391–398.

20. Camp, B. W, Swift, W. J., & Swift, E. W. Authoritarian parental attitudes and cognitive functioning in preschool children. PSYCHOLOGICAL REPORTS, 1982, 50, 1023–1026.

21. Fontenelle, S., & Alarcon, M. Hyperlexia: Precocious word recognition in developmentally delayed children. PERCEPTUAL AND MOTOR SKILLS, 1982, 55, 247–252.

22. Fujiki, M., & Willbrand, M. L. A comparison of four informal methods of language evaluation. LANGUAGE, SPEECH, AND HEARING SERVICES IN SCHOOLS, 1982, 13, 42–52.

23. Hughes, D., & Till, J. A. A comparison of two procedures to elicit verbal auxiliary and copula in normal kindergarten children. JOURNAL OF SPEECH AND HEARING DISORDERS, 1982, 47, 310–320.

24. Larsen, S. C., Parker, R. M., & Hammill, D. D. Effectiveness of psycholinguistic training: A response to Kavale. EXCEPTIONAL CHILDREN, 1982, 49, 60–66.

25. Luick, A. H., Agranowitz, A., Kirk, S. A., & Busby, R. Profiles of children with severe oral language disorders. JOURNAL OF SPEECH AND HEARING DISORDERS, 1982, 47, 88–92.

26. Wardrop, J. L., Anderson, T. H., Hively, W., Hastings, C. N., Anderson, R. I., & Muller, K. E. A framework for analyzing the inference structure of educational achievement tests. JOURNAL OF EDUCATIONAL MEASUREMENT, 1982, 19, 1 18.

27. Woolfolk, R. L., Lehrer, P. M., McCann, B. S., & Rooney, A. J. Effects of progressive relaxation and meditation on cognitive and somatic manifestations of daily stress. BEHAVIOUR RESEARCH AND THERAPY, 1982, 20, 461–467.

28. Barclay, L. K. Using Spanish as the language of instruction with Mexican-American Head Start children: A re-evaluation using meta-analysis. PERCEPTUAL AND MOTOR SKILLS, 1983, 56, 359–366.

29. Butler, S. R., Marsh, H. W., Sheppard, M. J., & Sheppard, J. L. Predicting reading achievement from kindergarten to third grade—Implications for screening. THE AUSTRALIAN JOURNAL OF EDUCATION, 1983, 27, 288–303.

30. Craft, D. H. Effect of prior exercise on cognitive performance tasks by hyperactive and normal young boys. PERCEPTUAL AND MOTOR SKILLS, 1983, 56, 979–982.

31. Eskenazi, B., & Diamond, S. P. Visual exploration of non-verbal material by dyslexic children. CORTEX, 1983, 19, 353–370.

32. Gittleman, R., & Eskenazi, B. Lead and hyperactivity revisited: An investigation of nondisadvantaged children. ARCHIVES OF GENERAL PSYCHIATRY, 1983, 40, 827–833.

33. Hasbrouck, J. M. Diagnosis of auditory perceptual disorders in previously undiagnosed adults. JOURNAL OF LEARNING DISABILITIES, 1983, 16, 206–208.

34. Kashani, J. H., McGee, R. O., Clarkson, S. E., Anderson, J. C., Walton, L. A., Williams, S., Silva, P. A., Robins, A. J., Cytryn, L., & McKnew, D. H. Depression in a sample of 9-year-old children: Prevalence and associated characteristics. ARCHIVES OF GENERAL PSYCHIATRY, 1983, 40, 1217–1223.

35. Siegel, L. S. Correction for prematurity and its consequences for the assessment of the very low birth weight infant. CHILD DEVELOPMENT, 1983, 54, 1176–1188.

36. Ramshaw, J. E., & Stanley, G. Psychological adjustment to coronary artery surgery. BRITISH JOURNAL OF CLINICAL PSYCHOLOGY, 1984, 23, 101–108.

37. Richman, L. C., & Eliason, M. Type of reading disability related to cleft type and neuropsychological patterns. CLEFT PALATE JOURNAL, 1984, 21, 1–6.

[497]

Illness Behaviour Questionnaire. Psychiatric patients; 1983; IBQ; 8 scores: 7 scales (general hypochondriasis, disease conviction, psychological vs. somatic perception of illness, affective inhibition, affective disturbance, dental, irritability) and Whiteley Index of Hypochondriasis; 1 form (3 pages); manual, second edition (61 pages); price data available from publisher; administration time not reported; I. Pilowsky; the Author.*

[498]

Ilyin Oral Interview. Junior high and secondary and adult students; 1972–76; IOI; designed to assess the ability of non-native English speakers to communicate verbally with content and structural accuracy; no validity data; tentative norms, publisher recommends use of local norms; individual; 1 booklet containing Forms Bill, Tom, (23 pages) and manual (22 pages); answer score sheet (1 page); 1984 price data: $15.95 per test book and manual; $5.50 per 50 answer score sheets; specimen set free on request; (5–30) minutes; Donna Ilyin; Newbury House Publishers, Inc.*

See T3:1128 (1 reference).

Review of Ilyin Oral Interview by THOMAS W. GUYETTE, Director of Speech Pathology, Children's Rehabilitation Unit, The University of Kansas Medical Center, Kansas City, KS:

The Ilyin Oral Interview (IOI) is designed to test the ability of second language learners to "use English orally in response to hearing it." This test is intended to be used to (1) determine placement in English as a Second Language classrooms, (2) help determine appropriate job placement, (3) document progress in the acquisition of English, and (4) provide diagnostic and remedial information. The test consists of two alternate forms with 50 items on each form. The order of items on the test is reported to be based on the difficulty of each item for second language learners. The Ilyin Oral Interview (IOI) is administered by having the student answer questions in complete sentences about sequences of pictures. The utterances are scored on the basis of semantic appropriateness, grammatical structure, and intelligibility. An utterance receives zero points if it is semantically inappropriate or unintelligible; 1 point if appropriate and intelligible but contains one or more grammatical errors; and 2 points if there are no grammatical errors, semantic errors, or intelligibility problems.

There are two areas where problems might arise with the scoring system. First, speech errors are scored only when they interfere with the intelligibility of communication in context. Judging the intelligibility of an utterance often presents problems related to agreement. The ability to understand speech with errors can vary significantly across individuals. Yorkston and Beukelman (1978, 1981) present data on dysarthric speakers which demonstrate that the interjudge estimates of intelligibility for the same sample of speech can vary between 0% and 90%. The author of the IOI has not demonstrated that scorer agreement can be obtained. Neither interjudge nor intrajudge reliability data are presented. Second, there may be scorer reliability problems when determining whether information conveyed is semantically appropriate but contains a grammatical error (score one instead of zero). As grammar plays a role in conveying information it is not always clear how to make this distinction. Again, no scorer reliability information is presented but the author does suggest the need for such reliability studies.

The IOI Manual also suggests that patterns of test scores can be used diagnostically to differentiate between production and comprehension deficits. Given the design of this test it is unclear how valid distinctions between comprehension and production can be made. Since each response requires both comprehension (the student must understand the question or command) and production (the student must formulate an answer) to be correct, errors in a response could result from either a comprehension deficit, a production deficit, or a combination of both.

Several studies are presented on the reliability and validity of this test. The test lacks reliability data in two areas. First, since two forms are presented, the equivalence of these forms needs to be demonstrated (American Psychological Association, 1974). Second, since one use of the test is to demonstrate progress in the acquisition of English, it would be important to know how much variation is related to different administrations across time (American Psychological Association, 1974). Several studies examining the internal consistency of the test items suggest adequate reliability in this area.

The results of several validity studies are also presented. These studies compare scores on the IOI with other evaluation procedures. Correlations between these procedures range from .31 to .85. However, many of these correlations have sample sizes below 20 and since no significance values are provided, these data are difficult to interpret. It is disturbing that the lowest correlation (.31) occurred between teacher ratings of conversational ability and the IOI in the largest sample (78 subjects). Overall, more validity data are needed.

In conclusion, problems related to scoring, reliability, and validity have been discussed. More research is needed to establish the claims made by the test. I would agree with the author that the results "are still tentative and should be treated with caution."

REVIEWER'S REFERENCES

American Psychological Association, American Educational Research Association, National Council on Measurement in Education. STANDARDS FOR EDUCATIONAL AND PSYCHOLOGICAL TESTS. Washington, DC: APA, 1974.

Yorkston, K. M., & Beukelman, D. R. A comparison of techniques for measuring intelligibility of dysarthric speech. JOURNAL OF COMMUNICATION DISORDERS, 1978, 11, 499–512.

Yorkston, K. M., & Beukelman, D. R. Assessment of intelligibility of dysarthric speech. C. C. Publications, Inc., Tigard, OR, 1981.

[499]

Imagery of Cancer. Cancer patients; 1978; IMAGE-CA; a combination of guided imagery, relaxation, patient drawings, and structured interview to evaluate the process of disease; 15 scores: vividness of the cancer cell, activity of the cancer cell, strength of the cancer cell, vividness of the white blood cell, activity of the white blood cell, relative comparison of numbers of cancer cells to white blood cells, relative comparison of the size of cancer cells to white blood cells, strength of the white blood cell, vividness of the medical treatment, effectiveness of the medical treatment, concreteness vs. symbolism, overall strength of imagery, estimated regularity, clinical opinion, total; individual; 1 form; record and scoring sheet (5 pages); handbook (197 pages); 1982 price data: $25.70 per complete kit including tape cassette and 25 record and scoring sheets; $8.45 per 25 record and scoring sheets; $7.50 per tape cassette; $9.75 per handbook; administration time not reported; Jeanne Achterberg and G. Frank Lawlis; Institute for Personality and Ability Testing, Inc.*

[500]

Impact Message Inventory: Form II. College students and adults 1976–79; self-report inventory; assesses "momentary emotional and other engagements of one person by another during ongoing transactions in counseling/psychotherapy and other dyads"; 15 subscales: Dominant, Competitive, Hostile, Mistrusting, Detached, Inhibited, Submissive, Succorant, Abasive, Deferent, Agreeable, Nurturant, Affiliative, Sociable, Exhibitionistic; reliability and validity data based on earlier form and not included in test materials; no norms; 1 form ('76, 4 pages); preliminary manual ('79, 16 pages); price data available from publisher; administration time not reported; Donald J. Kiesler, J. C. Anchin, M. J. Perkins, B. M. Chirico, E. M. Kyle, and E. J. Federman; Consulting Psychologists Press, Inc.*

See T3:1130 (1 reference).

TEST REFERENCES

1. Perkins, M. J., Kiesler, D. J., Anchin, J. C., Chirico, B. M., Kyle, E. M., & Federman, E. J. The Impact Message Inventory: A new measure of relationship in counseling/psychotherapy and other dyads. JOURNAL OF COUNSELING PSYCHOLOGY, 1979, 26, 363–367.

Review of Impact Message Inventory: Form II by FRED H. BORGEN, Professor of Psychology, Iowa State University, Ames, IA:

The Impact Message Inventory (IMI) is not the usual kind of "test." It does not purport to measure characteristics of the respondent, but rather how the respondent views another person in a dyadic relationship. As such, it is a rating scale to assess an interpersonal environment or impact. As a rating of a stimulus situation, it has something in common with environmental assessment scales, teacher rating scales, or counselor rating scales.

The IMI is introduced as containing "words, phrases and statements which people use to describe how they are emotionally engaged or impacted when interacting with another person." The IMI contains 90 items, with 30 each grouped under three different kinds of stems designed to elicit (1) direct feelings, (2) action tendencies, or (3) cognitive attributions. An example of the first kind of item is: "When I am with this person he makes me feel...appreciated by him." The respondent then fills in a box with a number from 1 to 4, reflecting agreement from "not at all" (1) to "very much so" (4). The inventory is designed to measure the 15 interpersonal styles of Leary (1957) and Lorr and McNair's Interpersonal Behavior Inventory (IBI). These dimensions are intended to represent a circular or circumplex order. Each of the 15 subscales is measured by six items, two from each section of the inventory.

The Perkins et al. (1979) paper was the only published paper about the IMI available to me for this review. While this paper presents a very condensed description of the development of the inventory, I also had access to an expanded, unpublished version of the Perkins et al. (1979) paper. The first edition of the preliminary manual is skimpy, detailing only the purposes of the inventory, the scoring, and a normative conversion table for raw scores. The manual contains no evaluative psychometric data, while the inventory development and initial evaluative data are presented in Perkins et al. (1979), especially the expanded unpublished version.

The inventory was carefully developed to measure the 15 dimensions of Lorr and McNair's IBI. Perkins et al. (1979) wrote items for each of the dimensions to yield an initial set of 259 items in Form I of the IMI. Then ratings from 451 undergraduates were used to derive the final items for the 90-item Form II of the IMI. A paragraph was written to characterize a prototypic ideal type for each of the 15 dimensions. The undergraduates were divided into 15 groups, and each group read one description and then responded to the IMI-Form I in terms of the impact of that hypothetical person. Each subgroup was divided into odd and even subgroups for validation and cross-validation of item statistics that were used to select the final items. The available information suggests that this was a reasonable and creative approach to providing an empirical basis for scale construction.

Scale length is a source of concern. Each scale contains only 6 items, and they are distributed across the three conceptually mixed perspectives. Perkins et al. (1979; p. 365) characterize the internal consistency reliabilities of the 15 subscales as "very high," but their statistical approach is an unconventional one certain to give inflated values. They call their approach Cattell's Q technique, but appear to be doing something quite different, especially when one studies the expanded version of their paper. Q technique involves correlating people over variables or items. What they have done is to group (average) their data for each of the 15 subgroups of undergraduates, and then proceeded with conventional *r*-technique analyses of items and scales. This is a defensible approach of using group-aggregated data, but it is misnamed as Q technique. All the evaluative data they present for Form II are of this kind, including item-scale correlations (their internal reliability coefficients) and factor analysis of the 15 scales. Such relationships will be higher (probably substantially so) for grouped data than for data for individuals. Consequently, their report implies the inventory has high reliability when used with individuals, when in fact relevant data have not been presented. The data they present speak to the likely high reliability when used with means for groups of respondents.

An additional design feature leads Perkins et al. (1979) to produce data that probably inflate the psychometric quality of the instrument. Specifically, their reliability and factor analytic studies of the final Form II are based on the same subjects that were used in the item analysis. While the group was split into validation and cross-validation groups for item analysis, it was recombined for the final evaluative analyses, thereby probably capitalizing on error variance to some degree.

In the expanded version of the Perkins et al. (1979) paper, they show the intercorrelations of the 15 subscales. Some are so high as to suggest that 15 distinct dimensions have not been successfully derived from the 90-item pool. For example, Dominant correlates .94 with Competitive, and Agreeable correlates .95 with Nurturant.

Kiesler is a leading figure in the study of counseling and psychotherapy. He is responsible for important conceptual insights and the IMI deserves to be seen in that light. The IMI derives from an innovative theoretical perspective, which is best articulated in the Anchin and Kiesler (1981) volume. In Kiesler's chapter therein he gives the best description of his concept of an Impact Message (p. 274 ff.). This is a conceptual notion imbedded in the interpersonal communications view of human relationships. It is complex and subtle, and not easily modeled by traditional psychometrics. While the psychometric data reviewed are not impressive to this reviewer, the conceptual base and research implications are seen as important. Research applications of the IMI are promising and should be encouraged. Other measurement approaches in the important research area of interpersonal communication can be examined in the Anchin and Kiesler (1981) volume.

Additional data are needed to justify the use of the inventory for individual assessment. Evidence at the individual (not group) level is needed for reliability, structure and dimensionality, and validity.

REVIEWER'S REFERENCES

Leary, T. F. INTERPERSONAL DIAGNOSIS OF PERSONALITY. New York: Ronald Press, 1957.

Perkins, M. J., Kiesler, D. J., Anchin, J. C., Chirico, B. M., Kyle, E. M., & Federman, E. J. The Impact Message Inventory: A new measure of relationship in counseling/psychotherapy and other dyads. JOURNAL OF COUNSELING PSYCHOLOGY, 1979, 26, 363–367.

Anchin, J. C., & Kiesler, D. J. HANDBOOK OF INTERPERSONAL PSYCHOTHERAPY. New York: Pergamon, 1981.

Review of Impact Message Inventory: Form II by STANLEY R. STRONG, Professor of Psychology, Virginia Commonwealth University, Richmond, VA:

This review is based on the new research manual for the Impact Message Inventory (IMI). The manual describes in detail the theoretical bases of the inventory, its development, and the results of 30 studies that explore the inventory's reliability, validity, and research applications. While originally constructed to characterize patient-therapist relationships in psychotherapy, Kiesler suggests that the inventory would be useful to characterize the interpersonal behavior of late adolescents and adults in two person interactions such as between husbands and wives, friends, acquaintances and strangers. Also, he suggests that the inventory has applications in psychotherapy studies of process and outcome and in supervision of therapy trainees.

The IMI generates a description of a target person's interpersonal behavior on the basis of the subjective reactions or impacts the person's behavior evokes in another with whom the person interacts. The inventory is intended to tap variance associated with the behavior of the target person, the reaction or perceptual style of the respondent other who completes the inventory, and the nature of the behavioral interchange between them. The IMI is based on interpersonal theory, which asserts that styles of interpersonal behavior and personality are ordered circularly around the dimensions of interpersonal control and affiliation. Behavioral styles are hypothesized to have lawful interrelationships such that in two person interactions the behavioral styles of the interactants evoke predictable and consistent responses from each other. Each party's behavior is hypothesized to evoke subjective effects or impacts in his or her interactant which partially determine the interactant's subsequent behaviors. The person filling out the IMI does not describe the other's behavior but rather describes the impact of the other's behavior on his or her subjective experience while relating to the other.

The IMI is based on Lorr and McNair's (1965) Interpersonal Behavior Inventory, an inventory on which persons rate their own or another's interpersonal behavior. The items of the Lorr and McNair inventory were combined into 15 paragraphs, one for each of the inventory's 15 scales, and statements describing the subjective impacts or reactions to the descriptions were generated. Final items for the 15 scales of the IMI were empirically derived from college students' endorsements of the items based on their reactions to the paragraphs. The resulting scales empirically form a roughly circular pattern around the control and affiliation axes theoretically defining interpersonal space.

As a theoretically derived inventory, the internal consistency of the scales is perhaps the most important indicant of reliability. In studies based on college student responses to the paragraph descriptions of the 15 styles and on therapist responses to outpatients in intake interviews, internal consistency reliabilities have been found to be satisfactorily high for the 15 scales and for combined scales representing the four poles of interpersonal behavior: dominance, submissiveness, friendliness, and hostility. Studies have found interreactor agreement among respondents to the same target person to range from 0% to 86%. To some extent, low interreactor agreement represents true variance associated with perceptual differences among respondents. But it may also represent error variance. While persons may experience subjective impacts while interacting with others, it is unlikely that they are systematically aware of them. Rather, it is likely that people focus their attention on construing the characteristics of the interactant, a task to which subjective impacts contribute, but do so out of awareness. Kiesler suggests that respondents can be sensitized to their subjective impacts evoked by the behavior of others. Such sensitization can reasonably be expected to increase true variance in IMI scores. Studies of interpersonal behavior using the IMI have found the inventory to be sensitive to many variations in target persons' behaviors, including assertive and nonassertive behaviors, behaviors associated with various behavioral disorders, personality differences, and methods of delivering information about treatment in medical settings. Meaningful differences have been found to be associated with variations in the characteristics of respondent groups. Further, differences on IMI scales have been found to be related to important outcome variables, such as response to dental surgery.

The psychometric characteristics of the IMI correspond reasonably well to the expectations of interpersonal theory, and the results of studies using the inventory have been significant and provocative, making the IMI a promising instrument for use in research on interpersonal behavior in a wide variety of settings. Studies are needed to determine if the IMI contributes information different from other measures of interpersonal behavior, such as the Interpersonal Check List (Laforge & Suczek, 1955), the Interpersonal Behavior Inventory (Lorr & McNair, 1965), and the Interpersonal Adjective Scales (Wiggins, 1979).

Not enough is known about the IMI to recommend it for use in clinical work. Such applications not only require further validity studies, but also normative data on which to base judgments about the meaning of an individual's scores on IMI scales relative to other individuals. Development of such norms is problematic since they must not only account for the characteristics of the target persons whose impacts on others are being evaluated, but also the characteristics of the responders who record their subjective reactions to the target person's behavior. Even so, for those willing to develop personal norms of their own reactivity to the interpersonal behavior of others, use of the IMI could provide useful information in the task of developing clinical understanding of clients and others. The IMI is a promising instrument for use in research on interpersonal behavior and has considerable potential for eventual applications to interpersonal diagnosis and psychotherapy.

REVIEWER'S REFERENCES

LaForge, R., & Suczek, R. F. The interpersonal dimensions of personality: III. An interpersonal check list. JOURNAL OF PERSONALITY, 1955, 24, 94–112.

Lorr, M., & McNair, D. M. Expansion of the interpersonal behavior circle. JOURNAL OF PERSONALITY AND SOCIAL PSYCHOLOGY, 1965, 2, 823–830.

Wiggins, J. S. A psychological taxonomy of trait-descriptive terms: The interpersonal domain. JOURNAL OF PERSONALITY AND SOCIAL PSYCHOLOGY, 1979, 37, 395–412.

[501]

Incentives Management Index. Sales managers, 1972–79; IMI; practices and attitudes regarding motivational needs of subordinates; companion to the Sales Motivation Survey; based on Maslow's need hierarchy; 5 scores: basic, safety, belongingness, ego-status, self-actualization; no data on reliability or validity; 1 form ('79, 17 pages); user's guide (no date, 8 pages); 1984 price data: $4 per test; administration time not reported; Jay Hall and Norman Seim; Teleometrics Int'l.*

[502]

Incomplete Sentences Task. Grades 7–12, college-age adolescents; 1979–80; IST; self-administered projective and psychometric test; "designed to detect potential emotional problems that might, for example, interfere with classroom learning"; 3 scores: hostility, anxiety, dependency; 2 levels labeled School Form (2 pages) for grades 7–12, College Form (2 pages) for college-age adolescents; manual ('80, 37 pages); 1984 price data: $16 per complete set including 30 tests; $10.50 per 30 tests; (15–20) minutes; Barbara Lanyon; Stoelting Co.*

Review of Incomplete Sentences Task by BERT P. CUNDICK, *Professor of Psychology, Brigham Young University, Provo, UT:*

The Incomplete Sentences Task (IST) consists of 39 incomplete sentence stems which can be scored for Hostility (18 items), Anxiety (10 items), and Dependency (11 items). These characteristics were selected because of "their importance in a number of theories of personality and because they are seen to be central in the adjustment of children of junior high school age." Two forms of the test are provided: a form for grades 7 through 12 and a second form in which minor changes in wording on 11 items have been made for use with a college population. Each item is identified as to the scored characteristic. Items receive a 0, 1, or 2 score. Scoring examples for each item are provided in a manual appendix.

Three tables are provided for converting raw scores to percentile scores. Separate sections in each table give the data for boys and girls. The first table is based on responses from 557 junior high school students from the Pittsburgh area. The third table is based on responses from 300 college students taking an introductory psychology class at Arizona State University. The second table is for senior high school students; however, no norm data was collected for this group. It is merely an average of the norms for grades 7 through 9 and the college students. The norms appear to be strictly convenience samples and appear adequate for initial test development but should be improved if the test is to have widespread usage. The test is an outgrowth of the senior author's research while obtaining her degrees. The use of the IST with senior high school and college-age students appears to be an afterthought in an effort to expand a promising effort with children to other populations.

Estimates of reliability were obtained on three 25-item preliminary criterion measures obtained from 3 judges on 32 students. Intraclass correlation coefficients are reported to range from .29 for the hostility score to .54 for the anxiety score. Internal consistency is dealt with by presenting factor loadings on 75 initial criterion items. The authors do not report traditional internal consistency reliability (e.g., coefficient alpha) for the final scores, nor do they report any test-retest data that might give users data on whether the scores are really measuring a persisting trait. The limited number of items measuring anxiety (10) and their low item-total correlations certainly call into question whether anxiety is adequately measured.

Attempts to validate the test consisted primarily of obtaining judges' ratings and taking those rated as "high" and those rated as "low" on a particular characteristic and comparing their responses. This was done first on each item in the construction stage of the test and was done again in a cross-validation study for the three total scores. The cross-validation attempt was commendable and showed significant differences for each of the three characteristics between the 2 extreme groups. However, it does appear that anxiety is intermeshed with dependency. It was not possible for this reviewer to know the exact nature of the judges' ratings. The instructions given to the judges and the instrument used to obtain them were not described. The reliability of these ratings were not reported but two or three independent judges were used for each group assignment.

The relationship between the three characteristics and IQ and GPA are also reported for a cross-validation group. The reported correlations are, respectively, –.22 and –.29 ($p < .05$) for hostility, –.28 and –.29 ($p < .01$) for dependency, but only –.11 and –.08 for anxiety (nonsignificant). Even the statistically significant correlations here are probably not psychologically significant. Another study ($N = 47$) with the college form shows significant correlations between judges' ratings and scores (.63 to .69), whereas self ratings were not significantly related to test scores. Again one is left to speculate on the nature of the judges' ratings.

The construction of the IST was a thorough undertaking that is well described in the manual. More representative norms would be a significant improvement, as would data on the reliability and standard error of specific scores. If one wishes to obtain responses directly from respondents using a sentence completion format, this appears to be a useful instrument. The validation studies cited utilized teacher ratings as a measure of concurrent validity. One could go directly to teacher rating instruments such as the School and Behavior Checklist or the Walker Problem Checklist and obtain direct ratings from teachers and regard the child's sentence completion responses as a potential source of error. The usefulness of the IST over such rating devices must be shown in future research to apply to a range of practice beyond the school. It does not relate well to school achievement, but the rated characteristics do appear to be homogenous and might be found useful in situations where measures of hostility and dependency and perhaps anxiety are desirable.

Review of Incomplete Sentences Task by DAVID M. DUSH, Program Evaluator, Midland-Gladwin Community Mental Health Services, Midland, MI:

The Incomplete Sentences Task (IST) is a personality assessment and screening test for junior and senior high school students and, with minor revisions in a second form of the test, for college students. It consists of 39 sentence stems scored for Hostility (18 items), Anxiety (10 items), or Dependency (11 items). These dimensions were chosen as indicators of "potential emotional problems that might, for example, interfere with classroom learning." Each response is scored as 0 (does not indicate), 1 (suggests), or 2 (definitely indicates) its respective personality characteristic. The manual provides 3 to 13 sample answers for each level of scoring for each stem to assist in reliable scoring. Summed scores for Hostility, Anxiety, and Dependency can be referenced to normative data in the manual for conversion to percentiles.

The construction of the IST has several features that set it apart from most preceding incomplete sentence tests. First, it focuses on a small number of specific, behaviorally anchored variables. Secondly, it utilizes stems that are highly structured, which probably aids reliability but may also increase the transparency of the test and limit the extent to which it remains "projective." Lastly, normative data are provided, grouped by age and sex.

The IST's nature rests heavily upon its rational-empirical method of construction. The authors first developed a criterion test of 138 brief behavioral rating phrases assumed to be manifestations of classroom hostility, anxiety, and dependency. This was reduced to 25 phrases in each category according to the "judgments made by" 5 child clinical psychologists and 3 school teachers. The details of development and refinement are somewhat vague. An initial study of 205 ratings of 90 junior high school students by 59 teachers produced low to modest intraclass correlation coefficients (.29 to .54). Factor analysis was used to reduce the criterion test to its final 50-item form. Notably, the second factor of the solution loaded on both "anxiety" and "dependency" ratings, and was discarded from consideration. These criterion analyses suggest a relatively weak and perhaps blurred criterion test, which may limit the validity and efficiency of the IST, especially since the IST stems purposely resemble the criterion ratings very closely.

Fifty initial sentence stems were completed by 228 junior high students who had also been rated by teachers on the criterion test. Stems discriminating ($p < .05$) high or "extreme high" from low criterion scores were retained for the final IST. Cross validation with 100 students revealed that hostility, anxiety, and dependency scores significantly discriminated extreme groups on the criterion test. However, discriminative validity remains unclear, since dependency scores discriminated the anxiety criterion groups better than the dependency criterion groups. Hostility and dependency had low correlations with IQ and GPA (–.22 to –.29).

The manual does not report sufficient data to establish the IST's validity. No data is provided to demonstrate the percent correct classification one can expect using the IST as a screening test. The IST was apparently not factored analyzed, and there is cause to question whether the items would pattern themselves as proposed. The IST scales were found to correlate discriminatively (.63 to .69) with 5-point ratings of hostility, anxiety, and dependence by relatives or friends for 47 college volunteers. However, no data is provided to compare the IST with any other personality variables, any clinical criterion (such as discriminating normals from diagnostic groups), or any other external criterion other than the criterion ratings that the authors developed themselves.

The reliability and normative data are also problematic. Correlations of IST items to their summed scale score are provided, but these refer to summed scores from an earlier, longer version. Interrater reliability figures of .86 to 1.00 for individual items are reported, but these are for two unspecified sets of 12 of the 39 items. The critical data concerning interrater reliability for summed scale scores, test-retest reliability, and internal consistency are not given, and too little is said of the requirements for rater training or the resiliency of the test to rating or test-taking biases. Normative data for grades 10 through 12 are produced by averaging the data from junior high and college students, which imposes additional assumptions upon the IST's applicability with high school students. The normative tables are also restricted by lack of thorough stratification of samples on variables such as SES, geographical region, and type of school.

The manual conveys the impression that the IST is ready for real-life clinical application, given routine precautions. This seems premature on the many counts cited above. Among tests of its type, however, the IST shows careful development in many respects, and sound conceptualization. It can be easily and flexibly administered, and promises to tap domains that are verifiable and relevant to the concerns and decisions of school personnel. It is presently viewed as a promising test for research applications and clearly warranting further psychometric study and development.

[503]

Independent Living Behavior Checklist. Behaviorally impaired adults; 1979; ILBC; criterion-referenced; 6 areas: mobility skills, self-care skills, home maintenance and safety skills, food skills, social and communication skills, functional academic skills; no validity data; no norms; individual; manual (196 pages plus test); other test materials must be supplied by examiner; 1985 price data: $8 per manual including 1 pad of 10 skills summary charts; $2 per 10 skills summary charts; administration time varies according to objective; Richard T. Walls, Thomas Zane, and John E. Thvedt; West Virginia Rehabilitation Research and Training Center.*

Review of Independent Living Behavior Checklist by JEAN DIRKS, Psychologist, Southgate Regional Center for Developmental Disabilities, Southgate, MI:

The Independent Living Behavior Checklist is designed to assess the living skills of developmentally disabled clients and to guide school personnel and staff personnel in setting training goals for the developmentally disabled. The Checklist appears applicable primarily for very high functioning clients (e.g. Mildly Retarded) who will eventually be able to assume their own care in regard to food preparation, clothing care, and apartment maintenance.

One strength of the Checklist is that the Checklist items are clearly worded and have objective scoring criteria. In addition, such areas as cooking and social skills are broken down into smaller, highly specific component skills which could easily be used as goals of training programs.

Unfortunately, however, there are several major drawbacks to the Checklist which limit its usefulness as an assessment instrument. Some of these drawbacks are its extreme length (343 items) and the paucity of normative data or statistical data. For example, there is no standardization sample, and reliability data is based on only five clients and a small subset of the Checklist items. In some cases, the excessive length of the Checklist is contributed to by overlapping items. For example, there are five separate items on opening a savings account, making a savings account deposit, making a savings account withdrawal, opening a checking account, and making a checking account deposit; yet all of these seem to involve the same skill.

Another drawback is the proposed alternating assessment and training strategy for usage. The example in the manual involving a hypothetical client indicates that a client should be assessed on the first several items in each of the six Checklist areas, and remedial training of the tester's choice should then be instituted on most of the items which the client cannot perform. Only when this training has been successful does the tester then proceed with assessment on the next several items. Alternating assessment and training follows in this fashion.

This alternation means that the assessment will not be completed for many months—i.e. until much of the training has been successful. Another problem with the alternation is that training itself may be instituted inappropriately, since the items within a Checklist area are not arranged in order of increasing difficulty. For example, "easy" items involving hand washing, hair combing, and urinating in the toilet come on the Checklist after "harder" items involving purchasing of clothes, using an electric iron, and selecting matching clothes. If the tester followed the procedure in the manual of instituting training on earlier items before beginning training on later items, then clients would in some cases receive training on more difficult skills before they had been trained on easier skills.

In general, the Checklist is aimed at higher functioning clients. However, although lower functioning clients (e.g. Profoundly, Severely Retarded) will not be able to live in "independent" living situations, they may nevertheless be able to cope with semi-independent living situations or non-institutional settings such as group homes, foster families, etc. In order to broaden the applicability of the Checklist, it would have been helpful if more items suitable for lower functioning clients could have been included, and if simple skills (such as the Checklist item for "client takes off and puts on clothes") could have been broken down into still simpler components (e.g. "client puts on clothes with physical prompts when clothes are oriented by staff," "client puts on clothes with verbal prompts when clothes are oriented by staff," and "client orients own clothes and puts them on independently").

In summary, because of the various drawbacks, and particularly because of the lack of normative data or data from standardized pilot testing, the Checklist is not recommended for use as an assessment instrument. It could be helpful in setting training goals for higher functioning clients, but it is less useful for routine assessment purposes.

Review of Independent Living Behavior Checklist by LOUIS J. FINKLE, Severely/Profoundly Handicapped Program, School of Education, James Madison University, Harrisonburg, VA:

The Independent Living Behavior Checklist (ILBC) is a 218-page book consisting of 343 criterion-referenced objectives written in a behavioral format of condition (actually pre-condition), behavior, and standard (actually criterion). This strict format allows the user to make "yes-no" clinical judgements with a minimum of ambiguity for objectives in all six skill areas that define its content (see above).

A request for behavioral checklists was sent to 883 state schools and rehabilitation facilities resulting in the receipt of more than 200 checklists. The ILBC is a result of this survey plus the creation of new skill objectives derived from the authors' work with many vocational rehabilitation clients.

A quick survey of client progress in the six skill areas is possible using the skill objectives profile. The profile is constructed by dividing the number of skill objectives mastered in an area by the total number of applicable objectives, then multiplying by 100 to yield a percentage.

The ILBC can be used as a progress management system as long as the client is in need of monitoring. It defines the extent and degree to which a client can function independently. Areas of deficit can then be identified to develop ongoing training programs. Since the ILBC is not considered a standardized test, the traditional "teaching to the test" controversy is not applicable.

"The ILBC simply defines the degree to which a client or trainee, using whatever adaptive devices required, can function without the constant aid and supervision of other persons." The strengths of this instrument stem from its focus on specific independent living skills and providing an unambiguous measure of the client's level of functioning.

Reliability concerns applicable to similar forms of behavioral checklists center on stability and inter-observer agreement. The stability factor was tested by videotaping five clients attempting to perform five skills from each of the skill areas. The 25 scores were recorded at initial entry time. Two weeks later the same videotape was scored by the same observers. Using this procedure, the authors calculated the overall mean stability of the ILBC as 98%. The inter-observer factor was tested by computing inter-rater reliability during both initial and subsequent videotaping of skill demonstrations. Reliability agreements ranged from 96% to 100% in all skill areas.

Content validity was addressed by sampling the universe of independent living skills. From a field of checklists ($N = 200$ plus), 53 closely related instruments were selected to cross-reference the contents of the ILBC. Inferences were made to suggest that the ILBC samples and measures the objectives deemed appropriate to independent living of handicapped persons.

The major strengths of the ILBC are the conciseness of its contents, inclusion of behaviorally stated objectives (complete with pre-conditions, behaviors, and criteria), and ease of summary chart record-keeping. Conciseness is a known blessing to anyone who has suffered the burdens of administering complicated assessments. The use of behavioral objectives and adequate record-keeping are now required by policies and laws dealing with handicapped populations. Recording and verifying exact behaviors at initial assessment, beginning phases of implementation, and upon reaching mastery level is done simply and neatly with the ILBC.

The major weaknesses are in its own conciseness and sequences. Although most checklists are sequential (easy-to-complex, order of skills, developmental, mastery sequence, etc.), the skills are representative and clustered. For example, the assessment of mobility skills in the ILBC does not include directions (toward, left, right, north, south), body orientation (vertical, bending, twisting), hazard avoidance (thresholds, dangerous areas) or recovery (slipping, falling, rolling, balancing); yet it does include skills entitled Cabinet-Counter I, II and III!

In summary, the ILBC is an extremely well done assessment in a field replete with checklists and assessments. Having been involved with several competing instruments, I must admit that this is one of the cleanest, well-prepared, and concise instruments dealing with daily living skills necessary for independent living. The ideal use of the ILBC would not be as a guide for future training (as implied in its format), but as an assessment to determine the progress of clients in programs which continue to use the 200-plus other checklists for training!

[504]

Industrial Reading Test. Grade 9 and over vocational students and applicants or trainees in technical or vocational training programs; 1976–78; IRT; ability to comprehend written technical materials; Forms A, B, ('76–77, 10 pages); manual ('78, 30 pages); distribution of Form A restricted to business firms; separate answer sheets (IBM 805/OpScan) must be used with reuseable booklets for Form A or B; 1982 price data: $10 per 25 test booklets; $5.75 per 50 IBM 805/OpScan answer sheets; $1.75 per hand scoring key; $2.85 per manual; $4.50 per specimen set; 40(45) minutes; Psychological Measurement Division; The Psychological Corporation.

Review of Industrial Reading Test by DARRELL L. SABERS, Professor of Educational Psychology, The University of Arizona, Tucson, AZ:

The Industrial Reading Test (IRT) was developed for the purpose of measuring reading ability in industry and in vocational schools. It is intended to be a power test of reading comprehension, and the time limit of 40 minutes is intended to be adequate for most examinees to complete the test.

The weakness of the IRT evolves from the statement from the manual which says, "The IRT is designed so that students or applicants will find the material relevant and meaningful." To make the material relevant and meaningful to the student, the authors used reading passages that contain information which is general knowledge to many (if not most) adults. As a result, the items do not require that the examinee obtain information from reading the passage. This may not contradict the statement in the manual that good performance on the test is not dependent upon previous knowledge of the subject matter; however, neither is good performance on the test dependent upon comprehension of the passages.

This reviewer reprinted the 38 items without the passages and administered them to ten workers between the ages of 17 and 52 from various occupations. The scores from these workers (who had no access to the paragraphs) ranged from 18 to 29, comparable to average scores for the groups which are reported in the manual. Six items were answered correctly by all ten of the workers who had not read the passages, and another nine items were missed only once or twice. On the other hand, there were only four items that were answered incorrectly by as many as eight out of the ten workers. The IRT suffers from a dearth of passage dependent items (that is, items the examinees will get wrong if they do not comprehend the passage).

The manual for the IRT is complete and honest. Statistical data are plentiful and sufficiently impressive. Good information regarding the development of the test, adequate reliability data, and many tables of information on criterion-related validity are included. Test scores are correlated with grades in a variety of vocational programs and with many other tests. Even data not supportive of the validity of the IRT are presented. For example, correlations between the IRT and three achievement tests (Ohio trade tests) in electronics, machine trades, and welding support an argument that IRT measures achievement (prior knowledge) rather than reading comprehension.

The instructions to examinees—including the appropriate directions to answer all items—are clear. An examiner will find the test easy to administer and score, and the manual presents adequate information on interpreting the results. However, all the norm data and the other information presented in the manual are of no use if the test does not measure reading comprehension.

One who believes that a test of reading comprehension need only assess whether a student can read a multiple choice item in order to select the keyed response may find the IRT acceptable. However, given this reviewer's opinion that a test of reading comprehension should assess whether an examinee can read the passages over which the items are written, the IRT cannot be recommended. The potential user of a reading comprehension test should look elsewhere for a measure. Even though it will be difficult to find a test with as much material relevant to industrial applicants, an effort should be made to find a test that measures reading comprehension.

[505]

Infant Rating Scale. Ages 5, 7; 1981; IRS; ratings by teachers for screening and early intervention; 2 levels; manual (25 pages); profile/record form (4 pages) for both levels; 1982 price data: $2.25 per 20 tests; $2 per 20 profile/record forms; $1.50 per manual; $2 per specimen set; administration time not reported; Geoff A. Lindsay; Hodder & Stoughton Educational [England].*

a) LEVEL 1. Age 5; 6 scores: language, early learning, behaviour, social integration, general development, total; 1 form (4 pages).

b) LEVEL 2. Age 7; 6 scores: language/education, fine motor skills, behaviour, social integration, general development, total; 1 form (4 pages).

Review of Infant Rating Scale by CARL J. DUNST, Director, Family, Infant and Preschool Program, Western Carolina Center, Morganton, NC:

The Infant Rating Scale (IRS), a British developed screening instrument, consists of two teacher completed checklists designed to identify children with early learning difficulties. Level 1 is used with 5-year-olds, and Level 2 with 7-year-olds. Each level includes 25 items which are rated on a five-point scale from above average performance (no problem) to below average performance (problem). For example, the Articulation item is rated on the following point scale: (1) very rarely makes articulatory errors; (2) good articulation, occasional errors; (3) satisfactory; (4) many words mispronounced; (5) very poor articulation, difficult to understand or does not talk. Two things are immediately apparent upon close inspection of the individual IRS items. First, the items are very practical and are precisely the types of behavior teachers use to make judgements regarding learning assets and deficits. In terms of face validity, the IRS must surely be judged favorably. Second, the items appear to be very easy to score. Short-term test-retest reliability seems to reflect this. In a study of 49 children rated two weeks apart by their teachers, stability coefficients for the 25 items ranged from .65 to .93 (median=.85). The long-term stability of the IRS was examined in a study of children (N=916) administered the Level 1 and Level 2 scales approximately 2 years apart. The stability coefficients for the scale items ranged from .23 to .54 (median=.44). Thus, as is generally true, reliability decreased with increased intervals between measurement occasions.

The 25 IRS items are divided into five subscales: Language (expressive and receptive), Early Learning/Fine Motor (including drawing, writing, fine-motor coordination, and attitude toward learning), Behavior (including temperament, attitude to teacher, kindness to peers, approach to learning, and attention/distractability), Social Integration (participation in class activities, acceptance by peers, and desire to interact with peers), and General Development (gross motor skills, response to new situations, and overall teacher concern). The division of the items into these a priori subscales is generally supported by factor analysis. Four factors were obtained in a study of the construct validity of the IRS: Language (e.g., articulation, vocabulary, sentence construction, comprehension, and expression), Child Behavior (e.g., temperament, attitude to teacher, kindness to peers, and approach to learning), Fine-Motor/Basic Skills (e.g., drawing, writing, reading, and numbers), and Social Behavior (child's relationships with his/her peers). The General Development subscale items tended to load moderately on the four principal factors.

The IRS yields three separate scores: individual item scores (25), subscale scores (5), and total score (1). The extent to which a child is showing specific and/or global learning related problems is made by determining what percentage of the standardization sample (N=1,342) fall below, at, or above the score(s) attained by the child. Determination of learning problems is based on the assumption that 2% of the standardization sample would be expected to have severe learning problems and be considered "high risk," and 13% would have some learning related problems and be considered "moderate risk." These percentages are based on the findings of two large-scale British studies which found that in the general population, one in six children (15%) had special educational needs, of which 2% had severe learning problems. Comparisons of a child's strengths and weaknesses can also be made by constructing a profile of abilities for the different subscales or individual items. The manual includes numerous examples along with four case studies to illustrate the procedures used in scoring and interpreting IRS findings for both inter- and intra-child comparisons.

The procedure for determining at-risk status on the IRS may be open to criticism for several reasons. First, the assumptions regarding the 2% and 13% cutoffs for determining, respectively, "high risk" and "moderate risk" status are not supported by the data from the IRS standardization sample. The percentage of children receiving "high risk" scores on the individual IRS items for Level 1 varied from 0 to 3.5, and the percentage receiving "moderate risk" scores varied from 3.3 to 21.8. Consequently, scale item scores have different meaning depending upon which items have been rated as learning problems. The author warns against use of item scores for differential diagnosis in the test manual; yet, the illustrative examples use the scale scores for this purpose. Second, because subscale scores are derived from item scores, the percentages of children having ratings between 0–2% and 3–13% could potentially also have different meanings with respect to severity of learning problems. Further analysis of the IRS data would seem warranted to determine the extent to which subscale scores and derived percentile ranks have similar or different meanings. Inasmuch as the standard errors of measurements for subscales range from .06 to .25, it would appear that similar percentile ranks in fact have different meanings.

Since the IRS is intended to be a screening device for assessing the presence of potential learning problems, the criterion validity of the scale is of crucial importance. The predictive validity of the IRS has been examined in several studies. In one investigation, the IRS (Level 1) subscale scores were correlated with the results of the Group Reading Test with measurements taken two years apart. The correlations obtained were .26, .24, .51, and .56, respectively, for the Behavior, Social Integration, Language, and Early Learning subscales. Total scores correlated .51 with reading scores. Both the Level 1 and Level 2 IRS scales were also correlated with the Primary Reading Test (PRT) scores, with measurements taken four and two years apart, respectively. PRT scores correlated significantly with IRS Level 1 Total scores (r =.48), Language scores (r =.51), and Early Learning scores (r =.58). Similar findings were reported for comparisons made with other measures of academic achievement. Taken together, the above results indicate that Total scores and both Language and Early Learning subscale scores are the best (but moderate) predictors of reading related learning abilities.

A second study examined the relationships between the IRS and several different measures of academic achievement for two "at-risk" groups of children (N=40 and 28) and a group of "not-at-risk" children (N=37); at-risk status was determined from IRS Total scores. Comparisons between the groups at 5 years of age revealed that the at-risk and not-at-risk groups differed significantly on the English Picture Vocabulary Test, the WPPSI vocabulary scale and geometric design subtest, the Frostig Position in Space subtest, and the Standard Reading Test visual and auditory discrimination subtests. The same differences were found between groups at 7 years of age on selected WISC-R subtests, the Schonell Spelling Test, and the Neale Analysis of Reading Ability test. Correlations between the IRS item scores at 5 years and the attainments on the criterion measures made at 7 years were, on the average, between .50 and .60. These correlations are probably somewhat inflated since the subtests comprising the sample were chosen in the first place because of the extremity of their scores on the IRS. A step-wise multiple regression analysis with Neale Reading age scores at 7 years of age as the criterion measures, and the IRS and the above described tests taken at 5 years of age as the predictive measures, revealed that IRS scores accounted for 54% of the variance whereas the other predictive measures accounted for only 5% of the variance. Again, the substantial *r* of .73 between IRS scores and reading age scores is probably spuriously high for the reason given above; nonetheless, the robustness of the IRS as a predictor of reading abilities is quite impressive.

The ability to predict which individuals would subsequently fail or pass reading using "risk" status on the IRS as the predictor dictor variable was examined in a third study of 480 children. Both reading failure and "at-risk" was defined, respectively, as scores below one *SD* from the mean on the Group Reading Test and IRS. For 80–90% of the cases, IRS Language and Early Learning subscale scores and Total scores predicted true negatives (children passing reading who had been "not-at-risk"). However, in only 32–48% of the cases did "at-risk" status predict reading failure. This is less than what would be expected by chance! Thus, although the IRS is a good predictor of intra-group rank orderings on criterion academic achievement measures (predictive validity), it is not a very good predictor of actual cases who will subsequently fail reading. This perhaps has to do with the procedures used for determining "at-risk" status, a problem discussed above. A discriminant analysis using actual reading failures/passes as the criterion and the IRS items scores, subscale scores, and total scores as the predictors, might shed light on the appropriate cutoff points for actual "at-risk" status.

SUMMARY. This test is a screening instrument designed to identify children with early learning difficulties. It is a well standardized, reliable, and valid instrument. Its major strengths are its ease of administration and scoring and emphasis on the assessment of practical learning-related behaviors. Its major weakness is the lack of objective criteria for determining "at-risk" status for subsequent learning problems. Because of the latter, extreme caution should be taken in relying on IRS scores for identifying specific children that might have future learning delays or difficulties. Its use is best restricted to the description of current learning-related behavior characteristics. When used appropriately, and with the cautions raised in this review in mind, the IRS should prove to be a valuable assessment tool for aiding teachers in the development of interventions designed to remediate early learning problems. The use of the IRS for this purpose is highly recommended.

[506]

The Infant Reading Tests. Ages 4.5–7; 1979; IRT; 2 levels; no norms; (15–25) minutes per test; Alan Brimer and Bridie Raban; Educational Evaluation Enterprises [England].*

a) PRE-READING TESTS. 3 tests; 1984 price data: £14.25 per set with 25 of each test, manual, and key; £.75 per manual (11 pages).

1) *Pre-Reading Test* 1. Temporal-spatial coordination; 1 form (6 pages).

2) *Pre-Reading Test* 2. 3 scores: sound discrimination (beginning, middle, end); 1 form (6 pages).

3) *Pre-Reading Test* 3. Shape discrimination; 1 form (2 pages).

b) READING TESTS. 3 tests; £10.50 per set with 25 of each test, manual, and key; £.75 per manual (11 pages).

1) *Reading Test* 1. Word recognition; 1 form (2 pages).

2) *Reading Test* 2. Sentence completion; 1 form (2 pages).

3) *Reading Test* 3. Reading comprehension; 1 form (4 pages).

[507]

Informal Evaluation of Oral Reading Grade Level. Ages 5–11 and adolescents and adults with reading difficulties; 1973; 2 scores: oral comprehension level, reading level (independent, instructional, or frustration); no data on reliability and validity; no norms; individual; 1 form (11 pages); instruction booklet (3 pages); notation sheet (4 pages); 1983 price data: $7.20 per 2 tests, 25 notation sheets, and instructions; administration time not reported; Deborah Edel; Book-Lab, Inc.*

Review of Informal Evaluation of Oral Reading Grade Level by LYNN S. FUCHS, *Assistant Professor, Peabody College, Vanderbilt University, Nashville, TN:*

The basic format of the Informal Evaluation of Oral Reading Grade Level is similar to that of standard informal reading inventories (IRIs): Based on samples of reading performance across a range of graded passages, the examiner draws inferences concerning a student's reading and listening comprehension levels. According to the *Standards for Educational and Psychological Tests* (1974), such an informal evaluation qualifies as a "test," and its publication warrants the issue of a manual that provides information concerning the instrument's development, technical characteristics, administration, scoring, and interpretation. Unfortunately, the 3-page instruction book, the only accompanying material of the Informal Evaluation of Oral Reading Grade Level, fails to qualify as such a manual. It omits most necessary supporting information and frequently lacks conceptual soundness in the information presented, all of which makes meaningful and accurate interpretation of results difficult.

With respect to the development of the instrument, only one piece of information is included and it is relegated to a footnote, which (*a*) states that reading passages were graded using Fry's Graph for Estimating Reliability and (*b*) provides a percentage of easy words in the first four passages. No data to document actual readability scores of the passages are provided; no information concerning how paragraphs were developed is presented; no description of pilot studies is reported. Given insufficient information on the instrument's development along with an absence of data on the technical characteristics of the test, the examiner has no basis upon which to assume that the test scores are reliable and valid.

Furthermore, directions for administration and scoring, the major focus of the test's supporting document, are inadequate. No guidelines concerning testers' experience and training are provided, an omission with potentially serious implications given (*a*) documented scorer inaccuracy in coding miscues and (*b*) lack of information on interscorer reliability. Too many judgments are left to the examiner. Despite suggestions that examiners allow students time to figure out words and correct errors and that testers terminate reading when students experience extreme difficulty, no guidelines with which to formulate these decisions are provided. There are no instructions about what constitutes basals and ceilings on student performance and no information on how to deal with inconsistent performance from passage to passage. Whereas instructions are provided for moving students through successively easier passages when they encounter problems, there is no mention of the need to move students through higher passages until frustration level is reached. Is the examiner assumed to know this from previous experience with IRIs? If so, again some statement concerning testers' experience is useful.

The directions to the Informal Evaluation of Oral Reading Grade Level suffer not only from serious omission but also from conceptual difficulties. No rationale is provided either for deviations from traditional practice, such as the use of unusual criteria for word recognition accuracy for independent and frustration levels, or for the omission of comprehension criteria for calculating reading levels. Although comprehension performance is not used in determining reading levels, the examiner is instructed to ask a "few" questions after the student reads each passage. The purpose for asking these questions is unclear, except that on the notation sheet the examiner indicates whether comprehension was "good" or "poor," a judgment for which no guidelines are given. Additionally, only prototypic questions are provided, which are described as "helpful in investigating comprehension." Given (*a*) demonstrated difficulty in writing comprehension questions that reliably and accurately predict students' reading levels on the same passages (Peterson, Greenlaw, & Tierney, 1978), (*b*) no taxonomy or guidelines for determining how to classify inferential and factual questions or to determine the appropriate proportions for various types of questions, and (*c*) no information concerning whether question-answering should constitute a recall or recognition task, listening comprehension scores derived from the administration of this test are of questionable use.

Finally, there are no directions for completing the notation sheet, and no information on how to interpret scores. The *Standards* specify that such information should be provided to persons who lack the training usually required to interpret test results. Yet, the meaningfulness or seriousness of the reading miscues that the examiner rates on the notation sheet never is explained, and no guidance is provided on how to use diagnostic information gleaned during testing for instructional purposes.

Commercial IRIs have been criticized because they lack the curricular validity that is essential to IRIs: With commercial inventories, it is often difficult to translate obtained instructional levels into placements within curricula that may incorporate widely divergent materials. On the other hand, a potential advantage of commercial inventories is more careful development of passages, questions, and procedures and more thorough investigation of the reliability and validity of such instruments. Unfortunately, the Informal Evaluation of Oral Reading Grade Level fails to fulfill this potential, because it is remiss in providing documentation for such development and investigation. Testers interested in IRIs should consider alternative instruments such as carefully teacher-prepared, curriculum-based inventories or better developed commercial IRIs.

REVIEWER'S REFERENCES

American Psychological Association, American Educational Research Association, National Council on Measurement in Education. STANDARDS FOR EDUCATIONAL AND PSYCHOLOGICAL TESTS. Washington, DC: American Psychological Association, Inc., 1974.

Peterson, J., Greenlaw, M. J., & Tierney, R. J. Assessing instructional placement with the IRI: The effectiveness of comprehension questions. JOURNAL OF EDUCATIONAL RESEARCH, 1978, 71, 247–250.

Review of Informal Evaluation of Oral Reading Grade Level by MARY BETH MARR, Assistant Professor of Education, State University of New York at Albany, Albany, NY:

This test is designed to assess an individual's grade level performance on oral reading and corresponding comprehension tasks. The intent is that with this knowledge a teacher can select materials and begin reading instruction at an appropriate level. The test consists of a series of graded passages (one passage per grade level) ranging in difficulty from primer to 8th-grade reading level.

This test has several serious limitations. First, no reliability or validity data are available, which causes one to question the utility of the test. Second, while the author has admirably adapted several passages from existing books and magazines, she has controlled for passage comprehensibility by using only a readability formula. Thus, passage difficulty was estimated by examining the number of sentences and the average number of syllables per 100 words, rather than by considering other significant factors such as content, text structure, narrative or expository form, etc. (see Meyer, 1981, for a discussion of text factors which influence comprehension). Third, the comprehension assessment is too haphazard. The author lists 10 general questions in the manual which the examiner may want to use, but requires that only four of these questions be asked per passage. Criterion performance is based on correct responses to three of the four questions. Also, the questions vary in their assessment of literal and inferential comprehension. In short, the author fails to control question type across the passages. Thus, the examiner may be less than systematic in selecting questions to assess comprehension, resulting in inaccurate comprehension assessment (i.e., inflated or deflated comprehension scores). Lastly, performance on this test is measured at such a general level (e.g., good/poor comprehension and the number of reading errors per 100 words) that at best it provides only passage placement information (i.e., the matching of the reader to the text for instructional purposes).

Other limitations of the test, although minor, warrant attention. The system for coding oral reading errors differs from standard scoring procedures; thus, the examiner would need to develop proficiency with this new system before using the test. Further, the types of oral reading errors described in the test manual do not match with those listed on the notation sheet used by the examiner. Hence, the author must assume the examiner has knowledge of the possible error types independent of those described in the test manual.

In summary, while this test is designed to assess oral reading and comprehension proficiency for placement in grade level materials, the nature of the testing tasks (reading passages aloud, answering comprehension questions, and the coding of oral reading errors) has the potential to provide information comparable to that obtained on a traditional teacher constructed or commercial informal reading inventory (IRI). However, the performance scores on this test are used only to rate comprehension as good or poor and to note the number, rather than the type, of oral reading errors per passage. As a result, the information elicited from the test is overgeneralized while the testing remains time consuming. Further, since the author does not provide validity or reliability data on this instrument, one might just as well use an IRI which requires approximately the same amount of testing time, but addresses the limitations noted above and can provide much more reading diagnostic data as well, particularly for placement in a reading series.

REVIEWER'S REFERENCES

Meyer, B. J. F. Basic research on prose comprehension: A critical review. In D. Fisher and C. Peters (Eds.) COMPREHENSION AND THE COMPETENT READER, New York: Praeger, 1981.

[508]

Information System Skills. Job applicants; 1983; ISS; predicts success in operating terminal based information systems; 5 scores: reasoning, form recognition, clerical speed and accuracy, manual speed, total; 1 form (13 pages); manual (no date, 17 pages); 1984 price data: £3.90 per 10 test booklets; £1.20 per set of scoring keys; manual free on request; £1 per specimen set; 66(76) minutes; Malcolm Morrisby; Educational & Industrial Test Services Ltd. [England].*

[509]

Information Test on Smoking and Health. Grades 9–16 and adults; 1984; for educational or research purposes only; no data on reliability and validity; no norms; 1 form (4 pages); no manual; price data available from publisher; administration time not reported; H. Frederick Kilander; Glenn C. Leach, Publisher.*

[510]

Initial Communication Processes. Severely handicapped pupils birth through developmental age 3 years; 1982; ICP; consists of 2 components: observational scales to screen, and objectives bank for selecting appropriate instructional objectives to aid in the planning of learning activities; individual; 10 scales: Auditory Skills, Visual Skills, Manual Fine Motor Skills, Oral Vocal Motor Skills, Object Play Skills (manipulative, symbolic), Problem Solving Skills, Affective Development, Communication Skills (comprehension, expression); 1 form; scales book (24 pages); objectives bank (29 pages); manual (39 pages); progress monitoring log (4 pages); 1983 price data: $24.95 per complete starter set; $10.25 per 5 scales books; $9.75 per objectives bank; $10 per 20 progress monitoring logs; $7.90 per manual; Terris Schery and Ann Glover; Publishers Test Service.*

Review of Initial Communication Processes by DAVID L. WODRICH, Institute of Behavioral Medicine, Good Samaritan Medical Center, Phoenix, AZ:

The Initial Communication Processes (ICP) begins with the laudable mission of bringing psychometric rigor to understandardized, criterion-referenced assessment of basic skills among severely developmentally delayed children. The authors contend that standardization will allow more accurate determination of intra-individual differences, and consequently better focused instruction, and will make possible the detection of small incremental changes over time. A variety of problems prevent attainment of these goals.

First, the ICP expends effort and time (average one hour, 20 minutes) primarily to produce a profile (quartile scores) across 10 skill areas (called scales). This information is then to direct instruction toward deficits or to provide a baseline for reassessment. Unfortunately, no data are presented about standard error of measurement for various scales; thus the magnitude of differences necessary to assume true skill differences is unknown. Moreover, because many scale distributions are extremely skewed, a difference of one or two raw score points frequently moves pupils from the first to fourth quartile.

Second, adequate validity, a prime goal of the ICP, lacks substantiation in the test manual. To achieve the stated goal of skill measurement across several areas, content validity is central. But the authors provide too little information about where items came from, how they were assigned to scales, and how feedback from local psychologists, program specialists, and national experts was used to revise a pilot form of the test. The authors, however, do present explicit descriptions of the domains for each scale. Criterion-related validity consists merely of statistically significant ANOVAs comparing scores for various groups of children (e.g., autistic vs. trainable mentally retarded), and similarly significant ANOVAs for mental age, type of handicapping condition, and teachers' behavioral ratings. If the authors deemed criterion-related validity important, they should have located reasonable criterion measures: perhaps the Bayley for global developmental level and some narrow-band special ability tests for the various scales.

Third, while the ICP describes itself as primarily observational, in many instances "structured situations" are required, these in fact being the equivalent of administering items from scales such as the Gesell or Bayley. No test kit materials exist, nor are extensive, explicit administration or scoring guidelines available. Objective administration and scoring in such situations seem a great deal to expect of special education teachers or instructional aides, for whom the test is designed, even though the authors present interrater reliability coefficients generally in the acceptable .90 range for the scales. Additional studies of interrater reliability are in order using rank and file classroom special education teachers.

Fourth, the ICP is unsuited for interindividual, norm-referenced comparison, and indeed the authors advocate no such use. Derived scores are reported by type of disability (e.g., trainable mentally retarded, severe/profoundly retarded) and by estimated range of mental age (e.g., less than two years mental age, more than two years mental age). Unfortunately, the manual provides no operational definitions for the categories, nor any acceptable method of determining mental age. Examiners are to "estimate" pupils' mental age or to obtain mental age findings from other tests. It is unclear why a total mental age was not derived from performance on ICP test items, if one is, in fact, required for producing derived scores for each of the scales.

Fifth, with the exception of a clearly written Introduction, the manual is consistently tedious to read and occasionally inscrutable. Teachers and instructional aides will be confused by the method of test construction and logic used to support it. At a practical level, a cumbersome system of locating derived scores within a series of "profiles" will leave users confused and somewhat uncertain about whether scores for each scale are really being compared with the same standardization sample.

Finally, the word "communication" in the test's title is misleading: the ICP contains visual, motor, cognitive, and affective content as well as measurement of communication skills. The authors' assertion that these skills are precursors to communication overlooks the fact that these skills are precursors to almost all subsequent development.

These shortcomings notwithstanding, the ICP may add something to the classroom. The ICP does provide an accompanying set of instructional objectives organized into the same scales as the test, and teachers charged with delineating instructional goals will appreciate this feature. Also of worth, an additional recording sheet clearly lists objectives and provides a visual method of following instructional efforts and progress. The ICP's test items are empirically scaled for difficulty (though five of the ten scales do not meet acceptable standards) and do have known and acceptable evidence of internal consistency (coefficient alpha values generally in the .80 range or better). These latter two facts are probably the primary advantages over informal, teacher-made classroom assessment.

In summary, the ICP attempts to standardize classroom assessment of severely delayed children by producing a norm-referenced profile. Uncertainty about validity, lack of standard error of measurement data, and a confusing manual and table for derived scores will result in many teachers concluding the instrument is not convenient or time efficient. There is little clear psychometric justification for abandoning criterion-referenced assessment in favor of this tool.

[511]

Initial Placement Inventory. Grades 1–8; 1980; IPI; designed to place students in SERIES "r" Macmillan Reading Program; criterion-referenced; no data on reliability; selected levels to cover grades 1 through 8 in 3 areas; 1 form (62 stencils); individual record form, group record form, (1 page); teacher's manual (8 pages); price data available from publisher; administration time not reported; Madeline A. Weinstein; Macmillan Publishing Co., Inc.*

a) SILENT READING. 3 scores: number of correct answers, reading level, placement level.

b) WORD RECOGNITION. Individual.

c) ORAL READING. Individual; 4 scores: number of decoding errors, reading level, number of correct comprehension questions, reading level.

[512]

The Instant Words Criterion Test. Elementary students; 1980; criterion referenced test of students' sight reading abilities with 300 common words with and without suffixes; item scores only; no data on reliability; no norms; no suggested standards of mastery for item and total scores; individual; 1 form ('80, 4 pages plus instructions for administration and scoring); no manual; 1983 price data: $8 per package of 40 tests; (15–20) minutes; Edward Fry; Jamestown Publishers.*

Review of The Instant Words Criterion Test by DAVID J. CARROLL, School of Education, University of the West Indies, Bridgetown, Barbados, West Indies:

This test is "instant" in the sense that it covers the 300 words which occur most commonly in English. These, according to the author, must be "recognised instantly for any kind of fluency or comprehension facility." This is in itself a tenable point of view; this review will discuss how far the test does what it sets out to do, as well as the possible objections to the premise.

The test is criterion-referenced in the sense that all of these 300 words have to be known by any reader of English. Therefore, if any word is not known it must be taught; therefore, the test is used to define the programme of instruction that will be followed—any word that a student fails has to be taught. Repeated testing is advised; there is, however, only one form of the test, by definition. No data are quoted for the test-retest reliability of the items. As a result we cannot know how often pupils who "know" a word fail on it; the author admits that some caution has to be exercised, stating that "newly taught words must be read correctly on three testing periods separated by one week each." Neither are there any estimates of scorer reliability.

The test is intended for individual administration. Administration is on the whole simple; the instructions are even simpler. No explanation is given of "missed," the word used to describe a failure. Neither is there any indication given of how much time should be allowed to the pupil to answer each item, which is surely important in view of the word "instant" in the title of the test and the implied assumption. No instructions are given on how to administer the suffix test. The reviewer's instinctive reaction is that the suffix test would need to be expanded from its present limited length by the teacher using the test, but there is no indication of this. It could be maintained that teachers are now sufficiently sophisticated to be able to cope with this and to know how to use the test without elaborate instructions; this reviewer is, however, doubtful.

This reviewer also has reservations about several other aspects of the test. First, the name "instant words," and the front page of the test, suggest that these words should be recognised "instantly." There is no indication in the instructions for administration that this is intended; if it were, hesitation would have to count as failure. One may, however, doubt whether it is possible to have a test of this kind which is speeded.

Second, re-testing seems to be a doubtful proposition where there are no parallel forms. Children frequently learn to recite books which they have had read to them repeatedly, without necessarily being able to "read" them. In just the same way, they may learn to recite such a list of words as are included in this test, without being able to read the words when they meet them elsewhere. This possibility could be reduced if it were possible to produce alternate forms with scrambled word order. Thirdly, and most importantly, it seems appropriate to question how far ability to read single words aloud represents actual reading skill.

There are several reasons for having doubts. The principle of selection is purely that of frequency of occurrence. No distinction is made between lexical and non-lexical items. Regular forms, plurals, past tenses, etc. are treated as "suffixes," while irregular forms (e.g., are, be, been, is) are not. If these irregular forms are sufficiently common, they appear in the list as well as the headwords. This inevitably means that there are some oddities. The test has do, does, don't, and did, feet but not foot, children but not child, and some quirks of order; for instance, example precedes eat in the list. There is no indication of an item-analysis to demonstrate that the actual order of difficulty for pupils is the same as the order adopted, but rather this order was determined by the "quick survey test." In other words, if pupils can do three words in a particular survey group, they are not tested on earlier words. This procedure would be justified if there were clear evidence of an order of difficulty, not merely of frequency. It also presents problems because it means that many of the words in the early groups are non-lexical—prepositions, articles, demonstratives, question words, and the like—whereas the later groups are composed largely of lexical items. All of these will tend to reduce attention to meaning.

Unlike some other tests which involve single words being read aloud, this test does not purport to be a test of general reading skill. The same author has produced tests of the ability to "sound out" unfamiliar words, and to make sense of sentences/paragraphs. This is, therefore, a test with limited objectives, and these limited objectives explain the absence of many features that one would expect to find in a group test which would be used to produce valid, reliable estimates of general performance such as norms, validation data, reliability coefficients, and so on. However, some estimate of test-retest and scorer reliability should have been made, and more specific instructions about timing and what constitutes a right or wrong response should have been given. Some justification is also needed of the choice of frequency rather than either "complexity" or "natural order" as the organising principle for the test. With these reservations, the test is a useful classroom measure for those following the kind of organisation advocated by the test constructor in their teaching of reading.

However, for those not following Dr. Fry's model, the test has much more limited interest, except as a vehicle for testing assumptions. Although the words chosen may be among the most frequently used in fluent native writing, or indeed in children's books, there is no guarantee that they are the ones most used by learners. It may be that they have other strategies. In fact, this possibility is implicitly admitted by the author of the test: "Younger students need nearly three years of schooling before they can read all 300 Instant Words." If this is so, can we accept that during that period they do not have "any kind of fluency or comprehension facility?" It may be that these 300 words are merely secondary indicators of a different kind of development which it is therefore pointless to teach directly. Frequency, furthermore, while itself a useful indicator, tells one nothing about purpose, and therefore nothing about how the language item is used, or what it is for. In the absence of emphasis on this, and on the effect of context on a pupil's ability to read the words, the information provided by the test must remain partial.

Review of The Instant Words Criterion Test by JOHN ELKINS, Reader in Special Education, Schonell Educational Research Centre, University of Queensland, St. Lucia, QLD, Australia:

This brief and inexpensive test relies upon a 1-page account to serve as a manual. As the subtitle indicates, the test is basically a word list, claimed to contain the most common 300 words in English written text, and constituting, with common suffixes, 65% of such text. No references are given to support this claim, but an inspection suggests that these words are indeed basic sight vocabulary. Nonetheless, they may not correspond to the vocabulary of particular basal reading schemes. The first 12 words from each successive 100 words may be used as a Quick Survey to minimize testing time on the Complete Diagnostic Test. Testing procedure requires the child to read from one copy while the examiner notes performance on a second copy. The use of a complicated record form as a stimulus sheet is an undesirable feature of this test. Since criteria for cessation of testing are vague, usually ranging between five and ten errors, the intended interpretation of test results must be subjective. Indeed, the rationale appears to be that teachers should instruct students systematically in the 300 words, the test being used to assess their knowledge of basic sight vocabulary. It is recommended that success on three occasions 1 week apart be demanded as evidence of mastery.

Unlike most tests, where items are neither publicly known or deliberately taught, it is recommended that students and parents be given copies of the test to improve student learning of this basic reading vocabulary list. One might question the extent to which inferences about overall reading ability can be drawn from performance on the Instant Words Criterion Test, especially if extensive coaching has taken place. It is also recommended that the same 300 words can form the basis of oral spelling items. There are no comments provided on reliability or validity. Clearly, the validity of the test is seen to lie in the selection of the 300 words. No concurrent or predictive data are given, nor are studies cited in which the clinical utility of the test is investigated. The literature on correlations between word reading tests and other types of reading measures suggests that rather high associations are typical. However, the low difficulty level of the items in the Instant Words Criterion Test might result in lower reliability when used with other than beginning readers.

In summary, the Instant Words Criterion Test cannot be easily assessed using criteria applicable to either psychometric or criterion-referenced tests other than to regard it as extremely inadequate. However, it may prove to be a useful tool for teachers and reading specialists, providing that their use of this test is guided by an understanding of the role of basic sight vocabulary in the development of reading proficiency. Its virtues lie mostly in the listing of common words and its potential for diagnostic interpretation. Judged as a test, it is sadly deficient in most technical aspects.

[513]

The Instant Words Recognition Test. Primary grades and remedial reading situations; 1971–77; criterion-referenced test; item scores only; no norms; no suggested standards of mastery for item or total scores; Forms 1, 2 ('71, 1 page); manual ('77, 5 pages); 1983 price data: $8 per package of 30 tests and manual; administration time not reported; Edward Fry; Jamestown Publishers.*

For a review by Priscilla Drum, and an excerpted review by Paula A. Fuld of the 1971 edition, see 8:780.

Review of The Instant Words Recognition Test by JAMES A. POTEET, Associate Professor of Special Education, Ball State University, Muncie, IN:

The Instant Words Recognition Test requires the student to listen to a word, find it in a set of five words, and put an X on it. There are two tests, specified as Form 1 and Form 2, consisting of 24 words for each of two levels: a "lower" and an "upper" level. The test words were selected from Fry's graded list of 600 words that should be recognized instantly by students in grades one through four. Thus, as the name of the test implies, the test assesses a recognition of a sample of these "instant words."

The top sheet of the response form, which the student marks, is carbonized and thus transfers the student's mark to the bottom sheet. The examiner separates the two sheets and inspects the bottom sheet to determine the number of correct responses as indicated by placement in a shaded area. Counting the number of marks in the shaded areas makes scoring straightforward and simple. The scoring sheet has different sizes of circles whose meaning is not explained. On one form of the scoring sheet, each item is coded to the specific list within each grade level from which the test words were selected.

According to the author, this test is an individually or group administered criterion-referenced test used to determine a starting point for teaching the "instant words" and to measure general reading achievement. The 600 instant words are listed in the manual by approximate grade level. The source, definition, or meaning of the list of "instant words" is not mentioned. No criterion of mastery is suggested for any age or grade level.

Knowing the number of words correctly identified does not, as the manual suggests, allow a teacher to determine a starting point in teaching the list of instant words. Nor does the test measure "general reading achievement" as suggested in the manual. The instructions are confusing to the student. Telling a student to place a mark "on top of" a word often results in the mark being placed directly above the word in the space between the lines of words. Consequently, the location of the mark on the carbon response sheet does not lie in the properly shaded area for scoring. The instructions could be changed to "put an X directly on the word like this" as a demonstration is given.

In summary, this test, with its confusing instructions, unclear interpretations, and little information regarding reliability or validity, does not provide results which allow it to be used to meet its stated purposes. Essentially, the test would not have to be used to determine which "instant words" to teach. The teacher would simply ask the student to read the entire list of instant words and proceed to teach those words that were not recognized. Used in this manner, the list would serve as its own criterion-referenced assessment device.

Review of The Instant Words Recognition Test by STANLEY F. VASA, Professor, Department of Special Education, University of Nebraska-Lincoln, Lincoln, NE:

The test consists of two levels of a criterion-referenced scale designed to measure recognition of selected words from two lists of 300 words developed by the author. A subject is required to respond to a word, which is pronounced in isolation, in a sentence, and again in isolation, and to identify that word from a list of five words. The recording system for the scale is easy to follow and is self-scoring by the use of pressure-sensitive answer sheets. The author reports that the purposes of the scale are twofold: to determine a starting point in teaching instant words, and to measure general reading achievement.

The test is relatively easy to administer and should require no more than 10 minutes to complete for an individual or group of children. The manual of directions does not report whether the entire scale or only a certain number of items are to be administered. No guidance is provided as to which list of instant words should be used instructionally after completing the test and scoring the number of items correct.

A dearth of information is available to the test user about the development of the 24-word test. The author reports that the test items were arranged in serial order from easy to hard; however, no information or data is provided to support the claim. Little insight is provided about the relationship of instant words recognized from oral presentation and overall reading achievement.

Evidence provided for the support of the test as a measure of general reading achievement includes a correlation with the Stanford Achievement Test of .77 and the Iowa Test of Basic Skills at .73. This information would have been more helpful if the data collection on the IWRT had been more thorough. These estimates were based on a study of only 153 first-grade students. No students from other grade levels were included in these correlational studies; however, it is implied in the manual of instruction that the test could be used with populations other than first graders. Word lists accompanying the test are labeled as grades one through four. There also is no evidence that the scale was administered to a sample of slow learners, although the author states the scale would be appropriate for use with such a population.

SUMMARY. The IWRT is useful as a criterion-referenced test for a limited number of teachers who wish to obtain a sampling of a student's instant sight-word recognition from a listing of 600 words provided by the author. Although the author claims several other purposes, there does not seem to be support for them. Of particular concern is the suggestion that the test may be used to compare performance between students, provide a ranking of students, and serve as a general reading achievement measure. The test does not meet several expected standards for this purpose. Concerns center on the development of test items, the lack of information on the standardization sample, and the indications of concurrent and predictive validity provided by the author.

Overall, the IWRT appears to have relatively little merit as a reading diagnostic tool. Its value would be in sampling the instant word list developed by the author. The use of the scale for any more detailed or demanding grouping or instructional guide would be foolhardy and subject to many erroneous assumptions on the part of the unknowing tester.

[514]

Instructional Styles Inventory. Instructors; 1976–79; may be used either in conjunction with or independent of Learning Styles Inventory (T3:1310); self-report inventory; 17 scores in 4 areas: conditions (peer, organization, goal setting, competition, instructor, detail, independence, authority), content (numeric, qualitative, inanimate, people), mode (talking, readings, iconics, direct experience), influence; no validity data; no norms; 1 form ('76, 4 pages); guide ['77, 20 pages]; profile sheet ['79, 2 pages]; separate answer sheets must be used; 1983 price data: $32.95 per starter set including 15 inventory booklets, 25 answer sheets, 25 profile sheets, and 1 guide; $1.50 or less per inventory booklet; $.12 or less per answer sheet; $.25 or less per profile sheet; $5 per guide; $12.95 per specimen set; (25–40) minutes; Albert A. Canfield and Judith S. Canfield; Humanics Media.*

Review of Instructional Styles Inventory by THOMAS B. BRADLEY, Associate Professor of Special Education, Shippensburg University, Shippensburg, PA:

The Instructional Styles Inventory was designed to assess 17 dimensions of instructional style grouped into four clusters. It may be used in conjunction with the Canfield Learning Styles Inventory or independent of it. When used with the Learning Styles Inventory the authors claim that it is possible to compare the style preferences of instructors and learners.

The inventory consists of 25 items. The respondent ranks each of four alternatives from most preferred (1) to least preferred (4). Instructions are explicit and concise; an example item presented on the cover of the inventory clearly demonstrates the correct method of ranking alternatives.

Scoring is facilitated by the format of the answer sheet and the detailed instructions provided in the guide which accompanies the inventory. However, two points of confusion do exist. The fourth area is labeled "Influence" in the guide while it is referred to as "Responsibility" on the profile sheet. Also, in computing this "Influence/Responsibility" factor, alternative C is not included in the calculation. While the directions for the computation are clear, no explanation for this omission is provided. Some uncertainty may arise as a result. A brief explanation inserted in the guide at this point would alleviate this potential for confusion.

Percentile equivalents of raw scores are provided for male and female respondents based on *N*s of 428 and 373 respectively. No other data on this reference group is provided for the person utilizing the test. The implicit assumption is that little of the variation in styles is attributable to factors other than sex of the instructor. This is an extremely questionable assumption. Instructional style would seem to be very much affected by such factors as the instructor's area of expertise (e.g., natural science vs. behavioral science vs. humanities), age, theoretical orientation, etc. Much more needs to be done to develop a stratified reference group in order to improve the usefulness of the inventory.

Examination of reliability data raises several questions. Since this inventory is very brief, one would expect that if a test-retest reliability coefficient were to be used to demonstrate profile stability over time, a significant test-retest interval would be utilized (i.e., a minimum interval of four weeks). The authors chose to use a one-week interval; thus the reported reliability coefficients (which range from .81 to .96) are best interpreted with caution, since these reliability estimates were obtained under conditions which maximized the correlation coefficients.

The limited number of items (typically 5) that are summed to produce the dimension raw scores is another problem. The larger the number of items that measure a given factor, the greater the probability that random errors will counterbalance. Merely doubling the number of items to be summed for each dimension to 10 would lead to a noticeable increase in reliability. The cost to be paid for that positive outcome, however, would be increased administration time to approximately one hour.

Despite these technical reservations, the reliability data tentatively indicate a satisfactory level of stability.

The major problems with the inventory are those concerned with validity-related issues. Several very serious problems are evident. First, there is the issue of item format. Respondents must rank alternatives from most preferred to least preferred with no opportunity to indicate relative degree of preference. There is little evidence to indicate that rankings assigned for one item are comparable with rankings for another item.

Since the respondent is forced to rank each alternative on the predetermined scale of 1 to 4, his/her apparent choices may merely indicate that other rankings were not available. For example, a respondent may prefer ranking two alternatives equally high, a third moderately low, and the fourth extremely low; or he/she may wish to rank two alternatives moderately high and two alternatives just slightly lower. All possible rankings, however, are forced into the 1 to 4 ranking scheme whether or not that scheme validly reflects reality.

Another validity-related issue concerns the self-report format of the inventory. Valid measurement will result only if the individual knows his/her own instructional behaviors and preferences and only if he/she is willing to relate these behaviors and preferences honestly. Assuming that this knowledge, willingness, and honesty are characteristic of the intended respondents is untenable. This is especially true in the absence of any research with this inventory that compares response patterns with actual classroom practices.

The authors allude only indirectly to validity by referring to research using the Instructional Styles Inventory. This research indicates that the closer the match between style preferences of students and faculty, the more effective the teaching/learning relationship. Only one such study is reported that supports this conclusion. It is referred to as a "Major Applied Research Project for Ed.D. degree." Certainly one unpublished study is not a strong statement for validity of the inventory.

The Instructional Styles Inventory is a test with satisfactory reliability, but with inadequate evidence to suggest that it measures what it purports to measure. Yet this reviewer is left with a positive impression of the test's potential usefulness because of its thoroughness of coverage. Few competing assessment devices can match the ease of administration and scoring on the one hand and the detail of the profiled results on the other. However, before this inventory can play a major role in research or instructional improvement, serious efforts will be required to develop evidence of its validity. Reliability studies that meet more stringent criteria would also be helpful.

Review of Instructional Styles Inventory by C. DEAN MILLER, Professor of Psychology, Colorado State University, Fort Collins, CO:

The Instructional Styles Inventory was designed to obtain scores on 17 dimensions which are directly comparable to equivalent dimensions on the Learning Styles Inventory published by Humanics Media. The inventory may be used to analyze a teacher's preferred instructional style or to make comparisons between a teacher's style to that of an individual student's learning preference or to a group or class profile of students' preference structure. The results may be helpful in that teachers may gain additional insight and understanding of the approaches and beliefs which underlie their choice of teaching strategies. Additional information pertaining to the teacher's beliefs about the relative importance of interpersonal relations, organization of instructional materials, goal setting, competition, and authority in facilitating learning may be obtained by the user. Four modes or approaches to teaching may provide users with additional information pertaining to their perceptions of the relative importance of lecturing, reading, use of visual materials other than reading, or direct experience to promote and facilitate learning. The inventory also addresses the question of who is responsible for learning. Five items in the inventory focus on such issues as student responsibility for learning, student responsibility for adjusting or adapting to teaching strategies, or improvement or enhancement of learning by varying instructional procedures.

The authors do not provide a theoretical foundation or rationale underlying the development of the inventory. References to four empirical studies were included in the manual. The brief summaries of the four studies provide interesting and potentially significant and helpful information, but without adequate detail to enable potential users to judge the merit or worth of each set of findings and related implications.

No validity studies were reported in the manual. Test-retest correlation coefficients were reported for 62 students enrolled in two management classes. Seven days separated the two testing sessions. Correlations for 21 scales ranged from .81 to .96.

Administration of the inventory is not difficult or complicated. Helpful suggestions for administering and scoring the instrument are provided in the manual. The profile sheets contain normative information for male and female instructors. By studying the descriptive information which is provided in the manual, the interpretation of the scores and profiles may become more meaningful and helpful to the individual teacher.

Even though the inventory appears to have some good potential, lack of a theoretical or conceptual framework and the absence of extensive empirical data limit the confidence a user may have in the information provided by the instrument. However, the reviewer is of the opinion that teachers who complete the inventory may benefit a great deal from learning about their preferred styles and strategies and recognize the possibility that their preferences are likely to match the preferences of some students and mismatch the styles of other students. In the absence of sufficient empirical data from which to evaluate the inventory, it seems advisable to consider the inventory as being primarily for experimental use and to stimulate teachers' awareness of the beliefs on which they base their instructional strategies.

[515]

Instrument for Disability Screening, [Developmental Edition]. Primary grade children; 1980; IDS; ratings by teachers; 9 scores: hyperactive/aggressive, visual, speech/auditory, reading, drawing/writing, inactivity, concepts, psychomotor development, total; no norms; individual; 1 form (4 pages); no manual; separate answer sheets may be used; price data available from author; (5–15) minutes; James R. Beatty; the Author.*

See T3:1161 (3 references).

Review of Instrument for Disability Screening, [Developmental Edition], by NORMAN A. BUKTENICA, Professor and Chair, Education Department, Moorhead State University, Moorhead, MN:

The Instrument for Disability Screening (IDS) is clearly in developmental stages. It is a screening device that is being developed to identify children who are classified as learning disabled. The format is that of the teacher rating separate children in eight categories on a five-point continuum.

Having no manual, rationale, or standardization data, it is difficult to review the merits or potential of the IDS. Therefore, one must question the theoretical base, the underlying assumptions of the instrument, and the existence of the types of children it is to identify.

The author is making attempts at standardization, but at the time of this writing the data have not yet been released. Some attempts at determining reliability are reported. Factor analysis of the original 80 items, when used with a sample of 400 children, identified 48 items that could be represented in 10 factors. Kuder-Richardson Formula 20 was applied to each of the 10 factor-obtained subscales to reveal reliability coefficients ranging from .51 to .80. In a subsequent study with 100 selected children, almost all of the 61 children labeled as learning disabled were differentiated from the remaining "normal" children by teacher ratings on the IDS. It is difficult to determine the validity of that study because the teachers knew the labeled and non-labeled children prior to the rating, and the KR-20 reliability coefficient for one subscale dropped to –.05. There are no reported validity studies but in personal communication the author reported that validation efforts are in progress.

The IDS cannot be considered a standardized instrument at this time. Perhaps it can be used as a research instrument, but the lack of evidence for validation and the absence of norms deems it unwarranted for use as a screening instrument at this time.

Review of Instrument for Disability Screening, [Developmental Edition], by STEVEN I. PFEIFFER, Pediatric Psychologist, Child Development Center, Department of Pediatrics, Ochsner Clinic, and Department of Psychology, Tulane University, New Orleans, LA:

Screening instruments are specifically intended to test a large number of children in order to identify those high-risk youngsters who would benefit from further evaluation and subsequent early intervention. Screening instruments are not designed to either label or place children in remedial programs, but rather as an essential first step in locating those children who most likely are handicapped. The primary problem with screening instruments is that their abridged format increases the number of false positives (children identified as disabled when no handicapping condition exists), as well as false negatives (children who are disabled but who are not identified as handicapped on the instrument). Thus, predictive utility remains a particularly thorny issue.

James Beatty has been developing a learning disability screening instrument over the past eight years, beginning with an 80-item, eight-factor questionnaire in 1975 that he entitled Classroom Screening Instrument. This teacher-scored form has undergone a number of revisions, presently consists of 65 items and eight factors, and has been renamed Instrument for Disability Screening (IDS). Beatty acknowledges that "the IDS is still in the developmental stage and that continuing research is being conducted on the instrument" (J. R. Beatty, personal communication, March, 1982).

Beatty (1975) earlier pointed out that the majority of existing instruments used for the early diagnosis of learning disabilities were originally developed for very specific problems, and not extensive enough to serve as comprehensive screening batteries. His goal was to develop "adequate screening instruments which will detect children with potential learning disabilities prior to comprehensive diagnostic testing" (1975).

The IDS was "developed through an extensive review of the literature and evaluated individually by a panel of 12 experts" (Beatty, 1979). The questionnaire, in its present developmental form, is completed by the child's teacher and scored on a five-point scale (behavior has never been observed, seldom, occasionally, frequently, typically). The 65 items cluster into eight factors: "Hyperactive/Aggressive" (11 items), "Visual" (8), "Speech/Auditory" (10), "Reading" (7), "Drawing/Writing" (6), "Inactivity" (7), "Concepts" (8), and "Psychomotor Development" (8). The four-page scoring sheet is neatly laid out, attractively displayed, and intended for computer scoring. Teachers are instructed on the scoring sheet to rate the frequency of occurrence of each of the 65 statements, based on their observations "in the classroom, on the playground, or during other school activities." Completion of a questionnaire should take no more than 10 minutes per child. No specific age range is provided, but the instrument seems most appropriate for primary level students.

To Beatty's credit, he has subjected the screening instrument to rigorous examination. The original questionnaire was administered to 400 children in grades 1, 2, and 3 who were identified as learning disabled by their teachers. A series of factor analyses was performed on the original instrument, resulting in a 48-item, ten-factor revision. The factors of "Body/Motoric" and "Social Emotional" were eliminated, and four new factors were added: "Inactivity/Lack of Concentration," "Neurological Disability," "Laterality Disability," and "Anxiety." Internal consistency for the revised instrument was obtained on a second sample of 100 children in grades 1 through 3 (61 classified as learning disabled by their teachers and 39 screened by their teachers as normal), with KR-20 reliability indices ranging from .10–.89 for the ten factors.

A second study (Beatty, 1979) sought to validate the revised instrument by correlating scores on the questionnaire with independent measures of the hypothesized ten traits. The monotrait-heteromethod validity correlations supported seven of the ten factors, and raised questions about the validity of three: "Anxiety," "Laterality Disability," and "Neurological Disability." Beatty also explored whether the instrument could discriminate between the 39 normal and 61 learning disabled students earlier described in his 1975 study. He found that 98 of the 100 children were correctly classified by the questionnaire.

The present instrument consists of eight factors, and it was not reported why, after dropping "Anxiety," "Laterality Disability," and "Neurological Disability," Beatty added the factor "Psychomotor Development" (which was one of the eight original factors). There is no available data at this time on the reliability, validity, or norms for the most recent revision of the DSI.

Although Beatty is to be commended for stressing the developmental nature of his questionnaire, and his insistence that the validation of the DSI must be a continual process (1979), his validation studies suffer from three serious flaws that diminish the present status of the screening instrument. First, in both studies Beatty identified his learning disabled population by simply having the classroom teachers diagnose the students as either learning disabled or normal. Written guidelines were provided to assist the teachers in interpreting the term "learning disability," (1975), but Beatty failed to acknowledge either: (1) the contamination/bias in having the same persons first label the students as learning disabled or not, and then complete questionnaires on the same children, or (2) that learning disabilities are a complex and often difficult-to-define set of syndromes that require more specialized, comprehensive, and in-depth diagnosis by an interdisciplinary group of professionals. Also, since the 39 normal and 61 learning disabled children were both initially diagnosed and subsequently rated on the DSI by the same teachers, it would be very surprising if these persons did not obtain the highly successful discriminations that were reported!

Second, Beatty neglected to employ a control group of normal children in his original validation study, and used a small control group in his follow-up research. This raises serious questions concerning whether the instrument is, in fact, appropriate to be administered to entire classes, or if the eight factors hold up for all children.

Third, in Beatty's (1979) most recent validation study, it is unclear how the 39 normal and 61 learning disabled youngsters were initially defined, and whether a diagnostic procedure independent of the teachers' DSI ratings was used to dichotomize the sample into the two groups. Additionally, the author does not specify who scored the children on the independent marker variables or how they were rated. It appears that the same teachers not only completed the DSI on the 100 students, but rated the youngsters on the marker variables as well.

Apart from the above-mentioned methodological issues inherent in the validation studies, six points bear mentioning that will require careful consideration as the DSI undergoes further revision. First, since the DSI is a screening instrument, it should be modified to include preschool and kindergarten levels, when early intervention is most useful. Second, it is unclear how much contact a teacher would minimally require before being able to validly complete the questionnaire. Third, the five-point rating scale is an elaboration of the original dichotomous scoring system, and the refinement is a plus. However, it would seem difficult to this reviewer for a teacher to meaningfully differentiate among the middle three scale points (seldom, occasionally and frequently), and this warrants empirical investigation. Fourth, as earlier mentioned, Beatty does not report why he eliminated the "Anxiety" factor from the first revision, and it would seem that consideration for a "Social/Emotional" set of items is warranted. Fifth, there are a number of problems with the items themselves. For example, some lack the clarity required of questionnaires (e.g., "Explodes for no apparent reason"), while a number of others are duplicative (e.g., "Often is aggressive toward peers or adults"—"Appears aggressive in comparison to behavior of peers"; and "Squints frequently"—"Rubs eyes frequently"—"Appears to have visual difficulties in comparison to peers"). Furthermore, the grouping of a few items is conceptually questionable, even if empirically justifiable. For example, "Has poor recall of materials presented orally in class" is placed within the "Speech/Auditory" factor, but appears to more accurately represent a "Memory" problem. Sixth, the DSI needs to be tried out with a heterogeneous group of children so that criteria for establishing "at risk," "borderline," and "not at risk" cutoff scores can be established, as well as reliability and validity data.

The DSI is in its developmental stage, and appears to hold promise as a screening instrument for learning disabilities. Its ease of scoring, brevity, and conceptual clarity make it potentially competitive with existing devices (such as the Individual Learning Disability Classroom Screening Instrument and the First Grade Screening Test). However, much more extensive and careful research and test development will be required before the DSI can be used for individual decision-making.

REVIEWER'S REFERENCES

Beatty, J. R. The analysis of an instrument for screening learning disabilities. JOURNAL OF LEARNING DISABILITIES, 1975, 8, 58–64.

Beatty, J. R. Construct validation of an instrument for screening learning disabilities. JOURNAL OF LEARNING DISABILITIES, 1979, 12, 58–65.

[516]

Interest Determination, Exploration and Assessment System. Grades 6–12; 1977–80; IDEAS; self-scorable; 14 scores: mechanical/fixing, electronics, nature/outdoors, science, numbers, writing, arts/crafts, social service, child care, medical service, business, sales, office practices, food service; 1 form ('78, 12 pages); manual ('80, 16 pages); 1984 price data: $19 per 25 booklets; $2.75 per manual; $3.50 per specimen set; (20–40) minutes; Charles B. Johansson; NCS Interpretive Scoring Systems.*

Review of Interest Determination, Exploration and Assessment System by M. O'NEAL WEEKS, Professor of Family Studies, University of Kentucky, Lexington, KY:

The Interest Determination, Exploration and Assessment System (IDEAS) is a vocational interest inventory developed by the author of the Career Assessment Inventory (CAI). Because it was designed primarily for people interested in careers that do not require a baccalaureate education, the CAI has been referred to as a "blue collar" version of the Strong-Campbell Interest Inventory (Bodden, 1978). Similarly, IDEAS is designed to explore the vocational interests of the non-college-bound student. Since all 112 items in IDEAS were taken directly from CAI, IDEAS is simply a shortened version of CAI.

IDEAS has several advantages over the longer, more complex, machine scored CAI: It is short, simple, easy to administer, self-scorable and can be interpreted by the student. Since the student can score his/her own inventory and is also given instructions for its interpretation, including an interest profile with normative scores (separate interest profiles are provided for grades 6 through 8 and grades 9 through 12), he/she is given immediate feedback from taking the inventory.

Some of the advantages of IDEAS are also its major weakness: it is too brief and simplistic to be used as a serious assessment of one's vocational interests. As a counseling tool it is, at best, a preliminary indicator of general directions of vocational interests. The manual reports "overall, good concurrent validity" for IDEAS, a statement based on its ability to differentiate individuals in occupations and career programs closely related to the interest scales from individuals in occupations and career programs not related to the interest scales. However, IDEAS has limited utility as a predictor for vocational choice and/or future vocational success. As one possible application of IDEAS, the manual recommends that it be used in conjunction with career programs and guidance units in social studies classes. Such usage as a stimulus for class discussion and for further vocational exploration seems very appropriate, provided its users are cautioned not to allow their IDEAS profiles to weigh too heavily on vocational choices.

The manual is extremely well done for such a brief and simple inventory, largely because IDEAS was drawn directly from CAI, on which the author appears to have done extensive research. The information on content validity, construct validity, concurrent validity, and reliability of IDEAS is very well presented and impressive. The correlations between IDEAS scales and the longer CAI scales were very high (.91 and above). IDEAS also fared well in comparisons to the Strong-Campbell Interest Inventory and the Minnesota Vocational Interest Inventory (r=.80 and above). Because of its validity, reliability, and ability to discriminate groups according to vocational interest, IDEAS can be recommended for use as a data collection inventory for research comparing groups at the sixth-grade level or above.

The descriptive information on the normative populations is limited to sample sizes and gender and grade level of subjects. There is no information regarding the socioeconomic status, educational performance levels, ethnic makeup, or geographical regions of the samples. With this one limitation, the manual measures up well to the *Standards for Educational and Psychological Tests*.

The students' directions for taking, scoring, and interpreting IDEAS are generally clear and adequate, with two minor exceptions. At one point the student is instructed to "copy each circled number onto the line to its right," but there are boxes rather than lines to the right, which may be somewhat confusing to students. The other minor criticism is that in the inventory itself some subjects which may be considered somewhat esoteric are parenthetically and briefly explained but others are not. For example, "study astronomy" is followed by "stars and planets" in parentheses whereas "study ecology" has no such accompanying descriptors.

In conclusion, IDEAS is a well developed, well constructed, and validated inventory. It is easy to administer, score, and interpret. The major weaknesses are that IDEAS is appropriate for use only with populations interested in vocations that do not require a college education, and it has limited utility as a basis for in-depth vocational counseling and decision making. As a precursor of more extensive vocational testing, as a stimulus for discussion of vocational interest, and as an instrument for collecting research data, IDEAS has much to recommend it.

REVIEWER'S REFERENCES

Bodden, Jack L. Review of the Career Assessment Inventory in THE EIGHTH MENTAL MEASUREMENTS YEARBOOK, 1978.

[517]

Intermediate Measures of Music Audiation. Grades 1–4; 1978–82; IMMA; advanced version of Primary Measures of Music Audiation; 3 scores: tonal, rhythm, composite; 1 form; manual ('82, 46 pages); profile (no date, 1 page); 7 1/2 ips test tape, 7-inch reel for tonal and rhythm parts; answer sheets for tonal, rhythm, ('78, 2 pages); price data available from publisher; (20) minutes for each part; Edwin E. Gordon; G.I.A. Publications, Inc.*

[518]

Interpersonal Behavior Survey. Grades 9–16 and adults; 1980; IBS; distinguishes assertive behaviors from aggressive behaviors; 21 scores: denial, infrequency, impression management, general aggressiveness—rational, hostile stance, expression of anger, disregard for rights, verbal aggressiveness, physical aggressiveness, passive aggressiveness, general assertiveness—rational, self-confidence, initiating assertiveness, defending assertiveness, frankness, praise, requesting help, refusing demands, conflict avoidance, dependency, shyness, plus additional scores (general aggressiveness—empirical, general assertiveness—empirical) and 10 short-form scores; norms consist of means and standard deviations; 1 form (8 pages); manual (78 pages, including test, answer sheet, and profile); separate answer sheets must be used; 1983 price data: $7.10 per 10 test booklets; $9.70 per scoring keys; $5.10 per 50 answer sheets; $5.10 per 50 profiles; $8.90 per manual; $24.75 per specimen set; (40–50) minutes; Paul A. Mauger, David R. Adkinson, Suzanne K. Zoss (test), Gregory Firestone (test), and J. David Hook (test); Western Psychological Services.*

Review of Interpersonal Behavior Survey by STEPHEN L. FRANZOI, Post-Doctoral Fellow, Training Program in Social Psychology, Indiana University, Bloomington, IN:

Unlike many measures reviewed in the *MMY*, the Interpersonal Behavior Survey (IBS) has a professional look to it that commands immediate attention. Once the reader wades through the 61-page manual describing the survey's development, reliability, and validity (including an 18-page guide to interpreting an IBS profile), the initial impression of a quality piece of work is not diminished. This is not to say that the IBS is problem-free; it is not. However, it is a survey distinguishing assertive behaviors from aggressive behaviors and, in this regard, appears to be successful. It also has been developed with a good deal of technical skill that has resulted in a solid foundation for future refinements that may prove necessary.

In their explanation of scale construction, the authors state in the manual that "item-level factor analysis" was used to develop the IBS scales. In fact, only 6 of the 24 scales were derived using factor analytic procedures. Those six scales are Hostile Stance, Expression of Anger, Self-Confidence, Initiating Assertiveness, Defending Assertiveness, and Frankness. Factor analysis of the item-summed scales resulted in the aggressive scales and the assertive scales loading on different factors. This finding, in concert with the finding that the intercorrelations between the scales of assertiveness and aggressiveness are in the predicted low range ($r < .10$), indicates that they are basically independent response classes (i.e., measuring different behavioral tendencies).

While these studies appear to verify that the aggressiveness scales measure different behavior patterns than the assertiveness scales, there is no evidence reported in the manual separating the individual aggressiveness measures from one another. This is also the case for the assertiveness measures. In fact, there is a good deal of item overlap between the eight aggressiveness scales and also between the nine assertiveness scales. One wonders whether there is empirical justification for eight different scales measuring different types of aggressiveness and nine different scales measuring different types of assertiveness; fewer scales may more accurately describe aggressive and assertive tendencies. Since they do not report item factor analyses of the total IBS there is no way to determine whether these different scales are indeed measuring different behavioral tendencies.

Long and short versions of the following IBS scales are available: General Aggressiveness, Expression of Anger, Disregard for Rights, Verbal Aggressiveness, Physical Aggressiveness, General Assertiveness—Rational, Frankness, Praise, Requesting

Help, and Refusing Demands. The longer versions were developed using internal consistency item analysis procedures and have better reliability than the short versions.

The reliability characteristics of the IBS were determined using a test-retest format over both a 2-day and a 10-week period and by assessing the internal consistency of each scale. The test-retest reliabilities range from the low .70s to the mid .90s and compare well with other scales in the field. The IBS scales appear to have adequate internal consistency, except for the Refusing Demands scale, where the reliability coefficients for the long and short versions were .33 and .11.

The validity of the IBS scales is presently based on their relations with a number of other self-report scales. In general, these relations are in the expected direction and thus support the scales' validities. For example, the General Assertiveness, Rational scale (SGR) correlated .47 with the Dominance scale of the California Psychological Inventory in a sample of college students. The SGR also correlated .63 with the Dominance scale of the Edwards Personal Preference Schedule (EPPS) in a sample of guidance graduate students, .64 with the College Self-Expression Scale, and .45 with the Assertion score of the Conflict Resolution Inventory. In terms of the SGR's discriminant validity, it was found to have minimal correlations with the Aggression scales of the Buss-Durkee Hostility Inventory (BDHI), the Interpersonal Check List (ICL), and the EPPS. The General Aggressiveness, Rational (GGR) scale correlated .57 with the Aggression scale of the EPPS, .47 with the Aggression scale of the ICL, and .65 with the Total Hostility scale of the BDHI. The discriminant validity of the GGR scale is shown by the lack of sizable correlations with the scales discussed above measuring assertiveness.

Taking these findings as a whole, a tentative conclusion is that the IBS generally has good reliability and internal consistency. Further studies suggest that the IBS scales are valid measures of aggressiveness and assertiveness. However, thus far the evidence for IBS validity is based on correlations with other self-report measures; what is now needed are studies to discover whether the aggressiveness and assertiveness scales are significantly related to observed aggressive and assertive behaviors respectively and not merely to other self-report measures. At present, this is where the IBS scales most need empirical verification.

There are a total of 272 items in the IBS. Clear instructions are provided, and the items consist of relatively brief statements that are answered using a true-false format. Items were written in everyday language and in the present tense, and require no more than a 6th-grade reading level so that a broad range of populations can be assessed. To guard against biases due to sex-role stereotypes, sexist language was avoided in the writing of the IBS items. One potential problem with the scale items is that in six of the scales there is an imbalance (25% vs. 75%) in the number of items scored in the true versus false direction. This imbalance in the number of true and false items measuring the presence or absence of a behavioral tendency makes those six scales (Physical Aggressiveness, Self-Confidence, Praise, Refusing Demands, Conflict Avoidance, and Dependency) more susceptible to response sets by subjects.

The results of an investigation of the effects of age, sex, race, and socioeconomic class on the IBS scales has turned up response differences. For example, subjects from the lower socioeconomic level score higher than those from the middle socioeconomic level on two aggressiveness scales, and the reverse is true on most of the assertiveness scales. Because of these demographic differences, special norms may need to be used for the scales most susceptible to these effects. The authors discuss this possibility in the manual and appear to be cognizant that additional research is needed here.

SUMMARY. The scales comprising the survey generally have good reliability and adequate convergent and discriminant validity with established assertiveness and aggression measures. The authors have taken care in scale construction and have conducted a number of studies to test its reliability and validity. While there are still some questions left unanswered about the IBS, particularly the number of separate scales measuring different types of assertive and aggressive behaviors, available data indicate it should be a useful instrument in the study of these two general behavioral categories.

Review of Interpersonal Behavior Survey by ROBERT R. HUTZELL, Clinical Psychologist, Veterans Administration Medical Center, Knoxville, IA:

The Interpersonal Behavior Survey (IBS) is a true/false, self-report inventory developed to assess assertiveness and aggressiveness as separate behavior classes. In addition to general assertiveness and general aggressiveness scores, the inventory measures subclasses of assertiveness, subclasses of aggressiveness, components of interpersonal relationship style, and types of instrument validity.

The IBS Administration Booklet is divided into three parts, with Part I alone or Part I + II constituting shorter versions of some of the scales. Part I (items 1–38) requires less than 10 minutes to complete and incorporates one validity scale, the short version of a general assertiveness scale, and the short version of a general aggressiveness scale. Part I + II (items 1–133) requires less than 1/2 hour and allows scoring of either the short or long version of all nine assertiveness scales, seven of the eight aggressiveness scales, two of the three validity scales, but none of the relationship scales. Completion of all three parts (all 272 items) requires roughly 45 minutes and allows full scoring of all the survey scales.

In many ways, the IBS reflects the current nature of the field; since 1970 assertion has received substantial clinical and experimental attention, yet many basic issues remain unresolved and not even a universally agreed upon definition of assertion has been established. The IBS scales apparently were developed and expanded through theses and dissertations using a variety of methods that are not adequately documented in the manual. Some of the scales were developed rationally, some empirically, and some through factor analysis. Some of the scales have considerable item overlap.

The IBS is distinct from the bulk of the paper-and-pencil assertion inventories available to date in several respects. First, many assertion scales confound assertion and aggression while others appear to measure only assertion and leave it to the test administrator to deal with the issue of aggression; but the authors of the IBS have recognized the importance of developing comparable measures of assertion and aggression. Second, the IBS subclasses of assertion and aggression reflect our current knowledge that neither assertion nor aggression are unidimensional. Third, while most assertion scales have been designed for use with rather limited populations, the IBS was designed for more universal use. Fourth, and viewed here as a deficit, the IBS appears to have been developed from the trait theory of assertion/aggression while the situation-specific theory, often underlying other assertion inventories, appears the most tenable explanation of assertion/aggression in the current literature. Last, the length of the full IBS is substantially greater than that of many other assertion inventories. (Although 10 of the IBS scales have short versions, half of those short versions are only one to three items shorter than their long version.)

The currently available information appears to support the reliability of the IBS. Internal consistency coefficients (coefficient alpha) are reasonable, though not exceptional, ranging from .52 to .88 ($M=.71$) for the full versions of the scales at cross-validation. Test-retest reliability information is encouraging, with correlations ranging from .71 to .96 ($M=.89$) at a 2-day inter-test interval and from .80 to .93 ($M=.89$) at a 10-week interval. Differences between scale means from first to second testing did not show statistical significance.

On the other hand, there are three noteworthy problems with the reliability information currently available. First, some of the full version scales and all three relationship scales are omitted from most of the reliability data. Second, all reliability estimates are limited to college student samples. Third, based upon standard error of measurement calculations from the reliability data, the authors suggest that a *T* score differing by more than 5 points from a previous *T* score for the same scale should be considered evidence of behavioral change. Yet, many of the scales are composed of very few items (range: 6 to 55 items for full version scales) and a change of 5 or more *T*-score points is produced by a change of only 1 raw-score point. (In the case of one scale, an increase of 2 raw-score points can move the respondent's score from approximately the 25th percentile to approximately the 75th percentile.)

Validation of the IBS has followed three directions, but as with the reliability data, the validity data often do not include the complete IBS or other necessary information. Factor analytic investigation appears to support the premise that the IBS scales of assertion and aggression evaluate separate response classes. A second method of validation, investigation of the correlation of IBS scores with the scores of other personality, assertiveness, and aggressiveness inventories, is presented more thoroughly in the manual than other validity data; the overall results suggest a reasonable degree of empirical validity as well as construct validity for many of the IBS scales. A third method of validation, concurrent validation of some of the IBS scales against 42 specified subject groups (e.g., lacrosse players, assaultive prisoners, students faking good, psychiatric inpatients), has been conducted, but the results are presented in too incomplete a manner to be useful at this time. Validation of the IBS against behavioral criteria is conspicuously absent, and such validation is indispensable because we know that individuals may possess an assertive behavioral repertoire and yet behave unassertively.

A relatively large section of the IBS manual is devoted to the interpretation and use of the IBS profile. Raw-score means and standard deviations for many (but not all) scales are presented for community residents, college students, community and college-student black persons, and high school students. *T*-score equivalents and percentiles are available for female community residents and for male community residents. The discussion of profile validity/invalidity is clear and particularly useful. The discussion of profile interpretation can help test interpreters to develop quite plausible descriptions of the IBS respondents, but before the descriptions can be accepted there must be substantial additional validation work.

In sum, considerable work has gone into the development of the IBS. Its assets include the minimal time requirements for several of the scale's short versions, inclusion of potentially relevant relationship scales and instrument validity scales, the distinction of assertion from aggression, assessment of subclasses of assertion and aggression, non-restriction to a single target population, and some data which suggest a reasonable degree of reliability and validity. Its deficits include its apparent adherence to a trait model of assertion when the situation-specific model appears more tenable, its overall length (if the complete IBS is administered), the large quantity of reliability and validity data missing from the manual, the lack of behavioral validation, and the lack of validity information regarding profile interpretation.

As a psychometric instrument, it is clear that considerable research on the IBS remains to be completed and published. On the other hand, potential consumers of assertion instruments will find that the IBS has been constructed and documented more carefully than the bulk of paper-and-pencil and behavioral assertion assessment devices available today. It is this author's recommendation that persons who will be selecting an assertion assessment instrument give favorable initial consideration to the IBS, comparing it with the alternative assertion instruments before making the decision as to which to select for their specific situation. It is this author's recommendation that the IBS developers settle upon a working version of the IBS and gather thorough information on the reliability, validity, and interpretation of that version; the end-product will be an updated and more complete IBS Manual.

[519]

Interpersonal Conflict Scale. Adults; 1981; experimental edition; "designed for the reporting of perceived feelings to statements about spouse behavior"; 8 scores: agreement in thinking, communication, disagreement in behavior, perception of the other's feelings, companionship and sharing, emotional satisfaction, security, recognition; tentative norms; one 80-item form (4 pages) and two alternate 40-item forms (2 pages), separate forms for males and females; teacher's and counselor's guide (12 pages); 1984 price data: $5 per 5 female and 5 male copies of any form; $4 per specimen set; (10–15) minutes; Carol Hoskins and Philip Merrifield; Family Life Publications, Inc.*

Review of Interpersonal Conflict Scale by STANLEY R. STRONG, Professor of Psychology, Virginia Commonwealth University, Richmond, VA:

The Interpersonal Conflict Scale (ICS) is intended to identify marital partners' specific areas of lack of need fulfillment, conceptually linked by the authors to areas of conflict in marital interactions. The authors state that use of the ICS decreases the time necessary to identify areas of lack of need fulfillment and conflict in marital counseling and focuses discussion in counseling on highly specific aspects of the marital relationship where better understanding and communication are needed.

The manual of the ICS presents no validity information supporting possible facilitative effects of the use of the ICS in counseling beyond their apparent clinical belief that it does so. All of the reliability and validity data presented stem from one study in which 52 persons took the ICS twice in one day, along with the Locke and Wallace Marital Adjustment Scale. In that study, the test-retest reliabilities of the eight scales of the ICS were reasonably high. Based on a two-factor solution of the matrix of intercorrelations of the scale scores, the eight scales were assigned to two combination scales labeled Interaction and Emotional Needs. Rudimentary norms based on the 52 persons are presented for scores on the two combination scales. The two combination scales are rather highly intercorrelated, making their separate use questionable. Unfortunately, many of the eight basic scales are also rather highly intercorrelated, raising questions about their individual use in identifying specific areas of lack of need fulfillment and conflict. Internal consistency reliability for individual scales would be important to the recommended use of the scale scores as indicants of specific areas of a lack of need fulfillment and conflict, but none is presented.

Beyond the content of the items, the only evidence for the validity of the ICS is the relationships of the two combination scales to the Locke and Wallace Marital Adjustment Scale, which are reasonably high. Relationships of the eight basic scales to the Locke and Wallace test are not presented. The interpretation of the two combination scales is based on their discrimination of high and low scorers on the Locke and Wallace test. Just how the distribution of scores on the Locke and Wallace was divided into high and low score groups is not presented.

The authors do not present enough information about the psychometric characteristics of the ICS, its validity in identifying areas of need and conflict, or the utility of using the ICS in counseling to recommend it for use in marital counseling. The preliminary results of the study the authors present suggest that the ICS may be worthy of further research to establish its psychometric characteristics and validity for use in marital counseling.

[520]

Interpersonal Language Skills Assessment: A Test of Pragmatic Behaviors, Preliminary Version. Ages 8–14; 1983; ILSA; "a system for structured observation of the interpersonal language skills of individual youngsters" while playing a standard table game; group must consist of 3 or 4 players who know each other; players must be of the same sex and should be at similar level of overall functioning; 3 scores: negation, inadequate communication, complex comments; no data on reliability and validity; tentative norms consist of means only; 1 form (6 pages); transcript form (2 pages); manual (83 pages); tape recorder necessary for sample of interpersonal communication; price data available from publisher; (15–30) minutes; Carolyn M. Blagden and Nancy L. McConnell; LinguiSystems, Inc.*

[521]

Interpersonal Style Inventory. High school and college and adults; 1977–82; ISI; 15 scores: directive-nondirective, sociable-detached, help seeking-self sufficient, nurturant-withholding, conscientious-expedient, trusting-cynical, tolerant-hostile, sensitive-lacks awareness, independent-conforming, rule free-rule bound, deliberate-impulsive, orderly-casual, persistent-lacks perseverance, stable/relaxed-anxious, approval seeking-admits frailties; norms for college students only; Form E ('77, 9 pages); manual ('82, 49 pages); separate answer sheets must be used; 1982 price data: $9.50 per 25 reusable booklets; $4.50 per 50 answer sheets; $2.50 per manual; $3.30 per specimen set; (40–50) minutes; Maurice Lorr and Richard P. Youniss; Maurice Lorr.*

See T3:1173 (1 reference).

Review of Interpersonal Style Inventory by JOHN DUCKITT, Chief Researcher, Institute for Sociological and Demographic Research, Human Sciences Research Council, Pretoria, South Africa:

The Interpersonal Style Inventory (ISI) is designed to describe personality in terms of 15 bipolar trait dimensions of self-report. In fact, the title is something of a misnomer. Five of the scales are concerned with traits such as anxiety and impulse control, and in general the interpersonal emphasis is not notably greater than in comparable personality inventories. Why these particular 15 traits are regarded as appropriate and adequate to represent the domain of human personality is, apart from a cursory reference to Murray's needs and "research on the interpersonal circle," never clarified. However, this lack of an explicit theoretical rationale is, of course, by no means peculiar to the ISI. On balance, despite a manual and test materials so plagued with errors and deficiencies that their publication must be regarded as premature, preliminary indications are that the ISI does not compare unfavourably in terms of its basic psychometric properties with highly sophisticated inventories designed along similar lines such as the Personality Research Form and Jackson Personality Inventory.

Each of the 15 component scales are composed of 20 items with equal numbers keyed for true and false responses to suppress the effect of acquiescence. In general, the formulation of the items is clear and straightforward and appears to conform adequately to the scale definitions. However, at least three items (numbers 17, 30 and 73) in the question booklet are marred by errors of a magnitude sufficient to cause irritation or even confusion to respondents (e.g., item 30 reads "I have cheated a little at sometime when at school"). In addition, the print becomes somewhat indistinct at times and item 282 was barely decipherable in the booklet provided for review. The separate answer sheets are hand-scored without a template, with the items sequenced such that each scale is scored from two rows with false responses only counted in one and true in the other. Scoring in this way did require a good deal of concentration, however, and the provision of a template would seem to be advisable.

One of the 15 scales is a Marlow-Crowne type social desirability scale (termed Approval-Seeking). Apart from being regarded as a personality dimension of interest in its own right, it is suggested that *T* scores of over 70 on this scale be suspect for faking good and rejection of the protocol considered. No empirical basis, however, is cited for the efficacy of this cutoff point, nor is there any discussion of the possibility of faking bad. On the basis of several factor analytical studies, the 15 scales group neatly and usefully into five broader second-order constructs (Interpersonal involvement, Socialization, Autonomy, Control, and Stability). The primary scales are grouped according to these second-order factors on the profile sheet, which also automatically expresses entered raw scores in the form of *T* scores. The *T* scores are derived from normative samples of 354 male and 411 female college students from "12 diverse settings." Although the manual describes a second set of norms for high school students no norm tables are provided for this sample and it would seem that this data was collected with an earlier form of the ISI (Form D). The manual unfortunately does not report the score distributions for the normative student sample. However, the maximum *T* scores for certain scales tend to be rather low (e.g., amongst females it is only 62 for Persistence), suggesting quite skewed distributions. It is not clear whether this reflects the limited nature of the normative samples or rather low ceilings for certain scales.

The ISI was developed through a series of studies and revisions. Initially, items to measure the carefully defined constructs were generated according to a number of criteria. These included an endorsement frequency of between 10 and 90%, rated fidelity to scale definitions, and judged social desirabilities within a moderate range which balanced out over each scale. Finally, four major factor analytical studies were conducted using small item parcels, half scales, or quarter scales. These studies indicated excellent factorial stability of the primary factors. Scale intercorrelations reported for the normative samples also confirm that the scales are substantially independent of each other, with no intercorrelations greater than .50 and the mean intercorrelation between all scales (with sign disregarded) being .21 for both men and women.

The attempt to suppress social desirability response bias would also appear to have been successful. The mean correlation of scales with the ISI's own social desirability scale was only .24 (with sign disregarded). The scale reliabilities also appear to be excellent. Alpha coefficients are given separately for men and women, and of the 30 coefficients only that for Approval-Seeking (for the female sample) sinks marginally below .70, with most being above .80. Mean alphas are .82 for both men and women. The test-retest stabilities over a 2-week period ranged from .80 to .95, with a mean of .87.

Several sources of evidence for the validity of the ISI scales are described in the manual. One of these sources consists of correlations between the ISI scales and a number of other self-report inventories and does by and large reveal a pattern of associations consistent with the conceptualization of these scales. However, strictly speaking, this data is probably better regarded as clarifying the labels and meanings attached to scales than as establishing validity per se. Much more pertinent to the issue of validity are a series of studies described in the manual in which the ISI was used to differentiate various groups of interest. Some of these findings, such as a substantial difference between the mean Rule-Free scale scores of left-wing political activists and a norm group (r $=.74$), seem clearly supportive of scale validities. In most cases, however, the validity implications of these studies are not as clear. The interpretation of the findings often seems to be post hoc. Findings are reported extremely cursorily, sometimes only by discriminant function analyses. Some negative findings seem to be glossed over (e.g., Nurturance did not predict the frequency of altruistic acts). In several cases the citations in the text for what appear to be unpublished studies, do not even appear in the reference list.

Finally, the mean correlation of the ISI scales with self-ratings in two samples were .54 and .55 (ranging from .26 to .77), and correlations with peer ratings varied from .21 to .57 with a mean of .41. However, although these coefficients, in general, seem reasonable, remarkably little information about these unpublished studies is given in the manual. Not even the sample size for the peer rating study is specified. This makes it rather difficult to evaluate how much reliance can be placed on these findings. Moreover, since only the correlation of each scale with its equivalent self or peer rating is given, an assessment of discriminant validities is not possible.

Overall, although some findings seem reasonably promising, the validity of the ISI at present remains largely an unanswered question. For this reason, and because of its limited normative base, it cannot yet be recommended for applications such as counselling which require the interpretation of individual test profiles. Nevertheless, its generally excellent psychometric properties suggest that it should have promise as a research instrument. The immediate priority, however, would appear to be a thorough-going revision of the manual and careful editing of the test materials prior to their reissue.

Review of Interpersonal Style Inventory by STUART A. KARABENICK, Professor of Psychology, Eastern Michigan University, Ypsilanti, MI:

The Interpersonal Style Inventory (ISI) represents the culmination of nearly two decades of development by Lorr and his associates (e.g., Lorr, 1975; Lorr & McNair, 1963, 1965; Lorr, O'Connor, & Siefert, 1977; Lorr & Youniss, 1973). It is a rationally and empirically constructed instrument based on the "interpersonal circle" by which qualitatively different traits are rank orderable without a beginning or end point—in other words, a closed sequence of ordered variables. Similar to other rationally constructed devices, the set of traits is derived from Murray's need system. The ISI focuses primarily on interpersonal behavior styles in a variety of social situations, but it includes scales to measure impulse control and "characteristic modes of dealing with work and play." The stress is on normal traits, but an emotional stability dimension is included.

There are 14 bipolar dimensions and a social approval (lie) scale, each with 20 statements and each balanced for acquiescence. There are five higher-order derived dimensions: (1) Interpersonally Involved vs. Interpersonally Avoidant; (2) Socialized vs. Unsocialized; (3) Autonomous vs. Dependent; (4) Organized/Controlled vs. Impulsive Expressive; and (5) Stable vs. Anxious.

The current form (E) is the latest in a series of four revisions. Its true/false response format makes it easy to administer compared to the Edwards Personal Preference Schedule (EPPS), for example, and the manual claims there have been no problems of administration with ages from 14 to 84 years. The 300 items require approximately 45 minutes to complete. Scoring is simplified in that scale items are repeated in the same sequence throughout the inventory.

The manual describes its potential uses as (1) self-insight, especially with regard to an individual's behavior in social settings; (2) counseling and therapy for diagnosis, structuring of individual and group therapy, and as a supplement to "standard measures of behavior disturbance"; (3) personnel guidance (assuming cooperative clients); and (4) research. The ISI is considered preferable for research in comparison to criterion-derived devices by virtue of its rational scale construction, homogeneous scale content, and exhaustivity of dimensions, at least in the interpersonal domain.

The manual presents an elementary guide to the use and interpretation of scores and profiles with all of the necessary normative data for T-score conversions. Two sets of norms (college and high school) are presumably available for this purpose but only the college norms (411 women and 354 men in 12 diverse settings) are presented, separately for men and women. The college sample was used to demonstrate a high level of reliability. Scale homogeneity (alpha) estimates range from .68 (Defensiveness) to .89 (Help-seeking) for women and from .72 (Defensiveness) to .89 (Help-seeking and Directive) for men, with a mean over all scales and sexes of .82, which is comparable to other similar inventories (e.g., the Personality Research Form [PRF], with split-half reliabilities from .50–.89).

Much of the manual is devoted to scale construction and construct and criterion validity. Several studies, each with credible samples (generally above 200 of each sex) are reported which document the theoretical basis for item selection, initial item generation, factor structure, and profile differences between selected criterion groups. Scale construction followed 11 steps: (1) dimensions selected "to represent the domain of interpersonal behavior" with the addition of dimensions concerned with impulse expression and control and emotional stability; (2) constructs formulated as to appropriate behaviors, attitudes, beliefs, and stimulus situations that elicit the behaviors; (3) item generation—including stress on simplicity of language, unidimensional representation, and intermediate endorsement level; (4) item refinement by inspection—by five graduate students; (5) equalization of response key to reduce acquiescence bias; (6) scales balanced to provide a moderate level of social desirability (mean=5.0 on a 9-point scale) on each; (7) creation of a social desirability scale; (8) selection of 10 true and 10 false keyed items for each scale; (9) scale refinement over a series of four studies; (10) internal consistency and stability estimation; (11) generation of norms.

Most of the information on development that is briefly summarized in the manual is available elsewhere in published form. The factor analyses used principal components, Cattell's scree test to determine factor retention, and Varimax rotation. Analyses use subscale (half or quarter) rather than items to increase reliability. Scale development is not always easy to follow because the number and content of scales change in successive forms. No rationale is given for these successive inclusions and exclusions.

Concurrent validity is established by relations with other inventories with similar dimensional properties, including the Eysenck Personality Inventory (EPI), 16 Personality Factor Questionnaire (16PF), Orientation and Motivation Inventory (OMI), Defense Mechanism Inventory (DMI), Washington Sentence Completion Test (SCT), Bentler Personality Inventory (BPI), Jackson Personality Inventory (JPI), Comrey's Personality Scale (CPS), and the EPPS. Several expected relationships between scales are documented along with complete tables of correlations of the ISI with 16PF, OMI, and DMI scores. The major study reported in this section summarizes Lorr, et al. (1977), which compares the ISI (Form C), Jackson's PRF, the CPS (see above), and the EPPS. After converting each inventory to ISI response format, they were independently factor analyzed, the 11 to 16 factors obtained were then used to derive scale scores that were, in turn, factor analyzed. The ISI loaded on each of the 12 derived factors, of which 9 are included in the current form (E). By comparison, the PRF loaded on 9 of the factors in the college sample, the CPS 6, and 5 for the EPPS.

Another comparison between the ISI and the BPI, JPI, Edwards Personality Inventories, and a set of Factor-Referenced Temperament Scales is presented in the manual but no data are presented. Instead, the "author and a colleague" inspected the inventories and provide judgments that each ISI (Form E) scale is equivalent in item content to at least one scale on one of the other inventories.

The manual reports several criterion validity studies that are summarized with differing levels of detail. These report successful attempts at differentiating between criterion groups "in expected directions." It must be noted that some of the studies use earlier forms of the ISI and may not bear directly on the present form.

A single convergent validity study compared self and peer ratings with ISI scale scores using a self-rating form of the ISI composed of phrase pairs that describe each pole of the bipolar dimensions. Two samples of college students (total $N=109$) rated themselves and each other. Correlations between ISI scale scores and self-ratings range from .33 (Conscientious) to .76 (Orderly), averaged across samples, with a mean of .55. Peer rating correlations range from .21 (Trusting) to .57 (both Sociable and Persistent), with a mean of .41. No significance levels are given.

To summarize, the ISI is rationally based on a circular ordering of interpersonal and style dimensions derived in part from Murray's system of needs. It appears comparable in reliability to other similarly constructed inventories. There is reasonable evidence of convergent validity based on self and peer ratings, and some evidence to indicate that criterion groups are differentiated on a number of ISI dimensions. The same form can be administered to a wide age range, and scoring is simplified. The manual is for the most part readable, although some sections (describing test development) are unclear. Thus, the ISI might be recommended for the purposes that the author suggests. Nevertheless, some points should be noted. First, the inventory has been through several forms, and much of the evidence for its psychometric properties is based on earlier forms. Thus, some of the dimensions have received more thorough examination than others. Second, there is considerable overlap among the ISI and similarly constructed inventories. We might agree with Lorr, et al. (1977) that it is desirable to have "a set of standard reference measures of personality dimensions" for basic and applied research. However, why the ISI should be preferred over other measures is a question that remains to be answered. About the only evidence we have relating to this issue is that the ISI (Form C at least) loaded more exhaustively in a factor analytical study than inventories of similar construction and dimensionality. Given that we have available a set of inventories all of which have acceptable reliability and concurrent validity (in the sense of comparisons with other similar inventories), what is needed are studies that compare criterion validity. One advantage of the ISI is its focus on the interpersonal domain. Its greatest liability at the present time would appear to be that even after many years of development more data are required before recommending the ISI over similar inventories currently available (e.g., the PRF or EPPS).

REVIEWER'S REFERENCES

Lorr, M., & McNair, D. M. An interpersonal behavior circle. JOURNAL OF ABNORMAL AND SOCIAL PSYCHOLOGY, 1963, 67, 68–75.

Lorr, M., & McNair, D. M. Expansion of the interpersonal behavior circle. JOURNAL OF PERSONALITY AND SOCIAL PSYCHOLOGY, 1965, 2, 823–830.

Lorr, M., & Youniss, R. P. An inventory of interpersonal style. JOURNAL OF PERSONALITY ASSESSMENT, 1973, 37, 165–173.

Lorr, M., O'Connor, J. P., & Seifert, R. F. A comparison of four personality inventories. JOURNAL OF PERSONALITY ASSESSMENT, 1977, 41, 520–516.

[522]

Intrex Questionnaires. Psychiatric patients; 1980–83; to measur the patient's perceptions of self and others; based on trait x state x situation philosophy and Structural Analysis of Social Behavior (SASB); test is one of several services available at cost to health care providers; 8 cluster scores in each of 3 areas: focus on others, focus on self, introjection; 7 subtests: Introject—Best, Introject—Worst; Significant Other Person—Best, Significant Other Person—Worst, Mother When Rater Was Aged 5–10, Father When Rater Was Aged 5–10, Mother and Father When Rater Was Aged 5–10, ('80–'83, 12–23 pages); user's manual ('83, 44 pages); answer sheets ('80–'83, 12 pages); price data available from publisher; scoring services and computer programs for local scoring and interpretation are available; 5–8 hours for complete battery; Lorna S. Benjamin; Intrex Interpersonal Institute.*

[523]

Intuitive Mechanics (Weights & Pulleys). Engineering students and industrial workers; 1956–59; ability to visualize internal movement or displacement of parts; limited reliability and validity data; 1 form ('56, 3 pages); manual ('59, 9 pages); scoring key ('59, 3 pages); 1982 price data: $4 per 20 test booklets; scoring key free; $1.50 per manual; $3 per specimen set; (3) minutes; L. L. Thurstone and T. E. Jeffrey; Human Resources Center, The University of Chicago.*

Review of Intuitive Mechanics (Weights & Pulleys) by WILLIAM A. OWENS, Director, Institute for Behavioral Research, The University of Georgia, Athens, GA:

Intuitive Mechanics (Weights & Pulleys) is a paper-and-pencil test designed to measure mechanical aptitude or comprehension. The test booklet contains one page of instructions and examples and two pages of test items, 16 per page. The items themselves are line drawings involving various arrangements of weights and pulleys to be judged as either stable or unstable on the basis of whether the system would move or remain stationary if "released." A subject responds to a given problem by placing an "X" on the test booklet in one of two parentheses beneath the problem. The test is timed and is, thus, a measure of the speed and accuracy with which a subject can visualize movement, or its absence, within a configuration.

Test format and directions are clear and unambiguous; three examples are provided and these seem representative. The manual is clearly written and no special sophistication is required of the examiner. Testing time is three minutes, and total time for administration is estimated at six minutes. The scoring key is a template in test format with holes punched where correct responses should appear.

In his factorial study of mechanical aptitude Thurstone identified five factors, one of which requires the subject to visualize the movement of parts or elements within a configuration. According to the authors, Weights and Pulleys was especially developed to measure this factor. Unfortunately, no data are provided regarding the criteria for item selection or the correlation of either test scores or factor scores with any external criterion or criteria. It is thus difficult to evaluate the success of the development effort.

In relation to reliability, the authors cite estimates of .60 and .85 for two shorter forms of the test given to engineering freshmen. However, the nature of these estimates is not specified. Clearly, any internal estimate would be inflated by the substantial speeding involved; whereas, alternatively, no time interval is stated to imply a retest or parallel forms estimate. Overall, it must be apparent that the authors have simply not presented adequate data to permit a fair evaluation of test reliability.

With respect to the all-important issue of validity, the manual contains only a lone reported correlation of .40 between Weights and Pulleys and a companion test known as Mechanical Movements. This fragmentary implication of some construct validity is the only evidence cited, and must be regarded as clearly inadequate.

A table for converting raw scores to normalized standard scores is provided based on a sample of over 900 persons of mixed occupational affiliation. Both the conversion and the qualitative interpretation of score levels are well addressed, but the mixed norms offer clear ambiguities in evaluating the score of a member of a particular occupational group.

In summary, some vital questions regarding the basic validity and reliability of Weights and Pulleys remain to be answered, other than inferentially. Until this has been done the test must necessarily be accorded a more restricted endorsement than can be rendered to such well documented devices as Bennett's Tests of Mechanical Comprehension.

[524]

Inventory of Individually Perceived Group Cohesiveness. Group members grades 5 and over; 1979–80; IIPGC; "self-report, 20-item measure of an individual's perceptions of cooperation, control and task influence processes operating in a group"; 4 scores: cooperation, control, task influence, total; no norms in manual; 1 form ('79, 2 pages); manual ('80, 8 pages); 1984 price data: $13.25 per complete set including 30 record form and feedback sheets; $7.50 per 30 record form and feedback sheets; $6.50 per manual; 15(20) minutes prior to and/or immediately after any type of group session; David L. Johnson; Stoelting Co.*

Review of Inventory of Individually Perceived Group Cohesiveness by GEORGE W. HOWE, Assistant Professor of Psychology, Department of Psychology and Human Development, Peabody College of Vanderbilt University, Nashville, TN:

The Inventory of Individually Perceived Group Cohesiveness (IIPGC) is a 20-item measure asking people who have just participated in a group discussion to rate that group concerning its emphasis on a variety of domains, including "discussion," "different ideas," "involvement," and "setting priorities." Scores are summed to provide an overall index of perceived group cohesiveness and three subscale indices of what the authors label "influence regarding the task," "cooperation," and "expectational control." While the measure is designed as a self-report instrument, the authors report using it as a rating form for independent observers, although they report no evidence for interrater agreement. The authors give no explicit definition of the general construct of cohesiveness, or of the three subscale components; nor do they provide any theoretical framework as context for such definitions.

In searching the Social Science Citation Index from 1974 through April, 1984, I could find no published study using the IIPGC, other than that which introduced the measure (Johnson & Ridener, 1974). The Instruction Manual and an unpublished technical report (Johnson, 1977) report IIPGC scores from 177 people participating in 27 groups; however, the participants and groups were extremely heterogeneous, ranging from a group of 10 third graders in a Brownie troop to a small professional staff of three in a Family Service agency who had been meeting together weekly for 6 months prior to data collection. Meaningful norms based on a stable and clearly defined population are therefore not available. I would also question whether the general idea of "group cohesion" can be meaningfully applied in the same way across such a diverse range of group situations. No test-retest coefficients are available to provide evidence for stability of the measure, although the authors inappropriately attempt to interpret insignificant changes in group means as evidence for stability.

Evidence for validity of the measure is almost nonexistent. While a number of the studies reported in the technical report include independent ratings of cohesion by observers, no data are presented on how well these ratings related to IIPGC ratings by group members. The original study, using measures of self disclosure and behavioral observation of group interaction with three groups of 23 undergraduates, provided some minimal evidence of measure validity, showing the IIPGC correlated substantially with the self-report measure of self disclosure, and that observations of self-initiated participation correlated with IIPGC scores for males, though not for females (Johnson & Ridener, 1974). This study also found evidence of internal consistency for the measure, reporting a reliability coefficient of .90. This level of internal consistency may easily be due to halo effect or social desirability response set, which have yet to be ruled out. This is consistent with the author's anecdotal report in the technical manual that group members across studies tended to rate the groups as more cohesive than did independent observers (Johnson, 1977).

Given the absence of clear construct definition, and the extremely minimal evidence concerning reliability and validity, I suggest this measure be considered as having little more than face validity at present. It may have some limited value as a tool for focusing group discussion around group process, but has no valid use as an assessment instrument.

REVIEWER'S REFERENCES

Johnson, D. L., & Ridener, L. Self-disclosure, participation, and perceived cohesiveness in small group interaction. PSYCHOLOGICAL REPORTS, 1974, 35, 65–66.

Johnson, D. L. TECHNICAL REPORT, Number 2, Summary of Field Studies and Uses of Inventory of Individually Perceived Group Cohesiveness (IIPGC). Institute of Human Resources, 1977. Available from Stoelting Co.

Review of Inventory of Individually Perceived Group Cohesiveness by ANDREW F. NEWCOMB, Assistant Professor of Psychology, University of Richmond, Richmond, VA:

The first, and possibly most important, comment that can be made about this test is the lack of information available about the instrument. The test is accompanied by only a five-page manual—seven pages if you count the sample answer sheets.

The test consists of a 20-item, self-report measure that is purported to assess the respondent's perceptions of cooperation, control, and task influence in group interaction. Unfortunately, an especially meager amount of information is provided on the rationale of the instrument and the selection of the test items. For example, no report is made of the internal consistency of these respective scales nor of their relative independence. Equally problematic is the author's contention that the total score on the instrument is presumed to reflect a measure of group cohesiveness. First, the three scales of cooperation, control, and task influence consist of 7, 5, and 8 items, respectively, and therefore make disproportionate contributions to a total group cohesiveness score. Second, little rationale is provided as to why the sum of these three measures is indicative of group cohesiveness.

Although the test author offers a one paragraph "opinion" to the contrary, it appears that the IIPGC may reflect little more than a 20-item measure of interpersonal attraction. The author provides very limited support for the validity of the three subscales and the overall group cohesiveness scale. Most importantly, no evidence is provided that the instrument assesses group processes independent of interpersonal attraction.

Information on the reliability of the instrument is equally limited. Five studies are reported in which a total of 23 subjects ranging in mean age from 16.3 to 58.3 years served as participants. Due to the small sample size in each study (range of 3 to 7 subjects), *t*-tests for correlated samples were used to assess test-retest reliability and no significant differences were reported. The absence of test-retest differences based on this methodology is not very surprising in light of the limited power provided by the small sample size and the relatively large standard deviations associated with many of the group scores. What was surprising was the report of a "KR 20 split-half reliability estimate." First, the application of this procedure seems unusual as dichotomous data does not result from the scoring procedures recommended by the test author, and the assignment of weights to response categories would appear awkward in the present circumstances. Second, the reported reliability coefficient of .90 for the entire test would appear to be contrary to what would be expected if the test did indeed assess the three independent domains of cooperation, control, and task influence. In fact, the large reliability coefficient is much more consistent with the notion that the test is assessing a single construct. Unfortunately, as noted previously, there is little indication as to what construct is being measured.

Normative information on the test is equally sparse. The test manual provides only a single paragraph summary of the various populations that the IIPGC has been used to study. Also included is a statement that "some interesting differences in total score, cooperation, control, and task influence scores across school-age, adult, and professional groups as well as differences among members', leaders', and observers' perceptions of cohesiveness have been reported." The reader is asked to compare this conclusion with a referenced technical report where a descriptive account of 22 studies with populations ranging from children to adults and sample sizes ranging from 3 to 14 is provided. Inasmuch as normative data is an essential component to the use of this test, the inclusion of this information in the test manual, with a 1979 copyright date, would appear to be not only appropriate but also necessary.

The test manual also includes two very brief and separate statements on the time of administration and the scoring of the test. Again these sections are far from informative and point out further weaknesses of the test. First, the author suggests that the test is "usually given to individual respondents either prior to and/or right after a group session." Unfortunately, this is the only instruction provided and no rationale is offered as to the relative merits of these different administration times or when in a series of group sessions this instrument should be employed. Second, the author suggests that scoring the test is a quick and easy process, yet no scoring templates are available. Third, in the section on scoring procedures, the author proposes that the test can be completed by "group members (fifth grade level up), trained observers, evaluators, and researchers." Not only does it appear that this information is misplaced in the manual, but no information is provided on the differential reliability of these different respondents.

In sum, the IIPGC appears to be a test with little more than a limited theoretical rationale and some suggestion of face validity. The internal consistency, independence, reliability, and validity of the three subscales has not been demonstrated nor has adequate reliability and validity information on the total group cohesiveness measure been obtained. Further administrative, scoring, and normative information is also required. Although the value of an instrument to assess the group processes of cooperation, control, and task influence as well as total group cohesiveness is not questioned, the value of the IIPGC in completing this task is quite questionable.

[525]

Inventory of Interests. Adolescents and adults; 1971; designed for use by counselors; ratings in 2 areas:

occupations, subjects for study; no data on reliability and validity; no norms; 1 form (8 pages); no manual; 1985 price data: $14.50 per 25 tests; $3.50 per specimen set; Spanish edition ('71) available; administration time not reported; Guidance Testing Associates.*

Review of Inventory of Interests by JAMES D. WIGGINS, Professor and Coordinator, Agency and School Counseling Programs, University of Delaware, Newark, DE:

The Inventory of Interests is divided into two main sections. The first lists 136 occupations under 14 headings that generally parallel divisions in the now-outdated 1965 *Dictionary of Occupational Titles*. The second section is strictly for persons interested in post-high school education and lists 56 majors. The Spanish Edition seems to be a direct translation of the English version.

It quickly becomes clear that the publisher's claim is true that the listings "are based on apparent relations among the occupations rather than on statistical evidence." A simple reading of occupations in the *Occupational Outlook Handbook* or in any commercially published source would provide as much, if not more, assistance. While the publisher (no authors are listed) may claim that the Inventory is for the counselor's use, this handicaps the competent interviewer who needs some psychometric assurance that there is some rational basis for using this instrument.

The occupational listings under the various headings are of unequal length, ranging from 21 under Craftsman to 6 under Operator of Machines. When the occupations were transposed to the commonly used Holland classification system, the problems with the Inventory become more apparent. By occupational area, there were 53 Realistic, 9 Investigative, 21 Artistic, 17 Social, 19 Enterprising, and 8 Conventional. The other 9 items could not be categorized. The chances of expressing an interest in skilled trades (Realistic) become high simply due to the large number of listings in that area, while scientific and service interests are virtually ignored. The relatively large number of choices in the Artistic area, where fewer than 3% of the population is employed, also seems to reflect the biases of the Inventory's authors.

The listings under the second section, Subjects for Study, correspond to similar ones found in many college guides. On both sections, responses to each item are expressed in a X–0–1–2 format, with the 0–1–2 responses ranging from no interest to strong interest in a specific occupation or subject for study. The X denotes not having enough information to express a like or dislike for the occupation. Responses are recorded in a confusing summary profile; I decoded the instructions with great effort.

The competent counselor can use simple interview techniques or locally-prepared instruments to obtain more comprehensive information than is offered by this outdated Inventory. For about the same cost, the Vocational Preference Inventory is definitely a better choice as it offers a psychometrically sound, theoretically based instrument. The Strong-Campbell Interest Inventory and The Self-Directed Search are more expensive but offer more explorational alternatives to students and counselors alike.

As no research is presented to show the effects of using the Inventory, it is presumed that they are unknown. No validity or reliability coefficients are available. Also, no gender-based data are available, but the large number of stereotypically male occupations listed should be another warning sign to the prospective user.

Finally, the sexist wording (salesman, fireman, and masculine pronouns) will be enough to keep most counselors from experimenting with the Inventory. Such wording would be easy to change but the total Inventory is deficient in many other ways. It is outdated, atheoretical, and limited in scope and cannot be recommended for use by students or counselors.

REVIEWER'S REFERENCES

Department of Labor. DICTIONARY OF OCCUPATIONAL TITLES. Washington, DC: U.S. Government Printing Office, 1965.

Department of Labor. OCCUPATIONAL OUTLOOK HANDBOOK. Washington, DC: U.S. Government Printing Office, 1982.

[526]

Inventory of Language Abilities. Grades K–2 and handicapped children in special classes; 1972; ILA; a component of the MWM Program for Developing Language Abilities; behavior checklists in 11 areas: auditory reception, visual reception, auditory association, visual association, verbal expression, manual expression, auditory memory, visual memory, grammatic closure, visual closure, auditory closure and sound blending; no data on validity and reliability; no norms; individual; 1 form; record booklet (16 pages including instructions for administration and scoring and profile); no manual; class grouping chart (1 page); 1984 price data: $15 per 25 inventories; administration time not reported; Esther H. Minskoff, Douglas E. Wiseman, and J. Gerald Minskoff; Educational Performance Associates, Inc.*

Review of Inventory of Language Abilities by RITA SLOAN BERNDT, Research Associate Professor, Department of Neurology, University of Maryland Medical School, Baltimore, MD:

DESCRIPTION. This instrument is not a test, "but rather a device for channelling the teacher's observations to behaviors relevant for screening possible language learning disabilities."

It consists of 11 checklists, each containing 12 examples of possible behaviors that a child could exhibit. Teachers simply go through the checklist for each child and note those that s/he has observed. Scoring is done by adding the number of checks for each checklist, with a (presumably arbitrary) cutoff of 50% for a determination of "possible learning disability" in that area.

CRITIQUE. This checklist system cries out for some documentation, but none is provided. On what basis were these items chosen? Is there any theoretical or empirical rationale for the selection of the items? How is the teacher supposed to interpret vague descriptions such as "often confuses different words" or "has difficulty matching pictures"? How often and how much difficulty? As a consequence of this poor specification, interrater reliability must be very low. No documentation of any kind of reliability is provided.

There are many specific problems with the items themselves. Some of them are useless without a specific test. An example is the item "Has difficulty learning abstract words (e.g., 'invisible'), but not words with visual representations." One hopes that anyone in the field of child language development knows that word frequency and word length (in syllables) are important factors in acquisition. Both of these tend to be highly correlated with concreteness. Without a specific test wherein words of different levels of concreteness are selected and matched on these other variables, no conclusions can be drawn about a child's difficulty in learning abstract vs. concrete words.

Other items are very peculiar and seem unlikely to be related to the presence of learning disabilities (e.g., doesn't observe changes such as change in teacher's hair color, doesn't recognize landmarks such as water fountain on the way to the bathroom). The authors may have some reason for including these kinds of items; if so, they should share them with the reader.

In conclusion, there are three major reasons that this instrument is without value as an informal screening for learning disabilities: (1) There is no evidence that these checklist items are related to the presence of learning disabilities. (2) The items themselves are so poorly conceived and specified that interrater or test-retest reliability would be expected to be very low. This is obviously of crucial importance if the instrument is to be of value. (3) A good classroom teacher does not need this checklist to determine that a child needs to have a formal screening for learning disabilities. Any teacher who cannot rely on his or her own observations and intuitions would probably have a difficult time applying this lengthy and cumbersome system.

[527]

Inventory of Perceptual Skills. Special education students; 1983; IPS; performance measure of visual and auditory skills for use in instructional planning; 11 scores: visual (discrimination, memory, object recognition, visual-motor coordination, total), auditory (discrimination, sequencing, memory, blending, total), total; no data on reliability; no norms; individual; student record booklet in 2 parts: part 1 filled by examiner (4 pages), part 2 filled by student (3 pages); stimulus cards (10 cards); instruction manual (18 pages); student workbook (19 pages); 1983 price data: $15 per complete kit including 10 student record booklets; $9 per 10 student record booklets; $2 per set of 10 stimulus cards; $1.50 per student workbook; $3 per instruction manual; (15) minutes; Donald R. O'Dell; Stoelting Co.*

[528]

Inventory of Self-Hypnosis. College and adults; 1978; adaptation of Harvard Group Scale of Hypnotic Susceptibility, Form A; self-administered instructions designed to teach self-hypnosis; 13 ratings: head falling, eye closure, lowering left hand, immobilization of right arm, finger lock, rigidity of left arm, hands moving together, inability to shake head, vivid imagining of a fly, eyelids glued shut, touching left ankle, blanketing fog, total; no data on reliability and validity; no norms; Form A plus instructions (29 pages); response sheet (1 page); separate answer sheets must be used; 1984 price data: $2 per inventory; $8.75 per 50 answer sheets; (60–90) minutes; Ronald E. Shor; Consulting Psychologists Press, Inc.*

Review of Inventory of Self Hypnosis by THOMAS R. COLEMAN, Director, Mental Health, Lafene Student Health Center, Kansas State University, and RODNEY K. GOODYEAR, Associate Professor of Counseling and Student Personnel Services, Kansas State University, Manhattan, KS:

The Inventory of Self-Hypnosis was developed to provide an empirical measure of hypnotic susceptibility when trance and subsequent suggestions are self-induced. The instructions and suggestions are an adaptation of the Harvard Group Scale of Hypnotic Susceptibility, Form A. The inventory manual addresses itself to the subject and gives step-by-step instructions which lead the subject into a trance state. Twelve suggestions including a post hypnotic suggestion are then self-administered and the subject reports his/her own responses to the suggestions. The inventory yields a single score of susceptibility. The subject is expected to keep track of time either by counting breaths or through the use of a timer. A description for the construction of the timer is provided in the back of the manual.

One of the major strengths of the inventory is that which is shared by its parent, the Harvard Group Scale, and its grandparent, the Stanford Hypnotic Susceptibility Scale, namely, that it provides a structured, standardized procedure by which responsiveness to hypnotic suggestion may be studied. This is the first and only such instrument for the objective study of self-hypnosis, and therein lies its usefulness.

Because of the close tie to the Harvard Group Scale, the author assumes that the validity and reliability established for the Harvard Scales can be applied to the Inventory of Self-Hypnosis and hence no reliability or validity data are provided. The assumption, however, is faulty because the measures and procedures used by the two scales are quite different. Although theory and some preliminary research suggests strong positive relationships between self and hetero hypnosis, one cannot equate the procedures used for induction or the methods of self-observation. The Harvard Group Scale requires the subject to attend to external source of direction and provide a self report, while the Inventory of Self-Hypnosis requires the subject to direct him/herself from within, while at the same time responding to the suggestions and then providing a self-report of responsiveness. The procedure used in the Inventory of Self-Hypnosis requires much more active involvement with several interruptions throughout the procedure, particularly if a timer is used. Thus, the self-hypnotic task is more complex, requiring the subject to assume several ego states at once: those of director, experiencer, and observer. Clearly, standardization norms and reliability and validity data are needed to enhance the credibility and thus the usefulness of this Inventory. When such norms are established, the inventory should prove helpful to those needing a standardized format with which to study self-hypnosis and suggestibility.

[529]

Inventory of Teacher Concerns. Teachers, 1981; behavior checklist for identifying student strengths and weaknesses; criterion-referenced; item scores only; no data on reliability and validity; no norms; 1 form (1 page); classroom inventory (1 page); directions for administration (9 pages); 1983 price data: $8.75 per complete set (includes 35 individual inventories, 1 classroom inventory, and directions for administration); administration time not reported; John W. Wick and Jeffrey K. Smith; American Testronics.*

[530]

Inwald Personality Inventory. Law enforcement applicants; 1980; IPI; behavioral characteristics and psychological fitness; 26 scales: Guardedness (GD), Rigidity (RT), Alcohol (AL), Drugs (DG), Substance Abuse (SA), Driving Violations (DV), Job Difficulties (JD), Trouble With Law & Society (TL), Antisocial Attitudes (AS), Hyperactivity (HP), Absence Abuse (AA), Illness Concerns (IC), Treatment Programs (TP), Anxiety (AN), Type "A" (TA), Phobic Personality (PH), Lack of Assertiveness (LA), Obsessive Personality (OB), Depression (DE), Loner Type (LO), Interpersonal Difficulties (ID), Family Conflicts (FC), Sexual Concerns (SC), Spouse/Mate Concerns (SP), Undue Suspiciousness (US), Bizarre Experiences/Thoughts (BE/BT); norms consist of means and standard deviations; 1 form ('80, 13 pages); manual ('83, 52 pages); separate answer sheets must be used; 1983 price data: $1.50 per test booklet; $9.50 per manual; $30 per specimen set; scoring service, $18.50 or less (prepaid answer sheets include processing fee); norms provided for over 100 cases scored; administration time not reported; Robin Inwald; Hilson Research Inc.*

Review of Inwald Personality Inventory by BRIAN BOLTON, Professor, Arkansas Rehabilitation Research and Training Center, University of Arkansas, Fayetteville, AR:

The Inwald Personality Inventory (IPI) was designed for the purpose of generating relevant information about the personality characteristics and behavioral patterns of candidates for positions in law enforcement occupations. The specific objective of the instrument is to contribute to the identification of unsuitable applicants for training as police officers, correction officers, and security guards. The author properly advises potential users of the IPI that it should be considered as only one component in the candidate selection process. With this entirely appropriate recommendation in mind, it is necessary to look to the manual for evidence that the IPI can, in fact, enhance the effectiveness of the officer candidate assessment procedure.

The 26 scales that comprise the IPI are grouped into four sets: Validity Measure (i.e., Guardedness), Acting out Behavior Measures (e.g., Alcohol, Antisocial Attitudes), Internalized Conflict Measures (e.g., Phobic Personality, Loner Type), and Interpersonal Conflict Measures (e.g., Lack of Assertiveness, Undue Suspiciousness). The rationale for the selection and organization of the 26 scales is presented in a single, brief paragraph which states in effect that it was the author's judgment that these particular scales are important in the psychological evaluation of law enforcement officer candidates.

In fact, the nature and content of the scales and their arrangement into four categories seems reasonable to this reviewer. Furthermore, careful psychometric studies have indicated that the rational approach to construction of personality inventories is as valid typically as the more time-consuming and expensive statistical approaches (i.e., empirical keying and factor analysis). But the test developer has an obligation to describe the psychological model or personality theory upon which the instrument is premised. Why is this set of 26 scales optimal for the selection of law enforcement officers? Why are each of these 26 scales included and not others for which reasonable cases could also be made? The IPI manual should provide answers to these questions.

Assuming that an acceptable psychological rationale for the IPI does exist, the next question that requires attention concerns the source of the 310 true/false items that the 26 scales are scored on. The only information given is that the items came from over 2,500 pre-employment interviews with law enforcement candidates. The manual does not describe the item-writing guidelines, nor does it indicate whether any item analyses were carried out on preliminary samples to select the "best" items. A cursory examination of the Test Book suggests that the items are similar to those comprising numerous other personality inventories and personal history questionnaires.

One type of item included in the IPI, which purports to measure actual behavior, is really a biographical inventory question (e.g., "I have collected unemployment," "I smoke marijuana on social occasions," "I have been divorced," and "I have been fired from a job"). However, the majority of the IPI items are typical personality inventory fare (e.g., "I love taking risks," "I have often thought that life is not worth the effort," "Sometimes I feel I cannot breathe," and "Troubles seem to follow me."). The difference between "behavioral" items and "personality" items is the basis for the highly questionable claim that IPI scales "can differentiate between individuals who express pathological or socially deviant attitudes and those who *act* on them." At the very least, this diagnostic distinction assumes that respondents have considerable insight into their personal functioning and that they are not motivated to portray themselves favorably, both highly dubious assumptions.

In addition to lack of detailed information about the basis of the 26 scales, the manual does not specify the procedure by which the 310 items were allocated to the scales. This is particularly important to know because many of the items are scored on more than one scale (i.e., the 310 items are scored a total of 490 times on the 26 scales). While this is not an unusual occurrence for empirically-keyed scales developed from a common item pool, it is not necessary or desirable in rationally constructed instruments. Among the problems caused by multiply-scored items are reduced dimensionality of the instrument and, consequently, diminished differential validity against multiple criteria.

Unfortunately, the dimensionality of the IPI cannot be determined accurately from the data provided in the manual. The rotated factor matrices include only one half or fewer of the 26 scales and the intercorrelation matrices are not given. The results that are presented are not promising, however. Just three factors explain the common variance of the IPI scales, and the first factor accounts for about two-thirds of the total variability of the profile.

Raw scores on the 26 IPI scales are converted to *T*-scores using norms for police officer candidates and correction officer candidates, separately for males and females, and by race for correction officer candidates. Norms are also provided for hired police officers and hired correction officers. The normative groups are large, carefully described, and appear to be suitable for the intended purposes of the IPI. The *T*-scores are presented graphically on a standard profile form, with the obtained scores incorrectly displayed as vertical bars with the baseline at zero. The computer-scored summary report also includes a printout of "critical items," which are the items endorsed in the positive or problematic direction, organized by scales.

The scale interpretations given in the manual appear to be based on literal translations of the content of the items that compose the scales. For example, on the Job Difficulties scale, "elevated scores may indicate: Past difficulties holding jobs, history of being terminated from jobs, problems with coworkers or bosses, and/or spotty employment record." And on the Depression scale, "elevated scores may indicate: Expressed discouragement and depression. Perceived difficulty coping with daily stresses, and difficulty achieving personal goals. General dissatisfaction with progress in life." The other scale interpretations are similar in format and decriptive focus.

The publisher also provides a computer-generated narrative report that consists of the score profile, critical item printout, and a series of statements derived mainly from the scale interpretations described above. The manual includes virtually no information on the development of the narrative report statements, except to say that they are largely based on item content, but also reflect clinical impressions and interpretations based on test results and interviews with officer candidates. A computer report should incorporate results from the correlational patterns with established instruments, as well as scale-specific criterion relationships, using data from the background review, candidate interviews, and subsequent performance in training and on the job.

Test-retest reliability coefficients were calculated for samples of 321 male and 171 female correction officer candidates who completed the IPI twice with a 6- to 8-week interval between administrations. Reliabilities ranged from .58 for Sexual Concerns to .87 for Driving Violations for males and from .60 for Illness Concerns to .79 for Antisocial Attitudes for females. For the male sample 10 scales have reliabilities lower than .70 while 13 scales fall below this value for females. Several of the scales are more reliable for males than for females. Although the reported reliabilities are lower than desirable for a screening instrument, it is reasonable to think that they would be higher with a more appropriate 1- to 2-week interval between administrations.

The manual summarizes the results of several studies that compared the predictive validity of the IPI and the MMPI against various performance criteria for samples of hired, probationary correction officers and law enforcement officers. In addition to termination after one year, three criteria were dichotomized into "acceptable" and "problematic" categories: absence, lateness, and disciplinary interviews. Discriminant equations were calculated using all 26 IPI scales and, separately, 15 or 16 standard MMPI scales.

For samples of male and female officers, with males divided by race, the proportions of correct classification of retained and terminated officers ranged from 72% to 89% for the IPI and from 62% to 80% for the MMPI. The proportions of correct classifications using the three dichotomized variables ranged from 63% to 82% for the IPI and 57% to 73% for the MMPI. Because the IPI prediction equations were based on more scales, it would be expected that shrinkage on cross-validation samples would be greater for the IPI than for the MMPI. In fact, this anticipated outcome was confirmed by the results of a study reported in the manual, in which the proportions of correct classifications for the three dichotomous criteria were almost the same for both instruments, and also considerably lower, ranging from 52% to 64%.

The finding of similar predictive ability of the IPI and the MMPI is surprising, considering the inclusion of scales in the IPI designed to measure behavior patterns critical to successful performance of law enforcement officers. The implication is that the traditional pathology scales are at least as important in predicting behavioral criteria such as absence, lateness, and disciplinary actions for persons in their field. It would be helpful to examine the regression equations for the IPI and the MMPI to pursue this issue further, but they are not presented in the manual.

A redundancy analysis of the IPI and the MMPI would provide a direct assessment of the relationships among the scales, as well as the total overlap of the two instruments. The author could easily conduct this analysis from existing data because the manual reports IPI-MMPI intercorrelations based on almost 2,500 correction officer candidates. The MMPI scales that are consistently related to IPI scales are K, Pt, and Sc. The important question, however, is what the IPI can contribute to the law enforcement candidate selection process that traditional instruments such as the MMPI cannot.

In addition to the investigations that are summarized above, the validity section of the manual reports several other studies (i.e., prediction of nine job performance criteria for a sample of male police officers, a comparative study of phobic outpatients, correlations between the IPI and five panel interview ratings for correction officers, and correlations with independently obtained biographical information). Despite the reviewer's critical comments, it should be emphasized that the validity research program for the IPI is well above average for a new instrument. The goal of future research should be to identify subsets of scales that are optimally predictive of officer job performance, such as citizen complaints regarding use of unnecessary force, discharge of firearms in the line of duty, and medical conditions possibly due to stress reactions.

To summarize, the Inwald Personality Inventory is a standardized questionnaire designed specifically for use in the selection process for law enforcement officer applicants. While the general idea is reasonable, the rationale and construction of the instrument are not adequately described. In particular, multiply scored items and low dimensionality may be serious shortcomings of the IPI. The normative data is good, the reliability of the scales is probably adequate, but the incremental validity of the IPI has not yet been documented. The computer-generated narrative report cannot be recommended at this time. Until the manual is appropriately revised and further research data is presented, the IPI should be used only on an experimental basis as an adjunct to the regular candidate assessment process.

Review of Inwald Personality Inventory by JON D. SWARTZ, Associate Dean for Libraries and Learning Resources, Professor of Education and Psychology, Southwestern University, Georgetown, TX:

This new self-report inventory is described by its author as being "designed specifically to aid law enforcement agencies in selecting new officers who satisfy specified 'psychological fitness' requirements. Like other personality measures...the IPI contains several distinct and sometimes overlapping scales, designed to measure behaviors, attitudes, and characteristics of various personality types....it documents combinations and patterns of historical life events which studies suggest correlate significantly with occupational failure in law enforcement."

The Inwald Personality Inventory (IPI) is a 310-question inventory, presented in a true-false format, with the questions "designed to reflect your feelings about yourself and life in general." The 26 scales (25 original, 1 validity) have been constructed to identify a variety of personality/behavioral characteristics in applicants for law enforcement positions. Developed with the express purpose of directly questioning law enforcement candidates about their admitted past and present behaviors, rather than inferring those behaviors from personality indicators, the IPI is not intended to be the sole source for evaluating psychological fitness; instead, it is suggested that the IPI be used "as one component in a psychological screening program, utilizing a series of validated assessment tools and procedures." (The total screening procedure advocated by Inwald and associates consists of a clinical interview, a stress measure, and a battery of tests that includes the IPI.)

IPI test items were developed from pre-employment interviews with over 2,500 law enforcement candidates. These items include not only critical characteristics used in clinical diagnoses but also self-revealing statements made by applicants during actual interviews. Thus, the population for whom the instrument was designed made specific contributions to the content of the battery. The language of the inventory is timely and deals with common experiences and familiar lifestyles (e.g., "I can get along with most people I meet.").

There are many things to like about the IPI. The manual is well done and reveals a test created according to professional standards. There are separate sections on reliability, validity, and standardization (norms on 7,733 police/correction officers and officer candidates are included). Extensive tables present normative data by sex, ethnicity, and job category (police officer candidates, hired police officers, correction officer candidates, and hired correction officers); varimax rotated factor analyses by sex and position (police officer, correction officer) are provided; test-retest reliability coefficients across the 26 scales are shown to range from the low .60s to the high .80s over 6- to 8-week intervals. Significant correlations, ranging from .20 to .72, are reported between appropriate scales on the IPI and the MMPI, CPI, 16 PF, FIRO-B, FIRO-F, STAI, and EPPS, using groups ranging from 139 to 1,880 individuals; the results of validation studies (presented by sex, ethnicity, and job performance variables) are presented along with three construct validity studies of "some of the more clinically-oriented scales" with law enforcement candidates and "previously-diagnosed phobic, depressive and/or anxious individuals." These data are quite impressive, showing several of the IPI scales to be acceptably reliable and valid for certain uses (e.g., selected IPI scales have been shown to have greater predictive validity than the MMPI in classifying "positive" and "negative" behaviors).

On the other hand, of course, there are the inevitable difficulties with all tests of this type (i.e., response sets/response styles). Moreover, in addition to the generic problems of all self-report inventories, the IPI has some unique problems—many due to its being such a new instrument. For example, the bibliography included in the manual is meager (only 12 entries, and 10 of these by Inwald and her associates). And all but one of the references listed are to papers presented at association meetings rather than to articles published in referred journals. (The only publication listed reporting research on the IPI is a monthly newsletter of the Washington Crime News Services.) In evaluating any new test it is necessary to go beyond the findings reported in a manual. Even if one is willing to accept a test author's findings at face value, the judicious user of any new assessment instrument will "test the test," drawing his or her own conclusions about its usefulness in specific settings and for particular purposes. Another negative factor in evaluting the IPI is its cost. The scoring services and test materials are quite expensive for a paper-and-pencil test of this type: a single Narrative Report, a computer printout of results with responses grouped according to scales, is $18.50.

In conclusion, the Inwald Personality Inventory is a promising new psychological screening device for the criminal justice field. Despite its newness, the findings reported so far are very encouraging; and there is no comparable instrument of which this reviewer is aware. Even if the IPI is only partly as good as the findings reported in the manual indicate, Inwald and her associates will have made a significant contribution. Given the economics of hiring and training increasingly large numbers of law enforcement personnel in this country, the IPI certainly deserves a close look from those responsible for selecting low-risk candidates for law enforcement positions. Further research is needed, of course, including cross-validation studies in a variety of agencies.

[531]

Iowa Parent Behavior Inventory. Parents; 1976–79; IPBI; ratings by parents of their behavior in relation to their child; no validity data; no norms; 2 forms; manual ('79, 41 pages, includes both forms and a score sheet); 1984 price data: $.10 per test; $3 per manual; administration time not reported; Sedahlia Jasper Crase, Samuel G. Clark, and Damaris Pease; Iowa State University Research Foundation, Inc.*

a) MOTHER FORM. 1977; 6 scores: parental involvement, limit setting, responsiveness, reasoning guidance, free expression, intimacy; 1 form (4 pages).

b) FATHER FORM. 1977; 5 scores: parental involvement, limit setting, responsiveness, reasoning guidance, intimacy; 1 form (4 pages).

TEST REFERENCES

1. Elrod, M. M., & Crase, S. J. Sex differences in self esteem and parental behavior. PSYCHOLOGICAL REPORTS, 1980, 46, 719–727.

Review of Iowa Parent Behavior Inventory by VERNA HART, Professor of Education, University of Pittsburgh, Pittsburgh, PA:

The Iowa Parent Behavior Inventory was developed to assess parental behaviors as part of the North Central 124 Regional Project, a study assessing rural areas. The investigators continue to work with the instrument.

The inventory, in its current phase of development, has both strengths and major weaknesses. The strengths are the ease of administration of the paper and pencil test, the shortness of the test (36 items), the fact that the inventory looks for actual behaviors rather than attitudes, and the inclusion of forms for both mothers and fathers.

The negative aspects of the inventory currently outweigh the positive. The manual neglects to mention several points needed regarding the construction of the instrument. Forty original items were developed, one-half relating to utilization of behavior and the other half to non-utilization of behavior. To these items were added 10 additional statements and then 17 more, for a total of 67. No information is provided as to the manner in which the additional 27 items were constructed. The total 67 items were factored and reduced to 36. These 36 items are distributed between the mother and father forms with 22 of the 36 items in common. Both the mother and father forms assess five similarly titled factors but the father form is missing the three items that make up the free expression factor found in the mother form. Although the factors are similarly titled and 22 of the 36 items in each form are identical, factor loadings on the two versions differ on all but one item.

The authors spend time justifying their initial use of a 1–99 format for scoring the items. As part of the first revision, the respondent who is not sure of the answer scores the item as a 50. This midpoint previously meant only that the parent behaved that way half the time.

The scoring format has been changed to a 5-point scale, despite the authors' earlier emphasis on the need for the 99-point format and its use in the development of the inventory. This reviewer could find no references using the shorter format, and contact with the first author substantiated the fact that what little has been published, as well as manuscripts ready for publication, has used the 1–99 format. The current inventory format includes only the shorter scoring format.

Validity of the instrument presents a problem. The original 40 items were written and edited by faculty in the Department of Child Development at Iowa State University. Although this might provide face validity evidence for the original 40 items, nothing is stated about the remaining items. No information is provided about other attempts to validate the items or the total instrument. Although some information is provided regarding the reliability of the two forms, it is difficult to interpret it because of sparse and incomplete information.

Subjects for the study are presumed to be parents of children in the Regional Project. Information provided in the manual appendix refers to the Regional Project rather than the inventory and includes information about the children of the project and not about the parents involved. Even then, the information does not match the information provided in the text of the manual. The numbers of subjects do not match, no information is provided regarding the control group mentioned, and ages of the children involved are given in the appendix but no information is provided about the ages of the children's parents or specific numbers of children at different target age groups. According to this description, there were to be 40 children from each of three age groups: 3 to 3 1/2, 6 to 6 1/2, and 9 to 9 1/2—a total of 120 children and their families per station. Information provided in the text of the manual indicates that the first revision of the inventory was administered to 393 mothers and 371 fathers. Since an intact family was stated as a criterion for subjects, the discrepancy between numbers provided in the description of subjects and numbers tested should be discussed.

The description of the sample states that the subjects must have lived on a farm of at least 10 acres for the past 5 years, lived at least 30 miles from the nearest center of 100,000 or more people, and lived in a homogeneously rural area. This makes the representativeness of the sample confined to a very limited population. Also, for purposes of subject selection, an urban population was defined as those living in urbanized areas of 2,500 inhabitants or more.

Information regarding the total score is not provided in the manual. When queried about the use of the score, the investigators stated that it depends on the intent of the individual investigators. There are no norms for comparison purposes.

The negative aspects of the test negate its use for most research purposes. The authors continue to work with the instrument and are revising the manual. It is hoped this revision will be of greater use than the current one. In the meantime, the Caldwell HOME Inventory contains several of the same factors as the Iowa Parent Inventory but has been studied longitudinally for its effect on development and shows a substantial relationship between HOME scores and children's mental test scores throughout the preschool years. Unfortunately, HOME is limited to the first 6 years of age and necessitates a home visit as well as an interview with the parent. Thus, if the authors can perfect the Iowa Parent Inventory, this short easy-to-administer paper and pencil test should find a ready market because of the current interest in parental involvement in early education, intervention, and socialization of young children.

Review of Iowa Parent Behavior Inventory by RICHARD L. WIKOFF, Professor of Psychology, University of Nebraska at Omaha, Omaha, NE:

PURPOSE AND NATURE OF THE TEST. The Iowa Parent Behavior Inventory is a pencil and paper inventory designed to assess behaviors of parents which are felt by the authors to be "salient in the parent-child relationship." The specific population targeted is not clearly stated, although it is implied that it was designed for parents residing on farms. The exact manner in which children were chosen was not reported. It was stated that the children were subjects from "the NC-124 regional project Life Span Analysis of Rural Children's Mental and Social Development" but this project is never described. An appendix titled "Description of Subjects" gives the criteria for inclusion in the NC-124 project, but the manual does not indicate how the subjects were chosen from this pool and does not present any demographic data about the subjects.

Six scales are presented for mothers and five for fathers. Each scale consists of items to be rated from 1 to 5. A response of 1 indicates that the parent almost never behaves that way and 5 indicates that the parent almost always behaves that way. A rating of 3 indicates that the parent behaves that way about half of the time or is not sure how often he or she behaves that way.

PRACTICAL EVALUATION. The instrument is not designed for general use. The manual consists of 40 pages duplicated from the original typewritten copies. It was written more in the style of a journal article than a test manual. There are no directions for administration. Scoring is relatively simple, although it would be time consuming if the inventory were administered in large numbers. The items are all scored in the same direction rather than half of them being reverse scored as recommended when using the summative model. The manual does not address examiner qualifications or training needed to use the instrument. The inventory has face validity but would be easy to fake. The socially desirable responses are obvious.

TECHNICAL EVALUATION. Norms are not given. During the development of the inventory, a scale of 1 to 99 was used instead of the 1 to 5 scale. Means and standard deviations for the former scale are given but not for the scale that is recommended.

Two types of reliability are reported for each of the scales. These are referred to as "total variance" reliability and "unique variance" reliability, the latter a misnomer. The authors reportedly used the Spearman-Brown formula for calculating these estimates of reliability. The method used is not clear and the results are questionable since the Spearman-Brown formula is not a reliability formula, but is a method for estimating the reliability of a test increased by any given length. If a split-half method was used the method of division is not reported. For this type of data, Cronbach's alpha would have been more appropriate. The reliability coefficients reported range from .56 to .86. These are inadequate for use with individuals and several are not even acceptable for group use. The sample sizes were just barely acceptable (393 mothers and 371 fathers). There was no attempt made to cross-validate the scales and there were no indications of stability.

Validity is never discussed in the manual. Some attempts were made to provide for content validity, but neither criterion-related nor construct validity were addressed. The items were subjected to a factor analysis, but the results are poorly reported. Varimax rotation was used, which is supposed to provide an orthogonal factor structure. Nevertheless, the authors presented a factor correlation matrix with correlations ranging from .04 to .50 for the mothers and from .26 to .61 for the fathers. The factor method used was not clear since the authors stated that they used a noniterative least squares method, which implies a principal components solution, but then said that they used the highest correlation in the row in the diagonal, which implies the principal factors solution which is an iterative procedure. Inadequate data was reported concerning the factor analysis. The method used to choose the number of factors was not adequately explained. Neither communalities nor percents of variance explained were given.

The theoretical basis for the inventory was weak. The literature reviewed might be appropriate for a journal article but was not suitable for a manual.

SUMMARY. This inventory is inadequate in every way. The manual would not be acceptable to this reviewer as a journal article, let alone as a marketable inventory. The manual does not adequately present the theory and rationale for the instrument. The population is not clearly delineated and the manner in which subjects were chosen is not clear. No demographic information is given regarding the subjects actually used. It presents its factor analytic results incompletely and poorly. Reliability was dealt with in a questionable manner and the results reported are unacceptable. Cross-validation of the items was not done. Validity was never discussed except for some indirect attempt at content validity. Much of the information described as "Essential" in the *Standards for Educational and Psychological Tests* was not reported. It is the reviewer's opinion that the inventory should not be used for any purpose until considerably more developmental research has been conducted.

[532]

Iowa Social Competence Scales. Ages 3–6, 6–12; 1976–82; ISCS; adaptation of Devereux Elementary School Behavior Rating Scale; ratings by parents for "measuring social behavior (competencies) of normal children"; 2 levels; no reliability data on combined preschool form; no norms; manual ('82, 46 pages); 1983 price data: $.10 or less per scale; $1 per manual; administration time not reported; Damaris Pease, Samuel G. Clark, and Sedahlia Jasper Crase; Iowa State University.*

a) PRESCHOOL. Ages 3–6; 1979; 3 forms.

1) *Mother.* 5 scores: social activator, hypersensitive, reassurance, uncooperative, cooperative; 4 pages.

2) *Father.* 5 scores: social activator, hypersensitive, reassurance, socially inept, attentive; 3 pages.

3) *Combined.* Suitable for either mother or father; 3 scores: social activator, hypersensitivity, reassurance; 4 pages.

b) SCHOOLAGE. Ages 6–12; 1979; 2 forms.

1) *Mother.* 6 scores: task oriented, disruptive, leader, physically active, affectionate toward parent, apprehensive; 2 pages.

2) *Father.* 5 scores: capable, defiant, leader, active with peers, affectionate toward parent; 3 pages.

TEST REFERENCES

1. Pease, D., Clark, S., & Crase, S. J. The Social Competency Scale for preschool-age children: Its development and factorial validity. EDUCATIONAL AND PSYCHOLOGICAL MEASUREMENT, 1981, 41, 851–861.

2. Wirth, S., & Pease, D. Convergent and discriminant validity of the Iowa Social Competency Scale for preschool children. EDUCATIONAL AND PSYCHOLOGICAL MEASUREMENT, 1983, 43, 305–314.

[533]

Iowa Tests of Basic Skills, Forms 7 and 8. Grades K.1–1.5, K.8–1.9, 1.7–2.6, 2.7–3.5, 3, 4, 5, 6, 7, 8–9; 1955–83; ITBS; previous edition still available; development of 1982 norms ('83, 30 pages); 1984 price data: $3 per development of 1982 norms; scoring service available from publisher; A. N. Hieronymus, E. F. Lindquist, H. D. Hoover, and others; Riverside Publishing Co.*

a) PRIMARY BATTERY: LEVELS 5–8. Grades K.1–1.5, K.8–1.9, 1.7–2.6, 2.7–3.5; 1978–79; 4 levels; Form 7 skills chart (no date, 1 page); practice test ('78, 8 pages); practice test guide, Levels 5 and 6 ('82, 4 pages); practice test guide, Levels 7 and 8 ('78, 8 pages); report to parents ('78, 4 pages); $18–$30 per 25 MRC scorable tests; $12–$15 per 25 hand-scorable tests; $51.75–$72.60 per 25 NCS scorable tests; $6 per 25 practice tests and 1 teacher's guide; $8.82 per MRC scoring masks; $.75 per response keys; $3.45 per 25 reports to parents; $4.98 per teacher's guide of any one level; $.75 per teacher's guide for practice tests.

1) *Level* 5. Grades K.1–1.5; 5 scores: listening, vocabulary, word analysis, language, mathematics; machine-scorable ('79, 16 pages) and hand-scorable ('79, 20 pages) forms; teacher's guide ('79, 16 pages); (150) minutes.

2) *Level* 6. Grades K.8–1.9; 6 scores: listening, vocabulary, word analysis, reading, language, mathematics; forms and teacher's guide same as for Level 5; (160) minutes in 6 sessions.

3) *Level* 7. Grades 1.7–2.6; 2 batteries; forms and teacher's guide same as for Level 5.

(*a*) Basic Battery. 9 scores: vocabulary, word analysis, reading comprehension (pictures, sentences, stories), skills (spelling), mathematics skills (concepts, problems, computation); (136) minutes.

(*b*) Complete Battery. 15 scores: 9 scores from Basic Battery plus listening, language skills (capitalization, punctuation, usage), work study skills (visual materials, reference materials); (235) minutes.

4) *Level* 8. Grades 2.7–3.5; details same as for Level 7.

b) MULTILEVEL EDITION: LEVELS 9–14. Grades 3, 4, 5, 6, 7, 8–9; 1978–79; social studies and science supplement for research use only; 2 forms plus practice test ('78, 6 pages); practice test guide ('78, 8 pages); 6 levels; 2 batteries; teacher's guide ('79, 96 pages); social studies and science directions (no date, 4 pages); preliminary technical summary ('79, 38 pages); percentile norms—large cities ('80, 56 pages), Catholic schools ('80, 56 pages), high socioeconomic ('80, 44 pages), low socioeconomic ('80, 44 pages); pupil profile chart ('78, 1 page); profile chart for averages ('78, 1 page); $29.85 per 35 social studies and science tests; $24.15 per 100 practice tests; $.75 per right response key; $4.98 per set of MRC scoring masks; $21 per 100 MRC answer sheets; $68.31 per 250 NCS answer sheets; $9.39 per 100 practice test answer sheets; $4.50 per 35 pupil profile charts; $3.99 per 35 profile charts for averages; $2.28 per technical summary; $3.99 per percentile norms; $4.50 per teacher's guide; $1.17 per social studies and science directions.

1) *Basic Battery.* 6 scores: vocabulary, reading, spelling, math (concepts, problems, computation); 2 editions; (139) minutes.

(*a*) Battery Booklet Edition. Grades 3–9; Form 7 ('78, 56 pages); $2.19 per test.

(*b*) Separate Booklet Edition. Grades 3, 4, 5, 6, 7, 8–9; Form 7 ('78, 94 pages) for each level; $39 per 35 tests of any one level.

2) *Complete Battery.* 11 scores: same 6 scores as in Basic Battery plus capitalization, punctuation, usage, visual materials, reference materials; 2 editions; (244) minutes.

(*a*) Battery Booklet Edition. Grades 3–9; Form 7 ('78, 96 pages) and 8 ('78, 97 pages); $3.24 per test.

(*b*) Separate Booklet Edition. Grades 3, 4, 5, 6, 7, 8–9; Form 7 ('78, 94 pages) for each level; $39 per 35 tests of any one level.

See T3:1192 (97 references); for reviews by Larry A. Harris and Fred Pyrczak of Forms 5–6, see 8:19 (58 references); see T2:19 (87 references) and 6:13 (17 references); for reviews by Virgil E. Herrick, G. A. V. Morgan, and H. H. Remmers, and an excerpted review by Laurence Siegel of Forms 1–2, see 5:16. For reviews of the modern mathematics supplement, see 7:481 (2 reviews).

TEST REFERENCES

1. Bruning, R. H., Burton, J. K., & Ballering, M. Visual and auditory memory: Relationships to reading achievement. CONTEMPORARY EDUCATIONAL PSYCHOLOGY, 1978, 3, 340–351.

2. Meyer, R. A. Mathematical problem-solving performance and intellectual abilities of fourth-grade children. JOURNAL FOR RESEARCH IN MATHEMATICS EDUCATION, 1978, 9, 334–348.

3. Prigge, G. R. The differential effects of the use of manipulative aids on the learning of geometric concepts by elementary school children. JOURNAL FOR RESEARCH IN MATHEMATICS EDUCATION, 1978, 9, 361–367.

4. Richman, L., & Harper, D. School adjustment of children with observable disabilities. JOURNAL OF ABNORMAL CHILD PSYCHOLOGY, 1978, 6, 11–18.

5. Dean, R. S. Predictive validity of the WISC-R with Mexican-American children. JOURNAL OF SCHOOL PSYCHOLOGY, 1979, 17, 55–58.

6. Kent, J., & Ruiz, R. A. IQ and reading scores among Anglo, Black, and Chicano third- and sixth-grade schoolchildren. HISPANIC JOURNAL OF BEHAVIORAL SCIENCES, 1979, 1, 271–277.

7. Plake, B. S., & Hoover, H. D. The comparability of equal raw scores obtained from in-level and out-of-level testing: One source of the discrepancy between in-level and out-of-level grade equivalent scores. JOURNAL OF EDUCATIONAL MEASUREMENT, 1979, 16, 271–278.

8. Thompson, B. Predictive validity of a measure of learning potential. MEASUREMENT AND EVALUATION IN GUIDANCE, 1979, 12, 77–81.

9. Bell, C., & Ward, G. R. An investigation of the relationship between Dimensions of Self-Concept (DOSC) and achievement in mathematics. ADOLESCENCE, 1980, 15, 895–901.

10. Charles, R. I. Exemplification and characterization moves in the classroom teaching of geometry concepts. JOURNAL FOR RESEARCH IN MATHEMATICS EDUCATION, 1980, 11, 10–21.

11. Curiel, H., Stenning, W. F., & Cooper-Stenning, P. Achieved reading level, self-esteem, and grades as related to length of exposure to bilingual education. HISPANIC JOURNAL OF BEHAVIORAL SCIENCE, 1980, 2, 389–400.

12. Knifong, J. D. Computational requirements of standardized word problem tests. JOURNAL FOR RESEARCH IN MATHEMATICS EDUCATION, 1980, 11, 3–9.

13. Haller, E. J., & Davis, S. A. Teacher perceptions, parental social status and grouping for reading instruction. SOCIOLOGY OF EDUCATION, 1981, 54, 162–174.

14. Plake, B. S., Loyd, B. H., & Hoover, H. D. Sex differences in mathematics components of the Iowa Tests of Basic Skills. PSYCHOLOGY OF WOMEN QUARTERLY, 1981, 5, 780–784.

15. Whaley, J. F. Readers' reactions to temporal disruption in stories. NATIONAL READING CONFERENCE YEARBOOK, 1981, 30, 191–195.

16. Wixson, K. K. The effects of postreading questions on children's comprehension and learning. NATIONAL READING CONFERENCE YEARBOOK, 1981, 30, 243–248.

17. Beck, I. L., Perfetti, C. A., & McKeown, M. G. Effects of long-term vocabulary instruction on lexical access and reading comprehension. JOURNAL OF EDUCATIONAL PSYCHOLOGY, 1982, 74, 506–521.

18. Blaha, J. Predicting reading and arithmetic achievement with measures of reading attitudes and cognitive styles. PERCEPTUAL AND MOTOR SKILLS, 1982, 55, 107–114.

19. Cooper, H., Findley, M., & Good, T. Relations between student achievement and various indexes of teacher expectations. JOURNAL OF EDUCATIONAL PSYCHOLOGY, 1982, 74, 577–579.

20. Cummings, O. W. Differential measurement of reading comprehension skills for students with discrepant subskill profiles. JOURNAL OF EDUCATIONAL MEASUREMENT, 1982, 19, 59–66.

21. Ansley, T. N., & Forsyth, R. A. Relationsip of elementary and secondary school achievement test scores to college performance. EDUCATIONAL AND PSYCHOLOGICAL MEASUREMENT, 1983, 43, 1103–1112.

22. Borkowski, J. G., Ryan, E. B., Kurtz, B. E., & Reid, M. K. Metamemory and metalinguistic development: Correlates of children's intelligence and achievement. BULLETIN OF THE PSYCHONOMIC SOCIETY, 1983, 21, 393–396.

23. Burlingame, K., Hardy, R. C., & Eliot, J. Study of horizontal line-mazes. PERCEPTUAL AND MOTOR SKILLS, 1983, 57, 1103–1109.

24. Day, K. C., & Day, H. D. Ability to imitate language in kindergarten predicts later school achievement. PERCEPTUAL AND MOTOR SKILLS, 1983, 57, 883–890.

25. Demo, D. H., & Savin-Williams, R. C. Early adolescent self-esteem as a function of social class: Rosenberg and Pearlin revisited. AMERICAN JOURNAL OF SOCIOLOGY, 1983, 88, 763–774.

26. Popovics, A. J. Predictive validities of clinical and actuarial scores of the Gesell Incomplete Man Test. PERCEPTUAL AND MOTOR SKILLS, 1983, 56, 864–866.

27. Raphael, T. E., & McKinney, J. An examination of fifth- and eighth-grade children's question-answering behavior: An instructional study in metacognition. JOURNAL OF READING BEHAVIOR, 1983, 15, 67–86.

28. Rowan, B., & Miracle, A. W., Jr. Systems of ability grouping and the stratification of achievement in elementary schools. SOCIOLOGY OF EDUCATION, 1983, 56, 133–144.

29. Hoover, H. D., & Kolen, M. J. The reliability of six item bias indices. APPLIED PSYCHOLOGICAL MEASUREMENT, 1984, 8, 173–181.

Review of Iowa Tests of Basic Skills, Forms 7 and 8, by PETER W. AIRASIAN, Professor of Education, Boston College, Chestnut Hill, MA:

The Iowa Tests of Basic Skills is a well-respected and widely used test battery intended to provide "comprehensive and continuous measurement of growth in the fundamental skills: vocabulary, reading, the mechanics of writing, methods of study, and mathematics." The multilevel battery contains 11 subtests and is designed for use in grades 3 to 9. The ITBS and their supporting materials have most of the positive attributes one would expect from a test series that has been in existence for 45 years. Among the new features of Forms 7 and 8 of the battery are the addition of a mathematics computation subtest and a reduction in the amount of testing time required to complete the battery.

INTERPRETIVE MATERIALS. The materials which support the tests are extensive, of high quality, and properly cautious. The Teacher's Guide is well-written and contains the detailed information a test user would need to select, administer, score, and interpret the tests. The section of the Teacher's Guide on "Preparation for Testing" provides a clear rationale for standardized administration procedures as well as explicit suggestions for preparing for and carrying out testing. In addition to these suggestions, a pamphlet entitled "How Are Your Basic Skills?" and a practice test are provided to help prepare examinees for taking the ITBS.

Directions for each subtest are detailed and appropriate for the intended age levels. The "Interpretation of Test Results" section of the Teacher's Guide, a most crucial section of any set of interpretive materials accompanying a test, describes well the types of norms and scoring service reports available from the test. The discussion of grade equivalent scores identifies common misinterpretations of these indices. This reviewer does have some reservations about the utility of the skill level scores and interpretations available to users, which he will discuss in the validity section of this review.

The Teacher's Guide devotes one section to "Use of Test Results in Improving Instruction." The user is cautioned that many of the uses of the ITBS cited in this section are simply suggestions from the authors for using test results. The suggestions are not validated strategies proven to improve student learning. The final sections of the Teacher's Guide contain norms tables and a clearly detailed list of the skills objectives measured by each test in the battery.

A Preliminary Technical Summary provides information of a more technical nature on the standardization sample, item selection procedures, validity, and reliability of the ITBS. In addition, this document provides detailed information about the steps taken to insure fairness to all students who might take the tests. As with the other interpretative materials available, the technical information is clearly presented.

ITEMS. All 11 subtests of the ITBS utilize multiple choice items. The geneology of the items, from the initial identification of skills to be tested to the writing, editing, trying out, reviewing, and selecting of the items themselves, is excellent. Before final selection, the items were subjected to review by a national team representing five racial and ethnic groups in order to obtain a judgment of each item's cultural fairness. Subsequent to these judgments, statistical analyses were conducted to identify and eliminate items that manifested a male-female or black-white bias.

For the most part, the test items appear to measure the skills objectives they were designed to measure. Two points, however, should be noted regarding the match between items and objectives. First, if a user is to make meaningful inferences about pupil achievement, it is crucial that the user be certain that his or her local objectives match those of the ITBS. The Teacher's Guide properly points out the importance of this match and encourages users to verify it before using the battery. Second, the items in the Language section subtests, because of the constraint imposed by multiple choice items, do not measure directly whether a pupil uses correct spelling, capitalization, punctuation, and grammar in his or her own writing production. Rather the items in these subtests measure these skills indirectly, by asking examinees to select correct and incorrect examples of usage. These sections test knowledge of rules, not the pupil's use of these rules in practice.

The two Work Study Skills subtests, visual materials and reference materials, contain large numbers of charts, graphs, tables, and other pictorial representations. The quality of the reproductions is outstanding. The only minor quibble one might have regarding the appearance of the tests is with the comparatively small size of the printing for items intended for pupils taking levels 12, 13, and 14. Overall, however, the development of the items, their relation to the skills that the tests are designed to measure, and the quality of the reproduction in the tests are outstanding.

NORMS. The tests were normed in the Fall of 1977 on 12,000 to 18,000 pupils per grade. School districts were stratified by size, region, and community socioeconomic status. A total of 165 school districts were sampled. Subsamples of about 3,000 students per grade were retested to provide spring norms. The norming sample was sufficiently large and representative of both majority and minority pupils. Fall, winter, and spring norms were provided, although the genesis of the winter norms is not clear. Special percentile rank norms are also available for region of the country, Catholic schools, large city schools, and school districts of high and low socioeconomic status. Raw scores on the ITBS are converted to either developmental scores (grade equivalent scores, age equivalent scores, standard scores) or status scores (percentile ranks, normal curve equivalents, stanines).

VALIDITY AND RELIABILITY. The within-grade Kuder-Richardson 20 reliabilities for the 11 subtests and total scores are high, generally greater than .85, with many exceeding .90. The K-R 20 reliability of the composite score for each level of the test is .98. The standard errors of measurement for each subtest and level are reported in the Technical Summary, a helpful interpretive guide to the user. It is unfortunate that the use of the standard error in interpreting scores is not described—with examples—in the section of the Teacher's Guide that deals with the interpretation of results. Also, it would be helpful to have test-retest reliability information additional to the long term (one, two, and three years) stability estimates obtained in a series of studies carried out on the 1974 version of the ITBS. Overall, the reliabilities of the ITBS are high, but more should be stated about the use of reliability and standard error information in test score interpretation.

While the content validity of an achievement test battery rests ultimately upon the judgment of the user regarding the match between local curriculum and the test content, there is little question that the ITBS contain content that is generally representative of school curricula in grades 3 to 9. This does not mean, of course, that every item or subtest is content valid for every school or classroom, but within the confines imposed by the construction of a nationally normed, nationally used test, the authors of the ITBS have done about all that can be expected to identify relevant and representative content to test. Moreover, the description of item selection and the skills objectives listed in the Teacher's Guide afford the user sufficient information to make the content validity determination vis-a-vis his or her own setting.

The test is somewhat lacking when it moves beyond content validity into other validity realms. Part 1 of the Teacher's Guide lists seven different purposes for the battery, including: to determine developmental levels of pupils in order to adapt instructional materials, to diagnose individual's qualitative strengths and weaknesses, to identify readiness skills for instructional placement, to provide information for grouping, and to diagnose group strengths and weaknesses. Each of these uses requires a different type of inference from the test data and each of these different inferences, in turn, requires its own validation. The validity section of the Technical Summary addresses the validity of only a few of these test score uses.

For example, in sections of the Teacher's Guide reference is made to the diagnostic uses of the test score information, particularly within subtests at the skill objective level. One of the available scoring formats provides objective-by-objective performance indications for each pupil in a class and for the class as a whole. While such information may be helpful to teachers, the user is cautioned that the usefulness of the test results for diagnosing pupil skill objective level performance or planning instructional placement or remedial activities has not been validated explicitly. There are relatively few items measuring each skill objective. No reliability information is provided at the skill objective level, although it may be assumed that skill level reliabilities will be considerably lower than the subtest reliabilities discussed above. The user may wish to make diagnostic use of the ITBS skill level results, but he or she should do so with the above limitations in mind. If the authors wish such instructionally related inferences to be made from the test results, they should devote more attention to the validity and reliability of the tests for these purposes.

The authors indicate that the ITBS are designed to assess a construct related to a pupil's general functioning skills, not to a pupil's factual content recall. The construct validity of the battery is addressed by examining three types of information: interrelationships among subtests in the battery, long term stability of the scores, and the relationship of scores on the battery to scores on other measures of achievement and ability. The authors are correct when they indicate that one should expect subtest scores on the test battery to be interrelated. The question for the ITBS and for all other achievement batteries on the market is, however, what level of relationship is desired? If the relationships among scores on subtests are very high, one may question the uniqueness of the separate subtests. If the relationships among subtest scores are very low, one may question the existence of the general verbal ability construct which seems to underlie paper and pencil, group administered tests. It should be noted that these issues are concerned with what underlying trait or traits the test is measuring and therefore are issues of construct validity. Very few test authors have good answers to the question of the desirable relationship among subtests on an achievement battery, which is acceptable given the present-day state of the art in testing. However, test authors might reasonably be expected to raise the issue for users who might not be aware of it.

The intercorrelations among both subtests and total scores of the ITBS are moderate to high. As expected, correlations of scores between subtests are lower than correlations between total scores, with the former ranging from the mid .50s to the mid .70s with most in the .65 area, and the latter being in the .70 to .85 range. Approximately 35 to 50% of the variance between any two subtests is shared, while approximately 50 to 70% of the variance between any two of the vocabulary, reading, language, study skills or mathematics total scores is shared. These are substantial overlaps among the test areas. Certainly these high intercorrelations raise questions about the distinctness of the 11 subtest scores obtained from the battery and therefore about their diagnostic usefulness. Overall, evidence for the independence of the subtests is moderate at best.

The ITBS does correlate with other measures of ability and achievement. Studies reported in an earlier ITBS manual indicate that the multiple correlation of the battery (for grade eight) with high school grade averages was around .60, .73 with ACT composite score, and .41 and .49 respectively for two studies of first year college grades. The correlations of the ITBS with the Cognitive Abilities Test are quite high, on the order of .60 to .80. In fact, the correlations of the ITBS with ability test scores are higher than the multiple correlations of the ITBS and high school and college grades.

The battery has criterion-related validity with other achievement and ability measures. However, criterion-related validity is not construct validity and the issue of what construct or constructs the ITBS assess is not answered satisfactorily in the interpretive materials available. As test constructors strive to move from items which test recall of content to items which assess more general understandings, concepts, and skills—as the ITBS does—they risk constructing tests which measure general ability rather than achievement. There clearly is overlap between a pupil's measured ability and achievement, and perhaps the final answer to the question of whether any test assesses a pupil's achievement or a more general underlying trait such as verbal ability rests with the local user, who knows the student and the curriculum he or she has followed. The construct validity of the ITBS is not satisfactorily established, either to indicate clearly what the tests assess or to use the results from different subtests for differential diagnosis and instructional planning. In fairness, however, it must be reemphasized that these limitations are not specific to the ITBS, but rather are limitations which characterize virtually all published achievement test batteries.

SUMMARY. The ITBS, Forms 7 and 8, are well constructed and well documented tests, certainly among the best available to users seeking a broad-range achievement battery. The procedures followed in test construction and standardization are exemplary. The norming sample was sufficiently large and representative. The documentation for the tests is complete, readable, and informative. The authors are suitably cautious where appropriate and take pains to point out to the user possible misinterpretations of particular scores and norms.

The claimed usefulness of subtest and skill level scores for making diagnostic and placement inferences about pupils needs to be subjected to explicit validation. The test does an excellent job of providing information about the general performance of pupils in a variety of basic skill areas. It may be less valuable for other suggested uses. Overall, the ITBS is one of the best standardized achievement test batteries available and is recommended for use by those whose curriculum objectives correspond to the tests' skill level objectives and for those seeking a general indication of pupils' performance in a variety of important basic skill curriculum areas.

Review of Iowa Tests of Basic Skills, Forms 7 and 8, by ANTHONY J. NITKO, Professor of Education, University of Pittsburgh, Pittsburgh, PA:

The Iowa Tests of Basic Skills (ITBS) measure pupils' growth in broadly defined skill areas such as listening, vocabulary, reading, language, work-study, and mathematics. In addition, there are supplementary subtests for social studies and science. The basic purposes for which the battery is designed are to facilitate (*a*) within classroom decisions such as diagnosing strengths and weaknesses, and individualizing instruction; and (*b*) decisions external to the classroom such as identifying strengths and weaknesses of a group (grade level, building, or school system), and ascertaining the effectiveness of curricular or instructional innovations.

The rationale for including each ITBS subtest is carefully explained in the Manual for School Administrators. The information provided about each subtest goes well beyond that typically provided for standardized survey tests: Nuances of content selection and placement are clearly explained and research is summarized in appropriate ways to explain how the developers arrived at each decision in the test construction process. For example, the reasoning behind the selection of specific item formats within subtests is carefully explained, usually by citing research studies conducted by faculty members and/or students at the University of Iowa that help to settle empirical questions about the type of procedures that better measure each basic skill area. The test user is a clear beneficiary of this ongoing research and development program.

A major change in Forms 7 and 8 is the revision of the mathematics skills subtests: The Problem Solving Subtest is revised, there is a new Computation Subtest, and a separate Concepts Subtest is provided. The Concepts Subtest covers 34 basic concepts over Levels 9 through 14 in six areas: numeration, number sentences, whole numbers, fractions, decimals, and geometry and measurement. Teachers are warned (in the Teacher's Guide) that before individualizing testing by assigning different test levels to different students, the concepts at the test level should be compared with the concepts taught during the year; otherwise the test level selected will be out of phase with the student. The Problem Solving Subtest has been changed in significant ways: Now the concepts and arithmetic operations needed to solve problems at a particular test level "have been introduced at least a year prior to the grade for which a level of the test is primarily intended." This is an appropriate change that should help a teacher to gain a clearer view of a student's ability to apply mathematical knowledge to realistic problems. The items on the Problem Solving Subtest cover three broad categories: single-step addition and subtraction, single-step multiplication and division, and multiple-step problems involving combinations of operations. The Computation Subtest covers whole numbers, fractions, and decimals, and crosses these with each of the four arithmetic operations. The Teacher's Guide appropriately warns that subtests measure general tendencies, not specific discrete skills. Once a general weakness has been identified (e.g., multiplication of fractions), it is necessary for a teacher to follow up with more sharply focused diagnostic tests to pinpoint a pupil's difficulty.

In addition to the regular battery, the ITBS has supplementary subtests in social studies and science for Levels 9 through 14. This supplement is primarily concerned with measuring background information in these subject areas. Basic skills which students use to learn in social studies and science (e.g., reading comprehension, use of reference materials, and understanding maps, graphs, and tables) are measured in the basic battery. Although the intent of these supplements is to measure students' knowledge of and ability to apply generalizations and principles, the test user should not assume the supplements are content free or independent of the curriculum used. Some science and social curricula will emphasize certain specific information or applications and neglect others. Thus, it is most important for the persons deciding on whether to use these supplements to carefully compare the local curriculum content and objectives and the kinds of knowledge and skill represented by the items. Further, potential users should study the technical terminology and general vocabulary used in the supplementary subtest items; frequently, the vocabulary level of the items seems to be higher than necessary. Students with lower verbal ability, but with good enough grasp of a generalization or principle to apply it to practical problems, may lack the requisite verbal skills needed to comprehend what some items are asking.

The ITBS has two excellent manuals: the Teacher's Guide and the Manual for School Administrators. A feature of the Teacher's Guide is that for each subtest, the Guide presents a taxonomy of skill objectives tested and a list of suggestions for teaching the skill. These suggestions and objectives should be very helpful to a teacher who is seriously concerned with reviewing the test results of each pupil and planning an instructional strategy. However, if a classroom teacher is to use the test results as an aid in individualizing instruction, it will be necessary for the school administration to provide the teacher with an analysis of each student's subskill performance. (It seems unlikely that teachers will have the time available to do this subskill analysis by hand.) The publisher provides two excellent computer-prepared reports for this purpose: the Student Criterion-Referenced Skills Analysis and the Pupil Item Response Record. Note that item scores and subskill scores based on clusters of items are not very reliable so that teachers will need to supplement these reports with information from their own observations and classroom knowledge of each pupil before making final decisions.

The suggestions for teaching each skill can be criticized because they are not specific prescriptions for teaching each of the subtests' microskills. However, this reviewer believes the suggestions to be at an appropriate level of specificity for this type of test. The suggestions, numbering about 15 per subtest on the average, form a coherent set of pedagogical principles for teaching in a particular developmental skill area. Teachers who learn and remember these principles should be able to apply them in specific ways when developing individualized lesson plans. The Guide also provides teachers with a bibliography of books and other printed materials useful for teaching in each of the basic skill areas.

The Manual for School Administrators is an excellent source for using the ITBS for administrative purposes. It is essential to consult this manual as part of the process of deciding whether to adopt this test. The Manual clearly spells out how to use the test for a variety of administrative purposes and explains how to use the support materials available from the publisher. The Manual should be "must" reading for elementary and junior high school instructional leaders (e.g., principals and coordinators).

The data presented in the Manual for School Administrators and in the Preliminary Technical Report indicate differences in performance between male and female students and between black and white students. In general, females perform better than males on most subtests. (However, the top 10% of the males tend to outperform the top 10% of the females in all areas except Language Usage and Use of Reference Materials.) An attempt was made to reduce potential gender and racial bias of test items during the development phase by having panels of judges review items for possible bias and offensiveness. Items were revised on the basis of these judgments. Although judges' ratings of items were reasonably reliable, there appeared to be little relationship between the judgment of the items' degrees of bias and the subsequent empirical difference between black and white student performance on the items. In another study, a special matched sample was constructed and used to study the performance of black/white and male/female groups. The manual and preliminary technical report provide extensive summaries of this data for Level 13 (grade 7). These data indicate the following: (*a*) disregarding race, females score slightly higher than males; (*b*) on the average, male and female distributions have essentially the same standard deviation; (*c*) on the average, blacks score substantially lower than whites; (*d*) the average standard deviation for black students' distributions is smaller than for white students' distributions; (*e*) the average KR20 reliabilities for males and females are approximately the same; (*f*) the average KR20 reliability for blacks is substantially lower than for whites; (*g*) the average standard errors of measurement for blacks and whites are the same; and (*h*) regardless of gender, the average subtest intercorrelation is lower for blacks than it is for whites.

The Manual indicates that the lowered reliability coefficients for blacks are the result of the smaller standard deviations for this group, a fact supported by the equal standard errors of measurement for the subgroups. The lower intercorrelations among the subtests for the black students are due in part to lower reliability, but the correlations are likely to remain lower even after correction for the attenuating effects of unreliability. The pattern among the reported intercorrelations appears to be roughly the same among the various subgroups, however. Factor analytic studies are not reported. Such studies would shed light on the question of whether the ITBS can be interpreted in the same way for each subgroup with whom it is used. Potential users of the ITBS are urged to follow the cautious advice of the test developers: "Procedures for evaluating achievement tests for possible bias are essentially the same as those used in evaluating the relevance of tests for individual pupils. It involves the same considerations previously suggested for evaluating test validity for the local school" (i.e., to carefully review each item to see if it is relevant to the local curriculum and what has been taught in class).

The ITBS appears to measure the growth or development of global cognitive skills that require relatively long periods of time for students to acquire. This contrasts with other basic skills tests that are constructed specifically to measure a few narrowly defined specific behaviors (cf., the IOX Basic Skill System). Such contrasts should alert the test user who is considering purchasing a basic skills test that the choice depends in part on the particular educational viewpoint that is adopted. When basic skills tests are to be used for program evaluation, the issue of the sensitivity of the test to the measurement of slowly acquired or quickly acquired cognitive skill becomes especially important because a test measuring global abilities is less likely to be sensitive to the specific effects of short-term instructional interventions than a test designed to measure the specific behaviors toward which the intervention is directed. It seems likely, however, that the ultimate goals of schooling include the learning of global cognitive abilities that students can use to perform a wide range of intellectual tasks. The ITBS seems more closely related to such ultimate goals.

SUMMARY. The ITBS is an excellent basic skills battery measuring global skills that are likely to be highly related to the long-term goals of elementary schools. The developers set an industry standard for the clear documentation of their choice of content and objectives to be measured and for their use of a well-documented ongoing empirical research program that supports both important test development decisions and the validity of the basic skills interpretation of the test results. The Teacher's Guide and Manual for School Administrators are of very high quality; if they are read and followed, improved instruction should result as well as improved test interpretation. In terms of technical quality, the ITBS is clearly the best basic skills battery of its kind. Before purchasing the test, however, the user should carefully follow the advice in the ITBS Manual: "The most valid achievement test for your school is the one that defines most adequately your objectives of instruction....To what extent this ideal has been attained in the Iowa Tests of Basic Skills is something that you must decide for yourself on the basis of a careful and critical item-by-item examination of the entire test battery."

[534]

Iowa Tests of Educational Development, [Seventh Edition]. Grades 9–12; 1942–81; ITED; previous edition still available; 9 scores: correctness and appropriateness of expression (Test E), ability to do quantitative thinking (Test Q), social studies (Test SS), natural sciences (Test NS), literary materials (Test L), vocabulary (Test V), sources of information (Test SI), total, reading total; Forms X-7, Y-7, ('79, 74 pages); 2 overlapping levels (grades 9–10, 11–12) in a single booklet; manual for teachers, counselors and examiners ('79, 47 pages); examiner's directions for testing ('79, 15 pages); manual for administrators and testing directors ('80, 58 pages); answer keys, norms and conversion tables ('82, 38 pages); score interpretation sheets ('82, 4 pages); separate answer sheets must be used; 1983 price data: $41.25 per 25 copies of either test; $19.80 per 100 answer sheets, 4 examiner's directions for testing and 1 norms and conversion tables booklet; $5.50 per 25 score interpretation sheets; $2.05 per norms and conversion tables booklet; $3 per manual for administrators and testing directors; $2.20 per manual for teachers, counselors, and examiners; $.90 per examiner's directions for testing; $4.10 per specimen set; rental and/or scoring service available from publisher; 245(280) minutes; prepared under the direction of Leonard S. Feldt, Robert A. Forsyth and E. F. Lindquist with the assistance of Stephanie D. Alnot and Paul S. Belgrade; Science Research Associates, Inc.*

See T3:1193 (14 references); for reviews by C. Mauritz Lindvall and John E. Milholland of an earlier form, see 8:20 (15 references); see T2:20 (85 references); for reviews by Ellis Batton Page and Alexander G. Wesman of earlier forms, see 6:14 (23 references); for reviews by J. Murray Lee and Stephen Wiseman, see 5:17 (9 references); for a review by Eric Gardner, see 4:17 (3 references); for reviews by Henry Chauncey, Gustav J. Froehlich, and Lavone A. Hanna, see 3:12.

TEST REFERENCES

1. Forsyth, R. A., & Ansley, T. N. The importance of computational skill for answering items in a mathematics problem-solving test: Implications for construct validity. EDUCATIONAL AND PSYCHOLOGICAL MEASUREMENT, 1982, 42, 257–263.

2. Lawson, A. E. Formal reasoning, achievement, and intelligence: An issue of importance. SCIENCE EDUCATION, 1982, 66, 77–83.

3. Ansley, T. N., & Forsyth, R. A. Relationsip of elementary and secondary school achievement test scores to college performance. EDUCATIONAL AND PSYCHOLOGICAL MEASUREMENT, 1983, 43, 1103–1112.

4. Hood, J., & Dubert, L. A. Decoding as a component of reading comprehension among secondary students. JOURNAL OF READING BEHAVIOR, 1983, 15, 51–61.

5. Jepsen, D. A., & Dustin, R. A simulated measure of adolescent career information-seeking behavior. MEASUREMENT AND EVALUATION IN GUIDANCE, 1984, 17, 32–39.

Review of Iowa Tests of Educational Development, [Seventh Edition] by EDWARD KIFER, Associate Professor of Education, University of Kentucky, Lexington, KY:

The precursor of the latest editions of the Iowa Tests of Educational Development (ITED) were developed in the 1940s under the able direction of E. F. Lindquist. That was a time when a general education was considered of utmost importance and attempts to operationalize and measure its broad outcomes were issues of highest priority.

Despite the fact that since then both testing and curriculum have taken a decided turn toward being more technical, narrow, and behavioristic, the Iowa Tests, in this case Forms X-7 and Y-7, maintain the tradition of attempting to measure broad educational outcomes. As stated in a Test Manual for Administrators and Testing Directors, the tests measure: "abilities that are important in adolescent and adult life and that constitute a major part of the foundation for continued learning. These skills include the ability to recognize the essentials of good writing, to solve quantitative problems, to analyze discussions of social issues critically, to understand nontechnical scientific reports and recognize sound methods of scientific inquiry, to perceive the subtle meanings and moods of literary materials, and to use sources of information and common tools of learning."

The manual states further that the tests are measures of abilities, or achievements, that are appropriate for "virtually all high school students, regardless of the particular courses they are taking or the curriculum they are following." The "abilities" vs. "achievements" terminology represents evident confusion about what to label the tests; the manual uses both kinds of language, calling it at once a measure of ability but also a measure of general achievement.

Given such worthy purposes, such a broad test, and such a diverse sample for which it is deemed appropriate, there should be no question about where and how such tests should be fitted into a testing program. That may not be the case, however. As tests have become increasingly (and wrongly, I believe) relied on as measures of outcomes of schooling, there has been corresponding technical interest in showing that achievement test items measure directly the content of the curriculum. Since the ITED is not intended to be either a representative or systematic sample of any particular content area, but rather a means to assess outcomes of having been educated in a traditional sense, it may be construed as a test battery that departs from the direction that many current tests are now taking.

The Seventh Edition of these tests, developed and tested from 1972 through 1978, continues to attempt to measure broad, general outcomes of education. It is similar to the Sixth Edition in the amount of time it takes to administer (slightly over 4 hours) and the scores it reports: correctness of expression, quantitative thinking, social studies, literary materials, general vocabulary, natural sciences, sources of information, an overall or composite score, and a total reading score. It is different from previous editions because each subtest contains two sets or levels of items: one set is focussed on 9th and 10th graders and contains items that are "easier and less sophisticated," according to the manual; and one set is focussed on 11th and 12th graders and contains items that are "more difficult" and "more similar in content to previous editions." Despite the presence of these two levels, scaling techniques have been used to equate the scores; standard scores, growth scale values, and percentile ranks have been made comparable for the two levels. Similarly, scores from this version of the tests have been equated with scores of previous versions. However, because of changes in our educational system, score interpretations that suggest precise comparisons between versions cannot be made.

The manual describes how the test was constructed, the various validities and reliabilities, interpretations of the scores, and reporting services offered by Science Research Associates. It is readable, informative, and a model for reasoned interpretation of scores. It quite rightly emphasizes the limitations of these tests, as well as any other tests, for assessing what it is that students know or learn. It also stresses quite correctly the importance of viewing test results in the context of the classroom, school, or school system from which they came.

The section on validity is straightforward, with an emphasis on the content validity of the tests. Here the test writers must rely on a philosophic defense of what is contained in their tests since the tests are not designed to have content validity in a strict sense. There may be no evidence, for example, to suggest that typical, day-to-day instruction in various content areas of the school emphasizes the kinds of skills that are required to answer correctly the items on these tests. That, of course, may reflect more the limitations of modern curriculum than the limitations of these tests, since the skills that are measured by the tests are arguably important.

If the skills measured by the test are part of the curriculum only insofar as certain teachers emphasize them, or are "there" in an amorphous and indirect way, evidence for content validity is not easily obtained. The tests may not have "content validity" as strictly defined since they sample no particular subject matter in a systematic way. They may have no "instructional validity" since they are not related directly to how teachers go about the task of educating the young. Their content validity, then, resides in the quality of the items and the importance of the things that are being measured. As a strict constructionist I would have to say the tests lack content validity; as an educator I would say the items appear to be "getting" at those things which I believe are extremely important educational outcomes.

Other types of validity discussed in the manual are criterion-related and construct validity. The manual makes these secondary to issues of content validity but reports a variety of studies that show substantial correlations between scores on these tests and various other achievement measures as well as relationships between these scores and other types of criterion measures. While the evidence is appropriate and necessary in order to understand better what the tests are, I was concerned with the datedness of the research references. Of the almost 70 sources cited in the manual, fewer than 10% of them were published after 1970 and none after 1980. More recent evidence about how these tests function would be desirable and should be published in a concise and easily understood form.

As one might expect from a long and sophisticated test battery, the reported reliability coefficients are impressively high. The internal consistency measures are around .9 and above. Coefficients reflecting relationships between parallel forms of the tests administered in consecutive years range from about .7 to .9, with the composite score having the highest coefficient for all samples. These coefficients are surely adequate. Nevertheless, I believe additional types of analyses to help the users of tests to understand the conditions under which score changes might increase, or the students for which score changes might more likely occur, are both desirable and necessary.

It appears that procedures for constructing norms and the samples of students who were tested produced national norms that are both appropriate and usable. Scores from the tests are reported in a variety of ways including scaled scores, both local and national percentile ranks, a profile of percent correct, and growth score values (GSVs). These GSVs, however, are more properly interpreted as average differences between adjacent grade levels than growth over time of individuals since they are based on cross-sectional rather than longitudinal data.

Scores on the various subtests are highly correlated (around .7 and above) reflecting, I believe, the emphasis on reading in all parts of the test. Each of the subtests requires the ability to read well, and although attempts have been made to control the difficulty or readability of the items, I was taken by the density of the prose on all subtests. The test manual cautions the test user to use care in interpreting scores, and to use other means of assessment, for those students who are considered slow or deficient readers. That warning, I believe, must be taken seriously. Although the test manual suggests that liberal time allotments have been made so each student should be able to complete each part of the test, additional caution should be used in interpreting scores when students, for whatever the reasons, fail to complete any parts of the test.

The Manual for Administrators and Testing Directors provides ideas and concrete examples of how these scores might be used to evaluate educational programs. This section shows how test scores, item responses, and score profiles could be used to draw inferences about the effectiveness of a curriculum and includes proper cautions about keeping the results in perspective. The manual fails to point out, however, that a school system need not give these tests to all students in order to gather this evidence. In fact, random samples of students would provide comparable information for less cost and take less testing time.

Should a school or school system wish to get information about what might be construed as broad outcomes of schooling with a heavy dose of reading, the Iowa Tests of Educational Development are appropriate to consider. In that case, the potential user should carefully scrutinize the items to decide whether the kinds of skills that are emphasized in the test are compatible with the goals of the school or system. A congruence between what is being measured and what is considered desirable in terms of outcomes of instruction is a necessary prerequisite for their adoption. If more narrow assessments of the curriculum are desired, other tests and test batteries may be more appropriate.

Review of Iowa Tests of Educational Development, Seventh Edition, by JAMES L. WARDROP, Associate Professor of Educational Psychology, University of Illinois at Urbana-Champaign, Urbana, IL:

The Iowa Tests of Educational Development (ITED) consist of seven tests: Correctness and Appropriateness of Expression, Quantitative Thinking, Social Studies, Natural Sciences, Literary Materials, Vocabulary, and Use of Sources of Information. Each test has two overlapping levels, Level I primarily for grades 9 and 10 and Level II for grades 11 and 12. Although easier than former editions of the ITED, Level I is not intended as a test of "minimum competencies" only.

From the fourth to the fifth edition of the ITED, testing time had been decreased by about half. This latest revision restores 50 minutes to the testing time, primarily through the addition of a subtest titled Ability to Interpret Literary Materials. The Reading Comprehension test from earlier versions has been eliminated, but comprehension passages and items are incorporated in the Natural Science and the Social Studies tests. In addition, the Language Arts test, with subscores for Usage and Spelling, has been replaced by a test titled Correctness and Appropriateness of Expression, with no subscores.

High school achievement batteries share a common feature: they are limited to assessing the subset of general skills and understanding that is not specific to any particular curriculum. The tests must be as applicable to students pursuing a college-preparatory curriculum as to those whose studies are vocationally oriented. Consequently, those unique and specialized learnings that should be a part of each pupil's high school education are not—and cannot be—well represented. Supplementing these general achievement batteries with course-related tests is important.

As is typical with high school achievement batteries, the authors of the ITED have attempted to focus on the skills necessary for the achievement of long-range educational goals that are common to all students. Items requiring the application of knowledge and skills are more common than in other batteries, although many items involving knowledge and literal comprehension are also to be found. Although the battery has been reorganized and the test of Ability to Interpret Literary Materials added, the tests continue to cover essentially the same content areas as did earlier versions.

CONTENT. The ITED subtests are rather traditional in form and content. Correctness and Appropriateness of Expression is essentially a proofreading test; the test of Ability to do Quantitative Thinking consists almost entirely of "story problems," with virtually no mathematics content that has not been introduced by grade 8; Social Studies and Natural Science each have two parts, "concepts and background" and "reading materials"; Ability to Interpret Literary Materials is a reading comprehension test, with content taken from literary sources and questions emphasizing inference and interpretation; and Vocabulary is a test requiring the choice of synonyms for words in a (phrasal) context.

STANDARDIZATION. The standardization procedure for this latest revision was bizarre. Although reference is made to "the broad national base of the normative high school data for the ITED" or "the percentage of a nationwide sample of students...who answered the item correctly," a diligent search finally led to the discovery that this seventh edition was not administered to a representative national sample. Apparently, the "Standardization" was accomplished in two stages.

The first stage was an "equating study" involving approximately 6,100 students from 20 schools, of which 13 were from Iowa, and 7 from other parts of the country. Note that this is not the equating study described in the Manual for Administrators and Testing Directors. The purpose of this study was to equate forms X-7 and Y-7 to the previously standardized form Y-5, using equipercentile equating. Given the changes in format and organization from the fifth to the seventh editions, equating for some scales required considerable creativity. (For example, Test L: Ability to Interpret Literary Materials, had no counterpart in the fifth edition, so it was equated to the latter's Reading Comprehension Test.)

After the equating study had been completed, "Representative Samples" of examinees from Iowa "were selected so that their scores reproduced the national norms." Score distributions for these samples "were used to estimate test reliability, standard error of measurement, and other test characteristics for a 'national' sample of examinees." (Note the quotes around "national"; they do not appear anywhere else in the manuals and materials for the ITED.) In addition, "Data from the *national* samples were used to calculate the national percentile bands" [emphasis added].

Statistical legerdemain is not an acceptable substitute for the use of proper standardization procedures. The major flaw in equipercentile equating is that it can be applied to any pair of tests and yield reasonable looking results, no matter how badly the assumption that the two tests are measuring the same trait has been violated. "Representative" samples of Iowa high school students whose score distributions reproduce some kind of estimated national norms do not qualify as "national samples" or provide a "broad national base."

The manuals and other materials accompanying this edition of the ITED give the impression that norms and test characteristics are based on a national standardization that simply was not carried out.

RELIABILITY. Reliability data for the ITED subtests and composites are reported in two places. In the Manual for Administrators and Testing Directors, a single reliability estimate is reported for Forms X-7 and Y-7 at each grade level. These values range from .87 to .94 for individual subtests, with 18 of the 28 coefficients in the .90s. In the Technical Supplement to Answer Keys, Norms, and Conversion Tables, separate reliabilities are reported for the two forms for both fall and spring testing. Here, subtest reliabilities range from .85 to .94, and 77 of the 112 values are in the .90s. Stability estimates are not available, and the claim that "it is administratively impossible to obtain parallel-forms correlations based upon representative groups of students" is unconvincing. Correlations between "parallel forms administered in consecutive years" for a college entrant sample are in fact reported for Forms X-6 and Y-6, although it is not apparent that these values are relevant to the seventh edition.

VALIDITY. The publishers claim that "content validity is by far the most important category for achievement tests." Such a claim is surely not consistent with contemporary thinking in measurement. Particularly for a subtest labeled "Quantitative Thinking," intended "to measure the student's ability to employ appropriate quantitative reasoning," or for the Vocabulary test, which "can serve as one of the best predictors of future success in school work," construct and criterion-related validities are at least as important as content validity. For the most part, content validity is treated by the presentation of item classification by content and skill categories. There is no clear description presented of the content domains from which items were derived, because the tests are concerned with the general educational development of students more than with the specific material presented in high school courses. It is the vagueness of domain specification that constitutes the major limitation of the evidence for the ITED's content validity.

The Manual for Administrators and Testing Directors presents additional validity information consisting primarily of correlations with other indicators (e.g., high school grades, subject-area achievement measures, ACT subtests, college freshman grades). Some of these correlations are treated as evidence for criterion-related validity, others for construct validity. Indeed, Lindvall's criticisms in the *8th MMY* (8:20) of the presentation of validity data for the fifth edition of the ITED apply without modification to the current edition.

Although well over 200 correlation coefficients are presented to describe the relationship of the ITED to other measures, they are all based on the third through sixth editions of the battery. No criterion-related validity data are presented for the current edition. Of course, it takes time to accumulate data about external corrrelations for an achievement battery, so the fact that few such data are available shortly after its release should not be viewed too harshly. On the other hand, it seems unlikely that validity coefficients for the 1952 or 1962 editions have much relevance to judging the utility of this 1980 edition.

SCORES AND USES. The material on using test results is as well done as I have seen. It provides some specific examples, some good general advice, and carefully-worded suggestions for how to interpret various pieces of information about student performance. Various derived scores are available, including standard scores, percentile ranks, and "growth scale values." These latter scores are described as "equal-interval, expanded standard score scales" used for both the SRA Achievement Series and the ITED. Although labeled as a "growth" scale, these scores are based on cross-sectional data, not longitudinal.

A variety of score reports is available. In general, these reports provide information that school administrators and teachers should find useful. Unfortunately, raw scores are not provided on any of these reports.

SUMMARY. The ITED have one of the most impressive pedigrees of all standardized test batteries. The first edition appeared over 40 years ago, and over the decades some of the leading professionals in educational measurement have been associated with these tests. It is disconcerting, then, to note the deficiencies of this seventh edition: (1) the various pieces of information needed to evaluate the test are located in diverse places throughout the several publications describing the battery, and the organization of this information sometimes seems capricious; (2) unnecessary inconsistencies can be found in different discussions of the same topic; (3) evidence for "criterion-related" and "construct" validity is based entirely on previous editions of the battery, editions published from 1952 to 1972; and (4) no national standardization was carried out for this latest edition, even though it differs considerably in content and organization from the previous edition.

For this reviewer, the most serious concern is with the misleading presentation of information about the development of national norms for the seventh edition. (In addition to the earlier illustrations in this review, see the section on "Derivation of Norms" in the Manual for Administrators and Testing Directors, p. 52.) Only a careful and diligent reading of all materials allows one to recognize that the national standardization was carried out using the *fifth* edition, and that norms for the seventh edition were derived on the basis of a study equating the seventh edition to the fifth. The equating study itself involved what is certainly an unrepresentative sample of 20 high schools.

One is left with the impression that this seventh edition of this venerable battery has been too casually produced. Publishers and developers seem to have relied too much on historical reputation and the tradition of high quality associated with previous editions, rather than to have invested the time, expertise, and resources necessary to maintain the high quality of the ITED. There is much that is good about these tests, and a lot of good thinking and sound advice are represented in the various manuals and other publications accompanying them. The deficiencies noted in this review are correctable, but there is no "easy fix."

A careful review and rewrite of the manuals, some reconceptualization of the nature of the evidence for the various sorts of validity, the estimation of short-term stability of scores, and an adequate national standardization program would restore the ITED to a position of eminence among high school achievement batteries.

[535]

IOX Basic Skill System. End of grades 5 or 6, grades 9–12; 1978–79; "minimal competency assessment"; criterion-referenced; 3 tests: Reading, Writing, Mathematics; 2 levels; 1983 price data: $6.95 per 50 answer sheets; $3.95 per teacher's guide; $3.95 per test manual; $2.50 per specimen set of either level; IOX Assessment Associates.*

a) ELEMENTARY LEVEL. End of grades 5 or 6; 1979; Forms A, B, (9–11 pages); test manual (16 pages); teacher's guide (18–20 pages) for each test; separate answer sheets (NCS) must be used; instructional material available; $37.50 per 25 tests; (40–45) minutes per test.

b) SECONDARY LEVEL. Grades 9–12; 1978; Forms A, B, (8–13 pages); test manual (14 pages); teacher's guide (18 pages) for each test; separate answer sheets (NCS) must be used; practice exercises and instructional material available; $42.50 per 25 reading tests; $37.50 per 25 writing or mathematics tests; $29.95 per set of practice exercises (spirit masters) including duplicable answer sheet and teacher's guide; $29.95 per set of instructional audio-cassette tapes; (45–50) minutes per test.

Review of IOX Basic Skill System by ANTHONY J. NITKO, Professor of Education, University of Pittsburgh, Pittsburgh, PA:

The IOX Basic Skill System serves two purposes: to guide instruction and to certify minimum competence. Unlike basic skills survey tests, the IOX Basic Skill Tests test a small number of specific skills in each of three content areas. There are two levels of tests: At the elementary level (fifth and sixth grade) seven skills in reading, eight in writing, and six in mathematics are assessed; at the secondary level (12th grade) five reading skills, four writing skills and four mathematic skills are assessed. Although there are fewer skills tested at the secondary level, they are more encompassing than the skills tested at the elementary level.

Both typical survey tests of basic skills and the IOX Basic Skill Tests explicitly state that test information should be used by teachers to guide instruction. A fundamental difference between the two types of tests is the breadth of the skill domain each measures and advocates that students learn. The IOX Tests represent the narrower domain.

In order to identify a potential domain, the developers of the IOX tests reviewed the types of skills several states wanted to include in minimum competency graduation programs. Certain of these competencies were selected and reviewed by panels of educators. A revised final list formed the basis for developing the secondary level tests. The skills on the elementary level tests were selected because the developers believe the skills facilitate learning of the broader skills on the secondary level tests.

Each of the skills measured by the IOX tests is defined by an IOX Test Specification that describes in an elaborate technical way all potentially useful test items. This technical description for each skill consists of four parts: (1) an elaborated statement similar to a behavioral objective, (2) a sample of the item format to be used, (3) a list of rules for writing item stems and accompanying interpretive materials, and (4) a list of rules for writing the response alternative for the multiple-choice items. Sometimes an IOX Test Specification includes a content supplement describing the particular content eligible for testing (e.g., types of prefixes and suffixes permitted in the word meaning subtest). Item writers followed the specifications' rules to generate test items. IOX Test Specifications are available as supplemental booklets.

Although each IOX Test Specification defines a large pool or domain of potentially useful items, an additional restriction is placed on the domain: The items must pass statistical muster in the field trials. In order to be included in the test for a specific skill, the secondary level test items had to have similar levels of difficulty and exhibit reasonable levels of discrimination (in the traditional norm-referenced sense). Further, they had to remain stable over a 1-week testing interval. An additional requirement for the elementary level items was that they meet the criteria of the one parameter latent trait (Rasch) model. Thus, although not articulated in the IOX Test Specification booklets, these statistical criteria become part of the domain definition.

The tests are printed as two forms, A and B. The developers strongly urge that if the test is used for purposes of deciding high school graduation, *both* forms should be used, a suggestion with which this reviewer wholeheartedly agrees. There are too few items in the separate forms, and data presented in the Test Manual demonstrate that at the secondary level there are considerable form-to-form subtest differences.

The developers recommend that scores be reported on a skill-by-skill (i.e., subtest) basis in order to facilitate diagnosis and instruction. Reliability data reported in the secondary level Test Manual, however, lead this reviewer to recommend that educators use more than scores on these IOX subtests to make decisions about minimum competence on each skill. With few exceptions there are 10 items per subtest (if both forms are used). Internal consistency reliability within subtests is relatively low. Test-retest (1-week interval) reliabilities range as follows: .40–.82 (mean=.60) for the reading subtests, .63–.81 (mean=.74) for the writing subtests, and .65–.87 (mean=.75) for the mathematics subtests. (It should be noted that these data are based on sample sizes of approximately 50 students and that the samples exhibit low variability in scores.) Although diagnosis and remediation are good principles to follow, decisions for individual students will have to be guided by additional information and teacher judgment.

The validity information provided for the IOX Basic Skill Tests is of two types: content validity (called "descriptive validity" in the Test Manual) and curricular relevance (called "domain-selection validity" in the Manual). Content validity is judged by asking whether the test items constitute a representative sample from the test developer's domain. When both Form A and Form B are used, the items do seem to represent the developers' domain, as this domain is articulated in the IOX Test Specifications. (This statement is qualified, however, by noting that some statistical culling of items has been done.) Curricular relevance is judged by each user of the test, rather than by the test developer. The question asked is whether the items in the test constitute a representative sample of what a school district considers to be the important minimum competency skills. The developers support their selection of skills by reporting that the skills appearing on the test were among those minimum competencies most highly rated in a survey of teachers and administrators. Such a statement, however, is more of a guide for marketing than it is a judgment of the relevance of the test for a particular school district. It is essential, therefore, that any person seriously considering adopting these tests carefully review the items in order to decide whether they represent what that person has in mind as "minimum competency."

No evidence is provided to establish the construct validity of these tests, although construct interpretations abound. The developers mention "probable generalizability," for example, by which they mean that if a student passed an IOX Basic Skill subtest, that student is likely to pass any other test measuring that skill. Another construct interpretation used by the developers is "teachability." Here the developers mean that the test measures skills that can be improved by direct instruction. Both of these construct interpretations are amenable to empirical verification, but no data are provided, other than the developers' suggestion that these interpretations can be made for IOX Basic Skill Tests.

An integral part of the IOX Basic Skill System is a separate Teacher's Guide that describes for each area (Reading, Writing and Mathematics) the specific subtests (skills) and offers teaching suggestions. The Skill Description section is a simplified explanation of the domain articulated in the IOX Test Specification booklets. It provides teachers with a clear description of the specific types of test items that will appear on the test. The Instructional Guidelines section identifies the subskills that make up the broader skill tested and suggests teaching strategies and activities. The Instructional Guidelines section seems to be a bit thin, however. More helpful teaching suggestions are given in the teacher's guides of achievement survey batteries such as the California Achievement Test and the Iowa Tests of Basic Skills. Teachers are advised to review sources other than the IOX Teacher's Guides for suggestions on how to teach basic skills.

The elementary level has tables of percentile ranks for fifth- and sixth-grade students. This reviewer recommends that these percentile ranks not be used because it is not clear what norm group the data represent, and these percentile ranks are estimated from the field trials in which each student took only 10 items, rather than taking the entire test. The developers recognize these problems and state that percentile ranks should be interpreted "with considerable caution, especially for extremely high and extremely low scores."

SUMMARY. The IOX Basic Skill Tests measure a very limited number of very specific reading, writing, and mathematical skills. A potential test user should recognize that these tests measure only minimal skills. If a school system teaches only these minimal skills, children are likely to be unprepared to compete in a highly technological society.

The skill subtests seem not to be reliable enough for differential diagnosis using only test scores. Persons contemplating using the IOX Basic Skill Tests for purposes of diagnosis and instruction are advised to take into account all additional relevant educational information when interpreting subtest scores.

The IOX Basic Skill Tests developers are to be commended for the careful and extensive way they have defined the precise nature of the domain from which test items are sampled. An additional commendation is given for the clear explanation of the domains in the Teacher's Guides. With knowledge of these domains and with some thoughtful preparation, teachers should be able to teach students how to perform well on any item sampled from an IOX Test Specification.

Review of IOX Basic Skill System by GUS P. PLESSAS, Professor of Education, California State University, Sacramento, Sacramento, CA:

The IOX Basic Skill System originated with the IOX Basic Skill Tests at the secondary level as minimum competency measures for high school graduation. Linked to these tests, as part of the overall design, is an elementary level battery of performance measures. Its chief purpose is to assess prerequisite abilities to successful achievement on the IOX Secondary Basic Skills Tests of reading, writing, and mathematics. Both levels of IOX tests include in most instances 5 items for assessing each skill in Form A and a similar number in Form B so that an average of 10 items are used for each skill assessment when both forms are given together.

Testing procedures and test information are provided in a manual for each school level of IOX measures. Instructions are written in a clear and precise style, providing an examiner with succinct guidelines for test administration. Also conveniently included is a concise description in performance terms of skills measured in the IOX series.

For ease of administration, the test format is plain and simple. Directions for examiners are straightforward and easy-to-follow; test items are legible and clear-cut.

Of practical use to a classroom teacher would be the Teacher's Guide, which accompanies the tests and elaborates each assessment area in terms of skills covered as well as related instructional strategies including suggested activities for teaching.

Central to the effective use of the IOX System is knowing the content of the tests and its relevance to the objectives of a school program. The manual states that "the IOX Basic Skills Tests were formulated so that educators can organize instructional sequences which will have a high likelihood of promoting the important skills measured in the tests." Here we can ask, then, what insights can be gained from the results of IOX if the skills assessed are not related distinctly to program objectives of a given school? This question implies that a school should examine critically any measure of minimal competency for similarity in content and purpose with those of its curriculum. Such an independent examination is crucial to the choosing of any tests, and especially one that is deliberately constructed to yield measurements that are directly interpreted in terms of specific performance standards. What type of test is best? The answer depends mainly on the purpose of testing. Appraisals of minimum competency are best when an administrator or teacher wants to know if a student has acquired a particular skill or knowledge as taught in a given program. In other words, such a test should determine the extent to which individuals in a group have learned or mastered a given unit of instruction.

Of serious concern relative to the significance of IOX test scores is whether the tests give consistent or reliable results. Put another way, how sure can an examiner be that the obtained IOX scores of test takers are actually true scores and that they would not vary greatly under repeated testing conditions?

Consider, for example, the reliability data for IOX Basic Skills Tests, Secondary Level. First, the number of items for each skill for each form is 5, but the test authors recommended combined-form, 10-item tests to achieve higher reliability values than those which would emerge from the use of either Form A or B alone. In the words of the authors, "the two forms of a particular test are strongly recommended to be used and scored together, rather than separately, in order to provide at least 10 items per skill."

Second, for individual assessment, such as that employed in making a pass or fail judgement on competency performance of a given skill by a given student, a test should have a reliability coefficient of at least .90. Data on the test-retest reliabilities of the Basic Skills Tests, Secondary Level, disclosed that not one variable attained a reliability of .90, but instead the median value is .70 with a range of .40 to .87 among the 13 competencies tested. If administrators only wish to compare test results of one school with another, these reliabilities are not as important as they would be for judgments about a single individual. But low reliability values place limits on test validity as well.

The validation of the IOX measures was limited to "descriptive" validity (content validity) and "domain-selection" validity. Thus, the accuracy with which the IOX tests measure what they purport to measure is not validated against any external criteria. It is wise, therefore, to inspect carefully the test items in the light of both content validity and face validity in terms of what it is one wants to measure for minimal competency.

The authors offer several ways to establish criteria for setting standards on the various tests (e.g., a percent correct for each skill, etc.). But in reality the test user must determine the level of success demanded before a student is allowed to "pass" a test. In the secondary level manual the authors state that "because the IOX Basic Skills Tests were developed with considerable speed....there was insufficient time to gather the array of comparative student performance data which the IOX staff would have preferred." In sum, the IOX Basic Skill System may or may not yield desired information, depending on the test user's circumstances. An important consideration is the school's ability to decide exactly what should be measured in the light of school program content and objectives. Where these coincide, the IOX system should be considered. But all decisions about cutoff scores and further testing are left to the user of the IOX measures. It seems that a locally created minimum proficiency test would serve a consumer just as well as the IOX system, for there is nothing new or unique about the IOX test or test items.

[536]

The IOX Basic Skills Word List. Grades 1–12; 1980; "a resource for reading instruction and readability determination"; 1 form (60 pages, contains word lists which are organized cumulatively for grades 1 through 12 as well as grade-level-by-grade-level); 1983 price data: $14.95 per book; IOX Assessment Associates.*

Review of The IOX Basic Skills Word List by MARIAM JEAN DREHER, Assistant Professor of Curriculum and Instruction, College of Education, University of Maryland, College Park, MD:

The IOX Basic Skills Word List (BSWL) is not a test but rather a graded list of words intended to be used as a resource in teaching and testing basic skills and in determining readability levels. BSWL is accompanied by a list of rules indicating the changes that can be made in a word without changing its grade level (e.g., beginning with the sixth-grade list, an affix can be added to a root word). The word list is prefaced by four pages explaining its uses and how it was generated.

DEVELOPMENT. Unlike other graded word lists which use only one criterion for selecting words, BSWL used three criteria: "(1) the frequency with which words occur in reading textbooks, (2) the frequency of words in generally read materials, and (3) children's demonstrated familiarity with particular words." In fact, the BSWL combines three existing word lists each based on one of the above criteria. The authors of BSWL started with the *EDL Core Vocabularies* (Taylor et al., 1979), which assign words to a grade level based on their frequency of occurrence in nine basal reading series. They then compared the EDL list to *The Living Word Vocabulary* (Dale & O'Rourke, 1976) which places words at a grade level according to their familiarity to children at that grade level. If the placement on the EDL list matched the grade placement on the familiarity rating, the word was retained on that grade level list. However, if an EDL word did not meet the familiarity criterion, then it was moved to a higher grade level. Next, the BSWL authors incorporated word frequency in students' general reading materials by checking their list against Sakiey and Fry's (1979) *3,000 Instant Words*. (These words are the 3,000 most frequent words from the Carroll, Davies, and Richman [1971] list of the most frequent words in samples of reading materials to which students in grades 3 through 9 are exposed.) Any words from the Sakiey and Fry list that were not already on the list were added to ensure that words important in general reading would be included. In short, BSWL is basically the EDL list with levels adjusted for familiarity and modified as needed to include words important in general reading.

USES. The authors state that BSWL is to be a teaching resource; it is to tell teachers which words their students need to master at each grade level. This claim seems reasonable since the list reflects not only the words that students in a particular grade are likely to need (based on frequency of occurrence) but also the words that the average student in a grade is likely to know (based on familiarity ratings). Thus, teachers concerned with basic skills can check their students' knowledge against the "average" provided by the list. Children who do not know the words can be instructed on them. However, no mention is made of effective ways of teaching vocabulary words to children. While it may not be appropriate to include such strategies, it probably would be appropriate to mention the need for effective strategies and to cite sources which teachers could refer to (e.g., Johnson & Pearson, 1978). Such sources seem important since vocabulary is often "taught" by having children copy dictionary definitions (Durkin, 1983).

In addition to its use as an instructional resource, another BSWL purpose is to determine readability levels for test items. Since it takes into account both word frequency and familiarity ratings, BSWL seems to have great potential for readability use. Indeed, BSWL grew out of a need to write test items at a precise reading level. The BSWL authors argue that for the best results, test items should be written at a designated readability level; teachers would then know which words their students need to master in order to handle the items. To develop tests at a particular level, teachers are told to use BSWL as a guide. No explicit procedure is stated, but apparently items of known readability can be constructed by using only words at or below the designated BSWL grade level. This type of item control is important because it would allow teachers to match item readability with students' reading level and would thus help ensure that basic skill test results reflected the skill tested and not vocabulary knowledge. However, readability is not only a matter of considering individual words, but could vary depending on how those individual words were put together in sentences and larger units. Reading difficulty is affected by such factors as syntactic structure and logical ordering of ideas as well as vocabulary (Davison & Kantor, 1982). Consequently, the BSWL authors should at least note the need to consider other factors influencing a test item's difficulty once it has been generated using the word list.

Finally, BSWL is also said to be useful for determining readability levels of instructional materials. But this use needs to be clarified. The authors state that if instructional materials appear inappropriate for a certain grade level, "then the grade level of questionable words can be quickly ascertained through the use of the Basic Skills Word List." This procedure would tell teachers the level of the *words* in question. However, BSWL is supposed to be useful for determining the level of *instructional materials*, that is, passages as well as individual words. But exactly how would teachers determine the level of a passage? Are they to check the level of "questionable" words and then assign the passage the same level? How reliable an estimate would this procedure yield? What if the questionable words are at different levels? What if one teacher selects different words from a passage than another teacher? Although the importance of determining the readability of instructional materials is stressed, no other explanations or examples are given on how to use the BSWL for this purpose. But several further questions remain. For example, what if a teacher does not have any particular questionable words, but simply wants an estimate of the material's level? Does he or she look up the grade levels of all the words in a passage and then take an average? Or perhaps a passage is automatically assigned a readability level equal to the list level of the hardest word in the passage. Just what percentage of words at a given level must a passage contain to make it that level? BSWL authors criticize current readability formulas, but they are vague in explaining how BSWL is to be used to solve the problems cited.

SUMMARY. By blending three different word lists, BSWL provides a unique resource indicating what vocabulary words most children at each grade level know and what they are likely to need in reading. Thus, teachers can check their students' knowledge against a basic vocabulary list for a particular level and can provide instruction on the words their students have not mastered. BSWL is also a good guideline to help teachers control the readability level when they write basic skills test items. But teachers must not assume that the readability of an item can be guaranteed by using only words from a designated level. Teachers should screen items carefully since the difficulty of individual vocabulary words is not the only determinant of readability. Finally, the very brief preface needs to be expanded so that the authors can clarify and validate their claims that the list is useful for determining the readability of instructional material.

REVIEWER'S REFERENCES

Carroll, J. B., Davies, P., & Richman, B. WORD FREQUENCY BOOK. New York: American Heritage Publishing Company, 1971.

Dale, E., & O'Rourke, J. THE LIVING WORD VOCABULARY—THE WORDS WE KNOW. Elgin, IL: Dome Press, Inc., 1976.

Johnson, D. D., & Pearson, P. D. TEACHING READING VOCABULARY. New York: Holt, Rinehart and Winston, 1978.

Sakiey, E., & Fry, E. 3,000 INSTANT WORDS. Providence, RI: Jamestown Pubs., Inc., 1979.

Taylor, S. E., Frackenpohl, H., White, C. E., Nieroroda, B. W., Browning, C. L., & Birsner, P. E. EDL CORE VOCABULARIES IN READING, MATHEMATICS, AND SOCIAL STUDIES. New York: McGraw-Hill, 1979.

Davison, A., & Kantor, R. N. On the failure of readability formulas to define readable texts: A case study from adaptations. READING RESEARCH QUARTERLY, 1982, 17, 187–209.

Durkin, D. TEACHING THEM TO READ (4th ed.). Boston: Allyn and Bacon, 1983.

Review of The IOX Basic Skills Word List by SUSANNA W. PFLAUM, Dean, Honors College, University of Illinois at Chicago, Chicago, IL:

This word list book was developed as "a resource for reading teachers who are attempting to enhance their students' fundamental reading skills" and also "to permit the more rigorous determination of readability levels for both instructional materials and testing devices." According to the directions, teachers may use the word lists for diagnosis and to select words for direct teaching. Because, as the authors maintain, readability formulas do not reflect vocabulary concerns sufficiently, this word list provides needed guidance on word levels, particularly in basic skills instructional and testing materials. The words to be included were selected from four sources: the *EDL Core Vocabularies in Reading, Mathematics, Science, and Social Studies* (Taylor, 1979), which provided the frequency of usage in reading texts; *The Living Word Vocabulary—The Words We Know* (Dale & O'Rourke, 1976), which provided an index of student knowledge of words and numbers per grade; and *Word Frequency Book* (Carroll, Davies, & Richman, 1971), which indicated frequency of use. Frequency of use was also checked with 3,000 *Instant Words* (Sakiey & Fry, 1979) under an incorrect assumption that the Carroll et al. source did not rank their 5,000,000 words by frequency. The total of 7,318 words are distributed unevenly across the grades with the primary grade number apparently determined by level of words introduced in reading materials, beginning with 341 in grade 1. This is a conservative estimate and more representative of basal reading series of the later 1960s and early 1970s than more recent ones. The determination of word load for grades 5 and above was based on words that are known by students as reported in the Dale and O'Rourke study (1976). Thus, in the middle grades, there are 971 at grade 5, 884 at grade 7, 325 at grade 9, and 393 at grade 11, for example.

The IOX Word List represents a very useable source for teaching and testing. Its usefulness for readability determination is less obvious. Since the corpus is so small, one would have difficulty determining difficulty of written text, even of test materials. Other weaknesses include the error about the Carroll et al. study and the decision to include few words at the secondary level, thereby limiting the potential usefulness at those levels to an extreme minimum for vocabulary development.

REVIEWER'S REFERENCES

Carroll, J., Davies, P., & Richman, B. WORD FREQUENCY BOOK. New York: American Heritage Publishing Company, 1971.

Dale, E., & O'Rourke, J. THE LIVING WORD VOCABULARY—THE WORDS WE KNOW. Elgin, IL: Dome Press, Inc., 1976.

Sakiey, E., & Fry, E. 3,000 INSTANT WORDS. Providence, RI: Jamestown Pubs., Inc., 1979.

Taylor, S. EDL CORE VOCABULARIES IN READING, MATHEMATICS, SCIENCE, AND SOCIAL STUDIES. New York: McGraw-Hill, 1979.

[537]

The IPAT Anxiety Scale Questionnaire. Ages 14 and over; 1957–76; ASQ; also called IPAT Anxiety Scale; title on test is Self Analysis Form, 1976 Edition; total score plus 7 optional scores (recommended only for experimental use): covert anxiety, overt anxiety, 5 component scores (apprehension, tension, low self-control, emotional instability, suspicion; reliability, validity, and norms data based on 1957 edition; no norms for part scores; 1 form ('76, 4 pages); handbook ('76, 106 pages); 1984 price data: $4.75 per 25 tests; $.85 per scoring stencil; $5.75 per handbook; $6.95 per specimen set; (5–10) minutes; Raymond B. Cattell, Samuel E. Krug (manual), and Ivan H. Scheier (manual); Institute for Personality and Ability Testing, Inc.*

South African adaptation: Ages 15 and over; 1968; adaptation by Elizabeth M. Madge; Human Sciences Research Council [South Africa].*

See T3:1197 (48 references); for reviews by Richard I. Lanyon and Paul McReynolds, see 8:582 (85 references); see also T2:1225 (120 references) and P:116 (45 references); for a review by Jacob Cohen of the earlier edition, see 6:121 (23 references); for reviews by J. P. Guilford and E. Lowell Kelly and an excerpted review by Laurance F. Shaffer, see 5:70.

TEST REFERENCES

1. Cochrane, N., & Neilson, M. Depressive illness: The role of aggression further considered. PSYCHOLOGICAL MEDICINE, 1977, 7, 283–288.

2. Cox, R. J., & McGuinness, D. The effect of chronic anxiety level upon self control of heart rate. BIOLOGICAL PSYCHOLOGY, 1977, 5, 7–14.

3. Haskell, S. D. Desired family-size correlates for single undergraduates. PSYCHOLOGY OF WOMEN QUARTERLY, 1977, 2, 5–15.

4. Egeland, B. Preliminary results of a prospective study of the antecedents of child abuse. CHILD ABUSE & NEGLECT, 1979, 3, 269–278.

5. Lion, J. R. Benzodiazepines in the treatment of aggressive patients. THE JOURNAL OF CLINICAL PSYCHIATRY, 1979, 40, 70–71.

6. Hauri, P. Treating psychophysiologic insomnia with biofeedback. ARCHIVES OF GENERAL PSYCHIATRY, 1981, 38, 752–758.

7. Shirom, A., Eden, D., & Kellermann, J. J. Effects of population changes on psychological and physiological strain in kibbutz communities. AMERICAN JOURNAL OF COMMUNITY PSYCHOLOGY, 1981, 9, 27–43.

8. Dodez, O., Zelhart, P. F., & Markley, R. P. Compatibility of self-actualization and anxiety. JOURNAL OF CLINICAL PSYCHOLOGY, 1982, 38, 696–702.

9. Lapierre, Y. D., Tremblay, A., Gagnon, A., Monpremier, P., Berliss, H., & Oyewumi, L. K. A therapeutic and discontinuation study of clobazam and diazepam in anxiety neurosis. THE JOURNAL OF CLINICAL PSYCHIATRY, 1982, 43, 372–374.

10. Pecknold, J. C., McClure, D. J., Appeltauer, L., Allan, T., & Wrzesinski, L. Does tryptophan potentiate clomipramine in the treatment of agoraphobia and social phobic patients? BRITISH JOURNAL OF PSYCHIATRY, 1982, 140, 484–490.

11. Plante, T. G. Concurrent validity for an Activity Vector Analysis index of anxiety. PERCEPTUAL AND MOTOR SKILLS, 1982, 55, 1043–1047.
12. Sameroff, A. J., Seifer, R., & Elias, P. K. Sociocultural variability in infant temperament ratings. CHILD DEVELOPMENT, 1982, 53, 164–173.
13. Payne, F. D., & Futterman, J. R. "Masculinity," "Femininity," and adjustment in college men. JOURNAL OF RESEARCH IN PERSONALITY, 1983, 17, 110–124.
14. Busch-Rossnagel, N. A., Peters, D. L., & Daly, M. J. Mothers of vulnerable and normal infants: More alike than different. FAMILY RELATIONS, 1984, 33, 149–154.

[538]

IPMA Fire Service Tests. Prospective fire service personnel; 1973–80; distribution restricted to persons who have completed a Test Security Agreement with the publisher; no reliability data; no validity data for tests *b–j*; validity information not in test materials, but is available from The Selection Consulting Center, 5777 Madison Avenue, Suite 820, Sacramento, CA 95841, for *a* only; no norms; 10 tests; no manual; separate answer sheets must be used; 1984 price data: basic rental fee, $30 per candidate; $6.50 per test booklet (member), $8 per test booklet (nonmember); scoring service, available; International Personnel Management Association.*

a) FIREFIGHTER. 1973; 84 items in 4 areas: decision-making and reasoning ability, understanding instructions, mechanical aptitude, reading ability; 2 forms labeled B-1(M), B-2(M), (38 pages); (120) minutes.

b) FIRE INSPECTOR. 1974 ; 1 form (28 pages); 2 levels.

1) *Fire Inspector*. 125 items in 8 areas: reading comprehension, records and reports, public speaking, interviewing, combustible materials, fire inspection hazards, fire prevention, public relations; (135) minutes.

2) *Senior Fire Inspector*. 60 items same as in 1 plus 35 additional items in 4 areas: fire safety, supervision, evidence, building inspection; (180) minutes.

c) FIRE DRIVER. 1974; 110 items in 13 areas: fire combat, automotive terms, ventilation, automotive maintenance, ladders, public relations, fire hazards, gauges, hydraulics, automotive operations, forcible entry, salvage, hoses; 1 form (24 pages); (135) minutes.

d) RADIO OPERATOR. 1974; 1 form (27 pages); 2 levels.

1) *Radio Operator*. 100 items in 9 areas: reading comprehension, vocabulary, arithmetic, filing, English usage, pronunciation, radio operation, electricity, radio I (terminology, principles, equipment, trouble shooting); (120) minutes.

2) *Senior Radio Operator*. 30 items same as in 1 plus 30 additional items in 2 areas: supervision, radio II (terminology, principles, equipment, trouble shooting); (150) minutes.

e) FIRE ENGINEER. [1968]; 100 items in 3 areas: automotive terminology/operations, fire equipment/combat and first aid, pumps/gauges/hydraulics; 1 form (24 pages); (120) minutes.

f) FIRE SERVICE SUPERVISOR (SERGEANT/LIEUTENANT). [1974]; 150 items in 13 areas: fire combat, equipment, first aid, inspection, hazards, building construction, sprinklers, alarms, salvage, supervision, reports, training, hydraulics; 1 form (24 pages); (165) minutes.

g) FIRE SERVICE ADMINISTRATOR (CAPTAIN). 1974; 150 items in 3 areas: combat equipment/fire combat/combat command/fire chemistry, inspection/building construction/salvage/sprinklers/alarms/hazards, supervisors/administration/training/report writing; 1 form (32 pages); (150) minutes.

h) FIRE SERVICE ADMINISTRATOR (BATTALION CHIEF). 1974; 175 items in 3 areas: combat equipment/techniques/command, inspection/building construction/alarm systems/extinguishers/hazards, supervision/administration/training/public relations/report writing; 1 form (37 pages); (180) minutes.

i) FIRE SERVICE ADMINISTRATOR (DEPUTY CHIEF). 1974; 175 items in 15 areas: reading comprehension, vocabulary, fire combat, combat equipment, physical, hydraulics, first aid, automotive, prevention and protection, sprinklers and alarms, arson, public relations, training, performance evaluation, supervision; 1 form (39 pages); (195) minutes.

j) FIRE SERVICE ADMINISTRATOR (CHIEF). 1974; 150 items in 22 areas: reading comprehension, special problems, combat techniques, fire command, pumpers, extinguishers, training, fire inspection, records and reports, combat equipment, hydraulics, fire chemistry, supervision, planning, NBFU Standards, fire hazards, public relations, education, fire training, budget, personnel, administration; 1 form (35 pages); (165) minutes.

Review of IPMA Fire Service Tests by LAWRENCE ALLEN, Professor and Chair, Department of Psychology, University of South Alabama, Mobile, AL:

Only one of the 10 IPMA Fire Service Tests deserves favorable comment. The documentation presented by IPMA to justify the use of the entry level Firefighter Test is substantive. Although there is no manual for this test, a sufficient number of validation studies have been conducted to warrant the use of the test. The most thorough of these validation studies appears to be the one conducted by the Selection Consulting Center. Over 70 agencies in California and Nevada participated in this project. One of the major results of this validation study was that the IPMA Firefighter Test was equally predictive for Whites, Blacks, and Spanish-surnamed applicants.

The original Firefighter Test needs updating, and IPMA has produced two new tests, the B-3 and B-4 Firefighter Tests. IPMA states that a technical report is currently under preparation that will give full information on the job analysis, test development, and validation research for these new tests. It is recommended that the B-3 and B-4 Firefighter Tests not be used before the technical report is available for examination.

This reviewer has supervised the administration of the original IPMA Firefighter Test to 237 applicants on one occasion and to 323 applicants on another occasion two years later and found that the test had significant adverse impact against black applicants. Although these results could be attributed to applicant sampling, it is suggested that potential users of entry-level firefighter tests consider using the new Firefighter Selection Test published by Psychological Services, Inc., of Los Angeles, California. This reviewer supervised the administration of this test to 563 applicants in the same city where the IPMA Firefighter Test had been discontinued and found that the Firefighter Selection Test had less adverse impact against black applicants when compared to the IPMA Firefighter Test. In addition, performance of female applicants was much better on the Firefighter Selection Test. Although the evidence is incomplete, early results also indicate that the Firefighter Selection Test is a better predictor of firefighter performance than its IPMA counterpart.

The nine IPMA promotional Fire Service Tests were all constructed prior to 1975 and have almost no documentation to justify their use. There are no test manuals for these promotional tests. It is difficult to imagine that a professional association that claims to represent 55,000 personnel managers and professionals in federal, state, and local government, and that has been supplying the public sector with written tests for over 30 years, and who currently rents over 100,000 tests per year to jurisdictions in every state of the nation as well as to governmental organizations in Canada, does not provide users of its Fire Service Tests with test manuals. Test manuals are designed to provide test users with information describing a test's rationale, development, technical characteristics, administration, and interpretation. It is improper for a test publisher not to provide a test manual or similar document for the users of a test. The *Standards for Educational and Psychological Tests* consider it "essential" for a test publisher to furnish a manual for every test that the publisher produces.

The only information that IPMA gives to support the use of the nine promotional Fire Service Tests is described in its Catalogue of Test Services. This document briefly describes IPMA tests and gives rental prices and instructions for ordering tests. IPMA states that reading lists containing the source materials used to develop promotional tests are available for all nine promotional Fire Service Tests except Radio Operator. IPMA also states that additional "documentation" is available to justify the use of the Fire Sergeant/Lieutenant Test, Fire Captain Test, and Fire Battalion Chief Test. This additional documentation turns out to be nothing more than a list of the tests' questions by number with a citation for the book and page number from which the test question was taken.

Such limited information about the nine promotional tests is practically useless. Test users need definitive information about a test's validity, reliability, norms, etc., to help them in determining the possible value of a particular test for their use. The sketchy data presented by IPMA to justify the use of its nine promotional Fire Service Tests have limited, if any, value for test users.

An inspection of the nine promotional tests as a group leaves the impression that the job analysis procedures used to construct these tests would not meet current professional standards. The subject areas in the tests do not appear to have been weighted properly (as reflected by the number of questions for each subject area) and certain critical subject areas appear to have been omitted. For example, the Fire Sergeant/Lieutenant Test is obviously classified by IPMA as a supervisory level test, but there are only 12 questions out of 150 on the test that relate to supervision practices. Job analyses performed by fire service officials in different parts of the nation have documented that subordinate performance evaluation is an important function of supervisory personnel in the fire service, but there are only 4 performance evaluation questions on the Fire Sergeant/Lieutenant Test, none on the Fire Battalion Chief Test, and only 3 such questions out of 150 on the Fire Captain Test.

Matters become even more ludicrous when the Fire Chief Test is examined. A job analysis for this position would certainly document the important management function of planning, but the Fire Chief Test has only 5 questions out of 150 about planning. There are also 5 questions each on pumpers, extinguishers, inspection, hydraulics, and several other subject areas that belong on fire service tests much lower on an organization's chain of command.

It is also interesting to note that there are 10 reading comprehension questions on the Fire Chief Test and the Radio Operator Test, 5 reading comprehension questions on the Deputy Chief Test, 15 such questions on the Fire Inspector Test, and no reading comprehension questions on the remaining five tests. What are we to make of this? It is inconceivable that job analyses for these nine tests could produce such a hodgepodge of reading requirements.

Close scrutiny of the nine promotional tests reveals that many of the questions are outdated. For example, the two major book sources used by IPMA to develop test questions for the Fire Captain Test and the Fire Battalion Chief Test have copyright dates of 1962 and 1967. In addition, many of the test questions for the nine promotional tests are vague and poorly worded. Some test questions are repeated verbatim in different tests. For example, this reviewer counted 25 test questions that were exactly the same on both the Fire Captain Test and the Fire Battalion Chief Test. A person doesn't have to be a psychometrician to know that this is an unsound professional practice for a series of sequential promotional tests. Additional comments and observations could be made about the defects and problems inherent in using these nine promotional tests, but it is not necessary.

In summary, there are three recommendations. First, test users looking for a suitable entry-level firefighter test should consider the new Firefighter Selection Test published by Psychological Services, Inc., or the new B-3 and B-4 Firefighter Tests by IPMA, if the technical report under preparation by IPMA subsequently provides the data needed to justify the use of the B-3 and B-4. Although the original IPMA Firefighter Test has served a purpose, IPMA should probably discontinue its publication.

Second, there is a simple recommendation for test users considering use of the nine promotional Fire Service Tests. Don't. Individually and as a group they are inadequate.

Third, this reviewer strongly urges IPMA and similar publishers of test materials for the public sector (especially police and fire departments) to take a more responsible approach to test development. Although the primary responsibility for the improvement of testing should probably rest on the shoulders of test users, test developers should carry their share of the load.

[539]

IPMA Police Service Tests. Prospective police service personnel 1973–79; distribution restricted to persons who have completed a Test Security Agreement with the publisher; reliability data for *a* only; no validity data for tests *c–j*; validity information not in test materials, but is available from The Selection Consulting Center, 5777 Madison Avenue, Suite 820, Sacramento, CA 95841, for *b* only; norms for *a* only; 10 tests; no manual; separate answer sheets must be used; 1984 price data: basic rental fee, $30 per candidate; $5.75–$7 per test booklet (member); $7–$8.50 per test booklet (nonmember); scoring service $15 per order; International Personnel Management Association.*

a) MULTIJURISDICTIONAL POLICE OFFICER EXAMINATION. 1976–79; MPOE; 150 items in 10 areas: verbal comprehension, spatial scanning, visualization, semantic ordering, memory for ideas, spatial orientation, problem sensitivity, induction, memory for relationship, paired associates memory; 2 forms labeled MPOE (165.1) ('76, 62 pages), MPOE (165.2) ('78, 70 pages); technical report ('76, 194 pages); study guide ('76, 38 pages); $1 per study guide; $15 per technical report; (150) minutes.

b) POLICE OFFICER. 1973; 71 items in 4 areas: human relations, decision-making and reasoning ability, data and rule interpretation, reading comprehension; 1 form (20 pages); (90) minutes.

c) POLICE DETECTIVE. 1974; 165 items in 15 areas: reading comprehension, crime classification, patrol, search and seizure, arrest, interrogation, identification, criminology, crime prevention, vice, courts and trials, fingerprints, supervision, public relations, juvenile delinquency; 1 form (38 pages); (180) minutes.

d) IDENTIFICATION OFFICER. [1972]; 100 items in 4 areas: fingerprinting (equipment, classification, filming, techniques), tabular interpretation, filing, photography (equipment, papers, film, errors, exposure, records and reports, processing); 1 form (26 pages); (105) minutes.

e) POLICE RADIO DISPATCHER. 1974; 120 items in 14 areas: reading comprehension, abstract reasoning, arithmetic calculations, filing skill, tabular interpretation, pronunciation, terminology, radio equipment, radio dispatching, radio operations, radio logs, radio communications, radio repairs, radio symbols; 1 form (30 pages); (120) minutes.

f) POLICE SUPERVISOR (CORPORAL, SERGEANT). 1974; 145 items in 10 areas: patrol (techniques, traffic, accident), investigation, first aid, civil disturbance, juvenile delinquency, drugs, courts and trials (evidence, search and seizure, arrest, warrants, testimony), community relations, report writing, supervision (training, leadership); 1 form (22 pages); (150) minutes.

g) POLICE ADMINISTRATOR (LIEUTENANT). 1974; 145 items in 16 areas: patrol, crime prevention, criminology, identification, interrogation, investigation, vice, juvenile delinquency, riot control, courts and trials, evidence, supervision, public relations, records and reports, uniform crime reports, reading comprehension; 1 form (34 pages); (165) minutes.

h) POLICE ADMINISTRATOR (CAPTAIN). 1974; 170 items in 17 areas: accident investigation, traffic, investigation, identification, interrogation, patrol, vice, crime prevention, courts and trials, administration—coordination, administration—planning, administration—budgeting, administration—general, uniform crime reporting, public relations, training, supervision; 1 form (39 pages); (210) minutes.

i) POLICE ADMINISTRATOR (ASSISTANT CHIEF). 1974; 200 items in 25 areas: reading, vocabulary, criminology, patrol, search and seizure, arrest, evidence, courts and trials, interrogation, office organization, identification, vice, probation and parole, crime prevention, reports, work assignments, supervision, personnel, employee relations, public relations, training, juvenile delinquency, special problems, patrol organization, administration; 1 form (46 pages); (210) minutes.

j) POLICE ADMINISTRATOR (CHIEF). 1974; 180 items in 29 areas: reading comprehension, tabular interpretation, crime classification, patrol, search and seizure, arrest, stolen property recovery, evidence, courts and trials, interrogation, investigation, accident investigation, traffic, criminology, identification, fingerprints, crime prevention, juvenile delinquency, vice, reports, special problems, supervision I, training, personnel I, public relations, administration, crime statistics, supervision II, personnel II; 1 form (44 pages); (145) minutes.

[540]

Irrational Beliefs Test. Adults; 1968–77; IBT; based on Ellis' Irrational Belief System; for research use only; 11 scales: Demand for Approval, High Self Expectations, Blame Proneness, Frustration Reactive, Emotional Irresponsibility, Anxious Overconcern, Problem Avoidance, Dependency, Helplessness, Perfectionism, Full Scale; no norms; Form A ('77, 3 pages); manual ('68, 90 pages); profile (no date, 1 page); 1983 price data: $40 per 100 tests; $8 per 100 profile sheets; $2.50 per manual; $3.50

per specimen set; administration time not reported; R. Garner Jones; Test Systems International, Ltd.*

TEST REFERENCES

1. Smith, T. W., & Brehm, S. S. Cognitive correlates of the Type A coronary-prone behavior pattern. MOTIVATION AND EMOTION, 1981, 5, 215–223.

2. Rohsenow, D. J., & Smith, R. E. Irrational beliefs as predictors of negative affective states. MOTIVATION AND EMOTION, 1982, 6, 299–314.

3. Thurman, C. W. Effects of a rational-emotive treatment program on Type A behavior among college students. JOURNAL OF COLLEGE STUDENT PERSONNEL, 1983, 24, 417–423.

4. Smith, T. W., Houston, B. K., & Zurawski, R. M. Irrational beliefs and the arousal of emotional distress. JOURNAL OF COUNSELING PSYCHOLOGY, 1984, 31, 190–201.

Review of Irrational Beliefs Test by JAYNE E. STAKE, Associate Professor of Psychology, University of Missouri-St. Louis, St. Louis, MO:

According to Albert Ellis, emotional disturbance is caused by negative, irrational beliefs that are learned early in life and that are accepted without question by the individual. Ellis identified 10 irrational beliefs that he found to be common among his psychotherapy patients. The Irrational Beliefs Test (IBT) was developed to measure these 10 beliefs. The total scale contains 100 items; 10 items are included for each of the 10 beliefs.

Following is a list of the irrational beliefs measured by the IBT: (1) It is a dire necessity for one to be loved and approved by virtually every significant other person in one's community; (2) one should be thoroughly competent, adequate, and achieving in all possible respects if one is to consider oneself worthwhile; (3) certain people are bad, wicked, or villainous, and they should be severely blamed and punished for their villainy; (4) it is awful and catastrophic when things are not the way one would very much like them to be; (5) human unhappiness is externally caused, and people have little or no ability to control their sorrows and disturbances; (6) if something is or may be dangerous or fearsome one should be terribly concerned about it and should keep dwelling on the possibility of its occurring; (7) it is easier to avoid than to face certain life difficulties and self-responsibilities; (8) one should be dependent on others and needs someone stronger than oneself on whom to rely; (9) one's past history is an all important determiner of one's present behavior, and because something once strongly affected one's life, it should indefinitely have similar effect; (10) there is invariably a right, precise, and perfect solution to human problems, and it is catastrophic if this perfect solution is not found.

Responses to the IBT test items are made on 5-point scales ranging from "Strongly Agree" to "Strongly Disagree." The items are arranged in rotating order so that the last digit of the test item corresponds to the number of the belief measured by the item. Direct and reversed items are interspersed to avoid the development of acquiescent or negative response sets. The IBT may be either computer or hand scored.

TEST CONSTRUCTION. The IBT was originally designed for research purposes, but it has also been used as a clinical assessment tool. The author began his development of the scale by writing 40 items for each of the 10 irrational beliefs. Twenty items indicated the presence of the belief; 20 indicated the absence of the belief. From the original pool of 400 items, a panel of three judges selected 20 items for each of the irrational beliefs. This panel included the author himself, a nonpsychologist naive to psychometrics, and an expert in psychometrics.

The 200 items were administered to a group of 131 undergraduates, approximately 60% of whom were females. Responses from the sample were subjected to a factor analysis, although the number of subjects was far below the number typically recommended for 200 variables. Fifteen factors were extracted, including 10 corresponding to the intended subscales. In some instances items loaded higher on a factor other than the one for which it was intended; in these cases the item was rekeyed to the factor for which it had the highest loading.

A final group of 100 items was selected from the 200 items on the basis of (1) high item-total correlations, (2) low item-item correlations, and (3) high factor loadings. In a factor analysis of the final 100 items, the mean factor loading ranged from .35 for items associated with Belief 7 (Problem Avoidance) to .63 for items associated with Belief 1 (Demand for Approval), with an overall mean of .42. Hence, factor loadings were in the low to moderate range, indicating a loosely identifiable factor structure.

TEST VALIDATION. The 100-item scale was administered to 105 junior college students, 73 college seniors, 177 adults (ages 18 to 60) from unspecified sources, and 72 patients from a state mental hospital. These subjects also completed the Sixteen Personality Factor Questionnaire and a 25-item symptom measure developed for the validation of the IBT.

Responses were again factor analyzed, this time with close to the recommended sample size. Mean factor loadings were lower in this cross-validation, ranging from .25 for the scale of items associated with Belief 4 (Overreaction to Frustration) to .43 for the scale of items associated with Belief 6 (Anxious Overconcern), with an overall mean of .33. In 51 instances items loaded more than .225 with a scale other than the one for which it was intended. This lack of clear factor divisions is due in part to the fact that irrational thoughts are interconnected and therefore frequently coexist. Given the interconnectedness of irrational thoughts, greater subscale distinctiveness may not be possible.

Two estimates of internal consistency were obtained. By Hoyt's method, internal consistency ranged from .45 for Scale 8 (Dependency) to .72 for Scales 1 and 6 (Demand for Approval and Anxious Overconcern), with a mean value of .61. By Guilford's method the range was .66 for Scale 8 to .80 for Scale 1, with a mean of .74. The test-retest coefficients ranged from .67 for Scale 4 (Overreaction to Frustration) to .87 for Scale 2 (High Self-Expectations), with a mean of .80. The test-retest coefficient for the total scale was .92. Hence, the scales vary considerably in their internal consistency and stability but the total scale does show good reliability.

Correlations were obtained between the IBT scales and each of 25 items on a self-report measure of symptoms. Correlations between individual scales and reported symptoms were consistently significant and in the low to moderate range, except that Scales 8 (Dependency) and 10 (Perfectionism) failed to correlate with symptoms above a chance level. The total score and Scale 6 (Anxious Overconcern) correlated higher with symptom endorsement than the other individual scales; correlations between the total score and symptom endorsement ranged from .24 ("I don't feel close to other people") to .47 ("Life seems dreary and difficult").

The IBT scales were also correlated with the 16 scales of the Sixteen Personality Factor Questionnaire (16PF). All IBT scales except 8 (Dependency) and 10 (Perfectionism) were significantly related to the 6 clinical scales of the 16PF, which measure anxiety, depression, rigidity, and emotional lability. Correlations were highest for IBT Scale 6 (Anxious Overconcern) and for the total IBT score. Correlations between total score and the 6 clinical scales of the 16PF ranged from .29 to .53. Furthermore, the IBT scales yielded lower, primarily nonsignificant relationships with the 10 nonclinical scales of the 16 PF.

Discriminant validity was tested by comparing scores of the 72 state hospital patients with scores of the 117 nonhospitalized adults. The full scale and the subscales discriminated between these two groups at the .01 level of significance or better, except for Scale 1 (Demand for Approval), 4 (Overreaction to Frustration), and 8 (Dependency).

In summary, the IBT total score shows satisfactory reliability and validity. The total score has yielded moderate correlations with self-reports of anxiety and depression and has successfully discriminated between hospitalized and nonhospitalized adults. In most cases, Scale 6, which taps Anxious Overconcern, correlated as well with pathology as did the full scale. Hence, it appears that Scale 6 might serve as a short form of the IBT. In contrast, Scale 8 (Dependency) failed to correlate with symptom endorsement or mental health status. These findings may reflect a problem with Scale 8, since this scale has fairly low internal consistency. An alternative explanation of the failure of the scale to predict maladjustment is that Ellis' premise, that reliance on others leads to pathology, is incorrect.

The IBT is a useful research tool for exploring and testing Ellis' theoretical assumptions. The test can also be used as an overall measure of a patient's irrational beliefs. There is no evidence, however, that the individual scales can provide a differential diagnosis of patient problems.

[541]

Item Analysis of Slosson Intelligence Test. Children and adults; 1978; to aid in screening for strengths and weaknesses in the major areas of learning; 1 form (1 page); manual (14 pages); 1983 price data: $4 per 50 score sheets; $8 per specimen set; Slosson Educational Publications, Inc.*

Review of Item Analysis of Slosson Intelligence Test by ROBERT LESLIE HALE, Assistant Professor of Education, Pennsylvania State University, University Park, PA:

The reason behind the development of the Item Analysis of the Slosson Intelligence Test is quite simply stated on the first page of the manual: "Since there have been many requests across the country for an item analysis of the Slosson Intelligence Test, one was developed." This single statement represents all the information concerning the development and technical standards which the user is given for this instrument. Certainly, this is inadequate information under any standard of test development and publication. Users have a right to expect information regarding the development of the Item Analysis and its technical properties including reliability and validity. In the case of this material, where techniques such as profile, pattern, factor, or cluster analysis may appropriately have been used to establish the groupings of the items, the exact technique(s) used should have been reported. If, on the other hand, armchair speculation was the technique of choice, then that too should have been reported. There simply isn't any reason to leave users totally in the dark. To the manual's credit, it states that the item analysis procedure gives "only an indication of strengths and weaknesses in learning and should be followed by further appropriate testing. This is not to be considered a diagnostic test." However, no indication is given of how appropriate follow-up testing should be conducted.

To use the Item Analysis score sheets, one simply administers and scores the Slosson Intelligence Test (S.I.T.) and marks the Item Analysis Score sheet noting which items are passed or failed two years above or below either the subject's chronological or mental age (two-year rule). The marked items are subsequently interpreted as possible strengths or weaknesses in terms of eight areas of classification: (1) Information, (2) Comprehension, (3) Arithmetic, (4) Similarities and Differences, (5) Vocabulary, (6) Digit Span, (7) Auditory Memory of Sentences, and (8) Visual-Motor. Users are told on page 1 that the two-year rule applies when either the mental or chronological age is used as the base from which the determination is made. However, users are not told what to do if a person's scores are two years below his or her chronological age, but are not two years below his or her mental age. On page 3 the author indicates that the two-year rule and both chronological and mental age should be used with children of average intelligence or better. "With average intelligence or better if items are failed two years below chronological age or mental age, the categories should be considered significant."

Examples are included in the manual which further confuse this issue. In Example 2, a child with above average intelligence is presented. The child is described as having weaknesses in Digit Span and Auditory Memory for Sentences. This child has a mental age of 9 years 3 months (9–3) and a chronological age of 7–11. Using the child's mental age and the two-year rule, any item failed below 7–3 would be considered a weakness and any item passed above 11–3 should be considered as a possible strength. In this example, failed items 4–8 and 4–10 were considered weaknesses while failed item 6–2 was not considered. If chronological age was used as the base, then items failed below 5–11 would be considered weaknesses and items passed above 9–11 should be considered strengths. Using chronological age clears up the failure to consider item 6–2 as a weakness. However, this child reportedly passed item 10–0, which under the two-year rule should have been considered a possible strength. Using this example as a model, users are left with the impression that the base from which the two-year rule determinations can be made may be either mental age, chronological age, either mental age or chronological age, or both. In Example 4 another child with above average IQ is considered to have strengths in all items passed two years above his chronological age. Thus, the two examples use different rules for determining the base to which the two-year rule is applied. No rationale for using one or the other age is given. The child in Example 5 is mentally retarded (IQ=63), and the child's mental age is used exclusively as the age for which comparisons are made. This reviewer suspects that there may be relationships between variables like IQ and the two-year rule which could lead to differential interpretations of successes and failures depending on the overall level of general intelligence. Again, no information is provided with respect to these concerns.

In addition to the difficulties inherent in even hypothesizing strengths and weaknesses based on a child's success or failure on a single item, it should be noted that other authors have also item analyzed the S.I.T. (Boyd, 1974; Fudala, 1979). There are disagreements among all three item classifications. As pointed out by another reviewer (Bohning, 1980) there is no evidence that the two-year rule is based on any statistically significant difference criterion. However, even if the two-year rule provided statistically significant item differences, one would further need to ask questions about the degree of abnormality these differences represented and if they are valid for identifying any remedial techniques which might be advantageously incorporated into the child's learning program. None of this has been attempted.

In summary, the Item Analysis of the Slosson Intelligence Test does not have supporting empirical evidence concerning its utility and does not provide the user with any technical information concerning its development. Without this kind of information, and with the knowledge of the limited reliability and validity inherent in single items, readers should be cautioned against using this material.

REVIEWER'S REFERENCES

Boyd, J. E. Use of the Slosson Intelligence Test in reading diagnosis. ACADEMIC THERAPY, 1974, 9, 441–444.

Fudala, J. B. Differential evaluation of students with the S.I.T. ACADEMIC THERAPY, 1979, 15, 61–64.

Bohning, G. Item Analysis of Slosson Intelligence Test: A review. PSYCHOLOGY IN THE SCHOOLS, 1980, 17, 339.

Review of Item Analysis of Slosson Intelligence Test by MARK D. RECKASE, Director, Resident Programs, The American College Testing Program, Iowa City, IA:

The Item Analysis of Slosson Intelligence Tests consists of a manual and score sheets that classify the items from the Slosson Intelligence Test into eight content categories. These categories include: (*a*) information, (*b*) comprehension, (*c*) arithmetic, (*d*) similarities and differences, (*e*) vocabulary, (*f*) digit span, (*g*) auditory memory of sentences, and (*h*) visual-motor. The manual gives brief directions for using the item classifications for gross screening "for strengths and weaknesses in the major areas of learning" and five examples of the use of the procedure. The directions instruct the user to administer the intelligence test and score the results. The score sheet is then analyzed to determine which items that were more than two years below the examinee's chronological or mental age were passed or failed. Items either passed or failed that were more than two mental age levels above the examinee's chronological or mental age level are also noted. The content classifications of the identified items are then determined, and the results are interpreted as an indication of the strengths and weaknesses of the examinee. The examples given in the manual demonstrate the use of the test in the areas of learning disabilities and reading. The manual suggests that the procedure can be used by "classroom teachers, reading specialists, speech clinicians, learning disability teachers, psychologists, and other responsible school staff." No other qualifications are listed for the users of the Item Analysis.

A procedure based on the interpretation of individual item responses in various content categories requires substantial information to support its use. First, a clear description of the procedure used to determine the item classifications is required so that the reasonableness of the classifications can be judged. Also, a definition of each content classification is needed so that a judgment can be made as to whether the items accurately reflect that universe of content. The manual gives no information of this type and, in fact, does not even state the qualifications of the person who produced the classification scheme or who did the classification of the items. This information would seem to be the minimum that would be required for this type of procedure. The manual is woefully inadequate in this regard.

A second type of information that is necessary to support the use of this procedure is evidence to show that the analysis of the individual items does give useful information. It would be particularly helpful to have data showing that those individuals who miss an item that is more than two mental age levels below their score really do tend to have a deficit in the content area identified more often than individuals who do not miss the item. The frequency of incorrect responses to those items for examinees without a deficit would also be useful since such data would serve as a base rate. The manual does not report any information of this type. In fact, no information supporting the validity of the procedure is given at all.

The reliability of the procedure for identification of persons with strengths and weaknesses is also not reported. Information concerning whether a person would miss the same item on a retest would be especially pertinent to the use of the procedure.

Given that the Item Analysis of Slosson Intelligence Test is totally devoid of supporting documentation, it is very difficult to judge the value of the procedure. The lack of documentation, plus the fact that the analysis of individual item responses is questionable at best, forces a conclusion that this procedure should be avoided unless the user is willing to obtain the information required to validate its use. This is information that the publisher should have provided.

[542]

Jackson Vocational Interest Survey. High school and over; 1976–77; JVIS; "developed to assist high school and college students and adults with educational and career planning"; 34 basic interest scale scores: creative arts, performing arts, mathematics, physical science, engineering, life science, social science, adventure, nature-agriculture, skilled trades, personal service, family activity, medical service, dominant leadership, job security, stamina, accountability, teaching, social service, elementary education, finance, business, office work, sales, supervision, human relations management, law, professional advising, author-journalism, academic achievement, technical writing, independence, planfulness, interpersonal confidence; 1 form ('77, 16 pages); manual ('77, 108 pages); profile ('77, 2 pages); separate answer sheets/cards (hand scored/machine scored) must be used; 1983 price data: $17.25 per 25 test booklets; $4.25 per 25 hand scored answer sheets; $4.25 per 25 profiles; $10.50 per manual; $16 per examination kit; scoring service, $7 or less per test for extended report (12 page computer report), $3.25 or less per test for basic report (4 page computer report), available from publisher (cost includes answer cards, printed reports, interpretive guide, and mailing interpretive reports); (45–60) minutes; Douglas N. Jackson; Research Psychologists Press, Inc.*

See T3:1204 (1 reference).

Review of Jackson Vocational Interest Survey by CHARLES DAVIDSHOFER, Associate Professor of Psychology, Colorado State University, Fort Collins, CO:

The Jackson Vocational Interest Survey (JVIS) is a recently developed instrument designed to assess broad areas of vocational interest. It represents a departure from more traditional interest measures in that the basic unit of measurement used in the JVIS is the scale rather than the test item itself. Additionally, Jackson employed sophisticated factor analytic and multivariate statistical procedures that were not practical prior to the availability of high-speed computer technology.

The JVIS consists of 34 basic interest scales which assess either a respondent's preferences for specific work related activities (e.g., law, elementary education) or preferences for work environments requiring various specific behaviors (e.g., planfulness, independence). Each of the 34 scales contains 17 items presented in an ipsative format. In contrast to most ipsative tests, the JVIS does not employ a pairwise comparison among all 34 variables, but instead pairs each variable with only 17 others thus producing a 17 x 17 matrix. Consequently, a high score on one interest dimension does not imply that it was more preferred than all of the other interest areas, but only more preferred than the 16 dimensions against which it was paired. The manual does not present a clear rationale for how the pairing was done, but it is interesting to note that if Holland's hexagonal classification is applied to the scales of the JVIS, it appears that in general the interest areas that are least related are the ones paired on the test. It is not surprising, therefore, that there is excellent separation among the 34 interest areas measured.

One of the most desirable features of the JVIS is the availability of hand scoring. The answer sheet matrix is constructed to provide 17 raw scores and 17 column scores corresponding to the 34 basic interest areas measured. A separate profile sheet permits the conversion of raw scores to standard scores for interpretive purposes. Rather than employing a traditional *T*-score distribution, however, Jackson uses a different constant to arrive at a distribution with a mean of 30 and a standard deviation of 10. This change may lead to greater score misinterpretation by counselors more familiar with *T* scores. The arguments offered in the manual for the adoption of this scoring system are not sufficiently compelling to offset this possible shortcoming.

The profile sheet allows comparisons of the respondent's interest scores with those of a norm group comprised of adolescents in grades 9–12 and college students. The exact composition of this group is not clearly stated in the manual, but it appears that it represents a fairly random sample of middle to upper class adolescents and young adults. How representative it is of lower socioeconomic classes is unknown.

A more serious objection to the use of this combined norm group concerns the inclusion of such a heterogeneous age sample. No data is given showing whether the younger students demonstrated significantly different interest profiles from those in the college-age group, but previous research has shown that certain interest dimensions are earlier developing (e.g., art, science) while others develop later in life (e.g., business, social service). It is not clear what effect combining such diverse age groups might have in masking such developmental aspects of interests.

The psychometric properties of the JVIS are a model for modern interest measurement. Great care was taken in the development of the scales to remove unwanted variance due to such sources as social desirability and lack of factorial purity. Consequently, the resulting scales appear to provide measures of the broad interest areas implied by each scale. Reliability estimates, as reported in the manual, are very acceptable. Long term estimates, however, are not available due to newness of the test.

Evidence for the validity of the JVIS is still rather sparse. Early studies suggest that it can discriminate among college students in different majors along intuitively predictable lines. Similarly, a few of the occupational groups tested with the JVIS produce profiles with high interest scores in predictable areas. Some of the moderately high interest scores are more problematic, however, as evidenced by chemists scoring moderately high on the social worker cluster. Much more research needs to be done on occupational profiles before the predictive validity of the test can be adequately demonstrated.

The JVIS manual provides a good description of the actual derivation of the test, but does not enumerate the theoretical basis upon which Jackson initially derived the test items. A particularly laudable feature of the manual is the inclusion of the actual scale items, which provides the user with a definite aid in understanding the nature of each scale. This is especially helpful with the work style scales and those work role scales which cut across several occupational groups, since it is not always intuitively obvious from the scale name what the underlying interest dimension actually entails.

The manual offers suggestions for score interpretation which are generally useful and appropriate. The discussion of the meaning of low scores, however, is particularly problematic. The manual states that low scores should be viewed as indications that those activities have been rejected, disliked, and avoided. This interpretation cannot be justified on the basis of an ipsative test. More precisely, the respondent has chosen other interests in preference to those indicated by low scores, but it is entirely possible that the examinee has many strong interests all of which cannot emerge on an ipsative test because of the forced-choice nature of the task.

In summary, the JVIS appears to be one of the better ipsative interest measures available. Its shortcomings are outweighed by its sound factorially-pure scales. As an instrument for use with adolescents early in the career decision-making process, it should facilitate exploration and minimize occupational stereotyping because of its emphasis on work roles and styles. Although it may well represent an improvement over the Kuder Occupational Interest Survey, it will not supplant the Strong-Campbell Interest Inventory. The impressive predictive validity data on the Strong-Campbell clearly distinguish it as the leader in the field, a status that only extensive empirical research on the JVIS may one day challenge.

Review of Jackson Vocational Interest Survey by RUTH G. THOMAS, *Associate Professor, College of Education, University of Minnesota, St. Paul, MN:*

The Jackson Vocational Interest Survey (JVIS) is a 289 item instrument designed to measure occupational interests in a way that is claimed to be different and superior to other existing vocational interest measures.

The JVIS is hand or machine scorable. The availability of hand scoring may be a distinct advantage to some users. Instructions for hand scoring are explicit; a special answer sheet format has been developed to make hand scoring easier. It should also be pointed out that hand scoring yields only the 34 basic interest scale scores while machine scoring provides, in addition, 10 occupational theme scores, administrative indices, and compares an individual's scores to college students enrolled in various majors and to those of persons in 32 occupational clusters.

The instrument is described as being appropriate for use with college and high school students and out of school persons who are making career and educational decisions, for use in college orientation and testing programs and employee classification and selection, and for research in vocational interests, psychology of work, and student characteristics.

Directions for administering the survey are detailed and comprehensive. Qualifications for administering and interpreting the JVIS are not spelled out. The manual demands more than passing knowledge of psychometric concepts and procedures.

The survey is described as taking about one hour to complete—a distinct disadvantage when compared with other vocational interest inventories requiring half that time and when fatigue and attention factors are considered. Reading level is described as approximately seventh grade. No substantiation for this claim is made. The sophisticated terminology used in some items indicates that the reading level may be considerably higher and also raises questions regarding potential socio-economic and educational level bias (e.g., invest in municipal bonds, using an atom smasher, arranging for competitive bids).

A consistent and frustrating characteristic of the manual is that it describes procedures, groups, and ideas in very general terms, leaving out details that are essential to formulating a clear understanding of what is being described and to assessing appropriateness of procedures or validity of claims. Organization is also problematic in that it is necessary to peruse several sections located in different parts of the manual to obtain all the information that is provided concerning a particular aspect of the survey.

Separate and combined norms for males and females are provided for a normative sample of high school and college students. From approximately 8,000 students on whom JVIS scores were obtained 1,000 individuals were selected by computer to yield a norm group composed of 500 males and 500 females. Procedures for selection of the 1,000 students are ambiguously described, leaving a question about representativeness of the final sample. High school students were Canadian (Ontario province) and drawn from grades 9–13. College students were freshmen entering Pennsylvania State University and students of undesignated status in colleges located in the continental U.S., Hawaii, and Ontario. The number and proportions of Penn State freshmen, other college students, and high school students in the final norm group sample of 1,000 are undefined, leaving questions of potential geographic, age, and socioeconomic bias unanswered.

Means on the 34 JVIS basic interest scales for a separate group of students admitted to Pennsylvania colleges and universities in 1976 are also provided which present additional information but add to concerns about geographic bias in the norms.

While sections of the manual regarding interpretation and scale construction are extensive, information critical to clearly understanding and assessing the rationale for the approach used in scale construction, how decisions about the set of interest dimensions to be included were made, the source of items, and exactly how the items were paired in the forced choice format is incomplete. Twenty-six scales focus on work roles; eight scales concern work styles which are described as interests in working environments emphasizing certain behaviors.

Procedures described for factor analysis of items are complex, elaborate, and are not written at a level which would be understandable to many potential users. The reader is constantly referred to other sources in very general discussions of intricate item analysis procedures. While the references to more detailed sources are appropriately provided for users who want to investigate the procedure in more depth, enough detail and clarity should be provided in the manual for the user to have a clear idea of the specific nature of procedures used.

A forced choice format was chosen to reduce response bias. The concept employed is similar to that used in the Kuder Occupational Interest Survey. However, the JVIS items are unlike the Kuder items in several ways. JVIS items present two instead of three options. JVIS items also force choices between categorically dissimilar options. For example, the respondent is asked to choose between being considered trustworthy and responsible and neatly arranging tools. Some items have multiple objects so that a person might respond negatively to one aspect of the item and positively to another aspect of the same item. These problems are discussed in detail by Juni and Koenig (1982). While such item characteristics may not affect the ability of the JVIS to predict the criterion of occupational interest, the potential difficulties the items may present to respondents should be considered.

Test-retest reliability coefficients are reported for the basic interest scales, for scale profiles based on 172 university students, and for scores on ten general occupational themes based on 54 university students. Internal-consistency reliability coefficients for the JVIS scales are based on 1573 high school students. A means of determining individual reliability is also provided. In general, reliability coefficients are acceptable and provide some indication that the item problems described earlier may not influence reliability unduly.

The manual is especially confusing and ambiguous in its discussion of profile development and validation. Predicted JVIS standard scores on the thirty-four basic interest scales are provided for 189 occupational groups composed of males and 89 occupational groups composed of females. Profiles for 52 occupational groups are also included. No description of the sample nor explanation of how the 52 occupational groups were selected is given.

Validity data presented is primarily concerned with concurrent and construct validity. Studies reported concern a variety of criteria including occupational success, occupation of employed persons, choice of academic college by entering freshmen ratings, Strong Vocational Interest Blank scales, and vocational preferences in experiments. Predictive validity for the JVIS on criterion measures relevant to occupational satisfaction is not established at present.

A serious question must be raised about why one would choose to use this measure requiring twice the administration time over other measures which are better established in terms of norms and interpretability, offer choice of an item format that is similar but less troublesome, and provide work roles scale scores, occupational theme scores, and an indication of individual reliability. It would seem to be the usefulness of the JVIS occupational cluster profiles and basic interest scales and the JVIS predictive efficiency that would have to be the critical factors in choosing the JVIS over the Strong or the Kuder. Unfortunately, we do not have much information at present about these factors.

REVIEWER'S REFERENCES

Juni, S., & Koenig, E. Contingency validity as a requirement in forced-choice item construction: A critique of the Jackson Vocational Interest Survey. MEASUREMENT AND EVALUATION IN GUIDANCE, 1982, 14(4), 202–207.

[543]

Jacobsen-Kellog Self Description Inventory II. College student and adults; 1983 (no date on test materials); SDI-II; 5 scores: attribution of positive traits, attribution of negative traits, denial of positive traits, denial of negative traits, total; reliability and validity data available in various journal reprints and included in test materials; norms for college students only; 1 form (6 pages); answer key (5 pages); no manual; 1983 price data: $1 per test and answer key; administration time not reported; Leonard I. Jacobsen and Richard W. Kellog; Leonard I. Jacobsen.*

[544]

Jansky Diagnostic Battery. Age range not indicated; no date on test materials; ratings in 4 areas: oral language, pattern matching, pattern memory, visuo motor organization; no data on reliability and validity; individual; no norms; no manual; 1985 price data: $25 per complete set; administration time not reported; Jeannette Jansky; the Author.*

[545]

Jenkins Activity Survey. Employed adults ages 25–65; 1965–79; JAS; a measure of type A behavior, the coronary prone behavior pattern; 4 scores: type A, speed and impatience, job involvement, hard-driving and competitive; author recommends use of local norms; Form C ('79, 4 pages); manual ('79, 30 pages); hand scoring instructions ('79, 10 pages); 1984 price data: $18 per 25 tests; $5.50 per manual; $6.50 per specimen set; scoring service available; (20–30) minutes; C. David Jenkins, Stephen J. Zyzanski, and Ray H. Rosenmen; The Psychological Corporation.*

See T3:1206 (1 reference).

TEST REFERENCES

1. Bloom, L. J. Psychology and cardiology: Collaboration in coronary treatment and prevention. PROFESSIONAL PSYCHOLOGY, 1979, 10, 485–490.

2. Jenni, M. A., & Wollersheim, J. P. Cognitive therapy, stress management training, and the Type A behavior pattern. COGNITIVE THERAPY AND RESEARCH, 1979, 3, 61–73.

3. Millon, T., Green, C. J., & Meagher, R. B., Jr. The MBHI: A new inventory for the psychodiagnostician in medical settings. PROFESSIONAL PSYCHOLOGY, 1979, 10, 529–539.

4. Bunnell, D. E. Individual differences in alpha rhythm responsivity: Inter-task consistency and relationships to cardiovascular and dispositional variables. BIOLOGICAL PSYCHOLOGY, 1980, 10, 157–165.

5. Forsman, L. Habitual catecholamine excretion and its relation to habitual distress. BIOLOGICAL PSYCHOLOGY, 1980, 11, 83–97.

6. Frankenhauser, M., Lundberg, V., & Forsman, L. Dissociation between sympathetic-adrenal and pituitary-adrenal responses to an achievement situation characterized by high controllability: Comparison between Type A and Type B males and females. BIOLOGICAL PSYCHOLOGY, 1980, 10, 79–91.

7. Gastorf, J. W., & Teevan, R. C. Type A coronary-prone behavior pattern and fear of failure. MOTIVATION AND EMOTION, 1980, 4, 71–76.

8. Carver, C. S., DeGregorio, E., & Gillis, R. Challenge and Type A behavior among intercollegiate football players. JOURNAL OF SPORT PSYCHOLOGY, 1981, 3, 140–148.

9. Fazio, R. H., Cooper, M., Dayson, K., & Johnson, M. Control and the coronary-prone behavior pattern: Responses to multiple situational demands. PERSONALITY AND SOCIAL PSYCHOLOGY BULLETIN, 1981, 7, 97–102.

10. Francis, K. T. Perceptions of anxiety, hostility and depression in subjects exhibiting the coronary-prone behavior pattern. JOURNAL OF PSYCHIATRIC RESEARCH, 1981, 16, 183–190.

11. Gotay, C. C. Cooperation and competition as a function of Type A behavior. PERSONALITY AND SOCIAL PSYCHOLOGY BULLETIN, 1981, 7, 386–392.

12. Hicks, R. A., & Hodgson, J. A. Type A-B behavior and the overt and covert hostility levels of college students. PSYCHOLOGICAL REPORTS, 1981, 48, 317–318.

13. Hicks, R. A., & Schretlen, D. Changes in level of Type A behavior in college students over a four-year period. PSYCHOLOGICAL REPORTS, 1981, 49, 22.

14. Hicks, R. A., McNicholas, G. A., & Armogida, R. E. Iride pigmentation, sex, and Type A behavior. THE PSYCHOLOGICAL RECORD, 1981, 31, 43–46.

15. Smith, T. W., & Brehm, S. S. Cognitive correlates of the Type A coronary-prone behavior pattern. MOTIVATION AND EMOTION, 1981, 5, 215–223.

16. Burke, R. J., & Deszca, E. Preferred organizational climates of Type A individuals. JOURNAL OF VOCATIONAL BEHAVIOR, 1982, 21, 50–59.

17. Herbertt, R. M., & Innes, J. M. Type A coronary-prone behavior pattern, self-consciousness, and self-monitoring: A questionnaire study. PERCEPTUAL AND MOTOR SKILLS, 1982, 55, 471–478.

18. Hicks, R. A., & Pellegrini, R. J. Sleep problems and Type A-B behavior in college students. PSYCHOLOGICAL REPORTS, 1982, 51, 196.

19. Kelly, J. A., Bradlyn, A. S., Dubbert, P. M., & St. Lawrence, J. S. Stress management training in medical school. JOURNAL OF MEDICAL EDUCATION, 1982, 57, 91–99.

20. Kelly, K. R., & Stone, G. L. Effects of time limits on the interview behavior of Type A and B persons within a brief counseling analog. JOURNAL OF COUNSELING PSYCHOLOGY, 1982, 29, 454–459.

21. Ketterer, M. W. Lateralized representation of affect, affect cognizance and the coronary-prone personality. BIOLOGICAL PSYCHOLOGY, 1982, 171–189.

22. Loewenstine, H. V., & Paludi, M. A. Women's type A/B behavior patterns and fear of success. PERCEPTUAL AND MOTOR SKILLS, 1982, 54, 891–894.

23. Matthews, K. A., & Carra, J. Suppression of menstrual distress symptoms: A study of Type A behavior. PERSONALITY AND SOCIAL PSYCHOLOGY BULLETIN, 1982, 8, 146–151.

24. Matthews, K. A., Krantz, D. S., Dembroski, T. M., & MacDougall, J. M. Unique and common variance in structured interview and Jenkins Activity Survey measures of the Type A behavior pattern. JOURNAL OF PERSONALITY AND SOCIAL PSYCHOLOGY, 1982, 42, 303–313.

25. Morell, M. A., & Katkin, E. S. Jenkins Activity Survey scores among women of different occupations. JOURNAL OF CONSULTING AND CLINICAL PSYCHOLOGY, 1982, 50, 588–589.

26. Retzlaff, P. D. Verbal estimation, production, and reproduction of time intervals by Type A individuals. PERCEPTUAL AND MOTOR SKILLS, 1982, 55, 331–334.

27. Rhodewalt, F., & Comer, R. Coronary-prone behavior and reactance: The attractiveness of an eliminated choice. PERSONALITY AND SOCIAL PSYCHOLOGY BULLETIN, 1982, 8, 152–158.

28. Sanders, G. S., & Malkis, F. S. Type A behavior, need for control, and reactions to group participation. ORGANIZATIONAL BEHAVIOR AND HUMAN PERFORMANCE, 1982, 30, 71–86.

29. Strube, M. J. Time urgency and Type A behavior: A methodological note. PERSONALITY AND SOCIAL PSYCHOLOGY BULLETIN, 1982, 8, 563–565.

30. Strube, M. J., & Ota, S. Type A coronary-prone behavior pattern: Relationship to birth order and family size. PERSONALITY AND SOCIAL PSYCHOLOGY BULLETIN, 1982, 8, 317–323.

31. Suinn, R. M. Intervention with Type A behaviors. JOURNAL OF CONSULTING AND CLINICAL PSYCHOLOGY, 1982, 50, 933–949.

32. Williams, R. B., Jr., Lane, J. D., Kuhn, C. M., Melosh, W., White, A. D., & Schanberg, S. M. Type A behavior and elevated physiological and neuroendocrine responses to cognitive tasks. SCIENCE, 1982, 218, 483–485.

33. Yarnold, P. R., & Grimm, L. G. Time urgency among coronary-prone individuals. JOURNAL OF ABNORMAL PSYCHOLOGY, 1982, 91, 175–177.

34. Young, L. D., & Barboriak, J. J. Reliability of a brief scale for assessment of coronary-prone behavior and standard measures of Type A behavior. PERCEPTUAL AND MOTOR SKILLS, 1982, 55, 1039–1042.

35. Hansson, R. O., Hogan, R., Johnson, J. A., & Schroeder, D. Disentangling Type A behavior: The roles of ambition, insensitivity, and anxiety. JOURNAL OF RESEARCH IN PERSONALITY, 1983, 17, 186–197.

36. Johnston, D. W., & Shaper, A. G. Type A Behaviour in British men: Reliability and intercorrelation of two measures. JOURNAL OF CHRONIC DISEASE, 1983, 36, 203–207.

37. Ruberman, W., Weinblatt, E., Goldberg, J. D., & Chaudhary, B. S. Education, psychosocial stress and sudden cardiac death. JOURNAL OF CHRONIC DISEASE, 1983, 36, 151–160.

38. Smith, J. C., & Sheridan, M. Type A (coronary-prone) behavior and self-reported physical and cognitive reactions to actual life stressors. PERCEPTUAL AND MOTOR SKILLS, 1983, 56, 545–546.

39. Thurman, C. W. Effects of a rational-emotive treatment program on Type A behavior among college students. JOURNAL OF COLLEGE STUDENT PERSONNEL, 1983, 24, 417–423.

40. Zurawski, R. M., & Houston, B. K. The Jenkins Activity Survey measure of Type A and frustration-induced anger. MOTIVATION AND EMOTION, 1983, 7, 301–312.

41. Smith, T. W. Type A behaviour, anger and neuroticism: The discriminant validity of self-reports in a patient sample. BRITISH JOURNAL OF CLINICAL PSYCHOLOGY, 1984, 23, 147–148.

Review of Jenkins Activity Survey by JAMES A. BLUMENTHAL, Assistant Professor of Medical Psychology, Department of Psychiatry, Duke University Medical Center, Durham, NC:

The Type A behavior pattern is a behavioral syndrome that has been demonstrated to be associated with increased risk for the development of coronary heart disease (CHD). Individuals displaying this pattern are characterized by extremes of competitiveness, striving for achievement and personal recognition, aggressiveness, haste, impatience, explosiveness and loudness in speech, and feelings of being under the pressure of time and challenge of responsibility. Type A individuals need not manifest all aspects of this profile to be classified as possessing it. However, Type A individuals display a predominance of these features, while individuals manifesting the converse, Type B behavior are identified by the relative absence of these characteristics.

Initially, the Type A behavior pattern was assessed by a standard behavioral interview which has become known as the Structured Interview (SI). Behavior pattern classification was based upon subjective clinical judgements by trained raters. In a large-scale prospective, epidemiologic study known as the Western Collaborative Group Study (WCGS), individuals classified as Type A by the interview method were observed to have roughly twice the incidence of CHD compared to their Type B counterparts.

The Jenkins Activity Survey (JAS) was developed in an attempt to duplicate the clinical assessment of the Type A behavior pattern by employing an objective psychometric procedure. The JAS is a self-administered, multiple-choice questionnaire that yields a composite Type A scale score and three factor analytically-derived subscales: Speed and impatience, Job involvement, and Hard-driving and competitive. It was initially developed from an item pool based upon the structured interview and questions from clinical experience that discriminated interview-determined Type A from Type B individuals.

The manual presents a brief historical overview of the concept of "coronary-prone" behavior and various approaches to the measurement of Type A. It describes the development of the JAS beginning with the experimental 64-item questionnaire designed in 1964 to the present 1979 version. The current Form C consists of 52 of the items included in its predecessor, Form B. Some minor modifications in the format of the JAS were made to facilitate administration and scoring of the instrument. However, the items composition and scoring algorithms for each scale are identical to the third (1969) edition and the subsequent (1972) Form B revision. Consequently, all reliability, validity, and clinical data based on the 1969 edition, Form B, and the present Form C are considered together.

The normative data (*T* scores, Centiles) published in the manual are based on the 1969 JAS scores of the WCGS participants. The sample consisted of 2,588 employed middle class males ages 48 through 65 years at the time of testing. The Type A scale for the 1969 edition was derived from discriminant function procedures using as criterion groups those subjects who had scored strongly Type A and B on the previous editions of the test. Similarly, three factor scales were also derived from discriminant function procedures. The JAS was standardized to have mean of 0.0 and standard deviation of 10.0 for all four scales. Positive scores indicate Type A behavior, while negative scores denote Type B behavior. In addition to data from the WCGS population, means from other populations (usually white, middle class males) are also included in the manual.

The Type A scale consists of 21 items, while Speed and impatience (Factor S), Job involvement (Factor J) and Hard-driving and competitive (Factor H) contain 21, 24 and 20 items respectively. There are a number of items that overlap between different scales, and are assigned different scale weightings. The manual characterizes the correlations between the Type A scale and Factor S (.67), H (.58), and J (.42) to be rather modest, and the authors claim that the three factor scores make independent contributions to the assessment of Type A tendencies.

Reliability estimates for the JAS Type A scale appear to be adequate. For example, estimates of item reliabilities derived from squared multiple correlation coefficients range from .27 to .75, with the corresponding internal consistency reliability coefficient for the Type A scale reported to be .85. Test-retest reliability estimates generally range between .60 and .70 for retest intervals of from six months to four years. However, most of the correlations are based upon significant modifications in the items in the 1965 and 1969 versions of the JAS. The authors claim that the consistently high correlations between scores derived in the 1965 and 1969 editions indicate the relative equivalence of the several editions of the JAS. Alternate forms of the JAS are not currently available, however.

Several kinds of validational evidence are presented. Concurrent validity has been established by comparing JAS scores to Type A ratings based upon the structured interview. Despite a statistically significant association between the two measures, as many as 30% of respondents are classified differently by the JAS and interview, and correlations between the JAS and interview in younger populations (e.g., college students) are less than .50. Recently, a comparison of the JAS and the interview method revealed that sources of common variance appear to be in measures of self-reported pressured drive and hostility and verbal competitiveness. The source of unique variance in the interview is the subject's speech style, while the source of unique variance in the JAS is self-reported time pressure. Evidence for the predictive validity of the JAS comes primarily from the prospective findings of the WCGS. Analysis of JAS Type A scores of 2,750 healthy men showed the Type A scale to distinguish the 120 future clinical cases of CHD from those men who subsequently remained healthy. Men scoring in the top third of the distribution (> +5.0) incurred 1.7 times the incidence of CHD over a four-year interval compared to those scoring in the lowest third (< −5.0). Numerous studies have also found patients with CHD to score higher on the JAS Type A scale than patients without CHD. However, compared to the interview, the power of the JAS Type A scale to predict CHD in the WCGS is clearly weaker than the interview, and none of the three subscales relate to any clinical manifestations of CHD. Other studies have shown the JAS to be related to increased rates of reinfarction and more extensive coronary atherosclerosis. It should be noted, however, that these results have not always been confirmed by other research groups, and more research is needed to document the relationship of the JAS to other clinical endpoints.

The JAS has been used concurrently with a number of standard psychological inventories, including the California Psychological Inventory (CPI), State-Trait Anxiety Inventory (STAI), Gough Adjective Checklist (ACL), Thurstone Temperament Schedule (TTS), Guilford-Zimmerman Temperament Survey (GZTS), and Strong Vocational Interest Blank (SVIB). Only the General Activity scale of the GZTS, the Active Scale of the TTS, and the Occupational level scales of the SVIB correlated with the JAS Type A scale .40 or greater. In several correlational studies, the JAS has also been shown to have negligible associations with measures of psychopathology, emotional distress, or psychiatric diagnoses.

The JAS has several major shortcomings. The norms cannot be considered representative of any population of broad general interest. The standardization sample did not include women, young or elderly, or persons with low socioeconomic status. While experimental versions of the JAS have been developed for individuals who are female, unemployed, elderly (Form N) and in college (Form T), these editions lack sufficient reliability and validity information and are not available for general use. Revisions of the norms on the basis of a more representative sample would be worthwhile. Local norms or norms for specific populations (patients in rural settings, minorities, individuals with low socioeconomic status, patients in cardiac rehabilitation programs or family clinic settings, etc.) may be more suitable.

Many users may be disappointed by the susceptibility of the JAS to test-taking attitude. Measures of response set such as defensiveness or social desirability are not included, and the items are readily transparent. The hand-scoring system is also difficult because of the complex weighting system employed. Consequently, hand scoring is tedious and time consuming and is not recommended.

Reliability data is limited but adequate. However, the validity data is too tentative at the present time. While the JAS items include an adequate sampling of the Type A behavior pattern, other potential coronary-prone behaviors such as feelings of helplessness, anger, depression, job dissatisfaction, and lack of social support are not included. Consequently, the terms "Type A" and "coronary prone" cannot be considered equivalent. In addition, since Type A is currently viewed as a behavioral predisposition elicited by appropriate environmental demands, assessment of relevant situational influences is lacking and would appear warranted.

Agreement between the JAS and structured interview is less than acceptable, especially for certain groups such as women, people who are retired, unemployed, or in school. Indeed, the authors acknowledge that the JAS misclassifies too many subjects to allow its use in clinical settings. In addition, evidence that the JAS can accurately predict new cases of CHD is lacking. While the JAS has been shown to be associated with increased prevalence of CHD in population studies in the U.S. (and recently Europe), an individual score offers little prognostic value in a clinical setting, even when combined with traditional risk factors. Moreover, while determination of hypertension, hyperlipidemia, or diabetes is important for subsequent treatment, determination of Type A scores does not aid in modification of the behavior pattern.

While the authors offer several clinical vignettes, the JAS scores do not permit any precise descriptive or diagnostic information about personality functioning. Indeed, a major limitation of the JAS is a lack of information about how scores translate into overt behaviors for a given individual. Subcomponents of the Type A behavior pattern such as hostility or anger, hastened behavioral tempo, and feelings of time pressure may best be evaluated by employing other instruments.

The limitations of the Type A construct should also be noted. While an extended critique is beyond the scope of the present discussion, Type A is not considered a typology in the traditional sense, although a certain underlying consistency of behavior is implied. More work is needed to clarify the conceptual basis for understanding Type A behavior. Since it has been estimated that 50–70% of the general population may be classified as Type A, and the incidence of CHD is extremely low (roughly 3% in the middle aged U.S. population), the predictive value of the instrument is obviously limited.

In summary, the JAS is still in an experimental phase, and norms, reliabilities, and validities are tentative. The primary positive features of the JAS are its easy to read booklet and test instructions, its relative brevity (it requires approximately 15 minutes to complete), its objective scoring system, and a well-documented record of its use in a variety of clinical and research settings. On the other hand, the test has several undesirable features including a complex scoring system, lack of safeguards against test-taking attitude, and limited practical utility. The JAS represents a valuable contribution to the advancement of research in the area of coronary heart disease, and is currently the most widely used instrument to assess Type A behavior. However, use of the JAS should be limited to experimental or clinical research. Clinical judgment remains the method of choice for assessment of the Type A behavior pattern, and for selecting appropriate individuals at risk for developing CHD.

[546]

JIIG-CAL Occupational Interests Guide. High school and college students; 1980; also called Job Ideas and Information Generator—Computer Assisted Learning; revision of the still-in-print APU Occupational Interests Guide; one component of a program including a job file and computer programs; self-ratings on 2 of six sections chosen by the student (unskilled, semi-skilled, skilled craft, skilled technician, semi-professional, graduate professional) yielding six preference scores: interest in practical work/using your hands/science and engineering, working with living things, clerical/secretarial/saleswork including business and some aspects of law, work involving neatness and an eye for colour and shape, interest in working with people in need, interest in working where you meet people including acting and writing; 1 form (15 pages); manual (132 pages); classroom guide (26 pages); information booklet (19 pages); report form (2 pages); answer sheets M (4 pages, for hand scoring), K (4 pages); distribution restricted to persons who have completed a training course; separate answer sheets must be used; supplementary directions (2 pages) for each type of answer sheet; 1983 price data: £4.50 per 20 tests; £2.25 per 20 answer sheets of either type; £5 per set of scoring templates; £2.25 per 20 instructions for answer sheets; £2.50 per 20 report form booklet; £10 per manual; £2.25 per classroom guide; £15 per specimen set; (120–180) minutes; S. J. Closs (classroom guide, manual, and test materials), P. R. MacLean, and M. V. Walker (classroom guide); Hodder and Stoughton Educational [England].*

Review of JIIG-CAL Occupational Interests Guide by JO-IDA C. HANSEN, Director, Center for Interest Measurement Research and Professor of Psychology, University of Minnesota, Minneapolis, MN:

The JIIG-CAL System (Job Ideas and Information Generator—Computer Assisted Learning) is a British career guidance program developed by researchers working on career guidance at Edinburgh University and by computer specialists working on computer assisted learning at the Educational Computer Center, London Borough of Havering.

The two major components of the JIIG-CAL System are (*a*) an interest inventory called the Occupational Interests Guide and (*b*) a Job File.

OCCUPATIONAL INTERESTS GUIDE. The interest inventory is designed to measure six types of interests. The interest factors are assigned the numbers 1 through 6 (e.g., Type 1, Type 2) rather than descriptive names. Each interest Type is subdivided into six levels (labeled A through F) that relate to length of training required for jobs in that Type and at that level. Five interest definitions are given for each Type, based on combinations of adjacent levels: AB, BC, CD, DE, and EF. The definitions do not reflect previously developed theories of interests and the author offers no theory or data of his own to justify the various levels that he has combined into single Types.

The respondent chooses the two adjacent levels he/she deems most relevant to his/her interests (e.g., AB or BC or EF) and, then, responds to 60 pairs of items (120 separate activities) that represent the six Types at the two designated levels. In other words, the respondent completes only 1/3 of the total item pool of the inventory. The usefulness of this design is dependent on the respondent's ability to correctly select his/her training level; unfortunately, the author does not present data to support the claim that most clients can select the appropriate level prior to career exploration.

Development and validation of the inventory are not described in any of the JIIG-CAL materials except for the brief statement that "The classification of interests developed by the writer was based initially on a comprehensive review of the available literature....This has been followed by successive research analyses." No hint is given about the nature of the research analyses; no reliability data (internal consistency or test-retest) are reported; nor are any concurrent, predictive, or construct validity data presented.

Raw scores are not standardized and samples are not presented for comparison purposes. The Information Booklet indicates that the Occupational Interests Guide is unisex but only masculine pronouns are used in reference to clients or counselors and no data are presented to indicate sex fairness of the inventory.

The inventory may be hand scored but the procedure is quite complex, involving, for example, corrections for response sets. Computer scoring, which is available for the inventory, offers the advantage of eliminating the inevitable hand scoring errors and at the same time allows the inventory results to be integrated with the Job File.

The basic computer output (profile) provides interpretive information for each Type at the training level selected by the student when he/she completed the inventory, along with an interpretive comment (strong dislike, dislike, don't mind, like, strong like) summarizing the respondent's interest in each of the six Types. A more extensive computer output matches the interest profile with the Job File.

JOB FILE. The Job File is accessed by a complex set of computer programs which operate a large and comprehensive file of job information. First, the student completes an information card; next, the computer makes 108 comparisons between the respondent's characteristics and the job characteristics for 417 occupations. The printout includes the 10 jobs at each of the respondent's two previously selected training levels that are most suitable based on the respondent-job characteristic comparison. Along with the 20 job titles, the printed output includes a basic description, the required qualifications, and the relevant skill requirements for each job.

Although the Job File of the JIIG-CAL is potentially useful for career guidance programs, the dearth of information on scale construction, reliability, and validity for the Occupational Interests Guide should deter counselors from selecting the JIIG-CAL for use with their students.

Review of JIIG-CAL Occupational Interests Guide by DAVID O. HERMAN, Vice President, Measurement Research Services, Inc., New York, NY:

The JIIG-CAL Occupational Interests Guide (Guide) has a number of unique qualities that set it apart from other career interest inventories in print, and make it worthy of serious evaluation. While these innovative aspects are of much interest and result from extensive developmental effort, their implications are not in all cases favorable, as this review will show.

The Guide provides scores on six interest scales, based on the examinee's preferences among various work activities. Actually the true number of scales measured is greater than six because each scale has up to five different meanings, depending on the student's preferred occupational level. The Guide thus measures interests with greater specificity than first appears.

This is accomplished by arranging the 180 items of the Guide in six sections of 30 each, each item consisting of a pair of statements that describe job-related activities. Within each section the items are appropriate to a narrow range of occupational levels, where levels are defined by one's "qualifications" (with regard to the British system of the number and type of school examinations passed), the length of job training required, and the amount of post-secondary education needed. Students respond only to the items in two adjacent sections of their choice—those that are most relevant to their own wishes and plans. Holding testing time to a minimum in this way makes for a kind of efficiency not found in other interest inventories. On the other hand, much depends on students' ability to choose realistically the sections they will respond to; for instance, students with high potential but low goals will probably miss out on valuable information.

Another consequence of responding to selected sections of the Guide should be mentioned. As noted earlier, the nature of the six interest types is not constant across levels, and in some cases the contrast between the lowest and highest level of an interest type is surprising. The description of Type 6, for example, includes "showing people where to go and giving directions" at the lowest level and, at the highest, "writing books and articles." The manual states that between levels the transitions are gradual and that within levels the scales are homogeneous. Inspection of the scale contents at different levels supports the manual's claim. Still it would be helpful to see empirical evidence of internal consistency and low intercorrelation of the scales within levels. Such information may be available elsewhere for earlier versions of the Guide, but it is not given in the otherwise comprehensive manual for the full JIIG-CAL System of which the Guide is a part.

A second unique quality of the Guide is that students respond twice to each item. First they rate individually both statements of an item pair on a three-point scale (Like; Don't Mind; Dislike), and then indicate which of the two activities they prefer. The scoring procedures yield both absolute preference scores from the three-point ratings, and ipsative preference scores from the forced choices. A summary score that combines the absolute and ipsative scores is also computed together with several other derived scores and indexes. These make possible a number of specialized interpretations regarding, for example, response sets and mutually inconsistent scores. Without doubt these and other interpretations based on the highly derived scores make interesting and challenging work for the counselor, and document the complexity of interest patterns in many youngsters. Whether all this is worth the trouble can only be answered by local experience regarding counselors' ability and willingness to use the information generated about each student, the students' ability to use this information, how much the rather fine-grained analyses of student responses add to the quality of career decisions, and so forth.

A curious aspect of the Guide as it now exists is that when responses are to be computer-scored, students mark their answers on a separate answer document which, however, is not machine-readable. The responses must then be keypunched from the answer document, or else copied from the answer sheet onto special cards from which the marks are optically readable. This arrangement may be an accommodation to the type of optical scanning equipment available in England but, whatever its purpose, most schools in the United States would want a system that permits students to mark their answers a single time onto a machine-readable document.

The items of the Guide are generally worded clearly, and most should be understood by high school students. A few would present difficulty to students in this country, such as, "Take patients to an operating theatre on a trolley" (terms with different British and American meanings), and "Fix slates on roofs" (rare activity in this country). Spellings are British.

The Guide may be hand-scored, but the procedure is lengthy (about ten minutes per answer sheet for an experienced scorer) and involved. Some of the steps are self-checking but many possibilities for error remain. In the reviewer's opinion all hand-scoring should be independently checked.

Different reports are prepared for the student and the counselor. The student report presents a rough profile, without numerical scores, of the individual's interests in each of the six scales. By contrast the adviser's report swarms with information: three scores on each interest scale (sometimes with corrections for various types of response sets), indications of response inconsistency and of unanswered questions, and more. This report is densely packed and most counselors would benefit from training in its use.

The manual and other supporting materials are admirably complete in presenting descriptions of the Guide and the JIIG-CAL System, directions for administration and for the handling of materials, discussions of response sets and their detection, and interpretations of results to students. The unusually thorough materials for teachers and counselors reflect the authors' care, of course, but also the difficulties of using the Guide competently. Certainly the Guide yields far more than scores on six interest scales, and considerable skill and experience will be needed to exploit it fully.

To summarize, the JIIG-CAL Occupational Interests Guide has several attractive features. Students respond to a subset of items, which permits flexible and efficient use of testing time. Computer-scoring provides ingenious objective measures of several types of response bias (though "hard" evidence of their validity is not given in the manual). The counselor's report presents extensive data about the student's scores and response characteristics that invite detailed exploration of the student's interest pattern. And except for its lack of psychometric backup, the manual is a model of thoroughness. These strengths should attract adventurous counselors in this country to give the Guide a trial on a pilot basis.

Even so, the Guide cannot be recommended for routine counseling use in the United States. The British flavor of some items would confuse many students here. Parts of the student directions for choosing the appropriate sections of the Guide to respond to are stated in terms of the British system of academic qualifications, which is unknown to students in this country. Machine-scoring requires some clumsy transcription of item responses, and hand-scoring is a treacherous maze of clerical procedure. And finally, some counselors will be discouraged by the complexities of using the Guide results effectively.

[547]

Job Activity Preference Questionnaire. Business and industry; 1972–81; JAPQ; restructured and simplified version of the Position Analysis Questionnaire used for measuring vocational preferences and experiences; weighted combinations of 150 items into 16 dimensions of work: making decision/communicating and having responsibility, operating vehicles, using machines—tools—instruments, performing physical activities, operating keyboard and office equipment, monitoring and/or controlling equipment and/or processes, working under uncomfortable conditions, working with art-decor entertainment, performing supervisory duties, performing estimating activities, processing written information, working with buyers—customers—salespersons, working under hazardous conditions, performing paced and/or repetitive activities, working with aerial and aquatic equipment, catering/serving/smelling/tasting; 1 form ('80, 12 pages); administrator's guide ('81, 39 pages); separate answer sheets (NCS) may be used; 1985 price data: $1.75 per test book; $.15 per answer sheet; $5 per administrator's guide; information on scoring and statistical services available; administration time not reported; Robert C. Mecham, Alma F. Harris (test), Ernest J. McCormick (test), and P. R. Jeanneret (test); PAQ Services, Inc.*

Review of Job Activity Preference Questionnaire by NORMAN G. PETERSON, Vice President, Personnel Decisions Research Institute, Minneapolis, MN:

The Position Analysis Questionnaire (PAQ) is a job analysis questionnaire that has been carefully developed over a number of years. It enjoys a good reputation and is widely used. The Job Activity Preference Questionnaire (JAPQ) is a modification of the PAQ and is intended to provide an analysis of a person's vocational preferences or experiences. The author of the administration and interpretation guide (note it is not labeled a manual) for the JAPQ states: "The computer processing system [applied to JAPQ responses] may be used to match information about a person with job profiles, job aptitude requirements, expected compensation and job prestige predictions based on relationships empirically derived." Unfortunately, that is the extent of the information the reader is given about these empirical relationships. The words reliability and validity do not appear in the table of contents nor in the index, and if they appear anywhere in the "guide," they are well hidden.

THEORY OR RATIONALE, DEVELOPMENT, RELIABILITY AND VALIDITY EVIDENCE. Apparently, the rationale or theory underlying the JAPQ is something like this: (*a*) thousands of actual jobs have been described in PAQ items by persons knowledgeable about the jobs; (*b*) factor analysis of responses to these job-descriptive items has yielded 16 dimensions (shown above), and other analyses have yielded a wealth of other information as well; (*c*) persons can use these same items (actually "restructured and simplified" in some unspecified way) to describe their vocational preferences and/or experiences; (*d*) these responses describing personal preferences or experiences can be compared to the job descriptive information already on file; and (*e*) this comparison yields information about the suitability or match between the person and the job. I say "apparently" above because the guide contains no adequate description of the theory or rationale behind the JAPQ. No studies of any sort are cited. Indeed, there is no list of references at all. At a minimum, the development and psychometric characteristics of the PAQ, the parent instrument, ought to be summarized and supported by appropriate references, and the way in which the PAQ was modified to give rise to the JAPQ should be fully described.

Communication with the author of the manual revealed the following: A respondent's ratings of preference or experience on JAPQ items are weighted and scored according to a factor analysis of ratings that described jobs on the PAQ, not according to a factor analysis of preference or experience ratings on the JAPQ. The preference or experience scores derived in this manner are then referred to norms based on job description ratings from the PAQ. There appear to be serious problems with this methodology. First, it is assumed that the factor structures of personal, vocational preferences or experiences are identical to the factor structure of descriptions of existing jobs. Second, it is assumed that the scale properties of ratings of vocational preferences or experiences are identical to that of ratings of job descriptions. Thus stated, these do not seem to be defensible assumptions. Certainly, research aimed at investigating these assumptions should be carried out and reported in the manual.

Although standard errors of measurement appear in graphic form on some of the computer printouts for the JAPQ, nothing further is reported about the reliability or stability of JAPQ responses. No data on the validity of JAPQ scores with regard to occupational choice, tenure, satisfaction, or other occupational outcomes are given.

In sum, the manual or guide does not present adequate theoretical grounds or even a rational argument for the use of the JAPQ. No reliability or validity evidence is presented. The basis for normative statements is not given. Nothing is said about the development of the JAPQ, other than it is a restructured and simplified version of the PAQ.

SCORING, INTERPRETATION, AND COMPLETION OF THE JAPQ. What the JAPQ does have is computer scoring with many printouts. The JAPQ cannot be scored by the user; it must be sent to the publisher for scoring on their computer. Of the 17 pages of text in the guide, 10 are devoted to describing the printouts. Even though that section is labeled "Interpretation of JAPQ Results," it would be better labeled "How to read the JAPQ Printout." With regard to career planning and guidance, the guide devotes not quite two pages. These are not sufficient in detail and they come at the end of the manual. They might be better placed near the front. There are innumerable scores and ranks and percentages sprinkled throughout the JAPQ printouts. The explanations of these are sometimes difficult to understand, due primarily to terseness and, in some cases, a lack of correspondence between illustrative figures and explanations in the text. The instructions for completion of the JAPQ itself are admirably short, but they ask a lot of the respondent. First, the respondent is asked not to "relate your responses directly to any specific job or occupation." Instead, respondents are asked to indicate their level of interest "in the activity or situation as a part of any job that you might consider." Finally, they are asked to "assume that an opportunity would be available for you to get any required education or training." This seems to be a fairly complicated set of instructions to hold in one's head, especially when compared to instructions for other vocational preference inventories. Furthermore, there is apparently only one set of instructions for the JAPQ—intended to instruct the respondent to indicate preferences. There is no alternative set of instructions with regard to responding in terms of job experience. Yet, the JAPQ is scored and printouts are supplied for experience responses.

SUMMARY. The concept of basing a vocational guidance instrument on data derived from large-scale job analytic research is appealing, as has been pointed out by Dunnette and Borman (1979). Such an instrument would have "realism" built into it and would be able to supply a great deal of information about occupations. The JAPQ holds out this promise, but, at least as described in the current manual, does not deliver. It may be that the various scores and interpretations derived from JAPQ responses are reliable, valid, and rest on a strong theory or rationale, but virtually no evidence or even pertinent information about these matters is given in the manual. In addition, Dunnette and Borman also point out several "thorny" methodological issues beyond those mentioned in this review that require attention before a vocational guidance instrument based on a job analysis system can be considered useful. For now, users would be better off to use any of the more well-recognized and completely documented vocational interest inventories.

REVIEWER'S REFERENCES

Dunnette, M. D., & Borman, W. C. Personnel selection and classification systems. ANNUAL REVIEW PSYCHOLOGY, 1979, 30, 477–525.

Review of Job Activity Preference Questionnaire by PAUL R. SACKETT, Assistant Professor of Psychology, University of Illinois at Chicago, Chicago, IL:

The Job Activity Preference Questionnaire (JAPQ) is an instrument for measuring job interests for career planning and guidance purposes. It is intended for career guidance and job placement use in many settings including secondary schools, colleges, personnel departments, and rehabilitation organizations. The instrument is a modification of the well regarded job analysis tool, the Position Analysis Questionnaire (PAQ). While the PAQ measures the extent of use or importance of various job elements (e.g., using written materials, using mathematics) for a particular job, the JAPQ measures a respondent's preference for (and, optionally, experience with) each job element. JAPQ responses are matched against the PAQ data base of 1,781 position titles, and the jobs and job families whose requirements most closely match the respondent's preferences (and/or experiences) are identified. Thus, two major features differentiating the JAPQ from other career interest instruments are (1) the matching of respondent preferences for involvement with various job elements with job analyst ratings of job requirements rather than with the preferences of job incumbents, and (2) the matching of respondent preferences with an extensive array of jobs rather than with a relatively small number of jobs or job families. The Work Interest Questionnaire (WIQ) is a simplified version of the JAPQ designed for administration using a microcomputer. Differences between the two will be noted as appropriate.

This review will focus in turn on the instruments themselves, on the scoring system, and on the psychometric data provided for the instruments.

The 150-item JAPQ seeks respondent preferences for the extent of involvement with or the importance of activities, abilities, work situations, interpersonal contacts, equipment usage, decision making, and responsibility. Several issues concerning the instrument deserve mention. First, many of the job elements are quite abstract, and are followed by an illustrative example. For example, one item asks the respondent to indicate the preferred degree of importance of "physically handling objects, materials, animals, human beings, etc. (loading or unloading trucks, farming activities, taking care of babies in a nursery, etc)." A respondent focusing on the examples rather than the abstract job elements may find responding difficult if one example is seen as desirable and another undesirable.

Second, there is no way a respondent can indicate indifference to a job element. For most items, respondents are asked how much they would like to use the job element or how important would they like the job element to be, using scales ranging from not at all/no importance to very extensive/very important. A respondent who feels that the presence or absence of a job element would not affect the desirability of a given job must nonetheless specify a desired level of that element.

Third, though the language has been simplified from the post-college graduate level of the PAQ, both the publisher's estimate and the Dale-Chall readability formula suggest that the JAPQ requires a 10th- to 11th-grade reading level. This is higher than other interest inventories, such as the Strong (9th grade) or the Kuder (6th grade). The JAPQ data base includes the full occupational spectrum and is clearly intended for use with a wide range of respondents, including high school students who are not college bound. Readability may be a problem for a significant portion of the intended audience. The WIQ deals with this problem successfully. Its 150 items directly parallel the JAPQ; however, both the items and the instructions have been simplified (e.g., "feeding—offbearing" has been replaced with "inserting—removing materials"). Finally, the JAPQ itself contains typographical errors (e.g., a missing right parenthesis, printing "place" where "plane" is intended).

The JAPQ is suitable for individual or group administration. Time to complete (not mentioned in the manual) is estimated by the publisher to be about 30 minutes. Responses are made on a separate answer sheet which is mailed to the publisher for analysis. Responses are matched with the 1,781 job PAQ data base and a complex computer printout is produced. Only select key aspects of the output can be mentioned here. First, a percentile score for each of 16 dimensions of work (e.g., making decisions, operating vehicles, working under hazardous conditions) is provided. The scores indicate the percentage of positions in the data base requiring less of that dimension than the respondent prefers. The dimensions are the result of factor analysis of the PAQ; the factorial structure of the JAPQ is not reported. Second, the 200 jobs in the data base which most closely match the respondent's preferences are listed and ranked. For each of these jobs, goodness of fit on each dimension is presented. Third, the top 200 jobs are categorized according to the 9 major occupational classes and 84 occupational divisions used in the *Dictionary of Occupational Titles* (e.g., law, art, domestic service, forestry, construction), thus identifying the general job categories providing the best match.

Fourth, respondents can specify that jobs requiring specific levels of certain job elements be excluded from consideration. For example, a person in a wheelchair can specify that jobs requiring the element "climbing" be excluded. The 200 best fitting jobs which do not require climbing would then be listed. Fifth, General Aptitude Test Battery scores or their equivalent may be input, if available, and incorporated into the matching process. Ability requirements for all jobs in the data base have been estimated; an estimate of how well the respondent would perform on each of the top 200 jobs is given. Sixth, the JAPQ can optionally be completed in terms of past experience, as well as preference, and the top 200 jobs based on experience matching can be listed. A combined ranking based preference, experience, and ability is provided if the experience or ability options are used. Finally, a respondent can specify *D.O.T.* occupational divisions in which he/she has a particular interest; all jobs in the data base from these divisions will be listed and goodness of fit on each dimension will be indicated.

While the analyses are sophisticated and potentially very useful, the information is presented on a densely packed computer printout that is extremely difficult to interpret. The printout is not self-explanatory and would not be meaningful to the respondent. Thus the process of providing feedback to the respondent becomes a difficult and time consuming task for the counsellor. In addition, the administration manual contains serious errors. In several places, the text explaining sample printouts does not match the printout at all, thus making it even more difficult for a potential user to learn to interpret the printout.

Administration and scoring of the WIQ differs significantly from that of the JAPQ. The WIQ can be administered and scored using a microcomputer. Due to disk storage limitations, matching is done using a 400 job data base. Alternatively, a data base containing about 250 jobs requiring college degrees or one requiring high school degrees can be used. If the WIQ is instead completed using the standard answer sheet and mailed to the publisher for scoring, the full 1,781 job data base can be used. The WIQ computer generated report is more interpretable than the JAPQ printout, although still confusing in places. While adding several interesting features, such as occupational outlook projections for the jobs listed, several important features of the JAPQ are not available, such as the job exclusion feature discussed above and the combining of preference, experience, and ability in ranking jobs.

The manual does not present any psychometric data for the JAPQ or WIQ. There are no reliability studies, validity studies, or normative data. No evidence is offered to support suggestions made in promotional materials that the JAPQ can be used in business settings to improve job satisfaction and reduce turnover. According to a personal communication from the publisher, 3-week test-retest reliabilities for the JAPQ at the item level averaged .54 with a range from –.01 to .80 using a sample of 71 high school juniors. Whether the simplified WIQ produces more acceptable reliability figures remains unknown. The publisher also claims moderate success in predicting tenure and performance in 3 separate studies. These studies need to be made available for public scrutiny.

In summary, the tie to the extensive PAQ data base which represents the full occupational spectrum in this country makes the JAPQ/WIQ a very promising instrument for assessing job interests. At present, the instrument can only be recommended for research use until a more interpretable reporting system is devised, until the errors in the manual are eliminated, and until evidence is provided as to stability of results over time and as to the relationship between job preferences as measured by the JAPQ/WIQ and outcomes such as satisfaction, performance, and tenure.

[548]

Job Awareness Inventory. Average and special needs students in grades 10–12; 1980–81; JAI; "criterion-referenced"; 5 scores: occupations, do you know how to, general information, interview actions, total; no norms; no suggested standards of mastery; Forms A ('81, 8 pages, pretest), B ('81, 7 pages, posttest); teacher instructions ('80, 7 pages including answer key); 1983 price data: $32.95 per complete set including 10 pretests, 10 posttests, and teacher instructions; administration time not reported; Teen Makowski; Mafex Associates, Inc.*

Review of Job Awareness Inventory by CHARLES DAVIDSHOFER, Associate Professor of Psychology, Colorado State University, Fort Collins, CO:

The Job Awareness Inventory (JAI) is described in the manual as a criterion-referenced test about knowledge of the world of work. As a psychological assessment instrument, however, it leaves much to be desired. A more appropriate description of this inventory would list it as a questionnaire useful in orienting junior and senior high school students about the world of work.

The manual for the JAI contains only minimal information needed to administer and score the inventory; it provides no data on the development of the instrument, its validity, appropriate age levels for use, or the norms used in determining the raw score to T score conversion charts. The manual reports on only one very inadequate estimate of its reliability. Consequently, the pamphlet that accompanies the JAI is not really a test manual, but rather a set of teacher instructions.

The JAI consists of two forms (A and B) which according to the instructions are to be used for pre- and posttesting respectively. Changes in scores over time are expected to reveal mastery of the career material presented during the interim. Since no data are given to indicate the comparability of the forms, it cannot be concluded that score increases actually reflect greater mastery of the material. It is possible that Form B could be either easier or more difficult, making interpretation of score changes virtually impossible.

It is essential to know the demographic data on the norm groups used in developing the scoring tables. It cannot be determined from the information provided in the instructional booklet whether there is an age or time difference already built into the scoring tables. In the absence of such data, meaningful interpretation of JAI scores is impossible.

An inspection of the scoring tables given show that apparently a "T score" of 50 always is equivalent to the midpoint of the number of items possible on each part of the test. In terms of the correct definition of a T score distribution, this makes no sense. Whatever meaning is to be attached to these "T scores," it definitely is not that normally attributed to a score with a mean of 50 and a standard deviation of 10. The accompanying instructional booklet needs to be revised to clear up this discrepancy.

The only study reported on the JAI is presented as evidence of the stability of the inventory. This test-retest study involved 13 subjects over a 10-day period. The composition of this group is not specified. Given the small unspecified sample used, little can be determined about the reliability of this questionnaire.

In summary, the JAI does not meet the criteria established for psychological tests, yet the content of this instrument has excellent face validity and would appear very useful in motivating junior and senior high school students to begin thinking seriously about their future careers. The items appear to be quite easy, suggesting that the ceiling of this questionnaire might easily be reached by students in their junior or senior year of high school. Therefore, the JAI would probably be most useful with students in grades 7 through 10 or with high school juniors and seniors of below average intellectual ability. There is also a strong suggestion in the instructional booklet that it has potential value for students with special needs or handicapped students.

At this point in its development, the JAI would appear to function best as an instructional aid for use in various career education and guidance programs.

[549]

A Job Choice Decision-Making Exercise. High school and college and adults; 1981; JCE; a behavioral decision theory approach to the measurement of need for Affiliation, need for Power, and need for Achievement; reliability and validity studies available upon request from publisher; 3 scores: affiliation, power, achievement; norms consist of means and standard deviations; 1 form (18 pages); scoring guide (84 pages); no manual; 1985 price data: $4 per exercise booklet; $25 per scoring guide; scoring service, $5 per exercise booklet; administration time not reported; Michael J. Stahl and Adrian M. Harrell; Michael J. Stahl.*

[550]

The Job Descriptive Index. Employees; 1975; JDI; manual title is *The Measurement of Satisfaction in Work and Retirement*; 5 scores: work, pay, supervision, promotions, people or co-workers; 1 form (6 pages); manual (190 pages); 1985 price data: $34 per 100 tests; $5 per scoring key; $18 per manual; scoring service available, consult publisher; administration time not reported; Patricia Cain Smith, Lorne M. Kendall, and Charles L. Hulin; Bowling Green State University.*

TEST REFERENCES

1. Dunham, R. B., Smith, F. J., & Blackburn, R. S. Validation of the index of organizational reactions with the JDI, the MSQ, and faces scale. ACADEMY OF MANAGEMENT JOURNAL, 1977, 420–432.

2. Herman, J. B., & Gyllstrom, K. K. Working men and women: Inter- and intra-role conflict. PSYCHOLOGY OF WOMEN QUARTERLY, 1977, 1, 319–333.

3. Ivancevich, J. M. Different goal setting treatments and their effects on performance and job satisfaction. ACADEMY OF MANAGEMENT JOURNAL, 1977, 20, 406–419.

4. Miles, R. H., & Petty, M. M. Leader effectiveness in small bureaucracies. ACADEMY OF MANAGEMENT JOURNAL, 1977, 20, 238–250.

5. Sarata, B. P. V. Job characteristics, work satisfactions, and task involvement as correlates of service delivery strategies. AMERICAN JOURNAL OF COMMUNITY PSYCHOLOGY, 1977, 5, 99–109.

6. Brief, A. P., & Aldag, R. J. The job characteristic inventory: An examination. ACADEMY OF MANAGEMENT JOURNAL, 1978, 21, 659–670.

7. Brief, A. P., Van Sell, M., & Aldag, R. J. Job scope-employee reaction relationships: Methodological considerations. JOURNAL OF MANAGEMENT, 1978, 4(2), 27–32.

8. Cherniss, C., & Egnatios, E. Participation in decision-making by staff in community mental health programs. AMERICAN JOURNAL OF COMMUNITY PSYCHOLOGY, 1978, 6, 171–190.

9. Golembiewski, R. T., & Yeager, S. Testing the applicability of the JDI to various demographic groupings. ACADEMY OF MANAGEMENT JOURNAL, 1978, 21, 514–519.

10. Johns, G. Task moderators of the relationship between leadership style and subordinate responses. ACADEMY OF MANAGEMENT JOURNAL, 1978, 21, 319–325.

11. McNichols, C. W., Stahl, M. J., & Manley, T. R. A validation of Hoppock's job satisfaction measure. ACADEMY OF MANAGEMENT JOURNAL, 1978, 21, 737–742.

12. Feild, H. S., & Caldwell, B. E. Sex of supervisor, sex of subordinate, and subordinate job satisfaction. PSYCHOLOGY OF WOMEN QUARTERLY, 1979, 3, 391–399.

13. Kim, J. S., & Schuler, R. S. The nature of the task as a moderator of the relationship between extrinsic feedback and employee responses. ACADEMY OF MANAGEMENT JOURNAL, 1979, 22, 157–162.

14. Kopelman, R. E. Directionally different expectancy theory predictions of work motivation and job satisfaction. MOTIVATION AND EMOTION, 1979, 3, 299–317.

15. Schriesheim, C. A. The similarity of individual directed and group directed leader behavior descriptions. ACADEMY OF MANAGEMENT JOURNAL, 1979, 22, 345–355.

16. Weed, S. E., & Mitchell, T. R. The role of environmental and behavioral uncertainty as a mediator of situation-performance relationships. ACADEMY OF MANAGEMENT JOURNAL, 1980, 23, 38–60.

17. Lee, C., & Schuler, R. S. Goal specificity and difficulty and leader initiating structure as strategies for managing role stress. JOURNAL OF MANAGEMENT, 1980, 6, 177–187.

18. McCabe, D. J., Dalessio, A., Briga, J., & Sasaki, J. The convergent and discriminant validities between the IOR and the JDI: English and Spanish forms. ACADEMY OF MANAGEMENT JOURNAL, 1980, 23, 778–786.

19. O'Reilly, C. A., III. Individuals and information overload in organizations: Is more necessarily better? ACADEMY OF MANAGEMENT JOURNAL, 1980, 23, 684–696.

20. Petty, M. M., & Bruning, N. S. Relationships between employees' attitudes and error rates in public welfare programs. ACADEMY OF MANAGEMENT JOURNAL, 1980, 23, 556–561.

21. Schuler, R. S. A role and expectancy perception model of participation in decision making. ACADEMY OF MANAGEMENT JOURNAL, 1980, 23, 331–340.

22. Sgro, J. A., Worchel, P., Pence, E. C., & Orban, J. A. Perceived leader behavior as a function of the leader's interpersonal trust orientation. ACADEMY OF MANAGEMENT JOURNAL, 1980, 23, 161–165.

23. Wexley, K. N., Alexander, R. A., Greenawalt, J. P., & Couch, M. A. Attitudinal congruence and similarity as related to interpersonal evaluations in manager-subordinate dyads. ACADEMY OF MANAGEMENT JOURNAL, 1980, 23, 320–330.

24. Drory, A. Organizational stress and job attitudes: Moderating effects of organizational level and task characteristics. PSYCHOLOGICAL REPORTS, 1981, 48, 139–146.

25. Ferratt, T. W., Dunham, R. B., & Pierce, J. L. Self-report measures of job characteristics and affective responses: An examination of discriminant validity. ACADEMY OF MANAGEMENT JOURNAL, 1981, 24, 780–794.

26. Strasser, S., Dailey, R. C., & Bateman, T. S. Attitudinal moderators and effects of leaders' punitive behavior. PSYCHOLOGICAL REPORTS, 1981, 49, 695–698.

27. Yeager, S. J. Dimensionality of the Job Descriptive Index. ACADEMY OF MANAGEMENT JOURNAL, 1981, 24, 205–212.

28. Agriesti-Johnson, C., & Broski, D. Job satisfaction of dietitians in the United States. JOURNAL OF THE AMERICAN DIETETIC ASSOCIATION, 1982, 81, 555–559.

29. Fulk, J., & Wendler, E. R. Dimensionality of leader-subordinate interactions: A path-goal investigation. ORGANIZATIONAL BEHAVIOR AND HUMAN PERFORMANCE, 1982, 30, 241–264.

30. Graen, G. B., Liden, R. C., & Hoel, W. Role of leadership in the employee withdrawal process. JOURNAL OF APPLIED PSYCHOLOGY, 1982, 67, 868–872.

31. Hulin, C. L., Drasgow, F., & Komocar, J. Applications of item response theory to analysis of attitude scale translations. JOURNAL OF APPLIED PSYCHOLOGY, 1982, 67, 818–825.

32. Khoury, R. M., & Khoury, D. C. Job satisfaction and work performance of police. PSYCHOLOGICAL REPORTS, 1982, 51, 282.

33. Lester, D. Job satisfaction, cynicism, education and belief in an internal locus of control in police. PSYCHOLOGICAL REPORTS, 1982, 50, 1214.

34. Lopez, E. M. A test of the self-consistency theory of the job performance-job satisfaction relationship. ACADEMY OF MANAGEMENT JOURNAL, 1982, 25, 335–348.

35. Parasuraman, S. Predicting turnover intentions and turnover behavior: A multivariate analysis. JOURNAL OF VOCATIONAL BEHAVIOR, 1982, 21, 111–121.

36. Parsons, C. K., & Hulin, C. L. An empirical comparison of item response theory and hierarchical factor analysis in applications to the measurement of job satisfaction. JOURNAL OF APPLIED PSYCHOLOGY, 1982, 67, 826–834.

37. Parsons, C. K., & Hulin, C. L. Differentially weighting linear models in organizational research: A cross-validation comparison of four methods. ORGANIZATIONAL BEHAVIOR AND HUMAN PERFORMANCE, 1982, 30, 289–311.

38. Podsakoff, P. M., Todor, W. D., & Skov, R. Effects of leader contingent and noncontingent reward and punishment behaviors on subordinate performance and satisfaction. ACADEMY OF MANAGEMENT JOURNAL, 1982, 25, 810–821.

39. Schneider, B., Reichers, A. E., & Mitchell, T. M. A note on some relationships between the aptitude requirements and reward attributes of tasks. ACADEMY OF MANAGEMENT JOURNAL, 1982, 25, 567–574.

40. Bateman, T. S., & Organ, D. W. Job satisfaction and the good soldier: The relationship between affect and employee "citizenship." ACADEMY OF MANAGEMENT JOURNAL, 1983, 26, 587–595.

41. Bruning, N. S., & Snyder, R. A. Sex and position as predictors of organizational commitment. ACADEMY OF MANAGEMENT JOURNAL, 1983, 26, 485–491.

42. Ganster, D. C., Hennessey, H. W., & Luthans, F. Social desirability response effects: Three alternative models. ACADEMY OF MANAGEMENT JOURNAL, 1983, 26, 321–331.

43. O'Brien, G. E. Skill-utilization, skill-variety and the job characteristics model. AUSTRALIAN JOURNAL OF PSYCHOLOGY, 1983, 35, 461–468.

44. Parsons, C. K. The identification of people for whom Job Descriptive Index scores are inappropriate. ORGANIZATIONAL BEHAVIOR AND HUMAN PERFORMANCE, 1983, 31, 365–393.

45. Sekaran, U. How husbands and wives in dual-career families perceive their family and work worlds. JOURNAL OF VOCATIONAL BEHAVIOR, 1983, 22, 288–302.

46. Smith, H. W., Winer, J. L., & George, C. E. The relative efficacy of simulation experiments. JOURNAL OF VOCATIONAL BEHAVIOR, 1983, 22, 96–104.

47. Somers, M. J., & Lefkowitz, J. Self-esteem, need gratification, and work satisfaction: A test of competing explanations from consistency theory and self-enhancement theory. JOURNAL OF VOCATIONAL BEHAVIOR, 1983, 22, 303–311.

48. Dean, R. A., & Wanous, J. P. Effects of realistic job previews on hiring bank tellers. JOURNAL OF APPLIED PSYCHOLOGY, 1984, 69, 61–68.

49. Fansher, T. A., & Buxton, T. H. A job satisfaction profile of the female secondary school principal in the United States. NASSP BULLETIN, 1984, 68, 32–39.

Review of The Job Descriptive Index by JOHN O. CRITES, Research Professor, Department of Graduate Education, Kent State University, Kent, OH:

A carefully constructed and widely used measurement of job satisfaction, the Job Descriptive Index (JDI) originated in the Cornell Studies of Satisfaction. Designed to operationally define five separate components of job satisfaction, the JDI consists of the following scales: (1) Work on Present Job, (2) Present Pay, (3) Opportunities for Promotion, (4) Supervision on Present Job, and (5) People on Your Present Job. Each scale is composed of adjectives ("Boring") and short phrases ("Good opportunities for promotion"), ranging from 9 items (Pay and Promotion) to 18 items (Work, Supervision, and Coworkers), with a total of 72 items. Computation of total score, however, is not recommended by the authors in the scoring instructions for the JDI:

> The subscales are discriminably different, have loaded on separate group factors with no general factor in repeated factor analytic studies, and do not intercorrelate highly despite their high reliabilities.

In contrast to the judgment of others that job satisfaction is multi-faceted, the authors have maintained that:

> Numerous studies have clearly indicated that there are several discriminably different areas of job satisfaction. Measures of these sub-areas should be relatively independent, and the workers should be able to discriminate among them (Smith, Kendall, & Hulin, 1975, p. 25).

Factor analyses of job satisfaction suggest, however, that there may be a general factor as well as more discriminable group factors, although there has been considerable controversy around the methodologies used in these studies and the interpretation of their results. More recently, Schriesheim and Kinicki (unpublished manuscript, 1984, p. 25) cite the same issue, concluding that although the JDI possesses discriminant validity, "studies clearly show that the JDI typically has a moderate degree of subscale intercorrelation." By "moderate" is meant correlations which have a modal tendency in the .30s and low .40s, although some range as low as .08 and as high as .76. Smith et al. (1975, p. 78) acknowledge that "nearly all the scale intercorrelations are quite high," but they attribute them largely to common method variance and to "the interdependence of certain job aspects from one setting to another." Their commitment is clearly to a multiple group factor model of job satisfaction. An alternative conceptual scheme has been proposed by Crites (1969, p. 495):

> Theoretically, it would seem that the "hierarchical" model might have greater potential heuristic value, since it is difficult to conceive of highly satisfied or dissatisfied workers as being differentially satisfied with the various aspects of their vocations. But it may be that those of moderate overall job satisfaction are more satisfied with certain features of their work than with others.

With the availability now of refined hierarchical factor analytic methods (Wherry, in press), these competing models can be empirically tested.

Another theoretical as well as practical issue with the JDI concerns the extent to which the items in it are descriptive or evaluative. In their initial conceptualization of the JDI, the authors clearly wanted the items in it to be descriptive—hence its title, the Job Descriptive Index. Illustrative of such items are these: routine, hot, challenging, "on your feet," and simple. An immediate problem with purely descriptive items, however, is how to score them, at least rationally (e.g., do workers *want* a challenging job?). At the start of their work Smith and her associates appeared to prefer an empirical approach, which they called "triadic scoring." It "built in" the evaluative dimension of job satisfaction by asking workers to describe what they considered their "best" and "worst" jobs, as well as their present jobs, using items which Smith et al. (1975, p. 156) state were "in large part descriptive of the job, rather than purely evaluative." But this "triadic scoring procedure did not improve the performance of the scales in several studies, as compared with a direct scoring procedure" (Smith et al., 1975, p. 150). The latter was first defined as follows: "An item was scored positively for all workers if it was endorsed more frequently for the best job than for the worst job, and it was scored negatively for all workers if endorsed otherwise" (Smith et al., 1975, p. 35). This direct scoring procedure was evidently changed, however, in the later development of the JDI, with the present scoring weights (3 = Yes to a positive item, 3 = No to a negative item, 1 = ? to any item) being derived from comparisons of satisfied and dissatisfied workers defined by upper- and lower-halves on a total score calculated from item weights which ranged from 1 to 3 (Smith et al., 1975, p. 79).

These emendations in the scoring procedure evidently also involved a shift from purely descriptive items, to largely descriptive items, to mostly evaluative items, at least as rationally determined. Schriesheim and Bird (unpublished manuscript, 1984) asked 64 judges to classify JDI items as either evaluative or descriptive or both, and they found that "the mixture is about two-thirds evaluative and one-third descriptive." Thus, what began as the Job Descriptive Index now appears to have become the Job "Evaluative" Index. The implications for the theory underlying the JDI are significant. Smith et al. (1975, p. 19) explicate the theoretical foundations for the JDI as follows:

> We want a measure which will reflect to a certain extent each subject's frame of reference. We also want the measure to reflect actual job-to-job and situation-to-situation differences in the worker's activities. A third consideration dictated by our model of job satisfaction is that the anchors or end points of the worker's subjective job continuum should be reflected in the resulting scale.

Given the original triadic scoring system, with descriptive item content, the JDI would have been true to this essentially ideographic model, which Smith et al. (1975, p. 13) relate to Helson's concept of adaptation level; but with the change to weights obtained from group differences on what are judged as mostly evaluative items, the entire rationale seems to have imperceptively shifted to a nomothetic frame of reference.

These are issues and problems with the JDI which need discussion and dialogue as soon as possible. Their salience is highlighted by this observation by Schriesheim and Kinicki (unpublished manuscript, 1984, p. 2) in their recent review of the JDI:

> Job satisfaction is the most commonly investigated variable in industrial-organizational psychology (Locke, 1976), with over three quarters of all recent studies using satisfaction as either an independent or dependent variable (Schriesheim & Skaret, unpublished manuscript, 1976). While many satisfaction measures exist, the Job Descriptive Index (JDI; Smith, Kendall, & Hulin, 1975) is used more than half the time (Yeager, 1981), a figure which is at least five to six times as great as the next most commonly used instrument (O'Connor, Peters, & Gordon, 1980; Schriesheim & Skaret, unpublished manuscript, 1976). Thus, the JDI is highly central to the study of industrial-organizational psychology.

It is unusual that an instrument used this much and obviously central to one of the principal fields of psychology (1) has no manual and (2) is hand-scored. Certainly it is incumbent upon the authors, or someone, to at least bring the materials on the JDI up-to-date and in accordance with the *Standards for Educational and Psychological Tests*. Even more important is a critical analysis of how closely the JDI measures the theoretical constructs originally posited for it, given its current items and scoring procedures. In an earlier review of the JDI, Crites (1969, pp. 490) concluded that it had "promise as the measure of job satisfaction of the future, because of its sophisticated conceptualization and its 'discriminant and convergent' validity." This conclusion still obtains, but the "future is now": to evaluate how much of its promise the JDI has fulfilled requires that it be systematically updated.

REVIEWER'S REFERENCES

Crites, J. O. VOCATIONAL PSYCHOLOGY: THE STUDY OF VOCATIONAL BEHAVIOR & DEVELOPMENT. New York: McGraw Hill, 1969.

Smith, P. C., Kendall, L. M., & Hulin, C. L. THE MEASUREMENT OF SATISFACTION IN WORK AND RETIREMENT: A STRATEGY FOR THE STUDY OF WORK ATTITUDES. Bowling Green, OH: Bowling Green State University, 1975.

Locke, E. A. The nature and causes of job satisfaction. In M. D. Dunnette (Ed.), HANDBOOK OF INDUSTRIAL AND ORGANIZATIONAL PSYCHOLOGY. Chicago: Rand McNally, 1976.

Schriesheim, C. A., & Skaret, D. J. ARE WE BUILDING AN ADDITIVE SCIENCE OF ORGANIZATIONS? NO! Unpublished paper, Department of Organizational Behavior, Graduate School of Business Administration, University of Southern California, Los Angeles, 1976.

O'Connor, E. J., Peters, L. H., & Gordon, S. M. The measurement of job satisfaction: Current practices and future considerations. JOURNAL OF MANAGEMENT, 1980, 4(2), 17–26.

Yeager, S. J. Dimensionality of the Job Descriptive Index. ACADEMY OF MANAGEMENT JOURNAL, 1981, 24(1), 205–212.

Schriesheim, C. A., & Bird, B. J. The evaluation-description controversy and the Job Descriptive Index (JDI): A theoretical and empirical analysis. Unpublished manuscript, 1984.

Schriesheim, C. A., & Kinicki, A. J. THE MEASUREMENT OF SATISFACTION BY THE JOB DESCRIPTIVE INDEX (JDI): A REVIEW. Unpublished paper, Management Department, College of Business Administration, University of Florida, 1984.

Wherry, R. J., Sr. CONTRIBUTIONS TO CORRELATIONAL ANALYSIS. New York: Academic Press, in press.

Review of The Job Descriptive Index by BARBARA A. KERR, Assistant Professor of Educational Psychology, University of Nebraska-Lincoln, Lincoln, NE:

PSYCHOMETRIC PROPERTIES. In many ways the Job Descriptive Index (JDI) is an exemplary instrument, the development of which was marked by cautiousness and psychometric rigor. The JDI is a set of five scales which measure five aspects of job satisfaction. Smith, Kendall, and Hulin (1975) define job satisfaction as "the feelings a worker has about his job" (p. 6), which are derived from a comparison of expected outcomes received from the work environment and actual outcomes. Smith et al. reviewed factor analytic studies and conducted their own research and interviews to discover the major factors influencing job-related feelings. Job satisfaction seemed to best be characterized by (1) nature of the work, (2) details of remuneration, (3) the nature of promotional opportunities, (4) characteristics of supervision, and (5) the co-workers on the job. The work, supervision, and co-workers subscales contain 18 items each, while the pay and promotion subscales have 9 items each. All the items included in each subscale are presented together under a heading (which labels the particular aspect of satisfaction being measured). Each item is a short word or phrase (e.g., "hot" for work satisfaction; "lazy" for supervision satisfaction), and the response categories used are "Yes," "?," and "No." The instructions ask respondents to put a "Y" beside an item if it describes the particular aspect of the job, an

"N" if the item does not describe the aspect, and a "?" if they cannot decide. Positively worded items are scored 3, 1, 0, and negatively worded items are scored 0, 1, 3 (for Y, ?, and N, respectively).

Based on research which showed that satisfaction has both descriptive and evaluative components, Smith et al. included a combination of items which merely described aspects of the work environment with items which allowed value judgments about the environment.

The JDI possesses good content validity, impressive construct validity, and adequate reliability. Smith et al. (1975) and Smith, Smith, and Rollo (1974) factor analyzed the JDI with a variety of samples selected from widely differing occupations. Golembiewski and Yeager (1978) factor analyzed the JDI with five demographic subdivisions of the hierarchy of a large corporation and with a single, very large sample ($N = 2{,}261$). All of these studies showed the five-factor conceptualization of satisfaction, including both evaluative and descriptive components, was fairly well supported. Occasionally subscales split into two or three separate factors, but this can be accounted for by the breadth of both the item sampling and the construct. Also, contextual differences across job situations of the various samples may account for the splitting of factors.

The JDI has consistently been shown to be highly correlated with independent variables which are theoretically meaningful, including the job satisfaction dimension of life satisfaction (Iris & Barrett, 1972), leader consideration (Hunt & Liebscher, 1973), and positive leader reward behaviors (Keller & Szilagyi, 1976). That the JDI has concurrent validity seems very well supported.

Evidence from a review of JDI research by Schriesheim and Kinicki 1984 indicates good predictive validity for a number of "job withdrawal" behaviors such as absenteeism and turnover. Strong convergent and discriminant validity are also reported. Very few instruments in industrial-organizational psychology have received the attention of researchers to the degree that the JDI has. That this intense scrutiny has revealed high performance of the JDI for all forms of validity is supportive of its excellent construct validity overall.

With respect to reliability, the JDI has not obtained extraordinarily high internal consistency coefficients; however, it has performed adequately given the brevity of the test and the sensitivity of the test to short-term changes in the work environment. Smith et al. (1975) reported an average corrected reliability coefficient for the five scales of .79 for split-half estimates of internal consistency. Higher internal consistency reliabilities were found for each of the scales: work (.84), pay (.80), promotion (.86), supervision (.87), and co-workers (.88). Further research has continued to show moderate internal consistency.

Test-retest reliability over brief periods (two and six weeks) has been shown to be fairly high (Schriesheim & Tsui, 1981). Longer-term tests of reliability, which may be misguided in the case of the JDI (job satisfaction scores *should* change over long periods), have shown low to moderate reliability coefficients (Smith et al., 1975).

Schriesheim and Kinicki (1984) have reviewed the psychometric properties of the Job Descriptive Index thoroughly and astutely. Their review was very helpful to this brief synopsis, and the reader is referred to their paper for the details of each study noted here. They conclude, "All in all, these conclusions indicate that the JDI is a high-quality measuring instrument, and that there is no existing measure of job satisfaction with as much positive evidence concerning its validity and reliability."

PRACTICAL PROPERTIES. The practical strengths of the Job Descriptive Index are numerous. First of all, the fact of its popularity ensures that users will be able to communicate and to compare information about job satisfaction with other users; a widely used measure contributes to progress in understanding of work satisfaction by providing a common language and frame of reference. When an instrument is as psychometrically sound as the JDI, its popularity is all the more important. Second, the JDI is easy to administer. The very short answer booklet requires from 5 to 10 minutes for the average person to complete. The JDI is useable in mass quantities. Manual scoring is easy with scoring keys that slip into booklets conveniently, although comparing raw scores to norms is not. The simple language makes possible the use of the JDI with populations with only eighth grade educations and only basic reading fluency in English. (A Spanish version is also available). The JDI has the advantage of not being too slick, unlike many instruments in this field, and therefore is probably non-threatening to test-takers who suffer from test anxiety.

The major practical problem that exists with the JDI is the absence of a concise manual. A photocopy of the out-of-print *The Measurement of Satisfaction in Work and Retirement*, written by Smith, Kendall, and Hulin (1975) to describe the entire project, is available to the test buyer for use as a manual. Although it is an interesting and highly readable account of psychometric research, it is very difficult to locate the appropriate norms and brief validity and reliability information. There are a great many tables of norms, stratified by combinations of sex with income, education, job tenure, community "prosperity," and community "decreptitude." The average user probably needs norms for sex, sex x income, and sex x job tenure, and several short summaries of validity and reliability information as provided by Schriesheim and Kinicki (1984).

Two problems arise in relation to intepretation of scores. The first is that the five scale scores cannot and should not be summed up as a global measure of job satisfaction. Smith et al. give warnings about this in their book and in a paper included in the test kit; however, review of the JDI literature will show that this caution has been ignored as often as it has been attended to. An even stronger statement should be added, possibly to every scoring key. Here, again, a manual would be useful to spell out the reason why the JDI does not measure the entire universe of affective responses to the job environment. Second, the JDI does not include a means of controlling for social desirability (the tendency to report oneself in a favorable light) or for leniency (the tendency to report perceptions of others that are overly positive.) Therefore, in research or practice where these may be important confounding variables, another measure of these tendencies needs to be used in order to understand and correct bias.

Finally, one of the JDI's major strengths—its simplicity—may be one of its main problems. It may be too simple for talented adults or for adults in very high-level positions. Recent research on gifted/talented adults (Kerr & Kaufman, 1983) shows that the response of the talented adult to underemployment may be extremely complex, involving more and different factors in his or her dissatisfaction than the five factors proposed by Smith et al. It is possible that for the talented adult, satisfaction in the job is much less related to pay, promotion, and co-workers and much more associated with the qualities of the actual work such as the degree of creativity and self-actualization possible. Smith et al.'s supervision factor may be completely irrelevant to this group; research on "leadership substitutes" (Kerr & Jermier, 1978) seems to show that talented individuals who are highly identified with a profession find supervision, no matter how bad or good, to be neutral in its impact. Extensions of the JDI and its methodology to this group would probably prove fruitful.

REVIEWER'S REFERENCES

Iris, B., & Barrett, G. V. Some relations between job and life satisfaction and job importance. JOURNAL OF APPLIED PSYCHOLOGY, 1972, 56, 301–304.

Hunt, J. G., & Liebscher, V. K. C. Some relations between job and life satisfaction and job importance. JOURNAL OF APPLIED PSYCHOLOGY, 1973, 9, 59–77.

Smith, P. C., Smith, O. W., & Rollo, J. Factor structure for blacks and whites of the Job Descriptive Index and its discrimination of job satisfaction. JOURNAL OF APPLIED PSYCHOLOGY, 1974, 59, 99–100.

Smith, P. C., Kendall, L. M., & Hulin, C. L. THE MEASUREMENT OF SATISFACTION IN WORK AND RETIREMENT: A STRATEGY FOR THE STUDY OF ATTITUDES. Bowling Green, OH: Bowling Green State University, 1975.

Keller, R. T., & Szilagyi, A. W. Employee reactions to leader reward behavior. ACADEMY OF MANAGEMENT JOURNAL, 1976, 19, 619–627.

Golembiewski, R. T., & Yeager, S. Testing the applicability of the JDI to various demographic groupings. ACADEMY OF MANAGEMENT JOURNAL, 1978, 21, 514–519.

Kerr, S., & Jermier, J. M. Substitutes for leadership: Their meaning and measurement. ORGANIZATIONAL BEHAVIOR AND HUMAN PERFORMANCE, 1978, 22, 375–403.

Schriesheim, C. A., & Tsui, A. S. Development and validation of a short satisfaction measure for use in survey feedback interventions. Unpublished manuscript, 1981.

Kerr, B. A., & Kaufman, F. Counseling talented adults. Paper presented at National Association for Gifted Children, Philadelphia, PA, 1983.

Schriesheim, C. A., & Kinicki, A. J. THE MEASUREMENT OF SATISFACTION BY THE JOB DESCRIPTIVE INDEX (JDI): A REVIEW. Unpublished paper, Management Department, College of Business Administration, University of Florida, 1984.

[551]

Job Skills Tests. Job applicants and industrial workers; 1981–83; 4 tests; "evaluate the ability of industrial workers to perform (various) operations"; norms consist of percentile equivalents only; price data available from publisher; Ronald T. Ramsay; Ramsay Corporation.*

a) READING. 1983; "ability to read a passage and answer questions about the passage"; Forms A, B, (6 pages); test manual (13 pages); 30(35) minutes.

b) ORAL DIRECTIONS. 1983; "ability to follow directions"; Form A (3 pages); test manual (15 pages); administration time not reported.

c) MEASUREMENT. 1981–83; "ability to measure"; Form A ('81, 3 pages); test manual ('83, 12 pages); administration time not reported.

d) ARITHMETIC. 1983; "arithmetic skills"; Form A (3 pages); test manual (11 pages); 20(25) minutes.

[552]

Job-Tests Program. Adults; 1947–81; battery of aptitude tests, personality tests, and performance appraisal forms used in various combinations in different jobs in business and industry; 4 series; price data available from publisher; Industrial Psychology, Inc.*

a) APTITUDE-INTELLIGENCE TEST SERIES. 1947–81; 15 tests; Joseph E. King (1–8, 10–15) and H. B. Osborn, Jr. (9).

1) *Office Terms.* 1947–81; tests ability to understand the special terms used in business.

2) *Numbers.* 1947–81; tests ability to work rapidly and accurately with numbers.

3) *Perception.* 1947–81; tests ability to perceive details in and recognize differences in words and numbers quickly.

4) *Judgment.* 1947–81; tests ability to figure out solutions to problems.

5) *Fluency.* 1947–81; tests ability to think of words rapidly.

6) *Parts.* 1949–81; tests ability to see the whole in relation to its parts.

7) *Memory.* 1948–81; tests ability to remember visual, verbal, and numerical materials.

8) *Sales Terms.* 1948–56; tests ability to understand words and information in the sales and contact fields.

9) *Factory Terms.* 1948–57; tests ability to understand words and information in the factory and mechanical fields.

10) *Tools.* 1948–76; tests ability to recognize pictures of common tools, equipment, and machines.

11) *Precision.* 1948–57; tests ability to see details in pictures, to recognize differences and likenesses rapidly.

12) *Blocks.* 1948–56; adapted from Army General Classification Test; tests ability to visualize objects on the basis of three dimensional cues.

13) *Dimension.* 1948–56; tests ability to visualize objects when seen from different angles.

14) *Dexterity.* 1949–56; tests ability to perform routine motor tasks rapidly; three paper and pencil subtests: Maze, Checks, Dots.

15) *Motor.* 1948–56; tests ability to coordinate eye and hand movements in a specific motoric task; motor apparatus required.

b) EMPLOYEE ATTITUDE SERIES. 1954–60; 3 tests; R. B. Cattell, J. E. King (1–3), and A. K. Schuettler (1–2).

1) *CPF (Contact Personality Factor).* 1954; test of extroversion versus introversion, or contact versus noncontact personality; also published by Institute for Personality and Ability Testing as Form A of IPAT Contact Personality Factor Test.

2) *NPF (Neurotic Personality Factor).* 1954; tests general stability, emotional balance, lack of neurotic tendencies; also published by Institute for Personality and Ability Testing as IPAT Neurotic Personality Factor Test.

3) *16 PF (Sixteen Personality Factor).* 1956; measures 16 basic factors of personality; Industrial Edition A.

c) JOB TEST FIELD SERIES. 1960–81; 28 recommended test batteries (Junior Clerk, Numbers Clerk, Office Machine Operator, Contact Clerk, Senior Clerk, Secretary, Unskilled Worker, Semi-Skilled Worker, Factory Machine Operator, Vehicle Operator, Inspector, Skilled Worker, Sales Clerk, Salesperson, Sales Engineer, Scientist, Engineer, Office Technical, Writer, Designer, Instructor, Office Supervisor, Sales Supervisor, Factory Supervisor, General Clerk, Dental Office Assistant, Dental Technician, Optometric Assistant).

d) MERIT RATING SERIES. 1957; developed to aid management in obtaining a reliable and accurate rating of an employee's job performance or efficiency, from the immediate supervisor; provides strengths and weaknesses on such performance traits as quantity, quality, job knowledge, personal work-habits, potential, etc.; 5 forms tailored to each of the major job families.

1) *Clerical.*
2) *Mechanical.*
3) *Sales.*
4) *Technical.*
5) *Supervisor.*

See T2:1078 (12 references); for reviews by William H. Helme and Stanley I. Rubin, see 6:774; for a review by Harold P. Bechtoldt of the Factored Aptitude Series, see 5:602; for a review by D. Welty Lefever and an excerpted review by Laurance F. Shaffer of an earlier edition of this series, see 4:712 (1 reference).

[553]

Jobmatch. Pupils geared toward non-academic occupations; 1982; a self-assessment program for career guidance and counseling based on the Job Disposition Questionnaire (JDQ); 40 profile scores compared to dispositional profiles of particular occupations; individual; questionnaire (8 pages); teachers guide (33 pages); profiles book (42 pages); job facts book (50 pages); answer sheet (2 pages); price data available from publisher; (60) minutes; Industrial Training Research Unit; Macmillan Education [England].*

Review of Jobmatch by GEORGE DOMINO, Professor of Psychology, University of Arizona, Tucson, AZ:

Jobmatch is a self-assessment package for use in career guidance with high school age students who are not pursuing a college education, but are directly entering the work force. The package consists of four booklets: (1) the Jobmatch Questionnaire (also referred to as the Job Disposition Questionnaire or JDQ) consisting of 49 multiple choice questions, each with 2 or 3 alternatives; (2) the Match Yourself booklet, which is a series of 40 templates bound together, which the client uses to score the JDQ; (3) the Inform Yourself booklet, also for use by the client, which gives for each of the 40 occupations assessed a brief description of what the job involves (e.g., "The chef or cook is in charge of preparing and cooking food."), what the preferences of individuals in that occupation are, what qualifications and training are needed, and some photographs showing the occupation in action; (4) a Teacher's Guide to Jobmatch, aimed for the professional rather than the client, and serving as manual.

On the surface the Jobmatch package is attractively done, with booklets clearly identified, modern looking graphics, and clear and concise writing. There are a few minor problems such as the omission of number 18 from the answer sheet, a picture of a pegboard on booklet covers which implies a fit between a particular person and a specific job, a lot of photographs in booklet 3 that are unessential (do we really need three photographs of women working at sewing machines to understand what a sewing machinist does?), and some wordings that reflect the British origin of this instrument ("place a tick in the appropriate box").

There are a number of positive aspects to Jobmatch that need to be pointed out. The client is intimately involved in the whole process and thus as an active participant is presumably better motivated. The questions in the JDQ cover four aspects: the physical environment (e.g., preference for working indoors or outdoors), the social environment (e.g., preference for contact with people), work content (e.g., tools used), and working method (e.g., degree of self-scheduling). With few exceptions, the questions are reasonable and ask the client to make meaningful comparisons, rather than to select among occupational titles. The manual underscores the importance of establishing rapport, of not using Jobmatch in isolation, and not perceiving Jobmatch as a test or predictive instrument. Finally, Jobmatch is also available in two computer versions, one interactive and one scorable by computer.

Now for the bad news. No information is given in the manual on how the JDQ items came to be, and why these particular ones were retained. No information is given on how the particular 40 occupations were selected. The 40 scales were developed in the same manner as those for the Strong Vocational Interest Inventory (i.e., the responses of individuals in a particular job were compared with those of the general population, and items showing a statistically significant difference, as determined by chi-square, were retained). A distinction is made in the manual between these significant items (called profile items) and a subset of these significant items which showed significantly greater endorsement by the specific occupational group (called key items). A table is given identifying the key items, but if the reader is interested in the composition of a particular scale (i.e., the profile items), these must be identified through use of the template.

The manual indicates that subjects in specific occupational groups were under 30, on the job for at least 6 months, and considered to be satisfactory employees. A table of sten norms indicates that there were 1,084 male workers and 801 female workers, but at no point is the size of each occupational group indicated (were there 2, 20, or 200 plumbers?) nor are additional demographic data given. A detailed example of the Bricklayer scale is given, indicating there were 68 bricklayers, but no indication for the other 39 groups.

Reliability data are scanty, and all that is presented is a test-retest study over an interval of 2 weeks for a group of 91 schoolchildren (neither age, grade, nor other information is given). The results show 25% changed responses, which the authors interpret as fairly normal, but the profile scores remained "encouragingly stable," with Spearman rho's between .62 to .88. One wonders why reliability studies with more appropriate adult samples were not carried out, or why measures of internal consistency were not computed.

Validity studies "have been carried out" but the only evidence presented are the scores of selected occupational groups on each scale. Presumably, the selected groups are those scoring highest and lowest on each scale, but this is not indicated. On most if not all scales, the appropriate group scores highest, but there are some puzzling patterns. For example, the second highest scoring group on the Nurse scale are motor vehicle mechanics (the analogy here is tempting), while farmers score higher than forestry workers on the Forestry Worker scale.

Jobmatch seems a good beginning, sophisticated in its packaging, but leaving much to be desired in its contents. Aside from the applicability to the American work force, Jobmatch has some potential, but much more technical information needs to be made available.

[554]

The John Test. Non-native speakers of English; no date on test materials; "a test of oral proficiency for ESL placement"; shortened version available; no norms, publisher recommends use of local norms; individual; 4 scores: comprehension, connected discourse, asking questions, total; 1 form (no date, 3 pages); guide for using (no date, 5 pages); score sheet (no date, 1 page); 1983 price data: $5 per complete set; (10) minutes; Language Innovations, Inc.*

[555]

Joliet 3-Minute Speech and Language Screen. Grades K, 2, 5; 1983; 5 scores: receptive vocabulary, grammar (evoked sentences), articulation, voice, fluency; individual; manual (33 pages including reproducible individual screen form, class record form, plus 8 vocabulary plates per level); 1984 price data: $19.95 per test kit; (3) minutes; Mary C. Kinzler and Constance Cowing Johnson; Communication Skill Builders.*

Review of Joliet 3-Minute Speech and Language Screen by ROBERT E. OWENS, JR., Professor of Speech Pathology, State University of New York at Geneseo, Geneseo, NY:

The Joliet 3-Minute Speech and Language Screen (J3MSLS) attempts to fill the need for a practical test with which to screen large numbers of children quickly. Thus, the authors have prepared short receptive vocabulary and elicited sentence imitation tasks. Other aspects of speech and language, such as phonology, fluency, and voice, are embedded within these tasks. Test data are recorded on a reproducible test score form.

The "Receptive Vocabulary" portion of the J3MSLS, consisting of only eight items for each of the three grade levels for which the test is designed, follows the testing format of the Peabody Picture Vocabulary Test. As such, the test provides no data on a child's depth of understanding of the words presented. The child merely points to pictures named by the tester. The author's procedures for initial selection of Receptive Vocabulary items are vague and no item validity data are provided. In addition, the black and white line drawings used to illustrate each item are not always clear. For example, visual acuity would be very important when trying to find a black and white "cardinal" from among three other birds. On another plate, birds supposedly demonstrating "migrate" are only tangential to the landscape in the illustration.

With large numbers of children and rapid scoring, there is also the potential to misscore the Receptive Vocabulary items. Neither the score form nor the test plate contain any letter designation as a key, although the test manual contains a vocabulary key section.

The "Evoked Sentences" portion of the J3MSLS screens in 10 sentences those syntactic forms which the authors' clinical experience has demonstrated to be most frequently produced incorrectly. Errors are scored for words omitted, substituted, added, transposed, or contracted, or for unintelligible words. Although the error rules are word-related, at least one example uses the possessive "s" marker. This raises the question of morphological markers, especially as they relate to dialectal differences. Obviously, the 3-minute administration time does not include time for determining such complex scoring issues. The test does allow for dialectal differences, however, but 20 more speakers of a dialect must appear within the screened population so that the test administrator can determine which dialectal variations should not be counted as errors.

Although standardized on 2,587 children, the test cutoff scores for these children are not reported in relation to other speech and language instruments. In addition, the geographic location of this norming sample is not described. From the original sample, 586 children were chosen at random for pass/fail score and in-depth correlational studies. This subsample of children was given the Peabody Picture Vocabulary Test and the Carrow Elicited Language Inventory. These results are reported as group means to demonstrate the validity of group scores, but the predictive strength of the J3MSLS is not addressed in this analysis. Item analysis would be particularly helpful in the evoked sentence portion of the test. Such analysis would have provided more information on individual test item validity.

Socioeconomic, sexual, and racial-ethnic differences of the subsample were also analyzed using the Cochran Q test. Socioeconomic factors were significant at a confidence level of .01 for high-mid/low differences on both the Vocabulary and Grammar portions of the test. Mid/low and sexual variables reflected significant differences only in the Receptive Vocabulary portion. With the social-ethnic categories, the greatest significant differences were between Hispanic-other and "white" groups for both Vocabulary and Grammar. These data are not translated into possible error score adjustments. If this random sample accurately reflects the overall standardization sample, then that sample is approximately 46% Black or Hispanic-other and approximately 43% low socioeconomic level.

The authors randomly selected 113 children for retesting. No significant differences were found between the two administrations at any of the grade levels (Salvia & Ysseldyke, 1981). Other subgroups were not analyzed, and no data on interexaminer reliability are presented.

In summary, the J3MSLS provides a quick but limited instrument for speech and language screening of large numbers of school-age children. Other tests, such as the Northwest Syntax Screening Test, take considerably longer to administer and only assess one area of language. This remark is not meant to imply that the J3MSLS screens all areas of speech and language. Important areas for school-age children, such as figurative language and pragmatics, are not assessed. In addition, the value of sampling 10 short imitated sentences must be questioned as a measure of expressive language use. It is also unfortunate that the test targets only grades K, 2, and 5. It is this reviewer's experience that public school speech-language pathologists face their major screening task with first-grade students. Still, the J3MSLS is a useful standardized screening tool. In addition, the use of reproducible score forms is commendable.

REVIEWER'S REFERENCES

Salvia, J., & Ysseldyke, J. E. ASSESSMENT IN SPECIAL AND REMEDIAL EDUCATION. Boston: Houghton Mifflin, 1981.

[556]

The Jones-Mohr Listening Test. Persons in educational and training programs; 1976; "a tape-assisted learning program"; no data on reliability and validity; no norms, authors recommend establishment of local norms; Forms A, B, (2 pages); facilitator's guide (28 pages); cassette tape (Form A and B) necessary for administration; 1983 price data: $44.95 per complete set including 25 copies of each form; $4 per 25 tests of either form; (20–25) minutes per form; John E. Jones and Lawrence Mohr; University Associates, Inc.*

TEST REFERENCES

1. Boice, R., Hanley, C. P., Shaughnessy, P., & Gansler, D. Eyewitness accuracy. A general observational skill. BULLETIN OF THE PSYCHONOMIC SOCIETY, 1982, 20, 193–195.

Review of The Jones-Mohr Listening Test by LEAR ASHMORE, Professor of Speech Communication and Education, The University of Texas at Austin, Austin, TX:

The Jones-Mohr Listening Test was, according to the authors, designed primarily to provide feedback to persons on their listening accuracy, motivate them to work on listening, and provide a research and evaluation tool. Through their work as facilitators in human relations training, the authors focus on three basic skills: listening, self-expression, and responding. They feel that listening is a most important skill in effective interpersonal relations and that the skill can be trained and evaluated. Apparently as a result of their experiences in training, the authors felt a need to develop a listening test structured in emotional intentions.

Specifically, the listening test was developed "to facilitate and evaluate skill building using emotionally laden statements." Actors read sentences in a manner which is supposed to convey various emotions. For each sentence read, four statements are presented from among which the listener is to determine the one which best represents the intended meaning of the actor. Interpretation of emotion is a somewhat precise activity, but this is what is required of the listener. According to the manual, no norms have been developed for this test. The best which may come from the test is the idea that we have different reactions to material delivered in some kind of emotional manner which may interfere with or facilitate the listening process.

The authors provide a format for administering the test and using the results for training. The stimulus items are recorded on tape and on a response form and the four response options are on the response form. The scoring is a simple count of agreement between the intended meaning of the stimulus and the presumed "correct" response. As indicated, the emphasis is on training and not on evaluation.

In the 1950s there was a considerable interest in and research on listening behavior, primarily on the part of Ralph Nichols at the University of Minnesota. Through the years since 1950 there have been spurts of interest in listening skill, mainly concerned with the importance of listening and ways to improve listening. In a 1983 publication, *Perceptive Listening*, coauthored by Dr. Nichols and published by Holt, Rinehart, and Winston, no mention is made of the test currently under review. The omission may be an indication that the test has been used primarily in education and human relations training and its usefulness as a measure of listening skill has not been realized.

In summary, the Jones-Mohr Listening Test seems to be more of a training procedure than a testing procedure of listening. Also, it uses interpretation of emotional intent of what is said as the measure of listening. There is no evidence to confirm or deny its usefulness in human relations training or the improvement of listening skills.

Review of The Jones-Mohr Listening Test by JOHN F. SCHMITT, *Assistant Professor of Communicative Disorders, The University of Alabama, Tuscaloosa, AL:*

Two of the stated purposes of the Jones-Mohr Listening Test are to provide immediate feedback to listeners on their listening accuracy and to provide a listening instrument for use in research and evaluation studies. Unfortunately, the test does neither. The other two purposes are to demonstrate to human relations workshop participants that their listening skills need improvement and then to motivate such participants to improve their listening skills. These two purposes may be met in part, but not because the instrument is a reliable or valid one. The test is recommended by the authors for group administration, but there is no mention of minimum or maximum group size or intended ages.

Since no reliability and validity data are provided, one would expect the test to have at least face validity. However, the test lacks face validity because it does not measure what it is intended to measure. There also are no indications that the test has either content or construct validity. The potential user should have information at least on alternate forms reliability, but none is given. The test is designed to assess listening, which the authors characterize as "the core skill in interpersonal relations." However, the test assesses listening outside the natural context of interpersonal interaction. Nonverbal aspects of communication also are not included, thereby omitting that aspect of communication felt to be responsible for the majority of the perceived meaning and underlying emotion of a message.

At least six specific problems emerge from an analysis of the procedures used to develop the test. First, the authors employed actors who pretended to express the target emotions of the 30 items of the two test forms. The result is that a number of stimulus sentences sound very much as if they are being read by actors rather than spoken by persons actually expressing the intended meanings and emotions. There are several stimulus items with unnatural pause boundaries, such as breaks within major sentence constituents rather than between them. The result is that the normal suprasegmental features of speech are violated. Second, there is no evidence that individual test items actually reflect the intended meaning and emotion. Also, there is no evidence that the one correct choice of four for each sentence is correct to the exclusion of the other three, despite the statement in the manual that incorrect responses were chosen "to be as different from this (intended response) as possible." As an example, the correct response to hearing "I could have crawled into a hole" is "I felt so ashamed" and not "I was really embarrassed." It is easy to see that a person could listen very attentively and still be "incorrect" in determining the appropriate answers.

Third, one of the main reasons that many listeners would be expected to score poorly on the test is attributable to the method of stimulus item selection. Without stating a rationale, the authors selected 150 acceptable items from an initial pool of 300. Of the 150 selected items, 60 met the criterion of having 44% of the graduate students who heard each item choose what the authors felt was the correct answer when given the test. Thirty items each were assigned to Forms A and B. The criterion of 44% correct is indeed low and shows that even the trial groups could not judge correct answers with an acceptable degree of consistency. Fourth, the test actually may be more valid for visually-impaired than normally-sighted persons, since the listener is deprived of the normal visual cues to intended meaning that seeing the face of the speaker provides. At best the test represents an atypical listening task. Fifth, several stimulus items represent the vernacular of which younger listeners may be more likely to be aware than older listeners. Examples are "Yeah,

I can really get off on that idea" and "I can't get up for any more studying." This is odd because it is assumed that the test is designed for adult listeners. Sixth, in the manual the authors state that an individual may be expected to score either higher on the second form than the first as a result of practice, or lower on the second form as a result of boredom. Therefore, a potential user of the test has little idea of how test takers might perform on the two versions of the test.

Administration of the Jones-Mohr Listening Test is simple. A group of persons is to listen to 30 stimulus sentences on audio cassette tape. The listeners have approximately 10 seconds to circle on a test sheet the one choice of four sentences that represents the intended meaning of the spoken sentence. After all 30 sentences have been heard the test administrator either can tell the participants the correct answers or can have them listen to the answers on tape. The authors observe quite appropriately that taking both forms of the test prior to administering it will make the test administrator more empathic with participants.

Each test score is classified as either excellent, good, fair, or poor, according to ranges of raw scores that appear in the manual. No justification is given for these four descriptors. It also is interesting to note that although the criterion for originally including an item on the test was that 44% of the graduate student sample responded correctly, an overall score of 44% on the test would categorize the participant as only a "fair" listener. The authors suggest that users develop their own charts for tallying group scores toward the goal of eventually establishing norms. They provide no tally sheets for this purpose, although a simple model appears in the manual.

The test is to be used in training listening skills and in conjunction with the materials of the Pfeiffer and Jones Series in Human Relations Training, a series that is co-edited by the first author of the Jones-Mohr Listening Test. There are three sample training designs that all include the test as the entry point for training. In the manual are brief outlines that a facilitator can follow in designing either a 1-hour, 3-hour, or 2-day workshop to improve listening skills. Users of the test are invited to employ it in research on intended emotions by changing the statements on the response sheet to the names of feelings such as anger, grief, surprise, and depression. The invitation presumes that the emotion indicated by the authors for each sentence is actually the dominant underlying emotion associated with the taped utterance. This may be true but has not been demonstrated.

The test represents a good idea that is lacking in proper execution. The test is confounded by a number of factors and seriously flawed by the lack of any reliability and validity data. The only mention of such data is that the authors invite researchers to use the test and then forward such data to them. The test cannot be considered to have even face validity because, among other reasons, there is no validity demonstrated for individual items or the test as a whole. The authors are correct in stating that the test is useful for generating discussion among group members. However, the discussion most likely will center on the low scores that members achieved and on disagreements about what the correct answers to individual items actually should be. That this test can be used to identify good and poor listening skills and then to improve such skills has yet to be shown.

[557]

Jordan Left-Right Reversal Test, Second Revised Edition. Ages 6–12, 9–12; 1973–80; visual reversals of letter and number; 2 levels in 1 booklet ('74, 4 pages); manual ('80, 54 pages); 1982 price data: $6 per 25 tests; $10 per manual; (20) minutes for level 1, (25) minutes for levels 1 and 2; Brian T. Jordan; Academic Therapy Publications.*

See T3:1224 (2 references); for reviews by Barbara K. Keogh and Richard J. Reisboard, and excerpted reviews by Alex Bannatyne and Alan Krichev, see 8:434 (5 references).

Review of Jordan Left-Right Reversal Test, Second Revised Edition, by MARY S. POPLIN, Assistant Professor, Faculty in Education, Claremont Graduate School, Claremont, CA:

The Jordan Left-Right Reversal Test (Levels 1 and 2) purports to measure directionality perception involving letter, word, and number reversals. This untimed test requires approximately 20 minutes to administer to groups or individuals. Raw scores in Level 1 (ages 5–8) are derived by counting the errors a child makes when asked to identify reversed letters (from an array of 27 upper case letters, 11 of which are reversed) and numerals (5 of 14 are reversed). Raw scores in Level 2 (ages 9–12) are computed by counting the number of errors made by children in identifying reversed letters embedded in words, e.g., "bepth for depth" (affecting 39 of 100 words) and whole word reversals embedded within sentences, e.g., "The girl chewed some mug," (14 reversed words in 20 sentences). Raw scores, representing both errors of commission and omission, are then converted to percentile and/or developmental age scores. Normal and abnormal limits are indicated on the conversion tables.

The standardization sample consisted of over 4,000 5- to 12-year-old children representing eight states, urban and rural areas, public and private schools, various socio-economic levels, and white and non-white races (though specific numbers and sampling details are not provided). Test-retest reliabilities for both levels are adequate (.83 to .98).

No information is provided on internal test reliabilities.

Validity was established by correlating the Jordan with the Bender-Gestalt Test and the reading subtest of the Wide Range Achievement Test. The correlations, while significant, were computed on a group of children from a wide age range (6 to 12 years). Additionally, analyses of variance on a sample of 325 children (ages 6 to 12) indicated that a normal group achieved significantly different scores on the Jordan from those of a group that had been diagnosed as having neurological disabilities. One might expect such significance given sample size and range, and the similarities of items on the Jordan with those of the Bender and WRAT. For example, reversals of figures are scored on the Bender as well as the Jordan. Additionally, the reading subtest of the WRAT involves context-less word recognition while the Jordan's emphasis is also word recognition separate from considerations for comprehension. There is little information given about the method of determining neurological disabilities except that the children were enrolled in schools for the neurologically impaired.

The test manual, first published in 1972 (Level 1) and updated and expanded in 1974 (see 8:434), was revised again in 1980. The only revisions noted in the 1980 manual are nine pages of remediation exercises. The exercises are directed toward improving awareness of body parts and space directionality, using visual-kinesthetic learning aids, and providing simple exercises for "right-left" directionality. This brings up the most critical question regarding this instrument, i.e., why would one want to give such a test?

The test's reported purposes include (*a*) being a part of the diagnostic battery used to detect learning disabilities, (*b*) acting as a screening instrument to help with the early identification of "possible neurological dysfunction which may be manifest in the area of reading," and (*c*) identifying children who need "remedial training for directionality of perception, regardless of reading level." Researchers in special education long ago challenged the notion that problems in visual perceptual abilities were inextricably linked to learning disabilities (Vellunti-no, Smith, Steger, & Kasman, 1975; Larsen, Rogers, & Sowell, 1976; Torgeson, 1977). In partial response to the inability of researchers to validate the visual perception hypothesis, the federal government in 1977 omitted mention of assessing psychological processing and perceptual abilities (visual perception being one of these) as part of the official criteria used to diagnose learning disabled students for special education services (P.L. 94–142). It is not surprising that the author fails to mention this fact since the 1980 manual cites no research published after 1972.

Many test manuals and test reviews addressing the early identification of potential school failures begin with the assumption that early identification is adventitious. First of all, as acknowledged by the author, left-right reversals are normal for young children. Secondly, also acknowledged by the author, not all children who reverse letters, numerals, and words have reading problems. So how can a test of reversals, no matter how well constructed, assist in identifying children who will have problems? Disregarding the fact that there is little evidence to indicate early interventions with the learning disabled are successful, there is still the potentially damaging effect of a first grader being labelled by such an instrument and subsequently monitored by school personnel. One would think the possibility of large number of false positives (i.e., identifying normal children as potential problems) far outweighs its usefulness in first grade screening. In addition, the relationship between left-right reversals and neurological dysfunction remains elusive.

Addressing the third purpose, one can only wonder why anyone would remediate "problems" that do not present reading or other school difficulties for the student. More importantly, efficacy studies of various visual perception training programs provide little evidence that this type of remediation is effective in improving either visual perception abilities or academic skills (Mann, 1971; Hammill, 1972). Although the previously mentioned studies did not utilize the Jordan, they have been conducted using tests that measure similar visual perception abilities.

Recent theories and research in reading highlight the futility of attending to the more mechanical aspects of word recognition, much less to something as hypothetical as visual perceptual constructs. Specifically, even good readers might easily miss many of Jordan's reversals since more efficient readers rely so heavily on predictability and context and automatically correct minor errors (Goodman, 1975; Singer & Ruddell, 1976; Smith, 1978). To view reading as an ability composed of numerous visual and auditory perception tasks distorts both the measurement and remediation of reading problems. Aside from the tenuous relationship between reversal recognition and academic achievement, there is evidence that left-right reversals, even in children's writing, have little value in predicting academic failure (Simner, 1982). This test is just one more example of instruments that encourage educators to attend to minute, inconsequential aspects of reading and writing.

In summary, the Jordan Left-Right Reversal Test is a reasonably well constructed, reliable measure of children's ability to recognize letters, word, and numeral reversals. Although the test might be used experimentally to measure certain aspects of neurological maturity, its application to the prediction, diagnosis, and remediation of learning disabilities is not recommended. Educators who wish to measure reading problems should measure abilities more related to reading.

REVIEWER'S REFERENCES

Mann, L. Perceptual training revisited: The training of nothing at all. REHABILITATION LITERATURE, 1971, 32, 322–327.

Hammill, D. D. Training visual perceptual processes. JOURNAL OF LEARNING DISABILITIES, 1972, 5, 552–559.

Goodman, K. S. READING PROCESS AND PROGRAM. Urbana, IL: National Council of Teachers of English, 1975.

Vellutino, F. R., Smith, H., Steger, J. A., & Kasman, M. Reading disability: Age differences and the perceptual deficit hypothesis. CHILD DEVELOPMENT, 1975, 46, 493–497.

Larsen, S. C., Rogers, D., & Sowell, V. The use of selected visual perception tests in differentiating between normal and learning disabled children. JOURNAL OF LEARNING DISABILITIES, 1976, 9, 85–90.

Singer, H., & Ruddell, R. B. THEORETICAL MODELS AND PROCESSES OF READING. Newark, DE: International Reading Association, 1976.

Public Law 94–142. Additional procedures for evaluating specific learning disabilities. FEDERAL REGISTER, December 29, 1977, 20 USC, 1411 note.

Torgeson, J. K. The role of nonspecific factors in the task performance of learning disabled children. JOURNAL OF LEARNING DISABILITIES, 1977, 10, 33–40.

Smith, F. COMPREHENSION AND LEARNING. New York: Holt, Rinehart and Winston, 1978.

Simner, M. L. Printing errors in kindergarten and the prediction of academic performance. JOURNAL OF LEARNING DISABILITIES, 1982, 15, 155–159.

Review of Jordan Left-Right Reversal Test, Second Revised Edition, by JOSEPH TORGESEN, Associate Professor, Department of Psychology, Florida State University, Tallahassee, FL:

The Jordan Left-Right Reversal Test is a simple, easy to administer test of children's ability to recognize letter and word reversals. Younger children (5 to 8 years) are required to indicate which of a list of single letters and numbers are presented in a reversed form. Older children (9 to 12 years) have the additional tasks of recognizing both reversed letters presented in lists of words and reversed words presented within sentences. Number of errors can be converted into percentile and age level scores.

The test was standardized on a national sample of 4,350 children, ages 5 through 12, who were taken from regular classroom settings. Although the test manual suggests that the sample included children from urban and rural, public and private schools as well as all levels of socio-economic status, no documentation is provided regarding the actual characteristics of the sample on these dimensions. The manual also provides no indication of how many children at each age level were tested. The sample did include 10% non-white minority children.

Test-retest reliabilities were reported at each age level between 5 and 12. Based on a sample of 260 children, Level 1 (individual letter and number reversals) had one month test-retest correlations ranging from .87 to .98, with an average of .93. On Level 2 (reversed letters within words, and reversed words in sentences) test-retest reliabilities for 230 children at a 2-week interval ranged from .83 to .91, with an average of .88. At least for Level 1, this test meets acceptable standards of reliability for individual diagnostic purposes.

Although the psychometric characteristics and standardization procedures for this test are generally quite good, the data on validity and the general rationale for its use are questionable. The basic validity data consist of comparisons between samples of "neurologically impaired" and normal children as well as correlations with reading level and performance on the Bender Visual-Motor Gestalt Test. While these relationships are all in the expected direction, what they mean for interpretation of the Jordan test is unclear. For example, the author suggests that the test may be measuring, at least partially, a neurologically based tendency for children to reverse visual images of letters. However, there is little support for this idea in recent studies of letter reversals in children (Staller & Sekuler, 1976). The author also suggests that the tendency to reverse letters may actually be a unique cause of poor reading. The primary evidence for this assertion is taken from the fact that poor readers make more reversals than good readers at all ages. However, other research shows that while poor readers make more reading errors of all kinds than good readers, the total proportion of errors attributable to reversals is no greater in poor than in good readers (Shankweiler & Lieberman, 1972).

One problem in the test manual is that there is no attempt to incorporate recent research to help test users to understand the meaning of letter and number reversals in children. The problem of test rationale and construct validity is particularly important when considering the remedial implications of poor scores on this test. The author devotes one chapter in the test manual to a discussion of remedial techniques for children who have problems with reversals. Although many of these suggestions involve direct instruction in letter and word reading and thus may help children to read better, other techniques are focused on remediating general problems in the perception of left-right and orientation in space. An overwhelming amount of research (Arter & Jenkins, 1979) has shown this latter type of instruction to be ineffective in improving the basic academic skills.

In sum, this test is a good measure of children's abilities to recognize letter and word reversals. However, the author's contention that the test should occupy a unique place in a battery of tests used to diagnose or screen for reading disabilities is unsupported. There is no evidence, for example, that the test makes a unique contribution (independent of IQ and other well established tests like the Bender Gestalt) to the prediction of reading problems. If one wants to obtain a good estimate of how deviant a given child is with respect to the ability to recognize correct orientation of letters and words, this is a good test to use. However, the rationale for this type of assessment as a guide to the remediation of reading problems is unclear.

REVIEWER'S REFERENCES

Shankweiler, D., & Lieberman, I. Y. Misreading: A search for causes. In J. F. Kavanagh & I. G. Mattingly (Eds.), LANGUAGE BY EAR AND BY EYE. Cambridge, MA: MIT Press, 1972.

Staller, J., & Sekuler, R. Mirror-image confusions in adults and children: A nonperceptual explanation. AMERICAN JOURNAL OF PSYCHOLOGY, 1976, 89, 253–268.

Arter, J. A., & Jenkins, J. R. Differential diagnosis-prescriptive teaching: A critical appraisal. REVIEW OF EDUCATIONAL RESEARCH, 1979, 48, 517–555.

[558]

Joseph Pre-School and Primary Self-Concept Screening Test. Ages 3–6 to 9–11; 1979; identifies children, at an early age, who may later develop learning problems; may be used with non-verbal children; 1 score: Global Self Concept; Item Dimension Chart relating to self concept dimensions of Significance, Competence, Power, General Evaluative Contentment, and Virtue; Confusion index; norms consist of median Global Self Concept scores for age groups 3–6 to 4–6, 4–7 to 5–11, and 6–0 to 9–11, suggested classifications for these scores, and percentages in each classification; individual; 1 form (4 pages); manual ('79, 66 pages); 1982 price data: $48 per complete kit including manual, 25 student record books, 16 wooden blocks, ball, picture story card and 6 kindergarten size pencils; $11 per 25 record forms; $11 per 25 parental questionnaires; $11 per manual; (5–7) minutes; Jack Joseph; Stoelting Co.*

Review of Joseph Pre-School and Primary Self-Concept Screening Test by KATHRYN CLARK GERKEN, Associate Professor, School of Human Development, University of Texas at Dallas, Richardson, TX:

This test requires a child to draw his/her face on a drawing of the same sex child. The child is then asked to respond to 15 questions, 13 of which are demonstrated by dichotomous sets of pictures. The manual is thorough and easy to understand. However, when the manual is revised, the author should eliminate the use of sexist language, a few minor typing errors, and incorrect reference citations.

The test is recommended in the Special Education Assessment Matrix (1981) as one of the best available for measuring the self-concept of young children. This evaluation of the instrument is warranted because there are so few satisfactory measures for determining self-concept perceptions, especially within the preschool age range. However, the evaluation does not report any limiting factors or cautions against possible misuse of the test. Not even a general warning is given about the necessity for interpreting all self-concept data with caution. The test has weaknesses as well as strengths that should be addressed.

The author reports that he attempted to conform to the guidelines set forth by the *Standards for Educational and Psychological Tests*. Some evidence for this is found in the manual, which begins with information regarding the rationale for the test. A theoretical base is presented, and the author provides support for the theory from professional literature. The author also clearly states the nature and purpose of the test and defines terms when necessary. One may not agree with all of his potential uses for the test, but they are explained fully.

The description of test development is generally clear; the only area that is not clear is item selection. The author states that the original items were selected on a "rational face validity basis" in order to tap five theoretical self-concept dimensions. His source for the items is not clear. It appears that he selected the dimensions and then used his own experiences to determine what kinds of questions should be asked to tap the dimensions. He does provide more detail regarding the pictorial presentation of the items, and he should be commended for his empirical determination of how young children might pictorially represent the selected items/situations. Empirical data were used to determine the final version of the test. However the children in the preliminary analyses did not represent the entire age range of the test.

The author reports that the pictures are used to insure that the child understands the questions, and he has allowed for a "confusion" score if a child cannot discriminate between pairs of pictures for each item. Although the author reports that the pictures were drawn as clearly as possible, this reviewer believes some ambiguity could be eliminated, and more importantly the overall quality of the drawings could be improved. The drawings are laminated and that feature should be maintained. However, new pictures should be drawn which contain the same child's face and body. The pictures now vary considerably in their attractiveness.

The directions for administering and scoring this test are very clear; there should be few procedural errors by examiners. An entire chapter, including several illustrated examples, focuses on the interpretation of the test. The author presents and explains each item in turn and indicates which items are seen as good predictors of the Global Self-Concept Score. However, he does not provide the raw data which would indicate the number of children in each age group who responded negatively to each item, nor the statistics describing the empirical relationship of each item to the Global score. The author classified the Global scores into five categories and interpretation is based on where the child's score falls. The author reports the median Global Self-Concept Score attained for each age group, but he also needs to report the mean and standard deviation and the raw data indicating how many children in each age group fell into each of his classification categories. He states that children whose scores fall into the last two categories need additional evaluation and/or self-concept remediation. He should also emphasize the need for validating this classification. In addition, he should exercise caution in suggesting that the Diagnostic Dimensional Evaluation be used to determine the specific areas in which a child needs remediation. It is doubtful that one would want to plan a remediation program based principally on the child's negative response to one or more items that the author has determined on a subjective/ theoretical basis belong to a specific dimension. There is no evidence of a statistical analysis to determine if the test items do "cluster" in five or even two groups. Additional statistical information is needed in this chapter.

The other area in which the author must provide more cautions is his suggestions for doing a qualitative analysis of the Identity Reference Drawing. Before interpreting a child's completion of a face drawing, one should keep in mind the plethora of literature that questions the validity of the analysis of human figure drawings. The author provides a table which indicates the frequency of occurrence for each emotional indicator, relative to each normative age group. It would be helpful to see the raw data for the table, and to know how many of the pictures drawn by children who were diagnosed as emotionally disturbed contained emotional indicators. This reviewer is also concerned about the author's suggestion that examiners should eventually feel comfortable in interpreting test scale indices without benefit of background information. It would certainly be unethical as well as negligent to make "blind" interpretations of such data.

This test is norm referenced and was standardized on 1,245 children residing in Illinois. Approximately 91% of the children were white and 9% non-white. The diversity of socioeconomic representation, schools, and classrooms is discussed. Raw data would be helpful in determining the racial, socioeconomic, urban/suburban/rural, school, and classroom breakdown. The author states that the heterogeneous nature of the sample appears to generally reflect the demographic makeup of the United States. No verification of his statement is presented since there are no data for the sex, SES, and urban/suburban/rural breakdown. It is clear that the percentages of whites and non-whites in the sample are not representative of the 5- through 9-year-old population in the United States in 1980 (Public Bureau of Census Report) in which 78% of the children were white, 14.9% were black, 9.2% were Hispanic, etc. Cautions should be presented regarding the representativeness of the sample.

The author does provide evidence of reliability and validity for the test. However, additional information is needed. A test-retest reliability coefficient of .87 was reported for a population of 18 preschoolers. He also reports KR-20 coefficients ranging from .59 to .81, with a median correlation of .73. The population on which these correlations were obtained was not described. An item-analysis in which item-discrimination coefficients ranged from .30 to .70 as a function of item and age level is also reported.

In his discussion of validity the author discusses both construct and criterion-related validity. Construct validity was established by comparing Global Self-Concept Scores to the scores obtained on two self-concept rating scales completed by teachers. However, the author must keep in mind that construct validity is not established in a single study. One way to begin is to formulate hypotheses about the characteristics of those who have high scores on the test in contrast to those who have low scores. Shavelson et al. (1976) suggest identifying two populations expected to differ on the construct and then determine whether or not their scores actually do differ. In his discussion of concurrent validity, the author reports significantly different Global scores for preschoolers placed in self-contained special education classes vs. preschoolers in regular education classes.

In summary, this test is indeed one of the best self-concept measures available for young children. The test is compact and relatively inexpensive, except for the cost of the pictures. The manual is well written, directions are very clear, the test was standardized in a reasonable size population, and the author has attempted to provide evidence of reliability and validity. However, even if it is one of the best instruments available, this does not mean it is ready for all the suggested uses. Additional research and cautious interpretation is needed, especially if one accepts that the self-concepts of young children are global, undifferentiated, and situation specific (Shavelson et al., 1976). In its present state, this test is most useful as a research tool or interview guide.

REVIEWER'S REFERENCES

Population profile of the United States: 1980. PUBLIC BUREAU OF CENSUS REPORT, Report Series P20, #363.

Shavelson, R. J., Hubner, J. J., & Stanton, G. C. Self-Concept: Validation of construct interpretations. REVIEW OF EDUCATIONAL RESEARCH, 1976, 46(3), 407–441.

Special Education Assessment Coalition. SPECIAL EDUCATION ASSESSMENT MATRIX. Monterey, CA: McGraw-Hill, 1981.

Review of Joseph Pre-School and Primary Self-Concept Screening Test by CATHY FULTZ TELZROW, Coordinator for Program Development, Cuyahoga Special Education Service Center, Maple Heights, OH:

This instrument is designed to provide a measure of the self-concept of children ages 3.6 to 9.11 via a child-interview format. The administration of the Joseph Pre-School and Primary Self-Concept Screening Test (JPPSST) begins by asking the subject to draw his or her own face on a same-sex line drawing. This Identity Reference Drawing (IRD) is intended to establish the self focus for the remainder of the interview, and it also may be evaluated qualitatively for emotional indicators, although such responses are not included in the global self-concept score. Following the completion of the IRD, the examiner presents the subject with 15 pairs of dichotomous questions. All but two of the pairs of questions are accompanied by line drawings which exemplify the verbal statements. In each case the child is asked to indicate which of the choices is most like him or her, either with a verbal response or by pointing to an appropriate picture. For example, the third item is presented as follows: "One of these boys (girls) has a teacher who doesn't like him (her) very much and the other boy (girl) has a teacher who likes him (her) a lot. Now which one happens to you the most?" Separate illustrative pictures are used for male and female subjects.

Each of the 15 items may be scored on a 3-point scale; a score of 2 is given for selection of the positive choice, a score of 1 if the child cannot decide or demonstrates ambivalence, and a score of 0 for selection of the negative item. In addition, 12 of the 13 items on which pictures are used may be scored on a confusion index in the event the child is unable to discriminate between the illustrations.

A global self-concept score is computed by summing the subject's score across the 15 items. These scores are interpreted in light of five levels of self-concept classification: high positive, moderate positive, watch list, poor, and high risk negative. Score distributions across these five categories differ for three age groups: 3.6 to 4.6, 4.7 to 5.11, and 6.0 to 9.11. Scores for older subjects are reported to be adjusted due to the tendency for social desirability response set bias.

In addition to the global self-concept score and the associated self-concept classification, scores for children whose responses place them in the Poor or High Risk Negative categories may be analyzed further using the Diagnostic Dimensional Evaluation. This procedure associates each item with five constructs determined by the test author to be related to self-concept: Significance, and its derivative, Virtue; Competence, and its derivative, Power; and General Evaluative Contentment.

A final rating can be provided by an independent observer's evaluating the subject's self-concept on an 11-point scale. The test author suggests that this index, when used in conjunction with the JPPSST, can provide some indications of children who may tend toward defensive or perfectionistic behavior.

There is little specific information provided in the test manual regarding item selection except for general guidelines concerning the need to utilize situations within the range of comprehension and experience of young children, and the desire to choose items of face validity to the five self-concept constructs mentioned above. The test user should be aware of the potentially threatening nature of some of the items (e.g., those that ask whether a parent likes the subject or a sibling better), especially for parents. It is recommended that the nature of the items and the purpose for such a test be explained thoroughly to parents prior to the test administration. The test author's failure to mention such a procedure in the manual is unfortunate.

The test materials are generally well-designed and easy to use. The manual is exceptionally thorough, and the author is to be commended for his attention to both the theoretical and the pragmatic aspects of the instrument. Three minor criticisms should be noted, however. Although the procedures for completing the Diagnostic Dimensional Evaluation are described in the manual, these directions could be summarized on the record form, thus facilitating the calculations. Space for this notation could be provided by eliminating the independent rater's question from the record form. Finally, the Item Response Summary forms pictured in the test manual are evidently no longer published, since they were not in the test kit reviewed nor are they listed in the publisher's catalog. In lieu of this form, subtotal notations could be added to the bottom of each column of items on the record form to facilitate scoring.

Technical data for the JPPSST are favorable. The standardization sample of 1,245 children in urban, rural, and suburban regions of Illinois was 91% white and 9% black and other minorities. Each of the three normative age groups included approximately 8% handicapped children.

Test-retest reliability for a small sample ($N = 18$) of preschool children was reported at .87. Kuder-Richardson reliability coefficients ranged from .59 to .81, with a median of .73. Concurrent validity for the JPPSST was demonstrated by comparisons with two teacher rating scales of self-concept (Inferred Self-Concept Judgement Scale $r = .51$; Behavior Rating Form, $r = .65$). JPPSST scores in the Poor or High Risk Negative categories correctly identified poor academic achievement four years later for 83% of preschool children and 70% of kindergartners, which was significantly different from chance at the .001 level.

To summarize, the JPPSST may represent one of the best child-interview self-concept measures available. The test is founded in self-concept theory and reports favorable reliability and validity results. In addition, it is a brief, easily administered instrument which represents a useful screening tool for social-emotional disabilities in young children.

[559]

Jr.-Sr. High School Personality Questionnaire. Ages 12–18; 1953–84; HSPQ; 18 scores: 14 primary factor scores (reserved vs. warm hearted, dull vs. bright, affected by feelings vs. emotionally stable, undemonstrative vs. excitable, obedient vs. assertive, sober vs. enthusiastic, disregards rules vs. conscientious, shy vs. adventurous, tough-minded vs. tender-minded, zestful vs. circumspect individualism, self-assured vs. apprehensive, sociably group-dependent vs. self-sufficient, uncontrolled vs. controlled, relaxed vs. tense), plus 4 second-order factors (introversion vs. extraversion, low anxiety vs. high anxiety, tender emotionality vs. tough poise, dependence vs. independence); no norms for second order factors; Forms A, B, C, D, ('68, 8 pages, authors recommend administration of 2 or more forms); manual and norms ('84, 101 pages); answer-profile sheet ('73, 2 pages); profile ('73, 1 page); separate answer sheets (hand scored, machine scored) must be used; 1985 price data: $9 per 25 reusable test booklets; $6.50 per 50 machine-scorable answer sheets; $5.50 per 50 hand scored answer sheets; $5 per scoring stencils; $6.50 per 50 hand-scored answer-profile sheets; $5.50 per 50 profiles; $6 per second-order worksheet; $9.25 per manual and $15.25 per specimen set; standard report scoring service, $16 or less per interpretation depending on amount ordered; (45–60) minutes per form; Raymond B. Cattell, Mary D. Cattell, and Edgar Johns (manual and norms); Institute for Personality and Ability Testing.*

British adaptation: Ages 13–15; 1973; supplement by Peter Saville and Laura Finlayson; NFER-Nelson Publishing Co. [England].

South African adaptation: Ages 13–18; 1967; adaptation by E. M. Madge; Human Sciences Research Council [South Africa].

See T3:1233 (22 references), 8:597 (68 references), and T2:1253 (37 references); for reviews by Robert Hogan and Douglas N. Jackson, see 7:97 (53 references); see also P:136 (29 references); for reviews by C. J. Adcock and Philip E. Vernon of an earlier edition, see 6:131 (17 references); see also 5:72 (4 references).

TEST REFERENCES

1. Harris, W. J., Drummond, R. J., & Schultz, E. W. An investigation of relationships between teachers' ratings of behavior and children's personality traits. JOURNAL OF ABNORMAL CHILD PSYCHOLOGY, 1977, 5, 43–52.

2. Power, C. N. Effects of student characteristics and level of teacher-student interaction on achievement and attitudes. CONTEMPORARY EDUCATIONAL PSYCHOLOGY, 1977, 2, 265–274.

3. Henry, S. E., & Kilmann, P. R. Student counseling groups in senior high school settings: An evaluation of outcome. JOURNAL OF SCHOOL PSYCHOLOGY, 1979, 17, 27–46.

4. Forman, S. G., & Forman, B. D. Family environment and its relation to adolescent personality factors. JOURNAL OF PERSONALITY ASSESSMENT, 1981, 45, 163–167.

5. Holmes, C. B., Persinger, B. D., Jr., & Busenbark, J. P. Personality traits of edgers and non-edgers on the Memory-For-Designs test. JOURNAL OF CLINICAL PSYCHOLOGY, 1981, 37, 405–408.

6. Cattell, R. B., Schuerger, J. M., & Klein, T. W. Heritabilities of ego strength (Factor C), super ego strength (Factor G), and self-sentiment (Factor Q) by Multiple Abstract Variance Analysis. JOURNAL OF CLINICAL PSYCHOLOGY, 1982, 38, 769–779.

7. Kawash, G. F. A structural analysis of self-esteem from pre-adolescence through young adulthood: Anxiety and extraversion as agents in the development of self-esteem. JOURNAL OF CLINICAL PSYCHOLOGY, 1982, 38, 301–311.

8. Woolfson, R. C. Psychological correlates of solvent abuse. THE BRITISH JOURNAL OF MEDICAL PSYCHOLOGY, 1982, 55, 63–66.

[560]

Judgement of Occupational Behavior—Orientation. Grades 6–adult; 1981; commonly called JOB-O; 9 scales: Education, Interest, Inclusion, Control, Affection, Physical Activity, Hands/Tools/Machinery, Problem-Solving, Creating/Ideas; 1 form (19 pages); manual (20 pages); 1982 price data: $1.25 per test; $1 per manual; Spanish and Vietnamese editions available; (60–80) minutes; Arthur Cutler, Francis Ferry, Robert Kauk, and Robert Robinett; CFKR Career Materials, Inc.*

Review of Judgement of Occupational Behavior—Orientation by BRUCE J. EBERHARDT, Assistant Professor of Management, University of North Dakota, Grand Forks, ND:

The primary purpose of Judgement of Occupational Behavior—Orientation (JOB-O) is "to start the student in the process of self-awareness, career-awareness, and career exploration." As an instrument used to initially whet the student's curiosity in the area of career exploration, the JOB-O has several commendable features. However, it is highly questionable whether this inventory can adequately satisfy many of its other suggested uses. The authors claim that completion of the JOB-O is a comprehensive process including "self-assessment of educational and career interests; comparison of the self-assessment with 120 job titles, selection of job titles that best match personal needs; research of job facts provided for in the answer insert; and, tentative, or final career decision-making." This is a great deal to ask from an inventory composed of only nine items.

The inventory is made up of two basic parts. The first part "is a reusable assessment booklet that contains nine self-assessment variables, all directions for self-administration, and the coding of 120 job titles in accordance with the nine variables." The second part is a "consummable answer insert that has nine boxes in which to place responses to the nine variables." The answer insert also includes facts about all the jobs in the inventory and a decision-making format.

The self-assessment section of the inventory consists of nine variables. The first two items ask students to indicate their educational aspiration and their preferred interest area category. The next seven items reflect characteristics of various work situations. Response alternatives of "usually or often," "sometimes or occasionally," and "seldom or rarely" allow students to state how frequently they would desire these characteristics to be present in their own jobs. Student responses to these nine variables are compared to numerically coded scales for 120 job titles. Information for the coding of the job titles was obtained from the *Dictionary of*

Occupational Titles (*DOT*) and the *Occupational Outlook Handbook*'s (*OOH*) classification systems.

As mentioned previously, JOB-O has several commendable features. First, the self-assessment and self-scoring format provides immediate feedback to students. This is one of the few advantages of this instrument, compared to more extensively researched instruments. However, the accuracy of the self-scoring has not been reported, even though a study on self-administration and scoring of the Self-Directed Search (SDS) indicated that this is a legitimate concern. It should be noted that, although the inventory is designed to be self-administered and self-scored, the authors highly recommend that an administrator lead the students through each step "by reading with the students, the questions and directions, and explain the content when necessary." It appears that this recommendation is appropriate only if the administrator is concerned with keeping a group of students working at the same pace, since the reading level of the questions and directions should be quite manageable for most individuals completing the inventory. In response to a survey question, 98% of a large sample of high school students (grades 9 to 12) indicated that the reading level of JOB-O was "average to very easy."

A second commendable and potentially motivating feature of the instrument is the job information which is provided for each of the 120 job titles. This information includes the following: number of people employed, yearly number of job openings, yearly pay (low and high), job outlook, kind of training, years of training, and job cluster. This information comes from the latest publication of the *OOH* and other Department of Labor sources. According to the authors, "This minimum amount of information is sufficient to give the student an awareness of vital facts upon which to base decisions, and yet, not so much that it confuses the issue, but leads to further research. Field testing indicates a high degree of satisfaction with the Insert Folder. Its simple layout makes job research possible for those who might have reading and/or graphics problems."

The 120 job titles selected for JOB-O are chosen from those jobs which will be in demand in the next decade according to U.S. Department of Labor reports. The inventory is updated every two years to conform to the national job trends as stated in the *OOH*. Job titles are added or deleted on a periodic basis in accordance with job outlook predictions. Administrators are instructed to inform students that job outlook predictions are based upon national labor information and that they may vary according to geographic location and economic fluctuations.

These positive features are easily overridden by the relative lack of technical data which are presented. No norms are provided, even though the authors state that observational data have been gathered from 3.5 million students who have taken the inventory. This lack of normative data on various student populations, specifically males and females, is unfortunate in that a large majority of the jobs represented appear to have been those traditionally dominated by males.

The reporting of reliability and validity data is quite sketchy and, in some cases, nonexistent. The authors state that "in a test-re-test of JOB-O given in 1973 (two week time duration) there was a 90% correlation of obtained job titles ($N=76$)." Not only has the inventory undergone several revisions since then, but in addition no information is given concerning the nature of the sample. A study in which no significant differences were found between subject responses to the present inventory and the Kuder OIS (Form DD) was cited as evidence for the inventory's construct validity. Again, no information about the size and nature of the study sample is provided.

Particularly upsetting is the absence of concurrent and predictive validity data. An unpublished study is cited which concluded "there is more support for the concurrent validity of JOB-O than the SDS (Holland)." As before, no information about the nature of the sample is given. The inventory user must trust the inferences made by the test developer. In regard to predictive validity, the authors state that "no claim is made for predictive validity, although data is available for a ten-year study." They suggest that such a study is currently in progress. According to the authors, the inventory "makes no claim of prediction, rather it shows a student how personal needs match a variety of occupations." However, without some evidence of predictive capabilities, such matches have questionable utility. If JOB-O lacks predictive validity, students could be misled in their career exploration by being encouraged to explore some occupations which are not appropriate for them.

One other potential problem with the inventory involves a suggested and implied use of the JOB-O. The manual which accompanies the inventory suggests that at the secondary, college, and adult levels, it can be used for final job decisions. Also, the last page of the answer insert is headed with the statement, "It's Decision-Making Time!!" Even though the inventory booklet warns that the JOB-O does not measure ability or aptitude, suggesting that a student should or could make career decisions based only upon the information provided in the inventory is potentially dangerous.

CONCLUSION. The authors have developed an inventory that might have some potential for encouraging career exploration, especially at the high school level. However, because little concrete evidence is presented for concurrent or predictive validity, JOB-O should be used with considerable caution because of a potential danger in leading students in the wrong direction in their career exploration.

[561]

Junior Eysenck Personality Inventory. Ages 7–16; 1963–70; JEPI; 3 scores: extraversion, neuroticism, lie; 1 form ('65, 3 pages); preliminary manual ('63, 11 pages); preliminary norms ['69–'70, 2 sheets]; 1983 price data: $4.50 per 25 tests; $2 per set of scoring keys; $2 per manual; $3 per specimen set; Spanish edition available; [15–20 minutes]; Sybil B. G. Eysenck; EdITS/Educational and Industrial Testing Service.*

See T3:1229 (24 references), 8:596 (36 references), and T2:1252 (14 references); for reviews by Maurice Chazan and Robert D. Wirt and excerpted reviews by Gertrude H. Keir and B. Semeonoff, see 7:96 (19 references); see also P:135 (7 references).

TEST REFERENCES

1. Forrest, R. Personality and delinquency: A multivariate examination of Eysenck's theory with Scottish delinquent and non-delinquent boys. SOCIAL BEHAVIOR AND PERSONALITY, 1977, 5, 157–167.

2. Powell, G. E. Psychoticism and social deviancy in children. ADVANCES IN BEHAVIOUR RESEARCH AND THERAPY, 1977, 1, 27–56.

3. Ackerman, P. T., Elardo, P. T., & Dykman, R. A. A psychosocial study of hyperactive and learning-disabled boys. JOURNAL OF ABNORMAL CHILD PSYCHOLOGY, 1979, 7, 91–99.

4. Hansford, B. C., & Neidhart, H. M. A view of fifteen-year-old girls in Australian schools. ADOLESCENCE, 1980, 15, 633–641.

5. Macmillan, A., Kolvin, I., Garside, R. F., Nicol, A. R., & Leitch, I. M. A multiple criterion screen for identifying secondary school children with psychiatric disorder. PSYCHOLOGICAL MEDICINE, 1980, 10, 265–276.

6. Maqsud, M. Eysenck's theory of personality and child-adult emotional attachments. MOTIVATION AND EMOTION, 1981, 5, 75–83.

7. Dorman, C. Personality and psychiatric correlates of the Halstead-Reitan tests in boys with school problems. CLINICAL NEUROPSYCHOLOGY, 1982, 4, 110–114.

8. Francis, L., Pearson, P. R., & Kay, W. K. Eysenck's personality quadrants and religiosity. BRITISH JOURNAL OF SOCIAL PSYCHOLOGY, 1982, 21, 262–264.

9. Nyborg, H., Eysenck, S. B. G., & Kroll, N. Cross-cultural comparison of personality in Danish and English children. SCANDINAVIAN JOURNAL OF PSYCHOLOGY, 1982, 23, 291–297.

10. Eysenck, S. B. G., & Saklofske, D. H. A comparison of responses of Canadian and English children on the Junior Eysenck Personality Questionnaire. CANADIAN JOURNAL OF BEHAVIOURAL SCIENCE, 1983, 15, 121–130.

[562]

Kaufman Assessment Battery for Children. Ages 2.5–12.5; 1983; K-ABC; intelligence and achievement; nonverbal scale available for hearing impaired, speech- and language-disordered, and non-English speaking children ages 4.0–12.5; 16 subtests with a maximum of 13 administered to any particular child: 10 mental processing subtests: Magic Window (ages 2.5–5.0), Face Recognition (ages 2.5–5.0), Hand Movements (ages 2.5–12.5), Gestalt Closure (ages 2.5–12.5), Number Recall (ages 2.5–12.5), Triangles (ages 4.0–12.5), Word Order (ages 4.0–12.5), Matrix Analogies (ages 5.0–12.5), Spatial Memory (ages 5.0–12.5), Photo Series (ages 6.0–12.5), and 6 achievement subtests: Expressive Vocabulary (ages 2.5–5.0), Faces and Places (ages 2.5–12.5), Arithmetic (ages 3.0–12.5), Riddles (ages 3.0–12.5), Reading/Decoding (ages 5.0–12.5), Reading/Understanding (ages 7.0–12.5); individual; 1 form consists of 3 easels: Easel 1 (187 pages), Easel 2 (204 pages), Easel 3 (273 pages); individual test record (12 pages); administration and scoring manual (272 pages); interpretive manual (352 pages); 1983 price data: $135 per complete kit; $152.50 per complete kit in vinyl carrying case; $168 per complete kit with special test plates of easily cleaned plastic (Special Edition); $185.50 per complete Special Edition kit in vinyl carrying case; $9.75 per 25 individual test records; $9 per administration and scoring manual; $10 per interpretive manual; $20 per carrying case; $3.50 per sampler kit; (35) minutes for age 2.5, (40–45) minutes for age 3, (45–55) minutes for age 4, (50–60) minutes for age 5, (60–70) minutes for age 6, (75–85) minutes for ages 7.0–12.5; Alan S. Kaufman and Nadeen L. Kaufman; American Guidance Service.*

TEST REFERENCES

1. Naglieri, J. A., Kaufman, A. S., Kaufman, N. L., & Kamphaus, R. W. Cross validation of Das' simultaneous and successive processes with novel tasks. THE ALBERTA JOURNAL OF EDUCATIONAL RESEARCH, 1981, 27, 264–271.

2. Herbert, W. Intelligence test: Sizing up a newcomer. SCIENCE NEWS, 1982, 122, 280–281.

3. Kaufman, A. S., Kaufman, N. L., Kamphaus, R. W., & Naglieri, J. A. Sequential and simultaneous factors at ages 3–12 1/2: Developmental changes in neuropsychological dimensions. CLINICAL NEUROPSYCHOLOGY, 1982, 4, 74–81.

Review of Kaufman Assessment Battery for Children by ANNE ANASTASI, Professor Emeritus of Psychology, Fordham University, Bronx, NY:

NATURE AND USES. The Kaufman Assessment Battery for Children (K-ABC) is a clinical instrument for assessing cognitive development. Its construction incorporates several recent developments in both psychological theory and statistical methodology. The K-ABC also gives special attention to certain emerging testing needs, such as use with handicapped groups, application to problems of learning disabilities, and appropriateness for cultural and linguistic minorities. The authors rightly caution, however, that success in meeting these special needs must be judged through practical use over time. They also point out that the K-ABC should not be regarded as "the complete test battery"; like any other test, it should be supplemented and corroborated by other instruments to meet individual needs, such as the Stanford-Binet, Wechsler scales, McCarthy scales, or neuropsychological tests.

The 16 subtests are grouped into a mental processing set and and achievement set, which yield separate global scores. The former are further grouped into those requiring primarily sequential processing of information and those requiring simultaneous processing, with separate global scores for each. This differentiation was suggested by available research on information-processing styles, as well as by its relevance to the diagnosis of learning disabilities and its implications for the design of remediation programs—illustrated in chapter 7 of the Interpretive Manual.

The mental processing subtests include a predominance of spatial and perceptual tasks, which should be helpful in identifying learning disabilities and neurological impairments. Provision is also made for a nonverbal scale, comprising six of the mental processing subtests that can be administered in pantomime and require only motor responses. The achievement subtests, although concerned with concrete and abstract vocabulary, reading, arithmetic, and general information, are much less closely linked with school learning than are tests traditionally given the achievement label. In the arithmetic subtest, for example, the child looks at a series of pictures of a family visit to the zoo and responds by counting and carrying out simple numerical operations with the objects in each picture. Reading comprehension is demonstrated by performing the actions described in each sentence that the child reads.

The entire K-ABC makes extensive use of pictorial and diagrammatic material, with a minimum of verbal responses. The layout of materials is ingenious and designed to facilitate use. Administration and scoring are relatively simple in comparison with other available individual instruments. Chapter 6 in the Interpretive Manual includes an excellent discussion of the cycle of hypothesis generation and hypothesis testing that is the essence of the clinical approach to diagnosis. It should prove valuable to the experienced clinician, but it does not substitute for professional training—nor was it meant to.

DEVELOPMENT AND STANDARDIZATION. The item and subtest analyses followed in developing the battery were extensive and thorough. Preliminary analyses in separate studies were followed by the major effort on the national sample of 782 children; and the final selections were "fine-tuned" with data from the standardization sample. Analyses cover item difficulty and discrimination, item bias, internal consistency within subtests, and factor analyses of subtests.

The K-ABC was standardized on a national sample of 2,000 children (aged 2–6 to 12–5), stratified within half-year groups for sex, geographic region, parental education, ethnic category (White, Black, Hispanic, other), and community size. About 7% of the sample was drawn from children placed in special education programs for various mental or physical disabilities, as well as for the gifted and talented. An additional 469 Black and 119 White children were tested in order to develop special sociocultural norms for race and parental education; these norms may be used, together with the general norms, as a supplementary interpretive aid. All scores are expressed as normalized standard scores and as percentile ranks. Provision is made for using the error of measurement in identifying specific areas of strength and weakness and in evaluating significance of differences among the four global scores. Conversions to stanines, age equivalents, and grade equivalents (where appropriate) are also available.

RELIABILITY AND VALIDITY. Odd-even reliabilities within one-year age groups averaged in the .70s and .80s for subtests; for global scores, the averages were in the high .80s and .90s. Test-retest reliabilities were computed within age groups spanning 3 or 4 years, retested after intervals of 2 to 4 weeks. For subtests, these reliabilities ranged from .59 to .98, clustering in the .70s and .80s; for global scores, they ranged from .77 to .97. In general, reliabilities were higher for the achievement than for the mental processing tests.

In addition to the validity built into the tests through the item and subtest analyses, several analyses conducted on the standardization sample contributed to construct definition. Data are provided from factor analyses of subtests, age differences, internal consistency of global scales, and correlations with other instruments. Supplementary data are incorporated from 43 studies by other investigators. Concurrent and predictive validity (6- to 12-month interval) against standardized achievement tests were investigated in several small groups of both normal and exceptional children. The correlations vary widely, but most appear promising, and the patterns of correlations with subtests tend to fit theoretical expectations. Analyses by ethnic groups yielded closely similar validities for Blacks, Hispanics, and Whites.

INTERPRETIVE HAZARDS. The use of the "mental processing" and "achievement" labels opens the way for possible misinterpretation of scores. Although the differentiation between these two sets of subtests is undoubtedly useful for diagnostic purposes and was generally supported by statistical analyses (especially at the older ages), the differentiation is not as basic as may be supposed by the casual reader. The excess meanings that have become associated with so-called aptitude and achievement tests are difficult to dislodge. The authors obviously do not themselves accept such excess meanings. The opening chapter of the Interpretive Manual clearly states that the K-ABC is not a "measure of innate or immutable abilities" and points out that "All cognitive tasks are seen as measures of what the individual has learned." It is noteworthy that some mental processing subtests correlate higher with an achievement subtest than with other mental processing subtests, and the two global mental processing scores correlate higher with the global achievement score than they do with each other. In the discussion of clinical interpretation, subtests across the two categories are grouped in terms of shared abilities and influences affecting performance.

Despite the cautions and supporting data, however, statements appearing elsewhere in the manual may inadvertently strengthen some popular stereotypes. For example, the manual reports that "The Sequential and Simultaneous Processing Scales were constructed to measure intelligence" and the K-ABC separates "problem-solving ability from achievement." When confronted with such statements, the reader may well forget that children's experiential history will influence the quality of their information-processing and problem-solving strategies, as well as their performance on "achievement" tests. Simplified descriptions of the K-ABC given in promotional material also tend to emphasize the distinction and to identify "intelligence" with performance on the mental processing scales. There is thus a danger that (*a*) the K-ABC may be misused, by examiners with insufficient background in psychology, in an effort to obtain ready answers to urgent practical questions, and (*b*) popular stereotypes regarding intelligence and achievement tests may mar the sophisticated individual case studies for which the battery was presumably designed.

SUMMARY. The K-ABC is an innovative cognitive assessment battery, whose development meets high standards of technical quality. When used by a qualified professional, it is a promising instrument for dealing with important practical testing needs. It should, however, be presented to the testing community with suitable cautions against probable misuses.

Review of Kaufman Assessment Battery for Children by WILLIAM E. COFFMAN, E. F. Lindquist Professor Emeritus, College of Education, University of Iowa, Iowa City, IA:

In a summary evaluation of the individual tests discussed in *Essentials of Psychological Testing, Third Edition*, Cronbach (1970) noted that the Wechsler (WAIS, WISC, WPPSI) was at that time the dominant individual test but that most of his comments would apply also to the Stanford-Binet. He then made the following comments: "The Wechsler's virtues are those of an aid to clinical observation rather than of a scientific measuring instrument. It is primitive in conception, embodying tasks that clinicians found useful in the early days of testing. Since these tasks were originally devised, psychological theory has advanced on many fronts; this theory did not enter into the design of the Wechsler and enters only indirectly into the profile organization and the interpretation. Measurement theory also has made advances by means of which a more efficient test could surely be engineered" (p. 252). He then made this prediction: "Very likely the test series that someday replaces Wechsler's will retain several of his tasks, but it can be expected to introduce new tasks tied to well-defined theoretical constructs" (p. 253). The Kaufman Assessment Battery for Children is such a test series. Whether or not it will replace the WISC-R and the Stanford-Binet is still an open question. It is, however, a very strong candidate, and the school psychologist or clinician who aspires to keep in touch with developments in the field will certainly want to consider the battery and the substantial body of evidence contained in its accompanying Interpretive Manual and Administration and Scoring Manual before selecting an individual test of ability.

Some indication of the complexity of the frame of reference from which the K-ABC was developed may be gathered simply by examining the reference list of 20 pages included in the Interpretive Manual. A detailed study of the manual reveals that in selecting the stimulus material and in organizing the subtests into scoring units, the authors have been guided by theoretical constructs growing out of research in cognitive psychology, that in selecting analytical procedures for examining tryout data they have been guided by developments in measurement theory, that in choosing to adapt materials or to break new ground they have probed the research and clinical literature related to tests already in use, and that in making the inevitable compromises between the ideal and the feasible they have been sensitive to the needs of both the educational and the clinical settings for which the battery was being designed. As a result, they appear to have made remarkable progress in achieving their stated goal of developing a test battery that rests on a strong theoretical and research base, that provides separate measures of information processing styles and knowledge base, that may provide useful guides for educational intervention, that is more than an adaptation of approaches common to existing measures, that is easy to administer and objective to score, and that is appropriate for a variety of subgroups of the children and youth of the country.

As with any new test battery, the data available at the time of publication of the first manual for the K-ABC are not as complete as many potential users might wish; nevertheless, the amount of supporting data that are presented is certainly more complete than is typical of newly published measures. In fact, the manual is so comprehensive that there is a danger that potential users will be tempted to scan it quickly and accept the basic claims while neglecting to note the careful qualifications the authors include with each suggestion for application. This is, first of all, a clinical instrument, and there is a danger that inexperienced users will be tempted to use the numbers the battery generates to provide simple answers to troublesome questions of selection, classification, and remedial treatment rather than to engage in the agonizing struggle with ambiguity required for the development of sound clinical judgment. A careful study of the authors' guidelines will insure resistance to the temptation.

TEST DEVELOPMENT. The development of the K-ABC involved serious thought based on deep study of theories of ability generated by research in cognitive psychology, neuropsychology, and related disciplines and also the application of analytical methods characteristic of modern psychometrics. At an early point in the process, the decision was made to develop two scales of intellectual functioning based on the growing conviction that there exist two basic types of information processing, one requiring the subject to manipulate stimuli one at a time (sequential) and the other requiring manipulation of stimuli all at once (simultaneous), and that it was the method of processing rather than the particular content being processed that was of primary importance. Furthermore, it was decided that the measures of intellectual functioning should be as independent as possible of the knowledge base developed through alertness to the environment and through schooling, although a good measure of the latter was also desirable. The battery, then, consists of subscales organized to produce four scores: a score for simultaneous processing, one for sequential processing, a general mental processing score based on a composite of the two, and a separate score for achievement.

The route to these four scores was a long and involved one. Altogether 50 possible mental processing and achievement tasks were generated and tried out in pilot studies. The 20 most promising were screened in systematic field studies. Analytical procedures included classical and latent trait item analysis; sex and race bias studies, both statistical and judgmental; factor analytic studies designed to assess the construct validity of the theoretical model; and extensive questionnaire studies that probed the field experience of the examiners who administered the experimental tests. Surviving this process were 16 subtests so arranged as to produce the four desired scores for children ranging in age from 2 1/2 to 12 1/2. Not all subtests are administered at all ages, but evidence is provided that supports the argument that the subtests that are administered produce scores on continuous scales across the age range. Beginning at age 4, it is also possible to administer selected subscales to obtain a nonverbal combined mental processing score for handicapped children for whom tests involving languages are judged inappropriate.

NORMS. Norms for the battery are based on administration of the tests to representative samples of 100 children at each 6-month age interval from 2 1/2 to 12 1/2, a total of 2,000 individuals. In contrast to other norming studies, the sampling frame provided for proportional representation of exceptional children. Instead of basing the norms for each age interval on only the 100 individuals at that age, the procedure adopted involved the generation of within group standard scores, smoothing and merging the distributions of these scores, and the production of norms based on this merged distribution. The effect of this procedure was to reduce markedly the sampling error of the norms.

The resulting norms tables relate raw scores for the four major scales to normalized standard scores with means of 100 and standard deviations of 15. Similar score scales are generated for each of the subscales within the Achievement series. For the mental processing subscales, which are less reliable than the others, scores are reported on scales with means of 10 and standard deviations of 3.

A variety of supplementary norms are provided, some requiring the testing of additional subjects. Sociocultural norms are provided based on a cross-tabulation by race (black-white) and by parental education (less than high school education, high school graduate, and one or more years of college or technical school). There are supplementary norms for out-of-level testing at ages 4 1/2 and 5 (the ages at which there is a change in the kinds of subtests included in the battery). For those who prefer percentile ranks or stanines to standard scores, conversion tables are provided. In each case, the limitations of the norms provided are carefully set forth in the manual. The user who does not attend to these cautions will have to bear responsibility for misuse or overinterpretation.

PSYCHOMETRIC CHARACTERISTICS. Although much of the manual is concerned with clinical indications provided by the tests, strong evidence is also provided that the measures have sound psychometric qualities. Internal consistency reliabilities (split-half) for the several subscales range between .62 and .92 and those for the global scales range from .89 to .97 with most in the .90s. Retest coefficients of similar magnitude are reported for somewhat smaller and less representative samples. Even the reliability coefficients based on administration of alternate levels for the Age 4 and Age 5 levels are within the same range. Standard errors of measurement are reported for all scales at all age ranges, and users are cautioned to interpret differences among scores in terms of the probability that the differences might arise as a result of chance fluctuation. Of particular note are tables based on a variety of significance levels. The test user can thus decide what level to use.

As one might expect, when subtests are intercorrelated, the coefficients are positive and significant; however, intercorrelations are clearly lower than would be possible given the reliabilities of the subtests. Each subtest is making a distinct contribution.

The authors base their claim of validity for the battery primarily on evidence of construct validity. The arguments in succession are: (1) Scores on each subtest are higher for successive age groups. (2) Internal consistency coefficients for the Mental

Processing Composite and for the Achievement Scale (the correlations of subscales with total less the subscale) are high enough but not too high. (3) Factor loadings for the subtests are higher with the scale to which they have been assigned than with other scales. (4) The several scales for the battery have high correlations with other tests designed to measure similar constructs and low correlations with scales designed to measure other constructs. (5) Patterns of scores for various groups of exceptional children identified by other means (learning-disabled, mentally retarded, behaviorally disordered, physically handicapped, high risk preschool children, hearing-impaired, gifted) are generally what one would expect on the basis of the rationales for the several subtests. (6) Black-White and Hispanic-White differences are generally smaller than for the WISC-R. The 37 tables supporting the argument draw on data from the norming study and from 43 other studies, many of which were encouraged and given modest support by the publisher of the K-ABC. Most of these involve only small samples, but the overall picture is one of consistent findings. It is likely that as other studies accumulate, the picture with respect to construct validity will become clearer and may possibly suggest alternate constructs as valid.

CLINICAL INTERPRETATION. Almost half of the 283 pages of text in the Interpretive Manual for the K-ABC are devoted to helping the user know what can be done to make sense of the test results once scores are available and what the implications are for educational or psychological follow-up. The authors make clear that the objective should be not simply to describe the patterns of scores but rather to try to reach an understanding of why patterns that do occur are as they are. They caution that in many cases all that can be expected will be the generation of hypotheses that will have to be checked against additional data based on other measures or on intensive case studies. One comes away from study of this part of the manual with the conviction that clinical interpretation is complex, difficult, and often frustrating; that patterns of test scores can lead to meaningful interpretations by clinicians with the training and experience of the Kaufmans but may be much less valid for the typical test user; and that one can expect examples of gross misuse of the K-ABC to arise just as they have with respect to the WISC-R and the Stanford-Binet. On the other hand, claims by the authors are carefully qualified, the need for continuing skepticism on the part of the user is emphasized, the dangers of trying to interpret differences that might be reflecting simply random variation are reiterated throughout the text of the manual, and systematic procedures for avoiding such are described in detail.

Of particular significance is the emphasis on the basic complexity of each of the individual subtests. The user is encouraged to begin the interpretation in the context of the simultaneous/sequential processing theory and the mental processing/achievement contrast, but there is also encouragement to group subtests in other ways and to relate patterns to other theories; the user is also discouraged from attempting interpretations based on unique elements of individual scales until attempts to find common elements among subtests have been exhausted. To build a meaningful context for such an approach to interpretation, the authors have included a variety of illustrative cases.

It is doubtful that all users of the battery will accept the Kaufmans' interpretations of the cases. For example, Cronbach has taken a look at the tests and sees them as measures of "fluid" ability, "crystallized" ability, and "efficiency in attending and rehearsing, essentially independent of reasoning or knowledge" (Cronbach, 1984, p. 223). Keith and Dunbar, on the basis of factor analyses of some of the standardization samples, argue that if one leaves out the two reading subtests, what is left provides measures of non-verbal reasoning, verbal reasoning, and verbal memory (Keith & Dunbar, in press). Whether or not such differences in theoretical orientation will lead to different prescriptions for classification or treatment is a question to be answered by further systematic research.

The final chapter of the Interpretive Manual outlines the author's beliefs about the relationship between scores on the mental processing scales and prescriptions for remedial instruction in reading, spelling, and arithmetic. The argument is supported by some published studies; however, a number of those cited show that other theoretical approaches have been relatively unsuccessful rather than that the recommended procedures actually produce the desired results. The detailed suggestions for approaches to instruction are thus more in the nature of interesting hypotheses than acceptable recipes. A sound evaluation must await further research.

REVIEWER'S REFERENCES

Cronbach, L. J. ESSENTIALS OF PSYCHOLOGICAL TESTING, THIRD EDITION. New York: Harper & Row, 1970.

Cronbach, L. J. ESSENTIALS OF PSYCHOLOGICAL TESTING, FOURTH EDITION. New York: Harper & Row, 1984.

Keith, T. Z., & Dunbar, S. B. Hierarchial factor analysis of the KABC: Testing alternate models. THE JOURNAL OF SPECIAL EDUCATION, in press.

Review of Kaufman Assessment Battery for Children by ELLIS BATTEN PAGE, Professor of Educational Psychology and Research, Duke University, Durham, NC:

The introduction of the Kaufman Assessment Battery for Children (K-ABC) has affected testing practice with more impact than any intelligence test in recent memory. The advertising campaign has been remarkable, both in professional publications and in popular TV appearances. The authors and publishers argue that the K-ABC addresses important mental processes not adequately tested before. Some advocates have made claims of having solved profound and ancient testing problems. Moreover, the K-ABC is an attractive and appealing test, has many game-like features, is not difficult to administer, and is not too subjective in its scoring. Typical testing time for preschool children is estimated to be around 45 minutes, and about an hour and a quarter for school aged children.

GIVING THE K-ABC. In the examination kit, everything fits inside an attractive carrying case. The major items inside are the three "easels" for the various sets of tests. These easels open like notebooks, but then are propped up in testing, so that the child looks at one display, while the tester follows instructions on his own side of the "easel." For example, for an Expressive Vocabulary item (ages 2–6 to 4–11), there is a color picture of a common object facing the child, while the tester is instructed to ask, "What is this?" The tester notes the child's answer on the Test Record and then flips the easel page over the top, presenting the child with a new display, and the tester with a new expected answer. In general, this easel method nicely separates the two displays, and permits an easy passage from item to item, and from one subtest to the next.

The K-ABC yields five major scores: Sequential Processing, Simultaneous Processing, Mental Processing Composite, Achievement, and Nonverbal. Sixteen subtests contribute in various ways to the five scores. The score for Sequential Processing is determined from subtests including Hand Movements, Number Recall, and Word Order. The Simultaneous Processing score is based on subtests which include Magic Window, Face Recognition, Gestalt Closure, Triangles, Matrix Analogies, Spatial Memory, and Photo Series. The Achievement score subtests are Expressive Vocabulary, Faces and Places, Arithmetic, Riddles, Reading/Decoding, and Reading/Understanding. The Nonverbal score is derived from the other scales. The Mental Processing score is a composite of the Simultaneous and Sequential scales.

DETERMINING THE SCALES. Much of the claim of new contributions to testing is dependent on the five scales, their meaning, and their assumed superiority to the scales yielded by previous intelligence tests for children.

The authors describe the scales as follows: "The Sequential Processing and Simultaneous Processing Scales represent two types of mental functioning that have been identified independently by cerebral specialization researchers...and by cognitive psychologists....Sequential processing places a premium on the serial or temporal order of stimuli when solving problems; in contrast, simultaneous processing demands a gestalt-like, frequently spatial, integration of stimuli to solve problems with maximum efficiency. The K-ABC Mental Processing subtests were deliberately designed to minimize the role of language and verbal skills for successful performance, and to include stimuli that are as fair as possible for boys and girls from diverse backgrounds."

The Kaufmans explicitly tie their battery to older tests of "intelligence," but stake out claims to overcome some of the criticisms of intelligence testing. They state: "Critics of standardized intelligence tests have frequently proposed 'solving' these problems by eliminating the tests or replacing them with unnormed procedures such as criterion-referenced measures, informal assessment techniques, and test-teach-test paradigms. That was not our solution. Rather, we delineated the areas of greatest need...and then attempted to develop a test battery to meet these perceived needs. Our primary goals for the K-ABC were: (1) to measure intelligence from a strong theoretical and research basis; (2) to separate acquired factual knowledge from the ability to solve unfamiliar problems; (3) to yield scores that translate to educational intervention; (4) to include novel tasks; (5) to be easy to administer and objective to score; and (6) to be sensitive to the diverse needs of preschool, minority group, and exceptional children. At all times the essence of test development was to blend the new with the known, to combine innovation with adaptations of tasks with proven clinical, neuropsychological, and empirical validity."

RELIABILITY. There is currently only one form of the K-ABC; therefore, estimating reliability is inevitably troubled. On the one hand, measures of internal consistency will be confounded with set, mood, tester influence, and the other uncontrolled variables of a given session. On the other hand, test-retest reliabilities will be inflated by using only the same items, and by other influences of the two sessions with the same material.

In any case, the reported split-half reliabilities for the subtests range from .72 to .92. The reported test-retest reliabilities for subtests range from .59 to .98. These last are particularly questionable, since the test-retest reliabilities were based on raw scores (making no allowance for age), small numbers of children (no group larger than 92), and with the children grouped into just three age brackets (2–6 to 4–11, 5–0 to 8–11, and 9–0 to 12–5). True reliability within age, then, would be confounded by the difference between ages.

For the four global scales of the K-ABC, the reported internal consistencies ranged from .84 (Simultaneous scores for preschool children) to .97 (Achievement scores for school-age children). The test-retest reliabilities (computed with the small *N*s) ranged from .77 (Sequential and Simultaneous scores for preschool children) to .97 (Achievement scores for older school-age children).

A very small sample ($N=41$) was used to check alternate-level reliabilities and produced high coefficients, but these should probably not be taken too seriously for the K-ABC as a whole.

There is an abundance of tabled information in the Interpretive Manual (IM), gathered under these difficult conditions, to help estimate errors of measurement. But these must be taken, here as with most other standardized tests, with a large grain of salt: such error estimates are artificially small, since they are based on reliabilities which are quite inflated.

STANDARDIZATION SAMPLE. There is abundant information in the IM about the methods used to develop the K-ABC and apply it to a national sample of 4,000 children. With exceptions to be discussed later, these conform to the best current practice. The documentation is commendable.

VALIDITY OF THE SCALES. Although the authors state that there is "abundant" evidence for the "sequential-simultaneous dichotomy" coming from a wide range of research and theorizing, particularly hemispheric research (e.g., Luria, 1966; Das et al., 1975), they also acknowledge that investigations of normal individuals pose enough problems to "preclude firm conclusions about the functions of each hemisphere." But they summarize that there is "widespread support for the existence of an important processing dichotomy—one that is connoted by the terms sequential and simultaneous."

Of course, from the viewpoint of the counselor working with a normal child, the important question is not where the processes are carried out, but how well. And the processes are important or not, not on the basis of their brain locus, but on the basis of their relevance to a child's success in school and in life. What the tester wants from such a test, then, is a measure of intelligence, as might be validated by factor analyses of this and other test batteries, and by external measures of success. And if there are to be breakdowns of the whole measure into parts, these should have maximum relevance for the prediction of some other measures or experiences. In short, we are interested in the psychometric performance of the K-ABC global scores: the Sequential, Simultaneous, Mental Processing Composite, Achievement, and Nonverbal.

RELATIONS AMONG K-ABC TESTS. There is no preordained way of building an intelligence test from scratch. Binet worked partly by brilliant insight, partly by trial-and-error, to develop tasks which would be useful in measuring this intriguing trait. But it was left for Spearman and others to make clear that virtually all cognitive tasks, no matter how different superficially, measure in common an underlying ability, often called *g*, for general ability.

The Kaufmans insist that their battery measures two different traits. The Mental Processing Composite is intended to measure "the total intelligence in the assessment battery." They say that their Achievement Scale is close to the "crystallized abilities," while their Mental Processing scales together resemble the "fluid abilities" described by Horn and Cattell (1966). If their description is granted, their own "intelligence" excludes the crystallized abilities and most of the verbal. Whatever intelligence is used in acquiring vocabulary, number skills, and reading comprehension, they would assign not to "the child's present level of intellectual ability," but to "evidence of past acquisitions." They acknowledge that this definition "represents a break from other intelligence tests."

How well do their correlation data support their separation? The Kaufmans chose not to look for *g* (i.e., general abilities factor) in their total battery, presenting only varimax rotations. But Jensen (in press) has indeed looked for *g* in the complete K-ABC matrix, and found the larger *g* loadings to be from the Achievement tests. This was true both for the pre-school and the school-age samples, with a mean *g*-loading being in the high .70s for Achievement subtests, but only in the high .50s for Mental Processing.

If we assume, then, that the best estimate of intelligence is the *g* factor, found as an unrotated first component from a matrix of good cognitive tests, we would have to conclude that the K-ABC is mislabeling "intelligence" and confusing the user about the obtained scores.

RELATIONSHIPS WITH OTHER INTELLIGENCE TESTS. Nor is this the end of the K-ABC problems with construct validity: It is also apparent that the correlations with the classic intelligence tests (WISC-R and S-B) are decidedly higher, on the average, for the Achievement subtests than they are for the Mental Processing subtests.

On what grounds, therefore, should the K-ABC scoring system be defended? The authors argue that their Achievement measures are "acquired factual knowledge" and that their Mental Processing (MP) measures are "ability to solve unfamiliar problems." Yet at the same time they welcome the mantle of measuring "intelligence," and acknowledge that there are "frequent empirical findings of little racial bias in intelligence tests" (Wigdor & Garner, 1982). How, then, to justify the exclusion of those K-ABC subtests which best agree with the historical standards of intelligence testing, the best available measures of *g*?

The simplest amendment of this situation would be in scoring: Why not standardize a composite which includes the Achievement score as well? Or would that deflate a substantial portion of the current claims for uniqueness?

SEPARATION OF THE MENTAL PROCESSING SCALES. In addressing the distinction between Sequential and Simultaneous scores, Jensen (in press) used only the correlations among the Mental Processing subtests, looking for common factors among them. An average of about 44% of the total MP variance was specific to the subtest, that is, contributing neither to the *g*-factor nor to the Sequential or Simultaneous scales. And an average of about 37% of the variance of the MP subtests contributed to *g*! This meant that only around 7% was left to be of use in differentiating Sequential from Simultaneous. Once again, this is not impressive evidence for the two claimed scales of Mental Processing. And, as we know, the variance specific to the individual subtests has little psychometric or educational meaning.

When the same correlation matrix was tested (Willson et al., 1983) with confirmatory factor analysis, the results appear more reassuring about the K-ABC factor structure. Under a highly constrained analysis (a LISREL-like analysis using SAS matrix procedures), when only two factors were permitted and only the MP tests were involved, there were "strong loadings" of subtests on the constrained factors. But their clean-looking factor structure was forced to obtain that clean look. And indeed, the authors report that Achievement subtests did load on the MP factors, and that tests of significance rejected the constrained models as inadequate. In short, this analysis is not really a contradiction of the Jensen findings. Only a tiny portion of the MP total variance goes into separating Sequential from Simultaneous; much more of it goes to the *g* factor; and this *g* factor is most strongly found in the so-called Achievement Scale.

MINORITY TESTING. One of the K-ABC's stated goals is "to be sensitive to the diverse needs of preschool, minority group, and exceptional children." Much public attention, through ads in professional publications, and TV talk-show interviews with the authors, has been directed to the apparent narrowing of the usual gaps between samples of white and black, and of Anglo and Hispanic. The IM provides rich tables, based on the MP scales, for comparisons by sex, parent, education, race, and ethnic group. These tables do show much smaller group differences than, for example, the one standard deviation so often seen between U.S. blacks and whites.

Yet the K-ABC publishers are put in a somewhat awkward position on the black-white difference. On the one hand, the tremendous media blitz is greatly helpful in marketing the K-ABC. On the other hand, they acknowledge quietly what virtually all serious testing scholars do, and what has been supported by the National Academy of Sciences panel (Wigdor & Garner, 1982): that traditional tests are not culturally biased against blacks, neither internally, in the selection of items, nor externally, against common important criteria. Thus the publishers use a more subjective language about the minority advantages of the K-ABC, with words such as "thoughtful," "humanistic," and most frequently "sensitive."

NARROWING THE GAP WITH TRADITIONAL TESTS. It is not difficult to design a test with a smaller or greater racial difference, so long as that goal is set in item selection and score computation. The WISC-R usually shows a black-white difference of over one standard deviation for the full-scale IQ. Yet, Jensen (in press) points out that if we used only three subtests from the standardization sample, we could reduce the black-white difference to less than four-tenths of a standard deviation. Similarly, if we weighted all WISC-R factors equally and took the mean as full-scale IQ, we would shrink the black-white difference over 70%. The question is not whether we can narrow the apparent difference in resulting test scores, but what the test score now means for the individual child.

For instance, what would happen to the black-white difference reported by the IM if the K-ABC included the Achievement Scale (which as we have seen is the most highly *g*-loaded Scale) in its calculation of an overall scale? With the information provided, it is hard to know for certain, but we may assume that the combination would markedly increase the black-white difference. This would take place because, when tests are intercorrelated, their summing spreads out the new scores rapidly in a strong relationship to the average intercorrelation. In the case of the MPC and Achievement Scales, we know from Table 4.9 that for school-age children the correlation between the two global scales is .74. Much of this relation would be based on the *g* factor, which could be expected to increase the estimated black-white difference.

EXAMINING OTHER EVIDENCE. Unfortunately, there are lapses in the presentations of other materials. We are told that the school-age black sample performed "4 to 6 points" below the preschool black sample on the four major K-ABC scales. Yet Table 4.36 compares the K-ABC with the WISC-R, so far as the black-white difference is concerned, on the basis of noncomparable samples loaded against the WISC-R. The K-ABC includes the preschool sample, where blacks did relatively well, but the WISC-R has only school-age youngsters, where blacks did relatively less well. Thus the comparison is unfair, and the unwary reader might be quite misled.

Also, the black sample, used by the K-ABC for these comparisons, is itself biased toward the higher parent-education level (as pointed out by Bracken, in press, and observable in Table 3.7). The under-high-school blacks are decreased by about 10% compared with the U.S. black population, and the over-high-school blacks are increased by about 12%. These proportions, again, favor the K-ABC by narrowing the black-white difference.

There are no really new testing principles in the K-ABC which would account for the smaller minority differences which their tables show. Rather, the K-ABC has been designed to emphasize the skills on which blacks have performed best on the traditional tests, have weighted these highly in the chosen "intelligence" portion, have excluded from this portion virtually all the vocabulary and other verbal tests, and have diminished the influence of the more complex nonverbal tests, which together with the verbal have frequently been the (justified) core of intelligence testing. In addition, they have used a minority sample upwardly biased, have presented comparisons with other tests that are markedly unfair, and have not made possible the study of black-white difference which would result from the full K-ABC Battery, including the *g*-loaded Achievement Scale. In presenting the test and Interpretive Manual this way, they may have weakened the general utility of the K-ABC, so far as its predictive and construct validities are concerned.

SUMMARY. The new Kaufman Assessment Battery for Children represents a remarkably ambitious effort to dominate the next generation of intelligence testing for children. Ironically, part of the effort is to sidestep the (admittedly misguided) attacks on testing, and to combine the respectability and power of the traditional tests (the Stanford-Binet, WISC-R, Peabody, etc.) with language and rationales more "sensitive" to the test critics. Thus we find apparent contradictions proliferating in the Interpretive Manual: avoiding "intelligence" in the title, but claiming to measure both aspects of it; basing the principal scales on brain laterality, yet disavowing "the so-called innate potential"; denying that other tests are culturally biased, but seeming to argue that the K-ABC is less so; acknowledging that the Achievement Scale is similar to Cattell's "crystallized intelligence," but implying that it is measuring only "factual information."

But such ironies are not limited to the K-ABC. There is a similar kind of ambivalence in much of standardized testing today, where we recognize that our abilities are partially confounded with our environments, and our achievements are indeed enhanced by our native abilities. One revealing way of studying such influences, of course, is to estimate the heritability of scales on the basis of the variance between and within families. It will be most interesting to see what the results are with the K-ABC, when such estimates are eventually made. One prediction is that the K-ABC Achievement Scale, loaded as it is with *g*, will be at least as heritable as the Mental Processing Composite. If so, what will that say about the present theories underlying the K-ABC?

The K-ABC is a remarkably attractive set of instruments. With its spirit of play in many of the subtests, its rather trendy language, and extraordinary advertising, the K-ABC will almost surely become a popular, if expensive, addition to psychological testing. However, no user should imagine that it has somehow overcome the traditional problems and rather arbitrary nature of such tests. No one should imagine that there is some intrinsic superiority in the K-ABC over its major competitors (it remains to be seen whether it is even as useful). And no one should imagine that it has really solved the problem of lower scores for minorities.

Surely, no one should believe that the K-ABC has captured something of large educational or psychological meaning in the Sequential-Simultaneous distinction. To the contrary, the subtests contribute only a tiny part of their variance to any such factors. Most of their variance goes to supporting the general (*g*) factor, and to the specific subtests. For predictive and counseling use, it may turn out that the Achievement Scale will be the best intelligence measure of the Battery, even though denied that status by the authors. Hopefully, in a new, future edition, there may be an overall composite score (perhaps "Development Scale"?), which may become the most useful score of the Battery.

REVIEWER'S REFERENCES

Horn, J. L., & Cattell, R. B. Refinement and test of the theory of fluid and crystallized general intelligences. JOURNAL OF EDUCATIONAL PSYCHOLOGY, 1966, 57, 253–270.

Luria, A. R. HIGHER CORTICAL FUNCTIONS IN MAN. New York: Basic Books, 1966.

Das, J. P., Kirby, J., & Jarman, R. F. Simultaneous and successive syntheses: An alternative model for cognitive abilities. PSYCHOLOGICAL BULLETIN, 1975, 82, 87–103.

Wigdor, A. K., & Garner, W. R. (Eds.) ABILITY TESTING: USES, CONSEQUENCES, AND CONTROVERSIES. PART I: REPORT OF THE COMMITTEE. PART II: DOCUMENTATION SECTION. Washington, DC: National Academy Press, 1982.

Willson, V. L., Reynolds, C. R., Chatman, S. P., & Kaufman, A. S. CONFIRMATORY ANALYSIS OF SIMULTANEOUS, SEQUENTIAL, AND ACHIEVEMENT FACTORS ON THE K-ABC. Annual Meeting of the National Association of School Psychologists, Detroit, 1983.

Bracken, B. A critical review of the Kaufman Assessment Battery for Children (K-ABC). SCHOOL PSYCHOLOGY REVIEW, 1985, 14, 21–36.

Jensen, A. R. The black-white difference on the K-ABC: Implications for future tests. JOURNAL OF SPECIAL EDUCATION, 1984, 18, 377–408.

[563]

Kaufman Infant and Preschool Scale. Ages 1 month–48 months and mentally retarded individuals whose preacademic functioning age does not exceed 48 months; 1979; KIPS; tasks in 3 areas: general reasoning, storage, verbal communication; individual; 1 form; evaluation cards (22 pages); evaluation booklet (10 pages); instruction manual (40 pages); 1984 price data: $195 per complete kit including 10 evaluation booklets; $8 per evaluation cards; $22 per 10 evaluation booklets; $14 per instruction manual; (20–30) minutes; H. Kaufman; Stoelting Co.*

Review of Kaufman Infant and Preschool Scale by ROY A. KRESS, Professor Emeritus of Psychology of Reading, Temple University, Philadelphia, PA:

In recent years the growth in the number of preschool training facilities and an emphasis on early intervention for children at high risk has brought about a need for an evaluation instrument appropriate for cognitive assessment in the infant and preschool child. Typically evaluators have used developmental scales which assume a congruent relationship between cognitive and developmental functioning. Although this relationship may be a highly positive one in most normally maturing children, it is evidently not so with high risk children nor with the mentally retarded.

Recognizing this disparity between cognitive functioning and developmental functioning, the Kaufman Infant and Preschool Scale (KIPS) attempts to provide an assessment of cognitive functioning which could be used for program planning on an individual basis. The instrument can be used with individuals of any age so long as the test preacademic functioning age (PAFA) obtained does not exceed 48 months. The scale attempts "to identify early high level cognitive deficits and assets leading to the provision of appropriate programming" and early intervention.

The 86 behavioral tasks used to assess a current functioning level are representative of three theoretical areas of cognitive development: General Reasoning, Storage, and Verbal Communication. The tasks are distributed over five maturational stages of early development: Infancy I (birth to 6 months), Infancy II (6 to 18 months), Early Childhood I (18 months to 3 years), Early Childhood II (3 to 4 years) and Play Age (+ 4 years).

The scales are quite easily administered by anyone familiar with individual testing procedures. Examiner instructions are succinct and clear enough for the experienced examiner. In some instances the author indicates that parental report of behavior appropriate to an item may be acceptable although he encourages repeated observations over several sessions whenever possible. In administration, basal and ceiling levels are established with credit (including partial, where applicable) for all items passed in each of the three areas. This total is weighted to arrive at a PAFA score which, when divided by the chronological age, yields a Preacademic Functioning Quotient (PAFQ). When older subjects are tested the maximal divisor is 16 years (192 months). Calculation by months is suggested throughout. Of special interest are the scatter analysis profiles, examination of which should be helpful in intervention programming.

Standardization was achieved using a population of 304 white children, ranging in age from 1 to 48 months, from two midwest medical clinics. An additional population of 91 mentally handicapped children was obtained from two rehabilitation centers. Application of t tests for sex differences yielded non-significant results except at the 36- to 48-month age range. This difference ($p < .01$) is explained away as being "due to the possible biased nature of the sample." Reliability coefficients using the Spearman-Brown Formula are significant and range from .88 to .98, with a median reliability of .93. Validation is established by inference, "comparing means and standard deviations of the KIPS samples with means and standard deviations of group IQ tests which were administered in this geographical area" to children in grades 1 and 2—a questionable procedure.

The KIPS does appear to fill a void now present for those working with preschool age children of a high risk nature. The maturational tasks are representative of high level cognition and appear to be logically and progressively more difficult in nature. They are representative of the type of cognitive tasks which can be taught. Since KIPS is not intended to be predictive, but to measure only current-level functioning, it could be used to monitor progress as the result of curricular treatment of such children. However, the standardization population was small, obviously biased, and the validation procedure highly questionable, all of which suggest caution in employing this instrument for any purpose other than that for which it was developed.

Review of Kaufman Infant and Preschool Scale by PHYLLIS ANNE TEETER, Assistant Professor of Educational Psychology, University of Wisconsin-Milwaukee, Milwaukee, WI:

The Kaufman Infant and Preschool Scale (KIPS) is an assessment instrument designed "to provide a measure of early high level cognition, and to indicate possible need for intervention." Although the KIPS was not developed as a diagnostic tool, the author indicates that useful clinical information can be gathered concerning a child's level of cognitive development. The KIPS reportedly separates general developmental abilities (such as motor and self-help skills) from high level cognitive functions (such as general reasoning and communication abilities). While general development is expected to parallel that of high level cognitive maturation in normal children, the author states that for many exceptional children this is not the case. It is the author's contention that traditional assessment devices are adequate for children without serious mental handicaps, but these measures are not appropriate for "the infant at high risk for either maturational or emotional problems or for the mentally retarded with a mental age below three or four." Traditional measures tend to overestimate abilities for "at risk" children because development is often determined by motor and self-help skills. Therefore, the KIPS was designed to better evaluate "high level cognitive" abilities separate from motor skills for "at risk" populations and to provide guidelines for curricular or remedial programming.

The KIPS was originally designed for children between the ages of 1 month and 4 years, but was found to be effective for all individuals who show a "preacademic functioning age" (PAFA) equal to or below 4 years. Accordingly, the author reports that the KIPS can be used for all mentally retarded individuals regardless of chronological age if the PAFA is less than 4 years. It can also be used with older children and adults with a PAFA above 48 months if the examiner is mainly interested in programming needs and not in determining a cognitive developmental quotient.

The KIPS is composed of 86 items derived from developmental research and from the author's experiences in child neuropsychology. The items are arranged in a hierarchy based on maturational expectancies. The items are weighted differentially so that a preacademic functioning quotient (PAFQ) can be derived. The items measure three basic areas of "high level cognition," including General Reasoning, Storage, and Verbal Communication.

The General Reasoning area consists of items to assess "early maturation processes in learning to adjust to and overcome environmental barriers." The tasks are Piagetian in nature. For example, item 18 at the 4+ level asks, "Which is bigger: A mouse or a cat; a cow or an ant; a spoon or a door?" (Two of the three must be correct to receive credit.) The items in the Storage area measure "attention span, concentration and memory." Performance on these items can be affected by anxiety and emotional factors as well. The items in the Storage area assess the child's ability to use recall for thinking. The author states that when memory is impaired the individual is likely to show "adaptive difficulties." An example at the 3- to 4-year level is: "Listen carefully while I say some words and then you say them: 'The black dog ran after the cat'." Finally, the Verbal Communication area is comprised of items measuring reasoning and memory abilities which are necessary for adequate verbal communication and expressive language skills. For example, item 30 at Level 3 to 4 years requires the child to: "Verbally demonstrate interrelationships in pictures with more than one word responses. Responds to 'tell me what you see' or 'make up a story'."

The test items are presented in five age ranges: 0 to 6 months, 6 to 18 months, 18 months to 3 years, 3 to 4 years, and 4+ years. Given the nature and degree of developmental changes one expects across these age ranges, these levels seem to be too large to be meaningful. Also there are sometimes too few items at each age level for a reliable measure of the child's abilities. For example, there are only 2 tasks required at the 3- to 4-year range in the General Reasoning area.

The test materials include an evaluation manual with printed stimuli and a variety of toys, blocks, balls, and pegs. Administration procedures are fairly general and many items do not have standardized instructions. It is also sometimes difficult to know which test materials are to be used for specific test items. For example, item 2 at the 18 months to 3 year level reads: "Recognizes and/or names familiar objects. Must name or point to 2 or 3 pictures for 1/2 score. Must name or point to all 5 for full credit." Although there is a table of contents for the Evaluation Card Manual with a brief description of the item, there are no numbers corresponding to test items. It would be helpful if the directions in the test manual included the card numbers for stimulus materials. In general, the test materials seem to be more interesting for the older age ranges, as many of the items below the 18-month level require no special materials at all.

Scoring procedures for the KIPS are presented in a clear and precise manner. There are no time limits for this test. While most items are scored based on observation of test performance, informants can be used to determine some abilities. It is possible to receive $^1/_2$ credit on some items where skills are emerging, but most items are scored as (+) full credit or (–) no credit. A preacademic functional quotient (PAFQ) is calculated only for children with a preacademic functional age (PAFA) of 4 years or less. The PAFQ is a ratio determined by dividing PAFA by the chronological age.

The standardization sample for the KIPS consisted of 304 children in the 1 month to 4 year range. These children were selected from two medical clinics in Wisconsin. A second group of 91 mentally handicapped individuals was also selected and ranged in age from 1 month to 55 years. While all subjects were Caucasian, there was no information presented about the socioeconomic status of the two groups. Performance differences based on sex were found for children from the general sample between the ages of 36 to 48 months. The author explains that this significant difference is "due to the possible biased nature of the sample as parents with children ages 3 and up would be aware of their children's deficits, and not be overly anxious to have [these deficits] reaffirmed." Why this would differentially affect males and females is not known, and why children in the general sample may be suspected to have problems is not explained. Also the author does not indicate which group performed better.

Split-half reliabilities for the general group ranged from a low of .58 in the 36 to 48 month group for General Reasoning, to a high of .89 in the 18 to 36 month group for Verbal Communication. When these coefficients were corrected with the Spearman-Brown Prophecy Formula to provide an estimation of the reliability for the full length of the test, reliabilities ranged from an .88 in the 36 to 48 month group to .95 for the 6 to 18 month and the 18 to 36 month groups. The standard error of measurement was highest in the 1 to 6 month group (5.51) and in the 36 to 48 month group (5.11). Reliabilities for the mentally retarded group were estimated at .98 for two subgroups aged 1 to 48 months: Group 1 with a PAFQ in the 55 to 84 range, and Group 2 with a PAFQ less than 55. Because the author collapsed the groups for the special sample, differences in reliabilities across ages cannot be determined. The author also reported reliabilities for two older groups in the special sample: 48 to 72 months, and 19 to 55 years. However, because the sample sizes were small (17 and 25 respectively), and the age ranges were so wide, these data are of questionable value for older children and adults regardless of their functional abilities. The author does not report test-retest or interrater reliabilities, which would be useful.

Means and standard deviations for PAFQs were reported for the general and the special groups. Again age ranges for the mentally retarded group were collapsed. Because one of the major purposes of this instrument is to assess high level cognitive abilities for "at risk" children, and because the tasks are developmental in nature, the treatment of these data make it difficult to effectively analyze the PAFQ. In essence, it is almost impossible to use the KIPS as a norm-referenced test with special populations. In fact, given the data reported, it is impossible, as recommended in the manual, to ascertain "the level of early high level cognition in three basic areas, from which one is able to program." Separate means and standard deviations were not reported for the three basic areas for either the general or the special sample. At best the KIPS can only be used as a criterion-referenced instrument to determine if certain skills have been attained. However, it is not possible to estimate when these skills should be present because of the way these data were analyzed.

Intercorrelations indicate that the three basic cognitive areas are fairly redundant and highly related. This is especially true for the 18 to 36 month group, where correlations range from .75 for Verbal Communication with General Reasoning, to .87 for Verbal Communication with Storage. Correlations drop noticeably but are still appreciable for the 1 to 6 month and the 36 to 48 month groups (.56 to .69).

Validity coefficients were calculated with the KIPS and the Academic Aptitude Test for grade 1, and the Otis-Lennon IQ Test for grade 2. The manual is unclear in its presentation of these data. It is difficult to know why the author did not use one of the other developmental tests available for this age range rather than group IQ tests. Also it is not clear why children in grades 1 and 2 were used, as the major thrust of the KIPS is aimed at children under the age of 48 months.

The test manual provides a classification table for determining the severity of mental retardation based on the PAFQ. There are also expectancy grade levels provided for children 6 years of age to adulthood. The author indicates that this table can be used to "ascertain if there is significant growth, and if such is in accordance with expectation." The author does not specify how these expectancy levels were derived. The classification-prediction method presented seems unwarranted because it does not appear to be empirically derived; children between the ages of 6 to 16 years were not used in the standardization of the KIPS. Test users are cautioned against using this procedure.

In summary, the KIPS is an instrument designed to measure "high level cognition" in three basic areas for "at risk" individuals. However, because the standardization sample for the mentally retarded group was small, the utility of this scale for special populations is questionable. Test users are advised to use the KIPS as a criterion-referenced rather than as a norm-referenced measure of development. Although three areas are represented, individual scores cannot be derived for the different cognitive abilities. In general, the validity of the KIPS as a measure of developmental maturation has not been determined. Also the small number of items across age ranges and the restricted standardization sample limit the usefulness of this instrument. The KIPS does not seem to be a significant improvement over other developmental scales presently available.

[564]

Keegan Type Indicator. Adults in organizational settings; 1980–82; KTI; measures perception, judgement, and relationship styles based on Jungian typology; 3 scores: extraversion vs. introversion, sensation vs. intuition, thinking vs. feeling; no data on reliability and validity; no norms; Form B ('82, 4 pages, includes scoring instructions); answer sheet (no data, 1 sheet); user's manual ('80, 13 pages); instructor's manual ('80, 21 pages); price data available from publisher; administration time not reported; Warren J. Keegan; Warren J. Keegan and Associates Press.*

[565]

Keele Pre-School Assessment Guide. Children in nursery school; 1980; KPAG; experimental form; criterion-referenced; ratings by teachers or counselors in 5 areas: social behavior, cognition, physical skills, socialization, language; no data on reliability and validity; no norms; individual; 1 form; manual (36 pages); record form (8 pages); 1984 price data: £3.85 per 25 record forms; £1.90

per manual; administration time not reported; Stephen Tyler; NFER-Nelson Publishing Co. [England].*

Review of Keele Pre-School Assessment Guide by CATHY W. HALL, Assistant Professor of Psychology, Fort Hays State University, Hays, KS:

The Keele Pre-School Assessment Guide (KPAG) is an informal measure of language, cognition, socialization, and physical skills of preschool children. It is not a test of intelligence or general aptitude. The assessment guide was developed in England for utilization with preschool populations. The authors chose to make the KPAG a highly flexible screening device, and to adapt it in such a way that a child's score would not provide information as to his/her standing in relation to other children of the same age range in the standardization sample. The major stated purposes of the KPAG are to plot the progress of individual children, to be a curriculum guide for preschoolers, and to serve as a final record of a child's preschool developmental level. The test fulfills these purposes, but the potential utility of the KPAG is perceived by this reviewer as extremely limited.

The test, the manual, and the record forms of the KPAG allow for only broad interpretations of test results. Although the tasks measured by the KPAG are stated to be in order of ascending difficulty, there is no way to determine a child's level of functioning in relation to his/her age range.

There is only very minimal information concerning the standardization of the KPAG, which involved "over one hundred children in preschool settings." There are no specifications as to age ranges, number of children per age range, socioeconomic status, minority representation, demographic information (other than England) or the type of preschool/nursery setting.

Another major drawback is the fact that there is not a standardized form of administration; in fact, those utilizing the KPAG are encouraged to "adapt" the guide as they feel necessary. Items are in the form of suggestions as to how a particular skill could be assessed. Observation is the primary means of assessment for Section I—aspects of a child's behavior. The assessment criterion for Section II—Language, Cognition, Socialization, and Physical Skills—are unstructured and the examiner is given the option of "modifying" the assessment procedure as she/he sees fit. Since the test can be utilized as a series of criterion assessments, the possibility of interrater error within the broad guidelines of administration should be noted. The only note of caution in the manual is that "once criteria have been established,...they should be adhered to reasonably closely."

There are no specific validity or reliability data presented for the KPAG. The manual also provides only minimal information for interpretation of test results. There is no specific information as to who should administer and/or interpret the test results, although it would seem that a teacher or teacher's aide with at least some background in test administration would be adequately qualified. Interpretation of the data obtained from the KPAG remains as loose as the assessment procedure.

Items utilized on the KPAG are from various sources, including psychological tests, developmental guidelines, and the authors' own research. The manual provides only minimal information on how items were selected for inclusion in the assessment guide. The authors also make the items of the KPAG highly flexible as well. They condone the substitution of items if the examiner feels other items may be of greater relevance. This brings up major concerns. If wide substitution does occur, the validity of the test is highly questionable.

The KPAG can provide broad guidelines for the nursery school curriculum, but the assessment guide is of little benefit if standardization, validity, and reliability data are lacking. It might be more advantageous to choose another measure if more than just a broad curriculum guide is required. The KPAG has the potential to become a very useful assessment guide, but far more work is needed than has presently been done to make it a valid assessment instrument. The title is correct in referring to it as an experimental edition.

Review of Keele Pre-School Assessment Guide by ROBERT F. MCMORRIS, Professor of Educational Psychology and Statistics, State University of New York at Albany, Albany, NY:

The Keele Pre-School Assessment Guide (KPAG) has two sections. The first contains 7-point rating scales concerned with social behavior; space provided under each scale allows further description of the child's behavior. The second section contains four clusters of items: Cognition, Socialization, Physical Skills, and Language. The 15 items each contain five skills arranged in order of difficulty. According to the manual, "The level of skill attained by the child in each area may be portrayed by plotting his performance on the circular chart at the end of the record form. Each segment of the chart represents a different area of skill and each concentric ring a particular level of difficulty. An item placed near the centre of the circle is therefore easier than one on the periphery. Items on the same concentric ring are of approximately equivalent difficulty."

How might the instrument be employed? The author describes five benefits for pre-school inventory use: (1) "ascertainment of the needs of individual children; (2) identification of progress and the next step in the learning process; (3) transmission of information to other caring adults; (4) provision of evidence of progress for parents; and (5) evaluation of current practice."

The KPAG is labeled an assessment guide and not a test. In the entry preceeding the reviews, the KPAG was termed "experimental form" and "criterion-referenced." With the first term the potential user receives a vital caution. Bases for the development of the KPAG are inadequately delineated. The author's assertions about uses and properties seem moderately reasonable, but data relevant to these assertions are not provided. In the absence of data, how should one interpret the results, whether from a criterion-referenced or norm-referenced point of view? Just what does this test measure? The remainder of the review is addressed to questions an interpreter might raise and to responses especially to two of those questions.

IS IT A MEASURE OF INTELLIGENCE? Appearing in capital letters in the manual is the statement: "The KPAG IS NOT A TEST OF INTELLIGENCE OR OF GENERAL APTITUDE." The child's development and proficiencies are outlined, but no score or set of scores is provided, nor is a fixed format of presentation required. Nevertheless, a profile is presented for Section 2, implying worthwhile, even diagnostic, information about cognitive development. To what degree are the behaviors like these tapped on intelligence tests?

To find out, a content comparison was made with two major intelligence tests. Obviously the comparison depends on assumptions of what is being measured with each instrument and whether the processes are comparable. Granting those caveats, Susan Zaret and I estimated proportions of the KPAG tasks similar to tasks included on the Binet and the Wechsler Preschool and Primary Scale of Intelligence (WPPSI), respectively, to be approximately 2/5 and 2/5 for Cognition, 1/2 and 1/10 for Physical Skills, 0 and 0 for Socialization, and 1/2 and 1/2 for Language. These estimates are derived from examination of each of the 75 skills (i.e., 15 items at 5 skills each), and are based on likely written comments in the intelligence testing as well as the actual scoring.

Frequently some, although not all, of the skills within an item were rated as comparable to an intelligence measure. For example, in the Space and Time item of the KPAG, the first skill (Differentiates night and day) seems related to WPPSI Information question 9 about what shines in the sky at night; the third skill (Knows some names of the days of the week) seems moderately related to WPPSI Information question 18 about the number of days in a week; but the fourth skill (Differentiates between left and right) seems less specifically related to any WPPSI item.

We expect any reader who compares the KPAG with a major intelligence test such as the Binet or WPPSI may arrive at somewhat different estimates than ours, but would agree that two or three KPAG clusters have considerable overlap as well as considerable divergence and uniqueness compared with the intelligence test. The KPAG, then, is not an intelligence test but seems to contain considerable content in common with intelligence measures.

CLUSTERING OF ITEMS. The author grouped the 15 items in four clusters, labeled Cognition, Physical Skills, Socialization, and Language, but did not supply a rationale or data to support this grouping. To help estimate the appropriateness of the clusters, this reviewer asked 10 faculty members and advanced graduate students to sort the 15 items into three to seven clusters and to label each cluster. (Copies of Section 2 were cut into items; the four cluster labels were removed.)

Sorters used three to six clusters, and provided various labels. Sortings were examined using target partition analysis (Ambrosino, McMorris, & Noval, 1979; Pfeiffer, Pruzek, & Sherry, 1975). The author's conceptualization received reasonable support; items tended to cluster more within the KPAG categories than between categories. No pair of items between categories was grouped together by more than 3 of the 10 sorters. The number of sorters who grouped pairs of items within categories averaged 4 (Cognition), 7 (Physical Skills), 6 (Socialization), and 8 1/3 (Language). Not surprisingly, only one pair of items received a perfect 10.

Language, then, was the most secure grouping, with Cognition least secure. Within the Cognition category, two or three of the items 1, 2, and 3 (Space and Time, Objects, and Sorting) tended to be clustered, as were 4 and 5 (Memory and Number). Item 6 (Problem Solving) was only moderately related to each of the other five. Among the labels for the first three items were recognition of physical properties, relational concept development, and seriation perception; three sorters classified items 4 and 5 as numerosity or numerical.

Although these results are somewhat unreliable due to the limited number of sorters, they help to both question and support the four clusters featured at the end of the instrument. Two related questions not addressed with the sorting are (1) whether the five skills in each item are unidimensional, and (2) whether the same rating across scales indicates equivalent development. For example, does a 4 represent more of the same ability or set of abilities, and not different abilities, than does a 3 or a 2 on the same five-skill item; and does a 4 in one item represent the same level of ability as does a 4 in another item? The first question concerning unidimensionality can be illustrated both by referring to the Space and Time item discussed above and by asking whether the Drawing and Writing abilities involved in copying letters (4) are the same as in drawing more complex human figures and other pictures (3).

CONTENT AND OTHER VALIDITY QUESTIONS. Validity questions additional to those considered in the two previous sections start with choice of content. Many items have a Piagetian base, and many a Gesellian basis—to name two. My colleagues were quite supportive of the content; suggestions for expansion included more number concepts and positional words (e.g., first and second). Perhaps the items reflect the objectives of representative preschools, but such educational importance of the instrument is not substantiated. Do preschools emphasize these skills? What commonly emphasized skills are omitted from the instrument? Are the KPAG skills necessary for success beyond the pre-school years? If those questions are not answered affirmatively, use of the instrument, especially as a curriculum guide, is questionable at best. (A stated purpose of the KPAG is to "provide an outline of and suggestions for activities in a preschool setting.")

Other appropriate information would include longitudinal data, correlations among items and among skills, difficulties of the skills, cross-cultural comparisons, and correlations with other instruments. Reports of use could be documented and use of construct labels supported.

The domains for criterion-referencing should be better specified (e.g., what is meant by "Properties of Objects"?). Limitations inherent in having a small number of tasks per domain appropriate for any given child should be described (e.g., to screen for disability, skills such as "Conserves continuous quantity" are too difficult, reducing the number of items effective for that use).

RELIABILITY. No reliability data are presented. Would immediate retesting give similar scores? Would two examiners tend to agree? Are differences across scales or differences in time reliable? Related to differences across time, since the examiner shows the child the correct response to many items after the item was missed, later testing could reflect such instruction as well as other learnings, practice effect, maturity, and measurement error.

STANDARDIZATION. Were all testing materials supplied in a kit its weight and cost would be prohibitive, and it would probably include a slide and a tricycle as well as jigsaw puzzles and blocks. All materials are supplied by the school, and would differ from school to school, affecting generalization and reliability of scaling negatively but the child's and the examiner's comfort positively. Directions for scoring are brief; minimum requirements for examiners are not specified. The term flexibility appears frequently in the manual.

SUMMARY. The KPAG allows assessment of just over 80 skills at reasonable cost. The measure is not an intelligence test, although some scales overlap considerably with leading intelligence tests. Fortunately, no summary score is given. The grouping of scales seems generally appropriate, and skills within a scale seem generally to proceed from simple to more complex. The circular profile provides a summary for 75 of these skills, but with the danger that the measure may therefore be considered a formal test and not a semiformal guide. No data are provided on questions of validity, reliability, or interpretability, so use of this developmental instrument may be premature. The price is right, but whether interpretations would be right is currently conjecture. It is hoped that the author and others will provide data to support its proposed interpretations.

REVIEWER'S REFERENCES

Pfeiffer, R. A., Pruzek, R. M., & Sherry, J. R. TARGET PARTITION ANALYSIS: BACKGROUND, RATIONALE, PROBLEMS AND PROSPECTS. Paper presented at the meeting of the Psychometric Society, Iowa City, 1975.

Ambrosino, R. J., McMorris, R. F., & Noval, L. K. Partitioning methods for detecting misconceptions of content and test items. JOURNAL OF EDUCATIONAL MEASUREMENT, 1979, 16, 187–195.

[566]

The Kendrick Battery for the Detection of Dementia in the Elderly. Ages 55 and over; 1979; battery should be repeated six weeks after initial testing; individual; 2 tests; manual (20 pages); 1984 price data: £8.65 per Object Learning Test; £4.45 per 25 record forms; £5.45 per manual; £6.45 per specimen set; (10–15) minutes; Andrew J. Gibson and Don C. Kendrick; NFER-Nelson Publishing Co. [England].*

a) OBJECT LEARNING TEST. A test of memory recall; Forms A, B, (4 cards).

b) DIGIT COPYING TEST. A test of speed performance; 1 form (2 pages).

TEST REFERENCES

1. Kendrick, D. C. Administrative and interpretive problems with the Kendrick Battery for the Detection of Dementia in the Elderly. BRITISH JOURNAL OF CLINICAL PSYCHOLOGY, 1982, 21, 149–150.

2. Skelton-Robinson, M., & Telford, R. Observations on the Object Learning Test of the Kendrick Battery for the Detection of Dementia. BRITISH JOURNAL OF CLINICAL PSYCHOLOGY, 1982, 21, 147–148.

Review of The Kendrick Battery for the Detection of Dementia in the Elderly by JOSEPH D. MATARAZZO, Professor and Chairman, Department of Medical Psychology, School of Medicine, Oregon Health Sciences University, Portland, OR:

The Kendrick Battery for the Detection of Dementia in the Elderly is suitable only for adults aged 55 and older and consists of two short and simple tests which together can be administered in 10 minutes or less. The first test, the Object Learning Test (OLT), consists of 4 large cards (40 x 35 cm), each of which contains black and white drawings of a number (10, 15, 20, and 25, respectively) of familiar objects (e.g., comb, chair, horse, spoon, gun, doll, pen, etc.). The subject is asked to recall as many items as possible after exposure (30–75 seconds) of each of the four cards; the score is the sum of the total number recalled. This test has an alternate form, thereby facilitating its use in assessing change in cognitive functioning over time in the same individual. The second test, the Digit Copying Test (DCT) contains 2 sheets of paper (2 trials) each with the same 100 digits randomly placed in rows of 10 per line. The subject is asked to copy as many of the 100 digits as possible in each 2-minute trial. The correlation between the alternate forms of the OLT is .91. The immediate test-retest reliability between trials 1 and 2 of the DCT is .97, and the 24-hour test-retest reliability of the OLT is .92 and .91 for Forms A and B, respectively. The intercorrelation between the OLT and the DCT was .18 and not significant in the standardization sample of 99 normal elderly subjects, .30 (*p* of .05) in 46 elderly depressed patients, and .53 (*p* of .01) in 43 unequivocally dementing patients.

The two Kendrick tests are grounded on a theory of cognitive-physiological arousal and were chosen to assess cognitive abilities which are sensitive to age changes (i.e., immediate recall of briefly perceived data, and speed of processing and recording information). In the test manual Gibson and Kendrick cite a validation study which reports the ability of the Battery to discriminate, without false positives or false negatives, non-dementing (normal) elderly subjects from dementing elderly subjects; a second study which showed that the Battery could discriminate normal, depressed, and dementing elderly patients; a third concurrent validity study involving patients on medication but whose results unfortunately required a change in Kendrick's earlier arousal-based theory; and a fourth study which utilized factor analysis and revealed the construct validity of the Battery. A fifth validity study by Gibson et al. (1980) showed that the present Battery cannot efficiently differentiate between elderly, long-stay psychiatric patients and the elderly groups in the three standardization samples discussed above.

The strengths of this two-test battery include its brevity (10 minutes) and the large print and picture size which are especially well-suited for the elderly groups for which it is intended. Additional strengths are the alternate form of the OLT, and the age-scaled norms for both OLT and DCT (expressed as quotients with a mean of 100 and standard deviation of 15) for age groups 55 to 64, 65 to 74, and 75 and older. Also considered as additional strengths are the reliability and validity data published in the manual, including the use of base rates and the resulting values of Kappa coefficients as indices of the discriminatory power of the Battery across normal and nonnormal elderly groups.

On the negative side, the scoring of the two tests by use of cutoff norms for converting the raw score on each test to a binary normal or nonnormal score for each age (with different cutoff scores for initial test versus retest raw score) constitute a cumbersome procedure for a busy clinician, and will require careful quality control of clerical assistants in research laboratories. The Battery's recommended use as an instrument to record test-retest changes during a 6-week interval limits its usefulness. The requirement that each patient be examined twice is difficult to meet in well-monitored research studies, and next to impossible to meet in the real world of neuropsychological assessment of hospitalized patients. Fortunately, however, and in common with batteries of similar tests, the Kendrick Battery may also be used when only a single testing is desired, and with outpatients as well as inpatients.

Used in isolation in its present form, this Battery quite likely yields information comparable to that which is obtained from the use of only a two-test battery consisting of the Digit Span and the Digit Symbol subtests of the WAIS-R; or any two-test combination of the Paired Associates test of the Wechsler Memory Scale, the Graham Kendall Memory for Designs Test, the Bender Gesalt Visual Reproduction Test, or the Category and Trails Tests of the Halstead-Reitan Battery, or other comparable two-test batteries. In many cases the use even of a single test yields important information. Thus, even a 10-minute, two-test battery such as the Kendrick will provide useful information. However, given the demonstrable complexity and very large individual differences in brain-behavior relationships, even an 8-hour battery with 20–25 individual tests (e.g., the Halstead-Reitan Battery), will in some cases barely provide the clinical neuropsychologist with the data required to make a differential diagnosis in the individual patient. Therefore, it is my opinion that the Kendrick Battery quite likely will remain a research instrument, inasmuch as batteries made up of individual tests (e.g., The Category Test, Trails A and B, Digit Symbol and Digit Span) already exist for clinical use and have considerably more published validity data. Filskov and Boll (1981) provide an excellent review of such test batteries. Too few clinical tests currently exist for select populations and for the assessment of specifiable aspects of pathology. Thus a low-cost battery designed to assess the progress of dementia in individuals 55 years and older seems to me to merit more research.

REVIEWER'S REFERENCES

Gibson, A. J., Moyes, I. C. A., & Kendrick, D. Cognitive assessment of the elderly long-stay patient. BRITISH JOURNAL OF PSYCHIATRY, 1980, 137, 551–557.

Filskov, S. B., & Boll, T. J. (Eds.), HANDBOOK OF CLINICAL NEUROPSYCHOLOGY. New York: John Wiley & Sons, 1981.

Review of The Kendrick Battery for the Detection of Dementia in the Elderly by K. WARNER SCHAIE, *Professor of Human Development and*

Psychology, The Pennsylvania State University, University Park, PA:

One of the major problems facing the clinical psychologist dealing with elderly clients is the issue of differential diagnosis between various forms of senile dementia and normal aging or functional pathology. There does not seem to be any royal road toward this objective. But we do know that instruments designed to provide differential diagnoses in young adults will generally be most unsatisfactory (cf. Schaie & Schaie, 1977). The Kendrick Battery therefore deserves attention, since it is one of the few cognitive tests designed especially for an elderly population. In its original form it consisted of two parts, the Synonym Learning Test (SLT), in which subjects are taught the meaning of new words, and the Digit Copying Test (DCT), a measure of psychomotor speed. The present version of the battery represents a response to the finding that the Synonym Learning Test was too stressful for work with older persons. A replacement test was constructed that requires subjects to recall familiar objects depicted by black-and-white line drawings. Two alternate forms have been provided for the new Object Learning Test (OLT).

The primary objective for this battery is to differentiate between persons likely to suffer from unspecified types of senile dementia from those not so affected. The authors raise the important caveats that the test should not be used for initial hospital diagnosis after 3 weeks of institutionalization, that its diagnostic utility may be impaired by the use of anxiolytic, antidepressant, or antipsychotic drugs, and that results for persons with a verbal IQ below 70 may be misleading. It is also important to note that the most successful discriminations obtained with this test involve repetition of the battery 6 weeks after the initial testing.

Reliability and validity studies for the test involving two samples ($N=188$ and 102) of dementing and non-dementing examinees are quite impressive. Accurate assignment was possible for 96% of the examinees on the first administration, and for 100% of the examinees when examining test-retest patterns, using the cutoff criteria specified in the manual. Validity studies examining performance on the Kendrick Battery by elderly depressives, however, have produced conflicting results. The authors may be correct, however, in claiming that these difficulties may be a problem of differential treatment histories since tricyclic anti-depressant medication as well as lower activity level will reduce performance on the test. No data have been reported on the predictive validity of the test with respect to either senile dementia or depression.

This is a test which is simple to administer, requires limited amounts of time, has clear scoring and interpretation procedures, and provides reasonably acceptable age norms for persons 55 to 64, 65 to 74 and those above 75. A number of problems remain. For example, in view of substantial gender differences in the abilities underlying this battery, differences which have been found to persist into old age (cf. Schaie, 1983), it would be useful to have separate norms for men and women. Also, there is a question whether the cutoff scores provided would be applicable in American clinical samples, and particularly in various ethnic groups. But those are matters for further research. In the interim, the Kendrick Battery would seem to provide a useful addition to the geroclinician's armamentarium in dealing with the perplexing topic of differentiating senile dementia from normal aging or other functional pathologies.

REVIEWER'S REFERENCES

Schaie, K. W., & Schaie, J. P. Clinical assessment and aging. In J. E. Birren & K. W. Schaie (Eds.), HANDBOOK OF THE PSYCHOLOGY OF AGING. New York: Van Nostrand Reinhold, 1977.

Schaie, K. W. LONGITUDINAL STUDIES OF ADULT PSYCHOLOGICAL DEVELOPMENT. New York: Guilford Press, 1983.

[567]

Kent Infant Development Scale. Ages 2–13 months; 1978–81; KID; ratings by parent or caregiver; 6 scores: cognitive, motor, social, language, self-help, full scale; individual, 1 form ('78, 16 pages); manual ('79, 22 pages); profile ('81, 2 pages); separate answer sheets must be used; 1982 price data: $60 per kit including 5 test booklets, 10 information fact sheets, 10 answer sheets, computer scoring and 10 print-outs; $1 per test booklet; $5 per prepaid computer-scored answer sheet; $5 per 25 answer sheets; $17.50 per set of scoring templates; $5.50 per 10 profile sheets; $10 per manual; $7.50 per specimen set; Spanish edition available; Jeanette Reuter, Lewis Katoff, and Virginia Dunn (manual); Kent Developmental Metrics.*

See T3:1246 (1 reference).

Review of Kent Infant Development Scale by CANDICE FEIRING, Assistant Professor of Pediatrics, Rutgers Medical School—UMDNJ, New Brunswick, NJ:

The Kent Infant Development Scale (KID) is an instrument to assess the developmental status of normal, at risk, and handicapped children. Overall, considering the empirical work on reliability and validity of the KID, psychometrically sound estimation of developmental ages for research or clinical purposes can be achieved through use of this scale. The internal consistency of the items in each of the five domains is quite high; alpha coefficients are: cognitive .97, motor .99, social .97, language .95, self help .96, and full scale .99. In addition to high internal consistency, the five domains and full scale score are all highly related. This indicates that each domain, rather than being a separate dimension of developmental age, is a redundant measure of the child's developmental status. This suggests the full scale KID score should be used as a total estimate of development (the items contributed by each scale making the instrument more reliable) rather than using domain scores separately as measures of particular skills. It should also be noted that an Inconsistency Scale for the KID is being developed in order to detect those caregivers who are not consistent (either within or across time) in their response to the KID.

Test-retest reliability studies with normal and handicapped children indicate consistency in measurement over short time intervals. Although the sample size in such studies was small for normal (20–40) as compared to handicapped (100–120) groups, reliabilities were always very high. Test-retest reliability for normal infants ranged between .88 and .90 while test-retest reliability for a severely handicapped sample ranged between .96 and .99. Interjudge reliability between 20 mothers and fathers ranged between .85 and .95. For a sample of 112 severely handicapped children interjudge correlations between caregivers familiar with the child (parents or nonrelative adults) ranged between .95 and .99.

The few concurrent validity studies on the KID show encouraging results. In a sample of 38 normal children, developmental ages estimated from the total KID Scale and the Bayley Scales of Infant Development were similar and 60% of the correlations between the two instruments were higher than .70. On a sample of 121 severely handicapped children the full scale score of the KID yielded a validity coefficient of .86 with the Bayley Scales of Infant Development. This concurrent validity is especially good considering the Bayley is a set of behavior performance items administered by an unfamiliar tester while the KID is a caregiver report measure.

Finally, predictive validity on a sample of 30 normal children indicated that the KID measure administered at 1 year was correlated .32 with the Minnesota Child Development Inventory administered at 4 years. While this relationship is not high and only accounts for 10% of the variance, it is within an adequate range considering the large time interval between testing and the apparent lack of predictive power of other measures from infancy to childhood (Lewis & Starr, 1979).

Overall, and especially in regard to tracking the growth of handicapped children within the first year of mental development, the KID appears to be a good, reliable, and valid instrument. The full scale KID Scale can serve as a good general index of developmental level. The individual scales of cognitive, motor, social, language, and self help have face validity but have not been shown to have sufficient psychometric differentiation from each other to be used as separate indices of particular skills.

REVIEWER'S REFERENCES

Lewis, M., & Starr, M. D. Developmental continuity. In J. Osofsky (Ed.), HANDBOOK OF INFANT DEVELOPMENT. New York: Wiley, 1979.

[568]

Kerby Learning Modality Test, Revised 1980. Ages 5, 6–8, 8–11; 1978–80; KLMT; diagnostic test for screening of perceptual modality functioning; 13 scores: visual (discrimination, memory, closure, motor coordination, total), auditory (discrimination, memory, closure, motor coordination, total), motor (visual, auditory, total); 1 form; 3 levels: kindergarten ('80, 11 pages), primary ('80, 15 pages), intermediate ('80, 14 pages); manual ('80, 39 pages plus tests, answer sheet, record sheet and scoring keys); separate answer sheets must be used with intermediate level only; 1983 price data: $69.80 per complete set including 10 tests of each level; $22.60–$27.80 per kit including 10 tests of any one level; $5.90 per 10 kindergarten test booklets; $6.10 per 10 primary test booklets; $6.10 per 10 reuseable intermediate test booklets; $2.35 per set of primary scoring keys; $5.80 per set of intermediate scoring keys; $9.50 per 100 answer sheets; $9.80 per tape cassette for each level; $9.50 per 100 record sheets; $7.20 per manual; (25–45) minutes; Maude L. Kerby; Western Psychological Services.*

Review of Kerby Learning Modality Test, Revised 1980, by THOMAS J. KEHLE, Professor and Director of School Psychology, and NICKI N. OSTROM, Research Associate, Department of Educational Psychology, University of Utah, Salt Lake City, UT:

The Kerby Learning Modality Test (KLMT) is a group screening test which purports to measure strengths and weaknesses in the perceptual modalities of vision, hearing, and motor activity. The intent is to identify children's "modality preferences" and perceptual learning disabilities. The terms "perceptual modality" and "learning modality" are used interchangeably because it is assumed that learning must take place through the perceptual channels. The three forms of the test are designed to be administered, scored, and interpreted by the regular classroom teacher. Recommendations are included in the manual for remedial activities and for teaching to modality preferences.

The design and interpretation of the KLMT rest upon definitions of learning disability which stress perceptual processing deficits. However, the conceptualization of learning disability upon which the test is based is neither clearly articulated nor critically discussed in the test manual. Potential users of the KLMT should be aware that definitions and diagnostic approaches to learning disability stressing perceptual process deficits are controversial. Further, studies of the effectiveness of remedial activities which focus upon perceptual process deficits rather than upon academic skills have yielded widely disparate results with learning disabled children. The single, unpublished study reported briefly in the KLMT manual of the efficacy of KLMT-based remedial activities suffers from a small number of subjects, inadequate description of design and analysis, and does not provide sufficient information to justify adoption of the recommended remedial activities. No evidence is presented to justify recommendations for teaching to perceptual modality preferences.

The KLMT interpretation guidelines for teachers outlined in the manual suggest that children ages 6 to 11 who score below the 28th percentile on any of the three perceptual modality scores are to be identified as possessing a disability and targeted for referral and remedial activities. Children scoring below the 39th percentile are considered to have a perceptual modality "weakness." The identification of such large numbers of children in regular classrooms as possessing perceptual modality disabilities or weaknesses is justified by the author on the basis of agreement with other selected estimates of the incidence of learning disabilities which place incidence levels at "5% to 25% of the school population." The author also argues that identification of perceptual disability in the underachieving student lessens teacher tension and improves teacher/student rapport to the extent that many students' behavioral and learning problems improve without specific methodological changes. Both justifications would be difficult to substantiate on the basis of thorough literature reviews. In fact, the author cites few references to substantiate them and the literature cited is far from comprehensive.

With regard to the potentially large proportion of children identified as disabled when tested with the KLMT, several inconsistencies are noted. While the manual states that children ages 6 to 11 scoring below the 28th percentile on any of the three perceptual modality scores should be considered disabled, only 25% of the 1975 standardization sample was identified as disabled. It is also stated in the manual that 8–23% of the children in various age groups in the normative sample showed some disability as identified by the KLMT. The lack of agreement between interpretive guidelines and reported incidence in the standardization sample is not explained. An additional norm table provided for sixth graders (12-year-olds), not included in the standardization sample, adds to concerns regarding incidence levels. According to the manual, of 43 children comprising a sample of sixth-grade public school children "typical of the U.S. population," 52% were found to have a perceptual modality disability on the KLMT, and 40% of these 43 children had both a perceptual modality disability and a "scholastic disability" as well. The value of a screening instrument which finds at least 28% of all children tested to have a perceptual modality disability is, to say the least, questionable.

The KLMT is described as a diagnostic, as well as a screening, test. However, several questions must be raised with regard to what the test is diagnosing. Perceptual processing tasks involve cognitive activity and correlate with general intelligence to varying degrees. No studies are reported in the manual which examined the diagnostic validity of the KLMT when controlling for individual differences in intelligence. This is a most serious deficiency. According to the manual, the IQ range of children included in the standardization sample was 75 to 137, and children with "below average IQs" were eliminated from the sample. Thus, IQs falling between 75–137 were considered to be at least average. However, this is an exceptionally wide range of IQs, spanning about four standard deviations and including approximately 95% of the total population. Individuals with IQs in this range will demonstrate extreme differences in intellectual performance. Subtests, particularly at the kindergarten level of the KLMT, which require the identification of similarities and differences, may be expected to draw upon reasoning skills and thus reflect general intelligence to some extent. An analysis of the relationship between IQ scores, KLMT performance, and academic achievement should be an essential component of the effort to determine whether the KLMT actually measures and isolates perceptual processing deficits, as the test manual claims.

Test-retest reliability was based on Spearman rank order correlation coefficients on relatively small numbers of kindergarten ($N=71$), primary ($N=57$), and intermediate level ($N=59$) children. The total group coefficients reported are quite high, ranging from .89 to .97. Similarly, alternate-form reliability was based on a small sample ($N=56$) but evidenced comparably high coefficients. Alternate forms were also evaluated after a 2-year interval. The correlations were moderate to high, but were based on unacceptably small sample sizes ($N=23$). The standard error of measurement is not defined; consequently, confidence intervals cannot be established.

Several unpublished studies of criterion-related and construct validity are reported in the KLMT manual. No information is reported regarding predictive validity. Attempts to demonstrate that the KLMT in fact measures specific perceptual modality functions are unconvincing. While the test author has made rather extensive efforts to provide validity information, a critical reading of the studies reported is difficult because the statistical techniques and other technical information are often omitted. For example, to test the hypothesis that low auditory modality scores were related to poor reading achievement, the standardized achievement test scores of students having KLMT disabilities were compared with national achievement test norms. According to the manual, "Results seemed to show that" specific modality disabilities were related to poorer performance in expected achievement areas. However, detailed information is not reported regarding the statistical tests employed, the size of the effect, the number and age of subjects, etc. Other validity studies suffer from small sample sizes, imprecise study design, and amateurish techniques. For example, the criterion validity of the KLMT is defined by the author as percent of agreement with clinic or psychologist's diagnoses of a reported *N* of 74 children who were presumably referred for evaluation of suspected learning disabilities. Using this procedure, 82% agreement was noted between the KLMT and clinic or psychologist's diagnoses with respect to specific type of modality disability. Similarly, agreement between an indication of a KLMT disability and placement in remedial reading classes was noted to be 76% on the basis of a total *N* of 38.

The kindergarten KLMT was compared to the Slingerland Screening Tests by converting the children's scores to percentile ranks on both instruments and calculating the Spearman rank order correlation. These correlations were .99 for the visual and auditory subtests, and .98 for the motor subtests. The author attributes these high correlations to the fact that the same modalities were tested by both instruments and that both instruments were normed on the same populations. The author fails to note that these correlations are somewhat greater than the reported test-retest reliability coefficients.

In summary, the basic premise of the KLMT rests on the assumption that certain children with normal cognitive ability markedly underachieve in academic areas due to deficits in visual, auditory, or kinesthetic perceptual modalities. The author argues that the 15-minute administration of the KLMT will adequately identify the offending modality and consequent teaching strategies can be designed and employed to attenuate the deficit.

There is no evidence presented to ensure that the KLMT was in fact measuring perceptual modalities. It is reasonable to assume, on the basis of the item content of the KLMT, that the instrument measures varying degrees of general cognitive ability. In addition, inadequate evidence is presented to support the efficacy of instructional strategies derived from KLMT data. The lack of sensitivity to appropriate methodology and reporting procedures regarding reliability and validity further adds to serious reservations regarding the instrument's utility.

In the reviewers' opinion, the numerous problems inherent in the rationale and development of the KLMT preclude its use as an effective diagnostic screening inventory.

[569]

Khatena-Torrance Creative Perception Inventory. Ages 12 and over; 1976; 13 scores: creative perception index (2 scores), environmental sensitivity, initiative, self-strength, intellectuality, individuality, artistry, acceptance of authority, self-confidence, inquisitiveness, awareness of others, disciplined imagination; 1 form, 2 tests: What Kind of Person Are You? (WKOPAY), Something About Myself (SAM), (2 pages); manual (71 pages); scoring worksheet (2 pages); 1984 price data: $42 per complete set including 30 copies of each test and scoring worksheets; $24.75 per 30 copies of each test and scoring worksheets; $24.75 per manual; (10–30) minutes; Joe Khatena and E. Paul Torrance; Stoelting Co.*

TEST REFERENCES

1. Raina, M. K., & Vats, A. Creativity teaching style and pupil control. GIFTED CHILD QUARTERLY, 1979, 23, 807–811.
2. Clements, R. D., Dwinell, P. L., Torrance, E. P., & Kidd, J. T. Evaluation of some of the effects of a teen drama program on creativity. THE JOURNAL OF CREATIVE BEHAVIOR, 1982, 16, 272–276.
3. Tindall, J. H., Houtz, J. C., Hausler, R., & Heimowitz, S. Processes of creative problem solvers in groups. SMALL GROUP BEHAVIOR, 1982, 13, 109–116.

Review of Khatena-Torrance Creative Perception Inventory by PHILIP E. VERNON, Professor of Educational Psychology, University of Calgary, Calgary, Alberta, Canada:

Both Torrance and Khatena are prolific contributors to the study of creativity in normal children, college students, and adults (as distinct from the highly talented). They are authors of several tests in this area, the best known being the Torrance Tests of Creative Thinking. The Khatena-Torrance Creative Perception Inventory (KTCPI) consists of two separate tests of creative self-perceptions: What Kind of Person Are You (WKOPAY) and Something About Myself (SAM). These two new tests consist of paper and pencil inventories, "based upon the rationale that creative functioning is reflected in the personality characteristics of the individual." Biographical questionnaires, dealing largely with childhood and adolescent interests and other background data, have yielded promising results (e.g., Anastasi and Schaefer's test). But the present instruments call more for self-assessments. The authors have surveyed the literature and come up with several personality characteristics which have been found to differentiate between more and less creative persons. These characteristics have been turned into 50 pairs of traits in the WKOPAY, e.g., "Which best describes you?—(*a*) Imaginative, (*b*) Critical." One member of each pair has been judged to relate more to the creative personality than the other. As in most forced-choice instruments, many subjects may find the choices unreal, since they cannot answer merely on the basis of social desirability. The second test, SAM, also contains 50 items; but these are simply statements about the subject's personality which have to be accepted or rejected as true. Each test can be answered in about 5 to 15 minutes, and there are no time limits. They can be hand-scored quite quickly. The tests have been used with children down to 10 years, but are mainly designed for adolescents and adults.

As well as the total scores or Creative Perception Indices, both sets of items have been factor analyzed to yield 5 and 6 clusters of items, which provide subscores for such traits as Self-confidence and Intellectuality. The various clusters are made up of 5 to 12 items; hence some of them must be low in internal consistency. But in fact no uses are suggested for these scores (e.g., for personality diagnosis), so it is difficult to see their purpose.

Both the total and cluster raw scores can be converted to standard scores with a mean of 5 and a standard deviation of 1. There seems to be little or no change with age in these scores, and most sex differences are small. Hence the same norms are used for adolescent and adult males and females.

It is somewhat surprising to find the standard scores on 3 of the 11 clusters ranging only from 6 to 3, indicating that the raw score distributions must have been rather far from normal. Since the correlations between the factor scores of SAM are mostly quite low, this would suggest poor internal consistency for the total scores. Actually, when the SAM is given to adolescents, the median item-total correlation is only .29, though for adults the figure is higher (.38). Nevertheless the authors claim very high internal consistencies for the total scores, and even retest reliabilities averaging .86 over 1- to 4-week time intervals. As the scoring is objective, there is no problem of marker unreliability.

The appendix to the manual gives 36 tables of norms, reliabilities, correlations with other tests, etc. As evidence for the content validity of their tests, the authors submit that this was ensured by choosing items derived from previous research. However, this does not guarantee that the particular item-pairs or statements, as printed in the tests, are equally valid. The logical makeup of the item factors or clusters is put forward as an argument for construct validity. But this is doubtful, since the stronger the subfactors, the lower must be reliabilities of the Creativity Indices.

Support for criterion-related validity is mainly based on numerous positive correlations found with other creativity tests. But as several of the tests referred to are quite unfamiliar, their names are of little help in evaluating validity. Also, most of the tests likewise involve self-report questions; hence positive intercorrelations are only to be expected. As Campbell and Fiske pointed out 25 years ago, correlations in the personality area between different traits measured by the same method (e.g., questionnaires) are apt to be higher than correlations between the same trait measured by different methods. A few of Khatena and Torrance's correlations range up to .75, but many others are relatively low. More acceptable as evidence (since it comprises different methods) are the correlations with the Torrance Tests of Creative Thinking. The WKOPAY gives a coefficient of .57 for males, though only .33 for females. WKOPAY and SAM themselves correlate .46 and .60 in two groups of students.

As in any personality questionnaire, our answers depend more on our own self-concepts of our traits, and on their social desirability, than on our actual behavior as observed by others. Hence the correlations between supposedly different self-report tests are largely determined by whether we interpret the tests as measuring the same, or different, traits. Thus it is unfortunate that the manual for the two tests tells the subjects that they will be "given the chance to see how creative they are." This will naturally reinforce the tendency to answer the items according to their conception of their own creativity. The SAM is also poorly designed in that all the items are worded in the same direction, so that the total score is just the sum of items accepted. Obviously this will be affected by the acquiescence response set. And some subjects are likely to guess that all items are meant to describe creativity and can therefore raise their scores as high as they like.

More solid grounds for claiming validity seem to be provided by the mean scores of different groups. Thus among ordinary elementary school teachers the mean WKOPAY score was 21.6. In groups of teachers attending classes in creativity and also among parents of gifted children, the means reached 35 (standard deviations around 7.0). However, the interpretation of this finding is ambiguous since such subjects are very likely to regard themselves as highly creative. Moreover, the teachers may have already been taught something about the traits of creative persons, and will therefore be able to boost their scores.

In conclusion, the two tests have the same advantages, such as ease of application, scoring, and norming, as any self-report personality test; but also show the same weaknesses in a rather high degree. They are probably inferior to autobiographical inventories, whose items have been empirically validated, and which depend more on memory for facts than on self-judgments. The construction of both tests is open to some criticism, and the available data on validity is unconvincing. One would agree with the authors that the tests could be useful in classes for teachers of gifted children, where they could be applied, and then scored and discussed by the students themselves. Also, the authors show that they are aware of some of the limitations of the tests by refering to them, in the manual, as a "Research Edition."

[570]

Kindergarten Language Screening Test. Grade K; 1978–83; KLST; norms consist of means and standard deviations; individual; 1 form; test form ('78, 4 pages); manual ('83, 16 pages including test); 1984 price data: $29.95 per test kit including manual and 40 test forms; $6.95 per 40 test forms; (10) minutes; Sharon V. Gauthier and Charles L. Madison; C.C. Publications, Inc.*

[571]

Kipnis-Schmidt Profiles of Organizational Influence Strategies. Organizational members; 1982; POIS; 6 or 7 scale scores (friendliness, bargaining, reason, assertiveness, sanctions [Form S only], higher authority, coalition) for each of 2 areas: first attempt to influence, second attempt to influence after resistance; Forms M (Influencing Your Manager), S (Influencing Your Subordinates), C (Influencing Your Co-Workers), (14 pages); trainer's manual (17 pages); respondent's guide (9 pages); 1984 price data: $45 per 10 tests; $45 per 10 respondent's guides; $55 per specimen set containing one of each form, respondent's guide, and trainer's manual; (20–30) minutes; David Kipnis and Stuart M. Schmidt; University Associates, Inc.*

[572]

Kit of Factor Referenced Cognitive Tests. Various grades 6–16; 1954–78; formerly called the Kit of Reference Tests for Cognitive Factors; for research use only; 72 factor-referenced cognitive tests; guide ('78, 114 pages); manual ('76, 227 pages); 1985 price data: $30 per complete set including tests and manual; $20 per tests; $10 per manual; tests compiled and manual written by Ruth B. Ekstrom, John W. French, Harry H. Harman, and Diran Dermen; Educational Testing Service.*

a) FACTOR CF: FLEXIBILITY OF CLOSURE.
1) *Hidden Figures Test.*
2) *Hidden Patterns Test.*
3) *Copying Test.*

b) FACTOR CS: SPEED OF CLOSURE.
1) *Gestalt Completion Test.*
2) *Concealed Words Test.*
3) *Snowy Pictures.*

c) FACTOR CV: VERBAL CLOSURE.
1) *Scrambled Words.*
2) *Hidden Words.*
3) *Incomplete Words.*

d) FACTOR FA: ASSOCIATIONAL FLUENCY.
1) *Controlled Associations Test.*
2) *Opposites Test.*
3) *Figures of Speech.*

e) FACTOR FE: EXPRESSIONAL FLUENCY.
1) *Making Sentences.*
2) *Arranging Words.*
3) *Rewriting.*

f) FACTOR FF: FIGURAL FLUENCY.
1) *Ornamentation Test.*
2) *Elaboration Test.*
3) *Symbols Test.*

g) FACTOR FI: IDEATIONAL FLUENCY.
1) *Topics Test.*
2) *Theme Test.*
3) *Thing Categories Test.*

h) FACTOR FW: WORD FLUENCY.
1) *Word Endings Test.*
2) *Word Beginnings Test.*
3) *Word Beginnings and Endings Test.*

i) FACTOR I: INDUCTION.
1) *Letter Sets Test.*
2) *Locations Test.*
3) *Figure Classification.*

j) FACTOR IP: INTEGRATIVE PROCESSES.
1) *Calendar Test.*
2) *Following Directions.*

k) FACTOR MA: MEMORY, ASSOCIATIVE.
1) *Picture—Number Test.*
2) *Object—Number Test.*
3) *First and Last Names Test.*

l) FACTOR MS: MEMORY SPAN.
1) *Auditory Number Span Test.*
2) *Visual Number Span Test.*
3) *Auditory Letter Span Test.*

m) FACTOR MV: MEMORY, VISUAL.
1) *Shape Memory Test.*
2) *Building Memory.*
3) *Map Memory.*

n) FACTOR N: NUMBER FACILITY.
1) *Addition Test.*
2) *Division Test.*
3) *Subtraction and Multiplication Test.*
4) *Addition and Subtraction Correction.*

o) FACTOR P: PERCEPTUAL SPEED.
1) *Finding A's Test.*
2) *Number Comparison Test.*
3) *Identical Pictures Test.*

p) FACTOR RG: REASONING, GENERAL.
1) *Arithmetic Aptitude Test.*
2) *Mathematics Aptitude Test.*
3) *Necessary Arithmetic Operations.*

q) FACTOR RL: REASONING, LOGICAL.
1) *Nonsense Syllogisms Test.*
2) *Diagramming Relationships.*
3) *Inference Test.*
4) *Deciphering Languages.*

r) FACTOR S: SPATIAL ORIENTATION.
1) *Card Rotations Test.*
2) *Cube Comparisons Test.*

s) FACTOR SS: SPATIAL SCANNING.
1) *Maze Tracing Speed Test.*
2) *Choosing a Path.*
3) *Map Planning Test.*

t) FACTOR V: VERBAL COMPREHENSION.
1) *Vocabulary I.*
2) *Vocabulary II.*
3) *Extended Range Vocabulary Test.*
4) *Advanced Vocabulary Test I.*
5) *Advanced Vocabulary Test II.*

u) FACTOR VZ: VISUALIZATION.
1) *Form Board Test.*
2) *Paper Folding Test.*
3) *Surface Development Test.*

v) FACTOR XF: FLEXIBILITY, FIGURAL.
1) *Toothpicks Test.*
2) *Planning Patterns.*
3) *Storage Test.*

w) FACTOR XU: FLEXIBILITY OF USE.
1) *Combining Objects.*
2) *Substitute Uses.*

3) *Making Groups.*
4) *Different Uses.*

See T3:1257 (78 references) and T2:561 (103 references).

TEST REFERENCES

1. Nelson, B. A., & Chavis, G. L. Cognitive style and complex concept acquisition. CONTEMPORARY EDUCATIONAL PSYCHOLOGY, 1977, 2, 91–98.
2. Becker, J. P., & Young, C. D., Jr. Designing instructional methods in mathematics to accommodate different patterns of aptitude. JOURNAL FOR RESEARCH IN MATHEMATICS EDUCATION, 1978, 9, 4–19.
3. Coward, R. T., Davis, J. K., & Wichern, R. L. Cognitive style and perceptions of the ideal teacher. CONTEMPORARY EDUCATIONAL PSYCHOLOGY, 1978, 3, 232–238.
4. Raskin, A., Gershon, S., Crook, T. H., Sathananthan, G., & Ferris, S. The effects of hyperbaric and normobaric oxygen on cognitive impairment in the elderly. ARCHIVES OF GENERAL PSYCHIATRY, 1978, 35, 50–56.
5. Young, C. D., & Becker, J. P. The interaction of cognitive aptitudes with sequences of figural and symbolic treatments of mathematical inequalities. JOURNAL FOR RESEARCH IN MATHEMATICS EDUCATION, 1978, 10, 24–36.
6. Webb, N. L. Processes, conceptual knowledge, and mathematical problem-solving ability. JOURNAL FOR RESEARCH IN MATHEMATICS EDUCATION, 1979, 10, 83–93.
7. MacKenzie, A. J. The effect of training in categorization on free recall: Some implications for Jensen's two-level theory. INTELLIGENCE, 1980, 4, 333–348.
8. McLeod, D. B., & Adams, V. M. Aptitude-treatment interaction in mathematics instruction using expository and discovery methods. JOURNAL FOR RESEARCH IN MATHEMATICS EDUCATION, 1980, 11, 180–234.
9. McLeod, D. B., & Briggs, J. T. Interactions of field independence and general reasoning with inductive instruction in mathematics. JOURNAL FOR RESEARCH IN MATHEMATICS EDUCATION, 1980, 11, 94–103.
10. Witt, S. J., & Cunningham, W. R. Family configuration and fluid/crystallized intelligence. ADOLESCENCE, 1980, 15, 105–121.
11. DuRapau, V. J., Jr., & Carry, L. R. Interaction of general reasoning ability and processing strategies in geometry instruction. JOURNAL FOR RESEARCH IN MATHEMATICS EDUCATION, 1981, 12, 15–26.
12. Magaro, P. A., & Smith, P. The personality of clinical types: An empirically derived taxonomy. JOURNAL OF CLINICAL PSYCHOLOGY, 1981, 37, 796–809.
13. Pijning, H. F. Effective learning strategies in the acquisition of psychomotor skills. INTERNATIONAL JOURNAL OF SPORT PSYCHOLOGY, 1981, 12, 183–195.
14. Guttman, R., & Shoham, I. The structure of spatial ability items: A faceted analysis. PERCEPTUAL AND MOTOR SKILLS, 1982, 54, 487–493.
15. Hertzog, C., & Carter, L. Sex differences in the structure of intelligence: A confirmatory factor analysis. INTELLIGENCE, 1982, 6, 287–303.
16. Kellerman, J. M., & Laird, J. D. The effect of appearance on self-perceptions. JOURNAL OF PERSONALITY, 1982, 50, 296–315.
17. Kerr, N. H., Foulkes, D., & Schmidt, M. The structure of laboratory dream reports in blind and sighted subjects. THE JOURNAL OF NERVOUS AND MENTAL DISEASE, 1982, 170, 286–294.
18. Mitchell, J. L., & Drewes, A. A. The rainbow experiment. JOURNAL OF THE AMERICAN SOCIETY FOR PSYCHICAL RESEARCH, 1982, 76, 198–215.
19. Parkes, K. R. Field dependence and the factor structure of the General Health Questionnaire in normal subjects. BRITISH JOURNAL OF PSYCHIATRY, 1982, 140, 392–400.
20. Simon, E. W., Dixon, R. A., Nowak, C. A., & Hultsch, D. F. Orienting task effects on text recall in adulthood. JOURNAL OF GERONTOLOGY, 1982, 37, 575–580.
21. Bouma, A., & Ippel, M. J. Individual differences in mode of processing in visual asymmetry tasks. CORTEX, 1983, 19, 51–67.
22. Frank, B. M. Flexibility of information processing and the memory of field-independent and field-dependent learners. JOURNAL OF RESEARCH IN PERSONALITY, 1983, 17, 89–96.
23. Harshman, R. A., Hampson, E., & Berenbaum, S. A. Individual differences in cognitive abilities and brain organization, Part 1: Sex and handedness differences in ability. CANADIAN JOURNAL OF PSYCHOLOGY, 1983, 37, 144–192.
24. Owens, W., & Limber, J. Lateral eye movement as a measure of cognitive ability and style. PERCEPTUAL AND MOTOR SKILLS, 1983, 56, 711–719.
25. Thomas, C. R. Field independence and Myers-Briggs thinking individuals. PERCEPTUAL AND MOTOR SKILLS, 1983, 57, 790.
26. Yeo, R. A., & Cohen, D. B. Familial sinistrality and sex differences in cognitive abilities. CORTEX, 1983, 19, 125–130.
27. Mueller, J. H., Heesacker, M., & Ross, M. J. Likability of targets and distractors in facial recognition. AMERICAN JOURNAL OF PSYCHOLOGY, 1984, 97, 235–247.

[573]

Knowledge and Attitudes of Drug Usage. Grades 4–6, 7–12; 1973; "an IOX measureable objectives collection"; utilizes knowledge, direct report, indirect, archival, observation, and planning information measures; no data on reliability and validity; no norms; 2 levels; manual (108 pages, includes all items necessary for administration); 1983 price data: $10.95 per manual; IOX Assessment Associates.*

a) INTERMEDIATE LEVEL. Grades 4–6; 4 objectives: drug experience, school description check list, life decisions, facts about drugs (2 alternate forms), plus basis of belief measure; (10–30) minutes per objective.

b) SECONDARY LEVEL. Grades 7–12; 8 objectives: drug use inventory (personal opinions), drug experience, school description check list, problems—problems, life decisions, facts about drugs (2 alternate forms), teacher observation form, community drug report, plus basis of belief measure; (10–30) minutes per objective.

Review of Knowledge and Attitudes of Drug Usage by GARY W. LAWSON, Associate Professor of Psychology, Director of Doctoral Studies in Chemical Dependency, School of Human Behavior, United States International University, San Diego, CA:

The Knowledge and Attitudes of Drug Usage 4–12 is a 108-page booklet consisting of 12 objectives and a variety of 12 measures designed to assess the attainment of the listed objectives. The objectives consist of two groups divided by grade level (grades 7 through 12 and grades 4 through 6) and subdivided into Direct Measures, Indirect Measures, Knowledge of Drugs, Observation Measures, and planning information. All of these were designed to gather data about drug availability, usage, and student attitudes about drug use in a given school population.

The major problem with this material is that it assumes that the teacher or school system already has a plan to achieve the objectives. It appears to be the last half of a drug education curriculum where no first half exists. For a review of a complete program see DiCiccio et al. (1984). The people who wrote the material seem to know a great deal about writing and measuring objectives and very little about drugs, drug use, and school systems. There are also no normative data, and no reliability and validity data. However, the manual does mention an attempt to achieve content validity by having a consultant review the content for accuracy.

Field testing for the measures was done on a "small sample of subjects." The manual did not mention sample size or demographics. The field tests were apparently done for the establishment of time requisites for test administration.

Several of the measures are similar to the Adolescent Alcohol Involvement Scale, a scale that was recently reviewed. The reviewers of this scale suggested that the scale not be used until it is revised to ensure that individual items as well as the scale produce meaningful results (Riley & Klockars, 1984).

Because the measures in this booklet are to be done anonymously and used to gather group rather than individual information, no such recommendation will be made for them. However, because of a lack of information on score interpretation, any conclusions based on the use of these measures should be tempered with caution. For example, on one measure the manual says that "a high score on this measure is interpreted as one indicating a high predisposition to use of legal drugs," yet it fails to mention what score would be considered high.

In the final analysis the Knowledge and Attitudes of Drug Usage 4–12 may be somewhat useful as a pre-post measure for those who have a plan or the skills to write a plan to achieve the listed objectives. However, it could be assumed that such a person or persons would also have the skills and knowledge to write their own more personalized objectives and measures of those objectives. Without some additional information on how to achieve the 12 objectives and on how to respond to the data after it is collected, and without some normative data for comparison, this material will not be widely used or particularly useful.

REVIEWER'S REFERENCES

DiCicco, L., Biron, R., Carifio, J., Deutsch, C., Mills, D. J., Orenstein, A., Re, A., Unterberger, H., & White, R. E. Evaluation of the CASPAR Alcohol Education Curriculum. JOURNAL OF STUDIES ON ALCOHOL, 1984, 45, 160–169.

Riley, K., & Klockars, A. J. A critical reexamination of the Adolescent Alcohol Involvement Scale. JOURNAL OF STUDIES ON ALCOHOL, 1984, 45, 184–187.

Review of Knowledge and Attitudes of Drug Usage by BARRIE G. STACEY, Senior Lecturer in Psychology, University of Canterbury, Christchurch 1, New Zealand:

The manual provides a set of measures which could be used by school personnel to obtain "a comprehensive picture of the drug use incidence in their particular area." The word "drug" refers to alcohol, tobacco, medically prescribed drugs, illegal drugs, and solvents (used as drugs). The authors intend school personnel to select those measures, or items drawn from measures, that meet their instruction or evaluation needs. The emphasis is upon user flexibility. For example, if a user is not concerned with "Life Decisions," this measure may be omitted from the set. Or if a user does not consider alcohol to be a problem, items dealing with alcohol may be deleted from the measures. The authors hope that such flexibility will make the set useful to persons of diverse moral persuasions. They suggest that the set could be used to evaluate school drug education programs.

The measures were produced for two age ranges: school grades 4 through 6 (intermediate level), and grades 7 through 12 (secondary level). They can be grouped into several categories: (*a*) knowledge measures which assess information possessed by the respondent, (*b*) direct report measures about drug usage in the respondent's social milieu, (*c*) an indirect measure indicating the respondent's tendency to deal with situations by using a legal drug, (*d*) an archival measure which requires a school staff member to gather data on local drug-related problems, (*e*) an observation measure which requires teachers to cooperate in observing and recording drug activities among their pupils, and (*f*) a planning information measure based upon school pupils rating the credibility of various sources of drug information. Because frank answers to certain items carry legal penalties, the authors emphasize the need for complete anonymity in administration so that a given answer sheet cannot be traced to a particular person. They also believe anonymity will tend to counteract the faking of answers by respondents. They provide directions for the administration and scoring of each measure. The various scoring procedures are uncomplicated.

The account of the development of this set of measures is vague and uninformative. The authors made use of published research and local sources of drug information. They employed specialist consultants to review the accuracy of the substantive information conveyed by the measures in an attempt to achieve content validity. They asserted "the validity question is primarily one of content accuracy." Beyond this the authors are unconcerned with the reliability and validity of the measures. They do not present the results of their field testing on "a small sample of subjects." The "wariness of school personnel" in taking responsibility for administering the set of measures is mentioned without being discussed. Guidelines for the interpretation of measure results are presented, but are completely inadequate. It is difficult to avoid the impression that the authors expect school personnel to undertake further developmental work on this set of measures, including their administration to samples of subjects for purposes of local standardization.

In terms of the conventional criteria utilized in the evaluation of tests and measures, the manual, which includes the set of measures, is completely inadequate. The authors stated that further field studies would be undertaken and that "desirable revisions" would be performed. It would have been preferable for them to have undertaken further studies and produced a manual that met higher professional standards before publishing their set of measures. At present the set appears to be of little practical value. In the reviewer's judgment, it places an unrealistic burden on school personnel who may want to use it, especially with reference to the interpretation of measure scores. Further, the manual directions may encourage naive school personnel to interpret mechanically the measure scores on the basis of idiosyncratic notions.

[574]

Knox's Cube Test. Ages 3–8, 9 and over; 1980; KCT; non-verbal mental test; attention span and short-term memory; no data on reliability and validity; norms for ages 3–18 only; individual; 2 levels labeled Junior Test Form, Senior Test Form, (3 pages); manual (53 pages); 1982 price data: $23 per complete set including 15 tests (specify level); $5.75 per 15 tests (specify level); $11 per KCT blocks; $8.75 per manual; administration time not reported; Mark H. Stone and Benjamin D. Wright; Stoelting Co.*

TEST REFERENCES

1. Stenner, A. J., & Smith, M., III. Testing construct theories. PERCEPTUAL AND MOTOR SKILLS, 1982, 55, 415–426.

2. Stone, M. H., & Wright, B. D. Measuring attending behavior and short-term memory with Knox's Cube Test. EDUCATIONAL AND PSYCHOLOGICAL MEASUREMENT, 1983, 43, 803–814.

Review of Knox's Cube Test by RAYMOND S. DEAN, Director of Neuropsychological Assessment Laboratory and Assistant Professor of Medical Psychology, Washington University School of Medicine, St. Louis, MO:

Knox's Cube Test represents the latest of several versions of a measure first introduced by Knox in 1914. Originally intended as a non-verbal test of mental ability, it is purported to measure "attention span and short-term memory which are independent of language development and educational exposure." Such a statement may be somewhat misleading, since the test is one of visual short-term memory for spatial location, not short-term memory in isolation. Moreover, short-term memory in general becomes more difficult to assess by a single method or material after preadolescence (Dean, 1982), a fact which is evident in the score x age curves presented in the manual. This fact may also be seen in numerous investigations which have offered data indicative of decreasing intercorrelations between memory tests with increasing age to adulthood (e.g., Reed & Reitan, 1963). Also, since most tests measure attention, and since there is no mechanism to separate memory and attention, individual examination of either seems difficult. In this same context, some data exist which indicate that performance on cube imitation tasks may be adversely affected by higher levels of anxiety (e.g., Sterne, 1966).

The materials consist of 4 one-inch black cubes which are affixed to a naturally finished strip of wood. After the examiner has tapped out one of 26 prearranged patterns, the subject must attempt to imitate the order in which blocks were originally tapped. A Junior Test Form (ages two through eight years) and a Senior Test Form (nine years and above) of the measure are available. Although these separate forms are offered, they differ only in the point at which the examiner begins to administer the 26 items. Although it is not stated in the manual, the administration should not exceed 15 minutes. The simplicity of administration and non-verbal response requirements have always been major attributes of such cube imitation tests. As such, the test has appeal in examining subjects with impaired verbal and motor abilities.

In what amounts to a non-verbal memory span task, the total number of correct and incorrect attempts are summed after five consecutive failures. These scores are interpolated for "median taps," "median reverses," "median distances," and a normative age equivalent in whole years. The layout of the consumable four-page protocol and scoring are appalling. If the examiner has the fortitude to learn the rather obscure data manipulation system, it becomes evident that the subject's performance may only be compared to a simple whole year age equivalent score. Although four examples are reported in the manual, how one interprets the results beyond the age equivalent score and error type is not clear. Moreover, a ceiling exists at age 18 years or when 16 correct items is reached. With numerous investigations showing a substantial relationship between age and performance on measures of cortical functioning for older (> 50 years), healthy adults (Reitan, 1956; Vega & Parsons, 1967), the interpretation of this instrument for older adults suspected of cognitive dysfunction is tenuous at best. In sum, with little reference data by which an individual can be compared, the measure may be more heuristically viewed as a clinical procedure.

The choice of items and the "normative information" reported comes about through an integration of the data derived from past versions of the test using the Rasch (1960) method. While I am not as enamored as the authors with the assumptions which must be made to utilize the Rasch model, the compilation of data gleaned from past versions, in which materials and procedures differ, represents a major concern. Although Rasch (1960) may well offer a systematic method of initial item selection, this does not reduce the necessity for formal investigations which examine the stability of scores and at least the concurrent relationship with other measures purporting to measure similar constructs. How this specific version of the Knox Cube Test relates to outside criteria is not broached in any significant manner.

The inability to determine standard score equivalents offers a major obstacle to comparison with specific measures of short-term memory in other modalities and hence poses difficulties in interpretation. Obviously, better standardization with a normal population is needed. Unfortunately, much of the data one would wish to have at hand in considering this test are not available in the manual. Such features as sex differences, reliability of finished test, and the correlation of this version with other forms are among the most obvious problems. For example, if in fact this is a measure of mental ability, it would be useful to show how the results of this test relate to measures of intelligence, ability, short-term memory, and the like. As it stands now, one has no idea how the Rasch method of "calibrating" items on an ability continuum holds up under realistic testing. Although Babcock's and Levinson's versions of this test are not without difficulties, I find them to be superior from a standardization point of view to the present adaptation. Frankly, it is not clear why this version was developed other than the fact that "even Babcock's version is 15 years old." If the authors are correct and the ability as measured by prior versions of this test does not change over time, then it is hard to understand why the authors have gone to such elaborate lengths to revise this test.

On balance, the Rasch (1960) method and the authors' (Wright & Stone, 1979) interpretation of it represent a viable method of defining difficulty parameters of items to be included in a single test. However, although this methodology may be useful in defining a difficult vector of items, further information is necessary to meet minimum standards of test usage. Without these data, the test user is placed in a quagmire of data on prior versions of the test which may or may not be helpful in interpreting the scores resulting from this form of the test. It is difficult to recommend use of this test for other than experimental purposes. While the measure may have utility in defining short-term visual memory for spatial location, this has not been shown in the manual or references provided.

REVIEWER'S REFERENCES

Reitan, R. M. The relationship of the Halstead Impairment Index and the Wechsler-Bellevue total weighted score to chronologic age. JOURNAL OF GERONTOLOGY, 1956, 11, 447–481.

Rasch, G. PROBABILISTIC MODELS FOR SOME INTELLIGENCE AND ATTAINMENT TESTS. Copenhagen: Danmarks Paedogogiske Institute, 1960.

Reed, H. B. C., & Reitan, R. M. A comparison of the effects of the normal aging process with the effects of organic brain damage on adaptive abilities. JOURNAL OF GERONTOLOGY, 1963, 18, 177–179.

Sterne, D. M. The Knox Cubes as a test of memory and intelligence with male adults. JOURNAL OF CLINICAL PSYCHOLOGY, 1966, 22, 191–193.

Vega, A., & Parsons, O. A. Cross-validation of Halstead-Reitan tests for brain damage. JOURNAL OF CONSULTING PSYCHOLOGY, 1967, 31, 619–625.

Dean, R. S. Neuropsychological Assessment. In T. Kratochwill (Ed.), ADVANCES IN SCHOOL PSYCHOLOGY—VOL II. New Jersey: Lawrence Erlbaum, Inc., 1982.

Review of Knox's Cube Test by JEROME M. SATTLER, Professor of Psychology, San Diego State University, San Diego, CA:

Tapping procedures have long been used to measure attention and short-term memory. As early as 1914, Knox developed a tapping test to measure the mental ability of immigrants. Other psychologists including Pintner, Patterson, Yerkes, Drever, Collins, Arthur, Amoss, Goodenough, and Babcock were soon to follow in developing versions of the tapping test, named after its founder as Knox's Cube Test. The present version by Stone and Wright is the latest attempt to standardize Knox's Cube Test.

The test is relatively simple to administer. Four 1-inch black cubes are fastened about 1 inch apart to a wooden board. A fifth unattached cube is used by the examiner to tap out various patterns. The patterns range from a 2 cube pattern (e.g., tapping cubes 1 and 3) to an 8 cube pattern (e.g., tapping cubes 3, 1, 2, 4, 3, 2, 1, and 4). Cubes are tapped at the rate of one per second. Credit is given when the examinee reproduces the same pattern as that of the examiner. The physical abilities needed to take the test include adequate vision and some motor control.

There are two forms of the present version of Knox's Cube Test. The Junior Test Form is for ages 2 through 8 years. It contains 16 items that range from a 2- to a 6-cube series. The Senior Test Form is for ages 9 and older and contains 22 items, which range from a 3- to an 8-cube series. Twelve items are common to both forms. Both forms have two practice series, and the test is discontinued after five consecutive failures. The raw score, which is the number of series performed correctly, is transformed to an age norm that ranges from 3 to 18 years.

The norms for Knox's Cube Test are based on the results of all studies with the test from 1915 to 1978 for which age norms were available. The norms were obtained by Rasch scaling procedures. The populations used in the norm group are extremely heterogenous and diverse, including mentally retarded, deaf, middle-class school children, and many subjects whose background is unknown. The failure to use a current representative national sample seriously limits the usefulness of this version of Knox's Cube Test.

A further serious shortcoming in using the test is the failure of the authors to present any information about its reliability or validity. It is inexcusable for both the authors and publishers to allow this potentially useful test to be published without supplying reliability and validity coefficients by age groups.

Other difficulties include the following: (*a*) the manual states that the test is adequate for age 2 years and older, yet the norms begin at age 3 years; (*b*) standard scores that are familiar to most users are not provided, thus again seriously limiting the usefulness of the test; (*c*) on the report form, four types of scores are provided, in addition to age norms: MITs (mastery units), median taps, median reverses, and median distances; again the manual fails to indicate how these scores can be used meaningfully; (*d*) error boundaries are defined as those that are 1 1/2 scores above and below the obtained score. However, the statistical basis for establishing these error boundaries is not described in the manual; and (*e*) no norms are provided for adults.

On the positive side, the manual contains a comprehensive survey of all prior revisions and available data. The authors have also "linked" all prior versions to a common calibrated item bank. Because of this, it is possible to administer earlier versions of the test using the item bank.

There is a need for a well-standardized nonverbal test of short-term memory, but the present version of Knox's Cube Test fails to meet minimally acceptable psychometric standards. Serious inadequacies include the nonrepresentative norm group and the failure to present any reliability or validity coefficients. Future studies could indicate that the norms are adequate and that the test has adequate reliability and validity. However, until such research is available, extreme caution must be used in employing Knox's Cube Test for any decision-making purpose.

[575]

Kohn Problem Checklist. Children ages 3–6 in preschool program; 1979; ratings by teachers or other observers; 2 factor scores: apathy-withdrawal, anger-defiance; no reliability or validity data in manual; individual; 1 form (4 pages, includes rating instructions); combined rating and scoring manual for this and Kohn Social Competence Scale ('79, 38 pages, includes copies of both instruments); scoring form (1 page); 1985 price data: $12.50 per specimen set (including manual and specimen tests); administration time not reported; Martin Kohn, Barbara Parnes, and Bernice L. Rosman; Martin Kohn.*

TEST REFERENCES

1. Kohn, M. The Kohn Social Competence Scale and Kohn Symptom Checklist for the preschool child: A follow-up report. JOURNAL OF ABNORMAL CHILD PSYCHOLOGY, 1977, 5, 249–263.

2. Sprafkin, C., Serbin, L. A., & Elman, M. Sex-typing of play and psychological adjustment in young children: An empirical investigation. JOURNAL OF ABNORMAL CHILD PSYCHOLOGY, 1982, 10, 559–568.

Review of Kohn Problem Checklist by JAMES L. CARROLL, Associate Professor of Educational Psychology, Arizona State University, Tempe, AZ:

The Kohn Problem Checklist (formerly the Kohn Symptom Checklist) consists of 49 problem behaviors that teachers are to use as a basis for rating preschool students. Kohn Problem Checklist (KPC) items were written to describe clinical symptoms which might be displayed in the preschool setting. The present 49-item version of the KPC takes five minutes or less to complete and represents a slight revision of a 58-item scale first used in 1965. For the child's behavior during the preceding week the teacher is instructed to rate each item as "not at all typical" (0), "somewhat typical" (1), or "very typical" (2). Item ratings are then summed for two factor scores. Factor I items (25) are labelled Apathy-Withdrawal and include such items as "Seldom smiles" and "Has an aloof and distant manner." Factor II has 24 items and is labelled Anger-Defiance. Items in this factor include "Seeks attention through rowdy or 'show-off' behavior" and "Says he/she is going to kill himself/herself." The two factors accounted for 51% of the common variance and for 25.5% of the total variance of the initial 58-item KPC.

Interrater reliability coefficients (Spearman-Brown corrected) on four occasions with sample sizes between 496 and 1,110 ranged from .53 to .69 (mean r=.61) for Factor I and from .69 to .83 (mean r=.77) for Factor II. While Factor II ratings appear to have moderate interrater reliability, the Factor I interrater reliability coefficients are marginal. In some presentations (e.g., Kohn, 1977a), the interrater reliabilities between pairs of teachers are reported to be .73 for both factors. This coefficient, however, is for scores "obtained by summing the ratings of all items that were most highly loaded on respective factor dimensions" (Kohn, 1977b). The smaller figures reported above are the better estimate of interrater reliabilities to be obtained by future users of the KPC. Stability coefficients were moderate for ratings by the same teacher in the same setting over a 6-month interval (Factor I r =.60, Factor II r =.73). For 6-, 12-, and 18-month intervals with different teachers and classrooms, stability coefficients for Factor I were .46, .43, and .35 respectively, and for Factor II were .54, .54, and .47 respectively.

Kohn and associates have produced an impressive array of validation studies for the KPC and the Kohn Social Competence Scale (KSCS). Factor I and Factor II scores are highly correlated with corresponding factors on the Kohn Social Competence Scale (r's range from –.69 to –.84), and with factor scores from the Schaefer Classroom Behavior Inventory (Factor I with Factor I, –.81; Factor II with Factor II, –.76). Coefficients for noncorresponding factors of the KPC and KSCS ranged from –.22 to –.38. The difference between corresponding and noncorresponding relationships indicates substantial independence of the two factors of social emotional functioning. Beyond these indications of convergent validity, however, most of the validity results reported by Kohn and associates are for factor scores for the pooled KPC and KSCS. That is, since the Factor I and II items of the KPC are like the negative end of the same factors on the KSCS, Kohn and associates have "generally used both instruments and pooled the respective factor scores for enhanced reliability." For a summary of validation studies for the pooled factor scores, see reviews for the Kohn Social Competence Scale.

The KPC when pooled with the KSCS appears to be a very useful tool for research on the social-emotional functioning of preschool children. Any use of the KPC for screening or treatment planning should be regarded as experimental. At present the interrater reliability of Factor I of the KPC is marginal for such use. No standardization has been attempted, and use of the sample conversion tables in the rating and scoring manual for normative purposes is inappropriate. Kohn recommends construction of local norms, and this recommendation is underscored by large KSCS score differences between a recent Seattle sample and the Kohn sample for which standard scores are reported in the manual (Demers & Skell, 1981). Also, most validation information available for the KPC is inextricably tied to pooled KPC-KSCS factor scores. For screening purposes a unidimensional global impairment rating such as the one used by Kohn as a dependent variable (well functioning=1, moderately-well functioning=2, poorly functioning=3) appears to identify at least as well as the KPC those children in need of further individual assessment. In any case, those further individual results rather than the screening data should be the basis for preventive or remedial intervention.

REVIEWER'S REFERENCES

Kohn, M. The Kohn Social Competence Scale and Kohn Symptom Checklist for the preschool child: A follow-up report. JOURNAL OF ABNORMAL CHILD PSYCHOLOGY, 1977, 5(3), 249–263. (a)

Kohn, M. SOCIAL COMPETENCE, SYMPTOMS AND UNDERACHIEVEMENT IN CHILDHOOD: A LONGITUDINAL PERSPECTIVE. Washington, DC: Winston-Wiley, 1977. (b)

Demers, R. Y., & Skell, R. Mean scores for Kohn Social Competence found markedly different in two samples. DEVELOPMENTAL PSYCHOLOGY, 1981, 17(4), 463–464.

Review of Kohn Problem Checklist by BERT O. RICHMOND, Professor of Counseling and Human Development Services, University of Georgia, Athens, GA:

A Rating and Scoring Manual for the Kohn Problem Checklist and Kohn Social Competence Scale comes in mimeographed form with a copyright date of 1975 and a revised edition date of 1979. The most recent date of research with the instrument, as cited by the authors, is 1977. The inventory is really three inventories in one: (1) Kohn Problem Checklist, (2) the 73-item Social Competence Scale, and (3) the 64-item Social Competence Scale. This review will focus on the Kohn Problem Checklist.

The Kohn Problem Checklist was developed as part of a research project and contains 49 phrases considered indicative of significant child behavior in a classroom. The scale is to be used with children from 3 to 6 years of age. The rater is asked to base judgment on the child's behavior during the last week and is asked to circle the number (0—not typical, 1—somewhat typical, or 2—very typical) that best describes the child's behavior.

The administration and scoring instructions are clearly presented. The items appear to have some content validity because they are descriptive of typical actions or attitudes of children in the 3- to 6-year age range. Not all of the items are stated in explicit behavioral terms. For example, item 22, "is self-conscious," leaves some question regarding the behavior to be rated.

The manual reports, but provides no data, on a factor analysis of the scale that resulted in two factor scores. Thus, a score for each item is placed in the appropriate factor column resulting in two final factor scores for each child. The factors emerging are labeled: (1) Apathy-Withdrawal, and (2) Anger-Defiance. There is a high correlation between factor scores on the Problem Checklist and the Social Competence scales, so it is possible to pool scores from the two instruments. A conversion chart is provided in the manual to pool factor scores. The authors maintain that the Social Competence Scale is "bi-polar and measures degrees of health as well as degrees of disturbance," whereas the Problem Checklist is "uni-polar and only differentiates disturbance from its absence." Stated correlations of –.75 between factors 1 and of –.79 between factors 2 on the Social Competence Scale and the Problem Checklist belie the notion that they are measuring behaviors very different from one another. The negative correlations simply suggest that the scales are constructed in different ways.

The lack of criterion-related validity in the manual is very evident. The manual also has no data on stability or reliability of the instrument, although the availability of such data is alluded to in separate studies by the authors. The absence of data on factor analysis or other item analysis interpretations is also evident.

Little interpretation of the meaning of high or low factor scores on the Problem Checklist scale is provided. Provisions are made and tables provided for combining both Problem Checklist and Social Competence scores into one score. Similarly, it is recommended that ratings of more than one teacher or observer could be pooled to provide a "more reliable" rating for the child. There is no explanation of mean scores obtained by children of different age, race, sex, or socioeconomic groups.

In summary, this instrument appears to have been developed for a research study by the authors. Explicit directions are provided for administration and scoring. However, the absence of technical, statistical, and psychometric data limits its usefulness. It is packaged in a mimeographed, stapled form that does not facilitate understanding or accessibility. Although the items appear to have been developed with some care and with attention to theoretical considerations, no description of such theoretical development is provided. Sufficient statistical and normative data must be provided for this scale to be useful to professionals who work with children. Data on the size and characteristics of the sample on which the scale was standardized, mean scores, standard deviations, and data on factor scores should be the minimum expected.

[576]

Kohn Social Competence Scale. Children ages 3–6 in half-day, full-day preschool programs; 1979, ratings by teachers or other observers; 2 factor scores: interest-participation versus apathy-withdrawal, cooperation-compliance versus anger-defiance; no reliability or validity data in manual; individual; 2 forms; 2 levels; combined rating and scoring manual for this and Kohn Problem Checklist ('79, 38 pages, includes copies of both instruments); 1985 price data: $12.50 per specimen set (including manual and specimen tests); administration time not reported; Martin Kohn, Barbara Parnes, and Bernice L. Rosman; Martin Kohn.*

a) 73-ITEM SOCIAL COMPETENCE SCALE. Children ages 3–6 in full-day preschool programs; 1 form (6 pages); scoring form (1 page).

b) 64-ITEM SOCIAL COMPETENCE SCALE. Children ages 3–6 in half-day preschool programs; 1 form (5 pages); scoring form (1 page).

TEST REFERENCES

1. Kohn, M. The Kohn Social Competence Scale and Kohn Symptom Checklist for the preschool child: A follow-up report. JOURNAL OF ABNORMAL CHILD PSYCHOLOGY, 1977, 5, 249–263.

2. Humphrey, L. L., & Kirschenbaum, D. S. Self-control and perceived social competence in preschool children. COGNITIVE THERAPY AND RESEARCH, 1981, 5, 373–379.

3. Sprafkin, C., Serbin, L. A., & Elman, M. Sex-typing of play and psychological adjustment in young children: An empirical investigation. JOURNAL OF ABNORMAL CHILD PSYCHOLOGY, 1982, 10, 559–568.

4. Begin, G. Convergent validity of four instruments for teachers' assessing social competence of kindergarten children. PERCEPTUAL AND MOTOR SKILLS, 1983, 57, 1007–1012.

Review of Kohn Social Competence Scale by JAMES L. CARROLL, Associate Professor of Educational Psychology, Arizona State University, Tempe, AZ:

The Kohn Social Competence Scale (KSCS) is a teacher rating measure of children's social functioning in a preschool environment. A 73-item, seven-point rating scale was designed for research with children in full-day preschool programs, and a modified 64-item, five-point rating scale is available for children in half day kindergarten or preschool programs. On either scale the teacher is instructed to rate statements according to frequency of occurrence, (from never to always) during the past week. Items vary in observability and concreteness from "child hits teacher" to "child is quarrelsome."

Teachers can complete either the full-day or half-day rating scale in less than 15 minutes per student. Student scores are then transferred to a scoring form so that factors and valences are appropriately separated. The KSCS yields two factor scores. Factor I is labelled Interest-Participation vs. Apathy-Withdrawal. Positive items for this factor are said to suggest interest, curiosity, and assertiveness, while negative items reflect withdrawal, lack of interest, and failure to elicit peer cooperation (Kohn & Rosman, 1972). Factor II is named Cooperation-Compliance vs. Anger-Defiance. Positive items for this factor indicate living within the classroom structure and complying with teachers' requests. Negative items indicate disturbance of classroom routine and defiance of teacher suggestions. Initially 90 items were selected from a pool of 200 items by factor analysis. Further selection and revision preceded use of the 73-item scale in a large sample, longitudinal study from 1967 through 1971. Using data from a longitudinal study of over 1,200 students enrolled in 90 public day care centers in New York City as well as data from several cross-sectional studies, Kohn (1977) reviewed reliability and validity studies for the KSCS. Reliability coefficients for pairs of teachers averaged .73 for Factor I and .78 for Factor II. The two factors are significantly related (r =.33). Stability coefficients were moderate for ratings by the same teacher in the same setting over a 6-month interval (Factor I r =.66, Factor II r =.75). For 6-, 12-, and 18-month intervals with different teachers and classrooms, stability coefficients for Factor I were .50, .41, and .35 respectively, and for Factor II stability coefficients were .57, .52 and .48 respectively.

Extensive validity data are available for the sample in the New York day care study (Kohn, 1977). In the New York City sample, Kohn found congruence between corresponding factors of the KSCS and factor scores from the Classroom Behavior Inventory of Schaefer and Aaronson. The factors have been shown to be differentially related to achievement during the primary grades (high Apathy-Withdrawal predicts lower academic attainment). Kohn has also reported prediction of behavior ratings over a 5-year span and differentiation between normal and emotionally/behaviorally disordered children. However, the generalizability of those findings has been called into question by Demers and Skell (1981), who compared a Seattle day care sample to the illustrative data in the scoring manual for the KSCS. Scores for the two groups were quite different, with Skell's subjects obtaining the healthier scores. For example, for Factor I the boys in Kohn's sample scored a mean of 7.0, and boys in Skell's study averaged 128.5. For girls, the mean Factor I scores for Kohn's sample was 20.2 and for Skell's sample 135.4. Demers and Skell suggested that differences in teachers in the two systems, and changes in cultural norms since the test was written (1965) and revised (1967) were possible explanations of the differences in scores. They concluded that the differences indicated a need for reevaluation of the KSCS. It should also be noted that validity findings reported to date are for factor scores based on a combination of KSCS and Kohn Problem Checklist (KPC) scores rather than for the KSCS alone. This should not detract from the validation of the factors for theoretical purposes, but may caution researchers to use the procedure Kohn and associates found effective. "In our work we have generally used both instruments and pooled the respective factor scores for enhanced reliability" (Kohn, 1977a).

As Kohn and associates have reported, the KSCS is a useful research measure. In particular, the pooled KSCS/KPC factor scores have been useful in research on the two factor model of social-emotional functioning.

For applied preschool screening purposes Kohn and Rosman (1973) recommended use of a combination of Factor I and Factor II scores for the pooled KSCS and KPC. This results in a rating scale composed of 113 (half-day) or 122 (full-day) items and requiring approximately 20 minutes for rating and approximately 5 minutes for scoring. This scale yields a unidimensional score for which no meaningful norms are available. Kohn recommended that tables provided in the manual be used for illustration only; although the sample is large, it represents only New York City public day care children from 1967 to 1971.

For social-emotional screening purposes a rating of global functioning by preschool teachers appears to predict future functioning as well as the lengthy screening measure. In Kohn's studies, for example, a one-item, 3-point rating of global functioning (1 for well functioning, 2 for moderately-well functioning, or 3 for poorly functioning) was used as a dependent variable. This global rating and a one-item, 2-point referral rating (0=no treatment necessary, 1=in treatment or referral necessary) add significantly to prediction of variance in elementary school global functioning and referral measure (grades 1 through 4 averaged). It is recommended that such brief screens be used so that those who are poorly functioning and/or in treatment or in need of referral will receive more extensive individual assessment. These brief screening items can be applied more often by more observers and are especially to be recommended in preschools where the frequency of social-emotional disturbance may be considerably lower than in Kohn's New York City day care sample.

REVIEWER'S REFERENCES

Kohn, M., & Rosman, B. L. A social competence scale and symptom checklist for the preschool child. DEVELOPMENTAL PSYCHOLOGY, 1972, 6, 430–444.

Kohn, M., & Rosman, B. L. Cross-situational and longitudinal stability of social-emotional functioning in young children. CHILD DEVELOPMENT, 1973, 44, 721–727.

Kohn, M. SOCIAL COMPETENCE, SYMPTOMS, AND UNDERACHIEVEMENT IN CHILDHOOD: A LONGITUDINAL PERSPECTIVE. Washington, DC: Winston-Wiley, 1977. (a)

Kohn, M. The Kohn Social Competence Scale and Kohn Symptom Checklist for the preschool child: A follow-up report. JOURNAL OF ABNORMAL CHILD PSYCHOLOGY, 1977, 5(3), 249–263. (b)

Demers, R. Y., & Skell, R. Mean scores for Kohn Social Competence found markedly different in two samples. DEVELOPMENTAL PSYCHOLOGY, 1981, 17, 463–464.

Review of Kohn Problem Checklist and Kohn Social Competence Scale by RONALD S. DRABMAN, Professor and Director, Psychology Training Program, The University of Mississippi Medical Center, Jackson, MS:

The Kohn Social Competence Scale (KSCS) and the Kohn Problem Checklist (KPC) are teacher rating scales designed to assess the social-emotional functioning of 3- to 6-year-old children. The KPC consists of 49 items which are rated by a teacher on a scale of "not at all typical," "somewhat typical," or "very typical," in terms of a child's behavior "during the most recent week." The test categorizes a child on two negative factors: Apathy-Withdrawal and Anger-Defiance. A high score indicates a high degree of symptomatology. The test comes with clear and concise instructions for scoring and even prorating for missing responses.

The KSCS contains 73 items for full-day programs and retains 64 of these items for half-day preschool or kindergarten programs. Children are scored for the most recent week on a 1 (never) to 7 (always) scale. This test categorizes a child on two factors. Factor One is called Interest-Participation versus Apathy-Withdrawal, and Factor Two is Cooperative-Compliance versus Anger-Defiance. This instrument also comes with well written scoring and interpretive directions (including prorating).

The KPC focuses on presence or absence of pathology and can be completed quickly. The KSCS is more comprehensive and measures a wider range of behavior.

Psychometrically, both tests are relatively sophisticated. They have been used in a number of studies by Kohn and his colleagues. Both scales have been shown to have adequate interrater reliability. Psychometric studies also indicate that the factors are relatively independent, and are similar to factors on other tests which purport to answer similar questions (e.g., Peterson-Quay Behavior Problem Checklist). The reliability across classrooms and over time is moderate but reasonable.

Discriminant validity studies have shown that 97% of those identified as disturbed on the Kohn Checklist were true positives. This is an impressive statistic. Kohn has also produced data indicating the factors are both moderately stable and predictive of risk over a 5-year period. This also is impressive.

Kohn clearly has developed an assessment instrument that is both reliable and valid. It is certainly a reasonable research tool. The criticism of this work has to do with incremental validity and with usefulness.

In terms of incremental validity, there is no evidence presented that these scales do a better job than other similar scales. The Kohn scales have formidable competitors. The Achenbach & Edelbrock Child Behavior Checklist and Quay & Peterson's Revised Behavior Problem Checklist offer the possibility of obtaining more information than the "Broad-band" factors identified by Kohn. Also, there is little evidence that these scales do better than simple global ratings by teachers (e.g., "Pick out the children in your room that are emotionally disturbed").

The other problem is usefulness. The authors of instruments like these need to gather information that will tell clinicians that therapy which produces changes in these behaviors will lead to a reasonable prediction of reduced problems. Scores on these factors are clearly indicative of current and predictive of future problems. However, what is needed is some indication that therapy which reduces scores on these factors will reduce current and future problems. Although logically this should be the case, it may well not be. Perhaps children who score high on these factors possess other qualities which while generally correlated with these factors are not measured by this scale. In that case, a change in test score might not be predictive of improved outlook. Until this information is available the Kohn instruments and those like them will not have fulfilled their promise.

[577]

Kraner Preschool Math Inventory. Ages 3–0 to 6–6; 1976–77; KPMI; criterion-referenced test which measures quantitative concepts acquisition and a norm-referenced subtest (Math/Screen) derived from KPMI which measures mathematics language development; 1 form; 2 parts, KPMI and Math/Screen Test; manuals ('76, '77), instructions, and test materials included in a three-ring notebook; 1983 price data: $53 per examiner's kit including manual, 25 scoring forms, classroom record sheet, 5 instructional record forms, and 25 Math/Screen Test booklets; $15 per additional forms (specify form); Robert E. Kraner; DLM Teaching Resources.*

a) KPMI. Ages 3–0 to 6–6; 1976; criterion-referenced; no scores, 7 areas: counting, cardinal numbers, quantities, sequence, positional, directional, geometry/measurement; no norms; 2 standards of mastery for each item, the earliest age in which 50% and 80% of the standardization sample responded correctly; individual; 1 form ('76, 245 pages); manual ('76, 22 pages).

b) MATH/SCREEN TEST. Ages 5–6 to 6–6; 1977; norm-referenced; 8 scores: numeral recognition, numeral comprehension, comparisons, sequence, position, direction, geometry/measurement, total; 1 form ('77, 4 pages); manual ('77, 18 pages); (10–15) minutes.

See T3:1266 (1 reference).

Review of Kraner Preschool Math Inventory by MARILYN J. HARING-HILDORE, Associate Dean, School of Education, University of North Carolina at Greensboro, Greensboro, NC:

The Kraner Preschool Math Inventory (KPMI) and its related, group-administered instrument, MATH/SCREEN, are nicely packaged and may appeal to potential users on that basis. However, serious weaknesses characterize both of these tests and raise questions as to their desirability and usefulness. These weaknesses, which may well be fatal flaws, will be explored in greater detail and prior to elaborating strengths because this reviewer believes the strengths should not be considered redeeming qualities.

Validity issues received little or no attention in the development of these inventories. The manual states that the KPMI was developed through an "informal survey" of such sources as research, lesson plans, and instructional materials, which yielded 153 specific concepts in seven major areas. This process is inadequate for inferring validity of the instrument for measuring quantitative concepts. Further, we cannot know if the three items constructed to probe each of the concepts are valid. Compounding the validity question was administration of the KPMI to 273 children in one geographic location after which the author arbitrarily established the Receptive Age as the earliest age interval at which 50% of that severely limited sample responded correctly on two of three trials testing a concept. Also, he established the Mastery Age as the earliest interval in which 80% of the sample responded correctly. These designations of Receptive and Mastery Ages are norms for interpreting each individual's performance on the test, but these norms are based on a sample which is far too small and too geographically restricted for that purpose. Unfortunately, test users are not cautioned in the manual about the seriousness of sample limitations in developing norms.

Many of the same criticisms of validity and norms also apply to MATH/SCREEN, inasmuch as it was developed by selecting the 21 most discriminating items from the KPMI with a sample of 188 students in one county. However, a .96 correlation between MATH/SCREEN scores and teacher ratings for 94 students appears to be some evidence of validity for that group test. This is the only validation study reported by the author and does not constitute adequate evidence of validity.

Yet another weakness apparent in the KPMI and MATH/SCREEN is the lack of data on reliability. When working with young children, it seems especially important to address issues of internal consistency and stability of responses over time. The author did make some assumptions concerning reliability when he selected two correct trials out of three as the criterion for success (and, presumably, reliable performance) on an item. However, that criterion is not particularly stringent when compared to five successes in eight trials, which is a common criterion in programs for shaping behavior. Reliability studies are essential if the KPMI and MATH/SCREEN are to become usable.

Despite these serious weaknesses, some aspects of the manual and tests are well done. In particular, the manual (which includes items to be administered individually on the KPMI) is an attractive package which is well organized and has clear instructions. Sections which are especially well done are suggested uses for the two tests, respectively, with cautions against labelling students who do not perform well. Rationales for development of the tests also are convincing. Finally, test users are provided with forms for individuals, classrooms, and general instruction which would be helpful in actually using test results to focus instruction.

In summary, the Kraner Preschool Math Inventory and MATH/SCREEN have serious flaws related to validity, norms and reliability that overshadow strengths which in comparison are of a minor, but appealing, nature (e.g., usability of the manual and of accompanying forms). These tests are of limited usefulness until these major weaknesses have been addressed.

Review of Kraner Preschool Math Inventory by EDWARD A. SILVER, *Associate Professor of Mathematics, San Diego State University, San Diego, CA:*

There are very few tests of young children's acquisition of quantitative concepts. The Kraner Preschool Math Inventory (KPMI) provides a vehicle for assessing children 3 to 6 years of age with respect to their attainment of common quantitative notions that are often assumed to be mastered by the time children begin first grade.

The manual discusses the differences between norm-referenced and criterion-referenced tests (CRT) and explains the rationale for developing this test as a CRT. However, no rationale is given for establishing the mastery criterion as two-out-of-three correct responses on three parallel items.

The discussion of test administration and scoring procedures is far too brief. Although the manual states that there is no required sequence of test items, some suggestions to the user regarding selection and sequencing of items would be in order. For example, since the manual establishes both a Receptive Age and a Mastery Age for each item, one might use the Mastery Age information in order to establish a graded sequence of questions within a topic cluster. A five-year-old child might be given an item with a Mastery Age of 4 years, 6 months; if the child were successful, one could proceed through a sequence of items with the same or older Mastery Ages, and if the child were unsuccessful, one could move down through a sequence of items to younger Mastery Ages. The ceiling level of the item sequence would be determined by the Receptive Age information.

A procedure similar to that suggested above would eliminate the need for administering superfluous items. It would be useful if the manual identified one recommended procedure for sequencing the items or several possible alternative procedures.

The testing program includes individual record sheets, class record sheets, and instructional record sheets. The manual suggests that these can be used to organize and use test results, but there is no discussion of how this is to be done. There are no suggestions made regarding planning for students who make certain errors or exhibit certain error patterns. Furthermore, the manual is silent on the issue of interpretation of test results. It is well known that the interpretation of a subject's performance, especially a young child's performance, is related to the extent of training and experience of the individual examiner or interpreter, yet no guidance is given by the KPMI manual.

In addition to the lack of useful information in the manual, there are several details of administering this test which are sure to perplex the novice, and perhaps even the experienced, examiner. For example, the individual record form is deficient in that it is impossible to conveniently mark different errors that could occur on different trials of an item. For one cluster of items, the directions appear on the back of the page on which the task is presented, thus creating an awkward situation. For some items, the directions are confusing or nonstandard; for example, asking a subject to "count to the first ball" or tell "which arrow tells you to go up?" (instead of "points up?"). Moreover, adoption of the easel design used by the Keymath Diagnostic Arithmetic Test would be an improvement over the current test binder format.

Despite the shortcomings noted above, the directions for most of the items are straightforward and the illustrations are attractive and realistic. All illustrations are black and white; the use of full color would enhance the visual effect.

The manual provides a brief description of the procedures used in test development and standardization. Users should be advised that the standardization sample consisted of 273 children, but that only 44 of the children were younger than 5 years old. Thus, one should be especially cautious in using the Receptive Age and Mastery Age information for children younger than 5 years old. No information is given concerning the validity or reliability of the KPMI.

Although the test covers a fairly wide range of quantitative concepts, no rationale is given for including one concept or excluding another. For example, the concepts "tall" and "tallest" are tested, but "taller" is not tested. In general, comparative forms of adjectives are not tested. One wonders why fundamental notions of one-to-one correspondence are not tested in a preschool mathematics inventory, or why a graded sequence of questions is not used to probe certain concepts. Research on the effects of task variables on children's performance suggests that relatively small changes in the presentation format of a given item can result in large changes in performance on the item. It is too easy to overestimate or underestimate a child's competence with respect to a given concept on the basis of one or two items, each presented in a similar format.

Although most of the items seem to be appropriate to assess knowledge of the relevant concept, there are some items that are questionable. For example, the same behavior on the part of the subject would be sufficient for mastery of both the concept "each" and the concept "all." The items lack the subtlety needed to distinguish between the two concepts; of course a skillful examiner could modify the directions so that mastery of these concepts might be more adequately examined.

The section of the test that might be regarded by first grade teachers as most important is that dealing with counting. Items are presented that examine rote, rational, serial, and ordinal counting abilities. The importance of mastery of rational counting to success in early number work is well established. KPMI provides an item that asks a child to count a set of 20 objects that appear on the test page. In scoring the child's performance on this item, the examiner is told simply to mark a plus if correct or a minus if incorrect and to circle the numbers missed. No mechanism is provided to record the type of error made by the child. The child could miss this item because she or he fails to say a number in the rote sequence, or says a number out of sequence, or recites a number name from the rote sequence without assigning it to an object in the collection being counted, or counts an object more than once. If this item is to have any diagnostic value, the information regarding the type of error must be recorded. The individual scoring record should be modified to allow for the recording of such information for the counting items and for most of the other items on the test.

Since this test was designed for use with young children it is surprising that the items do not involve manipulable quantities. One would expect improved performance on many of the items if subjects could physically manipulate the quantities involved in the question. However, since this is a test of readiness for first grade mathematics, instruction in which is usually dominated by textbooks and workbooks, perhaps it is appropriate that the test items be non-manipulative in nature.

In summary, the Kraner Preschool Math Inventory is a test of quantitative vocabulary for children 3 to 6 years of age. No information is provided about the test's reliability and validity. Furthermore, the standardization sample was inadequate with respect to 3-year-olds and 4-year-olds. In its present form, KPMI would appear to have limited diagnostic utility, and even less usefulness for the purposes of curriculum planning or program evaluation. Nevertheless, KPMI represents a first step in an important direction—the assessment of preschool children's attainment of quantitative concepts. If careful attention is given in the next revision to the numerous flaws and deficiencies in individual items, scoring procedures, and test administration procedures, subsequent editions of this test could be quite useful to administrators and teachers interested in young children's quantitative competence.

[578]

Krantz Health Opinion Survey. College; 1980; HOS; measures preferences for different health-care treatment approaches; 3 scores: information, behavioral involvement, total; norms consist of means and standard deviations; 1 form (no date, 2 pages); manual (14 pages, includes test); available free of charge from author; administration time not reported; David S. Krantz, Andrew Baum, and Margaret V. Wideman; David S. Krantz.*

See T3:1267 (1 reference).

TEST REFERENCES

1. Wallston, K. A., Smith, R. A., King, J. E., Forsberg, P. R., Wallston, B. S., & Nagy, V. T. Expectancies about control over health: Relationship to desire for control of health care. PERSONALITY AND SOCIAL PSYCHOLOGY, 1983, 9, 377–385.

Review of Krantz Health Opinion Survey by JAMES A. BLUMENTHAL, Assistant Professor of Medical Psychology, Department of Psychiatry, Associate, Department of Medicine, Duke University Medical Center, Durham, NC:

The Krantz Health Opinion Survey (HOS) is a 16-item questionnaire designed to assess individual differences in preferred role in health care procedures. The scale was based upon the notion that patients can be distinguished on the basis of their preferences for active participation in their medical management and in their desire for information regarding their condition and treatment. The scale is described in a single publication by Krantz, Baum, and Wideman (1980). There is no manual, and interested users are asked to write to the senior author for instructions for administration and scoring.

The authors provide a relatively detailed description of the development of the scale. The initial item pool of 40 statements was adapted from a questionnaire (Linn & Lewis, 1979) designed to measure physicians' attitudes towards self-care. The items had acceptable face validity and measured different attitudes and reported practices regarding health care. The 40-item test was administered to 200 college undergraduates and those items with correlations with the total score of less than .20 or with narrow distributions of response alternatives were eliminated. A revised 26-item scale was then administered to 159 undergraduates and a principal components analysis yielded a 9-item Behavioral Involvement scale (Scale B) concerning attitudes towards self-treatment and active behavioral involvement, and a 7-item Information scale (Scale I) measuring the desire to ask questions and to be informed about medical decisions. The remaining 10 items did not correlate with either scale and were eliminated. Thus, the HOS consists of 16 items requiring dichotomous (agree/disagree) judgements.

A limited set of reliability data is available. Point-biserial item correlations based on 200 cases ranged from .16 to .47 for the Total score and from .24 to .59 for the assigned subscales (B and I). The Total HOS score is reported to have a Kuder-Richardson 20 reliability of .77. Reliabilities for scales B and I are .74 and .76, respectively. The Total HOS score has a 7-week test-retest reliability of .74.

Normative data for the HOS also are limited. The scale was administered to three small samples of college undergraduates including unselected residents of a college dormitory ($N=56$), students reporting to a college infirmary for minor illnesses ($N=81$), and students enrolled in a medical self-help course ($N=12$). While the ages of the subjects were not mentioned, virtually all of the data apparently were obtained from subjects less than 21 years old. Norms for men and women are not presented separately despite the fact that the females tended to obtain higher scores on all the scales than their male counterparts. The authors state that scores are correlated with educational level and the HOS may not be suitable for uneducated individuals. Individual HOS subscales have a strong, positive correlation with a Total HOS score but are generally unrelated to each other or to such measures as Rotter's I-E scale, Spielberger's STAI, Ullman's Repression-sensitization scale, or the Hypochondriasis scale from the MMPI. The HOS is moderately ($r = .31$) correlated with the Wallston Health Locus of Control scale although the authors claim that the two instruments are "probably measuring independent processes." Investigations into response bias have not been systematically performed, although the correlation of the Crowne-Marlowe Social Desirability Scale and the Total HOS Scale is only −.03.

Validity data are considered preliminary. The content validity of the HOS may be less than ideal since some items are redundant (e.g., I usually don't ask the doctor or nurse many questions about what they're doing during a medical exam; I usually ask the doctor or nurse lots of questions about the procedures during a medical exam), and several content areas (e.g., questions about prognosis or side effects, preventive behaviors, etc.) are untapped. Convergent validity (i.e., is the factor structure reproducible in other populations?) is also in need of further investigation. Several cross-validational studies are available, however. Students voluntarily enrolled in a medical self-help course scored higher on Scale B and the Total HOS scale than a group of freshmen dormitory residents. In addition, a group of clinic users scored lower than the dorm residents on the B scale but not the Total scale. Analysis of a subset ($N=54$) of dorm residents who retrospectively rated their number of visits to the clinic revealed that low B scores were associated with more clinic visits. Finally, in a study of 81 undergraduates who visited the college medical office with medical complaints, high I scores and high Total scores were associated with more questions asked during an initial interview with a nurse clinician; high scores on all three scales were associated with more attempts at self-diagnosis; and high Total scores were associated with a tendency for some students to request specific medications during their medical examinations. Surprisingly, when the interval between symptom onset and the clinic visit was considered, there was no relationship between B scale or Total scale scores and latency to report to the clinic, and the I scale was actually negatively ($r = -.28$) correlated with latency. The authors argue that the B and I scales measure different response tendencies; thus the total HOS score is useful particularly when behaviors representing a composite of behavioral involvement and information seeking tendencies are considered.

Despite the author's claim that the scales are able to "predict" behavior, the data reported in their manuscript are unconvincing. Rather, it can be said that individuals scoring at the upper and lower ends of the distribution on the HOS can be distinguished by certain behavioral tendencies. In particular, high I scorers tend to be inquisitive and ask questions during medical examinations and high B scorers tend to have distrusting attitudes towards health care professionals. However, it should be reported that in a recent study of patients undergoing dental extraction surgery (Auerbach, Martelli, & Mercuri, 1983), subjects who obtained high scores on the I scale showed a much better adjustment when they received specific rather than general information about the procedures before surgery. More empirical studies of this sort would be welcome.

In summary, this instrument is still in a developmental stage. It is doubtful that the norms will prove of much value to most users in clinical settings since the normative groups are all college students with only minor medical problems. Further research is necessary to establish better normative data and to evaluate the significance of the test scores for such important outcomes as responses to treatment, compliance, preventative behaviors, and patient satisfaction. The interrelationship of patient attitudes to physician attitudes should also be explored. For example, what would be the outcome of the pairing of a physician who discourages active involvement and the asking of questions on the part of the patient with a patient who has a high need for information and active involvement in his/her health care? Despite its limitations, there are no real alternatives to the HOS. For those interested in assessing individuals' receptiveness to information and self-care in treatment situations and in assessing general attitudes towards physicians, the HOS is probably worth considering particularly in research settings. It is difficult to fully evaluate the value of the HOS since it is not currently widely used, and available validity data are limited. However, the HOS has potential use in a variety of situations and certainly deserves further study.

REVIEWER'S REFERENCES

Linn, L. S., & Lewis, C. E. Attitudes toward self-care among practicing physicians. MEDICAL CARE, 1979, 17, 183–190.

Krantz, D. S., Baum, A., & Wideman, M. V. Assessment of preferences for self-treatment and information in health care. JOURNAL OF PERSONALITY AND SOCIAL PSYCHOLOGY, 1980, 39, 977–990.

Auerbach, S. M., Martelli, M. F., & Mercuri, L. G. Anxiety, information, interpersonal impacts, and adjustment to a stressful health care situation. JOURNAL OF PERSONALITY AND SOCIAL PSYCHOLOGY, 1983, 44, 1284–1296.

[579]

Kuhlmann-Anderson Tests, Eighth Edition. Grades K, 1, 2–3, 3–4, 5–6, 7–9, 9–12; KA; 1927–82; seventh edition still available; 6 scores: 3 raw scores (verbal, non-verbal, full) and 3 derived scores; 7 levels labeled K, A, BC, CD, EF, G, and H; Levels K, A, and BC (grades K, 1, 2–3): 1 form ('81, 19 pages) for each level, 2 editions (hand-scorable, machine-scorable), manual of directions ('82, 39 pages) for each level, answer key for hand scoring ('82, 2 pages) for each level; Levels CD, EF, G, and H (grades 3–4, 5–6, 7–9, 9–12): 1 form ('82, 13–14 pages) for each level, manual of directions ('82, 33–39 pages) for each level, STS Scor-Vue ('82, 1 page) for each level, separate answer sheets (NCS Trans-Optic) must be used; 1983 price data: $16 per 20 machine scorable tests and 1 manual of directions (specify Level K, A, BC); $10 per 20 hand-scorable tests, 1 manual of directions, and class record sheet (specify K, A, BC); $10 per 20 reusable tests, 1 manual of directions and class record sheet (specify CD–H); $10 per 50 answer sheets (specify CD, EF, G, H); $2.50 per school scoring kit (specify CD–H); $1 per answer key (specify K–BC); $.50 per class record sheets; $4.50 per manual of directions; $4.50 per technical manual (specify K–BC, CD–EF, or G–H); scoring service, $1 per booklet, $.75 per pupil per answer sheet; 28(60–75) minutes in 2 days for Levels K–BC, 35(60–75) minutes for Level CD, 40(60–75) minutes for Levels EF–H; F. Kuhlmann (fourth and earlier editions) and Rose G. Anderson; Scholastic Testing Service, Inc.*

See T3:1272 (13 references) and T2:398 (53 references); for reviews by William B. Michael and Douglas A. Pidgeon, and an excerpted review by Frederick B. Davis of the seventh edition, see 6:466 (11 references); see also 5:348 (15 references); for reviews by Henry E. Garrett and David Segel of an earlier edition, see 5:302 (10 references); for reviews by W. G. Emmett and Stanley S. Marzolf, see 3:236 (25 references); for a review by Henry E. Garrett, see 2:1404 (15 references); for reviews by Psyche Cattell, S. A. Courtis, and Austin H. Turney, see 1:1049

TEST REFERENCES

1. Thorton, C. D. An evaluation of the Mathematics-Methods Program involving the study of teaching characteristics and pupil achievement in mathematics. JOURNAL FOR RESEARCH IN MATHEMATICS EDUCATION, 1977, 8, 17–25.

2. Prentky, R. A., Lewine, R. R. J., Watt, N. F., & Fryer, J. H. A longitudinal study of psychiatric outcome: Developmental variables vs. psychiatric symptoms. SCHIZOPHRENIA BULLETIN, 1980, 6, 139–148.

Review of Kuhlmann-Anderson Tests, Eighth Edition, by MICHAEL D. HISCOX, Director, Interwest Applied Research, Portland, OR:

When one considers that the first edition of the Kuhlmann-Anderson tests was published in 1927, it seems likely that we are discussing tests of quality and enduring value. Tests that are unreliable, poorly formatted, or which fail to provide useful information do not stay in publication for nearly 60 years. The issue, therefore, is less one of whether the Kuhlmann-Anderson tests are good tests, but whether their intent and construction make them optimal for a specific application.

The publisher specifies that the test series is designed to measure an individual's academic potential "through assessing cognitive skills related to the learning process." This sounds much like an "intelligence" (IQ) test. But while traditional mental ability tests focus on innate powers and attempt to minimize the effect of acquired experiences, the Kuhlmann-Anderson tests care principally about the relationship of the assessed skill to subsequent performance. Thus, whereas most mental ability tests struggle to avoid "contamination" from the examinees' acquired powers and learning, the Kuhlmann-Anderson handles the issue aggressively by saying the distinction between innate and acquired is unimportant.

Is such an approach correct? Does, in fact, this test measure academic potential? And will it be valid for the purposes for which users will employ it? Such questions are not conclusively answered. Predictive validity studies offer some guidance, as do correlations between the Kuhlmann-Anderson and other "intelligence" tests. But in the end, the user still has to use the test information in an appropriate way, and the test's Manual of Directions offers insufficient information on how and why the test works.

These qualms aside, one quickly recognizes that the Kuhlmann-Anderson tests are of uniformly high quality. Formatting and printing of the test booklets seem perfect; test takers are unlikely to have any difficulty maintaining their place as the test proceeds. The drawings and figures used in the test items are well done—detailed enough to be complete but without extraneous features. Appropriate samples and directions are provided. In short, there is little to criticize about the test booklets.

The test authors ask the user to show some faith regarding their selection of the items. Certainly the efficacy of item types in previous editions of the test is a legitimate reason for their use; it is not, however, a particularly satisfying criterion for a user. When one reviews a math test, there is a way to categorize items as suitable or unsuitable by the appropriateness of their content. Unfortunately, all but the very most sophisticated users of the Kuhlmann-Anderson tests will simply have to trust that the items are appropriate measures of academic potential, for there is no way for them to judge this, and the manuals offer little elaboration.

The answer sheets (and machine-scorable booklets which, with this Eighth Edition, now go to grade 3) are also without major flaw. There is, however, a curiosity with the hand-scorable versions: the student is instructed to complete an information grid of bubbles which, while necessary for machine scoring, seems a waste of administration time for hand scoring. Separate answer sheets can also be hand scored using transparent plastic overlays. Perhaps the only criticism of the scoring process involves the hand-scorable booklets. These are scored using reduced-size copies of the booklet pages as a key; the pages may, however, have been reduced too much, making it difficult to quickly locate the correct answer.

The Manual of Directions for each level is generally well done. Each provides a section describing the test, a set of administration directions, directions for scoring, information on interpreting the results, and an appendix containing the tables needed to find the derived scores. Two of the sections are very well done; the test directions are extremely clear and easy to follow, and the directions for scoring are concise but specific enough to avoid confusion. Each of the remaining sections has a minor problem. The charts in the appendix could profit from the inclusion of additional grid lines to make extracting the information easier and potentially more accurate. The introductory section does not adequately introduce the user to the appropriate uses of the test. And the section on test interpretation describes all of the information derived from the test but does not tell the reader what to do with the results. In fact, by far the greatest weakness of the manuals is that while the Kuhlmann-Anderson tests deal with the amorphous topic of "academic potential," the test materials give virtually no guidance about how to appropriately apply the results of the testing. Neither are there caveats about potential misuses of the data.

The key score from administration of the Kuhlmann-Anderson is the Cognitive Skills Quotient—the CSQ. This score is designed to be interpreted in the same manner as an IQ score (in-age mean of 100, standard deviation of 15). Beginning with this Eighth Edition, verbal and non-verbal (as well as full battery) CSQs are provided. The testing also yields an expanded standard score suitable for measuring growth over a period of time. The manual contains tables giving guidance on the amount of standard score increase one might expect. Tables of age-related norms allow comparisons of individual CSQs to others of the same chronological age, and tables of grade-related norms allow individual standard scores to be compared to others at the same grade level. Obtaining this information is relatively easy, given the helpful text and reasonably clear tables.

The full test reliabilities are certainly acceptable, particularly given the reasonable length of the test. KR20 reliabilities for the full test CSQ scores range from .90 at the A level to .97 at the H level. The reliabilities for the verbal and non-verbal scores at each level are, of course, lower. In fact, the KR20 for the verbal CSQ at level K is .81; at Level A it is .83. Given these results, the manual correctly calls for caution in using the verbal estimates at these two levels. (All other coefficients are in the .88 range or higher.) The last column of the reliability chart gives the standard error of measurement associated with each level, and the accompanying text does an adequate job of describing to the lay user how to apply this statistic. (Additional technical data are contained in a technical manual which was in rough draft form as this review was completed.)

In summary, one finds the Kuhlmann-Anderson tests to be high quality tests which are straightforward to administer and score. It is unfortunate that there is not better guidance on appropriate and inappropriate uses of the test given in the Manual of Directions; there is, after all, some potential for misuse of the test results by naive users. And, of course, one must come to grips with the mission of these tests as an indicator of "academic potential" and, further, must have a valid need for such information. But if such a need exists, the nearly 60-year history of the test suggests that the Kuhlmann-Anderson tests are an appropriate tool.

Review of Kuhlmann-Anderson Tests, Eighth Edition, by RONALD C. RODGERS, President, Rodgers and Associates, Wilmette, IL:

The eighth edition of the Kuhlmann-Anderson Tests (K-A) illustrates both the best and the paradoxical in measures of academic potential. This series of seven coordinated tests offers carefully crafted items, effective presentation of directions for administering and scoring the tests, and several improvements over the seventh edition which should make it still easier to use.

The introductory section of the Manual of Directions for each level illustrates the paradox inherent in such measures with its efforts to offer a "conceptual distinction between the K-A and traditional mental ability (IQ) tests." The manual attempts to distinguish this series of measures as "much less concerned with the question of whether or not skills assessed are inborn or acquired" than "traditional IQ tests." Unfortunately, there still appears to be little evidence to support claims that this is significantly different from other IQ tests on conceptual grounds. It may have to be sufficient that this is a very good addition to traditional attempts to measure "academic potential" within the limits of paper and pencil tests. Reference in the manual to "out-of-level" use of these tests also appears to illustrate this paradox; the need to rely on a lower level than that indicated by a student's assigned grade level affirms that acquired skills are all that can be measured as predictors of potential learning capability.

There are several potentially significant changes in the eighth edition. First, this edition offers seven levels instead of eight by merging three levels into two for grades 2 through 4. The new version also offers machine-scorable booklets for the lower grades (K through 3), but the manual notes that this required "considerable modifications of item types" without specifying what these changes were.

Unfortunately, it is impossible to assess the impact of changes such as these on the eighth edition at the time of this review because no technical manual is anticipated before the fall of 1984 (and perhaps later, according to the publisher). Another potentially significant change, noted with just a passing reference in the directions for interpretation, is that the eighth edition relied on item response theory ("specifically, the Rasch model") to develop its expanded score scale. Therefore, no information about the standardization samples or procedures in the application of new measurement and scaling strategies will be available until publication of the technical manuals. While some technical information is included in the Manual of Directions for each level, it is still a serious omission to have offered a test based on new methods for scaling and with "considerable modifications of item types" without a comprehensive technical manual to support its contentions about validity and comparability with earlier editions.

As a result, this review is limited to examination of the structure of the tests and the content of the Manual of Directions for each level. Actually, only two sections differ from level to level in these manuals: the specific directions for administering each level, and norms tables in the appendices. This points to one of the improvements which might be appropriate in future editions. All seven levels rely on sample class record sheets and score reports from grade 12, but it should take relatively little time and effort to offer examples specific to each level. While this may seem to be a minor matter for test developers and editors, experience has shown that teachers and school administrators who select and use tests such as these take great comfort in being able to rely on examples which use students as similar as possible to those they are testing.

Each level of the K-A begins with an excellent practice section, especially in the case of the tests for students in the early grades (K through 3). Another improvement for future editions, however, might be to include a specific warm-up and practice session at the beginning of the second session for levels K, A, and BC. The manual advises the test administrator to follow "the initial procedures as before" on the second day, but few of these procedures are appropriate to repeat. The insertion of a few sentences of special directions and additional practice items to remind pupils how to mark answer sheets and cope with the testing situation might help reduce artificial test anxiety for these children. A similar potential source of unnecessary anxiety is in a sample item in test BC-4, which offers words with opposite meanings. The first sample item begins "The first word is wrong" to offer the opposites "right/wrong," but the same purpose may be achieved with a sample which uses "left/right" without introducing unnecessary anxiety for second- and third-grade students.

Another area of concern in reviewing the application of a new or novel scaling technique before publication of the technical manual is the impact of the degree of overlap between adjacent levels. Within the verbal sections of these tests, from 14 to 30 items are common to adjacent levels, often with entire subtests appearing in both levels. In some cases, items with the same content appear in a more complex format or with an additional foil. Traditional test development practice compels that these be examined and reported as separate items entirely, yet they comprise most of the connection between level EF and levels BC and CD. In nearly all cases, common items between adjacent levels are confined to one or two subtests within the verbal score, but data typically reported in the technical manual must support the assumption that these function as common elements within a single domain rather than as entirely discrete constructs.

Similar issues arise for the non-verbal scores and links between levels. In addition, a few of the subtests (especially in the last two parts of Level BC) may be confounded by excessive sensitivity to speededness. While it may be an indication of "learning potential" to discover how quickly a child can recognize numbers and relationships, the time limits in these two tests may create a handicap for the student who has not yet mastered the mechanics of marking an answer sheet rapidly despite exceptional numerical skills.

In summary, the eighth edition of the Kuhlmann-Anderson Tests offers another excellent attempt to measure academic potential, especially in the lower and middle grades. Practitioners who still prefer to use such measures are likely to be pleased with this edition unless extraordinary surprises which alter the validity or quality of the tests emerge in the as yet unpublished technical manuals. The care with which this and earlier editions have been prepared suggests that such an occurrence is unlikely, but it would still be reassuring to repeat this review when complete information about the impact of changes in this edition is available.

[580]

Kundu Introversion Extraversion Inventory. Adults; 1976; KIEI; 1 form (4 pages); manual (8 pages); separate answer sheets must be used; 1982 price data: Rs. 225 per 25 reusable test booklets; Rs. 250 per 100 answer sheets; Rs. 100 per manual; (20–40) minutes; Ramanath Kundu; the Author [India].*

[581]

La Prueba Riverside de Realización en Español. Grades K, 1, 2, 3, 4, 5, 6, 7, 8; 1984; Spanish edition of The 3-R's Test; "designed to determine the degree to which students are literate in Spanish, and to assess the achievement of students whose primary language is Spanish"; 9 levels; teacher's guide and technical summary ('84, 88 pages); parent letter ('84, 2 pages); 1984 price data: $31.02 per 25 tests for levels 6–8; $35.01 per 25 tests for level 9; $39 per 35 tests for levels 10–14; $9 per 35 MRC answer sheets; $6.60 per 35 parent letters; $8.01 per manual; Nancy S. Cole, E. Roger Trent, and Dena C. Wadell; Riverside Publishing Co.*

a) LEVEL 6. Grade K; 3 scores: reading, mathematics, composite (average of 2 previous scores); Form A (12 pages), MRC scorable; instructions for administration (13 pages); (80) minutes in 2 sessions.

b) LEVEL 7. Grade 1; 3 scores: same as for Level 6; Form A (12 pages), MRC scorable; instructions for administration (12 pages); (85) minutes in 2 sessions.

c) LEVEL 8. Grade 2; 5 scores: reading, mathematics, composite (average of 2 previous scores), social studies, science; Form A (24 pages), MRC scorable; instructions for administration (14 pages); (140) minutes in 4 sessions.

d) LEVEL 9. Grade 3; 6 scores: reading, language, mathematics, composite (average of previous 3 scores), social studies, science; Form A (27 pages), MRC scorable; instructions for administration (10 pages); (165) minutes in 3 sessions.

e) LEVEL 10. Grade 4; 6 scores: same as for Level 9; Form A (23 pages); instructions for administration (10 pages) for Levels 10–14; separate answer sheets (MRC) must be used; (165) minutes in 3 sessions.

f) LEVEL 11. Grade 5; 6 scores: same as for Level 9; Form A (23 pages); separate answer sheets (MRC) must be used; (165) minutes in 3 sessions.

g) LEVEL 12. Grade 6; 6 scores: same as for Level 9; Form A (23 pages); separate answer sheets (MRC) must be used; (165) minutes in 3 sessions.

h) LEVEL 13. Grade 7; 6 scores: same as for Level 9; Form A (23 pages); separate answer sheets (MRC) must be used; (165) minutes in 3 sessions.

i) LEVEL 14. Grade 8; 6 scores: same as for Level 9; Form A (22 pages); separate answer sheets (MRC) must be used; (165) minutes in 3 sessions.

[582]

The Lake St. Clair Incident. Adults; 1977–78; LSC; to examine group and individual decision-making processes, help individuals and groups perceive and evaluate their interactions and styles of communicating, and utilize the instrument to simply have fun or create an environment; 3 scores: autocratic, consultive, consensual; no data on reliability and validity; norms consist of means and standard deviations; individual in part; 1 form ('78, 6 pages); manual ('77, 22 pages); 1983 price data: $1.50 per test booklet; $5 per manual; $9.95 per specimen set; (65–80) minutes; Albert A. Canfield; Humanics Media.*

Review of The Lake St. Clair Incident by JACK L. BODDEN, Staff Psychologist, Olin E. Teague V.A. and Associate Professor of Psychiatry & Behavioral Science, Texas A&M University College of Medicine, Temple, TX:

The Lake St. Clair Incident is really not a measurement instrument in spite of the fact that three "scores" can be derived from it. This point must be kept in mind so that the reader will not mistakenly assume that inclusion in *The Ninth Mental Measurements Yearbook* means that the Lake St. Clair Incident is some sort of test or scale.

As the author points out, the Lake St. Clair Incident is a survival or consensus exercise of the sort that was very popular in social psychology classes or communication groups in the late 60s and early 70s. As such, it is a device or vehicle for stimulating group involvement with and discussion of decision-making. It is not in any sense a measure of decision-making quality, style, or other decision-making construct. In fairness, it should be noted that the author does not make any exaggerated or inappropriate claims for the Lake St. Clair Incident.

Like other such exercises (e.g., The NASA Moon Mission), the Lake St. Clair Incident presents individuals with a problem (in this case, a small group of people are on a cabin cruiser which begins to sink in Lake St. Clair). Participants in the exercise are then given a list of 15 items such as a flashlight, rope, bottle of brandy, etc., and are asked to rank the items as to their importance in surviving the accident. The manual suggests that participants be instructed to make three separate rankings under three different sets of instructions. Initially, the ranking is made alone without any opportunity for discussion with other participants (referred to as the Autocratic Decision). The second ranking is made after group discussion (referred to as the Consultative Decision). A final ranking is made with the team members being instructed to achieve a common solution (the Consensual Decision). All three rankings are to be made within time limits specified in the manual.

The three "scores" are generated by comparing the participants' rankings with the "Expert's Rankings" given in the manual. Scores represent the absolute (irrespective of sign) differences between the rankings of the participant and the "experts." Team averages, as well as "gain" and "loss" scores across the three conditions, are also calculated. These "scores" are presumably to give the participants something concrete to discuss.

Since the Lake St. Clair Incident is not a true measurement instrument there is no psychometric information provided; there is no reliability and validity data in the manual. The manual does contain some rudimentary normative data in the form of means and standard deviations, as well as high and low scores obtained with an undefined sample of persons who have completed the exercise.

In summary, if one is interested in getting people actively involved with the subject of decision-making, as opposed to measuring some leadership-related construct, then the Lake St. Clair Incident is probably a good choice. It does appear to have some advantages over other survival/discussion exercises. For instance, it involves a realistic, plausible situation which can and does happen rather frequently (unlike trips to the moon or being stranded on a desert island). This is important for leaders of such discussion groups because it is difficult to get people to be serious about what they would do if they were going to be on the moon. It also has the advantage to having "expert rankings" made by experienced Coast Guard personnel, along with their rationale for the rankings.

[583]

Language Assessment Battery. Grades K–2, 3–6, 7–12; 1976; LAB; 3 levels; 2 editions: English, Spanish; technical manual (48 pages); separate answer sheets must be used; 1984 price data: $1.95 per scoring key (needed only for *b* and *c*); $9.24 per 35 Digitek answer sheets; $5.67 per technical manual; $11.61 per specimen set of both editions; prepared by Board of Education of the City of New York; Riverside Publishing Co.*

a) LEVEL I. Grades K–2; 3 tests: Listening and Speaking, Reading, Writing; individual; test booklet for test 3 (4 pages); examiner's directions for administering (18 pages); picture stimulus booklet (15 pages); $11.28 per 35 tests; $2.85 per examiner's directions for administering; $2.19 per picture stimulus booklet; (5–10) minutes.

b) LEVEL II. Grades 3–6; 4 tests: Listening, Reading, Writing, Speaking; test 4 individually administered; test booklet for test 1, 2, and 3 (11 pages); examiner's directions for administering (16 pages); picture stimulus card (2 pages); $19.95 per 35 tests; $2.19 per examiner's directions for administering; $.72 per picture stimulus card; (40–50) minutes.

c) LEVEL III. Grades 7–12; 4 tests: Listening, Reading, Writing, Speaking; test 4 individually administered; test booklet for test 1, 2, and 3 (11 pages); examiner's directions for administering (16 pages); picture stimulus card (2 pages); $19.95 per 35 tests; $2.19 per examiner's directions for administering; $.72 per picture stimulus card; (40–50) minutes.

Review of Language Assessment Battery by KATHLEEN BARROWS CHESTERFIELD, Research Associate, Juarez and Associates, Los Angeles, CA:

The principal problem of the Language Assessment Battery (LAB) is a lack of clarity as to the purpose for which the series is designed. Its stated aim is to determine the "effectiveness" of a child in English and Spanish. The term "effectiveness," however, is never defined, nor is it apparent what the test is attempting to measure. The word "effectiveness" would seem to imply that the object of interest is language as it is used for communicative purposes, i.e., the ability of a Spanish-speaking child to function successfully in an all-English classroom. The test items, however, do not seem particularly relevant either to the classroom or home situation. Many of the test items at all levels focus on recognition of isolated sounds (LAB Listening II & III) and on the production and recognition of words taken in isolation. One must question whether such skills as word-naming and discrimination between minimal pairs are valid indicators of language "effectiveness." As has been emphasized in modern testing theory in the field of second language acquisition, the various phonological, syntactic, and semantic units of language occur naturally within the larger context of discourse. Any test which claims to evaluate functional language should reflect some pragmatic value and demand the use of discourse processing skills reflecting language in use. There are, however, few items in the LAB which do this, despite the claim to measuring "effectiveness."

An additional difficulty with the series is the limited norm population—a "representative sample" of New York City students, one group of monolingual English-speaking children and the other a group of Spanish-literate children. Norming the English test on a sample of monolingual English-speaking children is a laudable and seldom taken procedure, especially given the underlying aim of the test to identify those children who are capable of "surviving" in an all-English classroom. Limiting the sample to Hispanics literate in Spanish, however, severely reduces the representativeness. By norming the test only to monolingual English students and Spanish-literate children, a mid range of language dominance often referred to as the "balanced bilingual" has been ignored. Though the Technical Manual claims that such a piloting was scheduled on a national level for 1976–77, the results of this projected administration are as yet unpublished. The lack of such data raises questions not only about the range of language proficiency for which the test is suitable but also about the equivalency of the Spanish and English versions.

It is also important to note that the test was designed to maximize discrimination at the low end of the score distribution (i.e., it is best at identifying students who are not "effective" in English). The test is easy—grammatical forms such as the subjunctive in Spanish are not included until Levels II and III. The time invested in testing students could be more effectively utilized if a test were used which might perform the multiple tasks of discriminating along the entire scale of language proficiency/dominance.

The series also suffers from severe geographical and cultural limitations, reflected in both the limitation of the norm group to New York City and the content of the test items. Despite a few items dealing with Mexican culture and history, the majority of the culture-related items were written specifically for students of Puerto Rican descent. The Spanish LEVEL II test, for example, refers to Puerto Rican historical and sports figures. Similarly, vocabulary which is regionally specific is employed in the listening section. No instructions are given in the administration manual on adjusting for regional differences in vocabulary. Perceived more positively, the idea of adapting the content of the text to the cultural background of the students is notable, despite the fact that it may prevent or limit its application to the wider Hispanic community outside of the New York City area. Also, in attempting to keep up to date and relevant in content, the test constructors have included items reflecting current health and life style concerns such as smoking.

In terms of general administrative factors, instructions for the administration of the test are clearly and concisely written. Information is lacking, however, as to the procedures for actual scoring of the test. The Examiner's Directions for Administering provides examples of possible correct responses, but no samples are given of incorrect responses. How does the scorer, for example, deal with misspelled words or with inappropriate articles accompanying correct nouns? Furthermore, all directions to examiners for the Spanish version of the test are in English. The lack of bilingual directions may present no problems in school districts in which the examiners are fully bilingual teachers, but it is probable that the Spanish version of the battery may be used in situations where test examiners are not literate in English.

Finally, the format of the test is generally uninteresting. The pictures, which are black and white, are lacking in originality and would not seem to stimulate the students' interest, especially at the levels of K through grade 2. Similarly, the tasks required of the students, such as pointing to the hammer, seem equally unmotivating. Use of more colorful graphics and unusual cartoon characters might help in insuring optimum student motivation.

In summary, due to the cultural content of the items and the limited norm group, the LAB would not seem appropriate for general use. It would appear to have some utility in identifying Spanish-speaking students of Puerto Rican descent who are nonfunctional in English classrooms either in the New York City area or in areas of similar ethnic makeup. It does not meet the designer-stated goal of determining "effectiveness," however, if such a goal includes identifying students along the entire scale of English language proficiency, while at the same time assessing pragmatic skills which are relevant to the classroom situation.

[584]

Language Assessment Scales. Grades K–5, 6–12 and over; 1981–82; LAS; 6 or 7 scores: minimal pairs, lexical, phonemes, sentence comprehension, oral production, total, observation of pragmatic language (optional); individual; test administered in part by tape cassette; Forms A, B, ('81, 22 pages); 2 levels: I (grades K–5), II (grades 6–12 and over); administration manual ('81, 15 pages); scoring and interpretation manual ('81, 42 pages); technical report ('81, 142 pages) for Form A; supplement ('82, 40 pages) for Form B; 1983 price data: $44.95 per complete examiner's kit including 50 test booklets for either level; $27.50 per 50 test booklets and cue pictures; $12.50 per cue picture booklet; $8.25 per audio cassette; $1.95 per administration manual; $9.50 per scoring and interpretation manual; $19.95 per technical manual; $4.95 per supplement; Spanish edition ('81) available for Form A only; (20–30) minutes; Edward A. De Avila and Sharon E. Duncan; Linguametrics Group.*

See T3:1281 (4 references).

TEST REFERENCES

1. Johnson, D. M. Natural language learning by design: A classroom experiment in social interaction and second language acquisition. TESOL QUARTERLY, 1983, 17, 55–68.

Review of Language Assessment Scales by LYN HABER, Associate Professor of Psychology, University of Illinois at Chicago, Chicago, IL:

The Language Assessment Scales (LAS) measure the degree to which a student displays the oral language proficiency of a normal monolingual speaker. There are both English and Spanish versions of the test, so that, for a bilingual child, it is possible to determine the degree to which each of his languages approximates monolingual proficiency. The measure can be used to sort out those children eligible for bilingual classrooms. It can also be used as a research instrument to correlate oral language proficiency with other linguistic and cognitive capacities.

There is one Spanish LAS for children grades K through 5 (Level I) and another for grades 6 through 12+ (Level II). For evaluating English, two alternative forms (A and B), are available at Levels I and II. The entire LAS includes student test booklets and tape recordings for English and Spanish Levels I and II; a manual on administration of the LAS, another manual on scoring and interpretation; a researcher-oriented description of the theoretical and technical specifications of the LAS (Form A); and a description, in draft form, of the validity and reliability of Form B, Level I. Taken together, the latter two documents contain an impressive amount of evidence on the reliabilities and validities of the LAS.

Each LAS contains seven subtests, the last two of which are optional. Phonology is assessed by (1) Minimal Pairs, an auditory discrimination task (recognition); and (2) Phonemes, a repetition task in which the target phoneme is embedded in single words and in phrases. The Lexicon (3) is assessed by a naming task. Syntax is measured by a picture recognition task called Sentence Comprehension (4); by Oral Production (5), where the student retells a story; and optionally, for children grades seven and over, by Written Production (6): having retold the story verbally (5), the student now writes it. Pragmatics (7), also optional, is a score derived from an observation form to be completed by an adult other than the examiner (e.g., the teacher).

The LAS is administered individually. The five subtests which are given to every student require at least 20 to 30 minutes. Of these five subtests, all but Lexical Items are tested using the LAS cassette tapes.

The only norms of the test are that monolingual first graders pass virtually all of the items on Level I in their respective languages, and all monolingual seventh graders pass the items on Level II.

If this test is to be used only to decide whether a child has the proficiency of a monolingual first grader (Level I), or seventh grader (Level II), then this is a powerful test, though it has some serious practical difficulties of administration and scoring. If the test is to be used for a more fine-grained analysis of language proficiency or to predict future school achievement, then the test is inadequate not only for these practical reasons, but because of serious theoretical and methodological difficulties in test construction.

Those who want to use the test to identify children eligible for bilingual classrooms, or to obtain a measure of the degree to which a child approximates the oral proficiency of a monolingual, must overcome some very real practical problems. Few personnel have the proper qualifications to administer the LAS. The tester must speak the test language fluently as a first language; and reliable scoring of the test requires either in-service training or extensive work with someone already trained; it cannot be self taught.

The LAS authors rightly stress that reliable results can be obtained only if testing is performed in quiet and nondistracting settings. Because the test uses pre-recorded tapes, and it is time consuming and difficult to replay an item, this kind of testing environment is critical. For many schools it is also nonexistent.

Several minor annoyances with the LAS concern administration of the test. All of the student's responses are entered into a test booklet, usually by the examiner. However, when Comprehension (4) is tested, the student is to point to, or mark an "X" on the picture matching the sentence. Does the examiner hand the booklet to the student for this test? Another awkwardness in administration concerns the size of the pictures. The pictures used in the Lexical, Comprehension, and Oral Production subtests are quite small, making it difficult for the tester to see what the student points to and at the same time record the response unobtrusively. Administration would be faster and smoother if a set of large laminated cards were included. The student could then turn these over one by one and respond while the tester quickly notes his/her answers.

The Oral Production subtest presents a more serious problem of administration, in that the tester is required to write down in the Student Test Booklet EXACTLY what the child says (emphasis the test authors'). If phonetic notation is needed, the transcription cannot be done at the time of testing: this is a prohibitively lengthy task. Assuming a transcription is made during the actual storytelling, either the student must slow down (an artificial and invalid testing procedure), or the tester is likely to make a loose transcription.

The most serious practical problems with the LAS concern scoring. According to the scoring manual, "a Phonemes item is correct if the student is able to repeat the item in such a fashion that s/he would not be misunderstood or ridiculed." In the context stimuli, the target phoneme appears two or even three times (e.g., /p/ in "the peppers are picked," or /ae/ in "He sat on a mat,") but the item is to be marked either acceptable or failed. How is a response to be scored if the student produces both an acceptable and an unacceptable /p/ or /ae/? The manual does not say. Of the five obligatory subtests, Minimal Pairs, Phonemes, Lexicon, and Sentence Comprehension are weighted equally, and Oral Production is weighted four times more heavily. No explanation is offered for this procedure, nor are any multivariate analyses reported in which this weighting is shown to produce the best fit with variables such as present school performance or teacher ratings.

The most important and innovative subtest is Oral Production. However, no set of principles defining the scoring is provided, so that even speech pathologists with wide testing experience would not be able to derive a reliable score. In place of a scoring manual, the authors resort to presenting 140 examples, 70 each in English and Spanish, at Levels I and II from children aged 5 to 17, in the Scoring and Interpretation Manual.

In summary, the LAS in its present form presents almost overwhelming practical problems if used to identify children for bilingual classrooms. Some of these are unrealistic demands in real-world settings, such as the requirements for fully fluent, highly trained testers, and for quiet testing space. However, many of the practical problems with the LAS itself could be solved.

The LAS contains many unnecessary items. It could be pruned to include just those syntactic forms which differ in English and Spanish children at relevant age levels. The Minimal Pairs subtest could be eliminated altogether; the Phonemes subtest could be eliminated or restricted to the few relevant for English versus Spanish speakers. A much simpler scoring procedure could be worked out for the Oral Proficiency subtest if only a binary distinction between proficient and nonproficient speakers were made (instead of the present five levels of proficiency). For example, the child who uses sentences, in contrast to unconnected phrases, is a proficient speaker.

Serious methodological and theoretical difficulties in test construction prevent use of the LAS to specify a quantitative description of a child's present language proficiency, let alone to predict future school achievement, or as a basis for intervention.

The LAS contains a number of poor test items, many of which are shown to be problematic by the authors' own research (see the Theoretical and Technical Specifications Manual). For example, in the Minimal Pairs subtest, /hw/ versus /h/ and "especially" versus "specially" in the English versions, and "todo" versus "toro" and "acosar" versus "acusar" in the Spanish version, are failed by about half the native monolingual children tested, and therefore cannot be used to differentiate proficient and nonproficient child hearer-users of the language.

The Phonemes task contains several errors. For example, in English Level II, Form B, the phoneme /c/ is modeled in isolation in the word "chess," and in context in the phrase, "He ate sandwiches for lunch." The speaker on the tape, like many native English speakers, pronounces "sandwiches" with /j/. In English Level I, Form A, the pronunciation /hw/ is modeled in isolation and in context for the words "white" and "wheat." Since this phoneme is rarely used in native English monolingual dialects, it should be dropped. Also, while some of the contexts used to model the target phoneme are plausible sentences, others are semantically silly or even syntactically anomalous: for example, "My father is further," "There's white and wheat" (English Levels I and II, Form A). Pronunciation and memory load are thus confounded. Since pronunciation is the issue here, surely the test sentences should be constructed to be meaningful. In Lexical Items, the same objection holds true for "dinosauro" in the Spanish version.

The Sentence Comprehension task, strongly reminiscent of Carrow's (1973) Test for Auditory Comprehension, is the weakest section of the LAS. Statistically, there are several items failed by many first grade monolingual children, both English and Spanish. Some items are failed even by older monolinguals. Since there are only 10 items tested, it is important that only valid ones be included. Poor scores on many of these items should probably be attributed to the drawings, which are sometimes ambiguous and are singularly unappealing. It is important in this context to test comprehension of language, not whether the child can solve ambiguities in poorly drawn cartoons. They badly need revision.

The Sentence Comprehension section sometimes tests vocabulary rather than syntax. At Level II, instead of probing comprehension of language, some of the stimuli are language puzzles, requiring a good memory and the ability to solve problems. For example, consider this stimulus from English Level II, Form A: "There are three pictures of little boys. Point to the picture where there is only one little boy who is not standing." Or this one: "Point to the picture which shows no more than one boy who is sitting and one barefoot girl talking on the telephone to a friend who cannot be seen in the picture."

Doubts can be raised about more general issues of test construction; for example, is Minimal Pairs (auditory discrimination) a useful subtest in a test of Oral Proficiency? The authors explain that "a low score on this subscale is an indication that the student may have difficulty understanding (decoding) words and sentences in instructional and other conversations." There are no data to this effect.

The test authors assert that the LAS results can be used to predict future school achievement (such as reading and math) in an English-only classroom; they further assert that it can be used as a basis for a plan of action for individualized remediation or small group instruction. No data to justify these assertions are provided in any of the manuals, though respectable correlations between the LAS and current school achievement are provided. No longitudinal data were collected at all, so correlations with future school performance remain an unknown.

While the authors do not explicitly claim that the LAS score is a quantitative measure of oral language proficiency, the labels attached to a child's score denote such a claim. The LAS cannot be used meaningfully to describe level of proficiency. If a child receives a total score of 72, so his oral proficiency level is 3, or "limited speaker," the clinician or teacher has no information about his level of language development relative to age. Specifically, this is because there are so many flawed items in the various subtests, and demands for nonlinguistic skills (such as problem solving); and especially because no statistical rationale is provided for the weighting of the various subtests. Another reason is that few test administrators will be properly trained to score Oral Proficiency, the most heavily weighted of the various subtests.

The authors do not refer to the proficiency criteria in use at the Foreign Service Institute, where the U.S. Government does much of its foreign language training. The same five levels are used there as in the LAS. The Foreign Service Institute has found that it requires lengthy disciple training to become a reliable scorer in this system; but, given adequate training, scorers are reliable within and among themselves, and the system is the finest known to this reviewer. However, because this system is meant to be independent of age, complexity of the content is not scored. The naive scorer tends to score content rather than form.

A second serious limitation in the quantitative interpretation of an individual's score, this one theoretical, concerns the basis of the norm of the test. All proficiency of Level I is with respect to a monolingual first grader. Consequently, nothing can be said about the development of language proficiency that would be expected as a function of age or grade through the elementary school years.

As a measure of oral language proficiency, the LAS has two outstanding virtues. First, it includes in "oral proficiency" measures of phonological, lexical, and syntactic knowledge. Second, to measure oral proficiency, the LAS relies most heavily on the student's spontaneous (yet controlled) utterances. Many measures of "oral proficiency" rely on nonverbal responses (which are far easier to record and score). Most tests that do use oral responses involve a repetition task, production of single words, or at best single sentences. Although the LAS oral proficiency task represents a highly structured and thus somewhat artificial context, in that the student retells a story, this task seems far better than either a spontaneous sample (which is subject to too many variables to be reliable) or the highly artificial and limited measures typically used. The researcher who wants to correlate normal first graders' language (measured as proficient on the LAS) with other cognitive skills, can clean up the problematical test items and have at his disposal not only a wealth of widely and carefully normed data, but one of the finest measures of oral proficiency known to this reviewer.

REVIEWER'S REFERENCES

Carrow, E. TEST FOR AUDITORY COMPREHENSION OF LANGUAGE: ENGLISH/SPANISH. Austin, TX: Learning Concepts, Fifth Edition, 1973.

[585]

Language Facility Test. Ages 3 and over; 1965–80; LFT; identical with Language Facility Test ('68) except for slight changes in manual; measures language and grammar in English or Spanish; 2 scoring systems (9-point qualitative scale for evaluating communication in primary language, error analysis for standard English) for verbal responses to 12 pictures; norms available for ages 3–15; individually administered in English or Spanish; 1 form ('77, 4 pages); manual ('77, 45 pages); manual supplements: Spanish version ('76, 13 pages); selected dissertations and technical reports ('80, 53 pages); stimulus pictures ('65, 12 pictures); 1983 price data: $22.50 per complete test set; $12 per 100 answer booklets; $2.50 per manual; (10–15) minutes; John T. Dailey; Allington Corporation.*

See T3:1282 (1 reference); for a review by Nicholas Anastasiow of an earlier form, see 7:955 (1 reference).

Review of Language Facility Test by CHARLES STANSFIELD, Associate Director/Language Programs, Educational Testing Service, Princeton, NJ:

The test reviewed is the second edition of the Language Facility Test (LFT). The test measures oral language "facility," a concept which developed as a reaction to the language deficit theory, which was current during the 1960s. The LFT is designed to measure facility in English as spoken in the home. Responses are rated without reference to standard English syntax, vocabulary, pronunciation, or environmental knowledge. The test requires children to describe 3 pictures, which are selected by the examiner from among 12 plates that are included in the test kit. The pictures are in one of three formats: (*a*) photographs of a teacher and children interacting in a migrant farm worker's preschool; (*b*) line drawings of a child in leisurely pose with little background detail or environmental stimuli; and (*c*) representations of paintings by the Spanish masters, Goya, Murillo, and Velasquez. Responses are recorded in writing by the examiner and ratings are assigned to responses for each picture on a scale of 0–9. Thus, the range of possible scores on the test is 0–27. The Test Administrator's Manual describes procedures for scoring responses. The response categories range from "no response," which is scored as a 0, to "well-organized story with imagination and creativity," which is scored as a 9. The manual gives sample responses for each plate and for each age group on which the test was normed (ages 3 to 15 years).

The second edition of the LFT includes a Spanish translation of the Test Administrator's Manual. Although standard Spanish is utilized, it is occasionally apparent that the translator was not familiar with use of Spanish to describe testing procedures. The word "examiner" is translated as conductor instead of the correct term examinador, and the phrase "to give a test" is incorrectly translated as conducir un examen instead of dar un examen.

A considerable amount of information on the reliability and validity of the test is reported in a manual supplement which draws on information in a dozen dissertations and reports involving the instrument. It is to the test author's credit that both favorable and unfavorable findings are included in the supplement.

A review of the studies cited indicates the reliability of the LFT is higher than that which is ordinarily obtained by measures of oral language. For a sample of 630 nine-year-old students in Washington, D.C. elementary schools, the average inter-correlation between ratings on the separate individual plates was .70. Using the Spearman-Brown prophecy formula, this suggests that a three-picture form of the test has a reliability of .88. A study of 56 mentally retarded children in the Baltimore Public Schools reported a test-retest reliability coefficient of .85. In a study of deaf students, the correlation between scores on two administrations was .76. When one considers that these scores represent pre- and posttreatment measures, it is probable that the true test-retest reliability of a single three-picture form is about equal to that projected by the Spearman-Brown formula. The interrater reliability is also quite adequate. A study of 116 Texas students enrolled in a Head Start program produced a correlation between raters of .92. Studies involving samples larger than 100 subjects show interrater correlations of between .88 and .94.

Although the reliability of the test is substantiated by independent research, its validity is not. None of the concurrent validity coefficients reported by the author is comforting. Based on a sample of 630 subjects, some of the correlations between LFT and other language proficiency assessments were: Metropolitan Reading Readiness (.12), Peabody Picture Vocabulary Test (.37), Gates Reading Test (.02), and teacher ratings (.22). Studies by other researchers show that the LFT correlates .25 with the Peabody Picture Vocabulary Test, .28 with the Metropolitan Reading Readiness Test, .18 with teacher ratings, and .01 with parent ratings. The low correlations between the LFT and other language measures may indicate that the LFT is measuring something other than language. In a study of 104 black students involving 26 measures the LFT showed non-significant correlations (.03 and .12) with the other language measures employed, but a significant correlation (.30) with a measure of creativity.

While the LFT may indeed be measuring something, it does not appear to be empirically verified as a valid measure of language competence or proficiency. In order to score high on the rating scale, the child needs to be capable of describing situations and drawing inferences. The plates do not facilitate this since they depict only a single picture. Less creative children are likely to name objects in a single picture without telling a story. A cartoon or picture sequence would be more effective. In order to improve upon the test as a language proficiency measure, while utilizing the current pictures, a tape recorded story based on the picture could be played to each child, who could retell the story in his own words. This use of story retelling would reduce the degree to which the test taps creativity to an acceptable level.

The current version of the LFT confuses language proficiency with cognitive development, which it measures through the construct of linguistic creativity. On the basis of professional testing standards it should not be used as a language proficiency assessment instrument without further evidence supporting its validity for an intended application.

[586]

The Language Imitation Test. Educationally subnormal children; no date on test materials; LIT; experimental instrument; 6 subtests: Sound Imitation, Word Imitation, Syntactic Control 1, Syntactic Control 2, Word Organisation Control, Sentence Completion; no norms; individual; record form (no date, 4 pages); manual (no date, 41 pages); 1985 price data: £3.85 per 25 record forms; £5.25 per manual; £5.35 per specimen set; administration time not reported; Paul Berry and Peter Mittler; NFER-Nelson Publishing Co. [England].*

TEST REFERENCES

1. McLeavey, B. C., Toomey, J. F., & Dempsey, P. J. R. Nonretarded and mentally retarded children's control over syntactic structures. AMERICAN JOURNAL OF MENTAL DEFICIENCY, 1982, 86, 485–494.

Review of The Language Imitation Test by RITA SLOAN BERNDT, Research Associate Professor, Department of Neurology, University of Maryland Medical School, Baltimore, MD:

SUMMARY. The purpose of this test is to provide a supplementary profile of the language abilities of the severely educational subnormal, and it is suggested that it be used in conjunction with other tests. The premise underlying the development of The Language Imitation Test is that the child brings a knowledge of language into operation when imitating words, sounds, or sentences. The pattern of errors produced is interpreted as an indication of the level of linguistic development on which the child is operating. The test itself consists of six subtests, with varying levels of complexity within each.

Scoring is based on a complex system, which varies from subtest to subtest. No norms are provided.

CRITIQUE. This test is an admirable attempt to obtain separate estimates about a child's functioning on different aspects of language processing. The scoring procedure requires attention to preservation of meaning, for example, as distinct from preservation of sentence form. Although one must applaud this view of language as a componential system that may show a selective disruption of its components, it is a difficult problem to develop a scoring system that reflects this view. This test fails to provide a scoring system that would adequately capture a selective disruption of a single component, should it occur. In subtest 4, for example, the omission of a negative morpheme (here for some reason expressed as the phonologically minimal bound morpheme "-n't") is an error both of form and of meaning. Although the authors recognize this, their solution is not satisfactory. A quantitative score is not going to capture the difference between this type of omission and some other.

There are two factors that could make this test more valuable, despite problems with the scoring system. First, if reliable norms were available, the test could serve as a reasonably quick screening test to place a specific child in relation to some group. Since the theoretical underpinnings of this instrument are at best debatable (i.e., that repetition is an indication of language competence), the inclusion of norms would have added some needed pragmatic support to a theoretically shaky rationale. Without such norms, the test seems to add little to the kinds of exercises a good clinician can devise in a few minutes.

A second possible way this test could be made more useful would involve the addition of a comprehension measure, linked to these sentence types. The relationships between a child's comprehension of particular sentences, and his/her ability to repeat them, is undoubtedly worth knowing. A child who could understand more than s/he could repeat would almost certainly suffer from a different functional deficit than a child who could repeat more than s/he could understand.

In summary, there are some kernels of good ideas in this test and its supporting materials. In its present form, however, it would seem to offer little of value to the practicing clinician.

[587]

Language Inventory for Teachers. Grades 1–12; 1982; LIT; checklist for use by teachers to assess written and spoken language; no data on reliability; no norms; individual; 1 form (6 pages); manual (111 pages); 1984 price data: $6 per 25 tests; $12 per manual; $12 per specimen set; (45–60) minutes; Arlene Cooper and Beverly A. School; Academic Therapy Publications.*

Review of Language Inventory for Teachers by MARCEE J. MEYERS, Associate Professor of Education, University of North Carolina-Wilmington, Wilmington, NC:

OVERVIEW. The Language Inventory for Teachers (LIT) is a criterion-referenced instrument for assessing spoken and written language skills and developing related instruction. The manual clearly describes this purpose with detailed examples of its application to individual educational program (IEP) development. According to the authors, the LIT is intended for use with special education students with the exception of children manifesting speech articulation or serious language difficulties. Special qualifications required for administration and interpretation are minimally identified; the manual states only that the inventory "should be administered by a professional who can be alert to specific student needs."

The checklist consists of 579 items classified according to five spoken language and eight written language goal statements. The authors suggest that these goals provide a hierarchy of language development useful for lesson planning. Neither the theory underlying the inventory nor the nature of the language characteristics assessed is clearly described. Initially the manual states that the LIT is "based on sound principles of learning, the acquisition of language, the use of language, and language as it relates to efficient learning at school." This statement, without specific examples of these learning and language principles, is clearly inadequate. The authors do state that the "conceptual framework upon which this inventory is predicated was drawn in chart form by Dr. Thom Cooper" and also that these charts of concept domains describe "the scope of language." The narrative section of the manual does not explain this model, its development, or its application. Furthermore, there does not appear to be a definite relationship among all the goals and the concept domains. If in fact Cooper's theoretical framework is sound, applicable to test construction, and useful for curriculum development as implied in the manual, the rationale for the model and more elaborate explanation of its components should be provided for test users. No references are even suggested for background reading.

ADMINISTRATION AND SCORING. The LIT manual and checklist form are poorly written, making administration procedures ambiguous. Numerous misprints make both the manual and checklist form difficult to use. This reviewer noted 14 misspelled words in the booklet, 3 cases of omitted words or punctuation that make the test items confusing, 7 examples of incorrect numbering on the checklist form, 5 tense errors in the test items, and 3 instances in which the test items are incorrectly referenced to their corresponding pictures.

In addition, several ambiguities are found in the questions and scoring procedures in the manual. Three of the test items never state whether the student or examiner should read the stimulus material. One question is incomprehensible to the reviewer because of careless placement of quotation marks and parentheses and incomplete instructions. In a few instances, abbreviations are used for language structures without any indication of their complete label; the following sentence pattern is included with no explanation: Sub. + is + Lod. Adv. (or Prep. Phrase). For one matching item, directions specify that the student should write letters of words to match numbered words, while the format suggests just the reverse (writing numbers to match lettered words).

On the checklist form, additional ambiguities exist. One item objective states that the student will use "N-V (to be) -N sentences (A dog is an animal)"; however, this behavior is never elicited by the directions or corresponding questions. Some of the checklist items do not seem to match the corresponding language goals; in several cases, for example, general information and mathematical skills are assessed.

The organization of the manual and checklist also creates a problem for test administration and scoring. The goals are included in the manual for the written language items, but not the spoken language items; this omission makes the classification of test items confusing. Several sentence patterns are listed throughout the checklist without explanation of their purpose or use. The checklist form does not have the appropriate number of blanks for recording student responses in numerous cases. For one test item, it is impossible to show the stimulus picture and ask the related questions simultaneously because the picture is printed on the back page of the questions. Use of the checklist form for recording responses to all written language items is virtually impossible because of problems with sequencing, overlap, and general organization.

Finally, the manual suggests the use of M (mastery), P (partial mastery), and N (needs instruction) for marking the checklist. Examples are provided for Mastery, but only a limited number for Partial Mastery. In summary, the directions are not presented with sufficient clarity or detail to allow smooth administration or accurate scoring.

INTERPRETATION. The LIT manual presents a list of variables that should be taken into account in interpreting performance. However, the variables listed—hearing loss, visual deficits, speech difficulties, and interference from bilingual homes—seem somewhat limited as factors affecting spoken and written language performance. The manual alerts the teacher to only three types of student errors: omissions, overgeneralizations, and limited carryover of rule. The lack of a more inclusive description of errors seriously compromises the usefulness of the manual. Although the applications suggested for using inventory results to generate IEP goals and objectives provides a practical approach for language assessment and instructional planning, there are several omissions in the specific IEP examples; one goal, two performance statements, and three educational tasks are incomplete. In one case, the evaluation procedure and criterion were vague rather than objective; the procedure was "teacher judgment" and the criterion was "improved performance."

TECHNICAL INFORMATION. The test manual does not describe fully the development of the LIT. One sentence suggests that the test is based on sound learning and language principles, but no explanation of the rationale, specifications followed in writing items, or related research is included. No norms are provided other than a list of goals and expected grade levels for development. All that the authors say is that "goals can be assessed and should be evaluated by the teacher in terms of peer comparison" and that "teacher knowledge of local norms is invaluable while assessing student skills." There is not one word in the manual pertaining to validity of the LIT.

SUMMARY. This reviewer cannot recommend the LIT until further information is provided and the *Standards for Educational and Psychological Tests* are addressed. Elaboration is needed on the underlying theory, inventory development, validity, and reliability. Furthermore, corrections need to be made and ambiguities clarified. The format of the checklist and manual should also be reorganized to facilitate administration, scoring, and interpretation. If these revisions and additions were made, it would be possible to determine if the inventory is appropriate for the stated purpose and application.

[588]

Language Proficiency Test. Grades 9 and over; 1981; LPT; 6–9 scores: aural/oral (commands, short answers [optional], comprehension [optional]), reading (vocabulary, comprehension), writing (grammar, sentence response, paragraph response, translation [optional]); reliability and validity for reading comprehension subtest only; no norms; short answer and aural/oral comprehension subtests individually administered; 1 form (12 pages); manual (29 pages); 1984 price data: $22.50 per test kit including manual and 10 tests; $15 per 10 tests; $7.50 per manual; $7.50 per specimen set; (80–100) minutes; Joan Gerard and Gloria Weinstock; Academic Therapy Publications.*

Review of Language Proficiency Test by JOHN M. KEENE, JR., Coordinator of Placement and

Proficiency Testing, Evaluation and Examination Service, The University of Iowa, Iowa City, IA:

The Language Proficiency Test, according to its authors, is a nine part English Language test for grade nine and above that "assesses a wide range of language ability yet uses materials that are not demeaning to the older student." The manual states the test is "especially suited to students who use English as a second language (ESL), learning handicapped students, and others with low-level language skills." The test is intended for placement and diagnosis of specific language deficiencies and is designed for criterion-referenced interpretation.

The organization consists of three major sections covering aural/oral skills, reading skills, and writing skills. Each section contains a set of subtests: aural/oral (commands, short answers, and comprehension), reading (vocabulary and comprehension), and writing (grammar, sentence response, paragraph response, and translation). Items are arranged in order of increasing difficulty within subtests.

Administration time is approximately one and a half hours. Seven of the subtests can be administered in group situations, while two subtests require individual administration. The administrator and the student mark directly in the test booklet provided. The test booklet contains a profile sheet for interpretation of subtest scores. Machine readable answer sheets are not available. Scoring procedures vary among subtests, but all raw scores are converted to an adjusted score that can range between 0 and 100.

The manual is brief, providing a description of the test, instructions for administration and scoring, a section on interpretation, and a set of four case studies illustrating the use of the instrument. There are no norms of any kind provided. Reliability data consists of a test-retest reliability coefficient (2-week interval) of .87 for 46 high school students. The reliability was computed only for the Reading Comprehension subtest, one-ninth of the total test. Validity data also is sparse. The correlation for the same 46 students between the Language Proficiency Test and the Barnel-Loft Multiple Skill Series is .77. The manual does not indicate whether this coefficient is based on total test or an individual subtest score.

The authors of this test have attempted to measure the breadth of English Language skills in a very small sample of behaviors. Because measurement of language skills in this type of situation is very dependent on specific word meanings, problems arise. In the Oral/Aural Commands section, the student is given 10 command sentences to respond to. Six of these 10 items deal with the concepts of books and writing (e.g., "Draw a circle on the bottom of the page."). If a student does not understand a single word concept, he will miss most of the section. A larger sample, with more items, would help alleviate this problem.

Item construction, especially in the Reading Comprehension section, could use some attention. The Reading Comprehension items are multiple choice items presented after short passages. Often the item stems are not complete questions and responses are not ordered as they should be. For instance, when a question asking for a time period is asked, the responses are (A) five months, (B) one year, (C) two months, (D) two weeks. This problem occurs in several places. There is no need to introduce such confusing format in a test of basic comprehension.

The scoring process for the Reading Comprehension subtest is rather unique. This subtest consists of 40 multiple choice items divided equally among 10 passages. The passages are arranged from easiest to most difficult according to the Fry Readability Formula. The student is asked to complete questions for all 10 passages. Scoring is accomplished by summing the number correct until reaching the first passage where three of four items are incorrect; no correct answers beyond this point are included in the score. The rationale behind this scoring procedure is not provided. Since readability indices are not 100% reliable, and familiarity of content may be quite important in this task, a great amount of information can be lost with this scoring procedure.

The interpretation section of the manual provides a scheme for placement based on percent correct; the authors warn these are only guidelines. A great deal of caution needs to be used in interpreting the nine adjusted subtest score scales and profile provided through use of the scoring procedures. The use of a 100-point scale when only five questions are asked (e.g., Oral/Aural Comprehension subscale) may allow instructors interpreting the profile to believe a greater difference exists than really does exist. A student not comprehending one statement receives a score of 20 less than one who comprehends all. Users may want to ignore the adjusted score scale and profile provided.

The manual stresses the placement nature of this instrument. The instrument is geared more toward diagnosis of potential problems and to indicate areas where further testing is needed. The use of this instrument to make decisions about students in any form cannot be recommended until adequate validity and reliability evidence is provided. At that point, because of the small behavior sample for most of the subtests, only very general screening functions can be recommended.

[589]

Language Sampling, Analysis, and Training, Revised Edition. Children with language delay; 1974–77; no data on reliability; no norms; individual; no reading by examinees; 1 form, 6 parts ('74); revised manual ('77, 60 pages including sample worksheets); visual and verbal stimuli for eliciting language sample determined by examiner; tape recorder recommended to record responses; 1982 price data: $17.50 per 25 sets of worksheets; $5.50 per 3 sets of worksheets and handbook; $4.25 per handbook; Dorothy Tyack and Robert Gottsleben; Consulting Psychologists Press, Inc.*

a) TRANSCRIPTION SHEETS. 1 form (4 pages); $8 per 50 worksheets; (30–90) minutes.

b) WORD/MORPHEME TALLY AND SUMMARY. 6 scores: 3 totals (sentences, words, morphemes) and 3 means (words/sentence, morphemes/sentence, word-morpheme index); 1 form (1 page); $4.25 per 50 worksheets; (10) minutes.

c) SEQUENCE OF LANGUAGE ACQUISITION. Assessment of 6 areas: noun phrase constituents, verb phrase constituents, constructions, complex sentences, negation, questions; 1 form (4 pages); $8 per 50 worksheets; (30) minutes.

d) BASELINE AND GOAL DATA. 1 form (2 pages); $4.25 per 50 worksheets; (20) minutes.

e) TRAINING WORKSHEET. 1 form (2 pages); prices same as for *d*; (10) minutes.

f) SCORE SHEET. 1 form (1 page); prices same as for *d*; used during training lesson.

Review of Language Sampling, Analysis, and Training, Revised Edition, by MARGARET C. BYRNE, University of Kansas, Lawrence, KS:

The purpose of this procedure is to analyze 100 utterances of an individual according to a specific grammatical system in order to plan an intervention program for those who need it. It is recommended for language-delayed individuals whose utterances range from two to six words.

The procedure is based on Chomsky's theory of acquisition of sentence structures and their underlying rules. The structures that Tyack and Gottsleben analyze are those that Morehead and Ingram found to be the most frequently occurring in children's speech. The latter organized the structures in the developmental sequence that they identified in their research.

When the language sample has been gathered, it is transcribed on a form that permits analysis of the number of words and morphemes per utterance, the form (a word or an affix), and the constructions (linear arrangement in which the forms occur). The clinician then calculates the word-morpheme mean; assigns the sample to a linguistic level (I to V); completes the sheets, Sequence of Language Acquisition, with all the correct and incorrect noun phrase constituents, noun phrases, verb phrases, combinations of noun and verb phrases, complex sentences, negation, questions, modals, particles, copula, present progressive tense, present tense 3rd person singular, and past tense, as indicated.

After the sample has been completely analyzed in this fashion, the clinician then prepares the Baseline and Goal worksheet. It provides the direction of the intervention program.

This method of language sampling analysis provides an excellent picture of the individual's grammatic performance in a 100-utterance sample. If the sample is typical of the person's language use, then its analysis will indicate the linguistic level and the direction for therapy that is developmentally oriented. If the sample is not adequate, or the clinician wishes to use a remedial rather than a developmental approach, this system will not be useful.

The major concern of clinicians who utilize this format is the fact that it is so time-consuming. The authors provide no estimate, but the completion of the paper work, after the sample has been transcribed, may take several hours. Also, the analysis is syntactic and provides no information about the semantic or the pragmatic aspects of communication.

SUMMARY. This procedure for analyzing a language sample in order to determine the developmental level and plan an intervention program has a firm theoretical basis. It provides a very detailed grammatical analysis of the language output of individuals whose average utterance contains two to six words. It is a time-consuming procedure. The Elicited Language Inventory may be preferable for those at the one- to three-word level; and the Developmental Sentence Analysis for those in the four- to six-word category.

[590]

Language Sampling and Analysis. Ages 1.5–14.5; 1978; LSA; supplement to Utah Test of Language Development; helps pinpoint language problems and measures an individual child's language change or development; individual; Form B—language sample data sheet, Form C—summary analysis sheet, (1 page); manual (22 pages); 1983 price data: $20 per kit including 50 language sample data sheets and 25 summary analysis sheets; $4 per 50 additional language sample data sheets; $2.50 per 25 additional summary analysis sheets; $50 per combination of UTLD kit and LSA kit; Merlin J. Mecham and J. Dean Jones; Communication Research Associates, Inc.*

[591]

Laterality Preference Schedule. Children and adults; 1978; LPS; 6 scores: general laterality, visually guided activity, visual, auditory, strength, foot use; reliability and validity data, for preadolescent children only, not included in test materials; norms, for adults only, consist of means and standard deviations; 1 form (5 pages, including normative data); no manual; 1982 price data: $20 per 100 tests; administration time not reported; Raymond S. Dean; the Author.*

See T3:1289 (6 references).

TEST REFERENCES

1. Dean, R. S., & Smith, L. S. Personality and lateral preference patterns in children. CLINICAL NEUROPSYCHOLOGY, 1981, 3(4), 22–28.

2. Dean, R. S., & Hua, M. S. Laterality effects in cued auditory asymmetrics. NEUROPSYCHOLOGIA, 1982, 20, 685–690.

Review of Laterality Preference Schedule by PATTI L. HARRISON, Research Associate—Test Division, American Guidance Service, Circle Pines, MN:

The Laterality Preference Schedule (LPS) assesses individuals' lateral preference for the performance of everyday activities, such as hopping, listening on the telephone, and holding a glass. Based on the premise that simple handedness is an inadequate representation of cerebral dominance, the LPS provides an indication of the different lateral systems used in peripheral activities and estimates degrees of cerebral specialization (Dean, 1982). The LPS offers a multifactor measure which views lateral dominance on a continuum.

GENERAL DESCRIPTION. The LPS is a 49-item self-report questionnaire which requires the respondent to indicate right-left preferences for activities involving the eye, ear, foot, arm, or hand. A score for each item is based on one of five choices selected by the respondent: left always, left mostly, left and right equally, right mostly, and right always. A total score and scores for six factors are obtained by summing the item scores. There is the possibility of a response set existing for the item scores, especially since the items pertaining to eye, ear, foot, etc. are grouped together.

Brief normative data are attached to the questionnaire and indicate mean scores and standard deviations for the six factors obtained from a sample of 256 male and female undergraduates. Unfortunately, a technical manual is not available for the LPS. The user must review and integrate various research reports for additional interpretive information: for example, mean factor scores and standard deviations for normal children (Dean, Schwartz, & Smith, 1981); performance of poor readers (Dean, 1978a, 1980); and cerebral patterns in psychiatric disorders (Dean, 1984b).

DEVELOPMENT. The LPS is the result of an extensive development which began with 153 items (Dean, 1982). About 100 undergraduates responded to the items; two days later, the students again responded to the items and were asked to physically perform the tasks assessed by the items. The final 49-item scale was obtained by eliminating any items which did not exhibit correlations of .80 or higher between initial response and two criteria (second response and actual performance). After the final scale was completed by 1,000 undergraduates, factor analysis identified six factors which accounted for 91.9% of the variability of the scale.

RELIABILITY. Moderate to good stability coefficients are reported for the LPS. With a sample of preadolescent children and a 4-week interval between test administration, Dean (1978b) found a correlation of .91 between total LPS scores. Coefficients of .69 to .93 for the six factor scores were obtained with a sample of undergraduates and a 1-week interval between test administrations (Dean, 1982). Internal consistency reliability coefficients are not reported for LPS.

VALIDITY. Validity information for the LPS is abundant and provides promising evidence for the practical utility of the scale and the ability of LPS scores to distinguish groups of individuals. Dean, Schwartz, and Smith (1981) found that learning disabled children were significantly more bilateral than normal children on the visually guided activity, visual preference, and foot use factors of the LPS, although no differences were found for the total score summed across factors. Dean (1978a, 1980) reports that poor readers with adequate vocabulary skills were significantly more bilateral than normal readers or poor readers with inadequate vocabulary. Dean (1979, 1980) indicates that more bilateral scores on the LPS are associated with higher Verbal than Performance IQs. In a study investigating levels of anxiety and emotional stability of children, the visually guided factor emerged as the most salient dimension (Dean & Smith, 1982); and depressive and schizo-affective patients obtained more bilateral scores than schizophrenic patients on the visually guided activity and visual preference factors (Dean, 1984b).

Using the visually guided activity factor to identify individuals with bilateral preference patterns, the author of the LPS provides evidence for the effects of different task presentations on learning. Dean and Hua (1982) found that instructions to shift attention to the directed ear significantly increased recognition of stimuli for bilateral individuals. Dean and Schwartz (1982) indicate that shortening the visual span of text lines increased comprehension and recall for bilateral readers and Dean (1984a) reports that instructions to image and visual interference had little effect on bilateral individuals' passage recall.

SUMMARY. The Laterality Preference Schedule is an easily administered scale which appears to have potential as a valuable tool. The author of the LPS provides evidence of the complex nature of cerebral lateralization and, with carefully planned research, supports the utility of the scale in studying different lateral systems. However, the use of LPS scores is difficult with the limited normative data and lack of specific guidelines for interpretation. A technical manual which summarizes research conducted with the scale and indicates suggestions for interpretation of scores or patterns of scores is clearly needed.

REVIEWER'S REFERENCES

Dean, R. S. Cerebral laterality and reading comprehension. NEUROPSYCHOLOGIA, 1978, 16, 633–636. (a)

Dean, R. S. Reliability and predictive validity of the Dean Laterality Preference Schedule with preadolescents. PERCEPTUAL AND MOTOR SKILLS, 1978, 47, 1345–1346. (b)

Dean, R. S. Cerebral laterality and verbal-performance discrepancies in intelligence. JOURNAL OF SCHOOL PSYCHOLOGY, 1979, 17, 145–150.

Dean, R. S. Cerebral lateralization and reading dysfunction. JOURNAL OF SCHOOL PSYCHOLOGY, 1980, 18, 324–331.

Dean, R. S., Schwartz, N. H., & Smith, L. S. Lateral preference patterns as a discriminator of learning difficulties. JOURNAL OF CONSULTING AND CLINICAL PSYCHOLOGY, 1981, 49, 227–235.

Dean, R. S. Assessing patterns of lateral preference. CLINICAL NEUROPSYCHOLOGY, 1982, 4, 124–128.

Dean, R. S., & Hua, M. S. Laterality effects in cued auditory asymmetries. NEUROPSYCHOLOGIA, 1982, 20, 685–690.

Dean, R. S., & Schwartz, N. H. INCREASING COMPREHENSION IN THE MIXED LATERAL ADULT READER. Paper presented at the annual convention of the American Psychological Association, Washington, DC: August, 1982.

Dean, R. S., & Smith, L. S. Personality and lateral preference patterns in children. CLINICAL NEUROPSYCHOLOGY, 1982, 3, 22–38.

Dean, R. S. Cerebral laterality effects in the dual processing of prose. CONTEMPORARY EDUCATIONAL PSYCHOLOGY, 1984, 9, 384–393. (a)

Dean, R. S. LATERAL PATTERNS IN SCHIZOPHRENIA AND AFFECTIVE DISORDERS. Paper presented at the annual convention of the National Academy of Neuropsychology, San Diego, CA: October, 1984. (b)

Review of Laterality Preference Schedule by JOHN E. OBRZUT, Professor of Educational Psychology, University of Arizona, Tucson, AZ:

The Laterality Preference Schedule (LPS) was designed as a screening measure of cerebral laterality for preadolescent children and adult populations. Laterality as measured in the LPS refers to a specific behavioral characteristic such as degree of hand preference. The unique contribution of the LPS is that each of the behavioral characteristics is viewed as a continuous variable rather than as an arbitrary dichotomy. Recently it has become clear that generalized patterns of lateralization (e.g., hand preference) may not represent dominance at the cortical level (Kinsbourne & Hiscock, 1981). In fact, there is evidence that simple handedness may not be as sensitive to cerebral dysfunction as discrepancies of eye/hand (Dunlop, Dunlop, & Fenelon, 1973) or ear/hand (Bryden, 1967) preferences. For example, data have been offered in support of less coherently lateralized cerebral systems for language disabled children but few differences of generalized patterns across tasks (Dean, Schwartz, & Smith, 1981). Thus, it is deemed more advantageous to view differences in lateral preference for the individual as a function of the particular cerebral system under investigation.

The Laterality Preference Schedule is an easily administered 49-item self-report measure that Dean has found to have some utility in assessing a respondent's lateral preference on a number of tasks involving the eyes, ears, arms, hands, legs, and feet. The inventory requires the respondent to indicate on a five-point Likert scale his/her preference from right-always to left-always for each item. A laterality score is calculated for each item using weights for each response category: right always=1, right mostly=2, both equally=3, left mostly=4, left always=5. Thus, scores extend from 49 (all items scored right always) to 245 (all items scored left always). Subscales of the LPS have also been isolated on the basis of factor analysis. Dean (1982a) states that using a principle component solution for the responses of 1,000 normal adults, six factors emerged from the 49 items of the measure. The six dimensions have been labeled by Dean as: Factor I—General Laterality (13 items), Factor II—Visually Guided Activity (17 items), Factor III—Visual (5 items), Factor IV—Auditory (5 items), Factor V—Strength (5 items), and Factor VI—Foot Use (4 items). Normative data for adults are provided for each of the six factors by sex and are located at the end of the inventory. Subjects can be tested in small or large groups with 4–20 subjects per group. Scoring should follow standard procedures as outlined in the manual, which may be obtained from the author upon request.

In initial attempts at estimating reliability and predictive validity, the author has reported a correlation of .83 between items of the LPS and manual performance in the laboratory with a group of 50 normal preadolescents (25 boys and 25 girls), and a temporal stability correlation of .91 when children were retested 4 weeks after its initial administration (Dean, 1978). Stability of factor scores for adults over a one-week period was found to range from .69 to .93 (Dean, 1982a). Predictably, those factors with the fewest number of items proved the least stable over time. Besides finding a similar six-factor structure for both males and females, males presented a significantly more anomalous pattern in their lateralization for general handedness, strength, and those tasks requiring visually guided fine motor activity. These results suggest that although the factor structure seems to warrant consideration of the LPS as a multifactor measure, the lack of stability and predictive utility of some factors may limit the use of the entire measure in neuropsychological research.

In fact, several studies have indicated that Factor II, which requires visual guidance in task performance, may be the most sensitive to other measures of cognitive (Dean, 1979; Dean, Schwartz, & Smith, 1981) and personality dysfunction (Dean & Smith, 1981). Therefore, most of the available studies have taken this into consideration and have used Factor II as the predictor of cerebral laterality.

While some of the evidence has been generated on groups of learning-disabled and normal children, other data has been gathered on young adult (undergraduate) populations. More specifically, cerebral laterality as inferred with the LPS has been shown to relate to various configurations of verbal-performance discrepancies in learning-disabled children (Dean, 1979), with seventh grade difference-poor readers (Dean, 1980), and with scores of the Trait Anxiety Inventory for Children on a normal preadolescent group and the Sixteen Personality Factor Questionnaire on a normal adolescent group (Dean & Smith, 1981).

On the other hand, adult populations have been used to study the comprehension effects after manipulating the spatial configuration of prose materials with readers who differed in lateral dominance (Dean & Schwartz, 1982), the degree to which the concreteness of auditorially presented prose material would interact with one's lateral preference (Dean, 1982b), and the effect of cued attention on perceptual asymmetries in those who differed in their lateral preference. One study even examined the patterns of laterality for psychiatric groups of schizophrenic, schizoaffective, and unipolar depressives.

Overall, Dean has accomplished the goal of developing an instrument of lateral preference which has a large number of objectively scored items. The major strength of this endeavor is that the inventory appears to have good-to-moderate stability on certain factors (e.g., Factor II) and also seems to have adequate differential utility for practical or research purposes. However, one obvious weakness is that most if not all of the validation research has been conducted by the author and colleagues. Replication by other researchers is necessary in order to enhance validity of the measure. In general, the practitioner should be cautioned that a technical manual with reliability and validity data is lacking, and normative data is limited to preadolescent children and college undergraduates. Finally, Dean points out that while the LPS is a reliable estimate of children's lateral preference patterns, it is by no means a clinical measure of neurological functioning. Keeping these cautions in mind, the practitioner will find this instrument a valuable asset in clinical practice or neuropsychological research.

REVIEWER'S REFERENCES

Bryden, M. P. An evaluation of some models of laterality effects in dichotic listening. ACTA OTO-LARYNGOLOGICA, 1967, 63, 595–605.

Dunlop, D. B., Dunlop, P., & Fenelon, B. Vision laterality analysis in children with reading disability: The results of new techniques of examination. CORTEX, 1973, 9, 227–236.

Dean, R. S. Reliability and predictive validity of the Dean Laterality Preference Schedule with preadolescents. PERCEPTUAL AND MOTOR SKILLS, 1978, 47, 1345–1346.

Dean, R. S. Cerebral laterality and verbal-performance discrepancies in intelligence. JOURNAL OF SCHOOL PSYCHOLOGY, 1979, 17, 145–150.

Dean, R. S. Cerebral lateralization and reading dysfunction. JOURNAL OF SCHOOL PSYCHOLOGY, 1980, 18, 324–332.

Dean, R. S., Schwartz, N. H., & Smith, L. S. Lateral preference patterns as a discriminator of learning difficulties. JOURNAL OF CONSULTING AND CLINICAL PSYCHOLOGY, 1981, 49, 227–235.

Dean, R. S., & Smith, L. S. PERSONALITY AND LATERAL PREFERENCE PATTERNS IN CHILDREN. Unpublished manuscript, 1981.

Kinsbourne, M., & Hiscock, M. Cerebral lateralization and cognitive development: Conceptual and methodological issues. In G. W. Hynd and J. E. Obrzut (Eds.), NEUROPSYCHOLOGICAL ASSESSMENT AND THE SCHOOL-AGE CHILD: ISSUES AND PROCEDURES. New York: Grune & Stratton, Inc., 1981.

Dean, R. S. Assessing patterns of lateral preference. CLINICAL NEUROPSYCHOLOGY, 1982, 4, 124–128. (a)

Dean, R. S. CEREBRAL LATERALITY EFFECTS IN THE DUAL PROCESSING OF PROSE. Unpublished manuscript, 1982. (b)

Dean, R. S., & Schwartz, N. H. INDUCING COMPREHENSION IN THE BILATERAL READER. Unpublished manuscript, 1982.

[592]

The Laurita-Trembly Diagnostic Word Processing Test. Grades 1.9–4.9, 5.0–college; 1979; criterion-referenced; 4 scores: raw, word count, vertical word processing, horizontal word processing, derived from 6 areas: vowel discrimination, direct phonic processing, indirect structural processing (long vowel, short vowel), prefixes and suffixes (long vowel, short vowel); no data on reliability and validity; no norms; 1 form; 2 levels: test materials exactly the same for both levels, only the directions are different; manual (73 pages, includes test stimulus materials); student answer sheet (no date, 3 pages); individual progress chart (no date, 1 page); 1982 price data: $24.95 per set of testing materials; administration time not reported; Raymond E. Laurita and Phillip W. Trembly; L & T Educational Materials, Inc.*

Review of The Laurita-Trembley Diagnostic Word Processing Test by LINNEA C. EHRI, Professor of Education, University of California, Davis, Davis, CA:

The Laurita-Trembley Diagnostic Word Processing Test (DWPT) is essentially a spelling dictation test administered to students from first grade through college. Since some effort is required to understand how the test works, a summary is helpful. The authors propose a 15 by 5 matrix which they allege characterizes the spelling patterns of almost all English words. Represented horizontally are vowel patterns (5 short, 10 long). Represented vertically are consonant patterns ordered by level of consonant difficulty (5 levels). This matrix is printed on a student progress chart and each cell contains a number indicating the total number of English words having each spelling pattern. Information about students' knowledge of these spelling patterns is obtained by administering the DWPT. The test includes 64 words sampling various categories in the matrix: 17 words measuring knowledge of each vowel pattern embedded in the easiest consonant context, single letters (Level I); 6 words measuring consonant blends (Level II); 5 words measuring digraphs (Level III); 12 words measuring inflections (Level IV); 24 words measuring prefixes and suffixes (Level V). Vowels in the words from Levels II through V are limited to short i and long a-e patterns, and spellers are told to use these letters. Based on students' ability to spell the small sample of words in each category or at each level, inferences are drawn about their potential for learning the spellings of all the words in those categories or levels. For example, if students spell "reef" correctly, this is interpreted to indicate that they have the potential for mastering all 33 words in the Level I "ee" category. Once learning potential is determined, then students receive instructions on all the words in the category until they can write each word correctly from dictation. This instructional objective is perhaps not unreasonable at the lower three levels since the numbers of words in the categories range form 1 to 104. However, at the higher levels, the numbers grow to 1,356 in the Level V "ee" category, making mastery exceedingly time consuming. When instruction is completed in a category, the DWPT is readministered to assess progress.

This test has a number of serious weaknesses that limit its value. Evidence indicating that the test is reliable and valid is not presented. Also some logical problems and inconsistencies are apparent in the description of the program.

Research findings about the development of spelling skill have not influenced the conceptualization of spelling difficulty levels. For example, studies of the emergence of vowel knowledge indicate that children learn to spell short vowels before long vowels (Guthrie & Seifert, 1977; Mason, 1976; Morris, 1981). However, the DWPT matrix ignores this. Vowel categories are represented as 15 stages with short and long vowels mixed. The term "stage" is a misnomer since the order of the vowels (1 to 15) is not intended to mean anything about acquisition order.

Assertions about the nature of spelling knowledge and how it is acquired are documented not by evidence but simply by references to the authors' "strong" beliefs and feelings. Since many of the assertions are questionable, there is a need for evidence. It is claimed that students' success in spelling the sample words on the DWPT indicates whether they have the potential for learning to spell a host of other unsampled words. This needs to be demonstrated, particularly since this inference underlies the design of spelling instruction. It is not clear that higher levels of spelling difficulty are indeed more difficult than lower levels and require prior mastery, particularly the ordering of blends before digraphs. Also, it is not clear that perfect performance in spelling words in any category is the appropriate criterion to use in designing instruction. Errors due to carelessness might disrupt a perfect score. Perfect scores, particularly in spelling inflections, might mean that students have already mastered the category, making followup instruction a waste of time.

The diagnosis-instruction-assessment cycle has a logical flaw. In order for students to indicate that they are ready for instruction in a spelling category, they must be able to pass all the sample items in that category on the DWPT. However, because instruction is limited to that category of words spelled correctly, it will not enable students to exhibit readiness for instruction in any new categories since these categories were not taught. In fact, any gains made during instruction will not even be apparent when the DWPT is readministered since students could already spell all of the sample words in this category before instruction began.

In actuality, the authors do not adhere to their own conceptualization of the test and its relationship to instruction. They acknowledge that perfect performance in a category on the DWPT may mean either that students have the potential for learning those words or that they have already learned the words. Allowing this second interpretation of test scores erodes the value of the test as a basis for designing instruction. Although general directions in the manual indicate that instruction is supposed to focus on words in categories spelled successfully on the DWPT, the sample case of John Doe reveals that instruction may also be provided in unsuccessful categories. This option discredits the importance of the author's concept of learning potential in designing instruction.

One procedure used to conduct the test may weaken its effectiveness. This is the procedure of telling students that all the words in a forthcoming group will be spelled with a particular vowel letter (a or i). The problem is that the words in these sets contain other vowel letters as well (e.g., shadier, retrograde). This may prove confusing and interfere with performance.

There are problems in the sample of words selected for the test. The authors do not state how the particular words were chosen. Was frequency of occurrence considered? This is known to influence spelling accuracy. Particular words may not be good exemplars of the patterns being measured. ROVE may not tap knowledge of the long vowel O-E pattern since E may be added for another reason, to prevent an illegal final V spelling (Venezky, 1970). WHIP may not tap knowledge of digraphs since some dialect speakers do not pronounce "whi-" differently from "wi-." The word PICKET is not appropriate for tapping knowledge of inflections since it does not contain any in its spelling. These instances suggest that great care was not taken in selecting words to exemplify categories on the DWPT.

The authors do not explain how they arrived at the numbers indicating the size of each word category in their matrix of potential words to be taught. What word list was used? The total number of words across categories in the matrix is 14,531. This falls far short of the total number of words in English. Test users are told to teach these words, yet the words are not listed in the manual. Users are told to find their own or purchase other materials published by the authors.

There are more sources of regularity in English word spellings than are captured by the authors' matrix (Venezky, 1970). For example, the vowel categories at Level I neglect to include diphthongs (i.e., ow, oi), the vowel sound in "look," and the long e vowel spelled Y or EY at the ends of words. The authors' claim about measuring "the entire range of categorical abilities involved in spelling" is thus exaggerated.

In sum, use of the DWPT is not recommended. No information on reliability or validity is presented. The test is designed primarily according to the strong beliefs of the authors, not according to evidence. The test purports to diagnose learning potential, to direct the design of instruction to a mastery criterion, and to evaluate the effectiveness of this instruction. However, in actuality it does not and in fact cannot do these things due to logical flaws in the design of the program. The authors need to clarify what their test is really measuring, to demonstrate this with evidence, and to eliminate the inconsistencies in their conceptualization of the test and its use.

REVIEWER'S REFERENCES

Venezky, R. L. THE STRUCTURE OF ENGLISH ORTHOGRAPHY. The Hague: Mouton, 1970.

Mason, J. M. Overgeneralization in learning to read. JOURNAL OF READING BEHAVIOR, 1976, 8, 173–182.

Guthrie, J. T., & Seifert, M. Letter-sound complexity in learning to identify words. JOURNAL OF EDUCATIONAL PSYCHOLOGY, 1977, 69, 686–696.

Morris, D. Concept of word: A developmental phenomenon in the beginning reading and writing processes. LANGUAGE ARTS, 1981, 58, 659–668.

Review of Laurita-Trembley Diagnostic Word Processing Test by GERALD S. HANNA, Professor of Educational Psychology and Measurement, College of Education, Kansas State University, Manhattan, KS:

The Laurita-Trembley Diagnostic Word Processing Test consists of 64 dictated words that examinees attempt to write correctly. These items sample from a matrix of word categories organized into five strata ranging in complexity from simple phonic processing to complex structural processing. The horizontal dimension of this matrix is divided into 15 vowel forms. Interpretation of test performance focuses upon the Individual Progress Chart's display of the 75 cells of this matrix. One would expect the rationale for this two-dimension instructional model upon which the test focuses to be carefully built upon a substantial foundation of theory and research literature. It is not. Rather, the rationale is argued from the limited vantage of authorial belief and opinion.

Only about 15,000 words are covered by the categories of the instructional model. It is unclear whether the categorical system encompasses so few words or whether only a sample of the classifiable words were sampled. Nor are the words listed. Thus, the domains sampled by the test are ill defined. This renders criterion-referenced interpretation of such scores as the word count difficult at best.

The first section of the test provides a one-item sample for each Level I category; this is used to record on the Individual Progress Chart the vowel discrimination performance for the 15 Level I cells. The next two-item section re-samples one of the Level I cells; it is unclear how this section is to be used. Next are six Level II items. Since generalization is made to all 15 Level II cells, it is puzzling that these words are all drawn from the same cell. The same sampling imbalance characterizes the section that assesses Level III as well as the final four sections on long and short vowels respectively in Levels IV and V.

The title indicates that the test is diagnostic. The normal pattern of diagnostic tests is to assess mastery of each of several well defined content domains. Instead, the test is designed to determine "the potential number of words an individual can learn to process." Performance that leads to checking off a cell in the Individual Progress Chart is deemed to show, at the very least, that the student is ready to learn all the words in the category and, at most, that the examinee has mastered all of these words. That is quite a range of possible meanings!

Performance that does not lead to checking off a cell apparently signifies that the examinee is not ready to learn the words in the cell. This seems odd in view of the demand that all words in a section must be correctly spelled before the corresponding cell may be checked off. Wouldn't correct spelling of, say, four out of the five words for Level III at least suggest readiness? Also odd for a diagnostic test is the absence of any suggestions for analyzing examinee spelling errors beyond simple right-wrong scoring.

The instructional sequence recommended for Level I is first to teach all the words in those cells for which the single-item-per-cell sample was answered correctly and then to proceed to the remaining Level I cells. The topic of the notoriously poor reliability of individual test items is not addressed. Sticking our heads in the sand and ignoring this problem does not lead to competent test development or to professional test use.

Pre- and postinstruction use of the instrument is strongly urged. In view of this and the manual's suggested uses of the test for accountability assessment, prudent users should be concerned about potential practice effect, test x instruction interaction, and instructional overemphasis of the 64 words that are sampled (i.e., teaching to the test, which taps only 6 of the 60 Level II–V cells). An alternate form of the test could attenuate all of these threats to valid assessment of growth. It would have been an easy matter to construct several alternate forms of this supply-type spelling test. Regrettably, none exist. Also omitted are item analysis and normative data.

The need is universal for tests (1) to have acceptable reliability for each interpreted subscore and (2) to be accompanied by data thereon. Since the Laurita-Trembley does not yield near-perfect scores for its intended audience, assessment of the internal consistency and/or short term stability of scores for its interpreted subparts would create no special problems. The total absence of reliability data is deplorable.

No validity data are provided. With respect to the essential topic of content validity, there is no explanation of the method or rationale of word sampling. Sampling imbalance was noted above, and the test's dictated sentences contain over twice as many male as female references. Regarding the critical topic of construct validity for the authors' self-professed radical approach, no data are provided. Some important topics, such as the instructional efficacy of the model upon which the test is based, might be troublesome to investigate; yet such research would certainly supply a needed and useful supplement to authorial opinion and belief. The neglect of other more easily researched topics, such as the discriminant validity of scores from the test's several separately interpreted sections, seems indefensible.

In summary, the Laurita-Trembley Diagnostic Word Processing Test is based upon a rationale that has not been anchored to theoretical or research literature, is accompanied by inadequate instructions for scoring and interpreting, is highly vulnerable (because of having only one form) to abuse in accountability assessment as recommended by the manual, is unaccompanied by reliability data, requires untenable belief on faith in the reliability of subsets of items containing as few as one item, and is not supported by citations of information or research that would support belief in any kind of validity. Clearly, the instrument falls short of prevailing standards of test development, research, and reporting. The reviewer is unable to recommend it for any applied purpose.

[593]

Law Enforcement Assessment and Development Report. Applicants for law enforcement positions; 1981; LEADR; computer-based analysis of Cattell's 16 Personality Factor Questionnaire with respect to individual's suitability for law enforcement work; 5 profile dimensions: performance potential, emotional maturity, integrity/control, intellectual efficiency, interpersonal relations; 16 PF Form A ('78, 10 pages); manual ('81, 42 pages); profile report (4 pages); separate answer sheets must be used; 1982 price data: $20 per complete kit including 1 prepaid processing package; $9.25 per manual; scoring service, $25 or less per report; (45–60) minutes for 16 PF; Rita Dee-Burnett, Edgar F. Johns, and Samuel E. Krug; Institute for Personality and Ability Testing, Inc.*

Review of Law Enforcement Assessment and Development Report by LAWRENCE ALLEN, Professor and Chair, Department of Psychology, University of South Alabama, Mobile, AL:

The Law Enforcement Assessment and Development Report (LEADR) is a four-page computer-based psychological report that claims to identify individuals who are most likely to become successful law enforcement officers. LEADR, published by the Institute for Personality and Ability Testing (IPAT), purports to measure five psychological dimensions important for success in law enforcement work: performance potential, emotional maturity, integrity/control, intellectual efficiency, and interpersonal relations.

In its promotional literature IPAT states that the LEADR score roster "gives you the concise, quantitative information you need to choose the most psychologically fit candidate." IPAT maintains that appropriate user settings include the military, federal associations, state police, nuclear power security, and private investigative agencies. The promotional literature also states that the LEADR manual "fully documents the basic research and technology on which the report was developed and validated."

In reality, LEADR is one of several interpretive reports that have been developed from Cattell's 16 Personality Factor Questionnaire (16PF). Other adaptations of the 16PF have been prepared for assessment purposes in such contexts as career development, marriage counseling, and the evaluation of business executives. LEADR purports to analyze the results of the 16PF with respect to how the person may be expected to function in law enforcement work.

Persons responsible for the objective selection of law enforcement personnel who anticipate that the LEADR might significantly help them in the selection process are in for serious disappointment. The LEADR materials and manual appear substantive at first glance, but close inspection of the manual reveals serious problems.

The claim that LEADR identifies individuals who are the most likely to become successful law enforcement officers is not substantiated by documentation in the manual. The literature review in the manual relating the 16PF to police work is certainly not impressive. There are only four studies cited, and they include small samples. The results of these studies are inconclusive, but the manual attempts to present these studies as support for using LEADR.

Reliability data in the LEADR manual were taken from the Administrator's Manual for the 16PF and from data in IPAT research files. The reliability data are not impressive for the six samples presented, and four of the samples included only high school or college students. It is interesting to note that the fourth sample was test-retest with a 9-week interval using Form C of the 16PF. LEADR uses only Form A. It is common knowledge in the 16PF literature that the four forms of the 16PF (A, B, C, D) are not equivalent, and the correlations between forms and even pairs of forms are so low that data gathered with one form or pair of forms may not be generalizable to all forms.

The LEADR manual uses construct validity as the basis for using LEADR. The data presented are totally inadequate. Much of the data presented come from group profiles taken from the 1970 16PF handbook. Some attempt to present criterion-related validity data is made, but the criteria used do not reflect law enforcement performance adequately, and the resulting coefficients are not significant in most cases.

The manual takes each of the five psychological dimensions "measured" by LEADR and attempts to make a case for the validity of each. The case is made better for some than others, but the data presented do not provide the evidence needed to justify the use of LEADR as a selection device for law enforcement personnel.

It is interesting to note that each of the LEADR dimensions, except the performance dimension, was constructed by combining various traits from the 16PF on a rational basis. There is little information presented in the manual to explain the allocation of the traits to the four dimensions of emotional maturity, integrity/control, intellectual efficiency, and interpersonal relations. The use of a rational basis for the allocation of traits to these dimensions seems ironic and questionable, especially since Cattell relied so heavily on factor analysis in the original development of the 16PF.

A major data deficiency in the LEADR manual is the lack of adequate job analysis information for law enforcement settings. Even if the manual contained reliability and validity data to support the use of LEADR, it is still necessary for the IPAT to provide some method or mechanism for potential users of LEADR to demonstrate that the local law enforcement setting is similar to the validation samples. If LEADR had been properly validated using a criterion-related validity strategy on representative national samples, it would not be difficult to establish the mechanism for showing that LEADR was suitable for use in a particular law enforcement agency setting. It should also be noted that there is no evidence in the manual to substantiate the claim in the promotional materials that "appropriate user settings include the military, federal associations, state police, nuclear power security, and private investigative agencies." The manual does say that the five LEADR dimensions "emerge fairly consistently in careful job analyses of law enforcement positions," but no definitive empirical evidence is presented to support the statement.

The manual states that the most appropriate use of LEADR is "to use the quantitative information it contains along with other data in preparing an objective ranking of candidate suitability." There are no instructions in the manual explaining how to use the percentile scores of the five dimensions in the selection process except for general statements like "It is not the goal of the LEADR program to establish predetermined score levels for candidate disqualification." If IPAT is going to make sweeping statements in its promotional literature maintaining that LEADR scores give test users the concise, quantitative information they need to choose the most psychologically fit candidate, then the manual should document the evidence to substantiate the claim and also should include some recommendation about how to use the five profile scores. Should the scores be combined in some manner or should they be left as separate scores? How should the scores be combined with other data in the selection process?

The selection of law enforcement personnel is probably the most challenging and potentially volatile area of personnel selection in the public sector today. Professional standards and the law mandate that employers must not discriminate on the basis of race, sex, religion, or national origin. The employer bears the burden of proof to show that test scores are related to job performance, and it is also the employer's responsibility to minimize "adverse impact" for black applicants and females. Lawsuits are common in cases of police selection, and most of the lawsuits charge racial or sexual discrimination against employment tests. LEADR, even though named a report, is technically and legally considered a test.

The LEADR manual contains very little information about the test performance of blacks and females, and the data that it does contain are not encouraging. In the sample cited in the manual there was a statistically significant difference between whites and blacks for three of the five LEADR dimensions. The LEADR manual should have extensive research data concerning the test performance of females and minorities.

The Ethical Principles of Psychologists state that the public offering of an automated interpretation service is considered as a professional-to-professional consultation. Although the manual states that LEADR is available only to individuals qualified to act on the information it contains, the content and tone of the LEADR promotional materials suggests a marketing strategy that could result in persons obtaining and using LEADR in law enforcement selection programs who do not understand the limitation of personality reports like LEADR. This could lead to serious problems, especially for those who overestimate the value of the narrative statements in the report.

In summary, the claim made by IPAT that LEADR identifies individuals who are most likely to become successful law enforcement officers is not substantiated by empirical data. The promotional materials for the report are misleading and border on sensationalism. Technical data presented in the manual do not warrant use of the instrument except on an experimental basis only. Certainly there is a need for identifying misfits in police selection as well as those individuals who have the personality characteristics for successful police work, but there are no simple ways for gathering such data. Using a psychologist or other competent professional is still the safest and most thorough way to select qualified law enforcement officers.

[594]

Law School Admission Test. Law school entrants; 1948–85; LSAT; test administered 4 times annually (March, June, September, December) at centers established by the publisher; LSAT total score plus an unscored writing sample; preparation material ('84, 32 pages); general information booklet ('84, 32 pages); 1985 price data: 12-month subscription service fee, $70 per candidate (includes fee for all tests taken within 12-month period, unlimited LSAT law school reports, and Prelaw Handbook or Canadian Law Schools Admission Handbook); 210(270) minutes per LSAT, 30(40) minutes per writing sample; administered by Law School Admission Services; Law School Admission Council.*

See T3:1292 (6 references), 8:1093 (7 references), and T2:2349 (7 references); for a review by Leo A. Munday of earlier forms, see 7:1098 (23 references); see also 5:928 (7 references); for a review by Alexander G. Wesman, see 4:815 (6 references).

TEST REFERENCES

1. Powers, D. E. Long-term predictive and construct validity of two traditional predictors of law school performance. JOURNAL OF EDUCATIONAL PSYCHOLOGY, 1982, 74, 568–576.

2. Stone, E. W. A plan for the special preparation of attorneys in effective writing skills. JOURNAL OF NEGRO EDUCATION, 1983, 52, 314–331.

Review of Law School Admission Test by GARY B. MELTON, Associate Professor of Psychology and Law, University of Nebraska-Lincoln, Lincoln, NE:

Virtually all American law schools require applicants to take the Law School Admission Test (LSAT). The LSAT is part of a program sponsored by the Law School Admission Council (LSAC); the program consists of national test dates, a registration procedure, standard testing centers, and a data assembly service which reports individual LSAT scores in conjunction with undergraduate grades and average LSAT scores and grades of other applicants from the same undergraduate institutions. The LSAC sponsors ongoing research about the LSAT and other factors in admissions; it also provides individual law schools with data to conduct their own validity studies and establish their own norms. Member schools set policy for the LSAT. A new edition of the LSAT is introduced at each regular testing date.

The LSAT has changed substantially since it was reviewed by Munday in *The Seventh Mental Measurements Yearbook* (7:1098). Since summer 1982 the LSAT has differed from former versions in several ways. First, instead of a 200–800 scale, scores now range from 10 to 48 with a mean of 30.5 and a standard deviation of 8.0. According to the 1984–85 LSAT preparation material, the change in scaling was taken to minimize the effects on scaled scores of a few points in raw score. Presumably, there had been concern about test consumers' overreifying differences of a few points on the 200–800 scale. Second, the Writing Ability test has been dropped, although a standardized, unscored writing sample is required. Third, the structure and content of the test is quite different. Only one of the four current subtests (Reading Comprehension, 28 items, 35 minutes) was present in the version reviewed by Munday. Other subtests include: Analytic Reasoning, 25 items, 35 minutes; Issues and Facts, 37 items, 35 minutes; Logical Reasoning, 26 items, 35 minutes. As in previous versions, only a total score is awarded.

Test-retest reliability for the LSAT is unreported. Kuder-Richardson 20 reliability is .93. K-R 20 reliabilities for the subtests are not reported. Mean item-subtest biserial correlations for the four sections range from .49 to .54. Subtest-total correlations vary from .81 to .85.

The subtests appear to be largely unspeeded, and the use of K-R 20 is probably appropriate. The percentage of test takers completing all items ranges from 83.0% on Analytical Reasoning to 97.5% on Issues and Facts. At least 96.2% completes three-fourths of the items on each subtest.

Validity studies on the LSAT have generally involved prediction of law school grades. The LSAC has expressly denied the appropriateness of any use other than law-school admissions. The 1984–85 General Information Booklet includes such a disclaimer: "The LSAT is designed to assist law schools in assessing the academic ability of their applicants. The LSAT was not designed, nor is it intended to be used, to predict success in the practice of law. No study purporting to show a correlation between LSAT scores and success in the practice of law is known to LSAC or LSAS [Law School Admission Services, the operating arm of LSAC]."

However, in a 7-state study, Carlson and Werts (1976) found the LSAT actually to be a better predictor of performance on examinations for admission to the bar (Multistate Bar Examination, .51;

locally produced essay examinations, .36) than of law school grades (first year, .31; second year, .31; third year, .26). Indeed, the LSAT was almost as valid in predicting performance on the MBE as were law school grades (.58), a rather curious finding in view of the fact that the MBE is essentially an achievement test.

Largely as a result of the substantial differences in selectivity among law schools, predictive validity of the LSAT varies markedly across schools and, within schools, across time. According to the General Information Booklet, validity studies were conducted in 139 of the 172 LSAC member schools during 1982. Correlations between LSAT scores and first-year law school grades varied from .06 to .71. These results are consistent with Schrader's (1976) review of more than 600 validity studies conducted between 1948 and summer, 1976, which showed widely variable correlations (mean=.34). Using this sample, Linn (1982; Linn, Harnisch, & Dunbar, 1981) found that 34% of the variance in validities was predictable simply from knowledge of the LSAT standard deviation in the populations studied.

Many of the published studies and discussions of validity of the LSAT in the past decade have focused on group differences, especially differences in predictive validity across racial and ethnic groups (e.g., Breland, 1975; Hathaway, 1984; Linn, 1975, 1982; Linn, Harnisch, & Dunbar, 1981; Linn & Hastings, 1984; Linn & Pitcher, 1976; Pitcher, 1976; Powers, 1977; Schrader & Pitcher, 1974). Generally, these studies have shown overprediction for minority-group applicants, although perhaps as a result of statistical artifacts (Linn & Hastings, 1984). However, a recent study suggests that the finding of overprediction may itself be an artifact of focus upon *first-year* law school grades. Hathaway (1984) found the correlation between LSAT and law school grades for minority students to drop from .51 (first year) to .27 (second year) to .17 (third year). These results, which are based on a single school (Columbia), should not be overemphasized, but they certainly bear further investigation with a more extensive sample.

There has been surprisingly little research on the constructs measured by the LSAT. All four subtests appear to measure verbal reasoning skills. The most facially valid is probably Issues and Facts, in which test takers are presented with a set of facts, a dispute, and two legal rules. They are asked to determine relevance to the dispute of a series of questions about the case and to identify conflicts between the rules in answering the questions. This task bears similarity to the case method employed in legal education, especially the first year. However, in experimental versions, Issues and Facts actually was found to be substantially less valid predictively than the LSAT as a whole, although more valid than a similar subtest (Principles and Cases) which it replaced (Pitcher, McPeek, & Binkley, 1976). The best predictor in Pitcher et al.'s study was Reading Comprehension, which actually may be the closest analogue to the task of analysis of the meaning of judicial opinions, even though the subtest does not include passages from legal writings.

This point raises the question, apparently still unanswered, posed in the two previous *MMY* reviews of the LSAT: is a separate law aptitude test really needed? Although "thinking like a lawyer" may be significantly different from the reasoning skills nurtured in graduate studies, it is not at all self-evident that aptitude for the former cannot be predicted by the Graduate Record Examination as well as, or better than, the LSAT. This hypothesis deserves empirical investigation.

In summary, the LSAT is a moderately valid predictor of law school grades, especially when used in combination with undergraduate GPA, as the LSAC advises. The LSAC program provides law schools with far more systematic admissions data, with respect to both individual student selection and school-based validity criteria for admissions, than they would probably be able or willing to generate on their own. However, particularly in view of the small proportion of variance in law school performance now predicted by the LSAT, attention should be given to the possibility that other verbal aptitude tests may be better predictors.

A final caveat is that most of the extant validity studies used the old LSAT. This fact is unsurprising in that the class taking the LSAT in 1982 has yet to graduate. However, because of the magnitude of changes in the new version, care should be taken in applying studies of former editions.

REVIEWER'S REFERENCES

Schrader, W. B., & Pitcher, B. Prediction of law school grades for Mexican American and Black American students [Report No. LSAC-74-8]. In REPORTS OF LSAC SPONSORED RESEARCH: VOLUME III, 1975-1977 (pp. 715-741). Princeton, NJ: Law School Admission Council, 1974.

Breland, H. M. DeFunis revisited: A psychometric view [Report No. LSAC-75-2]. In REPORTS OF LSAC SPONSORED RESEARCH: VOLUME III, 1975-1977 (pp. 55-105). Princeton, NJ: Law School Admission Council, 1975.

Linn, R. L. Test bias and the prediction of grades in law school. JOURNAL OF LEGAL EDUCATION, 1975, 27, 293-323.

Carlson, A. B., & Werts, C. E. Relationships among law school predictors, law school performance, and bar examination results [Report No. LSAC-76-1]. In REPORTS OF LSAC SPONSORED RESEARCH: VOLUME III, 1975-1977 (pp. 211-322). Princeton, NJ: Law School Admission Council, 1976.

Linn, R. L., & Pitcher, B. Predictor score regions with significant differences in predicted law school grades from subgroup regression equations [Report No. LSAC-7-2]. In REPORTS OF LSAC SPONSORED RESEARCH: VOLUME III, 1975-1977 (pp. 323-337). Princeton, NJ: Law School Admission Council, 1976.

Pitcher, B. Subgroups validity study [Report No. LSAC-76-6]. In REPORTS OF LSAC SPONSORED RESEARCH: VOLUME III, 1975-1977 (pp. 413-488). Princeton, NJ: Law School Admission Council, 1976.

Pitcher, B., McPeek, W. M., & Binkley, M. The validity of two experimental item types—Issues and Facts, and Artificial Language [Report No. LSAC-76-3]. In REPORTS OF LSAC SPONSORED RESEARCH: VOLUME III, 1975-1977. Princeton, NJ: Law School Admission Council, 1976.

Schrader, W. B. Summary of law school validity studies, 1948–1975 [Report No. LSAC–76–8]. In REPORTS OF LSAC SPONSORED RESEARCH: VOLUME III, 1975–1977 (pp. 519–550). Princeton, NJ: Law School Admission Council, 1976.

Powers, D. E. Comparing predictions of law school performance for Black, Chicano, and White law students [Report No. LSAC–77–3]. In REPORTS OF LSAC SPONSORED RESEARCH: VOLUME III, 1975–1977 (pp. 721–775). Princeton, NJ: Law School Admission Council, 1977.

Linn, R. L., Harnisch, D. L., & Dunbar, S. B. Validity generalization and situational specificity: An analysis of the prediction of first-year grades in law school. APPLIED PSYCHOLOGICAL MEASUREMENT, 1981, 5, 281–289.

Linn, R. L. Admissions testing on trial. AMERICAN PSYCHOLOGIST, 1982, 37, 279–291.

Hathaway, J. C. The mythical meritocracy of law school admissions. JOURNAL OF LEGAL EDUCATION, 1984, 34, 86–96.

Linn, R. L., & Hastings, C. N. Group differentiated prediction. APPLIED PSYCHOLOGICAL MEASUREMENT, 1984, 8, 165–172.

[595]

An LD Program That Works. Learning disabled children; 1979; approaches for implementing a learning disabilities program based on the Midland School in New Jersey; no data on reliability and validity; no norms; individual; 1 form, 2 parts: screening test (23 pages), evaluation (15 pages); manual ('75 pages, includes program, screening test, and evaluation); other test materials must be supplied by examiner; 1982 price data: $9.95 per manual; administration time not reported; Edward G. Scagliotta; Mafex Associates, Inc.*

Review of An LD Program That Works by BARBARA K. KEOGH, Professor of Education, University of California-Los Angeles, Los Angeles, CA:

"Screening for Foundational Learnings" is the screening component of "An LD Program That Works," an educational program for learning disabled pupils. There are four other components in the program: (*a*) administrative organization of the educational environment, (*b*) techniques for changing child behavior selected from traditional behavior modification approaches, (*c*) a format for evaluating and reporting child progress, and (*d*) projected goals, primarily vocational arts and personal adjustment training for exceptional pupils. While the various components of the overall program are presumably interrelated, the functional relationships and interactions are not described.

The screening test, the focus of this review, fails to meet conceptual and psychometric criteria reasonably expected of test developers. Rather than a coherent assessment system, the test is a set of discrete items grouped in four major categories which are titled: Dominance, Physical Growth and Development, Perception Screening, and Academic Learnings. Items in the first two categories are similar to those found in commonly used developmental tests, and include assessment of eye, hand, and foot preference, identity of body parts, ability to kick, button, string beads, cut, skip, and the like. The Perception Screening category contains the largest number of items and purports to assess a variety of components such as children's body awareness (draw a person), knowledge of body parts and functions, tactile-kinesthetic awareness, spatial relations, and figure-ground discrimination. Digits, stories, and nonsense syllable memory tests are considered figure-ground measures in this test. Another Perception Screening subsection includes shape recognition and identification of size, position, color, and texture. The fourth major category of the test, Academic Learnings, consists primarily of standard reading, spelling, and mathematics tests and formal and informal educational tests.

The test is poorly organized and is mechanically awkward. Each of the four major components of the test is formatted and scored differently. Some require a correct/incorrect decision, some a rating from 0 (no attempt made) to N (normal pattern). For the most part there are no norms or interpretative guidelines for individual items or categories of items. The digit, story, and nonsense syllable memory sections have chronological age score expectancies which the author suggests can be used to classify children's performance as ranging from "defective" to "superior." The source of the expectancies or scoring norms is unspecified. No information about the psychometric properties of the test or about interpretation and application of its content are provided. The rationale for selection and placement of items is unclear both theoretically and empirically. Many items could well be placed in any one of three major sections of the test. Further, a number of items are better suited for assessing preschool developmentally delayed children than learning disabled pupils of school age.

The test is also conceptually limited. Its appropriateness for screening learning disabled children is not addressed. This is particularly troubling, as the program as a whole is presumably for learning disabled pupils. However, the author has not provided a definition or description of the pupils he considers learning disabled. The educational needs of learning disabled pupils are also unspecified. Thus, it is not possible to link the screening test to educational practices. The range and diversity of personal and educational attributes subsumed within the learning disabilities category makes specification of both subject and program variables imperative. The material provided by the author does neither.

Both the predictive and concurrent/diagnostic validity of the test are questionable. Consider first the problem of predictive validity. A number of authors (Beckman-Brindley & Bell, 1981) have discussed problems of early identification of children with educational risks. Longitudinal evidence such as that provided by Werner, Bierman, and French (1971) documents the uncertainty of prediction of risk outcome without taking into account a number of personal, social, and economic variables. There is little in this screening test to argue for its predictive validity, and one must question its use as a screening device for identifying potentially learning disabled children. The diagnostic validity of the screening test for concurrent educational use is also uncertain. Restrictions in the use of tests for educational decision making are well known (Salvia & Ysseldyke, 1978). The evidence linking particular test items to specific educational interventions is limited at best. Given the weak conceptual underpinnings of the screening test as a whole, and the limited validity and reliability of the individual items, the educational use of this test is suspect.

In summary, there is little to recommend this screening measure for applied or research purposes with learning disabled pupils. In its present form the test is mostly a potpourri of items found in other developmental and/or educational tests. The test is poorly organized conceptually and mechanically. The backup material provided is extremely limited. Twelve of the 13 references in the manual are pre-1970. The potential limits of the tests are not discussed by the author, and there is no empirical evidence to support the efficacy of the test or the program. The other components of the program provide neither instructional nor administrative insights. Thus, despite its title, which implies that this is a program that works for learning disabled pupils, I cannot recommend its adoption.

REVIEWER'S REFERENCES

Werner, E. E., Bierman, J., & French, F. THE CHILDREN OF KAUAI: A LONGITUDINAL STUDY FROM THE PRENATAL PERIOD TO AGE TEN. Honolulu: University of Hawaii Press, 1971.

Salvia, J., & Ysseldyke, J. E. ASSESSMENT IN SPECIAL AND REMEDIAL EDUCATION. Boston: Houghton Mifflin, 1978.

Beckman-Brindley, S., & Bell, R. G. Issues in early identification. J. M. Kauffman & D. P. Hallahan (Eds.) HANDBOOK OF SPECIAL EDUCATION. Englewood Cliffs, New Jersey: Prentice-Hall, 1981.

Review of An LD Program That Works by J. LEE WIEDERHOLT, Professor of Special Education, University of Texas, Austin, TX:

Out of necessity this review must be brief. This is because even though the title of the booklet states that this is "An LD Program that Works," there is not one shred of evidence presented to support this claim. The first chapter reviews some of the issues in educating the learning disabled. Out of the seven references used to substantiate the views presented, the latest reference is 1972. Since a great deal of significant research has been conducted in the last decade, the chapter is sorely lacking.

Chapter II contains activities to assess a student's Dominance, Physical Growth and Development, Perception, and Academic Learnings. No data on reliability or validity are presented. It is of interest to note that out of approximately 24 pages only one page is devoted to Academic Learnings, and teachers are encouraged to use the Wide Range Achievement Test to supplement their assessment of academics. Chapter III contains a brief discussion of self-contained classrooms, modified block systems, and independent study. Chapter IV reviews strategies such as traditional behavior modification programs and modeling to change child behavior. The fifth chapter presents forms for evaluating and reporting child progress. These are presented without any data on their usefulness. The final chapter describes vocational arts and projected goals for older students.

While the title of the booklet may be grandiose, there are some interesting ideas presented that might be new and useful to unsophisticated or beginning teachers. However, what is presented is unsubstantiated and much of it is simply inappropriate for teachers in the 1980s.

[596]

Leader Behavior Description Questionnaire, Form 12. Supervisors; 1957–63; LBDQ-12; revision of Leader Behavior Description Questionnaire with 10 additional scores; for research use only; employee ratings of a supervisor; 12 scores: representation, demand, reconciliation, tolerance of uncertainty, persuasiveness, initiation of structure, tolerance of freedom, role assumption, consideration, production emphasis, predictive accuracy, integration, superior orientation; scores based upon responses of 4 to 10 raters; no norms; 1 form ('62, 6 pages); manual ('63, 15 pages); 1984 price information: $4 per 25 questionnaires; specimen set free on request; (20) minutes; original edition by John K. Hemphill and Alvin E. Coons; manual by Ralph M. Stogdill; current edition by Bureau of Business Research, Ohio State University; Administrative Science Research, Ohio State University.*

See T3:1296 (16 references); for a review by Robert L. Dipboye, see 8:1175 (101 references); see also T2:2452 (19 references) and 7:1147 (48 references).

TEST REFERENCES

1. Dessler, G., & Valenzi, E. R. Initiation of structure and subordinate satisfaction: A path analysis test of path-goal theory. ACADEMY OF MANAGEMENT JOURNAL, 1977, 20, 251–259.

2. Schriesheim, C., & Von Glinow, M. A. The path-goal theory of leadership: A theoretical and empirical analysis. ACADEMY OF MANAGEMENT JOURNAL, 1977, 20, 398–405.

3. Johns, G. Task moderators of the relationship between leadership style and subordinate responses. ACADEMY OF MANAGEMENT JOURNAL, 1978, 21, 319–325.

4. Sheridan, J. E., & Vredenburgh, D. J. Predicting leadership behavior in a hospital organization. ACADEMY OF MANAGEMENT JOURNAL, 1978, 21, 679–689.

5. Valenzi, E., & Dessler, G. Relationships of leader behavior, subordinate role ambiguity and subordinate job satisfaction. ACADEMY OF MANAGEMENT JOURNAL, 1978, 21, 671–678.

6. Schriesheim, C. A. The similarity of individual directed and group directed leader behavior description. ACADEMY OF MANAGEMENT JOURNAL, 1979, 22, 345–355.

7. Sheridan, J. E., & Vredenburgh, D. J. Structural model of leadership influence in a hospital organization. ACADEMY OF MANAGEMENT JOURNAL, 1979, 22, 6–21.

8. Lee, C., & Schuler, R. S. Goal specificity and difficulty and leader initiating structure as strategies for managing role stress. JOURNAL OF MANAGEMENT, 1980, 6, 177–187.

9. Niebuhr, R. E., Bedeian, A. G., & Armenakis, A. A. Individual need states and their influence on perceptions of leader behavior. SOCIAL BEHAVIOR AND PERSONALITY, 1980, 8, 17–25.

10. Sgro, J. A., Worchel, P., Pence, E. C., & Orban, J. A. Perceived leader behavior as a function of the leader's interpersonal trust orientation. ACADEMY OF MANAGEMENT JOURNAL, 1980, 23, 161–165.

11. Weed, S. E., & Mitchell, T. R. The role of environmental and behavioral uncertainty as a mediator of situation-performance relationships. ACADEMY OF MANAGEMENT JOURNAL, 1980, 23, 38–60.

12. Bunting, C. Leadership style and the instructional role of the principal. PSYCHOLOGY IN THE SCHOOLS, 1982, 19, 570–572.

13. Butters, M. A., & Gade, E. M. Job satisfaction and leadership behavior of residence hall assistants. JOURNAL OF COLLEGE STUDENT PERSONNEL, 1982, 23, 320–324.
14. Christiano, D. J., Jr., & Robinson, S. E. Leadership and cognitive style of college student leaders. JOURNAL OF COLLEGE STUDENT PERSONNEL, 1982, 23, 520–524.
15. Dorminy, F. N., & Brown, S. E. Job satisfaction of high school assistant principals as related to their perceptions of principals' behavior as leaders. PERCEPTUAL AND MOTOR SKILLS, 1982, 55, 387–390.
16. Knoop, R. A test of path-goal theory: Work values as moderators of relations of leaders and subordinates. PSYCHOLOGICAL REPORTS, 1982, 51, 39–43.
17. Michaels, C. E., & Spector, P. E. Causes of employee turnover: A test of the Mobley, Griffeth, Hand, and Meglino model. JOURNAL OF APPLIED PSYCHOLOGY, 1982, 67, 53–59.
18. Parsons, C. K., & Hulin, C. L. Differentially weighting linear models in organizational research: A cross-validation comparison of four methods. ORGANIZATIONAL BEHAVIOR AND HUMAN PERFORMANCE, 1982, 30, 289–311.
19. Yukl, G. A., & Van Fleet, D. D. Cross-situational, multimethod research on military leader effectiveness. ORGANIZATIONAL BEHAVIOR AND HUMAN PERFORMANCE, 1982, 30, 87–108.
20. Podsakoff, P. M., Todor, W. D., & Schuler, R. S. Leader expertise as a moderator of the effects of instrumental and supportive leader behaviors. JOURNAL OF MANAGEMENT, 1983, 9(2), 173–185.
21. Larson, J. R., Jr., Lingle, J. H., & Scerbo, M. M. The impact of performance cues on leader-behavior ratings: The role of selective information availability and probabilistic response bias. ORGANIZATIONAL BEHAVIOR AND HUMAN PERFORMANCE, 1984, 33, 323–349.
22. Powell, G. N., & Butterfield, D. A. The female leader and the "high-high" effective leader stereotype. THE JOURNAL OF PSYCHOLOGY, 1984, 117, 71–76.

[597]

Leadership and Self-Development Scale. College; 1976–79; 9 scores: assertiveness, risk taking, self-concept, setting goals, decision making, obtaining a followership, conflict resolution, group roles, evaluation; no reliability and validity data; norms consist of a mean total score for a sample of 25 college women attending a leadership and self-development workshop; 1 form (no date, 2 pages); no manual; mimeographed research report ('76, 20 pages); 1984 price data: free upon request from publisher; administration time not reported; Virginia Hoffman and Patricia B. Elmore; Patricia B. Elmore.*

See T3:1298 (2 references).

Review of Leadership and Self-Development Scale by ROBERT R. MCCRAE, Research Psychologist, Section on Stress and Coping, Gerontology Research Center, National Institute on Aging, NIH, Baltimore City Hospitals, Baltimore, MD:

The Leadership and Self-Development Scale is an ad hoc measure created to test the effectiveness of a leadership workshop for college women. Available information tells us nothing about the source or rationale of the items, nor are any data provided on reliability or validity of the scale. We are told, however, that the 25 items in the test are supposed to measure 9 distinct aspects of leadership, ranging from conflict resolution to risk-taking; and that scores were significantly higher after the workshop than before in a sample of 22 women nominated as having leadership potential.

As a psychometric device, this scale is an unknown quantity, and there is no basis for advocating its use in any context. In particular, potential users should not be persuaded that the test "works" by the fact that scores increased on retest. As reported, the study shows only that something changed between pretest and posttest. Because no control group was used, we can't attribute the change to the intervention; and because no validity evidence is offered to tell us what the scale really measures, we don't know what changed. For example, the authors also found that their workshop increased pro-feminist attitudes; perhaps the so-called leadership scale is only another measure of this ideology.

Ad hoc scales are not necessarily bad; sometimes they are needed to measure characteristics in special situations in which no standard instruments are fully appropriate. But it is usually possible to supplement the new scale with a few established measures of relevant constructs to bolster its interpretation. For example, the Rosenberg Self-Esteem scale or the Ascendance scale of the Guilford-Zimmerman Temperament Survey might have been used in the present study. Would they too have shown increases as a result of the workshop? Would they correlate with the Leadership and Self-Development Scale? Their inclusion in this study would have strengthened our confidence in the effectiveness of the intervention as well as providing a basis for evaluating the validity of the proposed scale.

The authors of the present scale have failed to analyze completely even the data they have. Certainly it would have been possible to calculate the internal consistency of the scale and its retest reliability for 22 subjects. The authors could also have reported the correlation between their scale and the feminist issues scale in order to demonstrate discriminant validity.

In the absence of these data, the scale is simply a collection of items. Anyone wishing to use them would have to begin the process of validation from scratch, and, on their face, there is little reason to start with this set of items. Although some of them ask directly about self-assessments of leadership ability, many others are ambiguous. Is the better leader one who goes along with group consensus, or resists it? One who delegates authority broadly or keeps tight control? Probably the answer depends on the task and the group, and no matter how this scale is intended to be scored, it is unlikely to measure leadership for all occasions.

The researcher interested in studying or promoting leadership will probably not find any single instrument that is tailor-made for his or her requirements—certainly not the Leadership and Self-Development Scale. As the list of its subscales suggests, a broad range of personality traits and interpersonal styles are relevant to leadership, and a battery of tests is probably needed. The researcher should recognize in advance that any findings are unlikely to be generalizable to other leadership contexts. It is also wise to recall that some of the qualities known to be associated with leadership, such as intelligence and extraversion, are highly stable dispositions which may be useful in identifying leaders, but are unlikely to increase as a result of short-term interventions.

[598]

Leadership Appraisal Survey. Adults in organizational settings; 1971–79; to be used in conjunction with the Styles of Leadership Survey; subordinates' ratings of leader practices and attitudes; scores in 5 areas: philosophy, planning, implementation, evaluation, total; no data on reliability and validity; 1 form ('79, 11 pages, includes scoring instructions); user's guide (no date, 4 pages); 1984 price data: $4.50 per survey; administration time not reported; Jay Hall; Teleometrics Int'l.*

[599]

Learning Ability Profile. Grades 5–16 and adults; 1975–78; LAP; 5 scores: total and 4 derived scores (certainty, problem solving, flexibility, frustration); norms consist of means and standard deviations; Forms A, B, ('78, 10 pages); revised manual ('76, 132 pages); supplement to revised manual ('78, 24 pages); separate answer sheets must be used; price data available from publisher; (90–120) minutes; Margherita M. Henning; Harvard Personnel Testing [Canada].* (U.S. distributor: Wolfe Computer Aptitude Testing.)

TEST REFERENCES

1. Fabi, B. A concurrent validity study of the Learning Ability Profile against college grade point average: Some Canadian data. EDUCATIONAL AND PSYCHOLOGICAL MEASUREMENT, 1983, 43, 859–863.

Review of Learning Ability Profile by PHILIP M. CLARK, Professor of Psychology, The Ohio State University, Columbus, OH:

The Learning Ability Profile (LAP) purports to be a measure of "inductive and deductive reasoning, and cognitive and problem solving skills." Stimulated by a desire to help eliminate "the vestiges of past unequal opportunities in education and employment," it is designed in such a way as to deemphasize the importance of educational background, although it does assume minimal literacy and minimal computational skill. It may be administered in groups and is intended primarily for use with adults employed in government or industrial settings, although it is also recommended for several educational uses.

LAP consists of 80 multiple-choice items which include pictorial, symbolic, arithmetic, verbal, and letter analogies as well as number and letter series. An unusual feature of this test is that each of the four choices in each item is graded from most to least desirable, and the format provides test-takers with immediate feedback as to the adequacy of their answers.

Though no explicit correlations with other measures of general ability are provided, LAP Total appears to be the score most comparable to overall ability. In the norms presented, this score increases with amount of education. The four additional scores (certainty, problem solving, flexibility, frustration) are said to "provide some analyses dealing with personality, as well as ability factors in task performance." The manual does not identify the items used in computing either the index of problem solving or the index of flexibility; it does state that this information "will be made available to researchers on an individual basis only."

The manual provides preliminary normative data based upon some 730 subjects drawn from several restricted populations. Included are Albuquerque, New Mexico elementary school students; students from selected English classes in an unidentified New Mexico high school "located very near the Mexican border"; some post high school technical school students; some undergraduate and graduate students from two large California universities; and some self-selected adults including some New Mexico MENSA members. Additional normative data are combined with these basic data in the supplement, making a total norm group of 1,358. It is unclear where and how most of the 628 additional subjects were obtained. The subjects are categorized as to ethnic group (Black, Hispanic, American Indian, Oriental, and Other), level of education, sex, and age. The total of 1,358 is somewhat misleading in terms of the stated primary purpose of the measure, since the minority groups are badly underrepresented at important age levels. The manual supplement assures all users of LAP that they will continue to receive data for underrepresented subgroups until all include 30 or more cases. What information is given on geographical representativeness suggests that the normative data are far too limited to support their general applicability.

Unfortunately, the manual for this test is poorly organized and unnecessarily repetitive. Information as to validity, reliability, how the items were generated, and how the basic aims of the measure are realized is hard won despite section headings which appear to promise an organized approach to the presentation of such information.

The most striking single fact about this test is that no explicit correlational or other adequate statistical data are presented in the manual or its supplement to support the claims that LAP Total and the various subscores are, indeed, measuring what they purport to measure. Means presented by educational level do indicate that LAP Total scores increase as educational level increases. But the apparent nonrepresentativeness of the group on which the presented norms are based limits the meaningfulness even of this modest indicator that the test is a measure of "learning ability."

It is unclear how the 80 items in the test were generated, though the manual does indicate that some of them are similar to those found on standardized multiple-choice tests. Although it is indicated that three physical scientists and three social scientists determined the order of quality of responses and level of difficulty for each item, there is no indication as to how these experts proceeded except that they functioned "independently." Furthermore, there is no indication that such a panel was involved in determining the adequacy of the items for measuring either the overall construct "learning ability" or any of the subscales. In fact, while there is a section of the manual headed Reliability and Validity, there is no systematic evidence presented to support the concurrent, predictive, or content validity of the instrument as a whole or any of its subscales. Several "Case Reports" are provided in the manual and its supplement suggesting how the LAP may be used in counseling and assessment. In these discursive thumbnail sketches occasional mention is made of scores obtained on such measures as the WAIS, which allow for scattered random comparisons with the LAP profiles provided. Such references are clearly unsystematic and inadequate for establishing validity. The supplement makes brief mention of validity studies carried out by users of LAP in various settings, and the comment is made that "Preliminary results made available to us indicate high predictive validity of LAP in all research using LAP." Data related to this important assertion are conspicuously absent.

No correlational data are presented to establish either the equivalence of the two forms of LAP or the stability of the test over time. The manual attributes this lack to the novel testing methodology which would, it claims, preclude an estimate of practice effect, and also to difficulties in getting organizations to cooperate in the administration of ability tests. An unconvincing argument is made that Forms A and B are equivalent on the basis of an analysis showing that the mean for 20 subjects who took Form A was not significantly different from the mean of 20 subjects equated for educational level who took Form B. Uncorrected odd-even coefficients of .90 and .91 on the two forms suggest acceptable internal consistency for LAP Total. No reliability data are reported for the four subscores.

SUMMARY. The LAP appears to be the result of noble motivation and includes several interesting and potentially worthwhile features (e.g., immediate feedback as to the adequacy of each response and an attempt to measure flexibility within the context of such a test). However, the almost complete lack of demonstration of the test's validity, the inadequacy of its norming data, the failure of the manual to deal effectively with important reliability issues, and the general lack of clarity of the manual lead this reviewer to conclude that the LAP should not be used for the purposes suggested by its publishers.

[600]

Learning Disability Rating Procedure. Grades K–12; 1981; LDRP; 11 scores: IQ, reading decoding, listening comprehension, comprehension variance, socially inappropriate behavior, expressive verbal language development, learning motivation, expressive writing development, independent work level/distractibility, severe discrepancy level, total; individual; 1 form (no date, 4 pages); manual (42 pages); 1984 price data: $14 per test kit including 25 rating forms; $6 per 25 rating forms; $8 per manual; $8 per specimen set; Gerald J. Spadafore and Sharon J. Spadafore; Academic Therapy Publications.*

Review of Learning Disability Rating Procedure by ROBERT J. ILLBACK, Director of Student Services, Fort Knox Dependent Schools, Fort Knox, KY:

The Learning Disability Rating Procedure (LDRP) is a group rating process through which decision-making teams attempt to determine the probability and likely severity of a youngster's learning handicap. The scale is predicated on the notion that many children are classified as learning disabled with minimal regard for the criteria established by Public Law 94–142, the Education for All Handicapped Children Act of 1975, which sets national policy for the identification of these children. In this regard, the scale attempts to address a major problem, which has been well documented elsewhere (Adelman, 1979; Lovitt & Jenkins, 1979; Yoshida, Fenton, Maxwell, & Kaufman, 1978). The authors' approach is interesting and somewhat innovative, in that it forces decision makers to consider preordained variables in specified ways, within the context of parameters delineated by the Federal guidelines. Unfortunately, the authors have focused precious little effort in the development and validation of the procedure, and what results is a process of entirely undetermined usefulness. Test users will be unable to draw meaningful conclusions based on the data obtained from this instrument, and it cannot therefore be recommended. The remainder of this review will detail the major problems which confront prospective users.

The LDRP is accompanied by a manual which is rather brief and superficial in its attention to a range of important test information. The authors describe some of their own views about current problems in identification of learning disabled children, but do not cite any of the relevant literature, such as research on multidisciplinary team decision making (e.g., Ysseldyke, Algozzine, & Mitchell, 1982; Pfeiffer, 1980), and the current state of knowledge about learning disabilities (Hallahan & Bryan, 1981). Thus, the context and theoretical rationale for the procedure are not clear. The 10 variables which are chosen by the authors, and especially the operational definitions of these, therefore appear arbitrary and arguable. It is not clear that the authors used standard item selection and analysis procedures in test development.

Administration of the LDRP is accomplished in group decision-making situations, with each person rating the child in question on each of the 10 variables following a general discussion. When disagreement exists, a rating of 3 or 4 is to be assigned. Then the group leader is to total the ratings and divide by the number of participants, yielding a mean value for each variable. The mean values are then added to obtain a total rating. These total scores are then to be compared with a four-category (poor candidate to excellent candidate) table which purports to predict the likelihood of needing special education and related services.

Substantial problems exist in this process, all of which contribute to its probable unreliability. For example, teams are notorious for having conflicting perspectives on children's problems, and the process does not deal with the likelihood that extreme variability will exist for some teams. Additionally, for most of the variables, the authors do not meaningfully control for the technical adequacy of standardized test data which are to be used to make relevant determinations (e.g., IQ score, achievement scores, behavior observations). Further, some of the guidelines are purely indefensible, such as deriving reading decoding and listening comprehension scores based on short performance samples of undetermined reliability and validity. Finally, ambiguity abounds, and there is a high probability of scoring errors.

Normative data are equally unconvincing. One hundred eighty-three students, all of whom had already been classified as learning disabled, were rated (presumably by their teachers). The authors provide means, but no data on the variability of these ratings. Also, there is not a shred of information about the demographics of the sample, nor are we told how the sample was obtained. Importantly, no data are available on a normal distribution of school children, for comparison purposes. The authors also attempt to provide normative data through asking a sample of 46 experts (also of undetermined origin) to provide ratings on an imaginary, stereotypical learning disabled child (contrary to considerable evidence that this population is extremely heterogeneous), and these data are presented within the norm table as well (again, only mean values). The authors inappropriately cite differences between the first and second set of ratings as evidence that learning disabled children are being overly identified. For all intents and purposes, the LDRP normative data are unusable (but the authors offer no cautions for their use).

The reliability of this procedure is also unknown. The manual describes an interrater reliability study, based on a total number of 5 students, in which 4 raters were able to obtain agreement at the 82% level. No data about the procedures' stability, internal consistency, or standard error are available. One validity study is provided in the manual, in which 30 elementary- and secondary-level learning disabled, mentally retarded, and emotionally disturbed students (10 of each, again of unknown origin) were rated, and a main effect was found for the learning disabled children. This study suffers from severe methodological and statistical problems. The manual does not address issues of content, criterion-related, or construct validity in any systematic fashion.

In sum, when essential and minimum standards of measurement practice are applied, the LDRP comes up short. Test users are therefore encouraged to explore alternatives to the use of the LDRP. One such alternative would be the Pupil Rating Scale, which is based on a far more adequate set of validation data and which is more behaviorally grounded. For reviews of the Pupil Rating Scale, see 1019, 8:439, Colligan (1977), Reeves and Perkins (1976), and Proger (1973).

REVIEWER'S REFERENCES

Proger, B. B. The Pupil Rating Scale: Screening for learning disabilities. JOURNAL OF SPECIAL EDUCATION, 1973, 7, 311–317.

Reeves, J. E., & Perkins, M. L. The Pupil Rating Scale: A second look. JOURNAL OF SPECIAL EDUCATION, 1976, 10, 437–439.

Colligan, R. C. Concurrent validity of the Myklebust Pupil Rating Scale in a kindergarten population. JOURNAL OF LEARNING DISABILITIES, 1977, 10, 317–320.

Yoshida, R. K., Fenton, K. S., Maxwell, J. P., & Kaufman, M. J. Group decision making in the planning team process: Myth or reality? JOURNAL OF SCHOOL PSYCHOLOGY, 1978, 16, 237–244.

Adelman, H. Diagnostic classification of LD: Research and ethical perspectives as related to practice. LEARNING DISABILITY QUARTERLY, 1979, 2, 5–15.

Lovitt, T., & Jenkins, J. Learning disabilities research: Defining populations. LEARNING DISABILITY QUARTERLY, 1979, 2, 46–50.

Pfeiffer, S. I. The school-based interprofessional team: Recurring problems and some possible solutions. JOURNAL OF SCHOOL PSYCHOLOGY, 1980, 18, 338–394.

Hallahan, D. P., & Bryan, T. H. Learning disabilities. In J. M. Kaufmann & D. P. Hallahan (Eds.), HANDBOOK OF SPECIAL EDUCATION. Englewood Cliffs: Prentice-Hall, 1981.

Ysseldyke, J. E., Algozzine, B., & Mitchell, J. Special education team decision making: An analysis of current practice. PERSONNEL AND GUIDANCE JOURNAL, 1982, 308–313.

[601]

Learning Efficiency Test. Ages 6 and over; 1981; LET; 6 scores (ordered immediate recall, unordered immediate recall, ordered short term recall, unordered short term recall, ordered long term recall, unordered long term recall) for both visual memory and auditory memory; individual; 1 form (4 pages); manual (79 pages); stimulus cards for visual memory subtest (47 cards); 1984 price data: $26.50 per complete kit including 25 record forms; $6 per 25 record forms; $8.50 per set of stimulus cards; $12 per manual; $12 per specimen set; (10–15) minutes; Raymond E. Webster; Academic Therapy Publications.*

Review of Learning Efficiency Test by ROBERT G. HARRINGTON, Assistant Professor in

Educational Psychology & Research, The University of Kansas, Lawrence, KS:

The Learning Efficiency Test (LET) is an individually administered, diagnostic instrument developed on the premise that there is a relationship between deficits in the visual or auditory modalities and children's inabilities to read or to solve math problems at grade-appropriate levels. This issue is controversial and as yet unresolved in the research literature. The extent to which some relationship exists between processing deficits and subsequent learning is unclear. Whether the relationship is causal or not remains unsubstantiated. Conclusive documentation that remediation of visual or auditory deficits will improve reading or math skills is unavailable. The cautious examiner needs to take these factors into consideration in deciding whether to use this instrument as part of a psychoeducational assessment.

The purpose of the LET is to examine how efficiently students, ages six through adult, retain bits of information presented through either the visual or auditory sensory modalities. For each of these subtests, both ordered and unordered recall are assessed under three recall conditions: immediate recall, short term recall, and long term recall. The test attempts to approximate actual classroom learning conditions by providing learning and memory tasks accompanied by controlled verbal interference. Verbal interference is achieved by having the child count out loud or repeat a meaningless sentence before being asked to recall a string of letters. This verbal interference is meant to test the student's ability to retain information in short-term memory (STM) and to transfer it from STM to long-term memory (LTM). It is questionable whether this type of verbal interference can serve as an appropriate analog of the types of interferences and disruptions to the learning process occurring in the classroom. This is a problem in ecological validity shared by many individually administered diagnostic-prescriptive instruments. The manual appropriately points out that this test is not designed for use with students who are severely hearing impaired, deaf, trainable mentally retarded, or severely and profoundly mentally retarded. The auditory subtests of the LET may be administered to blind or visually impaired students.

How the LET was designed is clear. The content validity of the test appears good. The material to be remembered for the LET is comprised of serial strings of nonrhyming or phonetically nonconfusable consonants which were constructed by randomly selecting letters from a list of 11 consonants. Letter sequences such as these are preferable to digits because the response domain is enlarged. Because there are only 9 digits compared to 26 letters, when letters are used the probability of correctly guessing is decreased. This represents an improvement over some previous instruments such as the Visual Aural Digit Span (VADS) which relies on digits as stimulus elements. The serial strings in the LET range in length from two to nine letters. During administration the letter strings are presented visually and orally to the student. "Different serial strings are used for each type of presentation to reduce the effects of practice or repetition on performance." A string of nine letters was selected as the maximum length on the basis of research which shows that the average adult remembers about seven items, plus or minus two; and the average adolescent can retain about six items, plus or minus one, in short-term memory. Thus, sequences which extend up to nine items can reasonably be expected to assess the full range of memory ability.

Standard directions for administration and scoring are simple and explicitly described in the manual. Six scores are obtained for both the visual and auditory subtests by allotting one point for each letter recalled in the last string of each recall condition. Scores for each condition may range from 0 to 9. Tables are provided to convert these raw scores into standard scores with a mean of 10 and standard deviation of 3. Such standard scores should permit an examiner to compare a particular child's performance to other children of the same chronological age. Because the range of possible raw scores is restricted from 0 to 9 a problem arises, however. For example, a raw score of 8 or 9 converts into a standard score of 19 for all children ages 6 through 14 on practically all of the six subtests in the auditory and visual modalities. From ages 14 through 17 a raw score of 4 converts into a standard score of 7 on ordered immediate auditory recall and raw scores of 0, 1, or 2 all convert into a standard score of 1 from ages 14 through 17. It seems that the limited range of possible raw scores has diminished this test's ability to discriminate. A table is also provided to convert the standard scores to percentile ranks but because of the narrow range of raw scores the resulting conversion to percentiles is also highly inadequate. Students with the same raw scores but varying in age may be placed in the same percentile rank. The standard error of measurement of a standard score on the LET is plus or minus 2 at the 95% confidence level. This means that the probability is 95% that a student's true score lies within this interval. On the LET, however, a standard score of 10 plus or minus 2 means that the child's true score may range from the 25th percentile to the 75th percentile. Obviously, this is not very helpful information. The restricted range of raw scores has distorted the significance of the standard error of measurement. A final table in the manual displays the standard errors of measurement of differences between standard scores. This reflects how much of a difference between two standard scores represents a significant difference. This measure is also difficult to interpret because of the narrow range of raw scores.

The LET was standardized on 575 public school students between the ages of 5 years, 0 months and 18 years, 11 months living in Connecticut, Rhode Island and Massachusetts. The sample was restricted to the northeast and did not represent a national sample. For this reason, examiners must be very cautious in applying these norms in other sections of the country. Students with organically, physically, or emotionally based learning problems were excluded from the sample as were children with IQs below 85. The test manual states that a range of urban-rural and socioeconomic backgrounds was sampled. Representative percentages of Caucasians, Blacks and Hispanics were included. Only one set of norms is provided for males and females because no significant sex differences have been found on the LET.

Test-retest reliability was determined using a small sample of 40 secondary students with learning and behavior problems. The intervals between tests ranged from one to six weeks, with a mean retest interval of 3.68 weeks. Test-retest reliability coefficients range from .81 to .97, with a median of .94. A larger sample size including a broader range of ages would have been more appropriate. Evidence of the diagnostic validity of the LET is provided by an examination of the patterns of intercorrelations of the Visual Memory and Auditory Memory subtests for different types of students including average, emotionally disturbed (ED), learning disabled (LD) and educably mentally retarded (EMR). The manual suggests that ED and LD students show greater inconsistency than the average EMR students in information processing abilities across the visual and auditory modalities. The intercorrelations between the groups were not always so distinctively different as to be convincing, however. Furthermore, no research data was presented to substantiate the claim that LD or ED students should be expected to perform inconsistently across these tasks. In order to demonstrate predictive validity two multiple step-wise correlation analyses were performed for groups of average, LD, ED and EMR students. For both reading and mathematics the LET does show some predictive validity but because of the limited information provided about sample characteristics it may be difficult to generalize these results. Specifically, correlations of the LET with reading achievement range from .50 to .92; for math achievement the correlations range from .49 to .93.

The test manual provides some guidelines for interpretations of test results. Behaviors and patterns the examiner should look for when analyzing the student's performance on the LET are adequately described. Specific strategies for remediation of various information deficits are also included. Unfortunately, some of the suggestions do not always seem based on sound teaching principles. For example, it is suggested that in order to spell the word "automobile," the word should be divided into five bits of information each containing two letters: au, to, mo, bi, le. By rehearsing these smaller bits of information the child is expected to eventually remember how to spell the whole word. It would seem that memorizing words is a very inefficient approach to learning to spell.

SUMMARY. The LET represents some major improvements in test design and item selection over previous tests of this type. Because of the narrow range of raw scores, however, the diagnostic-prescriptive usefulness of this test seems to be quite limited. The test's psychometric properties, including reliability and validity, require further substantiation. While the relationship between memory deficits and learning problems remains unclear, tests of this type may provide useful supplemental information for developing a child's educational program. Before this objective can be met the LET needs to undergo further research and revision.

[602]

Learning Environment Inventory. Grades 7–12; 1982; LEI; students' perceptions of the social climate; 15 scale scores: cohesiveness, diversity, formality, speed, material environment, friction, goal direction, favoritism, difficulty, apathy, democracy, cliqueness, satisfaction, disorganization, competitiveness; norms consist of means and standard deviations based on a 1967 and 1969 sample, no norms for grades 7–9; 1 form (4 pages); combined manual (57 pages) for this and My Class Inventory; separate answer sheets must be used; price data available from publisher; (20–50) minutes; Barry J. Fraser, Gary J. Anderson, and Herbert J. Walberg; Western Australian Institute of Technology [Australia].*

TEST REFERENCES

1. Shaughnessy, J., Haladyna, T., & Shaughnessy, J. M. Relations of student, teacher, and learning environment variables to attitude toward mathematics. SCHOOL SCIENCE AND MATHEMATICS, 1983, 83, 21–37.

Review of Learning Environment Inventory by JAMES R. BARCLAY, Professor of Educational and Counseling Psychology, University of Kentucky, Lexington, KY:

The Learning Environment Inventory (LEI) is a survey attitudinal instrument based on a test of 18 scales originally devised by Walberg in 1968 (Classroom Climate Questionnaire), modified in 1968, and finalized in 1969. It consists of 15 scales designed to provide information about the nature of the environmental "press" and relationships within the classroom. It was basically standardized on secondary school students and the "North American" sample included mainly students tested in

Montreal together with a few schools in Boston. The standardization data is based on 1,048 students tested in various subject areas in 1969.

Four tables are presented in the manual. One provides the means and standard deviations for individuals and classes, the second one provides alpha coefficients of reliability and also test-retest data ($N = 139$), a third the intercorrelations between scales for 149 physics classes, and a fourth lists a number of studies done by various researchers.

From there on, the manual comments in quick succession on many studies. These comments assert that the instrument: (1) possesses predictive validity against a variety of outcome variables; (2) shows relationships to the Moos Classroom Environment Scales; (3) has been used in studies in Israel, India, Brazil, Thailand, and Indonesia; (4) can be used as a criterion of curriculum effectiveness; (5) shows relationship to teacher personality variables; and (6) can be used to distinguish between rural and urban school environments. The final contribution of this rapid research summary is to cite a massive meta-analysis in which there were 734 correlations, 12 studies, 10 data sets, 823 classes in eight subject areas, and 17,805 students tested in four nations. The outcome of this massive study is reported as verifying 31 of 36 hypotheses made by one of the authors (Herbert J. Walberg).

Unfortunately, most of this information is highly compacted and convoluted without any supporting statistical data or summaries. Though many relationships are affirmed by the authors, readers are referred to studies which document the assertions. Users who might wish to know the relationship to achievement, intelligence, socioeconomic status, or other variables have the alternatives of accepting the authors' contentions or plowing through numerous references to find the information they are looking for.

Though both individual and group means and standard deviations are cited there are no other norms such as *T* scores or percentiles. This may be because the range of the standard deviation is extremely small for class means (.75 to 2.58) and not much wider for individual scores. Since both classroom and individual means are cited anywhere from 14.18 to 20.36, slight differences in scores on any of the seven item scales will represent rather massive differences in standardized scores or percentiles.

The test construction was originally based on factor analytic studies, but nothing further is cited in the manual about the details of contruct validity. There are no concurrent correlations relating to the scales, and predictive validity is asserted but the conditions and time lengths of such predictions will have to be ferreted out of specific research studies.

Unquestionably a great deal of research has been done with this instrument, but research alone does not constitute the sole criterion of usability. What can this instrument be used for? Users will want to know how it can be used. The authors favor class means rather than individual profiles. But what does a class mean signify on these scales? What kinds of specific suggestions can the authors make for interventions which would ostensibly "improve" the class profile? Still further one could question whether a class mean signifies anything in the real world. The perceptions of a classroom environment are made up of many students who think differently, process information differently, and may disagree on specific variables in accordance with their social power in the classroom, their previous level of achievement, and their background learning and experience. Thus, the overall effect of these individual differences would cancel out each other yielding rather homogenous means and narrow standard deviations.

Perhaps in the research the authors have criterion-type profiles of students of different background, intelligence, achievement, etc., but this is not reported in the manual. The normative sample is based largely on students in Montreal with a few schools from Boston. This can hardly constitute a representative "North American" sample. Moreover, the standardization data is 15 to 16 years old.

In summary, as a manual this is a very deficient effort. It really represents a kind of overview of research which has been done with this instrument—without the presentation of any supporting data. A manual should provide the kinds of data which users need to make decisions. Though unquestionably the assessment of classroom environment is an important task in modern education research, it is simply not sufficient to state means and standard deviations and cite research studies. Professionals such as school psychologists, counselors, and researchers attuned to psycho-educational change will not find information in this manual which will help them to determine whether the instrument will evaluate what they are looking for.

Potentially, this instrument may have value if research with individual differences is reported, methods of identifying deficits detailed, and the power potential of alternative interventions described. For the present, the use of the instrument is more appropriate for researchers who are seeking answers to some of these questions. If the meaning of some of these scales could be related to behavioral observations or alternative methods of evaluation such as the multi-method, multi-trait approach, and if these results can be expressed simply and directly, then the instrument would have a wider range of applications and uses.

Review of Learning Environment Inventory by JAMES C. REED, Neuropsychology Services, Wayland, MA:

The Learning Environment Inventory (LEI) is an inventory designed to measure the learning environment of a class. It consists of 105 statements to which the student responds by circling one of four answers: strongly disagree, disagree, agree, strongly agree. From these 105 statements, 15 scales can be generated. These 15 scales can be used to assess the perception of an individual student or to measure the learning climate of a class. Individual observation of classroom activities can be expensive and time-consuming. Hence, one part of the rationale for the development of this instrument was to provide a low-cost paper-and-pencil measure of classroom interactions that teachers could administer.

The LEI has been used nationally and internationally, and the authors provide a 6-page bibliography which contains studies in which the instrument has been used. The authors attempt to justify the inclusion of each scale on the basis of theoretical consideration and/or prior research. For example, for the Cohesiveness Scale (feeling of intimacy), the authors indicate that this variable has been found to be positively related to learning criteria. They do not document this statement, but they do refer to several studies that relate Cohesiveness to various class and course properties. Justification for the other scales is presented similarly.

There are several questions to ask. First, how reliable are individual scales that are based on 7 items each? Two studies, with *N*s of 464 and 1,048 respectively, list alpha coefficients that range from .54 to .86 for the various scales. For the reliability of group means, intraclass correlations for groups are reported. For two studies with *N*s of 29 and 64 the values range from .31 to .92. The authors state, "Taken together, the results...suggest that all LEI scales possess satisfactory reliability." Another way of interpreting the findings is to say that almost any individual scale may be suspect.

A second question of importance is how independent the separate scales are. The scale intercorrelations based on class means vary from .00 to .77. The median of the average mean correlation with the other scales is .32, and the highest mean correlation is .40. Of course, there is overlap in what is being measured, but the values indicate that the scales are reasonably independent.

Another question of some importance is: how stable is the social environment or learning climate of a class? Based on an *N* of 139, test-retest (the intervening time interval was not reported) reliability coefficients for individuals varied from .43 to .73. The magnitude of these values suggests that there is some stability to the learning environment, but at the same time, the learning environment is not etched in stone; far from it.

Is this test easy to administer and to score? For both questions the answer is yes. The directions for administration are simple and clear. Scoring may be done either by computer or by hand, and examples are provided.

Are the results easy to interpret? Can an individual classroom teacher learn something about the perceptions of the students and the learning climate which he/she helps create? The reliability of the individual scales varies widely and there is some question about the stability of the learning climate. Furthermore, a sensitive, experienced teacher is probably aware of class mood, student interaction, and perception. Nevertheless, with judicious use and with conservative interpretation, the LEI does provide a vehicle for constructive inquiry into possible directions to move in order to modify social factors that may influence learning.

In summary, the LEI is an instrument for measuring various aspects of the learning climate that may influence the acquisition of knowledge and development of skills and behaviors in students. For researchers, the scale has been used extensively on a national and international basis. There is a wide body of previous knowledge to which the results of an individual investigation can be related. For a particular teacher or school administrator, it provides an easy-to-use guide, which, if used conservatively and cautiously, may provide insight into the social structure of a particular class. For a short, group-administered test, the reliabilities appear adequate. It also has the limitations of such short group-administered tests; it is part of the nature of the beast.

[603]

Learning Preference Inventory. Grades 3–12 and young adults; 1978–80; LPI; identifies learning styles based on Jungian typology; 6 preference scores: sensing-feeling, sensing-thinking, intuiting-thinking, intuiting-feeling, introversion, extraversion; no data on reliability or validity; no norms; 1 form ('78, 4 pages); scoring and instruction sheet (no date, 2 pages); user's manual ('80, 66 pages); 1982 price data: $55 per complete kit; $2.50 per inventory (includes scoring/instruction sheet); $8.95 per user's manual; administration time not reported; Harvey F. Silver and J. Robert Hanson; Hanson Silver & Associates, Inc.*

[604]

Learning Screening. Grades 1, 1–2, 2–3, 3–4, 4–5, 5–6, 6–9; 1981; LS; upward adaptation of Rapid Exam for Early Referral; 7 scores: performance and learning ranks for each of 3 areas (math, spelling, reading), total rank; 7 levels; 1 form for each level (24 pages, student booklet); reading card (1 sheet); cassette audiotape (includes directions for administration); class ranking form (15 pages); manual (29 pages); 1985 price data: $36.50 per 25 student booklets (includes reading cards, specify level); \$20 per cassette audiotape (specify level); \$2.50 per class ranking form; \$5.95 per manual; \$16.95 per specimen set; 3(10) minutes per child for 10 days; Harold P. Kunzelmann and Carl H. Koenig; Charles E. Merrill Publishing Co.*

[605]

Learning Staircase. Developmental ages 1–7; 1976; criterion-referenced; "designed to answer the needs of early childhood special education classes"; 20 content areas (modules): adjectives, auditory memory, auditory perception, body image, classification, colors, fine motor, gross motor, number concepts, preverbal, reading readiness, same and different, sequence, spatial relationships, time, toilet training, verbal comprehension, verbal expression, visual memory, vocabulary; no data on reliability and validity; no norms; inventory individually administered; 1 form; inventory booklet (23 pages) labeled Assessment Inventory System; teacher's guide (76 pages); parental report form (24 pages); 1983 price data: \$59 per complete set including 568 task cards for 20 modules, assessment inventory systems for 20 children, 20 parental report forms, 100-sheet grid pad, teacher's guide; \$15 per 100-sheet grid pad, 25 Assessment Inventory System forms, and 25 parent report forms; (15–20) minutes per module; Lila Coughran and Marilynn Goff; DLM Teaching Resources.*

Review of Learning Staircase by CURTIS DUDLEY-MARLING, Assistant Professor of Education, University of Colorado at Denver, Denver, CO:

The Learning Staircase is an instructional program which, according to its authors, is designed for early childhood special education classes but may also be useful for some non-handicapped students lacking various skills. The program is divided into 20 content areas or modules. Modules contain sequences of activities presented on individual activity cards. Each activity card contains a behavioral objective, an age norm, suggested methods and materials for teaching the objective, and a criterion for determining mastery of the objective. There are 568 activity cards in all. The Learning Staircase can be used as a total instructional program or as part of a larger program.

The Learning Staircase was designed to be a "complete and comprehensive curriculum" and, as such, makes the assumption that it addresses skills important to children's linguistic, cognitive, and social development. The authors of this program would not claim the Learning Staircase addresses all of the skills handicapped children need to learn. The authors obviously do assume, however, that the behavioral objectives for each of the modules represent important developmental accomplishments.

In order to determine a starting point for individual children taking part in the Learning Staircase program, the authors recommend observation of each child, talking with parents, and the administration of the Assessment Inventory System. The Assessment Inventory System is criterion-referenced and the tasks are taken directly from the activity cards for each module. The manual provides procedures for establishing children's basal and ceiling ages for each module. The modules the child needs are determined by comparing their basal age to their mental age (if available) for each module. The basal age is also used to estimate children's entry level within modules.

The Assessment Inventory System was designed as part of the Learning Staircase program. Those choosing the Learning Staircase for school programs will find the Assessment Inventory System the most appropriate test to use for the purpose of planning instructional programs. Since it is criterion-referenced it provides precise statements of children's functioning within the Learning Staircase program. It also helps teachers determine the "scope and sequence" of instructional activities. The Assessment Inventory System is useful only in conjunction with the Learning Staircase program and, therefore, its utility and validity depends on the utility and validity of the overall Learning Staircase program.

The authors of the Learning Staircase do not provide a strong rationale for the selection and sequence of activities and modules. The selection of items appears to have been made on the basis of conventional wisdom rather than any scientific selection process or developmental model. Some items and modules were included because the authors believe they represent important prerequisites to other modules. For example, the Auditory Memory module is divided into four levels: imitating noisemaker sounds, repeating words, sentence imitation, and following directions. The authors assert that these activities represent a hierarchical sequence but fail to support this assertion. They also note a relationship between deficits in short-term memory and difficulty imitating sentences and conclude that speech and language problems may be the result of this difficulty. Part of the justification for including the Auditory Memory module rests on the authors' implied assumption that a causal relationship exists between short-term memory and language development. However, they fail to support this assumption. It is at least as plausible that delayed language development influences performance on short-term memory tasks. The failure to justify the selection of modules and activities is the major failing of the Learning Staircase.

In conclusion, pre-school teachers should select the Assessment Inventory System for use in their program only if they choose to use the Learning Staircase as an instructional program. The Assessment Inventory System could provide some useful information apart from the Learning Staircase program but it is not so useful that it would justify the expense of purchasing the entire program. If teachers do choose the Learning Staircase program, because it is consistent with their view of children's cognitive development, then the Assessment Inventory System is a very useful adjunct. However, the Learning Staircase represents a narrow, fragmented view of development which is not consistent with most contemporary models of development and, therefore, cannot be recommended.

Review of Learning Staircase by BARBARA K. KEOGH, Professor of Education, University of California, Los Angeles, CA:

The Learning Staircase is designed for use by teachers or intervenors who work with young handicapped children. The Assessment Inventory System (AIS) is the diagnostic and evaluative component of the program. The stated purpose of the AIS is to assess individual children for instructional purposes, rather than for classification. The program as a whole is criterion-referenced. Most assessment items are matched with instructional tasks. Both assessment and instructional components are based on specific items commonly found in developmental or readiness tests.

AIS items are organized according to Learning Staircase modules (e.g., auditory memory, body image, number concept, etc.) and according to developmental level or age expectancy within module. AIS items and Learning Staircase tasks are similarly numbered so it is possible to go directly from assessment items to corresponding instructional tasks. The latter are represented singly on five by eight inch cards. Each card contains the description of a task (e.g., "the child identifies his own body parts"), the level of expected performance, a method of instruction broken down into specific steps, a listing of material to be used in instruction, and a criterion for successful performance. Tasks cards are color-coded according to age of expected performance for normally developing children. The number of items in modules varies from six on the sequence module to eighty-one on the fine motor module. Range of items according to age expectancies also varies, with the visual-memory module containing items appropriate for children in the 2 through 7 year developmental age range and the same-different module appropriate for children who have developmental ages ranging from 4 to 6 years.

The AIS is to be individually administered by the diagnostician starting at the estimated ability level of the child. Each item is scored correct or incorrect. A basal age within each module is determined by working backwards until reaching three successful items; a ceiling is determined by three successive failed items. Basal and ceiling scores for each module may be transferred to a profile sheet (contained in the Learning Staircase packet). Individual grids are available for recording AIS findings and teachers' instructional plans.

The AIS gets mixed marks based on commonly accepted criteria of test adequacy. On the positive side, AIS items are easily translated into instructional goals and practices. Within modules the items tap abilities or competencies across a reasonable age range, and items are appropriate for assessing handicapped young children. AIS information about individual children can be gathered through formal testing, observation, or parent report, and assessment can be carried out in the educational setting by teachers or intervenors.

On the negative side, there are problems of construct validity, of psychometric adequacy of items and modules, and of lack of supporting information. Although the authors note that the system has been field tested in five school districts, no summarizing efficacy data are reported. From a developmental perspective the abilities or constructs presumably tapped by the 20 modules are frequently not comparable and are likely not independent. Naming a module or a set of items does not ensure construct validity. The user must be cautious when making inferences about children's developmental characteristics based on AIS module titles. From a measurement perspective, interpretation is limited because modules contain different numbers of items, similar items appear in several modules, and the order or sequence of items is sometimes questionable. Item order becomes important as basal and ceiling scores are presumably useful for determining individual children's educational needs and for documenting their progress. Characteristic of criterion-referenced approaches, the Learning Staircase and the AIS are self-contained. Interpretations or inference from assessment data are limited to the specific content covered.

The link between assessment and instruction is a strong point in this system. From the standpoint of educational interventions with young handicapped children, the program as a whole contains a number of useful techniques for classroom teachers. The specificity of items and the suggested instructional steps may provide beginning intervenors with practical techniques, at the same time allowing a range of options for experienced teachers. Although the number and specificity of items are potential strengths, intervenors may also find the system redundant and cumbersome. Other criterion-referenced systems appropriate for assessing young handicapped children (e.g., The Carolina Developmental Profile or the Portage Guide to Early Education) tend to be shorter, to be tighter conceptually, and to have had broader clinical-educational use. Rather than a test, the Learning Staircase, including the AIS, might best be viewed as an inventory of techniques and instructional tasks. The program as a whole is clinically rather than theoretically based, and its potential value lies in its practicality. The effectiveness of the Learning Staircase will depend upon the insight and skill of intervenors in selecting from this inventory of tasks.

[606]

Learning Style Identification Scale. Grades 1–8; 1981; LSIS; ratings by teachers; 4 scores obtained by rating 4 areas: intrapersonal information, extrapersonal information, cognitive development, self-concept; 1 form (4 pages); manual (65 pages); 1984 price data: $24.50 per 30 tests and manual; $8.65 per 30 rating, scoring, and profile forms; [10–20] minutes; Paul J. Malcom, William C. Lutz, Mary A. Gerken, and Gary M. Hoeltke; Publishers Test Service.*

Review of Learning Style Identification Scale by MICHAEL W. PRATT, Associate Professor of Psychology, Mount Saint Vincent University, Halifax, Nova Scotia, Canada:

Though the Learning Style Identification Scale (LSIS) is entitled a "learning style" assessment, the authors do not refer to cognitive style or modality preferences of the child as this term is commonly used in the educational literature. Rather, they define learning style in an extremely broad fashion as "the method students use to solve any problem that they encounter in their educational experiences." Based on a vaguely-sketched theoretical framework, the authors specify four separate learning styles dependent on the individual's level of "receptivity" to "interpersonal" vs. "extrapersonal" sources of information. In turn, these two aspects of personal orientation are said to depend on level of self-concept and cognitive development, respectively. In contrast to this theory however, what is actually assessed in this test are rated frequencies of specific classroom behaviors (e.g., "daydreams in class"). While these may be elements of individual "styles," the use of the qualifier "learning" here is somewhat confusing, and the rationale relating these particular behavioral items to the theoretical framework is obscure.

The instrument consists of a 24-item behavior checklist, to be filled out by teachers or "other professional persons who work with or have responsibility for children and youth." Items are rated 1–5, depending on their perceived frequency of occurrence. These 24 items were selected from a larger pool, based on factor loadings for a sample of children mainly from grades 3 through 6. Four factors were extracted, with six items associated with each. Though unlabelled in the manual, these factors are broadly parallel in content to the factors extracted from other behavioral checklists, such as the Problem Behavior Checklist of Quay and Peterson, as the authors note.

The checklist is certainly easy to administer, and profiling from the item results is very readily accomplished. The information obtained on specific behaviors in the classroom could be quite useful. Furthermore, the manual provides generally sound discussion regarding procedures for working with children's classroom behavioral difficulties. Obviously however, the interpretive features of the style scales require consideration of technical information on matters of reliability and validity.

This information is limited so far. The test manual contains somewhat brief discussion of a series of unpublished studies conducted on the LSIS by the authors. Details of the samples involved, and aspects of the results, are not always described fully. Split-half and test-retest reliabilities were computed for the four major learning style classifications; these appeared generally adequate. However, interrater reliabilities were not assessed in these studies, providing no information on the generality of these "learning styles" or on agreement between different observers of the same child.

Serious gaps are present in the validity information provided on the test to date. Content validity is somewhat unclear, given the lack of relation between theoretical rationale and the behavioral checklist items. Though the authors caution that inattention to learning style problems can have serious consequences (including delinquency, for example), no information on predictive validity has been provided in the manual. Nor is any information given on criterion validity in relation to similar behavioral assessment procedures (e.g., the Teacher Referral Form of Clarfield or the Problem Behavior Checklist of Quay and Peterson, which has been extensively studied and validated on a wide variety of populations). This is a serious lack, given the evident parallels between the LSIS and other instruments of this sort.

Construct validity was addressed in a study examining the correlation between learning style scores and Piers-Harris Self-Concept scores, as well as the Iowa Test of Basic Skills and the aptitude scores from the Cooperative School and College Ability Tests, both measures of cognitive achievements. Although the rationale provided in the introduction would predict that Styles I, II, and III would show differential relationships to self-concept and cognitive measures, the results instead suggest negative relations for all three styles with all of these external measures. Other studies reported in the manual indicate that Styles I, II, and III are generally quite positively correlated (with many coefficients in the .60 to .70 range), whereas Style IV is substantially negatively related to the others. These results are disturbing with respect to the construct validity of these presumably distinctive styles. Finally, it appears that only about 60% of all students are readily classified in one of these four styles, using scores of one standard deviation above the mean as a criterion. The remaining children are labelled Style V, and seem to form a large, residual population about which little distinctive may be said.

A normative sample of students from grades 1 through 8 was administered the LSIS. Unfortunately, the representativeness of this sample is not addressed; they were drawn from two midwestern school districts, one urban and one rural. The authors have generated standard *T*-scores for each of the four learning styles and argue laudably for caution based on sampling limitations. However, any normative use of the test whatsoever requires confidence in the representativeness of the sample, and this issue needs to be addressed further.

In summary, the LSIS in its current form is a classroom behavior rating scale, rather than a measure of "learning style" as this term is usually used. The rationale for considering these ratings to be indices of global approaches to learning, as argued by the authors, is quite unclear. The manual presents limited information on validity to date, and the results provided do not support the differentiation of these styles very convincingly. Most critically, work is needed comparing this instrument with others of similar format and type, such as Quay's Problem Behavior Checklist. The PBC is a well-validated instrument for assessment of behavioral styles, and has been used widely in classroom settings. Until the theoretical and empirical issues regarding the distinctiveness of the LSIS as an index of "learning style" rather than general behavioral orientation are clarified, this test cannot be recommended for use.

Review of Learning Style Identification Scale by K. ANN RENNINGER, Assistant Professor of Education, Swarthmore College, Swarthmore, PA:

The Learning Style Identification Scale (LSIS) is an inventory for the identification of student learning style by means of teacher ratings of student behaviors. It also prescribes methods by which the teacher can tailor the learning environment to meet student needs. The LSIS was designed to "complement and supplement" other testing and instructional programs. As such, it offers teachers, counselors, and other school personnel a method for identifying and responding to a child's learning style. For this inventory, learning style is defined generally as a child's method of handling social and academic problems.

Five learning styles are identified, each of which is conceptualized as involving varied configurations of (*a*) intrapersonal and extrapersonal information, (*b*) cognitive development, and (*c*) self-concept. Briefly, students characterized as Learning Style I receive and use more intrapersonal than extrapersonal information, have relatively "high" self-concepts, and are "deficient" in cognitive development. Students characterized as Learning Style II receive and use little intrapersonal and extrapersonal information, have relatively "low" self-concepts, and are "limited" in cognitive development. Students characterized as Learning Style III receive and use more extrapersonal than intrapersonal information, have relatively "low" self-concepts, and are "nearly average" in cognitive development. Students characterized as Learning Style IV receive and use intrapersonal and extrapersonal information, have "high" self-concepts, and are "high" in cognitive development. Students characterized as Learning Style V receive and use intrapersonal and extrapersonal information, but less so than Style IV learners, have average self-concepts, and are "adequate" in cognitive development.

Because the styles are each conceptualized as a configuration of factors, they are not readily categorizable in terms currently used to classify students. This should serve to protect the student from unreflective labeling, at least until the style types are in more common use. On the other hand, it is important to note that only four learning styles (I, II, III, IV) represent distinct configurations of factors. The fifth represents a style which shifts among each of the other four styles. The fifth is also the style of a majority of students.

Several comments seem to be in order at this point. First, the LSIS is not specifically billed as an assessment device for limited populations, but in effect it is most useful for work with the small percentage of students who have distinct styles, such as those of Styles I–IV. Second, the authors' discussions of each style component raise two sticky conceptual issues: (*a*) What distinctions are being made between intra- and extra-personal information? and (*b*) Is cognitive development really meant to be synonymous with school achievement? Third, there is some contradiction in the authors' alternating perceptions of these styles as traits or processes. Distinguishing between traits and processes is important since identification of a student as having a particular learning style constrains the teacher's actions in adjusting the learning environment for a child with that style. No discussion is included of the need for teacher responsiveness to change in student style and consequent reassessments of student behavior.

PRACTICAL EVALUATION. The technical and administrative manuals are combined for the LSIS. This is both a positive and a negative feature. As a combined manual, the information included is more technical than that often received by most classroom teachers. It reviews theoretical bases for the author's conceptualizations, offers several pages of description on each learning style, and includes details on instrument construction, reliability, and validity. Its scope is a positive feature because teachers who take time to read through the manual will have a much better understanding of what the LSIS can offer them. However, it is doubtful that the amount of detail included in the manual will lead most teachers to spend the time requisite to this kind of understanding.

In general, the administrative component of the manual is clearly written. The authors suggest that "the student should be observed carefully over a period of at least several days. It may even be helpful to maintain a daily log...." However, there is no attempt to standardize the method of student assessment. Thus, despite their clarity, the instructions for rating student behavior raise serious questions about the reliability and validity of the scale.

The procedure for scoring is easily followed. A raw score is calculated and a conversion chart is used to determine a standard score ($M = 50$; $SD = 10$). The standard score for each style is then graphed. Following this, the student's predominant learning style is identified as being "at least one-half standard deviation above the mean and at least three points above the standard score for any other learning style." The manual urges caution in interpreting scores and profiles; however, possible sources of error are not addressed.

Following the administrative information are discussions of each learning style and appropriate teacher responses. The suggested teacher responses to student behavior are both practical and comprehensive. A narrative explanation of each learning style is accompanied by a description of the relationships between the factors characterizing that style. For example, a portion of the authors' explanation of Learning Style III includes this explanation of the relations between the factors of extrapersonal information, cognitive development, and self-concept: "A Style III learner tends to be thin-skinned. This evolves from the fact that when a student comes into conflict with the external environment and has no access to intrapersonal information, coping with degrees of rejection, disappointment, or criticism becomes difficult."

No actual documentation for the putative causal links between factors of extrapersonal information, cognitive development, and self-concept is cited. Since the prescribed teacher responses are based on the described links between these factors or characteristics, the user must keep in mind that these links may be somewhat tenuous.

Following the description of each student style is a description of appropriate teacher responses to the characteristics of that style. These follow directly from the statements made about the learner and cover both the affective and cognitive needs of the student. Thus, teachers of a Style III student are urged to: (*a*) require completion of all assigned tasks, (*b*) encourage use of problem-solving techniques, (*c*) develop a positive personal relationship, (*d*) promote success with peers, and (*e*) use behavioral objectives. Methods for accomplishing these goals are clearly explained and reflect a variety of theoretical perspectives. In addition, a case study of a child with the characteristics of that particular style is included. This case study provides a concrete illustration of the use of suggested teacher strategies.

TECHNICAL EVALUATION. Although the LSIS offers teachers more than style identification, the technical information for this instrument focuses only on the scale for determining learning style. No discussion of the validity of the suggested teacher responses is included.

According to the manual, initial development of the LSIS was based on teacher ratings for a sample of students from an urban population, within which "classes were selected to represent differing socioeconomic and racial characteristics of the district." It is important that subsequent revisions of this test include more specific information on the sample characteristics, including factors such as SES and cultural differences which might influence assessment of style.

The test-retest reliability of the LSIS appears to be adequate (coefficients range from .84 to .96). However, the retest occurred after only two weeks. Subsequent evaluation of reliability might allow for a longer period of time between test sessions.

In contrast to its reliability, the content validity of the LSIS appears somewhat questionable. The LSIS is constructed such that overt behaviors are used to assess an individual's cognitive and affective development. The assumption that overt observable behaviors can be validly used to infer levels of development in these areas raises questions about the nature of the learning styles described by the LSIS. In addition, no baseline for observation is determined, so there is no check on frequency of a given behavior relative to other behaviors for a child or in relation to other children.

Criterion-related validity for the LSIS, however, is good and suggests that the overt behaviors identified with each style do at least correlate with such well-established measures as the Piers-Harris Children's Self Concept Scale, the composite score of the Iowa Test of Basic Skills, and the scholastic aptitude scores from the Cooperative School and College Ability Tests.

SUMMARY. The LSIS offers teachers, counselors, and other school personnel methods for both identifying and responding to student learning styles. A strength of this measure is the link between style and subsequent teacher action. The scale itself does not seem to be immediately useful without this supplementary information. Unfortunately the lack of technical information on the validity of the techniques suggested is a limitation. Potential users of the LSIS should attempt to test the validity of both style identification and the follow-up techniques across a variety of learning situations to determine the usefulness of the LSIS for their particular purposes.

[607]

Learning Style Inventory. College and adults ; 1976; self-administered questionnaire; 4 scores: concrete experience, reflective observation, abstract conceptualization, active experimentation; technical manual (53 pages); self-scoring test and interpretation booklets (7 pages); 1984 price data: $30 per 10 self-scoring test and interpretation booklets; $10 per technical manual; administration time not reported; David A. Kolb; McBer and Company.*

TEST REFERENCES

1. Sadler, G. R., Plovnick, M., & Snope, F. C. Learning styles and teaching implications. JOURNAL OF MEDICAL EDUCATION, 1978, 53, 847–849.

2. Whitney, M. A., & Caplan, R. M. Learning styles and instructional preferences of family practice physicians. JOURNAL OF MEDICAL EDUCATION, 1978, 53, 684–686.

3. Wunderlich, R., & Gjerde, C. L. Another look at Learning Style Inventory and medical career choice. JOURNAL OF MEDICAL EDUCATION, 1978, 53, 45–54.

4. Geller, L. M. Reliability of the Learning Style Inventory. PSYCHOLOGICAL REPORTS, 1979, 44, 555–561.

5. Leonard, A., & Harris, I. Learning style in a primary care internal medicine residency program. ARCHIVES OF INTERNAL MEDICINE, 1979, 139(8), 872–875.

6. Torbit, G. Counsellor learning style: A variable in career choice. CANADIAN COUNSELLOR, 1981, 15(4), 193–197.

7. Peterson, B. K. The effect of tables and graphs on reader retention, reader reaction, and reading time. THE DELTA PI EPSILON JOURNAL, 1983, 25, 52–60.

[608]

Learning Styles Inventory [Creative Learning Press, Inc.]. Grades 4–12 and teachers; 1978; LSI; "a measure of student preference for instructional techniques"; 9 factor scores: projects, drill and recitation, peer teaching, discussion, teaching games, independent study, programmed instruction, lecture, simulation; 2 forms: student, teacher, (2 pages); manual (44 pages); 1983 price data: $18.50 per 30 student forms, 1 teacher form and computer scoring; $6.95 per manual; $7.50 per specimen set; computer analysis provides 14-page printout for each classroom of students; (30) minutes; Joseph S. Renzulli and Linda H. Smith; Creative Learning Press, Inc.*

Review of Learning Styles Inventory by BENSON P. LOW, Clinical Instructor of Psychiatry & Behavioral Sciences, University of Washington, Seattle, WA:

The Learning Styles Inventory (LSI) does not appear to be a useful measure of learning styles. Although attractively packaged with a plethora of computer printouts full of practical implications for classroom teaching, the LSI suffers from poor construction and questionable validity.

The LSI is conceptually weak in that it fails to establish its own raison d'etre: that matching teaching styles to pupil learning styles leads to increased learning (i.e., academic performance over and above simple "pupil satisfaction" with teaching). The authors did not, for unknown reasons, draw on the substantial body of educational literature covering this important topic.

Although the LSI Manual includes a section on "Construct Validity," the authors offer no data demonstrating conceptual convergence between their measure of learning styles and that of others. Instead, they describe the factor analytic procedures they used to identify the factors comprising the LSI. Construct validity remains problematic in the LSI.

The empirical validation studies carried out by the test authors and described in the LSI manual suffer from a number of major problems. First, the study sample was composed only of seventh-grade pupils, although the instrument is marketed as appropriate for pupils from grade 4 through 12. At best, the results of the validation study are only of limited generalizability. The data do not warrant the broad usage suggested in the manual.

Second, the subjects' LSI ratings were taken after only three class meetings. The test authors did not address the issue of how reliabile LSI ratings can be after such a limited exposure to the instructional format, when actual application conditions involve much longer and sustained exposures.

Third, the results of the validation study seem obscured by the authors' use of multiple regression techniques, which in the present case included three sets of correlated measures (learning style scores) as predictor variables. While the results themselves show a statistically significant multiple correlation between learning style scores and achievement, there is no evidence that matching learning style to instructional format itself results in improved academic achievement.

Finally, the validation study examined only three of the nine LSI scales. The authors offer no evidence for the empirical validity of the other six scales. This omission, combined with the limited study sample alluded to above, casts considerable doubt on the usefulness of the validation study in buttressing the authors' claims.

Pupil learning styles may well be a useful area of investigation and measurement, particularly in terms of their relationship to achievement. The LSI, despite its claims, has not been adequately field-tested, and appears to be of suspect validity as a measure of pupil learning style, especially as this relates to improved learning. I suggest that prospective users look elsewhere for such a measure.

[609]

Learning Styles Inventory [Humanics Media]. Grades 6 through post-graduate level; 1976–80; may be used either in conjunction with or independent of Instructional Styles Inventory (T3:1160); self-report inventory; 17 scores in 4 areas: conditions (peer, organization, goal setting, competition, instructor, detail, independence, authority), content (numeric, qualitative, inanimate, people), mode (listening, reading, iconic, direct experience), expectation; 1 form ('76, 4 pages); manual ('80, 89 pages); profile sheet ('76, 2 pages); separate answer sheets must be used; 1983 price data: $62.95 per starter set including 25 inventory booklets, 50 answer sheets, 50 profiles, and manual; $1.50 per inventory booklet; $.12 or less per answer sheet; $.25 or less per profile sheet; $12 per manual; $19.95 per specimen set; (25–40) minutes; Albert A. Canfield; Humanics Media.*

TEST REFERENCES

1. Altschuld, J. W., Lower, M. A., & Ross-Harrington, M. L. A study of the learning styles of remedial and nonremedial postsecondary technic students. JOURNAL OF INDUSTRIAL TEACHER EDUCATION, 1982, 19, 47–58.

Review of Learning Styles Inventory by JOHN BIGGS, Professor of Education, University of Newcastle, Australia:

The Learning Styles Inventory (LSI) may be administered, either to individuals or groups, in teaching/learning situations in school and business with a view particularly to matching learning and teaching styles. The definition of "learning style" is based on that of Travers (1973): "an attribute of the individual which interacts with instructional circumstances in such a way as to produce differential learning achievement." Four aspects of a learning situation are suggested to be particularly important in the definition of a learning style: (1) *Conditions*: those aspects that individuals find motivating—peer and teacher affiliation, organizational structure, facts and details, independence in goal setting and in working, competition, and submission to authority; (2) *Content*: nominating areas of prime intrinsic interest—numeric, verbal, inanimate, and people; (3) *Mode*: the form in which the learner prefers to receive information—by listening, reading, graphs/pictures, or direct experience; (4) *Expectation*: of success, or failure. There are, then, eight scales for conditions, four each for content and mode, and one for expectation (i.e., seventeen in all). Each scale is accessed by six independent items. The task is to rank four alternatives within each item, and the ranks are summed across the six items. However, as the total number of items is only 30, some items contribute to four scales simultaneously. Thus, while some scales are independent of each other, others are not; and as is seen below, this leads to some difficulty in interpretation.

There is probably quite good support in the psychological literature for postulating these particular aspects of learning style as useful constructs. What the author does not do, however, is demonstrate that his scales are anchored into those constructs.

One way of testing factorial validity would be to factor analyze the item intercorrelational matrix, but because items are not independent, it would be meaningless to do this. Scale intercorrelations are reported in the manual, and there are a number of negative correlations between scales, undoubtedly because of the ranking (if one ranks Numerics "1" as preferred content, then all other contents have to be ranked at "2" or less).

Split-half reliabilities are extremely high: no split-half is lower than .96. Such high figures are due in part to the non-independence of the scales, and also in part to the fact that several items within a scale are very similar in content, sometimes involving only minor alterations of wording.

Several validity studies are reported where different occupational groups differ significantly on scale scores (e.g., data processing students were found, inter alia, to be low on both pupil and teacher affiliation, and high on detail and organization). However, to be high on both affiliation scales necessarily involves low detail and organization scores: the scales are scored that way. The validity studies make general sense, but one cannot know whether the differences are due to low affiliation, or to high structure, or to both. Other studies show fairly obvious associations; for example, students scoring high on Numerics "tended to do better in mathematics." Some, but not all, of the studies cited found that matching student style with teacher style led to higher achievement.

One might ask the following questions: (1) Does the LSI meet adequate technical standards? The answer to this must be no, as it is currently presented. There are too many scales for too few items, and the method of scoring spuriously raises reliability figures and makes obtained differences between groups ambiguous to interpret. (2) Could the LSI be improved? Yes, by reducing the number of scales and using a different method of scoring. (3) Is the job the LSI sets out to do worthwhile? Yes, there should be an instrument that can match student and teacher preferences. It is a worthy goal, and it is a pity that the present format of the LSI is unsatisfactory. (4) Does any other instrument do this job? Yes, one is being developed at the University of Sydney: the Learning Preference Scale, with forms for students, teachers and parents. The scale assesses independent references for cooperative, competitive, and individualized learning situations (Owens & Barnes, in press). The advantages of this scale over the LSI are psychometric and logistic. The three classroom atmosphere constructs of cooperative, competitive, and individualized learning are easier to understand and use than the 17 conceptually and methodologically interrelated ones of Canfield.

This is an interesting and developing area. It is to be hoped that the present instrument will reappear in a more acceptable form in the future.

REVIEWER'S REFERENCES

Travers, R. M. W. (Ed.), SECOND HANDBOOK OF RESEARCH ON TEACHING. Chicago: Rand McNally, 1973.

Owens, L., & Barnes, J. The relationships between cooperative, competitive, and individualized learning preferences and students' perceptions of classroom learning atmosphere. AMERICAN EDUCATIONAL RESEARCH JOURNAL, 1982, 19(2), 182–200.

Review of Learning Styles Inventory by C. DEAN MILLER, Professor of Psychology, Colorado State University, Fort Collins, CO:

The author states in the forward that, "This manual does not attempt to review the theoretical foundations for the instrument, nor does it attempt to review the comparatively new literature on the effective aspects of learning," and "the instrument...should not be confused with other procedures which purport to measure fundamental, enduring, or factorially discrete characteristics of human cognition." The instrument has been developed using theories and concepts from four areas: (1) personality constructs which have been found to be associated with motivation, (2) fields or domains of educational interests, (3) preferred learning channel or modality, and (4) expectancy pertaining to level of performance. There is no single theoretical or integrated rationale underlying the construction of the test. The four areas are likely to appeal to many educational practitioners because they are all part of a familiar educational pedagogy which teachers believe is basic to effective teaching and learning.

The sophisticated educational practitioner will recognize quickly that the Learning Styles Inventory has not been developed from current theories and empirical studies of learning, memory, and retrieval. Instructors and counselors need to be aware that this self-report inventory should not be confused with specific aspects of human cognition which include the constructive act of learning, the characteristics of primary and secondary memory, and retrieval processes. Potential users of this inventory will be confronted with the dilemma of having an instrument which has considerable face validity in terms of traditional pedagogical practice and little or no face validity for current views of human cognition. This may be due to the fact that when the inventory was developed in the early 1970s it was current and reflected what at that time was considered to be theoretically sound rationales for understanding and facilitating learning.

The manual contains an outline of the concepts which were used in developing the inventory. These concepts were used to define the construct of learning styles. There is no information in the manual to determine how the specific content was selected or to determine if the items cover a representative sample of the domain or construct to be measured. However, the author's reference to personality or attitudinal values which seem to affect learning could be construed as a trait approach to defining learning styles. If learning styles are composed largely of personality traits, the question of content validity may not be relevant.

The method of contrasted groups was used extensively in reporting validity information. Based on the large number of statistically significant differences which were reported, there is substantial support for the existence of a wide variety of learning styles which are visible among groups selected on the basis of educational majors. The meaningfulness of these differences is lessened because the large sample sizes contribute to the large number of statistically significant differences. Two studies involving differences between achievers and nonachievers and between persistors and nonpersistors were reported as "rough examinations of the potential predictive values of the instrument."

No correlations with other tests of learning styles were reported. Additional consideration of the validity of the inventory is limited due to the lack of an underlying theoretical foundation and no testing of hypotheses in the validation process. For example, it isn't clear whether or not the author intends for the inventory to be used to predict academic achievement, or to assess learning styles for the purpose of improving instruction programs which in turn would improve academic achievement.

Split-half reliability coefficients ranging from .96 to .99 (first half vs. second half and odd numbered items vs. even numbered items) may be spuriously high due to the fact that the items are not independent of each other. No test-retest correlations were reported in the manual. Estimates of standard errors of measurement were not reported.

Both forms of the inventory were designed for use with students from grade 6 through university postgraduate levels and for use "in training situations in business, government, and industry." Over 2,000 subjects were used in developing separate norms for males and females. From 85 to 106 subjects were used in developing separate norms for high school males and females and for junior high school males and females. No norms were reported for sixth grade pupils or for training situations in business, government, or industry. Sampling procedures, number of sampling units, and demographic data such as age, ethnic composition, socioeconomic status, and geographic locale were not reported. The lack of well defined and clearly described populations seriously limits use of these norms.

Administration of the inventory is not difficult or complicated. Helpful suggestions are provided in the manual. Users are likely to encounter difficulty in computing the raw scores due to several errors in the example reported on page 12 of the manual.

Interpretation of scores is confounded by the author's use of personality or attitudinal values, affective variables, preferences, and interest in describing the inventory without defining what is meant by each of the descriptors. Users would need to be somewhat familiar with expectancies, learning modalities, and vocational interests in order to adequately interpret the scores and profiles. There are helpful and informative interpretations of the meaning and possible implications of strong preferences in utilizing the scores for instructional planning. However, the author correctly reports an "absence of rigorous research on the consequences of utilizing specific instructional formats with persons with differing learning styles profile scores."

Potential users need to be aware that the inventory and manual do not include information about comparatively new findings on effective schools and effective learning, as well as current theories and empirical studies of learning, memory, and retrieval. In the absence of extensive concurrent and predictive validity information, it might be advisable to consider the inventory as being for experimental use even though large numbers of subjects have completed the inventory. One of the potential benefits of using the inventory might be the knowledge a teacher could gain from examining the diversity of profiles of learning styles which tend to exist in any class of students.

[610]

Learning through Listening. Ages 10–11, 13–14, 17–18; 1976–80; 6 scores: content, contextual constraints, phonology, register, relationship, total; norms consist of means and standard deviations; 1 form consisting of either an open real or cassette tape; 3 levels labeled Test battery A, B, C; 2 parts: I, II, for each level, on opposite sides of same tape; teacher's manual ('80, 48 pages); spirit duplicator masters for pupils' booklets I and II ('79, 39 pages); 1983 price data: £7.95 per tape (open reel or cassette); £9.95 per spirit duplicator masters; £2.95 per teacher's manual; (28–37) minutes for Part I, (29–41) minutes for Part II with a 15–30 minute break between parts; Andrew Wilkinson, Leslie Stratta, and Peter Dudley; Macmillan Education [England].*

Review of Learning through Listening by ALLEN BERGER, Professor of Education, University of Pittsburgh, Pittsburgh, PA:

A distinct feature of Learning through Listening is that the tapes were professionally recorded by the British Broadcasting System and University studios in Birmingham, England. The three tapes, available in cassettes and reel-to-reel, are intended for the following groups: Battery A, 10- and 11-year-old children; Battery B, 13- and 14-year-olds; and Battery C, 17- and 18-year-olds. In England, according to the authors, these groups would correspond to pupils in the final year of primary school, third year of secondary school, and sixth form or colleges of further education, respectively.

Each tape (or battery) is composed of tests of content, contextual constraints, phonology, register, and relationships (except Battery C is without a test of phonology). The tests of content are "designed to measure the ability to follow and understand a piece of informal exposition"; contextual constraints "(originally tests of prediction)...the ability to infer missing parts of a conversation from what is actually heard"; phonology, "the ability to understand differences in meaning brought about by different emphases"; register, "the ability to detect changes in the appropriateness of the spoken language used"; and relationship, "the ability to detect the kinds of relationships existing between people from the language they employ."

Battery A and B each take approximately 60 minutes to administer; Battery C, about 80 minutes. Each battery is divided into two parts (each part being on one side of each tape), and the authors recommend separating the two parts "by a short break of 15 to 30 minutes" for each battery. The questions to which students respond on the tapes are also on duplicated sheets which students use to record their answers. The tapes include such things as telephone conversations, reflections of a dream, radio announcements, street conversations, lectures, and conversations among interviewers of candidates for a teaching position. Approximately half of the time students listen to a complete story and then respond to all the questions; in other parts, they respond to each item after each brief vignette. There are approximately 75 items in each battery; in Batteries A and B, students get a point for each item correctly answered; in Battery C, items may have multiple correct answers and points are subtracted for incorrect responses. Students are not told that they will be penalized for incorrect responses.

The talk on each tape is realistic with appropriate background sounds. The user must bear in mind that the test was made in England and consequently contains references to Heathrow Airport, the Commons, Duke of Edinburgh, England, Wales, Scotland, Australia, going to the pictures, the curriculum of the sixth forms, rugby, four-penny stamps, boot (of a car), telly, tea, ringing up (on the telephone), flat, Air Canada. Some students may not have heard the pronunciation of words like schedule and missiles or exclamations such as "Good Job!" or "Oh, Mummy!" Students in Commonwealth countries would be at home with these expressions and pronunciations, and with few exceptions it seems unlikely that the differences would seriously impede the instructional use of these tapes in the United States.

Of the 42-page Teachers' Manual, all but seven pages are devoted to answers to the exercises and a score conversion chart; test data are contained in approximately three of the seven pages at the beginning of the manual. Much is missing. The authors provide no definition of listening or any rationale for the selection of the kinds of tests which make up each battery. Under a heading called "Some test statistics," only the following sparse information is provided for Battery A: "To establish mean scores, reliability coefficients, and to assess its relationship with other measures, test battery A was administered to a group of 180 children drawn from the final year in five primary schools in the West Midlands. In this group boys numbered 93 and girls 87." Similar sparse information is given for Battery B and C.

In addition, the authors offer almost no interpretation for the statistical information that is provided. For instance, they include for each battery a table of correlations among subtest scores. The relatively low intercorrelations are a good sign that the subtests are tapping into different facets of listening comprehension. But no interpretation of the data can be found in the manual.

There is also no discussion of validity (or even mention of the word) except as implied in a notation that each of the batteries was administered to students along with a reading test and an intelligence test. The correlation coefficients for the reading, listening, and intelligence scores are presented, but no rationale is given for these comparisons. Even though comparing scores on listening and reading tests is common practice, this reviewer questions the logic of making such comparisons for the purpose of establishing test validity. The justification (when one is given) that listening and reading are receptive language arts is not that persuasive when one is using the scores to establish the validity of a listening comprehension test.

Split-half reliability coefficients, corrected by the Spearman-Brown formula, were .78, .83, and .84 respectively for Batteries A, B, and C. Reliability coefficients were not significantly different between boys and girls.

The instructions for scoring indicate that the administrator is to take the total score for each student and record it "on the front cover of Booklet I." For Battery A, this total raw score is the final score. For B, "Scoring is a double process. Raw scores should first be obtained for the whole test battery, and these should then be transformed into normalised and standardised scores by using the score conversion chart." For Battery C, "Scoring should be done in three stages. First raw scores should be obtained for each of the tests in the battery. Secondly these scores should be transformed to converted scores shown on the score conversion charts. Finally, total overall (converted) scores should be calculated for each of the test sessions and for the whole test battery." The rationale for these different scoring procedures is not provided. In short, while Learning through Listening might be recommended as a classroom activity, as a test it suffers from a paucity of useful explanatory and interpretive information from beginning to end.

[611]

Leeds Scales for the Self-Assessment of Anxiety and Depression. Psychiatric patients; 1976; self-rating scale; 4 scores: depression (general, specific), anxiety (general, specific); 1 form (no date, 1 page); manual (26 pages); 1983 price data: £4.75 per complete set including 25 questionnaires; £1.75 per 25 questionnaires; £1.00 per 2 scoring stencils; £2.00 per manual; £3.00 per specimen set; administration time not reported; R. P. Smith, G. W. K. Bridge, and Max Hamilton; Psychological Test Publications [England].*

TEST REFERENCES

1. Berg, I., Butler, A., Houston, J., & McGuire, R. Mental distress of mothers of young children in Harrogate. PSYCHOLOGICAL MEDICINE, 1984, 14, 391–399.

Review of Leeds Scales for the Self-Assessment of Anxiety and Depression by JOHN DUCKITT, Chief Researcher, Institute for Sociological and Demographic Research, Human Sciences Research Council, Pretoria, South Africa:

The Leeds Scales were developed as brief self-assessment measures of the severity of symptoms of clinical anxiety and depression. A large number of measures of anxiety and depression are of course currently available. For this reason it is important that potential users, in order to select the test most appropriate for their needs, should clearly distinguish symptom state scales of this kind from those instruments (like the State-Trait Anxiety Inventory) which assess depression or anxiety as enduring personality traits or transient affective states.

The scales consist of 15 items relating to various states of affect, symptomatology, and behavior printed on a single questionnaire sheet. Four response categories are used, which appear immediately below each item and are scored 0–3. Scale scores are obtained by summing over items.

The manual, apart from an appendix briefly describing the scales and scoring procedure, is largely derived from an original paper in the *British Journal of Psychiatry* (Snaith, Bridge, & Hamilton, 1976) which outlines the development and validation of the scales. The initial item pool consisted of 22 items and included the full 12 items of the Wakefield Self-Assessment of Depression Inventory, which had in turn incorporated the 10 items of the Zung Self Rating of Depression Scale found to be most frequently endorsed by depressed patients (Snaith, Ahmed, Mehta, & Hamilton, 1971). Further items were added to give somewhat broader coverage to the more common symptoms of anxiety and depression. However, no attempt was made to sample these symptoms comprehensively or to provide any rationale for the items actually used in terms of theory or diagnostic criteria.

Items were selected for the final scales on the basis of high correlations with psychiatrists' ratings of anxiety or depression and their effectiveness in discriminating rated anxiety and depression. Two 6-

item scales, termed General Anxiety and General Depression, were obtained in this way from a patient sample covering a wide range of diagnoses ($N = 137$). A 6-item scale of Specific Anxiety was obtained from ratings of anxiety in a sample diagnosed as suffering from anxiety neurosis ($N = 26$), and a 6-item scale of Specific Depression was obtained from ratings of depression in a sample diagnosed as suffering from endogenous depression ($N = 48$). The rationale for this procedure, that the severity of anxiety and depression need not necessarily be best indexed by the same set of symptom items in different disorders, does not seem unreasonable.

However, as it happens the Specific and General Scales overlap very substantially. Thus, the two depression scales share 5 of their 6 items while the anxiety scales share 4 of 6 items. Moreover, the differences in criterion correlations of the non-shared items were not large and were not shown to be statistically significant. In addition, no attempt was made in the cross-validation study to demonstrate the utility of separate sets of scales. The manual simply does not report whether the Specific scales predicted severity ratings for anxiety neurotics or endogenous depressives any better than the General scales. Overall, therefore, there seems little empirical justification for the use of the two separate sets of scales. Indeed, users might well choose to ignore the Specific scales and use only the General scales, developed from the larger sample, with little if any likelihood of losing predictive efficiency.

No evidence is reported either in the manual or from subsequent studies of the internal consistency or test-retest reliability of the scale scores. The manual does, however, report a cross-validation study revealing rather impressive correlations (.85 and .83 for the two General scales) between scale scores and psychiatrists' ratings of the severity of anxiety and depression in small samples of psychiatric patients. Tabulated scale scores for psychiatric patients rated mild to severe in depression or anxiety ($N = 43$) and normals recruited from hospital staff ($N = 50$) are the only normative data of any kind reported. A cutting point of between 6 and 7 on both General scales seems to differentiate excellently between cases and non-cases with false positive rates of 7.1 and 7.3% and false negative rates of 7.8 and 9.6%. However, these rates could well be misleading given the probable socio-demographic differences between patients and staff and since an unspecified number of normals who reported self-perceived "nervous problems" were discarded from that sample.

The discriminant validity of the scales seems rather dubious. The manual suggests a difference score (Specific Depression minus Specific Anxiety) as a "diagnostic" score to aid in differential diagnosis. However, the difference between the mean diagnostic scores of groups of anxiety neurotics and endogenous depressives was only statistically significant at the .025 level when age was controlled. In addition, although the correlation of the Anxiety and Depression scales is not reported in the manual, a figure of .70 has been obtained in a subsequent study (Forrest & Berg, 1982). Depending on the reliabilities, this could well be evidence for convergent rather than discriminant validity and raises the possibility that instead of indexing specific clinical syndromes both scales might be primarily reflecting generalized psychiatric impairment or distress.

In general, the Leeds Scales tend to be rather rudimentary in psychometric terms. They are inadequately balanced against acquiescence and ignore problems of faking, random or careless responding, and social desirability effects. Their reliability is unknown, adequate normative data is lacking, and there are a number of unanswered questions concerning their validity. Their senior author in correspondence with this reviewer has suggested that a more recent measure, the Hospital Anxiety and Depression Scale, has effectively superceded the Leeds Scales. However, very little validational work on this newer measure has yet been completed. At present prospective users seeking brief symptom state measures of anxiety and depression might be better advised to use the relevant subscales of the Symptom Check List-90 or the scaled General Hospital Questionnaire. In the case of depression the Self-Rating Depression Scale and the Centre for Epidemiologic Studies Depression Scale, though somewhat longer, are also, if not necessarily better measures, at least better known quantities.

REVIEWER'S REFERENCES

Snaith, R. P., Ahmed, S. N., Mehta, S., & Hamilton, M. Assessment of the severity of primary depressive illness: Wakefield Self-Assessment of Depression Inventory. PSYCHOLOGICAL MEDICINE, 1971, 1, 143–149.

Snaith, R. P., Bridge, G. W. K., & Hamilton, M. The Leeds Scales for the Self-Assessment of Anxiety and Depression. BRITISH JOURNAL OF PSYCHIATRY, 1976, 128, 156–165.

Forrest, G., & Berg, I. Correspondence: Leeds Scales and the GHQ in women who had recently lost a baby. BRITISH JOURNAL OF PSYCHIATRY, 1982, 141, 429–430.

Review of Leeds Scales for the Self-Assessment of Anxiety and Depression by H. J. EYSENCK, Emeritus Professor of Psychology, Institute of Psychiatry, University of London, England:

The Leeds Scales for the Self-Assessment of Anxiety and Depression consist of two short scales, rigorously item-selected and subjected to external validation in terms of ratings. Twenty-two items were employed in the analysis, and attempts were made to exclude items showing significant correlations with sex and age. Responses to each item were on a 4-point scale (i.e., "definitely," "sometimes," "not much," and "not at all"). It is doubtful whether the difference between "sometimes" and "not much" would be very meaningful to most subjects, as they seem almost equivalent in common usage. Symptoms of somatic reference were not included in the list, which seems a definite disadvantage. It has usually been found that as far as general neuroticism is concerned (of which both depression and anxiety are parts), psychological symptoms are correlated with introversion, somatic symptoms with extraversion; arbitrary exclusions of this kind tilt the balance of the test in one direction or the other without any clear rationale.

The procedure of validating the scales against clinical judgement, and the item analyses, have been reasonably well done, and the correlations are encouragingly high. From the point of view of substituting the scales for interview results, clearly a good case could be made out for the use of these scales. Whether this is worthwhile or not is a practical question to be settled by psychiatrists or clinical psychologists thinking of using the scales. From the point of view of the psychometrician, the scales have not been submitted to the kind of analysis which would be required in order to obtain scientifically significant evidence regarding their meaning and relationships. There is no matrix of intercorrelations between the items; there is no factor analysis; there is no correlation of the scales with each other; and there is no correlation of the scales with widely accepted fundamental dimensions of personality, such as neuroticism and extraversion-introversion. It is usual for anxiety and depression to correlate very highly, and factor analysis of the total matrix of intercorrelations would be required to decide whether or not it is very meaningful to separate the two scores in this fashion. Altogether no data are given on correlations between these scales and other widely used scales, such as the MMPI, the EPI, the 16PF, etc. Knowledge of this kind would be essential in order to assess the specific contribution of these scales.

The authors also make an interesting and unusual distinction between what they call Specific scales and what they call General scales. For an item to be included in the Specific scales, it had to have a high correlation with an independent measure of the severity of the illness, and also had to be shown to be scored highly by patients suffering from the severer degrees of the illness. Furthermore, for an item to be included in a given scale, it had to be shown that "higher scores were obtained by the patients in the relevant diagnostic group." The selection of items for General scales to measure the severity of depression and anxiety throughout all the diagnostic groups depended on the individual correlations with observer ratings of depression and anxiety which were derived from the Hamilton Depression and Anxiety Scales. The General and Specific scales are fairly similar, but they are not identical. Whether there is any value in this differentiation seems doubtful to the reviewer, but it is certainly an unusual feature which ought to be emphasised in the description of the scales.

As a general conclusion, it may be stated that within their limitations the scales may be clinically useful, but as instruments of scientific interest they fall far short of what is desirable. The item analyses performed and the correlations with external criteria are satisfactory, but internal analysis by way of item intercorrelations and factor analysis is completely missing. It should be added that the items used are not unusual, recurring in many well-known questionnaires (e.g., "I feel miserable and sad," "I am restless and can't keep still," "I get tired for no reason," "I get dizzy attacks and feel unsteady," "I feel tense or wound up," etc.). The similarity with existing items and scales makes it particularly necessary to report correlations with such scales, in order to tell the reader what novel information he can hope to obtain from the new scales that is not already contained in older and more established scales. Such information should certainly be provided in the next edition of the manual.

[612]

Lessons for Self-Instruction in Basic Skills. Adult basic education students grades 4–5, 5–6, 7–8, 9 and above; 1979; LSI; "multilevel programmed learning aids in reading, mathematics and English language"; keyed to the Tests of Adult Basic Education and California Achievement Tests; 53 scores in 3 areas: reading, mathematics, language; no data on reliability; no norms, guides for using scores to assign LSI materials; 53 mastery test forms, (1 page); 4 levels; teacher's manual (64 pages); student record sheets (2 pages) and lessons for self-instruction booklets for each of the 53 test forms; 1983 price data: $190 per reading class assortment; $190 per mathematics class assortment; $155 per language class assortment; $13.45 per examination kit; administration time varies; Edward B. Fry, Lawrence Carillo, Gracecarol Bostwick, Miles Midloch, Eleanor Szaszy, Leo J. Brueckner, Robert C. Cochran, Jennifer A. Hill, Marvyl Doyle, and Eileen Lothamer; CTB/McGraw-Hill.*

[613]

Let's Talk Inventory for Adolescents. Ages 9 to young adulthood; 1982; 8 scores: ritualizing (2 scores), informing (2), controlling (2), feeling (2); norms consist of means and standard deviations; individual; 1 form; manual (108 pages); picture manual (254 pages); 1985 price data: $9.95 per 25 record forms; $12.95 per examiner's manual; $30 per picture manual; (35–50) minutes; Elisabeth H. Wiig; Charles E. Merrill Publishing Co.*

[614]

Lewis Counselling Inventory. Adolescents in school; 1978; identifies those students in need of guidance and counseling; 8 scores: relationship with teachers, relationship with family, irritability, social confidence, relationship with peers, health, total, lie scale; tentative norms consist of means and standard deviations, authors recommend use of local norms; 1 form; 2 parts: part 1 (2 pages), part 2 (1 page, optional supplementary questionnaire); manual (29 pages); 1985 price data: £3.25 per 25 inventories (part 1); £1.70 per 25 optional supplementary questionnaires (part 2); £8.75 per set of scoring stencils; £6.95 per manual; £7.25 per specimen set (does not include scoring stencils); (10–15) minutes for each part; D. G. Lewis and P. D. Pumfrey; NFER-Nelson Publishing Co. [England].*

Review of Lewis Counselling Inventory by DEBORAH N. BAUSERMAN, Licensed Psychologist, Winchester, VA:

The Lewis Counselling Inventory is a self-report inventory for use with individuals or groups in secondary schools. The authors cite multiple uses for the inventory including (1) helping teachers to identify those in greatest need of personal counseling, (2) increasing a teacher's understanding of his class, and (3) aiding in research investigations of adolescents. Avoidance of time-consuming test administration and scoring is an important feature of this survey of social psychological attitudes, relationships, and perceptions. Additionally, the survey does not seek to identify self-perceived problems that are concerns of all adolescents, but rather those that discriminate between pupils with a high and low incidence of difficulties.

The inventory is composed of two sections. The first section contains a series of 46 statements, written at a reading level of about 10 $^1/_2$ years, in the following six areas: (1) Relationship with Teachers, (2) Relationship with Family, (3) Irritability, (4) Social Confidence, (5) Relationship with Peers, and (6) Health. A Lie scale (6 items) is also incorporated. The 46 items are either positive or negative indicating either the presence or absence of a need for guidance and counseling. Following the inventory is a short questionnaire that encourages the student to expand upon particular aspects of his self-perceived problems, thus providing a starting point for counseling.

Information provided on test development indicated that the current form of the inventory was derived from a factor analysis of the intercorrelations of a larger set of statements (113), origin unknown. Response set responding was discouraged through the use of a balance between negatively and positively worded statements. The 113 statements were administered to a sample of 1,477 secondary school pupils from 13 schools in northwest England. Unfortunately for the potential test user, little or no demographic information about the students is provided save for the fact that they were enrolled in three different types of schools (comprehensive, secondary modern, and grammar) whose characteristics may be unfamiliar to an American reader/test user.

Following factor analysis of the 113 x 113 correlation matrix, statements were selected for inclusion in the revised, current form of the inventory in terms of their loadings on the factors identified. The factors, especially at the second-order level, generally confirmed the six areas originally selected as the basis for item generation and scoring; however, these factors or "areas" of counseling need represented in the inventory are not completely independent.

Test-retest reliability over a period of 3 days was .87, and the standard error of measurement was 3.48. Concurrent validity evidence included correlation of .62 between the inventory and the IPAT Anxiety Scale; a self-report of the respondents in which 73% of the boys and 76% of the girls considered that the inventory provided an adequate picture of their problems; and correlations between teacher and student perceptions of .75 for Relationship with Teacher, .76 for Relationship with Family, and .76 for Relationship with Peers. Evidence for the construct validity of the inventory was poorly described and therefore not compelling. Results of other studies on the inventory were also represented, providing interesting information about subject variables such as age, sex, and intelligence. The authors provide tentative normative data with the wise suggestion that schools develop their own norms.

In summary, this reviewer's perceptions of the strengths and weaknesses of the Lewis Counselling Inventory are as follows. On a positive note, the inventory appears not to belie its claim of quick and easy administration. The test items are simple and straightforward, describing categories or areas of adolescent concern which would have obvious interest to counselors of the individual adolescent. As a tool for group study, however, the instrument would probably prove somewhat unwieldy. The user should also bear in mind two additional caveats: (1) the inventory was constructed specifically for use with British students, and (2) the inventory score is based on agree-disagree responses, not intensity, with the possible outcome that school counselors would fail to detect a number of students with severe but circumscribed problems. Given the presence of its unique capabilities and largely persuasive standardization studies, however, the Lewis Counselling Inventory may rightfully take its place as a useful counseling tool on a short list of related tests including the Bell Adjustment Inventory and the Mooney Problem Check List.

Review of Lewis Counselling Inventory by GERALD L. STONE, Professor of Counseling Psychology, and Co-Director, Stroud Center for Educational Services, College of Education, The University of Iowa, Iowa City, IA:

The Lewis Counselling Inventory was not constructed to discriminate between normal and maladjusted students. Rather "the purpose of this inventory is to provide teachers in secondary schools with a convenient instrument for identifying those pupils most in need of guidance and counselling." This brief inventory (10–15 minutes), developed in Great Britain for use in British secondary schools, consists of 46 statements to which a respondent can either agree or disagree. A reading level of 10 1/2 years or higher is required. The revised form, derived from factor analysis of the intercorrelations of a large set of statements, has six scales: Relationship with Teachers (8 items), Relationship with Family (7 items), Irritability (6 items), Social Confidence (7 items), Relationship with Peers (6 items), and Health (6 items). A lie scale (6 items) was added. A short questionnaire is provided that allows respondents to elaborate on particular aspects of their self-perceived problems. In addition, a manual has been prepared, although it has several limitations (e.g., use of sexist language).

The statements were compiled from the initial form and others devised (though not entirely) to fit into the above mentioned scales. According to the authors, the items selected reflect problems that discriminate between pupils with a high and a low incidence of such difficulties, although item analyses are not provided. Little specific information is provided concerning the sources of the statements, magnitude of each problem, or item analysis by sex and grade.

Although reliability assessments can be problematic due to rapid changes in the nature of perceived problems and the use of scales with a modest number of items, the authors report a test-retest reliability of .87 for the revised inventory after an interval of 3 days. Internal consistency coefficients for each scale ranged from .75 to .27. Some of the scales (Social Confidence, Relationship with Peers, and Health) have less than adequate internal consistency, raising questions about the use of separate scales. The authors also refer to unpublished findings of studies using the old inventory since the correlations between the old and new forms are substantial. The test-retest reliabilities for the total score, as reported in these unqualified studies, are satisfactory.

It would seem that one appropriate way to demonstrate the validity of a self-report counseling inventory is through intensive case studies in which an evaluation of problems reported and actual problems could be addressed. This has not been reported in the manual, but the authors do report some evidence from unpublished theses for the appropriateness of the old as well as the new counseling inventory. For example, teachers were asked to rate pupils on scales paralleling the problem areas of the old inventory. Correlations with the pupil's scores indicated significant agreements in three areas: Relationship with Teachers, Relationship with Family, and Relationship with Peers. In constructing the revised form, statements were administered to 1,477 British secondary school pupils. The interscale correlations indicated that the scales were relatively independent.

Tentative norms have been developed for use in British schools, but the authors recommend the development of local norms.

In summary, the authors do a commendable job in discussing the limitations and suggesting many cautions. In evaluating the Lewis Counselling Inventory, one is inclined to ask the following questions: Is the inventory suitable for use in schools in other countries? Are the scale scores necessary? What role does problem magnitude play? Are there sex differences? Do the factor analytic results hold up under cross-validation? Does the lie scale serve a useful function? Do other researchers in other geographical locations publish research relevant to the inventory? Are there recommendations for the use of the inventory in counseling? Is there evidence to indicate that the inventory is superior to simply asking pupils if they have a large number of problems?

The Lewis Counselling Inventory does not adequately address these questions. At present, the inventory is directed at the British school system. In terms of the United States, the inventory does not yet provide substantial evidence for replacing traditional inventories such as the Mooney Problem Check List nor does the inventory incorporate other dimensions of a problem such as magnitude (see STS Youth Inventory, T3:2327).

[615]

Lexington Developmental Scales. Ages birth–6 years; 1973–77; may be used by parents and volunteers; "particularly helpful in pre and post testing"; contains behavioral and experimental items rated by examiner in 4 areas: motor, language, cognitive, personal and social; no validity data for short form; no norms, authors suggest standards of mastery; individual administration to ages birth–2 years; long ('77, 96 pages) and short forms ('77, 51 pages, short form consists of items from long form, both forms include instructions for administration, standardization data, and a record sheet); record sheet, long form (10 pages); additional testing materials must be supplied by examiner; 1984 price data: $5 per long form; $1.50 per short form; (60) minutes in 2 sessions for children ages birth–2, administration time varies for older children; United Cerebral Palsy of the Bluegrass, John V. Irwin, Margaret Norris Ward, Ann B. Greis, Carol C. Deen, Valerie C. Cooley, Alice A. Auvenshine, Rhea A. Taylor, and C. A. Coleman; Child Development Centers of the Bluegrass.*

See T3:1322 (1 reference).

TEST REFERENCES

1. Leonard, L. B., Steckol, K. F., & Panther, K. M. Returning meaning to semantic relations: Some clinical applications. JOURNAL OF SPEECH AND HEARING DISORDERS, 1983, 48, 25–36.

Review of Lexington Developmental Scales by MICHAEL J. ROSZKOWSKI, Evaluation Specialist/Associate Professor of Psychology, The American College, Bryn Mawr, PA:

The Lexington Developmental Scales (LDS) is described by its authors as an instrument designed to provide a graphic portrayal of developmental status during the age range of birth through six years. It is claimed that the scale is appropriate for multiple uses, including screening, curriculum planning, assessment of an individual's developmental progress, program evaluation, profiling of a child's differential levels of development across various abilities, and as a means for training regarding developmental milestones.

The LDS is available in a long form and a short form. The long form is designed to be a curricular guide and a means of assessing developmental progress. The primary purpose of the short form is screening. The long form contains 424 descriptive statements that are subsumed under 47 items. Although the manual refers to both the former and the latter as "items," for the purpose of clarity it is probably better to call the former "subitems" or "anchors" and to restrict the term "item" to the latter. Each of the subitems/anchors has a developmental age assigned to it (i.e., 3, 6, 12, 18, 24, 36, 48, 60, or 72 months). The items are grouped under four topical scales, called "areas" in the manual. These areas are Motor (14 items), Language (13 items), Cognition (10 items), and Personal Social (10 items). These four areas, sometimes appearing under slightly different titles, are common to most infant/preschool developmental scales and adaptive behavior scales. The short form measures the same four areas, but does so with only half as many items as the long form.

The LDS contains two types of items, behavioral and experiential. Behavioral items—which are located primarily in the motor, language, and cognitive scales—are based on direct observation of the subject's performance at the time of the assessment. The experiential items, in contrast, require the assignment of a "rating" to the subject's functioning in behaviors that can only be observed through prolonged contact with the individual. These items are found primarily on the Personal-Social scale. The latter type of item is subject to a variety of rater-related problems (e.g., errors of halo, central tendency, leniency, harshness, recency, etc.) which, while common to all rating scales, need to be considered when interpreting the scores.

Instructions for administering the scale are clearly presented. Level of development is recorded on a record sheet that is intended to provide a graphic representation of the subject's developmental status on each of the items. Separate record sheets are provided for each of the four areas. At the top of each record sheet one finds the previously-mentioned ages distributed sequentially at equal intervals along a horizontal line from left to right. The subitems associated with each specified age level are contained in boxes that are below and to the left of these age anchors. The examiner is to place an "X" at the point on the scale that represents the individual's level of performance on the item, and afterwards to connect these X's to form a graphic profile of the subject's abilities.

I found two problems with the physical layout of this profile sheet. The first problem is that even though the intervals between these ages are not equal, they are equidistant from each other on the record sheet. It would be more appropriate if the intervals between these age anchors were proportional to their actual differences. The second problem concerns the placement of the subitems/anchors. I would have found it easier to learn the use of the protocol if the statements constituting the subitems were located directly below their assigned ages rather than to the left of these numerical anchor points, but this may just be a personal preference.

In addition to a plot of the developmental age (DA) on each item, the manual suggests that the computation of a developmental quotient (DQ) is possible for each item by dividing the DA by the chronological age and multiplying this number by 100. Similarly, area-level DAs and DQs can be calculated by averaging the age levels obtained on each of the items within a given scale.

The user of the LDS should realize that derived scores in terms of developmental norms are less preferable to derived scores based on relative standing (i.e., percentiles or standard scores). The DQ computed from this scale is probably subject to all the shortcomings associated with the "ratio IQ" score, and perspective users would be wise to acquaint themselves with the inherent limitations of such indices.

Inter-observer reliability is a very important consideration in evaluating the adequacy of any behavior rating scale. The manual accompanying the LDS reports that this aspect of reliability was investigated in two separate studies. The first study involved 40 children aged 0 to 2 years old and two teams of observers. The first team of observers, consisting of a teacher and a health educator, assessed infants in the 5- to 19-month age range. The second team, consisting of a teacher and a nurse, assessed subjects who were 11 to 25 months old. The independent assessments made by the two members of each team were compared and the resulting correlations are reported in Table 1 in the manual. It is not clear whether these reliabilities are based on DAs or DQs. For each of the four areas, reliability is reported at the item level and on what is described as a "total area" correlation. At first I thought that the "total area" correlations for each of the four domains referred to the reliability of the total score computed for each domain by summing and averaging the respective item scores (i.e., average DA or DQ), but it appears that in reality this figure is simply the average (i.e., mean) item reliability. One must wonder why correlations using domain scores as data points were not computed since scores based on average DA and DQ are allowed. The item-level reliabilities are very high, ranging between .87 and .98 with an average of .93–.94. This level of reliability surprised me since item-level data are typically far less reliable. Given the high item-level reliabilities, the Spearman-Brown prophecy formula suggests that summated area scores, were they to be computed, would have reliabilities that are very close to unity.

I must wonder whether comparable levels of inter-observer reliability could be achieved by other observers, and would suggest that further studies of inter-observer reliability in this age group be conducted, particularly since the above reliability study (1) involved a rather small number of judges, (2) was done on what seems to be the older version of the instrument (it had fewer items), and (3) could have been based on the correlation of DQs rather than DAs. (The use of DQs when assessing reliability in an age-heterogenous group can give rise to what have been called "spurious index correlations." That is, there could occur a substantial correlation between two sets of DQs even when the correlation between their respective DAs is essentially zero because chronological age is the common factor in the formula used to compute the DQ and thus age is being correlated with itself.)

A second inter-observer reliability study with a group of older children (two to six years of age) is also reported, but the actual design of it is not clear from the description offered in the manual. The derived reliability coefficients from this study are also given in Table 1. The "total area correlations" (i.e., item reliabilities) are again quite high (.85–.87) for all scales except Personal-Social, which has an average inter-observer reliability of .60. Further data from this study are presented in Table 2, but no accompanying textual explanation of the table is made. The details of this study are said to be available in the 1973 version of the manual, but without this information Table 2 is not really comprehensible.

Under the topic of reliability, the authors also discuss the relationship between the long and short versions of their instrument. They claim that the short and long forms provide comparable developmental ages and developmental quotients. As evidence for this statement, a table reporting "differences in the mean developmental ages" between the two forms as derived for two samples of children is presented. Although no statistical tests are made available, the authors contend that the differences in the mean developmental ages computed with the long and short forms, respectively, are small, and that the "short form may be safely substituted for the long form." However, given the data reported, it is really impossible to evaluate the accuracy of this conclusion. To do so, one would also need to know the standard deviations of the DAs of the short and long forms, the correlation between the short and long forms, and the correlation between the short form and the remaining items on the scale.

The authors of the LDS place an emphasis on the interpretation of profiles, yet they fail to consider the reliability of difference scores in their discussion of the topic of reliability. Generally, difference scores are less reliable than the scores from which they were derived, and therefore small differences should not be given undue importance. The manual fails to convey this point. It would be particularly helpful if the manual stated the minimum differences ordinarily needed before a difference could be considered significant. The precision of the difference scores may be lower than an uninformed consumer, such as a parent, may believe.

The manual does not report any studies regarding test-retest reliability or internal consistency reliability. No standard errors of measurement are available. These statistics would also be beneficial in further understanding the precision of the derived scores.

Validity is discussed in terms of content validity and criterion-related validity. Under content validity, the authors discuss the procedures they used to construct their instrument and the efforts that have been made to refine it. The test manual does an adequate job of describing the development of the scale. The tasks included in the scale were selected from various tests and texts dealing with child development. Although the origin of each item is not specified, it appears that the items were taken from the sources listed in the bibliography. For example, the form-drawing subitems in the Motor area appear to come from the Developmental Test of Visual-Motor Integration. The age levels associated with the tasks were also gleaned from citations in the literature; the developers of the LDS did not standardize their scale on their own normative sample.

It is acknowledged that difficulty was experienced in assigning age levels to many of the items because of conflicting reports in the literature. In such circumstances, the authors state that the age assigned to a task was based on the "greatest possible degree of agreement among the sources." I assume this means that either the different ages mentioned for a task were averaged, or more likely, that the most frequently cited age was used. For 10 of the tasks, no age norms appeared in the literature and the authors assigned age levels to them on the basis of their own experience.

Several studies relevant to establishing the criterion-related validity of the LDS are discussed. The first one is concerned with the relationship between chronological age and the LDS. To check whether the ages assigned to each subitem were correct, the author calculated mean DQs on the four scales of the LDS that were administered to a group of 90 children ranging in age from 6 months to 6 years. Although it is not stated explicitly, the authors apparently reasoned that if the age levels assigned to the tasks were correct, then the mean DQs for each age group and the total group should be equal to 100. A table showing the mean DQs for each age level and the total group is presented, but the accompanying standard deviations are not reported. It is claimed that the "developmental quotients are generally close to 100," which "suggest that the various items on the Lexington Developmental Scale are correctly placed with respect to chronological age."

I must question whether these data can in fact be used as supporting evidence. First, contrary to the author's interpretation, the average DQs are not really close to 100. If the sample sizes were larger, it would have been instructive to examine the standard deviations of the DAs and the DQs at each chronological age to see whether a DQ of 100 means the same thing at different chronological ages, as the authors of this scale presume. Moreover, I have to question the very logic of the analysis. The sample size is rather small and it may be unreasonable to expect the mean DQ of this sample to be 100 even if in the general population the mean DQ does fall at this point. A Guttman analysis (or even a simple correlation between age and the number of items passed) would have offered a more clear-cut test of the question of the appropriateness of the developmental sequencing of the subitems.

The relationship between the LDS and the Stanford-Binet is reported in a second study of criterion-related validity. The DQ from the Cognitive area had the largest correlation ($r = .84$) with the IQ from the Stanford-Binet. DQs derived from the other areas had lower but still substantial correlations with IQ (Language: .75; Motor: .68; Personal-Social: .67). The intercorrelations between the area DQs were also computed in this study, and were found to be high (average inter-area correlation equaled .82).

A third set of data, dealing with the correlation between the LDS and the Illinois Test of Psycholinguistic Abilities (ITPA) is also discussed under the topic of criterion-related validity. The psycholinguistic age (PLA) score from the ITPA correlated .74 with the LDS Language scale, .68 with the LDS Motor scale, and .61 with the LDS Cognitive scale. In this same sample of subjects, the correlation between the LDS Cognitive and LDS Motor scales was .68.

While the authors do not have a separate section of the manual dealing with construct validity, the pattern of these correlations is interpreted as evidence of the LDS's convergent and discriminant validity. Although these studies do increase one's understanding of what the LDS measures, I would suggest that more systematic designs, such as multitrait-multimethod analyses and factor analytic studies, are still needed in order to fully establish the scale's convergent and discriminant validity.

Given the present level of evidence regarding the LDS's psychometric characteristics, I see it more as an instrument useful for a qualitative rather than a quantitative description of a child's behavior. As such, I consider the LDS as more appropriate for curricular planning, assessment of developmental progress, and program evaluation rather than as a means of establishing a child's precise developmental age or quotient.

Review of Lexington Developmental Scales by ZONA R. WEEKS, Associate Professor of Occupational Therapy, Indiana University Medical Center, Indianapolis, IN:

The primary purpose of the Lexington Developmental Scales (LDS) is to assess developmental age level. It has been used for assessing behaviors, evaluating children's progress and classroom programs, identifying children needing further evaluation and diagnosis, determining program accountability, counseling parents, and as a training device in child development for persons working with young children.

The large manual, entitled The Lexington Developmental Scales (1979 revision), which contains the methods and criteria for administration of all items, extends through 6 years of age. It is divided into six scales of 360 items (Gross Motor, Fine Motor, Receptive Language, Expressive Language, Cognitive, and Personal-Social). The long and short form publications are titled The Lexington Developmental Scales (1977 revisions). They are divided into four scales of 424 items (Motor—gross and fine, Language—receptive and expressive, Cognitive, and Personal-Social). Quality printing and careful proofreading to eliminate typographical errors would improve the appearance of the large manual. In addition, left margins are too narrow on many of the administration instructional half-sheets, causing the item ages to be totally obliterated by the spiral binding. The manual appears to have been written primarily for the setting for which it was originally produced. Certain statements and words of advice are not applicable to many other facilities in which this scale could be used. It is reported that teachers, nurses, students, parents, or other interested personnel can administer and accurately score the LDS.

The scales consist of some items requiring direct, immediate observation (called behavioral items) and some items scored from records or parent interviews (called experiential items). Children may be observed during classroom activities or elsewhere over a period of several weeks and by more than one person. Special instructions are included for classroom teachers who will have the children over a period of time and may use items from the scales for teaching or evaluative purposes. The authors suggest that teachers may wish to use the scales for assessment at the beginning and end of the school year. Consistent color-coding of results by years is suggested.

Interjudge reliability for the four scales and for individual items of the long form is reported to be typically greater than .90, according to results of one study completed with children from birth to 2 years and another with children from 2 to 6 years of age.

Validity may be inferred, according to the manual, because (1) an extensive literature search was used to place individual test items at appropriate age levels, (2) experienced teachers and other experts judged the progression of items to be appropriate, and (3) developmental ages and chronological ages of the children tested showed substantial agreement. The authors point out that, while further experimental data supporting validity are needed, the relatively high correlations with chronological age, the Stanford-Binet, and relevant measures from a battery used at United Cerebral Palsy of the Bluegrass centers provide evidence for basic validity.

In summary, the LDS appears to be a relatively useful instrument providing teachers and others working with young children with helpful information.

[616]

Library Skills Test. Grades 7–12 and college freshmen; 1980–81; LST; 1 form ('80, 8 pages); manual ('81, 23 pages); separate answer sheets must be used; 1983 price data: $16 per 20 tests and 1 manual; $10 per 50 answer sheets; $3.50 per school scoring kit; $4 per specimen set; scoring service, $.80 per pupil; 30(40) minutes; Illinois Association of College and Research Libraries; Scholastic Testing Service, Inc.*

Review of Library Skills Test by ROBERT FITZPATRICK, Associate Professor of Industrial Relations, Saint Francis College of Pennsylvania, Pittsburgh, PA:

According to the manual, this test is "designed to locate students' strengths and weaknesses in working with library materials." The 45 items are apportioned among seven parts: (I) Using Library Terminology, (II) Interpreting Catalog Cards, (III) Arranging Call Numbers (using both the Dewey Decimal and the Library of Congress systems), (IV) Recognizing the Parts of a Book, (V) Interpreting an Index (Readers' Guide to Periodical Literature and New York Times Index), (VI) Using Reference Sources, and (VII) Distinguishing Bibliographic Forms. These parts and most of the items seem reasonable. Unfortunately, however, the manual provides no rationale for the choice of content, design of items, and distribution of items among the parts.

The test is legibly and attractively printed. The directions are clear. Examinees are to be told that there is no correction for guessing. However, there is no indication that the time limit should be announced in advance. Users may wish to add a statement about the time limit to the directions.

Norms and descriptive statistics are reported for 500 students in each grade from 7 through 12 and for 1,200 college freshmen. At each grade level, percentile rank and stanine are given for each total score and percent correct is reported for each item. Mean scores increase regularly from grade to grade as do percents correct for the items, perhaps indicating a degree of construct validity.

Internal consistency reliability (KR20 or coefficient alpha) and standard error of measurement are given for each grade level. The reliabilities range from .83 to .90 and the standard errors from 2.5 to 3.0. Internal consistency methods yield inflated estimates of reliability for speeded tests; however, this test is not highly speeded. It is appropriate to conclude that the total test score is reasonably reliable. Item or other part scores, however, are bound to be less so. The use of this test as a diagnostic instrument is questionable.

The manual seems to invite users to attempt diagnosis with the test. For each grade level, there is a page labeled "Instructional Needs Analysis." These pages, according to the manual, "are set up in work sheet form to help other schools compare their 'rights analysis' with those of the national norms group." The manual neglects to warn the user that the item results are less reliable than the overall scores and that the Needs Analysis may suggest remedial instruction when the real need is for more thorough measurement.

Another problem with the Needs Analysis is that some items are likely to be more difficult than others because of differences in item form or construction rather than because of differences in student knowledge of the relevant subject matter. For example, the two most difficult items involve what most of us would think of as a minor technicality in the referencing of a self-published book. These two items constitute the whole of Part VII, Distinguishing Bibliographic Forms. One might conclude that bibliographic forms are undertaught, but it seems more likely that the items are simply testing, in part, a rather obscure point. The problem is compounded when a teacher tries to make comparisons. Suppose that the teacher finds that only 25% of the eighth graders answer item 45 correctly, but checks and finds that the same percentage of the national sample of eighth graders answered it correctly. Since there are four answer options for this item, 25% is the expected outcome if all the examinees were guessing. How, then, should the result be interpreted?

In contrast, Part I, Using Library Terminology, contains 12 items; their difficulties for grade 8 range from 30% correct to 75% correct. Interpretation of difference here would be somewhat easier. Also, of course, the part score is undoubtedly more reliable than that of Part VII, and thus a better basis for interpretations.

On the whole, the Library Skills Test seems adequate for its purpose, if the user is able to carry the burden of understanding and interpreting scores. The test appears to have a reasonable degree of content validity, and there is some evidence of construct validity. Total scores are reasonably reliable. It is to be hoped that further studies and a more informative manual may be forthcoming.

[617]

Life Event Scales for Children and Adolescents. Ages 6–11, 12 and over; 1981; LES-C, LES-A; "quantify the environmental stress the child or adolescent has had to cope with in the recent past"; 4 scores: 3, 6, 9, 12 months; data on interrater reliability only; no data on validity; norms consist of 75th percentile scores only; 1 form (2 pages, includes scoring instructions); 2 levels: children, adolescent; no manual; price data available from publisher; administration time not reported; R. Dean Coddington; Stress Research Co.*

[618]

Life Skills, Forms 1 and 2. Grades 9–12 and adults; 1979–80; 3 scores: reading, mathematics, total; Form 1, 2, ('80, 24 pages); manual ('80, 22 pages); separate answer sheets (MRC, NCS 7010, carbon-backed, self-mark) must be used; 1984 price data: $36.09 per 35 tests; $15.45 per 35 MRC answer sheets; $27.12 per 100 NCS answer sheets; $20.61 per 35 self-mark answer sheets; $2.70 per manual; $2.88 per specimen set; MRC scoring service, $.76 per student (minimum charge $50 per order processed); (80–100) minutes; Kenneth Majer and Dena Wadell; Riverside Publishing Co.*

Review of Life Skills, Form 2, by GWYNETH M. BOODOO, Assistant Professor of Research and Statistics, The University of Texas Health Science Center at Houston, Houston, TX:

Life Skills is designed to assist schools in the measurement of student ability to apply basic reading and mathematical skills to daily problems. It is suitable for students in grades 9 through 12, and those enrolled in adult education programs. The test consists of two subjects, reading and mathematics. The reading test consists of 48 items measuring 14 objectives which are grouped into four areas: Follow Directions, Locate References, Gain Information, and Understand Forms. The Mathematics test consists of 50 items which measure 19 objectives grouped into four areas: Compute Consumer Problems; Apply Principles of Percentages, Interest, and Fractional Parts; Identify, Estimate, and Convert Time, Currency, and Measurements; Interpret Graphs, Charts, and Statistics. There are two forms of the test, Form 1 and 2. This reviewer only reviewed Form 2.

The above items were chosen from initial banks of 160 reading and 192 mathematics items using data from a tryout sample (May, 1978). The standardized editions (Forms 1 and 2) were then administered to a national sample of students (November, 1978) in grades 9 through 12, groups of inmates drawn from penal institutions, and persons enrolled in other adult educational programs. The results of this testing are not given or discussed.

The objectives used are listed in the examiner's manual as well as the number of items per objective. Reading through Form 2 of this test, this reviewer found the items to match objectives and appear to measure worthwhile life skills. Unfortunately, however, no justification is given for the inclusion of the specific life skills in the test. In addition, the development of the items is not disclosed. Thus, the content validity of this test is questionable. One question that should be answered is: How is this test different from other tests which measure basic competencies? "Life Skills" or "Functional Competencies" need to be further defined and placed in perspective with respect to basic skills and competencies expected of the high school graduate. Although the items on this test certainly possess face validity, it is questionable whether this test should stand alone, apart from basic mathematics and reading tests. It may be best used when given in conjunction with some such test as, for example, the California Achievement Test.

A large portion of the examiner's manual (6 of 22 pages) is devoted to the administration of the test, and to the use of three different answer sheets (MRC, self-mark, NCS 7010). The directions are clearly written and easy to follow. The test may be given in one sitting or over 2 days.

The first answer sheet format may be sent to The Riverside Publishing Company for scoring, with total score equal to number right. The answer sheet may also be handscored by referring to the key in the examiner's manual. The Riverside Publishing company provides both basic services (classroom summary, school summary, and district summary) as well as three optional services (school raw score frequency distribution report, student response analysis report, and item analysis summary report). Examples of each of the six services are clearly presented in the examiner's manual and will be useful for individual student, school, or district assessment on any test objective.

Parallel form reliability coefficients were based on a sample of 393 11th- and 12th-grade students in Spring, 1979. Given the number of items on the test, these coefficients were all low: Reading (.77), Mathematics (.79), and total test (.83). Parallel form reliabilities computed for each objective were low (.01 to .36 for Reading and .02 to .50 for Mathematics) and are probably due in part to the restriction of range of scores. Tables showing intercorrelations among the objectives on each subject are also given and are also low (Reading—.17 to .48, Mathematics—.03 to .50). The latter information leads this reviewer to question exactly what is being measured by this test. Is there some underlying unidimensional "life skills" construct present or is the topic more complex? With the lack of information on the test's development, it is not possible to even hypothesize an answer to this question. No validity section is present in the examiner's manual and no validity studies are reported.

In summary, Life Skills, Tests of Functional Competencies in Reading and Math, has face validity, and The Riverside Publishing Company offers some clear and usable services to aid the teacher in diagnosing a student's standing on functional competencies on the objectives measured by the test. Unfortunately, the authors of The Life Skills manual make no attempt to discuss or document evidence to support the validity of this test either by describing its development, defining life skills, or providing evidence of its predictive validity by using criteria which demonstrate use of these life skills. Until this is done, users should treat this test at best as a very crude first attempt to assess students' functional competencies in certain specific life skills.

Review of Life Skills, Forms 1 and 2, by PHILIP L. SMITH, Associate Professor of Educational Psychology, University of Wisconsin-Milwaukee, Milwaukee, WI:

The Life Skills Tests of Functional Competencies in Reading and Math are designed to assist schools in measuring the overall success of their teaching of basic skills, and in their identification of students who are in need of the school's help in developing these competencies. The test contains "items which replicate reading and mathematics problems encountered each day." Examples of such "problems" cited in the test rationale include understanding directions on consumer products, calculating living expenses, completing a job application, and understanding the provisions of an installment agreement. It is clear from the test rationale, and from examination of the test itself, that the Life Skills tests approach the measurement of functional competencies by attempting to replicate, through an objective test item format, tasks in reading and mathematics that a person is likely to encounter in daily life.

The Life Skills tests are designed for use in grades 9 through 12 and in adult education programs. There are two forms of the tests, each of which has a Reading and a Mathematics portion. The suggested administration time for each of the sections is 40 minutes, so that the entire test could reasonably be given in less than an hour and a half. All items are in a multiple choice format (many of which include the option "none of these" to reduce guessing) and are contained in a reusable test booklet.

The Reading section of the Life Skills covers 14 objectives under the major headings of (1) Follow Directions, (2) Locate References, (3) Gain Information, and (4) Understand Forms. The Mathematics section covers 19 objectives under the major headings of (1) Compute Consumer Problems; (2) Apply Principles of Percentages, Interest, and Fractional Parts; (3) Identify, Estimate, and Convert Time, Currency, and Measurements; and (4) Interpret Graphs, Charts, and Statistics. Each objective is covered by from one to four items. The Reading test contains a total of 48 items and the Mathematics test contains 50 items. Items were selected from a total of 352 items that were administered to 4,629 students from 23 school systems. A number of scoring services are offered by the publisher. Basic Services include a classroom summary of each student's performance on each item, a school summary of each classroom's performance on each objective, and a district summary of each school's performance on each objective. Optional services include school level raw score frequency distributions, individual student response analyses, and an item analysis at the classroom, school, and district levels. The administration instructions in the test manual are quite clear, making the Life Skills a test that would be fairly easy to administer by the classroom teacher. However, the manual for the test provides no indication for the user as to how the test results are to be used or interpreted (e.g., mastery, criterion-referenced, norm-referenced) and provides no guidance to the user as to how competence should be defined.

Information on reliability and validity reported in the manual was based upon 393 11th- and 12th-graders and is therefore rather limited. The Form 1 to Form 2 correlations between the Reading and Mathematics tests are reported as .77 and .79, respectively. Alternate form correlations between the Reading and Mathematics sections range from .67 to .74, which is only slightly lower than the alternate form reliabilities. An inspection of the test items reveals an obvious reading dependence for the mathematics items which may at least partially explain the large magnitude of these correlations relative to the score reliabilities. Reliabilities for individual objectives are reported as ranging from .50 to .01. While these low reliabilities are most likely due to the relatively small number of items associated with each objective, they do indicate that information at the objective level does not provide a sufficient basis for making decisions at the individual level. This is acknowledged in the manual. Inter-objective correlations range from −.17 to .48 in Reading and from .03 to .50 in Mathematics. These small correlations are probably due more to the unreliability of the objectives than to a lack of correlation in the underlying competencies assessed, however. The instability due to the reliability problem is further highlighted by the fact that, in some cases, the inter-objective correlations are higher than the reliability of either of the objectives involved. Of course, the relevance one attaches to this correlational information depends upon how the test is to be interpreted. If the test is intended as a mastery or criterion-referenced test, the correlational evidence might be viewed as less significant. However, the test manual provides no information regarding how the tests are to be used; consequently, these data need to be considered by potential test users.

The Life Skills tests are one of a number of the so-called competency tests available whose content focuses on "everyday tasks" and therefore claim to measure "functional literacy." As such, the test is one of the shorter that one may choose from in terms of the number of items represented, the types of skills assessed, and the length of administration time. This characteristic has an advantage but a number of drawbacks as well. The advantage is that the test is relatively easy to administer in a short period of time. The drawbacks include the questionable reliability, and the validity in terms of the types of skills assessed. If the test is intended for use as a district or state level competency exam, these drawbacks take on particular significance and the test should probably not be used for that purpose. Other tests on the market (e.g., Basic Skills Assessment Program, Addison-Wesley; Competency Testing Programs, CTB/McGraw-Hill) provide much more comprehensive treatment of the areas contained in the Life Skills tests, and include a broader array of tasks that can be considered in the domain of "functional competencies." If the test is used, its implications should probably not go beyond the classroom level for individual teacher use in diagnosis and remediation of (or an indication of difficulties in) the reading and mathematics areas covered in the test. But even at this level, the reported reliabilities for the objectives indicate that objective-level information is likely to be highly unstable and of little use for diagnostic or remedial purposes. An additional weakness of the test is that its manual provides no indication of how the test results should be used or interpreted. This is in contrast to a number of such tests that provide both norms (when appropriate) and detailed procedures for determining or deciding upon definitions of what adequate performance means.

In summary, while the Life Skills test provides a relatively short and easy method to assess limited aspects of "functional competency," the technical data available for the tests indicate that its results should not be used in making serious decisions at the individual student level. If decisions regarding competency, remediation, or diagnosis are intended from a measure of functional competency, the potential user is urged to consider the variety of alternatives that are available.

[619]

Life Style Questionnaire. Ages 14 and over; no date on test materials; LSQ; "interests, attitudes and likely behaviours of people at work"; 13 scales: Expressive/Imaginative, Logical/Analytical, Managerial/Enterprising, Precise/Administrative, Active/Concrete, Supportive/Social, Risk Taking/Uncertainty, Perseverance/Determination, Self Evaluation, Sensitivity/Other Awareness, Affiliation, Degree to Which a Vocation is Associated with Self Fulfillment, Degree of Certainty; no data on reliability; 1 form (9 pages); interim manual (26 pages); profile (1 page); percentile profile (1 page); separate answer sheets must be used; 1982 price data: £2.15 per questionnaire booklet; £4.20 per manual; 65p per set of answer sheet and profiles; £7.30 per specimen set; administration time not reported; James S. Barrett; Test Agency [England].*

Review of Life Style Questionnaire by ROBERT B. SLANEY, Associate Professor of Psychology, Southern Illinois University, Carbondale, IL:

This questionnaire was developed to provide information on the interests, attitudes, and likely behaviors of people at work. It is intended for use in vocational guidance, counseling, recruitment, selection, and related areas. It consists of 132 statements about work activities which are divided into 13 scales, 6 of which are concerned with vocational choice while the remaining 7 purport to measure attitudes or potential behaviors. Particular attention is supposed to be given to whether the attitude scale scores are consistent with the scores on the career scales.

Developed in England, the measure occasionally contains a word or phrase that may seem curious to American respondents (e.g., barrister for attorney, or the word tick, meaning mark or check, which appears repeatedly in the instructions). More importantly, the respondent is frequently distracted because the items vary a great deal in their level of specificity, grammatical structure, content, clarity, tense, and freedom from obvious errors. Although the items need revision they generally appear to have face validity. Still, when the manual declares that the face validity is "immense for counselors," this statement seems unduly generous as well as unscientific.

The instructions are straightforward and each of the instrument's statements is responded to by marking one of three small squares to indicate agreement, uncertainty, or disagreement. There is no time limit. Respondents are asked to record the time taken; however, no apparent use is made of this information. Most persons can complete the measure in 20 minutes. Scoring requires counting and simple addition and is also straightforward, although errors in counting seem easy to commit and a less crowded scoring sheet would be preferable.

Two profile sheets are available for displaying the results. One places raw scores (or easily converted scores) on 12-point scales that categorize interests and attitudes as weak, average, or strong. Although these categories may be connected to a table of raw scores collected on "36 male and 26 female students in Further Education with a bias to Fine Arts or Pure Science Courses," this connection is unspecified. The second profile sheet is based on percentiles. For these calculations one chooses either 104 15- to 19-year-olds, or 68 British managers. For both samples sex and origin are unspecified and no other information is provided. Notably, no breakdown is provided by sex for any of the samples and, therefore, no consideration is given to sex differences in relation to normed versus raw scores. The inadequate norm groups and the failure to acknowledge possible sex differences are both serious inadequacies for this measure.

The development of this instrument involved the construction of interest and attitude scales. The interest scales were developed from job descriptions in the Classification of Occupations and Dictionary of Occupational Titles and specifically avoided the use of job titles. No empirical support is cited or provided for this choice. The particular descriptions that were used were chosen to represent each of the career interest scales although the specific manner in which they were chosen is unclear. The six interest scales were apparently intended to be similar to the six Holland Categories. No data, however, are presented to examine these possible relationships.

The attitude statements were generated by three experienced vocational counselors. Their object was to create a "pool of descriptive sentences relating to important concepts." These sentences constitute the first five attitude scales.

It appears that at this point a pilot study was conducted on 50 subjects, sex and origin unspecified. Based on this initial trial, statements were "altered or changed where responses were biased." What constituted bias and who judged its presence or absence is not related. Whatever the process, it apparently represents the sum total of developmental work with one exception. The exception is that at some time, presumably after the "initial trial," the 2 final attitude scales were developed from items that had already appeared on 1 of the first 11 scales. One of these latter scales, scale M, is particularly interesting. Although referred to as the "Opinions Changing/Opinions Stable" scale or again as the "Degree of Certainty Scale," its purpose is actually quite different. The manual states that "a score on this scale is a reflection of the amount of prevarication shown when answering this Questionnaire."

With the above statement in mind, it becomes relevant to examine the data supporting the reliability and validity of the scales. In brief, the manual provides no data whatsoever in support of reliability or validity for this instrument. It states that data on concurrent validity exist but does not provide this data or say where to find it. The complete absence of such essential data is exasperating and strongly suggests that the measure is totally inadequate.

It is even more exasperating that even though the manual is thoroughly inadequate empirically, the author does not hesitate to imply that the measure is based on a considerable amount of clinical experience. Nor does he hesitate to make suggestions for interpretations that are totally devoid of research support. After reading the section entitled "Notes on Interpretation" it may be predictable, perhaps inevitable, that four case studies, along with their profiles, are provided. To illustrate what is probably the most offensive example, case 3 begins "Jean is a spinster in middle age." Perhaps not surprisingly, it is stated later that Jean, having led a sheltered life, has a score on the Unemotional/Sensitive scale that "gives some cause for concern."

Indeed, it can be readily agreed that there is reason for concern about Jean's score but not, however, in the sense intended by the manual. Rather, concern should be directed toward the possibility that Jean or anyone else, client or counselor, would take the results of this measure seriously, given its primitive development, its almost total lack of research, and its absolute lack of reliability and validity studies. Unless this instrument receives the very considerable amount of attention and effort that it requires for adequate development, there is no reason to consider it seriously as a measure of interests or attitudes. Clearly it is grossly inappropriate for its stated purposes. Given its present state, it would be inappropriate to recommend this measure for any use related to measurement.

[620]

Life Styles Inventories. Managers; 1973–82; self-concept and others' perception of the manager; 2 forms; additional instructional materials available; 1983 price data: $15 per Level I inventory plus manual; $35 per set of Level II testing materials including manual, 1 "self" inventory, and 5 "other" inventories; (30) minutes; J. Clayton Lafferty; Human Synergistics.*

a) LEVEL I: LIFE STYLES INVENTORY (SELF DESCRIPTION). 12 scores: humanistic-helpful, affiliative, approval, conventional, dependence, avoidance, oppositional, power, competitive, competence, achievement, self-actualized; self-administered; 1 form ('82, 8 pages); manual ('80, 63 pages).

b) LEVEL II: LIFE STYLES INVENTORY (DESCRIPTION BY OTHERS). 16 scores: same as for Level I plus 4 summary perception scores; administered to manager and 4 or 5 others; 1 form ('81, 6 pages); manual ('81, 50 pages); scoring service, $20.

TEST REFERENCES

1. Cooke, R. A., & Rousseau, D. M. The factor structure of level I: Life Styles Inventory. EDUCATIONAL AND PSYCHOLOGICAL MEASUREMENT, 1983, 43, 449–457.

Review of Life Styles Inventories by HENRY M. CHERRICK, Dean, College of Dentistry, University of Nebraska Medical Center, Lincoln, NE:

The Life Styles Inventories are a multi-level diagnostic system whose purpose, according to the "Interpretation Manual," is "to provide accurate, detailed information about healthy human behavior." The Inventories consist of two "levels": Level I, the Life Styles Inventory (Self Description), is an instrument which proposes to assess one's "self-concept." This instrument is intended to measure thinking styles, consequences of thinking, causes of thinking, and time utilization. The Life Styles Inventory (Self Description) requires the respondent to evaluate and score himself/herself on 240 different personality characteristics. These scores are charted on a percentile rank graph based on the responses of 7,376 subjects in the "general population" who have described themselves on the same 240 personality characteristics. The graph visually demonstrates the individual's personal "style" in comparison with the 7,376 subjects representing the general population. Percentile ranks are obtained for 12 different styles: Humanistic-Helpful, Affiliative, Approval, Conventional, Dependence, Avoidance, Oppositional, Power, Competitive, Competence, Achievement, and Self-Actualized. From the graph, "back-up styles" can be determined which represent secondary thinking patterns.

Level II, the Life Styles Inventory (Description by Others) is an instrument which proposes to provide a composite profile which represents how others perceive the examinee's behavior. Five individuals are selected with personal knowledge of the examinee, and they rate the examinee on the same 240 personality characteristics that appear in the Level I Inventory. The responses are forwarded to an independent scorer whose primary role is to assist in keeping the confidentiality of the process and to compute the average scores over the five raters for the same 12 styles defined earlier. The scores are again plotted on a percentile rank graph which in this case represents how 508 subjects in the general population were rated on the Level II Inventory by 3,299 different raters. Additional "Summary Perceptions," also portrayed graphically, show how one is generally perceived in terms of ability to accept feedback, ability to deal with people and job responsibilities, and potential for growth.

The Life Styles Inventories are educational in nature and represent the practical application of theories developed by the authors. Reported validity data are extremely weak. Documentation supporting the validity of the inventories consists of staff reports and vague references to ongoing studies. Statistical methods are not described. Methods used to establish reliability are also not stated.

Excellent preparatory materials are available and include a set of well illustrated and clearly written instructions. A self-explanatory interpretation manual is supplied for both Level I and Level II. Due to the complexity of the instrument, it may be difficult for individuals with less than a 12th grade education to understand and make effective use of it. The test utilizes an excellent method for maintaining confidentiality of the reported data.

In summary, the Life Styles Inventories represent an extremely thought provoking and interesting system which appears to have great potential and could have widespread applicability. However, although reliability and validity data are supposed to be available in "Staff Reports," the reporting of such data in the interpretive manuals is strikingly inadequate.

Review of Life Styles Inventories by LINDA M. DuBOIS, Assistant Professor of Adult Restorative Dentistry, University of Nebraska Medical Center, Lincoln, NE:

The stated purpose of Life Styles Inventories is "to provide accurate, detailed information about human behavior. Any significant change in behavior or attitude begins with an understanding of current life position." Throughout the Life Styles Manual, however, continuing references are made to effective leadership, management style, problem-solving ability, and occupational status. The apparent purpose of Life Styles Inventories is to provide a tool for improving interpersonal and, in particular, leadership skills. Consistent with this objective, the items primarily address social behaviors. At any rate, the purpose of Life Styles Inventories is not to address life styles in the conventional sense of socioeconomic, cultural, or alternative life styles.

Life Styles Inventories include two instruments titled Level I and Level II. Level I (Self-Description) contains 240 short descriptors on which an individual rates him/herself. The ratings must fall into one of three categories: like the individual most of the time, like the individual quite often, and essentially unlike the individual. Level II (Description by Others) contains the same 240 items; however, on Level II a coworker rates the aforementioned individual. Level II also contains four questions that are labeled Summary Perceptions.

Although most of the items appear straightforward, several items are ambiguous. Examples are: "wants to be trusted, but it's hard"; and "seems to understand others but doesn't." The 240 items are supposed to measure one of the 12 "thinking styles" listed above in the descriptive information preceding the reviews. The scores for each thinking style are calculated by totaling the ratings on 20 appropriate items. These scores are then plotted on a percentile rank scale based on "general population" norms. Only after plotting can the scores on each thinking style be compared with one another. The responses to the four questions under Summary Perceptions in Level II are interpreted individually.

Reliability figures are not specifically cited in the test manual. According to the manual, repeated use of this instrument rarely produces the same results because the instrument often motivates individuals to change themselves. The manual, however, does claim that the inventories have statistically acceptable "internal" reliability and that they contain "consistent factors." There are no actual data to substantiate these claims. The proposed internal reliability may be a result of item order rather than true reliability. The items are ordered such that every five consecutive items represent one thinking style. A less obvious pattern also exists in the representation of the thinking styles. Since item responses can often reflect the preceding response, the internal consistency reliability of this instrument, whatever the figures are, may be exaggerated.

Neither are validity data cited in the test manual, although the manual states that the instrument has been found valid in measuring an individual's self-perception. The question is avoided as to whether the instrument validly measures 12 distinct thinking styles. The thinking styles appear to be based in theory. In support of the instrument, the test manual explains the theory and supporting literature fairly well.

The accuracy of this instrument is susceptible to social desirability response set. Its only reasonable use is for individuals who are not threatened by responding honestly, and the test manual is appropriately directed to individuals who are interested in self-improvement.

In addition to discussion of theory, the manual should be commended for providing strategies for self-improvement. The effectiveness of these strategies is not clear and would depend greatly on the tenacity and commitment of the individual. The patterns of behavior modification suggested are not always sensitive to environmental differences. While many of the suggestions are effective in many circumstances, they are not universally so. Individuals interested in self-assessment would be misled if they relied totally on this instrument.

Considering both the nature and number of the items, this instrument has potential in helping a motivated individual identify shortcomings and improve his/her interpersonal skills and management performance. Because of inadequate reliability and validity and lack of sensitivity to the environment, this instrument is not appropriate for personality assessment, psychological diagnosis, or employment decisions.

[621]

Life Themes Inventory. Ages 14 and over; 1981–82; LTI; 14 primary outcome scales: 10 primary life themes (self-integration, self-sustenance, self-perception, self-gratification, self-mobilization, self-regard, self-discipline, self-discovery, self-idealism, self-purification) plus 4 grouped themes (intrapersonal, interactional, transpersonal, cumulative); 2 versions: diagnostic ('82, 27 pages), screening ('81, 9 pages); handbook ('82, 194 pages including sample test booklets); separate answer sheets must be used; 15 individual data analyses available in the report of results: 7 P-reports (indicators of psychological constructs) and 8 S-reports (indicators of answer/score patterns); 1983 price data: $26.25 per 10 diagnostic test booklets; $17.60 per 10 screening test booklets; $12.60 per 10 diagnostic answer sheets; $8 per 10 screening answer sheets; $28 per handbook; $9 per specimen set of both versions including 15 individual sample reports; scoring service, $77 per complete report package; (180) minutes per diagnostic version, (45) minutes per screening version; Kelly R. Bennett, William H. Seaver, and Gina Caeglio; Life Themes, Inc.*

[622]

Light's Retention Scale, Revised Edition 1981. Grades K–12; 1981; LRS; ratings by teachers and parents; a nonpsychometric instrument used as a counseling tool with a specific retention candidate; individual; 1 form (4 pages); manual (48 pages); parent guide (4 pages); 1982 price data: $6 per 25 recording forms; $6 per 25 parent guides; $7.50 per manual; (15) minutes; H. Wayne Light; Academic Therapy Publications.*

See T3:1328 (1 reference).

Review of Light's Retention Scale, Revised Edition 1981, by MICHAEL J. HANNAFIN, Assistant Professor, Division of Educational Psychological Studies, University of Colorado, Boulder, CO:

According to the author, Light's Retention Scale (LRS) is a nonpsychometric instrument designed to provide "an objective standard that aids the school professional in determining whether the elementary or secondary student would benefit from grade retention." The scale was derived from "a comprehensive review of the literature," much of which is cited or summarized in the scale manual. The scale was designed for use by teachers, counselors, school psychologists, principals, and other school personnel as one of a variety of indicators to be considered in student promotion and retention decisions.

The scale contains 19 categories ranging from "sex of student" to "student attitudes about possible retention." Each category includes a series of statement options to be used by the rater to determine which most accurately characterizes the student under consideration. Numerical weights, ranging from zero to five, are assigned to each statement option. Students are rated for all 19 scale categories, the numerical weights totaled, and the total score compared to score ranges provided in an interpretation table. The table includes six discrete scale ranges, each corresponding to descriptive statements regarding the likelihood of successful retention, ranging from "student should not be retained" to "excellent retention candidate."

Throughout the manual, the author cautions users against misuses of the scale. He makes a strong point to avoid uses as a test or as the sole or primary decision indicator. The author also provides understandable directions for prospective users, as well as issues and research summaries regarding retention factors. In these respects, the manual is clear, useful, and effective. This reviewer's concerns do not pertain to what has been included in the manual, but to what has been omitted.

Although an extensive bibliography and abbreviated reviews are included in the manual, no information directly related to scale development is available. The author's most direct reference to scale development is in the statement: "From the literature review, several areas were identified which clearly relate to the retention decision process, and the 19 categories used in this scale were developed." The scale appears to be the product of the author's analysis of a body of research rather than the product of systematic development and verification. The manual contains no information related to why the specific categories were included over other possible categories. Other details regarding the development of the scale are also excluded from the manual. For example, the author cautions "when any one item is given a score of 5, the chances of the child benefiting from retention are minimal, regardless of the overall score." Such statements require accompanying support, preferably evidential or research-based, in order to be substantiated. Specific information related to the development of the scale and the rationale supporting its uses are seriously lacking.

The manual is also lacking information regarding the validity and reliability of the scale. Specifically, the author has not addressed issues regarding content, construct, and predictive validity. These omissions are potentially serious shortcomings, especially with regard to predictive validity. Since the purposes of the scale are predictive in nature, the validity of the scale in forecasting retention candidacy must be established. The reliability of both category and overall scale ratings is also unreported. Of particular concern is the lack of reported interrater reliability, since the author recommends use across a variety of raters with different academic training and field experiences. If attempts to establish reliability and validity have been advanced, such information needs to be included in the manual; if attempts have not been advanced, the scale rests on questionable foundations and assumptions.

The author's claim that LRS is a "non-psychometric" instrument may be misleading. Numerical and measurement aspects are included both in the scale construction and in the score tabulation procedures. If the author's intent was to caution users against undue reliance on the scale as the primary source of decision-making information, the warning is well advised. It would be unfortunate, however, if the intent was to bypass necessary evaluative scrutiny. LRS was developed to include 19 categories based upon the author's review of research; whether or not these or other factors are significantly related to the construct of interest is not known. Statement options have been assigned differential numerical weights; the rationale affecting the differential assignment of weights has not been included. A total score is summed across the scale categories and compared with discrete score ranges; the rationale for the ranges and the corresponding implications for retention decisions are not provided. It is difficult, given the structure and procedures of the scale, to accept the notion that the scales should not be judged on a psychometric basis. While it may have been the author's intent to construct a scale with no psychometric properties, such properties are readily apparent, and currently unsupported, in the LRS.

Overall, Light's Retention Scale must be considered deficient from basic developmental and validational perspectives. The manual, while providing good procedural information regarding the uses of the scale and background information regarding the promotion-retention controversy, does not address several important concerns pertaining to the test itself. Furthermore, the scale appears to rely more heavily on a psychometric and measurement foundation than suggested by the author, and requires more systematic study to justify the procedures and uses suggested. The scale could become a valuable tool in arriving at retention-promotion decisions if carefully studied, validated, and researched. This promise, however, has yet to be fulfilled.

Review of Light's Retention Scale, Revised Edition 1981, *by PATTI L. HARRISON, Research Associate, Test Division, American Guidance Service, Circle Pines, MN:*

Light's Retention Scale (LRS) is a rating scale designed to assist school personnel and parents with decisions about grade retention. Although the manual for the scale indicates that the LRS "provides an objective standard" which can be helpful in determining whether a student will benefit from retention, the author warns that the instrument should not be used as a test and should never be used as the sole criterion upon which retention decisions are made.

GENERAL DESCRIPTION. The LRS consists of 19 categories related to successful or unsuccessful retention (e.g., gender, physical size, and amount of parent's school participation). Each category contains two to six items scored on a scale of 0 to 5. Lower scale values indicate the characteristic described by the item is related to successful retention. The user of the LRS selects one item in each category which most accurately describes the retention candidate. A total score is obtained by summing the scores of the selected items.

DEVELOPMENT OF THE SCALE. The LRS manual indicates that the 19 categories, items, and scores for items were selected after an extensive review of educational and psychological research investigating retention. A description and justification for each category is supplied in the manual. Although some of the categories are justified intuitively and are probably used informally by many school personnel and parents, the author does not provide strong rationale for the inclusion of each of the categories and, especially, the scores that have been assigned to items. The author presents a confusing array of research purporting to support the scale including summaries of contradictory research findings, statements or research reports which don't appear to support a category, and conclusions the author has drawn without research support.

Two categories of the LRS, in particular, should be viewed with caution. The items in the category "Student's Age" (e.g., "Student's birthday falls in the last half of the calender year (July 1st through December 1st) and is in the younger half of his or her present class") are inconsistent with some school districts' requirements concerning age at school entrance. Students are assigned scores in another category, "Experiential Background," according to their social or cultural background (e.g., experiences such as summer camp or church groups). The author offers little valid support for the inclusion of this questionable and highly controversial category.

DIRECTIONS FOR ADMINISTRATION. The directions for administration are brief and rather vague. Although the manual indicates that the LRS can be administered during parent and school staff conferences, no specific guidelines are given about how or to whom the scale is administered. It is unclear whether a parent or school staff member should complete the record form during parent conferences. If a school staff member administers the scale to a parent, it is not apparent in the manual whether the staff member should read the items aloud or discuss them informally with the parent.

GUIDELINES FOR INTERPRETATION. The manual provides a table containing descriptive categories (e.g., excellent retention candidate, poor retention candidate) for ranges of total scores obtained with the LRS. The author states that the categories were determined subjectively and warns that they should serve only as guidelines when making retention decisions. The user is also instructed to ignore the total score if any item with a score of 5 was selected, because a student with an item score of 5 will have little chance of benefitting from retention. For example, a student who is in seventh to twelfth grade receives a score of 5 on item 5 for the category "Present Grade Placement" and is automatically placed in the category of a student who should not be retained, regardless of the student's scores for items in other categories.

No normative, reliability, or validity data are provided for the LRS. Although the author stresses that the LRS should not be used psychometrically, the scores assigned to the items, the categorization of total raw scores, and especially the stringent interpretation of any items with scores of 5 require the standard psychometric support necessary for all instruments used in decision making. An important omission is the lack of any evidence that retention has been beneficial for students with low total scores and unsuccessful for students with high scores.

SUMMARY. The most positive feature of the LRS is its emphasis on considering a wide array of factors when making decisions about retention. The categories and items of the LRS can form the basis of discussions with school personnel and parents and should be useful when attempting to summarize the characteristics of retention candidates. However, users should be aware that statistical support is necessary for the development and interpretation of all scales, even those described as nonpsychometric counseling tools. Because of the great potential for misuse of this instrument, users should refrain from interpreting the numerical values of items or total scores.

[623]

Lindamood Auditory Conceptualization Test, Revised Edition. Preschool children and over; 1971–79; LACT; 3 scores: isolated sounds in sequence, sounds within a syllable pattern, total; no data on reliability of part scores; no norms for sounds within syllables score; individual; no reading by examinees; Forms A, B, ('79, 2 pages); manual ('79, 80 pages); set of colored blocks; tape cassette of directions for administering; examiner's cue sheet ('79, 2 pages) for both English and Spanish-speaking subjects; 1983 price data: $25 per complete set including 50 each of Form A and B tests, manual, cassette, 24 wooden blocks in 6 colors, and 2 examiner's cue sheets (English and Spanish); $7 per 50 sets of tests; (10–35) minutes; Charles H. Lindamood and Patricia C. Lindamood; DLM Teaching Resources.*

See T3:1332 (2 references); for additional information and reviews by Katherine G. Butler and James A. Till of an earlier edition, see 8:942 (5 references).

TEST REFERENCES

1. Hasbrouck, J. M. Diagnosis of auditory perceptual disorders in previously undiagnosed adults. JOURNAL OF LEARNING DISABILITIES, 1983, 16, 206–208.

Review of Lindamood Auditory Conceptualization Test, Revised Edition, by NICHOLAS G. BOUNTRESS, Associate Professor of Communicative Disorders, Child Study Center, Old Dominion University, Norfolk, VA:

The Lindamood Auditory Conceptualization (LAC) test is designed to evaluate auditory perception and conceptualization of speech sounds. It is an individually administered test which is appropriate for subjects of any chronological or functional age who have an understanding of the concepts of sameness and difference, numbers from one to four, and left-to-right progression, and contains a "Precheck" to determine this understanding. Specifically, the LAC evaluates not only the ability to discriminate one speech sound from another, but also the number and order/sequence of sounds within spoken patterns. Subjects are required to manipulate colored wooden blocks representing individual speech sounds in response to orally presented stimuli. The LAC Test is divided into two major categories: Category I is subcategorized into I-A and I-B and tests isolated sounds in sequence, while Category II tests sounds within a syllable pattern. Category I-A requires that the subject listen to ten 2- or 3-phoneme sequences and indicate what is perceived by placing the colored blocks in corresponding sequences which indicate how many sounds are heard and if they are the same or different. Category I-B replicates the activity of I-A with six phoneme sequences, but also requires the subject's placement of the blocks in the order indicated by the order of the orally presented sounds. Testing in Category I is discontinued with five consecutive subject errors, and resumed with Category II. In Category II, the subject must respond to 12 orally presented syllable patterns by altering a designated "Basic" block pattern through the adding, substituting, omitting, shifting, and repeating of blocks. When an error occurs, the examiner removes the Basic block pattern and begins a new pattern in accordance with designated "Error Alternate" patterns. In response to further errors, the examiner alternates between the Basic and Error Alternate patterns and discontinues testing when the subject makes five total errors. For purposes of interpretation, the authors present recommended minimum scores for subjects in kindergarten through sixth grade and from seventh grade through adult. Educational implications for speech, reading, and spelling processes are presented, as well as illustrative clinical case studies.

The LAC Test was initially administered to a population of 660 students in grades K through 12 of the Monterey Public Schools who represented a wide range of ethnic and socioeconomic groups. Students were randomly selected from populations representing various levels of classroom performance based upon teacher ratings, and were also administered the Reading and Spelling subtests of the Wide Range Achievement Test (WRAT). A second sampling of 52 students was done in the Pismo Beach, California Public Schools, with subsequent samplings of first grade, third grade, and college-level subjects. An examination of scores from the Monterey sample indicates that errors in Category I virtually disappear in subjects above fourth grade; no such information is provided regarding subject performance in Category II. For the LAC total test, scores of subjects above fourth grade tend toward the extremes of the distribution. Despite the heterogeneity of the population samples, no data is provided by the authors regarding the performances of ethnic minorities and subjects from lower socioeconomic levels, although two studies are alluded to in the test manual.

Test-retest reliability was determined with the Pismo Beach population of 52 subjects, while predictive validity was determined on the basis of comparison to WRAT Reading and Spelling combined scores in both Pismo Beach and Monterey populations. The test-retest reliability between alternate forms of the LAC Test was .96. Correlations of the LAC total test with the WRAT scores ranged from .66 to .81, with an average of .73, for grades K through 12 in the Monterey population, and from .72 to .78 in the Pismo Beach sample.

While the LAC Test appears to be of considerable value in predicting spelling and reading performance, there are questions which should be raised regarding its diagnostic value with respect to children's perception and production of phonemic units. Using Locke's (1980a) data regarding the most common phonemic confusions of children, the LAC test's I-A and I-B categories are found to contain only six phonemic contrasts which are regarded as being of diagnostic relevance. The remaining ten items, therefore, present phonemic contrasts which children typically do not confuse. Furthermore, the LAC Test should be evaluated with regard to the criteria provided by Locke (1980b) for efficient assessment of speech perception when treatment for a production disorder is appropriate. Locke-proposed criteria that would have relevance to the LAC Test include such considerations as allowing for the observation of the same phonemes in identical phonetic environments in production and perception, and requiring a response easily within a young child's conceptual capacities and repertoire of responses. Finally, for the purpose of more clearly delineating the relevance of the LAC Test in evaluating children's transcoding processes, studies of predictive validity should focus on comparisons of LAC Test results with speech and language test results.

REVIEWER'S REFERENCES

Locke, J. The inference of speech perception in the phonologically disordered child. Part I: A rationale, some criteria, the conventional tests. JOURNAL OF SPEECH AND HEARING DISORDERS, 1980, 45, 431–444. (a)

Locke, J. The inference of speech perception in the phonologically disordered child. Part II: Some clinically novel procedures, their use, some findings. JOURNAL OF SPEECH AND HEARING DISORDERS, 1980, 45, 445–468. (b)

Review of Lindamood Auditory Conceptualization Test, Revised Edition, by JAMES R. COX, Associate Professor of Audiology, University of South Carolina, Columbia, SC:

The LAC Test utilizes patterns of colored blocks to symbolize sound sequences. Prerequisite skills for successful performance on the test include concepts of same and different, numbers to four, left-right ordering, and first-last. The test includes a precheck to determine the presence of these skills. The test requires very little time to administer, and scoring is quite simple.

Administration of the LAC requires skill in pronunciation of the phonetic alphabet as well as ability to time presentations correctly (approximately two per second). A training tape is included with the test in order to assist in examiner preparation.

The examiner is instructed to sit beside the subject being tested and be sure the subject is able to see the face for visual cues. The reviewer finds this to be an awkward test arrangement.

The LAC is divided into two categories, each testing a different level of conceptualization: Category A, same-different and ordering, and Category B, tracking changes in syllable patterns. This division permits some delineation of specific areas of difficulty. In addition, the authors include an item analysis which can assist in further refining areas of difficulty.

The LAC was standardized on 660 students, K through 12, in Monterey, California. From this sample, recommended grade-level minimum scores were established. The authors state that the minimum grade-level scores are "higher than might appear adequate" for the lower grade levels from the data presented. They suggest that this raising of cutoff scores "is to aid in early identification of students whose auditory-conceptual judgement needs further development." There is no attempt to support this claim through data presented.

Test-retest reliability data of the LAC Test are presented for 52 students, grades K through 12, from Pismo Beach, California. These 52 students were administered Forms A and B of the test, with a minimum interval of four weeks between them. The resulting correlation coefficient was .96. The heterogenous nature of the reliability sample probably has elevated the reported reliability.

Predictive validity is presented utilizing LAC scores, WRAT Reading and Spelling subtests, Cooperative Primary Reading Test, and the Word Identification subtest of the Woodcock Reading Mastery Test. Correlations with WRAT combined scores ranged from .66 to .81, with an average of .73.

The authors present extensive material regarding the educational implications of the LAC Test based largely on clinical experience and including a number of individual case studies.

In summary, the LAC Test—Revised Edition presents a novel approach for evaluating auditory processing of aurally presented stimuli. The test is applicable for children in grades K through adult; however, children below 7 years of age may have difficulty with skills necessary to perform the required tasks. Examiner variability may significantly affect the obtained results since the test requires live-voice presentation of test items. Much of the data presented in the manual is based upon theory, not necessarily supported by controlled research.

The LAC Test would be most useful for classroom teachers. The test has limited utility for speech-language pathologists since the test does not require motor speech responses. Additionally, minimum scores are tied to academic grade level rather than to level of speech and language development.

[624]

Linguistic Awareness in Reading Readiness. Grades K–1; 1983; LARR; no norms; suggested standards for mastery provided; 3 parts; administrative manual (36 pages); class evaluation record (1 page) for each part; 1985 price data: £6.95 per manual; £9.95 per specimen set; (20–25) minutes for each part of test; John Downing, Douglas Ayers, and Brian Schaefer; NFER-Nelson Publishing Co. [England].*

a) PART I—RECOGNIZING LITERACY BEHAVIOUR. Forms A, B, (11 pages); £4.45 per 10 test booklets and 1 class record form.

b) PART 2—UNDERSTANDING LITERACY FUNCTIONS. Forms A, B, (8 pages); £3.95 per 10 test booklets and 1 class record form.

c) PART 3—TECHNICAL LANGUAGE OF LITERACY. Forms A, B, (7 pages); £3.95 per 10 test booklets and 1 class record form.

[625]

Listening Comprehension. Grades 1–3; 1976; 7 scores: following directions, sequencing, using content in listening, finding new ideas, forming sensory images from oral description, sensing emotion and moods through word usage and manner of delivery, making inferences and drawing conclusions; no data on reliability and validity; no norms; 1 form (15 pages, including 11 informal inventory spirit duplicating masters, teacher's key, and manual); games and activities (43 pages); 1982 price data: $5.90 per 11 spirit duplicating masters including manual and teacher's key; $5.40 per games and activities; no administration time reported; Susan Hohl and B. Cheney Edwards; Educators Publishing Service, Inc.*

Review of Listening Comprehension by WILLIAM A. MEHRENS, Professor of Educational Measurement, Michigan State University, East Lansing, MI:

Listening Comprehension is not a test; it is a set of seven informal inventories and a set of games and activities. The phrase "Informal Inventories" is displayed very prominently on the cover of the one booklet and in the Table of Contents. In the introduction the authors stress that the "inventories are only suggested guides. It is the responsibility of the teacher to adjust them to meet the needs of the children."

The Following Directions inventory is composed of 17 directions. Some of these 17 are very simple (e.g., touch your nose), and others get quite complicated and involve completing several different tasks. Teachers determine how much time to allow for the task(s) and determine their own scoring criteria and procedure.

The Sequencing inventory is composed of three parts: (*a*) numbering pictures according to the sequence in which they were heard (five questions); (*b*) numbering objects according to their order in a read sentence (five questions); and (*c*) sequencing events in time after listening to a short paragraph (three questions for each of three paragraphs).

The Using Context in Listening inventory consists of nine sentences with words missing. The child is to mark the picture of the missing word on an answer sheet.

The Finding Main Ideas inventory consists of eight short paragraphs each followed by one 3-option multiple choice question on the main idea.

Forming Sensory Images from Oral Description consists of having children draw a picture of what they have heard. This is done for each of three poems. Scoring is subjective and no time limit is suggested.

Sensing Emotion and Moods through Word Usage and Manner of Delivery consists of reading eight questions. The examiner reads each statement twice, once reflecting the mood described (e.g., How would an angry person say this?). The child is to choose the correct reading. A teacher's ability to read well is crucial for this inventory.

Making Inferences and Drawing Conclusions consists of ten questions requiring the students to make inferences after listening to a statement or paragraph.

There are no data on norms, reliability, validity, or the amount of time the seven inventories will take. The directions are not standardized, the scoring is subjective in places, and there are no suggestions on which of the three grades (1 through 3) may be most appropriate for which of the inventories. In places the questions are poorly worded. Some questions have no best answer (e.g., it was so cold outside I put on my [shoes, coat, shirt]). Certainly for the above question the answer might well be shoes or shirt for a warm climate during the summertime. At times the questions probably incorrectly assume students will know how to do what is asked if they listen (e.g., make a rectangle, write the number that comes after sixty-two). In places there are contradictions in the paragraphs being read (e.g., He is all grey with one white spot).

The Games and Activities booklet consists of "games and activities designed to teach or remediate listening comprehension." No evidence is presented that they do so.

In summary, this is not a test, the authors do not make such a claim, nor do they follow the *Standards for Educational and Psychological Tests*. I do not know why it is reviewed in this *Yearbook*. When some critic of standardized tests counts up the number of published tests that get poor reviews in this *Yearbook*, Listening Comprehension should not be counted. If one wants to measure listening comprehension, I would suggest something like the appropriate subtest of the Stanford Achievement Test.

[626]

Listening Comprehension Group Tests. Adult education students of English as a second language; 1981; LCGT; 2 tests; student picture booklet (31 pages); examiner's test manual (35 pages); technical guide (24 pages); separate answer sheets must be used; 1984 price data: $2.95 per student picture booklet; $5.95 per technical guide; $4.50 per examiner's test manual; Donna Ilyin and Susan Rubin (technical guide); Newbury House Publishers, Inc.*

a) LISTENING COMPREHENSION PICTURE TEST. Beginning and intermediate adult education students of English as a second language; LCPT; does not require reading or writing skills; $5.95 per 50 answer sheets including 2 keys; (20–40) minutes.

b) LISTENING COMPREHENSION WRITTEN TEST. Intermediate and advanced students of English as a second language; LCWT; $5.95 per 50 answer sheets; (40–50) minutes.

Review of Listening Comprehension Group Tests by ROGER A. RICHARDS, Professor of Communication and Chairman of the Department, Bunker Hill Community College, Boston, MA:

The two very different short tests which form the Listening Comprehension Group Tests (LCGT) are designed to measure English language skills of non-native speakers. The Picture Test requires "beginning and intermediate adult education students" of English as a Second Language (ESL) to select from five pictorial or one-word options the one which correctly answers a question read aloud by the examiner. The Written Test asks "intermediate and advanced" ESL students to write one-sentence answers to oral questions.

As described by the authors, the tests present a Catch-22 situation to prospective users. We are told that a student at the elementary level should take only the Picture Test, an intermediate student may take either or both tests, and an advanced student may take only the Written Test. But the first of the four suggested uses for both tests is "Placement of Students." All of this suggests that in order to use these tests to find out a student's skill level, we must first know the student's skill level!

Given that we must already have separated our students into elementary, intermediate, and advanced levels in order to administer the proper tests and that the suggested cutoff scores create four undefined levels (300, 400, 500, and 600, which we are told are "described in the San Francisco Community College Instructional Guide"), the only placement function that the LCGT might serve is to re-partition an already known three-level population into four mystery levels.

The situation is no brighter regarding other purported uses. We are told that both tests can be used for "Diagnosis of Student Needs." Yet no diagnostic procedures or tools are suggested for the Picture Test, not even a classification of items by skill or content. A "Sample Diagnostic Checklist Worksheet" is supplied for the Written Test, but it provides only 13 categories, most of which are too broad to be meaningful—for example, "Article," "Preposition," "Adverb," "Adjective," "Vocabulary," "Punctuation," and "Spelling."

The recommended use of the tests as a "Measurement of Achievement" is even less promising. Although the authors claim that "the LCGT has two forms (BILL and TOM) to use as pre- and posttests," the only differences between the forms are a re-sequencing of the questions within each set and the name change. We are thus offered two essentially identical tests for pre- and posttesting!

A further flaw in the overall design of the LCGT is the lack of standardization. In the Picture Test, the problem is that "teachers, aides, and other school personnel who speak English fluently" administer the test by reading from the provided script. The variations thus introduced can be considerable. Given the range of suggested administrators and the audience at which the test is aimed, we expect some advice on such details as timing of questions and proper enunciation, inflection, and volume. All we find is advice to read "in a normal conversational tone" and to "allow students enough time to think and mark answers." What is "enough time to think"? Why taping was not used to ensure uniformity of presentation is unexplained.

The Written Test suffers from lack of standardization, particularly in relation to the need for scorers to use judgment in awarding 2, 1, or 0 points for each of the 30 answers. Even though scoring criteria are fairly clear, individual scorers are likely to disagree to some extent. The manual is not very reassuring, offering only the vague report that "even in the small groups [sizes not specified], reliabilities were high ranging from .77–.89."

Among the crudest elements of the LCGT are the questions on the Picture Test. These are in the form of five-option multiple-choice items. Only at the lowest possible level of language comprehension, however, could more than three of the options be operable for any question—and sometimes only one answer is viable. The reason is that the five responses are of the apples-and-oranges variety. Choice (A) is always the word "YES" and (B) is always "NO." But (C), (D), and (E) are drawings—(E) being a drawing of one or two clocks in three of the six sets.

Let us consider what this means for a typical problem set: Question 5 asks, "Where does he get the bus?" The choices are (A) YES, (B) NO, (C) a drawing of a bus, (D) a drawing of a curb and "BUS STOP" sign, and (E) a clock showing the time as 8:00. One does not need to know very much English to eliminate "YES" and "NO," to know that one doesn't wait for a bus ON the bus, or to realize the 8:00 does not tell WHERE. The answer is thus a giveaway. The same is true of Question 6: "When does he get the bus?" On a test to find out whether or not people understand ANY English, such questions might be valid, but on one purporting to separate elementary from intermediate ESL students, the questions appear much too easy—as well as incompatible with prevailing standards for writing acceptable multiple-choice questions.

But perhaps this reviewer is too skeptical, for the Technical Manual reports a wide range of scores. In one group of 98 students at level 400 (levels run from 100 to 700), a range of 3 to 25 is reported for a shortened, 25-question version of the LCGT. It seems that only an intermediate student with severe hearing impairment could conceivably answer as few as three questions correctly.

The Picture Test's use of orally presented questions and pictorial answers to assess listening comprehension without contamination by reading or writing is a significant contribution to the testing of listening. But basic deficiencies in test design and construction preclude the use of the Listening Comprehension Group Tests in their present form. It is reassuring to note the statement in the Technical Manual that "the LCPT...is still in an experimental form." We must hope that the later forms will correct the errors that render the present version unacceptable.

[627]

The Listening For Meaning Test. Ages 3–0 to 18–11; 1981–82; LFMT; "understanding of spoken English through the recognition of pictures"; individual; 1 form; testing book ('81, 127 pages); record sheet (no date, 2 pages); administrative manual ('82, 12 pages); 1983 price data: £10.50 per complete set including testing book, administrative manual, and 50 record sheets; £7.10 per testing book; £2.40 per 50 record sheets; £1 per administrative manual; administration time not reported; M. A. Brimer; Educational Evaluation Enterprises [England].*

[628]

Living in the Reader's World: Locator Test. Adults at reading grade levels 2.0–6.0; 1983; to diagnose non-proficient reader's appropriate starting point in a 4-book adult education reading program; upward extension of the BCD Test; no data on reliability and validity; no norms, guidelines for interpretation; no manual, general directions part of test ('83, 62 pages); 1984 price data: $2.15 per test, including answer sheet; administration time not reported; Cambridge, The Adult Education Co.*

[629]

The Lollipop Test: A Diagnostic Screening Test of School Readiness. First grade entrants; 1981; criterion-referenced; 4 scores: identification of colors and shapes and copying shapes, picture description and position and spatial recognition, identification of number and counting, identification of letters and writing; no norms, publisher recommends use of local norms; individual; manual ('81, 14 pages); stimulus card booklet ('81, 7 cards); student test booklet ('81, 8 pages); 1983 price data: $.65 per student test booklet; $19.95 per specimen set of 5 student test booklets, 1 manual, and 1 set of stimulus cards; $14.95 per manual; (15) minutes; Alex L. Chew; Humanics Limited.*

Review of The Lollipop Test by ISABEL L. BECK, Professor of Education, Unit Co-Director, Reading and Comprehension Unit Learning Research and Development Center, University of Pittsburgh, Pittsburgh, PA:

The Lollipop Test has a .86 correlation with the Metropolitan Readiness Test (MRT). This is important because the stated purpose for the development of the Lollipop Test was to determine if a diagnostic screening test of school readiness could have concurrent validity with a widely used test of proven predictive validity, e.g., the MRT. Given that the Lollipop Test has high concurrent validity with the MRT, the author suggests that the Lollipop Test can be substituted for the MRT or used to provide supplemental information. This review, then, will focus on what advantages might be obtained by substituting the Lollipop Test for the MRT or any other such major readiness instrument and what additional information would be available if the Lollipop Test were used in addition to the MRT.

The Lollipop Test is an individual test that takes approximately 15 to 20 minutes to administer. The MRT is a group instrument that takes 105 minutes to administer. In terms of a typical teacher's classroom time, there would appear to be no advantage. For example, it would take about 150 minutes to administer the Lollipop Test to 10 children. Of course, if the groups were larger there would be even more savings in administrator time with the MRT. In terms of scoring, if the MRT is hand-scored it would probably take more time than the scoring for the Lollipop Test; however, the MRT does provide an option for machine scoring. Let me simply say there are no great advantages to be obtained in terms of saving teacher time by administering the Lollipop Test. On the other hand, if one is concerned with saving students' time, there is an advantage for the Lollipop Test. If this were the only advantage, it would certainly not weight any decision to use the Lollipop Test over the MRT given the history of careful design of the MRT. That is, the MRT manual provides for richer information than the Lollipop Manual regarding interpreting the tests, discussing content, construct and predictive validity, as well as reliability data. Given the time issue there seems to be nothing to recommend substituting the Lollipop Test for the MRT when one's purpose is predictive validity. However, if one needs to test several children instead of a classroom of children, or if a particular child could not function in a group testing situation, the Lollipop Test is a possible alternative.

Let's move now to a discussion of what advantages might be available if the Lollipop Test were used "as part of a readiness assessment battery" as suggested by the author. Since predictive validity can be established by the MRT, we look now to see how the Lollipop Test "assists the school in planning their overall instructional objectives, and to individualize instruction." By this statement, the author is presumably supporting his claim that the test is criterion-referenced. This test is no more criterion-referenced than the MRT. Consider the following. The Lollipop Test has four subtests, each of the first three subtests has a possible score of 17 points, and the last subtest has a possible score of 18 points, yielding a total of 69 points. The author notes that "the child's total score on this test is not as significant as the identification and remediation of his deficit areas." How does one determine the "deficit areas?" Presumably by the subtests. Let's consider just the first subtest titled "Identification of Colors and Shapes and Copying Shapes" and examine whether, as arranged, the test helps us with the identification of a student's deficit areas. The mean score for the first subtest of the sample population was 14.51. What do we know about the remediation we need to undertake for a child from the population who had a score of, say, 10?

An item analysis of the first subtest reveals that 6 of the 17 points come from color identification, e.g., "Show me a green lollipop," 5 points from shape identification, e.g., "Show me the rectangle," and 6 points from copying shapes. All the above is by way of pointing out that the teacher would have to do an item analysis to determine for a child with a score of 10 where his/her deficits were. Hence, the Lollipop Test is no more criterion-referenced than the MRT, i.e., a teacher could also do an item analysis for it.

A factor analysis of the Lollipop Test does not help. For instance, contrast the first and second factors. The first factor, labeled Visual-Perceptual Abilities, "seems to measure a child's ability to recognize symbols, including letters, numbers, and shapes." The second factor, labeled numeral ability, "appears to measure a child's ability to count and, to a lesser extent, to recognize and identify numbers and shapes." Although the items load on four different factors, the distinction among the factors and their relative contributions toward school readiness is less than clear.

In summary, then, there is nothing to recommend the Lollipop Test in terms of specifying distinct deficit areas any more than the MRT or other such instruments. It can be recommended as a test of predictive validity, if one wants a short, easily administered, individualized instrument. For typical classroom situations one might better use the MRT or Murphy Durrell.

Review of The Lollipop Test by JANET A. NORRIS, Instructor, Speech Pathology and Audiology, University of Nebraska-Lincoln, Lincoln, NE:

The Lollipop Test appears to have been developed primarily as a research project to determine if a short screening instrument could be developed which would have concurrent validity with the Metropolitan Readiness Test (MRT). The greater goal of developing a well constructed, comprehensive screening test which would be valuable in assessing children for readiness seems to receive secondary, or almost incidental attention.

The author provides an overview of several definitions of readiness and philosophies of developing readiness, but never really identifies those on which this test is based. He also does not establish the relationship of much of the literature cited in the manual to the construction or theoretical basis of this test. The closest statement offered as a rationale for item selection reads, "The types of tasks finally included in the design of the Lollipop Test...are also included on most of the readiness tests examined by this author." This is bothersome for two reasons. First, it assumes that just because other tests have selected certain types of items as appropriate for readiness assessment, they therefore are appropriate items. Second, if the items on the test are included on most other readiness tests, it appears futile and redundant to create another test.

A reasonable justification for another readiness test could lie in excellent test construction, but this was not evident from the test manual. There is no indication that any item analysis was performed which would provide indications of difficulty, appropriateness, or discriminating power of the items. The justifications for item design and development were (*a*) use of stimulus items which are familiar to children regardless of socioeconomic background and (*b*) provision of a format which is interesting to children. However, again the validity of these claims is based only on the subjective opinion of the author.

The validation of the test involved computing correlations between the Metropolitan Readiness Test (MRT), the Lollipop Test, and a "research designed" teacher rating scale for readiness skills. No information was provided on the construction, reliability, or validity of the teacher rating scale, for which only moderate correlations ($r = .58$) with the Lollipop Test were obtained. The total correlation between the Lollipop and MRT was $r = .86$. The author stated that this high correlation may have occurred because both tests are oriented strongly to visual-perceptual abilities. Significantly, among the lowest correlations were those between the subtests of the Lollipop Tests and the MRT Word Meaning and Listening subtests, which are the more verbally oriented subtests of the MRT. Thus while the Lollipop correlates highly with the MRT, it appears to be assessing some different skills, thereby making the authors suggestion that it may be substituted for the MRT highly questionable.

A factor analysis of items provided construct validity evidence for the subtest categories. Whether these constitute the most significant readiness skills is another issue. Reliability in terms of internal consistency was high. Test-retest reliability was not established.

The sample used for validation of the test consisted of a small, homogeneous group of 69 children. Any concurrent validity claims are based on this sample alone. The author suggests score ranges for interpretation of the results of the Lollipop Test based on this sample, but also encourages the development of local norms. He suggests in the administration and scoring manual that "children who score below 50, or demonstrate a marked deficit on any subtest(s), should be referred for further psycho-educational assessment." This minimum performance level, however, appears to be arrived at subjectively. He further suggests that the test should be viewed as a criterion-referenced instrument, and that results can be used to identify children who need additional readiness before first grade and to assist in planning overall instructional objectives and to individualize instruction. These purposes seem to extend beyond the capabilities of the test. At best, it is a screening device which looks at a very narrow range of skills related to readiness. It correlates well with the MRT and thus may provide some predictive ability, but it falls short of providing a well-rounded assessment device which can be used in curriculum development, and cannot function as a substitute for tests which look at a broader range of skills. The skills assessed on the Lollipop Test merely correlate with success in school; an inherent danger exists in viewing instruction in the areas of the few skills tested as contributing significantly to preventing or remediating reading deficits. Both test performance and school performance could be manifestations of some other skills which underlie both; additionally, other types of items not assessed by the Lollipop Test also contribute significantly to success in school, such as verbal skills, for which correlations between MRT and the Lollipop Test were low.

The above considerations are particularly noteworthy when it is observed that no recommendations are provided in terms of who can administer or interpret test results, other than a statement indicating that the test requires only a brief orientation period for the novice examiner. Instructions are clear and scoring is straightforward. Items involve both listening (decoding) and spoken (encoding) identification. The stimulus items are printed on heavy card stock utilizing bright colors and clear pictures and print. The binding is too tight so that pages don't turn well, and the space allotted for the child to copy or draw figures handicaps a lefthanded subject; the example figure may be covered by the child's hand while drawing, thus adding a visual memory factor to the task.

In summary, the Lollipop Test does not contribute any advantages over similar tests already available. Its poor test construction, lack of norms, narrow scope, and limited reliability and validity render it no more useful than a similar teacher constructed criterion-referenced test. The advantage of having packaged stimulus cards and response forms would seem to be offset by the relatively high expense of the response booklets. Finally, the stated purposes of this test in identifying and planning overall instructional objectives and individualized instruction for children should be viewed cautiously, given the limited number and type of items assessed.

[630]

London House Employee Attitude Inventory. Business and industrial employees; 1982; EAI; 7 survey scales: Theft Admissions, Theft Attitudes, Theft Knowledge and Suspicion, Drugs, Job Burnout, Job Dissatisfaction, Validity; 1 form (13 pages); test administration and analysis instruction manual (no date, 32 pages); 1982 price data: $18 per test; administration time not reported; London House Management Consultants, Inc.*

TEST REFERENCES

1. Jones, J. W., & Terris, W. The Employee Attitude Inventory: A validity study of theft by current employees. Paper presented at the 8th Annual Meeting of the Society of Police and Criminal Psychology, Nashville, October 1982.

Review of London House Employee Attitude Inventory by NEAL SCHMITT, Professor of Psychology and Management, Michigan State University, E. Lansing, MI:

According to the test manual, the Employee Attitude Inventory (EAI) "was constructed to predict theft and other forms of counterproductivity among current employees." Its purposes include (1) investigation of a specific theft or counterproductive behavior; (2) deterrence of theft; and (3) monitoring multiple business units. Apparently, its major use has been to identify potential problem employees or groups of employees who are then further interviewed as a means of detecting theft or dishonest behavior. Responses to 179 items provide seven scale scores. Eight items are open-ended; most of the remainder require responses on Likert-type scales. In addition, employees are asked to fill in a variety of personal history and company information and to sign a survey agreement.

A relatively small number of reliability and validity studies have been reported. Odd-even split half reliabilities corrected with the Spearman-Brown formula range from .65 to .88 in two studies including approximately 500 respondents. Interscale correlations ranged from .36 to .67 (absolute values).

Several validity studies are reported in a variety of organizations and for employees in a variety of occupations. All of the studies report statistically significant relationships; moreover, correlations in the .40s and .50s appear frequently. However, all studies are concurrent and the criteria include anonymous self reports, results of polygraph examinations, and/or supervisors' reports of dishonest behavior or their suspicions of such. Polygraph examinations are dependent on employee admissions of theft or dishonest behavior just as are scores on the EAI. Shortcomings of the polygraph examination are noted in the EAI manual, yet at least three of the validation studies used polygraph admissions as criteria against which to evaluate the EAI. Anonymous self reports are so nearly equivalent to Theft Admissions, Theft Attitudes, and Theft Knowledge/Suspicion subscales of the EAI, it is not surprising that high validity coefficients are observed. Supervisory rating criteria may also produce inflated validities since employees who have been discovered by their supervisors would have no motivation to conceal such action. Truly predictive studies of theft behavior are needed. They are of course difficult to conduct.

The manual contains a statement that norms are available for 5,000 to 6,000 current employees, but data are reported for only 2,895 of these persons. Perhaps more important, no description of this normative sample is presented; it is called a "General" sample.

One study relating the EAI to the Personnel Selection Inventory (PSI), another inventory of employee honesty or attitudes toward honesty, is presented. A canonical R of .82 is reported for a sample of 63 bus drivers, but there is no cross-validation. However, because of similarity in content, the EAI is likely correlated highly with the PSI, for which a larger set of validity evidence is available (Sackett & Harris, 1984).

Aside from the relatively weak evidence of validity currently available, any user should be aware of another potential problem. Issues concerning when it is appropriate to require employees to take polygraph examinations are certain to be raised when this instrument is used. While confidentiality is assured, the person's name along with various biographical and company information is requested. Further, the employee is asked to sign a survey agreement that he(she) understands and agrees that deliberate attempts to deceive or distort answers will be reported to the company. Even if the need for security overrides legal and ethical concerns associated with the use of this instrument, this coercive procedure has the potential to generate negative motivational and attitudinal reactions on the part of employees. Recently, Ryan and Sackett (1984) have found minimal negative reactions to such testing among a group of 184 college students. Finally, the potential for misuse of EAI scores would seem substantial. All the EAI validity studies report that some respondents whose EAI scores were high did not report theft/dishonest behavior nor was there other evidence of such (not surprising in any measure which is not perfectly valid). Employees are asked to include their names on the surveys and the directions to the respondents indicate scores will be available to high level company personnel. The reputation of honest employees may thereby be questioned.

In sum, there is some limited evidence of the validity of the EAI in the detection of personnel problems involving dishonest behavior. More rigorous predictive studies should be conducted and care should be taken to prevent potential misuse.

REVIEWER'S REFERENCES

Ryan, A. M., & Sackett, P. R. PRE-EMPLOYMENT HONESTY TESTING, FAKABILITY, TESTEE REACTIONS, AND COMPANY IMAGE. Paper presented at The American Psychological Association Convention, 1984.

Sackett, P. R., & Harris, M. M. Honesty testing for personnel selection: A review and critique. PERSONNEL PSYCHOLOGY, 1984, 37, 221–245.

Review of London House Employee Attitude Inventory by GEORGE C. THORNTON III, Professor of Psychology, Colorado State University, Fort Collins, CO:

The London House Employee Attitude Inventory (EAI) is designed to predict theft and other forms of counterproductivity among current employees. The wording and content make it appropriate for investigation of current employees, not job applicants. It should be used as a preliminary screening device in conjunction with other procedures and interpreted in the context of employees' total job performance.

The EAI contains 171 objective items, 8 write-in questions, and sections on personal history and company information. Responses to the objective questions are given on adjectively anchored, Likert-type rating scales in terms of frequency of occurrence, agreement, typical use, or actions recommended to the organization in the case of various employee offenses. The items cover employee activities, preferences, habits, behaviors, and thoughts. Most questions clearly refer to behavior at work, but some extend beyond the job. I found several items objectionable: they are quite personal in nature, referring to personal finances, problems with spouse or family, and loss of sleep. In addition, I found repugnant the numerous questions which ask the respondent to report his/her thoughts, ideas, and feelings about various topics. Consider this question: "Have you occasionally had ideas that you would not want your supervisor to know about?" Even the most honest person is put in a moral bind. We've probably all had such thoughts, but to admit it implies we have been thinking about some misbehavior and thus are likely to actually engage in that behavior.

Many of the questions have a "Big Brother" tone about them. They ask the respondent to report illegal acts, social pressures, and suspicions about coworkers. I understand the seriousness of company theft, the theory behind questions of this nature, and the need to curtail offenders, but I dislike the effect these particular questions will have on innocent employees.

There has been a variety of research conducted on the survey scales and their predecessors (Terris &

Jones, 1982). The EAI is one of a long line of inventories developed over the years by London House to predict theft and drug use among applicants, and to measure job burnout and job dissatisfaction. The theft scales are composed of items which were found to correlate with theft admissions (e.g., cash or merchandise) in response to specific-issue polygraph examinations. The allocation to the three different theft scales was done rationally. A limitation of this postdictive design is that questionnaire and polygraph responses were probably not independent, thus making the reported, non-crossvalidated correlations in the range of .16 to .44 somewhat questionable.

The drug use and burnout scales are modifications of earlier instruments validated against self reports of drug use, theft, stress reactions, and counter-productivity (e.g., arguments and mistakes). Much of the research was done anonymously, making generalizability to operational use questionable. No information was available on the job dissatisfaction or validity scales. It would be particularly helpful to know about the latter scale, because it is quite obvious current employees, particularly dishonest ones, would not be inclined to answer in a self-incriminating way. An area of much needed research is the transparency or fakability of the scales and the accuracy with which the validity scale detects lying.

This brings me to my major criticism—the manual is grossly inadequate in reporting information about the rationale and theory behind scale development, reliability and validity evidence, and other psychometric considerations. Much of that information does exist in a series of technical reports available from London House, but even these do not provide clear descriptions of the lineage of EAI scales so that a potential user can adequately judge the adequacy of the instrument.

There are many positive features of the EAI which deserve emphasis. Theft research is difficult due to the low incidence of criterion behavior and the natural reluctance of organizations to make visible any problems they have in this area. The developers have gone as far as anyone in studying the problem. Research has been conducted in several jobs and industries, including sales clerks, nurses, and Salvation Army collectors. Initial information suggests the EAI demonstrates no adverse impact against protected groups. London House maintains strict security over the materials and will sell the test only to trained examiners. It also provides convenient telephone service for on-line scoring and test interpretation. Follow-up reports are presented in a clear and easy-to-interpret format.

In summary, the EAI is one of the more recent additions to London House's long string of measurement devices for theft and counterproductivity. It covers a broader range of variables than other similar questionnaires (e.g., the Reid Report), although I am not aware of any evidence of their relative validity. The manual is quite disappointing. Through personal communication and study of technical reports one can learn about the tight security on the the instrument and the variety of research carried out, but the manual gives little information upon which a potential user can make an informed judgment. On the basis of coverage, administrative convenience, the encouraging indications from prior research on EAI predecessors, and tight security, I would endorse use of the instrument in conjunction with other procedures for theft investigation.

REVIEWER'S REFERENCES

Jones, J. W., & Terris, W. THE EMPLOYEE ATTITUDE INVENTORY: A VALIDITY STUDY ON THEFT BY CURRENT EMPLOYEES. Paper presented at the 8th Annual Meeting of the Society of Police and Criminal Psychology, Nashville, October 1982.

Terris, W., & Jones, J. Psychological factors related to employee theft in the convenience store industry. PSYCHOLOGICAL REPORTS, 1982, 51, 1219–1238.

[631]

London House Personnel Selection Inventory. Job applicants; 1975–80; PSI; 9 scores: 3 scores (percentile score, risk category, low risk confidence) for each of 3 areas (dishonesty, violence, drug abuse); 1 form ('80, 16 pages); manual (no date, 11 pages); 1983 price data: tests rented only; rental and scoring service, $14 and less per test; administration time not reported; London House Management Consultants, Inc.*

See T3:1339 (2 references).

Review of London House Personnel Selection Inventory by WILLIAM I. SAUSER, JR., Associate Professor and Head, Department of Management, Auburn University at Montgomery, Montgomery, AL:

According to its manual, the London House Personnel Selection Inventory (PSI) is intended to evaluate "attitudes, opinions, and experiences of...job applicants in three critical areas: Dishonesty, Violence, and Drug abuse." The PSI is administered to job applicants, either individually or in groups, on the premises of the employing company. Test booklets are then mailed to London House for coding and scoring, and a standardized Test Analysis Report is mailed back to the company. For faster turnaround, the PSI may be coded in the employment office; these codes are then transmitted by telephone to London House, the data are key-entered and analyzed, and the nine scores are provided while the caller is still on the line. Follow-up written reports are mailed to the employing company when the test booklets are returned to London House. To maintain test security, all test booklets, even those damaged or partially used, must be returned to London House. Directions for administering and coding the PSI are very clear; no special training is required to use it.

The test booklet itself is 16 pages long and contains, in addition to the test questions, instructions to the test-taker, a compliance notice regarding equal employment opportunity, a consent form, a short survey about the employing company, and a lengthy, detailed survey of the applicant's personal and employment history. The PSI items take a variety of forms, including rating scales, checklists, and open-ended questions. Only the rating scale items are coded and scored; thus the reason for including many of the questions is unclear to this reviewer. The items themselves are straightforward, but the response options do not always seem to fit the question stems. The PSI is not a timed test and no estimates of administration time are provided in the manual. However, given the length and detail of the survey, it appears that many respondents would require an hour or more to complete the PSI.

Interpreting the nine scores is a straightforward matter. The percentile scores simply rank the applicant in relation to the normative sample. The risk category scores rate the applicant as either low, borderline, or high risk based on past behavior, and the low risk confidence scores predict the probability that the applicant will avoid future problems in each area. The manual provides no information regarding the precision of these predictions.

Although no scoring keys or technical data are reported in the test manual, it does include abstracts of 21 cited studies of the PSI's reliability, validity, and fairness. A comparison of these abstracts with the full-length reports of each study (provided to this reviewer) reveal that the abstracts are accurate and are based on statistically significant research findings. The PSI appears to be a reliable and fair instrument; moreover, validity studies with a variety of designs, samples, and criteria have established that the PSI provides meaningful scores in all three areas.

A shortcoming of the PSI manual is that it does not warn the user of possible misuses of the test. The PSI elicits very sensitive information, and test administrators and coders should be told to keep all responses strictly confidential. The manual should also warn users not to make copies of test responses to place in application files, nor to base any decisions on individual item responses, since these have not been validated. The manual includes letters from an attorney attesting to the legality of using the PSI for selection purposes, but users should not be misled regarding the need to establish, through their own local studies, that the scores obtained by the PSI are job related, and/or that the PSI has no adverse impact on employment opportunities for protected groups.

In summary, the PSI appears to be a useful instrument for evaluating the risks, in terms of potential for dishonesty, violence, and drug abuse, associated with hiring job applicants. Although lengthy, the PSI is easy to administer and code, and its results can be obtained quickly and interpreted easily. Users of the test should, however, be given more explicit warning in the manual regarding potential misuses of the PSI.

[632]

London Reading Test. Ages 10–7 to 12–4; 1978–80; LRT; 2 parallel Forms A, B, ('80, 8 pages); teacher's manual ('80, 72 pages); practice test ('80, 1 page, same for both forms); 1985 price data: £4.95 per 25 tests; £2.05 per 25 practice sheets; £2.90 per manual; £3.25 per specimen set; (50–60) minutes; Margaret Biscoe, Ced Bradshaw, Sheila Clarke, Miles Halliwell, David Morgan, Theresa Nunn, Helen Quigley, Irene Zelickman, and Gloria Callaway (practice test); NFER-Nelson Publishing Co. [England].*

Review of London Reading Test by AMOS L. HAHN, Assistant Professor of Education, University of Texas, Arlington, TX:

This test was designed primarily as a survey/screening instrument for children who are ready to enter English secondary schools. The main purpose of this test is to predict future reading performance and to identify areas where children will need remedial help.

According to the test manual, Forms A and B are parallel in that the difficulty levels of the equivalent passages in each form are the same. Using the Flesch Reading Ease Score, the first passage of each form has a Flesch score of 90 (90% of the textbook material analyzed was more difficult than these passages), the second passage of each form was 75 (a medium level of difficulty), and the third passage of each form had a score of 65 (only 10% of the textbook material analyzed was more difficult than these passages).

The first and second passages in each form of this test assess reading ability using a cloze format. A practice cloze passage is provided to ensure that children understand that (*a*) only one word should go in each space; (*b*) no contractions are allowed; (*c*) all gaps are the same length, regardless of the length of the word to be inserted; (*d*) there is often more than one correct way of filling a gap; (*e*) if they can't immediately fill a gap the best strategy is to read to the end of the sentence, paragraph or passage and then go back to the gap in question.

Since the purpose of these cloze passages is not to assess readability of the passage but to sample the child's performance on a passage of known readability, this test established 75% acceptable responses as equivalent to the instructional reading level and 90% acceptable responses as equivalent to the independent reading level. Although these passages may be suitable for English children, the spelling, vocabulary, and content of these passages may be inappropriate for children in other countries. Several words use English spellings (e.g., colour, recognised, apologised) and other words are colloquial in nature (e.g., mum, lorry, swimming baths). Although these passages deal with everyday topics (e.g., snow, an accident, a mistake), the perspective of these stories is unique to the English culture. Children in the United States may not have sufficient background knowledge to understand these passages. The content of the practice passage is abstract in that it deals with a robot that plays on a school team. All of the cloze passages employ a narrative structure.

The third passage of each form consists of an expository passage (The End of Pompeii or Elephants). One passage is followed by 13 comprehension questions and the other by 14 comprehension questions. The questions were written to test comprehension in each of these five categories: literal comprehension, reorganization, inferential comprehension, evaluation, and appreciation. Although several of the questions in the first and second categories are text-based, other questions in these categories seem to be passage independent, in that children could answer these questions using prior knowledge. Questions in the last three categories ask children to do such things as find a word in the passage that means the same as "able to grasp objects" (prehensile), to respond to a saying such as "Elephants never ______," to write something else that has the name "Jumbo," and to write why they did or didn't enjoy the story. All of the answers to these questions are scored and used as part of the reading ability score.

The manual states in narrative form that the test was standardized using both urban and rural populations in England and Wales. Five thousand subjects were used to standardize Form A, and 1,000 from the original 5,000 subjects were used to standardize Form B. Test reliability was calculated using the Kuder-Richardson 21 formula (.95), and validity was established by correlating this test with other well-known standardized tests used in English schools. The only table listed in the Appendix is that highlighting the various test correlations.

Reading ability is calculated using the total score from this test, age of subject, and time of year test was administered. Tables provide standard scores ($M = 100$; $SD = 15$) by age for British schoolchildren. A raw score of 35 is considered the criterion raw score. All children scoring less than 35 points should be individually assessed by a remedial teacher upon entry into the secondary school.

In summary, this test was designed to predict future reading performance and to identify areas where children will need remedial help. Since this test was written for and standardized on children in England and Wales, such factors as prior knowledge, variant spellings, and culture-specific vocabulary make this test inappropriate for other populations of children.

Review of London Reading Test by DAVID M. MEMORY, Associate Professor of Education, Indiana State University, Terre Haute, IN:

The publisher of the London Reading Test (LRT) says that its "aim was to produce a survey/screener test which could be given to the children in the familiar, non-threatening surroundings of their primary school. The results are intended to convey as much information as possible about the child's level of attainment and pattern of abilities. The score will indicate which children may need remedial teaching in the secondary school. The secondary school can then proceed immediately with its own individual diagnostic procedures."

Efforts to make the LRT as non-threatening as possible make it different from most comparable American tests. The teacher's manual emphasizes that the test should be administered under normal classroom conditions with no previous notice of the testing given. Also, there is no time limit for completing the test, and no intimidating separate answer sheets are used. Finally, the front of the test booklet has a rather amusing illustration, and students can be allowed to color that illustration and one inside when they complete work on the test. Some measurement specialists might argue that these procedures and features would tend to produce inconsistencies in administration of the test and in performance by the students. On the other hand, one might contend that these procedures and features would indeed make students relaxed when taking the test and would lead to results that accurately reflect their abilities. In any case, this reviewer is unwilling to condemn these test characteristics. Instead, because of these characteristics he would treat the LRT more as an informal test than most standardized reading tests published in the United States and would interpret the results accordingly.

One feature of the LRT, however, may be related to more weaknesses than strengths; that is the use of the cloze procedure for two of the three passages on the test. Because of the relative unfamiliarity of this procedure to many students, the publisher is to be commended for providing a brief cloze passage as a practice test and insisting that use of it is an integral part of the assessment process with the LRT. Nevertheless, there are problems with the use of the cloze procedure in this test. For one, the publisher has arbitrarily said that a 90% score on a passage indicates that the passage is at the student's independent level and a 75% score indicates the instructional level. It is unclear how the developer used these criteria in norming this test, but that statement in the teacher's manual can only mislead users of the LRT. Another problem is the answer key for the passages, which, though it seems carefully prepared, does include some responses designated as wrong that seem reasonable. Also the directions for using the key are not entirely clear, although it is probably appropriate that the publisher instructs teachers to mark items incorrect when in doubt because low scores can only lead to individualized testing at the secondary level. Finally, another questionable feature of the cloze passages on the LRT is that they are accompanied by illustrations which could give helpful clues to some students who would otherwise be unable to fill in certain blanks or which might mislead some students who otherwise would respond correctly.

The last of the three passages on the LRT is used in a more traditional way, but it too has problems. It is the only one of the three passages on a nonfiction topic, and knowledge background is likely to have an unpredictable influence on performance. Some students might be good readers but just happen to know little about the single topic dealt with on the test. This problem is compounded because some of the items related to that passage assess nothing but knowledge background. An equally serious problem with this passage is that it is intended to be used for assessing a broad range of comprehension abilities, including inferential comprehension, evaluation, and appreciation, but it is also the most difficult of the three passages. As a result, the user of the LRT would not know whether poor performance on the items related to this passage indicates poor general reading ability or specific weaknesses in the areas assessed. Moreover, with only a very limited number of items of any particular type, the teacher cannot assume that a correct response is a reliable indicator of ability in a certain area or that an incorrect response is clear evidence of a problem. Another questionable characteristic of the LRT is the use of a wide variety of question formats with this passage and use of scoring criteria which, for example, penalize checking of the chosen answer when underlining is called for. In effect, this part of the test is above all an assessment of the ability to follow written directions, and the student who has trouble in that area will have difficulty demonstrating other abilities that he or she might have. For these reasons, the goal of identifying a pattern of abilities seems unrealistic with the LRT.

There are also problems in the area of score interpretation. For example, a cutoff raw score is suggested for identifying students who should be tested individually on entry into the secondary school, but the rationale for the particular score suggested is very weak. Fortunately, the user of the LRT is alerted that expertise will have to be developed in interpreting results on this test. Similarly, tables are provided to use in deriving reading ages comparable to those based on reading tests well known in Great Britain, but the basis for constructing those tables is open to question because the samples of students used were very small. Consequently, these tables should be used only with at least as much caution as is suggested in the teacher's manual. At this point the publisher's idea that each student's completed test booklet be passed on to the secondary school to aid in interpretation seems wise; reporting scores alone is not enough.

Despite these reservations about the LRT as a standardized test, this reviewer is at least somewhat impressed by the reliability and validity data reported by the publisher. For example, one value presented which appears to represent an alternate forms reliability coefficient is .86. Also, for the two standardization samples, KR21 reliability coefficients of .95 and .93 are reported. Finally, correlation coefficients in the .80 range between the LRT and other reading tests well known in Great Britain are offered as evidence of concurrent validity. Despite these reasonably impressive data, however, this reviewer is bothered that no item-total correlations or other indices of discrimination are provided. With the test poorly designed to be used in differential diagnosis, it would be reassuring to know which items assess a global reading ability. The absence of item analysis data makes that impossible.

In general, the LRT has several features that make it suited for the use for which it is intended—the transfer of reading ability information from the non-threatening environment of the primary school to the secondary school. However, as the publisher admits, not enough is known about the interpretation of performance on the test to rely on numbers alone. Rather, the LRT can probably be treated as an informal screening instrument that only serves to help the teacher determine which students should be tested more extensively on an individual basis.

[633]

Longitudinal Interval Follow-Up Evaluation, 2nd Edition. Individuals who have received treatment for depression; 1979–83; LIFE II; revision of LIFE ('79); "to provide a longitudinal picture of the subject's psychiatric course and psychosocial functioning over a six month period"; 5 areas: course of psychopathology, treatment for psychiatric conditions, medical illness and treatment, psychosocial functioning, monthly global assessments of symptoms and functioning; no norms; individual structured interview; interview protocol ('82, 12 pages); score sheet ('82, 10 pages); new episode/new condition report ('83, 17 pages); score sheet for new episode/new condition report (no date, 4 pages); procedure manual ('82, 12 pages); 1983 price data: no per-copy charge for LIFE II; a fee of unspecified amount is required for training; NIMH scoring services must be used; administration time not reported; Martin B. Keller,

Robert W. Shapiro, et al.; Boston Massachusetts General Hospital.*

TEST REFERENCES

1. Andreasen, N. C., & Hoenk, P. R. The predictive value of adjustment disorders: A follow-up study. THE AMERICAN JOURNAL OF PSYCHIATRY, 1982, 139, 584–590.

2. Keller, M. B., Shapiro, R. W., Lavori, P.W., & Wolfe, N. Recovery in major depressive disorder: Analysis with the life table and regression models. ARCHIVES OF GENERAL PSYCHIATRY, 1982, 39, 905–910.

[634]

Lorge-Thorndike Intelligence Tests, Multi-Level Edition. Grades 3–13; 1954–66; LTIT; 3 scores: verbal, nonverbal, composite; Form 1 ('64, 52 pages); overlapping Levels A (grade 3), B (4), C (5), D (6), E (7), F (8–9), G (10–11), H (12–13) in a single booklet; manual ('64, 95 pages); technical manual ('66, 33 pages); no norms or reliability data for composite score; most data on validity based upon the earlier edition; separate answer sheets (Digitek, MRC) must be used; 1984 price data: \$4.92 per test; \$162.81 per 500 Digitek answer sheets; \$20.70 per 35 MRC answer sheets, manual, and materials needed for machine-scoring; \$12.60 per MRC scoring stencil; \$6.90 per technical manual; \$6.90 per manual; scoring services information available from publisher; 62(120) minutes; Irving Lorge, Robert L. Thorndike, and Elizabeth Hagen; Riverside Publishing Co.*

See T3:1341 (54 references) and T2:400 (38 references); for a review by Carol K. Tittle, see 7:360 (95 references); see also 6:467 (11 references).

TEST REFERENCES

1. Richman, L., & Harper, D. School adjustment of children with observable disabilities. JOURNAL OF ABNORMAL CHILD PSYCHOLOGY, 1978, 6, 11–18.

2. Schwartz, S., & Wiedel, T. C. Individual differences in cognition: Relationships between verbal ability and memory for order. INTELLIGENCE, 1978, 2, 353–369.

3. Jensen, A. R., & Inouye, A. R. Level I and Level II abilities in Asian, White, and Black children. INTELLIGENCE, 1980, 4, 41–49.

4. Weller, L., & Levi, S. Social class, IQ, self concept and teachers' evaluations in Israel. ADOLESCENCE, 1981, 16, 569–576.

5. Humphrey, L. L. Children's and teachers' perspectives on children's self-control: The development of two rating scales. JOURNAL OF CONSULTING AND CLINICAL PSYCHOLOGY, 1982, 50, 624–633.

6. Joseph, C. A., Joseph, C. R., & Stone, D. R. Subsumptive process in cognitive equivalence transformations with pictures and words. PSYCHOLOGICAL REPORTS, 1982, 50, 575–582.

7. Mayer, V. J., & Richmond, J. M. An overview of assessment instruments in science. SCIENCE EDUCATION, 1982, 66, 49–66.

8. McKim, B. J., Weissberg, R. P., Cowen, E. L., Gesten, E. L., & Rapkin, B. D. A comparison of the problem-solving ability and adjustment of suburban and urban third-grade children. AMERICAN JOURNAL OF COMMUNITY PSYCHOLOGY, 1982, 10, 155–169.

9. Roberge, J. J., & Flexer, B. K. The Formal Operational Reasoning Test. JOURNAL OF GENERAL PSYCHOLOGY, 1982, 106, 61–67.

10. Curley, J. F., & Reilly, L. J. Sensory process instruction with learning disabled children. PERCEPTUAL AND MOTOR SKILLS, 1983, 57, 1219–1226.

11. Klose, A. E., Schwartz, S., & Brown, J. W. M. The imageability effect in good and poor readers. BULLETIN OF THE PSYCHONOMIC SOCIETY, 1983, 21, 446–448.

12. Popovics, A. J. Predictive validities of clinical and actuarial scores of the Gesell Incomplete Man Test. PERCEPTUAL AND MOTOR SKILLS, 1983, 56, 864–866.

[635]

Louisville Behavior Checklist. Ages 4–6, 7–12, 13–17; 1977–81; LBC; "social and emotional behaviors indicative of psychopathological disorders"; 13 to 20 scales; 3 levels; manual ('81, 90 pages); answer-profile sheet, 1981 edition ('81, 2 pages); 1983 price data: \$79.50 per complete set including 10 reusable tests and 20 answer-profile sheets of each level; \$27.50 per kit including 10 reusable tests and 20 answer-profile sheets of any one level; \$8.10 per 20 reusable tests; \$14.65 per set of scoring keys, 1981 edition; \$5.25 per 50 answer-profile sheets, 1981 edition; \$7.80 per manual; administration time not reported; Lovick C. Miller; Western Psychological Services.*

a) FORM E1. Ages 4–6; 1977–81; 20 scales: Infantile Aggression, Hyperactivity, Antisocial Behavior, Aggression, Social Withdrawal, Sensitivity, Fear, Inhibition, Intellectual Deficit, Immaturity, Cognitive Disability, Normal Irritability, Prosocial Deficit, Rare Deviance, Neurotic Behavior, Psychotic Behavior, Somatic Behavior, Sexual Behavior, School Disturbance Predictor, Severity Level; Form E1 ('77, 4 pages).

b) FORM E2. Ages 7–12; 1977–81; 19 scales: same as for Form E1 except Academic Disability replaces Intellectual Deficit, Learning Disability replaces Cognitive Disability, and School Disturbance Predictor is omitted; Form E2 ('77, 4 pages).

c) FORM E3. Ages 13–17; 1981; 13 scales: Egocentric-Exploitive, Destructive-Assaultive, Social Delinquency, Adolescent Turmoil, Apathetic Isolation, Neuroticism, Dependent-Inhibited, Academic Disability, Neurological or Psychotic Abnormality, General Pathology, Longitudinal, Severity Level, Total Pathology; Form E3 ('81, 4 pages).

See T3:1343 (1 reference).

TEST REFERENCES

1. Miller, L. C. Dimensions of adolescent psychopathology. JOURNAL OF ABNORMAL CHILD PSYCHOLOGY, 1980, 8, 161–173.

2. Adams-Tucker, C. A socioclinical overview of 28 sex-abused children. CHILD ABUSE & NEGLECT, 1981, 5, 361–367.

3. Adams-Tucker, C. Proximate effect of sexual abuse in childhood: A report on 28 children. THE AMERICAN JOURNAL OF PSYCHIATRY, 1982, 139, 1252–1256.

4. Tarte, R. D., Vernon, C. R., Luke, D. E., & Clark, H. B. Comparison of responses by normal and deviant populations to Louisville Behavior Checklist. PSYCHOLOGICAL REPORTS, 1982, 50, 99–106.

5. Robinson, E. A., & Anderson, L. L. Family adjustment, parental attitudes, and social desirability. JOURNAL OF ABNORMAL CHILD PSYCHOLOGY, 1983, 11, 247–256.

Review of Louisville Behavior Checklist by BETTY N. GORDON, Staff Psychologist, Division for Disorders of Development and Learning, Clinical Assistant Professor of Psychology, Department of Psychiatry, University of North Carolina, Chapel Hill, NC:

The Louisville Behavior Checklist (LBC) was designed as a screening instrument for use prior to a full clinical evaluation, to aid parents in communicating their concerns about their children. Administration is by parent report and requires a 6th-grade reading ability.

The LBC consists of three forms of 164 true/false items each for grades 4 to 6, 7 to 12, and 13 to 17 years. The original items from which the final checklist was developed were derived from the clinical literature, other behavioral inventories, and the complaints of parents during intake interviews at the Louisville Child Guidance Clinic. The forms for ages 4 to 6 (E1) and 7 to 12 (E2) years consist of 20 and 19 scales, respectively. The first 11 scales were derived from a factor analysis of data for 6- to 12-year-olds. The remaining scales were added on the basis of clinical judgement. E1 was developed by eliminating items from E2 which seemed inappropriate for younger children and replacing them with more appropriate items.

Form E3 for 13- to 17-year-olds was also developed from E2. Forty-eight items considered inappropriate for adolescents were replaced by more age appropriate items. This form was factor analyzed, revealing nine factors. Four additional scales were added on the basis of clinical judgement. Twenty-seven items which had been eliminated from the factor analysis because they occurred with low frequency and 18 items which did not load on any factor were added to various scales, also on the basis of clinical judgement.

Raw scores for each of the scales are converted to standard scores using tables presented in the manual by age and sex. A profile can then be obtained. Standard scores for E1 are based on a random sample of 287 parents from the Louisville, Kentucky, area. Differences in standard scores in this sample were found to be influenced by income and race. The standard scores for E2 were based on a sample of 236 parents also from Louisville and were found to vary depending on socioeconomic status and the child's IQ. There are no general population norms for E3. Clinical norms, based on cases referred to child psychiatry or juvenile detention psychological services, are given in the manual by age and sex for each of the three forms.

With the exception of two scales, split-half reliability is adequate for all three forms, ranging from .60 to .97. The two scales with poor internal consistency are Antisocial Behavior (.33) and Immaturity (.44) for girls only. Test-retest data indicate reasonable stability over 3 months for E1 and E2. No stability data are reported for E3.

Several types of studies on the validity of the LBC are reported. For E2, children referred to a child guidance clinic were found to have a higher mean score than the general population, indicating greater parent perception of symptomatic behaviors. Another study compared phobic, autistic, and learning disabled children with a sample from the general population and found that each group had a distinct profile on the LBC. A study of the predictive validity of E1 compared parent report on the LBC and teacher referral of children as socially or emotionally disturbed. The LBC correctly classified 74.3% of the children. However, while it identified the non-referred children quite accurately (86%) it identified the referred children only slightly better than chance (54%). Comparison of teacher and parent ratings for Forms E1 and E2 revealed low but positive correlations ranging from .10 to .54. However, many factors such as age, sex, level, and type of disturbance were found to affect this relationship.

Validity studies for E3 compared four small groups of children: general public, upper income private practice (type of practice was not specified), psychiatric outpatient and inpatient, and juvenile delinquents. The LBC was found to discriminate among these groups. The primary evidence given for construct validity for E3 is the factor analysis used in test construction.

The LBC has some advantages as a screening instrument, when used together with other sources of information. It appears to be a reasonably reliable and stable instrument and the authors have studied its usefulness with a variety of clinical populations. In addition, an attempt has been made to devise an instrument which has some continuity over quite a wide age span. However, interpretation of information gathered through use of the LBC would have to be extremely cautious because of some major flaws in its development and in the demonstration of its validity. First, only some of the scales have been derived by factor analysis; others were added on the basis of clinical judgement, and in the case of Form E3, items rejected by factor analysis were included where the author thought they best belonged. Second, Form E1 was not factor analyzed and it is not clear that the same factor structure would emerge for this younger age group as was found for E2. This reviewer found the section in the manual on test development extremely confusing to read. Many of the tables contained different numbers of scales or had different scale labels than the final instrument, making it difficult to evaluate the adequacy of test construction.

Third, the norms are based on a local population and may not be valid for other areas of the country. Additionally, although the standard scores for the normative sample were found to be dependent on race and socioeconomic status, they are presented by age and sex in the manual.

Finally, the evidence for validity of the LBC is weak, particularly for Form E3. In addition, this particular scale has no general population norms and no test-retest reliability data are reported. Further studies are needed on the predictive validity of the LBC and its use and stability over time. The author needs to investigate the primary validity question of any parent report measure: What is the relationship between responses to the LBC and the child's actual behavior and functioning? As an alternative, the reader is referred to the Achenbach Child Behavior Checklist (Achenbach, 1978), which shows promise of being a psychometrically sound instrument designed for similar purposes.

REVIEWER'S REFERENCES

Achenbach, T. The Child Behavior Profile: I. Boys aged 6–11. JOURNAL OF CONSULTING AND CLINICAL PSYCHOLOGY, 1978, 46, 478–488.

[636]

A Love Attitudes Inventory. Grades 12 and college; 1971; LAI; no data on reliability and validity; no norms; 1 form (4 pages); manual (17 pages); 1984 price data: $5 per 10 tests; $1 per manual; $2 per specimen set; administration time not reported; David Knox; Family Life Publications, Inc.*

See T2:821 (1 reference).

Review of A Love Attitudes Inventory by PHILIP H. DREYER, Professor of Education and Psychology, Claremont Graduate School, Claremont, CA:

A Love Attitudes Inventory (LAI) is an informal scale intended for teachers and discussion leaders who wish to measure attitudes toward love for the purposes of discussion and self-discovery. The LAI consists of 30 statements to which the subject responds by marking a 5-point scale ranging from "1" (strongly agree) to "5" (strongly disagree). The test can be self-scored by adding all responses. Low scores (from 30 to 90) indicate a person whose attitude tends to be "romantic," while high scores indicate a person whose attitude is "conjugal" or "realistic." The test form also includes questions about the subject's sex, age, marital status, and parents' marital status, as well as two open-ended questions about feelings and behaviors the subject thinks demonstrate love. A Discussion Guide provides numerous definitions of love and a brief commentary on how each item might be discussed and understood. No other norms or statistical interpretation of scores is provided.

For the purposes of this scale, the author states, "a dichotomy of romantic and non-romantic (conjugal) love was established" (Knox & Sporakowski, 1968). Instead of concise definitions of "romantic" and "conjugal" love, the author quotes numerous other writers to imply that "romantic" love is impulsive, emotional, intellectually distracting, sexual, and mystical, while "conjugal" love is the opposite of romantic love and is based on the need to escape loneliness and to achieve self-fulfillment through a relationship with another person. Beyond these statements, no theoretical basis for the construct "love" is provided and no distinction between love and other constructs, such as "liking" or "altruism," is provided. Furthermore, the context of this dichotomous view of love is the traditional male-female relationship (eros). No mention is made of love between parent and child (agape) or love between brothers or between sisters (philos).

In the literature provided with the test there is no information about reliability and very little about validity. In separately published research reports, however, the author reports two attempts to estimate reliability. The first was a retest procedure conducted over a 1-week time interval with 25 single, undergraduate students at Florida State University. This procedure yielded a "percentage agreement of 78.4" (Knox & Sporakowski, 1968). Whether this agreement was for total score or for individual items is not explained. The second was a split-half reliability estimate using the 27 "best" items found in a study of 100 high school students. Here the reliability coefficient, corrected by the Spearman-Brown formula, was reported to be .89 (Knox, 1970).

Evidence of content validity is discussed in terms of the development of the scale. Two hundred items were submitted to 10 "professionals in the field of marriage and family living....Eighty-five of the original 200 items were retained, based on a minimum acceptability of 70 percent agreement" when judges rated each item as "romantic" or "conjugal." These 85 items were then administered to "300 senior high school and college students" whose responses were divided into quartiles. Thirty of the best 40 items which discriminated between highest and lowest quartiles were retained in the final version of the LAI. The author reported that in general older students tended to have more "conjugal" or "realistic" attitudes towards love than younger students; that male college students had more "romantic" attitudes than females; and that the love attitudes of high school students appeared to be more a function of parents' marital status than anything else, with adolescents from intact parent marriages having more "conjugal" attitudes than students from homes where parents were divorced or deceased (Knox & Sporakowski, 1968; Knox, 1970).

The literature provided with the Love Attitudes Inventory provides little technical information about the scale and no norms against which to judge a person's score. Even more troublesome is that the published research about the LAI appears to be based on responses from a total of 300 high school and college subjects who were tested before 1970. There appears to be no additional work done to enlarge the standardization sample, to improve reliability, or to better estimate validity in the last 14 years since the test was published. These technical shortcomings, combined with a weak theoretical base for the definition of love itself, seem to make the LAI a poor choice as a research instrument.

In summary, the Love Attitudes Inventory lacks sufficient reliability, validity, and standardization to be recommended for use as a research instrument; however, as an informal scale to stimulate group discussion in a class on interpersonal relationships or family life, the LAI might be useful.

REVIEWER'S REFERENCES

Knox, D. H., & Sporakowski, M. J. Attitudes of college students toward love. JOURNAL OF MARRIAGE AND THE FAMILY, 1968, 30, 638–642.

Knox, D. H., Jr. Attitudes toward love of high school seniors. ADOLESCENCE, 1970, 5, 89–100.

[637]

The Luria-Nebraska Neuropsychological Battery. Ages 15 and over; 1980; uses cards adapted from Luria's Neuropsychological Investigation by Anne-Lise Christensen; 14 scores: motor, rhythm, tactile, visual, receptive speech, expressive speech, writing, reading, arithmetic, memory, intellectual processes, pathognomic, left hemisphere, right hemisphere; individual; 1 form; manual (128 pages); tape provided for rhythm subtest; administration and scoring booklet (36 pages); patient response booklet (8 pages); 1983 price data: $137.50 per set including manual, 5 administration and scoring booklets, 5 patient response booklets, 6 stimulus cards, tape cassette, and stimulus cards adapted from Luria's Neuropsychological Investigation by Ann-Lise Christensen; $14.50 per 6 stimulus cards plus a tape cassette; $17.40 per 10 administration and scoring booklets; $5.90 per 10 patient response booklets; $95 per stimulus cards adapted from Luria's Neuropsychological Investigation; $20 per manual; (90–150) minutes; Charles J. Golden, Thomas A. Hammeke, and Arnold D. Purisch; Western Psychological Services.*

See T3:1346 (8 references).

TEST REFERENCES

1. Lewis, G., Golden, C. J., Purisch, A. D., & Hammeke, T. A. The effects of chronicity of disorder and length of hospitalization on the standardized version of Luria's Neuropsychological Battery in a schizophrenic population. CLINICAL NEUROPSYCHOLOGY, 1979, 1(4), 13–18.

2. McKay, S., & Golden, C. J. Empirical derivation of experimental scales for localizing brain lesions using the Luria-Nebraska Neuropsychological Battery. CLINICAL NEUROPSYCHOLOGY, 1979, 1(4), 19–23.

3. McKay, S., & Golden, C. J. Empirical derivation of neuropsychological scales for the lateralization of brain damage using the Luria Nebraska Neuropsychological Test Battery. CLINICAL NEUROPSYCHOLOGY, 1979, 1(2), 1–5.

4. Golden, C. J., & Berg, R. A. Interpretation of Luria-Nebraska Neuropsychological Battery by item intercorrelation: Items 25–51 of the Motor Scale. CLINICAL NEUROPSYCHOLOGY, 1980, 2, 105–108.

5. Golden, C. J., & Berg, R. A. Interpretation of the Luria-Nebraska Neuropsychological Battery by item intercorrelation: Items 1–24 of the Motor Scale. CLINICAL NEUROPSYCHOLOGY, 1980, 2, 66–71.

6. Golden, C. J., Moses, J. A., Jr., Zelazowski, R., Graber, B., Zatz, L. M., Horvath, T. B., & Berger, P. A. Cerebral ventricular size and neuropsychological impairment in young chronic schizophrenics: Measurement by the Standardized Luria-Nebraska Neuropsychological Battery. ARCHIVES OF GENERAL PSYCHIATRY, 1980, 37, 619–623.

7. Hartlage, L. C., & Telzrow, C. F. The practice of clinical neuropsychology. CLINICAL NEUROPSYCHOLOGY, 1980, 2, 200–202.

8. Newlin, D. B., & Tramontana, M. G. Neuropsychological findings in a hyperactive adolescent with subcortical brain pathology. CLINICAL NEUROPSYCHOLOGY, 1980, 2, 178–183.

9. Osmon, D. C. An empirical look at the theory of brain function behind the Luria-Nebraska Neuropsychological Battery. CLINICAL NEUROPSYCHOLOGY, 1980, 2, 145–152.

10. Vicente, P., Kennelly, D., Golden, C. J., Kane, F., Sweet, J., Moses, J. A., Jr., Cardellino, J. P., Templeton, R., & Graber, B. The relationship of the Halstead-Reitan Neuropsychological Battery to the Luria-Nebraska Neuropsychological Battery: Preliminary report. CLINICAL NEUROPSYCHOLOGY, 1980, 2, 140–141.

11. Golden, C. J., Graber, B., Coffman, J., Berg, R. A., Newlin, D. B., & Bloch, S. Structural brain deficits in schizophrenia. ARCHIVES OF GENERAL PSYCHIATRY, 1981, 38, 1014–1017.

12. Voorhees, J. Neuropsychological differences between juvenile delinquents and functional adolescents: A preliminary study. ADOLESCENCE, 1981, 16, 57–66.

13. Chelune, G. J. A reexamination of the relationship between the Luria-Nebraska and Halstead-Reitan Batteries: Overlap with the WAIS. JOURNAL OF CONSULTING AND CLINICAL PSYCHOLOGY, 1982, 50, 578–580.

14. Crosson, B., & Warren, R. L. Use of the Luria-Nebraska Neuropsychological Battery in aphasia: A conceptual critique. JOURNAL OF CONSULTING AND CLINICAL PSYCHOLOGY, 1982, 50, 22–31.

15. Delis, D. C., & Kaplan, E. The assessment of aphasia with The Luria-Nebraska Neuropsychological Battery: A case critique. JOURNAL OF CONSULTING AND CLINICAL PSYCHOLOGY, 1982, 50, 32–39.

16. Golden, C. J., & Berg, R. Interpretation of the Luria-Nebraska Neuropsychological Battery by item interpretation: The Reading Scale. CLINICAL NEUROPSYCHOLOGY, 1982, 4, 176–179.

17. Golden, C. J., & Berg, R. A. Item interpretation of the Luria-Nebraska Neuropsychological Battery VIII. The Expressive Language Scale. CLINICAL NEUROPSYCHOLOGY, 1982, 4, 8–14.

18. Golden, C. J., Ariel, R. N., McKay, S. E., Wilkening, G. N., Wolf, B. A., & MacInnes, W. D. The Luria-Nebraska Neuropsychological Battery: Theoretical orientation and comment. JOURNAL OF CONSULTING AND CLINICAL PSYCHOLOGY, 1982, 50, 291–300.

19. Golden, C. J., Ariel, R. N., Moses, J. A., Jr., Wilkening, G. N., McKay, S. E., & MacInnes, W. D. Analytic techniques in the interpretation of the Luria-Nebraska Neuropsychological Battery. JOURNAL OF CONSULTING AND CLINICAL PSYCHOLOGY, 1982, 50, 40–48.

20. Golden, C. J., Berg, R. A., & Graber, B. Test-retest reliability of the Luria-Nebraska Neuropsychological Battery in stable, chronically impaired patients. JOURNAL OF CONSULTING AND CLINICAL PSYCHOLOGY, 1982, 50, 452–454.

21. Golden, C. J., Gustavson, J. L., & Ariel, R. Correlations between the Luria-Nebraska and the Halstead-Reitan neuropsychological batteries: Effects of partialing out education and postmorbid intelligence. JOURNAL OF CONSULTING AND CLINICAL PSYCHOLOGY, 1982, 50, 770–771.

22. Golden, C. J., MacInnes, W. D., Ariel, R. N., Ruedrich, S. L., Chu, C. C., Coffman, J. A., Graber, B., & Bloch, S. Cross-validation of the ability of the Luria-Nebraska Neuropsychological Battery to differentiate chronic schizophrenics with and without ventricular enlargement. JOURNAL OF CONSULTING AND CLINICAL PSYCHOLOGY, 1982, 50, 87–95.

23. Hale, R. L., & Foltz, S. G. Prediction of academic achievement in handicapped adolescents using a modified form of the Luria-Nebraska Pathognomonic Scale and WISC-R Full Scale IQ. CLINICAL NEUROPSYCHOLOGY, 1982, 4, 99–103.

24. Picker, W. R., & Schlottman, R. S. An investigation of the Intellectual Processes Scale of The Luria-Nebraska Neuropsychological Battery. CLINICAL NEUROPSYCHOLOGY, 1982, 4, 120–124.

25. Portnoff, L. A. A Case of Capgras' Syndrome assessed with the Luria-Nebraska Neuropsychological Battery. CLINICAL NEUROPSYCHOLOGY, 1982, 4, 153–155.

26. Puente, A. E., Heidelberg-Sanders, C., & Lund, N. Detection of brain-damage in schizophrenics as measured by the Whitaker Index of Schizophrenic Thinking and The Luria-Nebraska Neuropsychological Battery. PERCEPTUAL AND MOTOR SKILLS, 1982, 54, 495–499.

27. Reynolds, C. R. Determining statistically reliable strengths and weaknesses in the performance of single individuals on the Luria-Nebraska Neuropsychological Battery. JOURNAL OF CONSULTING AND CLINICAL PSYCHOLOGY, 1982, 50, 525–529.

28. Ryan, J. J., & Prifitera, A. Concurrent validity of the Luria-Nebraska memory scale. JOURNAL OF CLINICAL PSYCHOLOGY, 1982, 38, 378–379.

29. Shelly, C., & Goldstein, G. Intelligence, achievement, and the Luria-Nebraska Battery in a neuropsychiatric population: A factor analytic study. CLINICAL NEUROPSYCHOLOGY, 1982, 4, 164–169.

30. Shelly, C., & Goldstein, G. Psychometric relations between the Luria-Nebraska and Halstead-Reitan Neuropsychological Test Batteries in a neuropsychiatric setting. CLINICAL NEUROPSYCHOLOGY, 1982, 4, 128–133.

31. Spiers, P. A. The Luria-Nebraska Neuropsychological Battery revisited: A theory in practice or just practicing? JOURNAL OF CONSULTING AND CLINICAL PSYCHOLOGY, 1982, 50, 301–306.

32. Spitzform, M. Normative data in the elderly on the Luria-Nebraska Neuropsychological Battery. CLINICAL NEUROPSYCHOLOGY, 1982, 4, 103–105.

33. Webster, J. S., & Dostrow, V. Efficacy of a decision-tree approach to the Luria-Nebraska Neuropsychological Battery. JOURNAL OF CONSULTING AND CLINICAL PSYCHOLOGY, 1982, 50, 313–315.

34. Nolan, D. R., Hammeke, T. A., & Barkley, R. A. A comparison of the patterns of the neuropsychological performance in two groups of learning disabled children. JOURNAL OF CLINICAL CHILD PSYCHOLOGY, 1983, 12, 22–27.

35. Plaisted, J. R., Gustavson, J. L., Wilkening, G. N., & Golden, C. J. The Luria-Nebraska Neuropsychological Battery—Children's Revision: Theory and current research findings. JOURNAL OF CLINICAL CHILD PSYCHOLOGY, 1983, 12, 13–21.

36. Quattrocchi, M. M., & Golden, C. J. Peabody Picture Vocabulary Test—Revised and Luria-Nebraska Neuropsychological Battery for Children: Intercorrelations for normal youngsters. PERCEPTUAL AND MOTOR SKILLS, 1983, 56, 632–634.

37. Stambrook, M. The Luria-Nebraska Neuropsychological Battery: A promise that may be partly fulfilled. JOURNAL OF CLINICAL NEUROPSYCHOLOGY, 1983, 5, 247–269.

38. Bryant, E. T., Maruish, M. E., Sawicki, R. F., & Golden, C. J. Validity of the Luria-Nebraska Neuropsychological Battery. JOURNAL OF CONSULTING AND CLINICAL PSYCHOLOGY, 1984, 52, 445–448.

39. Bryant, E. T., Scott, M. L., Tori, C. D., & Golden, C. J. Neuropsychological deficits, learning disability, and violent behavior. JOURNAL OF CONSULTING AND CLINICAL PSYCHOLOGY, 1984, 52, 323–324.

40. Goldstein, G., & Shelly, C. Discriminative validity of various intelligence and neuropsychological tests. JOURNAL OF CONSULTING AND CLINICAL PSYCHOLOGY, 1984, 52, 383–389.

41. Sears, J. D., Hirt, M. L., & Hall, R. W. A cross-validation of the Luria-Nebraska Neuropsychological Battery. JOURNAL OF CONSULTING AND CLINICAL PSYCHOLOGY, 1984, 52, 309–310.

Review of Luria-Nebraska Neuropsychological Battery by RUSSELL L. ADAMS, *Professor of Psychiatry and Behavioral Sciences, University of Oklahoma Health Sciences Center, Oklahoma City, OK:*

Aleksandr R. Luria's theory of higher cortical functioning has received international acclaim. His conceptual schemes of the functional organization of the brain are probably the most comprehensive currently available. In contrast to the more psychometric and quantitative approach of most western clinical neuropsychologists, Luria, a Russian neuropsychologist, utilized unstructured qualitative techniques in assessing neurologically impaired patients. Luria's approach, which is similar in many respects to behavioral neurology, adds data helpful in the rehabilitation process.

Luria's techniques for evaluation of patients have not until recently found their way into the mainstream of the clinical practice of neuropsychology in this country. Reasons for this include the lack of standardization of his techniques, the difficulties involved in interpretation, and the problems in receiving adequate training in Luria's approach in this country. Perhaps the most important reason for this lack of widespread use, however, has been that Luria's methods have not been put to the experimental test necessary for acceptance in western neuropsychological circles. Reitan has noted that the only validation of Luria's work has been Luria and his colleagues' impression that his techniques are effective. No systematic validation studies have been undertaken with large groups of subjects.

Another reason for the lack of acceptance of Luria's work in this country had been the absence of a compendium of the techniques that Luria utilized in evaluating patients. However, in 1975 Ann-Lise Christensen, who studied with Luria, published such a compendium together with interpretive guidelines. She also employed a qualitative unstructured and dynamic approach to patient evaluation. On reading Christensen's operationalization of Luria's techniques, Luria is quoted as saying, "Of course, it is a vulgarization—but I've always wanted someone to do what you have done" (Christensen, 1975, preface).

Golden and his colleagues have undertaken the important and difficult task of attempting to integrate Luria's techniques into American clinical neuropsychology. Utilizing Christensen's test material, Golden divided his individual items into 14 scales, established the reliability and validity of the instrument, simplified interpretation to objective rules, determined performance of normal control subjects, and established cutoff levels for the various scales based on a regression equation. One of his most useful contributions is the development of procedures for adjusting scores for the influence of education and age on performance.

Golden and his colleagues have also recently developed lateralizing scales, localization scales, and factor derived scales. Golden's approach to interpretation is notably different from Luria's strongly advocated qualitative approach. Golden's tests take approximately two and one-half hours to administer to a relatively intact patient. Moreover, his tests do not require the bulky equipment of the Halstead Battery and can be administered at bedside. Golden and his colleagues have appropriately modified the battery and its interpretation on the basis of research findings, with apparently dynamic results. These efforts by Golden and his colleagues certainly merit congratulations.

The volume of research concerning the Luria-Nebraska Neuropsychological Battery (LNNB) is very impressive given its short history. However, never before in the history of clinical neuropsychology has so much controversy centered around one instrument. At least seven reviews and critiques written by five different neuropsychologists have criticized the LNNB from a number of different perspectives including the statistical methodology employed in validating the test and establishing its reliability, the procedures utilized in subject selection for validation purposes, the theoretical underpinnings, the clinical applications, and the premature publication of the test (Adams, 1980a, 1980b; Crosson & Warren, 1982; Delis & Kaplan, 1982; Spiers, 1981, 1982; Stambrook, 1983). Spiers (1982, p. 305) concluded that the LNNB has "failed to measure up to the standards that must be required of any new instrument purporting to offer comprehensive assessment of neuropsychological functioning." Adams (1980, p. 522) states that "Shifting patient demographics and diagnoses, invalid statistical analyses and over-dramatized claims of diagnostic accuracy are some of the many liabilities in the Luria-Nebraska reports to date." This current brief review includes the author's view of some of the more pertinent criticisms previously cited by others plus this reviewer's own impressions.

According to the manual, the battery was designed for persons 15 years or older; yet the author claims (without presenting data in the manual) that it is effective with adolescents past the age of 12. Obviously data are needed to substantiate this claim. The neurological group in the original study had an average age of 44.3 years (standard deviation 18.8 years). A child version is currently being developed, but as yet has not been published.

The methodological errors committed in the construction of the test are both numerous and substantive. For example, in the first validation study 285 consecutive *t*-tests on the same group of subjects were computed between 50 normals and 50 neurological subjects on individual item performance. Approximately one third of the items in the battery, according to the test manual, were scored "0" and "2." Performing *t*-tests on such dichotomous variables violates the basic normality assumption of the *t*-test. With such truncated scale distributions, significance levels cannot be accurately estimated. Moreover, performing 285 consecutive *t*-tests certainly would result in some of the items being statistically significant purely by chance. In this same study, a discriminant function analysis was run using 285 item scores with only 100 subjects. This low ratio of subject to variables grossly violates an assumption of discriminant function analysis and in fact will not run on many computer algorithms. A linear combination of the 30 best items derived from this discriminant function analysis separated the groups with 100% accuracy. This perfect hit rate is almost certainly an artifact of the inappropriate use of discriminant function analysis.

The neurological subjects utilized in the above mentioned study were significantly different ($p < .01$) from the controls on mean education. (neurological group education = 10.3 years; control group = 12.2). However, controlling for education on each item (rather than on each scale) through analysis of covariance did not significantly change the results. Using analysis of covariance on dichotomous data again violates a basic assumption of the technique and may be one reason for the negative findings. Age and education certainly do affect results on the basic scales and hence on many of the individual items comprising those scales. In a later study, Golden and his colleagues found a multiple correlation of .74 between the average Luria score and the combination of age and education. Thus the fact that these original neurological and control validation groups differed in education may well account for some of the original differences reported for individual items. A much better approach than analysis of covariance for controlling for these differences in age and education would have been to equate the groups on those variables and use nonparametric statistics for item analysis.

Subject selection of neurologically impaired patients was another significant problem in several studies. For example, one series of studies evaluated the ability of the LNNB to localize brain injury to the frontal, sensorimotor, temporal, and occipital-parietal areas in each hemisphere (Lewis, Golden, Moses, Osmon, Purisch, & Hammeke, 1979). The subjects were categorized as having localized lesions simply if more than 50% of the lesion was involved in one localized area and no more than 25% of the lesion in another area. Thus, presumably a patient could have 51% of his lesion in the temporal lobe and 24% and 25% respectively in the occipital-parietal and frontal areas and still be placed in the temporal area localized group. Moreover, patients with open or closed head injuries were included in the localized neurological group. Although Golden reports in this study that patients were eliminated if there was a question concerning localization, establishing definite localized lesions in closed head injury cases is questionable for many reasons including the possibility of contracoup injuries not picked up by available neurological tests. This inexact localization procedure brings into question the findings of that particular series of studies. The small number of cases in each localized group presents another problem. Only six patients were available in each of the four right hemisphere groups and nine patients in each of the left hemisphere groups.

Problems in scale development were present in another study in which Golden and his colleagues attempted to derive eight scales for localizing brain injuries (McKay & Golden, 1979). Using as few as three patients in one localized group (right sensorimotor group) and a maximum of 12 patients in the largest group (left frontal group), Golden and his colleagues statistically compared the performance of each of the eight localized groups with the performance of 77 normal patients on the individual items of his battery. In this way 2,152 *t*-tests were computed (8 x 269 = 2,152) on the same group of normal subjects. After determining which specific items statistically differentiated a given localized group from normal subjects, Golden combined these significant items into a localization scale. Thus, for example, a right sensorimotor scale was developed by including the 16 items which significantly differentiated the three right sensorimotor patients from normal controls.

By utilizing certain decision rules, no item was present in more than two scales and no two scales had more than two common items. Scores for each subject were then computed on the eight scales. Golden then reported that each locally impaired group of patients performed poorest on its corresponding localization scale and that 47 of the 53 patients performed poorest on a scale corresponding to their diagnosed affected area.

This finding is obviously contaminated by artifact. Any given localized group would perform poorly on a scale comprised of items which were originally selected because the localized group performed poorly on these items. Items were included in a scale for a localized group only if the patients in the group performed poorly in contrast to normals on any given item. The fact that so few patients were in each of the groups also strongly contaminated the results and capitalized on fortuitous association. The normal patient had an average of 41.3, which was statistically younger than two of the lateralized lesion groups. The left sensorimotor group and the right temporal group had mean ages of 60.7 years and 55.2 years respectively. Thus obtained differences between these two groups and normals could have been a function of age rather than a result of the localized lesion. In this same study, Golden and his colleagues stated that 10 of the 53 localized patients in their group probably had generalized damage in addition to or as a result of focal localized lesions. The inclusion of these 10 "generalized impaired patients" was an error for a study which was attempting to develop scales for localized impairment.

Another problem is that LNNB does not include items measuring certain deficits which are of importance in evaluating certain neurologically impaired patients. For example, although immediate verbal and non-verbal items are included on the Memory Scale, delayed memory items of the type measured by Russell's revised Wechsler Memory scales are not included. Many patients with dementia can recall material immediately after presentation but with delays of 15 to 30 minutes may not recall these items. However, the yet unpublished Form II of the LNNB does reportedly include an intermediate memory measure. The fact that the battery is in constant change does offer opportunities to correct deficiencies as they are discovered. Golden notes in the manual that the battery is a dynamic instrument that has been revised in the past and probably will be revised again as research warrants.

In fairness to the LNNB, several points need to be made. Although item analysis and scale development were based on flawed methodology, many of the findings have held up in cross-validation. This speaks to the robustness of the LNNB even in the face of methodological problems. It also exemplifies the importance of performing cross-validation studies. Unfortunately some of the methodological errors made in earlier studies were also repeated in these cross-validation efforts. Luria's techniques for evaluation of patients are based on over 40 years of clinical experience. The test items derived from this experience are apparently not only robust, but also hold promise for a better theoretical understanding of higher cortical functioning.

Golden has attempted to answer some of the criticisms directed at his test in a series of articles. However, it is the opinion of this reviewer that his response does not fully address many of these criticisms.

Several studies have reflected positively on the LNNB and do not, in this reviewer's opinion, contain serious methodological problems. In one study, blind interpretation of the LNNB by Golden was compared to blind interpretation of the Halstead Neuropsychological Battery by Oscar Parsons (Kane, Sweet, Golden, Parsons, & Moses, 1981). These two batteries were found to be roughly equivalent in the hands of the two experienced clinical neuropsychologists in discriminating between a mixed group of psychiatric and brain-damaged populations. Although overall hit rate was much less impressive than that reported in previous studies, the batteries did discriminate reasonably well in blind interpretation between these two traditionally difficult-to-discriminate groups. In this particular study, each battery achieved an overall hit rate of approximately 80%. The ability of Luria to separate brain-injured patients from pseudoneurological patients was also investigated by Malloy and Webster (1981). These independent investigators found that the test separated the two groups with an approximate 80% hit rate. This is impressive, given the difficult diagnostic cases. Thus cross-validation by independent investigators adds further evidence to the utility of the battery. In yet another study by the Golden group (Berg & Golden, 1981), the LNNB was given to 80 hospitalized patients, 22 of whom had ideopathic seizures, 18 had seizures secondary to brain trauma or other CNS disorders, and 40 had no CNS involvement. The decision rules listed in the manual were applied to the three groups. The hit rates for the various groups were as follows: ideopathic seizure group (77.3%), seizures secondary to brain injury group (88.9%), and normals (87.5%). These hit rates are impressive and are comparable to other studies utilizing the Halstead Battery.

Golden has provided statistical controls for the simultaneous influence of age and education on LNNB test results. Such controls have seldom been accomplished with other neuropsychological batteries and is one of the more significant contributions of Golden's work. Numerous investigators have reported that age and education affect the performance of most neuropsychological instruments.

Another significant contribution of the LNNB has been the interest it has stimulated in this country in Luria's approach. Future refinements of the battery plus greater use of the qualitative interpretation described by Luria and his colleagues hold promise for future research.

The simplicity of the objective rules listed in the manual could easily seduce one not thoroughly trained in clinical neuropsychology into misinterpreting battery results. Golden has warned that cookbook rules can be used for screening purposes but cannot be considered a full neuropsychological interpretation. Those interested in using the LNNB should be cautioned that the battery is not a substitute for basic training in clinical neuropsychology despite its apparent simplicity in interpretation. As Golden has pointed out, competent interpretation involves not only knowledge of his battery but a thorough grounding in clinical neuropsychology, Luria's Theoretical Model, and neurology. A qualitative interpretation of individual items can aid greatly in the evaluation process. Thus both qualitative and quantitative data can simultaneously be utilized in interpretation. Future research is needed to cross-validate many of the validation studies done by Golden and also to correct for some of the methodological errors cited. Although many of the criticisms cited are significant, the LNNB does hold promise for future development.

After citing a series of validity studies on the LNNB in the manual, Golden and his colleagues state "The authors are well aware that the validity studies summarized here are insufficient to gauge the full value and limitations of the battery, and further investigations and replications are needed." This reviewer concurs completely with this assessment. Much more research from independent investigators is needed. The results of these independent investigations will either confirm or disconfirm Golden and his colleagues' findings, and a full assessment of the approach will have to await these investigations. The reader is, however, cautioned about putting too much confidence in Golden's earlier claims following his initial validation work that the LNNB has an overall effectiveness rate of about 90% "matching or exceeding the accuracy rate of other tests available in neuropsychology today."

REVIEWER'S REFERENCES

Christensen, A. LURIA'S NEUROPSYCHOLOGICAL INVESTIGATION. New York: Spectrum, 1975.

Reitan, R. Neuropsychology—The vulgarization Luria always wanted. CONTEMPORARY PSYCHOLOGY, 1976, 21, 737–738.

Lewis, G. P., Golden, C. J., Moses, J. A., Jr., Osmon, D. C., Purisch, A. D., & Hammeke, T. A. Localization of cerebral dysfunction with a standardized version of Luria's Neuropsychological Battery. JOURNAL OF CONSULTING AND CLINICAL PSYCHOLOGY, 1979, 47(6), 1003–1019.

McKay, S., & Golden, C. J. Empirical derivation of experimental scales for localizing brain lesions using the Luria-Nebraska Neuropsychological Battery. CLINICAL NEUROPSYCHOLOGY, 1979, 1, 1–5.

Adams, K. M. An end of innocence for behavioral neurology? Adams replies. JOURNAL OF CONSULTING AND CLINICAL PSYCHOLOGY, 1980, 48(4), 522–524. (a)

Adams, K. M. In search of Luria's battery: A false start. JOURNAL OF CONSULTING AND CLINICAL PSYCHOLOGY, 1980, 48(4), 511–516. (b)

Berg, R. A., & Golden, C. J. Identification of neuropsychological deficits in epilepsy using the Luria Neuropsychological Battery. JOURNAL OF CONSULTING AND CLINICAL PSYCHOLOGY, 1981, 49(5), 745–747.

Kane, R. L., Sweet, J. J., Golden, C. D., Parsons, O. A., & Moses, J. A., Jr. Comparative diagnostic accuracy of the Halstead-Reitan and standardized Luria-Nebraska Neuropsychological Batteries in a mixed psychiatric and brain damaged population. JOURNAL OF CONSULTING AND CLINICAL PSYCHOLOGY, 1981, 49(3), 484–485.

Malloy, P. F., & Webster, J. S. Detecting mild brain impairment using the Luria-Nebraska Neuropsychological Battery. JOURNAL OF CONSULTING AND CLINICAL PSYCHOLOGY, 1981, 49(5), 768–770.

Spiers, P. A. Have they come to praise Luria or to bury him?: The Luria-Nebraska Battery Controversy. JOURNAL OF CONSULTING AND CLINICAL PSYCHOLOGY, 1981, 49(3), 331–341.

Crosson, B., & Warren, R. L. Use of the Luria-Nebraska Neuropsychological Battery in aphasia: A conceptual critique. JOURNAL OF CONSULTING AND CLINICAL PSYCHOLOGY, 1982, 50(2), 22–31.

Delis, D. C., & Kaplan, E. The assessment of aphasia with the Luria-Nebraska Neuropsychological Battery: A case critique. JOURNAL OF CONSULTING AND CLINICAL PSYCHOLOGY, 1982, 50(1), 32–39.

Spiers, P. A. The Luria-Nebraska Neuropsychological Battery revisited: A theory in practice or just practicing? JOURNAL OF CONSULTING AND CLINICAL PSYCHOLOGY, 1982, 50(2), 301–306.

Stambrook, M. The Luria-Nebraska Neuropsychological Battery: A promise that may be partly fulfilled. JOURNAL OF CLINICAL NEUROPSYCHOLOGY, 1983, 5, 247–269.

[638]

The Macmillan Diagnostic Reading Pack. Reading ages 5–6, 6–7, 7–8, 8–9 years; 1980; no data on reliability and validity; no norms; individual; 4 levels labeled Teach Yourself To Diagnose Reading Problems Stages 1, 2, 3, 4; manual (47 pages); test cards (15 separate cards); 1982 price data: £9.95 per examiner's kit including manual, 16 test cards and 10 copies of checklists per stage; £1.10 per package of 10 checklists per stage; administration time not reported; Ted Ames; Macmillan Education [England].*

a) STAGE 1. Reading ages 5–6 years; item scores in 3 areas: visual skills (32 key words, letter-matching, upper and lower case matching, visual memory recognition, visual memory reproduction), auditory skills (transcribing sounds, sound value of letters, auditory discrimination, short-term auditory memory), phonic blending (blending 2 and 3 letter words, auditory blending); 1 form (4 pages).

b) STAGE 2. Reading ages 6–7 years; item scores in 5 areas: key words (68 key words, 32 key words), phonic recognition (initial and final consonant blends and digraphs, consonant and vowel sounds), phonic blending (consonant blends and digraphs, blending 2 and 3 letter words), phonic spelling (spelling 2 and 3 letter words, transcribing sounds), oral reading (accuracy, comprehension); 1 form (4 pages).

c) STAGE 3. Reading ages 7–8 years; item scores in 5 areas: key words (68 key words, 32 key words), phonic recognition (long vowels and vowel digraphs, final and initial consonant blends and consonant digraphs), phonic blending (vowel digraphs, consonant blends and digraphs), phonic spelling (spelling of short vowel words containing consonant blends and digraphs, spelling 2 and 3 letter words), oral reading (accuracy, comprehension); 1 form (4 pages).

d) STAGE 4. Reading ages 8–9 years; item scores in 4 areas: phonic recognition (long vowels and vowel digraphs, final consonant blends), phonic blending (vowel digraphs, consonant blends and digraphs), phonic spelling (spelling of regular single syllable words, spelling of short vowel words containing consonant blends and digraphs), oral reading (accuracy, comprehension); 1 form ('80, 4 pages).

Review of The Macmillan Diagnostic Reading Pack by JANE HANSEN, Associate Professor of Education, University of New Hampshire, Durham, NH:

The Macmillan Diagnostic Reading Pack (MDRP) is a unique test because of its dual purpose: It is a diagnostic instrument plus a method for teaching practitioners about reading diagnosis. The author of the test conducted surveys which showed that teachers do not diagnose reading systematically because (*a*) they do not know how, or (*b*) diagnosis, as they know it, is too time consuming, and/or (*c*) there is not a single comprehensive instrument available. These issues are addressed in the MDRP. A considerable amount of readable information about the reasons for diagnosis is in the manual. Besides this general information, the suggested use of the MDRP is one of gradual independence on the part of teachers. Initially, it is suggested that teachers administer the tests individually to become familiar with them. Next they can administer many of the tests to small groups. Finally, they will be able to use their own instructional materials from daily teaching to diagnose children's reading problems. Thus, diagnosis will not be too time consuming.

Parts of this apparently well-conceived plan are not perfect. A repeated phrase is "remedial teaching," but it would appear that the author's viewpoint of diagnosis is one where diagnosis is necessary for all teaching, not just remedial. Therefore, the overall intent of diagnosis is fuzzy. A caution about his system of teaching teachers to diagnose is that some of the tests, in order to be administered to groups, require "a little ingenuity on the teachers part." Also the format of the materials is that of individual test cards, so even when a subtest could easily be adapted to group administration the teacher has to produce the materials. Finally, it is stated that teachers will be able to apply miscue analysis procedures to their own materials after administering the MDRP, but the information provided on how to do this is somewhat sparse. But all in all, what is conveyed by the manual title, *Teach Yourself to Diagnose Reading Problems*, is laudable. This is not a goal of other diagnostic instruments and is developed somewhat in the MDRP.

The author contends the MDRP is a comprehensive diagnostic instrument. It could be considered comprehensive by teachers who believe that reading is a hierarchical arrangement of skills that should be mastered in a cumulative fashion. The mastery of all the subskills is determined by criterion-referenced tests. The test is designed for primary students whom the classroom teacher wants to diagnose. It is labeled a "surface diagnosis" test because it is designed to give teachers help in determining instruction for nonsevere problems; if administration of the test or subsequent instruction reveals serious problems, then a student is to be referred to a specialist for further diagnosis.

Administration of the MDRP to a student begins by determining beforehand his/her approximate reading age. Then testing begins in Stage 1 by having students read a list of sight words (presented in alphabetical order). Performance on the word list determines which of various decoding subtests is given next. Finally, testing in Stages 2, 3, and 4 culminates by having students read a story. Such a testing pattern reflects the belief that ability to read is something which happens when a series of subskills have been mastered.

A hierarchical notion of reading development is reflected in remedial suggestions to teachers. In the manual there are lists of references, organized by subtests, to which teachers can go for ideas about how to teach the subskill in that subtest. When studying the manual, perusing the subtests, and scanning the organization of references for instruction it is easy to picture classrooms where students spend many days doing little actual reading; they spend those days working on isolated subskills.

Stage 1 includes no comprehension measure because it is a prereading test. However, listening comprehension, for example, could have been included. In the suggestions for instruction in this prereading stage there are no total-reading suggestions such as reading to children. The subtests in this stage are based upon a progression from visual to auditory to blending skills. The author states that visual skills precede auditory skills, but provides no empirical support for it. The letter-matching test is of curious practical value; for example, it may or may not be necessary for children to be able to find "SWZC" in a multiple-choice format as a prereading skill. Two of the auditory subtests are a version of Wepman's Auditory Discrimination Test and a digit-memory test.

The blending tests in all the stages are lists of short words for the students to read. Again, it would be plausible to suggest that this subtest could have been one where students read words in context. The author purposely isolates skills so that pure knowledge of a skill can be determined. This may disregard reality: a successful reader is one who can orchestrate several skills. Also, many of the words are strange words (e.g., hilt, dreg) which misses an important assumption in phonics: students are to apply phonic generalities to words that are a part of their reading vocabularies.

In Stage 2, 3, and 4 the recognition of consonant and vowel sounds is a test where the teacher pronounces a nonce (nonsense) word and the student points to it from among multiple-choice items. This is another example of a subtest that has questionable validity as a reading task.

The oral reading/comprehension portions are questionable in more than one respect. First, it is debatable to use only oral reading as a comprehension measure; this test has no silent reading component. Second, the teacher's ability to provide a miscue analysis of oral reading is emphasized as a goal of the MDRP. Unfortunately, the author does not appear to realize that repetitions which are self-corrections are not serious errors compared to errors which disrupt meaning and remain uncorrected. All "errors" are weighted equally when deducting points to arrive at the score. Third, the passage in Stage 2 is a poor passage. It is ambiguous and the questions are poor. They do not follow the sequence of the story and tap unimportant information. When only one passage is given, the soundness of the passage is critical.

In summary, it may be unfortunate that we are continuing to create new, fractionated diagnostic instruments which appear to be unenlightened by research. The majority of recent research contends that subskills (and researchers are uncertain about which ones are important) are all interrelated and should be taught as part of an overall reading process and not as steps in the overall reading process. For teachers who subscribe to the underlying assumptions of the MDRP, it will guide them in planning instruction in a hierarchical approach to reading. The author states, "Strengthen the subskills and reading will improve." This is a questionable hypothesis upon which to write a test in 1980. The MDRP, however, does represent a step forward in its attempt to teach teachers about reading diagnosis.

Review of The Macmillan Diagnostic Reading Pack by JAMES V. HOFFMAN, Assistant Professor, Department of Curriculum & Instruction, The University of Texas at Austin, Austin, TX:

These testing materials were designed to assist the teacher of reading in diagnosing reading problems. The focus is on what the author calls "surface diagnosis." At the surface level of diagnosis, an effort is made to describe reading performance, the strengths and weaknesses in vocabulary, word recognition, sentence and paragraph comprehension, and related abilities. Prolonged diagnosis is discouraged. Rather, there is an emphasis on teachers using this information to reinforce strengths and minimize weaknesses.

The procedures recommended for using the packet are highly structured, and few assumptions are made regarding teacher knowledge or skills. The title of the teachers' manual for the packet, *Teach Yourself to Diagnose Reading Problems*, is revealing of the style of writing, organization of the content, and level of complexity with which the topic is dealt. The author suggests that once teachers become familiar and practiced with the procedures for testing, then some of the diagnosis can be done in group settings.

The first step in diagnosis involves assessing the child's "reading age." There are no direct means provided in the test packet for accomplishing this. The author recommends some suitable standardized tests that can be used for this purpose. Based on the student's reading age, the examiner is sent to one of the four stages of assessment provided: Stage 1 (reading age 5 to 6 years); Stage 2 (reading age 6 to 7 years); Stage 3 (reading age 7 to 8 years); and Stage 4 (reading age 8 to 9 years). Within each of the stages the examiner is provided with a series of diagnostic tests to be administered following a procedural flow chart.

Stage 1 diagnosis takes the child through the reading of 32 key sight words, letter matching, visual memory, auditory discrimination, sound-symbol knowledge, and blending. Stage 2 diagnosis begins with the reading of 100 key sight words, followed by recognition of nonsense words, and then blending of short words with consonant blends and digraphs. After a short spelling test, a brief passage is provided for the child to read orally so that reading accuracy, use of context cues, rate of reading, and comprehension can be assessed. In Stages 3 and 4, more difficult tests are provided of phonics, structural analysis, and syllabication. There is also continued analysis of a student's oral reading.

The individual subtests seem reasonably well-constructed. Although the test packet was developed in England, there are only a few items (e.g., mack, hilt) which are peculiar to that context. The procedural flow chart is easy to follow, and checklists for each stage provide an easy means to record and summarize results.

A few areas, however, cause some concern. While the sequence of tasks on the flow chart make the steps in diagnosis easy to follow, they are interspersed with prescriptions which could lead to inappropriate instruction. In Stage 1, for example, if a student can't transcribe letters of the alphabet but does know their sound value, the teacher is directed to teach the transcription of letters. All other activity, diagnostic or instructional, comes to a halt until this skill is mastered. Only then does the teacher move on through the flow chart of activities with the student. In Stage 3, if the student can't apply structural analysis but can identify root words, then the teacher is directed to teach structural analysis. Again, all other activity apparently ceases. In this regard, the test goes well beyond diagnosis into specific instructional prescriptions. In both of the examples just given, if the teacher strictly adheres to the flow chart sequence, she or he may never have heard the child read from connected text.

At the end of Stages 2, 3, and 4, diagnosis is a "close analysis of pupil's oral reading." Unfortunately, the guidance provided for interpreting pupil performance is inadequate. We are asked to make a decision as to whether the child has "good oral reading strategies," yet no specific criteria are given for making this decision other than counting errors and estimating comprehension. The limited guidance provided in interpreting oral reading performance is surprising given the author's stated position that reading is much more than a simple decoding process. The author emphasizes the importance of the semantic and syntactic cue systems in reading, yet does not follow through with an assessment procedure which is balanced in terms of these areas.

Finally, there is little data provided relative to reliability and validity characteristics. Cutoff scores are given for making certain decisions on some subtests, but the basis for establishing these cutoff points is not discussed.

The greatest strength of the materials packet is that it is easy for a teacher to follow. In this regard, it might be useful as an introductory treatment of systematic diagnosis for beginning teachers. As a diagnostic test, however, I would recommend use of such tests as The Woodcock Reading Mastery Tests or the Diagnostic Reading Scales over this one. Both of these tests provide a more balanced assessment of the breadth of reading skills and, in addition, provide supporting data on reliability and validity characteristics.

[639]

The Macmillan Reader Placement Test. Grades 1 and over; 1967–72; part of Macmillan Reading Program; can be used as supplement to Macmillan Mastery Tests; criterion-referenced; 2 tests: Word Pronunciation, Oral Reading; no data on reliability; basis for score interpretation not presented; individual; Forms 1, 2 ('72, 62 pages); manual ('72, 8 pages); separate answer sheet-record booklet ('72, 23 pages) must be used; price data available from publisher; 20(25) minutes; Edward R. Sipay, Albert J. Harris and Mae Knight Clark; Macmillan Publishing Co., Inc.*

[640]

Maculaitas Assessment Program, Commercial Edition. ESL students in grades K–3, K–1, 2–3, 4–5, 6–8, 9–12; 1982; MAC K–12; provides information for diagnostic, selection, and placement decisions in ESL programs; 6 levels of batteries; individual; 1 form for each level; stimulus booklet (25–46 pages) for levels K–3, K–1, 2–3; oral expression rating sheet (4–6 pages) for levels K–3 through 9–12; student booklet (26–29 pages) for levels 2–3 through 9–12; writing sample (4 pages) for levels 4–5 through 9–12; writing ability rating sheet (3 pages) for levels 4–5 through 9–12; NCS answer sheet (2 pages) for levels K–3 through 9–12; scoring overlay (1 sheet) for levels 2–3 through 9–12; pupil profile sheet (2 pages) for levels K–3 through 9–12; ECL chart (4 pages) for levels K–3 through 9–12; sample test (37–49 pages) for levels 2–3 through 9–12; examiner's booklet (13–26 pages) for levels K–3 through 9–12; examiner's manual (141 pages); technical manual (298 pages); 1983 price data: $9.95 per stimulus booklet (specify level); $1.75 per oral expression rating sheet (specify level); $4.50 per student booklet (specify level); $.50 per writing sample (specify level); writing ability rating sheet (specify level); $.75 per NCS answer sheet (specify level); $1.95 per scoring overlay (specify level); $.50 per pupil profile sheet (specify level); $1.95 per ECL chart (specify level); $4.50 per sample test (specify level); $5.95 per examiner's booklet (specify level); $18.45 per examiner's manual; $32.50 per technical manual; $195 per sample set (all six batteries and manuals); Jean D'Arcy Maculaitis; The Alemany Press.*

a) BASIC CONCEPTS TEST. ESL students in grades K–3; 8 scores: color identification, shape identification, 2 number identification scores (counting, spoken), 2 letter identification scores (alphabet, spoken), relationship identification, total; (15–20) minutes.

b) MAC K–1. ESL students in grades K–1; 7 scores: 2 oral expression scores (asking questions, connected discourse), 3 listening comprehension scores (commands, situations, minimal pairs), vocabulary recognition, total; (25–30) minutes.

c) MAC 2–3. ESL students in grades 2–3; 16 scores: 2 oral expression scores (answering questions, connected discourse, 2 vocabulary knowledge scores (identification, noun definition), 4 listening comprehension scores (identifying words, counting words, answering questions, comprehending statements), 6 word recognition skills (alphabetizing, recognizing vowels and consonants, recognizing long and short vowels, using word families, determining singular and plural forms, recognizing silent letters), reading comprehension, total; (79–89) minutes.

d) MAC 4–5. ESL students in grades 4–5; 15 scores: 2 oral expression scores (asking questions, connected discourse), vocabulary knowledge, 4 listening comprehension scores (positional auditory discrimination, answering questions, comprehending statements, comprehending dialogues), 4 reading comprehension scores (recognizing homonyms, recognizing antonyms, recognizing abbreviations, reading outcomes), 3 writing ability scores (grammatical structures, pictorial, school information), total; (119–134) minutes.

e) MAC 6–8. ESL students in grades 6–8; 11 scores: 3 oral expression scores (answering questions, asking questions, connected discourse), 3 listening comprehension scores (answering questions, comprehending statements, comprehending dialogues), 2 reading comprehension scores (vocabulary, reading outcomes), 2 writing ability scores (grammatical structure, application forms), total; (108–123) minutes.

f) MAC 9–12. ESL students in grades 9–12; 11 scores: same as for MAC 6–8; (108–123) minutes.

[641]

Maferr Inventory of Feminine Values. Junior and senior high school, college and adults; 1955–79; MIFV; for research use only; perception of sex roles; 5 tests labeled forms (consisting of the same 34 items with differing directions and scrambled order); 2 levels;

typewritten manual ('79, 124 pages); score sheets (no date, 1 page); bibliography ('79, 23 pages); manual and score sheets are for adult level, but authors claim they may be used for developmental level also; additional statistical information available; 1985 price data: $4 per 25 copies of any one form; $1 per 25 score sheets; $15 per manual; $3 per bibliography; $3 per specimen set; (10–15) minutes per test; Anne G. Steinmann and David J. Fox, with Mary Toro; Maferr Foundation, Inc.*

a) MAFERR DEVELOPMENTAL INVENTORY OF FEMININE VALUES. Junior and senior high school; 1966; 5 tests: Female Self Perception, Female Perception of Ideal Woman, Female Perception of Man's Ideal Woman, Female Perception of Mother's Ideal, Female Perception of Father's Ideal; no data on reliability and validity; no norms; Forms A, B, C, M, P, (1 page).

b) ADULT INVENTORY. College and adults; 1955–79; 5 tests (3 for women, 2 for men): Women's Self-Perception, Woman's Ideal Woman, Woman's Perception of Man's Ideal Woman, Man's Ideal Woman, Man's Perception of Woman's Ideal Woman; Forms A, B, C, BB, G, ('68, 1 page); Finnish, French, German, Greek, Japanese, Portuguese, and Spanish editions available.

For reviews by Goldine C. Gleser and Lenore W. Harmon, see 8:607 (28 references); see also T2:1267 (11 references).

TEST REFERENCES

1. Allison, J. R. Roles and role conflict of women in infertile couples. PSYCHOLOGY OF WOMEN QUARTERLY, 1979, 4, 97–113.

2. Crovitz, E., & Steinmann, A. A decade later: Black-white attitudes toward women's familial role. PSYCHOLOGY OF WOMEN QUARTERLY, 1980, 5, 170–176.

Review of Maferr Inventory of Feminine Values by CAROL ADAMS, Clinical Director, Indian Rivers Mental Health Center, Tuscaloosa, AL:

The Maferr Inventory of Feminine Values is a scale developed by Steinmann and Fox to measure various perceptions of women's sex roles: women's perceptions of themselves regarding the feminine role (Form A), their perceptions of the ideal woman (Form B), and their perception of men's ideal woman (Form C); additionally included are men's perceptions of the ideal woman (Form BB), and of women's ideal woman (Form G). Descriptively, it consists of 34 statements which express attitudes toward women's behavior, goals, and values. They are responded to on a 5-point scale ranging from "strongly agree" to "strongly disagree." Half of the items represent a traditional sex-role orientation, in which a woman achieves satisfaction through the growth and accomplishments of her husband and children. The other half represents a liberal orientation, in which satisfaction is gained through autonomous achievement. Scores are calculated from a summation of difference scores between pairs of adjacent liberal and traditional items. Two possible groupings of items are suggested by the authors, one with four subscales and the other with five.

Generally, the Maferr Inventory is a clever idea with the potential for generating useful, timely information. It is based on the projective hypothesis that the role of women is sufficiently unclear that a woman's perception of it varies as a function of her concept of herself vis-à-vis the feminine role. The instrument is, unfortunately, psychometrically loose and can only be recommended for research use at this stage in its development.

Reliability and validity data are minimal. The manual reports a Spearman-Brown split-half reliability of .81, too low for use in an individual counseling setting. Evidence of content validity is the unanimous agreement of seven experts on the categorization of items as liberal or traditional. Although the manual states that Maferr scores correlate with "a wide variety of other tests," a description of these results would be helpful.

Recommendations for improving the psychometric integrity and usefulness of the instrument are as follows:

(1) The representativeness of the normative sample needs to be demonstrated. Perhaps further, cross-sectional data need to be generated. Although the authors admit that their samples roughly represent only the better educated segment of America, the provision of means and standard deviations encourages inappropriate comparisons.

(2) In the context of the ascendancy of feminist views in some circles, assurance should be offered that the increase in liberal perception of women over the past 20 years among college students is not contaminated by social desirability responding.

(3) Data on the effect, if any, of order of administration of the various forms would be useful.

(4) Test-retest reliability data are needed to assess the stability of scores over time.

(5) Item analyses or factor analyses are needed to assess and improve the unidimensionality of the scale. It is, of course, an empirical question as to whether liberal and traditional views of women's roles represent bipolar opposites of a unidimensional scale. The evolution of present masculinity and femininity scales (e.g., M and F of the Bem Sex Role Inventory) might suggest otherwise.

(6) The trichotomy of scores in the most recent verison of the manual (balanced, family-oriented, and self-oriented) is artificial and peculiar. Why, for example, should a balanced orientation consist of such a narrow range of scores (−4 to +4 on a possible range of 136 points)? Maintaining both liberal and traditional scores would preserve more information and permit an exploration of the relationship between these variables.

(7) Studies exploring the relationships between various forms of the Maferr and popular measures of sex-role orientation, such as the Bem Sex Role Inventory and the Extended Personal Attributes Questionnaire, would provide needed evidence of concurrent validity for the Maferr while helping to

integrate it into the mainstream of the sex-role literature.

[642]

Maferr Inventory of Masculine Values. Junior and senior high school, college and adults; 1966–79; MIMV; for research use only; perception of sex role; 5 tests labeled forms (consisting of the same 34 items with differing directions and scrambled order); 2 levels; typewritten manual ('79, 48 pages); score sheets (no date, 1 page); bibliography ('79, 23 pages); manual and score sheets are for adult level, but authors claim they may be used for developmental level also; additional statistical information available; 1985 price data: $4 per 25 copies of any one form; $1 per 25 score sheets; $10 per manual; $3 per bibliography; $3 per specimen set; (10–15) minutes per test; Anne G. Steinmann and David J. Fox, with Mary Toro; Maferr Foundation, Inc.*

a) MAFERR DEVELOPMENTAL INVENTORY OF MASCULINE VALUES. Junior and senior high school; 1966; 5 tests: Male Self Perception, Male Perception of Ideal Man, Male Perception of Woman's Ideal Man, Male Perception of Mother's Ideal, Male Perception of Father's Ideal; no data on reliability and validity; no norms; Forms H, D, E, M, P, (1 page).

b) ADULT INVENTORY. College and adults; 1966–79; 5 tests (3 for men, 2 for women): Man's Self Perception, Man's Ideal Man, Man's Perception of Woman's Ideal Man, Woman's Ideal Man, Woman's Perception of Man's Ideal Man; Forms H, D, E, DD, F, ('68, 1 page); Finnish, French, German, Greek, Japanese, Portuguese, and Spanish editions available.

For a review by Leonard D. Goodstein, see 8:608 (4 references); see also T2:1268 (1 reference).

TEST REFERENCES

1. Skrapec, C., & MacKenzie, K. R. Psychological self-perception in male transsexuals, homosexuals, and heterosexuals. ARCHIVES OF SEXUAL BEHAVIOR, 1981, 10, 357–370.

Review of Maferr Inventory of Masculine Values by STUART A. KARABENICK, Professor of Psychology, Eastern Michigan University, Ypsilanti, MI:

The Maferr Inventory of Masculine Values (MIMV) is intended to provide self and ideal male role descriptions. There are five forms with different orderings of the same 34 statements; the five forms are purported to measure male self perception, male perception of ideal man, male perception of woman's ideal man, male perception of mother's ideal, and male perception of father's ideal. Pronouns are altered as appropriate. Persons respond on a five-point Likert scale from strongly agree to strongly disagree. Scale construction is based on an assumption of opposing tendencies: family-home orientation (fulfillment through others), versus self-orientation (fulfillment through self-improvement and work outside of the home and family). These orientations parallel (but are by no means identical to) the "expressive" and "instrumental" dimensions used in contemporary sex-role research. However, the MIMV is structured as unidimensional and bipolar rather than bi-dimensional as operationalized by the Bem Sex Role Inventory and the Spence-Helmreich Personal Attributes Questionnaire, which allow the possibility for persons to be classified as high or low on both dimensions. The MIMV scoring system produces a single score which is the difference between the two orientations. Thus, persons are arrayed as family oriented on one pole, self oriented on the other, and "balanced" if their scores fall in the middle range. There is no provision for distinguishing between persons who strongly endorse both roles from those who reject them both. In addition to scoring system constraints, most of the items have directly juxtaposed the orientations (e.g., "The needs of a family come before a man's personal ambitions"), which forces an ordering.

The test manual reports that five subscales have sometimes been used in research: marriage and career, male and female relationships, attitudes toward fatherhood, personality and social characteristics, and self-realization. However, no statistical substantiation (e.g., factor analyses) is provided to justify the subscales nor are any specific references cited. One subscale (personality and social characteristics) is composed of items that describe behavior styles or characteristics (e.g., "I express my ideas strongly") rather than the family versus self roles in most other statements. Such items raise questions about scale homogeneity. (It should be noted that behavior styles or characteristics define the type of items of which the sex-role scales alluded to above are totally composed.) Since no information is given about relations among the subscales it is unclear why personality and social characteristics items should be construed in the same manner as those which, for example, concern attitudes toward fatherhood. No descriptive data are made available in the manual for the subscales.

Although presenting some interesting total scale information from various samples, the manual is quite deficient and in no way meets acceptable psychometric standards. There are no factor analytic studies or even test-retest reliability data. The only evidence of scale homogeneity is a split-half Spearman-Brown prophecy of .86, but there are no accompanying details about the type of split or the sample on which it is based. Content validity stems from judgments of eight psychologists and sociologists who classified the items as family or self-oriented, with final scale versions composed of items for which there was unanimous agreement (but again with no accompanying statistical substantiation). Studies of concurrent validity are described as in progress. Tables of common and deviant responses on each of the forms are presented. In some cases the statistics are based on the entire sample, in others only on undergraduates. Other tables show the percentages of respondents in various categories ranging from family to self-orientations.

It appears that the manual has changed little from the previous edition, with descriptive statistics based on the same 2,454 persons from 12 diverse subgroups (with no claim to representativeness). The manual states that additional data have been collected, but these are not included in the current edition. It is hoped that subsequent editions of the test manual will correct the deficiencies noted above. From the list of references provided it seems that substantial work has been conducted using the MIMV. The user is also referred to a more extensive bibliography available upon request. However, it would seem that much more information should be given in the manual itself without the potential user having to seek out original sources, many of which are not easily accessible. The scale would have greater potential as a research instrument if its psychometric properties were known. At present the user should be alert to the caveats listed above, perhaps the most important of which is the possible heterogeneity of the scale and the related difficulty of interpreting the total scale score.

In sum, the manual's deficiencies make it difficult to fully evaluate the instrument. Its use is recommended with caution and only if the investigator is fully apprised of its possible shortcomings.

Review of Maferr Inventory of Masculine Values by FRANK D. PAYNE, Professor of Psychology, San Jose State University, San Jose, CA:

The authors of the manual for the Maferr Inventory of Masculine Values (MIMV) begin by describing the inventory as an index of "male and female self-concepts and perceptions of masculine and feminine values toward the masculine role." What they mean by this is that the inventory was designed "to distinguish between family home oriented [sic] men, men who fulfill themselves in life through the intermediary of others (liberal); and self oriented men, men who seek fulfillment by actualizing in life their own potentialities and abilities (traditional)." Family-other-orientation versus self-orientation revolves around the degree to which the individual (*a*) "considers his own satisfaction more important than those of his wife and family," (*b*) "is outgoing socially," and (*c*) is "status seeking on his job." The manual provides no theoretical justification for the centrality of these three components to the masculine role or other-versus self-orientation, despite the speculative nature of at least some of the components. Readers might well question, for instance, whether being socially outgoing necessarily has anything to do with self-orientation.

In addition to the lack of any clearly articulated theory, the MIMV also was constructed without the benefit of even the most rudimentary form of item analysis. Consequently, there is no reason to believe that the items even form a scale. Indeed, inspection of the items reveals a curious blend of statements about general attitudes (e.g., "Modern fathers should bring up their boys and girls to believe in absolute equal rights and freedoms for both sexes") and declarations regarding behaviors and feelings ("I argue with people who try to give me orders"). The coverage also is quite broad; the authors themselves state that the items can be grouped into "Marriage and Career," "Male and Female Relationships," "Attitudes Toward Fatherhood," "Personality and Social Characteristics," and "Self-Realization." Even by the authors' own definition, some of the items appear to have remote connections with family-other- versus self-orientation (e.g., "I worry about what people think of me").

The scoring system, which requires that responses to adjacent pairs of items be entered in a specially constructed table, is unnecessarily complex and could have been replaced with a simpler 0 to 4 and 0 to –4 weighting system. The authors suggest three approaches to norm-referenced interpretation of scores, all of which use data from a very heterogeneous composite of 12 subsamples selected "because of availability and for research rather than normative purposes" or from several subsamples of college undergraduates taken from the total sample. The first approach to score interpretation that they advocate requires the reader to compute standard scores using means and standard deviations given in the manual and then convert these to percentiles using the normal distribution (assuming the user knows how). The authors justify this procedure by stating that the MIMV "is normally distributed for self perception." Although it is impossible from the data they provide to reject this statement for self-perception for the total sample, the data for other perspectives and for college undergraduates reveals substantial departures from even a symmetric distribution. Clearly there is insufficient justification for using the normal distribution to convert to percentiles.

The second approach to score interpretation involves application of a descriptive label to the respondent based on the interval on the raw score scale within which the individual falls. The authors give no explanation for their particular cutoffs, and they apply the same cutoffs to all five perspectives and to undergraduates, despite considerable differences in the underlying distributions.

The final approach encourages the reader to use tables of items that were endorsed by 75% or more of the sample or by 15% or less to arrive at an item-by-item interpretation of the extent to which the respondent holds "commonly held views" versus "relatively deviant views."

Information on reliability is limited to a one-sentence statement that split-half reliability "using the Spearman-Brown prophecy formula is estimated at .86." It is not clear whether this estimate is based on one of the 12 subsamples or on the heterogeneous total sample. Investigation of validity consists of a content appraisal in which eight "psychologists and sociologists" unanimously agreed that each item was self-oriented or family-home-other oriented.

In general, the manual for the MIMV is poorly written and contains numerous typographical errors, grammatical inaccuracies, spelling errors, and awkward or unclear sentences. The MIMV obviously suffers from overwhelming flaws, including the absence of even simple forms of item analysis, inadequate reliability and validity data, non-representative normative data, and a questionable approach to interpretation of scores. There is no justification for recommending the use of the MIMV even for research purposes.

[643]

The Major-Minor-Finder. Ages 16–adult; 1978–81; M-M-F; intended to assist with "a choice of a major that best suits the needs of the student"; no data on reliability or validity; self-administered and self-scored; 1 form ('81, 18 pages including 4 page answer insert folder); manual ('78, 18 pages); 1983 price data: $5.75 per set of testing materials including test, insert folder, manual, and college major handbook; $1.35 per reusable test (including 1 answer insert folder); $.20 per answer insert folder; $1.50 per manual; (65–70) minutes; Arthur Cutler, Francis Ferry, Robert Kauk, and Robert Robinett; CFKR Career Materials, Inc.*

Review of The Major-Minor-Finder by RODNEY L. LOWMAN, Assistant Professor of Psychology, North Texas State University, Denton, TX:

The Major-Minor-Finder (M-M-F) is intended primarily for college-bound students. It profiles the respondent on 11 variables which are then compared to analogous data for 99 college majors coded on the same dimensions. The M-M-F also provides a summary of jobs related to each major, including average salaries, the number of workers in the area, and the skills and interests presumed to be necessary for college and work success. A specific page number from the now outdated 1980–81 Occupational Outlook Handbook is provided for those wanting additional information on the occupational group.

The M-M-F takes some pains to note in its manual that it "was not originally constructed as a test," instead describing itself as a "career exploration instrument." This assertion places the measure at odds with contemporary thought about what constitutes a psychological test. Because the instrument relies on the match between measured characteristics of the person and those of the job, it is crucial that the person's self ratings, and those of the major area, be reliably and validly established. Unfortunately, the authors provide little evidence that the M-M-F meets this criterion.

The individual's vocational characteristics are assessed by selecting from two lists of occupational groups and courses the one he/she would most want to take in college, and by answers to nine Likert response format items concerning occupational interests (e.g., "How much interest do you have in reading, studying, and analyzing social studies materials"). It is claimed that all respondents find 5 to 10 majors which match their own characteristics on 6 of the 11 variables and that 6 "matches" are necessary for user satisfaction.

From a face and perhaps content validity perspective, the M-M-F's individual ratings may show some relevance, but the test authors provide no evidence to demonstrate that the instrument measures stable characteristics predictive of later choice of, or satisfaction with, majors or occupations. Rather, the primary criterion to evaluate the instrument's effectiveness seems to be user satisfaction with completing the measure and with the related career exploration experience. Respondents were reported to be nearly 100% satisfied with the results and responded "enthusiastically to the instrument and the process." Youthful exuberance aside, the M-M-F appears to have inspired little or no research testing any of its assumptions.

Normative data provided in the test manual is skimpy at best. The measure was "field tested" (not validated—remember it's not a "test") using 1,000 subjects, largely in the San Francisco area. The sample was obtained by an unspecified method said to be random and included 15% minorities, though the specific racial groups are not noted, nor are racial breakdowns provided for the normative data. The only reliability data provided for the M-M-F reported a test-retest reliability coefficient of .92 for nine preferred college majors in a sample of 120 retested after a 2-week interval.

If there is any value at all in the use of M-M-F, it lies not in the description of personal characteristics, but rather in its reasonably well organized condensation of massive amounts of occupational data. To be useful, such information must be continually updated, and careful attention needs to be directed to assuring that respondents are not prematurely led away from occupations with bleak outlooks or comparatively low salary levels when such professions or majors may constitute their "best fit." While the authors of the test make the usual recommendations supporting the need for adjunctive counseling for those who need it, the form lends itself to mass administrations in which such cautions may be ignored.

The information describing the occupations is too succinct in many cases, and wrong in others. For example, the Occupational Outlook Handbook (OOH) references cite an outdated version of this work. Review of one of the professions listed, psychologist, found the M-M-F stating there were 135,000 workers in the field while the 1982–83 Occupational Outlook Handbook stated there were 106,000. Also the M-M-F ignores subtypes of occupations (e.g., clinical vs. engineering psychologists) in its listing of skills required for success, so students may be left with the impression that they must possess all of the skills listed to be suited for this occupation. This defect is aided somewhat by use of a companion work, The College Major Handbook, available at extra cost from the same test publishers. However, since the primary value of the M-M-F lies in its occupational descriptive data, limitations in this area are not easily dismissed.

Still another major problem with the M-M-F is the absence of any apparent grounding in the research literature of how and when persons make career decisions. The test is said to be used mostly by high school students. Yet, research evidence suggests that vocational preferences are rather unstable during these years, so that the ratings assigned to the individual, particularly when measured with an instrument of uncertain validity, might well be misleading or prematurely deter the respondent away from certain college or major choices. The M-M-F also makes a conceptual leap from college major to occupation, assuming that the choice of major will be identical with that of occupation. While this may often be the case, it is by no means always so.

In short, as a general guide to career possibilities used by well trained counselors with access to extensive occupational reference libraries, the M-M-F may be of some value, particularly if the occupational data in the form are frequently (annually) updated. As a measure of individual respondents' characteristics, however, the M-M-F should be cautiously employed, if at all. Far better measures such as the Strong-Campbell and the Self Directed Search are available for this purpose. The burden of proof rests with the test authors to demonstrate that the self- and corresponding college major/occupational assessments derived from their instrument are accurate and reliable measures of vocationally significant constructs, and that the ratings predict later satisfaction with major or career choice. Satisfaction with completing the form is a poor substitute for validity.

Review of The Major-Minor-Finder by DARYL SANDER, Professor of Education, University of Colorado, Boulder, CO:

The Major-Minor-Finder (M-M-F) was developed in 1978 to meet what the publishers describe as a need for "career exploration instruments with the JOB-O format." Specifically, it aims to help college-bound youth with identification of at least two potential major fields of study in college. Rather than following the traditional psychometric practice of comparing measured likes and dislikes with those of persons in a given criterion group or occupation, the M-M-F asks students to rate their school interests in nine broad areas on a 1 to 6 scale (very high interest = 1 to 6 = none), then match their code with interest codes given for each of 99 college majors. The code also includes two additional elements—a single choice among seven fields of work and a single choice among seven general areas of study in which students believe they have interest and ability. No provision is made in the student code for "don't know" or "uncertain" responses.

The Occupational Outlook Handbook and college catalogs are credited with providing basic objective information upon which the 11-element codes for each of the 99 college majors were established. However, the publishers further acknowledge in the manual that "subjective judgment by experts was used in the final coding of the majors." No additional information is given about the psychometric properties of the code, about the experts who made the judgments, or the process used in translating narrative descriptions from college catalogs and the OOH into numerical codes. The lack of information may well concern potential users of the instrument since conceivably any inaccurate coding could result in faulty final choices of college majors and flawed decisions.

Once students have completed matching their code with those of the 99 college majors, they are directed to select the nine which are most highly matched. Then from this list of nine, students are directed to select three which they believe best match their own interests and abilities and to summarize information which is given in the instrument with respect to average income, job outlook, number of colleges offering that major, etc. From the three final choices, students are then directed to select two fields, one to be designated a major, the other a minor. The 99 college majors appear to be a fairly comprehensive selection of the most popular fields of undergraduate study despite several interesting omissions (e.g., communications, foreign languages, and restaurant and hotel management). No rationale is given for directing students to make an initial choice of nine potential fields of study. To further confuse the issue, the manual indicates that it is advisable for the administrator to tell students that they need not select nine, but only those in which they believe they have an interest. The manual indicates that 90% of those who use the instrument can complete the total task within 50 minutes. Because the instrument is self-scoring, the possibility exists for errors in calculation or in the transfer of information from one page to another. No data regarding accuracy of student self-scoring is given in the manual.

The publishers specifically disavow any intention of regarding the instrument as a "test," which may explain the absence of the usual technical psychometric details. The manual gives no information on measurement error or reliability except for a reminder that "no pretense is made that the assigned ratings are absolute." The M-M-F claims content validity based upon college catalogs and the OOH. Presuppositions about homogeneity of interests among college students pursuing any given major field of study are not addressed. Indeed, a carefully conceived rationale for this approach to interest measurement is badly needed.

SUMMARY. The M-M-F is offered by the publishers as a career exploration tool to assist prospective college students in narrowing their search for a major field of study. The simple format and direct approach utilized by the M-M-F will likely appeal to counselors and others who assist youth with college and career choice processes. However, until more data pertaining to the psychometric properties of the instrument become available, users are cautioned to limit their use to research or experimental programs.

[644]

Management Appraisal Survey. Employees; 1967–80; MAS; ratings of managerial practices by employees; companion instrument to Leadership Appraisal Survey; 5 scores: overall leadership style, philosophy, planning, implementation, evaluation; no data on reliability and validity; 1 form ('80, 9 pages); user's guide ('80, 4 pages); 1984 price data: $4 or less per survey; administration time not reported; Jay Hall, Jerry B. Harvey, and Martha S. Williams; Teleometrics Int'l.*

See T3:2351 (1 reference); for a review by Abraham K. Korman, see 8:1185 (8 references).

[645]

Management Effectiveness Profile System. Managers and co-workers; 1983; MEPS; originally called Management Practices Audit; perception of managerial behavior; 2 scores (self, other) in 15 management skill areas: setting goals and objectives, identifying and solving problems, planning effectively, organizing, making decisions, delegating, building teams, evaluating performance, developing subordinates, managing conflict, using time effectively, handling and preventing stress, demonstrating commitment, increasing trust, being results oriented; no data on reliability; no norms; administered to manager and 4 or 5 co-workers; 2 forms labeled Self Description, Description by Others, (8 pages); manual (69 pages); management skills profile (4 pages); scorer's worksheet (1 page); item-by-item feedback (17 pages); item-by-item tabulation worksheet (4 pages); separate answer sheets must be used; 1983 price data: $75 per set of testing materials; Human Synergistics.*

[646]

Management Inventory on Leadership and Motivation. Managers and manager trainees; 1974–79; MILM; measures knowledge of behavioral theorists (Maslow, Herzberg, McGregor, McClelland, and Likert); no data on reliability and validity; no norms; 1 form ('74, 4 pages); answer booklet ('74, 4 pages); manual ('79, 8 pages); 1983 price data: $20 per 20 test booklets and answer booklets; $1 per manual; $2 per review set; (20–30) minutes; Donald L. Kirkpatrick; the Author.*

[647]

Management Inventory on Managing Change. Managers; 1978–83; MIMC; "principles, facts, and attitudes that are basic to managing change effectively"; no data on reliability and validity; norms consist of means only; 1 form ('78, 4 pages); answer booklet ('82, 2 pages); manual ('83, 8 pages); 1983 price data: $20 per test and answer booklets; $1 per manual; (15–25) minutes; Donald L. Kirkpatrick; the Author.*

[648]

Management Inventory on Time Management. Managers; 1980; MITM; no data on reliability and validity; no norms; 1 form (3 pages); manual (8 pages); answer booklet (4 pages); 1983 price data: $20 per 20 tests and 20 answer booklets; $1 per manual; $2 per specimen set; (15–20) minutes; Donald L. Kirkpatrick; the Author.*

[649]

Manual Dexterity Test. Ages 16 and over; no date; MDT; 4 scores: speed, speed and skill, manual speed (average scale score of speed, speed and skill), manual skill (difference between speed, speed and skill scale scores); 1 form (5 pages); manual (15 pages); 1983 price data: £2.30 per 25 test booklets; manual free on request with order; £.50 per specimen set; 2.25(8) minutes; Educational & Industrial Test Services Ltd. [England].*

[650]

Marianne Frostig Developmental Test of Visual Perception, Third Edition. Ages 3–8; 1961–66; DTVP; 7 scores: eye-motor coordination, figure-ground discrimination, form constancy, position in space, spatial relations, total, perceptual quotient; 1 form ('63, 19 pages); demonstration cards ('63, 11 cards); administration and scoring manual ('66, 38 pages); monograph on 1963 standardization ('64, 37 pages); 1982 price data: $11.50 for examiner's kit including 10 test booklets, 1 manual, 1 monograph, 1 set of plastic score keys, and 1 set of demonstration cards; $11.50 per package of 25 test booklets; $1.75 per demonstration cards; $1.00 per set of 3 plastic score keys; $4.50 per manual and monograph; $6 per specimen set including test booklet, manual and monograph, demonstration cards, and set of paper score keys; (30–45) minutes for individual administration, (40–60) minutes for group administration; Marianne Frostig in collaboration with D. Welty Lefever, John R. B. Witlesey, and Phyllis Maslow (monograph); Consulting Psychologists Press, Inc.*

See T3:1371 (25 references), 8:882 (72 references), and T2:1921 (43 references); for reviews by Brad S. Chissom, Newell C. Kephart, and Lester Mann see 7:871 (117 references); for reviews by James M. Anderson and Mary C. Austin, see 6:553 (7 references).

TEST REFERENCES

1. Ysseldyke, J. E. Aptitude-treatment interaction research with first grade children. CONTEMPORARY EDUCATIONAL PSYCHOLOGY, 1977, 2, 1–9.

2. Steele, K., & Barling, J. Self-instruction and learning disabilities: Maintenance, generalization, and subject characteristics. JOURNAL OF GENERAL PSYCHOLOGY, 1982, 106, 141–154.

3. Tejani, A., Dobias, B., & Sambursky, J. Long-term prognosis after H. influenzae Meningitis: Prospective evaluation. DEVELOPMENTAL MEDICINE AND CHILD NEUROLOGY, 1982, 24, 338–343.

4. Butler, S. R., Marsh, H. W., Sheppard, M. J., & Sheppard, J. L. Predicting reading achievement from kindergarten to third grade—Implications for screening. THE AUSTRALIAN JOURNAL OF EDUCATION, 1983, 27, 288–303.

Review of Marianne Frostig Developmental Test of Visual Perception, Third Edition, by RICHARD E. DARNELL, Professor and Director, Physical Therapy Program, The University of Michigan-Flint, Flint, MI:

This test contains five different subtests related to visual perception: Subtest 1, Eye-Motor Coordination (16 items); Subtest 2, Figure-Ground (8 items); Subtest 3, Constancy of Shape (18 items); Subtest 4, Position in Space (8 items); Subtest 5, Spatial Relationships (8 items). It was designed to be useful as a screening tool with groups of nursery school, kindergarten and first-grade children, and as a clinical evaluative tool for older children who have severe learning difficulties. This test has been the subject of extensive research and has been thoroughly and insightfully reviewed in previous editions of the *Mental Measurements Yearbook* (7:871 and 6:553).

At first inspection of the manual, there is a sufficiently high correlation of test scores with age and sufficiently low intercorrelations between subtests to support the claim that the test is both a developmental and a differential appraiser of perceptual capacity. This conclusion is open to serious question from several perspectives.

The five subtests are not drawn from a conceptual model of perception. Therefore, there is no sense of whether or not these factors, taken separately or together, relate to perception. This lack of construct validity is exacerbated by overwhelming factor analytic research data indicating the lack of separate factors. No specific recommendations are provided for the interpretation of individual subtest scores, other than a global cut-off score below which a child should receive training. Furthermore, the reliability of individual subtest scores (especially 1, 3, 4) is inadequate for individual interpretation. Total score reliabilities are somewhat better but vary markedly from one age to another. The test is actually comprised of five tasks, one requiring simple motor skills, one requiring copying, and three requiring recognition, all measuring a single attribute which has a reasonable global relationship with age in normal development.

The test norms present some difficulty to the user. A total of 2,100 children were utilized from 3 to 9 years of age; however, the children included are overwhelmingly Caucasian and from households in the middle socioeconomic level. The use of these norms with minority group children is suspect. Further, expectations for children's performance may have changed since 1961–62 given the popularity of early childhood stimulation and enrichment programs. Norms are not distributed by sex. Although numerous studies exist which describe the test performance of children and adults with mental, physical and learning difficulties, data pertaining to these important populations are not included. The antiquated standardization of this test severely limits its usefulness. Future efforts in this area should address the need for a data base formulated in terms of "hits, misses, and false positives." Such data are essential in tests specifically designed for screening purposes.

The rationale given for the multiple test scores is that each score contributes to the understanding of test results; however, none of the scores when used alone is entirely satisfactory. Although cautions for the use of perceptual quotients are appropriately identified, one cannot help but wonder why the quotients were not discarded altogether. This is especially true given the availability of age related standardization curves in the manual for quick visual interpretation. The potential misinterpretation possible with quotients would appear to militate against their inclusion. However, the authors indicate that global perceptual quotient scores appear to have slightly higher predictability than perceptual age scores.

Both the 1965 standardization pamphlet and the 1966 scoring and administration manual are easy to read and understand. Minor clarifications and additional examples would enhance the scoring instructions.

Perhaps the major difficulty with this test is not related to its intrinsic qualities, but the manner in which it is employed. Despite the fact it can be administered in groups, this test should only be given by a skilled psychologist. Unacceptable reductions in reliability occur when performed by untrained examiners. The test should be administered only in conjunction with other tests. Physical, emotional, intellectual, and social factors can influence the capacity to perform on any test. However, of special concern for this test is attention to auditory, tactile, and kinesthetic factors which might influence outcomes. Visual acuity and field differences must be addressed prior to the administration of this test. Users should disregard the suggestion in the manual that there is a direct one-to-one relationship between the presence of a low score and the need to initiate training. Of special importance is the failure of the test developer to present sufficient evidence that the need for training in perception as indicated by test results, or its actual use as a perceptual training tool, results in significant changes in children's functioning. The author's statement that "reliability and validity studies support use of the test as the basis for remedial training programs in visual perception" is unsupportable in the research literature. Although the test has some predictive value in measuring academic achievement or readiness, it is not designed to identify specific classroom difficulties or skills.

This test is but one of many instruments which are based upon the concept that visual perception is critical to school learning. A significant amount of evidence exists which questions this assumption, especially in the area of reading. Hammill (1972) reviewed 43 studies concerning the relationship between visual perception and reading. Only 13 of these met minimal methodological criteria and of those 9 studies reported no significant relationship between measures of visual perception and reading. In a study investigating the capacity of various visual skills to predict future reading performance in urban schools, only first grade achievement was an adequate predictor of future performance (Wiederholt & Hammill, 1973). However, another longitudinal study did show that one Frostig subtest, Spatial Relations, had some predictive value (Wiederholt, 1971).

Applied judiciously, the Frostig Developmental Test of Visual Perception has value as a gross indicator of perceptual function. The test can be extremely helpful as part of a total testing sequence conducted by a trained examiner. To improve its effectiveness, this test should have its clinical application to atypical populations thoroughly standardized and it should be utilized in an appropriate manner and for appropriate purposes. Individual scores and test results should be viewed with great suspicion when used as a basis for differential intervention.

REVIEWER'S REFERENCES

Wiederholt, J. L. THE PREDICTIVE VALIDITY OF FROSTIG'S CONSTRUCTS AS MEASURED BY THE DEVELOPMENTAL TEST OF VISUAL PERCEPTION. Unpublished doctoral dissertation, Temple University, Philadelphia, 1971.

Hammill, D. Training visual perception processes. JOURNAL OF LEARNING DISABILITIES, 1972, 5, 552–559.

Wiederholt, J. L., & Hammill, D. Use of the Frostig-Horne perception program in the urban school. PSYCHOLOGY IN THE SCHOOLS, 1973, 8, 268–274.

Review of Marianne Frostig Developmental Test of Visual Perception, Third Edition, by DAVID A. SABATINO, Dean, School of Education and Human Services, University of Wisconsin-Stout, Menomonie, WI:

The Frostig Developmental Test of Visual Perception (DTVP) was developed and has remained in its present form since the publication of the standardized edition in 1963. The DTVP was developed to ascertain visual perceptual development in the diagnosis of learning disabilities. The preliminary work began in 1958, using a theoretical explanation of visual perception which accounted for specific abilities which were assumed by the test authors to be independent from one another. The subtests were differentiated by the authors into two groups; those requiring visual perceptual discrimination (the authors refer to that trait as recognition) and those which require copying. Subtests II, III, and IV require recognition, whereas Subtests I and V draw upon motor (visual-manual motor) performance. The five subtests are: Subtest I—eye-hand coordination, Subtest II—figure-ground perception, Subtest III—form constancy, Subtest IV—position in space, and Subtest V—spatial relationships.

The standardization process included pilot work in 1959 and 1960, which contributed to increasing the test ceiling and served as an item analysis. The present standardization sample was collected in 1961, and was based on sampling the visual-motor perceptual development of over 2,100 children ages 3 to 9 in California schools. The test was designed for use as an individually administered psychoeducational diagnostic device, and a group test useful for screening entire classes of children. That fact made it popular with pre-school and early school age populations.

A dilemma on the soundness of the DTVP occurred in response to the theoretical model upon which the test was constructed. The test authors assumed uniqueness of subtest measurement capability by the fact that age norms, or developmental growth, could be demonstrated for each of the five subtests. At issue was the degree to which the test measured independent traits.

TEST-RETEST RELIABILITY. The authors reported a test-retest reliability coefficient of .80 for the total test. The test-retest values for individual subtests dipped to .42. That fact immediately suggests that individual subtests are fairly unstable, so unstable that repeated measurement would produce widely divergent scores. The absence of suitable test stability greatly detracts from the author's claims for five unique and specific subtests, or independent trait measurements.

VALIDITY. The issue of what the subtests purport to measure and how valid the traits themselves are, has remained the major issue. In short, how unique are the five subtests, and do they measure abilities that exist in fact, or are test items merely given a name based on face validity? The authors drew heavily from their own work and also from a study by Corah and Powell (1963), in which the intercorrelations among five subtests were generally below .68 and more generally in the .18 to .60 range. That research seemingly established some construct validity, which was later questioned by several researchers.

The initial concurrent validity evidence was obtained by the authors and Getman (1961), reporting a high positive correlation between the test scores and academic success. However, only one test score seemed to have any particular strength in predicting language arts ($r = .46$) or math concept ($r = .41$) relationships. That subtest was Position in Space (Colarusso, Martin, & Hartung, 1975). The marked motor dependence evident in the test failed to relate to handwriting (Yost & Lesiak, 1980). Wood (1977) found it to be an excellent predictor of those students ready to enter and able to profit from reading related language arts instruction.

Allen (1968); Hammill, Colarusso, and Wiederholt (1970); Boyd and Randle (1970); Ohnnacht and Olson (1968) Sabatino (1973); and Sabatino, Abbott, and Becker (1974) contributed to the literature on the factorial structure of the Frostig test. The majority of these studies described a principal component which contained all five DTVP subtests. However, most of the factorial studies were weakened by less than appropriate sample sizes, and the parallel administration and treatment of related tests designed to measure the same traits. When given the opportunity for similar trait measures to cluster, the DTVP does show two principal components. One is a visual perceptual discrimination factor (Subtests II, III, and IV), with Position in Space being the most robust (highest loading) subtest. The second factor is composed of a visual motor component (Subtests I and V).

Frostig and her colleagues not only announced an era, but helped to develop it. The Frostig DTVP has been widely used and sharply criticized. Its critics insisted that its claims were widely exaggerated. The research concluded that Frostig's names for the traits which she attempted to measure were conjecture, not reality. Further, the test measured a single, or at best two global visual-motor cognitive processes. Certainly, the manual motor aspect and consequent motor dependence of the test has been a point of confusion as to precisely what the test measures. The test purported to measure the sought after perceptual process focusing on the visual input modality, but also included the motor response mechanism. Most assuredly the lower than desired reliability caused some of the data-related uncertainty observed in the research studies. For these reasons the test has not been a good screening device as a single source instrument.

The Frostig DTVP represents a psychometric era. It represents a period of time when test development defined learning characteristics, and statistics meant standardization of a measurement procedure, not a determinant for the worth of a test, or a practice. The era is gone and the test remains, a reminder that most specific cognitive processes remain unchartered because of the incompleteness of our theories and their complexity. In conclusion, the Frostig DTVP has not been updated to include the criticisms made by the vast body of research to date. To some extent it has fallen into decay. Does a better measure of visual perception exist? If it is desirable to measure the motor response and visual perceptual discrimination, the Beery and Buktenica Developmental Test of Visual-Motor Integration (T3:701) maintains fairly satisfactory test-retest reliability and should be considered.

REVIEWER'S REFERENCES

Corah, N. L., & Powell, B. J. A factor analytic study of the Frostig Developmental Test of Visual Perception. PERCEPTUAL AND MOTOR SKILLS, 1963, 16, 59–63.

Allen, R. F. Factor analysis of the Developmental Test of Visual Perception performance of educable mental retardates. PERCEPTUAL AND MOTOR SKILLS, 1968, 26, 257–258.

Ohnmacht, F. S., & Olson, A. CANONICAL ANALYSIS OF READING READINESS MEASURES AND THE FROSTIG DTVP. Paper presented at a meeting of AERA, Chicago, February, 1968.

Boyd, L., & Randle, K. Factor analysis of the Frostig Developmental Test of Visual Perception. JOURNAL OF LEARNING DISABILITIES, 1970, 3, 253–255.

Hammill, D. D., Colarusso, R. P., & Wiederholt, J. L. Diagnostic value of Frostig testing: A factor analytic approach. JOURNAL OF SPECIAL EDUCATION, 1970, 4, 279–283.

Sabatino, D., Abbott, J. C., & Becker, J. T. What does the Frostig Developmental Test of Visual Perception really measure? EXCEPTIONAL CHILDREN, 1974, 40, 453–454.

Colarusso, R. P., Martin, H., & Hartung, J. Specific visual perception skills as long-term predictors of academic success. JOURNAL OF LEARNING DISABILITIES, 1975, 8, 651–655.

Wood, N. E. Directed art, visual perception and learning disabilities. ACADEMIC THERAPY, 1977, 12, 455–462.

Yost, L. W., & Lesiak, J. The relationship between performance on the developmental test of visual perception and handwriting ability. EDUCATION, 1980, 101, 75–77.

[651]

A Marital Communication Inventory. Adults; 1968–79; MCI; norms consist of means and standard deviations; Form M (for males), F (for females), ('79, 4 pages); manual ('78, 9 pages); socioeconomic data sheet (no date, 2 pages) and scoring instructions (no date, 2 pages); 1982 price data: $4.50 per 10 tests (5M, 5F); $1 per manual; $2 per specimen set; (20) minutes; Millard J. Bienvenu, Sr.; Family Life Publications, Inc.*

See T3:1372 (3 references); for a review by Bernard I. Murstein, see 8:342 (6 references); see also T2:823 (1 reference) and 7:565 (1 reference).

TEST REFERENCES

1. Schumm, W. R. Theory and measurement in marital communication training programs. FAMILY RELATIONS, 1983, 32, 3–11.

Review of A Marital Communication Inventory by JOSEPH P. STOKES, Associate Professor of Psychology, University of Illinois at Chicago, Chicago, IL:

This inventory is designed to assess communication in marriage. Two forms, one for males and one for females, each contain 46 items that are answered on a 4-point scale ranging from "never" to "usually." Total scores can range from 0 to 138 (although the manual says 0 to 144), with higher scores reflecting better communication.

The manual suggests a number of ways to use the inventory: as a counseling aid, as a teaching exercise, and as a research tool. The inventory does seem useful in fostering discussion of problem areas of marital communication and thus might be helpful to a counselor or a trainer. The manual describes ways to use the inventory as a structured exercise in a marriage enrichment program.

The psychometric data presented for the inventory do not justify its use as a research tool. Although good split-half reliability is reported, the evidence for validity is weak. As Murstein pointed out in a previous *MMY* review, some of the data used to claim validity for the inventory are unrelated to validity. Specifically, the fact that 45 of the 46 items discriminate between the upper and lower quartiles on total score suggests some internal consistency but not validity. Further, the fact that two groups of subjects obtained similar means on the inventory does not argue for the validity of the measure.

Some evidence of validity is suggested by a reported study in which a group of 23 subjects who were receiving marital counseling scored lower on the inventory than a comparable group of 23 subjects without apparent marital problems. This difference could, however, reflect the fact that some of the items (e.g., "Is he (she) affectionate toward you?" and "Do you and your husband (wife) engage in outside interests and activities together?") seem to measure marital adjustment rather than marital communication per se.

Included with the inventory is a form to gather socioeconomic information from the respondents and a key for converting the information to socioeconomic class. Why these forms are included and how socioeconomic status is related to marital communication are not explained.

As an objective measure of marital communication this inventory has serious shortcomings. It does, however, appear to fulfill one of the stated objectives: to help the couple "communicate about their communication." In this way the inventory may be useful to counselors and trainers.

[652]

Marital Satisfaction Inventory. Married couples beginning counseling; 1979–81; MSI; self-report of marital interaction and extent of marital distress, 11 scales: Conventionalization, Global Distress, Affective Communication, Problem-Solving Communication, Time Together, Disagreement About Finances, Sexual Dissatisfaction, Role Orientation, Family History of Distress, Dissatisfaction With Children, Conflict Over Childrearing; norms consist of means and standard deviations; 1 form ('79, 7 pages); manual ('81, 65 pages); profile ('81, 1 page); separate answer sheets must be used; 1983 price data: $17.50 per kit including 2 reusable tests, 10 answer sheets and 5 profile forms; $8.40 per 10 reusable tests; $5.10 per 50 answer sheets; $5.10 per 50 profile forms; $7.85 per set of scoring keys; $7.75 per manual; administration time not reported; Douglas K. Snyder; Western Psychological Services.*

TEST REFERENCES

1. Snyder, D. K., & Regts, J. M. Factor scales for assessing marital disharmony and disaffection. JOURNAL OF CONSULTING AND CLINICAL PSYCHOLOGY, 1982, 50, 736–743.

2. Scheer, N. S., & Snyder, D. K. Empirical validation of the Marital Satisfaction Inventory in a nonclinical sample. JOURNAL OF CONSULTING AND CLINICAL PSYCHOLOGY, 1984, 52, 88–96.

Review of Marital Satisfaction Inventory by DAVID N. DIXON, Professor of Educational Psychology, University of Nebraska-Lincoln, Lincoln, NE:

The marital therapy field is occupied by people with diverse training and experiences. They differ greatly in their understanding of psychometric theory and the appropriate uses of assessment instruments with married couples or individuals.

The marital therapy field is also a developing field searching for methods of assessment and treatment for marital concerns. Numerous tests, inventories, and scales have been developed to fill the need for useful techniques. Unfortunately, many of the assessment instruments are poorly developed and should be avoided by the consumer. Development of assessment instruments in marital therapy can certainly be described as demonstrating a great deal of vigor without a corresponding level of rigor.

The Marital Satisfaction Inventory (MSI) is not one of the weak instruments. In fact it stands in bold contrast to most instruments purporting to measure marital satisfaction. Development of the MSI has proceeded in a sound, planful manner and its further development is apparent through continued published research.

There is an extensive manual for the MSI, with adequate reporting of scale development, reliability, and validity data. The 11 scales are well described and contain from 15 to 43 items per scale. Scale reliability is indicated by internal consistency coefficients ranging from .80 to .97, with a mean coefficient of .88. Test-retest reliability coefficients over an average interval of 6 weeks ranged from .84 to .94, with a mean correlation of .89. Administration time is reported as 30 minutes in a source other than the manual.

Validation studies generally indicate high correlations with other measures of marital satisfaction for those scales from the MSI that purport to measure general satisfaction. Individual scales are generally supported by comparison between criterion groups including general marital therapy samples, divorce court sample, wife abuse group, sexual dysfunction sample, and general population couples. The validational data for each scale are still somewhat limited, but the author and other researchers seem committed to strengthening the empirical basis for test interpretation. In fact, they cite the MMPI with its extensive validational research as a model for further development. Because of this limited base, however, empirical support for scale interpretations is lacking. The assessment and treatment implications for any particular *T*-score is at this point quite tentative. The author usually is careful to include appropriate cautions when suggesting potential uses or meaning of scales.

The content of the MSI and the suggested procedures for interpretation suggest a general model of marital dysfunction that is consistent with most major theories of marital therapy. Inclusion of a Conventionalization Scale to measure social desirability responding recognizes the prevalence of this phenomenon in therapeutic and enrichment situations. The Global Distress Scale measures general unhappiness and uncertain commitment to the marriage. The Affective Communication, Problem-Solving Communication, and Time Together Scales provide general indications of dysfunction as well as specific disruptions. Disagreement about Finances, Sexual Dissatisfaction, Role Orientation, Family History of Distress, Dissatisfaction with Children, and Conflict over Childrearing Scales all represent major areas of marital interaction and conceptually rich sources of information in treatment.

The manual for the MSI is clearly written, providing not only needed information but clear explanations of what the information means (e.g., explanation of types of reliability, approaches to test development). Factor analytic results are provided for both the entire inventory and each individual scale. A major strength is the provision of interpretive guidelines and case examples to demonstrate the interpretive approach.

A fault in the scale is the Profile Form. In an attempt to provide a graphic display of husband and wife scores for each scale, a color coding system is presented side by side for each scale. Confusion results over which score corresponds to the spouse's scores. Graphically there is little separation of scales and thus lines appearing to go up together may not always indicate agreement. In fact, an increase by the husband on a scale followed by an increase by the wife on the next scale may visually appear to indicate agreement. Because of this layout problem a general comparison of the agreement of profile by the "eyeball" method alone provides little information.

Another questionable decision was the inclusion of the Role Orientation Scale on the Profile Form. High scores on all other scales indicate greater dysfunction while high scores on Role Orientation indicate a nontraditional view of marital and parental roles. It would seem to be better not to present this scale graphically at all since it has a different interpretive meaning from other scales.

The MSI is presently a useful instrument for counseling with couples. The information provided is of benefit as an index of general marital dysfunction and of particular sources of marital discord. The MSI is sufficiently developed from a psychometric perspective to justify limited clinical use. Continued development will provide a richer empirical base for interpretation.

Review of Marital Satisfaction Inventory by E. M. WARING, Professor of Psychiatry, University of Western Ontario, London, Ontario, Canada:

From a psychometric perspective the Marital Satisfaction Inventory would appear to be the best available self-report instrument to broadly evaluate marital relationships. Internal consistency reliability, test-retest reliability, factor structure, and preliminary work on convergent and discriminant validity all appear extremely promising. The inclusion of a Conventionalization scale to suppress an important response style variance consistently reported in the marital self-report literature is an important step.

While the Marital Satisfaction Inventory may be the best available marital self-report questionnaire at this time, there remains considerable room for psychometric improvement. The content validity of the Role Orientation subscale is so low as to raise questions about its usefulness. This is also true of the content validity of the Family History of Distress and Dissatisfaction with Children subscales. Limitations include the fact that the test was not based or developed on some explicit psychological theory, but started with a series of questions from a variety of marital assessment interviews. Further research on convergent and discriminant validity with such tests as the dyadic adjustment scale of Spanier (1979) or the Waring Intimacy Questionnaire (Waring & Reddon, 1983) would be useful. The availability of standardized norms and the availability of item factor analyses are strong features of this scale. The length of the scale (280 items) is perhaps excessively long for research purposes or some clinical purposes. The factor analysis suggests that there is one major factor, which may be marital satisfaction; but again it would be useful to compare this general factor to the Locke-Wallace Marital Adjustment scale (1959) or other scales measuring the quality of marriage. The second two factors which might be interpreted as relating to "parenting" and "family or origin," may suffer from reliability problems as they are dependent on current perceptions of past relationships in the family and on changing behaviors and attitudes with reference to children. The author rightly points out that such variables as the family life cycle, education, race, and perhaps also income are covariants of marital satisfaction which need further research in larger normative samples.

In conclusion, although some limitations have been addressed above, the Marital Satisfaction Inventory would appear to be the best self-report inventory for global assessment of marital satisfaction currently available. The MSI should prove useful for counselors working with married couples beginning counselling and for whom evaluative data are needed on extent of conventionalization, overall level of marital distress, differences between spouses' perceptions of aspects of their relationship, general quality of communication and leisure time, and other marital functions. Further research will determine the test's utility as a research instrument and as a psychometric instrument capable of measuring change in therapy.

REVIEWER'S REFERENCES

Locke, H. J., & Wallace, K. M. Short marital-adjustment and prediction tests: Their reliability and validity. MARRIAGE AND FAMILY LIVING, 1959, 21, 251–255.

Spanier, G. B. The measure of marital quality. JOURNAL OF SEX AND MARITAL THERAPY, 1979, 5(3), 288–300.

Waring, E. M., & Reddon, J. R. The measure of intimacy in marriage: The Waring Intimacy Questionnaire. JOURNAL OF CLINICAL PSYCHOLOGY, 1983, 39(1), 53–57.

[653]

A Marriage Evaluation. Marital counselees; 1977; 6 scores: readiness before marriage, decision making, communication, values, personal growth in marriage, commitment and expectations; no data on reliability and validity; no norms; 1 form (4 pages); manual (8 pages); 1983 price data: $4.50 per 10 tests; $1 per manual; $2 per specimen set; (15–20) minutes; Henry C. Blount, Jr.; Family Life Publications, Inc.*

Review of A Marriage Evaluation by HOWARD J. MARKMAN, Associate Professor of Psychology, University of Denver, Denver CO:

This inventory consists of 60 items divided into six areas that are designed to assess a couple's readiness for marriage, decision making, communication, values, personal growth in marriage, and commitment and expectations. The inventory was designed to help counsellors gain a "rapid assessment of the strengths and weaknesses in a troubled marriage." While it is possible that the information gained from the marriage evaluation might be useful to a competent marital and family therapist, the inventory itself is a "nontest." The items were generated in a face-valid manner and no information is reported on the validity or reliability of the inventory. The lack of validity evidence, or even concern for validity, provides a strong argument against use of this scale. Researchers and clinicians interested in using marital assessment instruments that have at least some validity evidence are referred to E. Filsinger's (Ed.) *Handbook of Marital and Family Assessment*, Beverly Hills, CA: Sage Publications, 1983.

Review of A Marriage Evaluation by RICHARD B. STUART, Professor of Family and Community Medicine, The University of Utah, Salt Lake City, UT:

The stated purpose of this instrument is the clarification of similarities and differences in couples' problem perceptions as an aid in couple counseling. The instrument consists of six clusters of 10 questions each in the areas of: readiness before marriage, decision making, communication, values, personal growth in marriage, and commitment and expectation. Questions like "Are you committed to stay married?" are answered "Yes," "Not Sure," or "No." For the most part, items in each area have a general apparent relevance. However, inclusion of items like "Do you try to communicate understanding and empathy when your spouse is depressed?" is placed in the communication section and might be better located in the commitment section. Such item placements are not validated by any item or subscale analyses. The instrument is scored by totalling the number of items on which both partners answer identically, with differences of one or two scalar points apparently being treated as equal indicators of disagreement. Unfortunately, the manual contains some confusing guidelines for interpretation of these results, as there are indications that a low level of agreement is indicative of a clinical level of stress in each area; item content is thus confused with interspouse congruence in item response.

No measures of reliability or validity are offered. The author stresses that the instrument is useful in clinical planning, but users are offered no guidance on how it might be useful for this purpose or for assessment of marriage therapy outcome, cross-couple comparisons, or other related matters of general interest to scientifically-oriented marriage therapists.

In summary, this unstandardized measure offers a small step beyond unqualified clinical observation. Unfortunately, this step may lead to weaker assessment to the extent that the therapist relies upon a pencil-and-paper test of unknown analytic properties which may not be entirely congruent with the therapist's theoretical approach.

[654]

The Marriage Expectation Inventories. Engaged and married couples; 1972–79; MEI; no data on reliability and validity; no norms; 2 forms ('76, 8 pages); manual ('79, 15 pages); 1983 price data: $4.50 per 10 tests; $2.50 per manual; $3 per specimen set; GMI scoring service available (also called Marriage Climate Analysis); (120) minutes; Patrick J. McDonald, Ellen B. Pirro (inventories), Charles Cleveland (inventories), and Claudette McDonald (manual); Family Life Publications, Inc.*

a) FORM 1. Engaged couples; no scores, 9 areas: love, communication, freedom, sex, money, selfishness, religious expectations, relatives, expectations related to children.

b) FORM 2. Married couples; no scores, 8 areas: love, communication, freedom, sex, money, selfishness, religious expectations, relatives.

For a review of an earlier edition by James L. McCary, see 8:345.

Review of The Marriage Expectation Inventories by DAVID N. DIXON, Professor of Educational Psychology, University of Nebraska-Lincoln, Lincoln, NE:

The Marriage Expectation Inventory (MEI) is not a psychometric instrument, but a clinical tool for obtaining information from engaged and married couples. The forms require each person to provide open-ended responses to statements in either eight (married couples) or nine (engaged couples) areas of marriage. Two hours are taken to complete the form and a major amount of interview time was suggested to interpret the responses.

The MEI is not strongly tied to theoretical or empirical sources. Even the item stems purporting to elicit material about the areas of marriage seem little tied to any conceptual framework for a particular area. The lack of conceptual sophistication in the development of the instrument is perhaps revealed by a statement in the manual suggesting the practitioner's need for a model of communication. The authors state that "a very simple model can be used that is available from almost any textbook on the communication process."

The model for a practitioner discussed and illustrated in the manual is also quite simplistic. The model is little tied to any scientific knowledge base and assumes little, if any, professional training.

The interview transcripts that are included in the manual relate little to the MEI. They illustrate practitioner-couple interactions, but these interactions are not tied to responses or patterns of responses on the MEI. Thus, how the MEI was used to facilitate the interview process is largely unexplained.

The authors of the manual are inconsistent in their use of sexist language. At times they make certain that the counselor/practitioner/facilitator is referred to in a non-sexist manner, but several times the professional is only labeled as a male. This appears to be a result of careless non-attention to their writing rather than unawareness of the issue. Another example of carelessness is in the printing of Form II when item 53 is followed by items 57 and 58 from Form I.

The last page of the manual refers to a computer facilitated analysis of responses to the MEI. This is called the Marriage Climate Analysis (MCA) and costs $35.00 per couple. No psychometric data were provided on this scoring system. This scoring system moves the MEI from the realm of a clinical tool to that of a test. The MEI at this point in time has no supporting data as a testing instrument. The consumer is cautioned to be extremely dubious of the MCA until evidence is provided regarding development and psychometric properties.

In conclusion, the MEI can be used to facilitate discussion. The content of the instrument seems only weakly tied to major theories of marital interaction. The manual gives no information about how the items were developed nor how to interpret responses. Administration and interpretation of this instrument involves a major amount of time and effort. Other more theoretical and psychometrically sound approaches are recommended.

Review of The Marriage Expectation Inventories by E. M. WARING, Professor of Psychiatry, University of Western Ontario, London, Ontario, Canada:

This inventory contains 58 statements about engagement and marriage. Couples are expected to spend 2 hours writing down their thoughts and feelings in order to elaborate on these statements (e.g., "In our marriage, communication is so important that..."). The statements concern aspects of eight areas of marriage including love, communication, freedom, and sex; and nine areas related to engaged couples including expectations related to relatives and children. After spending 2 hours elaborating on these statements, the couple will read and discuss their elaborations with a facilitator or counselor.

It would seem that the test allows for each member of the couple to self-disclose attitudes, values, and opinions regarding various aspects of marital functioning and engagement. These disclosures may or may not have been discussed previously and may or may not present areas of differences of opinion or conflict. The presence of the counselor facilitates self-disclosure.

Since there is no standardization of responses, no norms, and no assessment of reliability and validity, this inventory cannot be considered a psychometric instrument. Like the Sentence Completion Test, it is a clinical tool to facilitate self-disclosure of attitudes, thoughts, values, and feelings but in a limited area relating to marriage and engagement.

Thus, in the circumstance of couples with enough motivation, honesty, and psychological mindedness to take the 2 hours out to complete this inventory, a model of facilitating self-disclosure about attitudes ensues with the counselor. This may be both useful in clinical assessment and may also be a form of counseling or therapy similar to Sidney Jourard's work on self-disclosure (Jourard, 1971).

In summary, the Marriage Expectation Inventories are not psychometric tests, but appear to be clinical assessment and therapy aids which may help in facilitating self-disclosure of attitudes towards engagement and marriage in couples who have both the time and commitment to elaborate their thoughts and attitudes and discuss them with the facilitator. However, whether couples in counseling are better served by focusing on their perceived areas of attitudinal differences or taking the time to cover 58 separate items in a broad and perhaps over-inclusive way would be up to the individual inclination of the counselor and educator.

REVIEWER'S REFERENCES

Jourard, S. M. SELF DISCLOSURE: AN EXPERIMENTAL ANALYSIS OF THE TRANSPARENT SELF. New York: Wiley-Interscience, 1971.

[655]

A Marriage Role Expectation Inventory. Adolescents and adults; 1960–1979; MREI; 9 scores: authority, homemaking, children, personality, social participation, sexual relations, education, employment and support, total; reliability data and norms are for the original form only (author recommends use of local norms); Forms M (for males), F (for females), ('79, 4 pages, identical except for wording changes); revised manual ('79, 10 pages); profile (no date, 1 page); 1984 price data: $4 per 10 tests (5M, 5F, profiles and key); $1 per manual; $2 per specimen set; (15–30) minutes; Marie S. Dunn in collaboration with J. N. DeBonis; Family Life Publications, Inc.*

See T3:1383 (1 reference); for a review by Robert C. Challman of an earlier edition, see 6:685 (6 references).

Review of A Marriage Role Expectation Inventory by HOWARD J. MARKMAN, Associate Professor of Psychology, University of Denver, Denver, CO:

This inventory consists of 71 items that are purported to measure traditional and companionship expectations of marital relationships. The items have been organized by the author into eight subscales including: authority, homemaking, children, personality, social participation, sexual relations, education, and employment and support. There are separate forms for males and females and the inventory can be administered in large groups. The inventory, as the name suggests, is designed to assess expectations of marriage held by premarital and married couples. There is a short manual that explains the uses of the Inventory, how to score it, and presents what little data there is on its reliability and validity. Supposedly, based on the results of the scale, the individual's expectations concerning marriage can be divided into traditional, moderately traditional, moderately companionship, and companionship orientations.

This inventory was designed for use in high school and college classes and in premarital counselling situations. As noted in the manual, its best use is as a "teaching aid." It is possible that as a teaching aid this inventory may be useful; however, as a test it is at best face valid, and at worst it may lead to incorrect conclusions about the respondent. No data are presented concerning any form of validity of the inventory; rather the manual lists a set of generally unpublished masters and dissertation studies in which the inventory was used. While it is possible that research may determine that this scale has some degree of validity, at the current time it remains of questionable value to the field of marital and family relationships. There are data on reliability reported for an older edition and results indicate that the reliability is within an acceptable range.

The test manual itself is replete with misspellings and other typos, and if the test was constructed with the same lack of attention to detail that the manual was, this provides even less reason to use this test in any research or counselling situation. In fact, its use as a teaching aid is not recommended, because generally students do not give informed consent to learn information about themselves in educational settings. In this case the information presented may be misleading and incorrect, thus amplifying the caution against use of this inventory as a test in educational settings.

To summarize, my overall evaluation of this inventory is negative. No evidence is presented for its validity as this concept is defined by the *Standards for Educational and Psychological Tests*. A better choice for researchers and clinicians interested in assessing marital expectations is Epstein and Eidelson's Relationship Belief Inventory (Epstein & Eidelson, 1981).

REVIEWER'S REFERENCES

Epstein, N., & Eidelson, R. Unrealistic beliefs of clinical couples: Their relationship to expectations, goals and satisfaction. AMERICAN JOURNAL OF FAMILY THERAPY, 1981, 9, 13–22.

[656]

Martinek-Zaichkowsky Self-Concept Scale for Children. Grades 1–8; 1977; MZSCS; a non-verbal, culture-free instrument measuring global self-concept; no data on reliability for grades 5–8; 1 form (28 pages); manual (26 pages); 1983 price data: $25 per 25 tests; $5 per manual; $7.50 per specimen set; (10–15) minutes; Thomas J. Martinek and Leonard D. Zaichkowsky; Psychologists and Educators, Inc.*

See T3:1386 (3 references).

TEST REFERENCES

1. Martinek, T. J., Cheffers, J. T. F., & Zaichkowsky, L. D. Physical activity, motor development and self-concept: Race and age differences. PERCEPTUAL AND MOTOR SKILLS, 1978, 46, 147–154.
2. Karper, W. B., & Martinek, T. J. Differential influence of various instructional factors on self-concepts of handicapped and non-handicapped children in mainstreamed physical education classes. PERCEPTUAL AND MOTOR SKILLS, 1982, 54, 831–835.
3. Martinek, T. J., & Karper, W. B. Entry-level motor performance and self-concepts of handicapped and non-handicapped children in mainstreamed physical education classes: A preliminary study. PERCEPTUAL AND MOTOR SKILLS, 1982, 55, 1002.
4. Smith, T. L. Self-concepts and movement skills of third grade children after physical education programs. PERCEPTUAL AND MOTOR SKILLS, 1982, 54, 1145–1146.

Review of Martinek-Zaichkowsky Self-Concept Scale for Children by GEORGE M. GUTHRIE, Professor of Psychology, The Pennsylvania State University, University Park, PA:

The Martinek-Zaichkowsky Self-Concept Scale for Children (MZSCS) consists of 25 pairs of cartoons of children, one of whom in each picture is marked by shading. The child's task is to choose and mark "the picture which is most like you." Four pairs of the pictures, for example, show children successful/unsuccessful in push-ups, children being rejected/accepted by peers, solving/not solving school problems, and afraid/not afraid of a dog. Drawing on the research of Piers, the authors developed three sets of cartoons for each of 25 situations. A group of 48 children, including non-English speaking children, were asked to describe each pair, and the 43 pairs that were most accurately described were retained. From this pool 25 were selected that had the highest correlations with scores on the Piers scale and the Coopersmith Self-Esteem Inventory. A factor analysis of the data on the 25 pairs yielded 5 factors, some of which were similar to those found by Piers. There is, however, only one score: the total number of positive self-ratings chosen. The norms, common for all ages and both sexes, show 75% of subjects scoring 18 or more out of 25, and 50% scoring 21 or more.

The authors speak of a global self-concept even though others have found many independent factors in self-concept measures. Their total score correlates .49 and .56 with the Piers scale and the Coopersmith inventory, respectively, but only .06 with teachers ratings. No other validity data are reported.

This is an interesting attempt to develop a somewhat disguised measure of the self-concept. It follows in the tradition of the Rosenzweig P-F Study and the Blacky Test. But it cannot be considered a measure of unconscious factors just because it does not require explicit self-reports by the subject.

With respect to uses the authors say, "Hopefully, it will eventually serve as an effective measuring tool for research purposes." Before these hopes can be realized much more foundational work needs to be done to develop a theory of the self-concept and develop valid indices of the concept as formulated. There is little evidence offered that the scale, as currently described, is measuring anything.

Review of Martinek-Zaichkowsky Self-Concept Scale for Children by DAVID R. WILSON, Coordinator of Psychology Services and Research & Evaluation, Brewer-Porch Children's Center, The University of Alabama, University, AL:

The Martinek-Zaichkowsky Self-Concept Scale for Children (MZSCS) is designed to be a "non-verbal, culture-free" measure of global self-concept, appropriate for use with first through eighth graders. It serves as an easily administered measure which requires neither reading ability nor understanding of the English language. There are 25 items, each consisting of two cartoon-like pictures which are bipolar representations of the item (e.g., one picture showing a child who is happy and one showing that same child sad). The administration format is indeed simple; the child is requested to check the picture which is most like him/herself. The instrument can be completed in 10–15 minutes (this reviewer found that 5 minutes is adequate if it is administered individually). The scale is scored by counting the number of positive pictures selected, a process which takes only a few seconds. This measure requires no reading ability, but the description of it as "culture-free" suggests a lack of awareness of the degree to which responses to items such as these are culture-bound.

The MZSCS was derived from the Piers-Harris Children's Self-Concept Scale (PHCSCS), which is one of the most widely used and best validated self-concept instruments. Those items with high factor loadings on the PHCSCS were selected as initial items on the MZSCS. The 25 items were selected from six factors on the PHCSCS, in addition to some items from Jersild's (1969) collection of statements related to children's concerns about themselves, but detail is lacking regarding exactly how these items were selected. Then three different sets of cartoon pictures were drawn to represent each of the 25 items. In order to determine if the meaning of the cartoons did concur with the intended meaning, a sample of 48 first through fifth graders was asked to describe the meaning of the pictures, and those items for which 92% or fewer of these judges concurred with the intended meaning were dropped. This left 43 items. An a priori decision was made to have no more than 25 items. The 43-item scale was then administered to 148 elementary school children, and the final scale items were selected based on their correlation with the PHCSCS and with the Coopersmith Self-Esteem Inventory (CSEI). Eighteen items were correlated with these measures, with a range from .35 to .50. Seven additional items were selected based on high subtest correlations, with no more detail about this selection process provided.

The scale has been demonstrated to have adequate internal consistency, with an overall Hoyt estimate of reliability of .88. The overall standard error of measurement was computed at 1.65. There was no investigation of the stability of this measure via test-retest administrations.

The authors state that content validity was built into the scale by selecting items related to the PHCSCS, and that pertained to Jersild's (1969) items. This process is adequate but this reviewer would have preferred more detail about the decision processes. In order to establish concurrent validity, the 25 items of the MZSCS were correlated with the PHCSCS (.49 with $N = 120$), the CSEI (.56 with $N = 86$), as well as with teacher ratings (.06 with N

= 120). These correlations suggest that the MZSCS is measuring a construct similar to that measured by the PHCSCS and the CSEI, but the magnitude of the correlation with the PHCSCS suggests that this scale should not be considered a Piers-Harris "short form." One major improvement (and this applies to all self-concept and related measures) would be some attempt to establish discriminant validity. Anyone who is developing or using a self-concept scale should have some theoretical notions regarding groups that should score either high or low on a self-concept measure. If this cannot be done, the utility of the measures themselves is subject to question. The process of a priori defining certain groups as likely to score either very high or very low, then administering the measure to see if the prediction is carried out, is necessary if construct validity is to be established. The difficulty here may be in the construct, not the measures.

Also helpful in further establishing the validity of this measure would have been the inclusion of some attempt to control for the social desirability factor. Research with the PHCSCS has found correlations with a social desirability scale to be in the range of .25 to .45. Piers states in the manual for the PHCSCS that this desire to look good is rather strong, particularly in young children, and may represent confusion between how they really act, and how they are supposed to act.

It would also have been helpful to have included information regarding correlations between the MZSCS and some measure of intelligence or academic achievement. Correlations between such measures and the PHCSCS have ranged from zero to .48. In using the MZSCS with emotionally disturbed children, this reviewer often wondered if the children were not simply engaging in the intellectual task of selecting which of the two options was appropriate.

The most serious deficiencies of this instrument relate to its utility and interpretation. The manual states that the major use of the MZSCS is screening to identify "children in need of special consideration" but decision rules about how such children should be selected are lacking. Some norms are provided, with a mean of 20.1 and a standard deviation of 4.04 for data from four geographic area groups (N = 1,171). The major problem in interpreting results is that the distribution is quite negatively skewed and very high or perfect scores are quite common. In order to aid interpretation, stanines and percentiles are provided, but because of the skewed distribution, a child could move from a percentile score of 45.9 to one of 66.4 by moving from a raw score of 20 to 22. The developers state in the manual that "The real value of the scale is that it measures those children who have a low self-concept, yet seem to function favorably in the presence of the teacher"; yet they also cavalierly dismiss the problem of faking good by stating that "This is irrelevant since teachers tend to readily identify those children with obvious psychological deficiencies." This scale will not discriminate among students with adequate or very positive self-concepts, since such a high percentage will have perfect or nearly perfect scores, and the authors are to be commended for stating this in the manual. But adequate evidence was not presented to indicate that this measure is more sensitive to individual differences at the lower end of the scale. In the reviewer's clinical use of this scale with 10 emotionally disturbed children in a residential treatment program, virtually all children received perfect scores, even though the scale was being used with children who are considered to have "low self-concept" by clinical staff. Admittedly, this is a small sample, but the norms presented in the manual indicate the same problem. This reviewer also administered the Piers-Harris to this sample of children, and found it to be much more sensitive to individual differences.

In conclusion, the MZSCS is an easily administered scale which requires no reading ability. Based on the findings regarding concurrent validity, it appears to be measuring roughly the same content area as other established instruments such as the PHCSCS. What the authors have failed to do is to provide a clear rationale for the use of this instrument, and beyond that, how results should be interpreted. They do caution against relying on only one score in attempting to identify children as having low self-concepts. In trying to develop a short and easily administered scale, they have also reduced its potential utility. If one is to choose only one measure of self-concept, whether for clinical or group uses, it would be preferable to rely on a measure such as the PHCSCS for which there is supporting data to indicate that it is more sensitive to individual differences. On the positive side, the scale does seem to be very non-threatening to children, due to its cartoon format. This suggests some clinical uses on an individual basis as a vehicle for discussion of how children perceive themselves.

REVIEWER'S REFERENCES

Jersild, A. T. IN SEARCH OF SELF. New York: Columbia University, Teachers College Press, 1969.

[657]

Martinez Assessment of the Basic Skills: Criterion-Referenced Diagnostic Testing of Basic Skills. Learning disabled and mildly to moderately mentally retarded children; 1983; no norms; individual in part; 6 tests; student profile (3 pages); administration manual (67 pages); 1984 price data: $69.95 per complete kit including 5 student profiles and 5 response and record booklets of each test; $7.95 per 5 response and record booklets; $2.30 per 5 student profiles; $19.95 per administration manual; David Martinez; ASIEP Education Co.*

a) PRIMARY LANGUAGE CONCEPTS TEST. Student response and record booklet (7 pages); (10) minutes.
b) COUNTING AND NUMERALS TEST. Student response and record booklet (7 pages); (20) minutes.
c) TIME TELLING TEST. Student response and record booklet (7 pages); (10) minutes.
d) SPELLING TEST. Student response and record booklet (8 pages); (45) minutes.
e) ARITHMETIC TEST. Student response and record booklet (23 pages); (20–45) minutes.
f) READING TEST. Student response and record booklet (27 pages); (20–45) minutes.

[658]

The Maryland/Baltimore County Design for Adult Basic Education. Adult nonreaders; 1982; commonly called the BCD Test; "diagnoses a student's strengths, weaknesses, and deficiencies in skill areas that are prerequisite to literacy"; 21 subtest scores in 5 areas: background knowledge, alphabet recognition and reproduction, auditory perception and discrimination, visual perception and discrimination, sight vocabulary; 1 form (34 pages including diagnostic profile summary); administrator's manual (123 pages including answer keys and summary profile); 1984 price data: $2.50 per test; $9.95 per manual; (120–180) minutes; Baltimore County Public Schools Office of Adult Education; Cambridge, The Adult Education Co.*

Review of The Maryland/Baltimore County Design for Adult Basic Education by MARY M. DUPUIS, Associate Professor of Education, The Pennsylvania State University, University Park, PA:

The Maryland/Baltimore County Design for Adult Basic Education, commonly known as the BCD Test, was designed to fill a gap in adult literacy assessment; it is described as "a strong diagnostic-prescriptive test instrument that could be used to pinpoint the problems that hindered the ABE student in his attempt to achieve literacy." The authors argue that tests giving a "reading grade level" below fourth grade, or those giving information on only a few skills, do not give sufficient diagnostic information for instructors to develop teaching plans.

The BCD Test, indeed, includes a number of subtests not found in typical ABE diagnostic instruments. However, many are similar to "readiness" tests given to pre-reading children. These subtests are adult level in interest and content, but deal with basic knowledge of the world and basic thinking processes. For example, among the 21 subtests are those that measure reading a calendar for appropriate days of the week and months and holidays; identifying common coin values given in pictures of a quarter and two dimes, two dimes and a nickel, and the like; and visual perception of symbols.

The areas of readiness found in most reading tests are covered in this one—letter recognition and writing the alphabet, for example. Words are presented for sight word recognition both in isolation and in context. In each case, the flash card has the word in isolation on one side and the word with a picture context on the other. The test builds to a final subtest in which the student reads two short paragraphs, filling in the blanks with appropriate information such as name, age, and employer. This cloze-type reading passage is both personal and specific to the reader.

This reviewer concludes that the subtests provide appropriate and important information for the ABE instructor and student. The test, in fact, includes areas of concern which have great value for ABE instructors, but are not included on other published tests.

The test is easy to administer for any classroom instructor with minimal training. All items and instructions are read aloud to the test-taker and the answers are on the pages of the test booklet. All pictures and symbols are on the same page (or the facing page) as the answer page. Thus, each subtest could be given separately. The test directions suggest that the total test be subdivided into several shorter sections. Five sets of subtests, referred to as Batteries A–E are suggested. Each battery can be given in small groups or individually except Battery E. This battery, Sight Vocabulary, requires one-to-one testing, using the flash cards provided to test sight words in isolation and in context plus the final egocentric paragraph-reading test. Number of items per subtest varies from a minimum of 5 to a maximum of 33. No time limit is imposed on any subtest.

The directions for administering and taking the test are clearly stated and easy to follow. For each subtest, the specific purpose (objective) is given, along with specific test-giving instructions. Instructions to be read to the test takers are also written clearly.

Tests are scored by using the answer key provided. Three levels of results are possible for each subtest: Strength (mastery of the skill), Weakness (student needs some remedial work), and Deficiency (student needs serious remedial work).

The number of errors in each level of performance is given for each subtest. A student profile sheet, given in the student booklet, is easy to fill in for each student. Reporting to the student and recording scores for student records are both easy to do.

In the Administrator's Manual, the error chart after each subtest is followed by a problem/prescription chart which suggests that for students scoring at the weakness or deficiency levels, a particular prescription is appropriate. Unfortunately, the only source of remediation suggested is a single text, published by the test publisher. The suggestion that a given deficiency area can be remediated only by that publisher's book is not warranted. In fact, increasing numbers of materials for ABE-level readers are available. The test publisher's claim to a significant new ABE test would be strengthened if several alternative sources for materials to remediate particular areas were included. As it is, the tests could be seen as pretests for a particular text series, rather than as an independent test for general use of ABE students.

So far, this review has been relatively positive. The BCD Test is criterion-referenced and measures areas not measured by other tests. It seems to fit the adult test taker in content and interest level, ease of administration, scoring, and time invested. However, when we turn to the technical data supporting the test, the results are negative. There is no technical data supporting the test. The test authors acknowledge the help of a nationwide test of content reviewers and field-test participants. However, at the present date no information related to that review or the field test is available. No reliability data is given, nor is there a discussion of validity in the Administrator's Manual. In sum, we have only the reviewer's or test buyer's knowledge of the area of competing tests to use in assessing content validity. Clearly, this is insufficient to justify the use of this test, except in an experimental way. This is a sad commentary on this test and adult education in general. Given the date of the test's formal publication, one would expect that this critical technical information would be available. Until it is, no serious recommendation for the general use of the BCD test can be made.

In summary, the BCD test presents five separate test batteries, including 21 subtests, which test a wide range of pre-reading skills for adult nonreaders. The administration and scoring of the test are appropriately simple. The subtests include several important areas not routinely measured by other tests. Therefore, the resulting diagnostic profile is highly useful to an ABE instructor. The lack of technical data supporting the test's construction and validation make it impossible to recommend this test for standard classroom use at this time.

Review of The Maryland/Baltimore County Design for Adult Basic Education by SHARON L. SMITH, Associate Professor of Education and Director of the Learning Skills Center, Indiana University, Bloomington, IN:

The Maryland/Baltimore County Design for Adult Basic Education (BCD) test is described in the Administrator's Manual as a "thorough inventory of a student's strengths, weaknesses and deficiencies in pre-reading skills that need to be mastered before the student begins a formal reading program." At the outset it should be noted that the significant terms in this description are defined by the test authors in terms of their own test: "strength," "weakness," and "deficiency" are categories determined by the number of errors made on each of the 21 subtests, and the subtests, in turn, define the skills a student supposedly should master. It is this circularity that makes the test not what it claims to be, a strongly diagnostic test, but rather an alternative to a teacher-made informal inventory of interpretive skills that might be associated with reading acquisition.

The subtests are organized into five batteries which can be administered in any number of sessions, though the recommended number is five—one for each battery. Total testing time is estimated at 2 to 3 hours. A survey of the contents of the tests indicates how the test authors have identified prereading skills:

Battery A, "Background Knowledge," includes tests to assess ability to (1) give personal information on a form, (2) use a calendar, (3) tell time, and (4) count coins.

Battery B, "Alphabet Recognition and Reproduction," includes tests for (1) recognizing printed letters and (2) cursive letters, (3) reproducing printed letters and (4) cursive letters, and (5) writing the alphabet in proper order.

Battery C, "Auditory Perception and Discrimination," includes tests of ability to (1) hear differences in pairs of words, (2) match letters to beginning sounds in words, and (3) count syllables in spoken words.

Battery D, "Visual Perception and Discrimination," includes tests for (1) understanding directional words such as "above," "right," "nearest"; (2) matching words in an array; and (3) finding nonmatching words in an array.

Battery E, "Sight Vocabulary," includes tests of ability to interpret (1) traffic signs, (2) words in isolation, (3) words in a pictorial context, and (4) words in an "egocentric" context (i.e., in paragraphs containing personal information about the student).

For each subtest an answer sheet, "error chart," and "prescriptive chart" are provided. The error chart determines level of performance (strength, weakness, or deficiency) according to the number of errors made. The prescriptive chart tells what to do if weakness or deficiency is detected, directing the teacher to particular activities according to particular errors. Many of these directives are to a workbook series also published by Cambridge, Entering The Reader's World. Others suggest such activities as bringing in a calendar, making flash cards, or listing the student's misspelled words.

The test is constructed to be administered by a classroom teacher rather than a test expert. This objective has produced detailed instructions for administration that virtually program the examiner. The procedure seems intended for teachers who either are very inexperienced or lack confidence. It does offer the advantage of a common testing experience across students which may foster the development of one's own sense of where students are with regard to the tasks prescribed.

There is no psychometric information in the Administrator's Manual, so no assessment of reliability can be made. Validity is documented simply by lists of "content reviewers" and "field-test participants" along with their institutional affiliations. In addition, it is stated that the test was developed by "adult education instructors and a reading specialist" under a Federal grant because there was no existing test that served their needs. What they needed was a "strong diagnostic/prescriptive test," and this, presumably, is the goal they have achieved with the BCD.

Prescriptive the test may be, but it is not truly diagnostic. The BCD may be a useful inventory of the student's ability to perform the tasks included, though one might question the necessity of taking 2 to 3 hours to administer it. But the only significance given for these tasks is their correspondence to lessons in the workbook series. Even its prescriptive role is limited to the closed system formed by the test and the workbook series. The test is primarily a means for placing the student in the materials, which begs the question of the validity of the whole package. If the objective is not to place the student within this instructional program, one might well prefer the more straightforward approach of using a clock, real money, pencil and paper, and other items in the environment for informal assessment.

One is left, finally, with the choice of accepting or questioning the test authors' assumptions that the subtests do indeed represent requisite prereading skills and that differentiating levels of performance for these skills are measured by the test. These are rather large assumptions to accept, and one must conclude that this test is more convenient than convincing.

[659]

Maslach Burnout Inventory. Staff members in human service and educational institutions; 1981; MBI; research edition; test title is Human Services Survey; 2 scores (frequency, intensity) for each of 3 subscales: Emotional Exhaustion, Depersonalization, Personal Accomplishment; norms consist of means and standard deviations; 1 form (2 pages); manual (22 pages); demographic data sheet (2 pages); 1983 price data: $4.25 per 25 test booklets; $4 per 25 demographic data sheets; $1.25 per scoring key; $6 per manual; $7.25 per specimen set; (20–30) minutes; Christina Maslach and Susan E. Jackson; Consulting Psychologists Press, Inc.*

TEST REFERENCES

1. Belcastro, P. A. Burnout and its relationship to teachers' somatic complaints and illnesses. PSYCHOLOGICAL REPORTS, 1982, 50, 1045–1046.

2. Schwab, R. L., & Iwanicki, E. F. Perceived role conflict, role ambiguity, and teacher burnout. EDUCATIONAL ADMINISTRATION QUARTERLY, 1982, 18, 60–74.

3. Belcastro, P. A., & Gold, R. S. Teacher stress and burnout: Implications for school health personnel. JOURNAL OF SCHOOL HEALTH, 1983, 53, 404–407.

4. Nowack, K. M., & Hanson, A. L. The relationship between stress, job performance, and burnout in college student resident assistants. JOURNAL OF COLLEGE STUDENT PERSONNEL, 1983, 24, 545–550.

5. Riggar, T. F., Godley, S. H., & Hafer, M. Burnout and job satisfaction in rehabilitation administrators and direct service providers. REHABILITATION COUNSELING BULLETIN, 1983, 27, 151–160.

6. Stevens, G. B., & O'Neill, P. Expectation and burnout in the developmental disabilities field. AMERICAN JOURNAL OF COMMUNITY PSYCHOLOGY, 1983, 11, 615–627.

7. Malanowski, J. R., & Wood, P. H. Burnout and self-actualization in public school teachers. THE JOURNAL OF PSYCHOLOGY, 1984, 117, 23–26.

8. West, D. J., Jr., Horan, J. J., & Games, P. A. Component analysis of occupational stress innoculation applied to registered nurses in an acute care hospital setting. JOURNAL OF COUNSELING PSYCHOLOGY, 1984, 31, 209–218.

Review of Maslach Burnout Inventory by JACK L. BODDEN, Staff Psychologist, Olin E. Teague V.A. and Associate Professor of Psychiatry & Behavioral Science, Texas A&M University College of Medicine, Temple, TX:

"Burnout" is one of those fashionable psychological topics that seems to be written about, talked about, and warned about almost daily in books, newspapers, and television programs, as well as in popular and professional periodicals. There seem to be many instant experts on the subject and they each have developed a scale which will inform the person completing it whether or not he/she is burned out. The Maslach Burnout Inventory (subtitled "Human Services Survey") seems to be an exception to this pop phenomena. It is an exception in that its authors have been involved in a systematic program of research on "burnout" for several years, and they have gone to some lengths to develop an instrument with which to measure the construct.

Burnout, according to the MBI authors, is a syndrome of emotional exhaustion/depletion and cynicism which often afflicts human service deliverers (e.g., teachers, therapists, and nurses). The authors further state that burnout has three principal components: (1) emotional exhaustion, (2) development of negative attitudes toward service recipients, and (3) development of a tendency to evaluate oneself negatively with regard to one's work.

The MBI is designed to assess the three components of the burnout syndrome described above, and as such it contains three scales: Emotional Exhaustion, Depersonalization, and Personal Accomplishment. Each scale is further subdivided into an expression of Frequency and Intensity, creating a total of six scale scores.

Development of the MBI follows a fairly standard pattern, beginning with a pool of items written to reflect the construct and ending up with scales based upon a factor analysis of the item pool. A fourth factor was identified but it is not included in the MBI as it contained only three items. The MBI consists of 22 items (9 items on the Emotional Exhaustion Scale, 5 items on Depersonalization, and 8 items on Personal Accomplishment Scale).

The authors claim that it takes approximately 20–30 minutes to complete the instrument. Each item statement must be responded to twice: once in terms of how often it occurs (Frequency) and once again in terms of how strongly it is experienced (Intensity). This format seems generally satisfactory but results in some awkward combinations (e.g., having to respond "How strong?" to "I can easily understand how my recipients feel about things" seemed a bit forced to this reviewer).

The test manual seemed fairly adequate, providing useful information about the concept of burnout and the development of the MBI. Reliability data is included in the manual and the coefficients reported are modest, ranging from .53 to .82 for test-retest stability (2- to 4-week interval). Alpha coefficients are somewhat higher, ranging from .71 to .90. The standard error of measurement for each subscale is also reported, and some appear high for scales having relatively low potential score ranges (e.g., *SEM* of 3.96 for Depersonalization [Intensity], a scale which has a potential range from 0 to 35).

Validity data presented in the manual is of the construct and concurrent variety, and it generally looks promising. For instance, the authors cite data which shows the expected relationships between a variety of peer/spouse ratings and scale scores. The coefficients are generally small but statistically significant. The data also show that MBI scores have modest but significant relationships with a measure of job satisfaction and little or no relationship with social desirability (as measured by the Crowne-Marlowe Scale).

Tables in the appendix of the manual report a variety of additional information such as item factor loadings and scale intercorrelations, as well as some demographic norms. In addition, the manual also has an interesting section designed to promote research using the scale. This brings up an important point. The authors clearly state in the manual that the MBI should be used for research rather than diagnostic purposes because there is insufficient justification to warrant its use for diagnosis. This reviewer certainly agrees with the authors' statement about the use of the MBI but feels that too many potential users might be tempted to ignore this caution and use the inventory for clinical purposes.

To press the issue a bit further, not only must much more research be done with the MBI (and other such scales) before we can make any treatment or employment-related decisions about individuals who are presumed to be suffering from burnout, but also there remain some unanswered questions about the construct itself. Specifically, it is debatable whether "burnout" is either unique to human service workers or that it is anything more than a new label for some old concepts. For example, today's popular psychology tells us that our work must not only provide for economic security but also (and more importantly) it must provide "meaning" and emotional fulfillment; if, perchance, a human service provider fails to experience a profound sense of meaning in his/her work then this may be taken as a symptom of an ominous-sounding condition we have chosen to call "burnout." A more conventional explanation might be that from time to time any form of work (not just human service) can become a burden, something we become bored with. Little is gained by resorting to the notion of "burnout," which connotes psychopathology.

In summary, whether or not the notion of burnout proves to be valid, Maslach and Jackson have made an important contribution by developing a potentially useful measurement tool for researcher's interested in the effects of chronic stress in human service occupations. The MBI certainly appears to be the best scale presently available for operationalizing this highly visible and somewhat controversial construct; however, I must reemphasize the point that it is still only a research instrument.

Review of Maslach Burnout Inventory by E. THOMAS DOWD, *Associate Professor of Educational Psychology, University of Nebraska-Lincoln, Lincoln, NE:*

The phenomenon of burnout has received increasing attention in the last few years, most notably in the human services professions. Burnout is a term used to denote physical and emotional exhaustion from a job-related stress, resulting in negative work attitudes, a poor professional self-concept, and a loss of concern for clients served. Thus, it is appropriate that instruments are being developed to measure the construct.

The Maslach Burnout Inventory is a 22-item scale designed to measure three aspects of burnout (emotional exhaustion, depersonalization, and lack of personal accomplishment) along two dimensions (frequency and intensity). The Emotional Exhaustion subscale measures feelings of being emotionally overextended and exhausted by work. The Depersonalization subscale measures an unfeeling and impersonal response towards service recipients. The Personal Accomplishment subscale assesses one's feelings of competence and successful achievement in work. Individual items reflect the taker's feelings towards job-related activities. A demographic data sheet is included with the manual, although its use is not well discussed in the manual.

DEVELOPMENT OF THE SCALE. The authors state that items were derived from previous interview and questionnaire data and from other scales, but give no other information. Three factor analyses on two separate samples yielded 25 items from an original 47-item scale, and four distinct factors. Three of the factors, which had eigenvalues greater than one, became the three subscales. The fourth factor, as yet unidentified, awaits additional research. There is a moderate correlation between the Emotional Exhaustion and the Depersonalization subscales, and no correlation between these subscales and Personal Accomplishment. There is only a moderate relationship between the frequency and intensity dimensions.

RELIABILITY. Reliability coefficients were based on samples other than those used in item selection. Internal consistency reliability coefficients ranged from .71 to .90. Standard errors of measurement ranged from 3.16 to 4.99. Test-retest reliability (2–4 weeks apart) ranged from .53 to .82. Reliability thus appears to be adequately demonstrated.

VALIDITY. Two items of validity data are provided in the manual, convergent and discriminant. There are several studies using separate samples which assess convergent validity. The authors have commendably provided a wide variety of validity studies using different criteria, including the comparison of scores on this inventory with ratings from outside observers (co-workers and spouses), hypothesized relationships between various job characteristics and burnout scores, hypothesized relationships between burnout and various personal reactions such as desire to leave one's job, and hypothesized relationships between burnout and difficulties with families and friends. There are also validity studies linking burnout scores to such stress outcomes as increased use of alcohol and other drugs and insomnia.

Discriminant validity studies are also described in the manual which showed that variance in burnout scores could not be accounted for by scores on general job satisfaction or that burnout scores were not distorted by a social desirability response set.

NORMS. There are no serviceable norms given for this scale in the manual nor is there any information as to where adequate normative data can be obtained. Only means and standard deviations are provided. This is a significant lack.

EVALUATION. Overall, the Maslach Burnout Inventory is a rather well-constructed instrument. Reliability and validity data are sufficient to demonstrate both the stability and meaning of the construct. The manual is very complete, describing the construction of the instrument, the derivation of the subscales, administration and scoring, and reliability and validity. There is even a section on suggestions for future research. The authors are appropriately cautious; for example, they have not scored the fourth factor, nor even as yet given it a name. It appears to represent a dimension of involvement with people and they suggest that further research be conducted on this subscale. Since the subscale correlations range from moderate to quite low, the authors have appropriately not combined the scores into a total burnout score. A deficiency in the manual, however, is the lack of normative data, nor is there any discussion of the existence of norms in other sources.

Another deficiency is in the lack of an explicit definition of burnout or of information describing the method by which the original items were generated. The authors do refer the reader to original sources on burnout, where presumably a precise definition exists. But there is no assurance in the manual that the items in the inventory actually sample the construct domain. Most of the items have an affective, or "feeling" flavor, and appear to revolve largely around the concept of emotional exhaustion. One can easily conceive of other types of items leading to other results. Indeed, another burnout inventory, the Staff Burnout Scale for Health Professionals, demonstrates exactly that.

A further example of the lack of information on and description of the original concept is the authors' scoring for both frequency and intensity. That this idea has much merit is shown by the difference in scores for each subscale. However, no information is given in the manual as to the rationale for this distinction.

Finally, what I missed was a clear distinction between burnout in human services (which is what this instrument measures), and level of occupational stress. No information is provided that leads to a conceptual or practical differentiation of these two constructs. Given the intuitive relationship, I am surprised that discriminant validity studies were not conducted immediately.

The Maslach Burnout Inventory is a well-constructed, well-researched instrument, which should be of considerable use in diagnosing problems in a wide variety of human service occupations. As more research continues to be done using this scale, it should be possible to relate the concept of burnout to a number of behavioral and attitudinal problems among human service workers and to devise appropriate remedial strategies.

[660]

Mastery: An Evaluation Tool: Selected Short SOBAR Reading Tests. Grades 3–9; 1975–76; "provides an alternative to the full-length catalog Mastery Test in SOBAR Reading"; criterion-referenced; 9 tests, with varying grade levels; no data on reliability and validity; no norms; administrator's manual ('76, 4 pages);

separate answer sheets must be used; 1983 price data: $23.45 per 25 tests, 1 examiner's manual, and 1 examiner's manual supplement (specify test); $22.20 per 100 answer sheets (for local scoring only); $9.05 per specimen set; scoring service available from publisher; (60–75) minutes per test; Center for the Study of Evaluation, University of California at Los Angeles; Science Research Associates, Inc.*

a) PHONIC ANALYSIS. Grades 3–5; 1975; 1 form (8 pages); examiner's manual supplement (7 pages).
b) STRUCTURAL ANALYSIS. Grades 3–9; 1 form (8 pages); examiner's manual supplement (3 pages).
c) STUDY SKILLS. Grades 4–9; 1975; 1 form (12 pages); examiner's manual supplement (3 pages).
d) VOCABULARY I. Grades 4–5; 1975; 1 form (7 pages); examiner's manual supplement (2 pages).
e) VOCABULARY II. Grades 6–7; 1975; 1 form (7 pages); examiner's manual supplement (2 pages).
f) VOCABULARY III. Grades 8–9; 1975; 1 form (7 pages); examiner's manual supplement (2 pages).
g) COMPREHENSION I. Grades 4–5; 1975; 1 form (16 pages); examiner's manual supplement (2 pages).
h) COMPREHENSION II. Grades 6–7; 1975; 1 form (16 pages); examiner's manual supplement (2 pages).
i) COMPREHENSION III. Grades 8–9; 1975; 1 form (17 pages); examiner's manual supplement (2 pages).

Review of Mastery: An Evaluation Tool: Selected Short SOBAR Reading Tests by ROBERT CALFEE, Professor of Education and Psychology, School of Education, Stanford University, Stanford, CA:

T. R. Carlson, reviewing SOBAR (System for Objective-Based Assessment—Reading) in *The Eighth Mental Measurements Yearbook* (8:766), described it as "an impressive and overwhelming set of assessment materials." A careful reading of the remainder of the review suggests that this remark may be rather tongue-in-cheek. The review is devastating:

> The materials provided do not explain how the 302 or so objectives were sampled. There is no statement of the authors' conceptualization of the reading process nor consideration of any reading model serving as a framework for the two catalogs.
>
> ...it is difficult for this reviewer to understand why SOBAR is to be preferred over the mastery-type tests that accompany many current reading programs [a fundamental point, in my opinion].
>
> Most achievement tests provide item difficulty information. Where such information is not available, as in the case of SOBAR, it is difficult to judge whether failure on an item is due to lack of mastery of an objective or to the difficulty of the item.
>
> The practice of having pupils read the directions independently is not a good practice—particularly if the directions are too difficult for many pupils.
>
> The items in Phonic Analysis are predominately spelling oriented....the decoys are so different from the correct response that it is difficult to understand how they would draw meaningful response from pupils....Some of the items involve mastery of unusual spellings.
>
> In summary, before considering use of either the "customized" or "catalog" versions of this assessment system, one should wait for forthcoming technical data assuring acceptable quality of the objectives and test items.

The short-form version of this system is not changed in any fundamental way from the earlier version, except for being shorter. All of the shortcomings identified previously by Carlson are still apparent. No technical data are provided. The objectives lack any coherent framework, and are presented at a level of detail that seems picayune: "Given a sentence with a verb omitted, the learner will identify the inflected verb form (*s* or *es* or *ies*) to correctly [sic] complete the sentence. [Item Number and Key: 34(B), 35(D), 36(C); Objective Identification Number IC29]"

Carlson's extensive critique of the Phonic Analysis section of the battery still has full force. Vowel digraphs are often the "test" of a decoding assessment, and SOBAR does rather poorly (e.g., the "silent" vs. "sounded" vowels in items 58 through 60; the terminology is curriculum-dependent, and is questionable as a guide to understanding the English spelling-sound system). Other strange examples are found in the vocabulary section, in which the student is tested on the symbols XII, %, and $ as vocabulary items, and is asked to decide whether the statement, "The shark's teeth were razors" corresponds best to teeth that are white, sharp, damaged, or silvery. Are not some razors silvery?

The main advantage of the short-form SOBAR over the version reviewed previously is that it is shorter. The lack of a conceptual framework, the absence of technical information, the complexity and arbitrariness of the items, and the availability of plausible alternatives all argue against the use of this system.

Review of Mastery: An Evaluation Tool: Selected Short SOBAR Reading Tests by ANNETTE B. WEINSHANK, Teacher-Collaborator, Institute for Research on Teaching, Michigan State University, East Lansing, MI:

SOBAR (System for Objective-Based Assessment—Reading) Short Catalog Tests are part of a larger SRA evaluation program called Mastery, An Evaluation Tool. The Mastery program builds objective-based, criterion-referenced tests for math and reading for grades 3 through 9.

SRA selects the objectives after examining major basal textbook series and state curriculum guides; choices are reviewed by teachers and curriculum specialists. There are 138 objectives grouped into five major categories: phonic analysis, structural analysis, study skills, vocabulary, and comprehension. (Twenty-four additional objectives for grades K through 2 deal only with letter recognition.) Each objective is tested with three items; mastery is defined as correctly answering all three. A catalog lists all the objectives under each category.

There are three variants of the SOBAR test system: (1) customized tests, in which a teacher selects objectives of interest from the catalog and SRA provides three test items for each objective; (2) grade-based catalog tests (K through 9), in which objectives are drawn from all categories and the associated test items are presented in one test booklet for each grade level; and (3) the Short Catalog Tests in which selected objectives are drawn separately from each category, with the associated test items presented in their own test booklet (e.g., structural analysis). This shorter version of the grade-based tests reportedly was developed in response to teacher requests for a faster, category-specific evaluation program.

All of this information, necessary for placing the Short Catalog Tests into a comprehensible context, was pieced together only after six long-distance telephone conversations with staff at the Chicago offices of SRA and the receipt of a packet of explanatory materials requested by this reviewer. The test packet itself comes only with the nine different booklets which make up the test, a listing for each test of the objective being assessed and the correct item answers for each, a cryptic four-page administrator's manual, and a set of machine scorable answer sheets. The entire packet provides no clue to the consumer about the larger system of SOBAR assessment and the place of the Short Catalog Tests within it, about the existence of a larger pool of objectives from which the test objectives were chosen, or about the suggested grade level(s) for which each of the tests is appropriate (they are merely labelled "Grades 3–9"). Three of the six phone calls were devoted just to finding someone who had information about recommended grade-level appropriateness.

An objective by objective examination of the tests reveals that the items testing phonic analysis objectives (recommended for use in grades 3 through 5) include listening for single consonant sounds, consonant blends, clusters, and digraphs, long and short vowel sounds, and vowel digraphs. Structural analysis test items (grades 3 through 9) include identifying compound words, contractions, singular and plural forms, inflected verbs, possessive nouns, tense, parts of speech, syllables, and punctuation marks. Study skills (grades 4 through 9) include demonstrating dictionary and library skills, and reading graphs, maps, and tables. Three test booklets are provided for items testing the vocabulary objectives (grades 4 through 5, 6 through 7, 8 through 9), with items testing the ability to identify synonyms, antonyms, homonyms, simile, metaphor, and personifications. (It is puzzling that of the 45 test items used across the 3 levels, 20 are identical.) Finally, test booklets at the same three levels are provided for assessing mastery of the comprehension skills of identifying title, main idea, detail, sequence, cause and effect, opinion, theme, and mood. Overall, neither the objectives nor the test items themselves are substantively different from those provided by basal series publishers to accompany their texts or by other commercially available test packages.

No normative data (i.e., data about typical performance across large numbers of students) is provided for the SOBAR system in general, or for the Short Catalog Tests in particular. (The grade-based catalog tests and the customized tests were both reviewed by Carlson in *The Eighth Mental Measurements Yearbook*, 8:766, 1978.) There is no data on validity, i.e., on how changes in performance on the objectives are related to changes in actual reading performance. There is no data on item difficulty and discrimination. This is particularly serious. In the absence of normative information about performance on each item, empirically based test improvement cannot take place. For example, if items that are too difficult for most students are not identified and replaced, students could appear not to have mastered curricular material when in fact it is the test item itself that is defective in some way. Similarly, test items are expected to discriminate between stronger and weaker students. On a well constructed item, weaker students will not perform better than stronger ones. If items that do not discriminate in the expected direction are not identified and replaced, weaker students could incorrectly be assumed to have mastered material when in fact they have not.

Conceptually, there is no explanation for how the objectives chosen from each category were determined. In the structural analysis test, for example, 20 out of a possible 43 objectives were tested. What rationale guided the inclusion of some objectives and the exclusion of others?

Overall, the SOBAR Short Catalog Tests are meager fare conceptually, substantively, and technically. Carlson's (8:766) conclusions are applicable here. "Minimally, data are needed on the sampling of objectives as well as on item reliability, validity, discrimination, relevance, and difficulty....Those seeking a criterion-referenced assessment system need to consider other instruments."

[661]

Mastery Test in Consumer Economics. Grades 8–12; 1984; performance objectives in 15 areas (consumer in the marketplace, consumer in the economy, personal money management, consumer credit fundamentals, wise use of credit, food buying, housing, transportation, furniture/appliances/clothing, personal and health services, banking services, saving and investments, insurance, taxes and government, consumer in society) and total score; no data on reliability and validity; no norms; 1 form (7 pages); administrator's manual (23 pages); 1985 price data: $24 per test kit including manual, 20 test booklets, and 20 answer sheets; $10 per 20 test booklets; $11 per 50 answer sheets; $4.65 per manual; $5 per specimen set; STS scoring service, $1 per student ($20 minimum); 30(35) minutes; Les Diabay; Scholastic Testing Service, Inc.*

[662]

Matching Familiar Figures Test. Ages 5–12, 13 and over; 1965; MFF; reflection-impulsivity; no data on reliability and validity; norms for ages 5–12 only; individual; 1 form; 2 levels: elementary ('65, 30 pages including answer key and directions for administering), adolescent/adult (no date, 32 pages including answer key and directions for administering); no manual; mimeographed development of norms booklet (no date, 37 pages); 1983 price data: $10 per test; $3 per mimeographed development of norms booklet; administration time not reported; Jerome Kagan (test) and Neil J. Salkind (norms booklet); Jerome Kagan.*

TEST REFERENCES

1. Brown, R. T., & Quay, L. C. Reflection-impulsivity in normal and behavior-disordered children. JOURNAL OF ABNORMAL CHILD PSYCHOLOGY, 1977, 5, 457–462.
2. Camp, B. W., Blom, G. E., Hebert, F., & van Doorninck, W. J. "Think aloud": A program for developing self-control in young aggressive boys. JOURNAL OF ABNORMAL CHILD PSYCHOLOGY, 1977, 5, 157–169.
3. Cullinan, D., Epstein, M. H., & Silver, L. Modification of impulsive tempo in learning-disabled pupils. JOURNAL OF ABNORMAL CHILD PSYCHOLOGY, 1977, 5, 437–444.
4. Saltz, E., Dixon, D., & Johnson, J. Training disadvantaged preschoolers on various fantasy activities: Effects on cognitive functioning and impulse control. CHILD DEVELOPMENT, 1977, 48(2), 367–380.
5. Brent, D. E., & Routh, D. K. Response cost and impulsive word recognition errors in reading-disabled children. JOURNAL OF ABNORMAL CHILD PSYCHOLOGY, 1978, 6, 211–219.
6. Butter, E. J., & Vallano, T. W. Auditory and visual cognitive styles and adult reading performance. PERCEPTUAL AND MOTOR SKILLS, 1978, 47, 995–998.
7. Williams, D. Y., & Akamatsu, T. J. Cognitive self-guidance training with juvenile delinquents: Applicability and generalization. COGNITIVE THERAPY AND RESEARCH, 1978, 2, 285–288.
8. Aman, M. G. Cognitive, social, and other correlates of specific reading retardation. JOURNAL OF ABNORMAL CHILD PSYCHOLOGY, 1979, 7, 153–168.
9. Carlson, J. S., & Wiedl, K. H. Toward a differential testing approach: Testing-the-limits employing the Raven Matrices. INTELLIGENCE, 1979, 3, 323–344.
10. Firestone, P., & Martin, J. E. An analysis of the hyperactive syndrome: A comparison of hyperactive, behavior problem, asthmatic, and normal children. JOURNAL OF ABNORMAL CHILD PSYCHOLOGY, 1979, 7, 261–273.
11. Glenwick, D. S., Croft, R. G. F., Barocas, R., & Black, H. K. Reflection-impulsivity in predelinquent preadolescents in a residential facility. CRIMINAL JUSTICE AND BEHAVIOR, 1979, 6, 34–40.
12. Glenwick, D. S., Croft, R. G. F., Barocas, R., & Black, H. K. Cognitive impulsivity and social status in predelinquent preadolescent males. SOCIAL BEHAVIOR AND PERSONALITY, 1979, 7, 209–215.
13. Ikegami, T. Cognitive style in children: The relation between reflection-impulsivity and Rorschach scores. PSYCHOLOGIA, 1979, 22(4), 207–221.
14. Inagaki, K., & Hatano, G. Flexibility of accuracy versus speed orientation in reflective and impulsive children. PERCEPTUAL AND MOTOR SKILLS, 1979, 48, 1099–1108.
15. Kendall, P. C., & Finch, A. J., Jr. Analyses of changes in verbal behavior following a cognitive-behavioral treatment for impulsivity. JOURNAL OF ABNORMAL CHILD PSYCHOLOGY, 1979, 7, 455–463.
16. Norton, G. R., & Lester, C. J. The effects of modelling and verbal cues on concept acquisition of moderate retardates. COGNITIVE THERAPY AND RESEARCH, 1979, 3, 87–90.
17. Radatz, H. Some aspects of individual differences in mathematics instruction. JOURNAL FOR RESEARCH IN MATHEMATICS EDUCATION, 1979, 10, 359–363.
18. Conners, C. K., & Taylor, E. Pemoline, methylphenidate, and placebo in children with minimal brain dysfunction. ARCHIVES OF GENERAL PSYCHIATRY, 1980, 37, 922–930.
19. Dillon, R. F. Cognitive style and elaboration of logical abilities in hearing-impaired children. JOURNAL OF EXPERIMENTAL CHILD PSYCHOLOGY, 1980, 30, 389–400.
20. Loper, A. B., & Hallahan, D. P. A comparison of the reliability and validity of the standard MFF and MFF20 with learning-disabled children. JOURNAL OF ABNORMAL CHILD PSYCHOLOGY, 1980, 8, 377–384.
21. Margolis, H., Leonard, H. S., Brannigan, G. G., & Heverly, M. A. The validity of Form F of the Matching Familiar Figures Test with kindergarten children. JOURNAL OF EXPERIMENTAL CHILD PSYCHOLOGY, 1980, 29, 12–22.
22. Paulsen, K., & Johnson, M. Impulsivity: A multidimensional concept with developmental aspects. JOURNAL OF ABNORMAL CHILD PSYCHOLOGY, 1980, 8, 269–277.
23. Quay, L. C., & Weld, G. L. Visual and auditory selective attention and reflection-impulsivity in normal and learning-disabled boys at two age levels. JOURNAL OF ABNORMAL CHILD PSYCHOLOGY, 1980, 8, 117–125.
24. Arizmendi, T., Paulsen, K., & Domino, G. The Matching Familiar Figures Test: A primary, secondary, and tertiary evaluation. JOURNAL OF CLINICAL PSYCHOLOGY, 1981, 37, 812–818.
25. Barratt, E. S., Patton, J., Olsson, N. G., & Zuker, G. Impulsivity and paced tapping. JOURNAL OF MOTOR BEHAVIOR, 1981, 13, 286–300.
26. Blumenthal, J. A., McKee, D. C., Williams, R. B., & Haney, T. Assessment of conceptual tempo in the Type A (coronary prone) behavior pattern. JOURNAL OF PERSONALITY ASSESSMENT, 1981, 45, 44–51.
27. Chadwick, O., Rutter, M., Brown, G., Shaffer, D., & Traub, M. A prospective study of children with head injuries: II. Cognitive sequelae. PSYCHOLOGICAL MEDICINE, 1981, 11, 49–61.
28. Cohen, N. J., Sullivan, J., Minde, K., Novak, C., & Helwig, C. Evaluation of the relative effectiveness of methylphenidate and cognitive behavior modification in the treatment of kindergarten-aged hyperactive children. JOURNAL OF ABNORMAL CHILD PSYCHOLOGY, 1981, 9, 43–54.
29. Cohen, R., Schleser, R., & Meyers, A. Self-instructions: Effects of cognitive level and active rehearsal. JOURNAL OF EXPERIMENTAL CHILD PSYCHOLOGY, 1981, 32, 65–76.
30. Copeland, A. P., & Hammel, R. Subject variables in cognitive self-instructional training. COGNITIVE THERAPY AND RESEARCH, 1981, 5, 405–420.
31. Holmes, C. S. Reflective training and causal attributions in impulsive mildly retarded children. JOURNAL OF CLINICAL CHILD PSYCHOLOGY, 1981, 10, 194–199.
32. Karmos, J. S., Scheer, J., Miller, A., & Bardo, H. The relationship of math achievement to impulsivity in mathematically deficient elementary school students. SCHOOL SCIENCE AND MATHEMATICS, 1981, 81(8), 685–688.
33. Meade, E. R. Impulse control and cognitive functioning in lower- and middle-SES children: A developmental study. MERRILL-PALMER QUARTERLY, 1981, 27, 271–285.
34. Messer, S. B., & Brodzinsky, D. M. Three-year stability of reflection-impulsivity in young adolescents. DEVELOPMENTAL PSYCHOLOGY, 1981, 17, 848–850.
35. Parrish, J. M., & Erickson, M. T. A comparison of cognitive strategies in modifying the cognitive style of impulsive third-grade children. COGNITIVE THERAPY AND RESEARCH, 1981, 5, 71–84.
36. Sampsel, B. D., Widaman, K. F., & Winer, G. A. Relation in children of psychological differentiation and reasoning by class inclusion. PERCEPTUAL AND MOTOR SKILLS, 1981, 53(2), 439–446.
37. Schleser, R., Meyers, A. W., & Cohen, R. Generalization of self-instruction: Effects of general versus specific content, active rehearsal, and cognitive level. CHILD DEVELOPMENT, 1981, 52, 335–340.
38. Sousley, S. A., & Gargiulo, R. M. Effect of conceptual tempo on kindergarten reading readiness. PERCEPTUAL AND MOTOR SKILLS, 1981, 53(1), 127–134.
39. Staton, R. D., Wilson, H., & Brumback, R. A. Cognitive improvement associated with tricyclic antidepressant treatment of childhood major depressive illness. PERCEPTUAL AND MOTOR SKILLS, 1981, 53(1), 219–234.
40. Braswell, L., Kendall, P. C., & Urbain, E. S. A multistudy analysis of socioeconomic status (SES) and the measures and outcomes of cognitive-

behavioral treatment with children. JOURNAL OF ABNORMAL CHILD PSYCHOLOGY, 1982, 10, 443–450.

41. Brown, R. T., & Wynne, M. E. Correlates of teacher ratings, sustained attention, and impulsivity in hyperactive and normal boys. JOURNAL OF CLINICAL CHILD PSYCHOLOGY, 1982, 11, 262–267.

42. Butler, E. J., & Snyder, F. R. Effect of order of presentation on simultaneous and sequential Matching Familiar Figures Tests. PERCEPTUAL AND MOTOR SKILLS, 1982, 55, 1259–1262.

43. Campbell, S. B., Szumowski, E. K., Ewing, L. J., Gluck, D. S., & Breaux, A. M. A multidimensional assessment of parent-identified behavior problem toddlers. JOURNAL OF ABNORMAL CHILD PSYCHOLOGY, 1982, 10, 569–592.

44. Davidson, W. B. Multimethod examination of field dependence and impulsivity. PSYCHOLOGICAL REPORTS, 1982, 50, 655–661.

45. Dillon, R. F., & Donow, C. The psychometric credibility of the Zelniker and Jeffrey modification of the Matching Familiar Figures Test. EDUCATIONAL AND PSYCHOLOGICAL MEASUREMENT, 1982, 42, 529–536.

46. Flintoff, M. M., Barron, R. W., Swanson, J. M., Ledlow, A., & Kinsbourne, M. Methylphenidate increases selectivity of visual scanning in children referred for hyperactivity. JOURNAL OF ABNORMAL CHILD PSYCHOLOGY, 1982, 10, 145–161.

47. Gargiulo, R. M. Reflection/impulsivity and field dependence/independence in retarded and nonretarded children of equal mental age. BULLETIN OF THE PSYCHONOMIC SOCIETY, 1982, 19, 74–77.

48. Gow, L., & Ward, J. The Porteus Maze Test in the measurement of reflection/impulsivity. PERCEPTUAL AND MOTOR SKILLS, 1982, 54, 1043–1052.

49. Gow, L., & Ward, L. Extension of the use of measures of cognitive style to moderately-severely retarded trainees in a field setting. PERCEPTUAL AND MOTOR SKILLS, 1982, 55, 191–194.

50. Hatano, G., & Inagaki, K. The cognitive style differences in the use of latency and the number of errors as cues for inferring personality characteristics. JAPANESE PSYCHOLOGICAL RESEARCH, 1982, 24, 145–150.

51. Junkala, J., & Talbot, M. L. Cognitive styles of students with cerebral palsy. PERCEPTUAL AND MOTOR SKILLS, 1982, 55, 403–410.

52. Kendall, P. C., & Braswell, L. Cognitive-behavioral self-control therapy for children: A components analysis. JOURNAL OF CONSULTING AND CLINICAL PSYCHOLOGY, 1982, 50, 672–689.

53. Laine, M. Theoretical note on reflection-impulsivity. PSYCHOLOGICAL REPORTS, 1982, 51, 84.

54. Moore, M. J., Kagan, J., Sahl, M., & Grant, S. Cognitive profiles in reading disability. GENETIC PSYCHOLOGY MONOGRAPHS, 1982, 105, 41–93.

55. Obrzut, J. E., Hansen, R. L., & Heath, C. P. The effectiveness of visual information processing training with Hispanic children. JOURNAL OF GENERAL PSYCHOLOGY, 1982, 107, 165–174.

56. Paulsen, K., & Arizmendi, T. Matching Familiar Figures test norms based on IQ. PERCEPTUAL AND MOTOR SKILLS, 1982, 55, 1022.

57. Salkind, N. J., & Shlecter, T. Comparability of the Kansas Reflection Impulsivity Scale for Preschoolers and the Matching Familiar Figures Test in kindergarten children. CHILD STUDY JOURNAL, 1982, 12, 1–5.

58. Schwartz, M., Friedman, R., Lindsay, P., & Narrol, H. The relationship between conceptual tempo and depression in children. JOURNAL OF CONSULTING AND CLINICAL PSYCHOLOGY, 1982, 50, 488–490.

59. Steele, K., & Barling, J. Self-instruction and learning disabilities: Maintenance, generalization, and student characteristics. JOURNAL OF GENERAL PSYCHOLOGY, 1982, 106, 141–154.

60. Sternberg, L., Waldron, P., & Miller, T. L. Cognitive tempo and cognitive level relationships among mentally retarded children. PERCEPTUAL AND MOTOR SKILLS, 1982, 55, 463–470.

61. Tolor, B., & Tolor, A. An attempted modification of impulsivity and self-esteem in kindergartners. PSYCHOLOGY IN THE SCHOOLS, 1982, 19, 526–531.

62. Walker, N. W. Comparison of cognitive tempo and time estimation by young boys. PERCEPTUAL AND MOTOR SKILLS, 1982, 54, 715–722.

63. Agarwal, A., Tripathi, K. K., & Srivastava, M. Social roots and psychological implications of time perspective. INTERNATIONAL JOURNAL OF PSYCHOLOGY, 1983, 18, 367–380.

64. Buchanan, J. P. An examination of Kagan's risk hypothesis for conceptual tempo. GENETIC PSYCHOLOGY MONOGRAPHS, 1983, 107, 135–142.

65. Clark, L. A., & Halford, G. S. Does cognitive style account for cultural differences in scholastic achievement? JOURNAL OF CROSS-CULTURAL PSYCHOLOGY, 1983, 14, 279–296.

66. Copeland, A. P., & Weissbrod, C. S. Cognitive strategies used by learning disabled children: Does hyperactivity always make things worse? JOURNAL OF LEARNING DISABILITIES, 1983, 16, 473–477.

67. Karkheck, R. H., & Hogan, J. D. Relation of selected variables to improvement of children's problem-solving abilities. PERCEPTUAL AND MOTOR SKILLS, 1983, 57, 961–962.

68. Klee, S. H., & Garfinkel, B. D. The computerized Continuous Performance Task: A new measure of inattention. JOURNAL OF ABNORMAL CHILD PSYCHOLOGY, 1983, 11, 487–496.

69. Lawry, J. A., Welsh, M. C., & Jeffrey, W. E. Cognitive tempo and complex problem solving. CHILD DEVELOPMENT, 1983, 54, 912–920.

70. Lopez, L. C. Relationship between birth order and reflection-impulsivity in college age students. PERCEPTUAL AND MOTOR SKILLS, 1983, 57, 596–598.

71. Ozawa, J. P., & Michael, W. B. The concurrent validity of a behavioral rating scale for assessing attention deficit disorder (DSM III) in learning disabled children. EDUCATIONAL AND PSYCHOLOGICAL MEASUREMENT, 1983, 43, 623–632.

[663]

Mathematics Anxiety Rating Scale. Grades 7–12, college and adults; 1972–79; 2 levels; 1985 price data: $60 per 100 tests; Richard M. Suinn; Rocky Mountain Behavioral Science Institute, Inc.*

a) MATHEMATICS ANXIETY RATING SCALE—A. Grades 7–12; 1979; MARS-A; 1 form (7 pages); information for users (3 pages); brief (2 pages); (20–30) minutes.

b) MATHEMATICS ANXIETY RATING SCALE. College and adults; 1972; MARS; 1 form (7 pages); information for users (5 pages); brief (2 pages); (40–50) minutes.

See T3:1405 (9 references); for reviews by William E. Kline and James A. Walsh of *b*, see 8:610 (3 references).

TEST REFERENCES

1. Hendel, D. D. Experiential and affective correlates of math anxiety in adult women. PSYCHOLOGY OF WOMEN QUARTERLY, 1980, 5, 219–230.

2. Bruch, M. A. Relationship of test-taking strategies to test anxiety and performance: Toward a task analysis of examination behavior. COGNITIVE THERAPY AND RESEARCH, 1981, 5, 41–56.

3. Plake, B. S., & Parker, C. S. The development and validation of a revised version of the Mathematics Anxiety Rating Scale. EDUCATIONAL AND PSYCHOLOGICAL MEASUREMENT, 1982, 42, 551–557.

4. Plake, B. S., Ansorge, C. J., Parker, C. S., & Lowry, S. R. Effects of item arrangement, knowledge of arrangement test anxiety and sex on test performance. JOURNAL OF EDUCATIONAL MEASUREMENT, 1982, 19, 49–57.

5. Gabel, D. L., & Sherwood, R. D. Facilitating problem solving in high school chemistry. JOURNAL OF RESEARCH IN SCIENCE TEACHING, 1983, 20, 163–177.

6. Saigh, P. A., & Khouri, A. The concurrent validity of the Mathematics Anxiety Rating Scale for Adolescents (MARS-A) in relation to the academic achievement of Lebanese students. EDUCATIONAL AND PSYCHOLOGICAL MEASUREMENT, 1983, 43, 633–637.

Review of Mathematics Anxiety Rating Scale by MICHAEL J. HANNAFIN, Assistant Professor, Division of Educational Psychological Studies, University of Colorado, Boulder, CO:

The Mathematics Anxiety Rating Scale (MARS) is a 98-item self-rating scale designed to assess fear and apprehension of college and adult-aged individuals to specific math-related situations. The items, which range from "Being asked to add up 976 + 777 in your head" to "walking to class and thinking about a math course," are rated on a discrete scale (1–5) with corresponding descriptions ranging from "not at all" to "very much." The items are easily rated, and total math anxiety scores are computed by summing the numerical ratings across all items. According to the author, the results may then be compared to normative data, used as a math anxiety screening criteria, employed as an experiment design tool in lieu of control groups, used in the construction of desensitization hierarchies for therapeutic interventions, or employed as a measure of therapeutic progress.

The MARS-A, an adolescent version of the MARS, is also a 98-item scale similar in content, format, normative data availability, and score tabulation procedures. The differences between MARS and MARS-A are very minimal, and are not explained or substantiated by the author. Apart from very minor and very infrequent word substitutions, the MARS and MARS-A are virtually indistinguishable. The author indicates that MARS-A can be used to screen individual students in order to plan for placements in special mathematics courses, to provide counseling, or to provide therapeutic intervention (based on desensitization hierarchies). The author also suggests appplications for program evaluation and research in mathematics anxiety.

This reviewer's reservations regarding the MARS and MARS-A focus on several concerns. As noted in an earlier review (8:610), scales of this type are prone to "faking" responses by raters. Furthermore, there is little differentiation between the MARS and MARS-A content. It seems potentially problematic to base the rationale, support, and projected uses of one scale on the merits of another—especially when unanswered questions exist regarding the original scale. There is also a lack of sufficient background and developmental data regarding the MARS. The author includes no information as to why 98 items—not more, not fewer—were selected for use. Finally, several of the proposed uses of the MARS and MARS-A appear to lack substantiation. In some cases, it appears that the validational efforts of the author are inconsistent with the proposed uses of the scale.

Test-retest reliability data for the MARS range from .78 to .85, with internal consistency reportedly .97. It is unclear, however, whether these reliability estimates were obtained for a 94-item version of the scale or for the present 98-item version. The scale may have undergone some revision, as discrepancies in the total number of MARS items have been reported (Richardson & Suinn, 1972; Suinn, Edie, Nicoletti, & Spinelli, 1972; Hendel & Davis, 1978; Brush, 1978). The author reports MARS-A reliability coefficients of .89 based on the split half method, and .96 for internal consistency. Without reported item development procedures, however, reliability estimates could be misleading. Since the inclusion of non-discriminating items can often artificially inflate the reliability of a scale, it is important to establish the discriminability and supportability of individual scale items. No such data are reported.

Evidence for the validity of the MARS was presented in the form of negative correlations with mathematics aptitude, and by post-intervention reductions in reported mathematics anxiety by treated versus untreated clients. The latter validational rationale could be suspect in that treatments designed to reduce any form of anxiety, mathematics or otherwise, are likely to result in corresponding reductions in generalized anxiousness.

Validational support for the MARS-A are reported using a similar rationale. The author also reports "highly significant" differences between the math achievement of high versus low math anxious students. In addition, a significant but moderate correlation ($r = -.28$) is reported between MARS-A scores and the number of mathematics and science classes taken by junior and senior high school students.

The uses proposed for both the MARS and the MARS-A may be overstatements of the potential of the scales. The author's recommendation for use as screening tools may be most appropriate. It is likely that the scales will be sensitive to situational math anxiety. Use as a research tool or as a pre-to-posttest measure of therapeutic effectiveness, however, may be more difficult to substantiate for several reasons. First, the mean score changes for untreated groups, reported in a single published study (Richardson & Suinn, 1973), ranged from +2.40 scale points to −19.92 from pre- to posttesting. The individual score variation from pre- to posttesting has ranged from +62 to −108 scale points, with a mean absolute variation of 25.56 points (Hannafin, 1972). Adjustments for untreated group score shifts would need to be considered before statements regarding group therapeutic effectiveness could be made. Secondly, there is reason to suspect that the scores of high anxious subjects will be more variable than the scores of typical or low anxious subjects. It may be invalid to project score variations for high anxious subjects based upon score changes for an overall population. Finally, the author suggests MARS or MARS-A items may be used in the construction of desensitization hierarchies. This proposed use requires validational and reliability studies beyond what is presently available. Group mean variation data tend to obscure much of the individual variability noted on a case-by-case basis. The construction of desensitization item hierarchies, especially when subsequent reponses to such items will be used as a measure of posttreatment anxiety, requires information regarding the specific item stability, item discriminability, and content validity of the scales. Validational data do not seem to support or qualify such recommended uses.

Overall, the MARS and MARS-A are considered appropriate for group screening and efforts to identify subjects with extreme or severe anxiety reactions in everyday mathematical situations. A number of shortcomings regarding reported development, reliability, and validity data of the scales make several of the author's recommendations for use suspect. While the MARS and MARS-A may be valuable and useful in the functions recommended by the author, the corresponding support and documentation needed to justify such claims are lacking.

REVIEWER'S REFERENCES

Hannafin, M. AN INVESTIGATION OF THE ITEM STABILITY OF THE MATHEMATICS ANXIETY RATING SCALE (MARS): A STUDY OF THE INDIVIDUAL AND GROUP REHABILITY COMPONENTS OF THE MARS. Unpublished Master's thesis, Fort Hays Kansas State College (Hays, KS), 1972.

Richardson, F. C., & Suinn, R. M. The Mathematics Anxiety Rating Scale: Psychometric data. JOURNAL OF COUNSELING PSYCHOLOGY, 1972, 19, 551–554.

Suinn, R. M., Edie, C. A., Nicoletti, J., & Spinelli, P. R. The MARS, a measure of mathematics anxiety: Psychometric data. JOURNAL OF CLINICAL PSYCHOLOGY, 1972, 28, 373–375.

Richardson, F. C., & Suinn, R. M. A comparison of traditional systematic desensitization, accelerated massed desensitization, and anxiety management training in the treatment of mathematics anxiety. BEHAVIOR THERAPY, 1973, 4, 212–218.

Brush, L. R. A validation study of the Mathematics Anxiety Rating Scale (MARS). EDUCATIONAL AND PSYCHOLOGICAL MEASUREMENT, 1978, 38, 485–490.

Hendel, D. D., & Davis, S. O. Effectiveness of an intervention strategy for reducing mathematics anxiety. JOURNAL OF COUNSELING PSYCHOLOGY, 1978, 25, 429–434.

Review of Mathematics Anxiety Rating Scale by THOMAS R. KNAPP, Professor of Education and Nursing, University of Rochester, Rochester, NY:

At the end of his review of the MARS in the *8th MMY*, Walsh evaluated the test as "deficient." (Kline was much kinder in his review.) Several years have now passed and the MARS-A version (for adolescents) has been added, but the instrument remains deficient. There is still no manual, the information regarding norms, validity, reliability, etc., is still scanty, and the user still does not know where the items came from.

Since the MARS-A has not been previously reviewed and since it suffers from many of the same deficiencies as its parent, the remainder of this commentary will be devoted to the adolescent version of the scale.

Although both the MARS and MARS-A contain 98 items, there is a bothersome non-parallelism of the items. The slight alteration in the wording of the first item from "Determining the amount of change" (MARS) to "Deciding how much change" (MARS-A) is understandable, as is the shift from "total up a column of figures" (MARS) to "add up a column of numbers" (MARS-A), but item 5 on MARS has no counterpart on MARS-A, item 14 on MARS is item 5 on MARS-A, items 94 and 95 on MARS-A are more appropriate for MARS, etc. The directions are also not parallel, with MARS referring to "fear or apprehension" and MARS-A referring to "tension or apprehension," followed later by "frightened by it nowadays" (MARS) vs. "made anxious by it nowadays" (MARS-A).

The norms data for MARS-A are better than for MARS ($N=1,313$ junior and senior high school students vs. $N=394$ college students at the University of Missouri), but the schools are not even partially identified. There are no test-retest reliability data provided for this version, coefficient alpha is called an index of internal "consistence," and the validity data referred to on the second page of the informational brief are based on four analyses of variance and one correlational study for which the numbers of students are unspecified and of which the interested reader can make little sense.

Both the MARS and the MARS-A need considerably more work before they can be recommended for clinical use. The author must update the information provided in the information for users, in the informational brief, and in the two articles cited in 8:610. (The document containing information for users of MARS refers to another article in the 1973 volume of the *Journal of Counseling Psychology* which was nowhere to be found.) Mathematics anxiety can be very debilitating and interest in the topic is currently strong. This test apparently has little or no competition. It is indeed unfortunate that the prospective user must wait for much further research.

[664]

Mathematics Attitude Inventory. Grades 7–12; 1979; MAI; 6 scores: perception of the mathematics teacher, anxiety toward mathematics, value of mathematics in society, self-concept in mathematics, enjoyment of mathematics, motivation in mathematics; no data on reliability; norms for grades 8 and 11 only; 1 form (no date, 3 pages); manual (25 pages); 1985 price data: $25 per 50 tests; $2 per scoring key; $15 per manual; (20–30) minutes; Richard S. Sandman; Minnesota Research and Evaluation Center, University of Minnesota.*

See T3:1410 (1 reference).

TEST REFERENCES

1. Bestgen, B. J., Reys, R. E., Rybolt, J. F., & Wyatt, J. W. Effectiveness of systematic instruction on attitudes and computational estimation skills of preservice elementary teachers. JOURNAL FOR RESEARCH IN MATHEMATICS EDUCATION, 1980, 11, 124–136.

2. Brassell, A., Petry, S., & Brooks, D. M. Ability grouping, mathematics achievement, and pupil attitudes toward mathematics. JOURNAL FOR RESEARCH IN MATHEMATICS EDUCATION, 1980, 11, 22–28.

3. Sandman, R. S. The Mathematics Attitude Inventory: Instrument and user's manual. JOURNAL FOR RESEARCH IN MATHEMATICS EDUCATION, 1980, 11, 148–149.

Review of Mathematics Attitude Inventory by HARVEY RESNICK, Director, Career Development and Placement Center and (adjunct) faculty, Department of Psychology, University of Hartford, West Hartford, CT:

The Mathematics Attitude Inventory (MAI) is a 48-item multi-dimensional self-rating scale. It is intended to measure the attitudes toward mathematics of secondary school students along each of the following dimensions: Perceptions of the Mathematics Teacher, Anxiety Toward Mathematics, Value of Mathematics in Society, Self-Concept in Mathematics, Enjoyment of Mathematics, and Motivation in Mathematics. Each item is scored on a four-point scale ranging from (1) "Strongly Agree" to (4) "Strongly Disagree."

The author states that "the MAI was developed as a research tool for the determination of group attitudes toward Mathematics and the changes in these attitudes." This reviewer questions the value of the instrument for determining change in attitudes. In fact, the test was developed as part of a large scale National Science Foundation project. It was administered to 5,034 students, two samples of 8th- and 11th-grade mathematics students from California and Indiana. The author provides no information on test-retest reliability nor any information about its use to measure change in attitudes.

The only reliability data provided is a measure of internal consistency, Cronbach's alpha coefficient. It ranges from .68 for the four-item "motivation" scale to .89 for the seven-item "enjoyment" scale. There is no additional reliability data presented for either the individual scales or for the test. The limited number of items for each scale, ranging from four to eight, would seem to undermine the reliability of the test, not only for individuals but for groups as well.

The author notes in two different parts of the manual that the test should not "be used to make decisions about individual students," because individual scores may be subject to "considerable error." Yet, norms are provided by grade and by sex, in terms of means, standard deviations, and percentile ranks for each of the 6 dimensions. This information, especially the presentation of percentile scores, may mislead the users of the test to use it for assessment of the individual student. Also, the availability of only 8th- and 11th-grade norm groups effectively restricts use of the MAI to these populations. The author overstates the case for extending the test from 7th to 12th grade, if the norms provided are to be used appropriately.

The manual states the MAI can be completed in 20 minutes by most students, although there should be no time limit set. This amount of time is sufficient, assuming that the student has no difficulty in reading. There may, however, be some difficulty, especially at the lower grade level, for the student who is not reading at or near grade level. The test is also made more lengthy by the inclusion of 10 items not scored on any of the six scales. These items were included in the administration of the test on which the norm tables are based. This does not seem to this reviewer to be a convincing reason to include them. The scoring is also made more confusing by including these 10 items; the scoring is already confusing because some items on each of the six scales need to be "scored the reverse of the student's marked answer." However, scoring is less an issue if the test is machine scored.

The only validity data presented is based on two separate factor analyses on the 48 items conducted for each of the 2,000+ student samples. The process of developing test items and sampling is described in detail, and care was taken by the test developer to select large representative samples of mathematics students in each of two states with the specified grade levels. On both of these, six common factors emerged. Thus, there is evidence for factorial validity; however, scale intercorrelations raise the question of whether the scales are measuring separate concepts. For example, the correlation of the Enjoyment of Mathematics scale and the Self-Concept in Mathematics scale was .66. It appears that there is sizeable redundancy between at least two of the scales, with a question remaining about the test's discriminant validity. No convergent or predictive validity data is available. Although the authors state they developed this test because no other similar test was available, there are tests available which measure constructs similar to those purportedly measured by the subscales of this test. For example, Suinn's Math Anxiety Rating Scale and Fennema and Sherman's Math Anxiety Scale appear conceptually similar to the Anxiety toward Mathematics subscale of the MAI. The lack of anything other than a factorial validity scale must undermine the confidence of prospective users.

SUMMARY. The MAI must be rated as seriously deficient, and its use without further test development cannot be wholly recommended. Reliability and validity data are scarce. Only a beginning attempt at establishing its validity is made by the use of factor analytic methods. More information from a broader grade and geographic sample is necessary to use the normative data in any way, even if there was further evidence of its reliability and validity. At this time the test should be used only cautiously as a secondary measure, and for research purposes only. It may well be that with further development and refinement this test could prove itself useful as a research tool.

Review of Mathematics Attitude Inventory by RICHARD F. SCHMID, Associate Professor of Education, Concordia University, Montreal, Quebec, Canada:

The Mathematics Attitude Inventory (MAI) provides the user with a short, easily-administered instrument for assessing group attitudes towards six factors which may influence the learning of mathematics. Scores are derived only for each separate factor. Because the test was developed for determining group attitude, the authors advise against individual score interpretation.

As an overall assessment, the instrument appears to be quite valid due to the discrete nature of the categories under consideration and the care taken in the validation process. Unfortunately, the authors do not specify how, when, or why it should be used. For example, reference is made in both the general and technical portions of the User's Manual to its use as a "research tool." However, it is never made explicit whether a classroom teacher should be advised to collect and "eyeball" the data, and/or if a researcher should use the MAI as a covariate, blocking variable, or predictor of performance.

The appropriateness of use of the MAI might be determined by an examination of its content validity. The instrument was constructed for a large-scale evaluation project because "existing attitude measures did not seem to be appropriate." In 1972 and 1976, a total of 5,034 8th- and 11th-grade mathematics students from throughout the states of California and Indiana were employed in samples stratified by community size. Factor analyses on each year separately, and combined, all produced the same six factors eventually used. Factorial validity was thus established. Face validity is evident by simple inspection of the test.

The MAI is economical to use; a manual and one copy of the instrument may be purchased for $15.00, and the price for 50 tests is $25.00. The authors suggest (ill-advisedly) a number of alternative ways to gather the student responses, when in fact the only valid method is to use the original form (if the norms are to be employed). The simplified scoring procedure is said to approximate Rummel's regression technique, and is indeed easy to complete. Scoring is made even easier by the straightforward instructions in the user's section.

The authors suggest substituting normed averages (which are provided) for unanswered items (on tests with fewer than one-half unanswered items). This reviewer feels that this procedure should be used with great caution for two reasons. First, an item(s) left unanswered is a comment in itself (especially involving those which are personal or address the teacher). Second, adding such scores causes an "average" result, thus leading to an uninformative interpretation.

The four-point scale which is used may not be particularly effective at discriminating differences among either individuals or groups. Such a narrow scale often produces respondents who tend to answer consistently either toward the center (2 or 3) or toward the ends of the scale (1 or 4). Almost any administration of 20 or more students will betray two distinct "personalities" (those with strong feelings and those virtually without). This tendency in and of itself could be an important moderator variable. Also, although items were constructed in both positive and negative forms, their distribution across factors is uneven (e.g., all anxiety items are negative). On the plus side, the items are well-written and unambiguous.

The norms tables (means, standard deviations, and percentile ranks for both grades, male and female) are easy to employ, but the problem again arises as to why the test is being used. This problem is perhaps inherent in most attitude inventories, where only extreme deviations are informative, yet are extremely unlikely. The MAI might be used as an assessment of change over time due to intervention, but then the norms are less relevant. Unfortunately, no test-retest reliability data are supplied, so even multiple administrations are problematic. The MAI could be constructively employed to compare control and experimental group reactions to longer term instructional programs.

It is worth noting that the Teacher and Enjoyment scales are somewhat negatively skewed, so that the median might be the more useful statistic, particularly where small groups are concerned. Finally, although the results were derived from orthogonal factors, intercorrelations among many of the scales are predictably high. For example, high negative correlations between the Self-concept and Enjoyment with Anxiety would be useful to the practitioner for intervention strategies, an issue not discussed by the authors.

In summary, the MAI appears to have good content validity, is easy and economical to use, and comes with a straightforward User's Manual, including norms. Unfortunately, the purpose for using the test is left ambiguous, and its scale system may fail to discriminate effectively except in extreme or special cases. The MAI should prove useful for interested researchers and for teachers with some knowledge of measurement techniques.

[665]

Mathematics 8–12. Grades 9, 10, 11, 12; 1983–84; Mathematics 8 currently not available, scheduled for publication in 1985; 5 scores: understanding, computation, application, factual recall, total; no norms for part scores; 1 form (11–12 pages) for each level; 4 levels: mathematics 9, mathematics 10, mathematics 11, mathematics 12; teacher's guide for grades 9–12 ('84, 29 pages); group record sheet ('84, 1 page) for each level; 1985 price data: £5.95 per 25 test booklets (specify level); £3.45 per teacher's guide for grades 9–12; £3.95 per specimen set including manual and one of each test booklet; (60–80) minutes for each level; Alan Brighouse, David Godber, and Peter Patilla; NFER-Nelson Publishing Co. [England].*

[666]

Mathematics Evaluation Procedures K–2. Grades K–5; 1980; criterion-referenced; 104 objectives in 3 areas: number (problem solving and graphs), shape, measurement (length, mass, volume, area, time, money, temperature); no data on reliability and validity; limited information regarding suggested standards of mastery;

individual; 1 form; manual (280 pages, includes test, child's response sheet and record sheet of child's responses); 1982 price data: A$13.50 per set of testing materials; administration time not reported; North Sydney Region Infants Mistresses' Council; Australian Council for Educational Research [Australia].*

Review of Mathematics Evaluation Procedures K–2 by JOHN COOK, Senior Educational Psychologist, County Psychological Service, Littlehampton, West Sussex, England:

These tests are the result of an initiative by a group of infant school headteachers in Sydney, Australia to develop a means of evaluating the mathematical progress of children from their earliest years in school to the age of about eight or nine years. They consist of a developmental sequence of mathematical objectives which parallel the early school mathematics curriculum.

This assessment technique may be used to help a teacher discover the reasons for a child's apparent slow progress, evaluate a child transferring into a school to establish his or her position vis-à-vis the curriculum, and/or monitor each child's progress in mathematics. Time of administration is likely to vary according to the reason for testing, but a reasonable estimation would be 15–20 minutes for a routine survey, while several sessions of similar length may well be necessary for a newcomer to the school.

The contents are divided into three mathematical areas or "strands": number, shape, and measurement. The major strand is number and consists of 40 objectives, each with several sub-problems. Items here range from the initial classification of objects by attributes (e.g., "show me the blue block") and progress through to problem arithmetic and the display of statistical information. The upper limit for problems is their application to the four rules of number using numerals not exceeding 20. Questions from this section are to be selected to match the achievement level found generally in the strand. The language used throughout the number strand is that of set theory and includes some quite difficult concepts (e.g., "element" and "partition") which may well be too much for some preconceptual children. However, the manual states clearly that set language need not be used; certainly all items are readily adaptable for use within a more traditional classroom. While this degree of flexibility may allow wider use of the instrument, it is likely to have a significant effect on its precision as a test. If a variety of instructions are possible, then how can a subsequent tester be sure that there has been a real change in the child's performance? Also, most sections of the number items contain an extra part for children who use structured apparatus of the Cuisenaire rod type. "Rod" children complete both "rod" and "non-rod" questions whereas children not familiar with this apparatus complete only non-rod questions. Clearly practice or fatigue effects are different for each of these groups of children and may therefore affect performance.

The second strand, shape, evaluates the child's development of the language and concepts of geometric shape. Items included range from describing plane shapes through symmetry to the beginnings of an appreciation of simple mechanics (e.g., why are bridge girders formed in triangles?).

The final strand, measurement, includes items on length (12), mass (12), capacity (11), area (5), time (5), money (7), and temperature (3). There is a strong Piagetian flavour to this strand, with many examples related to development of conservation. Because most of the children within the range of these procedures are at a preconceptual/transitional stage, there are a range of non-numerical concepts whose development can be included. Some of the language within the section is perhaps too Piagetian, causing potential problems in differentiating between a child's difficulty in grasping a concept and the failure of the tester to simplify sufficiently the words used and the structure of the language in the sentence (e.g., "Have these two pieces of clay still the same mass as the ball?").

The layout of questions within the test proper is good. Clear instructions are given on the preparation needed, the materials required, and the procedure to follow. An index of each of the objectives is provided, linked to the test page. General presentation of the Procedures, however, constitutes a major criticism of the work. The authors recognise that a book of this size is likely to cause anxiety in infants' school teachers. Nearly all respondents of a trial exercise, described in an appendix, expressed "horror, amazement or shock at the thickness of the volume." In this reviewer's opinion, greater cognisance should have been taken of this reaction. While certainly it is possible by means of introductory courses to move beyond this reaction to some of the excellent material contained within, it must be remembered that there are many teachers without such support. There is no point in producing a volume if potential buyers put it down after a quick perusal.

The material contained within the book has a confusing organization. Instead of placing the index to the contents of the tests immediately before the test instructions proper, it is placed between the contents page and the introduction. It might have been more appropriate to follow usual practice by making use of a test manual containing the general instructions for administration and notes for guidance. The description of the trial procedures and feedback would also be relevant in the manual. A separate booklet could contain the tests and instructions, preceded by the index. Ideally this should be in ring-type binding to lie flat on a table. Finally, there could be separate record sheets for each pupil.

It should be remembered that the Procedures are in no sense an attempt to obtain a normative assessment of an individual child. There are, therefore, neither figures for reliability or validity, nor any normative tables. Great care therefore needs to be taken when making any interpretation of the scores obtained.

In conclusion, the Mathematics Evaluation Procedures are an attempt to meet a need in a highly neglected area of the school curriculum, the development of mathematics in the first years at school. It is easy to be overcritical about a procedure of this type because it lacks the rigor of a more systematically designed, normed assessment. As the product, though, of a group of enthusiastic practitioners, responding to a need not being met by the test producers, they are worthy of support. However, in the present forms the Procedures are not designed to attract a major consumer, the infants' school teacher. With some changes in presentation, perhaps along the lines suggested above, the Procedures could provide a stimulating and valuable addition to the materials available to the teachers of children in their early years at school.

Review of Mathematics Evaluation Procedures K–2 by RICHARD LESH, Professor of Mathematics and Education, Northwestern University, Evanston, IL:

Unlike tests which are designed to identify children (or classes) that are exceptional (either above or below average), this test is designed to identify what is exceptional about individual students. It is intended to identify specific (dis)abilities or (mis)understandings of individual children. No attempt is made to produce normative information for ranking or comparing classes (or children), nor to compare individual children (or classes) with some "standard." In fact, no provision is made for calculating or recording a total score. Rather, the goal is to provide a diagnostic tool to inform instruction and remediation; i.e., it is a formative assessment of individual youngsters, with results that map easily into the "strands" that shape most popular textbooks and curriculum guides.

The test's 106 objectives are organized into three "strands," comparable to those that constitute the "core" primary mathematics curriculum in many countries. In fact, a sizeable representative sample of Australian teachers and curriculum specialists participated in the selection of the test's objectives, using popular curriculum guides as a base pool. This fact, together with an extensive trial period in which items were refined and response types were classified, gives the test considerable "face" validity.

The test's main strands are: number, shapes (i.e., elementary geometry), and measurement. The number strand emphasizes problem solving in concrete situations, and it also emphasizes graphing and representational skills; the measurement strand includes items related to length, area, volume, mass, time, money, and temperature. Many of the items involve the use of concrete materials and many are intended to focus on "higher order cognitive processes."

For each objective, a number of items (i.e., usually at least five) are suggested which focus on various understandings related to the underlying objective. Each item set is intended to provide a starting point for generating a diagnostic interview for teachers to use with individual youngsters. The goal is to identify the processes that individual students use to answer the questions. It is assumed that: (*a*) students who produce the same number of items correctly, for a given objective, may base their answers on qualitatively different concepts and processes, (*b*) two students may interpret the same stimulus (question, or item) in quite different ways, and (*c*) two students may use two different processes to produce the same answer to a given item. Consequently, the test is accompanied by a sample "response sheet" which focuses on the quality of "expected" response types, and suggestions for "follow-up" questioning procedures.

The response sheet is referred to as a sample because individual teachers are encouraged to tailor the entire test to their own instructional objectives, and to the needs of individual youngsters. It is not suggested that any child be given the entire battery of items. Rather, items are to be sampled to "focus in on" the specific understandings, skills, and abilities of individual children.

Because different students are intended to receive different sets of items, and because different students who receive the same item often may interpret it in different ways, "standardization" is not a relevant issue for the test as a whole, nor for individual items. Relevance to critical curriculum objectives is the main issue, and the test's selection of content is excellent. The objectives not only represent sensible choices among concept priorities, the items accompanying each objective reflect unusually diverse and creative ways to assess different factors that contribute to the meaningfulness of the underlying ideas.

Each test is set out in three columns. The first states the objectives being evaluated, the second lists the materials needed, and the third gives details concerning instructions to be given to the child, together with suggestions to the teacher concerning the possible significance of various response types. The materials are largely those found in classrooms; others are easily made by teachers or are available commercially. Nearly all of the items have obvious instructional analogues for instruction or remediation.

As a "handbook" for teachers to use to create diagnostic "clinical interviews" for children in grades K through 2, this test is as useful as anything I have seen. It focuses heavily on "understandings" underlying basic mathematical ideas; yet it also includes items dealing with memorization and basic facts. Its selection of content is excellent, and it could easily be used to structure monthly lesson plans in most K through 2 classrooms in many countries.

Because the test is intended to yield "in depth" assessments of individual children, teachers using the test may wish to use some sort of standardized test to select students for such individualized attention. A text which gives profiles of abilities and disabilities also could help guide the selection of interview items. In particular, because the diagnostic interview text has the potential of being especially useful for identifying the difficulties of children with learning difficulties (e.g., children with "learning disabilities"), it is important to select interview questions that do not exacerbate known nonmathematical disabilities.

[667]

Mathematics Topic Tests: Elementary Level. Grades 4–9; 1974–80; criterion-referenced; 7 tests; no norms; "if 80 per cent of a group give correct answers to an item or a group of items, it can be said to have reached mastery in this area"; no information presented on mastery levels for individuals; manual ('80, 16 pages); directions ('77, 4 pages); record sheet (1 page) for each test; optional inservice training package (2 film strips and cassettes); separate answer sheets must be used except for test 2; 1984 price data: $13.20 per 35 tests; $2.25 per scoring key per test; $5.75 per 35 answer sheets; $.70 per class record form; $2.25 per 35 individual record forms; $33 per training package; $3.55 per manual; $1 per directions; $6.55 per specimen set; (20–40) minutes per test; Frances Crook Morrison; published in cooperation with the Research Centre of the Ottawa Board of Education by Guidance Centre, University of Toronto [Canada].*

a) TEST 1, NUMBER AND NUMERATION. Grades 5–9; 40 item scores plus total; Form A ('74, 4 pages).

b) TEST 2, ADDITION AND SUBTRACTION WITH WHOLE NUMBERS. Grades 4–6; 32 item scores plus total; Form A ('74, 4 pages).

c) TEST 3, MULTIPLICATION AND DIVISION WITH WHOLE NUMBERS. Grades 5–8; 24 item scores plus total; Form A ('74, 4 pages).

d) TEST 4, OPERATIONS WITH FRACTIONS. Grades 5–7; 32 item scores plus total; Form A ('74, 4 pages).

e) TEST 5, MULTIPLICATION AND DIVISION WITH FRACTIONS. Grades 6–9; 31 item scores plus total; Form A ('74, 4 pages).

f) TEST 6, MEASUREMENT, GRAPHS, AND GEOMETRY. Grades 5–8; 33 item scores plus total; Form A ('78, 7 pages).

g) TEST 7, OPERATIONS WITH DECIMALS. Grades 5–8; 39 item scores plus total; Form A ('78, 4 pages).

For a review by Thomas E. Kieren of an earlier edition, see 8:282.

Review of Mathematics Topic Tests: Elementary Level by RICHARD LESH, Professor of Mathematics and Education, Northwestern University, Evanston, IL:

Each of the seven tests of the Mathematics Topic Tests: Elementary Level would be quick and easy for a teacher to use and score. Students record multiple choice responses on answer sheets which can be graded using perforated grid overlays. Compared with most multiple choice achievement tests, the items on this test are quite "rich"; that is, even though the items are heavily symbolic/computational in nature, most require multiple-step solution procedures or the use of more than one mathematical concept. Multiple-step, multiple-concept items can be strong assets of a test if some attempt is made to isolate the procedures or ideas that are used to arrive at answers. On this test, however, no such attempt is apparent. In particular, no attempt is made to identify or interpret incorrect answer choices; only correct answers are identified. If errors are made, no attempt is made to identify the likely sub-step or sub-concept that was the source of difficulty. These facts make the interpretation of incorrect answers virtually impossible. Students with identical scores on a given subtest could easily reflect qualitatively different levels of understanding, depending on which sub-steps and sub-concepts caused the errors.

On some competing multiple choice tests, an attempt is made to infer the processes that students use in multiple-step or multiple-concept items by "holding factors constant" in either the distractors or the item stems in a set of "similar" problems. No such procedure was apparent in the construction of this test.

Each of the seven tests is accompanied by a class record sheet and by an individual record form intended to facilitate the interpretation of each student's performance. On the record form for individual students, tersely stated "objectives," similar to those in most curriculum guides or textbook series, are given for most test items. For some items, the "objective" is simply suggested by giving a key word or phrase (e.g., associative law, addition with tens, etc.). However, because most of the items can be answered incorrectly for a variety of reasons, depending on which sub-step or sub-concept is the source of error, and because many of these error sources have little to do with the stated objective of the item, the diagnostic utility of the test is limited. It is unlikely that a teacher could specify a given student's difficulties based on error patterns in the test battery.

On both the individual record forms and the class record sheets, the items/objectives are organized under "strand" headings, which again are similar to those typically used to organize textbook and curriculum guide objectives. For example, for the "multiplication and division with fractions" test, the strand headings are: meaning of multiplication and division with fractions, multiplication with fractions, finding percents, division with fractions, multiplication and division with decimals, and problems. By providing a link between test results and common instructional materials, this organizational scheme apparently is intended to help teachers design appropriate instructional activities to meet individual and class needs that are identified by the test. Unfortunately, as stated above, because the items frequently are questionable indicators of the stated objectives assigned to them, they are equally difficult to sort into the suggested strands. For example, even the items which were intended to test topics like "the meaning of multiplication of fractions" tend to depend heavily on computational skill; interpreting difficulties on these items as indicators of deficient conceptual understanding (or meaning) is questionable.

Would the test be useful for ranking or comparing students within a given class? The guide suggests that 80% correct on a group of items can be interpreted as mastery in that area. Yet, for most strands on most of the subtests, which 20% of the items are missed may be quite significant. For reasons described above, students with scores far below 80% could be closer to "mastery" than many of their colleagues with "mastery level" scores.

Is the test useful for ranking or comparing whole classes? Because no individual or class norms are given, it is not possible to compare class performance with standardized scales of achievement. Comparisons among individual classes also may be misleading, especially if the classes represent schools with different mathematics curricula. Due to the brevity of the seven tests, compared with many standardized achievement tests, the content sampled is rather "narrow" and the selection of problem types is even more restricted. For example, on the "fractions" tests, items about percents and decimals are included, but items about ratios, rates, proportions, etc. are omitted. This means that performance can be expected to be influenced considerably by the topics emphasized or de-emphasized by instruction in particular classes.

A number of standardized mathematics achievement tests are available commercially. I can see few reasons to select this one.

Review of Mathematics Topic Tests: Elementary Level by EDWARD A. SILVER, *Associate Professor of Mathematics, San Diego State University, San Diego, CA:*

This series of tests was developed to provide single-topic tests that would be useful at more than one grade level and could be administered at one sitting. As such, these tests provide a useful alternative to the usual tests for grades 4 through 9, which typically survey all the work done at one or more grade levels. Since the topic areas are quite broadly defined, each test surveys a fairly wide range of content within the topic domain.

The manual and the booklet giving directions for administering and scoring the tests are both clearly written, with useful suggestions for establishing a conducive testing environment and for using the test results. Directions to the examiner, as well as the students, are straightforward. Although these tests are not strictly timed, information is given regarding the expected working time for the tests.

The manual describes the procedure used to develop the tests, including mention of several tryouts. The KR-20 reliability coefficients obtained during the tryouts ranged from .60 to .93, with a median of .85. The validity of each test was established by the test development committee, but the manual wisely suggests that the validity of a test depends mainly on the suitability of the test's contents for a particular user. Before deciding to use a test, potential users are urged to consult the table of specifications, located at the end of the manual, for the test being considered.

No rationale is given for setting the criterion for group mastery at 80%. Furthermore, there is no mention of an individual mastery criterion. On the other hand, the manual describes in detail a number of ways in which the test results of a classroom group could be used, such as identifying general strengths and weaknesses, examining changes in a class across time, or examining differences between classes or grade levels.

Although the manual is rich in information about interpreting group performance, it contains far less useful information about individual performance. No data on individuial performance are provided and the relationship between item responses, or response patterns, and individual students needs is not discussed. No instructional suggestions are given for students who exhibit certain error patterns, nor is information given so that error patterns could be easily identified. Nevertheless, it should be noted that the manual wisely suggests that performance on these tests should be only one method used to assess students' achievement and individual needs. It is suggested that other approaches, such as observing a student solve a problem and questioning about the methods used, might be used to supplement the individual information obtained from these tests.

Beyond the lack of useful information regarding individual performance, the most serious deficiency of this series of tests is the lack of attention to testing children's understanding of basic concepts in the topic areas. The manual claims that the tests provide a "balanced coverage of skills, understanding of concepts, and applications," but it is clear that the tests are devoted almost entirely to computational skills. This is especially true with respect to items on fractions in Tests 4 and 5 and on decimals in Test 7, but even the items on whole numbers in Tests 2 and 3 tend to ignore basic conceptual understandings. The diagnostic utility of the tests would be significantly enhanced if they gave more attention to conceptual understanding. Nevertheless, the computational items are reasonable and probably represent accurately the emphasis in most school programs. Furthermore, the word problems and other application problems are clearly written and relevant to the topic domain.

Potential users will want to consider carefully the units of measurement used in the tests. Some of the tests contain only metric units, whereas others contain only imperial units. Since Canadian schools have converted entirely to metric units, revisions are planned so that the series will be entirely metric. No information was given as to the expected date of completion for the metric revisions.

In summary, the Mathematics Topic Tests are single-topic tests that can be administered at one sitting. They provide a useful alternative to survey tests that sample from several content domains. The tests would appear to be very useful in providing information about group performance and less useful in diagnosing the mathematical needs of individual pupils.

[668]

Maudsley Personality Inventory. College and adults; 1959–62; MPI; for revised edition, see Eysenck Personality Inventory; 2 scores: neuroticism, extraversion; H. J. Eysenck.

a) BRITISH EDITION. 1959; 1 form (2 pages); manual (8 pages); 1985 price data: £1.50 per 20 tests; £1 per manual; administration time not reported; Hodder & Stoughton Educational [England].

b) AMERICAN EDITION. 1959–62; 1 form ('59, 2 pages, items identical with British edition); manual ('62, 21 pages); 1985 price data: $3.75 per 25 tests; $2 per set of hand scoring keys; $2 per manual; $3 per specimen set; scoring service, $.45 or less per test; (10–15) minutes; Robert R. Knapp (manual); EdITS/Educational and Industrial Testing Service.*

See T3:1419 (39 references), 8:611 (129 references), T2:1275 (273 references), and P:161 (149 references); for reviews by Arthur R. Jensen, James C. Lingoes, William Stephenson, and Phillip E. Vernon, and excerpted reviews by Edward S. Bordin, A. Bursil, and G. A. Foulds, see 6:138 (120 references).

TEST REFERENCES

1. Rassaby, E., & Paykel, E. S. Factor patterns in depression: A replication study. JOURNAL OF AFFECTIVE DISORDERS, 1979, 1, 187–194.

2. West, J. E., & West, E. D. Child abuse treated in a psychiatric day hospital. CHILD ABUSE & NEGLECT, 1979, 3, 699–707.

3. LaPointe, K. A., & Crandell, C. J. Relationship of irrational beliefs to self-reported depression. COGNITIVE THERAPY AND RESEARCH, 1980, 4, 247–250.

4. Arndt, W. B., Jr., & Ladd, B. Sibling incest aversion as an index of Oedipal conflict. JOURNAL OF PERSONALITY ASSESSMENT, 1981, 45, 52–58.

5. Harrell, T. H., Chambless, D. L., & Calhoun, J. F. Correlational relationships between self-statements and affective states. COGNITIVE THERAPY AND RESEARCH, 1981, 5, 159–173.

6. Eyre, S. L., Rounsaville, B. J., & Kleber, H. D. History of childhood hyperactivity in a clinic population of opiate addicts. THE JOURNAL OF NERVOUS AND MENTAL DISEASE, 1982, 170, 522–529.

7. Rounsaville, B. J., Weissman, M. M., & Kleber, H. D. The significance of alcoholism in treated opiate addicts. THE JOURNAL OF NERVOUS AND MENTAL DISEASE, 1982, 170, 479–488.

8. Rounsaville, B. J., Weissman, M. M., Wilber, C. H., & Kleber, H. D. Pathways to opiate addiction: An evaluation of differing antecedents. BRITISH JOURNAL OF PSYCHIATRY, 1982, 141, 437–446.

9. Shiomi, K. Relationship between reversible-figure latencies and scores of two personality inventories. PERCEPTUAL AND MOTOR SKILLS, 1982, 54, 803–807.

10. Wilber, C. H., Rounsaville, B. J., Sugarman, A., Casey, J. B., & Kleber, H. D. Ego development of opiate addicts: An application of Loevinger's stage model. THE JOURNAL OF NERVOUS AND MENTAL DISEASE, 1982, 170, 202–208.

11. Fawcett, J., Clark, D. C., Scheftner, W. A., & Gibbons, R. D. Assessing anhedonia in psychiatric patients. ARCHIVES OF GENERAL PSYCHIATRY, 1983, 40, 79–84.

12. Hirschfeld, R. M. A., Klerman, G. L., Clayton, P. J., & Keller, M. B. Personality and depression: Empirical findings. ARCHIVES OF GENERAL PSYCHIATRY, 1983, 40, 993–998.

13. Rounsaville, B. J., Glazer, W., Wilber, C. H., Weissman, M. M., & Kleber, H. D. Short-term interpersonal psychotherapy in methadone-maintained opiate addicts. ARCHIVES OF GENERAL PSYCHIATRY, 1983, 40, 629–636.

14. Thomas, C. R. Field independence and Myers-Briggs thinking individuals. PERCEPTUAL AND MOTOR SKILLS, 1983, 57, 790.

15. Woody, G. E., Luborsky, L., McLellan, T., O'Brien, C. P., Beck, A. T., Blaine, J., Herman, I., & Hole, A. Psychotherapy for opiate addicts: Does it help? ARCHIVES OF GENERAL PSYCHIATRY, 1983, 40, 639–645.

[669]

McCall-Crabbs Standard Test Lessons in Reading. Reading level grades 3, 4, 5, 6, 7, 8; 1926–79; fourth revised edition of McCall-Crabbs Standard Test Lessons in Reading; item and grade equivalent scores; no data on reliability and validity; tentative grade score norms for grades 3–8; 1 form; 6 overlapping levels labeled Books A, B, C, D, E, F (grades 3–8) in separate booklets; revised manual ('79, 16 pages); separate answer sheets may be used; 1983 price data: $17.15 per kit of 6 booklets and manual; $2.65 per test booklet; $3.65 per 30 student answer sheets; $1.25 per teacher's manual/answer key; 60 tests per booklet, 180 minutes for each booklet, 3 minutes for any one test; original test by William A. McCall and Lelah Crabbs Schroeder; revision by Robert P. Starr; Teachers College Press.*

Review of McCall-Crabbs Standard Test Lessons in Reading by BRENDAN JOHN BARTLETT, Senior Lecturer in Psychology and Special Education, Brisbane College of Advanced Education: Mt. Gravatt Campus, Brisbane, Australia:

Notwithstanding its title, the McCall-Crabbs Standard Test Lessons in Reading (revised, 4th edition) is more a package of reading exercises than a test of reading, or an instructional program in reading. The package lacks empirical support as test or instructional tool. It does not report standardization, reliability, or validity data. It has no definition of key constructs, and it contains no instructional content beyond provision of passages of text and accompanying questions. It does contain an extensive range of exercises which, if used by teachers employing their own theoretical models of reading and reading instruction, might prove useful as a teaching resource.

The McCall-Crabbs package consists of six booklets and a Teacher's Manual. Each booklet contains 60 exercises, one to a page. Exercises are in a common format; a passage of text is followed by eight multiple-choice items. At the bottom of each page is a conversion table from which a respondent's raw score can be converted to grade-equivalents. Each page is removable, so that teachers may choose to use a booklet either as a consumable or as a non-consumable commodity.

Booklets are sequenced to span grades three to eight, with exercises graduated in accord with norms obtained in an unpublished standardization. Succeeding books are intended for average readers at levels one grade higher. The smooth graduation of exercises has been affected somewhat by differences in variation of performances within and across exercises in the standardization sample.

Transformation of raw scores to grade-equivalent scores only limits the extent to which performance or change in performance may be measured and interpreted. This limitation is acknowledged in the manual. The grade-equivalent transformations were standardized against performances of a large norm-sample on the Gates MacGinitie Reading Tests (GMRT). Correlations between total GMRT score and scores on individual test lessons for McCall-Crabbs were used as the basis for concurrent validity derivations. Set against a conservative index (Spearman $r = .60$), 96 of 360 coefficients failed to reach criterion. The unpublished standardization report does not contain reliability data nor information on construct, content, or predictive validity.

The manual adequately describes administration and scoring of the test lessons. It provides general suggestions for how the package might be used as an instructional tool. However, in the absence of a McCall-Crabbs perspective on reading, and of definition of terms used throughout the manual (e.g., "reading ability," "reading skills," and "growth in reading"), the manual is deficient as an explanatory framework for the package. Thus, potential users have no ready empirical information to support the authors' view that students who complete exercises in the package will receive feedback "that can help sustain progress toward longer-range goals [in reading growth]." This reviewer was unable to find published reports on data collected to test this claim.

Content and format of the six booklets suggests a traditional view of instruction in reading comprehension; a passage of text is followed by questions about the text. In the hands of a teacher knowledgable about writer, text, and reader variables in reading comprehension, such content and format may prove a useful basis for instruction. However, if a potential user seeks information about such variables or help with instructional method, the McCall-Crabbs package is not an appropriate instrument.

On the admission of its authors the McCall-Crabbs Standard Test Lessons in Reading (revised, 4th edition) is not intended to be a precise measuring instrument. Certainly it is not. In addition, despite the appeal of attractive packaging, a wide range of text, and a familiar format, the instructional value of McCall-Crabbs is undetermined; it is also untestable other than pragmatically as each user develops constructs for those reading behaviors which might be influenced by the package.

[670]

McCarthy Individualized Diagnostic Reading Inventory, Revised Edition. Grades K–12; 1971–76; 3 levels of qualitative ratings of reading (independent, instructional, frustration) and item scores classified above or below 90% mastery criterion; no data on reliability and validity; no norms; individual; 1 form ('76, 14 pages); 4 pages: part 1 (placement for instruction in reading, fluency, comprehension, and thinking skills), part 2 (phonics, word recognition and study skills), part 3 (questionnaire concerning a student's reading interests and habits), part 4 (outline for planning individualized remediations); manual ('76, 17 pages); teacher administration booklet ('76, 16 pages); individual record form ('76, 5 pages); 1983 price data: $1.60 per pupil booklet; $4.90 per individual record form; $2.40 per information booklet; $5.90 per teacher administration booklet; (35–60) minutes for part 1, (35–40) minutes for part 2, administration time not reported for part 3; William G. McCarthy; Educators Publishing Service, Inc.*

Review of McCarthy Individualized Diagnostic Reading Inventory, Revised Edition, by JOYCE HOOD, Associate Professor of Educational Psychology, The University of Iowa, Iowa City, IA:

The McCarthy Individualized Diagnostic Reading Inventory is neither better nor worse than most other informal reading inventories available today. It has not been norm-referenced because its purpose is to describe performance on curricular materials intended to be representative of those available for instruction. However, evidence is not provided that the word lists and test passages are representative of instructional reading materials at the specified levels. Difficulty levels were assigned to test passages using Spache and Dale-Chall readability formulas, which have little meaning in relation to grade levels of current basal readers. The Spache formula expresses readability in relation to basal readers published in the 1950s. The Dale-Chall formula yields an estimate of the grade equivalents on norm-referenced tests which would be achieved by children who are capable of comprehending a given selection.

In addition to the word lists and passages provided for instructional placement, a variety of skills are to be assessed in parts 2, 3, and 4. In testing phonics, the examiner is encouraged to pronounce the part of the word not being tested. Then the child is asked to pronounce the tested element, which is underlined, and then to synthesize the word. The examiner may find it only moderately difficult to pronounce parts of bat and tub, but quite challenging to pronounce parts of tonsils and amongst. This is just one example to illustrate why this reviewer finds the selection of skills to assess in this inventory and the method of assessment to be of questionable value.

When the relatedness of test content to instructional materials is poorly documented, a test user must develop a clinical sensitivity to levels of test performance which suggest a child may be ready for instruction at a given level in a particular reading program. The selection of one of the many available tests to use is usually based on considerations of convenience and appearance. On neither of these considerations is McCarthy's inventory particularly noteworthy.

The best feature of this inventory is that the teacher administration booklet is laminated, which improves its durability. This should be done for the pupil booklet also, which is not predicted to survive many uses in its present form. The size of type in the word lists and reading passages included in the pupil booklet gets smaller as difficulty increases. This may have a negative effect on the performance of older, poorer readers who can judge their performance by the size of type.

The laminated teacher booklet is to serve as a reusable answer sheet. An examinee's responses are to be marked in washable felt-tip marker and removed after they have been analyzed. An individual record form is provided where test performance is to be summarized and much additional information is to be entered, including remediation plans. An examiner who completes this form would spend a lot of time thinking about a child's abilities, interests, and physical and psychosocial characteristics. Nevertheless, this reviewer would prefer to have a record of a child's actual test performance to file along with the examiner's interpretation.

Because of the amount of detail to be recorded on the individual record form, an instructor of a practicum course in remedial reading might ask students to use this test. However, since the test content is not clearly related to specific levels of instructional materials, the results of the test would be difficult for any but the most experienced clinicians to interpret. As an experienced clinician, this reviewer would prefer to use excerpts from actual instructional materials for individual diagnosis. McCarthy's inventory does not make up in convenience what it lacks in precision in terms of the relationship of test content to specific instructional materials.

Review of McCarthy Individualized Diagnostic Reading Inventory, Revised Edition, by ROBERT M. WILSON, Professor of Education, University of Maryland, College Park, MD:

The McCarthy Individualized Diagnostic Reading Inventory, hereafter referred to as MIDRI, consists of four parts. Part 1 has the characteristics of an informal reading inventory. It starts with a word recognition assessment to determine placement for starting the reading section. Silent reading is followed by oral reading which is followed by questions for comprehension. Part 2 has the characteristics of a criterion-referenced test, assessing phonics, word recognition, and study skills. Part 3 is in the form of an interview which can provide information about a student and his or her learning environment. Part 4 provides space to start a plan of instruction.

Part 1 of the MIDRI has some interesting qualities. The passages are long enough (between 65 and 154 words in length) to obtain a good sample of reading behavior. The examiner is encouraged to make qualitative notes on reading behaviors that go beyond the test performance scores. For example, characteristics of fluent reading and of creative-critical reading skills are to be recorded. In the testing of comprehension there are two recall questions, two interpretive questions, and four creative-critical questions for each passage. For the latter there are no correct answers. Appropriately, teachers are to use their judgement on the appropriateness of answers for creative-critical questions. The passages used to evaluate comprehension are mostly narrative. Many teachers will want the responses of their students to expository material as well. The addition of some expository passages might make future editions of the MIDRI even more attractive and useful. The Individual Record Form for part 1 provides space for easy recording of a reading fluency and reading comprehension profile on the first page.

Part 2 provides 29 tests of reading related subskills. The examiner is encouraged to use these tests selectively since all of the tests would not be appropriate for any one reader. On the Individual Record Form there is space for an indication of mastery (90% correct) and a space for the examiner's diagnostic observations.

Part 3 presents questions for the examiner to ask the student. While the questions are not likely to reveal many significant factors about the reader, it is interesting that an inventory would carry such a section. The examiner is directed to inquire about such things as reading topic preference, school subjects most enjoyed, and books the reader has enjoyed. Part 3 also directs the examiner to examine school records for educational and physical information about the reader. I found this section to be refreshing since it places the reader in a context and brings the diagnosis to life.

Part 4, the development of an instructional plan, is good to have with an inventory. Unfortunately it only provides minimal direction for the examiner and has no real guidelines. For example, Table 20 is entitled, "Plans to Involve Parents." However, only two suggestions about how that might be done are included. They are: (*a*) listen to the child read for a brief time daily and (*b*) attend to the child's health problems. There are numerous other ways that parents can help and I would recommend that some of them be included. For example, it might be suggested that parents try to: make reading enjoyable, establish a pleasant study environment, make good reading material available, and focus on the meaning aspects of reading.

In the Information Booklet the MIDRI is reported to be valid and reliable. Technical data to indicate how validity and reliability were determined was not included. In correspondence with the constructor of this test, however, the following validity information was obtained. The Controlled Vocabulary Word Lists for levels 1 through 6 were made up from words occurring in the highest frequency as found in five basal reader series. For levels 7, 8, and 9 the words were selected from three English literature books. Field testing activities were conducted prior to the publication of the tests. Two tests were correlated with scores from the Iowa Test of Basic Skills and the Stanford Reading Test. Correlations of .70 and .90 were reported.

The MIDRI has been carefully created. It carries features that direct the examiner to important aspects of diagnosis beyond test scores. It is to be used by examiners who are expected to make diagnostic decisions concerning the appropriateness of answers and the appropriateness of sections to be administered.

[671]

McCarthy Scales of Children's Abilities. Ages 2.5–8.5; 1970–72; MSCA; 6 scores: verbal, perceptual-performance, quantitative, composite (general cognitive), memory, motor; individual; 1 form; manual ('72, 217 pages); record form ('72, 8 pages); 1984 price data: $150 per set of testing materials including manual, 25 record forms, and 25 drawing booklets; $10 per 25 record forms; $12 per 25 drawing booklets; $12.75 per manual; (45–60) minutes; Dorothea McCarthy; The Psychological Corporation.*

See T3:1424 (60 references); for reviews by Jane V. Hunt, Jerome M. Sattler, and Arthur B. Silverstein, and excerpted reviews by Everett E. Davis, Linda Hufano and Ralph Hoepfner, R. B. Ammons and C. H. Ammons, and Alan Krichev, see 8:219 (29 references).

TEST REFERENCES

1. Reynolds, C. R. The McCarthy drawing tests as a group instrument. CONTEMPORARY EDUCATIONAL PSYCHOLOGY, 1978, 3, 169–174.

2. O'Donnell, J. P., O'Neill, S., & Staley, A. Congenital correlates of distractibility. JOURNAL OF ABNORMAL CHILD PSYCHOLOGY, 1979, 7, 465–470.

3. Ivimey, J. K., & Taylor, R. L. Differential performance of learning disabled and non-learning disabled children on the McCarthy scales, WISC-R, and WRAT. JOURNAL OF CLINICAL PSYCHOLOGY, 1980, 36, 960–963.

4. Arinoldo, C. G. Black-white differences in the general cognitive index of the McCarthy scales and in the full scale IQs of Wechsler's scales. JOURNAL OF CLINICAL PSYCHOLOGY, 1981, 37, 630–638.

5. Armstrong, K. A. A treatment and education program for parents and children who are at-risk of abuse and neglect. CHILD ABUSE & NEGLECT, 1981, 5, 167–175.

6. Reynolds, C. R., McBride, R. D., & Gibson, L. J. Black-white IQ discrepancies may be related to differences in hemisphericity. CONTEMPORARY EDUCATIONAL PSYCHOLOGY, 1981, 6, 180–184.

7. Strom, R., Hathaway, C., & Slaughter, H. The correlation of maternal attitudes and preschool children's performance on the McCarthy Scales of Children's Abilities. JOURNAL OF INSTRUCTIONAL PSYCHOLOGY, 1981, 8, 139–145.

8. Wilson, R. S. Mental development: Concordance for same-sex and opposite-sex dizygotic twins. DEVELOPMENTAL PSYCHOLOGY, 1981, 17, 626–629.

9. Arinoldo, C. G. Concurrent validity of McCarthy's Scales. PERCEPTUAL AND MOTOR SKILLS, 1982, 54, 1343–1346.

10. Bondy, A. S., Sheslow, D., Norcross, J. C., & Constantino, R. Comparison of Slosson and McCarthy scales for minority pre-school children. PERCEPTUAL AND MOTOR SKILLS, 1982, 54, 356–358.

11. Camp, B. W. Note on maternal authoritarian attitudes and cognitive performance in kindergarten children. PSYCHOLOGICAL REPORTS, 1982, 50, 603–607.

12. Earls, F. Application of DSM-III in an epidemiological study of preschool children. THE AMERICAN JOURNAL OF PSYCHIATRY, 1982, 139, 242–243.

13. Goldberg, T., & Benjamins, D. The possible existence of phonemic reading in the presence of Broca's aphasia: A case report. NEUROPSYCHOLOGIA, 1982, 20, 547–558.

14. LaVeck, B., & Hammond, M. A. Performance on the motor scale of the McCarthy Scales of Children's Abilities as related to home environment and neonatal reflexes. PERCEPTUAL AND MOTOR SKILLS, 1982, 54, 1265–1266.

15. Massoth, N. A., & Levenson, R. L., Jr. The McCarthy Scales of Children's Abilities as a predictor of reading readiness and reading achievement. PSYCHOLOGY IN THE SCHOOLS, 1982, 19, 293–296.

16. Mcloughlin, C. S., & Gullo, D. F. Perceptual, motor, memory, and quantitative elements of language behavior: Differences between 3- and 4-year-old performance. PERCEPTUAL AND MOTOR SKILLS, 1982, 55, 1038.

17. Naglieri, J. A. Interpreting WISC-R and McCarthy scatter: A caution. CONTEMPORARY EDUCATIONAL PSYCHOLOGY, 1982, 7, 90–94.

18. Naglieri, J. A., & Harrison, P. L. McCarthy scales, McCarthy Screening Test, and Kaufman's McCarthy short form correlations with the Peabody Individual Achievement Test. PSYCHOLOGY IN THE SCHOOLS, 1982, 19, 149–155.

19. Piersel, W. C., & Santos, L. Comparison of McCarthy and Goodenough-Harris scoring systems for kindergarten children's human figure drawings. PERCEPTUAL AND MOTOR SKILLS, 1982, 55, 633–634.

20. Simons, M. R., & Goh, D. S. Relationships between McCarthy Scales of Childrens Abilities and teachers' ratings of school achievement. PERCEPTUAL AND MOTOR SKILLS, 1982, 54, 1159–1162.

21. Spencer, M. B. Personal and group identity of black children: An alternative synthesis. GENETIC PSYCHOLOGY MONOGRAPHS, 1982, 106, 59–84.

22. Swartz, J. P., & Pierson, D. E. Cognitive abilities of sibling pairs: Evaluating the impact of early education. PSYCHOLOGICAL REPORTS, 1982, 51, 171–176.

23. Valencia, R. R. Predicting academic achievement of Mexican American children: Preliminary analysis of the McCarthy Scales. EDUCATIONAL AND PSYCHOLOGICAL MEASUREMENT, 1982, 42, 1269–1278.

24. Bracken, B. A., & Prasse, D. P. Concurrent validity of the PPVT-R for "at risk" preschool children. PSYCHOLOGY IN THE SCHOOLS, 1983, 20, 13–15.

25. Ellison, P. H. The relationship of motor and cognitive function in infancy, pre-school and early school years. JOURNAL OF CLINICAL CHILD PSYCHOLOGY, 1983, 12, 81–90.

26. Siegel, L. S. Correction for prematurity and its consequences for the assessment of the very low birth weight infant. CHILD DEVELOPMENT, 1983, 54, 1176–1188.

27. Valencia, R. R. Stability of the McCarthy Scales of Children's Abilities over a one-year period for Mexican-American children. PSYCHOLOGY IN THE SCHOOLS, 1983, 20, 29–34.

28. Valencia, R. R., & Rankin, R. J. Concurrent validity and reliability of the Kaufman version of the McCarthy Scales Short Form for a sample of Mexican-American children. EDUCATIONAL AND PSYCHOLOGICAL MEASUREMENT, 1983, 43, 915–925.

29. Wilson, R. S. The Louisville Twin Study: Developmental synchronies in behavior. CHILD DEVELOPMENT, 1983, 54, 298–316.

Review of McCarthy Scales of Children's Abilities by KATHLEEN D. PAGET, Associate Professor of Psychology, University of South Carolina, Columbia, SC:

Six years after the publication of the McCarthy Scales of Children's Abilities (MSCA), Salvia and Ysseldyke (1978) suggested that "it is only a matter of time before the MSCA becomes one of the most popular tests for assessing the abilities of preschool children" (p. 245). At the time when that statement was made, the MSCA was becoming the focus of extensive research and clinical attention. Rather than widespread acceptance and popularity, however, the conclusion from the research is one of caution—that the test should be used in some circumstances, and not others. While this is a reasonable conclusion to reach regarding the use of any test, the reaction to it relative to the MSCA is one of disappointment—primarily because the test hit the preschool testing scene with such verve and promise. Even so, the MSCA has major strengths that place it among the best of available broad-based diagnostic instruments for use with preschool children. Seen in this light, the MSCA contributes substantially to the preschool assessment repertoire of most psychologists whose awareness of its limitations should provide a realistic perspective within which to use it in an informed manner.

ADMINISTRATIVE AND TECHNICAL CONSIDERATIONS. One outstanding feature of the MSCA is its technical manual, an exemplary piece of work comprised of elaborate information about the test's psychometric soundness, the standardization process, norms tables, and guidelines for administration and interpretation. Although these are features that should be included in any test manual, the extent of detail provided for the MSCA creates a clear framework within which the test user can function comfortably. Even with the structure of the manual, however, proper administration of the 18 different subtests requires keen attention to detail acquired through considerable practice and careful readings of the manual, as well as the available textbook (Kaufman & Kaufman, 1977). Psychologists who have not had much experience with preschool children would also be wise to engage in several practice sessions with children spanning the age range from 2 1/2 to 8 1/2 years before embarking on formal administrations. This is particularly true for the motor subtests. Even with good training in individual testing, psychologists and other specialists who flawlessly administer the MSCA could make errors in scoring that would distort the interpretation of a child's profile.

Another very favorable aspect of the MSCA is the gamelike and nonthreatening nature of the materials. This particular feature is frequently mentioned by researchers and applied psychologists alike, with a striking contrast made with the more adult-oriented, test-like materials of the Wechsler Preschool and Primary Scale of Intelligence (WPPSI). Although the MSCA administration time (60–90 minutes) can sometimes stretch the ability of a preschool child to sit still, most children proceed easily through the subtests and seem to enjoy the activities. In addition to the attractive materials, the directions to the subtests are easily understood, and the sequence in which subtests are ordered serves to engage young children who are often shy, nonverbal, and distractible. Kaufman and Kaufman (1977) have noted that these features seem to enhance rapport with minority children, in particular. Additionally, the inclusion of gross motor subtests in the MSCA battery provides a nice break from the routine of table activities, although the skilled examiner must beware that the change sometimes stimulates an already active child to be more active.

The standardization procedures followed in the development of the MSCA norms were also exemplary. The test was standardized on a sample of 1,032 children stratified by race, geographic region, father's occupational status, and, informally, urban-rural residency, in accordance with the 1970 U.S. Census data. The major problem which has affected test users' confidence in the meaning of the scores is the exclusion of exceptional children from the standardization sample. Regarding the usefulness of the MSCA with exceptional children, the statements made in the manual are broad in their intent: "It is hoped that [the test] will provide better understanding of both normal children and those with learning disabilities," and that it "should be quite useful for assessing the strengths and weaknesses of mentally retarded children." Unfortunately, problems in understanding the meaning of scores for exceptional children relative to normal children have created the major obstacle to widespread acceptance of the MSCA.

Despite its obvious technical strengths, Kaufman and Kaufman (1977) outline 3 areas where the MSCA has technical limitations: (1) lack of social comprehension and judgment tasks, (2) problems in testing older school-age children, and (3) difficulties pertaining to scale interpretation. The first limitation can also be seen as a strength, because the absence of social intelligence questions also means that the MSCA has fewer culturally loaded items than its Wechsler predecessor. However, pertinent information related to school-age children's functioning (social comprehension, maturity, and judgment) is missing from the battery (Kaufman & Kaufman, 1977). Also problematic relative to the assessment of older children is the lack of verbal reasoning and abstract puzzle solving tasks.

Specific problems with the third category of limitations, that of profile interpretation, include overlap in content between some of the scales (the Memory Scale with the Verbal and Quantitative Scales) and a limited floor and ceiling. Because of this latter problem, test users should realize that assessment of older gifted students and younger retarded children is not a recommended procedure. Another caution for test users pertains to the lack of techniques in the manual for dealing with spoiled subtests, although in their textbook, Kaufman and Kaufman (1977) address this issue and offer a technique for estimating scores for any of the subtests. By way of summary, it can be said that the technical limitations of the MSCA apply primarily to older and very young children. For preschool children aged 3 to 6 1/2, the technical contributions and advantages of the battery far outweigh the disadvantages.

RELIABILITY. In the MSCA manual, McCarthy provides information on the internal consistency and stability of test scores, as they were obtained from the standardization sample. The internal consistency coefficients for the General Cognitive Index (GCI) averaged .93 across 10 age groups between 2 1/2 and 8 1/2 years. Mean reliability coefficients for the other five Index Scales ranged from .79 to .88. Confirmation of these findings appeared in a study by Shellenberger (1977) with a Spanish-speaking sample, which reported an average coefficient of .93.

As stated by Kaufman (1982), "the internal consistency of the MSCA seems beyond reproach, but stability is the key reliability issue for preschool children" (p. 122) because of the appreciable fluctuation in the test behaviors of young children. In this category, the MSCA also fares quite well. The manual includes information on test-retest reliability over a 1-month interval on a stratified sample of 125 children grouped into three age levels. The average coefficient for the GCI was .90, with correlations ranging from .69 to .89 for the other scales. Other studies of long and short-term stability (Bryant & Roffe, 1978; David & Slettedahl, 1976) resulted in stability coefficients for the GCI of .85 and .84, respectively. Stability coefficients of the cognitive scales ranged from .62 to .76 in the Davis and Slettedahl (1976) study, with the Motor Scale emerging as the only scale that lacked stability ($r=.33$). Whereas these stability data suggest adequate test-retest consistency for the GCI, the studies used small, homogeneous samples and included few children under age 5. Moreover, none of the investigators examined stability for exceptional children, although such children constitute a very large proportion of the children administered the MSCA. As concluded by Nagle in 1979, "longitudinal studies are still needed which will evaluate MSCA stability over several age ranges and time intervals."

VALIDITY. Without a doubt, most of the research on the MSCA has been done in an attempt to determine its validity; specifically, the construct validity of its factor structure, the relationship of GCI to IQ and other measures, its ability to discriminate among various groups of children and its ability to predict school achievement. Research interest has also addressed issues related to the MSCA's validity with minority populations.

FACTOR ANALYSIS. According to the manual, the content of the MSCA and the organization of the six scales were determined primarily through "intuitive and functional considerations" based on McCarthy's extensive teaching and clinical experience. Analyses of the standardization data for five age groups (Kaufman, 1975) and for separate groups of blacks and whites (Kaufman & DiCuio, 1975) have given generally good support for the construct validity of the battery for normal children (Kaufman & Kaufman, 1977, pp. 83–103), although each factor did not emerge for every age group. The results also provide evidence that a child's profile of MSCA Index scores reflect real and meaningful performance in domains of cognitive and motor ability. The major practical implication of these results for test users is that a child's strengths and weaknesses can be determined through the interpretation of differences on Scale Indexes, as proposed originally by McCarthy. Stated more simply, profile interpretation is a meaningful contribution that the McCarthy makes to the psychological assessment of very young children.

Again, the major limitation of these large factor analytic studies is that they were based totally on data for normal children instead of exceptional children to whom the McCarthy would more likely be administered. Smaller studies done with atypical groups (Keith & Bolen, 1980; Naglieri, Kaufman, & Harrison, 1981) generally confirm the overall results of the factor analytic data for normal children: good construct validity for the global score (GCI) and for the Verbal, Perceptual-Performance, and Motor Scales, and limited validity support for the Memory Scale. Since the Quantitative factor failed to emerge for either special population, the Quantitative Index should be interpreted with extreme caution and may not correspond to any real ability in children, particularly those below age 5 (Kaufman, 1982).

RELATIONSHIP OF GCI TO IQ. Despite McCarthy's emphasis that the GCI is not synonymous with IQ, a great deal of effort has gone into determining the concurrent validity of the MSCA through comparisons of the GCI with Binet and WPPSI IQ scores. Several studies have yielded no significant differences between GCI and Binet IQ for samples of kindergarten to first-grade children (Davis, 1975; Davis & Walker, 1976; Kaufman, 1973) and 2 1/2- to 8 1/2-year-old children from predominantly Mexican backgrounds (Davis & Rowland, 1974); or between GCI and WPPSI Full Scale IQ with the McCarthy sample. The discrepancies are somewhat larger for the Wechsler Scales than for the Binet (3 points instead of 2) (Kaufman, 1982). The results from these studies generally indicate that the MSCA measures abilities similar to those assessed by the Stanford-Binet and WPPSI. Contrasting results were found by Gerken, Hancock, and Wade (1978) and Phillips, Pasewark, and Tindall (1978) with statistically significant differences of 10 and 7 points emerging, respectively, between GCI and IQ for preschoolers with no apparent learning problem. These differences emerged despite significant correlations between GCI and IQ.

Differences as large as 15 points (with GCI lower than IQ) have been found for children diagnosed as "learning disabled" (DeBoer, Kaufman, & McCarthy, 1974), and "minimal brain dysfunction" children experiencing learning problems in school (Kaufman & Kaufman, 1974). Bracken (1981) cautions that these differences should not be interpreted exclusively to mean that the MSCA is particularly sensitive for identifying children with serious learning problems because of methodological issues in the DeBoer et al. (1974) and Kaufman and Kaufman (1974) studies. The issues that he cites include regression to the mean, WISC/WISC-R differences, and the use of the 1960 Stanford-Binet norms as opposed to the 1972 norms. Bracken (1981) adds that research designs are needed that have counterbalanced experimental procedures, an anchor group of normal children, and a total sample size large enough from which reasonable inferences can be made. With methodological improvements, the GCI-IQ differences may not be as dramatic as once believed, although statistically significant differences may still be found, as in Naglieri (1979).

Bracken (1981) cautions further that the MSCA should not be used for classification purposes although supporting it as a useful diagnostic tool. Kaufman (1982) reaches a different conclusion. Because of high correlations between the GCI and IQ and the fact that the McCarthy includes so many tasks that resemble subtests on conventional intelligence tests, it *is* legitimate, according to Kaufman (1982) to use the GCI as an estimate of mental functioning (for a child referred for a learning disability). Kaufman continues to say that examiners should keep the 2–3 point GCI-IQ differences for normal children in mind when interpreting individual profiles. Further, because current definitions of "normal" intelligence for a learning disabled child are not as rigid as they used to be, "professional judgment should enable a diagnostician to reach a diagnosis of a learning disability when all symptoms point to this conclusion except for a McCarthy GCI in the 70's or 80's" (Kaufman, 1982, p. 153).

The validity of the MSCA for use with retarded children has not been studied very extensively in the McCarthy literature. A total of only 30 retarded children have been tested on both the McCarthy and Binet and only 50 have been administered the McCarthy and Wechsler battery (see Kaufman, 1982, Tables 5.2 and 5.3 pp. 124–127). With discrepancies of about 20 points in favor of the Binet IQ over the GCI (Levenson & Zino, 1979a, 1979b; Naglieri & Harrison, 1979) and 6 to 8 points for Wechsler IQ's (Naglieri, 1979), preliminary results are discouraging, and the jury is still out regarding the use of the McCarthy for classification of individual retarded children. Furthermore, a potential limitation exists on the use of the MSCA with retarded children because of the test's limited floor. Although extrapolated GCIs have been developed (Harrison & Naglieri, 1978), Kaufman (1982) states strongly that they should be used only for research purposes until more abundant evidence is available for assessing mentally retarded children's functioning. Similarly, the extrapolated GCIs should not be used for individual assessment of gifted children. Therefore, McCarthy's original suggestion of reporting low GCIs as "below 50" and high GCIs as "above 150" should be used for individual assessments.

DISCRIMINATION AMONG GROUPS. Studies conducted to determine the ability of the MSCA to discriminate among various groups of children indicate that the Scale Indexes and the subtests are quite effective in discriminating between learning disabled and non-learning disabled groups (DeBoer et al., 1974; Goh & Simons, 1980; Knack, 1978; Taylor & Ivimey, 1980). Results of efforts to distinguish reading disabled from non-reading disabled children, however, have been mixed. While Johnson and Wollersheim (1976) found good and poor readers to perform similarly on the five Scale Indexes, Nagle, Paget, and Mulkey (1980) found the battery to be quite efficient in discriminating between the groups. In the latter study, the Verbal Index was the best discriminator of good and poor readers, followed by the Perceptual-Performance and Memory Indexes. Another study by Weiss (1977) supported the validity of the McCarthy for predicting potential reading problems.

PREDICTION OF SCHOOL ACHIEVEMENT. In addition to the prediction of specific reading problems, evidence is growing with normal and exceptional samples that the MSCA is an accurate estimate of general school functioning (Kaufman, 1982). In her initial study, McCarthy reported a moderate coefficient of .49 between the GCI and total score on the Metropolitan Achievement Tests (MAT) over a 4-month interval. Since that time, significant coefficients have been reported with standardized achievement scores (Harrison, 1979; Long, 1976; Loxley & Gerken, 1980; Naglieri, 1979, 1980; Taylor & Ivimey, 1980), teacher ratings of behaviors associated with learning problems (Schodlatz, 1978), and teachers' ratings of achievement (Goh & Simons, 1980). Impressive correlations with achievement were also obtained for the Spanish-speaking sample in the Shellenberger (1977) study. These studies indicate that the first standard of a good screening test, that is, the ability to predict school functioning, has been reached by the MSCA (Kaufman, 1982).

VALIDITY WITH MINORITY POPULATIONS. Evidence from research using the MSCA with black children generally endorses its use with black preschool children (Kaufman, 1982). This conclusion results from studies showing consistently that black preschoolers earn GCIs in the 90s and do not differ substantially from their white counterparts (Arinoldo, 1979; Kaufman & DiCuio, 1975; Kaufman & Kaufman, 1973a, 1975; Long, 1976; Perino & Ernhart, 1974). Black-white discrepancies on the MSCA at school-age levels have been greater than at preschool-age levels but are similar to racial differences on conventional IQ tests. Limited evidence from a Spanish-speaking group (Shellenberger, 1977) also supports the validity of the MSCA with that particular minority group.

SUMMARY. To summarize the extensive information on the MSCA, a realistic scenario seems appropriate. Consider the decision faced by a psychologist responsible for the evaluation of a young preschooler (age 3 to 6 1/2 years) suspected of having learning problems. In looking over other instruments suitable for preschool-age children, the psychologist finds the Stanford-Binet, the WPPSI, Columbia Mental Maturity Scale, and the Peabody Picture Vocabulary Test—Revised (PPVT-R). The psychologist considers its assets and finds that the MSCA has excellent psychometric properties, with a reliable and stable global score; that there is outstanding empirical support for the interpretation of scores from the General Cognitive, Verbal, Motor, and Perceptual-Performance Scales; that correlations with school achievement are strong; that the test appears to be nondiscriminatory with regard to race, and that it does differentiate between learning disabled and normal children. When compared to its limitations (the discrepancy of one SD between the GCI and Binet IQ for retarded children, the consistently higher Wechsler Full Scale IQs than GCIs, and the difficulty with interpretation of the Memory and Quantitative Indexes), the advantages in using the MSCA outweigh the disadvantages for evaluating a preschooler in this particular age range. Thus, when desiring an instrument that is meticulously constructed, appeals to young children, yields a profile of various skills with reliable and valid information about the child's current and future abilities, the psychologist is most likely to choose the MSCA. Although the literature points directly to the need for caution when evaluating a child with the MSCA for classification purposes, such caution should be exercised when evaluating any preschoolers with any instrument.

If the child in the above scenario were younger or older, then the psychologist would need to consider additional information. Because of the MSCA's limited floor, the Stanford-Binet would likely yield a more accurate picture of a 2 1/2-year-old's functioning, while the limited ceiling and the lack of tasks measuring social judgement, abstract problem solving, and verbal expression would likely lead to the decision to use the WISC-R for a child age 6 1/2 to 8 years.

The MSCA will stand the test of time as a useful aid in screening and diagnostic decisions if used in the informed manner depicted in the above scenario. Perhaps the best perspective to have consists of viewing the MSCA much like a good friend—having had time to understand it, we are learning how we can depend on it.

REVIEWER'S REFERENCES

Kaufman, A. S. Comparison of the WPPSI, Stanford-Binet, and McCarthy Scales as predictors of first-grade achievement. PERCEPTUAL AND MOTOR SKILLS, 1973, 36, 67–73.

Kaufman, A. S., & Kaufman, N. L. Black-white differences at ages 2 1/2 – 8 1/2 on the McCarthy Scales of Children's Abilities. JOURNAL OF SCHOOL PSYCHOLOGY, 1973, 11, 194–204.

Davis, E. E., & Rowland, T. A replacement for the venerable Stanford-Binet? JOURNAL OF CLINICAL PSYCHOLOGY, 1974, 30, 517–521.

DeBoer, D. L., Kaufman, A. S., & McCarthy, D. THE USE OF THE MCCARTHY SCALES IN IDENTIFICATION, ASSESSMENT, AND DEFICIT REMEDIATION OF PRESCHOOL AND PRIMARY AGE CHILDREN. Symposium presented at the meeting of the Council for Exceptional Children, New York, April, 1974.

Kaufman, N. L., & Kaufman, A. S. Comparison of normal and minimally brain dysfunctioned children on the McCarthy Scales of Children's Abilities. JOURNAL OF CLINICAL PSYCHOLOGY, 1974, 30, 69–72.

Perino, J., & Ernhart, C. B. The relationship of subclinical lead level to cognitive and sensorimotor impairment in black preschoolers. JOURNAL OF LEARNING DISABILITIES, 1974, 7, 616–620.

Davis, E. E. Concurrent validity of the McCarthy Scales of Children's Abilities. MEASUREMENT AND EVALUATION IN GUIDANCE, 1975, 8, 101–104.

Kaufman, A. S. Factor structure of the McCarthy Scales at five age levels between 2-1/2 and 8-1/2. EDUCATIONAL AND PSYCHOLOGICAL MEASUREMENT, 1975, 35, 641–656.

Kaufman, A. S., & DiCuio, R. F. Separate factor analyses of the McCarthy Scales for groups of black and white children. JOURNAL OF SCHOOL PSYCHOLOGY, 1975, 13, 10–18.

Kaufman, A. S., & Kaufman, N. L. Social-class differences on the McCarthy Scales for black and white children. PERCEPTUAL AND MOTOR SKILLS, 1975, 41, 205–206.

Davis, E. E., & Slettedahl, R. W. Stability of the McCarthy Scales over a 1-year period. JOURNAL OF CLINICAL PSYCHOLOGY, 1976, 32, 798–800.

Davis, E. E., & Walker, C. Validity of the McCarthy Scales for Southwestern rural children. PERCEPTUAL AND MOTOR SKILLS, 1976, 42, 563–567.

Johnson, D. A., & Wollersheim, J. P. A comparison of the test performance of average and below average readers on the McCarthy Scales of Children's Abilities. JOURNAL OF READING BEHAVIOR, 1976, 8, 397–403.

Long, M. L. THE INFLUENCE OF SEX, RACE, AND TYPE OF PRESCHOOL EXPERIENCE ON SCORES ON THE MCCARTHY SCALES OF CHILDREN'S ABILITIES. Unpublished doctoral dissertation, University of Georgia, 1976.

Kaufman, A. S., & Kaufman, N. L. CLINICAL EVALUATION OF YOUNG CHILDREN WITH THE MCCARTHY SCALES. New York: Grune & Stratton, 1977.

Shellenberger, S. A CROSS-CULTURAL INVESTIGATION OF THE VALIDITY OF THE SPANISH VERSION OF THE MCCARTHY SCALES OF CHILDREN'S ABILITIES FOR PUERTO RICAN CHILDREN. Unpublished doctoral dissertation, University of Georgia, 1977.

Weiss, L. I. THE UTILITY OF THE MCCARTHY SCALES OF CHILDREN'S ABILITIES IN THE IDENTIFICATION OF POTENTIALLY READING DISABLED KINDERGARTEN CHILDREN AND ITS APPLICATION TO THE MATURATIONAL LAG HYPOTHESIS. Unpublished doctoral dissertation, University of Southern Mississippi, 1977.

Bryant, C. K., & Roffe, M. W. A reliability study of the McCarthy Scales of Children's Abilities. JOURNAL OF CLINICAL PSYCHOLOGY, 1978, 34, 401–406.

Gerken, K. C., Hancock, K. A., & Wade, T. H. A comparison of the Stanford-Binet Intelligence Scale and the McCarthy Scales of Children's Abilities with preschool children. PSYCHOLOGY IN THE SCHOOLS, 1978, 15, 468–472.

Harrison, P. L., & Naglieri, J. A. Extrapolated general cognitive indexes on the McCarthy Scales for gifted and mentally retarded children. PSYCHOLOGICAL REPORTS, 1978, 43, 1291–1296.

Knack, T. M. ASSESSMENT OF LEARNING DISABILITIES IN YOUNG CHILDREN WITH THE MCCARTHY SCALES. Unpublished doctoral dissertation, University of Michigan, 1978.

Phillips, B. L., Pasewark, R. A., & Tindall, R. C. Relationship among McCarthy Scales of Children's Abilities, WPPSI, and Columbia Mental Maturity Scale. PSYCHOLOGY IN THE SCHOOLS, 1978, 15, 352–356.

Salvia, J., & Ysseldyke, J. E. ASSESSMENT IN SPECIAL AND REMEDIAL EDUCATION. Boston: Houghton Mifflin, 1978.

Schodlatz, D. R. THE VALIDITY OF THE MCCARTHY SCALES OF CHILDREN'S ABILITIES FOR SCREENING PREKINDERGARTEN CHILDREN AT RISK. Unpublished doctoral dissertation, Harvard University, 1978.

Arinoldo, G. BLACK-WHITE DIFFERENCES IN THE GENERAL COGNITIVE INDEX OF THE MCCARTHY SCALES AND IN THE FULL SCALE IQs OF WECHSLER'S SCALES. Unpublished doctoral dissertation, University of Georgia, 1979.

Harrison, P. L. MERCER'S ADAPTIVE BEHAVIOR INVENTORY, THE MCCARTHY SCALES, AND DENTAL DEVELOPMENT AS PREDICTORS OF FIRST GRADE ACHIEVEMENT. Unpublished doctoral dissertation, University of Georgia, 1979.

Levenson, R. L., & Zino, T. C., II. Assessment of cognitive deficiency with the McCarthy Scales and Stanford-Binet: A correlational analysis. PERCEPTUAL AND MOTOR SKILLS, 1979, 48, 291–295. (a)

Levenson, R. L., Jr., & Zino, T. C., II. Using McCarthy Scales extrapolated General Cognitive Indexes below 50: Some words of caution. PSYCHOLOGICAL REPORTS, 1979, 45, 350. (b)

Nagle, R. J. The McCarthy Scales of Children's Abilities: Research implications for the assessment of young children. SCHOOL PSYCHOLOGY DIGEST, 1979, 8, 319–326.

Naglieri, J. A. A COMPARISON OF MCCARTHY GCI AND WISC-R IQ SCORES FOR EDUCABLE MENTALLY RETARDED, LEARNING DISABLED AND NORMAL CHILDREN. Unpublished doctoral dissertation, University of Georgia, 1979.

Naglieri, J. A., & Harrison, P. L. Comparison of McCarthy General Cognitive Indexes and Stanford-Binet IQs for educable mentally retarded children. PERCEPTUAL AND MOTOR SKILLS, 1979, 48, 1251–1254.

Goh, D. S., & Simons, M. R. Comparison of learning disabled and general education children on the McCarthy Scales of Children's Abilities. PSYCHOLOGY IN THE SCHOOLS, 1980, 17, 429–436.

Keith, T. Z., & Bolen, L. M. Factor structure of the McCarthy Scales for children experiencing problems in school. PSYCHOLOGY IN THE SCHOOLS, 1980, 17, 320–326.

Loxley, L., & Gerken, K. C. The predictive validity of the McCarthy Scales vs. Stanford-Binet. NATIONAL ASSOCIATION OF SCHOOL PSYCHOLOGISTS CONVENTION PROCEEDINGS, 1980, 149–151.

Nagle, R. J., Paget, K. D., & Mulkey, M. S. Comparison of good and poor readers on the McCarthy Scales. NATIONAL ASSOCIATION OF SCHOOL PSYCHOLOGISTS CONVENTION PROCEEDINGS, 1980, 138–140.

Naglieri, J. A. McCarthy and WISC-R correlations with WRAT achievement scores. PERCEPTUAL AND MOTOR SKILLS, 1980, 51, 392–394.

Taylor, R. L., & Ivimey, J. K. Diagnostic use of the WISC-R and McCarthy Scales: A regression analysis approach to learning disabilities. PSYCHOLOGY IN THE SCHOOLS, 1980, 17, 327–330. (a)

Bracken, B. A. McCarthy Scales as a learning disability diagnostic aid: A closer look. JOURNAL OF LEARNING DISABILITIES, 1981, 14, 128–130.

Naglieri, J. A., Kaufman, A. S., & Harrison, P. L. Factor structure of the McCarthy Scales for school-age children with low GCIs. JOURNAL OF SCHOOL PSYCHOLOGY, 1981, 19, 226–232.

Kaufman, A. S. An integrated review of almost a decade of research on the McCarthy Scales. In T. Kratochwill (Ed.), ADVANCES IN SCHOOL PSYCHOLOGY, Vol. II. Hillsdale, NJ: Lawrence Erlbaum Assoc., 1982.

Review of McCarthy Scales of Children's Abilities by DAVID L. WODRICH, Institute of Behavioral Medicine, Good Samaritan Medical Center, Phoenix, AZ:

The McCarthy Scales of Children's Abilities (MSCA) is one of fewer than a handful of well-standardized, carefully developed, comprehensive ability measures suitable for preschoolers and early elementary school children. Critical comments about the instrument must be predicated on the recognition that as one of that small group, the MSCA is superior to the vast majority of measures that purport to assess mental abilities in this age range.

Essentially favorable technical, psychometric properties of the MSCA are presented in the test manual and have been thoroughly addressed in prior reviews (8:219). Unfortunately, the test manual appears essentially unchanged since its original publication in 1972. Thus, over a decade of research on the test's psychometric and clinical properties is left unavailable to the clinician in what now must be considered a dated and consequently inadequate manual. A manual supplement or revision is needed badly if clinicians are to fully understand and use research findings. One potentially significant addition to the manual appears in a brief footnote that indicates a post-publication study found some learning disabled children earned "General Cognitive Index" scores (the MSCA composite cognitive score, essentially equivalent to IQ) in the mental retardation range. This finding raises the possibility that the

MSCA overidentifies mental retardation, a prospect that may significantly limit the instrument's usefulness.

At the hands-on level, examiners find the MSCA reasonably easy to administer and score, although some time is required to produce derived scores. This instrument is perhaps the best suited of the available ability tests to capture and maintain preschoolers' attention. Nonverbal items precede items requiring speech, thus allowing the child time to "warm up." A series of game-like gross motor tasks is placed between more traditional items requiring attention and persistence; thus even young and restless children can be assessed in a single examination session.

The MSCA is less useful when the clinician reaches the interpretation and planning phase. While the MSCA provides the advantage of separate Verbal and Perceptual-Performance scores, each resulting from constituent tests of varied content, it also yields a Quantitative Index of questionable content validity and dubious clinical utility. For young children who do not yet count or possess number concepts, the Quantitative Index may be determined entirely by a single subtest, Numerical Memory. This subtest consists of short-term recall of number sequences, items generally assumed to reflect primarily non-cognitive factors. For older children, orally administered items dealing with number concepts, called Number Questions, begin to contribute to the Quantitative Index, but the content here is nearly identical to Wechsler's Arithmetic subtests, which are assumed to measure verbal abilities. One may wonder whether the MSCA would have been better organized without a separate Quantitative Index. The manual presents no compelling evidence for its inclusion.

To some extent, interpretation problems also accompany the two additional cluster or index scores: Memory and Motor. The Memory Index is entirely composed of tests that also contribute to the General Cognitive Index; the Motor Index includes both fine motor tasks that contribute to the General Cognitive Index and some gross motor tasks distinct from the General Cognitive Index. Still, the author felt each index to reflect interpretable clusters of abilities. Precisely what is measured and what these index scores mean is not entirely clear. The Memory Index appears comparable to the "Freedom from Distraction" (FFD) factor that emerges after Verbal Comprehension and Perceptual Performance factors are separated on tests such as the Wechsler Intelligence Scale for Children—Revised (these FFD items typically measure attention and short-term retention and replication; most are verbal in nature). Unfortunately, the manual contains no factor analytic data and presents no discussion of distractibility/concentration in relation to this index.

The Motor Index, while appealing because of its unique standardized assessment of gross motor as well as fine motor skills, also presents interpretation problems. For instance, does an average Motor Index score in a child with a General Cognitive Index in the mentally retarded range indicate less likelihood of subsequent mental retardation, or is the index measuring solely non-cognitive skills that add nothing to predicting later cognitive development? Clinically relevant data such as this, if provided in an updated manual, would greatly enhance the clinical utility of the MSCA.

The MSCA's selection of standard scores also does little to facilitate interpretation, and may make communication to non-psychologists especially confusing. This problem arises from the fact that Verbal, Perceptual-Performance, Quantitative, Motor, and Memory Indexes are reported as *T*-scores (mean = 50, standard deviation = 10). Interpretation and intertest comparison would have been facilitated if the author could have decided that the indexes would be either the equivalent of Wechsler subtests or IQs (mean = 10, standard deviation = 3; or mean = 100, standard deviation = 15). The General Cognitive Index score on the MSCA has a mean of 100 and a standard deviation of 16, but would have been more consistent with contemporary trends if a standard deviation of 15 had been selected. Much to the credit of the author, derived scores are not provided for the brief, unreliable constituent tests that compose the various indexes. Consequently, clinicians will be less tempted to overinterpret test data.

Viewed in perspective, many of the aforementioned criticisms are minor. All in all, the MSCA represents one viable clinical tool for assessing preschoolers. When a child 2 1/2 to 6 years evidences delays in expressive language, nonverbal, or motor spheres, the MSCA is an acceptable tool and perhaps the tool of choice. The Wechsler Preschool and Primary Scale of Intelligence is also acceptable for those 4 to 6 years; the Kaufman Assessment Battery for Children has too few subtests suitable for children without expressive language and thus is not preferred for language delayed preschoolers. Although standardized for those as old as 8 1/2, the MSCA must be considered a less desirable choice than the WISC-R because of that instrument's research base and its superior verbal items. Should preschoolers score in the mentally retarded range on the MSCA, corroboration of general cognitive deficits using the Stanford Binet or Wechsler scales may be deemed appropriate.

[672]

McCarthy Screening Test. Ages 4–6.5; 1978, 1970–78; MST; adaptation of the McCarthy Scales of Children's Abilities; criterion-referenced; percentile cut-off scores provided for classification as "at risk" for learning problems; 6 tests: Right-Left Orientation, Verbal Memory, Draw-A-Design, Numerical Memory, Conceptual Grouping, Leg Coordination; norms consist of percentiles; individual; manual ('78, 65 pages); record booklet ('78, 4 pages); drawing booklet ('78, 9 pages); 1982 price data: $44 per complete set including all necessary equipment, manual, 25 record forms, 25 drawing booklets, and carrying case; $6.60 per package of 25 record forms; $9.75 per package of 25 drawing booklets; $1.65 per "Roger" Card (left-right orientation); $2.15 per tape; $1.10 per white card; $14.75 per conceptual grouping blocks in box; $8.25 per manual; (20–30) minutes; The Psychological Corporation.*

See T3:1425 (2 references).

TEST REFERENCES

1. Umansky, W., Paget, K. D., & Cohen, L. R. The test-retest reliability of the McCarthy Screening Test. JOURNAL OF CLINICAL PSYCHOLOGY, 1981, 37, 650–655.

2. Naglieri, J. A., & Harrison, P. L. McCarthy scales, McCarthy Screening Test, and Kaufman's McCarthy short form correlations with the Peabody Individual Achievement Test. PSYCHOLOGY IN THE SCHOOLS, 1982, 19, 149–155.

3. Vance, B., Kitson, D. L., & Singer, M. Comparison of the Peabody Picture Vocabulary Test—Revised and the McCarthy Screening Test. PSYCHOLOGY IN THE SCHOOLS, 1983, 20, 21–24.

Review of McCarthy Screening Test by NADEEN L. KAUFMAN, Director Psycho-educational Clinic, California School of Professional Psychology, San Diego, CA:

DESCRIPTION AND PURPOSE. The McCarthy Screening Test (MST) is an individual measure designed to identify those youngsters who are most likely to require additional educational assistance during their early school years. It is comprised of six subtests taken directly from the McCarthy Scales of Children's Abilities (MSCA): Right-Left Orientation; Verbal Memory Part I; Draw-A-Design; Numerical Memory, Parts I and II; Conceptual Grouping; and Leg Coordination. Administration is estimated in the manual to require approximately 20 minutes, and may be accomplished by examiners who are psychologists, "other qualified professional personnel," or teachers and paraprofessionals who have been instructed in its use. Decisions based on test scores should be made by "qualified professional personnel" only, as stated in the manual. Scoring for the MST yields either satisfactory development status or a need for further assessment status with no total score available. Thus the test is not diagnostic, but merely a category placement device which lets the test interpreter choose which cutoff point he or she wishes to employ. Besides the examiner's printed matter, the test materials the child works with include one picture of a boy (for use in Right-Left Orientation); a drawing booklet with some printed designs and space for the child's own productions (Draw-A-Design); a set of 12 small blocks in 2 shapes, 2 sizes, and 3 colors (Conceptual Grouping); and a tape 9 feet long for the child to walk on (Leg Coordination). Much of the manual is reprinted from the parent instrument, the MSCA, with a brief set of pages written directly for the MST itself.

EVALUATION. The MST is a valuable contribution to the field of early childhood screening, and yet one is ultimately disappointed in all that the MST could have easily been—but isn't. Unlike so many other now-vogueish criterion-referenced tests (e.g., the Brigance Inventory of Basic Skills) the MST categorizations of "At Risk" or "Not At Risk" are based on sound normative data obtained from the parent MSCA. The manual, like the MSCA broader version, is very clearly written. The scoring of drawing tests is always difficult, but the MST elaborates a highly structured system for reducing the inherent problems of judging a young child's productions. But in addition to the numerous positive and unique features of the MST, the test user must balance this screening test's flaws and sins of omission. Therefore, the two biggest areas of concern revolve around the specific selection of the 6 MST subtests from the original 18 of the MSCA, and on the technical data deficiencies.

SELECTION OF THE SIX SUBTESTS. Given the age range of the MST, children 4 to 6 years, it is hard to understand why Right-Left Orientation was included. It can only be administered to children aged 5 and above, cutting out 12 of the 30 months of potential test subjects. The relationship between laterality confusion and learning disabilities is highly speculative, but when significant relationships occur, the populations are invariably older than the MST's target sample. In addition, Right-Left Orientation is highly influenced by chance responding: of the 12 possible points obtained, the mean score for 5- to 6-year-olds is 6.8, which is not very different from a chance score. Also important in evaluating its inclusion as one-sixth of the test is the fact that it is highly unreliable, with a test-retest correlation of .30 reported by Umansky, Paget, and Cohen (1981) and .32 in the manual itself. Whereas all the individual subtests have too low reliability values to justify separate interpretations (and the manual states this on page 9), Right-Left Orientation was certainly a poor choice.

Leg Coordination, a gross motor task which correlated trivially with the criterion in a predictive validity study, doesn't relate significantly to the other MST subtests either. Whereas it is certainly a fine area to observe as part of preschool screening, the information it yields for facilitation of the child's learning career is questionable. Both Leg Coordination and another MST selection, Verbal Memory Part I, were two of a total of only four MSCA subtests which produced significant sex differences (these two favoring females) (Kaufman & Kaufman, 1973b; Umansky & Cohen, 1980). Verbal Memory Part I, a rote repetition of unrelated words and sentences, overlaps in the area measured with another MST subtest, Numerical Memory (rote number repetition). Given the 18 parent subtests to draw from, the 6 present in the MST do not provide the most logical array of behavior samples. In fact, there is some research evidence that suggests that alternate subtest groupings may be more valid (Harrison & Naglieri, 1981).

PREDICTIVE VALIDITY. The key issue for a successful screening instrument to address is the support available to document that the screening test is indeed valid for its intended purpose. Can the MST pick out those youngsters likely to fail in their early school years? The answer is a resounding "no adequate evidence." The manual reports no study whatsoever in which the actual MST, administered by teachers, paraprofessionals, etc., is evaluated for its ability to select "At Risk" children. The only predictive validity mentioned in the manual involves two unreferenced studies which pulled out scores on the MST when the entire MSCA battery (administered by psychologists and with the MST subtests occurring in a very different test sequence) was the data source. Incomplete information, small sample size, and undefined standard of criterion render the assertion of a $^2/_3$ success rate wholly uninterpretable on one of these studies. The other study utilizing MSCA data (also employing a small sample of children from 5 to 6 years of age) viewed scores on the Metropolitan Readiness Test (MRT), 6 months subsequent, as the criterion. Whereas some of the reported coefficients of correlations reached statistical significance, few of them were of meaningful magnitude. The generalizability of these data taken from the MSCA is highly questionable, since there is no way of estimating the effects of a different test order and different set of examiner qualifications upon the results. Additionally, there must be doubt about the adequacy of the MRT being the sole criterion for such a heterogeneous group as "At Risk" youngsters. One large-scale study on the MST ($N=971$) retested those children selected as failures 1 to 2 months earlier. Of the 300 children labeled "At Risk" based on MST criteria, rescreenings gave indications of disappointing validity support: 49% classified "At Risk" on round one were classified "Not At Risk" a month later. Additionally, one-half of children referred by teachers for suspected learning difficulties were entirely missed by the MST (Umansky, Paget, & Cohen, 1981). Certainly far more validity evidence is necessary before one can feel confident that the MST can do what it purports to do.

OTHER CONSIDERATIONS. The MST has other flaws which are less serious in nature but worth noting. There are no exceptional children in the standardization sample, thereby eliminating from the reference group those youngsters for whom the screening test is specifically designed. Even more important is the fact that there is no standardization for the MST as it is presented; the normative data were drawn from the much larger MSCA battery with a different test order and different examiner qualifications. Raw scores for age 6 were derived by interpolation from the standardization scores for 5- and 6-year-olds, despite the fact that this represents a year of vast growth and developmental change for young children. The table presented for cut-off decision-making offers nine different criteria for determining "At Risk" status. (These criteria are based on the number of subtests failed and the percentile used to determine failure.) The end result is quite confusing. The criteria are applied to a sample of 75 children labeled with the vague and heterogeneous description "disabled"; more empirical support is urgently needed to understand the implications of these dichotomies. A classification system based on "number of subtests failed" is further questionable because the individual subtest scores are generally quite unreliable. The manual encourages the examiner to administer the rest of the full MSCA to a child selected as "At Risk"; yet a research study found little congruence between teachers' scoring of the complex Draw-A-Design subtest and psychologists' scores for the same children (Reynolds, 1978). Additionally, eliminating 3-year-olds from the age range is an unfortunate choice for a screening test, since this represents a very current need in the assessment scene.

On the other hand, the MST has some research support suggesting that it is less race biased than other cognitive preschool measures (Kaufman & Kaufman, 1973a). The availability of a flexible set of rules for the test user to employ in determining who shall be considered "At Risk" provides schools with a high degree of individual application precedures. The manual cautions test users against interpreting the individual subtest scores, and in general has easy-to-understand directions with sample completed record forms included. The lack of a total MST score prevents the averaging of subtest strengths and weaknesses which would have resulted in a meaningless global number; such acknowledgement of young children's normal scatter is indeed rare.

SUMMARY AND CONCLUSION. The MST has been shown to possess some apparent flaws as well as certain unique strengths relative to other preschool screening tools. Overall, however, the MST should be viewed as a highly valuable contribution to the assessment field. Given evidence that most other screening measures available lack empirical support (Lindsay & Wedell, 1982), the MST should certainly be considered an important screening device for identifying "At Risk" youngsters.

REVIEWER'S REFERENCES

Kaufman, A. S., & Kaufman, N. L. Black-white differences at ages 2–8 on the McCarthy Scales of Children's Abilities. JOURNAL OF SCHOOL PSYCHOLOGY, 1973, 11, 194–204. (a)

Kaufman, A. S., & Kaufman, N. L. Sex differences on the McCarthy Scales of Children's Abilities. JOURNAL OF CLINICAL PSYCHOLOGY, 1973, 29, 362–365. (b)

Reynolds, C. R. Teacher-psychologist interscorer reliability of the McCarthy drawing tests. PERCEPTUAL AND MOTOR SKILLS, 1978, 47, 538.

Umansky, W., & Cohen, L. R. Race and sex differences on the McCarthy Screening Test. PSYCHOLOGY IN THE SCHOOLS, 1980, 17, 400–404.

Harrison, P. L., & Naglieri, J. A. Comparison of the predictive validities of two McCarthy short forms. PSYCHOLOGY IN THE SCHOOLS, 1981, 18, 389–393.

Umansky, W., Paget, K. D., & Cohen, L. R. The test-retest reliability of the McCarthy Screening Test. JOURNAL OF CLINICAL PSYCHOLOGY, 1981, 37, 650–654.

Lindsay, G. A., & Wedell, K. The early identification of educationally "At Risk" children revisited. JOURNAL OF LEARNING DISABILITIES, 1982, 15, 212–217.

Review of McCarthy Screening Test by JACK A. NAGLIERI, Assistant Professor of Psychology, Ohio State University, Columbus, OH:

The concept of constructing a screening test by selecting individual subtests from a larger measure of intelligence is an excellent one. The greatest advantage of using a short form of a more comprehensive intelligence test is that instruments such as the McCarthy Scales of Children's Abilities and Wechsler Intelligence scales are psychometrically superior to locally constructed and less adequately normed screening devices. The McCarthy Screening Test (MST) is one such short form which is comprised of selected subtests of the McCarthy Scales of Children's Abilities (MSCA). The MSCA is an ideal choice because of its excellent construction and standardization and the fact that it is a child-oriented test that children enjoy. Many practitioners have seen that the MSCA materials greatly facilitate the development of rapport and interest with young children, who are typically difficult to examine, in a way that other tests for young people do not (e.g., Wechsler Preschool and Primary Scale of Intelligence).

The McCarthy Screening Test is an attractively packaged short form of the MSCA designed to screen children aged 4 to 6 in about 20 minutes. The MST consists of 6 of the 18 McCarthy subtests: Right-Left Orientation, Verbal Memory, Draw-A-Design, Numerical Memory, Conceptual Grouping, and Leg Coordination. Scores on these subtests are used to identify a child as "At Risk" or "Not At Risk" on the basis of how many of the six subtests are failed at either the 10th, 20th, or 30th percentile rank relative to the MSCA standardization sample.

While the MST is conceptually superior to nonstandardized and less carefully constructed measures, its effectiveness must be demonstrated empirically. Even though the MST's publisher states that the subtests were "chosen because they have proved to be useful in identifying children with learning disabilities and perceptual problems" (The Psychological Corporation MST brochure) there is a clear paucity of research on the MST that affirms this statement. These and other aspects of the MST are discussed below.

According to the MST Manual the tests comprising the MST were "selected so that they are generally representative" of the McCarthy Scales of Children's Abilities. This statement is misleading because the MST includes no subtest that can be viewed as mainly verbal. The only verbal subtest included in the MST is Verbal Memory and it did not emerge as part of the verbal factor in the 4 to 4 1/2-year-old age group and ranked fourth as a verbal subtest in the MSCA standardization sample factor analysis (Kaufman, 1975). It is illogical that a short form designed to be representative of the MSCA (which has an entire Verbal Scale) does not contain a good measure of verbal ability. Opposite Analogies or Verbal Fluency would have been better choices in this respect.

Selection of subtests for the MST was also guided by the desire to choose tasks that are "important in achieving success in school." However, it is hard to imagine why subtests such as Right-Left Orientation, Leg Coordination, and to a lesser extent Verbal Memory were chosen. Right-Left Orientation is a subtest that is highly influenced by chance, has very poor reliability (according to the MST Manual itself), and did not load significantly on any of the McCarthy Scales in the factor analysis of the standardization sample (Kaufman, 1975). Moreover, Right-Left Orientation is only administered to children 5 years of age and older, thereby eliminating it from the MST for nearly half the children the test was designed to evaluate. The selection of Leg Coordination is equally troublesome given that its reliability is quite low and females score higher on this subtest than males (Kaufman & Kaufman, 1973). Moreover, current research has indicated that the McCarthy Motor Scales Index has not evidenced good concurrent validity or added to predictions of achievement (Harrison, 1981; Naglieri & Harrison, 1982; Taylor & Ivemy, 1980). Therefore the inclusion of two motor subtests in the MST is not justifiable. Finally, a third subtest which was a poor choice for the MST was Verbal Memory because females outperformed males on this subtest (Kaufman & Kaufman, 1973) and it also has low reliability.

Perhaps the most convincing evidence against including Right-Left Orientation, Leg Coordination, and even Verbal Memory from the MST is provided in the MST Manual itself. As evidence of the MST's predictive validity using the Metropolitan Readiness Test as a criterion, correlation coefficients among the subtests of these measures are presented. At the .05 level of significance, Leg Coordination did not correlate with any of the

Metropolitan subtests and Right-Left Orientation only correlated 15% of the time. Similarly, none of the Verbal Memory correlations with the Metropolitan subtests were significant at $p = .01$. Apparently, The Psychological Corporation included these subtests for some reason, but it could not have been because of these correlations with the Metropolitan Readiness Test.

Examination of the MST subtest reliability coefficients reported in the manual is disappointing. The split-half correlations corrected by the Spearman-Brown formula for Draw-A-Design, Conceptual Grouping, and Leg Coordination ranged from .41 to .80 (Average $r = .77$, .70, and .63 respectively) and test-retest reliability coefficients for Right-Left Orientation, Verbal Memory, and Numerical Memory are .32, .54, and .69, respectively. These reliability coefficients should have led the test's publisher to choose more reliable MSCA subtests or use the sum of the six subtest scores rather than adopting a subtest by subtest pass/fail approach. Naglieri and Harrison (1982) report that using the sum of the subtest scores appears to result in higher correlation coefficients with achievement. The present MST dichotomous scoring system requires that a child be labeled as "At Risk" or "Not At Risk" on the basis of relatively unreliable component subtests.

ADMINISTRATION AND SCORING. The MST Manual, like its parent test the MSCA, provides concise guidelines for administration and scoring. The subtest procedures are presented clearly and the examiner's statements are printed in bold red type for easy identification. Nearly all the MST subtests are straightforward to administer and objective to score. The only subtest which is somewhat subjective and time consuming to score is Draw-A-Design. In the interest of time and to have made the MST more attractive to preschoolers, the Puzzle Solving subtest from the MSCA would have been a better choice.

As with most of the subtests, the overall computation of subtest test scores and the number of subtests failed at the pre-determined criteria is easy to complete, making scoring of the MST a rather uncomplicated task. The greatest difficulty involved in scoring lies in determining which of the nine possible criteria (one, two, or three subtests failed at the 10th, 20th, or 30th percentile) to use for identification as "At Risk" or "Not At Risk." Unfortunately, no guidelines are presented in the MST Manual. I view this as a potentially harmful omission since the use of the 30th percentile will result in the identification of children whose scores fall only one half of a standard deviation below the normative mean which in all probability is normal variability.

THE MST IN PERSPECTIVE. While the MST is a better choice as a screening test than many poorly normed and constructed instruments used across the country, there is another short form of the MSCA developed by Kaufman (1977) which preliminary research findings suggest outperforms the MST. Kaufman's short form of the MSCA was constructed to assure that the group of six subtests selected would be child-oriented, have similar subtest proportions as the General Cognitive Index that correlated well with the total McCarthy GCI, be easy to administer and score, not differentiate significantly by sex or race, and have sound psychometric qualities. Based on McCarthy standardization sample data, Kaufman selected Puzzle Solving, Word Knowledge, Numerical Memory, Verbal Fluency, Counting and Sorting, and Conceptual Grouping for his short form. This collection of subtests yields a total score that is converted to an Estimated GCI rather than an "At Risk" dichotomy. Research directly comparing the two short forms has suggested that although both short forms total scores correlate significantly with achievement, the Kaufman short form has better predictive validity and correlated consistently higher with achievement than the MST (Harrison & Naglieri, 1981; Naglieri & Harrison, 1982). Moreover, using a similar "At Risk" criteria for the Kaufman short form "resulted in a significantly smaller number of false negatives than did four of the nine MST criteria" (Harrison & Naglieri, 1981, p. 393).

SUMMARY. In conclusion, the concept of adopting a screening instrument from a well constructed and standardized test such as the McCarthy Scales of Children's Abilities is excellent. However, the selection of MST subtests is questionable, the dichotomous scoring system is inefficient and partly based on unreliable component tests, the MST includes two subtests that favor females, and some of the subtests do not appear to correlate with achievement test scores. Hence, I do not recommend that the MST be used as a screening test at this time. In its place I recommend Kaufman's short form of the MSCA. The advantages of the Kaufman short form are as follows: it does not discriminate by sex, it is composed of subtests that correlate better with the MSCA GCI, it appears to have better predictive validity, and it has better reliability than the MST.

REVIEWER'S REFERENCES

Kaufman, A. S., & Kaufman, N. L. Sex differences on the McCarthy Scales of Children's Abilities. JOURNAL OF CLINICAL PSYCHOLOGY, 1973, 29, 362–365.

Kaufman, A. S. Factor structure of the McCarthy Scales at five age levels between 2 and 8. EDUCATIONAL AND PSYCHOLOGICAL MEASUREMENT, 1975, 35, 641–656.

Kaufman, A. S. A McCarthy short form for rapid screening of preschool, kindergarten, and first grade children. CONTEMPORARY EDUCATIONAL PSYCHOLOGY, 1977, 2, 149–157.

Taylor, R. L., & Ivimey, J. K. Diagnostic use of the WISC-R and McCarthy scales: A regression analysis approach to learning disabilities. PSYCHOLOGY IN THE SCHOOLS, 1980, 17, 327–330.

Harrison, P. L. Mercer's adaptive behavior inventory, the McCarthy Scales of Children's Abilities and dental development as predictors of first grade achievement. JOURNAL OF EDUCATIONAL PSYCHOLOGY, 1981, 37, 78–82.

Harrison, P. L., & Naglieri, J. A. Comparison of the predictive validities of two McCarthy short forms. PSYCHOLOGY IN THE SCHOOLS, 1981, 18, 389–393.

Naglieri, J. A., & Harrison, P. L. McCarthy scales, McCarthy Screening Test, and Kaufman's McCarthy short form correlations with the Peabody Individual Achievement Test. PSYCHOLOGY IN THE SCHOOLS, 1982, 19, 149–155.

[673]

The McGuire-Bumpus Diagnostic Comprehension Test. Reading level grades 1.5–2.5, 2.5–3.5, 4–6; 1971–79; MBDCT; although designed as part of the Croft Inservice Program Reading Comprehension Skills, the test may be used independently; criterion-referenced; reasoning skills; 4 tests, 12 scores listed below; "mastery" (defined as 2 or fewer errors on each test) required on previous test before administering Tests B, C, and D; no data on reliability; no norms; Forms X, Y, ('79, 7 pages, spirit masters for local duplicating); 3 levels: early primary, primary, intermediate; early primary manual ('79, 52 pages); primary and intermediate manual ('71, 72 pages); individual record card ('79, 2 pages); class record chart ('71, 1 page); 1984 price data: $79.95 per complete kit; $34 per spirit master book; $12 per manual; $11.50 per set of individual progress cards; $3 per class record chart; (30–40) minutes; Marion L. McGuire and Marguerite J. Bumpus; Croft, Inc.

a) LITERAL READING. 4 scores: selecting details, translating details, identifying signal words, selecting the main idea.

b) INTERPRETIVE READING. 3 scores: determining implied details, identifying organizational patterns, inferring the main idea.

c) ANALYTIC READING. 3 scores: identifying the problem, developing hypotheses, determining relevant details.

d) CRITICAL READING. 2 scores: selecting criteria for judgement, making a judgement.

[674]

McLeod Phonic Worksheets. Reading level grade 3.5 and under; 1972–77; formerly called Domain Phonic Tests; criterion-referenced; 6 areas: initial single consonants, final single consonants, single vowels, consonant blends and digraphs, vowel blends, auditory discrimination; no data on reliability and validity; no norms; individual; 1 form ('77, 4 cards plus 1 student analysis sheet); no specific manual; administrative, descriptive, and interpretative information included in same booklet as tests and worksheets; corrective exercises (63 pages) on duplicating masters for use after testing; 1984 price data: $22 per complete kit (book form) consisting of 4 test cards, 5 record and analysis masters, 63 worksheet masters, and teacher's guide; administration time not reported; John McLeod and Joan Atkinson; Educators Publishing Service, Inc.*

[675]

Meadow-Kendall Social-Emotional Assessment Inventory for Deaf and Hearing Impaired Students. Ages 3–6, 7–21; 1983; SEAI; behavior checklist to be completed by adult informant; 2 levels; manual (37 pages); 1984 price data: $2 per inventory; $11 per manual; administration time not reported; Kathryn P. Meadow and others listed below; OUTREACH.*

a) PRE-SCHOOL. Ages 3–6; 5 scores: sociable/communicative behavior, impulsive dominating behaviors, developmental lags, anxious/compulsive behaviors, special items; 1 form (4 pages); scoring and norms sheet (2 pages); Kathryn P. Meadow in collaboration with Michael A. Karchmer, Linda M. Petersen, and Lawrence Rudner.

b) SCHOOL-AGE. Ages 7–21; 3 scores: social adjustment, self image, emotional adjustment; 1 form (6 pages, includes scoring and norm information); Kathryn P. Meadow in collaboration with Pamela Getson, Chi K. Lee, and Linda Stamper.

[676]

Meanings and Measures of Mental Tests. Ages 5 and over; 1979; provides cluster analyses of the Wechsler Intelligence Scale for Children (WISC) and the Revised form (WISC-R), the Wide Range Achievement Test (WRAT), and Wechsler Adult Intelligence Scale (WAIS); 1 form; 5 analysis sheets (2 pages); manual (116 pages); 1984 price data: $9.75 per 50 analysis sheets (specify for which tests); $21.70 per manual; $22.85 per specimen set (includes manual and copies of all analysis forms); Joseph F. Jastak and Sarah Jastak; Jastak Associates, Inc.*

Review of Meanings and Measures of Mental Tests by ROBERT L. HALE, Assistant Professor, College of Education, Program in School Psychology, Pennsylvania State University, University Park, PA:

In Meanings and Measures of Mental Tests, Joseph and Sarah Jastak attempt to explain their methods of clustering the scores of several of the Wechsler Intelligence Scales and their Wide Range Intelligence Scale. These solutions are usually in combination with the Wide Range Achievement Test. The test combinations which they discuss are as follows: WAIS & WRAT, WISC & WRAT, WISC-R & WRAT, WRIS-S (Wide Range Intelligence Scale—Short Form) & WRAT, and WRIS.

The manual begins by referring to some prominent researchers in statistics and test interpretation (e.g., A. Anastasi, J. P. Guilford, L. J. Cronbach, L. L. Thurstone, etc.). This may initially lead the reader to believe that the method of test interpretation which the Jastaks discuss will be based on established psychometric principles. However, by the time the reader has progressed a very few pages, the realization firmly sets in that this is a idiosyncratic clustering method. "Our assumed traits may not be as rigorous or parsimonious as are those claimed by factor analysis. However, they are based on clinically tested intuitions and the opinions derived from them." The authors do not discuss the various methods of cluster and/or factor analyses which might legitimately be used to develop test profiles. Indeed, the Jastak's lack of scholarship allows them to ignore research which disputes the efficiency of their procedures (Hirshoren & Kavale, 1976). Additionally, they fail to compare their cluster results with more traditional methods of subscale clustering (Cohen, 1957; Kaufman, 1975).

Within the Jastak clustering system, test results are broken down into three "factorial hierarchies." Each test, no matter what it is measuring or its content, is reportedly composed of global, lobal, and, obal factors. The authors relate that "Spearman's *g* is probably similar to our global." Lobal cluster variances are said to relate to group factors while "Obal variance is a residual measure of error and an untapped lobal reserve. It is unique to each subtest." While this discussion sounds very much like the common breakdown of subtest variance into common, factorial, specific, and error variance components, and, indeed, while some of their mathematical procedures parallel traditional procedures, the philosophical and mathematical extensions applied by the Jastaks to the initial data radically depart from accepted psychometric practice. As examples of the philosophical departure, the authors state that, "In our view, large error variances do not reduce the clinical potential of the subtest." As examples of the mathematical departure, Judd and Judd (1981) convincingly demonstrate that the net effect of the calculations, "is both to increase the scatter among the subtest scores and occasionally to shift subtest scores by large random amounts." These converted scores which are later used to make inferences about the subject's personality thus approximate random number tables. Other things which the Jastaks feel free to leave out are statements about the subjects used to develop some of their tables. For example, while they state that they used probability sampling, they do not report important subject characteristics such as minority representation, urban-rural status, geographic representation, etc. No evidence is presented concerning the reliability, abnormality, or validity of their reported profiles. In this author's view, this may be just as well, for the time spent calculating those psychometric properties would be a waste of time. There simply can be no validity in what are essentially random numbers turned into profiles.

In summary, if the reader wishes to purchase materials which lack scholarship, whose theoretical development is based on a flawed philosophy and suspect psychometric principles, which have no reported validity, etc., this is the one to buy. This material could be seen as rather harmless except for the fact that it is being promoted through advertisement and workshops and is being used. In this author's view, the results of using the Jastak system may harm children, adults, psychometrics, and psychology.

REVIEWER'S REFERENCES

Cohen, J. The factorial structure of the WAIS between early adulthood and old age. JOURNAL OF CONSULTING PSYCHOLOGY. 1957, 21, 283–290.

Kaufman, A. S. Factor analysis of the WISC-R at 11 age levels between 6 1/2 and 16 1/2 years. JOURNAL OF CONSULTING AND CLINICAL PSYCHOLOGY, 1975, 43, 135–147.

Hirshoren, A., & Kavale, K. Profile analysis of the WISC-R: A continuing malpractice. THE EXCEPTIONAL CHILD, 1976, 23, 83–87.

Judd, B., & Judd, B., Jr. The Jastak system: Dangerous nonsense. SCHOOL PSYCHOLOGY REVIEW, 1981, 10, 494–498.

Review of Meanings and Measures of Mental Tests by ELAZAR J. PEDHAZUR, Professor of Educational Psychology, New York University, New York, NY:

Because of the potential deleterious consequences of using the Meanings and Measures of Mental Tests (MMMT) it is probably best to begin with a warning: Don't use it! Had the publication of tests and manuals been subject to regulations similar to those applied to the production and distribution of drugs, chances are that it would have never been published.

The MMMT is a mixture of strange and erroneous notions about measurement, factor analysis, cluster, and profile analysis. When one begins with the premise "that any test—all tests—sample[d] the totality of human behavior" (Foreword), it is not surprising that one ends up "interpreting" test scores much as fortune-tellers "interpret" tea leaves, cards, or whatever it is they "see" in crystal balls. The MMMT could have been dismissed as not worthy of comment in the *Mental Measurements Yearbook*, except that it may beguile unwary practitioners with its scientific-sounding statements, buzz phrases, formulas, tables, and instructions about transformations and interpretations of scores on the WAIS, WISC, WRAT, and WRIS.

Essentially, the entire MMMT system (?) is built upon a set of tables in which correlations of subtest scores (e.g., on the WAIS and WRAT) with the mean of the subtests are reported for males and females. Referring to the square of such correlations, the authors maintain that: "it has been variously interpreted. There is no consensus as to what it measures or what part of behavior it elucidates." Actually, these correlations are loadings of the subtests on the first centroid extracted from the correlation matrix with unities in the diagonal, and their squares constitute a mixture of common, specific and error variance. The Jastaks, however, offer their own interpretation. Beginning with a statement that they have no doubt that the variance reflected by the squared correlation is not global, they decide to label it "lobal" variance. It is noteworthy that here, as well as in most other parts of the manual, the authors do not provide any evidence in support of their interpretations, claims, pronouncements, and generalizations. Instead, they keep referring to their clinical experience and intuitions. Thus: "based on clinically tested intuitions and the opinions derived from them" the authors decided that what they labeled lobal variances are associated with "personality traits outside the realm of intelligence." Moreover, "it was finally decided that the visible (sic) variances derived from mean correlation coefficients resembled Thurstone's group factors more closely than they resembled the Spearman *g*." But the Jastaks do not stop here. They maintain that not only are the lobals "true behavior variables closely related to the personality structure," but also that they "lead an existence of their own and are responsible for the many failures of bright and educated people to adjust to themselves and others; as well as for the many successes in social adjustment of inferior and neglected people all over the world."

On the basis of their "clinical experience" the authors arrive at a set of lobal clusters (e.g., Lexigraphic, Reality, Motivation, Depression). In impressive-looking tables that appear to have been constructed by sheer will power and whose validity is apparently based on the mere say-so of its authors, percentages of variance of the various subtests (e.g., WAIS, WRAT) are attributed to the various lobal clusters.

How does one arrive at a person's scores on the lobal clusters? Simple! Provided one is willing to suspend all disbelief, to ignore all one knows about measurement and data analysis, and to follow the Jastaks' arbitrary and inexplicable manipulations of numbers. First, one has to go through several steps of transforming the subtest scores. Among other things, one is instructed to apply "regression constants" which are nothing more than constants proportional to the correlation of each subtest with the mean of the subtests. Depending on whether the mean of the "regressed scores" for a given cluster is above or below 100, the user is instructed to add or subtract constants, referred to as "lobal cluster loadings," to the "regressed scores," and to then calculate means and standard deviations of the lobal scores based on two to four elements, depending on how many the Jastaks have decided belong to a given cluster.

Readers who are puzzled by the procedures described in the preceding paragraphs will find much more to puzzle about in the MMMT. Following are but a few examples. In addition to what the authors have designated as lobal variances (see above), they speak of obal and global variances. Obal variance, which is conceived of as "error variance plus a potential or unused lobal variance," is defined as $[1 - r^2]^2$, where r^2 is the lobal variance of the subtest. The authors maintain that: "Large obal variances usually indicate that the test's clinical value has not been fully exploited."

Then there is the global variance, or "what might be called the hidden proportions of the total variances....Within each individual protocol, they act in rigid unison thus concealing a significant effect on each test result." Why, one wonders, is the global variance "hidden"? Why is it "concealing"? Because, reason the authors, it is obtained by subtracting from 100 the sum of the lobal and obal variances of each subtest. And what does this hidden global variance signify? "The only behavior trait (sic) which has a uniform effect on test results is intelligence. Intelligence does not discriminate between different tasks and occupations....Whether we dig ditches, sell merchandise, design machines, build houses, or do scientific research, the share of intelligence in all these undertakings is uniform. That is why the global effect is hidden or invisible."

After the preceding statement one is not surprised by the authors' definition of intelligence; or by their statements about the proportions of variance due to heredity and environment, and the roles they play in behavior; or by their social moralizing (e.g., p. 38). They do not, however, deserve comment.

The most pernicious aspect of the MMMT is its prescriptions for the clinical interpretation of the lobal scores, their scatters, the highest and lowest score, and the like. The MMMT includes a section on the clinical interpretation of the lobal clusters that sounds as if it came from another era and another domain. Following are but a few, almost random, examples. A high score on the language cluster (average of Lexigraphic, Linguistic, and Semantic) is interpreted, among other things, as reflecting: "High degree of conformity. Accepts authority figures and their decisions. Strong self-concept in language situations." Low score on this cluster reflects: "Poor self-concept in classroom and formal learning situations. Feels threatened and inferior. Will try to avoid as much as possible. Stronger tendency to externalize any feeling of hostility."

High score on the Reality cluster: "Is appropriate and relevant in behavior. Is more objective than subjective in dealing with events....Has few extreme or unrealistic fears....Strong ego structure; lesser need for ego defenses."

High score on Psychomotor cluster: "Harmony and balance between mind and muscles. Muscular system is quickly responsive to the commands of the mind. Physical energy is mobilized quickly. Time and energy is used efficiently."

After offering similar characterizations of performance on the other clusters, the authors recommend that: "Their individual meanings may be recombined and interpreted by examiners in accordance with the definitions and explanations reviewed above." And why not? When one runs wild in "interpreting" individual clusters, what is there to stop one from interpreting some combination in such terms as "the predisposition toward aggression may be chronic, troublesome, and socially very destructive"? Moreover, one can pick and choose as the spirit moves one. Thus, sometimes a large scatter of scores on clusters reflects personality disturbances, and sometimes it is a small scatter that does so. And when things seem not to fit the arbitrary interpretations, it is always possible to point to environmental factors as being the cause.

It is difficult to imagine that there is a market for the MMMT among practitioners. If such a market exists, one hopes that it is a small one, and that it will rapidly diminish and disappear altogether. The potential damage of practitioners using the MMMT is incalculable.

[677]

Measure of Arousal Seeking Tendency. College; 1978; norms consist of means and standard deviations; 1 form (3 pages); no manual; 1985 price data: $12 per specimen set; administration time not reported; Albert Mehrabian; the Author.*

See T3:1438 (1 reference).

Review of Measure of Arousal Seeking Tendency by NORMAN S. ENDLER, Professor of Psychology, York University, Toronto, Ontario, Canada:

The Measure of Arousal Seeking Tendency is a 32-item self-report questionnaire which assesses a person's preference for highly arousing situations, life-styles, and work experiences. The scale is balanced for response bias in that 16 items are positively worded and 16 items are negatively worded. There is a 9-point scale for each item ranging from –4 (very strong disagreement) to +4 (very strong agreement), and a total score is computed for each subject by algebraic summation of the item scores. There is no manual and a specimen set consists of a one-page ditto describing the format and administration instructions for the questionnaire, a one-page scoring sheet, and two pages containing the questionnaire. The price for these four ditto pages is $12.00. This is outrageous!

The first page of the specimen set indicates that norms were obtained from 536 undergraduates, and for this sample total scores on the Arousal Seeking Measure had a mean value of 32 and a standard deviation of 29. No reliability or validity data are reported as part of this specimen set, nor is there any indication as to the purpose or use of this test or what it measures.

Mehrabian, the developer of this questionnaire, describes it in a little more detail in a journal article (Mehrabian, 1978). He indicates that Arousal Seeking assesses the degree of preference for high information rate situations and activities. For a sample of 325 University of California undergraduates the mean was 35, the standard deviation was 27, and the Kuder-Richardson reliability coefficient was .93. The scale correlates .13 with the Crowne and Marlow Social Desirability scale and –.08 with Stimulus Screening, a scale developed by Mehrabian and Russell (1973). Mehrabian (1978) distinguishes Arousal Seeking from Stimulus Screening, which was designed to assess the arousal reaction to high information rate as distinct from preference or lack of preference for high information rate. Mehrabian (1978), on the basis of his study, concludes that "Arousal Seeking is useful for assessing differences in individual reactions to preferred situations" (p. 730). There does not seem to be any cross-validation of this study, nor does there appear to be any other published literature on the Measure of Arousal Seeking Tendency.

An investigator interested in assessing the degree to which a person seeks out arousing (varied, novel, or complex) experiences would be well advised to use the Zuckerman, Kolin, Price, and Zoob (1964) Sensation Seeking Scale (SSS) rather than the Mehrabian Measure of Arousal Seeking Tendency. Until additional data are available, there is no basis for using the Measure of Arousal Seeking Tendency other than for exploratory research. Caveat Emptor!

REVIEWER'S REFERENCES

Zuckerman, M., Kolin, E. A., Price, L., & Zoob, I. Development of a sensation-seeking scale. JOURNAL OF CONSULTING PSYCHOLOGY, 1964, 28, 477–482.

Mehrabian, A., & Russell, J. A. A measure of arousal seeking tendency. ENVIRONMENT AND BEHAVIOR, 1973, 5, 315–333.

Mehrabian, A. Characteristic individual reactions to preferred and unpreferred environments. JOURNAL OF PERSONALITY, 1978, 46, 717–731.

Review of Measure of Arousal Seeking Tendency by JON D. SWARTZ, Associate Dean for Libraries and Learning Resources, Professor of Education and Psychology, Southwestern University, Georgetown, TX:

This new paper-and-pencil test is one of a number of instruments developed by Albert Mehrabian and his associates at UCLA in an ongoing research program focusing on the characteristics of a variety of personality constructs. Mehrabian describes his Measure of Arousal Seeking Tendency as being "useful for assessing differences in individual reactions to preferred situations (high-arousal seekers approach, work, and affiliate more than low-arousal seekers in preferred settings)" (Mehrabian, 1978, p. 717).

The brief questionnaire consists of 32 items designed to assess a person's preference in three areas: highly arousing situations, work experiences, and life style. Sixteen of the items are positively worded (e.g., "I sometimes look for ways to change my daily routine"), and 16 negatively worded (e.g., "It is difficult for me to get excited about scenery"). Subjects respond to each item by means of a 9-point scale, ranging from –4 (for very strong disagreement) to +4 (for very strong agreement). A total score is computed for each subject by summing algebraically the positively-worded items and then subtracting the algebraic sum of the negatively-worded items.

Mehrabian reports a sample of 536 undergraduate students yielded a mean of 32 and a standard deviation of 29. Previously, a sample of 325 undergraduate students had produced a mean of 35, a standard deviation of 27, and a Kuder-Richardson reliability coefficient of .93. Correlational data have provided evidence that this measure of arousal seeking is neither confounded with social desirability nor a measure of arousability (Mehrabian, 1978). On the other hand, very little work has actually been done so far with this instrument. There is no manual, and more detailed information on reliability, validity, and standardization (with separate norms by sex, age, ethnicity, etc.) is needed.

The construct of arousal seeking appears useful for assessing differences in individual reactions to preferred situations, and Mehrabian has made a good beginning on the development of a questionnaire for assessing individual reactions to some of these situations. The next step in the development of this potentially useful measure, and one recognized by its author, is to experiment with actual situations and experimental ratings of behaviors.

In conclusion, the empirical foundation for this new measure of individual reactions to preferred situations is meager. While interesting and potentially valuable, in its present form it is really only suitable for research purposes—and should be treated as such by those who use it. In the judgment of this reviewer, the establishment of the Measure of Arousal Seeking Tendency as a psychometric instrument remains to be demonstrated.

REVIEWER'S REFERENCES

Mehrabian, A. Characteristic individual reactions to preferred and unpreferred environments. JOURNAL OF PERSONALITY, 1978, 46, 717–731.

[678]

Measure of Child Stimulus Screening and Arousability. Ages 3 months to 7 years; 1978; ratings by parents; norms consist of a mean and a standard deviation; 1 form (3 pages); no manual; instruction sheet (1 page); 1985 price data: $12 per specimen set; administration time not reported; Albert Mehrabian and Carol A. Falender; Albert Mehrabian.*

See T3:1439 (2 references).

Review of Measure of Child Stimulus Screening and Arousability by STEVEN KLEE, Senior Child Supervisor, Department of Psychiatry, Beth Israel Medical Center, New York, NY:

This test represents a quick screening measure to assess stimulus screening and arousability in infants and children. As used in this context, stimulus screening refers to the degree to which an individual selectively attends to certain aspects of his/her environment. The degree to which someone screens will then determine level of arousability. Given this paradigm, nonscreeners block out less stimuli and are thus potentially more arousable than screeners. The authors state that arousability is just one aspect of the more general area of information processing. In addition, we are told that since this is a physiological attribute, stimulus screening is expected to be stable over time.

To its credit, this questionnaire is simple to administer and score. No administration time is given but the simple wording and small number of items should make administration time relatively short. However, parents filling out this form may find the 9-point scale ranging from −4 to +4 a little awkward to use. One additional strength is that response bias is reduced through the alternation of positively and negatively worded items.

Despite the ease of administration, this measure appears to have many shortcomings. The final version of this test evolved from four separate studies. However, the age ranges sampled in these four studies differed greatly. In two studies the range was from 3 months to 7 years, while one study sampled ages 4 months to 30 months and another 4 months to 22 months. The eventual norms provided were based on study 3, which sampled ages 3 months to 7 years. These norms are based on a relatively small sample of 157 children. While we are told that the correlation with sex was nonsignificant, additional information regarding this sample is not provided. Specifically, the breakdown with regard to sex and, more importantly, with regard to age, would be useful. We are left with a single mean for a huge age range with no indication as to how many children were sampled at each age range or how scores varied with age.

The authors report high internal consistency (KR20=.92) for the 46-item final version of this measure. However, it would have been interesting to see test-retest reliability information. Given the claim that arousability is a relatively stable trait, test-retest data could have provided valuable support for this claim.

The weakest support for this measure seems to come from the validity data. In study 4, observational data were correlated with parental ratings, and four significant correlations were obtained. There was a −.42 correlation with per cent of time mother picked up her child when crying, a −.42 correlation with per cent of time mother reported her child was a distraction, and a +.26 correlation with number of hours per day a child watched TV alone. The conclusions drawn from these results were that those children who screen less require more attention from the mother. The potentially most meaningful correlation of observer rating of arousability with parent's rating of child stimulus screening was significant but only –.26.

Another limitation of this validity study is that the mothers used (in all 4 studies) were recruited from either LaMaze or LaLeche classes. As such, it can be hypothesized that they represent a biased sample of mothers who may be showing more concern and interest in childbearing issues than the general population.

In conclusion, the authors make some predictions about how varying amounts of the environmental structure may affect screeners and nonscreeners. These predictions might be interesting to pursue in some supportive studies. However, the authors make no attempt to suggest situations in which the Measure of Child Stimulus Screening and Arousability would be useful.

Overall, this is a quick and easy measure to administer and score. Decisions as to where and when to use such a test may be difficult. Once administered there is a mean and standard deviation with which to compare a child's score. However, the user may have difficulty interpreting the meaning of this score and in making subsequent predictions about the child's behavior.

[679]

Measure of Individual Differences in Dominance-Submissiveness. College; 1978; norms consist of means and standard deviations; 1 form (3 pages); 2 editions: 48-item edition and a 40-item edition; no manual; directions sheet (1 page); 1985 price data: $12 per specimen set; administration time not reported; Albert Mehrabian; the Author.*

Review of Measure of Individual Differences in Dominance-Submissiveness by ROBERT H. DELUTY, Assistant Professor of Psychology, University of Maryland Baltimore County, Baltimore, MD:

Mehrabian and his colleagues (e.g., Mehrabian & O'Reilly, 1980; Mehrabian & Russell, 1974) have demonstrated persuasively that all emotional states can be described in terms of three orthogonal dimensions: arousal-nonarousal, pleasure-displeasure, and dominance-submissiveness. The Measure of Individual Differences in Dominance-Submissiveness (Mehrabian & Hines, 1978) was developed to serve as a general index of the third critical dimension of emotional states.

Mehrabian and Hines initially constructed a 457-item questionnaire to tap "all conceivable aspects of [the dominance-submissiveness] trait" (p. 479). Factor analyses were conducted to avoid a disproportionate representation of any content group (or similar set of groups) and to identify redundant or similarly worded items. Those items which had low correlations with social desirability and with trait pleasure and arousability (the other two basic measures of temperament) and which had high item-total scale correlations were retained. The resulting 48-item questionnaire is composed of 24 positively worded items (e.g., "I usually win arguments") and 24 negatively worded ones (e.g., "I avoid talking about touchy subjects"), thereby controlling for response bias.

The 48-item questionnaire has very high internal consistency; Mehrabian and Hines report a Kuder-Richardson formula 20 coefficient of .95. The questionnaire's test-retest reliability, however, has yet to be assessed.

Mehrabian and his associates (Mehrabian, 1978a; Mehrabian & Hines, 1978; Mehrabian & O'Reilly, 1980) have correlated the questionnaire with a wide variety of self-report measures. The questionnaire has impressive criterion and convergent validity, as evidenced by its high correlations with Jackson's (1967) measure of dominance (r =.82) and with Mehrabian's (1978a) semantic differential measure of trait dominance (r=.58). Its discriminant validity is illustrated in its independence from social desirability bias and in its low correlations with trait pleasure and arousability (Mehrabian & Hines, 1978). A 40-item version of the questionnaire, also balanced for response bias and correlating .99 with the 48-item version, has been found by Mehrabian and Hines to yield even lower correlations with trait pleasure and arousability.

The questionnaire's construct validity is amply demonstrated in a study by Mehrabian and O'Reilly (1980), in which a multiple regression analysis was used to analyze particular personality measures as a function of trait pleasure, arousability, and dominance-submissiveness. Dominance (as assessed by the 40-item version of the questionnaire) had highly significant beta coefficients in regression equations performed on certain personality measures. Among those personality dimensions for which dominance coefficients were significant and positive were extroversion (Eysenck & Eysenck, 1968), achieving tendency (Mehrabian & Bank, 1978), arousal seeking (Mehrabian, 1978b), and aggression, exhibition, endurance, and autonomy (Jackson, 1967); personality dimensions for which dominance coefficients were significant and negative were trait anxiety (Spielberger, Gorsuch, & Lushene, 1970), neuroticism (Eysenck & Eysenck, 1968), sensitivity to rejection (Mehrabian, 1970), and "harm avoidance" and succorance (Jackson, 1967). Mehrabian (1978a) has theorized that the dominance-submissiveness dimension ranges from feelings of being influential, powerful, or in control to extreme feelings of powerlessness or lack of control over one's environment; the findings of the multiple regression analysis provide support not only for the validity of the dominance-submissiveness measure but also for the construct underlying the questionnaire.

Although the findings obtained by Mehrabian and his colleagues are encouraging, more extensive validation of the questionnaire is still necessary. For example, the reliability, validity, and normative scores of the measure have been assessed only in studies using University of California undergraduates as subjects. The fact that Mehrabian and Hines (1978) found no significant sex differences on the questionnaire may tell us more about college students in Los Angeles than about actual differences in dominance-submissiveness between men and women. In addition, the questionnaire has only been validated using other self-report measures; it would be highly desirable if scores on the questionnaire could be correlated with objective, behavioral ratings of dominance and submissiveness.

The clinical utility of the questionnaire is unknown, since no study employing clinical populations has yet been conducted. One would predict that clinically depressed individuals, for example, would score significantly lower on the questionnaire than would normal controls. The use of the questionnaire as a clinical assessment tool and as a clinical outcome measure (e.g., to gauge the effectiveness of different therapies for depression) has yet to be explored, and would be a fruitful avenue for further research.

Mehrabian (1978a) has also developed a semantic differential trait-dominance scale which has high internal consistency as well as convergent and discriminant validity. Furthermore, while this scale takes approximately 3–5 minutes to complete, the dominance-submissiveness questionnaire developed by Mehrabian and Hines requires 15–20 minutes. The dominance-submissiveness questionnaire, however, does have higher internal consistency and its construct validity has been more thoroughly investigated. Future studies should examine which of these two measures is more highly correlated with behavioral indices of dominance and submissiveness and is a more sensitive clinical assessment tool and outcome measure. Given the fact that the measures do not correlate too highly with one another ($r = .58$) and that they take a relatively brief time to complete, a weighted sum of both measures might prove to be a most useful, comprehensive index of dominance-submissiveness.

In conclusion, the dominance-submissiveness questionnaire has very high internal consistency and impressive convergent, discriminant, and construct validity using self-report measures as external criteria. Although it is the most researched measure of dominance-submissiveness available, future studies are strongly recommended to assess its (1) test-retest reliability, (2) clinical utility, (3) predictive and concurrent validity using behavioral criteria, (4) norms for populations other than undergraduates, and (5) superiority over other dominance-submissiveness measures as a clinical and research tool.

REVIEWER'S REFERENCES

Jackson, D. N. PERSONALITY RESEARCH FORM MANUAL. Goshen, NY: Research Psychologists Press, 1967.

Eysenck, H. J., & Eysenck, S. B. MANUAL FOR THE EYSENCK PERSONALITY INVENTORY. San Diego, CA: Educational and Industrial Testing Service, 1968.

Mehrabian, A. The development and validation of measures of affiliative tendency and sensitivity to rejection. EDUCATIONAL AND PSYCHOLOGICAL MEASUREMENT, 1970, 30, 417–428.

Spielberger, C. D., Gorsuch, R. L., & Lushene, R. E. MANUAL FOR THE STATE-TRAIT ANXIETY INVENTORY. Palo Alto, CA: Consulting Psychologists Press, 1970.

Mehrabian, A., & Russell, J. A. AN APPROACH TO ENVIRONMENTAL PSYCHOLOGY, Cambridge, MA: MIT Press, 1974.

Mehrabian, A. Characteristic individual reactions to preferred and unpreferred environments. JOURNAL OF PERSONALITY, 1978, 46, 718–731. (a)

Mehrabian, A. Measures of individual differences in temperament. EDUCATIONAL AND PSYCHOLOGICAL MEASUREMENT, 1978, 38, 1105–1117. (b)

Mehrabian, A., & Bank, L. A questionnaire measure of individual differences in achieving tendency. EDUCATIONAL AND PSYCHOLOGICAL MEASUREMENT, 1978, 38, 475–478.

Mehrabian, A., & Hines, M. A questionnaire measure of individual differences in dominance-submissiveness. EDUCATIONAL AND PSYCHOLOGICAL MEASUREMENT, 1978, 38, 479–484.

Mehrabian, A., & O'Reilly, E. Analysis of personality measures in terms of basic dimensions of temperament. JOURNAL OF PERSONALITY AND SOCIAL PSYCHOLOGY, 1980, 38, 492–503.

Review of Measure of Individual Differences in Dominance-Submissiveness by DOUGLAS N. JACKSON, Senior Professor of Psychology, The University of Western Ontario, London, Canada:

This device is a 48-item self-report measure of dominance-submissiveness designed to measure the trait broadly, tapping all conceivable aspects. Mehrabian views this dimension as one of three orthogonal dimensions which can be employed to describe and measure all emotional states (the other two are pleasure-displeasure and arousal-non-arousal), with various combinations appropriate for particular states. Thus, anxiety is viewed as being associated with displeasure, arousal, and submissiveness, while elation and excitement are construed as being associated with pleasure, arousal, and dominance. In such a system it is important to design a measure which, in addition to meeting the usual psychometric standards, satisfies at least three conditions: (*a*) the three dimensions be uncorrelated, (*b*) they each be free of nuisance variance due to response biases and desirability responding, and (*c*) evidence be forthcoming which supports faithful representation of all facets considered important in the substantive or theoretical representation of each of the dimensions.

In regard to the last condition, the authors defined dominance-submissiveness extremely broadly. Their definition encompassed 64 content groups of relatively homogeneous items (e.g., shyness, ability to say "no," control over others, willingness to express opinions, and confidence in own ideas). An initial item pool of 457 items was reduced to 104 items, then augmented by 62 modified and new items to yield a 166-item form from which the 48 final items were chosen. Multiple criteria were used in item selection: (*a*) high item-scale correlations; (*b*) differentiation from the Marlowe-Crowne scale, putatively a measure of social desirability response set; (*c*) differentiation from measures of the other two dimensions; and (*d*) factor analyses to avoid disproportionate representation of any one content group or similar sets of content groups, and to avoid inclusion of similarly worded or redundant items. The shortest and most simply worded item from a set of similar items was chosen. The final set of 48 items contains a balance of positively and negatively keyed items, 24 of each, scored on a 9-point scale ranging from very strong agreement to very strong disagreement.

The authors' attention to internal consistency in scale development was reflected in the final scale, with a reported KR-20 reliability of .95, which is impressive given the attempt to sample diverse content. The authors also present evidence for the scale's discriminant properties. None of the correlations with the measure of desirability nor with the measures of stimulus screening (considered the converse of arousability or of trait pleasure) exceeded .14. Sex differences were negligible. Evidence of convergent validity was in the form of a .82 correlation with Jackson's Personality Research Form (PRF) Dominance scale. A correlation of .50 with an earlier Mehrabian arousal scale was discounted by the authors as merely reflecting the fact that arousal seekers seek not only to be exposed to high information and risk situations, such as dangerous sports, but to seek mastery and dominance over them.

The development of the Dominance-Submissiveness scale is, in many respects, a model of excellent scale development, but there are a few shortcomings. It would have been helpful if there had been an explicit rationale for the inclusion of the 64 facets, or in the absence of such a rationale, at least expert judgments regarding the relevance of each facet to the domain of dominance. Although many of the facets, such as assertiveness, bear an obvious link, others, such as persistence, politeness, and ability to concentrate, do not. It is possible that the authors were following Loevinger's dictum that the item pool should be drawn from an area of content defined more broadly than the trait expected to be measured, but in the absence of any indication of what they consider to be the boundaries of the content domain encompassed by the trait of dominance, one can only speculate regarding their intentions. The risk, of course, is that the gross tripartite classification of emotions into only three dimensions has resulted in the necessity of implicit scale definitions which are overly broad and all-encompassing. My own preference is for a wider array of personality and motivational dimensions which possess clear and distinct definitions.

A second reservation is in regard to the author's choice of a desirability scale as a means of controlling this potent source of nuisance variance. The Marlowe-Crowne scale might better be considered a scale for defensiveness, rather than desirability. In factor analytic studies it has been shown to load factors marked also by the MMPI Lie scale more than a factor defined by other desirability scales, such as those of Edwards and of Jackson and Messick. But even with this shortcoming, it is doubtful that desirability is a major problem with the Dominance-Submissiveness scale.

A third limitation of this scale is the limited evidence for external validity. Although a high correlation with the PRF Dominance scale is very encouraging, evidence for convergence with non-test criteria would not only be useful, but essential.

In spite of these reservations the Dominance-Submissiveness scale is a carefully developed device which deserves a place among research instruments, and, should further positive evidence of validity become available, among techniques available for more general personality assessment.

[680]

The Measurement of Language Development. Language impaired children ages 3–0 to 7–11; 1975; MLD; 5 scale scores (receptive scale, expressive scale, mean length of utterance, word order, semantic relations) for each of 8 subtasks (primary verbs, personal pronouns, negatives, indefinite pronouns, interrogatives, wh-questions, secondary verbs, conjunctions); individual; picture plates (219 pages); record form (6 pages); instructional manual (65 pages); 1983 price data: $46.50 per complete set (including 25 record forms); $13.25 per 25 record forms; $21.25 per set of picture plates; $16 per manual; administration time not reported; Carol R. Melnick; Stoelting Co.*

Review of The Measurement of Language Development by DIANE NELSON BRYEN, *Professor of Special Education, Temple University, Philadelphia, PA:*

According to the author, "The Measurement of Language Development (MLD) was designed as a progress indicator of language development for use with a variety of language impaired children," including the mentally retarded. Designed primarily as a pre-therapy and a follow-up progress measure and not as a screening or in-depth diagnostic tool, the MLD can be used in a norm-referenced fashion with children ages 3 years through 7 years 11 months, or in a criterion-referenced manner.

The MLD assesses receptive and expressive linguistic structures using 186 equivalent and contrastable items for each scale. Within each receptive and expressive scale there are eight subtasks, each measuring a different morphosyntactic structure (primary verbs—80 items, personal pronouns—52 items, negatives—14 items, indefinite pronouns—16 items, interrogatives—5 items, Wh-questions—10 items, secondary verbs—5 items, and conjunctions—4 items). While the structures vary, the vocabulary of each stimulus sentence remains familiar and concrete, and the sentence length is kept simple (from 3 to 9 morphemes). In addition, the MLD is designed to assess the mean length of utterance (MLU) according to Brown's (1973) criterion, word order retention, and the usage of semantic relations (e.g., agent-action-object, possession-attribution).

The test format for the expressive scale employs the familiar elicited imitation paradigm developed by Fraser, Bellugi, and Brown (1963) and used in the Northwestern Syntax Screening Test (NSST), accompanied by two line drawings as pictorial representations for each item. For the receptive scales, the test format is a pointing response to one of four line drawings (one pictorial representation of the stimulus sentence and three foils).

Scoring of the MLD, which is extensively described in the Instruction Manual, is based on the binary scoring of the 186 scorable items of each scale. A total score for each scale can be converted into a percentile rank based on 6-month chronological age intervals provided in the manual (or mental age intervals for the mentally retarded). The manual also provides examples of how to score individual items. Although normative data is not provided for scores obtained on the semantic relations, MLU, and retention of word order components of this test, instructions and examples of scoring are provided in some detail. In addition, case studies are provided which illustrate the interpretation of these scores and provide comparisons of pre-therapy and post-therapy scores representing client growth in receptive and expressive abilities on the eight targeted structures, MLU, semantic relations, and word order retention.

The receptive and expressive scales were standardized on 1,091 nonhandicapped and "standard" English-speaking children, ages 3 to 7 years 11 months. The standardization population was drawn from urban, suburban, and rural settings in Illinois, Indiana, and Wisconsin, and represented socioeconomic groups ranging from lower-middle to upper-middle class. Based on this population, norms were developed at 6-month intervals employing 5th, 10th, 20th, 30th, 40th, 50th, 60th, 70th, 80th, 90th, and 95th percentiles.

Four major studies, in addition to the normative study, were conducted by the author to determine the reliability and validity of the MLD (excluding the semantic relations, MLU, and word order retention components). These studies were conducted with nonhandicapped children (ages 3 to 7 years 11 months), language delayed, and trainable mentally retarded youngsters. Generally, the MLD has adequate concurrent validity when CA, scores from spontaneous language samples, and other frequently used clinical tests were used as criterion measures (coefficients ranging from .50 to .79). The receptive and expressive scales have adequate internal consistency (ranging from .74 to .96); however, the eight subtests vary in internal consistency (from .37 to .94), with the lowest internal consistency for the conjunction and secondary verb subtasks (which contain the fewest scorable items).

SUMMARY. Generally the MLD is a reliable and valid test measuring eight morphosyntactic structures in both receptive and expressive modes. However, it is questionable whether individual subtask scores should be used as independent measures due to their more variable and lower reliabilities. The MLD is clearly an improvement over the NSST on which it is based. The addition of the semantic relations, MLU, and word order retention components provides a potentially broader basis for in-depth assessment of these eight structures. Unfortunately, the author has not provided any data to support their reliability or validity. In view of this, these components should be used with caution. Because the MLD was standardized and normed on a middle-class population, caution must again be used when using this test with lower socioeconomic populations. Finally, attention must be paid to the test format itself. The elicited imitation paradigm used in the expressive scale provides the examiner with information concerning the child's knowledge of the particular structure being assessed. However, it does not assess the use of this linguistic knowledge in the child's spontaneous language. Furthermore, because the receptive scale relies on the child's ability to comprehend the meaning represented by the line drawings in addition to the meanings of the stimulus sentences, this test paradigm may pose additional problems to children with visual perception problems. This problem is further compounded by the fact that the intended meaning represented by the line drawings is not always clear to the viewer. Because of this, scores on both scales may be somewhat erroneous due to artifacts of the test paradigms themselves.

REVIEWER'S REFERENCES

Fraser, C., Bellugi, U., & Brown, R. Control of grammar in imitation, comprehension, and production. JOURNAL OF VERBAL LEARNING AND VERBAL BEHAVIOR, 1963, 2, 121–135.

Brown, R. A FIRST LANGUAGE: THE EARLY STAGES. Cambridge, MA: Harvard University Press, 1973.

Review of The Measurement of Language Development by DIXIE D. SANGER, Assistant Professor in Speech Pathology and Audiology, The University of Nebraska-Lincoln, Lincoln, NE:

The Measurement of Language Development (MLD) was designed to function as a progress indicator of treatment provided to children in language intervention programs. It includes an instructor's manual, a book of picture plates, and a six-page record form to code, analyze, and score the responses. The test uses an elicited imitation format primarily to assess receptive and expressive language, and also allows an examiner to determine mean length of utterance, word order, and semantic relations for eight selected types of grammatical relations. However, normative data are provided only for receptive and expressive language subscales, in 6-month intervals between the ages of 3 years 0 months and 7 years 11 months. The author suggests that the receptive and expressive subscales can be used either in a norm- or criterion-referenced manner.

The total MLD contains 186 scorable items, but it is noteworthy that the eight grammatical relations subtasks vary markedly with regard to the number of items in each: primary verbs (80 items), personal pronouns (52 items), negatives (14 items), indefinite pronouns (16 items), interrogative reversals (5 items), wh-questions (10 items), secondary verbs (5 items), and conjunctions (4 items). The author suggests that these are the grammatic categories most often addressed among language impaired children, but that primary verbs and personal pronouns usually are among the major goals of treatment for most language handicapped children. Although some of the subtasks contain as few as four paired stimulus items, the MLD does provide a speech-language clinician with a tool for keeping systematic records that can be used for charting receptive and expressive morphosyntactic structures and can be used for evaluating short-term goals and developing treatment objectives. Additionally, clinicians can find the number of morphemes and types of semantic relations coded next to all of the stimuli in the record form, which is helpful for tabulating, analyzing, and recording the information that is clinically significant.

The MLD is patterned along the imitation, comprehension, production (ICP) model in the sense that it is expected children will acquire language in that progression. The design and scoring of the MLD is similar to that of the Northwestern Syntax Screening Test (NWSST) and the Developmental Sentence Scoring (DSS) procedure. However, literature documentation in support of the theoretical foundation of the instrument is limited. Instead, the author has reported some concurrent validity evidence involving the NWSST and the ITPA Grammatic Closure subtest, Peabody Picture Vocabulary Test, Goodenough Draw-A-Man, and a spontaneous language sample. Interestingly, the MLD receptive and expressive normative data do not clearly substantiate the imitation, comprehension, production paradigm. In particular the central tendency data, reported in 6-month age intervals, reflects higher scores for the expressive performances than the receptive performances among the youngest five age intervals, a fact that clearly raises questions about the ICP model. Also, there are minimal differences between the mean scores on both of these scales, which could lead to the belief that testing expression is as effective as doing both reception and expression. The manual states that reception must always be tested first; however, based upon the data reported it is unclear why the author adopted such a position. Perhaps it would be reasonable to consider testing with the expressive scale first, and only if the resulting performance was notably deficient would there be a need to follow up with the receptive scale.

Scoring the receptive and expressive performances is simplified by requiring a (1) for correct responses and a (0) for incorrect answers, and several examples are provided in the manual to facilitate scoring the test accurately. Summary data on the total score are presented in terms of means, standard deviations, standard errors of measurement, range, and percentiles.

The standardization sample consists of 1,091 children ranging in age from 3–0 to 7–11 years, with approximately equal numbers of females and males drawn from lower middle to upper middle socioeconomic status samples. Also, the author reports that the normative sample contains children from rural, small town, urban, and suburban settings. The author has made a strong attempt to use a representative sample; however, only 30 black children are included in the norms and they reportedly spoke standard English. Consequently, it is doubtful that the norms would be suitable for children who do not use standard American English. The author is to be commended for obtaining standardization data on the instrument, particularly in view of the fact that MLD is not intended to be a screening or testing device, but is to serve as an indication of clinical progress after six or more months.

The Measure of Language Development would be a more attractive instrument if additional literature had been referenced to support its ICP approach and also the rationale for the eight grammatical relations subtasks, and if normative data had been provided on the five scoring scales (receptive performance, expressive performance, mean length of utterance, word order, and semantic relations retained) instead of for only the receptive and expressive performances.

The author claims that the MLD could be given to deaf children. However, clinicians should be careful when using the instrument with the acoustically impaired because of the possibility that different sign language systems may delete or emphasize specific lexical items. Also noteworthy is that the author reports other language features that can be observed such as semantic relations, mean length of utterance, and word order. However, the record form shows these as morphemes retained, word order, and semantic relations. This is a minor point but may result in some confusion to individuals without much experience with the instrument. Also of interest is that the section of the manual that discusses scoring is not clear, and there is an apparent typographical error (one of several in the manual) that leads to some confusion. Sophisticated clinicians will realize that any attempt to dichotomize language behavior solely into a correct or incorrect mold causes much information to be lost. It is possible for language behaviors to be analyzed qualitatively, which allows for evaluating the processes as well as the products.

The reported internal consistency coefficients for the receptive and expressive subtasks are considerably lower than the coefficient for the entire test, which leads to the opinion the test should be given in its entirety to improve reliability. When using a tool like the MLD, however, some estimate is needed of the amount of time it would reasonably take to administer the entire instrument. Most likely, the total instrument does not have to be administered at one time. However, such fragmenting could justify questions regarding the internal consistency of the various subtasks.

The entire instrument is packaged in a spiral-bound soft-cover book that is relatively easy to carry and use. The stimuli are simple black and white line drawings with the four receptive stimuli on one page and the two for the expressive production subtest on the back side. Future editions might consider printing a code or the word "receptive" or "expressive" on one of the lower margins of the respective pages. Also, some code needs to be included in the record form to designate which picture is the correct response for a given item. Conceivably a child could select an incorrect picture that an examiner considers correct, or a child might identify a correct picture that an examiner considers incorrect. A future edition of the MLD should consider renorming some of the pictures and providing definite scoring directions.

Reliability data reported by the author included internal consistency (Cronbach's alpha) coefficients and corrected split-half coefficients above .90 for the entire instrument. However, individual subtasks consistently varied from .42 to .94 for the receptive scale, and from .37 to .94 for the expressive scale. It seemed that the first two subtasks (primary verbs—80 items, and personal pronouns—52 items) carried the bulk of the information on reliability and that the last four to six subtasks probably were too variable to be considered reliable.

The overall impression of the MLD is that if it is to be used as a measure of clinical progress, it should be done so guardedly. The author is to be commended for developing a data-based, standardized instrument to help attain accountability and systematically chart progress. However, the MLD could be strengthened with more normative data and additional supporting references in the manual. The MLD is a tool which could provide a wide sample of information on linguistic development and be of assistance to clinicians in planning short-term objectives and keeping records of progress.

[681]

The Measurement of Moral Judgment. Ages 10 and over; 1984; dilemma interviews designed to measure moral development; 1 score dichotomized as moral stage (I to V) and moral type (A: heteronomous or B: autonomous); no norms; individual; parallel forms A, B, and C consist of 3 standard dilemmas each; The Measurement of Moral Judgment: Theoretical Foundations and Research Validation contains instructions for administering and scoring moral stage; The Measurement of Moral Judgment: Standard Issue Scoring Manual contains the 3 forms and procedures for assessing moral type; price data available from publisher; (10–15) minutes; Anne Colby, Lawrence Kohlberg, et al.; Cambridge University Press.*

See T3:1262 (2 references).

TEST REFERENCES

1. Arredondo-Dowd, P. M. The psychological development and education of immigrant adolescents: A baseline study. ADOLESCENCE, 1981, 16, 175–186.

2. Bear, G. G., & Richards, H. C. Moral reasoning and conduct problems in the classroom. JOURNAL OF EDUCATIONAL PSYCHOLOGY, 1981, 73, 644–670.

3. Bush, D. F., Alterman, A. I., Power, C., & Connolly, R. Moral reasoning in alcoholics and addicts: Structure vs. content. PERCEPTUAL AND MOTOR SKILLS, 1981, 52, 269–270.

4. Evans, C. S. Moral stage development and knowledge of Kohlberg's theory. JOURNAL OF EXPERIMENTAL EDUCATION, 1982, 51, 14–17.

5. Gibbs, J. C., Widaman, K. F., & Colby, A. Construction and validation of a simplified, group-administerable equivalent to the Moral Judgment Interview. CHILD DEVELOPMENT, 1982, 53, 895–910.

6. Krebs, D., & Gillmore, J. The relationship among the first stages of cognitive development, role-taking abilities, and moral development. CHILD DEVELOPMENT, 1982, 53, 877–886.

7. Nisan, M., & Kohlberg, L. Universality and variation in moral judgment: A longitudinal and cross-sectional study in Turkey. CHILD DEVELOPMENT, 1982, 53, 865–876.

8. Thornton, D., & Reid, R. L. Moral reasoning and type of criminal offense. BRITISH JOURNAL OF SOCIAL PSYCHOLOGY, 1982, 21, 231–238.

9. Walker, L. J. The sequentiality of Kohlberg's stages of moral development. CHILD DEVELOPMENT, 1982, 53, 1330–1336.

[682]

Measures of Achieving Tendency. College; 1975; norms consist of means and standard deviations; separate forms for males, females, (3 pages); manual (20 pages, includes test); 1985 price data: $28 per specimen set; administration time not reported; Albert Mehrabian and Lewis Bank; Albert Mehrabian.*

See T3:1442 (1 reference).

Review of Measures of Achieving Tendency by JAYNE E. STAKE, Associate Professor of Psychology, University of Missouri-St. Louis, St. Louis, MO:

Mehrabian developed the first version of the Measures of Achieving Tendency in 1968. These scales were intended to measure resultant achievement motivation, which is defined as the difference between the individual's motivation to approach success and his/her motivation to avoid failure. Resultant achievement motivation had traditionally been measured by a combination of a projective measure of motivation to achieve (the Thematic Apperception Test) and a questionnaire measure of test anxiety (the Test Anxiety Questionnaire). This TAT-TAQ measure was time consuming to administer and score, and it was plagued with problems of reliability and validity. Mehrabian's intention in developing the Measures of Achieving Tendency was to produce reliable, valid scales of resultant achievement motivation that would be convenient to administer and quick to score.

The first two scales that Mehrabian developed were a 34-item male scale and a 34-item female scale. Half of the items on each scale were written so that a positive response would indicate that the motive to achieve was greater than the motive to avoid failure, and half were written so that a positive response would express greater motivation to avoid failure than to achieve success. Responses were made on a 9-point Likert-type scale. Soon after developing these scales, Mehrabian introduced shortened versions of the scales; these versions were each composed of 26 items from the original scales. The original and shortened female scales correlated .92; the original and shortened male scales correlated .94.

In Mehrabian's description of his development of these scales he does not include any information regarding how the scale items were selected. The male and female scales differ on 11 items; he gives no rationale for the differences between the scales.

The reliability of the male and female scales has proven to be adequate. The test-retest reliability was .78 for the male scale ($N = 110$) and .72 for the female scale ($N = 111$). Kuder-Richardson reliability coefficients were .72 ($N = 102$) for the male scale and .61 ($N = 100$) for the female scale.

In terms of discriminant validity, the scales have not been significantly related to measures of affiliation, and correlations with measures of social desirability have been fairly low (from .31 to .34).

As indicated earlier, the Mehrabian scales were meant as an alternative to the TAT-TAQ measure of resultant achievement motivation. Low correlations (.25 to .29) have been found between the male scale and the TAT-TAQ measure. Hence, the Mehrabian scales are measuring something different from the TAT-TAQ measure and cannot be used as a substitute for it.

The Mehrabian scales appear to be more closely related to measures of adjustment and independence. Among males, the Mehrabian measure was found to be negatively related to Eysenck's Neuroticism Scale ($r = -.40$) and to be positively related to Rotter's I-E Scale. Males with an internal locus of control scored higher on the male scale ($r = .64$).

The male scale has been successful in predicting some achievement behaviors in experimental studies. High scorers have tended to attribute success to internal factors and failure to external factors. Also, high scorers have shown a preference for tasks described as difficult as opposed to tasks described as easy. However, the Mehrabian scales have not been found to relate consistently to college grades, test scores, or ability to recall failed items.

In sum, the Mehrabian scales developed in the late 60s have proven to have adequate reliability and discriminant validity. The male scale has been successful in predicting some achievement-related behaviors, but has failed to relate consistently to measures of performance. Also, there is little evidence for the validity of the female scale. When the validity of the female scale has been tested, coefficients have generally been lower than for the male scale.

Mehrabian revised his scales of achieving tendency in 1978. His goal for the revision was to obtain a single and broad-based measure that would be applicable to both sexes and that would be more reliable than the earlier versions. Mehrabian began with a pool of 255 achievement items and later added 99 new and revised items. From this pool he retained items that had a high correlation with the total achievement score, a low correlation with social desirability scores, and low overlap with other items. His final version of the scale contains 38 items. Nineteen items are worded so that a positive response indicates that the motive to achieve is greater than the motive to avoid failure; 19 items are worded in the opposite direction. Subjects respond to the items on 9-point Likert-type scales.

Mehrabian tested the 1978 version of the scale with a sample of 76 male and 66 female university undergraduates. The 1978 scale correlated .59 with the 1969 male scale and .68 with the female scale. The size of these correlations suggests that the 1978 scale represents a substantive change in Mehrabian's measure of achieving tendency.

There is evidence that the 1978 scale may have better psychometric qualities than the earlier scales. In the sample of undergraduates cited above, the Kuder-Richardson coefficient of internal consistency was .91, and the correlation between a measure of social desirability and the new scale was .02.

In this sample the mean for males was 55 ($SD=34$) and for females 46 ($SD=36$). More research is needed to test the usefulness of the 1978 scale for the prediction of achievement behaviors.

[683]

Measures of Affiliative Tendency and Sensitivity to Rejection. College students and adults; 1976; 2 scores: affiliative tendency, sensitivity to rejection; norms consist of means and standard deviations for college students only; 1 form (no date, 3 pages, including directions for administration and scoring); no manual; 1985 price data: $12 per specimen set; administration time not reported; Albert Mehrabian; the Author.*

See T3:1443 (1 reference).

Review of Measures of Affiliative Tendency and Sensitivity to Rejection by PETER D. LIFTON, Assistant Professor of Psychology, The University of North Carolina at Chapel Hill, Chapel Hill, NC:

Mehrabian (1970a, 1976) proposes two questionnaire personality measures concerned with interpersonal behavior. The first, a measure of Affiliative Tendency, is "designed to assess social skills conducive to positive and comfortable social exchanges" (Mehrabian, 1976, p. 200) and to predict affiliative behavior. It seeks to identify persons who are "confident and relaxed in social situations, put their social partners at ease, and have more friends" (Ksionzky & Mehrabian, 1980, p. 145). The second, a measure of Sensitivity to Rejection, is "designed to assess weaknesses in social skills" (Mehrabian, 1976, p. 200) and to predict conformity behavior. It seeks to identify persons who are "submissive and tense in social situations, create discomfort in those with whom they interact, and have fewer friends" (Ksionzky & Mehrabian, 1980, p. 145–146).

Information concerning the reliability, validity, and utility of these measures was pieced together from psychology journal articles written by Mehrabian and his colleagues. No test manual comprehensively documenting either measure presently exists. This poses difficulties not only in writing this review but, more importantly, for persons interested in using these measures.

DESCRIPTION OF MEASURES. The measures of Affiliative Tendency and Sensitivity to Rejection consist of 26 and 24 different alternately-weighted statements, respectively. Persons provide self-report responses using a 9-point Likert scale. Scores are obtained by first reversing the sign of responses to negatively weighted items, then computing the algebraic sum of the items for each measure.

Computation of scores in this manner fails to consider item endorsement rates. The presumption is that the endorsement rate for each item is identical and normally distributed. No evidence has been provided to support this presumption.

ITEM DEVELOPMENT AND SELECTION. Some items in the initial pool were gathered from other measures of affiliation and sensitivity to rejection. Most items, however, were newly written. New items were developed rationally based on theoretical considerations of affiliative and conformity behavior (cf. Mehrabian & Ksionzky, 1970). Therefore, potential users of these measures first should ascertain that their theoretical orientation is consistent with Mehrabian's orientation.

The procedure of item selection for each measure is problematic. According to Mehrabian (1970a, p. 418; 1976, p. 200), "the final measures...evolved from this initial large pool of items after several stages of selection and modification." This selection was based on factor analyses of data from four college student samples. For both the Affiliative Tendency and Sensitivity to Rejection measures "factor analyses of the data obtained from each of the four samples did not consistently yield the same factors" (Mehrabian, 1970a, p. 419). Despite this, homogeneous criterion keying (factor analysis) still was employed as the method for item selection. Furthermore, these factor analyses yielded measures of Affiliative Tendency and Sensitivity to Rejection consisting of 31 and 38 items respectively (Mehrabian, 1970a), not the current 26- and 24-item version (Mehrabian, 1976) which is the subject of this review. The basis for the deletion of items from the 1970 to 1976 version is unstated.

Both versions involved consideration of satisfactory test-retest reliability, independence from social desirability, and independence from the other measure as additional criteria for selecting items. The minimum cutoff points for what constituted a "reliable" and "independent" item are unstated.

RELIABILITY. The measures of Affiliative Tendency and Sensitivity to Rejection appear internally consistent, with Kuder-Richardson coefficients of .80 or higher. They also appear stable over time, with product-moment correlation coefficients approaching .90. However, the test-retest reliabilities reported for the 1976 version of the measures (Mehrabian, 1976, p. 201) actually are for the 1970 version (Mehrabian, 1970a, p. 420). This "oversight" by Mehrabian does not imply that the 1976 version is unreliable, only that the incorrect test-retest reliability coefficients were reported.

CONTENT VALIDITY. The measures appear to cover a representative sample of behaviors associated with affiliation and sensitivity to rejection. This is due to the rational, content-validational approach used in the development of items. Additionally, Mehrabian (1976) has demonstrated that items on each measure form factors representative of a spectrum of affiliative (e.g., preference for group activities, overt expression of affection toward others) and conformity (e.g., avoidance of arguments, timidity in social situations) behaviors.

CRITERION-RELATED VALIDITY. There is evidence to support the criterion-related validity of the measure of Affiliative Tendency. High scorers on this measure prefer more intimate seating arrangements (Mehrabian & Diamond, 1971a, b), are more self-disclosing (Ksionzky & Mehrabian, 1980), more interactive with strangers (Crouse & Mehrabian, 1977), perceive other persons as more affiliative (Solar & Mehrabian, 1973), and anticipate more positive consequences from social interactions (Mehrabian & Ksionzky, 1974) than low scorers. There is also evidence to support the criterion-related validity for the measure of Sensitivity to Rejection. High scorers on this measure are more vigilant, tense, and anxious when interacting with strangers (Crouse & Mehrabian, 1977; Mehrabian, 1971), more conforming (Mehrabian, 1970b), less self-disclosing (Ksionzky & Mehrabian, 1980), and anticipate more negative consequences from social interactions (Mehrabian & Ksionzky, 1974) than low scorers.

CONSTRUCT VALIDITY. The construct validity of both measures is marginal, though discriminant validity appears better established than convergent validity. The primary evidence for discriminant validity is the measures' significant but low level correlations with social desirability and non-significant correlation with each other. Additionally, Sensitivity to Rejection is inversely related to arousal and dominance with both measures inversely related to achievement and flexibility. Little evidence for either measures' convergent validity is presented other than a weak association with emotional empathy (Mehrabian, 1976).

The evidence for construct validity satisfies only the multitrait portion of Campbell and Fiske's (1959) multitrait-multimethod matrix. Data from the self-report questionnaires of Affiliative Tendency and Sensitivity to Rejection were compared with data from other self-report questionnaires. Until multimethod comparisons are performed, it is reasonable to attribute any significant correlations to similarity in method rather than similarity in psychological construct.

Overall, although Mehrabian's (1976) findings suggest support for the construct validity of the two measures, his findings are more preliminary than conclusive.

TARGET POPULATION. Subjects involved in the development, validation, and experimental studies using the measures of Affiliative Tendency and Sensitivity to Rejection were University of California, Los Angeles, undergraduates. There is no reason to believe these measures generalize beyond this population. As such, the utility of the measures for other populations may be limited, or at least has yet to be demonstrated.

CONCLUDING REMARKS. Mehrabian's (1970a, 1976) measures of Affiliative Tendency and Sensitivity to Rejection are psychologically intriguing but psychometrically unproven. The absence of a test manual contributes to the confusion concerning the item development, item selection, and reliability of the measures. Content and criterion validity are good, but construct validity, computation of scale scores, interpretation of scores, and general utility beyond a specific college population are questionable. Furthermore, Mehrabian and Ksionzky (1970, 1972) suggest that these two measures form a 2 x 2 typology descriptive of four types of persons. The contribution to personality psychology of typologies in general and this typology in particular remains uncertain.

REVIEWER'S REFERENCES

Campbell, D., & Fiske, D. Convergent and discriminant validation by the multitrait-multimethod matrix. PSYCHOLOGICAL BULLETIN, 1959, 56, 81–105.

Mehrabian, A. The development and validation of measures of affiliative tendency and sensitivity to rejection. EDUCATION AND PSYCHOLOGICAL MEASUREMENT, 1970, 30, 417–428. (a)

Mehrabian, A. Some determinants of affiliation and conformity. PSYCHOLOGICAL REPORTS, 1970, 27, 19–29. (b)

Mehrabian, A., & Ksionzky, S. Models for affiliative and conformity behavior. PSYCHOLOGICAL BULLETIN, 1970, 74, 110–126.

Mehrabian, A. Verbal and nonverbal interaction of strangers in a waiting situation. JOURNAL OF EXPERIMENTAL RESEARCH IN PERSONALITY, 1971, 5, 127–138.

Mehrabian, A., & Diamond, S. Seating arrangement and conversation. SOCIOMETRY, 1971, 34, 281–289. (a)

Mehrabian, A., & Diamond, S. Effects of furniture arrangement, props, and personality on social interaction. JOURNAL OF PERSONALITY AND SOCIAL PSYCHOLOGY, 1971, 20, 18–30. (b)

Mehrabian, A., & Ksionzky, S. Some determiners of social interaction. SOCIOMETRY, 1972, 35, 588–609.

Solar, D., & Mehrabian, A. Impressions based on contradictory information as a function of affiliative tendency and cognitive style. JOURNAL OF EXPERIMENTAL RESEARCH IN PERSONALITY, 1973, 6, 339–346.

Mehrabian, A., & Ksionzky, S. A THEORY OF AFFILIATION. Lexington, MA: Heath, 1974.

Mehrabian, A. Questionnaire measures of affiliative tendency and sensitivity to rejection. PSYCHOLOGICAL REPORTS, 1976, 38, 199–209.

Crouse, B., & Mehrabian, A. Affiliation of opposite-sexed strangers. JOURNAL OF RESEARCH IN PERSONALITY, 1977, 11, 38–47.

Ksionzky, S., & Mehrabian, A. Personality correlates of self-disclosure. SOCIAL BEHAVIOR AND PERSONALITY, 1980, 8, 145–152.

[684]

Measures of Individual Differences in Temperament. College students and adults; 1978; 3 scores: trait pleasure, trait arousal, trait dominance; norms consist of means and standard deviations for college students only; 1 form ('78, 6 pages, including directions for administration and scoring); no manual; 1985 price data: $12 per specimen set; administration time not reported; Albert Mehrabian; the Author.*

See T3:1444 (1 reference).

Review of Measures of Individual Differences in Temperament by JOHN B. GORMLY, Associate Professor of Psychology, Rutgers University, New Brunswick, NJ:

The test reviewed here is one of several tests developed by Mehrabian to assess multiple aspects of temperament. The present test has several desirable features. It measures three fundamental aspects of temperament—trait-pleasure, trait-arousal, and trait-dominance—in a way that yields scores that are statistically independent of each other. The scores, then, are ideal for use with multiple-correlation and multiple regression procedures. The independence of the scores was achieved by appropriate, successive development of the items which make up the test. The test is easy to administer, and the testee should be able to complete the test in less than 10 minutes. Scoring the test responses is similarly easy. Although the test was designed as a measure of trait behavior, a slight change in instructions converts the test to an instrument assessing state-pleasure, state-arousal, and state-dominance.

The test as it stands, however, has some serious deficiencies. First, it was developed using only college students. Consequently the normative information (means and standard deviations) is known only for undergraduates from University of California, Los Angeles. Second, the number of items for the arousal scale is quite small—8 items—and they do not have sufficient internal consistency to consider them to be measuring a unitary trait. Third, the stability of scores over even a brief period of time is unknown; it is only assumed that a person's response to the test has stable, trait-like properties. Fourth, the validity of the scales is essentially unknown. There are no data to demonstrate that the scores from this measure predict socially relevant behavior.

The deficiencies listed above should not be taken as a condemnation of this measure of temperaments. They simply indicate that this test is not yet sufficiently developed.

The format of Mehrabian's measure of temperament is an alternative to the format of most traditional measures of personality. Mehrabian's measure consists of pairs of polar adjectives that are separated by 9-point rating scales. Most measures of personality traits present the testee with statements to which the testee can respond with Yes/No, True/False, or some similar response. The alternative format used by Mehrabian is worth investigating.

It is well known after extensive investigation that only small correlations have been found between traditional measures of personality and behavior. It is highly unlikely that anyone is going to produce a new set of statements for traditional inventories that is going to improve their predictive validity; the range of these statements already in use is extensive. Nor is it likely that the statements of traditional inventories are going to be combined in a manner that produces new, more predictive scales. Research such as that reported by Hase and Goldberg (1967) has demonstrated that scales constructed rationally, factor analytically, and by the contrasted-groups method all yield approximately the same predictive values. Thus, it is time to experiment with rating scales as well as other formats of personality assessment. It is as an experiment with the format of personality assessment that Mehrabian's measures of temperament have their most promise.

In summary, this measure of temperament seems to measure two of the three traits it was designed to measure. The scales should be considered to be in their developmental stages because of lack of data on stability of the scores and lack of data on relationships between the scale scores and socially relevant behavior.

REVIEWER'S REFERENCES

Hase, H. D., & Goldberg, L. R. Comparative validity of different strategies of constructing personality inventory scales. PSYCHOLOGICAL BULLETIN, 1967, 67, 231–248.

[685]

Measures of Occupational Stress, Strain, and Coping. Employed adults; 1981; experimental form; 3 questionnaires; 1983 price data: $3 per 10 profiles; $10 per specimen set (must be purchased to obtain manual); (10–15) minutes for each questionnaire; Samuel H. Osipow and Arnold R. Spokane; Marathon Consulting & Press.*

a) OCCUPATIONAL ENVIRONMENT SCALES. OES; 7 scales: Role Overload, Role Insufficiency, Role Ambiguity, Role Boundary, Responsibility, Physical Environment, Full Scale Total; Form E-2 (4 pages).

b) PERSONAL STRAIN QUESTIONNAIRE. PSQ; 5 scales: Vocational Strain, Psychological Strain, Interpersonal Strain, Physical Strain, Full Scale Total; Form E-2 (3 pages).

c) PERSONAL RESOURCES QUESTIONNAIRE. PRQ; 5 scales: Recreation, Self-Care, Social Support, Rational/Cognitive Coping, Full Scale Total; Form E-3 (3 pages).

Review of Measures of Occupational Stress, Strain, and Coping by H. JOHN BERNARDIN, Director, Administrative Systems Center, Florida Atlantic University, Boca Raton, FL:

The *Standards for Educational and Psychological Tests* state that a test manual "should provide enough information for a qualified user to make sound judgments regarding the usefulness and interpretation of test scores. Research is required prior to the release of the test or test scores for operational use." On what is considered to be the most important standard of the *Standards* (Glaser & Bond, 1981), the Preliminary Manual for Measures of Occupational Stress, Strain, and Coping leaves much to be desired. An extremely limited amount of research has been conducted with the three scales and there is little (or nothing) to support an argument of construct validity. As the authors state, the scales are still in a developmental state and the manual is "preliminary."

Based on the data presented in the manual, there is little to justify the use of the three scales at the present time. They are in dire need of more supportive research as described by Campbell (1976). As will be delineated below, other scales with lengthy research trails and copious psychometric support would seem a safer bet for those interested in stress, particularly the organizational parameters of stress.

The authors claim that items for all scales were selected on the basis of the "greatest content validity." While it is unclear how this was actually accomplished, it is doubtful the procedures used approximate those described for "content validity" in the *Standards* or the proposed revision (Novick, 1981). The authors would probably be on much safer ground had they used the term "face validity" instead.

It is suggested that the instruments may be used as screening devices for the assessment of stress, strain and coping, an assessment of the organizational milieu, as a stimulus for counseling, and as a measure of the effects of stress management interventions. While these are all certainly noble objectives, the authors present virtually no data to support any of these applications and insufficient psychometric data to justify even a modicum of construct validity. Two (improperly referenced) unpublished studies are cited as support for the OES and the PSQ. However, not enough detail on these studies is provided to facilitate clear understanding of what the studies were about and how their results supported an argument for construct validity. For example, the authors state that in a study by Baldwin (1981), there was a "strong inverse relationship between stress (OES) and satisfaction." This is apparently interpreted as support for the construct validity of the OES. However, an alternative explanation for these results is that the OES is simply a reverse scored measure of job satisfaction. Since there are already several well-developed and extensively researched measures of job satisfaction, the burden is on any scale developer to show through factor analysis and multi-trait, multi-method analysis that something different (i.e., not job satisfaction) is being assessed by the new scale. Otherwise, in terms of the applications above, the lengthy research trails of the Job Descriptive Index (Smith, Kendall, & Hulin, 1969) and the Minnesota Satisfaction Questionnaire (Weiss, Davis, England, & Lofquist, 1966) certainly justify their continued use. Since reliability is essentially the correlation between two maximally similar methods and validity is the correlation between two maximally different methods (Campbell & Fiske, 1959), the evidence from an item comparison of the OES and measures of job satisfaction, and the results reported in Baldwin (1981), suggest that the OES may be just another measure of job satisfaction. It is the authors' responsibility to show that it is not.

A related issue has to do with a justification for the new measures of role overload, role ambiguity, and role boundary. There is a considerable body of research using one measure of those constructs (Rizzo, House, & Lirtzman, 1970). The authors should acknowledge that this measure exists, criticize it if they feel it is justified, and/or present data to show their measure is somehow better. Once again, in the development of new measures of old constructs, the burden is on the developers of the new scale to show that a new scale is in fact warranted based on psychometric criteria, ease of administration, or brevity. Rather, the impression is created in the authors' literature review that little has been done in the area of role theory since Kahn's (1974) paper. In fact, a great deal of research has been done with one set of scales operationalizing role ambiguity and conflict (viz., Rizzo et al., 1970). Other scales are also available. Given the paucity of psychometric data presented in the manual, particularly the lack of factor analysis and other construct validation research, there is no compelling reason at this time to justify the OES as a suitable or superior replacement. While Rizzo et al. noted that their scales needed further refinement, the manual for the OES does not even recognize their existence.

Some other problems with the OES have to do with the items involving physical characteristics. A single frequency rating on "high levels of noise" certainly simplifies a complicated relationship between parameters of noise and reactions to it. For example, the relevance of the noise to the task is an important variable. For irrelevant sounds, high frequency tones are distracting and probably stressful. Whether noise is continuous or intermittent is also important. The extent to which noise makes communication difficult is also critical. The use of a single item for "high noise" seems to make the simple assumption that high noise is stressful. Research tells us a lot more than that. A response of "occasionally" on the OES to exposure to high levels of noise can be interpreted to mean either sporadic or continuous "occasional" noise. The interpretation is important to our understanding of stress.

An important parameter missing from the OES is the extent of sleep deprivation caused by the job. This is a proven source of stress related to work scheduling. Unfortunately, the frequency of an "erratic work schedule" (the only item on the scale even remotely related to sleep deprivation) is subject to more than one interpretation. Items having to do with shift work would be informative since a large percentage of the U.S. work force operates under such systems.

SUMMARY. The other work environment scale now available which attempts to be comprehensive in its scope is the Work Environment Scale (WES).

Based on the evidence presented in the two manuals, a stronger case can be made for the use of the WES at this time. While the proposal to study stress from the three perspectives (represented by the three questionnaires) is admirable, far more data is needed to support the use of the scales at this time.

REVIEWER'S REFERENCES

Campbell, D. T., & Fiske, D. W. Convergent and discriminant validation by the multitrait-multimethod matrix. PSYCHOLOGICAL BULLETIN, 1959, 56, 81–105.

Weiss, D. J., Davis, R. V., England, G. W., & Lofquist, L. H. Manual for the Minnesota Satisfaction Questionnaire. MINNESOTA STUDIES IN VOCATIONAL REHABILITATION, XXI, 1966.

Smith, P. C., Kendall, L. M., & Hulin, C. L. THE MEASUREMENT OF SATISFACTION IN WORK AND RETIREMENT. Chicago: Rand-McNally, 1969.

Rizzo, J., House, R., & Lirtzman, S. Role conflict and ambiguity in complex organizations. ADMINISTRATIVE SCIENCE QUARTERLY, 1970, 60, 683–687.

Kahn, R. L. Conflict, ambiguity, and overwork: Three elements in job stress. In A. McLean (Ed.), OCCUPATIONAL STRESS. Springfield, IL: Charles C Thomas, 1974.

Campbell, J. P. Psychometric theory. In M. Dunnette (Ed.), HANDBOOK OF INDUSTRIAL AND ORGANIZATIONAL PSYCHOLOGY. Chicago, IL: Rand-McNally, 1976.

Baldwin, A. M. THE RELATIONSHIP BETWEEN GRADUATE ADMISSIONS VARIABLES AND PROFESSIONAL PERFORMANCE SATISFACTION AND STRESS IN MASTERS LEVEL COUNSELING GRADUATES. Unpublished Masters Thesis, University of Maryland, College Park, MD, 1981.

Glaser, R., & Bond, L. Testing: Concepts, policy, practice and research. AMERICAN PSYCHOLOGIST, 1981, 36, 997–1000.

Novick, M. R. Federal guidelines and professional standards. AMERICAN PSYCHOLOGIST, 1981, 36, 1035–1046.

Review of Measures of Occupational Stress, Strain, and Coping by KEVIN R. MURPHY, Assistant Professor of Psychology, New York University, New York, NY:

The Occupational Environment Scales (OES), the Personal Strain Questionnaire (PSQ), and the Personal Resources Questionnaire (PRQ) provide an integrated set of measures of stress (defined as the presence of various role pressures in the work environment), strain (defined as the affective and subjective response to stress), and coping resources (defined by the availability and use of various coping behaviors and sources of social support). As noted in the manual, stress, strain, and coping are intimately related; the strategy of developing an integrated set of measures of these three constructs is therefore eminently sensible. Preliminary data presented in the manual suggest that the authors have made considerable progress toward developing useful and compatible measures of stress, strain, and coping.

The preliminary test manual clearly states that the scales are still undergoing revision and that little is known about the construct validity of the current scales. The authors show the proper caution in describing the possible uses of their scales, noting that the scales are "probably most useful now for research purposes," and stating in no uncertain terms that the scales should *not* be used as an employment screening device. The authors also suggest potential applications of the scales once a substantial degree of construct validity is established. These applications include individual counseling, career counseling, and organizational assessments; this description of future application of the scales is very helpful in developing a clear picture of the constructs which the authors intend to measure.

The test manual presents test-retest reliability data, obtained in a small ($N=31$) sample, for earlier versions of the scales, and internal consistency reliability estimates, obtained in a fairly large ($N=201$) and occupationally diverse sample, for the current version of each scale. Full-scale coefficient alphas for the OES, the PSQ, and the PRQ were fairly high (.88, .92, and .83, respectively); internal consistency reliability coefficients for the various subscales ranged from .57 to .92, with a median of .75. Evidence of construct validity, however, is somewhat limited and conflicting. The authors cite studies indicating negative correlations between coping and PSQ (strain) scores, and between job satisfaction and OES (stress). The test manual also documents the positive correlation between OES (stress) and PSQ (strain) scores and negative correlation between both OES and PSQ and PRQ (coping) scores. However, examination of the intercorrelations among subscale scores, particularly stress and strain subscales, shows that the correlations between subscales which are designed to measure the same construct (e.g., stress) are not substantially higher than those between subscales which are employed in measuring different constructs. There are a number of analytic methods for assessing the convergent and discriminant validity of the subscales; it would be useful for future versions of the manual to include the results of multivariate analyses, such as a factor analysis, to bolster their arguments regarding construct validity.

Although the manual presents a useful description of the way in which the constructs and dimensions to be measured were selected and defined, descriptions of the technical process of test construction are ambiguous and incomplete. For example, the manual includes a brief description of the item selection process, but none of the item statistics are presented, nor is there any clear description of the sample from which item analysis data were obtained. There is a detailed occupational breakdown of the normative sample, but it is not clear whether this is the same sample which is used to provide reliability data. The manual implies that normative data and reliability data were obtained from the same sample, but the number of cases varies slightly from table to table.

There are two potentially serious defects in the current versions of the scales. First, 120 of the 140 items included on the three scales are worded so that a high score (items are rated on a 5-point frequency scale, where "5" indicates "Most of the Time") indicates a high level of stress, strain, or coping ability. A better balance of positively and negatively worded items would be useful in removing possible biases due to response sets such as acquiescence. Second, scale means on two of the coping subscales, Social Support and Rational/Cognitive Coping, are very high (41.09 and 37.70, respectively). As a result, a person who indicates that he or she often uses every one of the strategies listed in these scales (a scale score of "3") will be seen as seriously deficient in the availability or use of these coping responses. It seems clear that these subscales must be revised to lower their "floor" considerably.

There are some minor problems and puzzles in the preliminary test manual. For example, there is a minor error in the instructions for scoring the Role Ambiguity OES subscale. The instructions indicate that seven of the items should be scored in reverse directions; a careful reading of the items shows that an eighth item (item 21) should also be scored this way. Comparisons of the test-retest reliability estimates for the previous versions of these scales and internal consistency estimates for the current, and presumably improved, versions presents a somewhat troubling puzzle. The test-retest reliabilities are consistently higher than the internal consistency estimates. When one considers that items from the earlier version which failed to show internal consistency were not included in the current version of each scale, this result seems surprising indeed. It is possible that the test-retest estimates, which were obtained from a small sample, are spuriously high, but it is not clear whether this would explain the confusing pattern of results. It would be useful to know the coefficient alphas for the original version of each scale.

Although there is clearly work to be done, these scales seem to show considerable potential as measures of stress, strain, and coping. There is already evidence of adequate reliability for the scales and most of the subscales, and the authors seem to be actively engaged in accumulating and evaluating evidence of construct validity. Test users should exercise considerable caution in interpreting scores from the current versions of the scales, and should heed the manual's warnings regarding the use of these preliminary scales in making personnel decisions. It appears likely that the scales, particularly the PRQ, will undergo some modification before they reach their final form, and it is therefore too early to deliver a final evaluation of the scales. Given the progress to date, it is quite possible that the final versions of the Occupational Environment Scales, the Personal Strain Questionnaire, and the Personal Resources Questionnaire will represent technically adequate and useful measures of stress, strain, and coping.

[686]

Measures of Pleasure-, Arousal-, and Dominance-Inducing Qualities of Parental Attitudes. Ages 3 months–8 years; 1979; ratings by parents to measure pleasure, arousal and dominance levels experienced by the child; 3 scores: pleasure-inducing, arousal-inducing, dominance-inducing; norms for mother's ratings only; individual; 1 form (4 pages); 1985 price data: $12 per specimen set; administration time not reported; C. A. Falender and A. Mehrabian; A. Mehrabian.*

See T3:1448 (1 reference).

Review of Measures of Pleasure-, Arousal-, and Dominance-Inducing Qualities of Parental Attitudes by DOUGLAS N. JACKSON, Senior Professor of Psychology, The University of Western Ontario, London, Canada:

This is a scale for measuring parental attitudes regarding child rearing, based on the assumption that such attitudes create a well-defined emotional climate in which children are reared. The theoretical basis for the measurement of these attitudes derives from Mehrabian's formulation that there are three orthogonal dimensions of emotional states, namely, Pleasure-Displeasure, Arousal-Non-Arousal, and Dominance-Submissiveness. These dimensions in combination are regarded as forming a basis for describing any emotional state. These dimensions also are viewed as providing a basis for understanding parental attitudes in terms of their induction of an emotional climate for children. For example, the authors speculate that a generally rejecting and hostile parent habitually induces feelings of displeasure, arousal, and submissiveness in his/her child.

The questionnaire, based on a series of item analyses, consists of 18 Pleasure, 12 Arousal, and 16 Dominance items. Item selection was based on an unusually elaborate series of analyses based on three separate samples. The initial group of 178 items was chosen from content groups representing most aspects of maternal attitudes identified by previous investigators. These were organized into one of three categories corresponding to the emotion it was expected to elicit in children. Examples of positive attitudes corresponding to the Pleasure, Arousal, and Dominance dimensions are, respectively, preferences for spending time with the child, for open-ended rather than highly structured play activities and toys, and for allowing the child to decide what to eat. At each of the three stages in item analysis, the item pool was sharply reduced based on empirical analyses and then augmented with new or revised items prior to further analyses. The final keys were approximately balanced for positive and negative exemplars to control for response bias.

Reliabilities, based on the KR-20 formula, are reported for the three scales: .79 for Pleasure, .62 for Arousal, and .77 for Dominance. Since these estimates were based on the same sample from which the final sets of items were selected, the estimates are inflated by some unknown degree. The authors report evidence that the three dimensions are independent; none correlate higher than .14. No evidence of external validity is provided.

The three scales of parental attitudes offered here are based on a theoretical rationale and a careful program of item analyses. Reliability evidence is equivocal, and evidence of external validity from the original publication is lacking. Although the reviewer would not recommend these scales for individual assessment, they might be useful in research on parental attitudes as they affect emotional development. Such research, as well, might properly undertake evaluations of scale reliabilities and of convergent and discriminant validity.

Review of Measures of Pleasure-, Arousal-, and Dominance-Inducing Qualities of Parental Attitudes by CHARLES WENAR, Professor of Psychology, The Ohio State University, Columbus, OH:

The authors' goal is to develop an instrument for measuring parental attitudes which is more fruitful and more theoretically oriented than those extant. However, they fall considerably short of the mark and the report of their effort reveals a number of flaws.

Their review of competing measures is inaccurate in places, and their claim to have a theoretically based instrument (in contrast to the atheoretical instruments extant) is exaggerated. At best, their instrument has more of a conceptual basis than do purely empirical instruments but, aside from fleeting references to information processing, its theoretical underpinnings are not in evidence.

In their rationale, the authors assume a unidirectional relation between parental attitudes and children's emotions (e.g., authoritarian parents induce slightly unpleasant, rather low arousal, submissive feelings in children); this assumption runs counter to current interactional models which state that the same parental attitude can induce different affects and that affects in children can change parental attitudes. The authors' simplistic reasoning leads them subsequently to assume that statements assessing parental attitudes will, ipso facto, measure the inferred affective state in the child (e.g., that a parent who shields the child from strangers creates an experience of negative arousal in the child). No evidence is offered to support such an inference.

Such conceptual flaws are complemented by psychometric ones. The authors tried out items on three successive populations, in order to obtain items which correlated highly with one of the three attitudes—pleasure, arousal, and dominance—while having a low correlation with the other two. Yet they present no data showing that the third and final items more successfully met this criterion than the first and second set.

The population used for the three item analyses is inadequately described and, in all probability, biased. The description of the population used for norms is woefully inadequate, being limited to a single sentence.

The scales' reliabilities are admittedly only adequate, while validity is limited to evidence indicating the independence of the three scales. Thus, the scales have not been correlated with other measures of parental attitudes so that their similarity and uniqueness can be judged, nor is there any evidence that the scales measure the emotional climate or the affect in children which they claim to measure.

In sum, the scales measuring three parental attitudes are in a preliminary stage of development. Until more evidence is offered concerning their uniqueness, validity, and fruitfulness, there is little justification for their use. Finally, $12 seems a large sum of money to pay for a preliminary instrument with questionable norms.

[687]

Measures of Self-Concept K–12. Grades K–3, 4–6, 7–12; 1972; "an IOX measureable objectives collection"; criterion-referenced; uses direct self-report, inferential self-report, and observation; no data on validity; no norms; 3 levels; manual (139 pages, includes all items necessary for administration); 1984 price data: $10.95 per manual; IOX Assessment Associates.*

a) PRIMARY. Grades K–3; 10 objectives: self-appraisal (5 objectives: comprehensive, peer, school, family, general), television actors, the class play, parental approval, work posting, perceived approval situation; (10–20) minutes per objective.

b) INTERMEDIATE. Grades 4–6; 11 objectives: self-appraisal (same as *a* above), what would you do, parental approval, the class play, how about you, work posting, perceived approval situation; (10–20) minutes per objective.

c) SECONDARY. Grades 7–12; 9 objectives: self-appraisal (same as *a* above), what would you do, word choice, for all I know, perceived approval situation; (10–30) minutes per objective.

See T3:1449 (1 reference).

Review of Measures of Self-Concept K–12 by DORCAS SUSAN BUTT, Associate Professor of Psychology, University of British Columbia, Vancouver, B.C., Canada:

This unique proposal for the assessment of educational programs stems from a meeting of representatives from 40 states held in Washington, DC, in 1970. The goal was to develop measures to assess the effectiveness of educational programs in fostering positive emotional development, the latter being defined for the purposes of the project as self-concept development. The project employed "a criterion referenced approach in the development of items and measures." As a first step in this approach an educational objective "is formulated as clearly as possible, and its importance for the learner confirmed by appropriate judges." Test items are then selected to measure pupils' attainment of that objective. One can assess the attainment both before and after the educational treatment, being advisably cautious about attributing positive change solely to educational treatment. The writers of the manual are careful to point out that the measures are for use in group assessment only. They are not appropriate to use for individual evaluation.

The result of this cooperative effort and revision is a set of 9 to 11 objectives for each of three grade levels: K through 3 (primary), 4 through 6 (intermediate), and 7 through 12 (secondary). Examples of these objectives are: "Students will evidence positive self concepts about the self in general by expressing agreement with statements that describe a person with positive self esteem; and by indicating disagreements with statements that depict a person with negative self esteem"; "Students will display positive self concepts by indicating that others would choose them to play roles which carry positive images in a pretend play."

The philosophy behind this project is applaudable. The goals are positive (i.e., what is education doing for the self-concept development of the pupils?) and the self-contained manual is a welcome guide because all that one needs to use the program is in the one manual.

On the other hand, the absence of any validation data leaves all of the measures in a very embryonic, even if promising, state of development. To take one example: a child is instructed to imagine he/she has just kicked a small dog. Two questions follow: Would your mother disapprove of you? Would your mother dislike you? Presumably the child with the good self-concept will endorse the first item but not the second. Although psychological theory predicts a parent should be able to punish without withdrawing love, the reviewer posed these questions to a handful of small children and found that most of them would dislike themselves if they committed the act and thought their mother would also. Thus the interesting and provocative assumption behind this single question is deserving of much further study.

Unfortunately the work of the revision did not concentrate on validation of the measures but upon increasing the number of participants in each testing group and upon correcting for socioeconomic biases in the first edition. Subscales and items were then screened on the basis of subscale intercorrelations and item homogeneity and stability. Internal consistency and stability indexes comprise the only statistical table reported in the manual. These are adequate for affective measures.

In conclusion, the Measures of Self-Concept K–12 are in the formative stages only. This reviewer can see constructive teacher use of these materials if proper caution is exercised. This is an interesting grass-roots project, high on potential, and even higher on the need for validation data.

Review of Measures of Self-Concept K–12 by GEORGE F. MADAUS, Director, Center for the Study of Testing, Evaluation, and Educational Policy, Boston College, Chestnut Hill, MA:

IOX Assessment Associates Measures of Self Concept K–12 is a collection of scales designed to measure 30 self-concept objectives across three levels of schooling: primary (grades K through 3), intermediate (grades 4 through 6), and secondary (grades 7 through 12).

The collection grew out of IOX's work in the early 70s with Title III programs. As such it is very much a product of its time. With the present emphasis in most school districts on developing basic skills and cognitive outcomes one gets the distinct feeling that today these affective objectives get little explicit attention in many school systems.

The well written, very readable manual suggests that local school districts first should decide on the appropriateness of these objectives and scales for their particular educational situation. If systems decide to adopt the scales the manual cautions that they should be used only to evaluate the effectiveness of instructional programs designed to improve learners' self-concepts (or impede increasing negative development). The scales are not meant to be used to assess, or make decisions about, individual students. Since they are meant primarily for program evaluation, the gathering of anonymous group data and the use of item and person sampling is stressed.

Another suggested use is longitudinal studies to assess self-concept development over lengthy periods of time. However, it should be noted that the anonymity requirement would make such longitudinal tracking difficult in school systems with high rates of student turnover.

The manual states that the items and scales were developed using a criterion-referenced approach rather than a norm-referenced approach. In the former approach an objective is clearly formulated and confirmed by judges as appropriate for the intended purpose and the items are designed to measure it. The manual discusses the norm-referenced approach as one in which the primary purpose is to produce a test "which discriminates among individuals—to 'spread people out'—rather than to assess the degree to which they achieve a particular criterion objective." Interestingly, on page 8 of the manual IOX admits that in revising the items after a field tryout the "ability of items to discriminate among subjects provided the key revision index." This reviewer does not wish to quibble, but this inconsistency points out the difficulty of trying to make distinctions between criterion-referenced (CRT) and norm-referenced tests (NRT), particularly at the item development level, and further of using the CRT-NRT distinction in the affective area.

The items were carefully screened for objective match, and were subjected to small- and large-scale field tryouts. The field tryouts revealed high intercorrelations among subscales on the direct self-report measures. Consequently, the manual points out that the assertion that the subscales are measuring truly distinctive constructs is not warranted. Despite this caution, the items keys are given for general, peer, school, and family self-concept subscores at each of the three levels. The provision of the subscale keys almost assures that some user will employ the subscale scores to measure the four named constructs as if they were distinct.

Two reliability estimates were obtained: an internal consistency index and a test-retest stability estimate. The former range from .54–.78 at the secondary level; .57–.87 at the intermediate level; and .37–.62 at the primary level. The latter estimates are .31–.87 (secondary); .64–.91 (intermediate); and .29–.77 (primary). The manual cautions that the primary level measures yielded lower internal consistency and test-retest results than at the other two levels and therefore should be used with considerable caution. This reviewer concurs. Other than content validity, no other validity information is presented. Certainly more in the way of construct validity evidence is needed for these affective measures.

This reviewer found the primary level self-report instruments disturbing. First, despite anonymity (which in local situations can't always be guaranteed), asking a young child to answer "yes" or "no" to items like "Do members of your family pick on you?" or "Do your parents like you even if you have done something bad?" will almost certainly be viewed as offensive and/or intrusive by some parents. Second, and even more troubling, is whether children in grades K through 3 understand the concepts being measured by various items. For example, what does the following item convey to a first grader: "Do you like being just what you are?" If he/she has had a fight with an older sibling that morning, how will he/she respond to the item that asks, "Do members of your family pick on you?" This is not to nitpick individual items but to raise the issue of whether self-concept can be measured in a stable fashion with self-report items read aloud to very young children. This reviewer is far from convinced.

If a school system is seeking to evaluate programs designed to affect self-concepts, then they should certainly consider this IOX collection for use in program evaluation. However, they should adhere to the warnings regarding use in the manual and perform their own validity studies for any inferences they wish to make. They should use the primary level scales with utmost caution if at all.

[688]

Measuring the Skills of Composition. Grades 1–12; 1981; a teachers' guide for classroom evaluation of student writing; 4 ratings: narration, description, exposition, persuasion; no data on reliability and validity; norms based on several thousand student compositions for California statewide writing assessment; manual (82 pages); 1984 price data: $11.95 per manual, including instructions for designing test appropriate to grade level, and skill-specific scoring guides; administration time not reported; Elaine Lindheim, Carol Lettieri, and John Ruggles; IOX Assessment Associates.*

[689]

Mechanical Familiarity Test: ETSA Test 5A. Job applicants; 1950–84; "measure ability to recognize common tools and instruments"; norms consist of means and standard deviations; 1 form ('59, 4 pages); scoring key ('59, 1 sheet); for more complete information, see 399; 1984 price data: $12 per 10 tests and scoring key; (60–70) minutes; Psychological Services Bureau; Employers' Tests & Services Associates.*

For reviews of an earlier version of the ETSA Tests by Marvin D. Dunnette and Raymond A. Katzell, see 6:1025.

[690]

Mechanical Knowledge Test: ETSA Test 6A. Job applicants; 1960–84; "measure mechanical insight and understanding"; norms consist of means and standard deviations; Form 1A ('60, 4 pages); scoring key ('60, 1 page); for more complete information, see 399; 1984 price data: $12 per 10 tests and scoring key; (90–100) minutes; Psychological Services Bureau; Employers' Tests & Services Associates.*

For reviews of an earlier version of the ETSA Tests by Marvin D. Dunnette and Raymond A. Katzell, see 6:1025.

[691]

Medical College Admission Test. Applicants for admission to member colleges of the Association of American Medical Colleges and to other participating institutions; 1946–84; MCAT; administered 2 times annually (spring, fall) at centers established by the publisher; 6 scores: biology, chemistry, physics, science problems, skills analysis (reading, quantitative); interpretive manual ('77, 113 pages); student manual ('84, 75 pages); practice test instructions ('84, 6 pages); separate answer sheets must be used; 1984 price data: examination fee, $50 ($55 for foreign and Sunday administrations); $3 or $3.75 (first class) per interpretive manual; $7 per student manual; 390(450) minutes in 2 sessions; constructed under the direction of AAMC by the American Institutes for Research; program administered at the direction of Association of American Medical Colleges.*

See T3:1576 (40 references), 8:1101 (40 references), and T2:2355 (30 references); for reviews by Nancy S. Cole and James M. Richards, Jr. of earlier forms, see

7:1100 (57 references); for reviews by Robert L. Ebel and Philip H. DuBois, see 6:1137 (43 references); for a review by Alexander G. Wesman, see 5:932 (4 references); for a review by Morey J. Wantman, see 4:817 (11 references).

TEST REFERENCES

1. Hynes, K., & Givner, N. Relationship between retaking the Medical College Admission Test and admission into medical school. PSYCHOLOGICAL REPORTS, 1980, 50, 894.

2. Sade, R. M., & Stroud, M. R. Medical student attendance at lectures: Effects on medical school performance. JOURNAL OF MEDICAL EDUCATION, 1982, 57, 191–192.

3. Sarnacki, R. E. The predictive value of the premedical grade-point average. JOURNAL OF MEDICAL EDUCATION, 1982, 57, 163–169.

4. Yens, D. P., & Stimmel, B. Science versus nonscience undergraduate studies for medical school: A study of nine classes. JOURNAL OF MEDICAL EDUCATION, 1982, 57, 429–435.

5. Carline, J. D., Cullen, T. J., Scott, C. S., Shannon, N. F., & Schaad, D. Predicting performance during clinical years from the New Medical College Admissions Test. JOURNAL OF MEDICAL EDUCATION, 1983, 58, 18–25.

6. Donnelly, M. B., Fleisher, D. S., Long, S. Y., Chen, C., & Rosenfeld, P. S. Simple adding versus differential weighting of MCAT subtest scores. JOURNAL OF MEDICAL EDUCATION, 1983, 58, 581–583.

7. Gary, N. E., & Rosevear, G. C. Program for increasing enrollment of early acceptees in medical school. JOURNAL OF MEDICAL EDUCATION, 1983, 58, 929–933.

8. Jones, R. F., & Adams, L. N. The relationship between MCAT science scores and undergraduate science GPA. JOURNAL OF MEDICAL EDUCATION, 1983, 58, 908–911.

9. Keimowitz, R. I. The effects of increasing tuition on admissions, students, and faculty at an expensive private medical school. BULLETIN OF THE NEW YORK ACADEMY OF MEDICINE, 1983, 59, 575–589.

[692]

Medical Ethics Inventory. First year medical students; 1982; MEI; 6 scores: social, economic, theoretical, political, religious, aesthetic; reliability data reported are for first year psychology students; no norms; 1 form (no date, 13 pages); manual ('82, 42 pages, including test); separate answer sheets (NCS) must be used; 1984 price data: $20 per complete set; administration time not reported; Cynthia J. Stolman and Rodney Doran; Cynthia J. Stolman.*

[693]

Medical Sciences Knowledge Profile. Citizens or permanent resident aliens in the United States and Canada; publication date not available; MSKP; program of the Association of American Medical Colleges; test is administered once a year at centers throughout the United States and foreign countries; 8 scores: anatomy, behavioral sciences, biochemistry, introductory clinical diagnosis, microbiology, pathology, pharmacology, physiology; 1984 price data: $170 per administration; 1.5 days for entire test; National Board of Medical Examiners.*

TEST REFERENCES

1. Stimmel, B. The Medical Sciences Knowledge Profile Examination: Are the first two years of medical school really necessary? NEW ENGLAND JOURNAL OF MEDICINE, 1980, 302, 576–578.

[694]

Memory-For-Designs Test. Ages 8.5 and over; 1946–60; MFD; brain damage; individual; 1 form ('60, 15 cards); revised manual ('60, 43 pages); norms-scoring examples booklet ('60, 12 pages, reprinted from manual); 1983 price data: $17 per set of test materials including manual; $15 per set of design cards; $2.50 per norms-scoring examples booklet; $5 per manual; (5–10) minutes; Frances K. Graham and Barbara S. Kendall; Psychological Test Specialists.*

See T3:1462 (48 references), 8:613 (34 references), and T2:1277 (16 references); for a review by R. W. Payne, see 7:101 (26 references); see also P:163 (15 references); for a review by Otfried Spreen, see 6:140 (18 references); see also 4:69 (5 references).

TEST REFERENCES

1. Carlson, J. S., & Wiedl, K. H. Modes of information integration and Piagetian measures of concrete operational thought. INTELLIGENCE, 1977, 1, 335–343.

2. Jarman, R. F., & Das, J. P. Simultaneous and successive syntheses and intelligence. INTELLIGENCE, 1977, 1, 151–169.

3. Orvaschel, H., Mednick, S., Schulsinger, F., & Rock, D. The children of psychiatrically disturbed parents. ARCHIVES OF GENERAL PSYCHIATRY, 1979, 36, 691–695.

4. Leong, C. K. Cognitive patterns of "retarded" and below-average readers. CONTEMPORARY EDUCATIONAL PSYCHOLOGY, 1980, 5, 101–117.

5. Leber, W. R., Jenkins, R. L., & Parsons, O. A. Recovery of visual-spatial learning and memory in chronic alcoholics. JOURNAL OF CLINICAL PSYCHOLOGY, 1981, 37, 192–197.

6. Lyon, R., & Watson, B. Empirically derived subgroups of learning disabled readers: Diagnostic characteristics. JOURNAL OF LEARNING DISABILITIES, 1981, 14, 256–261.

7. Ashman, A. Cognitive processes and perceived language performance of retarded persons. JOURNAL OF MENTAL DEFICIENCY RESEARCH, 1982, 26, 131–141.

8. Marsh, G. G., & Hirsch, S. H. Effectiveness of two tests of visual retention. JOURNAL OF CLINICAL PSYCHOLOGY, 1982, 38, 115–119.

9. Ong, J., & Jones, L., Jr. Memory-for-Designs, intelligence, and achievement of educable mentally retarded children. PERCEPTUAL AND MOTOR SKILLS, 1982, 55, 379–382.

10. Guy, J. D., Majorski, L. V., Wallace, C. J., & Guy, M. P. The incidence of minor physical anomalies in adult male schizophrenics. SCHIZOPHRENIA BULLETIN, 1983, 9, 571–582.

11. Hinkle, J. S. Comparison of reproductions of the Bender-Gestalt and Memory-for-Designs by delinquents and non-delinquents. PERCEPTUAL AND MOTOR SKILLS, 1983, 57, 1070.

12. Shelton, M. D., Parsons, O. A., & Leber, W. R. Verbal and visuospatial performance in male alcoholics: A test of premature-aging hypothesis. JOURNAL OF CONSULTING AND CLINICAL PSYCHOLOGY, 1984, 52, 200–206.

[695]

Menstrual Distress Questionnaire. Adult women; 1968–77; MDQ; this instrument has also been administered to men with modifications in instructions and purpose; 8 scores: pain, concentration, behavior change, autonomic reactions, water retention, negative affect, arousal, control; norms consist of means and standard deviations for Form A only; Form A (3 pages), T (2 pages); manual ('77, 52 pages, includes Forms A and T); 1982 price data: $4 per manual; administration time not reported; Rudolf H. Moos; the Author.*

See T3:1466 (4 references).

TEST REFERENCES

1. Englander-Golden, P., Whitmore, M. R., & Dienstbier, R. A. Menstrual cycle as focus of study and self-reports of mood and behaviors. MOTIVATION AND EMOTION, 1978, 2, 75–86.

2. Good, P. R., & Smith, B. D. Menstrual distress and sex-role attributes. PSYCHOLOGY OF WOMEN QUARTERLY, 1980, 4, 482–491.

3. Benton, D. The influence of androstenol—a putative human pheromone—on mood throughout the menstrual cycle. BIOLOGICAL PSYCHOLOGY, 1982, 15, 249–256.

4. Brooks-Gunn, J., & Ruble, D. N. The development of menstrual-related beliefs and behaviors during early adolescence. CHILD DEVELOPMENT, 1982, 53, 1567–1577.

5. Matthews, K. A., & Carra, J. Suppression of menstrual distress symptoms: A study of Type A behavior. PERSONALITY AND SOCIAL PSYCHOLOGY BULLETIN, 1982, 8, 146–151.

6. Parlee, M. B. Changes in moods and activation levels during the menstrual cycle in experimentally naive subjects. PSYCHOLOGY OF WOMEN QUARTERLY, 1982, 7, 119–131.

[696]

Merrill Language Screening Test. Ages 64–85 months; 1980; MLST; 3 or 4 scores: expressive language, receptive language, elicited language, articulation (optional); no reading by examinees; 1 form (4 pages); examiner's manual (64 pages); administration cassette tape available; stimulus cards (6 pages); 1983 price data: $45 per set of testing materials including manual, package of 100 score forms, stimulus cards, and cassette; $15 per package of 100 score forms; $6.95 per examiner's manual; (5–8) minutes; Myrna Mumm, Wayne Secord, and Katherine Dykstra; Charles E. Merrill Publishing Co.*

Review of Merrill Language Screening Test by CAROLYN PELUSO ATKINS, Associate Professor of Speech Pathology, West Virginia University, Morgantown, WV:

The Merrill Language Screening Test samples the four basic areas of linguistic competence—pragmatics, syntax, semantics, and phonology. Interestingly enough, the instrument's entire framework revolves around a single stimulus story which provides continuity throughout the test.

There are several advantages to using the MLST. The first is its administrative versatility; it may be administered in any one of three story presentation modes: large group, small group, and individually. This should be particularly useful to the speech-language pathologist in a public school setting.

Secondly, the accompanying audio-cassette tape, which is intended to familiarize the examiner with the five parameters of judgment included in the expressive language portion of the test, provides clear, concise instructions and is relatively easy to follow. While listening to the language samples of four children telling the story of Peter the Parrot, the examiner is able to follow each child's script in the manual. An additional benefit for the examiner is being able to listen to a discussion of each child's language sample, which includes an elaboration of specific scoring procedures.

In addition to instructions for the examiner, the audio-cassette tape also provides two different speakers narrating the story of Peter the Parrot as well as several repetitions of one speaker telling the story. The examiner, then, can use this material to model his intonational patterns, pausing, and stress when he tells the story—or he can simply use the tape. However, the examiner is rightfully cautioned that since no data have been collected on the use of the audio tape for the telling of the story, any use of it for this purpose should be considered experimental.

Another advantage of the MLST is the inclusion of six stimulus illustrations to be used in the presentation of the MLST story. They are large and colorful as well as sequenced and logical. Moreover, the story does have a controlled semantic content and does follow a simple hierarchical arrangement of events which serves to aid the child's ability to recall the happenings. However, even with these controls, the child is able to paraphrase the original story using language structures which he has acquired while simultaneously viewing one large card picturing all six events at once in correct visual sequence. It is also noted that the MLST is the first standardized language assessment instrument to use the paraphrasing task.

While the manual does provide the examiners with fairly clear advice as to scoring the expressive portion (Section I) of the test, it seems that the scoring of communication competence—especially intonational and/or inflectional patterns—is more subjective in nature than is the scoring of complete sentences, utterance length, subject-verb tense agreement, and elaboration. It is stated that the child may either copy the manner of the examiner's presentation or create one of his own. However, if he models the examiner, who is to say that the examiner will provide a good model of intonation and inflection initially? This is assumed but may not necessarily be accurate in fact. One other important point to note in Section I is that the child is able to self-correct on subject-verb-tense agreement without being penalized. While this may also be the case with other screening assessments, the instructions on when to penalize are usually not that explicit.

Section II (receptive language) involves the subject's response to five wh-question forms generated from the MLST story. Therefore, not only is the child required to provide a response which is grammatically appropriate, he is also required to be correct in content. Thus, Section II does provide a unit cohesive with Section I.

In Section III (elicited language) the child is instructed to repeat five sentences which sample 10 syntactic structures (2 per sentence). In order to get a sentence repetition correct, however, the child must accurately repeat both syntactic structures in each sentence but receives only one point. The reason underlying this scoring procedure (that is, giving him five points when using 10 syntactic structures) is not addressed in the examiner's manual. Acceptable variations in sentence repetition include Black English dialect. Fortunately, both the test manual and the examination form provide the examiner with the specific Black dialect variations.

Also included in the MLST is an optional Articulation Screening Inventory containing five sentences relating once again to the MLST story. Since the child has just repeated sentences in Section III, repeating the articulation sentences should pose no problem. Sixteen phonemes are targeted. Again Black dialect variations are acceptable.

In conclusion, the MLST generally proves to be a valuable screening assessment. This is due largely to its administrative versatility, the accompanying audio-cassette which provides clear instructions to the examiner, the vivid stimulus materials, and the overall cohesiveness and uniformity of the instrument.

[697]

Merrill-Palmer Scale of Mental Tests. Ages 24–63 months; 1926–48; no data on reliability; individual; 1 form; 33 tests: Action Agent Test (modification of Action-Agent Association Test ['11] by R. S. Woodworth and F. L. Wells), Simple Questions, Repetition of Words and Word Groups, Obeying Simple Commands, Throwing a Ball, Straight Tower, Crossing Feet, Standing On One Foot, Counting Two Blocks, Folding Paper, Making a Block Walk, Drawing Up String, Identification of Self in Mirror, Cutting With Scissors, Matching Colors, Closing Fist and Moving Thumb, Opposition of Thumb and Fingers, Copying a Circle, Copying a Cross, Copying a Star, Sequin Form Board, Mare and Foal Picture Completion, Manikin, Stutsman Picture Formboard (1, 2, 3), Decroly Matching Game, Wallin Peg Boards, Fitting Sixteen Cubes in a Box, Stutsman Nested Cubes, Stutsman Pyramid Test, Stutsman Buttoning Test, Little Pink Tower Test; guide for administering ('31); record blank (no date, 4 pages); 1982 price data: $325 per set of testing materials including 50 record blanks and guide for administering; $9 per 50 record blanks; $14.50 per guide for administering; administration time not reported; Rachel Stutsman; Stoelting Co.*

See T3:1471 (8 references) and T2:507 (17 references); for a review by Marjorie P. Honzik, see 6:527 (16 references); for reviews by Nancy Bayley, B. M. Castner, Florence L. Goodenough, and Florence M. Teagarden, see 2:1406 (13 references).

TEST REFERENCES

1. Freeman, B. J., Ritvo, E. R., Tonick, I., Guthrie, D., & Schroth, P. Behavior observation system for autism: Analysis of behaviors among autistic, mentally retarded, and normal children. PSYCHOLOGICAL REPORTS, 1981, 48, 199–208.

2. David, O. J., Grad, G., McGann, B., & Koltun, A. Mental retardation and "nontoxic" lead levels. THE AMERICAN JOURNAL OF PSYCHIATRY, 1982, 139, 806–809.

3. Goodall, E., & Corbett, J. Relationships between sensory stimulation and stereotyped behaviour in severely mentally retarded and autistic children. JOURNAL OF MENTAL DEFICIENCY RESEARCH, 1982, 26, 163–175.

4. Stewart, M. A., & Culver, K. W. Children who set fires: The clinical picture and a follow-up. BRITISH JOURNAL OF PSYCHIATRY, 1982, 140, 357–363.

Review of Merrill-Palmer Scale of Mental Tests by JACK A. NAGLIERI, Assistant Professor of Psychology, Ohio State University, Columbus, OH:

The Merrill-Palmer Scale of Mental Tests is designed to measure the intellectual ability of children 1 1/2 to 5 1/4 years of age. This scale is comprised of about 90 items, organized in order of difficulty, and yields mental-age and IQ scores. The Merrill-Palmer measures mental ability using tasks that are mostly nonverbal and that emphasize speed of performance. In general, the scale reflects an approach to mental measurement popular during the early 1900s and because of this has several disadvantages vis-à-vis more recently developed and standardized instruments.

The Merrill-Palmer test items are organized into 6-month intervals from 18 to 71 months. The progression of items moves from tasks such as throwing a ball, cutting with scissors, matching colors, and counting two blocks to copying a star, buttoning four buttons in 42 seconds or less, and completing the Seguin form board in 39 seconds or less. In general, most of the verbal tasks require one word answers. Item difficulty for nonverbal tasks is increased by requiring the child to complete some of the same tasks within shorter time limits. Motor ability plays an important role.

The Merrill-Palmer materials reflect the era in which they were constructed. For example, the pictures and puzzles typify 1930 styles of dress. These outdated items present a problem in terms of relevancy to today's children. In addition, the sheer number of boxes and envelopes makes the examiner's task of finding the correct materials cumbersome at best. The use of a mental-age score and computation of an IQ on the basis of dividing mental age by chronological age is outdated. In general, the materials and test construction are not on par with current tests of intelligence.

A guide for administering the scale is included with the test materials. This manual of administration is a portion of a larger work (Stutsman, 1931) and contains 7 of the 14 original chapters. Included in the manual are the following chapters: General Directions, Language Tests, All-or-None Tests, Form Boards and Picture Tests, Other Tests of Motor Coordination, Computation of Total Score and Use of Norms, and Guide for Personality Observations. Little information regarding the standardization of the scale and no reliability or validity data are provided. Moreover, the manual is confusing and does not facilitate smooth administration. For example, the first item (Obeying Simple Commands) is not presented on the first page of directions for administration, but rather, the instructions are included in chapters based upon the content of the task. Hence, the examiner must move through different chapters of the guide to locate the directions for administration and scoring continuous items.

The standardization sample of the Merrill-Palmer included about 300 males and 300 females aged 1 1/2 to 6 1/2 tested in the early 1900s and therefore is clearly not an appropriate comparison group for children 50 years later. This sample was not stratified on a number of important variables (e.g., race, geographic location) and any score derived from the sample (e.g., mental age, percentile rank, or IQ) should be interpreted cautiously. Although the manual does not report reliability coefficients, other researchers have reported test-retest reliability coefficients ranging from .39 to .92 with a median of .60 (DeForest, 1941; Driscoll, 1933; Ebert &

Simmons, 1943; Kawin, 1934; Stutsman, 1934). Thus, the reliability of the scale may not be comparable to other tests such as the McCarthy Scales of Children's Ability or the Wechsler Preschool and Primary Scale of Intelligence.

The Merrill-Palmer Scale has not been restandardized, the characteristics of the 1931 standardization sample are not specified, the materials are outdated and cumbersome to administer, and the test does not appear to be constructed according to any theory of intelligence. I do not recommend its use in determining a child's level of intelligence. The test appears more appropriately used as a clinical measure of specific abilities rather than a measure of intellectual ability. Although some authors (Sattler, 1982; Thorndike & Hagan, 1977) suggest that the Merrill-Palmer appears most useful for children 1 1/2 to 4 years of age, I suggest that the Stanford-Binet or McCarthy Scales be used instead at ages 2 or 2 1/2 and above because of their better standardization samples, test validity, and reliability.

REVIEWER'S REFERENCES

Stutsman, R. MENTAL MEASUREMENT OF PRESCHOOL CHILDREN. Yonkers-on-Hudson, NY: World Book, 1931.

Driscoll, G. P. The developmental status of the preschool child as a prognosis of future development. CHILD DEVELOPMENT MONOGRAPHS. New York: Teachers College, Columbia University, 1933, No. 13.

Kawin, E. CHILDREN OF PRE-SCHOOL AGE. Chicago: University of Chicago Press, 1934.

Stutsman, R. Factors to be considered in measuring the reliability of a mental test, with special reference to the Merrill-Palmer Scale. JOURNAL OF EDUCATIONAL PSYCHOLOGY, 1934, 25, 630–633.

DeForest, R. A study of the prognostic value of the Merrill-Palmer Scale of Mental Tests and the Minnesota Preschool Scale. JOURNAL OF GENETIC PSYCHOLOGY, 1941, 59, 219–223.

Ebert, E., & Simmons, K. The Brush Foundation study of child growth and development: I, psychometric tests. MONOGRAPHS OF THE SOCIETY FOR RESEARCH IN CHILD DEVELOPMENT, 1943, 8, (2, Serial No. 35).

Thorndike, R. L., & Hagen, E. P. MEASUREMENT AND EVALUATION IN PSYCHOLOGY AND EDUCATION. New York: Wiley, 1977.

Sattler, J. M. ASSESSMENT OF CHILDREN'S INTELLIGENCE AND SPECIAL ABILITIES. Boston: Allyn and Bacon, 1982.

[698]

Meta-Motivation Inventory. Managers and persons in leadership positions; 1979; MMI; self-administered measure of personal and managerial style; 32 scores: motivation for achievement, perfection, assertiveness, independence, achievement, meta-achievement, deterministic, approval, conventional, dependent, avoidance, helplessness, need for control, persuasiveness, manipulation, reactive, authoritarian, exploitive, concern for people, cooperation, affiliation, humanistic, synergy, meta-humanistic, self-actualization, stress, repression, anger, judgemental, creativity, growth potential, fun scale; 1 form (8 pages); feedback book (56 pages); 1984 price data: $1.95 per inventory; $6.50 per feedback book; $10 per specimen set; administration time not reported; John A. Walker; Meta-Visions.* (Also distributed by Humanics Media.)

Review of Meta-Motivation Inventory by JOHN K. BUTLER, JR., Associate Professor of Organizational Behavior, Clemson University, Clemson, SC:

The Meta-Motivation Inventory (MMI) is a 60-item commercial test designed to be self-administered and self-scored. Its purpose is to assist people in assessing their progress in personal and managerial development by making them aware of where they stand, in terms of 32 different scores, in relation to a normative population. The scores are intended to provide feedback on personal and managerial styles concerning 20 subscales, each of which comprise three items. Four major scales (Determinism, Motivation to Achieve, Need to Control Others, and Concern for People) are each made up of the 15 items of five of the subscales. Eight additional scales, composed of various combinations of the 60 items, include Self-Actualization (16 items), Stress (22 items), Repression (9 items), Anger (8 items), Judgemental (14 items), Creativity (14 items), Growth Potential (11 items), and Fun (13 items).

The 58-page *Meta-Motivation Book* accompanying the MMI is not a test manual and does not pretend to be one. It is sprinkled with quotations from charismatic authors. It gives one-page discussions of the 32 dimensions tapped by the scales. For each dimension, the discussion includes a brief conceptual description of the dimension. For each of the 20 subscales, there is also (*a*) a description of the associated personal and managerial style and (*b*) suggestions for modifying or reinforcing behaviors associated with a high score on the subscale.

The *Meta-Motivation Book* also includes a number of 26-dimensional profiles with scores on the 20 subscales, the four major scales, the Self-Actualization scale, and the Stress scale. Some of the profiles show norms, obtained from 220 mid-level managers from a wide range of business organizations. Two of the profiles show normative scores for (*a*) managers reporting high and low stress and (*b*) expansive and constrictive respondents (yeasayers and naysayers). A third profile conceptually locates respondents according to their positions with respect to five popular management theories. Then there is a leadership profile, derived from normative descriptions of the ideal leader. Last of all is a blank profile for the purpose of comparing how respondents perceive themselves vs. how others see them.

In its present form, the MMI package seems to be a useful tool for self development programs, management development seminars, and coaching/counseling sessions. It was intended for these purposes; it was not intended for research and certainly not as a tool for helping managers make personnel decisions.

However, the MMI shows some promise as a research instrument for three reasons. First, standardization seems to have been successful. Responses from 5,000 managers confirmed the original norms for all scales except one, the reactive scale, which measured 0.6 of a point higher than the original norm. Second, reliability is acceptable for research purposes. Test-retest correlations for the subscales ranged from .54 to .90 with a mean of .77. Test-retest correlations for the four major scales, Self-Actualization, and Stress ranged from .84 to .87. However, no measures of internal consistency were reported. Third, validation attempts have been made and are convincing for some of the scales. Face validity is claimed on the merits of the clinical experience of the author. This claim might be extended to content validity as well. Concurrent validity is supported by the fact that 87% of the managers in the original norm study said that the results accurately described their personal and managerial styles. Evidence for convergent validity comes from statistically significant correlations, averaging over .50, on 12 scales that are shared with another well-established inventory. Construct validity is indicated for the Achievement Motivation scale by a significant positive correlation with income, and for the Stress scale by significant correlations with responses about short and long term medical symptoms, which are solicited on the back of the MMI. Further, the MMI discriminates between management levels, between female managers and female non-managers, and between top and bottom sales people.

The four-page, typewritten guide, from which the above psychometric information was obtained, is well written and makes no grand claims; but it omits several issues. Nothing is said about (*a*) the method of item analysis that was, presumably, used to select items from an original pool; (*b*) the method of assessing internal consistency of the scales; (*c*) scales that did not perform as expected; (*d*) intercorrelations among the scales; (*e*) multitrait-multimethod correlations with shared scales of other inventories; (*f*) factor analytic assessments of dimensionality.

Perhaps it is unfair to expect discussions of all these issues, considering the original intended purpose of the MMI. Face validity seems to be the most relevant standard for a management development tool, whose usefulness depends on the extent to which respondents accept the results. However, with the possible exception of the Stress scale, more evidence of validity needs to be documented before the MMI can be used with confidence for research.

The choice of other tests to compare with the MMI depends on what the MMI is. It is a personality inventory. The title comes from the fact that "motivation" is a more appealing word than "personality" to managers, the target market. This strategy seems proper enough in view of (*a*) Allport's suggestion that units of motivation are a subset of units of personality and (*b*) the proposition that motivation results from appealing to a personality dimension (need, interest, value, etc.).

The measurement-feedback-corrective action approach of the MMI package suggests comparisons with the Strong-Campbell Interest Inventory (SCII) and the Myers-Briggs Type Inventory (MBTI). All three, especially the SCII, deal with career choice. All three deal with understanding of self and others; and they suggest action steps to promote changes, if desired. The MBTI has a superior theoretical base; the SCII, a superior empirical base. The MMI compares unfavorably with the others in terms of norms, but is probably just as useful as the MBTI as a tool for management seminars.

The emphasis on motivation through need satisfaction suggests comparisons with the Porter Needs Satisfaction Questionnaire, the Manifest Needs Questionnaire, McClelland's application of the Thematic Apperception Test, the Personality Research Form (PRF), and the Job Choice Exercise (JCE). All of these share dimensions with the MMI. The first three seem to have reliability problems. The PRF has excellent psychometric properties and seems to be useful for counseling and research, but it is too long for management seminars. The JCE has not yet achieved the notoriety of the others, but might prove to be the best of all for research purposes. It is founded on behavioral decision theory. It allows within-subject tests of models. It could be a precursor of a new wave in measurement. However, the dimensions that can be investigated are limited by the number of cues that can be managed by respondents. Also, the scoring method of regressing decisions on cues detracts from face validity and precludes self scoring. Thus, the MMI stands alone among the others for its intended purpose.

Overall, the MMI package can make a contribution to management development programs. It emphasizes personal growth. It shows reliability, face validity, and some empirical validity. Much work has been done and continues to be done on the Stress scale. Work needs to be done to validate the other scales. The MMI is fun to complete. It appeals to managers' interests. It was designed to be self-scored. Its dimensions are concisely described in the accompanying book, which offers suggestions for changing or reinforcing personal and managerial styles.

Review of Meta-Motivation Inventory by DENISE M. ROUSSEAU, Associate Professor of Organization Behavior, Northwestern University, Evanston, IL:

The Meta-Motivation Inventory (MMI) is a self-scoring assessment device to provide feedback to people regarding their characteristic thinking styles. Its manual describes its purpose as personal development and points out that thinking styles can be predictive of physiological and psychological symptoms of strain, leadership effectiveness, and relations to others. Norms are provided based on a sample of 220 mid-level managers. Feedback is in the form of 20 discrete scales, four combinative indices each based on 5 subsets of these scales, and supplemental measures (e.g., Stress and Self-actualization) based on selected items from the various scales.

In evaluating an instrument whose stated purpose is personal development and enhanced awareness, the major issues include: (1) the soundness and coherence of the model upon which feedback is based; (2) the reliability and internal consistency of the scales used; (3) the construct validity of the scales, including (*a*) the extent to which scales tapping different thinking styles are different and distinct from each other (discriminant validity), and (*b*) the extent to which scales measuring similar concepts are related to each other (convergent validity); (4) where links are made between inventory scores and behavior, evidence of a correlation between these (criterion-related validity); and (5) relevance and appropriateness of the test to its target population(s).

The dimensions each scale and index assess are derived, according to the manual, from the concepts that need theorists such as Maslow, Herzberg, and McGregor have proposed. Twelve of the 20 MMI scales correspond to those assessed in J. C. Lafferty's Level I: Lifestyles Inventory. Lafferty and his firm, Human Synergistics, are acknowledged as contributors to the development of the instrument, and a technical report (Walker, no date) indicates that the MMI does share 12 dimensions with an unnamed "well-established self-report inventory" and that correlations between the shared items average over .50 (based on a sample of 30 managers). It can be inferred that the MMI and Level I have similar conceptual foundations.

The need theory orientation of the MMI does ground the instrument in an empirically-derived framework. It is, however, somewhat unclear how the 20 scales, four indices, and two composites are used to give feedback. The sheer number of dimensions and the lack of apparent distinction between some of the concepts (achievement/meta-achievement, persuasiveness/manipulation) could make the various scores somewhat cumbersome for purposes of feedback.

Technical reports (Walker, no date) provide some support for the reliability of the scales and indices. Test-retest reliabilities for the subdimensions were computed for a sample of 33 educators over a 6-week interval, resulting in a range of coefficients from .54 to .90 and an average coefficient of .77. No internal consistency reliabilities are available for these measures.

No technical report available to the author addressed the issues of construct validity. Thus it is unclear how distinct the 20 scales are from each other. The instrument contains 60 items that are used to compute 26 scores (and the manual makes mention of additional possible combinations), making the distinctiveness of all these dimensions questionable. Given the absence of internal consistency reliability information for the indices and composites, it is also unclear whether the scales can be meaningfully combined to form these summary measures. It should be noted that Walker (1980) argues for the face validity of the MMI because 87% of a sample of 120 people (nature of sample unknown) indicated that they felt the results were an accurate description of their personalities.

Criterion-related validity is addressed in technical reports supporting the MMI. Using measures of short- and long-term stress effects (included on the last page of the inventory along with demographic information), correlations are computed for certain scales and indices from the MMI and such conditions as fatigue, irritability, performance reduction, and forgetfulness (short-term stress effects), and cancer, high blood pressure and colitis (long-term stress effects). Significant correlations are reported for these effects and some of the MMI scales. However, since only selected correlations are reported, it is impossible to tell how well all the scales generally correlate with stress effects. Since the MMI scores and stress data are gathered at the same time, no evidence of predictive validity can be provided. Despite the manual's mention of the MMI's relevance to leadership and relations with others, no evidence is presented to substantiate this.

The target population for the MMI is somewhat unclear. The reading level is not high for the instrument itself, although some of the questions are "double-barrelled" (e.g., "I believe in running things myself and making people do the job right"/"People in authority often don't know what they're doing and impede my growth"). I did find the manual, and particularly the instructions for norming one's scores, hard to follow. The manual implies that the MMI is applicable to employees and, in particular, managers of organizations, but does not provide norms for specific groups. The general norms provided are based on a sample of 220 mid-level managers. Thus, the MMI appears to be targeted to the management population, but at this point in time, the database on which the norms rest does not appear to be extensive.

When faced with a need for a self-assessment instrument, I believe the MMI has potential, but inventories do exist that are at this point better researched and substantiated. The aforementioned Level I: Life Styles Inventory, with its established reliability, construct validity, and criterion-related validity, may be a better choice. The MMI suffers by comparison, not from negative evidence, but from a lack of research on certain key issues.

REVIEWER'S REFERENCES

Walker, J. A. STRESS RESEARCH SUMMARY. Plymouth, MI: author, 1980.

Walker, J. A. THE META-MOTIVATION INVENTORY: ADMINISTRATION, VALIDATION, AND RELIABILITY. Plymouth, MI: Meta-Visions, no date.

[699]

Metropolitan Achievement Tests, 5th Edition (1978). Grades K.0–K.5, K.5–1.4, 1.5–2.4, 2.5–3.4, 3.5–4.0, 5.0–6.9, 7.0–9.9, 10.0–12.9; 1931–80; MAT; 2 batteries; Irving H. Balow, Roger Farr, Thomas P. Hogan, and George A. Prescott; NCS materials must be scored locally by the purchaser; The Psychological Corporation.*

a) SURVEY BATTERY. Grades K.0–K.5, K.5–1.4, 1.5–2.4, 2.5–3.4, 3.5–4.9, 5.0–6.9, 7.0–9.9, 10.0–12.9; 1977–79; subtests in reading and mathematics (grades K.5–12.9) available as separates; partial batteries without science and social studies available (grades K.0–12.9); complete batteries available (grades 1.5–9.9); practice tests available (grades K.0–6.9); 8 levels; teacher's manual for administering and interpreting ('78, 101–158 pages) for each level; 1984 price data: $1.50 per directions for administering practice tests; $1.50 per class record sheet; $8 per specimen set of any one level.

1) *Preprimer*. Grades K.0–K.5; 4 scores: reading, mathematics, language, total; 3 editions; $13 per 100 practice tests including directions; $6 per manual; (100–205) minutes in 4 or 8 sessions.

(*a*) Hand Scored Edition. Form JS ('78, 16 pages); $26.50 per 35 tests including manual, 35 practice tests and directions; $6.50 per scoring keys.

(*b*) MRC Machine Scored Edition. Form JS ('78, 16 pages); $40 per 35 tests including manual, 35 practice tests and directions; scoring service, $1.31 and over per test ($50 minimum).

(*c*) NCS Machine Scored Edition. Form JS ('78, 16 pages); $40 per 35 tests including manual, 35 practice tests and directions.

2) *Primer*. Grades K.5–1.4; 4 scores: same as 1 above; 3 editions; $13 per 100 practice tests including directions; $6 per manual; (100–195) minutes in 4 or 7 sessions.

(*a*) Hand Scored Edition. Forms JS, KS, ('78, 15 pages); $25.50 per 35 tests including manual and class record; $6.50 per set of scoring keys.

(*b*) MRC Machine Scored Edition. Forms JS, KS, ('78, 15 pages); $38.75 per 35 tests including manual; scoring service, $1.31 and over per test ($50 minimum).

(*c*)NCS Machine Scored Edition. Forms JS, KS, ('78, 16 pages); $38.75 per 35 tests including manual.

3) *Primary* 1. Grades 1.5–2.4; 7 scores: reading, mathematics, language, basics total, science, social studies, complete total; 3 editions; $13 per 100 practice tests including directions; $6 per manual; (155–245) minutes in 4 or 8 sessions.

(*a*) Hand Scored Edition. Forms JS, KS, ('78, 27 pages); $26.50 per 35 tests including manual and class record; $8.50 per set of scoring keys.

(*b*) MRC Machine Scored Edition. Forms JS, KS, ('78, 27 pages); $40 per 35 tests including manual; scoring service, $1.31 and over per test ($50 minimum).

(*c*) NCS Machine Scored Edition. Forms JS, KS, ('78, 27 pages); $40 per 35 tests including manual.

4) *Primary* 2. Grades 2.5–3.4; 7 scores: same as for 3 above; 3 editions; $13 per 100 practice tests and directions; $6 per manual; (175–245) minutes in 4 or 7 sessions.

(*a*) Hand Scored Edition. Forms JS, KS, ('78, 24 pages); $26.50 per 35 tests including manual and class record sheet; $8.50 per set of scoring keys.

(*b*) MRC Machine Scored Edition. Forms JS, KS, ('78, 24 pages); $40 per 35 tests including manual; scoring service, $1.31 and over per test ($50 minimum).

(*c*) NCS Machine Scored Edition. Forms JS, KS, ('78, 24 pages); $40 per 35 tests including manual.

5) *Elementary*. Grades 3.5–4.9; 7 scores: same as for 3 above; 3 editions; separate answer sheets may be used; $18 per 100 practice tests including directions and 100 answer sheets; $6 per manual; (195–265) minutes in 4 or 7 sessions.

(*a*) Hand Scored Edition. Forms JS, KS, ('78, 24 pages); $31 per 35 tests including manual and class record sheet; $8.50 per set of scoring keys for test booklets; $4 per set of scoring keys for answer sheets; $19 per 100 answer sheets including 3 class records.

(*b*) MRC Machine Scored Edition. Forms JS, KS, ('78, 24 pages); $40 per 35 tests including manual; $4 per set of scoring keys for hand scoring MRC answer sheets; $19 per 100 answer sheets; scoring service, $1.31 and over per test (test booklets), $.99 and over per test (answer sheets), ($50 minimum).

(*c*) NCS Machine Scored Edition. Forms JS, KS, ('78, 24 pages); $40 per 35 tests including manual; $29 per 100 answer sheets.

6) *Intermediate*. Grades 5.0–6.9; 7 scores: same as for 3 above; Forms JS ('78, 24 pages), KS ('79, 24 pages); separate answer sheets (hand-scorable, MRC, NCS 7010, OpScan) must be used; $31 per 35 tests including manual; $4 per set of scoring keys for hand-scorable answer sheets; $4 per set of scoring keys for hand scoring MRC answer sheets; answer sheets: $19 per 100 hand-scorable, MRC, $29 per 100 NCS 7010; $18 per 100 practice tests including directions and 100 answer sheets; $6 per manual; scoring service for MRC answer sheets, $.99 and over per test ($50 minimum); (190–240) minutes in 2 or 5 sessions.

7) *Advanced* 1. Grades 7.0–9.9; 7 scores: same as for 3 above; Forms JS ('78, 24 pages), KS ('79, 24 pages); separate answer sheets (hand-scorable, MRC, NCS 7010, OpScan) must be used; prices same as for intermediate level; 185(235) minutes in 2 or 5 sessions.

8) *Advanced* 2. Grades 10.0–12.9; 4 scores: reading, mathematics, language, total; Forms JS ('78, 16 pages), KS ('79, 16 pages); separate answer sheets (hand-scorable, MRC, NCS 7010, OpScan) must be used; prices same as for intermediate level; 110 (140) minutes in 2 or 3 sessions.

b) INSTRUCTIONAL TESTS. Grades K.5–1.4, 1.5–2.4, 2.5–3.4, 3.5–4.9, 5.0–6.9, 7.0–9.9; 1977–80; practice tests listed with survey battery above can be used with corresponding levels of instructional tests; 6 levels; teacher's manual for administering and interpreting the reading and mathematics instructional tests ('78, 128–171 pages) for each level; teacher's manual for administering and interpreting the language instructional tests ('79, 106–123 pages) for each level; 1984 price data: $1.50 per class record sheet; $7 per manual; $8 per specimen set of any one test and level.

1) *Primer*. Grades K.5–1.5; 3 tests.

(*a*) Reading Instructional Test. 6 scores: reading comprehension, visual discrimination, letter recognition, auditory discrimination, sight vocabulary, phoneme/grapheme—consonants; 3 editions; (133–213) minutes in 4 or 8 sessions.

(1) Hand Scored Edition. Forms JI ('78, 19 pages), KI ('79, 19 pages); $28 per 35 tests including manual and class record sheet; $10 per set of scoring keys.

(2) MRC Machine Scored Edition. Forms JI ('78, 19 pages), KI ('79, 19 pages); $39 per 35 tests including manual and class record sheet; scoring service, $1.41 and over per test ($50 minimum).

(3) NCS Machine Scored Edition. Forms JI ('78, 19 pages), KI ('79, 19 pages); $39 per 35 tests including manual.

(*b*) Language Instructional Test. 4 scores: listening comprehension, spelling, study skills, total; 3 editions; (80–120) minutes in 2 or 4 sessions.

(1) Hand Scored Edition. Form JI ('78, 8 pages); $18.50 per 35 tests including manual and class record sheet; $4.50 per set of scoring keys.

(2) MRC Machine Scored Edition. Form JI ('78, 8 pages); $24 per 35 tests including manual and class record sheet; scoring service, $1.35 and over per test ($50 minimum).

(3) NCS Machine Scored Edition. Form JI ('79, 8 pages); $24.50 per 35 tests including manual.

(*c*) Mathematics Instructional Test. 4 scores: numeration, geometry and measurement, operations and problem solving, total; 3 editions; (115–185) minutes in 4 or 7 sessions.

(1) Hand Scored Edition. Forms JI ('78, 15 pages), KI ('80, 15 pages); $25.50 per 35 tests including manual and class record sheet; $8 per set of scoring keys.

(2) MRC Machine Scored Edition. Forms JI ('78, 15 pages), KI ('80, 15 pages); $39 per 35 tests including manual and class record sheet; scoring service, $1.41 and over per test ($50 minimum).

(3) NCS Machine Scored Edition. Forms JI ('78, 15 pages), KI ('79, 15 pages); $39 per 35 tests including manual.

2) *Primary I*. Grades 1.5–2.4; 3 tests.

(*a*) Reading Instructional Test. 6 scores: reading comprehension, auditory discrimination, sight vocabulary, phoneme/grapheme—consonants, vocabulary in context, word part clues; 3 editions; (140–200) minutes in 3 or 6 sessions.

(1) Hand Scored Edition. Forms JI ('78, 19 pages), KI ('79, 19 pages); $28 per 35 tests including manual and class record sheet; $10 per set of scoring keys.

(2) MRC Machine Scored Edition. Forms JI ('78, 19 pages), KI ('79, 19 pages); $39 per 35 tests including manual and class record sheet; scoring service, $1.41 and over per test ($50 minimum).

(3) NCS Machine Scored Edition. Form JI ('78, 19 pages), KI ('79, 19 pages); $39 per 35 tests including manual.

(*b*) Language Instructional Test. 7 scores: listening comprehension, punctuation and capitalization, usage, grammar and syntax, spelling, study skills, total; 3 editions; (130–190) minutes in 3 or 6 sessions.

(1) Hand Scored Edition. Form JI ('78, 20 pages); $22 per 35 tests including manual and class record sheet; $8.75 per set of scoring keys.

(2) MRC Machine Scored Edition. Form JI ('78, 20 pages); $33.50 per 35 tests including manual and class record sheet; scoring service, $1.35 and over per test ($50 minimum).

(3) NCS Machine Scored Edition. Form JI ('79, 20 pages); $32 per 35 tests including manual.

(*c*) Mathematics Instructional Test. 5 scores: numeration, geometry and measurement, problem solving, operations—whole numbers, total; 3 editions; (105–145) minutes in 2 or 4 sessions.

(1) Hand Scored Edition. Forms JI ('78, 16 pages), KI ('80, 16 pages); $25.50 per 35 tests including manual and class record sheet; $8 per set of scoring keys.

(2) MRC Machine Scored Edition. Forms JI ('78, 16 pages), KI ('80, 16 pages); $39 per 35 tests including manual and class record sheet; scoring service, $1.41 and over per test ($50 minimum).

(3) NCS Machine Scored Edition. Forms JI ('78, 16 pages), KI ('79, 16 pages); $39 per 35 tests including manual.

3) *Primary* 2. Grades 2.5–3.4; 3 tests.

(*a*) Reading Instructional Test. 6 scores: reading comprehension, sight vocabulary, phoneme/grapheme—consonants, phoneme/grapheme—vowels, vocabulary in context, word part clues; 3 editions; (152–202) minutes in 3 or 5 sessions.

(1) Hand Scored Edition. Forms JI ('78, 19 pages), KI ('79, 19 pages); $28 per 35 tests including manual and class record sheet; $10 per set of scoring keys.

(2) MRC Machine Scored Edition. Forms JI ('78, 19 pages), KI ('79, 19 pages); $39 per 35 tests including manual and class record sheet; scoring service, $1.41 and over per test ($50 minimum).

(3) NCS Machine Scored Edition. Forms JI ('78, 19 pages), KI ('79, 19 pages); $39 per 35 tests including manual.

(*b*) Language Instructional Test. 7 scores: listening comprehension, punctuation and capitalization, usage, grammar and syntax, spelling, study skills, total; 3 editions; (130–190) minutes in 3 or 6 sessions.

(1) Hand Scored Edition. Form JI ('78, 20 pages); $22 per 35 tests including manual and class record sheet; $10.50 per set of scoring keys.

(2) MRC Machine Scored Edition. Form JI ('78, 20 pages); $39 per 35 tests including manual and class record sheet; scoring service, $1.35 and over per test ($50 minimum).

(3) NCS Machine Scored Edition. Form JI ('78, 20 pages); $39 per 35 tests including manual.

(*c*) Mathematics Instructional Test. 5 scores: numeration, geometry and measurement, problem solving, operations—whole numbers, total; 3 editions; (103–145) minutes in 2 or 4 sessions.

(1) Hand Scored Edition. Forms JI ('78, 16 pages), KI ('79, 16 pages); $25.50 per 35 tests including manual and class record sheet; $8 per set of scoring keys.

(2) MRC Machine Scored Edition. Forms JI ('78, 16 pages), KI ('79, 16 pages); $39 per 35 tests including manual and class record sheet; scoring service, $1.41 and over per test ($50 minimum).

(3) NCS Machine Scored Edition. Forms JI ('78, 16 pages), KI ('79, 16 pages); $39 per 35 tests including manual.

4) *Elementary*. Grades 3.5–4.9; 3 tests.

(*a*) Reading Instructional Test. 7 scores: reading comprehension, sight vocabulary, phoneme/grapheme—consonants, phoneme/grapheme—vowels, vocabulary in context, word part clues, rate of comprehension; 3 editions; separate answer sheets may be used; (150–200) minutes in 3 or 5 sessions.

(1) Hand Scored Edition. Forms JI ('78, 19 pages), KI ('79, 10 pages); $28 per 35 tests including manual and class record sheets; $10 per set of scoring keys for test booklets; $5 per set of scoring keys for answer sheets; $30 per 100 answer sheets including 100 pupil objectives analysis sheets and 3 class record sheets.

(2) MRC Machine Scored Edition. Forms JI ('78, 19 pages), KI ('79, 19 pages); $39 per 35 tests including manual and class record sheet; $7 per set of scoring keys for hand scoring MRC answer sheets; $30 per 100 answer sheets including 3 class record sheets; scoring service, $1.41 and over per test (test booklet), $1.08 and over per test (answer sheet), ($50 minimum).

(3) NCS Machine Scored Edition. Forms JI ('78, 19 pages), KI ('79, 19 pages); $39 per 35 tests including manual; $32 per 35 answer sheets.

(*b*) Language Instructional Test. 7 scores: listening comprehension, punctuation and capitalization, usage, grammar and syntax, spelling, study skills, total; 3 editions; separate answer sheets may be used; (150–200) minutes in 3 or 6 sessions.

(1) Hand Scored Edition. Form JI ('78, 16 pages); $22 per 35 tests including manual and class record sheet; $10.50 per set of scoring keys for test booklets; $4.50 per set of scoring keys for answer sheets; $21 per 100 answer sheets including 100 pupil objectives analysis sheets and 3 class record sheets.

(2) MRC Machine Scored Edition. Form JI ('78, 16 pages); $33.50 per 35 tests including manual and class record sheet; $4.50 per set of scoring keys for hand scoring MRC answer sheets; $21 per 100 answer sheets including 3 class record sheets; scoring service, $1.35 and over per test (test booklet), $1.08 and over per test (answer sheet), ($50 minimum).

(3) NCS Machine Scored Edition. Form JI ('79, 16 pages); $32 per 35 tests including manual; $32 per 35 answer sheets.

(*c*) Mathematics Instructional Test. 6 scores: numeration, geometry and measurement, problem solving, operations—whole numbers, operations—laws and properties, total; 3 editions; separate answer sheets may be used; (125–175) minutes in 3 or 5 sessions.

(1) Hand Scored Edition. Forms JI ('78, 16 pages), KI ('80, 16 pages); $25.50 per 35 tests including manual and class record sheet; $8 per set of scoring keys for test booklets; $4 per set of scoring keys for answer sheets; $22 per 100 answer sheets including 100 pupil objectives analysis sheets and 3 class records.

(2) MRC Machine Scored Edition. Forms JI ('78, 16 pages), KI ('80, 16 pages); $39 per 35 tests including manual and class record sheet; $4 per set of scoring keys for hand scoring MRC answer sheets; $22 per 100 answer sheets including 3 class records; scoring service, $1.41 and over per test (test booklets), $1.08 and over per test (answer sheets), ($50 minimum).

(3) NCS Machine Scored Edition. Forms JI ('78, 16 pages), KI ('79, 16 pages); $32 per 35 tests including manual; $22 per 100 answer sheets.

5) *Intermediate*. Grades 5.0–6.9; 3 tests.

(*a*) Reading Instructional Test. 7 scores: reading comprehension, phoneme/grapheme—consonants, phoneme/grapheme—vowels, vocabulary in context, word part clues, rate of comprehension, skimming and scanning; Forms JI ('78, 16 pages), KI ('79, 16 pages); separate answer sheets (hand-scorable, MRC, NCS 7010) must be used; $28 per 35 tests including manual and class record sheet; $5 per set of scoring keys for hand-scorable answer sheets; $7 per set of scoring keys for hand-scoring MRC answer sheets; answer sheets: $30 per 100 hand-scorable including 100 pupil objectives analysis sheets and 3 class record sheets; $30 per 100 MRC including 3 class record sheets; $32 per 100 NCS 7010; scoring service for MRC answer sheets, $1.08 and over per test ($50 minimum); (154–204) minutes in 3 or 5 sessions.

(*b*) Language Instructional Test. 6 scores: punctuation and capitalization, usage, grammar and syntax, spelling, study skills, total; Form JI ('78, 16 pages); separate answer sheets (hand-scorable, MRC, NCS 7010) must be used; $22 per 35 tests including manual and class record sheet; $4.50 per set of scoring keys for hand-scorable answer sheets; $4.50 per set of scoring keys for hand scoring MRC answer sheets; answer sheets: $21 per 100 hand-scorable including 100 pupil objectives analysis sheets and 3 class record sheets; $21 per 100 MRC including 3 class record sheets; $32 per 100 NCS 7010; scoring service for MRC answer sheets, $1.08 and over per test ($50 minimum); (120–170) minutes in 3 or 5 sessions.

(*c*) Mathematics Instructional Test. 8 scores: numeration, geometry and measurement, problem solving, operations—whole numbers, operations—laws and properties, operations—fractions and decimals, graphs and statistics, total; Forms JI ('78, 16 pages), KI ('80, 16 pages); separate answer sheets (hand-scorable, MRC, NCS 7010) must be used; $25.50 per 35 tests including manual and class record sheet; $5 per set of scoring keys for hand-scorable answer sheets; $4 per set of scoring keys for hand scoring MRC answer sheets; answer sheets: $22 per 100 hand-scorable including 100 pupil objectives analysis sheets and 3 class record sheets; $22 per 100 MRC including 3 class record sheets; $32 per 100 NCS 7010; scoring service for MRC answer sheets, $1.08 and over per test ($50 minimum); (165–235) minutes in 4 or 7 sessions.

6) *Advanced* 1. Grades 7.0–9.9; 3 tests.

(*a*) Reading Instructional Test. 4 scores: reading comprehension, vocabulary in context, skimming and scanning, rate of comprehension; Forms JI ('78, 12 pages), KI ('79, 12 pages); separate answer sheets (hand-scorable, MRC, NCS 7010) must be used; $28 per 35 tests including manual and class record sheet; $5 per set of scoring keys for hand-scorable answer sheets; $7 per set of scoring keys for hand scoring MRC answer sheets; answer sheets: $30 per 100 hand-scorable including 100 pupil objectives analysis sheets and 3 class record sheets; $30 per 100 MRC including 3 class record sheets; $32 per 100 NCS 7010; scoring service for MRC answer sheets, $1.08 and over per test ($50 minimum); 74(104) minutes in 2 or 3 sessions.

(*b*) Language Instructional Test. 6 scores: same as for intermediate level; Form JI ('78, 16 pages); separate answer sheets (hand-scorable, MRC, NCS 7010) must be used; prices and time same as for intermediate level.

(*c*) Mathematics Instructional Test. 8 scores: same as for intermediate level; Forms JI ('78, 16 pages), KI ('80, 16 pages); separate answer sheets (hand-scorable, MRC, NCS 7010) must be used; prices and time same as for intermediate level.

See T3:1473 (89 references); for reviews by Norman E. Gronlund and Richard M. Wolf and an excerpted review by Joseph A. Wingard and Peter M. Bentler of an earlier edition, see 8:22 (41 references); see also T2:22 (20 references) and 7:14 (25 references); for reviews by Henry S. Dyer and Warren G. Findley of an earlier edition, see 6:16 (16 references); for a review by Warren G. Findley, see 4:18 (10 references); see also 3:13 (7 references); for reviews by E. V. Pullias and Hugh B. Wood, see 2:1189 (3 references); for reviews by Jack W. Dunlap, Charles W. Odell, and Richard Ledgerwood, see 1:874. For reviews of subtests, see 8:283 (1 review), 8:732 (2 reviews), 6:627 (2 reviews), 6:797 (1 review), 6:877 (2 reviews), 6:970 (2 reviews), 4:416 (1 review), 4:543 (2 reviews), 2:1458.1 (2 reviews), 2:1551 (1 review), 1:892 (2 reviews), and 1:1105 (2 reviews).

TEST REFERENCES

1. Rourke, B. P., & Orr, R. R. Prediction of the reading and spelling performances of normal and retarded readers: A four-year follow-up. JOURNAL OF ABNORMAL CHILD PSYCHOLOGY, 1977, 5, 9–20.

2. Bruning, R. H., Burton, J. K., & Ballering, M. Visual and auditory memory: Relationships to reading achievement. CONTEMPORARY EDUCATIONAL PSYCHOLOGY, 1978, 3, 340–351.

3. Hoy, E., Weiss, G., Minde, K., & Cohen N. The hyperactive child at adolescence: Cognitive, emotional, and social functioning. JOURNAL OF ABNORMAL CHILD PSYCHOLOGY, 1978, 6, 311–324.

4. Turner, R. R. Locus of control, academic achievement, and follow through in Appalachia. CONTEMPORARY EDUCATIONAL PSYCHOLOGY, 1978, 3, 367–375.

5. Knifong, J. D. Computational requirements of standardized word problem tests. JOURNAL FOR RESEARCH IN MATHEMATICS EDUCATION, 1980, 11, 3–9.

6. Patchen, M., Hoffman, G., & Brown, W. R. Academic performance of black high school students under different conditions of contact with white peers. SOCIOLOGY OF EDUCATION, 1980, 53, 33–51.

7. Pihl, R. O., Parkes, M., Drake, H., & Vrana, F. The intervention of a modulator with learning disabled children. JOURNAL OF CLINICAL PSYCHOLOGY, 1980, 36, 972–976.

8. Winsberg, B. G., Bialer, I., Kupietz, S., Botti, E., & Balka, E. B. Home vs hospital care of children with behavior disorders: A controlled investigation. ARCHIVES OF GENERAL PSYCHIATRY, 1980, 37, 413–418.

9. Obrzut, J. E., Hynd, G. W., Obrzut, A., & Pirozzolo, F. J. Effect of directed attention on cerebral asymmetries in normal and learning-disabled children. DEVELOPMENTAL PSYCHOLOGY, 1981, 17, 118–125.

10. Becker, W. C., & Gerstein, R. A follow-up of follow through: The later effects of the direct instruction model on children in fifth and sixth grades. AMERICAN EDUCATIONAL RESEARCH JOURNAL, 1982, 19, 75–92.

11. Fletcher, J. M., & Satz, P. Kindergarten prediction of reading achievement: A seven-year longitudinal follow-up. EDUCATIONAL AND PSYCHOLOGICAL MEASUREMENT, 1982, 42, 681–685.

12. Massoth, N. A., & Levenson, R. L., Jr. The McCarthy Scales of Children's Abilities as a predictor of reading readiness and reading achievement. PSYCHOLOGY IN THE SCHOOLS, 1982, 19, 293–296.

13. Nimmer, D. N. The use of standardized achievement test batteries in the evaluation of curriculum changes in junior high school earth science. SCIENCE EDUCATION, 1982, 66, 45–48.

14. Obrzut, J. E., Hansen, R. L., & Heath, C. P. The effectiveness of visual information processing training with Hispanic children. JOURNAL OF GENERAL PSYCHOLOGY, 1982, 107, 165–174.

15. Roberge, J. J., & Flexer, B. K. The Formal Operational Reasoning Test. JOURNAL OF GENERAL PSYCHOLOGY, 1982, 106, 61–67.

16. Simon, M. J. Use of a vigilance task to determine school readiness of preschool children. PERCEPTUAL AND MOTOR SKILLS, 1982, 54, 1020.

17. Steele, K. J., Battista, M. T., & Krockover, G. H. The effect of microcomputer assisted instruction upon the computer literacy of high ability students. GIFTED CHILD QUARTERLY, 1982, 26, 162–164.

18. Summers, E. G., & McClelland, J. V. A field-based evaluation of Sustained Silent Reading (SSR) in intermediate grades. THE ALBERTA JOURNAL OF EDUCATIONAL RESEARCH, 1982, 28, 100–112.

19. Swanson, B. The relationship between attitude toward reading and reading achievement. EDUCATIONAL AND PSYCHOLOGICAL MEASUREMENT, 1982, 42, 1303–1304.

20. Tittler, B. I., Friedman, S., Blotcky, A. D., & Stedrak, J. The influence of family variables on an ecologically-based treatment program for emotionally disturbed children. AMERICAN JOURNAL OF ORTHOPSYCHIATRY, 1982, 52, 123–130.

21. Crowell, D. C., Hu-pei Au, K., & Blake, K. M. Comprehension questions: Differences among standardized tests. JOURNAL OF READING, 1983, 26, 314–319.

22. Dodendorf, D. M. A unique rural school environment. PSYCHOLOGY IN THE SCHOOLS, 1983, 20, 99–104.

23. Hatchette, R. K., & Evans, J. R. Auditory-visual and temporal-spatial pattern matching performance of two types of learning-disabled children. JOURNAL OF LEARNING DISABILITIES, 1983, 16, 537–541.

24. Lovrich, D., & Stamm, J. S. Event-related potential and behavioral correlates of attention in reading retardation. JOURNAL OF CLINICAL NEUROPSYCHOLOGY, 1983, 5, 13–37.

25. Sheppard, J. L., & Sheppard, M. J. Spotlight screener as a predictor of first-grade reading achievement. THE AUSTRALIAN JOURNAL OF EDUCATION, 1983, 27, 164–172.

26. Stanovich, K. E., Feeman, D. J., & Cunningham, A. E. The development of the relation between letter-naming speed and reading ability. BULLETIN OF THE PSYCHONOMIC SOCIETY, 1983, 21, 199–202.

27. Chandler, C. L., Weissberg, R. P., Cowen, E. L., & Guare, J. Long-term effects of a school-based secondary prevention program for young maladapting children. JOURNAL OF CONSULTING AND CLINICAL PSYCHOLOGY, 1984, 52, 165–170.

28. Meyer, L. A., Gersten, R. M., & Gutkin, J. Direct instruction: A project follow through success story in an inner-city school. THE ELEMENTARY SCHOOL JOURNAL, 1984, 84, 241–252.

29. Morris, D., & Perney, J. Developmental spelling as a predictor of first-grade reading achievement. ELEMENTARY SCHOOL JOURNAL, 1984, 84, 441–457.

30. Ziomek, R. L., & Schoenenberger, W. J. The relationship of Title I student achievement to program and school attendance. THE ELEMENTARY SCHOOL JOURNAL, 1984, 84, 232–240.

Review of Metropolitan Achievement Tests, 5th Edition (1978), by EDWARD H. HAERTEL, Assistant Professor of Education, Stanford University, Stanford, CA:

The fifth edition of the Metropolitan Achievement Tests (MAT) provides a comprehensive system of "survey" tests for measuring achievement in reading, mathematics, and language at grades K through 12, as well as science and social studies at grades 1.5 through 9.9. It continues the tradition of sound test construction, extensive norming and validation, and exemplary documentation established by earlier editions of the MAT. In addition, the 1978 edition introduces a separate set of "instructional" tests in reading, mathematics, and language for grades K.5 through 9.9. These instructional tests are intended for criterion-referenced as well as norm-referenced interpretation, and include at least three items testing each of numerous specific objectives. They yield scores in three to seven subareas for each of reading, language, and mathematics, as well as scores by objective. The briefer "survey" tests in all subject areas are intended primarily for norm-referenced interpretation.

Numerous interpretive aids are provided to assist teachers, principals, and district administrators in using test results, in addition to the usual range of pupil, classroom, building, and system summaries of raw and derived scores. One of these is an estimated Instructional Reading Level (IRL) for each pupil, keyed to many popular basal reading series. For each IRL, specific skills are highlighted as being of "high importance," others are designated "some importance" or "low importance." Teaching suggestions (introduce, practice, or apply) are given for each pupil for each skill tested in the reading instructional battery. Test booklets are available which combine the MAT Survey battery with corresponding levels of the Otis-Lennon School Ability Test, and OLSAT scores yield scaled-score predicted achievement ranges for each subject area, for individual students. Other special reports include a pre/post evaluation report and matched case summary combining data from fall and spring test administrations. Finally, as an aid in norm-referenced interpretation at the building or system level, data on parent education for a sample of students in each building (collected using a standard form) can be used to generate an SES Predicted Achievement Report, showing expected mean scaled scores by grade and subject area as a function of each school's "Parent Education Index."

The best of tests can be misused, especially when they are intended to provide information for as many audiences and types of decisions as is the MAT. With each of the many interpretive aids the authors provide comes a potential for abuse. The Teacher's Manual for Administering and Interpreting each of the tests, and the Administrator's Guides, are appropriately cautious, and the careful reader of these documents should not go far astray; but the computer-generated reports themselves may invite overinterpretation. For example, the Teacher's Manuals for the Reading Instructional tests explain that skill importance ratings are based solely on Instructional Reading Level, and while they reflect patterns of emphasis in most basal readers, "Clearly, the local curriculum and instructional priorities should take precedence over these generalized ratings....In addition, a check...against actual test performance may indicate different priorities for individual pupils." Nonetheless, the computer-generated Pupil Instructional Analysis lists skills of high, some, or low importance for each pupil, and the manual's cautions may easily be overlooked. Even more is asked of the teacher in deciding whether to trust a pupil's estimated IRL: "Teachers can get some idea of the accuracy of the estimate by looking at the pupil's performance by grade level of the reading passages....A great deal of confidence can be placed in an IRL [where the] pattern...is fairly typical"(i.e., performance on easy passages is good and performance on more difficult passages is poorer). Elsewhere, the manual states that IRL estimates "based on very atypical patterns...should be interpreted very cautiously" and suggest the need for further evaluation. While teachers can find a breakdown of number correct by passage grade level in some of the (optional) score reports, it is likely that many will neglect to examine response patterns across passages, and will accept the IRL estimates uncritically.

The MAT tests themselves are of excellent quality. Item Response Theory was not used in item analysis and selection, but test development and validation practices for this newest edition of the MAT nonetheless advance the state of the art in achievement testing. While more sophisticated statistical models for item response data might have permitted the use of smaller norming samples, more accurate estimation of standard errors, and more elegant derivation of standard score scales across forms and levels, the quality of the final product could not far exceed what has been achieved by classical methods.

Development of content specifications, item writing, tryout, and revision are well-documented in the MAT Special Report series, and followed established procedures, including procedures to minimize gender and ethnic bias or stereotyping. As a check on the content validity of the final tests, teachers of pupils in the norming sample at each grade level were asked to answer a questionnaire concerning the test's match to their own objectives in each content area, and whether they taught each objective on the tests. Their responses, summarized in the Special Report series, indicate that most teachers found the tests closely matched their own objectives in all content areas, and that the objectives in the instructional tests represent a core of content common to most districts' curricula. This may be all that can be asked of a published test intended for use nationwide. However, it does not answer the question of how much additional, related content taught by each teacher is left untested. Users of the MAT, or any other standardized battery referenced to specific objectives, must bear in mind that any atypical content emphasized in their curriculum is unlikely to be covered adequately.

In the areas of reading, language, and mathematics, the extensive content validation of the instructional tests also assures the content validity of the survey tests. These survey tests (for grades K.5 through 9.9) are systematic samples of the items included in the corresponding instructional tests. For reading comprehension, the survey and instructional tests are identical. In the areas of science and social studies, content validity is more difficult to determine. These areas are more broadly defined, and as the authors observe, there is greater variability among districts in curricula for science and social studies than for reading, mathematics, or language. The difficulties of domain definition are especially evident at the primary and elementary levels. Prospective users should review the content of these tests very carefully. The science tests sample a diverse collection of natural phenomena, from evaporation to cocoons, as well as skills like interpreting graphs and comparing lengths. Almost all items seem appropriate, and likely to be taught in at least some classrooms, but it is difficult to say just what content domain the total score refers to. In social studies, the problem is even more severe. Many of the social studies items appear to test facts or vocabulary most likely to be acquired out of school, and the range of content is so broad that, at the primary level especially, social studies is little more than a test of general information.

Extensive norms are provided for this edition of the MAT, including percentile ranks and stanines for both fall and spring administrations for pupils, buildings, and systems; scaled scores comparable across forms and levels (though not across content areas); grade equivalents; Instructional Reading Levels for reading scores; and fall and spring item p values. As with earlier editions of the MAT, norms are based on separate, matched samples tested in fall and spring. Some normative data are also reported for each objective on the instructional tests, and for item clusters spanning related objectives on the survey tests. KR-20 reliabilities and standard errors of measurement are nearly all over .80, with many over .90. Teacher's manuals report (inappropriate) KR-20 estimates for speeded subtests, but appropriate alternate-form reliabilities for these subtests are provided in the Special Reports, and are acceptably high. Failure to report alternate-form reliabilities for the remaining subtests is unfortunate, especially for the instructional tests, where items are classified according to objective. If items testing the same objective are quite homogeneous, an internal consistency reliability estimate like the KR-20, which disregards this internal structure, may be lower than the correlation between alternate forms constructed according to the same test blueprint.

Reliabilities for single objectives, or for separately-scored item clusters on the survey tests, are not reported. While objectives or item clusters should be sufficiently reliable to support classroom- or building-level interpretations, objective or cluster scores for individuals should be interpreted very cautiously, and corroborated with other data.

The number-correct criterion levels specified for mastery of each objective are probably reasonable, but are nonetheless arbitrary, and rigid interpretations of mastery patterns for individuals or mastery proportions for classrooms should be avoided. For item clusters on the survey tests, criterion levels are set at the national median number correct, which appears entirely arbitrary. Unless criterion levels are established or justified locally, master/nonmaster interpretations of item clusters should be avoided.

Integration of the MAT with the Otis-Lennon School Ability Test (OLSAT) is supported by test booklets, scoring and reporting services, and empirical norms combining the two instruments. Reported correlations between the tests are high, but well below their respective reliabilities, indicating that the ability and achievement tests measure distinct, but related, attributes. When the tests are used together, a scaled-score Predicted Achievement Range (PAR) in each MAT subject area can be calculated from OLSAT performance. According to the Special Reports, "Students scoring outside the PAR in either direction are those who show discrepancies between measured achievement and ability that are significant and deserve the attention of the teacher and/or counselor." These PARs are calculated in such a way that roughly one-third of all students' scores on each MAT subtest will fall outside the PAR, with 23% below the range and 10% above the range. In effect, the authors are asserting that at any given OLSAT ability level, those in the bottom quartile on the MAT are underachievers and those in the top decile are overachievers. The comparison of ability and achievement test performance can certainly be of value, especially in cases of poor academic performance where higher ability is suspected, and the joint norming of these tests is of value for such cases. However, routine screening and labeling of one child in three as significantly discrepant is of questionable value.

District administrators will probably welcome the introduction of the SES Predicted Achievement Report, especially in systems where schools vary markedly in socioeconomic status. This optional report indicates whether each school's average test scores in each subject area are below, within, or above ranges predicted from that school's Parental Education Index. Comparisons can also be made for the entire school system. As with the OLSAT PARs, these predicted achievement ranges are defined such that predetermined proportions of all schools fall in different ranges. For the SES report, the majority of all schools will show deviations that are "noteworthy" or "somewhat above (or below) expectation," and one in five, the top decile and the bottom decile at any given PEI, are described as showing "extreme" or "very substantial" deviations.

While the procedures used to derive the PEI and predictions based on it are reasonable and clearly described, some cautions are in order concerning its interpretation. First, the ranges developed, from "negligible difference" out to "extreme" in either direction, are arbitrary labels based on something like the percentile rank of the school among those with the same PEI. Second, PEI is only one of many demographic variables related to school achievement. A school well below its predicted score ranges might be at or above expectation if other factors like transiency or pupil language background could also be taken into consideration. These caveats are set forth clearly in the Special Report on the SES predicted achievement report, and any user of this service is urged to read that Special Report carefully. One final caution must be stated. The predicted achievement levels in this report reflect present differences in student achievement according to parental education, but the way things are is not the way they ought or need to be. Relating group achievement differences to out-of-school factors in itself neither explains nor excuses them, and it would be unfortunate if reports like this one encouraged complacency rather than renewed efforts to develop the potential of individuals from all backgrounds.

In summary, the fifth edition of the MAT is soundly constructed, validated, and normed. The scoring services provide a wide range of useful reports tailored to the various needs of teachers, principals, and district administrators. The new series of criterion-referenced instructional tests is a useful addition, and should be of considerable value, especially at the classroom level. Content validity should not be assumed, however, until test materials are compared to the local curriculum, especially for the science and social studies survey tests. Caution must be taken not to overinterpret some of the reports. Routine use of the OLSAT with the MAT would appear to be of limited value. The user who reads the relevant sections of the MAT manuals and Special Reports should be well equipped to use the MAT and its many scoring services and interpretive aids appropriately.

Review of Metropolitan Achievement Tests, 5th Edition (1978), by ROBERT L. LINN, *Chairperson, Department of Educational Psychology, University of Illinois at Urbana-Champaign, Champaign, IL:*

The Metropolitan Achievement Tests (MAT) have been widely used since the publication of the first edition in 1937. The 1978 edition, which is the focus of this review, is the fifth edition in this series. Many of the laudatory comments of reviewers of earlier editions of the MAT (e.g., Gronlund, 1978; Wolf, 1978) apply as well to the fifth edition. Some of the criticisms of earlier editions also apply, but several of the perceived shortcomings of earlier editions have been remedied.

The most significant change from earlier editions was the introduction of the "two component system." The two component system consists of a set of survey tests and a set of instructional tests. The survey component includes eight overlapping batteries of tests that span the full range of grades K through 12. Tests in reading, mathematics, and language are included in the survey battery at all levels. The five complete survey batteries designed to cover the middle of the first through the ninth grade also include tests in science and social studies. The survey component of the fifth edition is the most nearly comparable of the two components to earlier editions of the MAT. Two new batteries have been added to cover grades not covered by the fourth edition. These are the Preprimer Battery (grades K.0 to K.5) and the Advanced 2 Battery (grades 10.0 to 12.9). Science and social studies tests have been added to the Primary 2 (grades 2.5 to 3.4) and Elementary Batteries (grades 3.5 to 4.9). The new tests are somewhat longer at the Primer (grades K.5 to 1.4) and Primary I (grades 1.5 to 2.4) levels, but significantly shorter than their fourth edition counterparts at the higher levels. For example, administration time of the complete Advanced 1 Survey Battery has been cut by 80 minutes, from 265 to 185 minutes. The shorter new tests yield fewer scaled scores (e.g., a single mathematics total score rather than a total score plus the computations, concepts, and problem solving subscores reported for the fourth edition).

The second major component of the MAT is called the instructional component. The Metropolitan Instructional Tests are closely coordinated with reading, mathematics, and language tests of the Survey Battery, but are generally three to four times as long and provide more intensive coverage in each area. A carefully constructed list of instructional objectives is assessed with at least three items per objective. The objectives are also assessed by the Survey Battery, but frequently with only a single item per objective. For each instructional test, scale scores are reported for several subtests which are said to represent "the major [instructional] strands in the content area at a particular level." There are six levels of each instructional test which together are designed to span grades K.5 to 9.9.

Tests are often intended to serve a variety of sometimes incompatible functions. Brevity may be desired and is reasonably consistent with the goals of global evaluation of student performance and the monitoring of group performance. But brevity is incompatible with the goal of providing detailed information needed for purposes of instructional planning. Too frequently, attempts are made to make a single test serve too great a variety of functions. The necessary compromises result in a product that falls short of what would be accomplished by tests designed for a more limited array of purposes. The two component system of the MAT is a praiseworthy response to this dilemma. The global functions of a survey battery are accomplished with greater efficiency without compromising the dependability of the more detailed information provided by the instructional tests.

It is customary for a review to include comments on features such as appearance of the tests, clarity of directions for administration, quality of the interpretive materials and score reports, and adequacy of the normative data. Little will be said about these features here, however. As was true of earlier editions, the MAT gets high marks on these characteristics. It is a highly professional product with clear directions, a panoply of score reporting options, and ample, clearly written interpretive materials. The representativeness of the norms, like those provided by other publishers, is questionable due to their dependence on voluntary participation of schools. But the quality of those norming procedures that were under the control of the publisher, such as sample design and the substitution of alternates within strata for nonparticipants, are in keeping with the state of the technology. As was recently noted by Baglin (1981), all publishers face an increasingly difficult problem of unknown magnitude caused by nonparticipation, which not only makes comparisons across tests meaningless but gives a somewhat mystical quality to the meaning of "national" in national norms.

VALIDITY. The most important questions regarding any test are those of validity. The Teacher's Manuals note that content validity is of primary importance for an achievement test. They also note that, due to variations in curriculum from school to school, the content validity of the MAT must be judged in terms of the curriculum of the individual school where the tests are to be used. These are reasonable conclusions; however, as will be argued below, other types of validity questions need to be addressed in evaluating some of the claims for and recommended uses of the tests. Some of these additional questions will be considered after the issue of content validity is considered.

The basic approach to content validity for the MAT began in a fairly standard way with the usual review of textbooks and curriculum materials. Based on this review and input from curriculum experts, a "Compendium of Instructional Objectives" was developed for each test. The objectives have a high degree of specificity, with items such as "Can find sums to 18 using three addends" and "Can identify past tense verbs." The items designed to measure each objective are identified by number in the Compendium. The percentage of teachers in the spring standardization sample who reported that they taught each objective during the specified grade of school is available in the MAT Special Report series. These results lend credence to the belief that the objectives generally match what is being taught in the grades for which the tests were designed. The Compendium of Instructional Objectives with the listing of items measuring each objective should greatly facilitate the review of the content validity for the curriculum of each school. If the match is not found to be good, one might reasonably ask: "Why not?" and "Is the fault with the test or the curriculum?"

The vocabulary of the tests is carefully controlled based on Harris and Jacobson's (1972) Basic Elementary Reading Vocabularies. Possible contamination of reading skills with mathematics performance, for example, is reduced by generally limiting the vocabulary to a level one year lower than the grade at which the test is typically used. The now customary practice was followed of using reviews by panels and statistical analyses to identify and eliminate possible sources of ethnic and gender bias. As judged by the ratio of male to female nouns and pronouns, the 1978 edition is markedly more balanced than the 1970 edition (see Special Report No. 15).

By normal standards, the content validity of the MAT for widely shared instructional objectives is quite good and ample information is provided to assist school personnel in evaluating the degree of content validity for a particular school. For some claims and recommended uses of the tests, however, more than content validity is needed. Consider, for example, the following description of the instructional component: "It is an instructional planning tool that provides detailed prescriptive information on the educational performance of individual pupils in terms of specific instructional objectives." Prescription implies that the test results should direct instruction in ways that will remedy the weaknesses that are identified. The Teacher's Manuals do indeed provide teachers with many suggestions of activities to help correct identified weaknesses (e.g., "Pictorial representations of fractional regions should be helpful"). The advice is seemingly sensible and may, in fact, represent effective teaching strategies. But there is a lack of empirical support for the validity of the prescriptions.

It is undoubtedly too much to expect that experimental evidence be provided to support each prescription. On the other hand, a systematic program of test validation should include efforts to document the efficacy of the prescriptions. Logical analysis, summarization of existing instructional research, and special studies are needed in such a validation process. Content validity alone is not sufficient.

CRITERION-REFERENCED INTERPRETATIONS. Both the survey and instructional components are said to be designed to yield criterion-referenced as well as norm-referenced information. The Teacher's Manual suggests that correct responses to at least two out of three items measuring a particular objective be used as the criterion of "acceptable performance." Criterion-referenced interpretations of the 1970 edition were questioned by both Gronlund (1978) and Wolf (1978). Their questions regarding the appropriateness of criterion-referenced interpretations due to the small number of items per objective and the effects of the use of item statistics in the selection of items remain unanswered for the 1978 edition.

RELIABILITY. The KR-20 reliability coefficients of the tests are comparable to those of other high quality achievement tests of similar length. Very limited evidence is provided of alternate form reliability over a 10- to 14-day interval. The evidence provided is at the expected level, i.e., roughly .90 for reading comprehension and substantially less for shorter tests such as Skimming and Scanning, with values around .75. In view of the fact that about 70% of the school systems in the standardization sample tested in both the fall and the spring, it is puzzling that stability coefficients are not reported for fall-to-spring testing.

Reported standard errors of measurement are based on KR-20 coefficients. Coefficients based on alternate form reliability estimates would be preferable. It would also be desirable to have estimates of standard errors of measurement for different score regions as are provided for some tests (e.g., the Iowa Tests of Basic Skills and the Comprehensive Tests of Basic Skills). The assumption that the standard error of measurement is uniform throughout the score range is not tenable. Separate estimates for different score regions provide a better basis of judging the probable error for students whose scores fall at different points on the range of scores spanned by a test of a given level.

GROUP NORMS. The 1970 edition of the MAT was criticized for not providing school norms (Wolf, 1978). Both building and system norms are available for the 1978 edition. Adjusted building and system norms are also available based upon an index of parent education. The percentage of fathers and mothers who are college graduates and the percentage who did not complete high school are used to produce an SES Predicted Achievement Report against which the observed mean scale scores for a building or system can be judged. These adjustments provide a better basis for comparing schools or systems than the usual unadjusted group norms.

PREDICTED ACHIEVEMENT RANGE. It has become popular for publishers to use ability tests in conjunction with achievement tests to report "expected" or "anticipated" achievement scores against which observed student achievement can be compared. For the MAT this type of report was made possible by the joint standardization of the MAT with the Otis-Lennon School Ability Test. Rather than reporting point estimates of expected achievement, however, "predicted achievement ranges" are reported. Student achievement is identified as higher than predicted if the observed score is 1.25 or more standard errors of estimate above that predicted from the Otis-Lennon. A cutoff of .75 standard errors of estimate is used for identifying achievement that is lower than predicted. The remainder of the scores are considered to be in the typical range. Nationally, about 23% of the students fall in the lower than expected range, about 10% in the higher range, and the remaining 67% in the typical range. The use of just three broad categories seems preferable to more precise estimates given the high likelihood of misinterpretation of expected achievement scores. Nonetheless, it would be desirable to have more emphasis given to the dependability and instructional validity of the predicted achievement ranges.

TECHNICAL REPORTS. The bulk of the technical backup for the MAT is provided in a series of Special Reports rather than a single Technical Manual. Most of the desired technical information can be found in one or another of these reports. It would facilitate technical reviews, however, if the information in these reports were brought together and organized into a Technical Manual.

SUMMARY. Like the earlier editions in this series, the 1978 edition of the MAT has much to recommend it. The two component system makes it feasible to satisfy two different purposes better than would be possible with either component alone. The Compendium of Instructional Objectives provides an excellent basis for schools to evaluate the tests and an aide in interpretation. Of course, the MAT also has its shortcomings. Most notable of these is the limited evidential basis of support for some of the suggested interpretations. Validation needs to be conceived more broadly than only content validity. This is particularly true for the prescriptive uses of the instructional tests.

REVIEWER'S REFERENCES

Harris, A. J., & Jacobson, M. D. BASIC ELEMENTARY READING VOCABULARIES. New York: Macmillan, 1972.

Gronlund, N. E. Review of the Metropolitan Achievement Tests. In O. K. Buros (Ed.), THE EIGHTH MENTAL MEASUREMENTS YEARBOOK. Highland Park, NJ: The Gryphon Press, 1978.

Wolf, R. M. Review of the Metropolitan Achievement Tests. In O. K. Buros (Ed.), THE EIGHTH MENTAL MEASUREMENTS YEARBOOK. Highland Park, NJ: The Gryphon Press, 1978.

Baglin, R. F. Does "nationally" normed really mean nationally? JOURNAL OF EDUCATIONAL MEASUREMENT, 1981, 18, 97–108.

[700]

Metropolitan Readiness Tests, 1976 Edition. First half K, second half K and first grade entrants; 1933–76; MRT; 2 forms; 2 levels; 2 editions (hand scored, MRC scored); practice test ('74, 4 pages); parent-teacher conference report ('76, 4 pages) for each level; 1984 price data: $26 per 35 hand scored tests; $49.50 per 35 MRC scored tests; $7.50 per specimen set; MRC scoring service, $1.57 and over per test; Joanne R. Nurss and Mary E. McGauvran; The Psychological Corporation.*

a) LEVEL 1. First half K; 1974–76; 9 or 10 scores: auditory memory, rhyming, visual skills (letter recognition, visual matching, total), language skills (school language listening, quantitative language, total), total, copying (optional); no reliability data or norms for copying score; Forms P, Q, ('74, 25 pages); interpretation manual ('76, 31 pages); directions for administering ('76, 29 pages) for each form; (105) minutes in 7 sessions.

b) LEVEL 2. Second half K and first grade entrants; 1933–76; previous edition still available; 4 to 6 scores: auditory skills, visual skills, language skills, total, quantitative skills (optional), copying (optional); no data on reliability for part scores; norms consist of means and standard deviations for part scores, no norms for copying score; Forms P, Q, ('74, 23 pages); interpretation manual ('76, 30 pages); directions for administering ('76, 29 pages) for each form; (110) minutes in 5 sessions.

See T3:1479 (73 references), 8:802 (111 references), and T2:1716 (55 references); for reviews by Robert Dykstra and Harry Singer of an earlier edition, see 7:757 (124 references); for a review by Eric F. Gardner and an excerpted review by Fay Griffith, see 4:570 (3 references); for a review by Irving H. Anderson, see 3:518 (5 references); for a review by W. J. Osburn, see 2:1552 (10 references).

TEST REFERENCES

1. Reynolds, C. R. A factor analytic study of the Metropolitan Readiness Test. CONTEMPORARY EDUCATIONAL PSYCHOLOGY, 1979, 4, 315–317.

2. Scheuneman, J. A method of assessing bias in test items. JOURNAL OF EDUCATIONAL MEASUREMENT, 1979, 16, 143–152.

3. Kirschenbaum, D. S., De Voge, J. B., Marsh, M. E., & Steffen, J. J. Multimodal evaluation of therapy versus consultation components in a large inner-city early intervention program. AMERICAN JOURNAL OF COMMUNITY PSYCHOLOGY, 1980, 8, 587–601.

4. Eastman, B. G., & Rasbury, W. C. Cognitive self-instruction for the control of impulsive classroom behavior: Ensuring the treatment package. JOURNAL OF ABNORMAL CHILD PSYCHOLOGY, 1981, 9, 381–387.

5. Smith, S. R., Trueblood, C. R., & Szabo, M. Conservation of length and instruction in linear measurement in young children. JOURNAL OF RESEARCH IN SCIENCE TEACHING, 1981, 18, 61–68.

6. Ensminger, M. E., Brown, C. H., & Kellam, S. G. Sex differences in antecedents of substance use among adolescents. JOURNAL OF SOCIAL ISSUES, 1982, 38(2), 25–42.

7. Glazzard, P., Tollefson, N., Selders, J., & Barke, C. R. The predictive validity of the Kindergarten Teacher Rating Scale. EDUCATIONAL AND PSYCHOLOGICAL MEASUREMENT, 1982, 42, 687–693.

8. Webb, K., Clark, S., & Crase, S. J. A cross-model assessment of reading achievement in children. EDUCATIONAL AND PSYCHOLOGICAL MEASUREMENT, 1982, 42, 671–680.

9. Wheeler, J. W., Jr., & Nelson, D. L. Developmental trends in the phonemic organization of individual words. AMERICAN JOURNAL OF PSYCHOLOGY, 1982, 95, 223–233.

10. Day, K. C., & Day, H. D. Ability to imitate language in kindergarten predicts later school achievement. PERCEPTUAL AND MOTOR SKILLS, 1983, 57, 883–890.

11. Morris, D., & Perney, J. Developmental spelling as a predictor of first-grade reading achievement. ELEMENTARY SCHOOL JOURNAL, 1984, 84, 441–457.

Review of Metropolitan Readiness Tests, 1976 Edition, by MICHAEL M. RAVITCH, Associate Professor of Education, Director of Medical Education, Northwestern University, Chicago, IL:

The fourth edition of the Metropolitan Readiness Tests is intended to assess students' preparedness in verbal and quantitative skills. Level I is aimed at beginning through middle kindergarten children, while Level II is aimed at kindergarten and grade 1 students. Level I yields scores for "Visual Skills" (Letter Recognition, Visual Matching) and for "Language" (School Language and Listening, Quantitative Language). Level II includes four skill areas: Auditory (Beginning Consonants, Second-Letter Correspondence), Visual (Visual Matching, Finding Patterns), Language (School Language, Listening), Quantitative (Quantitative Concepts, Quantitative Operations). For some reason, the Auditory Memory and Rhyming subscales are not included in a "skill area" for Level I. The teacher's manual (Level I) on Interpretation and Use of Results argues that these two subscales are important but do not "constitute a sufficiently meaningful, well-defined, auditory cluster." If some items are included, why not include enough to have a "skill area"?

Grouping of subscales into skill categories is of questionable value. First of all, the manual indicates that the validity of the instrument is intended to be based on content (expert judgment of test constructors) and prediction of achievement as measured by later achievement tests. No evidence is given of scaling or factor analytic studies to portray skill areas as general traits or abilities. Indeed, a quick analysis of the correlations among subscales, corrected for attenuation in subscale reliabilities, would yield interscale correlations of .80 or higher. Therefore, to the extent that correlational data indicate whether scales are measuring general or specific traits, these scales appear to measure a common general trait. It seems appropriate to identify these separate subscales by their content, but it is not clear what is gained by labeling "skill areas."

In general, the technical data on the tests are complete and informative. Tables provide normative data on raw scores, percentile ranks, and stanines for the different testing samples of students. Tables are given separately for Form P and Form Q, for beginning of kindergarten and for middle of kindergarten (Level I), and for end of kindergarten and for beginning of grade 1 (Level II). The well written manual provides guidance in using the norm tables and in broad interpretations of the results for individual students, with cautions about implications of performance at chance level, about the use of tests with bilingual or learning-disabled children, and about the need to incorporate teachers' classroom observations of students' performances in decisions about students. The manual makes clear the test is not intended to be diagnostic of specific deficiencies or disabilities, but rather is intended to provide a general assessment of reading readiness. The sections on interpreting and using test results are particularly well written. The sample class records, with related explanations of how one might evaluate the students' performances, should be helpful to teachers using the MRT for the first time. The manual provides appropriate cautions about interpretation of subscales, since the reliability of individual subscales is often quite low, although the reliability of the overall test is much higher.

The samples of students used in the different phases of norm development and assessment of reliabilities included over 10,000 pupils from 40 participating school districts; a second evaluation of items included over 17,000 students from 92 school districts. Information on the gender, ethnicity, geographic distribution, and school level of the children is helpful to personnel at the school district level and in individual schools who wish to determine the extent to which normative data should apply to the particular students being tested. A stratified random sample of school systems was selected, stratifying on six levels of school system enrollment and five levels of socioeconomic status. The sampling unit was the school district. The approach to sampling was carefully explained, and is consistent with good testing practice.

Information on the reliability and validity of the test is clearly presented. Split-half, KR-20, and alternate form reliability estimates are given for Forms P and Q separately on each of the "skill areas": the Visual Skill area (Levels I and II), the Language Skill area (Levels I and II), the Auditory Skill area (Level II), and the Quantitative Skill area (Level II). Statistics are given for students tested at different times of the year and are given separately for Form P and Form Q. The extensive tables on reliability and correlation show correlations between fall and spring testing on subscales and among subscales.

In most regards, the presentation of the statistics is a model for test developers to follow. One omission is any treatment of sources of measurement error beyond that usually addressed in classical test theory. Specifically, these tests are administered by teachers to small groups of students at a time. Instructions are given orally by the teacher, albeit from a very carefully written manual with explicit instructions on test administration. Are students' scores susceptible to differences among examiners administering the test? The alternate form reliability is also an indication of the stability of the test over a short period of time; we do not know the extent to which alternate form reliability is affected by variability in students' performances on different occasions as opposed to the differences between forms. It is curious that the order in which the tests were given affects alternate form reliability. The statistics demonstrate the difficulty in developing perfectly parallel forms of a test.

In addition to the test, useful materials for parent-teacher conferences are included. These materials give examples of the kinds of questions that were asked on the test with suggestions to parents for ways in which they can help children develop the skills which were tested and which are considered essential for reading. An additional instrument, which is most likely to be useful for kindergarten or preschool children, is the Early School Inventory. The Inventory includes sections on Physical Development, Language Development, Cognitive Development, and Social-Emotional Development, all which are easy for the teacher to carry out and provide rough indicators of the student's development. Information is also obtained through an interview with parents.

SUMMARY COMMENTS. The Metropolitan Readiness Tests should continue to retain a place among the most widely used batteries for assessment of school readiness. Users familiar with previous versions will find the same quality in the tests and in the accompanying manuals. The statistical information provided with the test is appropriate and informative, and speaks to the quality of the instrument.

[701]

The Michigan Picture Test—Revised. Ages 8–14; 1953–80; MPT-R; 4 scores: tension, verb tense, direction of forces, combined maladjustment index, plus 4 tentative test variables: psychosexual level, interpersonal relationships, personal pronouns, popular objects; individual; 1 form ('80, 15 cards, 4 for boys only and 4 for girls only); manual ('80, 75 pages); 1982 price data: $19.50 per set of test pictures; $10 per 50 record forms; $16.50 per manual; $44.50 per specimen set; (60) minutes; Max L. Hutt; Grune & Stratton, Inc.*

See P:455 (11 references); for reviews by William E. Henry and Morris Krugman, and excerpted reviews by Laurance F. Shaffer and Edwn S. Shneidman of an earlier edition, see 5:150 (7 references).

Review of the Michigan Picture Test—Revised, by DEBORAH N. BAUSERMAN, Licensed Psychologist, Winchester, VA:

The Michigan Picture Test—Revised (MPT-R) represents a refinement and updating of an earlier version which first appeared in 1953 and essentially follows the trail first blazed by the Thematic Apperception Test. The intent of the author was "to develop a thematic, apperceptive test suitable for elementary school children that was capable of differentiating those with emotional maladjustment from those whose emotional adjustment was satisfactory." The studies presented by Hutt suggest that the MPT-R may be reasonably viewed as a screening test for the purposes of group differentiation; however, the claim that it is a tool "highly adaptable for several diagnostic purposes" is somewhat overblown given the extent of standardization to date.

The types of problems typically revealed in the stories are classified as: (1) interpersonal conflicts with peers, (2) intrafamilial conflicts, (3) conflicts with authority figures, (4) conflicts involving danger in physical activities, (5) conflicts in the psychosexual sphere, (6) conflicts in school situations, (7) feelings of personal inadequacy, (8) problems concerning the self-percept, (9) conflicts involving the expression of aggressive needs, and (10) problems in social situations. While the list of personality areas is not inclusive of all possible problem areas, it appears to be sufficiently broad to elicit relevant information concerning individual differences.

Beginning with 1,000 pictures, 65 were studied "experimentally" (in a manner not described) before selecting the final 15 cards comprising the test. These final 15 cards also met unspecified empirical criteria and covered "certain areas of developmental conflict that were considered to be critical in the patterns of adjustment of contemporary children."

Participants in the standardization study were drawn from two separate pools—17 public schools and 11 state child guidance clinics in Michigan—for a total of 700 children in grades 3, 5, 7 and 9. The sample was described as being "representative of the entire state in socioeconomic levels and...with differing cultural backgrounds." The description of the sampling procedure was lacking in information about: (1) the distribution of SES levels and ethnic/cultural groups, (2) the present sample in comparison with the U.S. population, and (3) the author's reason for stating that the test may usefully be administered to children in *ALL* grades of school. Also, of potential interest is that the author used the data from the clinic sample only for the analysis of the validity of several test variables and not for the purpose of obtaining normative data, with no explanation given.

The criterion measure for the MPT-R was an 11-item scale, the Rating Scale for Pupil Adjustment, which was designed to measure emotional adjustment and school functioning. This scale was completed by teachers who had known the children for at least 3 months. Unfortunately, no information was presented regarding the psychometric properties of the scale; neither was a rationale discussed for the definition of adjustment as the upper third or maladjustment as the lower third of the score distribution of the group which was administered the scale.

Of eight objective test variables culled from research and theory and selected for analysis, three variables were found to discriminate significantly between well-adjusted and poorly adjusted children. The three variables are combined to form a Combined Maladjustment Index; preliminary studies of the reliability and validity of these variables are discussed. The remaining five variables are discussed in a later section as variables which "may provide useful leads for the clinician and may merit further research study."

The three discriminating objective test variables are defined as follows: (1) the Tension Index (e.g., expressed needs of love, extrapunitiveness, submission, personal adequacy), (2) Verb Tense, a potpourri of hypothetical intellectual, emotional and defensive functioning, and (3) Direction of Forces, an index which is reminiscent of Rotter's IE Scale. As mentioned above, preliminary study of reliability and validity of these variables was undertaken, although not consistently. For example, interrater reliability was studied for two of the three variables while test-retest reliability was only determined for one variable, the span of time not specified. The only validity data presented was concurrent validity data, the author admitting "much more remains to be done in cross-validation." A chief shortcoming of the MPT-R as studied by the author was the finding that the test generates "some false positives." Hutt states, for instance, that "a child with a critical score on the Tension Index has a 55 percent probability of falling in the well-adjusted group and a 78 percent probability of falling in the poorly adjusted group in grade 3." The reviewer questions the utility of a test with such characteristics.

To conclude, the MPT-R may be viewed as a test with both advantages and disadvantages for the user. One advantage is that the methods of scoring the test variables do not require distortion of the holistic quality of the spontaneous story productions offered by children. Also, the test is flexible in that it may be used either in its short form as a screening tool or in its full length form for analysis of individual children. One disadvantage is that while it strives to objectify the scoring of projective or thematic material, it is at this date somewhat weak in the case it presents regarding standardization criteria. In addition, as a screening tool it appears to be rather cumbersome, failing to meet the ideal requirements of screening tools such as brevity, economy, and ease of administration and interpretation. For example, the test responses must be tape-recorded, transcribed, and then analyzed by a psychologist; this would limit its usefulness as a tool in school systems. Given the overlap between the MPT-R, TAT and CAT, this reviewer has reservations that a demonstrably clear and significant gain would be acquired in the use of the MPT-R at this stage of its development.

Review of Michigan Picture Test by HERBERT G. W. BISCHOFF, School Psychologist, Psychology Resources, Anchorage, AK:

The revision of the Michigan Picture Test (MPT-R) is the result of numerous requests for the MPT after it became unavailable. The Michigan Picture Test—Revised joins a host of other recently revised assessment instruments giving credibility to the notion that the MPT has, in some regards, withstood the test of time.

The revised version of the MPT contains all but one of the original stimulus cards. The current 15-card set includes four pictures for use with boys only and four for use with girls only, with the remaining cards (including a blank) used for both sexes. Four core cards may be used for the "screening" of emotional maladjustment. The revised test manual is newly organized to focus on more effective clinical application. New is a section on "qualitative analysis" of test protocols. In some cases, "the original statistical data have been reanalyzed and presented in clearer form." These are the only real changes from the original MPT.

By utilizing the same pictures as the original MPT, the author has avoided the task of restandardization and consequently the original data retain their shortcomings. The revision does not address previous criticisms. The 1951 standardization sample of 700 students throughout Michigan does not serve to represent today's multi-ethnic, multi-cultural group of youngsters. For the 1980s, the MPT-R pictures appear somewhat dated (mostly in dress) and lacking in ethnic variability. Although the author indicates that he is in the process of updating and extending the norms, current users should be cautioned that their clinical judgment of responses may, in all likelihood, make for a more accurate interpretation than the dated and limited normative data reported in the manual.

Eight variables were identified from an analysis of the original standardization data. Four were found to be useful in discriminating between well and poorly adjusted children (Tension Index, Verb Tense, Direction of Forces, and a Combined Maladjustment Index made up of the previous three variables). Selection of these variables was "based upon the research evidence available in the literature as well as upon theories of child development and of psychopathology in children." Substantial revisions in almost all major child development theories since the early 1950s would appear to warrant reconsideration of the original eight variables.

The MPT-R manual is attractive, easy to read, and well organized. Chapters cover test development and clinical application. The Scoring and Interpretation chapter reflects the author's efforts to objectify the scoring of this apperceptive test. The scoring system provides definition, steps in scoring, normative data, and helpful examples. The Qualitative Analysis section serves to highlight the importance of clinical judgment by paying attention to responses that reflect conflict and evidence projective phenomena and high emotional states.

In summary, the MPT-R will likely accomplish its goal of providing interested clinicians access to a new MPT. Without updated normative data, integration of more recent theoretical concepts of child development, and further reliability and validity data, this revision might more accurately be described as a new printing or a second edition. Krugman's review of the MPT in *The Fifth Mental Measurements Yearbook* (5:150) raised many concerns left unanswered by this revision. Notably, his concern over the utility of the MPT in light of the more effective Rating Scale for Pupil Adjustment (MPT-R Appendix B), used as a criterion measure for the MPT, has not been addressed. Also, the discriminative value of the variables, earlier found lacking, cannot increase through the reanalysis of old data. Additionally, concern continues that the Tension Index yields too many false positives, the research on use of verb tense is still not reported, and it is unclear whether significant differences among grade levels have been found on the Direction of Forces variable.

The hard work demonstrated in the development of the MPT has not continued to the same degree in the development of the MPT-R. The promises held in the MPT have not been fulfilled in its revision. The changes in the MPT-R appear cosmetic, and the MPT-R has value only to the skilled clinician willing to interpret children's responses to pictures as accurately reflecting their emotional reactions and adjustment.

[702]

Michigan Prescriptive Program in English. Persons striving to obtain 10th grade equivalency or pass the G.E.D. Test; 1973–75; a pretest is administered and scored and a prescribed course of study is implemented to help the student correct problem areas; no data on reliability and validity; no norms; 1 form (no date, 8 pages); no manual; instruction sheet (no date, 2 pages); study materials ('75, 74 pages); response and prescription sheets ('75, 7 sets of each); separate answer sheets must be used; 1983 price data: $1.50 per test booklet; $1 per answer key; $2 per response and prescription sheet booklet; $4.50 per English study materials; no administration time reported; William E. Lockhart; Ann Arbor Publishers, Inc.*

Review of Michigan Prescriptive Program in English by GAIL E. TOMPKINS, Assistant Professor of Education, The University of Oklahoma, Norman, OK:

The Michigan Prescriptive Program is designed to help students study for and pass the high school equivalency GED English Test. The Program includes two components: (1) a pretest covering grammar, usage, and spelling skills needed for the GED Test, and (2) a study guide.

The pretest covers 38 grammar and usage skills including calendar terms, irregular verbs, subjective complements, double negatives, and apostrophies. A section on spelling is also a part of the test. One to four test items are included for each grammar and usage skill, and there are nine test items on spelling. The accompanying study guide provides lessons covering the same grammar, usage, and spelling skills. The lesson on spelling reviews three basic spelling rules (the I-E rule, double final consonants, and words ending in "E").

The pretest includes 97 items presented in a multiple choice format. For each item, students are directed to locate a specific word (i.e., an adverb), choose the correct spelling, or identify an error (i.e., a word improperly capitalized). Five choices are provided for each item. Students record their answers on response sheets. Students complete the test at their own pace; there are no time limits. The test can be given to individuals or groups.

Scoring is quick and easy. A transparent answer key overlay is provided to simplify the scoring. The number of correct answers for each skill is recorded on a prescription sheet to form the student's individual prescription. Students are directed to use the study guide and review each skill in which they did not correctly answer all questions.

The study guide is organized with a separate lesson for each skill. A lesson includes three parts: (1) an explanation of the skill, (2) two sets of exercises, and (3) answers for the exercises. Students use the study guide independently. According to the Program, direct instruction by the teacher is not needed.

Instructions for using the Program are limited to approximately one-half page at the front of the study guide. However, they adequately explain the procedures involved in using the Program. These instructions are directed to the teacher or the examiner. There are no general instructions or other information provided for the students.

A brief section on "Background Information" is also included at the front of the study guide. The author explains that "When study is completed...a standardized achievement test should be administered. A tenth grade level indicates good chances of success on the GED Test." In addition, he explains that "A student who gets a total of about 70 right on the English test should be about ready for the G.E.D. English Test." The author does not provide any statistical data to support these statements.

The pretest and study guide are clearly written and are easy to follow, although the study guide does lack pictures or other interest-capturing designs. The author cautions that "Seventh grade reading level, or close to it, is necessary for a person to use the study materials without lots of tutoring help."

No information is provided about how the pretest and study guide were developed. There is also no information about the students who have used the Program.

The major weakness of this Program is the lack of statistical data on the Program's effectiveness. No information is provided with the Program to suggest that any studies have been done to provide data on the Program's reliability or validity. Research is also needed to provide support for the claim that a student with a score of 70 or higher should be ready for the G.E.D. English Test.

In summary, the Michigan Prescriptive Program provides a good review of grammar, usage, and spelling skills. It is a flexible program that is designed to meet students' individual needs. However, the lack of statistical data regarding the Program's effectiveness severely limits the value of the Program.

[703]

Michigan Prescriptive Program in Mathematics. Persons striving to obtain 10th grade equivalency or pass the G.E.D. test in math; 1978–79; a pretest is administered and scored and from the results a prescribed course of study is implemented to help the student correct problem areas; no data on reliability and validity; no norms; 1 form ('79, 12 pages); no manual; instruction sheet (no date, 2 pages); study materials ('78, 202 pages); response and prescription sheets ('79, 7 sets of each); separate answer sheets must be used; 1983 price data: $1.50 per test booklet; $8 per study materials; $2 per response and prescription sheet booklet; $1 per answer key; no administration time reported; William E. Lockhart; Ann Arbor Publishers, Inc.*

Review of Michigan Prescriptive Program in Mathematics by RONALD A. BERK, Associate Professor of Educational Research, The Johns Hopkins University, Baltimore, MD:

This program consists of a 70-item multiple-choice test and a corresponding set of mathematics study materials that are to be used in preparation for the high school equivalency G.E.D. math test. Since the scores from the placement test or pretest serve to guide the prescription, their validity and reliability are pivotal to the whole program. The test results furnish diagnostic information based on which items are answered incorrectly and predictive information on how well a person needs to perform in order to pass the G.E.D. test. As a preview to the quality of the pretest, it is sufficient at this point to note that there is no technical manual for the test and no evidence of validity and reliability studies reported elsewhere. The details are described next.

The 70 test items are keyed to 53 mathematics skills. The list of skills is the only definition of the domain given. There are no objectives or a table of specifications. This is unfortunate because the skills are uneven in level of specificity and are not expressed as behaviors. For example, they range in specificity from "subtract whole numbers," "change fractions to percents," and "find volume of rectangular solid" to "theorems," "set theory," "signs," and "slope." These latter topics are ambiguous from both the perspectives of item construction and score interpretation. Based on a review of the skills and the items, it is estimated that about a third of the test measures comprehension and application level skills according to Bloom's taxonomy, and the remainder are at the knowledge level. There is no rationale given for this particular distribution. In addition, the relationship between the skill distribution and that represented on the G.E.D. test is not reported. Certainly the correlation should be high if the pretest is to be of any value.

In regard to item construction, there is no description of the procedures used to write the items or sample them from the domain so that they represent a predefined body of mathematics content. No systematic review of the items was evidenced in order to establish their congruence with the domain. Further, there was no attempt to avoid sex role stereotyping or to consider the proportionate representation of women and minorities in the items and the prescriptive exercises. Among the items citing people, those people in all instances are males. For example, one item partitions the occupations of senators into businessmen, lawyers, and other occupations. The prescriptive materials contain a disproportionate number of exercises with males depicted in stereotypic tasks. In those exercises citing females, they are portrayed as cake bakers, babysitters, and grocery shoppers. No studies of sex, racial, or ethnic bias were reported.

The lack of information on item generation also raises questions concerning test length. There was only one item written per skill for most of the topics, regardless of the level of specificity. Two items were constructed for each of the fractions, decimals, and percent topics, with no reason given for the discrepancy. One or two items is clearly an inadequate foundation for any individual decision making, diagnostic or otherwise. Chance errors, carelessness, or measurement errors could account for any single incorrect answer.

As if the preceding problems are not serious enough, the author does not supply the results of any technical analyses of the items or test in terms of item analysis statistics and validity and reliability coefficients. In the Instructions for Using the Michigan Prescriptive Program, it is stated that a "score of about 45 right on the math test shows the student can probably pass the G.E.D. math test." The "Fact Sheet" claims that there will be an "average math gain of 1.5 years...in a total of 24 clock hours of study [and a] gain of 3–5 years in math...is achieved by highly motivated students." Yet no validity evidence is provided to support these predictions. Such statements also define the extent of the information given to the user on how to interpret the scores. The specific use of the scores is restricted to locating the prescriptive exercises corresponding to each item answered incorrectly on the pretest.

In summary, the non-psychometric approach to structuring the Michigan Prescriptive Program and the author's insensitivity to sex role stereotyping render the pretest worthless as a diagnostic tool and diminish the value of the prescriptive material as a study guide in preparation for the G.E.D. math test. Inasmuch as there is no evidence of the effectiveness of the pretest and the exercises in fulfilling the purposes for which they were developed, the program cannot be recommended to students or adults.

Review of Michigan Prescriptive Program in Mathematics by MARILYN N. SUYDAM, Professor, Mathematics Education, The Ohio State University, Columbus, OH:

The focus of this "program" is the study material which will supposedly help adults pass a high school equivalency test. One is to take the pretest and then do the pages in the study material which correspond to the items missed. Claims are made on an accompanying fact sheet that "Average math gain is 1.5 years...in a total of 24 clock hours study," "Gain of 3–5 years in math...is achieved by highly motivated students," and "Thirty hours is usually enough time for math study regardless of beginning score." Each of these claims is interesting—but on what they are based is unknown, since no data are provided. One has no way of ascertaining their validity. Moreover, "When study is completed..., a standardized achievement test should be administered" to provide an indication of success on the G.E.D. If more work is needed, "the study materials can be gone through again." Thus, the emphasis is on drill and practice.

The paucity of information about the test as well as the study materials is a major fault. The fact sheet consists of one page about the program (e.g., "Test administration is simple.") and on the reverse are instructions for using the program (e.g., "Let the student read the test directions and ask for help when necessary"). The fact sheet asserts that "Another test measures each of 49 important items in math" (in addition to an English test); it would be interesting if one could ascertain what the 49 important items are on the 70-item test—or which of the 53 skill areas assessed are not included by those 49 important items.

Covered are computation with whole numbers, fractions, and decimals (19 items) and with denominate numbers (4 items); other fraction skills (8 items); percent (7 items); equations and inequalities (4 items); geometry (5 items); area and other measurement topics (8 items); graphs (3 items); and a variety of topics including interest, square root, set union, and Roman numerals (12 items). The supposition is that these topics correspond to those on the G.E.D., although no evidence is provided in support of this.

The test items and response sheets are numbered from 1 to 70. The answer key is numbered from 200 to 298—with only even numbers used except for three items. Why the numbers differ is not made clear—and this makes it very confusing to check a response with an item, a difficulty compounded by the fact that the acetate answer key does not have holes punched in it to allow you to mark incorrect answers. Apparently you must write the number on a separate sheet, and no allowance is made for the natural inclination to see why you got the item incorrect. Obviously, the numbering on the study material corresponds to that on the answer key.

As you examine the key, it appears that there are double answers to some 17 items, but that turns out to be a result of the shift of item numbers (for instance, items 4 and 5 on the test are item 206 on the answer key and study material). Five answer choices are given for most items, but only four for four items.

The study material is essentially a "this-is-how-to-do-it-now-practice" type, with answers for practice exercises. Items on the pretest are not reviewed, even though this might be helpful in some cases (e.g., with graphs).

Adults who have been away from mathematics classes for several years often need review of mathematical content before taking an equivalency test. These materials could serve that purpose. However, the lack of any data on the validity and reliability of the test, and on the success of these materials in helping students pass an equivalency test, is a major shortcoming. The correlation of pretest items to study material, or even their relation to equivalency test items, is not sufficient. One needs to know how well they do what it is said they do.

[704]

MILCOM Patient Data Base System. Medical patients; 1980; self-administered health questionnaire and physical examination record; item scores only; health history questionnaire available as separate; no data on reliability and validity; no norms; individual; 1 form (7 pages, includes 4-page health history questionnaire with carbonless answer sheet to be completed by the patient plus 3-page physical examination record to be completed by the physician); 1984 price data: $88 per 100 questionnaires; $75 per 100 health history questionnaires; Spanish edition of health history questionnaire available; (15–30) minutes; Miller Communications, Inc.*

[705]

Mill Hill Vocabulary Scale. Ages 11–14, 14 and over; 1943–82; MHVS; revision of 1958 edition; intelligence; all forms (except Short Form) contain response form for the Standard Progressive Matrices; 4 forms; new manual ('82, 53 pages); 1983 price data: £6.10 per 50 tests; £4.50 per manual; (15–20) minutes; J. C. Raven, J. Raven, and J. H. Court; H. K. Lewis & Co. Ltd. [England].*

a) DEFINITIONS FORM. Ages 11 and over; consists of all words from both forms of the Junior and Senior forms below; 1 form ('82, 4 pages).

b) JUNIOR FORM. Ages 11–14; Forms 1, 2, ('82, 4 pages).

c) SENIOR FORM. Ages 14 and over; Forms 1, 2, ('82, 4 pages).

d) SHORT FORM. Ages 11 and over; consists of every fifth word from Definitions Form above; 1 form ('77, 2 pages); £3.35 per 50 tests; J. C. Raven.

See T3:1485 (29 references) and T2:402 (32 references); for a review of an earlier edition by Morton Bortner, see 6:471 (16 references); see also 4:303 (7 references); for a review by David Wechsler, see 3:239 (3 references).

TEST REFERENCES

1. Wolff, S., & Chick, J. Schizoid personality in childhood: A controlled follow-up study. PSYCHOLOGICAL MEDICINE, 1980, 10, 85–100.
2. Huxley, P. J., Kenna, J. C., & Brandon, S. Partnership in transsexualism. Part I. Paired and nonpaired groups. ARCHIVES OF SEXUAL BEHAVIOR, 1981, 10, 133–141.
3. McCartney, J., & O'Donnell, P. J. The perception of drinking roles by recovering problem drinkers. PSYCHOLOGICAL MEDICINE, 1981, 11, 747–754.
4. Hertzog, C., & Carter, L. Sex differences in the structure of intelligence: A confirmatory factor analysis. INTELLIGENCE, 1982, 6, 287–303.
5. Lykken, D. T. Research with twins: The concept of emergenesis. PSYCHOPHYSIOLOGY, 1982, 19, 361–373.
6. Bamber, J. H., Bill, J. M., Boyd, F. E., & Corbett, W. D. In two minds—Arts and science differences at sixth-form level. BRITISH JOURNAL OF EDUCATIONAL PSYCHOLOGY, 1983, 53, 222–233.
7. Bradley, B., & Mathews, A. Negative self-schemata in clinical depression. THE BRITISH JOURNAL OF CLINICAL PSYCHOLOGY, 1983, 22, 173–181.
8. Pears, E., Bowman, R., Kincey, J., & Gautam, R. Does prostacyclin prevent cognitive deficits after open heart surgery? PSYCHOLOGICAL MEDICINE, 1984, 14, 213–214.

[706]

Miller Assessment for Preschoolers. Ages 2–9 to 5–8; 1982; MAP; screening tool to identify children who exhibit moderate developmental problems; 6 scores: foundations, coordination, verbal, non-verbal, complex tasks, total; individual; 1 form; 6 developmental levels (ages 2–9 to 3–2, 3–3 to 3–8, 3–9 to 4–2, 4–3 to 4–8, 4–9 to 5–2, 5–3 to 5–8); record booklet (4 pages); drawing booklet (4 pages); item score sheet (2 pages) for each developmental level; examiner's manual (220 pages); 1983 price data: $225 per complete kit in carrying case; $6.25 per 25 item score sheets; $6.25 per 25 record booklets; $6.25 per 25 drawing booklets; $2.50 per labels for kit box; $22.50 per examiner's manual; (20–30) minutes; Lucy Jane Miller; The Foundation for Knowledge in Development.*

Review of Miller Assessment for Preschoolers by DENNIS J. DELORIA, Senior Scientist, MOBIUS Corporation, Alexandria, VA:

The Miller Assessment for Preschoolers (MAP) is an important new screening test for identifying children who exhibit moderate "preacademic problems" which may affect one or more areas of development, but who do not have obvious or severe problems. The authors do not recommend it for populations not included in the normative sample, such as children for whom English is not the primary language, or children with known physical, mental, or emotional dysfunction.

The MAP is exemplary in many ways, beginning with its long and careful development history. Since 1972 its authors examined 115 preschool tests, reviewed 177 sources of research and theory, and prepared and tested five editions of the MAP. This included over 800 items administered to several independent samples totaling over 4,000 preschool children. The last of these samples was a randomly selected, stratified national sample of 1,200 preschoolers.

The MAP is optimized for detecting preschoolers with potential problems. Most tests are developed to equally differentiate children at all ability levels, from high to low, consequently sacrificing precision at the lowest levels of performance. The MAP, on the other hand, demonstrates considerable precision for identifying differences among the lowest 25% of children, but has little precision for the upper 75% (i.e., normally performing children). This difference is strikingly demonstrated by low correlations between the MAP and the WPPSI (.27), and the ITPA (.31). The MAP is clearly not interchangeable with either of these.

The 27 performance items comprising the MAP "core" represent a broad range of behavioral domains. They include variations of items that have been widely used for decades (such as the draw-a-person), but they also include many neurologically-based items that are more familiar to the medical profession than to the educational or psychological professions. These items should be little influenced by a child's cultural environment, so we might expect the test to be more culture-fair than most when used with children who are not white middle-class. Non-white ethnic groups were included in the normative sample in proportion to their incidence in the U.S. population, but unfortunately the MAP Manual does not report separate results for the different ethnic groups. Among all groups there was a disproportionate share of well-educated, professionally-employed parents in the norm sample.

If desired, the MAP items can be grouped into five subscores for more detailed interpretation (with lower reliability than the overall score, of course), and the manual even provides assistance in interpreting individual item scores (with lower reliability yet). Particularly when coupled with the optional Supplemental Observations this results in an unusually rich set of information for use in assessing specifics of a child's performance.

The MAP was designed to be used at two levels. The 27 "core" items were designed to be administered by examiners possessing minimal training. According to the manual, examiners can include psychologists, physicians, occupational and physical therapists, speech pathologists, nurses, and teachers. But at another level it also has an optional set of Supplemental Observations that can be used by clinically-trained examiners and those taking an accredited MAP training seminar. The Supplemental Observations were completed during the norming of the MAP and an appendix is included in the manual to assist in interpretation; however, no statistics are presented about them and the manual cautions that the appendix is not sufficient by itself to permit interpretation of the Supplemental Observations.

A child must take all 27 items before a total score can be calculated. In order to properly adjust the difficulty of the items to a given child, the child's exact age must be determined in advance of the testing session, and appropriate versions of the 27 items selected. This is made into a relatively simple task by the layout of the scoring notebook provided with the test kit, in spite of the large number of objects that must be used in administering the test. The item preselection lowers the risk of subjecting a child to a long sequence of failures at the end of the session. The manual stresses that the assessment should be fun for the child, and directs the examiner to constantly reinforce the child, helping him or her to feel the job has been done exceptionally well even if the child appears to be functioning below normal.

Obvious care has been taken by the MAP developers to make the test materials easy to use and to minimize examiner mistakes. The materials are stored in a sturdy plastic case with labeled shelves, grouped into sets for each item, and kept in plastic containers. When used as recommended, all materials in the case are in full view of the examiner, but out of sight of the child. Everything needed by the examiner is provided except a stopwatch. If one considers that over 100 individual pieces make up the kit, the overall organization is impressive.

Care has been taken in planning the scoring process as well. The child's response to each item is recorded on a color-coded score sheet which immediately indicates the level of performance. Children scoring in the red areas are in the bottom 5%; those scoring in the yellow areas are in the bottom 25%, but above the lowest 5%; and all others are in the green, (normal) group, encompassing the top 75%. Separate score sheets are provided for each of the six age groupings. A simple and effective notebook indexing system keeps the item prompts and score sheets for a given age group in full view, eliminating page-turning during the testing session. Detailed scoring criteria insure a high level of standardization.

The manual is one of the few for preschool screening tests that closely follows recommendations given in the APA-AERA-NCME *Standards for Educational and Psychological Tests*: all the essential procedures and resulting statistics from the MAP's extensive development are described, including detailed norms and several types of reliabilities and validities; appropriate and inappropriate uses of the MAP are described; and the manual repeatedly cautions against overinterpretation of the results.

The development of an assessment device like the MAP is never finished, but the results to date are reassuring. One major area of research not yet completed is the MAP's ability to predict future child performance. The MAP Manual appropriately cautions that the test's predictive ability is unknown at this time. A major followup of about 500 children from the original normative sample is scheduled to begin in the Fall of 1984, when the children will be in the first, second, and third grades. As is true with other major tests, it is likely that dozens of independent research studies will be conducted over time using the MAP, extending our understanding of the test in important ways. The MAP clearly merits this kind of independent effort.

In summary, the MAP appears to be the best available screening test for identifying preschool children with moderate "preacademic" problems. I recommend it over the widely used Denver Developmental Screening Test for this purpose. It is short, carefully developed, and well standardized. It fills a clear need for professionals working with preschoolers and will quite likely play a major role for many years. The cost of the MAP is moderately high, but examiners seeking a high-quality screening test should not allow that to deter them from choosing it.

Review of Miller Assessment for Preschoolers by WILLIAM B. MICHAEL, Professor of Education and Psychology, University of Southern California, Los Angeles, CA:

Based on at least 10 years of painstaking research involving more than 4,000 children and 800 trial items, the Miller Assessment for Preschoolers (MAP) is a 30-minute, individually administered developmental test that is intended to identify potential learning disabilities of not too severe a nature in children between 2 years, 9 months and 5 years, 8 months of age. Initial developmental efforts included experimental tryout of items and their later revision or elimination on the basis of critical review and statistical analyses. Then a research form of 512 items was developed during 1979 and 1980 and standardized on a randomly chosen stratified population of 1,200 preschoolers from nine United States Census Bureau Regions. Accompanied by extensive item analyses with 600 children that had been judged as normal and with 90 children exhibiting preacademic problems, this standardization led to the selection of a core of 27 items that comprise the MAP Final Edition. In addition to this core of 27 items to identify children at risk in future school learning, the MAP provides, as a secondary goal, the Supplemental Observations—highly structured clinical information that may be helpful in describing in qualitative terms a child's weaknesses and strengths and in suggesting possible courses of remediation.

Derived from an exhaustive review of the professional literature as well as from the test author's clinical experience as an occupational therapist, the theoretical background or framework underlying the 27 core items may be characterized in terms of (*a*) the threefold classification of abilities hypothesized to be represented, (*b*) each of the performance indexes within the ability classification, and (*c*) a designation of the items corresponding to each performance index. Within the first classification of Sensory and Motor Abilities, the Foundations Index examines major or basic motor tasks and sensations essential to activities of higher complexity (Stereognosis, Finger Localization, Hand-Nose, Romberg, Stepping, Supine Flexion, and Kneel-Stand); the Coordination Index reflects increasingly complex motor tasks that join basic sensory and motor factors (Tower, Motor Accuracy, Tongue Movement, and Articulation); and the Combined Foundations and Coordination Indexes portray an integration of the Foundations and Coordination Indexes (Vertical Writing, Walks Line, and Rapid Alternating Movements). For the second classification hypothesized to represent Cognitive Abilities, the Verbal index comprises association, comprehension, expression in a verbal context, memory, and sequencing (General Information, Follow Directions, Sentence Repetition, and Digit Repetition); the Non-Verbal Index consists of memory, performance, and sequencing (Sequencing, Block Tapping, Object Memory, Puzzles, and Figure-Ground). In the instance of the third classification referred to as Combined Abilities, the Complex Tasks Index puts together sensory, motor, and cognitive abilities that are required for an interpretation of spatial-visual information (Block Designs, Draw-A-Person Game, Imitation of Postures, and Maze). Associated with this theoretical framework is a specification table in the MAP manual describing the relationship between items and a defined behavioral domain—a table affording at least some rudimentary evidence of the content validity of the MAP.

A careful examination of the highly detailed manual of more than 200 pages reveals that despite the recency of publication of the MAP Final Edition, a great deal of effort already has been expended within what would be considered a highly constricted time frame (*a*) to furnish numerous data regarding the reliability and validity of the test, (*b*) to provide necessary information concerning how to administer and to score each item, and (*c*) to assist the user in the interpretation of each item score and of each Performance Index score. Throughout the manual, a considerable amount of caution is exercised concerning the extent to which the user may make definitive judgments from the scores provided by the items or by sets of items within a given Performance Index. In other words, the test author has exhibited a welcome degree of modesty regarding the utility of the test in its current form. The only possible exception would be a potential underestimation of the amount of skill that may be required on the part of the examiner, who surely should have had a great deal of supervised preliminary experience prior to giving the test to a child in a formal setting.

Although the author has been unable to do predictive validity studies because children in the standardization sample have not reached school age, initial efforts with a few small samples have been undertaken to provide some evidence of factorial validity and criterion-related validity. There is some question concerning just how appropriate the estimates of criterion-related validity are in view of the fact that the other measures selected against which to validate the MAP reflect quite different constructs and theoretical orientations.

Preliminary evidence for the reliability of the MAP generally has been favorable. For sets of items associated with the five Performance Indexes, estimates of interrater reliability varied between .84 (Coordination) and .99 (Non-Verbal), with the Total MAP score yielding a value of .98. Estimates of stability in terms of percentages of examinees who did not switch a final scoring category upon retest ranged from 72 for the Coordination Index to 94 for the Non-Verbal Index, with the Total MAP score registering a value of 81. Two estimates of internal-consistency reliability ($N = 1{,}204$) were .79 (Spearman-Brown) and .79 (Guttman). Initial data pertaining to the standard error of measurement are still fragmentary.

A particularly strong feature of the MAP has been the detailed information presented in the manual for the administration and scoring of each of the items. Typically, one to four pages of narrative outlining any required materials, the procedure to be followed, and the scoring directions relevant to designated age groups appear in the manual for each of the core items. To minimize administration effort and to increase accuracy of scoring, matching Cue Sheets and Item Score Sheets have been furnished for each of the six age groups entering into the normative process.

Another helpful feature is the interpretive information provided in diagrams in the manual. In long rectangular blocks corresponding to a given item and age group are shaded areas representing percentile bands or intervals that are coded red, yellow, or green. The red area indicates that the child is functioning at or below the 5th percentile of the normative group; the yellow, between the 6th and 25th percentile; and the green, above the 25th percentile. Qualitatively speaking, the red, yellow, and green intervals are interpreted as revealing, respectively, that the child (*a*) appears to need further evaluation, (*b*) should be watched carefully, and (*c*) seems to be within normal limits. Parallel information has been furnished for each Performance Index as well as for the Total score.

In the reviewer's judgment the MAP Final Edition is an extremely promising instrument which should find wide use among clinical psychologists, school psychologists, and occupational therapists in assessing mild to moderate learning disabilities in preschool children. It is to be anticipated that with the accumulation of additional reliability, validity, and normative data, this instrument will take its place along with a handful of others in providing much needed information concerning the learning potentialities of both the so-called normal and learning-disabled preschool child.

[707]

Millon Adolescent Personality Inventory. Ages 13–19; 1976–82; MAPI; 20 scales: Introversive, Inhibited, Cooperative, Sociable, Confident, Forceful, Respectful, Sensitive, Self-Concept, Personal Esteem, Body Comfort, Sexual Acceptance, Peer Security, Social Tolerance, Family Rapport, Academic Confidence, Impulse Control, Societal Conformity, Scholastic Achievement, Attendance Consistency; Clinical Form, Guidance Form, ('82, 3 pages, NCS scorable, questions are the same for both forms—the difference lies in the type of interpretive output report); manual ('82, 72 pages); 1983 price data: $10.50 and less per Guidance Interpretive Prepaid Form; $15 and less per Clinical Interpretive Prepaid Form; $9.50 per manual; (20–30) minutes; Theodore Millon, Catherine J. Green, and Robert B. Meagher, Jr.; NCS Interpretive Scoring Systems.*

Review of Millon Adolescent Personality Inventory by DOUGLAS T. BROWN, Professor of Psychology, James Madison University, Harrisonburg, VA:

The Millon Adolescent Personality Inventory (MAPI) was developed, according to the authors, "for the purpose of identifying, predicting and understanding a wide range of psychology attributes characteristic of adolescents." The authors recommend that it be utilized as a component in testing for counseling and academic advising as well as clinical assessment and intervention in mental health settings. The intent of the instrument appears to be that of providing a system for diagnostic classification of adolescents while at the same time providing personality descriptions for counseling purposes. The test has three basic dimensions including Personality Style, Expressed Concerns, and Behavioral Correlates. Each of these dimensions contains subscales which are listed above. The first eight scales comprising the Personality Style dimension were derived using Millon's personality theory. This theory postulates eight basic personality styles which are based on the adolescent's perception of the sources of reinforcement (positive and/or negative) and the coping mechanisms used to deal with various types of reinforcement (active versus passive coping mechanisms). Personality styles, therefore, are various combinations of reactive and/or proactive behavior patterns such as "passive detached," "active detached," or "passive dependent." Millon has chosen to label these patterns with the personality style factor names listed above. The Expressed Concern dimension, which also comprises eight scales relating to developmental concerns of adolescents, appears to be founded on several accepted tenants of developmental theory. While not explicitly stated by the authors, these scales appear to be derived from developmental tasks suggested by Havighurst and Erickson. The third and final dimension of Behavioral Correlates, according to the authors, consists of empirically derived scales using methodology similar to that employed in developing the MMPI. These scales are used to provide a probability estimate that a subject belongs to "a troubled group" in a nonclinical population.

The MAPI consists of 150 items which are written at a sixth-grade reading level. It is administered using a NCS mark sense protocol and consists of two forms, the clinical form and the guidance form. These are differentiated only at the time of scoring and interpretation. The test publisher strongly suggests that the test be scored by NCS employing their automated assessment system. No materials are provided for manual scoring of the instrument.

Computer output provided by NCS on both the clinical and guidance forms includes validity and reliability data, verbal descriptions of personality style, descriptive statements of expressed concerns scales, and verbal descriptive statements of the behavioral correlate scales. In addition, a profile of Base Rate scores for each of the subscales is provided. The authors have elected to use Base Rate or cutoff scores as opposed to standard scores because of the assumption that the underlying traits being measured are not normally distributed throughout the population. The clinical interpretive report, in addition to the above information, contains a listing of problem areas such as "social alienation," "behavioral problems," or "emotional difficulties." Each of these areas appears to be triggered by key items which are then printed out very much like the critical items in the MMPI. In addition, a paragraph is provided which reviews treatment implications.

The Millon has a well-written, comprehensive manual. The authors make the point that the test has been developed using an established, theoretical rationale, while also employing external validation techniques. The fact that the test is written in language which can be readily understood by adolescents adds significantly to its credibility. This aspect alone distinguishes it from other instruments which have been adapted for adolescent use such as the MMPI and the CPI. The test construction procedures used for the MAPI are systematic and well thought out. For example, the statistical procedures used for item and scale selection are based on the actuarial model of assessment in which it is assumed that behavioral traits exist in the general population in a distribution which is unknown. The purpose, then, of test construction and standardization is to determine the nature of that distribution.

The manual presents test-retest reliability coefficients together with Kuder-Richardson internal consistency data. These range from .45 to .84 with most subscale reliabilities in the .60s and .70s. While the MAPI standardization sample is relatively large (2,000+ subjects), the reported reliability data is based on *N*s of 105 or less. The authors also report factor analytic data based on the intercorrelation matrix of all 20 subscales using an *N* of 1,138. Finally, the authors present concurrent validity data between the MAPI and other commonly used tests such as the CPI, 16PF, and the EPPS. No concurrent validity information is presented comparing the MAPI to the adolescent norms of the MMPI.

The MAPI has a number of weaknesses. Millon's Theory of Personality Style is sketchy, at best. Given the importance that the authors attach to this theory, a more comprehensive and understandable description of it would be helpful to the test user. As a result of this difficulty, some of the scale descriptions are unclear and inexact. This requires the test user to constantly reread and reinterpret the manual in order to arrive at some reasonable conceptualization of the meaning of certain subscales. The validation procedures used for the Behavioral Correlate Scales is unclear with regard to the clinical populations chosen to contrast with normal adolescents. It would have been helpful if the authors had classified these populations in some way, such as utilization of the DSM-III diagnostic criteria. The authors utilize two scales for determining the reliability of a given administration (reliability index and adjustment score). The reliability scale contains three items which have high face validity. While the authors maintain that this scale is successful in identifying individuals who produce unreliable test results, it is difficult to believe that a three-item scale in and of itself can be reliable. The adjustment score is designed to be similar to the *F* scale on the MMPI. Corrections from this scale are applied to the expressed concerns scales. While the authors maintain that the adjustment scores increase diagnostic accuracy, it is not clear from the manual how this task is empirically accomplished.

It is impossible to evaluate the procedures used for scoring this instrument since no data are provided by the manual which detail precisely how scoring is accomplished. One must simply trust NCS to machine score and interpret the instrument without being able to review the statistical procedures and decision rules used by the computer for making various determinations.

Finally, the factor analytic data presented in the manual, while interesting, is not particularly supportive of the underlying structure of the instrument. This is not surprising since the instrument is not based on traditionally accepted factor analytic test construction techniques. One wonders, therefore, why this information was presented.

In summary, the MAPI represents an excellent addition to the instrumentation available for use with adolescents. It fills a void in the area of personality assessment. The statistical procedures utilized in its standardization are modern and in keeping with the multivariate actuarial model of test development. While the personality theory underlying the instrument is weak, the developmental framework on which the Expressed Concerns are based is well founded. The manual is written in a manner which will be understood by professional psychologists. However, it is doubtful that nonpsychologists will be able to interpret the meaning of this instrument successfully without significant additional statistical and theoretical training. Thus the author's suggestion that the test should find broad use among guidance counselors and social workers trained at the masters level is questionable. It is more likely that the most common users would be school and clinical psychologists who would use the MAPI as part of their psychological test battery for diagnosis and treatment planning.

Review of Millon Adolescent Personality Inventory by THOMAS A. WIDIGER, Assistant Professor of Psychology, University of Kentucky, Lexington, KY:

The Millon Adolescent Personality Inventory (MAPI) is a 150-item, true-false questionnaire with eight "personality style" (PS) scales, eight "expressed concern" (EC) scales, and four "behavioral correlate" (BC) scales. The inventory requires only a sixth-grade reading level and can be completed in less than 20 minutes. Hand scoring templates are not available and cannot be constructed without violating copyright restrictions. The MAPI can be scored only by National Computer Systems (NCS) through the purchase of either the Clinical Interpretive or the Guidance Interpretive computer automated, narrative reports.

The MAPI items and scales were designed to be particularly relevant to the adolescent population. This is an appealing feature in comparison to other inventories (e.g., the MMPI or the California Psychological Inventory) that were designed for adult populations but have been applied to adolescent populations. Millon has also developed an adult clinical inventory that would likely be comparable to the MAPI.

Construction of the MAPI was guided by the psychometric recommendations of Loevinger (1957) and the personality theory of Millon (1969). Providing a measure of expressed concerns and personality styles is consistent with the current multiaxial format for clinical evaluation (Spitzer, Williams, & Skodol, 1980). Items for the PS and EC scales were selected on the basis of their explicit sampling of relevant traits and attitudes. Scale construction also considered point-biserial correlations between items and scale totals. According to the manual, "Items that showed high correlations (usually .30 or more) with any scale other than a theoretically incompatible one were added as an item to that scale." Independent clinical ratings of the personality styles and expressed concerns of 430 adolescents were collected to determine their base rates and to set scale cutoff points for clinical interpretation to correspond to these base rates, but these data were apparently not used to empirically evaluate the differential predictive validity of the PS and EC items or scales. No cross validation of the cutoff points was reported. In contrast, the items for the four BC scales were based solely on empirical data and were not subject to initial theoretical-substantive analysis.

The MAPI also includes three validity measures: (*a*) an "adjustment score" that consists of altering the score on particular EC scales depending on which PS scale is highest, (*b*) a three-item "reliability index" that makes direct inquiries regarding the reliability of the subject's responses, and (*c*) a three-item "validity index" of nonsensical items to detect random responders. No data regarding the adjustment score or the reliability index were presented. It is not clear why adjustments for denial and exaggeration tendencies are made only for the EC scales, and why these adjustments are based on the PS scales. It is also unclear if the reliability index works. If persons are not answering honestly, whether they would become honest in response to the item, "I'm not answering these questions honestly at all," is suspect. If persons are not paying attention, will they pay attention to the item, "I haven't been paying much attention to the questions on these pages"? This simple and direct approach might work, but it would be best to report supportive data. The paucity of empirical support for 16 of 20 MAPI scales is a matter of concern. Lanyon (1984) put it bluntly: "Because validity data are essentially lacking, publication at this time is premature" (p. 687). There are supportive data concerning the convergent and discriminant relationship of the scales to other inventories (Meagher, Zuskar, Millon, & Green, 1978), and Millon (1969, 1981) presents a sophisticated and scholarly literature review to support his taxonomy of personality styles, but there might not be enough basis to warrant the commercial production of a computerized interpretive program.

It is ironic that an inventory that has a weak empirical foundation is available only through a computer automated report. The authors suggest that the possibility of scoring errors, time consumption, and fallible nature of clinical prediction argue against publishing hand scoring templates. They state that "Clinical guidance decisions that are based on deductive inference only, as opposed to statistically derived and empirically demonstrated relationships, are subject to more than a modest degree of interpretive error." However, because the NCS report is based primarily on "deductive inference" and not on empirically demonstrated relationships the potential advantages of an automated report are weakened. Furthermore, hand scoring templates might stimulate additional clinical and research interest that is inhibited by the relatively expensive computer scoring.

An additional concern is the large amount of scale overlap (at times greater than 40%). The authors indicated that this overlap ensures structural validity (i.e., the scales relate in a manner predicted by the theory). Although it is true that uncorrelated scales would be inconsistent with the natural covariation of personality styles, expressed concerns, and behaviors, correlations built in by item overlap can be equally problematic. For example, one cannot use the MAPI to independently test hypotheses regarding personality styles and expressed concerns without artifactually obtaining relationships suggested by Millon's (1969, 1981) theory. In fact, many of the scale intercorrelations exceed the scales' test-retest and Kuder-Richardson reliabilities (although at times this appears to be unrelated to item overlap).

A final warning concerns the base rate scores. The cutoff points for each scale were chosen to select the percentage of persons with each personality style, attitude, or behavior that was equal to the base rate for each of the above constructs in a sample of 430 adolescents (325 outpatient and 105 inpatient) "drawn from diverse and representative settings." The frequency of correct decisions is maximized when the cutoff points for an inventory are adjusted according to the local base rate (Meehl & Rosen, 1955). However, if the test consumer's local base rate differs from the derivation sample, which is likely, the cutoff points will not be optimal. Furthermore, test consumers cannot determine the degree of inaccuracy or make their own adjustments because the derivation base rates and sample characteristics were not reported.

SUMMARY. According to Millon, "What appears to be needed for those working with adolescents...is some mechanism, a Rosetta Stone if you will, for decoding the mystery of these divergent behaviors and moods, a tool that will illuminate these matters in ways relevant to their resolution." The MAPI appears to be a potentially useful inventory for describing an adolescent's current personality style, expressed concerns, and behavioral correlates. The constructs measured by the MAPI appear to be topical and more useful to clinicians working with adolescents than other current personality inventories. However, commercial production has preceded adequate empirical evaluation. The MAPI scales have little empirical foundation. The personality and expressed concern items were selected on the basis of their apparent sampling of theoretical constructs (face validity), the cutoff points for the scales were chosen on the basis of unspecified base rates, and the percentages of correct decisions resulting from use of the cutoff points have not been cross validated. The MAPI should be given serious consideration by clinicians working with adolescents, particularly if they are relying on inventories that are more appropriate to an adult population. However, interpretive conclusions from the MAPI should remain tentative until additional empirical support is available.

REVIEWER'S REFERENCES

Meehl, P., & Rosen, A. Antecedent probability and the efficiency of psychometric signs, patterns, or cutting scores. PSYCHOLOGICAL BULLETIN, 1955, 52, 194–216.

Loevinger, J. Objective tests as instruments of psychological theory. PSYCHOLOGICAL REPORTS, 1957, 3, 635–694. (Monograph supplement 9.)

Millon, T. MODERN PSYCHOPATHOLOGY: A BIOSOCIAL APPROACH TO MALADAPTIVE LEARNING AND FUNCTIONING. Philadephia, PA: W. B. Saunders, 1969.

Meagher, R. B. J., Zuskar, D. M., Millon, T., & Green, C. J. The development of a scale assessing self-discontent in an adolescent psychological inventory. MEASUREMENT AND EVALUATION IN GUIDANCE, 1978, 11, 136–142.

Spitzer, R. L., Williams, J. B. W., & Skodol, A. E. DSM-III: The major achievements and an overview. AMERICAN JOURNAL OF PSYCHIATRY, 1980, 137, 151–164.

Millon, T. DISORDERS OF PERSONALITY: DSM-III. AXIS II. New York: Wiley, 1981.

Lanyon, R. Personality assessment. ANNUAL REVIEW OF PSYCHOLOGY, 1984, 35, 667–701.

[708]

Millon Behavioral Health Inventory. Physical and behavioral medicine patients ages 17 and over; 1981–82; MBHI; 8th-grade reading level required; machine scorable only; 17 to 20 scores in 3 to 4 areas: basic coping style (introversive, inhibited, cooperative, sociable, confident, forceful, respectful, sensitive), psychogenic attitudes (chronic tension, recent stress, premorbid pessimism, future despair, social alienation, somatic anxiety), prognostic indices (pain treatment responsivity, life threat reactivity, emotional vulnerability), plus scores for patients exhibiting specific disease syndromes: psychosomatic correlates (allergic inclination, gastrointestinal susceptibility, cardiovascular tendency); 1 form ('81, 4 pages); manual, third edition ('82, 44 pages); 1984 price data: $16.50 and less per test, scoring and reporting service included; $10 per manual; $17.50 per specimen set; (20) minutes; Theodore Millon, Catherine J. Green, and Robert B. Meagher; NCS Interpretive Scoring Systems.*

TEST REFERENCES

1. Millon, T., Green, C. J., & Meagher, R. B., Jr. The MBHI: A new inventory for the psychodiagnostician in medical settings. PROFESSIONAL PSYCHOLOGY, 1979, 10, 529–539.

Review of Millon Behavioral Health Inventory by MARY J. ALLEN, Professor of Psychology, California State College, Bakersfield, Bakersfield, CA:

This 150-item true-false questionnaire yields 20 scores plus a three-item validity scale and is intended for use with "physically ill" or "behavioral medicine" patients.

ADMINISTRATION AND SCORING. The test is self-administered and can be hand-scored (no scoring keys are available, but sufficient information is in the manual to make your own) or machine-scored. Machine scoring provides a profile and Interpretive Report similar to MMPI narrative reports. Instructions specify that subjects are to mark "False" if they cannot decide on an answer. It is not clear if omits are scored as "False" or ignored. The percentage of False responses contributing to each scale ranges from 0 to 81% (median=23%), suggesting that subjects with acquiescent response sets would tend to have elevated profiles. Ten or 15 point corrections in the psychogenic attitude scores are made if specified coping style scores are the highest. No empirical justification or validation for these specific adjustments are described and unreliability of profile shape is not taken into account.

TEST DEVELOPMENT. Sixty-four core items for the eight Basic Coping Styles, 83 core items for the six Psychogenic Attitude scales, and 3 items for the validity scale were selected based upon professional agreement and (for the coping scales) item-scale correlation patterns consistent with theory. These 150 items were administered "in a large number of medical settings" to develop the empirical scales. The three Psychosomatic Correlates Scales were begun by isolating 134 allergic inclination, 212 gastrointestinal, and 197 cardiovascular tendency patients and having "physicians, nurses, and/or other health personnel who knew them for a period of time" judge whether psychosocial factors exacerbate their symptoms on a 4-point scale (from "definitely" to "doubtfully"). Items that discriminated between the two extreme groups were selected in two-thirds of the sample and cross-validated in the remaining third. Only items that "held up" were retained as core items. Similar techniques were used for the Pain Treatment Responsivity and Life Threat Reactivity scales (two of the Prognostic Index Scales).

It is not clear what percentage of each of the groups were placed in the two extreme categories, so the cross-validation samples may have been very small. The type of analysis used (presumably over 150 chi-square tests for each scale) and the *p*-level considered significant were not given. A predominance of women or older subjects in the "definitely" category may have confounded these scales with gender or age. This apparently was not examined. It is not clear how many raters judged the patients, if interrater reliabilities were examined, or if any physical evidence supported the validity of the diagnoses or judgements. The Emotional Vulnerability scale was composed of items that discriminated for psychological disturbance on the Millon Clinical Multiaxial Inventory.

At this point an unspecified number of items comprised each of the 20 scales. Analyses of item-scale correlation patterns added items to each scale with theoretically reasonable patterns. Since it is not clear what percentage of the items were added to each scale in this way, the scales (especially the empirical ones) are more difficult to interpret. The manual states that each of the empirical scales was cross-validated at least once and "some of the scales have 'held up' as effective discriminators." The need for more careful and systematic validity analyses is essential because of the heavy reliance on face validity judgments in all stages of test development.

NORMS. The test developers state that "the use of the MBHI should be limited to populations that are not notably different in background from the samples employed to develop the instrument's base rate norms," implying that the manual will carefully describe this group. Unfortunately, this was not done. Most of the norms apparently are based on 752 subjects (45% male, 40% patients, 82% white). The physical problems of the patient groups are not specified, nor are the ages or geographical location of any of the norm groups.

All of the scales, except for the six psychogenic attitude ones, are converted to base rate (BR) scores (numbers ranging from 0 to 115). BR 75 and BR 85 are arbitrarily designated as suggesting the "presence" or "prominence" of a trait. The manual states that these cut scores maximize hit rates for classification, but no data on hit rates and false positives among non-patients and patients are provided. The manual reports that the six psychogenic scores are transformed to *T* scores, "suggesting a normalized distribution." The standard 50 ± 10 *T* scores obviously were not used, the scores are interpreted like BRs, and the actual shapes of the distributions are not described. There is no information provided on how the BRs correspond to the probabilities of exhibiting a trait. Does a BR of 115 suggest a 100%, 50%, or 5% chance?

BRs are different for men and women. Although the authors suggest that other moderator variables may affect the BR, no data are presented on differences among medical, health history, age, or ethnic groups. It seems likely that these variables would affect scale interpretations. Since no normative data are presented (e.g., percentiles or standardized scores), the test user has no information about how typical a score may be for men or women in general or for the patient category under consideration.

RELIABILITY. Although single scores can be interpreted, the authors state that "profile interpretation is the primary method of evaluating MBHI results." Profile analysis is most reasonable with highly reliable, uncorrelated scales. Test-retest reliabilities for "a general population" of unspecified size and undefined characteristics (e.g., age, gender, ethnicity, regionality) over a mean time interval of 4.5 months (range not given) are from .59 to .90 (median=.82). Reliability information for the target population (medical patients) is not provided, but since "reliability data are contaminated by changes in life circumstances," one would expect these reliabilities to be lower. Kuder-Richardson Formula 20 reliability estimates are from .66 to .90 (median=.82). I can only assume that reliability estimates were based on raw scores. Since the transformation to BR scores is non-linear (a change in one raw score point translates into a change of from 0 to 35 BR points), it is not clear what the reliabilities of the BR scores are.

Reported correlations among the scales are high, based on a sample of 337 patients and 224 non-patients (diagnoses, age, gender, etc., unspecified). If correlations for a "preliminary version" of the Pain Treatment Responsivity Scale (relation to the final PP scale not given) are omitted, virtually half of the interscale correlations are at least .60, with about 20% over .80. Some intercorrelations are as high as reliabilities allow. For example, scales 3 (Cooperative) and 6 (Forceful) correlate –.93 and have estimated reliabilities of about .7 or .8. Each of these scales consists of 33 items; 25 of these items are in common (but reverse scored). Scales 2 (Inhibited) and E (Social Alienation) correlate .92, have estimated reliabilities of about .85, and have 24 items in common. Because scales are so highly correlated it is not surprising that the reported factor analysis yields a first factor that accounts for "more than half of the variance" and three factors that account for 93% of the variance. It appears that 2–3 scores might be substituted for the 20 and yield a more reasonably interpreted profile.

INTERPRETATION. The authors recommend a profile analysis, but do not explicitly or implicitly discuss the reliability or standard errors of relevant difference scores. The computer narrative interpretation is based upon empirical and theoretical rationale so that "100 percent of all possible MBHI profiles can be interpreted." No evidence is provided for the validity of the computer interpretation. Since the test interpreter is likely to be a physician or nurse without psychometric sophistication, providing a profile of moderately reliable, highly intercorrelated scores and a narrative without explicit reference citations seems a dangerous practice.

The manual reports correlations with a variety of other published tests based upon a variety of samples (again, not specified). It is not clear why the selected scales were chosen and if "unexpected" correlations were omitted. Moderate (about .5) correlations between MBHI scales and various depression scales were common. Several validity studies were reported, with mixed results. Clearly more work in this area is required.

SUMMARY. The MBHI manual inadequately describes test construction, norming procedures, and test interpretation. The 20 clinical scales have moderate reliability in a non-patient sample and unknown reliability among patients. The reliability of the BR scores is unspecified. The scales correlate rather highly with each other, making the suggested profile analyses difficult, and they appear to measure only two or three dimensions. Empirical evidence for the validity of the computer narrative interpretation and the usefulness of the test in medical settings should be more firmly substantiated.

Review of Millon Behavioral Health Inventory by RICHARD I. LANYON, Professor of Psychology, Arizona State University, Tempe, AZ:

The rapid development of health psychology as a field and the high degree of interest in assessment questions are indications that there is a need for a high quality psychometric instrument specifically geared toward assisting professionals to make decisions about persons with physical health problems. The Millon Behavioral Health Inventory (MBHI), a 20-scale inventory with 150 items, was designed to meet this need. The publisher's advertising brochure describes the MBHI as "an unprecedented tool," "the single tool that does the work of many. Better." "Never, before the MBHI, has such a comprehensive inventory been available for application in such a wide range of medical settings." The brochure praises the "no-compromise refinement" in scale development through a "triple validation" procedure, and mentions "cross-validation in clinics, HMO's, and rehabilitation centers."

The first 8 scales of the MBHI represent concepts of "basic coping styles" in Millon's own theoretical scheme, although unfortunately the reader is provided with no information about this scheme, and is thus unable to evaluate its potential utility. The remaining 12 scales, 6 for psychogenic attitudes, 3 for psychosomatic correlates, and 3 for prognostic indicators, have no theoretical or conceptual framework, but are said either to reflect the findings in the literature on a topic or to have been derived empirically.

The section in the manual on the actual mechanics of scale development and construction is inadequate and in places inconsistent. The section on the construction of the 20 scales occupies less than three pages, and the material is all very general in nature. Because there is nothing that is specific to individual scales, it is impossible for the reader to determine the potential strengths or weaknesses of any one of them. A table of scale intercorrelations shows that more than one third of the intercorrelations are .70 or higher, indicating a high degree of redundancy among the scales and concepts. This is not unexpected since there are only 150 items for 20 scales, so that each item appears on an average of 4.6 different scales. The redundancy is further demonstrated in a factor analysis, which shows that fully 15 of the 20 scales load .40 or more on the first factor, with 10 of these loadings above .70.

The exact nature and size of the samples on which the MBHI was constructed and normed are not specified in the manual. It appears that a group of 752 males and females, a mixture of patients and nonpatients, was utilized both for construction and for representing the final norms. Norms for the six psychogenic attitude scales are expressed in traditional *T*-score form; however, for the remaining 14 scales, the prevalence or base rate of each characteristic was estimated and incorporated into a transformation, resulting in something called "base rate scores," which are not directly comparable with *T*-scores. The table of norm distributions does not reveal any obvious differences between *T*-scores and base rate scores, however.

It has to be concluded that the MBHI was not constructed with a high degree of psychometric care, despite the manual's statements to the contrary. The major support for its utility must therefore come from post-constructive empirical validity evidence, involving cross-validation data from studies of its actual use. The only systematic validity data given in the manual consist of correlations between the first 14 scales and several other inventories, including the MMPI, CPI, Beck Depression Inventory (BDI), and SCL-90. The highest correlates involve the MMPI Depression and Hypochondriasis scales, the BDI, and CPI scales related to social skills. Although relatively few of the total number of correlations are reported, these data do provide an initial basis for establishing the empirical meanings of the scales.

Aside from these correlations with other paper-and-pencil inventories, validity data are almost entirely absent from the manual, and do not appear to have been published elsewhere. Two pages of "Recent Research Projects" in the manual describe the findings of several unpublished theses and dissertations which have used the MBHI. But these do not provide systematic data on the test's empirical validity; rather one of them describes the construction of one of the scales, while two others describe the outcome of treatment programs for chronic pain and sexual dysfunction respectively. Ironically, the pain treatment study does not mention the patients' scores on the Pain Treatment Responsivity scale!

At the request of this reviewer, the publisher of the MBHI provided copies of a number of unpublished (and in some cases, incompleted) research studies on the MBHI. These studies tend to show mixed and sometimes limited utility for the MBHI in making predictions and discriminations related to such factors as attendance at a cardiovascular exercise facility, weight loss among obese patients in treatment, coronary bypass surgery, and pain management. Also sent by the publisher was a page entitled "On the validation of the MCMI, MBHI, and MAPI," addressing and justifying the current lack of published validation data. The relevant parts of this page stated that (1) in the construction phase of each inventory, "the equivalent of over 40–50 publishable studies, condensed and summarized in each test's manual, were carried out before publication of each inventory...reported in Chapters 4 and 5 of each test manual"; and (2) "a substantial number of publications will be forthcoming in the near future." These claims and promises should not obscure the fact that adequate construction and validity information is not contained in the manual, even though it is already in its third edition. Incidentally, there is no Chapter 5.

The validity question is also troublesome because of the computer interpretation system that must be used. Hand-scorable answer sheets and profile forms are not available, leaving the user little option but to utilize the publisher's services at $16.50 per single test, or $13.75 each for 2–24 tests (as of 1984). The manual does contain material on interpretation, but this consists mostly of favorable comparisons between patient case notes and corresponding paragraphs from the computer-produced interpretive report. Because there are so few empirical data to support the computer reports, users must accept them almost entirely on faith. This is an even more untenable situation than where computer interpretations are offered for an established and validated test such as the MMPI; there, at least the test's capabilities are known, even if the quality of a particular program is not. With the MBHI, there are two unrelated and unanswered validity questions: pertaining to the test itself, and pertaining to the computer interpretation program.

In sum, the difficulties with the MBHI at the present time are serious enough that this reviewer recommends against its use until either systematic validity data for the automated interpretations are made available, or the necessary materials and information are provided so that it can be used by hand at one's own risk.

[709]

Millon Clinical Multiaxial Inventory. Adults receiving psychotherapy or participating in psychological assessment; 1967–81; MCMI; report discusses relationships between the more transient DSM-III clinical disorders (Axis I) and the more enduring personality disorders (Axis II); 20 scores: 8 basic personality styles (schizoid, avoidant, dependent, histrionic, narcissistic, antisocial, compulsive, passive-aggressive), 3 pathological personality syndromes (schizotypal, borderline, paranoid), 6 symptom disorders scales of moderate severity (anxiety, somatoform, hypomanic, dysthymia, alcohol abuse, drug abuse), 3 symptom disorder scales of extreme severity (psychotic thinking, psychotic depression, psychotic delusions), plus 2 additional correction scales which provide a means to identify and adjust possible test-taking distortion; Form C ('76, 4 pages); manual ('77, 81 pages); profile/interpretive sample report ('81, 4 pages); 1984 price data: $5.05 or less per 25 tests; $6 per 25 hand scored answer sheets; $36 per set of answer keys with manual; $3.50 per 25 profiles; $11 per manual; $17.75 per specimen set; NCS scoring service, $6 or less per test; (20–40) minutes; Theodore Millon; NCS Interpretive Scoring Systems.*

See T3:1488 (3 references).

TEST REFERENCES

1. Green, C. J. The diagnostic accuracy and utility of MMPI and MCMI computer interpretive reports. JOURNAL OF PERSONALITY ASSESSMENT, 1982, 46, 359–365.

Review of Millon Clinical Multiaxial Inventory by ALLEN K. HESS, Associate Professor of Psychology, Auburn University, Auburn, AL:

The Millon Clinical Multiaxial Inventory (MCMI) is a 175-item true-false inventory which appears designed to answer the question: "Which type of chronic psychopathology does the respondent have?" The second major impression this inventory casts is the ineluctable comparisons with the MMPI that are made in the MCMI Test Manual, and that anyone considering this instrument will make.

The MCMI is a direct operationalization of Millon's taxonomy proposed in *modern psychopathology* (1969). This carefully constructed test never received the attention it merited. The text presents a taxonomy which is to account for (1) severity of the disorder, (2) covariation or clustering of signs, (3) a four (source of reinforcement) by two (active-passive) matrix of disorders, (4) a circumplicial set of related pathognomonic signs, (5) continuity between the premorbid personality and severe impairment, and (6) the separation between biological, situational, and personality factors. This formidable agenda of two major impressions and six items, plus the criteria in the *Standards for Educational and Psychological Tests*, are the benchmarks for our consideration of the MCMI.

The MMPI originated as an attempt to distinguish those whom insulin coma therapy would benefit from those who would be non-responders. This goal was soon translated into providing a part of the clinical intake for treatment planning, and from that goal, a burst of Kuhnian puzzle-solving activities began that has not yet slackened. The MMPI was applied to problems (e.g., Pharisaic virtue, success in baseball) far from its origins. The MMPI authors and Oscar Buros anticipated the MMPI's replacement by instruments capitalizing on psychometric and theoretical advances in the ensuing four decades. Millon attempts to do just that.

A 73-page manual introduces the conceptual goals of the MCMI and describes its scales. The scales are divided into three content sets: Basic Personality Styles, or premorbid, everyday functioning characterizing the patients; Pathological Personality Syndromes, or descriptions of patients showing chronic or episodic severe pathology in their overall personality; and Symptom Disorders, or reactive, often dramatic displays accentuating the Basic Personality Styles but in more intense forms.

The various scales of the MCMI are listed in the descriptive entry preceding this review. Each of the basic personality and pathological syndrome scales is further described by five features. For example, Scale 1: Schizoid (Asocial) is composed of affectivity deficit, mild cognitive slippage, interpersonal indifference, behavioral apathy, and perceptual insensitivity. And each element is further defined (e.g., for affectivity deficit the manual states, "exhibits intrinsic emotional blandness; reports weak affectionate needs and an inability to display enthusiasm or experience pleasure").

Chapter 2 of the manual provides clear instructions for administration. It advises the reader of the intentional unavailability of scoring templates (they can be constructed from Appendix D) and the availability of machine scoring and automated interpretative reports. The balance of chapter 2 discusses norms and base rate scores. Information regarding geographical location, socioeconomic status, sex, and age of the patient groups but not of the normative, non-clinical or "normal" group, are presented. The test uses base rate scores rather than standard scores in accord with some two to three decades of psychometricians calling for use of base rates. However, a clearer exposition is needed of how base rate scores were generated and how they are to be used. While a base rate score approach is laudable, its unfamiliarity to most test consumers requires more explanation. This is especially so since the MCMI is designed for diagnostic use; however, one person may use it with inpatient clients while another may use it for outpatient screening. Thus two samples with entirely different base rates may be subjected to the same cutting scores, yielding classification accuracy rates different from those in the manual. Separate sample base rates for different groups are not presented, although Tables III:1 and III:2 present base rate syndrome data for MCMI construction samples.

Chapter 3, "Interpretation," describes classification accuracy of the scales, which range from the 78% level to the 97% level for the MCMI construction sample. These figures are comparable for the cross-validation sample. The chapter then presents a code typing procedure, commonly occurring code types, and three case examples. The chapter concludes with a discussion of automated reports. The manual claims that because of the power of the actuarial-theoretical Millon system, "100 percent of all possible MCMI profiles can be interpreted." This is based on the notion that quantitative descriptive ratings were obtained in the MCMI's construction, and where these leave gaps, the clinically based theory bridges the gaps. It is the nature of formistic or typal models to more or less approximate an ideal type, or to meet or miss inclusion in a group's criterion set. However, in carving nature to joint, any system meets human variation and the system's gaps become more apparent. The MCMI needs more field trials before we can determine how many of the 100% of interpretable profiles truly fit their types. For example, organic and retarded conditions come to mind as two clinical syndromes that need to be screened by means other than the MCMI.

The chapter then discusses the automated reports, available only through National Computer Systems. The reports are sets of statements providing leads to be checked by the clinician. The basis for the combinations of statements is not specific.

Chapter 4 describes the MCMI's construction and, with chapter 5, which describes reliability and validity data, ought to appear before chapter 3, Interpretation. A well articulated discussion of the theoretical bases of the MCMI is presented. Recapitulation of the Millon typal theory shows "personality," "clinical," and "psychopathology" to have largely overlapping, if not identical, meanings for Millon. Contrary to the temper of our time, the MCMI is unabashedly trait and pathology oriented. Positive aspects of personality are absent. States appear as modifier variables of pervasive, deeply etched personality styles, serving to either accentuate or attenuate these styles.

The significant item overlap between scales is described as appropriate to a clinical model whereby scales ought to share variance and join together in syndromes. Yet this overlap plays havoc with statistical analyses. For example, chapter 5's factor analysis shows Scales 8, C, A, H, D and CC to load .892 or better on Factor 1. Yet of Scale A's 37 items, all but 4 appear on at least one of the other five scales. Thirty-three (89%) of Scale A's items are shared, making the meaning of the loadings questionable. The proposed cluster or pattern analysis projects will be based on such overlapping scales (36.65 items per scale, 175 total items, 20 clinical scales, and 2 validity scales), with their built-in exaggerations of shared variance.

Reliability studies in chapter 5 show 1-week test-retest reliability coefficients of an .87 average for Basic Personality Scales, .85 for Pathological Personality Syndromes, and .81 for Symptom Disorder Scales. Test-retest coefficients for 5-week intervals average .82, .77, and .67 for the three sets of scales. The latter are theoretically expected since Symptom Disorders are by nature reactive or transient. Kuder-Richardson 20 coefficients average .83, .90, and .82 for Basic Personality Styles, Pathological Personality Syndromes, and Symptom Disorders Scales, respectively. These are admirable considering the set of different components constituting a disorder tapped by a scale.

The balance of chapter 5 concerns validity studies. The MCMI correlates with the Symptom Distress Checklist-90 (SCL-90), the Psychological Screening Inventory (PSI), and the MMPI (basic scales plus Wiggins Content Scales) in theoretically expected and clinically meaningful patterns. Fake good, fake bad, and random response profiles are presented, as are ratings by clinicians of the usefulness of the MCMI automated report and two widely used MMPI Interpretative Report programs. The chapter concludes with research suggestions.

The MCMI is an excellent experimental test designed to describe psychopathology. It leaves many questions open, which speaks against its clinical use as it exists. Two caveats are (1) that it should be used with other instruments, and (2) that its profligate use of "red flag" diagnostic terms throughout the manual and the report may lead the user to view the client solely as pathological. Certainly clients who see their own report will react adversely.

The MCMI presents a rich research agenda. Longitudinal studies of profile types are warranted. Scaling studies are necessary to determine whether Symptom Disorders are more intense forms of Personality Styles. The circumplicial model of Personality Styles needs testing. The Millon typology is much like a Chinese medicine cabinet. There are rows and columns of drawers. It is the underlying theory which places a drawer's contents close to or far from other medicines, and the combinations which render potent potions. Millon's theory of the active-passive and sources of reinforcement matrix is untested. Do active-detached and active-independent types differ in behavior as shown by research? Such research to test Millon's theory will determine the potency of the MCMI.

Ironically, Millon concludes the manual by calling for research on responses to therapeutic modalities including drug therapies. We have come full circle from the origins of the MMPI to the agenda of the MCMI.

REVIEWER'S REFERENCES

Millon, T. MODERN PSYCHOPATHOLOGY. Philadelphia: Saunders, 1969.

Review of Millon Clinical Multiaxial Inventory by THOMAS A. WIDIGER, Assistant Professor of Psychology, University of Kentucky, Lexington, KY:

The Millon Clinical Multiaxial Inventory (MCMI) is a 175-item, self-report inventory that provides scores on 20 clinical scales and two "Correction Scales" (including a Validity Index). It was published in 1977 and was heralded by Butcher and Owen (1978) as the most recent challenger to the MMPI.

ADVANTAGES. The MCMI's construction was explicitly guided by the substantive, structural, and external considerations of construct validity formulated by Loevinger (1957) and by a consideration of weaknesses of the MMPI. Whereas the MMPI has been criticized for its inordinate length, inclusion of many unused items, and absence of any theoretical rationale for scale overlap (Dahlstrom, 1972; Norman, 1972), the MCMI is considerably shorter and the scale overlaps were guided by Millon's (1969, 1981) theoretical system. MCMI items were evaluated in terms of their ability to differentiate between particular clinical groups and a general psychiatric population and their sampling of relevant theoretical constructs. Butcher and Owen (1978) suggested that the explicit representation of traits and symptoms might make the MCMI susceptible to dissimulation. However, the MCMI includes a "Weight Factor" that is used to detect denial and exaggeration tendencies and to make appropriate scoring adjustments. The Weight Factor is based on the degree of deviation from the mid-range of the composite raw score total, and has been successful in detecting "faking good" and "faking bad" in nonclinical respondents. There is also a "Validity Index" consisting of four nonsensical items, but it is so brief and obvious that it could only serve to detect an occasional random responder.

A major advantage of the MCMI over the MMPI is its apparent relationship to the current diagnostic nomenclature. Although the MMPI continues to be a very popular inventory, its items, scales, and popular profile codes are based on the antiquated DSM-I. Considerable changes have occurred in the form and content of psychiatric diagnosis (Spitzer, Williams, & Skodol, 1980), and the MMPI's relationship to the DSM-III taxonomy is subject to question (e.g., Winters, Weintraub, & Neale, 1981). There is now considerable emphasis on the diagnosis of personality disorders (Frances, 1980), a task for which the MMPI is not well suited. No other self-report inventory is as closely related to the Axis II diagnoses as the MCMI. Each of the 11 personality scales of the MCMI is entitled by a respective Axis II diagnosis; elevations on the personality and clinical syndrome scales are considered to be diagnostic of the Axis II and Axis I disorders; and the computer automated Interpretive Report by the National Computer Service (NCS) provides diagnoses on Axes I, II, and IV. The personality and clinical syndromes measured by the MCMI are clearly more relevant to current practice than the MMPI. The apparent congruency between the MCMI and DSM-III is bolstered by Millon's (1983b) membership on the American Psychiatric Association's Advisory Committee for the Personality Disorders. According to the MCMI manual, "Since the author of the MCMI was a member of the task force that developed the DSM-III, much of what evolved in the committee's deliberations reflected the diagnostic conceptions the author employed in formulating the theory that underlies the MCMI."

DISADVANTAGES. The above advantages, however, have at times been overstated and oversold. For example, although the scale overlap does ensure that the scales will relate in a manner suggested by Millon's (1969, 1981) taxonomy, "when 20 scales averaging 37 items per scale are scored from a common pool of only 171 items, the psychometric consequences of such a high degree of scale redundancy will almost certainly be unfavorable" (Wiggins, 1982, p. 211). For instance, one cannot use the scales to independently measure the relationship among disorders or between disorders and external variables since covariations suggested by Millon's (1969, 1981) theory are built into the tests through the item overlap among scales (Widiger & Kelso, 1983).

There are also major problems with the interpretation of the MCMI scale scores. In the MCMI manual Millon describes three methods of MCMI interpretation: (*a*) single scale diagnostic decisions, (*b*) clinical profile interpretations, and (*c*) automated computer reports. In the first approach one would diagnose either the presence or the prominence of a syndrome when it achieves a "base rate score" greater than 75 or 85, respectively. The base rate score is a conversion of the raw score "by known personality and syndrome prevalence data." Simply put, the base rate score is an adjustment to the cutoff point to maximize correct classification by considering the effect of a base rate on the frequency of true positives and false positives (Meehl & Rosen, 1955). Disorders with low base rates will require relatively higher cutoff points and disorders with high base rates will require lower cutoff points. This is a sophisticated approach, but the cutoff scores employed by Millon and the NCS will not optimize accurate diagnosis when the local base rates differ from the base rates obtained in Millon's normative sample (Butcher & Owen, 1978). "An inflexible cutting score should not be advocated for any psychometric device" (Meehl & Rosen, 1955, p. 201). If the local base rate differs from the normative sample (e.g., 35% dependent, 12% antisocial, and 25% passive-aggressive), the cutoff points will no longer optimize accurate diagnosis. The MCMI would be improved by employing alternative cutoff points that varied according to the local base rate.

The second method of interpretation, clinical profile interpretation, involves a rational interpretation of the pattern of scale scores based on the theory and research regarding the MCMI. Millon acknowledges that the ability to interpret an MCMI profile is dependent upon the empirical validity of the inventory, the veridicality of the theory, the skill of the clinician, and the clinician's experience with the MCMI, all of which are subject to question. Furthermore, although the manual does provide "the steps and logic for using the configural pattern of scores on the MCMI as a basis for profile interpretation," up until recently one has not been able to obtain the scale scores necessary for single scale or profile interpretation. Hand scoring templates have not been available, the weight factor adjustment for denial and exaggeration tendencies is not presented in the manual, and one could not purchase a test booklet without first paying for the NCS automated computer report. There was little point in suggesting single scale or profile interpretation in the manual if one was required to purchase in advance the NCS Interpretive Report (approximately $17.00 per report purchased singly). The NCS, however, now intends to produce hand scoring templates and a scores-only computer report (K. Moreland, NCS, personal communication, April 11, 1984). Both will likely be available by the time this review is published.

The NCS Interpretive Report is a clinically sophisticated, comprehensive report, but it may be oversold. The report provides DSM-III Axis I and Axis II diagnoses, but there has never been any published research to support this usage of the MCMI (Lanyon, 1984). In the studies that derived and cross-validated the scale cutoff points, clinicians were given narrative descriptions of Millon's (1969) personality types. The clinicians did not have available, nor could they have been aware of, the DSM-III disorders and their diagnostic criteria. There has been no research published in the test manual or any journal that has indicated the extent to which the MCMI is predictive of DSM-III disorders. The only psychodiagnostic research published outside of the test manual is by Green (1982), which simply demonstrated a face validity for the NCS report. Data concerning the relationship between the MCMI and DSM-III should have been collected and reported prior to the presentation of the MCMI as a measure of DSM-III.

The MCMI could still be a good measure of DSM-III disorders if the DSM-III were based on Millon's (1969, 1981) taxonomy but this does not appear to be true. DSM-III eschewed any particular theoretical orientation (Spitzer et al., 1980). Axis II is in fact more of a collection of opposing theoretical orientations than a reflection of a single perspective. The Antisocial diagnosis reflects Robins' influence, the Avoidant reflects Millon, the Borderline reflects Kernberg and Gunderson, the Schizotypal reflects Rosenthal, Wender, and Kety, and the Narcissistic reflects the recent psychoanalytic literature (Frances, 1980; Gunderson, 1983; Spitzer, Endicott, & Gibbon, 1979; Widiger & Frances, in press). Inspection of the MCMI scale items clearly indicates that they sample the Millon (1981) personality types but often fail to adequately sample the Axis II disorders. Millon (1981) has in fact acknowledged disparities between his Aggressive and Negativistic types and the DSM-III Antisocial and Passive-Aggressive disorders, respectively. In addition, the NCS (1984, p. 5) report has added a disclaimer that "although the diagnostic criteria utilized in the MCMI differ somewhat from those in the DSM-III, there are sufficient parallels to recommend consideration of" DSM-III diagnoses. It would be even better to refrain altogether from identifying the NCS (1984) printout as a "DSM-III Report," from titling the MCMI scale with the names of the Axis II disorders, and from suggesting that scale elevations are diagnostic of DSM-III disorders. The MCMI might be a better measure of DSM-III than the MMPI, but it was constructed and validated as a measure of Millon's (1969, 1981) taxonomy, not DSM-III.

SUMMARY. The development of the MCMI followed a sophisticated model of test construction, with close attention given to substantive, structural, and external validity. The inventory provides measurements of syndromes of current interest to clinicians, and it is likely to be a better measure of DSM-III disorders than the MMPI. However, the positive features of the MCMI have been overstated. First, although the scale overlap is helpful in ensuring structural validity, it also prevents independent empirical validation of alternative theoretical predictions. Second, the cutoff points are optimal only when the local base rates are equivalent to Millon's derivation sample. Third, the MCMI was constructed and validated as a measure of Millon's taxonomy but has been presented as a measure of DSM-III without enough data to support this interpretation. Nevertheless, despite these concerns and limitations the MCMI has considerable potential. There is a need for independent research regarding its concurrent and predictive validity, particularly with respect to DSM-III disorders, but with additional empirical support it should become a useful alternative to the timeworn MMPI. It will not likely ever replace the MMPI, but this will be due to the superior tradition and empirical foundation of the MMPI and not to any unique faults in the MCMI.

REVIEWER'S REFERENCES

Meehl, P., & Rosen, A. Antecedent probability and the efficiency of psychometric signs, patterns, or cutting scores. PSYCHOLOGICAL BULLETIN, 1955, 52, 194–216.

Loevinger, J. Objective tests as instruments of psychological theory. PSYCHOLOGICAL REPORTS, 1957, 3, 635–694. (Monograph supplement 9.)

Millon, T. MODERN PSYCHOPATHOLOGY: A BIOSOCIAL APPROACH TO MALADAPTIVE LEARNING AND FUNCTIONING. Philadelphia: W. B. Saunders, 1969.

Dahlstrom, W. G. Whither the MMPI? In J. N. Butcher (Ed.), OBJECTIVE PERSONALITY ASSESSMENT: CHANGING PERSPECTIVES. New York: Academic, 1972.

Norman, W. T. Psychometric considerations for a revision of the MMPI. In J. N. Butcher (Ed.), OBJECTIVE PERSONALITY ASSESSMENT: CHANGING PERSPECTIVES. New York: Academic, 1972.

Butcher, J., & Owen, P. Objective personality inventories: Recent research and some contemporary issues. In B. B. Wolman (Ed.), CLINICAL DIAGNOSIS OF MENTAL DISORDERS. A HANDBOOK (pp. 475–546). New York: Plenum, 1978.

Spitzer, R. L., Endicott, J., & Gibbon, M. Crossing the border into borderline personality and borderline schizophrenia. ARCHIVES OF GENERAL PSYCHIATRY, 1979, 36, 17–24.

Frances, A. The DSM-III personality disorder section: A commentary. AMERICAN JOURNAL OF PSYCHIATRY, 1980, 137, 1050–1054.

Spitzer, R. L., Williams, J. B. W., & Skodol, A. E. DSM-III: The major achievements and an overview. AMERICAN JOURNAL OF PSYCHIATRY, 1980, 137, 151–164.

Millon, T. DISORDERS OF PERSONALITY: DSM-III. AXIS II. New York: Wiley, 1981.

Winters, K. C., Weintraub, S., & Neale, J. M. Validity of MMPI codetypes in identifying schizophrenics, unipolars, and bipolars. JOURNAL OF CONSULTING AND CLINICAL PSYCHOLOGY, 1981, 49, 486–487.

Green, C. J. The diagnostic accuracy and utility of MMPI and MCMI computer interpretive reports. JOURNAL OF PERSONALITY ASSESSMENT, 1982, 46, 359–365.

Wiggins, J. S. Circumplex models of interpersonal behavior in clinical psychology. In P. C. Kendall & J. N. Butcher (Eds.), HANDBOOK OF RESEARCH METHODS IN CLINICAL PSYCHOLOGY (pp. 183–221). New York: Wiley, 1982.

Gunderson, J. DSM-III diagnosis of personality disorders. In J. Frosch (Ed.), CURRENT PERSPECTIVES ON PERSONALITY DISORDERS (pp. 20–39). Washington, DC: American Psychiatric Press, 1983.

Millon, T. The DSM-III: An insider's perspective. AMERICAN PSYCHOLOGIST, 1983, 38, 804–814.

Widiger, T., & Kelso, K. Psychodiagnosis of Axis II. CLINICAL PSYCHOLOGY REVIEW, 1983, 3, 491–510.

Lanyon, R. Personality assessment. ANNUAL REVIEW OF PSYCHOLOGY, 1984, 35, 667–701.

National Computer Systems. MILLON CLINICAL MULTIAXIAL INVENTORY. DSM-III REPORT. Minneapolis: Author, 1984.

Widiger, T.A., & Frances, A. Axis II personality disorders: Diagnostic and treatment issues. HOSPITAL AND COMMUNITY PSYCHIATRY, 1985, 36, 619-627.

[710]

Minimum Essentials Test. Grades 8–12 and adults; 1980–81; MET; 4–5 scores: basic skills (reading, language, mathematics, plus optional writing), life skills; reliability data for Form A only; no validity data; norms included in test materials for grades 8–12 only; Forms A, B, C, ('80, 20 pages); teacher's manual ('81, 20 pages); technical manual, report 1 ('81, 14 pages); directions for administration ('80, 13 pages); answer key for all forms ('80, 3 pages); separate answer sheets must be used; 1983 price data: $24.85 per 35 tests and 1 directions for administration; $1.30 per answer key; $7.95 per 35 answer sheets; $1.90 per directions for administration; $4.35 per technical manual; $4.30 per teacher's manual; $6.50 per test review kit; scoring service, $.15 per student label, $.65 per student for class list; 45(50) minutes for basic skills section, 45(50) minutes for life skills section, 20(25) minutes for optional writing test; William K. Rice, Jr., Thomas R. Guskey, Carole Lachman Perlman, and Marion F. Rice; American Testronics.*

Review of Minimum Essentials Test by DAVID A. FRISBIE, Associate Director, Evaluation and Examination Service, University of Iowa, Iowa City, IA:

The focus of the Minimum Essentials Test (MET) is implied in the title: assessment of the basic skills deemed essential for graduation from high school. The manual indicates that a major purpose is to "assist school personnel in the early identification of students who will have trouble achieving standards of minimum competence at the time of graduation." A component of the Comprehensive Assessment Program, the MET is intended to be used to place students, to identify those in need of remediation, or to examine students on completion of a basic skills course.

TEST CONTENT. The Basic Skills Test is composed of subtests in Reading, Language, and Mathematics; the separate Life Skills Test represents applications of the basic skills in practical situations. There is also an optional writing exercise. Perhaps the most formidable task facing one who needs to select a test like the MET is judging the degree of fit between the local curriculum objectives and the objectives represented by the test items in the MET. The objectives chosen by the authors as the basis for the test development were selected because they were considered "necessary for an adult to master in order to cope in society." But these important objectives are not specified in the test manuals; only content classification tables are used in each area. The table for the Life Skills Test shows only such areas as communication, finance, and transportation. The table needs to be expanded to show how many items in communication, for example, require skills in each of the three basic skills areas. A related concern is the lack of content parallelism between the "parallel forms." For example, the Reading subtest in Form A has 11 items measuring literal comprehension but Form B has only 9. In Life Skills, the forms have 7, 5, and 8 items, respectively, in the "Health, Safety, and Nutrition" category. In light of this weakness and the fact that no data are supplied to show the equivalence of the parallel forms, Forms B and C are not recommended for use.

The four-choice multiple-choice items used throughout all tests are mostly straightforward and technically sound. However, 5 of the 50 life skills items contain flaws that result in more than one correct answer (4 items) or no correct answer. For example, a table shows the number of calories in 3 ounces of ground beef and an item asks how many calories in an ounce. The response choice "not given" is correct because the calorie count for one ounce, in a strict sense, is "not given" in the table. Another example shows a sample credit card monthly statement, including values for minimum payment and new balance. The question asks what minimum payment the recipient of the bill "should" make. The amount corresponding to the new balance is what many would think "should" be paid, as a minimum, to avoid finance charges. If the questions asked the minimum amount "required" instead, the authors' intended answer would be correct.

Test booklets are nicely formatted and efficient for examinees to use. The layout is familiar for experienced test takers, type size is very readable, and the use of color introduces variety. The general vocabulary level seems appropriate and no obvious sex or ethnic bias is present in the items. The tests are easy for typical students but they are sufficiently short in length that well prepared students are not likely to become bored.

TECHNICAL ASPECTS. Estimates of internal analysis (K-R 20) for the tests and subtests within grade levels are in the .80 to .90 range. Since equivalent forms estimates are not available, the MET should not be used for retesting purposes. Also, the publisher has not provided evidence that the MET can be used to classify examinees consistently as master and non-master when used as a minimum competency test.

As might be expected, test and subtest intercorrelations are moderately high. For example, the range of correlations across grades 8 to 12 between the Basic and Life Skills tests is .72 to .78. These values seem acceptable in view of the intended test purposes and the relatively high verbal component associated with each. The average test and subtest scores increase for successive grade levels, but generally only by fractional amounts. For grades 8 and 12, the mean difference on the Reading, Language, and Mathematics subtests is only 2.5–3.0 items, a much smaller range than might be expected on a well-designed norm-referenced achievement battery. But these are short tests (24 and 26 items) intended for both norm-referenced and criterion-referenced purposes. These data provide additional evidence that a single test cannot be expected to maximize one's ability to make both types of test score interpretations.

Though several stages of item tryout and pilot testing were employed, the test manual fails to specify the criteria used for selecting items for the final test forms. As a result, it is not known if the selection procedures optimized norm-referenced or criterion-referenced score interpretations.

The norm group described in the technical manual was selected using a two-stage sampling of districts and schools and was tested in fall 1979. The manual refers to the group as nationally representative. However, the large urban school representation is dominated by private (Catholic) systems rather than public ones. The presentation of test norms seems inconsistent with the major purpose for which the tests are intended, assessing minimum competence. Their greatest value may be as a referent for local districts that need to check the reasonableness of a criterion score they have established to represent minimum competence. The tests were not intended to be norm-referenced measures and the technical data supplied give little support for such use. A table of district-level mean score norms might be useful information for districts that need to use a criterion score with the MET.

ASSOCIATED DOCUMENTS AND SERVICES. Except for the absence of information about Forms B and C, the technical manual is comprehensive. However, the details one might expect to find about test development procedures, including item selection, standardization, and statements of objectives, are missing. The language used is simple and readable; it is not laden with statistical or psychometric jargon. The manual for administration appears to be satisfactory in every respect—complete, uncomplicated, and easy to use.

A case approach is used in the score interpretation section of the teacher's manual to describe how various score combinations might be interpreted and what action might be taken. Users may need more assistance than is provided to explain criterion-referenced interpretations to parents who are so accustomed to norm-referenced approaches. In addition, the manual could be expanded to show how each of the seven different types of scores available might be used and what cautions should be exercised in using them.

Students may respond to items in the test booklet, on a separate answer sheet, or on plain paper when hand scoring is to be done. Directions for hand scoring are simply written and usable; however, scoring stencils are not available. It appears that hand scoring of booklets or plain paper would be time consuming and subject to error. Standard machine scoring services, class lists, and student labels are available from the publisher. Because the Basic Skills subtests are recommended for group diagnostic purposes, a report of group means or percent scores for content subcategories would be a useful addition to current services.

Overall the MET might be useful as a minimum competency assessment tool by schools that can determine that test content matches well with the local basic skills curriculum. A careful review of the test items would be required to make this judgment. The parallel Forms B and C cannot be recommended for use because of the lack of content parallelism and absence of data regarding the equivalence of the three test forms. Established achievement batteries are likely to be superior to the MET when norm-referenced scores are needed or when diagnostic information is required.

Review of Minimum Essentials Test by LINDA A. LAGOMARSINO, Psychologist, Apache Junction Unified School District #43, Apache Junction, AZ:

The Minimum Essentials Test (MET) is a multiple-choice test developed to assess the achievement levels of students in grades 8 through 12 and adults in basic academic areas. This is a timed test that includes sections on reading (24 items), language (26 items), math (24 items), an optional writing test, and 50 items that require the application of these skills to practical life situations (i.e., reading a utility bill, interpretation of an airline schedule, and directions for medication). The reading difficulty of this measure was reported to be approximately at a sixth-grade level. According to the authors, three parallel forms are available. However, two of these are "reserved as secure forms." Tests may be hand scored by the user or machine scored by the publisher. Scores are available in stanines, percentages, percentiles, and normal curve equivalents. In addition, local percentiles and local stanines are also reported. According to the teacher's manual, the MET is designed to separately assess an individual's achievement levels in basic skills and the proficiency to apply these skills to life situations. This parallel assessment provides useful information regarding appropriate instructional programming for individuals and groups of students.

Three manuals accompany the MET. The Teacher's Manual describes the organization and content of the test as well as hand-scoring procedures, suggestions for interpretation of scores, and educational uses. The second manual, Directions for Administration, is explicit, well written, and clearly delineates standard administration procedures. Instructions are provided for advance scheduling and preparations through mailing computer-scored answer sheets to the publisher.

Less satisfying is the Technical Manual, which describes the development and pilot testing of the three parallel forms of the MET. Various analyses of the original data were mentioned (internal consistency estimates, item difficulty, point biserial coefficients, correlations with other tests in the Comprehensive Assessment Program, and Rasch). However, the results of these analyses were not offered. Standardization procedures appear to be comprehensive and well described. The standardization sample included 16,787 eighth- to twelfth-grade students from public and non-public schools and 457 individuals from military installations. The manual includes tables presenting information on the geographic region, school district enrollment, ethnic background, and socioeconomic status of the students participating. There was no mention of gender. Demographic information appears to be as representative as possible for the variables used.

All information presented in tables represent performances on Form A only of the MET. Four tables present the numbers of items for each skill category (e.g., question numbers 2, 14, and 15 assess the student's ability to select a topic sentence from a reading passage). Four tables present the mean raw score, standard deviation, and standard error of measurement by grade level (8 through 12). These statistics are available for each subtest on Form A. No such information was offered for the performances of adults.

Internal consistency coefficients for each test section by grade level range from the mid .80s to .95. These reliabilities were derived using KR-20 procedures. Subtest intercorrelations range from the mid .40s to the mid .80s. All correlation coefficients are reported for Form A only. No statistical information was offered for the alternate forms B and C. The lack of statistical information on test-retest and parallel form reliability seems a significant omission.

No validity information was reported in the Technical Manual. According to the author, additional technical reports will be released as validity data become available.

SUMMARY. The MET is an achievement measure in a multiple-choice format suitable for high school students and adults. Content includes reading, math, language, and typical life situations requiring the application of these skills. Standard procedures for administering this test are clearly presented. It appears that standardization procedures were adequately representative and generated a sufficient amount of data to establish more than the minimal reliability that is reported. It is unfortunate that the results of the statistical analyses which were purportedly conducted were not reported in the Technical Manual. Until that information is made available, this instrument should not be used to make recommendations or program placement decisions.

[711]

Minneapolis Preschool Screening Instrument. Ages 3–7 to 5–4; 1980; MPSI; screening test to identify children with handicapping conditions; norms consist of means and standard deviations; individual; 1 form; record sheet (2 pages); manual (69 pages); 1983 price data: $35 per complete test kit including 30 response forms; $3.50 per 30 response forms; (12–15) minutes; Robert Lichtenstein; Minneapolis Public Schools.*

[712]

Minnesota Child Development Inventory. Ages 1–6; 1968–74; MCDI; observations by mother; 8 scores: general development, gross motor, fine motor, expressive language, comprehension-conceptual, situation comprehension, self help, personal-social; 1 form ('72, 7 pages); manual ('74, 2 pages) for females; separate answer sheets (NCS) must be used; 1985 price data: $8 per 10 tests; $6 per 25 answer sheets; $15 per set of scoring stencils; $6 per 25 profiles (male or female); $10 per manual; $11 per specimen set; $8 per audio cassette; scoring service available from NCS Interpretive Scoring Systems; administration time not reported; Harold R. Ireton and Edward J. Thwing; Behavior Science Systems, Inc.*

See T3:1492 (6 references); for a review by William L. Goodwin, see 8:220 (3 references).

Review of Minnesota Child Development Inventory by JANE A. RYSBERG, Assistant Professor of Psychology, California State University, Chico, CA:

The child-service worker quickly discovers that each client consists of two individuals: (1) the child with his/her constellation of capacities, attitudes and motives; and (2) the child as perceived by parents and teachers. Many instruments exist which can adequately assess the abilities of the first client. The second assessment is often gained by an interview with the child's parents. It may be difficult to elicit an accurate picture of a child's present capacities via the interview, making it an inefficient use of time for both the parent and the professional.

Several different interview impediments may exist. The child-service worker and the parent may not share a common vocabulary; the parent may be able to describe a child's common activities but be unable to evaluate these behaviors against an age norm. Parents may be unaware of how to respond to the interviewer's questions, and may describe the child's best performance rather than a typical one. Finally, parents may be unwilling to present their child in a poor light, and may tell an interviewer more about who they would like the child to be than who s/he is.

Therefore, the Minnesota Child Development Inventory (MCDI) was designed as a supplement to a parental interview. Its primary purpose is to identify children whose development is below expectation for their age and sex. In addition, the MCDI may be used as an assessment tool when the child is temporarily unavailable or untestable. THE MCDI allows mothers to summarize their experiences with their children using a simple "yes-no" format.

The MCDI has seven developmental scales—Gross Motor, Fine Motor, Expressive Language, Comprehension-Conceptual, Situation Comprehension, Self Help, and Personal-Social. The General Developmental scale is composed of items from the other seven scales. The scale areas and their items were derived from the child development literature, psychological tests, and mothers' perspectives. Factor analytic techniques were not used in the construction, and so some of the scales are highly correlated.

The normative sample is carefully described in the manual—as well it should be. The demographics suggest, and the authors concur, that this instrument is suited for use with white, middle-class, non-handicapped children from intact families of successfully employed fathers and unemployed mothers.

The MCDI profile is presented as percent below age level. The authors caution against making direct interpretations from this profile on a scale. The degree to which a child is below an age expectancy, discriminability of a particular scale, and the number of scales scored at below age expectations must be considered. These cautions are not followed by validation figures. What are the behavioral distinctions between being below age expectations on two scales as opposed to four? What performance will be observed in a child who falls 20% below age range as opposed to one who falls 35% below age range? An attempt to define behavioral functioning is made by comparison of these percent below age level scores and IQ scores. The basis of this comparison is unclear, and the only example refers to subnormal intellectual performance.

Reliability was assessed only by the split-half method. Test-retest data would also be informative. Perhaps the authors consider this data superfluous, partly because the mothers in the normative sample had so little difficulty responding to the Inventory.

In summary, the Minnesota Child Development Inventory is a useful adjunct to a test battery which includes a parental interview. The MCDI will give the professional and the parent a common currency of exchange. If this instrument is used alone, its limitations in terms of reliability and validity must be remembered. In addition, the Inventory is most appropriately used with the same population which benefits most from psychoanalysis—white and middle class.

[713]

Minnesota Clerical Test. Grades 8–12 and adults; MCT; 1933–79; 2 scores: number comparison, name comparison; 1 form ('33, 6 pages); revised manual ('79, 22 pages); 1983 price data: $10 per 25 tests, $2.50 per scoring stencil; $3 per manual; $4 per specimen set; 15(20) minutes; Dorothy M. Andrew, Donald G. Paterson, and Howard P. Longstaff; The Psychological Corporation.*

See T3:1493 (5 references), T2:2135 (23 references) and 6:1040 (10 references); for a review by Donald E. Super, see 5:850 (46 references); for reviews by Thelma Hunt, R. B. Selover, Erwin K. Taylor, and E. F. Wonderlic, see 3:627 (22 references); for a review by W. D. Commins, see 2:1664 (18 references).

TEST REFERENCES

1. Fossum, J. A. The effects of positively and negatively contingent rewards and individual differences on performance, satisfaction, and expectations. ACADEMY OF MANAGEMENT JOURNAL, 1979, 22, 577–589.

2. Judd, L. L. Effect of lithium on mood, cognition, and personality function in normal subjects. ARCHIVES OF GENERAL PSYCHIATRY, 1979, 36, 860–865.

Review of Minnesota Clerical Test by MICHAEL RYAN, Clinical Psychologist, West Side Family Mental Health Clinic, Kalamazoo, MI:

The Minnesota Clerical Test purports to measure the elements of speed and accuracy needed to perform various clerical activities. Specifically, it evaluates those areas which require an individual to process numerical and/or linguistic material quickly and accurately. The test is divided into two subtests: Number Comparison and Name Comparison. Each subtest consists of 100 identical pairs and 100 dissimilar pairs which are composed of digits or letters. Dissimilar pairs generally differ in regard to one digit or letter. Identical and dissimilar pairs are distributed randomly and the examinee is required to check only the identical pairs.

The total test is administered in 15 minutes and may be given individually or in a group setting. Instructions for scoring are straightforward and clear. The score on each subtest is achieved by subtracting the number of incorrect items from the number of correct items.

In 1979 a revised manual for the Minnesota Clerical Test was published. The purpose of the manual was to present new psychometric data in a format more congruent with modern standards of test construction. This manual presents new norms for 10 vocational categories. Detailed percentage charts are provided as are means and standard deviations for each group. In addition, a table with the means and standard deviations for 31 vocational categories is included. The authors should be commended for their effort to include ethnic minority representation in the new norms.

The norms, however, remain confusing to use. Lack of definition of the normative categories makes it difficult to determine the norm group with which an examinee should be compared. Because of the marked differences in performances between groups, the selection of the proper norms is critical. More general norms or a more specific description of each norm group is indicated. Furthermore, the normative sample was obtained primarily in eastern states;

only six norm groups were sampled from the South or the West.

In addition to the reports of reliability and validity included in the previous manuals, the new manual contains summaries of more current studies. The newer reliability studies concur with past studies in indicating that the Minnesota Clerical Test has test-retest coefficients ranging from .81 to .87. Furthermore, the authors should be commended for providing a concise yet useful discussion of the test's reliability.

Three types of validity studies were provided in the new manual. In these studies the Minnesota Clerical Test was correlated with the following criteria: measures of job performance, measures of training outcome, and scores from other tests. The job performance of directory assistants, clerks, clerk-typists, and bank-tellers was correlated significantly with scores on the Minnesota Clerical Test. Ratings of course success and grade point average in business schools also produced significant correlations. The manual indicates that the Minnesota Clerical Test is highly related to other tests of clerical ability such as the Short Employment Tests, General Clerical Tests, and Personnel Tests for Industry.

The new manual forthrightly provides validity studies with non-significant results. Furthermore, every attempt has been made to include relevant statistics and information concerning the ethnic background of the subjects in each study. With a test as old and well-researched as the Minnesota Clerical Test, the authors have been able to provide a wide range of different studies composed of diverse populations and criteria. However, the authors have failed to provide detailed information concerning the specific attributes of the jobs, courses, and tests which constitute the criterion measures. Furthermore, the manual lacks a discussion of the significant vs. the non-significant validity studies. The discussion plus a careful definition of the criteria are critical to understanding exactly what the Minnesota Clerical Test measures.

In summary, the Minnesota Clerical Test is recommended to assess perceptual speed and accuracy as it relates to traditional clerical tasks. It is easily administered and scored and a wealth of reliability and validity data is available. However, updated and interpretable norms are needed to facilitate the interpretation of the results and a more detailed discussion of the test's validity is needed to more clearly delineate what the instrument measures.

Review of Minnesota Clerical Test by RUTH G. THOMAS, Associate Professor of Education, University of Minnesota, St. Paul, MN:

The Minnesota Clerical Test (MCT), first developed in 1931 as a measure of perceptual speed and accuracy relevant to clerical work, has remained virtually unchanged. The manual which accompanies the test has undergone several revisions, the most recent being published in 1979.

Directions for administration and scoring of this test are simple and clear. Since it is a speeded test, accuracy of timing in administration is important. No special qualifications for administering and interpreting the test are indicated beyond thorough familiarity with the directions.

While the 1979 manual is somewhat more comprehensive than the previous 1959 edition, no information regarding test development or the rationale underlying the construct measured is provided. The test's applications and appropriate audiences are clearly identified as selection of people for a range of clerical jobs and as providing information for the counseling of individuals considering training programs for clerical positions.

Norms presented in the 1959 manual are presented in an appendix. New norms for persons employed in clerical positions, clerical trainees, clerical job applicants, and students enrolled in clerical and business programs are provided by sex and race. Data for the norm groups was reported between 1974 and 1976 but the manual does not indicate whether data was actually collected during this time period or earlier. The degree to which the normative samples are purposeful and representative is difficult to discern since sample selection procedures are not described. Neither is it possible to determine whether or not data collection presented the potential for bias since the conditions are not described. Norms do encompass various clerical jobs at several types of institutions and in different geographic locations. However, the limited range of types of institutions and the predominance of norm groups composed of employees in a single institution suggests that representativeness of these norms is limited. Female norm groups predominate.

The primary value of the new norms is that they expand the industrial norms and, assuming that the reported data was actually collected in the early to mid-1970s, update previously available norms.

New stability reliability coefficients are reported (.81 and .83 for the numbers test; .86 and .87 for the names test) which are more consistent and are, on the average, higher than those previously reported. The new coefficients likely reflect the four-day interval between test administration versus intervals of several weeks or months for coefficients reported in previous editions.

New criterion-validity data is provided with respect to job performance and earnings of employed persons and grade point average, course success, and task performance of students. Most job performance measures involved job performance ratings completed by supervisors or by undesignated persons. Two job performance measures involved job productivity.

Four coefficients of correlation between job productivity measures and the MCT scores are significant and are more consistent than are coefficients reflecting correlations between job performance ratings and MCT scores. The latter coefficients range from –.12 to .88 and likely reflect lack of reliability in the criterion measure. Student criterion data are too limited to identify patterns. Six criterion coefficients are predictive and involve time spans of six months and two years; the rest appear to be concurrent; only two of the predictive coefficients are significant.

New construct validity data is also summarized showing significant correlation between the MCT and tests of intelligence, clerical aptitude, verbal and numerical scores and typing speed. There was little relationship between the MCT and tests of judgment, reasoning, and comprehension.

No rationale for the appropriateness of criterion measures is given although their limitations are discussed. Criterion measures are described in very limited one-line footnotes.

The major weakness in the criterion validity data is the questionable reliability of job performance ratings. Many aspects of clerical job performance would be assessable by techniques that are more objective and more focused in nature than are supervisor ratings, which are typically based on a wider range of variables than those assessed on the MCT. The preponderance of supervisor rating data used in reporting validity of the MCT needs to be counterbalanced by more objective and focused measures.

In summary, the revisions in the 1979 manual have improved the usefulness of the MCT. The test has the advantages of being relatively short, easy to administer, and reliable. However, test developers and publishers need to go further in establishing predictive validity and norms that are clearly representative of relevant groups.

Ref
Z
5814
.P8
B932
1985
Vol. 1

97495

Also by Sheila Miyoshi Jager

Ruptured Histories: War, Memory, and the Post-Cold War in Asia
(with Rana Mitter, eds.)

Narratives of Nation-Building in Korea: A Genealogy of Patriotism

BROTHERS AT WAR

BROTHERS AT WAR

The Unending Conflict in Korea

SHEILA MIYOSHI JAGER

W. W. NORTON & COMPANY
NEW YORK LONDON

Ketchikan Public Library
Ketchikan, AK 99901

Copyright © 2013 by Sheila Miyoshi Jager

All rights reserved
Printed in the United States of America
First Edition

For information about permission to reproduce selections from this book,
write to Permissions, W. W. Norton & Company, Inc.,
500 Fifth Avenue, New York, NY 10110

For information about special discounts for bulk purchases, please contact
W. W. Norton Special Sales at specialsales@wwnorton.com or 800-233-4830

Manufacturing by Courier Westford
Book design by Kristen Bearse
Production manager: Devon Zahn

Library of Congress Cataloging-in-Publication Data

Jager, Sheila Miyoshi.
Brothers at war : the unending conflict in Korea / Sheila Miyoshi Jager. — First edition.
pages cm
Includes bibliographical references and index.
ISBN 978-0-393-06849-8 (hardcover)
1. Korean War, 1950–1953. 2. Korean War, 1950–1953—Influence. 3. Korea (North—Foreign relations—Korea (South) 4. Korea (South—Foreign relations—Korea (North) I. Title.
DS918.J34 2013
951.904'2—dc23
2013012760

W. W. Norton & Company, Inc.
500 Fifth Avenue, New York, N.Y. 10110
www.wwnorton.com

W. W. Norton & Company Ltd.
Castle House, 75/76 Wells Street, London W1T 3QT

1 2 3 4 5 6 7 8 9 0

FOR JIYUL

Contents

Abbreviations Used in Text

AEC: Atomic Energy Commission
ASPAC: Asia-Pacific Council
CCP: Chinese Communist Party
CPKI: Committee for the Preparation of Korean Independence
CPV: Chinese People's Volunteer
DMZ: demilitarized zone
DPRK: Democratic People's Republic of Korea
IAEA: International Atomic Energy Agency
ICRC: International Committee for the Red Cross
JCS: Joint Chiefs of Staff
KATUSA: Korean Augmentation to the United States Army
KCIA: Korean Central Intelligence Agency
KCP: Korean Communist Party
KDP: Korean Democratic Party
KMAG: Korean Military Advisory Group
KPG: Korean Provisional Government
KPR: Korean People's Republic
KSC: Korean Service Corps
LST: landing ship tank
LWR: light-water reactor
MACV: Military Assistance Command Vietnam
NAM: Nonaligned Movement
NKPA: North Korean People's Army
NKWP: North Korean Workers' Party
NPT: Nuclear Nonproliferation Treaty
NVA: North Vietnamese Army
PDS: Public Distribution System
PLA: People's Liberation Army
POW: prisoner of war
PRC: People's Republic of China
ROK: Republic of Korea
SACEUR: Supreme Allied Commander Europe
SCA: Soviet Civil Administration
SCAP: Supreme Commander for the Allied Powers
SKWP: South Korean Workers Party
SOFA: Status of Forces Agreement
TF: Task Force
UNC: United Nations Command
UNRC: United Nations Reception Center
UNCURK: United Nations Commission for the Unification and Rehabilitation of Korea
USAFIK: United States Army Forces in Korea
USAMGIK: United States Military Government in Korea
VPA: Vietnam People's Army
WFP: World Food Program

Acknowledgments

My first opportunity to study the Korean War in depth came in 2006 when I was offered a two-year research fellowship at the U.S. Army War College in Carlisle, Pennsylvania. Affiliated with the War College is the U.S. Army Military History Institute, which houses the largest collection in the United States of oral history archives on the Korean War. One of the major benefits I saw of working with oral histories at the onset of this project was the visceral connection I was able to make with the subjects of my research. Although oral histories are not always reliable and must be handled with care, they are invaluable for re-creating the mood and emotions of the battlefield that underlay the actions and attitudes of the soldiers who fought there.

I was also fortunate during my research at the Institute to run into a group of South Korean researchers from South Korea's Truth and Reconciliation Commission (TRC). The South Korean government had established the Commission in 2005 to investigate various incidents in Korean history, and in particular numerous atrocities committed by various government agencies during Japan's occupation of Korea, the Korean War, and the successive authoritarian governments. The Commission was disbanded in 2010. As I sat down with the TRC researchers one evening over coffee, I discussed my project, and they offered their help. As the primary researcher on the Commission at that time, Suh Hee-gyŏng not only shared with me thousands of pages of unpublished and published reports and photos of the Commission's findings, but also helped me navigate the daunting Korean bureaucracy in securing permission to use them. She also provided invaluable assistance in assembling materials pertaining to the mass killings that occurred early on during the Korean War. Kim Dong-ch'un, former standing commissioner of the Commission, also provided important materials; it was he who showed me what I regard as one of the most haunting photos of the war, the remains of 114 bodies discovered at Buntegol, Chŏngwŏn, Ch'ungbuk province, in 2007, which appears in this book.

I am also indebted to Balázs Szalontai for sharing some of his unpublished work with me. The book is much richer because of it. Katalin Jalsovszky, the archivist at the Hungarian National Museum, quickly and efficiently helped me to secure some rare North Korean photos of the war. I am thankful to Balázs and Chris Springer, who brought these amazing photos to my attention. John Moffett, librarian at the Needham Institute in the United Kingdom, was helpful in taking the time to locate, scan, and send dozens of photos of Joseph Needham's trip to China in 1952. Mitchell Lerner steered me to some of his and other recent work on the USS *Pueblo* incident from which the book has greatly benefited. Choe Yong-ho of the Korea Institute of Military History, Ministry of National Defense, Republic of Korea, helped me to track down books, articles, and data on Korea's involvement in the Vietnam War. Raymond Lech generously provided me with copies of transcripts of pretrial interviews, appellate reviews, memos, and letters concerning U.S. Korean War POWs. Ray allowed me to borrow this extraordinary collection—filling more than fifteen boxes—to use at my leisure before he deposited them at the U.S. Army Military History Institute, where the collection now resides. New materials about the war from the Soviet, Chinese, East German, Hungarian, and Romanian archives, all available online at the web site for the Cold War International History Project at the Woodrow Wilson International Center for Scholars, have enabled scholars to adopt a truly multinational approach in their study of the cold war. We now know more about the views of "other" major players in the cold war than ever before. This book is a direct beneficiary of the tremendous contributions the Wilson Center has made to advancing cold war scholarship. Finally, I would like to acknowledge Oberlin College for granting me a two-year leave during which time the bulk of the research for this book was done. I also benefited greatly from three summer research grants awarded by Oberlin for travel to Korea and other research libraries in the United States. I consider myself lucky to be teaching in such a supportive academic environment. My colleagues Ann Sherif, Pauline Chen, and Qiusha Ma have been not only wonderful mentors but also supportive friends.

During the writing phase of the project, Daniel Crewe, my editor at Profile Books in the United Kingdom, read so many drafts of this book that I have lost count. Several of the major sections of the present text were completely revised and rewritten in response to his suggestions and questions. Allan R. Millett, who read an early draft of the book, was pointed in his critical comments but made it all that much better. Retired U.S. Army Colonel Don Boose also read through an earlier draft of the manuscript and provided excellent feedback, especially on the later chapters. For her enthusiastic and unfailing support of this project, I am grateful to my editor at W. W. Norton, Maria Guarnaschelli, and her assistant, Melanie Tortoroli: Maria, for having such faith and insight into the book even as the manuscript grew longer, and Melanie, for helping me at critical points in the rewriting and for keeping everything else on track. I would also like to acknowledge my copy editor, Mary Babcock, whose meticulous attention to every detail of the book helped to improve it tremendously. Kim Preston and Bonnie Gordon have seen me through some of the more grueling stages of the book's evolution, and I also wish to thank them here for their warm friendship and support.

My older kids, Isaac and Hannah, also contributed to this project early on: Isaac, now a cadet at West Point, for spending an entire summer with me at the Military History Institute pouring over after-action reports and writing them up, and Hannah, for her computer wizardry in organizing all my books, papers, computer files, and photos. In addition, both helped care for their younger siblings, Emma and Aaron, when mom was at work in the attic, good deeds for which I am thankful. All four kids grew up with this book, patiently tolerating my own "unending" obsession with the war without too much complaint while also providing the necessary perspective as only one's children can do.

My greatest debt is owed to my husband, Jiyul, without whose contribution this book might never have been written. We covered a great deal of ground together; his help in surveying a broad range of materials, reading and rereading through numerous drafts of the manuscript, and above all, his enthusiasm for debating—and often correcting—the finer points of Korean War history, made the final product a much better book. These conversations became part of our daily routine and contributed to the overall richness of our daily lives. For that, I will always be grateful.

A note on source, transliteration, and naming convention: Considerations of space have precluded the inclusion of a separate bibliography. The notes include the full citation of each source when it appears for the first time in a particular chapter. Throughout the text, I have employed the McCune-Reischauer system of romanization for all Korean words and names, with the exception of well-known nonstandard romanized names, such as Syngman Rhee, Park Chung Hee, Kim Il Sung, and Kim Jong Il. As a rule, Chinese names are romanized according to the pinyin system. Korean, Chinese, and Japanese personal names are, with the exception of Syngman Rhee, written with family name first and given name last.

Sheila Miyoshi Jager
Oberlin, Ohio
December 2012

BROTHERS AT WAR

Introduction

The War Memorial, Seoul. (PHOTO BY AUTHOR)

MY INTEREST IN THE KOREAN WAR began with a visit to a memorial. In the summer of 1996 my family relocated to South Korea when my husband, a U.S. Army officer, was assigned to work at the U.S. embassy in Seoul. Just a few minutes away from the main gate of the Yongsan U.S. Army base, where we lived, is the War Memorial, and over the next four years I made frequent trips to visit it. Ostensibly, it commemorates South Korea's military war dead, but other wartime events, including Korea's thirteenth-century struggles with the Mongols and sixteenth-century defense against the Japanese, are also represented in the exhibitions. Inclusion of these earlier conflicts appears to reinforce the idea that the Korean War was part of the nation's long history of righteous struggle against adversity—in this case, South Korea's struggle against

North Korean communists. Situated on five acres along a wide boulevard that bisects the army base, the War Memorial encompasses a rare, large open space in crowded Seoul. Originally conceived and planned under the No T'ae-u (Roh Tae-Woo) administration (1988–93), the complex opened its doors in 1994. It includes a museum as well as an outdoor exhibition area featuring tanks, airplanes, statues, and a small amusement area for children. It has become a popular destination for school field trips.

What struck me most about the memorial was the paradox of what it represented. How does one commemorate a war that technically is not over? While the Korean War, at least for Americans, "ended" in 1953, the meaning and memories of the war have not been brought to closure in Korean society because of the permanent division of the peninsula. How does one bring closure to a war for which the central narrative is one of division and dissent, a war whose history is still in the process of being made?

In South Korea, the official view of the Korean War has always had, unsurprisingly, an anti–North Korean character. One striking feature of the memorial, however, is the relative absence of depictions of the brutal struggle between the North and the South. Although its purported task is to memorialize the war, the main purpose of the memorial appears to be to promote reconciliation and peace. There are few exhibits of bloody battle scenes, but most conspicuously is the lack of any reference to known North Korean atrocities committed during the war. The successive purges of South Korean sympathizers after the North Korean People's Army occupied Seoul in June 1950 and the execution of prisoners of war are represented nowhere. Evidence of the widely publicized executions of an estimated five thousand South Korean civilians during the last days of the North Korean army's occupation of Taejŏn in September 1950—an event highlighted in the history books from previous South Korean military regimes—is also missing. For a war that was particularly remembered for its viciousness, the memorial seems to be promoting a tacit kind of forgetfulness. This is in sharp contrast to earlier representations of the conflict that proliferated during the cold war, when North Korean brutality played a central role in the story of the war.

It was not difficult to understand why this sudden shift in memory had occurred. By the time the memorial had opened its doors, the cold war had ended and South Korea had come out on top. Following its global coming-out party during the 1988 Seoul Olympics, South Korea had clearly "won" the war against the North, but it could not afford to bask in its glory if it wanted to foster North-South rapprochement and the reunification of the peninsula. The memorial's designers were thus faced with the dilemma of how to memorialize a brutal war while at the same time leaving open the possibility for peninsular peace.

When I returned to the Memorial a decade later, the pendulum of politics in South Korea had swung sharply to the Right. The conservatives had gained power and opposed improving relations with the P'yŏngyang regime. I was in Seoul in 2006 when North Korea test-fired missiles, including a long-range Taep'odong-2 with the theoretical capacity to reach the continental United States. These acts of defiance were followed by the testing of North Korea's first nuclear device on October 9, 2006, and then again on May 25, 2009. South Koreans were furious. When the conservative presidential candidate Yi Myŏng-bak (Lee Myung-bak) assumed office in 2008, he abruptly renounced the policy of engagement with the North that previous administrations had pursued. The North responded with vitriolic attacks against the new South Korean government. Relations between the two Koreas spiraled downward from there. By then, it had become quite apparent that the Korean War would not end as optimistically as the War Memorial planners had hoped. Rather, the memorial itself had become part of the history of the war, one "phase" of its never-ending story.

That initial visit to the War Memorial in 1996 spurred me to think more closely about the war. Eventually, I made the memorial the subject of several essays and book chapters and then finally undertook a major research project on the Korean War itself. This entailed exploring the policies and actions of all the major players of the war, including the sixteen UN countries that sent troops to aid South Korea, the military history, and a wide variety of popular and academic writings about the conflict. But I never lost sight of my original fascination with the war and its continuing and evolving impact on the two Koreas and on the rest of the world.

Since the late nineteenth century, the Korean peninsula has been a focal point for confrontation and competition among the Great Powers. First China, then Japan, Russia, and the United States in succession, exerted some form of control over the peninsula. No other place in the world has assumed such symbolic importance to these four countries. The Second World War, however, left only two Great Powers vying for influence over Korea: the United States and the Soviet Union (formerly Russia).

But by then the Koreans had already divided themselves into partisan camps under the tutelage, and with the support, of these two patrons. Two antagonistic regimes were born: communists in the North and conservatives in the South, each with dreams of reunifying the Korean peninsula under their rule, but without any means of achieving this ambition on their own. Their diverging visions of what kind of modern nation Korea was to become made the possibility of conciliation and unity increasingly remote and exploded into war in 1950.

The main issues over which the war was fought had their origins immediately after Korea's liberation from Japan in 1945. The division of the peninsula at the 38th parallel by the United States and the Soviet Union gave rise to a fractured polity whose political fault lines were exacerbated further by regional, religious (Christians versus communists), and class divisions. Open fighting among these groups eventually claimed more than one hundred thousand lives, all before the ostensible Korean War began. Prior to the founding of the Republic of Korea in August 1948, the Americans organized a constabulary force in their zone to augment the national police, primarily to conduct counterinsurgency operations against leftist guerillas. While the record of their operations remains controversial, the security forces successfully suppressed the insurgency by the spring of 1950. The decision by North Korea's leader, Kim Il Sung, with the backing of Joseph Stalin, to launch a conventional attack across the 38th parallel on June 25, 1950, thus resumed the fighting by other means.

The Korean War, in the midst of the rapidly developing cold war, reestablished China, now Communist China, as a Great Power, setting up a triangular struggle over the peninsula between the United States, the Soviet Union, and Communist China. The irresolution of the Korean War, owing to the lack of a peace treaty, with only a military armistice signed in 1953, stoked the fire of simmering confrontation and tension between North and South Korea as well as their Great Power overseers. But the most important fuel that kept the flame of confrontation alive was the implacable nature of the two Korean regimes. This is all the more remarkable as Korea had been unified since the seventh century.

Today, the essentially continuous war between the Koreas threatens to reach beyond their borders, as North Korea continues to develop nuclear weapons and long-range missiles. How did we get to this point? This book is the story of Korean competition and conflict—and Great Power competition and conflict—over the peninsula: an unending war between two "brothers" with ramifications for the rest of the world. If a resolution to the conflict is ever to be found, this history must be understood and taken into account.

I develop two major but overlapping themes in this book. The first one emphasizes the evolution of the war through time. Because the Korean War technically ended in an armistice and not a peace treaty, it continued to influence regional events even though the significance of the war dramatically changed. Hence, the conflict evolved from a civil war in 1948–49 to an international war from June 1950 to 1953, to a global cold war after 1953, only to undergo yet another transformation in the late 1960s, when the focus of the conflict was no longer on containing communism per se, but ensuring the region's stability. By the mid-1970s, the stalemated Korean War kept American forces in South Korea because the conflict had ironically become a source of regional stability during a period of significant changes in Asia: Sino-American rapprochement, the Sino-Soviet split, and increasing Sino-Vietnamese tensions. Although the Korean War continued to be waged as a series of "local wars" along the demilitarized zone (DMZ) dividing the North from the South, the nature of the conflict had fundamentally changed since the armistice. In the post–cold war period, the Korean War was defined by a series of crises over the North Korean nuclear weapons program and the potential collapse of the North. Should fighting ever resume on the Korean peninsula, it will not resemble the first phase of the war. No one will mistake another North Korean attack on the South as a communist challenge or a war by proxy.

As much as the war has transformed over the years, it has also stayed very much the same. By titling this book *Brothers at War*, I highlight the second major theme: the continuous struggle between North and South Korea for the mantle of Korean legitimacy. It was this competition, after all, that had given rise to Kim Il Sung's ambition to reunify the peninsula by force in June 1950. Although Kim did not succeed in this endeavor, he never gave up on his dream of "liberating" the South. By the late 1960s, when it appeared that South Korea was winning the legitimacy war against the North, owing to the South's rapid economic growth and greater international stature, Kim embarked on a series of provocative actions in the hope of toppling the South Korean regime. These events were remarkable for the brazenness in which Kim tried to co-opt his allies, the Soviet Union and China, to back him in starting a second Korean War. While these efforts ultimately failed, they reveal Kim's increasing desperation to undermine the South's growing global stature and influence. By the 1990s, few people could deny that North Korea had lost its legitimacy war with the South. The contrast between the two "brothers" could not have been more stark. Today, North Korea is an aid-dependent nation, wracked by hunger, repression, and a looming legitimacy crisis. This book puts this legitimacy struggle in a longer historical perspective to consider how the fraternal conflict has influenced, and continues to influence, East Asia and the world.

This book is also a military history of the war. The critical importance I give to military campaigns and operations arises from my conviction that it was during the life-and-death struggles in Korea that cold war antagonisms were hardened and perceptions of the enemy were formed. I argue that these perceptions were just as important in understanding American and Chinese behavior after the armistice, for they continued to influence America's view of China and China's view of America. Certainly, the two "lost" decades in Sino-American relations between the outbreak of the war in 1950 and Nixon's opening to China in 1972 came about because of attitudes forged by both parties during the war.

At the same time that the Korean War influenced the cultural perceptions of the enemy, it transformed society at home. When the armistice was signed in 1953, the United States, for the first time in its history, emerged staunchly anticommunist, with a large permanent standing army, a huge defense budget, and military bases around the world. The war did much to forge a new China too. China had lost nearly half a million men, but Mao Zedong emerged with his reputation intact and his power greatly enhanced. Emboldened by his success, Mao applied what he learned during the war to building his communist utopia at home, stoking the flames of Sino-Soviet competition in the process. The war significantly transformed the two Koreas as well. The military on both sides of the DMZ became the strongest, most cohesive, best-organized institutions in Korean life. For the first time since the twelfth century, a military regime took power in South Korea in 1961, marking the beginning of its extraordinary path toward economic development and the source of its eventual "triumph" in its legitimacy struggle with the North.

Something about North Korea invites people to view it hermetically, not unlike the way Westerners wrote about the "Hermit Kingdom" after their travels to Korea in the nineteenth century. "It can hardly be a cause of surprise," observed the German businessman and traveler Ernst Oppert in 1879, "that a system so strictly and severely carried out, combined with a reputation for inhospitality not altogether undeserved, would have been thought sufficient to deter others from any attempt to form a closer acquaintance with this country. It naturally follows that foreigners have found it next to impossible to collect any reliable information on the subject there, and Corea has remained to us like a sealed book, the contents of which we have yet to study."[1] Similar observations could be made about North Korea today. The place is uniformly characterized in the West as "bizarre," "erratic," or simply "baffling." North Korean experts also tend to isolate and insulate North Korean uniqueness, focusing on Kim Il Sung's cult of personality and the regime's Stalinist-Confucian system. For many, the regime's behavior is explained either as a ruthless ploy to maintain its hold on power and privilege or as a "rational" response to the legitimate threats posed by hostile foreign powers, namely, the United States.[2] Both interpretations have focused on the actions of the regime in which North Korea's ongoing legitimacy war with the South plays little or no role.

North Korea's main security threat, however, is not the United States. It is the prosperity, wealth, and prestige of South Korea. The greatest challenge of the North Korean regime is not how it will feed its own people; it is how it will come to terms with its own humiliating defeat. South Korea's miraculous story of economic growth and democratic progress threatens the regime's hold on power precisely because the more North Koreans know about the South, the less likely they are to put up with the conditions of poverty and repression at home. It is the regime's pending legitimacy crisis that drives it to act in "irrational" ways. This is why it explodes nuclear devices, launches missiles, fires on South Korean naval vessels, and shells remote islands. A North Korean poster sums up these anxieties: "We will reckon decisively with anyone, anywhere who meddles with our self-respect."[3] Any reforms that would make North Korea look more like the South cannot be accepted, for they would undermine the entire legitimacy of the regime and spell the end of the Kim dynasty.

More than sixty years after North Korea invaded South Korea, the first major hot war of the cold war has yet to end. The fighting resolved nothing of the internal Korean issues that had caused the war in the first place, and the status quo ante was restored. Today, the Korean peninsula remains roughly divided where the conflict began, and the DMZ that separates North and South Korea is the most heavily fortified border in the world. Two million soldiers face each other along a two-and-a-half-mile-wide strip of land straddling the 155-mile-long Military Demarcation Line. President Bill Clinton once called the DMZ "the scariest place on earth." This is hardly an exaggeration. Should fighting break out again on the Korean peninsula, the ramifications on the region and the world would be catastrophic. There is also reason to hope, however, that given the regional powers' experience in dealing with this sixty-year-old conflict, they will eventually come up with a solution to finally end it. China is the key and has the best potential to bring this about.

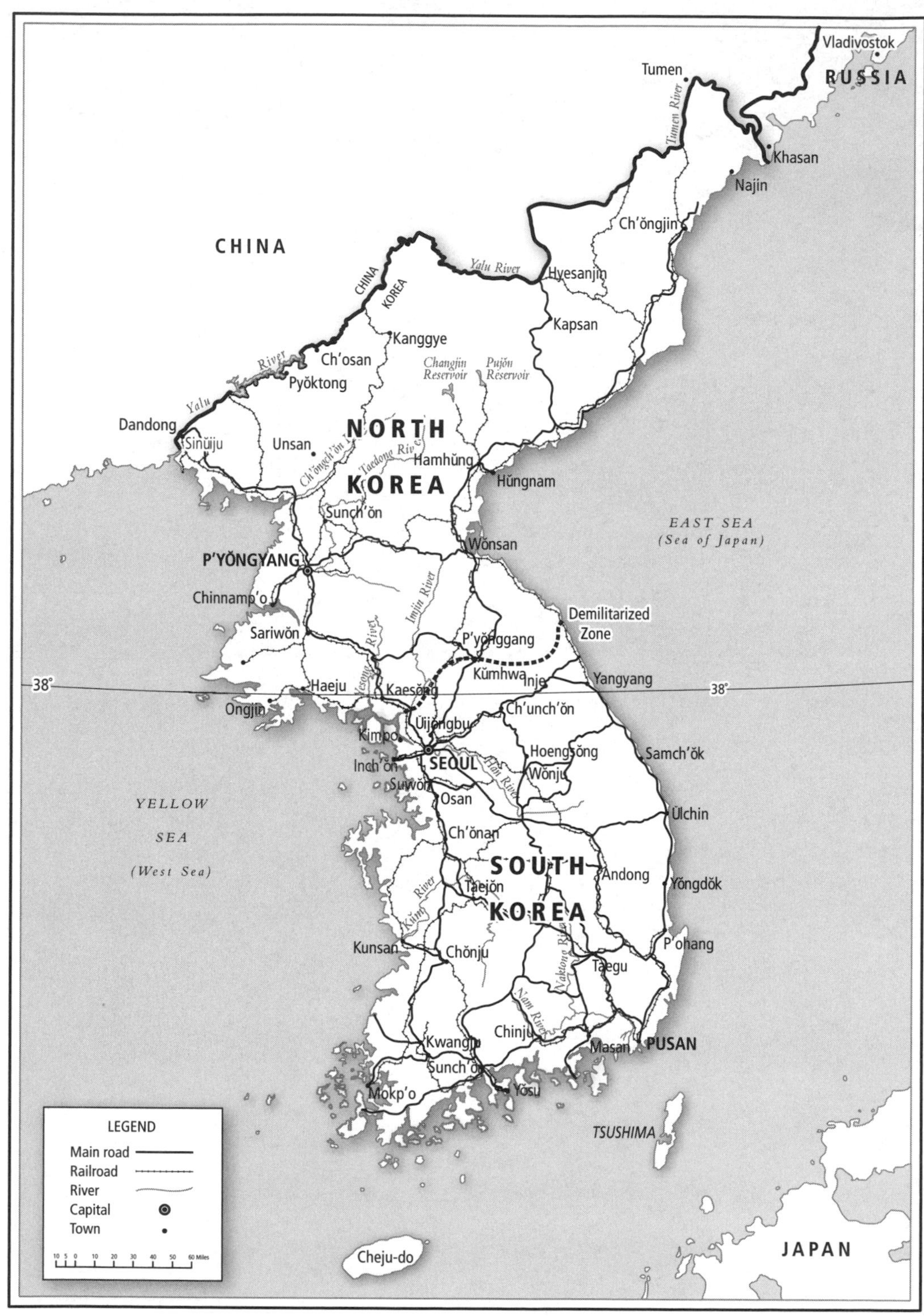

Korean peninsula

PART I

THE WAR

In 1943, in the middle of World War II, President Franklin D. Roosevelt, Premier Joseph Stalin, and Prime Minister Winston Churchill discussed the fate of Korea at the Cairo Conference, in anticipation of Korea's liberation from Japanese rule. Roosevelt hoped to grant Korea independence "in due course" after a period of trusteeship under the Allied Powers. This did not sit well with the Korean people. The Korean nation had been in existence far longer than any of the Allied Powers. By the seventh century, Korea was a unified nation with its own language, culture, monarchy, state bureaucracy, and centuries of high civilization comparable to that in neighboring China and Japan. Korea had been an independent nation for over a thousand years when Japan annexed it in 1910.

Korea's fate after World War II was not decided by a trusteeship, but by military conditions on the ground. Roosevelt anticipated there would be heavy losses in defeating the Japanese forces in China and Korea. Hoping to leave those operations to Soviet forces, he agreed at the Yalta Conference in February 1945 that for entry into the war against Japan, Stalin would get the southern Sakhalin and the Kurile Islands, the lease of ports at Dairen [Dalian] and Port Arthur [Lüshun], and control of key railroads in northeast China, formerly Manchuria. At the Potsdam Conference in July 1945, news of the successful testing of the atomic bomb significantly dampened President Harry Truman's enthusiasm for a quick Soviet entry into the war. Japan surrendered virtually overnight in August soon after the atomic bombings of Hiroshima and Nagasaki, coupled with rapid Soviet advances in Manchuria. Truman, who had become president after Roosevelt's death in April, proposed that the occupation of Korea be shared, divided along the 38th parallel. To his surprise, Stalin agreed. Although the entire peninsula had been his for the taking, Stalin was focused more on consolidating control over Eastern Europe. Control over the northern half of Korea was enough to secure Soviet interests without unduly antagonizing Washington. Eventually, the two zones were to be united under a trusteeship, but as the cold war heated up in Europe, it soon became clear that no reconciliation between the superpowers, and their respective zones, would be possible.

Violent upheavals by communists and leftists plagued the American zone. In the face of Soviet opposition, a UN-sponsored election for a national assembly was conducted but only in the South in May 1948. The new national assembly chose an aging and fiery nationalist, Syngman Rhee, to be the first president of the

Republic of Korea. Four months later, in September 1948, the Democratic People's Republic of Korea was established in the north, headed by a young former Soviet Army captain and anti-Japanese guerilla fighter, Kim Il Sung. By the end of 1948, two antithetical and antagonistic regimes were formed, each with its own vision of Korea's future.

Stalin gave Kim Il Sung the green light to launch the invasion of South Korea, which took place at dawn on June 25, 1950. Within a week, American forces, under the UN flag, were committed in the fighting. Kim Il Sung's war of liberation had turned global, and China's entry in October 1950 risked expansion into World War III. The unfinished war, the first hot war of the cold war, intensified global confrontation and competition between the United States and the Soviet Union. Paradoxically, the new international order that resulted from the fighting significantly reduced the possibility of a world war by establishing a stable balance of power that neither side was willing to upset.

CHAPTER ONE

Liberation and Division

Shortly before noon on August 15, 1945, Kim Eun-kook turned on the radio. His grandfather told the young boy that an important announcement was to be broadcast at noon and that they would listen to it together. The day before, the police had come through his neighborhood in Hamhŭng city to remind everyone to listen to the radio because the emperor would be speaking. "The emperor was going to say something about a 'fantastic weapon' invented by Japan," the old man told the boy. The weapon was supposed to "wipe out the Americans in no time" and win the war for Japan.

Eun-kook and his grandfather sat together on the veranda while they listened to the crackling notes of the Japanese national anthem. Although they had been reminded by the police to face the radio and touch the floor with their foreheads when the emperor spoke, they did no such thing. Both remained sitting upright and cross-legged. Then the emperor spoke. Eun-kook translated the speech for his grandfather because the old man could not understand Japanese. At first the young boy had a hard time making sense of the emperor's words. Neither he nor his grandfather, or any of the emperor's subjects for that matter, had ever heard the voice of the emperor before.

"Well, what is he saying?" asked the old man. "Has he said anything important yet?" The boy shook his head. The emperor spoke in a complex form of Japanese that few people could understand. Eun-kook turned up the volume. Suddenly, he straightened up, jolted by what he had just heard. He told his grandfather that the emperor had just announced that Japan had lost the war and would surrender unconditionally to the Allied Powers. The old man grasped the boy and began sobbing. Hearing the cries, the boy's grandmother ran out to the veranda. She too began weeping openly when she learned the news. Before the emperor had finished speaking, Eun-kook abruptly turned off the radio. He ran outside and took down the Japanese flag that hung by the door. Showing it to his grandmother, he asked what he should do with it. "Burn it," she said.[1]

End of Empire

For tens of millions of Koreans who listened to the Japanese emperor's announcement that afternoon, August 15 was a day of joyous celebration, marking freedom from thirty-five years of colonial servitude. Despite the fervor of the moment, however, liberation carried a heavy price. Korea was not liberated by Koreans, and so Korea was subjugated to the will and wishes of its liberators. While thousands of Japanese flooded the trains and ferries to go back to Japan, the Americans and Soviets took control. American planners had only a vague notion of what would happen to Korea after Japan's collapse. Korea had never been important to the United States. Forty years earlier, President Theodore Roosevelt had taken a cold-eyed, realistic view of the situation in northeast Asia. He had accepted Japan as the regional hegemon and praised Japan's success and progress from a feudal state to world power in less than four decades. Roosevelt's recognition of Japan's "special interest" in Korea after it defeated Russia in the Russo-Japanese War (1904–5), a war he helped end by negotiating a peace treaty, for which he received the Nobel Peace Prize, had facilitated Korea's colonization. For this Japan had agreed to recognize America's special interest in the Philippines.

Theodore Roosevelt's complicity in Korea's colonization would be rectified in 1945 by his cousin's vision of a free and independent Korea. After World War II, Franklin Delano Roosevelt (FDR) embraced a new world order that would fundamentally transform the status of Japanese and European colonies. He advocated the virtues of representative democracy, aid to the oppressed, free trade, and open markets. But before full independence could be granted to Korea and other former colonies, FDR envisioned a period of trusteeship by the Allied Powers to oversee internal affairs and prepare them for independence and self-rule. He was also careful to ensure that postcolonial nations would not orient themselves against American interests. Although at first opposed, Churchill agreed, because the Cairo Declaration did not specifically infringe on

Britain's own colonial holdings and named only Korea for trusteeship. The Declaration, published on December 1, 1943, contained the first Great Power pledge by the United States, Great Britain, and China to support Korean independence "in due course." Stalin responded positively about the trusteeship idea when FDR told him about it at their meeting in Tehran shortly after the Cairo Conference, but Stalin thought the period of trusteeship should be as short as possible.[2]

The proposal, however, was ill defined and lacked specifics on how a joint trusteeship in Korea was supposed to work. In the end, it was not resolved through an agreement, but by military events on the ground. More than FDR's grand design for a new world order, it was the sudden collapse of Japan that would determine Korea's future, as well as the post–World War II order in Asia. At Yalta in February 1945, as the end of World War II approached, FDR and Stalin agreed that Soviet forces would liberate Korea while the Americans would invade the Japanese mainland.[3] Stalin expected much in return for liberating Manchuria and Korea. American General Douglas MacArthur, the Supreme Commander for the Allied Powers (SCAP) for the Japanese occupation, warned, "They would want all of Manchuria, Korea, and possibly parts of North China. The seizure of territory was inevitable, but the United States must insist that Russia pay her way by invading Manchuria at the earliest possible date after the defeat of Germany."[4] Roosevelt tacitly agreed. Without consulting Churchill or the Chinese leader Chiang Kai-shek (Jiang Jieshi), FDR made a secret deal with Stalin conceding the Kurile Islands, the southern half of Sakhalin, and special privileges in Manchuria for Soviet entry into the war against Japan.[5]

By the time the Potsdam Conference was held in July following Germany's surrender, the situation had changed dramatically, owing to the death of FDR in April and the success of the atomic bomb program. The main goal of the Potsdam Conference was to establish a vision for the postwar world order, but the bomb's existence had complicated matters between the United States and the Soviet Union. American Secretary of War Henry Stimson told President Harry Truman at the conference that the atomic bomb would be ready in a matter of days for use against Japan. Truman then approached Churchill to discuss what they should tell Stalin. If they told him about the bomb, he might try to enter the war against Japan as soon as possible. The bomb provided the possibility of circumventing a costly invasion of Japan, and the need for Soviet help became far less pressing. Truman decided to tell Stalin as late as possible and to describe it in the vaguest terms, not as an atomic bomb but as "an entirely novel form of bomb."[6]

Stalin, however, had already known of the bomb's existence for some time.[7] Andrei Gromyko, the Soviet ambassador to the United States at the time, recalled that Stalin was angry at the Americans' apparent lack of trust. "Roosevelt clearly felt no need to put us in the picture," Stalin later told Gromyko. "He could have done it at Yalta. He could simply have told me the atom bomb was going through its experimental stages. We were supposed to be allies."[8] Stalin told Truman that his forces would be ready for action by mid-August. With the atomic bomb on the table, however, Stalin secretly decided to advance the date of the attack by ten days, as Truman and Churchill had feared. He would outmaneuver the Americans, who had hoped to force Japan's surrender without the Soviet Union's entry into the war. At 11 p.m. on August 8, two days after "Little Boy" was dropped on Hiroshima, the Soviet Union declared war on Japan. Soviet forces began crossing into Manchuria an hour later on August 9. For just a week's worth of fighting, the Soviet Union reclaimed the territory lost in the Russo-Japanese War. Truman had lost the race to induce Japan's surrender before Soviet tanks rolled into Manchuria.[9]

Japan's sudden collapse caught everyone by surprise. The fate of the Korean peninsula suddenly became of interest to the Americans. The Soviet advance through Manchuria was so rapid that it would be able to occupy all of the Korean peninsula before the Americans could get there. It was one thing to give up Korea to save American lives and quite another to simply hand it over to the Soviets. The United States realized that talks of joint trusteeship would be moot if the Soviets occupied all of Korea. The Americans decided to approach the Soviets with a proposal to divide the peninsula into American and Soviet zones of occupation, with the ultimate goal of creating a unified Korea under joint American and Soviet tutelage. But before such a request could be offered, a decision on where to divide the peninsula had to be made. This task fell on two U.S. Army colonels from the War Department staff, Charles Bonesteel, future commander of U.S. and UN forces in Korea in the late 1960s, and Dean Rusk, future secretary of state under Presidents John F. Kennedy and Lyndon B. Johnson. Using a *National Geographic* map and working late into the night under great pressure, they chose the 38th parallel. Rusk later recalled that "we recommended the 38th Parallel even though it was further north than could realistically be reached . . . in the event of Soviet disagreement," but to the surprise and relief of everyone, Stalin agreed.[10]

Why did he agree when Soviet forces could have easily occupied the entire peninsula? Rather than territorial gain, Stalin's main concern was to eliminate Japanese political and economic influence in the region. "Japan must forever be excluded from Korea," stated a June 1945 Soviet report on Korea, "since a Korea under Japanese rule would be a constant threat to the Far East of the USSR."[11] Stalin accepted a divided occupation in Korea because the Americans could help in neutralizing Japan. Japanese victory in the Russo-Japanese War had forced Russia to forfeit its interests in Korea and Manchuria for nearly half a century and to give up Russian territory in southern Sakhalin. Japan's demise gave Stalin the chance to regain Russia's pre-1905 position in the Far East. As Stalin triumphantly noted in a radio speech on September 2, the date of Japan's formal surrender, "The defeat of the Russian troops in the period of the Russo-Japanese War left grave memories in the minds of our people. It fell as a dark stain on our country. Our people trusted and awaited the day when Japan would be routed and the stain wiped out. For forty years we, the men of the older generation, have waited for this day. And now this day has come."[12]

Red Army in Korea

The first weeks of Soviet occupation did not bode well for the Koreans. The soldiers were not the Red Army's finest and lacked discipline. The initial wave of Russian troops behaved with widespread and indiscriminate violence toward the local population. Within days of their arrival, disturbing reports of rape and pillage filtered into the American zone from beleaguered Japanese and Korean refugees.[13] Harold Isaacs of *Newsweek* described a harrowing visit to Sŏngdo city, about fifty miles north of Seoul and now known as Kaesŏng, which the Russians had mistakenly occupied and then retreated from as it lies south of the 38th parallel. During their ten-day stay, the Russians had thoroughly ransacked the city's shops, wineries, and warehouses.[14] Moscow claimed northern Korea's economic resources as compensation for its week-long war against Japan. Industrial complexes in North and South Hamgyŏng provinces were particularly hard hit as Russian forces dismantled steel plants, textile mills, and dock facilities and shipped the parts back to the Soviet Union.[15]

Reports of the Soviet pillaging led many Americans to believe that support for the Russians in northern Korea would be short-lived. Remarkably, however, Korean resistance to Soviet occupation did not last long. Stalin ordered the commander of the Soviet occupation force to take control of the situation and "to explain to the local population . . . that the private and public property of the citizens of North Korea are under the protection of Soviet military power . . . [and] to give instruction to the troops in North Korea to strictly observe discipline, not offend the population, and conduct themselves properly."[16] By late September 1945, discipline markedly improved, and the harassment of the local population ended as the Soviet occupiers quickly began to establish control over their zone.[17] Ethnic Koreans already in service with the Soviet government and others were mobilized to help with the administration of the Soviet zone. While the occupation of northern Korea found the Soviets almost as unprepared and untrained for the task as the Americans were in the south, the available pool of these Soviet Korean citizens who were committed communists, spoke both Korean and Russian, and understood the political and cultural nuances of Korean society made the transition to Soviet-occupied northern Korea a fairly easy one.

The history of the Soviet Korean community is intimately intertwined with the turbulent history of Russo-Japanese relations. Although Korean emigration to the Russian Far East goes back to the mid-nineteenth century, the flow increased significantly after the Russo-Japanese War and Japanese colonization of the peninsula. Tens of thousands of Koreans during this period fled the Japanese colony and sought refuge in Russia. Following the Russian Revolution of 1917, many Korean communists joined the Bolsheviks in Russia's civil war. Japan's invasion of Manchuria in September 1931 and Stalin's pledge to aid Chiang Kai-shek's Nationalist forces against the Japanese further consolidated Soviet Koreans behind the Soviet regime in their fight against Japan. In 1932, all Soviet Koreans were granted Soviet citizen-

Ethnic Korean families living in the Soviet Far East, like Hum Bung-do and his wife (above), were the first among many ethnic minorities to be subjected to the hardships of deportation by the Soviet leadership in 1937. Their resettlement in Kazakhstan and Central Asia also offered a partial solution to depopulation in these areas. Forced collectivization, famine (1931–33), epidemics, and other hardships had killed some 1.7 million people in Kazakhstan alone. These losses created severe labor shortages, which were partly filled by the new Korean settlers. (COPYRIGHT KORYO SARAM: *THE UNRELIABLE PEOPLE*)

ship, but it did not spare them from Stalin's Great Purge of the late 1930s. Japan's invasion of China in 1937 was used as a pretext to forcibly relocate, at great human cost, the entire Korean community away from the Soviet Far East on the suspicion that they were instruments of the Japanese.[18] Between September and November 1937, some 180,000 Koreans were involuntarily resettled in the Soviet interior in Kazakhstan and Uzbekistan.[19] It was from these same communities that Stalin later recruited ethnic Koreans to help administer the Soviet zone.

The first cohort of Soviet Koreans arrived in P'yŏngyang in September 1945 to help set up the Soviet Civil Administration (SCA), the Soviet military government for the northern zone. "We call this period the 'Age of the Translators,'" wrote Lim Ŭn, a former North Korean official who defected to the Soviet Union in the 1960s. "The interpreters were powerful ambassadors of the Soviet Army Headquarters."[20] By quickly replacing top colonial Japanese and Korean officials and civil servants, the Soviets righteously claimed a sharp break from the colonial past. Marshal Aleksandr M. Vasilevsky, the commander in chief of the Soviet forces in the Far East, put Korean anti-Japanese sentiments to work on behalf of his troops. On August 9, the same day the Soviets invaded Manchuria, Vasilevsky issued an "Appeal by the Commander-in-Chief of the Soviet troops in the Far East to the People of Korea" that linked Korea's anti-Japanese colonial struggle to Russia's struggle against Japan:

> The dark night of slavery over the land of Korea lasted for long decades, and at last, THE HOUR OF LIBERATION HAS COME! The Red Army has, together with the troops of the allied armies, utterly destroyed the armies of Hitler's Germany, the permanent ally of Japan . . . Now the turn of Japan has come. Koreans! Rise for a holy war against your oppressors . . . Remember, Koreans, that we have a common enemy, the Japanese! Know that we will help you as a friend in the struggle for your liberation from Japanese oppression![21]

While the occupation was overseen by Soviet officers, law and order was maintained by a Soviet Korean bureaucracy that worked directly with the Korean population. Soon after liberation, several hundred self-governing People's Committees sprang up throughout the country, in both the north and the south, to help secure law and order in the immediate aftermath of liberation, but they quickly evolved into local governing groups with their own peacekeeping duties. Rather than banning them as the Americans had done in their zone, the Soviets used them by turning them "into core institutions of the pro-Soviet regime."[22]

Senior Soviet officers in Korea were not specialists in foreign affairs, let alone experts on Korea, but many of the key officers were, interestingly, veterans of the Russo-Finnish War of 1939–40, a fact that would later have consequences when the operational plan for the invasion of South Korea was formulated. Marshal Kirill Meretskov, who commanded the

Soviet forces attacking Manchuria and Korea and then became chief of the SCA, was a senior commander in the Finnish War and was personally chosen by Stalin for his proven ability in that conflict. "The wily man of Iaroslavl [Meretskov's headquarters in the Finnish War] would find a way of smashing the Japanese," Stalin said.[23] Another veteran of the Finnish War who played a key role in the occupation was Maj. Gen. Nikolai Lebedev. A political officer with limited military training, Lebedev participated in the liberation of Manchuria and northern Korea and became the head of the SCA in 1947. The most important personage was another Finnish War veteran, Col. Gen. Terentii Fomich Shtykov, head of the Soviet delegation to the United States–Union of Soviet Socialist Republics Joint Commission on Korea, the brainchild behind the creation of the SCA, and the first Soviet ambassador to North Korea. Khrushchev, future leader of the Soviet Union, described him as "brilliant."[24] Shtykov was known as Moscow's "Mr. Korea." He was, according to the historian Charles Armstrong, "instrumental in formulating Soviet policy toward Korea, had direct access to Stalin, and exercised close supervision of the political events in northern Korea."[25] Lebedev later said that "there was not an event in which Shtykov was not involved."[26]

With the Soviet Koreans working directly with the populace, Soviet authorities were able to control their zone unobtrusively while promoting Soviet policies. Yet, despite their central role in running the Soviet zone, the Soviet Koreans' influence over the Korean people was limited. Most of them had been born and raised in the Soviet Union and therefore had few if any close personal ties to the land or the people. Thus, there was an early recognition of the need for an indigenous Korean leader who had legitimacy in the Korean community while still being receptive to Soviet influence. The Soviets' first choice was Cho Man-sik. A devout Christian and nationalist who commanded great respect for his refusal to adopt a Japanese name in the 1940s, Cho was perhaps the most admired political figure in all of Korea and thus could have been an effective Soviet proxy.[27] Since the communist movement in northern Korea was virtually nonexistent, its main strength being in the south, there was no pool of Korean communists for the Soviets to choose from. The Soviets hoped to leverage Cho's popularity and prestige to put together a broad coalition of leftists and nationalists as a base of support for their policies and plans to create a pro-Soviet regime.

It was soon apparent, however, that Cho was not amenable to such an arrangement. Yu Sŏng-ch'ŏl, a Soviet Korean who later became chief of the North Korean army's Operations Bureau, recalled that Cho opposed Soviet policies and "refused to cooperate with the Soviet Occupation Forces." Even after Cho's refusal, "the Soviet Occupation Forces tried to recruit Cho through many different people. However, they were never successful in their attempts, and [because of] this the Soviets lost interest."[28]

The other logical choice was Pak Hŏn-yŏng, one of the key leaders of the Korean Communist Party (KCP). But Pak was from Seoul and was neither well known nor completely trusted in the north. "The decisive cause of Pak's failure," wrote Lim Ŭn, "was that he was unable to get 'a sign of wings' [a check mark next to his name] from Stalin." The Soviets also discounted Korean communists who had fought with the Chinese communists in the Chinese civil war, because they could not be trusted. Kim Mu-chŏng, more commonly known simply as Mu Chŏng, was perhaps the most prominent member of this faction. He participated in and survived the Long March with Mao Zedong in 1934–35 and was considered by his contemporaries as a "matchless star." "He won popularity as he was an eloquent speaker of great resources," observed Lim Ŭn. But it was precisely because of his strong ties to the Chinese communists "that the Soviets felt that they could not trust him."[29] This left one final group of Korean communists who might be tapped, the small band of former anti-Japanese guerillas in Manchuria who had found refuge in the Soviet Far East. Among them was a boyish thirty-three-year-old captain in the Soviet Army named Kim Il Sung. Yu Sŏng-ch'ŏl recalled that Kim had "considerable authority among the . . . partisans who, along with Kim, had risked their lives conducting anti-Japanese resistance operations . . . in Manchuria."[30]

Compared to Cho Man-sik, Pak Hŏn-yŏng, and Mu Chŏng, Kim Il Sung had far less experience as either a political leader or a military commander. The 88th Brigade at Khabarovsk, to which Kim Il Sung had been assigned as a young Soviet captain, was a reconnaissance unit that infiltrated into Japanese areas to gather information.[31] Yu, who met Kim in the 88th Brigade, recalled only one instance when Kim directly commanded a reconnaissance mission: "On June 4, 1937, Kim Il Sung led a group of some 200 partisans . . . across the border in an assault on the border village of Poch'ŏnbo killing several Japanese police and retreating after obtaining rations and funds from landlords there." A month after the Japanese surrender, Kim Il Sung and Yu Sŏng-ch'ŏl arrived in Wŏnsan. "At the time," recalled Yu, "I was not quite sure how the Soviets intended to use us in North Korea, but I believe there was no definite plan. Even at this time, none of us was thinking that Kim Il Sung would become the new leader of North Korea."[32] Still, visible interest in Kim Il Sung was shown when Col. Gen. Ivan Chistiakov, commander of the Soviet occupation army, personally greeted him. The first sign of Kim's rising star came at a mass rally in mid-October to honor the Soviet Army. It was there that Kim was introduced to the citizens of P'yŏngyang. Cho Man-sik was also asked by the Russians to give his blessing to the event by appearing alongside Kim.

By all accounts the event was a flop. When Lebedev, chief of the SCA, opened the rally and presented Kim as a national hero and an "outstanding guerilla leader," many were astonished and even angry. O Yŏng-jin, Cho Man-sik's personal secretary, recalled the public's reaction:

> [The people had anticipated a gray-haired veteran patriot] but they saw a young man of about 30 with a manuscript approaching the microphone . . . His complexion was slightly dark and he had a haircut like a Chinese waiter . . . "He is a fake!" All of the people gathered upon the athletic field felt an electrifying sense of distrust, disappointment, discontent, and anger . . . There was the problem of age, but there was also the content of the speech, which was so much like that of the other communists whose monotonous repetitions had worn the people out.[33]

The Soviet authorities were alarmed and bewildered by the negative reaction, but they stuck with their choice and thereafter "placed enormous emphasis on improving Kim Il Sung's image through propaganda activities."[34]

In late 1945, Chistiakov announced that the People's Committees would be allowed to participate in political affairs if they interacted with proper Russian authorities.[35] This was followed by a requirement for all "anti-Japanese parties and democratic organizations" to register with the SCA and provide a roster of its members. The SCA was thus able to identify "activists" and control organizations that were deemed potentially subversive. Parties identified as anticommunist or sympathetic to the United States were banned.[36] Many Koreans reacted with outrage. In addition, contrary to the hope that the People's Committees would abolish the state purchase of grains, a policy the Japanese had forced on Korean farmers, no such reforms occurred. Instead, on August 20, the People's Committees officially announced plans for the state to purchase grain. For the average North Korean farmer, very little had changed before and after liberation.[37]

On November 23, riots broke out in Sinŭiju, a northwestern city on the Yalu River. Secondary-school students demonstrated against "the provincial police headquarters, People's Committee, and the provincial [communist] party headquarters calling for the removal of Communist and Soviet military rule." One account stated that "the police and Soviet troops opened fire killing 23 students and wounding some 700."[38] Soon after the uprising, a stream of people began to flow to the south. From early December 1945, six thousand refugees a day poured into the American zone, straining the U.S. military command's ability to handle them.[39] Student riots in the port city of Hamhŭng on the east coast in March 1946 exacerbated the situation.[40] By July 1947, the *New York Times* reported, nearly two million refugees had moved south from the Soviet zone.[41]

The Soviets welcomed this exodus, for it removed much of the anti-Soviet and anticommunist factions in their zone. Still, the uprisings in Sinŭiju and elsewhere were warnings to Kim Il Sung and his Soviet backers of the potential hazards from social unrest. Lebedev was particularly alarmed by reports of scattered violence. Political opponents shot and killed the chairman of a township People's Committee in the county of Haeju, and an ex-landlord attempted to murder a peasant committee member in the same province. There were reports of water tanks being poisoned and a food depot set on fire.[42] The Soviet response was to tighten control over political groups and activities. Kim Il Sung declared that social and political unrest had occurred because the Korean Communist Party (KCP) had weak ties to the masses. He called for the merging of "democratic forces" in northern Korea to create a united front. New members needed to be properly screened and trained, and old members vetted to purge reactionary elements. Local cells were brought under centralized party control. By December 1945, the contours of the future North Korean regime had already begun to take shape.[43]

General Hodge Goes to Korea

The Americans faced greater difficulties in governing their zone despite the initial goodwill of the Koreans. Many Koreans were familiar with the American missionaries who had been in Korea since the mid-nineteenth century. Moreover, a large number of prominent Korean leaders in the south, as in the north, were devout Christians. Few believed that American soldiers would act like the Russians and expected, with tremendous excitement, the prospect of independence and freedom.

The goodwill quickly evaporated soon after Lt. Gen. John R. Hodge and his XXIV Corps arrived in September 1945. A capable and blunt-speaking field commander, Hodge went to Korea with the simple goal of disarming the Japanese and sending them back to Japan. With the trusteeship plan still not fully settled, American policy in East Asia was focused not on the occupation of Korea, but on the occupation of Japan. The focus on Japan would have lasting implications for Korea. General MacArthur adopted an "enlightened" policy, treating the Japanese not as America's conquered foe, but as a new and liberated friend. Arriving

Parade welcoming the Americans on September 16, 1945. Many of the welcoming parades also featured Soviet flags as the Korean people were not sure whom their liberators would be. (U.S. NATIONAL ARCHIVES AND RECORDS ADMINISTRATION)

in Tokyo at the end of August, MacArthur believed that the occupation should make maximum use of existing institutions to govern "from above" while seeking to induce radical changes "from below." America, he said, would lead the Japanese by example. Setting out to reform the Japanese of their "backward" and "feudalistic" culture, MacArthur sought to reweave Japan's political, social, cultural, and economic fabric and revise the very way the Japanese thought of themselves. It was a role he relished.[44] But America's occupation policy for Japan had confusing implications for Korea. If the Japanese were to be reformed and treated as friends, where did that leave the Koreans, victims of Japan's brutal colonial regime?

Hodge did not give much thought to the question since his primary concern was to disarm and repatriate the Japanese. He was also unsure of the reception he and his troops would receive when they arrived in Korea. Colonel Kenneth Strother of the XXIV Corps staff recalled Hodge's uneasy reaction: "At the time and in the atmosphere which had been generated by four years of combat with the Japanese, the thought of trusting the lives of a small group of American soldiers to the Japanese Army [in Korea] was startling." Moreover, there had also been some doubt as to whether the Japanese were in full control of the situation in Korea. "The Japanese government was having plenty of trouble between their surrender and the arrival of the American occupation forces," observed Strother. "As we later learned, a conspiracy against the government to prevent national surrender developed on August 16 into an open revolt by the garrison troops of Tokyo. This was put down with bloodshed, leaving serious question as to the attitude we might expect in the Japanese troops stationed in Korea."[45] The precarious state of affairs in liberated Korea and the potential for violence led Hodge to decide that he would have to rely on incumbent Japanese officials to carry out the essential functions of governance. To his relief, Hodge and his men were received peacefully and courteously, dispelling fears that they might face a hostile or unstable situation in Korea. However, the Koreans reacted with outrage when Hodge announced that Japanese officials, including the hated Governor General Abe Nobuyuki, would continue to administer the American zone. Hoping to placate their anger, Hodge announced that "Abe's position would be analogous to that of the Emperor of Japan," meaning that he would "merely be a figurehead." For a people who had been oppressed by this "figurehead" for the last thirty-five years, these were hardly reassuring words.[46]

On September 9, Hodge and Abe signed the formal surrender document. As Abe reached over to sign with the pen, he began to tremble. "His complexion suddenly took on an alarming green cast," recalled Strother. Turning his head away, Abe "vomited quietly in his handkerchief before affixing his own signature." Hodge was deeply affected. As a professional military man, Hodge respected the Japanese as loyal soldiers and empathized with the pain of their defeat. Earlier, Abe had requested that he and his family remain in the official residence for a few extra days because his wife was ill with pneumonia. Strother recalled that "Hodge, a stern-looking, tough talking man, replied with obvious compassion that the Abes could stay in residence as long as they wanted."[47] Such acts of compassion toward the Japanese, mostly because Japanese cooperation was essential, enraged the Koreans. They deeply resented the Americans treating the Koreans as a conquered people while conferring with the Japanese on the future of their country. They also questioned American motives. Just what kind of liberators would allow a defeated nation to remain in power? What kind of deal was being struck? The situation smacked of the Great Power jostling over Korea that had occurred at the end of the nineteenth century and had led to subjugation under Japan.

The Americans soon realized that retaining Japanese officials was harming their ability to govern. MacArthur wrote to Hodge, "For political reasons it is advisable that you should remove from office immediately: Governor-General Abe, Chiefs of all bureaus of the Government-General, provincial governors and provincial police chiefs." He concluded, "You should furthermore proceed as rapidly as possible with the removal of other Japanese and collaborationist Korean administrators." This was easier said than done. Could the Americans govern without the Japanese? H. Merrell Benninghoff, the State Department political advisor to Hodge, thought that the "removal of Japanese officials is desirable from the public opinion standpoint," but they must be relieved "only in name [because] there are no qualified Koreans for other than the low-ranking positions, either in government or in public utilities and communications." The question was how long Hodge and his staff would have to rely on the Japanese. Benninghoff pointed out a possible way out: "Seoul, and perhaps southern Korea as a whole, is at present politically divided into two distinct political groups. On the one hand there is the so-called democratic or conservative group, which numbers among its members many of the professional and educational leaders who were educated in the United States or in American missionary institutions in Korea. In their aims and policies they demonstrate a desire to follow the western democracies." On the other hand, "there is the radical or communist group. This apparently is composed of several smaller groups ranging in thought from left of center to radical. The avowed communist group is the most vocal and seems to be supplying the leadership." Benninghoff believed that the U.S. Army Military Government in Korea (USAMGIK) would be able to work with the so-called conservative group. He also optimistically concluded, "Although many of them have served with the Japanese, that stigma ought eventually to disappear."[48]

Early in the occupation, USAMGIK had attempted to be neutral in its treatment of the various and often hastily organized Korean political groups. But this policy proved to be increasingly difficult. For practical purposes, the Americans needed Koreans who spoke English, but "it so happened that these persons and their friends came largely from the moneyed classes because English had been a luxury among Koreans." They were therefore part of the privileged conservatives far removed from the masses.[49] The Americans also needed Koreans who supported the occupation's aims, which meant that these Koreans required American support to remain in power. The "radical" group identified by Benninghoff did not fit either of these categories.

Ironically, it was the Japanese who were largely responsible for the viability of the so-called "radical" group. On August 14, Abe met with Yŏ Un-hyŏng, a moderate leftist who was rumored to be a member of a Korean communist group in Shanghai. Abe said that the Japanese were planning to surrender the following day, and asked Yŏ to organize a group to help maintain order. Yŏ agreed. Within a few weeks, the organization that was meant to keep the Koreans in line during the transition period until the arrival of the Americans had transformed into a self-declared and de facto Korean government. Two days before the Americans' arrival, Yŏ declared that his newly established organization was not only a political party but also the government of the Korean People's Republic (KPR). The KPR group attracted many populist and left-leaning nationalists whose paramount concern was not ideology, but the establishment of an independent Korean state.[50]

On the morning of September 8, three leading members of the KPR group, including Yŏ, went to meet Hodge. Yŏ viewed the American occupation command as a transitional authority between the Japanese colonial government and the newly established KPR. The members had come to offer their services as a liaison between the American military command and the Korean people. They were also emphatic about removing the Japanese from Korea as quickly as possible. Hodge, ironically, refused to meet them because the KPR group was formed with Japanese support. He considered it "unwise to give even the slightest possible appearance of favoring any political group."[51] In a double irony, it also became apparent that the allegedly "pro-Japanese" KPR was not supported by the Japanese, who considered Yŏ to be a "political opportunist with communist leanings." The Americans were warned that the KPR was "better organized and more vocal" than any other political group in Korea, and that "the nature and the extent of actual communist (Soviet Russia) infiltration cannot be stated with certainty, but may be considerable."[52]

More alarming was the KPR's unwillingness to cooperate with USAMGIK. By mid-September, the KPR began organizing numerous subsidiary groups throughout the country. The group released political prisoners, assumed responsibility for public safety, and organized food distributions. In addition, the KPR called for a national election as early as March 1946. Realizing that the authority of the occupation was being undermined by the KPR, Maj. Gen. Archibald Arnold, the military governor of Seoul, issued a strongly worded statement against the organization for "confusing and misleading" the Korean people. He declared that "there is only one Government in Korea south of the 38 degrees north latitude"; it is the government "created in accordance with the proclamations of General MacArthur, the General Orders of Lieutenant General Hodge and the Civil Administration order of the Military Governor." Arnold also mocked the KPR's "self-appointed 'officials,' 'police,' groups, big (or little) conferences," which he said were "entirely without any authority, power or reality," and warned the KPR leaders that the "puppet show" must end. "Let us have no more of this," he declared. "For any man or group to call an election as proposed is the most serious interference with the Military Government, an act of open opposition to the Military Government and the lawful authority of the Government of Korea under the Military Government."[53]

Arnold's proclamation appalled the KPR leaders. While his statement was meant to show who was in charge, its demeaning tone and condescending language resulted in further alienating the KPR and ordinary Koreans from the Americans. In response, the KPR published *The Traitors and the Patriots.* The pamphlet began with an exposure of allegedly pro-Japanese officials who were advising USAMGIK. It attacked the notion that USAMGIK was the only legitimate government south of the 38th parallel. The KPR, the pamphlet asserted, "was the duly constituted organ of the people," and Arnold's statement was condemned as an "insult to the Korean people."[54]

By mid-October 1945, Hodge understood that the KPR could have no future role under the American occupation. USAMGIK gave its support to the Korean Democratic Party (KDP), the group of conservatives first identified by Benninghoff. What the Americans needed most at this time was bilingual, educated, and above all, cooperative allies to deal with rising discontent and revolutionary sentiments. Hodge was less worried about the KPR's leftist ideology than its deliberate attempts to subvert his authority. A crackdown on the KPR soon ensued. His willingness to accept leftist organizations as long as they did not challenge USAMGIK's authority also reflected MacArthur's tolerance of leftists and communists in Japan at the time.

Hodge miscalculated in thinking that disbanding the KPR would end the challenges to USAMGIK's authority. Many Koreans were by now deeply disillusioned by the failed expectations of liberation. Especially critical was land reform and rice supply. USAMGIK seized Japanese-owned land but did not turn it over to Korean farmers. Theoretically, former Japanese land was to be held in escrow for redistribution as part of a land reform plan, but lack of planning led to rumors that the land would be given to wealthy landlords, those who had collaborated with the Japanese, and supporters of the American occupation. Many Koreans believed that the Americans were reestablishing the same system of land ownership and political dictatorship that had prevailed under the Japanese. Furthermore, in the fall of 1945, USAMGIK abolished the price controls on rice. The bumper crop in 1945 led many to expect that for the first time in decades, Koreans would have an ample supply of rice since no rice would be sent to Japan, as had been the practice during the colonial period. But just the opposite result occurred. With price

General Hodge broadcasting to the United States about the conditions of American troops in Korea, April 18, 1948. (U.S. NATIONAL ARCHIVES AND RECORDS ADMINISTRATION)

controls gone, speculators bought up the rice they could find, driving up the price. Greedy farmers withheld rice in anticipation of greater profits. USAMGIK did little to stop the hoarding, while hungry Koreans demanded that price ceilings be reinstituted. In March 1946, the Americans were forced to issue directives for rationing, but these controls only reminded Korean farmers of the former Japanese system. To make matters worse, the average Korean received only half the amount of rice he or she had received under the Japanese.[55] "As a result of its handling of the rice problem, the Koreans arrived at a complete loss of faith in the Military Government," lamented an attorney who served in Korea during this period.[56]

The Americans also had a problem the Soviets did not: the repatriation of several hundred thousand Japanese soldiers and civilians.[57] In October alone, more than eighty-eight thousand were evacuated, creating enormous administrative and logistical pressures on the relatively small American force. Meanwhile, hundreds of thousands of Korean refugees from the Soviet zone and Manchuria added to the south's economic plight. "The refugee crisis," stated an embassy report, "is making living conditions increasingly hard. Three-quarters of the population of Korea is now in our hands and the Koreans are looking to us for a solution to their problem."[58] Inflation, black markets, scarcity of consumer

The rice shortage in Pusan came to a head on the evening of July 6, 1946, when a mob of hungry people attempted to break into a rice distribution center. (U.S. NATIONAL ARCHIVES AND RECORDS ADMINISTRATION)

goods, and an unbalanced wage scale added to the economic and political confusion in the American zone.

The morale of the Americans was a problem as well. Charles Donnelly, an economic advisor to the U.S. Army Forces in Korea (USAFIK was the overall military command in Korea and oversaw USAMGIK), noted that "the shortage of typewriters, stencils, and chairs is scandalous."[59] Empty shelves in the post exchange glumly revealed the reality of being at the end of a long supply line from the United States. One reporter counted the following items for sale in early December: "ten cartons of cigarette, five bars of candy, six toothbrushes, several packages of razor blades, and a few pads of writing paper, all for 500 soldiers." Americans, who "just a few weeks ago were selling cigarettes to the Koreans, are now buying them back at a high cost . . . grumbling soldiers and officers are complaining that folks at home don't seem to care, now that the war is over, whether we are getting supplies or not."[60] Another chronic problem was theft. "Thievery here is rampant," Donnelly complained. "My felt hat was stolen from my office. Miss Carol's handbag with sixty dollars in it was taken from her desk while she was in the restroom. Simon lost his hat and top coat. A resident in the Bizenya [a hotel] awoke to find that his room was literally stripped of everything except the bed in which he was sleeping." Relations between the Americans and the Koreans were increasingly strained. The Koreans resented the occupation while the Americans increasingly disliked the Koreans because they acted "like difficult spoiled children." "The Koreans are unwilling to take the time to develop political and economic know-how," wrote Donnelly. "All they want is for Americans to get out of their country so that they can run it by themselves."[61] By the end of 1945, the Americans were struggling to gain control over an increasingly chaotic and demoralizing situation. Something had to be done.

CHAPTER TWO

Two Koreas

Prior to 1945, Stalin had been vague in committing to a joint trusteeship for Korea, and now that the Soviets had successfully set up a relatively stable, friendly, and well-functioning government in their zone, he became less enthusiastic. The Soviets were barely responsive to American initiatives to unify the economy or to relax travel restrictions between the two zones. Hoping to exchange a trainload of supplies for coal, Hodge was shocked to learn that the Soviets not only refused to send the coal, but also kept the train.[1] The Americans faced far greater economic and political turmoil than the Soviets. Hodge and his staff identified the uncertainty of Korea's future as the greatest source of political discontent. Establishing an independent, united, and democratic Korea was clearly a priority. The turmoil provided an ideal condition for leftist and communist groups to flourish. Edwin Pauley, an advisor to President Truman who visited Korea in early 1946, warned Truman that "communism in Korea could get off to a better start than practically anywhere else in the world. The Japanese [had] owned the railroads, all the public utilities including power and light as well as all of the major industries and natural resources." Now the communists could "acquire them without any struggle of any kind." For this reason "the United States should not waive its title or claim to Japanese external assets located in Korea until a democratic (capitalist) form of government is assured."[2] But how was such a government to be established? Joint trusteeship leading to independence seemed to be the only viable option to avoid a divided Korea. Until an agreement was concluded with the Soviets, however, USAMGIK would be forced to tighten control, build closer relationships with more conciliatory groups like the KDP and prevent a takeover by the leftists. While Washington was considering trusteeship with the Soviets, Americans on the ground were strengthening their control over their zone and hence deepening the division between the two zones.

The contradiction frustrated the Americans in Korea. They were critical of the trusteeship idea. William Langdon, Hodge's political advisor, pointed out the obvious: that Koreans of all political persuasions would protest fervently against it. "After one month's service in liberated Korea and with background of earlier service in Korea," Langdon wrote to the secretary of state in Washington, "I am unable to fit trusteeship to the actual conditions here or to be persuaded of its sustainability from moral and practical standpoints and, therefore, believe we should drop it." As an alternative, Langdon proposed a trusteeship plan to begin in the American zone. He noted that during the transition period between USAMGIK and the formation of an independent Korean government, the Soviets should be invited to participate in the process. But if the Soviets were not forthcoming, the United States should carry out the plan in the southern zone. The deteriorating political situation in the south required immediate action for transition to independence with or without the Soviets. "It is imperative that the U.S. act," warned Langdon, as "[only such actions] will convince the Korean leaders that our intentions of their independence are genuine and in this way we can win their support in fighting communism, unrest, and the hostility of the masses toward us."[3]

Hodge and his staff, as well as MacArthur and his staff, agreed with Langdon. The issue boiled down to promising Koreans their independence by backing political leaders and groups conciliatory to American interests. But whom? The KDP's leaders had always had the ears of the Americans, but the group's political power base was weak due to its lack of contact with the masses and past associations with the Japanese. Someone without links to the colonial regime, but with nationalist standing among the Koreans, was needed. KDP leaders suggested Syngman Rhee (Yi Sŭng-man). In many ways, Rhee was the perfect candidate. He had spent much of his life overseas, mostly in the United States, where he earned a PhD from Princeton in 1910. After a two-year stint in Seoul as a Christian educator and missionary, he returned to the States in 1912. In 1919 he was elected the first president of the Korean Provisional Government (KPG), a government in exile in Shanghai. He went back to the United States in 1925 after being expelled by the KPG and remained there until the end of World War II. While in the States, he was politically active in the Korean independence movement. He was fluent in English as well as untainted by association with the colonial regime. Rhee was seventy years old in 1945, but vigorous. He was also difficult, stubborn, and fiercely patriotic. Francesca Rhee, his Austrian wife whom he met in Geneva in 1933, wistfully wrote in a letter to a friend, "When I married Dr. Rhee, I married Korea."[4]

Rhee's stint as president of the KPG was marked by strife. He tried hard to get American recognition of the KPG as the legitimate government of Korea during the colonial period. Some in the State Department found him and other KPG leaders "personally ambitious and somewhat irresponsible" and downplayed the clout of the KPG "even among exiles."[5] Nevertheless, Hodge and his advisors were eager to embrace him, believing that the legitimacy Rhee could bring to the KDP and the promise of Korean independence might be enough to stem the tide of political chaos in their zone. The State Department, however, still intent on pursuing trusteeship, dragged its feet. With backing from the War Department and MacArthur, however, Hodge prepared to create a governing body in the American zone. In any case, Hodge knew that the Soviets had already created a de facto government in the north, whether the State Department wanted to admit this or not. In the end, Washington settled on a two-track policy, building up "a reasonable and respected government" in the south that would deepen the division between the two zones, while pursuing trusteeship in the hope that the two could eventually be reunited.

After much pressure, the Soviets agreed to discuss trusteeship. In mid-December 1945, the U.S. secretary of state and foreign ministers from Great Britain and the Soviet Union met in Moscow to discuss a variety of post–World War II issues. Korea was high on the agenda. The Moscow Decision that came out of the conference included provisions for establishing a unified Korean government through Soviet-American cooperation to end zonal occupations. A joint commission formed from the Soviet and American occupation authorities was to formulate recommendations for establishing a single government. However, in preparing its recommendations, the agreement stated, "the Commission shall consult with the Korean democratic parties and social organizations." Once a provisional government was established, the Soviet Union,

Members of the U.S.-U.S.S.R. Joint Commission. From left to right: Brig. Gen. John Weckerling; Col. Koruklenko; Mr. Tunkiv, Dr. Arthur Bunce; Lt. Gen. John Hodge, Col. Gen. Terentii Fomich Shtykov; Maj. Gen. Albert E. Brown; Maj. Gen. Nikolai Lebedev; Calvin M. Joyner; B. M. Balasonov; William R. Langdon; and Col. Lawrence L. Lincoln, June 1, 1947. (U.S. NATIONAL ARCHIVES AND RECORDS ADMINISTRATION)

China, Britain, and the United States would oversee it in a trusteeship for a period of up to five years.

Not surprisingly, the plan was greeted by wild protests in the south. Schools were closed down, as were factories, stores, and public transportation, while people demonstrated in the streets. Hodge, who had predicted the violent reaction, called on Song Chin-u, a leading member of the KDP, and asked him to endorse the trusteeship plan. A haggard Song tentatively agreed. The next morning, Hodge awoke to the dreadful news that Song was dead. He had been shot in the head in front of his house.[6]

Other southern Korean leaders protested and claimed independence from the Americans. Rhee, publicly distancing himself from Hodge, spoke out against the Moscow Decision. He declared that the "self respect of his nation would not permit the acceptance of this decision or of anything short of full independence."[7] Kim Ku, a staunch rightist and the last president of the KPG in Shanghai, called for a general strike and insisted on immediate recognition of the KPG. Left-wing groups were similarly outraged. The KCP denounced trusteeship. Opposition by the Right and the Left opened the possibility for a powerful coalition to challenge the trusteeship plan. On New Year's Day 1946, southern communist party leader Pak Hŏn-yŏng signed a public anti-trusteeship statement with members of the Kim Ku group. That same day, Pak met with Hodge to tell him directly his opposition to trusteeship. A huge "Citizens Rally against Trusteeship and for the Acceleration of National Unification" was planned for January 3. For the first time since liberation, the Right and the Left joined in a common cause to oppose the American and Soviet plan.[8]

But the cooperation did not last. Pak was summoned to P'yŏngyang on January 2. He returned a changed man. He told party members that the North Korean leadership had decided to support the Moscow Decision and trusteeship. Although many members balked, Pak made support of trusteeship an issue of party loyalty. In an extraordinary about-face, the January 3 rally, planned as an anti-trusteeship demonstration by Pak and other Korean communists, became a rally in support of the Moscow Decision. Moderate leftists were stunned and appalled. It was evident that Soviet authority wielded far greater control over the northern zone and the Korean communist movement than had been previously thought. Compared to the Americans' unsuccessful efforts to get the KDP and other conservative groups to support trusteeship, the Soviets were able, within a matter of a few days, to quickly put their house in order. This was the turning point the Americans needed to stabilize their zone.

Fierce opposition to trusteeship in the south temporarily united the moderate Left and the Right. A full-blown anticommunist/anti-Soviet movement enabled the Right to mobilize popular support for its policies for the first time. The communists were now painted as servants of a foreign, anti-Korean, anti-independence pro-Soviet regime. While the trusteeship controversy temporarily bolstered the American zone by fracturing the Left, and provided greater legitimacy to the KDP and other right-wing groups, the controversy had even greater consequences in the Soviet zone, where it created a political crisis and the end of challenges to the regime.[9]

On January 1, 1946, the chief of the SCA, Maj. Gen. Andrei Romanenko, asked Cho Man-sik to publicly endorse trusteeship and promised that he would be made the first president of Korea if he did so. Cho refused and was arrested, never to be heard from again. It was rumored that he was executed in October 1950 along with other political prisoners soon after the Inch'ŏn landing.[10] Cho's arrest was followed by a roundup of other Korean nationalist leaders as the Soviets made an all out effort to create a pro-Soviet proto-government in the north. In early February, the Soviets oversaw the creation of the Central People's Committee as a provisional government. Kim Il Sung became its chairman, making him, in effect, the interim premier. "Parting with Cho Man-sik without regret, Shtykov made up his mind to support Kim Il Sung as the head leader of democratic Korea and suggested this to Stalin," Lim Ŭn recalled.[11] With Cho Man-sik out of the way and the arrest of other "reactionaries," there was no longer a viable opposition leader or party in northern Korea.

The opening weeks of 1946 also saw dramatic changes to the situation in the American zone. Hodge realized the benefit of the KDP and other right-wing groups using the Moscow Decision as a catalyst for political unity. He allowed the belief to circulate in the south that it was the Soviets, not the Americans, who advocated trusteeship. Never in favor

The first formal meeting of the American-Soviet commission in Seoul. General Hodge is seated on the left, with General Shtykov in the middle and a female interpreter on the right, January 16, 1946. (U.S. NATIONAL ARCHIVES AND RECORDS ADMINISTRATION)

of the trusteeship idea, Hodge stepped out of bounds of his authority by openly siding with the Right in its opposition to the Moscow Decision. Shtykov was angry that Hodge had allowed newspapers in the American zone to falsely report that it had been the Soviets who forced trusteeship down Washington's throat. On January 22, the Soviet newspaper *Izvestia* published a strongly worded article accusing the southern rightists of "fermenting enmity against the Soviet Union."[12] Four days later at a press conference, Shtykov provided a detailed history of the trusteeship idea, declaring that it was "the Americans who had called for 'guardianship' for Korea for at least five years and possibly ten years, but that the Soviets opposed this and succeeded in obtaining adoption of the Russian plan."[13] Embarrassed over the flap, the State Department asked Hodge to clear up the "misunderstanding" and announce that Shtykov's account was essentially correct. Hodge sent back a blistering response: "It [the State Department request] is in itself complete evidence that the Department has paid little attention either to the information painstakingly sent in from those actually on the ground [in Korea] as to the psychology of the Korean people or to the repeated urgent recommendations of the commander and State Department political advisors . . . Just after the quelling of the revolt and riots brought about by the announcement of the trusteeship, our position here was the strongest since our arrival."[14]

Hodge was right. It was his opposition to the Moscow Decision that had temporarily elevated USAMGIK's status among Koreans in the south. Going against the will of the people by endorsing trusteeship would have destroyed American credibility and led to further chaos. He saw no hope in any future cooperation with the Soviets through a joint trusteeship plan or on any other basis. Hodge's remedy for Korea was to create a separate government in the south that would give the Koreans the independence they craved while shielding it from the "ruthless political machinery" in the north. Contrary to State Department officials, Hodge understood that the Moscow Decision was unworkable.

Hodge did not have to wait long for his view on the trusteeship to be vindicated. In the weeks leading up to the first meeting of the U.S.-U.S.S.R. Joint Commission tasked to establish an interim government, set for March 20, tensions had been building. On March 5, Winston Churchill delivered his fiery speech in Fulton, Missouri, in which he warned that "an iron curtain has descended across the [European] Continent." An angry Stalin fired back in an interview with *Pravda* that Churchill was nothing more than "a second Hitler." He defended his actions in Eastern Europe, stating that "it was only natural that the Soviet Union would welcome friendly nations on its borders." Picking up on Stalin's words about "friendly" nations, Hodge warned the Soviets before the first meeting that "the purpose of the American delegation is to see that a government [in Korea] corresponds to the views of the majority, not the minorities, no matter how vocal and well organized they are, or how energetic they may be in their political activities."[15] Clearly, Hodge was worried that the Soviets would favor "friendly" groups amicable to Soviet interests and exclude right-wing organizations from participating in the interim government.

Shtykov's opening speech proved Hodge correct. The Soviet officer attacked what he called "reactionary and anti-democratic groups" in the south that were offering "furious resistance" to the creation of "a democratic system in Korea." He called for a "decisive battle" against them. The criterion to determine whether a group was reactionary or anti-democratic was to be based on its support for the Moscow agreement. In other words, groups that opposed the Moscow Decision, which meant all right-wing and moderates in the south, were to be excluded from participating in the provisional government.[16] The Americans were stunned. After six weeks of fruitless discussion, the Joint Commission adjourned. Trusteeship seemed dead, and the path to permanent division appeared more certain than ever. Chistiakov later defended the Soviet position by stating that the reestablishment of Korea as an independent state required "the liquidation of the ruinous after-effects of long Japanese domination in Korea." Since the Soviet delegation was "guided by the aims and spirit of the Moscow Decision," whose purpose was to oversee the liquidation of Japanese influences, "it would therefore not be right to consult on the question of methods of fulfilling the Moscow Decision with those parties which had voiced opposition to this plan for Korea."[17] By insisting that all "pro-Japanese/anti-democratic" forces be *excluded* from the political process, the Soviets would be assured that Korea would rest in "friendly" hands. "If they [pro-Japanese forces] seize power in the [Korean] government," Shtykov told Hodge, "the government would not be loyal to Russia, and its officials would be instrumental in organizing hostile actions on the part of the Korean people against the Soviet Union."[18] These concerns underscored the extent to which the Russians feared the resurrection of Japanese power.

Failed Revolution

Suspension of the Joint Commission ushered in a period of armed struggle in the American zone. Pak Hŏn-yŏng returned to Seoul in July 1946 with instructions from Shtykov to merge the main leftist parties in the south to form the South Korean Workers Party (SKWP). In late September, a rail strike in Pusan spread throughout the American zone. More strikes followed, by postal employees, electrical workers, printers, and laborers in other industries. Students joined in, and USAMGIK faced its first real major crisis. By the end of September, the strikes became violent. On the evening of October 1, the Autumn Rebellion (also known as the Taegu Uprising) began. The police fired on striking workers at the Taegu railway station, killing one. An angry crowd assembled in front of the city police headquarters. Major John Plezia, an American advisor who was inside the headquarters, called for help from nearby American units. By the time American troops arrived, mob attacks had spread to other police stations. The next day, violence continued with vehemence. "It was open season on the police and all other natives who held jobs with the U.S. Military Government," stated one eyewitness account. "Mobs killed them on the streets, stormed police boxes and public offices and rooted them out of their homes and hiding places for slaughter." Rioters ransacked the homes of Korean officials, looting and killing. Hodge declared martial law and a crackdown. Thousands of alleged leftists were arrested. As order was restored over the following weeks, policemen and their rightist allies exacted revenge.[19]

The Americans believed that the communists and, in particular, Pak Hŏn-yŏng had instigated the strikes. Shtykov's diary clarified the Soviet involvement. The Soviets did not instigate the strikes, but their occurrence "provoked the intervention of Soviet leaders in the north." Shtykov provided advice and funneled large sums of money to support the general strike and the Autumn Rebellion. As unsettling as the uprising was for the Americans, it proved to be counterproductive for the communists. The riots resulted in loss of popular support for the Left and the emergence and rise of more extreme and less accommodating organizations from the Right. "There are no moderate groups in Korea anymore," Francesca Rhee lamented to a friend. "There are only Rightists and communists."[20] The forced merger of the Left into the SKWP had also alienated many moderate leftists, and the base of communist support shrunk to extremist groups. The successful repression of the uprising also revealed that the communists did not have the organizational strength necessary to bring about a revolution in the south. This, in turn, consolidated the forces of the Right, which became more powerful than ever before.

The most significant development was that the extreme violence perpetrated by both sides laid bare the pretense that reconciliation between the northern and southern zones was even possible. Although the United States and the Soviet Union were still officially bound to follow the Moscow Decision and the trusteeship plan, Syngman Rhee and other right-wing politicians began to actively petition to form a separate government in Seoul. "If anyone says Dr. Rhee should unite with the Reds or anyone else," wrote Rhee in a letter to his friend and advisor Robert Oliver, "tell him that Dr. Rhee will never cooperate with smallpox."[21] In January 1947, Rhee publicly repudiated the Moscow Decision. In a long and bitter diatribe against the Joint Commission, Rhee warned the Americans, "We will not accept the plan for a four power trusteeship for our country . . . It is ridiculous to believe that a nation with a 4,000 year old history of independence needs to be shepherded through a period of 'political tutelage.'"[22]

Hodge was in a difficult position. The political complications were accompanied by deteriorating living conditions in the American zone. Meanwhile, the Russians were simply biding their time. "They [the Russians] are playing now a game of waiting, a game of out-waiting us with the idea that we will tire and get out," Hodge told the U.S. House Appropriations Committee in May.[23] The Russian position had produced a deadlock. Southern rightist groups would never allow themselves to be excluded from the Joint Commission process, yet the Soviet position on excluding them was immutable. General Chistiakov expected his intransigence to pay off in terms of growing instability in the American zone. The longer the Joint Commission dragged on, the stronger the rightists' pressure in the south. The stalemate was bound to result in the splintering of the moderate center and confrontation between the Americans and the extreme Right. "If this trend continues," stated a 1947 interagency report, "it is apparent that our position in Korea will soon weaken to a point where it may become untenable. The Korean people are daily growing more antagonistic in their attitude toward the Military Government, toward U.S. objectives in Korea, and even toward the U.S. itself." The only alternative to continuing beyond the impasse was to form a separate government in the south, in effect creating an independent South Korea, but such a course was fraught with difficulties. Recognizing Korean independence in the southern zone would not solve its basic economic problems. "Only unification and a program of outside aid in rehabilitation can do that," wrote one political advisor, and the United States was "the only reliable source for such aid." In addition, the United States would have to establish safeguards to ensure that an independent southern Korea would not fall under Soviet domination, which meant a continued presence of American troops.[24] Two years after the liberation of Korea, the Americans still lacked a clear policy on their interest there. Unanswered was a basic question: Was the survival of a noncommunist Korea of sufficient importance to U.S. interests to undertake the risks, economic burden, and responsibility of supporting a separate South Korean regime? The unspoken consensus seemed to be "no," but many thought abandoning Korea would hurt American credibility and prestige in the emerging cold war environment.

In late September 1947, at the final Joint Commission meeting, Shtykov made a surprising proposal. He said the Koreans should be given the opportunity and responsibility for forming their own government. The Soviets were prepared to withdraw their troops from the northern zone if the Americans agreed to withdraw all their troops from the south.[25] The joint withdrawal could take place as early as 1948. The proposal seemed to provide a way for the Americans to extricate themselves from the Korean quagmire. A mutual withdrawal of troops would still preserve American prestige since it could be explained that the Koreans were getting what they had always wanted: independence. But it would also mean abandoning Korea to a likely bloody civil war and the all-but-certain takeover of the peninsula by the communists.

The Soviet proposal was studied in Washington for nearly three weeks. The Pentagon, tired of footing the bill for the occupation, had long called for a graceful exit. Korea was of little strategic value, defined as defending Japan, and the occupation was costly.[26] The State Department, however, believed that the loss of Korea would undermine America's prestige and threaten Japanese and Pacific security. It had been a year since Churchill's "Iron Curtain" speech at Fulton and George Kennan's "Long Telegram" warning of the Soviet aim to dominate the world. Communist parties were growing in France and Italy. In a weak and divided China, the Soviet Union was in position to exert greater influence than any other country. The Truman Doctrine, established in March 1947, committed U.S. support for democracies and fighting communism worldwide. How, then, could the Americans abandon Korea to the communists? On October 17, the Russians received their answer:

> In view of the continued inability of the Soviet and the United States Delegations in the Joint Commission to agree on how to proceed with their work and the refusal of the Soviet Government to participate in discussion on this problem with the other Governments adhering to the Moscow Agreement on Korea, the United States Government considers it obligated to seek the assistance of the United Nations in order that, as the Secretary of State said on September 17, "the inability of two powers to reach an agreement" should not further delay the early establishment of an independent, united Korea.[27]

The Americans thus passed the issue to the United Nations. Under UN auspices, elections for a national assembly were scheduled for May 1948, and the assembly would in turn select the president. The Soviets were invited to participate in the northern zone, but they refused, claiming that the UN could not guarantee fair elections. The specter of a permanently divided Korea was becoming a reality.

Yŏsu, Sunch'ŏn, and Cheju-do

In April 1948, Kim Il Sung hosted a conference in P'yŏngyang with southern political leaders to discuss Korea's future. It was his response to the UN's approval of separate elections in the South. He declared that Koreans must not allow other Great Powers to decide their fate. Sensing a ruse to postpone the elections, Rhee refused to attend. His rivals, the right-wing Kim Ku and moderate Kim Kyu-sik, however, agreed to go. Rhee was proved correct; the conference was a Soviet ploy. The conference "agreement" was announced with great fanfare, but it offered nothing that the Soviets had not put forth before, reiterating the same proposals laid out to the Americans in September 1947. The agreement did add one major new item that was bound to raise the ire of southern leaders: "separate elections in South Korea, if held, cannot express in any way the will of our nation, and will be regarded as a fraud."[28] Kim Ku, the staunch anticommunist and nationalist, had risked his political career by going to P'yŏngyang. He returned to Seoul disgusted. Charges of being soft on communism dogged him. A year later, a South Korean military officer, Lt. An Tu-hŭi, assassinated him.[29]

By the fall of 1946, after the Autumn Rebellion, the need for a larger indigenous security force in the American zone was apparent. Hodge envisioned an upgraded and larger security force consisting of an army of forty-five thousand, a navy and coast guard of five thousand, and a national police of twenty-five thousand.[30] While the War Department and the State Department generally backed the idea, Secretary of State George Marshall was concerned about the Soviet reaction. In 1946, the Americans were still committed to negotiating some kind of modus vivendi with the Russians, and he thought the establishment of a separate army would be interpreted as an attempt to create a separate regime. Hence, instead of "army," the ground force would be called the Korean Constabulary.

One of the men chosen to work in organizing the Constabulary was Capt. James H. Hausman, an infantry officer who had become battle-hardened in Europe during World War II. He was thirty-two years old and, at over six feet tall, an imposing figure. He was not a career officer, but a prewar sergeant. Trying to find a place for himself in the post–World War II army, Hausman had volunteered for occupation duty in Japan. He went instead to Korea as an advisor in the Military Advisory Group (commonly known in 1949 as KMAG, for Korean Military Advisory Group) that assumed responsibility for helping to organize the newly created Korean Constabulary. As an alternative force with no direct links to the hated Japanese colonial regime—a lasting legacy that the Korean police were hard-pressed to deal with—the Constabulary would help bring order to the American occupied zone without having all the obvious residual colonial associations attached to it. Volunteers accepted into the Constabulary would be chosen based on ability and merit. However, under pressure to recruit rapidly, background checks were often perfunctory. This situation would later have serious repercussions for the Constabulary and the nation. As Hausman later admitted, "We actually created a safe haven for many communists [and] we suffered the ill-effects of this many times in the months and years ahead."[31]

The Constabulary's first test came in early April 1948. While Kim Ku and Kim Kyu-sik were fuming in P'yŏngyang, a storm had gathered in the southern island of Cheju-do. On April 3, 1948, communists and leftists attacked the local government, police, and rightist youth organizations. The SKWP had ordered them to take actions to disrupt the planned general elections on May 10. Pak Hŏn-yŏng, the head of the SKWP, emphasized that actions be limited to disruptive activities to avoid bloodshed. Despite this, the rebellion became violent and spread throughout the island. It also received substantial outside help. Colonel Rothwell Brown, an American advisor, reported that the SKWP had infiltrated "over six thousand agitators and organizers" from the mainland and, with the islanders, established cells in most towns and villages. In addition, he estimated that "sixty to seventy thousand islanders had joined the party," and they were, for the most part, "ignorant, uneducated farmers and fishermen whose livelihood had been profoundly disturbed by the post-war difficulties."[32]

Thousands of police and Constabulary troops were sent to the island under orders from USAMGIK, but they could not end the unrest by election day. By May 10, the violence had become so rampant that few people dared to go to the polls. "During election week," wrote one Korean observer, "there were fifty assorted demonstrations, disorders, arson cases, and attacks, in addition to attacks on three government buildings."[33] The voting on Cheju-do was declared invalid, as the voting rate was only 20 percent, compared to the nearly 90 percent turnout on the mainland.

The end of the voting did not stop the mayhem. Instead, it became more vicious and widespread, eventually developing into a full-blown insurgency. Reports of atrocities began to surface with increasing frequency. "Stories were told of raided villages where there were found the bodies of hanged women or women and children run through with spears.

Korean students in Seoul pass out election handbills to passersby on May 4 in preparations for the elections on May 10, 1948. (U.S. NATIONAL ARCHIVES AND RECORDS ADMINISTRATION)

Voters marking their ballots during the UN-supervised elections on May 10, 1948. (U.S. NATIONAL ARCHIVES AND RECORDS ADMINISTRATION)

Tales of villages utterly wiped out kept coming in," wrote an American observer. "A number of rightist and police were also kidnapped, then hanged or beheaded."[34] A violent pacification campaign ensued. Government forces established fortified strategic hamlets manned by local militia, and conducted sweeps to locate the insurgents. Innocent civilians were invariably caught up in the sweeps.

The establishment of the Republic of Korea (ROK) on August 15, 1948, did little to curb the violence on Cheju-do. At the founding ceremony, President Rhee, selected by the newly elected National Assembly, urged the audience not to forget the division of the nation and that it would be his mission to reunify the peninsula. Meanwhile, vigilance against the forces of "alien philosophies of disruption" must be forcibly put down.[35] By August 15, the operation to put down the insurgents had reached a feverish pitch. In the hunt for the agitators, whole villages became targets, innocent suspects were beaten and hanged, and women and children massacred. A reign of terror largely perpetuated by government forces, the police, and the Republic of Korea Army (ROKA, as the Constabulary was renamed after the founding of the republic) gripped the island. "There was the occasion when ROKA personnel on Cheju-do speared to death about twenty civilians (allegedly communists) without benefit of a trial," remembered Hausman.

> Unfortunately, a picture was taken later and was given to Ambassador Muccio [first U.S. ambassador to the ROK]. I might add, a Korean Military Advisor Group sergeant had witnessed this act and he was plainly recognizable in that picture. I was ordered to report to the Ambassador. When confronted with the facts of the picture, I told the Ambassador that this was a good sign because in the past, similar groups of two hundred or more had been summarily executed and now the number was down to twenty. This was progress! I won't repeat the Ambassador's reply to me. I wouldn't want to give you the impression that he was short-tempered and uncouth.[36]

Meanwhile, in the Soviet zone, the DPRK was founded on September 9, 1948, an uneventful affair that provided a study in contrasts: a cohesive, peaceful, and highly disciplined North against the increasingly chaotic, violent, and unstable South.

As the turmoil on Cheju-do grew worse, a battalion in the 14th Regiment of the ROK Army stationed at the southern port city of Yŏsu received orders in mid-October to deploy to the island. For some time Hausman had been wary of the 14th Regiment because of doubts about its political reliability. There were a number of red flags that should have made him even more cautious. Rumors of leftists and SKWP members infiltrating its ranks abounded. The regimental commander, Maj. O Tong-gi, a fervent anticommunist, had also just been sacked, providing an opportunity for leftists and communists to organize a mutiny. On October 19, on receipt of the deployment order, the regiment mutinied. By the following morning, mutinous soldiers had murdered their officers, gathered thousands of supporters, seized control of Yŏsu, and then occupied the nearby city of Sunch'ŏn. "People's Courts" meted out summary justice. The Cheju-do Rebellion had now spread to the mainland, presenting the first major challenge to the newly established ROK. Brigadier General William Roberts, chief of KMAG, having great confidence in Hausman, selected him over more senior officers to go to Kwangju city, in the southwest, to take operational control of the suppression campaign. At Kwangju, Hausman was told that the 4th Regiment had also apparently mutinied. The 4th Regiment had been ordered to help suppress the rebellion in Sunch'ŏn, but it had disappeared en route. Meanwhile, underground members of the SKWP and local People's Committees began taking over parts of Kwangju. "In essence," wrote Hausman, "all hell had broken loose and we had nothing to stop the onslaught."[37]

On October 21, Hausman received the first good news: the "lost" 4th Regiment had not mutinied after all and was "found" in the hills west of Sunch'ŏn. Hausman organized a patchwork of ROK Army units to reclaim the city and put down the rebellion. Sunch'ŏn was retaken on October 23. ROK soldiers discovered that the mutineers had massacred as many as five hundred police and civilians, including women and children. Elmer Boyer, an American missionary living in Sunch'ŏn at the time, recalled what happened before the ROK Army units arrived:

> Most of the police were killed and hundreds of civilians. In one pile of bodies, where they had been shot, bound and tied in bunches of about ten, I counted ninety-eight persons . . . In the police yard, there were about eighty bodies . . . Just below our house, twenty-four were shot. I buried these and another Christian young man together in a long grave near here.[38]

By October 28, most of the towns and villages held by the rebels were recaptured. The Korean police exacted revenge. Keyes Beech, reporting for the *Chicago Daily News*, was in Sunch'ŏn days after the city fell and recalled the scene: "Before each square stood police, some attired in old Japanese uniforms and wearing swords. One by one, the citizens were called forward, to kneel before the police. Every question was punctuated by a blow to the head or back, sometimes with a rifle butt, sometimes from the edge of a sword. There was no outcry, no sound at all except for the barked questions and the thud of blows. That was what made the scene so terrifying, the utter, unprotesting quietness."[39] Many identified as rebels were summarily executed.[40]

By the spring of 1949, the last of the original leaders of the Cheju-do Rebellion were eliminated. The police killed Yi Tŏk-ku in early June and hung his mutilated body on a cross. Later that month, Kim Chi-hoe, "the greatest guerilla leader" and a native of Cheju-do, was killed. "When his capture appeared imminent," remembered Hausman, "we issued strict instructions to bring his body to Seoul (It was customary to mutilate bodies and display them for people to see) . . . One morning, I found a square five-gallon gas tank in my office. On inspection, I found it contained one highly bloated head, Kim Chi-hoe's." By the end in June 1949, an estimated thirty thousand had been killed in Cheju-do, many of them innocent civilians massacred by government forces.[41] The last of the American troops, except for KMAG, left South Korea in July 1949. It was nearly a year since the ROK had been established. KMAG, authorized with five hundred officers and soldiers as advisors and trainers, including Hausman, continued the task of building, organizing, and training the young ROK security and military forces. But the Soviets had been ahead of the Americans, by withdrawing from North Korea the previous fall and leaving behind a Soviet military advisory group to help build the North Korean armed forces.

Not surprisingly, Rhee was anxious about the departure of the Americans and especially how the United States would regard an invasion by the North. "In case of an attack by outside powers," he asked, "would the Republic of South Korea be able to count upon all-out military aid?"[42] President Truman made no promises, but he tried to calm the old man's fears by requesting from Congress a $150 million aid package. The suppression of the uprisings, especially Yŏsu-Sunch'ŏn, was seen as a success

ROK Army Chief of Staff Maj. Gen. Ch'ae Pyŏng-dŏk ("Fat Chae") addresses officers of the newly created ROK Army. Captain James Hausman is in the dark uniform, on the right, September 26, 1949. (U.S. NATIONAL ARCHIVES AND RECORDS ADMINISTRATION)

for the fledgling nation, although low-level guerilla war continued until early 1950. More importantly, the uprising had revealed and allowed the purging of leftists and communists in the ROK Army who could have caused far greater difficulties in the future. In Cheju-do, the SKWP had been prematurely forced into an armed struggle that it was unable to win.

Kim Il Sung's dream of reuniting the peninsula under his rule by provoking a general uprising in the South had been thwarted. Having twice failed to foment an internal revolution in the South, with the Autumn Rebellion in 1946 and the Cheju-do Rebellion in 1948–49, Kim now considered another way to communize the South. In March 1949, Kim Il Sung went to see Stalin.

CHAPTER THREE

Momentous Decisions

Kim's trip was his first official visit to Moscow after the establishment of the DPRK. His main goal was to obtain Stalin's approval and support to use force for reunification. "Now is the best opportunity for us to take the initiative into our own hands," he told Stalin. "Our armed forces are stronger, and in addition, we have the support of a powerful guerilla movement in the South. The population of the South, which despises the pro-American regime, will certainly help us as well." Although Stalin did not oppose the idea on principle, he remained unconvinced that the conditions were right. American forces were still in the South, and North Korean forces were not yet strong enough. Moreover, Stalin believed that the Americans would intervene, setting the stage for a direct U.S.-Soviet confrontation that he wanted to avoid at all costs. "You should not advance south," he told Kim. Instead, he advised patience, to wait for the South to attack first. "If the adversary has aggressive intentions, then sooner or later it will start the aggression. In response to the attack you will have a good opportunity to launch a counterattack. Then your move will be understood and supported by everyone."[1] Kim returned to P'yŏngyang disappointed but not despairing. Stalin had not categorically rejected Kim's plan, but had merely qualified his support based on the right conditions. Kim would simply have to be patient and wait for the right opportunity.

While Kim was brooding about the future, the Chinese civil war, which had raged for almost two decades, was finally coming to an end. The war had reached a turning point by December 1947 after Nationalist forces suffered a series of disastrous defeats. "[A year earlier] our enemies were jubilant," wrote Mao, "and the U.S. imperialists, too, danced with joy . . . Now [they] are gripped by pessimism."[2] Stalin began to have doubts about how he approached the Chinese situation. Writing to Yugoslav leader Milovan Djilas in early 1948, he admitted that he had erred in supporting the Nationalists and demanding Mao's cooperation with Chiang Kai-shek. Mao, he told Djilas, had been right all along.[3] A year later, as the People's Liberation Army (PLA) routed the Nationalists, Stalin made what amounted to a public apology. He told Liu Shaoqi, Mao's second in command, that "all victors are always right . . . you Chinese comrades are too polite to express your complaints. We know that we have made a hindrance to you, and that you did have some complaints . . . We may have given you erroneous advice as the result of lacking understanding of the true situation in your country."[4]

The speed of the Nationalist collapse astonished everyone. By May 1949, Chiang abandoned the mainland for the island of Formosa (Taiwan). On October 1, Mao proclaimed the birth of the People's Republic of China (PRC) from the Gate of Heavenly Peace (Tiananmen), the entrance to the Imperial Palace, and the beginning of a new era in China's history. "The Chinese people, comprising one quarter of humanity, have now stood up," he triumphantly declared. "[Today] we have closed our ranks and defeated both domestic and foreign oppressors through the People's War of Liberation and the great people's revolution, and now we are proclaiming the founding of the People's Republic of China. Ours will no longer be a nation subject to insult and humiliation."[5] The next day the Soviet Union became the first country to establish diplomatic relations with Beijing, severing its ties with the Nationalists. Not long thereafter, Mao began to prepare for his first visit abroad, to Moscow.

Mao urgently needed economic and technical assistance from the Soviet Union to rebuild a nation ruined by decades of war. He also needed Moscow's military umbrella while the People's Liberation Army (PLA) concentrated on suppressing the last pockets of internal resistance and liberating Taiwan. Stalin's ill-treatment of the Chinese Communist Party (CCP) had not been forgotten, however, and Mao knew that Stalin was not likely to meet his needs without some kind of quid pro quo. Months earlier Mao had explained to Anastas Mikoyan, a senior member of the Soviet Politburo sent by Stalin on a fact-finding mission, that the policy of "leaning to one side" would involve a degree of diplomatic isolation and dependence on Russia. Yet, Mao had been careful not to cast Stalin's "help" as Chinese dependence, but in the spirit of friendship

North Korean leader Kim Il Sung (hatless, looking to the left) and Pak Hŏn-yŏng (second from the right, with glasses) are greeted by Soviet officials in Moscow, March 1949. (LIBRARY OF CONGRESS)

and allegiance to a common cause. "You must lean to one side," Mao had said. "To sit on the fence is impossible. In the world, without exception, one either leans to the side of imperialism or to the side of socialism."[6] Mao was acutely aware that he had to make good on his promise to the Chinese people to establish a new, proud, and independent China, a China that had finally "stood up." Mao was trying to maintain a delicate balance. Although he needed Soviet help, he would not allow his country to be subservient to Soviet interests and policies. The new China had to expunge the last remnants of its "century of national humiliation."

The first test of Mao's balancing act came in late 1949 when he met Stalin for the first time since the founding of the PRC. Arriving in Moscow on a bitterly cold afternoon in mid-December, his welcoming ceremony had been curtailed due to the weather, and Mao was asked to provide the Soviets with a copy of his arrival speech instead of delivering it in person at the station. The speech outlined Mao's main objective: Soviet economic, technical, and military assistance. Mao also expected the Soviets to abrogate the Sino-Soviet Treaty of Friendship signed with Chiang Kai-shek in August 1945 as an appendix to the Yalta accords, which most

Chinese saw as a national disgrace for it gave Moscow extraterritorial rights in China.[7]

Mao and Stalin met on the evening of December 16. According to the Soviet version, Mao began by stating his goal of replacing the 1945 treaty with a new one. Stalin pointedly refused: "As you know, this treaty was concluded between the USSR and China as a result of the Yalta Agreement," and therefore the terms of the treaty involved other parties (the United States and the United Kingdom) and could not be changed or abrogated without their consent. Mao and Stalin did not meet again for five days. Meanwhile, Mao waited in Stalin's dacha a few miles outside of Moscow. He had been left alone to brood in isolation. "Since Stalin neither saw Mao nor ordered anyone else to entertain him," Nikita Khrushchev later recalled, "no one dared to see him."[8] On December 21, Mao was invited to attend ceremonies marking Stalin's seventieth birthday. Stalin then subsequently canceled talks that had been scheduled for two days later. Mao was furious. "I have only three tasks here," he shouted to his bodyguard. "The first is to eat, the second is to sleep and the third is to shit!"[9] Mao cabled home on January 2, 1950, that "up to now, I have had no chance to go out to speak face to face with any [of the Soviet leaders] alone."[10]

This clash of wills might have gone on longer had it not been for Western press reports that the Soviets were mistreating Mao. Some even speculated that Mao was under house arrest. This prompted Stalin to send a Soviet correspondent to interview Mao. Mao indicated that he would stay in Moscow as long as it would take to get a new treaty. "The length of my sojourn in the USSR," Mao said, "partly depends on the period in which it will be possible to settle questions of interest to the People's Republic of China. These questions are, first and foremost, the existing Treaty of Friendship and Alliance between China and the USSR."[11] Stalin at last decided to meet Mao and to negotiate a new Sino-Soviet treaty. When Mao saw Stalin on January 22 and asked about Yalta, Stalin responded, "To hell with it. Once we have taken up the position that the treaties must be changed, we must go all the way. It is true that for us this entails certain inconveniences and we will have to struggle against the Americans. But we are already reconciled to that."[12]

Several explanations have been proposed for why Stalin changed his mind. Britain's recognition of the PRC in early January had given

Stalin pause. Others—Sweden, Denmark, Switzerland, and Finland—followed, fueling Stalin's paranoia that China might tilt toward the West. While congressional conservatives in the United States denounced London's decision, many in the State Department, including Secretary of State Dean Acheson and George Kennan, who was in charge of planning, thought the United States should follow suit. Nonrecognition would simply drive the Chinese communists closer to the Soviets.

Stalin also saw that the Truman administration was backing away from Chiang Kai-shek, which signaled the possibility of U.S.-PRC relations. Acheson, Kennan, and others in the State Department thought the United States should sever ties with the corrupt Chiang regime, but Truman took an ambiguous position. Truman reaffirmed both the Cairo Declaration of December 1943 and the Potsdam Declaration of July 1945, which promised the restoration of Taiwan, formerly a Japanese colony, to "China," but he would not formally end Washington's commitment to Chiang. The United States, he declared, "had no desire to obtain special rights or privileges or to establish military bases on Formosa or to detach Formosa from China." Washington would send no military aid to Chiang or continue any involvement "in the civil conflict in China."[13] Acheson's presentation at the National Press Club on January 12, 1950, further clarified the extent and limit of U.S. interest and policy in East Asia. Acheson accused the Soviet Union of acting to annex parts of China, a "process that is complete in Outer Mongolia . . . and nearly complete in Manchuria." He reconfirmed America's hands-off policy regarding the future of Taiwan, while excluding, fatefully as it turned out, South Korea from America's defensive perimeter in the western Pacific. Britain's recognition of the PRC, Truman's assurances of neutrality in China's civil war, and Acheson's affirmation of Washington's hands-off policy vis-à-vis Taiwan gave Stalin the impression of an emerging relationship between China and the West and the United States in particular.[14] Stalin thus had to reconsider his relationship with Mao. If the United States was willing to allow China to "liberate" Taiwan without interference, it could eventually lead to the normalization of Sino-American relations and a wedge in Sino-Soviet relations. And that was unacceptable to Stalin.[15]

A final consideration for Stalin was Japan. By late 1949, as the cold war intensified, the Americans had adopted a "reverse course" policy in

Japan that, through economic revitalization and remilitarization, aimed to turn Japan into an anticommunist bulwark in northeast Asia. Stalin was fearful of a remilitarized Japan. "Japan still has cadres remaining," Stalin told Mao, "and it will certainly lift itself up again, especially if Americans continue their current policy." Mao seized on Stalin's thoughts: "Everything that guarantees the future prosperity of our countries must be stated in the treaty of alliance and friendship, including the necessity of avoiding a repetition of Japanese aggression."[16] Both Mao and Stalin saw Japan as a serious potential threat, perhaps even greater than a threat from the United States. Russian enmity with Japan went back to the nineteenth century, and China had suffered two ruinous wars in 1894–95 and 1931–45 that were then, and remain today, fresh in the memory of the Chinese people.

On February 14, 1950, Foreign Ministers Zhou Enlai and Andrei Vyshinsky signed the "Treaty of Friendship, Alliance and Mutual Assistance" as Stalin and Mao looked on.[17] The negotiations had been difficult. Stalin had balked at Mao's request for a Soviet commitment to aid China in the event of an American attack; Stalin would agree only on the condition that a war was formally declared. Mao had also been irritated by Stalin's demands for special privileges in Xinjiang in western China and Manchuria in the northeast. Despite these and other compromises, Mao basically obtained what he had wanted and was satisfied that he had the basis to establish a new place for China in the world, one that would instill pride in all Chinese.[18] Soon after Mao's departure, Stalin invited Kim Il Sung to Moscow.

War Drums

Kim was supremely confident in the spring of 1950. North Korea was politically and economically stable, and his regime was firmly in control. He was also sure that with Soviet support he could successfully use force to reunite the peninsula. There was little doubt that the NKPA was better trained and equipped than its southern counterpart. Although Stalin had not given approval for an invasion of the South during Kim's March-April 1949 visit, he promised to significantly increase military assistance to create a modern military force. Over four hundred Soviet advisors were authorized by January 1950. All were officers, with the majority (72 percent) being lieutenant colonels.[19] The NKPA, as well as the small navy and air force, was organized, trained, and prepared for war by a far more professional and experienced cadre of advisors than the ROK armed forces, for the vast majority of the Soviet advisors were veterans of the epic battles of the eastern front in World War II.[20] The NKPA's professional capacity and battle readiness increased further in the late spring of 1950, when Mao allowed the transfer of tens of thousands of ethnic Korean veterans who had fought for him in the Chinese civil war.

Eager to start a war that was certain of a quick victory, Kim Il Sung approached Shtykov in mid-January 1950 and told him that the time had come "to take up the matter of the liberation of Korea." He was becoming restless. "Thinking about reunification makes it impossible for me to sleep at night," Kim confided. Shtykov noted that Kim "insists on reporting to Stalin personally to gain permission for North Korea to attack the South."[21] Stalin's response was brief and to the point: "An operation on such a large scale demands preparation. It is necessary to organize the operation in such a way as to minimize risk. I am ready to see the man."[22] An excited Kim, along with Pak Hŏn-yŏng, who had moved to North Korea to join forces with Kim around August–September 1948, when the two separate Korean states were established, departed for Moscow on March 30. At their meeting, Stalin told them that the international environment had "sufficiently changed to permit a more active stance on the unification of Korea." He was optimistic that the communist victory in China was an important psychological blow to the West, proving "the strength of Asian revolutionaries and shown the weakness of Asian reactionaries and their mentors in the West." He also believed that China would help in the quest for unification. In apparent reference to the Koreans in the PLA, he told Kim, "China has at its disposal troops which can be utilized in Korea without any harm to the other needs of China." Furthermore, the Soviet Union's possession of the atomic bomb, successfully tested in August 1949, and its treaty alliance with China would make "the Americans even more hesitant to challenge the Communists in Asia." Nevertheless, Stalin was still worried about the possibility of an American intervention. Kim reassured Stalin on this point. Since the "USSR and China are behind Korea and are able to help," Kim reasoned, "the Americans will not risk a big war." Moreover, "the attack will be swift and the war will be won in three days," and the Americans will not have enough time to even deliberate about intervention. As for China, Kim did not want Mao's help. "We want to rely on our own force to unify Korea," Kim said emphatically.[23]

Stalin asked if there would be support in the South for such an invasion. Kim assured him that the "guerilla movement in the South has grown stronger and a major uprising can be expected." Pak added that "200,000 party members will participate as leaders of the mass uprising." Stalin remarked that they "should not count on direct Soviet participation in the war because the USSR had serious challenges elsewhere to cope with, especially the West." He told Kim to secure Mao's commitment to help as a condition for his assent to an attack. Stalin warned them, "If you should get kicked in the teeth, I shall not lift a finger. You have to ask Mao for all the help."[24] Stalin had transferred the burden of decision to Mao. He thought that regardless of the outcome, the Soviet Union would benefit. Success meant a communist Korea that expanded Russia's "friendly" borders. A failure, conceivable only if the United States intervened, would result in Chinese assistance to North Korea and a Sino-American confrontation that would end all possibilities of a Sino-American rapprochement. This is what Stalin had feared most, and Kim's invasion could help prevent it. Stalin had everything to gain by supporting the invasion plan and appeared to have little to lose. Still, Stalin premised his support of Kim's war on his calculations that the United States would not intervene.

Kim went to see Mao in mid-May 1950. Rather than try to persuade him to commit to supporting the plan, Kim matter-of-factly "informed Mao of his determination to reunify his country by military means." The war would be won quickly, Kim assured Mao, and Chinese help would not be needed. Peng Dehuai, later the commander of Chinese forces in Korea, recalled that Mao disagreed with Kim's proposal because he thought that the Americans might intervene, but Mao could not reject it since Kim had presented it as a fait accompli approved by Stalin.[25] Having just concluded the Sino-Soviet treaty, which was seen as essential for the PRC's future, Mao felt he could not refuse. Mao also needed Stalin's help to "liberate" Taiwan, and he could not use the argument about possible American intervention in Korea to oppose Kim's plan since a similar argument could be used to deny Soviet support for the invasion of Taiwan. Mao, reluctantly, gave his support.[26]

Endgame

While Kim and Stalin were meeting in April, Paul Nitze was finishing an explosive secret report on the future of America's military and national security posture. Nitze had recently replaced George Kennan as the director of policy planning at the State Department, and over the course of the winter of 1949–50 he had produced National Security Council Paper 68 (NSC 68), which eventually became, through its proposal for military buildup and containment of communism, the American master plan for the cold war. In the document delivered to President Truman in April, Nitze and his staff introduced an ominous theme from the very beginning: "The assault on free institutions is world-wide now, and in the context of the present polarization of power, a defeat of free institutions anywhere is a defeat everywhere . . . Thus unwilling our free society finds itself mortally challenged by the Soviet system." Nuclear weapons were insufficient to thwart this ominous threat, as the Soviets were expected to achieve nuclear parity by 1954. Dramatic measures, a massive military buildup, would be required to counter the Soviet challenge. The cost would be $40 to $50 billion a year, three times the annual defense budget that Truman and the War Department had estimated for the early 1950s.[27]

Truman was not persuaded. NSC 68 might dramatically point out the perilous state of American security against a theoretical Soviet threat, but with midterm elections coming up in the fall of 1950, he was resistant to expanding defense expenditures when Americans still expected continuation of the peace dividend from the victory in World War II. Truman set off in May to Washington state, where he was scheduled to speak at the ceremony dedicating the Grand Coulee Dam. He did not mention during the two-week trip the possibility of a major Soviet threat or that it may require a national call to arms. On the contrary, he projected confidence and hopefulness about the global situation and America's security. At his weekly press conference on June 1, Truman assured the American people that the world was "closer to peace than at any time in the last five years."[28] NSC 68 was politely ignored.

Stalin was encouraged by Truman's talk about peace and prosperity. The Americans, he surmised, were simply tired of war and had also withdrawn their forces from Korea the year before. Nevertheless, with planning for the invasion rapidly moving forward, Stalin remained cautious about American intentions. Stalin rejected Kim's request for Soviet advisors to operate ships for an amphibious assault, a request that Shtykov advised should be granted. When Shtykov conveyed another request from Kim on June 20, the eve of the attack, for Soviet advisors to be assigned to frontline combat units, Stalin admonished the ambassador. "It is necessary to remind you that you are a representative of the USSR and *not* of Korea," he wrote. "Send necessary numbers of our advisors to headquarters and to army groups dressed in civilian uniforms posing as *Pravda* correspondents. You will be held personally responsible if any of these men were taken prisoner."[29] Stalin wanted to minimize the risk of Soviet casualties or prisoners lest it lead to a direct U.S.-Soviet confrontation in Korea.

On June 15, Shtykov informed Stalin that the operational plan, written by the Soviet advisory group, was ready. The attack would start in the early morning on Sunday, June 25 (the evening of June 24, Washington time). "At the first stage, formations and units of the NKPA will begin action on the Ongjin peninsula [on the far western end of the 38th parallel] like a local operation and then deliver the main strike along the western coast of Korea to the South," he related.[30] Key to the plan was to disguise the attack as a counteroffensive reacting to a South Korean provocation. The offensive would then spread eastward along the 38th parallel over the following days. In its overall conception, the plan was similar to Russia's attack on Finland in 1939, which was not surprising since most senior Soviet officers in North Korea were veterans of the Finnish War. As in Korea, the Finnish plan had contained a ruse, the shelling of a Russian village near the Finnish border, Mainila, before the start of the Soviet invasion. A Soviet mobile artillery unit had been secretly deployed deep into the woods near the Soviet-Finnish border and had shelled Mainila. Soviet troops, located near Mainila, had then reported receiving Finnish artillery fire. This had become a pretext, albeit fabricated, for a general attack against Finland. General Vladimir Razhubayev, chief of the Soviet Advisory Group from early 1951 to 1953, stated that in North Korea "the People's Central Committee was full of experts who were working on a way to pull a similar pretext off." Shtykov himself had led a major part of the invasion force against Finland.[31]

As June 25 approached, Stalin received alarming news from Shtykov, who relayed an urgent message from Kim that "the Southerners have learned the details of the forthcoming advance of the NKPA." Kim urged modification of the plan. "Instead of a local operation at the Ongjin peninsula as a prelude to the general offensive," relayed Shtykov to Stalin, "Kim Il Sung suggests an overall attack on 25 June along the whole front line." Stalin approved "an immediate advance along the whole front line," but he stipulated that it still must be made to look like a counterattack.[32] The stage was set for the invasion, but Stalin and Kim failed to foresee how the United States and the rest of the world would view it. The two leaders also completely failed to consider the possibility that they would be testing the effectiveness of the collective security mechanism of the newly established United Nations.

CHAPTER FOUR

War for the South

The opening shots of the attack in the predawn hours of Sunday, June 25, 1950, surprised few, and yet all were caught unprepared. Localized skirmishes and even major actions along the parallel had occurred with regularity over the previous year, and nothing in the way the North Korean attack began gave any indication that it was different this time. Almost nightly, the North Koreans infiltrated patrols to probe, ambush, or take prisoners. The South Koreans retaliated with their own patrols. These actions sometimes involved hundreds of men. Not infrequently, artillery duels were waged. A year earlier, North Korean shelling near Kaesŏng, located just south of the parallel, was of such ferocity that the American Methodist Mission there was forced to stay in a shelter for three days.[1] Border skirmishes had continued unabated since January, but in May, border incidents suddenly dropped off sharply, making Capt. Joseph Darrigo of KMAG suspect that something was afoot. North Korean farmers were evacuated from the border zone. Captain Darrigo reported his concerns to his superior, Lt. Col. Lloyd H. Rockwell, but it was lost in the cacophony of similar warnings that had become almost routine in Seoul and Washington.[2]

The five hundred U.S. military advisors of KMAG were under the leadership of Brig. Gen. William Roberts, who was nearing his mandatory retirement in July. KMAG's mission was to train and build functioning ROK security forces, especially the army. It was a daunting challenge requiring patience and skill. But Roberts was an optimist. The ROK Army had, after all, been battle-tested in the Yŏsu-Such'ŏn uprisings and in the numerous clashes along the border. It had proved its loyalty and its mettle. Roberts reported to Washington that the ROK Army could meet any test the North Korean army might impose on it.[3] The optimistic assessments were also voiced by the ambassador to South

Korea, John Muccio, who confirmed that progress in military training had been "heartening," and the ROK Army "had kept pace" with the North Koreans.[4] The official view from Washington was summed up by Republican Senator H. Alexander Smith (New Jersey), a recent guest of Ambassador Muccio, who reported that the ROK forces were "thoroughly capable of taking care of South Korea in any possible conflict with the North."[5]

President Syngman Rhee disagreed. He interpreted the stream of positive assessments of the fledgling army, which had no tanks, no heavy artillery, and no fighter aircraft, as a deceptive ploy to deny him military aid and equipment. He complained to Muccio and Roberts that the ROK Army was woefully underequipped to repel a North Korean attack. In Washington, however, denial of Rhee's repeated requests for more arms was thought to be prudent and justified. There was legitimate concern that the difficult and fiercely patriotic Rhee might start a war of reuni-

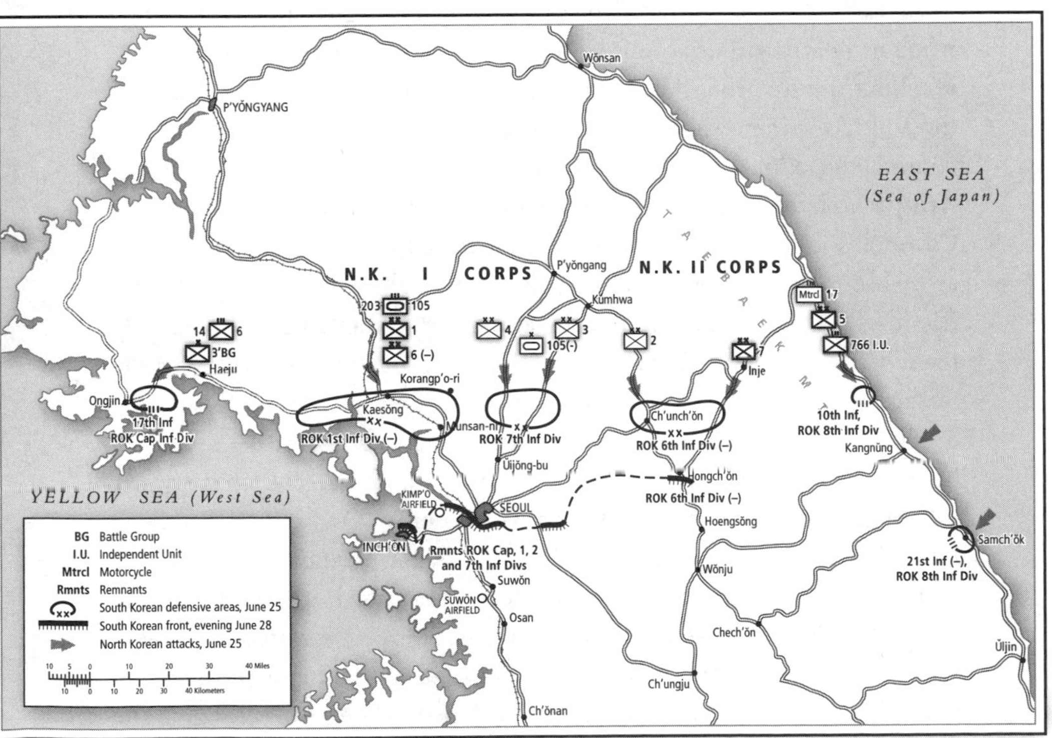

North Korean Invasion, June 25–28, 1950. (MAP ADAPTED FROM ROY B. APPLEMAN, *SOUTH TO THE NAKTONG, NORTH TO THE YALU* [U.S. GOVERNMENT PRINTING OFFICE, 1960])

fication on his own if he were given the tanks, artillery, and aircraft he demanded. A week before the outbreak of war, Muccio wrote to Acheson, "The Korean Army has made enormous progress during the past year. The systems and institutions set up through the instrumentality of KMAG are now such that reductions in advisory personnel can well be made," and he recommended a 50 percent reduction by the end of 1950.[6] More important was a definitive shift in reducing South Korea's strategic value to the United States. Democratic Senator Tom Connally (Texas), chairman of the Senate Committee on Foreign Relations, told a reporter that "I am afraid it [the United States abandoning South Korea] is going to be seriously considered because I'm afraid it is going to happen, whether we want it to or not."[7] The praises heaped on the ROK military provided political cover for drawing down American commitments. Rhee had reasons to be concerned.

Captain Darrigo was the only American officer at the 38th parallel on the morning of June 25. He was the KMAG advisor to a regiment of the ROK First Division, and he lived in Kaesŏng. Darrigo jumped out of bed when he heard artillery shells land nearby, ran to his jeep, and sped away, reaching the division's headquarters in Munsan, about twenty miles to the south, to sound the alarm. Unfortunately, the very capable division commander, Col. Paek Sŏn-yŏp, perhaps the best officer in the ROK Army who later became its first four-star general, was absent. Lieutenant Colonel Rockwell, chief KMAG advisor to the ROK First Division, was also absent. He had gone to Seoul for the weekend to visit family and friends. By the time they were notified later that morning and hurriedly made their way back, Kaesŏng had fallen and NKPA tanks were rolling toward Seoul.

The NKPA conducted six sequenced thrusts across the 38th parallel, beginning in the Ongjin Peninsula on the west and then rolling eastward. KMAG advisors with the ROK 17th Regiment on Ongjin had also been jolted from their beds by artillery. Without heavy weapons, the regiment had little chance. At first, many ROK soldiers fought bravely. "Acting without orders from their officers," recalled Paek, "a number of them broke into suicide teams and charged the T-34s clutching explosives and grenades. They clambered up onto the monsters before touching off the charges."[8] But the futility of the "human bomb" attacks soon led to "T-34 fear," and the troops began to run away. "The symptoms of the disease were straightforward," Paek later wrote. "As soon as the men even heard the word 'tank' they fell into a state of terror."[9]

When news of the North Korean invasion reached Washington in the early evening of Saturday, June 24, many officials, including Truman and Acheson, were away for the weekend. Truman was at his home in Independence, Missouri. Acheson called from his country house in Maryland to inform the president of the news. He also told Truman that he had requested an emergency session of the UN Security Council.[10] While Truman returned to Washington, the UN Security Council met and unanimously adopted an American resolution calling for the immediate cessation of hostilities and the withdrawal of North Korean troops. There was no Soviet vote, and hence no veto, because the Soviet representative had walked out earlier that year to protest the UN's refusal to seat the PRC in the council instead of Taiwan. Truman gathered his principal advisors for a crisis meeting. All agreed that the Soviet Union was involved. Acheson recommended that MacArthur be instructed to airdrop supplies, food, ammunition, and weapons to strengthen the South Korean forces. No direct U.S. military involvement was discussed, as it was still widely believed that the ROK Army was capable of handling the NKPA. This belief was reinforced by the first of many cables from Ambassador Muccio: "The Korean defense forces are taking up prepared positions to resist northern aggression. There is no reason for alarm."[11]

Muccio's reports became more ominous the following day: "I earnestly appeal to Department to back up to such extent as may be necessary KMAG's appeal for additional ammunition. Without early receipt of such ammunition and assuming hostilities continue at present level, is feared most stocks in Korean hands will be exhausted within ten days time."[12] Faced with bleaker reports about the situation on the front, and with rumors running wild that the NKPA was about to take Seoul, Muccio ordered the evacuation of American civilians. On the morning of Tuesday, June 27, nearly seven hundred American women and children boarded a Norwegian ship at Inch'ŏn and sailed for Japan. More Americans were evacuated the following day, and Muccio went to Suwŏn, twenty-five miles south of Seoul. Rhee and the ROK government had departed earlier that morning and were on their way farther south to the city of Taegu. Ordinary Koreans were on their own. Some stayed, but many left, becoming faceless actors in innumerable tragedies on the refugee trail. In just two days, Seoul was in chaos and its residents in full flight.

Not everyone was eager to leave the city, however. Four American journalists, Keyes Beech of the *Chicago Daily News*, Frank Gibney of *Time*, Marguerite Higgins of the *New York Herald Tribune*, and Burton Crane of the *New York Times*, arrived on one of the last evacuation planes from Tokyo on June 27 to cover the fall of Seoul.[13] They were greeted at ROK Army headquarters by Col. W. H. Sterling Wright, KMAG's acting chief, and a skeleton crew of KMAG officers. KMAG's chief Brig. Gen. Roberts had departed just days before to retire and his replacement had not yet arrived. Despite the bleak situation, Wright was hopeful. He and others had been bolstered by MacArthur's message earlier that day that "momentous events are in the making."[14] It was after midnight when the group finally decided to turn in. Colonel Wright suggested that Marguerite Higgins, together with a group of other KMAG officers, accompany him to his quarters in the KMAG housing area. Meanwhile, Beech, Gibney, and Crane went with Maj. Walter Greenwood, who offered the men a place on the sofa and floor to sleep. But no sooner had they closed their eyes when they were awakened by the phone. Beech heard Green shout, "They are in the city! Head for Suwŏn!" It was raining hard that night as Gibney, Beech, and Crane jumped into their jeep. "The whole city was on the move," recalled Beech. "It was toward the Han River Bridge."

The pitiful human mass, wet and trudging through the dark, created an eery scene. Caught in the streaming mobs of people, oxcarts, trucks, and bicycles, the three reporters saw Capt. James H. Hausman ahead of them as they approached the bridge. Suddenly everything came to a halt. "We sat in the jeep waiting," Beech recalled. "Then it seemed that the whole world exploded in front of us. I remember a burst of orange flame; silhouetted against the flame was a truckload of Korean soldiers. The truck lifted into the air. I felt our own jeep in motion, backwards."[15] Crane and Gibney were wounded by flying glass and bled from their heads, but they were conscious and able to walk. Beech noticed the truckload of soldiers whose vehicle had shielded them from the blast. All of the soldiers were dead, their bodies strewn haphazardly in heaps on the ground. And so were hundreds of other innocent people who had died in the explosion or who had simply drowned in the dark river waters below. Someone had blown up the Han River Bridge with people still on it.

Hausman's group had been luckier. They were safely across the river when the bridge blew. "It was a tremendous explosion," he recalled, "Our jeep actually left the road, vertically."[16] Meanwhile, Wright and Higgins, who had not yet crossed the bridge, were unharmed although they now found themselves, like Gibney, Crane, and Beech, trapped on the wrong side of the Han River. Fortunately they were able to make it safely across on makeshift rafts. The KMAG party, including the four American journalists, had come through the ordeal miraculously, without loss of life.

The premature destruction of the bridge was not only a humanitarian disaster but a military one as well. Seoul was still in ROK hands at the time, and trapped on the northern side of the Han River were over thirty thousand ROK soldiers. Colonel Paek, whose men had fought heroically to hold back the attack, was devastated: "I cried tears of blood on that day. I saw no way to rescue the men of the proud ROK 1st Division, scattered as they were over miles of threatening terrain."[17] Brigadier General Yu Chae-hŭng, commander of the ROK Seventh Division, led just over one thousand men to safety. The other two ROK divisions that were still relatively intact, the ROK Sixth Division in Ch'unch'ŏn to the east and the Eighth at Samch'ŏk on the East Sea, were now isolated and utterly helpless.

On June 28, three days after the attack, the ROK Army could account for only twenty-two thousand men of the nearly hundred thousand that had made up its rolls on the twenty-fifth. Most of its heavy weapons, transport, and supplies were lost. General Roberts's "best doggone shooting army outside of the United States" was not just defeated, it was destroyed.[18]

MacArthur's survey team, sent to assess the situation and led by Brig. Gen. John Church, landed in Suwŏn on June 27, just hours before the fall of Seoul. Church was shocked by the utter chaos. Hausman, who had just arrived in Suwŏn, related the horrific story of the Han River bridge explosion and the ROK Army's dire predicament. Church notified Tokyo that "it will be necessary to employ American ground forces" to reestablish ROK positions at the 38th parallel and to recapture Seoul.[19] That evening, MacArthur radioed Church that a senior officer would be arriving the next morning. That senior officer turned out to be MacArthur himself. A distraught Rhee greeted MacArthur. Church and

Wright briefed them on the deteriorating situation. Returning to Tokyo that evening, MacArthur cabled Washington: "The only assurance for holding the present line and the ability to regain later the lost ground is through the introduction of United States ground combat forces into the Korean battle area. Unless provision is made for the full utilization of the Army-Navy air team in this shattered area, our mission will at best be needlessly costly in life, money and prestige. At worst, it might even be doomed."[20] But Truman had already decided to intervene. Later, he said that committing American troops to combat in Korea was the most difficult decision of his presidency, more so than the decision to use the atomic bomb against Japan in 1945. He did not want to get into a war, but he thought that failure to act in Korea could lead to another world war, this time with the Soviet Union.

On June 27, congressional leaders, the secretary of state, the secretary of defense, and the Joint Chiefs of Staff (JCS) joined Truman for a meeting. He informed them that that morning he had authorized the use of air and sea forces. The congressional leaders approved that the crisis be managed on the basis of presidential authority alone, without calling on Congress for a declaration of war. That evening, the UN Security Council passed Resolution 83 authorizing the use of force to halt North Korean aggression, testing for the first time the UN principle of collective security. In the days leading to the UN resolution, the American people's anxiety and doubt over what to do about Russia's "testing" of America's resolve in Korea had suddenly given way to a new clarity and sense of purpose. Three days later, on June 30, Truman authorized the deployment of American ground forces.

The response of the American people, the media, and Congress was overwhelmingly positive. The press unanimously praised Truman for his "decisiveness" and his "bold and courageous decision." The *Christian Science Monitor*'s Washington Bureau chief, Joseph Harsh, gushed, "Never before have I felt such a sense of relief and unity pass through the city."[21] Truman had drawn the line, and the American public firmly backed him. Yet, there was still confusion concerning exactly what the crisis was all about. At a June 29 press conference, Truman was asked whether the United States was at war. "We are not at war," Truman replied. A reporter asked, "Would it be correct . . . to call this a police action under the United Nations?" "Yes," replied Truman, "that is exactly what it amounts to."[22] Calling Korea a "police action" would later haunt Truman when the bloody and brutal reality of a full-blown war became apparent. Throughout the hot months of July and August 1950, American soldiers were stunned and humiliated as they were repeatedly thrown back by the North Korean "bandits." For the time being, however, Truman's euphemism served to downplay the seriousness of the crisis and provided the illusion that the "police action" would be a relatively quick and simple affair.[23]

Less than six days after the North Korean attack, American soldiers were committed to the fighting. The former Japanese colony that few had ever heard of and had been on the periphery of America's postwar interests suddenly became the epicenter of America's first armed confrontation against communism. Truman had drawn the line in Korea between freedom and slavery. Haphazardly and fatefully, Korea's localized civil war morphed into a war between the centers of power in the post–World War II order.

Desperate Days

The first American troops arrived in Korea confident that the North Koreans could be stopped quickly. Virtually nothing was known about the enemy, but everyone thought that once the North Koreans saw that they were fighting Americans, they would retreat in panic. Overconfidence and arrogance ruled the day. "We thought they'd back off as soon as they saw American uniforms," Lieutenant Philip Day recalled. Lieutenant John Doody echoed the sentiment: "I regarded the episode as an adventure that would probably last only a few days."[24] Their first encounter with the NKPA abruptly exploded their illusions. More important, the confrontation between the world's most powerful nation and a nation of "bandits" was a brutal wake-up call to Washington, for it showed just how much American military readiness had deteriorated. America's precipitous demobilization and slashed defense budgets after World War II, the peace dividend, and the "soft" occupation in Japan exacted an unforgiving outcome in the violence of combat. It was glaringly apparent that despite its vaunted nuclear supremacy, America was unprepared to fight a conventional war.

MacArthur selected the Twenty-Fourth Infantry Division as the first unit to deploy. The division and its commanding general, Maj. Gen. William Dean, seemed well suited for the job. Dean was the only one of the four division commanders in the Eighth U.S. Army, the American occupation force in Japan, to have commanded troops in combat. He had also served as commanding general of the Seventh Infantry Division and as military governor of South Korea under Lt. Gen. John R. Hodge from 1947 to 1948. Dean took command of the Twenty-Fourth Division after the dissolution of USAMGIK following the elections in May 1948. MacArthur instructed Dean to send a battalion task force, as quickly as possible, to be followed by the remainder of the division. Dean chose the 1st Battalion of the 21st Infantry Regiment commanded by Lt. Col. Charles Smith as the core of the task force. Smith had fought in the Pacific in World War II and was considered the most experienced and competent of the battalion commanders in the division. But the unit was only at two-thirds strength and most of the soldiers had no combat experience, having joined after World War II. The unit also lacked training, owing to the "soft" occupation duty in Japan. The equipment was in poor shape, and antitank weapons were inadequate against the tanks of the NKPA. Task Force (TF) Smith was the best that MacArthur could send, a unit of ill-trained, undermanned, underequipped, and underexperienced men.[25] Dean's instructions to Smith were simple: "Contact Brig. Gen. John Church and if you can't locate him, go to Taejŏn and beyond if you can . . . Good luck to you and God bless you and your men."[26]

Brigadier General Church greeted TF Smith at Taejŏn on the morning of July 2. Brimming with confidence, Church assured Lieutenant Colonel Smith that all that was required to stop the NKPA was a few Americans who would not run from tanks. Smith was ordered to block the enemy north of the village of Osan. The NKPA's primary avenue of attack was along the main road from Seoul, which ran through Osan and farther south through Taejŏn and Taegu to Pusan. It was the only avenue of attack from the Chinese border to the southern coast that was free from the mountains dominating most of the peninsula. To this day, this corridor is the key line of communication and transportation and therefore the backbone of South Korea's bustling economy. It was also the traditional invasion path through the peninsula whether coming from the north or from the south. The Mongols in the thirteenth century and the Manchus in the seventeenth century followed it going south; the Japanese followed it north during their invasion in the sixteenth century. The NKPA, in other words, was using a well-worn path. As TF Smith deployed north of Osan, the Twenty-Fourth Infantry Division's 34th Infantry Regiment, led by Col. Jay Lovless, arrived in P'yŏngtaek south of Osan. Dean deployed the regiment around P'yŏngtaek to block any enemy that got through TF Smith.

Smith and his men caught sight of the North Korean soldiers on the morning of July 5. Over thirty tanks rolled toward their positions. The Americans fired recoilless rifles and bazookas at point-blank range, but to their surprise, even direct hits had no effect. The artillery battery attached to TF Smith destroyed four of the tanks, but still nearly thirty had gotten through and headed south toward the 34th Infantry Regiment digging in at P'yŏngtaek. By early afternoon, Smith ordered a withdrawal. Soon thereafter, "things slowly began to go to pieces," Lt. Philip Day recalled. "All crew served weapons were abandoned, as well as all the dead and some 30 wounded. Confusion rapidly became rampant."[27] A quarter of the unit, 150 men, was lost at Osan.[28]

Reports that TF Smith was overrun reached Lovless the next morning. Fearful that the understrength battalion at P'yŏngtaek might not be able to hold, Lovless ordered it to fall back to Ch'ŏnan, about eight miles farther south. Meanwhile, a battalion at Ansŏng to the east fell apart. Dean was furious that P'yŏngtaek was abandoned without a fight, and he ordered Lovless to go back, but it was too late because P'yŏngtaek had already been taken by the NKPA. By this time, Ch'ŏnan's defenses rapidly fell apart, and the hasty withdrawal from P'yŏngtaek and Ansŏng now turned into a frantic flight. The men abandoned equipment, weapons, and comrades who had been killed or wounded. "I was thoroughly disgusted with this exhibition," recalled John Dunn. "It was more than a lack of aggressiveness and initiative, it bordered on cowardice."[29] Dunn, who was taken prisoner at Ch'ŏnan, spent the rest of the war in a POW camp. It took just a few days for the cocky and confident American soldiers to become a disoriented mob of terrified men.

As bewildered American and ROK troops were flung back, MacArthur decided to commit the whole of the Eighth U.S. Army. Lieutenant General Walton "Johnnie" Walker, its commander, was known as a "GI's

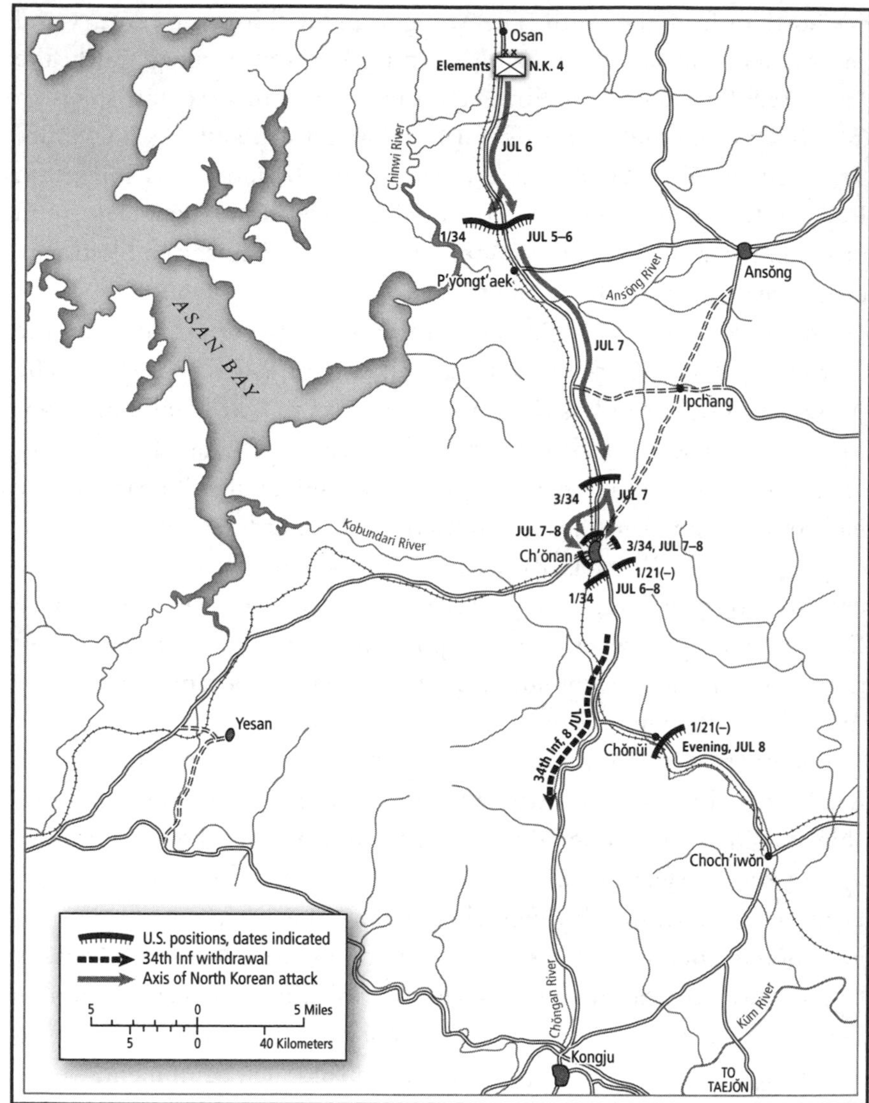

Delaying actions, 34th Infantry Regiment, July 5–8, 1950. (MAP ADAPTED FROM ROY B. APPLEMAN, *SOUTH TO THE NAKTONG, NORTH TO THE YALU* [U.S. GOVERNMENT PRINTING OFFICE, 1961])

general." A modest and unpretentious man who "smiled infrequently and rarely voiced a remark worthy of being remembered," Walker made a personal assessment of the situation by visiting Dean at Taejŏn in early July.[30] His assessment was crucial in MacArthur's decision to use all of the Eighth Army. Walker's operational control included the remnants of the ROK Army, conceded by President Rhee on July 14.[31] The unified U.S.-ROK forces gave hope of establishing a coherent defense.

Much has been made of the ROK Army's poor performance, but this ignores the heroic efforts made to successfully rebuild the ROK Army on the run.[32] The South Koreans were able, against great odds, to piece their shattered forces back together while fighting a delaying action without collapsing, despite their inferiority in men, arms, equipment, and training. "We started greatly under-strength and bereft of heavy weapons and equipment and were obliged to reorganize, replenish and even re-arm while keeping ahead of a pursuing enemy," recalled Paek Sŏn-yŏp. "In what I regard as one of the minor miracles of the war, some four or five thousand of the men we lost crossing the Han rejoined the division during our withdrawal to the Naktong [River]."[33] ROK forces reached their prewar strength by the end of August.[34] Kim Il Sung later acknowledged that "our greatest mistake was failing to encircle and completely annihilate the enemy, and giving them enough time to reorganize and reinforce their units while withdrawing."[35]

Walker's immediate task was to delay the enemy advance. In the west, location of the NKPA's main effort, Walker established a defensive line along the south bank of the Kŭm River. In the east, Walker used the mountains and the narrow coastal corridor to delay the North Korean advance. The purpose of the delay was to buy time for reinforcements, not only from the United States, but also from over a dozen other UN nations, to arrive and set the conditions for a counteroffensive. The Kŭm River was the first defensible river line south of the Han along the path of North Korea's advance. Less than fifteen miles beyond it was Taejŏn, the first major city after Seoul along the invasion route. Walker wanted Dean's Twenty-Fourth Division to hold the Kŭm River line to protect Taejŏn, a key nexus of road and rail networks. But Dean's forces could not hold, and the North Koreans easily penetrated the Kŭm River line and then began assaulting Taejŏn on July 20. Whereas Dean's tactical sense called for withdrawing from Taejŏn as it was being surrounded, he was ordered to hold on to gain time for reinforcements to arrive from Pusan. It was a fateful delay. Dean became trapped as NKPA forces closed in from all sides. Escaping the city on foot, he survived in the mountains for thirty-six days before being captured, and spent the rest of the war as a POW. Dean was the highest-ranking POW, and in January 1951, Truman, not knowing whether he was alive, awarded him the Medal of Honor.

By the end of July, the Twenty-Fourth Division was in very bad shape. It had lost more than half of its men.[36] It had been a desperate, agonizing, and bitter month. Many soldiers felt that their leaders, from Truman on down, had failed them. They had been told that their sojourn in Korea would be an easy affair, a mere "break" from the boredom of the occupation in Japan. Moreover, the difficulty of identifying friend from foe, because some NKPA troops infiltrated UN lines by disguising themselves in the same white-cotton clothes that refugees wore, led American troops to commit appalling deeds, including shooting at women and children, because they did not know what else to do.

Near the village of Nogŭn-ri, about a hundred miles southeast of Seoul, several hundred refugees were killed in late July by soldiers of the 7th Cavalry Regiment from the First Cavalry Division and by American aircraft. The American soldiers, who believed North Korean soldiers were hiding among the villagers, had told the villagers to gather by the railroad tracks. There are contradictory accounts of what happened next. One Korean witness recalled spotting an American plane that suddenly swooped down and strafed the area. An American soldier recalled receiving fire from the refugee group.[37] Whatever triggered the mayhem, the terrified villagers ended up in a nearby tunnel, where they sought cover and ended up trapped.[38] Yang Hae-chan, nine at the time, recalled that they were "fired upon by American soldiers, bullets rained down on the crowd."[39] Another eyewitness said they were "packed tightly inside with little or no room to move," and recalled having to "drink bloody water from the stream that flowed through one of the tunnels." The killing lasted several days, and "dead bodies were piled up on the tunnel entrance" to protect those inside from the oncoming fire. Two hundred and forty-eight people, including many women and children, are alleged to have been killed in the incident.[40]

Early August brought more despair but also new hope. American and ROK forces set up a defense line behind the Naktong River. It was a thinly held front and the last line of defense. On the map, the Pusan perimeter looked like a tiny toehold at the southeastern corner of the peninsula. Walker dramatically declared, "There will be no Dunkirk, there will be no Bataan . . . We must fight until the end . . . I want everybody to understand that we are going to hold this line. We are going to win."[41] The soldiers were exhausted, bitter, and dispirited. The monsoon season had just ended, but it was abnormally hot and dry. Lack of water forced the soldiers to drink from paddies and ditches, causing severe cases of dysentery. Yet, despite the exhaustion, the heat, and the sickness, Walker's line held.

One key to this success was the delaying action of the ROK Sixth Division, which had put up a tenacious fight in Ch'unch'ŏn thirty miles east of Seoul against overwhelming odds.[42] A KMAG advisor recollected that the Sixth Division was driven from the city but "counterattacked and recaptured Ch'unch'ŏn and then held it for five days until ordered to withdraw because of failure along the rest of the front."[43] Shtykov reported on June 26 to Gen. Matveyev Zakharov, head of a special mission from the Soviet General Staff to oversee the operations, that "the invasion ran into trouble from the beginning especially because the Soviet plan did not take into account the severe terrain that slowed down mechanized units and especially the unexpectedly courageous defense of the ROK 6th Division at Ch'unch'ŏn."[44] The ROK Sixth Division's delaying actions threw off the NKPA's timeline and probably bought time for the establishment of the Pusan perimeter and the arrival of UN reinforcements.[45]

Shtykov was worried. He wrote to General Zakharov that NKPA units were operating on an ad hoc basis without direction from senior staff. The quality of staff work was poor, "[the command staff] does not have battle experience," he complained, and "after the withdrawal of Soviet military advisers they organized the battle command poorly, they use artillery and tanks in battle badly and lose communications."[46] On June 28, Shtykov reported to Stalin that without more Soviet advisors on the ground, "it would be difficult for the NKPA to conduct smooth operations."[47] On July 8, Shtykov cabled Stalin to convey Kim Il Sung's personal appeal for more Soviet advisors for frontline units: "Being confident of your desire to help the Korean people rid themselves of the American imperialists," Kim pleaded, "I am obliged to appeal to you with a request to allow the use of 25–35 Soviet military advisers in the staff of the Front of the Korean Army and the staffs of the 2nd Army Group, since the national military cadres have not yet sufficiently mastered the art of commanding modern troops."[48] Kim confided to Shtykov that without the advisors, "the invasion would fail." Shtykov wrote to Stalin "that he had never seen Kim Il Sung so dejected and hopeless."[49] Stalin acquiesced. That Stalin would have allowed Soviet advisors to serve in the front lines and risk a direct confrontation with Americans revealed how critical the situation had become.[50] By mid-July, the NKPA had largely lost its momentum.

The next Eighth Army unit to arrive was the Twenty-Fifth Infantry Division, which included the all-black 24th Infantry Regiment. Following the Twenty-Fifth was the First Cavalry Division in mid-July and the 5th Regimental Combat Team from Hawaii, which arrived on July 25. The Second Infantry Division followed in early August and then a provisional U.S. Marine brigade. With these reinforcements, a defensive line was established along the Naktong River in southeastern Korea. The Eighth Army was responsible for the seventy-mile western flank of the Pusan perimeter, while the ROK Army was responsible for the fifty-five miles of the front on the northern boundary. With overextended supply lines and increasing UN strength, North Korea estimated that it had about a month at most to break the Pusan line and bring the war to a conclusion in its favor. Throughout August and early September, the NKPA maintained unrelenting pressure, but the perimeter held.

War for the North

As the situation in Korea stabilized, Truman sent W. Averell Harriman, a senior White House advisor, to Japan. Truman had been disturbed by MacArthur's highly publicized trip at the end of July to Taiwan, where he had met Chiang Kai-shek and publicly praised the generalissimo's "indomitable determination to resist communist domination."[51] Secretary of State Acheson was upset, but he put MacArthur's trip down to politics. "Before 1950 General MacArthur had neither shown nor expressed any interest in Formosa," wrote Acheson. "But the General was not deaf to political reports coming to him from the United States, particularly those emanating from the Republican right wing, which found our Far Eastern policy repulsive and occasionally mentioned the General as the charismatic leader who might occasionally end the obnoxious Democratic hold on the White House."[52] It was well known that MacArthur had looked favorably on Chiang's offer of Nationalist troops for Korea, but Truman rejected the offer for fear of drawing China into the war. Truman told Harriman to tell MacArthur to stay clear of Chiang Kai-shek and to find out MacArthur's future plans for Korea.[53] Harriman returned with an encouraging report. Concerning Chiang Kai-shek, MacArthur would do as the president ordered. For the war, Harriman reported on MacArthur's plan for victory with a bold amphibious landing at Inch'ŏn, behind enemy lines, to surround and destroy the North Korean forces.

MacArthur's audacious plan carried great risks. The greatest were Inch'ŏn's tremendous tides of thirty feet or more and the lack of suitable landing beaches. The landing could take place only at high tide, which lasted just two hours. General Omar Bradley, chairman of the JCS, thought it was the riskiest plan he had ever seen. General Joseph "Lightning Joe" Lawton Collins, army chief of staff, thought the plan should be modified by making the landing site at Kŭnsan instead of at Inch'ŏn. Kŭnsan was located 130 miles south of Inch'ŏn. Geographically, it was more hospitable and accommodated more easily the amphibious landing MacArthur proposed. But it was precisely the "impracticalities" of the operation that could ensure Inch'ŏn's success, MacArthur argued, "for the enemy commander will reason that no one would be so brash as to make such an attempt."[54] The Joint Chiefs were not convinced. Secretary of the Army Frank Pace Jr. noted that "the almost universal feeling of the Joint Chiefs was that General MacArthur's move was very risky and had very little chance of success."[55] Whether MacArthur was angered by the reluctance of the Joint Chiefs or simply frustrated by the events in Korea, he almost lost all support for the Inch'ŏn plan when he challenged Truman's Far East policy in late August. In response to an invitation by the Veterans of Foreign Wars to send a message to its annual convention, MacArthur chose to address the thorny issue of Taiwan. As he did during his trip to the island a few weeks earlier, MacArthur argued for Taiwan's strategic value and attacked those who opposed supporting Chiang Kai-shek. "Nothing could be more fallacious than the threadbare argument by those who advocate appeasement and defeatism in the Pacific that if we defend Formosa, we alienate continental Asia," he declared. Drawing on his claim of intimate knowledge of the "Oriental mind," he concluded,

"Those who speak thus do not understand the Orient. They do not grant that it is in the pattern of Oriental psychology to respect and follow aggressive, resolute and dynamic leadership, to quickly turn on a leadership characterized by timidity or vacillation."[56] Widely covered by the media, MacArthur's message represented exactly the kind of dabbling in politics that Truman had warned MacArthur against. Truman, however, appeared swayed in favor of the Inch'ŏn plan by a strong memorandum of support from Lt. Gen. Matthew B. Ridgway, the U.S. Army's deputy chief of staff for operations and administration and a World War II hero, who had gone to Japan with Harriman.[57]

MacArthur chose his chief of staff, Maj. Gen. Edward Almond, to command the landing force, X Corps, for Inch'ŏn. Almond had a relatively undistinguished record as a division commander in World War II, and the appointment surprised many, including Almond himself. Almond was concerned about his ability to execute two jobs, as MacArthur's chief of staff and as commander of X Corps. "Well, we'll all be home by Christmas," MacArthur reassured him. "It is only a short operation. You'll continue as my Chief of Staff and you can get any assistance you like."[58] Almond was a fiercely driven and competitive man with an all "consuming impatience with incompetence,"[59] but he inspired little affection from his peers or subordinates. The mutual dislike between Almond and Maj. Gen. O. P. Smith, the commanding general of the First Marine Division assigned to X Corps, was well known. Smith, a cautious commander who believed that "you do it slow, but you should do it right," was deeply suspicious of Almond. He later told the commandant of the Marine Corps, Gen. Clifton Cates, that he had "little confidence in the tactical judgment of [Almond's] X Corps or in the realism of their planning."[60] Their poor relations would have tragic consequences later in the war.

Despite the doubts and worries, the landing was a great success. At high tide early on September 15, the marines easily seized the small island of Wŏlmi-do, which controlled access to Inch'ŏn. The main force from the First Marine Division landed that afternoon in the next high-tide cycle. The landing caught the North Koreans by surprise; only a token force of two thousand North Korean soldiers defended the Inch'ŏn area. Within three days nearly seventy thousand men were put ashore.[61]

The Joint Chiefs and General Walker assumed that X Corps would be placed under the Eighth U.S. Army, but MacArthur kept it directly under his own control. MacArthur's decision to divide the command surprised many. "When MacArthur insisted on keeping the X Corps under his own control, the feeling was that the Eighth Army was being slighted in favor of MacArthur's 'pets,'" recalled Ridgway. "While there was never any open expression of jealousy or unwillingness to cooperate, there was no mistaking the fact that the atmosphere of mutual trust so necessary to smooth cooperation was lacking."[62] The arrangement had lasting consequences. "The relationship between Almond and Walker was horrible," recalled Col. John Michaelis. "I used to be in Walker's office, briefing him or something, and the phone would ring. 'Walker this is Almond.' This is a two-star general talking to a three-star general. 'I want you to do so and so.' And Walker would ask, 'Is this Almond speaking or Almond speaking for MacArthur?' They just couldn't get along."[63] Walker resented Almond's special access to MacArthur. "Walker was very suspicious of Almond," remembered Maj. Gen. John Chiles, Almond's operations officer. "He thought Almond was putting words in MacArthur's mouth because he was close to MacArthur and Walker wasn't."[64] Almond's position was an unenviable one. William McCaffrey, a regimental commander in X Corps, recalled that "Almond's complete mystical faith in General MacArthur and his duties to his troops placed him in an extraordinary position of inner conflict."[65] This inner conflict became notably manifest in Almond's relationship with his subordinate commanders, who felt that he was unresponsive to their needs and fighting conditions, because his greater goal was always to please the "big man" in Tokyo.

By September 25, the marines had entered Seoul. MacArthur declared it retaken even though less than half of the city was in UN hands. MacArthur's gamble had paid off. The North Korean army, faced with encirclement and annihilation, rapidly retreated and disappeared "like wraiths into the hills."[66] For MacArthur, success of the Inch'ŏn plan and the liberation of Seoul were both a vindication and a professional triumph. Doubts expressed by General Omar Bradley, Collins, and other members of the JCS had fed into MacArthur's paranoia that Washington was conspiring against him. But everything had gone just as MacArthur said it would. His honor and reputation had been strengthened to epic proportions. He saved South Korea. It was *his* brilliant plan that

General MacArthur addresses guests at a ceremony held at the Capitol Building in Seoul to restore the capital of the Republic of Korea to its president, Syngman Rhee (in the background with glasses). (U.S. NATIONAL ARCHIVES AND RECORDS ADMINISTRATION)

would bring victory. MacArthur was indignant when the Joint Chiefs questioned his authority to restore Syngman Rhee's government, which, they said, "must have the approval of a higher authority." "Your message is not understood," replied MacArthur. "The existing government of the Republic has never ceased to function."[67] The Joint Chiefs simply allowed the matter to rest. It was the first of a series of MacArthur's actions in Korea that the JCS failed to directly challenge. Ridgway later remarked, "A more subtle result of the Inch'ŏn triumph was the development of an almost superstitious regard for General MacArthur's infallibility. Even his superiors, it seemed, began to doubt if they should question *any* of MacArthur's decisions."[68] The more troubling result of Inch'ŏn, however, was that MacArthur ceased to have any doubts about himself.

South Korean prisoners shot by retreating North Korean troops, October 6, 1950. (U.S. NATIONAL ARCHIVES AND RECORDS ADMINISTRATION)

Savage War

Soon after Seoul's liberation, disturbing reports of North Korean atrocities began to surface. "Everywhere the advancing columns found evidence of atrocities as the North Koreans hurried to liquidate political and military prisoners held in jails before they themselves retreated in the face of the U.N. advance," stated the official U.S. Army history.[69] The Associated Press reported that "mass graves, large and small, are being found daily in South Korean communities."[70] The *Washington Post* called a massacre site at Yangyŏng, thirty-five miles south of Seoul, "Red Buchenwald," reporting that "in this Korean Red murder camp, 700 Korean civilians including children were executed."[71] The *New York Times* conveyed that at "Chunghŭng, near Kunsan, Communist soldiers armed with bamboo spears last Monday impaled eighty-two men, women and children after they took the village food supply."[72]

The *Jefferson City Post* reported that "seeing the massacre stung the imagination." It was a "coldly calculated massacre. Each man had been shot individually. Many apparently were clubbed to make sure they were

Captured North Korean soldiers guarded by ROK Military Police remove the bodies of sixty-five political prisoners of the North Korean army that had been dumped into wells in the city of Hamhŭng, North Korea, October 19, 1950. (U.S. NATIONAL ARCHIVES AND RECORDS ADMINISTRATION)

UN forces make another grim discovery of a North Korean massacre near Hamhŭng, where roughly three hundred bodies were taken out of a tunnel, October 1950. (U.S. NATIONAL ARCHIVES AND RECORDS ADMINISTRATION)

In the courtyard of the Taejŏn central police station, a film crew records the oral testimony of a survivor of the Taejŏn massacre, October 31, 1950. These on-site recordings by survivors played an important role in creating the Taejŏn massacre as an iconic symbol of Red terror in both American and South Korean memories of the war. (U.S. NATIONAL ARCHIVES AND RECORDS ADMINISTRATION)

dead. One man had a hatchet sticking to his head."[73] An American survivor of a massacre in Chinju related how the North Koreans had first made them dig their own graves before mowing them down with machine guns. "They tied us all together and shot us," said Pvt. Carey Weinald. "I played dead."[74] North Korean soldiers and local leftists wantonly killed thousands. Women, the elderly, and children were not spared. In one especially brutal incident at Muan county on October 3, families selected for execution were bound and taken to the shore, where the adults were killed with knives, clubs, bamboo spears, and farm implements and then thrown into the sea. Children under ten were thrown into a deep well. The majority of those killed were women and children.[75]

The North Korean massacres at Taejŏn prison became endowed with particularly powerful symbolic significance. The official U.S. history of the war described what had happened in Taejŏn as "one of the greatest mass killings of the entire Korean War," estimating that five to seven thousand civilians and soldiers had been slaughtered.[76] Private Herman

Nelson described the horror of what he saw when he entered the prison: "After a GI thought he saw a body in an open well in the prison camp, an American officer ordered the well searched. A total of twenty-nine dead American soldiers were fished out of the well." Over the next few days, more gruesome discoveries were made: "We discovered a church basement full of women slaughtered by the North Koreans. It was the same sickening sight we had witnessed a few days earlier."[77] Yi Chun-yŏng, who had been a South Korean prison guard at Taejŏn prison before the North Koreans came, vividly recalled the scene when he returned to the prison in early October:

> I entered the prison and walked around and discovered the corpses. They were black and covered with flies. I was speechless. I couldn't believe how cruelly these civilians were killed . . . Some had been shot and others seemed to have been killed by a blunt force that had cracked open their skull. I went to wells and found them full of bodies. We considered what to do . . . We obtained seven suspected communist prisoners and told them to line up the bodies. But the bodies were so decomposed that when we tried to pick them up, the flesh just slipped off. If they were clothed we could have picked them up by their clothing, but most were naked. The communist prisoners asked to be killed rather than handle these bodies, so we returned them to jail. I went to the Taejŏn City Hall to ask for help . . . By the next day, they had mobilized 300–400 people to clear up the bodies. I had them dig holes in the hill behind the prison to bury them . . . It took 2–3 days to do it. At first I thought of burying them individually, but there were just too many bodies, so we buried them in groups in larger holes. I don't have an exact count, but it was between 400–500 people.[78]

The discovery of mass murder solidified in the minds of Americans and others that they were dealing with an "unnatural" enemy, one who had "no regard for human life" or who observed "no rules of war or humanity." Like the "Mongolian hordes" of Asia's past, this enemy "fights with a blend of Asiatic fatalism and Communist fanaticism." "We are facing an army of barbarians in Korea," wrote Hanson Baldwin of the *New York Times*, "but they are barbarians as trained, as relentless, as reckless of life, and as skilled in the tactics of the kind of war they fight as the hordes of Genghis Khan." The North Korean "hordes," like their Russian masters, inherited the particular "Mongolian penchant for cruelty" and used "weapons of fear and terror."[79]

If the horrors of Taejŏn were a glimpse of an enemy not bound by laws of warfare, it was also apparent that the South Koreans were just as brutal. "[The South Korean security forces] murder to save themselves the trouble of escorting prisoners to the rear," wrote an appalled John Osborne of *Time* and *Life*. "They murder civilians simply to get them out of the way or to avoid the trouble of searching and cross examining them. And they extort information . . . by means so brutal that they cannot be described."[80] The *New York Times* reported on July 13 that twelve hundred suspected communists had been executed by the South Korean police since the outbreak of hostilities, an estimate that was woefully inadequate. In the early days of the war, little effort was made by North or South Koreans to hide their atrocities. Telford Taylor, the former chief counsel for prosecution at Nuremberg, incensed by what he was reading in the newspapers, wrote to the *New York Times* that "it seems apparent, if we may take the press accounts at face value, that the atrocities have not all been the work of the North Koreans. The laws of war and war crimes trials are not weapons like bazookas and hand grenades to be used only against the enemy. The laws of war can be 'law' in the true sense only if they are of general application and applied to all sides." He concluded, "We will make ourselves appear ridiculous and hypocritical if we condemn the conduct of the enemy when at the same time troops allied with us are with impunity executing prisoners by means of rifle butts applied to backbones."[81]

The commission of atrocities by South Koreans was not the only issue that would make the Americans appear "ridiculous and hypocritical" to the world. From the beginning, the Americans faced a moral dilemma over what to do with the thousands of Korean refugees. It was a different kind of war from World War II, where the enemy was clearly identifiable on the battlefield. North Korean soldiers easily mixed with the refugees by disguising themselves in the ubiquitous white-cotton peasant clothing. "Time after time an American soldier would pass an innocent-looking bearded Korean farmer hoeing a rice paddy only to be confronted with the same figure throwing grenades at him in a dawn attack," wrote Marguerite Higgins.[82] In late July, the Associated Press reported an announcement by the South Korean government that civilians found making "enemy-like actions" would be executed.[83] "The enemy has used the refugees to his advantage in many ways," reported Ambassador Muccio on July 26, "by forcing [the refugees] south and so clogging the roads as to interfere with military movements, by using them as a channel for infiltration of agents, and most dangerous of all, by disguising their own troops as refugees, who after passing through our lines proceed, after dark, to produce hidden weapons, and then attack our units from the rear. Too often such attacks have been devastatingly successful." Muccio also described a meeting at the South Korean Home Ministry on July 26 between American and South Korean officials where they concluded that leaflets warning people not to proceed south, and that if they did, they risked being fired upon, would be dropped north of the U.S. lines. "If refugees do appear from north of US lines they will receive warning shots, and if they then persist in advancing they will be shot."[84] These instructions were consistent with eyewitness accounts. No one willingly wanted to shoot innocent civilians, particularly women and children, but the nature of the war often forced American soldiers to do so. Colonel Paul Freeman, a regimental commander, admitted in an interview twenty years later, "This was the first time we had really encountered Communist cruelty . . . When we first met some of these North Korean attacks, they were driving civilians, elderly people, in front of them as shields. We had a very difficult time making our men fire into them. But if we didn't fire into them, we were dead. I mean our people were dead. This was a very hard thing to do."[85]

Another measure involved air strikes. "We heard numerous stories about American planes strafing civilians," recalled H. K. Shin, who was just sixteen when he joined the ROK Military Police.[86] One observer recalled that the First Cavalry Division's commanding general, Maj. Gen. Hobart Gay, ordered a "scorched earth" policy: "In any withdrawal, all rural structures would be leveled, burned to the ground. No cover would be left for the enemy. Further, after a posted period, any Koreans found in the area between UN lines and the enemy would be considered hostile and shot on sight."[87] Distinctions between civilians and soldiers were blurred, and the brutality of the violence disturbed even the most seasoned soldier. "Much of this war is alien to the American tradition and shocking to the American mind," observed John Osborne. "The attempt to win it is to force our men in the field to commit acts and attitudes of the utmost savagery." This was not, he thought, "the inevitable savagery of combat in the field, but savagery in detail, the blotting out of villages where the enemy *may* be hiding, the shooting and shelling of refugees who *may* include North Koreans . . . or who *may* be screening an enemy march upon our positions."[88]

Some of the worst atrocities were committed by South Koreans against South Koreans. In July 1950, the South Korean military and police conducted mass executions of suspected leftists before the arrival of the North Korean army.[89] At Chŏngwŏn in central South Korea, the police killed hundreds of suspected communists. Pak Chŏng-gil, a young boy at the time, remembered the "perfidious" activities of the fleeing South Korean police: "I think they killed several thousand people there. Every day for seven straight days I saw four trucks in the morning and three trucks in the afternoon loaded with people." The trucks, he said, all came back empty at night. At Nanju, in the southwest, police officers disguised as North Koreans stormed the village. When the people welcomed them, they were rounded up, taken to a field, and summarily executed.[90] These and other massacres throughout South Korea in 1949 and 1950 demonstrated that the end of the Cheju and Yŏsu-Sunch'ŏn Rebellions had not stopped the fratricidal bloodshed. South Korean

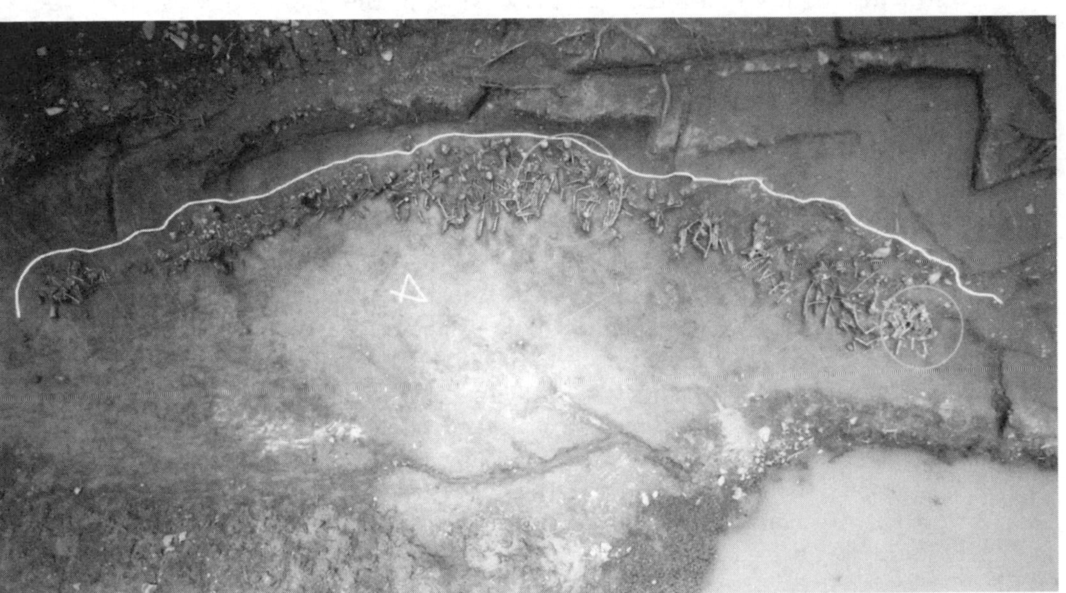

Remains of 114 Bodo League victims executed in July 1950 at Chŏngwŏn, Ch'ungbuk province, excavated by the Truth and Reconciliation Commission in 2007. Remains of the victims reveal that they had been shot to death. (ROK TRUTH AND RECONCILIATION COMMISSION)

security forces purged the army of leftists and communists and did their ruthless best to rid the countryside of communist guerilla groups formed by the remnants of the Yŏsu-Sunch'ŏn rebels who had escaped into the mountains. Caught in the roundup of suspected leftists and communists were innocent civilians, including women and children who were summarily executed in the thousands in the name of fighting the communists. It is estimated that at least a hundred thousand South Koreans were killed in the summer of 1950. Most were members of the Bodo League (*kungmin podo yŏnmaeng*, National Guidance League), ostensibly created by the Rhee government in the summer of 1949 to rehabilitate leftists, but in reality it was a form of totalitarian state control of the people. Its logic required hapless and often illiterate farmers and fishermen to be enticed to join the league with promises of jobs, food, and other benefits to meet the quota imposed from Seoul. When North Korea invaded, the South Korean regime hastily took measures to eliminate those who might help the communists, and Bodo League members, mostly innocent of leftist leanings, were arbitrarily and summarily executed all over the country. Indeed, the hundred thousand estimate might be on the conservative side, as there were three hundred thousand members on the rolls of the league on the eve of the North Korean invasion.[91]

In an interview in November 2007, Chŏng Kwang-im recounted how her young farmer husband, who had joined the Bodo League in 1949, was summarily arrested and executed at Taejŏn:

> One day the police came and asked where my husband, Pak Man-ho, was and I told them that he went away to make some money. They then arrested me. I spent the night in the jail. The next morning my husband came to the police station with our two children who had been crying for me all night. After he arrived they called for me. They gave me the children and took my husband without any chance for us to talk. At the urging of other people I awaited outside the prison. Around five in the morning a siren rang and trucks came. They loaded the trucks with prisoners, one at a time. We didn't know where they were being taken to. I heard later they were taken to Sannae village.

Pak was executed in a remote valley near Sannae village. Chŏng later went to recover his remains, but she could not find him because the bodies had rapidly decomposed in the July heat. She never remarried and

The remains of twenty-nine bodies were unearthed at the third site of the Kolryŏnggol, Sannae, Taejŏn in 2007. They were found face down with their knees bent, which suggests that the victims were killed execution-style. (ROK TRUTH AND RECONCILIATION COMMISSION)

lived a life of suffering with her two sons, ostracized by her husband's past as an alleged communist sympathizer.[92]

Many American advisors, concerned and revolted by what they saw, filed reports with photographs. But the senior-level American response was decidedly ambivalent. Lieutenant Colonel Rollins Emmerich reported on the situation in Pusan, which had never fallen into enemy hands. He discovered that the local ROK Army commander, Col. Kim Chŏng-wŏn, planned "to execute some 3,500 suspected Communists." He told Colonel Kim that the enemy would not reach Pusan soon and that "atrocities could not be condoned." But "Colonel Kim was told that if the enemy did arrive to the outskirts of Pusan he would be permitted to open the gates of the prison and shoot the prisoners with machine guns." Emmerich faced a similar situation in Taegu, where he managed to persuade South Korean authorities not to execute forty-five hundred prisoners. Taegu soon was threatened by the presence of North Koreans on its outskirts, and hundreds of the prisoners were executed. Donald Nichols, an air force intelligence officer, witnessed, photographed, and reported on the execution of eighteen hundred prisoners in Suwŏn, just south of Seoul. A North Korean press report that a thousand prisoners were executed in Inch'ŏn in late June 1950 was corroborated by an Eighth Army report on the execution of "400 Communists" there. Attempts were made to restrain the South Koreans, but the authorities receiving these reports, including MacArthur, were ambivalent. He had received numerous reports of the killings and atrocities committed by South Korean forces under his command, but he deferred to Ambassador Muccio, who merely asked the South Korean government to execute humanely and only after due process. MacArthur considered the situation a Korean "internal matter" and took no action.[93]

Ironically, one of the most egregious massacres by the South Koreans took place in the very vicinity where the North Koreans were accused of committing their most heinous war crimes. In early July, three weeks before Taejŏn fell to the NKPA, South Korean security forces executed thousands of suspected communists and leftists. Details of this incident have only recently been reported in South Korea. "After receiving news of the North Korean attack on Taejŏn," reported the *Wŏlgan chosŏn*, a prominent South Korean monthly, in June 2000, "high ranking government and prisoner officials were too busy retreating to worry about the prisoners at Taejŏn prison." As a result, "the responsibility ultimately fell on lower-ranking prison officials who did not want their men butchered alone by the revolting prisoners."[94] Yi Chun-yŏng, the Taejŏn prison guard who saw victims of North Korean killings in October, recalled the chaotic events in the days before the city fell. "We received a phone call from the Chief Prosecutor of the Justice Ministry and were ordered to execute all the leaders and officials of the Communist Party." Seeking confirmation, Yi found the justice minister at the train station getting ready to evacuate south. The minister coolly told Yi "to tell the Commandant in charge to take action based on his own judgment." Yi was furious. "If there hadn't been others around, I would have shot him then and there," Yi recalled indignantly. "The nation was in peril because people like him didn't take any responsibility for any decision."[95] Minutes later, the minister was gone, taking one of the last trains out of Taejŏn.

There were only twenty-two men to guard and control the thousands of prisoners. Most were political prisoners charged with communist and leftist leanings. The local military police unit, led by Lt. Sim Yŏng-hyŏn, had arrived. Sim directed the prison guards to identify for execution any prisoners who had violated the Special Security Law, who had been involved in the 1948 Yŏsu-Sunch'ŏn Uprising or the 1948–49 Cheju-do Rebellion, or who had been indicted for spying, and anyone else who had received a sentence of ten years or more. But time was short and they could not complete the sorting. In the end, all prisoners were executed. "The Commandant said that [executing all the prisoners] may become a political problem in the future, but there was nothing that could be done about the situation as there was no time to sort through all their backgrounds."[96] The prisoners, men and women, with their hands tied behind their backs, were loaded onto trucks. "Men from nearby villages were mobilized to dig trenches." The prisoners were driven to various sites in the outskirts of the city and "taken to the trenches in groups of about ten. They were forced to kneel at the trench and bow their heads. The firing team was composed of military and civilian policemen. They put the barrel against the back of the head and fired."[97] "Even at point blank range, some were not killed outright," Yi recalled. "Lt. Sim ordered me to confirm the executions and finish off those who were not dead. I was carrying a 45 caliber pistol unlike other guards who had smaller caliber pistols. I shot those who were still alive and squirming as I walked by them. I did as I was ordered." There was one moment, however, that Yi will never forget:

> As I walked by I heard behind me, "Sir, sir, I am not dead yet, please, sir, shoot me." I turned around and saw a man who had worked in the mess hall. He had been imprisoned for theft and had one year left to serve out his ten year term . . . Why didn't he say, "Hey you bastard, I am not dead. Shoot me, you bastard." Why did he call me "sir" instead? He had no hostility towards me, and I suddenly felt a rush of anguish and respect for this man. He asked me to shoot him because he was suffering and I did.[98]

Yi later blamed higher authorities for what happened: "I don't regret the death of communists who were convicted and sentenced to death, but the others . . . I wonder what kind of people led our nation who allowed them to be executed as well."[99] Although scattered reports about the mass executions managed to find their way into the foreign media, few stories ever reached the mainstream press because they were dismissed as communist propaganda. Alan Winnington, a British journalist for the communist *Daily Worker*, wrote what he had witnessed in Taejŏn when he arrived there with the NKPA:

Civilians about to be executed by South Korean security forces, Taejŏn, July 1950. (U.S. NATIONAL ARCHIVES AND RECORDS ADMINISTRATION)

> Try to imagine Rangwul Valley, about five miles south-east of Taejon on the Yongdong road. Hills rise sharply from a level floor of 100 yards across and a quarter of a mile long. In the middle you can walk safely, though your shoes may roll on American cartridge cases, but at the sides you must be careful for the rest of the valley is thin crust of earth covering corpses of more than 7,000 men and women. One of the party with me stepped through nearly to his hip in rotting human tissue. Every few feet there is a fissure in the topsoil through which you can see into a gradually sinking mass of flesh and bone. The smell is something tangible and seeps into your throat. For days after I could taste the smell. All along the great death pits, waxy dead hands and feet, knees, elbows, twisted faces and heads burst open by bullets, stick through the soil . . . All six of the death pits are six feet deep and from six to twelve feet wide. The biggest is 200 yards long. Local peasants were forced at the rifle point to dig them, and it was from these that I got the facts. On July 4, 5 and 6, all prisoners from the jails and concentration camps around Taejon were taken in trucks to the valley, after first being bound with wire, knocked unconscious and packed like sardines on top of each other. So truckloads were driven to the valley and flung into pits. Peasants were made to cover the filled sections of the pits with soil.[100]

Few believed him at the time. When the city was retaken, victims of the earlier massacre perpetrated by the ROK forces were conflated with victims of the North Korean killings. Buried beneath the story of the

North Korean slaughter, literally, was the forgotten story of the South Korean carnage. The raw brutality of a civil war wracked by deep and polarized ideological divide and decades of pent-up personal animosities exploded in the first few months of the war, causing a wound in Korean society, North and South, that remains raw to this day. The tides of cruelty continued with the tides of war as North and South Koreans tried to outdo each other in eliminating suspected collaborators and sympathizers of the other side as the front line moved north and south. In the context of the cold war, where clear lines between the "free world" and the "slave world," and "civilization" and "barbarism," needed to be starkly drawn, the messy civil war in Korea, with its moral ambiguities and vengeful deeds, had to be simplified. Historical forgetting, selective reporting, propagandistic self-deception, and a truly savage war and war crimes played major roles in the demonization of the other side. While the Western press continued to report on North Korean atrocities, particularly the merciless treatment of American POWs, critical coverage of South Korean brutality and U.S. operational excesses largely disappeared. Already, in the opening weeks of the war, a subtle yet distinct process of "forgetting" was beginning to take place.

CHAPTER FIVE

Uncommon Coalition

At the end of August 1950, UN ground forces began to arrive in Korea, starting with the first contingent of British troops. The passage of UN Security Council Resolution 83 on June 27, 1950, obligated UN member states to consider sending assistance "to the Republic of Korea as may be necessary to repel the armed attack and to restore international peace and security in the area." Fifty-one member states were part of the United Nations upon its founding in 1945, and by the time of the Korean War, only eight more had joined. Out of these fifty-nine nations, forty-eight offered or sent forces or aid to South Korea. Seven non–UN member states also sent aid, bringing the total to fifty-five nations. Japan was under Allied occupation when the war started, but it was a critical support base for the war and was thus a member of the coalition. Germany was also under occupation but provided nonmilitary aid. Adding South Korea brought the final count of the coalition to fifty-eight. Of these, twenty-two nations, including one non–UN member, with "boots on the ground" in Korea formed the core of the coalition. Never before in modern history had so many nations committed themselves to a common political and military endeavor as they did during the Korean War (see appendix).[1]

There was a fundamental difference in the way the coalition in Korea was organized and operated compared to coalitions in other wars, such as the two world wars and the more recent conflicts in Iraq and Afghanistan. Coalitions formed in wars before and after the Korean War normally consisted of discrete national units under national command, with coalitional integration or command and control achieved only at the highest level of command. For example, in World War II, the major Allied forces in the European theater of operations did not mix different nationalities below the corps level, except for very minor exceptions for specialized operations. In Korea, necessity, expedience, improvisation, and politics demanded a wholly different kind of coalition.

The unique character of the Korean coalition arose from a number of factors. First, the South Korean military was placed under UN/U.S. control because of its severely depleted and disorganized state after the first two weeks of fighting.[2] Second, as an extension of the first, two pools of manpower were provided to UN/U.S. forces. One comprised the tens of thousands of Korean men known as KATUSA (Korean Augmentation to the United States Army) soldiers assigned to U.S. units, an arrangement that was later expanded to include British, Australian, Canadian, French, Dutch, and Belgian units. Most of the KATUSA soldiers were integrated down to the lowest level, the squad of some dozen men. The other pool of manpower was the Korean Service Corps (KSC), civilian laborers who were organized and led by ROK Army leaders to provide dedicated support to all UN/U.S. units. The ratio of laborers to soldiers was roughly one to two. Finally, non-U.S./Korean UN ground forces were sent not as large units or with a complete support structure and thus could not operate independently. Britain, Turkey, and Canada sent brigades (3,000–5,000 men), but most non-U.S./Korean UN ground forces were battalion size (about 1,000 men). All units were integrated into American divisions and corps. By 1952, every American division and corps had KATUSA soldiers and at least one UN battalion or brigade. The British Commonwealth ground forces (United Kingdom, Australia, Canada, New Zealand, and India) did combine into a single division in the summer of 1951, an arrangement unprecedented for the Commonwealth, but it was subordinated to a U.S. corps and relied on American logistical support. The flow of campaigns and battles from late 1950 to mid-1951, under constant reorganization and re-subordination, led to complex mixes of nationalities.[3]

By the end of 1950, ten nations (in the order of arrival: the United Kingdom, the Philippines, Australia, Turkey, Thailand, the Netherlands, France, Greece, Canada, and New Zealand) had sent ground combat forces to join the Koreans and the Americans. Four more nations (Belgium, Luxembourg, Ethiopia, and Colombia) sent combat forces by the middle of 1951. Medical units from five other nations (Sweden, India, Denmark, Italy, and Norway) arrived by the end of 1951, while the United Kingdom, Canada, Australia, and New Zealand significantly increased their contingents. By the end of 1951, the total strength of the non-U.S./ROK force was 35,000. This would grow to nearly 40,000 by July 1953.[4]

The British Commonwealth forces formed the majority of the coalition forces, about 60 percent (21,000–24,000). These forces went through several stages of reorganization, from the Commonwealth Brigade of British, Australian, Canadian, and Indian units in 1950 to, with reinforcements in 1951, the unique First Commonwealth Division formed in the summer of 1951. The unprecedented formation of the Commonwealth Brigade and the Commonwealth Division created political and high-level military difficulties, but at the lower level it was a relatively smooth process done efficiently and effectively, owing to a shared military heritage and culture and the use of English as a common language. The assignment of the Norwegian mobile army surgical hospital (NORMASH) also was done without significant problems. The Commonwealth units were the only forces besides the U.S. military that established a separate logistical system, easing the burden of support from the Eighth U.S. Army, which still had to provide fuel and fresh food.

Integrating an Army

The arrival of the 5,000 men of the Turkish Brigade in October 1950, however, posed far greater challenges. As soon as the situation stabilized after the victory at Inch'ŏn, a centralized transition and training center, the United Nations Reception Center (UNRC), was established near Taegu to help "clothe, equip, and provide familiarization training with US Army weapons and equipment to UN troops." As the first UN troops to be processed, the Turks, during their three-week stay, provided the UNRC a much clearer picture of the kinds of problems the American commanders would be facing in commanding an international coalition. For example, bathing proved to be an unexpected challenge. "When showers were set up, it was found out that only one Turkish soldier at a time would bathe, until the problem of their unexpected modesty was solved by the soldiers themselves. Each man formed an individual cubicle by wrapping shelter halves around himself."[5]

Language differences also posed a formidable barrier. Greek, Turkish, Thai, French, Flemish, Spanish, and Dutch as well as a number of other

South Korean children present flowers to a Turkish officer (center) in charge of the first contingent of Turkish troops on their arrival in Pusan, October 18, 1950. (U.S. NATIONAL ARCHIVES AND RECORDS ADMINISTRATION)

dialects "were among the tongues used in the UN ground [combat] units." Added to these difficulties were the "Swedish, Norwegian, Italian, and several regional languages used by medical units supporting the combat forces." Although the language barriers were never completely overcome, English was the lingua franca, and the burden of translation was left to UN units that "provided English-speaking personnel to translate training materials, operational orders and supply instructions into their own languages."[6]

Feeding the Turks was a special challenge, for most of them were Muslims and forbidden to eat pork. The Eighth Army devised a porkless diet manufactured by a Japanese fish cannery. The Turks also procured their "own stronger brand of coffee." Since the staple of the Turkish diet was bread, they were given "three times the amount of bread issued to a US regiment as well as greater quantities of vegetable oil, olives, vinegar, dehydrated onions, and salt."[7]

As with the Turks, culinary differences with the units from other countries initially posed great problems and stressed the U.S. ration

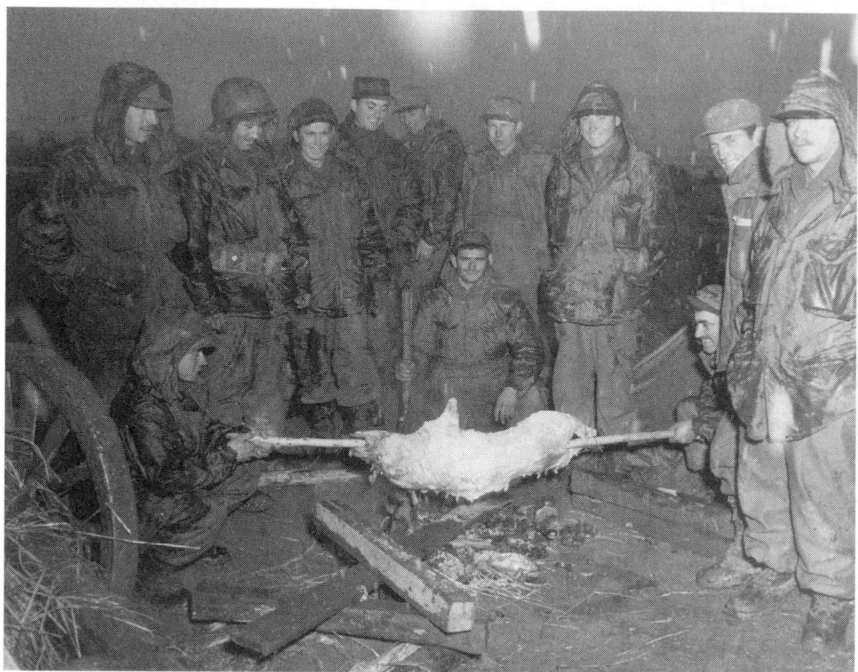

Troops in the Greek army prepare for a pork barbecue behind UN lines in Korea. Like other nationalities, the Greeks had their own unique dietary requirements, such as olive oil, raisins, and special flour, which were provided in sufficient quantities through their own channels. (U.S. NATIONAL ARCHIVES AND RECORDS ADMINISTRATION)

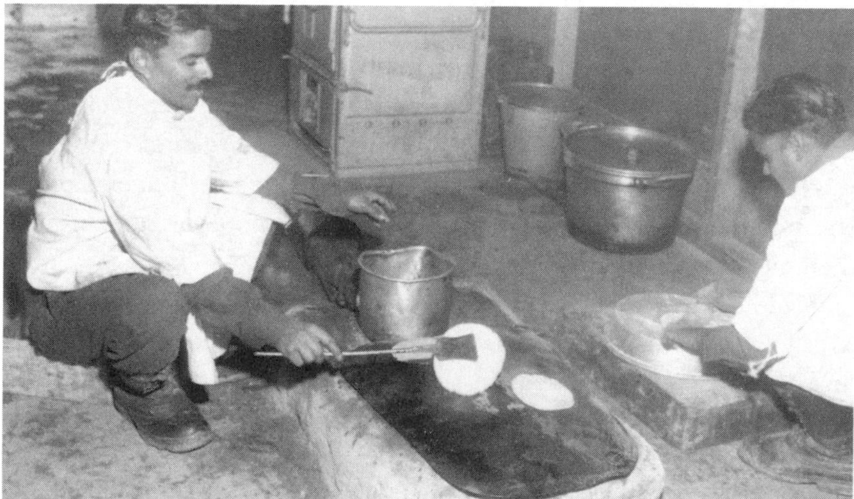

Indian cooks prepare traditional "chapati" flat bread. Unlike troops from Asian and European nations, which required large quantities of rice and potatoes, respectively, Indian troops required large quantities of wheat. (U.S. NATIONAL ARCHIVES AND RECORDS ADMINISTRATION)

system. It was difficult, for example, to get the Thai to eat "any sort of food except rice and pots of boiled vegetables, thick with peppers and hot sauces." The Greeks did not eat corn, carrots, and asparagus and required olive oil for cooking. The Indians were mostly vegetarians. The Filipinos required additional rice, while the Belgians, French, and Dutch consumed greater quantities of bread and potatoes than the Americans did. The Greeks required special meals for religious days: "On Good Friday, they desired no meat in their rations, whereas for Greek Orthodox Easter, they required fifteen live lambs for their traditional feasts."[8]

Clothing also produced its share of difficulties. The Thai, Filipino, and Greek soldiers required smaller clothing. A major challenge was combat boots. "It must be remembered that some of these troops were accustomed to wearing sandals, and therefore their feet were wide at the ball and narrow at the heel," noted an American officer. Ethiopians were generally taller than Americans and their feet longer and narrower.[9]

The most critical area, weapons and ammunition, was not a major issue. Most UN troops, except for the Commonwealth units, were given American arms. Some contingents arrived already familiar with the U.S. Army, its procedures, and weapons. The Philippine army had been trained by the United States for many years, while the Greek army had recently undergone intense American training and equipping under Lt. Gen. James Van Fleet, to fight its communist insurgency. Van Fleet's assumption of command of the Eighth Army a few months after the Greek battalion's arrival no doubt provided an additional level of comfort to the Greeks.

The greatest challenge of the coalition, however, was integrating the ROK Army with the Eighth U.S. Army. Until the breakout from the Pusan perimeter in September 1950, ROK Army units were kept together at their own part of the front and controlled through the ROK Army headquarters. When the Eighth Army was reorganized for the breakout, the ROK First Division was assigned to an American corps, thus beginning the process of integrating ROK units with American forces.[10]

The need for men was so great in the summer of 1950 that the KATUSA program expanded rapidly, and by September over 19,000 KATUSA soldiers were assigned to the Eighth Army and X Corps.[11] Integration of these Korean soldiers presented major difficulties at all

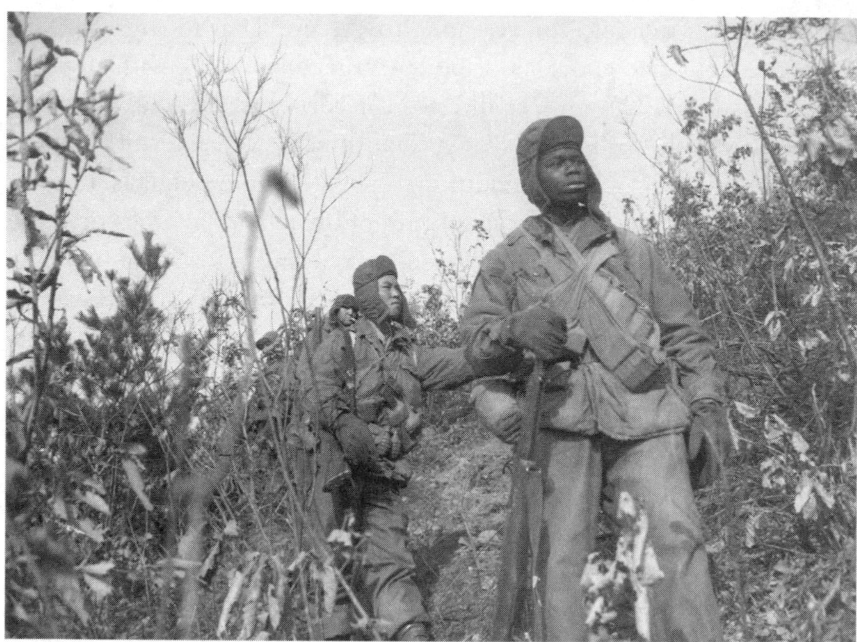

American and KATUSA soldiers of the 27th Infantry Regiment advance toward Chinese forces at Kyŏngan-ri February 17, 1951. (U.S. NATIONAL ARCHIVES AND RECORDS ADMINISTRATION)

levels of command. The success of the Inch'ŏn landing demonstrated the surprising efficiency of UN operations even at this early phase in the war. While most accounts of the operation have focused on the epic battles of the U.S. X Corps and its two American divisions, the First Marine Division and the U.S. Army Seventh Infantry Division, what is rarely noted is the role that the Korean soldiers and marines in the two divisions played in the events. The simpler arrangement was the attachment of the ROK Marine Corps Regiment to the U.S. First Marine Division.[12] Such an attachment was routine and natural, and the regiment fought as a unit. However, the situation in the Seventh Division was quite different, because fully one-third of the division was composed of KATUSA soldiers.

The Seventh Division had been on occupation duty in Japan at reduced strength. It became further depleted when men were transferred to the Twenty-Fourth and Twenty-Fifth Infantry Divisions as they deployed to Korea in July 1950, thereby reducing the Seventh to less than half strength by late July. Essentially the division was not combat ready.[13] Two measures were taken to bring it up to strength after it was selected for the Inch'ŏn operation. First, a large portion of the replacement flow from the United States was sent to the division. Second, MacArthur requested that the South Korean government provide Korean recruits to make up for the remaining shortfall. In mid-August nearly 9,000 Koreans arrived at Yokohama, Japan, "stunned, confused, and exhausted."[14] General "Johnnie" Walker reported to MacArthur, "They are right out of the rice paddies, and have nothing but shorts and straw hats."[15] Many had literally been dragged off the streets and arrived in Japan "in their native civilian clothes, white baggy cotton pants, small white jackets, [and] rubber shoes," according to Maj. Spencer Edwards, the Seventh Division's replacement officer.[16] They had less than a month to become soldiers and get ready for an amphibious landing, one of the most complex and riskiest of military operations. In three weeks, 8,600 Koreans were clothed, equipped, and trained, however minimally, to join the 16,000 Americans of the Seventh Division embarking for Inch'ŏn.[17] The challenges and obstacles were huge. Few, if any, spoke English. They had no military background or experience. Stocks of small-size uniform items were quickly exhausted. For many, the standard American rifle (the M1) was too long. Instead of forming all-Korean units, they were apportioned throughout the division at the rate of a hundred men per company or battery and integrated to the lowest echelon. Given that a standard company or battery may have about two hundred men, this was an enormous challenge. A buddy system of pairing individual Koreans with an American was used for assimilation, training, and control.[18] The operational risks of the Inch'ŏn plan were magnified by the huge tactical risk of employing a division composed of the greenest troops, American and Korean, in which a third of the fighting force did not understand English.[19]

Fortunately, the First Marine Division, which landed first, was able to quickly secure a beachhead, allowing the Seventh Division to land without fighting for one. The Seventh Division soon entered combat to cut off the North Korean army's retreat and to liberate Seoul. Their actions on the battlefield were predictably mixed. Major Edwards recalled that "some of the ROKs participated heroically and some of them disappeared at the first sign of danger. The great majority behaved just as any other troops with less than three weeks' training would have—they just didn't know what was going on." Korean civilians watched in amaze-

Korean Service Corps (KSC) laborers, near Suwŏn, February 5, 1951. In addition to the KATUSAs serving in U.S. units, the other pool of manpower was the KSC. Affectionately referred to as the "A-Frame Army" by American soldiers because of their wooden backpacks, at its peak the KSC had over 130,000 Koreans who were organized to provide direct support to non-Korean soldiers. The unarmed members of the KSC moved ammunition, supplies, and food to the front lines, traversing steep and rugged terrain that was otherwise inaccessible by vehicles. They also helped in the evacuation of wounded and deceased soldiers and the construction of defensive positions. (U.S. NATIONAL ARCHIVES AND RECORDS ADMINISTRATION)

KSC laborer, near Suwŏn, February 5, 1951. (U.S. NATIONAL ARCHIVES AND RECORDS ADMINISTRATION)

ment as thousands of Koreans marched through the streets wearing the patch of an American unit that had been part of the occupation force in South Korea between 1945 and 1949. By the end of the Inch'ŏn-Seoul operations on October 3, the Seventh Division had suffered 572 casualties, of which 166 were KATUSA soldiers. By this time, thousands of other KATUSA soldiers had been assigned to and were fighting in all U.S. Army divisions.[20]

Japanese nationals also played an important role in these operations. The majority of the landing ship tanks (LSTs) that the First Marine Division used at Inch'ŏn, thirty-seven of forty-seven, were, in fact, manned by Japanese crews.[21] Furthermore, twenty Japanese minesweepers were contracted to help clear mines along the coastal areas. One was sunk during mine-clearing operations in Wŏnsan Harbor.[22] Japanese nationals thus participated directly in combat operations. One Japanese national was even listed as an exchanged POW after the armistice.[23] In addition to providing LST crews and minesweepers, Japan was literally the unsinkable base of support for the fighting. Nearly all military forces and supplies to Korea came from or transited through Japan. It also provided bases for air and naval operations.[24] Troops were trained there before deployment, were treated there after being wounded, and played there during R&R leave. Japanese firms provisioned the UN forces and repaired their equipment.

Calling the Eighth Army a "U.S. Army" was thus a significant misnomer by the summer of 1951. More appropriate would have been the "UN Army in Korea" since less than half of its half-million men were Americans. Indeed, more than 50 percent of the fighting force were Koreans, of whom 20,000 were integrated into U.S., French, Dutch, and Belgian units. Some 28,000 soldiers from nineteen other nations joined them. The Eighth Army's strength increased to nearly one million men by the time of the armistice, with 300,000 Americans, 590,000 Koreans, and 39,000 soldiers from other nations.[25] No U.S. division since August 1950 was purely American, as KATUSA soldiers filled the ranks through all echelons.[26] The U.S. divisions also had at least one UN battalion or brigade attached. Every U.S. corps had at least one ROK division. I Corps was probably the most diverse, composed of U.S. Army, ROK, and British Commonwealth divisions, which also included Turkish, Greek, and Norwegian contingents. Furthermore, since the summer of 1950 all non-

Korean UN ground units were supported by the ROK Army's KSC. At its height the Eighth Army's KSC had 130,000 men to support 300,000 non-Korean soldiers.[27]

Common Cause

So why had all these nations come together under the UN flag to fight in Korea? Although each nation had its own reason to participate in the war, there was a broad commonality of factors, especially for the nations that sent combat forces. First and foremost, the war was seen as a test for the young United Nations and the concept of collective security it was supposed to uphold. Invoking the UN also invoked its most important member, the United States, and support to the UN also implied support for the Americans. Demonstrating this support became critical in the aftermath of World War II, for the United States emerged from the war as the most powerful and prosperous nation in the world, a world devastated by the destruction of that war and the ensuing strife and unrest of postcolonial struggles for independence, many involving indigenous communist movements. Communist insurgencies in Malaya for the United Kingdom and Indochina for France were particularly troubling. The United States had also been helping the Philippines battle its growing communist threat. In 1949, the Dutch pulled out of Indonesia, conceding defeat in the Indonesian War of Independence. Its new president, Sukarno, was sympathetic to communism. Most noncommunist member states of the United Nations thus felt an obligation to uphold the UN Charter and its principle of collective security. No member state felt this obligation more keenly than the three Western permanent members of the Security Council: the United States, the United Kingdom, and France. Anticommunism and collective security were major shared ideologies of the nations that sent aid to Korea, especially those that deployed combat forces. The line was to be drawn against communism in general and against the Soviet Union in particular.

But idealistic ideology alone could not produce the kind of assistance the war called for, as most nations lacked the resources to provide it. Furthermore, many nations either were dependent on or wanted American assistance or commitment for economic development and security.

Soldiers of the Argyll and Sutherland Highlanders arrive in Pusan. Originally, the British government had decided to mobilize and deploy the Twenty-Ninth Infantry Brigade, a unit in the British strategic reserve force, but the brigade would not be ready on time. As a result, the Twenty-Seventh Brigade from Hong Kong was sent to Pusan as a quick stop measure until the Twenty-Ninth Brigade could be deployed. Only two of the brigade's three battalions, the Argyll and Sutherland Highlanders and the Middlesex battalions, were sent, however. In order not to deplete the Hong Kong garrison completely, the Leicesters were left behind. Arriving on August 29 to bolster the Pusan perimeter, the Twenty-Seventh Brigade was the first non-U.S. UN ground force to enter the war. (U.S. NATIONAL ARCHIVES AND RECORDS ADMINISTRATION)

Britain was particularly keen to maintain a "special relationship" with the United States and to secure an American commitment for Western European security. France, already deeply embroiled in a protracted war with Ho Chi Minh's forces in Indochina, was eager to obtain American assistance for its own "cold war struggle" in Asia. France had convinced the Americans that, far from fighting a selfish colonial war, it was in fact defending the principles of freedom against communist world dictatorship. For its efforts in Korea and in Indochina, President Truman believed that France was entitled to a generous measure of American military and financial assistance since "these were two fronts in the same struggle."[28] Many nations reasoned that providing a contribution, especially combat forces, would serve not only their idealism but also, by getting in America's good graces, their national interests. Largely

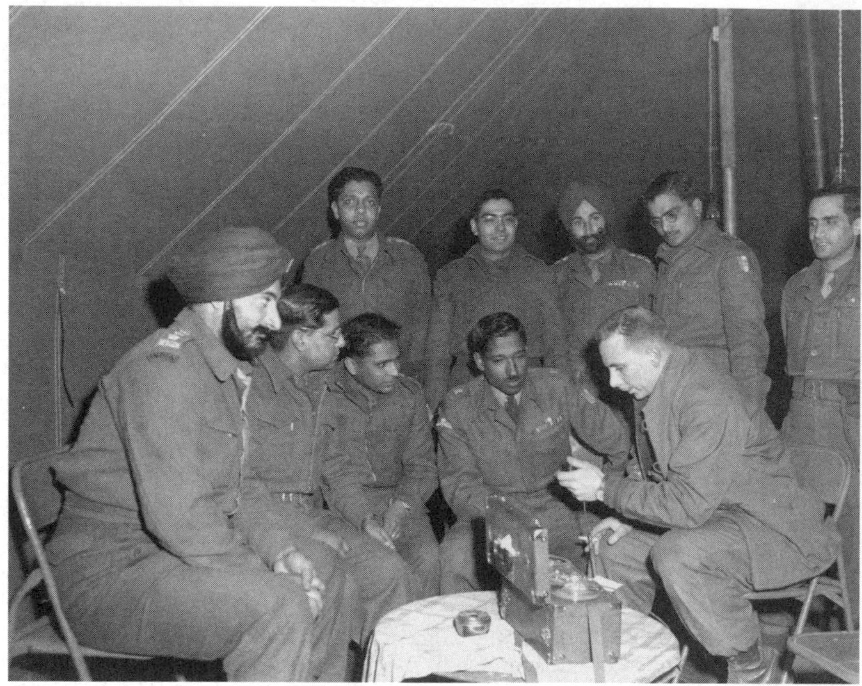

On November 20, 1950, the 60th Indian (Parachute) Field Ambulance, a mobile army surgical hospital, arrived and became part of the Twenty-Seventh Brigade. Britain pressured India for a large combat force, but Prime Minister Jawaharlal Nehru wanted to position India, which had only recently won its independence in 1947, as a leader of the underdeveloped countries in the UN and nonaligned with any major power. Nehru decided to contribute a medical unit as a commitment to the UN rather than to the Commonwealth, a symbol of its noncombatant status. The 60th Field Ambulance was an elite regular unit with personnel who were veterans of the Burma campaign during World War II serving in the British army. (U.S. NATIONAL ARCHIVES AND RECORDS ADMINISTRATION)

because of their participation in the Korean War, Greece and Turkey, for example, were admitted to NATO in 1952. This was a triumph especially for Turkey, which had struggled to be accepted as part of Europe. Its large contribution in Korea, the legendary Turkish brigade, served to prove Turkey's commitment to the West and its willingness to make sacrifices to uphold it.[29]

For Thailand, participation in the war helped to solve the special problem it had faced following the Second World War. Thailand had been a member of the Axis after signing an armistice with Japan in December 1941. Fighting in Korea largely "rehabilitated" the Thai in the eyes of the

A group of smiling Turkish officers pose with Korean Boy Scouts who welcomed their arrival at Pusan, October 19, 1950. (U.S. NATIONAL ARCHIVES AND RECORDS ADMINISTRATION)

free world. Japan's role in the Korean War was not so much as a willing participant, since it was still under American occupation in 1950, as it was of an unsuspecting bystander of a conflict from which it reaped tremendous benefit. The war was, as Prime Minister Yoshida Shigeru once famously proclaimed, "a gift from the gods." A war boom, stimulated by U.S. procurements for the war, put Japan's economy back on track. Japanese industrial production during the conflict also laid the technological foundation for the subsequent development of the country's industry.[30] Japan's central role in enabling the support of the UN forces created a paradox regarding the ending of the Allied occupation and the restoration of sovereignty. At first, military necessity made it preferable to delay any plans for Japanese independence until the Korean War was over. The Americans needed Japan's full compliance for their war efforts in Korea. However, as the level of occupation forces dwindled and Japanese civil society became crucial in maintaining military support for the Korean War, the logic of denying the Japanese their independence was turned on its head as the Americans began to realize the necessity for placating, and even appeasing, the Japanese people as a prolonged occupation could degrade their cooperation and support. Nothing could have done this more powerfully than the end of the occupation, which occurred in April 1952. At the same time, even though the Japanese postwar constitution, drafted by the Americans, specifically forbade the maintenance of a military, the Korean War convinced both the Americans and the Japanese that Japan needed to be rearmed to defend itself against the communist and Soviet threat. Japan regained not only sovereignty, but a military as well. [31]

India, too, provided an interesting case. Although it sent a military medical unit that served with the Commonwealth forces, its motive was not to strengthen ties with Britain or the United States. Rather, India wanted to demonstrate its nonaligned and nonbelligerent policy. In line with this position, India agreed to chair the Neutral Nations Repatriation Commission, which later oversaw the repatriation of POWs from both sides and provided a brigade-size custodial force to supervise the POW exchange after the armistice was signed. It also accepted a significant number of POWs from both sides who did not want to be repatriated to their countries. India's record in Korea helped to validate its nonalignment policy and its position as a leader of the Nonaligned Movement (NAM) during the height of the cold war. [32]

Ultimately, the most important outcome of the Korean War for all these nations was the legitimization of the United Nations. The failure of the League of Nations to confront Japan after it invaded Manchuria in 1931 had loomed large for many UN members. The successful coalition that fought in Korea erased doubts that the UN might be an equally empty promise; it had become a credible and effective international organization for peace and cooperation. For most countries that sent military forces to Korea, it was the first time in their history to participate in a war in a foreign land not for conquest, occupation, or defense of colonial territory. MacArthur's spectacular victory at Inch'ŏn, however, would test the promise of that noble endeavor when UN forces were ordered to cross the 38th parallel into North Korea.

CHAPTER SIX

Crossing the 38th Parallel

By the end of September 1950 the mandate of the original UN Security Council resolution had been fulfilled: the aggressors had been repelled and the original boundary restored. However, unfulfilled was the second and more ambiguous mandate of the June 27 resolution, which called for restoration of "international peace and security in the area." Many assumed that this required establishing conditions ensuring that another attack could not be mounted after UN forces withdrew—in other words, for the UN to eliminate North Korea and reunify Korea. Yakov Malik, the Soviet permanent representative to the UN, challenged this interpretation and the meaning of restoring "international peace and security in the area." Malik argued that peace and security could be restored only if Korea was reunified, and this required the withdrawal of all foreign troops to allow the Koreans to work out their own reunification. To avoid a Soviet veto in the Security Council, the United States turned to the General Assembly to introduce a resolution providing political guidance for military operations in Korea. The resolution called for the establishment of "conditions of stability" throughout Korea with a unified government followed by "a prompt withdrawal of troops." The Soviets opposed the resolution, and so did India and Yugoslavia, who argued that it exceeded the original limited objective of repelling the invasion. The resolution passed on October 7.[1]

The resolution stipulated that UN forces "should not remain in any part of Korea longer than necessary once the goal of achieving stability and a unified democratic Korea had been attained." It did not explicitly call for UN forces to cross the 38th parallel, and this ambiguity reflected the delicate nature of the political situation surrounding the "artificial dividing line." Most members of the UN, including the United States, sought to evade the issue by playing down the significance of the 38th parallel, "to allow the UN commander to be guided by tactical considerations when he reached the parallel."[2] In any case, General MacArthur had already received authority to conduct military operations north of the 38th parallel even before the UN resolution was passed.

On September 27, MacArthur received the crucial directive from the Joint Chiefs of Staff authorizing his advance into North Korea. It stated, "Your military objective is the destruction of the North Korean Armed Forces. In attaining this objective you are authorized to conduct military operations . . . north of the 38th Parallel in Korea, provided that at the time of such operation there has been no entry into North Korea by major Soviet or Chinese Communist Forces, no announcement of intended entry, nor a threat to counter our operations militarily in North Korea." The directive explicitly stated that "under no circumstances, however, will your forces cross the Manchurian or USSR borders of Korea," and included a prohibition: "As a matter of policy, no non-Korean ground forces will be used in the northeast provinces bordering the Soviet Union or in the area along the Manchurian border."[3] But the directive was complicated by the new secretary of defense, George Marshall. Marshall wrote to MacArthur, "We want you to feel unhampered tactically and strategically to proceed north of the parallel. [However] announcement [of this] . . . may precipitate embarrassment in the U.N. where evident desire is not to be confronted with necessity of a vote on passage of 38th Parallel, rather to find you have found it militarily necessary to do so." Marshall wanted MacArthur to recognize the political sensitivity of crossing the "artificial line" and to cross the line only under absolute military necessity while keeping it low key. MacArthur's reply, however, gave cause for concern. "Parallel 38 is not a factor in the military employment of our forces . . . in exploiting the defeat of the enemy forces, our own troops may cross the parallel at any time," he wrote back. "Unless and until the enemy capitulated, I regard all of Korea open for our military operations."[4]

While the UN and the Truman administration were deliberating over the issue of the 38th parallel, the ROK Third Division simply crossed it on the clear autumn day of October 1, a week before the UN resolution was passed. Colonel Kim Chŏng-sun, the commander of the lead regiment, later recalled, "It was overwhelming. I thought that that damned

American soldiers gaze at portraits of Stalin and Kim Il Sung. Such portraits were commonly found in villages and towns liberated by UN forces, November 7, 1950. (U.S. NATIONAL ARCHIVES AND RECORDS ADMINISTRATION)

line, which had separated our people and the country for so long, was about to crumble, and we would be reunified. We were all so excited that we practically ran across the 38th Parallel."[5] There had been strong indications that ROK troops would cross the line regardless of UN authorization, as President Syngman Rhee had repeatedly stated that he had no intention of halting his forces at "the artificial border" and they would stop only at the Yalu River on the Chinese line. "We have to advance as far as the Manchurian border until not a single enemy soldier is left in our country," announced Rhee at a mass rally on September 19.[6]

This climactic moment was followed by a remarkable phase of pursuit. By October 10, ROK forces had captured Wŏnsan, the major port city on the east coast. On October 17, they occupied the northern cities of Hamhŭng and Hŭngnam and thereby secured North Korea's main industrial hub on the east coast. Meanwhile, in the west, UN forces advanced rapidly against little opposition, and ROK units entered the city of Ch'osan on the Yalu River on October 26. In a little over a month since the Inch'ŏn landing, the tide of war had completely turned.

Lessons of History

In 1592, the Japanese military ruler Toyotomi Hideyoshi launched an invasion of the Korean peninsula. Intent on building a great East Asian empire, Hideyoshi set his sights on Ming China. Control of the Korean peninsula was necessary to secure the invasion route into China. The Japanese invasion force landed just off Pusan and then advanced up the Pusan-Taegu-Seoul corridor. After taking Seoul, the soldiers marched to Kaesŏng, meeting little opposition.[7] Once in Kaesŏng, however, the Japanese did not advance farther north as a unified force. Instead, Hideyoshi divided his army. Konishi Yukinaga commanded the western force, which continued northward through flat open terrain to P'yŏngyang and beyond to the Yalu River. Katō Kiyomasa led the eastern force, which advanced to the northeast through a mountainous and wild region toward the Tumen River on the Manchurian border. Petty rivalries put the two commanders at odds, and the result was that the two armies operated without coordination. Hideyoshi's decision to divide his army was a fatal one. With Katō side-tracked in the wilderness of northeastern Korea, the strength of Konishi's thrust toward P'yŏngyang and beyond, strategically the more important axis, was effectively cut in half. Eventually, the Japanese faced a dilemma. They needed more men to secure the peninsula, but the Korean navy's successful interdiction of shipping prevented reinforcements. Faced with the approaching winter, Konishi hunkered down in P'yŏngyang while his army was whittled away by hunger, disease, and the cold. Katō's army, meanwhile, was scattered across northeastern Korea. It was at this moment, when the Japanese forces were at their weakest, that Ming China attacked, turning the tide of the war.[8]

Substitute the UN for Japan, MacArthur for Hideyoshi, Walker for Konishi, and Almond for Katō, and you have exactly what happened in Korea in late 1950. MacArthur divided his command like Hideyoshi, sending the Eighth Army up the western half of North Korea, while the weaker ROK forces advanced along the eastern coast, and the X

Corps embarked to conduct an amphibious landing at Wŏnsan on the east coast. The forces would link up at the "waist" of the Korean peninsula, a line stretching from P'yŏngyang to Wŏnsan, and then advance north, still under separate commands.[9] General Omar Bradley, chairman of the JCS, later wrote, "Too many North Koreans had slipped through the trap [of the encirclement between the X Corps forces advancing east and south after the Inch'ŏn landing and the Eighth Army advancing northward], perhaps a third of the 90,000 North Korean troops in South Korea . . . The military textbook solution to the existing problem was 'hot pursuit.' That is, to drive forward at utmost speed with all the UN forces at hand before the North Koreans could dig in defensively."[10] Instead, MacArthur stopped the pursuit, pulled the X Corps from the lines, loaded it aboard ships, and sent it on a long voyage to the other side of the peninsula to conduct a landing of dubious value. Walker's Eighth Army, tired from months of fighting and strung out from attacking and moving from Pusan, was left to continue the pursuit. As it turned out, ROK forces occupied Wŏnsan a week before the X Corps's amphibious "assault." Another week of delay was caused by mines in the harbor. When the X Corps finally landed, on October 25, they discovered to their dismay that even Bob Hope's USO show had beaten them to Wŏnsan, much to MacArthur's embarrassment and chagrin.

Pilgrimage to Wake

At this moment Truman decided to meet MacArthur, for the first time. MacArthur was upset by the president's "summoning." Ambassador John Muccio later recalled, "The general appeared irked, disgusted, and at the same time somewhat uneasy" during the plane ride there. "In the course of his exposition, he used such terms as 'summoned for political reasons' and 'not aware that I am still fighting a war.'"[11] The two met on October 15 at Wake Island in the middle of the Pacific, the site of a heroic American stand against the Japanese in the opening days of World War II. Truman's main concern was the possibility that China would enter the war. MacArthur assured Truman that Chinese intervention was unlikely, and even if they did decide to fight, UN forces would be able to handle it and "the victory was won in Korea."[12] During the meeting, neither Truman nor his advisors questioned MacArthur's declarations. At one point, Assistant Secretary of State Dean Rusk, alarmed by the superficiality of the questions posed by the president and the speed in which he was firing them off, passed a note to him suggesting he slow down. Truman scribbled a reply back, "Hell no! I want to get out of here before we get into trouble!"[13] MacArthur's answer to the most important issue facing Truman, and indeed the future postwar world order, was not challenged.

So why did Truman travel so far to meet MacArthur? Truman's own explanation was that he had sought a better rapport with MacArthur and wanted a chance to explain to him in person the goals of U.S. foreign policy. "Events since June had shown me that MacArthur had lost some of his contacts with the country and its people in the many years he had been abroad," Truman later wrote. "I had made efforts through Harriman and others to let him see the world-wide picture as we saw it in Washington, but I felt that we had little success. I thought he might adjust more easily if he heard it from me directly."[14] If this had been Truman's intention, it had clearly failed. The meeting had created more friction than friendship. MacArthur turned Truman down for lunch, saying that he needed to get back to Tokyo as quickly as possible. "Whether intended or not," Bradley later wrote, "it was insulting to decline lunch with the President, and I think Truman was miffed, although he gave no sign."[15] Truman and MacArthur said good-bye before lunchtime that same morning. The president had been on Wake Island for just five hours. They never saw each other again.[16]

After returning from the meeting, MacArthur removed all restraints on the advance of UN forces. It was a violation in spirit of the September 27 directive from the Joint Chiefs. In response, the JCS meekly queried MacArthur, who replied that "the instructions contained in [my message to my subordinate commanders to advance north] were a matter of military necessity." As for the provision to use only ROK forces, "not only are the ROK forces not of sufficient strength to initially accomplish the security of North Korea, but the reactions of their commanders are at times so emotional that it was deemed essential that initial use be made of more seasoned and stabilized commanders." MacArthur saw "no conflict with the directive . . . dated 27 September, which merely enunciated the provision as a matter of policy." He continued that "the necessary latitude for modification was contained also in [the message] dated 29

September from the Secretary of Defense [Marshall] that he should 'feel unhampered . . . to proceed north of the 38th Parallel.'" He concluded haughtily that "this entire subject was covered in my conference at Wake Island."[17]

The die was cast. "As in the case of the Inch'ŏn plan, it was really too late for the JCS to do anything about the order," Bradley recalled.[18] While all seemed aware that something was terribly amiss, there was no consensus over what should be done about it. "We were all deeply apprehensive," recalled Dean Acheson. "We were frank with one another, but not quite frank enough." Had Marshall and the JCS proposed a halt at the P'yŏngyang-Wŏnsan line, the "waist" of the peninsula, Acheson continued, "disaster would probably have been averted."[19] But such a stance would have meant a fight with MacArthur, and everyone, it seemed, was more afraid of MacArthur than they were of a potential conflict with the Chinese. As UN forces advanced deeper into North Korea, Chinese troops were massing along the Manchurian border, just as they had done nearly 360 years earlier when the Ming army had lain in wait for the approaching Japanese.

"If War Is Inevitable, Let It Be Waged Now"

Ten days after the Inch'ŏn landing, Gen. Nie Rongzhen, the acting chief of staff of the PLA General Staff and military governor of Beijing, dined with K. M. Panikkar, India's ambassador to China. The conversation quickly turned to Korea. "General Nie told me in a quiet and unexcited manner that the Chinese did not intend to sit back with folded hands and let the Americans come to the border," recollected Panikkar. "This was the first indication that I had that the Chinese proposed to intervene in the war." Panikkar impressed on Nie, "a pleasant-spoken man, friendly and ready to discuss matters with an air of frankness," how destructive a war with the United States would be, how "the Americans would be able to destroy systematically all the industries of Manchuria and put China back by half a century." But Nie "only laughed." "We have calculated all that," he told the ambassador. "They may even drop atom bombs on us. What then?" Not long after this conversation, Premier Zhou Enlai spoke on the first anniversary of the founding of the PRC, on October

1, and warned that the Chinese people "will not tolerate foreign aggression and will not stand aside should the imperialists wantonly invade the territory of their neighbor." Just after midnight on October 3, Panikkar was abruptly awakened. Zhou had sent a message for him to come to his residence at once. Zhou explained that China had reached a decision regarding Korea. "If the Americans cross the 38th Parallel," Panikkar recalled, "China would be forced to intervene in Korea. Otherwise, he was most anxious for a peaceful settlement."[20]

Panikkar's cable to New Delhi was passed through London to Washington, where it was retransmitted to MacArthur. MacArthur considered the warning a bluff: the Chinese had not intervened when the tide of war was in their favor, so why would they enter when the tide was against them? Truman was skeptical, but his skepticism was less an issue of strategy than of credibility. The problem with the Indian ambassador's warning, according to Truman, was that "Mr. Panikkar had in the past played the game of the Chinese Communists fairly regularly, so that his statement could not be taken as that of an impartial observer. It might very well be no more than a replay of Communist propaganda." Furthermore, a key vote on the UN resolution was due the following day, and "it appeared quite likely that Zhou En-lai's 'message' was a bald attempt to blackmail the United Nations by threats of intervention in Korea."[21]

As Panikkar's message was being considered in Washington, Kim Il Sung, facing imminent defeat, was close to panic. He and Pak Hŏn-yŏng had been completely wrong about the South Korean people's reaction. A senior North Korean communist cadre, Lim Ŭn, remarked, "We all steadfastly believed the boasting of Pak Hŏn-yŏng that once we first occupied Seoul, the 200,000 South Korean Worker's Party (SKWP) members, who were in hiding throughout South Korea, would rise up and revolt, toppling the South Korean regime." Kim had no contingency plan for failure. When the anticipated revolt did not happen, Kim threw all his troops into the attack to try to end the war as quickly as possible. "He was engrossed only in marching forward," according to Lim.[22]

Kim faced total defeat since his forces were cut off by the landing at Inch'ŏn. He begged Stalin for help, pleading to him on October 1, "We are determined to overcome all the difficulties facing us so that Korea will not be a colony of the U.S. imperialists . . . This notwithstanding, if the enemy does not give us time to implement the measures which we plan, and, making use of our extremely grave situation, steps up its offensive operations into North Korea, then we will not be able to stop the enemy troops solely with our own forces. Therefore, dear Iosif Vissarionovich, we cannot help asking you to provide us with special assistance."[23] Stalin wrote to Mao and Zhou that he had warned the North Koreans to expect an amphibious landing at Inch'ŏn and "had admonished the North Koreans to withdraw at least four divisions from the South immediately." But the North Koreans had failed to heed his warning and now "our Korean friends have no troops capable of resistance in the vicinity of Seoul." Stalin concluded, "I think that if in the current situation you consider it possible to send troops to assist the Koreans, then you should move at least five-six divisions toward the 38th Parallel at once," adding that "the Chinese Divisions could be considered as volunteers, with Chinese in command at the head, of course."[24]

Mao's reply was unexpected.[25] Going back on his initial promise to aid the North Koreans, Mao wrote that his forces were not strong enough to take on the Americans: "We originally planned to move several volunteer divisions to North Korea to render assistance to the Korean comrades when the enemy advanced north of the 38th Parallel. However, having thought this over thoroughly, we now consider that such actions may entail extremely serious consequences." Mao explained that a clash with the United States would ruin his plans for peaceful reconstruction. He believed it would be better "to show patience . . . and actively prepare our forces" for a moment when the situation was more advantageous. Mao added, "Of course, not to send out troops to render assistance is very bad for the Korean comrades," but while the Koreans will "temporarily suffer defeat, [this] will change the form of the struggle to partisan war."[26]

Stalin asked Mao to reconsider. He thought the Americans would not start a major war and would agree on a settlement that favored the communists. Under such a scenario, China might also resolve the Taiwan issue. A passive "wait and see policy" as Mao suggested would be counterproductive: "China would fail to get back even Taiwan, which at present the United States clings to as its springboard, not for Jiang Jieshi [Chiang Kai-shek] who has no chance to succeed, but for themselves or for a militaristic Japan." Stalin then made his most compelling argument for Chinese intervention: "If a war is inevitable, then let it be waged now, and not in a few years when Japanese militarism will be restored as an ally of the USA and when the USA and Japan will have a ready-made bridgehead on the continent in a form of the entire Korea run by Syngman Rhee."[27]

Mao spent many sleepless nights that early October trying to decide. He convened an urgent meeting of the Politburo Standing Committee to tell its members he had decided in favor of intervention, but he met strong opposition. Lin Biao, Mao's old comrade in arms during the civil war, was firmly against it. China, he said, was not ready for such a monumental undertaking. What the country needed was to recuperate after decades of warfare. Nor had the Chinese revolution been fully completed, as there were still more than a million "bandits" roaming the countryside and party control was not completely secure. And, he argued, the PLA's outdated arsenal was no match against the Americans and would lead to a great slaughter. For Lin Biao, the wiser and safer decision was to accelerate the buildup of the Chinese air, naval, and artillery forces and to assist North Korea in fighting a guerilla war without direct intervention.[28] Mao's response echoed Stalin's, that if the Chinese did not fight the Americans now, they might be forced to do so at a later date. Since America's plan to occupy North Korea was part of a grand strategy to dominate the whole of East Asia, the task of defending China would be that much harder if the Americans gained a foothold on the Korean peninsula. Given the deployment of the U.S. Seventh Fleet to the Taiwan Straits and MacArthur's belligerence toward China, Mao was convinced that such a confrontation was only a matter of time.

He also appealed on moral grounds: "It would be shameful for us to stand by seeing our neighbors in perilous danger without offering any help."[29] China would lose face before its North Korean comrades, many of whom had fought in the PLA. Moreover, if China did not help North Korea, the Soviet Union might do nothing if China were in peril, and "internationalism would be empty talk."[30] General Peng Dehuai, a brilliant military leader and another of Mao's close civil-war comrades, summed up the main thrust of Mao's argument: "The tiger wanted to eat human beings; when it would do so would depend on its appetite."[31] Mao prevailed. Stalin wrote, "Mao expressed solidarity with the main ideas of my letter and stated that he would send nine, not six, divisions to Korea."[32] Mao had also based his decision to enter the war on the understanding that China would receive air support from the Soviet Union.

On October 8, the day after the UN passed the resolution empowering UN forces to unify Korea, Mao cabled Kim Il Sung: "In view of the current situation, we have decided to send volunteers to Korea to help you fight against the aggressors."[33] China, it was decided, would enter the Korean War on October 19.

Just as the Korea question seemed to be finally settled, it took another startling turn. While Mao was deciding about China's intervention in Korea, Stalin was considering what, if any, involvement there should be for the Soviet Union. The Politburo agreed with him that a direct confrontation with the United States must be avoided, even if it meant abandoning North Korea.[34] The best option was a proxy in the form of China. When Zhou went to Moscow to finalize the details of Sino-Soviet military cooperation in Korea, he was shocked to learn from Stalin that the Soviet Union would seek to avoid all direct involvement in the conflict. It would not provide Soviet air forces to protect Chinese troops in Korea as promised earlier.[35] Zhou told Stalin that the decision would put the Chinese in a quandary as to whether to proceed without the promised air cover. He cabled Mao and the CCP leadership and asked them to reconsider the decision to intervene in light of the Soviet "betrayal."[36]

Mao suspended his intervention order, and the Politburo convened to deliberate. As before, two main points were raised: China was unprepared for a conflict with the Americans, and the intervention could not be done without Soviet help.[37] "Comrade Mao Zedong remained undecided even when our forces reached the Yalu River," recalled Nie Rongzhen. "He racked his brain and indeed thought about this many times before he made up his mind."[38] An exhausted Mao, who had not slept for days, finally decided to proceed with the intervention. His reasoning had not changed: the UN forces would not stop at the Yalu and war with the United States was inevitable. The others conceded, and Mao informed Zhou in Moscow that "the consensus is that it is still advantageous to send our troops to Korea."[39]

Chinese troops began crossing the Yalu on October 19, embarking on a risky venture that would determine the fate of China and its revolution. Stalin's "betrayal" clarified for Mao the limits of the Sino-Soviet alliance and reinforced the slide toward an eventual Sino-Soviet split. The betrayal also strengthened Mao's determination to be self-reliant in national security.[40] Domestically, Mao's "far-sighted" and "brilliant" decision to confront the American "imperialists" in Korea would lead to his complete monopoly on power and the radicalization of China's political and social affairs. Once China's external enemies were defeated abroad, Mao would turn to China's "internal" enemies at home. Less than two weeks after crossing the Yalu, the Chinese People's Volunteer (CPV) army launched an attack that would determine the course of China's future for decades to come.

First Strike

In less than two weeks, 200,000 Chinese soldiers crossed the Yalu River into North Korea undetected by the United Nations Command (UNC).[41] On October 25, the Chinese initiated their first major attack. The main effort, in what Peng Dehuai called "First Phase Offensive," was against the Eighth Army. Peng targeted the ROK Army sectors for they were weaker and more vulnerable. ROK II Corps, part of the Eighth Army that occupied the eastern half of the army's area of operations, received the first blow. Within a few days, II Corps was largely destroyed, and all of the Eighth Army was put in peril. By early November, however, General Walker was able to rally his troops and establish a defense line along the Ch'ŏngch'ŏn River north of P'yŏngyang. The Chinese also engaged the X Corps on Korea's east coast, but only on a limited scale. General Almond ordered the X Corps, scattered widely in the rugged mountains of the northeast region, to mop up remnants of the NKPA and reach the Yalu as quickly as possible. A short but bloody engagement with the Chinese took place in early November near Changjin (Japanese: Chosin) Reservoir, but the Chinese forces mysteriously disappeared as quickly as they had appeared, instilling a false sense of security.[42]

Despite the scale of the Chinese actions and their consequences in the Eighth Army sector, MacArthur's chief of intelligence, Maj. Gen. Charles A. Willoughby, refused to believe it was a major intervention. He estimated that about 16,500, but no more than 34,000, Chinese were in Korea.[43] Willoughby's lack of alarm was not only supported by MacArthur, but also shared by Walker and Almond. According to Walker, the "Chinese" presence had merely indicated the introduction of North Korean reinforcements taken from China.[44] This assessment

First group of captured Chinese held near Hamhŭng, October 30, 1950. (U.S. NATIONAL ARCHIVES AND RECORDS ADMINISTRATION)

was repeated in MacArthur's report to the UN, which concluded that "there is no such evidence that Chinese Communist units, as such, have entered Korea."[45] Considering the damage inflicted on the Eighth Army, these assessments were excessively optimistic, if not delusional. MacArthur provided the JCS with his personal "appreciation" of the situation and presented four possible scenarios to explain the sudden appearance of the Chinese: first, a full-scale invasion; second, covert military assistance; third, permitting volunteers to help North Korea; or fourth, provisional intervention predicated on encountering only ROK units in the border provinces. He thought "the last three contingencies, or a combination thereof, seem to be the most likely condition at the present moment." MacArthur "warned against hasty action and specifically discounted the possibility that the intervention of the Chinese Communists was a 'new war' "[46]

Privately, however, MacArthur seemed to have had some doubts. On November 6, he told his air commander, Lt. Gen. George Stratemeyer, to plan for a bombing campaign of North Korea. "General MacArthur wanted an all-out air effort against communications and facilities with every weapon to stop and destroy the enemy in North Korea," wrote Stratemeyer in his wartime diary.[47] A key target was the bridge over the Yalu River at Sinŭiju, to stop or delay the flow of Chinese troops. Recognizing the political sensitivity of the mission, Stratemeyer contacted Air Force Chief of Staff Gen. Hoyt S. Vandenberg, who in turn got in touch with Deputy Secretary of Defense Robert A. Lovett and Secretary of State Acheson. They agreed that such a mission was unwise due to the risk of accidentally bombing Chinese territory, which could provide a casus belli for China and perhaps even the Soviet Union. Moreover, such action violated the U.S. commitment not to take any action that would affect Manchuria without prior consultation with the British. Truman, who was in Independence to cast his vote on Election Day, November 7, received an urgent call from Acheson. He told Acheson that he would "approve this bombing mission only if there was an immediate and serious threat to the security of our troops." Truman also asked Acheson to find out "why MacArthur suddenly found this action necessary" since his earlier cable had given no hint that such drastic actions were being contemplated. The JCS canceled the mission less than two hours before the bombers were scheduled to take off. MacArthur was requested to "forward his estimate of the situation and his reasons for ordering the bombing of the Yalu River bridges."[48] It was the first time the JCS had countermanded an order from MacArthur.

MacArthur's reply was unexpected. In a sudden and inexplicable change from his report just a few days earlier, MacArthur wrote that "men and material in large force are pouring across all bridges over the Yalu from Manchuria. This movement not only jeopardizes but threatens the ultimate destruction of the forces under my command." "The only way to stop this reinforcement of the enemy is the destruction of these bridges and the subjection of all installations in the north area supporting the enemy advance to the maximum of our air destruction," he declared. "I cannot overemphasize the disastrous effect, both physical and psychological, that will result from the restrictions which you are imposing. I trust that the matter [will] be immediately brought to the attention of the President as I believe your instructions may well result in a calamity of major proportion for which I cannot accept the responsibility without his personal and direct understanding of the situation."

The JCS was jolted by the cable's accusatory and hysterical tone. Bradley recollected that "we had little choice but to authorize the mission." Truman agreed.[49]

Two days later, MacArthur again changed his tune. "The introduction of Chinese Communist forces in strength into the Korean campaign had completely changed the overall situation," he wrote on November 9, but he had every confidence that with his superior airpower he could interdict Chinese reinforcements from Manchuria and destroy those already in Korea. MacArthur was now so confident that he planned to resume the offensive on November 15 to occupy all of North Korea.[50] On November 7, the JCS had received the startling report that Chinese and North Korean troops had completely broken contact with UN forces and "disappeared." These developments appeared to support MacArthur's initial assessment that the Chinese had intervened only in moderate numbers and, having been successfully "rebuffed," lost their nerve for further fighting.[51] The JCS decided that MacArthur would "continue military operations in accordance with current directive," but the directive should be "kept under review." "We read, we sat, we deliberated," recalled Bradley, "and, unfortunately, we reached drastically wrong conclusions and decisions."[52] The JCS was lulled by MacArthur's optimistic predictions of a quick victory, the sudden disappearance of the Chinese, and "wildly erroneous" estimates of the scale and intent of the Chinese intervention.

If the Americans appeared blissfully ignorant of China's real intentions, the North Koreans were downright unhappy. China's entrance had significantly marginalized Kim Il Sung and North Korea, which now played only a supporting role. Keenly aware of his diminishing influence, Kim had hoped to reorganize his forces with the help of the Soviet Union even as China was preparing to launch its second offensive at the end of November. Ambassador Shtykov wrote to Stalin with a plea from Kim Il Sung: "Our North Korean friends will withdraw to Manchuria with the personnel for organizing nine divisions . . . Once again, our comrades in North Korea are requesting that ninety Soviet advisors and education and training specialists remain with them to help them organize the nine divisions and establish education and training institutions. The North Koreans state that if they do not have this help, it will take them a year before they can prepare for combat on their own."[53] Kim believed that with Soviet help he could reconstitute his tattered NKPA in time to make a difference in the outcome of the war. His fear of Chinese domination of the Korean peninsula was understandable. Given the long history of Chinese interventions in Korea, Kim was loath to give China control over military operations.

Disgusted by the turn of events, Stalin refused to help, deciding instead to distance himself from Korean military matters all together. When Shtykov told Kim that his request had been denied, "he was silent for a moment," then turned to Pak Hŏn-yŏng and said, "How can matters have come to this?"[54] To add to Kim's misery, Stalin replaced his team in North Korea. First to go was Gen. Nicolai Vasiliev, chief of the Soviet Military Advisory Group, who was replaced by Gen. V. N. Razuvaev. Ambassador Shtykov was recalled at the end of December, demoted to lieutenant general in early 1951, and then forced to retire, a precipitous fall reflecting Stalin's displeasure at his performance. Shtykov's departure had far-reaching consequences for future North Korean–Soviet relations. He had been Stalin's personal envoy to North Korea since 1945 and had enjoyed direct access to the Soviet dictator. Razuvaev, who also replaced Shtykov as ambassador while remaining chief of the Soviet Military Advisory Group, did not enjoy the same close relationship with Stalin. With Shtykov gone, Kim Il Sung no longer had a valuable ally with a direct line to Stalin. To Kim's dismay, Mao became the new conduit to the Soviet leader. North Korea had been treated as an independent agent by Stalin since 1945, but with the Chinese entering the war, North Korea became relegated to a satellite of China. A perceptible split between Kim and Stalin was beginning to emerge, sowing the seeds for future conflict and driving Kim to seek a more independent path from the Soviet Union.

CHAPTER SEVEN

An Entirely New War

The war in Korea was on everyone's mind as Americans sat down to enjoy their Thanksgiving feast. Truman reminded the American people "in church, chapel and synagogue, in their homes and in the busy walks of life, every day and everywhere, to pray for peace."[1] Cardinal Francis Spellman of New York made a plea "for clothing, blankets and money for the destitute in Korea."[2] Americans, Commonwealth soldiers, and other UN allies in Korea, some of whom had never eaten turkey, were treated to a lavish Thanksgiving dinner. The logistics of transporting tens of thousands of frozen turkeys, then thawing, cooking, and serving them on the front lines was an immense undertaking. And just so the American people would know what would be served, newspapers published the menu. Many soldiers later said it was the best meal they had ever eaten.

Army's Holiday Menu[3]

Roast turkey
Cranberry sauce
Sage dressing and giblet gravy
Snowflake potatoes and candied sweet potatoes
Fresh green peas and whole kernel corn

Waldorf salad
Lettuce, Thousand Island dressing
Ice cream and pumpkin pie
Mincemeat pie. Fruitcake.

Parker house rolls
Bread
Butter

Mixed shelled nuts
Fresh fruit

Coffee
Fruit punch

The lavishness of the meal enhanced the optimism of the moment. Everyone thought the war was just about over and the "boys" would be home for Christmas. MacArthur stated that "regardless of Chinese intervention, the war will be finished by the end of the year."[4] The meal was as much a victory feast as it was a tribute to the sacrifices of the UN forces. Few knew that for many of these soldiers it would be their last good meal for months and for some, their last Thanksgiving meal.

The Eighth Army and X Corps resumed their advance the next morning. With MacArthur's reassurance that the war would be over by the end of the year, there was little else on anyone's mind but the upcoming Christmas holidays that promised a trip home. Everything had been

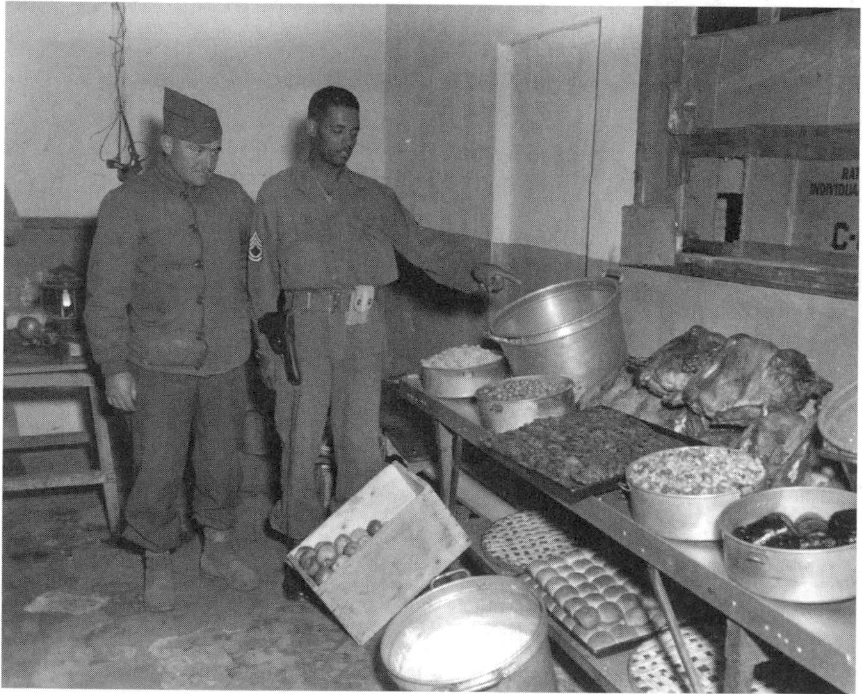

Inspecting Thanksgiving dinner preparations at a mess hall, November 23, 1950. (U.S. NATIONAL ARCHIVES AND RECORDS ADMINISTRATION)

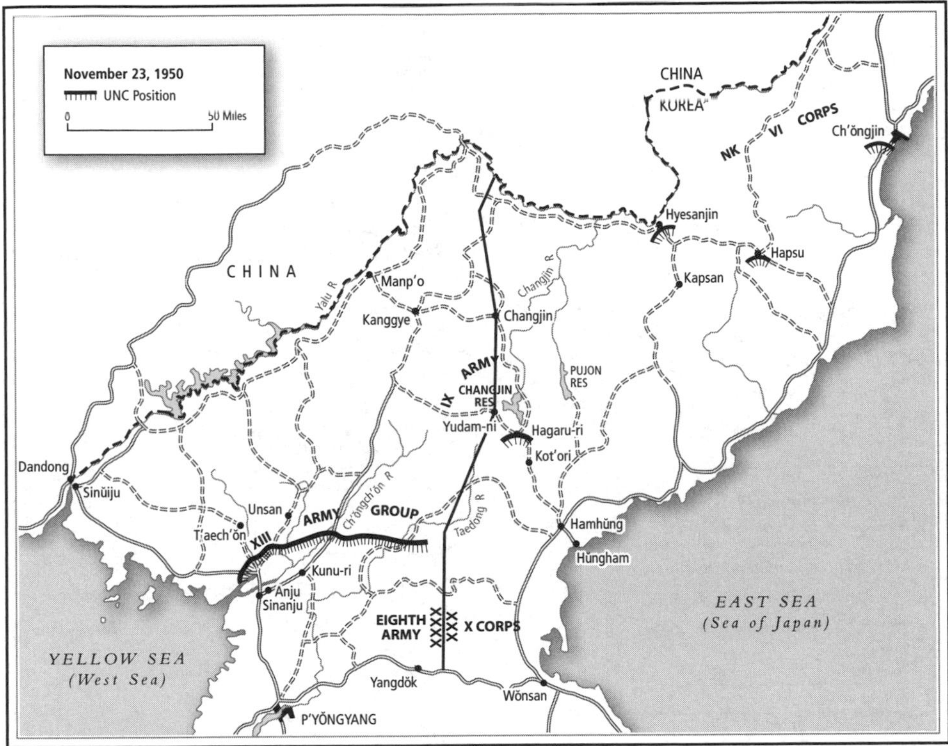

The battlefront, November 23, 1950. (MAP ADAPTED FROM BILLY C. MOSSMAN, *EBB AND FLOW*, U.S. GOVERNMENT PRINTING OFFICE, 1990)

going remarkably well. MacArthur was certain that Stratemeyer's bombing campaign had destroyed all significant targets between the UN front lines and the Yalu River. Stratemeyer recalled MacArthur's visit to Korea on November 24: "[He] was thrilled with the entire operation as was everyone in his party."[5] When IX Corps commander Maj. Gen. John Coulter told him that his troops were eager to reach the Yalu, Earnest Hoberecht of the United Press overheard MacArthur's reply: "You can tell them when they get up to the Yalu, Jack, they can all come home. I want to make good my statement that they will get a Christmas dinner at home."[6] No one suspected, least of all MacArthur, that at that very moment almost 400,000 Chinese troops were about to strike.

The CPV attacked ROK II Corps, again, on the evening of November 25. The gravity of the situation was not immediately apparent to General Walker. By nightfall, he received disquieting news from ROK II Corps that its divisions had encountered strong CPV "resistance." Walker made

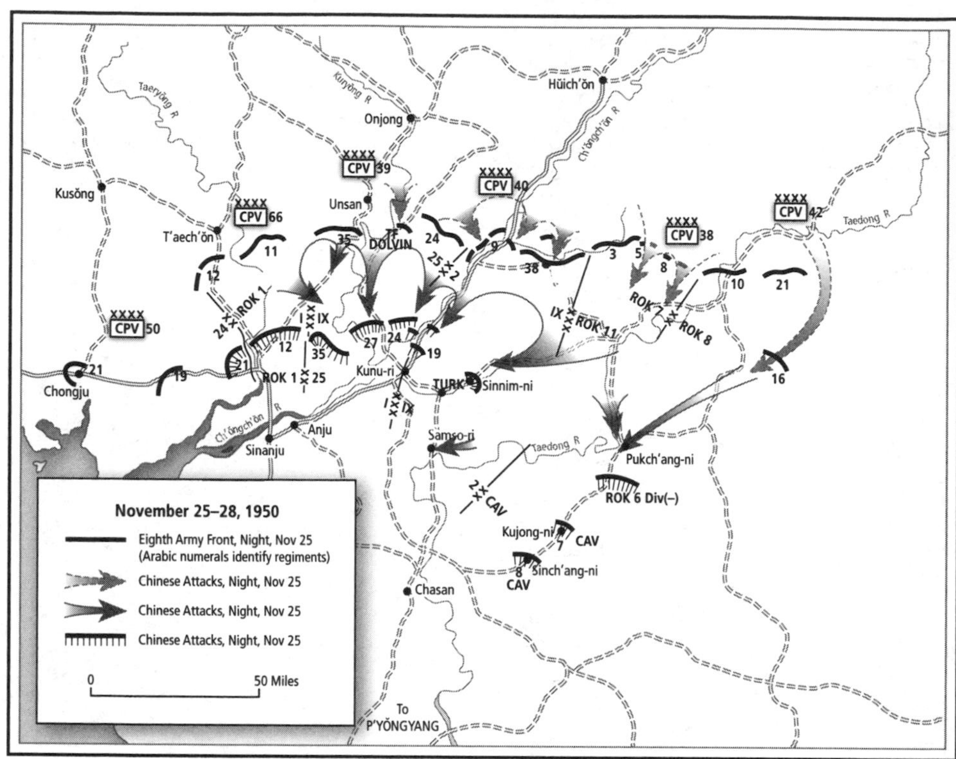

Battle of the Ch'ŏngch'ŏn, second Chinese offensive against the Eighth Army in North Korea, November 25–28, 1950. (MAP ADAPTED FROM MOSSMAN, *EBB AND FLOW*)

no effort to reinforce the South Koreans.[7] He soon realized that ROK II Corps was under a strong CPV attack that threatened to expose the army's eastern flank. As ROK forces collapsed, the CPV began encircling the Eighth Army. In the face of the irresistible Chinese onslaught, Walker ordered the Eighth Army to break contact and retreat to more defensible terrains north of Seoul. Within ten days the Eighth Army had retreated 120 miles.

In the eastern sector, a large CPV force was planning to launch an attack against the X Corps, whose units were widely dispersed over hundreds of square miles of freezing barren mountains. The core of X Corps, the First Marine Division with elements of the Seventh Infantry Division, was scattered around the Changjin Reservoir. On November 27, the X Corps resumed its advance northward, unaware of the disaster that was unfolding against the Eighth Army. The winter of 1950–51 turned out to be one of the harshest on record. Temperatures were so cold that soldiers were routinely afflicted with frostbite, weapons did not function, vehicles and generators did not start, artillery shells failed to explode, and food always arrived frozen. Treating the wounded was particularly challenging. "Everything we had was frozen," recalled Chester Lessenden, a medic. "Plasma froze and the bottles broke. We couldn't use the plasma because it wouldn't go into the solution and the tubes would clog up with particles. We couldn't change dressings because we had to work with our gloves on to keep our hands from freezing." The journalist Keyes Beech wrote that "it was so cold that men's feet froze to the bottom of their socks and the skin peeled off when the socks were removed."[8] Two weeks earlier, Maj. Gen. O. P. Smith, the First Marine Division commander, had confided his deep concerns about the precariously exposed deployment of X Corps to the commandant of the Marine Corps. General Almond, he angrily vented, was pushing Smith to advance too fast and without taking the necessary precautions. This resulted in the division being strung out along a sixty-mile dirt road dominated by high grounds on both sides under harsh winter conditions, a situation Smith thought resulted from an unsound operational plan. "Time and again I have tried to tell the Corps Commander [Almond] that in a Marine division, he has a powerful instrument, but that it cannot help but lose its full effectiveness when dispersed," Smith fumed.[9]

Disaster struck on the night of November 27, and thus began one of the greatest epic tales of tragedy and triumph in the annals of American military history.[10] The CPV hit the widely dispersed X Corps everywhere simultaneously. Piecemeal destruction of the First Marine Division was prevented by Smith's decision to concentrate the bulk of his division at three key villages around and near the Changjin Reservoir: Yudam-ni, on the northern side; Hagaru-ri, on the southern side about ten miles from Yudam-ni; and Kot'o-ri, a farther ten miles south of Hagaru-ri. It was another fifty miles from Hagaru-ri to Hŭngnam port, which was the X Corps's main port for supply and evacuation, should it be necessary. Smith ordered the marines on the western side of the reservoir to fall in on Yudam-ni, and the task force from the Seventh Infantry Division, commanded by Col. Allan MacLean, on the eastern side to fall back to Hagaru-ri. On the morning of November 28, Almond made an impromptu visit to Hagaru-ri to confer with Smith and then visited the Seventh Division task force. Almond told MacLean to take the offen-

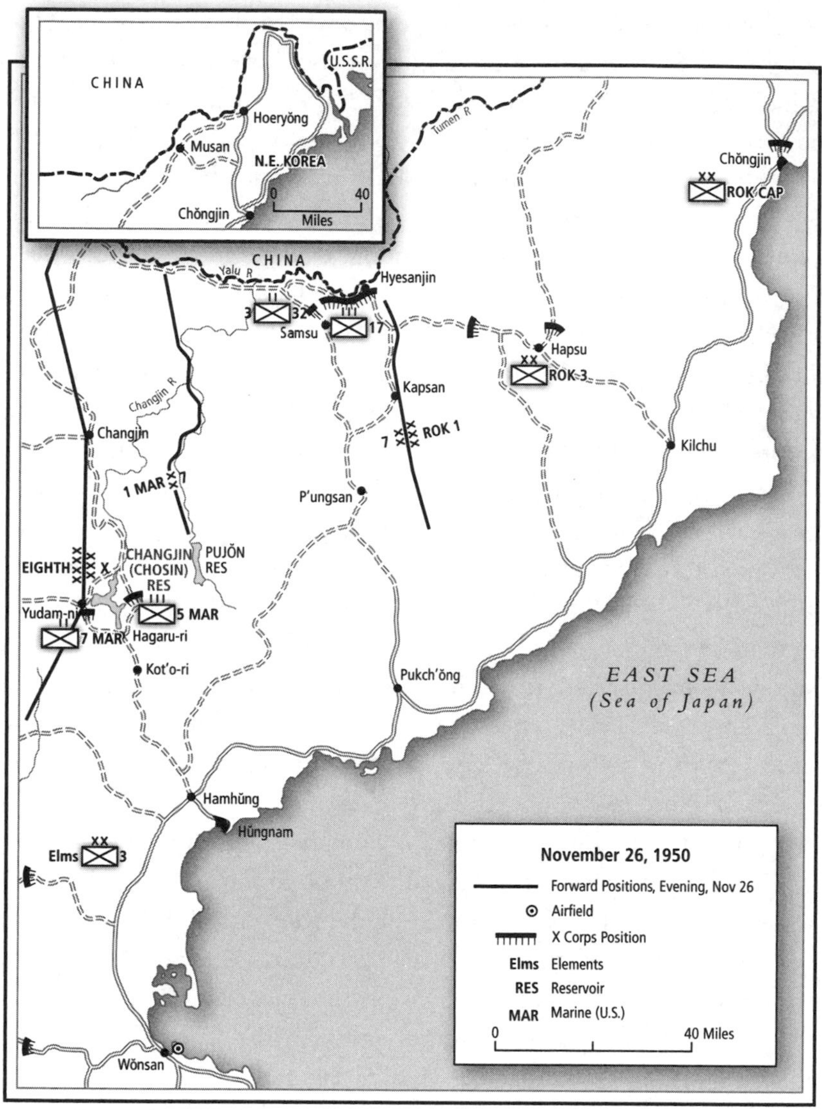

The X Corps zone, North Korea. (MAP ADAPTED FROM MOSSMAN, *EBB AND FLOW*)

sive. "The enemy who is delaying you for the moment is nothing more than remnants of Chinese divisions fleeing north," Almond assured him. "We're still attacking and we're going all the way to the Yalu. Don't let a bunch of Chinese laundrymen stop you."[11] However, with dire reports from the Eighth Army, MacArthur knew something was wrong and sent an alarmist cable to the JCS proclaiming that America now faced an

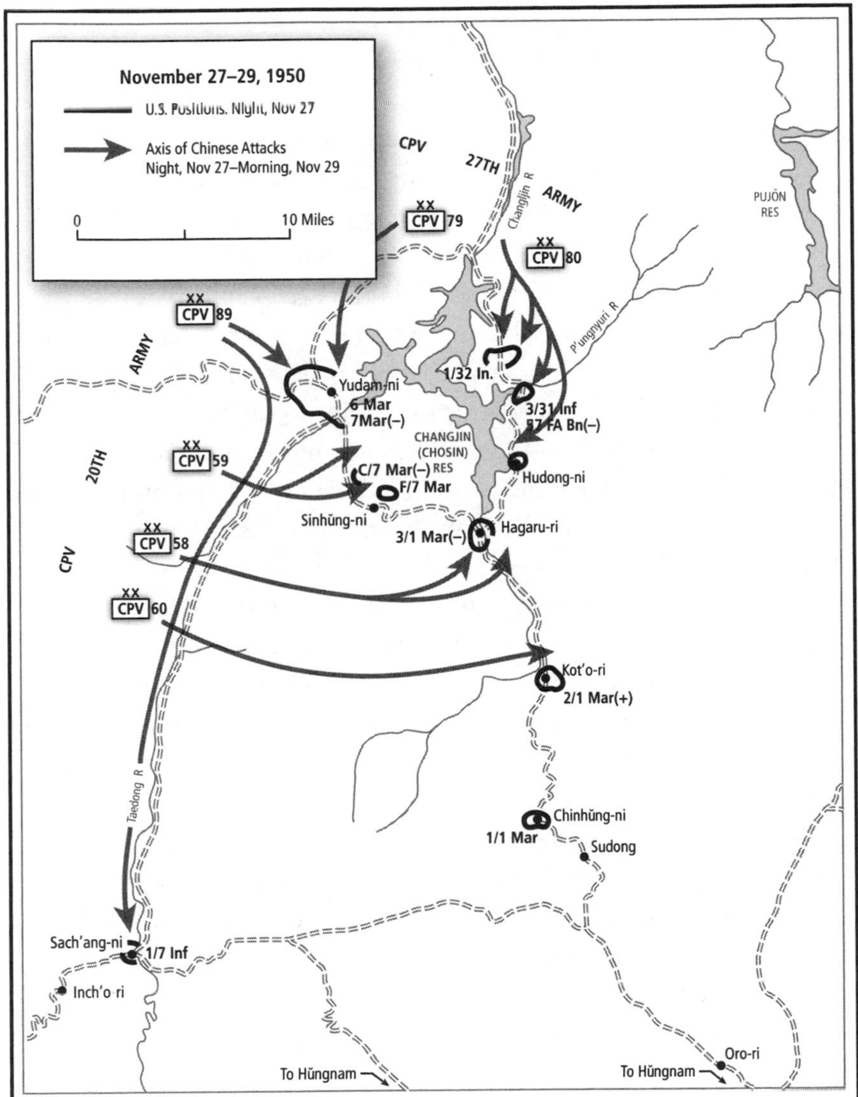

Battle of the Changjin Reservoir, North Korea, November 27–29, 1950. (MAP ADAPTED FROM MOSSMAN, *EBB AND FLOW*)

"entirely new war." It had finally dawned on him that the Chinese had come in with both feet. He ordered an immediate withdrawal.

It was almost too late. During the night of November 28–29, the CPV besieged MacLean's strung-out force. He ordered withdrawal at 2:00 a.m. "The snow was coming down in earnest," recalled Maj. Hugh

Robbins, "and the footing had become extremely slippery. Columns of foot soldiers had formed on the road on each side of the vehicles and had moved out in front . . . Many vehicles, which simply could not start because of the cold, had to be left behind, but none of the wounded was without transportation." As the task force made its way south toward Hagaru-ri, MacLean was killed. Lieutenant Colonel Don Faith, a battalion commander under MacLean, took charge. The task force continued its treacherous march toward Hagaru-ri. Faith called for close air support to hold off the Chinese, and marine aircraft responded with napalm. But tragedy struck as some of the napalm hit the task force. "It hit and exploded in the middle of my squad," recalled Pvt. James Ransone. "I don't know how in the world the flames missed me . . . Men all around me burned." Soon thereafter, Faith was killed and his command fell apart. "It was everyone for himself," recalled Staff Sgt. Chester Bair. "The chain of command disappeared." Over the next few days, survivors of the task force came limping, stumbling, and crawling across the great sweep of ice covering the reservoir to Hagaru-ri. The marines there used sleds to help them. A marine recalled, "Some of these men from Faith's outfit were dragging themselves on the ice, others had gone crazy and were walking in circles." "I was disoriented, exhausted, nearly frozen, hungry, and vomiting blood," remembered Sergeant Bair. "The temperature at night was 20 or more degrees below zero. The wind was so strong it was hard to stand or walk on the ice."[12] The marines rescued about a thousand of the original twenty-five hundred troops of the task force. Of these, only four hundred were fit enough to continue to serve. The rest were evacuated to Japan.

As the disastrous drama unfolded on the eastern side of the reservoir, on the western side the marines successfully fell back to Yudam-ni. They were then ordered to withdraw farther south and join the marines at Hagaru-ri. Afterward, the whole force was to withdraw still farther south to Kot'o-ri to rejoin the rest of the First Marine Division and then move to Hŭngnam for evacuation. The marines from Yudam-ni broke through the Chinese forces and arrived at Hagaru-ri on December 4–5, creating a surge of confidence that they were going to survive the ordeal after all. Smith made headlines around the world when he refused to call the withdrawal a retreat. "Retreat hell!" he said. "We are not retreating. We're just advancing in a different direction."[13] The truth of the matter was that there was no front or rear, and therefore nowhere to retreat to. What the marines were doing *was* attacking in another direction.[14] The epic withdrawal of the marines at Changjin Reservoir became a cause for celebration. Headlines announced that calamity had been miraculously averted. "Marines Return Full of Fight after a Nightmare of Death," announced the *New York Times*.[15] "Marine Guts Turn Disaster into Day of Moral Triumph," blazed the *Washington Post*. Jack Beth reported for the paper that "American Marines walked out of 12 days of freezing hell. These thousands of Leathernecks did it on guts. They turned their encirclement into one of the fightingest [*sic*] retreats in military history."[16] *Time* magazine wrote admiringly, "The running fight of the Marines and two battalions of the Army's 7th Infantry Division from Hagaru . . . was a battle unparalleled in U.S. military history . . . It was an epic of great suffering and great valor."[17]

The "triumph" might have been as much due to Chinese miscalculations as the bravery of the Americans. Had the Chinese hit Hagaru-ri on the night of November 27, they could have isolated the marines and soldiers to the north and thus destroyed in piecemeal most of the First Marine Division and the Seventh Division task force. Smith later told the *New York Times*, "They knew all about us all right, where we were and what we had, but I can't understand their tactics. Instead of hitting us with everything at one place, they kept hitting us at different places. Had the Chinese decided to knock out the small Marine garrison at Hagaru-ri, the task of regrouping the forces into a full division would have been made immeasurably more difficult."[18] What Smith did not know is that the CPV had also taken a terrible beating from the cold, had suffered from lack of food, and had been tremendously hampered by UN air attacks. Tens of thousands of soldiers of the CPV Ninth Army Group died from freezing. The Chinese soldiers were supposed to have been issued winter uniforms, but many did not get them. They wrapped themselves in cotton scarves or covered themselves with "carpets."[19] Moreover, incessant UN air attacks limited movement to the nights. "We have no freedom of activities during the daytime," General Peng complained to Mao. "Even though we have several times of the armed strength to surround them on four sides, fighting cannot end in a night."[20]

Two weeks into the Chinese offensive, Mao worried about the adequacy of the CPV logistical network. "Are you entirely sure about supplying our army's food and fodder by drawing on local resources?" an anxious Mao wrote to Peng. "Have the railroad lines from Sinŭiju and from Manp'o to P'yŏngyang been under rush construction? When will the construction be completed? Is it really possible for both railroads to transport all military supplies to the P'yŏngyang area?"[21] The answers were apparent by the end of December, when the offensive began to run out of steam. Marshal Nie Rongzhen, who oversaw CPV logistics, described in his memoirs how he had stockpiled supplies, but that the "preparations had not been sufficient."

> During the Second Campaign, we had originally planned that two armies plus two divisions could handle campaign responsibilities in the western sector of the advance. But because we couldn't transport the required amounts of rations up to the front, we were forced to cancel the two extra divisions . . . In the eastern sector, the troops which entered Korea had not made sufficient preparations and faced even greater difficulties. Not only did these troops not have enough to eat, their winter uniforms were too thin and could not protect their bodies from the cold. As a result, there occurred a large number of non-combat casualties. If we hadn't had these logistical problems as well as certain other problems, the soldiers would have wiped out the U.S. First Marine Division at Changjin Reservoir.[22]

By late December, over a hundred thousand men in the X Corps, Americans and South Koreans, and, in a humanitarian triumph of the Changjin epic, more than ninety-eight thousand refugees were evacuated.[23] After great pressure, Almond approved the evacuation of refugees despite concerns over the presence of communist infiltrators. One of the approximately two hundred ships assembled for the evacuation at Hŭngnam was the SS *Meredith Victory*, a merchant ship built during World War II. Commanded by Capt. Leonard LaRue, the vessel was later credited with "the greatest rescue operation by a single ship in the history of mankind." As a cargo ship, the *Meredith Victory* was designed to accommodate fewer than sixty people, but Captain LaRue and his crew somehow managed to load fourteen thousand refugees on board. After a harsh three-day journey, the refugees, who had suffered cold, hunger, and lack of facilities, and grown by five newborns, were landed at Kŏje island on Christmas Day. There was not a single casualty, and the *Meredith Victory* became known as the "Ship of Miracles."[24]

North Korean refugees attempting to board U.S. Navy ships at Hŭngnam, December 1950. (U.S. NATIONAL ARCHIVES AND RECORDS ADMINISTRATION)

"Defeat with Dignity and Good Grace"

China's intervention shocked the American public. "The nation received the fearful news from Korea with a strange-seeming calmness," *Time* wrote. "It was the kind of fearful, half-disbelieving matter-of-factness with which many a man has reacted on learning that he has cancer or tuberculosis." Unlike Pearl Harbor, which had "pealed out like a ball of fire," the numbing facts of the defeat in Korea "seeped into the American consciousness slowly." Days passed before it became apparent that UN forces had met a "crushing defeat." The disaster and its implications became the subject of endless shocked conversations. "Some of them were almost monosyllabic, men meeting on the street sometimes simply stared at each other and then voiced the week's oft-repeated phase, 'It looks bad. Very bad.' "[25]

It did not take long for recriminations to follow. There were "peeved cracks" about MacArthur's "home by Christmas" remarks, as well as criticism of the Truman administration. While most Americans accepted that war with China, perhaps even World War III, was now inevitable, it was MacArthur who had the greatest difficulty coming to terms with the disaster. Almost immediately, he launched a public attack on the administration. In late November he "cast discretion to the wind" and publicly expressed his frustration and resentment. He began with a written statement in the *New York Times* justifying his march north. "Every strategic and tactical movement made by the United Nations Command has been in complete accordance with United Nations resolutions and in compliance with the directives under which I operate," MacArthur insisted. "It is historically inaccurate to attribute any degree of responsibility for the onslaught of the Chinese Communist armies to the strategic course of the campaign itself." The next day, in an interview with *U.S. News & World Report*, MacArthur criticized the limitations the Truman administration had placed on "hot pursuit" and the bombing of Manchurian bases as "an enormous handicap, without precedent in history." MacArthur also wrote to Hugh Baillie, president of United Press International, and came close to questioning the motives of allies, particularly the British, by suggesting that their "selfish" and "short-sighted" vision had been responsible for withholding support for his forces.[26]

Truman was predictably angry. Of this latest incident of MacArthur "shooting off his mouth," Truman later wrote in his memoir that "he should have relieved General MacArthur then and there." The reason he did not "was that I did not wish to have it appear as if he were being relieved because the offensive failed. I have never believed in going back on people when luck is against them and I did not intend to do it now." Nevertheless, MacArthur "had to be told that the kinds of public statements he had been making were out of order."[27] On December 5, the president issued two directives that, though generally applicable to all "officials of the departments and agencies of the executive branch," were really meant for MacArthur. The first required that "all public statements by U.S. government personnel, civilian and military, had to be cleared in advance by the State and Defense Departments." The second ordered all officials and commanders to "exercise extreme caution in public statements . . . and to refrain from direct communication on military or foreign policy with newspapers, magazines, or other publicity media in the United States."[28] While Truman never directly blamed MacArthur for the failure of the UN forces, he did blame the general "for the *manner* in which he tried to excuse his failure."[29] Everyone in his administration had a share in the blame for the disaster, but MacArthur alone was unable to deal with the defeat with "dignity and good grace." He had panicked, lashed out at the administration, and then lapsed into a profound depression.

The JCS met on December 3 to discuss the situation in Korea. MacArthur had written to the JCS that unless ground reinforcements "of the greatest magnitude" were promptly sent, hope for success "cannot be justified and steady attrition leading to final destruction can reasonably be contemplated." For Bradley and the rest of the JCS, "this message and all it conveyed was profoundly dismaying. It seemed to be saying that MacArthur was throwing in the towel without the slightest effort to put up a fight."[30] The JCS seemed paralyzed about what to do and unable to leap beyond MacArthur's doom and gloom.

In the end, it was the State Department that took control of the situation. It was thought that perhaps the United States should try to negotiate a cease-fire with the Russians. George Kennan, who was recalled from leave at the Institute for Advanced Study in Princeton to be an advisor to Secretary of State Acheson, counseled that engaging in negotiations with the Russians at such a time of weakness would do more harm than good, since "they would see no reason to spare us any of the humiliation of military disaster." "The prerequisite to any satisfactory negotiation . . . is the demonstration that we have the capability to stabilize the front somewhere in the peninsula and to engage a large number of Communist forces for a long time."[31] UN forces had to stand firm to exert pressure on the enemy to force a cease-fire. Kennan, aware that Acheson was surrounded by "people who seemingly had no idea how to take defeat with dignity and good grace," composed a note to raise the secretary's spirits and strength to face what would no doubt be a trying period:

> Dear Mr. Secretary:
>
> There is one thing I would like to say in continuation of our discussion yesterday evening. In international, as in private, life what counts most is not really what happens to someone, but how he bears what happens to

> him. For this reason almost everything depends from here on out on the manner in which we Americans bear what is unquestionably a major failure and disaster to our national fortunes. If we accept it with candor, with dignity, with a resolve to absorb its lessons and to make it good by redoubled and determined effort—starting all over again, if necessary along the pattern of Pearl Harbor—we need lose neither our self-confidence nor our allies nor our power for bargaining, eventually, with the Russians. But if we try to conceal from our own people or from our allies the full measure of our misfortune, or permit ourselves to seek relief in any reactions of bluster or petulance or hysteria, we can easily find this crisis resolving itself into an irreparable deterioration of our world position—and of our confidence in ourselves.[32]

Acheson, moved, read the note to his staff. "We were being infected by a spirit of defeatism emanating from headquarters in Tokyo," Acheson declared. The essential problem facing Washington's political leaders was how to begin "to inspire a spirit of candor and redouble and determine our effort." Acheson thought that the main issue was that "the Korea campaign had been cursed . . . by violent swings of exuberant optimism and the deepest depression and despair . . . what was needed was dogged determination to find a place to hold and fight the Chinese to a standstill." This would be better than to consider withdrawal from Korea.[33] Secretary of Defense George Marshall agreed. Acheson met with Truman and the matter was settled. Kennan recalled, "We lunched with Secretary Acheson. He had just been talking with the President. The President's decision was, as always in great crises, clear, firm and unhesitating. He had no patience, Mr. Acheson told us, with the suggestion that we abandon Korea. We would stay and fight as long as possible."[34]

Truman asked Army Chief of Staff J. Lawton Collins to go to Tokyo and Korea to assess the situation. Collins reported that although the military situation "remained serious, it was no longer critical." The Eighth Army and X Corps were "calm and confident," Collins recalled. "Throughout my visit, [Walker] seemed undismayed. While the situation was tight, I saw no signs of panic and left the next morning for the X Corps reassured that the Eighth Army could take care of itself." Further, he anticipated "no serious trouble" in evacuating the X Corps from Hŭngnam. Collins concluded that the best solution was to evacuate the X Corps to Pusan, and the Eighth Army "should be gradually withdrawn toward Pusan," where the united force could hold a defensive line "indefinitely." Collins's assessment was greeted "like a ray of sunshine."[35]

While the crisis was unfolding, British Prime Minister Clement Attlee arrived in Washington on the afternoon of December 4 for urgent talks with Truman. The British were alarmed by Truman's mention of the possible use of atomic weapons in Korea. If the prospect of a third world war in Korea was not enough to deal with, now came the unwelcome visit from "a Job's comforter" in the form of Attlee. Acheson found Attlee "persistently depressing," whose thoughts resembled "a long withdrawing, melancholy sigh." As soon as Attlee was reassured by Truman "that alarm over the safety of our troops would not drive us to some ill-considered use of atomic weapons," the real purpose of his trip emerged. What Attlee wanted was to end the war in Korea so that the United States could "resume active participation in security for Europe." He also wished that Britain be allowed "some participation . . . in any future decision to use nuclear weapons." To end the fighting in Korea, Attlee urged Truman and Acheson to consider giving China UN membership and cutting Taiwan loose. Attlee argued that the UN position in Korea was so precarious that a price must be paid to extricate UN forces out of that conflict. Giving China a seat at the UN and withdrawing from both Korea and Taiwan would not be too high a price to pay, Attlee argued, for "there was nothing more important than retaining the good opinion of Asia." Moreover, China was not a Soviet satellite, and if handled properly, "it might become an important counterpoise to Russia in Asia and the Far East."[36]

Acheson vehemently disagreed. "To cut, run and abandon the whole enterprise was not acceptable conduct. There was a great difference between being forced out and getting out," he responded.[37] Furthermore, the security of the United States was more important than anyone's "good opinion," and the preservation of America's defenses in the western Pacific and the Asian people's confidence in America also provided "a path to securing their good opinion." The only way to fight communism, he said, "was to eliminate it." In the end, the British agreed to stay the course in Korea and accepted the United States' refusal to rush to negotiations with China. In return, Truman implicitly agreed to keep the fighting limited and to abandon any plans for Korean unification. Truman also privately assured Attlee that he was not considering

Alarmed by rumors that the United States might use atomic weapons in Korea, British Prime Minister Clement Attlee (center) makes an urgent visit to Washington for talks with President Truman, December 4, 1950. (TRUMAN LIBRARY)

use of the atomic bomb and agreed to a broad pledge of close U.S-UK consultations on all global crises.[38] Truman had, in effect, promised not to risk World War III without consulting the British. Talks with Attlee ended with a clear consensus, but they stirred up consternation in other circles. Republican Senator William Knowland from California, a severe critic of Truman and a strong supporter of Chiang Kai-shek who was known as the "Senator from Formosa," said he saw "the making of a Far Eastern Munich."[39] Korean President Rhee stated he was "tremendously disappointed" that the Truman-Attlee conference ended "without a call for complete mobilization of the democratic world to fight against communism," and thought that "it would have been better if the United Nations had not helped us at all if we are to be abandoned now."[40] But the furor eventually died down. UN forces would stay in Korea until a truce was negotiated. Once the front stabilized, a political basis for negotiations to end the conflict could begin. What no one could have guessed was just how long the negotiations would take.

Meanwhile, as the X Corps was evacuating, the Eighth Army continued to fall back. General Walker ordered the evacuation of P'yŏngyang on December 3 and a "scorched earth policy" to destroy everything that might be of use to the enemy. Corporal Leonard Korgie, one of the last Americans to abandon the city, recalled the scene:

> We went through P'yŏngyang at night and the whole city looked like it was burning. In one place, the engineers burned a rations dump about the size of a football field. God, it was a shame to see it in a land of hunger all the food going up in smoke. There was U.S. military equipment everywhere. I don't know how much was destroyed . . . I believe we set on fire most of the villages we passed through. We weren't going to give the Chinese too many places to shelter in during the rest of the winter.[41]

While the measure was to deny the enemy shelter and supply, the more immediate impact of the wholesale destruction of towns and villages was on the civilian population. North Korea was already a barren land with few resources, and the measure created an enormous refugee crisis in the middle of a harsh winter. When word spread that UN forces would not defend P'yŏngyang, three hundred thousand people living there fled. Barges and small boats ferried people across the Taedong River, but the UN forces destroyed many of these to prevent the refugees from crossing and clogging the roads the military needed for its own withdrawal. The civilians were also barred from crossing over bridges, so they sought alternative crossing routes. Some made their way over the ruins of the great steel bridge destroyed by American bombers earlier that summer. Others tried to wade across through freezing water. It was clear that nothing but inhumane suppression by force could deter the refugees.[42] Captain Norman Allen recalled his torment about the refugees' plight:

> The refugees, awful moments there, deep memories. So pitiful, so desperate; they also hampered our movement by day and threatened our positions at night. Oh my God, what to do about them? The problem drove me wild. Once there were hundreds of them in one valley, maybe four hundred yards wide. We were tied in on the road with a company of another battalion. They came right up to our lines and we had to fire tracers over their heads to stop them from overrunning us . . . Shortly thereafter, both companies began receiving incoming mortar fire. The

other company reported one of its platoons was overrun by the enemy who had mixed with refugees . . . When our road block reported that the refugees were pressing in on them and the pressure was growing, the men requested permission to fire. I asked who the refugees were, men, women, what? They replied: "Mostly women and children, but there are men dressed in white right behind them, men who look to us to be of military age." I paused. The pause went on. The roadblock came on again, urgent,

Fearing communist reprisals, refugees crawl perilously over the shattered girders of a bridge across the Taedong River in their desperate attempt to flee P'yŏngyang once it became clear that UN troops would not defend the city, December 4, 1950. (U.S. NATIONAL ARCHIVES AND RECORDS ADMINISTRATION)

desperate, requesting permission to fire . . . I instructed the roadblock to fire full tracer along the final protective line, then to fall back to the high ground . . . I could not order firing on those thousands upon thousands of pitiful refugees.[13]

Some soldiers did open fire, and aircraft sometimes strafed the refugees. Hong Kyŏng-sŏn and his grandmother were among the refugees. Hong, a nineteen-year-old student and a Christian, had been part of the crowd that welcomed the UN liberation of the city in October. The news that the Americans had decided to abandon the city just three months later was an unbelievable shock. An even greater shock occurred when they were strafed by an aircraft with South Korean markings.[44] At Chinnamp'o, a port thirty miles southwest of P'yŏngyang, UN forces were trying to evacuate the thousands of refugees who had streamed in. But of the fifty thousand refugees, only twenty thousand could be evacuated. On December 3, U.S. Navy Transport Squadron 1, which was en route to Japan from Inch'ŏn, was ordered to divert to Chinnamp'o to aid in the evacuation. The following morning, five ships reached the port and began loading the refugees. Lt. Jim Lampe, an officer in the squadron, had been born in Korea in a missionary family and had gone to school in P'yŏngyang as a child. His return to North Korea was a homecoming. Lampe was ordered to help evacuate those who had worked for the UN forces, as they would be the most likely targets for retribution. But, as Lampe wrote to his wife, this proved to be exceedingly difficult:

I had the police form a line of all those who worked for us, who hadn't gotten out on the junks, to form a line, four abreast, with their families, along the pier area, to be taken to an LST by our small boats. It was morning now and that line was the most pathetic thing I had ever seen. We got into trouble when a group of several thousand who hadn't worked for us, but wanted to get out, crashed through the guards and into the line . . . Each of these people had a pitiable small bundle with them [and] each thought that their life depended on their getting on one of those boats. Noon passed . . . all but twelve of our guards were pulled out and we backed down to the loading ramp. The crowd had absolutely no semblance of order now; it was just a solid mass of people, several thousand, all pushing . . . Women, the old ones, young girls and half naked babies in the cold, all crying, pleading . . . The last boat out. I felt like a monstrous murderer. A devil with a gun and pistol condemning these people to death . . . I was ashamed and embarrassed to be leaving and these helpless ones

> had to stay. I had to actually kick my foot free from a woman's hand as I stepped in the boat. I felt like killing these people for making me feel like a murderer, and I wanted to blow my brains out for being the murderer. Big, warm, well-armed American! . . . I vowed never to go near Chinnamp'o again. How could I look at these people in the eyes![45]

The refugees themselves also had to leave the more unfortunate behind. H. K. Shin remembered one tragic scene in which a small child, perhaps a year or two old, was crying at the side of the road next to her dead mother while a stream of refugees passed by. He recalled, "People passed by the child and dead mother shaking their heads as a desperate gesture of hopelessness and pity, but no one stopped to help the crying child. War had forced them to close their hearts and care for their own burdens."[46]

December Massacres

The reaction in Seoul to the fall of P'yŏngyang was deadly. In the seemingly endless cycle of violence and retribution that characterized the war since it began, the South Korean government rounded up suspected "enemies" for summary execution. By the second week of December, mass executions of alleged communists by South Korean security forces took place on a large scale. An earlier period of retributive atrocities had taken place after the success of Inch'ŏn. The *London Times* on October 25, in a story titled "Seoul after Victory," reported that "290 men and women and seven babies were detained . . . They squatted on the floors, unable to move or to lie down . . . (and) were beaten to insensibility" with rifle butts and bamboo sticks, and tortured "with the insertion of splinters under the finger nails." The story concluded that while "the scene described has been, as is still being, repeated throughout Korea," UN forces "feel either too helpless to intervene or believe attention drawn to the reprisals would be excellent material for Communist propaganda."[47] The daily executions after the fall of P'yŏngyang became too egregious to ignore. According to Western news sources, eight hundred persons described as convicted communists, collaborators, saboteurs, and murderers were executed during the second week of December alone. "A wave of disgust and anger erupted through American and British troops who either have witnessed or heard the firing squads in action in the Seoul area," reported the *Washington Post*.[48] A worried Muccio reported to Acheson that "17 persons had been killed, according to a British report, in a 'brutal,' and 'criminal fashion' raising concerns about the international backlash against the Rhee regime."[49]

The British were also alarmed. A December 19 cable from the Foreign Office reported that "a massacre of 34 prisoners including women and children by South Korean police was witnessed by men of the Northumberland Fusiliers," causing deep consternation among the British troops.[50] Private Duncan, one of the witnesses, wrote to his member of Parliament.

> Sir:
> I wish to report an incident that occurred at a place three miles north of Seoul in Korea on December 12, 1950. Approximately forty emaciated and very subdued Koreans were taken about a mile from where I was stationed and shot while their hands were tied and also beaten by rifles . . . I myself saw the graves and also one of the bodies as they were very cruelly buried. The executioners were South Korean military police and the whole incident has caused a great stir and ill-feeling among the men of my unit . . . I write to tell you this as we are led to believe that we are fighting against such actions and I sincerely believe that our troops are wondering which side in Korea is right or wrong. Also my own feelings are so strong that I felt I must make known to someone of power this cruel incident.[51]

Other eyewitness accounts, like those of Fusilier William Hilder, were widely quoted by news organizations: "A truckload of prisoners was shot less than 150 feet from the camp where the British were eating their breakfast. The guards led them in groups of 10 into the trenches and then shot them in the back of the head. The women were screaming and the men wailing . . . Some of the guards went around with a machine gun firing bursts into those who didn't die immediately. I walked away when the kiddies were shot. I didn't like to see it."[52]

President Rhee and other South Korean officials denied the killing of children, calling the reports "irresponsible and vicious slander," but the on-site response was immediate and intense.[53] Brigadier Tom Brodie, commander of the British Twenty-Ninth Infantry Brigade, was so incensed that he ordered his men to shoot any South Korean policemen attempting to carry out executions on the so-called Execution Hill, which was near his troops' encampment. Brodie vehemently said that "he would not have people executed on my doorstep. My officers will stop executions in my area or within view of my troops."[54] Father Patrick O'Connor of the *Catholic News Agency* of Washington, D.C., and Father George Carroll, two priests in Seoul, sought to stop the executions by appealing directly to Rhee. Constantine Stavropoulos, principle secretary of the United Nations Commission for the Unification and Rehabilitation of Korea (UNCURK), demanded that Cho Pyŏng-ok, South Korea's Home Minister, conduct an immediate investigation. UNCURK was created in October 1950 in anticipation of a reunified Korea as a result of UN operations. It was charged with overseeing the unification, reconstruction, and security of Korea as directed by the UN General Assembly. It arrived in Korea only days before the massive Chinese intervention at the end of November.[55] The American mission requested that UNCURK itself conduct an investigation, which it did. The investigation largely confirmed the reports.[56] Eventually, Rhee, who had initially ordered the executions speeded up, backed down and, conceding to international pressure, suspended the mass executions.[57] Muccio reported, "Owing to public furor caused by second day's executions and foreign correspondents cabling stories of mass executions without trial . . . government has suspended executions for time being."[58]

Nevertheless, the credibility and legitimacy of the South Korean government, and by extension, the UN intervention, had already been badly damaged. Journalist René Cutforth reported on an Australian officer's reaction to the inhumane and dire conditions of the Sŏdaemun (West Gate) Prison, which summed up the general mood: "This, my God, is a bloody fine set-up to waste good Australian lives over. I'm going to raise hell!"[59] It was a sentiment shared by many who seriously questioned their country's involvement in what was obviously a vicious civil war. The American public was angered and disgusted. Allen Neave of Highsville, Maryland, wrote to the *Washington Post* reflecting the prevalent feeling:

> It has been said that the United Nations Troops are now fighting in Korea to preserve, among other things, decency. Are South Korean massacres more decent than others? Those same South Koreans are imploring the

> United Nations to hold off the bloody hordes from the North. Why? So that they can match, drop for drop, the quantity of mother's and children's blood spilled? Surely some of my buddies are not fighting for this!![60]

International outrage forced Rhee to order an "inquiry into the conduct of the executions." He also gave assurances to the British that "no further executions in the British area" would be carried out and that "the lieutenant in charge of the firing party is being held for court martial proceedings." Rhee announced that he had accepted UNCURK's recommendation for the mitigation of death sentences. He also announced amnesty for political prisoners.[61] Finally, he assured the UN that "in the future, all executions will be carried out individually and not in groups of persons."[62]

James Plimsoll, the Australian representative to UNCURK, was pleased by "the very satisfactory response" regarding the amnesty and future ROK policy on prisoners. Nevertheless, he could not help but wonder "to what extent this policy was actually being carried out." In a February 1951 report to Canberra, Plimsoll admitted that "the Commission has no way of being sure that mass executions are not occurring; and the United States Embassy is equally in the dark." Being in the dark, however, was exactly where the UN wanted to be. There were, after all, practical matters to consider in the conduct of the war. Although everyone deplored the mistreatment of prisoners, the UN was limited in what it could do to prevent it in the future because UN forces had come to depend on South Korean security forces to "check the infiltration of North Korean spies and agents, and in fighting guerillas in some regions." Undermining their morale at such a critical time would make an already precarious situation worse. Internal reform of the security forces was needed, Plimsoll believed, not international censure. Plimsoll explained, "Some members of the Commission wanted a scathing report on the executions to be submitted to the General Assembly of the United Nations, but the majority opposed this." He concluded, "No advantage can be gained by an act which might weaken the international support now being accorded the United Nations' effort in Korea." Plimsoll's assessment was largely shared by MacArthur's staff. Public condemnation of the executions could undermine the UN war effort and threaten the safety of UN troops. Humanitarian concerns had to give

Thousands of terror-stricken Koreans pack all the roads leading southward, fleeing the advance of the communists. In this picture, two families combine their efforts in a cart pulled by the fathers and pushed by the mothers and older children, January 5, 1951. (U.S. NATIONAL ARCHIVES AND RECORDS ADMINISTRATION)

way to the military realities on the ground, which required cooperation with the South Koreans, who were responsible for the major share of the fighting. After the initial public outcry died down, MacArthur imposed censorship on all media dispatches of UN operations.[63]

"Revolt of the Primitives"

Confusion over the morality of the war, uncertainty over the reasons why American soldiers were fighting and dying, and fear of World War III with China's intervention led to increasing alarm and skepticism in the American public that translated into an angry backlash against the Truman administration and against Acheson in particular. Truman's approval rating plummeted to an all-time low, and his critics attacked him with increasing ferocity. In mid-December congressional Republicans overwhelmingly voted for the removal of Acheson from his office. Republican Senator Joseph McCarthy of Wisconsin asserted that "the Korea deathtrap" could be laid squarely at "the doors of the Kremlin and those who sabotaged rearming, including Acheson and the President."[64] Even those who were disgusted by McCarthy's anticommunist scare tactics questioned Acheson's continued effectiveness. Walter Lippmann, whose liberal "Today and Tomorrow" column in the *New York Herald Tribune* was enormously influential, called on Acheson to resign, charging that the administration's actions had led to "disaster abroad and disunity at home."[65] Nor did the revered George Marshall escape the barrage of attacks. Senator William Jenner, Republican from Indiana, accused him of playing the "role of a front man for traitors." As a result, he said, the government had been turned into a "military dictatorship, run by communist-appeasing, communist-protecting, betrayer

Harry Truman (center) with Dean Acheson (left) and George Marshall, in good spirits despite an extremely difficult December. In one of his press conferences at the height of the attacks, Acheson was asked how the attacks were affecting him. He replied with a story of a poor fellow who had been wounded during the Indian wars in the West. "He was in bad shape," said Acheson, "scalped, wounded with an arrow sticking into his back, and left for dead. As the surgeon prepared to extract the arrow, he asked the man, 'Does it hurt very much?' to which the wounded man replied, 'Only when I laugh.'"[66] (TRUMAN LIBRARY)

of America, Secretary of State Dean Acheson."[67] Acheson weathered the "shameful and nihilistic orgy" of abuse with humor. "Humor and contempt for the contemptible," wrote Acheson, "proved as always, a shield and buckler against the 'fiery darts of the wicked.'"[68]

While humor enabled Acheson to endure what John Miller of the *London Times* had called "a revolt of the primitives against intelligence," his only real protection against the vicious attacks was the complete confidence of Truman.[69] On December 20, four days after he declared a state of emergency because the United States was in "great danger created by the Soviet Union," Truman delivered an impassioned defense of his secretary of state. "How our position in the world would be improved by the retirement of Dean Acheson from public life is beyond me," Truman declared. "If communism were to prevail in the world, as it shall not prevail, Dean Acheson would be one of the first, if not the first, to be shot by the enemies of liberty and Christianity."[70] Truman knew that Acheson's departure would not be the end of "the revolt of the primitives," but would merely become an invitation for further attacks against his administration, because the source of the anger was not Acheson or even the administration's foreign policy, but the hysterical fear of communist subversion heightened by China's unexpected entrance into an unpopular war.

The campaign against Acheson and Truman exacted a heavy toll. It tore at the fabric of American democracy and threatened to widen the war to mainland China. "[The McCarthyites] were operating on the principle that there can be no such thing as an honest difference of opinion, that whoever disagreed with them must be a traitor," wrote Elmer Davis of *Harper's Magazine*.[71] Thus, while fighting a war against communism abroad, Americans were engaged in a "cold civil war" at home. The result, according to Acheson, was that "the government's foreign and civil services, universities, and China-studies programs took a decade to recover from this sadistic pogrom."[72] The situation could have been far worse, however, had it not been for the new commander of the Eighth Army, Lt. Gen. Matthew B. Ridgway, who was able to quickly reverse the situation in Korea. Ridgway's leadership prevented a defeat in Korea that would surely have allowed anticommunist forces to paralyze America's democratic institutions and give credence to MacArthur's belligerent calls to expand the war to China and hence World War III. Ridgway could offer only the possibility of a limited victory, but the stabilization of the battlefield eventually led to the demise of the "revolt of the primitives."

Wrong Way Ridgway

Ridgway's appearance in Korea was the result of a traffic accident in which General Walker was killed on his way to Ŭijong-bu north of Seoul.[73] Before his death, serious questions had been raised about Walker's leadership. His decision to abandon P'yŏngyang without a fight was seen as "one of the most important tactical mistakes of the war."[74] With uncontested airpower and strong armor forces, the Eighth Army had a good chance of turning back the Chinese. Some correspondents thought the withdrawal was an "uncontrolled bug-out," nothing like the measured, successful retreat and evacuation of the X Corps. Walker became despondent; his professional reputation was now stained by the disastrous retreat while his leadership during the desperate days of the Pusan perimeter seemed all but forgotten.[75]

Walker's apprehension about his future was warranted. Only a few weeks earlier General Collins had had a discussion with MacArthur about replacing Walker with Ridgway. When news of the tragic traffic accident reached MacArthur and the Joint Chiefs, Collins was able to obtain almost immediate clearance for Ridgway's assignment. Three days after Walker's death, Ridgway was on his way to Tokyo. MacArthur and Ridgway had been acquaintances for years, but they were never particularly close. Ridgway had served under MacArthur at West Point in 1919 when the latter was the superintendent of the academy. Unlike his flamboyant boss, Ridgway was known for his no-nonsense, hands-on approach. His trademark habit of strapping a hand grenade to the webbing harness on his chest was interpreted as showmanship, but Ridgway explained that "[The grenades] were purely utilitarian . . . Many a time in Europe and Korea, men in tight spots blasted their way out with hand grenades."[76] If anything, the grenades symbolized his view of himself as both a leader and a common soldier.

MacArthur greeted Ridgway warmly at their first meeting, in Tokyo on the day after Christmas 1950. Ridgway asked whether he might go on the offensive should an opportunity present itself. MacArthur simply replied, "The Eighth Army is yours, Matt. Do what you like with it."[77] MacArthur's latitude for Ridgway, something that he had not extended to either Walker or Almond, was not so much a reflection of special confidence as it was an indication of his troubled state of mind. MacArthur had become deeply despondent over the consequences of China's intervention. He had staked his reputation on the Chinese not entering, or if they did, that he could easily deal with them. "The Red Chinese had made a fool of the infallible 'military genius'," Bradley later observed.[78] Now the situation appeared close to hopeless. What else could MacArthur do but give Ridgway his full support? MacArthur was unsure that UN forces could hold the Chinese back, and he continued to urge expanding the war to mainland China. The Joint Chiefs, however, strongly disagreed. Their directive of December 29 stated that "Korea is not the place to fight a major war" and that MacArthur must continue to defend while "inflicting such damage to hostile forces in Korea as is possible." Instead of following the directive, MacArthur challenged the Joint Chiefs, arguing that the Chinese war-making capacity should be crippled by air and by a naval blockade. He also urged acceptance of Chiang Kai-shek's offer of Nationalist troops. MacArthur presented the JCS with two alternatives: expand the war to China or withdraw to Japan. In arguing for the former, he risked World War III, a risk the Truman administration was not willing to take.

While the JCS and MacArthur sparred, Ridgway was planning to go on the offensive. He thought the notion of withdrawing to Japan absurd. UN forces had complete control of the skies and the seas and had vastly superior weapons and logistical support at its disposal. There was no reason why the Eighth Army could not get back on its feet. "My morale was at the highest of all times," he later confided. "I didn't have the slightest doubt that we would take the offensive. It was just a question of giving us a little time."[79] Upon his arrival in Korea on December 27, Ridgway called on Ambassador Muccio and President Rhee. Muccio was deeply worried about the rumors that UN forces were preparing to evacuate to Japan. Ridgway reassured both men that he and the UN were staying. He told them that "he planned to go on the offensive again as soon as we could marshal our forces."[80] Ridgway then toured the front, in an open jeep in freezing weather, and within forty-eight hours had met every corps commander and all but one division commander. He did not like what he saw, later writing, "Every command post I visited gave me the same sense of lost confidence and lack of spirit. The leaders, from ser geants on up, seemed unresponsive, reluctant to answer my questions."[81] The challenge was infusing this demoralized force with renewed spirit. His first step was to take formal control of the X Corps and unify the UNC under him. As William McCaffrey, Almond's deputy chief of staff, recalled, "Ridgway told him [Almond] how things were going to go in Eighth Army from now on. Almond got the point, and that's how it went. There wasn't any question as to who was the army commander. Ridgway straightened out that ridiculous situation the first day."[82]

Ridgway made other major changes as well. Major General Coulter of the IX Corps, who had performed badly when the Chinese attacked, was promoted out of his position. Ridgway retained his friend Maj. Gen. Frank Milburn, commander of I Corps, who also did not do well, but kept him under close rein. Officers who did not perform up to standard or who were deemed wanting were sent packing. Once, Ridgway attended a briefing given by Colonel Jeter, the I Corps operations officer, who was briefing his plans for "defending in successive positions." Ridgway interrupted him and asked what his attack plans were. Puzzled, Jeter said there were no attack plans since the Eighth Army was in retreat. Ridgway relieved him on the spot.[83] News of Jeter's fate spread quickly among the ranks. While some within I Corps staff resented Ridgway's treatment of Jeter, it did have the kind of shock effect that the new commander had hoped for. Ridgway made it clear that he intended to move the Eighth Army forward, not backward. Thus was born a grudging nickname that, while originally intended as an insult, soon became a badge of honor: "Wrong Way Ridgway."

While dramatic changes were made at the top, Ridgway also sought to inspire transformation from the bottom. He visited the troops, listened to their complaints, and shared in their hardships. "It is the little things that count," he recalled of his efforts to uplift his soldiers. One soldier had complained to him that there was never enough stationery to write letters home, so the general "had somebody send up a supply of stationery." Ridgway became known for passing out extra gloves. "Any soldier up there, you know, the temperature is down below or around zero and his hands are cold and raw, and sure would like to have a pair of gloves;

a thousand and one little things like that." Ridgway was strict about officers setting good examples. "I never would permit a senior officer to ride about in an automobile, I mean of any kind. He had to be in an open jeep with the top down for safety. That does the GI good too, to see his commander up there, as cold as hell."[84] Blessed with a phenomenal memory, Ridgway astonished his soldiers by remembering their names. According to one account, Ridgway could recall "without hesitation four or five thousand names, half of whom were enlisted men."[85] It was his acute attention to detail, and to the names and needs of his men, that made Ridgway's leadership so effective, especially with soldiers who believed that they had been ill treated, betrayed, and forgotten. His aide-de-camp, Walter F. Winton Jr., recalled,

> If you had been a betting man, you would not have bet an awful lot on the United Nations Forces at this juncture in history. A short summation of the situation: weather terrible, Chinese ferocious, and morale stinko. The Eighth Army Commander, General Ridgway, took hold of that thing like a magician taking hold of a bunch of handkerchiefs out of a hat, like so . . . He didn't turn the Army around by being mean to people, by shooting people, by relieving people, by chopping people's heads off, or by striking fear; quite the opposite. He breathed humanity into that operation . . . He effected gradual and orderly relief. He kept alive the old spirit of the offensive, the spirit of the bayonet; call it what you will. Talk about practicing what he preaches. During the time he was in command of the Eighth Army, in Korea, I can hardly think of half a dozen days when he was not under hostile fire. This impressed me. The troops knew it and once they got the idea that somebody was looking out for them, and not for himself, the miracle happened.[86]

As Ridgway was breathing new life into his army, the Chinese continued their long trek south. Rest halts were few. It was deathly cold. Almost everything had to be carried on men's backs or by pack animals since they had little motorized transport. Each man carried rations for about a week consisting of soya flour, tea, rice, some sugar, and perhaps a small can of meat.[87] The lengthening supply line meant that replenishing even these meager supplies became more difficult. Hunger became endemic. UN air raids disrupted the CPV's march and supply lines, and the bombing of villages left few places for the soldiers to seek shelter. One Chinese soldier recalled, "One night it was reported to me that an entire squad's post collapsed in the snowstorm. When I rushed to the squad's

Generals Matthew B. Ridgway (left) and Edward Almond, February 15, 1951. (U.S. NATIONAL ARCHIVES AND RECORDS ADMINISTRATION)

post in the trench, I was dumbfounded by the scene, all nine unconscious and covered by layers of snow. As those bodies under the thin uniforms began to turn cold, I also realized that their food bags were empty. None of them survived to participate in the offensive attack."[88]

By January 1951, the Chinese army was badly in need of a rest. General Peng, cautious by nature, understood the limitations of his army and what he could achieve against a technologically superior force with near-total command of the skies. He was wary of underestimating the enemy. After the CPV's victorious second campaign in late November, Peng requested permission to regroup his forces and rest over the winter. Logistical problems, hunger, cold, and exhaustion had made it almost impossible to continue. "Let [the troops] stop in areas dozens of *lis* north of the parallel, allowing the enemy to control the parallel, so that we will be able to destroy the enemy's main force the next year," Peng wrote to Mao. But Mao was impatient and wanted the third offensive to begin as soon as possible, by no later than early January, much earlier than what Peng thought wise or feasible. "Our army must cross the 38th parallel," Mao wrote back to Peng in mid-December. "It will be

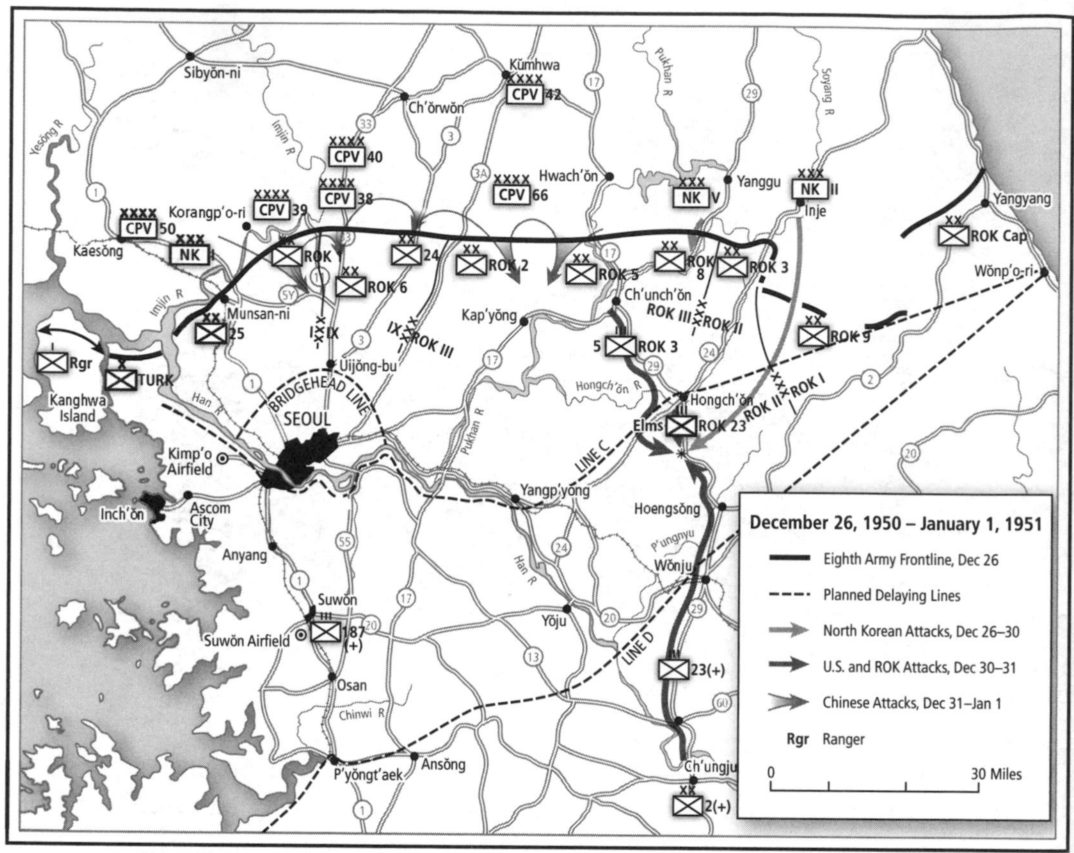

Chinese third offensive, December 1950–January 1951. (MAP ADAPTED FROM MOSSMAN, *EBB AND FLOW*)

most unfavorable in political terms if [our forces] don't reach the 38th parallel and stop north of it." Peng warned Mao of "a rise of unrealistic optimism for a quicker victory from various parts" and suggested a more prudent advance.[89] Peng continued to press his case to Mao, laying bare the full horror of what his army was facing in Korea: "Most of the overcoats for the various corps have not yet arrived, nor have the cotton-padded shoes for the 42nd Army." By this time, the shoes had been mostly worn out, and some of the soldiers had been forced to go barefoot. "Cooking oil, grain, and vegetables are either unavailable or late in arrival, and the physical strength of our army unit has weakened, with increasing numbers of sick soldiers." The situation was going from bad to worse, Peng warned Mao. "If there is no remedy for quick relief, the war will be protracted."[90] But Mao could not be persuaded to postpone the offensive. Peng arrived at a compromise solution: he would scale down the size of the military operation and stop whenever it became necessary.[91] The CPV would adopt a "gradual plan of advancement."[92] He knew that UN morale was low, but there were still a quarter of a million UN forces, and Peng worried that as they began to dig in, it would become increasingly costly to assault them and their wall of firepower. Mao finally agreed.

The CPV attack pushed UN forces across the Han River.[93] Seoul fell on January 4, the third time the city had changed hands since the war began. While the withdrawal was not without some disorder, Ridgway had by this time, less than ten days after his arrival, revived the Eighth Army's spirits. Ridgway established a strong defensive line about sixty miles south of Seoul. After Seoul's fall, Peng pushed south for a few more days and then ordered a general halt. His exhausted soldiers were simply in no condition to continue, and he feared that UN forces were trying

Refugees again flee from Seoul, January 5, 1951. (U.S. NATIONAL ARCHIVES AND RECORDS ADMINISTRATION)

to lure his army into vainly assaulting fortified positions. Peng's forces, including the NKPA, withdrew several miles to rest and regroup. When the third offensive ended, China had "only 280,000 poorly supplied and very exhausted troops facing 230,000 well-equipped UN and ROK forces."[94] Peng's forces had been reduced in half, and the winter months were making it difficult to get supplies through to those who remained.[95] Zhang Da, who was only seventeen years old when he enlisted to fight in Korea, remembered that many soldiers continued to "suffer severe frostbite to their hands and their feet." The food was also very poor, with the main staple being "baked dry flour with rice, sorghum or ship biscuits."[96] A captured diary written by a Chinese officer vividly recounted what Peng and his army were up against during that harsh winter:

> Difficulties: 1) We have been troubled on the march due to icy roads. 2) we are exhausted from incessant night marches. To make matters worse, when we should be resting during the day, we cannot take a nap due to enemy air activity. 3) Due to a shortage of shoes, almost all the soldiers are suffering from frostbite. 4) We have had to cross rivers with our uniforms on during combat, which has resulted in severe frostbite. 5) The fighting is becoming critical due to lack of ammo and food. 6) Lack of lubrication causes untimely rifle jams when firing. 7) We have had to carry heavy equipment on our backs, we are always heavily burdened when marching. 8) The physical condition of the soldiers has been getting worse as they have to hide in shelters all day long, and fight only at night or during enemy air assaults. 9) When reconnoitering at night disguised in civilian clothing, it is very difficult to carry out the mission because of language difficulties.
>
> Morale of the soldiers of our unit: Enemy air strikes frighten the soldiers most of all. The most unbearable labor they have to endure is to carry heavy equipment on their backs when climbing mountain ridges. Their conviction that they will win the war is wavering.[97]

On January 11, Mao instructed Peng to reorganize the CPV and defend Seoul, Inch'ŏn, and the areas north of the 38th parallel, while the NKPA was to be resupplied and continue their attack south. Kim Il Sung was delighted. Kim, Pak Hŏn-yŏng, and Peng met to discuss the new plan. Peng was wary. He thought Kim's focus on expanding territory without destroying the enemy was pointless. Furthermore, sending the North Koreans ahead alone assumed that the communists held the advantage and that UN troops would eventually retreat from the peninsula, something Peng did not believe was likely to happen. He knew that the NKPA was not strong enough to destroy the UN forces on its own, and with the latter's well-defended positions and superior firepower, the NKPA would surely fail. But Pak countered that the UN forces need not be annihilated, only *pursued.* Recent reports from Moscow indicated that the UN forces would soon withdraw from the peninsula. All they needed was a little prodding. Peng retorted that a few more American divisions would have to be destroyed before the UN forces withdrew. Kim responded by suggesting again his idea of sending NKPA forces south now and CPV forces to follow after resting for a month. Peng impatiently "raised his voice" and emphatically declared that "they [Kim and Pak] were wrong and that they were dreaming." "In the past, you said that the US would never send troops," he fumed. "You never thought about what you would do if they *did* send troops. Now you say that the American army will definitely withdraw from Korea, but you are not considering what to do if the American army doesn't withdraw." He scolded the Koreans for "hoping for a quick victory," which was "only going to prolong the war" and "lead . . . to disaster." Peng concluded that "to reorganize and re-supply, the Volunteer Army needs two months, not one day less, maybe even three [months]. Without considerable preparation, not one division can advance south. I resolutely oppose this mistake you are making in misunderstanding the enemy. If you think I am not doing my job well, you can fire me, court martial me, or even kill me." When Stalin was informed of the heated exchange, he sensed a crack in the alliance and sided with Peng. "The leadership of the CVA [Chinese Volunteer Army] is correct. Undoubtedly the truth lies with commander Peng Dehuai."[98]

While the Chinese halted, MacArthur continued his calls to widen the war with China. What disturbed the JCS most, however, was MacArthur's "negative and defeatist tone about the Eighth Army," painting the bleakest possible picture of the situation in Korea. This was all the more puzzling since it was in sharp contrast to the optimistic reports from Ridgway. "It indicated," wrote Bradley, "that MacArthur might well be completely out of touch with the battlefield." MacArthur reported that the UNC was not strong enough to hold Korea and protect Japan. He reported gloomily that his troops were "embittered" and tired and that "their morale will become a serious threat to their battlefield efficiency unless the political basis upon which they are asked to trade life for time is clearly delineated, fully understood, and so impelling that the hazards of battle are cheerfully accepted."[99]

MacArthur's message of potential doom was received grimly in Washington. Truman was deeply disturbed.[100] Rusk later remarked that "when a general complains of the morale of his troops, the time has come to look at his own." Acheson, unconvinced by the general's ominous predictions, was also suspicious and privately concluded that MacArthur was "incurably recalcitrant and basically disloyal to the purposes of the Commander-in-Chief."[101] The JCS told MacArthur to hold out as long as possible and to withdraw to Japan if no other recourse was available, while the administration considers contingency military and nonmilitary courses of action against China. Generals Collins and Vandenberg then flew to Japan and Korea on a fact-finding mission. What they found surprised and heartened them. Ridgway was optimistic and confident. Both men were impressed with how Ridgway had revived the Eighth Army. There was no doubt in their minds that the UN forces could and would stay and fight in Korea. "Morale very satisfactory considering condition," reported Collins to Washington. "On the whole, Eighth Army now in position and prepared to punish severely the enemy."[102] It was their opinion that, short of Soviet intervention, the Eighth Army could continue operations in Korea without endangering the security of either itself or Japan. From then on, there was no further discussion about blockading or bombing China. Ridgway had made that option moot.

But Ridgway's success was also MacArthur's failure, for it undercut his power to direct and influence events in Korea. The JCS distrusted MacArthur and sought information on Korea directly from Ridgway, as MacArthur was seen as untrustworthy. "There was a feeling," wrote Bradley, "that MacArthur had been 'kicked upstairs' to chairman of the board and was, insofar as military operations were concerned, mainly a prima donna figurehead who had to be tolerated."[103] MacArthur had become what he feared most: ignored and irrelevant. He was stung by public criticisms characterizing his actions in Korea as "a momentous blunder," a "gross miscalculation," and a "great tragedy."[104] As the war in Korea stabilized in January 1951, MacArthur had probably already decided that he would challenge the president in order to regain the influence and power he had lost after the Inch'ŏn landing. He would gamble his career and reputation in a public spat with the increasingly unpopular Truman administration to redeem his honor and kick-start a new career in politics. It was a calculated risk and one that only MacArthur, courageous, flamboyant, brilliant, but supremely egotistical, could have taken.

Lost Chances

On January 14, Mao cabled Peng his estimate on the future intentions of the UN forces: they could, under pressure from the CPV and NKPA, retreat from the peninsula after "symbolic" resistance; or they could retreat to Taegu and Pusan, wage a stubborn defense as in 1950, and then retreat. Either way, Mao thought, "they will finally retreat from Korea after we have exhausted their potential."[105] It was now Mao's turn to underestimate the enemy. His drastic miscalculation about American tenacity and its ability to spring back from defeat cost the Chinese the opportunity to gain a greater victory at far less cost than what they would get later, after another two and a half years of war. The success of the third offensive, and especially the recapture of Seoul, had convinced Mao that China now held the upper hand. China's victories, just like MacArthur's success at Inch'ŏn, had made Mao hungry for total victory in Korea. This overconfidence led him to reject the UN Cease-Fire Commission's peace plan, which included many of Beijing's earlier demands. Presented to the UN on January 11, the plan proposed a five-step program: (1) cease-fire; (2) a political meeting for restoring peace; (3) a withdrawal by stages of all foreign forces; (4) arrangement for an immediate administration of all Korea; and (5) an establishment of an "appropriate body" composed of the United States, the United Kingdom, the Soviet Union, and China to settle Far East problems, including the status of Taiwan and China's representation in the UN.

This was a poor deal for Washington, for the "appropriate body" charged with settling affairs in Korea was clearly stacked against the United States. The United Kingdom was likely to support a motion to seat the PRC instead of Taiwan in China's seat at the UN, as it had promoted such a shift since the founding of the PRC. China's admission to the UN would lead to a complete loss of UN support for Taiwan. This would not play well domestically, since the Truman administration was already under fire for having "lost" China, and the "primitives" were getting louder in their calls for Acheson's head. The cease-fire, proposed to take place at the 37th parallel, therefore farther south than the 38th, would also yield considerable new territory to North Korea, including Seoul. South Koreans would undoubtedly oppose it bitterly. Acheson recalled, "The choice whether to support or oppose this plan was a murderous one threatening, on the one side, the loss of the Koreans and the fury of Congress and press and, on the other, the loss of our majority and support in the United Nations." Nevertheless, Acheson decided to gamble by recommending support, calculating that the Chinese would reject it. After painful deliberations, Truman supported the recommendation. Acheson later wrote, "The President—bless him—supported me even this anguishing decision."[106] As Acheson and Truman "held their breath," the Chinese unequivocally rejected the UN cease-fire plan. Acheson's gamble, which he admitted had almost brought the administration to "the verge of destruction domestically," had paid off.[107]

With China's rejection of the cease-fire, Washington could claim the moral high ground, for it was China's decision to continue the war. On January 20, a resolution condemning China as an aggressor was introduced in the UN. Britain and other allies thought the condemnation of China was gratuitous, but Acheson, with an eye toward American public opinion, lobbied unapologetically for the resolution.[108] It was a triumph of poker-player diplomacy and Acheson had played his cards beautifully. China was now thrust into a pariah status as an aggressor, while the Truman administration suffered little domestic political consequences. Getting the British to support the resolution had been a particularly hard sell, but with Acheson's private assurances that the administration would not use the resolution as an excuse to widen the war, the British finally agreed. The UN General Assembly resolution condemning China passed on February 1.

Meanwhile in Korea, Ridgway was taking his own great gamble. He launched a probe in mid-January to find the CPV, which seemed to have disappeared. He was wary of a possible trap and repeating the mistake of November, when MacArthur recklessly urged an advance to the Yalu. There were other concerns as well. The Russians had greatly built up the Chinese air force in recent weeks. By January 1951, some estimates gave the Chinese as many as 650 combat aircraft.[109] The question on everyone's mind was whether this new airpower would be used against UN forces. Ridgway considered two options: dig in and wait for the Chinese to make their next move, or take the initiative and go on the offensive. Unsurprisingly, Ridgway chose to go on the offensive, even though the Eighth Army was not completely recovered. Run right, his plan would have an incalculable psychological benefit. He needed to show his soldiers, and the badly mauled ROK forces, that the Eighth Army was no longer in retreat. He also desperately needed to know about the enemy: "There were supposed to be 174,000 Chinese in front of us at that time but where they were placed, in what state of mind, and even that they were there at all was something we could not determine. All our vigorous patrolling, all our constant air reconnaissance had failed to locate any trace of this enormous force."[110]

Ridgway's probe discovered the Chinese withdrawing. Furthermore, the feared Soviet-backed Chinese air force had failed to materialize. Ridgway's actions made clear to Mao and Kim that Peng's calculation had been correct: the UN forces were not defeated nor would they withdraw from the peninsula without a fight. Thus, by the end of January 1951, the communists' euphoria about the war began to decline sharply. While tensions between America and its allies, and especially with Britain, had eased significantly by early 1951, relations between Stalin and Mao were strained. Mao realized that Stalin was doing his utmost to keep the Soviet Union out of direct participation in the war.[111]

On January 25, Ridgway launched a general offensive that caught Peng by surprise. Peng reported on February 4, "We are obliged to begin the 4th phase of operations. The battle begins under unfavorable conditions. Our period of rest is interrupted and now, when we are not yet ready to fight."[112] The fourth phase of the Chinese offensive might have been forced to be launched prematurely, but at least the UN forces did not know where the attack would come.

By early February, the Eighth Army had reestablished full contact with the CPV, but it did not know if the Chinese were establishing a defensive line or preparing a counteroffensive, and if so, where. Intelligence indicated that Chinese forces had shifted from the west to the mountainous central region. Ridgway could not be sure where the Chinese might strike along this central region, but the most likely path of

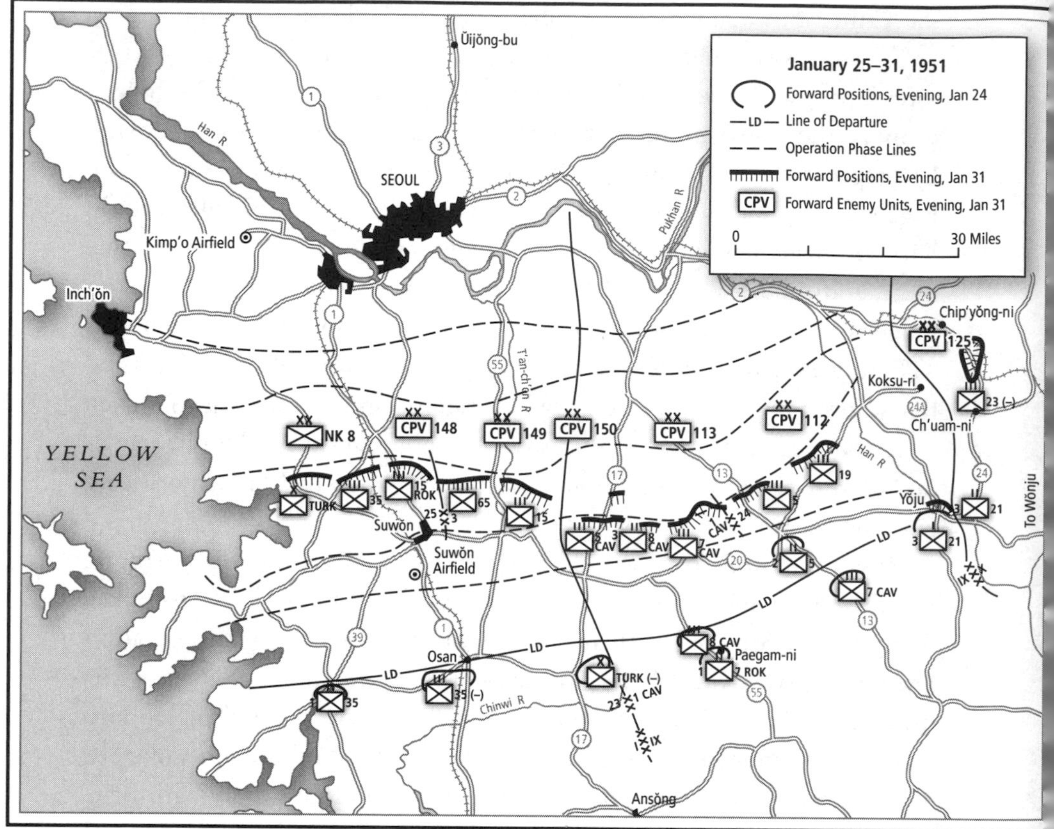

First phase of the UN counteroffensive, January 25–February 11, 1951. (MAP ADAPTED FROM MOSSMAN, *EBB AND FLOW*)

enemy advance would be down the Han River valley toward Wŏnju. Chinese control of Wŏnju would allow them to be within striking distance of Taegu. And once Taegu was taken, the Chinese would be poised to take Pusan. Major action was anticipated for the X Corps, which was deployed in the central region.[113] Ridgway was thus prepared to go to the defensive, taking advantage of the rugged terrain in the central region. His objective was "to advance and then hold along the general line Yangp'yŏng-Hoengsŏng-Kangŭng" from west to east. Ridgway intended to dig in behind this defensive line and slaughter Chinese forces during their attempt to cross it.[114]

On February 5, the X Corps launched its offensive. The attack plan was to move about thirteen miles north of Hoengsŏng to Hongch'ŏn to disrupt North Korean forces that could threaten the X Corps. Almond's plan of advance placed the lightly armed and weaker ROK divisions of his command in the lead, followed by the heavier American units. The result of this disposition proved to be disastrous. On February 11, three CPV divisions hit the ROK Eighth Division in a frontal assault in broad daylight and destroyed it within hours. Its collapse imperiled the U.S. Second Infantry Division at Hoengsŏng. "Our people fought desperately to extricate themselves from certain destruction," recalled one veteran. "On the afternoon of February 13, I received an order to proceed [south] to Wŏnju immediately. Upon my arrival late in the day, I was informed of the catastrophe suffered by our people and the expectation that the Chinese would resume their attack the next morning."[115] A tally of casualties a few days later revealed a disastrous outcome: over 1,500 Americans and Dutch (the Netherlands Battalion was attached to the Second Division) killed, wounded, and missing and nearly 8,000 casualties for the ROK Eighth Division.[116] UN losses at Hoengsŏng were so appalling that MacArthur's headquarters (Far East Command) tried to suppress the story. When the Seventh Marines passed through the same area later in March, they were shocked to discover corpses still littering the battlefield. It was, recalled Bill Merrick, "like an enormous graveyard."[117] More than 250 bodies of American and Dutch soldiers, including the Dutch battalion commander, Marinus den Ouden, were recovered. Many of the bodies had been looted of shoes and clothes, and several had been bound and shot in the back. Sickened by the sight, the marines erected this sign:

MASSACRE VALLEY.
SCENE OF HARRY TRUMAN'S POLICE ACTION.
NICE GOING, HARRY.

Meanwhile, another drama was unfolding at the little town of Chipyŏng-ni, fifteen miles northwest of Wŏnju. Colonel Paul Freeman, commander of the Second Division's 23rd Infantry Regiment, received the news of X Corps's withdrawal to Wŏnju with a sense of foreboding. The disaster at Hoengsŏng opened Freeman's right flank, exposing his forces to encirclement. Freeman's request for permission to withdraw was denied by Ridgway, an unusual skip-echelon command since Ridgway went over the heads of the corps and division commanders. He

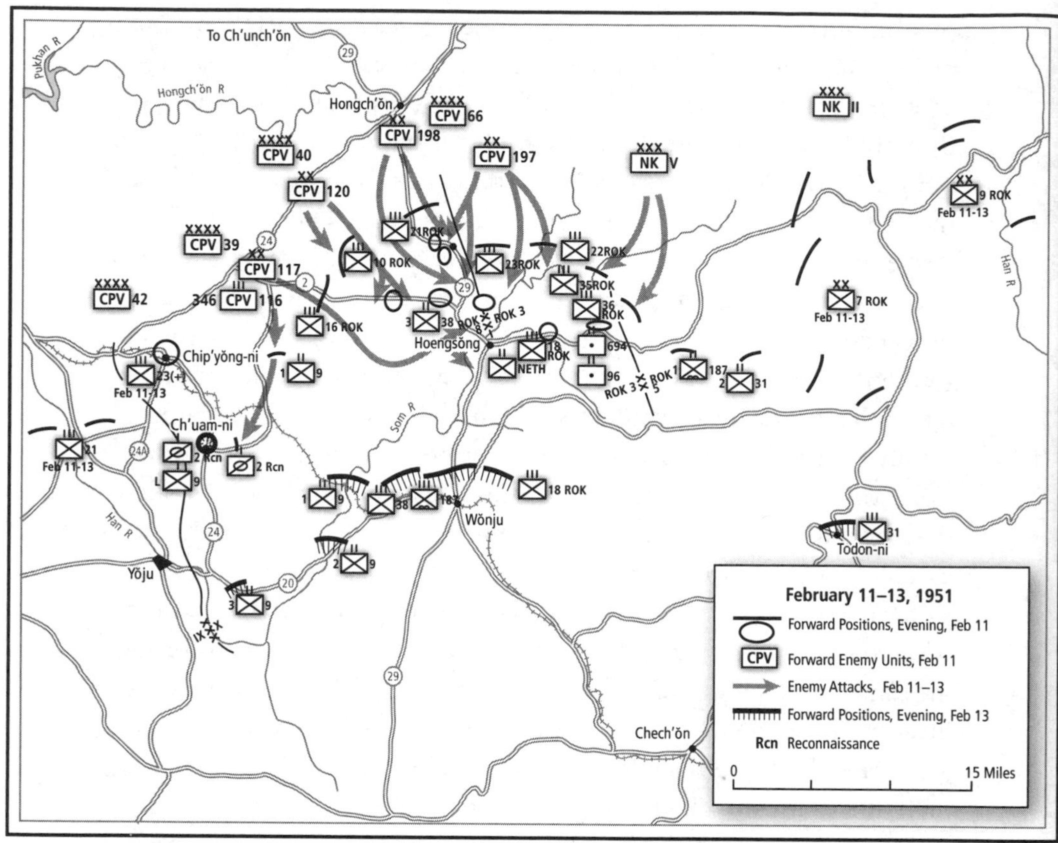

Battle of Hoengsŏng, February 11–18, 1951. (MAP ADAPTED FROM MOSSMAN, *EBB AND FLOW*)

ordered Freeman to stay and hold Chipyŏng-ni, which was now the vital "left shoulder" holding back the CPV penetration. As important rail and road hubs, both Wŏnju and Chipyŏng-ni had to remain in the hands of the Eighth Army.

The crucial battles for Wŏnju and Chipyŏng-ni demonstrated the UN force's enormous advantages, which proved decisive in defeating the CPV. Control of roads and railways with abundant motor transport meant that troops could be rapidly repositioned and supplies could flow unimpeded. Extensive communications provided the capacity to respond quickly to developing situations and close air-ground coordination. The battle of Wŏnju in mid-February in particular, which was known as the "Wŏnju shoot" for the prodigious use of artillery by UN forces, was a devastating blow for the communists and a major turning point of the war. From then on, Peng realized that the opportunity for quick and decisive victory in Korea had passed. The fourth offensive that had begun with a bloody bang against UN forces on February 11 at Hoengsŏng ended just fifteen days later with the bloody defeat of the CPV at Wŏnju and Chipyŏng-ni. Chinese losses were staggering. The better part of fourteen CPV divisions was destroyed.[118] An anguished Peng went to see Mao. "I explained to Chairman Mao that the Korean War could not be won quickly," Peng later wrote. "The Chairman gave a clear instruction for conducting the War to Resist U.S. Aggression and Aid Korea, 'Win a quick victory if you can; if you can't, win a slow one.'"[119]

CHAPTER EIGHT

Quest for Victory

By the end of February 1951, the Eighth Army was again on the offensive and advancing steadily. On March 15, Seoul, now a devastated city, was abandoned by the enemy without a fight, and changed hands for the fourth time in less than nine months. Unlike the festive mood that had surrounded the recapture of the city in September, there were no ceremonies and no grand speeches to mark the occasion. The ROK troops who first entered the city simply took down the North Korean flag and raised their own at the Capitol Building. The war-beaten residents appeared almost too weary to notice. Soon, the issue of whether to cross the 38th parallel once again became a matter of discussion. The political and military situation was entirely different from what it was in September 1950. The kind of sustained drive into North Korean territory after Inch'ŏn appeared unlikely against the still-formidable Chinese force. Nevertheless, MacArthur pressed for unifying the peninsula and taking the war to China. On February 15, he asked for the removal of military restrictions, to permit bombings to disrupt the supply line from the Soviet Union into North Korea. The JCS denied the request. On February 26, MacArthur asked for authorization to bomb the hydroelectrical power facilities along the Yalu. The JCS did not give it to him, for "political reasons." A frustrated MacArthur issued a public statement on March 7, in direct violation of Truman's gag order on public discussion of policy matters, predicting that the "savage slaughter" would continue and the war would evolve into one of attrition and indecisiveness unless Washington's policies changed.

The first opportunity to bring an end to the war came in March when the exhausted Chinese forces abandoned Seoul and retreated north, allowing the UN forces back to the 38th parallel. With status quo ante bellum essentially restored, the UNC, as George Kennan had predicted, was finally in a position to negotiate a settlement from "something approaching an equality of strength." On March 20, the Joint Chiefs informed MacArthur that the president was about to implement a peace initiative: "Strong UN feeling persists that further diplomatic efforts towards settlement should be made before any advance with major forces north of 38th parallel," they wrote. "Time will be required to determine diplomatic reactions and permit new negotiations that may develop." Rather than responding directly to the initiative, MacArthur simply reiterated his earlier position: "I recommend that no further military restrictions be imposed upon the United Nations Command in Korea . . . The military disadvantages arising from restrictions . . . coupled with the disparity between the size of our command and the enemy ground potential render it completely impracticable to attempt to clear North Korea or to make any appreciable effort to that end." The JCS was puzzled by the cable. His "brilliant but brittle mind" seemed to have snapped, recalled Bradley, but no one in Washington was prepared for what MacArthur did next.[1]

The General and the Statesman

On March 24, MacArthur issued a public statement that challenged the pride of China and the authority of his Washington superiors, sabotaging any chance for a peace settlement. MacArthur's "communiqué" began by taunting China for its lack of industrial power and poor military showing against UN forces. More seriously, he raised the possibility of a widened war: "The enemy, therefore, must by now be painfully aware that a decision of the United Nations to depart from its tolerant effort to contain the war to the area of Korea, through an expansion of our military operations to his coastal areas and interior bases, would doom Red China to the risk of imminent military collapse."[2] He concluded with words that seemed calculated to upstage the president: he, MacArthur, personally "stood ready at any time" to meet with the Chinese commander for a settlement. The White House and the State Department were bombarded with queries by allied leaders and the press demanding to know whether there was now a new direction in U.S. policy in Korea. The French newspaper *Le Figaro* mocked MacArthur's negotiation offer as "an olive branch with a bayonet hidden amongst the leaves." London's *Daily Telegraph* observed that "the U.N. General Assembly becomes embarrassed, resentful or merely incredulous when General MacArthur . . . speaks again of carrying the war to the Chinese mainland." Soviet Foreign Minister Andrei Vyshinsky probably best summed up the general reaction of the foreign press when he announced that MacArthur was "a maniac, the principal culprit, the evil genius" of the war.[3]

That evening, Deputy Secretary of State Robert A. Lovett, Dean Rusk, and others gathered at Acheson's home to discuss the uproar that MacArthur had created. Lovett, Acheson recalled, "was angrier than I had ever seen him." The general, he said, "must be removed at once." Acheson shared Lovett's anger: "[MacArthur's statement] can be described only as defiance of the JCS, sabotage of an operation of which he had been informed, and insubordination of the grossest sort to his Commander-in-Chief." The following day, Lovett, Acheson, and Rusk met with Truman. "The President," recalled Acheson, "although perfectly calm, appeared to be in a state of mind that combined disbelief with controlled fury."[4] In his memoirs, Truman confided that he decided that day to relieve MacArthur, although it was not yet clear to him when and how he would do it. "[MacArthur's statement] was an act totally disregarding all directives to abstain from any declarations on foreign policy . . . By this act MacArthur left me no choice. I could no longer tolerate his insubordination." Yet, despite the seething anger in the room, the president coolly asked the group to check his directive prohibiting comments on policy to see if there was any ambiguity. They told him it was crystal clear. Truman then instructed Lovett to send a priority message to MacArthur "that would remind him of his duty under the order."[5] Given the circumstances, Truman's mild reprimand appeared to be yet another instance of Washington's leaders caving in to MacArthur. The general had, after all, violated the December order repeatedly, including his statement earlier in March predicting a "savage slaughter" in Korea, and nothing much was said then. Despite his "controlled fury," Truman appeared to be wavering again.

However, it was different this time. Truman's outward restraint was due to not only his sense of caution, but also what others called "political guile." As during other crises, Truman refused "to act impulsively or irresponsibly, whatever his own feelings."[6] His ability to remain cool, calm, and collected under fire was a trait that his staff had come to admire.[7] On this occasion, there was an additional motive. For all his anger, Truman understood that MacArthur remained an enormously popular figure. The mood of the country favored the general, not the president. A mid-March Gallup poll showed the president's public approval rating at an all-time low of just 26 percent. War casualty figures were appalling and further soured the national mood (the Defense Department reported that the United States had suffered a total of 57,120 casualties since June 1950).[8] People were becoming fed up with the war, and MacArthur at least spoke of a way to victory and end. Patience was required to bring down MacArthur. Premature or rash action would hurt only Truman and his administration. Thus, far from being timid, Truman's calm rebuke was actually a calculated response aimed, in Acheson's words, at "laying the foundation for a court-martial."[9]

Truman did not have to wait long. In early April, House Minority Leader Joe Martin took the floor with an explosive revelation. A long-time MacArthur admirer, Martin told the House that he had sent the general a copy of a speech he had made in February. Martin called for the use of Nationalist Chinese forces in Korea and accused the administration of a defeatist policy. He asked for MacArthur's views "to make sure my views were not in conflict with what was best for America."[10] MacArthur's response carried no stipulation of confidentiality, and Martin announced it dramatically in Congress: "It seems strangely difficult for some to realize that here in Asia is where the Communist conspirators have elected to make their play for global conquest, and that we have joined the issue thus raised on the battlefield . . . if we lose the war to communism in Asia the fall of Europe is inevitable, win it and Europe most probably would avoid war and yet preserve freedom."[11]

The Martin letter and renewed doubts about MacArthur's loyalty could not have come at a more inopportune time. The Joint Chiefs had just received alarming intelligence that the Soviet Union was preparing for a major military move. "One suggestion," recalled Bradley, "taken with utmost seriousness, was that they would intervene in Korea. Another was that they might attempt to overrun Western Europe."[12] It appeared that the situation in Korea had reached a new crisis point. In conveying these reports to Truman, Bradley also provided the JCS's recommendation that MacArthur be authorized to retaliate against air bases and aircraft in China in the event of a "major attack."[13] He convinced Truman that the Chinese and the Russians might be preparing to push the United States out of Korea and that the air force needed to be prepared to respond quickly. Deeply shaken, Truman called for the chairman of the Atomic Energy Commission (AEC), Gordon Dean, who controlled all nuclear warheads, and told him that he had decided to deploy bombers and atomic warheads to the Pacific because of the serious situation in Korea.[14] Dean recalled, "He [Truman] said that if I saw no objection, he would sign the order directing me to release to the custody of General Vandenberg, Chief of Staff, USAF, nine nuclear ****[*sic*]."[15] Truman said that he was not giving the air force a green light to drop the nuclear bombs; he still hoped the need to use them would never arise. He was sending them as a contingency, and no decision would be made without consulting the National Security Council's special committee on atomic energy. The next day, the 99th Medium Bomb Wing was ordered to pick up atomic bombs for trans-shipment to Guam. By this time, Truman and Acheson had approved a draft order to MacArthur authorizing him, in the event of a "major" air attack on UN forces originating outside of Korea, to retaliate against air bases in China, but not with nuclear weapons without Truman's release.

MacArthur never received the order. Bradley later explained, "I was now so wary of MacArthur that I deliberately withheld the message and all knowledge of its existence from him, fearing that he might, as I wrote at the time, 'make a premature decision in carrying it out.'"[16] MacArthur had lost Bradley's trust. By sending nuclear bombs and approving a directive that conditionally authorized their use, Truman strengthened the argument for MacArthur's relief: if nuclear weapons were to be used in Korea, it was absolutely essential to have a trustworthy commander in the field. Furthermore, Truman had shown that although he disapproved of MacArthur's public statements, he was willing to consider the strategic concepts underlying them.[17] While Truman and the JCS were in agreement with MacArthur on what had to be done in case of an attack, they were also in agreement that MacArthur was the wrong person to be entrusted with such a difficult mission.[18] It was this confluence of events—MacArthur's letter to Martin, the crisis in Korea, and the decision to deploy nuclear weapons—that led to the conclusion to dismiss MacArthur. Acheson, Bradley, George Marshall, and Averell Harriman (the "Big Four") unanimously agreed that MacArthur should be relieved of duty.[19]

Truman insisted that MacArthur be notified with courtesy and dignity. Secretary of the Army Frank Pace Jr. was en route to Japan and Korea, and Marshall decided to have him deliver the order of relief personally to MacArthur on the morning of April 12 (evening of April 11, Washington time) before it was publicly announced. But a chain of actions made the notification neither courteous nor dignified. On the evening of April 10, the information had leaked, and the *Chicago Tribune*, a staunch critic of the Truman administration, queried for confirmation and details. An emergency White House meeting considered whether to stick to the original plan or to make an immediate announcement. The fear was that the *Tribune* would notify MacArthur, and he might try to trump the president by dramatically resigning before the public announcement. The risk could not be taken. A special press conference was called at 1:00 am on April 11, Washington time, to tell the reporters, bleary-eyed and bewildered, of the extraordinary news. Although an attempt was made to inform MacArthur shortly before the press conference, radio broadcast of the order reached Tokyo first.[20] MacArthur learned of his dismissal from his wife, Jean, after she was notified by a member of the personal staff who had heard the news on the radio. MacArthur was seventy-one years old and had been in Asia for fourteen years. Ridgway was chosen to replace him.

Ridgway did not know of his promotion until a reporter congratulated him. Flustered, the general shrugged it off. Not long thereafter, he received official word from Secretary Pace and the next day flew to Japan for his last meeting with MacArthur. Ridgway recollected, "He was entirely himself, composed, quiet, temperate, friendly, and helpful to the man who was to succeed him."[21] Nevertheless, MacArthur's rancor against Truman was palpable. He told Ridgway that an "eminent medical man" had confided to him that "the President was suffering from malignant hypertension" and that "this affliction was characterized by bewilderment and confusion of thought." Truman, MacArthur declared, "would be dead in six months."[22]

MacArthur left Tokyo amid much emotional fanfare. The Japanese Diet passed a resolution praising him. Prime Minister Yoshida and other top officials publicly expressed their gratitude for his "outstanding" service to Japan. Throngs of Japanese densely lined the route from the embassy to the airport to offer their farewells. A nineteen-gun salute was rendered and a large formation of jet fighters flew in formation over the airport in his honor.[23] "The farewells were an ordeal," commented William Sebald, the American ambassador to Japan. "Many of the women were sobbing openly, and a number of the battle-hardened men had difficulty suppressing their tears."[24] MacArthur turned and waved to the crowd one last time before boarding his famed *Bataan.* "You'd think he was a conquering hero," said one observer, "not at all a demeanor of a man who'd just been fired."[25]

MacArthur received a tumultuous reception on his return to the United States. It was his first visit to the continental United States in fourteen years. He was greeted with one of the biggest ticker-tape parades ever staged in New York, and he delivered a stirring farewell speech to a joint session of Congress that Congressman Dewy Short of

Japanese crowds line the road to the airport to say good-bye to General MacArthur, April 16, 1951. (U.S. ARMY MILITARY HISTORY INSTITUTE)

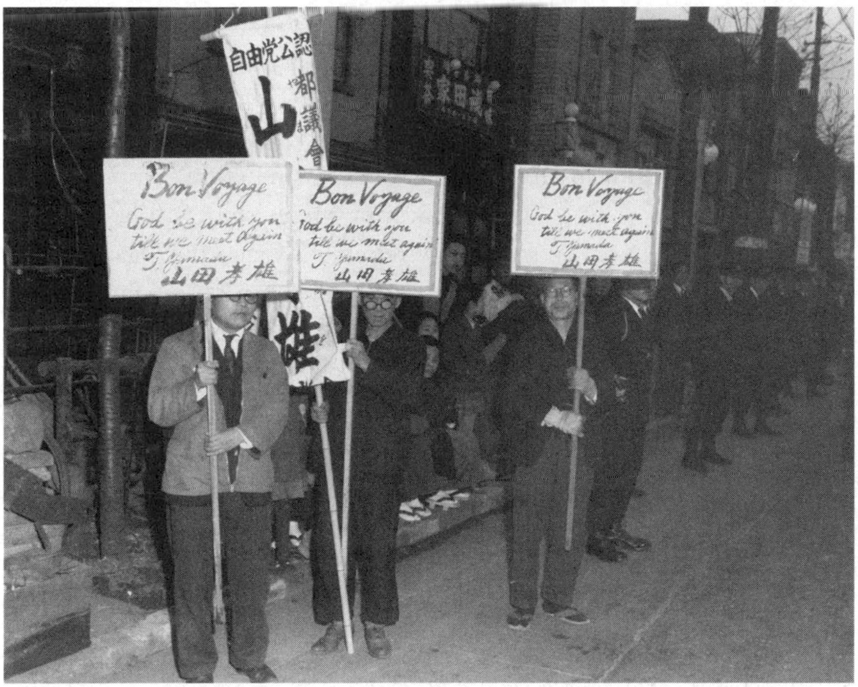

"Bon Voyage" and "God Be with You" from Japanese well-wishers, April 16, 1951. (U.S. ARMY MILITARY HISTORY INSTITUTE)

Missouri characterized as "the voice of God."[26] The reaction to MacArthur's firing was stupendous. In San Gabriel, California, students hanged an effigy of Truman. In Ponca City, Oklahoma, a dummy representing Acheson was soaked in oil and then burned. At MacArthur's birthplace in Little Rock, Arkansas, citizens lowered the flags to half mast. In Lafayette, Indiana, workers carrying signs "Impeach Truman" paraded in the rain. Senator Richard Nixon from California reported that he had received more than six hundred telegrams on the first day of the news of MacArthur's recall, and most were in favor of impeachment of Truman. "It is the largest spontaneous reaction I've ever seen," said Nixon, who demanded MacArthur's immediate reinstatement. Before the day was over, the White House had received seventeen hundred telegrams about MacArthur, three to one against his removal.[27] Republicans spoke threateningly of "impeaching" the president. Pro-administration voices, however, were heard in the two houses of Congress, both controlled by the Democrats, Truman's party. House Speaker Sam Rayburn spoke for many of the president's supporters when he declared, "We must never give up [the principle] that the military is subject to and under the control of the civilian administration."[28]

Throughout Europe, MacArthur's dismissal was greeted as welcome news, as the Europeans had long feared his mercurial ambition and desire to widen the war. "The removal of MacArthur will be received with dry eyes; yes with extraordinary relief," reported the Danish newspaper *Afterbladet*, which described Truman's decision as "the most daring during his career." The French, reported Janet Flanner in *The New Yorker*, were "solidly with Truman." Britain's Conservative leader Winston Churchill expressed his approval, stating that "constitutional authority should control the action of military commanders." Ironically, the Russians and the Chinese also approved. But the most impressive support for Truman's decision was the weight of editorial opinion at home. The *New York Times*, *New York Herald Tribune*, *Washington Post*, *Boston Globe*, *Atlanta Journal*, *Minneapolis Tribune*, and *Christian Science Monitor* all endorsed his decision. Truman remained calm throughout the political storm because, as he later confided, "I knew that once all the hullabaloo died down, people would see what he was." As he anticipated, the "hullabaloo" did subside. After Senate hearings investigating MacArthur's dismissal had shown that Truman's decision to relieve the general had been unanimously backed by Secretary of Defense Marshall and the JCS, public opinion turned in favor of the president. In mid-May, Democratic National Committee Chairman William Boyle pronounced that "the public 'furor' over MacArthur's dismissal appeared to be subsiding," and that the Senate hearings had "helped to blow away much of the fog and bring out the facts."[29]

Spring Offensive

While the Truman administration settled on limiting the war, the Chinese decided to make one last effort to drive UN forces out of the peninsula. Although the defeats at Wŏnju and Chipyŏng-ni had demonstrated that a quick victory would be elusive, Mao believed that success was possible with sufficient forces. He thought a million men could do it. This was nearly three times the number of soldiers who had pushed back the UN forces the previous fall and winter.[30] The spring offensive from mid-April to mid-May 1951 would be the last effort for a communist victory and the largest campaign of the Korean War. Peng had reservations about the logistical capacity to support such a massive offensive, but he agreed with the plan, believing that it was more favorable for the CPV to fight now than later, because "the enemy is tired, its troops have not been replenished, its reinforcements have yet to gather, and its military strength is relatively weak."[31] By launching the spring offensive, the CPV could "regain the initiative."[32]

Lieutenant General James Van Fleet replaced Ridgway as the commander of the Eighth Army just before the spring offensive was launched. Only days after taking over, he would be in charge of defending against the massive communist assault. Van Fleet was coming off a highly successful assignment in Greece. In the post–World War II period, Greece had become fertile ground for communism. With Moscow's support, Greek communists initiated an insurgency. At first, Britain provided military and economic assistance, but by early 1947 the British had run out of resources, bankrupted by World War II, the loss of colonies, and the crisis it supported in Europe. Britain asked the United States to accept responsibility for continuing the aid, and it did, thus establishing the Truman Doctrine in March 1947 that committed the United States to help fight communism around the globe. Van Fleet arrived in Greece in late February 1948 to revamp the Greek army, which, among other things, "lacked an offensive spirit" and was shot through with "incompetent older officers."[33] He did such a remarkable job that by August 1949 the Greek army was able to put the communist insurgents on the run. It was a great victory for the Truman Doctrine and a personal triumph for Van Fleet.

Truman and others saw the situations in Korea and Greece as similar, and so it was thought that Van Fleet's success in Greece might be replicated in Korea. Both countries were poor, peninsular with mountainous terrain, and wracked by a brutal civil war with communists who were supported by border states (Soviet support for the Greek communists had been channeled through Yugoslavia, although Tito's split from Stalin closed this route and was a major factor in the defeat of the insurgency). The long-term solution for Korea, like Greece, was thought to be the creation of reliable and effective indigenous security forces that could stand up to the communist threat. Bittman Barth, who served under Van

Fleet in France in 1944, recalled that Van Fleet inspired his men with "quiet self-assurance" that transmitted "a feeling of confidence." The Greeks "admired him tremendously," as would the South Koreans, who later honored him with the epitaph "Father of the ROK Army."[34]

Ridgway told Van Fleet, when he arrived on April 14, that although he would give Van Fleet "the latitude and high respect his ability merited," he would keep a tight rein on operations in Korea: "I undertook to place reasonable restrictions on the advances of the Eighth and ROK Armies. Specifically, I charged Van Fleet to conduct no operations in force beyond the Wyoming Line [the farthest line of advance of UN forces, located slightly north of the 38th parallel] without prior approval of GHQ. I made my wishes unmistakably clear to General Van Fleet with respect to the tactical latitude within which he was to operate."[35] Ridgway's decision to closely oversee Eighth Army operations was warranted because he was concerned that Van Fleet might share MacArthur's view on the war and might, perhaps inadvertently, initiate actions that could widen it. One of Ridgway's first official acts as the new head of Far East Command was to issue a "directive" to his senior commanders that succinctly laid out the basic principles on which the war was to be waged to support the UN and U.S. policy for limiting the war:

> The grave and ever present danger that the conduct of our current operations may result in the extension of hostilities, and so lead to a worldwide conflagration, places a heavy responsibility upon all elements of this Command, but particularly upon those capable of offensive action. In accomplishing our assigned missions, this responsibility is ever present. It is a responsibility not only to superior authority in the direct command chain, but inescapably to the American people. It can be discharged ONLY if every Commander is fully alive to the possible consequences of his acts; if every Commander has imbued his Command with a like sense of responsibility for its acts; has set up, and by frequent tests, has satisfied himself of the effectiveness of his machinery for insuring his control of the offensive actions of his command and of its reactions to enemy action; and, in final analysis, is himself determined that no act of his Command shall bring about an extension of the present conflict . . . International tensions within and bearing upon this Theater have created acute danger of World War III. Instructions from higher authority reflect the intense determination of our people, and of all the free peoples of the world, to prevent this catastrophe, if that can be done without appeasement, or sacrifice of principle.[36]

Ridgway also issued a more specific "Letter of Instructions" to Van Fleet designed "to prevent expansion of the Korean conflict." He instructed Van Fleet that "your mission is to repel aggression against so much of the territory (and the people therein) of the Republic of Korea, as you now occupy and, in collaboration with the Government of the Republic of Korea, to establish and maintain order in said territory . . . Acquisition of terrain in itself is of little or no value."[37] Bradley later wrote, "It was a great relief to finally have a man in Tokyo who was in agreement with the administration's views on containing the war."[38]

The spring offensive was launched on April 22, just eight days after Van Fleet's arrival. The communist forces struck in two tremendous and simultaneous blows: a main effort in the west by Chinese troops and a supporting attack in the east, through rugged mountains, by the North Koreans. In the west, 250,000 Chinese attacked the I and IX Corps with the aim of capturing Seoul by May 1. Most of the units of the two corps were American, but I Corps also included the Twenty-Ninth British Brigade, and each corps had an ROK division, which, given its weaker strength, proved to be an Achilles' heel. The ROK Sixth Division in the IX Corps was overwhelmed and collapsed, threatening the U.S. Twenty-Fourth Division to its west and the First Marine Division to its east with envelopment. The collapse of the ROK Sixth Division symbolized for many, then and since, the weakness of the ROK Army. Some blamed the inadequacy of the unit's weaponry and training against overwhelming Chinese force, but many others blamed poor leadership and cowardice. It was an ignoble fate for a division whom some credited for having saved the nation by mounting an effective and stubborn defense in the Ch'unch'ŏn area in the opening days of the war, an action that threw off the North Korean schedule and bought time for UN forces to arrive.

The First Marine Division, with an exposed flank, was forced to fall back. The U.S. Twenty-Fourth Division's exposed eastern flank posed an even more serious challenge. It appeared that the Chinese plan was a wide envelopment of Seoul from the east in concert with the main thrust from the north. Fortunately, the Twenty-Seventh Commonwealth Infantry Brigade, consisting of British, Canadian, Australian, New Zealand, and Indian units, made a heroic stand at Kapyŏng and checked the eastern arm of the offensive. In the west, the Chinese attack concentrated on the weakest part of the front line, the sector held by the ROK First

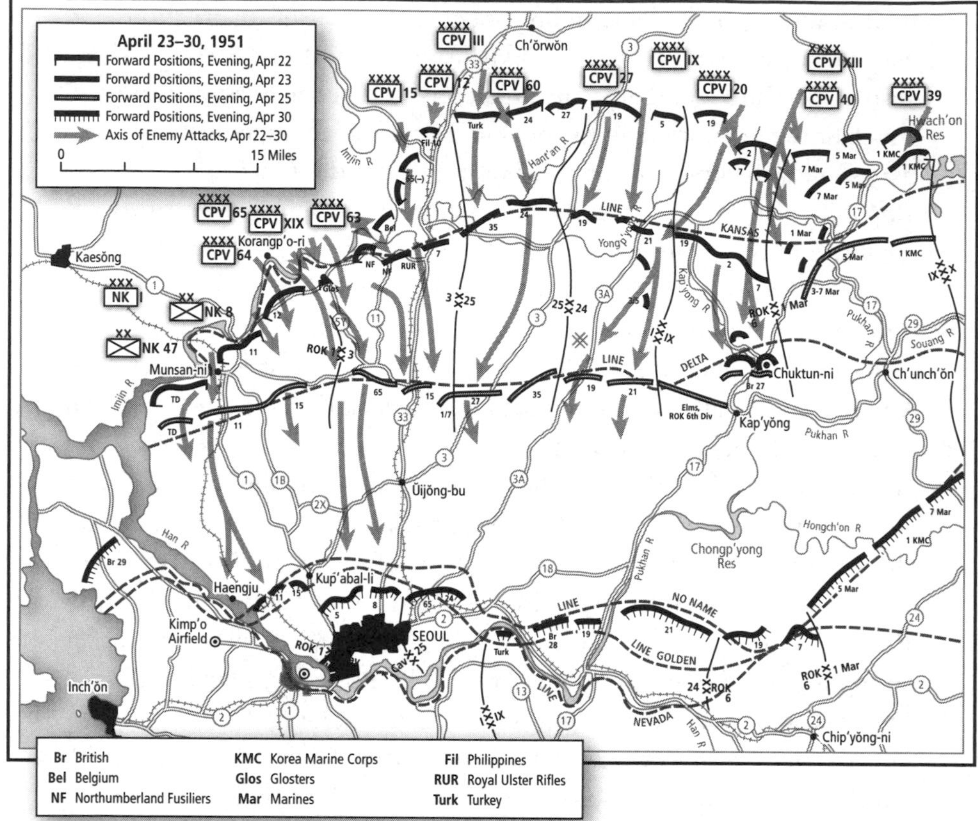

Chinese spring offensive, April 22–30, 1951. (MAP ADAPTED FROM MOSSMAN, *EBB AND FLOW*)

Division occupying the westernmost end. To its eastern flank was the British 29th Infantry Brigade. These forces held the gates to Seoul, and if they collapsed, not only Seoul but the entire front would be in danger of being rolled up.

The capture of Seoul seemed to be the communists' main objective. Though Ridgway had not changed his view about not holding real estate just for its own sake, he believed that for psychological and symbolic reasons, Seoul had become an overwhelming stake for Mao, especially after the defeats at Wŏnju and Chipyŏng-ni. Ridgway instructed Van Fleet to make a strong stand for Seoul: "I attach considerable importance to the retention of Seoul. Now that we have it, it is of considerable more value, psychologically, than its acquisition was when we were south of the Han."[39] Van Fleet agreed and thought that losing the capital would also have a deleterious effect on ROK forces. "Seoul had been given up twice before," Van Fleet later recalled. "I felt that to give it up a third time would take the spirit out of a [Korean] nation. It would destroy morale completely to lose their capital."[40] The war devolved to a battle for Seoul. Given the CPV's logistical shortcomings, Van Fleet estimated that holding them up for several days north of Seoul with delaying or blocking actions would be sufficient to exhaust their supplies and give the UN force enough time to establish a strong defensive line. This critical mission largely fell on the British 29th Brigade with its attached Belgian battalion. It was deployed widely along the Imjin River at the most traditional crossing point, where armies had swept north and south through the peninsula over the past centuries. It was no different this time, as the main thrust of the Chinese pointed at the heart of the brigade. Due to the wide front that the British and Belgians had to hold, the line was not continuous, islands of companies being separated by wide-open stretches. Holding back the Chinese main assault would be a difficult if not an impossible task.

Magnificent Glosters

The British 29th Brigade had arrived in Korea in early November 1950, just in time to be initiated into the war with the Chinese intervention and the UN retreat. As with all British formations, its units possessed long and proud martial histories, going back as far as the seventeenth century, and had served in some of the most storied and exotic corners of the British Empire. Many of the soldiers were reservists who had been in World War II, and at an average age of thirty, many were married with children when they were called back to duty. The Belgian battalion with its Luxembourg platoon was attached to the brigade on the eve of the battle at Imjin River.

The Chinese struck on the night of April 22. In the initial assault, the Belgian battalion was surrounded and cut off. For twenty-four hours the Belgians' situation was precarious, but they held off the Chinese until they could be rescued and fall back. The next day, two British battalions, the Glosters (1st Battalion of the Gloucestershire Regiment) and the Royal Ulster Fusiliers, were besieged by Chinese forces. The incredible mobility of the Chinese on foot over the rough terrain enabled them to surround these units by infiltrating through the open stretches in the line. By mid-morning the battalions were forced to contract to hilltop perimeters. The Chinese also put terrific pressure on the ROK First Division, which was covering the British brigade's western flank. While it did not collapse like the ROK Sixth Division, it was nevertheless driven back several miles, exposing the Glosters' flank. The Glosters, anchoring the brigade's western end, found themselves in considerable difficulty as the Chinese completed their encirclement. The battalion, having suffered many casualties, was tightly ensconced atop a single hill, Hill 235. Its commanding officer, Lt. Col. James Carne, inquired about a possible withdrawal before the noose became too tight. Brigadier Tom Brodie, the brigade commanding officer, told Carne to stay put and hold out for just a few more hours. "I understand the position quite clearly," Carne replied. "What I must make clear to you is the fact that my command is no longer an effective fighting force. If it is required that we shall stay here, in spite of this, we shall continue to hold."[41]

Brodie assured Carne that a rescue mission was on its way. By this time, however, the Chinese had penetrated so far behind the lines that a rescue mission was increasingly becoming unfeasible. Ammunition, food, water, and medical supplies were running dangerously short. The men were more thirsty than hungry. "The heat of the day and the loss of sweat in the march up to the night position made them thirsty, and there was no water," recalled Capt. Anthony Farrar-Hockley, the battalion's adjutant. Aerial resupply was attempted, but the perimeter was small and located atop a steep hill surrounded by the Chinese, making accurate air drops nearly impossible. One pilot asked if "there (was) any means of marking a dropping zone." Farrar-Hockley said he felt like shouting over the radio, "Tell them to aim for a high rock with a lot of Chinese around it!" Many of the bundles rolled down the hillsides to the Chinese. Substantial air support was also committed, but it did not relieve the situation.[42]

Early on the morning of April 25, after nearly three days of intense fighting, the 29th Brigade received orders to withdraw. Carne explained the situation to his men and told them that the battalion could not carry on as a unit. He gave them the option of surrendering or fighting their way out as separate groups. All opted to make their way out. Three of

Top of Gloster Hill (Hill 235) shortly after the battle. (SOLDIERS OF GLOUCESTERSHIRE MUSEUM)

the four companies along with the staff at battalion headquarters headed south directly toward the UN line. Very few made it through, and most of them were captured, including Carne. The fourth company's commander, Capt. Mike Harvey, decided on a counterintuitive route and proceeded north. This took his men straight into the Chinese rear, where they were able to swing around to the west and then south toward the UN line. For the next few miles Harvey and his group did not encounter any Chinese. Adding to their good fortune, they were spotted by a UN aircraft, which began guiding them homeward through the hills. Suddenly, they came under heavy fire from the Chinese, but then they saw American tanks just ahead of them down the valley. As they raced toward the tanks, however, the Americans mistook them for Chinese and opened fire, killing six. Horrified, the aircraft pilot flew frantically over the tanks and dropped a note from the sky. Realizing their mistake, the Americans ceased their fire, and the Glosters rushed forward for cover behind the tanks. The Americans were heartsick over their mistake. The lieutenant in charge asked how many were killed. Captain Harvey did not want to make the Americans feel any worse than he had to, so he did not answer.[43]

Of the original 699 men, only 77 made it out.[44] A large number were captured and spent over two years in POW camps. Van Fleet described the Glosters' action as "the most outstanding example of unit bravery in modern warfare." Although there was much recrimination about who was responsible for the debacle—some blamed Brodie for not giving the withdrawal order earlier, while others blamed Carne for not communicating more clearly the dire situation—Van Fleet concluded that the loss of the Glosters had not been in vain: "This is one of those great occasions in combat which called for a determined stand," he later wrote. "The loss of 622 officers and men saved many times that number."[45] The British 29th Brigade had held for sixty crucial hours, which had not only severely gutted the Chinese force but also seriously disrupted their schedule and momentum. It had also bought enough time to establish a firm defense line to protect Seoul. On the night of April 27–28, the Chinese made one final effort, but they were unable to overcome the defense

Glosters taken prisoner are on a break while on their way to a POW camp on the Yalu River. (SOLDIERS OF GLOUCESTERSHIRE MUSEUM)

Brigadier Tom Brodie, commander of the British 29th Brigade, unveiling a memorial to the men who lost their lives during the battle at Imjin River, July 5, 1951. (U.S. NATIONAL ARCHIVES AND RECORDS ADMINISTRATION)

line or sustain their attack. By April 29, there was a palpable diminution of the offensive. "After we had turned back the enemy's first greatest onslaught by April 28," recalled Van Fleet, "we dug in and waited for him to come. We waited and waited and he did not come."[46] Despite the huge losses, the Chinese had not yet given up hope. Turning their sights eastward, they planned a "second phase" of the spring offensive.

Victory Denied?

Detecting the CPV's shift eastward, Van Fleet thought the Chinese were planning to attack down the Pukhan River valley to envelope Seoul from the southeast.[47] Unexpectedly, the offensive was launched on May 16 much farther to the east than Van Fleet had estimated. Massive CPV and North Korean forces struck UN forces situated from the central region to the east coast. Van Fleet had placed his units mainly to defend Seoul and now faced an all-out attack on his weaker eastern sector. The main

CPV effort was against X Corps and ROK III Corps, with a supporting attack against ROK I Corps deployed by the east coast. The four ROK divisions in X Corps and ROK III Corps rapidly collapsed. This exposed the U.S. Second Division's right flank in a replay of the events of November 1950, when the collapse of the ROK Sixth Division placed the entire Second Division in a similar predicament that had led to its virtual destruction. The objective of the attack in the east was uncertain, but one possibility was to advance to Pusan. "This was a startling development," recalled General Almond.[48]

The communist offensive met initial success, especially in the exploitation of the gap opened by the collapse of the ROK units. U.S. units to the west of the gap and ROK units from I Corps to the east were forced to fall back, creating a large bulge in the UN lines. But the shoulders held with rapid reinforcements and a shifting of forces from the western sector. Punishing artillery and air attacks exacted an enormous toll on the Chinese troops. By the third day, the offensive began to wane. Sensing the enemy's exhaustion and with Ridgway's urging, Van Fleet and Almond formed a counteroffensive plan that would, if successful, turn the game around and surround the bulk of the communist forces. IX Corps supported by I Corps would attack from the west and cut off lines of communication, supply, and, most importantly, reinforcement or withdrawal routes in the western half. X Corps, supported by ROK I Corps, would attack in the east to cut off similar lines in the eastern half. It was a bold plan nearly worthy of the Inch'ŏn operation in its ambition and objective. If successful, the entire eastern half of the front would be torn wide open, and a majority of the communist forces neutralized.

On May 20, merely four days after the communist offensive started, the western attack was initiated, joined by the eastern attack on May 23. Peng decided on May 21 to cut his horrendous losses and not only halt the offensive, but rapidly pull his forces back to a line about ten miles north of where they had started, because it was more defensible. The UN attacks were overly cautious and slow and allowed the bulk of the enemy to escape. By July 1, UN forces had pushed the communists back twenty-five to fifty miles north all across the front, establishing a line that more or less remained static for the next two years, until the armistice.

Despite the failure to completely destroy the attacking communist forces, the outcome was a triumph for the UN forces in general and the

U.S. Army, and especially X Corps, in particular. During the opening days of the counteroffensive, wrote Van Fleet, UN forces "offered no resistance at all in the east or along the coast." He concluded, "The Red soldier in that advance must have thought it was a very easy war." However, on the third day, "we launched a counterattack in the main area of battle and instead of being outflanked by the Reds who had poured down the mountains and roads east for as much as 50 miles, we pinched them off and disposed of them at leisure."[49] Van Fleet had beaten the Chinese at their own game.

The success of the counteroffensive presented an opportunity to destroy the Chinese army and, by extension, a chance to win the war. Years later, Van Fleet would bitterly recall that the chance to end the war in May–June 1951 was squandered. This was not November 1950,

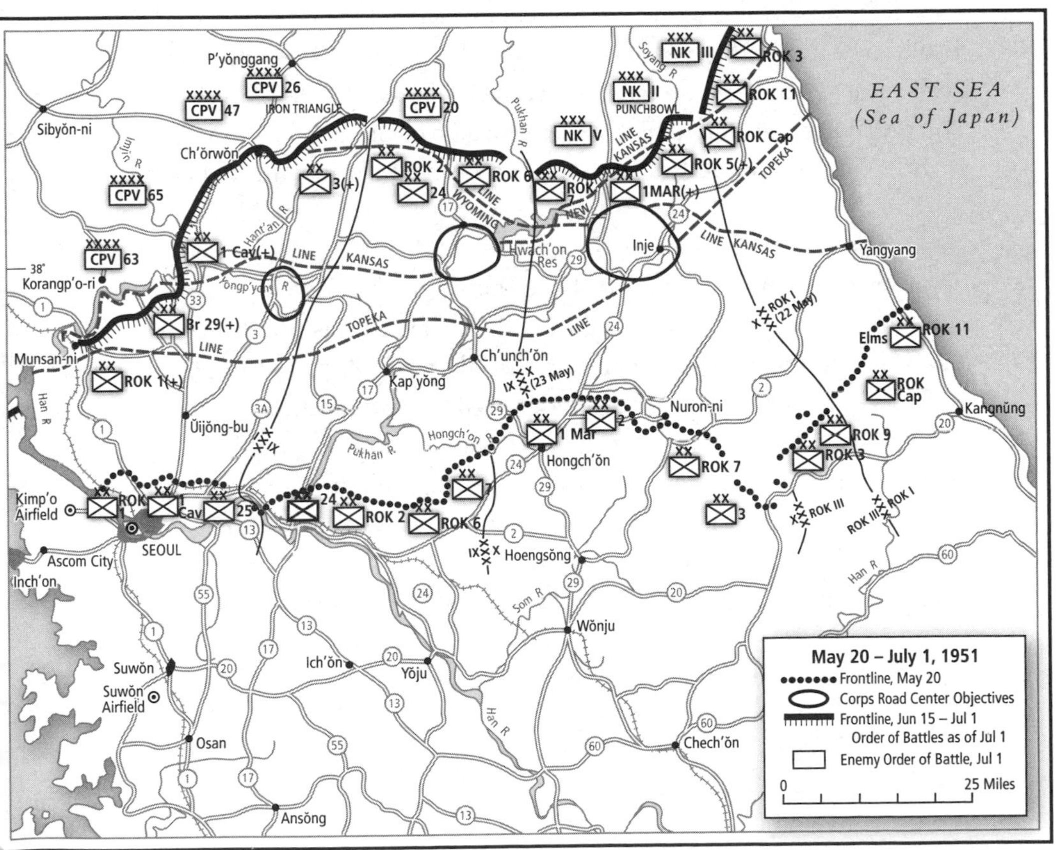

Eighth Army advance, May 20–July 1, 1951. (MAP ADAPTED FROM MOSSMAN, *EBB AND FLOW*)

when MacArthur had made his foolhardy plunge to the Yalu to face a fresh, strong, and eager Chinese army. After the huge casualties and deprivations suffered by the Chinese forces since the winter, Van Fleet believed they were tired, weak, and perhaps morally defeated. "The mission to which we had been assigned, to establish a defensive line across the peninsula, was accomplished," recalled Van Fleet, "though we could have readily followed up our successes and defeated the enemy, but that was not the intention of Washington."[50] Sensing Van Fleet's frustration, Ridgway wrote to him, "Because of this particularly sensitive period politically, I would like you and your most senior officers . . . meticulously to avoid all public statements about the Korean situation which pass beyond the purely military field."[51] Ridgway did not want another MacArthur-esque fiasco. Had the political will existed, a military victory might have been possible since the communist front lay wide open. "We met the attack and routed the enemy," Van Fleet later wrote. "We had him beaten and could have destroyed his armies. Those days are the ones most vivid in my memory, great days when all of the Eighth Army, and we thought America too, were inspired to win."[52]

But Washington and its allies wanted only to bring the fighting to an end. No one could determine for sure what Mao would do if UN forces once again advanced to the Yalu. Surely, the Chinese forces would regroup and continue the fight. Then there was the issue of what Stalin might do if the war was extended to China. There was also little likelihood that North Korean communists would have simply accepted their defeat. Given the nature of the vicious civil war that preceded June 1950, disaffected Korean communists, northern and southern, would undoubtedly have taken up arms and continued the fight in an insurgency. With objectives to bring about "an end to the fighting, and a return to the status quo" achieved, Acheson told the Senate on June 7 that UN forces would accept an armistice. It was time to end the Korean War.

CHAPTER NINE

The Stalemate

Secretary of State Dean Acheson was cautious but receptive to the overture for a cease-fire and an armistice from the Soviet ambassador to the UN, Yakov Malik, on June 23, 1951. There were doubts about the Soviets' sincerity, but Acheson nonetheless responded quickly to seize an opportunity to end the fighting.[1] General Ridgway was more skeptical. Although he found the prospect of a cease-fire "not unwelcomed," he deeply distrusted the communists. He sent a message to "all commanders" in the field lest they began to let down their guards. "Two things should be recalled" about the Soviets, he warned: "One is the well-earned reputation for duplicity and dishonesty," and "the other is the slowness with which deliberative bodies such as the [UN] Security Council produce positive action." He cautioned General Van Fleet to "personally assure yourself that all elements of your command are made aware of the danger of such a relaxation of effort and that you insist on an intensification rather than a diminution of the United Nations' action in this theater."[2]

Ridgway was right to be cautious. In light of recent evidence, the Soviet proposal appears to have been disingenuous. In a cable to Mao in early June, Stalin stated that the best strategy to pursue was "a long and drawn out war in Korea." By then, the Eighth Army's successful counteroffensive had seriously disrupted the communist forces. A cease-fire would have been advantageous to the communists, as it would have allowed the Chinese and the North Koreans to rest and regroup. "The war in Korea should not be speeded up," Stalin advised Mao, "a drawn out war, in the first place, gives the possibility to Chinese troops to study contemporary warfare on the field of battle and in the second place, shakes up the Truman regime in America and harms the military prestige of the Anglo-American troops."[3] Given the fighting and casualties suffered since October, the Chinese leadership probably thought they had learned enough. But Mao's exchanges with Stalin indicate that he was willing to continue the war. His reaction to a potential end of hostilities appeared ambivalent.[4] Although Mao responded favorably to an offer made by Ridgway, as the UNC commander, on June 29 to discuss an armistice, Mao's message to Stalin two weeks earlier gave no indication that Mao was thinking about an armistice at all. "The position at the front in June will be such that our forces will be comparatively weaker than those of the enemy," he wrote. "In July we will be stronger than in June, and in August we will be even stronger. We will be ready in August to make a stronger blow to the enemy."[5]

In June, Mao's intention was to use the operational pause during armistice negotiations to rebuild his forces and eventually resume the offensive, but his communications in July and August indicated that he was willing to conclude an armistice if it was accomplished in a manner that would not undermine China's prestige.[6] Mao was anxious to avoid unfavorable armistice terms that would threaten not only his leadership position, but the revolution itself. The Chinese regime was careful in how it presented the new strategy of ending the war to the Chinese people. On July 3, the Central Committee issued "Instructions on the Propaganda Affairs Concerning the Peace Negotiations in Korea," which began with the point that "peace has been the very purpose of the CPV's participation in the anti-aggression war in Korea."[7] The United States was to be portrayed as the weaker party, "that it was the American leadership who had solicited negotiations and an armistice" and not China.[8] Mao already viewed the war as a victory for China: it had fought the world's greatest superpower to a standstill, and he was not about to sabotage this perception. The British reporter and communist sympathizer Alan Winnington noted, "This is the first time Oriental Communists have ever sat down at a conference table on terms of equality with Americans, and they intend to make the most of it."[9]

Ridgway had no interest in enhancing China's or Mao's prestige. He identified several points that he did not like in Beijing's response accepting his June 29 proposal for a meeting to discuss an armistice. The most important clause was: "We agree to suspend military activities and to hold peace negotiations," meaning, first stop fighting and then talk.[10] In passing Beijing's message to the JCS, Ridgway wrote that a suspension of military activities would "gravely prejudice the safety and security of UN forces" and would be "wholly unacceptable." For their part, Chinese leaders believed that the fighting thus far had taught the Americans that neither side could achieve military victory, and therefore assumed that suspension of fighting and restoration of the 38th parallel as the border would be acceptable.[11]

Both sides had valid concerns. But whereas Mao was seeking ways to preserve and enhance China's and his prestige, using the armistice negotiations with the world's most powerful nation for domestic propaganda purposes, Ridgway had no intention of compromising on anything. Why should he yield anything to the Chinese when the UN forces were strong and had the advantage? When armistice negotiations started in July, Ridgway told the UN team's chief delegate, Vice Adm. C. Turner Joy, that the basic UN position was an "implacable opposition to communism." In his "Guidance Memo," Ridgway instructed the delegates that they were "to lead from strength not weakness." Ridgway concluded that if UN negotiators could "cap the military defeat of the Communists in Korea" with skillful handling of the armistice talks, "history may record that communist military aggression reached its high water mark in Korea, and that thereafter, communism itself began its recession in Asia."[12]

Truce Talks

Each side's negotiating team consisted of five principal military delegates. Admiral Joy, commander of U.S. Naval Forces Far East, led the UN team, which included Maj. Gen. Paek Sŏn-yŏp, the commanding general of the ROK I Corps, who represented the ROK but only as an observer. On the communist side, the senior delegate was Lt. Gen. Nam Il, the NKPA's chief of staff and a veteran of the Soviet Army in World War II, where he participated in some of the greatest battles including Stalingrad. The Chinese, however, took control of all major policy decisions at the talks, but only after coordination with Moscow. The initial meeting was held on July 10 at Kaesŏng. The UN team soon realized that it had been a mistake to agree to meet in this ancient capital city. The supposed "neutral zone" was a facade as it was full of Chinese and North Korean

The UN delegation arrives at the negotiation site in Kaesŏng, July 10, 1951. (U.S. ARMY MILITARY HISTORY INSTITUTE)

soldiers. The situation was particularly galling for Ridgway, because UN forces had held Kaesŏng before the talks and withdrew to make it "neutral." He also appeared to be unaware of Kaesŏng's symbolic importance to the North Koreans until after the talks began. Over a thousand years earlier, Kaesŏng had been the capital of the ancient kingdom of Koguryŏ, whose territory encompassed all of North Korea as well as a large part of Northeast China. Koguryŏ was conquered by a southern kingdom, Silla, in the unification wars of the seventh century. Silla's ancient territory was now part of South Korea. For North Korea, seeing itself as part reincarnation of Koguryŏ and engaged in another war of unification, Kaesŏng symbolized, if not the possibility of a reversal of that ancient defeat, at least the continued preservation of the northern "kingdom."

It was soon apparent that the Kaesŏng arrangement was a propaganda stage rather than a sincere venue for talks. The UN delegation was required to arrive bearing a white flag as if in surrender and to be escorted by communist troops, journalists, and photographers. The UN press corps, much less soldiers, were prevented from entering the area. The UN, or more specifically, the Americans, were portrayed as coming to Kaesŏng to plead for peace. The talks got off to a predictably rocky start. "At the first meeting of the delegates," recalled Admiral Joy, "I seated myself at the conference table and almost sank out of sight. The communists had provided a chair for me which was considerably shorter than a standard chair." Meanwhile, "across the table, the senior Communist delegate, General Nam Il, protruded a good foot above my cagily diminished stature. This had been accomplished by providing stumpy Nam Il with a chair about four inches higher than usual." Other indignities followed. During a recess, Joy was threatened by a communist guard "who pointed a burp gun at me and growled menacingly." Joy's courier, who had been instructed to carry an interim report to Ridgway, was halted and forcibly turned back. A guard posted "conspicuously besides the access doorway wore a gaudy medal which he proudly related to Col. Andrew J. Kinney was for 'killing forty Americans.'" Joy had had enough. On July 12, the UN delegation walked out. The talks resumed three days later after the armed communist personnel were withdrawn.[13]

After much haggling over the physical arrangement of the negotiation room, the discussion finally turned to the agenda. The UN delegation presented three main items: establishment of a truce line, exchange of POWs, and an enforcement mechanism for the armistice. The communists agreed to these but added one more: the withdrawal of all foreign armed forces from Korea. Joy rejected this item as a political matter, which it was, and not appropriate to the armistice talks, which were limited to military matters. A few days later the communist side agreed to drop the withdrawal issue after the UN team stood uncompromisingly firm against its inclusion. The communists then raised the stakes by proposing that the 38th parallel be the line of truce and that a cease-fire be declared during the negotiations. When the talks started, UN forces were in possession of a significant amount of territory in good defensible terrain north of the 38th, especially in the eastern and the central regions. Using the 38th as the truce line would be highly disadvantageous to the UN. Mao confided to Stalin that "it is possible there will be some divergence," but "our proposal is extremely just and it will be difficult for the enemy to refute."[14] Since the 38th had been recognized as the boundary before the war, the communists advocated that it be simply restored. The UNC rejected the proposal outright, stating that the 38th parallel "has no significance to the existing military situation."[15] A proposed cease-fire was also rejected as it was seen as a ruse to build up and strengthen the communist forces.

The communists were angered by the UN response. General Nam described the UN position as "incredible," "naïve and illogical," and "absurd and arrogant." Nam then proposed the 38th parallel as the truce line with a twelve-mile-wide demilitarized zone, in contrast to the UN's proposal for a twenty-mile-wide zone. The talks deadlocked. A perturbed Mao wrote to Stalin for advice. A month had passed, and no progress had been made. The truce line was, thus far, the only issue discussed. Mao had come to believe that "from the entire course of the conference and the general situation outside the conference, it is apparent that it is not possible to force the enemy to accept the proposal about the 38th parallel." He concluded, "We think that it is better to think over the question of cessation of military operations at the present front line than to carry on the struggle for the 38th Parallel and bring the conference to a breakdown."[16] Under pressure from Washington, the UN team made a concession: to accept the communist proposal for a twelve-mile-wide demilitarized zone. The communists stated that they were considering the line of military contact, as proposed by the UN, for the truce line.[17]

The communists abruptly broke off the talks on August 23, alleging that an American aircraft had bombed a neutral area near Kaesŏng. They also alleged that a few days earlier "enemy troops, dressed in civilian clothes, made a raid on our security forces in the neutral zone in Kaesŏng," killing a Chinese soldier and wounding another.[18] The UN delegation refuted the allegations after its own investigations.[19] Yet, given Mao's earlier message to Stalin that he wanted to avoid a breakdown in the negotiations "at all costs," it is difficult to understand why such incidents would have been staged. It is likely that the ground raid was the work of South Korean partisans conducted without coordination or permission from the UNC. The ROK Army and partisan operations had been responsible for a number of previous violations in the area, and it is possible that President Rhee, who vociferously opposed the talks, ordered them to disrupt the negotiations. Mao wrote to Stalin in late August that "the enemy, in justifying himself, stated that this was [committed by] partisans from the South Korean partisan detachment active in our region, and therefore he does not take any responsibility

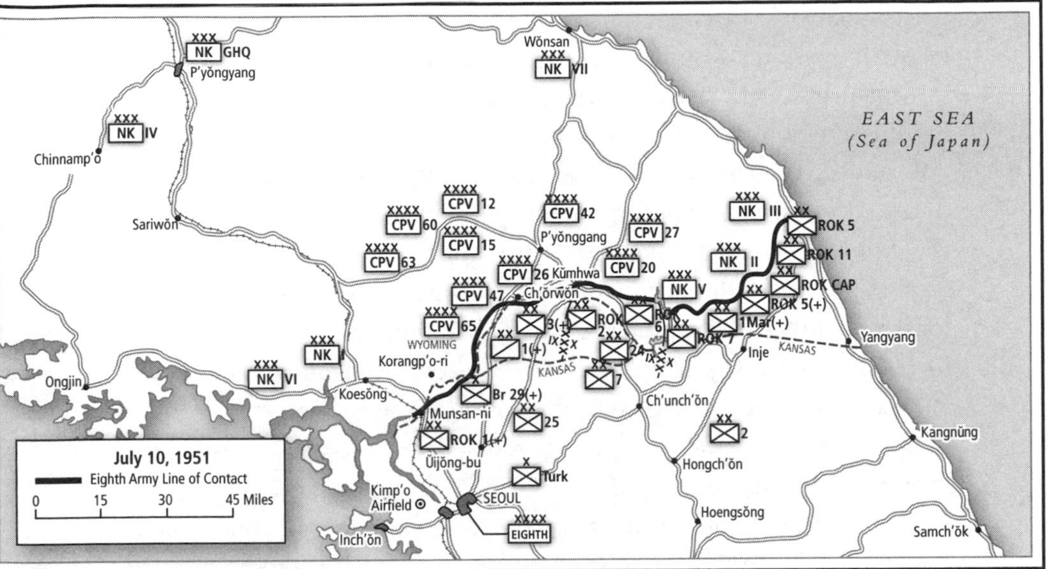

The front line in early July 1951. (ADAPTED FROM WALTER G. HERMES, *TRUCE TENT AND FIGHTING FRONT*, U.S. GOVERNMENT PRINTING OFFICE, 1996)

for it . . . The negotiations will not be resumed until we receive a satisfactory answer."[20]

The talks remained suspended for the next two months, during which time the UNC conducted a series of limited-objective attacks that pushed the front line north an average of fifteen miles. In the meantime, Ridgway had been fighting a less visible, but no less hotly contested battle with Rhee. The old patriot was adamantly opposed to a truce of any kind. In mid-July, Rhee pressed Ridgway to continue the war to victory. Van Fleet alerted Ridgway to "rumors to the effect that the ROK Army was prepared in the event of any settlement along the 38th parallel, to continue the fighting regardless of the consequences." Ridgway then reminded Rhee that "if the UN troops were withdrawn from Korea, the country would be united in slavery."[21] Truman warned Rhee that "it is of the utmost importance that your Government takes no unilateral action which would jeopardize the armistice discussions."[22] Truman implied that should Rhee continue to oppose the talks or threaten unilateral action, the U.S. and other UN forces were prepared to withdraw from Korea. Temporarily chastised, Rhee nevertheless continued to disrupt the armistice talks in other ways, hoping that the UN team's mounting frustration with the communists would eventually lead to the end of the negotiations and a resumption of an all-out effort to "win" the war.

Meanwhile, other nations, especially the British, were pulling Washington in the opposite direction, urging a more flexible stance to get the talks moving and an armistice signed.[23] India proposed that the foreign ministers of the major powers meet to get the talks back on track.[24] While the Truman administration had no intention of broadening the number of participants in the negotiations, Washington was also aware that the longer the talks dragged on, the greater the pressure of "world opinion" to resolve matters quickly. To make matters even more complicated, Ridgway insisted that the site of negotiations be moved from Kaesŏng to a neutral zone. The communists refused, accusing the Americans of "creating a pretext for breaking off negotiations." The impasse finally ended in early October when the Chinese agreed to move the venue to P'anmunjŏm, south of Kaesŏng, in no-man's land between the two sides. The talks resumed later in October, with the truce-line issue at the top of the agenda. Despite pressure from the allies, Ridgway showed no flexibility in terms that now included the return of Kaesŏng to UN control in exchange for territory on the east coast.[25]

Facing another deadlock, the communists made a surprising offer. In what many rightly viewed as a breakthrough and a major concession, they offered to accept the battle line, instead of the 38th parallel, as the truce line, provided the UN agreed to its implementation immediately. In effect, they proposed that the fighting stop before other issues are resolved and an armistice is put into effect. The UN team rejected the offer. Suspending all military operations would mean a de facto ceasefire, which would end any leverage the UN might have to influence the communists' behavior. "The agreement to this proposal," argued Ridgway, "would provide an insurance policy under which the communists would be insured against the effects of the UNC military operation during the discussions of other items on the agenda."[26] If the proposal was accepted, the communists could indefinitely drag on negotiations on the remaining agenda items without fear of UN military reprisal.

Washington was upset at Ridgway's rejection. The UN team's rigid position threatened to drag the war on unnecessarily and was affecting public support for it. An opinion poll in October 1951 revealed that 67 percent agreed with the proposition that the war in Korea was "utterly useless." Senator Robert Taft (Ohio), a Republican presidential candidate for 1952, attacked the administration: "Stalemated peace is better than a stalemated war we had better curtail our losses of 2,000 casualties a week in a war that can't accomplish anything."[27] The British, America's most important ally, in particular, were concerned by what they perceived as "American intransigence."

With public and official opinion in the United States and abroad swinging in support of the communist proposal, the State–Defense committee that oversaw the negotiations in Washington informed Ridgway, through the JCS, of the following: "Throughout we have taken as basic principle that the demarcation line should be generally along the battle line. Communists now appear to have accepted this principle. We feel that in general this adequately meets our minimum position re DMZ [demilitarized zone]." Regarding Ridgway's concern that the communists would drag on the negotiations indefinitely while a de facto cease-fire was in effect, the message proposed provisional acceptance "qualified by a time limitation for completion of all agenda items."[28] This meant that the truce line would become void if an armistice was not completed within the deadline.

But Ridgway was still not amenable. He was convinced that without the leverage of constant UN military pressure, the communists would lose a sense of urgency and incentive to make progress in the talks and would continue to strengthen their forces during the respite. The service chiefs disagreed. They felt that the provisional truce was not a de facto cease-fire and certainly did not affect air and naval actions. The truce-line agreement was finalized on November 27 over Ridgway's strong objections. It would expire if other issues were not finalized by December 27. After nearly six months of frustrating negotiations, the first significant agreement had finally been reached. The talks now turned to the remaining agenda items: an armistice enforcement mechanism and the exchange of POWs.

Voluntary Repatriation

Admiral Joy requested an exchange of POW rosters and immediate admission of representatives from the International Committee of the

Red Cross (ICRC) to the communist POW camps. Neither side knew the names or precise number of prisoners held by the other side. Ridgway was initially instructed to seek a POW exchange on a one-for-one basis until all UN prisoners had been returned, and then repatriate the remaining communist prisoners. But there were problems with this scheme. Dean Rusk pointed out that the UNC held about 150,000 prisoners, mostly North Koreans, compared to "less than 10,000 United Nations personnel in enemy hands," and thus the repatriation of all communist POWs "would virtually restore intact to North Korean forces equivalent to the number it possessed at the time of the aggression."[29] This was a moot point under the Geneva Convention, which required repatriation of all POWs by the detaining powers. Although the United States had yet to ratify the 1949 convention, it felt bound to abide by its provisions. However, there was undoubtedly a desire to find a way to limit or delay the reconstitution of the NKPA. Ambassador Muccio raised a related point to Acheson: the long-standing ROK claim that forty thousand of the POWs were South Koreans who had been forced to serve in the NKPA.[30] But how could one distinguish between a genuine and committed North Korean soldier, an anticommunist North Korean conscript, an impressed South Korean civilian, a North Korean who may pretend to be an impressed South Korean, and a pro-North South Korean who had willingly joined the NKPA but claimed otherwise? The situation was further complicated, because at least half of the Chinese prisoners appeared to have been former Nationalist soldiers who were impressed into the CPV.

Brigadier General Robert McClure, the U.S. Army chief of psychological warfare, suggested that prisoners be repatriated voluntarily. Citing moral and humanitarian considerations, McClure was concerned that Koreans and Chinese who had been impressed into the NKPA and the CPV would be "sentenced to slave labor, or executed" upon their return. He pointed out the propaganda value of allowing prisoners to choose where they wanted to be repatriated. A significant number of Chinese prisoners seeking repatriation to Taiwan instead of China "would be a formidable boon to Washington's Asian policies."[31] Furthermore, "if word of it got around, it might encourage other disaffected Chinese soldiers to surrender."[32]

The plan was forwarded to the National Security Council. Acheson vigorously objected to it. While he recognized "the possible psychological warfare advantages of the proposed policy," it was "difficult to see how such a policy could be carried out without conflict with the provisions of the 1949 Geneva Convention which the United States and the Unified Command has expressed its intention of observing in the Korean conflict."[33] The Geneva article pertaining to the treatment of POWs required that all "prisoners of war shall be released and repatriated without delay after the cessation of hostilities."[34] There the matter would probably have died had it not been for Truman's strong interest in the issue. Truman opposed an all-for-all exchange since it was "not on an equitable basis." Nor did he want to send back prisoners who had surrendered or cooperated with the United Nations, "because he believed they [would] be immediately done away with." Truman's position was strongly supported by a State Department counselor, Charles Bohlen, who "personally witnessed the anguish of Russian prisoners forcibly returned home from German prison camps at the end of World War II, many of whom committed suicide rather than reencounter Stalinism."[35] Truman's position, tinged with emotionalism and humanitarianism as well as cold war ideology, violated the Geneva Convention, which had no provisions for either the need for equity in the number of POWs exchanged or exceptions to the all-for-all arrangement. In retrospect, the Geneva code was too black and white, a reaction to the huge numbers of unrepatriated and abused German and Japanese POWs held by the Soviet Union after the end of World War II and the forcible repatriation of Soviet prisoners who did not want to go back and wound up executed. It did not consider the possibility that some POWs did not want or could not be repatriated for legitimate reasons.[36]

But many had reservations about voluntary repatriation. The JCS pointed out that the enemy POWs had been captured while they fought against UN forces, and thus "we had no obligation to let them express their wishes, much less give the other side any pretext for retaining UN troops."[37] General Bradley favored returning all prisoners, "including, even if necessary, the 44,000 ROK personnel [forcibly impressed into the NKPA]."[38] Ridgway was also against voluntary repatriation: "We [the UN team] believe that if we insist on the principle of voluntary repatriation, we may establish a dangerous precedent that may be to our disadvantage in later wars with communist powers," he argued. "Should they ever hold a preponderance of POWs, and then adhere to their adamant stand against any form of neutral visit to their POW camps, we would have no recourse if they said none of our POWs wanted to be repatriated."[39] In early December it was agreed that, at least initially, the UN maintain its position on one-for-one exchange, which would allow the UNC to retain certain classes of prisoners who did not wish repatriation.

The POW rosters were exchanged in mid-December, and each side had cause to complain. North Korea had boasted of capturing over 65,000 ROK prisoners in the early months of the war, and by the end of 1951 the ROK Army identified over 88,000 missing, and yet the North Korean roster contained the names of a little over 7,000 ROK POWs. Part of the discrepancy could be accounted for by the thousands of former ROK Army soldiers who were classified as North Koreans and were therefore among the NKPA POWs. Still, there were tens of thousands who remained unaccounted for. Furthermore, the 4,400 UN POWs listed by the Communists contrasted sharply with the nearly 12,000 Americans and several thousand other UN soldiers identified as missing.[40] Likewise, the communists protested that over 40,000 of their soldiers were missing from the UN list. They claimed 188,000 missing while the UN roster listed only 132,000 (95,000 North Koreans, 21,000 Chinese, and 16,000 South Koreans who joined the NKPA). The UNC claimed that 37,000 were determined to be South Korean civilians impressed into the NKPA and were reclassified as civilian internees and thus not included on the roster. The communists protested "that it was not the place of residence but the army in which a man served that determined whether he should be repatriated or not."[41] While both sides cried foul, the striking disparity in the number of POWs made one thing clear: the communists were unlikely to accept the proposal for an initial one-for-one exchange, followed by repatriation of the remaining prisoners. A decision was therefore made to put the voluntary repatriation principle on the table.

The proposal was introduced in early January 1952, with a predictably explosive reaction from the other side. Maj. Gen. Yi Sang-ch'o, a member of the communist delegation, branded the proposal as "a barbarous formula and a shameful design," which they "absolutely cannot accept."[42] The communists accused the UNC of forcibly holding prisoners and "bluntly violat[ing] the regulations of the Geneva Joint Pledge on POWs' Rights."[43] After weeks of acrimonious exchange, Joy gloomily concluded that "the commies will never give up in their determination to bring about the unconditional release and repatriation of all of their POWs."[44] The thirty-day time limit on the truce line expired on December 27. As Ridgway had feared, the communists had rested and strengthened their forces during the month-long respite. It appeared that the continuation of a stalemated war was inevitable.

With another deadlock, voluntary repatriation faced, according to U. Alexis Johnson, a "serious rearguard defection in the Pentagon."[45] Robert Lovett, who had become secretary of defense in September 1951 after Marshall retired, searched for another solution. Admiral William Fechteler, chief of Naval Operations, and General Hoyt Vandenberg, air force chief of staff, were now firmly opposed to voluntary repatriation. Joy also expressed doubts, believing that the communists would never concede on the issue. He raised the ethical issue of a policy that would prolong the suffering of American POWs instead of seeking their immediate release: "Voluntary repatriation placed the welfare of ex-communist soldiers above that of our own United Nations Command personnel in communist prison camps"[46] However, with Truman still adamantly in favor with the support of the State Department, Lovett agreed not to oppose the idea when discussing it with the president.[47] Prime Minister Churchill, who replaced Attlee in October, also agreed with voluntary repatriation for the same reasons Truman wanted it, and played a key role in building a consensus for the policy in the international community. Other European leaders were concerned about the legality and practical implementation of voluntary repatriation, but key allies from the British Commonwealth, Canada and Australia in particular, were assuaged in their doubts by Churchill's strong support. Doubters also included British Foreign Secretary Anthony Eden, who reminded Churchill that humanitarianism worked both ways and that British prisoners should not be forgotten. How could the British government back a policy that would seek to put the welfare of communist prisoners before that of their own citizens languishing in enemy camps? Churchill, however, was undeterred. In time, Eden came around. "I did not know that our legal grounds were so poor," he wrote at the time, "but this doesn't make me like the idea of sending these poor devils back to death any worse."[48]

The crucial challenge was selling it to the communists. The first task

North Korean prisoners who wanted to remain in the South, June 25, 1952.
(U.S. NATIONAL ARCHIVES AND RECORDS ADMINISTRATION)

was to find out how many communist POWs would opt for repatriation. U. Alexis Johnson, who was visiting Ridgway in early February, wrote, "Hints dropped by communist correspondents at Panmunjom, and other data led us to believe that, as Ridgway put it, numbers and nationalities of the POWs returned, rather than the principles involved, appears to be the controlling issue."[49] If the number of those wanting repatriation was high enough, the communists might be amenable. Ridgway's staff estimated that about 16,000 would choose not to be repatriated, leaving about 116,000 who would.[50] When the communists were given these figures in early April, they did not balk and instead proposed that the issue be deferred until both sides determined the exact number of prisoners to be exchanged. The UNC had reached a point of no return. By agreeing to carry out the screening process, the UNC was now fully committed to the principle of voluntary repatriation and would henceforth be honor-bound not to return those who had identified themselves as anticommunists.

The results of the UN screening were as unexpected as they were astonishing. "Our procedures," recalled Johnson, "were actually designed to favor repatriation. Within the camps, we publicized a command offer of amnesty to all POWs who chose repatriation, stressing that refusing to go home might open their relatives to reprisals, made clear that those refusing repatriation might have to stay on Kŏje Island [UNC POW camp] long after others had gone home, and promised nothing about what eventually would become of them." The screening revealed that only 70,000, a little over half, wanted to return home, rather than the estimated 116,000. The communists angrily denounced the result when informed of it in late April. With the number of non-repatriates so large, even Johnson admitted, "The possibility of their ever accepting voluntary repatriation seemed remote."[51] Eager to keep the talks going, the UN team responded that they were prepared to return all 70,000 immediately in exchange for the 12,000 UN POWs in an all-for-all arrangement. As for those who did not want repatriation, it was proposed that they be screened again by a neutral international organization.

The communists refused, recessing the talks indefinitely. "We believed that world opinion needed to follow closely what was going on at the negotiations," wrote Chai Chengwen, a staff member of the communist delegation. "The people who wanted an early end to the war should know where the obstacles really lay." On May 9, 1952, the *People's Daily* published a prominent editorial where "voluntary repatriation" was interpreted as "forced repatriation" *against* the communist side. "They said that releasing all the prisoners would mean enhancement of our military manpower," observed Chai. "Our answer was that the Americans' argument showed that what they really were concerned with was not prisoners' rights and happiness, but competition in combat forces and military power."[52] The situation seemed insoluble. Sending back those who did not want to be repatriated would mean certain death or imprisonment. The impasse meant either an indefinite prolongation of the existing stalemate or renewed attempts to end the war quickly through drastic action. "So there we sit," wrote a sullen Walter Lippmann, "or rather, there sit the unhappy prisoners of war, waiting."[53]

CHAPTER TEN

"Let Them March Till They Die"

The first large group of Western prisoners was captured in early July 1950. Among them were fifty-eight Western missionaries, including Rev. Larry Zellers, a Methodist missionary from Texas who had come to Korea fresh out of college to teach English at the Methodist Mission in Kaesŏng, and Bishop Patrick Byrne, an American who along with his secretary, Father William Booth, had willingly stayed in Korea when the war started. "Byrne's only concern was with the question of where he could serve the Church best," recalled Father Philip Crosbie, an Australian who was captured at Ch'unch'ŏn. "Since a Church overrun by communists would have more need of such aid as he could offer, he decided to remain in his headquarters in Seoul."[1] Father Byrne had a remarkable record of missionary work in Japan and Korea. He was the director of the Maryknoll Mission in Kyoto when World War II started in the Pacific, but he was not detained by the Japanese. When the war ended he was transferred to Korea to become the bishop.[2]

Commissioner Herbert Arthur Lord, a fluent Korean speaker, had come to Korea in 1909 at the age of twenty-one, on the eve of Japan's annexation of Korea. In 1935, he was sent to British Malaya and then to Singapore, where he was taken prisoner by the Japanese in 1942 and interned until the end of the war. He returned to Korea in 1949, nearly sixty years old, to run the Salvation Army branch there. At the outbreak of the war, he remained in Seoul to continue his work. He, along with the French missionaries Father Paul Villemot, Mother Beatrix Edouard, and Mother Eugenie Demeusy, was taken into custody by the North Koreans in early July. Father Villemot was eighty-two years old and in poor health. Mother Beatrix was a frail woman of seventy-six who had spent most of her life in Korea looking after Korean orphans. Within days of the invasion, these Western missionaries found themselves in a school located on the outskirts of P'yŏngyang that had been transformed into a concentration camp for prisoners.

They were soon joined by over seven hundred American soldiers. Among them was Maj. John Dunn, who had been captured at Ch'ŏnan. At the camp, Dunn met Capt. Ambrose Nugent, who had been taken prisoner near Osan. Nugent had been beaten, starved, threatened, and marched on foot from Seoul. He was forced to take part in the first of many propaganda broadcasts that would later haunt him after the war. In early October, the prisoners were moved north to the city of Manp'o. They were aware that something dramatic had happened. News filtered in that UN forces had landed at Inch'ŏn and were moving north. Elated, they thought they would be freed any day, and excitedly prepared for liberation. "We took it for granted that our captors would keep us in Manp'o until the United Nations Forces could reach us," recalled Father Crosbie. "It seemed that the only other way they could prevent our early liberation would be to take us across the Yalu to Chinese territory, and we reasoned that the Chinese would not want us on their hands."[3] Much to their surprise and disappointment, however, they were told that they would be going north with the retreating NKPA. The North Koreans, it seems, had use for them.

Death March

After P'yŏngyang was captured by UN forces in mid-October, the prisoners were marched to the Yalu River to go by boat to a village more than a hundred miles away. But the boats never arrived. "The organizing abilities of our captors were the subject of much bitter criticism as we plodded back with our loads to our old home," recalled Father Crosbie.[4] In Manp'o they met their new commandant, known simply as "The Tiger." For the next nine days, the prisoners would endure a bitter ordeal that left few survivors. The Death March, as it later became known, began with a warning from the Tiger. On the evening of October 31, he told the prisoners that they had a long walk ahead of them and that they must proceed in military formation. Commissioner Lord voiced concerns for the entire group. "He pointed out that many of the party would find it impossible to march like soldiers, and at a military pace; that for some the attempt would surely be fatal." The Tiger roared, "Then let them march till they die! That is a military order."[5] And so, at dusk, the prisoners—diplomats, soldiers, elderly missionaries, women, and seven children, all captured at the start of the war—set out on a march toward Chung'an-ni. No one was prepared or equipped to handle a long march or deal with the approaching winter. Nearly everyone was still wearing the same summer clothes they had worn when captured in July. Major Green, who had been captured with Nugent and Dunn near Osan, recalled that "a lot of the guys didn't have clothing and a lot of them were barefooted, and a lot of people had dysentery." "We began in the evening," recalled Father Booth. "We camped in a cornfield not far outside of Manp'o. It was bitterly cold at the time and we slept, or tried to sleep, on the ground." The next morning it began to snow. Chilled to the bone, the first of many prisoners began to fall out. Nugent recalled that "the merciless pressure was especially weakening for the many who were suffering from severe dysentery, which seemed to be rife among the GIs." When the marching finally stopped for the day, the prisoners had to spend another night in the open, huddling against each other for warmth.[6]

Over the next few days, more prisoners, too weak to go on, were left by the side of the road. When the Tiger saw what was happening, he halted the march. The prisoners had been organized into five groups, with an American officer responsible for each. The Tiger ordered the group leaders to step forward and told the five men they would be executed for disobeying orders. Lord pleaded for their lives, explaining that the guards had given permission to leave behind those who could not keep up and that they would be picked up later by oxcarts. The Tiger scoffed and decided to execute one of the officers and singled out Lt. Cordus Thornton of Longview, Texas. As he stepped forward, Thornton whispered to Lord, "Save me if you can, sir." In a scene burned into the memory of everyone on the Death March, the Tiger convened an impromptu court-martial, found him guilty, and pronounced death. One witness vividly recalled what happened:

> "There, you have your trial," The Tiger announced. "In Texas, sir, we would call that a lynching," Lieutenant Thornton responded . . . The Tiger asked Thornton if he wished to be blindfolded. Hearing an affirmative answer, The Tiger handed a small towel to a guard. Another towel

> was used to tie the victim's hands . . . The Tiger moved smartly to face the victim and ordered him to turn around. Pausing for a moment, The Tiger pushed up the back of Thornton's fur hat. But like Father Crosbie, I had seen too much already, my eyes snapped shut just before The Tiger fired his pistol into the back of Thornton's head. When I opened my eyes, I saw that the brave young man lay still without even a tremor. The Tiger knew his business well. Quickly putting away his pistol, The Tiger called for Commissioner Lord to come to his side and translate. "You have just witnessed the execution of a bad man. This move will help us work together better in peace and harmony." In that brief speech, The Tiger managed to outrage both the living and the dead.[7]

Thornton's death had a salutary effect on the prisoners. Perhaps it was the sheer bravery and dignity with which Thornton had faced his death that inspired them. During the long march many showed great acts of kindness. Monsignor Thomas Quinlan and someone else assisted Father Charles Hunt, a large Anglican priest with a foot problem who found it difficult to keep up with the march. "Monsignor and his partner were supporting Father Hunt's upper body, while the lower lagged behind about three feet"[8] Natalya Funderat, "a stout Polish woman who was having great difficulty keeping up, was helped for a time by Commissioner Lord, who tied a rope around her waist and pulled her along like a farmer with an ox."[9] Sagid, a seventeen-year-old Turkish boy, was lugging a large suitcase full of clothes for his youngest brother, Hamid. He was the oldest of six children of the Salahudtin family, who had come to Korea as traders. All of them walked except Hamid, who was just one year old. Father Byrne had come down with a serious cold. At night, the others tried their best to warm him with their bodies and protect him from the winter air. The French consul and his staff carried Mother Beatrix for a time. By the fourth day the old woman simply could not go on. When the Korean guards pushed the old woman to get up, Mother Eugenie pleaded with them. She told them the woman they were beating "was seventy-six years old and had spent nearly fifty of those years in caring for the sick and the poor orphans of their country." Her appeals were in vain. She was executed for exhaustion.[10]

After nine days the group arrived at Chung'an-ni, later known as Camp 7, where they were quartered in an old school. By then, winter had arrived and temperatures dropped to below freezing. Surveying the sick and dying prisoners, the Tiger believed that exercise would cure their health problems, and ordered everyone outside the next morning. Lord and Quinlan vainly tried to reason with the Tiger that exercise under such conditions was madness. The Tiger responded by placing his pistol to Lord's head. Father Villemot was carried out into the freezing cold even though he could barely stand. He weakly went through the motions but died three days later. The Combert brothers, both French priests, who had arrived in Korea at the turn of the century, died two days later. More deaths followed. Father Byrne died on November 25. Father Canavan told the others, "I'll have my Christmas dinner in heaven" and passed away on December 6. Almost everyone was suffering from dysentery. The room that Major Green occupied was so crowded that when the guards wouldn't let people out, they ended up defecating on themselves and on the people around them. Beatings were also a regular occurrence. Green recalled that "one of their favorite methods was to have a man kneel and kick him in his chin, and they took some of the guys that they got it in for and would make them kneel down against the building and butt their heads against the building till they gave out, fell over."[11] But more than the starvation diet, the illness, the continual beatings, and the deplorable sanitary conditions, it was the "merciless grinding down of men, the dehumanizing process that went on, the attempt to turn human beings into sheep" that Father Crosbie recalled most vividly.[12] Many of the prisoners began to lose the will to live. Camp 7 was the first of many POW camps that sprang up along the Manchurian border during the winter of 1950–51. But unlike other camps, which would be administered by the Chinese or jointly by the North Koreans and the Chinese, Camp 7 was run solely by the North Koreans at least until October 1951. The death rate was appalling. Approximately two-thirds of the 750 men, women, and children who marched in October were dead by the following spring.[13] At this rate, no prisoners would soon be left alive at Camp 7.

Valley Camp to Camp 5

While Major Dunn, Captain Nugent, Father Booth, and other prisoners were out in the cold cornfields near Manp'o at the end of October, Maj. Harry Fleming, an American regimental advisor in the ROK Sixth

Division, reached the Yalu. He was the only American during the war to look across the Yalu into China. Farther south, another advisor was fighting for his life. Major Paul Liles had only recently arrived in Korea and was assigned to advise a sister regiment to Fleming's in the ROK Sixth Division. Liles reached his regiment while the unit was heavily engaged with the Chinese. "The first battle with the Chinese was already going on when I arrived," he later recalled. "The battle went on all night . . . and the next morning it became obvious that we were cut off by a road block in the rear." The ROK soldiers panicked at being surrounded, and the regiment soon fell apart. Liles was able to evade the Chinese for three days, but then was captured.[14]

Meanwhile, Fleming was contemplating victory as he stood on the banks of the Yalu. He firmly believed that the war was over. "I listened to the radio from Seoul," he recalled later. "I heard speeches that were being made as to the tremendous victory by the United Nations in Korea, and our morale was pretty good." That afternoon, however, Fleming received the disturbing message that "[someone] told me that the Second Regiment [Liles's], which was my support regiment, had been completely decimated in battle, with great loss, and that my regiment was to return to a place called Unsan which was about 75 miles to our rear, and there, rejoin the Division." As news of the disaster began to hit him, he realized how vulnerable he and the regiment really were: "We had extended our supplies and communications to the point where we just had no contact with the rear whatsoever except through radio." For the next four days, the regiment fought their way south. Surrounded and out of supplies, Fleming and his party were overtaken by a Chinese patrol. "My interpreter, a Korean by the name of Quan, hit the ground with me," Fleming recalled. Fleming had fainted temporarily but had come round just in time to see his assistant, Captain Roesch, struggling with a Chinese soldier. "He [the Chinese soldier] stood over Captain Roesch with this burp gun and opened it up into him, killed him." Shortly thereafter, Fleming was captured.[15]

Fleming was taken to a collection point called Valley Camp. Located ten miles south of the Manchurian border, the compound, like so many other camps, was originally constructed by the Japanese as living quarters for Korean miners during the colonial period. Each of the mud-walled houses, with three small rooms and a kitchen, housed roughly sixty prisoners. "This meant that the width that each individual had on the floor was so narrow that everyone on one side of the room had to lie on the same side at the same time. You could not lie on your back and when you moved everyone had to move in unison." There were about 750 men at Valley Camp. "At this time," recalled Fleming, "I had marched quite a ways, and I hadn't much to eat, and what I had had, I couldn't eat, except on very rare occasions. Water was practically non-existent." Food consisted of cracked corn twice a day and a few frozen turnips. The weather was bitterly cold. Fleming found Liles in the camp, but he was desperately ill. "At the time," recalled Fleming, "Major Liles was more dead than alive from ulcers on his legs, and a general debilitated condition." Both men agreed that while Liles was the senior officer, Fleming was physically better able to take command and organize the prisoners.[16]

The camp was jointly administered by the Chinese and the North Koreans, and the first thing Fleming did was to meet with them to seek permission to visit the entire camp. He did not get far with the North Korean commander, Maj. Kim Dong-suk. Kim insisted that the UN soldiers were not POWs, but war criminals, and should be treated as such. But the Chinese camp commander, Yuen, who was apparently the senior or at least had greater authority than his North Korean counterpart, was more pliable and agreed that Fleming could visit the various compounds within the camp to determine what was needed to improve living conditions. Fleming was shocked by his tour: "Actually the men were suffering from hunger such as we were at the time, [*sic*] were having hallucinations about food, and I actually got many requests, believe it or not, for things such as chocolate bars, or candy and other things."[17] Everything was filthy, and the men were covered in lice. All suffered from dysentery and many had pneumonia. There was also a serious discipline problem. The Chinese promoted this by causing dissent between the officers and the enlisted men. "The first statement the Chinese made to us," recalled Liles, "was that 'you are no longer members of your armed forces' and to the enlisted men they told them that they wouldn't have to follow the order of their officers."[18] In their desperate situation, however, the prisoners welcomed the strong leadership that Fleming provided.

One of the first things that Fleming did was to enforce sanitation.

The soldiers were told to relieve themselves in a make-shift latrine instead of anywhere, as they had been doing. Water had to be boiled before drinking it. This was a difficult rule to enforce since boiling water was time-consuming and took more energy than most could muster on their starvation diet. A lice-picking routine was also enforced. Fleming's measures soon began paying off. Of the approximately 750 prisoners at Valley Camp, only 22, or just 3 percent, died.[19] Captain Sidney Esensten testified after the war that "the morale of this camp was pretty good and I think that is why our death rate was so low."[20] But there was a price to be paid. Liles recalled, "Major Kim offered to improve rations only if the officers would sign surrender leaflets. We refused."[21] They did, however, sign a leaflet announcing the entry of the Chinese into the war. Soon there were more demands to endorse a pro-communist propaganda. "Kim repeated his warning that all who refused to cooperate would perish," Fleming later testified. "The younger, stronger officers believed that U.S. forces would arrive to rescue us in a few weeks, and we should tell Kim to go to hell." But Liles was not so sure: "I had seen on the roads, on the mountainous terrain, the complete absence of U.S. aircraft after 1 December 1950. I predicted a long hard struggle for UN forces before they could again reach the Yalu. My fellow officers called me a traitor, saying I had lost my faith in my own troops. I was more concerned with keeping myself and my men alive, however, than in preserving my own honor and reputation, priceless though it had been, because I was the senior officer."[22] The price for better treatment was the acceptance of some sort of "accommodation" with the communist authorities.

After a two-month stay at Valley Camp, the prisoners marched six miles to Camp 5 at Pyŏkdong in mid-January 1951. It was much larger than Valley Camp, accommodating approximately three thousand men. In the following months, POWs from other temporary camps were transferred to Camp 5. The majority of them came from a temporary collection site called "Death Valley," so named because of its high mortality rate. Many of the prisoners there had been captured at Kunu-ri at the end of November, where the Second U.S. Infantry Division was nearly destroyed. "The men were more or less down to an animal stage," recalled Lieutenant Erwin. "They would sit and watch with a wolfish look and if a man was unable to eat, or anything like that, they would always grab it away from him."[23] Men died rapidly at Camp 5. "The camp held about 3,200 by the end of January 1951," Liles later said. "At this time, the death rate at Pyŏkdong (Camp 5) was 7 per day average, and the corpses were collected by a Korean bullock cart, reminding me of stories of the Great Plague in London."[24]

Unlike Valley Camp, Camp 5 was administered only by the Chinese. The conditions, however, were far worse, and once again Fleming began the task of organizing the men to care for themselves. Many compounds did not establish a common latrine. Starvation was making men unruly, hostile, and then passive. Captain Charles Howard, a survivor of Camp 5, recalled, "You don't think as clearly as you would under normal conditions. A man's instinct goes back to self-preservation and I know my own personal thoughts were devoted mostly to food. I didn't think too much about home or my wife, family, because I was primarily interested in food."[25] Some men eventually had no desire for food or life and simply laid down and died. Despite the dire conditions, Fleming attempted to bring order and discipline to alleviate the situation. He organized details to make clean water available, sleeping arrangements so the men would have equitable sleeping space, and a kitchen to control rations so all would have their fair share.[26]

In late January, Major Kim, the former commandant of Valley Camp, made an unexpected visit. He told the Chinese commandant that he needed twenty prisoners to take with him to P'yŏngyang for ten days to make radio broadcasts. Although the prisoners had already guessed at Kim's sinister motivations, he assured them that those selected for the trip would be able to broadcast letters to their families. He also promised that they could broadcast the names of the POWs in Camp 5. This was especially enticing to the prisoners, since the North Koreans had not yet released such a list to the ICRC. Ten officers and ten enlisted men, including Liles and Fleming, were selected. Among the other officers were Lieutenant Erwin and Captain Galing, both of whom had come to Camp 5 from Death Valley, and Capt. Clifford Allen, a black officer who had recently arrived at Camp 5 from Bean Camp, another notorious collection center where an estimated 280 of 900 prisoners had died. As dawn broke on the cold winter day of January 30, 1951, the twenty prisoners from Camp 5 set off by truck for the 110-mile ride to P'yŏngyang. They would not return to Pyŏkdong until nearly a year later.

Camp 10

While prisoners at Camp 5 and Camp 7 were slowly starving to death, another group of captured soldiers were in a comparatively better situation. In December 1950 about 250 prisoners captured at the Changjin Reservoir were brought to Kanggye, where they were housed in what once was a large village. There were no barbed wires or any enclosures around Camp 10, only a Chinese soldier who stood guard at each house. Camp 10 was administered solely by the Chinese. The prisoners were provided sufficient food, clothing, and medical attention to sustain a reasonably comfortable life. Only twelve prisoners at Kanggye died, most from battle wounds, between December 1950 and March 1951, a remarkable figure considering that nearly twice that many prisoners died every day at Death Valley and seven daily at Camp 5 during the same period. The reason for the high survival rate at Camp 10, however, had less to do with Chinese benevolence than with experimentation of new methods of thought and behavior modification. The Chinese wanted to know whether they could turn loyal UN soldiers into loyal communists. These experiments, later popularized in the Western press as "brainwashing," attempted to control the prisoners' minds through psychological pressure, social conditioning, and reward. The articles published in the camp newsletter, *New Life*, starting in January 1951, contained pro-communist and anti-American themes. The experiment seemed to be working. The newsletter featured articles like "Truman a Swindler," "Truth about the Marshall Plan," "We Were Paid Killers," and "Capitalism and Its Aims," and appeared to have been written by the prisoners voluntarily. With "proper" guidance and training, it seemed that UN soldiers could be transformed into pliant communists. At least, this is what the Chinese believed, and they diligently set about working with the prisoners at Camp 10 to accomplish this task.

Prisoners at Camp 10 were told that they were not prisoners but "students," that "they were fools for being in Korea, for being duped into it, and had no business there." The Chinese dangled the idea of early release, "the quicker you learn what we have to teach you, the sooner you will be released and sent back to your lines."[27] The men were organized into ten-man squads, each with a leader who was responsible for overseeing the group's "education." Private Theodore Hilburn of the First Marine Division later testified, "[The squad leaders] would give us these papers and books and they would mark off a column for us to read and study and he [Camp Commandant Pan] would have the squad leader read to us and then would have us discuss it. They called it going to school."[28] The prisoners were also required to attend larger meetings run by the Chinese. The first such meeting occurred on December 22 with a Christmas party for the prisoners. They were given hot white rice and pork, an expensive treat given that the Chinese soldiers on the front had far worse rations. "The party was held in a large warehouse," recalled Marine Sgt. Leonard Maffioli. "They had a banner tacked up on all four walls with 'Fight For Peace' and such slogans as that. They had two Christmas trees with little candles burning on them."[29]

The Chinese also distributed presents, a few pieces of candy, a handful of peanuts, and a pack of cigarettes. Music was played. Some of the prisoners even danced. After the festivities, the Chinese asked for volunteers to give a speech. Master Sergeant William Olson, a veteran of Omaha Beach in Normandy in 1944 who had served in the army for seventeen years, was the first to stand up. Olson told the assembled POWs that they were lucky to have been captured by the Chinese, who had given them food, warm clothing, and tobacco. Conditions at the camp were far better than what Allied POWs had experienced under the Nazis. He praised China's lenient policy and thanked his captors. The speech was short, but it elicited considerable reactions among those who heard it. "I was shocked to tell the truth," recalled Master Sgt. Chester Mathis, "that he would get up and talk like that in that short a period because we hadn't received any indoctrinations or lectures to speak of, and I was really amazed."[30] Lieutenant Charles Harrison recounted, "There seemed to be a general feeling of anger, confusion and distrust amongst everybody."[31] The following week, parts of Olson's speech, entitled "If the Millionaires Want War, Let Them Take up the Guns and Do the Fighting Themselves," was published in *New Life*.

> The Germans were Christians. But they did not allow us to spend our Christmas happily. The Chinese do not observe Christmas, but they have arranged this fine party for us. The Nazis beat their prisoners. They spat on us and forced us to stand for intolerably long hours at a time. Some of us who could not stand this torture would urinate in their trousers. BUT

> THE CHINESE HAVE GIVEN US WARM CLOTHES, BEDDING AND EVEN HAND TOWELS. THEY HAVE SHARED THEIR FOOD WITH US AND GIVEN US THE BEST THEY HAD. This has taught me a lot of things, I can tell you. When I get home this time, they would not get me in the army again. If the millionaires want war, let them take up guns and do the fighting themselves.[32]

Many prisoners wrote articles for *New Life.* The general approach to the indoctrination program was to do just enough to survive. "I think I could best explain this passive attitude in the little bits of advice that we were able to get from Major McLaughlin," recalled Harrison. "He told us that to save lives he saw nothing wrong with going along with the program to a certain extent."[33] To McLaughlin, the senior officer at Camp 10, the articles appearing in *New Life* were merely a "parody of Communist ideology." None of the prisoners were physically threat-

American POWs at an unidentified camp, undated. (U.S. ARMY MILITARY HISTORY INSTITUTE)

ened. "There were no threats of violence," recalled Joseph Hammond, "just subtle hints that if we learned and studied their so-called truth, we would be released to go home."[34] On March 1, after four months, Camp 10 was closed, and the remaining prisoners were transferred to other POW camps. The experiment appeared to be a success. Prisoners would cooperate with the right amount of pressure and incentives applied incrementally and persistently. Plans were made to expand the "reeducation" program to other camps.

Camp 12

Fleming, Liles, Allen, and the other seventeen prisoners from Camp 5 arrived in P'yŏngyang on February 1. Over the next several months, they were interned in various locations in and around the capital city and then settled at Camp 12. They had to attend "indoctrination" classes for three weeks and, as at Camp 10, conduct daily readings and discussions. But conditions were much worse than those at Camp 10. Fleming recalled, "It was through these conditions of life, these predatory conditions of life I should say, that the communists reduced us to a very, very servile state; where they almost got us to the point that we would do anything they wanted us to do, because we had nothing to fall back on, no strength left, and no source of strength. When a man is sick and starving and freezing, he loses his ability to rationalize."[35]

After the indoctrination period the prisoners were asked to make propaganda radio broadcasts. Fleming stated that they were told "that anyone who refused would be marched back to Pyŏkdong [Camp 5], which was a distance of 160 miles. In our weakened condition, it was tantamount to death." Everyone agreed to make the broadcasts, although only five, including Fleming, were selected to participate. The main theme was that "the United States foreign policy should return to that of the Roosevelt era of 'good-will all over the world'." Liles later testified that "the broadcast was cleverly written by Major Fleming and was purposely very vague and nebulous."[36] To the prisoners' great disappointment, they were unable either to broadcast the names of POWs at Camp 5 as had been promised or to read letters to their families.

The prisoners at Camp 12 were the victims of the most intense indoctrination pressure endured by any POW in North Korea. Between February and December 1951, POWs at Camp 12 made over two hundred propaganda radio broadcasts. Some contained outright lies, such as Fleming's statement that all POWs had received treatment that "[was] in strict accordance with the principles of humanity and democracy." Other broadcasts were critical of the United States, accusing it of a "grave error in interfering in Korean internal affairs" and demanding that UN forces "should leave at once." An appeal "inviting UN troops to surrender and promising kind treatment by the communists" was broadcast in late spring during the Chinese offensive. A broadcast in mid-December addressed an Eighth Army report (Hanley Report) that accused the Chinese of killing 2,513 American POWs and 250 other UN prisoners since November 1950 and the North Koreans of killing at least 25,000 South Korean POWs and 10,000 North Korean "reactionaries." Outraged by the report, which later proved accurate, the Chinese forced the prisoners at Camp 12 to denounce it. Most, if not all, of the POWs later profoundly regretted what they had done. Major Clifford testified after the war, "I was ashamed of the whole recording. I was very pointedly, very, very pointedly, ashamed of any portion of the recording that referred to the Korean War. So far as my name and identity was concerned, I shouldn't have even done that."[37]

There was a constant fear of being purged. Nothing frightened the men at Camp 12 more than the threat of being sent to a camp known as "The Caves."[38] Lieutenant Bonnie Bowling described the Caves as a place of horror where prisoners were sent to die. "The conditions were such that I don't know anyone who stayed there more than six months and survived," recalled Capt. Lawrence Miller.[39] Lieutenant Chester Van Orman remembered passing the camp on his way to get rations: "There were many Korean, South Korean, bodies that were frozen and laid up on the ground over the entrance of the caves."[40] Captain Allen remembered the Caves as nothing more than "holes in the ground with mounds of dirt piled on top." The prisoners there "were skeletons, living skeletons or walking corpses . . . The Caves was a place where life absolutely could not be maintained."[41] Captain Anthony Farrar-Hockley of the Glosters was one of a handful who survived the Caves. After his capture during the battle at Imjin River, and several failed escape attempts that led to a stay at the notorious interrogation and torture center called Pak's Palace, where two of his ribs were cracked under torture, the British officer was brought to the Caves. "Except when their two daily meals of boiled maize were handed through the opening," wrote Farrar-Hockley later, "they [the prisoners] sat in almost total darkness. A subterranean stream ran through the cave to add to their discomfort, and, in these conditions, it was often difficult to distinguish the dead from the dying."[42] The exact number of men who died will never be known.

The beginning of the armistice talks in July 1951 brought significant changes in the treatment of the POWs. There was now concern over the number of POW deaths. The communists realized that if conditions were not changed, few, if any, prisoners would be alive by the time the armistice was signed. "The only time we started getting food," recalled Lt. Col. John Dunn from Camp 7, "was after we were turned over to the Chinese, and that was after the peace talks had started. Up to that time, we were practically living on nothing." He added, "When they were winning the war, they were a pack of raving animals. They had no respect for anything and would not hesitate a moment about killing a man . . . The period up until the time these negotiations started was characterized by mass starvation . . . After that period, they just started feeding people."[43] By the end of 1951, when POW rosters were exchanged, deaths at the camps had all but ceased. "Life at Camp 5 seemed pretty good," according to Liles, who had returned after Camp 12 was disbanded in December. "Food was excellent (compared to what we had been eating). POWs got rice, steamed bread, pork and potato soup . . . POWs had blankets, warm winter clothes, were fat and healthy."[44] Beginning in 1952, the Chinese permitted the prisoners to write two censored letters home every month, their first communication with their families since their capture. Together with the better food, clothing, and medical care, the prisoners entered a new period of relative "normalcy" in which daily existence in the POW camps became tolerable.

As their physical conditions improved, the POWs faced a new challenge: the increasing attempt to attack their minds. The Chinese began to systematically apply lessons from Camp 10 at all camps. They pitted prisoners against each other, creating an insidious division between the so-called progressives (collaborators) and the reactionaries (recalcitrants). These divide-and-conquer tactics worked wonders for the communists, as they preyed on weaker prisoners to perform their propaganda work, which in turn exacerbated the social isolation they felt among their

This photo was taken by Wang Nai-qing, a former Chinese POW guard at Pyŏkdong (Camp 5). Although the picture is undated, it is clear that it was taken in late 1951 or sometime in 1952 when conditions in the camp had markedly improved. The prisoners are well dressed and look generally well fed and healthy. (COURTESY OF WANG NAI-QING)

peers. But the most insidious aspect of the divide-and-conquer tactics was that whoever had collaborated with the enemy in the past now found themselves stuck in the role of the so-called progressives. This included the prisoners from Camp 12, all of whom had been captured during the fall and winter of 1950–51 and therefore had experienced firsthand the horrors of the POW camps before the conditions changed for the better. For prisoners captured later on, and especially those captured after the truce talks started, it was easy to overlook the intense physical and mental deprivations of the POWs captured earlier. Moreover, almost every POW had collaborated to some degree to survive, whether it was participating in study group sessions or signing unknown documents, but censoring others as "progressives" helped many of them cleanse their own sense of guilt. Some even found a new status. Major Harold Kaschko later recollected, "In late 1952 the food and camp conditions improved sufficiently that a number of prisoners became self-proclaimed heroes, brightening their own reputation by spattering on others."[45]

Soon after Camp 12 prisoners were moved to Camp 5, Fleming, Allen, and other officers were transferred to an officer's compound, Camp 2, located about ten miles northeast of Pyŏkdong at the village of Pingchŏng-ni. Camp 2 was the only POW camp for officers. The 350 officers there were quartered in a large school that also included a spacious yard. The compound was enclosed by barbed wire and guarded by two hundred Chinese soldiers. After arriving at Camp 2, the officers from Camp 12 immediately sensed that something was wrong. They were greeted by their fellow officers with hostile, stony stares. When one of the newcomers, Maj. David McGhee, went up to a group of Americans, he was asked, sarcastically, "So how's everything in Traitors' Row?" It was an indication that the prisoners from Camp 12 would be "treated as pariahs."[46] In the case of McGhee, the question seemed particularly unfair. McGhee was a survivor of both Pak's Palace and the Caves. He had been sent to the Caves because he had refused to make broadcasts. Yet now he was labeled a collaborator and traitor simply because he had been at Camp 12. "The thing that the men held most against us," McGhee later testified, "was that we had gone to that group voluntarily, or you might say, with our eyes open. Its announced purpose was propaganda, we had volunteered to go, and it was resented specifically, or most intensely, by the company grade officers [lieutenants and captains]."[47]

Also taken by Wang Nai-qing, this photo shows UN POWs attending a typical study lecture session at Pyŏkdong (Camp 5). (COURTESY OF WANG NAI-QING)

Major Nugent, whom Liles later described as a "physical and mental wreck" at the time, was similarly disdained. Captain Waldron Berry later testified about Nugent: "I do not recall ever having spoken to him," he said contemptuously. "His reputation as a collaborator effectively precluded any conversation with him so far as I was concerned."[48] Captain John Bryant recollected that "collectively, [we] had a very low opinion of Nugent and perceived him with the same lack of trust and confidence as was reserved for other members of Traitors' Row," adding, "My personal opinion was that Nugent, or other officers who were members of Traitors' Row . . . were unfit to be officers of the United States Armed Forces."[49] The prisoners from Traitors' Row did their best to cope with the ostracization. Liles became withdrawn and depressed. Fleming also withdrew and spent most of his time in the camp "library," rarely speaking to other prisoners. Captain Allen reacted with anger: "Camp 5 and Camp 2 were living much better than Camp 12 . . . We [at Camp 12] were the worst off bunch, and still, we were the ones who were called traitors, which is a nasty name. There were a lot of loud mouths there, a lot of self-professed patriots, waving the Flag and calling other people nasty names."[50]

By early 1952, deep factional divisions within the camps had emerged. The result was a mini-war of suspicion among the prisoners that played havoc on their morale. "Throughout the thirty-two months that I was prisoner the things that we discussed or things we would plan would invariably get out to our captors," recalled Lieutenant Chester Van Orman. "It resulted in people getting mighty suspicious of one another."[51] Many thought the Chinese planted rumors or provided special treatment to a particular prisoner to arouse suspicion, to keep the prisoners divided. Only the British officers appeared to be immune from the communists' tactics. Lieutenant Sheldon Foss thought their "discipline was better than ours and they were, for the most part, a unit. I know some British officers who are still alive and to my knowledge never went along with them [the Chinese]. These included Colonel Carne, commanding officer of the Gloucestershire Regiment; Major Joseph Ryan who was with the Royal Ulster Rifles; and Major Sam Weller of the Gloucestershire Regiment."[52]

Fleming, Nugent, and many other POWs emerged from their captivity emotionally shattered and with intense resentment against communism. Commander R. M. Bagwell later noted that "on many occasions in private conversation with Fleming, we discussed the communist menace,

Major Ambrose Nugent, Fort Sill, Oklahoma, January 1955. Nugent was court-martialed in 1955 on charges that he collaborated with the enemy by making propaganda broadcasts and signing leaflets urging American soldiers to surrender. After the six-week trial ended, he was cleared of all charges and promoted to lieutenant colonel. Nugent retired from the Army in 1960 and died in 1988 at the age of seventy-eight. (U.S. NATIONAL ARCHIVES AND RECORDS ADMINISTRATION)

and he shared my feelings, he had an extreme dislike bordering on hatred for any part of that system."[53] Similarly, Nugent "was outspoken in his hatred [of the communists]," Maj. Filmore Wilson McAbee later testified. "He appeared to have an intense, almost pathological hatred for them."[54] Despite daily exposure to communist doctrine, very few UN prisoners emerged from their prison camp experience transformed into communists.

Return of the Defeated

Return of the Defeated (*Toraon p'aeja*), a unique and incisive personal account of a South Korean POW's experience, was published in 2001. Its author, Pak Chin-hŭng, had been a soldier in the ROK Sixth Division in the very same regiment where Maj. Harry Fleming had served as its chief American advisor. It was the only UN unit to reach the Yalu River. Pak was nineteen years old when he voluntarily enlisted in the army. At the time of his enlistment he had been a first-year medical student at the Taegu medical school. Fifty years later, at the age of seventy, Pak published his memoir. It was one of a small handful of memoirs written by former South Korean POWs that began to be published in the wake of democratization in the 1990s.[55] That Pak had waited so long to write had been as much due to political necessity as personal choice. South Korea until the early 1990s was authoritarian, virulently anticommunist, and inhospitable to former South Korean soldiers who had ended up as POWs in communist prison camps. They were suspected of being sympathetic to communism or worse: being closet communist spies. South Korea's democratization allowed Pak to freely revisit his past, but he did not take much satisfaction from it. He is a man consumed by bitterness and regret at having been long rejected by the country he so loyally served.

Pak's regiment was under a Chinese onslaught in late November 1950. After two days of grueling fighting, he faced the unpleasant realization that the officers in his unit had deserted. Pak was captured by the Chinese at Tŏkch'ŏn. After being interrogated, he was marched north to a former Japanese coal mine in Hwap'ung that was used by the NKPA as a temporary holding camp for prisoners. The Chinese forced Pak to carry wounded Chinese soldiers through the arduous mountain paths, but he did not mind. He was impressed by their commitment not to leave their wounded behind. Certainly, this contrasted sharply with his own experience when his officers simply got up and abandoned him and the hundreds of wounded at Tŏkch'ŏn.

At Hwap'ung, the Chinese handed the South Korean prisoners over to the North Koreans. Living conditions were deplorable, but the North Korean guards were hardly better off. Prisoners were given just 150 poorly cooked kernels of corn per day. They were bitterly cold, sick, and starving. Nevertheless, Pak was able to take comfort in the warm camaraderie among the prisoners. "There was no discrimination based on rank, age or authority or wealth," he wrote. "We all shared equally." One day, Pak unexpectedly found a pot of salt hidden in the ceiling. This was literally manna from heaven. All the prisoners had been suffering from salt and vitamin deficiency. He informed the others in his room and carefully divided the salt equally among them. "I could not believe how delicious the salt tasted," Pak later recalled. "It was unbelievably delicious. Sweet, salty, just beyond words. I put a kernel of corn in my mouth, licked the tip of my finger and carefully picked up one grain of salt and put it in my mouth. We could hardly describe how delicious the corn tasted!"[56]

In January 1951, life at Hwap'ung came to an abrupt end and the prisoners made an arduous winter march north to Camp 5 in Pyŏkdong, the same camp to which the Americans from Camp 12 would be transferred. Pak recalled "the death march to Pyŏkdong as the most difficult time of my life. None of us had an overcoat and the cold wind swept down from the mountains and up the valley. We constantly fell. We had to shorten our stride to prevent from falling, but that meant jogging rather than walking." When they arrived, the camp was already full of prisoners. South Korean prisoners were separated from other UN soldiers, but they all lived under the same deplorable conditions. They were given a starvation diet of two meals a day consisting of roughly seventy corn kernels. The death toll of South Korean prisoners was horrendous, twenty to fifty per day according to Pak. But their deaths were not wasted. "When someone died, all his clothes would be taken off and divided among the living. The dead were disposed completely naked," Pak wrote. Even the lice-infested clothing from typhoid victims was prized among the prisoners. Since typhoid is transmitted by lice, wearing these clothes was a dangerous undertaking. Pak came up with a simple solution. Every night he would take off one pair of clothes to hang outside, and by the morning the lice were frozen to death. "They don't fall off easily, so I have to beat the clothes with a stick. This is how I killed them. On very cold nights, even the eggs died. It was much more efficient and effective than catching them by hand."[57]

In the midst of the misery, the North Korean guards still insisted on calling the prisoners "Liberated Soldiers," liberated from American imperialism. Like other UN prisoners, South Korean prisoners were forced to undergo "ideological educational studies," but they were meant to appeal more to the stomach than to the mind. "During these study sessions we expected propagandistic lectures with extravagant claims. But they weren't . . . the gist of the sessions was: don't stay here starving, volunteer for the People's Army. Fight for the fatherland and eat rice and meat. They didn't try to agitate or incite us. It wasn't coercive like asking those to volunteer to step forward. They used persuasion." In other words, the prisoners could risk dying of disease and starvation in the camps, or they could join the NKPA and risk dying on the battlefield for their nation and their people with glory and honor. In the meantime, they would also be better fed and clothed. Pak was conflicted about what to do. If he stayed in the camp, he thought he would certainly die if conditions did not improve. On the other hand, he thought about the future. If he joined up with the NKPA, he would never be able to see his family again. Moreover, what kind of life could he expect in North Korea? There was certainly no chance of him ever becoming an officer. How would he, a former South Korean soldier, expect to be treated in North Korea? Still, the offer was tempting as he was consumed by thoughts of food. "The only thing I wished for was to eat. I only thought about food. I could not stop thinking about rice no matter how hard I tried. I was unable to feel sadness or any other emotion. I was becoming an animal but so was everyone else."[58]

Not surprisingly, many prisoners signed up. "Most argued that it would be better to volunteer and live rather than stay in the prison camps and die of starvation or typhoid," Pak lamented. Pak did not volunteer. The painful choice was made all the more poignant when Pak learned that an old classmate from medical school in the same camp decided to join. Pak was shocked by the news. His classmate told him, "How can we survive here. Every day 20 to 50 of us die. How can I survive until the end? We don't know when the war will end, and if we stay we will surely die. I want to join so I can live."[59] Pak tried to persuade his friend that the war would soon be over and reminded him about his family back home. What about his future in North Korea? But his friend's mind was made up. As a last favor, he asked Pak to visit his family if Pak survived the war. He wanted his mother and father to know what had happened to him. Pak memorized his address.

> After I was repatriated and returned home, the very first place I went to was his house. He hadn't told us, but he was married and had a daughter. When I conveyed the news everyone broke down in tears. I left his house in a hurry . . . I felt horrible, as if I had committed a sin by surviving and returning home.[60]

Pak remembered a similarly tragic encounter just before he was repatriated. His train stopped at Sariwŏn on the way to P'anmunjŏm in August 1953. A North Korean private approached him and said, "I can't return home even though I used to be a prisoner of the People's Army like you, because I volunteered. Please tell my family that I am alive."[61] Pak couldn't forget his tear-streaked face.

In the summer of 1951, South Korean prisoners were moved to another camp located near the town of Anbyŏn in the northern part of Kangwŏn province. The camp was an abandoned school, and unlike Camp 5 the floors were covered with wood. "It seemed like paradise compared to the hell of Pyŏkdong camp," recalled Pak.[62] The prisoners were issued unmarked North Korean uniforms and were fed boiled corn instead of the rock-hard uncooked kernels they had eaten before. They were put to work. Owing to the threat of UN air attacks during the day, they worked only at night. They loaded sacks of rice and corn on a rail car, which they then pushed across a wooden bridge. On the other side, other prisoners transferred the cargo onto freight cars. These were then pushed into a tunnel to avoid detection from the air. Before dawn the rails were disassembled for the same reason. At dusk, the rails were reassembled and the cycle was repeated. Through these laborious measures, supplies continued to get through to the front lines.

Given the stable situation and relatively good living conditions, Pak and a group of prisoners, calling themselves the "Resurrection Band" to signal their "rebirth" as free men, began planning an escape. They would live off the land. They had stolen bayonets and grenades and hid them under the roof tiles. A few days before the plan was to be executed, however, "lightning struck" when one of the men betrayed the group.[63] The group was apprehended and interrogated, and Pak, as the alleged leader of the plot, was sent off to P'yŏngyang to be questioned further. In retrospect, it may have been a blessing for Pak that the plan had failed. Unlike American, British, and other non-ROK UN POWs whose chances of a successful escape were limited by their conspicuous appearance, Pak probably could have made it to UN lines. He spoke the language, blended into the surroundings, and otherwise could roam the countryside relatively anonymously. Yet, it was precisely this advantage that became a huge liability for South Korean POWs. Once captured, or recaptured, there was nothing he could do to actually prove his national loyalty. Tragically, many ROK POWs who had successfully made their escape to the South were again incarcerated, this time in UN POW camps, as suspected North Korean spies and infiltrators.

Pak told of one such story involving a Mr. Cho. Like Pak, Cho joined the ROK Army at Taegu and fought with the ROK Sixth Division. He was captured by the Chinese and then sent to a North Korean prison camp. To his surprise, the commandant of the camp turned out to be a close high school classmate. This classmate had fled to the North in 1948 following the suppression of the Yŏsu-Sunch'ŏn Rebellion. He recognized Cho immediately. Deeply moved to see an old friend, the North Korean officer helped Cho escape. After an arduous trek south, Cho reached UN lines held by Americans. "But the Americans treated him as a North Korean soldier and took him prisoner," wrote Pak. "He ultimately ended up classified as a North Korean and was sent to Kŏje Island!"[64] Cho's family tried everything they could to get him released, writing petitions to various agencies and producing his South Korean army serial number as evidence of his service in the ROK Army, but to no avail. Cho was identified as a North Korean POW. He was finally able to return home through the anticommunist prisoner release in July 1953 that had been secretly engineered by President Rhee to sabotage the armistice.

And then there were those who were forced to remain in North Korea as virtual slaves. Many of the ROK prisoners were unaware that an armistice had even been signed. "One day I found it rather strange that I could not hear the sound of airplanes overhead," recalled Cho Ch'ang-ho, who was able to escape and return to South Korea in 1994 after nearly fifty years of detainment in a political camp in Manp'o and forced labor in various mines in North Korea. "Later, I found out the reason the skies had fallen silent: the war was over."[65] In his memoir, *Return of a Dead Man* (*Toraon saja*), published in 1995, Cho claimed that thousands of South Korean POWs were as oblivious to the war's end as he was.[66] Kim Kyuhwan, a POW who escaped to the South in 2003, testified that he had been forced to work in a mine for thirty-five years and had no idea when the war ended. "Six hundred and seventy South Korean POWs were confined to hard labor at the Aogi coal mine in 1953," he wrote. "There are no more than 20 left now. Over the past five decades, many have died in working accidents, and others have died of old age."[67] According to former POWs who escaped, most South Korean prisoners were sent to work in mines in the hinterlands of the northeast along the Chinese border, the most remote part of North Korea. Since 1994, sixty-five former South Korean POWs have escaped to South Korea through China.[68]

At the end of the war, 11,559 UN POWs were repatriated, including 3,198 Americans and 7,142 ROK soldiers. According to official figures from the South Korean Ministry of National Defense, however, 41,971 South Korean soldiers remained unaccounted for.[69] Assuming that the 41,971 had not been killed in action, what had happened to the missing soldiers? An intriguing Soviet embassy report dated December 3, 1953, was recently discovered in the Soviet archives by a Chinese scholar.[70] The report stated that 42,262 ROK soldiers "voluntarily" joined the NKPA, while 13,940 were forced to stay in North Korea after the war as laborers, coal miners, and railway workers. According to a former South Korean POW who escaped to the South in 1994, 30,000 to 50,000 ROK POWs were forcibly held by North Korea and unrepatriated. Another source puts that number at 60,000.[71] Thus the number of South Korean POWs who were forcibly held back and unrepatriated ranged from 13,940 to 60,000, depending on the source. These figures do not include the South Koreans who "voluntarily" joined the NKPA, which, as the Soviet report pointed out, were in the tens of thousands, even though one can hardly describe the choice made by starved and abused prisoners to survive by joining the NKPA as "voluntary." Thus, the Soviet figure of 42,262 "voluntary" nonrepatriates seems rather meaningless. Nevertheless, if the figures are correct, the document does provide insight into the enormous number of South Koreans who were not repatriated after the war. If the December 1953 Soviet report is taken at face value, then a minimum of 56,202 South Korean POWS (42,262 + 13,940) were not repatriated, voluntarily or forcibly, and this is a far higher number of unaccounted South Koreans than the official Ministry of National Defense figure of 41,971. The individual and familial tragedies that lie behind these enormous numbers are staggering.

Considering the fate of many thousands of South Korean POWs, Pak was one of the lucky ones. He had survived and was repatriated in August 1953. At the time, however, he did not feel so lucky. He was elated to hear that he was going to Inch'ŏn when he boarded a bus at P'anmunjŏm. But when he was told that he and his fellow prisoners would continue their journey by ship, his joy suddenly turned to fear. The ship took him and others to Yongch'o Island off South Korea's southern coast. Yongch'o had been a POW camp for North Korean prisoners. Pak's fear turned into rage: "We couldn't believe it!! How could we be placed in a camp for North Korean POWs!"[72] Yongch'o served as a holding camp for the South Korean authorities to screen repatriated prisoners for their political "purity." Over the next few months the "released" prisoners found themselves prisoners once again, this time by their own government. They felt lonely, anxious, and betrayed, having been given no information when they might return home. For all Pak knew, he would be waiting out the rest of his life on this small, rocky, isolated island. But the worst was his deep sense of betrayal. He had done nothing wrong. He had served his country loyally. What did all his suffering mean if his country did not even recognize his sacrifice?

Adding insult to injury and fueling the sense of betrayal was Pak's back pay for the three years he was a prisoner. The amount came to a little more than a few dollars. Furious, Pak "wanted to throw on the ground the pittance I received as compensation for the thirty-three months of suffering." Not wanting to handle the money himself, he asked a fellow prisoner to buy something with it. "I thought the money was unlucky and didn't want to put it in my pocket, but when I saw what he came back with from the camp store, I could only sigh. He held one bottle of cheap liquor and a few cans of meat."[73] This was what three years in a North Korean prison camp was worth to his country, he thought. He and his friends drank the cheap wine "made with potato liquor and food coloring" and fell into a deep, troubled sleep. He had blown his three years of back pay in one night of drunken slumber.

Not long thereafter, prisoners began committing suicide. Rather than fling themselves off the cliffs of the island where their bodies would be swept away by the ocean, they chose the most gruesome method possible, hanging themselves in the latrine. "I saw an unbelievably shocking sight. How could this happen, I thought! I reopened my closed eyes and saw my fellow prison-mates hanging on ropes. Not just one or two, but 10 of them! I couldn't tell who they were. Nobody moved but simply stared at the hanging figures. Another 7–8 prisoners hung themselves the next day and another 4–5 the following day." The camp commandant prevented the suicides by increasing security and surveillance, but this only heightened the stress on the prisoners as they now had less freedom to move about: "All we did was eat and let time flow by."[74]

Confined to barracks on this isolated island in the middle of nowhere, Pak slumped into a deep depression. One day he was informed of the screening process that the detainees would have to go through. The screening would determine whether they were ideologically "fit" to reenter South Korean society. "In the 1950s, everyone thought that if you had been exposed to communism, even for a few days, you could be turned into a communist," complained Pak. "This is something we all had to go through."[75] The prisoners were uneasy. If the screening process determined that a prisoner was a communist, they would have no future in South Korea. Their fate hinged on the decision of the screener. To his relief, Pak passed the screening. He was determined to be "ideologically sound" and could leave Yongch'o Island and his life as a POW. He was given a two-week leave to visit his family in Taegu, and was to report to the recruiting office at Tongnae, near Pusan, where he would be given his new assignment. Despite his three-year service in the war, he would not be discharged from the army.

At home in Taegu, Pak realized the great gulf that now existed between himself and his former life. Some childhood friends invited him to a coffee shop to talk about old times. When he arrived, he felt out of place. His classmates were dressed in stylish clothes and wore their hair long. They laughed easily and freely. When Pak asked them how they had passed the war years, they told him that they had avoided military service so that they could continue their studies. How was it possible that he was the only one of the group who had volunteered? "I was the only fool here," he thought to himself. To make matters worse, a policeman approached them and singled Pak out. Someone had reported him as a suspicious character, and the policeman wanted to see his identification papers. He said that he had left them at home. A commotion ensued. Pak was humiliated and indignant: "How dare they who didn't serve in the army much less seen a battlefield, living safely in the rear, ask me, who had not only fought in the war but had suffered as a POW, for identification papers!" The next evening, still boiling with anger, he thought of his classmates. "I thought of their easy-going laughing faces. Some welcomed me while others secretly jeered. I also thought about the contemptuous looks of the young women at the coffee shop. I thought about the disabled veteran in shabby clothes with a crutch who came into the coffee shop. He didn't even have a prosthetic leg so one of his pants legs flopped around. He had given one of his legs for his country but became a beggar. Compared to those who avoided military service, he was condemned to live in the shadows of society for the rest of his life. I could only pity him."[76]

After his two-week leave, Pak reported for duty to his new unit and was sent to the DMZ. The cold and deprivation reminded him of his days in the prison camps. "I could barely contain my hunger," he remembered. "I could barely put up with my misery and self-pity. How did I wind up like this, suffering like this in this mountain valley while others were studying."[77] He had given so much for his country, and yet others who had shirked their duty were living comfortably at home. How could this be? Pak was at last discharged from the army in March 1954. He decided that he would try to forget the past. He would resume his medical studies and become a doctor. He would not let the trauma of war and his bitterness ruin his life.

Then, one day in 1995, Pak read about a POW who had escaped from North Korea. After the fall of the Soviet Union in 1991 and the death of Kim Il Sung in 1994, it appeared that North Korea was on the verge of collapse. Escapees and defectors trickling out of the country began to tell stories of famine and extreme hardship. South Korea, too, was undergoing a period of unprecedented transition. Kim Dae-jung was elected president in 1997, the first opposition leader to be elected in South Korean history. Kim initiated a new policy to engage North Korea (Sunshine Policy), ushering in a period of unprecedented cooperation between the two Koreas. Pak no longer had to suffer the stigma of silence that he felt imposed on him by South Korea's former military dictatorships. Ironically, though, in the new age of North-South rapprochement, the South Korean government did not want to publicize any harsh criticisms of North Korea for fear that it might wreck the delicate negotiations between the two countries. And so Pak's story remained "undesirable."

Pak began writing about his experiences as a South Korean POW for an obscure daily, *Yŏngnam Today*, in 1999. He felt as if he and other POWs had been doubly forgotten, first by the anticommunist military regimes and then by a democratic South Korean government that was focused on establishing a close relationship with P'yŏngyang. The South Korean government was not interested in pursuing old wounds from the past. Pak's anger was suddenly rekindled. Why wasn't the government doing more to locate former South Korean POWs and demand their release from the North Korean regime? Why wasn't more being done to obtain from the North Korean regime an accurate accounting of the tens of thousands of South Koreans who had disappeared after the war? Why were the South Korean people forgetting the war crimes committed by the North against their own citizens?

Pak read about a former POW, Yang Sun-yŏng, who had escaped to South Korea from the North in 1997. He was owed back pay for the time he was a POW, and the government offered him 2,200,000 won, or about $1,600, for the forty-four years and six months of imprisonment. "I could not suppress my anguish when I heard about this," wrote Pak. "It amounted to 45,393 won [$33] per year or just 3,782 won [$2.78] per month. That was the pay for an enlisted soldier back then." Couldn't the government have found another way to compensate him adequately? "How was it," he asked, "that the government could give hundreds of millions of won to prevent a bank from going under, but give Yang a mere pittance for his 44 years of hardship as a POW?"[78] Pak could not understand. Did his and other former South Korean POWs' service and suffering for their country mean so little?

Yang was furious too. He refused to accept the compensation money.

CHAPTER ELEVEN

Propaganda Wars

When the armistice talks stalled over the POW issue in the fall of 1951, incendiary raids reminiscent of those during World War II were carried out against the North with such effectiveness that Air Force Chief of Staff General Hoyt Vandenberg complained, "We have reached the point where there are not enough targets left in North Korea to keep the air force busy."[1] Charles Joy, chief of the Korean mission of CARE (Cooperative for Assistance and Relief Everywhere) and witness to World Wars I and II, wrote, "In twelve successive years of relief work in different parts of the world, I have never seen such destitution and such widespread misery as I have seen here."[2] Similar observations were made by the Hungarian chargé d'affaires, Mária Balog, who reported in February 1951,

> Korea has become a pile of ruins. There are no houses or buildings left [presumably in P'yŏngyang]. Cities and villages have been blown up, or destroyed by bombings, or burned down. The population lives in dugouts in the ground. The people are literally without clothes or shoes. They cannot even be sent to work, at least until the weather starts warming up. There is no food. Cholera, which the Soviet physicians managed to eradicate in the last five years, may emerge, since it occurred in a district of P'yŏngyang as late as last summer . . . They are not prepared against these epidemics; there is no medicine and there are not enough medical personnel. There is no soap.[3]

The rapid descent into the hell of an all-out war left many Americans stunned. Freda Kirchwey, senior editor of *The Nation*, angrily observed, "Someday soon the American mind, mercurial and impulsive, tough and tender, is going to react against the horrors of mechanized warfare in Korea . . . liberation through total destruction cannot be the answer to the world's dilemma."[4] An appalled Harold Ickes of the *New Republic* wrote,

"They [Koreans] had welcomed us to South Korea with shouts of joy. We were deliverers, bringing aid and comfort and unity. Apparently we were bringing other things, wounds and dismemberment and death. Bombs falling from the air or bullets from machine guns being fired into a hurrying or huddled mass, cannot distinguish between the sexes, or between the ages and infants."[5] Upton Sinclair, the Pulitzer Prize–winning author and social activist, worried that devastation by bombing was counterproductive because it fomented a "hatred of Americans in Asia."[6] In Britain, prominent clergymen protested the use of napalm. Emrys Hughes, a renowned Welsh Labour politician, requested permission to exhibit photographs of the P'yŏngyang bombings in the House of Commons, where a similar exhibition of the "Mau Mau atrocities" in Kenya had been allowed in the past, but the request was denied.[7]

In the end, what determined the debate on the bombing was not the moral argument, but the acceptance by both American and European leaders that the destruction of North Korea was necessary to prevent a greater evil, the possibility of another world war. "Korea is merely one engagement in the global contest," ran an editorial in the *Washington Post*. "If we can punish the Chinese severely enough in Korea, a settlement

Napalm victims, February 4, 1951. (U.S. NATIONAL ARCHIVES AND RECORDS ADMINISTRATION)

P'yŏngyang, 1953. By the end of the war, only three major buildings remained standing. "The gleaming-white building of the bank stands out grotesquely in the center of the city, one of the few buildings that can still be restored. It was used as a hospital by the [UN] interventionists who had evacuated in too great a hurry to blow it up. But beyond it, all the way to the railway station, there is nothing but ruins, a forest of semi-demolished walls and blackened chimneys."[8] (COURTESY OF THE HUNGARIAN NATIONAL MUSEUM).

can be achieved . . . This sober analysis carries little of the glitter or glib promises of the MacArthur formula. But it shows a lot more regard for military risks and realities."[9] With the war at a stalemate by the fall of 1951, Western leaders were of the opinion that bombing campaigns were necessary to punish the communists and force them to the negotiating table. Despite the destruction of North Korean cities, towns, and villages, the success of the bombing was measured by its utility in forcing a settlement and thus preventing a larger war.[10]

Tunnel War

To a certain extent, the air campaigns were effective in achieving that goal. UN strategic bombing had added to the communist difficulty in sustaining the war. Coping with relentless attacks from the air, Chinese logistical problems multiplied as battle lines moved southward. The UN air interdiction campaign against North Korean rail and road networks was particularly devastating to the Chinese forces.[11] General Hong Xuezhi, deputy commander of the CPV force in Korea and also its chief of logistics, recalled that "on 8 April 1951, American napalm bombing runs set 84 rail cars afire, destroying 1,500 tons of grain, 408,000 uniforms, and 190,000 pairs of boots." As much as 40 percent of all supplies had been destroyed in the bombing raids, and CPV troops were going hungry.[12] During the fifth campaign (April 22–June 10), Marshal Nie Rongzhen, who oversaw CPV logistics at the Central Military Commission headquarters in Beijing, described the Chinese troops as "unable to break through enemy lines in the Xianli Sector because they didn't have food or bullets and they stopped the attack for three days and lost the initiative."[13] With all railways virtually gone, the CPV was forced to resort to trucks, donkeys, and corvée labor to transport supplies from the Yalu to the front, facing great hazards. The countryside had become a moonscape of huge craters filled with water. Trucks operating at night without lights for fear of detection or being attacked by night bombers often drove into the craters, wrecking the vehicle and sometimes killing the driver. General Hong complained, "Even with a hundred men it took forever to fill in a crater."[14]

With the front virtually static and under constant air attack, the Chinese were forced to go underground. Tunnels, bunkers, and trenches became the backbone of China's defensive strategy. Each soldier "had a rifle in one hand and a shovel in the other," wrote General Hong. The tunnels were constantly expanded under arduous conditions. "The big 'orchestra' composed of our soldiers and commanders played a new 'movement' in constructing tunnel fortifications," recalled Yang Dezhi, an army group commander. "This approach meant operating inside the mountains, dealing with rocks, sandy grit, and cave-ins. Lacking technology or advanced tools, we were depending largely on our hands. Pickaxes were worn down so that they ended up looking like rounded iron blocks about the size of a hammer . . . broken glass and metal plaques were also used at tunnel entrances to reflect sunshine inside during the daytime . . . They worked so hard that their palms blistered, then became thick and badly calloused." By August 1952 the Chinese had dug 125 miles of tunnels and 400 miles of trenches. By the end of the war the Chinese had built an astonishing 780 miles of tunnels that formed underground cities. On August 4, 1952, almost two years after China entered the war, Mao optimistically reported, "The problem of food, that is, how to guarantee the provision lines, had been for a long time a real question. We did not know, until last year, that digging up grottos for storing food was the solution. Now we are aware of it. Each of our divisions has enough food for three months. All have their storage and ceremonial halls. They are well off."[15]

Despite satisfaction with the underground facilities ("one could find all kinds of facilities, such as dorms, canteens, and latrines . . . There was also what our soldiers called the underground mansion 'our club hall'"), life was difficult and stressful.[16] Under constant air attack, soldiers spent weeks underground. Coping with the darkness was a challenge. Meager light was provided by oil lamps made from tin cans and shell casings, and keeping the lamps lit used up precious cooking oil. Smoke from the lamps caused headaches and dizziness in the congested and poorly ventilated space. Moreover, the lack of sunlight and poor diet led to nutrient deficiencies with serious effects such as night blindness and diarrhea. Urgent calls were made for shipments of proper food, but "because the shipments were small in quantity, the troops vast in numbers, these shipments were a drop in the bucket and the problem was not solved." A solution was found through a local Korean folk remedy. Korean peasants showed that night blindness could be cured by drinking bitter "pine needle tea." The already denuded Korean landscape became ravaged even more by marauding Chinese soldiers searching for the proper nourishment. Tadpoles became a favorite dietary supplement as they were a rich source of vitamins and also helped cure night blindness. General Hong recalled "taking a handful of the little tadpoles from a crater, pop them into a tea pot with some water, best with some sugar but okay without, and gulp them down alive three times a day, and in two days you begin to see results. We got every unit mobilized to play with this clever beverage . . . once again, the night returned to us."[17]

Although the constant bombardment from the air had slowed the communist advance, and thus stalemated the war, it did little to force the communist leadership to a settlement. Despite the destruction, there was little evidence of a collapse of will. As in World War II, intensive strategic bombing could inflict catastrophic damage on a society without defeating it.[18] The Chinese and the North Koreans had simply adapted. It soon became clear that the stalemate war could not be won on the battlefield. Rather, it would have to be waged in the court of world opinion. For the communists, this would entail an all-out effort to win condemnation of the United States by discrediting the integrity of the UN war effort in Korea as well as undermining the legitimacy of the principle of nonforcible repatriation.

American Bugs

In early 1951, intelligence reports describing a devastating epidemic sweeping across North Korea reached General MacArthur's desk. The reports recounted many cases of communist soldiers and civilians dying from a mysterious disease whose symptoms appeared to resemble the bubonic plague. As the Eighth Army advanced northward to recapture Seoul, verification of these reports became a priority. The bubonic plague can sweep though a population like wildfire, blazing a path of death that is difficult to extinguish. A bubonic plague north of Seoul would obviously impact on potential future UNC operations. MacArthur directed Brig. Gen. Crawford Sams, his chief of public health and welfare, to find the truth. It would be a difficult and hazardous task since the allegedly infected area was in enemy territory. Moreover, no one, including Sams, had firsthand experience with the plague. "Not too many of our doctors in America have seen the bubonic plague, and so far as I knew there were none in the Far East at the time," Sams later wrote. Several reports stated that hospitals in the Wŏnsan area were filled with plague patients. Sams "felt that he should go to Wŏnsan in an attempt to investigate these cases for himself." Thus began one of the most astonishing episodes of the war.[19]

The journey posed seemingly insurmountable challenges. Sams decided to enter behind enemy lines by sea. He would travel to near Wŏnsan by ship at night and then get ashore on a row boat. Once he was on land, the journey to find a patient would become more perilous, since he was "an Occidental among Orientals in the dead of winter" and thus without vegetation for cover. He would have to kidnap the patient, take him to the coast, put him on a rubber raft, and then transport him to a waiting ship. "We could then . . . make our laboratory determination."[20] The operation had to be done quickly and surreptitiously. It seemed like an impossible task, but given the importance of the mission, Sams decided that he had to take the risk. For twelve days in March, Sams tried various ways of getting ashore. Ten teams of Korean agents had been sent in advance to support the operation from ashore, but nothing had been heard from them for several days, and apparently all of them had been captured or killed and the mission compromised. Sams recollected, "Unfortunately, in the torturing which preceded death or execution of these agents, apparently some yielded to such fantastic pressure as the oriental mind can devise in torture, and the communists were aware of the fact that I was trying to get into Korea from that location." The odds of success appeared nil, and any sane mind would have canceled the operation. But providence struck as the last team of agents, apparently safe, made contact, and Sams decided to proceed.

Sams and Yun, a Korean commando, approached the shore south of Wŏnsan by a little village called Chilso-ni. Yun made contact with the advance team. Over the next few days, Sams hid in a cave while Yun and the other agents scouted nearby villages for victims of the plague. Although unable to capture a patient, Sams was nevertheless able to determine, through the agents who had actually seen many sick people, that there was indeed an epidemic, but it was not the plague. Rather, it appeared to be "a particularly virulent form of smallpox, known as hemorrhagic smallpox." The "Black Death," as the epidemic was called, "was as fatal as the bubonic plague except that it was a different disease" and could be more easily controlled through immunization inoculations and medical treatment.[21]

Sams returned safely with the good news. The communists were furious that Sams had avoided capture. "They executed some twenty-five people in the little village of Chil-So-Ri whom they suspected of having collaborated with us and our agents," Sams later wrote. But more significantly for the course of the war, Sams's mission incited a new but still largely uncoordinated charge by the communists that would later erupt into one of the most explosive issues of the Korean War: the accusation that UN forces were engaged in biological warfare. On May 4, 1951, the *People's Daily* reported that Sams's mission was "to spread the plague" and that the ship that had taken him to Wŏnsan was a biological warfare vessel designed to "carry out inhuman bacteriological experiments on Chinese People's Volunteers."[22]

Biological or germ warfare was not a new issue in China. During the Second Sino-Japanese War (1937–45) the Japanese established a number of units in occupied China where they worked on developing biological weapons using Chinese prisoners and internees as subjects for gruesome experiments. The most important activity took place at Unit 731 in Harbin commanded by Lt. Gen. Ishii Shirō. The Americans granted Ishii, his subordinates, and members of other Japanese biological warfare units immunity from prosecution for war crimes in exchange for the technical information they had gathered. In the emerging cold war environment, a calculated determination was made that rebuilding Japan, rather than punishing Japanese war criminals, would better serve the long-term security interests of the United States and the free world. In one of the most blatant cases of injustice, Ishii's men, their past hidden, became ostensibly respectable members of Japanese society as deans of medical schools, senior science professors, university presidents, and key technicians in industries.[23] The Soviets put to trial in Khabarovsk the few members of Unit 731 they had captured. The biological warfare methods that the Chinese alleged that the Americans used were *precisely* the same as those described in evidence and testimonies that came out at the trials.[24]

After raising the issue of bacteriological warfare in early 1951 following General Sams's extraordinary mission to North Korea, the communists backpedaled. By mid-May 1951, charges of bacteriological warfare almost disappeared from the communist press. With the prospect of a truce, continuing the accusations seemed unwise. By July 1951, when the armistice talks began, they were dropped completely. It was not until early 1952, after truce talks became deadlocked, that the communists once again raised the charges of bacteriological warfare. In February 1952, North Korean Foreign Minister Pak Hŏn-yŏng accused the United States of repeatedly dropping large numbers of insects carrying cholera and other diseases. The Chinese followed up with charges of their own. In a front-page editorial, the *People's Daily* condemned "the appalling crimes of the American aggressors in Korea in using bacteriological warfare." The accusations gained worldwide publicity with Premier Zhou's statement on February 24 that called on all nations to condemn the "U.S. Imperialists War Crimes of germ warfare."[25] The communists claimed that one thousand biological warfare sorties were flown by UN aircraft between January and March 1952 in northeast China.

In early April the *People's Daily* began publishing eyewitness accounts of germ warfare attacks. An account by a Chinese journalist described how a twin-engine plane had sprayed germ-carrying "poisonous insects" near Xipuli, China, on March 23. Another report relayed how a British reporter witnessed insects being released from an American plane on April 2 in the same area.[26] Between mid-March and mid-April, germ warfare allegations with descriptions of strange insects and mysterious airborne voles filled China's media as the country went on a nationwide insect and rat extermination campaign. The communists also imple-

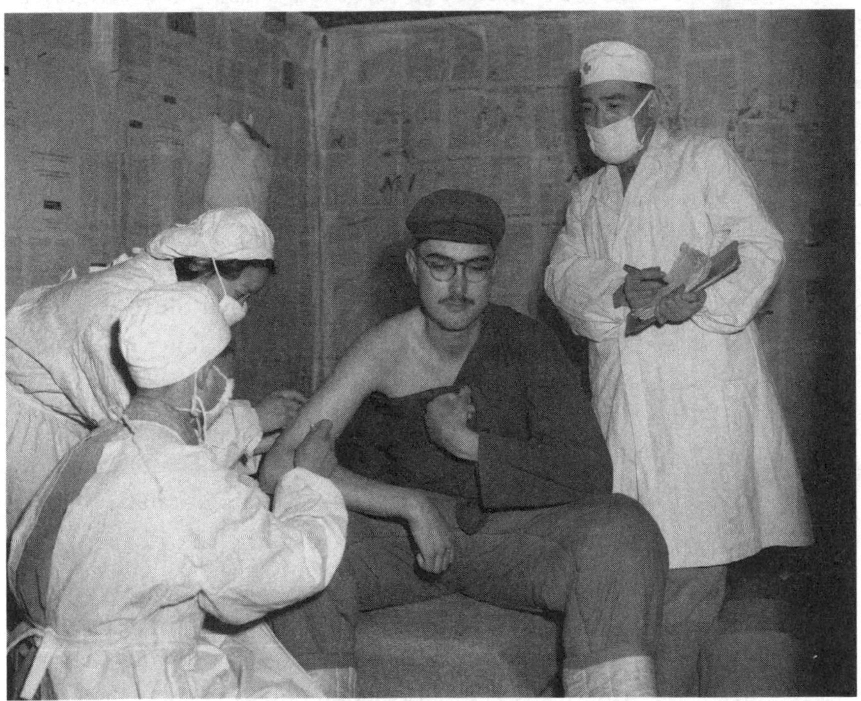

Lieutenant Ralph R. Dixon, prisoner of war, gets inoculated at a POW camp, April 3, 1952. Facing a long and protracted war, Mao inaugurated the Patriotic Hygienic Campaign in 1952 to mobilize thousands of students, housewives, and workers to reduce the incidence of disease and to "crush the enemy's germ warfare." In addition, hundreds of thousands of Chinese citizens, including UN POWs, were inoculated against the dreaded disease. Mao also instigated a widespread purge of counterrevolutionaries during this same period. Those who were not immediately executed were systematically "cleansed" of their bourgeois ideology and their "disease-laden" Western inclinations in reeducation camps that began to spring up throughout the country. (U.S. NATIONAL ARCHIVES AND RECORDS ADMINISTRATION)

mented a national inoculation campaign. By October, 420 million people had been inoculated against smallpox. "In our large towns and seaports," wrote Fan Shih-shan, general secretary of the Chinese Medical Association, "small pox has been completely wiped out . . . Constant measures taken to destroy rodents and fleas, mass vaccination of local populations, early diagnosis, efficient isolation and energetic treatment have succeeded in controlling the disease."[27]

During his captivity in North Korea, Gen. William Dean experienced firsthand the effects of this national campaign when he too was vaccinated. "Everybody, soldiers, civilians, adults and children, received four separate inoculations and revaccination," recalled Dean. "They were monster shots and all of North Korea had fever and sore arms."[28] American POWs languishing in prison camps along the Yalu were also informed of the germ warfare. William Banghart at Camp 5 recalled that "the bacteriological warfare orientation given to us by the Chinese" consisted of "an elaborate display of pictures, photostatic copies of confessions or statements made by [air force pilots] Lieutenants Quinn and Enoch, and a great quantity of printed matter . . . One thing I remember clearly is the report I read on the pictorials supplied to the company libraries by the Chinese concerning a Japanese war criminal called Shirō Ishii, who had been released from military prison in Japan and flown to the U.S. where he was supposed to have conferred with President Truman and MacArthur. Every man in the company was given a written test on his feelings on Bacteriological Warfare."[29] One popular slogan was, "One fly, one American soldier; the enemy drops them, we will eliminate them!"[30] Political cartoons depicting U.S. imperialism as the Grim Reaper riding the back of a housefly reinforced the notion that the American enemy, and anyone associated with him, was an enemy of China.[31] Slogans such as "Resist Germ Warfare and American Imperialism" were calculated to stir hatred for the Americans as disease-laden pests.

The innumerable eyewitness accounts of germ attacks, the lure of war memory, the power of rumor, the fear of epidemic diseases, and the reality of a frustrating war transformed charges of germ warfare into a belief that gripped the Chinese public in terror. Whipped into frenzy, Chinese farmers, housewives, students, and factory workers became citizen-soldiers ready to battle against the unseen and disease-bearing American enemy. This enemy came in many forms. As early as 1949 the

CCP leadership had begun launching a campaign to rid the new nation of its counterrevolutionary forces in the guise of the "Suppress Counter-revolutionary Campaign." The CCP arrested thousands of religious sect leaders, alleged Nationalist spies, and gang leaders, and executed many hundreds. A wide-scale program was launched to crack down on beggars, prostitutes, and criminals. The war in Korea ("Resist America, Aid Korea") merely intensified the CCP dread of these "internal" enemies. The germ warfare charges arose simultaneously with several new campaigns launched in 1952 that were aimed at the professional classes. The "Three-Anti campaign" and "Five-Anti campaign," which began at the end of 1951 and in January 1952, respectively, were designed to undermine the authority of China's capitalists and business managers as well as the rural landlords.[32] In February 1952, the CCP also inaugurated the "Patriotic Hygiene Campaign," which mobilized housewives, students, and workers, equipped with gauze masks, cotton sacks, and gloves, to fight against the American-delivered germs. "Let us get mobilized," Mao wrote in a memorial to the National Heath Conference in Beijing. "Let us attend to hygiene, reduce the incidence of disease, raise the standards of health, and crush the enemy's germ warfare."[33]

At the same time, the "Thought Reform Campaign" began penetrating institutions of higher learning and professional services. Intellectuals, who had previously thought of themselves as benignly apolitical, or even progressive, were now forced to publicly announce their allegiance. Thought reform classes included not only instructions in proper work ethic, but also the abandonment of "Western influenced elitism."[34] Between February and July 1952, germ warfare was transformed from a regional military-related issue in northeast China into a national mobilization campaign aimed to rid China of all "foreign" influences. Foreign jazz was banned in early 1952. The teaching of English ceased.[35] In the hunt for American germs, anyone remotely associated with America—the Nationalists, capitalists, religious leaders, Western-trained intellectuals, businessmen, or managers—was considered a menace to the national body-politic and caught in the same net as insects and rats. In radio broadcasts, mass meetings, and daily newspapers, the Chinese state called on its citizens to expose evildoers, confess crimes, and eliminate poisonous germs from their homes and workplaces.[36]

The publication of confessions by captured American pilots intensified the popular hysteria. Some wondered why the POWs were even kept alive. In a widely distributed brochure prepared by the China Medical General Association entitled "General Knowledge for Defense against Bacteriological Warfare," the linkage between the war against germs at home and the war against enemies abroad was made explicit. In both cases, the best defense was vigilance and the eradication of "impure" elements within Chinese society in order to maintain the nation's health. "It is possible to defend against bacteriological warfare," the brochure stated. "Under the leadership of Chairman Mao and the Communist Party, we can overcome any kind of weapon, because it is the men holding the weapons, and not the weapons [themselves], that can decide the victory and defeat of the war."[37] By linking American germ attacks with a disease prevention movement aimed to rid China of both its biological and its political impurities, the CCP leadership was able to transform popular dread of American germs into fear of China's internal enemies that would eventually lead to the persecution of hundreds of thousands of Chinese businessmen, intellectuals, and landowners.[38]

The hallmark of Mao's design to purge counterrevolutionaries was his decree on February 21, 1951, which extended the death penalty or life imprisonment to virtually any kind of antigovernment activity. What exactly constituted that activity, however, was never clearly defined. Arrests and purges soon became routine occurrences. The Hong Kong newspaper *Wah Kiu Yat Po* reported that more than "20,000 persons had been killed in the southeastern districts of Kwangsi [Guangxi], a troublesome southern province," in March 1951 alone.[39] The same newspaper reported the arrests of thousands of people in northeast China. "Mao said that in the struggle against counterrevolution 650,000 persons were executed in the country," recounted V. V. Kuznetsov, Soviet ambassador to the DPRK, noting as an aside that "some number of innocent people apparently suffered."[40] The goal of the "purification" campaigns was to eliminate entire groups of people from the fabric of Chinese society, and the fear of American bugs provided the perfect pretext to do it.

While Chinese and North Korean officials had little trouble persuading their people that biological warfare was real, persuading the international community was a far more difficult task. The Soviet Union leveled charges of biological warfare through the UN and took the lead in this task. The first official U.S. denial came on March 4, 1952. Secretary of

State Dean Acheson angrily stated, "We have heard this nonsense about germ warfare in Korea before [in 1951]," and denied the charges "categorically and unequivocally." He said he welcomed "an impartial investigation by an international agency such as the Red Cross."[41] General Matthew Ridgway told Congress on May 22 that the allegations "should stand as a monumental warning to the American people and the Free World about the extent to which the communist leaders will go in fabricating, disseminating and persistently pursuing these false charges."[42] A week after calling for an investigation, Acheson sent a request to the ICRC requesting an on-site investigation, under the auspices of the UN, of the allegedly affected areas as soon as possible. Neither China nor North Korea responded to the ICRC's request for such an inspection. Three additional requests were made, and when they were all ignored, the ICRC considered their request rejected. The only acknowledgment made of the requests was at the UN, where Soviet delegate Yakov Malik formally rejected them on behalf of China and North Korea. Malik charged that a UN-sponsored ICRC investigation would be biased in favor of the United States and the West, and therefore an impartial investigation could not be guaranteed. The UN Political Committee, however, approved the ICRC investigation in early April. It was only on the verge of this expected approval that the Soviet Union offered to withdraw the charge of biological warfare "as proof of its sincere striving for peace."[43]

Although the Soviets dropped the charges, the drama was not over. The allegations by the communists had stirred anger among many of America's leading scientists. Unable to conduct on-site investigations, they examined whatever evidence was available, in this case nine photographs published by the *People's Daily* of the alleged insects and voles dropped by the Americans as disease vectors. Scientific experts discredited the photographs as fakes.[44] Under pressure of widespread skepticism in the noncommunist press, CCP leaders were unable to let the allegations simply drop because they had staked their regime's reputation and the basis for national "purification" campaigns on the charges. The ICRC and the UN's World Health Organization were deemed untrustworthy, but an investigation by neutral outsiders with Chinese oversight would be acceptable. For such an investigation to be legitimate, however, the Chinese government needed a credible group of Western scientists to verify its claims.

To lead the international group, the Chinese invited Joseph Needham, a Cambridge University don from the United Kingdom. Needham was a polymath, one of those exceptionally rare individuals who could rightly be called a Renaissance man. Needham's scientific credentials were impeccable. He was at the time one of the world's leading scientists, a pioneering biochemist who had written leading works on biochemistry and embryology. But he also possessed special qualifications in dealing with Chinese matters and especially Mao's Communist China. He was an avowed leftist and rejoiced in Mao's victory and the establishment of the PRC, believing that a communist utopia would follow. This view would be tempered later, especially after the Cultural Revolution of the late 1960s to early 1970s, but in 1952 no such suspicion entered Needham's mind. In 1942, the British government posted Needham to wartime China to head a new office in Chongqing, the Sino-British Science Cooperation Office, as a sort of cultural attaché to help spread British goodwill and material assistance among the Chinese academic community. He had never been to China, but had developed a lifelong passion for the country in the late 1930s, even learning the language fluently enough to read classical texts. He stayed for four years and during that time traveled the country widely, amassing a huge amount of material on the history of science and technology in China and establishing a wide network of contacts in the Chinese scientific community. The material he collected formed the basis for a monumental project on the study of scientific and technological developments in China that would prove not only the vastness of China's achievements but also the indebtedness of the world to China's genius. It would put to rest the prevailing view that China was backward and had contributed little to the development of mankind. The first volume of his work, *Science and Civilization in China*, was published in 1954. It is arguably the most important study of China's scientific history ever undertaken and from a man who was trained neither as a historian nor as a Sinologist.

When Mao invited Needham to investigate the biological warfare allegations, he was in the midst of writing the first volume of his work, and he enthusiastically accepted the chance to return to China and to meet his old acquaintances, including Zhou Enlai.[45] Needham was intrigued about the allegations since he had been convinced earlier that the Japanese had used fleas to spread plague in China. He also had to

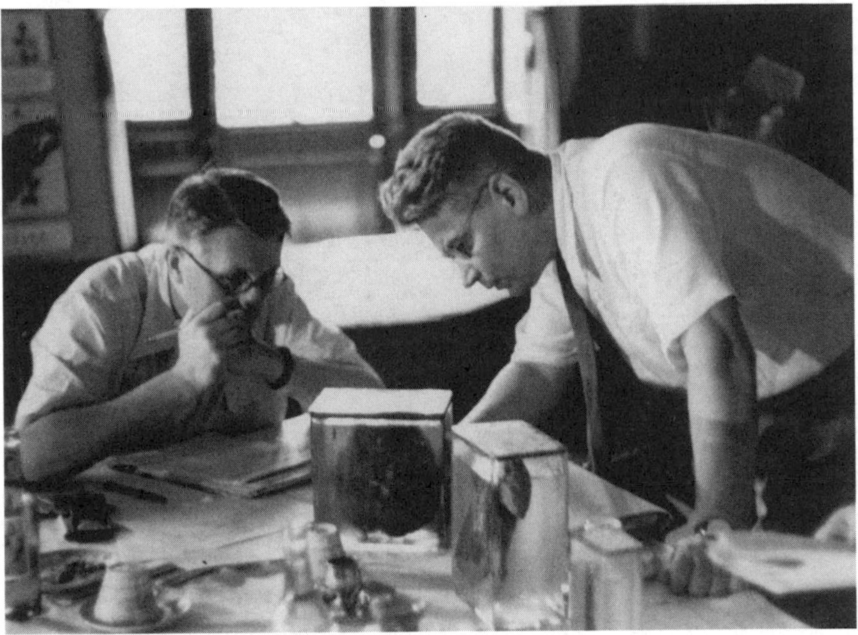

Joseph Needham (seated) and N. N. Zhukov-Verezhnikov examining specimens, 1952. (NEEDHAM RESEARCH INSTITUTE)

wonder about the connection between the alleged outbreak of "inexplicable" illness in 1951 and the American decision to grant amnesty to Japanese scientists involved in biological warfare in exchange for their experimental data. Needham looked forward to employing his scientific and language skills in the service of the struggling new regime.

Another key expert invited by the Chinese was N. N. Zhukov-Verezhnikov, a bacteriologist and vice president of the Soviet Academy of Medicine who was also intimately familiar with Ishii's Unit 731 program. Zhukov-Verezhnikov had served as a medical expert in the Khabarovsk trials of members of Unit 731. Needham and Zhukov-Verezhnikov, along with four other left-leaning Western scientists from Italy, France, Brazil, and Sweden, constituted the International Scientific Commission, formed by the Soviet-bloc World Peace Organization in the spring of 1952, to investigate allegations of germ warfare. The team arrived in June and worked tirelessly over the summer. Their report presenting the findings of Chinese scientists, with commentaries and final conclusions by the commission, was issued on September 15, 1952.

It confirmed everything China had claimed: "These [biological weap-

Members of the International Scientific Commission (left to right): Olivo Oliviero (Italy), Jean Malterre (France), N. N. Zhukov-Verezhnikov (USSR), Andrea Andreen (Sweden), Samuel Pessoa (Brazil), and Joseph Needham (UK). (NEEDHAM RESEARCH INSTITUTE)

ons] have been employed by units of the U.S.A. Armed Forces, using a great variety of different methods for the purpose, some of which seem to be developments of those applied by the Japanese army during the Second World War."[46] Curiously, although commission members had significant scientific credentials and were responsible for writing, organizing, translating, and editing the final report, they themselves conducted no direct scientific investigations. Instead they heard testimonies and viewed a vast array of evidence presented to them by Chinese scientists, including an amazing variety of supposed vectors—voles, spiders, nonbiting flies, and other insects.[47]

Needham appeared to put particular stake in the reputation of the dozens of Chinese scientists who had participated in the investigations and submitted the evidence, writing later that "they were first rate bacteriologists . . . and of whom I know well personally and can vouch for."[48] At the same time, he appeared blissfully unaware that the germ warfare investigations were taking place in the midst of a tense climate of political repression, "Thought Reform," reeducation, and the execution of

Plague lab, 1952. After spending the summer of 1952 investigating claims of bacteriological warfare presented by Chinese scientists, the International Scientific Commission published a 665-page report on September 15. Archibald Vivian Hill, the 1922 Nobel laureate in physiology and medicine, summed up the Western reaction to the report by proclaiming it to be "a prostitution of science for the purposes of propaganda." As for Needham, he was proclaimed a persona non grata by the British academic establishment. Needham was also blacklisted by the U.S. State Department and banned from travel to the U.S. until the mid-1970s. (NEEDHAM RESEARCH INSTITUTE)

hundreds of thousands of counterrevolutionaries.[49] Neither Needham nor the other Western scientists considered how politics might have compromised scientific truth. Nor did they seem aware that Chinese bacteriologists and entomologists were under intense pressure to cook the evidence and back the government's claims of American germ warfare. Needham simply could not believe that profound political changes might have influenced the conclusions of the scientists with whom he had become and remained close. He told Dr. Alfred Fisk, an American scientist and colleague, "If anyone insists on maintaining that a large number of scientists or scholars who were excellent men before automatically becoming scoundrels on the same day that a government such as that of Mr. Mao Tse-tung [Mao Zedong] comes into power (a government which, by the way, I am convinced has the support of the overwhelming majority of the people), I do not argue with him."[50]

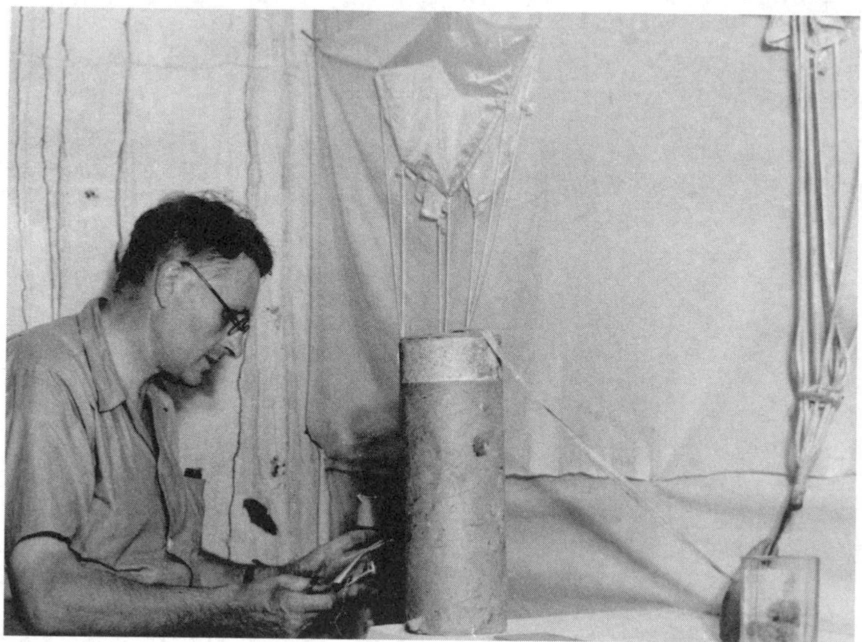

Joseph Needham examining an alleged biological warfare canister dropped from American bombers. (NEEDHAM RESEARCH INSTITUTE)

In his field notes, however, Needham hinted that many of these exhibitions might have been staged for his benefit. He was uncertain of what he might find when he visited Gannan county, the site of the first reports of purported droppings of germs. After he was invited to observe a technician in full protective gear examining microscopic slides that had been set up in a mobile bacteriological laboratory, he later wrote to his wife, "I have the feeling that this may have been a mise-en-scene for one person."[51] Nevertheless, he gave the Chinese the benefit of the doubt.[52] At a press conference following his return home, Needham was asked "what proof he had that samples of plague bacillus actually came from an unusual swarm of voles as the Chinese had claimed." "None," he answered. "We accepted the word of the Chinese scientists. It is possible to maintain that the whole thing was a kind of patriotic conspiracy. I prefer to believe the Chinese were not acting parts."[53]

Curiously, there were no epidemics in China or North Korea in 1952. The head of the UN World Health Organization, Dr. Brock Chisholm, noted that "North Korean and Chinese reports of epidemics in enemy territory . . . did not indicate the use of germ warfare because bacteriological weapons would bring far heavier casualties than indicated by the accounts of epidemics." He concluded that if germ warfare had been waged, "millions of people would die suddenly" and there would be "no mystery as to whether bacteriological weapons had been used."[54] Alternatively, one could also conclude that the hygienic measures put in place were done quickly and widely enough to have prevented epidemics from biological weapons. However, the Western public dismissed the whole episode as a hoax, yet another example of the dangers of communism and how a communist regime promoted lies over truths by subordinating science to politics. It was not simply the cynicism of the untruths that was unsettling, but the darker power of what those untruths revealed about the enemy. "The alarming thing," the *New York Times* wrote, "is the demonstration that the power we are fighting is not simply a great, militant and aggressive empire on the make, it is the power of *evil*. It could be said of the ruling mind in Russia that it has lost

Members of the International Scientific Commission with Korean and Chinese officials. Needham, with glasses, is seventh from the left. Kim Il Sung is seventh from the right, summer 1952. (NEEDHAM RESEARCH INSTITUTE)

the sense of truth. To this mind anything it desires is good, and any lie is truth that serves its end."[55]

In January 1998 the Japanese newspaper *Sankei shinbun* uncovered twelve Soviet-era documents. They provided the first evidence that the biological warfare allegations had been fabricated. The documents describe how the North Koreans and the Chinese, with Soviet help, created false evidence.[56] One document described how the hoax was carried out. General Razuvaev, the Soviet ambassador to the DPRK, reported, "With the cooperation of Soviet advisers a plan was worked out for action by the Ministry of Health . . . False plague regions were created, burials of bodies of those who died and their disclosure were organized, measures were taken to receive the plague and cholera bacillus. The adviser of MVD [Ministry of Internal Affairs] DPRK proposed to infect with the cholera and plague bacilli persons sentenced to execution, in order to prepare the corresponding [pharmaceutical] preparations after their death."[57]

What was the reason for the elaborate hoax? Chinese commanders in the field made the initial charges. Mao ordered scientific investigations to confirm the reports before making them public, but the North Koreans prematurely made their charges before the tests were completed. Mao realized that the charges were false, but he decided to take advantage of the opportunity to discredit and embarrass the United States, to maintain China's revolutionary momentum while purging its internal enemies.[58] This happened while the armistice talks were deadlocked over the issue of voluntary repatriation of POWs, and thus allegations of germ warfare could also be exploited for their propaganda value to gain an edge at the talks. Domestically, it came at an opportune moment for Mao. Fear of political impurity and invisible enemies could help mobilize the nation under Mao's leadership to be prepared for a protracted war. Mao exhorted the people to report pro-American attitudes in the intellectual and business communities. The germ warfare campaign would make the link between American biological warfare and spiritual contamination of the Chinese body-politic direct and tangible. Internationally, the charges would expose the hypocrisy of the UN policy of voluntary repatriation. While such heinous war crimes are being committed, the insistence that POWs freely choose where they wanted to be repatriated after the war would appear calculated and shallow.

The Soviet Union went along with the hoax until the spring of 1953, when the Soviet delegation at the UN was ordered to "no longer show interest in discussing this question." Even more strikingly, Moscow told Beijing and P'yŏngyang that the Soviet government was now aware that the allegations claiming that the United Sates had used biological weapons were false. A May 1953 resolution of the presidium of the USSR Council of Ministers (which ran the Soviet Communist Party immediately after Stalin's death in March 1953) noted that "the Soviet Government and the Central Committee of the CPSU [Communist Party of the Soviet Union] were misled" and concluded that "the accusations against the Americans were fictitious." In order to remedy the situation, the resolution recommended that "publication in the press of materials accusing the Americans of using bacteriological weapons in Korea and China" cease and that "the question of bacteriological warfare in China (Korea) be removed from discussion in international organizations and organs of the UN."[59] Apparently, the Soviets had resolved to distance themselves from the hoax because it "damaged Soviet prestige."[60]

Regardless of the decisions made by the Soviet Union's new leadership to abruptly end the propaganda campaign, the allegations had already begun to die down by the summer of 1952. This is because another scandal, tragically of Washington's own making, did far more damage to America's image abroad and UN credibility on the POW repatriation issue than communist allegations of bacteriological weapons ever did.

Kŏje-do

On May 7, 1952, the new UN commander in chief, Gen. Mark Clark, landed at Haneda Airport in Tokyo. General Ridgway was glad to see him. After a year as commander of both the UNC and the Far East Command, Ridgway was relieved to be leaving. "The negotiations with the communists were my major concern throughout most of my remaining tenure in the Far East Command," Ridgway later wrote. "They were tedious, exasperating, dreary, repetitious and frustrating."[61] Ridgway was going to Paris to be the Supreme Allied Commander Europe (SACEUR), replacing General Dwight Eisenhower, who had decided to try for the Republican nomination in the 1952 presidential election.

Clark had become well known as commander of the Fifth Army in the Italian Campaign during World War II. He had also gained a reputation for being vainglorious. A former superior, Gen. Jacob Devers, described Clark as a "cold, distinguished, conceited, selfish, clever, intellectual, resourceful officer."[62] Clark would have to rely on all of those traits in dealing with the communists at P'anmunjŏm. He had no illusions about the difficulty he faced: "I had been in on much of the Korean planning in Washington and knew that this would be the toughest job of my career."[63] What Clark did not know was that on the very day of his arrival, he would be confronted with one of the biggest crises of the Korean War. On Kŏje Island (Kŏje-do), some thirty miles off the southeast coast of Korea and the site of the main UNC POW camp, Brig. Gen. Francis Dodd, the camp commandant, was taken hostage by North Korean prisoners. They threatened to kill him if their demands were not met.

By December 1951, there had been indications of serious problems in the camp. The first problem was overcrowding. Between September and November, over 130,000 prisoners had been taken, owing to the success of the Inch'ŏn operation. The UNC had not anticipated nor was it prepared to hold such a large number of prisoners. In January 1951, with the number of POWs reaching 140,000, the prisoners were consolidated into one complex of compounds on Kŏje-do to ease the task of holding them and to reduce the number of guards needed. The camp was originally designed to hold 5,000.[64] The prisoners were literally packed in with minimal fencing, which permitted them to communicate freely among themselves as well as with local villagers. Through sympathetic villagers and refugees, the Chinese and North Korean authorities were able to pass messages back and forth to the POWs. As a result, the communist prisoners received instructions from and coordinated with P'yŏngyang and Beijing to instigate mass demonstrations, riots, and other disturbances. The inadequate guard force was another major problem. There were simply not enough guards nor were they of a quality "to insure the alertness needed to detect prisoners' plots or to identify and isolate the ringleaders."[65] As a virtual civil war raged between the prisoners, with former Chinese Nationalist and anticommunist Koreans (many of whom had been forcibly enlisted in the NKPA) clashing with their pro-communist opponents, beatings, mock trials, and murders became a daily occurrence. The UN guards, especially the Americans charged

Pro–North Korean compound, May 31, 1952. The banner says, "Long live General Kim Il Sung, the acclaimed leader of our people and the supreme commander of the Korean People's Army." (U.S. NATIONAL ARCHIVES AND RECORDS ADMINISTRATION)

with administering the camp, were intimidated or indifferent and did not take actions to prevent the incidents.

In mid-February, a large riot broke out when thousands of staunch North Korean communists refused to allow UN personnel to enter their compound to conduct preliminary prisoner screening. "There were approximately 3,000 civilian Korean internees in Compound no. 62," wrote Sir Esler Dening, the first British ambassador to Japan after World War II, who was then serving as political advisor to the UNC. "Amongst them were a fairly high proportion of fanatical communists, and the Americans had reasons to believe that these latter were using strong arm tactics to coerce 'deviationists' (e.g. anti-communists) amongst the internees into line." The result was a clash between UN guards and the prisoners that resulted in the death of dozens of prisoners. The incident was the first real indication that something was terribly wrong at Kŏje-do. "Unfortunately, the episode is a very disagreeable one and I fear, brings the United Nations Command nothing but discredit," concluded Dening.[66] R. J. Stratton, chief of the China and Korea Department in the British Foreign Office, was sufficiently alarmed to ask Sir Oliver Franks, the British ambassador to the United States, to raise the issue with the U.S. secretary of state: "If you see no objection, it might be well to draw Mr. Acheson's attention informally to the possibility of repercussions in the House of Commons, which, as he knows, has a long tradition of humanitarian interest in cases of alleged brutality."[67] The implied "repercussion" pertained to continued British participation in the war.

Camp conditions deteriorated rapidly. P. W. Manhard from the American embassy reported that leaders in the pro-Nationalist Chinese compounds "exercise[d] discriminatory control over food, clothing, fuel, and access to medical treatment," and pro-Nationalist prisoners controlled former CPV soldiers by means of "beatings, torture, and threats of punishment." He feared that "mounting resentment among the Chinese POWs [against the pro-Nationalist leaders] constituted an increased threat to the security within the UN POW camp."[68] A detailed public report by UNCURK after the commission's visit in mid-March described a situation that was clearly out of control. G. E. Van Ittersum, the Dutch representative, wrote that "no American ever enters the compounds . . . In many compounds there is no sewage. Dead and seriously wounded people are hardly ever extricated."[69] Pro-communist compounds were strewn "with banners and placards with such slogans as 'Down with American Imperialism.'" General Dodd told the commission that "he did not have enough guards to have these signs removed." In another pro-communist compound the commission "found about 5,000 communist prisoners formed round a square beating drums and shouting communist songs." Dodd, "fearing a hostile incident," requested that commission members quickly withdraw. The commission was barred from entering a third pro-communist compound. The prisoners, he said, "had not allowed any American to enter the camp on the two previous days." Moreover, during the commission's visit, "this compound was being bombarded with stones thrown across the road from a non-communist compound." Unmistakenly shocked, UNCURK concluded, "The visit to Koje-do made clear to the commission members the possibility of further political disturbances." As for Dodd, "he is living on the edge of a volcano and on any day there might be fresh outbreaks of violence and more deaths."[70]

On the evening of May 6, members of Compound 76 asked for a meeting with Dodd to discuss their complaint over beatings by Korean guards and poor living conditions. Compound 76 contained some 6,400 North Korean prisoners who were categorized as "zealous communists" and had violently refused to be screened by UN personnel in April. In exchange for a meeting they agreed to be rostered and fingerprinted. UN personnel had not been able to enter the camp for many weeks, and Dodd was directed to complete a roster of the remaining POWs. Dodd agreed and arrived on the afternoon of May 7 with five guards. He spoke to the prisoners through the fence. Shortly after the meeting began, a work detail of forty prisoners was permitted to pass through the gate under the supervision of two guards. The gate was opened, allowing some of the prisoners talking with Dodd from the inside to step outside. The last few men of the detail suddenly rushed Dodd as they were about to pass the gate and dragged him inside. Bewildered, some of the American guards swung their weapons to their shoulders, but Dodd shouted, "I'll court-martial the first man who shoots." The prisoners closed the gates and then raised a sign painted on ponchos, about twenty-five feet in length, which read, in stilted English:

WE CAPTURE DODD AS LONG AS OUR DEMAND WILL BE SOLVED, HIS SAFETY IS SECURED. IF THERE HAPPEN BRUTAL ACT SUCH AS SHOOTING, HIS LIFE IS DANGER[71]

News of Dodd's kidnapping quickly reached Ridgway. Ridgway informed the Joint Chiefs that the prisoners were capable of a mass breakout, which might result in the capture of the island itself. An American infantry battalion and a company of tanks were immediately dispatched to the island. General Van Fleet appointed Brig. Gen. Charles Colson to take charge of the camp and to negotiate Dodd's release.

Soon after his capture, Dodd sent a message that he was unharmed but that he would be killed if force was used to try to rescue him. He passed on the prisoners' demand that two delegates from each of the other compounds be brought to Compound 76, "where a conference would be held to discuss grievances and settle the terms on which he would be released."

The next morning, May 8, Dodd was confronted by representatives from all compounds, Chinese and North Koreans. One by one they spoke, "each having prepared a good deal of evidence" for their accusations of violence and abuse allegedly suffered. It was an extraordinary account of "concentrated and unvarnished tale of murder, torture, and thuggery, rape (for there were delegates from the women's compound) and of the unrelieved brutality of the men under his [Dodd's] command."[72] One described how some prisoners had been beaten by other prisoners because they wanted to return to North Korea. Others displayed evidence of torture, claiming that the scars on their bodies had been inflicted by the South Korean guards. "The warehouse bookkeepers explained how the camp supplies were sold by ROK soldiers to the black market. Two female prisoners told their stories about frequent rapes and gang rapes by both guards and prisoners." The prisoners drew up a list of nineteen counts of death and injury caused by the South Korean guards. One Chinese prisoner recalled that "[Dodd] became nervous and sometimes seemed touched by the stories. He just said: 'I can't believe it. I can't believe it.'"[73] On May 10, three days after Dodd's capture, Colson received a statement written in Korean, with a poor but comprehensible English translation, that the prisoners said he must sign to secure Dodd's release.

> 1. Immediate ceasing the barbarous behavior, insults, torture, forcible protest with blood writing, threatening, confinement, mass murdering, gun and machine gun shooting, using poison gas, germ weapons, experiment object of A-bomb, by your command. You should guarantee PW's human rights and individual life with the base on the International Law.
> 2. Immediate stopping the so-called illegal and unreasonable volunteer repatriation of NKPA and CPVA [Chinese People's Volunteer Army] PW's.
> 3. Immediate ceasing the forcible investigation (Screening) which thousands of PW's of NKPA and CPVA be rearmed and falled in slavery, permanently and illegally.
> 4. Immediate recognition of the PW Representative Group (Commission) consisted of NKPA and CPVA PW's and close cooperation to it by your command. This Representative Group will turn in Brig. Gen Dodd, USA, on your hand after we receive the satisfactory declaration to resolve the above items by your command. We will wait for your warm and sincere answer.[74]

Colson was appalled. He could not sign such a document. He responded with a revised version. Dodd offered to modify Colson's draft so that it was acceptable to both sides. Over the next few hours, Dodd, Colson, and Senior Col. Lee Hak-ku, the POW spokesman, engaged in furious back-and-forth exchanges until a final statement was agreed upon.[75] That evening, Colson signed the document and Dodd was released.

It was now up to General Clark to clean up the Kŏje-do mess and make sure that it never happened again. "As Ridgway waved good-bye," remembered Clark, "I visualized him throwing me a blazing forward pass." Clark was unsure whether he was ready to catch the ball. Earlier that morning, Clark had written a public statement denouncing the text of the POW demands and of Colson's agreement. Clark was upset not only that Dodd and Colson had accommodated the prisoners' demands but also that Colson signed a letter containing incriminating language that could be used against the UN negotiators in P'anmunjŏm:

> I do admit that there have been instances of bloodshed where many PW have been killed and wounded by UN Forces. I can assure that in the future that PW can expect humane treatment in this camp according to the principles of International Law. I will do all within my power to eliminate further violence and bloodshed. If such incidents happen in the future, I will be responsible.[76]

Clark stated that "the allegations set forth in the first paragraph are wholly without foundation," and that "any violence that has occurred at Kŏje-do has been the result of the deliberate machinations of unprincipled communist leaders whose avowed intent has been to disrupt the orderly operation of the camp and to embarrass the UNC in every way possible."[77] Dodd also released a statement including an account of his capture. He ended it with a justification of sorts: "The demands made by the PWs are inconsequential and the concessions granted by the camp authorities were of minor importance."[78] Clark could not have disagreed more. Colson's statement and the entire Dodd affair had greatly damaged the UN position. Ridgway agreed: "The United Nations Command was asked to plead guilty to every wild and utterly baseless charge the Red radio had ever laid against us."[79] By admitting that there had been "instances of bloodshed" and that "prisoners of war had been killed or wounded by UN Forces," Colson had undermined the moral foundation of the UN, and in particular, the principle of voluntary repatriation, which was based on the assumption of fair and equal treatment. Dodd and Colson were punished by being demoted to colonel.[80]

Clearly changes had to be made at Kŏje-do. Clark sent Brig. Gen. Hayden Boatner, the "tough, stocky and cocky" assistant commander of the Second Infantry Division, to replace Colson. The compounds were broken up, and some prisoners and all civilian internees were moved to other camps. Routine inspections were enforced, and anti-UN or pro-communist banners and signs were forbidden. But the UNC had suffered a severe blow to its credibility. "At the time of the Secretary of State's statement in the House on the repatriation question on May 7, we had no reason to doubt the validity of the screening process," wrote Charles Johnston from the China and Korea Department of the British Foreign Office. "The revelations which we now have of the conditions in the camps must give us serious misgivings on the fairness and accuracy of the census." He concluded, "We still stand firmly on the principle of voluntary repatriation; but we must be sure that the factual foundation on which that principle rests is sound."[81]

Acheson told Foreign Secretary Anthony Eden in late May that "the incident on Kŏje Island had greatly weakened the moral position of the United Nations Command," and that it was "urgently necessary to restore this."[82] Johnston lamented that Britain's image had been tarnished by the whole affair. He was angry that the British had been kept out of the loop on the Kŏje-do incident. The Foreign Office, however, had been well aware of the troubling conditions on Kŏje-do for quite some time. In December 1951 it had raised concerns about the camp but had been rebuffed. "Is U.S. State Department now in a position to supply the authoritative statement on recent events on Kŏje requested in our telegram No. 2039 of 16 May?" Johnston demanded. "It would be regrettable and embarrassing if the results of the United Nations Command's enquiry into these recent disturbances on Kŏje were withheld from us, as were those on the 18 February and the 13 March riots."[83] From then on the Foreign Office insisted on being kept directly informed about the POW situation. Some members of the British House of Commons even began whispering that "the troubles of Kŏje-do would probably never have happened if the prison camps had been under British control." Many British officials were privately "scathing on the subject," although they did their best to hide their disdain publicly.[84]

It was only months later that Clark realized the full extent of the "civil war" and general lawless conditions that had existed at Kŏje-do. There were whisperings that Dodd and Colson had been unfairly scapegoated and that Ridgway and Van Fleet deserved much of the blame. But the anticipation of an imminent truce meant that the POW problem was largely soft-pedaled in the hope that a quick armistice would resolve all the problems. Any public revelation of the conditions at Kŏje-do, it was thought, would give the communists another excuse to delay the talks. The irony is that the armistice did not resolve the problems at Kŏje-do. Rather, the situation at Kŏje-do complicated the problem of reaching an armistice. The Dodd affair and everything that it revealed about the conditions of the camp had seriously compromised the principle of non-forcible repatriation. It gave the communists fodder for refusal based on claims that the screening process had been unfair. By May 1952, the war seemed to have reached a moral and physical stalemate. It would take a new American president to move the struggle forward, even at the risk of a nuclear war.

CHAPTER TWELVE

Armistice, at Last

President Truman's approval rating sank to 22 percent by February 1952. The war remained an unresolved nightmare, mired in petty haggling at P'anmunjŏm and punctuated by fierce battles over a landscape that resembled the horrors of World War I trench warfare. Many thought Korea was a conflict that was neither noble nor necessary. Edith Rosengrant of Springfield, Colorado, a widowed mother of six children, wrote a stinging letter to Truman, enclosing her son's posthumously awarded Purple Heart: "Soldiers need help when they are fighting . . . Dick's life was thrown away by his own country's cowardly leaders."[1] Halsey McGovern of Washington, D.C., lost two sons in Korea, Lt. Robert McGovern, who won the Medal of Honor, and Lt. Jerome McGovern, who won the Silver Star. They died within eleven days of each other in early 1951. Mr. McGovern took an even more dramatic and unprecedented action than Mrs. Rosengrant to express his bitterness. He notified the Pentagon that he would not accept the Medal of Honor, the nation's highest award for valor, or the Silver Star on behalf of his sons because the president was "unworthy" to "confer them on my boys or any other boys."[2]

Donna Cooper of Memphis, Tennessee, also returned the Purple Heart awarded to her fallen son, Pvt. Paul Cooper, who was killed in October 1951. She wrote:

> Dear Mr. President:
>
> Today I buried my first-born son. Having known the depth of his soul, I can find no place among his memories for the Purple Heart or the scroll. I am returning it to you with this thought: To me, he is a symbol of the 109,000 men who have been sacrificed in this needless slaughter, a so-called police action that has not and could never have been satisfactorily explained to patriotic Americans who love their country and the ideals it stands for. None of us appreciate the degradation and ridicule we have to suffer because of a pseudo war. If there had been a need for armed con-

Robert McGovern and Francis McGovern as students at St. Johns College High School in Washington, D.C. Robert McGovern was a member of Company A, 5th Cavalry Regiment, First Cavalry Division. He was awarded the Medal of Honor for his actions near Kamyangjan-ni on January 30, 1951. Eleven days later, his brother, Francis McGovern, posthumously earned the Silver Star for his actions near Kŭmwang-ni while serving with Company I, 9th Infantry Regiment, Second Infantry Division. (COURTESY OF CHARLES MCGOVERN)

> flict to preserve the American way of life, I could have given him proudly and would have treasured the medal. However, since there was nothing superficial in his whole life, I cannot mar his memory by keeping a medal and stereotyped words that hold no meaning and fail to promise a better tomorrow for the ones he died for.[3]

Recrimination and disillusionment over Korea, rabid McCarthyism, and personal attacks against Truman and Acheson brought with them a thirst for profound political change. Eisenhower's declaration of his candidacy for president in 1952 led many to express optimism that his experience in foreign policy and moderate position on domestic issues made him just the right person to replace Truman.

"I Shall Go to Korea"

Polls showed that the war was the foremost issue on the American people's minds, and the election would largely become a referendum on Korea. Eisenhower addressed the issue directly on October 24, when, in a blistering speech, he promised to forgo "the diversions of politics" and concentrate on the task of closing the war that "has been the burial ground for 20,000 American dead." Korea, he said, "has been a sign, a warning sign, of the way the Administration has conducted our world affairs" and "a measure, a damning measure, of the quality of leadership we have been given." If elected, Eisenhower declared dramatically, "I shall go to Korea." The speech drew high praise and rave reviews from the press. The *New York Times* hailed the speech and endorsed Eisenhower. For Emmet Hughes, Eisenhower's speech writer, "psychologically, this declaration ("I will go to Korea") probably marked the end of the campaign. Politically, it was later credited . . . with sealing the election itself."[4] Truman, however, thought using the tragic Korean situation for political gains was contemptible. "Ike was well informed on all aspects of the Korean War and the delicacy of the armistice negotiations," recalled the chairman of the JCS, General Omar Bradley. "He knew very well that he could achieve nothing by going to Korea."[5] Still, the speech was a masterful political stroke, for it put the Democrats on the defensive, and Eisenhower's promise to go to Korea, while not offering a specific policy proposal to end the war, nevertheless offered a chance at something new.

Eisenhower won in a landslide against Adlai Stevenson. Keeping his campaign promise, the president-elect announced that he would go to Korea on November 29. He was not yet sure how he would end the war, but he did possess one significant advantage. Republican critics such as Senators Robert Taft and William Knowland would be silent, at least for the time being, and this gave the incoming administration much greater freedom to maneuver.

As soon as news of Eisenhower's planned trip reached Seoul, President Syngman Rhee announced that he would be given a rousing reception, including a mass rally, parades, and dinners. Rhee saw the visit as an opportunity to convince the new president to resume the offensive to achieve Korean unification. Rhee thought Eisenhower would be sympathetic to the cause of "total victory" both as a military man and as a Republican. "I expect General Eisenhower to bring peace and unity to Korea," the South Korean president told the *New York Times*. "We are depending on him."[6] The JCS instructed General Clark to tell Rhee that there would be no public receptions or appearances for Eisenhower

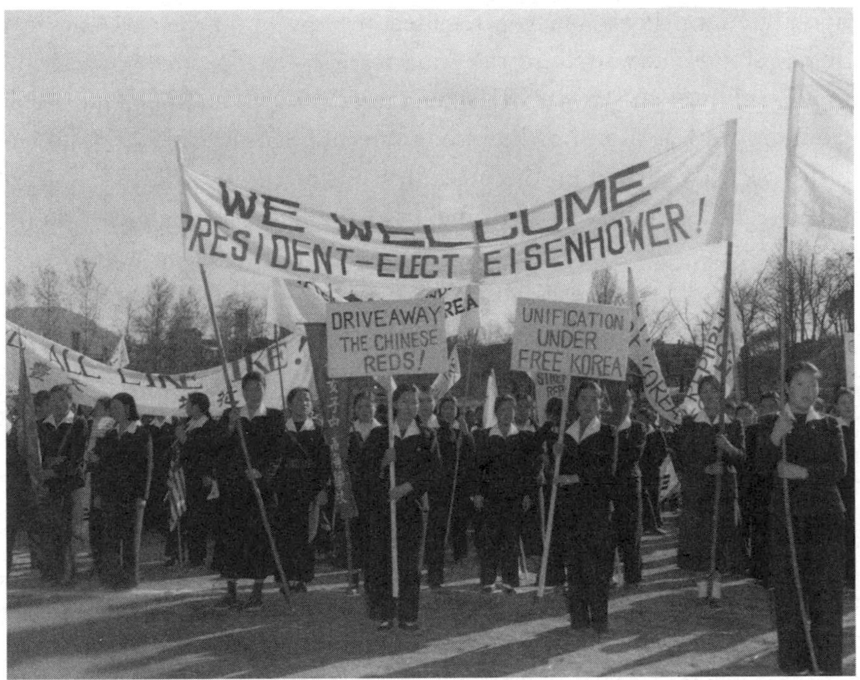

Korean civilians during a rally held in anticipation of President-elect Eisenhower's forthcoming visit to Seoul, November 25, 1952. (U.S. NATIONAL ARCHIVES AND RECORDS ADMINISTRATION)

because it was too dangerous. The visit would be brief, and Eisenhower's advisors cautioned him to avoid Rhee. "President Syngman Rhee is old and feeble," warned John Foster Dulles, Eisenhower's choice for secretary of state, before his trip. "His will is still powerful and he has three obsessions: (1) To continue power; (2) to unite all of Korea under his leadership; (3) to give vent to his life-long hatred of the Japanese." Dulles recommended "that political matters be discussed as little as possible with Rhee."[7]

Eisenhower's time in Korea consisted almost entirely of touring the front and visiting units. He saw his son John, who was serving in the Third Infantry Division. When Eisenhower declined to attend a welcoming ceremony in Seoul, Rhee refused to take no for an answer. On December 4, Rhee went to downtown Seoul where a large "U.S. President-Elect Eisenhower Welcome Rally" at the Capitol Building had been organized. A huge crowd bearing American flags and "Welcome Ike" banners had gathered to see and greet Eisenhower that afternoon. General Paek Sŏn-yŏp recalled the disappointment: "Rhee sat on the stand and waited for the Americans to change their minds and for Eisenhower to show up. I accompanied President Rhee and shook from the cold, as some one hundred thousand Seoul residents waited in bitter weather, sitting on the plaza in front of the Capitol. We waited for Eisenhower, but he never came."[8] Realizing that Eisenhower would not show up, Rhee went to the presidential residence to wait for the president-elect's courtesy call. Paek was furious. "Whatever the Americans' real reasons [for not meeting Rhee]," Paek later reflected, "this communication dealt a severe blow to the prestige of a sovereign head of state." Paek immediately got in touch with General Clark, telling him that in no uncertain terms he could not imagine a "greater affront" to South Korea. "If the president-elect does not visit President Rhee," Paek threatened, "you will insult President Rhee, of course, but you will also offend the Korean people. If a meeting between the two men does not materialize, any and all future cooperation between the ROK Army and the United States will be jeopardized." Taken back by the vehemence of Paek's response, Clark immediately got on the phone with his staff. A meeting was arranged.[9]

On December 5, the day the president-elect was due to depart, Eisenhower finally met with the South Korean president and his cabinet. The meeting lasted just forty minutes, and nothing substantive was discussed. Rhee nevertheless made sure that the meeting was recorded for posterity. General Clark recalled that the "newspaper people were there, including still and movie photographers. Rhee was certain he was going to have a fine record of the Eisenhower visit."[10] The old patriot needed to save face, but he was angry and confused. He had thought Eisenhower had a grand strategy to drive the communists out of Korea. Eisenhower made it clear, however, that he would not seek unification but rather a truce in Korea, and pursued an alternative strategy to end the war: "My conclusion, as I left Korea, was that we could not stand forever on a static front and continue to accept casualties without any visible result. Small attacks on small hills would not end the war."[11]

On December 5, as Eisenhower was flying from Seoul to Guam, MacArthur delivered a speech to the National Association of Manufacturers at the Waldolf Astoria Hotel in New York City, where he announced that he had come up with a solution on how to end the war in

Korea. Eisenhower was informed of MacArthur's proposal, and a meeting between the two men was quickly arranged. Despite mutual antipathy (MacArthur once dismissed Eisenhower as a "mere clerk, nothing more"), Eisenhower was curious to know what the old general had to say. They met in New York City on December 17. MacArthur handed him a copy of his "Memorandum for Ending the Korean War." The plan called for a two-party conference between the president and Stalin to "explore the world situation as a corollary to ending the Korean War" and to agree that "Germany and Korea be permitted to reunite under forms of government to be popularly determined upon." If Stalin refused such a meeting, the president should inform him that it was the intention of the United States "to clear North Korea of enemy forces . . . through the atomic bombing of enemy military concentrations in North Korea and sowing the fields with suitable radioactive materials . . . to close major lines of enemy supply and communication leading south from the Yalu." The president should also threaten to "neutralize Red China's capability to wage modern war." The memo, MacArthur explained, presented "in the broadest terms a general concept and outline." He would also "be glad to elaborate as minutely as desired."[12]

Eisenhower listened patiently and said, "General, this is something new. I'll have to look at the understanding between ourselves and our Allies in the prosecution of this war." Privately, Eisenhower was appalled. "He didn't have any formal peace program at all," Eisenhower later confided. "What he was talking about was the tactical methods by which the war could be ended."[13] But the nuclear question remained a central question when Eisenhower deliberated on how best to end the war. Sharp disagreements over how atomic weapons might be used became the focus of intense debate. The air force and the navy believed that atomic bombs might constitute sufficient pressure to force China to accept reasonable armistice terms. The army strongly disagreed. Army Chief of Staff Joe Collins noted that the Chinese and North Koreans were dug in underground across the front and provided poor targets for atomic weapons. Bradley was concerned that casualties in a new offensive would be so great that "we may find that we will be forced to use every type of weapon that we have."[14]

There was also concern about the impact of the use of nuclear weapons on the UN coalition in Korea. Between February and May 1953, the

National Security Council conducted a series of meetings that were far more "discursive than decisive" in an effort to find a way to end the war.[15] Notwithstanding interservice differences, the threat of Soviet retaliation, and the "disinclination" of allies to go along with a military proposal that included nuclear weapons, Eisenhower wanted to take a more "positive action against the enemy" and concluded that "the plan selected by the Joint Chiefs of Staff was most likely to achieve the objective we sought." The JCS plan included the option of employing atomic weapons "on a sufficiently large scale to insure success." Secretary of State Dulles, then on a trip to India, told Prime Minister Nehru that "if the armistice negotiations collapsed, the United States would probably make a stronger rather than a lesser military exertion, and that this might well extend the area of conflict." He also told Nehru that "only crazy people could think that the United States wanted to prolong the struggle, which had already cost us about 150,000 casualties."[16] Dulles's intent was for Nehru to pass the message to the Chinese that the United States was prepared to use nuclear weapons if an armistice agreement was not soon forthcoming. But Nehru apparently passed no such message to the Chinese and later denied having any role in conveying Washington's atomic warning.[17]

Whether Nehru's denial is to be believed or not, the Chinese were aware that Eisenhower was considering the nuclear option. The new American ambassador to the Soviet Union, Charles Bohlen, was instructed to "emphasize" to the Soviet foreign minister the "extreme importance and seriousness of the latest UNC proposals" by pointing out "the lengths to which the UNC has gone to bridge [the] existing gap" and "making it clear these represent the limit to which we can go." Furthermore, Bohlen was to point out that "rejection [of] these proposals and consequent failure [to] reach agreement in the armistice" would create a situation that Washington is "seeking earnestly to avoid."[18]

Most Americans and others around the world at the time believed that the threat of nuclear war coerced the communists to reach an armistice agreement. "We told them we could not hold it to a limited war any longer if the communists welched on a treaty of truce," Eisenhower told his assistant, Sherman Adams. "They didn't want a full scale war or an atomic attack. That kept them under some control."[19] But had nuclear coercion really worked in Korea? Was the threat of nuclear warfare the most important factor in forcing the communists to reach an armistice agreement?[20] The answer is, probably not. First, Chinese leaders were well aware of the potential of an American nuclear attack. Indian Ambassador K. M. Panikkar recalled that when Truman raised the possibility that atomic weapons might be used in Korea in late November 1950, "the Chinese seemed totally unmoved by this threat." General Nie Rongzhen told Panikkar early in the war that "the Americans can bomb us, they can destroy our industries, but they cannot defeat us on land. We have calculated all that. They may even drop atom bombs on us. What then? After all, China lived on farms."[21] The Eisenhower administration's alleged threat of nuclear war was also issued nearly two months *after* the communists had already made a significant compromise at P'anmunjŏm. An unexpected breakthrough occurred in March 1953 when the communists suddenly became conciliatory. On March 30, Zhou Enlai declared that the communists would agree to voluntary repatriation.[22] Whatever happened to change the communists' minds between October 1952, when the armistice talks were suspended, and March 1953, it could not have been the nuclear threats made in May. The forces of peace were already in motion in Korea *before* any alleged threat of nuclear war was made.[23]

What, then, had happened to change the communists' mind? Why had they finally come around on the POW voluntary repatriation issue after two years of fruitless talks? If not "atomic brinkmanship," what suddenly pushed them to the path toward peace?

Death of a Dictator

On March 4, 1953, the Soviet people awoke to the radio bulletin that Stalin was gravely ill. He had suffered from a "sudden brain hemorrhage" with loss of consciousness and speech.[24] The world soon learned that Stalin was dead. Power was assumed by a coalition of four men: Georgi Malenkov was appointed premier. Lavrenti Beria retained his position as minister of the interior, while V. M. Molotov, who had known Stalin longer than anyone else, became foreign minister. Nikita S. Khrushchev became Central Committee secretary. There was other startling news. Sweeping changes in the government and party hierarchies were announced.

In the months before his death, Stalin appeared intent on keeping the flames of the war burning bright. In August and September 1952, Stalin and Zhou met to discuss the war's course. Zhou wanted a settlement in Korea, but he approached the matter with Stalin cautiously, seemingly to agree with Stalin's hard-line stance while attempting to explore the possibility of a negotiated settlement. Zhou noted that "the [North] Koreans were suffering greatly" and were anxious to bring the war to a close. Stalin responded caustically that "the [North] Koreans have lost nothing except for casualties." The Americans, he said, "will understand this war is not advantageous and they will have to end it." He claimed that the "Americans are not capable of waging a large-scale war at all," because "all of their strength lies in air power and the atomic bomb." Stalin advised that "one must be firm when dealing with America"; patience was required to beat them. "The Americans cannot defeat little Korea," Stalin mockingly declared. "The Germans conquered France in 20 days. It's already been two years and the USA has still not subdued little Korea. What kind of strength is that?" Belittling America's alleged weakness was probably galling to Zhou since it was the Chinese, not the Russians, who were fighting and dying in Korea. Zhou stated that if the United States "makes some sort of compromises, even if they are small, then they should accept" them, but only "under the condition that the question of the remaining POWs will be resolved under mediation by some neutral country, like India, or the remaining POWs transferred to this neutral country, until the question is resolved."[25] Zhou was trying to find a way to end the impasse over the POW issue. But Stalin continued to discourage the Chinese premier's desire for flexibility. He reiterated his hard-line stance to Mao in late December.[26]

General Clark anticipated communist rejection of the proposal made on February 22, 1953, for the exchange of sick and wounded POWs: "There was dead silence for over a month," he recalled.[27] Three weeks after Stalin's death, the silence was broken. The communists not only agreed to exchange the sick and wounded but also proposed a resumption of the talks, which had been suspended for nearly six months. The communists had abruptly changed their tune and became conciliatory. Stalin's death was a turning point in the war, although few had been prepared for it.

Many had believed that post-Stalinist Russia would experience a great upheaval. "Some in the West predicted that the Soviet Union would surely undergo a bloodbath," recalled Ambassador Bohlen. But the predictions proved wrong. Within days of Stalin's death, it appeared that the so-called guardians of unity—Malenkov, Beria, Molotov, and Khrushchev—were firmly in charge.[28] They ushered in a striking shift in foreign policy. Malenkov announced a "peace initiative" in mid-March, stating that "there is no litigious or unresolved question which could not be settled by peaceful means on the basis of the mutual agreement of the countries concerned... including the United States of America."[29] A few days later, Radio Moscow admitted, for the first time since the end of World War II, that the United States and Great Britain had played a role in the defeat of the Axis Powers. Stalin's "Hate America Campaign" of 1952 was abruptly suspended.[30] During Stalin's final days, Moscow had been festooned with anti-American propaganda: "Placards portraying spiderlike characters in America military uniform . . . stared down at us from every fence throughout the city," George Kennan observed.[31] These disappeared. The Russians also agreed "to intervene to obtain the release of nine British diplomats and missionaries held captive in Korea since the outbreak of the Korean War." The changes were not confined to Korea. The Soviet government withdrew Stalin's 1945 claim to the Turkish provinces of Kan and Ardahan and control of the Dardanelles. After weeks of refusal, Moscow agreed to the appointment of Dag Hammarskjöld as the new secretary general of the United Nations. Moscow also proposed the possibility of a meeting between Malenkov and Eisenhower to discuss "disarmament and atomic energy control." On June 8, Molotov told the Yugoslav chargé d'affaires that Moscow wanted to send an ambassador to Belgrade, "the first move toward repairing the rupture with Tito."[32]

It was all breathtaking, but the biggest change was Moscow's desire to end the Korean War. On March 19, the Soviet Council of Ministers adopted a resolution that was a complete review of Soviet policy in Korea. In "tortuously convoluted language" that reflected the Kremlin's unease at fundamentally altering Stalin's Korea policy, the resolution declared,

> The Soviet Government has thoroughly reviewed the question of the war in Korea under present conditions and with regard to the entire course of events of the preceding period. As a result of this, the Soviet Government has reached the conclusion that it would be incorrect to continue the line

> on this question which has been followed until now, without making those alterations in that line which correspond to the present political situation and which ensue from the deepest interests of our peoples, the peoples of the USSR, China, and Korea who are interested in a firm peace throughout the world and have always sought an acceptable path toward the soonest possible conclusion of the war in Korea.[33]

The resolution outlined "statements that should be made by Kim Il Sung, Peng Dehuai, the government of the PRC, and the Soviet delegation at the UN" to quickly achieve an armistice.[34] Two weeks later, the communists responded positively to Clark's proposal for exchanging sick and wounded prisoners while also announcing their intention to obtain a "smooth settlement of the entire question of prisoners of war."[35]

Despite the breakthrough, Clark was suspicious: "I could not help but think, as I read the proposal to resume armistice talks, that perhaps it was the anesthetic before the operation."[36] The feeling was widely shared in Washington and London. Dulles, in particular, was highly suspicious of the new Soviet leadership and their "peace offensive." British Foreign Secretary Eden also shared the skepticism, arguing that what changes there seemed to be in Russian policy might be "tactical" moves to dupe the West. Eden, like Dulles, believed that the Soviet Union merely wanted to be more accommodating to gain time to consolidate the new leadership. The Kremlin, according to Dulles, was trying to "buy off a powerful enemy and gain a respite." Moreover, he argued, it would be an "illusion of peace" if there was "a settlement [in Korea] based on the status quo." The United States needed to make "clear to the captive people that we do not accept their captivity as a permanent fact of history."[37]

Despite Dulles's reservations, Eisenhower wanted to take advantage of the moment and responded with his own peace offensive in a speech on April 16. He called it "The Chance for Peace." Eisenhower said he welcomed the recent Soviet statement, but he could accept them as sincere only if the words were backed by concrete deeds. He called for a Soviet signature on the Austrian treaty, an agreement for a free and united Germany, and the full independence of the Eastern European nations. He also called for the conclusion of an "honorable armistice" in Korea. "This means the immediate cessation of hostilities and the prompt initiation of political discussions leading to the holding of free elections in Korea." In exchange, Eisenhower said, he was prepared to conclude an arms-limitations agreement and to accept international control of atomic energy to "insure the prohibition of atomic weapons."[38] There was no reference to Taiwan or China. It was an expression of the American vision of the conditions of peace in Europe and Asia. The persuasive power of the speech was essentially reactive, not proactive. For critics of the Eisenhower administration, the speech was more political posturing than an actual compromise effort to achieve détente with the Soviet Union.[39]

Still, the speech was well received. Sherman Adams called it "the most effective of Eisenhower's public career and certainly one of the highlights of his presidency."[40] Walter Lippmann commended the president for "seizing the initiative" and for beginning discussion and negotiations of the greatest complexity and consequence."[41] But nothing significant was achieved because of it. Moreover, incredibly, it was during this time that the Eisenhower administration began contemplating the use of nuclear weapons to achieve a quick end to the Korean War. Ambassador Bohlen in Moscow believed the United States had missed an important opportunity to fundamentally change its relationship with the Soviet Union after Stalin's death: "I wrote Dulles that the events could not be dismissed as simply another peace campaign designed solely or even primarily to bemuse and divide the West."[42] Three years of fighting an angry and frustrating war in Korea had embittered Americans against the Soviet Union, and thus it was probably no surprise that Bohlen's observations fell on deaf ears in Washington. The temporary thaw between the Americans and the Soviets after Stalin's death did not bring about measurable changes in their relationship, but it did make possible the exchange of sick and wounded prisoners in Korea. In mid-April an agreement was reached at P'anmunjŏm, and Operation Little Switch repatriated seven hundred UNC POWs and seven thousand communist POWs between April 20 and May 3. Only one item remained for resolution for an armistice: the selection of neutral nations to serve as custodians of the prisoners refusing repatriation. But this issue was relatively minor compared to previous hurdles. "Despite these annoyances," recalled General Clark, "progress toward an armistice appeared to be rapid. None of the disagreements that still existed appeared to be too difficult to overcome."[43]

Divided Nation

The talks at last reached the point of settlement in early June. The final issue of selecting neutral nations to supervise voluntary non-repatriates was settled when the communist side agreed to establish a Neutral Nations Repatriations Commission with five members—Poland, Czechoslovakia, Switzerland, Sweden, and India. These countries would share in the task of maintaining custody of the non-repatriates in their original places of detention. India would be in physical custody of the non-repatriates. Communist and UN authorities would question the non-repatriates for final verification that their decision was made voluntarily and free of coercion.[44] As the negotiators began working out the last details, Clark reported that "the resolution of the POW issue will now make the signing of the armistice agreement possible in the near future and possibly as early as June 18."[45]

After nearly two years of negotiations, peace was finally in sight. But one final obstacle remained: Rhee refused to get on board. "An armistice without national unification was a death sentence without protest," he declared.[46] After meeting Rhee just before the POW terms were agreed on, Clark reported that "he had never seen him [Rhee] more distracted, wrought up and emotional." Rhee had always held out hope that the armistice negotiations would fail. Clark later wrote, "My relations with South Korea's venerable, patriotic and wily chief of state had been excellent right up to the moment the United States indicated clearly it intended to go through with an armistice that might leave his country divided. Then I became a whipping boy for his bitterness and frustration."[47] Proclaiming the right of self-determination, Rhee insisted that peace must be restored by the Koreans themselves: "We reassert our determination to risk our lives to fight on to a decisive end in case the United Nations accepts a truce and stops fighting. This is imperative because the presence of Chinese Communist troops in Korea is tantamount to denying us our free existence."[48]

Washington had assumed that Rhee's threat to continue fighting alone was a bluff and that he would sign the armistice, and so the administration was caught off-guard by the emotional intensity of his opposition and the scale of popular support from the South Korean people.

Clark suggested a mutual security treaty to placate Rhee and the South Koreans. Eisenhower agreed and wrote to Rhee that while he empathized with the South Korean leader's "struggle for unification," the time had nevertheless come "to pursue this goal by political and other methods." The enemy "proposed an armistice which involves a clear abandonment of the fruits of aggression," and since the cease-fire line would follow the front lines, "the armistice would leave the Republic of Korea in undisputed possession of substantially the territory which the Republic administered prior to the aggression, indeed, this territory will be somewhat enlarged." He also agreed to negotiate "a security pact . . . which would cover the territory now or hereafter brought peacefully under the administration of the ROK" in addition to providing "substantial reconstruction aid to South Korea." He concluded, "Even the thought of a separation [between the United States and the ROK] at this critical hour would be a tragedy. We must remain united."[49] On June 18, Eisenhower received Rhee's reply. Rhee surreptitiously ordered the ROK Army to release twenty-seven thousand anticommunist North Korean prisoners held in its custody. Clark remembered that "all hell broke loose, at Rhee's order."[50]

The release of the prisoners had been carefully planned. The idea had originated with Rhee himself. Former prime minister Chŏng Il-kwŏn, a senior army commander at the time, recalled that the "release was planned in top secret between retired Maj. Gen. Wŏn Yŏng-dŏk [as provost marshal general in charge of the Korean guard force] and Rhee," and that he himself had been kept in the dark.[51] Only at the last minute was the plan disseminated to key subordinates. At 2:30 a.m. on June 18, Wŏn's men abetted the prisoners' escape by "cutting the barbed wire and killing the camp lights." Meanwhile, the Americans, under orders to fire only in self defense, tried to turn back the mass of prisoners with tear gas, "but the gas proved useless."[52] When news of the escape was made public, Rhee immediately acknowledged his role in the plan.[53]

Eisenhower was aghast at Rhee's perfidy: "What Syngman Rhee had done was to sabotage the very basis of the arguments that we had been presenting to the Chinese and North Koreans for all these many months. In agreeing that prisoners should not be repatriated against their will, the communists had made a major concession. The processing of the prisoners was observed by representatives of both sides. This condition was negated in a single stroke by Rhee's release of the North Koreans." Eisenhower immediately sent a warning to Rhee: "Persistence in your present course of action will make impractical for the UN Command to continue to operate jointly with you under the condition which would result there from. Unless you are prepared immediately and unequivocally to accept the authority of the UN Command to conduct present hostilities and to bring them to a close, it will be necessary to effect another arrangement."[54] But what other arrangements could there be? The South Koreans could not possibly win the war against China by themselves and yet they constituted the bulk of the UN fighting force. Rhee could order ROK forces to withdraw from the UNC. This possibility deeply worried the Americans and other UN participants. Rhee could sabotage not only the armistice but also the fate of the UNC, the credibility of the UN itself, and the idea of international collective security. Prime Minster Nehru laid out these concerns in a memo to the president of the UN General Assembly: "In view of [Rhee's] action,

Anti-armistice demonstrations, April 1953. (AP PHOTOS)

armistice terms become unrealistic and the United Nations has been put in a most embarrassing position which will undoubtedly affect their credit and capacity for future action." Furthermore, "Chinese and North Koreans can, with reason, object to signing any armistice terms which have not been and are not likely to be carried out." As a result, "the position of United Nations Command in Korea becomes completely anomalous and the question arises whether United Nations Policy must be subordinated to President Rhee's policy." Nehru suggested that the matter be taken up at once by the UN General Assembly since "the whole future of the United Nations is jeopardized."[55]

The South Korean people overwhelmingly supported Rhee's actions. On June 25, the third anniversary of the start of the war, Rhee appeared before a cheering crowd and vowed to unify the nation and "fight communism to the death." With "tears in his eyes," his voice "broken as the loudspeaker carried his words to the crowds and all over the nation through Seoul radio," he declared, "What we want, because we know we will die if we follow our Allies, is to be given the opportunity to fight by ourselves. We simply ask to be allowed to decide our fate by ourselves." The crowd roared and hysterically waved banners that said, "Don't sell out Korea" and "Down with the Armistice."[56] Daily anti-armistice demonstrations in Seoul and other cities and increasing bitterness threatened to sever U.S.-ROK relations. An alarmed Dulles wrote to Rhee,

> Dear Mr. President:
>
> I speak to you as a friend of your nation. As you know I have long worked for a free and united Korea. In 1947 and again in 1948 in the United Nations, I initiated for the United States steps which led to the establishment of your government and international acceptance of the proposition that Korea ought to be free and united [illegible] I pledged our nation's continuing support of that goal. Also, because aggression was an ever-present threat and because your people felt alone, I asserted that free world unity was a reality, and I concluded: "you are not alone." You will never be alone so long as you continue to play worthily your part in the great design of human freedom.
>
> That pledge of unity was hailed throughout South Korea. It was quickly put to the test, for within six days, the aggressor struck, within a few hours, the brave army of the Republic of Korea was overwhelmed by superior forces and the territory of the Republic of Korea was overrun. Then you pleaded for the help of the Free World. It came. The United Nations acted

> and the United States responded quickly and largely to its appeal on your behalf. We responded because we believed in the principle of free world unity.
>
> The principle of unity cannot work without sacrifice. No one can do precisely what he wants. The youth of America did not do what they wanted. Over one million American boys have left their homes and families and their peaceful pursuits, to go far away to Korea. They went because, at a dark hour, you invoked the sacred principle of free world unity to save your country from overwhelming disaster . . .
>
> Your nation lives today, not only because of the great valor and sacrifices of your own armies, but because others have come to your side and died besides you. Do you now have the moral right to destroy the national life which we have helped save at a great price? Can *you* be deaf when *we* now invoke the plea of unity?[57]

The call for unity and the moral outrage against Rhee's actions were echoed around the world. London's *Daily Mail* condemned Rhee for his "treacherous" and "insolent" act, which brought up "a simple, but all-important question: Who is to be in charge in South Korea, the United Nations or Syngman Rhee?" If an armistice failed to materialize, "such is the enormity of Rhee's offense," it declared. "He has demonstrated he is not to be trusted. He should be replaced by someone with a sense of responsibility. If necessary, his whole Government should be bundled out." London's *Daily Herald* was similarly outraged: "The present position is utterly intolerable and the disaster for the world would be incalculable." India's *Delhi Express* stated that "Rhee should be removed at once to a place far from the scene of mischief." The *Times of India* responded that "the situation calls for an all-out action to save peace," while Tokyo's *Jiji shimpō* suggested that the United States depose of "the unscrupulous dictator."[58]

Only the communists reacted coolly. They wanted to end the fighting. Their letter to Clark in early July included the usual vitriol against the Syngman Rhee "clique" for "unscrupulously violating the prisoner of war agreement," but the letter, signed by both Kim Il Sung and Peng Dehuai, nevertheless ended on an upbeat note: "To sum up, although our side is not entirely satisfied with the reply of your side, yet in view of the indication of the desire of your side to strive for an early armistice and in view of the assurances given by your side, our side agrees that the delegations of both sides meet at an appointed time to discuss the question of implementation of the armistice agreement and the various preparations prior to the signing of the armistice agreement."[59] An uncharacteristically generous response, it indicated the communists' determination to conclude an armistice. The communists also saw Rhee's provocative actions as an opportunity to splinter the U.S.-ROK alliance. In their assessment and response to the current state of armistice negotiations, the Soviet leadership suggested that the Chinese "achieve a common point of view with the U.S. on the issue of an armistice in order to isolate Rhee . . . and deepen the domestic and foreign differences of the American side." It was a policy that Kim Il Sung would continue to exploit in his future dealings with the United States. As the Chinese Deputy Minister of Foreign Affairs Wu Xiuquan later quipped, "In this case, a paradoxical situation will be created inasmuch as we and the U.S. are sort of acting together against Syngman Rhee."[60]

A grim Eisenhower opened an emergency National Security Council meeting on June 18 lamenting "the terrible situation" for UN forces. How could UN forces "conduct the defense of South Korea while ignorant of what ROK forces in their rear would do next?" he asked. If the UNC was unable to trust Rhee, "how can we continue to provide ammunition for the ROK forces when we have no idea what their next move would be?"[61] Removing Rhee, an option considered, no longer seemed possible. He had gained enormous domestic prestige for his bold defiance. Getting rid of him could create a politically explosive situation that could lead to mass defections within the ROK Army. The only viable option was negotiation to get South Korea to agree to the armistice. Walter Robertson, the assistant secretary of state for East Asian and Pacific affairs, would lead the American team. U. Alexis Johnson, the deputy assistant secretary of state overseeing Japan and Korea policy, later said, "In Robertson, Rhee had met his match. Garrulous, earthy, charming as it was possible to be, Robertson could out-talk even Rhee; and his voice had the kind of soothing richness that could tame even this crochety monomaniac."[62]

Robertson was optimistic. Rhee told him that his arrival in Korea was "like a hand to a drowning man." Robertson reported to Dulles that Rhee was "a shrewd and resourceful trader" who was also "highly emotional, irrational, illogical, fanatic, and fully capable of attempting to lead his country into national suicide." Still, Robertson believed there was room for compromise. If the Americans could not persuade Rhee to accept an armistice, they would scare him into compliance. Eisenhower told the National Security Council on July 2 that "we can do all sorts of things to suggest to Rhee that we might well be prepared to leave Korea, but the truth of the matter is, of course, that we could not actually leave . . . We must only take actions which imply the possibility of our leaving."[63] The new Eighth Army commander, Lt. Gen. Maxwell Taylor, who replaced General Van Fleet in January 1953, announced on July 6 plans "for the withdrawal of American and British divisions from the battle line with or without the cooperation of the South Korean Army in the event of a truce being signed with the communists."[64] The story was picked up by newspapers around the world, including *The Times of London*, which reported, "An inspired dispatch from Washington even speaks of a possible withdrawal of American and allied forces; and the expectation in the United Nations is that, unless Mr. Rhee is brought to terms, the United Command will proceed to the signature of an armistice without him."[65] Patience and politicking paid off. On July 9, Rhee indicated that he was prepared to cooperate with the United States and not disrupt the armistice talks. In exchange, Rhee received "informal assurances" that the U.S. Senate would ratify the mutual security treaty and provide additional economic and military support. Rhee's bold move had paid off handsomely. Dulles later confided that "we had accepted it [mutual security treaty and aid] as one of the prices that we thought we were justified in paying in order to get the armistice."[66]

With the prospect for peace just around the corner, the communists decided to give Rhee a "bloody nose" just to make sure he would not try another ploy to disrupt the armistice agreement. On July 13 they launched their final offensive. ROK II Corps was driven back six miles and suffered more than ten thousand casualties. The communists had made their point. General Paek Sŏn-yŏp later noted, "The outcome of the Kŭmsŏng battle had dealt a serious blow to the President's prestige."[67] The attack undermined Rhee's credibility that ROK forces could face the Chinese alone. The Chinese had called Rhee's bluff, and thereafter there was no more talk of South Koreans going north.

There was one final obstacle to the signing of the armistice: inside the wooden building in P'anmunjŏm where the armistice was to be signed hung a copy of Picasso's *The Dove*, a painting that had been adopted by the communists as their symbol of peace. Clark ordered this "Red Symbol" removed. After a heated exchange, Picasso's *Dove* painting was finally covered up.

At 10:00 a.m. on July 27, 1953, Lt. Gen. William Harrison, the Eighth Army deputy commander who had replaced Admiral Joy as chief UN delegate in May 1952, and Lt. Gen. Nam Il signed the eighteen-page armistice agreement. They did so in twelve minutes and in complete silence. When finished, they simply got up and left without saying a word. "That's the way it had been throughout the negotiations," said Clark later. "Never during the talks did the delegates of either side nod or speak a greeting or farewell during the daily meetings."[68]

Immediately afterward, the document was taken to Clark at his forward headquarters in Munsan. Three hours after the signing in P'anmunjŏm, Clark sat down at a long table in front of newsreels and TV cameras to sign the document again. He then addressed the audience:

> I cannot find it in me to exult in this hour. Rather, it is time for prayer, that we may succeed in our difficult endeavor to turn this armistice to the advantage of mankind. If we extract hope from this occasion, it must be diluted with the recognition that our salvation requires unrelaxing vigilance and effort.[69]

Many in Korea shared Clark's ambivalence. "The cease-fire caused a measure of anguish in the officers and men of the South Korean army because it perpetuated the division of our nation," wrote Paek. "The lengthy armistice negotiations had given us enough time, however, to accept the reality that we could do nothing about it."[70] There were no victory celebrations in the United States, no cheering crowds in Times Square, no sense of triumph. "The mood," wrote one observer, "appeared to be one of apathy."[71] Yet Eisenhower considered the armistice to be one of his greatest achievements. He had promised to go to Korea and end the killing and this he did. Although Stalin's death and other events played a greater role in ending the war than either Eisenhower or Dulles ever cared to admit, the president had nevertheless put his prestige behind the settlement. He also knew that only a Republican president could have done it. The same settlement coming from a Democratic administration, especially one that had been blamed for "losing" China, would have had a far more divisive effect on the country.[72] Still, the armistice did not resolve the fundamental problem that had precipitated Kim Il Sung's invasion of South Korea. The nation remained divided.

Although the killing had stopped, the war continued, solidifying cold war arrangements for the next fifty years. The Korean War has officially outlasted the cold war, since no formal peace treaty between the belligerents has been signed, and it has persisted in influencing global events, giving birth to a new world order that would directly impact not only the politics and societies in America and China, but also those in the East Asian region and beyond.

PART II

COLD WAR

What impact did the Korean War have on the cold war? Since no peace treaty was signed to formally end the conflict, the Americans and the Chinese continued to view each other warily, setting the stage for another potential superpower confrontation in Asia. What lessons did the United States and China take away from the Korean War that helped them shape their respective responses to the growing conflict in Indochina? How did their experiences in Korea influence their domestic and foreign policies, especially with regard to the Soviet Union? Finally, how did South Korea become the unexpected beneficiary of this continuing cold war struggle, with lasting implications for its own ongoing legitimacy war with North Korea?

Although the fighting in Korea ceased in 1953, the war continued to shape events. The United States emerged staunchly anticommunist with, for the first time in its history, a large permanent standing army, an enlarged defense budget, and military bases around the world. The Korean War also did much to forge Chinese self-perceptions. The Chinese had lost nearly half a million men in Korea, but they had fought the world's greatest superpower to a standstill and emerged with their reputation and self-esteem greatly enhanced. The Korean War led to mass mobilization campaigns that aimed to eradicate the "impure" and "foreign" elements of Chinese society and inspire a politically motivated popular nationalism that Mao used to consolidate his power.

After a brief repose (1954–57) during which China cultivated a new international image to correspond with its claims of peaceful coexistence, as reflected in its role in ending the First Indochina War in Geneva in 1954, China once again reverted to themes of war, revolution, and mass mobilization in the wake of Khrushchev's denunciation of Stalin in 1956. In 1958, Mao started the Great Leap Forward movement for economic development, which led to widespread famine and the deaths of millions. He also initiated military actions against Taiwan in 1958 and India in 1959, partly to divert domestic attention away from the failure of the Great Leap.

China's new radicalism caused strains in the relationship between Mao and Khrushchev. China accused the Soviet Union of abandoning the true principles of Marxism-Leninism by seeking accommodation with the West. It was during this period that China provided substantial military aid to the Vietnamese communists in their struggle to "liberate" South Vietnam. The CCP's claim of leadership of the world revolutionary movement directly challenged the Soviet Union. To China's leaders, the Vietnam War essentially served a similar purpose in radicalizing the Chinese masses as the Korean War had done a decade earlier. In each case, "resisting America" became a rallying cry to mobilize the Chinese population along Mao's revolutionary lines.

Meanwhile, the responses by Presidents John F. Kennedy and Lyndon B. Johnson to the growing awareness of Chinese radicalism and the Sino-Soviet split informed Washington's view of the war in Vietnam and their retrospective view of the war in Korea. Both presidents believed Vietnam to be a test of whether Moscow's seemingly more benign form of communism or Beijing's radical Bolshevism would triumph in the international communist movement. Vietnamese communist success, it was believed, would dramatically encourage the radical national liberation doctrine espoused by China. The dominant assumption was that the Chinese communists were the vanguard of the most aggressive wing of world communism and had to be stopped. The crucial moment that led America down the path to tragedy in Vietnam took place in July 1965, when Johnson committed American power to seek a military solution.

The "lessons" of the Korean War played a significant role in Johnson's decision. Although Eisenhower had opposed American intervention in the First Indochina War on the grounds that he did not want a repeat of Korea, Johnson saw the lessons of that war quite differently. The frustrations of an indecisive victory in Korea had been tempered in time by the domino theory and the notion that the communist threat in Asia had, at least, been contained. The Korean War was now seen as an extension of the cold war and the global struggle against communism. Korea was held up as a model of how the battle line for freedom had been successfully drawn.

Along with the decision to deepen American commitment in Vietnam, Johnson sought to internationalize the war by seeking combat forces from other countries. South Korea's President Park Chung Hee responded positively. Major General Park had come to power in 1961 after a decade of economic stagnation. South Korea during the 1950s appeared to be losing its legitimacy war with the North. Mired in hopeless poverty and plagued by corruption, the gap in economic performance between the South and the North was increasing. In April 1960, a popular uprising, led by labor and student groups, overthrew the Rhee regime. The post-Rhee government floundered. In May 1961, Park Chung Hee and some thirty-six hundred troops staged a coup, steering the country into a new direction.

Park portrayed involvement in Vietnam to his own people as repayment to the free world for saving South Korea during the Korean War, but he also saw an opportunity to strengthen South Korea's security and economy. Washington provided an extensive list of economic and military incentives. Vietnam also furnished a compelling replay of the Korean situation that Park used to rally support for national construction and anticommunism. "Re-fighting" the communists in Vietnam provided South Korea the foundation for the nation's spectacular growth in the coming decades. South Korea's involvement in America's second major cold war struggle in Asia thus brought about enormous advantages for the Park regime, largely because the first struggle in Korea between the United States and China had remained unresolved.

In addition, Park abandoned Rhee's anti-Japanese attitude and normalized relations with Japan. In June 1965 the two countries signed the Treaty of Basic Relations, and South Korea obtained Japanese grants and loans for Park's modernization program. This step had troubling implications for Kim Il Sung, since Japan had recognized the ROK as the only lawful government in Korea. Moreover, the economic benefits accrued to South Korea for help in Vietnam led Kim to believe that South Korea would soon catch up to the North. Time was quickly running out if he was to achieve the "liberation" of South Korea.

Under these conditions and fearful that the South would soon surpass the North in economic and military power, Kim Il Sung began to embark upon a series of provocative actions against the South, setting the stage for a new "phase" of the Korean War.

CHAPTER THIRTEEN

Lessons of Korea

On August 5, 1953, Maj. Ambrose Nugent, former POW from Camp 12, arrived at Freedom Village in Munsan and began weeping uncontrollably. Released as part of Operation Big Switch (the final exchange of prisoners that took place between August 5 and December 23, 1953), Nugent felt elated and relieved, but also confused. "Having been a prisoner of war in the hands of the Asiatic Communists," he later recalled, "and having gone through these periods that we did over there—the death, the starvation, the deprivation, the threat of never being able to return home—reaching Freedom Village was like coming out of a black night. Over the course of the next month, I felt like I was dreaming."[1]

Awakening from that dream turned out to be far ruder than he, or any other prisoner of war, might have expected. Almost immediately after repatriation, the prisoners realized that they would not be going home as heroes, but as suspected collaborators. Even before their homecoming, journalists and military officers began painting a disturbing picture of undisciplined soldiers in Korea who were lacking in camaraderie and patriotism. As many as one-third of the prisoners were suspected of having collaborated in one form or another. Twenty-three American airmen, including a senior marine pilot, Col. Frank H. Schwable, had publicly confessed to germ warfare and other war crimes. Twenty-one American POWs had decided to remain with the enemy. Many prisoners had made public statements against the UN effort in Korea, with particular criticisms of America's conduct in the war. Fourteen former POWs, including Major Nugent, Lt. Col. Harry Fleming, and Lt. Jeff Erwin, all survivors of the 1950 winter death march, were court-martialed for their alleged collaboration with the enemy. Major William Mayer, an army psychiatrist and outspoken critic of the POW behavior, summed up what many Americans thought about the prisoners' "misconduct": "Too many of our soldiers in prison fell far short of the historical American standings of honor, character, loyalty, courage, and personal integrity." He concluded, "The fact that so many yielded to the degree that they did presents a problem of fantastic proportions and should cause searching self-examination by all Americans, both in and out of uniform."[2]

The lack of a clear victory in Korea made questions about the character flaws of the American soldier all the more urgent. What could explain the nation's less-than-total victory in its first confrontation with communism? Some devious force had to be at work, whether this was "Red" infiltration at home or a deep spiritual flaw within American society itself. Whatever the cause, Korean War POWs became associated with all that was wrong with American society: materialistic, pampered, and overindulgent ways had produced men wholly unprepared to face America's ideologically dedicated adversaries. By the end of 1953, Americans were inundated with daily anecdotal evidence of treason. Headlines like "The GIs Who Fell for the Reds," "The Colonel's Korean Turncoats," "Why Did the Captives Cave In?" or simply "The Rats" fed a growing sense of crisis that American society was somehow failing.[3]

Feminized Nation

These concerns were also taken seriously by the Department of Defense and the armed forces. In the aftermath of the POW "debacle," the secretary of defense's Advisory Committee on Prisoners of War was established in June 1955 to provide "recommendations on various aspects of the POW problem, which entailed provisions for a new Code of Conduct" as well as a "program of training and education to make the Code effective."[4] "We must view the communist treatment of prisoners of war as only another weapon in the world-wide war for the minds of men," declared Gen. John E. Hull, the new commander of the Far East Command, to the committee. The foundation of a soldier's strength, he announced, "lies not in armament and training alone" but is "derived in large part from his early environment which shapes his beliefs, builds his loyalty and molds his stature."[5] As symbols of an effete and indulgent society,

Korean War POWs became linked to deep anxieties about the American character. New measures to strengthen American society were therefore deemed necessary.[6] The Korean War experience sharpened Americans' anxieties about their nation's "apathy" in the face of the communist threat by painting the American struggle against these alien forces as a contest between two ways of life: freedom and individualism versus slavery and conformity.

Popular concerns over the apparent loss of manly vigor in the wake of the Korean War also found expression in popular cold war cinema. American films made during this period repeatedly returned to fear of an overwhelming "feminine" force that threatens American manhood/nationhood. *My Son John* (1952), for example, explores the unhealthy relationship between mother and son that eventually turned John into a communist.[7] Popular science fiction films of the 1950s reinforced these anxieties. As the film scholar Michael Rogin observed, "Biology is out of control in these films . . . and reproduction dispenses with the father."[8] In *The Thing from Another World* (1951) the aliens are able to quickly multiply, through detachable body parts. Likewise, in *Invasion of the Body Snatchers* (1956) the ovarian pods take over the body of their victims as they sleep. *Them!* (1954) literally makes the connection between communists and the matrilineal society of giant ants whose multiplying colonies threaten to overrun the free world.

Behind these anxieties lay the emergence of a strong and hostile China. Like the giant insects/aliens that made their appearance onto the Hollywood screen, the Chinese also became associated with these ant-like creatures in the popular mind, made all the more striking by their nocturnal fighting habits and their propensity to dig underground passages and build "nests." "They [the communists] continue unceasingly to burrow and tunnel to advance their positions against the citadels of freedom," Dulles once famously declared.[9] Moreover, because the end of the fighting in Korea had not settled the contest between freedom and slavery, it was feared that the Chinese would take the struggle to other parts of Asia.[10] It was this fear of the Chinese communist threat that had led the Truman administration to support the French in their effort to reestablish their former colonial power in Indochina after World War II. "The loss of Vietnam," Eisenhower was convinced, "would have meant the surrender to Communist enslavement of millions."[11] Secretary of State Dulles advocated a harsh approach to China, "a policy of containment through isolation" because it held out the promise of ultimately dividing Moscow from Beijing.[12] Chinese forced dependence on the Soviet Union, he believed, would inevitably lead to conflict between them. The Chinese would realize the drawbacks of their dependence, while the Soviets in turn would tire of supporting the Chinese. "My own feeling," explained Dulles, "is that the best way to get a separation between the Soviet Union and Communist China is to keep pressure on Communist China and make its way difficult so long as it is in partnership with Soviet Russia." Yugoslavia's Tito did not break with Stalin because the West was nice to him. "On the contrary, we were very rough on Tito."[13]

The policy also had the concomitant benefit of soothing the domestic forces of the right wing in Congress, which blamed the Truman administration for China's "fall" in 1949. The Eisenhower administration was very aware of the power of the Taiwan-China lobby and the need to cultivate a fervently anticommunist Chinese image to defend itself against potential attacks.[14] Such a policy also allowed the administration to pursue a partial improvement in Washington's relationship with Moscow.

Isolating China would also help to limit the status it gained from holding back the world's greatest superpower in Korea. In his speech before the Oversea Press Club on March 29, 1954, Dulles outlined the administration's position toward Communist China as well as the threat it posed to Indochina. The United States was opposed to recognizing China, he declared, and the reasons were simple: "Will it help our country," Dulles asked, "if by recognition we give increased prestige and influence to a regime that actively attacks our vital interests? Will it serve the interests of world order to bring into the United Nations a regime which is a convicted aggressor, which has not purged itself from that aggression, and which continues to promote the use of force in violation of the principles of the United Nations?"[15] Dulles also believed that by holding back on recognition with Beijing, the United States would enhance the prestige of the anticommunist leaders in Asia. For those "defenders of freedom" it was necessary to show a positive spirit that America and her anticommunist allies would stand strong against the forces of defeatism and tyranny. The new importance of Indochina after Korea thus became part of a developing concern about anti-Western and communist activity in the Third World.

As the architect of Eisenhower's foreign policy, Dulles was also aware that many of the "new nations" that had emerged since World War II "harbored mistrust and fear of the West."[16] Touting American values of freedom while supporting old colonial powers, like the French in Indochina, clearly presented a problem for the Eisenhower administration. And this is exactly what made the Chinese communists so dangerous. They were seen to be taking advantage of the fervor of anticolonialism and independence movements in Asia to enslave them under communism. Any accommodation with China, Dulles believed, would certainly "sow discouragement" among the anticommunist leaders in Asia, since communism would be seen as "the wave of the future"[17] The United States needed to confront the Chinese communists head-on in their battle for the Third World by showing that the "boundless power of human freedom" was stronger than the enslaving myths of communism.[18] "We should be dynamic, we should use ideas as weapons, and these ideas should conform to moral principles," Dulles declared. "That we do this is right, for it is the inevitable expression of a faith... But it is also expedient in defending ourselves against an aggressive, imperialistic despotism."[19] Smaller countries in Asia needed to be encouraged to take sides. They also had to be presented with a stark moral choice that any accommodation with the Chinese communists would mean turning their back on the self-evident truths of freedom and goodness. This is why the United States would remain implacably opposed to Communist China. "It . . . is one thing to recognize evil as a fact," Dulles announced on March 29, 1954. "It is another thing to take evil to one's breast and call it good. That we shall not do."[20]

Dulles's fear of the dynamism of the Chinese communists as the potential "wave of the future" was also a reflection of his anxieties about America's moral decline in the wake of the Korean War. The Chinese represented an "acute and imminent threat" precisely because they were "dizzy with success" and "have an exaggerated sense of their own power."[21] American reaction to this threat had been lukewarm, and he criticized the Truman administration for its "passive" policies. Although he was quick to commend Truman for his forthright decision to respond to the North Korean attack, he believed that the administration's response had merely been reactive. To counter this passive response, a new "policy of boldness" was required. "It is ironic and wrong that we who believe in the boundless power of human freedom should so long have accepted a static political role," he observed. "It is also ironic and wrong that we who so proudly profess regard for the spiritual should rely so utterly on material defenses while the avowed materialists have been waging and winning a war with social ideas, stirring humanity everywhere."[22]

The attempt to rally the nation by invoking themes of boldness and strength also deeply resonated with the American national character. The historian Rupert Wilkinson identified the national preoccupation with national vigor with what he called "the fear of winding down," which "rests on the traditional belief that Americans are people of energy and reach who nevertheless fear the loss of their vigor and competence."[23] Dulles claimed that to defend freedom in Asia, Americans needed to act boldly and thereby "seize the initiative."[24] "We were from the beginning a vigorous, confident people, born with a sense of destiny and of mission," he reminded the nation. "That is why we have grown from a small and feeble nation to our present stature in the world."[25] The anxiety that China might provide an alternative model emulated by other Asian nations thus propelled both Eisenhower and Dulles to proclaim that the United States must act boldly and repulse the Chinese hordes from sweeping over Vietnam and the rest of Southeast Asia. "The violent battles now being waged in Viet-Nam and the aggressions against Laos and Cambodia are not creating any spirit of defeatism," Dulles told the nation on April 19, 1954. "On the contrary, they are rousing the free nations to measures which we hope will be sufficiently timely and vigorous to preserve these vital areas from Communist domination."[26]

The call to action was also in response to a vulnerable Japan. Dulles was concerned over what a communist victory in Vietnam might mean for Japan's future growth. The "workshop of Asia" would be deprived of access to the vital raw materials—tin, tungsten, and rubber—from Southeast Asia that it needed. A communist victory could also undermine Japan's confidence in America's protection. "The situation of the Japanese is hard enough with China being a commie," Dulles declared. If Indochina fell, "the Japs would be thinking how to get on the other side." As he reassessed the repercussions of a communist victory, Dulles concluded that "the Indochina situation" was even "more important than Korea, because the consequences of loss there could not be localized, but would spread throughout Asia and Europe."[27] China's success in Korea had created a new "breeding ground" for communists. Although that "plague on freedom" had been temporarily stopped at the 38th parallel, this did not mean that the communists would not try and find other outlets to reproduce themselves. Admiral Arthur Radford, chairman of the JCS, spoke of Korea simply being "one tentacle" of Chinese communism "that has been denied the prize for which it was reaching." Indochina and then the rest of Southeast Asia were seen as the most viable other prizes. This region "was a very real part of the over-all conflict between the free world and Communism."[28]

Beyond the familiar imagery of communism as a "plague" on human freedom, the fear of a French loss in Indochina had awakened in the Eisenhower administration old fears associated with Japanese conquest, the Greater East Asia Co-Prosperity Sphere and the Yellow Peril. Vietnam was one of the launching pads for the Japanese conquest of Southeast Asia in World War II, and a communist victory in Vietnam could also provide a similar launching pad for other communist conquests. "Communist conquests, if Indochina falls," wrote the *U.S. News & World Report*, "may well follow the pattern set by the Japanese, as officials here see it. In 1940, Japanese 'protective forces' took over Indo-China after the fall of France. That gave Japan a base from which to seize other countries of Southeast Asia."[29]

Linked to concerns regarding American vigor, or lack thereof, was the administration's "New Look" policy, which focused on, among a variety of issues, the role of nuclear weapons both to deter and to defeat communist aggression. Dulles laid out the details of the New Look policy in the April 1954 issue of *Foreign Affairs*, where he explained that the capacity for instant retaliation was the most effective deterrent against a surprise attack. Asserting that the Chinese and the Soviets would always resort to battle conditions involving manpower, which favored them, Dulles observed that "the free world must devise a better strategy for its defense based on its own special assets." These assets included "air and naval power and atomic weapons which are now available in a wide range, suitable not only for strategic bombing but also extensive tactical use."[30] This did not mean, Dulles emphasized, turning every local war into a world war. It did mean, however, "that the free world must maintain the collective means and be willing to use them the way which most effectively makes aggression too risky and expensive to be tempting." In this way, "the prospective attacker is not likely to invade if he believes the probable hurt will outbalance the probable gain." Korea had been the first test of the policy of massive retaliation since, according to Dulles and Eisenhower, it was the threat of massive nuclear retaliation that had finally pushed the communists to settle the conflict. "The essential thing is that a potential aggressor should know in advance that he can and will be made to suffer for his aggression more than he can possibly gain."

Yet, for all his rhetorical power, which the journalist Richard Rovere once characterized as "one of the boldest campaigns of political persuasion ever undertaken by an American statesman," Dulles's repeated calls to "preserve" Indochina from the communists were ambivalently received by the American people.[31] To the administration, attempting to determine the best response to what looked to be, in mid-1954, the inevitable defeat of France in Indochina, a central question was whether Americans would support another war in Asia.

The "Never Again Club"

On March 13, 1954, the Vietnam People's Army (VPA) besieged and assaulted Dien Bien Phu, a major French strongpoint located in northern Vietnam and manned by ten thousand men. As the siege developed, it became clear that the French had underestimated the Communist Vietnamese strength. The possibility of a French defeat loomed, and such an outcome would be a decisive military and psychological victory for the communists. In late March, General Paul Ely, the French Armed Forces chief of staff, arrived in Washington. His mission was to secure American military aid in the form of bombers and a commitment of American air support in the event of a Chinese air attack.[32] Dulles and Admiral Radford were noncommittal about Ely's query regarding Chinese intervention, although the request for bombers was approved. According to Ely, however, he received a promise from Radford that he would push for an approval of airstrikes to relieve the siege. The plan, code-named VULTURE, called for massive strikes against the Communist Vietnamese positions from bombers based on U.S. carriers and in the Philippines.

Radford's plan generated little support among the Joint Chiefs. General Matthew B. Ridgway, then the army chief of staff, was the most vocal in his opposition. Ridgway thought that Radford saw Indochina as a place to "test the New Look" strategy of placing primary reliance on airpower and the threat of massive retaliation to deter communist aggression. To Ridgway, the war in Indochina was an uncomfortable reminder of Korea. He later recalled, "In Korea, we had learned that air and naval power alone cannot win a war and that inadequate ground forces cannot win one either. It was incredible to me that we had forgotten that bitter lesson so soon that we were on the verge of making the same tragic error."[33] Ridgway felt sure that "if we committed air and naval power . . . we would have to follow . . . immediately with ground forces in support." He responded with an "emphatic and immediate 'No'" when asked for his view on the desirability of U.S. military intervention.[34] There was also the question of possible Chinese intervention in Indochina and the widening of the war, which might lead to World War III. UN forces had narrowly escaped this fate in Korea, and Ridgway saw no reason to test that possibility again in Indochina. For him, "no more Koreas" also meant "no more unilateral intervention close to the Chinese border."[35]

To Ridgway and other members of what later became known as the "Never Again Club," the lessons of Korea proved to be a strong incentive against involvement in Vietnam. Vice Admiral A. C. Davis in the office of secretary of defense, for example, warned that "involvement of US forces in the Indochina War should be avoided at all practical costs," because, as he warned, "one cannot go over the Niagara Falls in a barrel only slightly."[36] It was a sentiment echoed throughout the country. One reader wrote to the editor of the *New York Times*,

> We, the American people, have only recently finished (I hope) with the Korean War. This so-called police action cost us over 100,000 casualties and an increased cost of living with higher prices, that we can ill-afford. After reading Secretary Dulles' March 29 statement on Indochina, I wonder if we are going to be again dragged into another "Korea" in Indochina, with more casualties and sacrifices.[37]

Similar concerns were expressed by members of Congress. Many of them opposed the limited air and naval intervention proposed by Dulles and Radford on the ground that such a venture would be a repeat of Korea. Senate Majority Leader William Knowland expressed the unanimous concerns of his fellow congressmen when he said that there should be no congressional action until the administration has secured the commitment of political and material support from America's allies. "We want no more Koreas with the United States furnishing 90% of the manpower," he stated. However, if "satisfactory commitments" could be obtained, "the consensus was that a Congressional resolution could be passed, giving the president power to commit armed forces to Indochina."[38] In effect, Congress insisted that the United States could intervene only as part of a coalition. Dulles later dubbed this plan "United Action." The idea was to create a coalition composed of the United States, the United Kingdom, France, Australia, New Zealand, Thailand, and the Philippines for the joint defense of Indochina and the rest of Southeast Asia against the communist threat. This would also allow the United States to take control of the Indochina situation from the French while at the same time "remove the taint of waging the war for French colonialism."[39] Cooperation from the British and French was vital to the plan's success.

Dulles flew to Europe in April in a frantic round of "shuttle diplomacy" before the Geneva Conference, set up to resolve the Indochina crisis, opened on the twenty-sixth. He had hoped to persuade the British to answer his call for "United Action" to save Indochina, while holding out the prospect of U.S. intervention to France if it remained committed to the fight in Indochina and resisted a negotiated settlement in Geneva. French Foreign Minister Georges Bidault refused, saying that such a commitment would jeopardize the success of the Geneva negotiations. British Foreign Secretary Anthony Eden also made it clear that no decision regarding Dulles's proposal of "United Action" would be made before the Geneva meeting. The looming memory of Korea informed his view: "I did not believe that anything less than intervention on a Korean scale, if that, would have any effect in Indo-China," he later wrote. "If there were such intervention, I could not tell where its consequences would stop." Echoing Omar Bradley's famous dictum made at the MacArthur hearings in 1951, Eden concluded, "We might well find ourselves involved in the wrong war against the wrong man in the wrong place." Eden was also wary of the administration's motives: "Once President Eisenhower had been assured that the United Kingdom would participate in this declaration, he would be prepared to seek Congressional approval for intervention." Prime Minister Churchill shared Eden's concerns. He later confided to Eden, "What we were being asked to do was to assist [Dulles] in *misleading* Congress into approving a military operation." If the United Kingdom acceded to this latest American proposal, "we should be supporting direct United States intervention in the Indo-China war, and, probably, later American action against the Chinese mainland." The best Eden could do was to promise Dulles to revisit the issue in the event that the talks at the upcoming conference failed. More cautious than either Dulles or Radford, Eisenhower was forced to concur: "Without allies . . . the leader is just an adventurer like Genghis Khan."[40]

The Geneva Conference

The prospect of sitting down with the Chinese in an international forum meant to confer both legitimacy and prestige on the PRC was extremely distasteful to the Eisenhower administration.Earlier in 1954 in Berlin, when Soviet Foreign Minister V. M. Molotov proposed a conference in Geneva with representatives from the United States, France, Britain, the Soviet Union, and China to both conclude the Korean War with a peace treaty and end the Indochina War, the Americans at first refused.[41] Dulles, in particular, wanted nothing to do with a conference that provided China equal status. But the deteriorating events in Indochina had forced his hand. Dulles had to go to Geneva if he hoped for cooperation from the French and the British, but not without taking some heat from the Republican right wing and the China lobby, which characterized the conference as nothing more than a "second Yalta" and an "appeasement to communism."

In the weeks leading up to the Geneva Conference, Dulles had thus been forced to walk a fine line between not doing anything that might enhance China's prestige and building an international consensus about Indochina and Korea. By the time the conference began on April 26, it was also clear that the United States, France, and Britain were on the defensive. "One only has to look across the room to poor Bidault, pale, apprehensive, doomed, to see how far we have fallen back since last year," observed Evelyn Shuckburgh, Eden's private secretary. "The serried ranks of yellow faces and blue suits, the confident hand-shakes between Molotov and Premier Zhou Enlai after the latter's speech, the ashen anger of Dulles" demonstrated that it was the Chinese who were now on top. Dulles's proposal "to reactivate the UN Neutral Nations Commission for Korea and try to unite the country, by the withdrawal of Chinese troops from North Korea," was met with predictable resistance from the communists. Even the British were perturbed by Dulles's "moralistic denunciations" of the Chinese, which failed to further the discussions. According to Shuckburgh, Eden was "concerned" by the fact that "with regard to the Korea issue, no reasonable proposition has yet been put forward from the Western side—nor can be, because the Americans felt obliged to give further run to the ridiculous South Korean proposal of elections in North Korea only." Very quickly, it had become apparent that no solution to Korean unification would be forthcoming.[42]

Nevertheless, the Korean War overshadowed the events. As during the armistice negotiations at P'anmunjŏm, symbolism became extremely important. U. Alexis Johnson, who served as the coordinator of the U.S. delegation, recalled that he was under considerable pressure "to satisfy Dulles' stringent and convoluted seating requirements" aimed to deny China its due status as an equal participant of the conference. "This was China's first major international conference, but we did not want to give its government any added status." Dulles refused, for example, "to sit at a table with Zhou Enlai, thus requiring an auditorium-type seating arrangement"[43] The secretary of state also purportedly refused to shake hands with Zhou. Zhou never forgot the rebuke, and the incident was often recounted to visitors with "an air of injured innocence."[44] Despite American attempts to marginalize the Chinese, however, the Communist Vietnamese victory at Dien Bien Phu on May 7 significantly enhanced China's hand. The French defeat and the rising crisis in Algeria made the French even more desperate to extract themselves from Indochina. The victory also made the British more skeptical of military intervention.[45] Eden stalwartly refused to answer Dulles's call for United Action. Chinese Vice Foreign Minister Wang Bingnan recalled that "when the news of Dienbienphu [*sic*] came we spread it to each other. We were very much encouraged and felt more confident in solving the Indo-China issue."[46] With the aim of breaking the American policy of isolation toward China by adopting a moderate line, Chinese leaders hoped to win over British and French support on Indochina by driving a wedge between them and the United States.[47]

To a large extent, the Chinese were successful. Nevertheless, Zhou and other Chinese leaders were still concerned that the Americans might intervene unilaterally. According to Khrushchev, who had by then become the de facto leader of the Soviet Union, "Zhou Enlai told him before the Geneva Conference that 'China could not meet Ho Chi Minh's demands to send Chinese troops to Vietnam.'" Zhou had also told Ho that "we've already lost too many men in Korea—that war cost us dearly. We're in no condition to get involved in another war at this time."[48] After fighting in Korea, the Chinese wanted to focus on domestic affairs and rehabilitate their economy. Although the French defeat had raised the possibility that the Communist Vietnamese might be able to end the war more or less on their own terms, the Chinese nevertheless pressed their Vietnamese allies into accepting a divided Vietnam to settle the conflict. The Vietnamese were also pressured into agreeing to proposed elections that would eventually unify all of Vietnam. Rather than driving for maximum advantage for their Vietnamese comrades, the Chinese pushed them hard for a compromise solution. Eventually, and not without some resentment, Ho accepted the 17th parallel as a temporary dividing line. Nationwide elections were scheduled to follow in 1956.

The Geneva Conference had thus ended the First Indochina War, although the Korean War remained without resolution. And it was the Korean War experience that had played a decisive role in President Eisenhower's decision *not* to intervene in Indochina in 1954. That decision also began to raise doubts about his New Look strategy and its reliance on "massive retaliation." It had become clear to Dulles and Eisenhower that the threat of massive retaliation would not have saved the situation in Indochina. America and her allies would not risk nuclear war over interests that were, despite all the heated rhetoric, still considered peripheral. Thus, Eisenhower's reaction to the Indochina situation was actually very much in line with Truman's reaction to Korea. Richard Rovere wrote in 1956, "About all that seems to be left of the New Look now is a budget that strengthens the Air Force at the expense of ground forces. But if the worst happens in Indochina, where atomic bombs would be useless as crossbows, the ground forces will have to be restored to their former strength—and then some."[49] Rovere would be proved right.

Eisenhower's Warning

"How can a liberal society provide for its military security when this requires the maintenance of professional military forces and institutions fundamentally at odds with liberalism?"[50] This paradox, first posed by Samuel Huntington in his classic work *The Soldier and the State*, became particularly acute after the Korean War when U.S. foreign policy shifted its emphasis from political and economic "containment" of communism to military security from it.[51] For Huntington, there were three possible answers to this dilemma: The first was to return to the pre-1940 pattern of civil-military relations, that is, "cutting military forces to the bone, isolating military institutions from society, and reducing military influence to negligible proportions." In this way, American society would remain true to its liberal tradition based on the idea that military and democratic values were antithetical and that a large standing army posed a threat to liberty. However, the pursuit of liberty would be realized at the expense of the nation's military security.

The second solution was "to accept increased military authority and influence but to insist that military leaders abandon their professional outlook and that military institutions be reformed along liberal lines." The drawback of this solution was that while it would provide for the continuation of liberalism in American society, it might have to accomplish these goals at the expense of military effectiveness. Finally, the third solution was for society to adopt "a more sympathetic understanding and appreciation of the military viewpoint and military needs." This would require, however, "a drastic change in the basic American liberal ethic."[52] Although none of these solutions was followed exclusively, it was the third solution—the militarization of American society—that was ultimately adopted in the aftermath of the Korean War. Why?

At first, Eisenhower had tried to adhere to the traditional American stance that military and democratic values were antithetical. He recognized early on in his presidency the threat that a large standing army and huge defense expenditures posed to American society. As a staunch Republican, he accepted his party's time-honored view that balanced budgets and low taxes were essential factors in maintaining a healthy economy. Vowing to put the nation on the course to achieve both security and solvency, Eisenhower aimed to eliminate the national deficit, racked up during the Truman administration, by targeting defense for major cuts. For him, "the foundation of military strength, was economic strength."[53] Eisenhower's New Look policy would thus rely almost exclusively on nuclear weapons at the expense of a large permanent standing army. The principle of "massive retaliation" would make war obsolete since, as the American military strategist Bernard Brodie put it, "war and obliteration are now completely synonymous."[54]

But beyond the concern for balanced budgets, Eisenhower was also fearful that huge defense expenditures would lead to America's slide toward becoming a "garrison state." Would America have to become a garrison state in order to fight one? The New Look was Eisenhower's answer to this paradox and to the heightened tensions between the military imperatives of security and the maintenance of a liberal society.

Yet Korea had shown that atomic weapons did not make war obsolete. As Ridgway, Taylor, and other military leaders would later argue, a "properly balanced" force was necessary to prepare for a wide range of contingencies, and only such a force could claim real credibility as a deterrent.[55] Moreover, committing the nation to a strategy that reduced war to the threat of annihilating entire civilian populations also meant that force was no longer an instrument of policy, since such a strategy undercut the very purpose of war itself. Such sentiments, widespread among army leaders during the mid-1950s who deplored the way that nuclear weapons had "corrupted American thinking about war," had given rise to a fierce backlash against the New Look among army leaders. As a result of the New Look, wrote one Army officer,

> we have accepted civil destruction as an object of war and a means of war where formerly it was an incident of war. The question raised is not of humanity but of reality—whether we have forgotten that war is still a political instrument which must have political objectives and methods... This error leads to the brutalization of war without purpose, to a preoccupation with mass destruction, to the neglect of political realities.[56]

Ultimately, Eisenhower's New Look failed. By relying on nuclear weapons, Eisenhower had attempted to balance military imperatives and democratic values, but the solution proved unworkable. His strategy of massive retaliation had offered only two choices: the initiation of general nuclear war—Armageddon—or compromise and retreat.[57]

Thus when John F. Kennedy came into office in 1961, the stage was set for a new defense policy. Although Kennedy was not adverse to the use of nuclear weapons, the main tenet of his defense strategy, Flexible Response, was the resurgent role that the army would play "to put out a brushfire war before it becomes a conflagration." Kennedy believed that the security of the free world required that the United States "have military units capable of checking Soviet aggression at any scale of violence."[58]

Flexible Response also aimed to reinvigorate U.S. global power through the expansion of the range of options available to policy makers, by demonstrating a U.S. willingness to fight non-nuclear wars. During President Kennedy's first year in office, military outlays rose 15 percent. Between 1961 and 1962, the army's budget increased, and 207,000 soldiers were added to its rolls. The number of active-duty divisions increased from eleven to sixteen. Kennedy also dispatched additional ground troops to West Germany "to bolster U.S. commitment to NATO." In 1961, he dispatched four hundred American Green Berets to South Vietnam; by 1963, there were sixteen thousand American military personnel in that country, a huge increase from Eisenhower's nine hundred advisors.[59] Whereas Eisenhower had tried, and failed, to resolve the fundamental tensions in civil-military relations through reliance on nuclear weapons, Kennedy had opted to resolve these same tensions by adopting Huntington's third solution: making American society more militarized.

Military influence during this period had indeed extended throughout the government, and from there to virtually every area of American life. Few developments more dramatically symbolized the new status of the military than the links forged between the business community and the armed forces. While military spending helped to revive the flagging aviation industry in New England, it also contributed enormously to the economic boom of the American West. Civic and local leaders in places like California, Colorado, New Mexico, and Utah organized sustained efforts to capture a large share of the defense budget, which in turn shaped, often dramatically, the growth patterns in those regions. The *Denver Outpost*, for example, began tracking the economic benefits of government procurements, which included more than $1.5 billion for metal mining in western states.[60] Utah's defense industry complex, in particular, grew very rapidly. By 1963, the state was receiving $408 million in defense contracts, an absolute gain of 1700 percent since the outbreak of the Korean War, and the largest gain recorded by any state for the same period.[61] These expenditures helped to reopen hundreds of mines, add new jobs, and increase the state's income, all of which in turn laid the foundation for new industries.[62] A similar dynamic affected California, which dominated the fast-growing military aviation, missile, and electronics industries that accounted for the bulk of military procurements. Nearly 25 percent of all persons employed in manufacturing, equivalent to one out of every fifteen of those employed in the state, worked in the defense industry.[63]

Although traditional isolationists like Republican Senators Robert Taft and William Jenner would continue to hammer away on the point that the national purpose was "to maintain the liberty of our people" rather than "reform the entire world or spread sweetness and light and economic prosperity to peoples who have lived and worked out their own salvation for centuries," the Korean War had made these isolationist views largely irrelevant.[64] The Great Debate of 1951, between the Old Right "isolationists" like Senator Taft and the cold war liberal interventionists like Dean Acheson, had by 1961 been firmly settled in favor of the new ideology of national security, which had made it impossible for the United States to retreat from globalism or to reduce its defense spending to the comparatively modest levels of the pre–Korean War period.[65] The influential columnist James Reston of the *New York Times*, in describing the Korean War as a major turning point in American history, wrote that the United States was going to have to live with permanently higher defense budgets, less spending on nondefense programs, and a large peacetime army." "Whether we like it or not," observed Reston of America's new global identity, "we have inherited the role played by the British" of maintaining world peace, and "this role must be organized, not on a temporary, but on a permanent basis."[66]

Eisenhower was keenly aware of the problems that Korea raised. He had won the 1952 presidential election by promising to end the fighting there, but he knew the conflict was not over. The unfinished war would continue to shape events, channeling American policy and state-making into a direction that he feared was wrong for the country. In his farewell address to the nation on January 17, 1961, one of the most important presidential speeches ever given in American history, Eisenhower conceived his good-bye to America as a warning. "A vital element in keeping the peace is our military establishment," he told the nation. "Our arms must be mighty, ready for instant action, so that no potential aggressor may be tempted to risk his own destruction." But the new role of the military in American society raised troubling questions. One was the rising defense budget. "We annually spend on military security more than the net income of all United States corporations," he noted, and the conjunction of "an immense military establishment and a large arms industry is new in the American experience." Eisenhower continued, "We recognize the imperative need for this development. Yet we must not fail to comprehend its grave implications." Then he warned,

> In the councils of government, we must guard against the acquisition of unwarranted influence, whether sought or unsought, by the military industrial complex. The potential for the disastrous rise of misplaced power exists and will persist. We must never let the weight of this combination endanger our liberties or democratic processes. We should take nothing for granted. Only an alert and knowledgeable citizenry can compel the proper meshing of the huge industrial and military machinery of defense without peaceful methods and goals, so that security and liberty may prosper together.[67]

Eisenhower's warning went largely unheeded. The militarization of American society and the ever-growing military-industrial complex had become the Korean War's enduring legacy.

CHAPTER FOURTEEN

Deepening the Revolution

The Chinese people emerged from the ashes of the Korean War supremely confident. The war had imbued them with a sense of national pride for having fought the greatest superpower to a standstill and affirmed Mao's promise that China would indeed overcome its "century of national humiliation." Mao declared "a great victory in the war to resist U.S. aggression and aid Korea"[1] Recognizing China's new status, Khrushchev assumed a solicitous stance toward Mao and China by ending all unequal agreements between the two nations and by providing Beijing with the necessary economic and military assistance to help China get back on its feet. Khrushchev welcomed the emergence of a strong communist neighbor. The historian William Taubman noted that between 1953 and 1956, "the Soviets agreed to build, or aid, in the construction of 205 factories and plants valued at about $2 billion, with $727 million financed with Soviet credits, all at a time when the Russians themselves suffered shortages."[2] The scale of Soviet largesse was impressive: technological support to initiate or upgrade 156 industrial projects for the First Five-Year Plan; giving up the Soviet share in four Soviet-Sino joint ventures; a corps of experts to tutor the Chinese in everything from road construction to factory management; and blue prints of entire factories.[3] In 1955, Moscow provided nuclear technology, purportedly for peaceful purposes.[4] Moscow even offered to give Beijing a sample nuclear bomb in 1957.[5] "We gave everything to China," recalled Khrushchev. "We kept no secrets from the Chinese."[6]

Besides helping China economically, Soviet leaders were also generous in offering diplomatic and military support. The Soviets insisted on Beijing's participation in the 1954 Geneva Conference on Indochina and Korea. When Mao began shelling the offshore islands of Jinmen (Quemoy) and Mazu (Matsu) in late 1954, during the First Taiwan Strait

Crisis, Khrushchev backed him, even though he was trying to improve relations with the West. The Chinese were also invited to attend the founding meeting of the Warsaw Pact in 1955.[7] Khrushchev later wrote, "We considered the people of the Soviet Union and China to be brothers, and we felt this world was useful not only for us but also for the international communist movement."[8]

But Khrushchev was disappointed with the outcome of Soviet generosity. Even when the Sino-Soviet relationship was at its most harmonious during the mid-1950s, growing tensions were becoming apparent. This happened because Mao was no longer willing to play second fiddle to Khrushchev as he had done with Stalin. He had never forgotten that Stalin had reneged on his promise to provide crucial air support at the start of China's entry into the Korean War, leaving Mao's forces to face the Americans alone. In Mao's view, China had earned its newfound respect and international prestige from the Chinese blood spilled on the battlefields of Korea, and he sought to uphold the memory of these enormous sacrifices by asserting China's equality, and indeed, superiority, with the Soviet Union. No amount of aid or solicitous treatment from Khrushchev would diminish Mao's desire to show just who ruled the roost.[9]

Khrushchev's memories of his first visit to Beijing in 1954 are replete with resentments. For example, when he offered to withdraw Soviet troops from Port Arthur and Dairen and restore the two ports to China, Mao insisted that the Soviets leave their heavy artillery behind. Surprised, Khrushchev refused to do so without payment.[10] Khrushchev had also raised the question of Chinese guest workers coming to Siberia, to help with the cutting of timber. "We thought it was of mutual interest and to some degree would be of assistance to China," wrote Khrushchev, but Mao's reply angered him. "Everyone looks at China as a kind of reserve source of labor," Mao said. "In China this attitude toward the Chinese people is considered insulting." The matter was quickly dropped, though Khrushchev resented Mao's haughtiness. "It seemed to me that Mao could not reconcile himself to the circumstances necessary for healthy relations among socialist countries, circumstances in which each country and each ruling party hold a position of equality with all the others," Khrushchev later declared. "He was aspiring to hegemony of the world Communist movement!"[11]

It was the Polish and Hungarian crisis of 1956 that had brought these private tensions into public awareness. Khrushchev had not consulted the Chinese in advance about his secret speech at the Twentieth Congress in 1956 that denounced Stalin. While Mao had his own grievances against Stalin, he believed it was unwise to undermine the cult of personality. "Mao had an almost mythical faith in the role of the leader," observed Mao's personal physician, Li Zhisui. "He was China's Stalin, and everyone knew it. He shared the popular perception that he was the country's messiah." Khrushchev's attack against Stalin raised uncomfortable questions about Mao's own leadership style and "cult of personality," which was by then well orchestrated throughout the country. Li observed, "For Mao to agree to the attack against Stalin was to admit that attacks against himself were permissible as well." Just as important, Mao saw foreign manipulation in the denunciation. "Mao saw Khrushchev's attack as playing into the hands of the Americans, the imperialist camp," Li later wrote. He also quoted Mao as saying that "[Khrushchev] is just handing the sword to others, helping the tigers harm us."[12]

Khrushchev's handling of the Polish and Hungarian crises of 1956 merely reconfirmed Mao's view of the Soviet leader's deficiencies. His vacillation in the face of the crises, and his apparent reliance on Chinese advice to use force to crush the Hungarian rebellion made it seem, at least to the Chinese, as if they were coaching the Soviets, in a stark reversal of roles.[13] By the end of 1956, Mao began to harbor serious doubts about Khrushchev's competence to lead the communist movement, as Mao had come to believe that the Polish and Hungarian crises had been the direct outcome of Khrushchev's "foolish" denunciation of Stalin. "The sword of Stalin has now been discarded by the Russians," he proclaimed in November 1956, "and some people in Hungary have picked it up to stab at the Soviet Union and to oppose so-called Stalinism." Mao added that "we Chinese have not thrown it away." Mao was becoming increasingly critical of Khrushchev's principle of "peaceful coexistence" between the socialist and nonsocialist worlds. He accused Khrushchev of abandoning the class struggle. Mao asserted that "the Western world had simply used the Hungarian incident to mount an anti-Soviet, anti-communist tide," and he, not Khrushchev, was the more qualified to lead the communist revolution and to dictate the principles underlying the relations between and among socialist countries since he was the true Marxist-Leninist.[14] "Mao thought he was God," Khrushchev complained. "Karl Marx and Lenin were both in their graves and Mao thought he had no equal on earth."[15]

Mao could hardly hide his disdain for his Soviet hosts during his trip to Moscow in November 1957, the first since 1949–50. "The arrangements for Mao and his entourage had been made with the greatest care," reported Li Zhisui. Yet Mao received the Russian hospitality with contempt. "Look how differently they're treating us now," he snapped. "Even in this communist land, they know who is powerful and who is weak. What snobs!" Although two Russian chefs were assigned to him, Mao refused to eat the food they prepared, preferring instead "the Hunanese fare concocted by his favorite chef." Taken to see a performance of *Swan Lake* at the Bolshoi, Mao was immediately bored and announced at the end of the second act that he was leaving. He seemed, in the words of his physician, to be "deliberately refusing to appreciate Russian culture."[16] Khrushchev noticed Mao's "aloof manner." "You could already sense that he placed himself above the rest," Khrushchev angrily recalled. "Sometimes he allowed himself to do things that in general were impermissible, and he did it all without paying the slightest attention to others." The Soviet leader also complained that Mao flirted with his wife during the meetings, saying "indecent things to her laughing." Khrushchev was appalled.[17]

Relations between the two leaders worsened in 1958. Following the harsh crackdown of the failed Hundred Flowers campaign, which had been introduced in 1956 to encourage open criticism of the government and its policies, Mao launched the Great Leap Forward campaign, a new mass mobilization movement to consolidate his power and maintain China's revolutionary momentum.[18] Sino-Soviet tensions escalated during this period as Mao sought to both radicalize China's domestic policies and distance himself from Soviet economic practices. His realization of China's economic backwardness coupled with a new confidence to claim authority in the world communist hierarchy led him to launch the movement, which was intended to turn China into an industrialized power in just a few years. Mao wanted to prove that he was the true successor of Marx and Lenin.

It was at this moment, when Mao decided to assert China's independence from Moscow, that Khrushchev proposed a joint venture: establishment of a communication station on China's coast to serve not only

Soviet submarines in the Pacific but also a joint Soviet-Chinese submarine fleet. The Soviets would build the radio station themselves, but the technology would be "in the common interest of the entire socialist camp" since, as Khrushchev put it, "all military resources of the socialist countries were all serving one common cause, to be prepared to repel the imperialists if they unleashed a war against us."[19] Mao's reaction was unexpected. He accused the Soviet Union of "big power chauvinism" and charged them with "looking down on the Chinese people." Furthermore, "if the Soviets wanted joint ownership and operation of a submarine fleet," Mao sarcastically told Soviet Ambassador Pavel Yudin, "then let us turn into joint ownership and operation of our army, navy, air force, industry, agriculture, culture, education." Or better still, "[you] may have all of China's more than ten thousand kilometers of coastline and let us only maintain a guerilla force." Mao told Ambassador Yudin, "Please report all my comments to Comrade Khrushchev . . . You must tell him exactly what I have said without any polishing so as to make him uneasy. He has criticized Stalin's [policy] lines but now adopts the same policies as Stalin did."[20]

Alarmed by Yudin's report, Khrushchev rushed to Beijing. Between July 31 and August 3, 1958, the two leaders met four times. Khrushchev was mistaken in thinking a personal visit would smooth Mao's ruffled feathers, for Mao treated him shabbily if not with contempt. "Mao returned the extravagant hospitality given him in the Soviet Union [in 1957] with a slap in Khrushchev's face," observed Li Zhisui.[21] After four days of intensive meetings, an agreement on the construction of the long-wave radio station was eventually signed, but it had been hard fought and revealed the growing discord between the two leaders. Mao would later recall that "the overturning [of our relations with] the Soviet Union occurred in 1958, and that was because they wanted to control China militarily."[22]

Even more alarming than Mao's boorish behavior during the 1958 meetings from Khrushchev's point of view was his view of nuclear war. "Mao regarded as the top priority not the question of peaceful coexistence, but the question of preparing for war with the aim of crushing our enemies in a war, no matter how great the losses such a war might bring to the socialist countries." Mao was not afraid of nuclear war: "The size of the population is decisive, as in the past, in deciding the balance of forces. We have plenty of people . . . There is no country that can succeed in defeating us." Khrushchev was stunned by Mao's bravado. Mao advised that if there was an attack on the Soviet Union, the Russians should offer no resistance. Instead, "you should withdraw gradually," Mao told Khrushchev. "Retreat for a year or two or three. You would force the enemy to extend his lines of communication and thereby weaken him. Then, with our combined forces, we would attack him and crush him." "But where would Soviet forces retreat to?" asked an astonished Khrushchev. "Didn't you retreat as far as Stalingrad? For two whole years you retreated, so why can't you retreat for three years to the Urals or Siberia?" Was Mao playing the fool simply to annoy the Soviet leader? Khrushchev couldn't be sure. Mao's wild rants about preparing for nuclear war worried Khrushchev: "If he [Mao] actually believed that his arguments made sense in terms of military strategy, it's hard to believe that an intelligent person would be capable of thinking that way. To this day, it remains a total mystery to me. I still don't know whether he was being provocative or was simply incapable of thinking clearly."[23]

The talks ended abruptly. Khrushchev had originally planned to stay a week but left after only three days. Mao's churlish behavior and his talk of Soviet forces retreating to the Urals in the event of a nuclear attack had angered and confused him. According to Li Zhisui, however, this had been Mao's intention all along: "The chairman was deliberately playing the role of emperor, treating Khrushchev like the barbarian come to pay tribute. It was a way, Mao told me on the way back to Beidaihe, of 'sticking a needle up his ass.'"[24]

If Khrushchev returned to Moscow believing that the worst of his troubles with Mao were over, he had been sorely mistaken. On August 23, 1958, the Chinese began bombarding the offshore Taiwanese islands of Jinmen and Mazu, initiating the Second Taiwan Strait Crisis without any advanced warning to Moscow. In response, the Americans mounted a massive show of force in the Taiwan Strait. Dulles announced Washington's intention to defend the offshore islands. A Sino-American war would very likely draw in the Soviet Union. Khrushchev secretly sent Foreign Minister Andrei Gromyko to Beijing to find out what Mao was up to. He was relieved by Gromyko's report. Mao's intention was not to provoke a war with the United States, but rather to draw the world's attention to the Taiwan question and to divert American strength from the rest of the world. With these assurances, Khrushchev sent a letter to Eisenhower declaring his country's solidarity with Beijing. The Soviet Union would abide by the Sino-Soviet Treaty of 1950 and would regard an attack on China as an attack on itself.[25] Khrushchev thought as well that the show of solidarity would reduce the threat of war since he believed that Washington would not risk conflict, one that could go nuclear, over Taiwan. Still, Khrushchev was infuriated by Mao's actions. It appeared that Mao's intent was to derail Khrushchev's pursuit of détente with the United States and to undermine his quest for "peaceful coexistence." The shelling may have been Mao's way of declaring war on Khrushchev's "revisionism" and announcing his independence from the Soviet regime. These assumptions proved correct. Mao later confided to Li Zhisui: "The islands are two batons that keep Khrushchev and Eisenhower dancing, scurrying this way and that." For Mao, "the shelling of Quemoy and Matsu was pure show, a game to demonstrate to both Khrushchev and Eisenhower that he could not be controlled, and to undermine Khrushchev in his new quest for peace."[26]

More important than international considerations, however, was Mao's main concern in the summer of 1958 on how to propel the Great Leap Forward movement into its most radical phase, the communization and militarization of the entire Chinese population.[27] On August 17, at a meeting of the Politburo of the CCP, Mao discussed the idea of shelling Jinmen and Mazu. The crisis would help in the mobilization effort of the Great Leap Forward, Mao reasoned, for "tension can help increase steel as well as grain [production] . . . To have an enemy in front of us, to have tension, is to our advantage."[28] Wu Lengxi, the director of Xinhua (New China News Agency) and editor of *People's Daily*, the two main propaganda organs, recalled, "Chairman Mao said that the bombardment of Jinmen, frankly speaking, was our turn to create international tension for a purpose." That purpose was to mobilize the people and to re-create the revolutionary fervor of the civil war and Korean War days. "The shelling of Jinmen-Mazu was a continuation of the Chinese civil war," Mao explained. "No foreign country or international organization should be allowed to interfere in China's affairs."[29] By linking the 1958 Taiwan Strait crisis and the Great Leap Forward, Mao wanted to galvanize the people by evoking their nationalist pride and profound victim mentality. Jinmen and Mazu were part of China's territory that had been "lost" as a result of imperialist aggression (by

Japan and later by the United States), Mao explained. They therefore needed to be recovered. "Taiwan keeps the pressure up," Mao told Li Zhisui. "It helps maintain our internal unity. Once the pressure is off, internal disputes might break out."[30] In the meantime, significant fissures had opened between Beijing and Moscow. Khrushchev departed Beijing after his visit in the summer of 1958, having grave doubts about Mao's "methods for building socialism" and his capacity to deal with the capitalist world in "a rational, cooperative way."[31]

The Tragic Demise of Peng Dehuai

The man who had led Chinese forces in Korea had never been shy about bringing bad news to Mao. Peng Dehuai had always been honest with Mao. When Mao pushed Peng to pursue and drive UN forces from the Korean peninsula during the winter of 1950–51, Peng protested, stating that doing so was foolhardy and would lead to certain defeat. He halted his army near the 38th parallel instead, insisting that his men needed to regroup and rest. Nine years later, Peng warned Mao that he was pushing his people too hard and too fast: grain targets were unrealistic; there was excessive reliance on production of steel of dubious quality from backyard furnaces; the people were exhausted. Peng's conclusion that disaster was looming came from firsthand observations. In October 1958, Peng traveled to the northwestern province of Gansu, which he had liberated from Nationalist forces almost a decade earlier. What he saw shocked him. At an infantry school, classes and training had been canceled because all instructors and students were laboring at backyard furnaces, with "their clothes black as soot." The school staff told him that houses and fruit trees were used for fuel. He saw fields with ripe crops ready for harvest and inquired why they were being left to rot. The reply he received was that there were not enough people to harvest because they had to work at the furnaces. At an iron and steel works, Peng saw "smashed cooking vessels being used as raw materials simply to produce more iron. Useless lumps of it were lying resting on the ground." The whole operation was "futile," Peng told the local cadre and "compared it to beating a gong with a cucumber."[32] Although they agreed, they told him their quota had to be filled.

Peng visited his home province, Hunan, where he met with old friends in his home village, Wushi, not far from Mao's birthplace in the same county, Xiangtan. It was the first time he had visited since the 1920s. The mood of the people was somber. He met aged peasants who were angry, even mutinous. "The youth can tighten their belts; the old can grit their teeth," said one farmer, "but babies? They can only cry." They hated the daily militarized routine, the forced communal living, and the destruction of family life that had been the center of Chinese society for millennia. There was not enough food. He was shown a "dish of vegetables with a few grains of rice" as a typical meal. Peng could see from their physical condition that they were not deceiving him. The cadres, they explained, were under constant pressure to outdo rival communes, which led to chronic exaggeration of crop yields. A set percentage of the yield was taken for provisioning the cities, and when this was applied to the exaggerated yields, there was virtually nothing left for the farmers. The Great Leap was a huge lie. "The old folk indicated to Peng that they could cope with natural disasters, but man-made ones were another matter."[33]

Assessing the success or failure of the Great Leap was not in Peng's portfolio as defense minister, but so great was his distress, especially what he witnessed in his own home town, that Peng decided to write a private letter to Mao on his observations. "By the evening of July 12, I had formed the opinion that serious disproportions had now emerged in China," he later wrote. "This became the burden of my letter dated July 14, 1959. In that letter, I merely set out in general terms several relatively important issues, but made no comment on the causes that had given rise to these problems, indeed, at that time I could not explain the causes." The letter was hand-delivered to Mao at Lüshan, where the Central Committee, the highest authority of the party, was meeting to discuss the Great Leap.

Peng was not prepared for the fury of Mao's response. Instead of handling the letter as a private communication from a trusted colleague, Mao copied and circulated it to the 150 senior cadres attending the meeting. Mao attacked Peng, "declaring that the letter constituted an 'anti-Party program of right-wing opportunism'."[34] He presented a stark choice to the Central Committee: side with Peng and he, Mao, would "go away to the countryside, to lead the peasants and overthrow the government," or side with Mao. He added a direct challenge to the leaders of the PLA. If they did not want to follow him, he would raise another army, a truly Red one this time, and continue the revolution.[35] They sided with Mao, and Peng was censured. Virtually overnight, Peng had become persona non grata. He was forced to move out of his large home to a half-ruined house. For the next six years he lived under virtual house arrest cleaning sewers and collecting refuse.

On December 28, 1966, at the start of the Cultural Revolution, Peng was arrested. His niece said he was continuously beaten and tortured. "During the decade of trouble, uncle was subjected to harsh persecution," she wrote. "After the CPC [Communist Party of China] Central Committee had reviewed uncle's case, I came across one document . . . prepared for the group for the Cultural Revolution." The document described Peng's tragic demise:

> Yesterday, at the Peking Aviation Institute, there was a meeting of struggle with Peng Dehuai attended by 30–40 people. Peng Dehuai was at the meeting and was beaten several times. He was wounded in the forehead, and there were internal injuries in the regions of the lungs: tomorrow there will be a new round . . . After the meeting of struggle on July 19, 1967, Peng lay on the bed to rest, he had chest pains and difficulty in breathing, groaned constantly and in the evening could not even spit. When he was ordered to write down material, he said: "I cannot write now." On the 22nd—today—the pain in his chest expanded in every direction and became even more serious. He had difficulty getting up off the bed . . . and could not speak. The doctor diagnosed two broken ribs, a rapid pulse and high blood pressure, and there were internal injuries.[36]

By the time of his death on November 29, 1974, Peng was unable to speak and had to be fed intravenously.[37] The old revolutionary and hero of the Korean War died of untreated pneumonia in an empty, unheated building at the Municipal Party Committee headquarters in Beijing.[38]

Meanwhile, Peng's predictions about the Great Leap had come true. The Soviets had warned Mao of the coming disaster, but Mao did not want to listen. "They wanted to show us how to build communism," Khrushchev later quipped. "Well, all they got was a stink, nothing else."[39] In 1957, the average annual amount of grain per person in the countryside was 450 pounds. The following year, it dropped to 443 pounds and then to 403 pounds in 1959, and in 1960, it was 348 pounds, a drop of 112 pounds per person in just three years.[40] The result was famine on a grand scale. An estimated 45 million Chinese people starved to death between 1959 and 1962.[41] In the wake of the crisis, the distrust between Moscow and Beijing deepened while the specter of a radical and hostile China increased the fear and loathing of Mao's regime in Washington. From Mao's perspective, however, his management of the crisis had been masterful. He had successfully promoted domestic mobilization by provoking international tensions. Mao's handling of China's domestic and external policies in the late 1950s was a foretaste of what was to come.[42] That is, in the same way Mao used the Korean War to consolidate his power and spur on the revolution, he used succeeding international crises to further that revolution. The next "opportunity" came in Vietnam.

Khrushchev, Korea, and Vietnam

Khrushchev visited Mao in September 1959 immediately following his twelve-day visit to the United States. He and Eisenhower had agreed, in their meeting at Camp David, that "the question of general disarmament is the most important one facing the world today."[43] The visit had made a positive impression on Khrushchev, who later insisted to his skeptical colleagues that Eisenhower was a reasonable "good hearted" man who could be dealt with through personal diplomacy.[44] Mao had not been consulted about the U.S. trip, and he wondered whether "peaceful co-existence" and talks about general disarmament concealed a secret agreement at China's expense. In China, Khrushchev spoke of the "Camp David spirit" of cooperation between East and West, which Mao perceived as an insult since Khrushchev was visiting to celebrate the tenth anniversary of the founding of the PRC and to give homage to the Chinese Revolution and China's victory over foreign imperialism.[45] At Eisenhower's request, Khrushchev asked Mao to release five U.S. citizens held on espionage charges. His awkward mediation further antagonized Mao. As the historian Sergey Radchenko noted, "The Soviet leader lacked the tact to understand that Mao needed no one, least of all Khrushchev, to deal with the West."[46]

Khrushchev and other Soviet leaders became increasingly alarmed by what they considered Mao's "Stalinist tendencies." Mikhail Suslov, a powerful and influential member of the Soviet Politburo, reported on the 1959 meeting, with stinging criticism of Mao's leadership style:

> One should not omit the fact that . . . mistakes and shortcomings in the field of domestic and foreign policy of the Communist Party of China are largely explained by the atmosphere of the cult of personality of com. [comrade] Mao Zedong. Formally, the CC [Central Committee] of the Communist Party of China observes the norms of collective leadership, but in effect the most important decisions are made single-handedly, and thus are often touched by subjectivism, and in some instances are simply not well thought through. Glorification of com. Mao Zedong is visibly and unrestrainedly on the rise in China. In the party press one can increasingly find such statements as "we, the Chinese, live in the great epoch of Mao Zedong," comrade Mao Zedong is portrayed as a great genius. They call him the beacon illuminating the path to communism, the embodiment of communist ideas. The name of com. Mao Zedong is equated with the party, etc. One presents the works of com. Mao Zedong in China as the last word of creative Marxism, of the same rank as the works of the classics of Marxism-Leninism. In effect, the works of com. Mao Zedong are at the foundation of all educational work in the party and in the last two–three years has been reduced to the study of Mao's works. All this, unfortunately, pleases com. Mao Zedong, who, by all accounts, himself has come to believe in his own infallibility. This is reminiscent of the atmosphere that existed in our country during the last years of I.V. Stalin.[47]

Tensions in Sino-Indian relations complicated the situation between Mao and Khrushchev. Prime Minister Nehru's accommodation of the Dalai Lama in the spring of 1959 after a failed Tibetan uprising against Chinese rule had led to a Sino-Indian clash along the Indo-Tibetan border. Khrushchev's decision to maintain a neutral position in the dispute further infuriated Mao, for whom the neutrality indicated that Moscow "had virtually adopted a policy to support India's position."[48] In February 1960, both sides publicly aired their differences at a Warsaw Pact meeting in Moscow. The purpose of the meeting had been to endorse Khrushchev's policy of peaceful coexistence and disarmament proposals in advance of the Soviet leader's big-four summit meeting with Eisenhower scheduled for that spring. Chinese delegates opposed peaceful coexistence, condemning it as being merely a "bourgeois pacifist notion."[49]

The two sides were now on record with "diametrically opposed analysis of world affairs and prescriptions for bloc policies."[50] Two months later, on April 22, 1960, Mao publicly attacked the Soviet Union's foreign policy, using the occasion of the ninetieth anniversary of Lenin's birth to extrapolate on his themes of war and revolution. Citing Lenin, Mao declared that war was the "inevitable outcome of systems of exploitation and the source of modern wars is the imperialist system." As long as imperialism existed, "wars of one kind or another will always occur." Furthermore, "in the light of bloody facts both of the historical past and of the modern capitalist world," peaceful coexistence between capitalist and socialist worlds was a chimera, a myth created by communist revisionists like Khrushchev.[51] Lashing out against Soviet "revisionism," he accused Khrushchev of pursuing policies that were ideologically incompatible with the teachings of Marx and Lenin. Moreover, unlike the Soviet Union, which was unwilling to support national liberation struggles in the Third World, China was the natural ally of the oppressed peoples.

An open clash followed as both sides began canvassing support among other communist parties. For the first time, Khrushchev publicly denounced Mao by name at the Romanian Party Congress in June 1960, calling him an "ultra-Leftist, ultra dogmatist and left wing revisionist who, like Stalin, had become oblivious to any interests but his own."[52] The next month, Khrushchev notified Mao that he would be withdrawing all Soviet advisors and experts from China. Ratified agreements on economic and technological aid were suspended, and hundreds of cooperative scientific and technological projects came to an abrupt halt mid-completion. Khrushchev also reneged on his promise to provide a sample atomic bomb. Mao was shocked and furious.[53] Several weeks after the Soviets withdrew, the CCP leadership left Beijing to escape the summer heat at a seaside resort. Mao vented his anger to the Vietnamese leader Ho Chi Minh, who joined him there:

> Khrushchev can cooperate with America, England and France. He can cooperate with India and Indonesia . . . He can even cooperate with Yugoslavia, but only with China is it impossible on the grounds that we have divergent opinions. Does that mean that his views are identical with America, England, France and India to allow whole-hearted cooperation? [He] withdraws the experts from China and doesn't transfer technology, while sending experts to India and giving technology. So what if China doesn't have experts? Will people die, I don't believe it.[54]

Nikita Khrushchev, Mao Zedong, and Ho Chi Minh at a banquet in Beijing celebrating the tenth anniversary of communist rule in China, October 1, 1959. China's support of Vietnam's struggle began to take a radical turn in 1962 and early 1963 that further strained relations with the Soviet Union. Competition with Moscow for influence in Vietnam drove the two nations further apart but also made the situation difficult for Hanoi, which was now forced to navigate between two contending powers. Moreover, after the catastrophe of the Great Leap Forward, Mao saw an opportunity afforded by the crisis in Vietnam to strengthen his hold on power. In the same way that Mao used the crisis in Korea to instigate the Thought Reform Campaign and the Patriotic Hygiene Campaign to mobilize the masses and consolidate his hold on power, the Chinese leader used the tensions caused by the war in Vietnam to attack Soviet "revisionists" and launch the Cultural Revolution. (AP PHOTOS)

Ho had come to China hoping for assistance for the armed struggle in South Vietnam. Throughout the late 1950s, Mao had counseled Ho on the wisdom of adopting the Bandung line of peaceful coexistence, a policy first advocated by Zhou Enlai in Bandung, Indonesia, when Zhou and Ho met in April 1955. When in 1958 an increasingly frustrated Vietnamese Politburo formally requested China's help in reviving a revolutionary war to bring about a communist victory in the South, Chinese leaders advised caution: "The realization of revolutionary transformation in the South was impossible at the current stage."[55] By the fall of 1959, however, Mao had softened his position because of increasing tensions with the Soviet Union, and agreed to provide the military aid Ho requested. Nevertheless, Chinese leaders were uneasy that Ho might prematurely escalate the conflict from guerilla war to conventional war. It would be better to wage a protracted guerilla war "for three to five years, even eight or ten years."[56] Chinese leaders were wary of provoking a wider war with the Americans in Vietnam. China's policy toward

Vietnam underwent a major shift in late 1962 and early 1963, owing to increased military support to Saigon from the Kennedy administration. The North Vietnamese feared that American forces would attack the North. Alarmed, Mao substantially increased military aid.[57]

In addition, China's economy had begun to recover by the end of 1961, and Mao felt personally vulnerable. The myth of his "eternal correctness" had been called into question for the first time by the disaster of the Great Leap Forward. His colleagues favored more moderate policies by allowing family households to grow produce in their own private plots, offering more freedoms and status to intellectuals, and moderating China's foreign policy toward its principle antagonists, namely, the Soviet Union, the United States, and India.[58] Mao feared the influence of Soviet-style "revisionists" within his own ranks. Moreover, the abrupt withdrawal of Soviet aid in July 1960 had cast China into deep isolation from the rest of the world. Mao believed that his apocalyptic vision of the inevitable struggle between the forces of revolution and reaction was in the process of being fulfilled. He was not about to be marginalized on the eve of this fateful struggle.

Finally, the lessons of the Korean War had instructed Mao on the profound linkage between war and revolution. Renewed militancy abroad would serve his purpose by creating militancy at home. Throughout 1962–64, Mao repeatedly emphasized that the Chinese people were facing reactionary forces both from within and from outside their country. They needed to be prepared for the inevitable war. "In our country, we must . . . admit the possibility of the restoration of reactionary class," Mao declared at the Central Committee's Tenth Plenum in September 1962. "We must raise our vigilance and properly educate our youth . . . Otherwise, a country like ours may yet move toward its opposite. Therefore, from now on, we must talk about this every year, every month, every day . . . so that we have a more enlightened Marxist-Leninist line on the problem."[59]

Although Mao's emphasis on war and revolution played an important role in plotting his comeback, it was the debate over Vietnam policy where Mao attempted to gain an advantage in any challenge to his authority. Vietnam crystallized the essential tenets of Mao's revolutionary ideology: his rejection of the possibility of peaceful coexistence and his view of China's new and central role as supporter of Third World liberation movements. The contest between Mao's revolutionary goals and the more moderate policies favored by so-called revisionists was brought to a head during the spring and summer of 1962, when Wang Jiaxiang, head of the CCP's International Liaison Department, openly challenged Mao. Wang had been deeply affected by the failures of the Great Leap. While he was convalescing from an illness in Canton, he received a report about the mass starvation in Hunan Province and "became emotional and wept." Believing that the CCP needed to concentrate on China's domestic problems and adopt a more moderate line to reduce international tensions, Wang warned the party's leadership against becoming involved in another war with the United States, this time in Vietnam. He criticized the tendency to overrate the dangers of world war and underestimate the benefits of peaceful coexistence. As for supporting revolutionary movements in Asia, Africa, and Latin America, Wang advocated reducing the costs of foreign entanglements. "At times like the present economic crisis, China had to consider very carefully what it spent overseas and not go overboard."[60]

Wang Jiaxiang's ideas came under heavy attack by Mao during a conference of party members held in Beidaihe in August 1962. The Chinese leader condemned Wang for promoting the policy of "three reconciliations and one reduction" as appeasement to imperialism, revisionism, and international reactionism, and reduction of assistance to support anti-imperialist forces in other countries.[61] He rejected the idea that the "Soviet Union of today" would be "China's tomorrow," saying that he sought a different future for China.[62] By the end of 1962, Mao was able to reassert his control over China's foreign and domestic policies. His decision to censure Wang and other revisionists, including future leader Deng Xiaoping, came hand in hand with the adoption of a more radical policy toward Vietnam.[63]

However, when the United States launched its first air strike against North Vietnam in August 1964, Mao wanted to avoid the apparent mistake he had made in Korea by selecting the wrong channel to convey China's warning. Mao did not want a direct Sino-American clash. The Chinese believed that one of the reasons why the Americans had ignored the warning in October 1950 against crossing the 38th parallel in Korea was because the Truman administration did not trust the messenger, Indian Ambassador Pannikar, who was thought to be anti-American and thus unreliable.[64] This time Mao chose an American ally, Pakistan, through its president, Ayub Khan, who was scheduled to visit Washington the following spring, to deliver a warning. Zhou Enlai asked Khan to convey to President Lyndon Johnson that "if the United States expands the war, the war will gradually be expanded to China. We are prepared both materially and spiritually."[65] The Americans would not dismiss a message coming from their Pakistani ally so quickly.

But the visit was unexpectedly canceled. The Chinese attempted other channels. They sent the warning for Washington to Burmese leader Ne Win and Cambodia's Prince Norodom Sihanouk. On April 20, Zhou himself delivered the message in a speech to leaders of the NAM in Bogor, Indonesia, at a gathering to mark the tenth anniversary of the Bandung Conference. He stated that "if the United States bombs China, that means bringing the war to China. The war has no boundary. This has two meanings. First, you cannot say that only an air war on your part is allowed, and the land war on my part is not allowed. Second, not only may you invade our territory, we may also fight a war abroad." In order to emphasize the seriousness with which the Americans should take China's warning, Zhou declared that "the Korean War can be taken as evidence." On May 16, Zhou reassured a visiting Vietnamese National Liberation Front (Vietcong) delegation of China's solidarity with their cause, telling them that "we will go to Vietnam if Vietnam is in need, as we did in Korea." Finally, the British senior diplomat in China, chargé d'affaires Donald Hopson, was summoned to a rare meeting on May 31 with Foreign Minister Chen Yi. Chen told Hopson that he would be "grateful" if Hopson could pass on the warning to the Americans.[66]

The Korean analogy thus set the stage for escalating the war in Vietnam for the purpose of radicalizing the Chinese masses and leading them toward the Cultural Revolution. At the same time, warnings to the Americans *not* to expand the war to China were based on the lessons of Korea and were clear indications that Mao wanted to avoid another Korean-style confrontation.[67] What Mao did not anticipate was how his Vietnam policy would lead to the complete breakdown of Sino-Soviet relations. Ironically, their joint support of North Vietnam contributed to the growing acrimony between them. As China plunged into the chaos of the Cultural Revolution, Mao faced the possibility of a war with the Soviet Union.

CHAPTER FIFTEEN

Korea and Vietnam

I would suggest to you that if we had not gone into Korea, I think it would have been very unlikely that we would have gotten into Vietnam.

—GEORGE BALL, July 1986[1]

We are duty-bound and obliged to defend a friendly ally from Communist aggression, just as the 16 allies of the free world, led by the United States, saved us in the Korean War of 1950.

—PARK CHUNG HEE, February 1965[2]

By 1965 the Sino-Soviet split had become obvious. But these new developments did not mean that the communist threat to the free world had diminished in any way. Both the Kennedy and Johnson administrations saw the split and Sino-Soviet competition in the communist world as actually leading to greater efforts on the part of Moscow, and Beijing, to exert communist control over the Third World. "We see stepped up attempts to subvert, to undermine, and to spread Communist revolution," the elder statesman W. Averell Harriman observed.[3] Staunch anticommunists like W. W. Rostow echoed the same theme: "The impulse in Moscow to seek the expansion of Communist power is so deeply rooted and institutionalized that Soviet leaders will feel an almost historic duty to exploit gaps in the capacity, unity and will of the West."[4]

It is not surprising that the Kennedy administration saw the fate of Vietnam tied to new concerns about communist activities in the Third World. These concerns were carried over into the Johnson administration after Kennedy's death in November 1963. In a key speech on April 7, 1965, Johnson explained why America had to be involved in Vietnam. Directly, America had a moral duty to honor the pledge made at the Geneva Conference in 1954 to protect Vietnamese independence. More broadly, Vietnam was part of the American commitment to protect the free world order, and stopping the communist threat in Vietnam was especially vital to halting the Chinese threat to that order. "The central lesson of our time is that the appetite of aggression is never satisfied. To withdraw from one battlefield means only to prepare for the next," Johnson passionately stated.[5] William Bundy, assistant secretary for Far Eastern affairs, echoed the charge:

> We recognize the profound implications of the Sino-Soviet split and the possibility that it may lead to greater tensions between the U.S.S.R. and Communist China in the northern regions. But we doubt that the U.S.S.R. has yet abandoned her Communist expansionist aims, and certainly not to the point where in the foreseeable future she could be relied upon to play a constructive role in assisting other nations to defend themselves against Communist China . . . And let us recognize too that, to the extent that Soviet policy has changed, or may change in the future, this will be in large part due to the fact that we, in partnership with other free-world nations, have maintained a military posture adequate to deter and to defeat any aggressive action. We do not aim at overthrowing the Communist regime of North Vietnam but rather at inducing it to call off the war it directs and supports in South Vietnam . . . If Hanoi and Peiping prevail in Vietnam in this key test of the new communist tactics of "wars of national liberation," then Communists will use this technique with growing frequency elsewhere in Asia, Africa and Latin America.[6]

America's challenge in Vietnam was to prevent these "wars of national liberation" from spreading. When asked in April 1965 how Americans could hope to compete with China in influencing Southeast Asia, "which is virtually a Chinese backyard," Secretary of State Dean Rusk replied, "Why not? These countries in Southeast Asia have a right to live out their own lives without being overrun by the outside . . . their national existence depends upon it. If we were to abandon that idea then the great powers would—what? Revert to the jungle?"[7] For Rusk the problem of South Vietnam essentially boiled down to a replay of the war in Korea: North Vietnam, with the backing of China and the Soviet Union, was waging a war of aggression against a sovereign state.

In 1954, as senator, Johnson, along with Senator Richard Russell Jr., the chairman of the Senate Armed Services Committee, had been the loudest and strongest opponent of American military intervention in Indochina. And yet, as president, Johnson embarked on a series of intervention actions in Vietnam, the sort he had advised Eisenhower against a decade earlier. Why? Why had the "lessons" of Korea, which had provoked such a strong reaction by members of the "Never Again Club" and Congress *against* American involvement in Indochina in 1954, now emerged as a preeminent consideration *for* intervention in 1965?

Part of the answer had to do with the fact that perceptions of the Korean War had changed. The frustrations over the inconclusive and protracted nature of the war in Korea had, by the mid-1960s, been tempered by time, while the communist threat in Asia had at least been contained. The Korean intervention was viewed through the prism of the wider global cold war struggle and was eventually cast as an American victory.[8] Korea had become an example where the battle line for freedom had been successfully drawn and had stood firm.

Lyndon B. Johnson: Refighting the Korean War

By the time of President Kennedy's death, in November 1963, there were sixteen thousand American advisors and support troops in Vietnam. Three weeks earlier, the president of South Vietnam, Ngo Dinh Diem, was killed in a military coup that had been quietly sanctioned by Washington. Johnson had inherited a chaotic and unstable situation in Vietnam made all the more difficult because his interests and strengths were not in foreign affairs but domestic policy. According to McGeorge Bundy, who served as the national security advisor to Kennedy and Johnson, Johnson's main concern during the first months of his presidency was the upcoming 1964 presidential elections, which "served as powerful deterrent for Johnson to take any definitive action regarding American commitment to Vietnam." For a year Johnson was tremendously constrained, as he could ill afford a major escalation of the Vietnam conflict during an election year, but neither could he afford to lose South Vietnam and be blamed for a communist victory on his watch. "My own impression, then and through the early summer, was that he [Johnson] wanted firmness and steadiness in Vietnamese policy, but no large new decisions," Bundy recalled.[9]

The opportunity to show his serious commitment to Vietnam came on August 2, 1964, when the North Vietnamese attacked an American destroyer in the Gulf of Tonkin. Two days later, new gunboat attacks were reported. Although doubts were later raised about whether a second attack had actually occurred, Johnson responded by ordering retaliatory raids against North Vietnam. The incident provided Johnson with enough leverage to extract from Congress almost unlimited authority to escalate American involvement in Vietnam. The Gulf of Tonkin Resolution that Congress passed gave the president the authority to respond to any armed attack against the United States without congressional approval. Johnson attempted to quell concerns over this unprecedented presidential power by reassuring the American public that "we still seek no wider war." In a speech on August 5, he declared, "To any who may be tempted to support or to widen the present aggression, I say this: there is no threat to any peaceful power from the United States of America. But there can be no peace by aggression and no immunity from reply."[10] The resolution provided the president with just enough political cover to convince the American people that he was tough on communism without appearing overly belligerent.

Johnson won a landslide victory that November. Domestic political considerations continued to shape his decisions on Vietnam. On the one hand, he feared that Vietnam would drag down his domestic agenda. He was keenly aware that the stalemated war in Korea had prevented Truman from seeking a second term. At the same time, he thought that "losing" South Vietnam to the communists would damage his power and America's credibility and standing in the free world. The Vietcong had stepped up their military pressure, and by the spring of 1965 it appeared that all of South Vietnam was on the verge of being overrun by the communists. The choice was remarkably stark: withdraw or escalate. The Korean analogy largely informed how Johnson thought about the two issues.[11]

Advocates of a negotiated neutralization of South Vietnam and eventual American withdrawal included two influential Democratic senators, Richard Russell of Georgia and Wayne Morse of Oregon. Russell was convinced that the U.S. mission in Vietnam was doomed and that negotiations and withdrawal were the only viable options. He warned the president that Vietnam "would be a Korea on a much bigger scale and worse." He also heeded the historical lessons of the French colonial wars. "The French reported that they lost 250,000 men and spent a couple of billions of our dollars down there and just got the hell whipped out of them." When Johnson brought up the subject of bombing North Vietnam, Russell retorted, "Bomb the North and kill old men, women and children? . . . Oh hell! That ain't worth a hoot. That's just impossible . . . We tried it in Korea."[12] Senator Morse was also pessimistic about the American ability to make any headway in Vietnam. He had voted against the Tonkin Resolution, one of just two senators who chose to defy the president, and challenged every major assumption underlying Johnson's Vietnam policies. "The policy of what we called helping the Government of South Vietnam control a Communist-inspired rebellion has totally failed," he wrote in February 1965. "I do not foresee a time when any Government in South Vietnam that is dependent upon the United States for its existence will be a stable or popular one." Instead,

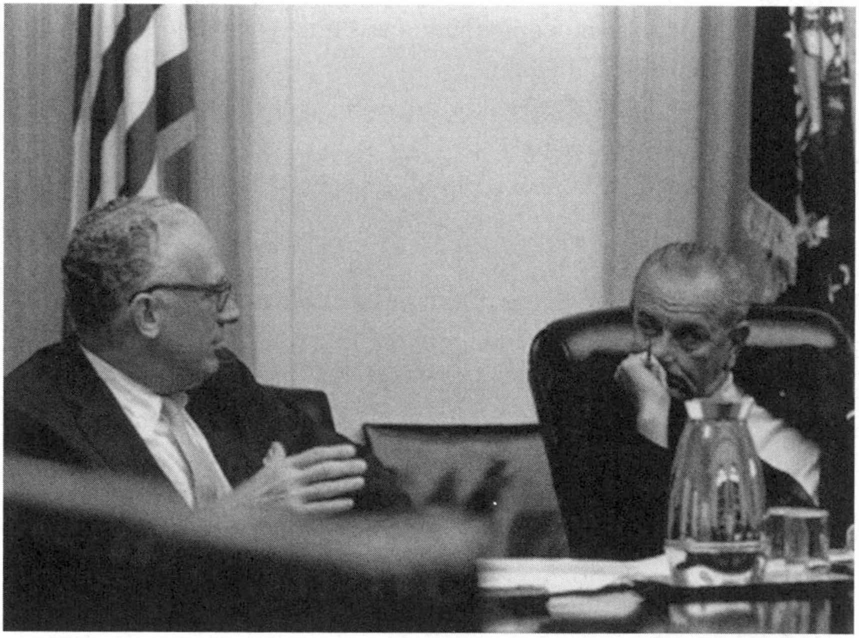

George Ball and President Johnson, July 14, 1966. During the Second World War, Ball had been a member of the United States Strategic Bombing Survey (USSB) team that was charged with studying the effects of bombing Germany and Japan. The survey found that "the German capacity to produce armaments of war had increased through the end of 1944 despite progressively expanded allies sorties." In addition, it found that the resolve of both the German and the Japanese population to resist the enemy had not been broken. The conclusion of the survey disturbed Ball and would later affect his thoughts about the bombing of North Vietnam.[13] (LBJ PRESIDENTIAL LIBRARY)

Morse advised, "we should be seeking some kind of settlement that will carry out the 1954 objective of removing foreign domination from the old Indo-China, but this time with an effective guarantee of international enforcement."[14]

Undersecretary of State George W. Ball agreed. As Johnson's "favorite dove," Ball had been an early and consistent opponent of American escalation.[15] Having worked closely with the French during the Indochina war, he had seen firsthand the futility of that conflict. He was also deeply alarmed by the resolution. Sensing that Johnson would win a landslide victory and worried that a decision on Vietnam was fast approaching, Ball wrote his thoughts in October 1964 in a long memorandum titled "How Valid Are Our Assumptions Underlying Our Vietnam Policies."[16]

The main thrust of the memorandum was to show that the Korean War analogy was wrong and even dangerous in thinking about Vietnam. In a section titled "South Vietnam Is Not Korea," Ball argued that Seoul in 1950 had a stable government ruled by a leader who wielded strong political control over the population. This was not the case in South Vietnam in 1964. In South Korea, Americans had fought under a United Nations mandate. No such mandate existed for South Vietnam. Moreover, the Korean War had begun with a massive invasion and was fought as a conventional war. In South Vietnam there was no such clear-cut invasion, only a "slow infiltration that many nations regarded as an 'internal rebellion.'"[17] "In approaching this problem," he wrote, "I want to emphasize one key point at the onset: the problem of South Vietnam is *sui generis*. South Vietnam is not Korea, and in making fundamental decisions it would be a mistake to rely too heavily on this Korean analogy."[18] Instead, Ball argued that the far more valid, and sobering, comparison was the French experience in Indochina between 1945 and 1954. Based on that, he favored a gradual withdrawal of American military forces from South Vietnam.

When Johnson finally gave the memorandum serious consideration in February 1965, it was already clear that Ball never had a chance. Johnson had already made up his mind that an American withdrawal from Vietnam was not a viable option. "It was useless for me to point out the meaning of the French experience," Ball later wrote. "They thought the French experience was without relevance. Unlike the French, we were not pursuing colonialist objectives but nobly waging war to support a beleaguered people. Besides, we were not a second-class nation trying to hang on in Southeast Asia from sheer nostalgic inertia; we were a superpower—with all that implies."[19] Since the purported goal was to help the South Vietnamese defend themselves against communist tyranny, how could moral comparisons between French and American aims in Vietnam even be considered? The strongest arguments for withdrawal, however, actually came from the military. The Joint Chiefs had found themselves in the same position as Ball with regard to the escalation of the war. Johnson's military advisors warned him that "it would take hundreds of thousands of men and several years to achieve military stalemate." If war was to be waged there, then Johnson was urged to mobilize the reserves "and commit the United States to winning the war."[20]

This was essentially the same argument that General Ridgway had given to President Eisenhower in 1954: if the United States was not prepared to pay the cost in blood and treasure that would be incurred by a guerilla war in Vietnam, then such a war *must* be avoided. In effect, the arguments against escalation by both Ball and the JCS wrestled with the Korean War analogy in different ways to make a similar point. Ball said the war in Vietnam was fundamentally *different* from the Korean situation because Saigon in 1964 was not Seoul in 1950. He warned that a war to prop up a failing regime in the face of the Vietcong's increasing success would result in the loss of American prestige. The Joint Chiefs, on the other hand, worried that Vietnam was too much *like* Korea because it would lead to another inconclusive and stalemated war. It might also risk another war with China and lead to World War III.

The president weighed his options carefully before deciding his next move. However, it was the domestic political implications of the Korean War analogy that vexed Johnson the most. "For LBJ," McGeorge Bundy later confided, "the domino theory was really a matter of domestic politics." Vietnam was "an American political problem, not a geopolitical or cosmic matter."[21] Very simply, Johnson did not believe that his administration could survive the loss of South Vietnam. His credibility was at stake. "I am not going to be the President who saw Southeast Asia go the way that China went," he told Henry Cabot Lodge, U.S. ambassador to South Vietnam, shortly after assuming power.[22] As a product of Texas of the 1950s, Johnson was defined by the Korean War era and the fear of appearing "soft" on communism. "Those fears and suspicions of the

Communists had never entirely left him," David Halberstam observed, "and they colored the way he understood the challenge of Vietnam."[23]

At the same time, Johnson was keenly aware that Truman's real fall from grace was brought about by the stalemate in Korea. Eisenhower had capitalized on the Korean tragedy to secure his landslide victory in 1952. "It looks to me like we are getting into another Korea," a distraught Johnson told McGeorge Bundy in the spring of 1964. "I just don't think it's worth fighting for 10,000 miles away from home and I don't think that we can get out. It's just the biggest damn mess I ever saw." Bundy tried to reassure the president. He could fight in Vietnam and still protect his domestic agenda. "Thirty-five thousand soldiers had died in the Korean conflict over a three year period, at a rate roughly comparable to the death toll in Vietnam," he said. "Yet there was no protest." The Korean War had been "a hard choice but incontestably right, both in morals and politics."[24] The American people would see it that way too.

Bundy's assumptions are revealing. The notion that the American people would simply accept the war in Vietnam as a necessary replay of Korea demonstrated the extent to which the legacy of that war still informed the Johnson administration's foreign policy. Bundy declared that "to abandon this small and brave nation to its enemy and to the terror that must follow would be an unforgiving wrong... [It] would shake the confidence of all these people in the value of the American commitment."[25] What Bundy had failed to address, however, was that the times had changed: the two apparent monolithic constructions of the 1950s were in the process of breaking apart. An overt rebellion by France was taking place in one camp, while another rebellion by China was taking place in another. It was now possible for a member of the Western bloc to be either "American" or "Gaullist" just as it was possible for a member of the Communist Party to be "Russian" or "Chinese."[26] So where did this leave the notion of credibility underlying the domino theory and America's policy in Vietnam?

Years later McGeorge Bundy admitted that he should have challenged the logic of the domino theory when he had the opportunity as national security advisor. In his memoirs, President Johnson claims to have harbored no such doubts. His primary concern had always been how the fate of South Vietnam would adversely affect his domestic agenda.[27]

In February 1965, Johnson ordered a limited bombing campaign of

North Vietnam called Operation Rolling Thunder. Six changes of government in South Vietnam had already occurred in 1964, and three more took place in the spring of 1965. The Vietcong saw their opportunity and had stepped up military pressure, pushing South Vietnam to the verge of collapse. Johnson made the fateful decision of introducing a substantial number of ground troops in March, to protect U.S. air installations. Subsequently, more troops were added to conduct offensive operations in the areas around U.S. air bases. A critical moment of decision had finally been reached. Disastrous South Vietnamese military defeats in the spring led to a series of crisis-driven inspection visits and White House meetings to determine what if anything should be done. By the summer of 1965, the Pentagon requested an increase of 100,000 troops, bringing levels there to 175,000 to 200,000. In six months, the Pentagon projected the need for another 100,000.[28] By the end of 1966 the number was 385,000 and by 1968, at its height, the total U.S. commitment stood at 536,000 military personnel.

Johnson later wrote that his decision to gradually increase the levers of war was due to fear of China's reaction; calling up the reserves and publicly committing the United States to a full-scale war in Vietnam might have precipitated another Korea-like confrontation. Yet it was clear from the beginning that Chinese leaders had sought to avoid a direct Sino-American clash and would only intervene if the United States had invaded North Vietnam. The Chinese had learned from the Korean War experience too, and repeatedly and publicly communicated their intentions so that there would not be any confusion.[29] Moreover, as Ridgway and others later argued, if Johnson had been really worried about such a confrontation, he should have clearly stated the main objectives of the war at its onset. "With our aims loosely described only as 'freedom for the people to choose their way of life' or as 'standing up to communism,'" Ridgway later complained, "we have drifted from a point where we were told, a scant two years ago, that our military task would be largely accomplished and our troops withdrawn by December 1965, to a point where the faint outline of half-million troop commitment becomes a distinct possibility. And even that commitment is not offered as a final limit."[30]

The accumulation of difficulties and the costs of the war also meant that the stakes rose. When his liberal allies began to abandon him,

Johnson felt betrayed. What he had failed to realize was how much the world had changed since the Korean conflict. Had Johnson been truly convinced that the fall of South Vietnam posed an imminent threat to America's national security, as Truman believed about South Korea, he would have embarked on a full-scale commitment to the war from the very beginning. That he failed to do so, deciding instead to wage a major war virtually in secret, speaks volumes not only about his growing doubts regarding the "lessons" of Korea, but also about his impotence in challenging their main assumptions.

Park Chung Hee's Crusade

While a handful of nations sent token forces to Vietnam to join in support of the United States, they did not come close to duplicating the "Uncommon Coalition" of the Korean War. The largest and most meaningful partner was South Korea, which provided both substantial military support and political coverage for the Americans. The height of South Korea's involvement reached its maximum strength in 1968, with over 50,000 military and 15,000 civilian contract workers. The ten-to-one ratio of U.S. to South Korean manpower is misleading because, in fact, 20 percent of the infantry combat forces under U.S. control were South Koreans, a situation rarely appreciated or acknowledged. As during the fighting in Korea, most of the Americans were part of the tail—a tail that also supported the Koreans—while the majority of the Koreans were part of the teeth. Moreover, as U.S. forces began to draw down in 1968, and would be almost all out by early 1973, the South Koreans remained in force until after the Paris Peace Accords were signed in January 1973, effectively serving as the rear guard of the American withdrawal.[31]

These military efforts were led by Gen. Park Chung Hee, who came to power in May 1961, a year after the South Korean people toppled Syngman Rhee in a watershed event known as the April 1960 Revolution. Postwar South Korea in the 1950s was a terribly depressing place, a "hopeless case of poverty, social anomie and political instability."[32] The war had devastated the country. Although Rhee had leveraged South Korea's strategic position in the cold war to wheedle hundreds of millions of dollars in military and economic aid from the United States, he

Park Chung Hee (seated), as a Manchurian Army officer. (SAEMAŬL UNDONG CENTRAL TRAINING INSTITUTE)

had little to show for his efforts, as much of the aid was siphoned off to line the pockets of corrupt officials. Nearly a decade after the war, the country, with its tiny domestic market and thoroughly aggrieved population, still lacked sources of domestic capital. The North Korean threat, which had justified the stationing of large numbers of American troops in South Korea, was not only a military security concern. In 1961, North Korea's gross national product (GNP) per capita was $160, twice that of the South, posing dire psychological and political threats as well.[33] A review of U.S. policy toward South Korea in 1957 revealed that it was then "the largest beneficiary of American aid in the third world." The Americans wanted to reduce this dependence but could not do so until South Korea became able to grow its economy. Postwar South Korea seemed headed to a future of poverty, dependence, corruption, and despair.[34]

Yet one substantive outcome of the war was the creation of a modern South Korean military that had swelled from 100,000 in 1950 to well over

600,000 by 1953. The once-fledging force was transformed by the war into an experienced modern formidable fighting organization. It was also adept at solving large-scale logistical problems. This allowed ROK military leaders to boast that their level of managerial skills was "ten years ahead of the private sector." In addition, the military could claim that it was the most democratic institution in South Korean society. Many of its leaders were of humble origins, "and its organization acted as the melting pot for men of diverse social and economic backgrounds."[35] The South Korean military was, in the words of one historian, "the strongest, most cohesive, best-organized institution in Korean life," and by 1961 it had decided to make its power known.[36]

Park Chung Hee became the chosen agent to lead his nation out of its current crisis. After graduating at the top of his class from the military academy of the Japanese puppet state Manchukuo in Manchuria in 1942, he was selected to spend two years at the Japanese Military Academy near Tokyo, where he graduated in 1944. He was then assigned to the Eighth Manchurian Infantry Corps, essentially a Japanese-controlled unit, where he fought anti-Japanese guerilla bands, many manned by Koreans. After Korea's liberation in 1945, Park joined the Korean Constabulary, which subsequently became the ROK Army. His link to the Japanese colonial regime as a soldier in the Japanese military would haunt him after he became president, but it was his membership in the leftist SKWP that almost cost him his life. In the hotbed of postliberation politics, Park followed his older brother, an ardent communist, and became a member of the party. He was later caught up in the purging of leftists and communists from the ROK Army after the Yŏsu-Sunch'ŏn Rebellion in late 1948. Arrested, interrogated, and facing a death sentence, he was saved by then Colonel Paek Sŏn-yŏp, also a graduate of the Manchukuo military academy and in charge of rooting out leftists in the ROK Army, and by KMAG advisor Capt. James H. Hausman. Both sensed something extraordinary about the future president. After serving time in prison, Park returned to work for the ROK Army as a civilian. Given his spotty background, he would probably not have amounted to much had it not been for the outbreak of the Korean War, which gave him the much-needed opportunity to prove his loyalty to South Korea. Just fourteen months after his discharge and days after the North Korean invasion, Park was reinstated into the ROK Army as a major.[37]

Park, however, was not a communist but rather an ardent nationalist and pragmatist. He easily overthrew the corrupt and ineffective government of Rhee's successor, Chang Myŏn, in a bloodless military coup on May 16, 1961. Chang had come to power after the April Revolution, but his administration also floundered. When Park took over, he immediately issued a "revolutionary platform" that called for the eradication of "all social corruption and evil," the creation of a new "national spirit," and a "self-supporting economy." Park sought to change it all, justifying his actions in terms of a "surgical operation." "The Military Revolution is not the destruction of democracy in Korea," he declared in March 1962. "Rather, it is a way of saving it; it is a surgical operation intended to excise a malignant social, political and economic tumor." Koreans, he said, must embark on a "new beginning" by bringing an end to Korea's long history of "slavish mentality" toward strong foreign countries, including the

Thousands of citizens jam City Hall Plaza in Seoul to pledge their support for the military government's anticommunist and austerity programs, May 1961. (AP PHOTOS)

United States, and achieving national independence. In this he shared with his North Korean nemesis, Kim Il Sung, the same drive for economic and military self-sufficiency that they both linked to overcoming the people's historical "subservient" mentality toward foreign powers. Just as Kim had steadfastly worked to increase his independence from the Soviet Union and China, Park sought to gain independence from the Americans by "eradicating the corruption of the past and by strengthening the people's ability to be autonomous."[38]

The coup was wildly popular. Most people enjoyed seeing corrupt officials and businessmen being paraded down the street with dunce caps and sandwich cards declaring "I am a hoodlum" and "I am a corrupt swine." Park's cleanup efforts were so effective that even liberal skeptics greeted the coup with unabashed admiration. The liberal monthly journal *Sasanggye* published the kind of laudatory reaction to the military's "clean-up" operation that was typical. It congratulated the coup leaders "for making the citizens respect the law, reinvigorating sagging morale, and banishing hoodlums."[39] At the same time, however, Park needed these businessmen "hoodlums" to help him jump-start the flagging economy, so he offered them a deal: no jail time if they invested their "fines" in building up new industries to sell products in foreign markets. Park wanted to build an export-based economy. His efforts paid off, and in 1963 he legitimately won the presidential election, marking the end of the junta that had led the nation since the May 1961 coup. This in turn provided him with the political legitimacy he needed to govern effectively and with the U.S. backing he would have to rely on to help fund his national development program. But Park and the nation needed time to recover. What Park feared most was the withdrawal of American troops from the Korean peninsula before South Korea was ready to stand on its own against North Korea. His fears were not unwarranted. In 1961, President Kennedy had seriously considered reducing U.S. forces in South Korea.

The Vietnam War provided the opportunity for Park to begin to realize his goal of achieving national independence and security, even though the price of this autonomy meant aligning South Korea's interests with U.S. security interests in East Asia. Although Park had railed against his country's dependence on Washington, he was quick to recognize the enormous opportunities afforded by South Korea's commitment

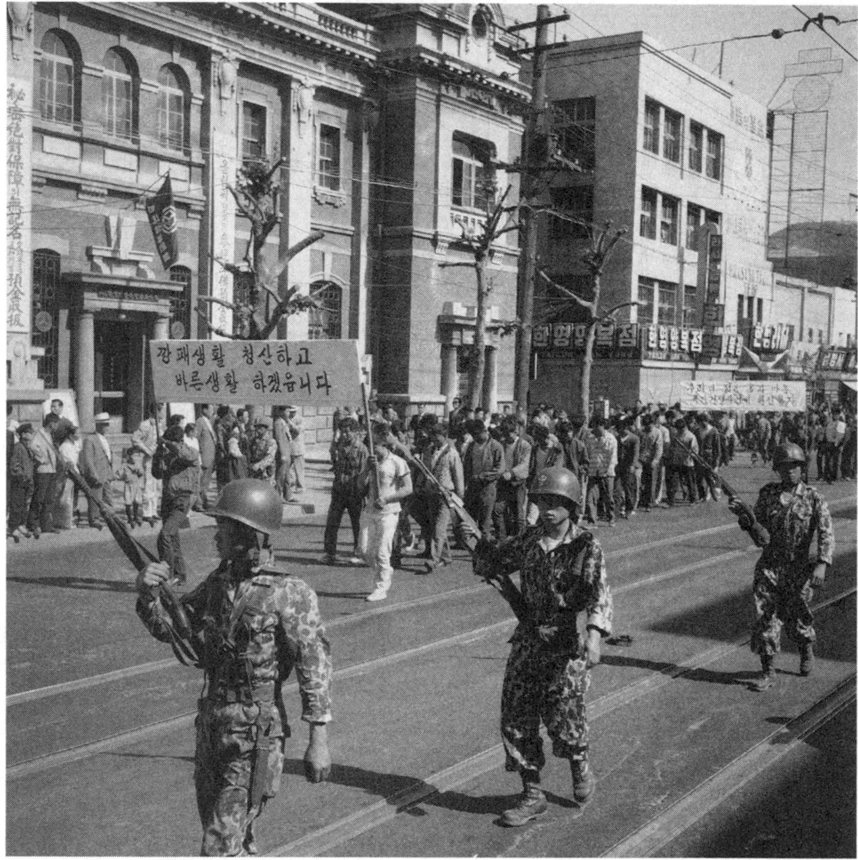

"Hoodlums" are paraded through the streets on May 23, 1961. The sign reads, "We will give up our hooligan lifestyle and lead a clean life." (AP PHOTOS)

of a large combat force to the war in Vietnam. There was the public relations of joining an idealistic and moral anticommunist crusade as a member of the free world. There was also the leverage, from the commitment of Korean blood, he could use to maximize U.S. economic and military aid to fulfill the national priority of securing Korea's autonomy. At the same time, by rallying the nation in support of another war against communism, Park reopened old wounds. His crusade in Vietnam and the ongoing threat from North Korea would become powerful sources of domestic mobilization in support of his economic and national security policies. Park would refight the Korean War in Vietnam to win the nation's economic autonomy from the United States and to secure itself from the threat of another war with the North.

Korea's interest in Vietnam goes back to 1954, when Syngman Rhee offered to send a division to Vietnam in the wake of France's disastrous defeat at Dien Bien Phu in May. Two months later the French were out with the signing of the Geneva Accords. Rhee's motivation was twofold. The most obvious was to demonstrate Korea's appreciation for the help it had recently received from UN forces in the Korean War. The other motive was more personal: "a burning desire to mobilize an anticommunist front in Asia under his leadership and to court U.S. opinion," as characterized by Ellis O. Biggs, U.S. ambassador in Seoul at the time.[40] Given Rhee's character, it seems rather certain that the latter motive was the dominant one, as he had been under a cloud in American and world opinion, especially over his actions in the final months before the armistice. The Americans at first favorably considered Rhee's offer but ultimately rejected it, owing to the difficulties of supporting the force in Vietnam, but more important was the potential political backlash from the American public, who might question why U.S. troops remained in Korea if South Korea could afford to send forces to Vietnam.[41]

Park also made an early offer of troops, in mid-November 1961, during his visit to Washington, the first by a South Korean head of state. It had barely been five months since the coup, and Park was still a general and the chairman of the junta known as the Supreme Council for National Reconstruction. The CIA's report on his communist ties before the Korean War raised suspicions, but the Kennedy administration gambled that he was the genuine article, and therefore someone who could lead Korea into a democratic and self-reliant nation. Park's visit was a personal triumph and solidified and legitimized his position as Korea's leader. He was greeted upon his return by a wildly cheering, flag-waving crowd of half a million lining the road from the airport.[42] The State Department informed the American embassy in Seoul that "Chairman PAK's [*sic*] visit successful in achieving results hoped for . . . Chairman made very good impression on U.S. officials with whom he came in contact. Appeared dedicated, intelligent, confident, fully in command his govt, and quite aware of magnitude of problems he faces . . . Informal visits elsewhere in U.S. . . . enhanced favorable image of Chairman among Americans generally and together with Washington visit received generally very good press."[43] In response to President Kennedy's question on whether Park had any thoughts about Vietnam, Park responded that he realized the situation was grave and that his country stood ready to assist the United States in sharing the burden to resolve it.[44] Park's motives are uncertain but are suggested by the circumstances of the infancy of his regime, its shaky legitimacy, and the desire to be in America's good graces not only to ensure continued aid but also to reverse its decline, the principle objective of his trip. But there was no explicit American request for troops nor was any given, and by mid-1962 aid levels had gone down, and the United States was considering again a partial drawdown of forces in Korea.[45]

The continuing uncertainties in Korea itself did not help. The junta was still the government, although elections were promised by the end of 1963. Also causing significant problems were the negotiations over the normalization treaty with Japan. Normalization of relations with Japan was an emotional and enormously unpopular issue with the Koreans, who periodically staged mass demonstrations against it. The end of Japanese colonialism was too recent, and the grievances too much to overcome with a simple treaty. But for Park, opening the gates to Japanese grants, loans, and technology was key to fulfilling his economic plans, so he was determined to finalize the treaty. After much uncertainty, a general election was held in November 1963 to choose a president and representatives to the National Assembly. The elections seem to have been fair according to reporting from the American embassy.[46] Park won the presidency, and his party won the majority of seats in the Assembly. Having retired from the army before the elections, Park now had a genuine civilian government, and a political base to achieve his vision for "National Restoration."

After a suspension of talks, owing to the political uncertainties in Korea, negotiations with Japan resumed in early 1964. With the stability of a newly elected civilian government in South Korea, which also represented continuity of the previous junta regime, the Japanese felt secure enough to continue the talks. It also helped that Park was sympathetic to Japan, not only because he had been an army officer in the Japanese colonial regime, but also because he looked to Japan's modernization path since the mid-nineteenth century as a model for Korea. Although Japan saw little to gain from normalizing ties with Korea, indeed it would have to pay compensation for its actions during the colonial period, the United States exerted extraordinary pressure since 1961 on both sides to conclude a treaty. This policy was based purely on the aim of creating a Northeast Asian anticommunist bulwark anchored by Japan and with Korea on the mainland. Ideally, Japan would replace the United States as a proxy of containment in the region, and normalization of Japanese–South Korean relations was sine qua non to getting there.

One final set of issues animated this situation. By the early 1960s Japan had essentially fully recovered from World War II economically. Trade with the United States was a key to sustaining its rapid economic growth. But the economic success of Japan's export machine began to cause friction with its former overseer, and numerous trade and tariff issues began to affect U.S.-Japanese relations. There was also the question of Okinawa, which remained under U.S. occupation and which Japan wanted to get back as soon as possible (it did so in 1972). Improving trade relations with the United States to stay on the path to greater prosperity and reclaiming Okinawa were the two overriding Japanese foreign policy goals at the time.

In 1964–65 the Vietnam War and the Japan-Korea normalization treaty converged. The American escalation and need for troops from Korea, Korea's eagerness to reverse the trend of American aid and open the gates to Japanese funds and technology, and Japan's desire to smooth trade relations with the United States and resolve the Okinawa situation dynamically interacted, creating a situation of great complexity. The best outcomes for Park were a close and beneficial relationship with the United States through support in Vietnam, to ensure South Korea's security, and a treaty with Japan to kick-start economic development.

The opportunity came when Park was asked for a contribution of military aid as part of President Johnson's More Flags campaign in April 1964. Korean support in Vietnam could serve three main purposes, according to historian Jiyul Kim: "to further cement U.S.-ROK relations through alliance and aid; to serve as insurance for that relationship should the normalization talks with Japan break down; and, to increase Korea's and Parks' regional and international importance and influence."[47] Park's offer was a modest one—a mobile army surgical hospital (of 130 personnel) and a ten-person Taekwondo instructor team—but these personnel represented almost a third of the total response (500 from a dozen countries) to the More Flags campaign. Only Australia, with its 167 advisors, exceeded the Koreans in number.[48] By adopting an option for increasing military pressure if North Vietnam remained intransigent in negotiations, a new plan approved by Johnson in December 1964 paved the way for the escalations of 1965.[49] The plan also meant a renewed American effort to solicit additional international assistance. Park, to American elation, agreed to provide a 2,000-person engineer unit for civic projects.[50] This was a substantial addition to the 23,000 Americans in Vietnam at the end of 1964. The renewed U.S. pleas to get "More Flags" from other countries did not do well. South Korea was the only nation to answer the call.[51]

At the end of April 1965, Johnson approved the next dramatic escalation, additional ground forces consisting of nine U.S. battalions (a division), three ROK battalions (a regiment), and an Australian battalion, with the possibility of a further twelve U.S. battalions (division plus regiment) and six ROK battalions (two more regiments to make a ROK division).[52] A Korean contingent thus became an integral and vital part of the overall plan. The deployment of the ROK and Australian forces was not yet confirmed, but 50,000 more Americans were put in the pipeline to join the 23,000 already in Vietnam, to bring the total to almost 75,000. By early June, the military situation had seriously deteriorated, and the Americans anticipated a large-scale Vietcong offensive that threatened to overrun South Vietnam. General William Westmoreland, commander of Military Assistance Command Vietnam (MACV), the top U.S. command in Vietnam, made an urgent request for a further 100,000 soldiers, consisting of thirty-four U.S. battalions (almost four divisions), nine ROK battalions (one division), and one Australian. Westmoreland's plan to use this force to stabilize the situation and then go on the offensive was approved.[53] It was this request that led to intense deliberations and a decision in July 1965 to approve Westmoreland's request for 100,000 troops, then another 100,000 in early 1966, and the possibility of several hundred thousand more beyond, thus decisively committing and escalating the American intervention in Vietnam and opting for a military solution. The number of soldiers in MACV ballooned from 23,000 Americans, 140 Koreans, and 200 Australians in early 1965 to 180,000 Americans, 21,000 Koreans, and 1,500 Australians by the year's end. By the end of 1966 the command would include 385,000 Americans, 45,000 Koreans, and 5,000 Australians, as well as a small force from New Zealand.[54]

In May 1965 Park made a state visit to Washington, his first as presi-

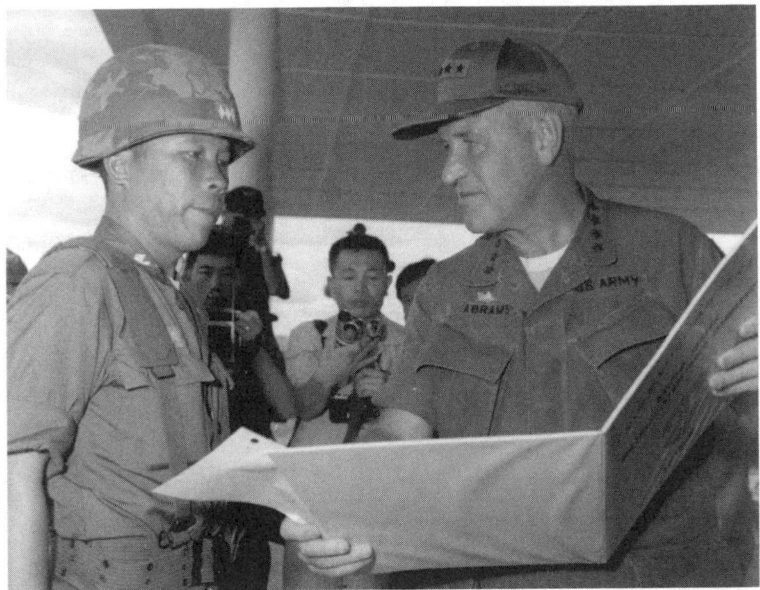

General Creighton Abrams, a U.S. commander in Vietnam, presents the U.S. Presidential Unit Citation to the commander of the Cavalry Regiment of the ROK Capital "Tiger" Division, for actions performed by its Ninth Company, Qui Nhon, Vietnam, September 9, 1968. (U.S. NATIONAL ARCHIVES AND RECORDS ADMINISTRATION)

dent. Dean Rusk recalled later, "There was a personal rapport between President Johnson and President Park."[55] Park provided strong assurances that Korea would be able to send a military division to Vietnam even though no official request had been made, much less approved by the ROK National Assembly. Furthermore, negotiations over the normalization treaty with Japan had progressed sufficiently enough so that a final agreement was imminent. Park could now envision the realization of his grand plan for South Korea.

Nevertheless, doubts about sending South Korean troops to South Vietnam still lingered over the potential cost in lives and the reduced sense of security until the deployed troops could be replaced (and they eventually were, many times over). In a dramatic legislative special session in mid-August 1965, members of the minority party, who opposed both the treaty and the troop bill, resigned and walked out in protest after the majority party, Park's party, forced the treaty legislation to a plenary vote. It passed almost unanimously in their absence. The following day the troop bill also passed unanimously. Interestingly, the troop

Soldiers of the South Korean White Horse Division (Ninth Infantry Division) with Vietnamese prisoners near a village in the Hon Be mountains near Tuy Hoa, November 30, 1966. (AP PHOTOS)

bill was debated before the vote, and pointed questions were raised about the nature of the war and whether it could be won, the same questions that George Ball had raised in opposing escalation. It was an indication that what ultimately mattered was not stopping communism in Vietnam per se, but the leverage that the deployment could provide in obtaining concessions from the United States.[56]

The Korean division-size contingent consisting of two army regiments and a marine brigade deployed just two months later. In 1966, in line with another large expansion of American forces, the More Flags campaign was laid out again. The Koreans responded with another division of 24,000 men. The terms for deploying the second division, emphasizing economic incentives rather than military aid, were qualitatively different from the terms of the first deployment. According to U.S. Ambassador William Porter's testimony to the Senate in 1970, the total direct benefit of the war to South Korea between 1965 and 1970 was approximately $930 million, a significant portion of foreign exchange earnings and of the GNP.[57] By the end of the war, over 5,000 South Koreans had died and 11,000 had been wounded in Vietnam.[58]

When Park came to power in 1961, South Korea was one of the poorest nations in the world in terms of per capita GNP, and it was completely dependent on the United States. By the end of 1966 South Korea was well on its way to becoming a self-sufficient regional economic and political power. James C. Thomson, a key Asia policy advisor on the National Security Council, wrote in June 1966 that "political instability, economic doldrums, and isolation from its neighbors have given way to robust and relatively stable democracy, economic take off, and full participation both in [the] Viet-Nam war and Asian regional arrangements."[59] Two months later in Seoul, Ambassador Porter observed that Korea had "traditionally been a country which looked backward rather than forward, looked inward rather than outward, evaded or deflected relationships with other countries rather than initiated or influenced them . . . [but now] to a new self-confidence has been added a new outlook and a new attitude toward the outside world in which Korea now conceives of herself as playing an important part."[60]

For the first time since the opening of Korea in the late nineteenth century, the nation had garnered the world's respect. The year 1966 was a watershed for South Korea and a personal triumph for Park, owing to the country's role in the Vietnam War and the normalization treaty with Japan. Economically the GNP growth rate increased from 2.2 percent in 1962 to 12.7 percent in 1966, starting a trend for one of the longest sustained periods of high growth of any nation in history.[61] By the end of 1966, the South Korea–Japan trade was the largest in volume in Asia. Complementing the market was U.S. economic aid, which increased from $120 million in 1962 to $144 million in 1966. With regard to security, the ROK armed forces' rapid program of modernization, including new weaponry for ground, air, and naval forces, significantly boosted the nation's capacity to defend against any renewed North Korean hostility. U.S. military aid increased from $200 million in 1961 to $247 million in 1966 and reached $347 million in 1968. Washington also gave a firm promise not to draw down U.S. forces without consultation.[62] Of great symbolic importance was the signing of the Status of Forces Agreement (SOFA) in July 1966, which defined Korean jurisdiction over U.S. troops. Until the agreement was signed, American forces essentially operated under extraterritorial rules. Koreans, therefore, had no legal right to prosecute any crimes committed by American soldiers against a Korean. The State

Department observed that "the question of even-handed treatment was particularly important in early 1965 when we were asking the Koreans to participate to a greater extent in the struggle in Viet-Nam . . . our actions relating to the SOFA were designed to assist the ROK evolve from a client state into a self-reliant and self-confident ally."[63] Perhaps the greatest value to ROK security was the combat experience gained by its armed forces in Vietnam.

The political and diplomatic achievements of 1966 were perhaps even more impressive. In June 1966, Seoul hosted the inaugural meeting of the Asia Pacific Council (ASPAC), with delegations from all noncommunist Asian nations. It was the culmination of Park's dream for it had been his initiative, a venue for South Korea to take a leading role in a new regional organization dedicated to fighting communism and focused on China. ASPAC did not last long—it disbanded in 1975 after the fall of Saigon and the establishment of U.S.-China ties—but it was able to provide one of the strongest statements of Asian-Pacific (Australia and New Zealand were members) support for the U.S. policy in Vietnam. James C. Thomson gleefully reported, "A plethora of regional and sub-regional cooperative initiatives has evolved: *ASPAC, ADB* (Asia Development Bank, to be organized in November) . . . , which hold great promise for future Asian resolution of the region's own problems. Most important, our own view that our presence in Viet-Nam was buying time for the rest of Asia *is now shared by the Asians themselves.*" President Johnson credited Park on the idea for the conference in his memoirs.[64]

At the end of October 1966, after a swing through Southeast Asia, his second for the year, Park participated in the Manila Conference hosted by Johnson "for a review of the war . . . and for a broader purpose—to consider the future of Asia" with countries that had forces in Vietnam. Johnson continued his Asian trip with a state visit to Korea the following week, the first by a serving U.S. president. He reassured the Koreans that the United States was making all possible efforts to harden Korean defenses by modernizing its armed forces and that "the United States has no plan to reduce the present level of United States forces in Korea."[65] It was a triumphal moment for Park. In November the Asia Development Bank was established in Tokyo, with South Korea as one of the charter members.[66] By the end of 1966, though still poor and underdeveloped, South Korea and Park bathed in the glow of these international achievements. Security, prosperity, and influence were now within reach and the possibilities for the future seemed limitless. Vietnam had given South Korea an opportunity to refight the battle against communism, and in the process had laid the foundation for South Korea's spectacular economic growth.

It was under these circumstances that Kim Il Sung, wary that the South would soon catch up to the North, declared renewed provocations to foment a communist revolution in the South. Embarking on a Korean-style "Vietnam strategy" of infiltrating spies and armed guerillas into the South, with the aim of establishing revolutionary bases and inciting instability there, Kim also began to invest a large amount of his nation's resources on a military buildup. It was the beginning of a new phase of the Korean War marked by intense competition and conflict between the Kim Il Sung and Park Chung Hee regimes for the mantle of Korean legitimacy.

PART III

LOCAL WAR

By 1968, the strategic environment that led to America's involvement in Korea and Vietnam had drastically changed. The "surprise" Tet Offensive in January 1968 shocked the American public and turned them against the war. A dispirited President Johnson decided to forgo running for a second term, halt the bombing of North Vietnam, and begin peace talks. At the same time, the threat of monolithic communist power was receding following the Sino-Soviet split, Sino-American rapprochement, and the withdrawal of U.S. forces from Vietnam by early 1973. It was in this new political and strategic environment that the Korean War entered a new phase. This period, from the late 1960s to the late 1980s, saw an intensified "local" struggle between the two Koreas that had little or no impact on the world at large. Faced with a precipitous decline in its economic fortunes, and realizing that South Korea was overtaking North Korea economically, Kim Il Sung launched a series of provocative actions in 1968 and 1969 against South Korea and the United States in a last-ditch effort to foment a South Korean revolution and achieve reunification under his control. The most daring acts were a commando raid to assassinate President Park (which failed) and the capture of the USS Pueblo, within three dramatic days in late January 1968. In October 1968, more than a hundred North Korean commandos landed on the east coast to organize the local peasants and fishermen to spark a communist revolution. In April 1969, the North Koreans shot down an unarmed U.S. reconnaissance plane, killing several-dozen Americans. Between 1967 and 1969, the DMZ was declared a combat zone because of increased North Korean military actions.

The localized confrontations amounted to a competition—economic, military, and psychological—between the two systems and their competing visions of modern Korea. By the late 1960s, peaceful reunification of Korea on P'yŏngyang's terms seemed unlikely. In addition, continued U.S. military presence in South Korea, the strengthening of the South Korean military, and Japan's rapid growth were serious threats to Kim's increasingly shaky regime. With the U.S. and significant South Korean forces committed in Vietnam, Kim saw a chance to try again for reunification by force. Neither the Soviet Union nor China had any interest in Kim's plans. Only once did the situation briefly become of global concern again. This was the ax murder incident in 1976, when North Korean soldiers killed two U.S. officers at the Joint Security Area in the DMZ. The U.S. military response was an overwhelming preparation for large-scale military confrontation.

Kim's provocations had severe repercussions for U.S.-ROK relations. Washington's lukewarm response to the North's attempt on Park's life contrasted with its hyperreaction to the capture of the USS Pueblo. Both responses were based on Washington's desires not to risk renewed fighting in Korea when it was bogged down in Vietnam, and to get the Pueblo crew released. The Nixon doctrine, announced in July 1969, also shocked Park. It essentially stated that nations must rely primarily on their own capacity to secure their defense rather than rely on U.S. power. Park began to think that South Korea must be prepared to defend itself without American support. These feelings were reinforced by Nixon's détente policy with China and the Soviet Union, dramatically demonstrated with a visit to China in February 1972 and to Moscow in May 1972. Soon thereafter, Nixon forced South Vietnam to accept the Paris Peace agreement signed in January 1973, which marked the end of American involvement in Vietnam. For Park, these events signaled America's betrayal of its three principal anticommunist partners in Asia: Taiwan, South Vietnam, and South Korea. In the 1970s Park embarked on a major effort to build up heavy industries tied to an indigenous arms industry. North and South Korea also intensified their diplomatic competition around the world by trying to upstage the other in claiming to be the more legitimate Korean regime.

It was during this "local" phase of the war that America's first post–Vietnam War president was elected to office. Soon after announcing his candidacy in 1975, Jimmy Carter called for a phased and eventually complete withdrawal of U.S. forces from South Korea. Carter's rationale was based not only on a perception of low North Korean threat and the adequacy of South Korean military capacity, but also on his disgust over the Park regime's human rights abuses. Ultimately, President Carter was unable to fulfill his campaign promise. The North Korean threat turned out to be much greater than had previously been known. In addition, the American presence in South Korea had become an indispensable source of regional stability during a period of intensified conflicts among communist nations over national interests and historical issues in Asia. Carter's plan was privately opposed by the Soviet Union and China. Beijing, paranoid about the Soviet threat, was particularly nervous because it saw the removal of American forces as tempting the Soviets to reassert their long-standing interest over the Korean peninsula. The Russians wanted continued American presence to maintain the precarious balance of influence over North Korea and to restrain Kim Il Sung from restarting the war. Ironically, the unfinished Korean War had become necessary to maintaining the peace on the Korean peninsula.

CHAPTER SIXTEEN

Legitimacy Wars

One of the more remarkable feats of Kim Il Sung was that he was able to survive the Korean War at all. The North Korean people rightly wondered what the war had accomplished other than the complete destruction of their country. "So many men of military age perished in the war," wrote the historian Balázs Szalontai, "that women far outnumbered men in North Korea until the 1970s." While soldiers sought refuge from the incessant bombing campaigns in the damp and overcrowded tunnels, they also faced another enemy that proved just as deadly: tuberculosis. It is estimated that as many as a quarter of a million demobilized NKPA soldiers had serious infections. Considering that the total troop strength at the start of the war was roughly 135,000, this is an appalling number. "In the last six months of the war," wrote one North Korean physician, "more people died of tuberculosis than on the front."[1]

The number of civilian deaths from tuberculosis is not known, but without proper equipment—one North Korean hospital treating fifteen hundred tuberculosis patients did not have a single X-ray machine—or adequate medical staff, civilians must have succumbed to the disease by the tens of thousands. One study calculated that the total population of the DPRK in 1949 stood at 9.622 million, but owing to either death or emigration, it decreased by 1.131 million during the war.[2] Hundreds of thousands of acres of farmland had also been decimated, along with nearly three-fourths of residences. Seventy percent of North Korea's trains and 85 percent of its ships had been destroyed during the war, making the country's transportation system almost inoperable.[3]

Despite such destruction, the country had survived, but the North Korean people were aware that it was no thanks to the NKPA or Kim Il Sung. Chinese troops had carried the main burden of the war, while the NKPA had been reduced to a mere supporting role. Chinese influence in North Korean affairs had predictably increased, giving rise to tensions and resentment among North Korean leaders. Ironically, it was the Chinese role in the war that provided new opportunities for Kim to maintain his grip on power. The Soviet Union's domination of North Korean society since 1945 had been severely curtailed by the war and by the Chinese presence on the peninsula. Kim used this situation to his own advantage. Many Soviet Koreans had served as general officers in key positions both during and after the war, and there was a predictable backlash against them, a logical outcome of defeat since Soviet Koreans had never been entirely accepted into North Korean society.

The first sign of Kim's new strategy to strengthen his leadership position was his decision to attack Hŏ Ka-i (Alexei Ivanovich Hegai), the highest ranking Soviet Korean in the North Korean government and a founding member of the North Korean Workers' Party (NKWP). Hŏ was removed from his post as first secretary when China entered the war, and demoted to deputy prime minster, a significant drop in status and power. Taking advantage of the temporary leadership vacuum in the Soviet Union after Stalin's death in March 1953, Kim decided to get rid of Hŏ. On July 2, 1953, Hŏ was found dead, allegedly by his own hand, but the suicide had the appearance of a setup.[4] Shortly after the armistice, Kim also began to target the Yanan faction, Koreans who had served with the Chinese communists during their civil war. Although he was selective in purging leaders of this group, given that Chinese forces continued to remain in North Korea until the late 1950s, Kim nevertheless was bold enough to take on Gen. Mu Chŏng (Kim Mu-chŏng), the best-known member of the Yanan faction, for his alleged role in the unsuccessful defense of P'yŏngyang in October 1950. Mu, however, was able to avoid the fate of a mysterious suicide; he was simply expelled from the party and later sought asylum in China, where he remained for the rest of his life.[5]

Although the removal of Hŏ Ka-i and Mu Chŏng weakened Chinese and Russian influence, Kim waited until 1956 to embark on a wholesale purge of either group, as he was not yet prepared to alienate them and risk cutting off aid or even direct intervention. The South Korean communists who had moved north, however, had no such foreign protector and were thus the first to be completely purged. A week after the armistice was signed, the first show trials began in P'yŏngyang. On August 3,

In the front row, from left to right, Ch'oe Yŏng-gun, Pak Hŏn-yŏng, and Kim Il Sung, P'yŏngyang, 1952. This photo was probably taken by a foreign visitor, which explains the odd composition with Kim barely in the frame. It may also be indicative of the low esteem Kim was held at the time. Also noteworthy is the prominent display of both Stalin and Mao in the background. Fearful of plans to oust him from power, Kim instigated a full-scale attack against the Domestic faction in 1953. This group had originally hailed from the south, and its members had been prominent leaders in the South Korean Workers Party (SKWP) before they were purged or moved north after the ROK's founding in 1948. Foreign Minister Pak Hŏn-yŏng, the most prominent member of the domestic faction, was arrested in 1953. Accused of being an American spy, he was tried and executed in 1955. (COURTESY OF THE HUNGARIAN NATIONAL MUSEUM)

twelve leading members of the SKWP were tried on counts of espionage, sabotage, and conspiracy. Four days later they were found guilty, and in one fell swoop, Kim Il Sung had managed to eliminate the entire southern faction from the North Korean leadership.[6] The North Korean leader spared the leader of the group, his close associate Pak Hŏn-yŏng, however. He was placed in solitary confinement and "tried" two years later. On December 15, 1955, Pak was sentenced to death and executed.

August Purge

In 1955, Kim Il Sung introduced the guiding philosophy of his regime, which remains to this day the foundational political tenet of North Korea. Addressing the Presidium of the Supreme People's Assembly, the highest organ of power according to the North Korean Constitution, on December 28, Kim delivered his first speech about *chuch'e* (literally translated as "master of one's body" or "self-determination").[7] He spoke of the need to study Korean history and culture. Why were Koreans looking at foreign landscapes and studying foreign literature when Korea had its own rich beauty and literary traditions? he asked. He attacked the *Nodong sinmun* newspaper, the NKWP organ, for blindly copying headlines from *Pravda*, and condemned its former editor, Ki Sŏk-bok, a Soviet Korean, for harboring "a subservient attitude toward the Soviet Union." Kim also accused Soviet Koreans of being "dogmatic and fundamentalist in their emulation of the Soviet Union" by their strict adherence to the Moscow line. "To make revolution in Korea we must know Korean history and geography as well as the customs of the Korean people," he declared. "Only then is it possible to educate our people in a way that suits them and to inspire in them an ardent love for their native place and their native motherland."[8] The speech was significant in other ways as well. References to the "glorious Soviet Army that liberated Korea" and "the Soviet Union, savior of all oppressed nations," that had been part of the standard history of North Korea were gone. The "little Stalin" who was "expected to act under the wise protective shadow of the 'big Stalin' in Moscow" was replaced by a man of "unusual naïve spontaneity," loving, innocent, and sincere, in short, a man who embodies truly Korean virtues.[9]

By early 1956, an all-out campaign to weaken Soviet political influence had begun in earnest. Contacts by Soviet Koreans with the Soviet embassy were discouraged. Special permission to meet with "foreigners," a code word for the Russians, had to be obtained. The number of Korean-language Radio Moscow programs was cut in half. The role and presence of the Korean Society for International Cultural Exchange, the primary conduit for spreading Soviet culture, were greatly diminished. "Local branches were closed down, the collection of personal membership fees halted and control of its profitable publishing section was transferred to the Ministry of Culture." Later that spring, the NKWP Central Committee ordered the end of all performances of Russian plays in Korean theaters. The Institute of Foreign Languages, the primary source of Russian-language education, was closed. Russian was no longer taught to college students. Also notable was that the "Month of Soviet-Korean Friendship" was not celebrated in 1956. It had been one of the largest events in North Korea since 1949 and had not even been canceled during the war.[10] Finally, Kim declared that "his partisan activities to have been the vanguard of the Korean communist revolution," sidelining the vital roles that the Soviet Union and the Soviet Koreans had played in the creation of the NKWP.[11] Soviet embassy official S. N. Filatov observed that many Soviet Koreans were growing increasingly worried about the situation in North Korea. According to Filatov, "praise of comrade Kim Il Sung is especially widespread in both oral and print propaganda in Korea and if anyone comments on this matter, they are subject to punishment." Soviet contribution to the liberation of Korea, and its vital role in the founding of the NKWP, were being seriously distorted.[12]

The first overt challenge to Kim's anti-Soviet moves came during the Third Congress of the Workers' Party of Korea, held in P'yŏngyang in late April 1956. Emboldened by Khrushchev's speech in February 1956 denouncing Stalin, critics of the regime began to mobilize themselves against Kim Il Sung's dominance of the NKWP.[13] Pak Ŭi-wan (Ivan Park), a Soviet Korean and the vice premier and minister of light industry, was a leading member of this group."[14] Ch'oe Ch'ang-ik, a prominent leader of the Yanan faction, also began making moves against Kim. He complained that the group's great contributions to the revolutionary

Ch'oe Ch'ang-ik addresses the Third Congress of the Workers' Party of Korea in April 1956. Ch'oe was an early challenger of Kim's personality cult, and he pressed for economic reforms. He was later executed in 1960. (COURTESY OF THE HUNGARIAN NATIONAL MUSEUM)

struggle against Japan and the war effort against the Americans were not being properly recognized by the North Korean leadership.

The biggest source of concern, however, was not simply the marginalization of Soviet Koreans or the Yanan faction, but the distinct "lack of criticism or self-criticism within the North Korean leadership." Opponents of the regime had become wary of Kim's growing personality cult and the uncritical acceptance of his economic directives. "There is no collective leadership in the Korean Worker's Party," Yi Sang-jo, the North Korean ambassador to the Soviet Union, complained. "Everything is decided by Kim Il Sung alone, and the people fawn over him."[15]

The challenge came during the August 1956 NKWP plenum, where Yun Kong-hŭm, another leading member of the Yanan faction, directly criticized Kim. "Yun said that the CC [Central Committee] of the KWP does not put the ideas of Marxism-Leninism into practice with integrity and dedication," Pak Ŭi-wan later recalled. But Kim's supporters vigorously counterattacked. Calling Yun "a dog," they defended Kim and asserted that "the democratic perversion inside the party" was the "legacy of Hŏ Ka-i and did not pertain to the practical work of Kim Il Sung." Yun was immediately condemned as a "counterrevolutionary," and Kim demanded that he be "removed from the ranks of the CC, expelled from the party and put on trial."[16] Soon thereafter, Yun and his band of rebels fled to China. Their "coup" had failed. It was a defining moment for the Great Leader. He had successfully withstood an internal challenge from the party.

Backlash against Kim's foes, real and imagined, ensued. The opposition appealed directly to the Soviet Union and China for help. Ambassador Yi wrote to Khrushchev on September 5 requesting that he send "a senior official of the CC CPSU [Communist Party of the Soviet Union] to Korea to convene a CC Plenum of the [North Korean] Workers Party . . . [where the] intra-party situation is to be studied . . . and comprehensive and specific steps worked out directed at removing the shortcomings in our party."[17]

Concerned by the developments in North Korea, Khrushchev and Mao decided to act. On September 23, a joint delegation led by Soviet statesman Anastas Mikoyan and the Korean War Chinese commander Peng Dehuai arrived in P'yŏngyang. Peng's contempt for Kim Il Sung was well known. The two had clashed many times during the war, and

Peng, according to a 1966 Soviet report, was "not ashamed to express his low opinion of the military capabilities of Kim Il Sung."[18] Mao was also disdainful of the North Korean leader. According to one Soviet official who accompanied Mikoyan to P'yŏngyang, Mao told Mikoyan that Kim started an "idiotic war and himself had been mediocre."[19] The entire episode was an excruciatingly humiliating experience for Kim Il Sung. He was forced to convene a new party plenum in September, where he had to criticize himself and revoke his decisions from the August plenum and reinstate purged opposition leaders.[20] He was also warned against further purges. When the delegation left a few days later, it appeared that a thoroughly chastised Kim had been forced to mend his ways and embark on a new course.

But Kim was unexpectedly saved by events in Eastern Europe. Stalin's death in 1953 and then Khrushchev's dramatic denunciation of the man and his policies in early 1956 set in motion Eastern European reform movements to gain independence from Soviet domination and liberalization of its political-economic system. Events moved rapidly. Violent public demonstrations in Poland that summer reached a climax in mid-October with the selection of a previously purged moderate communist leader, despite Khrushchev's personal opposition and threat of intervention. Developments in Poland inspired Hungarian students, whose spontaneous demonstrations in support of the new Polish leader sparked a nationwide uprising. Khrushchev faced a mounting crisis in two of the most important members of the Soviet bloc. The new Polish leader was able to assure Khrushchev that greater autonomy and reform did not mean giving up communism or leaving the Soviet orbit, and obtained a modus vivendi. Khrushchev's concession in Poland was also encouraged by his increasing concern over the much larger and more dangerous situation developing in Hungary. By the end of October, reform forces had led an armed insurrection, which violently overthrew the government and announced its intention to withdraw from the Warsaw Pact. A few days later Soviet troops already stationed in Hungary intervened and crushed the uprising, at a cost of twenty thousand Hungarian lives. Several hundred thousand Hungarian refugees fled to the West. Mao, who had bristled at Khrushchev's denunciation of Stalin, had advised a violent suppression of the Hungarian revolt. The limits of Khrushchev's liberalization had been crossed, and the Soviet Union tightened its grip over central Europe.[21]

Fortunately for Kim, the Soviet intervention in Hungary created a backlash in North Korea against the exonerated rebels in the September plenum. The Soviet reaction in Europe raised the possibility of a similar reaction by the Kremlin against North Korea. Would the North Korean rebels who had demanded Kim's removal and called for political liberalization be crushed too? The timing of the Hungarian crisis was fortuitous in other ways as well. China was undergoing its own domestic political turmoil with the launching of its Anti-Rightist campaign. It would be difficult for Mao to support those who railed against the personality cult in North Korea that Mao had embraced for himself in China. Moreover, following the events in Hungary, the Chinese leader began to have second thoughts about the wisdom of backing North Korean dissidents against Kim. Khrushchev's de-Stalinization initiatives had seriously called into question the competence and wisdom of Soviet leadership. Mao was also wary of seeing Kim Il Sung replaced by those who might develop strong ties with the Soviet "revisionists." Hence, by November 1956, Mao had decided to firmly reject these initiatives. There would be no Hungarian Revolution in China nor would China support a similar revolution in North Korea.[22]

Khrushchev was caught by surprise by the events in Hungary and Poland. They were cautionary tales on the dangers of liberalizing too rapidly. He also decided to reject the North Korean dissidents' plea for help. In supporting the status quo, Khrushchev could at least take satisfaction that Kim had eliminated the Yanan faction, an act that presumably increased the Soviet Union's position. Moreover, he could not be sure that in the event of Kim's removal, the new North Korean leader would favor the Soviets over the Chinese. The Soviet leader had little appetite to risk another confrontation with Mao over Korea. For all these reasons, Khrushchev decided not to interfere in North Korea's domestic affairs. "The small spark of the Hungarian uprising was possibly sufficient to burn the buds of the North Korean democracy," observed the Soviet Korean Hŏ Chin, who later fled to the Soviet Union.[23] Henceforth, the purge of real and imagined supporters of the Korean opposition "gained official recognition and unconditional approval."[24]

The scale of the purge between 1958 and 1959 was large. Nearly one hundred thousand "hostile and reactionary elements" were rounded up, imprisoned, and executed. Andrei Lankov noted that this number represented roughly the number of "enemies" exposed between 1945 and 1958. Therefore, "within just nine months of 1958–1959, more people were persecuted on political grounds than during the *entire* first thirteen years of North Korean history."[25] Kim emerged from the August 1956 challenge unscathed and strengthened. Recalling these events in 1965, he saw the moment as a decisive one in North Korean history. It was the moment, he said, when the party had triumphed over "outside forces": "At that time the handful of anti-Party factionalists and die-hard dogmatists lurking within our Party challenged the Party, in conspiracy with one another on the basis of revisions and with the backing of outside forces."[26]

Military Line

By 1961, Kim Il Sung was firmly in control of North Korea. Such a turn of affairs would never have been tolerated under Stalin, but Khrushchev really had no alternatives. When the Hungarian ambassador to North Korea, Jozsef Kovacs, asked Vasily Moskovsky, the newly appointed Soviet ambassador, why the Soviet Union acquiesced to Kim's behavior, he was told that the Soviets were forced to accommodate Kim Il Sung's "idiosyncrasies" because of the Soviet Union's antagonistic relationship with China. "In the policy of the KWP and the DPRK one usually observes a vacillation between the Soviet Union and China," he told Kovacs. "If we do not strive to improve Soviet-Korean relations, these will obviously become weaker, and at the same time, the Chinese connection will get stronger, we will make that possible for them, we will even push them directly toward China."[27] The Sino-Soviet rivalry over North Korea, as elsewhere in the world, was seen as a zero-sum game.

In December 1962, Kim adopted a "military line" that called for "modernizing and strengthening North Korea's military capacity" to reunify the peninsula through an unconventional war unlike the conventional war he tried in 1950.[28] It was the culmination of Kim's thinking about developments in the South since Park Chung Hee's coup in May 1961. Unlike his predecessors, Rhee and Chang, Park was a military man. His ambitious vision for South Korea based on accelerated economic development and expanded military capability was linked to what was undoubtedly a much more competent strategic vision toward the North and the future of the peninsula. Kim thought it inevitable, given Park's background, his vision, and the South's much larger population, that time was running out to reunify the peninsula under his terms. Moreover, ominous signs of economic stagnation in North Korea were beginning to appear in the mid-1960s, owing to faulty economic policies and greatly increased spending on the military. This happened precisely as the South Korean economy began to take off under Park. By the late 1960s it became clear that it would simply be a matter of time before South Korea would catch up with the North, economically and militarily. The longer North Korea waited, the stronger South Korea would become. The North Korean regime, it was reported, was following with "growing anxiety the developments in South Korea where younger, more flexible state leadership has been able to bring the country [back] from the brink of total collapse after the fall of Syngman Rhee."[29] The North Korean Seven-Year Plan (1961–67), introduced with great fanfare in September 1961, was therefore designed to build up the North Korean economy and military to fulfill the goals of the "military line" policy in order to initiate a new war to communize the South. This war was compelled by the ongoing legitimacy wars between Kim in the North and Park in the South. Since each leader claimed to be creating their version of a prosperous and internationally respected nation, the question became which nation, the North or the South, was representative of the "true" Korea. Kim had to make sure to win this legitimacy war before South Korea became too strong to challenge him on that front. "Unification cannot be delayed by one hour," he declared in 1966. "Liberation of the South," he stated, was "a national duty."[30]

During the 1950s, it appeared that North Korea was winning this contest of legitimacy. With the help of the Soviet Union and other socialist states, it had achieved rapid economic strides, recovering from the war and reconstructing the nation. In fact, North Korea had attracted so much attention as a "model" socialist state that many wealthy Korean families living in Japan decided to return to the socialist fatherland and begin a new life there.[31] North Korea's GNP was also higher than the South's and would remain so until the mid-1960s. Nevertheless, there were already signs that this growth rate could not be sustained. Production rates began to slow down or, in some cases, were reversed.[32] Internal deficiencies in the North Korean system and overdependence on foreign aid accounted for much of the decline. The Soviet Union financed the lion's share of nonrepayable assistance, although China also contributed huge sums of aid both during and after the war.[33] This aid had played a decisive role in Kim's reconstruction plans, but it did little to help establish a strong foundation on which to build North Korea's economy, which was becoming overpoliticized. "The issue of political guidance was of single and exclusive importance in resolving any problem," complained one Hungarian official. "The rise of careerists and people of that ilk, and the thrusting of the few technical experts into the background and their designation as politically unreliable on fictitious charges, is a common occurrence."[34] As the pace of economic growth slowed, industrial output declined further. One analysis noted that "in 1966, industrial output had declined 3% over the preceding year, the first time in North Korea."[35]

By this time, it had become clear that Kim's *chuch'e* economy had reached its limits.[36] His dream of creating an autarkic economy turned out to be an unrealizable and self-contradictory enterprise because it led to more dependency, not less. As the historian Erik van Ree pointed out, a country that tries to produce almost everything it needs "spends a tremendous amount of energy in the task of supplying the domestic market." This, in turn, causes problems with productivity and inefficiency. Moreover, the limitation of a small domestic market like North Korea's also makes it very difficult to specialize. Without specialization, it becomes impossible to pursue a vigorous export policy and to take advantage of the international markets. The result is a lack of innovation and a scarcity of funds.[37] Consequently, North Korea had no alternative but to rely on the influx of large amounts of foreign aid as its only strategy for economic growth. But even large influxes of foreign funds could not offset the inevitable slowdown of North Korea's economy, which was caused by the strict adherence to the orthodox Stalinist concept of all-around development and national self-sufficiency.[38] Ironically, Kim's *chuch'e* economy required continuing inputs of foreign funds with no expectation of repayment, the exact opposite of the independent national economy achieved by South Korea.[39] Yet, despite all these problems, the North Korean leadership "thwarted any attempt to reformulate political and economic concepts even within the given socialist model."[40]

At the same time, Kim began to mobilize the entire population for work. In 1958, he launched the *ch'ŏllima* movement, which was based on the massive use of "voluntary labor." The historian Balázs Szalontai noted that "generally speaking, at the end of 1958, people had to do four to five hours of unpaid work every day, in addition to the eight-hour workday." In an ambitious speech Kim Il Sung gave at the Workers' Congress in September, the North Korean leader declared that the Five-Year Plan (1956–61) should be filled in just three and a half years. Agricultural cooperatives pledged to increase harvests, while factories also promised to double their 1958 outputs in just one year. Yet, for all the back-breaking labor, basic living standards hardly improved. Part of the reason for this was the low quality of the yields. In some cases, North Korean factories were mass-producing products that were defective, and yet they continued to produce them anyway to fulfill abstract quotas.[41] While the mobilization campaigns put tremendous strain on the already overworked population, they did not overcome the problems of productivity and inefficiency inherent in a collectivized system.

As the Park regime's political and economic fortunes rose rapidly by the end of 1966, owing to the Vietnam War and the normalization treaty with Japan, the number of incidents along the DMZ underwent a dramatic intensification in 1967, "reaching about 360 by September as opposed to a total of 42 in 1966."[42] Szalontai reported that by July of that year, Kim Il Sung was already preparing for the assassination of Park Chung Hee. Kim's new militant strategy also appeared to be behind his decision to promote military cadres within the NKWP in October 1966, which was then followed by a massive purge of many high-ranking officials as well as several prominent party members in 1967. It is likely that the purge of these leaders was linked to their disagreements with Kim's new militant strategy.[43]

As Kim was escalating his attacks against the South, the battle for legitimacy also took on an international dimension as Park began to directly challenge Kim in the forum of world opinion. Both leaders engaged in diplomatic wars to secure support for their regime in the form of special goodwill missions that crisscrossed the continents and oceans. "The Korean Question" of establishing a unified and democratic Korea through peaceful means had been an agenda item since 1947, but it took on far more significance by the mid-1960s because of the wave of decolonization and new member states in the UN after World War II.[44] From 51 member states at its founding in 1945, the UN had expanded to 122 by 1966.[45] South Korea saw the UN as the most important venue for settling the Korean question and for gaining its legitimacy by becoming a full member.[46] Thus, starting in 1966, South Korea made extraordinary efforts to garner the maximum number of votes for the UN resolution approving South Korean membership by dispatching goodwill missions worldwide, but in particular to young nations in Asia, Africa, the Middle East, and Latin America. North Korea countered with missions of its own starting in 1968, albeit on a smaller scale. Sometimes a keystone cops–like scene took place when a South Korean mission would arrive just as a North Korean mission was departing, or vice versa.[47]

Most importantly, the legitimacy battle waged between the Kim Il Sung and Park Chung Hee was linked to the political question of foreign presence, and especially military forces, in South Korea. Kim had always insisted that the withdrawal of all foreign troops from the Korean peninsula was a prerequisite to achieving peaceful reunification. He had much to gain from this position since the Soviet troops had departed from North Korea in 1948, and the Chinese had by 1958. Furthermore Kim claimed to have purged all those who had worked with the Japanese during the colonial period, while South Korea's Park had himself served in the Japanese army. Kim also claimed that while North Korea had achieved true national autonomy, South Korea was still a "puppet" controlled by and living under the yoke of "foreign occupation." By casting the struggle between North and South Korea in terms of a struggle for national sovereignty, Kim asserted the existence of a "revolutionary movement in South Korea" ready at any moment to topple the Park regime.[48]

Kim seems to have truly believed that the Park regime could be toppled from within. His plan first called for finishing the North Korean revolution by completing its military-industrial base. Simultaneously, the military part of the campaign would begin through the use of unconventional forces (special operations, agitators, and guerillas) to harass the Americans "on every front," including off the peninsula, to strain their commitment to the South by stretching their forces worldwide and thereby break the U.S.-ROK alliance.[49] Once the South Koreans were free of their "puppet master," they would be liberated either by

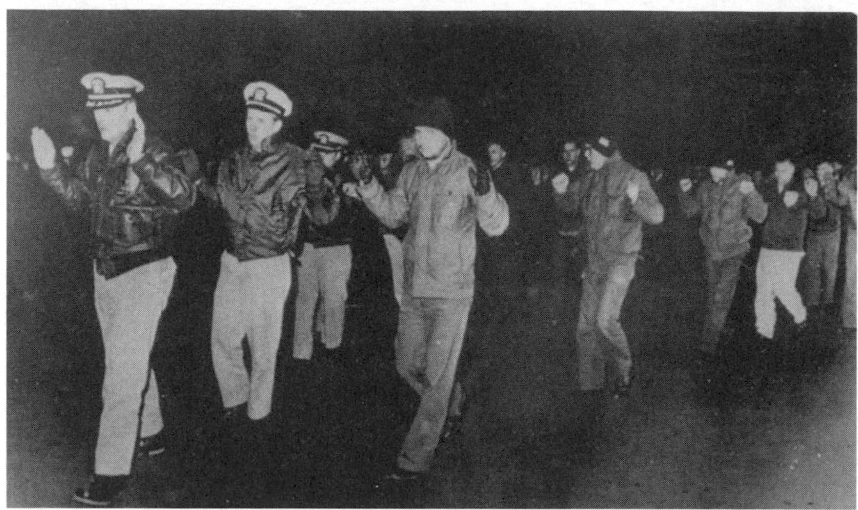

In this photo, released by the U.S. Navy, crew members of the USS *Pueblo* are seen in captivity. This photo has become an iconic image in North Korean propaganda and is repeatedly used in North Korean posters to show North Korea's "triumph" over a humiliated United States. (AP PHOTOS)

fomenting a revolution or through a conventional invasion.[50] Kim had formulated a fantastically ambitious plan. While completing military and economic goals, he also meant to reunify the peninsula.[51]

The consequences of the new policy were immediate and startling. The share of the military budget "rose from an average of 4.3 percent during 1956–1961 to an astonishing annual average of 31.2 percent in 1967–69."[52] The expansion of the defense sector caused shortages of manpower and raw materials in the nondefense sector of the economy. Production quotas lagged far behind the unrealistic targets of the Seven-Year Plan, and Kim was forced to ask for more Soviet aid. Eager to encourage North Korea's disengagement from China, the Soviets obliged. While Kim "took the Soviet Union for a cow he could usefully milk in order to keep his regime afloat," the Soviet Union was satisfied that it could "keep the North Koreans from the Chinese embrace."[53]

On January 21, 1968, North Korea tested the limits of Soviet friendship when it sent thirty-one commandos across the DMZ on a mission to assassinate Park at his official residence, the Blue House. Two days after the failed assassination attempt, North Korea raised the stakes even higher with the capture of the USS *Pueblo* and its crew off the North Korean coast but still in international waters. Its seizure provoked a condemnation by the Johnson administration and raised the possibility of renewed full-scale fighting on the Korean peninsula.[54]

The Blue House Raid and the Pueblo Incident

"The key question," wrote the *New York Times* on January 28, 1968, was "why did they do it?" Why did North Korea risk war with the United States and invite international condemnation to capture a ship that posed little threat?[55] "What made the *Pueblo* incident particularly disturbing was that it came after more than a year of stepped up North Korean military pressure against South Korea," the *New York Times* continued. There was as yet a lack of understanding or appreciation of Kim's new campaign. There were speculations that Kim was laying the groundwork for greater military action "so that seizure of the *Pueblo* . . . may be a way of testing the readiness of the United States, embroiled as it is in Vietnam, to resist a broadened North Korean offensive," or perhaps the attack was a way "to divert both the United States and South Korea from the Vietnam effort?" Had the Russians and the Chinese put them up to it? The Russians, after all, stood to gain a "great deal from capture and the study of the *Pueblo*'s electronic equipment." There was little doubt in Washington that the attack on the *Pueblo* was part of a coordinated action linked to the broader context of the cold war and Soviet ambitions. The most likely explanation was that it had been prompted by the Soviet Union "to increase pressure on Washington to move to the negotiating table in Vietnam." In his statement to the nation on January 26, President Johnson related the crisis to the "campaign of violence" against South Korean and American troops near the DMZ over the previous fifteen months. Johnson suggested that the attack on the *Pueblo* "may also be an attempt by the Communists to divert South Korean and United States military resources which together are resisting the aggression in Vietnam." Although he did not mention the Soviet Union directly, it was clear that he believed that a conscious effort had been made to open up a second front in Asia. "The attempts to divert American efforts in Vietnam would not succeed," he declared. "We have taken and are taking precautionary military measures [that] do not involve a reduction in any way of our forces in Vietnam."[56]

Contrary to his assessment of Soviet and North Korean intentions, however, the war in Vietnam was not foremost on Kim Il Sung's mind when the *Pueblo* was seized. Rather, it was the failed Blue House raid two days earlier that preoccupied him. Kim had sent commandos to South Korea in January 1968 with an order to assassinate Park Chung Hee. The attempt was a shortcut measure to "liberate" South Korea. Kim had hoped that the assassination would create the necessary political instability in the South to provide an opportunity for pro-North "revolutionary forces" there to usurp power, thus leading to reunification under his rule.[57] Ironically, the operation failed through the commandos' uncharacteristic humanitarian action. A day out from reaching their target, they had been hiding during daylight in the woods when four South Korean woodcutters discovered them. The standing procedure in such a case would have been to kill the witnesses, but after some intense discussion the commandos let the woodcutters go, with a firm warning not to report their discovery to the security forces.

The North Koreans would later come to regret their decision. Immediately after being released, the woodcutters went straight to the police. A massive manhunt was launched. The thirty-one commandos were

Seoul high school students carry a placard depicting the captured USS *Pueblo* that says, "Return the Pueblo now!" The rally was attended by more than a hundred thousand people, with demonstrators burning an effigy of Kim Il Sung. (AP PHOTOS)

nearly on the doorsteps of the Blue House when they were found. In the ensuing firefight and pursuit, all the commandos were killed except one, who was later captured. Sixty-eight ROK soldiers, policemen, and civilians and three American soldiers were killed in the hunt for the would-be assassins. Kim's gamble had backfired, as huge anti–North Korean demonstrations were mounted in Seoul and a wave of anticommunist hysteria swept through the country. On January 30, a hundred thousand students in Seoul braved a nipping cold day to stage a protest against the North Korean regime. The rally included the appearance of "women whose sons had been killed by the Communists and several South Korean veterans of the war in Vietnam who went to the platform and ceremonially nicked their forefingers to write anti-Communist slogans in blood." At the same time, a ten-foot straw effigy of Kim Il Sung was burned.[58] To make matters worse, the surviving North Korean commando, Kim Sin-jo, promptly confessed, provided details of the operation, and repented.[59] That same day, thousands of students, parents, and teachers from Poin Technical High School and Kangwŏn Middle School in Kangwŏn province held anticommunist rallies to "denounce the barbarous armed provocations of North Korea" and burned an effigy of Kim Il Sung.[60] The *Kangwŏn ilbo* summed up the defiant mood: "Although the Blue House raid and the *Pueblo* incident were indeed worrisome, we should not shake in fear for this is exactly what North Korea wants." Instead, the paper proclaimed confidence in the people's patriotic spirit: "As we saw with the Blue House raid, our people are thoroughly armed with anti-communism."[61] The Czech embassy in P'yŏngyang reported with a sense of awe how the South Korean government immediately capitalized on the spontaneous anti–North Korea demonstrations, even by leftist laborers, students, and intellectuals, to achieve its main objective: "to turn public attention from criticizing the government, army and police to a more acceptable matter—against the DPRK, which was a complete success."[62]

The failure of the Blue House raid had profound political implications for Kim. The vehement reaction against the raid demonstrated quite clearly that South Koreans had no desire to be "liberated" by the North. Moreover, the myth of a South Korean revolutionary force ready and willing to topple the Park regime and unify the peninsula under Kim's leadership was shattered. It was the second time that Kim had severely miscalculated South Korea's reaction to a North Korean probe.[63] Mortified by the public criticism, Kim responded by blaming the entire affair on South Korean partisans. Less than forty-eight hours later, the *Pueblo* was seized.

The seizure of the *Pueblo* was done without prior knowledge of the Soviet leadership, contrary to White House assumptions. On January 24, North Korean Deputy Foreign Minister Kim Chae-bong simply announced to a group of stunned "fraternal" ambassadors in P'yŏngyang that an American intelligence ship had been captured. Soviet Premier Alexei Kosygin was furious. He later complained that the Soviet Union "learned about [the details of] the *Pueblo* affair only from the press."[64] He was also uncertain about North Korean intentions, but assumed that the seizure was simply a pretext to divert attention from the failed operation in South Korea.[65]

Whether the *Pueblo* had actually trespassed into North Korean waters, as the North Koreans claimed, was viewed as largely irrelevant. American intelligence ships freely operated "near Soviet military bases and the Soviets freely monitored US communications off the American shores." In the April 1968 Soviet Communist Party plenum, General Secretary Leonid Brezhnev, who succeeded Khrushchev after the latter's ouster in 1964, stated that the *Pueblo*'s seizure was "unusually harsh" by international standards.[66] Rather, the bigger issue for the Soviet leader was whether North Korean "adventurism" would lead to war with the United States. Shortly after the *Pueblo*'s seizure, Brezhnev expressed concern that although "comrade Kim Il Sung assured [us] that the [North Korean] friends did not intend to solve the problem of uniting North and South Koreas by military means, and in this connection [did not intend] to unleash a war with the Americans . . . several indications appeared recently that, seemingly, suggested that the leaders of the DPRK have begun to take a more militant road." He was worried that "the North Koreans did not appear to show any inclination toward settling the incident." More alarming still, "DPRK propaganda took on a fairly militant character." The North Korean people are told that "war could begin any day." Brezhnev also noted that the country was on "full mobilization" and that "life, especially in the cities was changed in a military fashion." In addition, "an evacuation of the population, administrative institutions, industries, and factories of Pyongyang" had already begun.[67]

Provoking the United States into a war could have been a primary motive behind the seizure. On January 31, Kim wrote to Kosygin expressing his confidence that the Soviets would come to his aid in the event of a war. "Johnson's clique could at any time engage in a military adventure in Korea," he wrote. "The policy of the American imperialists is a rude challenge to the DPRK, and the Union of Soviet Socialist Republics, who are bound together by allied relations according to the treaty of friendship, co-operation and mutual help between the DPRK and the USSR; [it is] a serious threat to the security of all socialist countries and to peace in the entire world." He concluded that "in case of the creation of a state of war in Korea as a result of a military attack by the American imperialists, the Soviet government and the fraternal Soviet people will fight together with us against the aggressors," and they "should provide us without delay with military and other aid and support, to mobilize all means available."[68]

This brazen attempt to co-opt the Soviet Union into a war with the United States greatly alarmed Brezhnev, who decided that the time had finally come to put Kim Il Sung in his place. "To bind the Soviet Union somehow, using the existence of the treaty between the USSR and the DPRK [as a pretext] to involve us in supporting such plans of the Korean friend about which we knew nothing" was intolerable.[69] On February 26, Brezhnev told North Korean Deputy Premier and Defense Minister Kim Ch'ang-bong, who had come to Moscow instead of Kim Il Sung at Brezhnev's request, that the Soviets would not support a war. "We still base ourselves on the assumption that the Korean comrades maintain a course of peaceful unification of Korea, for we are not aware of [any] changes [to this course]," he told Kim Ch'ang-bong. Moreover, although "we indeed have a treaty, we would like to stress that it has a defensive character and is an instrument of defending the peace loving position of North Korea." He asked North Korea to settle the *Pueblo* incident and the return of the crew "by political means without much delay." Kim Il Sung was forced to acquiesce and soon sent assurances that he was pursuing a political solution, although he confessed it could be protracted. Kim had backed away from war.[70] Still, Kosygin was concerned that the Soviets were getting their information on the *Pueblo* talks only through the open press and were "not aware of the considerations and plans of the DPRK government with regard to further development of events." Kosygin ended with a promising incentive: "We do not have secrets from you, and we tell you everything frankly." If the North Koreans are cooperative, the Soviets would do their best "to relieve the economic difficulties" caused by a decreased flow of goods from China.[71] Brezhnev was less conciliatory, warning the North Koreans that "the DRPK could lose serious political gain obtained at the early stages of this incident."[72]

China's attitude toward the situation is less clear. At the time, China was embroiled in the Cultural Revolution. Since 1965, Sino–North Korean relations had been severely strained because of Kim's entirely pragmatic decision to side with the Soviets in the Sino-Soviet dispute. The fall of Khrushchev from power in October 1964 had temporarily thawed relations between China and the Soviet Union, but when Khrushchev's successor, Leonid Brezhnev, sent Premier Kosygin to China to smooth over differences, disputes concerning joint action and aid to North Vietnam renewed tensions. Beijing, only reluctantly and with constant delays, allowed railway transit of Soviet aid to North Vietnam through Chinese territory.[73] Kim repeated Soviet and North Vietnamese complaints that China was blocking Soviet shipments. It was only natural that North Korea sided with the wealthier Soviet "revisionists" as opposed to the poorer Chinese "dogmatists." On January 21, 1967, North Korea issued its first official statement criticizing Chinese policies. It branded Mao's dictatorship as more disastrous to international communism than Khrushchev's revisionism. The Chinese responded by branding the DPRK as another revisionist regime. That year, clashes between Chinese Red Guards and ethnic Koreans in China's Northeast became particularly grisly and ominous when Korean bodies were displayed "on a freight train traveling from the Chinese border town of Sinŭiju into the DRPK, along with graffiti such as 'Look, this will be also your fate, you tiny revisionists!' " Open retaliation against the Chinese provocations was too risky. Instead Kim strengthened his personality cult and his brand of communism in opposition to the Cultural Revolution. He told a Soviet visitor on May 31, 1968, that North Korea's relationship with China was "at a complete standstill."[74] Kim knew he could not count on Chinese support in a war against the Americans.

The problem Kim faced was how to defuse the *Pueblo* crisis without losing face with his own people. He knew that simply releasing the crew without an official apology from the United States would severely weaken his position and power by undermining his reputation as a fearsome revolutionary fighter who had the courage to stand up to foreign powers. It might even lead to his overthrow. Since the mid-1950s, North Korean domestic propaganda had dwelt increasingly on the virtues of national self-determination by touting North Korea's economic success made "without foreign assistance." Kim's talk of self-reliance, which he contrasted to the "lackey" regime in the South, meant that resolving the crisis without an official American apology—in effect, admitting he had backed down to U.S. pressure—would be quite impossible.

The Soviets understood the North Korean leader's dilemma. Over the following months, while Kosygin worked quietly to keep North Korean belligerence from turning into a military confrontation, he also pressured the Americans to yield to North Korean demands for an official apology, which he conveyed to Llewellyn Thompson, U.S. ambassador to Moscow and a longtime Russia hand. Thompson praised Kosygin for acting with "a distinct tone of restraint" in trying to negotiate an end to the crisis, citing his willingness to be a mediator between the two countries.[75] "There were enough conflicts in the world already and there was no need to have a new one," Kosygin told Thompson.[76] Thompson was convinced that the Soviets did not want war.

The result of the delicate triangular finessing and balancing of North Korean, Soviet, and American interests was a long and drawn-out negotiation. North Korea stood its ground not to back away from demanding official admission of "hostile acts and intrusion" into North Korean territory, a "proper apology" and guarantee "against future similar incidents" as a condition for the release of the crew. The Americans balked: "We know, and can prove, that at least some of the documents which they [the North Koreans] have given us are falsified," Dean Rusk told President Johnson. "I firmly believe that we should not admit incursions which we are reasonably certain did not occur."[77] Johnson agreed. He desperately wanted to secure the release of the crew, but without forsaking America's honor and credibility. The impasse was on.

Confessions

The ordeal for the *Pueblo*'s crew, a complement of eighty-three men, contained its share of drama, violence, surprise, and humor. Captain Lloyd

"Pete" Bucher, the commander of the ship, did not know what to expect when they were taken to P'yŏngyang. Some of the men had been injured, and one man, Duane Hodges, was killed in a brief firefight. Bucher, battered and beaten, wondered in his prison cell whether he and his men could withstand the harsh interrogations that would no doubt follow. The ship's intelligence value was staggering. It was full of the most sensitive electronics and classified documents. The men had tried to destroy them, but there was simply too much and too little time. The crew also included specialists who had intimate knowledge of intelligence capabilities and operations. Their personnel files, on the ship and captured, could tell exactly what their specializations were and where they had served.[78]

Bucher was soon taken to the interrogation room. He was relieved when he was not asked about the *Pueblo* ship's equipment, documents, or crew. Instead, the excitable Korean colonel, whom Bucher later nicknamed "Super-C" (for Super Colonel), handed him a confession to sign. "I took advantage of the opportunity to glance through it, catching among the rest of stilted English-Communist composition some specific reference to my admitted association with the CIA in provoking North Korea into a new war. And to promises of great rewards to myself and my family if I succeeded in this infamous mission." Bucher refused to sign and braced himself for a "painful pummeling."[79] Over the next few days, Bucher "puzzled a great deal about the nature of the questions the interrogators had concentrated on so far, wondering why they had asked so little oriented towards obtaining technical information, military intelligence. Instead they seemed completely hung up on a propaganda line for purely political purposes when dealing with me."[80] Other crew members were similarly mystified. Bucher's executive officer, Lieutenant Edward R. Murphy, wondered whether the North Koreans had really "comprehended the importance of their capture. Their questions indicated little interest in the equipment aboard." He observed that they had shown "only undisguised amazement that such a small ship had such a large crew."[81] They seemed to be concerned only with using the *Pueblo* and its crew for propaganda purposes rather than extracting intelligence. "We seemed to be entirely in the custody of propaganda, not intelligence specialists," observed Bucher. "It became obvious to me that the Korean communists had not the slightest intention of going after information of real intelligence value from us."[82]

Initially, Bucher thought the North Koreans were biding their time until Soviet interrogators arrived. They never did. Instead, the North Koreans just repeated their demand for signed confessions and letters of confession and apology to the Korean people, family members, newspaper and magazine editors, political leaders, and the White House. Eventually, Bucher decided to comply. The strain had become too much to bear when the stakes of compliance seemed so low. He was sure that no one in the United States would believe the crew's worthless "confessions." Bucher considered breaking the Code of Conduct, but he did not believe that endangering the life of his men was worth refusing to sign worthless pieces of propaganda. He was not betraying any secrets, after all. He encouraged his men to include in their confessions and letters verbal subterfuges, especially in personal letters to family members, to indicate that they had been written under duress. The subterfuges included mentioning nonexistent relatives, using outlandish or fictitious names, and referencing nonexistent possessions. For example, Bucher concluded his second letter to his wife, Rose, by telling her to send his greeting to his relative "Cythyssa Krocasheidt."[83] When Super-C requested names of influential leaders who "would work on your government for an apology," the men suggested writing to "labor leader Jimmy Hoffa and the Reverend Dr. Hugh Hefner."[84] Visual subterfuge was also used. A group picture inserted in a letter to one family member showed some of the men making the "Hawaiian hand gesture" by extending the middle finger. The prisoners had convinced their captors that the gesture was meant as a good luck sign. The trick worked until one day a family member, puzzled by the picture, released it to the local paper, which was then picked up by the national press. The North Koreans were furious to discover its true meaning.[85]

Meanwhile, the men continued to wonder what the North Koreans hoped to accomplish. Bucher and his men were forced to listen to lectures, lasting hours, about "America's imperialistic sins," the Korean War, the Vietnam War, the CIA, South Korean traitors, the miseries caused by the United States, and so on. It seemed like an attempt at brainwashing, the sort they had heard about from the Korean War, but it was not particularly intense. Sometimes they were asked questions that any ordinary map or encyclopedia could have easily answered. Questions pertaining to the *Pueblo* were even more baffling. The North Koreans wanted to know, for example, about all the supplies that Lieutenant Stephen Harris had ordered for the ship, including the exact amounts and quantities. Harris made them up, and his interrogator "wrote down faithfully every nonsensical figure he gave them."[86] But what they seemed most intensely curious about was American society and social mores, especially sex. James Layton recollected, "If they had questioned the Americans as closely on military matters as they did on American women, the entire U.S. Navy's communications system would have been in jeopardy."[87]

The North Koreans worked hard to keep the prisoners the focus of domestic attention, staging public appearances solely for popular consumption.[88] There was apparently no interest in appealing to the outside world, including Soviet and Chinese audiences. The prisoners appeared in film and television productions that would be seen only by North Koreans. They were taken on public excursions, a concert, a theater production, and even a circus performance, where they were more part of the show for the North Korean public than of the audience. They were featured in "press-conferences" and wrote regularly for the *Nodong sinmun,* the official NKWP newspaper. Bucher and his men did their best to undermine the propaganda. In one joint letter to the Korean people, entitled "Gratitude to the People of Korea for Our Humane Treatment," Bucher inserted this dig at their North Korean captors:

> We, who have rotated on the fickle finger of fate for so long . . . we of the *Pueblo* are sincerely grateful for the humane treatment we have received at the hands of the Democratic People's Republic of Korea and we not only desire to paean the Korean People's Army, but also to paean the Government and the people of the Democratic People's Republic of Korea.[89]

It was only in the last month of their captivity, when the North Koreans caught on to the true meaning of the "Hawaiian hand gesture," that they punished the prisoners mercilessly. By then, however, the game was getting old. After nearly one year in captivity, the prisoners were losing their effectiveness as a propaganda tool. "The North Koreans had exhausted their propaganda efforts," Lieutenant Murphy later explained. "We were no longer an asset to them."[90] The Americans were also becoming increasingly impatient. Something had to be done.

The solution to the crisis came from an unlikely source. James Leon-

Pueblo crew showing the "Hawaiian hand gesture" of good luck. (AP PHOTOS, KCNA)

ard, the country director for Korea in the State Department, had discussed the frustrating situation with his wife, Eleanor. Every American proposal had been rejected, and North Korea would not back down on their demand for the "Three A" solution ("admit, apologize, assure"). Eleanor suggested that "if you really make it clear beforehand that your signature is on a false document, well, then, you remove the deception."[91] Leonard thought it worth a consideration and took the proposal to Rusk, who in turn discussed it with President Johnson. They could not see how it could possibly work, but thought it was worth a try. The proposal was made on December 15, and two days later it was accepted.[92]

The Americans were stunned. In effect, the Americans had agreed to sign a Korean-drafted document of apology "for grave acts of espionage" after branding it an outright lie. Moreover, they had repudiated the document with the full and prior knowledge of the North Koreans, who "had agreed beforehand that the United States would proclaim their document false and would sign it to free the crew and *only* to free the crew."[93] Rusk called the resolution bizarre: "It is as though a kidnapper kidnaps your child and asks for fifty thousand dollars ransom. You give him a check for fifty thousand dollars and you tell him at the time that you've stopped payment on the check, and then he delivers your child to you."[94] General Charles Bonesteel, commander of U.S. forces in Korea, noted, "It is difficult to explain its rationality. I don't know whether they've gotten bored with the crew, or possibly thought they had diminishing value as propaganda there."[95] Walt Rostow, who served as Johnson's special assistant for national security affairs, thought the North Koreans were simply "nuts."[96]

But the "nutty" resolution made perfect sense within the context of North Korea's domestic politics. It satisfied Kim Il Sung's one and only condition: a signature on a piece of paper that proved to his isolated domestic audience that he was a great revolutionary fighter who was both feared and respected by the United States. The signed confession was also important in "proving" that, in contrast to the southern "lackey regime," North Korea was strong and brave enough to force the world's greatest military power to bow to its demands. Since the confession mattered only to his own people, who had no access to other sources of information, Kim did not care whether it was discredited by the rest of the world. In the ongoing legitimacy wars with South Korea, this was all that mattered.

On December 23, 1968, as snow fell on the barren hills surrounding P'anmunjom, the remains of Fireman Apprentice Duane Hodges were taken over the Bridge of No Return. Bucher followed, and then the rest of the crew. As the men were repatriated where the armistice had been signed fifteen years earlier, North Korean radio announced the nation's triumph. The American apology represented the "ignominious defeat of the United States imperialist aggressors and constitutes another great victory of the Korean people who have crushed the myth of the mightiness of United States imperialism to smithereens." It was also announced that the ship would not be returned, but "confiscated."[97] Today, the *Pueblo* currently resides on the banks of Taedong River in P'yŏngyang, where it has become a favorite tourist destination.

CHAPTER SEVENTEEN

Old Allies, New Friends

The end of the *Pueblo* crisis was one of the few positive moments in a year, 1968, marked by domestic and global upheavals. First and foremost among American domestic issues was the failing situation in Vietnam, where hundreds of young Americans were dying each week with no indication of progress in the war. American cities were wracked by racial riots. The assassinations of Martin Luther King and Robert Kennedy symbolized a loss of hope for a better future. The rest of the world was hardly doing better. Social and political unrest and anti–Vietnam War riots paralyzed major cities in Europe, Asia, and Latin America. The Czechoslovakian attempt to rise up for democracy and to escape the grip of the Soviet Union was violently crushed by Soviet forces in August 1968. Through it all, the *Pueblo* drama played in the background. "When news first came of the *Pueblo*'s seizure," went a *New York Times* editorial, "fear swept the nation that the incident would lead to a new war on the Asian continent. Fortunately, good sense in Washington prevented that tragedy."[1] The *Chicago Tribune* shared in the nation's relief that the crew had finally come home: "Despite the unprincipled manner in which the release was affected, we are sure everybody in the country will feel a warm glow that the men are finally free."[2] The agreement also received favorable international reactions. Most nations dismissed the apology as meaningless. The *Times of London* described the outcome "as a triumph of patience and diplomacy." The *Berliner Morgenpost* editorialized, "Only a malicious observer could maintain that the American confession had any truth."[3]

The South Korean reaction, however, was different. The failure to forcefully respond to North Korean provocations, and the bizarre conclusion of the *Pueblo* affair, led many South Koreans to begin to question America's commitment to their security. Their fears were first aroused by

Washington's lackluster response to the attempted assassination of President Park. "The incursion into the very heart of the city was what shocked South Koreans the most: it brought the North Korean menace very close." Coming just two days later, the seizure of the *Pueblo* had similarly galvanized the South Korean public, which staged daily demonstrations against the North Koreans."[4] Some of the protests were also directed toward the American government. General Charles Bonesteel reported on January 27 that there was "an expression of strong feeling at all levels of the republic, that US at our governmental level had taken no adequately drastic action following attempted attack on President and Blue House. However, seizure *Pueblo* we had reacted drastically." Park was personally offended and angry. "The depth of feeling over this is very deep," Deputy Secretary of Defense Cyrus Vance told President Johnson after Vance visited Seoul in early February to placate Park. "It was considered a personal affront and a loss of face," because "the raiders got within 300 yards of Blue House," adding "Park wanted to react violently against North Korea." These feelings were compounded by Washington's unprecedented decision to engage in closed negotiations with North Korea without a South Korean presence. On February 7, demonstrators near P'anmunjŏm were turned back by American soldiers who "fired shots in the air," and the next day, a thousand high school students, with posters demanding "Away with Bootlicking Conferences," staged demonstrations in front of the U.S. Information Service Centers at Taegu and Kwangju.[5]

The chairman of the National Assembly's Foreign Affairs Committee, Pak Chŏn-kyu, charged that his nation "was being cut off from discussion of vital interest to its welfare." William Porter, U.S. ambassador to South Korea, reported, "Much ill-feeling had been created by division of the country years ago and current [secret] US talks with NK touching on sovereignty of the country make it impossible to predict how ROK people will react . . . If there is another incident, however, ROK will have to act. They are preparing limited retaliation measures." President Park believed that Johnson did not comprehend or appreciate the magnitude of the threat that South Korea faced. "Indefinite efforts for peaceful solutions will only bring advantages to them rather than to us," he wrote to Johnson on February 5. "I can say through our own experiences that the Communists should be taught a lesson that any aggressive action cannot escape due punitive action."[6]

Tensions between Allies

Park's call for retaliatory action might have been given a more sympathetic ear in Washington a decade earlier. Growing difficulties in Vietnam, however, made it impossible for the Johnson administration to risk another confrontation in Asia. Washington's passive reaction to the Blue House raid had thus opened up a rift. When Johnson decided to reject Park's call for military action following the *Pueblo*'s seizure, American officials in Seoul began to wonder whether U.S.–South Korean relations had reached a crisis point. "I have been deeply disturbed over last several days at growing irrationality in certain areas ROKG [South Korean government] most especially in President Park himself," reported General Bonesteel on February 9. "Inputs in last day have confirmed that Park is almost irrationally obsessed with need to strike now at North Koreans, with sort of 'après moi le deluge' philosophy accentuated by our secret talks with NK at Panmunjom." Bonesteel thought Park might order unilateral air strikes without consulting or informing the United States. "We are taking all feasible preventive measures, which cannot be 100 percent . . . and I feel, or at least hope, ROK Chiefs of Staff would disobey such orders."[7]

The sudden tension also complicated the war in Vietnam. Only a few weeks earlier Park had agreed to send another ten thousand men to Vietnam. He not only withdrew his commitment in the wake of the Blue House raid and the *Pueblo* seizure, but also hinted that he might consider a withdrawal of South Korean troops from Vietnam to shore up defenses at home. To make matters far worse, the Vietcong launched the Tet Offensive in the early morning hours of January 30, 1968, a week after the *Pueblo* was seized, which demonstrated that far from being on the verge of defeat, the communist insurgency was stronger than ever and put in jeopardy any assessment that the Americans were winning or that the war was even winnable. The prospect of losing fifty thousand men in the aftermath of the offensive left Johnson and his staff "aghast."[8] A South Korean retaliatory attack would severely complicate American foreign policy. "We certainly did not want them [the South Koreans] to start another Korean War by launching an attack," recalled Dean Rusk. "After all, we were heavily involved in Vietnam."[9] Ironically, Johnson and

Brezhnev found themselves in almost exactly the same position as Truman and Stalin had just before June 1950: two belligerent Korean regimes intent on war. The Korean War risked going global all over again.

But Brezhnev had no intention of repeating Stalin's mistake. And Park ruled over a country very different from the impoverished and backward nation governed by Rhee. "We have tended to be pleased about economic progress in South Korea over the past few years," Ambassador Porter wrote to William Bundy on February 27, 1968, "and our satisfaction at this has to some degree obscured the fact that we have concurrently been nourishing a tiger, which is becoming difficult to restrain and confine."[10] This "tiger" could not be appeased by mere soothing words. Park demanded increased military assistance to improve his defensive capabilities at home if South Korean troops were to remain in Vietnam. In early February, Johnson asked Congress to pledge $100 million in special military aid to South Korea. "We need to give whatever aid is necessary to South Korea," he told congressional leaders. "They are among our best allies."[11]

Johnson sent Vance, the president's "soft-spoken troubleshooter," as a special emissary in mid-February to prevent Park from taking action against the North while convincing him to keep his troops in Vietnam. The situation was extremely tense. Vance found Park to be "moody, volatile and . . . drinking heavily." Park was still fuming over the fact that Washington "did not permit any retaliatory action on the attack on Blue House." The raid on the Blue House "had an unfortunate psychological effect on him," Vance continued. "He felt that both he and his country had lost face and his fears for his own safety and that of his family were markedly increased."[12] During the four-and-a-half-hour meeting on the morning of February 12, an angry Park immediately put Vance on the defensive. "These incidents are clearly preparatory steps for an invasion," Park declared. He believed it was necessary to "threaten the North with retaliatory action" in order to make the North Koreans "recognize and apologize for their illegal behavior and obtain their guarantee never to repeat such actions."

Vance responded that he duly "understood the point" of forcing the North to apologize. But, he added, "a warning of retaliation can only be given when one is ready to follow through with it."

"Are you saying there is a difference in severity between an attempt to

President Johnson's personal representative, Cyrus Vance, visits Seoul for talks with Park Chung Hee, February 12, 1968. (U.S. NATIONAL ARCHIVES AND RECORDS ADMINISTRATION)

assassinate a nation's president and his family in Seoul and the bombing of P'yŏngyang?" Park retorted.

"Of course, the killing of the president and his family is an unthinkable act," Vance responded. "But from the world's perspective they will not think of that act as equivalent to the bombing of a city and from that point of view there is a difference."

"They came to assault the presidential residence armed with anti-tank guns and mines!" Park exclaimed. "This cannot be interpreted as anything but an attempt to bring down our country. What would the U.S. do if this happened in the United States?"

"An air attack is a clear attack of aggression," Vance responded calmly. "The UN will recognize it as such. A guerrilla attack is I believe something quite different. I believe these things must be dealt with case by case."

"What is the American government's policy toward the present crisis?" a furious Park shot back. "Don't retaliate, don't give warning, are we to wait to consult each other for every other incident before we decide to do anything!"[13]

Fortunately, cooler heads prevailed when Vance again met with Prime Minister Chŏng Il-kwŏn two days later. Vance told Chŏng that any unilateral South Korean military action would necessitate the immediate withdrawal of American forces because it was "not our interest, or in the interest of the Republic of Korea, to have another all-out war in Korea." But he also warned that "if we fail to reach agreement on the issues before us, there would be serious US domestic reactions in respect to Korea." After some "gasps and sputtering," an agreement between the two sides was finally reached. The South Koreans agreed there would be "no reprisals for the Blue House or *Pueblo*." There would also "be no reprisals in the future without consulting" the Americans. They would "stand by during the closed door sessions with North Korea." In addition, Vance secured "an understanding that they would keep their troops in South Vietnam." The price for restraint and continued support in Vietnam, however, was, as expected, very high. "Park has a large shopping list," Vance reported. It included six Phantom fighter-bomber squadrons and small arms and equipment for one million men in the newly created homeland defense force; four new airfields; expansion of existing airfields; and no reduction in military aid. These measures would require over one hundred million dollars in new funds.[14]

Johnson was prepared to pay the cost. He urged Congress to follow as closely as possible the ROK requests, despite the concerns of some of his military advisors that such a large military procurement might actually embolden Park to take future unilateral actions against the North. The president, however, believed that the overall goal of the wish list was not "to improve combat effectiveness but to maximize the political and psychological impact on South Korea."[15] It was, in effect, an expensive way to give Park and the South Korean people an assurance that the United States was not going to abandon them. On July 8, 1968, Congress approved the wish list with some minor adjustments, for a total aid package of $220 million.[16] The administration also promised to increase business opportunities in South Vietnam for South Korean firms. Park was thus able to reap tremendous benefits from the *Pueblo* crisis despite what he deemed the "ignoble" conclusion of the affair. Kim Il Sung had come away with a worthless piece of propaganda while Park Chung Hee had secured hundreds of millions of dollars in U.S. aid.

Ultimately, Kim's gamble failed. The Blue House raid and the *Pueblo* crisis further strengthened the Park regime, not weakened it. The crisis also made clear that neither the Soviet Union nor the United States was willing to back their respective Korean allies in restarting the Korean War.

Park Chung Hee and Richard Nixon, who was on a private visit, in Seoul, 1966. Nixon's decision to visit Seoul and meet with Park Chung Hee in the run-up to his bid for the presidency in 1968 was indicative of the new status and prestige that South Korea enjoyed as a close ally of the United States. Following years of political reorganization after his narrow defeat to John F. Kennedy in 1960, Nixon won the presidency in 1968 promising to end the Vietnam War. (U.S. NATIONAL ARCHIVES AND RECORDS ADMINISTRATION)

China, embroiled in the Cultural Revolution, also had no appetite for another war on the Korean peninsula, especially if the fighting involved a regime friendly to the Soviet Union. The war that had ushered in the global cold war in June 1950 had thus evolved, by the end of the 1960s, into a series of localized "guerilla" conflicts, mostly along the DMZ.

Opening to China

"It is not often that one can recapture as an adult the quality that in one's youth made time seem to stand still; that gave every event the mystery of novelty; that enabled each experience to be relished because of its singularity."[17] So wrote Henry Kissinger about his first meeting with Chinese Premier Zhou Enlai. On July 9, 1971, Kissinger, President Richard Nixon's national security advisor, secretly arrived in Beijing for a historic meeting that would change the world and pave the way for the normalization of Sino-American relations. Even before his presidency, Nixon had contemplated the possibility of establishing relations with China. In an October 1967 *Foreign Affairs* article titled "Asia after Viet Nam," the arch anticommunist who had established his career during the McCarthy era made a startling proposal to bring China into the folds of the international community. "Taking the long view, we simply cannot afford to leave China forever outside the family of nations, there to nurture its fantasies, cherish its hates and threaten its neighbors," Nixon wrote. "There is no place on this small planet for a billion of its potentially most able people to live in angry isolation."[18]

Shortly after assuming the presidency in 1969, Nixon set out to implement his China policy. The idea was not to improve relations with China at the expense of the Soviet Union, but rather to create a more stable balance of powers by establishing a triangular relationship among the three greatest powers. "We moved toward China," Kissinger later wrote, "to shape a global equilibrium. It was not to collude against the Soviet Union, but to give us a balancing position to use for constructive ends—to give each Communist power a stake in better relations with us."[19] More immediately, Nixon believed a Beijing amicable to Washington could pressure Hanoi to negotiate an end to the Vietnam War.

By 1969, a significant shift in China's security strategy had also begun to occur. The 1968 Soviet invasion of Czechoslovakia, and the outbreak of clashes along the Sino-Soviet border the following year, had led Mao to seriously consider the possibility of a Soviet invasion. It was one reason why Mao approved high-level secret contacts with the United States. He did not encounter internal opposition to his radical new approach toward the United States, but he was nevertheless mindful of the need to prepare the public and the CCP for dramatic changes. In response to a *Time* interview with Nixon in September 1970, which revealed that the president hoped to visit China one day, Mao related through a trusted American intermediary, the journalist Edgar Snow, that he "would be happy to talk to him, either as a tourist or as a president."[20] In April 1971, the pace of change picked up dramatically when Mao invited the American Ping-Pong team to Beijing. The event was a tremendous success. "You have opened up a new chapter in the relations of the American and Chinese people," Zhou Enlai told the players.[21] For the Chinese leadership, the United States was increasingly thought of as a strategic partner to deter the Soviet Union. In this, Mao shared with Nixon a similar approach to triangular diplomacy: "My enemy's enemy is my friend."[22]

Kim Il Sung's reaction to China's sudden shift was at first one of bewilderment. By the time the *Pueblo* affair had run its course, Kim had decided to mend his relations with China. A high-level North Korean delegation was, in fact, in Beijing during Kissinger's secret trip, although the North Koreans were unaware of it at the time.[23] Zhou Enlai flew to P'yŏngyang on July 14, 1971, to personally brief Kim on Nixon's upcoming visit. Kim rationalized the extraordinary development by interpreting Nixon's visit as evidence of America's "accelerating decline" in the face of Chinese power and as representative of a triumph for China and for all small nations fighting against foreign imperialism. "The United States had attempted to isolate China," Kim declared triumphantly at a mass rally, "but China developed into a mighty anti-imperialist revolutionary power in Asia, and the American blockade came to a shameful end." Nixon's visit "proved the bankruptcy of America's anti-Chinese policy." It also represented a "march of the defeated to Beijing."[24]

President Richard Nixon and Premier Zhou Enlai at a state dinner in the Great Hall of the People, Beijing, February 28, 1972. (U.S. NATIONAL ARCHIVES AND RECORDS ADMINISTRATION)

While gloating over America's "defeat," Kim announced his willingness to establish contact with Washington and Seoul.[25] This was an abrupt change in North Korean policy, but after the *Pueblo* incident Kim believed that Nixon's China trip might have gains for North Korea. He now thought the Chinese could assist in securing the withdrawal of American troops from South Korea. A Soviet diplomat in P'yŏngyang observed in early 1972 that North Korean anti-Americanism "solely rests on the U.S. presence in South Korea." If the Americans were to withdraw, "the position of the DPRK vis-à-vis the United States would change as well."[26] Kim could ride on the coattails of "America's humiliation."

In Seoul, Park was deeply dismayed and distressed by the news. The Nixon administration had not notified the Koreans (or the Japanese for that matter) of Nixon's upcoming visit before it was made public. The Sino-American rapprochement was part of a pattern of perceived American betrayals that began with the lackluster response to the 1968 Blue House raid and continued with the establishment of the Nixon Doctrine in 1969, which essentially stated that nations must rely on their own capacity to secure defense rather than on American power. It was also clear by this time that Nixon was ready to do anything to pull U.S. forces out of Vietnam, especially in order to win reelection in 1972. South Vietnam could be betrayed. And establishing ties with China required cutting ties with Taiwan, and so Taiwan would also be betrayed. Park was convinced that the United States was now in the process of abandoning South Korea. Many South Koreans shared these sentiments, as summed up in this editorial in the *Kangwŏn ilbo*:

> For twenty-seven years since World War II, the issue of who has legitimate claim over mainland China, the Nationalists of the Republic of China or the Communists, has been a global issue. Until last year, the Nationalists were recognized as having that legitimacy, but this was shattered by Nixon's visit. Under the power and influence of the U.S., the USSR and Japan, Communist Chinese legitimacy over mainland China has now become a reality in international politics. It is the realization of the "strong eats the weak" principle at work.[27]

The withdrawal in early 1971 of twenty thousand of the sixty-two thousand American troops from South Korea over Park's objections had already intensified the feelings that South Korea would be the next country to be "eaten." Such foreboding was further intensified during

Park's conversation with Ambassador Lam Pham Dang on November 3, 1972. Lam, chief of South Vietnam's Observation Delegation to the Paris Peace Accord talks that began in 1968, had been sent to South Korea by South Vietnamese President Nguyễn Văn Thiệu to convey his country's concerns regarding the terms of the peace accord that was about to be signed by the United States and North Vietnam (it was signed on January 23, 1973, in Paris). Of utmost concern was that the accord did not require the withdrawal of North Vietnamese troops from South Vietnam. "An agreement that doesn't require North Vietnam to withdraw north of the 17th parallel is meaningless," Park told Lam. He also told Lam that Philip Habib, U.S. ambassador to the ROK, had conveyed to him that the Americans were forced to accept this agreement because the peace accord would collapse without it. "I told him [Habib] that if an accord is reached without North Vietnamese troops withdrawing from the south then all of South Vietnam will eventually be taken over by the enemy." Lam shared Park's dismay. Both men wondered whether the U.S. position was constrained by the upcoming presidential elections (on November 7) and whether the U.S. government would change its position after Nixon was reelected. Park was also vexed by Lam's account that the Americans seemed to be prepared to sign the accord only with the North Vietnamese, effectively leaving South Vietnam out in the cold.

"If the U.S. and North Vietnam sign the agreement without South Vietnam's signature, do you see it as being valid?" Park asked.

"I believe the U.S. will stop all military actions based on such an agreement," Lam told Park. "But it will not be able to explain why 40,000 Americans died in Vietnam."

To add to the uncertainty of the situation, Lam confided that before his departure from Saigon, "Dr. Kissinger strongly warned me not to reveal that the U.S. negotiated the terms of the accord without prior consultation with the South Vietnamese during my trip."[28] Apparently, South Koreans were supposed to be kept out in the cold as well. Park was left to make sense of this betrayal and what it might mean for South Korea.

Responding to these events, Park decided that he needed to buy time to strengthen his nation, and in 1971 he quickly moved to approve secret visits between emissaries of Kim Il Sung and himself. Yi Tong-bok, a former member of the ROK National Assembly (1996–2000) who had served in key government positions dealing with North Korea, recalled that the decision to accept the offer for dialogue "had very much to do with a reduced confidence in the United States . . . many officials in the South Korean government as well as the private sector became very worried about the possibility of some kind of political deal between Washington and Beijing about Korea, struck across our shoulders."[29] An inter-Korean dialogue was seen as a temporary measure for Park to build up the country, thus "forestalling the reckless acts of Kim Il Sung."[30] For Kim, believing that the time of U.S. withdrawal from the Korean peninsula was near, talk of peaceful reunification was intended merely as a ploy to oust Park from power. "There are many people in South Korea who want peaceful reunification," confided one North Korean official to the Romanian leader Nicolae Ceaușescu in September 1972. "If we extend our talks, it is likely that at the next presidential elections, Park Chung Hee is eliminated and the position of the president is occupied by the New Democratic Party . . . It is only then that we will be able to create a democratic unified government, through free general elections in both North and South Korea."[31] Kim's plan, in other words, was to lay the foundations for the gradual communization of the South. From the onset, it was clear that neither leader had any illusions that inter-Korean dialogue would lead to peaceful reconciliation.

To no one's surprise, the talks led nowhere and were suspended after only one year. Nixon's historic visit to China took place in February 1972, and three months later he visited Moscow, securing his triangular diplomacy. Kim quickly comprehended that Sino-American rapprochement would not open the path to Korean reunification under his terms as he had hoped. Mao had no interest in jeopardizing his new relationship with the United States by backing the possibility of renewed fighting on the peninsula. Kim had deceived himself with his simplistic assessment of Nixon's visit as simply a "knee-fall before the grand Chinese power." He had, instead, given Park the breathing room he needed to respond to the changing global situation. Even the Bulgarians complained about North Korea's parochial foreign policy perspectives. "The Nixon visit was interpreted as forced upon the American president [and in this way] the Korean leadership attempts to hide from its people the parallel interests of China and the United States," observed one Bulgarian official. "It is pursuing its nationalistic course and fails to notice the anti-Soviet aspect of rapprochement between the Chinese leadership and the United States."[32] Kim, it appeared, did not grasp the full significance of Nixon's "triangular diplomacy" even though he played it so well himself.

Meanwhile, Park tightened his grip on power while pushing forward with his modernization plans. Riding the nationwide wave of fear and apprehension, Park declared martial law. On October 17, 1972, he dissolved the National Assembly and promulgated a new constitution that effectively made him president for life. Inspired by Japan's 1868 revolution, the Meiji *Ishin* (restoration), which ushered in Japan's modernization, Park called his new system *Yusin*, the Korean pronunciation of *Ishin*, thus evoking "restoration" and "revitalizing reforms."[33] While most histories of the period focus on elite Seoul-centered intellectual and student criticism of *Yusin*, in the countryside there appears to have been an overwhelming feeling that *Yusin* was, in fact, an appropriate response to the threats and crises then facing the nation. Although there are no hard numbers to back this claim, a cursory overview of many of the local Korean newspapers published at the time does provide a good feel for what the ordinary Koreans, mostly farmers and fishermen, thought about *Yusin*. Editorials and letters that appear in the *Kangwŏn ilbo* from 1972 to 1974, for example, are almost all overwhelmingly positive. A poem written by a ninth grader in Kangwŏn-do about *Yusin* is indicative of the kind of heart-felt response that frequently appeared in this local paper:

Oh October *Yusin*
You have come to do a great deed
While we flounder against the storm winds.

You will heal the wounds
Made by the devil's nails.

The days go by silently
But our thirty million souls suffer from insecurity and anxiety
Oh, October *Yusin*
You've come to sooth us with a new law.
We will face the future firmly united
At this historical moment

Oh October *Yusin*
You will secure for us
Great benefit, glory and peace.[34]

Park justified his actions on the grounds that South Korea must be united and strong to deter or survive another North Korean attack. The *Yusin* system also sought to achieve political, socioeconomic, and security reforms to maintain South Korea's independence in a changing international environment.[35] Park saw the ultimate aim of *Yusin* as restoration of "the prestige and strength of the Korean nation" that had been lost when Korea lost its sovereignty to Japan in 1910.[36] With an ambitious plan for developing an economy based on heavy industries with the capacity to indigenously produce armaments, Park sought to promote his nation's self-reliance and independence. In 1974, Park authorized a program to develop nuclear weapons technology, but he suspended it in July 1976 under intense U.S. pressure.[37] Ultimately, Park recognized that maintaining a strong alliance with the United States was the most effective deterrent to war, so he would continue to pursue greater self-reliance, but under the protection of the United States.

In the meantime, with hopes for North-South reconciliation now dead—along with Kim's dream of riding the wave of Sino-American rapprochement to achieve his own unification dreams—both Park Chung Hee and Kim Il Sung began concentrating their efforts on developing their nations at home. At the same time, they resorted to fighting the war abroad, through active diplomacy. For Kim, this meant weakening the Park regime through propaganda and diplomatic means and rejecting any action that might confer legitimacy on the ROK, including vigorously opposing South Korea's efforts to gain admission to the United Nations, either independently or under a two-Korea policy. In 1973 alone, Kim Il Sung sent delegations to over eighty countries, and by the mid-1970s ninety member states worldwide recognized the DPRK, almost equaling the number that maintained diplomatic relations with the ROK.[38] In response, Park found it necessary to develop ties with nonaligned member states, since they played a key political force in the UN. But these efforts proved difficult because of Kim's aggressive diplomatic maneuverings and the ideological, anti-imperialist worldview that North Korea naturally shared with other Third World nations.[39] It was another indication of just how "local" the Korean War had become.

CHAPTER EIGHTEEN

War for Peace

The operation was scheduled to begin at 7:00 a.m. As squadrons of fighter jets circled ominously overhead, a sixty-man security platoon of American and South Korean soldiers equipped with side arms and ax handles advanced into the truce village at P'anmunjŏm. The platoon was accompanied by a sixteen-man tree-cutting detail. B-52 strategic bombers from Guam were circling farther south, while three batteries of American 105mm howitzers were stationed north of the Imjin River. A mile from P'anmunjŏm, an ROK infantry reconnaissance company, armed with M16 rifles, mortars, and machine guns, was deployed just outside the Joint Security Area, ready to pounce at the first sign of trouble. Altogether 813 men were involved in the operation. Forty-five minutes later a message was flashed to higher headquarters that the mission was accomplished without incident: a forty-foot-tall Normandy poplar tree had been cut down.[1]

The operation was the climax of a week of tension that began on August 18, 1976, when North Korean soldiers attacked with axes a group of American and South Korean soldiers who were in the Joint Security Area at P'anmunjŏm. The Americans and South Koreans were preparing to prune a tree to clear the line of sight from a guard post. Before they began their work they suddenly found themselves confronted by a large group of angry and armed North Koreans. One South Korean later recalled, "Suddenly they swarmed out of nowhere crowding the Americans, beating them with clubs and kicking them." By the time the attack was over, two American officers, Capt. Arthur Bonifas and Lt. Mark Barrett, were dead of massive head injuries. Four other Americans and five South Koreans were also wounded. The Americans had not fired a shot. "We wanted to avoid escalating any incidents," an American official explained.[2] Within hours, Kissinger was on the phone with

UNC soldiers cut down a poplar tree near the Bridge of No Return, August 21, 1976. (U.S. NATIONAL ARCHIVES AND RECORDS ADMINISTRATION)

the American ambassador in Seoul, Philip Habib: "I want retaliatory action," he told Habib. "We cannot have Americans killed. I hope that is clear."[3] Cooler heads prevailed once the poplar tree was cut down, its removal being a symbol of American resolve and the mass of military power placed on alert a demonstration of its strength. Nevertheless, it was unclear whether the tree cutting would represent the entirety of the American response to the attack. While Kissinger and other American officials believed that the killings were premeditated, they were equally convinced that North Korea did not want to start another war.

Why did the North Koreans commit this heinous attack? The most plausible reason is that it was an act of impulsive passion by North Korean guards who have long been inculcated with hatred for the United States and Americans.[4] However, while the actual killing of the American soldiers may not have been planned, the weight of intelligence, "including the number of Korean reinforcements ready prior to the incident," suggests that it was a calculated political ploy instigated for either domestic or international reasons.[5] On the domestic front, a series of crises had befallen North Korea by 1976. It had been unable to pay back its foreign loans from Japan and European nations, amounting to $1.8 billion, and was on the verge of defaulting. P'yŏngyang had asked for a two-year moratorium, but the debt led to a 63 percent decline in foreign exports during the first five months of 1976.[6] As the economy went into sharp decline, North Korea eventually defaulted. The ax attack may have been an effort to divert domestic attention away from North Korea's failing economy. In addition, there was also the matter of Kim Il Sung's successor. Earlier in the year, Kim had named his son, Kim Jong Il, as his heir apparent. Raising tensions and the threat of renewed war might have been a way for the elder Kim to rally public support for his son during a moment of national crisis. On the international front, the attack could have been staged to draw the world's attention to the Korean situation, as part of a propaganda campaign to condemn the American presence in South Korea and thus eventually force a withdrawal. Within hours of the attack, Kim Jong Il asked the Conference of Nonaligned Nations, meeting in Sri Lanka, to pass a resolution condemning the American presence in South Korea. Kim's "ax diplomacy" could have provoked an American reaction that might have been used to rally support for North Korea at the United Nations. The conference did, in fact, pass the resolution.[7]

As more details of the incident surfaced, however, it became clear that the North Koreans had severely misjudged the situation. No North Koreans had been killed, and the brutal nature of the murders suggested that the North Koreans had been the deliberate instigators of the attack. World opinion swung against North Korea. American reaction had also been swift and strong. The tree-cutting operation unequivocally conveyed the message that Washington was prepared to go to war if necessary. Kim soon issued a statement saying that the killing of the two Americans was "regretful" and that both sides should take steps to ensure that such incidents do not happen again. It was an unprecedented act of contrition for the Great Leader. Washington's initial reaction to Kim's "apology" was harsh. "This expression represented a backhanded acknowledgement that they are in the wrong," Kissinger announced. "However, we do not find this message acceptable because there is no acknowledgement for the brutal, premeditated murder of two Americans."[8] But then Washington abruptly softened its stance. It had concluded that raising further tensions would be counterproductive, and accepted Kim's "conciliatory" message.

South Koreans were appalled by Washington's sudden turnaround. With confidence in American security commitments at its lowest point since the fall of South Vietnam in 1975, they had looked for signs that the Americans would get tough with P'yŏngyang. "In order to guard peace we have to show the North Koreans very strong resolve," Park Chung Hee declared in response to the news that Washington had accepted Kim's "regrets."[9] O Se-yŏng of the opposition New Democratic Party expressed similar concerns, saying he was "worried that the North Koreans may accept it [the American response] as further evidence of their success in their continuous provocations."[10] Washington's decision not to pursue further retaliatory action against North Korea simply reconfirmed in most South Koreans' minds that the American commitment to their security was waning and that they might soon have to face North Korea on their own.

For Americans at home, the brutal killings had, more than any other North Korean provocations since the *Pueblo* seizure, showed them how quickly they could become involved in another Asian land war. In a speech to the Senate on September 15, 1976, Senator George McGovern (D-South Dakota) stated that "the tree cutting incident proved that U.S. forces sent to Korea a generation ago could trip this generation into another war in the wrong place at the wrong time." He then called for the withdrawal of all U.S. forces and the "avoidance of further identification with that disreputable tyrant [Park Chung Hee]."[11]

McGovern's reaction was shared by the first post–Vietnam War president, Jimmy Carter. Carter too was troubled by the "tripwire" danger created by the U.S. forces. He was also deeply troubled by the human rights abuses of the Park regime. For these reasons he was determined to fulfill a campaign pledge to "withdraw our ground forces from South Korea on a phased basis over a time."[12] But keeping this campaign promise proved to be nearly impossible. By the end of his presidency, Carter was forced to confront the reality that an American withdrawal from Korea could have a dangerous impact on the security and stability of the vital Northeast Asian region. The unending Korean War and its unremitting confrontation sparked by continued American presence, paradoxically, now played a vital role in keeping the peace.

Withdrawal

After the trauma of Nixon's resignation in 1974 and South Vietnam's fall in 1975, which was still shocking even if anticipated, the political mood in the United States was deeply skeptical of the government and against further American military ventures in Asia. There was a yearning for moral and righteous governance. Jimmy Carter promised to build "a new world order based on a U.S. commitment to moral values rather than an inordinate fear of communism." The policy, first articulated in May 1977, made human rights a primary issue in how America conducted foreign affairs. Carter based his new approach on his faith in the universality of democracy and American values and principles: "We are confident that democracy's example will be compelling . . . We are confident of our own strength . . . through failure we have now found our way back to our own principles and values, and we have regained our lost confidence."[13] A month later, Carter articulated what this morality-oriented foreign policy might mean for Korea: the withdrawal of U.S. ground forces from South Korea. The mutual defense treaty and commitment of American airpower would remain, but U.S. troops would go home.

On January 26, 1977, six days after his inauguration, Carter ordered a broad review of U.S. policy toward the Korean peninsula, which was set down in Presidential Review Memorandum/NSC 13 (PRM 13).[14] Key national security agencies and officials were tasked to "analyze current developments and future trends bearing on our involvement in Korea," including "possible course of action dealing with . . . the reduction in U.S. conventional force levels on the peninsula."[15] Despite the seemingly open-ended nature of the review, however, officials in the new administration were shocked when Secretary of State Cyrus Vance told the group that the president's mind had already been made up: the group was directed to study not *whether* ground forces should be withdrawn, but *how* it should be carried out.[16] William Gleysteen Jr., Carter's ambassador to South Korea, recalled his dismay: "Some participants threatened to refuse cooperation; others threatened to publicize the issue, perhaps by way of Congress. The angry, fractious session ended in chaos."[17] By asking for recommendations on implementation rather than an assessment of the soundness of the decision, Carter thwarted any opposition to his plan. They thought that for a candidate who had campaigned on the platform of openness and against the overreaching of presidential power, Carter was doing exactly the opposite. In the end, the review group decided to continue by not only framing the study "consistent with the President's instructions," but also allowing the option "to argue for a minimum of withdrawals."[18] Privately, they were concerned that Carter did not understand the risks inherent in a U.S. withdrawal. Doubts would be raised, including by the North Koreans, about whether the U.S. would really fight in the event of another war. This ambiguity could increase the risk of war, as it did in 1949 when the American forces withdrew from the Korean peninsula. Moreover, Carter had announced his plan without any preconditions. There was no incentive for the North Koreans to guarantee that they would not again attempt to use military force against the South by such measures as a nonaggression pact or a reduction in their forces.

Defenders of Carter's plan argued that troop withdrawal was hardly a novel idea. In 1971, Nixon, over the strong objections of the Park regime, had withdrawn the twenty thousand men in the Seventh Infantry Division, of the approximately sixty thousand U.S. troops then on duty in Korea. There was also talk of reducing the remaining U.S. ground combat unit, the Second Infantry Division, to a single brigade. The difference, of course, was that Nixon did not call for the complete withdrawal of U.S. ground forces. This distinction was critical because without troops on the ground, the United States would have an option to intervene in the event of another war or not. Although the Carter administration publicly declared its commitment to South Korea's defense since "the President cannot evade the choice of going to war or not because our Air Force will still be there," privately the president acknowledged that the withdrawal plan would remove the tripwire that would automatically involve the United States in any renewal of fighting. Senator Larry Winn of Kansas stated the concern over the tripwire situation at a House hearing on the ax murder incident: "You don't usually start a war with an ax."[19] The problem was that in Korea you very well could.

These fears were spelled out in another presidential review, Presidential Review Memorandum/NSC 10 (PRM 10), completed on February 18, 1977, which stated that "once the U.S. land forces are out of Korea, the U.S. has transformed its presence in Asia from a land-based posture to an off-shore posture. This . . . provides the U.S. flexibility to determine at the time whether it should or should not get involved in a local war." With the troops gone, "the risk of automatic involvement . . . is minimized. However, should the U.S. decide to intervene, military forces would be readily available." Thus unlike PRM 13, which focused on *how* the withdrawal of U.S. forces should be carried out, PRM 10 provided an acceptable rationale for withdrawing the ground troops. As for deterring North Korea from launching another invasion, "North Korea must take into account powerful U.S. air and naval assets in any decision to attack the South." Nevertheless, its predictions were grim. The North Koreans could not win "a sustained combat" against the South, the report said, but even with U.S. supply comparable to the "initial air and naval support at D-Day," it was possible "that they could at least temporarily attain their most likely major objective, the capture of Seoul."[20]

Within the State Department, Vance's deputies were divided about the withdrawal plan. There was general consensus that given its robust economy, South Korea would be able to make up for a U.S. withdrawal by increasing its military budget, but among the foreign and defense policy community, the reaction was universally negative. Carter's national security advisor, Zbigniew Brzezinski, recalled little support for the idea. The Joint Chiefs of Staff adamantly opposed the withdrawal, fearing that its net effect "could be dangerous for deterrence."[21] Meanwhile, Carter sent Vice President Walter Mondale to Japan in February 1977 to inform the Japanese of his determination to withdraw American ground troops. In yet another slap in the face to the Koreans, the South Koreans received no such courtesy visit.

Many in the Carter administration had serious doubts about the withdrawal plan and also thought that the process of implementing the major policy change was flawed. "No real consultations had been held with any Asian ally; no major strategic or national advantage to the United States had been clearly enunciated or postulated; no extraction of advantage of concessions from those who threatened the stability of Northeast Asia and their vital role to U.S. interest had been obtained." Carter had merely decided that it was "time to go" and seemed to have persuaded himself that it would not result in disaster. Caught between loyalty to the president and a growing perception that the plan carried unnecessary risks to American security, many of the president's advisors simply hoped that the withdrawal process would drag out sufficiently long "so that if concerns did prove real, there would be time for policy adjustments before the U.S. had gone too far."[22]

The public façade of support for Carter's plan broke wide open when Maj. Gen. John Singlaub, chief of staff of U.S. Forces Korea, told the *Washington Post* in May 1977 that "if U.S. ground troops are withdrawn on the schedule suggested, it will lead to war."[23] He was relieved of his duties because his statements were "inconsistent with announced national security policy and have made it difficult for him to carry out" his duties.[24] Singlaub's testimony before a House subcommittee soon thereafter that his views were shared by the military and the diplomatic community created a political firestorm on Capitol Hill. The controversy that had been brewing within the administration for months had been blown wide open. What particularly disturbed conservative leaders like Senators Barry Goldwater and Strom Thurmond was that the administration was pushing a major policy move without congressional or national debate. Goldwater stated on the Senate floor, "The official announcement by the Pentagon said that public statements by General Singlaub . . . were inconsistent with announced national security policy. What I would like to know is where was this official policy defined and announced by the President or by the Pentagon? I can't find such a policy declaration. It has not been presented to the Armed Services Committee of which I am a member . . . and so far as I know it has not been presented in the Committee on Foreign Affairs."[25] Republican critics charged Carter with attempting to hastily and carelessly fulfill an ill-considered campaign promise. Carter had underestimated the obstacles he would face in Washington. He had also misjudged the limits of his powers as the president.

Backlash

Critics of the withdrawal plan loudly voiced their concerns. They pointed to strategic considerations beyond just the risk of a North Korean attack. A precipitous withdrawal of troops from Korea would raise doubts in Japan about America's commitment to Japan's security. Senators Hubert Humphrey (D-Minnesota) and John Glenn (D-Ohio) reported to the Senate Foreign Relations Committee that Japan might expand its military, which could "shatter the fragile balance that now exists in East Asia."[26] The withdrawal might also lead Japan to accommodate Soviet power in the Pacific. China, too, might begin to question American credibility as an Asian-Pacific power willing and able to counterbalance the Soviet Union. Such an uncertainty about America could undermine, as one official put it, the "Chinese interest in normalizing relations with the United States and increase the risk of Sino-Soviet accommodation." South and North Korea would no doubt react to the American withdrawal with an arms buildup and might embark on developing nuclear weapons. The human rights situation in South Korea was likely to worsen. Without American leverage on the Seoul regime, President Park "will undoubtedly use the phase out as further rationalization to intensify repression of his domestic opponents." This was the reason why virtually "the entire South Korean opposition is against American withdrawal."[27] Richard Stilwell, a retired Army general and former commander of the UNC in Korea, summed up the majority opinion in the defense and foreign policy community when he said that "disengagement of American troops entails the gravest of risks, not only on the peninsula but also in Northeast Asia and far beyond," and that the modest investments of men and resources "provide a deterrent that effectively thwarts the North Koreans."[28]

As doubts and opposition to the withdrawal plan became more vocal, Carter responded by sending Secretary of Defense Harold Brown to Seoul to revise the withdrawal schedule. To compensate for the loss of American troops he also promised $1.9 billion in military aid that would be "provided in advance of or parallel to the withdrawals."[29] The military aid package was an essential component of the withdrawal plan. By providing the Park regime with assistance to develop the capacity to defend itself, Carter hoped to assuage fears that South Korea was being abandoned. In December 1977, the State Department published a report that South Korean security would not be harmed by the American withdrawal if it were accompanied by military aid.[30] The aid package, however, required congressional approval, and Korea in the year 1977 was a very unpopular country. Angered and frightened by the abrupt manner in which Carter had announced his withdrawal plan without prior consultation, Park turned to bribing American officials in an effort to buy congressional votes in its favor. The "Korea-gate" scandal, as it came to be known, was a desperate attempt at influence peddling by a regime that was certain it was being abandoned. By the end of 1977, four full-scale congressional investigations of the bribery scandal were under way. Support for South Korea in Congress plummeted so drastically that Carter's proposal to leave weapons behind as insurance when U.S. troops pull out "could not now pass the House." The Korea-gate investigation had paralyzed all legislative actions on Korea. Representative Clement Zablocki, chairman of the House International Relations Committee, announced that "it would be futile to begin hearing this year because of the fall-out from the Korean influence peddling."[31] Robert Rich, the State Department country director for Korea, summed up the feeling on Capitol Hill: "Congress probably could not have passed a bill stating that Korea was a peninsula in North East Asia."[32]

Another obstacle that Carter ran into was self-inflicted. By publicly and relentlessly chastising the Park regime for its human rights abuses, Carter had undercut American popular support for South Korea. It was difficult for him to argue that with the withdrawal of U.S. troops the repressive regime should be provided with a large compensatory military package. Moreover, Carter's emphasis on human rights had emboldened Park's domestic critics. "It's a contest of nerves to see how far we can go," said one opponent of the regime. "With Carter talking human rights, Park doesn't dare arrest all of us. It would mean another whole year of embarrassing sham trials."[33] Questions were raised as to whether the withdrawal should proceed during a period of such political turmoil, as many now believed that North Korea might take advantage of the situation. "We do not face just a frontal, all-out invasion from the North, but a general strategy of revolution in the South," said Kim Kyŏng-wŏn, Park's special assistant for foreign affairs. "The appearance of instability as well as the actual fact would make us run the risk of misleading North Korea to believe that their theories are confirmed. This is a real enough danger."[34] Many in Washington agreed.

While criticism of the withdrawal plan mounted and it became clear that Congress was not going to approve enhanced military aid to South Korea, Senators John Glenn and Hubert Humphrey, two staunch allies of the president, returned from an extensive trip in Asia. The purpose of the trip was to study the withdrawal question as it related to the whole strategic and diplomatic equation in Northeast Asia. Their report, issued on January 8, 1978, created a stir in Congress. It concluded that "the President's decision to withdraw troops from Korea will have a critical impact on the peace and stability of East Asia." With regard to the tripwire effect, "the United States will gain the option not to become involved in another ground war in Asia; but the United States maintaining its commitment, U.S. naval and Air Force personnel would undoubtedly be involved if war broke out."[35] In other words, the best way to ensure that the United States avoided a new Korean War was to prevent such a war from happening in the first place.

But the most devastating, and compelling, finding was the strong opposition to the withdrawal by both China and the Soviet Union.[36] The late 1970s was a period of intense regional change and realignments within the communist world, including China's new relationship with the United States, continuing hostility between China and the Soviet Union, and increasing tensions between China and Vietnam. Instability on the Korean peninsula was the last thing any of the regional powers wanted. Although neither China nor the Soviet Union publicly opposed the withdrawal plan for fear of alienating North Korea, owing to their political rivalry with each other, the report concluded that "both value relations with the United States and Japan above Korean ambitions for reunification." It also found that both countries "seek to disassociate themselves from Kim Il Sung's more rash actions and view the U.S. security commitment to Seoul as a useful ingredient in keeping peace on the peninsula and restraining Japanese rearmament." In particular, the Chinese, paranoid about the Soviet threat, feared that the removal of American forces from the Korean peninsula might tempt the Soviets to reassert their long-standing Russian interests over the peninsula. Humphrey and Glenn observed that "U.S. force reduction, in and of itself, will not lead China to abandon its basic foreign policy strategy of developing a U.S. connection. But it will raise some troublesome implications in Peking [Beijing]. It is widely believed that the Chinese tacitly support a U.S. military presence in South Korea as an element of the strategic counterweight to the threat of Soviet 'encirclement' of China." As for the Soviet Union, "Soviet national interest is best served by a divided, not a unified Korea. Unpredictable Kim could draw the Soviet Union into a conflict with the United States," which is why the Soviet leaders want American troops to remain in the South despite their public utterances to the contrary. The report noted that "Soviet media still refers to 'two Korean states' and the USSR has yet to endorse North Korea's claim to be the 'sole sovereign state' on the Korean peninsula." As for Japan, "it views East Asia strategic politics as tripolar, with the United States, the Soviets and the PRC determining its future . . . the situation in Korea is the vortex of these relationships and thus Japan views its own fate inextricably linked to that of Korea." This is why the Japanese government "was disheartened by Carter's campaign pledges and confidence in the US is at a low point." A withdrawal from Korea would damage Japan's "confidence in the U.S. determination to defend Japan." Under these circumstances, "the rearmament of Japan might develop a situation that would shatter the fragile balance that now exists in Asia." Similar sentiments were voiced by Taiwan, the Philippines, Singapore, Thailand, and Australia. Singapore's President Lee Kuan Yew was particularly critical: "The withdrawal from Korea is part of President Carter's plan for a decreased U.S. presence in Asia."[37]

In South Korea, as expected, the reaction was universally negative. Even staunch domestic opponents of the Park regime were against the withdrawal. The report noted that "every dissident interviewed opposed U.S. troop withdrawal. The Korean National Council of Churches in a recent position paper stated bluntly 'we would like to make clear our belief that the plan to withdraw American troops will deal a death blow to our people's churches in their struggle for freedom, justice and human rights.' They fear that without strong American presence there will be no restraining the government."[38] The regional powers agreed that a sudden American retreat would send the world a political message that the United States was disengaging from an area of potential conflict and abandoning allies.

While these alarming findings were being absorbed by Congress and the administration, behind-the-scene developments would eventually kill the withdrawal plan altogether. A main assumption of the plan was that even after the withdrawal, the military balance of power still favored South Korea. Its larger population, twice that of the North, was seen as a distinct advantage in its long-run economic and military competition with the North.[39] In late 1975, however, John Armstrong, a young army intelligence analyst at Ft. Meade, Maryland, made a startling discovery. Working with imagery of North Korean forces taken by aircraft and satellites, Armstrong determined that North Korean tank forces were nearly double the amount of previous estimates. His initial findings led to a larger effort to completely reassess North Korea's military strength. After two years, the team of three-dozen analysts under Armstrong confirmed a huge increase in North Korean military capability over the previous decade. Ground forces increased by 40 percent, from 485,000 to 680,000, the first time the NKPA had fielded a force larger than the ROK Army. The North Koreans possessed more than a two-to-one advantage in tanks and artillery, and the bulk of this larger force was positioned closer to the DMZ than previously thought and "in such a configuration to suggest offensive intent." The findings electrified the intelligence community, and senior officials recognized the stark implications of the study for Carter's pullout plan. In January 1979, the results of the study became front-page news in the *New York Times* and the *Washington Post*.[40]

Carter questioned the validity of the new assessment (and would continue to do so well after the end of his presidency) and still pressed for withdrawal. The normalization of relations with China on January 1, 1979, raised the possibility of a Sino-American initiative to finalize a settlement between North and South Korea that would permit the withdrawal. During his visit to the United States in late January, Deng Xiaoping, who had succeeded Mao in 1978, two years after the latter's death, agreed to help arrange North-South talks, but when North Korea refused to compromise on the terms of those talks, Deng said that he would not put pressure on North Korea. Carter's scheduled trip to Tokyo in June for the G7 summit provided an opportunity for a visit to Seoul to discuss the situation with Park. Carter's aides proposed such a visit, hoping the outcome would convince Carter that the withdrawal plan was premature. Carter was reluctant to meet Park, whom he despised for his human rights record, much less to discuss the withdrawal plan. Nevertheless, he agreed to make the visit but tied it to an unexpected proposal: a three-way summit with Kim Il Sung and Park in the DMZ. It was an idea born from the Camp David Accords, which had concluded the previous September between Israel and Egypt. Carter would attempt to end the Korean War through diplomacy. A North-South settlement would allow him to keep his campaign promise, since the long-term presence of American troops after North-South rapprochement would be unnecessary.

It was an idealistic, if not hopelessly naive, proposal that failed to take into consideration the long and aggrieved history between the two nations, the regional implications of a withdrawal, and the opposition to withdrawal by China, Japan, and the Soviet Union. White House aides thought it might be seen as a "flaky" stunt. Ambassador Gleysteen, who grew up in China with missionary parents, said he "nearly fell out of my chair" and "exploded with surprise and anger." A visit meant to symbolize close relations between the United States and South Korea would "be turned into a circus of events featuring Park's most feared enemy." Asia experts in the State and Defense Departments were also horrified, realizing that such an event would be seen by the South Koreans as "the first steps toward a Vietnamese solution for Korea." It would lead to further suspicion in South Korea that the United States was in the process of abandoning an old ally. It would also allow Kim to create a wedge between the Americans and the South Koreans. Park would never agree to such a summit, and the proposal itself would poison the relations between the two allies. Gleysteen said that if Carter went ahead with these plans, he would resign. Through Brzezinski, Carter was convinced to quietly drop the plan without the South Koreans ever knowing about it.[41]

Like so many of his initiatives, Carter's policies were not part of an overall strategic design. Each foreign policy initiative, as one observer put it, "was considered a sacred goal."[42] Focused on the human rights issue and the tripwire effect, Carter failed to understand the complex history of Korea's unending war, and America's continued involvement in it, and how that situation had paradoxically become the basis for maintaining the peace.

To Seoul

The meeting with Park had initially been proposed as a mechanism to adjust and refine the withdrawal proposal. Ambassador Gleysteen was hopeful: "With fingers crossed, I believed we were over the hump in getting President Carter to suspend his troop withdrawal." By this time, Carter was about the only person in Washington who favored the withdrawal. Instead of a trilateral summit, Carter accepted a trilateral meeting by lesser diplomats. Gleysteen proposed that "if the president were to tell Park that we would accommodate his concerns by a significant alteration of our troop withdrawal plans, then on that basis of the confidence generated by such a declaration, we could tell him we wished to explore with him the possibility of announcing in Seoul a proposal for a trilateral summit at a later time."[43] Although most of his aides opposed the idea of a trilateral meeting with North Korean diplomats, Park agreed. He saw a possible way to end or reduce the scope of the withdrawal plan, and he was convinced that the North Korean leader would reject the proposal anyway. As it turned out, Park was correct about Kim's reaction, but he miscalculated President Carter's.

On the evening of June 29, 1979, Carter arrived in Seoul after having just finished the G7 summit meetings in Tokyo. Ham Su-yŏng, commander of the presidential guard, recalled later that "the treatment Park received from the [American] visitors was insulting." Because of security concerns, the Secret Service did not notify the Koreans about Carter's exact time of arrival. This meant that Park was forced to wait for nearly an hour at the airport. Moreover, the accompanying press corps was allowed to debark the plane first. As a result, Park, who was short in stature, "was forced to fight his way through a crowd of reporters before finally greeting the U.S. President."[44] After a brief handshake, Carter abruptly departed. In a remarkable defiance of protocol that amounted to a slap in the face against Park, Carter immediately flew to Camp Casey, the headquarters of the U.S. Army's Second Infantry Division near the DMZ, for his first night, rather than stay at the state guesthouse in Seoul. It was an inauspicious start for the visit.

Carter traveled back to Seoul the next morning to meet Park at the Blue House. Gleysteen had advised Park not to bring up the withdrawal issue, at least not right away, in order to set a positive tone for the meeting. Park ignored this advice. Leading off the first session, he delivered "a long, school marmish lecture on the North Korean threat."[45] He asked for U.S. withdrawal plans to be halted: "The most honest desire of every Korean is to avoid the recurrence of war. What is the surest guarantee against the recurrence of war? Continuation of the U.S. presence and end to withdrawals." Park also addressed the president's human rights concerns: "I have great admiration for your human rights," he began, but "every country has unique circumstances. You cannot apply the same yardstick to countries whose security is threatened as to countries whose security is not." He pressed the point on security:

> You went to the front line area, Mr. President, and drove back to Seoul. Our capital is only 25 miles from the DMZ. Right across the DMZ hundreds of thousands of soldiers are poised. We have suffered a tragic war . . . Some time ago several members of Congress came to call on me. I told them that if dozens of Soviet divisions were deployed at Baltimore, the U.S. Government could not permit its people to enjoy the same freedoms they do now. If these Soviets dug tunnels and sent commando units into the District of Columbia, then U.S. freedoms would be more limited. We support human rights policy. Respect for human rights is also our concern. I want as much freedom for our people as possible. But the survival of 37 million people is at stake, and some restraint is required.[46]

Carter became furious while Park continued talking for nearly an hour. One of Carter's aides noticed his habit of "working his jaw muscles" to stifle his anger. Passing a note to Vance and Defense Secretary Brown, Carter wrote, "If he goes on like this much longer, I'm going to pull every troop out of the country."[47]

After the meeting, Vance, Brown, Gleysteen, and Brzezinski rode together to the ambassador's residence. Carter vented his anger toward Gleysteen, asking why Park, "in the face of North Korea's huge buildup, was unwilling to increase his country's defense expenditure at least to the American level of 6 percent of the GDP and why Park was so resistant to some real measure of political liberalization." Carter accused his aides of conspiring against him and threatened to continue the withdrawal. Gleysteen tried to defend Park, saying that although his behavior during the session was "ill-advised," he was obviously "upset by Carter's refusal to reassure him about the troop issue." Moreover, the ambassador pointed out that comparing the defense expenditures of the United States with those of South Korea was misleading; South Korea was still a developing nation "and was already carrying a very heavy defense burden." He reminded Carter that in the past "we deliberately refrained from pushing Korea too hard on military expenditures for fear of strengthening the military and their authoritarian tendencies." Vance and Brown joined on Gleysteen's side while Brzezinski remained conspicuously silent. Witnessing the heated exchange through the rear window of the presidential limousine, Nicholas Platt, the National Security Council expert on Asia, turned to a companion and said, "There goes your Korea policy; it's all being decided right there now!"[48]

The mood of the next day's meeting improved considerably after Vance and Gleysteen were able to secure from Park a promise that he would spend more than 6 percent of GDP on defense. Park also said that he "understood" Carter's views on human rights and would make more efforts at liberalization. Carter agreed to reconsider the withdrawal plan and to deal "satisfactorily" with the military question when he got back to Washington. He then made an unusual effort to reach out to Park, asking the South Korean leader about his religious beliefs. Park replied he had none. Carter said, "I would like you to know about Christ," and "proposed to send Chang Hwan (Billy) Kim, an American-based Baptist evangelist who fashioned himself as the Korean Billy Graham, 'to explain our faith'."[49] Despite the initial setback, the summit had been a success. Gleysteen recalled Park's ebullient reaction after Carter's departure: "After Air Force One was airborne, Park, normally rather dour and distant in manner, looked at me, laughed in appreciation, and gave me a big bear hug, an act of spontaneity that astounded his attendants." On July 5, Park sent a message through his Korean CIA chief, Kim Chae-kyu, that he would be releasing 180 political prisoners over the next six months. On July 20, Brzezinski announced that Washington would suspend troop withdrawals from South Korea until 1981, the start of what would have been Carter's second term, in order to reassess the military balance on the peninsula.[50]

That chance did not come. In a sweeping reversal of Carter's policies, his successor, Ronald Reagan, increased the number of American forces in Korea to forty-three thousand, the highest level since 1972. Carter's futile efforts showed that even a resolute president was unable to sever the link between the United States and the Korean peninsula. His two-and-a-half-year withdrawal program ended with a reduction of only three thousand men. Meanwhile, in Seoul, Carter's criticism of Park's human rights record dealt a severe blow to the South Korean president's standing among his own people. The result would lead to another chapter in the unending Korean War.

CHAPTER NINETEEN

End of an Era

LIKE A LONE MAGNOLIA BLOSSOM BENDING TO THE WIND

Under heavy silence
Of a house in mourning
Only the cry of cicadas
Maam, maam, maam
Seem to long for you who is now gone

Under the August sun
The Indian Lilacs turn crimson
As if trying to heal the wounds of the mind

My wife has departed alone
Only I am left
Like a lone Magnolia blossom bending to the wind
Where can I appeal
The sadness of a broken heart

—PARK CHUNG HEE, August 20, 1974,
composed the day after his wife's state funeral[1]

Park Chung Hee awoke every morning to the picture of his wife, Yuk Yŏng-su. On a table under her portrait rested two vases of fresh chrysanthemums and next to them, in a wooden box, was a book about the late First Lady written by the celebrated poet Pak Mok-wŏl. Park missed her dreadfully. In the years after her death, Park had been under a great deal of strain. After a long period of rapid growth, South Korea was experiencing rising political unrest aggravated by an economy that was now stagnant, owing to the 1973 oil crisis and a worldwide recession. Carter's criticism of the regime's human rights record had also emboldened Park's critics. Park's aides were concerned that he was becoming emotionally unstable.

The tragedy took place at the National Theatre on August 15, 1974.

Park was giving a speech to commemorate the twenty-ninth anniversary of the nation's liberation from Japan when shots rang out. Yuk Yŏng-su slumped to the floor. The bullet, fired by a Japanese North Korean assassin, Moon Se-kwang, was meant for Park. Many believed that Park was unable to recover from the shock, and his leadership suffered as a consequence. "Park's power and handling of power changed when she died," observed his biographer Cho Kap-je. "He appeared to become more and more a shell of a man lacking his previous substance. His ability to balance his personality and the use of power had diminished considerably in the last years of his life."[2]

By the time of his death, Park was increasingly isolated. In the 1960s he had been able to travel freely, interacting with people without too much restraint, but since the assassination of his wife, his movements had become severely restricted, depriving him of human contact. Yuk also had had a humanizing influence on him, and without her he felt lost,

Park Chung Hee with his wife, Yuk Yŏng-su, celebrating Park's forty-ninth birthday, on September 30, 1966. Yuk was Park's second wife; the two had married on December 12, 1950, in the midst of the most harrowing phase of the Korean War. Yuk's father was against the match, but Yuk married Park anyway without her father's blessing or approval. (SAEMAŬL UNDONG CENTRAL TRAINING INSTITUTE)

vulnerable, and insecure. In Park's bedroom side drawer, he kept two rifles. "The man who had gained power by the gun," observed Cho, "felt that someday the gun would be turned on him."[3]

That day came sooner than anyone had expected. On the evening of October 26, 1979, while dining in the company of his associates, Kim Chae-kyu, the chief of the Korean Central Intelligence Agency (KCIA), and Ch'a Chi-ch'ŏl, Park's powerful head of Blue House security, Park was shot to death. His demise came not from the hands of a North Korean assassin, but from Kim, an original member of the revolutionary group that took power in May 1961 and one of Park's closest colleagues and advisors. During the investigation and trial, Kim espoused the view that the violent demonstrations and political unrest wracking the nation were an indication of growing public dissatisfaction with Park's rule, and that he believed the time was ripe for a democratic revolution.

However, the real motive for the assassination was something more prosaically personal. Friction between Kim and Park was exacerbated by Kim's growing resentment of Park's body guard, Ch'a Chi-ch'ŏl, who became more powerful and influential after he became the Blue House security chief in 1974 in the wake of Yuk Yŏng-su's death. "That night, it appeared that Kim Chae-kyu was only thinking of killing the president and he had no plan of action for what to do afterwards," wrote Cho Kap-je. "The fact that he had no idea about which command center was most effective for carrying out a coup d'etat shows that the assassination was not premeditated and was a more spontaneous decision."[4] Kim had shot Ch'a first before turning his gun on Park, allegedly saying, "Sir! The reason why the political situation is a mess is because you are served by this worm of a man [Ch'a]!" Subsequent investigations supported the conclusion that Park's murder was a crime of passion and not the result of a conspiracy.[5]

Park's assassination opened a new era of uncertainty in South Korean politics. By the time of his death, vocal critics of the Park regime were demanding greater freedom and democracy. At the same time, the reality of the unending war marked by frequent and violent military confrontations along the DMZ and costly terrorist actions instigated by Kim Il Sung's regime made the possibility of a transition to democracy in the South very unlikely.[6]

Kwangju Uprising

For a time after Park's death, it looked as if Kim Il Sung's cherished dream of fomenting revolution in the South might happen. Taking advantage of the atmosphere of uncertainty following the events of October 26, opposition politicians and student activists began to loudly voice their demands to lift martial law and hold direct presidential elections. The large-scale release of dissidents in July that Park had agreed to during Carter's visit had emboldened Park's critics, and they demanded immediate changes to the *Yusin* constitution. Meanwhile, government and military leaders argued that the *Yusin* charter must remain in effect until the late president's successor could be chosen, to ensure stability and security. Acting President Ch'oe Kyu-ha, a "soft-spoken" former diplomat and Park's prime minister, was formally elected interim president on December 6. But Ch'oe had no independent political backing, and the real power lay with the military.

That power asserted itself on the night of December 12, when Gen. Chŏn Tu-hwan (Chun Doo Hwan), who had taken control of South Korea's intelligence apparatus since Park's assassination, staged a coup. Ambassador Gleysteen and the senior U.S. commander in Korea, Gen. John Wickham, stood by essentially as spectators, having little leverage over the unfolding events. "The era of America's paternal influence over the ROK had passed," Wickham concluded. "Since the United States had significantly reduced its military deployment . . . and had recently threatened to withdraw even those forces, ROK leaders doubted the reliability and continuity of America's commitment." Although President Carter had spent his entire presidency pressuring South Korea to liberalize and reduce the influence of the military, in the end he got exactly the opposite.[7] The events of December 12 put an end to any hope for the emergence of democratic and civilian rule. The South Korean people were outraged.

Chŏn had at first blamed the unrest on a "minority" of student radicals, professors, and intellectuals. However, with daily protests continuing unabated for months on end, he suddenly changed his tune and on May 13 played the North Korea card. Widespread arrests of students and oppositional leaders followed, and martial law was declared on

South Korean soldiers on guard in downtown Kwangju, May 23, 1980. The Kwangju uprising was a pivotal moment in South Korea's struggle for democracy. Swept up by a tide of demonstrations following the death of Park Chung Hee and the military coup that brought Chŏn Tu-hwan to power, the brutality of the new regime's response outraged many Korean citizens. The Kwangju Uprising also tainted South Koreans' view of the United States due to Washington's alleged role in the suppression of the uprising, thus giving rise to fervent anti-Americanism, especially among students. While student dissidents began questioning the U.S. role in Korean affairs, they also began challenging their nation's traditional hostility toward North Korea. (AP PHOTOS)

May 17. The citizens of Kwangju rose up in anger when they received news that Kim Dae-jung, who had almost defeated Park in the 1972 presidential elections, was arrested in the early morning hours of May 18. Kwangju was the capital city of Kim's home region, the South Chŏlla province in southwestern Korea, and Kim was their local hero. This region had been neglected during the economic boom of the 1960s and 1970s because Park had concentrated on developing the southeastern region of Korea, where he was born. Resentment over regional favoritism fueled the anger evoked by the arrest of Kwangju's favorite son. Its citizens responded by seizing weapons from local police, turning the city into a fortress, while demanding the release of Kim and the restoration of democracy. Chŏn responded by ordering the city surrounded by army units. He then unleashed them to retake control. The outcome of the battle between well-armed and organized regular soldiers, many with combat experience in Vietnam, against a hastily assembled citizen militia armed with only a hodge-podge collection of light weapons was predictable.

The city was retaken on May 27. Official government estimates of the number of civilians killed ranged from 170 to 240, but the actual number was likely higher. The brutal put down and killings fueled an intense national opposition to the Chŏn regime, especially from students. Rumors of U.S. complicity also fanned anti-American sentiment.[8] But it was the magnitude of state violence and the complete devastation of democratic forces and processes after the Kwangju uprising that drove many South Korean dissidents and intellectuals to search for the origins of their nation's predicament. While Kim Il Sung continued his efforts to disrupt South Korean society with a new emphasis on terrorism, these students looked to North Korea for answers to their nation's problems.

Students and the Politics of Legitimacy

One way students did this was by openly embracing North Korea's version of the ongoing war between the two Koreas. Accepting Kim Il Sung's view of the conflict as that between Korean revolutionary nationalists in the North and American "imperialists" and their "lackey" South Koreans meant that South Korea was seen as a "puppet" creation of the Americans. Students' embrace of this North Korean line also recycled Kim's *chuch'e* ideology (*chuch'eron*), which stressed North Korea's self-reliance and active resistance to foreign powers.[9] By the mid-1980s, *chuch'eron* had gained widespread influence among student dissidents and intellectuals.

This influence was manifested in two important ways. First, students began to directly challenge and subvert decades of cold war rhetoric that portrayed North Korea as *the* enemy of the South. The officially accepted relationship between friend and foe that had been part of the established South Korean line since the Korean War was turned upside down in *chuch'eron.* Instead, the *real* enemy of the people was the United States, not North Korea. These dissidents saw the U.S. decision to divide, occupy, and establish a military regime in southern Korea as a direct expression of imperialist ambitions in the Korean peninsula. They also questioned the very legitimacy of the South Korean state by playing up Kim Il Sung's resistance to the UN foreign-sponsored elections in 1948, on which the ROK claimed its legal basis. Moreover, whereas state-sponsored histories saw North Korea's menace solely in political and ideological terms, students argued that the United States, the "new" enemy, posed a threat that was much more radical and fundamental. The American capitalist culture represented an invasive force that threatened to undermine the very core of Korean national identity. The decadent individualism of the West, which these dissidents associated with consumerism, sexual promiscuity, and crime, presented external threats that required a nationalist strategy to combat.

Second, the students' rejection of the established South Korean view of North Korea as the main "enemy" forced them to come up with new ways of depicting the North-South relationship. Interestingly, they did this by drawing on a traditional canon of Confucian morality tales about women's steadfast loyalty during periods of loss and forced separation from their husbands. The eighteenth-century *Tale of Ch'unhyang*, Korea's most renowned love story, was especially influential. It concerns the love between the son of an upper-class family named Yi Myong-nyŏng and the daughter of a socially despised *kiseang* (female entertainer) named Ch'unhyang. After their engagement, Yi is called to duty in the capital far away from Ch'unhyang. Shortly thereafter, Ch'unhyang is sent to prison when she refuses the advances of the evil local governor. Finally, her husband returns, rescues her, and punishes the evil governor, and they live happily ever after. Every Korean, North or South, is familiar with this tale. Indeed, it has been the subject of numerous books, dramatic performances, movies, and cartoons in both Koreas.[10]

Students thus used the Ch'unhyang narrative in their portrayal of the division. As an exemplary model of Korean virtues, unwavering, faithful, and determined to undergo whatever tribulations required to resist the forces of evil, the loyal Ch'unhyang came to represent South Korea. Ch'unhyang remains true to her husband (North Korea) by defiantly resisting political authority and not succumbing to the advances of the lascivious evil governor (the United States). Implicit references to the Ch'unhyang story appeared repeatedly in student illustrations and pamphlets. Images of two lovers about to fall into each other's embrace or of a happy couple triumphantly running across the DMZ revealed the connection between marital union and a reunified nation. Indeed, to think of North and South Korea as lovers, struggling to overcome the division of the peninsula, challenged decades of cold war rhetoric.

If marriage represented the unification of the two Koreas and the end of the war, then the division of the peninsula was often compared to

"The Road to Unification," illustration of a man and woman embracing in the shape of the Korean peninsula, used in a Seoul National University student pamphlet, April 1989. (AUTHOR'S COLLECTION)

rape. Rape signaled the breakdown of the marital bond and thus symbolically came to stand for the nation at war with itself. During colonial times, rape was often used to evoke Korea's experience under Japanese colonialism. It was also rooted in the real-life experiences of thousands of Korean women who were forcibly and systematically recruited by the Japanese government to serve as prostitutes (euphemistically referred to as "comfort woman") for Japanese soldiers during World War II. In both colonialism and the division, the image of the violated woman carried with it the values of purity against filth, and of chastity against foreign contamination. A famous poem by the "resistance" poet Kim Nam-ju, "Pulgamjŭng" (1988), shows how prostitution, rape, and violence become interrelated themes in their symbolism for the division:

My elder sister
Is our liberated country's lady of the night.
To borrow one highly venomous tongue,
She is a widely gaped vulva like a
Chestnut burr under the boots of the U.S. Eighth Army.

My little sister is our modernized country's new woman.
To borrow an expression of a common boy,
She is a widely open tourist vulva under the Japanese yen.

How deep did we lapse by rotting.
Not awakening no matter how much [we are shaken].
Not feeling no matter how much [we are pinched].
Ah, my half-piece country,
After 36 years of broken waist, when will you open your eyes from
Your long, long humiliating sleep . . .[11]

The title "Pulgamjŭng," meaning frigidity, refers to a woman's guilt or fear of becoming pregnant or contracting a venereal disease. Rape constituted not only a threat to the marital bond but also a crisis of maternity and female reproduction. For many student dissidents, the danger of Western, and specifically American, cultural contamination was perceived as a threat to the integrity and purity of the Korean nation. To defend the nation's inner "core," Korean women needed to resist the advances of the lascivious foreign male. The reality of American military presence in South Korea exacerbated this perceived crisis. The murder of a Korean prostitute by an American soldier in November 1992 provoked a national outrage igniting large demonstrations in Seoul. Students demonstrated for a full week while even taxi drivers refused to serve American soldiers. The accidental death of two schoolgirls caused by two American soldiers ten years later, on June 13, 2002, caused a similar wave of anti-Americanism that No Mu-hyŏn (Roh Mu-hyun) rode to the presidency in 2003.[12]

The focus on sweeping South Korea clean of America's "putrefying influence" was, of course, a central theme of Kim Il Sung's *chuch'e* ideology. In contrast to North Korea, which was deemed clean and pure and had established itself "without reliance on foreigners," the South was deemed polluted in every way. The description of South Korea in the North Korean novel *Encounter* (*Mannam*) was standard North Korean propaganda: "[South Korea was] the flashiest of American colonies . . . but look under the silk encasing and you see the body of what has degenerated to a foul whore of America." South Korea has been "covered in bruises from where it has been kicked black and blue by the American soldiers' boot."[13] Similar preoccupations with purity and pollution also appeared in South Korea's dissident rhetoric, combining calls for the two Koreas' "national rebirth" with the hope for deliverance from the war and division perpetuated by the United States. This rallying cry for a "liberated" and reunified Korea during a 1989 student demonstration in Seoul was typical of student hyperbole during this period:

> Youth! You who vigorously strike the bell of freedom at dawn, stomp out the dark shadows of the Stars and Stripes with bloody cries, and with longing for the sun-shining Mt. Paektu, work for the independence and reunification of this land. Only then will spring arrive joyously. Let us finish together the incomplete revolution so that we can live in a better world.[14]

The idea that students were struggling toward spring merely recycled North Korean propaganda about the "unfinished" revolution. Korea's spring meant a return to the nation's pristine origins before the peninsula was divided and before the South went from a Japanese colony to an American one. Appropriating Kim Il Sung's propaganda, student

Hours before taking to the streets to do battle with riot policemen, usually at the entrance of the university gate, students put on musical performances, dances, and historical dramas about key events in Korea's modern history. On the occasion of the ninth anniversary of the Kwangju uprising, students at Chŏnnam University in Kwangju recounted those events in a musical performance. Kwangju, May 18, 1989. (AUTHOR'S COLLECTION)

dissidents thus offered a vision of South Korea's *true* liberation from all foreign powers by embracing the *chuch'e* idea as their own.

The naiveté of these fanciful musings aside, by focusing on the virtues of Koreaness versus foreignness, student dissidents had idealized the North Korean regime. North Korean officials were no doubt heartened by the spectacle of South Korean students hurling Molotov cocktails at riot policemen dressed in full battle gear on the streets of Seoul, for it reconfirmed the regime's old propaganda line that the South Korean people were chafing under the yoke of American imperialism and longed to be liberated by their northern brethren. Even as late as the 1980s, Kim Il Sung had still not relinquished the dream of fermenting a nationalist revolution in the South.

In the legitimacy wars between North and South Korea, South Korean student dissidents had thus clearly sided with the North. In their embrace of Kim Il Sung's *chuch'e* thought, which became de rigeur within the mainstream of the student movement during the 1980s, they also condemned the United States and the American-backed "puppet" regime in the South as the main enemy.

Although some of this revolutionary rhetoric later softened and became absorbed into mainstream South Korean society well into the turn of the twenty-first century, it would take P'yŏngyang's economic collapse and the exposure of its nuclear ambitions to rid many South Koreans of their romantic illusions.[15]

PART IV

AFTER THE COLD WAR

The collapse of East European communism and the dissolution of the Soviet Union in 1989–91 spelled disaster for North Korea, which to survive had relied extensively on Soviet aid and concessional pricing for trade. The reality of an impoverished and isolated North Korea was laid bare at a time when South Korea was basking in the afterglow of hosting the 1988 Summer Olympics. The changing geopolitical environment and the stark contrast between the South and the North led South Korea's President No T'ae-u (Roh Tae-woo), elected in 1987, to pursue rapprochement with the communist world, including North Korea. No's Nordpolitik policy aimed to establish close relations with North Korea's allies and thereby induce it to open up to the world. Although Nordpolitik saw considerable diplomatic and economic success, it did not open up the North.

When it was discovered that Iraq had failed to disclose its nuclear program in the aftermath of the first Gulf War in 1991, Hans Blix, the director of the International Atomic Energy Agency (IAEA), the UN agency responsible for enforcing the Nuclear Nonproliferation Treaty (NPT), decided to get tougher in demanding that NPT signatories establish acceptable inspection regimes as soon as possible. North Korea became the first test case, one that the North had not expected. This led to conflicts between North Korean officials and IAEA inspectors and the eventual withdrawal of North Korea from the NPT in March 1993. The possibility of a second Korean War loomed ominously on the horizon.

War was averted when former president Jimmy Carter helped to broker a deal between the United States and North Korea. North Korea agreed that it would abandon its nuclear program if the United States and other allies agreed to provide two light-water reactors (LWRs) for power generation. Signed in October 1994, the Agreed Framework also outlined steps for normalization of relations between the United States and North Korea and assurance that the Americans would never threaten North Korea with nuclear weapons. In 1994, North Korea experienced two catastrophes: the beginnings of a devastating famine and the death of Kim Il Sung. Unable to feed its own people but refusing to initiate necessary reforms, North Korea resorted to provocations and brinkmanship to survive. After discovering that North Korea had secretly begun a uranium enrichment program, the United States declared the Agreed Framework void, and construction of the LWRs stopped. In 2006, North Korea surprised the world by testing a nuclear device. A second nuclear device was tested in 2009. Following the sinking of a South Korean ship in March 2010, allegedly by North Korea, North-South relations have deteriorated to the lowest point in years. North Korea experienced another blow in December 2011 following the unexpected death of Kim Jong Il and the anointment of his younger son, Kim Chŏng-ŭn (Kim Jong-un), as successor. Isolated and impoverished, the P'yŏngyang regime is transitioning under the watchful eye of its only ally and benefactor, China. So what is next for North Korea? How will the Korean War finally end?

CHAPTER TWENTY

North Korea and the World

On the morning of July 9, 1994, North Koreans woke up to hear that "there will be a critical announcement at noon on TV. Everybody must watch it." When the hour arrived, twenty-one million anxious North Koreans gathered around television sets to see a solemn official, dressed in black, read a prepared statement:

> We, the working class, collective farmers, People's Army soldiers, intellectuals, young students, Central Committee of the Party, Military Commission of the Party, National Defense Commission of the DPRK, Central People's Committee, and Administration Council report with mournful heart to the people that the General Secretary of the Chosun Workers' Party, Premier of the DPRK and Great Leader, Comrade Kim Il Sung, passed away unexpectedly at 2AM on July 8, 1994.

The cause of Kim's sudden demise was a massive heart attack. At the time of his death, North Korea was a failed state. It was, as one observer wrote, "an island of stagnation in a sea of East Asian growth."[1] For most of North Korea's existence, Kim Il Sung had been able to rely on the support of both China and the Soviet Union. Following the turmoil of the Cultural Revolution and Sino-American rapprochement, North Korea depended almost exclusively on the largesse of the Soviet Union, which until 1984 provided more than $1 billion in foreign aid and credits annually, mostly in soft loans that P'yŏngyang did not repay. An Eastern European scholar noted, "A distinctive feature of the creditor-debtor relationship . . . was continuous long-term loans extended by the Soviet Union and frequent deferral of North Korean repayment."[2] North Koreans could not even "produce enough clothing for themselves."[3]

The pattern of defaulting on loans was characteristic of North Korea's trade regime and foreign policy to secure continual and concessional foreign capital. According to the economist Nicholas Eberstadt, this system is distinguished by a "political conception of international economic relations wherein goods and services are understood to flow not so much through voluntary commercial exchange between contractually equal partners, but through a struggle between states and systems." In other words, North Korea viewed the loans not as contractual obligations, but as rewards, "as a sort of tribute from abroad."[4] The North's peculiar triangular relationship with the Soviet Union and China had encouraged this pattern to develop and continue. The "tributary" system, however, ended rather abruptly after the fall of the Berlin Wall in 1989, the dissolution of the Soviet Union in 1991, and the end of the cold war in Europe. Russia and China's abandonment of the "friendship price" system and demand for hard currency for exports resulted in a steep decline in the North Korean economy. The DPRK had fallen into a classic poverty trap. Stagnant economic growth stifled investments to grow the economy. The North's economy was degraded by a lack of innovation and by a dependence on imported raw materials with no resources to pay for them.

Meanwhile, South Korea was booming, its success highlighted by the 1988 Summer Olympics in Seoul, which marked a turning point in the city's status and relationship with the world. South Koreans dramatically showcased to billions around the world that they were no longer the "poverty-stricken Asian war victim" of the past, but a vibrant, rich, and modern society. The contrast with the North could not have been more striking.[5] Furthermore, South Korea had just made a peaceful and successful transition to democracy. On December 16, 1987, after nearly three decades of authoritarian rule, South Koreans chose their first democratically elected president, a former general and Chŏn Tu-hwan's close friend No T'ae-u. This transition was in large part due to students who came together with ordinary citizens during the summer of 1987 to demand a direct presidential election. After weeks of protests, Chun's chosen successor, No T'ae-u, conceded to these demands. But during the election a split in the opposition led to No's victory with just 36 percent of the popular vote. Nevertheless, the election had been fair and democracy secured. The election and the Olympics symbolized South Korea's political and economic coming of age. For the first time in over five decades, the South could claim victory in its legitimacy war with the North. But could this victory end the war?

The time had come to find out. On July 7, 1988, four months after his inauguration and on the eve of the Seoul Olympics, President No announced a new approach to relations with North Korea. In his memoirs, No wrote that he had "agonized over how to resolve the stand-off with the North" and then thought of how the Qin emperor had defeated his enemies at the end of the Warring States period (BCE 475–221) and unified China. "The strategy used by Emperor Qin called for 'establishing close relations with distant states in order to destroy the enemy nearby.'" No therefore "decided to invoke this strategy of making friends with distant enemies." Nordpolitik, as the policy was known, signaled South Korea's new openness to communist nations around the world and led to the South's predominance over the North in a changing international climate. "We would follow the road to P'yŏngyang through Eastern Europe, Moscow and Beijing."[6]

Hungary was the first communist country to respond and establish diplomatic relations. In a dramatic reversal of fortunes, South Korean aid was a key factor. South Korea offered a loan of $625 million to help Hungary's struggling economy. Full diplomatic relations were established on February 1, 1989, over P'yŏngyang's vociferous objections. The Soviet Union soon followed. Until Mikhail Gorbachev came to power in 1985, South Korea was little known and not of any significant concern to the Soviet Union. After the success of the Seoul Olympics, Moscow took steps to establish relations with South Korea. In 1989, trade offices were opened in Moscow and Seoul, and direct sea and air routes established between the two countries.[7] Politically, in a dramatic turnaround, Moscow dropped its opposition to South Korean membership in the United Nations. These developments were, naturally, distressing to the North Korean regime. Hoping to halt Moscow's drift toward Seoul, Kim Il Sung invited Gorbachev to P'yŏngyang. Gorbachev was scheduled to visit China in the spring of 1989, and Kim asked him to stop on his way to Beijing. But despite Kim's desperate pleas, Gorbachev declined.

The rejection was a blow to Kim, who had wanted to obtain Moscow's reassurance of continued support. Gorbachev's trip to China was also disturbing because it signaled the beginning of a closer relation between Moscow and Beijing. North Korea had survived by playing the two communist powers against each other, but this leverage would no longer be available. Gorbachev further inflamed Kim's anxieties by announcing, while in China, his new friendship with Seoul. It was no comfort to Kim that Gorbachev viewed better relations with South Korea as having no effect on Moscow's relations with the North since the main purpose of his Korea policy was "helping the peace process on the Korean peninsula."[8]

In May 1990, Gorbachev met with his senior foreign policy advisor Anatoly Dobrynin, the legendary Soviet ambassador to the United States from 1962 to 1986. He instructed Dobrynin to convey to President No the message that Gorbachev was willing to meet him in San Francisco in June after his summit meeting with President George H. W. Bush in Washington. He also asked Dobrynin to explore the possibility of obtaining a major loan from South Korea. Dobrynin recalled that Gorbachev simply said, "We need some money." The San Francisco meeting was confirmed, and when No and Gorbachev met, the Soviet leader gave his commitment to "peaceful reunification" of the Koreas and the two discussed the normalization of relations between their countries. At the press conference after the meeting, an ebullient No told reporters that "as a result of today's meeting, the cold war ice on the Korean peninsula has now begun to crack." He reaffirmed that "Seoul did not wish to isolate North Korean regime" and that the ultimate goal of Nordpolitik was to induce North Korea to open up to the world.[9]

Events moved quickly after the meeting in San Francisco. On September 30, 1990, Moscow and Seoul established full diplomatic relations. This was originally supposed to have taken place on January 1, 1991, but the Soviets decided to move the date forward due to the extremely rude treatment they received from P'yŏngyang. "The communiqué stated the date of normalized relations as '1 January 1991,'" No recalled, "and Foreign Minister Shevardnadze, with his own pen, crossed it out and wrote '30 September 1990' right at the foreign ministers meeting." It was, the South Korean president wrote triumphantly, "a gift from an angry Shevardnadze."[10]

The Soviet Union also agreed to stop all military aid and cooperation with North Korea in return for South Korea's economic assistance. "The Soviet Union kept its promise and thereafter not a single Soviet fighter jet, tank or missile was shipped to North Korea," No later remarked. "As a result, for $1.4 billion in economic loans, South Korean security gained tens of billions of dollars worth of security."[11] Gorbachev explained his reasons for the abrupt change in North Korean policy in his memoir: "It was clear that we could not, for obsolete ideological reasons (i.e. because of our ties with North Korea), continue opposing the establishment of normal relations with his [No's] country which showed an exceptional dynamism and had become a force to be reckoned with, both in the Asia-Pacific region and in the wider world."[12]

China also moved toward a closer relationship with South Korea. In May 1991, Chinese Premier Li Peng announced that China would not oppose admission of both North and South Korea to the United Nations. This was another huge blow to Kim Il Sung. Since the only possible veto against South Korean membership was the Soviet Union, which had already announced its support for Seoul, Kim had no choice but to follow the winds and announce that North Korea would apply for UN membership too. Kim had long opposed dual membership for North and South Korea, but it was now evident that the world considered the two Koreas as separate sovereign entities. Adding to North Korea's woes was China's announcement in early 1992 that it would normalize relations with Seoul. On August 24, 1992, China and South Korea established diplomatic relations. The previous December the Soviet Union had dissolved.[13]

The dramatic transformation of the geopolitical situation around the divided peninsula at the end of the 1980s and in the early 1990s appeared to spell the doom of the North Korean regime. Its economy in shambles, traditional sources of support all gone, and its founding and inspiring leader dead, few believed that the anachronistic regime could survive much longer. Even South Korean students became disillusioned, knowing full well that Kim's utopia was a chimera and the South had won the war. Yet, despite these setbacks, North Korea did not collapse, nor does it appear likely that it will any time soon. The regime continues to present itself to its people as a defiant power that, in stark contrast to the "Yankee colony in the south," embodies the true spirit of the self-reliant Korean nation. The tenaciousness with which it still clings to the myth of its greatness and fearlessness in the face of great odds defies easy predictions about its future. North Korea's refusal to go the way of other communist states demonstrates the enduring legacy of Kim Il Sung as well as the power of the unending Korean War to shape contemporary events.

Showdown

What is the secret to the extraordinary enduring power of North Korea and the first and only communist dynasty, the Kim family regime? Traditional, historical, and ideological factors—the traditional patriarchal and hierarchical social structure of Korea's Confucian past, Korea's history of isolationism, and the fierce anti-imperialist nationalism that developed during the colonial period—account for part of the answer, but part also lies in Kim Il Sung's strategy for national survival, which provided just enough material sustenance to avert collapse. The strategy was characterized by a unique "aid-maximizing economic strategy" whereby external aid rather than development and economic growth became the indispensable foundation for national viability.[14] Although Kim Il Sung touted self-determination (*chuch'e*) as the fundamental principle of his regime, it was a policy that in reality required dependency. One of the more extraordinary features of Kim's foreign policy was his uncanny ability to navigate between Great Power interests to achieve his own ends. He was the original author of the Korean War, but it was Stalin who made it possible and Mao who largely fought it. After the war, he was able to secure his position by playing China and the Soviet Union against each other, as well as obtain vast amounts of economic aid from both powers. The end of the cold war closed North Korea's sources of support, but Kim again showed his extraordinary ability to leverage competing interests for his gain, this time by playing the nuclear card.

The North Korean nuclear program began in 1985 after three decades of lobbying the Soviet Union for help. During the 1960s and 1970s, the Kremlin had been unwilling to support North Korea's repeated requests for a nuclear power plant because of its suspicion of Kim Il Sung's belligerent intentions. Since P'yŏngyang was hardly a cooperative ally, this refusal was understandable. North Korea's worsening economic condition was another reason for the refusal. The plan was expensive, and North Korea had no means to pay for it. The DPRK made another request in early 1976, even as highly contentious negotiations over North Korea's debt were taking place in Moscow.[15]

Given the frosty relationship between the two communist countries, the dire state of the North's economy, and the long-term pattern of

North Korean belligerence, why did the Soviet leadership finally change its mind and approve of nuclear cooperation with the P'yŏngyang regime in 1985? A major reason was renewed cold war tensions and the increasing international isolation of the Soviet Union during this period. Following the Soviet invasion of Afghanistan in December 1979, the United States decided to increase diplomatic, military, and economic pressures on the Soviet Union during a period when it was already suffering economically. Sino-Soviet relations were also at a standstill. While Moscow's relations with China and the United States worsened, North Korea's strategic importance to the Soviet Union increased. As one observer put it, "Nuclear cooperation between Moscow and P'yŏngyang was one carrot that the Chinese could not match."[16] At the same time, since the Soviets knew they could not maintain effective control over the P'yŏngyang regime, they wanted to be sure that Kim Il Sung's hands were "tied by as many international agreements as possible."[17] The Soviet Union thus agreed to supply four LWRs in 1985, but only if North Korea joined the NPT, which it did in December of that year. The NPT required signatories to sign a safeguard inspection agreement within eighteen months that permitted inspections to identify violations.

However, due to a mix-up in paperwork, the inspection agreements were never signed. By then, the prospects of North Korea receiving the Soviet reactors had dimmed, owing to the waning fortunes of the Soviet economy. Kim Il Sung was stuck with the treaty commitments but without the Soviet reactors. He was thus forced to embark on an indigenous nuclear program at a place called Yŏngbyŏn. It was not until 1991, after the Persian Gulf War (code-named Operation Desert Storm), that pressure to inspect the North Korean nuclear facilities became an international issue. Until then, the IAEA had limited inspections of civilian nuclear sites that NPT signatories had voluntarily reported, but the Gulf War crisis revealed that Iraq, an NPT signatory, had undisclosed secret nuclear sites. Facing "withering criticism" for ineffectiveness and timidity, the IAEA and its new director, Hans Blix, decided to get tough. North Korea became its first target.[18]

When North Korean officials refused to allow the inspection of two installations at Yŏngbyŏn that American intelligence had identified as potential sites for secret nuclear activity, a showdown with the IAEA became inevitable. The IAEA told the North Koreans that if these installations were not open to inspections it would ask the UN Security Council to consider sanctions. The situation, thought Blix, tested the credibility and standing of the IAEA, but more important, allowing North Korea to ignore the required inspections could fundamentally undermine the NPT and the global nonproliferation program. On March 12, 1993, P'yŏngyang made the stunning announcement that North Korea intended to withdraw from the NPT rather than submit to inspections. Three days later, the IAEA Board voted to hand the matter over to the UN Security Council and ordered their inspectors home.

With this defiant act, North Korea had seized the initiative. It was now up to the United States, South Korea, and the international community to persuade P'yŏngyang not to withdraw from the NPT. The United States offered to improve political and economic relations and give security assurances if North Korea remained in the NPT and allowed IAEA inspections. When it became clear that the negotiations were going nowhere, the new Clinton administration decided to ask the United Nations to lay the groundwork for economic sanctions. The move came hours after North Korea threatened war in March 1994 if Washington and Seoul mounted a pressure campaign. In an ominous exchange between North and South Korean officials, captured on video, the North Korean delegate warned his South Korean counterpart that "Seoul is not far away from here. If a war breaks out Seoul will turn into a sea of fire." The statement was so extraordinary that the South Korean government broadcasted it on national television, instantly enflaming anti–North Korean passions. Realizing that the comments had backfired, Kim Il Sung went out of his way to disown the "sea of fire" comment, saying that it had been a "mistake" by the negotiator.[19]

Just three months after his inauguration, in January 1994, President Bill Clinton faced the first international crisis of his administration. As the United States pushed for UN Security Council sanctions against North Korea, the P'yŏngyang regime repeatedly denounced the move, declaring "sanctions are a declaration of war." China and Russia became concerned as the United States and North Korea inexorably moved toward direct confrontation. Prime Minister Li Peng warned that "pressure . . . can only complicate the situation on the Korean peninsula, and it will add to the tension."[20] Russia was also reluctant to support UN sanctions for similar reasons, and it proposed as an alternative a forum with the two Koreas, China, the United States, Japan, Russia, and the IAEA "to work out a balanced approach to denuclearization and international guarantees for North Korea." The Americans were "miffed" mostly because the negotiation track had been tried in vain for over a year and they thought such a conference would lead nowhere.[21]

Unlike the Americans, however, China and Russia had been dealing directly with North Korean recalcitrance for over forty years; both countries had successfully thwarted previous North Korean plans to restart another war on the Korean peninsula. They also understood what Washington apparently did not: that the crisis was neither unique nor isolated but linked to a long series of provocations aiming to bolster Kim Il Sung's hold on power during a period of political uncertainty. The North Korean leadership would view UN sanctions as an international slap in the face that directly challenged the myth of Kim Il Sung as a fearsome and respected leader. It was to uphold and strengthen this myth that had been behind the capture of the *Pueblo* in 1968. Neither China nor Russia wanted to humiliate Kim Il Sung in front of the world. They feared destabilizing the regime, for its collapse would likely result in millions of refugees crossing the Chinese and Russian borders, a calamitous event. If necessary, China and Russia were willing to exercise their veto power in the UN Security Council to stop a sanctions resolution. "It's an international rule now to solve all issues through dialogue," declared Zhang Tingyan, China's ambassador to South Korea. "Why should the North Korean nuclear problem be an exception? China cannot agree to sanctions or any other measures."[22]

Japan too opposed sanctions for a variety of domestic concerns. Sanctions would require stopping the substantial flow of money sent by ethnic Koreans in Japan to their relatives in North Korea. These remittances were estimated to be roughly $600 million annually. Such an action could expose Japan to a severe backlash from pro-North residents, including the possibility of violent acts and terrorism.[23] If the North launched another attack, U.S. bases in Japan would undoubtedly be targeted with missiles. A war or a North Korean collapse also raised the specter of a massive influx of refugees.

South Korea, fearing both war and North Korean collapse, even if the latter resulted in fulfilling the long-cherished dream of reunification, was ambivalent about sanctions as well. Attitudes toward reunification had changed after South Koreans learned the economic and social cost of German reunification. "On the one hand, the absolute majority wants to see reunification," said Kil Jeong Woo, director of policy studies at the Research Institute for National Unification (RINU), a government think tank in Seoul. "That's the emotional side. On the economic side, after witnessing the German experience, we should be more realistic." With estimates for the costs of absorbing North Korea ranging from $200 billion to more than $1 trillion over a decade, many South Koreans had trepidations over what reunification might mean for their newfound prosperity. RINU calculated in 1994 that "raising North Korea's economic level to 60 percent that of the South would take 10 years and cost $40 billion each year, an amount equal to one-eighth of South Korea's annual economic output." Rather than a "big bang" approach to unification, which could result in millions of refugees streaming across the border, the South Korean government began emphasizing "stability, not unity."[24]

In pressing for UN sanctions, the Clinton administration was thus swimming against a strong current of opposition. With Chinese and Russian vetoes of a sanctions resolution certain, North Korea was under no pressure to compromise. Ironically, the same regional concerns that had frustrated Carter's efforts to withdraw U.S. ground troops from South Korea in the 1970s also complicated Clinton's attempts to get tough over the North Korean nuclear program. No one in the region wanted to upset the fragile balance of power on the Korean peninsula and risk another conflict. This was the dilemma that the Clinton administration faced when Kim Il Sung raised the ante and precipitated a showdown that would lead the United States and North Korea to the brink of war.

Defueling Crisis

On April 19, 1994, North Korea notified the IAEA of its intention to withdraw spent fuel rods from a nuclear reactor in Yŏngbyŏn, but without IAEA monitoring. The announcement was a direct rebuff of both the United States and the UN, which had repeatedly warned North Korean authorities not to take this action. Plutonium could be extracted from the rods at a reprocessing plant in Yŏngbyŏn to provide P'yŏngyang with the main ingredient for a nuclear weapon. Secretary of Defense William Perry declared that Washington would seek sanctions if the fuel rods were withdrawn without IAEA scrutiny, calling the situation "a very substantial near-term crisis." The estimate was that there was enough plutonium in the eight thousand rods for four or five nuclear weapons. The removal of the rods without IAEA monitoring posed another serious problem. In essence, the IAEA would not be able to determine the history of previous refueling operations and thus the total number of rods available for reprocessing and the total amount of plutonium North Korea might have accumulated. The agency complained that if the withdrawal was not monitored, "it would result in irreparable loss of the agency's ability to verify that plutonium-laden fuel was not being diverted for use in nuclear weapons." In 1986, for example, the CIA estimated that the Yŏngbyŏn reactor had been shut down for up to 110 days. It was unclear how many of the eight thousand rods might have been replaced at that time, but CIA estimates put the amount of plutonium that might have been obtained to be enough for one or two nuclear bombs. When the actual unloading of the fuel rods began in early May of 1994, the IAEA sent a team led by Dmitri Perricos to witness the operation. According to Perricos, the unloading process was "a big mess," which he believed was deliberate to keep the world guessing on how much plutonium the North possessed, in a high-stakes game of brinkmanship.[25]

The Joint Chiefs were particularly incensed and were asking, in effect, "How long are we going to let them walk all over us?" The Clinton administration once again pressed for UN sanctions, but the difficulty in devising and winning support for sanctions, especially from China and Russia, undercut the message of resolve that the United States sought to convey. In secret, a military option was now put on the table. On June 10, Secretary Perry presented to President Clinton a detailed contingency plan for bombing Yŏngbyŏn. Military considerations included reinforcing military forces in Korea and the region to deter any North Korean military action in response to UN sanctions. These options ranged from two thousand personnel to fill out wartime headquarters staff, to a major force of fifty thousand troops, four hundred aircraft, and fifty ships, an option that would require a reserve call-up and the evacuation of U.S. and foreign noncombatant personnel from South Korea. Clinton was told that renewed war could result in 52,000 U.S. and 490,000 South Korean military casualties in the first ninety days, in addition to a large number of civilian casualties. Furthermore, the inevitable collapse of the

North Korean regime would send millions of refugees flooding across Asia, with destabilizing effects in China, South Korea, and Japan.[26]

On June 16, Clinton and his advisors considered the military options. Perry reminded the group of the danger of starting a cycle of measures and countermeasures that a military contingency to deter North Korean action against sanctions could spark. He evoked Barbara Tuchman's account in *The Guns of August* of such a cycle propelled by "cross-purposes, misunderstandings and inadvertence" in the days leading to World War I. Could this cycle be stopped? The meeting was in its second hour when Clinton was informed that former president Jimmy Carter was on the line from P'yŏngyang. Carter had offered his services to Clinton in a last-ditch effort to resolve the crisis and went to P'yŏngyang ostensibly as a private citizen in response to a standing invitation to visit that Kim Il Sung had extended. Robert Gallucci, assistant secretary of state for political-military affairs, stepped out of the Cabinet Room to take the call. Carter told Gallucci that Kim Il Sung had agreed not to expel the IAEA inspectors and to keep the monitoring equipment in place in return for resuming talks and no sanctions. Kim, in effect, had promised to freeze his nuclear program. He would not place new fuel rods in the reactors, nor would he reprocess the irradiated ones that had already been removed. Carter said that he planned to describe the progress he had made with the North Korean dictator on CNN. Stunned, Gallucci returned to the meeting with the amazing news.[27]

There was skepticism over whether Carter had obtained anything new. Kim did not say he would stop reprocessing or stop producing plutonium. "What we have here is nothing new," one White House official complained. "The problem is that North Korea now has a former president as its spokesperson." The most serious concern was his unexpected public call to "stop the sanctions activity in the United Nations." "In my opinion, the pursuit of sanctions is counterproductive in this particular and unique society," Carter declared. "I don't think the threat of sanctions has any effect at all on North Korea as far as damage to its society or economy is concerned. The declaration of sanctions would be considered by [North Koreans] as an insult to their country . . . and a personal insult to their so-called Great Leader [Kim Il Sung] by branding him a criminal." Kim had played a weak hand brilliantly. Carter's opposition to sanctions and his public pronouncement presented a powerful case to the world. Carter's words humanized the North Korean dictator, making him look rather grandfatherly and quite reasonable; they also fed into the North Korean myth of Kim's respectability during a period of political crisis for the North Korean regime. Carter seemed oblivious to how his efforts might be perceived. By lending respectability that Kim craved, Carter had undercut the strength of the American negotiating position. "President Kim Il Sung understood that I was speaking as a private citizen, not as a representative of the U.S.," Carter later insisted.[28] To most people, Carter was anything but a private U.S. citizen.

Back in Washington after the two-day visit, Carter declared the crisis "over." Although few believed this was the case, since there was still no formal agreement, the visit did provide a breakthrough: the chance to step back from the brink of war and the possibility of a North-South Korean summit. Before he entered North Korea, by ground across the DMZ on June 15, he had met with South Korean President Kim Yŏng-sam, who gave Carter a trump card to play—a proposal for a North-South summit without any preconditions. Carter brought up the proposed summit during a boat ride he and his wife, Rosalynn, took with Kim. On the seven-hour journey down the Taedong River, Kim and Carter "had an interesting conversation," which included discussion on an "unprecedented meeting between him [Kim Il Sung] and South Korean president Kim Young Sam [Kim Yŏng-sam] to be arranged by me at an early date." Thus, quite suddenly, the momentum toward military confrontation was halted. Carter later insisted that North Korea would have gone to war had the United States pursued UN sanctions, conducted an air strike, or sent significant military reinforcement, but in light of North Korea's long history of provocations and backing down when confronted with Armageddon, this seems unlikely. In retrospect, Carter's mission bought time for North Korea, but it also bought time for the Clinton administration to avert a catastrophic showdown on the Korean peninsula. Clinton seized the opportunity made by Carter to negotiate a new deal with P'yŏngyang. Kim Il Sung had survived once again.[29]

Accord

The death of Kim Il Sung in July 1994 did not seriously affect the results of the Carter mission. The U.S.-DPRK nuclear talks began the next day, and the Americans were relieved that the Great Leader's unexpected demise did not change North Korea's desire for a deal nor alter its basic negotiating position. What did change was the prospect for a North-South summit. After weeks of debate on whether an official condolence should be announced, Seoul not only decided not to offer such a condolence but also announced that arrests would be made to anyone who publicly expressed such a sentiment. The stern announcement by the Unification Ministry had followed a North Korean announcement inviting South Korean mourners to come to P'yŏngyang to pay their respects to the Great Leader. The North guaranteed their safety, declaring "they could enter either through Panmunjom [*sic*] or through a third country." The North's invitation to those who found "it hard to repress their bitter grief" was angrily denounced by Seoul. It decided to block a plan hatched by leftist students to send a condolence mission to P'yŏngyang. Seoul suspected that North Korea would use the invitation to exploit the students in order to shore up the regime's legitimacy at home, by showing its citizens how much South Koreans respected the Great Leader. Instead, on the day of Kim's funeral, Seoul released hundreds of Soviet documents, obtained by President Kim Yŏng-sam during a visit to Russia in early June, which conclusively revealed that Kim Il Sung was behind the North Korean attack on June 25, 1950.[30] P'yŏngyang resumed its anti–South Korean rhetoric, which had been suspended because of the anticipated summit. North-South relations rapidly deteriorated and hope for reconciliation evaporated.

Despite the North-South spat, U.S.-DPRK nuclear talks resumed in Geneva on August 5, 1994. By the time of Kim Il Sung's death, it was expected that Kim Jong Il would succeed him in the first dynastic succession in communist history. The short, plump, moon-faced man with a pompadour had a reputation for hard drinking and womanizing. A single portrait of him, a rarity in North Korea, is hung in the entranceway of the Yŏngbyŏn nuclear complex. Beyond the basic elements of the provisional agreement that Carter had negotiated with Kim Il Sung, freezing of the nuclear program and foregoing proliferation-prone nuclear facilities in return for two LWRs, there were a number of other items of concern to both sides. The most contentious issue was what to do with the eight thousand spent fuel rods that North Korea had removed in May. The United States wanted the rods to be moved to a third country so that the plutonium could not be extracted from them in the future.

Another issue was the dismantlement of North Korea's plutonium production facilities, the reactors, and the reprocessing plant. A final issue concerned international inspections of two key nuclear waste sites, which could reveal the amount of plutonium North Korea may already have accumulated. "There'll be no overall settlement until the question of the past has been settled," declared Gallucci, the U.S. official chosen to lead the negotiations with North Korea.[31]

The terms of the accord that was eventually brokered heavily favored North Korea. First, North Korea was not forced to relinquish its eight thousand spent fuel rods to a third country. Instead, the United States and North Korea were to "cooperate in finding a method" to "dispose of the fuel in a safe manner that does not involve reprocessing" in North Korea. There was no provision for dismantling the reactors or the reprocessing plant. Although North Korea agreed to stop work on two other reactors, it was allowed to keep the only working reactor operating until the two promised LWRs were "nearly" complete. Finally, on the most contentious issue, the IAEA's demand for "special inspections" of two nuclear waste sites, North Korea did not have to allow inspections until a significant portion of the LWR project was complete. The agreement did require North Korea to let the IAEA inspect the nuclear sites acknowledged by the North Koreans, "but only after the supply contracts for the LWR project are done." In effect, North Korea would remain in violation of the NPT until the shipment of these "key components" which might take a decade or more.[32]

IAEA officials were furious. North Korea would continue to possess nuclear spent fuel for years. This would leave open the possibility that if it ever renounced the agreement, it could kick out the international inspectors and resume its bomb project. The United States also agreed to supply five hundred thousand tons of heavy fuel oil "to make up for the energy foregone by North Korea before the LWRs came into operation."[33] In effect, the Americans agreed to a new foreign aid program that would help keep North Korean factories running and homes heated for years to come.

North Korea predictably hailed the Agreed Framework, signed on October 21, 1994, as a triumph of North Korean diplomacy. North Korea's domestic propaganda celebrated the agreement as an "abject Yankee surrender" that reinforced the image of cowering Americans who yielded to

North Korea's fearsome power. "America had no choice but to grovel."[34] Seoul was less enthusiastic. As part of the Agreed Framework, the South Korean government was supposed to build the promised LWRs. One aspect of the Agreed Framework was the establishment of a consortium of nations called KEDO (Korean Peninsula Energy Organization), which also included the United States and Japan, that was responsible for implementing the energy-related parts of the Agreed Framework. Although South Korea, as part of this consortium, had been tasked to build the LWRs, it had been given little say in actually formulating the main provisions of the agreement. Many South Koreans felt resentful. In particular, North Korea's rejection of South Korean reactors was especially galling. In the ongoing legitimacy war with the South, the concept of South Korea "aiding" North Korea, much less providing reactors, did not sit well with P'yŏngyang, which continued to belittle the South as puppets of Washington. President Kim Yŏng-sam was equally adamant that Seoul would not foot the bill for reactors from another country. Feeling aggrieved at having been left out of the negotiations, and fearing once again that the United States might sell Seoul short and conclude a separate deal with the North, Kim Yŏng-sam demanded South Korea's inclusion in the process.[35] In the end, Washington persuaded Seoul to accept a compromise. North Korea would accept South Korean reactors if no mention was explicitly made that they were from South Korea.

The Agreed Framework also received a skeptical response in the United States. President Clinton defended it with the argument that North Korea committed to freeze and "gradually" dismantle its nuclear program. More important, the agreement was seen as a necessary step to end North Korea's self-imposed isolation from the international community. Critics, however, insisted that the administration had made a bad deal. A *Washington Post* editorial opined, "How can such an agreement even be defended? . . . It pays North Korea, and handsomely, for returning to the nonnuclear obligations it took on and violated and ideally should not have been paid for at all . . . The accord sets an international precedent that lets the North Koreans keep hiding for years the very facilities whose inspection would show their nuclear cheating to date." The *New York Times* headline simply read, "Clinton Approves a Plan to Give Aid to North Koreans."[36] Faced with a choice between war or compromise, the Clinton administration had opted for compromise.

Three weeks after the agreement was signed, the Republicans took control of both houses of Congress in the fall elections in 1994. Predictably, the Agreed Framework was severely criticized by the new Republican majority. Senator Frank Murkowski of Alaska, the chairman of the Senate Subcommittee on East Asian Affairs, said he would block the United States from purchasing the promised heavy oil. "I don't support the administration's concessions which I find totally unacceptable," he declared. "We have given away the store. I don't know what we've gotten in return other than promises." Other prominent Republicans, including Bob Dole of Kansas and Jesse Helms of North Carolina, also lambasted the agreement. "It is always possible to get an agreement when you give enough away," said Dole.[37] Appropriating funds for the heavy oil was, according to one administration official, like "going through the rings of hell."[38] As a result, the shipments of heavy oil often arrived late. Work on the two LWRs also began falling behind schedule. With the nuclear crisis seemingly behind them, the Americans no longer considered North Korea all that important. Besides, conditions in North Korea were steadily declining. By 1995, reports from travelers and defectors recounted devastating stories of a terrible famine sweeping across the nation. North Korea appeared to be collapsing from within.

CHAPTER TWENTY-ONE

Winners and Losers

So had South Korea finally won its legitimacy war? Now a prosperous democratic society, how could South Koreans not feel proud of themselves and their accomplishments? The stark contrast between a rich and powerful South Korea and an impoverished and isolated North Korea erased any doubts which nation had emerged triumphant. Yet, at the same time that South Koreans basked in their victory over the North, commemorating the triumph proved tricky. This is because the most pressing issue at that time was to create a usable past that could make the future unification of the two Koreas possible. Recalling the horrors and frustrations of the war, and in particular, North Korea's brutal role in it, was no longer deemed tactful when the primary concern was to finally end the conflict and bring the two separated nations together. A new story of the war had to be constructed, one that would mobilize South Koreans in a tacit forgetfulness of North Korea's "criminal responsibility" for the war while simultaneously commemorating the war as a national tragedy.[1]

Triumph and Forgiveness

The first sign of this new approach occurred in 1994 when the War Memorial, a huge architectural complex located in central Seoul and one of the showpieces of No T'ae-u's presidential legacy, was opened to the public. Whereas earlier narratives of the war had placed the North Korean invasion and brutality at the center of the story, the memorial's various exhibits and displays aimed to promote collective forgiveness by excluding many brutal aspects of the war.[2] This message of forgiveness was clearly apparent in the most iconic structure of the War Memorial:

The Statue of Brothers, War Memorial, Seoul. (PHOTO BY AUTHOR)

The Statue of Brothers. Standing at one corner of the memorial precinct, the first thing that strikes the viewer about the statue is the enormous discrepancy in the size of the two figures. Embracing his smaller brother to his heart, the South Korean soldier's emotion-laden face stares intently at this younger North Korean while the latter looks up at him with admiring, grateful, and, one imagines, tearful eyes.

This theme of brotherly reunion is also reinforced by the cracked base, which is in the shape of an ancient Silla tomb mound. The ancient Silla kingdom unified the Korean peninsula in 668 CE when it conquered the northern kingdom of Koguryŏ. The historical analogy between the ancient past and the divided present is strikingly apparent. "My idea of using a Silla tomb as a pedestal," the statue's sculptor, Chae Yŏng-jip, remarked, "was not intended to evoke the idea of death. On the contrary, it was intended to evoke ideas of hope and rebirth, the cycles of history so to speak. The two brothers are reborn out of the womb of the past to be one again in the future." Rising out of the tomb, a reunified peninsula is reborn as a nation of brothers, although the South Korean elder brother is the more powerful and hence the more legitimate. In my interview with Chae, he remarked that the portrayal of the younger brother as weak and defenseless was deliberate, designed to show "the defeat of communism and the victory of South Korean democracy."[3] President No's reunification message was clear: South Korea's "forgiving embrace" of the North was predicated on the idea that the two Koreas would be united under the South, the authentic and legitimate Korea whose prosperity presented a clear contrast to the poverty-stricken North. Nevertheless, this reconciliation message was evoked on the basis of the South's "forgiveness" of the North, not its explicit triumph over it.

These ideas about reconciliation with the North reached full bloom during President Kim Dae-jung's ascendancy to political power in 1998. Kim was a devout Catholic, and his faith deeply influenced his worldview. In recalling President Park Chung Hee's persecution of him throughout his lifetime, for example, Kim wrote in his memoirs that it was his faith in God that had sustained him. "History only honors those who confess their sins before God, who forgive their enemies and who look after their neighbors."[4] Over and over again in his writings, Kim returned to the virtues of Christian forgiveness. When he became president, Kim declared that he bore no grudge or ill will against the former president or Park's successors, Chŏn Tu-hwan and No T'ae-u, stating, "Only a leader who holds the conviction that forgiveness is the ultimate victory can forgive with confidence."[5] To make good on his promise, one of Kim's first presidential acts was to propose building a memorial hall to honor Park Chung Hee. (It was opened a decade later, in 2012.) And in an unexpected act of clemency, Kim also pardoned Chŏn Tu-hwan and No T'ae-u, who had served just two years of their lifetime sentences in jail.[6]

It was precisely the "higher calling" of Kim's politics that most worried his critics. If love and forgiveness became the catchwords for Kim's attempts to reconcile with his former enemies, these same ideas became the mantra of his "Sunshine Policy" toward North Korea. Naming his new diplomatic efforts after Aesop's fable "The North Wind and the Sun," Kim rejected the idea of putting undue pressure on North Korea as a way to force it to open up to the world.[7] Rather, the essence of his policy was to engage P'yŏngyang out of its isolation by encouraging South Korean companies to do business with the North regardless of their political differences. The impact of this approach would be felt gradually as North Korea became penetrated and influenced by the lib-

Chairman Kim Jong Il meets President Kim Dae-jung, P'yŏngyang, June 12, 2000. Kim received the 2000 Nobel Peace Prize for his efforts to bring about a North-South rapprochement which culminated in the June 13–15, 2000, summit. However, his administration was later criticized when it was discovered that it had secretly paid the Kim Jong Il regime $500 million to attend the summit, causing a major political scandal that eventually led to the downfall of Kim's chief of staff, Pak Chi-wŏn, who was sentenced to prison for his role in the payment scandal. (AP PHOTOS)

eralizing affects of an economy integrated with the global economy. In time, it was hoped, North Korea would have become liberalized enough to make a more open relationship or even unification with South Korea possible.

That moment, it seemed, had finally arrived when Kim Dae-jung flew to P'yŏngyang to attend a historic summit on June 12, 2000. The North Korean leader, he reported, was not crazy after all, but quite sane and even witty. Kim Dae-jung was treated with all the reverence and respect as an "elder brother" should. When Kim returned to Seoul three days later to a hero's welcome, it appeared that the politics of forgiveness had actually worked.

If only it had been that easy. Amid the joyful calls for national reconciliation, a more sinister reality about North Korea was emerging, casting serious doubts on whether Kim Jong Il's regime could really be redeemed after all.

The North Korean Famine

"What is going on over there is simply beyond imagination," Dr. Hu Wanling, a researcher at China's Yanbian University and an ethnic Korean, told Jasper Becker, one of the first Western journalists to write about the North Korean famine. Like many residents living in the border region, Hu believed "hundreds of thousands have died from hunger and the worst is yet to come."[8] In August 1996, U.S. Congressman Tony Hall returned home stunned by what he saw during his four-day visit to North Korea. "Everyone is systematically starving together," he told reporters in Tokyo, it was "a slow starvation on a massive scale." Hall said the evidence included "families eating grass, weeds and bark; orphans whose growth has been stunted by hunger and diarrhea; people going bald for lack of nutrients and hospitals running short of medicine and fuel."[9] Interviews conducted by the humanitarian aid group Médecins Sans Frontières (Doctors Without Borders) in 1998 of scores of North Korean refugees hiding in China painted a dark picture of the most vulnerable victims of the famine: "Children are often too weak to come to class and teachers . . . desert the classroom to look for food . . . Some parents, unable to support their children, abandon them. Children and elderly can be seen lying on the street, too weak to stand."[10] Gangs of abandoned children were often seen at train stations. The trains had all but ceased to operate owing to lack of fuel or electricity, and the stations served as shelters. These children were called *kottjebi*, "flower swallow," because, like the migratory bird, they were in constant search of food and warmth. Hyŏk Kang, who escaped from North Korea in 1998, recalled that "about fifty children from all different backgrounds tried to survive like this, by stealing or begging for food around the station. Some of them lay lifelessly on the ground then dropped dead like flies. People gathered for a few minutes around the body of a child who had just died, as though to witness a spectacle, but then lost interest again almost immediately. In these times of famine, each person only thought of himself."[11]

In an interview with two former *kottjebi* conducted in 1999 by a reporter from the *Wŏlgan Chosŏn*, ten year old Im Ch'ŏl and his eight-year-old sister So-yŏn described their harrowing struggle for survival and their eventual escape to China. After their mother died, both children began living at the market.

> "Since we didn't have anything to eat at home we always stayed in the market," said Ch'ŏl. "The market seller would put down a straw mat to sit on and then throw it away at the end of the day. So you'd get a few of those to put over you when you slept. . . . The kids would fill up the market area because there were so many of them."
>
> "Could you tell me about your friends there and something about them?" asked the reporter.
>
> "Kim Chin-hyŏk was very smart. He was very good at his studies and had a real talent for math. He became a *kottjebi* after his mother disappeared. Although he was very brainy, he still couldn't get enough to eat, so what do you do? Since he didn't get enough to eat, he didn't have the strength to use his brain. He'd beg and then get beaten up and because he slept on the ground and didn't eat, he'd get sick all the time. So he died at the age of ten. He was one year older than me."
>
> "So where did he die? Did he die in the market?"
>
> "Of course he died in the market. Where else would he have died?"
>
> "How did he die?"
>
> "He was begging. Kids died all the time so we got used to it. When I woke up one morning, he couldn't get up. The market sellers don't like it when a *kottjebi* dies. You know the sacks they sit on? They put him in one of those and then put him on a cart used to carry hay on and dumped him near the mountain and came back. Then after that a kid named Chang Ch'ŏl starved to death. He was tall and he had very good penmanship. But good penmanship doesn't help you beg, does it? So he died too, just like Chin-hyŏk. So two of our good friends died. . . . "
>
> "So-yŏn, did you have friends in the market?"
>
> "Yes."
>
> "Tell me about them. What were your friends doing in the market, So-yŏn? Tell me their names."
>
> "I hung around with Hyang-ryo and we picked up scraps. We ate off the ground."
>
> "Where is Hyang-ryo now?"
>
> "She died."
>
> "How did she die?"
>
> "We were walking together and then she peed and died."
>
> Ch'ŏl recalled the day when his sister almost died. Her face began to swell up as did her hands and feet. Her brother managed to steal some noodles from one of the nearby noodle shops and he fed them to her. She eventually recovered.
>
> "That day, two girls lying beside So-yŏn died," he said. "One was six and the other was seven. They had swollen faces and feet just like

> So-yŏn, but they didn't have anyone to feed them and so their deaths were unavoidable. When I saw those two being taken away, it was like they were taking away two pigs. The men who took them to the mountains said to us, 'You puppies, if you die, this will happen to you too.' . . ."[12]

There were also grim rumors of cannibalism from escapees claiming to have firsthand knowledge. "People are going insane with hunger," said one former North Korean military officer who fled to China with his family. "They even kill and eat their own infants. This kind of thing is happening in many places," he said. Another North Korean claimed that in his home city of Wŏnsan, a husband and wife had been executed because they had murdered fifty children and stored their salted flesh in a hut.[13] Public executions for these crimes, including stealing government property, became commonplace by 1998, the worst year of the famine crisis. "Last March, they shot 13 people to death who ate humans or cows in Wŏnsan," said a refugee. "The criminals were dangled up high and people were forced to come and look at them. What an unimaginable tragedy! At the present time, Chosŏn [North Korea] is hell on earth."[14] Estimates of the number of deaths caused by famine between 1995 and 1998 range from 600,000 to 1 million, or roughly 3 to 5 percent of the population.[15] Interviews with North Korean refugees suggest that in the northern provinces, 25 percent of the population may have perished from starvation since they were the first to be cut off from the central distribution system. Reports that people were "dropping like flies," including observations of desperate behavior such as foraging for wild plants, tree parts, or anything remotely edible, are simply "too specific and too widespread to be dismissed."[16]

The rest of the world became aware of the food crisis only when North Korea launched the "let's eat two meals a day" campaign in 1991.[17] Over the ensuing years, while sparring with IAEA inspectors, the North Korean regime was fatally slow in responding to the growing food crisis. Much of this had to do with the peculiarities of the North Korean economic system, which was heavily dependent on socialist sources of aid for basic requirements.

Back in 1958, Kim Il Sung abolished private shops, and markets were strictly regulated as "relics of capitalism." Farmers essentially became state employees. They farmed state-owned cooperatives and were forced to sell their produce to the state at fixed prices. Some farmers were allowed to cultivate small private plots of land to grow vegetables and herbs, but in contrast to other communist states the allotted plots were far smaller and resulted in a dearth of privately produced food. It was believed that allowing farmers to cultivate larger private plots would lead to them to ignore their work obligations in the cooperatives.[18] Instead of markets and private shops, food was distributed through the Public Distribution System (PDS), which provided basic necessities at heavily subsidized rates as payment for work. Food rationing levels were determined by a combination of occupation and rank. The PDS reflected the stratification of North Korea's hierarchical system. Senior government and military officials and heavy laborers received the most food. At the bottom were children and the elderly.[19]

Implicit in this system of entitlement was also a political stratification (three-tiered) system, since class background was an important determinant of socio-political hierarchy. Two years after the 1956 coup that had almost toppled Kim Il Sung, the NKWP investigated the population to determine political reliability, which was largely based on family background. This in turn defined the opportunities available for higher education, housing, work assignments, and residency. At the bottom of the three-tiered system was the so-called hostile class. These included families who had been rich peasants or whose family origins hailed from South Korea or Japan. People of this rank were closely watched by neighborhood organizations called the *inminban*, literally "people's group," whose members reported anything suspicious. The second tier, the so-called wavering class, hailed from families of middle-class peasants, traders, or owners of small businesses. The upper tier, the core class, was composed of people whose families had traditionally been workers, soldiers, or party members. Only members of the core class, which constituted roughly 15 percent of the population, were able to live in P'yŏngyang, considered a privilege. By contrast, members of the hostile class were relocated to remote regions of the country beginning in the late 1950s, especially the northeast where most of North Korea's mines and infamous concentration camps were located. This stratified classification system would later have important implications for the famine, as it was precisely these parts of the country that experienced the severest deprivations.[20]

By most accounts, the PDS ceased to function properly by 1993, and the first regions to suffer were the remote northeastern North and South

Hamgyŏng provinces. "The rations stopped in 1993," recounted one refugee. "The government said that every district had to solve its own food problems."[21] This remote region was particularly dependent on the PDS because of its mountainous terrain and lack of agricultural land. The people were forced to go into the hills and mountains to forage for anything to eat. "Our village was feeding itself on weeds like wormwood and dandelion," remembered Hyŏk Kang. "Weeds, whatever kind, were boiled up and swallowed in the form of soup. The soup was so bitter that we could barely keep it down."[22] In 1995, North Korea took the unprecedented step of requesting international food aid, although the magnitude of the crisis was unknown to the outside world owing to the secretive and closed nature of the regime. International aid began to flow into the country in 1996, although these efforts were hampered by North Korean officials who barred aid workers from monitoring where the aid was going to ensure it was not being misdirected, for example, to the military. One of the most frustrating constraints for international aid workers was the denial of access to the parts of the country that needed the most help. Refugees all tell the same story: that most of the donated food did not go to the most vulnerable population and instead was skimmed off by corrupt officials and sold in the black market or funneled to politically influential groups. Good Friends, a South Korean organization involved in the aid program, estimated that as much as "50 percent of Korean aid went to non-deserving groups, including the military." A survey in 2005 of a thousand North Korean refugees showed that only "63 percent of the respondents reported even knowing about the *existence* of foreign humanitarian assistance."[23]

North Korea's restriction on monitoring the distribution of food aid posed an ethical dilemma for those involved in the effort. Could they continue to give aid when they could not ensure that it was going to the needy and not strengthening a repressive regime? One refugee said that he and others were told in their regular political study classes how Kim Jong Il "declared that although 30 percent of the population survived the famine, it would be enough to rebuild the country." When Kim was allegedly told in 1996 that three million had died of famine, he was suppose to have replied, "Be tough. No uprisings will be allowed. I will control military power. Have a strong heart. If the people revolt they will hang us, and if they don't, the South Koreans will."[24]

In 1998 most of the private nongovernmental international aid groups in North Korea withdrew, citing "inadequate access" and "their consequent inability to account for the eventual use of their aid supplies."[25] Their pullout, however, did not adversely affect North Korea's situation. They were but one of three main components of the humanitarian assistance to North Korea, the other two being the UN's World Food Program (WFP) and direct governmental aid. The largest donor was the United States, which gave food aid through the WFP. European countries, Japan, South Korea, and China also donated through the WFP. A U.S. Congressional Research Service report stated that from 1995–2008, "the United States has provided North Korea with over $1.2 billion in assistance, about 60% of which has paid for food and about 40% for energy."[26] In 2008, North Korea signaled that it was again facing food shortages. In May of that year, North Korea and the United States agreed on a protocol allowing for the distribution of up to five hundred thousand tons of food assistance.[27] In the ensuing years, food aid and concessional imports made up more than 90 percent of North Korea's imported grain.[28] North Korea has become an aid-dependent economy, with aid amounting "to approximately two-thirds of recorded merchandise exports, and aid together with revenue from illicit activities such as the exportation of missiles, drug and endangered species trafficking, and counterfeiting, have roughly equaled the total value of exports."[29]

Two countries, however, sent unconditional aid on a bilateral basis. China and South Korea provided "concessional sales," or grants of food, outside of the WFP. This policy met with criticism from some WFP donors and nongovernmental organizations, because it undermined efforts to establish an adequate monitoring system of food distribution. China and South Korea became, in effect, "the suppliers of last resort."[30] Beginning in 1995, South Korea had pursued a restrictive aid policy, but this changed with the inauguration of President Kim Dae-jung in February 1998, and especially after his historic summit with Kim Jong Il at P'yŏngyang in June 2000. Under Kim Dae-jung roughly three-fourths of South Korean food aid was sent with little demand for monitoring its distribution.

In addition to aid, Kim Dae-jung supported inter-Korean business projects aimed at developing economic engagement across the divided peninsula. It is unlikely that South Korean companies ever made any profits from these projects. Instead, they were more akin to providing state subvention for businesses agreeing to undertake projects that had little prospect for future gains. For example, Hyundai Corporation promised North Korea $942 million for the Kŭmgang-san (Diamond Mountain) tourism venture, but it took government funds to fulfill that promise. When it was later revealed that Kim Dae-jung's close associates had secretly transferred $500 million to North Korea in return for securing the June 2000 summit, questions were raised about the legitimacy of Kim's 2000 Nobel Peace Prize, and the South Korean public's feeling toward North Korea soured. The election of the conservative Yi Myŏng-bak as president in 2008 was, in part, a negative referendum on the Sunshine Policy.[31] In the United States, President George W. Bush's denunciation of North Korea as part of the "axis of evil" in his State of the Union Address in January 2002 effectively put an end to the Agreed Framework and the Clinton administration's engagement strategy toward the P'yŏngyang regime.

The Korean public's dissatisfaction with the engagement strategy was a function of how little the situation changed in North Korea. Major efforts to engage P'yŏngyang through subsidized trade relations did not lead to the kind of casual and spontaneous contact between ordinary North and South Koreans as it had been hoped. South Korea's two large-scale projects of economic engagement, Diamond Mountain and the Kaesŏng Industrial Park, were physically isolated from the rest of North Korea and have had little or no effect on liberalizing North Korea's economic or political stance. Moreover, industrial decline, spurred by lack of equipment, raw materials, and dilapidated infrastructure, resulted in large-scale unemployment. The 2009 WFP report on North Korea estimated that 40 percent of its factories stand idle and another 30 percent are operating well below capacity.[32]

Gulag Nation

The famine and the resulting relaxation of state controls in the 1990s unleashed drastic changes in North Korea. These changes did not result from any decision from the top, but rather from the chaotic circumstances at the bottom. As the old economic system began to fall apart, many North Koreans responded by engaging in surreptitious market activities, selling household items and setting up informal trade networks with Chinese merchants along the border. For the first time, markets began to appear in urban areas. The private markets (*changmadang*, literally "market grounds") grew rapidly as more and more entrepreneurial North Koreans sought alternative means to support themselves and their families. By the mid-1990s, even some luxury foods like fresh fruits and vegetables became available in the markets. Thus, during the death grip of the famine, more food became available, but only to those with hard currency. Corruption was also rife. Foreign-donated rice was sold on the black market by corrupt officials. Travel restrictions, even those to China, could be overcome with a bribe. Out of desperation and hunger, North Koreans reinvented the concept of a free market economy. In the 1990s, North Koreans would say that there were three types of people: "those who starve, those who beg and those who trade."[33]

But the rise of the free market system had dangerous political implications for the regime. Cross-border trade with China and the creation of dense business networks threatened to undermine the government's monopoly on information, especially about South Korea. Once the country was able to recover its equilibrium after the profound chaos created by the famine, mostly with the help of foreign aid and the large infusion of cash from South Korea during the lush "sunshine" years, the regime initiated a direct attack on the emerging market economy beginning in 2005. An indication of the new direction was the decision to reinstate the PDS. The anti-market campaigns were not limited to the food economy, however, but included escalating restrictions on market traders and border-crossing activities. In 2004 and 2007, the North Korean criminal code was changed to expand the definitions of economic crimes, to prohibit a wide range of standard commercial practices. Trading companies also came under greater scrutiny. In April 2008, a team of "200 investigators [was sent] to Sinŭiju in the name of an Antisocialist Conscience Investigation to inspect the books of foreign trade organizations" that impeded market activity. These ad hoc visits, becoming more frequent in the border regions, targeted "illegal internal movement, contraband, and cross-border trade." North Korean refugees living in China also came under greater scrutiny. In cooperation with the Chinese government, North Korean security began to hunt down these refugees to bring them back to North Korea, where they faced incarceration, torture, and even death. One of the major ramifications of the crackdown on private market activity was the expansion of the North Korean prison system and the growing incarceration of citizens for economic crimes.[34]

Prison labor camps, or *kwalliso*, were first established in North Korea after liberation from Japan to imprison enemies of the revolution, landowners, collaborators, and religious leaders. After the war, these places housed un-repatriated South Korean prisoners of war.[35]

Satellite imagery reveals the massive size of these camps. One camp is large enough to hold fifty thousand inmates.[36] There are six such camps in existence today occupying, according to a May 2011 Amnesty International report, "huge areas of land and located in vast wilderness sites in South Pyŏng'an, South Hamgyŏng and North Hamgyŏng Provinces." A comparison of these latest images with satellite images taken in 2001 also "indicates a significant increase in the scale of the camps."[37] Recent testimonials from North Korean refugees paint a dark picture of life in the camps: widespread deprivation of food, medical treatment, and clothing, along with torture and public executions. Perhaps the most notorious penal colony is *kwalliso* no. 15, or Yodŏk, made infamous by Kang Chŏl-hwan, who was incarcerated there as a child and then escaped to South Korea in 1992 and whose memoir, *The Aquariums of Pyongyang*, has been translated into French and English.[38] A distinctive feature of the North Korean penal system is that inmates and their families are typically incarcerated for long-term or life sentences. Most belong to the hostile and wavering classes, which include a large number of Japanese citizens of ethnic Korean origin who returned to North Korea in the 1950s and 1960s. Although encouraged by the Kim regime to move to North Korea, they were later deemed politically suspect because of their exposure to Japanese liberalism and capitalism. During the 1990s, North Korean students and diplomats, part of the core class, who had been assigned to or studied in Eastern Europe or the Soviet Union, also became suspect.

North Korean authorities continued to find new ways to criminalize market activity, which included the establishment of *kyohwaso*, or reeducation camps for less serious crimes, to supplement the *kwalliso* camps. Still, testimonials and memoirs of former prisoners of *kyohwaso*

Kwalliso no. 15 (Yodŏk). There are currently six operating *kwalliso* in North Korea containing between five thousand and fifty thousand prisoners, totaling between 150,000 to 200,000 people. The encampments themselves are self-contained closed compounds or "villages." A striking feature of the North Korean gulag system is "guilt by association," whereby family members of up to three generations, including children, are incarcerated along with the offending political prisoner. (COURTESY OF THE COMMITTEE FOR HUMAN RIGHTS IN KOREA)

paint a hellish existence of forced labor under brutal conditions, beatings, rampant disease, hunger, torture, and executions. "Everyone moved as a group," recalled Soon Ok Lee, who was released from *kyohwaso* no. 1 (Kaech'ŏn) in 1994 and eventually fled the country to South Korea via

Hong Kong in 1995. "Everyone had to eat, sleep, work or use the toilet at the same time. Until a team was called to use the toilet, team members could not relieve themselves. So new prisoners often wet their pants."[39] The work was brutal, with constant pressure to meet the daily quotas. "At 5:30 a.m. messengers distributed quotas to each prisoner. At 11 pm, the messenger gathered them back and examined each prisoner's activities to see if they had met their quota. Prisoners who could not complete their job had their food reduced to 240 grams (8.4 ounces) for one day of incomplete work, and 210 grams (7.4 ounces) after four days of incomplete work."[40] In camps involving hard labor like mining copper and logging, convicts worked ten to twelve hours a day. One study estimated that "below subsistence level food rations coupled with the harsh conditions and hard labor resulted between 1991 and 1995 in the deaths of one-quarter to one-third of the inmates."[41]

These camps were an important source of hard currency, for the products they made were exported. A former inmate recalled that "every few months, camp authorities trotted out their latest version of the 'Let's Earn Some Dollars for Kim Il Sung Campaign.' These crusades were intended to make us heave with enthusiasm at the idea of harvesting exotic hardwoods, gathering ginseng, or producing whatever else the Party thought might fetch a few dollars on the free and open market."[42] Inmates of *kwalliso* no. 15 (Yodŏk) made brandy (labeled "Yodŏk Alcohol"), textiles, and distilled corn and mined for gold among other things. *Kyohwaso* no. 1 made doilies for Poland, army uniforms for the Soviet Union, sweaters for Japan, and paper flowers for France. Another camp built refrigerators and bicycles.[43] A prisoner from *kyohwaso* no. 77 (Tanch'un) testified about its gold-mining operation: "2,000 out of roughly 7,000–8,000 prisoners died from mining accidents, malnutrition, and malnutrition related diseases" during his two years there in the late 1980s.[44]

A shorter-term detention/punishment system was set up recently to punish the growing number of "petty" criminals. Their crimes include leaving their village, traveling without authorization, not showing up for work, and leaving the country. North Koreans who are caught crossing the border into China or persons forcibly repatriated from China are brought to these detention facilities, where they face the same brutal treatment, hard labor, and subsistence rations as prisoners in the long-term camps. Although most prisoners were incarcerated for less than a year, the death rate was extraordinarily high. One study of former refugees who had been in these detention centers noted that "90 percent reported witnessing forced starvation, 60 percent reported witnessing deaths due to beating or torture, [and] 27 percent reported witnessing executions."[45]

One notable feature about the North Korean penal system is the pervasive experience of deprivation and terror encountered at all levels of contact with authority.[46] As the range of economic activities deemed criminal expands, so does the need to create more detention facilities. Subjecting prisoners to "horrific conditions" from the start may be the state's effort to deter criminal economic activity, but the system might also have led to an unintended effect: the rise of corruption. One survey of North Korean refugees showed that "85 percent of respondents reported that they needed to pay bribes to engage in market activity." If a bribe is not offered or is insufficient to prevent an arrest, officials can always extort money from those who wish to avoid incarceration or those seeking to get out of serving their time. And the more terrifying the incarceration experience, the higher the price to avoid it. In their exhaustive research on North Korea's penal system, Stephan Haggard and Marcus Noland observed that "corruption may act as a safety valve in a fraying socialist system; a means of maintaining support among cadre by providing them access to economic rents." In this predatory society, repression of the people by government, party, and security functionaries appears not to be harnessed by political or even ideological objectives but by private gain, which in turn maintains the regime and its predatory practices.[47]

The Japanese journalist Ishimaru Jiro, who tracks domestic changes in North Korea in his magazine *Rimjin-gang*, which publishes remarkable reports from and interviews by underground North Korean informers, noted that corruption is rampant at all levels of society. Despite the recent government crackdown on private markets (*changmadang*), they continue to flourish mostly because they create a necessary income for corrupt officials. "The government extorts a lot of money from the *changmadang*," related one anonymous office worker to a *Rimjin-gang* reporter.

> Suppose I am a shoe salesman at the market. As soon as I put shoes out on my street stall, a space about fifty centimeters [twenty inches] wide,

> guards will come and calculate my possible day's income according to the goods I have on display. Then they demand a street tax. Maybe that would be 300 to 400 won a day. In the case of a central *jangmadang* [*changmadang*], there are about 10,000 to 15,000 salespeople. Think about it. How much money can they pluck from a *jangmadang* if they take a few won from each merchant![. . .] When the government ordered the ban on the *jangmadang* in October and November of last year [2005], people said, "Everything will restart soon. Just wait for a month and the *jangmadang* will be active again." And it's true. After a month, things were back to business as usual.[48]

Extorting bribes from merchants in the markets or confiscating their goods through crackdowns is common practice among these officials. "If they don't do such things, they can't survive. In other words, they are parasites living off the markets, and in that, they are also excellent examples of the market's power."[49]

These predatory conditions were further exacerbated by North Korea's fiscal policies. In a move that was widely interpreted to consolidate his hold on power, Kim launched a disastrous currency reform in 2009 to crack down on the market economy. On November 30, the regime announced that the "old" 100 North Korean won would be equal to 1 "new" won. The aim of the reform was to punish the rising entrepreneurial class by annihilating private savings earned outside the officially sanctioned state economy. The result was runaway inflation, a widening food crisis, and further deterioration of the North Korean economy.[50]

While most of the world is well aware of the character of the regime and the human rights abuses that go on in North Korea, opening the country up to further scrutiny would expose this corruption and level of abuses on a much wider scale. The more pressure the North Korean regime faces to improve its human rights situation and instituting economic reforms, the harder it becomes to maintain the internal stability and order of the failed system. Since long-term survival of the regime is the leadership's foremost concern, it must continue the policy of national isolation and politics of terror if it is to maintain its hold on power.

How long can such a situation continue? In the short run, engagement with North Korea aimed at reducing the chances of a North Korean collapse through food and other economic aid is a reasonable and rational approach, especially in light of North Korea's continued belligerence and its testing of a nuclear device in 2006 and 2009. It is widely accepted that a renewal of fighting on the peninsula would be disastrous for the region. But what is the long-term prospect of this approach? The longer the North Korean regime continues to exist, the more decrepit its economy will become and the more desperate its people will grow. The contradictory impulses of propping up a failed regime while also seeking to secure stability and peace on the Korean peninsula has not been lost on P'yŏngyang's closest ally, China.

EPILOGUE

China's Rise, War's End?

Kim Chŏng-ŭn, front right, walks beside the hearse carrying the body of his late father, Kim Jong Il, during a funeral procession in P'yŏngyang on December 28, 2011. Behind Kim Chŏng-ŭn is Chang Sŭng-taek, Kim Jong Il's brother-in-law. (AP/KCNA)

ON THE MORNING OF December 28, 2011, hundreds of thousands of North Koreans lined the snow-covered streets of P'yŏngyang to bid farewell to their Dear Leader, Kim Jong Il.[1] The three-hour funeral event, which was broadcast live on North Korean television, showed wailing crowds of men and women as a tearful Kim Chŏng-ŭn, Kim's youngest son and chosen successor, trudged through the snow alongside the black limousine that carried his father's casket. The snowfall also gave the country's state-run media fresh material with which to eulogize the Dear Leader since his unexpected death was announced on December 19: "The feathery snowfall reminds the Korean people of the snowy days when the leader was born in the secret camp of Mt. Paektu and of the great revolutionary career that he followed through the snowdrifts." The reference to Mt. Paektu, the legendary site where Korea's mythical founder, T'an'gun, had descended from the Heavens and the place where Kim Il Sung had waged his battles against the Japanese, provided a fitting symbol to mark the end of the dictator's life. In his death, the snow imagery also showed the way forward to his rebirth: "The march in the new century of the *Juche* [*Chuch'e*] era," went the joint 2012 New Year's editorial, "is the continuation of the revolutionary march that started up on Mt. Paektu. Steadfast is the will of our service personnel and people to adorn our revolution, pioneered by Kim Il Sung and whose victory after victory they won following Kim Jong Il, with eternal victory following the leadership of Kim Jong Un [Kim Chŏng-ŭn]."[2]

Although the twenty-something Kim Chŏng-ŭn hardly seemed prepared to take over his father's mantle, having just been introduced to the Korean people in 2010, North Korean officials quickly rallied around their new king. But more important to the future of North Korea was that Chinese leaders did too. Just one day after the announcement of Kim Jong Il's death, China moved swiftly to assure its communist ally of its strong support amid the uncertain leadership transition. On December 20, President Hu Jintao visited North Korea's embassy in Beijing to offer his condolences while Foreign Ministry spokesman Liu Weimin offered a crucial endorsement to "Comrade Kim Chŏng-ŭn," calling on him to build a strong Communist country and realize permanent peace on the Korean peninsula."[3] At the same time, a number of PRC Central Committee members, including China's number two, Premier Wen Jiabao, paid their respects to the deceased leader at the embassy. Wen's remarks, in particular, reinforced the strong emphasis that China's leaders have placed on ties with North Korea:

> Comrade Kim Jong Il was the North Korean Worker's Party and country's great leader, and a close friend to the Chinese people. Since long ago, he developed the cooperative and friendly relations between China and North Korea, producing great achievements [in that area]. We believe that the Korean Worker's Party under the leadership of Kim Jong Eun [Kim Chŏng-ŭn] the North Korean people will certainly pass through their grief, pushing forward to new successes in socialist construction. The Chinese side wants to take the same road as the Korean side, in order to

> further and consolidate and develop the traditional friendship and cooperation between the two countries, striving together.[4]

South Koreans have been concerned about China's rise and growing influence in North Korea for some time. These concerns became clear in the summit meeting between former South Korean president No Mu-hyŏn and Premier Wen that was held on September 10, 2006, in Helsinki. They had come to attend the Asia-European Meeting forum in order to discuss pressing bilateral issues.[5] Press reports of the meeting reveal that the two leaders spent a good part of their time discussing ancient history, specifically the history of the Koguryŏ/Gaogouli kingdom. Koguryŏ was one of the three ancient kingdoms of Korea, along with Paekche and Silla, which existed between the third millennium and the seventh millennium AD.[6] At the height of its power in the fifth century, Koguryŏ encompassed a vast area in what is today Northeast China and North Korea. During his meeting with the Chinese premier, the South Korean president wanted to discuss recent reports by Chinese archeologists and historians who claimed that since Koguryŏ's former territory now resides within the current borders of the PRC, its history should be considered part of "Chinese history."[7] Official press releases of the meeting later revealed that President No "had expressed his dissatisfaction with some conclusion of the Chinese archeological teams and the publication of a provincial research center dealing with events some two thousand years ago."[8]

President No's concern over China's historical treatment of Koguryŏ began in 2002, following China's launching of its ambitious Northeast Asia Project. The ostensible aim of the project was to "strengthen the association between China proper [all of China] and the northeast region," which includes three provinces: Heilongjiang, Jilin, and Liaoning. But as the South Korean public soon learned, the Chinese government and scholars associated with the project appeared to be "conducting a systematic and comprehensive effort to distort the ancient history of Northeast Asia" by portraying Koguryŏ and the succeeding state of Parhae (Korean)/Bohai (Chinese) as Chinese, not Korean, kingdoms. In April 2004, the South Korean government lodged a formal protest following the appearance on the Chinese Foreign Ministry website that portrayed Koguryŏ as Chinese and removed references to Koguryŏ as

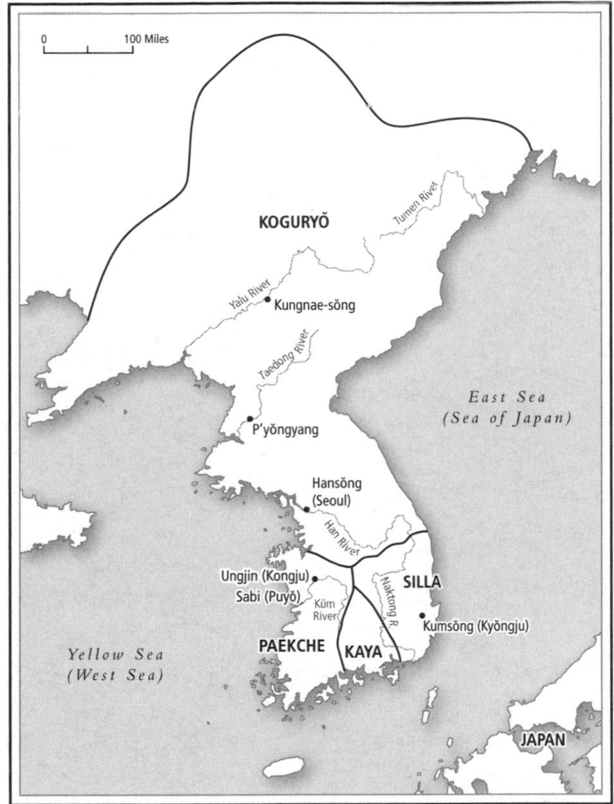

Map of the Three Kingdoms of Korea (AD 300–600) (Kaya was not a kingdom, but a confederation of tribes). In AD 660 Silla conquered Paekche with the help of T'ang China, and eight years later, in 668, Silla and the T'ang subdued Koguryŏ. Turning on its ally, the T'ang then invaded Silla in 674, but Silla was able to finally drive the T'ang from the Korean peninsula in 676, thereby achieving the unification of the peninsula. However, most of Koguryŏ's former territory in Northeast China was not included in Silla's unification.

being part of Korea's Three Kingdom era.[9] Beyond this bickering over history, however, the political ramifications of the dispute have been far-reaching. By claiming Koguryŏ as part of China's ancient past, the South Koreans charge, the Chinese government was surreptitiously undermining the legitimacy and political authority of North Korea whose territory was once part of Koguryŏ.

China's treatment of Koguryŏ has not been all that different from the way it has treated other ancient tribes and states that are now part of the PRC.[10] Knowing that the threat to the integrity of the Chinese nation has

China's Heilongjiang, Jilin, and Liaoning provinces and North Korea.

historically always come from internal challenges to its central authority, China launched an ambitious plan to exert control over its diverse ethnic population by promoting a common Chinese identity under the rubric of being a "multi-ethnic nation."[11] The link made between Koguryŏ and the Northeast provinces like Jilin, whose majority population is ethnic Korean, has clearly been a way to increase the notion of a Chinese identity among ethnic minorities.

But the Northeast Asia Project clearly has another aim: to construct a unitary national history and identity in the Northeast intended to pave the way for the economic intervention and integration of North Korea. Indeed, it is not coincidental that China's concern with Koguryŏ's history began in earnest in 2004 when Premier Wen announced that the Chinese government would embark on an ambitious economic development project for the Northeast provinces. According to Chinese government sources, Chinese investment in North Korea in 2006 topped $135 million and bilateral trade reached $1.69 billion, "an increase of almost seven percent over the $1.58 billion in bilateral trade in 2005."[12] Trade imbalance and North Korea's economic dependence also reached lopsided proportions, with imports from China of crude oil, petroleum, and synthetic textiles amounting to $2 billion while exports, consisting mainly of coal and iron ore, totalling just $750 million.[13] These investments are similar to the contributions to the DPRK's economy during the 1953–60 period, except that China now exerts far greater political leverage over the P'yŏngyang regime because North Korea now has no one to rely on but Beijing.

Despite China's increasing involvement in North Korea, however, Chinese leaders realize that merely propping up the regime without fundamentally transforming its economy will not resolve China's main security dilemma in the region: maintaining stability and peace on the Korean peninsula. Hence, China's ambitious efforts to develop North Korea to prevent the inevitable implosion of its economy while also shielding the North Korean regime from internal collapse. This "grand bargain" is certainly distasteful to the North Korean regime, which is used to getting its own way—thus, Kim Jong Il's decision to conduct a second nuclear test in May 2009. But when the Americans did not respond and the test instead resulted in even more punitive UN sanctions, the friendless regime was forced to make amends with China. "Despite their public rhetoric about the closeness of their ties," confided one observer, "officials in both China and North Korea each tell even American officials how much they dislike each other. North Korean officials have on numerous occasions suggested to American officials that it would be in the interest of our two countries to have a strategic relationship to counter China."[14] North Korean officials privately voiced their wariness of Beijing to South Korean diplomats, and worry about China's "increasing hold on precious minerals and mining rights in the DPRK [and] many oppose mineral concessions as a means to attract Chinese investments." According to one well-placed source, "Disputes with North Korean counterparts develop all the time . . . Investment disputes also occur between competing investors in China." In May 2010, the Saebyŏl Coal Mining Complex in North Hamgyŏng province sealed a contract with a Chinese enterprise. It promised to hand over an "unheard degree of discretion in affairs of personnel management, materials and working methods" to the Chinese. According to one source, the Chinese have been guaranteed "operational independence free from the control of the Saebyŏl party committee, and take 60 percent of net profits." North Korean workers appear to be happy with the arrangements, as they are now guaranteed steady wages and food. But others are far more pessimistic: "The purse strings in the border regions of our country have basically been handed over to China, and our 'socialist pride' is in the hands of China. Any factory where they produce even a small amount of goods has been invested in by the Chinese."[15]

North Korea's increasing dependence on China, however, does not mean that Beijing's leaders are able to exert complete control over their difficult neighbor. North Korea's second nuclear test in May 2009 strained relations between the two countries, but Chinese leaders also know from historical experience that such actions are geared more toward North Korea's domestic audience than the international community. Thus, despite his displeasure with North Korea over the nuclear test, Chinese Premier Wen nevertheless signed an ambitious co-development project with Kim Jong Il the following October.

The project, covering the Chinese cities of Changchun, Jilin, and Tumen, encompasses an area of seventy-three thousand square miles, but it is landlocked by Russia. Kim Jong Il agreed to lease the sea port at Rajin, a gateway to the Pacific, as well as sign on to various economic development projects. In December 2010, for example, China's Shangdi Guanqun Investment Company signed a letter of intent to invest $2 billion in the Rajin-Sŏnbong economic zone, which represents one of the largest potential investments in North Korea.[16] There are already reports that North Korean workers have been dispatched to begin the project, and plans are under way for the building of a new fifty-thousand-kilowatt hydroelectric power plant on the Tumen River.[17] North Korea and China have also recently signed an investment pact on building a highway and laying a railroad between Quanhae in Jilin and Rajin-Sŏnbong.

But more telling to the future relations between North Korea and China has been the swift reopening of the border after Kim Jong Il's passing. When Kim Jong Il's death was announced on December 19, most

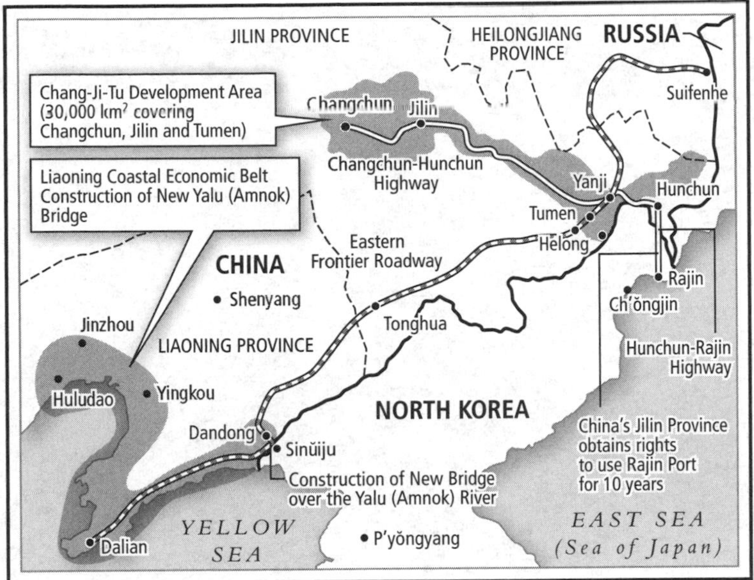

Changchun-Jilin-Tumen River (Chang-Ji-Tu) area.

people assumed that North Korea would close its frontier with China, at least for the short term. However, within forty-eight hours, "many border crossings sprang open again," underlying the reality that the new regime can ill afford to cut off its lifeline to China, even for a few days. Although China's strategy to encourage economic reforms in the North does not appear to be successful, the expansion of trade and investment has nevertheless "unleashed economic forces at least in the border region" as well as created a new group among the country's elite who have a vested interest in expanding trade.[18]

The pressing question that North Korea now confronts in the face of becoming a "fourth province of northeastern China" is how to sell it to the North Korean people. For a regime that has always touted *chuch'e* as the core principle of its nationalist ideology, such dependence would likely trigger a mass legitimization crisis. It would be hard to justify North Korea's *chuch'e* philosophy of self-determination and the regime's repeated denunciation of South Korean "flunkyism" while becoming an economic satellite of China. Hence, the regime's continued efforts to demonstrate its "independence" from China and create international crises to galvanize domestic public support for itself. This has become all the more urgent since Kim Jong Il's death. According to sources familiar

Arirang, North Korea's mass games in 2010, celebrating Sino–North Korean Friendship and the sixtieth commemoration of the "Victorious Fatherland Liberation War." (AP/KOREAN CENTRAL NEWS AGENCY)

with the North Korean situation, Kim Jong Il was "obsessed with creating political stability to allow orderly succession."[19] Chinese leaders, aware of the delicate situation, had tolerated Kim's antics because they understood he would never actually start a war.

But instigating crises in response to internal domestic turmoil, a familiar North Korean tactic, has done very little to mask the reality of China's growing influence over North Korean affairs. This is where the Korean War story plays a vital role in forging a new relationship between the two countries. In years past, the anniversary of the Chinese intervention in the Korean War, which occurred on October 19, 1950, had been worth just a few lines in the North Korean press, if it was mentioned at all.[20] In recent years, however, China's role in North Korea's Korean War commemorative culture has taken on a strikingly new and prominent role. In August 2010, North Korean officials announced that North Korea's mass games known as *Arirang*, the iconic gymnastic and artistic performance scheduled to be performed as part of the commemorative celebrations, would feature two entirely new scenes: "One of them represents the Korean People's Revolutionary Army and Chinese armed units fighting together against the Japanese imperialists during the anti-Japanese armed struggle. The other portrays the Chinese People's Volunteers joining the Korean army and people in the Korean War against the imperialist allied forces' invasion under the banner of resisting America and aiding Korea, safeguarding the home and defending the motherland." Performers "in Chinese clothes" danced with Chinese props, including "several dozen meter-long dragons, pandas and lions."[21]

If the inclusion of Chinese props and dress was not striking enough for a country that has not overtly acknowledged China's role in the conflict, a grand banquet to commemorate the sixtieth anniversary of the CPV's entrance into the Korean War was held on October 24, 2010. In his address to members of the visiting delegation of the CPV veterans,

On October 26, 2010, Kim Jong Il, center, laid a wreath in front of the grave of Mao Anying, Mao Zedong's eldest son who died during the Korean War. The CPV Martyrs Cemetery, located in Hoech'ang, South P'yŏngan province, has become an important site for ceremonial visits made by Chinese and North Korean officials. Premier Wen Jiabao visited the cemetery during his October 2009 visit to the DPRK. An official visit to the CPV Cemetery in September 2010 was one of the first major events after Kim Chŏng-ŭn was publicly introduced as his father's hereditary successor. In October 2012, DPRK state media reported that a memorial ceremony marking the completion of extensive renovation work of the cemetery was held to mark the sixty-second anniversary of the CPV entry into the Korean War. (AP/KOREAN CENTRAL NEWS AGENCY)

the North Korean vice president of the Presidium of the Supreme People's Assembly, Yang Hyŏng-sŏp, saluted "the CPV's brave men and our people and army [who fought] side by side, to carry forward the courageous spirit and collective heroism" and made "the Fatherland Liberation War a great victory, by gloriously defending Northeast Asia and world peace."[22] This was followed by an unprecedented official visit to the cemetery of Chinese soldiers killed during the Korean War, including Mao Anying, Mao Zedong's son.[23]

Even then, China's role in the war is construed as being one of "reciprocal obligation" since North Korea had once aided the Chinese in their war against Japan. "The tradition of ties of friendship between the peoples of the DPRK and China, sealed in blood in the joint struggle against U.S. and Japanese imperialisms, the two formidable enemies, has steadily developed on the basis of particularly comradely trust and sense of revolutionary obligation of the leaders of the elder generation of the two countries," explained the *Nodong sinmun*, the North Korean party daily, in its October 24, 2010, issue. In short, by equating China's aid against American "imperialists" in the Korean War with the aid of Korean revolutionaries in fighting Japan in China during World War II, North Korean officials drew attention to the *equality* of revolutionary comrades in arms based on the bonds of DPRK-China friendship "sealed in blood," rather than on any indication of super-power "dependence." The "ties of friendship between the people of the two countries" are thus presented in terms of a familial bond of obligation and respect between younger and older generations:

> Kim Il Sung visited China to participate in the function for founding the People's Republic of China in Juche [*chuch'e*] 38 [1949] and had his first meeting with Chairman Mao Zedong and Premier Zhou Enlai. Since then, the leaders of the two countries made great efforts to boost the friendly relations between the DPRK and China . . . In the new century, General Secretary Kim Jong Il paid several visits to China and Chinese party and state leaders including Hu Jintao visited the DPRK, deepening the friendly feelings and comradely fraternity and boosting the DPRK-China friendly and cooperative relations.[24]

What is remarkable about this passage is not only the parallel that is drawn between Kim Il Sung's visits to Mao and Kim Jong Il's visit to Hu Jintao, but also the attempts made to highlight Kim Il Sung's revolutionary struggle in Manchuria. Since Jilin, Heilongjiang, and Liaoning provinces once comprised the Japanese puppet state of Manchukuo, the regime's current "joint" cooperation with China to develop this area is presented as being *foreshadowed* by Kim Il Sung's "hard-fought revolutionary struggle" there. During his visit to Jilin province in August 2010, Kim Jong Il directly linked China's Northeast development project with his father's exploits in Manchuria:

> Jilin and Heilongjiang provinces are a witness to Korea-China friendship and a historical land dear to the Korean people as Comrade President Kim Il Sung waged a hard-fought revolutionary struggle against the Japanese imperialists together with Chinese comrades in this area, leaving indelible footsteps. He in his lifetime had often recollected this historical land and wanted to visit here again. Carrying his desire with us, we have come here today. Entering the northeastern area of China we have felt that this area, which had been trampled down ruthlessly by the Japanese imperialists, is now vibrant with life, enjoying a splendid development in political, economic, cultural and all other fields under the leadership of the Communist Party of China.[25]

Percy Toop, a Canadian tourist, photographed this painting on October 27, 2010, at the Rajin Art Gallery. Many experts believe it is a painting of Kim Chŏng-ŭn. What is remarkable is that the setting and layout are similar to those in depictions of the young Kim Il Sung.[26] (COURTESY OF PERCY TOOP)

This passage is immediately followed by nostalgic reminiscences of Kim Il Sung's revolutionary past, which seek, once again, to demonstrate the "unbreakable" bond of friendship between the two countries.

The explicit linkage made between Kim Il Sung's past exploits in Manchuria and China's future exploits in Heilongjiang and Jilin provinces also provides clues on how P'yŏngyang decided to approach the delicate transition issue. With Kim Il Sung's popularity still intact, it makes sense for the regime to bring the Great Leader back to life in the person of his grandson, Kim Chŏng-ŭn. Such a reincarnation myth would be an effective ploy to ensure a smooth succession, since the Great Leader's untimely death in 1994 has largely absolved him of responsibility for North Korea's disastrous predicament, the famine and the country's economic collapse. This "reincarnation" drama was meticulously planned, with North Korean propaganda skillfully playing up the uncanny resemblance between the Great Leader and his grandson. When official photos of Kim Chŏng-ŭn were first released to the public in October 2010, some North Korea watchers even suggested that Kim Chŏng-un may have undergone plastic surgery to look more like his grandfather. Footage released in the week following the announcement of Kim Jong Il's death showed Kim Chŏng-ŭn visiting a tank division using the same signature mannerisms as his grandfather—walking with his left hand in his pocket and using his right hand to gesture while talking. Kim Chŏng-ŭn also shares the same swept-back hairstyle and protruding belly as the elder Kim; even his gait is reminiscent of the Great Leader's.[27] If Kim Chŏng-ŭn, with Chinese help, can begin a kind of "return to the past," to the days of Kim Il Sung before the famine, he may prove to be a far more effective leader than his own father. Also telling was the decision to introduce the heir apparent at the sixty-fifth anniversary of the NKWP, on October 10, 2010. On the reviewing stand with Kim Chŏng-ŭn and his father was Zhou Yongkang, China's point man in North Korea who is helping to oversee the Northeast Asia Project.[28]

Having embraced Kim Chŏng-ŭn as his father's legitimate successor, China's leaders have signaled that they do not support any drastic change in either Sino-DPRK relations or North Korea's domestic policy, at least in the near future. China will continue to push for economic reforms while exerting pressure on P'yŏngyang's leaders for more access

Kim Jong Il, right, and his son Kim Chŏng-ŭn attend a massive parade to mark the sixty-fifth anniversary of the NKWP in P'yŏngyang, October 10, 2010. (AP PHOTOS)

and faster development of Chinese business interests, particularly in the mineral sector and large projects like at Rajin.

Not surprisingly, South Koreans have become increasingly alarmed by all this talk of Sino–North Korean relations "forged in blood." They remain deeply suspicious of Chinese influence in North Korea and are wary about China's "strategic plot to colonize North Korea economically."[29] Relations between the two countries were made even more tense after North Korea's sinking of the South Korean naval vessel *Ch'ŏn'an* in March 2010.[30] South Korea had initially believed that China, as its largest trading partner, would endorse its position in its quest to seek international justice for the attack. When China wielded its veto power as a UN Security Council member to force a watered-down statement that did not identify North Korean culpability, Seoul responded with anger. Relations between the two countries are currently at their lowest since they established diplomatic ties in 1992.[31] In retaliation for North Korean provocations, the Yi administration cut off all aid to North Korea, including food aid. However, by adopting a hard-line stance toward the Kim Jong Il regime, South Korea essentially surrendered its economic leverage over North Korea to China. Some South Korean lawmakers expressed concern: "I'm worried that North Korea is getting too close and familiar to China in a bid to push third-generation succession," said

Representative An Sang-su, chairman of the ruling Grand National Party. "Would we be able to stop North Korea, if it decides to be under the control of China?"[32]

But the reality is that few South Koreans today are ready to take on the burdens of unification. In the 1990s, more than 80 percent of South Koreans believed that unification was essential; in 2011, that number dropped to 56 percent. Roughly 41 percent of those in their twenties believe unification is imperative, and among teenagers, that figure drops closer to 20 percent.[33] This huge drop in support is in large part due to the failed promises of Kim Dae-jung's Sunshine Policy. In November 2010, the South Korean Unification Ministry released a white paper which declared that the policy was dead. "Despite outward development over the past decade," the white paper said, "inter-Korean relations have been under criticism from the public in terms of quality and process. They have in fact, become increasingly disillusioned with the North and more worried about security as the North continued its nuclear arms program." Furthermore, despite the massive aid from South Korea and inter-Korea exchanges and cooperation over the last decades, no "satisfactory progress has been made in the issue of separated families, South Korean prisoners of war and abduction victims." The paper concluded, "The North has made no positive change in proportion to the aid and cooperation from South Korea."[34]

Few South Koreans harbor illusions about the dire state of the North Korean economy or the tremendous costs of unification. South Koreans also worry about the toll unification will take on the fabric of their society. The Korean Employers Federation predicted that if North Korea collapsed, up to 3.5 million people could flood South Korea. "Even under a conservative estimate, up to 1.6 million North Koreans may move to South Korea, mainly because of the huge difference in wages and employment opportunity," the Federation said. "Such a wholesale movement of people could seriously disrupt the local labor market and cause other social problems."[35] While many older South Koreans give lip service to the ideal of a reunified peninsula, they qualify their support by talking about it taking place over the long term, and preferably after they are dead.[36]

Thus it appears that it will be up to China to drag North Korea into the twenty-first century and finally end the Korean War.[37] North Korean leaders understand this, which is why they have already begun to accommodate China into their national narrative and China's presence into Kim Il Sung's revolutionary past. Hence all the hoopla recently about the Korean War, Kim's Manchurian exploits, and the two countries' bilateral friendship "forged in blood." This does not mean, however, that the new Kim Chŏng-ŭn regime will cease making trouble for China. Since the stability and legitimacy of the regime still rest firmly on the myth of Kim Il Sung, his anti-imperialist exploits, and the principle of *chuch'e*, China knows that it must allow the regime to assert some independence if it is to avoid collapse. Just how much "independence" China will tolerate from its recalcitrant neighbor remains to be seen. Needing both to preserve his rule and to build a "strong and prosperous nation," Kim Chŏng-ŭn is now faced with resolving the perplexing contradictions of instituting vital economic reforms under Chinese guidance while at the same time preserving the *chuch'e* principle so crucial to the legitimacy of the regime during a delicate transition period.

Over one hundred years has passed since China was forced to leave the Korean peninsula after its humiliating defeat in the 1894–95 Sino-Japanese War. That war marked China's decline and Japan's ascendancy in East Asian affairs. In the long aftermath of the war fifty years later, in which China saved North Korea from certain defeat, a revitalized China has returned to the Korean peninsula to reclaim its once-dominant position in Asia. China's rise has many implications for the region, but one of them certainly is the role it will play in ending the war on the Korean peninsula.

The events connected to the ending of the Korean War will be momentous, and the uncertainties surrounding North Korea's potential economic collapse and China's absorption of North Korea's economy are disquieting, as much for the millions of hungry North Koreans as for the prosperous Koreans in the South. How will South Korea react to China's intrusion into North Korea? As for the United States, whose military might and economic power came of age both during and after the Korean War, the specter of a rising China is certainly unnerving, but more worrying, perhaps, than China's role in ending the war in Korea is what this might signal for China's new place on the world stage. Understanding and responding to these changes will require reflection on the lessons and legacies of the unending Korean War and the role this conflict has played, and will continue to play, in shaping the region's past and future.

Addendum

As this book was going to print, it was announced that Pak Kŭn-hye, Park Chung Hee's daughter, was elected president of South Korea on December 19, 2012. As the eldest daughter of Park Chung Hee and Yuk Yŏng-su, Pak Kŭn-hye took on the role of first lady after her mother was tragically killed in a botched assassination attempt on her father's life in 1974. Not only is Pak the first female leader in Korea's millennium-long history (if we do not count the few Silla queens who ruled between the third and seventh century CE), her election also signals another "return of the past" as she must now deal with Kim Chŏng-ŭn, Kim Il Sung's grandson, in the ongoing struggle between North and South Korea. How this legitimacy struggle plays out between the progenies of these two momentous leaders of Korea's history adds a new and ironic twist to the unending war in Korea and China's role in resolving this long-standing family feud.

Appendix

UNC COMBAT FORCES IN KOREA
(Most figures are estimates; conclusive personnel figures are notoriously elusive.)

COUNTRY	CONTRIBUTION AT MAXIMUM STRENGTH	PERSONNEL (NO.)		CASUALTIES (NO.)	
		Peak Ground Strength	Total for 1950-53	Killed/ Missing from All Services	Wounded from All Services
Australia	2 infantry battalions 1 fighter squadron 1 air transport squadron 2 destroyers/frigates 1 aircraft carrier	2,300	17,000	275	1,100
Belgium	1 infantry battalion	950	3,500	97	350
Canada	1 infantry brigade 1 air transport squadron 3 destroyers 1 dry cargo ship	6,200	25,000	309	1,202
Colombia	1 infantry battalion 1 frigate	1,100	6,000	210	610
Ethiopia	1 infantry battalion	1,300	3,500	122	566
France	1 infantry battalion 1 gun boat	1,200	4,000	271	1,008
Greece	1 infantry battalion 1 air transport squadron	1,300	5,000	194	459
Luxembourg	1 infantry platoon	50	90	7	21
Netherlands	1 infantry battalion 1 destroyer	820	5,300	120	645
New Zealand	1 artillery regiment combat team 1 truck transport company 2 frigates	1,400	4,500	39	79
The Philippines	1 infantry battalion combat team	1,500	7,400	128	300

COUNTRY	CONTRIBUTION AT MAXIMUM STRENGTH	PERSONNEL (NO.)		CASUALTIES (NO.)	
		Peak Ground Strength	Total for 1950-53	Killed/ Missing from All Services	Wounded from All Services
South Africa	1 fighter squadron (South Africa did not deploy a ground unit)	210	825	34	16
Thailand	1 infantry battalion 1 frigate 1 air transport flight	1,300	6,500	136	469
Turkey	1 infantry brigade	5,500	15,000	889	2,111
United Kingdom	2 infantry brigades 1 aircraft carrier 2 cruisers 4 destroyers 1 hospital ship 4 frigates 1 HQ ship	14,200	60,000	1,078	2,674
United States	Eighth Army Fifth Air Force Seventh Fleet	330,000	2,000,000	36,574 (7,296 missing as of January 30, 2013)	103,284

UNC MEDICAL UNITS (Non-U.S./ROK)

COUNTRY	UNIT	BEDS (NO.)	PERSONNEL (NO.)
Denmark	Hospital ship *Jutlandia*	360	200
India	60 Parachute Field Ambulance	1,000	345
Italy	Red Cross hospital	150	130
Norway	Mobile army surgical hospital	200	106
Sweden	Red Cross hospital	450	160

OTHER OFFERS

COUNTRY	AID	STATUS
Bolivia	30 officers	Not accepted
Costa Rica	Use of sea and air bases Volunteers	Accepted Not accepted
Cuba	Infantry company	Accepted but not sent
El Salvador	Volunteers	Not accepted
Iran	2 ambulance units	Offer withdrawn
Japan	Use of bases; R&R facilities	Note: Japan regained sovereignty in April 1952 but continued to provide key logistical and infrastructural support for the war
Lebanon	Infantry battalion	Offer withdrawn
Norway	Merchant ship tonnage	Accepted
Pakistan	Infantry regiment	Offer withdrawn
Panama	Free use of bases, roads, and merchant marine space Volunteers	Accepted Not accepted
Taiwan	3 infantry divisions, 20 C47s transport aircraft	Not accepted

HUMANITARIAN AND RECONSTRUCTION AID AS OF 1953

COUNTRY	AID (in 1953 U.S. dollars; the purchasing power of $1 in 1953 was $8 in 2010)
Argentina	$500,000 of corned beef
Australia	$200,000 of barley, $200,000 of medical supplies
Austria	$40,000 of medical equipment
Belgium	$60,000 of sugar
Brazil	$2.7 million cash
Burma	$50,000 of rice
Cambodia	$25,000 of food and timber
Canada	$6.9 million cash
Chile	$250,000 cash
China (Taiwan)	$635,000 of coal, food, DDT, and medical supplies

COUNTRY	AID (in 1953 U.S. dollars; the purchasing power of $1 in 1953 was $8 in 2010)
Cuba	$270,000 of sugar and alcohol
Denmark	$140,000 of medical supplies, $100,000 of sugar
Dominican Republic	$10,000 cash
Ecuador	$100,000 of rice
Egypt	$29,000 cash
El Salvador	$500 cash
Ethiopia	$40,000 cash
France	$75,000 of medical supplies
Germany	$47,000 of medical supplies
Greece	$85,000 of medical supplies, $36,000 of salt, and $31,000 of soap
Guatemala	$153,000 of timber
Honduras	$2,500 cash
Iceland	$45,000 of cod liver oil
India	$168,000 of jute bag
Indonesia	$100,000 cash
Iran	1,000 tons of oil—declined
Israel	$63,000 of medical supplies, $34,000 of food
Japan	$50,000 of clothing and medical supplies
Lebanon	$50,000 cash
Liberia	$25,000 of rubber
Luxembourg	$30,000 cash
Mexico	$350,000 of food and medical supplies
Netherlands	$263,000 cash
New Zealand	$280,000 of food, soap, and vitamins
Nicaragua	Rice and alcohol—Declined
Norway	$70,000 of soap, vitamins, and alcohol
Pakistan	$380,000 of wheat
Paraguay	$10,000 cash
Peru	$59,000 of cotton and wool
Philippines	$2.3 million of rice

COUNTRY	AID (in 1953 U.S. dollars; the purchasing power of $1 in 1953 was $8 in 2010)
Saudi Arabia	$20,000 cash
Sweden	$8,000 of medical supplies
Switzerland	$39,000 of medical supplies
Syria	$11,000 cash
Thailand	$4.4 million of rice
Turkey	Vaccines—declined
United Kingdom	$1.34 million of food, medical supplies, charcoal, and cloth
United States	$253 million of various aid in kind
Uruguay	$2 million cash, $250,000 of blankets
Venezuela	$150,000 of food, medical supplies, clothing, and blankets
Vietnam	$2,000 of rice

Sources: Compiled from *Yearbook of the United Nations*, 1951, 1952, 1953, 1954, 1955, available at http://unyearbook.un.org/ (accessed July 10–20, 2010); Paul M. Edwards, *The Korean War: A Historical Dictionary* (Scarecrow Press, 2003); James I. Matray, ed., *Historical Dictionary of the Korean War* (Greenwood Press, 1991); Gordon L. Rottman, *Korean War Order of Battle: United States, United Nations, and Communist Ground, Naval, and Air Forces, 1950–1953* (Greenwood Publishing, 2002), appendix D: Korean War Casualties; Stanley Sandler, ed., *The Korean War: An Encyclopedia* (Routledge, 1995); Allan R. Millett, "Appendix 2: Selected Statistics, Korean War," *Their War for Korea* (Brassey's, 2002), pp. 266–267; Anthony Farrar-Hockley, *The British Part in the Korean War* (Stationery Office, 1995), vol. 2, p. 491; Walter G. Hermes, *Truce Tent and Fighting Front* (U.S. Government Printing Office, 1966), p. 513; Republic of Korea Ministry of National Defense Institute for Military History Compilation, "6-25 chŏnjaeng t'onggye (Korean War Statistics)," available at www.imhc.mil.kr/imhcroot/data/korea_view.jsp?seq=4&page=1 (accessed October 28, 2012); http://www.dtic.mil/dpmo/summary_statistics/, accessed July 20, 2010, this is the official website of the Department of Defense's Defense Prisoner of War—Missing Person's Office (DPMO); Anne Leland and Mari-Jana Oboroceanu, *American War and Military Operations Casualties* (Congressional Research Service, February 26, 2010); Korea Institute of Military History, *The Korean War: Volume Three* (University of Nebraska Press, 2001), pp. 692–693; and Spencer C. Tucker, ed., *Encyclopedia of the Korean War: A Political, Social, and Military History* (ABL-CLIO, 2000); U.S. Department Of Labor, Bureau of Labor Statistics, Consumer Price Index, July 26, 2010, available at ftp://ftp.bls.gov/pub/special.requests/cpi/cpiai.txt (accessed August 15, 2010); Lawrence H. Officer and Samuel H. Williamson, "Purchasing Power of Money in the United States from 1774 to 2009," *Measuring Worth* (2010), available at http://www.measuringworth.com/ppowerus/ (accessed July 31, 2010).

Notes

Abbreviations

CWIHP: Cold War International History Project, Woodrow Wilson International Center for Scholars, Washington, D.C.

DASJA: Department of the Army Staff Judge Advocate

FEER: *Far Eastern Economic Review*

FRUS: United States Department of State, *Foreign Relations of the United States* (U.S. Government Printing Office, various years)

HUSAFIK: "History of the United States Armed Forces in Korea," unpublished manuscript available in the U.S. Army Center for Military History, Ft. McNair, Washington, D.C., and the Historical Office of Eighth U.S. Army at the Yongsan U.S. Army Base, Seoul, Korea

HMGK: *History of the United States Army Military Government in Korea*, unpublished manuscript available in the U.S. Army Center for Military History, Ft. McNair, Washington, D.C., and the Historical Office of Eighth U.S. Army at the Yongsan U.S. Army Base, Seoul, Korea

JFK: John F. Kennedy Library, Boston, Massachusetts

LBJ: Lyndon B. Johnson Library, Austin, Texas

MOFAT: Republic of Korea Ministry of Foreign Affairs and Trade (archives), Seoul, South Korea

MHI: U. S. Army Military History Institute, Carlisle, Penn. (archives)

NARA: National Archives and Records Administration, College Park, Md.

NKIDP: North Korea International Documentation Project, Woodrow Wilson International Center for Scholars, Washington, D.C.

NSF: National Security Files, at JFK and LBJ libraries

TRC: Truth and Reconciliation Commission, Republic of Korea

INTRODUCTION

1 Ernst Oppert, *A Forbidden Land: Voyages to the Corea* (G. P. Putnam's Son, 1882), p. 3.

2. U.S. policymakers generally have fallen into two main camps in their approach to North Korea. The so-called "optimists" believe that negotiating with North Korea is possible and that the reason the P'yŏngyang regime

has so far been unwilling to abandon its nuclear ambitions is due its legitimate fear for its own national security. By contrast, the so-called "pessimists" view P'yŏngyang actions far more cynically, identifying a familiar pattern of behavior with the outside world, which is to "start negotiations, squeeze aid out of the international community by making incremental concessions (while trying to cheat), and then walk away from talks and stage a provocation or two—only to return in exchange for more payoffs." For the pessimists, North Korea's main goal is to maintain its hold on power by any means possible, including using nuclear blackmail. See Andre Lankov, "Changing North Korea: Information Campaign Can Beat the Regime," *Foreign Affairs* (November/December 2009), pp. 95–97.

3 Quoted in B. R. Myers, *The Cleanest Race: How North Koreans See Themselves and Why It Matters* (Melville House, 2010), p. 149. Myers makes a similar point, that the threat to North Korea is the prosperity and well-being of South Korea and the legitimization crisis that will ensue if these facts become known among the North Korean population. However, unlike Myers, I do not foresee another attempt by the North at "liberating" the South anytime soon, as I make clear in the epilogue.

ONE: *Liberation and Division*

1 The story is told in Richard Kim, *Lost Names: Scenes from a Korean Boyhood* (University of California Press, 1988), pp. 164–166. Though written as fiction, the novel is based on Richard Kim's own childhood experience.

2 *FRUS: Diplomatic Papers, 1945, vol. 6: The British Commonwealth, the Far East* (1969), p. 1098; Bruce Cumings, *The Origins of the Korean War*, vol. 1: *Liberation and the Emergence of Separate Regimes, 1945–1947* (Princeton University Press, 1981), pp. 106–109.

3 Cumings, *The Origins of the Korean War*, vol. 1, p. 118.

4 United States Department of Defense, *The Entry of the Soviet Union into the War against Japan: Military Plans, 1941–45* (U.S. Government Printing Office, 1955), pp. 51–52.

5 Kathryn Weathersby, "Soviet Aims in Korea and the Origins of the Korean War, 1945–1950: New Evidence from Russian Archives," *CWIHP Working Paper 8* (November 1993), p. 10.

6 Winston Churchill, *The Second World War: Triumph and Tragedy* (Houghton Mifflin Harcourt, 1953), pp. 635–639; Tsuyoshi Hasegawa, *Racing the Enemy: Stalin, Truman, and the Surrender of Japan* (Belknap Press, 2006), p. 141.

7 The Soviets had been aware of the bomb through their wartime espionage operations in the United States. The Americans were later able to confirm this through the Venona Project, a highly secret intelligence operation involving interception of Soviet intelligence messages. At Potsdam, President Truman was not aware that the Soviets knew about the Manhattan Project. John Earl Haynes and Harvey Klehr, *Venona: Decoding Soviet Espionage in America* (Yale University Press, 2000); Richard J. Aldrich, *The Hidden Hand: Britain, America and Cold War Secret Intelligence* (John Murray, 2001); Stephen Budiansky, *Battle of Wits: The Complete Story of Code-Breaking in World War II* (Free Press, 2002).

8 Andrei Gromyko, *Memories* (Hutchinson, 1989), p. 109.

9 Hasegawa, *Racing the Enemy*, pp. 178–193; William Stueck, *The Korean War: An International History* (Princeton University Press, 1995), p. 18.

10 *FRUS, 1945*, vol. 6, p. 1039; Cumings, *The Origins of the Korean War*, vol. 1, pp. 120–121.

11 According to historian Kathryn Weathersby, the fate of Korea as a potential "springboard for Japanese invasion onto the Asian continent" and the Soviet Far East was a foremost concern for Stalin. These views were not challenged. The long-held assumption that debate within the Soviet government was limited is correct. She claims that in the hundreds of documents she has studied in the Soviet Central Committee and Foreign Ministry archives, she has never come across a "document indicating a policy debate of any kind." Thus, she concludes, we can assume that the June 1945 report accurately reflected the opinion from the top and that if "its recommendation had not already been approved, the authors would never have written it." Weathersby, "Soviet Aims in Korea and the Origins of the Korean War," p. 11; Cumings, *Origins of the Korean War*, vol. 1, pp. 120–121.

12 Radio Address of Generalissimo Stalin, Soviet Embassy Information Bulletin (Washington, D.C.), September 6, 1945. Quoted in Harold R. Isaacs, *No Peace for Asia* (MIT Press, 1947), p. 256. See also Max R. Beloff, *Soviet Policy in the Far East, 1944–1951* (Oxford University Press, 1953), p. 246.

13 *New York Times*, November 4, 1945.

14 Allan R. Millett, *The War for Korea, 1945–1950: A House Burning* (University Press of Kansas, 2005), pp. 48–50; Henry Chung, *The Russians Came to Korea* (Korean Pacific Press, 1947), p.45.

15 Cumings, *The Origins of the Korean War*, vol. 1, pp. 388–389; Richard E. Lauterbach, *Danger from the East* (Harper & Brothers, 1964), pp. 213–217.

16 Kathryn Weathersby, "Soviet Policy toward Korea: 1944–1946," PhD dissertation, Indiana University, 1990, p. 191.

17 Most scholars who studied the Soviet occupation of North Korea concluded that Soviet policies were well received owing to Soviet authorities' taking popular measures such as prosecuting collaborators, especially those who worked in the detested police, and confiscating Japanese farms and farms belonging to Korean landowners to redistribute them. Recent historians have revised this view of the Soviet occupation. They argue that the Soviet occupation was anything but popular. They also question the alleged discontinuity between the colonial and postcolonial regime in North Korea. These scholars make clear that the Soviet occupation was an *imperialist* occupation and that the Soviets continued many unpopular policies that were identical to Japanese colonial policy such as state purchase of grains. They also argue that many Korean mid-level managers and administrators who had worked for the colonial regime remained and worked for the new government. See Mitsuhiko Kimura, "From Fascism to Communism: Continuity and Development of Collectivist Economic Policy in North Korea," *Economic History Review* 52, no. 1 (February 1999); Kim Ha-yŏng, *Kukchejuŭi sigak eso pon hanbando* [The Korean Peninsula from an International Perspective] (Seoul: Ch'aek pŏlle, 2002); Chung'ang ilbo t'ŭkpyŏl ch'wijaeban, eds., *Pirok chosŏn minjujuŭi inmin konghwaguk* [Secret History of the Democratic People's Republic of Korea] (Seoul: Chung'ang ilbosa, 1992). For recent studies on the

Soviet occupation of North Korea, see Andrei Lankov, *From Stalin to Kim Il Sung: The Formation of North Korea, 1945–1960* (Rutgers University Press, 2002); Andrei Lankov, *Crisis in North Korea: The Failure of De-Stalinization* (University of Hawaii Press, 2005); Erik van Ree, *Socialism in One Zone: Stalin's Policy in Korea, 1945–1947* (Berg, 1989); *CWIHP Bulletin: New Evidence on North Korea*, no. 14/15 (Winter 2003/Spring 2004); Charles K. Armstrong, *The North Korean Revolution, 1945–1950* (Cornell University Press, 2003). The most comprehensive book in English on this period of North Korean history is Robert Scalapino and Chong-sik Lee's monumental two-volume *Communism in Korea* (University of California Press, 1972).

18 Chong-sik Lee and Ki-Wan Oh, "The Russian Faction in North Korea," *Asian Survey* 8, no. 4 (1968), p. 272.

19 Henry R. Huttenbach, "The Soviet Koreans: Product of Russo-Japanese Imperial Rivalry," *Central Asian Survey* 12, no. 1 (1993), pp. 59–69. See also German N. Kim, "The Deportation of 1937 as a Logical Continuation of Tsarist and Soviet Nationality Policy in the Russian Far East," *The Korean and Korean American Studies Bulletin* 12 (2001), pp. 19–43; Dae-sook Suh, ed., *Koreans in the Soviet Union* (University of Hawaii Press, 1987); Walter Kolarz, *The Peoples of the Soviet Far East* (Archon Books, 1969).

20 Lim Ŭn, *The Founding of a Dynasty in North Korea: An Authentic Biography of Kim Il-sŏng* (Tokyo: Jiyusha, 1982), p. 144.

21 Quoted in Van Ree, *Socialism in One Zone*, p. 59.

22 Lankov, *From Stalin to Kim Il Sung*, p. 12. Having good reason to fear reprisal, the Japanese approached local influential Koreans about organizing an interim governing body that could help keep law and order after liberation. Thus was formed the *Chosŏn kŏnguk chunbi wiwŏnhoe*, or Committee for the Preparation of Korean Independence (CPKI). Within weeks of liberation, the CPKI organized tens of thousands of Koreans into local branches aimed to maintain law and order. These self-governing groups, which sprang up throughout the country, eventually evolved into People's Committees. While the Americans disbanded these self-proclaimed governing groups in the South, in North Korea the Soviets chose instead to infiltrate and manipulate them and eventually allying with them to serve the interests of the pro-Soviet North Korean regime. See van Ree, *Socialism in One Zone*; Cumings, *The Origins of the Korean War*, vol. 1, pp. 267–350.

23 Van Ree, *Socialism in One Zone*, p. 54.

24 Nikita Khrushchev, *Khrushchev Remembers* (Little, Brown, 1970), p. 370.

25 Charles K. Armstrong, *The North Korean Revolution: 1945–1950* (Cornell University Press, 2003), p. 53.

26 Hyun-su Jeon with Gyoo Kahng, "The Shtykov Diaries: New Evidence on Soviet Policy in Korea," *CWIHP Bulletin: The Cold War in Asia*, no. 6/7 (Winter 1995), p. 69.

27 Lankov, *From Stalin to Kim Il Sung*, pp. 10–11; Scalapino and Lee, *Communism in Korea*, p. 238.

28 Yu Sŏng-ch'ŏl, "Testimony," installment 6, November 7, 1990, in Sydney A. Seiler, *Kim Il Sung 1941–48: The Creation of a Legend, the Building of a Regime* (University Press of America, 1994), p. 122.

29 Lim, *Founding of a Dynasty in North Korea*, p. 153. See also Lankov, *From Stalin to Kim Il Sung*, pp. 79–80.

30 Yu, "Testimony," p. 105.

31 North Korean propaganda purports that Kim Il Sung led the "Korean People's Revolutionary Army." This force never existed. Wada Haruki, *Kim Il-sŏng gwa manju hangil chŏnjaeng* [Kim Il Sung and the Anti-Japanese Struggle in Manchuria] (Seoul: Changjakkwa pip'yŏngsa, 1992), pp. 136–141. See also Lankov, *From Stalin to Kim Il Sung*, pp. 49–76; Suh Dae Sook, *Kim Il Sung: North Korean Leader* (Columbia University Press, 1988), pp. 37–47; Sydney A. Seiler, *Kim Il Sŏng, 1941–1948: The Creation of a Legend, The Building of a Regime* (University Press of America, 1994), pp. 29–41.

32 Yu, "Testimony," pp. 112–116.

33 Quoted in Scalapino and Lee, *Communism in Korea*, vol. 1, pp. 324–325, from O Yŏng-jin, *So kunjoŏng ha ŭi Pukhan: Hana ŭi chung-ŏn* [North Korea under Soviet Military Government: An Eyewitness Report] (Seoul: Chung'ang Munhwasa, 1952).

34 Yu, "Testimony," pp. 124–125.

35 Van Ree, *Socialism in One Zone*, p. 113; Scalapino and Lee, *Communism in Korea*, vol. 1, p. 331.

36 Scalapino and Lee, *Communism in Korea*, vol. 1, p. 332.

37 Mitsuhiko Kimura, "From Fascism to Communism: Continuity and Development of Collectivist Economic Policy in North Korea," *Economic History Review*, New Series, 52, no. 1 (February 1999), p. 77.

The Land Reform Act of March 5, 1945, was the first major action of the newly formed North Korean Provisional People's Committees. While land reform promoted the distribution of cultivated lands previously owned by the Japanese and a small number of Korean rural gentry to thousands of Korean tenant farmers, Soviet authorities still established price controls that forced these farmers to sell their produce at fixed low prices to state cooperative associations. Immediately after the completion of land reform, the new government also established 25 percent tax-in-kind, "which was to exact approximately 25 percent of the gross produce and constitute the sole burden upon the farmer." Thus, land distribution was just one part of the communist agrarian reform. The other major aspect of land reform was taxation and market policies, which remained essentially unchanged from the Japanese colonial era. See Scalapino and Lee, *Communism in Korea*, part II, pp. 1023–1025. There were other parallels between the colonial and the postcolonial agricultural landholding systems. As the essential element in a capitalist system, private ownership of land derives from the right of the owner to dispose of his property according to his own will. But despite becoming landowners on paper due to land reform, this right was denied to the North Korean farmer. Indeed, the 1945 Land Reform Act strictly *prohibited* the sale or lease of land transferred by deed. "The former tenant was given a legal document guaranteeing ownership of that land, but this had little meaning because of the strict constraints on the disposal of his property." See Kimura, *From Fascism to Communism*, pp. 76–77.

New scholarship on postliberation North Korea is emerging about the extent to which both Stalinist and Japanese imperialist fascism ideology became the main currents of North Korea's economic policy. After August 15, 1945, and despite the Soviet and North Korean leaders' rhetoric about "cleansing" their zone of former Japanese collaborators and influences, many Korean administrators and managers who had worked for the colonial regime at intermediate levels had, in fact, remained to work for the new government and only later defected or were expelled after it was firmly established. The continuity between Japanese and North Korea economic policy was largely due to the apparent sympathy between Soviet and Japanese ideas on economic planning. The conversion of Japanese communists to imperial fascism in the late 1930s had a substantial impact on policy making in the wartime Japanese economy. This conversion was most apparent in Manchuria, where many former Japanese Marxists played an important role in developing the strategic plans for the industries in the Japanese puppet state of Manchukuo. These same Soviet influences, which had helped to shape wartime Japanese economy in Manchuria, also dominated North Korea after 1945. Ibid., p. 82. See also Andrei Lankov, "The Demise of Non-Communist Parties in North Korea (1945–1960), *Journal of Cold War Studies* 3, no. 1 (Winter 2001), pp. 104–109. For a discussion of the relationship between Japanese fascism and North Korean communism, see Brian Myers, *The Cleanest Race: How North Korean See Themselves (and Why It Matters)* (Melville House, 2010), pp. 30–38. Leonid Petrov has also noted that many South Korean intellectuals who had been trained in Japan eventually settled in the north. For example, Paek Nam-ŭn (1894–1979) was a leading North Korean intellectual whose major works were all written in Japanese. It was only after liberation that he translated these works into Korean. After the founding of the Republic of Korea in 1948, Paek Nam-ŭn, and other Japanese-trained intellectuals like him, settled in P'yŏngyang, where they went on to be appointed to high positions within the NKWP and DPRK government. Paek himself held various high administrative posts throughout his career, including educational minister and president of the academy of science. Most of these intellectuals would later come to regret their decision to side with the North Korean regime, as they were later destroyed during the North Korean purges of the late 1950s. See Leonid A. Petrov, "Foreign and Traditional Influences in the Historiography of Paek Nam-un," *Proceedings of the Twelfth New Zealand International Conference on Asian Studies*, Massey University, November 19–26, 1997, pp. 205, available at http://www.north-korea.narod.ru/paek.htm (accessed July 26, 2012).

38 Scalapino and Lee, *Communism in Korea*, vol. 1, p. 336, fn 49. The Sinŭiju uprising on November 23 was the single largest anti-communist demonstration during the "liberation" period. The incident was sparked by the arrest of a school principal who had publicly criticized Soviet soldiers and Korean communists. The arrest became the catalyst for a series of bloody clashes between students and armed Soviet and Korean communists linked to internal Korean security forces, called *poandae*, which was commanded by Kim Il Sung. See Adam Cathcart and Charles Kraus, "Peripheral Influence: The Sinŭiju Student Incident of 1945 and the Impact of Soviet Occupation in North Korea," *Journal of Korean Studies* 13, no. 1 (Fall 2008); Armstrong, *North Korean Revolution*, pp. 62–64. The South Korean historian Kim Ha-yŏng has argued that the uprising was fueled by genuine expressions of popular anger,

which were both deep and widespread. According to her, Soviet occupation forces actually suppressed popular demands for democracy, and their success in doing so was in large part due to the fact that they were able to quickly gain full control over their zone. Moreover, their central aim was to recover the territory and influence that had been lost to the Japanese at the end of the Russo-Japanese War. The basis for Soviet policy toward the Korean peninsula was thus not revolutionary internationalism but the desire for imperialist expansion. Stalin's policy toward Korea, in other words, was simply following the tradition of the tsarist empire. See Kim Ha-yŏng, "The Formation of North Korean State Capitalism," trans. Owen Miller, *International Socialism: A Quarterly Journal of Socialist Theory*, June 1, 2006, available at http://www.isj.org.uk/?id=205 (accessed June 30, 2008). The original Korean version is Kim's *Kukchejuŭi sigak eso pon hanbando* [Korean Peninsula from an International Perspective].

39 *New York Times*, December 6, 1945.

40 Kim Hak-chun, *Pukhan 50 nyŏn-sa* [Fifty Years of North Korean History] (Seoul: Tong'a ch'ulp'ansa, 1995), pp. 96–97; Kim, *Kukchejuŭi sigak eso pon hanbando* [Korean Peninsula from an International Perspective], p. 257; Armstrong, *North Korean Revolution*, pp. 62–63.

41 *New York Times*, July 9, 1947.

42 Van Ree, *Socialism in One Zone*, p. 120.

43 Ibid., pp. 122–123; Scalapino and Lee, *Communism in Korea*, pp. 336–337.

44 John Dower, *Embracing Defeat: Japan in the Wake of World War II* (W. W. Norton, 1999), p. 78. See also D. Clayton James, *The Years of MacArthur*, vol. 3, *Triumph and Disaster, 1945–1964* (Houghton Mifflin, 1985), pp. 287–300.

45 Kenneth Strother, "A Memoir: Experience of a Staff Officer, Headquarters XXIV Corps in the Occupation of Korea, September–November 1945," Miscellaneous Collection S, MHI; James, *The Years of MacArthur*, vol. 3, pp. 287–300.

46 HUSAFIK, vol. 3, chap. 4, pp. 16–17.

47 Strother, "Memoir," pp. 13–14.

48 *FRUS, 1945*, vol. 6, pp. 1045–1050.

49 Ibid., p. 1135.

50 The Korean People's Republic (KPR) was an outgrowth of CPKI peacekeeping activities that had begun immediately after liberation with Japanese support. On September 6, 1945, CPKI members from Seoul and nearby provinces came together to announce the formation of the KPR. It was a direct response to the impending arrival of American occupational forces. CPKI leaders were eager to establish their own provisional government before the arrival of the Americans, "both to show that Koreans could run their own affairs and to forestall either a prolonged American tutelage or the installation in power of other Koreans who might gain American favor." Cumings, *The Origins of the Korean War*, vol. 1, p. 84; Millett, *The War for Korea, 1945–1950*, pp. 46–47.

51 U.S. Army Military Government in Korea (USAMGIK) G-2 Periodic Report no. 1, September 9, 1945, Headquarters XXIV Corps, "Activities of Left-Wing Korean Political Parties," p. 13, H. L. Wolbers Papers, box 1, MHI.

52 *FRUS, 1945*, vol. 6, p. 1064.

53 USAMGIK, "Activities of Left-Wing Korean Political Parties," pp. 15–17.
54 *New York Times*, October 30, 1945.
55 Cumings, *The Origins of the Korean War*, vol. 1, pp. 375–379.
56 Lauterbach, *Dangers from the East*, pp. 218–219.
57 *New York Times*, November 4, 1945.
58 *FRUS, 1945*, vol. 6, pp. 1142–1143.
59 Charles H. Donnelly, "U.S. Military Government in Korea (USAMGIK)," unpublished memoir, pt. 3, 1947–53, p. 960, Charles H. Donnelly Papers, MHI.
60 *New York Times*, December 8, 1945.
61 Donnelly, "U.S. Military Government in Korea," pp. 914, 957–958.

TWO: *Two Koreas*

1 Soon Sung-cho, *Korea in World Politics, 1940–1950, An Evaluation of American Responsibility* (University of California Press, 1967), p. 94.
2 Quoted in Cumings, *The Origins of the Korean War*, vol. 1, p. 200; Ambassador Edwin Pauley to President Truman, June 22, 1946, in *FRUS, 1946*, vol. 8: *The Far East* (1971), pp. 706–709. Truman was impressed with Pauley's letter; see his response, July 16, 1946, in *FRUS, 1946*, vol. 8, pp. 713–714; and in Harry Truman, *Years of Trial and Hope* (Doubleday, 1956), p. 366.
3 Cumings, *The Origins of the Korean War*, vol. 1, pp. 184–187; "Langdon to Secretary of State," November 20, 1945, in *FRUS: Diplomatic Papers, 1945*, vol. 6: *The British Commonwealth, the Far East* (1969), p. 1131.
4 Letter from Mrs. Rhee to Mrs. Frye, May 4, 1947, "Robert T. Oliver File," 79 #13011, Syngman Rhee Presidential Papers (hereafter "Rhee Papers"), Yonsei University, Seoul, Korea. For a complete catalogue of the Rhee papers, see Young Ick Lew and Sangchul Cha, comp., *The Syngman Rhee Presidential Papers: A Catalogue* (Seoul: Yonsei University Press, 2005).
5 "Memorandum of February 5 and May 14, 1945," in *FRUS, 1945*, vol. 6, pp. 1023, 1030.
6 Cumings, *The Origins of the Korean War*, vol. 1, p. 219; Millett, *The War for Korea, 1945–1950*, p. 69.
7 *New York Times*, December 29, 1945.
8 Erik van Ree, *Socialism in One Zone: Stalin's Policy in Korea, 1945–1947* (Berg, 1989), pp. 142–144; Cumings, *The Origins of the Korean War*, vol. 1, pp. 221–223; HUSAFIK, vol. 2, chap. 4, p. 78; Scalapino and Lee, *Communism in Korea*, vol. 1, pp. 276–277.
9 Cumings, *The Origins of the Korean War*, vol. 1, pp. 223–225; Scalapino and Lee, *Communism in Korea*, vol. 1, pp. 276–280.
10 Lim Ŭn, *The Founding of a Dynasty in North Korea: An Authentic Biography of Kim Il-sŏng* (Tokyo: Jiyusha, 1982), pp. 150–151; Scalapino and Lee, *Communism in Korea*, pp. 337–340; Van Ree, *Socialism in One Zone*, p. 143; Andrei Lankov, *From Stalin to Kim Il Sung: The Formation of North Korea, 1945–1960* (Rutgers University Press, 2002), pp. 23–24.
11 Lim, *Founding of a Dynasty in North Korea*, p. 152.
12 Van Ree, *Socialism in One Zone*, pp. 145–146.

13 *New York Times*, January 27, 1946.
14 Quoted in Cumings, *The Origins of the Korean War*, vol. 1, p. 227.
15 *New York Times*, March 11 and 13, 1946.
16 Stalin's instructions to the Soviet delegation stated "that the Commission must consult *only* with those democratic parties and organizations that fully and without any qualifications support the Moscow Decision." See Jongsoo James Lee, *The Partition of Korea after World War II: A Global History* (Palgrave Macmillan, 2006), pp. 96–102.
17 Memorandum, October 26, 1946, Major General Albert E. Brown Papers, Korea, 1946–47, box 3, MHI.
18 HUSAFIK, vol. 3, chap. 2, pp. 212–213. As Kathryn Weathersby demonstrates, briefing papers for the December 1945 conference reveal that Stalin was very concerned about the threat of a resurgent Japan and that his aim for Korea was to eradicate Japanese influence in the peninsula. "If Soviet policy is directed at the destruction of the military capability of the Japanese aggressors, at the eradication of Japanese influence in Korea, at the encouragement of the democratic movement of the Korean people and preparing them for independence, then judging by the activity of the Americans in Korea, American policy has precisely the opposite goal. The Americans have not only retained in Korea the old administrative apparatus, but have also left many Japanese and local collaborators in leadings posts. In the American zone, Japanese enjoy broad political rights and economic possibilities." The Soviets also were well aware that Rhee's political views were staunchly anti-Soviet, and they understood that should a government hostile to the Soviet Union come into power, they would not be able to safeguard their economic and strategic interests there. This concern was highlighted in another briefing report prepared for the December conference which concluded that "the Japanese military and heavy industry in North Korea must be transferred to the Soviet Union as partial payment of reparations, and also as compensation for the huge damage inflicted by Japan on the Soviet Union throughout the time of its existence, including damages from the Japanese intervention in the Far East from 1918–1923." Quoted in Kathryn Weathersby, "Soviet Aims in Korea and the Origins of the Korean War, 1945–1950: New Evidence from Russian Archives," *CWIHP Working Paper 8* (November 1993), pp. 17–20. See also Wada Haruki, "The Korean War, Stalin's Policy and Japan," *Social Science Japan Journal* 1, no. 1 (1998), pp. 5–29.
19 HUSAFIK, vol. 2, pt. 2, p. 29.
20 Hyun-su Jeon with Gyoo Kahng, "The Shtykov Diaries: New Evidence on Soviet Policy in Korea," *CWIHP Bulletin: The Cold War in Asia*, no. 6/7 (Winter 1995), pp. 92–96; Letter from Mrs. Rhee to Mrs. Frye, May 4, 1947, "Robert T. Oliver File," 79 #13011, Rhee Papers.
21 Rhee to Oliver, May 6, 1947, "Robert T. Oliver File," 79 #13011, Rhee Papers.
22 "Statement by Rhee," January 23, 1947, "Robert T. Oliver File," 79 #13004, Rhee Papers.
23 *New York Times*, May 29, 1947.
24 "Draft Report of Special Interdepartmental Committee on Korea, February, 25, 1947, *FRUS, 1947*, vol. 6: *The Far East* (1972), pp. 611–612.

25 Millett, *The War for Korea, 1945–1950*, p. 120.
26 James F. Schnabel and Robert J. Watson, *History of the Joint Chiefs of Staff*, vol. 3, part 1: *The Korean War* (Michael Glazier, 1979), pp. 13–14.
27 "Robert Lovett to V. M. Molotov," October 17, 1947, in *FRUS, 1947*, vol. 6, p. 837.
28 Lankov, *From Stalin to Kim Il Sung*, pp. 45–46; Andre Lankov, "What Happened to Kim Ku?" *Korea Times*, September 4, 2008; "Chronology of Activities of Opposition to the UN Election," Albert E. Brown Papers, Korea, 1946–51, box 3, MHI.
29 An justified the killing by stating that Kim Ku was acting on behalf of the Soviets. An was tried and given a life sentence, but he was pardoned in time to fight in the Korean War, survived it, and became a successful businessman in exile. Many had long suspected that Rhee was ultimately behind An's actions, but it was only in 1992 that An confessed to a major newspaper that Rhee's chief of security had been behind the assassination. In October 1996, at the age of seventy-nine, An was beaten to death by an attacker wielding a club inscribed with the words "Justice Stick." See Lankov, "What Happened to Kim Ku?" An's story took a final strange turn when a U.S. Army Counter Intelligence Corps (CIC) report from July 1, 1949, was discovered in the National Archives (NARA). It clearly states that An was a CIC informant and then an agent. He was also a member of a secret right-wing organization called the "White Clothes Society," whose leader, Yum Dong-jin, supported Rhee and opposed Kim Ku and was considered "our man in Seoul" by the CIC. This raised speculation that the U.S. government might have ultimately been behind the assassination. The CIC report by Maj. George Cilley can be found at http://www.korean-war.com/Archives/2002/06/msg00085.html (accessed August 1, 2010).
30 Allan R. Millett, "Captain James H. Hausman and the Formation of Korean Army, 1945–1950," *Armed Forces and Society*, no. 4 (Summer 1947), p. 510.
31 Ibid., pp. 507–513; James Hausman, John Toland interview transcript, p. 37, Hausman Papers, Yenching Library, Harvard University, Cambridge, Mass.
32 John Merrill, *Korea: The Peninsular Origins of the War* (University of Delaware Press, 1989), p. 67; Bruce Cumings, *The Origins of the Korean War*, vol. 2: *The Roaring of the Cataract, 1947–1950* (Princeton University Press, 1990), p. 254.
33 Merrill, *Korea*, p. 81.
34 HUSAFIK, pt. 3, p. 18.
35 Millett, *The War for Korea, 1945–1950*, p. 161.
36 James Hausman, "Notecards for a Speech on the Early Days of the Korean Constabulary," Hausman Papers. See also Donald Clark, "Before the War—Western Encounters with Korea," unpublished manuscript (author's personal copy), p. 31.
37 James Hausman, "History of the Rebellion, 14th Constabulary," Hausman Papers; Clark, "Before the War," p. 33.
38 Hausman, "History of the Rebellion, 14th Constabulary"; Donald Clark, *Living Dangerously in Korea: The Western Experience, 1900–1950* (Eastbridge, 2001), pp. 335–336.
39 Keyes Beech, *Tokyo and Points East* (Doubleday, 1954), p. 141. Also partly quoted in Cumings, *The Origins of the Korean War*, vol. 2, p. 265.
40 Cumings, *The Origins of the Korean War*, vol. 2, p. 265; Beech, *Tokyo and Points*

East, p. 141; Kim Kye-yu, "Naega kyŏkkun yŏsunsagŏn" [My Experience of the Yŏsu Sunch'ŏn Incident], *Chŏnan munhwa* 4 (1991), pp. 54–57.

41 Hausman, "Notecards for a Speech." The total number killed in Cheju-do is in dispute. Allan R. Millett, for example, doubts it was as high as thirty thousand, based on his own careful analysis. See Millett, *The War for Korea, 1945–1950*, p. 303, no. 74.

42 *New York Times*, May 7, 1949.

THREE: *Momentous Decisions*

1 Kathryn Weathersby, "Should We Fear This? Stalin and the Danger of War with America," *CWIHP Working Paper 39* (July 2002), pp. 3–5.

2 Mao Tse Tung, *Selected Works of Mao Tse-tung* (Foreign Language Press, 1977), vol. 4, pp. 160–163.

3 Sergei N. Goncharov, John W. Lewis, and Xue Litai, *Uncertain Partners: Stalin, Mao and the Korean War* (Stanford University Press, 1993), p. 24.

4 Shi Zhe, " 'With Mao and Stalin: The Reminiscences of Mao's Interpreter,' Part 2; Liu Shaoqi in Moscow," *Chinese Historian* 6, no. 1 (Spring 1993), p. 83. Mao's resentment of Stalin was palpable during his 1956 conversation with the Soviet ambassador: "When armed struggle against the forces of Chiang Kai-shek was at its height, when our forces were on the brink of victory, Stalin insisted that peace be made with Chiang Kai-shek, since he doubted the forces of the Chinese Revolution." "Mao's Conversation with Yudin, 31 March 1956," *CWIHP Bulletin: The Cold War in Asia*, no. 6/7 (Winter 1995), p. 165.

5 Mao, *Selected Works of Mao Tse-tung*, vol. 5, pp. 16–17.

6 Tony Saich, ed., *The Rise to Power of the Chinese Communist Party: Documents and Analysis* (East Gate, 1996), pp. 1368–1369; Chen Jian, *China's Road to the Korean War* (Columbia University Press, 1994), pp. 15–23, 33–57, 64–78.

7 Goncharov et al., *Uncertain Partners*, p. 85.

8 "Conversation between Stalin and Mao, Moscow 16 December 1949," *CWIHP Bulletin: The Cold War in Asia*, no. 6/7 (Winter 1995), p. 5; Goncharov et al., *Uncertain Partners*, pp. 85–88.

9 Sergei Goncharov, "The Stalin-Mao Dialogue," *Far Eastern Affairs*, no. 2 (1992), pp. 109–110. This article features Goncharov's interview with Ivan Kovalev, Stalin's personal envoy to Mao Zedong.

10 Goncharov et al., *Uncertain Partners*, p. 92.

11 *New York Times*, January 2, 1950; Goncharov et al., *Uncertain Partners*, pp. 92–93. See also Vladislav Zubok and Constantine Pleshakov, *Inside the Kremlin's Cold War: From Stalin to Krushchev* (Harvard University Press, 1996), pp. 60–62.

12 "Conversation between Stalin and Mao, Moscow, 22 January 1950," *CWIHP Bulletin: The Cold War in Asia*, no. 6/7 (Winter 1995), p. 8.

13 *New York Times*, January 5, 1950.

14 This interpretation is implied in Goncharov et al., *Uncertain Partners*. Also see John Lewis Gaddis, *We Now Know: Rethinking Cold War History* (Oxford University Press, 1998), pp. 72–73; William Stueck, *Rethinking the Korean War: A New Diplomatic and Strategic History* (Princeton University Press, 2002), p. 73. Lorenz Lüthi has argued, however, that despite the intricate maneuvers

between Mao and Stalin, there was never really a chance of China's rapprochement with the United States simply because Mao did not want it. Lüthi also rejects the notion that Mao was pretending to Stalin that such a rapprochement was possible or that he played the "American card" to get better terms from Stalin. See Lorenz M. Lüthi, *The Sino-Soviet Split: Cold War in the Communist World* (Princeton University Press, 2008). Chen Jian agrees, stating that America's "lost chance" with China is a myth and that the CCP's adoption of its anti-American policy had "deep roots" that went way beyond U.S. support for the Nationalists (p. 48). Sergey Radchenko similarly describes Mao as a "revolutionary realist" who "worked toward one goal alone: China's and his own power" (p. 69). Accordingly, Mao's ultimate goal was to restore the nation's independence and pride and to secure his control over China's state and society. Sergey Radchenko, *Two Suns in the Heaven: The Sino-Soviet Struggle for Supremacy, 1962–1967* (Stanford University Press, 2009); Chen Jian, *Mao's China and the Cold War* (University of Chapel Hill Press, 2001).

15 Gordon Chang, *Friends and Enemies: The United States, China and the Soviet Union, 1948–1972* (Stanford University Press, 1990), pp. 65–66.

16 "Minutes of Conversation between Stalin and Mao, Moscow, 22 January 1950," *CWIHP Bulletin: The Cold War in Asia*, no. 6/7 (Winter 1995), pp. 7–8.

17 Text of the treaty in John W. Garver, *Chinese-Soviet Relations, 1937–1945: The Diplomacy of Chinese Nationalism* (Oxford University Press, 1988), pp. 214–216.

18 Goncharov et al., *Uncertain Partners*, pp. 110–129. Mao also received another gift from Stalin: the Soviet leader provided Mao with a list of Chinese informers within the CCP who reported to Moscow. It was another instance of Stalin's many betrayals that resulted in the purge of hundreds of pro-Soviet communists in the CCP. See Zubok and Pleshankov, *Inside the Kremlin's Cold War*, p. 61.

19 An Sŭng-hwan, "Chupukhan ssoryŏn kunsagomundanŭi pukhangun chiwŏn hwaldong (1946–1953) [Soviet Military Advisory Group Support to the NKPA, 1946–1953]," in *Hanguk chŏnjaengsaŭi saeroun yŏngu* [New Research on Korean War History] (Republic of Korea Ministry of National Defense Institute for Military History Compilation, 2002), vol. 2, p. 371.

20 A list of the number of Soviet advisors assigned to the NKPA reveals the degree of effort to professionalize the NKPA at every level of its command structure in the months before the outbreak of the war:

Division level and higher (total 34)

- Commander (Shtykov)
- Chief advisor to NKPA Supreme Staff
- 10 functional branch advisors
- 18 Supreme Staff operations staff advisors (key group, responsible for war planning and execution)
- 5 division commanders' advisors

Advisors at brigade level and below (total 202)

- 15 brigade advisors
- 68 regimental advisors
- 8 battalion advisors
- 9 military school advisors

- 28 military school faculty advisors
- 39 advisors to various other units
- 6 medical advisors
- 29 military specialists

From ibid., pp. 370–371.

21 Vladamir Petrov, "Soviet Role in the Korean War Confirmed: Secret Documents Declassified," *Journal of Northeast Asian Studies* 13, no. 3 (1994), pp. 51; Kathryn Weathersby, "The Soviet Role in the Early Phase of the Korean War: New Documentary Evidence," *Journal of American–East Asian Relations* 2, no. 4 (Winter 1993), p. 429.

22 Petrov, "Soviet Role in the Korean War Confirmed," p. 51.

23 Weathersby, "Should We Fear This?" pp. 9–11.

24 Goncharov et al., *Uncertain Partners*, pp. 143–145; Weathersby, "Should We Fear This?" pp. 11–12. Also see Nikita Khrushchev, *Khrushchev Remembers: The Glasnost Tapes*, trans. and edited by Jerrold L. Schecter with Vyacheslav V. Luchkov (Little, Brown, 1990), pp. 86–87; Khrushchev, "Truth about the Korean War: Memoirs," *Far Eastern Affairs*, no. 1 (1991), pp. 63–69.

25 Weathersby, "Should We Fear This?" pp. 12–13; Goncharov et al., *Uncertain Partners*, p. 145.

26 Goncharov et al., *Uncertain Partners*, p. 146. Sources differ as to how reluctant Mao actually was regarding his support of Kim's invasion plans. According to Khrushchev and other Chinese officials close to Mao, it was Mao who convinced Stalin to back Kim because he firmly believed that the United States would not intervene. Thus, far from being manipulated into supporting the war, Mao, according to these accounts, was a strong advocate of Kim's war. See Chen Jian, *China's Road to the Korean War: The Making of the Sino-American Confrontation* (Columbia University Press, 1994), pp. 87–91; Krushchev, *Khrushchev Remembers*, p. 368.

27 The full text of NSC 68 can be found at http://www.fas.org/irp/offdocs/nsc-hst/nsc-68.htm (accessed January 20, 2009).

28 David McCullough, *Truman* (Simon & Schuster, 1992), p. 773; *Public Papers of the Presidents: Harry S. Truman 1950* (U.S. Government Printing Office, 1965), p. 152. For an assessment of the significance of this document, see Ernest R. May, ed., *American Cold War Strategy: Interpretating NCS 68* (St. Martin's Press, 1993).

29 Telegram from Stalin to Shtykov, June 20, 1950, cited in Petrov, "Soviet Role in the Korean War Confirmed," pp. 53–54. Petrov notes that when the NKPA captured Seoul, Stalin forbade General Vasiliev to go there because of its proximity to the front. He "did not want the United States, the United Nations and World opinion to catch him directly participating in the war," although at that time few doubted the degree and nature of Moscow's involvement. An Sŭng-hwan also noted how the Soviet advisory activity was restricted: "Advisors who went to North Korea just before and during the war travelled on their army or navy identification cards rather than with a passport and thus did not register with the Soviet Embassy. Advisors only wore civilian clothing and disguised themselves as *Pravda* correspondents." An, "Chupukhan ssoryŏn kunsagomundanŭi pukhangun chiwŏn hwaldong (1946–1953) [Soviet Military Advisory Group Support to the NKPA, 1946–1953]," p. 369.

30 Weathersby, "Should We Fear This?" p. 14.
31 "Interview of General Razhubayev by Aryuzunov, 29 May 2001," cited in An, "Chupukhan ssoryŏn kunsagomundanŭi pukhangun chiwŏn hwaldong (1946–1953) [Soviet Military Advisory Group Support to the NKPA, 1946–1953]," pp. 439–440.
32 Weathersby, "Should We Fear This?" pp. 14–15. See also Anatoly Torkunov, *The War in Korea, 1950–1953: Its Origins, Bloodshed and Conclusion* (Tokyo: ICF, 2000), p. 68.

FOUR: *War for the South*

1 Larry Zellers, *In Enemy Hands: A Prisoner in North Korea* (University Press of Kentucky, 1991), p. 1.
2 "Letter to Lt. Col. Roy E. Appleman from Joseph R. Darrigo," July 2, 1953, Clay Blair Collection, box 78, MHI; Roy E. Appleman, *South to the Naktong, North to the Yalu* (U.S. Government Printing Office, 1961), pp. 23–24.
3 Appleman, *South to the Naktong,* p. 20.
4 *FRUS, 1950,* vol. 7: *Korea* (1976), p. 49.
5 Quoted in Clay Blair, *The Forgotten War: America in Korea, 1950–1953* (Times Books, 1987), p. 55.
6 *FRUS, 1950,* vol. 7, pp. 121–122.
7 *U.S. News & World Report,* May 5, 1950, p. 30.
8 Paik Sun Yup (Paek Sŏn-yŏp), *From Pusan to Panmunjom: Wartime Memoirs of the Republic of Korea's First Four-Star General* (Brassey's, 1992), p. 8.
9 Ibid., p. 7.
10 Dean Acheson, *Present at the Creation* (W. W. Norton, 1969), pp. 404–405; Harry S. Truman, *Memoirs,* vol. 2: *Years of Trial and Hope* (Doubleday, 1956), p. 332; McCullough, *Truman,* pp. 774–775.
11 *FRUS, 1950,* vol. 7, p. 124; McCullough, *Truman,* p. 777; Truman, *Memoirs,* vol. 2, pp. 332–333.
12 *FRUS, 1950,* vol. 7, p. 129.
13 Marguerite Higgins, *War in Korea: The Report of a Woman Combat Correspondent* (Doubleday, 1951), p. 16.
14 Beech, *Tokyo and Points East,* p. 111; James Hausman, Toland interview transcript, pp. 32–33.
15 Beech, *Tokyo and Points East,* pp. 112–113.
16 Hausman, Toland interview transcript, p. 34.
17 Paik, *From Pusan to Panmunjom,* p. 18.
18 Quoted in D. Clayton James and Anne Sharpe Wells, *Refighting the Last War: Command Crisis in Korea, 1950–53* (Free Press, 1992), p. 138.
19 Blair, *Forgotten War,* p. 76.
20 Douglas MacArthur, *Reminiscences: General of the Army* (Naval Institute Press, 1964), p. 334.
21 *Christian Science Monitor,* June 29, 1950.
22 Anthony Leviero, "U.S. 'Not at War,' President Asserts," *New York Times,* June 30, 1950.
23 John Toland, *In Mortal Combat Korea, 1950–1953* (William Morrow, 1991), pp. 65–68.

24 Eric C. Ludvigsen, "An Arrogant Display: The Failed Bluff of Task Force Smith," *Army* (February 1992), p. 38.

25 A recent study by Thomas E. Hanson suggests that the American soldiers in Japan might have been better prepared than commonly believed. See his *Combat Ready? The Eighth U.S. Army on the Eve of the Korean War* (Texas A&M University Press, 2010).

26 Quoted in *Real Magazine*, October 1952.

27 Michael W. Cannon, "Task Force Smith: A Study in (Un)preparedness and (Ir)responsibility," *Military Review* 68, no. 2 (February 1988), p. 66.

28 Appleman, *South to the Naktong*, p. 75.

29 Letter from Dunn to Appleman, June 17, 1955, Clay Blair Collection, box 72, MHI.

30 *New York Times*, September 3, 1950.

31 Appleman, *South to the Naktong*, p. 110.

32 Comments critical of the ROK Army are found in most standard works in English on the Korean War such as Blair, *Forgotten War*; Appleman, *South to the Naktong*; Cumings, *The Origins of the Korean War*, vol. 2. Allan Millett, however, has sought to correct this bias by focusing on many of the ROK Army's accomplishments, especially at the beginning of the war when the ROK Capital Division and ROK First Division slowed the progress of the NKPA, thereby effectively thwarting Kim's Il Sung's victory drive to Pusan. See Allan R. Millett, *The War for Korea, 1950–1951: They Came from the North* (University Press of Kansas, 2010), pp. 195-201. See also Korean Institute of Military History, *The Korean War*, vol. 1 (University of Nebraska Press, 1999), pp. 374–410.

33 Paik, *From Pusan to Panmunjom*, p. 30.

34 Korea Institute of Military History, *Korean War*, vol. 1, pp. 299–300.

35 "Order from Supreme Commander, NKA, to All Forces, 15 Oct 1950," quoted in James F. Schnabel, *Policy and Direction: The First Year* (U.S. Government Printing Office, 1990), p. 114n.

36 Blair, *Forgotten War*, p. 141.

37 *Korea Times*, October 1, 1999.

38 There are conflicting accounts as to why U.S. soldiers fired on the refugees. Some accounts contend that ill-trained and besieged soldiers had simply panicked, while others believe that they had been ordered. So far, no evidence has been uncovered that U.S. soldiers were given *explicit* orders to shoot the refugees at Nogŭnri; ample evidence supports the contention that there was a policy in place regarding the shooting of refugees. See Sahr Conway-Lanz, "Beyond No-Gun-ri: Refugees and the United States Military in the Korean War," *Diplomatic History* 29, no. 1 (January 2005), p. 59; Charles J. Hanley, Sang-Hun Choe, and Martha Mendoza, *The Bridge at No Gun Ri: A Hidden Nightmare from the Korean War* (Henry Holt, 2001).

39 "One Korean's Account: Too Frighten to Cry," *U.S. News & World Report*, May 22, 2000, p. 52.

40 Department of the Army Inspector General, *No Gun Ri Review*, January 2001, pp. 149–150. An estimate of the number of deaths can be found in ibid., p. 191. The incident gained international attention as a result of a report by Charles J. Hanley, Sang-Hun Choe, and Martha Mendoza, published by the Associ-

ated Press in September 1999, that won the Pulitzer Prize in 2000. The AP team later published a much more extensive revision of their findings in *The Bridge at No Gun Ri.*

41 Donald Knox, *The Korean War*, vol. 1: *Pusan to Chosin, an Oral History* (Harcourt Brace, 1985), pp. 72–73.

42 Millett, *The War for Korea, 1950–1951*, pp. 94–96.

43 Narrative Report of the United States Military Advisory Group to the Republic of Korea, Office of the Chief, USMAG, 1946–1949, Provided by Col. Harold Fischgrund, (Ret.), KMAG, G3 Office, 1949. Copy obtained from Allan R. Millett.

44 Quoted in An Sŭng-hwan, "Chupukhan ssoryŏn kunsa komundangŭi pukhangun chiwŏn hwaldong (1946–1953) [Soviet Military Advisory Group Support to the NKPA, 1946–1953]," p. 443.

45 The soldiers of the ROK Sixth Division held firm and defended the city of Ch'unch'ŏn until noon, June 28. The speed of the North Koreans' advance was seriously retarded and their tight timeline thrown to the winds. As events turned out, the North Korean army failed to execute the most important component of the operation as devised by Soviet planners—the encirclement and destruction of the ROK Army. The Soviet planners had envisioned a smaller-scale version of the epic campaigns of encirclement fought on the eastern front during World War II. The destruction of the ROK Army, not territorial advance, was the key to rapid victory. But the North Korean encircling forces, delayed by the ROK Sixth Division, were unable to encircle Seoul from the east and south to cut off the retreat route of the bulk of the ROK Army, which was located north of Seoul. See Kim Jwang-so, "The North Korean War Plan and the Opening Phase of the Korean War: A Documentary Study," *International Journal of Korean Studies* (Spring/Summer 2001), pp. 26–27. See also Millett, *The War for Korea, 1950–1951*, pp. 95–96; Korean Institute of Military History, *The Korean War*, vol. 1, pp. 280–282.

46 "26 June 1950, Top Secret Report on Military Situation by Shtykov to Comrade Zakharov," *CWIHP Bulletin: The Cold War in Asia*, no. 6/7 (Winter 1995), pp. 39–40.

47 Cables from Shtykov to Stalin on June 28, 1950, are cited in An, "Chupukhan ssoryŏn kunsa komundangŭi pukhangun chiwŏn hwaldong (1946–1953) [Soviet Military Advisory Group Support to the NKPA, 1946–1953]," p. 443.

48 "8 July 1950, ciphered telegram, Shtykov to Fyn-Si (Stalin), transmitting letter from Kim Il Sung to Stalin," *CWIHP Bulletin: The Cold War in Asia*, no. 6/7 (Winter 1995), pp. 43–44.

49 Cables cited in An, "Chupukhan ssoryŏn kunsa komundangŭi pukhangun chiwŏn hwaldong (1946–1953) [Soviet Military Advisory Group Support to the NKPA, 1946–1953]," p. 449.

50 Ibid., pp. 449–451. An is convinced that Soviet advisors were sent to the front with North Korean troops during the first weeks of the war. He believes that Stalin most likely ordered the withdrawal of most of the advisors before June 25. However, by July 8, realizing that the war was not going well, he agreed to send the requested twenty-five to thirty-five advisors. With regard to the earlier July 4 Shtykov cable requesting assignment of two advisors per two Army Group headquarters, and movement of General Vasiliev and a

group of officers to the front headquarters in Seoul, Stalin replied only that it would be better for Vasiliev to remain in P'yŏngyang. An sees this as a silent consent for the assignment of the Army Group advisors. The South Korean historian Pak Myŏng nim cites as further evidence the testimony of North Korean POWs. See Pak Myŏng-nim, *Han'guk chongchaengui palbalgwa kiwŏn* [The Korean War: The Outbreak and Its Origins] (Seoul: Nanamch'ulp'an, 1996), vol. 1, pp. 196–197.

51 James, *The Years of MacArthur*, vol. 3, pp. 453–454.
52 Acheson, *Present at the Creation*, p. 422.
53 James, *Years of MacArthur*, vol. 3, pp. 456–458.
54 MacArthur, *Reminiscenses*, p. 349.
55 Former secretary of the army Frank Pace Jr., interview, March 23, 1975, p. 8, MHI.
56 Quoted in James, *Years of MacArthur*, vol. 3, p. 461.
57 Truman, *Memoirs*, vol. 2, p. 356.
58 Almond interview with Capt. Thomas Fergusson, March 28, 1975 (side 1 of tape 4), Edward Almond Papers, box 1, p. 20, MHI.
59 McCaffrey correspondence, September 10, 1978, Roy Appleman Collection, box 20, MHI.
60 O. P. Smith, "Summary of the Situation of 15 November Contained in Letter to Commandant of the Marine Corps," Clay Blair Collection, box 83, MHI.
61 Appleman, *South to the Naktong*, pp. 509–513.
62 Matthew B. Ridgway, *The Korean War* (Doubleday, 1967), p. 42.
63 Clay Blair's interview with Michaelis, April 4, 1984, Clay Blair Collection, box 77, MHI.
64 Oral reminiscences of Major General John H. Chiles, July 27, 1977, interview with D. Clayton James, Clay Blair Collection, box 77, MHI.
65 McCaffrey correspondence, September 10, 1978, Roy Appleman Collection, box 20, MHI.
66 Russell Spurr, *Enter the Dragon: China's Undeclared War against the U.S. in Korea, 1950–51* (Newmarket Press, 1999), p. 105.
67 James, *Years of MacArthur*, vol. 3, p. 482; Schnabel and Robert Watson, *The History of the Joint Chiefs of Staff*, vol. 3, part 1: *The Korean War*, pp. 229–230.
68 Ridgway, *Korean War*, p. 42.
69 Appleman, *South to the Naktong*, p. 587.
70 *New York Times*, October 6, 1950.
71 *Washington Post*, October 4, 1950.
72 *New York Times*, October 6, 1950.
73 *Jefferson City Post*, October 2, 1950.
74 *New York Times*, September 28, 1950.
75 TRC, *Truth and Reconciliation: Activities of the Past Three Years* (Seoul: Ch'ungbuk National University Museum, 2009), pp. 95–96.
76 Appleman, *South to the Naktong*, p. 587.
77 Account of Pvt. Herman G. Nelson in Richard Peters and Xiaobing Li, *Voices from the Korean War: Personal Stories of American, Korean, and Chinese Soldiers* (University Press of Kentucky, 2004), pp. 67–68.
78 Interview with Yi Chun-yŏng, a former guard at Taejŏn prison, November 21, 2007, TRC and Ch'ungbuk National University Museum in *Han'guk*

chŏnjaeng chŏnhu mingan in chipdan hŭisaeng kwallyŏn 2007nyŏn yuhaebalgul pogoso [2007 Report on the Excavations of Human Remains Related to Civilian Massacres before and during the Korean War] (Seoul: Ch'ungbuk National University Museum, 2008) (hereafter *2007 Report on Excavations*), vol. 2, pp. 255–256.

79 *New York Times*, July 14 and 27, 1950.

80 *Time*, August 21, 1950, p. 20.

81 *New York Times*, July 13 and 16, 1950.

82 Higgins, *War in Korea*, p. 89.

83 *New York Times*, July 26, 1950.

84 Muccio to Rusk, July 26, 1950, box 4266, 795.000 Central Decimal Files 1950-1954, RG 59, NARA. The letter, uncovered by the historian Sahr Conway-Lanz, resides in a collection of State Department documents on the Korean War. The document was first cited in Sahr Conway-Lanz, "Beyond No Gun Ri: Refugees and the United States Military in the Korean War," *Diplomatic History* 29, no. 1 (January 2005), p. 59. The letter appears to prove that there was an official policy regarding the shooting of refugees. The revelations are part of a larger probe on the UN handling of the refugee problem during the war. The issue of American killings of Korean civilians is an extremely polemical one and has riled nationalist passions in both the United States and South Korea. An early pioneer in presenting the ferocious nature of the war is Bruce Cumings, whose two-volume study titled *The Origins of the Korea War* is considered a landmark in Korean War historiography. See also Jon Halliday and Bruce Cumings, *Korea: The Unknown War* (Viking Press, 1988); Conrad C. Crane, *American Airpower Strategy in Korea, 1950–1953* (University Press of Kansas, 2000); Sahr Conway-Lanz, *Collateral Damage: Americans, Non-combatant Immunity, and Atrocity after World War Two* (Routledge, 2006). South Korean coverage of civilian killings started even before the September 1999 AP No Gun Ri report and was divided along political lines. In June 1999 the conservative monthly *Wŏlgan chosŏn* published, as part of a series marking the fiftieth anniversary of the beginning of the war, an article detailing the North Korean massacre of South Korean soldiers in hiding and patients at the Seoul National University Hospital in Seoul on June 28, 1950, immediately after the city was captured (pp. 118–130). When the AP report was published, the left-liberal newspapers immediately linked it to a wider issue of U.S. responsibility and culpability and strongly supported the call for apology and compensation. (See, for example, *Tong-a ilbo* articles on September 30 and October 1, 1999. Also see the October 15 interview with Stanley Roth, who was then the assistant secretary of state for East Asia, which portrays a recalcitrant, skeptical, and even defiant American attitude toward U.S. involvement in the killing of civilians during the war; and the *Chung'ang ilbo* story and editorial on October 1, which unequivocally points to U.S. culpability in No Gun Ri and other alleged massacres and pointedly calls for a U.S. apology and compensation for the alleged killings.) On the other hand, the conservative press, while covering the AP story, did so in a matter-of-fact manner that did not immediately point to U.S. culpability and instead highlighted the possible mitigating circumstances—such as untrained troops, fear of North Korean soldiers, and confusion caused by North Koreans disguised as

civilians—to try to conceptualize the incident as something comprehensible while acknowledging it as a tragedy that required an apology and compensation if proved true. (See for example, *Chosŏn ilbo* stories on September 30 and October 11, 1999, and its editorial on October 1, 1999.) The liberal press continued its attacks with further accounts of U.S. complicity in atrocities committed against South Korean civilians, with additional stories on the deliberate destruction of bridges (at Waegwan and Koryŏng) in early August 1950, which blocked refugees from moving south, and another air attack incident at Kwegaegul in January 1951. (See *Chung'ang ilbo*, October 15, 1999, for the Waegwan and Koryŏng story, and *Tong-a ilbo*, December 3, 1999, for the Kwegaegul story.)

85 General Paul Freeman, interview with Colonel James N. Ellis, November 29 and 30, 1973, U.S. Army Military History Research Collection, Senior Officers Debriefing Program, MHI.

86 H. K. Shin, *Remembering Korea 1950: A Boy Soldier's Story* (University of Nevada Press, 2001), p. 44.

87 O. H. P. King, *Tail of the Paper Tiger* (Caxton Printers, 1962), p. 359.

88 *Time*, August 21, 1950, p. 20.

89 In January 2000 a liberal journal in South Korea broke a major story based on newly discovered documents and photographs from the U.S. National Archives that graphically show the execution of eighteen hundred political prisoners by the ROK Military Police and the Korean National Police, an incident that was long believed to be true but unsupported by documentary evidence. The total number believed to have been killed was roughly eight thousand, although this figure is not corroborated by documentary evidence (*Han'gyorae 21*, January 20, 2000, pp. 20–27). Another liberal journal, *Mal*, stoked the flames of anti-Americanism further with a series of articles in its February 2000 issue that provide both documentary and photographic evidence of killings of civilian political prisoners, allegedly communists, by South Korean security forces in Seoul in April 1950 before the war began, at Taejŏn in early July 1950, and at Taegu in August 1950 and April 1951. Both stories strongly implicated the United States, with photos showing American officers calmly observing the executions. The April 1950 incident is made more significant by the fact that it occurred before the war while the country was under peaceful civilian control, and yet the executions were carried out by the ROK Military Police. Also implicated in the killings is Rhee, who is portrayed as being in cahoots with the United States because purging the Left strengthened his dictatorial hold on power. While not the last in this Left-Right debate about wartime culpability, one additional example demonstrates the unending cycle of the accusatory debate, the kind of cycle that the South Korean historian Pak Myŏng-nim calls for an end to. In June 2000, *Wŏlgan chosŏn* published a long article on the North Korean massacre of several thousand civilians and POWs, South Korean and American, at Taejŏn in late September 1950. It happened as the North Korean forces reeled back from the success of the Inch'ŏn landing (pp. 264–287). This was a direct counter to the liberal media coverage of the South Korean killings at Taejŏn in July 1950. The article also made a semantic distinction between *massacre*, which characterizes what the North Koreans committed, and *execution* of prisoners

by the South Korean police. The execution of political prisoners is indirectly justified, because their arrests, as menaces to national security, were legal under South Korean law at the time (and for a long time afterward). The debate is far from over. See Sheila Miyoshi Jager, “Re-writing the Past/Re-claiming the Future: Nationalism and the Politics of Anti-Americanism in South Korea,” *Japan Focus*, July 29, 2005, at http://www.japanfocus.org/products/details/1772 (accessed January 2010).

90 A compilation of oral histories of massacres can be found in the *2007 Report on Excavations.*

91 In late 2005, the South Korean government initiated an ambitious project, the TRC, to bring closure to the many open historical wounds that had been eating into the soul and fabric of the South Korean people and society. The TRC was modeled on the many other similar efforts around the world (most notably in South Africa and Rwanda) that had sprouted since the 1990s as the end of the cold war opened up space for repressed histories and memories to come out in the open. The TRC was charged with investigating and finding the truth of contentious issues from the colonial period, the period of authoritarian rule in the 1960s and 1970s, and the Korean War. Truth could begin the national healing process. The historical issues concerned were charged with domestic and international political implications. For the colonial period, the most contentious were collaboration and the assertion that collaborators were never brought to justice and had instead prospered under the right-wing rule that controlled South Korea for most of the postliberation period. The focus of the 1960s–1970s period was on the massive human and civil rights violations that undermined democracy. American support for that regime, based on cold war logic, is linked to the substantial anti-Americanism that exists today in South Korea. But it is the alleged killings and massacres by North Koreans, South Koreans, and Americans before and during the Korean War that have taken up most of the commission’s efforts. They are also the most sensitive and politically explosive issues attesting to the enduring impact of the civil conflict that still feeds deep antipathies and enmities in South Korean society. TRC findings of evidence of massacres in the South by South Korean security forces made headlines in the summer of 2008 when excavations of massacre sites, testimonies by perpetrators and witnesses, and gruesome photographs from American archives were revealed with the suggestion of American complicity or at least acquiescence. TRC, *Truth and Reconciliation.* Also see Charles J. Hanley and Jae-Soon Chang, “Summer of Terror: At Least 100,000 Said Executed by Korean Ally of US in 1950”; Jae-Soon Chang, “Hidden History: Families Talk of Korean War Executions, Say US Shares Blame”; Charles J. Hanley and Jae-Soon Chang, “U.S. Okayed Korean War Massacres”; Charles J. Hanley, “Fear, Secrecy Kept 1950 Korea Mass Killings Hidden,” all AP reports dated July 4, 2008, all available at http://japanfocus.org/-Charles_J_-Hanley/2827 (accessed December 2008). The main excavation report is a massive three-volume set, *2007 Report on Excavations.*

92 *2007 Report on Excavations*, vol. 2, pp. 319–335.

93 Chang, “Hidden History”; Hanley and Chang, “U.S. Okayed Korean War Massacres”; Hanley, “Fear, Secrecy”; Millett, *War for Korea*, pp. 160–161.

94 *Wŏlgan chosŏn*, June 2000, pp. 264–287. According to Kim Tong-ch'un (Kim Dong-choon), the former commissioner for the Sub-Committee of Investigation of Mass Civilian Sacrifice at the TRC, as many as three hundred thousand suspected communists and leftists may have been executed during the months of June to July 1950 alone. Kim Dong-choon, *Chŏnjaeng'gwa sahoe* [War and Society] (Seoul: Tolpaegae, 2000).
95 *2007 Report on Excavations*, vol. 2, pp. 239–241.
96 Ibid., p. 248.
97 Ibid., p. 236.
98 Ibid., p. 237.
99 Ibid., p. 259.
100 Alan Winnington, *I Saw the Truth in Korea* (People's Press Printing, 1950), pp. 5–6.

FIVE: *Uncommon Coalition*

1 The central pillar of the international coalition, the integration of U.S. and South Korean armed forces, continues to exist today as the foundation for the security of South Korea, a part of the legacy of the unending war.
2 The arrangement of the South Korean military being put under UN/U.S. control lasted until 1994, when peacetime operational command was transferred to South Korea, but wartime operational control still remained with the UN/United States and is not due to be transferred to South Korea until 2015.
3 UN naval and air forces entered the war before ground forces. Two days after the invasion U.S. air and naval forces based in Japan were committed. British naval forces based in Japan followed a day later. Australian air and naval units also based in Japan entered the war on July 1. By the end of July 1950, while the only UN ground forces were American, naval forces from Canada, France, and New Zealand and air forces from Australia and Canada had joined in the effort. By the summer of 1951, additional naval forces from the Netherlands, Thailand, and Colombia as well as a South African fighter squadron and a Greek air transport squadron had joined the coalition. The UN coalition's command structure for controlling air and naval units was straightforward. At the top, the U.S. Far East Command in Japan controlled the coalition as the UNC. The Far East Command's ground, air, and naval components controlled their respective coalition component forces. Air forces were simply organized because coalition contributions were few and small. These units were attached to matching U.S. Air Force units. Coalition naval forces were more substantial, with ships up to the size of aircraft carriers (United Kingdom and Australia) coming from eight nations. They were integrated into the U.S. Naval Forces Far East Command.
4 Walter G. Hermes, *Truce Tent and Fighting Front* (U.S. Government Printing Office, 1966), p. 513.
5 William J. Fox, *Inter-Allied Co-operation During Combat Operations* (Washington, D.C.: Office of the Chief of Military History, Department of the Army, 1952), pp. 10–14.
6 Ibid., pp. 84–85.

7 Ibid., pp. 158–159.
8 Ibid., pp. 155–158.
9 Ibid., pp. 150–155.
10 Appleman, *South to the Naktong*, p. 545.
11 David Curtis Skaggs, "The KATUSA Experiment: The Integration of Korean Nationals into the U.S. Army, 1950-1965," *Military Affairs* 38, no. 2 (April 1974), p. 55; Appleman, *South to the Naktong*, p. 547.
12 Appleman, *South to the Naktong*, p. 503n.
13 James F. Schnabel, *Policy and Direction: The First Year* (U.S. Government Printing Office, 1972), pp. 86, 165–166.
14 Appleman, *South to the Naktong*, p. 492.
15 Schnabel, *Policy and Direction*, p. 167.
16 Skaggs, "KATUSA Experiment," p. 53.
17 Schnabel, *Policy and Direction*, p. 168; Skaggs, "KATUSA Experiment," p. 53; Appleman, *South to the Naktong*, p. 492.
18 Skaggs, "KATUSA Experiment," p. 53; Appleman, *South to the Naktong*, p. 492.
19 Skaggs, "KATUSA Experiment," p. 53.
20 Appleman, *South to the Naktong*, pp. 503–509, 512, 520–523, 527–531, 541; Skaggs, "KATUSA Experiment," pp. 53–54.
21 Appleman, *South to the Naktong*, p. 501.
22 I am indebted to Col. Don Boose (U.S. Army retired) for pointing this out. James A. Field Jr., *History of United States Naval Operations, Korea* (U.S. Government Printing Office, 1962), pp. 232–240. These operations are also covered in more detail in Arnold Lott, *Most Dangerous Sea: A History of Mine Warfare and an Account of U.S. Navy Mine Warfare Operations in World War II and Korea* (U.S. Naval Institute Press, 1959). See also Tessa Morris-Suzuki, "Post-War Warriors: Japanese Combatants in the Korean War," *Asian Pacific Journal* 10, issue 31, no. 1 (July 30, 2012); Reinhardt Drift, "Japan's Involvement in the Korean War," in J. Cotton and I. Neary, eds., *The Korean War in History* (Manchester University Press, 1989), pp. 20–34.
23 Hermes, *Truce Tent*, p. 514.
24 Although there was some talk after the outbreak of the war to directly recruit Japanese soldiers for the war effort, this proposal was immediately squashed by General MacArthur, owing to the sensitive nature of the proposal. Given Stalin's heightened sensitivity about revived Japanese militarism, public evidence of direct involvement by Japan might have led him to risk full-scale Soviet involvement in Korea, something the Americans wanted to avoid at all costs. In addition, South Koreans were adamantly adverse to any Japanese involvement in the war effort because of their recent colonial experience. South Korean backlash and outright defections from the ROK Army were enough concerns to MacArthur that he emphatically stated that "no Japanese were to be employed with the army in Korea." That said, recent evidence suggests that some Japanese nevertheless fought alongside the Americans, although their numbers were quite small. Most had worked for American soldiers in Japan as male cooks, drivers, interpreters, or servants and then later followed their employers to Korea. See Tessa-Morris-Suzuki, "Post-War Warriors," pp. 2–5.
25 Hermes, *Truce Tent*, p. 513

26 And indeed, all U.S. Army units stationed in South Korea to the present day have KATUSAs.

27 Lt. Col. Russell L. Prewittcampbell, "The Korean Service Corps: Eighth Army's Three-Dimensional Asset," *Army Logistician* (March–April 1999), at http://www.almc.army.mil/alog/issues/MARAPR99/MS337.htm (accessed July 15, 2010); Hermes, *Truce Tent*, p. 513; Allan R. Millett, *The War for Korea, 1950–1951: They Came from the North* (University Press of Kansas, 2010), pp. 158–159. Another way to consider the multinational character of the UN army and the significance of the non-U.S. contributions is to quantitatively examine the allocation of the most important fighting elements in the war, the infantry battalions. These units formed the backbone of the front line and provided the overwhelming bulk of men who fought and died. Each nation had its own unique structure, but generally the units were roughly equivalent in terms of battlefield presence. From the beginning of the armistice talks to its conclusion two years later, the UN army nearly doubled in size. These increases were accounted for not only by the growth of the South Korean army but also by a 20 percent increase in U.S. forces and a near doubling of forces from other nations. In the summer of 1951 the Eighth Army had a total of 185 infantry battalions, of which 96 were Korean, 72 American, and 17 from other UN member states. Roughly 10 to 15 percent of all U.S., French, Dutch, and Belgian battalions were also manned by KATUSAs. In other words, conservatively, the KATUSA strength in the U.S. and UN battalions was the equivalent to about eight Korean battalions. The final tally of infantry battalions is then 104 ROK, 65 American, and 16 other nationalities. In percentage terms they are, respectively, 56, 35, and 9 percent. In early 1953, due to a shortage of men, the Commonwealth Division received 1,000 KATUSAs, now dubbed KATCOMs (Korean Augmentation to Commonwealth soldiers), who were integrated down to section (squad) level in the British, Canadian, and Australian infantry battalions. By the summer of 1953, the Eighth Army now had grown to 222 infantry battalions. The ROK number increased to 129, the American contributions stayed the same at 72, and the number from other UN nations increased to 21. The number of KATUSAs remained about the same but was now augmented by the KATCOMs in Commonwealth units. The Korean battalion equivalent in U.S. and other UN units was about 9. After adjustments for this, the final figures (and percentages) are 138 ROK (62 percent), 65 U.S. (29 percent), and 19 from other UN nations (9 percent). If we consider just the U.S. and other UN battalions, the 65 U.S. battalions in 1951 comprised 80 percent of the total (81 battalions), while in 1953 the same number of U.S. battalions (65) comprised 77 percent of the total (84).

A number of general observations can be based on these comparisons and trends from 1950 to 1953. First, the proportion of ROK to UN battalions increased from a little over half to two-thirds. Second, the proportion of U.S. battalions to other UN nations decreased a bit from 80 percent to 77 percent. More important, the share from other UN countries increased from 20 percent to 23 percent. This seems significantly out of proportion to the absolute number of men: 253,000 Americans to 20,000 other UN forces in 1951, to 300,000 Americans to 39,000 other UN forces by 1953. This discrepancy can be explained by the much higher number of Americans who were involved in support functions compared to the number of other UN forces. The "tooth to tail" ratio, in military parlance, was much lower for the American force, a circumstance exaggerated because, except for the Commonwealth units, other nations completely depended on the United States to provide their "tail."

28 Fredrik Logevall, *Embers of War: The Fall of an Empire and the Making of America's Vietnam* (Random House, 2012), pp. 282–283. See also Callum A. McDonald, *Britain and the Korean War* (Blackwell, 1990), pp. 1–4.

29 John M. Vander Lippe, "Forgotten Brigade of the Forgotten War: Turkey's Participation in the Korean War," *Middle Eastern Studies* 36, no. 1 (January 2000), p. 98.

30 Richard Samuels, *Rich Nation, Strong Army: National Security and the Technological Transformation of Japan* (Cornell University Press, 1996), p. 141; John W. Dower, *Embracing Defeat: Japan in the Wake of World War II* (W. W. Norton, 2000), pp. 541–546.

31 Roger Dingman, "The Dagger and the Gift: The Impact of the Korean War on Japan," *Journal of American–East Asian Relations* 1, no. 1 (1993), pp. 29–55; Akagi Kanji, "The Korean War and Japan," *Seoul Journal of Korean Studies* 24, no. 1 (June 2011), pp. 145–184; Akitashi Miyoshita, "Japan," *Encyclopedia of the Korean War*, vol. 1 (ABC-CLIO, 2000), pp. 284–285.

32 Jeffrey Grey, *The Commonwealth Armies and the Korean War* (Manchester University Press, 1988), pp. 182–183; Sri Nandan Prasad, *History of the Custodian Force (India) in Korea* (Historical Section, Ministry of Defence, Government of India, 1976).

SIX: *Crossing the 38th Parallel*

1 Schnabel and Watson, *The History of the Joint Chiefs of Staff*, vol. 3: *The Korean War, Part 1*, p. 244.

2 Ibid., pp. 242–244.

3 Schnabel, *Policy and Direction: The First Year*, p. 182.

4 Schnabel and Watson, *History of the Joint Chiefs of Staff*, vol. 3, p. 243.

5 Korea Institute of Military History, *The Korean War* (University of Nebraska Press, 2000), vol. 1, p. 762.

6 Appleman, *South to the Naktong*, pp. 614–615.

7 Samuel Hawley, *The Imjin War: Japan's Sixteenth-Century Invasion of Korea and Attempt to Conquer China* (University of California Press, 2005), p. 220. For an excellent overview of the Imjin Wars, see also Kenneth M. Swope, *A Dragon's Head and a Serpent's Tail: Ming China and the First Great East Asian War, 1592–1598* (University of Oklahoma Press, 2009); Stephan Turnbull, *The Samurai Invasion of Korea, 1592–1598* (Cassell & Company, 2002).

8 The war would continue over the next few years. While Ming China emerged victorious from the struggle, the heavy financial burden had adversely affected its military capabilities, thus contributing to its fall to the Manchus in 1644. Hideyoshi's misadventure had also cost the Japanese. After the war, Japan would not venture out into the world again until 1894–95, when it fought and won in another war against China.

9 James, *The Years of MacArthur*, vol. 3, pp. 348–349.
10 Omar N. Bradley and Clay Blair, *A General's Life* (Simon & Schuster, 1983), p. 567.
11 Quoted in James, *Years of MacArthur*, vol. 3, p. 503.
12 Ibid., pp. 503–505.
13 Dean Rusk, *As I Saw It* (W. W. Norton, 1990), pp. 168–169.
14 Harry S. Truman, *Memoirs*, vol. 2: *Years of Trial and Hope* (Doubleday 1956), p. 363.
15 Bradley and Blair, *General's Life*, p. 576.
16 McCullough, *Truman*, p. 808.
17 Schnabel and Watson, *History of the Joint Chiefs of Staff*, vol. 3, pp. 275–276; James, *Years of MacArthur*, vol. 3, p. 499. Six months later, General Collins cited this incident as the first instance when MacArthur violated a JCS directive. J. Lawton Collins, *Lightning Joe: An Autobiography* (Louisiana State University Press, 1979), pp. 179–181.
18 Bradley and Blair, *General's Life*, p. 579.
19 Dean Acheson, *Present at the Creation* (W. W. Norton, 1969), p. 468.
20 K. M. Panikkar, *In Two Chinas: Memoirs of a Diplomat* (George Allen & Unwin, 1955), pp. 108–110; *New York Times*, October 2, 1950; *New York Herald Tribune*, October 1, 1950.
21 Truman, *Memoirs*, vol. 2, p. 362.
22 Lim Ŭn, *The Founding of a Dynasty in North Korea: An Authentic Biography of Kim Il-sŏng* (Tokyo: Jiyusha, 1982), pp. 145, 181–184.
23 Alexandre Y. Mansourov, "Stalin, Mao, Kim and China's Decision to Enter the Korean War, September 16-October 15, 1950: New Evidence from the Archives," *CWIHP Bulletin: The Cold War in Asia*, no. 6/7 (Winter 1995), pp. 98, 112.
24 "Ciphered Telegram, Filippov (Stalin) to Mao Zedong and Zhou Enlai, 1 October 1950," *CWIHP Bulletin: The Cold War in Asia*, no. 6/7 (Winter 1995), p. 114.
25 This account of Mao's October 3 communication with Stalin, informing him of China's refusal to enter the war, is based on documents declassified after the fall of the Soviet Union. The message contradicts the purported Mao-to-Stalin message of October 2 that was published in 1987 in an official Chinese document compilation and had since been relied on for numerous scholarly accounts. The official account cites that Mao wrote to Stalin that the Chinese leadership had decided "to send a portion of our troops, under the name of [Chinese People's] Volunteers to Korea, assisting the Korean comrades to fight the troops of the United States and its running dog Syngman Rhee." However, Mao apparently did not send the cable, probably because of the divided opinion among the top CCP leadership. See Shen Zhihua, trans. Neil Silver, *Mao, Stalin, and the Korean War: Trilateral Communist Relations in the 1950s* (Routledge, 2012), pp. 149–158. For the texts of the two versions of Mao's October 2, 1950, telegram, and two interpretations of them, see Mansourov, "Stalin, Mao, Kim and China's Decision," pp. 94–119; Shen Zhihua, "The Discrepancy between the Russian and Chinese Versions of Mao's 2 October 1950 Message to Stalin on Chinese Entry into the Korean War: A Chinese Scholar's Reply," *CWIHP Bulletin*, no. 8/9 (Winter 1996/97), pp. 237–242.

26 "Ciphered telegram from Roshchin in Beijing to Filippov [Stalin], 3 October 1950, conveying 2 October 1950 message from Mao to Stalin," *CWIHP Bulletin: The Cold War in Asia*, no. 6/7 (Winter 1995), pp. 114–115.
27 "Letter, Fyn Si [Stalin] to Kim Il Sung (via Shtykov), 8 [7] October 1950," *CWHIP Bulletin: The Cold War in Asia*, no. 6/7 (Winter 1995), p. 116.
28 Chen Jian, *China's Road to the Korean War: The Making of the Sino-Soviet Alliance* (Columbia University Press, 1995), p. 185.
29 Xiaomin Zhang, *Red Wings over the Yalu: China, the Soviet Union and the Air War over Korea* (Texas A&M University Press, 2002), pp. 74–76.
30 Peng Dehuai, *Memoirs of a Chinese Marshal* (University Press of the Pacific, 2005), p. 473. See also Hao Yufan and Zhai Zhihai, "China's Decision to Enter the Korean War: History Revisited," *China Quarterly*, no. 121 (March 1990), p. 106.
31 Peng, *Memoirs of a Chinese Marshal*, p. 473.
32 Mansourov, *Stalin, Mao, Kim, and China's Decision*, p.101.
33 Chen Jian, "The Sino-Soviet Alliance and China's Entry into the Korean War," *CWIHP Working Paper 1* (June 1992), p. 29; Goncharov et al., *Uncertain Partners*, p. 279.
34 Mansourov, *Stalin, Mao, Kim, and China's Decision*, p. 100; Nikita Khrushchev, *Khrushchev Remembers* (Little, Brown, 1970), pp. 144–152.
35 There are different versions of what took place during the Zhou-Stalin meetings. See Chen, "Sino-Soviet Alliance," pp. 31–32; Mansourov, *Stalin, Mao, Kim, and China's Decision*, p. 103. See also Shen Zhihua, *Mao, Stalin, and the Korean War*, pp. 170–174; Zubok and Pleshankov, *Inside the Kremlin's Cold War*, pp. 67–69.
36 Mansourov maintains that Stalin never betrayed Mao and that the account of Stalin's betrayal is fictional. See Mansourov, *Stalin, Mao, Kim, and China's Decision*, p. 105.
37 Goncharov et al., *Uncertain Partners*, pp. 192–193.
38 Xiaobing Li, Allan R. Millet, and Bin Yu, eds., *Mao's Generals Remember Korea* (University Press of Kansas, 2001), p. 41.
39 Chen, "Sino-Soviet Alliance," p. 32.
40 Chen Jian, *China's Road to the Korean War: The Making of the Sino-American Confrontation* (Columbia University Press, 1994), pp. 222–223.
41 Anthony Farrar-Hockley, "A Reminiscence of the Chinese People's Volunteers in the Korean War," *China Quarterly*, no. 98 (June 1984), p. 295.
42 Clay Blair, *The Forgotten War: America in Korea, 1950–1953* (Times Books, 1987), pp. 387–390; Millett, *The War for Korea, 1950–1951*, pp. 305–306.
43 Blair, *The Forgotten War*, p. 391.
44 Appleman, *South to the Naktong*, p. 677.
45 Schnabel and Watson, *History of the Joint Chiefs of Staff*, vol. 3, p. 281.
46 James, *Years of MacArthur*, vol. 3, pp. 519–520; Truman, *Memoirs*, vol. 2, p. 373. The reason MacArthur seems to have discounted the possibility of a major intervention in Korea, despite ample evidence to the contrary, appears to be linked to his belief that the time had passed for the CPV to have derived any tactical benefits from entering the war at this time. A Far East Command daily intelligence published on October 28 sums up this view: "From a tacti-

cal viewpoint, with victorious U.S. Divisions in full deployment, it would appear that the auspicious time for such [Chinese] intervention has long since passed; it is difficult to believe that such a move, if planned, would have been postponed to a time when remnant North Korean forces have been reduced to a low point of effectiveness." See Schnabel and Watson, *History of the Joint Chiefs of Staff*, vol. 3, p. 281.

47 William T. Y'Blood, ed., *The Three Wars of Lt. Gen. George E. Stratemeyer: His Korean War Diary* (U.S. Government Printing Office, 1999), p. 257.

48 Truman, *Memoirs*, vol. 2, pp. 374–375.

49 Bradley and Blair, *General's Life*, pp. 585–589; Acheson, *Present at the Creation*, p. 464; Schnabel, *Policy and Direction*, pp. 243–246; James, *Years of MacArthur*, vol. 3, pp. 520–522.

50 Schnabel and Watson, *History of the Joint Chiefs of Staff*, vol. 3, pp. 301–302; Bradley and Blair, *General's Life*, pp. 590–591.

51 "Section 7: Chinese Communist Intervention in Korea 6 November 1950," *National Intelligence Council, Selected National Intelligence Estimates on China 1948–1976*, available at http://www.dni.gov/nic/NIC_foia_china.html.

52 Bradley and Blair, *General's Life*, p. 594.

53 An Sŭng-hwan, "Chupukhan ssoryŏn kunsa komundangŭi pukhangun chiwŏn hwaldong (1946–1953) [Soviet Military Advisory Group Support to the NKPA, 1946–1953]," p. 455.

54 Cited in ibid., p. 456.

SEVEN: *An Entirely New War*

1 *Washington Post*, November 23, 1950.

2 *New York Times*, November 23, 1950.

3 Ibid., November 21, 1950.

4 *Chicago Tribune*, November 23, 1950.

5 William T. Y'Blood, ed., *The Three Wars of Lt. Gen. George E. Stratemeyer: His Korean War Diary* (U.S. Government Printing Office, 1999), p. 299.

6 Toland, *In Mortal Combat Korea*, p. 281.

7 Blair, *The Forgotten War*, p. 440; Millett, *The War for Korea, 1950–1951*, pp. 336–337.

8 Beech, *Tokyo and Points East*, p. 196.

9 Oliver P. Smith, "Aide de Memoir . . . Korea, 1950–1: Notes by General O. P. Smith on the Operations during the First Nine Months of the Korean War," 1951, folder 3, pp. 604–610, PD 110, Collection Unit, Marine Corps Historical Center, Washington, D.C.; "Forgotten War," Clay and Joan Blair Collection, Alphabetical Files S-V, box 83, MHI.

10 There are many accounts of the battle of Changjin (Chosin) Reservoir, but the most recent is David Halberstam, *Coldest Winter: America and the Korean War* (Hyperion, 2007). The most detailed military histories of the battle are Roy E. Appleman's *East of Chosin: Entrapment and Breakout in Korea, 1950* (Texas A&M Press, 1987) and Millett, *The War for Korea, 1950–1951*.

11 Almond quoted by Martin Blumenson, "Chosin Reservoir," in Russell A. Gugeler, *Combat Actions in Korea* (U.S. Government Printing Office, 1987), pp. 69–70.

12 Donald Knox, *The Korean War*, vol. 1: *Pusan to Chosin, an Oral History* (Harcourt Brace, 1985), pp. 552–559; Roy E. Appleman, *Disaster in Korea: The Chinese Confront MacArthur* (Texas A&M University Press, 1989), p. 133.

13 *Time*, December 18, 1950, p. 26.

14 Max Hastings, *The Korean War* (Simon & Schuster, 1988), p. 159.

15 *New York Times*, December 11, 1950.

16 *Washington Post*, December 11, 1950.

17 *Time*, December 8, 1950, pp. 26–27.

18 *New York Times*, December 24, 1950; Appleman, *Disaster in Korea*, p. 328.

19 William Whitson, *The Chinese High Command* (Praeger, 1973), p. 96; John J. Tkacik Jr., "From Surprise to Stalemate: What the People's Liberation Army Learned from the Korean War—A Half Century Later," in Laurie Burkitt, Andrew Scobell, and Larry Wortzel, eds., *The Lessons of History: The Chinese People's Liberation Army at 75* (U.S. Army War College Strategic Studies Institute, July 2003), p. 303.

20 Quoted in Chester Cheng, "Through Chinese Eyes: China Crosses the Rubicon," *Journal of Oriental Studies* 31, no. 1 (1993), p. 11.

21 "Telegram, Mao Zedong to Peng Dehuai and Gao Gang, 2 December 1950," in Guang Zhang and Jian Chen, eds., *Chinese Communist Foreign Policy and the Cold War in Asia: New Documentary Evidence, 1944–1950* (Imprint, 1996), p. 211.

22 Quoted in Tkacik, "From Surprise to Stalemate," pp. 302–303.

23 Billy C. Mossman, *Ebb and Flow: November 1950–July 1951* (U.S. Government Printing Office, 1990), pp. 165–176.

24 Bill Gilbert, *Ship of Miracles* (Triumph Books, 2000), pp. 77–157.

25 *Time*, December 11, 1950, pp. 17–18. Fifty-five percent of Americans believed that the United States was in World War III. *Washington Post*, December 6, 1950.

26 *U.S. News & World Report*, December 8, 1950, pp. 16–22; Hugh Baillie, *High Tension* (Harper's & Brothers, 1959), pp. 225–226. See also James, *The Years of MacArthur*, vol. 3, p. 540; *New York Times*, December 1, 1950; Bradley and Blair, *A General's Life*, pp. 601–602.

27 Truman, *Memoirs*, vol. 2, p. 384.

28 James, *Years of MacArthur*, vol. 3, p. 542.

29 Truman, *Memoirs*, vol. 2, pp. 381–382.

30 Bradley and Blair, *General's Life*, p. 603; Matthew B. Ridgway, *The Korean War: How We Met the Challenge; How All-Out Asian War Was Averted; Why MacArthur Was Dismissed; Why Today's War Objectives Must Be Limited* (Doubleday, 1967), pp. 77–78.

31 James Chase, *Acheson: The Secretary of State Who Created the American World* (Harvard University Press, 1998), pp. 306–308; Acheson, *Present at the Creation*, pp. 476–477; George F. Kennan, *George F. Kennan: Memoirs 1950–1963* (Pantheon Books, 1972), pp. 27–35; John Lewis Gaddis, *George F. Kennan: An American Life* (Penguin, 2011), pp. 412–413.

32 Acheson, *Present at the Creation*, p. 476; Kennan, *George F. Kennan*, p. 31.

33 Acheson, *Present at the Creation*, pp. 476–477; Robert L. Beisner, *Dean Acheson: A Life in the Cold War* (Oxford University Press, 2006), p. 418; Kennan, *George F. Kennan*, p. 32.

34 Kennan, *George F. Kennan*, p. 33.
35 J. Lawton Collins, *Lightning Joe: An Autobiography* (Louisiana State University Press, 1979), p. 373; Bradley and Blair, *General's Life*, pp. 606–607.
36 Acheson, *Present at the Creation*, pp. 478–482; M. L. Dockrill, "The Foreign Office, Anglo-American Relations and the Korean War, June 1950–June 1951," *International Affairs* (Royal Institute of International Affairs) 62, no. 3 (Summer 1986), p. 466; Rosemary Foot, "Anglo-American Relations in the Korean Crisis: The British Effort to Avert Expanded War, December 1950–January 1951," *Diplomatic History* 10, no. 1 (Winter 1986), p. 49; *FRUS, 1950*, vol. 7: *Korea* (1976), pp. 1376, 1383, 1431–1432.
37 Acheson, *Present at the Creation*, p. 482.
38 *FRUS, 1950*, vol. 7, pp. 1462–1464, 1473–1475, 1479; Schnabel and Watson, *The History of the Joint Chiefs of Staff*, vol. 3, part 1, p. 379; William Stueck, ed., *The Korean War in World History* (University Press of Kentucky, 2004), p. 140; Beisner, *Dean Acheson*, p. 421.
39 Acheson, *Present at the Creation*, p. 485.
40 *Washington Post*, December 9, 1950.
41 Knox, *Korean War*, vol. 1, p. 659.
42 Appleman, *Disaster in Korea*, p. 318.
43 Knox, *Korean War*, vol. 1, p. 657.
44 Clark, *Living Dangerously in Korea*, p. 395. UN pilots charged with carrying out the strafing and bombing campaigns often justified these sorties by labeling civilians as "disguised troops" or as "supporters" of enemy activity. One pilot recalled, "If we saw civilians in the village, just because they look like civilians, from an airplane you can't tell whether he's a civilian or a soldier, anything in North Korea I consider an enemy. They're definitely not on our side, therefore I have no mercy . . . Anything supporting enemy troops is an enemy of ours; therefore, I consider it worthwhile to strike it." Sometimes, this view was justified. In one case, a pilot had spotted a group of people in a village in white clothing. The presence of women and children in the streets and their friendly waves made him hesitate. But he strafed them and received heavy fire in return from the "peaceful civilians." Raymond Sturgeon was more circumspect about his mission. Dropping napalm and strafing people was a "difficult job," "I can't say I enjoyed it. You're there and that's what you do . . . we were instructed to hit civilians because they did a lot of the work, but I just couldn't do it." John Darrell Sherwood, *Officers in Flight Suits: The Story of American Air Force Fighter Pilots in the Korean War* (New York University Press, 1996), pp. 104–106.
45 Quoted in Clark, *Living Dangerously in Korea*, pp. 393–394.
46 H. K. Shin, *A Boy Soldier's Story: Remembering Korea 1950* (University of Nebraska Press, 2001), p. 143.
47 "Seoul after Victory: Reverse Side to South Korean Rule," *London Times*, October 25, 1950.
48 Peter Kalischer, "2 U.S. Priests Protest as S. Koreans Kill Prsoners," *Washington Post*, December 17, 1950.
49 Muccio to Secretary of State, December 21, 1950, in *FRUS, 1950*, vol. 7, p. 1586.
50 "Atrocities and Trials of Political Prisoners in Korea, British Foreign Office

to Korea and Tokyo, and to Washington and United Kingdom Delegation, New York," December 19, 1950, Telegram no. 125, WO 371/84180, National Archives, Kew, UK.

51 Letter from Private Duncan to Member of Parliament, FO 371/92847, National Archives, Kew, UK.

52 *Washington Post*, December 17, 1950.

53 *New York Times*, December 19, 1950; *Washington Post*, December 18, 1950. Reports of the execution of children were never officially confirmed. Graves opened by UN investigators looking into the allegations did not find children's bodies. Ambassador Muccio also believed the reports to be false, writing on December 20 that "UNCURK had sent a military observer, Colonel White, Canada, to observe exhumation of bodies on December 17, which was conducted under orders of Home Minister and Justice Minister. Exhumation proved allegations re shooting of children wholly false." *FRUS, 1950*, vol. 7, p. 1579.

54 "Mass Executions of Reds in Korea End," *Washington Post*, December 22, 1950. See also "From Foreign Office to Korea," Telegram no. 129, December 21, 1950, WO 371/ 84180, National Archives, Kew, UK.

55 Donald W. Boose Jr., "United Nations Commission for the Unification and Rehabilitation of Korea," in Spencer C. Tucker, ed., *Encyclopedia of the Korean War: A Political, Social and Military History* (ABC-CLIO, 2000), pp. 681–683.

56 Millett, *The War for Korea, 1950–1951*, pp. 374–375. Recent reports provided by South Korea's TRC provide new evidence that children may have indeed been executed. In late 1950 and early 1951, the commission estimates that more than 460 people, including at least 23 children under the age of ten, were executed in Namyangju, about sixteen miles northeast of Seoul. The TRC also reported that children were among the victims in at least six other mass killings during this period. See Charles J. Hanley and Jae-soon Chang, "Children Executed in 1950 South Korean Killings," Associated Press, December 6, 2008. See also Kim Tong-ch'un, *Chŏnjaeng'gwa sahoe* [War and Society]. Kim headed the TRC from December 2005 to its closing in December 2010.

57 *Chicago Daily Tribune*, December 19, 1950.

58 Muccio to Secretary of State, December 20, 1950, in *FRUS, 1950*, vol. 7, p. 1580; *Chicago Tribune*, December 14, 18, and 19, 1950; *New York Times*, December 21, 1950; *Washington Post*, December 17 and 22, 1950.

59 René Cutforth, *Korean Reporter* (Allan Wingate, 1952), p. 52. For other descriptions of the conditions at Sŏdaemun Prison, see Martin Flavin, "Korean Diary," *Harper's Magazine*, March 1951.

60 *Washington Post*, December 21, 1950.

61 Muccio to Secretary of State, December 22, 1950, in *FRUS, 1950*, vol. 7, p. 1587.

62 James Plimsoll, Australian Representative to the UN Commission for the Unification and Rehabilitation of Korea, February 17, 1951, Departmental Dispatch no. 2/51 FO 371/92848, p. 3, National Archives, Kew, UK.

63 Plimsoll, Dispatch no. 2/51, pp. 4–6; *Washington Post*, December 27, 1950; Steven Casey, *Selling the Korean War: Propaganda, Politics and Public Opinion, 1950–53* (Oxford University Press, 2008), pp. 154–168. On December 22, the UNC instructed the Eighth Army Public Information Office (PIO) to check all stories emanating from Korea for security violations. Nevertheless, some

stories did get out. Reprisals against suspected leftists continued through early 1951. The most well-known massacre during this period, the Kŏch'ang Civilian Massacre, took place on the east side of the Chiri Mountains. Although the number of people reported killed during the incident varies widely, it attracted enough attention that Rhee ordered Defense Minister Shin Sŏng-mo and Home Minister Cho Pyŏng-ok to resign. Those who were directly involved in the massacre were later court-martialed and imprisoned. Kim Tong-ch'un, *Chŏnjaeng'gwa sahoe* [War and Society], pp. 301–302.

64 Cited in Richard Fried, *Men against McCarthy* (Columbia University Press, 1976), p. 102; Thomas Reeves, *The Life and Times of Joe McCarthy* (Madison Books, 1997), pp. 347–350.

65 Ronald Steel, *Walter Lippmann and the American Century* (Little, Brown, 1980), p. 474.

66 Dean Acheson, "Memories of Joe McCarthy," *Harper's Magazine*, October 1969, p. 120. Also see Acheson, *Present at the Creation*, p. 366.

67 Acheson, *Present at the Creation*, p. 365.

68 Acheson, "Memories of Joe McCarthy," p. 120; Acheson, *Present at the Creation*, p. 366.

69 Elmer Davis, "The Crusade against Acheson," *Harper's Magazine*, March 1951, p. 24.

70 *Washington Post*, December 20, 1950.

71 Davis, "Crusade against Acheson," p. 29.

72 Acheson, "Memories of Joe McCarthy," p. 124.

73 Almond Diary, December 27, 1950, Edward Mallory Almond Papers, box 10, MHI; Appleman, *Disaster in Korea*, pp. 390–397.

74 Appleman, *Disaster in Korea*, p. 314.

75 Halberstam, *Coldest Winter*, p. 486.

76 James Michener, Draft Article, December 29, 1951, MRP Official Correspondence, series 2, p. 25, MHI. Portions of the draft were later published under the title "A Tough Man for a Tough Job," *Life*, May 12, 1952, pp. 103–118.

77 Interview with Ridgway, March 5, 1988, Matthew B. Ridgway Papers, series 5, Oral Histories, 1964–1987, box 88, MHI; Ridgway, *Korean War*, p. 83.

78 Bradley and Blair, *General's Life*, p. 616.

79 Ridgway interview, "Troop Leadership at the Operational Level: The Eighth Army in Korea," Ft. Leavenworth, Kansas, May 9, 1984, series 5, Oral Histories, box 8, p. 7, MHI.

80 Ridgway, *Korean War*, p. 84.

81 Ibid., pp. 86–87.

82 Clay Blair Collection, box 68, MHI.

83 The Jeter story was well known. Clay Blair interviewed many soldiers who repeated it and it became another Ridgway legend. Blair, *Forgotten War*, p. 574.

84 Ridgway interview, "Troop Leadership at the Operational Level," p. 18.

85 Interview with Maj. Matthew P. Caulfield and Lt. Col. Robert M. Elton, August 29, 1969, Matthew Ridgway Papers, series 5, Oral Histories, box 88, MHI.

86 Interview with General Walter Winton, May 9, 1984, Matthew Ridgway Papers, series 5, Oral Histories, box 8, MHI.

87 Anthony Farrar-Hockley, "A Reminiscence of the Chinese People's Volunteers in the Korean War," *China Quarterly*, no. 98 (June 1984), p. 295.

88 Pingchao Zhu, "The Korean War at the Dinner Table," in Philip West, Steven Levine, and Jackie Hilt, eds., *America's War in Asia: A Cultural Approach to History and Memory* (M. E. Sharpe, 1998), p. 185.

89 Guang Zhang and Jian Chen, eds., *Chinese Communist Foreign Policy and the Cold War in Asia: New Documentary Evidence, 1944–1950* (Imprint, 1996), pp. 214–215; Xiobing Li, Allan R. Millett, and Bin Yu, eds., *Mao's Generals Remember Korea* (University Press of Kansas, 2001), p. 18.

90 Cited in J. Chester Cheng, "The Korean War through Chinese Eyes: China Crosses the Rubicon," *Journal of Oriental Studies* 31, no. 1 (1993), p. 13.

91 Ibid., p. 18.

92 Shen Zhihua, "Sino-North Korean Conflict and Its Resolution during the Korean War," *CWIHP Bulletin*, no. 14/15 (Winter 2003/Spring 2004), p. 10.

93 Ridgway, *Korean War*, p. 93.

94 Li et al., eds., *Mao's Generals Remember Korea*, p. 19.

95 Peng Dehuai, *Memoirs of a Chinese Marshall: The Autobiographical Notes of Peng Dehuai (1898–1974)* (University of Hawaii Press, 2005), p. 478.

96 Zhang Da, "Resist America, Aid Korea!" in Zhang Lijia and Calum MacLeod, eds., *China Remembers* (Oxford University Press, 1999), p. 27.

97 Cited in Roy B. Appleman, *Ridgway Duels for Korea* (Texas A&M University Press, 1990), p. 155.

98 Shen, "Sino-North Korean Conflict," pp. 15–16; Chen Jian, *Mao's China and the Cold War* (University of North Carolina Press, 2001), p. 94.

99 Bradley and Blair, *General's Life*, p. 619; full text of MacArthur's January 10 telegram (quoted in text) in Matthew Ridgway Papers, series 3, Official Papers, Eighth Army, Special Files, December 1950–April 1951, box 68, MHI.

100 Truman, *Memoirs*, vol. 2, p. 492.

101 Acheson, *Present at the Creation*, p. 515.

102 Collins, *Lightning Joe*, pp. 253–254.

103 Bradley and Blair, *General's Life*, p. 623.

104 *Washington Post*, January 15, 1951.

105 Chen, *Mao's China and the Cold War*, p. 94.

106 Acheson, *Present at the Creation*, p. 513.

107 Beisner, *Dean Acheson*, p. 423.

108 *New York Times*, January 13, 1951; Beisner, *Dean Acheson*, pp. 423–424; Bevin Alexander, *Korea: The First War We Lost* (Hippocrene Books, 1986), p. 388.

109 Robert F. Futrell, *The United States Air Force in Korea, 1950–1953* (U.S. Government Printing Office, 1988), p. 273; Blair, *Forgotten War*, p. 652.

110 Ridgway, *Korean War*, p. 105.

111 Evgueni Bajanov, "Assessing the Politics of the Korean War, 1949–1951," *CWIHP Bulletin: The Cold War in Asia*, no. 6/7 (Winter 1995), p. 90.

112 Quoted in Appleman, *Ridgway Duels for Korea*, p. 219.

113 Blair, *Forgotten War*, p. 669; Millett, *The War for Korea, 1950–1951*, pp. 398–399.

114 Ridgway telegram to GHQ, February 3, 1951, Clay Blair Collection, box 68, MHI.

115 Maj. Gen. George Craig Stewart, "My Service with the Second Division during the Korean War," p. 17, Clay Blair Collection, Forgotten War, Alphabetical Files S, box 77, MHI.

116 Blair, *Forgotten War*, p. 690; Paik Sun Yup, *From Pusan to Panmunjom: Wartime Memoirs of the Republic of Korea's First Four-Star General* (Brassey's, 1992), p. 125.
117 Gary Turbark, "Massacre at Hoengsŏng," *Veterans of Foreign Wars Magazine*, February 2001.
118 Blair, *Forgotten War*, pp. 711–712; Millett, *The War for Korea, 1950–1951*, p. 391.
119 Peng, *Memoirs of a Chinese Marshal*, pp. 479–480.

EIGHT: *Quest for Victory*

1 Bradley and Blair, *A General's Life* (Simon & Schuster, 1983), p. 626; Schnabel and Watson, *The History of the Joint Chiefs of Staff*, vol. 3, p. 468; *FRUS, 1951*, vol. 7: *Korea and China, Part 1* (1983), pp. 251–256.
2 *New York Times*, March 24, 1951.
3 *Washington Post*, March 27, 1951; Beisner, *Dean Acheson: A Life in the Cold War*, p. 427.
4 Acheson, *Present at the Creation*, p. 519.
5 Truman, *Memoirs*, vol. 2, pp. 441–442.
6 David McCullough, *Truman* (Simon & Schuster, 1992), p. 837.
7 "Collins Interview with Lt. Col. Charles C. Sperow," 1972, pp. 309–311, Senior Oral History Program Project, MHI.
8 McCullough, *Truman*, p. 837.
9 Acheson, *Present at the Creation*, p. 519.
10 *Washington Post*, April 6, 1951.
11 *FRUS, 1951*, vol. 7: *Part 1*, p. 299.
12 Bradley and Blair, *General's Life*, p. 630.
13 *FRUS, 1951*, vol. 7: *Part 1*, p. 309; Bradley and Blair, *General's Life*, p. 630.
14 Robert H. Ferrell, ed., *Off the Record: The Private Papers of Harry S. Truman* (Harper & Row, 1980), pp. 210–211.
15 Rogers M. Anders, ed., *Forging the Atomic Shield: Excerpts from the Office Diary of Gordon E. Dean* (University of North Carolina Press, 1987), p. 137.
16 Bradley and Blair, *General's Life*, pp. 630–631.
17 Roger Dingman, "Atomic Diplomacy during the Korean War," *International Security* 13, no. 3 (Winter 1988/89), p. 74; Daniel Calingaert, "Nuclear Weapons and the Korean War," *Journal of Strategic Studies* 11, no. 2 (June 1988), pp. 177–202; Steven Casey, *Selling the Korean War: Propaganda, Politics and Public Opinion, 1950–53* (Oxford University Press, 2008), pp. 230–231.
18 Anders, *Forging the Atomic Shield*, p. 140.
19 McCullough, *Truman*, p. 840.
20 James, *The Years of McArthur*, vol. 3, p. 600; Clay Blair, *The Forgotten War: America in Korea, 1950–1953* (Times Books, 1987), pp. 788, 794–797; Robert J. Donovan, *Tumultuous Years: The Presidency of Harry S. Truman, 1949–1953* (W. W. Norton, 1967), pp. 340–362.
21 Matthew Ridgway, *Soldier: The Memoirs of Matthew B. Ridgway, as Told to Harold H. Martin* (Harper, 1956), p. 223.
22 Mathew Ridgway Papers, series 3, "Official Papers," box 72, MHI.
23 James, *The Years of MacArthur*, vol. 3, pp. 602–603.
24 William J. Sebald and Russell Brines, *With MacArthur in Japan: A Personal History of the Occupation Ambassador William Sebald* (W. W. Norton, 1965), p. 235.

25 Frank Tremaine cited in "MacArthur," *American Experience*, PBS, Enhanced Transcript, p. 29, available at http://www.pbs.org/wgbh/amex/macarthur/filmmore/transcript/index.html (accessed October 1, 2010).
26 *Time*, April 30, 1951, p. 23.
27 *Life*, April 23, 1951, pp. 42–46.
28 *Time*, April 23, 1951, p. 28; James, *Years of MacArthur*, vol. 3, p. 610.
29 *Washington Post*, April 12, 1951; McCullough, *Truman*, pp. 846–847; James, *Years of MacArthur*, vol. 3, pp. 607–608; Merle Miller, *Plain Speaking: An Oral Biography of Harry S. Truman* (Berkley, 1974), pp. 311–312; *United Press International*, May 12, 1951.
30 General (Ret) Hong Xuezhi, "The CCPV's Combat and Logistics," in Xiobing Li, Allan R. Millett, and Bin Yu, eds., *Mao's Generals Remember Korea* (University Press of Kansas, 2001), pp. 131–132.
31 Shu Guang Zhang, *Mao's Military Romanticism* (University Press of Kansas, 1995), pp. 145–146.
32 Li et al., eds., *Mao's Generals Remember Korea*, p. 125.
33 Blair, *Forgotten War*, p. 807.
34 Paschal N. and Mary H. Strong, "Sabres and Safety Pins" [Oral History], p. 414, Clay and Joan Blair Collection, "Forgotten War," Alphabetical Files S–V, box 83, MHI; Bittman Barth, "Tropic Lightning and Taro Leaf in Korea" [Oral History], pp. 74–75, MHI.
35 Ridgway, *The Korean War*, pp. 162–164.
36 "Memorandum for Commanding General, Eighth Army," April 25, 1951, Matthew Ridgway Papers, series 3, Official Papers, CINC Far East, 1951–53, box 73, MHI.
37 Ridgway, "Ltr, CINCFE to CG Eighth Army, 25 April 1951, sub. Letter of Instructions," Matthew Ridgway Papers, series 3, Official Papers, CINC Far East, 1951–53, box 73, MHI.
38 Bradley and Blair, *General's Life*, p. 640.
39 "Instructions Given Orally to Colonel Paul F. Smith, in the Presence of Major General Doyle Hickey, Chief of Staff, GHQ, FEC," April 26, 1951, Matthew B. Ridgway Papers, series 3, Official Papers, Commander-in-Chief Far East, 1951–52, box 72, MHI.
40 Interview with General James A. Van Fleet by Colonel Bruce H. Williams, tape 4, March 3, 1973, p. 23, MHI.
41 Quoted in Anthony Farrar-Hockley, *The Edge of the Sword* (Frederick Muller, 1954), p. 49.
42 Ibid., p. 54.
43 E. J. Kahn, "A Reporter in Korea: No One but the Glosters," *The New Yorker*, May 26, 1951, p. 15; Barry Taylor, "Open Road Barred," *Military History* 7, no. 5 (April 1991), pp. 47–52; Brian Catchpole, "The Commonwealth in Korea," *History Today* (November 1988), pp. 33–39.
44 Blair, *Forgotten War*, p. 847.
45 Van Fleet to Ridgway, May 11, 1951, Matthew B. Ridgway Papers, series 2, Correspondence Official, Eighth U.S. Army, January 1951–June 1951, "N-Z," box 13, MHI.
46 *Life*, May 11, 1953, p. 132.
47 Blair, *Forgotten War*, p. 859; Millett, *The War for Korea, 1950–1951*, pp. 443–444.

48 Interview with Lieutenant General Almond (Retired) by Captain Fergusson, March 29, 1975, side 1, tape 5, p. 26, Edward Almond Papers, MHI.
49 *Life*, May 11, 1953, p. 132.
50 Van Fleet interview, p. 53. See also Van Fleet, "How we can win with what we have," *Life*, May 18, 1953, pp. 157–172.
51 Mathew Ridgway Papers, series 3, Official Papers, Commander-in-Chief Far East, 1951–52, box 72, MHI.
52 *Life*, May 11, 1953, p. 127.

NINE: *The Stalemate*

1 *FRUS, 1951*, vol. 7: *Korea and China, Part 1* (1983), p. 547.
2 Quoted in Blair, *The Forgotten War*, p. 925.
3 Stalin to Mao, June 5, 1951, *CWIHP Bulletin: The Cold War in Asia*, no. 6/7 (Winter 1995), p. 59.
4 *FRUS, 1951*, vol. 7: *Part 1*, p. 507.
5 Mao to Stalin, June 13, 1951, *CWHIP Bulletin: The Cold War in Asia*, no. 6/7 (Winter 1995), p. 61.
6 Kathryn Weathersby, "New Russian Documents on the Korean War," *CWIHP Bulletin: The Cold War in Asia*, no. 6/7 (Winter 1995), pp. 34–35.
7 Chen, *Mao's China and the Cold War*, p. 100.
8 Ibid., p. 101.
9 C. Turner Joy, *How Communists Negotiate* (Macmillan, 1955), p. 4.
10 Quoted in Blair, *Forgotten War*, p. 933.
11 Chen, *Mao's China and the Cold War*, p. 100.
12 Walter G. Hermes, *Truce Tent and Fighting Front* (U.S. Government Printing Office, 1988), p. 19.
13 Joy, *How Communists Negotiate*, pp. 4–9.
14 Mao telegram to Stalin, July 3, 1951, *CWIHP Bulletin: The Cold War in Asia*, no. 6/7 (Winter 1995), p. 66.
15 Hermes, *Truce Tent*, pp. 26–35.
16 Mao to Stalin, August 12, 1951, *CWIHP Bulletin: The Cold War in Asia*, no. 6/7 (Winter 1995), p. 68.
17 *FRUS, 1951*, vol. 7: *Part 1*, p. 745.
18 Mao to Stalin, August 27, 1951, *CWIHP Bulletin: The Cold War in Asia*, no. 6/7 (Winter 1995), p. 68; Stueck, *The Korean War: An International History*, pp. 228–229.
19 *FRUS, 1951*, vol. 7: *Part 1*, pp. 848–849, 850–852.
20 Mao to Stalin, August 27, 1951, p. 68.
21 Matthew B. Ridgway Papers, series 3, Official Papers, Commander-in-Chief Far East, 1951–52, box 72, MHI.
22 *FRUS, 1951*, vol. 7: *Part 1*, pp. 774–776.
23 Rosemary Foot, "Anglo-American Relations in the Korean Crisis: The British Effort to Avert Expanded War, December 1950–January 1951," *Diplomatic History* 10, no. 1 (Winter 1986), p. 66.
24 Shiv Dayal, *India's Role in the Korea Question* (Delhi: Chand, 1959), p. 143.
25 Stueck, *Korean War*, pp. 236–237.
26 Quoted in Blair, *Forgotten War*, p. 957; *FRUS, 1951*, vol. 7: *Part 1*, p. 1099.

27 *New York Times*, November 17, 1951.
28 *FRUS, 1951*, vol. 7: *Part 1*, p. 1093.
29 Ibid., p. 618.
30 Ibid., p. 622.
31 Foot, "Anglo-American Relations in the Korean Crisis," p. 88.
32 J. Lawton Collins, *War in Peacetime: The History and Lessons of Korea* (Houghton Mifflin, 1969), p. 340.
33 *FRUS, 1951*, vol. 7: *Part 1*, pp. 857–858.
34 The Geneva Convention of 1949, Convention (III) relative to the Treatment of Prisoners of War, Geneva, August 12, 1949, Article 118, available at http://www.icrc.org/ihl.nsf/FULL/375?OpenDocument (accessed January 2009).
35 U. Alexis Johnson (with Jeff Olivarius McAllister), *Right Hand of Power: The Memoirs of an American Diplomat* (Prentice-Hall, 1984), p. 133; Foot, "Anglo-American Relations in the Korean Crisis," pp. 88–89.
36 Hermes, *Truce Tent*, pp. 135–136. Among the many controversial decisions made at Yalta was the agreement that when World War II ended in Europe, Soviet citizens, regardless of their individuals histories, be sent back to the Soviet Union. Although the agreement reached at Yalta did not specifically state that the Allies must return Soviet citizens against their will, this was what happened in many cases. Rather than return to face the firing squad or the Gulag, many Soviet citizens who were forced to return committed suicide instead. For a heartbreaking account of the forced repatriation of Soviet citizens after the war, see Anne Applebaum's Pulitzer prize–winning book, *Gulag: A History* (Anchor Books, 2003), pp. 435–439.
37 Johnson, *Right Hand of Power*, p. 133.
38 *FRUS, 1952–54*, vol. 15: *Korea, Part 1* (1984), p. 401.
39 Allen Goodman, ed., *Negotiating while Fighting: The Diary of Admiral C. Turner Joy at the Korean Armistice Conference* (Stanford University Press, 1978), p. 137.
40 Hermes, *Truce Tent*, p. 141; Goodman, *Negotiating while Fighting*, p. 154. According to the Hanley Report of November 1951 on North Korean war crimes, compiled by Colonel James M. Hanley, chief of the Eighth Army's war crimes section, 2,513 U.S. POWs and more than 25,000 South Korean POWs were killed. See *Korean Atrocities: Report of the Committee on Government Operations Made through Its Permanent Subcommittee on Investigations by Its Subcommittee on Korean War Atrocities Pursuant to S. Res. 40* (U.S. Government Printing Office, 1954). The report can be accessed at http://www.loc.gov/rr/frd/Military_Law/pdf/KW-atrocities-Report.pdf.
41 Hermes, *Truce Tent*, p. 142.
42 Goodman, *Negotiating while Fighting*, p. 181; Major General (Ret) Chai Chengwen, "The Korean Truce Negotiations," in Xioabing Li, Allan R. Millett, and Bin Yu, eds., *Mao's Generals Remember Korea* (University Press of Kansas, 2001), p. 216.
43 Chai, "Korean Truce Negotiations," p. 217.
44 Goodman, *Negotiating while Fighting*, p. 208.
45 Johnson, *Right Hand of Power*, p. 135.
46 Joy, *How Communists Negotiate*, p. 152.
47 Johnson, *Right Hand of Power*, p. 135.
48 Anthony Eden, March 21, 1952, FO 371/99564, National Archives, Kew, UK.

49 Johnson, *Right Hand of Power*, p. 139.
50 *FRUS, 1952–54*, vol. 15: *Part 1*, pp. 76–77, 58–59.
51 Johnson, *Right Hand of Power*, p. 139.
52 Chai, "Korean Truce Negotiations," pp. 217–224.
53 *Washington Post*, February 26, 1952.

TEN: *"Let Them March Till They Die"*

1 Philip Crosbie, *March Till They Die* (Browne & Nolan, 1955), p. 54.
2 "Maryknoll Missionary Follows in Steps of Missionary Bishop in North Korea," *Catholic News Agency*, May 13, 2008.
3 Philip Crosbie, *Pencilling Prisoner* (Hawthorne Press, 1954), p. 98.
4 Ibid., p. 101.
5 Larry Zellers, *In Enemy Hands: A Prisoner in North Korea* (University Press of Kentucky, 1991), p. 85.
6 Nugent, vol. 4, Department of the Army Staff Judge Advocate (DASJA), p. 692. The bulk of primary sources were obtained from the DASJA through the Freedom of Information Act by Raymond B. Lech, to whom I am indebted for giving me access to them. The material consists of eighty volumes of transcripts of the fourteen U.S. Army court-martial proceedings. Each transcript is formally known by the name of the person being tried. The transcripts are now in the MHI; Nugent, vol. 8, DASJA, p. 2015; vol. 12, DASJA, pp. 139–140; Larry Zellers, *In Enemy Hands: A Prisoner of North Korea* (University of Kentucky Press, 1991), p. 88. Also see Raymond B. Lech, *Broken Soldiers* (University of Illinois Press, 2000).
7 Zellers, *In Enemy Hands*, pp. 90–91.
8 Ibid., p. 100.
9 Clark, *Living Dangerously in Korea*, p. 380.
10 Crosbie, *Pencilling Prisoners*, pp. 141–146.
11 "Testimony of Major Green," Nugent, vol. 8, DASJA, p. 2044.
12 Crosbie, *Pencilling Prisoners*, p. 181.
13 "Testimony of Major Booker," Nugent, vol. 8, DASJA, pp. 2144–2146.
14 Liles, vol. 4B, DASJA, pp. 1817–1818.
15 Fleming, vol. 11, DASJA, pp. 1418, 1477.
16 Ibid., pp. 1497–1500.
17 Ibid., p. 1516.
18 Liles, vol. 2, DASJA, p. 74.
19 "Testimony of Captain Sidney Esensten," Liles, vol. 2B, DASJA, p. 82; "Testimony of Anderson," Liles, vol. 2, DASJA, p. 428. See also Raymond B. Lech, *Broken Soldiers* (University of Illinois Press, 2000), pp. 42–48.
20 Liles, vol. 2, DASJA, p. 86.
21 Liles, vol. 1, DASJA, p. 143.
22 Ibid., pp. 1443–1444.
23 Erwin, vol. 4, DASJA, p. 1146.
24 Liles, vol. 1, DASJA, p. 144.
25 Erwin, vol. 3, DASJA, pp. 815–816.
26 Fleming, vol. 11, DASJA, p. 1544.
27 Olson, vol. 2, DASJA, pp. 29–30.

28 "Testimony of PFC Theodore Hilburn," Olson, vol. 3, DASJA, p. 133.
29 "Testimony of Staff Sergeant Leonard J. Maffioli," Olson, vol. 3, DASJA, p. 175.
30 "Testimony of Master Sergeant Chester Mathis," Olson, vol. 3, DASJA, p. 213.
31 Olson, vol. 3, DASJA, p. 88.
32 "General Court-Martial Order, 10 June 1955," Olson, vol. 2, DASJA, pp. 22–23.
33 "Harrison Testimony," Olson, vol. 3, DASJA, p. 104.
34 Olson, vol. 3, DASJA, p. 278.
35 Fleming, vol. 2, DASJA, p. 305.
36 Liles, vol. 5, DASJA, pp. 279–280.
37 Fleming, vol. 4, DASJA, p. 207; vol. 9, DASJA, p. 1061.
38 Lech, *Broken Soldiers*, p. 124.
39 Liles, vol. 2B, DASJA, p. 724; Lech, *Broken Soldiers*, p. 124.
40 Liles, vol. 3, DASJA, p. 944.
41 Ibid., p. 1053.
42 Farrar-Hockley, *The Edge of the Sword*, p. 192.
43 "Dunn Testimony," Nugent, vol. 5, DASJA, pp. 996–1024.
44 Liles, vol. 1, DASJA, p. 154.
45 "Testimony of Major Harold Kaschko," Liles, vol. 1, DASJA, p. 211.
46 Lech, *Broken Soldiers*, p. 147. "Testimony of Major David McGhee," Fleming, vol. 10, DASJA, p. 1163.
47 Fleming, vol. 10, DASJA, p. 1164.
48 Liles, vol. 1, DASJA, p. 148; "Affidavit of Captain Waldron Berry, 3 Nov 1954," Nugent, vol. 1, DASJA, p. 98.
49 "Affidavit of J. D. Bryant, Captain, United States Air Force, 3 Nov 1954," Nugent, vol. 1, DASJA, p. 98.
50 Fleming, vol. 9, DASJA, pp. 1150–1151.
51 "Testimony of Van Orman," Fleming, vol. 7, DASJA, p. 483.
52 Alley, vol. 4, DASJA, p. 205.
53 "Deposition of Comdr R. M. Bagwell, 10 Sep 1954," Fleming, vol. 4, DASJA, p. 2.
54 "Affidavit of Major Filmore Wilson McAbee, 22 Sep 1954," Nugent, vol. 1, DASJA, p. 354.
55 Cho Ch'ang-ho, *Toraon saja* [Return of a Dead Man] (Seoul: Chiho ch'ulp'ansa, 1995).
56 Pak Chin-hŭng, *Toraon p'aeja* [Return of the Defeated] (Seoul: Yŏksa pip'yŏngsa, 2001), p. 73.
57 Ibid., pp. 78–79, 91–92.
58 Ibid., pp. 94, 98–99.
59 Ibid., pp. 100–101.
60 Ibid., p. 102.
61 Ibid., p. 100.
62 Ibid., p. 104.
63 Ibid., p. 116.
64 Ibid., p. 121.
65 "Hardly Known, Not Yet Forgotten: South Korean POWs Tell Their Story," *Radio Free Asia*, January 25, 2007, at http://www.rfa.org/english/news/politics/korea_pow-20070125.html (accessed March 5, 2010).
66 Cho reiterated this claim in his testimony before the U.S. Congress on April

27, 2006. His testimony stated, "As a POW, I didn't even know that the war ended and the exchange of POWs had been occurred. I've learned that fact long after war ended. All of returned POWs whom I've met were not much different. They didn't know that the exchange of POWs had been occurred either." *North Korea: Human Rights Update and International Abduction Issues: Joint Hearing before the Subcommittee on Asia and the Pacific and the Subcommittee on Africa, Global Human Rights and International Operations of the Committee on International Relations, House of Representatives, 109th Congress, 2nd Session, April 27, 2008* (U.S. Government Printing Office, 2006), p. 43. This congressional hearing provides many more details about Cho's circumstances and stories of other ROK POWs' experience in North Korea.

67 "Hardly Known, Not Yet Forgotten," *Radio Free Asia.*

68 Cho Song-hŭn, *Han'gukchŏn kukkunp'oro silt'aepunsŏk* [An Analysis of the Actual Conditions of South Korean POWs] (Seoul: Kukpangbu kunsa p'yŏnch'an yŏnguso, 2006), p. 103.

69 Ibid., pp. 56–57. See also *2010 White Paper on Human Rights in North Korea* (Korea Institute for National Unification, 2010), pp. 480–485. http://www.kinu.or.kr/upload/neoboard/DATA04/2010%20white%20paper.pdf (accessed October 15, 2012). For an excellent description of the recent plight of former South Korean POWs, see Melanie Kirkpatrick, *Escape from North Korea: The Untold Stories of Asia's Underground Railroad* (Encounter Books, 2012), pp. 117–133.

70 "Soviet Embassy Charge d'Affaire to North Korea S.P. Suzdalev to Foreign Minister Molotov," December 2, 1953, in Yang Chin-sam, "Chŏnjaenggi chungguk chidowa pukhan chidobu saiŭi mosun'gwa kaltung [Contradictions and Discord between the Chinese and North Korean Authorities during the Korean War]," *Hanguk chŏnjaengŭi saeroun yŏngu* [New Research on the Korean War], vol. 2 (2002), p. 619. See also *Yonhap News*, June 16, 2005.

71 Cho, *Han'gukchŏn kukkunp'oro silt'aepunsŏk* [An Analysis of the Actual Conditions of South Korean POWs During the Korean War], pp. 94–95.

72 Pak, *Toraon p'aeja* [Return of the Defeated], p. 199.

73 Ibid., p. 204.

74 Ibid., pp. 218–219.

75 Ibid., pp. 211–212.

76 Ibid., pp. 226–228.

77 Ibid., pp. 232–233.

78 Ibid., p. 206.

ELEVEN: *Propaganda Wars*

1 *FRUS, 1951*, vol. 7: *Korea and China, Part 1* (1983), p. 176.

2 Sahr Conway-Lanz, *Collateral Damage: American, Noncombatant Immunity and Atrocity after World War II* (Routledge, 2006), p. 151. Biographical sketch of Charles Joy at http://www.harvardsquarelibrary.org/unitarians/joy.html (accessed April 6, 2009).

3 Quoted in Balázs Szalontai, "The Four Horsemen of the Apocalypse in North Korea: The Forgotten Side of a Not-So-Forgotten War," in Chris Springer and Balázs Szalontai, *North Korea Caught in Time* (Garnet, 2010), p. xii.

4 Freda Kirchwey, "Liberation by Death," *Nation*, March 10, 1951, p. 216.
5 Harold Ickes, "Sherman's Hell, Korea's Hell," *New Republic*, March 1951, p. 18.
6 Conway-Lanz, *Collateral Damage*, p. 155.
7 John Gittings, "Talks, Bombs and Germs: Another Look at the Korean War," *Journal of Contemporary Asia* 5, no. 2 (1975), p. 214.
8 Soviet journalist Vassili Kornilov, quoted in Springer and Szalontai, *North Korea Caught in Time*, p. 20.
9 *Washington Post*, May 16, 1951.
10 The belief that airpower could have coercive force by itself had existed since the invention of airpower in World War I. But World War II, the first time massive strategic bombing was employed to both destroy and terrorize, demonstrated that it had an opposite effect in both Germany and Japan. The bombing seemed to embolden the bombed even more to fight and resist. In Germany, war production actually increased toward the end of the war even as factories were destroyed. There is significant evidence as well that not even the atomic bombs, the ultimate strategic bombing, convinced the Japanese people to surrender. See, for example, *The U.S. Strategic Bombing Survey* (*USSBS*), a massive detailed assessment of the effects of bombing in Germany and Japan. The report, issued in the fall of 1945, concluded that strategic bombing had a decisive effect, but subsequent analyses concluded otherwise. A good introduction and summary as well as guides for finding the hundreds of *USSBS*s available can be accessed at http://www.ussbs.com/ (accessed May 7, 2009). Tsuyoshi Hasegawa, in *Racing the Enemy Stalin, Truman, and the Surrender of Japan* (Harvard University Press, 2006), argued that rather than the atomic bombs, the Soviet Union's entry into the war was the decisive factor that convinced Japan to capitulate. The debate over the efficacy of airpower still rages today, for example, whether air attacks deterred Serbia in Kosovo in 1999 and the efficacy of the "shock and awe" campaign against Iraq in 2003. Daniel Byman and Matthew Waxman provide good summaries of the advocates of Kosovo airpower in their criticism of it in "Kosovo and the Great Air Power Debate," *International Security* 24, no. 4 (Spring 2000), pp. 5–38.
11 Robert F. Futrell, *The United States Air Force in Korea, 1950–1953* (U.S. Government Printing Office, 1988), pp. 313–340; Robert A. Pape, *Bombing to Win: Air Power and Coercion* (Cornell University Press, 1996), pp. 147–149.
12 Quoted in John J. Tkacik Jr., "From Surprise to Stalemate: What the People's Liberation Army Learned from the Korean War—A Half Century Later," in Laurie Burkitt, Andrew Scobell, and Larry Wortzel, eds., *The Lessons of History: The Chinese People's Liberation Army at 75* (U.S. Army War College Strategic Studies Institute, July 2003), pp. 303–304.
13 Quoted in ibid., pp. 304–305.
14 Quoted in ibid., p. 308.
15 General (Ret.) Yang Dezhi, "Command Experience in Korea," in Xiaobing Li, Allan R. Millet, and Bin Yu, eds., *Mao's Generals Remember Korea* (University Press of Kansas, 2001), pp. 153–155; Tkacik, "From Surprise to Stalemate," p. 311.
16 Yang, "Command Experience in Korea," p. 154.
17 Quoted in Tkacik, "From Surprise to Stalemate," p. 313.

18 By the fall of 1951 eighteen of twenty-two major cities in North Korea had already been at least half obliterated. In early 1952, the Far East Air Force (FEAF) began to target power plants and dams along the Yalu River. The huge Suiho hydroelectrical plant was destroyed in June 1952. The Sukam and Chasan Reservoirs in South P'yŏngan province were destroyed in May 1953, causing huge floods that destroyed hundreds of villages and much livestock and food. See Conrad Crane, *American Airpower Strategy in Korea, 1950–1953* (University Press of Kansas, 2000), pp. 122–124. See also Michael S. Sherry, *The Rise of American Air Power: The Creation of Armageddon* (Yale University Press, 1987).

19 "Crawford Sams Memoir: Medic, 1910–1955," pp. 709–710, Crawford Sams Papers, box 1, MHI.

20 Ibid., p. 715.

21 Ibid., p. 716.

22 Ibid., p. 718; *Renmin Ribao* [People's Daily] published in English in *Foreign Radio Broadcasts*, May 4, 1952.

23 The pioneer work exposing the activities of Unit 731 and subsequent cover-up was done by John W. Powell. See his "Japan's Germ Warfare: The U.S. Cover-up of a War Crime," *Bulletin of Concerned Asian Scholars* 12, no. 2 (1980), pp. 2–17, and "Japan's Biological Weapons, 1930–1945: A Hidden Chapter in History," *Bulletin of Concerned Asian Scholars* 37, no. 8 (October 1981), pp. 43–52. See also Sheldon Harris, *Factories of Death: Japanese Biological Warfare 1932–45 and the American Cover-Up* (Routledge, 1994), p. 54.

24 Milton Leitenberg, "New Evidence on the Korean War Biological Warfare Allegations: Background and Analysis," *CWIHP Bulletin*, no. 11 (Winter 1998), pp. 187–188.

25 Ruth Rogaski, *Hygienic Modernity: Meanings of Health and Disease in Treaty-Port China* (University of California Press, 2004), p. 293.

26 *Renmin Ribao* [People's Daily] published in English in *Foreign Radio Broadcasts*, April 9, 1952.

27 Fang Shih-shan, "Effects of War on the Health of the People," *Chinese Medical Journal* 71, no. 5 (September–October 1953), p. 324.

28 William Dean, *General Dean's Story* (Viking, 1952), p. 276.

29 William E. Banghart, "Court Martial Papers," vol. 1, Department of the Army Staff Judge Advocate (DASJA), pp. 199–200, MHI.

30 Yang, "Command Experience in Korea," p. 166.

31 Rogaski, *Hygienic Modernity*, p. 295.

32 The Three-Anti campaign launched in late 1951 aimed to eradicate (1) corruption, (2) waste, and (3) bureaucracy. The Five-Anti campaign was launched in January 1952 to eliminate (1) bribery, (2) theft of state property, (3) tax evasion, (4) cheating on government contracts, and (5) stealing state economic information. The two campaigns evolved into an all-out war against the bourgeoisie. See also Rogaski, *Hygienic Modernity*, pp. 288–289; Jonathan Spence, *The Search for Modern China* (W. W. Norton, 1990), pp. 536–538.

33 Quoted in Simon Winchester, *The Man Who Loved China* (HarperCollins, 2008), p. 201.

34 Rogaski, *Hygienic Modernity*, pp. 288–289.

35 Lynn T. White, "Changing Concepts of Corruption in Communist China: Early 1950s versus Early 1980s," in Yu-Ming Shaw, ed., *Changes and Continuities in Chinese Communism* (Westview Press, 1988), pp. 327–330.
36 Rogaski, *Hygienic Modernity*, p. 289.
37 A. M. Halpern, "Bacteriological Warfare Accusations in Two Asian Communist Campaigns," in U.S. Air Force, *Project Rand Research Memorandum* 25 (April 1952), pp. 54–55.
38 Philip Short, *Mao: A Life* (Henry Holt, 2000), pp. 436–437.
39 *New York Times*, March 13, 1951.
40 "Telegram to V.M. Molotov from Beijing from the Ambassador of the USSR to the PRC, V.V. Kuznetsov, about the Results of a Conversation with Mao Zedong on 11 May 1953 [Not Dated]," *CWIHP Bulletin*, no. 11 (Winter 1998), p. 183.
41 *Department of State Bulletin*, vol. 26, pt. 1, April–June 1952, pp. 427–428.
42 Ibid., pt. 2, April–June 1952, pp. 925–926.
43 Milton Leitenberg, "New Russian Evidence on the Korean War Biological Warfare Allegations: Background and Analysis," *CWIHP Bulletin*, no. 11 (Winter 1998), p. 190. According to Kathryn Weathersby, in anticipation of Acheson's request to the chairman of the ICRC that the ICRC investigate the Chinese and North Korean charges of bacteriological warfare, Soviet Foreign Minister Andrei Gromyko began to immediately prepare for a strategy to refuse such a visit. Citing the Geneva Convention, which specified that "the parties participating in armed conflict would themselves investigate the facts of any alleged violation of the convention," Gromyko advised the North Koreans to refuse any proposal made by the ICRC to conduct on-site investigations. The Soviets at the highest level were also involved in helping the North Koreans avoid inspections proposed by members of the World Health Organization (WHO). When North Korean leaders received the third, and last, telegram from UN Secretary General Trygvie Lie on April 6 requesting that the WHO be allowed to visit North Korea for inspections, the ambassador to North Korea, V. N. Razuvaev, advised that the DPRK respond that "the proposal cannot be accepted because the World Health Organization did not have proper international authority." No doubt, it was because of intense international pressure to prove the truth of allegations, and to fend off further requests for inspections, that the International Scientific Commission, the group organized in 1952 by the Soviet-bloc World Peace Organization, was formed to provide its own on-site investigations. Kathryn Weathersby, "Deceiving the Deceivers: Moscow, Beijing, Pyongyang, and the Allegations of Bacteriological Weapons Use in Korea," *CWIHP Bulletin*, no. 11 (Winter 1998), p. 178.
44 *New York Times*, April 2, 1952.
45 Winchester, *Man Who Loved China*, p. 204.
46 *Report of the International Scientific Commission for the Investigation of the Facts concerning Bacteriological Warfare in Korea and China, with Appendixes* (Commission, 1952), p. 60.
47 Albert E. Cowdrey, "'Germ Warfare' and Public Heath in the Korean Conflict," *Journal of the History of Medicine and Allied Sciences* 39 (April 1984), pp. 169–170.
48 Quoted in Ruth Rogaski, "Nature, Annihilation, and Modernity: China's

Korean War Germ-Warfare Experience Reconsidered," *Journal of Asian Studies* 61, no. 2 (May 2002), p. 403.

49 Ibid., pp. 403–404.

50 Needham to Dr. Alfred Fisk, October 11, 1953, cited in Tom Buchanan, "The Courage of Galileo: Joseph Needham and the 'Germ Warfare' Allegations in the Korean War," *History* 86, no. 284 (October 2001), p. 513.

51 Winchester, *Man Who Loved China*, p. 206.

52 Rogaski, "Nature, Annihilation, and Modernity," p. 402.

53 Cowdrey, " 'Germ Warfare' and Public Health," p. 170.

54 *New York Times*, April 3, 1952.

55 Ibid., May 31, 1952.

56 Weathersby, "Deceiving the Deceivers," p. 177. See also Leitenberg, "New Russian Evidence on the Korean War Biological Warfare Allegations," pp. 185–199.

57 "Explanatory Note from Lt. Gen. V.N. Razuvaev, Ambassador of the USSR to the DPRK and Chief Military Advisor to the KPA, to L.P. Beria," April 19, 1953, *CWIHP Bulletin*, no. 11 (Winter 1998), p. 181; "Explanatory Note from Glukhov, Deputy Chief of the Department of Counterespionage of the USSR Ministry District and Former Advisor to the Ministry of Public Security of the DPRK, to L.P. Beria, Deputy Chairman of the USSR Council of Ministers," April 13, 1953, ibid., p. 180.

58 Weathersby, "Deceiving the Deceivers," p. 179; Chen Jian, *China's Road to the Korean War: The Making of the Sino-American Confrontation* (Columbia University Press, 1994).

59 "Resolution of the Presidium of the USSR Council of Ministers about letters to the Ambassador of the USSR in the PRC, V.V. Kuznetsov, and to the Charge d'Affaire of the USSR in the DPRK, S P. Suzdalev," May 2, 1952, *CWIHP Bulletin*, no. 11 (Winter 1998), p. 183.

60 Weathersby, "Deceiving the Deceivers," p. 177. For the text of the decision by the Council of Ministers to reach a negotiated settlement in Korea, adopted March 19, 1953, see *CWIHP Bulletin: The Cold War in Asia*, no. 6/7 (Winter 1995), pp. 80–82.

61 Matthew B. Ridgway, *The Korean War: How We Met the Challenge; How All-Out Asian War Was Averted; Why MacArthur Was Dismissed; Why Today's War Objectives Must Be Limited* (Doubleday, 1967), p. 204.

62 Stanley Sandler, *The Korean War: An Encyclopedia* (Routledge, 1995), p. 84.

63 Mark Clark, *From the Danube to the Yalu* (Harper & Brothers, 1954), p. 30.

64 Hermes, *Truce Tent*, pp. 233–235.

65 Ridgway, *Korean War*, p. 206.

66 "Sir Esler Dening to British Foreign Office, Feb 25, 1952," FO 371/99638, National Archives, Kew, UK.

67 FO 371/ 99638, April 11, 1952, National Archives, Kew, UK.

68 "Memorandum by P.W. Manhard of the Political Section of the Embassy to the Ambassador of Korea in Korea (Muccio)," March 14, 1952, in *FRUS, 1952–54*, vol. 15: *Korea, Part 1* (1984), pp. 98–99.

69 "Koje POW Camps," May 6, 1952, FO 371/99639, National Archives, Kew, UK.

70 "United Nations Commission Report," March 27, 1952, FO 371/99638, National Archives, Kew, UK.

71 "Summary of Events: Koje-do May 7 through May 10, 1952," FO 371/99639, National Archives, Kew, UK.

72 Wilfred Burchett and Alan Winnington, *Koje Unscreened* (Britain-China Friendship Association, 1953), p. 72. British journalists Burchett and Winnington were well-known communist sympathizers.

73 Zhao Zuorui, "Organizing the Riots on Koje," in Richard Peters and Xiaobing Li, eds., *Voices from the Korean War: Personal Stories of American, Korea and Chinese Soldiers* (University Press of Kentucky, 2004), p. 256. A fictionalized account of this scene also appears in Ha Jin's prize-winning *War Trash* (Pantheon Books, 2004). Ha cites Zhang Zhe-shi's *Meijun Jizhongying Qinli Ji* [Personal Records in the American Prison Camps] (Chinese Archives Press, 1996) as a source for his historical novel.

74 Hermes, *Truce Tent*, p. 250.

75 "Statement of Brig. General Francis T. Dodd," May 12, 1952, FO 371/99638, National Archives, Kew, UK.

76 Hermes, *Truce Tent*, p. 252.

77 Clark, *From the Danube to the Yalu*, p. 46.

78 "Statement of Brig. General Francis T. Dodd," May 12, 1952.

79 Ridgway, *Korean War*, p. 214.

80 Hermes, *Truce Tent*, pp. 253–254.

81 C. H. Johnston, "Conditions in Prisoner of War Camps under the Control of the United Nations Command," May 23, 1952, FO 371/99638, National Archives, Kew, UK.

82 "Record of the Conversation with Mr. Acheson at the United Nations Embassy, Paris," May 28, 1952, FO 371/99638, National Archives, Kew, UK.

83 "Telegram to F.D. Tomlinson from Charles Johnston," June 16, 1952, FO 371/99638, National Archives, Kew, UK.

84 "Confidential 1553/25/52," May 29, 1952, FO 371/99638, National Archives, Kew, UK.

TWELVE: *Armistice, at Last*

1 *New York Times*, January 30, 1952.

2 Ibid., January 12, 1952. Robert and Jerome McGovern's younger brother Charles set up a memorial web site in 2004: http://www.mcgovernbrothers.com/ (accessed December 3, 2011).

3 *New York Times*, February 21, 1952.

4 Emmet J. Hughes, *The Ordeal of Power: A Political Memoir of the Eisenhower Years* (Atheneum, 1963), p. 32.

5 Bradley and Blair, *A General's Life*, p. 656.

6 *New York Times*, November 23, 1952.

7 Memorandum by John Foster Dulles to Dwight Eisenhower, November 26, 1952, in *FRUS, 1952–54*, vol. 15: *Korea, Part 1* (1984), p. 693.

8 Paik Sun Yup (Paek Sŏn-yŏp), *From Pusan to Panmunjom: Wartime Memoirs of the Republic of Korea's First Four-Star General* (Brassey's, 1992), pp. 215–216.

9 Ibid., pp. 216–217.

10 Mark Clark, *From the Danube to the Yalu* (Harper & Brothers, 1954), p. 239.

11 Dwight D. Eisenhower, *Mandate for Change, 1953–1956* (Doubleday, 1963), p. 59.
12 Douglas MacArthur, *Reminiscences: General of the Army* (Naval Institute Press, 1964), pp. 410–411.
13 Eisenhower Oral History Interview, July 28, 1964, pp. 8–9, John Foster Dulles Oral History, Princeton University, Princeton, N.J.
14 *FRUS, 1952–54*, vol. 15: *Part 1*, p. 818.
15 Dingman, "Atomic Diplomacy during the Korean War," p. 81; Edward C. Keefer, "Eisenhower and the Korean War," *Diplomatic History* 10, no. 3 (Summer 1986); H. W. Brand, "The Age of Vulnerability: Eisenhower and the National Insecurity State," *American Historical Review* 94, no. 4 (October 1989); Rosemary Foot, "Nuclear Coercion and the Ending of the Korean Conflict," *International Security* 13, no. 3 (Winter 1988/89).
16 *FRUS, 1952–54*, vol. 15: *Part 1*, pp. 1061–1069.
17 Sarvepalli Gopal, *Jawaharlal Nehru: A Biography*, vol. 2: *1947–1956* (Jonathan Cape, 1979), p. 148; Escott Reid, *Envoy to Nehru* (Oxford University Press, 1981), p. 45.
18 *FRUS, 1952–54*, vol. 15: *Part 1*, p. 1103.
19 Sherman Adams, *First-Hand Report: The Story of the Eisenhower Administration* (Harper & Brothers, 1961), p. 49.
20 David Rees described Eisenhower's "Korea Plan" as the "first vindication of the massive retaliation theory." See also David Rees, *Korea: The Limited War* (St. Martin's Press, 1964).
21 K. M. Panikkar, *In Two Chinas: Memoirs of a Diplomat* (George Allen & Unwin, 1955), p. 108.
22 Vojtech Mastny, *The Cold War and Soviet Insecurity: The Stalin Years* (Oxford University Press, 1998), pp. 172–173.
23 Foot, "Nuclear Coercion and the Ending of the Korean Conflict," pp. 104–107. This does not mean that nuclear threats played no role in bringing the war to an end, but that the claims of its effectiveness, which Eisenhower had used to justify his New Look strategy, had been greatly exaggerated.
24 *New York Times*, July 12, 1953; also William Taubman, *Krushchev: The Man and His Era* (W. W. Norton, 2003), pp. 240–241.
25 Conversation between Stalin and Zhou Enlai, August 20, 1952, *CWIHP Bulletin: The Cold War in Asia*, no. 6/7 (Winter 1995), pp. 12–13; Kathryn Weathersby, "Stalin, Mao, and the End of the Korean War," in Odd Arne Westad, ed., *Brothers in Arms: The Rise and Fall of the Sino-Soviet Alliance* (Woodrow Wilson Center Press/Stanford University Press, 1998), p. 105.
26 Weathersby, "Stalin, Mao, and the End of the Korean War," p. 108. The historian Chen Jian, however, maintains that while Stalin's death might have played a role in changing Chinese attitudes toward the POW issue, it was "more an outgrowth of Beijing's existing policies based on Chinese leaders' assessment of the changing situation than a reflection of altering Soviet directives." After reassessing China's gains and losses in Korea during the spring of 1953, China's leaders had simply decided that nothing more was to be gained from the continuing conflict. By that time, China's social and political transformation under Mao and the promotion of the country's international prestige and influence had already been achieved. Nevertheless, while

domestic concerns certainly played a role in changing Chinese attitudes, this does not explain why these changes came so soon after Stalin's death. See Chen, *Mao's China and the Cold War*, pp. 115–116.

27 Clark, *From the Danube to the Yalu*, p. 241; Hermes, *Truce Tent*, p. 411.

28 "Death of Stalin," July 16, 1953, Office of Current Intelligence, Central Intelligence Agency (HR70-14), p. 3, available at http://www.foia.cia.gov/CPE/CAESAR/caesar-02.pdf (accessed February 3, 2008).

29 Royal Institute of International Affairs (RIIA), ed., *Documents on International Affairs, 1953* (RIIA, 1956), pp. 11–13.

30 Serhy Yekelchyk, "The Civic Duty to Hate: Stalinist Citizenship as Political Practice and Civic Emotion (Kiev, 1943–53)," *Kritika: Explorations in Russian and Eurasian History* 7, no. 3 (Summer 2006), pp. 551–552.

31 Quoted in Walter Isaacson and Evan Thomas, *The Wise Men: Six Friends and the World They Made* (Touchstone, 1986), p. 554.

32 Hermes, *Truce Tent*, p. 412; Charles E. Bohlen, *Witness to History, 1929–1969* (W. W. Norton, 1973), p. 348; Klaus Larres, "Eisenhower and the First Forty Days after Stalin's Death," *Diplomacy and Statecraft* 6, no. 2 (July 1995), p. 436.

33 Weathersby, "Stalin, Mao, and the End of the Korean War," p. 108; "Resolution, USSR Council of Ministers with Draft Letters from Soviet Government to Mao Zedong and Kim Il Sung and Directive to Soviet Delegation at United Nations, 19 March 1953," *CWHIP Bulletin: The Cold War in Asia*, no. 6/7 (Winter 1995), p. 80.

34 Weathersby, "Stalin, Mao, and the End of the Korean War," p. 108.

35 Hermes, *Truce Tent*, p. 412.

36 Clark, *From the Danube to the Yalu*, pp. 241–242.

37 Quoted in Larres, "Eisenhower and the First Forty Days after Stalin's Death," pp. 455–456; J. W. Young, "Churchill, the Russian and the Western Alliance: The Three-Power Conference at Bermuda, December 1953," *English Historical Review* 101, no. 401 (October 1986).

38 Eisenhower, "A Chance for Peace," April 16, 1953, available at http://usa.usembassy.de/etexts/speeches/rhetoric/ikechanc.htm (accessed March 2, 2009).

39 The speech appeared to be part of a larger psychological warfare campaign aimed to weaken and destabilize the new government in Moscow. See Larres, "Eisenhower and the First Forty Days after Stalin's Death"; Kenneth A. Osgood, "Form before Substance: Eisenhower's Commitment to Psychological Warfare and Negotiations with the Enemy," *Diplomatic History* 24, no. 3 (Summer 2000).

40 Adams, *First-Hand Report*, p. 97.

41 Walter Lippmann, "Today and Tomorrow," *New York Times*, April 20, 1953.

42 Bohlen, *Witness to History*, p. 352.

43 Clark, *From the Danube to the Yalu*, p. 256.

44 Hermes, *Truce Tent*, pp. 425–432.

45 Clark to JCS, June 9, 1953, in *FRUS, 1952–54*, vol. 15: *Part 1*, p. 1157.

46 *New York Times*, June 25, 1953.

47 Clark, *From the Danube to the Yalu*, pp. 257–258; U. Alexis Johnson (with Jeff Olivarius McAllister), *Right Hand of Power: The Memoirs of an American Diplomat* (Prentice-Hall, 1984), pp. 166–167.

48 *New York Times,* May 31 and June 9, 1953.
49 Eisenhower, "Letter to President Syngman Rhee of Korea concerning the Acceptance of the Panmunjom Armistice," June 7, 1953, in *Public Papers of the Presidents of the United States: Dwight D. Eisenhower, 1953* (U.S. Government Printing Office, 1960), p. 96.
50 Clark, *From the Danube to the Yalu,* p. 279; Stueck, *The Korean War: An International History,* pp. 335–336.
51 Chŏng Il-kwŏn, Oral History Interview, September 29, 1964, John Foster Dulles Oral History Project, Princeton University Library, Princeton, N.J. The detailed account of how the escape was planned can be found in Ch'oe Tok-sin, *Naega kyokkun p'anmunjŏm* [My Panmunjom Experience] (Seoul: Munhwasa, 1955). Ch'oe wrote that preparation for the release began in early June.
52 *New York Times,* June 21, 1953.
53 *Dong'a ilbo,* June 19, 1953; *New York Times,* June 18, 1953.
54 Dwight D. Eisenhower, *Mandate for Change, 1953–1956* (Doubleday, 1963), pp. 185–186.
55 "Korea: Action in General Assembly," FO 371/105505, National Archives, Kew, UK.
56 *Dong'a ilbo,* June 25, 1953; *New York Times,* June 25, 1953; Yi Han-up, *Yi Sŭng-man 90-nyŏn* [Syngman Rhee: 90 Years] (Seoul: Yonsei University Press, 1995), p. 141.
57 "Dulles Letter to Syngman Rhee June 24, 1953" (emphasis in original text), FO 371/105505, National Archives, Kew, UK.
58 "Public Opinion in Many Countries Demands the Removal of Rhee," FO 371/105505, National Archives, Kew, UK.
59 "Text of a Letter from Marshal Kim Il Sung and General Peng Te-Huai (Peng Dehuai) to General Clark, Handed Over at Panmunjom on July 8, 1953," letter dated July 7, 1953, FO 371/105508, National Archives, Kew, UK.
60 "Telegram: Of the Soviet Chargé to the PRC to the Chairman of the USSR Council of Ministers, 3 July 1953," Document 114, in James Person, ed., "New Evidence on the Korean War," Document Reader, NKIDP, June 2010.
61 *FRUS, 1952–54,* vol. 15: *Part 1,* pp. 1202–1203.
62 Johnson, *Right Hand of Power,* p. 168.
63 *FRUS, 1952–54,* vol. 15: *Part 1,* p. 1307; Edward C. Keefer, "President Dwight D. Eisenhower and the End of the Korean War," *Diplomatic History* 10, no. 3 (July 1986), pp. 267–289.
64 "General Taylor Announced That If the South Korea Decided to Fight Alone, He Would Withdraw US. Troops from the Front," FO 371/105508, National Archives, Kew, UK.
65 *Times of London,* July 3, 1953.
66 Cited in Stephen Jin-Woo Kim, *Master of Manipulation: Syngman Rhee and the Seoul-Washington Alliance, 1953–1960* (Seoul: Yonsei University Press, 2001), pp. 112–114.
67 Paik, *From Pusan to Panmunjom,* p. 241.
68 Clark, *From the Danube to the Yalu,* p. 295.
69 Ibid., p. 296.
70 Paik, *From Pusan to Panmunjom,* p. 245.

71 *New York Times*, July 28, 1953.

72 Stephen E. Ambrose, *Eisenhower*, vol. 2: *The President* (Simon & Schuster, 1984), p. 106.

THIRTEEN: *Lessons of Korea*

1 Nugent, vol. 14, DASJA, p. 3346. See explanation of source in note 6, chap. 10. The scene is also vividly portrayed in Raymond B. Lech, *Broken Soldiers* (University of Illinois Press, 2000), pp. 203–204.

2 Major William E. Mayer, "Why Did Many Captives Cave In?" *U.S. News & World Report*, February 24, 1956, p. 56; Eugene Kinkead, "A Reporter at Large: The Study of Something New in History," *The New Yorker*, October 26, 1957, p. 114.

3 Eugene Kinkead, *In Every War but One* (W. W. Norton, 1959), p. 18. Not everyone agreed with such dire assessments. Lieutenant Colonel Thomas Cameron, one of the army lawyers who participated in Operation Big Switch, asserted that all the talk about American POWs' failings in Korea was utter nonsense. Such harsh judgments about the prisoners' conduct, he claimed, were the result of Chinese propaganda, not American failings. "From what I've seen in my little corner of Big Switch the vast majority of the prisoners were victims of a damnable frame-up . . . The whole thing is mainly lies, clever lies!" (Nugent, DASJA, Appendix "Q," box 9-16). He thought the more serious issue was "the loss of faith and our distrust in the ability of American soldiers to resist Red ideology." Some of America's most prominent social scientists also stepped forward to take issue with popular characterizations of POW conduct during the war and their ominous implications for American society. Drs. Edgar Schein and Albert Biderman, both eminent scientists who were employed by the air force to investigate Korean War POW behavior, adamantly refuted popular condemnation of these soldiers' "moral" failing: "The behavior of the Korean War prisoners did not compare unfavorably with that of their countrymen or with the behavior of other nations who have faced similar trials in the past," they concluded. "It is our opinion that any serious analysis of American society, its strengths and weaknesses, should rest on historically correct data." See Albert Biderman, "The Dangers of Negative Patriotism," *Harvard Business Review* 60 (November 1962), p. 93. See also Biderman's *March to Calumny: The Story of American POWs in the Korean War* (Macmillan, 1963); Edgar H. Schein, "Brainwashing and Totalitarianization in Modern Society," *World Politics* 3, no. 3 (April 1959), pp. 430–441; H. H. Wubben, "American Prisoners of War in Korea: A Second Look at the 'Something New in History' Theme," *American Quarterly* 22, no. 1 (Spring 1970), pp. 3–19; Ron Robin, *The Making of the Cold War Enemy: Culture and Politics in the Military Intellectual Complex* (Princeton University Press, 2001), pp. 162–184.

4 Letter to Secretary of Defense Charles Wilson from Defense Advisory Committee on Prisoners of War, July 12, 1955, NARA, RG 341, box 441.

5 "Presentation to Secretary of Defense from Defense Advisory Committee on Prisoners of War," Part 5, "Conclusion" by General J. E. Hull, Vice Chairman, July 29, 1955, NARA, RG 341, box 441.

6 According to Allan R. Millett, 565 of 3,746 returned American POWs were investigated for possible violation of the Uniformed Code of Military Jus-

tice, with the most serious charges being murder and collaboration with the enemy. The majority (373) of the cases were dismissed on legal or administrative grounds. "Of the remaining 192, the Army convicted six officers and men of crimes and discharged 61 for unsuitability. The Marine Corps reprimanded one and put two on special assignment while the Air Force retired three officers and separated seven for 'misbehavior.'" Memo from Allan R. Millett to the author, June 14, 2011. Regarding the figures for the army, according to Raymond B. Lech in *Broken Soldiers*, the most authoritative and comprehensive study of U.S. Army POWs who were court-martialed, five officers and nine enlisted men were court-martialed, and eleven of them were convicted and punished (pp. 212–213, 264–276).

7 The classic cold war film *The Manchurian Candidate* (1962) also repeats the theme of the dysfunctional American family, represented here by a weak father, an intrusive mother, and an isolated son. In this film the mother is actually a communist agent whose manipulative relationship with her son almost results in the communist takeover of the U.S. government. Like *My Son John*, the *Manchurian Candidate* also sees momism/communism as a threat to the free man and the free nation. Michael Rogin, "Kiss Me Deadly: Communism, Motherhood, and Cold War Movies," *Representations* 6 (Spring 1984), pp. 12–17.

8 Ibid., p. 27.

9 John Foster Dulles, "Address before the Overseas Press Club of America, March 20, 1954," reprinted in *U.S. News & World Report*, April 9, 1954, p. 73.

10 Rosemary Foot, "The Eisenhower Administration's Fear of Empowering the Chinese," *Political Science Quarterly* 3, no. 3 (Autumn 1996), p. 513.

11 Dwight Eisenhower, *Mandate for Change, 1953–1956* (Doubleday, 1963), p. 333.

12 Foot, "Eisenhower Administration's Fear," p. 513.

13 John Lewis Gaddis, *Inquiries into the History of the Cold War* (Oxford University Press, 1987), p. 174.

14 Nancy Bernkopf Tucker, "Cold War Contacts: America and China, 1952–1956," in Harry Harding and Yuan Ming, eds., *Sino-American Relations, 1945–1955: A Joint Assessment of a Critical Decade* (SR Books, 1989), p. 238.

15 *New York Times*, March 30, 1954.

16 Gordon Chang, *Friends and Enemies: The United States, China, and the Soviet Union, 1948–1972* (Stanford University Press, 1990), p. 168.

17 Foot, "Eisenhower Administration's Fear," p. 514.

18 *Life*, May 19, 1952, p. 152.

19 Ibid., p. 154.

20 *New York Times*, March 30, 1954.

21 Ibid., March 22, 1955.

22 *Life*, May 19, 1952, p. 152.

23 Rupert Wilkinson, *The Pursuit of American Character* (Harper & Row, 1988), p. 777; Foot, "Eisenhower Administration's Fear," p. 515.

24 *New York Times*, April 17, 1953.

25 *Life*, May 19, 1952, p. 152.

26 *New York Times*, April 20, 1954.

27 Richard H. Immerman, *John Foster Dulles: Piety, Pragmatism, and Power in U.S. Foreign Policy* (Scholarly Resources, 1999), p. 88.

28 *U.S. News & World Report*, March 5, 1954, p. 55.
29 Ibid., April 16, 1954, p. 21.
30 John Foster Dulles, "Policy for Security and Peace," *Foreign Affairs* 32, no. 3 (April 1954), p. 358.
31 Ibid., pp. 358–359; Richard H. Rovere, *Affairs of State: 1950–1956, The Eisenhower Years* (Farrar, 1956), p. 193.
32 *The Pentagon Papers (Senator Gravel Edition): The Defense Department History of United States Decisionmaking on Vietnam* (Beacon Press, 1971), vol. 1, p. 97.
33 Matthew B. Ridgway, *Soldier: The Memoirs of Matthew B. Ridgway* (Harper & Brothers, 1956), p. 277.
34 Quoted in David H. Petraeus, "Korea, the Never Again Club, and Indochina," *Parameters* (December 1987), p. 64.
35 Yuen Foong Khong, *Analogies at War: Korea, Munich, Dienbienphu, and the Vietnam Decision of 1965* (Princeton University Press, 1992), p. 78.
36 Quoted in Petraeus, "Korea, the Never Again Club," p. 64.
37 *New York Times*, April 3, 1954.
38 Khong, *Analogies at War*, p. 76; *FRUS, 1952–1954*, vol. 13: *Indochina, Part 1* (1982), pp. 1224–1225.
39 George C. Herring, "Franco-American Conflict in Indochina, 1950–1954," in Lawrence S. Kaplan, Denise Artaud, and Mark Rubin, eds., *Dien Bien Phu and the Crisis of Franco-American Relations, 1954–1955* (Scholarly Resources, 1990), p. 42.
40 Anthony Eden, *The Eden Memoirs: Full Circle* (Casell, 1960), pp. 114–119; George C. Herring and Richard H. Immerman, "Eisenhower, Dulles and Dienbienphu: 'The Day We Didn't Go to War' Revisited," *Journal of American History* 71, no. 2 (September 1984), p. 361. See also Fredrik Logevall, *Embers of War: The Fall of an Empire and the Making of America's Vietnam* (Random House, 2012), pp. 549–554.
41 The armistice that was signed at end of the war on July 27, 1953, required a political conference within three months "to settle through negotiation the questions of the withdrawal of all foreign forces from Korea, the peaceful settlement of the Korean question." This timeline was obviously not met, nor was it clear whether it ever would be met.
42 Evelyn Shuckburgh, *Descent to Suez: Foreign Office Diaries, 1951–1956* (W. W. Norton, 1986), pp. 181–182.
43 U. Alexis Johnson, *The Right Hand of Power*, p. 204.
44 Ibid., p. 204. In his memoirs, Wang Bingnan denied that Dulles refused to shake Zhou Enlai's hand. See Zhai Qing, "China and the Geneva Conference of 1954," *China Quarterly*, no. 129 (March 1992), p. 119.
45 Shuckburgh, *Descent to Suez*, p. 198.
46 Quoted in Zhai, "China and the Geneva Conference of 1954," p. 110.
47 Chen Jian and Shen Zhihua, "The Geneva Conference of 1954: New Evidence from the Archives from the Ministry of Foreign Affairs of the Peoples Republic of China," *CWIHP Bulletin*, no. 16 (Spring 2008), p. 8.
48 Quoted in Zhai, "China and the Geneva Conference of 1954," p. 109. For a similar parallel Zhou made between the conflict in Indochina and China's war in Korea, see Logevall, *Embers of War*, pp. 596–597.
49 Rovere, *Affairs of State*, p. 199.

50 Samuel P. Huntington, *The Soldier and the State: The Theory and Politics of Civil-Military Relations* (Harvard University Press, 1957), p. 345.
51 John Lewis Gaddis, "Was the Truman Doctrine a Real Turning Point?" *Foreign Affairs* 52, no. 2 (January 1974), pp. 392–393.
52 Huntington, *Soldier and the State*, p. 346.
53 *New York Times*, September 26, 1952. Also, A. J. Bacevich, "The Paradox of Professionalism: Eisenhower, Ridgway, and the Challenge to Civilian Control, 1953–1955," *Journal of Military History* 61 (April 1997), p. 308.
54 Quoted in Andrew Bacevich, *The New American Militarism: How Americans Are Seduced by War* (Oxford University Press, 2005), p. 150.
55 Bacevich, "Paradox of Professionalism," pp. 151, 321.
56 Cited in ibid., p. 324.
57 Andrew Bacevich, *Washington Rules: America's Path to Permanent War* (Henry Holt, 2010), p. 61.
58 Ibid., pp. 62–65.
59 George T. McKahin, *Intervention: How America Became Involved in Vietnam* (Alfred Knopf, 1986), pp. 139–140.
60 Michael J. Hogan, *A Cross of Iron: Harry S. Truman and the Origins of the National Security State, 1945–1954* (Cambridge University Press, 1998), p. 472.
61 James L. Clayton, "The Impact of the Cold War on the Economies of California and Utah, 1946–1965," *Pacific Historical Review* 36, no. 4 (November 1967), p. 464.
62 Quoted in Hogan, *Cross of Iron*, p. 472.
63 James L. Clayton, "Defense Spending: Key to California's Growth," *Western Political Quarterly* 15, no. 2 (June 1963), pp. 284–288.
64 *New York Times*, January 5, 1951.
65 By 1955, a fundamental reorientation of NATO and of European security led not only to the granting of full sovereignty to West Germany but also to its rearmament and NATO membership. Germany's rearmament marked a sea change in British and in particular French attitudes. As the instigator of two world wars on the continent and the cause of the death of tens of millions of people, a rearmed Germany, much less making it an integral part of European security, was anathema. But the Soviet threat reinforced by the Korean War had reversed that position. The situation developed even more rapidly with regard to Japan. Japan's sovereignty and rearmament had already taken place a few years earlier, in 1952. In the process, the reversal of priorities in economic policy entailed repudiating many of the original ideals of "demilitarization and democratization" that had seemed so inspiring to a defeated Japanese populace in 1945. That earlier effort proved too radical in the context of the emerging realities of the cold war. By 1947 economic stagnation and social unrest gave rise to fears that the country was ripe for communism. American occupation took a "reverse course," abandoning programs for reform and the creation of a demilitarized and pacifist state. Purged politicians and industrialists from World War II were rehabilitated, the euphemistically named Self Defense Force was created, and a bold effort was made to bring Japan into the Western system of defense as part of the containment ring against communism. The war boom, stimulated by U.S. procurements, put Japan's economy back on track. Arms production and military procure-

ments dominated Japanese industrial production during the war years. Sales worth 7 million yen in 1952 grew to 15 billion by 1954. The impact of U.S. military contracts, however, went far beyond just sales figures. It laid the technological foundation for the post–World War II development of Japanese industry, which became globally dominant by the 1980s. See Samuels, *Rich Nation, Strong Army*, pp. 137–141; also Dower, *Embracing Defeat*, pp. 540–542.

66 *New York Times*, July 23, 1950.

67 President Dwight D. Eisenhower, Farewell Radio and Television Address to the American People, January 17, 1961, available at http://www.eisenhower.archives.gov/all_about_ike/Speeches/Farewell_Address.pdf (accessed December 10, 2011).

FOURTEEN: *Deepening the Revolution*

1 Mao Tse-Tung, *Selected Works of Mao Tse-tung* (Foreign Language Press, 1977), vol. 5, p. 115.

2 William Taubman, *Khrushchev: The Man and His Era* (W. W. Norton, 2003), p. 336.

3 Sergey Radchenko, *Two Suns in the Heavens: The Sino-Soviet Struggle for Supremacy, 1962–1967* (Woodrow Wilson Center Press, 2009), p. 10.

4 Chen Jian and Yang Kuisong, "Chinese Politics and the Collapse of the Sino-Soviet Alliance," in Odd Arne Westad, ed., *Brothers in Arms: The Rise and Fall of the Sino-Soviet Alliance* (Woodrow Wilson Center Press/ Stanford University Press, 1998), pp. 255–257; Taubman, *Khrushchev*, p. 336.

5 Taubman, *Khrushchev*, p. 337.

6 Quoted in Zubok and Pleshakov, *Inside the Kremlin's Cold War*, p. 217.

7 Taubman, *Khrushchev*, p. 337.

8 Sergei Khrushchev, ed., *Memoirs of Nikita Khrushchev*, vol. 3: *The Statesman, 1953–1964* (Pennsylvania State University Press, 2007), p. 417.

9 Chen Jian, *China's Road to the Korean War: The Making of the Sino-American Confrontation* (Columbia University Press, 1994), pp. 220–222; Thomas Christensen, *Useful Adversaries: Grand Strategies, Domestic Mobilization and Sino-American Conflict, 1947–1958* (Princeton University Press, 1996), p. 163.

10 Taubman, *Khrushchev*, p. 337.

11 Khrushchev, *Memoirs*, vol. 3, pp. 421–423. Mao listed his grievances against Stalin during a March 31, 1956, conversation with Soviet ambassador Pavel Yudin. For a transcript of that conversation, see *CWIHP Bulletin*, nos. 6/7 (Winter 1995–1996), pp. 164–167.

12 Li Zhisui, *The Private Life of Chairman Mao* (Random House, 1994), p. 115.

13 Taubman, *Khrushchev*, p. 339; Peter Vamos, "Sino-Hungarian Relations and the 1956 Revolution," *CWIHP Working Paper* 54 (November 2006), pp. 23–24.

14 Vamos, "Sino-Hungarian Relations," pp. 24–25.

15 Jerrold L. Schecter with Vyacheslav V. Luchkov, trans. and eds., *Khrushchev Remembers: The Glasnost Tapes* (Little, Brown, 1990), p. 153.

16 Li, *Private Life of Chairman Mao*, pp. 220–222.

17 Khrushchev, *Memoirs*, vol. 3, pp. 436–437.

18 Chen, *Mao's China and the Cold War*, pp. 202–203.

19 Khrushchev, *Memoirs*, vol. 3, p. 455.

20 "Minutes, Conversation between Mao Zedong and Ambassador Yudin, 22 July 1958," *CWIHP Bulletin: The Cold War in Asia*, no. 6/7 (Winter 1995), pp. 155–158.
21 Li, *Private Life of Chairman Mao*, p. 260.
22 Chen and Yang, "Chinese Politics and the Collapse of the Sino-Soviet Alliance," p. 270.
23 Khrushchev, *Memoirs*, vol. 3, pp. 459–461.
24 Li, *Private Life of Chairman Mao*, p. 261.
25 *FRUS, 1958–1960*, vol. 19: *China* (1996), pp. 145–153.
26 Li, *Private Life of Chairman Mao*, pp. 270–271; Taubman, *Khrushchev*, pp. 392–393.
27 Chen and Yang, "Chinese Politics and the Collapse of the Sino-Soviet Alliance," p. 271.
28 Chen, *Mao's China and the Cold War*, p. 180.
29 Wu-Lengxi, "Memoir, Inside Story of the Decision Making during the Shelling of Jinmen," *CWIHP Bulletin*, no. 8/9 (Winter 1996), p. 212.
30 Chen, *Mao's China and the Cold War*, pp. 202–203; Li, *Private Life of Chairman Mao*, p. 262.
31 Khrushchev, *Memoirs*, vol. 3, p. 485.
32 Roderick MacFarquhar, *The Origins of the Cultural Revolution*, vol. 2: *The Great Leap Forward, 1958–1960* (Columbia University Press, 1983), pp. 195–197.
33 Ibid., p. 197.
34 Quoted in Viktor Usov, "Peng Dehuai: Pages from Reminiscences: Confessions of a Chinese General," *Far Eastern Affairs* 5 (1987), pp. 138–139.
35 Quan Yanchi, *Mao Zedong: Man, Not God* (Foreign Language Press, 1992), p. 53.
36 Quoted in Usov, "Peng Dehuai," p. 141.
37 Jurgen Domes, *Peng Te-huai: The Man and the Image* (Stanford University Press, 1985), pp. 123–124; Short, *Mao*, p. 585. According to Usov, Peng died of lung cancer. "In 1974, the illness became acute, the cancerous growth spread to the lungs and caused him great pain, but no one would give him even a pain-killing injection," Usov, "Peng Dehuai," p. 141.
38 By 1978, however, following China's rapprochement with the United States, Peng's reputation began to be rehabilitated. By January 1979, China was swept by a "veritable avalanche of memoirs" in praise of the good general, marking the passing of an era that signaled an apparent "end" of the Korean War and of cold war antagonism between the two superpowers. Yet, while U.S-Sino rapprochement was welcomed by Chinese leaders, Peng's posthumous rehabilitation served to keep alive the memory of China's "victory" in Korea, which did so much to change Chinese perceptions of themselves and the world. Ibid., pp. 127–128.
39 Quoted in Radchenko, *Two Suns in the Heavens*, p. 12. Radchenko's portrayal of Khrushchev as the main culprit of the Sino-Soviet split, due to his insensitivity and his insistence to play the first fiddle, is contrasted to Lüthi's portrayal of the Chinese leader whose Great Power aspirations, personality, and ideology made peaceful coexistence between them impossible. Lorenz M. Lüthi, *The Sino-Soviet Split: The Cold War in the Communist World* (Princeton University Press, 2008).
40 Jonathan Spence, *The Search for Modern China* (W. W. Norton, 1990), p. 583.
41 Estimates of death by famine range from 15 to 32 million. However, the his-

torian Frank Dikötter disputes these numbers, believing that the magnitude of the disaster was much higher, from 43 to 46 million people. See his *Mao's Great Famine: The History of China's Most Devastating Catastrophe, 1958–1962* (Bloomsbury, 2010), p. 325.

42 Chen, *Mao's China and the Cold War*, p. 204

43 *Time*, October 5, 1959, p. 20.

44 Khrushchev, *Memoirs*, vol. 3, p. 169.

45 MacFarquhar, *Origins of the Cultural Revolution*, vol. 2, p. 269; Chen and Yang, "Chinese Politics and the Collapse of the Sino-Soviet Alliance," p. 273.

46 Radchenko, *Two Suns in the Heavens*, p. 14.

47 "M. Suslov, To Members of the CC CPSU Presidium," December 18, 1959, Document 24, in David Wolff, "One Finger's Worth of Historical Events," *CWIHP Working Paper* 30 (August 2000), p. 71.

48 Chen and Yang, "Chinese Politics and the Collapse of the Sino-Soviet Alliance," p. 273.

49 Strobe Talbott, ed. and trans., *Khrushchev Remembers: The Last Testament* (Little, Brown, 1974), p. 473.

50 MacFarquhar, *Origins of the Cultural Revolution*, vol. 2, p. 268.

51 Ibid., pp. 272–273.

52 Quoted in Philip Short, *Mao: A Life* (Henry Holt, 1999), pp. 503–504.

53 Shu Guang Zhang, "Beijing's Aid to Hanoi and the United States–China Confrontations, 1964–1968," in Priscilla Roberts, ed., *Behind the Bamboo Curtain: China, Vietnam and the World beyond* Asia (Stanford University Press, 2006), p. 260; Roderick MacFarquhar, *The Origins of the Cultural Revolution*, vol. 3: *The Coming of the Cataclysm, 1961–1966* (Columbia University Press, 1997), p. 356.

54 David Wolff, "In Memoriam Deng Xioaping and the Cold War," *CWIHP Bulletin*, no. 10 (March 1998), p. 149.

55 Chen Jian, "China's Involvement in the Vietnam War, 1964–69," *China Quarterly*, no. 142 (June 1995), p. 358.

56 Qiang Zhai, *China and the Vietnam Wars, 1950–1975* (University of North Carolina Press, 2000), p. 113.

57 Chen, *Mao's China and the Cold War*, p. 207; Zhai, *China and the Vietnam War, 1950–1975*, pp. 122–129.

58 MacFarquhar, *Origins of the Cultural Revolution*, vol. 3, p. 273.

59 Ibid., p. 283.

60 Ibid., pp. 269–273; Chen, "China's Involvement in the Vietnam War," pp. 361–362.

61 Chen, *Mao's China and the Cold War*, p. 211; Qiang, *China and the Vietnam Wars*, p. 115.

62 MacFarquhar, *Origins of the Cultural Revolution*, vol. 3, p. 334.

63 Chen, *Mao's China and the Cold War*, pp. 210–211.

64 James G. Hershberg and Chen Jian, "Informing the Enemy: Sino-American 'Signaling' and the Vietnam War, 1965," in Roberts, ed., *Behind the Bamboo Curtain*, p. 220.

65 Quoted in ibid., p. 221.

66 Ibid., pp. 224–227

67 The link between the impact of the Korean analogy and Chinese and Ameri-

can decision-making in 1965 is the subject of Hershberg and Chen's pioneering essay, "Informing the Enemy." The analysis set forth in this chapter draws heavily on this work. See also Chen Jian, "Personal-Historical Puzzles about China and the Vietnam War," in Chen Jian, Stein Tonnesson, Nguyen Vu Tungand, and James G. Hershberg, "77 Conversations between Chinese and Foreign Leaders on the Wars in Indochina, 1964–1977," *CWIHP Working Paper 22* (May 1998), p. 26.

FIFTEEN: *Korea and Vietnam*

1 Quoted in Khong, *Analogies at War*, p. 97. Ball was the under secretary of state, the second highest position in the State Department. In 1972, the position was renamed deputy secretary of state.

2 Sin Bum Shik, compiler, *Major Speeches by Korea's Park Chung Hee* (Hollym, 1970), p. 238.

3 W. Averell Harriman, "Sino-Soviet Conflict," *Proceedings of the Academy of the Political Science* 28, no. 1 (April 1965), p. 104.

4 W. W. Rostow, "The Third Round," *Foreign Affairs* 42, no. 1 (October 1963), p. 9.

5 The full text is available at the LBJ Presidential Library web site: http://www.lbjlib.utexas.edu/johnson/archives.hom/speeches.hom/650407.asp (accessed April 15, 2011).

6 William Bundy, "Progress and Problems in East Asia: An American Viewpoint," *Department of State Bulletin*, October 19, 1964, p. 537.

7 *U.S. News & World Report*, April 19, 1965, pp. 79–80.

8 Khong, *Analogies at War*, p. 114. Khong notes that in late 1952, 56 percent of Americans thought the war was a mistake while only 32 percent thought it worthwhile. By September 1956 the proportions began to reverse, with 41 percent thinking it a mistake and 46 percent considering it worthwhile. A poll in liberal Minnesota in March 1965 resulted in 67 percent thinking it had been worthwhile and only 16 percent, a mistake. See also John E. Mueller, *War, Presidents and Public Opinion* (John Wiley and Sons, 1973), pp. 170–171.

9 Quoted in Gordon Goldstein, *Lessons in Disaster: McGeorge Bundy and the Path to War in Vietnam* (Henry Holt, 2008), p. 98.

10 *New York Times*, August 6, 1964.

11 Of the many analogies evoked to justify America's involvement in Vietnam, it was "lessons" of Korea that played the most influential role in the U.S. decision in the summer of 1965. One study found that the Korean analogy and its perceived lessons in the minds of policy makers "can explain why the Johnson administration decided to intervene . . . and took the form that it did." The Korean analogy worked in two ways: one that pushed for action and the other setting the limits of that action. As in Korea, Vietnam was seen as a situation where international communism was threatening the free world. Furthermore, by 1965, in contrast to the opinion in the immediate aftermath of the armistice, the Korean War was seen as a case of success in fighting back and containing communism. The lesson for Vietnam was that not only were the political stakes high, to demonstrate the credibility and will of America and its allies to fight communism, but military intervention was just and necessary and could succeed in preserving peace and freedom.

However, the possibility of Chinese intervention constrained the options for intervention. In terms of strategy, this meant that an invasion of North Vietnam, crossing the 17th parallel, was not an option lest it provoke China's entry with combat forces. Reinforcing the Korean lesson was the lesson of Munich in the 1930s: that aggression must not be appeased. William Bundy, the author of the December 1964 decision for a new Vietnam strategy of escalation, stated publicly in January 1965 that "in essence, our policy derives from (1) the fact of the Communist nations of Asia and their policies [the expansionist policies of China and North Vietnam]; (2) the lessons of the thirties and of Korea; (3) the logical extension of that fact and these lessons to what has happened in Southeast Asia." And that "our action in Korea reflected three elements: a recognition that aggression of any sort must be met early and head-on . . . ; a recognition that . . . our vital interests [in Asia] could be affected by action on the mainland; [and] an understanding that . . . there must be a demonstrated willingness of major external powers both to assist and to intervene if required" (quoted in Khong, *Analogies of War*, pp. 99–100). See George Ball, *The Past Has Another Pattern* (W. W. Norton, 1983); Khong, *Analogies at War*; Ernest R. May, *"Lessons" of the Past: The Use and Misuse of History in American Foreign Policy* (Oxford University Press, 1973); Robert Jervis, *Perceptions and Misperceptions in International Politics* (Princeton University Press, 1976).

12 Quoted in Michael R. Beschloss, *Taking Charge: The Johnson White House Tapes, 1963–1964* (Simon & Schuster, 1997), pp. 367–369.

13 David L. Di Leo, *George Ball, Vietnam and the Rethinking of Containment* (University of North Carolina Press, 1992), p. 22; James A. Bill, *George Ball: Behind the Scenes in U.S. Foreign Policy* (Yale University Press, 1997); pp. 160–161.

14 *U.S. News & World Report*, February 15, 1965, p. 69.

15 James C. Thomson Jr., "How Could Vietnam Happen? An Autopsy," *Atlantic Monthly*, April 1968, p. 48.

16 George W. Ball, "Top Secret: The Prophecy the President Rejected," *Atlantic Monthly*, July 1972, pp. 36–49; Ball, *Past Has Another Pattern*, p. 380.

17 Ball, *Past Has Another Pattern*, p. 381.

18 Ball, "Top Secret," p. 37; Khong, *Analogies at War*, p. 107; Ball, *Past Has Another Pattern*, pp. 380–381.

19 Ball, *Past Has Another Pattern*, p. 376.

20 Larry Berman, *Planning a Tragedy: The Americanization of the War in Vietnam* (W. W. Norton, 1982), pp. 119-120.

21 Quoted in Goldstein, *Lessons in Disaster*, p. 139.

22 Tom Wicker, "The Wrong Rubicon: LBJ and the War," *Atlantic Monthly*, May 1968, p. 139.

23 David Halberstam, *The Best and the Brightest* (Random House, 1969), p. 592.

24 Quoted in Goldstein, *Lessons in Disaster*, pp. 137–138. Dean Rusk also frequently brought up the similarity between Korea and Vietnam in his private and public statements. "In Korea, the international community proved that overt aggression was unprofitable. In Vietnam, we must prove—once again . . . that semi-covert aggression across international boundaries cannot succeed." Even in his approach to the prosecution of the Vietnam War, Rusk drew on the Korean War analogy: "Rusk envisioned the desired end of the

Vietnam war as a negotiation which, as in Korea, would reaffirm the approximate status quo ante." See Thomas J. Schoenbaum, *Waging Peace and War: Dean Rusk in the Truman, Kennedy and Johnson Years* (Simon & Schuster, 1988), pp. 424–425.

25 Quoted in ibid., p. 195.

26 Roberto Ducci, "The World Order in the Sixties," *Foreign Affairs* 42, no. 3 (April 1964), p. 384. In January 1964, France extended diplomatic recognition to the PRC. French President Charles de Gaulle apparently had Vietnam in mind when he opted for recognition since everyone understood that China was a key player in resolving the conflict in Indochina. Recognition of China by France was also an affront to the domino theory and cast doubt on the whole rationale of credibility on which America's Vietnam policy was based. It was, as Averell Harriman bitterly complained to France's ambassador in Washington, "a slap in Lyndon Johnson's face." The move was interpreted as a deliberate insult to the United States in other ways, to demonstrate France's Great Power status and independence vis-à-vis Washington. According to one Western diplomat in Paris, "for de Gaulle, Vietnam is just another lever to cut American influence in Europe to a minimum." See Fredrick Longevall, "The French Recognition of China and Its Implications for the Vietnam War," in Roberts, ed., *Behind the Bamboo Curtain*, pp. 153–159. See also Ball, *Past Has Another Pattern*, p. 378.

27 Goldstein, *Lessons in Disaster*, p. 139; David S. Broder, "Consensus Politics: End of an Experiment," *Atlantic Monthly*, October 1966, p. 62; Doris Kearns Goodwin, *Lyndon Johnson and the American Dream* (Harper & Row, 1976), p. 169; Halberstam, *Best and the Brightest*, p. 501; Robert Dalleck, *Flawed Giant: Lyndon Johnson and His Times* (Oxford University Press, 1998), pp. 252–253.

28 Robert D. Dean, *Imperial Brotherhood: Gender and the Making of Cold War Foreign Policy* (University of Massachusetts Press, 2003), p. 228.

29 James G. Hershberg and Chen Jian, "Informing the Enemy: Sino-American 'Signaling' and the Vietnam War," in Roberts, ed., *Behind the Bamboo Curtain*, p. 231.

30 Matthew Ridgway, "On Viet Nam," in Marcus G Raskin and Bernard B. Fall, eds., *The Viet-Nam Reader* (Random House, 1967), p. 437. The article was originally published in *Look*, April 5, 1966.

31 Jiyul Kim, "U.S. and Korea in Vietnam and the Japan-Korea Treaty: Search for Security, Prosperity and Influence," MA thesis, Harvard University, 1991, pp. 24–30. Much of the discussion on South Korea and Vietnam in this chapter has relied on Jiyul Kim's thesis and the large amount of primary source materials he has made available to me for use in this study. I am indebted to his expertise, his critical review of this chapter, and for allowing me to extensively quote from his work.

32 Taehyun Kim and Chang Jae Baik, "Taming and Tamed by the United States," in Byung-Kook Kim and Ezra F. Vogel, eds., *The Park Chung Hee Era: The Transformation of South Korea* (Harvard University Press, 2011), pp. 60–61.

33 Ibid., p. 60.

34 Ibid., p. 62. Much of the blame for South Korea's stagnant economy also had to do with Rhee's monetary policy. Rhee resisted American efforts to devalue the South Korean currency, insisting that the won be valued at 500 won to the

dollar "despite American claims that the real value of the dollar was as much as twice that." This exchange rate impeded any growth in exports since the prices of Korean goods were too high to attract foreign markets. Meanwhile, import licenses, issued to businessmen by corrupt government officials, strengthened Rhee's hold on power. "Rhee continued to pursue such policies because, although they stunted economic development, they strengthened the power of his regime." See Gregg Brazinsky, *Nation Building in South Korea: Koreans, Americans and the Making of a Democracy* (University of North Carolina Press, 2007), pp. 35–36. For a comprehensive reference source on South Korea's development, see Edward S. Mason et al., eds., *The Economic and Social Modernization of the Republic of Korea* (Harvard University Press, 1980); LeRoy R. Jones and Il Sakong, *Government, Business and Entrepreneurship in Economic Development: The Korean Case* (Harvard University Press, 1980).

35 Yong-Sup Han, "The May Sixteenth Military Coup," in Kim and Vogel, eds., *Park Chung Hee Era*, p. 41.

36 Bruce Cumings, *Korea's Place in the Sun: A Modern History* (W. W. Norton, 1997), p. 302; see also Gregory Henderson, *Korea: The Politics of the Vortex* (Harvard University Press, 1968), pp. 334–360.

37 On Park's life story and the 1961 coup, see Han, "May Sixteenth Coup." For a discussion of Park's involvement in leftist movements and his arrest during the ROK Army purge of 1948, see Cho Kap-je, *Nae mudŏm e ch'imŭl paet'ŏra 2: Chŏnjaeg'gwa sarang* [Spit on My Grave, vol. 2: War and Love] (Seoul: Chosŏn ilbosa, 1998), pp. 215–238. When Park made his coup in 1961, his communist background had temporarily given rise to some worry in Washington. Park was listed in a 1948 CIA report of field-grade officers in the ROK Army who had been "confined for subversive activities." Shortly after the 1961 coup, doubts about Park's political affiliations were raised in a State Department report issued on May 31, 1961: "The declared position of the regime is anti-Communist and available evidence does not support allegations of Pak's continuing ties with the Communists. However, we cannot rule out the possibility that he is a long-term Communist agent, or that he might re-defect." *FRUS, 1961–1963*, vol. 22: *Northeast Asia* (1996), pp. 468–469. Also Bruce Cumings, *The Origins of the Korean War*, vol. 2: *The Roaring of the Cataract, 1947–1950* (Princeton University Press, 1990), p. 266; Kim Kyŏngnae, "Chŏnhyangjanya? aninya? In'gan Pak Chŏng hŭi ui chŏnhyang chubyon [Is he a convert from communism or not? The circumstances of the ideological conversion of Park Chung Hee]," *Sasanggye* (November 1963), pp. 102–110.

38 Cumings, *Korea's Place in the Sun*, p. 348; Kim Hyung-A, *Korea's Development under Park Chung Hee: Rapid Industrialization, 1961–79* (RoutledgeCurzon, 2004), pp. 73–75. The idea of national independence or autonomy (*minjokchŏk chajusŏng*) was the basis on which Park appealed to the public for mass support for his new economic initiatives. This idea referred to Park's pursuit of a "Korean-style" way of life and, especially, independence from the United States. In Park's second book, *Kukka wa hyŏngmyŏng'gwa na* [*The Nation, the Revolution and I*], published in September 1963, he was openly critical of U.S. aid policy and more generally of Korea's traditional reliance on foreign powers (*sadaejuŭi*). The May 16 Revolution, he declared, "was not simply a change of regime. It was a new, mature national debut of spirit" and "the end of

500 years of stagnation of the Chosŏn dynasty (1392–1910), the oppression and bloodshed of 35 years of Japanese rule and the nagging chronic disease bred by the residue of the Liberation." His revolution represented, he declared, "a national debut, inspired by the courage and self-confidence of a people determined never again to be poor, weak or dumb." The revolution, he asserted, was "our last chance for national renaissance." In building the groundwork for this "national renaissance," Park believed it was necessary to create a "spiritual revolution" as the basis for economic construction. These ideas later became the basis for his Secondary Economic Movement, which he launched in 1968. In a speech he gave at a national rally on September 18, 1968, he stated that "we must discard the mental habit of dependency and explore a brighter future image of the fatherland by uniting our strength." See Sheila Miyoshi Jager, *Narratives of Nation Building: A Genealogy of Patriotism* (M. E. Sharpe, 2003), pp. 79–80; Park Chung Hee, *Kukka wa hyŏngmyŏng'gwa na* (Seoul: Tonga ch'ulp'ansa, 1963), p. 22 (this book was later translated under the title *The Nation, the Revolution and I* (Seoul: Hollym, 1970)).

39 Kim, *Korea's Development under Park Chung Hee*, p. 74.

40 Kim, "U.S. and Korea in Vietnam and the Japan-Korea Treaty," pp. 22–23.

41 Ronald H. Spector, *Advice and Support: The Early Years of the U.S. Army in Vietnam, 1941–1960* (Free Press, 1985) p. 198.

42 Kim, "U.S. and Korea in Vietnam and the Japan-Korea Treaty," pp. 41–43.

43 Deptel (Department of State Telegram) 1426, December 4, 1961, National Security Files (NSF), Country, box 128, JFK Library. Quoted in Kim, "U.S. and Korea in Vietnam and the Japan-Korea Treaty," p. 41.

44 Memcon (Memorandum of Conversation), Park-Kennedy, November 14–15, 1961, NSF, Country, box 128, JFK Library, Boston, Mass.; Kim, "U.S. and Korea in Vietnam and the Japan-Korea Treaty," pp. 41–42.

45 Deptel 80 (Seoul), July 27, 1962, NSF, Country, box 129, JFK Library.

46 Seoul Embet 741, November 27, 1963, NSF, Country, box 254, LBJ Library, Austin, Tx.

47 Kim, "U.S. and Korea in Vietnam and the Japan-Korea Treaty," p. 140.

48 Stanley Robert Larsen and James Lawton Collins Jr., *Vietnam Studies: Allied Participation in Vietnam* (U.S. Government Printing Office, 1975), pp. 120–121. Tab C (Third Country Assistance to Vietnam) from "Position Paper on SE Asia," December 2, 1964, NSF, McGB [McGeorge Bundy] Memos to the Pres., box 2, LBJ Library.

49 Khong, *Analogies at War*, pp. 118–120.

50 Deptel 557 (Seoul)/Thomson to McGB, "The Week That Was," December 17, 1964, Thomson Papers, box 11, JFK Library.

51 Kim, "U.S. and Korea in Vietnam and the Japan-Korea Treaty," p. 143; see also *The Pentagon Papers (Senator Gravel Edition): The Defense Department History of United States Decisionmaking on Vietnam* (Beacon Press, 1971), vol. 3, pp. 417–423, 429.

52 *Pentagon Papers*, pp. 451–452; Memo McNamara to LBJ, April 21, 1965, NSF, McGB Memos to the Pres., box 3, LBJ Library.

53 William C. Westmoreland, *A Soldier Reports* (Doubleday, 1976), pp. 136–141; *Pentagon Papers*, pp. 413, 415, 467; William Bundy Oral History, tape 2, p. 29, May 29, 1969, LBJ Library.

54 Kim, "U.S. and Korea in Vietnam and the Japan-Korea Treaty," pp. 11–12, 160, 233–236.

55 Dean Rusk Oral History, interview 3, tape 1, p. 26, January 1970, LBJ Library.

56 *Kukhoe-sa: Chae 4, 5, 6 dae kukhoe* [History of the National Assembly: The 4th, 5th and 6th National Assembly] (ROK National Assembly, 1971), pp. 909–913; Kim, "U.S. and Korea in Vietnam and the Japan-Korea Treaty," pp. 201–202.

57 The terms of agreement for the second ROK division deployed in 1966 were detailed in the "Brown Memorandum" named after Winthrop G. Brown, who was the U.S. ambassador in Seoul at the time. The memo was first made public in the "Symington Hearings" of 1971 when the Senate examined U.S. security policy in Asia. The hearings also provided hard data on the economic benefits for Korea. *U.S. Security Agreement and Commitment Abroad*, vol. 2, pt. 6 (Korea), Hearings before the Committee on Foreign Relations, 91st Congress, 2nd Session (U.S. Government Printing Office, 1971), pp. 1549–1550, 1571, 1708, 1759–1761; see also Sejin Kim, "South Korea's Involvement in Vietnam and Its Economic and Political Impact," *Asian Survey* 10, no. 6 (June 1970), pp. 519–523.

58 Not much is known about North Korea's involvement in the Vietnam War. Balázs Szalontai, however, has uncovered evidence from the Hungarian National Archives of extensive involvement by the P'yŏngyang regime in North Vietnam's war effort. The logic of P'yŏngyang's support of Hanoi apparently stemmed from Kim Il Sung's attempt to undermine U.S. military strength in Asia. For this goal, P'yŏngyang was ready to provide North Vietnam with "substantial quantities of material assistance," which is astonishing given the fact that this was the same period when North Korea was beginning to experience serious setbacks to its own economy. According to Szalontai, "in 1966, P'yŏngyang gave Hanoi a total of 12.3 million rubles of economic and military aid, such as steel, diesel engines, explosives, iron plates, tractors, power generators, and irrigation equipment." The next year, "the value of North Korea aid rose 20 million rubles, including arms, pontoons and military uniforms." These amounts were comparable to what "the more developed East European countries gave to the Democratic Republic of Vietnam, or even exceeded the latter's individual contributions." Kim was apparently willing to provide this aid in order to help Hanoi withstand the massive increases in American combat troops in Vietnam that occurred during 1966. "The more successfully the North Vietnamese fought, the more U.S. troops were tied down in Vietnam, and the less able Washington was to resort to military measures in other countries," including the Korean peninsula. See Balázs Szalontai, "In the Shadow of Vietnam: A New Look at the North Korea's Blue House Raid and the Pueblo," *Journal of Cold War History* 14.4 (Fall 2012), pp. 122–166.

Kim Il Sung also dispatched dozens of North Korean pilots to fight in the Vietnam War. The details of this operation came to light only in 2007 when a Vietnamese newspaper reported that fourteen North Korean air force personnel killed in the Vietnam War had been buried in a special cemetery near Hanoi and had been subsequently disinterred and repatriated to North Korea in 2002. In a letter written to the newspaper, a retired North Vietnamese general who had worked with the North Koreans revealed that a total of

"87 North Korean Air Force personnel had served in North Vietnam between 1967 and early 1969, during which time the North Koreans lost 14 men and had claimed to have shot down 26 American aircraft." In 1966 North Korea agreed to provide pilots and support personnel to man a North Vietnamese Air Force regiment "consisting of two companies (ten aircraft each of MiG-17s) and one company of MiG-21s" that would be under the command of the North Vietnamese Air Force-Air Defense Command to help defend Hanoi against the intensified American bombing campaign called Rolling Thunder. In reality, however, they were volunteer soldiers who maintained their own sovereignty, commanding "their own forces with the assistance of representatives from our [Vietnamese] side." Although the North Vietnamese provided technical support as well as all housing, living supplies, transportation equipment, and medical support, this assistance was hardly comparable to the generous aid package Park was able to secure from Washington for his contribution to the war effort. As far as prestige and benefits accrued from their respective participation in the war, Seoul emerged the clear winner. See Merle Pribbenow, "North Korean Pilots in the Skies over Vietnam," NKIDP, e-Dossier No. 2 (November 2011), pp. 1–3, available at http://www.wilsoncenter.org/publication/nkidp-e-dossier-no-2-north-korean-pilots-the-skies-over-vietnam (accessed March 7, 2012).

59 Memo, JCT to Rostow, Subj: Elements of Progress in Asia, June 24, 1966, Thomson Papers, box 13, JFK Library.

60 *Administrative History, Department of State*, vol. 7 (East Asia), p. 2g, LBJ Library.

61 Alice H. Amsden, *Asia's Next Giant: South Korea and Late Industrialization* (Oxford University Press, 1989), p. 56.

62 John G. Roberts, "The Spoils of Peace," *FEER*, June 23, 1966, pp. 596–598; Charles Smith and Louise do Rosario, "Empire of the Sun," *FEER*, May 3, 1966, pp. 46–48.

63 *Administrative History, Department of State*, vol. 7 (East Asia), p. F4, LBJ Library; Kim, "U.S. and Korea in Vietnam and the Japan-Korea Treaty," p. 256.

64 *Administrative History, Department of State*, vol. 7 (East Asia), p. 2g, LBJ Library; Memo, JCT to Rostow, Subj: Elements of Progress in Asia, June 24, 1966, Thomson Papers, box 13, JFK Library; Lyndon B. Johnson, *The Vantage Point: Perspectives of the Presidency, 1963–1969* (Holt, Reinhart & Winston, 1971), p. 359. Also quoted in Kim, "U.S. and Korea in Vietnam and the Japan-Korea Treaty," pp. 256–257.

65 Seoul Embtel (Embassy Telegram) 2402, November 2, 1966, NSF, Country, box 255, LBJ Library; Kim, "U.S. and Korea in Vietnam and the Japan-Korea Treaty," pp. 257–258.

66 *Administrative History, Department of State*, vol. 7 (East Asia), p. 2g, LBJ Library; Kim, "U.S. and Korea in Vietnam and the Japan-Korea Treaty," p. 257.

SIXTEEN: *Legitimacy Wars*

1 Balázs Szalontai, "The Four Horsemen of the Apocalypse in North Korea: The Forgotten Side of a Not-So-Forgotten War," in Chris Springer and Balázs Szalontai, *North Korea Caught in Time: Images of War and Reconstruction* (Garnet, 2010), p. xix.

2 Nicholas Eberstadt and Judith Banister, *The Population of North Korea* (University of California, 1999), p. 133; Szalontai, "Four Horsemen of the Apocalypse in North Korea," p. xix.

3 Zhihua Shen and Yafeng Xia, "China and the Post-War Reconstruction of North Korea, 1953–1961," *NKIDP Working Paper* 4 (May 2012), p. 2, available at http://www.wilsoncenter.org/sites/default/files/NKIDP_Working_Paper_4_China_and_the_Postwar_Reconstruction_of_North_Korea.pdf (accessed May 31, 2012).

4 Andrei Lankov, *From Stalin to Kim Il Sung: The Formation of North Korea, 1945–1960* (Rutgers University Press, 2002), pp. 150–151. In a brief memoir written by Ho K'ai's daughter, Lila, entitled, "Appanŏn amsaldang hayŏtda [My Father Was Assassinated]," she accuses Kim Il Sung of murdering her father in 1953. Although her evidence is circumstantial, she cites the highly suspicious manner in which her father's body was disposed of. She writes that her mother was not allowed to see the body of her husband when she arrived at his residence in Harbin, where he allegedly committed suicide, and was told that her husband had already been buried. See "Biographies of Soviet Korean Leaders," Asian Reading Room, Library of Congress, at http://www.loc.gov/rr/asian/SovietKorean.html (accessed June 1, 2012).

5 Lim Ŭn, *The Founding of a Dynasty in North Korea*, pp. 193–203; Lankov, *From Stalin to Kim Il Sung*, pp. 91–93.

6 Lim, Founding of a Dynasty, p. 194; Lankov, *From Stalin to Kim Il Sung*, pp. 94–95.

7 In his memoir written after his defection to South Korea in 1997, Hwang Chang-yŏp, the self-proclaimed architect of *chuch'e* ideology, revealed the circumstances behind the creation of *chuch'e* thought. Born in 1922 and trained as a social scientist and philosopher in Japan (before 1945) and in Moscow (1949–53), Hwang began to devise an ultra-nationalistic ideology that emphasized Korea's unique national characteristics after the war. By revising the orthodox Marxist tenet of class struggle as the driving force of history, Hwang sought instead to show that Korea's history had to be viewed from the perspective of the "people" (*inmin*). Hwang saw the "people's " struggle against foreign powers to achieve independence and self-determination as the main agent of Korean history. In particular, the notion of opposing *sadaejuŭi*, or serving Great Powers, was deemed to be especially important in the Korean people's drive to achieve *chuch'e*. "I decided to use the term 'people,' because I thought that opposing *sadaejuŭi* was not so much linked to the use and adaption of Marxist-Leninist concepts of class struggle, but rather, it had to do with tenaciously upholding the (national) self-determination of the Korean people." The most salient features of *chuch'e* ideology promote hostility against foreign powers while encouraging the sovereignty of Korea's heritage and its people. But as Hwang later explained, *chuch'e* ideology was eventually transformed from its original concept of national self-determination to become "the justification and organizational system for Kim Il Sung's one-man dictatorship." The necessity to inculcate the populace with *chuch'e* had effectively made Kim Il Sung the *sole* keeper and protector of the people's independence and self-determination. For this reason, North Korean propagandists have continually emphasized how Kim Il Sung worked to promote

the idea that the Korean people "not depend on great powers and instead determine their own destiny through self-determination." See Hwang Chang-yŏp, *Hwang Chang-yŏp hoegorok: Nanŭn yŏksaŭi chillirŭl poatta* [Hwang Chang-yŏp Memoir: Witness to History] (Seoul: Hanŭl, 1999), pp. 337–356. In February 1997, Hwang and an aide defected to the South Korean embassy in Beijing and several weeks later arrived in Seoul. After his defection, his wife committed suicide and one daughter died under mysterious circumstances. His other three children, two daughters and one son, as well as his grandchildren are believed to have been sent to labor camps. After his arrival in South Korea, Hwang soon found himself in the cold. Under the new Sunshine Policy of President Kim Dae-jung (1998–2003) that called for engagement with North Korea, few South Koreans, least of all Kim Dae-jung, were receptive to his anti–North Korean message as they feared it would upset the North. As a result, Hwang found himself increasingly isolated. On November 20, 2000, Hwang accused his South Korean hosts of keeping him a virtual prisoner. Nevertheless, Hwang wrote numerous books as well as contributed to the *DailyNK*, an online paper established by North Korean exiles in South Korea. Hwang died in his home on October 19, 2010, of a heart attack. "Hwang Jang-yŏp Hold Press Conference to Explain Why He Defected from North Korea," at http://www.fas.org/news/dprk/1997/bg152.html (accessed January 7, 2012). Also Aidan Foster-Carter, "P'yŏngyang Watch: Hwang Chang-yŏp: An Enemy of Which State?" *Asia Times*, November 30, 2000, at http://www.atimes.com/koreas/bk30dg01.html (accessed January 7, 2012).

8 James F. Person, "We Need Help from the Outside: The North Korean Opposition Movement of 1956," *CWIHP Working Paper* 52 (August 2006), pp. 17–18.

9 Tatiana Gabroussenko, "Cho Ki-Ch'ŏn: The Person behind the Myth," *Korean Studies* 29 (2006), p. 67; Brian Myers, *Han Sorya and North Korean Literature: The Failure of Socialist Realism in the DPRK* (Cornell East Asian Series, 1994), pp. 140–141.

10 Andrei Lankov, "Kim Il Sung's Campaign against the Soviet Faction in Late 1955 and the Birth of *Chuch'e*," *Korean Studies* 23 (1999), pp. 60–62. See also Lankov, *Crisis in North Korea* (University of Hawaii Press, 2005), pp. 26–59.

11 Person, "We Need Help from the Outside," p. 18.

12 "Memorandum of Conversation with Vice Premier of the Cabinet of Ministers of the DPRK and Member of the Presidium, KWP CC Park Chang-ok," Filatov S. N., March 12, 1956, Document 1, in ibid., p. 58.

13 Khrushchev said in his secret speech at the Twentieth Party Congress of the Communist Party of the Soviet Union on February 25, 1956, "Stalin acted not through persuasion, explanation, and patient cooperation with people, but by imposing his concepts and demanding absolute submission to his opinion. Whoever opposed this concept or tried to prove his viewpoint, and the correctness of his position was doomed to removal from the leading collective and to subsequent moral and physical annihilation. This was especially true during the period following the 17th party congress, when many prominent party leaders and rank-and-file party workers, honest and dedicated to the cause of communism, fell victim to Stalin's despotism." Taubman, *Khrushchev: The Man and His Era*, pp. 270–277.

14 "Memorandum of Conversation with Vice Premier and Minister of Light Industry Bak Uiwan (Ivan Pak), 5 June 1956," *CWHIP Bulletin*, no. 16 (Fall 2007/Winter 2008), p. 473.
15 "Report by N. T. Fedorenko on a Meeting with DPRK Ambassador to the USSR Li Sangjo, 29 May, 1956," *CWHIP Bulletin*, no. 16 (Fall 2007/Winter 2008), p. 471.
16 "Memorandum of Conversation with Deputy Premier, Pak Ŭi-wan (Ivan Pak), September 6, 1956," translation in Person, "We Need Help from the Outside," pp. 77–78.
17 Letter to Khrushchev from Ambassador Yi Sang-jo via Deputy USSR Minister of Foreign Affairs N. Fedorenko, September 5, 1956, in *CWHIP Bulletin*, no. 16 (Fall 2007/Winter 2008), p. 488.
18 Documents published in Kathryn Weathersby, "From the Russian Archives: New Findings on the Korean War," *CWHIP Bulletin*, no. 3 (Fall 1993), p. 16.
19 Nobuo Shimotomai, "Pyeongyang in 1956," *CWHIP Bulletin*, no. 16 (Fall 2007/Winter 2008), p. 460.
20 James. F. Person, "New Evidence on North Korea in 1956," *CWHIP Bulletin*, no. 16 (Fall 2007/Winter 2008), pp. 448–449. For a description of the plenum as an attempt to replace Kim Il Sung, see Andrei Lankov, "Kim Takes Control: The 'Great Purge' in North Korea, 1956–1960," *Korean Studies* 26, no. 1 (2002), pp. 92–93.
21 John Lewis Gaddis, *The Cold War: A New History* (Penguin Press, 2005), pp. 107–110. Taubman, *Khrushchev: The Man and His Era*, pp. 294–299; Mark Kramer, "New Evidence on Soviet Decision Making and the 1956 Polish and Hungarian Crises," *CWIHP Bulletin*, nos. 8–9 (Winter 1996–1997).
22 James F. Person, "We Need Help from the Outside," pp. 49–50.
23 Hŏ Chin was the pseudonym for Lim Ŭn, author of *The Founding of a Dynasty in North Korea.* Quoted in Andrei Lankov, "Kim Takes Control: The 'Great Purge' in North Korea, 1956–1960," *Korean Studies* 26, no. 1 (2002), p. 102.
24 Ibid., p. 108.
25 Ibid., p. 105.
26 Kim Il Song, *Selected Works* (Foreign Language Publishing House, 1971), vol. 2, pp. 579–580.
27 Quoted in Balázs Szalontai, *Kim Il Sung in the Khrushchev Era: Soviet–DPRK Relations and the Roots of North Korean Despotism, 1953–1964* (Woodrow Wilson Center Press, 2005), p. 190.
28 B. C. Koh, "The *Pueblo* Incident in Perspective," *Asian Survey* 9, no. 4 (April 1969), p. 270; Daniel P. Bolger, "Scenes from an Unfinished War: Low Intensity Conflict in Korea, 1966–1968," *Leavenworth Paper* 19 (Combat Studies Institute, 1991), p. 3.
29 "Ministry of Foreign Affairs, Ministry of National Defense, Ministry of the Interior to the KPCZ CC [Communist Party of Czechoslovakia Central Committee] Presidium and the Czechoslovak Government File no.: 0200.873/68-3, 4 February 1968, Information about the Situation in Korea," Document 15, in Christian F. Ostermann and James F. Person, eds., *Crisis and Confrontation on the Korean Peninsula, 1968–1969: A Critical Oral History* (Woodrow Wilson International Center for Scholars, 2011), p. 186.

30 Bernd Schaefer, "North Korean Adventurism and China's Long Shadow, 1966–1972," *CWIHP Working Paper* 44 (October 2004), p. 19.

31 Most of the Japanese Koreans who immigrated to North Korea in the late 1960s and 1970s later regretted their decision. For a terrifying account of their experiences, see Kang Chol-hwan, *The Aquariums of Pyongyang: Ten Years in the North Korean Gulag* (Basic Books, 2001), and Tessa Morris-Suzuki, *Exodus to North Korea: Shadows from Japan's Cold War* (Rowman & Littlefield, 2007). In her in-depth and moving examination of the mass repatriation of Japanese Koreans (Zainichi) to North Korea, Morris-Suzuki reports that beginning in 1958, Kim Il Sung, together with leaders of Chŏngryŏn (General Association of Korean Residents in Japan), a pro–North Korean organization established in Japan in 1955, began coordinating, with international support, a vigorous propaganda campaign aimed to promote the mass repatriation of Zainichi to North Korea. Remarkably, among the 86,603 ethnic Koreans from Japan who eventually returned to North Korea between 1959 and 1985, the vast majority of them—some 97 percent—had originated from South Korea. While Kim Il Sung's interest in promoting this mass exodus stemmed in part from the labor shortage that North Korea was then experiencing, owing to the withdrawal of Chinese troops from North Korea in 1958, the repatriation of thousands of Zainichi to North Korea also provided the Kim regime with a propaganda victory. What better way to show the world the superiority of the North Korean system than to have thousands of Korean residents, originally from South Korea, "voting with their feet to return to the socialist North." The North Korean leadership certainly framed the repatriation issue in this way. In a meeting with Soviet Deputy Premier Anastas Mikoyan in mid-1959, Foreign Minister Nam Il boastfully proclaimed, "The emergence of the repatriation issue has brought political gains to the DPRK while Syngman Rhee has lost out. He is not only unable to accept [returnees] to South Korea, but on the contrary, is prepared to export unemployed people from South Korea to Latin America" (Morris-Suzuki, *Exodus to North Korea*, pp. 181–184). Sadly, while unknown numbers of those who left Japan for the DPRK would later end up in North Korean concentration camps, the mass exodus was hailed as evidence of the superiority of the North Korean system.

32 Joseph Sang-hoon Chung, " 'Seven Year Plan' (1961–1970): Economic Performance and Reforms," *Asian Survey* 12, no. 6 (June 1972), p. 529. One striking finding of more recent assessments of North Korea's economy is that the economic slowdown occurred much sooner, starting as early as the early 1960s. Comparison of growth rates between the two Koreas shows that only in the late 1950s was the growth rate in North Korea higher than that in the South. By the mid-1960s, South Korea's GNP per capita had already begun to surpass that of the North. These assessments run counter to the traditional view of high economic growth until the mid-1970s. See Byung-yeon Kim, Suk Jin Kim, and Keun Lee, "Assessing the Economic Performance of North Korea, 1954–1989: Estimates and Growth Accounting Analysis," *Journal of Comparative Economics* 35 (2007), pp. 564–582; Nicholas Eberstadt, *Policy and Economic Performance in Divided Korea during the Cold War Era: 1945–91* (AEI Press, 2010), pp. 78–80.

33 As one Soviet official stated, "The intensity of the two countries' rapproche-

ment was in direct proportion to the volume of all kinds of aid to the DPRK from the Soviet Union." Sergey S. Radchenko, "The Soviet Union and the North Korean Seizure of the USS *Pueblo*: Evidence from Russian Archives," *CWHIP Working Paper 47* (2005), p. 10. According to Russian sources, the Soviet Union rendered extensive aid to North Korea by November 1945. An aid package of 74 million rubles was provided in 1946; in 1947 that figure doubled to 140 million. After the war, in 1953 Moscow announced that it would grant 225 million rubles in free financial aid. The assistance dispensed by the Soviet Union and by other socialist states to North Korea accounted for 77.6 percent of all imports entering North Korea during 1954–56, which were financed through this free aid. For a detailed account of Soviet development aid to North Korea from 1945 to 1960, see George Ginsburg, "Soviet Development Grants and Aid to North Korea, 1945–1980," *Asia Pacific Community* (Fall 1982), pp. 43–63. According to Erik van Ree, the Soviets provided grants and credits roughly to the tune of $690 million for the period between 1953 and 1959. Long-term credits from Moscow between 1961 and 1976 were provided on at least eight occasions in the amount of approximately $300 million. Although assistance declined year by year, van Ree believes that Moscow may have provided P'yŏngyang assistance for the whole period of 1953–76, with credits and grants in the order of $1.3 billion. Soviet sources also suggest that "P'yŏngyang never repaid anything" (p. 68). The total of $1.3 billion average out to roughly $55 million in grants and aid per year that Soviet invested into North Korea's industry. North Korea's "economic miracle" was a chimera financed by foreign inputs from the Soviets and other communist bloc countries. See Erik van Ree, "The Limits of *Juche*: North Korea and Soviet Aid, 1953–1976," *Journal of Communist Studies* 5, no. 1 (1989); George Ginsburg, "The Legal Framework of Soviet Investment Credits to North Korea," *Osteuropa-Recht* 29, no. 4 (1983), pp. 256–277. Chinese documents uncovered from the PRC Ministry of Foreign Affairs archives also show the extensive amount of food aid China provided to North Korea after the war. From January 1954 to September 1955, for example, China transferred 300,000 tons of grain to North Korea. The Chinese also provided extensive monetary aid. In November 1953 Kim Il Sung arrived in Beijing to hammer out an economic pact with Chinese leaders that heavily favored North Korea: Beijing offered 800 million yuan in grants to be used for food, textiles, cotton, coal, reconstruction supplies, and other equipment. Kim also learned, "much to his delight," that the Chinese had "cancelled all of North Korea debts from the Korean War." China also became the largest supplier of consumer goods to North Korea, "flooding the market with clothing, toiletries and utensils." Apart from this aid and the delivery of important reconstruction equipment and supplies, perhaps the most important assistance P'yŏngyang received was from Chinese troops who were stationed in North Korea from 1953 to 1958. These soldiers made up for significant labor shortages and rebuilt infrastructure, and "their importance in reconstruction should not be underemphasized." See Adam Cathcart, "The Bonds of Brotherhood: New Evidence of Sino-North Korean Exchanges, 1950–1954," *Journal of Cold War Studies* 13, no. 3 (Summer 2011), pp. 27–51. China's aid also included the cancellation of North Korea's war debt, which amounted to 729 million Chinese yuan. According to Zhihua Shen and Yafeng Xia, "China's aid to North Korea in 1954 was equal to 3.4 percent of China's 1954 budget." See Shen and Xia, "China and the Post-War Reconstruction of North Korea, 1953–1961," p. 7.

34 "Report, Embassy of Hungary in North Korea to the Hungarian Foreign Ministry, August 1962," *CWIHP Bulletin*, no. 14/15 (Winter 2003/Spring 2004), p. 127.

35 Chung, " 'Seven-Year Plan'," p. 528. See also Scalapino and Lee, *Communism in Korea*, Part 2, pp. 1257–1262.

36 Ibid.

37 Van Ree, "Limits of *Juche*," pp. 55–56. Since domestic producers were protected from the foreign competition, there was no real incentive for increasing efficiency or productivity. In order to cope with these problems, North Korea was forced to resort to mass mobilization drives for longer working hours. This was essentially the strategy behind the *ch'ŏllima* movement that was launched in 1958, which was intended to promote rapid economic development. However, the mobilization of domestic labor alone cannot sustain a high level of growth in an economy limited by the constraints of a small domestic market that is bound to be monopolized by one or two producers. This is because there is very little incentive to improve productivity and efficiency through innovation in a seller's market. The result is decreased productivity and declining economic growth.

38 Erik van Ree, "Limits of *Juche*," p. 56. Van Ree also notes the irony that the *chuch'e* concept was original to North Korea. In fact, the idea behind all-around development and national self-sufficiency was in keeping with the standard, orthodox Stalinist concept of comprehensive economic development that was propagated after 1945. But this idea soon ran into trouble owing to the creation of unnecessary duplication of industries in the Soviet bloc countries. Although Khrushchev attempted to reverse this trend after 1953 by introducing the principle that small states should not strive for all-around development but instead begin a program of international specialization, North Korea never really got on board with that new program. As van Ree notes, "During the 1960s and 1970s, the construction of an autarkic, all-round economy remained the official goal." Ibid., p. 61; Sang-chul Suh, "North Korean Industrial Policy Today," in Robert A. Scalapino and Jun-yop Kim, eds., *North Korea Today: Strategic and Domestic Issues* (Center for Korean Studies, 1983), pp. 197–213.

39 By the 1970s, the Kim regime attempted to make some fundamental changes in its development strategy when it began to borrow heavily from Japan and Western Europe to finance the importation of new technology and foreign plants. However, it soon found itself unable to meet payments on external debts and defaulted. As a result of its debt problem, North Korea has been unable to obtain Western sources of credit since 1976. See Suh, "North Korean Industrial Policy Today," p. 213; Aidan Foster-Carter, "Korea and Dependency Theory," *Monthly Review* (October 1985), pp. 27–34.

40 Karoly Fendler, "Economic Assistance and Loans from Socialist Countries to North Korea in the Postwar Years, 1953–1963," *Asien: The German Journal on Contemporary Asia* 42 (January 1992), p. 4; V. Andreyev and V. Osipov, "Rela-

tions of the USSR and the European Socialist Countries with the DPRK in the 1970s," *Far Eastern Affairs* 1 (1982), pp. 52–56.

41 Szalontai, *Kim Il Sung and the Khrushchev Era*, pp. 121–123. The *ch'ŏllima* movement was modeled after Mao's Great Leap Forward. Like China, Kim also launched a patriotic hygiene campaign to eliminate the four "pests" (mice, sparrows, flies, and mosquitoes). The DPRK also introduced small-scale steelmaking projects, and in rural areas it "carried out the policy of merging cooperatives and operating mess halls," following China's practice of making "every citizen a soldier." See Shen and Xia, "China and the Post-War Reconstruction of North Korea, 1953–1961." Also, Scalapino and Lee, *Communism in Korea*, Part 2, pp. 1115–1120.

42 Balázs Szlontai, "In the Shadow of Vietnam: A New Look at North Korea's Militant Strategy, 1962–1970," *Journal of Cold War History* (forthcoming).

43 Ibid. Also Suh Dae-suk, *Kim Il Sung, the North Korean Leader* (Columbia University Press, 1988), pp. 231–234.

44 MOFAT: C21/F6/134, October 1967. The format for referencing MOFAT archival material, available only on microfilm, is microfilm roll number/file number/frame number, date.

45 Each year the UN General Assembly reaffirmed, through an overwhelming majority, its support for "The Korean Question" resolution. "Growth in United Nations Membership, 1945–Present," available at http://www.un.org/en/members/growth.shtml (accessed March 15, 2011).

46 See resolutions passed in 1965 and 1966: UN General Assembly, 20th Session (September–December 1965), Resolution 2132 (XX) "The Korean Question," December 21, 1965; UN General Assembly, 21st Session (September–December 1966), Resolution 2224 (XXI) "The Korean Question," December 19, 1966, available at http://www.un.org/documents/resga.htm (accessed March 15, 2011).

47 MOFAT: the following selected archival references to ROK/DPRK goodwill missions in 1967, 1968, 1970, and 1972 provide a good overview of the scale and variety of these missions especially those from South Korea.

1967 ROK Goodwill missions: C21/F6/1-146 (Middle East), October 17–November 7, 1967; C21/F7/1-372 and C21/F8/1-135 (East Africa), August 24–October 5, 1967; C21/F9/1-382 (West Africa), August 23–September 29, 1967; C22/F1/1-132 (Southeast Asia), August 13–September 9, 1967; C22/F2/1-39 (Central America), October 16–26, 1967.

1968 ROK Goodwill missions: C27/F4/1-111 (North Africa), January 22–February 1, 1968; C27/F5/1-236 (South/Southeast Asia), August 19–September 11, 1968; C27/F6/1-417 (Middle East), August 1–31, 1968; C27/F7/1-184 (Central America), August 1–24, 1968; C27/F8/1-258 (East Africa), August 1–September 8, 1968; C27/F9/1-284 (West Africa), August 1–September 1, 1968.

1968 DPRK Goodwill missions: D6/F18/1-15 (Africa), November 7–December 19, 1968; D6/F19/1-216 (Southeast/Southwest Asia), June 15–August 1, 1968.

1970 ROK Goodwill missions: C41/F5/1-66 (Middle East, Cyprus), July 9–August 6, 1970; C41/F6/1-155 (Latin America), July 23–August 15, 1970; C41/F7/1-23 (East Africa), July 25–August 19, 1970; C41/F8/1-62 (West Africa), July 23–August 17, 1970.

1970 DPRK Goodwill missions: D8/F31/1-142 (Africa), January 22–February 24, June 27–August 5, 1970.

1972 ROK Goodwill missions: C56/F9/1-221 and C56/F10/1-219 (Asia), July 8–23, 1972; C56/F10/1 189 (Middle East), December 5–21, 1972; C57/F11/1-66 (West Africa), December 5–18, 1972; C57/F5/1-209 (North Europe, Ethiopia), August 4–18, 1972.

1972 DPRK Goodwill missions: C56/F10/1-219 (ROK discussion of North Korean missions to East Europe, Middle East, Africa, Asia), July 8–23, 1972.

48 North Korean propaganda spread the message that South Koreans wished for nothing more than to rid themselves of their foreign "oppressors" and to be reunited with their northern brethren under the benevolent rule of Kim Il Sung. North Korea therefore needed "to be on constant alert and eventually seize the right opportunity to act." See Schaefer, "North Korean 'Adventurism'," p. 19. An East German report also confirms North Korean thinking: "More and more often they [North Koreans] repeat their readiness to act on the order of the party and the leader, to destroy the enemy and liberate South Korea. Ideological propaganda addressed to the population for armed liberation of South Korea has increased. At the same time, reports in the DPRK press about revolutionary movements and events in South Korea have proliferated. They are portraying a picture of a revolutionary upsurge already in motion." Quoted in ibid., p. 42.

49 The North Korean pilots and air defense forces sent to North Vietnam were part of this effort. According to a recently declassified CIA report, North Korea had offered an infantry division, but it was apparently rejected by Hanoi. CIA Intelligence Report, *Kim Il-Sung's New Military Adventurism* (TOP SECRET), November 26, 1968 (declassified with redactions on May 2007), p. 6, available at http://www.foia.cia.gov/CPE/ESAU/esau-39.pdf (accessed March 15, 2011).

50 Ibid., pp. 1–11; Bolger, *Scenes from an Unfinished War*, pp. 33–36.

51 B. C. Koh, "North Korea and the Sino-Soviet Schism," *Western Political Quarterly* 22, no. 4 (December 1969), pp. 957–958.

52 Chung, " 'Seven-Year Plan'," p. 538.

53 Radchenko, "The Soviet Union and the North Korean Seizure of the USS *Pueblo*," p. 10. The Soviet Union's abundant military aid for North Korea was an open secret. The *New York Times* reported in January 1968, for example, that "over the course of the last twelve months Moscow provided North Korea with 21 MIG 21 and 350 MIG-17 aircrafts, 80 MIG-15 fighters plus 80 IL-28 bombers." It also reported that "the North Korean army of 350,000 to 400,000 men is equipped almost exclusively with Soviet equipment, including medium tanks." *New York Times*, January 31, 1968. In 1968, Kim introduced a new slogan: "Vietnam is breaking one leg of the American bandit, we are breaking the other one." Quoted in Schaefer, "North Korean 'Adventurism'," p. 12.

54 *New York Times*, January 28, 1968.

55 Mitchell B. Lerner, *The Pueblo Incident: A Spy Ship and the Failure of American Foreign Policy* (University Press of Kansas, 2002), p. 99; also *New York Times*, January 28, 1968.

56 *New York Times*, January 27, 1968.

57 Radchenko, "The Soviet Union and the North Korean Seizure of the USS *Pueblo*," p. 12.

58 *New York Times*, February 1, 1968; *Chosŏn ilbo*, February 1, 1968.

59 A year later, Kim was pardoned and released. In 1970 he became a South Korean citizen. He is today a well-known Protestant minister and an outspoken critic of the North Korean regime. John M. Glikona, "The Face of South Korea's Boogeyman," *Los Angeles Times*, July 18, 2010.

60 *Kangwŏn ilbo*, January 30, 1968, p. 3.

61 Ibid., January 25, 1968, p. 2. The *Kangwŏn ilbo* was the only province-wide newspaper published in Kangwŏndo province until 1992, when the *Kangwŏn domin ilbo* was established. Kangwŏndo is the only province that was split in half by the 38th parallel and the DMZ. Its border with North Korea, rugged terrain, and coastline, which is contiguous with North Korea, made it vulnerable to frequent North Korean provocations, including infiltration, murder, kidnapping of farmers and fishermen, capture of fishing boats, and even an attempt to incite a revolutionary uprising. Kangwŏndo was and still is predominantly populated by farmers and fishermen. Their tight-knit communities, tied to the soil and the sea and the constant threat of North Korean provocations, fostered a deeply anticommunist and anti–North Korean attitude and values. Kangwŏndo remains today one of the most conservative areas of South Korea. What sets the *Kangwŏn ilbo* apart from the more established national newspapers published in Seoul is that because it is far away from Seoul, the seat of power, and its major concern was economic development and the success of farming and fishing, it received relatively little scrutiny from the central government. As a result its contents were more open and often critical of Seoul's policies during the authoritarian period of the 1960s–70s.

62 "9 February 1968, [from] The Embassy of Czechoslovak Socialist Republic SM-021712/68, Pyongyang, [to] Ministry of Foreign Affairs, [subject] Pueblo and American-South Korean Relations," Document 17, in Ostermann and Person, eds., *Crisis and Confrontation on the Korean Peninsula*, pp. 207–208.

63 The first time Kim had severely miscalculated was when he had assured Stalin that "200,000 South Korean partisans" would rise up to greet the NKPA after it launched its invasion of the South. During the spring of 1968, Park approved the creation of the Homeland Reserve Force (*hyangt'o yebigun*), a people's militia. Although primarily designed to deal with the increasing North Korean guerilla threat in the countryside, it was, in essence, the first nationwide mass mobilization of the Park era. The Homeland Reserve Force quickly grew to include 2.5 million citizens and "created a hierarchically organized armed men in every village, town, city, and county" (Jiyul Kim, "War, Diplomacy, Mobilization and Nationbuilding in South Korea, 1968," unpublished paper [Harvard University, 2004], p. 4). The militia proved to be invaluable in detecting North Korean guerilla infiltration activity. In addition, Park established "reconstruction villages" just south of the DMZ. These villages, inhabited by armed ex-soldiers and their families on the model of Israeli border kibbutzim, "created a band of fiercely loyal people squarely in the path of any likely northern infiltrators" (Bolger, *Scenes from an Unfinished*

War, p. 83). ROK soldiers were also directed to work with local villages, building roads and doing civil engineer projects. The aim of the new ROK civic-action effort was to promote closer ties between the military and the civilian population. One of the most important ROK civic-action efforts entailed the creation and dispatch of "Medical/Enlightenment Teams" into the harsh T'aebaek and Chiri Mountains, where many North Korean infiltrations had taken place. These teams conducted medical screenings, inoculations, and minor surgery while promoting anticommunism. The success of the Homeland Reserve Force can be measured by the complete failure of Kim Il Sung's last major infiltration effort, which occurred in October 1968, just ten months after the Blue House raid. One hundred and twenty members of the elite 124th Army unit landed at eight separate locations on the east coast of South Korea, between the towns of Samchŏk and Ulchin. Their aim was to create guerilla bases in the South, but the scheme collapsed thanks to local villagers who quickly alerted the police to the North Korean presence. A force of seventy thousand, including thirty-five thousand Homeland Reserve Force members, was mobilized to track down the intruders. Within two weeks, they had all been captured or killed. As General Bonesteel observed about the incident, "It was a losing game to begin with for the North because of a miscomprehension of the situation in the South." Bolger, *Scenes from an Unfinished War*, pp. 86–87; Kim, "War, Diplomacy, Mobilization, and Nation-Building in South Korea, 1968," pp. 26–27.

64 Radchenko, "The Soviet Union and the North Korean Seizure of the USS *Pueblo*," p. 14.

65 Schaefer, "North Korean 'Adventurism'," p. 22.

66 Radchenko, "The Soviet Union and the North Korean Seizure of the USS *Pueblo*," p. 14.

67 Ibid., Document 23, "Excerpt from a Speech by Leonid Brezhnev," April 9, 1968, pp. 62–64. Similar observations were made by the Romanian ambassador to the DPRK, N. Popa, about the general state of tension, troop movements, neighborhood anti–air defense drills, night alarms, and evacuation of major cities in North Korea. "The archives of central institutions, a significant part of the State Library and of the Academy, more than half of the machinery used in the Typographic Complex and probably many other factories have been moved out of Pyongyang." Telegram from Pyongyang to Bucharest, TOP SECRET, no. 76.051, February 27, 1968, in Mitchell Lerner and Jong-Dae Shin, *NKIDP e-Dossier* No. 5: "New Romanian Evidence on the Blue House Raid and the USS Pueblo Incident," Document 23, available at http://www.wilsoncenter.org/publication/nkidp-e-dossier-no-5-new-romanian-evidence-the-blue-house-raid-and-the-uss-pueblo (accessed April 24, 2012).

68 Radchenko, "Soviet Union and the North Korean Seizure of the USS *Pueblo*," Document 23, p. 65.

69 Radchenko, "Soviet Union and the North Korean Seizure of the USS *Pueblo*," p. 15. Documents from the Romanian archives reinforce this view. S. Golosov, second secretary of the Soviet embassy in P'yŏngyang, reported that "Soviet diplomats were extremely worried with respect to the unrestrained actions undertaken by the DPRK against the ROK (the January 21 attack in Seoul)

and against the USA, manifested in the capturing of the military vessel AGER-2 [the USS *Pueblo*]. The Soviet diplomat pointed out that if the DPRK continued to undertake such initiatives to speed up the reunification of the country, it would be possible for the Soviets to be presented with a fait accompli in the sense of the resumption of an all-out war." S. Golosov also complained to Romanian officials that "when we try to moderate this warmongering state of mind on many occasions, our position is not taken into account." Telegram from P'yŏngyang to Bucharest, TOP SECRET, no. 76. 017, January 25, 1968, in Lerner and Shin, NKIDP e-Dossier No. 5: "New Romanian Evidence," Document 5.

70 Radchenko, "Soviet Union and the North Korean Seizure of the USS *Pueblo*," Document 23, pp. 66–67.

71 Ibid., Document 24, "Record of Conversation between Chairman of the Council of Ministers of the USSR Aleksei Kosygin and North Korean Ambassador in the USSR Chon Tu-hwan," May 6, 1968, p. 70.

72 "Excerpt from Leonid Brezhnev's Speech at the April (1968) CC (Central Committee) CPSU (Communist Party of the Soviet Union) Plenum, April 9, 1968," Document 13, in Mitchell B. Lerner, " 'Mostly Propaganda in Nature:' Kim Il Sung, the Juche Ideology, and the Second Korean War," *NKIDP Working Paper 3* (December 2010), p. 97.

73 Qiang Zhai, *China and the Vietnam Wars, 1950–1975* (University of North Carolina Press, 2000), p. 150; Radchenko, "Soviet Union and the North Korean Seizure of the USS *Pueblo*," p. 160.

74 Schaefer, "North Korean 'Adventurism'," pp. 5–15.

75 Lerner, *Pueblo Incident*, p. 140.

76 Radchenko, "Soviet Union and the North Korean Seizure of the USS *Pueblo*," pp. 18–19.

77 "Memorandum from Secretary of State Rusk to President Johnson, Washington, March 14, 1968," in *FRUS, 1964–1968*, vol. 29: *Korea, Part 1* (2000), p. 665.

78 *New York Times*, January 24, 1968; Lerner, *Pueblo Incident*, p. 118.

79 Lloyd M. Bucher, *Bucher: My Story* (Doubleday, 1970), p. 231.

80 Ibid., p. 249.

81 Edward R. Murphy, *Second in Command: The Uncensored Account of the Capture of the Spy Ship Pueblo* (Holt, Rinehart & Winston, 1971), p. 162.

82 Bucher, *Bucher*, p. 311.

83 Ibid., p. 324.

84 Stephen Harris, *My Anchor Held* (Fleming H. Revell, 1970), p. 108.

85 *Time*, October 18, 1968, p. 38.

86 Ed Brandt, *The Last Voyage of the USS Pueblo: The Exclusive Story, Told by 15 Members of the Crew* (W. W. Norton, 1969), pp. 84–85.

87 Ibid., p. 176.

88 Lerner, *Pueblo Incident*, p. 119.

89 Bucher, *Bucher*, p. 344.

90 Mitchell B. Lerner, "A Dangerous Miscalculation: New Evidence from Communist-Bloc Archives about North Korea and the Crisis of 1968," *Journal of Cold War Studies* 6, no. 1 (Winter 2004), p. 20.

91 Trevor Armbrister, *A Matter of Accountability: The True Story of the* Pueblo *Affair* (Coward-McCann, 1970), p. 334.

92 Ibid., p. 335.
93 *New York Times*, December 23, 1968.
94 Lerner, "Dangerous Miscalculation," p. 19.
95 *New York Times*, December 26, 1968.
96 Lerner, "Dangerous Miscalculation," p. 19.
97 *New York Times*, December 23, 1968.

SEVENTEEN: *Old Allies, New Friends*

1 *New York Times*, December 23, 1968.
2 *Chicago Tribune*, December 24, 1968.
3 Lerner, *Pueblo Incident*, p. 221.
4 *New York Times*, February 18, 1968.
5 Lerner, *Pueblo Incident*, p. 131.
6 Cables and letters between Seoul and Washington, in *FRUS, 1964–1968*, vol. 29: *Korea, Part 1* (2000), pp. 315–330.
7 "Telegram from the Commander in Chief, United States Forces, Korea (Bonesteel) to the Commander in Chief, Pacific (Sharp), Seoul, February 9, 1968," in *FRUS, 1964–1968*, vol. 29: *Part 1*, p. 356.
8 Kim, "U.S. and Korea in Vietnam and the Japan-Korea Treaty," pp. 243–249; Lerner, *Pueblo Incident*, p. 133.
9 Lerner, *Pueblo Incident*, p. 133.
10 "Letter from the Ambassador to Korea (Porter) to the Assistant Secretary of State for East Asian and Pacific Affairs (Bundy), Seoul, February 27, 1968," in *FRUS, 1964–1968*, vol. 29: *Part 1*, p. 392.
11 Lerner, *Pueblo Incident*, p. 134.
12 "Memorandum from Cyrus R. Vance to President Johnson, Washington, February 20, 1968," in *FRUS, 1964–1968*, vol. 29: *Part 1*, pp. 384–385. Key U.S. cables and reports pertaining to the Vance visit are in *FRUS, 1964–1968*, vol. 29: *Part 1*, pp. 347–395. Records of the visit from the South Korean archives are in MOFAT, C28/10 (C21-1/7-7/7) and C28/F11 (C22-1/1).
13 MOFAT, "First Park-Vance, Park Meeting," C28/F10 (C21-1/7-7/7)/42-58, February 12, 1968.
14 The details of what South Korea wanted as printed in *FRUS* ("Notes of the President's Meeting with Cyrus R. Vance," February 15, 1968, in *FRUS, 1964–1968*, vol. 29: *Part 1*, pp. 378–379) appear to be incorrect with regard to one item. The *FRUS* transcript of Vance's meeting with Johnson immediately after his return states, "One million dollars to augment his anti-guerilla forces." In actuality, the issue concerned providing small arms and equipment for one million men of the homeland security forces. The more accurate details come from the letter Vance signed at the conclusion of his visit (MOFAT, "Letter from Cyrus Vance to Foreign Minister Ch'oe Kyu-ha," C28/F10 (C21-1/7-7/7)/243-244, February 15, 1968).
15 Lerner, *Pueblo Incident*, p. 136.
16 Ibid., pp. 134–166.
17 Henry Kissinger, *White House Years* (Little, Brown, 1979), p. 742.
18 Richard Nixon, "Asia after Viet Nam," *Foreign Affairs* 46, no. 1 (October 1967), p. 121.

19 Walter Isaacson, *Kissinger: A Biography* (Simon & Schuster, 1992), p. 336.

20 National Security Archive, *New Documentary Reveals Secret U.S., Chinese Diplomacy behind Nixon's Trip*, National Security Archive Electronic Debriefing Book 145, William Burr, ed., December 21, 2004, Document 4: "Front page of People's Daily, 25 December 1970, showing from left, Edgar Snow, interpreter Ji Chaozhu, Mao Zedong, and Lin Biao, at a reviewing stand facing Tiananmen Square on 1 October 1970," available at http://www.gwu.edu/~nsarchiv/NSAEBB/NSAEBB145/index.htm (accessed March 16, 2011).

21 Isaacson, *Kissinger*, pp. 338–339.

22 Philip Short, *Mao: A Life* (John Murray, 2004), p. 583.

23 Bernd Schaefer, "North Korean 'Adventurism' and China's Long Shadow, 1966–1972," *CWIHP Working Paper 44* (October 2004), p. 32.

24 Ibid., pp. 34–35.

25 Don Oberdorfer, *The Two Koreas* (Addison-Wesley, 1997), p. 12.

26 Schaefer, "North Korean 'Adventurism'," p. 38.

27 *Kangwŏn ilbo*, September 30, 1972, p. 2.

28 MOFAT, *Lam, Pham Dang, Visit of South Vietnamese Special Envoy*, C58/F5/77-87, November 2–4, 1972.

29 Christian F. Ostermann and James F. Person, eds., *The Rise and Fall of Détente on the Korean Peninsula, 1970–1974*, History and Public Policy Program, Critical Oral History Conference Series (CWIHP, 2011), pp. 14–15.

30 Seongji Woo, "The Park Chung-hee Administration amid Inter-Korean Reconciliation in the Détente Period: Changes in the Threat Perception, Regime Characteristics and the Distribution of Power," *Korea Journal* (Summer 2009), p. 54. The South Koreans had good reason to worry. In his conversation with Zhou Enlai on July 9, 1971, Kissinger gave hope that North Koreans would have something to gain from a Sino-U.S. rapprochement: "If the relationships between our countries develop as they might, after the Indochina war ends and the ROK troops return to Korea, I would think it quite conceivable that before the end of the next term of President Nixon, most, if not all, American troops will be withdrawn from Korea." "Memcon (Memorandum of Conversation), Zhou Enlai-Kissinger 9 July, 1971," in *FRUS, 1969–1976*, vol. 17: *China 1969–1972* (2006), p. 390. See also Bernd Schaefer, "Overconfidence Shattered: North Korean Unification Policy, 1971–1975," *CWIHP Working Paper 2* (December 2010), p. 6.

31 James Person, "New Evidence on Inter-Korean Relations, 1971–1972," Document 28 (September 22, 1972), *NKIPD Document Reader* 3, CWIHP, October 15, 2009.

32 Schaefer, "Overconfidence Shattered," p. 31. Also Schaefer, "North Korean 'Adventurism'," p. 37.

33 See Yong-Jick Kim, "The Security, Political, and Human Rights Conundrum, 1974-1979," in Kim and Vogel, eds., *Park Chung Hee Era*, 2011), pp. 457–482; see also Ch'oe Ho-il, "Kukga anbo wigiwa yusinch'eche [National Security Crisis and the Yusin System]," in Cho Yi che and Carter Eckert, eds., *Han'guk kundaehwa, kichŏkŭi kwachŏng* [Modernization of the Republic of Korea: A Miraculous Achievement] (Seoul: Wŏlganchosŏnhoe, 2005), pp. 149–179. Ch'oe makes the interesting point that South Korea's economic suc-

cess was a direct result of the threat posed by North Korea and that rapid industrialization under Park's *Yusin* system can aptly be described as "crisis development." This situation was not unlike what Japan's leaders experienced at the end of the nineteenth century when Commodore Mathew Perry and his armed "black ships" sailed into Edo (Tokyo) Bay in 1853. Japan's new Meiji leaders quickly recognized the Western threat to their nation and, in response, launched the Meiji Revolution in 1868. Not surprisingly given his background as a former lieutenant in the Japanese Kwantung Army, Park saw himself as a "Korean" Meiji reformer and considered his *Yusin* system to be the Korean equivalent of Japan's Meiji Revolution.

34 Yi P'il–nam, "The October *Yusin*," *Kangwŏn ilbo*, February 27, 1973.

35 Oberdorfer, *Two Koreas*, p. 37.

36 Kim Hyung-a, *Korea's Development under Park Chung Hee: Rapid Industrialization, 1961–79* (Routledge, 2004), p. 139.

37 Recent evidence indicates that the nuclear program continued under cover and in reduced scale in response to President Carter's threat to withdraw all U.S. forces from Korea. See Sung Gul Hong, "The Search for Deterrence: Park's Nuclear Option," in Kim and Vogel, eds., *Park Chung Hee Era*, pp. 483–510; Peter Hayes and Chung-in Moon, "Park Chung Hee, the CIA, and the Bomb," Nautilus Institute, September 23, 2011, available at http://www.nautilus.org/publications/essays/napsnet/reports/Hayes_Moon_ParkChungHee_Bomb (accessed October 10, 2011).

38 Schaefer, "Overconfidence Shattered," p. 28.

39 Pak Ch'i-young, *Korea and the United Nations* (Springer, 2000), pp. 49–50. The Nonaligned Movement (NAM) originated at the Asia-Africa Conference held in Bandung, Indonesia, in 1955. The conference, convened at the invitation of the prime ministers of Burma, Ceylon, India, Indonesia, and Pakistan, brought together leaders of twenty-nine states, mostly former colonies, from the two continents of Africa and Asia to discuss "similar problems of resisting the pressures of the major powers, maintaining their independence and opposing colonialism and neo-colonialism, specially western domination." In 1961, it was formally established as an intergovernmental organization of states that represented nearly two-thirds of the United Nations' members. See http://www.nam.gov.za/background/history.htm, the official NAM web site (accessed April 15, 2011).

EIGHTEEN: *War for Peace*

1 John Singlaub, *Hazardous Duty: An American Soldier in the Twentieth Century* (Summit Books, 1991), pp. 376–379; *New York Times*, August 25, 1976; *Time*, August 30, 1976, pp. 42–43; *Newsweek*, August 30, 1976, pp. 50–52.

2 *New York Times*, August 19, 1976.

3 "Response to Ax Killing, Memorandum of Telephone Conversation, August 18, 1976," *The United States and the Two Koreas from Nixon to Clinton (1969–2000)*, item K000213, Digital National Security Archives (accessed February 2, 2010).

4 I am indebted to retired U.S. Army Col. Don Boose for this point. Colonel Boose served at the Joint Security Area as a member of the UN Command Military Armistice Commission and was present in the Joint Security Area

when the ax incident took place, and participated in its investigation and negotiations with the North Koreans. He stated, "Having studied the incident intensely, I am convinced that the murder of the two U.S. officers was not planned, but was the result of a fight instigated by the NKPA guard force officer on the scene that got out of hand. The most compelling evidence is that the North Koreans were totally unprepared to take advantage of the incident for propaganda purposes and were unprepared to deal with any military escalation that might have resulted." Comment for the author, July 13, 2011.

5 "Minutes of Washington Special Actions Group Meetings, Washington, August 19, 1976, 8:12-9:15 a.m.," Document 285, Chapter 6, in *FRUS, 1969–1976*, vol. E-12: *Documents on East and Southeast Asia, 1973–1976*. Available only online at History.state.gov/historicaldocuments/frus1969-76ve12/d285 (accessed November 16, 2011).

6 *New York Times*, August 11, 1976.

7 Ibid., August 29, 1976. During the first half of 1976, P'yŏngyang took several steps to heighten international tensions. In February, two North Korean diplomats publicly announced that the DPRK possessed nuclear weapons. On April 7, two North Korean tanks entered the DMZ and remained there for four hours, "an act unprecedented since the 1953 armistice." The killing of the two American soldiers in August was thus the culmination of a series of provocative actions timed to coincide with the NAM conference in Sri Lanka. Such provocations were, as the historian Balázs Szalontai has observed, "often planned well in advance and were carefully coordinated with diplomatic maneuvers, indicating that KWP leaders were more rational actors than it is sometimes assumed." See Balázs Szalontai and Sergey Radchenko, "North Korea's Efforts to Acquire Nuclear Technology and Nuclear Weapons: Evidence from Russian and Hungarian Archives," *CWIHP Working Paper 53* (August 2006), pp. 13–15.

8 *New York Times*, August 22, 1976.

9 Ibid., August 25, 1976.

10 Ibid., August 23, 1976.

11 Robert Rich, "U.S. Ground Forces Withdrawal from Korea: A Case Study in National Security Decision Making," *Executive Seminar in National and International Affairs*, U.S. Department of State, Foreign Service Institute, June 1982, p. 6.

12 *New York Times*, June 24, 1976; Don Oberdorfer, "Carter's Decision on Korea Traced Back to January 1975," *Washington Post*, June 12, 1977.

13 *U.S. News & World Report*, June 6, 1977, p. 17; *New York Times*, May 23, 1977. Also, James V. Young, *Eye on Korea: An Insider Account of Korean American Relations* (Texas A&M Press, 2003), pp. 41–42.

14 Presidential Review Memorandum (PRM) 13 available at http://www.fas.org/irp/offdocs/prm/prm13.pdf (accessed April 1, 2011).

15 "Top Secret, Presidential Directive, May 5, 1977," *The United States and the Two Koreas from Nixon to Clinton (1969–2000)*, item K000228, Digital National Security Archives; Oberdorfer, *Two Koreas*, p. 87.

16 Oberdorfer, *Two Koreas*, p. 87; Cyrus Vance, *Hard Choices: Critical Years in America's Foreign Policy* (Simon & Shuster, 1983), p. 128.

17 William Gleysteen Jr., *Massive Entanglement, Marginal Influence: Carter and Korea in Crisis* (Brookings Institute Press, 1999), p. 22.

18 Ibid., p. 23.

19 *Deaths of American Military Personnel in the Korean Demilitarized Zone: Hearing before the Subcommittees on International Political and Military Affairs and International Organizations of the Committee on International Relations, House of Representatives, 94th Congress, 2d Session, September 1, 1976* (U.S. Government Printing Office, 1976), p. 22.

20 PRM 10 *Comprehensive Net Assessment Force Posture Review*, February 18, 1977. PRM 10 was one of the largest strategic reviews of the cold war. Neither the PRM 10 task force reports nor the overview reports have been declassified. Portions of the report and its findings have been published as an annex to the final PRM 10 report. See PRM 10 (February 18, 1977), available at http://www.fas.org/irp/offdocs/prm/prm10.pdf (accessed April 1, 2011); Joe Wood and Philip Zelikow, "Persuading a President: Jimmy Carter and American Troops in Korea," *Kennedy School of Government Case Program*, Harvard University, C1-96-1319.0, p. 7; Rowland Evans and Robert Novak, "PRM 10 and the Korean Pull-out," *Washington Post*, September 7, 1977; PRM/NSC-13 (January 26, 1977), p. 23, available at http://www.fas.org/irp/offdocs/prm/prm13.pdf (accessed April 1, 2011). For an excellent overview of PRM 10, see Brian J. Auten, *Carter's Conversion: The Hardening of America's Defense Policy* (University of Missouri Press, 2009), pp. 154–165.

21 Wood and Zelikow, "Persuading a President," p. 9.

22 Rich, "U.S. Ground Forces Withdrawal from Korea," p. 14. See also Vance, *Hard Choices*, pp. 127–130.

23 *New York Times*, May 26, 1977; Oberdorfer, *Two Koreas*, p. 89.

24 *Time*, May 30, 1977, p. 14.

25 *New York Times*, May 29, 1977.

26 *U.S. Troop Withdrawal from the Republic of Korea, a Report to the Committee on Foreign Relations, United States Senate*, by Senators Hubert H. Humphrey and John Glenn, January 9, 1978 (hereafter the *Humphrey and Glenn Report*), 95th Congress, 2d Session (U.S. Government Printing Office, 1978), p. 13.

27 *New York Times*, July 2, 1977.

28 Ibid., May 30, 1977.

29 Oberdorfer, *Two Koreas*, p. 91.

30 Wood and Zelikow, "Persuading a President," p. 15.

31 *Washington Post*, October 28, 1977. See also Chae-Jin Lee, *A Troubled Peace: U.S. Policy and the Two Koreas* (Johns Hopkins University Press, 2006), pp. 98–103, and Kim Han-cho, *Robisŭt'ŭ Kim Han-cho ch'oe ch'o kopaek koria geit'e* [*Very First Confessions of Lobbyist Kim Han-cho*] (Illim wŏn, 1995). Although ten members of Congress and several Korean businessmen, including Pak Tong-sŏn and Kim Han-cho, were implicated in the scandal, in the end only U.S. Congressman Richard T. Hanna (D-CA) and Kim Han-cho were convicted by the U.S. Department of Justice for their roles in the affair. (Pak was granted immunity in exchange for his testimony). Kim Han-cho served a six-month prison sentence in the United States and later wrote a memoir about his experiences. In it, he blamed Kim Hyŏng-uk, one of Park Chung Hee's close associates and KCIA director from 1963–1969, of

offering false testimony against him. Kim Hyŏng-uk also implicated Park Chung Hee in the lobbying scandal. Nevertheless, no definitive evidence has ever been uncovered directly linking the South Korean president to illegal lobbying activities, and is it still unclear how much Park Chung Hee knew about the affair. On October 7, 1979, Kim Hyŏng-uk disappeared in Paris. It was widely rumored that he was killed by ROK agents. See Chong Hŭi-sang, "Kim Hyŏng ukŭn naega chukyŏtta" ["I Killed Kim Hyŏng-uk"), *Sisa chŏnŏl*, December 18, 2005, http://www.sisapress.com/news/articleView.html?idxno=23992 (accessed December 17, 2012).

During his testimony, Kim Hyŏng-uk heavily criticized Park. Kim was also going to publish his memoirs, which would have been extremely damaging to Park, so the latter tried to silence him with a bribe. Kim took Park's money but still gave a friend in New York the only copy of the manuscript. Excerpts of the manuscript were originally published in Japan. The entire manuscript was eventually smuggled into South Korea and published in 1985. See Kim Hyŏng-uk, *Kim Hyŏng-uk heorok* [*Memoir of Kim Hyŏng-uk*], 3 vols. (Tosŏ ch'ulp'an ach'im, 1985). For the complete transcripts of the congressional hearings, including Kim Hyŏng-uk's testimony, see Committee on International Relations, *Investigation of Korean-American Relations: Hearing before the Subcommittee on International Organizations*, 95th Cong., 1st sess., in seven parts from June 22, 1977, to August 15, 1978 (Government Printing Office, 1978), http://catalog.hathitrust.org/Record/002939983 (accessed December 17, 2012).

32 Quoted in Oberdorfer, *Two Koreas*, p. 92.

33 *New York Times*, April 10, 1977.

34 Ibid., March 11, 1977.

35 *Humphrey and Glenn Report*, p. v; Rich, "U.S. Ground Forces Withdrawal from Korea," p. 22.

36 China's strong opposition to the withdrawal plan was made clear in a report from the Hungarian embassy in P'yŏngyang in July 1975: "We know from Soviet and Chinese sources that—primarily in China—Kim Il Sung considered the possibility of a military solution. According to the Chinese ambassador, the DPRK wants to create the kind of military situation in South Korea that came into being in South Vietnam before the victory. Taking advantage of the riots against the dictatorial regime of Park Chung Hee, and invited by certain South Korean [political] forces, the DPRK would have given military assistance if it had not been dissuaded from doing so in time. This dissuasion obviously began as early as [Kim Il Sung's visit] in Beijing [April 18–26, 1975], for it is well-known that—primarily in Asia—*China holds back and opposes any kind of armed struggle that might shake the position of the USA in Asia* [author's emphasis]. A new Korean War would not be merely a war between North and South [Korea]. With this end in view, during the Korean party and government delegation's stay in Beijing, the Chinese side strongly emphasized the importance of the peaceful unification of Korea." Document No. 26, "Report, Embassy of Hungary in North Korea to the Hungarian Foreign Ministry, 30 July 1975," in Szalontai and Radchenko, "North Korea's Efforts to Acquire Nuclear Technology and Nuclear Weapons," pp. 52–53.

37 *Humphrey and Glenn Report*, pp. 9–16.

38 Ibid., pp. 9, 62.
39 Rich, "U.S. Ground Forces Withdrawal from Korea," p. 3.
40 Oberdorfer, *Two Koreas*, p. 103. In a similar intelligence assessment of the military balance on the Korean peninsula, the CIA warned that "the static mili tary balance between North and South Korea alone now favors the North by a substantial margin" and that "the US military presence in South Korea represents an in-place affirmation of the US commitment to help to defend the South and remains a key factor in the balance of deterrence on the Korean peninsula." "Military Balance on the Korean Peninsula (Secret)," CIA NFAC (National Foreign Assessment Center), May 10, 1978, in *The United States and the Two Koreas from Nixon to Clinton (1969–2000)*, item K00259, Digital National Security Archives.
41 Oberdorfer, *Two Koreas*, pp. 101–105; Rich, "U.S. Ground Forces Withdrawal from Korea," p. 22; Gleysteen, *Massive Entanglement*, p. 43.
42 Michael A. Ledeen, "Trumping Asian Allies," *Harper's Magazine*, March 1979, p. 28.
43 Gleysteen, *Massive Entanglement*, pp. 38–43; Oberdorfer, *Two Koreas*, p. 105.
44 Cho Kap-je, *Nae mudŏm e ch'imŭl paet'ŏra: Ch'oin ŭi norae* [Spit on My Grave: Hymn of a Great Man] (Seoul: Choson ilbosa, 1998), vol. 1, p. 108.
45 Gleysteen, *Massive Entanglement*, p. 46.
46 "Conversation between President Carter and South Korean President Park Chung Hee, July 5, 1979," in *The United States and the Two Koreas from Nixon to Clinton (1969–2000)*, item K00317, Digital National Security Archives (accessed March 2, 2010).
47 The scene is vividly painted by Oberforder, *Two Koreas*, p. 106.
48 Gleysteen, *Massive Entanglement*, pp. 47–48.
49 Oberdorfer, *Two Koreas*, p. 108.
50 Gleysteen, *Massive Entanglement*, p. 50.

NINETEEN: *End of an Era*

1 Chŏng Chae-gyŏng *Wiin Pak Chŏng-hŭi* [The Great Man Park Chung Hee] (Seoul: Chipmundang, 1992), pp. 295–296.
2 Cho, *Nae mudŏm e ch'imŭl paet'ŏra: Ch'oin ŭi norae* [Spit on My Grave: Hymn of a Great Man], pp. 62–63.
3 Ibid., p. 20.
4 Ibid., p. 169.
5 Ibid., p. 119. According to the South Korean Joint Investigation Team of the Martial Law Command that investigated the incident, Kim Chae-kyu did not give instructions to mobilize military units nor were other KCIA men alerted to his plan. The official report concluded that Kim's anger at the president's reprimands over his handling of the political turmoil in Pusan and Masan, together with his deep hatred of Ch'a Chi-ch'ŏl, whom he saw as having an unhealthy and negative influence on Park, drove Kim to kill both men. On the other hand, Kim allegedly also told his attorneys that the assassination was premeditated because he was intent on preventing bloodshed in Seoul, where large demonstrations were expected in the wake of the political turmoil in Pusan and Masan. For an excerpt of the report in English, see *New*

York Times, November 7, 1979. A detailed account of the assassination and its aftermath is recounted in Cho's *Nae mudŏm e ch'imŭl paet'ŏra* [Spit on My Grave].

6 Between 1966 and 1972 North Korean forces caused the deaths of 329 South Korean military, 91 civilians, and 75 American military personnel. North Korean terrorism continued into the 1980s with devastating results. On October 9, 1983, North Korea attempted to assassinate President Chŏn Tu-hwa), Park's successor, and his cabinet members in Rangoon, Burma (Myanmar). The president survived the attack, but four members of his cabinet, including two senior presidential advisors and the ambassador to Burma, were killed in the blast. In September 1986, a North Korean bomb at Seoul's Kimp'o International Airport killed five and wounded thirty. A year later, on November 29, 1987, two North Korean agents planted a bomb on Korean Air flight 858 bound for Seoul from Abu Dhabi. It exploded in mid-flight, killing all 115 on board. North Korea was condemned as a terrorist state by the international community. See Narushige Michishita, "Calculated Adventurism: North Korea's Military-Diplomatic Campaigns," *Korea Journal of Defense Analysis* 16, no. 2 (Fall 2004), pp. 188–197; Joseph S. Bermudez Jr., *Terrorism: The North Korean Connection* (Crane Russak, 1990), p. 43.

7 John A. Wickham, *Korea on the Brink: From the "12/12/ Incident" to the Kwangju Uprising, 1979–1980* (National Defense University, 1999), pp. 61–65; Oberdorfer, *Two Koreas*, pp. 117–119.

8 Oberdorfer, *Two Koreas*, 125; Wickham, *Korea on the Brink*, 128. Nearly a decade later, after an extensive investigation due to enormous political pressure from South Korean and American human rights activists and politicians, the U.S. government concluded that Ambassador Gleysteen and General Wickham had no prior knowledge of nor aided and abetted the December 12 coup, the declaration of martial law, or the Kwangju crackdown, and that they had tried their utmost to prevent political and human rights abuses through the unauthorized and misuse of military forces. See *U.S. Government Statement on the Events in Kwangju, Republic of Korea, in May 1980* issued by the American embassy in Seoul on June 19, 1989, available at http://seoul.usembassy.gov/p_kwangju.html (accessed July 30, 2011).

9 For a detailed examination of student *chuch'e* ideology (*chuch'eron*), see Sheila Miyoshi Jager, *Narratives of Nation Building in Korea: A Genealogy of Patriotism* (M. E. Sharpe, 2003), especially chaps. 4 and 6. I am grateful to M. E. Sharpe for allowing me to use portions of these and other chapters in this book. Copyright, 2003, M. E. Sharpe. All rights reserved. Reprinted by permission of M. E. Sharpe, http://www.mesharpe.com/.

10 The link between national unification and romantic reunion is laid out in detail in Sheila Miyoshi Jager, "Woman, Resistance and the Divided Nation: The Romantic Rhetoric of Korean Reunification," *Journal of Asian Studies* 55, no. 1 (1996).

11 Kim Nam-ju, Nongbuŭi pam [The Farmer's Night] (Seoul: Kidok Saenghwal Tongjihoe, 1988). Translation in Jager, *Narratives of Nation Building*, pp. 69–70.

12 Sheila Miyoshi Jager and Jiyul Kim, "The Korean War after the Cold War: Commemorating the Armistice Agreement in South Korea," in Sheila Miyo-

shi Jager and Rana Mitter, eds., *Ruptured Histories: War, Memory and the Post-Cold War in Asia* (Harvard University Press, 2007), pp. 262–265.

13 Quoted in B. R. Myers, *The Cleanest Race*, pp. 155–156.

14 Jager, *Narratives of Nation Building*, p. 103.

15 On how these perceptions of North Korea were absorbed in mainstream South Korean society, see Jager and Kim, "Korean War after the Cold War." In *Swiri* [Shiri] (1999), for example, Korea's first Hollywood-style big-budget blockbuster, the reunification drama is examined from the perspective of a doomed love story between a South Korean security agent and a secret North Korean agent. *Joint Security Area* (2000) and *Taegguki* [T'aegukki] (2004), both also blockbuster hits, explored the Korean War in terms of the relationship between brothers. Like *Swiri*, both films were sympathetic in their portrayal of North Korea.

TWENTY: *North Korea and the World*

1 Nicholas Eberstadt, *The End of North Korea* (American Enterprise Institute Press, 1999), p. 118.

2 Karoly Fendler, "Economic Assistance from Socialist Countries to North Korea in the Postwar Years: 1953–1963," in Han S. Park, ed., *North Korea: Ideology, Politics, Economy* (University of Georgia Press, 1996), p. 166.

3 *Christian Science Monitor*, July 10, 2003.

4 Eberstadt, *End of North Korea*, p. 100.

5 After P'yŏngyang's unsuccessful attempts to persuade the Soviet Union and other Soviet-bloc countries to boycott the Seoul Olympics, Kim suggested that North Korea co-host the games and asked for a fifty-fifty split of all events. Seoul and the International Olympic Committee (IOC) rejected the proposal but, under pressure from North Korea's allies, suggested instead that North Korea be allowed to host some events, including table tennis and fencing. North Korea responded that the offer was insufficient. As negotiations stalled, the IOC and Seoul eventually decided to go ahead with their planning without P'yŏngyang's participation. Angered by this turn of events, North Korea decided to disrupt the games and on October 7, 1987, sent two highly trained espionage agents to destroy Korean Air flight 858. The plane blew up on its way from Abu Dhabi to Seoul, killing all 115 persons on board. In wake of the bombing of flight 858, North Korea was placed on a list of countries practicing terrorism, further deepening its international isolation. See Oberdorfer, *Two Koreas*, pp. 180–186; see also Kim Hyun-hui, *The Tears of My Soul* (William Morrow, 1993).

6 No T'ae-u, *No T'ae-u hoegorok* [Memoirs of No T'ae-u], vol. 2: *Chŏnhwangiŭi taejŏllyak* [Grand Strategy of a Turning Point] (Seoul: Chosŏn nyusŭ p'resu, 2011), p. 140.

7 Carolyn Ekedahl and Melvin Goodman, *The Wars of Eduard Shevardnadze* (University of Pennsylvania Press, 1997), p. 216.

8 Oberdorfer, *Two Koreas*, p. 207.

9 Quoted in ibid., pp. 209–212.

10 No T'ae-u, *No T'ae-u hoegorok* [Memoirs of No T'ae-u], vol. 2, p. 209.

11 Ibid., p. 217.

12 Mikhail Gorbachev, *Memoirs* (Doubleday, 1995), p. 544.
13 Oberdorfer, *Two Koreas*, p. 246.
14 Eberstadt, *End of North Korea*, p. 100.
15 Document No. 30, "Report, Embassy of Hungary in North Korea to the Hungarian Foreign Ministry, 15 April 1976," in Balázs Szalontai and Sergey Radchenko, "North Korea's Efforts to Acquire Nuclear Technology and Nuclear Weapons: Evidence from Russian and Hungarian Archives," *CWIHP Working Paper 53* (August 2006), p. 56.
16 Szalontai and Radchenko, "North Korea's Efforts to Acquire Nuclear Technology and Nuclear Weapons," p. 29.
17 Ibid., p. 21.
18 Oberdorfer, *Two Koreas*, pp. 254–255, 267–269; International Institute for Strategic Studies (IISS), *North Korea's Weapons Program: A Net Assessment* (Palgrave Macmillan, 2004), pp. 34–35.
19 " 'Sea of Fire' Threat Shakes Seoul," *Financial Times*, March 22, 1994; *Washington Post*, May 1, 1994.
20 *New York Times*, March 23, 1994.
21 *Washington Post*, May 1, 1994.
22 *New York Times*, March 19, 1994; Peter D. Zimmerman, "Nuclear Brinkmanship Redefined," *Los Angeles Times*, June 5, 1994.
23 *Washington Post*, April 6, 1994; Oberdorfer, *Two Koreas*, p. 319.
24 *New York Times*, July 24, 1994.
25 *Washington Post*, May 19 and 20, 1994; Oberdorfer, *Two Koreas*, p. 309.
26 *Washington Post*, May 19, 1994; Joel Wit, Daniel Poneman, and Robert Gallucci, *Going Critical: The First North Korean Nuclear Crisis* (Brookings Institution, 2004), p. 205; Oberdorfer, *Two Koreas*, p. 315.
27 Wit et al., *Going Critical*, pp. 227–228; Oberdorfer, *Two Koreas*, pp. 306, 332.
28 Wit et al., *Going Critical*, p. 228; *Washington Post*, June 18, 19, and 20, 1994; Myers, *The Cleanest Race*, p. 142; *New York Times*, June 19, 1994.
29 Jimmy Carter, *Sharing Good Times* (Simon & Schuster, 2004), pp. 129–130; Oberdorfer, *Two Koreas*, p. 336.
30 *New York Times*, July 15, 1994; Oberdorfer, *Two Koreas*, pp. 344–345.
31 Myers, *Cleanest Race*, p. 51; *New York Times*, August 31, 1994.
32 *Washington Post*, November 23, 1994; Oberdorfer, *Two Koreas*, pp. 352–354.
33 Oberdorfer, *Two Koreas*, p. 357.
34 Myers, *Cleanest Race*, p. 144.
35 *Chosŏn ilbo*, September 4, 1994; *Washington Post*, September 5, 1994.
36 "The Content of the Korea Accord," *Washington Post*, October 21, 1994; "Clinton Approves a Plan to Give Aid to North Koreans," *New York Times*, October 19, 1994.
37 *New York Times*, November 26, 1994.
38 "Kim's Nuclear Gamble," *Frontline*, PBS, 2003, directed by Marcela Gaviria and written by Martin Smith.

TWENTY-ONE: *Winners and Losers*

1 Sheila Miyoshi and Jiyul Kim, "The Korean War after the Cold War," in Jager and Mitter, eds., *Ruptured Histories*, p. 242. I am grateful to Harvard University Press for giving me permission to reprint portions of this chapter in this book. Copyright, 2007, Harvard University Press. All rights reserved. Reprinted by permission of the present publisher, Harvard University Press, http://www.hup.harvard.edu/.

2 A detailed treatment of the War Memorial can be found in my "Monumental Histories: Maniless, the Military and the War Memorial," *Public Culture* 14, no. 2 (Spring 2002), pp. 387–409; *Narratives of Nation Building in Korea: A Genealogy of Patriotism* (M. E. Sharpe, 2003); and Jager and Kim, "Korean War after the Cold War." I am grateful to Duke University Press for giving me permission to reprint portions of my article "Monumental Histories" in this book. Copyright, 2002, Duke University Press, http://www.dukeupress.edu/.

3 Jager, *Narratives of Nation Building*, pp. 136–138. The interview with Chae Yŏng-jip was conducted by the author on March 25, 1997. See also Jager and Mitter, eds., *Ruptured Histories*, pp. 248–249.

4 Kim Dae-jung, *Tashi saeroŭn sichakŭl wihayŏ* [Again, in the Interest of a New Beginning] (Seoul: Kim Yongsa, 1998), p. 173; Jager, *Narratives of Nation Building*, p. 144.

5 Kim, *Tashi saeroŭn sichakŭl wihayŏ* [Again, in the Interest of a New Beginning], p. 116; Jager, *Narratives of Nation Building*, p. 144.

6 Former President Chŏn Tu-hwan had been sentenced to life in prison and No T'ae-u to seventeen years in 1995 during Kim Yŏng-sam's administration, for their role in the 1979 military coup that brought Chŏn to power. They were also tried and found guilty for their role in the brutal suppression of the Kwangju uprising in May 1980 as well as for the collection of million-dollar bribes.

7 In Aesop's tale, the North Wind and the Sun boast that each is more powerful than the other. To settle the question, they both agreed that the one who could first strip clothes off a wayfaring man would be declared the victor. The North Wind tried first. Blowing with all his might, the blast succeeded only in making the traveler wrap his cloak closer around him. It was then the Sun's turn. Shining his rays on the earth, the traveler soon began to take off one garment after another, until at last, overcome with heat, he undressed altogether. Persuasion is stronger than force.

8 Jasper Becker, "Letters Highlight Horror of Famine: Victims Caught in Desperate Struggle for Help as Worse Feared to Be Yet to Come," *South China Morning Post*, May 12, 1997.

9 "Scores of Children Dead in North Korea Famine," *CNN World*, April 8, 1987, available at http://articles.cnn.com/1997-04-08/world/9704_08_korea.food_1_food-crisis-food-and-medicine-pyongyang?_s=PM:WORLD (accessed May 30, 2011).

10 Médecins Sans Frontières (Doctors Without Borders), "North Korea: Tes-

timonies of Famine," August 1, 1998, available at http://www.doctorswithoutborders.org/publications/article.cfm?id=1468 (accessed May 30, 2011).

11 Hyŏk Kang, *This Is Paradise: My North Korean Childhood* (Abacus, 2007), p. 125. For other testimonials about life in the North Korean gulags see Blaine Harden, *Escape From Camp 14: One Man's Remarkable Odyssey from North Korea to Freedom in the West* (Viking, 2012). See also Barbara Demick's masterful *Nothing to Envy: Ordinary Lives in North Korea* (Spiegel & Grau; 2009) and Melanie Kirkpatrick, *Escape from North Korea: The Untold Story of Asia's Underground Railroad* (Encounter Books, 2012).

12 So Kae-mal, "Im Ch'ŏl-Im-So-yŏn onuiŭi yuksŏng chŭngŏn (nogŭm t'aep'u nokch'wi kirok)" [Oral testimony of brother and sister, Im Ch'ŏl and Im So-yŏn (transcript of a taped interview)] *Wŏlgan Chosŏn*, September 1999, pp. 304–319. After living in the market for several months, Chŏl decided to make the hazardous journey to China with his sister. After crossing the Tumen River in April 1999, they were eventually taken in by a Chinese family. The secret interview took place somewhere in China.

13 Jasper Becker, "North Koreans Turning to Cannibalism, Say Refugees," *South China Morning Post*, October 1, 1997.

14 Andrew S. Natsios, *The Great North Korean Famine: Famine, Politics, and Foreign Policy* (United States Institute of Peace, 2001), p. 220.

15 Given the secrecy of the North Korean regime, it is not surprising that estimates of the number of deaths by famine vary enormously. North Korean officials put the estimated number of deaths between 1995 and 1998 at 220,000, but interviews with party defectors have said that that number is greatly deflated, suggesting that internal estimates range from 1 to 1.2 million. The South Korean nongovernmental organization Good Friends Center for Peace, Human Rights, and Refugees puts the number of famine-related deaths as high as 3.5 million, or 16 percent of the population (Good Friends Center for Peace, Human Rights, and Refugees, "Human Rights in North Korea and the Food Crisis," March 2004). A team from Johns Hopkins School of Public Health working from 771 refugee interviews sought to determine the mortality rates in North Hamgyŏng province, which was widely seen as the most affected province. The study concluded that nearly 12 percent of the province's population had died of starvation. Extrapolating from these numbers for the whole country (which the Johns Hopkins team did not do) would yield an estimate of more than 2.6 million deaths, which is certainly too high given that not all provinces were affected as traumatically as North Hamgyŏng province. See Stephan Haggard and Marcus Noland, *Hunger and Human Rights: The Politics of Famine in North Korea* (U.S. Committee for Human Rights in North Korea, 2005), p. 18, available at http://www.hrnk.org/download/Hunger_and_Human_Rights.pdf (accessed May 30, 2011); Bradley Martin, *Under the Loving Care of the Fatherly Leader* (Thomas Dunne Books, 2004), pp. 557–573; see also Amnesty International, "Starved of Rights: Human Rights and the Food Crisis in the Democratic Republic of Korea (North Korea)," January 17, 2004, p. 9, available at http://www.amnesty.org/en/library/info/ASA24/003/2004 (accessed May 30, 2011). In 1994, the North Korean government reportedly stopped sending food ship-

ments to these remote northeastern provinces, which were highly dependent on the PDS. The failure of already poor domestic production of food was also compounded by severe floods in 1995 and 1996. As a result, mortality rates from the famine vary considerably according to region. Médecins Sans Frontières, "North Korea: Testimonies of Famine"; Haggard and Noland, *Hunger and Human Rights*, p. 17; Natsios, *Great North Korean Famine.*

16 Scott Snyder, "North Korea's Decline and China's Strategic Dilemmas," United States Institute of Peace Special Report (October 1997), p. 2, available at http://www.usip.org/files/resources/SR27.pdf (accessed May 31, 2011).

17 Amnesty International, "Starved of Rights," p. 9.

18 Andre Lankov, *North of the DMZ: Essays on the Daily Life in North Korea* (McFarland, 2007), p. 315.

19 Haggard and Noland, *Famine in North Korea*, pp. 53–54.

20 Ibid., pp. 54–55. This sociopolitical classification system, or "*sŏngbun*," impacts every facet of people's daily lives, from housing and food to education and healthcare. *Sŏngbun* literally means "ingredient" or "material substance," and North Koreans use the term to refer to one's sociopolitical background based on one's family history. Whereas other societies practice "discrimination based on religion, ethnicity and other factors, the primary source of discrimination in North Korean society is defined by the regime to be one's presumed value as a friend or foe to the Kim regime" (p. 6). It is also the root cause of discrimination and humanitarian abuses in North Korea. In his exhaustive study of the *sŏngbun* system, Robert Collins demonstrates how the institution of *sŏngbun* has created "a form of slave labor for a third of North Korea's population of twenty-three million citizens and loyalty-bound servants out of the remainder" (p. 1). See Robert Collins, *Marked for Life: Sŏngbun, North Korea's Social Classification System* (The Committee for Human Rights in North Korea, 2012), http://www.hrnk.org/uploads/pdfs/HRNK_Songbun_Web.pdf (accessed November 1, 2012); Chon Hyun-joon, Lee Keum-soon, Lim Soon-hee, Lee Kyu-chang, and Hong Woo-taek, *White Paper on Human Rights in North Korea* (Korea Institute for National Unification, 2011), pp. 220–227.

21 Médecins Sans Frontières, "North Korea: Testimonies of Famine," p. 7.

22 Kang, *This Is Paradise*, p. 89.

23 Haggard and Noland, *Hunger and Human Rights*, p. 28.

24 Jasper Becker, *Rogue Regime: Kim Jong Il and the Looming Threat of North Korea* (Oxford University Press, 2005), pp. 205–206.

25 Amnesty International, "Starved of Rights," p. 18.

26 Mark E. Manyin and Mary Beth Nikitin, "U.S. Assistance to North Korea," Congressional Research Service Report for Congress, July 31, 2008, available at http://www.fas.org/sgp/crs/row/RS21834.pdf (accessed May 31, 2011).

27 World Food Program, "Emergency Operation Democratic People's Republic of Korea (1 September 2008–30 November 2009)," Executive Summary, pp. 5–6, available at http://one.wfp.org/operations/current_operations/project_docs/107570.pdf (accessed May 31, 2011).

28 Haggard and Noland, *Hunger and Human Rights*, p. 16.

29 Marcus Noland, "Between Collapse and Revival: A Reinterpretation of the

North Korean Economy," paper presented at a conference on Economic Development in North Korea and Global Partnership, Cheju, South Korea, March 15–16, 2001, p. 1, available at http://www.iie.com/publications/papers/paper.cfm?ResearchID=401 (accessed May 31, 2011).

30 Haggard and Marcus, *Hunger and Human Rights*, p. 17.

31 Nicholas Eberstadt, *The North Korean Economy: Between Crisis and Catastrophe* (Transaction, 2007), p. 170; "South Korea Mourns Kim Dae Jung's Death," *Bloomberg Businessweek*, August 18, 2009, at http://www.businessweek.com/blogs/eyeonasia/archives/2009/08/south_korea_mourns_kim_dae_jungs_death.html (accessed May 31, 2011); Haggard and Noland, "Sanctioning North Korea: The Political Economy of Denuclearization and Proliferation," *Peterson Institute for International Economics Working Paper Series* (July 2009), pp. 17–18, available at http://www.iie.com/publications/interstitial.cfm?ResearchID=1268 (accessed May 31, 2011).

32 Stephan Haggard and Marcus Noland, "North Korea's External Economic Relations," *Peterson Institute for International Economics Working Paper Series* (August 2007), p. 19; Haggard and Noland, "Sanctioning North Korea," p. 3; World Food Program, "Emergency Operation," p. 2.

33 Lankov, *North of the DMZ*, p. 320.

34 Stephan Haggard and Marcus Noland, "The Winter of Their Discontent: Pyongyang Attacks the Market," Peterson Institute for International Economics (January 2010), pp. 3–9, available at http://www.piie.com/publications/pb/pb10-01.pdf (accessed May 31, 2011). For the most up-to-date examination of the North Korean surveillance and prison system, see Ken E. Gause, *Coercion, Control, Surveillance, and Punishment: An Examination of the North Korean Police State* (The Committee for Human Rights in North Korea, 2012), http://www.hrnk.org/uploads/pdfs/HRNK_Ken-Gause_Web.pdf (accessed November 1, 2012).

35 The adoption of the three-tiered political structure of loyal, wavering, and hostile classes in the 1950s led to whole groups of citizens being imprisoned for political crimes based solely on family ties. "Group punishment in the form of incarceration of extended family and confiscation of property is a distinctive feature of the management of political crimes" in North Korea, a tradition that goes back to feudal times when "three generations" were punished along with the condemned. David Hawk, *The Hidden Gulag: Exposing North Korea's Prison Camps* (U.S. Committee for Human Rights in North Korea, 2003), p. 27, available at http://www.hrnk.org/download/The_Hidden_Gulag.pdf (accessed May 31, 2011); Helen-Louise Hunter, *Kim Il Sung's North Korea* (Praeger, 1999), pp. 3–13.

36 Stephan Haggard and Marcus Noland, "Economic Crime and Punishment in North Korea," *Peterson Institute for International Economics Working Paper Series* (March 2010), p. 4, available at http://www.piie.com/publications/wp/wp10-2.pdf (accessed May 31, 2011).

37 Amnesty International, "Images Reveal Scale of North Korean Political Prison Camps," May 3, 2011, available at http://www.amnesty.org/en/news-and-updates/images-reveal-scale-north-korean-political-prison-camps-2011-05-03 (accessed June 1, 2011).

38 Chŏl-hwan Kang, *Aquariums of Pyongyang: Ten Years in the North Korean Gulag*

(Basic Books, 2001). Since his 2003 publication, *The Hidden Gulag*, David Hawk wrote a second edition that chronicles in greater detail the conditions of Camp 15 as well as other political penal labor camps, owing to a substantial increase in the amount of available testimony from former prisoners. In 2002 and 2003 there were roughly three thousand former North Koreans who resettled in South Korea. That number has increased to over twenty thousand in 2009–10. These testimonies, together with many more and clearer-resolution satellite photographs, corroborate and reconfirm the findings and analysis of the first edition. See David Hawk, *The Hidden Gulag*, 2d ed. A Report by the Committee for Human Rights in North Korea (Committee for Human Rights in North Korea, April 2012), available at http://hrnk.org/wp-content/uploads/HRNK_HiddenGulag2_Final_Web_v4.pdf (accessed April 13, 2012).

39 Hawk, *Hidden Gulag* (2003), p. 44; Soon Ok Lee, *Eyes of a Tailless Animal: Prison Memoirs of a North Korean Woman* (Living Sacrifice Book, 1999), p. 60.

40 Lee, *Eyes of a Tailless Animal*, p. 60.

41 Hawk, *Hidden Gulag* (2003), p. 53.

42 Kang, *Aquariums of Pyongyang*, p. 92.

43 Becker, *Rogue Regime*, p. 87.

44 Hawk, *Hidden Gulag* (2003), p. 48.

45 Ibid., pp. 56–58; Haggard and Noland, "Economic Crime and Punishment in North Korea," p. 12. Numerous witnesses have also offered detailed accounts of pregnant women forced to undergo abortion and infanticide upon their repatriation to North Korea. According to David Hawk, North Korean officials have made no secret of racially motivated abortions and infanticide forced upon Korean women in order to prevent them from giving birth to "half-Chinese" babies. There also appears to be little difference between forced abortions and infanticide as many of the fetuses are born viable. According to one account from a sixty-six-year-old grandmother who was held in a detention center in Sinŭiju after being forcibly repatriated in 1997, all the babies she was assigned to help deliver were killed shortly after birth. "The first baby was born to a twenty-eight-year-old woman named Lim who had been married to a Chinese man," she recalled. "The baby boy was born healthy and unusually large, owing to the mother's ability to eat well during pregnancy in China." She then "assisted in holding the baby's head during delivery and cut the umbilical cord." However, when she held the baby "and wrapped him in a blanket, a guard grabbed the newborn by one leg and threw him in a large plastic-lined box." When the box was full of babies, it was taken outside and buried. See David Hawk, *The Hidden Gulag*, 2nd ed., (2012), pp. 122–125.

46 Hawk, *Hidden Gulag*, 2d ed. (2012), p. 121.

47 Haggard and Noland, "Economic Crime and Punishment in North Korea," pp. 12–16; Shin Joo Hyun, "Bribery and Extortion Are Common in North Korean Commerce," *DailyNK*, December 31, 2010, at http://www.dailynk.com/english/read.php?cataId=nk01500&num=7196 (accessed May 31, 2011). When bribery becomes the unofficial exchange between state officials and the population, a certain equilibrium in the system is maintained. In this case, the dictator who is unable to pay government officials a living wage "condones corruption as the price he must pay to maintain his loyalty." At

the same time, however, government officials such as police officers and security agents are granted more discretionary power when they deal with cracking down on informal market activities. Since market traders understand that police and other government officials have the power to punish, they are incentivized to bribe their way out of arrest or harsh punishment. "Equilibrium is established between government officials and market participants as bribe-takers and bribe-givers, respectively, and even strong collusion may develop." However, such a system is fragile, since members of the police and other officials may want to increase the amount of bribes they receive, thus increasing the discontent among the population. Byung-Yeon Kim, "Markets, Bribery, and Regime Stability in North Korea," *East Asia Institute Security Initiative Working Paper* 4 (April 2010), p. 21.

48 Ishimaru Jiro, *Rimjin-gang: Reports by North Korean Journalists within North Korea* (Asiapress, 2010), pp. 97–98.

49 Ibid., p. 170.

50 Although the reform effectively wiped out all private savings from black-market operators, it also caused hyperinflation. Merchants with goods for sale wanted to convert their merchandise into hard currency like Chinese yuan or U.S. dollars or into durable items such as rice. Those who wanted to buy goods were unable to do so since the retail prices for all goods skyrocketed. The situation caused open dissension among the North Korean populace, the first time that such open and public criticism of the regime had ever occurred. The regime later publicly acknowledged that the currency reform was a massive failure and pinned the blame on Pak Nam-gi, director of the Planning and Finance Department of the KWP. Pak was arrested in January 2010 and executed by firing squad two months later. See Ishimaru, *Rimjin-gang*, p. 175; "N. Korean Technocrat Executed for Bungled Currency Reform: Sources," Yonhap News Agency, March 18, 2010; Scott Snyder, "North Korea Currency Reform: What Happened and What Will Happen to Its Economy?" paper presented at the 2010 Global Forum on North Korea Economy, Korea Economic Daily and Hyundai Research Institute, Seoul, Korea, March 31, 2010, available at http://asiafoundation.org/resources/pdfs/SnyderDPRK-Currency.pdf (accessed March 25, 2012).

EPILOGUE: *China's Rise, War's End?*

1 An earlier version of this chapter was previously published in the online *Asia-Pacific Journal* 9, no. 2 (January 24, 2011), available at http://japanfocus.org/-Sheila_Miyoshi-Jager/3477. I am grateful to Mark Selden, the journal's coordinator, for granting me permission to reuse portions of the article in this book.

2 "DPRK Leading Newspapers Publish Joint New Year Editorial," Korea Central News Agency (KCNA), January 1, 2012, at http://www.kcna.co.jp/item/2012/201201/news01/20120101-15ee.html (accessed January 2, 2012).

3 Stephanie Ho, "China Recognizes Kim Jong Un as North Korea's Next Leader," Voice of America, December 19, 2011, at http://www.voanews.com/english/news/asia/China-Recognizes-Kim-Jong-Un-as-North-Koreas-Next-Leader-135914943.html (accessed December 22, 2011).

4 Adam Cathcart, "Beijing-P'yŏngyang: Developments in and around North Korea from the Chinese Media," *Sino-UK*, December 22, 2011, at http://sinonk.wordpress.com/2011/12/22/beijing-pyongyang-developments-in-and-around-north-korea-from-the chinese-media/ (accessed January 7, 2012).

5 Andrei Lankov, "The Legacy of Long-Gone States: China, Korea and the Koguryo Wars," *Asia-Pacific Journal*, September 28, 2006, p. 1, available at http://www.japanfocus.org/-Andrei-Lankov/2233 (accessed May 1, 2011).

6 Traditional dating of Koguryŏ is 37 BC–AD 668, but recent archeological evidence suggests that state formation on the Korean peninsula occurred around AD 300, much later than 37 BC. This means that the Three Kingdoms of Koguryŏ, Paekche, and Silla were established after the Chinese Han Lelang period (108 BC–AD 313), when Han Dynasty commanderies occupied the northwestern part of the Korean peninsula and introduced to Korea the most important "traits of civilization," including intensive wet rice agriculture, iron technology, and writing. These traits of civilization spread to other parts of the peninsula to create the basis for the emergence of new Korean states that comprised Koguryŏ, Paekche, and Silla. Sarah Milledge Nelson, *The Archeology of Korea* (Cambridge University Press, 1993); Gina Barnes, *State Formation in Korea: Historical and Archaeological Perspectives* (Curzon, 2001); Hyung Il Pai, "Lelang and the Interaction Sphere: An Alternative Approach to Korean State Formation," *Archaeological Review from Cambridge* 8, no. 1 (1989), pp. 64–75.

7 Yonson Ahn, "Competing Nationalisms: The Mobilization of History and Archeology in the Korea-China Wars over Koguryo/Gaogouli," *Asia-Pacific Journal*, February 9, 2006, p. 2, available at http://www.japanfocus.org/-Yonson-Ahn/1837 (accessed May 1, 2011).

8 Lankov, "The Legacy of Long-Gone States," p. 2.

9 Ahn, "Competing Nationalisms," p. 5.

10 Lankov, "The Legacy of Long-Gone States," p. 5.

11 Sheila Miyoshi Jager, "The Politics of Identity: History, Nationalism and the Prospect for Peace in Post-Cold War Asia," U.S. Army Strategic Studies Institute (April 2007), pp. 21–22, available at http://www.strategicstudiesinstitute.army.mil/pdffiles/pub770.pdf (accessed May 1, 2011).

12 Bonnie Glaser, Scott Snyder, and John S. Park, "Keeping an Eye on an Unruly Neighbor: Chinese Views of Economic Reform and Stability in North Korea," *United States Institute of Peace Working Paper* (January 3, 2008), p. 10, available at http://www.usip.org/files/resources/Jan2008.pdf (accessed May 1, 2011).

13 Scott Snyder, "Pyŏngyang Tests Beijing's Patience," *Comparative Connections* (July 2009), p. 5, available at http://csis.org/files/publication/0902qchina_korea.pdf (accessed May 1, 2011).

14 Choe Sang-hun, "South Korea Risks Driving North into China's Embrace," *International Herald Tribune*, April 29, 2010, p. 2.

15 Min Cho Hee, "Chinese Take Complete Control of Mines," *DailyNK*, May 11, 2010, at http://www.dailynk.com/english/read.php?cataId=nk01500&num=6352 (accessed May 1, 2011).

16 "Company's $2 Billion Pledge Would Mark One of the Largest Deals with

Neighbor; Pact Was Signed after Yeongpyeong Shelling," *Wall Street Journal*, January 19, 2011.

17 "China's Industrial Expansion near North Korea Stirs Fears," *Korea Times*, August 7, 2010; "Kim Jong Il's China Visit Was about Economy," *Korea Times*, September 6, 2010. The ambitious plan that emerged in 1991 aims to convert an area from the Chinese town of Yanji to the Sea of Japan and from Ch'ŏnjin in North Korea to Vladivostok in Russia into a $30 billion trade and transport complex. The goal is to create a free economic zone in Northeast Asia over the next twenty years involving China, the two Koreas, Russia, and Japan. While the development project poses great potential economic benefits, implementing it has been very complicated because of political issues and the fact that the area in question will require border countries to relinquish some of their land if the overall project is to succeed. Mark J. Valencia, "Tumen River Project," *East Asian Executive Reports* 14, no. 2 (1993), available at http://www1.american.edu/TED/tumen.htm (accessed May 1, 2011); Joseph Manguno, "A New Regional Trade Bloc in Northeast Asia?" *China Business Review* 20 (March/April 1993).

18 Jeremy Page, "Trade Binds North Korea to China," *Wall Street Journal*, December 24, 2011. For China's failed efforts to put North Korea on the path to economic reform, see Stephan Haggard, Jennifer Lee, and Marcus Noland, "Integration in the Absence of Institutions: China-North Korea Cross-Border Exchanges," *Peterson Institute for International Economics Working Paper Series* (August 2011), available at http://www.iie.com/publications/wp/wp11-13.pdf (accessed December 26, 2001). Also see Carla Freeman and Drew Thompson, "The Real Bridge to Nowhere: China's Foiled North Korea Strategy," *United States Institute of Peace Working Paper* (April 22, 2009), available at http://www.usip.org/files/resources/1%282%29.PDF (accessed December 26, 2011).

19 The April 27, 2009, cable from the American embassy in Seoul, in "U.S Embassy Cables: Reading the Runes on North Korea," *Guardian*, November 29, 2010, at http://www.guardian.co.uk/world/us-embassy-cables-documents/204174 (accessed May 1, 2011).

20 Tessa Morris-Suzuki pointed out that the North Korean Victorious Fatherland War Museum portrays the war as a battle between the United States and North Korea, with almost no reference to the involvement of any other countries in the war: "The emphasis throughout is on US imperialism and aggression, and the war, in short, is narrating as a resounding victory of the DPRK over the United States" (p. 11). Tessa Morris-Suzuki, "Remembering the Unfinished Conflict: Museums and the Contested Memory of the Korean War," *Asia-Pacific Journal* (July 27, 2009), available at http://www.japanfocus.org/-Tessa-Morris_Suzuki/3193 (accessed May 1, 2011). However, as B. R. Myers has pointed out, this does not mean that China's contribution to the war has been completely ignored. Chinese visitors, for example, are taken to specific exhibits that do acknowledge their country's enormous sacrifice in the war, but these exhibits are off-limits to North Koreans, who "are taken on another route where they see and hear no mention of it." Myers, *The Cleanest Race*, p. 130.

21 "Arirang Has a New Scene Reflecting DPRK-China Friendship," *Korean Central News Agency of the DPRK* (hereafter *KCNA*), October 22, 2010, at http://

www.kcna.co.jp/item/2010/201010/news22/20101022-12ee.html (accessed May 2, 2011).

22 "DPRK Arranges Banquet to Mark Entry of CPV into Korean Front," *KCNA*, October 24, 2010, available at http://www.globalsecurity.org/wmd/library/news/dprk/2010/dprk-101024-kcna04.htm (accessed May 2, 2011).

23 "Floral Tribute Paid to Mao Anying and Fallen Fighters of the CPV," *KCNA*, October 24, 2010. One interesting (and amusing) side note regarding Korean War memory: During the White House state banquet hosted on January 19, 2010, in honor of President Hu Jintao, the Chinese pianist Lang Lang played "My Mother Land," which was a very popular song during the Korean War. The song encouraged the Chinese to fight the American invaders. See http://news.backchina.com/viewnews-124030-gb2312.html (accessed May 3, 2011).

24 *Nodong sinmun*, October 24, 2010.

25 Speech of Kim Jong Il at Banquet," *KCNA*, August 30, 2010, at http://www.kcna.co.jp/item/2010/201008/news30/20100830-23ee.html (accessed May 4, 2011).

26 According to the Korea scholar Rüdiger Frank, the building in the picture appears to be the Catholic church on the bank of the Songhua River in Jilin City. He suggests that the painting is linked to the increasingly frequent allusions to Kim Il Sung's youth in Northeast China in what is clearly a campaign to emphasize traditional Sino–North Korean closeness. "So the painting might actually be part of the new policy of emphasizing the two countries joint revolutionary past" (p. 3). On the other hand, he is not entirely convinced that this is, in fact, a painting of Kim Chŏng-ŭn. Rather, it appears to be a portrait of a young Kim Il Sung in Northeast China. Frank Rüdiger, "Harbinger or Hoax: The First Painting of Kim Jung Un?" *Foreign Policy*, December 9, 2010, at http://www.foreignpolicy.com/articles/2010/12/09/harbinger_or_hoax_the_first_painting_of_kim_jung_un (accessed May 2, 2011). Other North Korea experts, however, are convinced that the portrait was indeed the first glimpse of the new leader Kim Chŏng-ŭn. See Mark McKinnon, "North Korea's Kim Jong-un: Portrait of a Leader in the Making," *Globe and Mail*, December 4, 2010.

27 *Korea Times*, January 6, 2012.

28 *Dong-a ilbo*, October 11 and 13, 2010; *Telegraph*, October 5, 2010; Aidan Foster-Carter, "North Korea: Embracing the Dragon," *Asia Times*, October 28, 2010.

29 *New York Times*, April 29, 2010. For an excellent overview and analysis of South Korea's reaction to China's economic influence in North Korea and the political challenges of future Sino-South Korean relations, see Scott Snyder, *China's Rise and The Two Koreas: Politics, Economics, Security* (Lynne Rienner Publishers, 2009).

30 South Korean President Yi's current position toward North Korea is that it must apologize for the *Ch'ŏn'an*'s sinking and the Yŏnp'yŏng shelling before serious negotiations can resume. Since North Korea has refused to acknowledge its responsibility for the sinking of the South Korean corvette and has justified the shelling of the island as a retaliatory move, Yi will presumably have to wait a long time.

31 *Korea Times*, September 9, 2010.

32 Ibid., November 2, 2010.

33 Chico Harlan, "South Korea's Young People Are Wary of Unification," *Washington Post*, October 17, 2011. Every year the Institute of Peace and Reunification Studies at Seoul National University conducts extensive polling data on unification issues. In the 2010 survey, South Koreans of all ages were asked about their views on the personal benefits from unification. The responses were startling, with 75.2 percent of South Koreans replying that unification would have no or very little impact for them personally, while just 3.6 percent responded that it would benefit them "very much" and 21.2 percent "somewhat." These results compare with the findings in 2008, in which 72.3 percent replied "very little" or "none at all." In 2009, the percentage was higher, at 76.1, most likely due to North Korea's decision to test a nuclear device on May 25 of that year. See *2010 T'ongil ŭisik chosa* [2010 Investigation on Perceptions on Unification], Institute of Peace and Unification Studies, Seoul National University, 2010, available at http://tongil.snu.ac.kr/xe/index.php?document_srl=6147 (accessed March 18, 2012).

34 *Choson ilbo*, November 18, 2010.

35 *Korea Times*, January 27, 2012.

36 Andre Lankov, "South Korea Harbors Unification Heresy," *Asia Times*, September 9, 2011.

37 Foster-Carter, "How North Korea Was Lost to China," *Asia Times*, September 10, 2010.

Index

Page numbers in *italics* refer to illustrations and maps.